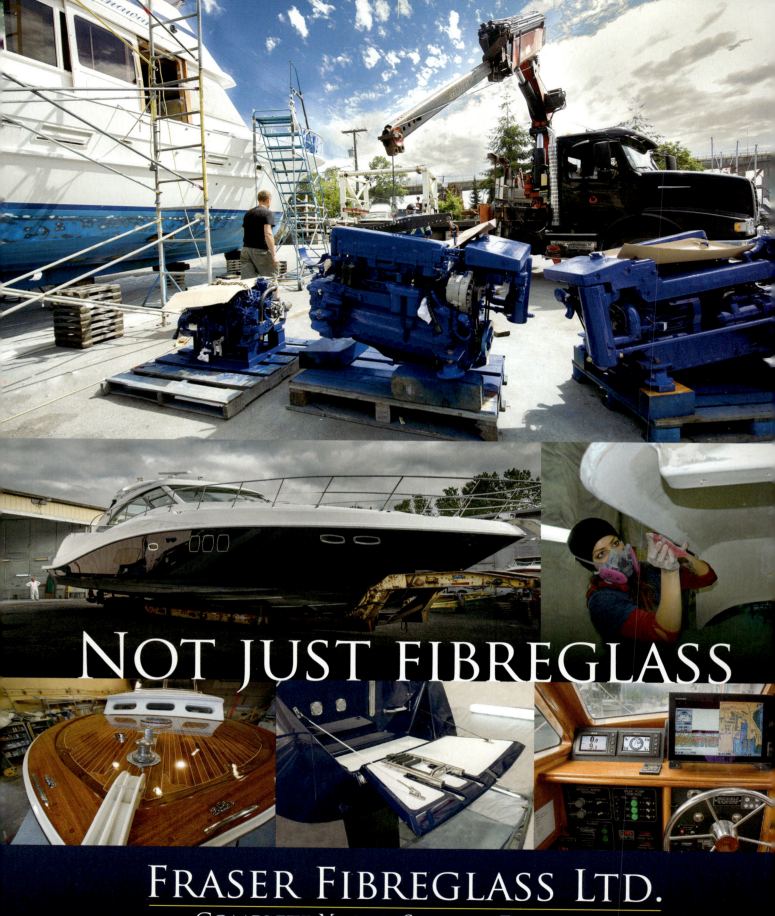

WAGGONER CRUISING GUIDE 2020

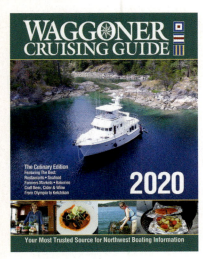

*Our cover photo of a Nordhavn afloat in clear, blue-green water was captured by Mike Beemer, while leading a Waggoner Guide Flotilla to Desolation Sound. The featured 47-foot Nordhavn, **Si Senora**, is owned by Bill Nolan and Anne Gordon, anchored and stern-tied in beautiful Prideaux Haven.*

TABLE OF CONTENTS

4	Locator Maps
7	Messages from the Editors
8	Field Correspondents
9	About the Waggoner Cruising Guide
10	Culinary Destinations - 2020 Edition Theme
18	How to Cruise the Pacific Northwest
24	Floatplane Travel
26	U.S. and Canadian Customs Information
32	Boardings and Homeland Security
34	Interpreting Northwest Weather
40	Differences between U.S. and Canadian Charts
43	Buoys, Beacons, and Ranges
45	VHF Radio Procedures
48	State and Provincial Parks and Public Wharves
49	What Recreational Boaters Need to Know About VTS
52	Cellular, Internet and Satellite Communications
55	Smartphone Apps for Cruisers
57	Swimming Pools of the Inside Passage
58	About Anchoring
60	ELCI Shore Power
64	Chartering and Flotilla Cruising
66	Developing an Itinerary to Delight the Entire Crew
68	Provisioning
71	Potable Water
72	Fishing and Shellfish Collecting
74	Maintaining Your Boat Like A Pro
76	Boating from Inn to Inn
80	Whale Wise - Viewing Whales and Marine Mammals
88	Speed Limit and No Wake Zones
91	VHF Channels
92	Contact Phone Numbers - Conversion Tables

INDEXES

499	Index to Places, Parks, Marinas and Anchorages
510	Advertiser Index
511	Sidebar Features Indexes

CRUISING AREAS

94	South and Central Puget Sound	340	Johnstone Strait
138	Hood Canal	352	The Broughtons
145	North Puget Sound	375	North Vancouver Island
188	Strait of Juan de Fuca	387	West Coast of Vancouver Island
194	San Juan Islands	428	Rounding Cape Caution
225	Gulf Islands	431	Northern B.C. Coast
274	Strait of Georgia	477	Haida Gwaii
284	Vancouver, Mainland B.C. and the Sunshine Coast	487	Crossing Dixon Entrance
316	Desolation Sound and Discovery Passage	492	Arriving in Ketchikan

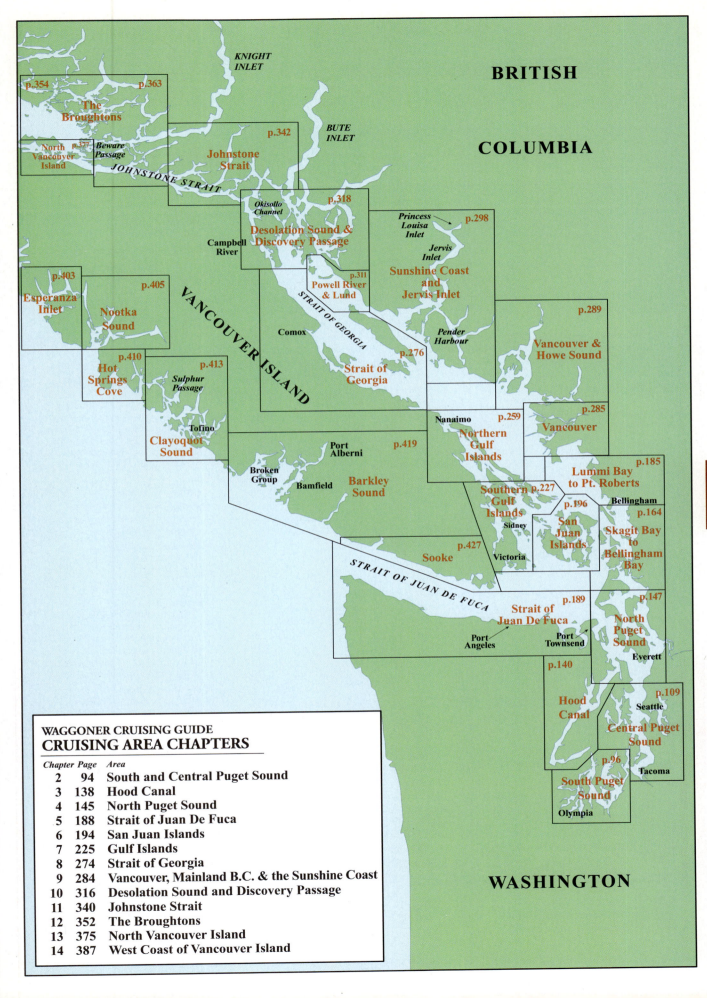

We want to hear from you!

Your comments, suggestions and corrections are invited. We appreciate hearing from anyone who finds errors in this publication.

We are interested in ideas about what you would like in future editions of the Waggoner Cruising Guide. There are a number of members of the Waggoner community who contribute to our website. Our readers are interested in your experiences and tips. We post cruising reports, pictures, video, updates about changes in specified areas, and tips that range from anchoring to restaurants to technical issues.

Contact us through our website www.WaggonerGuide.com, or by telephone, mail, or e-mail at WaggonerCruisingGuide@gmail.com.

CAUTION

This book was designed to provide experienced skippers with cruising information about the waters covered. While great effort has been taken to make the Waggoner Cruising Guide complete and accurate, it is possible that oversights, differences of interpretation, and factual errors will be found. Thus none of the information contained in the book is warranted to be accurate or appropriate for any specific need. Furthermore, variations in weather and sea conditions, a mariner's skills and experience, and the presence of luck (good or bad) can dictate a mariner's proper course of action.

The Waggoner Cruising Guide should be viewed as a reference only and not a substitute for official government charts, tide and current tables, coast pilots, sailing directions, and local notices to mariners. The Waggoner Cruising Guide assumes the user to be law-abiding and of good will. The suggestions offered are not all-inclusive, but are meant to help avoid unpleasantness or needless delay. Maps are not for navigation. Maps do not show all navigation marks, obstacles, hazards, and structures. Maps are for reference only.

The publisher, editors, and authors assume no liability for errors or omissions, or for any loss or damages incurred from using this publication.

Copyright © 2020 by Waggoner Media Group
Published by FineEdge.com

All rights reserved. Except for use in a review, no part of this book may be reproduced or utilized in any form or by any means, electronic or mechanical, including photocopying, recording, or by any information storage or retrieval system without written permission of the publisher.

Printed in the United States of America
Spiral Edition ISBN: 978-1-7341312-1-5

Library of Congress information available upon request.

Direct advertising inquiries to:
Waggoner Media Group
PO Box 726
Anacortes, WA 98221 USA
Phone (425) 780-5015
Fax (360) 299-0535
Email: WaggonerCruisingGuide@gmail.com
www.WaggonerGuide.com

Book Sales U.S.
Fine Edge Nautical Publishing
PO Box 726
Anacortes, WA 98221 USA
Phone (360) 299-8500
Fax (360) 299-0535
Email: orders@FineEdge.com
www.WaggonerGuideBooks.com

WAGGONER CRUISING GUIDE

Founding Editor
Robert Hale

Editor/Publisher
Mark Bunzel

Managing Editors
Lorena Landon
Leonard Landon

Associate Publisher
Karla Locke

Art Director & Production
Sara White

Advertising Production
Melanie Haage, Karla Locke,
Tony Locke, Sara White

Field Correspondents
Mary Campbell, Melissa Gervais, Deane & Arlene Hislop, Dan & Karin Leach, Jim Norris & Anita Fraser, Bob & Shino Posey, John Shepard

Correspondents/Contributors
Bruce & Margaret Evertz, Gil & Karen Flanagan, Gill Graham, Robert & Marilynn Hale, Jennifer & James Hamilton, Steve & Elsie Hulsizer, Tom Kincaid, John & Lorraine Littlewood, Kevin Monahan, Duart Snow, Rob & Jean Warner, Whale Wise

Office
Marie Wagner

Proofreading
Mary Campbell, Lara Dunning, Brett Oemichen

Reference Maps
Melanie Haage, Leonard Landon

eBooks
Tony Locke, Nettie Adams

Photography
Mike Beemer, Danielle Fellin Bernardo, Peter Brown, Mark Bunzel, Mary Campbell, Deane Hislop, Lorena Landon, Dale Miller, Jim Niehaus, Jim Norris, Don Odegard, Brett & Sue Oemichen, Jim Redmond, Sara White

Government Data
BC Parks, BC Parks Forever Society, Canada Customs, US Customs, First Nations, National Weather Service, WA Dept. of Fish & Wildlife, WA Parks, WA Dept. of Ecology

Book Sales Canada
Chyna Sea Ventures, Ltd.
Unit 4, 147 E. Fern Rd.
Qualicum Beach, BC, V9K 1T2
Phone: (250) 740-1184
Fax: (250) 740-1185
Toll Free: 866-627-8324
Email: orders@ChynaSea.com
www.ChynaSea.com

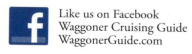
Like us on Facebook
Waggoner Cruising Guide
WaggonerGuide.com

Twitter
@TheWaggoner

Hungry For Boating Experiences

This year we are celebrating the culinary experience. Food is a big part of our boating experience in the Northwest and on the Inside Passage. We have excellent choices and options from world-class gourmet restaurants, incredible farmer's markets, and wonderful bakeries. Opportunities to catch and prepare fresh salmon and halibut, as well as prawns and Dungeness crab, abound in the Pacific Northwest waters. The Inside Passage has seen an increase in wineries, breweries, cideries, and now distilleries, along with coffee roasters proud of their special blends. With our 2020 culinary edition, we encourage you to further explore the many incredible food destinations during your travels.

We expect to see more boats out on the water in 2020. We estimate that one boatbuilder, producing the Ranger Tug and Cutwater boats, has launched and sold over 1200 boats in the last 5 years alone. We have already seen the impact of more boats on the water. Making reservations during the peak season is now routine practice. Don't forget to reserve your table at restaurants too. This Waggoner Cruising Guide will make it easier to plan your itinerary for a fun-filled season of activities and adventure.

Our goal is to be "*The Most Trusted Source for Northwest Boating Information*." We continue to expand this trusted boater's guidebook with helpful information; this 2020 record breaking edition has 512 pages. The Waggoner is now available online in eBook form. Our online articles at Waggoner eNews enable boaters to read about the latest information; you can sign up for eNews on our website. We just started our new podcast series called Waggoner Currents. You can now listen to valuable boating information from your Waggoner Experts in your car, or at home. Last year, over 1200 seats were sold for our Waggoner Seminars and the number will double in 2020. Our local area boaters are hungry for information and training. And our flotillas continue to be in high demand; watch for more about flotilla opportunities and planned rendezvous. We look forward to seeing you out on the water

Mark Bunzel, Editor & Publisher

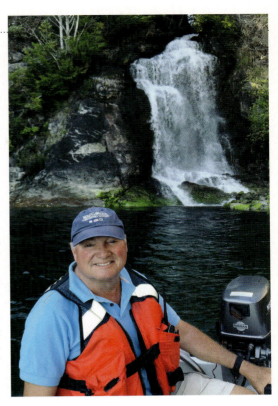

What's New in the 2020 Waggoner Cruising Guide?

Each year we are often asked the question – "What's new and exciting?" And each year we are happy to provide the same answer, "much has changed, and important information for boaters has been added to the Waggoner." This year is no exception. Our good economy and brisk boat sales have put marinas on the fast-track for providing new docks, new services, and upgrades to their facilities. You'll find many changes at marinas documented in the 2020 Waggoner edition. The Waggoner Team spends the summer out on the water each year, checking marinas first-hand, and searching for new destinations to include in the Waggoner Cruising Guide.

Hiking the many trails found throughout the islands of the Pacific Northwest is a favorite pastime among boaters. We have included many of these hiking trails on our new reference maps. We have also revealed some lesser-known beach access areas that offer trails with spectacular views from the above mountaintops. As always, you'll find updated information throughout every chapter of the 2020 Waggoner Cruising Guide, highlighting marinas, anchorages, trails, and helpful information for transiting challenging passages and rapids.

Waggoner Reference Maps and Dock Diagrams continue to receive positive feedback from our readers. Many of the reference maps have been enhanced and 12 new reference maps have been added to this year's edition. Boaters find these maps invaluable, with detail for boaters that can't be found elsewhere. Dock diagrams allow boaters to more easily find their slip assignment, and reference maps help boaters plan their itinerary, while noting important speed zone areas and restricted areas. Weather Maps have been enhanced to clearly delineate weather forecast areas as heard on the VHF weather channel

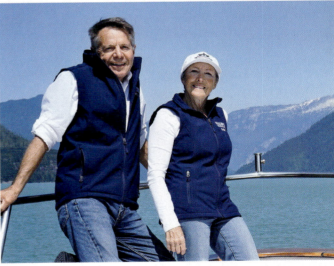

2020 Edition Theme. There's something special about arriving for dinner by boat, or preparing fresh caught salmon over a barbeque, or enjoying a special culinary event with other boaters. Some of the most unique dining experiences can be found among the islands of the Pacific Northwest, where farm-to-table food is the norm. During the summer cruising season, Managing Editors Lorena and Leonard Landon, and Editor/Publisher Mark Bunzel, searched out some favorite eateries accessible by boat, plus made some new discoveries. Yes, *Culinary Destinations* is our chosen theme for 2020. While there are many dining choices available to boaters, we have shared some of those special venues that stand out as unique experiences. You'll find 18 food-theme related sidebars scattered throughout the 2020 Waggoner Guide. Don't miss our list of favorite Bakeries and Farmers Markets in Chapter 1, where you will also find two excellent recipes from the Waggoner recipe contest. Chapter 1 is the best resource for "How to Cruise the Pacific Northwest," and contains the latest information regarding radio communications, clearing customs, weather resources, and much more.

Lorena & Leonard Landon, Managing Editors

Meet our Field Correspondents

Mary Campbell came late to boating but has been making up for lost time. For the last 25 years, she has been sailing the Inside Passage, originally in her Colvin junk schooner and, for the last 10 years, in her Cascade 36. Retired, she spends each summer on the boat. Her travels have taken her through Southeast Alaska, across the Gulf of Alaska to Seward and the Katmai region; she has circumnavigated Vancouver Island and been captivated by the native villages of Haida Gwaii. She's also sailed in warmer climates, including the Sea of Cortez, the Pacific Coast of Mexico, Australia's north and east coasts, and parts of Indonesia. Still, her favorite cruising destinations are Prince William Sound and Haida Gwaii. Their pristine beauty and rugged coastlines present a last frontier of coastal cruising. Mary appreciates the challenge of cruising where the sight of another boat is a welcome surprise, and where the wildlife outnumbers the humans.

Melissa (Missy) Gervais has been boating for 20 years and is a member of the Royal Vancouver Yacht Club. She enjoys anchoring out in B.C.'s beautiful marine parks and taking photos of the many special, scenic destinations found in British Columbia. Her dog, Jonathan, is a companion aboard her 34-foot power boat, *As You Wish*. Melissa enjoys cruising the Gulf Islands and Sunshine Coast during vacation time from her active career with Pacific Yacht Systems. Melissa, who often goes by Missy, hosts a blog site which includes marine products, a photo gallery, and an events calendar geared to women boaters — missygoesboating.com. She also writes articles for Northwest Yachting Magazine.

Deane and Arlene Hislop call Anacortes their home. Between the two of them, they have over 75 years of Pacific Northwest boating experience, with the last 24 years cruising together. They enjoy visiting the many marinas and secluded coves that dot the inland waters of the Pacific Northwest. Deane and Arlene can be found cruising year-round between Olympia and northern Vancouver Island, spending more than 100 nights a year aboard their 381 Meridian, *Easy Goin'*. They enjoy meeting other boaters, exploring new locations, sampling local cuisine and collecting information, experiences and images for boating publications. Deane is a freelance writer and photographer specializing in recreational boating. His work has appeared in regional, national and international publications. Deane's images have also been featured in advertisements, websites and on magazine covers.

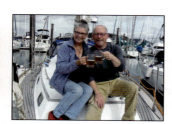

Dan and Karin Leach are retired and live aboard their Passport 40 in Anacortes. Dan started sailing when he was a kid. His high school graduation gift from his dad was a 15 foot sailboat and a copy of Joshua Slocom's *Sailing Alone Around the World*. Karin started sailing in 2004 when Dan said, "Hey, we should get back into sailing…only on bigger boats." She took lessons so that if he got hit by the boom, she could at least get back home. They've been cruising the waters between Washington and Alaska ever since. Karin is still perfecting her small oven bread recipes. Dan just wants to keep everything on the boat in working order and keep Karin happy. According to Dan, "Girls stay if the heater and the head work." Dan and Karin cruise the NW waters from spring to fall and land cruise in their RV from fall to spring.

Anita Fraser and Jim Norris have been boating nearly their entire lives, having been engaged in commercial fishing, marine research, and more recently as active recreational boaters. They are Great Loop veterans, completing "The Loop" in 2008 on a 32-foot Grand Banks. Since 2010 they have cruised extensively between their home port of Port Townsend and Glacier Bay, Alaska on their 42-foot Krogen, *Spirit Quest*. Their northern trips have included the west side of Vancouver Island and Haida Gwaii. They have also cruised as far south as San Diego, spending a winter in Oxnard, California. Each year they explore their favorite destinations and personal secret places in Northern B.C. and Southeast Alaska.

Bob and Shino Posey owned a PT 38 Trawler for many years in which they explored the Pacific Northwest and BC's lower mainland. Bob started boating with runabouts in the 60's. They currently own a 24-foot Sea Sport Explorer, based in Anacortes, which provides flexibility in planning a variety of cruising destinations. They spend most summers cruising the San Juan and Gulf Islands and enjoyed a recent trip to Chatterbox Falls in Princess Louisa Inlet. During the 2018 boating season, Bob and Shino trailered their boat to Prince Rupert BC and cruised the Inside Passage to Southeast Alaska where they rendezvoused with family members near the southern tip of Baranof Island.

John Shepard started sailing, racing, and instructing as a teenager in San Diego. As a Naval junior, John had free use of boats that provided recreational opportunities for servicemen, and he took full advantage sailing and racing in the waters of Southern California. John first started cruising the Pacific Northwest with a trailerable boat, exploring rivers, lakes and bays. Inspired by reading Jonathan Raban's book, *Passage to Juneau*, John purchased a Cal 35 Cruiser sloop, named *Hadley*. John undertook refurbishing s/v *Hadley*, making extensive repairs and refits. In 2017, with projects nearly complete, a fast-moving boat appeared out of the fog near Double Bluff on Whidbey Island and clipped his starboard stern. Thankfully the stern quarter and transom were mostly fiberglass repairs; a quick maneuver had helped avoid a more serious collision. Happily, *Hadley* was repaired over the winter and was ready in 2018 to once again weave through island passages in all sorts of weather and cross the straits that make up our water playground of the Pacific Northwest.

LEGEND

	Lateral Buoys (R/G) No Light		Structures		Trail
	Mid-Channel Buoys				Road
	Lateral Lights (R/G)		Land		Boundary lines
	Lateral Buoys (R/G) Lighted		Water		Railroad
	Non-Lateral Lights (W/Y)		Shallow water		Curvilinear Route
	Non-Lateral Buoys Lighted		Tidal area dries at chart datum (zero tide)	①	Key to Text
	Non-Lateral Buoys No Light		Restricted Area - No entry or limited operation area	⚓	Anchorage
	Mooring Buoy	No Anchoring Zone	Warning text		Lighthouse
	Lateral Daymark Beacon Lighted		Special use area as described with each instance		Dock/float
	Range Markers	NO WAKE / 5 KNOTS	Speed Limit		Linear Moorage
Beacon - shape and color as indicated		+++	Rock awash at chart datum	✖	Stern-tie anchor pins
		✱ ✱ ✱	Rock which covers and uncovers	Even # Slips / Odd # Slips	Even/Odd Slip Number Direction Indicator

ABOUT THE WAGGONER CRUISING GUIDE

Waggoner Guide (pronounced [wagənər] not [wagənir]) has been guiding boaters to the spectacular Northwest destinations since 1994. It provides the reader with information about marinas, anchorages, passages, and attractions from Olympia, Washington to Ketchikan, Alaska. It is referred to by boaters as *The bible for northwest cruising*. This all-inclusive guidebook is updated annually.

Waggoner Guide strives to be the most up-to-date cruising guidebook with the most accurate information. The writing style is intended to be as concise, factual, and informative as possible.

How the book is organized. The first section of the book, referred to as 'Front Matter,' contains valuable information that helps boaters plan and execute a successful trip. This Chapter 1, Front Matter has instructional material regarding customs, weather, anchoring, communications and other pertinent how-to information.

The body of the book is divided into chapters by geographic cruising area, starting in the south at Olympia, Washington and progressing north to Ketchikan, Alaska. Keeping with the south to north organization, material within each chapter generally progresses northward. Each chapter begins with an overview of the area followed by detailed information for each marina along with passages and designated anchorages. Ports, harbors, and cities with multiple boating facilities also begin with an overview description to help the reader become familiar with the area.

Reference maps for the chapter's coverage area are located at the beginning of the chapter with additional reference maps found throughout the chapter. A Legend of symbols used on Waggoner Guide reference maps can be found in this section. Area reference maps indicate destinations with numbers, which correspond to the numbered text for marinas and significant anchorages. Reference maps are not for navigation and do not show all navigation aids, beacons, marks, lights, and hazards. Maps are not to scale and are for reference purposes only. Boaters should carry up-to-date electronic charts and/or paper charts.

You will also find 'Local Knowledge' and 'Sidebars' within many of the chapters. Local Knowledge provides helpful tips and warnings regarding shoals, rocks, tides and current for specific locations, which may not be depicted on navigational charts. Short articles, called Sidebars, relate personal experiences that are informative and helpful to the reader. Sidebars also provide historical background for a number of destinations, enlightening the imagination and purpose of why we go there in the first place.

The Year's Theme. Some of the Sidebars in the Waggoner Guide focus on a chosen theme for the year. *The Culinary Experience* was chosen as this year's theme. Boaters can find some excellent restaurants among the islands of the Pacific Northwest, where fresh farm-to-table foods are the norm. Nestled in coves and forested areas, these dining venues offer a special experience. This year's edition includes 15 food related sidebars that are unique to the boating lifestyle. In this chapter, you will also find a list of favorite "Bakeries of the Inside Passage," and two contest winner recipes.

How the Book is Made. The Waggoner Guide Team of Northwest boaters, cruise Northwest waters and the Inside Passage to Alaska each year, gathering updates for marinas, anchorages, and passages found in the Waggoner Guide. The Waggoner Team, along with experienced Field Correspondents and knowledgeable contributors, provide the many hundreds of updates included in each year's edition of the Waggoner Cruising Guide. While it is not possible to physically go to every anchorage or marina each year, every effort is made to get the latest information directly from marinas by phone or other means. Editorial work begins in September to incorporate these changes and updates, including new reference maps and photos. Editors, proof readers, and designers of maps, ads, and page layout spend untold hours preparing copy for final proofs, while meeting our print deadline. The much-anticipated announcement of the current edition of the Waggoner Guide is provided in our 'eNews.' Copies of the Waggoner Cruising Guide are made available at the Seattle Boat Show, where boaters enthusiastically purchase the new edition and begin making plans for their next adventure. Copies are also available at retailers throughout Washington, B.C., and Alaska and at the Anacortes Waggoner Book Store.

How to send us Comments and Feedback. The Waggoner Team invites your comments, suggestions and corrections. We appreciate hearing from our readers regarding ways we can improve our publication. Your ideas for future editions are always welcome along with your experiences and tips, which inform and help other boaters. Contact us through our website, www.WaggonerGuide.com, or by telephone (360) 299-8500; you can also find us on Facebook.

WaggonerGuide.com and eNews. At WaggonerGuide.com, we have a dedicated team of experienced boaters and travel experts who share a variety of articles each month about boating in Washington, British Columbia, and Southeast Alaska. Some of the topics include maintenance tips, cruising destinations, boat reviews, and on-the-water reporting. You'll also find boating seminar announcements, guidebook updates, access to free downloads, and our collection of boating and nautical-themed books in the Waggoner Store.

A great way to stay tuned into WaggonerGuide.com is to subscribe to Waggoner eNews. This newsletter is sent out twice a month and contains our latest boating related articles. It also gives you access to our eNews subscriber-only downloads. All of our content is geared toward you, our reader, who lives and breathes boating in the Pacific Northwest

To enroll in Waggoner eNews, visit WaggonerGuide.com. You'll find the subscribe button on the right column. Or, visit our Facebook page at https://www.facebook.com/WaggonerCruisingGuide and in the left-hand column, you'll find the Subscribe to eNews tab.

Advertisers. Advertising helps provide the best cruising information at the best price to you the cruising public; advertisements often provide more extensive information about the facility that is not part of the mission of the Waggoner Guide. Advertising helps us keep in touch with the marinas and service providers, who provide information about what is coming for the next cruising season. This symbiotic relationship helps the Waggoner Team stay in communication with the Marine Trade Industry and provide guidance regarding cruisers' needs. Combined ads, called Community Market Place, inform our readers of local events, farmers' markets, and other local points of interest.

eBooks. Waggoner Cruising Guide is available in a seven volume eBook series from Amazon. Volume 1 of the series is Chapter 1 of the guidebook, which includes how to go cruising topics. Volumes 2 through 7 cover the cruising area from Olympia, WA to Ketchikan, AK and are organized by common cruising areas. You can purchase Volume 1, along with one or more of the cruising area volumes where you plan to cruise. See WaggonerGuideBooks.com for more information.

2020 WAGGONER CRUISING GUIDE

CULINARY DESTINATIONS

We have come a long way since the days of hardtack and limes when it comes to eating aboard, while out at sea. This 2020 edition of the Waggoner Cruising Guide explores the world of food in the realm of boating, from fine dining and dockside cafes, to contest winning recipes, sea harvested ingredients, and sea-aged rum. This year's theme sidebar articles include some of the most memorable food related boating experiences. Needless to say, research for this theme proved to be some of the most enjoyable.

"The Culinary Experience," this year's Waggoner Cruising Guide theme, explores the world of eating pleasures for the boating enthusiast. Food related sidebar articles are found throughout the 2020 Waggoner edition. Shown below are six thumbnail images of the 15 Theme Sidebars throughout the guidebook; look for the distinctive cedar-board background to discover these theme sidebars, or see the Theme Sidebar Index in the back of the guide.

While there are many culinary options for boaters, we have included some of the

Ajax Cafe

Ajax Cafe reopened in early 2019 after being closed for several years for needed repairs to the historic 1800's Samual Hadlock home. The Cafe picked up where it left off, with great food and good times, it's a testament to the quality and patronage found at Ajax Cafe. Boaters will find anchorage and a day-use dock in front of the Cafe. Hats on the Cafe walls are for guests to wear; it's all part of the fun at Ajax.

Westcott Bay Oyster Farm

The Westcott Bay Oyster Farm offers a one-of-a-kind experience. Visitors can purchase fresh mussels, clams, and oysters directly from the Farm. Farm personnel can even show you how to shuck and slurp; or if you prefer, they can barbecue your order of fresh shellfish. Picnic tables overlook the bay and oyster beds. Boaters can anchor in Westcott Bay or Garrison Bay, and arrive by dinghy at the Farm's designated dinghy guest dock.

Woodstone Manor

Cruising the islands instills a casual air and relaxed feel, without having to give up elegant charm. There are numerous first-class dining venues found throughout the islands of the Pacific Northwest. Woodstone Manor is one of the latest fine-dining destinations. The Inn will pick guests up at Montague Harbour, providing boaters the opportunity to enjoy some incredible cuisine at a beautiful manor house overlooking the countryside.

more unique opportunities and culinary experiences. Bakeries are a favorite stop for boaters, too; don't miss the best "Bakeries of the Inside Passage" listed in Chapter 1, along with recipes from our recipe contest.

Of course, seafood is ever present when boating the Inside Passage. Salmon is an all-time favorite, and you would be hard-pressed not to find a grill aboard a pleasure boat. Eventually, everything finds its way onto the grill, meats and seafood are the most obvious; but we have seen potatoes, tomatoes, zucchini squash, peppers, and carrots; just about everything except peas (they tend to fall through the grate). We've even seen cinnamon buns warmed on the grill in the morning; it seems that everything tastes better when grilled.

Food and boating, what a great combination! Our appetites always seem to be bigger after a day on the water. We don't know if it's the fresh breeze or warm sun. Tending lines and sails certainly works up that end of the day appetite. Exploring the island trails, likewise, encourages the appetite. Refreshing drinks are a great way to get things going for a nice barbecue, or dinner out.

Bon Appétit!

A HISTORY OF THE WAGGONER

About 1584 the Dutch pilot Lucas Janszoon Waghenaer published a volume of navigational principles, tables, charts, and sailing directions, which served as a guide for other such books for the next 200 years.

These "*Waggoners*," as they came to be known, met with great success, and in 1588 an English translation of the original book was made. During the next 30 years, 24 editions of the book were published in Dutch, German, Latin, and English. Other authors followed the profitable example set by Waghenaer. Soon, American, British, and French navigators had Waggoners for most of the waters they sailed.

The success of these books and the resulting competition led to their eventual demise. In 1795 the British Hydrographic Department was established, and charts and sailing directions were issued.

We hope you find this new Waggoner to be as useful as the Waggoners of old. *Waggoner* is an ancient name with a proud history. Use and enjoy.

OUR MISSION

The Waggoner mission is to provide essential boating information for Northwest waters in an easy-to-use format. Through printed publications, digital media, and instructional materials, Waggoner endeavors to empower the boating public to discover the rewards of cruising these waters. We encourage all boaters to explore the beautiful waterways of the Pacific Northwest. Waggoner strives to be the go-to source of boating information for cruising the Northwest and Inside Passage.

SERVE THE READER

Although its coverage was limited initially, this book had one quality boaters seemed to recognize: it was written for them. The book contained factual, unbiased information about Pacific Northwest cruising and marine facilities, and it was easy to read and use.

The first Waggoner Cruising Guide laid the groundwork for each succeeding annual edition. Today, the guide has grown in size and coverage area (now Olympia, WA to Ketchikan, AK), with the addition of many timely articles, tips and stories. It's beginning philosophy of "serve the reader" has continued over the years and it shows on every page.

  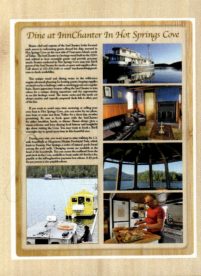

Laughing Oyster

Word has it that the long-time favorite Laughing Oyster establishment is for sale; but not to worry, the owner/chef is committed to finding the right person to carry on the traditions and excellent seafood dishes at the Laughing Oyster Restaurant. Guests can sit outside on the large deck or inside, where you'll find an atmosphere of relaxed elegance. Intimate dinner menus and scheduled special buffet dinners, with live music, continue to be popular at this restaurant perched above the Okeover Harbour Authority docks.

Cluxewe

Cluxewe is a real find, nestled above a beach along the shores of Broughton Strait, north of Port McNeill. Boaters can anchor their dinghy off the beach; or arrive by courtesy van or taxi via the back-country roads. After a great meal, stroll the beach and enjoy the sunset; watch the eagles soar. Chef Pankratz creates beautifully prepared braised meats, lamb, and seafood dishes with style, using seasonal flowers and herbs. Guests are treated to the full experience at Cluxewe.

InnChanter

If you are anchored at Hot Springs Cove, on the west side of Vancouver Island, chances are the heritage vessel InnChanter is anchored there too. Shaun, the captain and chef, treats his B&B overnight guests with tasty, creative meals; fresh fish is often part of the fare. Boaters can join other guests aboard this 1920's refitted vessel for breakfast, lunch, or dinner, with advanced reservations. Shaun always gives a warm welcome and loves sharing local history. A guest dinghy dock is available at the InnChanter.

Bakeries of the Inside Passage

SLUYS POULSBO BAKERY
18924 Front St. NE, Poulsbo, WA
360-779-2798 www.sluyspoulsbobakery.com
The big window, displaying freshly baked goods, combines the visual appeal with the sweet smells to draw you into the shop. Cakes, pies, cinnamon rolls, tarts, cookies, and breads are among the tasty treats from which to choose. Everything is hand-made in this family owned and run bakery.

HOLLY B'S BAKERY
211 Lopez Rd., Lopez Island, WA
360-622-8133 www.hollybsbakery.com
This local community bakery uses locally grown and milled flour from Skagit Valley to create their delicious butterhorns, croissants, cinnamon rolls, cookies and breads. Days and hours of operation vary, so call ahead.

BAKERY SAN JUAN
775 Mullis St, Friday Harbor, WA
360-378-5810 www.bakerysanjuan.com
This place has it all, everything from cakes, cookies, fresh pastries, to breads and pizzas. Make it a full meal here with their deli sandwiches, specialty beers, and wine.

ROSES BAKERY & CAFE
382 Prune Aly, Eastsound, Orcas Island, WA
360-376-4292 www.rosesbakerycafe.com
Artisan crusty breads are one of their specialties, along with tasty sweet baked goods. Pair one of their breads with a variety of cheeses or deli meats to make a perfect lunch. They also have fine wines.

SIDNEY BAKERY
2507 Beacon Ave, Sidney, BC
250-656-1012 www.sidneybakery.com
A must stop when visiting Sidney, this family-run bakery has been in operation for 108 years, serving a wonderful selection of sweet treats and breads. Pies, cakes, pastries, donuts, and buns.

TRUE GRAIN BREAD
1725 Cowichan Bay Rd., Cowichan, BC
250-746-7664 www.truegrain.ca
Their wide selection of breads are made from BC grown and milled grain. Their croissants are excellent and their cookies are some of the best.

CHEMAINUS BAKERY
2875 Oak Street, Chemainus, BC
250-246-4321 www.facebook.com
The display cases are filled with delicious pastries, croissants, cookies, cheese cake, and much more. A wall is filled with a variety of different breads, including baguettes.

EMBE BAKERY
174 Fulford-Ganges Rd., Ganges, BC
250-537-5611 www.facebook.com/embebakery/
Much more than a bakery, Embe's has delicious deli items. The bakery is a great place to shop for breads, pies, cakes, muffins, donuts, and cinnamon rolls. Be sure to check out their quiche and meat pies.

VANILLA LEAF BAKERY
4605 Bedwell Harbour Rd., Pender Island, BC
250-629-6453 www.vanillaleafbakery.com
Buy the whole loaf or get one of their sandwiches made with their breads in this Bakery & Café, located a half-mile from Port Browning Marina, in the Driftwood Shopping Centre. Sweets include pastries, muffins, cookies, seasonal specialties, and much more.

OLD TOWN BAKERY
510 1st Avenue, Ladysmith, BC
250-245-2531 www.oldtownbakery.ca
This is the place to go for cinnamon buns. They have one of the widest selections of different cinnamon buns; combinations with nuts, fruits, and flavors. Watch them prepare fresh pies, cakes, cookies, and Cornish pasties. This is a busy bakery.

RED'S BAKERY
1010 Commercial St., Nanaimo, BC
250-755-6533 www.facebook.com/RedsBakeryNanaimo/
Come here to be tempted by their many different dessert items. Pies, cakes, dessert bars (of course Nanaimo Bars), tarts, and cookies, will test your willpower.

CHURCH STREET BAKERY
221 A Church Street, Comox, BC
250-890-2300 www.churchstreetbakery.ca
Their wood fired brick oven is the hub of this local bakery that uses local sources for their wonderful baked goods. Sourdough breads are one of their specialties. Sweet treats include muffins, scones, croissants, caramel sticky buns, and more. Ask about their tapas night and pizza menu. Seating is available indoor and outdoor. There's a rush in the mornings for baked goods.

NANCY'S BAKERY
1451 Hwy 101, Lund, BC
604-483-4180 www.facebook.com
If cinnamon rolls are your thing, then this is a must-stop bakery. They have a great selection of different types of cinnamon rolls; just don't expect to find the "mini" variety, these are meal size. Their specialty breads are excellent..

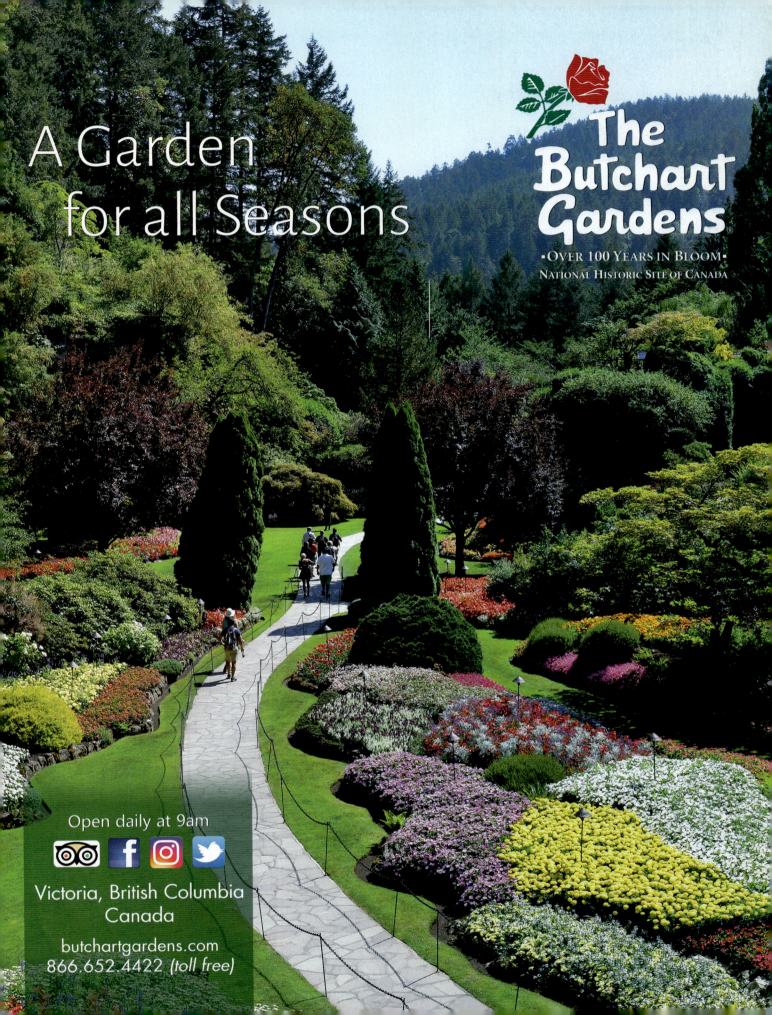

Farmers Markets
Olympia, WA to Campbell River, BC

The Olympia Farmers Market
Thursday-Sunday; 10 am – 3 pm
Days & Hours vary in shoulder season
Percival Landing & Swantown Marina

Gig Harbor Waterfront Farmers Market
Thursdays; 3 pm – 7 pm
June 1 – August 31
Skansie Brothers Park near Arabella's

Tacoma's Broadway Farmers Market
Thursdays; 10 am – 3 pm
May – August
Days & Hrs. vary in shoulder season

Des Moines Farmers Market
Saturdays; 10 am – 2 pm
June – September
Des Moines Marina waterfront

Seattle's Pike Place Market
Open daily; 9 am – 6 pm
Sundays; until 5 pm
85 Pike Street

Bremerton Farmers Market
Thursdays; 4 pm – 7 pm
May to mid-October
Evergreen-Rotary Park

Port Orchard Farmers Market
Saturdays; 9 am – 2 pm
mid-April to mid-October
Port Orchard Waterfront Park

Poulsbo Farmers Market
Saturdays; 9 am – 2 pm
April-October and
Nov. - Dec. 10 am – 2 pm
18901 8th Ave NE

Kingston Farmers Market
Saturdays; 9 am – 2 pm
mid-May to late-November
every other Sat. in shoulder season
Old Dutch Church; 272 Wall St

Everett Farmers Market
Sundays; 11 am – 4 pm
mid-May to mid-October
Hewitt & Wetmore Avenues

Coupeville Farmers Market
Saturdays; 10 am – 2 pm
April – October
Community Green, NW Alexander

Anacortes Farmers Market
Saturdays; 9 am – 2 pm
May-October
Days & Hrs. vary in shoulder season
Depot Arts Center, 7th St & R Ave

Port Angeles Farmers Market
Saturdays year-round; 10 am – 2pm
Front & Lincoln Streets

Bellingham Farmers Market
Saturdays; 10 am – 3 pm
April – December
Days & Hrs. vary in shoulder season
Depot Square, 1100 Railroad Ave

Lopez Island Farmers Market
Saturdays; 10 am – 2 pm
mid-May to mid-September
Village Road in town

Orcas Island Farmers Market
Saturdays; 10 am – 3 pm
May – August

Eastsound Village Green
San Juan Island Farmers Market
Saturdays; 9:30 am – 1 pm
mid-April to mid-October
Days & Hrs. vary in shoulder season
Friday Harbor, 150 Nichols Street

Victoria Public Market
Open Daily; 10 am – 6 pm
Sundays until 5 pm
1701 Douglas Street

Sidney Street Market
Thursdays; 5:30 pm – 8:30 pm
June – August
Beacon Av (mostly crafts)

Salt Spring Island Market
Saturdays; 9 am – 4 pm
April – October
Ganges, Centennial Park

Chemainus Wednesday Market
Wednesdays; 10 am – 3 pm
late May to mid-September
Waterwheel Park

Silva Bay Market
Sundays; 10 am – 2 pm
July – August
Gabriola Is., 3415 S. Rd.

Lasqueti Island Market
Saturdays; 10 am – 1 pm
mid-June through August
Legion Grounds, False Bay

Nanaimo Farmers' Market
Saturdays; 9 am – 2 pm
May – September
Pioneer Plaza, waterfront

Comox Valley Farmers' Market
Saturdays; 9 am – 1 pm
Valley Exhibition Grounds
Native Sons Hall in shoulder season

Pier Street Farmers Market
Sundays; 10 am – 2:30 pm
May – August
Campbell River, Pier Street

RADAR REDEFINED
Solid-State Doppler Tracking
It's The NXT Generation

It's the comfort of knowing you are safe. It's Doppler Radar echoes changing color, showing which targets are a threat to you. It's instant tracking of up to 100 moving targets. It's Furuno's Bird Mode tracking birds to find the best fishing grounds. It's the all-new NXT Solid-State Doppler Radar for NavNet TZ-touch & TZtouch2.

Target Analyzer™ function, facilitated by Doppler technology, immediately alerts you to targets (displayed in red) that pose a threat to your vessel.

RezBoost™ beam sharpening displays higher resolution targets, similar to those from a large open array antenna.

DRS4D-NXT and DRS6A-NXT
Solid-State Doppler Radars

Experience The NXT Radar at Youtube.com/FurunoVideo

EMERALD HARBOR MARINE
VESSEL SYSTEMS & SERVICES

2601 W. Marina Place, Suite T
Seattle WA 98199

Phone (206) 285-3632
www.emharbor.com
info@emharbor.com
www.FurunoUSA.com

Theme Recipe Grand Prize Winner

Spicy Mint Lamb Balls with Tomato Sauce

1 medium onion, diced
¼ cup cream
1 egg yolk
1 teaspoon ground cumin
½ teaspoon ground cinnamon
½ teaspoon red pepper flakes
½ cup panko crumbs
½ cup each of chopped mint and basil, with additional for sauce and garnish
salt and pepper
1 lb. ground lamb

Mix all ingredients except the lamb. Gently combine in the lamb with your hands. Form into 12 golf ball sized meatballs. Refrigerate while preparing the tomato sauce.

Tomato Sauce
1 medium onion, diced
4 tablespoons olive oil, divided
1 teaspoon ground cumin
½ teaspoon red pepper flakes
2 cloves garlic, chopped
1 28 oz. can of crushed tomatoes
½ cup red wine
salt and pepper

Sauté onion in 2 tablespoons of olive oil over medium heat until translucent, then add the spices and cook until fragrant. Add the garlic and cook for about one minute. Add the diced tomatoes and red wine, turn heat to low and let sauce simmer for 10 minutes or so while cooking the meatballs.

Heat remaining 2 tablespoons of olive oil in a large skillet over medium heat. When the oil starts to shimmer place the meatballs in the pan so that they are not touching. Cook without stirring for approximately five minutes until browned then flip and cook for another five minutes on the second side.

Add a handful of the reserved chopped mint and basil into the tomato sauce, stir and pour over the meatballs in the skillet. Simmer over low heat for approximately 10 minutes. Spoon over your favorite pasta or rice and garnish with remaining chopped mint and basil. Bon appétit!

Janet McKinnon
Seattle, WA

Theme Recipe First Prize Winner

Potato Bowl with Black Bean Sauté

Potato bowls take the best aspects of stuffed baked potatoes and make them an easy cruising meal. A hot water bath minimizes propane usage and lets you take a short paddle or shore walk while the potatoes "cook." They're also endlessly variable, with the use of different vegetables. The recipe includes some of my favorite ingredients. You can also prep for two meals at one time by boiling twice the number of potatoes and using half the next day for a breakfast egg-skillet, or a lunchtime potato salad.

    2–3 large potatoes, unpeeled, cut in 1-inch cubes
    1 tablespoon extra-virgin olive oil
    1/4 onion, diced
    1/2 bell pepper, diced
    4–6 mushrooms, diced or sliced
    1/2 15-ounce can black beans, drained
    1/2 teaspoon ground cumin
    1/2 teaspoon ground coriander
    salt and freshly ground pepper to taste
    1/4 cup sharp cheddar cheese, grated
    1/4 cup prepared salsa
    1/4 cup sour cream
    2 tablespoons fresh cilantro, chopped

Add the cubed potatoes to a large saucepan and fill it with water, covering the potatoes by at least 1/2 inch. Cover and bring to a boil over high heat, skimming off any foam that forms just before it comes to a boil. Once the water has boiled, remove the covered pot from the heat, wrap the pot in towels. Let the potatoes sit for 1 hour; check for doneness and drain. If they are not tender, replace the lid on the pot and let the potatoes sit until the water cools to lukewarm before draining.

Heat the oil in a skillet over medium heat. Add the onion and sauté for about 5 minutes until soft. Add the pepper, continue cooking another 2–3 minutes, and then add the mushrooms; sauté another 1–2 minutes until they start to soften. Stir in the beans and spices, and then add the potato cubes; cook, stirring for about 5 minutes, until warmed through. Divide into bowls. Top each serving with a handful of cheese, a couple spoon scoops of salsa, a dollop of sour cream, and a sprinkle of cilantro. Serves 2.

We make our own Grilled Tomato Chipotle Salsa while on land and always pack some for our cruising trip. Any prepared salsa can be substituted, or make a quick fresh salsa using 2 cloves minced garlic, 1/2 minced jalapeño, 1 diced medium tomato, and a splash of lime juice.

    Julie Laing
    Bigfork, Montana

How to Cruise the Pacific Northwest

Inside Passage. The Inside Passage is one of the best cruising grounds in the world. The distance from Olympia, Washington to Ketchikan, Alaska is about 600 miles as the crow flies. On a boat, meandering through fjords and between islands, the distance multiplies. Most of these waters are protected; open water passages are relatively short, and anchorages are plentiful.

Wildlife is outstanding. Whales—orcas, humpbacks, grays, and more—are regularly spotted. Bald eagles are everywhere. Bears snatch salmon from seaside rivers or forage on the beach. Porpoises, seals, sea lions, sea otters, and myriad other life call the Inside Passage home.

Natural beauty overwhelms. The great volcanoes of the Cascade mountains are visible throughout Puget Sound and the San Juan Islands. Sandstone in the Gulf Islands, eroded by wind and water, forms fascinating patterns and shapes. Magnificent, glacier carved fjords run deep into British Columbia's interior. Waterfalls plunge thousands of feet from snow-covered peaks all the way to the waters' edge.

We have impressive cities, too. Seattle, Victoria, and Vancouver are easily visited by boat and have every amenity imaginable. Smaller cities like La Conner, Anacortes, Sidney, Cowichan Bay, Ladysmith—even Port McNeill, Port Hardy, Prince Rupert, and Ketchikan farther north—roll out the red carpet for visiting boats. They have restaurants, shops, and museums to explore or enjoy.

Small resorts and marinas, many family run, dot the coast. Some are as simple as local logs felled, milled, and lashed together to form a dock. Others have spas and high-end restaurants. Potluck dinners and happy hours are common at the smaller marinas.

You won't go hungry cruising this area. Bigger towns have grocery stores. Many marinas stock the essentials for their guests. Farmers markets, local bakers, artisan cheese makers, and craft wineries, breweries and now a few distilleries operate along the Inside Passage. Seafood, of course, is plentiful. Cruisers catch salmon, halibut, lingcod, prawns, and crab. They pick oysters and harvest sea asparagus.

The history is rich. Yaculta and Alert Bay have superb museums detailing the history of Native cultures. In Ketchikan, Totem Bight State Park has a remarkable collection of totems. Cruisers can follow in the footsteps of Capt. George Vancouver's 1790s expedition and the early expeditions of the Spanish explorers, during which many of the waterways and land masses in this area were named. Opportunities to enjoy the arts are readily available; in this book we describe the full range of museums at destinations along the way. Tacoma alone has six museums and a zoo, all within easy walking distance from the docks.

The variety of experiences, the majesty of the vistas, and the splendor of the wildlife and the variety of attractions in our towns and cities on the water keep us cruising.

HOW TO CRUISE TOPICS
Inside Passage
"Gates" and Their Effect
Chartering
Trailering a Boat
Anchoring vs. Marinas
Moorage Reservations
Have Flexible Expectations
About the Boat
Be Self-reliant
Best Months
GPS Chartplotters, Charts and Books
It Takes Teamwork
Use FRS Radios
Don't be Cheap
What to Bring & How to Equip the Boat
Cruising Tips & Techniques

"Gates" and Their Effect. The Pacific Northwest is a series of cruising areas separated by what we call "gates"— significant bodies of water that must be crossed. Although gates define our experience and abilities, they also serve as natural stopping points. Some cruisers stay in Puget Sound because the Strait of Juan de Fuca and San Juan Channel is a gate. Some stay in the Gulf Islands because the Strait of Georgia and Dodd Narrows crossing is a gate bringing concerns about the sea state conditions. Some go no farther than Desolation Sound because Johnstone Strait and the reversing tidal rapids north of Desolation Sound are gates. And some stay

Nordhavn 52

"Making your boating dreams come true."

Frank Durksen and James Knight - over 50 years of combined experience in premium yacht sales and service.

At Yacht Finders International we specialize in Passage-Making Trawlers, and quality power yachts.

Frank Durksen
theyachtfinder@gmail.com
360-770-8685

James Knight
james@nordhavnonly.com
561-262-4279

AAA YACHT FINDERS International

1.800.704.2628 • www.findyachts.com

south of Cape Caution because the ocean swells of Queen Charlotte Sound can be looked at as a gate. Gates exist all the way up the coast, all the way to Alaska.

Once beyond a gate and in a given cruising area, the waters are protected. Fortunately, summer weather usually is agreeable. With a study of the tide and current books, a close eye on the winds, an understanding of the weather, and a properly-equipped boat, the gates can be negotiated in safety, and often in comfort. The farther one decides to explore, the more time is needed. For the dedicated summertime Northwest cruiser, time is the principal element limiting cruising choices.

Chartering. The most popular charter boat waters run from the San Juan Islands to Desolation Sound, a distance of approximately 160 miles. These waters include the San Juan Islands, the Canadian Gulf Islands, the cities of Victoria and Vancouver, Howe Sound, Princess Louisa Inlet and the ever popular Desolation Sound. Most charters are for a week or two. It would take years of careful planning and repeat visits for a regular charter cruiser to see all there is to see in this area. For more information see *Chartering* in Chapter 1.

Trailering a Boat. Trailering is faster and more affordable than running a boat on its own bottom, and it avoids difficult passages across open water—the "gates" described earlier. Trailer boats can be towed to all the cruising grounds from Puget Sound to the far end of Vancouver Island. Even the sounds and inlets of the west coast of Vancouver Island can be seen easily and safely. Some people trailer all the way up Vancouver Island, launch at Port Hardy, and—watching the weather carefully—cruise north past Cape Caution to Rivers Inlet and beyond.

Many boats are trailered from the B.C. Interior to launch at Bella Coola or Prince Rupert. It's a long drive, but the waters they get to are some of the finest in the world. From Prince Rupert, you can cruise north into Southeast Alaska, which is not accessible by road. Another option is to tow the boat and trailer onto the ferry. Although expensive, both the BC Ferries and the Alaska Marine Highway ferries allow trailered boats.

Anchoring vs. Marinas. Compared with the waters farther north, Puget Sound has relatively few good anchorages. Most Puget Sound cruising is from marina to marina, or hanging off state park buoys. The San Juan Islands and Canadian Gulf Islands have many marinas and many anchorages. Desolation Sound is mostly anchorages with a few marinas. State and provincial marine parks dot the waterways from Puget Sound to Desolation Sound, many but not all, with mooring buoys. The Broughtons have a wide variety of marinas and many, many anchorages. West Coast Vancouver Island and the waters north of Cape Caution have a few marinas but mostly anchorages. It is possible to cruise the Inside Passage all the way to the top of Vancouver Island and stay only at the dock in a marina. For more information, see *About Anchoring* in this chapter.

Moorage Reservations. Many marinas accept advance reservations for transient moorage. Reserving moorage in advance is always a good idea and highly recommended during the busy summer season. A telephone call is the most universally accepted means for making reservations. Increasingly, some marinas have online reservation services available on their website and a few accept email requests. Some marinas require a credit card to confirm a slip reservation while others do not. Ask about their policy for charging your credit card and about their cancelation policy in case weather or unexpected delays cause a change in plans. Some marinas charge for no-shows. Ask about your slip assignment; a few marinas assign a slip at the time of reservation. Others request that you contact them by VHF radio or cell phone upon arrival.

BOATERS: THE PUMPOUT GUY IS READY FOR YOU!

Get your onboard holding tank emptied for free on Lake Washington, Portage Bay, Duwamish River and at select marinas at Gig Harbor and Liberty Bay

This service is provided courtesy of Washington State Parks, Washington Sea Grant and the Pumpout Guy. **Let's work together to protect the waters we love!**

To arrange: pumpoutguy.com, 206.437.6764 or radio, VHF Ch 68

For more information see pumpoutwashington.org

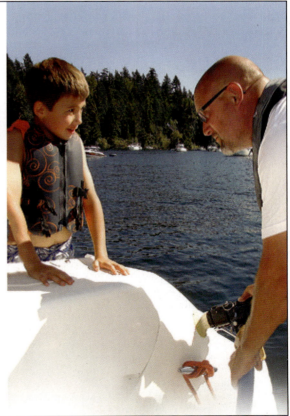

HOW TO CRUISE THE PACIFIC NORTHWEST

It's best to contact the marina directly for slip reservations. However, there are three third-party online marina slip reservation providers where you can review marinas, check moorage rates, and request a reservation. These third-party providers are growing in popularity but still list a relatively small number of marinas in the NW. For more information about these marina booking services, see Third-party Moorage Reservation Services in this chapter. There are some websites that purport to have slip booking relationships with local marinas but do not. Check with the marina first before contacting any third-party web provider.

Have Flexible Expectations. Marina facilities run the range from elegant to, shall we say, rustic. Managements span the same range. A person who expects 5-star facilities and service at every stop will be disappointed. Especially in the remote areas, the docks and other facilities can be rather on the rough side. Service at the Native villages up the coast, for example, is provided on their terms, in their way, and that's different from the city approach most Waggoner readers are accustomed to. When we're out cruising we have found it helpful to relax and take things as they come. We appreciate the places that do things our way, but we get along with the places that don't.

The one area we have less patience with is cleanliness. We think public washrooms, showers and laundry areas should be clean and in good condition, always. If we could have one message for marina operators, it would be, *keep those areas sparkling.*

About the Boat. Northwest cruising is coastal cruising in generally protected waters, so blue-water ocean voyaging vessels are not required. But the waters can get rough. Whether power or sail, good Northwest cruising boats are strongly built and seaworthy. Lightweight pontoon boats or open ski boats that are so popular on inland lakes are not well suited to these waters.

The weather can be cool and often wet. Northwest cruising powerboats tend to have large cabins and ample window area. Northwest cruising sailboats tend to have dodgers across the fronts of the cockpits or even full cockpit enclosures. Winds often are light and on the nose—"noserlies"—so sailboats should have good power.

Most Northwest cruising boats are equipped with cabin heat. It could be heat generated while the engine is running, a diesel heater or diesel furnace, or electric space heaters on the dock's shore power. Heat can add comfort when it is raining, on a cool night, or when cruising in the off-season.

GPS and chartplotter are standard equipment on Northwest cruising boats. A chartplotter, whether a dedicated marine unit, computer software on a PC or pad/tablet, or app software on your smartphone makes it easy to always know your position.

AIS (Automatic Identification System) is increasingly popular and common-place on Northwest boats. AIS receivers display vessel name, course, speed, and closest point of approach for nearby boats equipped with an AIS transponder, which broadcasts the vessel's boat information, course, and speed. Large commercial and pleasure craft, ferries, cruise ships, and freighters, all broadcast AIS signals. Increasingly, pleasure boats of all sizes are equipped with AIS transponders as well.

Radar has grown better and prices are trending down. Newer digital radar systems require less power, are lighter and often plug right into a chartplotter. Most important, the new digital radar units are very sensitive and provide a better resolution and presentation in color. Since fog and rain clouds can lower visibility to near-zero any time of the year, cruising boats in the Northwest often end up with radar. Autopilots take the uncertainty out of steering in fog and make long passages less tiring. They too are quickly added.

Dinghies and tenders and convenient dinghy launching/ recovery systems are important. When anchored or tied to a mooring buoy, the dinghy will be used to travel to shore. Some cruisers use their dinghies extensively for exploring and fishing.

Substantial anchoring systems are important. See the *About Anchoring* section of Chapter 1 for more information.

The minimum size for a cruising boat probably is in the 18- to 20-foot range, and that's pretty minimum. Most mom-and-pop cruising boats fall into the 25- to 50-foot size range, with the majority in the 32- to 50-foot range—large enough to be comfortable, small enough to be handled by two people.

Waste Discharge. There are three types of discharge from a boat that are regulated in both U.S. and BC waters: black water or sewage; gray water from sinks and showers; and bilge water from the vessel's bilge areas. Details of the regulations vary by jurisdiction but the objective is the same, to keep potentially damaging discharge from entering the sea.

Today, most boats with marine toilets are equipped with a Type III Marine Sanitation Device (MSD) or holding tank that stores black water for later disposal at a shore side pumpout facility. Some vessels are equipped with Type I or Type II MSDs where black water is treated before being discharged overboard. No Discharge Zones (NDZ) are areas where discharge of untreated, and in the case of Washington State waters, treated black water, may not be discharged overboard. All of Puget Sound waters up to the Canadian border are an NDZ, where no black water may be discharged. Free pumpout stations are located at marinas, fuel docks, and public docks throughout the area. There are 14 NDZs in BC waters, located in confined waters such as small bays and harbors where the exchange of sea water is limited. See the No Discharge Zones sidebar in this chapter for a list. Pumpout facilities are easily found on BC's inside waters up to Campbell River and Desolation Sound areas. From Campbell River north to Prince Rupert, pumpout facilities are few and far between. West Coast Vancouver Island has very few. Some pumpouts in BC are free while some charge for their use.

Gray water discharge from onboard sinks and showers is generally not restricted or regulated, and it is okay to discharge overboard. Most boats have no facility for holding gray water. Fortunately, there are only two known locations where it is requested that gray water not be discharged. Eagle Harbor in Washington State, and Pirates Cove in BC, request 'no gray water discharge.' As a practical matter, most people understand that few boats have facilities for holding gray water and simply ask for voluntary measures to limit the amount of gray water discharge — detergents, soaps, shampoo, and other potentially damaging liquids.

Bilge water containing oils, antifreeze, and other hazardous liquids may not be discharged overboard. Some used motor oil disposal locations also accept bilge water. Improved bilge pumps are now available that detect oil in the bilge and protect against accidental discharge of oil and oily bilge water.

Be Self-reliant. Don't venture out with the idea that if things go wrong, you can always call the Coast Guard. An important part of good seamanship is being able to handle whatever's thrown at you. Calling the Coast Guard is for true emergencies.

HOW TO CRUISE THE PACIFIC NORTHWEST

Best Months. The prime cruising months begin in April and end by October, with July-August the most popular. Boats are used year-round in Puget Sound. On winter weekends Puget Sound's popular ports are surprisingly busy. Cabin heat is a must in the winter. As mentioned above, cabin heat is almost a must the rest of the year.

North of Puget Sound, pleasure boating is best done between early May and late September. Really dependable summer weather (little rain, long days of glorious sunshine) normally doesn't arrive in the Northwest until July. September can be an outstanding cruising month. The crowds are gone and the weather can be perfect.

Use caution when cruising during the winter months. Storms lash the British Columbia coast. A Northwest boat with a warm and dry pilothouse is the way to enjoy winter cruising. Some, with flexible schedules, cruise year round. It takes a good understanding of the weather, and a warm, dry boat. There are many resources available to understand the weather and help keep you from an unexpected surprise. See the *Interpreting Northwest Weather* section of Chapter 1 for our approach and suggestions for understanding the weather.

About GPS Chartplotters, Charts and other Publications. To keep this book informative and up-to-date, we have stuck our nose into many ports, bays, and coves along the coast. In the process we have become unyielding advocates of chartplotters, charts, and navigation publications. Properly used, charts not only keep a boat out of trouble, they allow one to enter areas you wouldn't want to try without the chart.

With advancements in electronic charting in recent years, more mariners are asking whether carrying paper charts is still worthwhile. For years, we would not leave the dock without a set of paper charts. Even with computer navigation and a complete selection of electronic charts, it seemed wise to have paper charts as a backup.

But times are changing. Tablets and smartphones, with built-in GPS receiver systems and robust batteries, provide excellent redundancy. Low cost, highly effective chartplotting software is available for most tablet platforms. Many of these Apps make updating charts easy. If relying on a tablet or smartphone as a backup, consider carrying an extra battery pack. They're inexpensive and greatly extend battery life.

When using electronic charts, be aware that hazards can disappear at certain zoom levels. We always examine our route at several zoom levels to ensure that it is free of hazards.

Whatever form of charts you decide to carry, keep them updated. While rocks haven't changed location, navigation aids do change. Recently, for example, significant buoyage changes were made in Swinomish Channel. In British Columbia, some buoys were determined as unnecessary or redundant and were removed to meet budget goals. New charts reflect the change whether on paper or on new electronic updates. A five year old (or older) chartplotter may have very old charts and not reflect navigational updates.

Many cruising guides cover the Inside Passage and each offers a different point of view. We carry as many as we can fit, and keep several open at the helm. The U.S. Coast Pilot and Canadian Sailing Directions are good resources to have aboard, but they are focused on large commercial craft navigation.

Accurate tide and current tables are essential. Many electronic charting packages include tide and current data. However, we've found these are often inaccurate because they are based on old or estimated data. Note: Both U.S. and Canadian government tide tables are not corrected for Daylight Saving Time, so you'll have to make the corrections manually. Capt'n Jack's, covering Puget Sound, and Ports and Passes, covering Olympia to Prince Rupert and Southeast Alaska, are excellent and inexpensive, and times are corrected for Daylight Saving Time. Ports and Passes is updated each year with official government data. We have found some chartplotter tides and currents information to be off by as much as 45 minutes. Full disclosure: We are also the publishers of Ports and Passes.

U.S. Coast Guard Local Notices to Mariners, Canadian Notices to Shipping, and Canadian Notices to Mariners provide updated information on navaids and regulatory changes. U.S. and Canadian light lists are useful, too. Both of these can be found online, search on "local notice to mariners."

We do not understand the mentality of the owner that will make a major investment in a boat and fuel, then hold back on charts and other navigation information. At the other extreme is the person who has very little invested, and won't buy navigation information because it costs too much compared to the value of the vessel. *Remember:* the rocks, tides and weather are indifferent to how much the boat cost. They treat all boats equally.

It Takes Teamwork. Like many boating couples, we work together as a team, checking and doublechecking routes, depths, and charted hazards along a chosen course. If we question or doubt our path, we come to a stop until the safest course can be verified before continuing on. This is not the time for wounded pride or "I told you so's," it's a matter of successfully accomplishing the task at hand, and the opportunity to learn and grow as a team. Everything looks different on the water, so it's easy to mistake land marks and aids to navigation. The more experienced you are as a team, the better off you will be when the going gets tough, or when you are faced with a true emergency. Both partners should know how to use the radio, handle the helm, navigate, and manage sea conditions for a safe arrival into port. Docking and line-handling should be shared responsibilities. It's a good idea to schedule time for practice as well as a shake-down cruise for boat maintenance checks. The more comfortable you become with your own skills and know what your boat can handle, the more fun you will have. On a power vessel, it is imperative to conduct engine room checks, requiring a confident partner to take over the helm. Extended excursions or overnight passages for both power and sail, require taking turns at the helm so your partner can get some rest. The more you learn, the more opportunities you will have for new adventures farther afield. Share the experience.

Use FRS Radios. Inexpensive, handy, no license required. If cruising with other boats, they keep needless chatter off VHF channels. Headsets improve communication between skipper, first mate and crew, and reduce the need for shouting when docking. Couples credit headsets with saving a relationship by avoiding yelling.

Don't Be Cheap. It's bad form to use a private marina's facilities and not pay for the privilege. Even if a direct charge is not made, usually something can be purchased. When we overnight at a marina, we pay the moorage, just as our readers do. We're glad the marina is there, and we want it to be there for the future. We are pleased to do our part.

WHAT TO BRING AND HOW TO EQUIP THE BOAT.

Carry Tools and Spares. Our tool box is in the main cabin, available for immediate access. It seems like we are in that box at least once a day, usually for something minor, but it has to be fixed. Carry all owner's manuals, extra engine oil, transmission fluid, hydraulic fluid, coolant, and distilled water (for the batteries), spare V-belts, ignition parts, impellers and filters. Carry a spare raw water pump. The list of tools and spares has no end. You can't prepare for everything, but you can prepare for likely problems.

HOW TO CRUISE THE PACIFIC NORTHWEST

Carry Self-amalgamating Tape. This is stretchy tape that sticks to itself but not to what it's wrapped around. Usually it is available in black or white. The black is stronger. We have used self-amalgamating tape to repair a leaking high pressure fuel line, and to repair a broken oven door handle. The stuff is magic.

Carry Shore Power Cords & Adapters. If your boat has 30 amp shore power, you will need adapters for 15 amp, 20 amp and 50 amp outlets. It hasn't happened often, but there have been times when the nearest power receptacle was more than 50 feet away. We carry a second 50-foot shore power cord.

First Aid. Nobody knows when an accident might occur (that's what makes it an accident). In many areas you will need to be self-reliant. It could be hours or even the next day before medical aid might be available at your location. Carry a comprehensive medical kit and know how to use it. Carry spare medication for many of the common ailments. Call the Coast Guard if you do have a medical emergency. The U.S. Coast Guard has a medical professional on duty somewhere (it might be Kodiak, AK); they can be patched through for medical advice if needed. If you have guests onboard, ask if there are any medical issues or allergies. While your cruising may be recreational boating, the captain has responsibility for crew and guests.

Clothing. Except for some areas of Desolation Sound in the summer, most of the waters of the Northwest are cold. Even during warm weather you may welcome a sweater or jacket. Layering clothing works well. Rain gear is essential on sailboats.

On an enclosed powerboat, rain gear makes exploring shoreside attractions more pleasant when it is raining. Rubber boots are useful. Shoreside attire can be as nice as you want; most people do fine with comfortable sports clothes.

CRUISING TIPS & TECHNIQUES.

Shore Power Connection. Since not all docks have breakers to turn off individual outlets, we turn the boat's 110-volt switch to OFF before we hook up or unplug shore power. If the dock power has its own breaker, we turn it to OFF, too. When everything is hooked up, we turn the dock switch to ON, and then the boat switch.

Update Credit Cards. Credit and debit cards seem to be the preferred form of payment on both sides of the border. Even the remote areas have some means of accepting credit or debit cards. Some credit card companies have a very favorable exchange rate and withdrawing cash at ATMs may be cheaper than exchanging money beforehand. Before traveling out of the country call your credit card companies to tell them where you will be and the dates of your trip. Otherwise they might (will) refuse a charge, usually at the most awkward moment. Getting it straightened out is exasperating.

Public Toilets. Take your own paper to public toilets. Especially outhouses at parks and campgrounds. We speak from experience.

Pets. Keep pets on leash, and clean up after them. Many people cruise with pets. Some marinas are more pet-friendly than others. Use the designated pet-walking areas. Don't let the dog lift his leg against the water faucet or power box. Carry plastic bags and clean up if the pet doesn't make it to the potty area.

Assisting Others. When helping arriving boats, follow the skipper's instructions. When we take a line we hold it loosely, awaiting instructions. Most skippers have a plan that will stop the boat and lay it alongside the dock. A bow line pulled tight at the wrong time can ruin the plan: the bow swings toward the dock and the stern swings away. Obviously, if the landing plan has failed and the boat is being swept off, the dock crew goes into action. Even then it's a good idea to confirm with the skipper rather than acting on one's own.

Mooring Buoys. It's often easier to pick up mooring buoys from the stern or mid-ships, not the bow. If the bow of the boat is very high off the water it may be impossible to loop a line through a mooring buoy ring. Carry a line aft to a low point of the hull (it may be the swim step), loop it through the ring on the buoy, then carry the line back to the bow. You may want to cleat or tie off one end of the line amidships to keep control of it throughout the process.

Mooring buoys are often limited to small or medium sized boats. State and provincial park buoys are generally limited to boats 45 feet and under. Maximum boat size on some mooring buoys depends upon wind speeds. Rafting on mooring buoys is often limited and sometimes not allowed. For specifics see the *State and Provincial Parks and Public Wharves* section of Chapter 1 and the write-up for your planned destination.

Squeaky Fenders. De-squeak fenders with dishwashing soap. Joy, Ivory Liquid, whatever is handy seems to work. Slather it on. One application lasts for hours.

Use Scoot-Gard. This is the bumpy, rubbery material carried on big rolls at the marine store. It keeps things from sliding around. We use it for drawer and shelf liners. The microwave oven and the laptop computer with our charting and navigation program sits on it. Whenever we want something to stay where we put it but don't want to bolt or tie it into place, we use Scoot-Gard. It's inexpensive and it works.

Boat Cards. Consider making a boat card. One of the joys of cruising is the people you meet along the way. Boat cards are like business cards for your boat, and make it easy to stay in touch with people you meet.

FLOATPLANE TRAVEL ALONG THE INSIDE PASSAGE

For cruisers who need to travel home during a cruise, need parts shipped to them, or want to have guests join them in remote areas, floatplane travel can be a good option.

Floatplane flying provides a new perspective for boaters. If you can, sit in a window seat, or even the co-pilot seat up front. Take a small map, or this book, and pick out the islands as you fly by. The view is unforgettable—especially on a sunny day, the islands unfold dramatically. Currents are visible. Sometimes whales are spotted, and the pilot may even spend a few moments circling for a better view. On cloudy days you'll fly low—300 to 500 feet above the water.

Be prepared for a flight to have several stops along the route. If transiting from one country to the other, there will be a stop for customs clearance.

Many marinas offer boat watching service, perfect for when owners fly home. Some can even clean, fuel, and provision boats. For time-strapped cruisers, these services can be useful.

Floatplane operators are accommodating. We've seen floatplanes deliver parts and people to boats in remote anchorages.

The cost to use a floatplane service may initially appear high, but the time savings and convenience are huge. Consider that it's only a 3-hour flight from Port McNeill, near the north end of Vancouver Island, to Vancouver or Seattle.

THE BEAVER

For airplane buffs, a floatplane ride can be particularly thrilling. The venerable de Havilland DHC-2 Beaver is among the most widely used floatplanes in the northwest. De Havilland began producing the Beaver in 1948, and built nearly 1700 of them during a 19-year production run. Although the last Beaver was produced in 1967, operators and enthusiasts alike still appreciate its unparalleled combination of short field performance, durability, and versatility. Kenmore Air, Pacific Coastal, NW Seaplanes, Seair, Inland Air, and Tofino Air all operate Beavers. Pilots rave about flying them.

Equipped with a powerful engine (450 h.p. for piston Beavers) and a large wing optimized for short takeoff and landing distances, Beavers can reach places other planes can't. They can carry things other planes can't, too. De Havilland engineers designed the Beaver with doors wide enough to accommodate a 45-gallon drum and the ability to carry 2100 pounds of payload. Piston Beavers cruise at about 100 knots burning about 23 gallons of fuel per hour—enviable economy compared to many powerboats. Some operators have upgraded the original piston power plant to a newer turbine engine, increasing speed, payload capacity, and range.

FLOATPLANE TRAVEL ALONG THE INSIDE PASSAGE

The Beaver is so popular that well maintained examples have actually appreciated in value. When new, Beavers sold for about $50,000. Today, they can fetch more than $500,000.

KENMORE AIR
(866) 435-9524
Seattle (Lake Union or Kenmore)
to Sullivan Bay and Port McNeill

NW SEAPLANES
(425) 277-1590
Seattle (Renton) to Hakai Pass
and many points in between

FRIDAY HARBOR SEAPLANES
(425) 277-1590
Friday Harbor and San Juan Islands

PACIFIC COASTAL AIRLINES
(800) 663-2872
Victoria, Vancouver, Comox, Campbell River, Powell River, Port Hardy, Bella Bella, Masset

HARBOUR AIR VANCOUVER
(800) 665-0212
Victoria to Gulf Islands and
Sunshine Coast

SEAIR SEAPLANES
(800) 447-3247
or
(866) 692-6440
Vancouver to Gulf Islands
and Nanaimo

INLAND AIR
(888) 624-2577
Prince Rupert, North B.C.,
Haida Gwaii

TOFINO AIR
(866) 486-3249

WILDERNESS SEAPLANES
(800) 343-5963
B.C. Central Coast

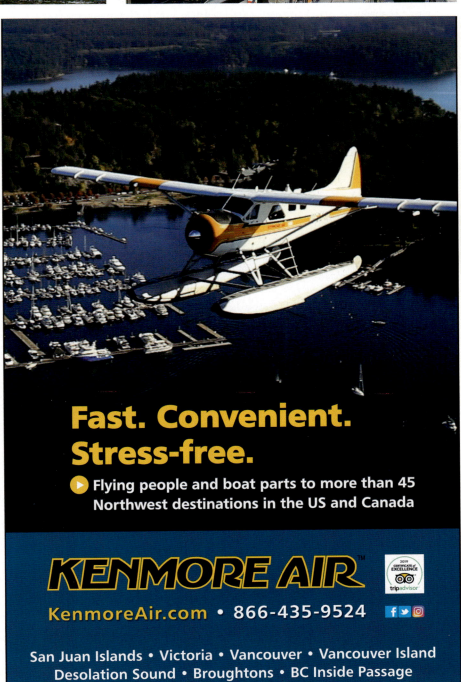

Fast. Convenient. Stress-free.

▶ Flying people and boat parts to more than 45 Northwest destinations in the US and Canada

KENMORE AIR™
KenmoreAir.com • 866-435-9524

San Juan Islands • Victoria • Vancouver • Vancouver Island
Desolation Sound • Broughtons • BC Inside Passage

U.S. AND CANADIAN CUSTOMS INFORMATION

U.S. / CANADA BORDER CROSSING
Customs must be cleared whenever the U.S.-Canada border is crossed in either direction. Generally, the process is quick and straightforward; but if the skipper isn't prepared with the proper information, it can be time consuming. It is extremely important to follow all the rules and be polite. While customs officers are trained in courtesy and usually are cordial, they have at their disposal regulations that can ruin your day. Take border crossing seriously, failure to follow the rules can have onerous consequences. Prepare ahead of time by inventorying items on board that need to be declared. Declare everything that must be reported, have a written list, don't trust your memory. Follow all the rules and report to customs as soon as possible after crossing the border. We know of an instance where a pleasure boater had their vessel seized by customs officials for failure to report their arrival in a timely manner. Their boat was finally returned, but only after paying a fine of $1,000. Another boater neglected to sign their new passport, which caused some significant delays and anxiety for family members. Be prepared and follow the rules so border crossings are non-events.

All vessels are required to clear with Customs when arriving in either the U.S. or Canada from a foreign port. Canadian and U.S. vessels do not need to clear out when leaving Canada. U.S. vessels do not need to clear out when leaving the U.S., except if the vessel is being exported. Canadian vessels with a U.S. Cruising License do not need to clear out when leaving U.S. waters. All non-U.S. flagged vessels (including Canadian) without a U.S. Cruising License are required to check-out when leaving U.S. waters.

Customs hours, rules, and requirements can and do change with short notice throughout the year. We urge readers to check the U.S. Customs and Border Protection (CBP) website www.cbp.gov and Canada Border Services Agency (CBSA) website www.cbsa-asfc.gc.ca for the latest. Check the Waggoner Guide website www.WaggonerGuide.com for border crossing updates.

Passports. If you don't have passports, we encourage you to get them. Lacking a passport, carry proof of citizenship such as an enhanced driver's license, enhanced identification, birth certificate, certificate of citizenship or naturalization, and photo ID. Standard (non-enhanced) drivers licenses are not proof of citizenship and are not accepted for border crossing. Citizens of some countries need visas as well. Carry birth certificates for all minors aboard — you may be asked for them.

Trusted Traveler Programs. Canada and U.S. have a number of Trusted Traveler Programs that expedite border crossings for boaters when all on board the vessel are enrolled in one of these programs. Nexus is a joint Canada and U.S. program that is recognized on both sides of the border and can expedite customs clearance going either direction. Most other programs are singular to one side of the border or the other.

Nexus. With Nexus, each person applies online and then contacted to set an appointment for an interview by both Canadian and U.S. customs agents at the Vancouver, B.C.; Blaine, WA or Seattle, WA CBP offices. The card is good for 5 years, and the cost is $50 U.S. or CDN per person. From start to finish, the entire process takes several months. If you cross the border by car along with your card, you'll have the additional benefit of using the Nexus lanes at the border. For general information or to begin the application process, U.S. citizens can go to www.cbp.gov, and Canadians go to www.cbsa-asfc.gc.ca.

Clearance Numbers. A clearance number will be issued to you when you have successfully completed reporting to the respective U.S. or Canadian customs agency. Keep a record of your clearance number, along with the date, time and location of clearance. You may be asked for this number later. Canada requires that foreign flagged vessels post their clearance number on a dockside viewable window while in Canadian waters. Keep a record of interactions with border officers. If you have received permissions or instructions from a customs officer via telephone, record the date and time of the conversation along with name or badge number.

Contact Customs or Coast Guard.
If unforeseen circumstances don't allow you to report to customs authorities as soon as possible after crossing the border, telephone customs authorities and report your circumstances. If you don't have cellular coverage, hail the Coast Guard on VHF and report your situation. This applies to crossing the border in either direction and with both Coast Guard agencies.

Don't Cross Border with Marijuana. Even though recreational marijuana may be legal in both British Columbia and the State of Washington, it is illegal to transport marijuana in any quantity across the Canada-U.S. border in either direction.

Be sure to have your passports ready when clearing customs.

CANADIAN CUSTOMS INFORMATION

CANADA BORDER SERVICES AGENCY (CBSA) Proof of citizenship and identification, such as Canadian or U.S. passport, U.S. Passport card, Trusted Traveler Program cards (Nexus and Sentri), State or Provincial issued enhanced driver's license, is required of all on board when entering Canada. If you are bringing a child other than your own into Canada, carry a notarized statement authorizing you to take the child into Canada and proof that the person signing the statement has custody of the child. The letter should include parents' or guardians' addresses and phone numbers. Canada Border Services Agency website has a sample letter.

Reporting to Canada Customs. All vessels arriving in Canada from a foreign country must clear Border Services immediately after the vessel comes to rest. The master, or the master's designated representative, must report to Border Services in-person or by telephone from a Border Services direct land line phone, or by calling (888) 226-7277. No one else may leave the vessel, and no baggage or merchandise may be removed from the vessel. You must report at a designated port of entry unless you have Nexus or Canpass. At some locations, Border Services officers will be present; at many other locations you will report by telephone. Even if you report by telephone, your boat may be subject to inspection. To avoid delays, have the following information ready when you report:

- Vessel name, length, and Coast Guard documentation number or state/province registration number

- Number of people on board
- Names, addresses, citizenship, birth dates and passport numbers of all passengers
- Purpose of the trip
- Number of pets on board – proof of vaccination needed
- Declare if you have cash over $10,000
- Length of absence from Canada (Canadian boats); Length and purpose of stay in Canada (U.S. boats)
- Quantity and type of alcoholic beverages
- Declare all goods being imported, including firearms

Once cleared, either by phone or by an officer, you will be given a clearance number. Post your clearance number in both side windows. Log this number with the date, time, and place of clearance. Vessels are subject to re-inspection while in Canadian waters, usually by RCMP officers when their patrol boat reaches a marina. The officers are well trained and polite, but be sure you don't have anything on board you shouldn't have.

Nexus. If all passengers aboard a boat have a Nexus permit, a vessel can clear Canada Border Services Agency by calling, toll-free, (866) 996-3987 at least 30 minutes and up to 4 hours before arriving at a designated CBSA or Nexus reporting station. The vessel must physically check in at a designated CBSA or Nexus reporting station. At the time of Nexus call-in, the Border Services officer will ask for the vessel's identification number, vessel's intended reporting station, estimated time of arrival (ETA), purpose of the trip, and length of stay. You must appear at the appointed reporting station before your declared ETA and wait at the station until the ETA. If no officer is present at the reporting station before the ETA, you may continue on your way, without further action. We usually take a photo, with date and time stamp, of ourselves and our boat at the reporting station – just in case. In the accompanying list of designated reporting stations, note that some are for Nexus/Canpass vessels only and can only be used by vessels where all on board have Nexus or Canpass.

Canpass-Private Boats. Canpass-Private Boats program was discontinued in 2018. New applications for the program are no longer being accepted. Those with valid and unexpired Canpass cards can continue to use them until the expiration date.

Firearms Restrictions. You may not bring switchblades, most handguns, automatic weapons, anti-personnel pepper spray or mace into Canada. Under certain circumstances, some long guns are allowed. Bear spray, if labeled as such, is permitted if declared. A Non-Resident Firearm Declaration Form is needed to bring firearms into Canada. Call the Canadian Firearms Centre at (800) 731-4000 for a copy of the form, or download one from www.cfc-cafc.gc.ca. The cost is $25 CDN, and it is good for 60 days. All weapons and firearms must be declared to CBSA.

B.C. POINTS OF ENTRY

Designated B.C. Points of Entry for Pleasure Craft Reporting
All locations contact Canada Border Services Agency
Toll-free (888) 226-7277 (7 days a week, 24 hours a day)

Bedwell Harbour: May 1 to Friday before Victoria Day
9:00 a.m. to 5:00 p.m.
Friday before Victoria Day to Labour Day
8:00 a.m. to 8:00 p.m.
Labour Day to Sept. 30
9:00 a.m. to 5:00 p.m.
Oct. 1 to Apr. 30 (Canpass/Nexus only)

Cabbage Island: (Canpass/Nexus only)

Campbell River: Coast Marina; Discovery Harbour Marina

Galiano Island: Montague Harbour Marina (Canpass/Nexus only)

Mayne Island: Horton Bay (Canpass/Nexus only)
Miners Bay (Canpass/Nexus only)

Nanaimo: Nanaimo Port Authority Basin–E Dock
Summer 8:00 a.m. to 5:00 p.m.
Winter 8:00 a.m. to 4:30 p.m.
Townsite Marina (Canpass/Nexus only)

North Pender Is.: Port Browning Marina (Canpass/Nexus only)

Prince Rupert: Lightering Dock
++ Cow Bay Marina
Fairview Govt. Dock
Prince Rupert Rowing and Yacht Club
Rushbrooke Government Dock

Saltspring Is.: Ganges Harbour–Seaplane Dock
First floating breakwater (Canpass/Nexus only)
Royal Victoria YC Outst.(Canpass/Nexus only)

Sidney: Canoe Cove Marina
Port Sidney Marina
Royal Victoria YC Outstation
Tsehum Marina
Van Isle Marina

Ucluelet: 52 Steps Dock June 1–Sept 30 only
8:00 a.m. to 10:00 p.m.
Oct. 1–May 31 (Canpass/Nexus only)

Vancouver: False Creek Fisherman's Wharf
Steveston Harbour Authority (Canpass/Nexus)
Royal Vancouver Yacht Club–Coal Harbour
Harbour Green Dock

Victoria: Oak Bay Marina
Royal Victoria YC (Cadboro Bay)
Raymur Point CBSA Dock

White Rock: White Rock Government Dock
Crescent Beach Marina

2020 WAGGONER CRUISING GUIDE

U.S. AND CANADIAN CUSTOMS INFORMATION

Food Restrictions. Food restrictions are subject to change without notice. Check the CBSA website at www.cbsa-asfc.gc.ca for updates. Canadian customs has an interactive website where you enter the food item you are planning to bring into Canada, and after selecting options regarding the item's origin and planned use, you will get an Approved or Not Approved determination. See the CBSA website for a link to this Automated Import Reference System (AIRS) website. Other than restricted foods, you can carry quantities of food appropriate for your stay. Be aware of the following restrictions and limitations:

- No houseplants (including potted herbs)
- No apples, no pitted fruit (apricots, plums, peaches) Cherries are sometimes okay
- Potatoes from US are allowed – 1 bag per person of US #1 commercially packaged
- All firewood is prohibited

Liquor & Tobacco Restrictions. Not more than 1.14 liters (38.5 oz.) of hard liquor, or 1.5 liters of wine, or a total of 1.14 liters of wine and liquor, or 24 12-ounce bottles of beer or ale per person of legal drinking age (19 years old in B.C.). Not more than 1 carton of cigarettes and 2 cans (200 grams) of tobacco and 50 cigars or cigarillos, and 200 tobacco sticks per person 19 or older without paying duty and taxes on the excess amount.

If in doubt, call (204) 983-3500 for inspection.

Duty-free Limits. Canadian residents returning to Canada may be eligible for a personal exemption on duty for goods brought into Canada. An exemption on goods up to $200 CDN is allowed for out-of-country stays of more than 24 hours. The exemption for stays of 48 hours or more is $800 CDN and may include alcohol and tobacco items. See the CBSA website for full details.

Declare All Items. If in doubt, declare it to CBSA. This is especially true for food items. If you are not sure, simply declare it and let the CBSA officer make the decision. It is always best to inform CBSA agents of items that you have on board. Failure to declare items can result in fines and penalties.

Pets. Owners of dogs and cats must bring a certificate issued by a licensed U.S. or Canadian veterinarian clearly identifying the pet and certifying that it has been vaccinated against rabies during the previous 36 months.

Currency. Cash or other monetary instruments in excess of $10,000 CDN per boat must be reported. For current rules and regulations, check out the Canada Border Services Agency website at www.cbsa-asfc.gc.ca.

U.S. CUSTOMS INFORMATION

U.S. CUSTOMS AND BORDER PROTECTION (CBP) CBP requires approved identification, such as a U.S. or Canadian passport, U.S. Passport card, Trusted Traveler Program cards (Nexus and Sentri), I-68, State or Provincial issued enhanced driver's license, for entry to the U.S. We recommend that everyone aboard have a passport.

Reporting to U.S. Customs. You must report arrival and obtain clearance from U.S. CBP at a designated point of entry; OR by using the CBP ROAM smartphone App; OR if all on board are enrolled in Nexus, I-68, or Global Entry, clearance may be conducted by calling (800) 562-5943. Whether in-person, by ROAM App, or by voice call, have the following information at-hand in order to avoid delays:

• Name, date of birth and citizenship of all persons on board (including passport number or citizenship identification)
• Name of the boat and vessel registration or documentation number
• Nexus BR Number
• Vessel homeport and current location
• CBP user fee decal number (30 feet in length and over), or Cruising License Number for foreign flagged vessels (including Canadian vessels).
• Canadian customs clearance number for U.S. flagged boats.
• Estimated length of stay in U.S. for Canadian vessels and other foreign flagged vessels.
• For U.S. vessels, date you departed U.S. and how long you were in Canada

Designated Washington U.S. Ports of Entry. Arrivals requiring an in-person report may be made at any of the following Ports of Entry: Friday Harbor, Roche Harbor, Port Angeles, Point Roberts, and Anacortes. All other ports require appointments to be made in advance for in-person inspections (during regular business hours only). Don't assume that if you call for an appointment you will get one. To save time and avoid problems, clear U.S. Customs at one of the five designated Ports of Entry. If you arrive after normal business hours, call (800) 562-5943 for further instructions. Local customs office numbers are listed later in this section. I-68s are available at all locations listed.

Entering Alaska. All vessels entering Southeast Alaska from a foreign country must clear U.S. Customs. Vessels my clear customs by reporting in-person in Ketchikan; OR with the CBP ROAM App; OR by telephone if all on board are enrolled in Nexus, I-68 or Global Entry. For detailed instructions on clearing U.S. Customs in Alaska, see *Chapter 19 – Arriving in Ketchikan.*

CBP ROAM APP. ROAM is an official CBP smartphone App that can make your arrival reporting within U.S. waters a lot easier and may expedite your U.S. customs clearance requirements. New as of 2019, boaters can check-in with CBP using the App as soon as they enter U.S. waters and have cell phone coverage. CBP officers access your boat and traveler information with the App and can open a video chat with you to obtain and verify information if needed. CBP will then either clear you for entry with a clearance number, or direct you to a designated U.S. Port of Entry for further processing. Those approved for entry do not need to report in-person at a Port of Entry. CBP ROAM is available for clearance 24/7. Check with CBP to confirm hours of operation.

You don't need to be a member of a Trusted Traveler program to use ROAM; it can be used by U.S. and foreign travelers. The ROAM App can be used when entering at Washington and Alaska Ports of Entry for pleasure craft. The App supports iOS and Android phones and tablet mobile devices. The App works best with 4G or LTE service and is reported to also work with 3G service. Boaters needing a Cruising License, or who must pay duty, will need to report in-person to a Port of Entry. For more about the App and its use, see the www.cbp.gov website or www.WaggonerGuide.com.

Clearing by Telephone. Boaters with nothing to declare normally can clear U.S. Customs by telephone, if all on board have Nexus, I-68s or Global Entry. With Nexus, I-68 or Global Entry, you can call the Small Boat Reporting Office after entering U.S. waters, at (800) 562-5943 to report arrival and request clearance. When calling underway, call from an area with good reception. While you report, slow to idle speed to reduce background noise and remain in the good reception area. The Small Boat Reporting Office operates from 7:00 a.m. to 10:00 p.m. from May through September, and from 7:00 a.m. to 8:00 p.m. the balance of the year. If you enter the U.S. outside these hours, you must remain aboard your boat until you can clear.

Indications are that clearing by telephone with the Small Boat Reporting Office's 800 number will be replaced by ROAM App in the future.

I-68. The I-68 Permit is valid for 1 year from the date of issue. U.S. citizens, Lawful Permanent Residents, Canadian citizens and Landed Immigrants of Canada who are nationals of Visa Waiver Program countries are eligible to apply. The cost is $16 per person, $32 for families. Apply at CBP offices within the Puget Sound area. Bring proof of citizenship, such as a passport, certified copy of your birth certificate, and photo ID. Vessel information also helps. Each person applying

must appear. Children under 14 can be listed on parents' I-68.

Small Vessel Reporting System (SVRS). The Small Vessel Reporting System program was replaced in 2018 with the CBP ROAM App. SVRS program is no longer available.

Processing Fee (CBP Decal). Pleasure vessels 30 feet in length or more must pay an annual processing (user) fee of $29.47 to enter or re-enter the United States. U.S. vessels less than 30 feet are not subject to the fee, provided they have nothing to declare. Payment is required at or before the vessel's first arrival each calendar year. If you report by telephone, they charge your credit card. A non-transferable decal will be issued upon payment. Renewal notices for the next year's decal are mailed or emailed in the autumn. Vessels with a valid Cruising License do not have to pay this fee and do not require a decal. Order your sticker before you need to enter the U.S. Even if you have Nexus, I-68 or Global Entry preclearance, lack of a current-year sticker may direct you to a designated port of entry for inspection. User Fee stickers are not sold at CBP offices, but can be ordered online at https://dtops.cbp.dhs.gov, or by phone (317) 298-1245, or email decals@cbp.dhs.gov.

Cruising License. A Cruising License (sometimes referred to as a Cruising Permit) is available to Canadian and most foreign flagged vessels. A Cruising License saves time and money for foreign flagged vessels frequenting U.S. waters. Foreign vessels without a Cruising License must complete form CBP-1300 and pay a $19.00 (cash only) Navigation Fee upon entering U.S. waters, and each subsequent movement between U.S. ports, and upon exiting U.S. waters. With a Cruising License, you only need to complete form CBP-1300 and pay the Navigation Fee once at the vessel's initial reporting and clearance with CBP.

To get a Cruising License, foreign vessels upon entering U.S. waters must report to one of the designated CBP Ports of Entry where they submit form CBP-1300 and pay the $19.00 fee. CBP will inspect the vessel and process CBP-1300. A Cruising License can then be requested. There is no charge for the Cruising License. Vessels with a Cruising License do not need the $29.47 CBP decal. Cruising Licenses are good for up to one year or upon surrendering to CBP when leaving U.S. waters. Cruising Licenses cannot be extended and are available only when the vessel reports and clears-in at a CBP Port of Entry. Foreign flagged vessels made outside of the U.S. must wait 15 days after expiration of their Cruising License before requesting a new one. During this 15-day period, the vessel may enter and depart U.S. waters by submitting a CBP-1300 and paying $19.00

2020 WAGGONER CRUISING GUIDE

U.S. AND CANADIAN CUSTOMS INFORMATION

upon entry, exit, and movement. Vessels made in U.S. are exempt from this 15-day waiting period.

Cruising Licenses do not affect customs reporting requirements. Foreign vessels with a Cruising License are required to report their movement by reporting their arrival at designated ports in SE Alaska. Foreign vessel movement within Washington's inside waters are not required to report their movement after the initial reporting entry into Washington's U.S. waters. Vessels must report and clear in with CBP upon entry to U.S. waters by reporting in person; OR by reporting arrival with the CBP ROAM App; OR by telephone with one of the trusted traveler programs like Nexus. You will need your Cruising License number when reporting in with CBP.

Food Restrictions. Food restrictions are subject to change without notice. See www.WaggonerGuide.com for updates and for a downloadable copy of CBP information regarding food products that may not be brought into the U.S. For specific food related questions, contact an Agricultural Specialist at (360) 332-8661 or (360) 988-2971. As a general guideline, any food you bring into the U.S. must be made or grown in Canada or the U.S., and labeled as such. Potatoes should be kept in original commercial packaging. Don't bring fresh tropical fruits or vegetables in, even if you bought them in the U.S. CBP recommends declaring all meat and produce when entering the U.S. If declared, prohibited goods will be seized but no fine will be levied. Subject to change without notice, use the following list to minimize problems:

- No sheep, lamb or goat in any form; this includes pet food
- Beef, pork, chicken, turkey and meat products from Canada are allowed
- Keep pet food in original packaging
- No fresh citrus, regardless of where you bought it
- No fresh produce (vegetables or fruit) grown outside the U.S. and Canada
- Canned fruits and vegetables, however, are unrestricted regardless of origin; leave labels/stickers on cans
- No tomatoes
- No garlic, chives, green onions, leeks, and other green Allium vegetables from Canada
- No cut flowers or potted plants (they are subject to so many restrictions that it's better to leave them in Canada and avoid the hassle)
- Seafood is okay
- Dairy products are okay
- Eggs are usually okay
- All firewood is prohibited; boaters with firewood may be required to return to Canada to dispose of it

Pets. Dogs and cats must be healthy. The requirement for evidence of rabies vaccination for dogs coming from certain countries was removed in 2018. Birds are subject to USDA Veterinarian inspection to enter or re-enter. It is usually not advisable to bring birds across the border.

Currency. Cash or other monetary instruments in excess of $10,000 U.S. per boat must be reported.

Duty-free Limits. U.S. residents outside of the U.S. less than 48 hours can import merchandise up to $200 in value per person without duty. If the stay is more than 48 hours, the limit is $800 per person. For ease and simplicity, try to restrict what you bring back home to products made or grown in Canada (sometimes even that isn't sufficient). For the latest customs information, go to the U.S. Customs and Border Protection website pages for pleasure boats at www.cbp.gov/travel/pleasure-boatsprivate-flyers/pleasure-boat-overview.

Declare All Items. If in doubt, declare the item to CBP. This is especially true for food products. If you are not sure, simply declare it and let the CBP officer make the decision. It is always best to inform CBP agents of items that you have on board. Failure to declare items can result in fines and penalties.

Clearing customs at Roche Harbor on San Juan Island

Pilotage Exemption for Foreign Flagged (other than U.S. or Canadian) Vessels. Foreign flagged vessels (other than Canadian) in Washington waters are required by Washington State law to have an exemption in order to operate without a professional Pilot. To request an exemption, download and submit an application from the www.pilotagewa.gov website or call the Washington Board of Pilotage Commissioners at (206) 215-3904.

Aquatic Invasive Species (AIS) Prevention Permit. As of 2018, most boats operating in Washington State waters that do not have a Washington State registration sticker need to purchase and carry an AIS Prevention Permit. Dinghies are exempt. Permits can be purchased online or at any Washington State Department of Fish and Wildlife license retailer. The permit is good for one year. For more details, see the AIS Prevention Permit sidebar in this chapter.

U.S. POINTS OF ENTRY

Anacortes (360) 293-2331
Office at Cap Sante Marina
8:00 a.m. to 8:00 p.m. Summer
8:00 a.m. to 5:00 p.m. Off-season
closed 1 ½ hours mid-afternoon)

Friday Harbor (360) 378-2080
Customs booth at the dock with phone
Office at Spring & First Streets
8:00 a.m. to 8:00 p.m. Summer
8:00 a.m. to 5:00 p.m. Off-season

Point Roberts (360) 945-5211
or (360) 945-2314
Customs Dock near Fuel Dock
8:00 a.m. to 8:00 p.m. Summer
8:00 a.m. to 5:00 p.m. Off-season

Port Angeles (360) 457-4311
Office Boat Haven
8:00 a.m. to 9:00 p.m. Summer
8:00 a.m. to 5:30 p.m. Off-season

Roche Harbor (360) 378-2080
Customs dock at Roche Harbor Marina
8:00 a.m. to 8:00 p.m. Summer
8:00 a.m. to 5:00 p.m. Off-season

Ketchikan (907) 225-2254
Call and wait for agent at assigned slip
6:00 a.m. to 6:00 p.m. Summer

Other Customs Offices
(by appointment only, call 24 hours ahead for availability and instructions):

Bellingham (360) 734-5463

Blaine (360) 332-6318

Everett (425) 259-0246

Port Townsend (360) 385-3777

Seattle (Boeing Field) (206) 553-0667

Tacoma/Olympia (253) 593-6338

U.S. AND CANADIAN CUSTOMS INFORMATION

U.S. Customs – ROAM App Available in Washington and Alaska

New in 2019, U.S. Customs and Border Protection (CBP) ROAM App can be used when entering at state of Washington and Alaska Ports of Entry. The App can make your arrival reporting with U.S. Customs a lot easier. **R**eporting **O**ffsite **A**rrival – **M**obile, **ROAM** App, is an App that can be used at Washington pleasure craft Port of Entry locations including Anacortes, Point Roberts, Friday Harbor, Roche Harbor, and Port Angeles. In Alaska the App can be used at Ketchikan and Wrangell Ports of Entry. This official CBP App will support Apple iOS and Google Android phones and tablet mobile devices. Travelers entering U.S. waters can check-in using the App, and CBP officers can initiate a video chat for information verification, or an interview if required. If approved for entry, boaters do not have to report in-person at a Port of Entry.

To use the ROAM App, input your biographic, vessel, and trip details into the App. Then submit your arrival for CBP Officer review by pressing the App's **Report Arrival** selection on your mobile device. A CBP Officer may initiate a video chat to further interview travelers. Once the CBP Officer reviews the information, you will receive a notification and email with your clearance status and next steps, if applicable. The App needs to have cellular data connection or Wi-Fi service to report and process your arrival. The App works best with 4G or LTE cell service. However, boaters are successfully using it on 3G as well.

The ROAM App can be used by U.S. and foreign travelers to report arrival. You don't need to be part of a trusted traveler program to use ROAM. Reporting arrival in-person at one of the Port of Entry locations is still available. Travelers requiring a Cruising License, or who must pay duties, will need to report in-person to CBP at the nearest Port of Entry. Travelers with I-68 or Nexus may still report by calling the CBP Small Boat Reporting Office; however, this option may be replaced by ROAM at some future date.

To install and prepare the App, you will need an iOS or Android phone or tablet with camera. You will also need an email address. The App is free and available from the Apple App Store and the Google Play Store. To get started:

1. Download and install the App from the Apple App or Google Play store.
2. Setup a Login.gov account (if you don't already have one). Login.gov is a U.S. General Services Administration website and service, providing a single sign-in account to multiple participating government programs. If you are enrolled in Nexus you probably already have a Login.gov account. You can create an account from the ROAM App or at the Help menu selection at Login.gov website. You will need to provide an email address.
3. Open the App and sign-in with your Login.gov account.
4. Add information about your mode of transportation – your boat (make, year, registration number, length). You can add and save information for more than one boat.
5. Add information about the travelers who will be on your boat when reporting in with ROAM. The App has a feature to populate the traveler information by scanning each person's travel document. Travel documents accepted include: Passport, Passport Card, Nexus, Enhanced U.S. Drivers License, Global Entry, Birth Certificate (kids 15 and under), Permanent Resident Card.
6. With the App, take a picture of each person's travel document.

That's it. You're now ready to use ROAM App to report your arrival into U.S. waters.

To use the ROAM App and report arrival:
• Report Arrival as soon as possible after entering U.S. waters. Report Arrival requests made outside of U.S. waters will be rejected.
• Ensure that you have a good cell signal and that you will be able to maintain cell coverage.
• Open and sign-in to the ROAM App.
• Press the **Report Arrival** selection, then select the mode of transportation (boat) and select travelers from saved profile information and designate one of the selected travelers as the vessel master.
• Answer all questions with further details and items to declare.
• Press the **Submit** selection - you will get a tracking number - this is NOT your clearance number and you are not done.
• The app goes into pending status while CBP officers on the other end process the information. Be patient, this may take a while before receiving a response.
• You will next get a response from the App with a clearance number, or instructions for further processing, which may include going to the nearest CBP Port of Entry for in-person processing.
• Your clearance number will show on the App and in a message to the email address on your Login.gov account profile.

For more about ROAM on the CBP website, see www.cbp.gov/travel/pleasure-boats-private-flyers/pleasure-boat-overview/roam.

[Leonard Landon]

2020 WAGGONER CRUISING GUIDE

Boardings

"Welcome Aboard" – may not be the first thing that comes to mind when someone in uniform steps aboard your vessel. However, if we are prepared, it's more likely that we will be ready to welcome these agents of safety and law enforcement when we are out cruising. There are a number of different agencies and agents that may board recreational vessels.

U.S. Agencies. On the U.S. side of the border, the Coast Guard (USCG) routinely boards vessels to check for compliance with required devices and safety equipment. If underway and approached by a USCG patrol vessel for boarding, the officer may want you to slow down, but continue underway. They will come alongside and board while underway; however, you may choose to come to a stop. An officer will board and conduct a standard safety inspection. Their inspection includes checking for proper vessel documentation, personal floatation devices, and vessel safety equipment. The inspection takes about 15 to 30 minutes and includes a 'results form' with any deficiencies noted on the signed form. Any deficiencies noted on the form must be addressed and acknowledged by the Coast Guard. If there are no deficiencies, you will receive the same signed form noting the successful inspection. Keep this form on the vessel as it serves to waive any subsequent inspection boarding within the next 12 months.

State police, county sheriff, city police, and port authorities have on-the-water patrol boats for safety, search and rescue, and law enforcement. Agents of these departments can and do board recreational vessels. Unlike the U.S. Coast Guard's once-a-year limit on vessel boarding, there is no limit for these other law enforcement agencies.

Retain the paperwork from a boarding, it will save you from future boardings for one year.

Canada Agencies. On the Canadian side of the border, Canadian Coast Guard does not have maritime or law enforcement responsibilities and does not perform vessel inspections. Royal Canadian Mounted Police (RCMP) and city police have law enforcement responsibilities. RCMP does not routinely board vessels for marine safety inspections.

When cruising near the U.S. and Canada international border, you may be stopped and boarded by agents of the respective border patrol (U.S. Customs and Border Patrol, and Canadian Border Services Agency). They patrol the border crossings with their high-speed boats.

While fishing, crabbing, or prawning, agents from wildlife departments from Washington, Alaska, or British Columbia may board your vessel to check for compliance with seafood-collection rules and laws.

Preparation. While there are no guarantees, responsible cruisers can reduce their chances of boarding by keeping their boats clean, orderly, and in good condition; running the boat cautiously and competently, consistent with weather and sea conditions; doing nothing that would invite closer scrutiny. A current Coast Guard Auxiliary voluntary safety inspection sticker in the window might be a help. Consider doing your own inspection before the boating season to make sure you have all of your documentation, flares and approved life jackets or PFDs, placards and other items in order. For the complete list, you can search USCG Vessel Safety Checklist on the internet and find the same list used by the Coast Guard. Expect more checks by small boats. We watched armed USCG personnel in a mid-20-foot inflatable check the boats on moorings in Fossil Bay (Sucia Island) and board one of them.

Have all required boat documentation, licenses, and other paperwork ready in the event you are boarded. It is helpful to have a folder with the most current official documents. Keep a second folder for copies of original documents in the event you need to leave a copy with an official. Record each boarding event in your log, including the agent's name and authority. These agents help keep our cruising waters safe; thank them with a smile.

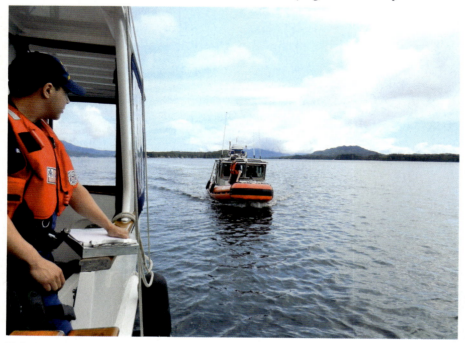

U.S. Coast Guard may want to board your vessel while remaining underway.

U.S. Homeland Security

Here are some do's and don'ts, drawn from material published by the U.S. Coast Guard and expanded upon by our own experiences.

Keep your distance from all military, cruise line or commercial shipping. For U.S. naval vessels, slow to minimum speed within 500 yards, and do not approach any U.S. naval vessel within 100 yards. Violation of the Naval Vessel Protection Zone is a felony offense. If you must pass within 100 yards of a U.S. naval vessel, you must contact the vessel or its Coast Guard escort vessel on VHF 16. The only exceptions to these requirements would be in a congested area, where there is no way to give this kind of room, or in a narrow channel, such as the mouth of the Snohomish River in Everett, which fronts on the Navy base there. In such cases, navigate slowly, predictably, and obey all instructions.

Observe and avoid all security zones. Also avoid commercial port operation areas, especially those that involve military, cruise line, or petroleum facilities. Observe and avoid other restricted areas near dams, power plants etc. Violators will face a quick, determined, and severe response. Translation: You risk being blown out of the water. The buoyed security zone protecting the Trident submarine base at Bangor, in Hood Canal, is a good example. The restricted area is patrolled by four high-speed small craft, at least two of them with impressive guns mounted on the decks. Although we give the security zone a wide berth as we go by, it is obvious that we are being watched. When we increase our speed from 8.5 knots to 16 knots one of the patrol craft will turn abruptly and run on a parallel course at our speed until we pass the far boundary. We thought about taking photos of the base with at least one of the patrol boats in view, but decided it would be prudent to motor along as predictably and innocently as possible.

Don't stop or anchor beneath bridges or in the channel. If you do, you can expect to be boarded by law enforcement officials.
Be alert for anything that looks peculiar or out of the ordinary. Report suspicious activities to local authorities, the Coast Guard, or port or marina security. Do not approach or challenge those acting in a suspicious manner. Suspicious behavior includes:

- Suspicious persons conducting unusual activities near bridges, refineries, or around high security areas on or near the water
- Individuals establishing roadside stands near marinas or other waterfront facilities
- Persons photographing or making diagrams of things, such as the underside of a bridge, the area around nuclear powerplants, and waterfront facilities near what might be high-risk vessels
- Unknown or suspicious persons loitering for long periods of time in waterfront areas
- Suspicious persons renting or attempting to procure or "borrow" watercraft
- Suspicious vendors attempting to sell or deliver merchandise or drop off packages in waterfront areas

Always secure and lock your boat when not on board. Do not leave your boat accessible to others. Always take the keys with you. **When storing your boat, make sure it is secure and its engine is disabled.** If the boat is on a trailer, make the trailer as immovable as possible.

Be Prepared for a Vessel Boarding. Expect to see U.S. Coast Guard surveillance and vessel boardings. The physical size and geographic complexity of Northwest waters make these waters difficult to patrol and quite "porous" for vessels doing illegal things. More "assets," as the military calls them, are being deployed here.

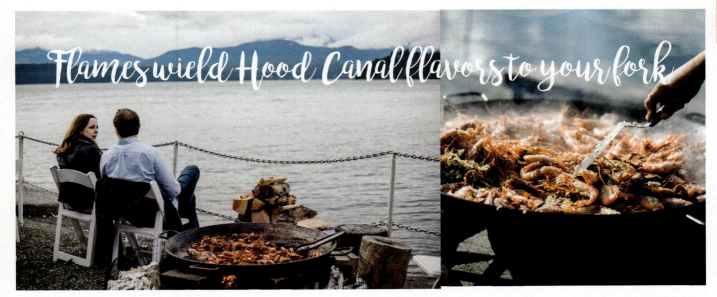

SEASONAL, WEEKLY, ALA CARTE MENU, PRIVATE EVENTS, MONTHLY CANAL COOKOUTS

MARINE VENUE OF
ALDERBROOK RESORT & SPA
5101 E HWY 106, UNION, WA 98592
360.898.3500

INTERPRETING NORTHWEST WEATHER

Weather is one of the biggest fears of many boat crews. There is a lot of information available when you know how to get it, know how to understand it and evaluate it in order to make an effective go, or no-go decision.

Weather on the Internet, Cell Phone and VHF WX. At the Waggoner Guide, we have developed a means of using all of the weather information available to avoid getting into an uncomfortable situation. Many boaters do not realize how you can use the internet to gather a good picture of the weather. No internet available? If you have cell phone coverage, you can call for weather and buoy reports. Out in a very remote area? If you have VHF WX coverage, you can gather the right information you need over the radio; it just takes a little more effort. In remote areas of Haida Gwaii and Northern B.C., you can use satellite based systems such as Garmin InReach, Iridium Go, and Globalstar Sat-Fi to access weather information. There is a description of this system in the *Cellular, Internet and Satellite Communications* section of this chapter.

Weather Overview. First, start by using the internet to view weather information days before your intended departure. Use the NOAA Ocean Prediction Center, Pacific Region, Current Surface Analysis and then the 24, 48, 72, and 96 hour forecasts to look at the weather patterns as they develop and cross the Pacific Ocean.

We look at the High and Low pressure systems and how they are forecast to move; typically from west to east. While this is offshore weather, it provides an indication of the weather systems that will pass over Puget Sound and the Inside Passage. Often in July and early August, a large high pressure system will sit offshore resulting in good weather for an extended period of time. This is called the Pacific High and typically offers favorable conditions.

Next, we look at the isobar lines over the coastal areas where we will be cruising. The isobar lines show the change in barometric pressure over a distance. Tighter isobar patterns show areas of wind and its counterclockwise direction around a low. We look for areas of big lazy (widely separated) isobars around a high indicating limited wind. Looking at the weather charts gives us a visual overview of the weather and the systems that will be affecting our route over the next couple of days. Even if we do not have access to the internet while en route for a few days, we have the overview. To add to the overview, we look at one of the visual services on the internet, www.windy.com. This website puts the weather prediction models into motion, where you can see the wind patterns circulating and how they flow across the Pacific. You can also see a visual of the offshore wind and sea conditions.

Another popular weather App for mariners is PredictWind. It too presents a lot of visual information when an internet connection is available.

The Forecast. We then look at the NOAA Marine Forecasts for US waters, and when traveling north into British Columbia, we look at the Environment Canada Marine Pacific reports and forecasts. We compare the forecast in text format with the NOAA Surface Analysis charts. They should coincide. Even the 48-hour forecast should coincide with the forecast results. We take notes and start worksheets for the upcoming days.

Weather and Sea Conditions Worksheet. A worksheet to facilitate collecting and organizing weather and sea conditions information is available as a free download at the Waggoner Guide Store, free eBook section, Weather Checklist. This worksheet also includes a detailed description of the format and order of information presentation on VHF weather channels and telephone broadcasts. Recording the VHF WX forecasts with your smartphone allows you to replay relevant portions of the forecast.

Weather Reporting Stations. Using the two *Weather Reporting Stations* reference maps in this section, note and record the weather reporting station names along your day's route on the worksheet. Next, gather the weather reports for these stations from either the internet, by calling on a cell phone to the numbers shown on the weather maps, or by listening on the WX VHF. The worksheet list of weather reporting stations keeps us focused on the stations we care to record from the continuous audio format. When listening to the WX channels, listen for the station names along the route. The weather worksheet has outlines of the Continuous Marine Broadcasts for both U.S. NWS and Environment Canada. They are different. The outline will help you determine where you are in the sequence of a WX broadcast.

We start with the synopsis for the area. Next, we record the relevant station reports and then the lighthouse and buoy reports, with particular attention to the reported wind direction, speed and sea condition.

Check the Tides and Currents. Next, look up in a Tide and Current Guide to determine whether you will be cruising with a Flood or an Ebb current, and the time of slack. This will be useful to understanding the sea state as the day progresses. Avoid wind opposing current situations. This information is not included in a weather forecast and must be understood by the mariner using a tide and current guide or software to understand the sea state. Rather than just a go or no-go situation, we may see that it is best to delay a departure for a couple of hours for a more

favorable current situation. Lastly, see where we are in the lunar cycle by looking up the phase of the moon in the Tide and Current guide. A full moon or a new moon means tides and currents will be at their strongest, and slack will be very short for tidal rapids.

Once all this information is gathered, you can develop a picture of the weather for your departure and route for the day. You will understand where the weather systems are and the resulting conditions for your route. You will know areas of wind; you can check to see if there will be wind opposing a current and determine your strategy. You can see if the forecast matches the conditions reported in a lighthouse or buoy report. If the forecast does not match, beware.

You and Your Boat's Tolerances. Next is comparing forecast conditions and observations with tolerances for your vessel and especially for your crew. You can minimize surprises while underway by gathering and evaluating as much information as possible from as many sources as possible. Gather the information described above and there should not be too many surprises while underway, though Mother Nature is known to shift plans.

It's always a good idea to have fail-safe contingency plans or duck-in points if things change. For crossing the Strait of Georgia or Cape Caution, you can look to see if you have an opposing, beam-to, or following sea. This may change your go or no-go tolerances or the direction on your route.

Go-NoGo Checklists. Checklists to aid in evaluating conditions for a Go or NoGo decision are located in four chapters describing the passages: Strait of Juan de Fuca; Strait of Georgia; Cape Caution; and Dixon Entrance. These checklists summarize the more important conditions to consult before making that all important decision to proceed with the passage or wait for more favorable conditions. The lists include specifics for the area including weather forecasts, names and numbers for weather buoys, and names of lighthouse and weather station locations to consult when evaluating conditions. The checklists are intended to be summarized lists.

Checklist items are grouped into these topic areas: Tides & Currents; Weather System Predictions; Weather & Seas Forecasts; Observations & Present Conditions; Go-NoGo Decision; Fail-Safe Contingency Plans. The heading line for each category includes a brief notation (Internet; Phone; Satellite; VHF) listing the sources for current information.

Underway – Monitor and Log Actual Conditions. At regular intervals along your planned route, make log entries noting the wind and sea conditions you encounter.

INTERPRETING NORTHWEST WEATHER

The Current Surface Analysis Chart for September 16, 2016 shows High Pressure over the area from Seattle up through the Strait of Georgia.

Big lazy isobar lines indicate light wind.

Note how this is consistent with both the U.S. National Weather Service (NWS) and Canadian Environment Canada text forecasts on the right side of this page.

Current Surface Analysis Chart

National Weather Service Forecast Synopsis for Northern Waters

On this 24-Hour Surface Forecast we can see the Low pressure system moving in from offshore and the isobars bunching up tighter.

The text forecasts show the wind and waves picking up as the Low comes ashore on Saturday through Saturday night. You can use this information to make a go or no-go decision.

From this you can see that it would be best to go north on Friday. If you cannot leave then you should most likely wait until Sunday.

24-Hour Surface Analysis Chart

National Weather Service Summary Forecast for Northern Waters

This 48-Hour Surface Forecast shows that another low is approaching with forecast seas of 2 feet. Tuesday's forecast returns to about 1 ft. seas.

48-Hour Surface Analysis Chart

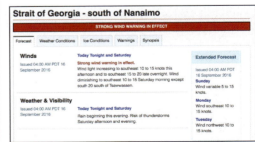
Environment Canada Forecast Strait of Georgia - South of Nanaimo

2020 WAGGONER CRUISING GUIDE

INTERPRETING NORTHWEST WEATHER

Record how your boat handled the different seas. If your actual conditions are significantly different from forecast expected conditions, note this in your log and always be prepared to use your contingency plans. Sometimes the best option is to head to a safe port and wait for better conditions.

Planned vs Actual. After arriving at your destination, review your log of actual conditions encountered along your route, to help develop experience with the forecasting tools. Make log entries to record how the vessel and crew managed with the day's actual conditions and note the forecast conditions. This will help develop experientially based interpretation of forecast weather for future trips and make the next go or no-go decision easier. For example, what will a forecast of 15 to 20 knot winds with five to six foot seas with a Dominant Wave Period (interval) of 12-15 seconds feel like, and how will your vessel handle it.

For a better understanding of weather. Consider learning more and taking a weather course. The Waggoner Guide and our Seattle Boat Show University or Cruisers College programs offer courses with weather experts, from 3-hour seminars to multi-day courses. Understanding the weather is a fascinating part of boating. The rewards when you get it right are substantial for you and your crew.

Passage GO-noGO Worksheet

Day's Passage:

Date: _____ From: _____ To: _____

Sunrise: _____ Sunset: _____ Lunar Cycle Stage _____

Location	Time	Heading	Tidal Current Flood/Ebb
From			
To			

Weather Forecast Synopsis Notes:

_____

_____

_____

Forecast by Reporting Station in Direction of Day's Passage:

1. _____ _____

2. _____ _____

3. _____ _____

Lightstation and Buoy Reports:

1. _____ Wind Dir & Speed _____ Sea Condition _____

2. _____ Wind Dir & Speed _____ Sea Condition _____

3. _____ Wind Dir & Speed _____ Sea Condition _____

COLLECTING WEATHER FORECASTS AND OBSERVED WEATHER INFORMATION

Via Internet

Environment Canada	weather.gc.ca/marine/
NOAA National Weather Svc.	www.weather.gov/sew
National Data Buoy Center	www.ndbc.noaa.gov
Ocean Prediction Center	www.opc.ncep.noaa.gov
	ocean.weather.gov

Via Telephone

Seattle	206-526-6087
Vancouver	604-666-3655
Victoria	250-363-6880
	250-363-6492
Comox	250-339-0748
Alert Bay	250-974-5305
Prince Rupert	250-624-9009
Tofino	250-726-3415

Via VHF Radio Continuous Broadcasts

(– see this section for Format & Order)

WX1	Seattle, Neah Bay, Cape Lazo, Alert Bay, Eliza Dome, Klemtu
WX2	Saltspring Island, Nootka, Calvert Island, Mt. Gil, Dundas, Island
WX3	Olympia, Mt. Helmcken, Bowen Island
WX4	Puget Sound, San Juan Islands
WX8/21B	Mt. Park, Discover Mtn., Holberg, Mt. Ozzard, Mt. Hays, Kitimat

COLLECTING WEATHER BUOY INFORMATION

Via Internet

U.S. NOAA National Weather Svc. www.weather.gov/sew
National Data Buoy Center www.ndbc.noaa.gov

Via Telephone

(Have Buoy numbers from maps on following pages)
Dial-A-Buoy 888-701-8992 or 301-713-9620

COLLECTING LIGHTSTATION REPORTS

Hourly reports originate from observations provided by Canadian Coast Guard staffed lightstations. Reports are normally taken during daylight hours. Reports generally conform to the format and coding below. The "Issued at" field at the top of the report indicates the Universal Time Coordinated (UTC) and date of the observation. (subtract 8 hours, or 7 hours during daylight savings, for local time)

Via Internet

Environment Canada   weather.gc.ca/marine/

Format and Order of Lighstation Report:

Name|Sky|Visibility|Weather|Wind Direction|Wind Speed|SeaState|Swell|Remarks

Sample Reports: CARMANAH OVC 15 RW E 22G30 2FT CHP
MCINNES   CLDY 15 CLM 1FT CHP LO SW
BOAT BLUFF PC 15 NW04 RPLD

Name: Station Identification Name

Sky: Sky Conditions – CLR (clear); CLDY (cloudy); PT CLDY (party cloudy); X (obscured); -X (partially obscured)

Visibility: Visibility measured in miles

Weather: Weather Elements – R (rain); RW (rain showers); S (snow); SW (snow showers); -L (drizzle); F (fog); T (thunder); A (hail);

Wind Direction: Eight compass points – N, S, E, W, NE, NW, SE, SW

Wind Speed: wind speed and sometimes gusts in knots; or CLM for calm.

Sea State: Wave height reported in feet; and sea state - SMTH (smooth); RPLD (ripped); CHP (chop); MOD (moderate); RUF (rough)

Swell: Direction and state of swell – LO (0 to 2 meters); MOD (2 to 4 meters); and HVY (greater than 4 meters)

Remarks: Abbreviations such as (OCNL RW- for occasional light rain shower)

www.WaggonerGuide.com

INTERPRETING NORTHWEST WEATHER

VHF WEATHER REPORT BROADCASTS ORDER – SAMPLE WEATHER BUOY REPORT

U.S. NOAA NATIONAL WEATHER SERVICE - The following numbered list is the order of information presented on NWS VHF continuous broadcasts.

1. Introduction
   - Date and time the forecast was prepared
   - Name of forecast area
     - Puget Sound and Hood Canal
     - Admiralty Inlet
     - Northern Inland Waters (including San Juan Islands)
     - East Entrance Strait of Juan de Fuca
     - Strait of Juan de Fuca
     - Pacific Waters - West Coast Vancouver Island

2. Marine Synopsis
   - An overview for an area, delivered by day

3. Hourly Observations Roundup
   - Weather conditions including wind speed (in knots), wind direction and barometric pressure (in millibars)

4. Marine Observations and Buoy Reports
   - Wind and sea conditions

5. Marine Forecast by area of Washington
   - Forecast winds, seas, and sky conditions for current and next three days
   - Special advisories such as Small Craft and Gale Warnings

ENVIRONMENT CANADA - The following lists the order of information presented on VHF weather channels in Canadian waters.

1. Introduction
   - Date and time the forecast was prepared
   - Warnings
   - Name of forecast area
     - Juan de Fuca Strait – East Entrance
     - Juan de Fuca Strait – Central
     - Haro Strait
     - Strait of Georgia – South of Nanaimo
     - Strait of Georgia – North of Nanaimo
     - Howe Sound
     - Johnstone Strait

2. Weather Summary by Area
   - Summary by area

3. Marine Weather Forecast Statement
   - Forecast winds, seas, and sky conditions for Today, Tonight, and Tomorrow
   - Special advisories such as Small Craft and Gale Warnings

4. Technical Marine Synopsis
   - Weather systems summary and position
   - Forecast weather systems 24 hour movement

5. Extended Marine Forecast for Pacific Water
   - Forecast conditions for 2 – 5 days
   - Delivered by area
     - Juan de Fuca Strait – East Entrance
     - Juan de Fuca Strait – Central
     - Haro Strait
     - Strait of Georgia – South of Nanaimo
     - Strait of Georgia – North of Nanaimo
     - Howe Sound
     - Johnstone Strait

6. Automated Reports - Weather conditions from automatic reporting stations.

7. Ocean Buoy Reports
   - Wind direction, speed, combined seas, and barometric pressure from buoys.

8. Lighthouse Weather Reports
   - Wind and sea conditions updated hourly by lighthouse operators

9. Local Marine Weather Reports

10. Special Reports
    - Special notices - such as status Military exercise areas like - Whiskey Golf (WG)

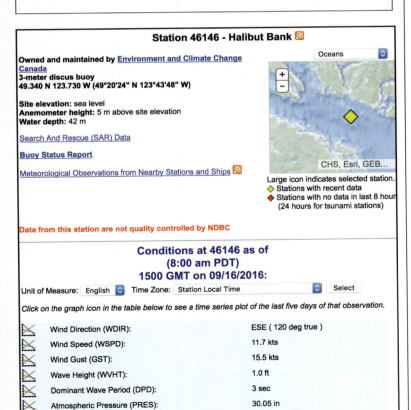

Halibut Bank - Buoy Report with actual conditions of wave heights of 1 foot or less. A DPD of 3 seconds warns of light chop.

INTERPRETING NORTHWEST WEATHER

WEATHER REPORTING STATIONS
WASHINGTON, BRITISH COLUMBIA, AND SE ALASKA

Weather Reporting Stations - South

Weather Reporting Stations - North

Differences Between U.S. & Canadian Charts

Canada and the United States are two separate nations, and their charts, while similar in many ways, have important differences.

U.S. charts are in fathoms and feet; most Canadian charts are metric. *With all charts, read the chart title and margin information to see if the chart is metric, fathoms and feet, or feet.* Metric charts show soundings and heights in meters. A meter (spelled metre in Canada) equals 39.37 inches, or 3.28 feet. Two meters equals 6 feet 7 inches, or just over one fathom. The difference is significant. Don't confuse fathoms with meters.

Waters appear to be deeper on U.S. charts of Pacific Northwest waters. This difference is important wherever the water is shallow, and is the result of the two countries using different *chart datums*.

Depths on a chart are measured from the chart datum, also called the reference plane or **tidal datum**. On Canadian charts, the chart datum is either Lowest Normal Tides, or Lower Low Water, Large Tide. For that reason, you don't find many "minus tides" in Canadian tide tables.

On U.S. charts of Pacific Northwest waters, however, the chart datum is Mean Lower Low Water. Mean Lower Low Water is the mean, or average, level of the lower of the two low tides each day. Since the U.S. chart datum has half the lower waters above it and half below it, U.S. tide books show minus tides.

It's not a question of whether the tide drops lower in Canada or the U.S. It's a question of where the depth is measured from. U.S. charts start their measurements from a point higher than Canadian charts. The difference can be as much as 1.5 meters, or almost 5 feet.

Example: Assume that you are in the U.S., skippering a sailboat. The sailboat's keel draws 5 feet, and you want to anchor overnight in a bay with a charted depth of one fathom (6 feet). According to the tide table, low tide will be minus 1.5 feet at 0700. Knowing that your boat, with its 5 feet of draft, would be aground in 4.5 feet of water, you would look for a more suitable anchorage.

If this bay were in Canada, the chart would show a depth of perhaps just 1 meter (assuming a Lowest Normal Tide lower than the tide at 0700). The tide table would show a low tide at 0700 of perhaps 0.4 meters. You would add the 1 meter depth from the chart to the 0.4 meter low tide from the tide table, and get 1.4 meters of water at 0700. Since you draw more than 1.4 meters (55 inches), you would not anchor in the bay that night.

Important Exception: Both Canadian and U.S. charts show soundings in the other country's system when the charts cover both sides of the border. The U.S. chart would convert Canadian meters to U.S. fathoms, but would adopt the Canadian chart datum in Canadian waters. The Canadian metric chart would convert U.S. fathoms to meters, but would adopt the U.S. chart datum in U.S. waters. This is explained in the chart legends.

Clearances appear to be greater on U.S. charts. U.S. charts for Northwest waters measure clearances from Mean High Water. One-half the high waters are above the mean. Canadian charts measure clearances from Higher High Water, Large Tides. The same bridge, over the same waterway, would show less vertical clearance on a Canadian chart than on a U.S. chart. Metric Canadian charts show heights and depths in meters; Canadian charts in fathoms and feet show heights in feet and depths in fathoms. A Canadian metric chart might show a bridge clearance as "3," meaning 3 meters above Higher High Water, Large Tides. A U.S. chart would show a bridge clearance as "12" or more, meaning 12 feet or more above Mean High Water.

Puget Sound No Discharge Zone

All of Puget Sound waters up to the Canadian border are a State of Washington designated No Discharge Zone (NDZ). It is illegal to discharge any (treated and untreated) black water sewage in this NDZ. In 2018, state law established the NDZ to improve area water quality and aid in the state's Shellfish Restoration initiative. Gray water is not included in the new regulations and there is no change for gray water discharges from onboard sinks and showers.

The Vessel Sewage NDZ includes all Washington marine waters east of New Dungeness Light, at the east end of the Strait of Juan de Fuca, plus Lake Washington, Lake Union, and the waters that connect them to Puget Sound.

Compliance means using an approved marine sanitation holding tank, securing the overboard thru-hull in the closed position and using pumpout facilities. If you have a Type I or Type II Treatment Marine Sanitation Device, you will need to secure it in a manner which prevents discharge of treated or untreated sewage by closing the seacock and removing the handle, or using a wire-tie.

Washington State boaters already practice good stewardship of state waters. The vast majority of vessels have holding tanks for use at pumpout facilities. State enforcement agents are first emphasizing outreach and education for this new law.

DIFFERENCES BETWEEN U.S. & CANADIAN CHARTS

Canadian charts use more symbols to show buoys and tide rips. Canadian charts use symbols that approximate the shapes of buoys, with letters to indicate the buoy's characteristics. U.S. charts use a single diamond-shaped symbol for nearly all navigation buoys, with descriptive letters to indicate the buoy's characteristics.

For example, U.S. Chart 18421, Strait of Juan de Fuca to Strait of Georgia (1:80,000), shows the bell buoy marking Buckeye Shoal, north of Cypress Island, as:

U.S. Chart 18421

But on Canadian Chart 3462, Juan de Fuca Strait to Strait of Georgia (1:80,000), the buoy is shown as:

Canadian Chart 3462

Canadian charts may use arrows to show the location of the buoy or beacon. If other detail on the chart makes precise location difficult, the Canadian chart will offset the symbol slightly, in the direction of the preferred navigable water. The offset is indicated by an arrow pointing to the actual location of the buoy or beacon. Sometimes the arrow is easy to overlook.

Chart No. 1 cracks the code. Nautical charts are filled with important navigation information. Unfortunately, so much of the information is in the form of symbols, abbreviations and undefined terms that it can be confusing. Each country has published a book that shows each symbol and defines each term used on its charts. The U.S. book is titled *Chart No. 1*; and the Canadian book is titled *Chart 1*. The Canadian book is available from Canadian Hydrographic chart agencies. The U.S. book is produced by several private publishers. Copies are available at marine supply outlets.

The Canadian Coast Guard publication *The Canadian Aids to Navigation System* explains the Canadian buoyage and light system, and is highly recommended. A PDF version is available on the Canadian Coast Guard website. The cost for the print version is $7.50 (Cdn) from Canadian Hydrographic chart agents, nautical bookstores and chandleries.

The introduction pages of both these books are filled with essential information. Don't overlook them.

LARGE SCALE, LARGE DETAIL

Large scale, large detail, that's the easy way to remember the difference between small scale and large scale charts. A small scale chart shows a large part of the earth's surface, but in small detail. Conversely, a large scale chart shows a small part of the earth's surface, but of course in great detail. Yes, it's counter-intuitive and confusing, but that's how it is. In the Northwest, large scale harbor charts typically have scales of 1:6,000, 1:12,000, 1:24,000. Medium scale charts have a scale of 1:40,000. Small scale charts have scales of 1:73,000 or 1:80,000.

At a scale of 1:12,000, 1 inch on the chart equals 12,000 inches (1,000 feet) on the earth. At a scale of 1:80,000, 1 inch on the chart equals 80,000 inches (6,667 feet) on the earth. When you are looking for the rock or picking your way through a narrow channel, the larger the scale of your chart, the easier your task will be.

If the Waggoner Cruising Guide is obsessed with anything, it is with safe navigation and the tools needed to accomplish safe navigation. *Large scale, large detail*. It works.

RUNNING IN THE FOG

Fog is an unavoidable reality of summer weather in the Northwest and on the British Columbia coast. On the Strait of Juan de Fuca, Vancouver Island's west coast, Johnstone Strait, Queen Charlotte Strait and Sound, and the Central Coast, you can pretty much depend on encountering fog almost daily from mid-July through September and sometimes much later in the season. So learning to navigate safely in "low viz" is critical.

The American Meteorological Society's *Glossary of Meteorology* defines fog as a collection of water droplets suspended in the atmosphere near the earth's surface that affects visibility. In temperate coastal areas like ours, fog results when warm air cools as it passes over cold water, which causes water vapor to condense and saturate the air. Fog may form in the evening, overnight or early-morning hours, then dissipate as the day warms. It may start sneaking over the trees into your anchorage near the end of cocktail hour – and you know you will wake up to pea soup.

When you do – and you will if you venture far from Puget Sound or the Strait of Georgia – here are some thoughts to help you prepare for your next "low-viz" passage.

Go or no-go? Should you set out in poor visibility in the first place? If you don't really have to go, don't. Running in fog is a stress-inducing business that can take the fun out of cruising, and it can be dangerous. The wisest course may be to wait for the fog to burn off, as it always does sooner or later.

In weighing a decision to run in fog, consider how well you know the waters you'll be navigating – a run through home water is a completely different challenge from transiting an area for the first time. Are the waters you'll navigate unobstructed – or encumbered with hazards that radar may not help you avoid? How much vessel traffic – big and small – might you encounter? High-traffic areas of Puget Sound, the Strait of Georgia and the Inside Passage are subject to vessel traffic management systems. Do you know how to listen for VTS operators' instructions to mariners around you and call them for guidance?

Make a Plan B. Where will you go if it becomes too risky to continue…or your nerves fail you? Is there a harbor en route that is clear enough to enter safely even if you can't see a thing?

And consider this: if you cruise long enough and seriously enough you will probably have to run in fog someday. If you can do it safely, why not try? It can be a tremendous learning opportunity and confidence-booster.

Slow down. This sounds obvious – but some boaters have trouble doing this under any conditions. Reducing your speed increases the amount of time you have to spot obstacles, hazards or vessels and take evasive action. If you hit something at reduced speed, it will do less damage and hopefully you will avoid catastrophic damage.

Trust your equipment. It goes without saying that you should have complete confidence in your navigation suite – plotter, sounder, radar, AIS and, yes, paper charts – you should know how to use them and know their limitations. We rely on sight to orient ourselves in space and find our way. Deprive us of visual cues and we veer off course or ramble in circles, still convinced we're on course. Magnetic compasses have helped mariners for centuries, so trust yours. Better yet, the electronic compass built into your vessel's autopilot is even more accurate and enables your autopilot to steer a precise course for hours or days, freeing you to keep a closer watch.

Radar paints a clear picture of your surroundings, *as long you know how to read it.* It's a good habit to run with radar even in clear conditions so you can see how blips and images appear on screen in relation to vessels and objects around you while you can still see them. Add an AIS receiver/transceiver and you'll have a clear, precise reading of the course, speed and size of vessels you may not be able to see, especially the big, fast-moving ones.

However, it is the modern chartplotter running reliable electronic charts that brings safe passages in low visibility within reach of recreational mariners. Zoomed in to an appropriate level, a good plotter enables you to accurately pinpoint hazards you can't see and find safe water through them. Remember, not all obstacles on all charts are depicted precisely, so a margin of error is prudent! Set your radar range to the same scale as your plotter – or overlay it on the plotter if you can – so you can match charted features with radar for a clearer picture of your surroundings. Three-dimensional charts that show bathymetric data are better still. Use your plotter's predicted track feature to point your way past hazards.

Finally, use your VHF radio. Commercial vessels routinely broadcast their approach to points or channels which may bring them close to other traffic, so monitor Channel 16 and VTS channels. Follow their example and announce your intentions when you enter waters where you may meet other vessels; invite concerned craft to respond. If you spot a converging target on radar, call them to determine their intentions and discuss how to pass or cross safely.

Listen and look carefully. There is still a place for our own sharpened senses when we think we can't see diddly. In steamship days, skippers and pilots used to blow a whistle and listen for the time it took for echoes to return in order to determine their distance from shore. It makes sense to throttle back from time to time. Step on deck and listen for whatever you might hear: a horn, voices, a nearby outboard, birds calling, the lap of waves against the shoreline, the low thrum of really big engines…or nothing at all.

In restricted visibility, Collision Regulations require you to sound a single prolonged (four to six seconds) horn blast every two minutes if you are under way, and two prolonged blasts if you are stopped. Sound carries well across still water and in fog and sends a clear message to anyone around. Don't forget to use your nose, as well. Water smells different than land; the odor of guano may tip you off to a seabird colony on an isolated rock; a whiff of engine exhaust may warn you of vessels nearby.

Even when you're sure you can't see a thing, you often still can – if you look hard enough. Have your crew keep an intent bow watch for anything you may not see from the helm. Step outside and look around carefully yourself. The white hull of that lone sport fisher rolling in the chop may appear so faintly you aren't sure it's there. Or the superstructure of a container ship or ferry may float serenely through the top layer of the mist…and, hopefully, it won't be too close.

[Duart Snow]

Buoys, Beacons and Ranges

Red, Right, Returning means leave **Red** navigation aids off your **Right** hand when you're **Returning** from seaward. If the navigation mark is not red, leave it off your left hand when you're returning from seaward.

This is the general rule in U.S. and Canadian waters, with three subtle refinements:

• Safe water mark. A buoy with red and white vertical stripes that marks an approach or mid-channel. Unobstructed water surrounds this mark. Both inbound and outbound, it is good practice to leave this buoy to port.

• Preferred channel mark. A buoy or a beacon with red and green horizontal bands. This aid marks a channel junction or an obstruction. While the aid can be passed on either side, the color of the top band indicates the preferred or main channel.

• Isolated danger mark. An aid—either a buoy or a beacon—with black and red horizontal bands that marks an isolated danger (an example would be the Blakely Island Shoal Isolated Danger Buoy DS, west of Blakely Island in the San Juan Islands). These marks have navigable water all around, but should not be approached closely without caution.

Nuns. All red buoys marking channels are shaped as cones, and are called nuns. Most nun buoys are painted solid red. If the nun buoy has a green horizontal band painted on it, the buoy marks the meeting of two channels, with the left channel being the preferred, or main, channel. (If you leave the buoy to starboard, you will be in the left channel.) If lighted, the light will be red.

Cans. All green buoys marking channels are called cans. They are shaped like, well, cans. Most can buoys are painted solid green. If the can buoy has a horizontal red band painted on it, the buoy marks the meeting of two channels, with the right channel the preferred, or main, channel. If lighted, the light will be green.

Beacons. Buoys float, and are held in place by heavy anchoring systems, but beacons are permanent navigation aids attached to the earth. Beacons can be located on land, installed on docks or breakwaters, or mounted on pilings. A lighthouse is a beacon. A beacon not on land will be placed in shallow water outside a channel. Do not pass a beacon close aboard. Give it considerable room.

An unlighted beacon is called a daybeacon. A lighted beacon is called a minor light. A minor light marking the right side of a channel will carry a red light (Red, Right, Returning). A minor light marking the left side of a channel will carry a green light. If a minor light marks the meeting of two channels, it will be red if the left channel is preferred; green if the right channel is preferred.

Daymarks are the colored panels mounted on beacons. Red panels are triangle shaped; green panels are square. A triangle shaped red panel with a green horizontal stripe indicates the meeting of two channels, with the left channel the preferred, or main channel. A square panel painted green with a red horizontal stripe indicates the meeting of two channels, with the right channel the preferred channel.

Whenever a navigation aid is marked with a horizontal stripe of contrasting color, the color at the top of the aid indicates the preferred, or main channel.

Approaching a channel from seaward, buoys and beacons are numbered, beginning with the marks to seaward. Red buoys, daybeacons, and minor lights carry even numbers, such as 2, 4, 6, and so on. Green buoys, daybeacons, and minor lights carry odd numbers, such as 1, 3, 5, and so on. Depending on the channel, it might be appropriate to skip some numbers, so that buoy 6 is roughly opposite buoy 5, even if no buoy 4 exists.

Ranges. Ranges are used to help a boat stay in the middle of a narrow channel.

Ranges are rectangular panels standing vertically, each with a wide stripe running from top to bottom down the middle of the panel. Ranges are attached to the earth and arranged in pairs, one behind the other. The rear range board stands taller than the front range board. To use a range, steer until the rear range board appears to be on top of the front board. You can steer toward a range, looking ahead (leading range), or away from a range, sighting astern (back range).

Buoys and beacons are not selected and placed at random. They follow a plan, although to a newcomer the plan may at times seem obscure.

Despite the complexity of the buoyage and light system, you will find that as you understand it better your enjoyment afloat will increase. At some point you will want a thorough explanation of the entire system. For U.S. waters it will be found in the introduction to the Coast Guard Light List. For Canadian waters it will be found partly in the introduction to the Canadian Coast Guard List of Lights, Buoys and Fog Signals, and completely in the Canadian Coast Guard publication, The Canadian Aids to Navigation System. Latest editions of these publications should be aboard every boat. They are available at chart agencies and chandleries.

Red, Right Returning

RED, RIGHT, RETURNING from the sea means the conical red nun buoy marks the right side of the channel. Vessels returning from the sea upstream will leave red navigation aids to starboard. Red aids are assigned even numbers, beginning with No. 2 at the seaward end of the channel.

Nun Buoy

A GREEN CAN buoy marks the left side of the channel. Vessels returning from the sea or upstream will leave green navigation aids to port. Green aids are assigned odd numbers, beginning with No. 1 at the seaward end of the channel. Buoys and beacons can be lighted or unlighted.

Can Buoy

A BEACON, such as this light at Webster Point in Lake Washington, is attached to the earth, and should be given a good offing. Port-hand beacons carry square green dayboards; starboard-hand beacons carry red triangular dayboards.

Lighted Beacon

CYLINDRICAL WHITE RESTRICTED OPERATIONS BUOYS, such as this one, mark speed zones, restricted anchoring areas, fish habitats and other important information.

Restricted Operation Buoy

2020 WAGGONER CRUISING GUIDE

Nordic Tugs
A Tradition of Excellence

NT44

Reasons to Buy a Nordic Tug

Built in the USA to NMMA & ABYC standards
Fast trawler - Cruise up to 14-15 knots, 17-18 knots WOT
Comfortable luxury surrounded by strenghth & performance
Great efficiency at hull speed - typically 2-2.5 gph
Comfortable & spacious interiors
10 year structural hull warranty
Extensive sea-trial for every boat
High resale value
Decades of hull refinement
Hard chine bottom that reduces roll

NT40

NT 26' • NT 34' • NT 40' • NT 44' • NT 49' • NT 54'

Factory Direct Sales

360.757.8847   ext. 108 or 115   www.nordictugs.com   sales@nordictugs.com

VHF Radio Procedures

The VHF radio is an important piece of safety equipment, and VHF 16 should be monitored when the boat is underway. While monitoring, you will hear weather and safety warnings, and be aware of what's happening around you. A boat close by, for example, may be having problems and call for help. By monitoring your radio, you can respond.

Station Licenses, U.S. Vessels. Until 1996, U.S. pleasure craft were required to have station licenses for their marine VHF radios. In 1996, however, the requirement was dropped for pleasure craft under 20 meters (65 feet), operating inside the U.S. only. All U.S. vessels operating in foreign waters, including Canada, still need a U.S. station license. With the 1999 dropping of station licenses in Canada (see below), it was hoped that pleasure craft exempted from station licenses in the U.S. no longer would need a station license to travel in Canadian waters. It now appears that it would require an act of Congress—literally!—to exempt U.S. pleasure craft from needing a station license for Canadian travel, and that's not likely. As a practical matter, Canadian authorities do not enforce U.S. radio license laws, and U.S. authorities are not going to follow a boat into Canada. In other words, there's no enforcement. We have our station license, however, and would not be without it, enforcement or no enforcement. We recommend that our readers do the same. Apply for your station license at the same time you register for your Maritime Mobile Service Identity (MMSI) number. You will need this number to use the Digital Selective Calling (DSC) and emergency calling features all VHF radios have. You can register online at www.fcc.gov, using the Universal Licensing System (ULS). The online process is cumbersome, but the processing time is short. The forms are also available from the FCC at (888) 225-5322 (Monday through Friday), if you apply by mail. If you call, choose menu option 2, Licensing. The person who took our call was well-informed and helpful. A station license serves the entire vessel, regardless of the number of VHF radios the vessel has. The station license also covers the use of a tender's VHF radio (such as a handheld model) as long as the radio is used in tender service, and as long as it is not used on land. It's all right for two or more radios from the same vessel with the same call sign to talk to each other via handheld VHF radio. U.S. pleasure craft longer than 20 meters, and all U.S. commercial vessels, are required to have an FCC station licenses.

Station Licenses, Canadian Vessels. Beginning in March 1999, station licenses no longer were issued to Canadian vessels so long as 1) the vessel is not operated in the sovereign waters of a country other than Canada or the U.S.; 2) the radio equipment on board the vessel is capable of operating only on frequencies that are allocated for maritime mobile communications or marine radio navigation. Canadian vessels not meeting those two requirements must have station licenses.

Operator's Permit, U.S. The U.S. does not require operator's permits for VHF radio use within the U.S. For foreign travel, however, a Restricted Radio Operator's permit is required. The U.S. individual permit is issued for life, and costs $60. If you are from the U.S. and take a boat to Canada, you will need a Restricted Radio Operator permit. Use Schedule E of FCC Form 605 to apply, and Form 159 to remit payment. If you are applying for both a station license and a Restricted Radio Operator permit you will need a separate Form 159 for each application. The forms can be downloaded from www.fcc.gov, or you can apply electronically on the FCC website.

Operator's Permit, Canada. Canada requires each person operating a VHF radio to have a Restricted Operator's Certificate. For Canadian residents a test must be passed, but the certificate is free and issued for life. Training for the test and the issuing of certificates is handled by the Canadian Power and Sail Squadrons.

> **VHF RADIO TOPICS**
> Station Licenses, U.S. Vessels
> Station Licenses, Canadian Vessels
> Operator's Permit, U.S.
> Operator's Permit, Canada
> How to use the VHF radio
> The Low Power Switch
> When Not to Call on Channel 16
> DSC & GMDSS
> Mayday Hoaxes
> Contacting the Coast Guard by Cell
> Automatic Identification System

> **RADIO CHECK**
> U.S. and Canadian Coast Guard ask that VHF Radio Check requests be made on a working channel. In U.S. waters that would be channel 22A and in Canadian waters that would be 83A. Requests for radio check should never be made on channel 16.

Reliable voice, email and messaging communications for the Inside Passage to Alaska and beyond.

Enjoy the piece of mind that a satellite phone system can bring you on your next trip and stay in contact with those back home, for less than cellular roaming in many cases.

Satellite Communications Sales, Support, & Rentals

206.878.8270
www.ocens.com

2020 WAGGONER CRUISING GUIDE

VHF RADIO PROCEDURES

How to Use the VHF Radio. The easiest way to get a general sense of radio use is to monitor VHF 16, the hailing and distress channel; VHF 22A, the U.S. Coast Guard channel; VHF 83A, the Canadian Coast Guard channel, and the working channels. The VTS channels are good, too, because you'll be listening to professional mariners at work. VTS transmissions are brief and often informal, but you'll be listening to experienced people in action. On VHF 16 and the ship-to-ship working channels, you'll also hear inexperienced people. The difference will be obvious. To use the radio, call on the calling channel, VHF 16. When communication is established, switch to a working channel for your conversation. Except in instances of distress, you may not have a conversation on VHF 16. VHF 09 may be used for conversations; but because it is an alternate calling channel in the U.S., the conversations should be brief.

The Low Power Switch. VHF radios can transmit at 25 watts, their highest power rating, or at 1 watt, the low power mode. Handheld VHF radios usually have a maximum power of 5 watts and low power of 1 watt. Whenever practical, use the low-power mode. Other vessels a few miles away can then use the same channel without interference from you. The difference between high power and low power affects transmission distance only. Reception ability is unaffected. Handheld radios should use low power whenever possible. The battery lasts longer. When making a securite call, such as transiting Dodd Narrows or Malibu Rapids, be sure to have your VHF radio set on **LOW POWER** (1 watt). A securite call is for traffic safety purposes only and is not a call for right-of-way. Vessels traveling with the current are the 'stand-on' and vessels traveling against the current flow are the 'give-way.'

AIS display shows nearby vessels and potential conflicts. In this case it shows the fleet of sailboats at the start of the Swiftsure International Yacht Race.

When Not to Call on Channel 16. Large vessels in the VTS traffic lanes usually do not monitor VHF 16. They monitor the VTS channel for their area. In Puget Sound waters covered by Seattle VTS Traffic, large vessels also must monitor VHF 13, the bridge-to-bridge communications channel. Seattle Traffic covers all U.S. waters and the entire Strait of Juan de Fuca, including the Canadian side. If you are disabled in a traffic lane and a large vessel is bearing down on

CRUISERS COLLEGE
INCREASE YOUR NAUTICAL KNOWLEDGE AND DIY CLASSES

WATCH FOR OUR SEMINAR COURSES ON:
- Hands-on Diesel Engine Troubleshooting
- Troubleshooting Electrical Problems on Your Boat
- Taking Care of the Fiberglass Boat
- Troubleshooting Outboard Motors
- Troubleshooting Vessel Systems
- Marine Weather
- Cruising Essentials for Women
- Using New Technology for Navigation and Communications

To see a schedule of our up coming classes go to www.WaggonerGuide.com/CruisersCollege
Or call the Waggoner Guide office to register at 425.780.5015

Cruisers College is brought to you by

VHF RADIO PROCEDURES

you, call the vessel on the appropriate VTS channel (see VTS Radio Channels chart in the *What Recreational Boaters Need to Know About VTS* section in this chapter). If you are still unsure about what to do, call the Coast Guard on VHF 16 and ask them to contact the vessel for you, or to provide you with the correct channel.

DSC & GMDSS. DSC stands for Digital Selective Calling, and is part of the Global Maritime Distress and Safety System (GMDSS). Basically, if you have a DSC radio with a valid MMSI (Maritime Mobile Service Identity) number in its memory and push the covered red button, the radio will send an automatic digital distress message on VHF 70. This message contains the MMSI number, which is linked to a database that includes your name, vessel information, emergency contacts, and other information. If the vessel's GPS is connected to the VHF, or the radio is equipped with a GPS receiver, the radio also transmits GPS coordinates. For this to work, the radio must have the vessel's MMSI number stored in its memory. MMSI numbers are issued in the United States by the FCC or BoatUS, and in Canada by Transport Canada and Industry Canada. Important for U.S. vessels traveling to Canada: Officially, MMSI numbers issued by BoatUS are only for use in the United States. However, a BoatUS MMSI number will work in Canada, but the database information may not be available to Canadian authorities. The distress signal and your location, if your radio is connected to a GPS signal, will be transmitted to authorities and other DSC equipped vessels to alert other boats. Brief your crew before heading out on a passage on how to summon help using the red DISTRESS button on your VHF radio. Consider preparing a check-list for emergencies for your crew that includes summoning help on the VHF radio and even the location of your safety equipment. For more information on this critical topic,
see WaggonerGuide.com and search for the article on "Prepare Your Vessel for an Emergency." The article has many useful tips on how to prepare an emergency manual for use by your crew in case of an emergency.

Mayday Hoaxes. Each year, hoax Mayday calls cost the U.S. and Canadian Coast Guards millions of dollars ($2 million in Seattle alone) and in some cases put lives at risk. Sometimes the hoax is Junior playing with Grandpa's radio, sometimes it is the result of things getting too festive, sometimes the caller has a mental problem. Now that direction-finding equipment can locate the sources of radio calls, arrests can be made and penalties assessed. Radios are not toys, and hoax Mayday calls are not jokes. Large fines and even jail terms are the penalties.

LOCAL KNOWLEDGE

To Reach the Coast Guard by Cell or Smartphone App

U.S. Coast Guard Rescue Center Seattle
911 or (206) 220-7001

U.S. Coast Guard Rescue Center Juneau
(for all of southeast Alaska) 911
or (907) 463-2000

Canadian Coast Guard 911
or *16 or (250) 413-8933

Android and iOS smartphones can access and hail U.S. Coast Guard with their free official USCG App. The App has an emergency button as well as access to other helpful information.

Automatic Identification System (AIS). AIS is a VHF-based radio tracking system for commercial and recreational vessels. Vessels equipped with AIS transponders transmit their name, course, speed, MMSI number, vessel size, and destination. Vessels equipped with AIS receivers display information from surrounding vessels and warn of potential conflicts. Large commercial vessels are required to have Class-A transponders while recreational vessels optionally have Class-B transponders. In the past, the high cost limited AIS transponders to only larger recreational vessels and AIS receivers to some recreational boats. The cost to equip your boat with both transmit and receive continues to get more affordable all the time. AIS transmit is particularly valuable in low visibility situations and when operating near large commercial traffic. Vessel name and MMSI AIS information makes it much easier to call a nearby vessel regarding potential conflicts. The price to equip your vessel with an AIS receiver is very affordable and well worth the expense.

New AIS applications show up each season. Small AIS man-overboard devices that attach to lifejackets are available; when activated, show a MOB alert on all AIS equipped vessels nearby. AIS system design provides for a number of different message types that include virtual navigation aids, observed weather information, and local harbor/port information.

Vesper announced an AIS transceiver combined with a completely redesigned VHF radio. Cortex was anounced in late 2019 but is still awaiting FCC certifications in the U.S. This new device also incorporates vessel system monitoring.

SCOLDING ON THE RADIO

When a fellow boater does something that is dangerous or inconsiderate, proper VHF radio protocol does not allow the injured party to start yelling at "the boat that just went by" without identifying themselves – especially not on high power. If it's necessary to talk to the other boater – first switch to LOW POWER – then try to hail the boat by name and switch to a working channel.

Most people don't realize they're doing something wrong, so start by explaining the situation. Make sure it's a conversation and not a lecture. Explain the situation and listen to the response. A civil conversation is more likely to get results than an angry lecture. Make sure you are on a working channel and on low power.

SECURITÉ CALL INSTEAD OF BIG WAKE SCOLD

When a nearby boat is creating a large and potentially dangerous wake, instead of getting on the VHF radio and blindly scolding – do everyone a favor and issue a Securité call to alert other boats in the area. First switch to LOW POWER, then call: "Securité, Securité, this is the 34-foot sailing vessel WINDY– caution for a potentially dangerous wake from a fast-moving large black-on-white power boat in Mosquito Pass."

"Securité"
"Securité"
"Securité"

2020 WAGGONER CRUISING GUIDE

STATE AND PROVINCIAL PARKS AND PUBLIC WHARVES

The waters from Puget Sound north into B.C. are dotted with more than 200 state, provincial, and national parks, and in B.C., more than 220 public wharves.

Washington Parks. At the state level, parks are administered by the Washington State Parks and Recreation Commission and by the Department of Natural Resources (DNR). Usually, DNR sites are on the primitive side. State parks, which tend to be more developed, charge for moorage at buoys and docks. For docks and floats, expect to pay $.70 per foot, $14 minimum. Mooring buoys are $15. The dock or buoy fee applies after 1:00 p.m., payable for even a stop-and-go visit, such as walking the dog. *Unless otherwise marked, buoys are for boats 45 feet and less; boats longer than 45 feet are not allowed.* Rafting is allowed for boats 36 feet and less. Each rafted boat must pay a moorage fee.

State parks charge moorage fees year-round. Annual moorage permits are available and valid from January 1 to December 31, $5 per foot, $60 minimum. Contact Washington State Parks Information, (360) 902-8844 (Monday through Friday), or infocent@parks.wa.gov. Or check their informative website at parks.state.wa.us/435/Boating.

Campsite fees are paid in addition to dock or mooring buoy fees. Self-register ashore for moorage or campsites.

Boat launch sites. State parks with boat launches charge fees of $7. The launch fee includes the daily parking fee. Annual launch permits cost $80 and are valid for a year from date of purchase. Contact Washington State Parks, (360) 902-8844, or from parks.state.wa.us/435/Boating.

Reservations. Moorage is unreserved. Leaving a dinghy or other personal property at a buoy or dock does not reserve moorage. Rafting is permitted, but not mandatory. Rafting is allowed on buoys, within specified limits. Reservations (for campsites only) in all state parks are accepted. Call toll-free (888) 226-7688.

Department of Natural Resources parks generally are primitive or have few facilities, and most do not charge fees.

Washington Boater Education Card. All operators of boats with motors of 15 horsepower or more born after January 1, 1955 are required to have their Washington State Boater Education Card. Washington State Parks administers this program. See their website at http://boat.wa.gov/ or call (360) 902-8555.

If you are boating in Canadian waters for longer than 44 days a Canadian Operator Card, or the equivalent issued by a state in the U.S. is required. The Washington Boater Education Card qualifies for cruising more than 44 days, as do U.S. Coast Guard licenses such as Captain's or Mate's license.

Public docks provide access to parks and islands.

Canadian Boater Pleasure Craft Operator Card (PCOC). Canada has a similar program for its boaters, requiring boater education and certification. In B.C., several firms offer classes and testing services to prove competency. A special program called "Rental Boating Safety Checklist" is for power-driven rental boats and bareboat charter boats. Consult your Canadian charter company for more information and requirements.

B.C. Parks, Including Gulf Islands National Park Reserve Parks. Most B.C. marine parks have floats or mooring buoys, and safe, all-weather anchorages. Marine parks are open year-round. Some have no on-shore facilities, others have day-use facilities, picnic areas, and developed campsites. Most parks have drinking water. Overnight moorage fees ($12 for a buoy; $2/meter for dock moorage) are charged at a number of the more developed parks. No rafting is permitted on mooring buoys. No charge for anchoring, even with a stern-tie to shore. Tent sites are extra. Contact B.C. Parks General Information at www.env.gov.bc.ca/bcparks. For more information on the Gulf Islands National Park Reserve, contact (866) 944-1744, or see their website at www.pc.gc.ca. On the homepage select "Find a National Park" and select "Gulf Islands National Park Reserve."

Public Wharves. In British Columbia, public wharves provide moorage for commercial vessels (primarily the fishing fleet) and pleasure craft. Especially in the off-season, public wharves are filled with fish boats, leaving little or no moorage for pleasure craft. Facilities vary, from a dock only, to fully-serviced marinas. Most of the public wharves now are operated by local harbor authorities or their equivalents. Locally-run public wharves charge market rates, and may reserve space for pleasure craft. Moorage fees vary. Public wharves are easily identified by their red-painted railings.

NO DISCHARGE ZONES (NDZ)

PUGET SOUND - all of Puget Sound waters up to the Canadian Border are an NDZ No discharge of any (treated and untreated) black water in this zone. Compliance means using an approved sanitation device holding tank and having thru-hull valves secured with wire ties or zip ties. Gray water (from sinks and showers) is not included in these regulations.

BRITISH COLUMBIA - discharge of black water is not allowed in the following areas. Approved holding tanks are required in these areas. Macerator treatment systems, even if approved in the U.S., do not qualify. Unless otherwise noted, Gray water is not included in the regulations.

- Pirates Cove (no gray)
- Prideaux Haven
- Roscoe Bay
- Smuggler Cove
- Squirrel Cove
- Tod Inlet
- Victoria Harbour
- Carrington Bay
- Cortes Bay
- Gorge Harbour
- Ladysmith Harbour
- Mansons Landing
- Montague Harbour
- Pilot Bay

What Recreational Boaters Need to Know About VTS

Much of the information below is general in nature. It is intended to give recreational boaters a broad understanding of the Vessel Traffic Service (VTS) and how VTS can improve safety for all boats.

VTS is primarily for commercial vessels, although all power driven vessels 40 meters (131 feet) or longer, commercial or recreational, must be active participants. Active VTS participants are required to maintain radio watch on the assigned VTS channel for the waters they are in, and to call in at designated points with their location, course, speed, and estimated time of arrival (ETA) at the next call-in point. The VTS centers keep track of all active participant vessels and advise of any traffic that might interfere.

All power driven vessels between 20 meters (66 feet) and 40 meters (131 feet) must be passive participants, meaning they must keep a radio watch on the appropriate VTS radio channels.

Pleasure craft should monitor VTS. Although recreational vessels shorter than 20 meters are exempt from being active or passive participants in VTS, they must know how to keep out of the way of large, slow-maneuvering vessels. We keep our radio set on the VTS channel for the area we are cruising to hear where the large commercial vessels are operating.

Turn Point Special Operating Area. Turn Point is the northwest corner of the San Juan Islands' Stuart Island, where Haro Strait joins Boundary Pass. Turn Point is a blind corner. A recreational vessel could be completely unaware of a fast approaching ship on the other side. Monitor channel 11.

Separation Zones. The VTS lanes in Puget Sound, the Strait of Juan de Fuca, and the approaches to Haro Strait and Rosario Strait are divided into inbound and outbound lanes, with a separation zone between the two. The separation zones vary in width and are shown in magenta on the charts.

With the following precautions, pleasure craft are free to operate in the Puget Sound VTS lanes:

Pleasure craft, even vessels under sail, do not have right-of-way over VTS participant vessels and must not impede them in any way.

Wherever practical, pleasure craft should stay out of the VTS lanes, or at least minimize the length of time spent in the lanes. Large commercial vessels are required to remain in the VTS lanes unless cleared to do otherwise. It makes no sense to compete for that space.

If inbound in the VTS lanes, run in the inbound lane; if outbound, run in the outbound lane. Keep a lookout astern for overtaking vessels.

If crossing the VTS lane(s), try to cross at right angles to minimize the time spent in the traffic lanes. This is not always possible or practical, but it should be the objective.

Do not loiter or fish in the VTS separation zones.

Be aware of what is going on—ahead, astern, and to the sides. In the jargon this is called "situational awareness." Give large vessels lots of room. Make early and substantial course adjustments. Show them some side, meaning the side of your boat. (This is good practice whenever two vessels meet, regardless of size.)

If there's any doubt at all, cross behind a large vessel, not in front of it. A container ship traveling at only 11 knots needs more than a mile to come to a complete stop. Many container ships travel at 20 knots or more, which lengthens their stopping distance.

If you see a tug, look for a tow. Never, ever, pass between a tug and its tow. Leave ample room when crossing behind a tow.

Radio communication. While active VTS participants (large vessels and tugs with tows) are required to maintain radio watch on the appropriate VTS radio channel, such as VHF 14 in Puget Sound south of Bush Point, they are not required to monitor VHF 16, and many do not. Participants in Seattle Traffic waters also are required to monitor VHF 13, the U.S. bridge-to-bridge channel. Canada does not use VHF 13.

To contact a large vessel in Seattle Traffic

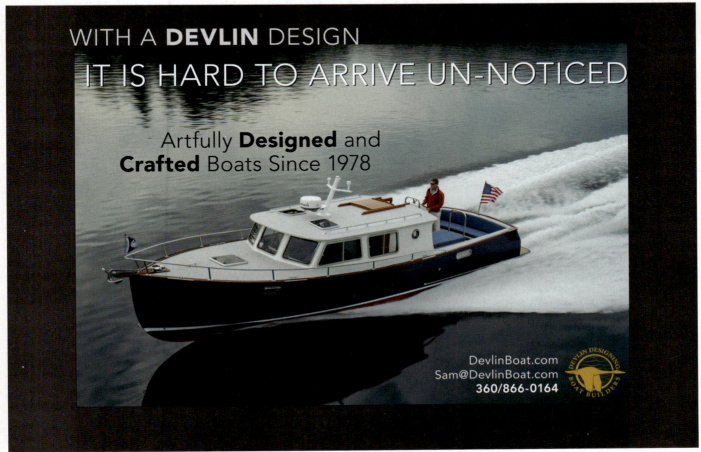

2020 WAGGONER CRUISING GUIDE

VTS Radio Channels - Puget Sound to Dixon Entrance

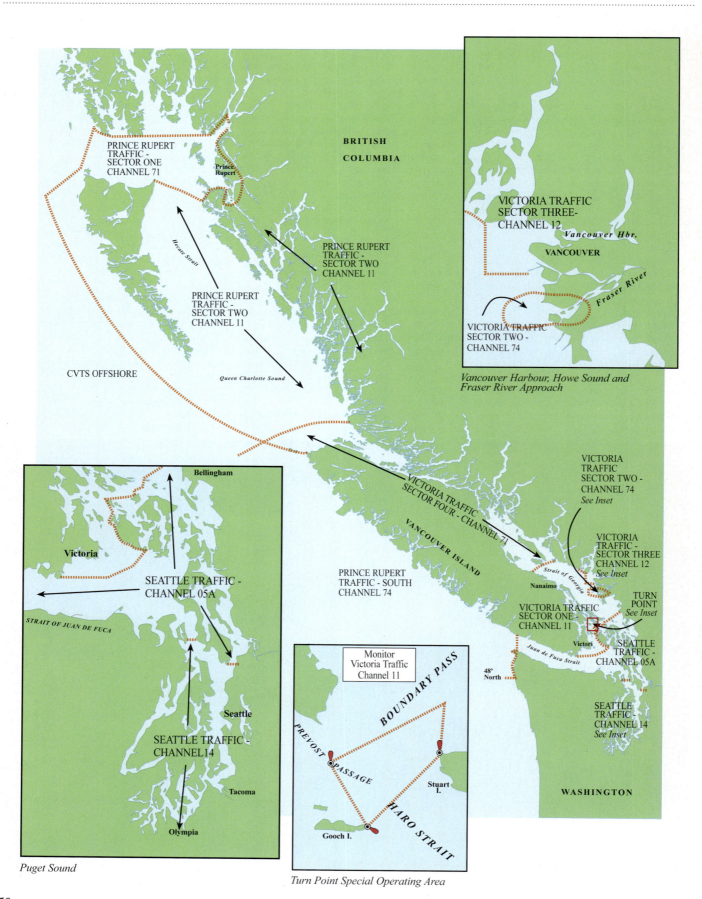

WHAT RECREATIONAL BOATERS NEED TO KNOW ABOUT VTS

VTS RADIO CHANNELS

TRAFFIC AREA	AREA DESCRIPTION	VHF CHANNEL
Seattle Traffic	Puget Sound west of Whidbey Island and south of Bush Point.	14
Seattle Traffic	Strait of Juan de Fuca (including Canadian waters), and Puget Sound north of Bush Point on the west side of Whidbey Island, including the San Juan Islands and Rosario Strait. Also the entire east side of Whidbey Island.	05A
Prince Rupert Traffic – South	West Coast of Vancouver Island & approaches to the Strait of Juan de Fuca.	74
Victoria Traffic – Sector One	Southern Area, Race Rocks (Victoria) to Ballenas Island/ Merry Island. This includes Haro Strait, Boundary Pass, the Gulf Islands, and the southern part of the Strait of Georgia, except for Vancouver Harbour and the Fraser River.	11
Turn Point Special Operating Area	Haro Strait/Boundary Pass. See map and text.	11
Victoria Traffic – Sector Two	Fraser River, Sand Heads to Shoal Point, New Westminster.	74
Victoria Traffic – Sector Three	Vancouver Harbour and approaches.	12
Victora Traffic – Sector Four	Ballenas Island/Merry Island north to Cape Caution. This includes the northern part of the Strait of Georgia and Inside Passage waters north to Cape Caution.	71
Prince Rupert Traffic – Sector One	Prince Rupert Harbour & approaches, including the north end of Grenville Channel, Chatham Sound, and all of Dixon Entrance to Langara Island.	71
Prince Rupert Traffic – Sector Two	Remainder of Zone. Hecate Strait, Cape Caution north to Alaska on the west side of Haida Gwaii.	11

waters call on VHF 13. In Canada VTS waters call on the appropriate VTS channel, such as VHF 11 in southern Strait of Georgia waters.

We have made such calls a few times with excellent results. Twice in narrow channels, the large vessel voluntarily reduced speed to lower its wake. One time it was a cruise ship in northern B.C.; the other time it was a deadly-looking U.S. warship at the mouth of Admiralty Inlet.

Consolidation of Canadian Marine Communications and Traffic Services (MCTS) Centres:

• Vancouver Coast Guard Radio consolidated to Victoria Coast Guard Radio

• Comox Coast Guard Radio consolidated to Victoria Coast Guard Radio

• Tofino Coast Guard Radio consolidated to Prince Rupert Coast Guard Radio

Monitor VTS channels. This is called being a passive VTS participant. Many of the transmissions are extremely brief: a vessel calls in and is off the air almost before you realize it. But by monitoring you'll learn that a ferry is departing the dock, or that a large vessel is about to emerge from a channel just around the next point, or that a container ship is calling in from 5 miles behind you, traveling at 22 knots.

These are good things to know, even in clear weather. In thick weather, at night or in fog, the information is invaluable. We have even called the VTS center ourselves, such as prior to a fog-bound crossing of Puget Sound. We kept our transmission brief, and made sure we weren't a pest. Their response advised us of any potentially conflicting traffic and was always helpful, polite, and professional.

VESSEL TRAFFIC SERVICE PHONE NUMBERS

Washington:
USCG Puget Sound Vessel Traffic Center (206) 217-6040

B.C.
Prince Rupert MCTS Centre (250) 627-3074 or (250) 627-3075

Victoria MCTS Centre (250) 363-6333

Cellular, Internet and Satellite Communications

Voice and data communications remain one of the priorities when cruising. Lately, with a multitude of smart and connected devices onboard, data communications have become a top priority for cruisers. Email, social media, weather information, financial transactions, marina slip reservations, and web browsing have all become essential elements of today's cruising. Cellular is the most cost effective solution for voice, messaging, and data communications in much of the Northwest cruising area. Satellite service provides the best geographic coverage, but at a higher cost. Wi-Fi internet service is available from a number of different free and for-fee providers. In more remote areas, service is not always available, or the service is slow and unreliable.

Cellular. In Washington waters, cruisers have a number of cellular providers to choose from, all with excellent voice, messaging, and data service. All of the Washington waters, except the western half of Strait of Juan de Fuca, have excellent cellular coverage. U.S. based cellular providers have a range of plans at reasonable rates. In 2017, reasonably priced plans were introduced with unlimited voice and data that include roaming in Canada. Today's cellular data speeds are good and service is very reliable. If you are on one of the newer rate plans, cellular is a cost effective way to handle your voice, messaging, and internet needs while cruising all of the Northwest waters. Be sure you have a voice, messaging, and data plan which includes roaming in Canada; if you don't, you may be shocked when you get the bill.

Three major cellular providers: Telus, Rogers, and Bell, operate in B.C. with voice, text messaging, and data coverage. Voice, messaging, and data coverage is complete from the U.S. border on the south, to Campbell River/Desolation Sound on the north. There is no coverage in Jervis Inlet and spotty in mountainous areas.

From Campbell River/Desolation Sound to Port McNeill, cellular coverage is spotty. Johnstone Strait has the better coverage, with little if any coverage in the passages and inlets off of the Strait. Coverage between Campbell River and Port McNeill keeps getting better each season.

Cellular towers high atop mountains near Port McNeill and Port Hardy provide coverage in much of Queen Charlotte Strait, and the edge of the Broughtons. But don't expect to get coverage within the Broughtons.

Between Port Hardy and Prince Rupert, cell coverage is limited to the area around the towns of Bella Bella/Shearwater, Klemtu, Hartley Bay, Kitimat, and Bella Coola. The area around Prince Rupert has good cell coverage that continues north to the U.S. border in Dixon Entrance.

Haida Gwaii has cell coverage in and around the city of Queen Charlotte, Sandspit, and Masset.

The west coast of Vancouver Island has coverage from Hot Springs south to and including Barkley Sound. Alberni Inlet has coverage in some areas. There is coverage in Quatsino Sound in the north.

Southeast Alaska coverage begins in Dixon entrance near Cape Fox but is spotty until you pass the entrance to Behm Canal on your way to Ketchikan. Four major U.S. cellular carriers provide voice, data, and messaging coverage in and around populated areas in Southeast Alaska.

Cellular service keeps getting better every season with more and better coverage in remote areas.

Cellular Amplifiers. Cellular amplifiers are a good addition when cruising north of Campbell River and Desolation Sound. From Campbell River north, there are fewer cell towers and the distances between them are much greater. Cellular signals emitting from the towers are powerful, but the return signals from your phone are relatively weak. A cell amplifier's main advantage is in boosting the signal from your phone so that the distant cell tower can "hear" your phone. The best amplifiers have an external antenna. Be sure and match the amplifier's frequencies to your phone, and the carriers for your planned cruising area.

Cruise ships have a predictable effect on cell service. In remote areas north of Campbell River and especially in southeast Alaska, cell phone service is noticeably degraded when a cruise ship or two are in the cell tower area. These remote systems, sized to limited cellular demand, are often swamped by the thousands of devices in the hands of cruise ship passengers.

Important: For emergency, distress, and rescue operations, cellular telephones are not substitutes for VHF radios. If you have a problem and need help, get on channel 16 and start calling. The Coast Guard and neighboring vessels will hear you and may be your closest and fastest aid.

Satellite Communications. Satellite today is more than just phones. Two satellite providers, Iridium and Globalstar, offer a number of equipment and service plans with voice, message, and data communication services. Satellite phones give you communication nearly everywhere. Prices of satellite phones have come down, but airtime is still more expensive than cellular. Satellite messaging and data services have recently become much easier to use with the introduction of Iridium Go and Globalstar Sat-Fi devices. These devices bring satellite communications to your smartphone, tablet, and PC. Both Iridium Go and Sat-Fi connect your smartphone, or any Wi-Fi enabled device, to the respective satellite system for voice, data, and messaging. The devices are easy to use and allow multiple devices to connect to the satellite service. Data speeds are slow to very slow, with bandwidth for simple email and light browsing. Some weather information services are available. Both Iridium and Globalstar services and devices have data compression features that make internet browsing possible. Satellite device rentals are available.

Satellite coverage is different for each of the two providers, so check the coverage before buying devices. Both Iridium and Globalstar have coverage throughout the Inside Passage waters.

Satellite Messengers. Satellite messengers like those from SPOT and Garmin offer an inexpensive way for cruisers to track and check in. Depending on the device and service plan selected, satellite messengers can send automated position reports, link to smartphones to send and receive text messages via satellite, or send a distress signal. Basic weather forecasts and marine weather forecasts are now available on Garmin's InReach device. Satellite messengers rely on private satellite constellations, not the internationally organized Cospas-Sarsat network that EPIRBs and PLBs use. SOS messages go through a private emergency center that passes on the message to government emergency services. Satellite messengers are not EPIRBs and should not

> **COMMUNICATIONS TOPICS**
> Cellular
> Cellular Amplifiers
> Satellite Communications
> Satellite Messengers
> Wi-Fi Internet
> Being a Good Wi-Fi Citizen
> Wi-Fi Amplifiers

The InReach system now offers weather information from Ocens.

Lewmar Windlasses

With ever-smaller fitting anchor winches, Lewmar has a wide product offering for boats between 18ft – 250ft. Using hard wearing, corrosion resistant materials on deck, coupled with powerful, under-deck motor solutions, our latest windlass designs focus on ease of use and reliability.

Featuring the New VX1, VX2/3 and HX1 Windlass Range with Hybrid Polymer Gypsies

The Lewmar Patent Pending hybrid gypsy, offers a 15% reduction in weight, is 5% stronger and offers an endurance life comparable to all metal gypsies. The Hybrid Gypsies greatest attribute is the sound! Quieter than any other comparable gypsy on the market! It is our quietest anchoring solution to date.

Classic Lewmar Windlasses

Fisheries Supply offers the complete line of V Series Vertical Windlasses, H Series Horizontal Windlasses, Pro-Fish Windlass, Pro-Series Windlass, Pro-Sport Windlass, CPX2 Vertical Windlass, Captive Reel Windlass & More.

Call us 800.426.6930   FisheriesSupply.com   1900 N. Northlake Way, Seattle

CELLULAR, INTERNET AND SATELLITE COMMUNICATIONS

Iridium Go

Globalstar Sat Fi2

take the place of an EPIRB, but they can provide low-cost communications far beyond cell phone service. Satellite messengers offer the coverage of satellite service at a lower cost.

Wi-Fi Internet. Wi-Fi may be one of the most universal and inexpensive means of accessing the internet when cruising. However, availability, speed, and reliability are often problematic. Most marinas have Wi-Fi available for their guests. How the marina provides this Wi-Fi service varies from marina to marina. The larger, popular marinas have in-house installed commercial grade Wi-Fi systems that are accessible, and reliable with bandwidth for most internet needs. Other marinas have contracted with commercial Wi-Fi providers such as Shaw-Go for commercial grade Wi-Fi service. A few marinas with commercial grade Wi-Fi systems offer high bandwidth, for a fee, as an alternative to their lower bandwidth free Wi-Fi. A number of marinas have in-house installed Wi-Fi, built from home-grade equipment connected to residential bandwidth internet service. In remote areas of B.C., where there are no landlines, marina Wi-Fi is via limited bandwidth Dish Satellite Internet providers. Satellite internet service is much slower and at a much higher cost than landline data service. Marina operators provide this service to guests at a high price; and it is metered. Every bit (pun intended) of data is a cost to the marina operator.

A decade ago, when a boat pulled into a marina moorage space, the boat might use one or possibly two Wi-Fi connection ports, and their usage consisted of simple emails and some limited bandwidth web browsing. But today, every person onboard has a smartphone that they want to connect to Wi-Fi, and they may have a tablet or PC. In addition, the boat has its own devices, including a chartplotter, wanting to connect. Young people onboard may have gaming devices as well. Then there's Fire TV that attemps to connect for streaming video or movies. Every piece of electronics today is Wi-Fi enabled. The demand for internet bandwidth has increased tenfold, putting an enormous strain on Wi-Fi systems.

Wi-Fi user expectations have changed dramatically; at home the average internet user has grown accustomed to large bandwidth internet connections with almost limitless amounts of data transfer. We all assume that any internet connection will be fast, available, and constant.

Marinas are challenged to keep up with this increasing demand. Remotely located marinas, where landline internet is not available, have an almost impossible task trying to meet demand with very limited bandwidth satellite internet connections.

How to be a Good Wi-Fi citizen. Adjust your expectations and your internet usage for Wi-Fi. Be prepared for internet access slower than you might be accustomed to; allow extra time for the online task and have an alternate plan. Most importantly, adjust your internet usage to minimize data transfer. Be especially aware of data upload, as upload speeds are the slowest on nearly every type of connection.

- Turn off automatic updates. Not always as simple and straight-forward as it sounds.
- On smartphones, tablets, and PC's, turn off automatic photo backup to cloud storage. Do you really need all 200 images uploaded to the cloud right now?
- Smartphones – almost all of the Apps on our smartphones are searching for App updates. This constant 'pinging' to check for updates is largely unnecessary internet traffic when we are out boating. So go through your Apps one-by-one and turn off updates. Each App is different.
- Don't even think of using Apps like Facetime, Netflix, Amazon Video, and gaming Apps.
- Limit your use: email with no attachments; Facebook, scrolling slowly and no video viewing; voice only Skype, no video; and limit smartphone usage when Wi-Fi is the only signal available.

Wi-Fi Amplifiers. When your assigned slip is far out on the end of the most distant dock, the marina's free Wi-Fi may not help you much if you don't have an amplifier onboard. Relatively inexpensive, Wi-Fi amplifiers boost the often weak marina signal. Amplifiers allow you to reach otherwise unusable Wi-Fi signals from the surrounding area. These include Wi-Fi from providers like Shaw and Xfinity. Wi-Fi amplifiers connect to an onboard Wi-Fi router to bring the amplified signal throughout your boat. Wi-Fi amplifiers often allow boats at anchor to use nearby Wi-Fi.

"For all your hardware, standing & running rigging needs"

NORTHWEST RIGGING

Standing Rigging • Lifelines • Cable Railings • Swaging
Running Rigging • Custom Rope Work • Splicing
Furler Sales & Installation • Hardware

www.nwrigging.com • 360.293.1154 • Anacortes

Smartphone Apps for Cruisers

There are literally any number of Apps for just about every topic imaginable. Android and iOS Smartphone Apps can help with so many boating related activities. But it's important to keep in mind that onboard dedicated marine systems should remain the primary systems. Apps are often free and easy to download and install. Free Apps can contain advertising. Occasionally, an enhanced version of the free App can be purchased for a small price. Apps can be very cost effective additions to onboard equipment and serve as excellent backup and augmentation to dedicated equipment like chartplotters, VHF radio, depth sounder, and radar. Increasingly, smartphone Apps are the human-interface through Wi-Fi to control and monitor equipment and devices on board; a good example is the Watchmate App listed below.

Apps are usually free and easy to download and install. Before becoming too dependent upon the App's information, learn where the App came from and where it gets its information. Tides and currents information is a great example. There are a number of Apps that display tides and currents for various Northwest locations. But where is the information coming from and how accurate is it?

Here are some of the more popular boater related Apps.

U.S. Coast Guard – This official App is configurable and saves your information as well as details of one or more of the boats you use. Once configured, you can use the App to: request Emergency Assistance; geo-locate the nearest NOAA weather buoys and view the latest conditions; file a float plan; report a hazard to navigation; report a problem with a navigation aid; report a marine life issue; consult navigation rules; request a vessel safety check; and report suspicious activity. Good information resource and an Emergency Assistance function that sends your Lat/Lon information to the Coast Guard.

Marine Traffic - Provides up-to-date marine traffic information. It works well for monitoring ship traffic or monitoring friends. It can be used to monitor commercial vessel traffic, including ferries, if you don't have an onboard AIS.

Barometer - There are a number of good barometer Apps for both Android and iOS that use the device's sensors to measure and, more importantly, track barometric pressure. Much better than tapping the glass face on the brass encased, wall mounted mechanical barometer.

U.S. Customs CBP ROAM – This official Customs and Border Protection App supports Android and iOS devices. Travelers entering the U.S. can check-in with the App, and CBP officers can initiate a video chat for information verification, or an interview if required. If approved for entry, boaters do not have to report in-person at a Port of Entry. The App that can be used at State of Washington and State of Alaska pleasure craft Port Of

---

A Tribute to Don Douglass and Reanne Hemingway-Douglass

"No one has done more to open up the entire West Coast for the recreational boater than this pair. By visiting and recording information about every nook and cranny from San Diego to Glacier Bay, they answered the question every captain looking at a chart asks; I wonder what that cove is like? I have used every one of their books and have found their chartlets and diagrams spot on. Their guides relieve anxiety . . . they give us confidence . . . and inspire us to explore. I think the sheer volume of their work impresses me the most. They literally explored every inch of this coastline in a systematic way, and still had time to write down the details of what they found. Whew!"

[Jim Norris]

When cruising the waters of our vast coastal and northern regions, we always marvel at the energy, commitment, and effort that went into researching and producing the Exploring Series guidebooks.

We at Waggoner Cruising Guide pay special tribute to Don Douglass (who passed away in the fall of 2018) and Reanne Hemingway-Douglass, who gave unselfishly so much of themselves for the enjoyment of the boating community. Can you imagine spending 35 years cruising the West Coast and Pacific Northwest waters, recording what each bay looks like, noting the best anchorage spots, and mapping each bay and cove? Don Douglass and Reanne Hemingway-Douglass did just that; not for their own benefit, but for the rest of us boaters who dare to believe that we, too, can venture beyond our comfort zone. Reanne, along with her husband Don, transited river bars, narrow passage ways, and endured violent seas; they persevered with strength and courage through it all, sharing their personal stories and collecting data for their guidebooks.

We were first introduced to the Douglasses through Reanne's book, *Cape Horn; One Man's Dream, One Woman's Nightmare*. We marveled at what they had accomplished. Their Exploring Series guidebooks empowered us to extend our own boating territory, cruising to Mexico and back, and cruising the isolated areas of the Gulf of Alaska. When the weather forecast started to talk about gale force winds, we knew we could go to their guidebooks for an accurate description of anchorage options; we knew they had been there and could trust their writeup.

Thank you Don and Reanne for showing us the extent of what our region has to offer, and for inspiring us to seek out our own adventures.

[Lorena Landon]

SMARTPHONE APPS FOR CRUISERS

Entry locations. Reporting Offsite Arrival – Mobile, ROAM App, is configurable and saves your profile information.

iNAVX – This very feature rich iOS and Android App has many of the functions found on full function chartplotters, including everything from real-time navigation on a full suite of downloadable nautical charts, to an anchor watch feature. Interfaces with Vesper's AIS Wi-Fi gateway and supports AIS transponders/receivers. Positioning, GRIB weather, routing, charting and tracking all combine to make this app a powerful navigation tool.

Anchor Watch – Both the free and charge version of this anchoring App are feature rich. The App uses the iOS or Android device's GPS receiver to track the boat's position relative to the set anchor and sounds an alarm if the position exceeds a preset set distance from the anchor. There are other anchor watch Apps available, but this one has the added feature that will send an SMS message to another phone (on shore) in addition to sounding an alarm on the device left on the boat.

PredictWind – This Android and iOS App displays a wind speed and direction forecast for the selected area. Users can choose from four different forecast models. PredictWind provides accurate and time-specific information in an hour by hour format for a seven day period. Geographical coverage is provided for the entire west coast up to the Gulf of Alaska. You can zoom in on the forecast map to see micro area forecasts; which can be very helpful in route planning. With the App, it's easy to navigate between wind, swell, rain, cloud, air and sea temperature forecasts in table, map and graph views. Android, iOS and Web App.

SailFlow – Graphical indicator of current wind conditions and predicted wind. The App is location-sensitive and presents a concise list of nearby stations with current conditions and hour by hour predicted winds for 7 days. Options include detailed and basic displays. Forecasts include sky conditions. Select from a number of prediction models. Android and iOS compatible.

Navionics – This Android, iOs and Web App is a valuable navigation tool.

The App is free and the cost for charts varies by geographic coverage area. The route planning feature allows the user to program settings for boat draft, speed, and fuel consumption; then choose either automatic routing from start to end points, or manually enter waypoints. The App calculates distance, time en route and total fuel required. Route planning is only one of many features and functions in this App. The use is intuitive and features are far too many to list here.

iSailor – A full-function Android and iOS App that is free but requires regional chart purchase. Locates position using Apple iOS Location or on phone GPS if available. Quick entry of waypoints. Vector maps. Route tracking. AIS provided through purchased internet access service.

VesselFinder – Map display of AIS information on vessels worldwide. With the pro version you can build your own fleet of vessels you follow. Current and historical data. Tracking information. Android and iOS compatible.

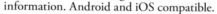

Wunderground – Android and iOS, this is the Weather Underground App, an extensive weather forecasts and conditions service. This is a good full info weather resource with data from a network of stations providing area forecasts, weather radar, satellite maps, and severe weather warnings. Local weather stations with camera images provide helpful information about localized conditions. Use the camera images from a station on the other side of the fog bound strait to discover if it's clear on the other side. Select from "Forecast on Demand" or "NWS" for forecast information source.

Windy – This Android, iOS, and Web App is one of the best wind, wave, and weather forecasting tools available today. Forecast wind and wave conditions are put into motion on a map display that can be zoomed out to see coming weather patterns and zoomed in to see localized conditions. Professional weather forecast model options including ECMWF, NAM 5km and GFS 22km; allow comparison of models to improve your weather data interpretation. Forecast information is in data and graphical display format with color and movement. 10 day forecasts show what's happening locally, regionally, and globally. Forecast conditions for ground level up to 13.5 kilometers let you see not only what is happening but what is steering the weather to you.

WatchMate – This App is the display and controls for the Vesper AIS transponder receiver device. The App is only useful in conjunction with the Vesper. We list this here because the App, in conjunction with the Vesper unit, has some well-done AIS traffic alarms and an excellent anchor watch feature. Android and iOS compatible.

Alltrails – This App helps all of us boaters find those often times little known walking paths, hiking trails, and pedestrian ways that are so important to boaters looking for exercise and just getting around without a car. The App is free and has complete information about the trails. Android and iOS compatible.

Swimming Pools Of The Inside Passage

Swimming pools are a welcome treat at a marina. Over the years we've had many readers request a list of boat-accessible swimming pools in the Northwest. As it turns out, there are many choices, from Hood Canal to Gorge Harbour, and most of the pools are heated. You just need to know how to find them. A warm summer sunny day is always better with a good swim.

PLEASANT HARBOR MARINA
The heated outdoor pool and hot tub are tucked among the trees above the marina. Open seasonally.

ALDERBROOK RESORT & SPA
The indoor heated pool is in a greenhouse adjacent to Hood Canal, with a beautiful view of the area.

ROSARIO RESORT & SPA
Three pools are located around the property. The family pool is adjacent to the marina. The adults-only pool is in front of the resort on a sun deck. A lap pool is tucked into the spa in the basement of the historic mansion.

LOPEZ ISLANDER RESORT & MARINA
Pool and hot tub are located across the street from the marina and main lodge building.

DEER HARBOR MARINA
The seasonal outdoor pool is up the hill and overlooks the marina.

SEMIAHMOO MARINA
The spa and pool are part of the Semiahmoo Health Club at the resort, and are available for a fee.

ROCHE HARBOR MARINA
The large heated pool is on the hill overlooking the marina. A dinghy dock provides access, or walk around from the main docks.

POETS COVE MARINA
The pool and hot tub overlooks the marina. Laundry is just a few steps away, so you can catch up with the wash while lounging at the pool.

PORT BROWNING MARINA
The pool is on the sloping hillside next to the pub. Kids love this pool.

OTTER BAY MARINA
The adults-only pool is just up the way, next to the main building and snack bar. The family pool is up the hill.

GANGES
The new community center has a pool and shower facility for visitors. Ask the marina for directions.

BRENTWOOD BAY RESORT & MARINA
The pool and hot tub are just outside the main building, overlooking the marina. The focus is on serenity and relaxation for adults.

BEACH GARDENS RESORT & MARINA
You can enjoy the indoor pool year round.

GORGE HARBOUR MARINA RESORT
The pool and hot tub overlook the marina and the harbor.

PENDER HARBOUR RESORT & MARINA
Moorage guests of the marina have access to all the resort's amenities, including the heated seasonal outdoor pool. The pool has a secluded private appeal.

ABOUT ANCHORING

One of the unique features of boating is the freedom of movement and independence to make any protected body of water home for a quick lunch stop or an overnight. Some people look forward to dropping anchor in an unfamiliar cove or bay. Many people do not share this enthusiasm. There are a few general principles that will help everyone anchor successfully. Cruising from dock to dock is fun, and no one can fault the conveniences. But a world of possibilities opens to those who have good anchoring gear and know how to use it.

Use good gear. Big, strong anchors work; small, cheap anchors don't. The most experienced cruisers seem to carry the biggest anchors. Well-equipped, wide-ranging boats carry all of the common designs: Bruce, CQR (plow), Danforth, Delta, Northhill, Rocna, Manson Supreme, and Ultra. Make sure your anchor is made of high quality steel. If it's wedged in a rock, you don't want it to bend. While Danforth style anchors are easiest to bend, within the limits of their design, they can be made strong and expensive, or weak and cheap. There are no strong, cheap Danforth style anchors. Read the sizing charts carefully, and size your anchor for storm conditions. Some sizing charts are written for 20-knot winds. Others are written for 30 knots. The Bruce chart is written for 42 knots and Rocna sizing is based upon 50 knots. When the wind comes on to blow hard at 3:00 a.m., you don't want a 20-knot anchor out there.

Pick your spot. Unless you're setting out a stern anchor or running a stern-tie ashore, plan on your boat swinging through an entire 360-degree circle. You don't want to bump up against a rock, a dock or another boat. Be sure to account for tidal changes. We've seen anchored boats aground at low tide because they didn't allow for drying flats or a sand bar in their swing circle. Other anchored boats will tend to swing as your boat swings, but not always. One night at Jones Island in the San Juans, swirling tidal currents had anchored boats swooping toward one another in a "dance of death."

Carry ample rode. For an anchor to bury and hold properly, you should pay out anchor rode at least five times the water depth. In 20 feet of water you would want 100 feet of rode out. In 60 feet of water you would want 300 feet out. Often, especially in crowded anchorages during high summer season, it will not be possible to anchor on 5:1 scope (five times the depth of the water). That is understood. In fact, the norm for most Northwest anchorages seems to be 3:1. But I've watched people put out 30 feet of rode in 20 feet of water, and wonder why the anchor wouldn't bite. For the deep waters of the Pacific Northwest, carry at least 300 feet of anchor rode, whether all-chain or combination chain and rope. Opinions vary about how much chain a combination rode should include, but no one would criticize you for having at least a foot of chain for every foot of boat length. Mark your rode well with something that is easily seen and clearly indicates the length. We have seen people with all chain that have no markers and therefore no way to know how much rode is out.

Rope or chain? For years we used a combination anchor rode—a length of chain backed up with 300 feet of top-quality nylon rope—and we anchored successfully. On a smaller boat with no anchor windlass, a combination rode is the way to go. When we moved to the 37-footer we found a new religion: all-chain. With all-chain, if we let out 100 feet of chain in 30 feet of water, 70 feet of chain will be lying on the bottom after the anchor is set. At a pound a foot, that's 70 pounds of chain that must be lifted off the bottom before we get to the anchor. During settled conditions we now get by with less scope, and our swinging circle is smaller. In storm conditions, of course, we're back to 5:1, or as close to 5:1 as we can manage.

Pay out all-chain rode as you move astern, not in a pile on top of the anchor. Use the clutch on your windlass to allow chain to pay out as you back-down. Initially, allow enough chain out to place the anchor on the bottom, then use movement astern to lay the chain along the bottom. Then secure the windlass clutch and begin to set the anchor.

Read the tide tables. If the overnight low tide isn't very low, a shallow anchorage can be just right. On the other hand, if the moon is either new or full (the two times during the month when the tidal range is the greatest) the shallow anchorage might go dry at low tide. You also want to know the maximum height of the tide during your stay. Set your scope for five times the water depth at high tide, or if you can't get five times, as much as you can get away with.

Set the anchor well. To get the best bury in the bottom, you want the angle between the anchor and the boat to be as flat as possible. After lowering the anchor, back well down before you set the hook. As you set, the rode should seem to stretch almost straight out from the bow. If the rode angles downward very much, you don't have enough scope out. When the anchor is set, you can shorten up to avoid swinging into other boats or onto a sandbar. You'll know, by the way, when the anchor is set. The anchor rode pulls straight and the boat stops. If you have any doubt as to whether the anchor is set, then it probably isn't. Weeds can foul an anchor, especially a Danforth style anchor, and many bottoms have weeds. Once the anchor is set, you don't have to pour on all 600 horsepower to prove your point. Anchors gain holding power through pulling and relaxing over time, a process called soaking. An anchor put down for lunch might be recovered with little effort. Left overnight it might feel as if it had headed for China.

Look at your chart. For happy anchoring you want a good holding bottom, appropriate depths, and protection. The nautical chart can help with all these needs. If the chart says Foul, don't anchor there. If the chart shows submerged pilings at the head of the bay, avoid the head of the bay. If the chart shows 200-foot depths right up to the shoreline, that's a bad spot. If it shows the bay open to the full sweep of the prevailing wind and seas, find another bay or you could be in for a rough night. I find the easiest anchorages to be in 20 to 50 feet of water, with a decided preference for the 20- to 30-foot depths. Approach slowly, take a turn around the entire area to check the depths, and decide where you want the boat to lie after the anchor is set. Then go out to a spot that will give you sufficient scope and lower the anchor. Back way down, set the hook, and shorten up to the desired location.

Anchor bridle snubber lines should be long enough and secured aft of the bow sprit.

www.WaggonerGuide.com

ABOUT ANCHORING

Anchor in the right places. Don't anchor in cable crossing areas or near charted underwater pipeline areas. Increasingly, some communities and locales are discouraging anchoring in or near eelgrass. Anchoring gear, especially anchor chain, can be harmful to eelgrass. Eelgrass areas are not generally charted so check the Waggoner Cruising Guide or check for signage on spar buoys in the area marked, "no anchoring."

Use an anchor watch. There are a number of GPS based anchor watch systems that monitor your boat's position and signal an alarm if the boat moves outside of a predetermined boundary circle. There are a number of Android and iOS smartphone Apps available with anchor watch features. Some chartplotters and chartplotter PC software have boundary circle features. For these anchor watch systems to work well, place the center of the boundary circle at the spot where you drop the anchor. This may mean taking the anchor watch system to the bow when you center the circle. After centering the boundary circle, set the radius of the circle equal to the scope, plus the distance from the bow roller to the place on the boat where the anchor watch will rest while anchored, plus an appropriate GPS error factor, plus any significant tidal exchange that increases your swing. Anchor watch systems monitor the boat's current location and sound an alarm if outside of the boundary circle. Some smartphone apps can also SMS text or email an alarm to another phone that goes ashore with you.

How to use a trip line. If there is any indication that your planned anchoring area is prone to fouling or snagging your anchor, use a trip line to help recover your anchor. Anchors prepared for trip lines have a small hole at the nose of the anchor, somewhere near the top and far forward. Before deploying the anchor, attach a length of line that is longer than the maximum tidal water depth at your intended anchoring location. To the other end of the line attach a small float or buoy. Later when you go to weigh anchor and it is snagged on something, use the trip line to help free the fouled anchor. The float or buoy also alerts other boaters of your anchor's location.

Bridles and Snubbers. Anchor bridles and snubbers are lengths of nylon line attached to a chain hook. When the hook is attached to a deployed anchor chain and the nylon lines are attached to cleats on the boat, the bridle acts as a shock absorber to keep the anchor from breaking loose and to reduce chafe on the bow roller. As the wind and waves raise the boat, flex in the nylon lines absorb shock loads to avoid pulling the anchor free. Attached aft of the bow, bridles help reduce the boat's wind sailing and reduce yawing. To be effective the snubber lines need to be at least 30 feet long and should allow the chain attachment point, when deployed, to be below the waterline. Several pre-made bridles are available at marine suppliers or make your own.

Carry a stern-tie. In some anchoring locations, where swing room is limited, you will set the anchor offshore, back toward shore to set, and take the dinghy in with a line from a stern cleat to a securing point on shore such as a rock, tree, or stern-tie pin. Boats line Tod Inlet, near Butchart Gardens, and Prideaux Haven, in Desolation Sound, tied this way. In many small bays, with limited swing room, it's the only way you can anchor. Sometimes you'll find a little niche for just your boat. We carry 600 feet of inexpensive polypropylene rope (because it floats) for stern ties. Some popular anchorages necessitating stern-tie have metal pins embedded in rock with rings or a length of chain, through which you can pass your stern-tie line. After passing the end through the ring, bring the end back to the boat. That way, when you are ready to depart, you can release and recover the stern-tie line without leaving the boat. When there are no stern-tie anchor pins, find something secure on shore to anchor your stern-tie line. Carry a disposable short length of rope, about 5 feet long, that can be looped around something solid on shore like a rock outcropping. As a last resort loop your stern-tie around a dead tree. Many parks in BC and Washington frown on using live trees.

Up-slope anchoring. Up-slope anchoring is used when the only convenient anchoring depths are near to shore. Up-slope anchoring involves dropping the anchor on the upsloping sea bottom as it shallows. Once the anchor is set, back-down toward the nearby shore and stern-tie to shore. The stern-tie holds the boat in a position where it is always pulling the main anchor up the slope and keeps the anchor set.

Secure the anchor rode to the boat. We have all heard stories about boaters losing their all chain anchor, when they discover that the end, buried under hundreds of pounds of rode in the anchor locker, was not attached to the boat. Be sure the end of your anchor chain is attached to the boat – but not hard attached. The anchor should be attached to a length of nylon rope that is secured to the boat. Instead of leaving this nylon rope buried under a pile of chain in our anchor locker, we coil the line and keep it high and dry attached to the side of the anchor locker. In the event the anchor is stuck or if you need to get away from the anchor quickly, the rope can be cut. Secure a floating buoy to the end of the nylon rope so that you can retrieve the anchor and chain later.

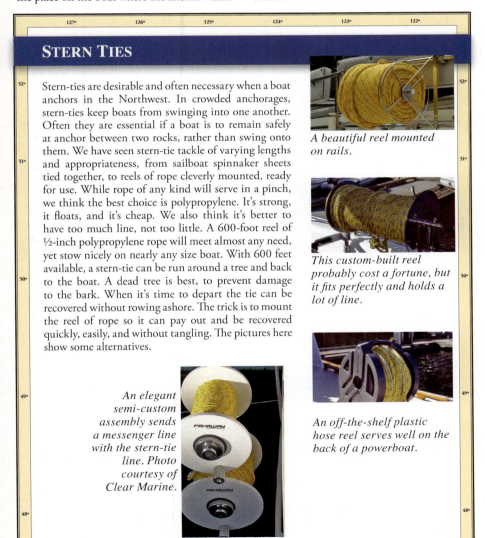

STERN TIES

Stern-ties are desirable and often necessary when a boat anchors in the Northwest. In crowded anchorages, stern-ties keep boats from swinging into one another. Often they are essential if a boat is to remain safely at anchor between two rocks, rather than swing onto them. We have seen stern-tie tackle of varying lengths and appropriateness, from sailboat spinnaker sheets tied together, to reels of rope cleverly mounted, ready for use. While rope of any kind will serve in a pinch, we think the best choice is polypropylene. It's strong, it floats, and it's cheap. We also think it's better to have too much line, not too little. A 600-foot reel of ½-inch polypropylene rope will meet almost any need, yet stow nicely on nearly any size boat. With 600 feet available, a stern-tie can be run around a tree and back to the boat. A dead tree is best, to prevent damage to the bark. When it's time to depart the tie can be recovered without rowing ashore. The trick is to mount the reel of rope so it can pay out and be recovered quickly, easily, and without tangling. The pictures here show some alternatives.

A beautiful reel mounted on rails.

This custom-built reel probably cost a fortune, but it fits perfectly and holds a lot of line.

An elegant semi-custom assembly sends a messenger line with the stern-tie line. Photo courtesy of Clear Marine.

An off-the-shelf plastic hose reel serves well on the back of a powerboat.

2020 WAGGONER CRUISING GUIDE

ELCI Protected Shore Power

ELCI Breaker with Test/Reset on Eaton Pedestal

What You Need to Know About New Shore Power. Since 2011, marinas and boat builders have been making changes to alternating current (AC) service on boats to eliminate the risk of electrical shock drownings (ESD) coming from current leakage. These changes will be noticeable to you, the boater, at the shore power pedestals at new or updated marinas. New or updated marina shore power will have fault protection that will "trip" the shore power breaker and turn off power to your boat if the device detects AC current leakage.

What is equipment leakage and how does it cause drownings? AC power has three wires, 1) Hot, 2) Neutral, and 3) Ground. The Hot and Neutral wires carry AC current, and the Ground is a safety wire. When operating correctly and with no electrical faults, the Hot and Neutral wires carry the current, and the Ground wire has no current. However, faulty boat wiring or appliances can cause current to "leak" and find a path other than the Hot and Neutral wires. The Ground wire is the safety net that is designed to safely carry this leaking current to a grounding point. On land, this is literally a stake in the dirt. On a boat, the Ground wire has several connections, one goes to the shore power connection and another goes to the boat's bonding system that electrically connects the boat's metal parts in the sea water. This bonding connection can allow faulty leaking current to energize the water around the boat. If someone enters this energized water, the person's body becomes a better conductor of electrical current than the surrounding water. The person then becomes immobilized by this current and drowns. Anyone entering the water to assist can also become a victim of ESD. The danger is greatest in fresh water, however; the danger exists in brackish water or a layer of fresh rain or river water over salt water. ESD danger is the reason swimming is not allowed in marinas.

Equipment Leakage Circuit Interrupter (ELCI) is the device that, when installed on the shore power pedestal and/or on your boat, will protect against ESD by detecting current leakage and turn off the AC shore power connection. On the marina shore power side of the connection, building code requires ELCI devices on all newly installed shore power service. In marinas that rebuild all the docks, all shore power is ELCI protected. However, often the marina rebuilds only a few of their floats, resulting in both old and new shore power service in the marina.

A typical household circuit is rated at 15 or 20 amps of current and most shore power connections are 30 amps or 50 amps. Electrical current leakage is measured in milliamps (1/1000 of an amp - mA). Household Ground Fault Circuit Interrupters (GFCI) in the average kitchen or bathroom trip at 15 mA of leakage. Very small amounts of electrical current can have serious effects on the human body.

CROW'S NEST YACHTS

SEATTLE | NEWPORT BEACH | SAN DIEGO | ANACORTES

Now Expanded in the NW to Anacortes

Crow's Nest Yachts features a robust brokerage yacht sales business under the ownership of three local yacht brokers since 2010. With more than 80 years combined experience in the industry. Dan Wood, Vic Parcells, and Dale Partna are the principals and are committed to serving yacht owners in the Northwest. Now Crow's Nest Yachts has opened a sales office in Anacortes near the Cap Sante Marina. Next time you are in Anacortes stop by and say hello. Read more on our Facebook page!

   For instant listing updates, follow us on social media!

CROW'S NEST YACHTS SEATTLE
(206) 625-1580 • seattle@crowsnestyachts.com

CROW'S NEST YACHTS ANACORTES
(360) 299-3988 • sales@crowsnestyachts.com

WWW.CROWSNESTYACHTS.COM

ELCI PROTECTED SHORE POWER

- 1 mA Barely perceptible, tingling
- 16 mA Painful shock, maximum current an average person can grasp and "let go"
- 20 mA Paralysis of respiratory muscles
- 100 mA Ventricular fibrillation threshold
- 2000 mA Cardiac standstill and internal organ damage

Building code for marina shore power calls for a 30 mA ELCI threshold at the pedestal and/or a 100 mA ELCI for a collection of pedestals on a dock.

Some marinas are installing 30 mA ELCI breakers at each pedestal, while others are installing one 100 mA ELCI breaker to protect a group of pedestals. If you trip the 30 mA pedestal breaker, power is only off to your boat. If you trip a 100 mA ELCI breaker, power will be off to all the boats in the group of pedestals served by that breaker. Your boat will not be popular with neighboring boats that are suddenly without power.

On the boat, American Boat & Yacht Council (ABYC) standards call for an ELCI device; so if your boat was built within the last five years, you most likely have ELCI protection. For older boats, an ELCI device can be added that will not only make your boat safer, it will ensure that you don't have problems when you plug into shore power at marinas with ELCI-protected shore power.

What to do if your boat trips the ELCI breaker. Your first visit to a marina with upgraded shore power may require some extra time and effort. Fortunately, this is normally a one-time process and you likely won't have problems at other ELCI equipped marinas. Before attempting your first-time connection to ELCI-protected power, make sure you know how to reset the ELCI breaker. Look for a reset that is separate from the traditional over-amperage breaker reset. If you don't find any evidence of an ELCI breaker and reset on the pedestal, it may be the 100 mA breaker ELCI breaker protecting a group of pedestals; in which case, you will need the marina staff help to reset.

If the ELCI breaker trips as soon as you bring shore power to your panel, then: 1. Switch off shore power on your breaker panel. 2. Turn off all AC panel breakers, including AC breakers on separate inverter panel, if equipped. Also turn off all main AC and inverter breakers (doublepole breakers – the ones where two breaker switches are tied together). 3. Reset the dockside ELCI breaker and then turn the breaker to ON. 4. If the ELCI breaker trips again, you likely have a boat wiring issue that will need to be addressed by a marine electrician. You will need to find shore power without ELCI-protection or go without shore power until the problem is fixed. 5. If the ELCI-breaker has not tripped, then on the boat's breaker panel, switch the power source to Shore Power. 6. Try different sequences of turning main double pole breakers on and individual circuit breakers on to discover what is causing the ELCI Breaker to trip. This may take some time as you will need to restart the process by resetting the on-shore ELCI breaker with each attempt. Having someone on the dock resetting the ELCI breaker helps to facilitate this trial and error process.

What is causing the ELCI Breaker to Trip? Reverse Y-splitters (adapters that combine two 30 amp receptacles into one 50 amp or two 50 amp into one 100 amp) are a known source of ELCI breaker problems and unless specifically designed for ELCI-protected power, will likely not work.

Inverters are also a possible source of ELCI breaker issues. Properly installed marine inverters may trip the ELCI breaker if other onboard AC breakers are switched on before the inverter completes its process of synchronizing with shore power. Marine inverters correctly tie or connect the boat's Neutral wire with the Ground wire when the boat is NOT connected to shore power and the inverter is creating AC power. When the inverter senses AC shore power, it begins a process of synchronizing with shore power and switching to pass-thru mode. Once this process is complete, the inverter breaks its Neutral to Ground connection and correctly leaves the boat's Ground and Neutral connected to the respective shore power connection. If other double-pole AC breakers are ON during this syncing process, amperage on the Neutral wire still connected to Ground wire may trip the ELCI breaker.

2020 WAGGONER CRUISING GUIDE

ELCI PROTECTED SHORE POWER

Wait for about 30 seconds after supplying shore power to the inverter before turning other main and individual breakers on.

Marine battery chargers are another potential cause of ELCI breaker issues. Try turning off or lower the amperage setting to provide a temporary solution.

Self-testing galvanic isolators may also be a cause of ELCI breaker problems. Replace with a newer galvanic isolator or disable the self-test feature of the device.

A possible source of an unwanted, problematic, neutral-to-ground connection occurs when home-store (non-marine) appliances are installed on boats. Inverters that are not designed for marine use are a source of ELCI problems, and improperly installed inverters may be a source of incorrect Neutral-to-Ground connection when the Neutral conductors are not separated into two busses; inverted and non-inverted. ABYC recommendations call for separating Neutral and Ground wires for inverter loads from non-inverted. A Neutral/Ground connection should only be present at a source of power. If you are still having problems, it's probably time to call in a qualified ABYC technician.

Do I Need an Isolation Transformer? An isolation transformer is not required in order to use ELCI-protected power sources. If your boat is properly wired and powered up correctly, there is no requirement for an isolation transformer. Isolation transformers all but eliminate the possibility of tripping dock ELCI breakers. They also bring other benefits and are generally a good addition to the boat. Transformers are available in a variety of different voltages and amperages ranging in price from $1,000 to $4,000. If an isolation transformer is installed within 10 feet of the boat's shore power inlet, an onboard ELCI breaker is not required in order for the boat to be ABYC compliant.

ELCI, RCD, GFCI, GFI Different or Same? All of these devices perform the same function of detecting amperage leakage by sensing an amperage imbalance on the Hot and Neutral wires. The difference is in the level of imbalance, or leaking amperage that trips the breaker.

Marinas with ELCI-protected Power. ELCI-protected breakers first appeared at new or rebuilt marinas in Southeast Alaska; North Harbor in Petersburg, Thomas Basin in Ketchikan, and some docks at Bar Harbor South in Ketchikan. In Washington State, Rosario Resort, Poulsbo Marina, Eagle Harbor Marina, and Eagle Harbor Waterfront Park City dock, have upgraded all their docks to ELCI-protected power. Roche Harbor, Point Roberts Marina, Friday Harbor, and Skyline Marina, have upgraded some of their docks. Salt Spring Marina, in Ganges Harbour, is one of the first in British Columbia with ELCI-protected power. In the Waggoner Cruising Guide, marinas that have upgraded their shore power are identified with the label "ELCI-protected power."

Onboard Blue Sea Systems ELCI and Over-amperage breaker

How to Prepare Your Boat. If you are having problems with upgraded shore power, the first place to look is your boat. Ground fault and amperage leakage technology has been around for many decades. One way to prepare your boat is to install an ELCI breaker on your boat. If there are any issues on your boat, an ELCI will bring them to your attention and will do so at your schedule. There are several options ranging in price from $160 to $750 for adding ELCI protection to your boat.

[Leonard Landon]

DERELICT VESSEL REPORTING

There comes a time when boats reach the end of their useful life; and unfortunately, these boats are often left abandoned to fade away with the past. Perhaps the owners don't have a means of transporting the vessel for proper disposal, or aren't aware of the options that are available. Abandoned boats, left ashore or in the water, can leak oil and other contaminates, polluting marine habitat and putting our waters at risk.

Reporting Derelict Vessels. If you see an abandoned or derelict vessel in Puget Sound waters, you can call 360-902-1574 to report the vessel's location and other pertinent details. In 2002, the Washington State Legislature passed the Derelict vessel Act which gave certain local and state agencies the authority and funding for the removal and disposal of derelict and abandoned vessels from waters in the state. Public entities authorized to remove derelict/abandoned vessels include DNR; Dept of Fish & Wildlife; Parks & Recreation Commission; Metropolitan park districts; Port districts; and cities or counties with ownership, management, or jurisdiction over the aquatic lands where the vessel is located. DNR can assist those entities in funding removal, including reimbursement of up to 90 percent of the cost of removal and disposal.

Procedures for Removal. Prior to taking custody of the vessel, the public entity must attempt to notify the vessel's owner; mail notice to the last known address; post intended action on the vessel; print notice in a newspaper in the county the vessel is located; and publish on DNR's website. The owner of a derelict or abandoned vessel is responsible for reimbursing the authorized public entity for all costs associated with the vessel's removal.

Public moorage facilities follow their own existing procedures for removal of abandoned vessels and can then request reimbursement from the Derelict Vessel Removal Account. Private moorage facilities may seize a vessel for nonpayment of rent, but they cannot receive Derelict Vessel Removal Program funds. A private moorage facility may contact the local Authorized Public Entity for removal of the vessel; the public entity is then eligible for the reimbursement funds.

British Columbia – Derelict Boat Reporting. British Columbia has similar derelict boat reporting and disposal programs. If you see a derelict boat in BC on the beach or in the water that does not appear to be an immediate hazard, you can choose from several sources to report the abandoned vessel in British Columbia:

- Canadian Coast Guard at 800-889-8852
- Transport Canada at 604-775-8867
- Dead Boat Disposal Society at 250-383-2086 (Qathet Regional District-Powell River)
- Capital Regional District (CRD) at 250-360-3030 (southern tip of Vancouver Island and Southern Gulf Islands)

Requested information may include exact location of the derelict vessel; vessel name and description, license number or other identifier; and photos.

CHARTERING

Bareboat or crewed; sail or power; small and intimate or large and luxurious; one week or one month; on your own or with a group; chartering is an excellent way to not only cruise the Northwest waters and the Inside Passage, but it's a great way to try different styles of cruising. It's also an option for those who routinely cruise Puget Sound and San Juan Islands, but have always wanted to cruise farther north. You could charter a boat in Comox B.C. and cruise Desolation Sound or The Broughton Archipelago. Or charter a smaller, faster boat and use on-shore accommodations for overnighting. See the *Cruising Inn to Inn* section of this chapter for more information on this option.

Charter cruising is really all about flexibility. If you do not own a boat, you can rent one and cruise some of the most beautiful destinations in the world. Already have a boat, but need a larger boat with extra staterooms for family and friends? You can rent one. Or, do you want to try cruising with a different design before you consider purchasing. No experience is required. The charter company can provide an instructor-skipper to teach you how to handle a boat, or you can hire the captain to guide you to the most beautiful places. First mates, chefs and naturalists are available too. The surprising thing is that chartering a boat is relatively inexpensive compared to staying at luxury inns and hotels. Your destination can change every day without having to pack and unpack your luggage between destinations. The trips are memorable for all the wildlife experiences, secluded anchorages, and the choice of fine dining destinations – right on the water.

Flexibility includes the type of boats from which to choose, everything from sailboats and power trawlers, to large yachts. Take a look at the different companies' websites and the variety of boats they offer. Often the search starts with selecting power or sail. Then how many people will be on the boat. How many staterooms will you need? Do your guests mind sharing a head (bathroom), or do you need individual en-suite heads for all cabins? The age of the boat may vary the price. Next, how much do you want to spend versus how much room do you need or want? The range can go from about 26 feet up to 65-foot yachts.

Some charter operators offer a stay-the-night-before option so you can get an early start cruising on the first day of your charter. This option allows you to get onboard, load your personal items, equipment, and provisions. You can sleep aboard the boat but may not leave the dock until the morning of your planned charter. This option is usually charged at half the daily charter rate.

You might consider an organized flotilla where you can travel with a group of like-minded mariners guided by a professional that knows the area. Activities are often arranged every day and you meet some of the greatest people in the world.

At the end of your charter you will be expected to do some basic cleaning to return the boat in good order. Wash the dishes and put things away in the galley; re-fill the fuel and water tanks; empty holding tank(s); and hose down the exterior of the boat.

Some charter operators offer concierge services where they will provision the boat for you, set an itinerary and help with trip planning, and cleanup the boat afterwards.

You can plan and take your dream trip without the cost of owning a boat. Or, if you live and boat in a different area of the world, charter a boat and enjoy Pacific Northwest and Inside Passage cruising.

AIS Made Easy!

Milltech Marine offers complete, low-cost AIS solutions for every need.

- AIS Receivers, Radios and Transponders including the latest 5-watt Class B AIS
- Featuring *smart*AIS™ solutions from Vesper Marine
- Free support and online resources

YOUR AIS EXPERTS
call us...
1-206-299-2217

Visit our online store: **www.MilltechMarine.com**

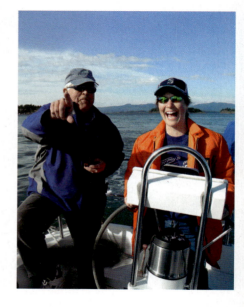

FLOTILLA CRUISING WITH NEW FRIENDS

There are many boaters who prefer cruising with other boats and crews as a group flotilla. For some, it is with a group of friends from a yacht club, a boat club, or with an organized commercial venture. They believe in safety in numbers, and often travel with one or more experienced crews to lead the group. Many use a flotilla trip as an opportunity to learn before they cruise on their own.

In the Northwest, there are several styles of flotilla cruises offered by different companies. They are all unique and have something different to offer. People who choose flotillas come in all ages, with varied boating experience. The common thread throughout is the opportunity for social interaction with other boaters, and the opportunity to gain a broader understanding of our Pacific Northwest waters.

Northwest Explorations in Bellingham, offers trips where customers charter a high-end yacht for multiple weeks with planned legs to Southeast Alaska, and planned legs for the return trip. Participants can purchase a chosen leg along the routes, depending on the amount of time you have to spend. Northwest Explorations supplies the boats, but you are captain and crew of your assigned vessel. Their fleet offers a variety of beautiful Grand Banks yachts and other brand yachts, including a DeFever and a Fleming 55. They call their flotilla trips "Mother Goose" flotillas, where most of the boats follow along together. A mother ship leads with crew, a naturalist, and a mechanic to support 5-8 boats. Activities are planned along the way. This format is ideal for those who live and boat in another area of the country or the world, or if you have limited time to take your boat up to Southeast Alaska. Northwest Explorations also offers flotilla trips to Desolation Sound

The Waggoner Cruising Guide has a flotilla program for the passage from Anacortes to Ketchikan in Southeast Alaska, and an additional flotilla from Anacortes to Desolation Sound. Boaters use their own vessels in this program. The group usually consists of 6-8 boats that vary in size and speed. Some boats stay clustered during each day's leg, while others choose to meet up at the end of the day at the designated rendezvous location. The complete trip is organized and planned around an itinerary with activities and education along the way, including weather and seamanship. This program offers seminar courses, conducted in the months prior to departure, to develop the skills needed for a confident passage home. Trip leaders prepare daily briefings and guide all the participants on the trip to help insure a safe, pleasant passage. Friendships are made on the flotilla trips that last a lifetime.

Jim Rard and Crew from Marine Servicenter offer a 12-week "Sail Alaska" program for power and sailboats. Participants learn while cruising to Alaska. Once in Southeast Alaska, Jim reveals his favorite destinations through organized special events and wildlife viewing. Imagine building and firing up a stone pizza oven and having homemade pizza cooked on hot rocks at a remote island in Southeast Alaska.

Slowboat, led by former Waggoner Guide Managing Editor, Sam Landsman, and experienced cruisers Laura Domela and Kevin Morris, Slowboat specializes in adventure cruising. Their flotilla program takes boaters to unique, out of the way destinations. They offer flotilla cruises to and from Southeast Alaska, destinations within Southeast Alaska, and the West Coast of Vancouver Island for beginner and experienced cruisers traveling with their own boats. They too work with the participants to share their knowledge for the unique situations presented in remote locations.

All flotilla cruisers say they come back from these trips with new skills, confidence, and many new friends from their time on the water.

DEVELOPING AN ITINERARY TO DELIGHT THE ENTIRE CREW

Planning an itinerary for you and your crew generates enthusiasm for the trip and establishes team effort. For many, trip planning is part of the fun, starting months before the actual trip. You can dream about what your cruise will be like through the islands or Desolation Sound.

Involving the crew. You can start by involving the crew with pre-trip research, or you create the first draft as Captain. Look through the many cruising guides available (we stock most in the WaggonerGuide.com store). Also look through past issues of magazines that cover the Northwest like *Pacific Yachting*, *Northwest Yachting*, *48 North* and *SEA* magazine to name a few. Start that short list of places you want to visit for the first time, re-visit, or see from a different point of view and share with guests who have previously never seen this beautiful area.

Everyone can prioritize activities and destinations based on their interests and work together to finalize the itinerary. Depending on how much time you have for the trip and knowing the distances involved, you can create an itinerary with reasonable expectations. Time should be factored in for provisioning, fuel stops, weather delays, and transiting any rapids along your route. Consider time for relaxing too. Those on a tight schedule might move to a different destination every day to see as much as possible. Others plan for a day or two, or plan short cruising legs to allow plenty of time to fully enjoy a destination.

A few questions to start. Asking a few basic questions will help you develop an itinerary. Many boaters have preconceived ideas about their anticipated cruise, or expect to see and do certain things they have in mind. A pre-planned itinerary, with some specifics, helps set the expectations for a pleasant and rewarding cruise. Consider:

How much time do you have, including the trip back? What speed do you expect to cruise at?

What do you want to see? This list could include wildlife, quaint villages, cannery ruins, museums, or simply relax at remote anchorages.

What activities do you want to do? Perhaps go fishing, swimming, or kayaking. Or you may prefer attending happy hours at the smaller marinas, or souvenir shopping when in town. Walking the beaches and hiking the trails found on many of the islands is always a favorite. You may have a crew that is split, where some will want to see the local museum, while others rummage through the shops in town. There are many locations that fit this criteria.

Are friends and family flying in to meet you? Options may include commercial airports, smaller community airports, or perhaps arriving by seaplane at more remote areas. You may want to factor in extra time for missed connections if you have guests arriving by plane.

Is this your first time cruising the Northwest? Are you planning a 1-week or 2-week bareboat charter? There are so many places to go and enjoy both near and far. Most people who are new to the area start by cruising among the San Juan Islands on a 1-week to 2-week itinerary, leaving from the charter bases in Anacortes or Bellingham. If you want to focus on the islands of British Columbia, there are bareboat charter companies in Sidney, Nanaimo and Vancouver. If you really just want to cruise Desolation Sound and the Broughton Islands area, there is a reputable charter company in Comox, BC where you can save a day or two by starting your cruise much closer to these areas.

Begin with the basics. With the basic information, we like to create an itinerary in a spreadsheet, or on a pad of paper. For those who like to work with spreadsheets, we have posted a few sample itineraries at www.WaggonerGuide.com/Itineraries. Start laying out a day on each line with a few notes.

There may be some special events such as the Saturday Market in Ganges, or the world-famous fireworks at Butchart Gardens. Your schedule may shift, so remain flexible. A 90-mile day of cruising may be too much, or a passage may miss slack at one of the tidal rapids.

At the Waggoner Guide, we like to start our itinerary with the "knowns" in place. For example, if we were planning a trip north to Desolation Sound, the Broughtons or Southeast Alaska and leaving from Anacortes, we know to plan for clearing Canadian Customs. We have three basic choices for clearance, heading north to Sidney, Bedwell Harbour, or Nanaimo. Nexus, i68 and Canpass holders will have many more options to clear Customs if the entire crew is registered in the programs.

Timing Dependencies. Typically we cross over to the Canadian Gulf Islands and work our way north through the protected waters of the islands. We then look at the times of slack water for Dodd Narrows, near Nanaimo. We record the time of morning and afternoon slack in our itinerary and then determine the approximate time and point of departure. It is a long day's cruise from Anacortes to Nanaimo at a cruise speed of 7-9 knots. If slack at Dodd Narrows is at noon, we probably will not be able to get there in time, especially if we need to allow nearly an hour to clear Canadian Customs in Bedwell Harbour. Instead we may elect to stay a day in the Gulf Islands and catch the morning slack at Dodd Narrows the following day, or plan for the evening slack and get to Nanaimo at around 7:00 p.m. This is where the different choices come into play. If you cannot get to Dodd Narrows in time, you can save an hour by planning to clear Canadian Customs in Nanaimo. This option would eliminate the stop at Bedwell Harbour (Poets Cove) and require an arrival at the Nanaimo Canadian Customs dock well before the closing time of 5:00 p.m. in the summers (4:30 p.m. in the off-season).

Why stop in Nanaimo? It is a good jumping off point for heading north to Campbell River or crossing over to the Sunshine Coast. The weather is typically better in the early morning when winds should be lighter. You can make the open water crossing before afternoon winds kick up. Nanaimo is also a good provisioning point. Markets and liquor stores near the marina allow you to stock up on food items that may have been restricted when clearing Canadian Customs.

There are other options you can build into the plan. When leaving from Seattle, you may need to allow a day to reach the Anacortes area or the San Juan Islands. Stopping in historic Roche Harbor or Friday Harbor may be a crew member's request. However, it may make more sense to save this stop for the return trip from Canada, since both locations are a U.S. Customs Port of Entry.

Any size. Any color. No excuses.

www.americantugs.com

PROVISIONING YOUR BOAT FOR A WELL FED AND HAPPY CREW

Quality food on board is a big part of the cruising experience. Having that perfect meal surrounded by magnificent scenery is part of what makes our boating lifestyle so special. It is a fine balance between meals that are fun to prepare and keeping life and chores on board simple.

A few questions to start. How long is your cruise plan? Looking at an itinerary, roughly how many nights will you be dining on board versus eating at many of the very good restaurants along the way? Do you have anyone on your crew who has special food needs, is a vegetarian, needs gluten-free or likes milk in their coffee? Fat-free milk or whole milk? Does anyone on the crew have any allergies, or food items they like every day? You can see where this is going. If you are doing the cooking - how much work are you prepared to do? Pancakes in the morning or frozen waffles? It begs the question - do you have maple syrup on board? Or, do you like to sleep in and leave breakfast items out for crew and guests to help themselves. Are you headed to Canada, or from Canada into the U.S.? Will you need to purchase some items once you get into Canada due to border restrictions?

How much space do you have in your refrigerator or on-board freezer? Do you have a refrigerator or are you working from a cooler with ice. Your menu planning will change based on what foods you can store safely.

Headed up to the Broughtons? Be prepared to have your favorite dish to share for pot luck Happy Hours. Sometimes they are full meals and sometimes they are appetizer Happy Hours with finger foods. You will want to have a few recipes that are quick and easy to prepare. My favorite item is a supersize box with six packages of brownie mix. I make

it more indulgent with chocolate chips and cream cheese. It is quick, easy and I have never come back to the boat with anything left on the plate. I carry lots of cream cheese on the boat and can quickly mix in smoked salmon or a spice mix to make a quick dip for crackers or chips. Wine, beer, spirits for mixed drinks - don't forget the mixers. A warm day in the islands on Taco Tuesday begs for a margarita or a cold Corona. Stock what you need, being mindful of the limits imposed by Customs on either side of the border.

Make up your list. Indicate whether you should buy items in Canada or the U.S. depending on which direction you are headed across the border. Chocolate, candy, and liquor are generally more expensive in Canada due to the taxes imposed. The selection of wines at retail is better in the U.S. and maybe you should just pay the duty of 90% of the value for a selection of good wines for your vacation cruise – that's right - almost double. Luckily many customs agents will average the value of your wine low when calculating the duty. Let them come up with a value. You can have a list of what is on board; but in reality, it is very hard to value liquor coming into the country. You will be surprised that an agent's estimate is probably lower than you might think.

Do not try to sneak extra alcohol into either country. We have seen too many bottles of very good liquor confiscated because the boater was not honest. Agents seem to be looking for liquor more than anything else. The irony is that laws go back to the thinking that one might be smuggling liquor into the country for profit, denying a country of duty and tax.

Don't forget the incidentals. A charcoal grill - needs charcoal and lighter fluid. Is your grill gas, do you need a supply of propane tanks? When cruising, you need to be self-sufficient. You do not have the ability to jump in the car and head to the store to purchase that missing ingredient or favorite food item. You could be a week or ten days between major grocery markets.

Pre-packaged Portions. One of our instructors and an excellent cook, Lynette Brower, likes to pre-prepare foods and place them into plastic bags for a complete meal. She keeps freezer bags filled with chicken or steaks broken down into portions for dinners. When she has guests; out come two bags. Often she will store the spices inside the bag along with the food item. By planning ahead with pre-packaged meals, time is saved and entertaining becomes more enjoyable.

Get rid of unnecessary packaging. Is your boat limited on storage space for food

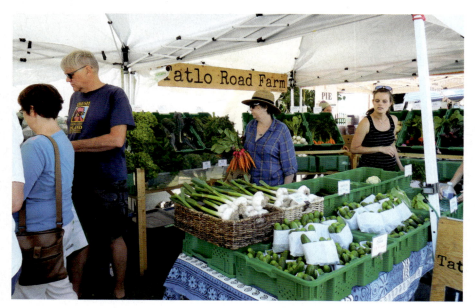

PROVISIONING YOUR BOAT FOR A WELL FED AND HAPPY CREW

or perishables? Consider removing food from boxes and bulky packaging. Mark the inner bag with a Sharpie. If it is a mix for preparation, cut the cooking directions from the box and tape it to the bag. Getting rid of the packaging before items are stored on your boat carries an additional benefit. Once north of Desolation Sound, getting rid of trash is a challenge and an expense. Many resorts charge by the bag or the pound to take your trash. Sometimes the trash needs to be stored for several days in a warm lazerette before it can be responsibly disposed. Getting rid of unnecessary packaging helps reduce trash.

Use plastic bins. A good system is to store dry food items in plastic bins sized to fit into the cabinets in the galley or other storage spaces. They can be segmented for how they are used. I have a bin for baking ingredients such as flour, sugar, baking soda and baking powder. The bin keeps the mess contained and supplies at-hand when doing a baking project. Bins keep canned goods from sliding around in rough seas and can be safely stowed.

Paper towels and paper plates are your friend. Unless you happen to be cruising on a mega-yacht, mealtime cleanup will be without a garbage disposal and dishwasher. Paper plates are a great option to reduce the dishwashing chore and reduce fresh water use (often a limited resource). You will likely be using more paper towels than at home. Paper towels make cleanup a breeze. It's best to wipe out greasy pots and pans rather than send oil and grease down the drain and into the sea water around your boat. Paper goods tend to be more expensive the farther north you go. Remember, everything has to be barged or flown in to the more remote locations.

Dining out. Options for dining-out disappear quickly the farther north you cruise. Beyond Desolation Sound restaurants are few and far between. Dining onboard is the rule, and it is important that you are prepared with the necessary items to make those tasty meals.

Don't overstock. In our experience, most people over stock their boats with food. It must be a comfort factor. There are plenty of places to purchase food items on the Inside Passage. Even the smallest marina markets try to support their guests with a means of purchasing food items and sometimes even fresh produce. We have not heard of anyone starving while out on a summer cruise. If anything, they come back refreshed and maybe even a pound or two content.

Keep it fun. Lastly, consider who is doing the cooking and cleaning up on your boat. It should not be the same person. This is a vacation in northwest paradise. Keep it light; keep it fun - and no galley slaves.

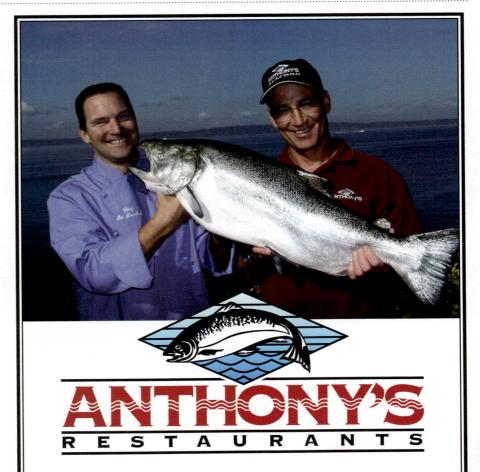

You're on the Water, and so is Anthony's!

Waterfront dining on the Puget Sound from Olympia to Bellingham and throughout the Northwest!

Anthony's opened our own seafood company in 1984 for the sole purpose of ensuring our guests only the highest quality northwest seafood. Complementing our seafood, Anthony's family-owned restaurants offer fresh seasonal produce from local farms, local microbrews and Northwest wines, enhanced with backdrops of scenic Puget Sound locations.

If you're cruising in Puget Sound, bring the crew ashore to the nearest Anthony's! Pick up your signature Anthony's Boater's Guide complete with moorage information for each location.

For additional information visit:
www.anthonys.com

Fisheries Supply
Marine Supplies Since 1928

Don't let a broken pump, clogged fuel filter or lost anchor ruin your vacation. Fisheries Supply has a full range of shipping options throughout the Pacific NW and Alaska, including custom solutions via Kenmore Air to almost anywhere in the San Juans, BC and the Inside Passage.

Largest Selection
of Marine Supplies in the Pacific Northwest

Same-Day Shipping
for Orders Placed by 2pm

Custom Shipping
to the San Juans, BC and Inside Passage*

*via Kenmore Air, certain restrictions apply

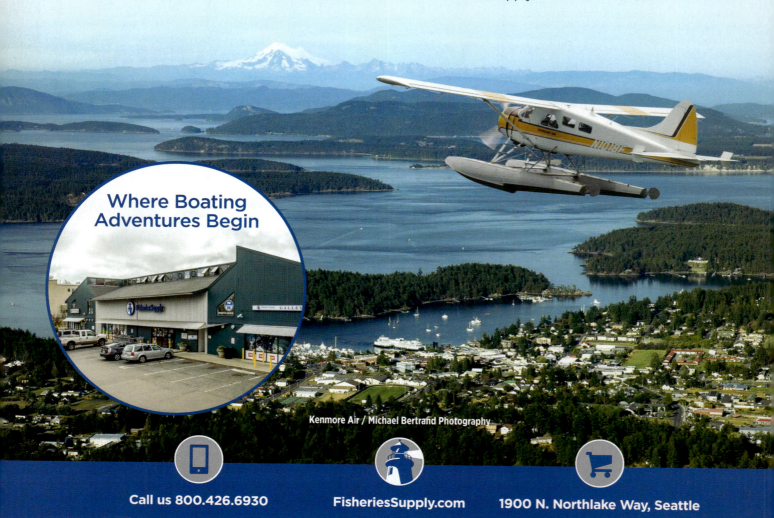

Kenmore Air / Michael Bertrand Photography

Where Boating Adventures Begin

Call us 800.426.6930   FisheriesSupply.com   1900 N. Northlake Way, Seattle

Potable Water, Can I Drink It?

"Is your water potable?" That's often one of the first questions boaters ask marinas when cruising the Northern BC Coast, the Broughton Archipelago and sometimes even in the Gulf Islands. Boaters often find a 'boil water' notice or 'not-potable' sign at water spigots and hose-bibs on the docks. But what does this mean to boaters and why has this sign been posted?

What is not-potable water? These notices indicate that the marina's private water system has not been certified by the Health Department as a public water system. Establishing a water system as a certified public water supply is an extensive and costly process, often not justifiable at remote, small marinas. Sometimes it requires a process for purification and exposure to UV light to kill certain bacteria. Sometimes the water is good and just needs to be tested regularly and sent in for certification. Water from private water systems may or may not be tested regularly but is used routinely, and may have been used for years with no ill effects. Remote resort locations like Pierre's Echo Bay Resort & Marina have been using the same well water for years with no ill effects. The hose bibs are marked non-potable and boil first; the water does have a slight brown tinge, but no one has reported problems with the water.

If other than owners are using or consuming water from a non-certified water system, the Government requires that a non-potable or boil notice be posted. The sign doesn't mean that the water is bad, but rather serves to inform guest users of the water source and allow the guest user to make a choice or further inquiries.

As boaters, what do we do with this information? Depending on your comfort level, there are several options for non-potable water:

- Simply don't use the marina water, use only the water from your onboard tank.

- Do your own checking – ask locals if they regularly use the water for household needs. After your evaluation, you may choose to use the local source.

- Before your trip, you may wish to purchase a 3-stage water filter (the third stage needs to be a ceramic filter) and use this filter system to filter the marina water when filling your tank.

- If you have a watermaker onboard, you may wish to use your own established procedures for making water and filling or re-filling your onboard tank.

- Another option is to sanitize the marina water put in your tank with a chemical additive. You will need to research and purchase these additives before your trip.

- Lastly, installing filters and a UV light sanitizing system to your onboard water system will ensure you have safe water no matter where you fill your water tank.

What is the brown color in the water? Additionally, boaters may have discovered that a few water sources on Northern BC Coast and in the Broughtons have a slight tannin or brown color to the water. While the water may be potable and not harmful, it certainly can be unappealing. Nature has its own filtration system that sometimes picks up coloring from cedar roots, resulting in the weak tea appearance to the water. This is an isolated issue, and nearly all of the marinas and water sources in the area have clear water.

In summary, small outlying marinas provide a surprising number of amenities for boaters, including acceptable sources of water. During their short business season, it's amazing what they can and do provide for the boating community. We encourage boaters to let them know how much we appreciate their facilities.

Spectra has engineered simplicity and reliability into watermaking. The best pump means the quietest and most efficient operation. There isn't even oil to change! Run it off the batteries, alternator or genset through a charger.

Whether your needs are 10 gallons a day or 10,000, we have a model for you.

And, of course, Spectra stands behind all its watermakers with the industry's best warranty.

When it comes to planning and installing a Spectra, the most experienced team anywhere is Emerald Harbor Marine.

Simply put, Spectra makes the most versatile, quiet, compact and efficent watermakers.

At Elliott Bay Marina in Seattle
206-285-3632
www.emharbor.com

2020 WAGGONER CRUISING GUIDE

FISHING AND SHELLFISH COLLECTING

How To Catch Dinner. If you love to eat salmon, halibut, rockfish, crab or prawns - you are boating in the right place. Washington, Alaska, and British Columbia all require licenses to harvest virtually any type of seafood. Washington and Alaska licenses can be purchased at sporting goods stores and other retail outlets, or online with a credit card. British Columbia licenses can be purchased at Independent Access Providers (check their website for a list), or online with a credit card. If you purchase online, consider how you will print the license; unless you have a printer onboard, it may be best to do it at home ahead of time.

Investing in Gear. Crabbing is inexpensive and fun for even an inexperienced crew. Crabbing gear is relatively easy to purchase at a few hundred dollars, but the costs go up from there. Catching prawns can be more costly, especially if you purchase a pot puller to pull the weighted traps up from 250-350 feet deep. Many have outfitted their boats or dinghies to target salmon with all the best equipment, spending thousands of dollars for downriggers, trolling motors, special rods, reels, lures and a fishfinder. Some salmon fishing enthusiasts even tow a special boat set up to catch salmon. There is a lot of money invested, and we don't dare ask how much

the investment totals compared to the cost of buying quality salmon at the market.

Charter Fishing. At the Waggoner Guide, we love to fish, or to put it more directly, we love to "catch" fish. Rather than investing a fortune "gearing up" to fish, we have gotten into the practice of hiring an expert with all the right equipment and going charter fishing for salmon or halibut once or twice a summer. Prices vary from reasonable to very expensive, ask before booking.

The experts know their local waters, where the fish are and how to fish. We nearly always fill our freezer with as much fish as we can handle and have a lot of fun. Your charter captain can conveniently issue fishing licenses for the charter, and has all the gear and fresh bait. Depending on the location, the charter captain also knows where to take the fish to be processed, flash frozen and stored in the freezer to be shipped home, where you can accept the shipment later.

Guests. We typically treat our guests to a fishing expedition in the Johnstone Strait areas, the Broughtons, Northern B.C. or in Southeast Alaska. A half-day charter will often do it; and with a good guide and good conditions, we limit out within the half-day charter and fill the freezer. We have also

found it is best to ask the charter captain when to fish. Many start out the day early in the morning. We have also had excellent results when our charter captain suggested fishing on the evening change of tide.

Finding a Good Charter. Ask around at the marinas you will be visiting. They know the good local fishing guides. You may want to book a charter well in advance of your stay at a marina. When the bite is on, reservations with the best charter captains fill up quickly. The charter captains will often pick you up at your marina or even at your boat on the hook at an anchorage with a fast boat to quickly get you to the best fishing spots in the area. Most charter captains I have fished with take real pride in finding fish and helping you land them on the boat. They want you to catch fish, take them home, and tell your friends!

Catching Fish Without Fishing. There is another technique we have found to catch fish without even dropping a hook in the water. It all starts with being nice to people. Most fisherman catch more fish than they can use. We have seen some excellent techniques among pleasure boaters to catch fish with fresh baked bread, cookies and pies carried down a dock full of commercial fishing boats during the season, offering a trade. Many guys use

THIRD-PARTY MOORAGE RESERVATION SERVICES

The world of internet booking service providers that offer moorage slip reservations services has arrived in NW cruising grounds. Three providers have been actively growing their list of marinas where you can review and book marina stays. Dockwa, Snag-A-Slip, and SwiftHarbour list marinas in Washington State and British Columbia. SwiftHarbour is based in Vancouver, BC, and Dockwa and Snag-A-Slip are U.S. companies.

All three have web, Android, and iOS Apps for using their service. These are all third-party booking services where you request moorage through the service. Confirmation of your requested moorage comes from the booking agent a short-time later, after the marina confirms the request back to the booking service company. All three services allow free browsing of their listed marinas. All of the booking services require a credit card for moorage deposit or payment; there may or may not be a reservation fee. Timing of charges to your credit card varies by booking service. Terms and conditions for cancellation, reservation changes, and no-show charges are governed by the marina's policy and not the booking service.

Marina listings with the service companies are not exclusive. You will find the same marina listed with more than one service; Pt. Roberts Marina in Washington is listed with all three booking services.

Snag-A-Slip

snagaslip.com; Annapolis, MD; (443) 808-2700

Snag-A-Slip lists approximately four marinas in Washington, from Gig Harbor to Pt. Roberts. U.S. East Coast based Snag-A-Slip has a much larger presence on the East Coast, where they

have many marinas listed. Snag-A-Slip advertises that you can check slip availability before booking moorage. Setting up a user account is optional, and moorage can be booked as a 'guest' to Snag-A-Slip. Listings are not limited to marinas, individual slip owners may list their slip for short- or long-term rental.

Dockwa

dockwa.com; Newport RI & Cambridge, MA; (401) 236-8304

Dockwa is one of the larger companies in this new business category, with many listings throughout the U.S., Caribbean, Bahamas, and Panama. In the NW, Dockwa lists about 18 marinas in Washington State. Boaters may browse their listed marinas freely. A free user account is necessary to make a reservation request. Moorage is booked, confirmed, and paid through Dockwa. Their services include solutions that help the marinas manage slip reservations and moorage payment.

Swift Harbour

swiftharbour.com; Vancouver, BC; (604) 670-4818

Swift Harbour is the local Northwest company that has made a presence in this online marina moorage reservations business category. Based in Vancouver, BC, they are the only provider listing marinas in British Columbia. They list about 20 marinas covering the cruising area from the Canada U.S. border on the Salish Sea through the Gulf Islands, and out the Strait of Juan de Fuca to West Coast Vancouver Island. Browsing the marina listings is open to all, and you will need a free account to book moorage. Booking confirmation from their service includes a welcome packet with marina information.

FISHING AND SHELLFISH COLLECTING

the traditional technique of walking down the dock with a six pack of beer or a 20-dollar bill, which usually lands a catch. Keep in mind, however, that some commercial operators are not allowed to sell fish to individuals unless the operator holds a special license.

Freeze the Bounty. Crab can be frozen and keeps well up to a year. Pack in freezer bags or vacuum bags with clean seawater or milk. When you are ready, defrost and squeeze the excess liquid out of the meat. Freezing in milk or seawater also works well for uncooked prawns. It keeps the meat from breaking down and getting freezer burn. While much of your catch may end up frozen for later, fresh fish, prawns and crab, consumed just an hour or two after coming out of the water is about as good as it gets.

Fishing Regulations. Fishing and shellfish collection have become much more complicated and onerous over the years. Laws not only require fishing licenses for specific species, at specific times, and for specific locations, but also set possession limits and storage requirements for fish and shellfish identification purposes. Field Correspondent Deane Hislop, and professional fisherman Gill Graham, share additional information below, regarding fishing in the waters of British Columbia.

SPORT FISHING IN B.C.

Know Before You Go. British Columbia Sport Fishing regulations cover 47 different management areas and vary from area to area, and from year to year, so it is important that anyone planning to wet a line, drop a pot, pick oysters or dig clams in British Columbia tidal water obtain the latest copy of the Department of Fisheries and Oceans (DFO) Canada, British Columbia Sports Fishing Guide from an authorized license dealer. Guides and licenses are also available online at www.pac.dfo-mpo.gc.ca. Beware, regulations can change during the season, so it is wise to monitor the website for any in-season revisions.

If you are going fishing or harvesting shellfish in tidal waters, you need a Tidal Waters Sports Fishing License. If you're going fishing in fresh waters for salmon or any other species, you're required to have a Non-Tidal Angling License issued by the Province of B.C.

Before going fishing, make sure you can answer these five questions:

1. Can I fish at this time, at this location?

2. Is the gear, and the manner in which I plan to use it, legal for catching fish, crab, shrimp or prawns?

3. What can I catch and keep, and in what amount?

4. Do I have the correct license (and supplementary salmon stamp if needed), and do I need to record my catch on the license?

5. How many fish, crab, shrimp, clams, oysters can I possess, and how am I allowed to clean, package and transport them to my residence?

Certain coastal areas are designated rockfish conservation areas (RCAs). Sport fishing is not allowed in RCAs. Gathering of invertebrates by hand picking or diving, or collecting crab, shrimp or prawn by trap, and smelt by gillnet may be allowed. Find out where B.C.'s RCAs are located at bcsportfishingguide.ca.

Reminders:

• Barbless hooks are required for all salmon and sea-run trout fishing. Treble barbless are acceptable in most areas.

• Know the size limit for the area fishing.

• In tidal waters, there's no limit to the number of fishing rods you can use.

• When filleting salmon, the tail must remain attached for the purpose of identification. The adipose fin or fin clip scar must also remain attached to determine if the fish is wild or hatchery.

• It's illegal to willfully snag hook a salmon. If you should foul hook a salmon, it must be released immediately.

• You must immediately record on your license all adult chinook you keep.

• Harvesting of northern abalone, an endangered species in B.C., is prohibited.

For more information on sport fishing in B.C., including seasons, limits, gear requirements and restrictions, go to bcsportfishingguide.ca.

Deane Hislop

Posession Limits. The number of fish or shellfish of any species that you are allowed to keep as your daily limit and in possession is determined by the area in which you are fishing. Knowing the number of the area you are in is imperative to staying within your limits and therefore legal.

The daily limits are what you are allowed to catch in one day, the in-possession limits are usually twice the daily limit. Once you have your possession limit you are done fishing, you must stop. The catch you eat, while still part of your daily limit, is not part of your possession limit. You may take or send your catch to your ordinary residence; once there, they are no longer part of your possession limit and you can fish again. However, the regulations are very clear on the explanation of your ordinary residence, and your boat is not included. The address on your driver's license is your ordinary residence.

Probably the most misunderstood, is the fact that if you are going to keep the crabs to take home, you cannot clean, cook and pick out the meat. The carapace, which is the shell on the top that you measure to determine his legality, has to be attached to the body. It is possible to lift it part way and clean out the innards, cook him, and then freeze him, however you cannot pick the meat from his shell. Technically, if you have frozen picked crab in your freezer, you committed an offence.

You can ship your catch to your ordinary residence, or someone else could take it home for you, however, there are certain criteria that have to be met to do this; check the regulations. Most importantly, remember the crabs have to have the carapace attached until they reach your residence. You cannot start catching more until your possession limit is in your ordinary residence.

Gill Graham

Rockfish Conservation Areas in B.C. Our coastal waters of British Columbia abound in wonderful delights from the sea. Rockfish species are one of these delicacies we can enjoy. Rockfish come in so many varieties, colors and shapes that a lot of people have no idea what they are catching. There are 37 varieties of Rockfish found on this coast. Yelloweye (red snapper) are rockfish. It is very important to know what species you are catching to stay within the regulations.

As man has learned over the ages, you just can't take and take and expect what you are taking to always be there. To protect our rockfish, Fisheries and Oceans Canada (DFO) designated protected areas for them in 2002. These areas are called rockfish Conservation Areas or RCAs. There are 16 RCA locations along our coast, and you should know where they are. Before you go fishing, go to bcsportfishguide.ca and locate the area in which you will be fishing and take note of the RCA locations in that area. You might be surprised where some of these RCAs are located. Know before you go. Inside an RCA, you are not allowed to put a line in the water that is targeting any fin fish. You cannot troll for salmon in an RCA since rockfish will go after a lure; you cannot jig for Ling Cod since rockfish will go for your jig. You can handpick or dive for shellfish (invertebrates), you can fish for crab or prawns, you can catch smelt by gillnet, in the area. If your gear is attached to a fishing rod with a hook, jig, or lure, it cannot go in the water.

Many rockfish live to be over 100 years old, that 15-pound yelloweye you just brought up from 250 to 300 feet could be that old. Unlike salmon, rockfish don't survive well with catch and release. That is why there is no size limit for rockfish. If you catch a rockfish, DFO regulations state you have to keep that fish. If you are in an area that allows one (1) rockfish per day, you have your one limit no matter how big he is, or if you like him or not, he is yours.

Gill Graham

2020 WAGGONER CRUISING GUIDE

MAINTAINING YOUR BOAT LIKE A PRO

The Waggoner Cruising Guide team takes boat maintenance very seriously. A breakdown can ruin your day, or even a week. For us and the boats in our flotilla trips, or when we are out researching for the Waggoner Guide, we cannot afford to breakdown. We certainly don't want a breakdown while underway in the remote areas of Northern B.C. or while crossing an open body of water like Dixon Entrance or rounding Cape Caution. You do not want to breakdown either. Time for summer cruising is a valuable commodity. The worst thing that can happen is when you have a breakdown and your family and friends are stuck waiting for repairs or parts. It is important to develop a maintenance program that is pro-active and preventative.

We have established a maintenance program that starts in the fall just after the cruising season ends. We begin by updating the list of our normal maintenance items such as taking an oil sample before changing the oil and filters. Coolant is inspected and changed. We inspect all systems to see what has broken or needs repair; we like to take care of this in the fall before the boat is laid up for the winter. Corrosives in used oil sitting over the winter can add to the wear on an engine.

It all starts with a checklist specifically tailored for our boat, identifying work to be done. After completing annual maintenance items, we start on upgrade items or refit. Scheduling work in the fall allows us to order needed parts that are often on sale during the winter months or available at boat show prices.

We also inspect our spares. When we purchase spares, the new spare is installed and the old part becomes the spare. This way we know the spare works and has all of the hardware it needs for installation. We carry a spare water pump – the old one stands by and ready to be installed. Parts stores are typically hard to find in our cruising areas. The old part probably has plenty of life in it for a temporary fix. We pack more spares for a single engine boat than we do for a twin-engine boat, where our second engine is our spare.

Look at spares as systems. For example, we do not believe in carrying a rebuild kit for the head. We do carry a complete, working pump assembly ready to be installed and carry spare duckbill valves. Rebuilding a pump for the head is not a pleasant task, nor would it go over well with the rest of the crew.

Our inspection checklist includes due dates for many items like hoses and belts. Dates are also set for various systems: the cooling system on the engine is sent out for flushing at a radiator shop every 5 years; the exhaust

BOAT SYSTEMS FOR INSPECTION AND SERVICE
- Engine Systems
- Control Systems
- Heat and Water Heater
- Electrical – Batteries, Inverters and Power Cables
- Fuel System – Filters and Tanks
- Water – Filters, Pumps and Tanks
- Heads and Waste systems
- Lighting – External and Internal
- Fire Suppression – All Extinguishers
- Emergency Kits, Flares and First Aid
- Electronics and Communications
- Charts and Cruising Guides
- Anchor Systems
- Galley and Refrigeration
- Dinghy
- Bedding and Soft Goods
- Accessories and Recreational Gear

Canadian Service Office at Canoe Cove.

MAINTAINING YOUR BOAT LIKE A PRO

Prefill new filter with clean oil when changing engine oil.

system is removed and inspected annually. If you have a stainless steel or ceramic coated exhaust system, the interval can be much longer. For gensets and small diesel auxiliaries, the exhaust systems may be very hard to remove and inspect. It may be cheaper to just replace the exhaust system at a cost for parts of about $200. The transmission oil cooler is replaced every 5 years. Some transmission coolers can be sent to a radiator shop to flush, pressure test and service. Soft goods such as dripless seals, sail drive boots, hoses, belts etc. are inspected every year; after 10 years they are all replaced. We service the windlass system with an inspection and lubrication annually. Every 5 years the windlass gets a major inspection, and every 10 years the windlass motor is sent out to a motor shop to be rebuilt. An anchor windlass is a single point of failure, keeping the windlass in great shape can save you from a real headache on the summer cruise.

Our maintenance checklist is divided among the boat's systems. The engine and propulsion systems are well understood, but we also breakdown our checklist into the other systems, such as the anchoring system, refrigeration, furnaces and heat, including the water heater. Electrical systems are checked – both 12V and 120/240V. Start and House Batteries are serviced and possibly replaced. We plan to replace batteries every 7-10 years for sealed batteries, and every 4-7 years for lead acid batteries, if they were properly maintained. And, remember when you replace battery banks, you need to replace all the batteries in the bank, even if just one is not performing to specifications. We even view the dinghy as a system and make sure the outboard is serviced and the fuel replaced annually. We check the dinghy's steering system, anchor system and the gear bag for first aid supplies and other safety items.

You do not have to do all the work, but often you do have to manage the work to make sure it gets done. If you elect not to do some things on your checklist, have your shop update your checklist and ask them to sign off on the inspection and service items to ABYC standards.

Determine what items on your checklist you want to work on and those you would prefer a marine professional handle. For example, inspecting and remarking your anchor chain may be a day project you want to do.

A boat is a complex series of systems, all working in a corrosive environment. Your boat's systems are in standby through most of the year, ready for those good months when you go boating. It is best for boats to be used on a regular basis; you may want to use your boat more often and go boating once or twice every other month, but with our busy lives that may not be practical. The key is to have a process for good routine maintenance built into your boat ownership to maximize fun with family and friends for an enjoyable cruise.

Maintenance courses are offered at the Seattle Boat Show University and Cruisers College programs.

BOATING FROM INN TO INN

Boating from Inn to Inn. There is a new trend in boating, using shore-side inns, hotels or cabins as extra staterooms. Many of these Inns are designed for visiting boating guests and are very cool. You can boat with friends or family and give them the option of staying onshore. Handy if your boat does not have that second or third stateroom. This is also handy if you would like a night ashore and some of the options like yurts or bubble homes are very interesting. If you have a fast speedboat with a cuddy cabin, you can run up the Inside Passage to Alaska in two long days or less. There are lots of options.

When we started seeing this trend, we recognized the opportunity for guests aboard a boat to enjoy the day's cruise with the option to stay overnight onshore at an inn, cabin, or hotel room. There are even boats and houseboats in marinas that you can rent for the overnight stay. Some of these options can be booked through the marina or even on Airbnb. Grandparents can now join the fun of a day's cruise with the family and spend the night ashore in a comfortable bed with a normal sized bathroom facility. With a little creative planning and the Waggoner Cruising Guide in hand, you can create a cruising itinerary with stays in marinas that have nearby shore-side overnight stays. Accommodations range from luxury inns and hotel rooms to other boats in the marina, yurts, and even camp sites where the kids can stay in a tent.

Downsize your boat. We also see a trend where some cruising couples are downsizing their boat. They have owned a 45 foot to 60 foot displacement trawler, allowing them to cruise for weeks

Artisan Suites on Bowen Island sits atop the hill above Snug Cove, close to shops.

April Point Resort, Spa & Marina near Campbell River

Roche Harbor Resort on San Juan Island is a great family destination.

Camp in luxury at Backeddy Resort & Marina near Egmont, BC.

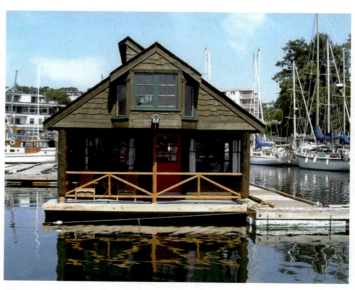
The cottage at Westbay Marine Village in Victoria

www.WaggonerGuide.com

BOATING FROM INN TO INN

or months at a time. They have done the long trips and now want to downsize to reduce their boating costs, allowing them to experience other types of travel. Rather than letting go of the boating scene, they change their boating style and purchase a smaller vessel with basic overnight accommodations for two. They buy a faster boat and plan their trips to quickly dash to different places and stay ashore for most of the time during their trip. One owner who downsized from a 45-foot semi-displacement trawler to a new 28-foot Sea Sport, with twin outboards, planned a four-day passage from Anacortes to Ketchikan. He and his wife stayed in cabins at Blind Channel and Echo Bay and then hotel rooms at Shearwater and Prince Rupert before arriving in Ketchikan. While their new 28-foot boat was not inexpensive, they saved on moorage, insurance, and general maintenance with a smaller boat.

A growing family or bringing grandchildren along. If your cute young children are growing into gangly teenagers, and a new larger boat with cabins for all is not in your future, consider lodging them off the boat ashore. There are many anchorages and marinas with camping areas and tent sites. It can be an adventure to arrive by boat and take the dingy to shore and set up camp. Some marina resorts have swimming pools, kayak rentals, and many recreational activities. Involve the kids in the planning. Let them research and make some of the choices on where to stay. This works for grandchildren too. The added benefit - with the kids ashore - you get your privacy back at the boat.

Seascape Waterfront Resort in Gowland Harbour near Campbell River

Hastings House has beautiful classic cottages overlooking Ganges Harbour on Salt Spring Island.

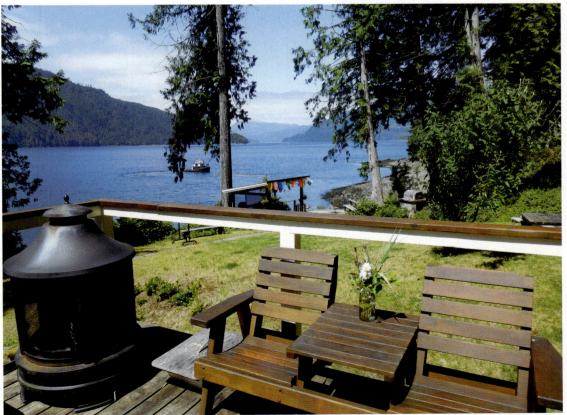

Denham Bay above Dent Rapids in Discovery Passage is a quiet, restful destination.

2020 WAGGONER CRUISING GUIDE

Garmin Chartplotters at Fisheries Supply

You probably already know how to use a Garmin chartplotter. *It's that intuitive.* Just turn it on and follow the simple menu. Everything is at your fingertips to easily plan your route and set your course. Most Garmin echoMAP™ and GPSMAP® chartplotters are available combined with built-in sonar capabilities. These include advanced HD-ID™ sonar, CHIRP sonar and Garmin ClearVü™ and SideVü™ scanning sonar, which provides the clearest scanning sonar images on the water.

Featuring touchscreen technology

GPSMAP® 8400/8600 Series
Now includes 10", 12" and 16" chartplotter/sonar combo models with full in-plane switching (IPS) touchscreen displays, support for traditional, scanning and Panoptix™ sonar, preloaded coastal charts and inland maps featuring Navionics® data and Auto Guidance technology.

GPSMAP® 10x2/12x2 Series
Choose from 10" or 12" chartplotter/sonar combos with traditional and scanning sonars, preloaded coastal charts and inland maps featuring integrated Garmin and Navionics® content, networking capabilities and Wi-Fi® connectivity.

For the complete offering of Garmin Chartplotters go to **fisheriessupply.com/garmin**

Call us 800.426.6930

FisheriesSupply.com

1900 N. Northlake Way

Isotherm Fridges and Freezers

Isotherm refrigerators and freezers are the result of careful research. Marine refrigerators operate under tough conditions: they must withstand violent movements, operate noiselessly, be thoroughly reliable and, perhaps the most important of all, consume an absolute minimum of battery power.

CRUISE Fridges
Isotherm CRUISE Marine fridges are available in Classic (panel), Elegance (silver), and Stainless Steel Models

CRUISE Freezers
Perfect complement to CRUISE fridges

DRAWER Fridges and Freezers
Easy access to food and drinks with the help of robust DRAWER technology

Travel Boxes
Transportable portable refrigerator/freezers

Clear & White Ice Makers
Isotherm offers two different models with two different technologies: clear ice and white ice

 Call us 800.426.6930

 FisheriesSupply.com

 1900 N. Northlake Way

WHALE WISE - VIEWING WHALES AND MARINE MAMMALS

Observing marine life, including whales breaching, feeding or on the hunt, is always a thrill to see. The diversity and complexity of marine life in our coastal waters is truly extraordinary. It's one of the reasons boaters come to the waters of Washington State and British Columbia. Unfortunately, increased vessel traffic and noise threatens some of the whale population along with other factors like pollutants and lack of prey.

Cetaceans & Pinnipeds. Some of the more common whales found in the Salish Sea and the Inside Passage are humpback, gray, minke and fin. These migratory whales are found in our waters almost year round from early spring to late fall. Their telltale exhalation blow can be seen from far away. Humpbacks and grays are the more frequently observed in our waters. However, it can be difficult to identify the species as they are all big and gray in color. Dall's porpoise are often seen in NW waters and are often mistaken for baby killer whales. Seals and sea lions are often seen hauled out on rocks and protected shorelines.

Killer Whales / Orca Whales. In the Northeast Pacific there are three types of killer whales (also referred to as orca whales): residents (salmon specialists), transients (marine mammal specialists), and offshore killer whales. Southern Resident Killer Whales are critically endangered with only 75 members remaining. Northern Resident and Transient Killer Whales are threatened but not endangered.

Research has shown that underwater noise and sudden loud spikes of noise impacts whale behavior and their ability to find food. This is especially the case for killer whales, the largest member of the dolphin family.

Killer whales are constantly on the move, traveling 70 to 100 miles per day in search of food. Boats that get too close to a whale can prevent the whale from having a successful catch of prey. Killer whales, like other marine mammals, are protected by law.

Laws and Guidelines. In WA and BC waters, marine mammals are protected by federal law that (in addition to other protections) requires vessels to remain a minimum distance of 100 yards and 200 yards if these mammals are resting or with young. These marine mammal protection laws have been in place for many years and govern boat and people proximity to marine wildlife.

U.S./Canada Laws & Guidelines. The declining population of Southern Resident Killer Whales prompted considerable attention and triggered efforts to protect them. The Salish Sea is a transboundary region overseen by Canada, U.S., and Washington State. New more restrictive laws governing the operation of vessels near whales came into effect in 2019 in BC and Washington State waters.

Washington State and BC laws regulating distances between boats and killer whales are similar, but there are some differences that should be noted between Washington and BC waters. Laws may vary that regulate vessel approach distances, viewing distances, approach speeds, and restricted access to certain waters.

If whales surface unexpectedly within 200 yards, slowly move away perpendicular to the whales' direction of travel. If they're within 200 yards, shut down until the whales are a safe distance away. Be aware that you can still be cited, even if the incident was not intentional. Positioning the boat directly ahead or behind a whale, including shutting down, is not permitted under law. U.S. and Canadian law requires vessels give 400 yards of clearance in front and behind whales. Traveling behind whales should also be avoided.

In addition to governing laws, BC and Washington have voluntary guidelines that boaters are asked to follow. This section is an overview and summary of regulations for these jurisdictions. See Chapter 6 *Whale Wise – Washington State* for laws and guidelines specific to Washington State waters. See Chapter 7 *Whale Wise – Gulf Islands* and Chapter 14 *Whale Wise – BC Juan de Fuca* for regulations and guidelines specific to BC waters.

SRKW Critical Habitat Areas. BC has declared areas of southern Gulf Islands, Strait of Juan de Fuca, and Pacific Ocean waters off Barkley Sound as Southern Resident Killer Whale Critical Habitat (SRKW), with more restrictive regulations. See the reference map in this section for details. Regulations specific to SRKW Critical Habitat and Southern Resident Killer Whales are in force from June 1st to October 31st.

Interim Sanctuary Zones. Three zones have have been established in Canadian waters, where general vessel traffic is prohibited from June 1 – October 31. Vessel traffic is not allowed: a) off the southwest shore of North Pender Island; b) off the southeast end of Saturna Island; and c) Swiftsure Bank at the east entrance to Strait of Juan de Fuca. These Interim Santuray Zones are subject to change; check Fisheries and Oceans Canada website www.pac.dfo-mpo.gc.ca for the latest information.

Judging Distance. Keep in mind that 200 yards is 600 feet or 2 football fields, so binoculars are your friend. Judging distance at sea can be challenging. It may be helpful to think in terms of boat lengths. For a distance of 200 yards, a 50-foot boat would need to stay twelve boat-lengths away, and a 30-foot boat would need to stay twenty boat-lengths away. For those used to visualizing distance in miles, one-quarter statute mile is 440 yards, and a half statute mile is 880 yards. Radar, especially digital radar, may be a useful tool for measuring distance from an object.

Enforcement. Regulations are strictly enforced by various officials or agencies of Washington State, and the Province of British Columbia. Law enforcement personnel may board your vessel if you are in violation of

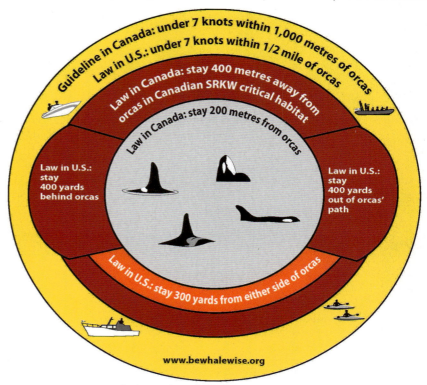

www.bewhalewise.org

WHALE WISE - VIEWING WHALES AND MARINE MAMMALS

whale watching regulations. In the U.S. that may be NOAA, Washington Department of Fish and Wildlife (WDFW), or the County Sheriff's Department. Canadian Fishery officers and BC Conservation officers provide enforcement in Canada.

Whale Warning Flag. While being good stewards of whale watching regulations, boaters can also help protect our whales by flying a 'Whale Warning Flag' when sighting whales. San Juan County is running a pilot project through the 2020 boating season. If you see this flag, slow to 7 knots or less, be prepared to adjust your course, and follow the whale watching regulations. If you would like one of these flags, contact Frances Robertson, Marine Program Coordinator for San Juan County, at francesr@sanjuanco.com. Don't forget to lower the flag once you or the whales have left the area.

Quick Guide To Regulations for Marine Mammal Viewing

Canadian/BC Regulations

- 400 meters from killer whales in SRKW areas
- 200 meters from killer whales in BC waters other than SRKW areas
- Vessels are prohibited from entering any of 3 Sanctuary Zones from June 1st to October 31st
  1. off East Pt. on Saturna Island
  2. southwest shore of North Pender Island
  3. Swiftsure Bank at the west entrance to Strait of Juan de Fuca.
- 7 knots or less (voluntary) slow zone within 1000 meters of killer whales
- Turn off depth sounders (voluntary) when not in use
- Engine off or neutral idle (voluntary) near killer whales
- 100 meters from non-killer whales, dolphins, porpoises, and other marine mammals; 200 meters if they are resting or with young

U.S./Washington Regulations

- 400 yards from the path (behind and in front) of Southern Resident Orcas
- 300 yards from Southern Resident Orca whales
- 7 knot speed limit within ½ mile of Southern Resident Orcas
- Disengage engine transmission if a Southern Resident Orca whale is within 200 yards
- 100 yards from non-killer whales, dolphins, porpoises, and other marine mammals; 200 yards if they are resting or with young
- Turn off echo / depth sounders (voluntary) when not in use
- Vessels are asked to avoid the Voluntary No-Go Zone on the West Side of San Juan Island, which extends ¼-mile offshore from Mitchell Bay to Cattle Point, and a ½-mile offshore at Lime Kiln Lighthouse.

Overview of 2019 management measures to protect Southern Resident killer whales

GET OUT OF YOUR COMFORT ZONE AND INTO OURS

Don't let fear of the unknown hold you back from fulfilling your dreams of adventure. With Nordhavn's track record of safe, successful ocean passages and circumnavigations, you can confidently take on the world and all that it has to offer. Made of bullet-proof fiberglass construction and rated to handle all offshore conditions, a Nordhavn is fearless...even if you aren't.

Nordhavn yachts offer peace of mind and body. Attentive space planning and elegant interiors (which you can design to your exact specification) evoke a luxuriously unfettered atmosphere. So with your Nordhavn, you'll always have the comforts of home no matter which far-reaching locale you happen to be in.

Not everything you're afraid of deserves fear. A Nordhavn allows you to pursue your passion with complete conviction.

For information on our line of Nordhavn yachts ranging from 47 to 120 feet, visit nordhavn.com.

NORDHAVN YACHTS NORTHWEST
Seattle, WA 206.223.2624   www.nordhavn.com   Anacortes, WA 360.209.9780

Edible Flowers

Did you know that there are many types of flowers you can eat? Yes, in fact, there are 75 different types of edible flowers. Edible flowers can be used in salads, soups, and pasta dishes, or used as garnishes and toppings. But where do you buy edible flowers? You can usually find 1-ounce packages (kept in the refrigerated section) of high-end groceries like Whole Foods. Of course, you will want to know about any potential allergies you may have. Be sure to confirm the edible genus and species if purchasing products at a farmer's market, and be sure to check for freshness. Edible flowers should be used as soon as possible, and kept in the refrigerator in an airtight container, with a damp paper towel.

Cooking with flowers is a creative and fun way to add color, taste, and appeal to just about any meal. This culinary practice has been used around the world for centuries, going back to Roman times and the ancient Greeks.

Here are a few edible flowers that have caught the attention of chefs:

Arugula. All parts of this flower are edible; the leaves, flowers, seeds, and sprouts. This flower is typically added to salads for a spicy flavor. Packed with proteins, minerals and calcium, they have a health benefit as well.

Bachelor's Button. The flowers of the Bachelor Button come in a variety of colors, and are mostly used as a decorative garnish for salads. The flowers have a mild peppery flavor.

Hibiscus. The roots and flower of the Hibiscus are both edible and taste similar to cranberry. The Hibiscus is often added to tea and soups. You can also stuff the flower petals with a rice mixture or cheese.

Bee Balm. The flower of the Bee Balm has a strong flavor and is used to make tea; it's also used in preparing jellies and even breads. It is reported that Bee Balm helps eliminate congestion.

Nasturtium. This edible flower has a sweet, pleasant flavor (the smaller flowers are best) and are used as a garnish for salads. The flower buds are used in cocktails. Nasturtiums are packed with nutrients, including vitamin C and iron.

Squash Blossoms. The edible blossoms of the squash are often seen in markets during the summer months. They can be used in salads or stuffed with goat cheese; or fried in batter stuffed with spices and ricotta cheese.

Pansy. The pansy, a common garden flower, is beautiful in appearance. The sepals and petals are edible, with a somewhat sweet flavor; use pansies that have only been grown organically. These flower petals are used in fruit salads, in cocktails, and added atop desserts and soups.

Violets. Both the leaves and flowers of the violet are edible, and contain iron, calcium and vitamins C and A. You can add the leaves to salads or prepare them as you would spinach.

samlexamerica®

Power Conversion Products Since 1991

MORE SOLUTIONS
SAFE | PROVEN | RELIABLE

Choose from the widest variety of power conversion products from one manufacturer.

Inverter/ Chargers

DC-AC Inverters

Solar Solutions

Power Supplies

Battery Chargers

 Best Customer Service in the Industry

 Technical Support

 Online Tools

1-800-561-5885
samlexamerica.com

AVAILABLE AT LFS MARINE & OUTDOOR
WASHINGTON STORES: Seattle • Bellingham
ALASKA STORES: Anchorage • Cordova • Dillingham • Dutch Harbor • Homer • Kenai • Sitka

800-426-8860 | **LFSMarineOutdoor.com**

IT WILL NEVER HAPPEN TO ME...

We never plan to fall in and end up in the cold waters of the Northwest; but it happens, and in most cases, everything ends up OK. Every once in a while, we hear about an accidental drowning.

It's wise to be prepared, just in case. Have you thought about how you will get a person out of the water on your boat? You have only about 15 minutes or less until the situation becomes critical and life threatening. That's 15 minutes to spot and find the individual, bring the boat alongside, and pull them into the boat. You should have equipment available like a Lifesling Overboard Rescue System ready to deploy, or a block and tackle, or the use of a davit system. Next, you'll need to get them to a safe spot on the boat and a means of warming them up. You may be doing this in rough sea conditions singlehanded; or YOU may be the one in the water, hoping your crew knows the procedures and how to use the equipment on board.

We recommend you practice the steps for a man overboard situation:
1. Instruct crew to keep eyes on the person overboard; arrest your forward motion.
2. Push the "Man Overboard" button on your Chartplotter or GPS.
3. Raise the RED safety cover on the Distress button on the VHF radio. Press the button for 3-4 seconds and make a Mayday Call on VHF 16 with the name of your vessel and that you have a Man Overboard situation with a person in the water. Give your lat/lon position.
4. Access the Man Overboard ring and line, or a Lifesling or other device, and deploy. Circle them to pull the float and line to them. Pull them to the side of the boat.
5. Deploy the swim ladder and assist climbing out of the water. They may not have the strength, and a line may have to be rigged to pull them out – most likely a davit system or block and tackle rigged to a high position on the boat, or use the boom and winch on a sailboat.
6. Once on the boat, begin warming the victim with blankets. Communicate the situation on VHF 16 and determine if additional help is needed.

We make it a practice to wear life jackets while on deck and keep a VHF handheld with DSC in a pocket, and flares in another pocket. The crew wears the CrewWatcher Man Overboard system, where their location can be displayed on the chartplotter. Most importantly, we have the Man Overboard procedure list in our Emergency binder at the helm.

See CruisersCollege.org for classes on Man Overboard situations

Mark Bunzel

SPEED LIMIT AND NO WAKE ZONES

Speed limit and boat wake control zones exist throughout our boating region. Almost none of these speed zones are depicted on our nautical charts. Often, but not always, the speed zones are marked by on-water buoys or signage along the shore. Signage for No Wake zones is often private to protect nearby docks or marinas. Speed limits and no wake rules are imposed by a variety of different jurisdictions, including federal government, state/provincial government, port authorities, county government, and local/city government. Some are suggested or requested speed and wake control areas.

Various controlling authorities police and enforce speed limit and no wake zones for the safety of people, boats, marinas, and shorelines. Speed limit and no wake zones are not normally depicted on charts and may or may not be marked with signs or buoys. There is a wide variety of different signage and buoys marking speed limit and no wake areas and some are more visible than others. That being said, boaters are expected to operate their vessels in compliance with these regulations.

In general:
- Speed should be reduced and wake minimized when within 100 yards/meters of shore.
- Reduce speed and minimize wake when near beaches, swimmers, kayaks, canoes, and divers.
- A "No Wake 5-knot speed zone" requires a speed that produces a minimized wake which may be less than the 5-knot maximum.
- Kill your transom wake by briefly halting outside a marina entrance.
- Big fast boats should be especially careful with their powerful large wakes.
- Speed limit laws in BC are often legislated in km/hour and have been converted and rounded.

NOTE: This is not a complete list but does include many of the commonly visited locations.

Puget Sound	Budd Inlet, Olympia	7-knot speed limit from Olympia Shoal to an East/West line at the North tip of Port of Olympia peninsula, where a 5-knot limit begins and extends south in both the east and west channels. No Wake speed limit in all City of Olympia waters.
Puget Sound	Amsterdam Bay, Anderson Island	5-mph No Wake speed is requested to protect shoreline.
Puget Sound	Foss Waterway, Tacoma	A No Wake speed limit exists throughout the Thea Foss Waterway.
Puget Sound	Commencement Bay, Waterways	5-mph speed limit in the Hylebos, Blair, St. Paul, Milwaukee, Sitcum, and Middle waterways off of Commencement Bay.
Puget Sound	Gig Harbor	5-mph No-Wake speed limit is enforced in Gig Harbor and 200 feet outside the entrance.
Puget Sound	Salmon Bay, Ship Canal, and Lake Union	7-knot No Wake speed limit is enforced from Hiram M. Chittenden Locks to Webster Point.
Puget Sound	Washington Narrows between Sinclair Inlet and Dyes Inlet	A Minimum Wake speed is requested to protect shoreline and boats moored at the marina.
Puget Sound	Liberty Bay, Poulsbo	5-knot speed limit on the north half of the bay; a marked buoy signals the south end of the speed limit zone.
Puget Sound	Keyport	An on-shore sign at the Keyport Naval Research facility marks a No Wake speed limit zone in front of the Naval facility docks.
Puget Sound	Eagle Harbor	5-knot speed limit begins at buoy
Puget Sound	Port Ludlow	5-mph No Wake speed limit is in effect throughout Port Ludlow and applies to all vessels, including dinghies.
Swinomish Channel	La Conner	A No-Wake Zone extends from Hole-In-The-Wall on the south end to the railroad swing bridge on the north end
Puget Sound & San Juan Islands	Orca Whales	A 7-knot No Wake speed limit is required and enforced within one-half nautical mile of Southern Resident Orca Whales within inland Washington waters.
San Juan Islands	Pole Pass	7-knot speed zone marked by white cylindrical buoys extends from just west of Pole Pass eastward almost to Bell Island and is enforced by the County Sheriff.
Southern Gulf Islands, Strait of Juan de Fuca, Fraser River Outlets	Killer (Orca) Whales	7-knot or slower speed is requested of all vessels when within 1 km (1/2 mile) of Killer (Orca) Whales.
Gulf Islands	Victoria Harbour	7-knot speed limit begins at Ogden Point and extends to Shoal Point, where a 5-knot speed limit begins and extends throughout the inner harbour.
Gulf Islands	Oak Bay, near Victoria	4-knot speed limit is in effect throughout the harbour area north of the breakwater and west of Mary Tod Island.

SPEED LIMIT AND NO WAKE ZONES

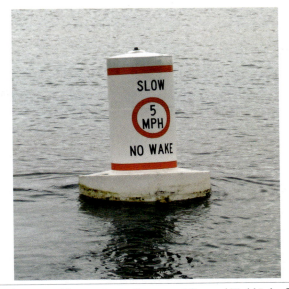

Gulf Islands	Brentwood Bay Todd Inlet	4-knot speed limit exists in Brentwood Bay and Todd Inlet from a line between the Brentwood Ferry Terminal to the northeast boundary of Gowlland Tod Provincial Park (approximately the unnamed point on the peninsula west of Daphine Islet.)
Gulf Islands	Pender Canal, between North Pender and South Pender Islands	5-knot speed limit exists from Ainslie Point to Mortimer Spit.
Gulf Islands	Ganges Harbour	5-knot speed limit zone throughout the harbour begins at a mid-channel buoy near Rock Point.
Gulf Islands	Tsehum Harbour, Sidney	A No Wake, speed limit of 4-knots is in force in Tsehum Harbour.
Gulf Islands	Birds Eye Cove/Maple Bay	A white buoy entering Birds Eye Cove from Maple Bay marks a 5-knot No Wake speed limit zone.
Gulf Islands	Nanaimo, Newcastle Channel	5-knot speed limit zone protects marinas along Newcastle Channel from Bate Pt. to Shaft Pt.
Gulf Islands	Nanaimo Harbour	5-knot speed limit is in effect within 150 meters of shore and when near or around anchored vessels, float planes, and beach areas.
Vancouver	False Creek	5-knot No Wake speed limit extends throughout False Creek Inlet and begins off Sunset Beach.
Vancouver	Vancouver Harbour	A voluntary 15-knot speed limit is requested in the waters around First Narrows, Lions Gate Bridge.
Vancouver	Coal Harbour	5-knot speed limit is enforced in Coal Harbour
Vancouver	Indian Arm, Deep Cove	5-knot speed limit is enforced in Deep Cove
Vancouver	Indian Arm, Bedwell Bay	5-knot speed limit is enforced in Bedwell Bay
Sunshine Coast	Princess Louisa Inlet	A no-wake speed limit is in effect throughout the inlet.
Desolation Sound	Pendrell Sound, East Redonda Island	3-knot speed limit is in effect throughout the north half of Pendrell Sound to protect seed oyster growing operations.
Desolation Sound	Gorge Harbour	A No Wake speed limit is in effect throughout the harbour.
Johnstone Strait	Cordero Channel, Cordero Lodge	A No Wake speed is requested when passing Cordero Lodge.
North Vancouver Island	Port Hardy	3-knot speed limit exists in the Inner Harbour
West Coast Vancouver Island	Bull Harbour	3-knot speed limit is requested inside the harbour
Northern B.C. Coast	Prince Rupert	5-knot speed zone is enforced within 600 yards of the harbour's south shore. There are no buoys marking the zone which begins at the Fairview Container Terminal and continues to Ritchie Point.
Northern B.C. Coast	Porpoise Harbour, Prince Rupert area	5-knot speed limit exists throughout the harbour
Northern B.C. Coast	Venn Passage, Prince Rupert area	Two 5-knot speed limit zones in Venn Passage: off the airport dock on Digby Island, and off the village of Metlakatla

2020 WAGGONER CRUISING GUIDE

AIS (Aquatic Invasive Species) Prevention Permit

Out-of-State Boaters Need A Washington State AIS Prevention Permit. Most out-of-state watercraft and floatplanes are now required to have an Aquatic Invasive Species (AIS) Prevention Permit when operating in Washington State waters. The $24 permit can be purchased online or at any WDFW license sales location throughout the state. Watercraft registered in the State of Washington automatically pay an annual fee as part of their registration and therefore do not need to separately purchase a permit.

Who Needs the AIS Prevention Permit? Operators of recreational vessels not registered in Washington, seaplane operators, and commercial transporters of watercraft are required to purchase and carry an AIS Prevention Permit. Permits can be purchased online or at any Fish and Wildlife license dealer. Online purchased permits are mailed and a temporary permit, good for 10 days, can be printed. Permits are valid for one year from date of activation.

The following are exempt from the required permit:

- Recreational vessels registered in Washington with a valid WA State registration sticker
- Small watercraft (Washington or out-of-state) that do not require state or country registration, such as canoes and kayaks
- Watercraft used solely as tenders to larger boats
- Vessels registered in Idaho or Oregon, when used in shared state waters
- U.S. and foreign documented commercial vessels
- Military, federal, tribal, state, and local government vessels used for government purposes

What's the Purpose of the Permits? AIS Prevention Permits were authorized in 2017. Fees from non-resident permits and resident vessel registrations help support the department's efforts to keep Washington's waters free of aquatic invasive species and manage infestations.

Invasive species such as zebra mussels and guagga mussels, European green crab and New Zealand mud snails (to name a few) are often spread by boats and trailers. Both marine saltwater and freshwater can harbor invasive species. WDFW's task of controlling invasive species in Washington waters is costly and permit and registration fees help fund the department's work.

What About Enforcement? This new permit has prompted a number of questions for boaters regarding enforcement of the permits and vessel inspections. WDFW's permit enforcement and inspection for invasive species is focused on boat trailers and boats transported overland.

- AIS Prevention Permits are for fundraising and do not automatically trigger vessel inspections
- Inspections of watercraft for aquatic invasive species are currently land-based, focused on trailered boats and boat trailers
- As of 2019, there were no on-water check/inspection stations for invasive species

Where to Get More Information. Aquatic Invasive Species is an important topic for all Northwest boaters. British Columbia, Washington, Oregon, and Idaho remain relatively free of invasive species. WDFW's efforts, along with those of similar agencies in neighboring states and provinces, are imperative to keep the region's waters free of invasive species. Increasing numbers and types of watercraft routinely on the move, make the containment job more difficult.

WDFW's website provides valuable information on this topic and a link to purchase the permit online. Please click through to learn more about their work and invasive species. Learn about some possible ways that both trailerable and non-trailerable vessels may unwittingly harbor and carry invasive species.

Aquatic Invasive Species Information https://wdfw.wa.gov/ais/ AIS Prevention Permit Information https://wdfw.wa.gov/licensing/ais_prevention/

[Leonard Landon]

VHF CHANNELS FOR PLEASURE CRAFT

WASHINGTON WATERS

05A VESSEL TRAFFIC SERVICE SEATTLE—Northern Puget Sound and Strait of Juan de Fuca. Vessels not required to participate are highly encouraged to maintain a listening watch. Contact with VTS is encouraged if essential to navigational safety.

06 INTERSHIP SAFETY. Only for ship-to-ship use for safety communications. For Search and Rescue (SAR) liaison with Coast Guard vessels and aircraft.

09 INTERSHIP AND SHIP-SHORE ALL VESSELS and CALLING & REPLY FOR PLEASURE VESSELS (optional, U.S. only). Working channel.

13 Vessel BRIDGE to Vessel BRIDGE, large vessels. Low power only. May also be used to contact locks and bridges BUT use sound signals in the Seattle area to avoid dangerous interference to collision avoidance communications between large vessels. Call on Channel 13 or by phone at 206/386-4251 for nighttime bridge openings (after 2300) in the Lake Washington Ship Canal, Seattle.

14 VESSEL TRAFFIC SERVICE SEATTLE—Southern Puget Sound. Vessels not required to participate are highly encouraged to maintain a listening watch. Contact with VTS is encouraged if essential to navigational safety.

16 INTERNATIONAL DISTRESS AND CALLING. Calling channel. Used only for distress and urgent traffic, for safety calls and contacting other stations. Listen first to make sure no distress traffic is in progress; do not transmit if a SEELONCE MAYDAY is declared. Keep all communications to a minimum. Do not repeat a call to the same station more than once every two minutes. After three attempts, wait 15 minutes before calling the same station. Pleasure vessels may also use Channel 09 for calling.

22A COAST GUARD LIAISON. A government channel used for Safety and Liason communications with the Coast Guard. Also known as Channel 22 US. The U.S. Coast Guard does not normally monitor 22A so you must first establish communications on Channel 16.

66A PORT OPERATIONS. Marinas in Puget Sound are being encouraged to use this common frequency for arranging moorage.

67 INTERSHIP ONLY FOR ALL VESSELS (U.S. only, Puget Sound.) Working channel.

68 INTERSHIP and SHIP-SHORE FOR PLEASURE VESSELS ONLY. Working channel.

69 INTERSHIP and SHIP-SHORE FOR PLEASURE VESSELS ONLY. Working channel.

70 DIGITAL SELECTIVE CALLING ONLY (No Voice) FOR DISTRESS AND CALLING.

72 INTERSHIP ONLY FOR ALL VESSELS (U.S. only, Puget Sound.) Working channel.

78A INTERSHIP and SHIP-SHORE FOR PLEASURE VESSELS ONLY (Not available in Canada). Working channel. Marinas in Puget Sound are being encouraged to use this as a secondary working channel.

BRITISH COLUMBIA WATERS

05A VESSEL TRAFFIC SERVICE SEATTLE—Strait of Juan de Fuca west of Victoria.

06 INTERSHIP SAFETY. Only for ship-to-ship use for safety communications.

09 INTERSHIP AND SHIP-SHORE. All vessels. Working channel.

11 VESSEL TRAFFIC SERVICE VICTORIA—Strait of Juan de Fuca east of Victoria; Haro Strait; Boundary Passage; Gulf Islands; Southern Strait of Georgia.

VESSEL TRAFFIC SERVICE PRINCE RUPERT—North of Cape Caution.

12 VESSEL TRAFFIC SERVICE VANCOUVER—Vancouver and Howe Sound.

16 INTERNATIONAL DISTRESS AND CALLING. Calling channel. Used only for distress and urgent traffic, for safety calls and contacting other stations. Listen first to make sure no distress traffic is in progress. Do not transmit if a SEELONCE MAYDAY is declared. Keep all communications to a minimum. Do not repeat a call to the same station more than once every two minutes. After three attempts, wait 15 minutes before calling the same station.

66A PORT OPERATIONS. Most marinas in southern B.C. will use this channel.

67 INTERSHIP AND SHIP-SHORE. All vessels. Working channel.

68 INTERSHIP AND SHIP-SHORE. Pleasure vessels. Working channel.

69 INTERSHIP AND SHIP-SHORE. Pleasure vessels. Working channel.

70 DIGITAL SELECTIVE CALLING ONLY (No Voice) FOR DISTRESS AND CALLING.

71 VESSEL TRAFFIC SERVICE COMOX—Northern Strait of Georgia to Cape Caution.

VESSEL TRAFFIC SERVICE—Prince Rupert, Dixon Entrance and Chatham Sound.

72 INTERSHIP. All vessels. Working channel.

73 INTERSHIP AND SHIP-SHORE. All vessels. Working channel.

74 VESSEL TRAFFIC SERVICE VICTORIA—Victoria-Fraser River.

VESSEL TRAFFIC SERVICE TOFINO—West of Vancouver Island.

83A COAST GUARD LIAISON. Primary Canadian Coast Guard Safety and Communications Channel. Also known as Channel 83 U.S. mode.

To contact the Canadian Coast Guard, use Channel 16 to call the station nearest you: Victoria, Vancouver, Comox, Prince Rupert or Tofino.

Even though you may use alternate communication means such as cellular phone, MONITOR VHF 16. The safety of yourself, your family and your friends is enhanced by a watch on 16 by all vessels.

RADIO EMERGENCY SIGNALS

MAYDAY	Vessel threatened by grave and imminent danger and requests immediate assistance.
PAN PAN	Urgent message concerning safety of vessel or person on board or in sight.
SECURITÉ	Message concerning safety of navigation or meteorological warning.
SEELONCE MAYDAY	Mayday in progress, do not transmit normal communications.
SEELONCE FEENE	Resume normal communications.

2020 WAGGONER CRUISING GUIDE

CONTACT PHONE NUMBERS & WEB ADDRESSES

U.S. COAST GUARD

U.S. Coast Guard Emergencies	**VHF CH 16 or call 911**
	(206) 217-6001 or (206) 220-7001
U.S. Coast Guard Emergency Juneau	**911 or (907)463-2000**
Cellular Phones Only	**911**
U.S. Coast Guard District Office: Seattle	(206) 220-7000
U.S. Coast Guard Smart phone App	

U.S. TOWING

Fremont Tugboat Co.	(206) 632-0151
TowBoatUS all locations 24-hour dispatch	(800) 888-4869
TowBoatUS Anacortes	(360) 675-7900
TowBoatUS Everett	(425) 344-3056
TowBoatUS San Juan	(360) 378-1111
(Friday Harbor & Roche Harbor)	
TowBoatUS Lake Washington	(206) 793-7375
TowBoatUS Oak Harbor	(360) 675-7900
TowBoatUS Olympia	(360) 790-9008
TowBoatUS Port Townsend	(360) 531-4837 or (360) 301-9764
TowBoatUS Port Hadlock	(360) 301-9764
TowBoatUS Seattle	(253) 312-2927
TowBoatUS Tacoma	(253) 312-2927
Marine Services Whidbey (Deception Pass)	(360) 675-7900

U.S. WEATHER INFORMATION NUMBERS

Seattle	(206) 526-6087
Dial-A-Buoy	(888) 701-8992
	(301) 713-9620

U.S. CUSTOMS CLEARANCE NUMBERS

For customs entry call:	(800) 562-5943
Anacortes	(360) 293-2331
Friday Harbor/Roche Harbor	(360) 378-2080
Point Roberts	(360) 945-5211 or (360) 945-2314
Port Angeles	(360) 457-4311
By Appointment Only:	
Bellingham	(360) 734-5463
Blaine	(360) 332-8511
Everett	(425) 259-0246
Port Townsend	(360) 385-3777
Seattle	(206) 553-0770
Tacoma/Olympia	(253) 593-6338
Ketchikan	(907) 225-2254

WA PARKS INFORMATION NUMBERS

WA State Parks Launch & Moorage Permit Program	(360) 902-8500
San Juan County Parks	(360) 378-8420
WA Department of Natural Resources	(360) 708-1692

CANADIAN COAST GUARD

Canadian Coast Guard Emergency Numbers	**VHF CH 16**
Cellphone	*16
Search and Rescue: Vancouver	VHF CH 16 or (800) 567-5111
Search and Rescue: Victoria	(250) 413-8933 or (800) 567-5111
Search and Rescue: Other areas	(800) 567-5111
Canadian Coast Guard District Office: Victoria	(250) 480-2600

B.C. TOWING

Vessel Assist Gulf Islands	(800) 413-8222
C-Tow	VHF CH. 07A or (888) 419-2869
Covers Victoria to the north end of Vancouver Island & the Tofino area	
Port McNeil	(250) 974-5305

CANADIAN WEATHER INFORMATION NUMBER

Vancouver	(604) 666-3655
Victoria	

CANADIAN BORDER SERVICES CLEARANCE NUMBER

All locations & CANPASS	
contact Canada Border Services Agency toll-free:	(888) 226-7277

CANADIAN PARKS INFORMATION NUMBERS

B. C. Parks General Information	(604) 582-5200
Gwaii Haanas National Park Reserve	(250) 559-8818
Gulf Islands National Park Reserve	(250) 654-4000 or (866) 944-1744

MARINE MAMMAL RESOURCES

San Juan County Marine Mammal Stranding Network is a collaborative program of the Whale Museum (Friday Harbor) and the National Marine Fisheries.
To Report a Stranding in San Juan County
Call 1-800-562-8832 or email hotline@whalemuseum.org
This hotline is a voicemail system that is checked frequently throughout the day. Leave your name and phone number.

NOAA Marine Mammal Disentanglement Network is a program for boaters to help entangled marine mammals in U.S. waters.
To report entangled whales call NOAA Fisheries hotline at (877) 767-9425.
NOAA 24/7 Hotline - To report injured or stranded whales, dolphins, porpoises, seals and sea lions, or to report incidents of marine mammal harassment:
Call NOAA's 24/7 hotline at (800) 853-1964.

BC Marine Mammal Response Network – handles marine mammal matters in B.C. waters; they ask that boaters report all injured, distressed and dead marine mammals and sea turtles.
Call their 24/7 hotline (800) 465-4336

FISHERIES & FISHERIES MANAGEMENT

Paralytic Shellfish Poisoning PSP shellfish closures can be expected without warning at any time during the season.

For PSP closures in Washington, phone (800) 562-5632. Washington State Dept. of Health Paralytic Shellfish Poisoning page: www.doh.wa.gov and search PSP. The website has a PSP fact sheet and links to PSP toxin closed areas of Puget Sound and San Juan Islands.

Washington State Dept. Fish and Wildlife information on fish and wildlife action plans: wdfw.wa.gov/conservation/cwcs/

Washington State Dept. Fish and Wildlife information fishing and shellfishing: wdfw.wa.gov/fishing/

U.S. Fish and Wildlife Service Fisheries and Habitat Conservation: www.fws.gov/fisheries/

For PSP closures in B.C., phone the Openings and Closures Toll Free Line: (866) 431-3474 or (604) 666-2828 in the Lower Mainland, or go to: www.pac.dfo-mpo.gc.ca/fm-gp/contamination/biotox/index-eng.htm

Fisheries Management Areas. Download map of Fisheries Management Areas to enable you to decipher closure areas at: www.pac.dfo-mpo.gc.ca

Rockfish Conservation Areas booklet contains chartlets of all conservation areas. Many people do not realize that RCA's prohibit ALL hook and line fishing, not just fishing for rockfish. To view or download a copy of the booklet, go to: www.pac.dfo-mpo.gc.ca

CONVERSION TABLES

TEMPERATURE (FORMULAS)

FAHRENHEIT TO CELSIUS
To convert temperature from Fahrenheit to Celsius:

(F° - 32) × .555 = C°

Example: Convert 40° F to C:
(40 - 32) = 8; 8 × .555 = 4;
thus 40° F = 4° C

CELSIUS TO FAHRENHEIT
To convert temperature from Celsius to Fahrenheit:

(C° × 1.8) + 32 = F°

Example: Convert 4° C to F:
(4 × 1.8) = 7.2; 7.2 + 32 = 39.2 (round to 40); thus 4° C = 40° F

QUICK REFERENCE

32° Fahrenheit = 0° Celsius
0° Fahrenheit = -17.8° Celsius

VOLUME

U.S. GALLONS TO LITERS
1 U.S gallon = 3.7854 liters

To convert U.S. gallons to liters, multiply U.S. gallons × 3.785.
Example: 40 U.S. gallons × 3.785 = 151 liters

To convert liters to U.S. gallons, divide by 3.785.
Example: 151 liters ÷ 3.785 = 39.89 U.S. gallons (round to 40)

IMPERIAL GALLONS TO LITERS
1 Imperial gallon = 4.546 liters

To convert Imperial gallons to liters, multiply Imperial gallons × 4.546.
Example: 40 Imperial gallons × 4.546 = 182 liters

To convert liters to Imperial gallons, divide by 4.546.
Example: 182 liters ÷ 4.546 = 40.035 (round to 40)

U.S. GALLONS TO IMPERIAL GALLONS
1 U.S. gallon = .833 Imperial gallons

To convert U.S. gallons to Imperial gallons, multiply U.S. gallons × .833.

Example: 40 U.S. gallons × .833 = 33.32 Imperial gallons

To convert Imperial gallons to U.S. gallons, multiply Imperial gallons × 1.20.

Example: 33 Imperial gallons × 1.20 = 39.6 U.S. gallons

LITERS AND QUARTS
1 liter = 1.0567 quarts, or 33.8 ounces
1 quart = .9467 liters, or 947 ml

SPEED

Convert knots to miles per hour: Knots × 1.15
Convert miles per hour to knots: MPH × .868

WEIGHT

1 kilogram (kg) = 2.2 pounds (lbs.)

1 pound = .4545 kilograms (454 grams)

1 U.S. gallon of fresh water weighs 8.333 lbs. or 3.787 kg

1 Imperial gallon of fresh water weighs 10 lbs. or 4.545 kg

1 liter of fresh water weighs 2.2 pounds or 1 kg

1 U. S. gallon of gasoline weighs 6.2 lbs. or 2.82 kg

1 Imperial gallon of gasoline weighs 7.44 lbs. or 3.38 kg

1 liter of gasoline weighs 1.64 lbs. or 0.744 kg

1 U.S. gallon of No. 2 diesel fuel weighs 6.7 pounds or 3.05 kg

1 Imperial gallon of No. 2 diesel fuel weighs 8.04 pounds or 3.66 kg

1 liter of No. 2 diesel fuel weighs 1.77 pounds or 0.8 kg

DISTANCE

1 inch = 2.54 centimeters

1 foot = .3048 meters

1 meter = 3.28 feet

1 fathom = 6 feet

1 fathom = 1.83 meters

1 cable = 120 fathoms

1 cable (British) = 0.1 nautical mile

1 statute mile = 5280 feet; 7.4 cables; 1.609 kilometers

1 nautical mile = 6076 feet; 8.5 cables; 1.852 kilometers

1 statute mile = 0.868 nautical mile

1 nautical mile = 1.15 statute mile

BAROMETRIC PRESSURE

2020 WAGGONER CRUISING GUIDE

South & Central Puget Sound

CHAPTER 2

SOUTH PUGET SOUND
Olympia • Case Inlet • Carr Inlet • Tacoma Narrows

CENTRAL PUGET SOUND
*Gig Harbor • Tacoma • Vashon Island • Seattle
Bremerton • Poulsbo • Bainbridge Island*

See Area Map Page 96 - Maps Not for Navigation

SOUTH AND CENTRAL PUGET SOUND

South Puget Sound begins at Olympia and ends at Tacoma Narrows. For scenic quality, relatively calm seas and solitude, South Puget Sound is an excellent region to explore. For some reason, Seattle boats that voyage hundreds of miles north often do not consider venturing just a few miles south. Yet South Sound is dotted with marine parks and served by enough marinas to meet most needs. We like South Sound and recommend it.

The waters are generally flatter in South Sound, good for cruising year-round. The channels are relatively narrow and have enough bends to minimize fetch and prevent most wind from creating large seas. Tide-rips, of course, still form where channels meet, and skippers must be aware of them.

Olympia is South Sound's only significant city. Getting away from civilization is easy, yet it is always close by. First-time visitors usually are surprised at the beauty of this area. Mt. Rainier, an inactive volcano 14,410 feet high, dominates many vistas. The islands and peninsulas tend to be either tree-covered or pastoral, with pockets of homes or commercial enterprise. Most marine parks have docks, buoys, and anchoring. The marinas are friendly and well-kept.

No Discharge Zone: All of the inside waters of Washington State from Puget Sound to the Canadian Border are a No Discharge Zone (NDZ). It is illegal to discharge any (treated and untreated) black water sewage. Gray water from showers and sinks is not covered by this restriction.

BUDD, ELD, TOTTEN INLETS

Budd Inlet. The mile-wide entrance to Budd Inlet is between Dofflemyer Point and Cooper Point. Approaching from the north, simply round Dofflemyer Point, where a white-painted light blinks every 4 seconds, and head for the Capitol dome.

Anchorage in Budd Inlet is along both shores in 10 to 20 feet, mud bottom, with Butler Cove and Tykle Cove preferred.

Launch Ramps: Swantown Marina has a 2-lane launch ramp. Boston Harbor also has a launch ramp and parking for tow vehicles and trailers.

The City of Olympia's Priest Point Park, on the east side of Budd Inlet, has one of the finest sand beaches in southern Puget Sound.

Olympia. Olympia is one of the most charming stops in Puget Sound, the more so because so few boats from central and northern Puget Sound ever visit. Olympia is an undiscovered treat for many northern boaters.

Moorage in Olympia is at five marinas: NorthPoint Landing, Port Plaza Dock, Percival Landing, West Bay Marina, and Swantown Marina. Fuel is available at Swantown Marina, Zittel's Marina, and Boston Harbor.

To get to the marinas, continue past Olympia Shoal, marked by lighted beacons on the shoal's east and west sides. From Olympia Shoal, pick up the 28-foot-deep dredged and buoyed channel leading to the harbor. A spoils bank from channel dredging is east of the channel. The spoils area is quite shoal and parts of it dry. Stay in the channel.

The channel branches at a piling intersection marker east of the privately-owned West Bay Marina. The dayboard on the marker is green on top, red on the bottom. The green top-color marks the main channel. If you leave the marker to port you'll proceed down the western leg past the Port of Olympia large ship docks, to Percival Landing, and to the Olympia Yacht Club at the head of the inlet. If you leave the marker to starboard, you'll take the eastern leg to the Port of Olympia's Swantown Marina and Boatworks. On both sides of each channel the water shoals rapidly to drying flats. The Olympia harbor has a no-wake rule.

West Bay Marina has a few guest slips and a restaurant, but no fuel dock. The Olympia Yacht Club has guest moorage for members of reciprocal clubs only. In the western channel, Percival Landing and the Port Plaza dock have guest moorage. In the eastern channel, the Port of Olympia's Swantown Marina has guest moorage.

A beautifully landscaped walkway surrounds the Percival Landing area. It's a popular place for strolling, with an excellent view of harbor activities. Good restaurants, a supermarket, a fish market, several micro-breweries, and a wine shop

Port of Olympia

2020 WAGGONER CRUISING GUIDE 95

SOUTH AND CENTRAL PUGET SOUND *Reference Only – Not for Navigation*

South Puget Sound

are nearby. Some boaters find the number of people walking just above their boats disconcerting, although we have found nights to be quiet. Swantown Marina, in East Bay, does not have the crowds walking by the boats but it's not as convenient for shopping and restaurant access.

Olympia is the state capital, and we urge a tour of the Capitol Campus and its buildings. Besides housing the largest chandelier ever made by Louis Comfort Tiffany, the Capitol dome, at 287 feet tall, is one of the tallest masonry domes in North America. The grounds are beautiful and the buildings are magnificent. Informative tours are conducted on the hour, 10:00 a.m. to 3:00 p.m. on weekdays, 11:00 a.m. to 3:00 p.m. on weekends. No charge for these tours.

Downtown Olympia has its own charm. Parts of it got stuck in the '50s. If you've seen the film "Pleasantville," you'll recognize the storefronts. The State Theater's tall art deco sign is not a bit out of place in Olympia's downtown. The Eastside Club Tavern was the inspiration for Moe's Tavern on "The Simpsons" TV show. Some of the restaurants have employees who have been there 20 to 40 years, and they're open every day of the year so regular customers have somewhere to go, even at Christmas.

About 20 antiques stores are located in the downtown area and near Percival Landing. Art galleries are springing up. If you need a jolt of caffeine, coffee roaster Batdorf & Bronson is just east of the farmers market. They have a tasting room, just like a winery, only with coffee. Samples are free, but we always buy at least a couple bags of coffee. We enjoy it.

Olympia Farmers Market. The Olympia Farmers market is located between Percival Landing and the Port of Olympia's Swantown Marina. The market is open Thursdays through Sundays from April through October. Hours are 10:00 a.m. to 3:00 p.m. The market is open weekends in November and December, and and Saturdays only January through March. Everything sold is grown or made locally, except for a few fruits that come from Yakima. Musicians perform on a covered stage, and take-out food is available from several outlets. No pets allowed. The market's roof is topped by a weathervane in the shape of a traditional flying pig.

Olympia hosts several festivals each year. For additional information visit: www.downtownolympia.com or www.visitolympia.com.

See Area Map Page 96 - Maps Not for Navigation

SOUTH AND CENTRAL PUGET SOUND

Hiking trails around Capital Lake are easily accessible from Percival Landing in Olympia.

Fuel. Olympia has a fuel dock at Swantown Marina with marine gas and diesel.

With all the services and shopping opportunities of a major city, combined with beauty and the friendliness of a small town, Olympia makes a truly pleasant destination for boaters exploring south Puget Sound.

 THINGS TO DO

1. Washington State Capitol. Take a short walk from the marinas for a free 60-minute tour of the architecturally magnificent legislative building.

2. Hands On Children's Museum. This children's museum has exhibits and an outdoor discovery center. A must-see for kids. Adjacent to Swantown Marina, 414 Jefferson St. NE, hocm.org, (360) 956-0818.

3. Olympia Farmers Market. One of the largest farmers markets in all of Puget Sound. It is open Thursday through Sunday, April to October, and limited days during the off-season. Located between Swantown Marina and Percival Landing.

4. Percival Landing Park. See classic boats, sculptures, and views of the Capitol on this landscaped walkway around the harbor.

5. Antique and specialty shops. More than 20 in the downtown area, a short walk from the waterfront.

6. Batdorf & Bronson Coffee Roasters. Taste the difference and learn the finer points of coffee.

① **Percival Landing.** 217 Thurston Ave., Olympia, WA 98501; (360) 753-8380; www.olympiawa.gov. Percival Landing has nice showers and restrooms. The park, with moorage, is adjacent to downtown Olympia near shopping, restaurants, and other facilities. Four hours day moorage, no charge. Guest moorage is along E float on the east side of the waterway. Water, 30 & 50 amp power are available on E float. Pumpout is on F float. D float, below the Olympia Oyster House restaurant on the west side, has limited space, no power or water. Register at The Olympia Center, east of E float. Group reservations available from October 1 to April 30.

The floats have access to toilets, showers, and portapotty dump. After-hours or weekends, self-register at the kiosk next to the parking lot. Cash or checks only at the kiosk, no credit cards. First-come, first-served. Maximum 7 days in a 30-day period. No manager is on site, so you may have to search for everything, including the registration kiosk. Good grocery shopping at Bayview Thriftway, west of the yacht club. The Harbor House meeting center was built as part of the Percival Landing renovation and is available for group gatherings up to 30 people. Call (360) 753-8380. There are also two outdoor pavilions.

Limited guest moorage during the Wooden Boat Show in May, and Harbor Days in early September, which includes tugboat races.

① **Port Plaza Dock.** 701 Columbia St. NW, Olympia, WA 98501; (360) 528-8049; marina@portolympia.com; www.swantownmarina.com. Monitors VHF 65A. This is a modern, all-concrete set of floats on the east side of the waterway leading to Percival Landing and Olympia Yacht Club. The docks are intended for day use but are available for overnight. Location is convenient to dining and shopping, 4 hours no charge. No water, no power. Self-register at the kiosk at the head of the ramp. Reservations accepted for a $5 non-refundable fee.

The Port Plaza itself is a work of art. The sculpted concrete work suggests waves. It's completely flat but very effective. Bronze shells, golf balls, drafting tools—all sorts of things are set into the cement. The more you look, the more you see.

704 Columbia St. NW
(360) 357-9700

① **NorthPoint Landing.** 1675 Marine Drive NW, Olympia, WA 98501; (360) 528-8000; www.portolympia.com. Small dock operated by the Port of Olympia, at the north end of the waterway leading to Percival Landing and Olympia Yacht Club. Day use only. Max 4 hour stay. No power or water. 4 feet of depth at zero tide. Anthony's Hearthfire Grill is adjacent to the dock.

1675 Marine Drive NE
(360) 705-3473

② **West Bay Marina.** 2100 Westbay Drive NW, Olympia, WA 98502; (360) 943-2022; westbaymarina@hotmail.com; www.westbay-marina.com. On the west side of Budd Inlet. Guest moorage to 40 feet; call ahead for availability. Facilities include 30 amp power, restrooms, showers, coin-operated laundry, pumpout. Use caution, docks are in disrepair and may be unsafe. Tugboat Annie's restaurant and pub, a longtime favorite, is on site.

③ **Swantown Marina.** 1022 Marine Drive NE, Olympia, WA 98501; (360) 528-8049; marina@portolympia.com; www.swantown marina.com. Certified Clean Marina. Monitors VHF 65A. This is the

The docks at Percival Landing Park

SOUTH AND CENTRAL PUGET SOUND *See Area Map Page 96 - Maps Not for Navigation*

Port of Olympia small boat moorage. Open all year, 70+ guest moorage slips for vessels to 100 feet. Fuel dock located on A Dock with diesel and ethanol-free gasoline. Nice restrooms, showers and laundry. Pumpout, portapotty dump, 30 & 50 amp power, garbage drop, waste oil dump, security patrols, well-tended grounds, free Wi-Fi, ice. Reservations accepted for $5. Dry boat storage, 2-lane launch ramp. Block and crushed ice at the Harbor Office. Groceries are a 15-minute walk away. The Olympia Farmers Market and downtown attractions are within walking distance.

The channel leading from the intersection beacon, with its green and red dayboard, can be confusing. If the weather is clear, you'll see a long, low 2-story condominium block on the eastern shore. Aim for those condominiums.

Guest moorage is on A-dock a short distance inside the entry next to the launch ramp. Register and pay moorage at the kiosk at the head of the ramp, or in the office at the head of I-Dock. Swantown Marina is parklike: clean, quiet, spacious and well-maintained.

Swantown Boatworks, (360) 528-8059, with 82-ton Travelift, is at the south end of the marina. Pettit Marine chandlery is located in the same building, offering marine repair services. Mechanics and marine personnel are located in adjacent offices.

Burfoot County Park. 6927 Boston Harbor Rd. NE, Olympia, WA 98506. Located a half-mile south of Dofflemyer Point. This is a 60-acre county park, open all year, day use only. Restrooms, picnic tables, trails, and play area. Anchoring or beaching only.

④ **Boston Harbor.** Boston Harbor is a halfmoon-shaped bay between Dofflemyer Point and Dover Point. Anchorage is limited but possible. Much of the bay is taken up by the Boston Harbor Marina.

④ **Boston Harbor Marina.** 312 - 73rd Ave. NE, Olympia, WA 98506; (360) 357-5670; www.bostonharbormarina.com. Phone ahead for slip assignment. Open all year with very limited guest moorage. Gas and diesel at the fuel dock. Best to call ahead regarding diesel. Guest moorage is located in front of the store on the west side of the 600 Dock and in unoccupied slips. Caution: the south end of the 600 Dock dries at low tide. The north docks, damaged by past storms, were replaced in 2019. 20 amp power, picnic area, beach access, free Wi-Fi, restrooms, but no showers. The launch ramp dries on minus tide. The store has groceries, ice, beer on tap, wine, fresh seafood, some marine supplies, gifts, clothing, and books. Sandwiches, soups, and soft-serve ice cream at the store. Rental kayaks and SUPs available.

This is a real neighborhood place, a throwback to when small marinas up and down Puget Sound served surrounding communities. The quaint old store is built on pilings, and there's not a level floor to be found. The store and docks are gathering places for locals, and a cheery bunch they are. On Fridays, from Memorial Day to Labor Day, live music with beer tasting is held on the pier. Breakfast is served on the pier Saturday and Sunday mornings from 10:00 a.m. to noon, summer season only. If you relax and just let it happen, you'll think Boston Harbor is a delight.

No-wake zone: Several white warning buoys off the mouth of Boston Harbor mark a no-wake zone. Please slow down. Wakes from passing craft play havoc with the moored boats.

Boston Harbor Marina

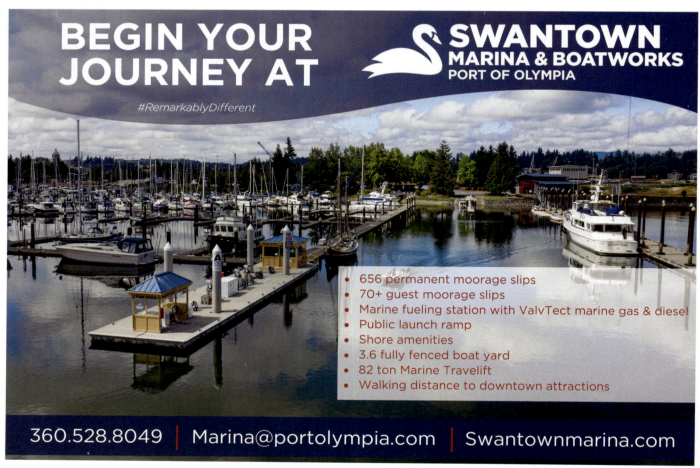

See Area Map Page 96 - Maps Not for Navigation

SOUTH AND CENTRAL PUGET SOUND

PEALE AND PICKERING PASSAGES AND CASE INLET

The store, gift shop, and fuel dock at Fair Harbor Marina re-opened with new owners in 2019.

Pickering Passage extends northward from Totten Inlet past the west sides of Squaxin Island and Harstine Island. A fixed bridge connects Harstine Island to the mainland with a mean high-water vertical clearance of 31 feet. A ferry service once crossed Pickering Passage between 1922 and 1969. The passage was named by Charles Wilkes during his 1838-1842 expedition in honor of the crew's Naturalist, Charles Pickering. The small marina located between Jarrell Cove and Dougall Point is private Indian Cove Marina.

Peale Passage runs along the east side of Squaxin Island. Shallow but passable depths. Squaxin Island is private. Protected anchorage can be found in the nooks off the eastern shore.

Jarrell Cove. Jarrell Cove is off Pickering Passage near the northwest corner of Harstine Island. Jarrell's Cove Marina and 43-acre Jarrell Cove State Marine Park occupy this pleasant, sheltered cove.

Eld Inlet. Eld Inlet is immediately west of Budd Inlet, and extends about 5 miles south from Cooper Point before it becomes aptly-named Mud Bay. Hold to a mid-channel course past Cooper Point, which has an extensive drying shoal northward from the point.

Eld Inlet has no marinas, but anchorage is good, mud bottom along both shores. Directly across the inlet is the waterfront activities center for The Evergreen State College. The center has a float and buildings to store canoes and other small craft used by students.

Frye Cove County Park. 4000 NW 61st Ave., Olympia, WA 98502. Just north of Flapjack Point in Eld Inlet. Open all year, day use only. Toilets, no other services. Anchoring or beaching only. Picnic shelters, barbecues, hiking trails.

⑤ **Hope Island Marine State Park.** (360) 426-9226. Junction of Totten Inlet and Pickering Passage. Boat access only. Trails crisscross the island leading through forest, meadows, and old orchards. Interpretive signs explain the island's history and ecology. Visitors rave about this park. The park has 3 mooring buoys on the west shore, 2 mooring buoys off the south shore and decent anchorage in 30 feet or less on the east side. Currents can run strong on either side of Hope Island; be sure your anchor is set well. Stay west and south of the red nun buoy on the southeast corner of Hope Island, which marks a nasty, charted shoal. Campsites, pit toilets, no fires, no pets. Pack out all garbage.

Totten Inlet. Enter Totten Inlet past Steamboat Island, connected to the the mainland by a causeway from Carlyon Beach. Homes and a private marina are on the island and mainland beach. The beach is marked by a quick flashing light. All of Totten Inlet is less than 60 feet deep. The inlet shoals to drying mud flats toward its south end, called Oyster Bay.

The entrance to **Skookum Inlet** is on the west side of Totten Inlet, about 3 miles southwest of Steamboat Island. Skookum Inlet is called "Little Skookum" by locals, to differentiate it from nearby Hammersley Inlet, which they call "Big Skookum." Little Skookum is a pleasant exploration, but not navigable beyond Wildcat Harbor except by dinghy. Little Skookum is one of south Puget Sound's major oyster growing areas.

HAMMERSLEY INLET & SHELTON

Hammersley Inlet extends westward about 6 miles to Oakland Bay and the city of Shelton. Note the shoal area that blocks the entire south side of the entrance to Hammersley Inlet. Enter Hammersley Inlet on the north shore past Point Hungerford, marked by a beacon with a flashing red light. As Chart 18457 shows, depths range from 10 to 30 feet. Currents to 4 knots flood in and ebb out. The strongest currents occur around Cape Horn, a sharp, constricted bend just inside the entrance. Be mindful of tugs with tows. This scenic passage is lovely and is worth the side trip. Follow the chart and keep an eye on the depthfinder. Moorage is at the Port of Shelton's Oakland Bay Marina, about a mile from Shelton.

Shelton. Shelton is the site of a major lumber mill, with rafted logs in storage in front of the town. Oakland Bay grows shallow north of Shelton, but is navigable at other than extreme low tide, and could offer anchorage on a mud bottom.

⑥ **Oakland Bay Marina** (Port of Shelton). 21 W. Sanderson Way, Shelton, WA 98584; (360) 426-6435; www.portofshelton.com. This marina is managed by the Shelton Yacht Club. Open all year, 120 feet of guest moorage, 30 amp power and pumpout. No fuel. The visitor dock is between the boat houses. Least depth 10 feet. Home to the friendly Shelton Yacht Club. Reciprocal moorage on a space available basis. Groceries, restaurants, and services are in town, about a mile away. The Port continues making improvements to the pier and uplands.

LOCAL KNOWLEDGE

SHALLOW AREA: A shallow spit at Jarrell Cove State Park extends from the point that protects the second park dock, the dock deeper in the cove. Boats sometimes cut the point too closely on low tides and go aground.

⑦ **Jarrell's Cove Marina.** 220 E. Wilson Rd., Shelton, WA 98584; (360) 426-8823. Open 7 days a week Memorial Day to Labor Day. The fuel dock has diesel and gasoline. In the winter, the store is closed and fuel is by appointment. Facilities include 3 RV sites, 30 amp power, restrooms, showers, laundry, pumpout, limited guest moorage. Get a slip assignment from the fuel dock before landing, even for a short stay. The store has groceries, beer, ice, some marine hardware, books, propane. The piña colada shaved ice sno-cones are popular with adults who might add a little something when they get back to the boat. Lots of other flavors available, too. Gary and Lorna Hink are the owners.

⑦ **Jarrell Cove Marine State Park.** 391 E. Wingert Road, Shelton, WA 98584; (360) 426-9226. Northwest end of Harstine Island. Open all year. This is a large, attractive park, with 650 feet of dock space on two docks, 14 mooring buoys (boats 45 feet and under). 30 amp power. Clean and well-maintained restrooms and showers, picnic shelters, RV sites and standard campsites. Except for the single buoy between the inner dock and shore, mooring buoys have minimum 10 feet of water at all tides. The inner end of the outer dock can rest on mud bottom on minus tides. The inner dock has 6 feet of water on zero tide. The outer end has sufficient depths for

SOUTH AND CENTRAL PUGET SOUND

See Area Map Page 96 - Maps Not for Navigation

most drafts on all tides. Fishing, clamming, hiking, and bird watching. This park is a wonderful off-season destination.

McLane Cove. Across Pickering Passage from Jarrell Cove. Protected, quiet, lined with forest. Anchorage in 10 to 20 feet.

⑧ **Stretch Island** has good anchorage in the bay south of the bridge to the mainland. The bridge has a mean high water clearance of 14 feet. The channel under the bridge dries at low tide.

⑧ **Stretch Point Marine State Park.** (360) 426-9226. On Stretch Island. Open all year, accessible only by boat. No power, no water, no restrooms or showers; no garbage drop, pack it in – pack it out. 5 overnight mooring buoys for boats 45 feet and under. Buoys are close to shore because of a steep dropoff. Swimming and diving, oysters and mussels, and a smooth sand beach. The rustic shelters behind the beach are private property and not part of the park.

Reach Island. At the southern end of Reach Island is Fair Harbor, the location of Fair Harbor Marina. The bay has limited anchorage. The channel north of the marina, under a bridge with a mean high water clearance of 16 feet, dries on a minus tide.

⑨ **Fair Harbor Marina.** 5050 E. Grapeview Loop Rd., P.O. Box 160, Grapeview, WA 98546; (360) 426-4028; airharbormarina19@gmail.com; www.fairharbormarina.com. Open during the summer months with side-tie guest moorage on an 88-foot dock; call ahead for space. Year-round permanent moorage. Concrete launch ramp, water, 20 & 30 amp power, garbage, Wi-Fi, restrooms and showers. Picnic areas. Owners Susan and Vern Nelson retired and the marina was purchased by Kelly and Cindy Granger in early 2019. The fuel dock and gift store have been reopened. The store offers sundries, ice cream, and a nice selection of artisan gifts. A charming pavilion at the head of the dock is available for weddings and special events. Three vacation cabins are planned for the near future.

Jarrell Cove

⑩ **Allyn Waterfront Park Marina (Port of Allyn).** P.O. Box 1, Allyn, WA 98524; (360) 275-2430; portofallyn@aol.com; www.portofallyn.com. Open all year, launch ramp, 250 feet of moorage for boats to 45 feet on a "T" shaped float at the end of a public pier. Restrooms on site; playground and picnic area nearby. The lovely gazebo is available to rent for special events. Potable water and power at the docks. The dock is exposed to winds. No fuel, but you can bring jerry cans to the gas station in town. Allyn is surrounded by shoal water, but can be approached by favoring the east side of the channel until opposite the wharf, then turning in. Depth at the mooring float is 5.25 feet at zero tide. Office hours are Monday through Friday, 11:00 a.m. to 4:30 p.m. Pay moorage at the office, or at the pay station. A waterfront park, 100-year-old church, grocery and liquor store, post office, restaurants, wine tasting room, kayak rentals, and the George Kenny School of Chainsaw Carving are a short walk ashore.

If you're experiencing a craving for a manly, heart-stopping burger and shake, visit Big Bubba's Burgers, an Allyn landmark, across the road from Waterfront Park. Golfing available at nearby Lakeland Village Golf Course.

Rocky Bay. The best anchorage is behind a small sandspit extending from Windy Bluff. Enter with caution and round the little rocky islet off the end of the spit before circling in to anchor.

Vaughn Bay. Vaughn Bay can be entered at half tide or higher. Take a mid-channel course past the end of the spit, then turn to parallel the spit until safe anchoring depths are found

Jarrell's Cove Marina has great snow cones. It's a popular stop.

See Area Map Page 96 - Maps Not for Navigation

SOUTH AND CENTRAL PUGET SOUND

Penrose Point State Park dock offers moorage for shallow draft vessels.

near the head of the bay, or east of the spit. Jet skis and water skiers sometimes roar around during the day, but they quit at sundown and leave the bay peaceful at night. A launch ramp is on the north shore of the bay.

Herron Island. Privately owned.

⑪ **McMicken Island Marine State Park.** (360) 426-9226. On Case Inlet, off the east side of Harstine Island. Open all year, day use only, no overnight camping. Toilets, and 5 overnight mooring buoys for boats 45 feet and under. Mooring buoys, are on the north and south sides of 11½-acre McMicken Island. The buoys on the north side are a little close to shore on minus tides. Self register and pay mooring buoy fee on shore. Anchorage is on either side of the island, good holding bottom.

A trail on McMicken Island leads to a nice view of the beach and surrounding waters. A sign says to watch for poison oak. An artificial reef is north of the island. Fishing, good clamming and oyster gathering, swimming. McMicken Island is accessible only by boat except on low tides, when it and Harstine Island are connected by a drying spit. The spit comes up quickly, and you could find yourself aground if you try to pass between the two islands. The park has no garbage drop and a "Pack it in–Pack it out" policy.

Harstine Island State Park. This park is across the bay from McMicken Island. Open all year, day use only. No power, water, or toilets. At low tide you can cross to McMicken Island State Park. Anchoring only. Clamming, beachcombing.

⑫ **Joemma Beach State Park.** (360) 902-8844 or (253) 884-1944 Formerly Robert F. Kennedy Recreational Area, southeast Case Inlet, just north of Whiteman Cove. Cascadia Marine Trail campsite, 500 feet of dock space in place from mid-May through mid-October, 4 mooring buoys (boats 45 feet and under), boat launch, vault toilets. No power, no showers. The docks are good. Camping and picnic sites (including a covered shelter) on shore. This 122-acre marine camping park is named after Joe and Emma Smith, who lived on the premises from 1917 to 1932. Red Rock crabbing has occasionally been reported as excellent, right at the dock. The docks are exposed to southeast storms.

DRAYTON PASSAGE, PITT PASSAGE, BALCH PASSAGE

Taylor Bay. Taylor Bay, on Anderson Island, offers limited anchorage near the entrance, but is exposed to southerlies.

Oro Bay has a shallow, well-marked entrance with good anchorage inside. Oro Bay has a tranquil, rural feeling about it. Entering, the first dock you come to is a Tacoma Yacht Club outstation. Burwell's Landing is a Bremerton Yacht Club outstation. The Oro Bay Marina is home to Oro Bay Yacht Club, with some reciprocal moorage.

Two major parks, managed by the Anderson Island Park District, are the highlights of Oro Bay. Jacobs Point Park, the newer of the two, occupies most of the peninsula between inner and outer Oro Bay. Historically a pioneer farm, Jacobs Point Park provides 82 acres of trails, woodlands and beaches. Access is via a wooden staircase located north of the two red buoys. Stay on the trails, poison oak abounds. Andy's Park at the northeast corner of the bay provides 180 acres of wetlands, tidal estuary, and forest with a 2-mile nature trail loop. Access to Andy's Park is from Eckenstam Johnson Road, or through Jacobs Point Park.

Amsterdam Bay indents Anderson Island and is very shallow. Safe anchoring depths are right in the middle, when that spot is not already occupied by local residents' boats. The shores are rural and picturesque. If low tide isn't too low, it's a good place to spend the night. Observe a 5 mph or lower no-wake speed to prevent damage along the shoreline.

⑬ **Eagle Island Marine State Park.** (360) 426-9226. Ten-acre island on Balch Passage, off north side of Anderson Island. Open all year, day use only, 1 overnight mooring buoy on the east side, 2 overnight mooring buoys on the west side. Mooring buoys for boats 45 feet and under, self-register and pay mooring buoy fee on shore. No toilets, power, or water. Boat access only. Avoid the reef, marked by a buoy, off the west side of the island. Fishing and clamming. Watch for poison oak. No fires, no garbage drop and a "Pack it in–Pack it out" policy, no camping.

Eagle Island is a lovely spot. Except for the current which can roar through, this is an excellent South Sound layover location. Lots of seals, a fine view of Mt. Rainier, and good anchoring on the east side. The island is covered with dense forest, but well-maintained trails lead through the trees. Correspondents James and Jennifer Hamilton call Eagle Island "a gem." Don't be oversold, but do expect a good place to spend some time.

Filucy Bay. Filucy Bay is a popular destination and a fine anchorage. Anchor inside the spit to the south of the entrance, or in the north section, farther in. The north section is wooded, quiet, and protected with good holding over a mud bottom. The view of Mt. Rainier from the entrance of Filucy Bay is stunning. Longbranch Improvement Club Marina welcomes visiting boaters. Homeowners around the bay shoot off impressive fireworks on the 4th of July, which can be seen from the Club Marina docks.

⑭ **Longbranch Improvement Club Marina.** 5213 Key Penninsula Hwy. S., Longbranch, WA 98351; (253) 307-1873 cell; dockmaster@licweb.org; www.licweb.org. Longbranch is a good South Sound stopover, and especially popular as a destination for boating club cruises. Open all year, but hours vary in winter. The marina has 760 feet of side-tie dock space for guest moorage; 30 amp ELCI protected power, water, ice, Wi-Fi, and garbage drop. Toilets, no showers. No charge for 4-hour day moorge. Advance notification for groups is requested. Group cruises stack the boats in tightly, and raft several deep. Check their website for the schedule of group cruises. The guest moorage bull rails are painted yellow. The docks have a large covered area with roll-down canvas sides, lights, tables, chairs, heaters, barbecues, book exchange. This marina has a warm, friendly atmosphere.

If you've anchored out, the dinghy dock is on the west side of the main dock, next to the ramp. Mechanic and divers are on call.

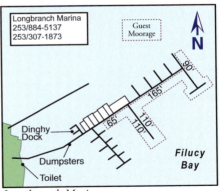
Longbranch Marina

2020 WAGGONER CRUISING GUIDE

SOUTH AND CENTRAL PUGET SOUND

See Area Map Page 96 - Maps Not for Navigation

Dances are held Memorial Day, July 4th, and Labor Day at the historic Longbranch Improvement Club Hall, located about a half-mile away. The dances are popular and usually sell out.

Pitt Passage is a winding, shallow passage between McNeil Island and the mainland. Because the passage is shoal, many skippers avoid it. Safe transit, however, can be made by following the navigation aids between tiny Pitt Island and McNeil Island. The waters west of Pitt Island are shoal.

Red, Right, Returning assumes you are returning from the north. This means that from the north, run an S-shaped course to leave the green can Wyckoff Shoal Buoys 1 and 3 to port, then turn east across the north side of Pitt Island to leave the red Daybeacon 4 to starboard. Continue between Pitt Island and McNeil Island, to leave the red nun Buoy 6 to starboard. Study the chart carefully before making your first run through Pitt Passage. Note how Wyckoff Shoal extends westward from McNeill Island almost across the mouth of the passage.

McNeil Island was a federal prison, and later a state prison, which closed in 2011. Field Correspondent, Mary Campbell, shares that local lore has it that during McNeil's time as a prison, escapees who made it to the other side of Pitt Passage found a warm bed and sandwiches at the home of a local grandma, who sent them on their way after they were rested and fed.

CARR INLET

Mayo Cove. Mayo Cove is pretty. The bay is shallow, however, and drying shoals are on either side. For exploring, take the dinghy part way up the inlet leading to Bay Lake.

Lakebay Marina & Resort. 15 Lorenz Road, Lakebay, WA 98349; (253) 884-3350. Located across Mayo Cove from Penrose Point Marine State Park. Beware that waters are shallow approaching the marina and park docks. Charts may not accurately depict water depths. A large sunken fish boat is reported to lie between the marina and the shoreline.

Over the last few years, the marina has fallen into an advanced stage of disrepair. Labor & Industries placed a non-occupancy notice in June 2019 due to needed electrical upgrades. The non-occupancy hold was lifted in July, allowing the marina to re-open. Water is available at the docks, no power. The fuel dock was not functional in 2019.

The historic wharf, once used as a Mosquito Fleet landing, has been placed on the Historic Registry. At press time, it was not clear what the future holds for Lakebay Marina, or when improvements might take place.

⑮ **Penrose Point Marine State Park.** (253) 884-2514. In Mayo Cove, west shore of Carr Inlet. Open for mooring and camping year-round. The 158-foot dock has 270 feet of side-tie space. The inner side of the dock grounds on lower tides. 8 mooring buoys for boats 45 feet and under – 3 buoys on the west side of Penrose Point in Mayo Cove, 5 buoys located on the east side of the Point. Self register and pay mooring fee on shore. Facilities include Cascadia Marine Trail campsite, picnic sites, restrooms, seasonal showers, pumpout, portapotty dump. No power. Standard campsites, 2.5 miles of hiking and biking trails, clamming, oyster picking, swimming, fishing. At low tide enter the cove with care, giving the spit a wide berth; stay west of the line of mooring buoys in Mayo Cove.

Von Geldern Cove. Von Geldern Cove is a shallow bay exposed to northerly winds. Anchorage is possible near the entrance. Most of the shoreline is residential. The town of Home, with a launch ramp, has some supplies. Take the dinghy under the bridge at the head of the bay and explore the creek until it's too shallow.

The town has an interesting past. Home was founded in the late 1800's by three men and their families, who wanted to establish a community based on an anarchist philosophy. Land was provided to those who became members of the community's Association and agreed to the anarchist ideals. The community later divided into factions and eventually dissolved in 1919.

Glen Cove is protected by a spit, but is very shallow and not recommended for overnight anchorage.

Rosedale. Rosedale is a small community tucked in behind Raft Island. Good anchorage. Enter the bay to the north of Raft Island, since a causeway connects the island to the mainland across the very shoal south side. The small and quaint Island View Market, with groceries and liquor, has a dinghy dock.

Cutts Island Marine State Park. (253) 265-3606. Open all year, day use only, 8 overnight mooring buoys for boats 45 feet and under. Correspondent Randy Wickers reported in 2019 that he tied his 42-foot Nordic Tug to one of the new-style buoys and dragged one-quarter mile. Self-register and pay mooring fee on shore. The mooring fee can also be paid at Kopachuk Park. Accessible by boat only. No power, no water, no toilets, no camping or fires allowed. Easy row to Kopachuck Marine State Park. Cutts Island is connected to Raft Island by a drying shoal. Watch your depths if you try to cross between Cutts Island and Raft Island. We are told that in bygone days, Cutts Island was a Native American burial ground, and its local name is Dead Man's Island. Watch for poison oak when hiking.

⑯ **Kopachuck Marine State Park.** (253) 265-3606. Three miles north of Fox Island, just north of Horsehead Bay. Open all year for day use and mooring. 2 overnight mooring buoys for boats 45 feet and under. Self-register and pay mooring fee on shore. Good bottom for anchoring, but unprotected. Underwater park with artificial reef for scuba diving. Kitchen shelters, picnic sites. Playground, trail, clamming, fishing. Swimming in shallow water off the beach area. The campgrounds are permanently closed due to hazardous trees.

Horsehead Bay. Horsehead Bay is an excellent anchorage, surrounded by fine homes. A launch ramp is near the harbor entrance. Good holding ground is a short distance inside the bay.

Hale Passage separates Fox Island from the Olympic Peninsula, and is crossed by a bridge with a mean high water clearance of 31 feet. A short distance east of the bridge, a green can buoy marks a drying, boulder-studded shoal. Pass to the north of the buoy. Currents run strongly through Hale Passage, with 1 to 2.5 knots common, flooding west and ebbing east. The ebb current is stronger than the flood.

Fox Island is connected to the mainland by a bridge with a mean high water clearance of 31 feet. Good anchorage can be found behind Tanglewood Island, which has a pavilion used by yacht clubs and other groups for special occasions. Residents of Fox Island are protective of their privacy, so it is a good idea to stay aboard unless invited ashore.

Wollochet Bay. Wollochet Bay winds a couple of miles into the mainland off Hale Passage. The shores of the bay are lined with homes, many with mooring buoys, but good anchorage can be found. The mouth of the bay is open to southerly winds. Inside, the waters are protected. Tacoma Yacht Club has an outstation near the head of the bay.

We've had good luck catching crab at the mouth of the bay.

A favorite pastime while visiting Wollochet Bay is launching the dinghy and exploring the saltwater marsh and estuary area at Wollochet Bay Estuary Park. The park, at the very head of the bay, has 854 linear feet of shoreline including the confluence of Artondale Creek.

Ketron Island. Privately owned.

Penrose Point State Park & Lakebay Marina

See Area Map Page 96 - Maps Not for Navigation

SOUTH AND CENTRAL PUGET SOUND

HENDERSON INLET, NISQUALLY, STEILACOOM, TACOMA NARROWS

Henderson Inlet extends about 5 miles south from Itsami Ledge. The inlet has been the site of major logging operations over the years, and a few log rafts remain along Woodard Creek; the log rafts have become habitat for pupping seals, and the old train trestle now affords cover for thousands of bats that emerge at dusk and fly to downtown Olympia. Anchorage is good along approximately half of the inlet before it becomes too shallow near the entrance to Woodward Creek.

⑰ **Zittel's Marina Inc.** 9144 Gallea St. NE, Olympia, WA 98516; (360) 459-1950; www.zittelsmarina.com. Open all year, hours may vary in the winter. Ethanol-free gasoline and diesel at the fuel dock. Guest moorage in unoccupied slips and side-tie up to 65 feet when available (don't count on availability), 30 amp power, launch ramp, restrooms, portapotty dump, showers. Haulout and repairs, limited marine supplies, boat rentals, groceries, bait and tackle. Owned and operated by Mike and Kathi Zittel.

Tolmie Marine State Park. (360) 753-1519. Eight miles northeast of Olympia. This 105-acre park is open all year for day use and overnight moorage, except closed for day use Mondays and Tuesdays in winter. Restrooms and showers. 5 mooring buoys for boats 45 feet and under are well offshore; beach and shallows extend out some distance. Self-register and pay mooring fee on shore. The underwater park for scuba diving includes sunken wooden barges. Hiking trails, picnic sites with barbecues, meeting room. Nice sandy beach. The park includes a small saltwater lagoon marsh area good for watching wildlife. No camping.

Nisqually Reach is the body of water south of Anderson Island, between the island and the mainland. The channel is marked by buoys along the extensive mudflats of the Nisqually River delta. The delta is a wildlife refuge, and is accessible by boat at half tide or better, by way of the Luhrs Beach launch ramp near Nisqually Head. Tom Kincaid has entered the river itself by dinghy, but from the water side the entrance is hard to spot. Opportunities for bird watching along the nature trail that skirts the wildlife refuge.

Steilacoom. Picnic area on a small pebble beach, launch ramp, and fishing pier adjacent to the ferry landing. A year-round 60-foot day-use dock available for hourly moorage, limited to boats 23 feet and under, adjacent to the ferry landing. Steilacoom, incorporated in 1854, is the oldest incorporated town in Washington. A museum, restaurants, and other services are nearby. Steilacoom Marina, at Gordon Point, is abandoned and dilapidated.

Zittel's Marina a convenient fuel stop on your way to or from Olympia.

Tacoma Narrows. All of the water in southern Puget Sound flows through Tacoma Narrows, with 4- to 6-knot currents or higher. Day Island Yacht Club, Narrows Marina, and Day Island Marina are on the east side of the south end of the Narrows. The Tacoma Narrows bridges, more than a mile long and 180 feet above the water, are two of the world's longest suspension bridges.

Back eddies form along the sides of the narrows, useful when transiting with an opposing current.

⑱ **Narrows Marina.** 9007 S. 19th St. Suite 100, Tacoma, WA 98466; (253) 564-3032; nmbt@narrowsmarina.com; www.narrowsmarina.com. Open all year except Christmas week, three days during Thanksgiving, and Easter Sunday. Ethanol-free gasoline and diesel at the fuel dock, restrooms, pumpout, guest moorage, long term parking, convenience store, tackle and live bait. Full service repairs on-site with a 9-ton lift.

Painted boards along the docks indicate where you can tie up. Green indicates free moorage for visits less than three hours. Blue indicates reserved guest moorage; call ahead for a slip assignment. The fuel dock is inside the breakwater in the northeast corner of the marina. Currents can run strongly at the docks.

The Boathouse 19 restaurant and Narrows Brewing Company are on site. The top of the bar at Boathouse 19 is made from the old Day Island Bridge and the table tops are from Nalley Valley pickle barrels. Narrows Brewing Company has a tasting room where you can bring your own food and sample a variety of beers.

Narrows Marina is a 10 minute taxi ride from Chambers Bay Golf Course, the site of the 2015 U.S. Open.

Days Island. If your destination is the Day Island Yacht Club at the back of the lagoon, run down the west side, close to Days Island and its boathouses. At lower tides this will be obvious, because a big drying shoal blocks the middle. Time your passage for mid-tide or higher. Least depth at zero tide is said to be 4 feet.

Titlow Park. Tacoma Narrows Waterway. Located on the Tacoma side, about 1 mile south of the Tacoma Narrows Bridge. Open all year, park with tennis courts and 'Spray Ground' (splash park). Restaurants a short walk away. Titlow Park is a marine preserve with excellent diving.

CENTRAL PUGET SOUND

LOCAL KNOWLEDGE

SPEED LIMIT: A no-wake speed of 5 mph or less is enforced within Gig Harbor and 200 feet outside the entrance.

Narrows Marina

2020 WAGGONER CRUISING GUIDE

SOUTH AND CENTRAL PUGET SOUND

See Area Map Page 109 - Maps Not for Navigation

Marinas, anchorages, and restaurants abound in gorgeous Gig Harbor.

⑲ **Gig Harbor.** www.gigharborguide.com. Gig Harbor is one of the most perfectly protected harbors in Puget Sound, and one of the most charming towns. The south shore is lined with moorages for the substantial commercial fish boat and pleasure boat fleets. The entrance to Gig Harbor is narrow, especially at low tide. Maintain a mid-channel course around the end of the spit.

Gig Harbor has overnight moorage, marine supplies, major repairs, and haulout. Anchorage is in 20 to 42 feet with good holding, although the bay shoals close to both shores and toward the head. In some areas, weed on the bottom can foul anchors.

The City of Gig Harbor maintains Jerisich Park (identifiable by the tall flagpole at its shoreward end) with a dinghy dock and long moorage float; 30 amp power, water and holding tank pumpout. The Gig Harbor Maritime Pier, 40-feet, next to Tides Tavern, has temporary moorage, restrooms and pumpout.

We enjoy walking Gig Harbor's village-like commercial streets. The harbor is lined with shops, galleries, and specialty shops, including antiques. Building architecture is turn-of-the-20th-century. At least two shops in town serve enormous ice cream cones and have chairs out front, where you can enjoy your treat in the shade. Several good restaurants, from casual to elegant. On the casual side, Tides Tavern, a short distance inside the mouth of the bay, is a longtime favorite. If you are lucky, you'll find room to tie the boat at their private dock. Tides Tavern personnel can come to your boat to take your order and deliver your meal dockside, a nice option for families. Anthony's, near the head of the bay, also has a dock. More likely, you'll take the dinghy or approach by land. The JW Trolley at the Gig Harbor Marina & Boatyard is a local Gig Harbor favorite for informal dining. Open 8:30 a.m. to dusk.

Finholm's Market and Deli, The Harbor General Store, and The Waterfront Natural Market offer some groceries within easy walking distance of the waterfront. Several supermarkets are uptown, best reached by bus or taxi. In the summer months, a trolley-themed bus service runs seven days a week, frequently between the waterfront and uptown areas.

For a great view of Gig Harbor and Mt. Rainier, the local Lions Club built an observation area called the Finholm View Climb. The stairway is at the head of the bay, across the street from Anthony's Restaurant. Lee's SUP & Kayak rentals are located in front of Anthony's Restaurant.

For a romantic time with someone special, grab your favorite refreshment and take a gondola tour of the harbor (gigharborgondola.com). A small snack box of cheese, fruit and chocolates is provided.

The beautiful Gig Harbor History Museum (www.harborhistorymuseum.org) is superb. Located at the west end of Harborview Drive, the main road along the waterfront.

⑲ **Gig Harbor Marina and Boatyard.** 3117 Harborview Drive, Gig Harbor, WA 98335; (253) 858-3535; www.gigharbormarina.com. Monitors VHF 69. Open all year with guest moorage in unoccupied slips, 30 amp power, water, garbage drop, and free Wi-Fi. Restrooms with showers. Reservations accepted. Full service boatyard with haulout to 50 tons. Their marine consignment and repair shop, called "Second Wave," is a fun place to find used and rare marine equipment; shop online at secondwaveattheboatyard.com or call (253) 509-0798. "The Club" building and classroom space are available for rendezvous and other events.

⑲ **Arabella's Landing.** 3323 Harborview Drive, Gig Harbor, WA 98335; (253) 851-1793; info@arabellaslanding.com; www.arabellaslanding.com. Open all year, 225 feet of guest side-tie moorage for boats up to 175 feet, six 50-foot slips, and one 60-foot slip; 30 & 50 amp power, water, Wi-Fi, restrooms, showers, laundry, secured gate, pumpout. ADA accessible. Reservations recommended.

Stan and Judy Stearns developed this classy marina, located a short distance past the city dock, close to shopping, restaurants, services, and groceries. Excellent concrete docks, beautiful grounds, and brick walkways. They have a well-trained crew to help with landings, make dinner reservations, or assist in finding someone to repair your boat if necessary. The moorage fee includes power, water, and showers. Group gatherings may make use of the clubhouse with

Gig Harbor

See Area Map Page 109 - Maps Not for Navigation   **SOUTH AND CENTRAL PUGET SOUND**

WE BOUGHT A MARINA

It all started with some beer and oysters on a hot summer day. Truly, that's how this story began for us. We took a ride on our Harley to Treasure Island to visit friends, and we gathered along the shoreline to enjoy oysters over a fire, along with a cold beer. I looked out over the canal and spotted boats lined-up in rows. I then proceeded to ask Bob, "what is that over there?" He replied, "Well that is Fair Harbor Marina." He went into detail about the marina and the events connected with the property. It was at this point Sue chimed in. "Oh, by the way, it's for sale and there is a wedding venue too." I paused, and turned to see the smile growing from one ear to the other on my wife's face. I didn't have a chance to react before "OH REALLY?!" shot past my head. I knew that this one statement had just started a chain-reaction in my wife's thought process. I must admit that I was also intrigued. This was in July, 2018, and then I found ourselves as new owners of the marina in March of 2019. So, like I said, beer and oysters.

Fair Harbor is a place for families, where Vern and Susan Nelson enjoyed their lives for 30 years. We want to continue that legacy and expand on it in the future. The fuel pumps were opened in May of 2019 to serve the boating public once again. The store was also reopened for guests to get ice cream on a hot summer day, along with bags of ice, cold beer and wine. Guests can also find great coffee and espresso in the morning. And yes, the shop now carries merchandise ranging from art, pottery and linens, to chap stick and sunscreen.

The venue for wedding services continues to be offered at Fair Harbor Marina. We feel that the beauty of this place has to be seen in person to be fully appreciated. Cindy and I are pleased to be members of this special community. Our goal is to create a fun and memorable family environment for all. Our gift in return is having a young man or woman come up to us on their wedding day and tell us, "I used to run down those docks to get ice cream from you in the store when I was a kid!"

We are honored with the great pleasure of creating lasting memories, whether it's from the new beginning of "I Do!" or "my mom and dad brought us here on our boat every summer!" We are glad to be part of such a wonderful story and look forward to welcoming the boating community year-round.

Kelly and Cindy Granger, Owners
Fair Harbor Marina, South Puget Sound

WAGGONER CRUISING GUIDE
A Nautical Information Company

Waggoner Cruising Guide
The "bible for NW Cruising" with 500 pages of information on the key marinas and anchorages covering Olympia to Ketchikan

Waggoner eNews and the WaggonerGuide.com
Twice per month we send out information on destinations, maintenance and events to over 9,000 boaters.

Ports and Passes
The top selling Tides and Currents guide.

Seminars through Cruisers College, Waggoner Seminars, and Seattle Boat Show University
Informative multihour and all day seminars on all of the critical subjects for cruising and boat maintenance. See WaggonerGuide.com/seminars for schedules and locations.

Waggoner Flotillas
Learn through participating in 2 and 3 week flotilla cruises to Desolation Sound, The Broughtons, and to Southeast Alaska, and now the British Virgin Islands.

Waggoner Trip Planning
We can help you plan your trip. We have been there and have the "inside knowledge" to help you plan your trip for the maximum enjoyment for you and your entire crew.

Cruising Maps
Maps of the top cruising areas from San Diego to Glacier Bay, Alaska

WaggonerGuide.com Bookstore
Books, cruising maps, Cruising Guides for all areas of the Northwest and the Inside Passage, or stop by our store in Anacortes.

Waggoner Guide to Cruising the Virgin Islands
We know the Virgin Islands too and have a special cruising guide for charter cruisers. We can help plan your trip too. Post hurricane info too.

WaggonerGuide.com — (425) 780-5015

2020 WAGGONER CRUISING GUIDE

Cruising the Shoulders

Prime cruising season in the Pacific Northwest is in July and August, that's when you find the largest number of boats out cruising. In the past, boating activity didn't get started until well after Memorial Day and dropped-off after Labor Day. More recently, boating activity starts earlier in the season and continues well into fall. There are several factors stretching the boating season into the shoulder months of spring and fall.

The Pacific Northwest and the Inside Passage have been discovered. More out-of-area boaters are enjoying the protected waters, mild climate, and the unique boater friendly destinations this area has to offer. Western Washington and specifically the Seattle metro area have seen an influx of people in recent years that are eager to enjoy the area's great boating. Add to this a vibrant economy, providing people with time and money to get out on the water, and you get a significant increase in boating activity seen over the last three to five years.

Spring and fall shoulder cruising seasons have much to offer the boater that has the flexibility to take advantage of these opportunities. Before Memorial Day and after Labor Day, there are so few recreational boaters out there that VHF channel 16 is almost silent. We sometimes switch to VHF weather channels to ensure the radio is working. There are far fewer boats during a shoulder season, easing competition for moorage, anchorage, and access to services. Yes, there are some trade-offs; marina staffing levels may be reduced, and hours and days of operation may be curtailed. In early spring, you may find marina facilities and staff that may not be completely ready for your visit. So, when cruising in shoulder season, be adaptable and flexible. You may need to leave a message and wait for a callback to your inquiry for moorage. You may have to arrive a little earlier and depart later to accommodate off-season office hours.

The rewards for cruising in the shoulder season are many. Prices are often reduced and availability is greater. Often people have more time to share insider information about places to visit or things to do. You may find other cruisers more eager to visit and share boating stories. You will get more use out of your annual state parks pass. You will have your choice of prime spots in popular anchorages.

For marina operators in the Broughtons and elsewhere, the boating season is unfortunately too short. Marinas welcome a longer season and tend to open earlier and stay open later if demand calls for it. Cruising the shoulder season can bring new friendships and new opportunities, and in the process, help to convince marinas to extend their season. Give it a try, get out there early and come back later in the season.

Which areas are best for shoulder season cruising? South, Central, and North Puget Sound are some areas that start the earliest and run much later in the season. These areas are effectively year-round boating destinations. Next, the San Juan Islands, Gulf Islands, Vancouver B.C. destinations are good early and late season areas. Desolation Sound, north to and including the Broughtons, tend to be later in the shoulder season with facilities ready for full operation around Memorial Day, and curtailing operations by mid-September. Because of resort fishing activity, West Coast Vancouver Island around Barkley Sound and Tofino get started earlier than Desolation Sound.

September and October can often be a surprisingly good time of the year to cruise the Pacific Northwest waters from Olympia to Desolation Sound. Despite the occasional early fall storms that will have you sheltered for a few days, there can be some excellent fall cruising with settled weather, gorgeous sunsets, and empty anchorages.

[Landons]

lounge, fireplace, and coffee service.

Enjoy Netshed No. 9 restaurant at the top of the docks for breakfast and lunch, and make reservations for a 5-star dinner at Brix 25. Ship to Shore Marine Supply, on site, has an excellent stock of marine supplies and kayaks which you may try out in their infinity pool. Arabella's has two Airbnb suites for their guests that want to stay ashore. See GigHarborAirbnb for reservations for the "The Sail Loft" and "The Cove Suite."

Bayview Marina, just east of Arabella's Landing, is under the same ownership, with 250 feet of dock, 30 & 50 amp power and water on the dock.

⑲ **Jerisich Dock.** 3211 Harborview Drive, Gig Harbor, WA; (253) 851-6170; www.cityofgigharbor.net. Open all year, 420 feet of first-come, first-served dock space, 30 amp power, seasonal water, free seasonal pumpout. Two mooring buoys for vessels 32 feet and under (no charge), but required to register. This is an attractive and well-used public dock and park, located just west of Tides Tavern on the downtown side of Gig Harbor. Maximum 3-night stay within a 10-day period. Pay overnight moorage fees at self-payment kiosk adjacent to the dock, credit and debit cards accepted. Dinghy dock is near shore on the west side. Restaurants, groceries, and a seasonal trolley café are all within walking distance. Check your tide table; close to shore you could touch at low tide.

The Welcome Plaza is located upland from the Jerisich Dock in Skansie Brothers Park. Restrooms and showers for visiting boaters are located at the plaza. The Splash Fountain is popular with children. A viewing deck, with tables and chairs, is located above the restrooms.

⑲ **Peninsula Yacht Basin.** 8913 N. Harborview Drive, Gig Harbor, WA 98332; (253) 858-2250; dockmaster@peninsulayachtbasin.com; peninsulayachtbasin.com. Open all year, no guest moorage, reciprocal privileges with Gig Harbor Yacht Club only. Maximum boat length 85 feet, 6-foot depth at zero tide, 20 &

Arabella's Landing

Gig Harbor Marketplace

RESTAURANTS, SHOPS & SERVICES

ANTHONY'S
Anthony's at Gig Harbor serves premium NW seafood and offers a spectacular view of the harbor and Mt. Rainier. Enjoy the view from our expansive deck. Downstairs in our Shoreline Room lounge is a lighter menu and a more casual dining experience.
253-853-6353 • 8827 Harborview Dr. N., Gig Harbor, WA 98335 www.anthonys.com

HARBOR HISTORY MUSEUM
Harbor History Museum creates opportunities to experience the heritage of the greater Gig Harbor communities by collecting, preserving, and sharing the rich history of the area. Artifacts, video kiosks, hands-on exhibits, computer interactives, and a small theater bring Peninsula history to life in our permanent galleries. In addition, the Museum provides 3-5 special exhibits throughout the year so there is always something new to see and experience for our members and visitors.
253.858.6722 ext. 5 • 4121 Harborview Drive, Gig Harbor, WA 98332 • www.harborhistorymuseum.org

HERITAGE DISTILLING CO.
Located in downtown Gig Harbor, Heritage Distilling Co.'s (HDC) Waterfront location serves as the perfect spot to kick off your Gig Harbor adventure. This newly expanded distillery and tasting room is open 7 days a week for spirits flights, cocktail kits, gifts, memberships & much more. While HDC serves as the hometown distillery for this maritime town, it is also notably known as being the maker of BSB® - Brown Sugar Bourbon, recently named "The World's Best Flavoured Whisky" by Whisky Magazine. This storefront thrives in the heart of the bustling downtown area within walking distance to Skansie Brothers Park, Gig Harbor Maritime Pier and many more Waterfront attractions perfect for the whole family.
Families Welcome - 3118 Harborview Dr, Gig Harbor, WA 98335
Call for delivery options: 253-514-8120 - HeritageDistilling.com

GIG HARBOR COMMUNITY EVENTS

Monthly First Saturday FREE Art Walk at various downtown galleries www.gigharborwaterfront.org
April - Annual Gig Harbor Paddlers Cup www.gigharborpaddlerscup.com
May - Street Scramble - An urban scavenger hunt! www.gigharborguide.com
May - Gig Harbor Beer Festival www.gigharborbeerfestival.com
June - Maritime Gig Festival www.maritimegig.com
June - Aug 14 Summer Sounds at Skansie Every Tuesday - Enjoy an outdoor concert! www.gigharborguide.com
July - Gig Harbor Wings and Wheels Air Show and Car Show www.freedomfair.com
July - Chalk the Harbor www.gigharborwaterfront.org
July - Peninsula Art Leauge's ArtFest www.peninsulaartleague.com
July - Gig Harbor Wine & Food Festival www.gigharborwaterfront.org
September - Race for a Soldier Half Marathon and 5K www.raceforasoldier.org
October - Gig Harbor Film Festival www.gigharborfilmfestival.org
November - Annual Girls Night Out www.gigharborwaterfront.org
November - Donkey Creek Chum Festival www.harborwildwatch.org
November - Turkey Trot www.gigharborturkeytrot.com
December - Lighted Boat Parade gigharboryachtclub.wildapricot.org/

Visit GigHarborGuide.com for events and information

SOUTH AND CENTRAL PUGET SOUND

See Area Map Page 109 - Maps Not for Navigation

30 amp power, restrooms, showers. Located on the north shore of Gig Harbor, next to Anthony's Shoreline Restaurant.

TACOMA AREA

Commencement Bay. The southern shoreline of Commencement Bay is mostly parks, interspersed with buildings, housing, restaurants, and other facilities. At least two restaurants provide moorage for their patrons. Following this shoreline southeastward leads to the Thea Foss Waterway.

Tacoma's Commencement Bay is busy with commercial traffic. Most visiting boats choose to moor at one of several marinas in the Thea Foss Waterway. Museums, restaurants, and other attractions are a short walk from the docks.

Point Defiance. Point Defiance marks the northern end of Tacoma Narrows and is noted for swirling currents and excellent salmon fishing. The entire point is a major Tacoma park, complete with trails, a zoo, aquarium, gardens, sports facilities, and picnic areas.

㉑ **Breakwater Marina.** 5603 N. Waterfront Drive, Tacoma, WA 98407; (253) 752-6663 (office); (253) 752-6685 (service); www.breakwatermarina.com. Certified Clean Marina. Open all year, 15 & 30 amp power, restrooms, showers, laundry, portapotty dump, pumpout, propane, store. Limited guest moorage for boats up to 45 feet, call ahead. Repairs available. The Tacoma Yacht Club, located across from Breakwater Marina, offers reciprocal moorage for participating yacht clubs.

㉑ **Point Defiance Boathouse Marina.** 5912 N. Waterfront Drive, Tacoma, WA 98407; (253) 591-5325; pointdefiancemarina.com. Certified Clean Marina and 5-Star EnviroStar rating. Open 7 days a week all year except Thanksgiving and Christmas. Guest moorage is on the dock between the ferry landing and the 8-lane boat launch, 72 hour maximum stay. Pay at the boat launch kiosk. Ethanol-free gasoline, restrooms, free pumpout, some 30 amp power, dry storage for small boats, boat rentals. Bait, tackle, snacks, souvenirs and gift items at Point Defiance Boathouse Tackle Shop. Public fishing pier. Anthony's Restaurant is at the east end of the marina.

The marina is within walking distance of the Point Defiance Zoo & Aquarium and Point Defiance Park. Bus service to greater Tacoma.

Ruston. Point Defiance below the community of Ruston is the Tacoma terminus of the ferry to Vashon Island. The Point Defiance Boathouse Marina and Anthony's at Point Defiance restaurant are west of the ferry dock. A large launch ramp, operated by the Parks Department, is east of the ferry dock. Long-term tow vehicle and trailer storage is available a couple of blocks up the hill from the launch ramp.

The small town of Ruston was the site of a smelter. The site has recently been redeveloped, and a substantial footbridge now leads to the ferry terminal. A half-mile east of Point Defiance is the impressive Point Ruston development, consisting of classy condos and apartments, shops, cafes, and a theater. A 'splash pad' overlooks the waterfront and pathway that connects Point Ruston to Point Defiance. Point Ruston is definitely worth a visit for the grand views, eateries, and park-like atmosphere.

Old Town Dock. Next to Jack Hyde Park (formerly Commencement Park). The docks are usable, but don't appear to get much traffic. Smaller boats only.

STRONG CURRENTS: Currents, especially on large tides, can run stronger than expected in Thea Foss Waterway. Plan landings and departures accordingly.

Thea Foss Waterway. The Thea Foss Waterway (formerly City Waterway) has gone through a major renewal and revitalization.

Just inside the mouth of the waterway, the Foss Waterway Seaport is a fascinating stop. It is housed in the century-old Balfour warehouse, once part of a mile-long row of wheat warehouses. The 300-foot-long by 150-foot-wide building is itself a museum exhibit. Displays inside include a lab, a working boat building shop, Willits canoe exhibit, marine biology exhibit, and an extensive display detailing Puget Sound's maritime history. Some 1200 feet of public floats make boat access easy.

Up on Pacific Avenue, the Union Railroad Station has been restored and rebuilt as the Federal Courthouse, and decorated with Dale Chihuly glass sculpture. The must-see Washington State History Museum, which shares the courthouse's beautiful architecture, is next door.

The Washington State History Museum is excellent. Allow at least two hours to see it; three or four hours is better. The museum is enjoyable for both children and adults.

At the head of the waterway, the Museum of Glass fronts on the waterway, immediately east of the courthouse and the Washington State History Museum.

The Chihuly Bridge of Glass connects the courthouse and history museum complex with the Museum of Glass. You can spend several hours there. The hot shop furnaces roar, and the crew may create a bowl, a vase, or candlestick holders before your eyes. Exhibits in the galleries rotate. The works on display are impressive.

The Tacoma Art Museum features regularly rotating exhibits, and the building itself is a work of architectural art.

LeMay-America's Car Museum, across the road from the Tacoma Dome, draws large crowds. More than 350 cars, trucks and motorcycles are on display, dating from the beginning of motorized transport. Open 7 days a week, 10:00 a.m. to 5:00 p.m. Check website for weekly events. Highly recommended.

Downtown Tacoma is very different from other Puget Sound cities. Many of the old buildings are beautiful, and some are historic. One building has a plaque commemorating Russell G. O'Brien, who on October 18, 1893, originated the custom of standing during the playing of the Star Spangled Banner. We learn the most interesting things when we walk around.

Guest Moorage: Dock Street Marina, with guest moorage, is in front of the Museum of Glass. Guest moorage is also available at Foss Harbor Marina. Side-tie guest moorage is

Commencement Bay

SOUTH AND CENTRAL PUGET SOUND

See Area Map Page 109 - Maps Not for Navigation

available at Foss Waterway Seaport.

No Anchoring Zone: All of the Thea Foss Waterway is a no anchoring zone.

Breweries: Area breweries include McMenamins Elks Lodge on 565 Broadway; Odd Otter Brewing at 716 Pacific; Pacific Brewing & Malting at 610 Pacific Ave.; and 7 Seas Brewing at 2101 Jefferson Ave.

Farmers Market: On Broadway between 9th and 11th Streets, a farmers market with 70 to 90 vendors. Thursdays, May through October from 10:00 a.m. to 3:00 p.m.

Light Rail: Light rail runs from the theater district at the north end of downtown Tacoma to a last stop, 2½ blocks from the Tacoma Dome and LeMay-America's Car Museum. At the museum district, the tracks are in the middle of Pacific Avenue, fronting the Washington State History Museum. The free trains are clean and safe. They run every 12 minutes from morning to evening.

Looking south in the Thea Foss Waterway, as seen from the 11th St. bridge

With the accomplishments and ongoing efforts of the Port of Tacoma, city leaders and others, The Foss Waterway and downtown Tacoma is a first class urban boating destination.

Things to Do

1. LeMay-America's Car Museum. This museum is housed in a dramatic building, just up from the waterfront. See over 350 cars, trucks and motorcycles on display in the world's largest auto museum.

2. Museum of Glass. With its iconic architecture near the waterfront and beautiful glasswork, this has become a key part of the Tacoma art scene.

3. Tacoma Art Museum. Art in Tacoma continues with photography, paintings, and Chihuly glass.

4. Washington State History Museum. Learn about Washington's past.

5. Tacoma Glassblowing Studio. See how glass art is made.

6. Point Defiance Zoo & Aquarium. See an Asian Forest Sanctuary, elephants and tigers. The large aquarium has octopi, sharks, and a beluga whale.

7. Children's Museum of Tacoma. The museum serves young children and their parents through self-directed play.

8. Daffodil Festival. See the annual Daffodil street parade held in early April, followed by the parade of boats all decorated in daffodils, held mid-April.

㉑ **Foss Waterway Seaport.** 705 Dock St, Tacoma, WA 98402; (253) 272-2750; info@fosswaterwayseaport.org; www.fosswaterwayseaport.org. Located at the mouth of Foss Waterway. Visitor moorage along 1200 feet of floating dock. From the middle gangway to the south end, 30 & 50 amp power and water are available. No power or water north of the middle gangway. No restrooms or garbage drop. Pumpout available April through September. Reservations only for groups. Payment is made at the Seaport office, or drop box after hours, 4 hour free

Thea Foss Waterway

Breakwater Marina

Tacoma Museums

Tacoma Art Museum

The art museum supports and preserves the region's art history through its collections, changing exhibitions, and learning programs. The Northwest perspective alternates between historical and contemporary artists. Free events and programs for all ages. The Tacoma Art Museum (TAM) is located at 1701 Pacific Avenue; open Tuesdays through Sundays from 10 a.m. to 5 p.m.; free on Thursdays from 5 p.m. to 8 p.m. (253-272-4258).

Washington State History Museum

This museum maintains three permanent exhibits relating to the history of the State of Washington, including Native American Tribes, the Progress through Statehood, Industrialization, and the War and Post-War Eras. The permanent Learning Center encourages visitors to learn more through interactive exhibits. The permanent Model Railroad, an 1,800 square-foot layout, depicts the rail lines from Tacoma's Point Defiance Park to the Cascades. Other exhibits are as scheduled. This excellent State history museum is located in the old railroad Union Station at 1911 Pacific Avenue; open Tuesdays through Sundays from 10 a.m. to 5 p.m.; till 8 p.m. on the third Thursday of each month (253-272-3500).

Museum of Glass

Visiting the Museum of Glass, provides the opportunity to view craftsman at work, heating and shaping glass into sculptures, vases, and works of art at the Hot Shop. The Museum's galleries exhibit rotating and permanent glass art, including those of the world-famous artist, Dale Chihuly. Group tours and private events can be scheduled. Don't miss this fascinating museum, within easy walking distance from the docks, at 1801 Dock Street; open Wednesdays through Saturdays from 10 a.m. to 5 p.m.; and on Sundays from noon to 5 p.m. (253-284-4750).

LeMay America's Car Museum

The LeMay Car Museum is one of the finest in the world, with exhibits displaying classic cars and rare cars from each period in time from the inception of the automobile. The stunning 165,000 square-foot facility houses in excess of 3,000 vehicles and thousands of artifacts. Meeting space, educational programs, and a café are available. Plan to spend the day at this exceptional museum located at 2702 East D Street, Tacoma; open 10 a.m. to 5 p.m. daily (253-779-8490).

Foss Waterway Seaport

The museum at the Foss Waterway Seaport dock celebrates the area's rich maritime history and serves as a maritime education and event center. Exhibits cover maritime and boating history, commerce and trade, unique stories of Tacoma, and other boating related history. Special events are held as scheduled, a special treat for the entire family. Open Wednesdays through Saturdays from 10 a.m. to 4 p.m.; and Sundays from noon to 4 p.m. (253-272-2750).

SOUTH AND CENTRAL PUGET SOUND   See Area Map Page 109 - Maps Not for Navigation

Tacoma Foss Waterway

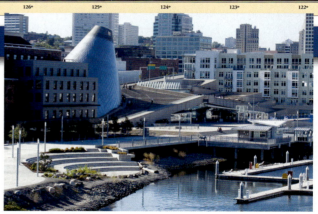
Museum of Glass and waterfront walk

For years Tacoma was an industrial port and not friendly to recreational boaters. The city waterfront had been neglected, facilities were limited and there wasn't much to do. The city was famous more for its pulp mills than its historic buildings, museums, and restaurants.

In the late 1980s Tacoma's political leaders got serious about rejuvenating their city. The Simpson Paper Mill spent tens of millions of dollars on renovations, reducing emissions and sweetening the air. In 1990 the University of Washington established its Tacoma campus, which now has more than 4000 students just up the hill from the Thea Foss Waterway. Tacoma Link light rail was built to help the growing population get around the city.

Foss Waterway Seaport

Much of Tacoma's redevelopment has been centered around the Thea Foss Waterway. In 1992 the former president of University of Puget Sound conceived of the idea for a glass museum. Working with Dale Chihuly, a Tacoma native, he proposed the glass museum be built in Tacoma. In 2002 the high-profile, 75,000 square foot Museum of Glass opened a few steps up from the Thea Foss Waterway. Exhibits show a variety of glass, from both Chihuly and other artists. The working hot-shop, visible to visitors, is a highlight.

Part of Tacoma's revitalization is the emergence of its museum district, conveniently located just upland from the Thea Foss Waterway. Above the Glass Museum is the outstanding Washington State History Museum, housed in a distinctive brick building. The Tacoma Art Museum is just north of the History Museum.

Seaport. The century-old Balfour Dock building was originally built for cargo arriving by rail and departing by sail. After a recent renovation, it now houses the Working Waterfront Maritime Museum. Inside you'll find notable classic boats and sailing vessels along with displays of boat building and restoration. The extensive guest dock along the waterfront offers four hours of free moorage, perfect when visiting the museum.

Looking south from the 11th Street bridge to the LeMay Museum

What would any progressive city be without a Children's Museum? The Children's Museum of Tacoma believes in the "Power of Play" and "Play to Learn", and play is the right of every child. The museum is new and bright, a fun place for kids. It moved to its current location on Pacific Avenue in 2012.

A single, discounted admission ticket to the Tacoma Art Museum, Museum of Glass, the LeMay-America's Car Museum and the Washington State History Museum. The pass is good for a seven day period while visiting Tacoma and includes a discount for the Foss Waterway Seaport. The Children's Museum of Tacoma is a "pay-as-you-will" museum.

Union Station

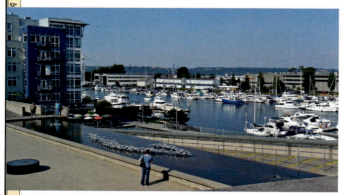
Tacoma Waterfront

Slightly further away is LeMay—America's Car Museum. Harold LeMay, now deceased, was a garbage pioneer. He started LeMay Inc. in 1942 and grew it into the 10th largest garbage hauler in the country. The wealth generated from his business endeavors allowed him to indulge his automotive hobby. Over time he and his wife collected more than 3,300 cars, trucks, and motorcycles—the largest private collection in the world. Today, more than 700 of his cars are on display in his namesake museum.

At the entrance to Thea Foss Waterway is Foss Waterway

Tacoma has grown into one of the region's best urban destinations with an esplanade, restaurants and museums to explore, all within a short walk from marinas of the Thea Foss Waterway.

See Area Map Page 109 - Maps Not for Navigation   **SOUTH AND CENTRAL PUGET SOUND**

stay. A dock for floatplanes is attached to the northwest end of the Seaport Facility; watch for floatplane activity.

㉑ **Foss Harbor Marina.** 821 Dock Street, Tacoma, WA 98402; (253) 272-4404; info@fossharbor.com; www.fossharbormarina.com. Certified Clean Marina. Monitors VHF 71. Open all year, ethanol-free gasoline and diesel at end of D dock. Visitor moorage to 95 feet in unoccupied slips. Restrooms, showers, laundry, water, fixed and slip-side pumpout, portapotty dump, 30 & 50 amp power, free Wi-Fi in lounge area, Wi-Fi on the docks for a fee, kayak and SUP rentals. The docks have recently been improved and are excellent. Store has expanded beer and wine selection, deli sandwiches, convenience groceries, bait, tackle, marine supplies. An indoor lounge and outdoor patio are available for customers. Convenient walk to downtown.

㉑ **Dock Street Marina.** 1817 Dock St., Tacoma, WA 98402; (253) 250-1906;

The dramatic highway 509 bridge is just south of Dock Street Marina.

info@dockstreetmarina.com; www.dockstreetmarina.com. Call ahead by phone for slip assignment. Certified Clean Marina. Concrete docks, security gates, 30, 50 & 100 amp power, water, slip-side pumpout, garbage, recycling drop, laundry, restrooms, free showers, free cable TV, some wheelchair access, kayak rentals. Complimentary bicycles for marina guests. This is the marina in front of the Museum of Glass. It is made up of two sets of docks—G and H docks are the southern, guest moorage docks. The permanent moorage 17th St. docks are immediately north.

The office, showers, and laundry are above the guest moorage docks, 30 slips 36-60 feet, with 127-foot pier ends. Concierge service. Pet-friendly. Moorage in the north docks is by assignment in unoccupied slips only. A 320-foot dock is in the north moorage.

Special events such as the Daffodil Marine Parade completely fill the marina. See their website for the complete list of special events. Rendezvous sometimes fill the marina, too. Reservations recommended, even in the off season.

Dock Street Marina is first-class, with an easy walk to many Tacoma restaurants and museums. Don't be surprised to find a courtesy newspaper in the cockpit on Sundays, or a red rose on Valentine's Day.

㉑ **Dock Street North Pier.** (253) 272-4352; This is the long concrete float north of Dock Street Marina. No power, water, or garbage, reservations 24-hours in advance. Watch your depths at zero tide or lower.

㉑ **Delin Docks.** 1616 East D St., Tacoma, WA 98421; (253) 572-2524; info@delindocksmarina.com; www.delindocksmarina.com. Certified Clean Marina. Open all year, 30 & 50 amp power, water, restrooms, free showers, laundry, pumpout, portapotty dump. These are nice docks with 30- to 60-foot slips, located immediately north of Johnny's Dock on the east side of Foss Waterway. They're primarily permanent moorage, although occasionally unoccupied slips might be used for guest moorage.

Note: Dock Street Marina and the Delin Docks are under the same management.

㉑ **Johnny's Dock.** 1900 East D St., Tacoma, WA 98421; (253) 627-3186; www.johnnysdock.com. Open all year with limited moorage to 55 feet, power, and water. Guest moorage primarily serves Johnny's Dock restaurant.

㉑ **Tacoma Fuel Dock.** 820 East D St., Tacoma, WA 98421; (253) 383-0851; (800) 868-3681, www.cbmsi.com. Fuel dock open

J&G MARINE SUPPLY

SOMETHING FOR EVERY BOATER From the Smallest Runabout to the Largest Cruiser

YOUR ONE STOP SHOP for

ELECTRONICS   SALES • SERVICE • INSTALLATION

Autopilots • Antennas • Chart Plotters • GPS • Inverters • Radars
Sat. Receivers • Sounders • VHF & SSB Radios

ComNav • ICOM • Digital Antenna • Shakespeare • SIMRAD
Furuno • Intellian • FLIR • Nobeltec • SI-TEX
Garmin • Big Bay Technologies • C-MAP • Northstar • KVH
Lowrance • Maretron • Magnum Energy • Raymarine • Standard Horizon • Rose Point
OceanLED

FIBERGLASS SUPPLIES

Polyester & Epoxy Resin • Cloth • Mat • Tape
Fillers • Cleaners • Waxes • Tools
 • Paint • Varnish • Sealants

and MARINE ACCESSORIES!

Anchors, Battery Switches, Bilge Pumps, Boat Hooks, Books
Charts— U.S. & Canadian, Crab & Shrimp Pots, Docklines
Fenders, Flares, Fuel Tanks, Heaters, Horns
Life Vests, Mooring Buoys, Paint & Varnish, Plumbing, Rod Holders
Shorepower Cords & Connectors, Trailer Accessories, Zincs

M-F 8:30-5:00   SAT 9-1:00

1690 Marine View Dr. Tacoma WA 98422

253-572-4217   800-381-4217

TACOMA MARKETPLACE

RESTAURANTS, SHOPS & SERVICES

 WASHINGTON STATE HISTORICAL SOCIETY
Our museum is dedicated to collecting, preserving and vividly presenting Washington's rich and storied history. We invite you to explore our interactive exhibits and high-tech displays, listen to theatrical storytelling, discover dramatic artifacts and learn about Washington State's unique people and places.
253-272-9747 • 1911 Pacific Ave. • www.washingtonhistor.org

 CHILDREN'S MUSEUM OF TACOMA
We encourage all ages to celebrate play with our playscapes and innovative design that celebrates imagination and encourages creativity. The museum has five main play areas – Woods, Water, Voyager, Invention and Becka's Studio. We are open Wednesday to Sunday from 10am to 5pm. Admission is by donation. Come play with us!
253-627-6031 • 1501 Pacific Ave. • www.playtacoma.org

 DOCK STREET MARINA
Dock Street Marina is Tacoma's only dedicated guest moorage facility. Located in front of the Museum of Glass and just steps away from the Chihuly Bridge of Glass that leads to more museums, shops and restaurants. Reservations recommended. Please call.
253-250-1906 • www.dockstreetmarina.com.

 FOSS WATERWAY SEAPORT
The Foss Waterway Seaport celebrates Tacoma's rich maritime heritage—past, present and future. Located on the waterfront in a century-old wheat warehouse built cargo arriving by " rail and departing by sail!" Features maritime heritage exhibits, land and boat based marine science, heritage boat shop and hands on activities for ages. Short term moorage, power & water. Home of Festival of Sail (tall ships) June 15 -18, 2017.
253-272-2750 ext 100 • 705 Dock Street •
www.fosswaterwayseaport.org

 LEMAY – AMERICA'S CAR MUSEUM
Celebrating America's love affair with the automobile. The four-level, 165,000 sq. ft. museum features rotating exhibits and 300 cars, trucks and motorcycles on display. Free Tacoma Link Light Rail from Union Station to the Dome District.
253-779-8490 • 2702 E. D Street • www.americascarmuseum.org

 MUSEUM OF GLASS
The world famous Museum of Glass is located at the south end of the Foss Waterway with adjacent guest moorage. Featuring multiple exhibitions and art installations, hands-on art studio, diverse educational programs, and a fully functioning glass blowing Hot Shop, the museum offers a unique and entertaining experience for all. Hours are 10am to 5pm, Tuesday through Sunday.
253-284-4750 • 1801 Dock St. • www.MuseumofGlass.org

 NORTHWEST YACHTNET BROKERAGE
Our brokers have the knowledge, contacts and yachting expertise to give you optimal service in any area that you require. NW Yachtnet Brokerage brokers complete the continuing education required to be "Certified Professional Yacht Brokers." Our highly skilled team will treat you with honesty and respect. We are here to make boating the enjoyable experience it is meant to be. We have offices in Tacoma, Seattle, Olympia, and Gig Harbor
1-888-641-5901 • www.nwyachtnet.com
1717 Dock Street (next to the Museum of Glass)

 ROCK THE DOCK
Always great food, friends and fun on the Thea Foss Waterway! Live music every weekend - never a cover charge. Dock side outdoor seating. Full menu on line, find us on Facebook or visit our website for a full calendar of events.
253-272-5004 • 535 Dock St. • www.RocktheDockPub.com

 TACOMA ART MUSEUM
Tacoma Art Museum serves the diverse communities of the Northwest through its collection, exhibitions, and learning programs, emphasizing art and artists from the Northwest and broader western region. We are open Tuesday to Sunday from 10am to 5pm.
253-272-4258 • 1701 Pacific Avenue •
www.tacomaartmuseum.org

TACOMA COMMUNITY EVENTS

April	Daffodil Festival • Sailing Schooner Zodiac Easter Brunch Cruises www.fosswaterseaport • Tacoma City Marathon
May	Apple Blossom Festival
June	NW Pinball Show • Festival of Sail (tall ships) * Scottish Highland Games • www.tacomagames.org
July	Freedom Fair • Tacoma Pride Festival - 2nd week in July Tacoma Food Truck Fest • www.metroparkstacoma.org/foodtruckfest
	Vintage Motorcycle Festival • www.americascarmuseum.org
August	Brew Five Three, Tacoma's Beer and Blues Festival www.broadwaycenter.org
Oct.	Tacoma Film Festival • www.TacomaFilmFestival.com
Nov.	Annual Holiday Tree lighting at the Broadway Center Day after Thanksgiving
Nov-Jan	Ice Skating Rink in Tacoma Polar Plaza

See Area Map Page 109 - Maps Not for Navigation   **SOUTH AND CENTRAL PUGET SOUND**

Trails in Des Moines Beach Park connect with the 2.4-mile Des Moines Creek Trail; all of this now connected with Des Moines Marina.

all year except Thanksgiving, Christmas, and New Year's Day. Summer hours 8:00 a.m. to dusk, winter hours 8:00 a.m. to 4:30 p.m. Monitors VHF 69, summer only. Gasoline, diesel, ice, frozen herring, soft drinks, snacks. Located on the east side of Thea Foss Waterway; look for the large Tacoma Fuel Dock sign. The uplands house Commencement Bay Marine Services and the Tacoma Youth Marine Center, training young people in the skills needed for work on boats and along the waterfront. A portion of fuel sales supports the Sea Scouts and Tacoma Youth Marine Center.

Hylebos Waterway. The Hylebos Waterway follows the north shore of Commencement Bay and includes a number of moorages, boat builders, and boat service businesses. The shores are lined with heavy industry of many kinds, not all of it scenic. Still, an interesting exploration.

Guest moorage is at Chinook Landing Marina, a short distance up the waterway.

㉒ **Chinook Landing Marina.** 3702 Marine View Drive Suite 100, Tacoma, WA 98422; (253) 627-7676. Monitors VHF 79. Certified Clean Marina. Open all year, guest moorage available. Snacks and ice cream at the office. This is an excellent facility, 30 & 50 amp power, restrooms, showers, laundry, free Wi-Fi, pumpout, portapotty dump, 24-hour security. Larger boats should call ahead for availability. No shops or restaurants nearby. The well-stocked J&G Marine Supply chandlery is located about a mile away.

Tyee Marina. 5618 Marine View Dr. Tacoma WA 98422; (253) 383-5321. Permanent moorage only.

Browns Point Park. Open all year, day use only. Picnic tables and a swimming beach. The lighthouse is the focal point, with free tours of the light keepers cottage on Saturdays 1:00 p.m. to 4:00 p.m., May to October. For more information call the Points Northwest Historical Society (253) 927-2536.

VASHON ISLAND, COLVOS PASSAGE, EAST PASSAGE, DES MOINES, BLAKE ISLAND

Colvos Passage. The current always flows north in Colvos Passage, so heading north on a flood tide is a good choice. Colvos Passage offers little to entice a boater to stop, although you can anchor off Olalla and dinghy to the little store for a snack.

Harper State Park. Located 1.5 miles west of the ferry landing at Southworth. Open all year, day use only. Anchoring only. The gravel launch ramp is usable at high tide only, but is the closest launch to Blake Island, 1 mile away.

Quartermaster Harbor. Quartermaster Harbor indents the south end of Vashon Island about 4 miles. It is protected on the east side by Maury Island, which connects to Vashon Island by a narrow spit of land. Dockton Park is a popular destination.

Anchorage is good throughout most of Quartermaster Harbor. Anchorage is no longer available off the village of Burton due to a field of private mooring buoys laid out by the State Department of Natural Resources (DNR). Anchorage is available farther to the east, or on the south side of Burton Peninsula.

The Quartermaster Yacht Club (members of reciprocal clubs welcomed) is at Burton, as is the Quartermaster Marina. The village of Burton has a well-stocked convenience store and several small shops. Taxi service is available on Vashon Island (Vashon Taxi (206) 434-1121).

Jensen Park, on Burton Peninsula, has a launch ramp, beach, picnic tables and barbecues. Vashon Watersports rents kayaks, canoes, and stand-up paddleboards at the park.

㉓ **Dockton Park.** 9500 SW Dock Road, Dockton, WA 98070; (206) 477-6150. Operated by King County Parks. Dockton is a popular 23-acre park on the west side of Maury Island in Quartermaster Harbor. The park has play equipment, trails, fire pits, picnic shelters, picnic tables, barbecue areas, and restrooms.

Docks at Dockton Park closed in May 2019 due to structural damage to the breakwater and finger piers. The affected areas are closed indefinitely until such time that repairs and/or dock replacements can be completed. Funds are currently being sought for improvements to the facility. A small area of the marina's main dock is open to boats for day-use on a first-come, first-serve basis free of charge. The park's land facilities and boat launch remain open.

About two blocks down 260th street, which runs eastward just above the dock, trailheads lead southward into 152-acre Dockton Forest, with one of the largest madrona forests in the area.

Anchoring Note: Holding can be fair to poor in the area north of the Dockton Park docks. If anchoring, be sure of your set.

Quartermaster Marina. 23824 Vashon Highway SW, Vashon, WA 98070; (206) 919-2318 (manager); (206) 463-3624 (office). Open all year, guest moorage in unoccupied slips. Call ahead for availability. Water, 30 & 50 amp power, restrooms, garbage drop, pumpout, Wi-Fi.

East Passage. Located between Vashon Island and the mainland. Large ships bound to or from Tacoma or Olympia use this route. Tidal currents flood south and ebb north, and normally are a little stronger in East Passage than in Colvos Passage on the west side of Vashon Island.

Dash Point State Park. 5700 SW Dash Point Rd., Federal Way, WA 98023; (253) 661-4955. Open all year, 398 acres, restrooms, showers, no power. Sandy beach, swimming, and primitive, partial utility, and full utility campsites.

Redondo. A launch ramp, with 2 floats and a floating breakwater, is operated by the city of Des Moines. Fishing pier with coffee hut. Highline Community College operates the Marine Science and Technology Center (MaST), open to the public Saturdays 10:00 a.m. to 2:00 p.m. Anchor out and take the dinghy in.

Saltwater Marine State Park. 25205 8th Place South #1, Des Moines, WA 98198; (253) 661-4956. Two miles south of Des Moines. Open all year, overnight camping. Two day-use-only mooring buoys. Restrooms, showers, no power. Artificial reef for scuba diving, and outside shower for scuba rinse-off. Sandy swimming beach. Vault toilets, primitive campsites, picnic tables and shelters, kitchen shelter, children's play equipment. Seasonal concession stand.

Maury Island Marine Park. 5405 SE 244th Street, Dockton, WA. This is a 300-acre park at the site of what once was a sand and gravel operation, 1.5 miles south of Point Robinson. Trails lead through the park. The anchorage, with fair holding, is well protected in a northerly breeze. Popular with locals. On

115

2020 WAGGONER CRUISING GUIDE   115

SOUTH AND CENTRAL PUGET SOUND

See Area Map Page 109 - Maps Not for Navigation

sunny days the winds are warmed as they cross Maury Island, making for good sunbathing. Operated by King County Parks.

Point Robinson. Point Robinson is surrounded by a 10-acre county park that can be approached by dinghy. The lighthouse is beautiful and the park has a nice beach, but no facilities for boaters.

Tramp Harbor, where Vashon Island joins Maury Island, has convenient anchoring depths, but only minimal protection from winds, particularly from the north. It is seldom used for overnight anchorage.

㉔ **Des Moines.** The City of Des Moines, between Tacoma and Seattle, is a good destination for clubs and groups. The Des Moines Marina has full services available.

Des Moines Beach Park is within easy walking distance of the marina.

㉔ **City of Des Moines Marina**. 22307 Dock Ave. S., Des Moines, WA 98188; (206) 824-5700; marinainfo@desmoinesmarina.com. The marina does not monitor VHF. Certified Clean Marina. Open all year. Gasoline, diesel, propane, 30 amp power, free Wi-Fi. Showers, no laundry. Plans are in the works to construct new shower, laundry, and office facilities. This 840-slip marina and public pier has 1500 feet of guest moorage, much of it side-tie, for boats to 100 feet. Maximum boat length in permanent slips is 62 feet. The parking lot is paid parking. Channel depth is 13 feet at zero tide. Stop at the fuel dock for directions to an empty berth. Free moorage for 4 hours. Restrooms, free showers, 2 free pumpouts. Reservations accepted for boats 32 feet and larger, or groups of 5 or more boats, 1 day in advance. Reservations also available through Dockwa.com. CSR Marine operates the repair yard, with a Travelift haulout to 25 tons.

Inside the breakwater at Des Moines Marina. Fuel dock is on the right, guest moorage on the left.

The marina can assist yacht clubs or rendezvous with planning and special needs, including free shuttle service upon request.

Des Moines Marina is the closest marina to Sea-Tac Airport. The marina can provide shuttle service to and from the airport.

The guest area has a 25×100-foot concrete activity float with shelter, and concrete moorage floats. An 80-foot-long ADA-compliant ramp available. The grounds are beautifully landscaped. Plans are underway to develop an attractive connection, with easy access, between the waterfront and downtown shops.

Services, including groceries, and several restaurants, are within walking distance of the marina. Shuttle service by request. The 670-foot public fishing pier runs east-west. To enter the marina, leave the fishing pier to port and turn to starboard at the north end of the breakwater. At low tide the entrance is tight, especially with opposing traffic. At the south end of the marina, Des Moines Yacht Club has guest moorage for visiting members of reciprocal clubs.

Farmers market on Saturdays, June through September. July 4th "Fireworks over Des Moines."

ANTHONY'S HOMEPORT RESTAURANT
421 South 227th St.
(206) 824-1947

Yukon Harbor offers good anchorage, well protected from the south but open to the northeast.

㉕ **Blake Island Marine State Park.** (360) 371-8330. Open all year, 475 acres with 1500 feet of dock space in the breakwater-protected marina. 24 mooring buoys for boats 36 feet and under ring the island. Pumpout, water, 30 amp power. No garbage drop and a "pack it in–pack it out" policy. Moorage is limited to 7 consecutive days. Buoys on the east side are exposed to wakes from passing ships. Self-register and pay mooring buoy fee on shore.

The marina is on the northeast shore of the island. To enter, follow the dredged channel marked by red and green beacons. Stay in the marked channel; the water is shoal on both sides of the beacons. Immediately inside the breakwater, one float is for the boat that

City of Des Moines Marina

SOUTH AND CENTRAL PUGET SOUND

Blake Island Marine State Park

brings guests to Tillicum on Blake Island, and another is for the State Parks boat. The rest of the floats are available on a first-come, first-serve basis. Expect to find them full during high season and on weekends year round.

Blake Island has primitive campsites, including a Cascadia Marine Trail campsite. An underwater reef is good for scuba diving. The park has picnic shelters, volleyball courts, nature trail, approximately 16 miles of hiking trails through dense forest, and 5 miles of shoreline to explore. The Tillicum restaurant venue is a replica of a Native Longhouse. It is open only when tours are scheduled, and features dinner with fish cooked on stakes facing an open fire. Tours include dinner and a show with dancing and masks, and compares favorably with the show at Alert Bay. Call Argosy Tours (888) 623-1445; (206) 623-1445. Internet search, Argosy Cruises Tillicum Excursion. Individuals arriving by private boat should call ahead for dinner reservations.

Wildlife is abundant, including a high raccoon population not fearful of people. They roam the grounds and docks day or night looking for food. As in all state parks, there is a policy not to feed the animals. Park rangers recommend securing all garbage, pet food and ice chests; yes they can open an ice chest. Do not leave hatches open or you might find an unwelcomed surprise in your salon.

Blake Island is just a short hop from Elliott Bay Marina or Shilshole Bay Marina. The park is accessible only by boat and is one of the most popular stops on Puget Sound. A gem of a park.

SEATTLE

Elliott Bay, the center of Seattle's shipping industry, is a busy ocean port. Keep a sharp watch for ferries coming and going from Colman Dock, for tugs with tows, and for commercial vessels of all kinds. Large vessels are slow to maneuver, and should always be given a wide berth. When there's any doubt at all, cross behind commercial vessels, not in front of them.

Piers 89, 90, and 91 in Smith Cove are heavily used by commercial ships. The Port of Seattle's grain terminal occupies part of the shoreline north of the regular commercial piers. Myrtle Edwards Park, including a fishing pier, stretches about a mile along the Elliott Bay waterfront. The piers on the central waterfront, too small for modern maritime commerce, have been converted to other uses, including a hotel, shops, museums, an aquarium, and places to sit and watch the harbor activity.

At Pier 36, south of the Colman ferry dock, the U.S. Coast Guard has its Seattle headquarters, including the Coast Guard Museum and Vessel Traffic Service.

Downtown Seattle is served by two excellent marinas: Elliott Bay Marina on the north shore below Magnolia Bluff, and Port of Seattle's Bell Harbor Marina at Pier 66. These two marinas make downtown Seattle easy and safe to visit.

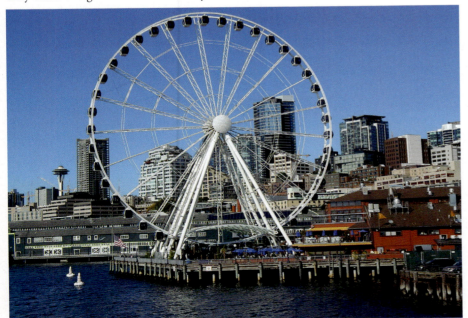
Ride the Great Wheel on the Seattle waterfront.

Seattle is often referred to as the "Boating Capital of America" and with little wonder. With abundant first-class visitor moorage, there is good reason to cruise to the Emerald City to find out what makes it so special.

Things to Do

1. Pike Place Market. Unique shops with many specialty food items, even the first Starbucks. You can see cheese being made at Beechers. Watch out for flying salmon in the market. Don't miss the nearby Olympic Sculpture Park.

2. Seattle Aquarium. See a coral reef, giant Pacific octopus, pinecone fish, and potbellied seahorses. Located at Pier 59, a few blocks south of Bell Harbor Marina.

3. Seattle Art Museum (SAM). Locally curated exhibits and rotating exhibitions from the best art collections of the world.

4. Fremont Farmers Market. Year-round on Sundays in this funky neighborhood. You never know what you might find.

5. Burke-Gilman Trail. Rent a bike and see Seattle from Shilshole to Kenmore, mostly along the city's lakefront. Some detours on streets through Ballard.

6. Seattle Center. Tour the Space Needle, or MoPop, the museum of pop culture formerly known as EMP—the Experience Music Project, and the Chihuly Garden and Glass Museum.

7. Pacific Science Center at Seattle Center. Enjoy the IMAX Theater, the Planetarium or unique exhibits. Great for kids and adults.

8. Tillicum, Blake Island. Take your boat to Blake Island State Park and make a reservation for a tribal salmon buffet dinner and show. Experience the Coast Salish people through storytelling and dance.

9. Center for Wooden Boats. Walk around the antique restored boats on South Lake Union. With membership and checkout, you can even rent a classic sailboat or powerboat for a cruise on the lake.

10. Museum of History and Industry (MOHAI). Located in South Lake Union. Many exhibits on Seattle's heritage.

11. Kenmore Air Tour. What better way to learn the islands and waterways of this spectacular cruising area than from the air? Stay local or take an extended flight from Lake Union to the San Juan Islands and back.

12. Museum of Flight. A short taxi ride away is one of the nation's best flight museums. The Concorde, WWII aircraft, a Space Shuttle Simulator, a Boeing 707 and 787, and more.

Anthony's Family of Restaurants

Anthony's family of restaurants has long been a favorite among Puget Sound boaters. Their waterfront locations are uniquely boat centric, with dedicated moorage for restaurant patrons, or are conveniently located at marinas that have transient guest space. You can boat just about anywhere in Puget Sound and not be far from an Anthony's restaurant.

Anthony's is always a sure bet, whose reputation is unsurpassed for consistently delivering quality seafood dishes, complemented with Northwest wines and local microbrews. It's not surprising they can deliver the highest quality of fresh seafood, since they manage their own wholesale seafood company, able to select the best seafood from around the Pacific Northwest, Alaska, and Hawaii.

You'll find the same high-quality meal preparation, too, no matter if you're dining at Anthony's upscale Dinner Houses, or at one of their more casual dining venues. Favorite dishes include the Alder Planked Wild Alaska Salmon, with smoked sweet red pepper beurre blanc; and the Northwest Cioppino with salmon, clams, mussels and lingcod, simmered in a tomato-herb broth. Other favorites include Mahi Mahi, Dungeness Crab Cakes, and Penn Cove Mussels. Meat lovers can choose cuts of Northwest beef, expertly prepared to your liking. And don't forget the seasonal berry creations, including strawberry lemonade, specialty cocktails, and the berry shortcake.

There are many Anthony locations throughout Puget Sound from which to choose, including Anthony's Hearthfire Grill in Olympia, Anthony's Pier 66 in Seattle, and Anthony's at Cap Sante Marina, to name a few. Casual Dining venues include Chinook's at Salmon Bay in Seattle, the Beach Café in Edmonds, and Anthony's Cabana at Anacortes, among others. Anthony's even has "To Go" Bars, like Woody's in Everett, a convenient option for a picnic or meal back at the boat.

Many of Anthony's restaurants have banquet rooms that can accommodate special celebrations, meetings, or boat club gatherings. "Finn the Food Truck," with rotating locations throughout Greater Seattle, can be booked for private special events; email finn1@anthonys.com or call (425) 531-8268. You have the option of customizing your own menu. Yes, Anthony's has come a long way since 1969, when founder Budd Gould opened his first restaurant in Bellevue, Washington.

The Gould family, consisting of several generations, along with the senior management team continue the legacy of providing quality restaurants and continue to give back to the communities in which they are located. Anthony's helps sponsor the Fishermen's Fall Festival and puts on the Seattle Fishermen's Memorial Banquet, among other worthy charitable events.

Next time your cruising Puget Sound waters, don't forget to stop at one of Anthony's restaurants to enjoy the fabulous views and fabulous food.

See Area Map Page 109 - Maps Not for Navigation   **SOUTH AND CENTRAL PUGET SOUND**

13. Seattle Zoo. An outstanding zoo for the day or an afternoon, just a cab ride away.

14. Seattle Children's Museum. Over 22,000 sq. ft. of hands-on exhibits for kids, ages 10 months to 10 years, to explore, and daily educational programs.

15. Seattle Great Wheel. Take a ride on one of Seattle's newest attractions. Great views day or night. Located at Pier 57.

㉖ **Elliott Bay Marina.** 2601 W. Marina Place, Seattle, WA 98199; (206) 285-4817; info@elliottbaymarina.net; www.elliottbaymarina.net. Monitors VHF 78A. Certified Clean Marina. This is a beautiful marina, immaculately maintained, open all year. The fuel dock has gasoline, diesel, free pumpout, and a store with convenience groceries. Contact the office for waste oil disposal. Guest moorage available in unoccupied slips for most vessels on a first-come, first-serve basis. Reservations recommended for larger vessels 50 feet and up. Contact the marina regarding availability. Boaters can submit requests for reservations through Dockwa.com for any size boat. The marina has free cable TV, 30 & 50 amp power, up to 100 amp on outside moorage; some 200 amp available. Restrooms, laundry, pumpout, free showers, free use of kayaks, SUPs and bikes, and excellent 24-hour security. Enter through either end of the breakwater.

The marina office is on the ground level of the main building, near Maggie Bluffs marina grill. Elegant dining at the Palisade restaurant is located upstairs. It's 5 minutes by cab or Uber to downtown Seattle. There is easy access to the Seattle public transportation system within walking distance.

The marina is headquarters for the Downtown Sailing Series; 10 informal races Thursday evenings during the summer, with barbecue and awards afterward.

Whole Foods Market and West Marine are about 1 mile away. A bike and walking path runs from the marina along scenic Myrtle Edwards waterfront park to the downtown waterfront. We took about an hour each way to walk between the marina and Pier 70. Seattle Yacht Club has an outstation (no reciprocal moorage) at the marina. Views of downtown, Mt. Rainier, Olympic Mountains.

㉗ **Bell Harbor Marina.** Pier 66, 2203 Alaskan Way, Seattle, WA 98121; (206) 787-3952; bhm@portseattle.org; www.portseattle.org. Monitors VHF 66A. Certified Clean Marina. Open all year, 30, 50 & 100 amp power, water, restrooms, free showers, garbage/recycling drop, pumpout, 24-hour security. Entrance at 47°36.55'N/122°20.85'W—look for the distinctive spire as a landmark. Moorage reservations can be made by telephone or email.

The Port of Seattle's Bell Harbor Marina, with 37 slips, is part of Seattle's Central Waterfront Development, and is an easy cruising destination. Depending on the mix, the docks will hold as many as 70 visitor boats, 30 feet to 70 feet. The waterfront, with the Seattle Aquarium, a variety of shops, and the Seattle Great Wheel, is just outside the marina. It's a safe, 2-block walk to the always interesting Pike Place Market.

Visitors can leave their boat at Bell Harbor and take in a game at Safeco Field for the Mariners or CenturyLink Field for the Seahawks or the Sounders. Three restaurants are just above the marina with many more restaurants and shops within walking distance.

Bell Harbor's facilities are top-notch, with excellent wheelchair access. The staff is professional and alert.

Because of rough water in Elliott Bay, the breakwater entry is narrow. Boats larger than 70 feet will find the entry and turning basin a little tight. The Port of Seattle provides approximately 1900 feet of outside pier apron devoted to large vessels including superyachts and cruise ships.

Bell Harbor Marina

Elliott Bay Marina

2201 Alaskan Way
(206) 448-6688

2020 WAGGONER CRUISING GUIDE

SOUTH AND CENTRAL PUGET SOUND See Area Map Page 109 - Maps Not for Navigation

East Waterway. Both sides of East Waterway are lined with docks for commercial vessels, most of them loading or unloading containers. The waterway is navigable to Spokane Street, where a fixed bridge and foul ground block further navigation.

West Waterway. West Waterway and the connecting Duwamish River make a splendid sightseeing voyage. Use large-scale Chart 18450.

Enter past busy Vigor Industrial shipyard (formerly Todd Shipyard) and the now-closed Lockheed Shipyard at the mouth, and motor along a fascinating variety of docks, ships, barges, small pleasure boats, mega-yachts, and abandoned hulks. Commercial buildings and the modest homes of South Park are on both sides.

You will go under the 1st Ave. S. Bridge, vertical clearance 39 feet, and past the former site of the Boeing Company's Plant 2, to the 16th Ave. S. Bridge (renamed the South Park Bridge). The famed Delta Marine facility, builder of commercial fish boats and megayachts, is a short distance beyond the 16th Ave. S. (South Park) Bridge.

Transient moorage is available at Duwamish Yacht Club (206-767-9330) for reciprocal yacht club members; one 45-foot side-tie at the end of B dock. The yacht club is located one-half mile past the 16th Ave. S. Bridge; vessel clearance 34 feet. Past Delta Marine and the Duwamish Yacht Club, a low bridge blocks progress to all but small, open boats.

Don Armeni Park and Seacrest Park are located between Harbor Island and Duwamish Head. Don Armeni Park has a 4-lane launch ramp with floats. Seacrest Park has a fishing pier.

1st Avenue South Bridge. The Duwamish Bridge, officially known as the 1st Ave. South Bridge, spans the Duwamish Waterway, carrying vehicle traffic on State Hwy 99. The two bridge spans open for marine traffic from 9:30 a.m. to 2:30 p.m. daily, including federal holidays, except Columbus Day. Bridge openings for marine traffic are not allowed Monday-Friday from 6:00 a.m. to 9:00 a.m. and 3:00 p.m. to 6:00 p.m. except for vessels of 5,000 gross tons or more.

To request an opening, call the bridge tender at (206) 764-4160, or call on VHF 13. Average opening time is 11 minutes; the far span is opened first. Vessel clearance, 39 feet.

Harbor Island Marina. 1001 Klickitat Way S.W., Seattle, WA 98134; (206) 787-3006; him@portofseattle.org; www.portofseattle.org. This Port of Seattle marina is located on the south end of Harbor Island and caters to long term tenants. No guest moorage.

South Park Marina. 8604 Dallas Ave. S, Seattle, WA 98108; (206) 762-3880; info@southparkmarina.com; www.southparkmarina.com. Moorage and dry boat storage. Repair services on site, with a team of independent service providers. Haulouts to

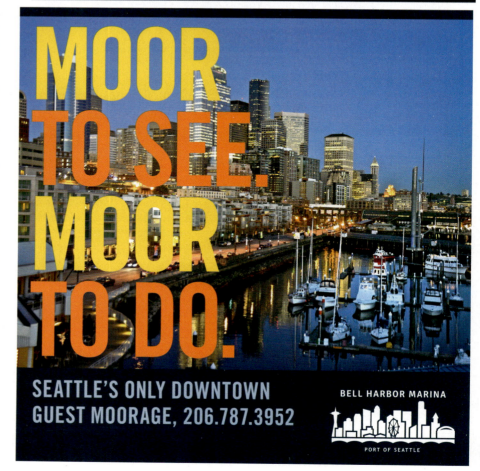

See Area Map Page 109 - Maps Not for Navigation

SOUTH AND CENTRAL PUGET SOUND

45 feet. Boat owners may do work on their own boat. 30 amp power, water, restrooms, showers, and laundry.

SHILSHOLE BAY

LOCAL KNOWLEDGE

Shallow Area: Do not stray south of the buoyed channel in Shilshole Bay. The water between the channel and Magnolia Bluff shoals rapidly.

Shilshole Bay indents the shoreline of Puget Sound north of West Point, and leads via a dredged channel to the Hiram M. Chittenden Locks (**Ballard Locks**) and the Lake Washington Ship Canal. Shilshole Bay Marina is north of the dredged channel, with entrances around the north and south ends of a long rock breakwater.

Lacking local knowledge, boats bound for the locks should follow the channel, marked by buoys, to the locks.

㉘ **Shilshole Bay Marina.** 7001 Seaview Ave. NW, Suite 100, Seattle, WA 98117; (206) 787-3006; (800) 426-7817; after hours call (206) 601-4089; sbm@portseattle.org; www.portseattle.org. Certified Clean Marina. Monitors VHF 17. Open all year, office hours 8:00 a.m. to 4:30 p.m., Monday through Saturday. This is a large, busy, well-equipped marina, operated by the Port of Seattle. The marina has guest moorage for more than 100 boats to 250 feet, 30, 50, & 100 amp power, restrooms and showers (upgraded in 2019), laundry, free cable TV on the guest docks, pumpout, portapotty dump. Take a short 1.7 mile bike ride or taxi to Ballard for shopping and a selection of dining options. Stop along the way and view the Ballard Locks. Waste oil disposal stations, recycling and garbage drop.

A complete boatyard (Seaview West) with 55-ton Travelift haulout is at the south end of the marina. The boatyard has repair-yard supplies and propane. A wide launch ramp is at the north end of the marina.

Coffee shop onsite and Duke's Seafood Restaurant. Walking distance to restaurants, a fast-food stand, and a West Marine store. Golden Gardens Park, with beach and picnic areas, is a short walk north of the marina.

The large Central Plaza, in front of the office building and adjacent to the guest docks, is nice for gatherings. Contact the office for event planning.

㉘ **Shilshole Bay Fuel Dock**. 7029 Seaview Ave. NW, Seattle, WA 98117; (206) 434-8241. Open 7 days a week except Thanksgiving and Christmas. Ethanol-free gasoline, diesel, kerosene. At the end of H dock, the Port of Seattle operates a pumpout, bilge pumpout, and portapotty dump at the outer end of the dock. Convenience store carries ice, beverages, snacks, local guidebooks. Friendly people, clean and efficient operation.

LAKE WASHINGTON SHIP CANAL

The Lake Washington Ship Canal connects the Hiram Chittenden Locks with Lake Washington, a distance of approximately 5.5 miles. Except for a marked course in the middle of Lake Union, a 7-knot speed limit is enforced all the way to Webster Point, at the entrance to Lake Washington. Most boats travel about 6 knots. If no bridge openings are needed, allow about 30 minutes between Lake Union and the locks, and about an hour between Lake Washington and the locks. The Lake Washington Ship Canal has fuel docks, ship repair yards, boatyards, and moorages. Keep an alert lookout for vessels pulling out or turning. This can be an active area.

LOCAL KNOWLEDGE

Sound Signals: For all of the bridges, the sound signal to request an opening is 1 long blast and 1 short. The bridge tender will answer with 1 long and 1 short blast if the bridge can be opened or 5 short blasts if it cannot.

Ship Canal Bridge Information. From west to east, the Lake Washington Ship Canal is crossed by the Ballard Bridge, vertical clearance 46 feet at the center; Fremont Bridge, vertical clearance 31 feet at the center; University Bridge, vertical clearance 45 feet at the center; and the Montlake Bridge, vertical

We're not just a marina.
We're a super fun destination.

SHILSHOLE BAY MARINA
PORT OF SEATTLE
Call us: 206 787 3006

2020 WAGGONER CRUISING GUIDE

SOUTH AND CENTRAL PUGET SOUND See Area Map Page 109 - Maps Not for Navigation

Shilshole Bay Marina

clearance 48 feet at the center.

Rush Hour Restricted Openings: The Ballard, Fremont and University Bridges do not open for recreational vessel traffic weekdays from 7:00 a.m. to 9:00 a.m. and 4:00 p.m. to 6:00 p.m., except holidays.

Nighttime Bridge Openings: The Ballard, Fremont and University Bridges are untended at night between 11:00 p.m. and 7:00 a.m. One crew, based at the Fremont Bridge, stands by to open bridges for vessel traffic. For openings call one hour ahead on VHF 13, or by telephone (206) 386-4251.

The Montlake Bridge is tended 24 hours a day, but between 11:00 p.m. and 7:00 a.m. vessels needing an opening must call ahead on VHF 13 or by telephone, (206) 720-3048.

㉚ **24th Avenue Landing.** At the foot of 24th Ave. NW on the north side of the Ship Canal, east of the locks. Open all year, day-use only up to 2 hours free of charge; no overnight stays. Dock has 300 feet of space, 40-foot maximum boat length. No power, water or showers. The Ballard business district is within walking distance.

㉚ **Ballard Oil Co.** 5300 26th Ave. NW, Seattle, WA 98107; (206) 783-0241; info@ballardoil.com; www.ballardoil.com. Open Monday through Saturday. Just east of the locks, on the north side of the Ship Canal. Diesel only. Set up to handle larger pleasure craft and commercial vessels.

㉛ **Salmon Bay.** The Port of Seattle's Fishermen's Terminal is located on the south side of the Lake Washington Ship Canal at Salmon Bay, a half-mile east of the locks. Although Fishermen's Terminal caters primarily to the large Seattle-based fishing fleet, guest and permanent moorage is available for pleasure craft. A short term guest float is located along the inner bulkhead at the head of the west wall, often used by boaters while dining at Chinook's restaurant. Major repair facilities are nearby, as are stores offering a variety of marine services and supplies.

㉛ **Salmon Bay Marine Center.** 2284 W. Commodore Way #100, Seattle, WA 98199; (206) 450-9100; www.sbmc.com. On the south side of the Ship Canal, this facility has 18 slips to accommodate vessels from 60 to 240 feet. Most slips are sold or on long term lease. Short term moorage for large vessels may be available by reservation. Slips are 30 feet to 45 feet wide with a minimum depth of 12 feet. Power is single and 3-phase 240/480 and 208 volt–200 amp. A 50-cycle transformer is available. Black water connection at each slip with gray water pumpout. Free Wi-Fi, parking, and 4 electric utility cars for dock use. Marine repair companies and several large yacht brokerages are in the shoreside building.

㉛ **Salmon Bay Marina/Port of Seattle.** 2100 W. Commodore Way, Seattle, WA 98199; (206) 787-3395; salmonbay@portseattle.

Hiram M. Chittenden Locks

The dredged, well-marked channel leading to the Hiram Chittenden Locks passes under the Burlington Northern bascule bridge. *Caution: Although Chart 18447 shows vertical clearance of this bridge to be 43 feet from mean high water, Local Notice to Mariners reports that the actual clearance may be closer to 41 feet. Clearance gauges have been installed at the draw.* The bridge is kept open unless a train is due. The opening signal is one long and one short blast, the same signal as for the Ballard, Fremont, University, and Montlake Bridges. Remember, though, if a train is due you will be ignored.

Your wait at the locks, in either direction, can be as short as zero or as long as several hours depending on the flow of commercial traffic.

Approaching From Puget Sound: If you are approaching from Puget Sound, you'll starboard-side tie to the wall on the south side of the channel under the railroad bridge; use gloves to protect your hands from barnacles, creosote, and tar. If traffic is heavy, as it often is at the end of fair weather summer weekends, you may end up port-side tying to the wall west of the railroad bridge. Normally, only large commercial craft tie to that wall, but if the waiting area is crowded, you may be there too. The current always flows from the lake into the Sound. Approach carefully and be ready with extra fenders. Wait your turn and do not crowd ahead. Government vessels and commercial vessels have priority over pleasure craft, and will be directed into the locks ahead of pleasure craft.

Red and green lights on the large and small locks signal when you can enter. Red light means no; green light means yes. A loud hailer system also announces directions to the traffic waiting to transit.

Lock attendants do not respond to most radio calls from pleasure craft, but if you must communicate with them, call on VHF 13, using the 1-watt low-power mode. If you need help, they will answer. If you're calling to complain, forget it.

There are two locks: a large lock 825 feet long and 80 feet wide, and a small lock 150 feet long and 30 feet wide. On a busy summer weekend, the large lock can take a half-hour or more to fill with vessels. Lock attendants will direct entering vessels to one lock or the other by light signals and the loud hailer. Each vessel should have bow and stern mooring lines at least 50 feet long with a 12-inch eye in one end. Fenders should be set out on both sides of the boat. You may be placed against the lock wall or rafted to another boat.

The lock attendants are conscientious, experienced, and helpful. They make eye contact with the helmsman of each vessel as it enters, and signal their intentions clearly. They are polite, but they give direct orders. Do exactly what they tell you to do. They have seen everything and know how to deal with problems.

If directed into the large lock, larger vessels will be brought in first and tied along the walls. Smaller vessels will raft off. Large vessel or small, be sure you have 50-foot mooring lines, bow and stern, in case you are put along the wall. The lock attendants will throw messenger lines to you. Tie your mooring lines to the messenger lines and they will take them to bollards on top of the lock wall.

There is usually some current in the locks, flowing from the lakes toward the Sound. Enter slowly but with enough speed for steerage. Once your lines are made fast, prepare to assist boats that lie alongside you. When the lock is closed and the water begins to rise, the vessels along the wall must keep a half-turn on their cleats and continuously take in slack. When the water has stopped rising, make all lines fast until you are told to leave.

If directed into the small lock, you will lie alongside a floating wall equipped with yellow-painted "buttons." Loop your bow and stern lines around the buttons, bring the lines back, and make them fast to cleats. The floating walls rise or fall with the water level, so you don't need to tend your lines during the transit. Caution: It is always possible that a floating wall could jam in its tracks. Stand by to slack your lines quickly if that happens.

When directed to do so, loosen your lines and move out of the locks slowly but with good steerage.

Approaching From The Lake: If you are westbound from the lake to the Sound, you still need 50-foot mooring lines, bow and stern, in case you lie along the wall of the large lock. However, you will be able to hand your lines to the attendant instead of tying them to messenger lines. Boats along the large lock wall will slack their lines as the water drops.

Planned 45-day LARGE LOCK closures:
February 12, 2020 – April 5, 2020
October 12, 2020 – December 3, 2020
February 12, 2021 – April 5, 2021
November 9, 2021 – November 24, 2021

SOUTH AND CENTRAL PUGET SOUND See Area Map Page 109 - Maps Not for Navigation

org; www.salmonbaymarina.com. Staff at Fishermen's Terminal respond to phone calls and email. Restrooms, showers, and laundry facilities, 30 & 50 amp power. This marina was purchased by the Port of Seattle in June of 2018 and is for full time leased moorage only. Seattle Marine & Fishing Supply, a large chandlery, is across the street. Walking distance to restaurants and Fishermen's Terminal.

㉚ **Covich-Williams Chevron.** Dock Office, 5219 Shilshole Ave. NW, Seattle, WA 98107; (206) 784-0171; www.covichwilliams.com. On the north side of the Ship Canal, next to Salmon Bay Sand & Gravel. Open weekdays 8:00 a.m. to 5:00 p.m., Saturdays until noon; closed Sundays. Gasoline, diesel, kerosene. Carries filters, absorbent products, antifreeze, environmental products, fuel additives.

㉚ **Ballard Mill Marina.** 4733 Shilshole Ave. NW, Seattle, WA 98107; (206) 789-4777; ballardmillmarina@gmail.com; www.ballardmillmarina.com. Open all year, no guest moorage, 28 to 60 feet. Restrooms, pumpout, 20 & 30 amp power, showers. East of Covich-Williams Chevron fuel dock on the north side of the Ship Canal. Free pumpout on the east dock. Stores, restaurants, marine supplies, haulout and repairs nearby.

㉛ **Fishermen's Terminal/Port of Seattle.** 3919 18th Ave. W., Seattle, WA 98119; (206) 787-3395; (800) 426-7817; ft@portseattle.org; www.portseattle.org. Monitors VHF 17, 24 hours a day, 30, 50 & 100 amp power, water, restrooms & showers, security cameras, free pumpout (sewage and bilge), recycling, waste oil dump. Major repair and supply facilities nearby. Restaurants, fish sales, shops, small grocery store, chandlery, postal service on site. The marina is on the south side of the Ship Canal, immediately west of the Ballard Bridge. Guest moorage welcomed, first-come, first-served, call for slip assignment. Make payment at building No. C15 located at 3919 - 18th Ave. West.

Dining: Chinook's at Salmon Bay is good for sit-down dining. A takeout seafood window is on the east side of the building. Tables and chairs are on the deck or in a covered area. An excellent fish market is in the front of the building. The Highliner Pub and the Bay Café also offer dining. The side-tie guest mooring float is in front of the restaurant building; complimentary 4-hour moorage.

Fishermen's Terminal

1900 W. Nickerson St.
(206) 283-4665

Lake Union is lined with ship and boat moorages, houseboat moorages, and boating related businesses. It's the center of Seattle's boat sales industry. In the middle of the lake, a speed range marked by 4 buoys, is for sea trials. Other than the speed range, a 7-knot speed limit is enforced. A launch ramp is on the north shore, east of Gas Works Park. Gas Works Park is easily identifiable by the painted remnants of an industrial coal gas plant. Tyee Yacht Club and Puget Sound Yacht Club have moorages on Lake Union. The large Fisheries Supply marine store is located near Gas Works Park. Guest moorage is limited on Lake Union.

The south end of Lake Union is the home of Northwest Seaport. Next door is the Center for Wooden Boats and lovely Lake Union Park with the Museum of History and Industry (MOHAI). Kenmore Air's seaplane base is on the southwest shore, just across from the park. Flight operations are in the center of the lake. A vertical line of lighted buoys north of the MOHAI building marks the runway. Aircraft taking off and landing will trigger flashing lights to indicate air operation. Be aware of floatplanes.

A major ship repair yard, Lake Union Drydock, is on the eastern shore near the south end of the lake. Ivar's Salmon House, a popular waterfront restaurant, is at the north end of the lake under the I-5 freeway bridge, with temporary moorage for tenders and small boats while dining.

Waggoner eBooks

The 2020 Waggoner Cruising Guide and the Ports and Passes - Tides and Currents Guide are available as eBooks.

Available by cruising areas.
Search for the books on Amazon
or WaggonerGuideBooks.com

360.299.8500 • www.WaggonerGuide.com

SOUTH AND CENTRAL PUGET SOUND

See Area Map Page 109 - Maps Not for Navigation

Morrison's fuel dock and convenience store are located at the east end of the Ship Canal where it meets Lake Union.

㉜ **Morrison's North Star Marine.** 2732 Westlake Ave. N., Seattle, WA 98109; (206) 284-6600; www.morrisonsfueldock.com. Open all year, 7 days a week. Fuel dock with ethanol-free gasoline and diesel, no guest moorage. Restrooms, free pumpout, water. Handles oil changes; call for appointment. Limited marine hardware, local charts, groceries, beer, wine, ice. Friendly and well-run.

㉜ **Nautical Landing Marina.** 2500 Westlake Ave. N., Seattle, WA 98109; (206) 464-4614; info@nautical-landing.com; www.nautical-landing.com. Open all year for permanent and guest use with 1900 feet of moorage, 30, 50 & 100 amp power, security, Wi-Fi, garbage and recycling drop. This facility is popular with superyachts and has services to match.

㉝ **MOHAI Docks** Center for Wooden Boats. Docks located in front of the Museum of History and Industry, on the south end of Lake Union, are managed by the Center for Wooden Boats (206-382-2628). The North Wall has 160 feet of side-tie moorage and one 60-foot slip. Overnight stays at $1.30 per foot. Reservations are available by phone. The Parks Department may be taking on more responsiblility for moorage along the North Wall in the near future. Two-week maximum stay. The small concrete Art Float in front of the gazebo structure is for human-powered craft only. The West Wall has 220 feet of side-tie moorage on a first-come, first-serve basis, no charge. Day-use only from sunrise to sundown. Overnight moorage is only for boats participating in special public viewings and programs.

㉝ **Chandler's Cove.** 901 Fairview Ave. N., Seattle, WA 98109. An 85-foot guest float at the north end of the pier, two-hour day moorage limit, no overnight stays. Several restaurants are in the area. It's an easy walk to the Center for Wooden Boats and the Museum of History and Industry (MOHAI).

A time-line for re-development of South Lake Union by Vulcan Inc. is currently undetermined and plans remain in limbo.

㉝ **H.C. Henry Marina.** 809 Fairview Place N., Seattle, WA 98109. Located on the south end of Lake Union. Short-term public moorage on the south side of H dock, 2-hour limit while dining at area restaurants, no overnight stays.

㉝ **Marina Mart.** 1500 Westlake Ave. N., Seattle, WA 98109; (206) 268-3322; www.marinamart.com. Permanent moorage only, no guest moorage.

Portage Bay. East of the University Bridge, vertical clearance 42 feet at the center, Portage Bay is the home of Seattle Yacht Club and Queen City Yacht Club. The University of Washington has several facilities along the north shore. The University Bridge opens to 1 long blast and 1 short.

Montlake Cut. East of Portage Bay, the Montlake Cut connects to Union Bay and Lake Washington. The cut is narrow. When boat traffic is heavy, boat wakes can be turbulent as they bounce off the concrete side walls. Slow, steady speeds are called for. The Montlake Bridge, which crosses the cut, has a vertical clearance of 46 feet at the center. The bridge opens to 1 long blast and 1 short.

Union Bay. Union Bay is just east of the Montlake Cut and connects with Lake Washington. The dredged channel is well buoyed. The University of Washington's waterfront activities center is on the north shore, and the arboretum is on the south shore. Except for the dredged channel, the bay is shoal.

LAKE WASHINGTON

Lake Washington, 16 miles long, defines the eastern border of Seattle, and washes the edges of Kenmore, Bothell, Kirkland, Medina, Bellevue, Mercer Island and Renton. Summer weekends will be busy. Watercraft of all types crisscross the lake and party-raft in the bays. Opening Day of Boating Season celebration in early May of each year fills the waters from Lake Washington to Portage Bay, with hundreds of decorated boats parading through the Montlake Cut. Seafair celebration weekend borders on madness.

The Lake Washington shoreline is filled from the waterline to the tops of the ridges with waterfront homes and mansions. Cruising the shores while admiring the elegant to modest homes is a perfect day-long experience. There is a 7-knot speed limit within 100 yards of shore, docks, and bridges throughout Lake Washington. Kirkland, Bellevue, Leschi, Madison Park, Juanita Bay, and Renton are some nice boater friendly day stops for lunch or dinner. Limited overnight guest moorage is available at marinas and public docks in Kirkland, Kenmore, Newport, and Renton. Restrictions on overnight anchoring on Lake Washington are enforced. Overnight anchoring is only allowed in Andrews Bay on the south end. At the north end of the lake, overnight anchoring is allowed in Juanita Bay; in Kenmore, off of Log Boom Park; and in fair weather, off St. Edwards Park.

See Area Map Page 109 - Maps Not for Navigation

SOUTH AND CENTRAL PUGET SOUND

Two floating bridges, I-90 and SR 520, cross Lake Washington and limit boater access to the south end of the lake with a maximum 70 feet of vertical clearance. Construction on the replacement SR 520 bridge floating span is complete. Work on the western connection to I-5 near Montlake continues. The replacement floating span does not have an opening section for boat traffic. Boat traffic passes under the fixed bridge at high-rises on either end along two navigation channels. Vertical clearance is 65 to 70 feet at the east high-rise and 42 to 49 feet at the west high-rise. Vertical clearances vary as the seasonal lake level is adjusted; higher water levels in spring and early summer, and lower levels in fall and winter. The I-90 floating bridge has a maximum vertical clearance of 34 feet at the west end and 37 feet at the east end. Least clearance at each end is 28 feet. The East Channel I-90 fixed bridge has a vertical clearance of 70 feet.

Sand Point. North from Webster Point, the first notable landmark is the former Naval Aviation base of Sand Point. Sand Point now includes Magnuson Park, which has a 2-lane launch ramp with floats. It is also the Northwest District headquarters for the National Oceanic and Atmospheric Administration (NOAA), which has a long piling pier along its north shore. Facilities west of NOAA are part of the park.

Guest moorage at the north end of Lake Washington can be found at Harbour Village Marina.

Kenmore. Kenmore offers two marinas: North Lake Marina, with permanent moorage slips, fuel dock, and repairs; and Harbour Village Marina with guest guest moorage. Kenmore is home to Kenmore Air, a major seaplane operation. Stay well clear of seaplane operating areas. Kenmore is at the mouth of the Sammamish River. Shoal water abounds. Find the buoys and stay in the dredged channel. The river is navigable by small, low, shallow-draft boats all the way to Lake Sammamish.

㉞ **Harbour Village Marina.** 6115 NE 175th St., Kenmore, WA 98028; (425) 485-7557; harbormaster@harbourvillage.net. Open all year with 400 feet of side-tie moorage on the outside of the breakwater. Office hours vary. 30 & 50 amp power, restrooms, and showers. Reservations online at www.dockwa.com. Caution for shallow water; follow the marked charted channel until abeam the marina.

㉞ **North Lake Marina.** 6201 NE 175th St., Kenmore, WA 98028; (425) 482-

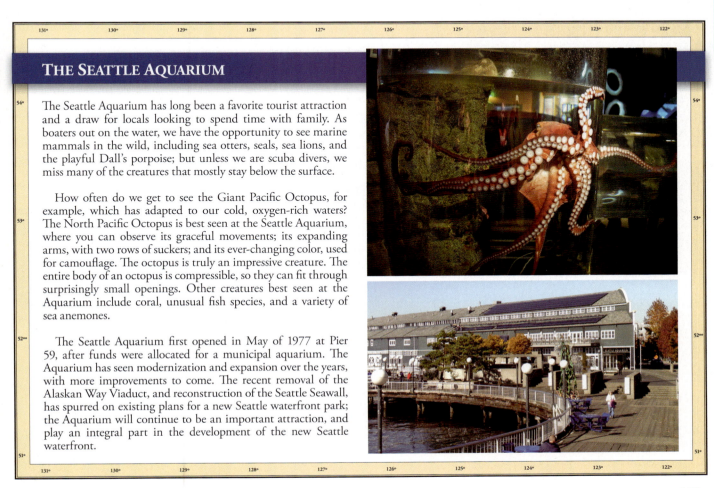

THE SEATTLE AQUARIUM

The Seattle Aquarium has long been a favorite tourist attraction and a draw for locals looking to spend time with family. As boaters out on the water, we have the opportunity to see marine mammals in the wild, including sea otters, seals, sea lions, and the playful Dall's porpoise; but unless we are scuba divers, we miss many of the creatures that mostly stay below the surface.

How often do we get to see the Giant Pacific Octopus, for example, which has adapted to our cold, oxygen-rich waters? The North Pacific Octopus is best seen at the Seattle Aquarium, where you can observe its graceful movements; its expanding arms, with two rows of suckers; and its ever-changing color, used for camouflage. The octopus is truly an impressive creature. The entire body of an octopus is compressible, so they can fit through surprisingly small openings. Other creatures best seen at the Aquarium include coral, unusual fish species, and a variety of sea anemones.

The Seattle Aquarium first opened in May of 1977 at Pier 59, after funds were allocated for a municipal aquarium. The Aquarium has seen modernization and expansion over the years, with more improvements to come. The recent removal of the Alaskan Way Viaduct, and reconstruction of the Seattle Seawall, has spurred on existing plans for a new Seattle waterfront park; the Aquarium will continue to be an important attraction, and play an integral part in the development of the new Seattle waterfront.

2020 WAGGONER CRUISING GUIDE

SOUTH AND CENTRAL PUGET SOUND

See Area Map Page 109 - Maps Not for Navigation

9465; susan@northlakemarina.com; www.northlakemarina.com. Open all year, closed weekends November through March. Ethanol-free gasoline at the fuel dock, no diesel. Permanent moorage only, no guest space. Parts, accessories, ice. Complete repairs available. Haulout to 20 tons.

Logboom Park. North shore of Lake Washington, Kenmore. Open all year, day use only moorage. Restrooms, no power, no showers. Trails, fishing pier, children's play equipment, picnic areas, and outdoor cooking facilities. The park is on the Burke-Gilman Trail, a walking and cycling trail that runs from Lake Union to the Sammamish River Trail. Note: Docks are in a state of disrepair and may be unsafe. Anchoring south of the park for up to 72 hours is allowed, watch for shallow water.

Saint Edward State Park. 14445 Juanita Drive NW, Kenmore, WA 98028; (425) 823-2992. Located on the northeast shore of Lake Washington, this 326-acre day-use park has trails and picnicking. Anchoring is possible off the park in fair weather for up to 72 hours. Beach landing only. A playground is located at the top of the bluff. A park pass can be purchased at the automated pay station. The historic brick building on the grounds served as a Catholic seminary in the 1930s, with hundreds of students in residence.

Juanita Bay. Anchorage for up to 72 hours is possible in Juanita Bay, which shoals gradually toward all shores. In nice summer weather, the bay is a crowded, popular, party-rafting destination. Off-season, the bay is quieter. The waterfront city park and estuary, at the head of the bay, provide paddling and beach-landing opportunities.

Kirkland. Kirkland is an outstanding cruising destination. The City of Kirkland's Marina Park visitor docks are well maintained, and connect directly with downtown. A good launch ramp is immediately north of the docks. If you enjoy tree-lined streets, superb dining, interesting boutiques and upscale galleries, you will not be disappointed. Kirkland is prosperous and it shows.

Next to Marina Park is the Kirkland Homeport Marina, which is primarily full-time, leased moorage; www.kirklandhomeportmarina.com.

A mile south of Marina Park is privately-owned Carillon Point Marina, with some guest moorage and access to restaurants and other businesses. Several restaurants in the area have their own docks for patrons.

㉟ **Marina Park.** 25 Lakeshore Plaza Drive, Kirkland, WA 98033; (425) 587-3300; www.kirklandwa.gov. Launch ramp adjacent. Open all year, 90 guest slips, restrooms, 30 amp power in some slips, Wi-Fi. No showers. This is a large and popular Lake Washington destination. Moorage is first-come, first-served and paid through electronic public pay stations located on the dock. Between 8:00 a.m. and 10:00 p.m. the first 3 hours free, ticket provided at pay station. Excellent access to downtown Kirkland. Nearby groceries, ice, and post office.

Use of the launch ramp can be purchased for a fee (each way) at the on-site pay station; a bollard in front of the ramp will lower upon payment. A key card for the season can be purchased from the city office at 123-Fifth Avenue. Use of the ramp is free from November 1st through March 31st. For additional information call (425) 587-3300.

Guest moorage can also be found along 150 feet of side-tie on the Second Avenue South Dock (Anthony's Restaurant), managed by the city. Check with Anthony's Restaurant for moorage while dining. The dock is located on the south side of a private marina. Make payment at the public pay station at the Marina Park.

ANTHONY'S HOMEPORT RESTAURANT
135 Lake Street South
(425) 822-0225

㊱ **Carillon Point Marina.** 4100 Carillon Point, Kirkland, WA 98033; (425) 822-1700; www.carillon-point.com. Certified Clean Marina. Open all year, guest moorage, 30 &

PACIFIC FIBERGLASS, INC.
Haulouts, Repair, Rejuvenation
(206) 789-4690

Whole Boat Care
Your boat is a lot more than fiberglass and so is our expertise. Sure, we'll fix your fiberglass or do the best LPU paint job. *And* take care of a mechanical issue like the steering system on this 47-footer. We'll get you back on the water.

On the Ship Canal at Canal Boatyard.
(206) 789-4690 • pacificfiberglass.com

SHIP CANAL BRIDGE OPENINGS

BRIDGE	HEIGHT	CLOSED HOURS	
Burlington-Northern Railroad Bridge	43 feet MHW		
Ballard Bridge	46 feet at center	Weekdays 0700-0900, 1600-1800 and Special Events	1-hour notice 2300-0700
Fremont Bridge	31 feet at center	Weekdays 0700-0900, 1600-1800 and Special Events	1-hour notice 2300-0700
University Bridge	45 feet at center	Weekdays 0700-0900, 1600-1800 and Special Events	1-hour notice 2300-0700
Montlake Bridge	48 feet at center	May 1- Aug. 31: Weekdays 0700-0900, 1530-1800; Sept. 1-April 30: Weekdays 0700-1000, 1530-1900	May 1-Aug 31: 1230-1530 and 1800-1830 opens only on the hour and half hour
SR 520 *West End*	44 feet	SR 520 replacement bridge no longer has an opening span.	
SR 520 *East End*	65 feet 70 feet	on the shore side of the channel on the deep water side of the channel	

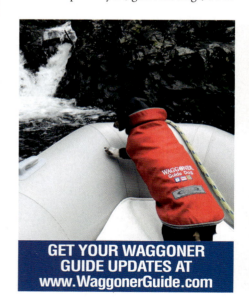

GET YOUR WAGGONER GUIDE UPDATES AT
www.WaggonerGuide.com

50 amp power, Wi-Fi, restrooms, showers, pumpout, portapotty dump. The public pier on the north end of the marina has 150 to 200 feet of side-tie, 2-hour tie-ups at no charge. The inside of the pier is for boats 32 feet and under and the outside of the pier is for larger vessels. Overnight moorage in unoccupied slips as available. This is a nice marina adjacent to a high-quality hotel with restaurants, spa, and shopping. Downtown Kirkland is 1.5 miles away by road.

㊱ **Yarrow Bay Marina.** 5207 Lake Washington Blvd. NE, Kirkland, WA 98033; (425) 822-6066; service@yarrowbaymarina.com; www.yarrowbaymarina.com. Open all year with ethanol-free gasoline and diesel, no guest moorage. Marine parts, restrooms, pumpout, haulout and repairs.

Cozy Cove and Fairweather Bay. Cozy Cove and Fairweather Bay are entirely residential, but anchorage is possible.

Meydenbauer Bay. Meydenbauer Bay is the home of Bellevue Marina and the Meydenbauer Bay Yacht Club, which has some moorage for reciprocal clubs. Meydenbeauer Beach Park underwent extensive renovation in 2017 and 2018. Downtown Bellevue, with outstanding shopping, is nearby. Anchorage is possible in Meydenbauer Bay, although the water is deeper than most pleasure craft prefer. The marina off Beaux Arts Village, a short distance south of Meydenbauer Bay, is reserved for Beaux Arts residents.

Bellevue Marina. 99th Avenue NE, Bellevue, WA 98004; (425) 443-1090 Dock Master. Small boat visitor moorage between Pier 2 and Pier 3, day use only up to 4 hours between 8:00 a.m. and 9:00 p.m. daily. Seasonal portable toilets. City park Rangers monitor the facilities.

Montlake Cut on Opening Day of Boating Season is a colorful parade of boating revelry.

Luther Burbank Park. 2040 84th Avenue SE, Mercer Island, WA 98040; www.mercergov.org. Open all year, day use only, dock space for 30 or more boats. Restrooms, no power, no showers. No anchoring. Park has picnic areas, swimming areas, trails, tennis courts, amphitheater.

East Channel Bridge. The I-90 fixed bridge over the East Channel on the east side of Mercer Island, has a vertical clearance of 65 feet.

㊲ **Newport Shores.** 3911 Lake Washington Blvd. SE, Bellevue, WA 98006; (425) 641-2090; www.seattleboat.com. Newport Shores has a large private marina (Seattle Boat-Newport), with an adjacent public launch ramp and fuel dock. Open all year, call or visit website for hours. Fuel dock with gasoline and diesel, located just south of the I-90 East Channel Bridge at Newport Yacht

Cruise with New Friends

Join us for a fun-filled passage to
Desolation Sound, The Broughtons, and to Ketchikan.

We organize activities along the way and teach you more about weather and how to cruise the area. Most of all, we have a lot of fun cruising and dining together. We take you to the best places along the way too.

Ask about our flotillas in the British Virgin Islands.

360.299.8500 • www.WaggonerGuide.com

Carillon Point, Kirkland

SOUTH AND CENTRAL PUGET SOUND
See Area Map Page 109 - Maps Not for Navigation

Gene Coulon park, with launch ramps, dockside eateries, and day-use moorage

Basin; snacks, beverages, and ice. Complete repairs available. Marine supplies and parts, new and used boats, self-serve storage. Haulout to 35 tons.

㊳ **Gene Coulon Memorial Beach Park.** 1201 Lake Washington Blvd., Renton, WA 98055; (425) 430-6700; www.rentonwa.gov. Open all year, day use only. Slips for small boats and side-tie for larger vessels. Restrooms, showers, no power. Pay at the automated pay box. Showers in summer only, at the swim center. Ivar's and Kidd Valley restaurants in the park. Eight lanes for boat launching, very well organized, credit and debit cards only. No overnight parking in winter. This is a big, attractive, and much-used park with picnic shelters, playground equipment, tennis courts, horseshoe pits, volleyball courts, grassy areas and beaches. It has a fishing pier and a paved walkway along the water. Popular with everyone, especially families. Located on the southeast shore of Lake Washington, next to Boeing's Renton 737 complex.

Rainier Beach. Has a launch ramp and a private marina. It is the home of the Rainier Yacht Club. Limited guest moorage for visiting members of reciprocal clubs.

Andrews Bay. 5895 Lake Washington Blvd. S., Seattle, WA 98118; (206) 684-4396; www.seattle.gov. Andrews Bay is a popular anchoring spot, with room for many boats. Nestled in between Seward Park on Bailey Peninsula and the mainland, it is one of the few authorized pleasure boat anchorages in Lake Washington. Signs on the Seward Park shoreline mark the anchorage area, denoted by buoys marked with the letter "A". Put the hook down in 25 to 50 feet, excellent mud bottom, 72-hour maximum stay in a 7-day period. There is a 3 knot speed limit in Andrews Bay. A Seattle Parks swim area with bathhouse and lifeguards is at the head of the bay. A large grassy playfield is adjacent. Miles of trails lead through dense forest. Excellent stop, especially for families.

㊴ **Lakewood Moorage.** 4400 Lake Washington Blvd. S., Seattle, WA 98118; (206) 475-6559; www.seattle.gov. Open all year. No guest moorage. Permanent moorage only.

Stan Sayers Memorial Park. www.seattle.gov. Open all year. Temporary, day use moorage only, not enough depth for larger boats. Restrooms, no power, no showers. Launch ramp with boarding floats. Tie up to the floats. This is the pit area for hydroplanes during the annual Seafair races.

RICH PASSAGE, PORT ORCHARD, BREMERTON, SILVERDALE

LOCAL KNOWLEDGE

HEAVY TRAFFIC: Rich Passage is the ferry route between Seattle and Bremerton. Keep a sharp lookout ahead and astern and stay well clear of the ferries. Naval vessels also use Rich Passage to and from the Bremerton Naval Shipyard.

Rich Passage is winding but well-buoyed. From the west entrance, the city of Bremerton and the Naval Shipyard are clearly visible. For security reasons, stay well off the Naval facilities.

Currents run to 2 knots at the east entrance and 5.5 knots at the west entrance, flooding west and ebbing east.

Manchester State Park. 7767 E. Hilldale, Port Orchard, WA 98366; (360) 902-8844; www.parks.wa.gov. Open 7 days a week year-round; 111 acres, day use and overnight camping. Restrooms, showers, no power. Anchoring only; a bit rough because of boat traffic in Rich Passage. Park is in a shallow cove, good for wading in summer and scuba diving offshore. Picnic tables and shelters with fireplaces, campsites, nature and hiking trails. Old gun battery and emplacements are fun to explore.

㊵ **Port of Manchester.** P.O. Box 304, Manchester, WA 98353; (360) 871-0500; www.portofmanchester.com. Open all year, 400 feet of guest dock space, restroom, no overnight moorage. Dock can be dry on zero or minus tide. A launch ramp is adjacent to the dock. Overnight parking allowed. No power or other facilities at the dock. A restaurant and pub are a short walk away.

Fort Ward Park. 2241 Pleasant Beach, Bainbridge Island, WA 98110; (206) 842-2306; www.biparks.org. Open all year. Anchorage is exposed to wind and wakes from passing boat traffic. Toilets, launch ramp and hiking trails. Because of strong currents in Rich Passage, the underwater park is for expert scuba divers only. Bird watching from 2 bird blinds. Remains of historic fort emplacements to explore. No camping.

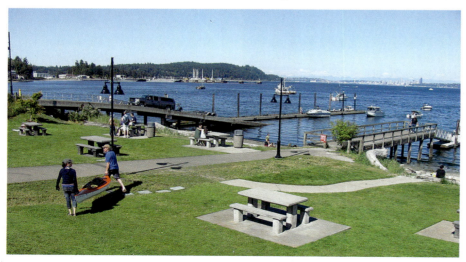
Manchester has an inviting sandy beach, day-use moorage, and spectacular views of Seattle.

See Area Map Page 109 - Maps Not for Navigation   **SOUTH AND CENTRAL PUGET SOUND**

Port Orchard. The city of Port Orchard has long been a popular destination for Puget Sound boaters. It has a number of marinas that welcome visiting boats, including one, Port Orchard Marina, that is operated by the Port of Bremerton. Port Orchard Yacht Club, which welcomes visiting reciprocal yachts, is west of the Port Orchard Marina. Several other marinas have permanent moorage. Anchorage is in 50 to 60 feet, mud bottom. A passenger ferry runs between Port Orchard and Bremerton. Water Street boat launch has long term parking for tow vehicles and trailers.

Downtown Port Orchard has several antique and collectibles shops, and restaurants. Seasonal farmers market, 9:00 a.m. to 3:00 p.m. on Saturdays, mid-April through mid-October. The Port Orchard Public Market is open daily with a variety of local food and beverage vendors. Concerts by the Bay are held at Marina Waterfront Park June through September.

Besides a walkable waterfront featuring family friendly activities, playgrounds, parks and an array of excellent dining and shopping options, there are many events and festivals year round, www.exploreportorchard.com.

㊶ **Port Orchard Marina.** 707 Sidney Pkwy., Port Orchard, WA 98366; (360) 876-5535; kathyg@portofbremerton.org; www.portofbremerton.org. Certified Clean Marina. Monitors VHF 66A. Enter the marina around the west end of the breakwater. The entrance is marked with navigation lights. Open 7 days a week all year, except for fall/winter holidays. Gasoline and diesel at the fuel dock, guest moorage in 50 slips (40-foot), and side-tie moorage along 1500 feet of inside breakwater with another 1500 feet available on the outside. The marina is well-managed and well-maintained, with clean restrooms and beautiful landscaping.

The marina has 30 amp power, water, restrooms, laundry, free showers, free pumpout, portapotty dump, and free Wi-Fi. An excellent children's play area is at the north end of the marina grounds. This is one of Puget Sound's popular destinations. Reservations accepted, 4 hours of day use free. It's one block to downtown Port Orchard. Repairs are nearby. Shuttle service by appointment.

Bremerton. The Bremerton waterfront was redeveloped several years ago and offers excellent facilities. The Bremerton Harborside Kitsap Conference Center, with a Starbucks, Anthony's Restaurant, and Cold Stone Creamery, overlooks the marina. The Hampton Suites Hotel is next door. Bremerton is doing its best to shed a dowdy image and make a name for itself.

Points of interest include the Naval Museum, the historic destroyer USS Turner Joy, and the attractive city boardwalk. Many boaters take the passenger ferry for the 10- to 12-minute ride to Port Orchard, where the dining, the seasonal farmers market, antiques shopping,

Port Orchard Marina

and boutiques are popular. Bremerton Marina is secured by a locked gate. Kitsap County buses in the adjacent transportation center can take you anywhere you wish to go, or take the ferry to downtown Seattle.

There is always something happening in Bremerton with its line-up of festivals and concerts. The Blackberry Festival is held Labor Day weekend, with booths ashore selling wonderful blackberry treats and more. We just happened to be there, and the festival was a hoot.

Located northeast of Bremerton, across Washington Narrows, is the popular Boat Shed restaurant (360-377-2600) adjacent to the Manette Bridge. The restaurant's 50-foot guest float is available while dining at the Boat Shed. Be prepared with fenders and lines. Current can run swiftly through Washington Narrows so plan accordingly.

LOCAL KNOWLEDGE

STRONG CURRENTS: Tidal currents can make boat handling tricky in Bremerton Marina. It is best to time arrival and departure to coincide with slack water.

㊷ **Bremerton Marina.** 120 Washington Beach, Bremerton, WA 98367; (360) 373-1035; kathyg@portofbremerton.org. www.portofbremerton.org. Monitors VHF 66A. Certified Clean Marina. Located next to the ferry dock. Open all year, except for fall/winter holidays. Guest moorage in 80 to 100 slips and 990 feet inside of side-tie dock space, 30 & 50 amp power, water, garbage, restrooms, free showers, laundry, free Wi-Fi, 2 portapotty dumps. Shuttle service by appointment. No fuel is available. The nearest fuel dock is at Port Orchard.

This quality marina has excellent docks and a breakwater to protect against ferry wakes. Fountain Park, a short walk to the other side

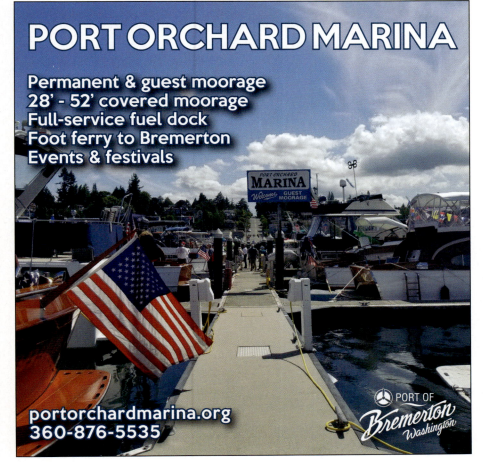

2020 WAGGONER CRUISING GUIDE

SOUTH AND CENTRAL PUGET SOUND

See Area Map Page 109 - Maps Not for Navigation

of the ferry dock, is lovely. The dramatic fin-like sculptures are fountains meant to resemble the superstructure (called the sail) of a modern submarine.

Washington Narrows connects Sinclair Inlet with Dyes Inlet. The narrows are crossed by two bridges with a minimum vertical clearance of 80 feet. Tidal currents, averaging over 2 knots, flood west and ebb east. Signs ask boaters to maintain minimum speed to reduce wake damage to the shore and to boats moored at the marina. A launch ramp with float and fishing pier is on the north side of the narrows about halfway along, part of the Lebo Street Recreation Area.

Bridgeview Marina. (360) 876-2522; Permanent moorage only, no transient space; pumpout is for moorage customers only.

Phinney Bay. Phinney Bay is the home of the Bremerton Yacht Club, with guest moorage for visiting reciprocal boats. Anchorage is good throughout the bay, which shoals toward each shore.

Ostrich Bay. Ostrich Bay offers good anchorage, mud bottom. The most popular anchorage is along the west side of the bay, facing dense forest. We have spent several pleasant nights at this spot. For some reason this entire area is overlooked. Even when the docks at Port Orchard and Bremerton are full on summer holiday weekends, Ostrich Bay has been almost empty.

Caution: Unexploded ordnance from years ago, when the Navy pier was used for loading munitions, has been found in the bay, especially in the vicinity of the pier.

Oyster Bay. A narrow but easily-run channel leads off Ostrich Bay into Oyster Bay, where perfectly protected anchorage is available toward the center of the bay. To enter, keep between the lines of mooring buoys and mooring floats on both sides of the channel. The channel shoals to about 6 feet at zero tide. Oyster Bay is surrounded by homes.

Dyes Inlet indents the Kitsap Peninsula northwest of Bremerton. Silverdale is on the north shore of Dyes Inlet and has a marina, waterfront park, boat ramp, and boardwalk. Dyes Inlet is connected to Sinclair Inlet via Port Washington Narrows.

㊸ **Silverdale Marina** (Port of Silverdale). P.O. Box 310, Silverdale, WA 98383; (360) 698-4918; portofsilverdale@wavecable.com; www.portofsilverdale.com. Open all year. Guest moorage along 1300 feet of wide, side-

Bremerton Marina

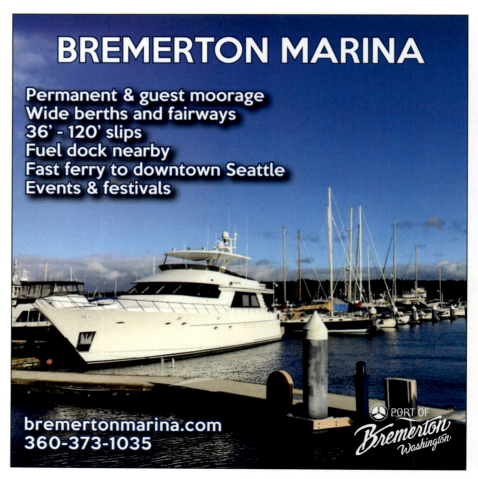

tie dock with a least depth of 10 feet at zero tide. No rafting. Moorage is on the honor system, but confirmed by security patrols that record the moored boats. Three-night maximum stay. Group reservations accepted online for a $75 fee. Restrooms, 30 amp power, seasonal potable water, pumpout, showers, 2-lane concrete launch ramp. No long-term parking. The pumpout operates 8:00 a.m. to 10:00 p.m., weekends, May to October.

The marina is adjacent to county-run Silverdale Waterfront Park. The park has picnic tables, restrooms, fire pits, children's play area, pavilion and a Veterans Memorial. Interesting shops and dining are in adjacent Old Town Silverdale. Complete shopping is at the Kitsap Mall about a mile away. The Trails shopping center is about 1.5-miles away. The nearby Clear Creek Trail & Interpretive Center is a good walk.

Whaling Days, a 3-day celebration the last weekend of July, draws big crowds, both from land and the water. Plan to anchor out. If you're on the dock, expect to be included in the carnival atmosphere. It's a big fair with live bands all weekend, activities for kids, outrigger canoe races, a fun run and more. See their website at www.whalingdays.com. Silverdale hosts the Kitsap Peninsula Water Trails Festival during the fourth weekend in June. Events include a 50K triathlon, kayak races, and waterfront activities.

BROWNSVILLE, POULSBO, NORTHERN PORT ORCHARD

Northern Port Orchard separates Bainbridge Island from the Kitsap Peninsula. Rich Passage and Sinclair Inlet are at the south end; Agate Passage is at the north. Brownsville and Poulsbo are the major marina destinations. The Agate Passage bridge has a vertical clearance of 75 feet. Currents in Agate Passage run to 6 knots on spring tides, flooding south and ebbing north.

Port of Brownsville

Bremerton harborside boardwalk leads to the USS Turner Joy.

LOCAL KNOWLEDGE

ROCK: A nasty rock, almost awash at zero tide, is inshore from the mooring buoys at Illahee Park, approximately between the buoy nearest the dock and shore. Thanks to Correspondents Al & Becca Szymanski, S/V Halona, for the report.

㊹ **Illahee Marine State Park.** 3540 NE Bahia Vista Drive, Bremerton, WA 98310; (360) 478-6460. Located 3 miles northeast of Bremerton. Open all year, mooring and overnight camping. Guest moorage with 356 feet of side-tie dock space, 5 mooring buoys for boats 45 feet and under. Restrooms and showers, no power. The dock is protected by a floating concrete breakwater. Park has 3 kitchen shelters, picnic tables, campsites, horseshoe pits, ball field, hiking trails, and portable toilet. Popular for fishing and sunbathing. Most services are in the upland area, reached by a steep trail.

㊺ **Port of Brownsville.** 9790 Ogle Rd. NE, Bremerton, WA 98311; (360) 692-5498; jerry@portofbrownsville.org; www.portofbrownsville.org. Certified Clean Marina. Monitors VHF 16, switch to 66A. Open all year, 7 days a week. Fuel dock has

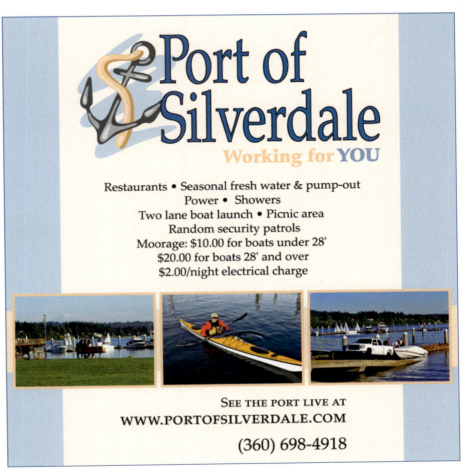

SOUTH AND CENTRAL PUGET SOUND See Area Map Page 109 - Maps Not for Navigation

The Port of Brownsville Marina is a popular venue for club events.

ethanol-free gasoline, diesel, and propane. Guest moorage in 25 24-foot slips, 20 40-foot slips, and 550 feet of side-tie moorage along the breakwater, 30 & limited 50 amp power, free Wi-Fi, restrooms, showers, laundry, book exchange, free pumpout, portapotty dump, in-slip pumpout service (MV Ms le Pew). Paved 2-lane launch ramp with ample parking.

Up on the wharf, a covered picnic/gathering pavilion, with tables, is inviting. Additional picnic tables are on the docks and in Burke Bay Overlook Park above the wharf, with barbecue. This is a popular destination for club cruises. Group reservations invited.

A breakwater marks the entrance to the marina. The channel and area around the fuel dock has been dredged to 9 feet at minus tide and well marked with green buoys to port on entrance, so you don't have to hug the south side of the dock. The Deli has snacks, beer, and wine selection. They make take-out food and can cater a gathering. This is a pleasant, friendly marina.

Groceries are available a short walk (city block) up the road at the Daily Stop.

Brownsville Appreciation Day: Fourth Saturday of September. Folksy and fun, small community at its best. Classic boats and cars, treasure hunt, unicycles, hot dogs and hamburgers. All proceeds (not just profits) divided among the local elementary schools.

Savory Treat: A short walk up the road from the marina, Sweeney's Country Meats has mouth-watering specialty meats. We tried a marinade jerky and some of the bacon. All were delicious and well worth a visit.

㊻ **Port of Keyport Marina.** P.O. Box 195, Keyport, WA 98345; (541) 760-0176; www.portofkeyport.com. Concrete docks with five 50-foot slips for guest moorage, first-come, first-served. Water, 30 amp power. No restrooms. Six hours free, 3-day maximum stay. Be mindful of the current when approaching the dock. Boat launch ramp. Make payment at the Keyport Mercantile, located upland. There are several restaurants in the area, and the must-see Naval Undersea Museum (360-396-4148).

A pedestrian gate, open 10:00 a.m. to 4:00 p.m., is about a quarter of a mile straight up Washington Street from the dock. The gate leads onto the Naval Base and the Naval Undersea Museum. You can view a simulation of a nuclear fast attack submarine, torpedoes and torpedo tubes, a Confederate mine from the Civil War, and learn the history of naval diving. The museum is open daily. Admission is free.

Fletcher Bay. Fletcher Bay is shallow and not a good anchorage.

㊼ **Manzanita Bay.** Manzanita Bay is a good overnight sheltered anchorage for Seattle-area boats. The bay is all residential and has no public facilities, but the holding ground is excellent. Observe the 5-knot no-wake speed limit beginning halfway down the bay. Although the bay is lined with lovely homes, the surrounding hills give a feeling of seclusion.

At the north end of the bay, Manzanita Landing, a former Mosquito Fleet landing, provides access to the trail system of Manzanita Park. From the landing take Manzanita Road NE to NE Day Road West. Walk east to the park, which is on the left (north) side of the street.

Liberty Bay. The entrance to Liberty Bay is past the Keyport Naval torpedo research and testing facility and around Lemolo Point. The Navy requests boats travel at no-wake speed past its facility. A power cable with 90-foot clearance crosses overhead. A sign on the beacon off Lemolo Point asks boaters to slow down in all of Liberty Bay; buoys post the speed limit. Much of Liberty Bay is covered by Wi-Fi. Three major marinas are along the north shore of Liberty Bay: a private marina; the Poulsbo Yacht Club; and the Port of Poulsbo Marina.

The private marina has no guest moorage. At the Poulsbo Yacht Club, reciprocal moorage is along the northwest perimeter of the floating breakwater. Some reciprocal moorage is still available on the inside of the older breakwater.

㊽ **Poulsbo.** Poulsbo, on Liberty Bay, is one of the most popular destinations on Puget Sound, partly because it is close to the major population centers, and partly because it is such a delightful place to visit. Settled originally by Scandinavians, the downtown business district still loudly (to say the least) maintains its Norwegian heritage. Everything most visitors need is available either near the

Poulsbo

134 www.WaggonerGuide.com

water or at the malls located on the highway about a mile away.

The waterfront portions of Poulsbo make for a lovely walk. Victorian homes and gardens have been restored and preserved to perfection.

Restaurants, bakeries and many shops that specialize in gifts, collectibles and home accessories are a few steps away in downtown Poulsbo. Dining and shopping are popular. Sluys Poulsbo Bakery, Boehm's chocolates and Mora's Ice Creamery are favorites. Longship Marine (360-779-2378) is one of the few remaining second-hand marine stores offering marine supplies and woodworking materials. The store is located in a historic building on the lower level, with an entrance that faces the marina. The interior has been beautifully remodeled. The store's previous location, next door on Anderson Parkway, is now a housewares shop.

The nearby Poulsbo Marine Science Center is fun for families. Don't miss the Maritime Museum on Front Street, showcasing the rich maritime history of Poulsbo and the Mosquito Fleet that transported supplies, mail and people to and from the islands. Special events include the Saturday Farmers Market, May - October; Viking Fest, 3rd weekend in May; Scandinavian Midsommer Fest, June; 3rd of July Celebration; Traditional Street Dance, August; Yule Fest, December and the Chip Hanauer Winter Rendezvous held the second weekend in February.

Looking for a great day trip or a weekend getaway? Look no further, Poulsbo has it all.

㊽ **Poulsbo Marina / Port of Poulsbo.** 18809 Front St., P.O. Box 732, Poulsbo, WA 98370; (360) 779-9905; (360) 779-3505 ext. 1 (for reservations) office@portofpoulsbo.com; reservations@portofpoulsbo.com (for reservations); www.portofpoulsbo.com. Monitors VHF 66A. Open 7 days a week, all year, except Christmas Day and New Year's Day. Register by 4:00 p.m. to get the combination for the showers and restrooms. The fuel dock has ethanol-free gasoline and diesel. The marina has 130 guest slips, 10-foot depths at low tide, and 30 amp ELCI-protected power on all docks. Side-tie on the end of E dock. The Port utilizes available permanent slips for guest moorage when available. Reservations accepted but may be limited during special events. Good restrooms and showers, laundry, pumpout, portapotty dump, launch ramp, free Wi-Fi. A meeting room and activity float are available. Groceries, fine restaurants and shops within walking distance.

If anchored out, dinghy tie-up is on the shore side of the dock closest to shore.

Agate Passage connects Port Orchard with Port Madison, and is crossed by a highway bridge with a vertical clearance of 75 feet. Currents in the pass run as high as 6 knots at spring tides, flooding south and ebbing north. The channel through the pass is well marked, but in general, a mid-channel course will serve. For some reason, many craft go through Agate Passage too fast, creating havoc for slower craft. Agate Passage isn't very long. Keep the speed down, look astern to judge your wake, and give fellow boats a break.

PORT MADISON AND BAINBRIDGE ISLAND

Miller Bay. Miller Bay indents the Northwest corner of Port Madison. It is very shallow and should be entered only at half tide or better, or with local knowledge. Like many bays on Puget Sound, Miller Bay has a drying shoal in the middle, so navigable water can be found only around the perimeter.

Mattson's Bay Marine. 20622 Miller Bay Rd. NE, Poulsbo, WA 98392; (360) 598-4900; mattsonsbaymarine@gmail.com. Open Tuesday through Saturday all year. Haulout to 30 feet, parts and complete repairs. Launch ramp, dry storage.

Suquamish. Suquamish is best known as the winter home of Chief Seattle and the former site of his Longhouse, the Old Man House village. With its restaurant and other cultural attractions, it makes a good day trip from Seattle.

The Suquamish community dock and float, just north of Agate Pass, provides short-term moorage for visiting boats. The east side of the float is exposed to chop from boat traffic and weather in outer Port Madison. If the protected space on the west side is not available, boaters can anchor and take the dinghy to the float. Good anchorage is northeast of the float. A boat ramp is south of the float; it's not usable at low tide.

Today, the town of Suquamish is the center of the Suquamish Indian Reservation. A community center across the street from the dock is patterned after the Old Man House. The Suquamish Museum is up the hill.

Visible above the community center is an impressive veterans memorial, with carved figures honoring Chief Kitsap, Chief Seattle, and Suquamish veterans.

From the veterans memorial, follow signs to Chief Seattle's grave in the Suquamish Tribal Cemetery behind the white church of St. Peter's Catholic Mission. The original gravestone placed by Seattle pioneers is still there, along with more recent Native carvings and inscriptions of Chief Seattle's words.

From Chief Seattle's grave, continue walking uphill to the Suquamish Museum. The museum is open 10:00 a.m. to 5:00 p.m., daily.

Since 1911, the Suquamish Tribe has been celebrating Chief Seattle Days on the third weekend of August. Activities include a traditional salmon bake, canoe races, baseball, drumming and dancing, and a memorial service honoring Chief Seattle.

Sully's Bistro & Bar is within easy walking distance of the dock. Agate Pass Cafe and Scratch Kitchen have closed.

Indianola. Indianola is distinguished by the long pier that served passengers and freight during Mosquito Fleet days. A float is installed during the summer to give access to the town, max boat size 30 feet, max stay 30 minutes. The float grounds on low and minus tides. The Indianola Country Store, just a few blocks from the pier, has been in business since the 1920s. It has a good selection of grocery items, beer and wine, and a popular deli.

Inner Port Madison. The inner, residential bay extends for about 1.5 miles into the north end of Bainbridge Island. This is where Port Madison Yacht Club and a large Seattle Yacht Club outstation (no reciprocals) are located. Anchorage is good throughout, with a wide bight about 0.75 mile inside the entrance. Shore access is possible from a dinghy dock at Hidden Cove Park just west of the SYC outstation. Farther in, Hidden Cove is a lovely spot. For Seattle area boats, this is an often-overlooked area to have a picnic lunch or a quiet night at anchor. The shores are private but the setting is idyllic.

Fay Bainbridge Park. www.biparks.org. South of Point Monroe on Bainbridge

Who can resist stopping in for fresh bakery treats at Sluys Bakery in Poulsbo?

SOUTH AND CENTRAL PUGET SOUND

See Area Map Page 109 - Maps Not for Navigation

Stroll the waterfront park from the Poulsbo Marina guest moorage floats.

Island. Open all year; exposed, anchoring only. Restrooms, showers. The park has 3 kitchen shelters, fireplaces, fire rings, a beach area, launch ramp, utility and primitive campsites, children's play equipment, horseshoe pits, fishing, clamming, and a concession stand in summer.

Murden Cove. Murden Cove has convenient anchoring depths, but little protection from winds. It's a long row to shore, partly over drying flats. The residential community of Rolling Bay is at the head of the bay.

LOCAL KNOWLEDGE

NO ANCHOR ZONE: The bottom around the south entrance to Eagle Harbor has been capped to prevent the spread of pollutants from a former creosote facility. Do not anchor in this area.

Eagle Harbor. Eagle Harbor is the location of the Winslow neighborhood of the City of Bainbridge Island. The entire island is considered the City of Bainbridge, which includes several neighborhood areas. Winslow is the western terminus of a ferry from downtown Seattle.

The neighboorhood of Winslow has a guest dock and boat launch at Eagle Harbor Waterfront Park. Anchorage in Eagle Harbor is available west of the Ferry Maintenance Yard, and at least 200 feet south of the marinas and east of the private tidelands. Anchorage up to 48 hours, no charge. Anchored boats must register at the Waterfront Park kiosk. An electronic self-registration payment kiosk for dock moorage and anchored boats is located at Eagle Harbor Waterfront Park.

Several marinas in the area provide guest moorage if a permanent tenant is away. All but one marina, Eagle Harbor Marina on the south shore, are on the town side of the harbor. Queen City Yacht Club, Meydenbauer Bay Yacht Club, and Seattle Yacht Club have outstations in Eagle Harbor. A pumpout station is located at Eagle Harbor Waterfront Park, and in-slip pumpouts are provided at Eagle Harbor Marina. At the west end of Eagle Harbor is the Dave Ullin Open Water Marina consisting of 16 private buoys, no public mooring.

We enjoy walking the streets of town, which offer boutiques, art shops, and a variety of good restaurants. The grocery store, within walking distance, has everything. The beautiful Bainbridge Island Museum of Art has a cafe. The Alehouse on Winslow, located next to the museum, has a nice selection of beer and cider on tap; patrons may bring in outside food. The grounds and gardens at Bloedel Reserve, on the north end of the island, are worth a visit. Kitsap Transit, at the ferry terminal, provides service during weekdays and Saturdays.

Eagle Harbor is entered through a marked channel past foul ground that extends south from Wing Point. Nun Buoy 2 is at the end of this foul ground, and the Tyee Shoal Beacon is a short distance south of Buoy 2. The ferries round Tyee Shoal Beacon, but other craft can use Buoy 2 safely, following the rule of Red, Right, Returning. Follow the markers all the way in. Shoal water extends out to the channel on both sides. Observe the 5-knot speed limit from Buoy 5. The far west end of the inner harbor is an Aquatic Conservancy area where power boats are not allowed.

No Discharge Zone. City requests no gray water discharge; use free showers ashore.

㊾ **Eagle Harbor Waterfront Park & City Dock**. 280 Madison Ave. N., Bainbridge Island, WA 98110; (206) 780-3733 or (206) 786-7627 (cell); www.ci.bainbridge-isl.wa.us. Open all year. 900 feet of guest side-tie moorage at the dock. Water, 30 & 50 amp ELCI-protected power, and pumpout. All moorage facilities are first-come, first-served. Washrooms, free showers, and garbage drop are located upland from the dock in the Waterfront Park. Rafting is required, no one is turned away; med-tie is an option. There is a nominal fee for stays up to 3 hours. Boat launch ramp is next to the dock. Payment for moorage is made at the electronic self-registration payment station located at the Park; shower code is shown on the receipt. Maximum 2-day stay in a seven-day period at the dock. Community volunteer kiosk hosts greet boaters and help answer questions.

A short quarter-mile walk north from the Waterfront Park brings you to the center of town and the grocery store on Winslow Way. Half-mile long Winslow Way is lined on both sides with small shops, restaurants, pubs, and a bakery. One block north of Winslow Way on Ericksen Avenue is the Bainbridge Island Historical Museum.

The cold water didn't deter these swimmers at Indianola.

See Area Map Page 109 - Maps Not for Navigation   **SOUTH AND CENTRAL PUGET SOUND**

㊾ **Winslow Wharf Marina.** P.O. Box 10297, 141 Parfitt Way SW, Bainbridge Island, WA 98110; (206) 842-4202; dave@winslowwharfmarina.com; www.winslowwharfmarina.com. Monitors VHF 09. Open Tuesday through Saturday, 9:00 a.m. to 5:00 p.m. Guest moorage in unoccupied slips. Maximum boat length 50 feet, 30 & 50 amp power, clean remodeled restrooms, free showers. Wi-Fi, laundry, book exchange, pumpout, portapotty dump. Reservations required. Chandlery Marine, a well-stocked marine supply store, has a little bit of everything, (206) 842-7245. Seattle Yacht Club and Meydenbauer Bay Yacht Club have dock space reserved for their members. The spaces are clearly marked, and non-member boats may not use them.

㊾ **Harbour Marina.** 233 Parfitt Way SW, Bainbridge Island, WA 98110; (206) 550-5340; info@harbour-marina.com; www.harbour-marina.com. Open all year. Unoccupied slips used for guest boats, call ahead for availability. Facilities include 30 amp power, restrooms, free showers, laundry, pumpout. Located directly below Harbour Public House, an English-style pub with beer, wine, and food. No kids allowed in the pub. Moorage for visiting the pub and Pegasus Coffee House is clearly marked. Close to the Waterfront Trail and a short walk to downtown.

㊿ **Eagle Harbor Marina.** P.O. Box 11217, 5834 Ward Ave. NE, Bainbridge Island, WA 98110; (206) 842-4003; harbormaster@eagleharbormarina.com; www.eagleharbormarina.com. Open all year. Primarily permanent moorage with limited guest moorage, call ahead. Marina has 30,

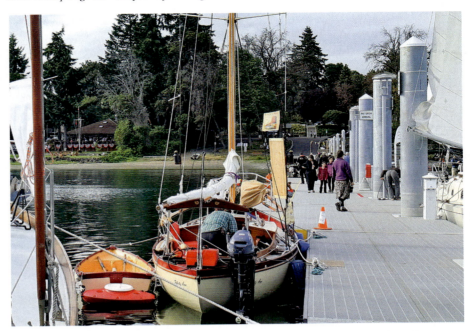

Popular City Dock in Eagle Harbor won't turn boats away, so plan for rafting and use the opportunity to make new friends.

50 & 100 amp ELCI-protected power. Restrooms, showers, laundry, pumpout, free Wi-Fi. Docks were recently replaced and upgraded, including monitored shore power, in-slip portable pumpout, year-round water, and security. This marina is on the south side of Eagle Harbor away from town; there are no restaurants or stores in the immediate area.

㊶ **Blakely Harbor.** In the late 1800's Blakely Harbor was the site of ship building activities and the Port Blakely Mill, one of the world's largest sawmills. Now it is a quiet residential neighborhood. Some stub pilings remain from the old docks. The head of the bay, including the old mill pond and ruins of the concrete powerhouse, is now the 40-acre Port Blakely Park, with shore access and a hiking trail.

Good anchorage in 35 to 50 feet can be found far enough into the bay to be well protected, yet still have a view of the Seattle skyline. A few homes line the harbor shore. Sunset on a clear evening is beautiful. Blakely Rock is 0.5 mile off; give it a good offing. Enter Blakely Harbour in the middle of the mouth of the bay. A drying reef extends from the north shore, and shoals are along the south side.

Eagle Harbor

Hood Canal

CHAPTER 3

HOOD CANAL
Dabob Bay • Pleasant Harbor • Alderbrook

Main street in historic Port Gamble

Hood Canal is a 65-mile-long glacier-carved fjord. Because the shorelines are fairly straight with few protected anchorages, Hood Canal is less used by pleasure craft than many other waterways. Most boaters don't realize that shrimping, oyster gathering, clamming and fishing can be outstanding. The shrimping season is short, usually in May, and on those days the boats are plentiful. In clear weather the views of the Olympic Mountains from Hood Canal are outstanding. Other than shrimpers and knowing fishermen, however, Hood Canal is largely undiscovered.

Several rivers flow from the Olympic Mountains into Hood Canal, and each has formed a mudflat off its mouth. Although the shoal off the Dosewallips River, a couple of miles south of Pulali Point, is marked, the shoals off the Duckabush, Fulton Creek, Hama Hama, and Lilliwaup rivers are not marked, nor is the extensive shoal off the Skokomish River at the Great Bend. Care must be taken to avoid running aground.

Pleasant Harbor and the Alderbrook Inn Resort can take larger boats, but many of the other marinas and parks on Hood Canal are aimed at trailerable boats. This has disappointed some people with larger boats.

No Discharge Zone: All of Hood Canal is a No Discharge Zone (NDZ). It is illegal to discharge any (treated and untreated) black water sewage. Gray water is okay.

Hood Head. Anchorage can be found behind Hood Head on the western shore of Hood Canal, but the water shoals rapidly to drying flats near the head of the bay.

Shine Tidelands State Park. Stretches 1 mile north of the Hood Canal Bridge into Bywater Bay on the west shore of Hood Canal. Day use only, toilets, no power, water or showers. Anchoring only, well offshore. Launch ramp, crabbing and clamming, hiking trails.

Bywater Bay. Anchor in 6 to 12 feet, good holding on a soft bottom with room to swing. The spit provides wave protection from north winds. A shallow draft boat can easily enter the lagoon in the undeveloped Wolfe Property State Park at the northwest corner of the bay. [Hamilton]

Port Gamble. Port Gamble is a fine anchorage, protected from wave action by a sandspit at the entrance. Anchorage in 18 to 30 feet is possible everywhere. Many people prefer the area just inside the spit. There is no guest dock or designated landing area.

Port Gamble is charming and historic. The remnants of the sawmill are being removed, and the town has been restored. A museum, restaurants and small shops are on the tree-lined main street. Port Gamble began as a sawmill company-owned town, founded in 1853 and operating until 1995. The Port Gamble Historic Museum (360) 297-8078 covers the history of the mill and town; open daily, May through September.

LOCAL KNOWLEDGE

DANGEROUS ROCKS: Sisters, two substantial rocks about 200 yards apart, lie 0.4 mile south of the Hood Canal bridge on the west side. The rocks dry at half tide. The southern rock is marked by a large lighted beacon, yet from time to time an unwary boat manages to go up on these rocks. For safety, if you have passed under the western end of the bridge, turn eastward at once and run parallel to the bridge to the middle before turning south into Hood Canal.

Hood Canal Floating Bridge. The east end of the Hood Canal Floating Bridge has 50 feet of vertical clearance. Clearance on the west end is 33 feet. The bridge can be opened for larger vessels, but it is not manned. To arrange an opening call (360) 779-3233, which connects to a State Department of Transportation office in Tacoma. They will take your name, telephone number, name of your vessel, date and time of desired opening, and whether you are inbound or outbound. They also will ask what width opening you need (300 feet or 600 feet). One hour's notice is needed to get a crew to the bridge and prepare it for opening. No bridge openings between 3:00 p.m. and 6:15 p.m. daily, from Memorial Day to Labor Day.

Salsbury Point County Park. Just off the northeast end of the Hood Canal Bridge. Day use only, restrooms, no power. Anchoring only, 2 launch ramps. Picnic tables, fireplaces, children's play area. Nature trail. Sandy beach for experienced divers only because of strong currents.

Kitsap Memorial Marine State Park. (360) 779-3205; Four miles south of Hood Canal Bridge. Open all year, day use and overnight camping, 2 mooring buoys for boats 45 feet and under. Self-register and pay mooring buoy fee on shore. Restrooms, showers, no power. Picnic sites, kitchen shelters, fireplaces. Standard campsites, swimming beach, playground, horseshoe pits, volleyball courts, baseball field. Buoys are exposed to tidal currents and wind.

Squamish Harbor. Squamish Harbor has convenient anchoring depths, but the harbor is quite open and has numerous rocks and reefs that must be avoided. It is seldom used for overnight anchorage.

Thorndyke Bay. Thorndyke Bay is too open to provide a snug anchorage.

LOCAL KNOWLEDGE

RESTRICTED AREAS: Boaters should take great care not to enter the Restricted Area in front of the Bangor Naval Station on the east side of Hood Canal, about 4 miles south from Vinland, which is patrolled constantly to keep passing vessels well away. The patrol craft are fitted with guns and are authorized to shoot. Best practice is to stay west of mid-channel when transiting this area. A second Naval Restricted Area is located off Point Whitney in Dabob Bay.

NAVAL OPERATING AREAS: Two adjoining Naval Operating areas cover a majority of Hood Canal, from South Point to Hazel Point. When transiting this area, boaters should monitor Channel 16. Look for Naval vessels flying a "Bravo" (red) flag during periods of Naval operations. A passage corridor outside the Operating Areas follows the west side of Hood Canal, hugging the eastern shoreline of Toandos Peninsula. Another Naval Operating & Exercise Area is in Dabob Bay, where flashing lights along the shoreline indicate the status of operations.

USS Henry M. Jackson returning to Bangor Naval Base on Hood Canal.

Naval Base Kitsap (Bangor). This is the location of Bangor Naval Station, homeport for a fleet of nuclear submarines. Several of these awesome machines often are visible to passing craft. Stay outside of the marked restricted area.

Seabeck Bay. Anchorage is possible behind Misery Point, with good protection from the south and west. The Seabeck General Store can be accessed by dinghy. The Olympic View Marina is for permanent moorage only.

Scenic Beach State Park. South of Seabeck. Open for day use all year and overnight camping in summer only. Anchoring only. Standard and primitive campsites. Kitchen shelter, fireplaces, fire rings, horseshoe pits, volleyball areas. Scuba diving, swimming, hiking, shellfishing.

Fisherman Harbor. Fisherman Harbor can be entered only at high water, but once inside offers protected anchorage in 5 to 15 feet. Follow the natural channel into the bay, then turn south and follow the spit until anchoring depths are found. All the land around the bay is privately owned. Years ago, we tiptoed into Fisherman Harbor in a sailboat at something less than high tide. It was careful going, with a close watch from the bow and a bit of luck, but the boat got in without touching. Less foolish souls should wait for higher water. [Hale]

Dabob Bay. Most of Dabob Bay is a Naval Operating & Exercise Area with 5 warning lights. Flashing amber lights indicate Naval operations are in progress; boaters may enter the area on an amber light but should keep well clear of Navy vessels. Flashing red lights indicate the area has been closed to navigation. If the lights turn red while you are inside the Operations Area, shut down engines and depth sounder until operations have ended. The 5 warning lights are located at Whitney Point, Pulali Point, and Sylopash Point on the west side of the bay; Zelatched Point on the east side of the bay; and at the north end of the bay on the southeast side of Bolton Peninsula. South of Pulali Point (western shore of Dabob Bay) is outside the Operating Area and includes Jackson Cove, where good anchorage can be found. Boaters should be aware of the Restricted Area just off Point Whitney, a charted no anchoring zone.

A State Department of Fish and Wildlife oyster research laboratory is at Whitney Point with a good launch ramp alongside. A breakwater-protected marina, Herb Beck Marina, is at the village of Quilcene.

Caution should be exercised when transiting Dabob Bay and Quilcene Bay to avoid the large number of shrimp pots during the season.

Broad Spit Park. On the east shore of Bolton Peninsula in Dabob Bay. Anchor on either side of the spit, depending on wind direction. Easy beach access, trails ashore. Lagoon that fills at high tide. Field Correspondent Jim Norris reports "We anchored two nights just north of Broad Spit in Dabob Bay. The wind was SE 20-25 all day. Given the full fetch of Hood Canal for waves to develop, I feared a nasty swell would bend around the spit and make life uncomfortable. Not so. The spit offered good protection from the waves, but not the wind. We swung around on the anchor, but no other motion in the boat."

Quilcene Bay. Anchor in 12 feet, good holding in mud along the east shore opposite the marina, with protection from moderate southerly winds.

① **Herb Beck Marina.** 1731 Linger Longer Rd., Quilcene, WA 98376; (360) 765-3131; www.portofpt.com/marinas/. Managed by the Port of Port Townsend. Monitors VHF

Pleasant Harbor Marina

HOOD CANAL

See Area Map Page 140- Maps Not for Navigation

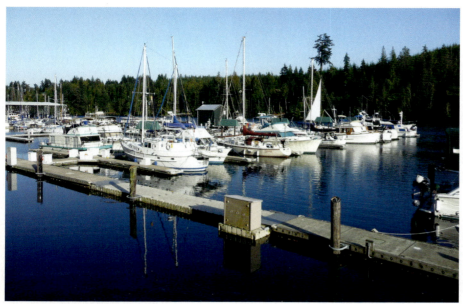

Pleasant Harbor Marina, a clean, attractive facility with guest moorage

66A. Open Tuesday through Saturday, 8:00 a.m. - 4:30 p.m. in the summers; hours and days may vary during the off-season. Ethanol-free gasoline and diesel at the fuel dock. Limited guest moorage to 40 feet, 20 & 30 amp power, water, showers, restrooms, pumpout, garbage drop. Reservations accepted. This is a small, rustic marina. Swimming is great in the summer at a designated area just south of the marina, with water temperatures above 70 degrees.

Dosewallips State Park. (360) 796-4415; South of Brinnon. Park open all year for day use and overnight camping. Accessible by kayak or canoe. Restrooms, showers. Hiking trails, picnic areas, standard, utility, and primitive campsites.

Pleasant Harbor. Pleasant Harbor is a major stopping point on Hood Canal with a good destination resort marina and a state park dock. Enter through a narrow channel with least depth of 8.5 feet at zero tide. Inside, there's room to anchor, 18 to 42 feet, mud bottom. Pleasant Harbor Marina has excellent facilities for visiting boaters. Home Port Marina of Pleasant Harbor (formerly, Pleasant Harbor "Old" Marina) has no guest moorage.

Pleasant Harbor is full of boats in May, when the annual shrimping season is under way. For dates, go to www.wdfw.wa.gov.

② **Pleasant Harbor Marina.** 308913 Hwy 101, Brinnon, WA 98320; (360) 796-4611; (800) 547-3479; reservations@phmresort.com; www.pleasantharbormarina.com. Monitors VHF 09 & 16. Open all year. Closed Thanksgiving and Christmas. Ethanol-free gasoline, diesel and propane at the fuel dock. The marina has approximately 60 guest slips and unoccupied slips as available, 30 & 50 amp power. Side-tie moorage to 150 feet. Facilities include clean restrooms and free showers, laundry, free Wi-Fi, on-site security, and free pumpout at the fuel dock. two toilets. A 2-hour tie-up near the fuel dock is available for store, restaurant, and pub customers.

The main building houses the marina office, restaurant, pub, and store. The store has a selection of gifts, clothing, some groceries, beer and wine. At the fuel dock you'll find ice cream, ice, crab and shrimp bait, and marine hardware.

A shuttle bus can take you to several local hikes that range in length from a 0.2 mile trail to a 130-foot-high waterfall, to a 3.5- mile loop of Dosewallips State Park.

This is a popular destination. Reservations strongly recommended, especially on weekends and holidays. Many of the permanent tenants spend considerable time at the marina, and life on the docks is quite friendly. Amenities include a barbecue and picnic area, swimming pool, hot tub, laser skeet range, and children's play area. Kayak, and SUP rentals. Live music May through September. Diane is the very capable manager.

② **Pleasant Harbor Marine State Park.** (360) 796-4415. Open all year for day use and overnight mooring. No camping. Dock has 120 feet of space, 3-night maximum stay, first-come, first-served. This is the first dock on the right as you enter Pleasant Harbor.

Triton Head. A state park launch ramp is at Triton Head, and anchorage is possible off this little bight.

③ **Triton Cove State Park.** (360) 796-4415; West side of Hood Canal, south of the Dosewallips River. Open all year, day use only. Vault toilet, no power, no showers. Concrete launch ramp, picnic area.

④ **Glen Ayr Resort.** 25381 N U.S. Hwy 101, Hoodsport, WA 98548; (360) 877-9522; office@garesort.com; www.glenayr.com. Open all year. Nice docks and friendly staff. Moorage for boats up to 24 feet, motel and townhouse guests have priority. Space for transient boaters, except during shrimp season. Restrooms, guest showers, laundry. No power at the docks. Attractive location and popular diving destination.

⑤ **Hoodsport.** Hoodsport is popular with scuba divers as a place to view the giant Pacific octopus. Local marine preserves such as Octopus Hole and Sund Rock offer divers the chance to see octopus, wolf eels, rockfish, anemones and other marine life.

The town has a grocery store, hardware store, restaurants, an espresso shop, a beauty salon, and gift shops. The Washington Department of Fish and Wildlife operates a fish hatchery in town.

⑤ **Port of Hoodsport.** P.O. Box 429, Hoodsport, WA 98548; (360) 877-9350; portmail@hctc.com; www.portofhoodsport.us. Six guest moorage slips for boats up to 16 feet, one outside 40-foot slip subject to wave action. No power, no water. Garbage drop and picnic area. Self-register and pay at the head of the dock for stays over 12 hours. Grocery store across the highway; other businesses are within walking distance.

Sunrise Motel & Resort. 24520 Hwy 101, Hoodsport, WA 98548; (360) 877-5301; sunrise@hctc.com; myweb.hcc.net/sunrise. An older resort open all year, no power, no laundry. Restrooms and showers in motel rooms. Maximum boat length 20 feet. Moorage for those staying ashore. Underwater park, scuba air station, barbecue, hot tub.

Potlatch Marine State Park. (360) 877-5361. South of Hoodsport. Open all year, day use and overnight camping and mooring. Restrooms, showers, no power. Five mooring buoys (boats 45 feet and under) are offshore in deep water, except the second buoy as you approach from the north. We are told this buoy swings into 5-foot depths at zero tide. Self-register and pay mooring buoy fee on shore. The park has a picnic area, an underwater park for scuba diving, hiking trails, campsites. Good wildlife-watching.

⑥ **Hood Canal Marina.** P.O. Box 305, 5101 E. Hwy 106, Union, WA 98592; (360) 898-2252; hoodcanalmarina@hctc.com; www.hood-canal-marina.com. Certified Clean Marina. Open all year. Fuel dock with ethanol-free gasoline and diesel, open daily 8:00 a.m. to 5:00 p.m., call ahead in off season; 30 amp power, free Wi-Fi, washrooms, and pumpout. Limited guest moorage, maximum 40-foot vessels. Call ahead for moorage. Moorages fill quickly in May during shrimp season. The Union launch ramp is adjacent and has off-site secured parking. The Union City Market, at Hood Canal Marina, offers food items, crafts, books and clothing.

PLEASANT HARBOR
— MARINA & RECREATION COMMUNITY —

CALL NOW
360-796-4611

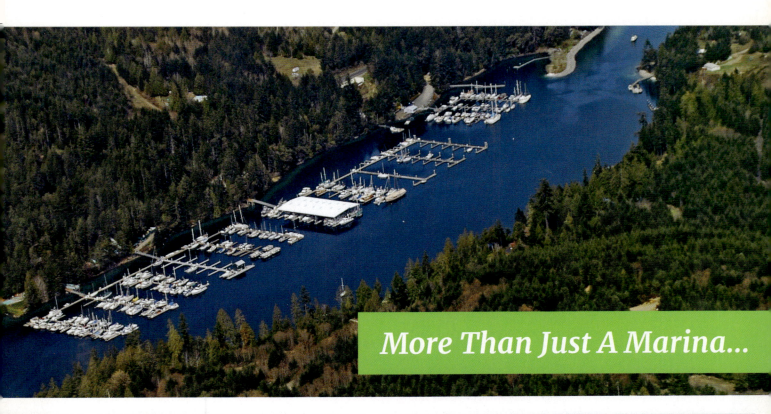

More Than Just A Marina...

YEAR ROUND MOORAGE

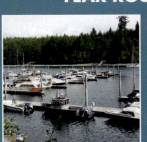

- 312 Slip Protected Marina
- 30 & 50 Amp Power
- Non-Ethanol Gas & Diesel
- Vacuum Pump Out
- Heated Pool & Hot Tub
- Permanent / Guest Moorage
- Groceries / Gift Shop

LODGING

- 4 Suites
- Queen Size Beds
- En-Suite Bathrooms
- Outside Deck with BBQ
- Heated Pool & Hot Tub
- TV + WiFi
- Full Kitchen

GALLEY & PUB

- Delicious Food
- Local Beers On Tap
- Local Wine Selection
- Roof Top Patio
- Live Music
- 3 Big Screen TVs

ACTIVITIES & ADVENTURES

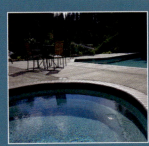

- Children's Play Area
- Laser Skeet Shooting
- Horseshoes
- Hiking
- Boating
- Lawn Games
- Shrimping/Crabbing

Play, Relax, Enjoy
www.pleasantharbormarina.com

HOOD CANAL See Area Map Page 140- Maps Not for Navigation

Docks at Alderbrook Resort & Spa

⑦ **Alderbrook Resort & Spa.** 10 E. Alderbrook Drive, Union, WA 98592; (360) 898-2200; (360) 898-2252; cindy.sund@alderbrookresort.com; www.alderbrookresort.com. Monitors VHF 16, then switch to a working channel. Open all year, 1500 feet of guest moorage. Restrooms, showers, 30 & 50 amp power, water, swimming pool and whirlpool spa, free Wi-Fi. Pumpout available, check for availability in advance. Seaplane dock. Kayak, paddleboard, hydrobike and seacycle rentals. The trawler *Twanoh* is available for scheduled trips and charters.

If you're looking for a quality resort experience, you'll find it here. The rooms are beautifully appointed, the grounds are immaculate, and the dining room is superb. Moorage is free while dining. They have an indoor pool, with a spa adjacent. Hiking trails surround the property. Everything you're looking for in a weekend getaway is here, including golf. Best to call ahead for reservations and prices.

⑧ **Twanoh Marine State Park.** (360) 275-2222. Eight miles west of Belfair. Open all year, day use and overnight camping and mooring, except no camping in winter. Has 200 feet of overnight and day-use moorage dock, 6 mooring buoys for vessels 45 feet and under. Self-register and pay mooring fees on shore. Restrooms, showers, pumpout, portapotty dump, power, no water. Be aware that water depth at the dock is only 3 feet at zero tide. This is a large and popular park, with launch ramp, playground, picnic areas, kitchen shelters, fireplaces. Launch ramp. Docks are removed from November through April. Standard, utility and primitive campsites, tennis courts, hiking trails.

⑨ **Summertide Resort & Marina.** P.O. Box 450, 15781 NE Northshore Rd. Tahuya, WA 98588; (360) 275-9313; www.summertideresort.com. Guest moorage, 20-foot maximum boat length. Reservations required. Restrooms, showers, Wi-Fi, no power. Launch ramp, RV spaces with hookups. Boat moorage is for those staying in one of the resort's rental cottages, or other upland accommodations; no overnighting aboard vessels at the dock. The store carries groceries, beer, wine, snacks, ice, bait, and tackle; boaters are welcome to stop for shopping at the store.

Belfair State Park. (360) 275-0668. Three miles southwest of Belfair on the north shore of Hood Canal. Open all year for day use and overnight camping. Restrooms and showers. Anchor far offshore, if at all. Drying mudflats restrict approach to small, shallow-draft boats only. Popular park, camping reservations required in summer.

⑩ **Port of Allyn North Shore Dock.** P.O. Box 1, Allyn, WA 98524; (360) 275-2430; www.portofallyn.com. Open all year with 240 feet of side-tie dock space. Water, 30 amp power, portable toilets, seasonal pumpout and portapotty dump, no showers. Overnight moorage, maximum 45 feet, 14-day limit in the summer. Self-registration payment box on-site. Launch ramp with credit, debit card payment, or pay on the website.

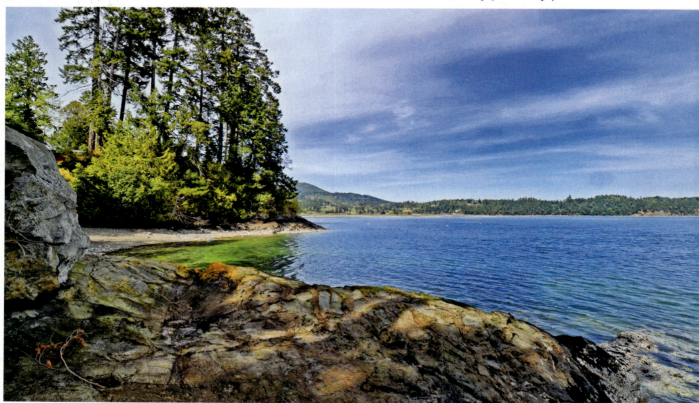

Hood Canal has splendid views and interesting beaches.

North Puget Sound

CHAPTER 4

NORTH PUGET SOUND
Kingston • Admiralty Inlet
Port Ludlow • Port Townsend

SKAGIT BAY TO BELLINGHAM BAY
Edmonds • Everett • Langley
Saratoga Passage • Coupeville
Oak Harbor • La Conner • Deception Pass
Anacortes • Bellingham

LUMMI BAY TO POINT ROBERTS
Semiahmoo Bay
Blaine • Point Roberts

NORTH PUGET SOUND　　　　　　See Area Map Page 147 - Maps Not for Navigation

North Puget Sound. For the sake of convenience, this chapter includes cruising grounds northward to Point Roberts, the U.S. territory located at the southern end of the Strait of Georgia. The cruising waters from Edmonds north to Deception Pass form what is meteorologically known as the "convergent zone," where weather and sea conditions can change. Whidbey Island, with Deception Pass, is the dominate feature of North Puget Sound, along with smaller surrounding islands, including Cypress Island and Vendovi Island. Major community destinations include Kingston, Port Townsend, La Conner, and Anacortes.

No Discharge Zone: All of the inside waters of Washington State from Puget Sound to the Canadian Border are a No Discharge Zone (NDZ). It is illegal to discharge any (treated and untreated) black water sewage. Gray water from showers and sinks is not covered by this restriction.

Kingston. Kingston, in Appletree Cove on the west side of Puget Sound, is the western terminus of the ferry run to Edmonds, and possibly the only city in Washington State where you can get an authentic French crepe at five o'clock in the morning while waiting for the ferry. A Port-owned marina, with a park, is located behind the breakwater. The park's meticulously maintained lawn and gardens are inviting. Kingston's tree shaded main street is lined with cafés with great food and colorful names, many with outdoor seating. Farther uptown is a grocery store and hardware store. On the north side of the ferry holding area a deck overlooks Puget Sound. A path leads to a Port-owned broad sandy beach filled with driftwood. It's a pleasant walk and great for families. On the the park grounds next to the marina a farmers market, quite popular, is open 9:00 a.m. to 2:00 p.m. Saturdays, May to mid-October. Concerts on the Cove, with a beer garden, are held Saturday evenings during July and August.

A pavilion on the park grounds, just up from the marina, is used for music concerts, gatherings, and weddings.

Anchoring is good south of the marina breakwater. Watch your depths. It gets shallow close to shore.

① **Port of Kingston.** P.O. Box 559, Kingston, WA 98346; (360) 297-3545; info@portofkingston.org; www.portofkingston.org. Monitors VHF 65A but prefers telephone calls. Open year-round, 47 guest slips to 50 feet, water and 30 & 50 amp power. At the deep water end of the guest dock, a float accommodates vessels up to 85 feet. The marina has restrooms, laundry, portapotty dump, free showers, free pumpout, in-berth pumpout on the guest dock, and free upgraded Wi-Fi throughout the marina. The fuel dock has ethanol-free gasoline, diesel and Delo lubricants. A dual-lane concrete launch ramp, with a float between the two lanes, is available. Parking (fee charged) for tow-vehicles and trailers. Two electric courtesy cars are available through the Port office for local trips to shopping several blocks away. They are fun to drive and popular; 30-minute usage recommended.

Four mooring buoys for boats to 40 feet are outside the breakwater north of the ferry dock. They are exposed to winds and wakes of passing boat traffic.

Moorage reservations are accepted with one day advance notice; call the Port office during business hours or see their website for a link to Dockwa.com for online reservations. Kingston is quite popular during the summer months, reservations are recommended. Slips marked "open" are first-come, first-served, and reserved slips are marked reserved.

Enter the marina around the end of the rock breakwater. Leave the two pilings that mark the edge of the dredged channel to port. Leave the red buoy marking the end of the breakwater to starboard. Guest moorage is in slips extending from the dock that runs parallel to the breakwater, plus the side-tie

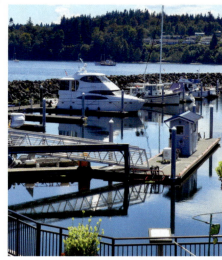

Port of Kingston marina with breakwater protected guest moorage and fuel.

Kingston

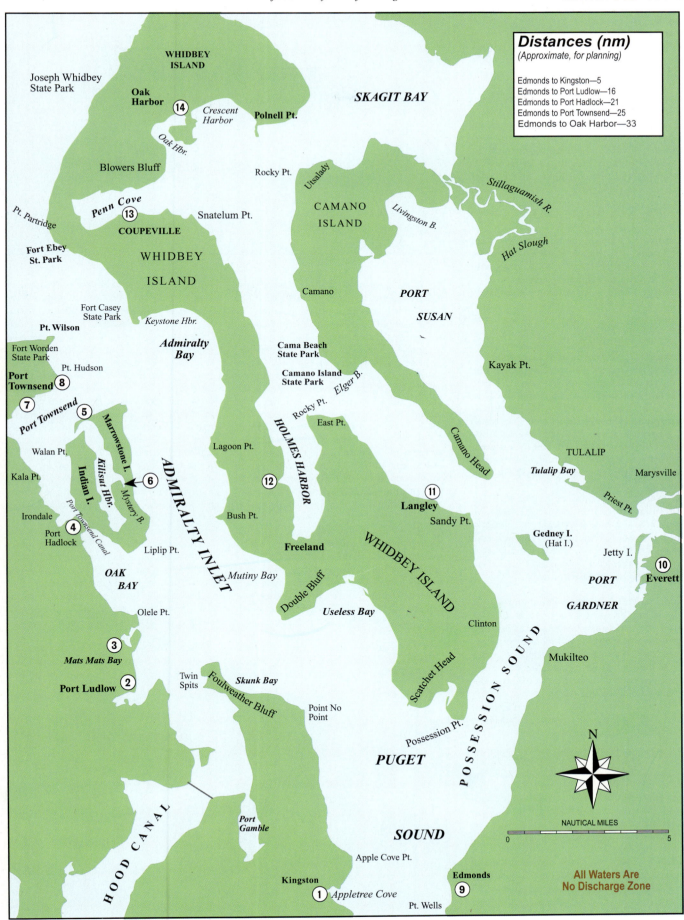

North Puget Sound

NORTH PUGET SOUND

float for larger boats at the outer end. The fuel float is at the shore end of the guest dock. Moor in any unreserved guest dock slip and register at the Port office. Gazebos, with picnic tables and power, are available for visiting boaters on a first-come, first-serve basis.

High-speed passenger ferry service to downtown Seattle. See the website for a schedule of music events and the weekend Farmer's Market. The nearby estuary is perfect for paddlers and bird watchers. The famous Christmas Lights, with over 150 sculptures and 500,000 lights, is a popular event during the shoulder season.

ADMIRALTY INLET

Admiralty Inlet begins at Point No Point in the south and ends at Point Wilson in the north. Admiralty Inlet is wide, deep, and straight, with no hazardous reefs or shoals. It makes up for this good design by often being the only patch of rough water for miles. Flood current or ebb, Admiralty Inlet waters swirl and lump up. If the wind is light, you'll see the swirls. If the wind is blowing, you'll be in the lump. Use the Bush Point current tables to predict the times of slack water, and the time and strength of maximum current.

If Admiralty Inlet is rough and you have to be there anyway, try to favor the eastern or western shores. The western shore is preferred. A suggested route is along Marrowstone Island, far enough off to avoid the rocks shown on the chart. Approach around Marrowstone Point inside the rough water just outside, and into Port Townsend Bay.

If you are northbound past Point No Point and you can see that Admiralty Inlet is rough (you can see it), head west across the south tip of Marrowstone Island, and go through Port Townsend Canal into Port Townsend Bay. Port Townsend Canal currents are based on the Deception Pass current tables.

Point No Point. Point No Point, on the west side of Puget Sound, is a popular salmon-fishing spot and a place where boats heading up-sound and down-sound tend to converge. Boat traffic can get heavy, especially when the salmon are running and the waters are literally covered with small sport fishing boats working along the tide-rip.

Watch out for this tide-rip. When a strong wind opposes a big tide, the waters off Point No Point can turn dangerous.

LOCAL KNOWLEDGE

NAVIGATION NOTE: Check your chart before entering the landlocked Port Ludlow inner harbor and be sure to pass between the two islets. Passing outside of either islet could put you aground.
SPEED LIMIT: A 5-mph "no wake" speed limit is in effect throughout Port Ludlow and applies to all vessels, including dinghies.

Port Ludlow

② **Port Ludlow.** Well-protected Port Ludlow indents the western shore of Puget Sound. It was once the site of a major Pope & Talbot sawmill, and now is a nice residential area, a destination resort and a marina. Anchorage is in the landlocked inner harbor, reached by passing between two little islands near the head of the bay. Deeper draft boats should watch the depth sounder closely when entering the inner harbor at low tide. The passage is shallower than the bays it connects. Good anchorage, mud bottom, is in about 15 feet. An 8-foot shoal area a short distance northeast of the entrance is noted on large scale Chart 18477. Anchorage can also be found south of the marina; note the charted cable area immediately west of the marina.

The inner harbor is a favorite destination in Puget Sound, protected from all winds. Upscale homes are set well back and often screened by trees, providing privacy and a lovely harbor charm. Meydenbauer Bay Yacht Club has an outstation on the peninsula that forms the inner harbor. A level, scenic one-mile pathway parallels Oak Bay Road, leading west from the marina to the Village Center which has a grocery, gift shop, and a pizza shop.

② **Port Ludlow Resort and Marina.** 1 Gull Drive, Port Ludlow, WA 98365; (360) 437-0513; (877) 344-6725; marina@portludlowresort.com; www.portludlowresort.com. Monitors VHF 68. Certified Clean Marina. Open 7 days a week, all year. Ethanol-free gasoline and diesel at the fuel dock. Concrete docks, some of which are beginning to show their age. Guest moorage in 50 slips and along 460 feet of dock, plus unoccupied slips as available, 30 & 50 amp power, water, restrooms, Wi-Fi, gazebo with barbecue, pumpout, portapotty dump, free showers. Pavilion tent for groups. Kayak, SUPs, and skiff rentals. Reservations recommended.

A resort restaurant and lounge are within walking distance. Locals speak highly of the restaurant. Free shuttle for marina guests to the resort's 18-hole golf course. The marina store carries convenience items, a few groceries, propane and limited marine hardware. Shops, medical services, and a post office are located in the nearby Village Center. Marine mechanics from Port Townsend may be available. With its large grounds, pavilion tent, dining and golf, this is a popular destination for groups and rendezvous.

The marina often runs cruise-in specials that include moorage, golf, and restaurant credit. Check the marina website.

③ **Mats Mats Bay.** A course between Port Ludlow and Mats Mats Bay should avoid Snake Rock, close to shore, and Colvos Rocks

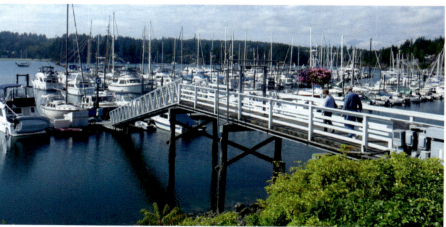
Port Ludlow Resort and Marina

148 www.WaggonerGuide.com

Dogs Onboard

There are really only two types of boaters—those who cruise with dogs, and those who don't. Those who don't think cruising with dogs is for the birds. The main reason we cruise with dogs lies at the heart of why we cruise in the first place. Cruising is about exploring, and on those routine shoreside jaunts, dog people come to know the terrain with an intimacy one wouldn't have thought possible. When our fellow-cruisers are

still abed, listening to the coffee perk while cold rain drums on the deck above them, we're ashore in full foul-weather gear, hiding under the dripping trees, while Buddy sniffs out the perfect spot to lift a leg. Led by The Nose, we hike to the ends of obscure trails—and beyond. We scramble over slippery rocks and dig up the coast's finest beaches. We come to know this extraordinary place in all its moods. Dogs initiate us into the world of wildlife, both living and dead. One night my wife Jan took our dachshund Rosie ashore for her evening visit. Suddenly, Spouse was leaping over rocks and crashing through bushes in hot pursuit of Hound, who was in hot pursuit of a rank-smelling wild goat. To Rosie, a city beast with a hunter's heart, the goat's scent trail must have seemed as wide as the I-5 freeway. Dead wildlife also has its attractions, especially if it's decaying and smelly. If you are a canine, getting in touch with your Inner Hunter means disguising your scent so your prey can't smell you coming. A beach walk is not complete without a roll on a dead crab, a seagull or fish carcass . . . or worse. On one occasion, for example, it was my turn to chase Rosie as she bounded over logs and disappeared around a bay. From afar I watched in horror as she sniffed the rotting remains of a seal, then looked at me for permission to roll. All I could do was yell "Nooooo!" at the top of my lungs. Rosie looked mighty put out but, incredibly, she left her prize untouched. Aboard the boat, settling down with Rosie in my lap gives me an ironclad excuse for not moving when my mate asks me to do something. In fact, it allows me to issue orders: "Could you pass up my sweater (my binoculars, my wine glass, my dinner . . .)?" It's not unknown for the crew of our little ship to have a debate about whose knee gets Rosie. These arguments are more frequent on chilly off-season cruises, when Rosie gives off the warmth of a modest cabin heater. What dogs really teach us is how to enjoy the simple things. When the trails have been walked, the beaches dug and the goats chased, it's time for us all to sit down together, to listen to the sounds or the silence, feel the tide turn, watch the birds fly and the sun set, and savor life on this coast in all its perfection. Yes, cruising with dogs is best.

-Duart Snow

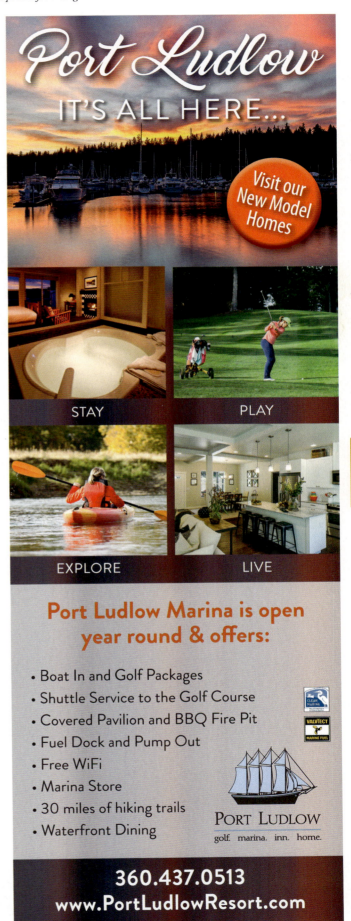

NORTH PUGET SOUND

and Klas Rocks, farther offshore. Colvos Rocks are marked by flashing lights at the north and south ends, and Klas Rocks by a diamond shape dayboard with a flashing white light. Snake Rock is not marked.

Mats Mats Bay has a dogleg entrance with a least depth of 5 feet at zero tide. A lighted range shows the center of the narrow channel. Buoys mark the channel. Pay attention to all buoys, and do not stray from the marked channel, especially at low water. Anchor in 18 feet in the middle or south part of the bay. The north end of the bay is shallow. The large number of boats on permanent moorings restrict anchoring options. Mats Mats Bay is well protected from almost any wind. A launch ramp is at the south end of the bay.

Oak Bay. Oak Bay, with convenient anchoring depths, is at the southern approach to Port Townsend Canal. Oak Bay County Park is on the west side of the channel, approximately one mile south of the entrance to the canal.

Oak Bay County Park. Northwest shore of Oak Bay. Open all year, restrooms, launch ramp, campsites, picnic tables, no power, no water. Anchoring or beaching only. Marked by a rock jetty. Swimming, scuba diving, clamming, crabbing.

Port Townsend Canal. Port Townsend Canal (also known as Hadlock Canal) runs from Oak Bay to Port Townsend Bay through a relatively narrow dredged channel. The canal is well marked, easy to transit, and spanned by a bridge with 58-foot vertical clearance. Currents run to 3 knots. Port Townsend Canal is a secondary station under the Deception Pass reference station in the current tables.

Port Hadlock and Irondale. The towns of Irondale and Port Hadlock are west of the northern entrance to Port Townsend Canal. Limited guest moorage at Port Hadlock Marina and a day-use dock at Irondale. Anchorage is good, sand bottom. Stay north of Skunk Island, due west from the marina.

④ **Port Hadlock Marina.** 173 Hadlock Bay Rd., Port Hadlock, WA 98339; (360) 385-

Ajax Cafe

Ajax Café is one of the most unique dining venues in all of Puget Sound, offering excellent cuisine and presentation. The Café is housed in the historic Galster House, built in the late 1800's, located within steps of the public dock at Irondale in the northwest corner of Port Hadlock. Boaters can tie-up at the dock or anchor out and arrive by dinghy. Boats can stay at the dock up to 4-hours while guests dine at Ajax and visit the adjacent Northwest School of Wooden Boatbuilding.

Today's Ajax Café was once the home of Samuel Hadlock, founder of Port Haldlock. Samuel came to Port Townsend Bay in 1870 after building the Tacoma lumber mill. He then built a new sawmill on the Port Hadlock waterfront around which was a general store, post office, hotels, and saloons. The Galsters later moved into the Hadlock home and lived there until 1949. Mr. Galster tended bar in the saloon located on the first floor of the house, now the Ajax Café.

Over the years, beginning in 1977, Ajax became known for its excellent meals and party atmosphere. Hats hang on the walls of the café, representing various periods of time and professions. Patrons are invited to select and don one of the hats, transforming their persona and character. There's something about this simple activity that starts conversations between people and even across the room — "oh, that hat is you," "you look great in that hat," "where are you from?" Soon the entire café is one big happy group of friends. Even the old record album jackets, used as menu covers, evoke conversation; we were presented with a John Denver album cover, which of course launched a conversation about snow skiing, piloting aircraft and other subjects. Photos of famous musicians and movie stars on the café walls complete the fun atmosphere of the then-and-now conversations.

When the Ajax Café closed in 2016 due to needed plumbing repairs, the community and the café's many patrons were heart broken. A campaign to raise funds and save Ajax soon ensued. Time was passing by and it was feared that Ajax might be lost, until the Northwest School of Wooden Boatbuilding began raising funds to purchase the house, make repairs, and provide a long-term lease for Ajax. After being closed for two years, the Ajax Café reopened on April 6, 2019 and picked up where they left off, with great food and good times. Most restaurants would never survive after a two-year closure. It's a testament to the quality of the cuisine and patronage found at Ajax Café.

The quality of the cuisine at Ajax's is due to the talented chef using fresh, local ingredients, including locally grown fruits and vegetables from local farms; home-made breads; and local beef and poultry. Chef Graham has a knack for creating juicy, flavorful dishes that leave you wanting to come back for more. Nightly specials include seasonal dishes and fresh seafood like the Northwest Fishermen's Stew with mussels, clams, prawns and fresh fish in a saffron bouillabaisse. I chose the baked, encrusted salmon placed over a risotto cake topped with a flavorful fruit/vegie sauce; and my husband chose the Pork tenderloin with tomatillo chutney and fresh prunes served with a three-potato au gratin. We topped off our culinary experience with a warm pear compote, a la mode. And, yes, we were left with the desire to return and try more of Ajax's tasty dishes.

The Ajax Café is open for dinner Tuesdays through Sundays, starting at 5:00 p.m.; call 360-385-1965 for reservations; you'll not want to miss this special venue with good food and fun times. Reservations are a must at this popular café.

PORT TOWNSEND MARKETPLACE

RESTAURANTS & SHOPS

ELEVATED ICE CREAM & CANDY SHOP
We use the freshest local Ingredients in our flavorful ice creams, ices and sherbets, and handcraft our own chocolates and truffles. See our assortment of dark chocolate bars, candies and gifts. We're open late during boating season! Just two blocks west
of Point Hudson.
360-385-1156 • 627 Water St. • www.elevatedicecream.com

THE FOUNTAIN CAFE
Downtown Port Townsend is a casual and intimate cafe known for its excellent lunches and dinners enjoyed in a cozy setting one block from the hustle and bustle of Water Street. This popular eatery is located in the entertainment zone around Haller Fountain, a historic landmark famous for its statuesque, nude maiden and her attending sprites.
360-385-1364• 920 Washington St.
www.fountaincafept.com

MARINE THRIFT
Marine Thrift is a place where builders, sailors, DIYers, and the curious can find amazing deals on hardware, tools, and all kinds of other interesting boat gear. We keep good materials out of the landfill and in circulation while ensuring costs of boating stay accessible to many.
360-379-5807 • 315B Haines Place, Port Townsend
info@marinethrift.com • www.nwmaritime.org/marine-thrift

THE SWAN HOTEL AND COTTAGES
Located on the water front near the Point Hudson Marina, the NW Maritime Center and Historic Downtown. The Swan features suite,
studio, and hotel-style rooms, as well as deluxe cottages. Within walking distance of most of Port Townsend's restaurants, shops & attractions.
360-385-1718 • 222 Monroe at Water Street
frontdesk@theswanhotel.com • www.theswanhotel.com

THE WINE SELLER
The Small Town Wine Shop With a Big City Selection, since 1982. Amazing selection of fine wines, champagne, beer & ale, ciders, gourmet foods, cheese, coffee, chocolate & cigars. Surprisingly competitive prices! Generous mixed-whole and 1/2 case discounts. Knowledgeable friendly wine specialists!! OPEN 7 DAYS a WEEK. Marina delivery available!
360-385-7673 • 1010 Water St. • www.PTwineSeller.com

THE WOODEN BOAT CHANDLERY
Everything for wooden boats and the people who love them. For boat owners, we have bronze hardware, copper nails, rope, oakum, varnishes and more. For boat lovers, we have NOAA charts, cruising guides, galley ware, maritime books, nautical gifts and toys, and affordable apparel and more.
360-379-2629 • 431 Water Street • Yellow Building at NW Maritime Center • woodenboatchandlery.com

PORT TOWNSEND COMMUNITY EVENTS

Event	Month
Strange Brew festival	January
Shipwrights' Regatta	February
WBF Maritime Swap Meet	April
Port Townsend Rhododendron Festival	May
Classic Mariner Regatta	June
Steampunk Festival	June
Raker's Car Show	June
Centrum's Jazz Festival	July
Centrum's Acoustic Blues Festival	July
Wooden Boat Festival	September
Crafts By the Dock Fair	September
PT Film Festival	September
Kinetic Skulpture Weekend	October
Holiday Craft Fair	November
Festival of Lights	December

6368; harbormaster@porthadlockmarina.com; www.porthadlockmarina.com. Permanent moorage marina with limited guest moorage in unoccupied slips, call for availability. 30 & 50 amp power, water, restrooms with showers. Laundry, garbage, pumpout and free Wi-Fi. Open all year.

Hadlock Public Dock. A Port of Port Townsend day-use dock, located at Irondale. 75 feet of side-tie guest moorage, with 4-hour maximium stay at no charge. The much loved Ajax Cafe, located upland, reopened for business in October 2018; dinners served Tuesday-Sunday with scheduled live entertainment; call (360) 385-1965 for reservations. The adjacent **Northwest School of Wooden Boat Building** is worth a visit. Guided tours of the school are offered to the public on the first Friday of every month, starting at 3:00 p.m. The tour is approximately an hour and a half, covering boat building techniques and the school itself, which attracts students from around the world.

Fort Townsend Marine State Park. (360) 385-3595. Open summers only, 367 acres, 3 mooring buoys for boats 45 feet or less, restrooms, showers, no power. The park has campsites, swimming, playgrounds, hiking trails, picnic tables, fire rings, and kitchen shelters. Self-guided nature trail, clamming, fishing and scuba diving. Self-register and pay mooring buoy fee on shore.

Kilisut Harbor. Kilisut Harbor is entered through a channel between Walan Point and the spit protecting the harbor. When approaching the entrance, stay clear of the Navy restricted area off Walan Point. The channel is well marked though shallow, averaging about 11 feet. Currents can run strongly. The channel swings past Fort Flagler State Park on the north shore, then continues through Kilisut Harbor to Mystery Bay. Mystery Bay State Park, on the north shore, has a long dock and mooring buoys. At the head of Mystery Bay is the village of Nordland, and a great old general store with its small dock. Mystery Bay is a voluntary no anchoring zone to protect local shellfish.

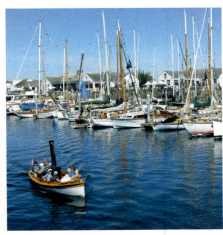

The Wooden Boat Festival in Port Townsend

An incredible variety of boats are seen in Port Townsend.

Port Townsend Boat Haven

Let Us Do Your Passage Planning

At the Waggoner Guide, we know the best places to go! We can take you to the most beautiful destinations as part of a flotilla, or help you plan the trip of your dreams.

Let us plan your itinerary and make all arrangements including moorage, coveted dinner reservations, and transfers for your crew.

Passage Planning for the Inside Passage, Virgin Islands and European Canal Boat trips.

902 - 8th Street Anacortes • 360.299.8500 • www.WaggonerGuide.com

NORTH PUGET SOUND

See Area Map Page 147 - Maps Not for Navigation

⑤ Fort Flagler Marine State Park. (360) 385-1259. On Marrowstone Island. Open all year, 784 acres, day use, overnight mooring and camping. Has 256 feet of dock space with 6-foot depths at zero tide (docks removed in winter), 6 mooring buoys for boats 45 feet or less, launch ramp. The current can run strongly through this area; allow for it when mooring. Restrooms, showers, portapotty dump, no power. Self-register and pay mooring fee on shore. Easy trails lead to old fortifications along the north shore of Marrowstone Island. Underwater park for divers. Snack and grocery concession. Boat rentals, fishing supplies. Standard, utility, and primitive campsites. Campsite reservations are a good idea in summer, call (800) 452-5687.

⑥ Mystery Bay Marine State Park. (360) 385-1259. In Kilisut Harbor on Marrowstone Island. Open all year, 10 acres, 683 feet dock space with 4.5-foot depth at zero tide, 7 mooring buoys for boats 45 feet or less. Pumpout, portapotty dump, toilets, launch ramp, no power, no showers. This park is open for day use only, but overnight mooring is permitted at the dock. The dock runs parallel to shore. Call Fort Flagler office for more information (360) 388-1259. Self-register and pay mooring fee on shore. The charming Nordland General Store is at the shallow end of the bay with a dock in front. Dinghy landing only.

Port Townsend. Port Townsend has two Port-owned marinas, Point Hudson Marina and the Port of Port Townsend's Boat Haven. Boat Haven is closer to a supermarket, but Point Hudson is closer to downtown.

Port Townsend is a major boatbuilding and repair center with craftsmen skilled in every nautical discipline. It is the home of the annual Wooden Boat Festival at Point Hudson Marina, held the weekend after Labor Day. Next to the Point Hudson Marina is the Northwest Maritime Center and the Wooden Boat Chandlery. Northwest Maritime Center often has boat building projects underway, visitors welcome. Wooden Boat Chandlery carries an array of nautical items. A Maritime Thrift Store for used gear is located in Boat Haven, 315 B Haines Place.

Port Townsend is a favorite destination. The commercial district is lined with imposing stone and brick buildings from before 1900. At that time, residents hoped Port Townsend would become the western terminus of the transcontinental railroad and the principal city on Puget Sound. Victorian homes, many of them beautifully restored and cared for, are on the hill above the business district. Port Townsend's upper business district is at the top of a long flight of stairs from the lower district on Water Street. The town of Port Townsend is a haven for writers, craftspeople and artists of all kinds. Tourists overwhelm the town during the summer, but that shouldn't keep anybody away.

Whether you're a woodenboat fan, history buff or antique collector, Port Townsend has a little bit of everything. Even with limited time to spare, the town's distinctive charm and spectacular views of Admiralty Inlet are enough to make the trip worth it. The Port Townsend Passenger Ferry, Puget Sound Express, runs between Port Townsend and Friday Harbor, May to late September, call (360) 385-5288 for reservations.

Point Hudson Marina

⑦ Port of Port Townsend Boat Haven. P.O. Box 1180, 2601 Washington Street, Port Townsend, WA 98368; (360) 385-2355; (800) 228-2803; info@portofpt.com; www.portofpt.com. Monitors VHF 66A. Open all year. Guest moorage along 900 feet of side-tie linear dock and unoccupied slips as available, 30 & 50 amp power, restrooms, showers, laundry, pumpout, portapotty dump, for-fee Wi-Fi, launch ramp. Garbage receptacles are locked. Make sure you get the code before carrying a load of garbage up the docks. Ethanol-free gasoline and diesel fuel at the fuel dock (The Fish 'N' Hole).

The marina is west of the ferry dock, and entered between a rock breakwater and a piling wavebreak. The first basin on the right has the Coast Guard float, home of the 87-foot Cutter *Osprey*, and slips for commercial vessels. The next basin is the recreational basin with combination fuel dock and registration dock, moorage slips, linear dock, launch ramps, and haulout facilities. Fuel/registration dock is on the right, after passing the Coast Guard float.

See Area Map Page 147 - Maps Not for Navigation

NORTH PUGET SOUND

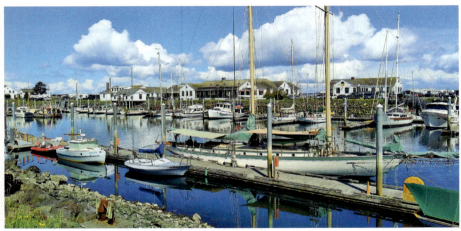

Point Hudson Marina is near the Northwest Maritime Center, a must see.

Call ahead or check-in at the marina office for guest moorage availability and slip or side-tie assignment, which may be in the recreational basin or commercial basin. The moorage office, in combination with the yard office, is located upland from C-dock. Vessels over 50 feet should call a day in advance. Spaces may be available through the marina for reciprocal yacht club members with Port Townsend Yacht Club. After hours, empty slips are marked on a map board at the top of the launch ramp and fuel dock. Temporary tie-up is just past the fuel dock towards the launch ramps, 1-hour limit.

Customs clearance by appointment only during standard business hours 8:00 a.m. to 4:00 p.m.; call (360) 385-3777. There is only one CBP agent stationed in Port Townsend in an office at Point Hudson. Please plan accordingly.

A hardware store and a large Safeway supermarket are across the highway. The local co-op market is a few blocks closer to town. The Chamber of Commerce Visitor Information Center is just beyond Safeway. Key City Fish, an excellent fish market, is in the boatyard area. Several good restaurants are nearby. More restaurants and a brew pub are in the Boat Haven. The main part of the town, with more restaurants and shops, is a 5-7 block walk.

A 300-ton Travelift and a smaller Travelift are available for haulout. Major boatbuilding and repair facilities and a chandlery (Admiral Ship Supply) are at the Boat Haven, and a West Marine store is nearby.

⑦ **The Fish 'N' Hole**. (360) 385-7031. Ethanol-free gasoline and diesel fuel, open all year. Located inside the Boat Haven breakwater. Floating store carries soda, snacks, ice, bait, tackle.

⑧ **Point Hudson Marina** & RV Park. P.O. Box 1180, Port Townsend, WA 98368; (360) 385-2828; (800) 228-2803; pthudson@portofpt.com; www.portofpt.com. Monitors VHF 09. Open all year, moorage slips to 70 feet. Water, 30 & 50 amp power, restrooms, showers, pumpout, laundry, for-fee Wi-Fi. Reservations recommended. Temporary tie-up is available for up to 4 hours, call ahead for space assignment. Ice, event facility, RV park and restaurants are on the property or nearby. The marina is within easy walking distance to town.

Enter the marina between two piling breakwaters that force the channel into a distinct bend, directly into the prevailing northwesterly summer winds. The limitation on the size of boats is mainly due to the turns required to enter the breakwater. The marina office is in a white building on the north side.

The Sea Marine haulout and boatyard facility is at the north end of the basin. There's no grocery store nearby, so Sea Marine has ice, propane, and beer. Three restaurants are in the historic white buildings on the north side of the harbor. Other marine businesses around the harbor include Hasse & Co. sailmakers, Brian Toss Rigging, and the Wooden Boat Chandlery located in the NW Maritime Center on the south side of the harbor entrance. The coffee shop at the Wooden Boat Chandlery has free Wi-Fi.

Customs clearance by appointment only during standard business hours 8:00 a.m. to 4:00 p.m.; call (360) 385-3777. There is only one CBP agent stationed in Port Townsend in an office at Point Hudson. Please plan accordingly.

Fort Worden Marine State Park. (360) 344-4400. North of Port Townsend. Open all year, 120 feet of dock space, 5 mooring buoys. Restrooms, showers and no power. The dock is protected by a wharf. Use the dock or a buoy—this is not a good anchorage, although a friend found good sand bottom in about 18 feet. He also reported that the wakes from passing ship traffic rolled him out of his bunk all night, and he won't overnight there again. Others say they've had no trouble at all. Underwater park for scuba diving. Boat launch with two ramps. Tennis courts, picnic areas, snack bar concession near moorage area. Hiking trails, swimming, fishing. Utility and primitive campsites. Campsite reservations taken year-round. Call (800) 452-5687. Self-register and pay mooring fees on shore.

Upland, the old officers' quarters can be rented overnight. Fort buildings house the Marine Science Center and the Centrum Foundation, which conduct workshops and seminars on the arts each summer.

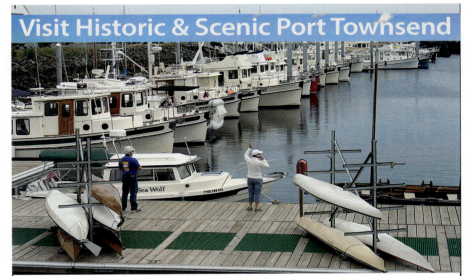

Stay at Point Hudson Marina & RV Park. Just steps away from the heart of downtown. Walk to shops, restaurants & more!

Reservations: 360-385-2828
PortofPT.com
pthudson@portofpt.com | VHF 09

Point Hudson Marina & RV Park

2020 WAGGONER CRUISING GUIDE

Ocean-Aged Rum and Bourbon

There is a theory that you can take a medium grade whiskey or rum and ocean age it in a cask that is agitated on a boat, and the flavor will improve significantly. Some say it has the same affect as aging the spirit 3x-5x. The color darkens and 2 years of aging tastes like 6 years, or as much as 10 years. Really? This requires some testing.

In the spirit of our 2020 Cuisine Edition, we are starting some serious research. Our cruising boats have quite a bit of motion during a summer's passage. Especially if we are going up and back on the Inside Passage. What if we purchased a wood cask and filled it with a medium grade spirit for one season, maybe two. Would a taste test show improvement with the "motion of the ocean?"

Where do you get an oak cask to age your rum or whiskey? The search is easy on Amazon, of course, where there is a good selection of oak aging casks. They come tastefully engraved with your boat's name and other details. The price is not too bad either – about $60 for a 2-liter model. Larger casks are available too.

Next, where to place the cask aboard the boat? I don't recommend the engine room, what with the heat and smells. I put mine up high in a storage area on the fly bridge to get the maximum motion, even while at anchor.

The next challenge will be clearing Customs. We called Canadian Customs, but it turns out they have not had this request before. We used a handy online duty calculator, since the duty varies by the purchase price and the proof of the spirit beyond the allowed 1.14 liters per person. I plan to carry the receipt for my cask as proof of its size, and the receipt for my rum purchase, no longer in the original bottle. US Customs allows you to bring back 1 liter per person, so aging 2 liters on a passage seems like a good idea. This will be an interesting experience crossing through both Canadian and US Customs: "Do you have anything to declare?" "Ah yes, I have a 2-liter cask of rum that is going through Ocean Aging."

We are not the first ones to do this. Jefferson's, a small batch distillery in Louisville, Kentucky, first started this experiment by sending 4 casks of whiskey on an ocean-going research vessel. After two years and four crossings of the equator, the results were a tasty and very dark colored spirit, apparently from the increased contact with the charred interior of the cask. Jefferson's Ocean Aged Whiskey is now very popular. To meet volume production, casks are now loaded into a container and placed on a round-the-world trip, returning back to New Orleans after almost a year at sea. Jefferson's has received rave reviews.

Locally, you can visit Von's 1000 Spirits in Seattle, not too far from the Pike Place Market and Bell Harbor. When you enter the restaurant and well known bar for spirits, you will see multiple barrels being rotated like a rotisserie with bourbon whiskey in an advanced state of aging. They call it BOSS Whiskey and claim by rotating the barrels 24/7 with the "Whiskey Whisperer" for three months – or 130,000 revolutions, it achieves a mystical flavor. They claim this accelerates the aging process by 25 times. We tested it and it is pretty good!

So, does the cruising motion at sea really produce better rum or whisky? Perhaps a taste comparison test may be in order at the end of the cruising season, with ocean-aged and non-ocean-aged grog. We will let you know. Stay tuned for more news this summer.

See Area Map Page 147 - Maps Not for Navigation

NORTH PUGET SOUND

LOCAL KNOWLEDGE

TIDE-RIP: The tide rip at Point Wilson can be dangerous to cruising boats. The bigger the ebb, the greater the chance for a tide-rip. A small ebb can produce no rip at all, particularly if the wind is light. Use the Bush Point current tables to predict the time of slack water and strength of maximum current. Those who think that a fast boat makes current tables unnecessary are wrong, and Point Wilson will prove them so.

Point Wilson. Point Wilson is the corner where Admiralty Inlet turns into the Strait of Juan de Fuca. On an ebb, a nasty tide-rip can build immediately north of Point Wilson, and stretch well across the mouth of Admiralty Inlet. If it's a big ebb and opposed by strong westerly winds, the seas in this area are not merely nasty, they are dangerous. They are high, steep and close together. They break. They are not long rollers; they are pyramid-shaped, and have no consistent pattern except for being ugly.

Since boats bound for the San Juan Islands or out the Strait of Juan de Fuca often schedule their passages to take advantage of the ebb, skippers must be aware of what can happen at Point Wilson, especially if a westerly is blowing. In such conditions, the wise approach is to favor the Whidbey Island side. The even wiser choice is to wait until slack water or the beginning of the flood. Better yet, wait for the wind to drop and then go at slack water.

For information on crossing the Strait of Juan de Fuca, see Chapter 5, Strait of Juan de Fuca.

WEST WHIDBEY ISLAND

South Whidbey State Park. On Admiralty Inlet on the Whidbey Island side, just south of Lagoon Point. Open all year, day use only. Campground closed October 15 to March 15. Restrooms, showers, no power. Anchoring in calm conditions or beaching only. Picnic sites, hiking trail, underwater park for scuba diving.

Anthony's Beach Cafe is a relaxed casual family affair located front and center at Port of Edmonds.

Fort Casey State Park. (360) 678-4519. Admiralty Head, adjacent to Keystone Harbor on Admiralty Inlet. Open all year, day-use and overnight camping, restrooms, no power, no showers. Has a 2-lane launch ramp with boarding floats. Not a good anchorage; beachable boats are best. Underwater park with artificial reef for scuba divers. Picnic areas, standard and primitive campsites. Lighthouse and interpretive center. Historic displays and remains of the old fort to explore. Guided tours during summer.

Fort Ebey State Park. (360) 678-4636. Open all year for day use and overnight camping. The park has restrooms and showers. Anchoring only, or small boats can be beached. Standard campsites, picnic sites. Interesting bunkers and gun batteries are in the old fort.

Joseph Whidbey State Park. (360) 678-4636. Northwest shore of Whidbey Island on Admiralty Inlet. Open April through September, day use only. Toilets. Anchor or beach only. One mile of sandy beach on Puget Sound. Picnic sites.

NORTHEAST PUGET SOUND

⑨ **Edmonds.** Edmonds, a prosperous community with a small-town feel to it, is about 8 miles north of Shilshole Bay on the east side of Puget Sound. Edmonds has a major rock breakwater-protected marina (the Port of Edmonds Marina) with excellent facilities for visiting boats. At the marina and in the town a short distance away you'll find a number of very good restaurants, antiques stores, a lively art scene, an historic 252-seat movie theater, art museum, performance theaters, and interesting shops and galleries. Edmonds "walks" well. This is an ideal destination for a weekend getaway, year-round. A courtesy van service to downtown Edmonds is provided for guests of the Port of Edmonds Marina. Don't miss Edmonds' many wonderful restaurants, including Chanterelle, The Cheesemonger's Table, and Daphnes Bar, among other fine dining establishments.

Port of Edmonds

VHF CH 69 • 425-775-4588 • PORTOFEDMONDS.ORG • INFO@PORTOFEDMONDS.ORG

2020 WAGGONER CRUISING GUIDE

NORTH PUGET SOUND See Area Map Page 147 - Maps Not for Navigation

Things to Do

1. Edmonds Waterfront Festival (June)

2. Marina Concert Series: Wednesday evenings and Sunday afternoons (June - mid-September).

3. Taste of Edmonds (Around the second week of August.)

4. Edmonds Public Art Walking Tour: 12 of 15 art pieces are in the city's central core.

5. Edmonds Historic Site Walking Tour: This self guided tour takes you past 29 sites in a one-square-mile section of the city's historic center.

6. Scratch Distillery: Learn about the distilling process for handcrafted vodkas and gin in a relaxed contemporary atmosphere. Tour & Tasting on Saturdays and Sundays.

7. Cascadia Art Museum The museum showcases American regional art from the mid-19th to the mid-20th century.

8. Edmonds Center for the Arts has theatre productions, comedy, film series, and live music.

9. Edmonds Segway Tours: Learn about Edmond's history or take a sunset tour. Book online or call (206) 947-5439.

⑨ **Port of Edmonds**. 336 Admiral Way, Edmonds, WA 98020; (425) 775-4588; info@portofedmonds.org; www.portofedmonds.org. Monitors VHF 69. Certified Clean Marina and Certified Clean Boatyard. Open 7 days a week all year. The fuel dock has ethanol-free gasoline & diesel. The marina has 500 feet of guest side-tie dock space, plus unoccupied slips when available. They can accommodate boats to 100 feet. The docks are served by 30 & 50 amp power, restrooms, showers, two pumpouts, a covered outdoor weather center, and public plaza. Used oil drop. Reservations accepted, with a fee.

Enter through the middle of the breakwater. Guest moorage and the fuel dock are immediately to the south. The marina has a large do-it-yourself work yard, a 10,000-pound public sling launch and a 50-ton Travelift. Close to two popular public beaches and a public fishing pier. An artificial reef for scuba diving (the first such site in the state) is next to the ferry dock just north of the marina. Fishing charters are available. It's a short walk to several restaurants. On Saturdays a market is set up near the downtown business district. The marina provides courtesy van service to downtown Edmonds. The marina personnel are friendly and helpful.

456 Admiral Way
(425) 771-4400

456 Admiral Way
(425) 771-4400

Possession Sound is on the southeast side of Whidbey Island between Possession Point and Mukilteo.

Mukilteo. (425) 263-8180. Mukilteo Lighthouse Park has a 4-lane launch ramp with floats in summer. It is exposed to ferry wakes and waves generated by winds on Possession Sound and Port Gardner. A launch fee is charged. Call for more information. Tucked behind the ferry wall and pilings next to Ivar's Restaurant are 3 seasonal, 24-foot Port of Everett floats for access to restaurants and other businesses ashore; caution is advised, floats shift forward and back between pilings. The Mukilteo Lighthouse is open for visitors April through September.

Gedney Island. (425) 327-2607. Gedney Island, known locally as Hat Island, is privately owned. The marina on the north shore is for Gedney Island property owners and their guests, and members from reciprocal yacht clubs.

CRUISERS COLLEGE
INCREASE YOUR NAUTICAL KNOWLEDGE AND DIY CLASSES

WATCH FOR OUR SEMINAR COURSES ON:

➤ Hands-on Diesel Engine Troubleshooting
➤ Troubleshooting Electrical Problems on Your Boat
➤ Taking Care of the Fiberglass Boat
➤ Troubleshooting Outboard Motors
➤ Troubleshooting Vessel Systems
➤ Marine Weather
➤ Cruising Essentials for Women
➤ Using New Technology for Navigation and Communications

To see a schedule of our up coming classes go to www.WaggonerGuide.com/CruisersCollege
Or call the Waggoner Guide office to register at 425.780.5015

Cruisers College is brought to you by

EVERETT MARKETPLACE
RESTAURANTS, SHOPS & SERVICES

ANTHONY'S HOMEPORT EVERETT
Located on Port Gardner Bay, the restaurant offers fresh northwest seafood with majestic views of Puget Sound islands and the Olympic Mountains. Lunch served Monday-Saturday, Sunday brunch and dinner served daily. Located at Everett Marina Village. Visitor moorage along the dock in front of the restaurant.
425-252-3333 • 1726 West Marine View Drive, Everett Marina Village
www.anthonys.com

ANTHONY'S WOODFIRE GRILL
Featuring specialties from its custom-built rotisserie, applewood-burning oven and applewood grill. Serving signature fresh northwest seafood selections, as well as northwest beef selections at lunch and dinner daily. Located at Everett Marina Village. Visitor moorage along the dock in front of Anthony's HomePort.
425-258-4000 • 1722 West Marine View Drive, Everett Marina Village
www.anthonys.com

BAYSIDE MARINE AND DRYSTACK
Offering consignment brokerage, used boat sales, parts and service for most major brands of pleasure boats and inside boat drystack. Keep your boat inside with secure rack storage with private dock and launching.
425-252-3088 • 1111 Craftsman Way •
www.baysidemarine.com

Calendar of Events

ALL SUMMER LONG:
Waterfront Farmer's Market
Music at the Marina
Jetty Island Days
Harbor Tours

APRIL
Everett Half Marathon

APRIL
Milltown Sailing Swap Meet

MAY
Opening Day of Boating

JUNE
Marina Cleanup Day

JULY
Fourth of July Celebration
Sail-In Cinema

AUGUST
Fresh Paint Festival of Artist at Work
Sail-In Cinema

SEPTEMBER
Mukilteo Lighthouse Festival
Wheels on the Waterfront Car Show

DECEMBER
Holiday on the Bay

Port of Everett
www.portofeverett.com/events
or 800-729-7678

Photos courtesy of Port of Everett

NORTH PUGET SOUND

See Area Map Page 147 - Maps Not for Navigation

Port of Everett Marina

Tulalip Bay. Anchorage is possible, but Tulalip Bay is very shallow, with a reef guarding the entrance and drying shoals inside. Several private floats and mooring buoys owned by members of the Tulalip Tribes often occupy the bay.

 LOCAL KNOWLEDGE

STRONG CURRENTS: Currents in the Snohomish River can be quite strong, particularly on an ebb tide. Allow for the current as you maneuver.

Night Lights: At night, lights ashore in Everett's Navy facilities make the entrance channel buoys very difficult to see and identify. A vessel approaching at night should be extremely cautious.

⑩ **Everett.** The Port of Everett Marina is home to a fishing fleet as well as private pleasure craft. Entry is about a mile upstream from the marked mouth of the Snohomish River. Information about moorage can be obtained from the fuel dock just inside the piling breakwater.

When you are in the river and approaching the marina entrance, watch for debris in the water and pay close attention to your navigation. Several aids to navigation, including one buoy marking a sunken ship, can be confusing. Although the channel can be entered between Lighted Buoy 3 and Light 5 off the south end of Jetty Island, the water between them is somewhat shoal. For complete safety we recommend entering by leaving Lighted Buoy 3 to port. The channel leads past the U.S. Navy homeport facilities.

The marina is a long hike from the central business district, but bus and taxi service are available.

Everett offers numerous activities of interest. The Everett Marina hosts a farmers market in Boxcar Park at the disabled-access dock, Sundays, 11:00 a.m. to 4:00 p.m. May through October. The Port of Everett hosts a summertime waterfront concert series at Port Gardner Landing June through August, from 6:30 p.m. to 8:30 p.m. on Thursday and Saturday. The Xfinity Arena at Everett (www.xfinityarenaeverett.com) brings big-name entertainment. For professional sports with an intimate feeling, take in a minor league baseball game and cheer on the Aquasox. The July 4 fireworks show is Puget Sound's largest outside Seattle, and right in the laps of the Everett moorage.

Across the river from the marina is a Port-owned float at Jetty Island, which has what is probably the largest pure sand beach on Puget Sound. The Langus Waterfront Park, with a good launching facility, is on the north shore of the main river channel, a short distance up the river from the Port of Everett Marina.

Farther up the Snohomish River, Dagmar's Landing is a large dry-land storage facility with a huge fork lift truck and a long float. A detailed chart or local knowledge are required before continuing beyond Dagmar's.

THINGS TO DO

1. **Boeing Aircraft Factory.** Take a 90-minute tour of the world's largest aircraft plant. Children must be at least 4 feet tall. A cab ride away.

2. **Flying Heritage Collection.** A remarkable collection of one-of-a-kind military aircraft from the past 75 years. Located at Paine Field, adjacent to the Boeing factory.

3. **Tulalip Casino Resort.** Adult gaming and good restaurants. The Tulalip Amphitheatre often has live music.

4. **Everett Performing Arts Center.** See performances at this beautiful performing arts center about 1.5 miles from the marina.

5. **Angel of the Winds Arena.** International shows and sporting events, ice skating. Located about 2 miles from the marina.

6. **Port Gardner Bay Winery.** A boutique winery with relaxed tastings. They also offer classes in winemaking. About 1.5 miles from the marina.

7. **Everett Farmers Market.** Every Sunday at Boxcar Park, just up from the marina.

8. **Port Gardner Landing.** Summer Concerts.

9. **Legion Memorial Golf Course.** Close to the marina.

⑩ **Port of Everett Marina.** 1205 Craftsman Way, Suite 105, Everett, WA 98201; (425) 259-6001; marina@portofeverett.com; www.portofeverett.com. Monitors VHF 16. Certified Clean Marina. Open all year, gasoline and diesel at fuel dock. Over 5000 feet of guest moorage with depths 10 to 16 feet, unoccupied slips used when available. Moorage is first-come, first-served, and self-pay stations are on the docks. Reservations accepted for group rendezvous. If staying less than six hours before 10 p.m., guest moorage is free. Water, 20, 30 & 50 amp power, restrooms, showers, laundry, multiple free pumpout stations, free portapotty dump, for-fee Wi-Fi.

Handicapped-accessible guest moorage available. Watch for strong currents when landing at the guest dock. The Port's Craftsman District has a Travelift haulout to 75 tons with yard storage, a boatyard for repairs and maintenance. The Travelift is at the east end of the moorage. The Jetty Landing launch, a 13-lane launch ramp (largest in the

See Area Map Page 147 - Maps Not for Navigation

NORTH PUGET SOUND

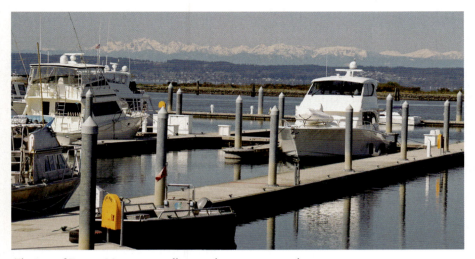
The Port of Everett Marina is excellent, with attractions nearby.

state), is just north of the marina.

The Port of Everett's North Marina offers a first-class 42-slip guest moorage facility. The concrete docks are wide, stable and heavily built. Power is 30 & 50 amp, with 100 amp at the end moorages. A pumpout line is built into the main docks with attachments at each slip. The basin has its own restrooms, showers, and laundry. The Port of Everett is a large, complete marina, with shops, full repairs, services nearby, and and two chandleries. An attractive marina village with a hotel, shops, a West Marine store and good restaurants is adjacent to the south mooring basin. The wheelchair-accessible float is next to the street in the east end of the south basin. The Waterfront Center Building on the north side of the marina has an inside coffee area, a brew-pub restaurant and a distillery. Harbor Marine, a complete marine supply store and chandlery, is on 10th Street between the north docks and the Jetty Landing launch ramps. They have added a snack bar and cafe with daily specials.

The Port of Everett has undergone substantial development of the uplands, including a hotel, apartments, and splash park. New docks were installed in 2019, and additional upgrades are planned for 2020.

1726 West Marine View Dr.
(425) 252-3333

1722 West Marine View Dr.
(425) 258-4000

Everett Marine Park. On the Snohomish River, north of the Port of Everett Marina. Open all year, 700 feet of overnight guest moorage, restrooms, pumpout, portapotty dump. Pay station on shore. No power, no showers. The park has a 13-lane launch ramp with boarding floats. An attendant is on duty summer and fall.

Jetty Island. (425) 257-8304; www.everettwa.org. Jetty Island is a lovely low sand island across the river from the Everett Marina and Everett Marine Park. Jetty Island is open all year. Two large docks provide space for a number of boats. Boats can overnight at the dock. Jetty Island has toilets but no showers, no power, and no water for boats. The toilets are closed in winter. Pay station on shore.

River currents can make landing at the docks challenging. Before approaching the dock, be sure your boat is well fendered, dock lines ready, and contingency plans agreed upon.

Jetty Island is a wildlife preserve with great birdwatching. The Parks Department offers nature programs during the summer, and runs boats from the launch ramp to the island, no charge, July 4 through Labor Day.

Snohomish River Delta. The Snohomish River Delta has three main mouths—Steamboat Slough, Ebey Slough, and the main river—each of which is navigable for all or part of its length. Cautious boaters can cruise the delta.

Contributing Editor Tom Kincaid has cruised all of this area, some of it several times, in a 30-foot sailboat, a 36-foot powerboat, and an outboard-powered dinghy. The waters are subject to tidal action. Drying flats are off the river mouths. Enter only during the hours of highest tides. The Snohomish River Delta is a fascinating place with wildlife, calm anchorages, and quiet.

Langus Waterfront Park. North shore of the Snohomish River. The park is open all year and has restrooms, but no guest moorage, power or showers. This is a City of Everett park with a 2-lane concrete launch ramp and boarding floats. A wide concrete float is for fishing and launching rowing shells.

Port Susan. Port Susan is surrounded by Camano Island to the west and the mainland to the east. A swampy waterway connects the northern end of Port Susan with Skagit Bay. Kayak Point in Port Susan is a Snohomish County Park. North of Kayak Point, Port Susan shoals to drying flats, through which meander the two mouths of the Stillaguamish River. At high tide it is possible to cross over these flats and enter South Pass to Stanwood, although the bridge just beyond Stanwood is very low.

Kayak Point County Park. 15610 Marine Drive, Stanwood, WA 98292; (360) 652-7992. Open all year, restrooms but no showers. Anchorage only close to shore. The anchorage is exposed to southerly winds. Launch ramp with boarding floats. Fishing pier, no overnight moorage at the pier.

Saratoga Passage. Saratoga Passage separates Camano Island from Whidbey Island. The

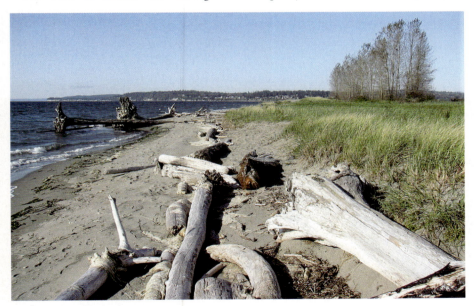
Jetty Island Wildlife Preserve is a short dinghy ride form Everett Marina.

NORTH PUGET SOUND

See Area Map Page 147 - Maps Not for Navigation

waters are better protected and often smoother than Admiralty Inlet, and the current is less. Boats running between Seattle and the San Juan Islands often choose this inside route via Deception Pass or La Conner when the wind and seas are getting up in Admiralty Inlet.

This is not to say the waters are always smooth. One year, Bob and Marilynn Hale ran into uncomfortable seas while southbound in Saratoga Passage during a 25-knot southerly storm, and were forced to run back to Oak Harbor for shelter.

Saratoga Passage is relatively free of dangers, but it does have two tricks: Rocky Point(s) and Holmes Harbor. A study of the chart shows two Rocky Points in Saratoga Passage. One is on Whidbey Island at the entrance to Holmes Harbor; the other is at the north end of Camano Island.

Southbound boats may be tempted to go straight into Holmes Harbor instead of turning southeast past the Whidbey Island Rocky Point. If you're not watching your chart, the appeal is quite strong. Follow the Camano Island shoreline.

Cama Beach State Park. (360) 387-1550. Twelve miles southwest of Stanwood. Open all year, anchoring only. Restrooms, showers, small store, 15 miles of hiking and biking trails, 24 cabins, 7 deluxe cabins and 2 bungalows. The Center for Wooden Boats runs the boathouse and boat rental operation, first-come, first-served. Many classic rowboats and sailboats are available for hourly or daily rentals. The workshops on shore may have a boat building project or two underway. See the CWB website (www.cwb.org) for information on classes offered at Cama Beach and available boat rentals. Advance contact is recommended for hours and days of operation (360) 387-9361 or cama@cwb.org.

Elger Bay. Elger Bay is a good anchorage, mud bottom, with surprisingly good protection from northerly winds. Watch your depths close to the head of the bay.

The historic village of Coupville offers shops, cafes, and a museum.

Camano Island State Park. (360) 387-3031. Fourteen miles southwest of Stanwood. Open all year for day use and overnight camping, first-come, first-served. Restrooms, showers, no power. Anchoring only. Launch ramp. Underwater park for scuba diving. Cabins, standard and primitive campsites.

⑪ **Langley.** The Langley Boat Harbor serves the delightful village of Langley. If the boat harbor is crowded, as it usually is during the summer, anchorage is good south and east of the harbor, unless strong northerly winds make the area uncomfortable. Langley Boat Harbor has a long history of being creative about getting another boat tied up. Their motto is, "We'll try to fit you in." Be sure you have fenders set on both sides.

The town of Langley itself has streets lined with historic buildings that house interesting shops, excellent galleries, fine restaurants, a whale museum, a craft brewery, and a vintage 250-seat movie theater. Langley is a good walking town. You'll find beautiful views of Saratoga Passage from the bluff above the marina. A couple blocks from the cozy commercial district is where the farms begin.

⑪ **Port of South Whidbey/Langley.** P.O. Box 872, Freeland, WA 98249; (360) 221-1120; harbormaster@portofsouthwhidbey.com; www.portofsouthwhidbey.com; Monitors VHF 66A. Guest moorage year-round. Approximately 1,100 feet of moorage. Docks D and E are located behind the outer breakwater; docks A, B, and C are behind the wall of the inner harbor. Depths shallow to approximately 8 feet at zero tide south of the breakwater. Check your depth.

Reservations accepted online 48 hours in advance, highly recommended during the peak season. Restrooms, showers, 20, 30, 50 & 100 amp power, launch ramp (higher tides only), pumpout barge, free Wi-Fi. Friendly service staff tries to help every boat dock. Nearby groceries, unique shops, boutiques, bakery, and laundromat are up the hill in town. Free shuttle to town in season. Crabbing for everyone at the upper wharf, and by reservation only off D and E docks at the marina.

Holmes Harbor. Holmes Harbor indents the eastern shore of Whidbey Island for about 5 miles in a southerly direction. It is deep and relatively unprotected from strong northerlies. The harbor has a good launch ramp at the head and anchorage along either shore. Honeymoon Bay is a good anchorage. Holmes Harbor is subject to williwaws, the unusually strong gusts of wind that spill across the lower portion of Whidbey Island.

Langley Boat Harbor with floating breakwater moorage and inner harbor docks

Langley Boat Harbor

See Area Map Page 147 - Maps Not for Navigation   NORTH PUGET SOUND

⑫ **Honeymoon Bay.** Honeymoon Bay is a favored anchorage on the west shore of Holmes Harbor. Private mooring buoys take up most of the good spots; but with a little diligence, satisfactory anchoring depths with adequate swinging room can be found. Honeymoon Bay is exposed to northerly winds.

Penn Cove. Penn Cove is about 10 miles north of Holmes Harbor. The cove extends nearly 4 miles west from Long Point, with the town of Coupeville on the southern shore. Anchorage is good along both shores and toward the head of the bay, but be aware that strong winds from the Strait of Juan de Fuca can blow across the low neck of Whidbey Island at the head of the cove. This is where the famous Penn Cove mussels come from. Watch for mussel-growing pens.

⑬ **Coupeville.** The town of Coupeville is served by the Coupeville Wharf, a 415-foot-long causeway on pilings extending over the beach to deep water. Coupeville is quaint, old, and friendly, with a variety of shops, galleries, and restaurants. A display of tribal canoes is 200 feet from the head of the wharf.

⑬ **Coupeville Wharf.** P.O. Box 128, Green Bank, WA 98253; (360) 678-6379. Open all year, 480 feet of dock space, first-come, first-served, free moorage before 5:00 p.m. Watch depths at low and minus tides. Gasoline and diesel at the fuel dock. There is also room to anchor in front of town. Pumpout, restrooms and showers are on the wharf, no power or water on the float. Free Wi-Fi is available on the float and throughout town. A gift shop, a coffee shop, and a restaurant are at the outer end of the wharf. The town's shops and restaurants are within easy walking distance. Island Transit, with stops nearby, offers free bus service to key points on Whidbey Island.

Oak Harbor Marina, with picnic tables along the water, is a good place for gatherings.

Captain Coupe Park. 602 NE Ninth St., Coupeville, WA 98239-0577; (360) 678-4461. Open all year with restrooms and nearby portapotty dump, no power, no showers. Anchoring only. A launch ramp with a float is installed in the summer. The park is one-quarter mile by water from Coupeville wharf. It's better to anchor closer to the wharf. Mud flats surround the launch area at low tide.

SKAGIT BAY TO BELLINGHAM BAY

⑭ **Oak Harbor.** Oak Harbor is a shallow and well protected port with a major, city-owned marina. The entrance channel is marked by red and green buoys and beacons, beginning with Buoy 2, about 0.6 miles offshore from Maylor Point. From Buoy 2 the entry channel runs northward into Oak Harbor, and makes a 90-degree turn to the east for the final mile that leads to the marina.

Do not pass between Buoy 2 and Maylor Point. The water there is shoal and littered with large boulders that have been known to tear stern drive units out of boats.

The only moorage is at the spacious Oak Harbor Marina. The marina has complete facilities and park grounds ashore for dog-walking, games, or strolling. It's a bit of a walk to town, and the nearest grocery store is 1½ miles away.

Anchorage can be found just outside the marina close to the entry channel. The bottom is soft; be sure your anchor is well set. A small float for dinghies is in front of the business district, about a 1-mile walk from the marina. The float dries at low tide.

Events: Holland Happening is the last weekend of April; the town's celebration of their Dutch heritage. Hydroplane races are held mid-August.

Festivals: Oak Harbor Music Festival is Labor Day weekend; free admission.

Taxi: (360) 682-6920 or (360) 279-9330.

LOCAL KNOWLEDGE

ENTRANCE CHANNEL: Shoals line each side of the channel all the way into Oak Harbor. You will go aground if you stray.

⑭ **Oak Harbor Marina.** 865 SE Barrington Dr., Oak Harbor, WA 98277; (360) 279-4575; csublet@ohmarina.org; www.ohmarina.org. Monitors VHF 16, switch to 68. Open all year (closed Sundays & holidays, October through March); twenty 40-foot slips on F-dock and side-tie along G-dock. Reservations accepted, with first night charged; non-refundable. The fuel dock has mid-grade ethanol-free gasoline, diesel and propane. 20 & 30 amp power, water, restrooms, showers, laundry, pumpout, porta-potty dump, and free Wi-Fi.

One set of restrooms and showers is on the lower level of the administration building at

Oak Harbor Marina

2020 WAGGONER CRUISING GUIDE

NORTH PUGET SOUND

Reference Only – Not for Navigation

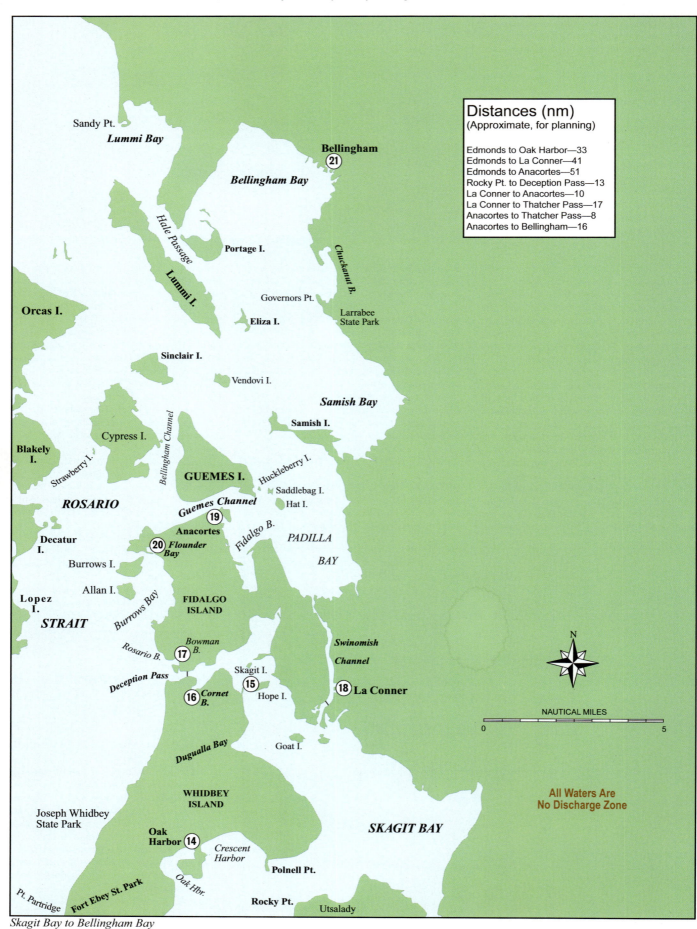

Distances (nm)
(Approximate, for planning)

Edmonds to Oak Harbor—33
Edmonds to La Conner—41
Edmonds to Anacortes—51
Rocky Pt. to Deception Pass—13
La Conner to Anacortes—10
La Conner to Thatcher Pass—17
Anacortes to Thatcher Pass—8
Anacortes to Bellingham—16

All Waters Are No Discharge Zone

Skagit Bay to Bellingham Bay

SWINOMISH CHANNEL

In October, 2013, the U.S. Coast Guard changed the buoyage in Swinomish Channel. The "change point," noting "return from the sea (Red Right Returning)" was moved to the center of La Conner. It previously was about 2 miles north of La Conner. Old charts do not reflect this change. Buoy R22 has been changed to G35; G23 to R34; R26 to G31; and G25 to R32.

Swinomish Channel current predictions and slack water timing are dependent upon tidal high and low water level differences and river outflow. Therefore, time of slack water and current flow can only be estimated. According to Ports and Passes, slack water occurs at La Conner Landing 2.0 to 3.5 hours after high or low tide; current flows north from 2.0 to 3.5 hours before and after high tide; current flows south from 2.0 to 3.5 hours before and after low tide. General rule of thumb is to use Seattle tides and add 30 minutes (adjust for daylight saving). Tides and helpful information for transiting the Swinomish Channel are found in Ports and Passes in the La Conner section.

The southern entrance to Swinomish Channel is just north of Goat Island. Do not turn into the channel until the range markers in Dugualla Bay, to the west, are in line. The channel is well marked but narrow, particularly if you meet a tug with a tow of logs. Check the range markers as you go. Rock piles lie immediately outside of the dredged channel. Tidal currents flow across the channel and can sweep a boat off course. Occasionally a deadhead log will imbed itself in the shallow bottom. At Hole in the Wall the channel bends sharply around a high rock outcropping. Swirling currents in this area call for close attention.

From Hole in the Wall to the railroad swing bridge to the north, the channel is a no wake zone. Be particularly mindful of your wake when passing through the town of La Conner.

Red, Right, Returning: The buoyage system for Swinomish Channel south of the town of La Conner assumes "return" is from the south. North of La Conner and in Padilla Bay, the dredged channel assumes "return" is from the north. Red navigation aids in Padilla Bay are on the west side.

Rainbow Bridge (now painted orange), located just south of La Conner, has an overhead clearance of 75 feet.

Swinomish Channel is dredged every four to six years, but it silts up between dredgings. Maintenance dredging of the channel was completed in November 2018. Keep in mind that the silting occurs at the same locations each time, so at low tide the wary boater can avoid them. Here are the troublesome shoaling areas:

1. West of Goat Island, the very entrance to Swinomish Channel is shoal. Especially on a low tide, swing wide and don't cut any of the entry buoys close. The channel leading past Goat Island is quite shoal. On very low tides deep draft vessels such as sailboats should wait for more water.

2. South of town at Shelter Bay, a shoal extends from the west side of the channel, approximately from the southernmost house north to the entrance channel of the Shelter Bay development. Favor the center of the channel.

3. About midway along the main La Conner waterfront, a shoal extends from the west side of the channel, approximately between the middle of the restaurants on the La Conner side and a tall pole with antennas on the west side. Favor the east side of the channel.

4. Just south of the highway bridges and the railroad swing bridge, at the location marked "Pipeline Area," sand accumulates on top of the pipeline to create another shoal.

5. The most troublesome shoal is opposite Buoy 29, north of the railroad swing bridge and the highway bridges. This shoal stretches across the entire channel.

Shelter Bay, with its private moorage, indents the western shore of Swinomish Channel just north of Hole in the Wall.

Then comes lovely Rainbow Bridge (actually it's orange), vertical clearance 75 feet in the center. North of Rainbow Bridge the town of La Conner stretches along the eastern shore of the channel. Three city public floats, La Conner Marina, and several privately-owned floats serve restaurants and other businesses along the town waterfront. Across from La Conner the Swinomish Indian Reservation occupies most of the west side of the channel.

Just north of La Conner is a point where the flood and ebb currents meet, ebbing south past La Conner and north toward Anacortes. The channel is marked by buoys and a range, but follows a generally northerly direction until

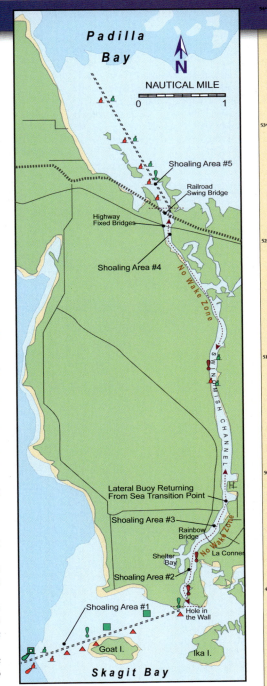

Swinomish Channel

it passes under a swinging railroad bridge and fixed highway bridges to enter Padilla Bay. The highway bridges have a vertical clearance of 75 feet. The railroad bridge is very low. Hundred-car-long crude oil trains headed to the local refinery can close the bridge for 20 minutes or more, holding up boat traffic. If you are there at the wrong time, consider dropping the anchor until the train has passed. Currents can be strong. Overhead power and telephone cables cross at several charted locations, with a minimum vertical clearance of 72 feet.

NORTH PUGET SOUND

See Area Map Page 164 - Maps Not for Navigation

the head of the docks. Additional restrooms, showers, and laundry are in buildings a short distance away. A floating restroom facility is on the guest moorage F-dock.

In the adjacent park, there are Bocce ball and Petanque courts. Free loaner bicycles at the marina.

Military and retired military (with DoD I.D.) can walk onto the Navy base area and use the Navy Exchange for shopping and provisioning. The Exchange is in one of the large buildings that formerly was a hangar. A seasonal convenience store is open in the summer.

A 100-foot-wide concrete launch ramp, built in 1942 to launch PBY Catalina patrol seaplanes, is at the south end of the marina. Extended parking for trailers and tow vehicles. Mariners Haven has repairs and a chandlery.

Oak Harbor Marina is protected by a floating concrete breakwater; guest moorage is in slips on the inside of this breakwater labeled F-dock, and along the float leading to shore, labeled G-dock. A dredged channel, 100 feet wide with a least depth of 12 feet at zero tide, leads along the west face of the breakwater and around the end, to side-tie moorage on G-dock. Water outside the channel is shoal. The safest approach to G-dock, north side moorage, is to head directly for the entrance light at the south end of the breakwater; then turn to port and proceed along the outside (west side) of the breakwater to the north moorage.

Running with a flood current under Deception Pass Bridge on the way to Cornet Bay

Crescent Harbor. Just east of Oak Harbor. The Navy facility along the western shore near the head of the bay has large old hangars that once housed PBY Catalina flying boat patrol aircraft. Crescent Harbor is exposed to southerly winds, but in northerlies or westerlies it's a good anchorage.

Rocky Point. Tidal currents meet off Rocky Point. North of the point they flood south out of Deception Pass and Swinomish Channel. South of the point they flood north out of Saratoga Passage.

Skagit Bay. Skagit Bay extends from Polnell Point and Rocky Point to Deception Pass. The bay becomes increasingly shoal toward the east due to Skagit River outflow. The navigable channel parallels the Whidbey Island shore, and is well marked by buoys. Use caution in this channel; buoys can be dragged out of position by tugs with tows. The village of Utsalady, with a launch ramp, is on the Camano Island side of the channel. Anchorage there is not protected from northerly winds and waves, but Correspondents James &

Cornet Bay

Bowman Bay

Deception Pass Marine State Park

166   www.WaggonerGuide.com

Jennifer Hamilton report anchoring through a southeast gale without difficulty.

⑮ **Skagit Island, Hope Island, Similk Bay.** Hope Island is part of Deception Pass Marine State Park with 4 mooring buoys on the north side and good anchorage, particularly along the south shore. Check the depths before using the buoys. No power, water, restrooms or showers. Trails lead around and through the island. Skagit Island, just to the north, has 2 mooring buoys along its north side. Self-register and pay mooring buoy fees on shore. Similk Bay is shoal but navigable in shallow draft boats. Anchorage is possible almost anywhere.

⑮ **Kiket Island / Kukutali Preserve.** Located just east of Skagit Island. Kiket Island is part of the Deception Pass State Park and jointly managed with the Swinomish Tribal Community reservation. The Island is open to the public for day-use only from dawn to dusk. Although technically an island, Kiket is connected to Fidalgo Island by a thin tombolo. Kiket Island can only be accessed by non-motorized boats. Access to Flagstaff Point on the west end of Kiket Island is restricted. Trails, a viewing platform, and pit toilets can be found on Kiket Island.

Strawberry Island. This small, undeveloped island is part of the Deception Pass Marine State Park and is seldom visited. Strawberry Island (east of Deception Pass) should not be confused with the island of the same name located west of Cypress Island.

⑯ **Cornet Bay.** Cornet Bay, tucked in behind Ben Ure Island, indents the north shore of Whidbey Island just east of Deception Pass. A dredged channel marked by pilings leads to Deception Pass Marina and a state park, both of which offer visitor moorage, and serve as a place to hole up while waiting for the tidal change. The passage west of Ben Ure Island should not be attempted except at high tide, and then only by shallow draft boats. The channel to a county dock at the south end of the bay is very shallow and should only be attempted with local knowledge. Vessel Assist towing and emergency rescue office nearby.

⑯ **Deception Pass Marina.** 200 West Cornet Bay Road, Oak Harbor, WA 98277; (360) 675-5411. Open all year. The marina has some slips reserved for visiting boats and uses unoccupied slips as available; contact by phone, no VHF. The docks have water and 30 amp power. Limited room for larger boats up to 65 feet. Ethanol-free gasoline, diesel, and propane at the fuel dock. The store carries convenience groceries, bait, tackle, charts, books, beer and wine. Restrooms, no showers (showers are available at the state park next door). Call ahead for availability of guest moorage. Nearby laundry and haulout.

⑯ **Deception Pass Marine State Park, Cornet Bay.** Open all year for day use and overnight moorage; first-come, first-served. Payment boxes on the floats and at a kiosk on shore. The park has 600 feet of side-tie dock space, restrooms, showers and pumpout, but no power. Two additional 100-foot floats are anchored offshore and not connected to land. A 5-lane launch ramp has boarding floats. Hiking trails and picnic areas nearby. Groceries, laundromat and services are at Deception Pass Marina. Park has campsites, but not near this area. On Ben Ure Island, a single cabin is available for rent. Reservations online or call (888) 226-7688.

Bowman Bay in Deception Pass State Park offers anchorage and scenic hiking trails.

LOCAL KNOWLEDGE

STRONG CURRENTS: Currents run to 8 knots in Deception Pass with strong eddies and overfalls. Dangerous waves can form when a big ebb current meets strong westerly winds. It is best to time an approach to enter the pass at or near slack water. Try to travel single-file.

Deception Pass. Deception Pass narrows to 200 yards at Pass Island, one of the anchors for the spectacular 144-foot-high bridge that connects Whidbey Island and Fidalgo Island.

Tidal current predictions are shown under Deception Pass in the tide and current books. An even narrower pass, Canoe Pass, lies north of Pass Island. Kayaks use Canoe Pass, but lacking local knowledge we wouldn't run our boat through it.

From the west, the preferred route to Deception Pass is just to the south of Lighthouse Point and north of Deception Island.

North of Lighthouse Point, **Bowman Bay**, also known as Reservation Bay, is part of Deception Pass State Park.

⑰ **Deception Pass Marine State Park, Bowman Bay** (Reservation Bay). Open all year for day use and overnight camping and mooring. Restrooms with showers, no power. Bowman Bay has a gravel 1-lane launch ramp. Standard campsites are on the north shore. The park has picnic sites and outdoor kitchens. An underwater park for diving is near the mouth of Bowman Bay, near Rosario Head. When entering take care to avoid Coffin Rocks and Gull Rocks, which cover at high tide. Safe entry can be made by staying fairly close to the Reservation Head side of the entrance.

A mooring float, approximately 100 feet long and not connected to shore, is located behind Reservation Head. On the east side of the bay, the 40-foot-long float at the park pier is for dinghies. The small buoys next to the pier are used as a race course for remote-controlled miniature sailboats.

Anchorage is also possible in the bay north of Rosario Head, but it is exposed to wave action from Rosario Strait.

⑰ **Deception Pass Marine State Park, Sharpe Cove.** Open all year for day use and overnight camping and mooring. The park has 160 feet of dock space, no power. Restrooms, showers, portapotty dump, picnic sites, kitchen. Campsites are east of Sharpe Cove. The onshore facility is the Walla Walla University Rosario Beach Marine Laboratory.

Shelter Bay Marina. 1000 Shoshone Drive, La Conner, WA 98257; (360) 466-3805; www.shelterbay.net; kemerson@shelterbay.net. Shelter Bay Marina is on the west side of Swinomish Channel just south of La Conner. Primarily permanent moorage, but some guest moorage space is available. Water, 30 & 50 amp power, pumpout, restrooms, showers, no laundry.

⑱ **La Conner.** The Port of Skagit's La Conner Marina, with two large moorage basins, is a short distance north of downtown La Conner. Both moorage basins have guest moorage and full facilities for visitors. Fuel is available adjacent to the marina at La Conner Landing, and propane is available at Boater's Discount marine supply store between the two basins.

The town of La Conner has three public floats for guest moorage for boats up to 45 feet, with stays of 24 hours, located along the quarter-mile long waterfront boardwalk.

Current in Swinomish Channel can be strong and difficult to predict. Allow for

La Conner Marketplace
Restaurants, Shops & Services

Calendar of Events

JANUARY
Skagit Valley Winter Birds Festival

FEBRUARY
Annual Smelt Derby

MARCH
Annual La Conner Daffodil Festival

APRIL
Skagit Valley Tulip Festival

MAY
Opening Day Boating Season Parade

JUNE
MoNA Auction

JULY
Hometown 4th of July Celebration

AUGUST
Annual Classic Boat & Car Show

OCTOBER
Festival of Family Farms
Annual Brew on the Slough –
La Conner's Beer Fest

NOVEMBER
Arts Alive!

DECEMBER
Community Tree Lighting
Lighted Boat Parade

Dates may change, check website
www.lovelaconner.com

Boardwalk photo courtesy of
La Conner Chamber of Commerce
Town photo courtesy of Aimee Beckwith

LA CONNER CHAMBER
A beautiful village on the banks of the Swinomish Channel. Shop, Dine, Art and Wine! Come experience the LaConner love. Located just 60 miles north of Seattle in the heart of Skagit Valley
360-466-4778 • 413 Morris Street,
La Conner, WA • www.LoveLaConner.com

LA CONNER BREWING COMPANY
Unique Northwest-style family-friendly brewpub featuring wood-fired pizzas, burgers and other fresh local pub fare served with our small-batch, hand-crafted beers. Wines and hard ciders available too. Enjoy by the fireplace or on the garden terrace.
360-466-1415 • 117 S. First Street,
La Conner, WA
www.LaConnerBrewery.com

LA CONNER MARITIME
Servicing, building and equipping boats for nearly 40 years, we take pride in our reputation as a friendly, professional boat yard that can handle every customer need from pressure washing the hull to rebuilding the engine.
360-466-3629 • 920 W. Pearle Jensen Way
La Conner, WA
www.LaConnerMaritime.com

LA CONNER LANDING FUEL DO[CK]
The friendliest and most convenient fuel dock around! Fuel up and pump out at th[e] same time. Quality marine diesel and etha[nol] free gas. Located on the Swinomish chan[nel] just north of town. Ice, bait, food and ma[rine] supplies. Hours vary by season.
360-466-4478 • 541 North 3rd Street,
La Conner, WA

NORTH PUGET SOUND

La Conner Marina

When you're going places

Port of Skagit

La Conner Marina is walking distance to great dining and shopping in the quaint town of La Conner. Enjoy your voyage through the Swinomish Channel en route to the picturesque San Juan Islands.

360-466-3118 | VHF 66A | www.portofskagit.com

Your Full-Service Repair and Refit Yard in Destination La Conner

- Haul outs to 110 tons
- 30,000+ SF heated, indoor work space
- Providing solutions for safe and reliable boating for over 30 years

service@laconnermaritime.com

- Long & Short Term Storage
- Gas & Diesel Repair & Repowers
- Paint, Fiberglass & Wood Repair
- Bow & Stern Thrusters
- Full System Service
- Wood Boat Specialist
- Heating Systems
- Sanitation Systems
- Electrical

MEMBER ABYC

NORTHERN LIGHTS   VOLVO PENTA   NAIAD DYNAMICS   ALEXSEAL

LA CONNER MARITIME SERVICE

See the Hide-A-Davit in action on our website!!

Hull Paint & Repair

Hydraulics & Systems Engineering & Installation

920 W. Pearle Jensen Way ▪ La Conner, WA 98257   (360) 466-3629 ▪ www.laconnermaritime.com

2020 WAGGONER CRUISING GUIDE

NORTH PUGET SOUND

See Area Map Page 164 - Maps Not for Navigation

current before landing anywhere along the channel.

The town of La Conner is thoroughly charming. It has excellent restaurants, galleries, museums, wine tasting rooms, and shops. During the summer, hordes of visitors arrive by car and tour bus. Even when crowded, the town is enjoyable. Free outdoor concert, parade, food vendors and fireworks on the 4th of July. On summer Sundays in Gilkey Square, live music from mid-June to August.

⑱ **La Conner Marina**. P.O. Box 1120, 613 N. 2nd St., La Conner, WA 98257; (360) 466-3118; www.portofskagit.com/la-conner-marina. Monitors VHF 66A. Open all year with 30 amp power on F-dock and 30 & 50 amp power on G-dock; water, free Wi-Fi, restrooms, showers, laundry, pumpout. Online reservations accepted two days in advance via Dockwa. Haulout to 82 tons. Complete repairs available through La Conner Maritime.

All shopping and services are within walking distance. A monorail launch can handle boats to 14,000 lbs. Trailers must be roller style, no bunks. A paved and lighted storage yard is available for trailers and tow vehicles.

The Anacortes Farmers Market is open Saturdays from 9 am to 2 pm, May to October.

This marina, owned by the Port of Skagit, is where most visiting boats tie up. F dock at the south basin has 1200 lineal feet of side-tie guest moorage. G dock at the north basin has another 1200 feet of side-tie moorage. E dock, near shore in the south basin, has 450 feet of guest moorage for the Swinomish Yacht Club. Reservations accepted. Unoccupied slips are used when available. If the moorage appears full, call anyway. They try to fit everybody in.

⑱ **La Conner Landing Fuel Dock**. P.O. Box 1020, La Conner, WA 98257; (360) 466-4478. Open all year. Summer hours from 8:00 a.m. to 6:00 p.m. daily. Hours and days vary during the fall and winter, call ahead. Fuel dock with ethanol-free gasoline and diesel, pumpout. The store has tackle, bait, ice, marine items, and snacks.

Caution: Strong current flows past the dock. Look for the directional sign on the fuel shed labeled 'CURRENT' with an arrow indicating which way the current is running.

⑱ **Town of La Conner Public Floats.** (360) 466-3125. The town of La Conner has three floats with first-come, first-serve moorage for vessels 45 feet and under for stays up to 24 hours. The three separate floats are along the waterfront boardwalk that parallels the Swinomish Channel. The street-end floats are located at Benton, Calhoun and Washington Streets. Larger vessels may be accommodated at Benton float with prior approval by calling ahead. Self-registration and cash payment at payment drop boxes located at each of the floats. Call for stays longer than 24 hours. No water, no power; public restrooms are available in town and near the La Conner Marina.

Caution: Strong current flows past the floats, check the current before approaching.

Padilla Bay. The well-marked channel through Padilla Bay is about 3 miles long between drying flats. Don't take any shortcuts until north of Beacon 2, which marks the edge of Guemes Channel. Deeper draft boats, such as sailboats, should hold to a mid-channel course, especially at low tide. To the west of the channel are long docks serving ocean-going tankers calling at the two major oil refineries in Anacortes. Often tankers, barges, or tug boats lie at anchor in the bay awaiting room at the docks.

Red, Right, Returning: In Padilla Bay, Red, Right, Returning assumes "return" is from the north. Red navigation aids are on the west side of the channel from Padilla Bay to La Conner. South of La Conner, red navigation aids are on the east side of Swinomish Channel. Approaching La Conner from north or south, remember Red, Right, Returning.

Saddlebag Island Marine State Park. Open all year for day use and overnight anchoring and camping. Boat access only. Anchorage is good off the north or south shore. Water depths are inconveniently deep on the west side, and inconveniently shallow on the east. Vault toilets, primitive campsites. Cascadia Marine Trail campsite. One-mile hiking trail. "Hot spot" for crabbing.

Huckleberry Island. North end of Padilla Bay, owned by the Samish Indian Nation. Open all year, day use only. No services. Undeveloped 10-acre island with anchoring or beaching only. No fires or camping. Pack out all garbage. Attractive to kayakers and scuba divers. Gravel beach on the southwest side of the island.

⑲ **Anacortes.** www.anacortes.org. Anacortes is a major boating center, with fishing and pleasure craft facilities in Fidalgo Bay and along Guemes Channel. The city's marine businesses can provide for a boater's every need, including food, fuel, and repairs. With seven haulout yards, Anacortes has the marine trades for any repair. For pumpout service, call PumpMeOut at (425) 903-3137.

U.S. Customs: Anacortes is a U.S. Customs port of entry with an office in the Cap Sante Marina harbormaster's building. There is no U.S. Customs dock. Call the marina office for a slip assignment and proceed to the slip. Then call the Anacortes Customs Office at (360) 293-2331 for instructions. Between 1:00 p.m. and 3:00 p.m. during the summer agents are apt to be 4 miles away at the Washington

La Conner

(360) 293-2565

MARINE SERVICES GROUP

YOUR ONE STOP SHOP FOR ALL YOUR BOATING NEEDS

Mechanical, Repair, Finishing, Electronics, Canvas and Upholstery

MEET THE FAMILY...

WE SELL AND SERVICE ALL BRANDS
BUT HERE ARE SOME OF OUR FAVORITES

Like us on Facebook | @msganacortes

1910 Skyline Way - Anacortes, WA 98221 | marineservicesgroup.com

ANACORTES MARKETPLACE

RESTAURANTS, SHOPS & SERVICES

CALENDAR OF EVENTS

JANUARY
First Friday Gallery Art Walk

FEBRUARY
First Friday Gallery Art Walk

MARCH
First Friday Gallery Art Walk
Anacortes Salmon Derby

APRIL
First Friday Gallery Art Walk
Spring Wine Festival
Island Chicks Antique & Vintage Show, Port Warehouse
Skagit Valley Tulip Festival
Anacortes Annual Quilt Walk

MAY
First Friday Gallery Art Walk
Anacortes Boat & Yacht Show

JUNE
Kids Fishing Derby
Chamber Gallery Art Walk
Anacortes Waterfront Festival, Cap Sante Marina

Dates may change, check website
www.anacortes.org
360-293-7911

ACE HARDWARE
Ace Hardware of Anacortes is your locally owned and operated hardware store, specializing in marine hardware, stainless fasteners, electrical, Craftsman Tools, fishing licenses, tackle, bait, rain gear and all your hardware needs.
360-293-3535 • 1720 Q Avenue, Anacortes, WA 98221 • 360-378-4622
www.AceAnacortes.com

Mary LaFleur

ALT INSURANCE GROUP
An all lines broker with a specialty niche in yacht insurance, Mary LaFleur has over 30 years in the insurance industry, represents over 30 insurance carriers, and is a life-long boater. "Most times we can save our boaters enough on their auto, home, commercial and RV insurance to put fuel in their tanks." Customer Service is second to none.
253-222-7519 • 360-899-4653
819 Commercial Avenue, Ste D,
mary@altinsurancegroup.com
www.altinsurancegroup.com

ANACORTES MARINE INSURANCE
One of only a few Insurance agencies in Washington State, offering direct access to the top Yacht Insurance markets in the world. Featuring CHUBB, REDSHIELD and PANTAENIUS, as well as PREMIER, SAFECO, and TRAVELERS, our experienced staff can find the best coverage/best pricing to fit your needs. Additional access to brokers allows us to handle all types of Marine-related Business Pursuits.
360-588-8112 • 1116 12th St
www.AnacortesMarine-Ins.com

ANTHONY'S
Anthony's at Cap Sante Marina - Lunch and dinner daily in a scenic waterfront setting, overlooking the marina with two view decks. Serving fresh northwest seafood from our own seafood company. Adjacent is The Cabana by Anthony's, a casual seafood restaurant with a classic "to-go fish & chips" bar. Both restaurants are steps from the marina.
360-588-0333 • 1207 Q Avenue •
www.anthonys.com

ANTHONY'S THE CABANA
The Cabana is located adjacent to Anthony's at Cap Sante Marina. The Cabana offers casual family-friendly dining as well as a classic fish & chip "to-go" bar for quick service dining. The Cabana has two full-size Bocce Ball courts available for guests while dining.
360-588-0333 • 1207 Q Avenue • www.anthonys.com/restaurants/detail/anthonys-cabana

THE BROWN LANTERN ALE HOUSE
Serving the locals & visitors to Historic Anacortes since 1933, just steps from the waterfront in the heart of oldtown. Featuring outstanding burgers, creative pub fare, 15 beers on draft, and over 50 different whiskies alone! See why we are voted the "Best Tavern in Anacortes" year after year. Now family friendly.
360-293-2544 • 412 Commercial Ave.
www.brownlantern.com

Statue Photo Courtesy of Anacortes Chamber of Commerce, Steve Berentson, photographer
Cap Sante & Mt Baker Photos Courtesy of Tony Locke Photography

Great experiences come in small islands

Relax and enjoy a weekend (or more!) on Fidalgo Island. With mild temperatures, lush forest lands to explore, and water that surrounds, staying here is a great way to spend your time away from home. Visit by car, ferry, plane or boat. Experience amazing restaurants, boutique shopping in historic downtown, nature viewing, multiple festivals across the year, live music, and so much more.

From Anchors to Zincs you can cover all of your boating needs in Anacortes! We have first class marinas and over 50 marine trades companies and professionals that are dedicated to providing quality parts and services. Let us help you buy, insure, store, moor, maintain, repair, and enjoy your boat, right here on beautiful Fidalgo island.

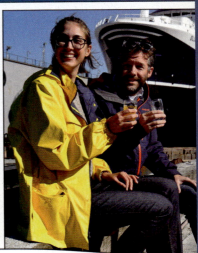

ANACORTES.ORG
360-293-3832

Download the app in Google Play or the Apple Store

ANACORTES MARKETPLACE

RESTAURANTS, SHOPS & SERVICES

CALENDAR OF EVENTS

JULY
First Friday Gallery ArtWalk
4th of July Parade
Shipwreck Day Anacortes

AUGUST
First Friday Gallery ArtWalk
Anacortes Arts Festival
Fidalgo Bay Day

SEPTEMBER
First Friday Gallery ArtWalk
Oyster Run Motorcycle Rally

OCTOBER
First Friday Gallery ArtWalk
Bier on the Pier
Anacortes Fall Boat Show
Trick or Treat Downtown

NOVEMBER
First Friday Gallery ArtWalk
Fall Vintage Market

DECEMBER
Tree Lighting,
Holiday Parade
Holiday ArtWalk
Lighted Boat Parade

Dates may change, check website
www.anacortes.org
360-293-7911

NORTH HARBOR DIESEL & YACHT SERVICE
North Harbor Diesel and Yacht Service has been in Anacortes since 1985. Come see us for boat storage, engine services, hull and bottom repairs, maintenance and modernizing. Open year round Monday–Friday, we are the region's premier boat yard.
360-293-5551 • 720 30th Street
www.northharbordiesel.com

ROCKFISH GRILL & ANACORTES BREWERY
The Rockfish Grill serves Northwest food including seafood and wood fired pizza made with fresh local ingredients. They proudly pour Anacortes Brewery beers made right next door. Live music weekly. Full bar. Family friendly.
360-588-1720 • 320 Commercial Avenue
www.anacortesrockfish.com

SALISH MARINE LLC
Marine maintaince and repair. Working Anacortes and Laconner.
360-707-1257 • 16840A Bennett Rd, Burlington, WA 98273
www.facebook.com/Salishmarine

SEATTLE YACHTS
Serving the Pacific Northwest for over 33 years, Seattle Yachts is the premiere dealership for trawlers, cruising sailboats and motoryachts, both new and brokerage. Now with 2 offices to serve you; one at Shilshole Marina in Seattle and the other at the Anacortes Marina.
844-692-2487 Ext 2
Anacortes Marina
2415 T Ave, Suite 112
www.SeattleYachts.com

MARINE SERVICES GROUP is the management company that owns and operates North Island Boat, Anacortes Marine Electronics, 3C Canvas, and Jensen's Shipyard. Our divisions work together to create and efficient "one stop shop" environment to repair and maintain every system within your vessel. With multiple locations and mobile capabilities, we can provide the same level of superior service from Everett to Bellingham and throughout the San Juan Islands.
Headquarters: 1910 Skyline Way • Anacortes, WA 98221 • 360.293.2565
www.marineservicesgroup.com

ANACORTES MARINE ELECTRONICS
At Anacortes Marine Electronics our NMEA and MEI certified technicians can troubleshoot, install, and network any component on your vessel. We specialize in designing and configuring custom navigation and communication packages that meet your individual needs and help you take full advantage of your boating season.
A Division of Marine Services Group
1910 Skyline Way Anacortes, WA 98221
360.293.2565
www.anacortesmarine.com

NORTH ISLAND BOAT
North Island Boat is a full-service boat yard open year-round. Our team of ABYC certified technicians are trained to service all brands and are equipped to handle any of your mechanical, gas, diesel, hydraulic, electrical, or shipwright needs. With mobile capabilities, we can provide service from Everett to Bellingham.
A Division of Marine Services Group
1910 Skyline Way Anacortes, WA 98221 • 360.293.2565
www.northislandboat.com

3C CANVAS
Our fabrication shop is dedicated to sewing, cutting, and bending your marine canvas and upholstery visions into reality. Using top of the line material to create custom fit designs, our canvas makers provide quality dodgers, biminis, enclosures, and covers for any vessel.
A Division of Marine Services Group
1910 Skyline Way Anacortes, WA 98221 • 360.293.2565
www.3ccanvas.com

NORTH HARBOR DIESEL
& Yacht Service Inc.

Service • Sales • Storage

AWARD WINNING YACHT SERVICE
- Complete diesel & gas Engine Services & Repowers
- Complete Interior Remodel & Design
- Custom Hull Modifications
- Fully Stocked Marine Store
- 22,000 Sq. Ft. Shop

SHORESIDE MARINA
- 5 Acres of dry outdoor storage
- Low monthly storage fees
- 4 Sea-Lifts - up to 65 Ft. & 45 Tons

360-299-1907
**For Shoreside Marina Information,
Call Robyn at 360-899-9274**

INSIDE PASSAGE YACHT SALES
Now located at North Harbor Diesel
We match perfect boats to individual buyers. It is our passion! New boats from Lindell Yachts, Parker, and Sargo. Large inventory of used boats from center consoles to cruisers and pilot houses. It's not about the boat…it's about the lifestyle.

360.468.4997 • InsidePassageYachtSales.com

360-293-5551
Anacortes, WA
NorthHarborDiesel.com
service@northharbordiesel.com

NORTH PUGET SOUND

See Area Map Page 164 - Maps Not for Navigation

State Ferry terminal, clearing arrivals on the international ferry from Sidney, B.C. You'll have to wait aboard for the agents to return. Otherwise, they will ask the captain to walk up to the Customs Office, Suite F, to the right of the harbormaster's office for clearance.

Fidalgo Bay is shallow. If you stray from the dredged and marked channels during low water, you could find yourself aground.

Four marinas are located on the Fidalgo Bay side of town. Three additional marinas are located on the west end of Fidalgo Island. From north to south on Fidalgo Bay, the first is Cap Sante Marina, owned by the Port of Anacortes, with guest moorage, fuel, water, electricity, pumpout and haulout facilities.

The second, behind a prominent breakwater, is Anacortes Marina, where Marine Servicenter has fuel, pumpout, 55 ton Travelift haulout, and repairs. Open seven days a week from 8:00 a.m. to 4:30 p.m. and 8:00 a.m. to 8:00 p.m. from Memorial Day weekend to Labor Day weekend. Permanent moorage only. Anacortes Yacht Charters and many bareboat charter boats are based in this marina. Follow the dredged channel to the marina entrance on the south side.

Next is the 360-foot-long dock and haulout ramp for Pacific Marine Center (360) 299-8820. Large vessels can be hauled out with their 200-ton Travelift and blocked in their extensive yard complex for maintenance and repairs. They also have multiple KMI Sea-lift machines for haulout on their ramp for vessels up to 65 feet. Limited moorage is available on their docks, typically reserved for repair or dry storage customers.

The fourth is Fidalgo Marina, where Cap Sante Marine has a 50 ton Travelift and the haulout ramp for North Harbor Diesel. The marina is protected by a piling breakwater, and is entered through the dredged channel marked by pilings extending from deeper water near Cap Sante.

Moving east to west, Dakota Creek Industries is a large shipyard on Guemes Channel with Syncrolift ship lift and drydock for vessels to 400 feet.

Next to the Guemes Ferry is Anchor Cove, a private marina with no transient moorage.

Lovric's Sea-Craft is on Guemes Channel, with two marine ways for haulout, and a small dry dock.

Skyline Marina is in Flounder Bay on the west side of Fidalgo Island, 3 miles from downtown Anacortes. It has some guest moorage and a DIY yard with 55 ton Travelift haulout and a stationary lift accommodating 16,000 pounds.

Farmers Market: Saturdays 9:00 a.m. to 2:00 p.m. next to the Depot Arts & Community Center; seasonal.

Events: Wine Festival, early April; Anacortes Waterfront Festival, early June at Cap Sante Marina; Shipwreck Day, July; Anacortes Arts Festival, early August; Oyster Run, late September; Bier on the Pier, early October. www.anacortes.org; info@anacortes.org; (360) 293-7911.

Things to Do

1. Charming downtown. Visit the shops, galleries, antique stores, and restaurants along Commercial Avenue.

2. W. T. Preston, an old snag boat, is part of the Anacortes History Museum. Located across from the north end of Cap Sante Marina.

3. Live music. On Fridays and some Saturdays in July and August, the Port of Anacortes hosts free concerts at Seafarers' Memorial Park.

4. Skagit Cycle. Rent a bike and ride the Tommy Thompson Trail, or just around town. Catch the Tommy Thompson Trail from R Avenue at Cap Sante Marina.

5. Cap Sante Park. Walk to the top and view Mt. Baker and the marina from this scenic vantage point. Sunsets from here are particularly beautiful. A steep switchback trail leads from the gazebo on the point at Cap Sante.

6. Seabear Smokehouse. Learn the difference in taste between smoked pink, king and sockeye salmon at their smokehouse and factory store at 30th Street and T Ave.

7. Crabbing. Fidalgo Bay often has great crabbing.

---

⑲ **Cap Sante Marina/Port of Anacortes.** 100 Commercial Ave., 1019 Q Ave., Anacortes, WA 98221; (360) 293-0694; (360) 661-5000; marina@portofanacortes.com; www.portofanacortes.com. Monitors VHF 66A. Formerly Cap Sante Boat Haven. Open all year with moorage to 120 feet. Call or radio ahead for slip assignment. There is a $5 fee for reservations. No fee for same-day reservations. The 18×120-foot fuel dock, with ethanol-free gasoline, and diesel is to port inside the breakwater. A high-volume fuel delivery hose is available. Propane at boat launch. The marina has 20 & 30 amp power with some 50 & 100 amp power available, ELCI protected shore power on docks A & B. 5 pumpout carts (free), 2 portapotty dumps, restrooms, showers, and laundry. Guest boaters are given an access code to the laundry. A pumpout float is located just inside the harbor entrance. Used oil dump near the office. Free Wi-Fi throughout the marina. Loaner wheelchair available. Complimentary bicycles with baskets are available for marina guests. A monorail launch can handle boats to 25,000 pounds. A small hoist and dry storage yard for hand launching small boats is in the North Basin on P-Q dock. Call (360) 293-0694. Most of the guest area marina floats have been replaced by wide, stable concrete floats, with wide slips and wheelchair accessible ramps to shore. The floats are first-

Cap Sante Marina

Anacortes

Cap Sante Marina

A year-round all weather marina, Cap Sante Marina in Anacortes is one of the boating capitals of the Northwest. Centrally located between Victoria, BC and Seattle, Cap Sante offers the ultimate location for guests planning to explore the region. Within walking distance to downtown, you can enjoy our many local restaurants, shops, festivities and amenities.

Cap Sante Marina | 1019 Q Avenue, Anacortes, WA 98221 | 360-293-0694 | VHF 66 US (66a)
www.portofanacortes.com | marina@portofanacortes.com

NORTH PUGET SOUND

See Area Map Page 164 - Maps Not for Navigation

class in every way.

Follow the dredged and marked channel, and enter between the arms of a piling breakwater due east of Cap Sante. The area to port just inside the breakwater, towards Seafarers' Memorial Park, is shoal and should not be attempted. The harbormaster's office and U.S. Customs office are just north of C & D floats.

This is a clean and popular stop, located in the heart of downtown Anacortes. Complete facilities, including many good restaurants, large Safeway and Marketplace grocery stores, well-stocked Ace Hardware and Sebo's hardware stores, and two marine stores (West Marine, Marine Supply & Hardware) are within walking distance. An esplanade leads from the marina to the Seafarers' Memorial Park and building, and around the marina to Rotary Park. A dock for dinghies is behind a small breakwater at Seafarers' Memorial Park. The lawn and beach areas are used as a kayak launch.

Cap Sante Marina is one of the top three most popular marinas (rated by marina moorage nights) in the state. It is considered the homeport of the San Juan Islands and is often used as a supply and provisioning jumping-off point for cruises into the islands and further north.

Skyline Marina

⑲ **Anacortes Marina**. 2415 T Avenue, Anacortes, WA 98221; (360) 293-4543. Primarily private moorage. Marine Servicenter, with fuel dock, haulout, and repairs, is located there. Enter through the dredged channel to the south opening in the pilings. Exit the marina through the north opening in the breakwater. Marine Servicenter's fuel dock, pumpout and a 55 ton Travelift are straight ahead when you enter the marina.

⑲ **Marine Servicenter**. 2417 T Avenue, Anacortes, WA 98221; (360) 293-8200; service@marinesc.com; www.marinesc.com. Open all year. Fuel dock with ethanol-free gasoline, diesel, propane, pumpout, portapotty dump, lubricants, engine oil. Complete repair facilities with yard and haulout to 55 tons.

⑲ **Fidalgo Marina**. 3101 V Place, Anacortes, WA 98221; (360) 299-0873. No guest overnight moorage, but a number of marine businesses are located there. Enter through the opening at the end of the dredged channel

on the north side. First, to starboard, is the dock with a 50-ton Travelift for Cap Sante Marine, a full-service boatyard for repairs and refits (360) 293-3145.

Next are the staging docks with temporary moorage for the marine repair businesses. The city dock has marked temporary hourly moorage but no overnight. The ramp at the end of the small basin is for the 45-ton capacity KMI Sea-Lifts for North Harbor Diesel's repair yard and dry storage yards, and Banana Belt Boats brokerage storage yard.

Guemes Channel. On an ebb tide, waters in Guemes Channel can be very rough, especially west of the mouth of Bellingham Channel.

Watch for the Guemes ferry, a small car and passenger ferry that makes frequent crossings between Anacortes and Guemes Island.

Next to the ferry dock is Anchor Cove Marina, a private condo marina with covered and open slips.

Farther west is Lovric's Sea-Craft (360) 840-3271, a commercial shipyard and moorage with large marine ways for haulout.

Ship Harbor was once the primary harbor for Anacortes and offers some protection and reasonable anchorage. Watch for ferry traffic from the busy Washington State Ferries terminal in Ship Harbor. *Cross behind the ferries, not in front.*

Guemes Island. Guemes Island has no facilities specifically for boaters, although anchorage can be found along the north shore. Anchorage also can be found on the eastern

NORTH PUGET SOUND

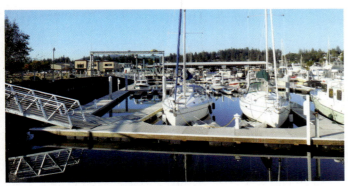

Skyline Marina in Fidalgo Bay is one of the closest marinas to the San Juan Islands.

shore in a tiny notch called Boat Harbor. A ferry connects Guemes Island to Anacortes.

Washington Park. www.cityofanacortes.org. West shore of Fidalgo Island on Guemes Channel. Open all year for day use and overnight camping. Restrooms, portapotty dump, showers. Anchoring or beaching only. Two-lane launch ramp, parking area, picnic tables, picnic shelters, fireplaces, campsites. Playground equipment. The loop road is 2.2 miles in length and is good for walking or jogging. The park has forested areas and viewpoints along the beaches overlooking Rosario Strait to Burrows Bay.

Flounder Bay. Flounder Bay has been dredged to provide moorage for the Skyline real estate development. Skyline Marina and several charter companies are inside the spit. Also a small chandlery, Travelift, and other facilities, including a large dry storage building. Entry is from Burrows Bay along a dredged channel marked by lighted pilings.

㉚ **Skyline Marina.** 2011 Skyline Way, Anacortes, WA 98221; (360) 293-5134; info@skylinemarinecenter.com; www.skylinemarinecenter.com. Open all year, guest moorage, 30 amp power (ELCI-protected power on some docks), laundry, showers. Reservations can be made through Dockwa.com. Fuel dock with ethanol-free gasoline, diesel and pumpout. A seaplane float is at the fuel dock. Propane and a coffee bar at the marina office.

Complete boat repairs and services are available. The yard has space for DIY repairs. A convenience store with grocery items is a block away. Other marine services nearby. Secure inside and outside storage for boats, vehicles, and trailers. Water taxi to the San Juan Islands. The marina is 4 miles from downtown Anacortes.

In 2017, the inner area around TA-TC docks was dredged and new docks installed. A 16,000 pound stationary lift was added and the nearby 55 ton Travelift area was rebuilt. A building housing a kayak tour operator, a marine brokerage, bareboat charter and other marine related businesses are located upland. The nearby North Island Boat Company (360-293-2565) accepts used oil.

Burrows Island State Park, Alice Bight. The anchorage has room for two or three boats. A beach area provides good dinghy/kayak landing access to the upland two campsites, with a pit-toilet. Most of the island is part of the Burrows Island State Marina Park, an undeveloped 330-acre park. The campsites are part of the Washington Water Trails system. There are no trails on the island except for the short piece up to the campsites. Most of the shoreline is steep cliffs. The Burrows Island Lighthouse is on the west tip of the island. The bight is open to the southeast through the northeast. Anchoring is exposed to weather from the south and more so from the southeast. Holding is good on a mud bottom; anchorage is more steep-to than charts indicate.

Allan Island. Allan Island is privately owned; no public access.

Cypress Island. Department of Natural Resources; paul.mcfarland@dnr.wa.gov. A park ranger told us he considers Cypress Island to be the "crown jewel" of the San Juan's, we agree. The island is nearly all public land, which is managed by the Washington State Department of Natural Resources. A network of trails leads through the Cypress Island Natural Resource Conservation Area and is one of the largest undeveloped island areas in the San Juan's. Approximately one-half mile of tidelands and marine bedlands that surround Cypress Island, Strawberry Island, and Cone Islands make up the Cypress Island Aquatic Reserve, overseen by DNR to conserve and minimize negative effects on aquatic habitats.

Best access is on the east side of the island at Cypress Head, Eagle Harbor, and Pelican Beach, where anchorage and approximately 25 DNR mooring buoys are located. Except for the Eagle Cliff Trail on the north end of the island, island trials and moorage buoys are open year-round. DNR mooring buoys are not subject to the state park's boat size limitations and are open to all, no rafting. Beach access is permitted at all these locations. Pit toilets are available on shore, along with campsites and trailheads. No water on the island and no

Cypress Island - Department of Natural Resources

NORTH PUGET SOUND

garbage service.

About a half-mile south of Pelican Beach, just past a small headland, two attractive little coves have room for one or two boats to anchor. Cascadia Marine Trail campsites are located at Pelican Beach and Cypress Head. Pets are allowed on leash, no bicycles.

Cypress Island has a fascinating history. Fishing villages once dotted the island, used seasonally by the Samish Tribe. In 1791, Spanish explorer Jose Narvaez arrived and named the island San Vincente. The name was changed to Cypress by Captain George Vancouver in 1792, when he mistook the island's juniper trees for cypress trees.

Pelican Beach. Located on the northeast side of Cypress Island, open all year. This DNR site has 6 mooring buoys, 5 campsites, compost toilets, a picnic shelter, fire pit, gravel beach, and interpretive signs. Numerous species of wildlife and birds can be observed. Public DNR beaches extend from the park around the north end of Cypress Island for 1.5 miles until just south of Foss Cove, where the north tip of the island is private property. The trailhead at Pelican Beach leads to the south and connects to year-round trails and the seasonal Eagle Cliff Trail. The Eagle Cliff Trail is closed from February 1 to July 15 to protect endangered wildlife.

Moorage is unprotected to the north. If anchored or moored to a buoy and the northerly wind comes in, you'll not want to stay. Current runs through the moorage and is subject to wakes from passing traffic.

Eagle Harbor. Located on the east side of Cypress Island towards the north end. Eagle Harbor is shallow, especially at low tide, but has 15 DNR mooring buoys. Use care in approaching all but the outermost of these buoys. The bay's shallow spots are truly shallow. Boaters should use caution and verify depths at lower tide levels. Convenient beach access to the island's trails. No fires, no camping. If you have sufficient depth, Eagle Harbor provides good protection. Views of Mount Baker are breathtaking.

Cypress Head. Located on the east side of Cypress Island, open all year with 4 DNR mooring buoys and 9 campsites, picnic sites, compost toilets and trailhead that connects to the island's trails. Many species of birds and wildlife, good fishing. Tide-rips at the south end of the island can cause wave action.

Deepwater Bay. Located on the southeast end of Cypress Island. Deepwater Bay is

Bookstores, cafes, and pubs make up the charming village of Fairhaven.

- Boat Parts & Supplies
- Kayak Rentals & Sales
- Outdoor Gear & Clothing
- Fishing, Crabbing & Shrimping Gear
- Pacific Northwest Gifts, Books & Maps
- Pet Friendly

Where your outdoor adventures begin!

Largest selection of SeaDog parts in Bellingham!

360.734.3336 or 800.426.8860
LFSMarineOutdoor.com

BELLINGHAM MARKETPLACE

RESTAURANTS, SHOPS & SERVICES

ANTHONY'S AT SQUALICUM HARBOR
Located in Bellwether on the Bay, offering spectacular views of the San Juan Islands. Serving fresh Northwest seafood from our own seafood company along with seasonal local produce - lunch, Monday through Saturday; Sunday brunch; and dinner served daily. Visitor moorage nearby on side-tie docks.
360-527-3473 • 360-647-5588 • 25 Bellwether Way, Bellingham
www.anthonys.com

ANTHONY'S HEARTHFIRE GRILL
On Squalicum Harbor in Bellwether on the Bay, offering guests spectacular views of the San Juan Islands. Serving premier northwest beef and fresh northwest seafood, this high-energy restaurant specializes in hearthfire cooking. Lunch and dinner served daily. Visitor moorage nearby on side-tie docks.
360-527-3473 • 7 Bellwether Way, Bellingham
www.anthonys.com

LFS MARINE & OUTDOOR
Located within easy walking distance of Squalicum Harbor docks. Boaters will appreciate the wide selection of fishing gear and crab pots, boat equipment and supplies, safety supplies, outdoor clothing, boots, and rain gear, plus Pacific Northwest gifts, nautical books, and cards.
Open Weekdays 8 to 5, Saturdays 9 to 5.
800-426-8860 • 360-734-3336 • 851 Coho Way Bellingham, WA 98225 • www.LFSmarineoutdoor.com

NW EXPLORATIONS
NW Explorations is a premier brokerage, charter and marine services company offering first class customer service in all areas. Whether you want to charter, buy/sell a vessel, or care for your existing boat, NW Explorations can help meet your needs.
360-676-1248 • 2623 South Harbor Loop Dr., Bellingham, WA 98225 • www.nwexplorations.com

SAN JUAN SAILING
A family run business for over 30 years, we strive to provide our guests with sail and power instruction, charters (sailboats, trawlers, motoryachts, sail and power catamarans), and brokerage services in a manner that consistently exceeds their expectations.
360-671-4300 • Gate 3, Squalicum Harbor, Bellingham
www.sanjuansailing.com

TRI-COUNTY DIESEL MARINE
We're factory trained and authorized for servicing the top brands covering maintenance, repair, and repower of marine propulsion and power generation. With over 100 years of combined experience, no job is too big or too small for our friendly team of professionals.
360.733.8880 • 2696 Roeder Ave. , Bellingham, WA 98225
care@tricountydieselmarine.com
www.tricountydieselmarine.com

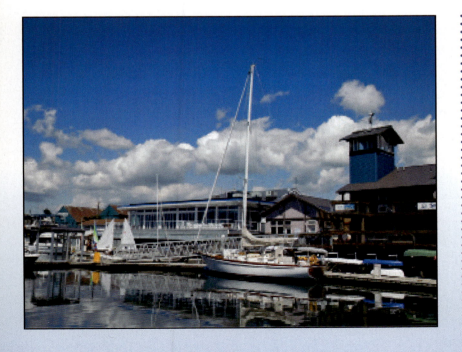

Harbor Events

May — Ski-to-Sea -

July — Haggen Family 4th of July - Fireworks & fair

April - Christmas — Farmers Market - Saturdays

September — Sea Feast

Contact the Port of Bellingham
www.portofbellingham.com • 360-676-2500

Maintenance tips

Basic engine service: Oil change, fuel filter change, refrigeration re-charge and diagnosis, battery maintenance, stuffing box adjustment, prop cleaning, and new zincs installed.

Inspect and service the tender: check for leaks in the inflatable, have the outboard serviced, ensure that all davit and hoist systems onboard are functioning.

Electronics: Ensure that all local charts are loaded onto nav-gear, and or charts are procured. Keep an updated version of the Waggoner Guide in the chart table.

Inspect and service all charging gear: High output alternator, regulator, inverter, and genset service.

NORTH PUGET SOUND

exposed to southerly winds, seas, and boat wakes. Several fish farm net pens are in the area. In 2017, strong currents collapsed one of the pens, releasing 300,000 Atlantic salmon

Secret Harbor. Located on the southeast end of Cypress Island, adjacent to Deepwater Bay. The head of Secret Harbor dries. DNR pit toilets and a kayak launch area are located at the head of the harbor, where you will find a trailhead to the island's network of trails.

Secret Harbor has a rich history. It was the home of a residential treatment facility for troubled youth that started in 1947. The isolated program on Cypress Island was successful at modifying the behaviors. The program and facility ran for more than 50 years at its island location; and except for supplies brought in by boat, it was self-sustaining. In 2005, the property was sold to the State of Washington and the program moved to the mainland where it provides best practices in the field of child welfare for boys and girls.

Strawberry Island. Strawberry Island, located west of Cypress Island in Rosario Strait, is an undeveloped public island that is managed by DNR. Strawberry Island is popular with kayakers. Strong currents and submerged rocks can make landing difficult; landings are best suited for kayaks rather than dinghies. An island with the same name located east of Deception Pass is part of Deception Pass State Park.

Vendovi Island. San Juan Preservation Trust, www.sjpt.org. Day use only, open April 1 through September 30, 10:00 a.m. to 6:00 p.m Thursday through Monday. No anchoring. A 70-foot dock (3-hour max stay) behind a rock breakwater is on the north shore. All visitors must sign in and review visitor guidelines at the head of the dock upon arrival. A public restroom is in the building at the top of the hill.

Sinclair and Eliza Islands. A piling breakwater protects a loading and unloading dock on the south shore of Sinclair Island, but there are no facilities specifically for pleasure boaters. Eliza Island is privately owned, with a private dock and float on the north side. Anchorage is possible several places around the island.

Larrabee State Park. (360) 676-2093. Seven miles south of Bellingham on Samish Bay. Open all year for day use and overnight camping. The park has restrooms and showers. This was Washington's first official state park, dedicated in 1923. It covers 2000 acres and is heavily used. Facilities include a launch ramp, kitchen shelters, picnic tables, standard, utility, and primitive campsites. Fishing, clamming, crabbing, scuba diving. Trails provide access to two freshwater lakes within the park. A 5.5-mile walking/bicycling trail connects with Bellingham.

Chuckanut Bay. Chuckanut Bay is a good anchorage with protection from prevailing

The day-use dock at Vendovi Island provides access to hiking trails and beautiful scenic vistas.

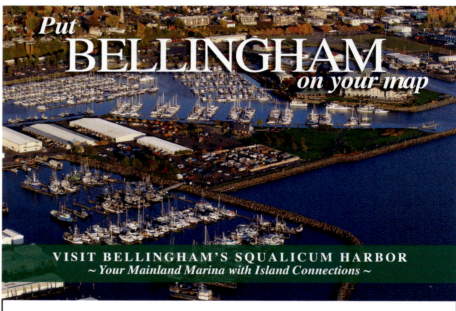

VISIT BELLINGHAM'S SQUALICUM HARBOR
~ Your Mainland Marina with Island Connections ~

A variety of restaurants, Hotel Bellwether, chandlery, trails and parks alongside our harbor and more than 1,000 feet of visitor dock space make Squalicum Harbor an ideal visitor destination.

- Friendly dockside service
- Several charter boat operations
- 4-lane boat launch open year-round
- Courtesy shuttle service and other ground transportation options
- Over-the-dock fuel service for bulk pricing
- Available Fuel Dock
- Diverse marine repair and supply services in the harbor
- Full Service Boatyard
- Restrooms, laundry and showers
- Holding tank pump-outs

- Closest U.S. port to Alaska
- Minutes away from the San Juan and Gulf Islands and midway between Seattle and Vancouver, B.C.
- An expanded Bellingham International Airport, providing more commercial flights to a growing number of destinations
- Outstanding visitor amenities:
  Vibrant downtown with entertainment, microbreweries, shopping, museum, seasonal farmers market
  Unsurpassed recreation opportunities – Mt Baker, golfing, bike trails

SQUALICUM HARBOR OFFICE: 722 Coho Way, Bellingham, WA 98225 • (360) 676-2542
squalicum@portofbellingham.com • www.portofbellingham.com

winds in the north or south arms. Enter close to Governors Point to avoid extensive rocky shoals that partially block the entrance. The land around the bay is privately owned. Correspondents James and Jennifer Hamilton anchored in Pleasant Bay, just inside Governors Point, during a southeast gale. "The winds howled up to 49 knots, but the water was reasonably calm. Good holding over mud." [Hamilton]

㉑ **Fairhaven Moorage.** (360) 714-8891; www.boatingcenter.org. Nine mooring buoys, a side-tie linear mooring system, and two boat launch ramps at Fairhaven are managed by the Community Boating Center. Moorage and boat launch May through October, 38-foot maximum. Launch ramps are tide-dependent and best suited to smaller boats. Pay moorage at the CBC office or pay box. Walk up to shops and restaurants in Fairhaven's lovely Victorian buildings. Just south of the business district you'll find a beautiful old park with mature plantings and great expanses of lawn. The Seaview Boatyard Dock (360) 676-8282 is located east of the Bellingham Cruise Terminal and guest linear moorage. The boatyard dock is used for staging in preparation for Travelift haulout.

㉑ **Bellingham.** Bellingham is the largest city between Everett and the Canadian border, and has complete facilities for commercial and pleasure craft. Moorage, fuel, marine supplies, and repairs are available at the Port of Bellingham's Squalicum Harbor. Bellingham Yacht Club and Squalicum Yacht Club are nearby. BYC has moorage for members of reciprocal yacht clubs.

Bellingham offers extensive moorage options, marine services, and waterfront parks.

The charming Hotel Bellwether is near the mouth of the Squalicum Harbor south basin, adjacent to the Marina Restaurant and shops. The port runs a courtesy shuttle to downtown grocery stores, and the historic Fairhaven area shops and restaurants.

Mooring buoys and a linear moorage system are at Fairhaven, in the south part of Bellingham Bay. Fairhaven is a delightful stop with turn-of-the-20th-century Victorian buildings, boutiques, a large bookstore and other interesting shops. Fairhaven is also the southern terminus of the Alaska Marine Highway Ferry System, (360) 676-8445. As with Squalicum Harbor, you can take a bus or taxi to downtown Bellingham. Many shops, restaurants and a supermarket are within walking distance in this historic area. The Bellingham International Airport is convenient for arriving or departing guests.

Bellingham's scenic surroundings and its proximity to the San Juan Islands alone would be enough to draw many boaters. Bellingham is a college town with incredible shopping opportunities including provisioning for the galley. Squalicum Harbor has comfortable moorage and is a convenient base for cruising.

Things to Do

1. Spark Museum of Electrical Invention. Over 1,000 radios and many other electrical devices on display; electrical show.

Port of Bellingham, Squalicum Harbor

NORTH PUGET SOUND

See Area Map Page 185 - Maps Not for Navigation

2. Bellingham Railway Museum. Model and actual trains, including a simulator.

3. Whatcom Museum. Art, photography, and a family interactive gallery. Downtown.

4. Historic Fairhaven. Good shopping and restaurants surrounded by period buildings. Peruse Village Books.

5. Bellingham Farmers Market. Held in Depot Square, a glass and steel building modeled after a railroad station, with beams and arches salvaged from a local highway bridge. Wonderful local vendors every Saturday from 10:00 a.m. to 3:00 p.m. One of the largest markets in the state.

6. Boundary Bay Brewery & Bistro. Across from the farmers market. Great beer garden and good food.

7. Mount Baker Theatre. Enjoy a performance in this magnificently restored art deco theater built in 1927.

8. Mindport. Not quite a science museum. Themes encourage creative play.

9. The Big Rock Garden. More than 37 sculptures in this 2.5-acre park. Local and internationally acclaimed artists represented. Near Lake Whatcom, a cab ride away.

LOCAL KNOWLEDGE

SHALLOW AREA: A shoal habitat enhancement bench (4-foot depth at zero tide) is along the breakwater protecting the western basin of Squalicum Harbor. The bench extends approximately 200 feet out from the breakwater and runs approximately 400 feet along the breakwater. White cylindrical can buoys mark the outer corners. From its outer edge, the bench slopes another 100 feet into Bellingham Bay until it meets the sea floor. Give the buoys a good offing when running along the face of the breakwater.

㉑ **Squalicum Harbor/Port of Bellingham**. 722 Coho Way, Bellingham, WA 98225; (360) 676-2542; squalicum@portofbellingham.com; www.portofbellingham.com. Certified Clean Marina. Monitors VHF 16, switch to 68. Open all year, guest moorage along 1000 feet of dock in two basins. Unoccupied slips are used when available, please call ahead. The marina has 20, 30 & 50 amp power (mostly 30 amp), restrooms, showers, laundry, pumpout, portapotty dump, and fee-based Ecco Wi-Fi. Three-day maximum stay in any 7-day period for visiting boats with longer stays subject to approval. The docks in both basins are gated for security. Restaurants nearby. Also chandleries and repair shops.

Seaview Boatyard runs the shipyard adjacent to the westernmost moorage basin. The yard has a 150-ton Travelift and a 35-ton Travelift.

Squalicum Harbor is divided into two moorage basins, each with its own entrance and guest moorage. The westernmost has restrooms located about halfway out the main pier, and onshore at the top of the dock ramp. Portable pumpout carts are kept at the restroom station.

In the eastern basin, guest moorage is just inside the breakwater entrance. Hotel Bellwether, with its dock, is located on the east side near the entrance. The hotel is part of a larger Port of Bellingham Bellwether development with park grounds, restaurants, boutiques, and a coffee shop. Seasonally, you can buy fresh fish right off the boat. A marine life tank (great for kids) also is near the streetside parking lot. A 3-lane launch ramp, with extended-term parking for tow vehicles and trailers, is just east of the east basin.

Harbor Marine Fuel. (360) 734-1710. Open all year. Fuel dock with diesel and gasoline (containing ethanol). Store carries motor oils. Located in northern Squalicum Harbor, behind the breakwater.

ANTHONY'S AT SQUALICUM HARBOR
25 Bellwether Way
(360) 647-5588

7 Bellwether Way
(360) 527-3473

㉑ **Hotel Bellwether.** 1 Bellwether Way, Bellingham, WA 98225; (360) 392-3178; reservations@hotelbellwether.com; www.hotelbellwether.com. Open all year, side-tie moorage along 220-foot concrete float, 30, 50 & 100 amp power. Larger boats tie outside, smaller boats tie inside. This is a classy small hotel, done to 5-star standards. Outstanding dining. Located just inside the mouth of the Squalicum Harbor east basin. Reservations required. Dog friendly.

Hilton Harbor Marina. 1000 Hilton Ave., Bellingham, WA 98225; (360) 733-1110; info@hiltonharbor.com. Fuel dock with gasoline only. Located at the south entrance to Squalicum Harbor at the foot of Hilton Avenue. Two 3 ton hoists, repairs. Oil disposal available.

LUMMI BAY TO PT. ROBERTS

Lummi Island. Lummi Island is high (1480 feet) and has no facilities specifically for visiting boaters. Anchorage is good in several places, including Inati Bay and along both shores of Hale Passage. A ferry connects Lummi Island to the mainland. Restaurants and other businesses are near this dock. The Lummi Nation's people haul their boats, including reef net boats, on the beach south of the ferry dock.

Inati Bay. Inati Bay is on the east side of Lummi Island, approximately 2 miles north of Carter Point. It is the best anchorage on Lummi Island, protected from all but northeasterly winds (rare in the summer) with good holding. There may be debris on the bottom left from the old Hood Canal caisson that was once moored here. A log boom chain is reported to

Fairhaven Village has a wide slection of eateries.

Fairhaven Moorage

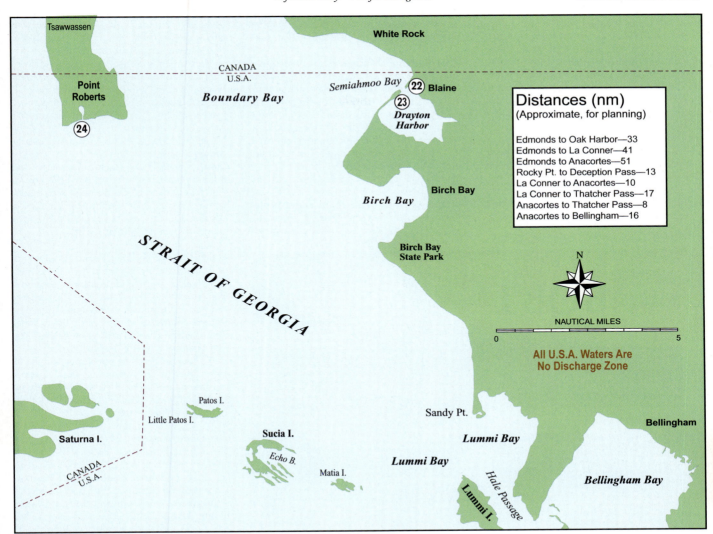

Lummi Bay to Point Roberts

lie on the north side of the bay near the rock wall. Member-only moorage at the Bellingham Yacht Club outstation property.

When entering Inati Bay, leave the white cautionary buoy well to starboard to avoid the rock that extends northward from the buoy. Stay close to the point of land on the south side of the entrance.

Lummi Island Recreation Site. Southeast shore of Lummi Island. Open all year, toilets, campsites.

Sandy Point. Sandy Point is a private real-estate development consisting of several canals with homes on them. No public facilities. Long docks serving a refinery and an aluminum plant extend from shore north of Sandy Point.

Birch Bay. Birch Bay at the southeastern end of Strait of Georgia is a large bay with excellent anchoring depths over a flat mud bottom. However, the bay is so large that it affords little protection from wind and waves. Open to the northwest, west, and southwest, Birch Bay is best used in calm conditions. Popular in the summer, you will find almost as many small craft as crab pot buoys. Large sections of the head of the bay are drying tidal areas. The cluster of buildings on the east shore marks the town of Birch Bay and the group of masts on the north shore marks the private Birch Bay Marina with no services for transient boaters.

Shoal Entry: The approach to Blaine through Semiahmoo Bay is shoal at all stages but high tide. Pay close attention to the buoys along the drying bank on the south side of the bay, and turn into the entrance channel before getting too close to the eastern shore.

㉒ **Blaine.** Blaine has two moorages in Drayton Harbor. One is owned by the Port of Bellingham; the other, Semiahmoo, is privately owned and has both permanent and guest moorage at this nice resort.

The Blaine Marina is on the east (port) side, with entry through an opening in the piling breakwater. Follow the signs to the guest moorage in the middle of the harbor.

The Semiahmoo Marina is on the west side of the entrance channel and has fuel. Both marinas have water, power, and other facilities ashore. The Port's marina gives access to the town of Blaine and a number of boating-related businesses and a good selection of restaurants. Semiahmoo Marina has access to two world-class golf courses. In the summer, Friday through Sunday, the classic foot ferry, *Plover*, operates between the two marinas or you can dinghy between the two.

With all that Blaine has to offer, no lack of things to do and fantastic sunsets, it makes a nice cruising destination.

Drayton Harbor is a sensitive shellfish harvesting area.

No Discharge Zone. Gray water okay.

㉒ **Blaine Harbor/Port of Bellingham.** P.O. Box 1245, 235 Marine Drive, Blaine, WA 98230; (360) 647-6176; blaineharbor@portofbellingham.com; www.portofbellingham.com. Monitors VHF 16, switch to 68. Certified Clean Marina. Side-tie guest moorage along 800 feet of wide dock, unoccupied slips up to 120' used when available. Services include 30 & 50 amp power, water, restrooms, showers, laundry, pumpout carts, portapotty dump, and fee-based Ecco Wi-Fi. Repairs, haulout, supplies available. Waste oil disposal. Two blocks to town. Concrete launch ramp with parking. Restaurants nearby. Courtesy shuttle to grocery store in town.

The side-tie guest (visitor) dock is served by a wide fairway for easy maneuvering. The shoreside facilities are built to a turn of the 20th century theme. The marina office is in the Boating Center building. A 65-person public meeting room, with kitchen, is also in this building at Gate 2. An attractive park with a children's playground and beach access is across the road on the north side of the spit. Walking distance to the Peace Arch at the border.

㉓ **Semiahmoo Marina.** 9540 Semiahmoo Parkway, Blaine, WA 98230; (360) 371-0440; moorageoffice@semiahmoomarina.com; www.semiahmoomarina.com. Monitors VHF 68. Open all year. Ethanol-free gasoline and diesel at the Semiahmoo Marina fuel dock, which offers a fuel discount for guests; propane, free pumpout. Guest moorage in unoccupied slips when available. One 50-foot slip is reserved for reciprocal yacht clubs. Call for availability for all guest moorage, reservations accepted. Services include 30 & 50 amp power, restrooms, free showers, laundry, pumpout, portapotty dump, Wi-Fi. Marina store with gifts, clothing, beer, wine, and marine items. Marina Cafe serves breakfast and lunch.

The Semiahmoo Resort has a hotel, spa with pool, restaurants and kayak, SUP, and bicycle rentals. It is a full resort with all the amenities. If you have bicycles on board or have rented a bike, you can ride the 1.2-mile scenic pathway to the Alaska Packers Association Cannery & Fishing Museum, located at 9261 Semiahmoo Parkway. Museum displays, housed in an original cannery building, include machinery and historic photos. Open weekends 1:00 p.m. to 5:00 p.m., Memorial Day through September.

The par 72 Semiahmoo course is outstanding. Day passes available for marina guests. Telephone (360) 371-7015.

㉔ **Point Roberts.** Point Roberts is a low spit of land extending south from Canada into U.S. waters. Although physically separated from the U.S., Point Roberts is U.S. territory and part of the state of Washington. The Point Roberts Marina is on the south shore. Enter via a dredged channel skirted by drying flats. The channel was last dredged in the fall of 2017. Four ocean-front parks, one located at each corner of 4.9 square mile Point Roberts, can be reached by bicycle. Bicycle rentals are available through Peddle Pushers Bike Rentals (360-990-0193).

㉔ **Point Roberts Marina Resort.** 713 Simundson Drive, Point Roberts, WA 98281; (360) 945-2255; prmarina@pointrobertsmarina.com; www.pointrobertsmarina.com. Monitors VHF 66A. Open all year. Fuel dock with mid-grade gasoline, diesel, propane, ice, beer & wine, fishing licenses, tackle, convenience items. The fuel dock is open daily during the summer season until 5:00 p.m., Sunday through Thursday; and until 8:00 p.m. on Friday and Saturday. Guest moorage in unoccupied slips. Phone ahead for slip

Blaine Harbor promenade.

Point Roberts Marina

See Area Map Page 185 - Maps Not for Navigation   NORTH PUGET SOUND

Drayton Harbor

assignment, reservations required. Services include 30 & 50 amp power, (ELCI-protected power on some docks), water, free Wi-Fi, restrooms, showers, laundry, garbage drop, free pumpouts. Used oil drop. The remodeled Compass Rose Bar & Grill at the marina is delightful, reservations recommended for large groups; (360) 945-7673. Other restaurants, golf and groceries are nearby. Haulout to 35 tons. Westwind Marine Services, with repairs and a chandlery, is in the main building and has seasonal hours.

Point Roberts is a U.S. Customs port of entry. The first dock to starboard has a direct-dial telephone to customs. Agents typically drive over from the Point Roberts border office. Summer hours 8:00 a.m. to 8:00 p.m., winter hours 8:00 a.m. to 5:00 p.m. Consider calling ahead at (360) 945-5211.

Lighthouse Marine County Park. (360) 945-4911; lthouse@pointroberts.net; www.whatcomcounty.us. Open for day use and overnight camping in summer, day use only in winter. On the southwest corner of Point Roberts. Anchor north of the park and row in, or moor at Point Roberts Marina and walk or ride a bike over. Facilities include boat launch ramp with seasonal staging float, campsites, picnic shelters, fire pits, barbecues, restrooms, showers, sand and gravel beach. Also a whale exhibit, playground, boardwalk, and picnic shelters. Whales can sometimes be seen from the park. A small public airstrip is along the eastern perimeter of the park.

2020 WAGGONER CRUISING GUIDE

Strait of Juan De Fuca

CHAPTER 5

CROSSING THE STRAIT OF JUAN DE FUCA
Sequim Bay • Port Angeles • Clallam Bay • Neah Bay

STRAIT OF JUAN DE FUCA

The Strait of Juan de Fuca is about 100 miles long and 12 miles wide. Depending on the weather, it can be flat calm or extremely rough. The typical summertime pattern calls for calm mornings with a westerly sea breeze rising by mid-day, increasing to 30 knots or more late in the afternoon. If this sea breeze opposes an outflowing ebb current, the seas will be unusually high, steep, and close together. Often, however, the "typical" weather pattern does not prevail, and the wind blows around the clock. Or, it can be calm, even on a warm summer afternoon. Weather reports must be monitored. If wind is present or predicted, we stay off the strait.

CROSSING THE STRAIT OF JUAN DE FUCA

The Strait of Juan de Fuca has a well-earned reputation for being rough at times. It's true that a boat crossing the strait can take a beating that its crew will not want to repeat, but often the crossing can be almost flat. If conditions truly are foul, alternate routes exist. The secret to an easy crossing lies in picking your times and not being foolhardy. Routes suggested below are approximate and for reference only. They assume good conditions and the absence of current. Since current is always present, appropriate course adjustments will be needed.

Summer weather pattern. During the high summer cruising season, the "typical" weather pattern calls for near-calm conditions in the early morning when the air over the entire region is cool. As the summer sun heats the land, air over the land rises and colder ocean air funnels down the Strait of Juan de Fuca to replace the rising land air. This is called a sea breeze, and it usually develops in the late morning or early afternoon. By late afternoon the sea breeze can be quite strong, creating short, high seas, especially on an ebb. After sundown, as air in the interior cools, the sea breeze dies away.

Given this pattern, early morning crossings are preferred. Carefully monitor the official weather reports and forecast. If the morning report says the wind already is blowing 15 to 20 knots, and more wind is expected, don't cross. Wait until the wind subsides or take an alternate route.

Fog can develop unexpectedly. Sometimes it is only a thin mist, other times it can be pea-soup thick. Normally when the wind moves in, the fog blows out.

LOCAL KNOWLEDGE

DANGEROUS TIDE RIPS. Ebbing tidal currents can set up dangerous tide-rips at Point Wilson, and at the south end of Rosario Strait, at Cattle Pass, and off Discovery Island. Do not underestimate the viciousness of these tide-rips. Whenever possible, plan your passage to transit these danger spots near the turn of the tide or on a flood.

Point Wilson Tide-Rip. One of the more frustrating pieces of water we face in the Northwest is the infamous Point Wilson tide-rip just off Port Townsend. The rip usually (but not always) forms on an ebb tide, and may or may not be accompanied by westerly wind. The patch of rough water can extend for several miles north and west of Point Wilson. Usually, the rip doesn't form until well into an ebb cycle, so timing your arrival to coincide with slack water is best.

If, however, your timing is off, you can pick one of two routes around it.

The first is to hug the Point Wilson shore as closely as you dare, keeping close to shore until you pass McCurdy Point.

The other route is to stay close to the Whidbey Island shore (avoiding the shoal water off Partridge Point and stay east of Partridge Bank) until past Smith Island before turning toward your destination.

Point Wilson to San Juan Channel. The most direct route from Point Wilson to Friday Harbor is via San Juan Channel. A direct course between the two intersects Smith Island. Shoals, covered with dense kelp, extend westward from Smith Island for nearly 2 miles. Partridge Bank, between Point Wilson and Smith Island, should be avoided. Heavy kelp is an obstacle, and if the wind is up, seas are worse in the shallow water over the bank.

At Point Wilson you'll set a course of approximately 301° magnetic until you're abeam the Smith Island light, where you'll turn to a course of 330° magnetic to fetch Cattle Pass. (From Cattle Pass to Point Wilson reverse the process: run 150° magnetic until the Smith Island light bears abeam to port, then turn to 121° magnetic to fetch Point Wilson.)

When using this route, it's best to time your arrival at Cattle Pass for shortly after the current turns to flood. The current can run hard through Cattle Pass, so it's best not to fight it. Use the San Juan Channel current predictions.

If you do it right, you'll carry the last of a dying ebb out Admiralty Inlet, past Point Wilson, and well across the strait.

Just before reaching Cattle Pass, the current will turn to flood, flushing you nicely through the pass and into San Juan Channel. Since you can have 2 to 4 knots of current in Admiralty Inlet, and a couple knots of current in the strait, riding the ebb can save considerable time, even in a fast boat. The less time you're exposed, the less time you have to meet trouble.

To Rosario Strait or Deception Pass. From the mouth of Admiralty Inlet, plot a course that leaves Point Partridge bell buoy off Whidbey Island to starboard. If you're bound for Rosario Strait, stay out of the traffic lanes as much as possible. As noted above, the mouth of Rosario Strait can be filled with dangerous tide-rips on an ebb tide. Be prepared to favor the eastern shore.

To Haro Strait (Roche Harbor). Leaving Point Wilson, run a course of approximately 301° magnetic until the Smith Island light is abeam to starboard. Then turn to approximately 305° magnetic to run toward

Strait of Juan de Fuca

2020 Waggoner Cruising Guide   189

Strait of Juan de Fuca

See Area Map Page 189 - Maps Not for Navigation

Strait of Juan de Fuca Go-NoGo Checklist

Tides & Currents - See Ports & Passes; Canadian Tides & Current Tables Vol. 5
- ☐ Phase of the moon – Spring or Neap Tide
- ☐ Flood or Ebb - Ebbing tidal currents can set up dangerous tide-rips at: Point Wilson, Cattle Pass, and South end of Rosario Strait

Weather System Predictions – via Internet or satellite
- ☐ Check NOAA Ocean Prediction Center forecasts for any approaching significant weather systems
- ☐ Check Windy.com, Predictwind.com, SiriusXM Marine, or Sailflow.com
- ☐ See Environment Canada and NWS NOAA forecasts for the Synopsis for East Entrance Juan de Fuca Strait, and Haro Strait

Weather & Seas Forecasts – via Internet, phone, or VHF
- ☐ See NWS NOAA Zone Area Forecasts for East Entrance Strait of Juan de Fuca, Northern Inland Waters Including San Juan Islands, and Admiralty Inlet; note wind speed and direction, wave height and interval, and trends
- ☐ See Environment Canada Forecast for Juan de Fuca Strait – East Entrance; Check for warnings, note wind speed, direction and trends

Observations & Present Conditions – via Internet, phone, or VHF
- ☐ Check Buoy Report for New Dungeness (46088); note wind and sea conditions
- ☐ Check Lighthouse and Station Observation Reports from Smith Island, Race Rocks, Port Townsend, Trial Island, and Entrance Island; note wind and sea conditions

Go-NoGo Decision
- √ Check wind direction in relation to direction of travel.
- √ Are you prepared to clear U.S. or Canada Customs?
- √ Is there a wind against wave or current situation?
- √ Are the more protected, but longer, alternate routes a better option?

Fail-Safe Contingency Plans
- √ Duck-in locations along the route: Dungeness Spit, and Oak Bay on Vancouver Is.

See *Chapter 1 Interpreting Northwest Weather* section for telephone numbers, website addresses, VHF channels, and buoy numbers.

Lime Kiln Point on the west side of San Juan Island. Once near Lime Kiln Point, follow the San Juan Island shoreline north.

If you're returning south from Roche Harbor, follow the San Juan Island coastline until you're a little south of Lime Kiln Point, then turn to approximately 125° magnetic until the Smith Island light is abeam to port. At Smith Island turn to 121° magnetic to fetch Point Wilson.

Both the flood and ebb currents run strongly along the west side of San Juan Island. Even in a fast boat it is best to make this passage with favorable current. The Canadian Hydrographic Service book, *Current Atlas: Juan de Fuca Strait to Georgia Strait* illustrates these current flows in convincing diagram form. *Waggoner Tables*, published annually, provide the time schedule for the Current Atlas.

To Victoria. From Point Wilson, a course of approximately 275° magnetic takes you 30 miles to Victoria. Returning from Victoria, a course of about 095° magnetic should raise Point Wilson in time to make late-run corrections for the effects of current. In slow boats, the trip between Victoria and Point Wilson usually can be made on a single favorable tide. In all boats, utilizing favorable current can save significant time.

Even the best plan can go awry. While over the years we have made many easy crossings of the strait (only a few have been "memorable"), it's important to understand that conditions can change with little warning. When you're several miles offshore and the wind decides to kick up, you can't pull over until things improve.

The Strait of Juan de Fuca is not to be feared, but it should be respected. Be sure your boat is seaworthy, well-equipped, and in excellent condition. Carry plenty of fuel. Check the typically easterly flowing offshore weather systems. Let the weather and tide and current tables set your plans. Don't be afraid to wait, but be confident enough to seize opportunities as they arise.

Discovery Bay. Discovery Bay is west of Point Wilson. It is somewhat protected from the Strait of Juan de Fuca by Protection Island, a wildlife refuge. Discovery Bay is open and unobstructed, surrounded by forest and farm lands, with a few waterfront communities. The bay is seldom used by pleasure craft as an overnight anchorage. Gardiner, halfway down the bay, has a launch ramp. The WorldMark Club dock, along the west shore near Port Discovery, is available for timeshare members only. A small private community marina is located on the east shore at Cape George.

Sequim Bay. Sequim Bay is a large, beautiful bay with a State park, marina, and anchoring opportunities. The bay is protected by Travis Spit, which extends from the eastern shore.

To enter, steer for the middle of this spit, then turn sharply west and run parallel to the spit before turning to the south at the tip of the spit. Current can run strongly in the channel during tidal exchange. The marked channel leads to the west of a shoal area just south of Travis Spit; favor the shore side of the channel when passing green channel markers 5 and 7.

Anchoring is possible in most of Sequim Bay with varying depths; one of the preferred is in a bight just south of John Wayne Marina on the west shore in 30 to 50 feet. Sequim Bay State Park is about 1.5 miles south of the John Wayne Marina entrance, on the west shore, with a moorage dock and mooring buoys for boats 45 feet and under.

Actor John Wayne, who often visited Sequim Bay aboard his yacht Wild Goose, donated 22 waterfront acres to the Port of Port Angeles on condition that the Port build a marina on the site.

Local Knowledge

SHOAL AREA: Sequim Bay has a large shoal in the middle of the entry channel with passage around the eastern and western sides. The marked channel, Red, Right, Returning to Sequim Bay, leads around the western side of the shoal area.

① **John Wayne Marina.** 2577 W. Sequim Bay Road, Sequim, WA 98382; (360) 417-3440; (no VHF); rona@portofpa.com; www.portofpa.com. Open all year, gasoline and diesel at the fuel dock; first-come first-served guest moorage in approximately 22 side-tie spaces on two floats, and assigned slips as available. Services include 30 & 50 amp power, water, clean restrooms and showers; free Wi-Fi, laundry, pumpout, portapotty dump, and launch ramps.

The Dockside Grill restaurant is ashore and is reported to be excellent. Picnic area and beach access are nearby. Check-in at the first float inside the breakwater. John Wayne Marina is operated by the Port of Port Angeles. For those desiring onshore accommodations, the John Wayne Waterfront Resort (360-681-3853) has cabins and camp sites a short walk away.

① **Sequim Bay Marine State Park.** (360) 683-4235; Sequim Bay Marine State Park occupies 92 acres along the western shore of Sequim Bay. Open all year, day use and overnight mooring and camping, 120 feet of dock space and 6 buoys (for boats 45 feet and under). Facilities include restrooms, showers, portapotty dump, picnic sites, campsites, kitchen shelters, and launch ramp. No power. The mooring buoys are in deep water. Self-register and pay nightly mooring buoy fee on shore. The water around the dock and mooring float is shallower. Watch your depths at low tide. Boarding floats at the launch ramp are removed in the winter. The Olympic Discovery Trail passes through the park and

See Area Map Page 189 - Maps Not for Navigation   STRAIT OF JUAN DE FUCA

is accessible for walking or bicycling; see the Olympic Discovery Trail sidebar for more information.

Dungeness Spit. Beautiful Dungeness Spit, 5.5 miles long, is the world's longest natural sand spit. The spit provides protection from westerly weather, and convenient anchoring depths along its inner edge before an attached cross-spit forces the channel south. Shallow draft boats can continue into the inner harbor, where there is a launch ramp and protected anchorage. Dungeness Spit is a wildlife refuge and open to hikers but has no public facilities.

② **Port Angeles.** Port Angeles is a substantial small city on a bay protected by Ediz Hook. The Port Angeles City Pier, with visitor moorage, is near the south end of the business district. Guest moorage with full services is available at the breakwater-protected Port of Port Angeles Boat Haven marina at the southwest corner of the bay and City Pier.

Port Angeles is a U.S. Customs port of entry. The *Coho* car and passenger ferry runs from Port Angeles to Victoria (www.cohoferry.com). It is possible to moor the boat in Port Angeles, take the *Coho* ferry as a walk-on passenger in the morning, tour Victoria, B.C. for the day, and return to Port Angeles in the late afternoon.

The outer end of Ediz Hook is a Coast Guard station. Just west of the Coast Guard station is the Port Angeles Pilot Station, where Puget Sound Pilot tenders shuttle pilots to ships bound to or from Puget Sound ports.

Port Angeles has a number of attractions. The walkable town has many shops and restaurants to explore. The Feiro Marine Life Center, on the city pier, focuses on the marine life in the Strait of Juan de Fuca. Open daily, 10:00 a.m. to 5:00 p.m. in summers and 12:00 p.m. to 5:00 p.m. in winters. In late June, free summer concerts begin on the pier, Wednesdays 6:00 p.m. to 8:00 p.m. The Juan de Fuca Festival with music, workshops and crafts is on Memorial Day weekend. For general tourist information see the North Olympic Peninsula Visitor & Convention Bureau website: www.olympicpeninsula.org. The Olympic Discovery Trail is accessible at both Port Angeles moorage locations.

Farmers market: Saturdays year-round, from 10:00 a.m. to 2:00 p.m. at the corner of Front Street and Lincoln Street.

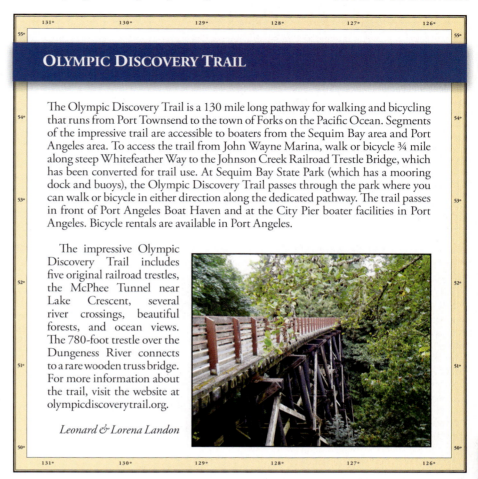

OLYMPIC DISCOVERY TRAIL

The Olympic Discovery Trail is a 130 mile long pathway for walking and bicycling that runs from Port Townsend to the town of Forks on the Pacific Ocean. Segments of the impressive trail are accessible to boaters from the Sequim Bay area and Port Angeles area. To access the trail from John Wayne Marina, walk or bicycle ¾ mile along steep Whitefeather Way to the Johnson Creek Railroad Trestle Bridge, which has been converted for trail use. At Sequim Bay State Park (which has a mooring dock and buoys), the Olympic Discovery Trail passes through the park where you can walk or bicycle in either direction along the dedicated pathway. The trail passes in front of Port Angeles Boat Haven and at the City Pier boater facilities in Port Angeles. Bicycle rentals are available in Port Angeles.

The impressive Olympic Discovery Trail includes five original railroad trestles, the McPhee Tunnel near Lake Crescent, several river crossings, beautiful forests, and ocean views. The 780-foot trestle over the Dungeness River connects to a rare wooden truss bridge. For more information about the trail, visit the website at olympicdiscoverytrail.org.

Leonard & Lorena Landon

John Wayne Marina

Port Angeles City Pier

2020 Waggoner Cruising Guide

STRAIT OF JUAN DE FUCA

See Area Map Page 189 - Maps Not for Navigation

Port Angeles Boat Haven

② **Port Angeles Boat Haven.** 832 Boat Haven Drive, Port Angeles, WA 98362; (360) 457-4505; pamarina@olypen.com; www.portofpa.com. Open all year, ethanol-free gasoline and diesel at the fuel dock, and high-volume fuel delivery for larger vessels. The marina has concrete docks, side-tie guest moorage, and a guest arrival float. Maximum boat length 164 feet. Services include 30, 50, and 100 amp power, restrooms, Wi-Fi, showers, waste oil disposal, pumpout. Security system with locking gates. Call ahead for after-hours arrival. Online reservations available through Dockwa.com. Excellent 2-lane launch ramp with ample room for tow vehicles and trailers. Customs clearance is available from a dedicated phone on the water side of the harbor office, (360) 457-4311. Haulout on a 70-ton Travelift. Groceries, doctor, post office, and laundry are nearby. The Castaway Restaurant, located on the northwest end of the moorage basin, is a full service restaurant and night club frequently featuring live music.

② **Port Angeles City Pier.** Foot of North Lincoln St., Port Angeles, WA 98362; (360) 417-4550; www.cityofpa.us. Six new floats, one of which is ADA accessible, were installed at Port Angeles City Pier in 2018. Guest overnight side-tie moorage available for boats up to 80 feet. No power, no water; first-come, first-served. A self-registration pay station is located near the docks. Maximum 10-day stay.

Crescent Bay. Crescent Bay is a possible anchorage if conditions on the Strait of Juan de Fuca become untenable. A little protection can be found close to the western shore, but swells can still work into the bay and make for an uneasy stay. Past the east end of Crescent Bay is the Salt Creek Recreation Area. Field Correspondent Jim Norris reports this is a great spot for tide pool exploring, with a nice beach.

Pillar Point. Pillar Point has a fishing resort with launch ramp and float but is not available for transient moorage. In a westerly the area close to and east of the point is a notorious windless spot—a "hole" in sailboaters' language. A Waggoner reader wrote to tell us anchorage is good along the eastern shore.

CLALLAM BAY AND SEKIU

Clallam Bay. Clallam Bay, with Sekiu on its western shore, is somewhat protected from westerlies and has convenient anchoring depths along the shore. A serious reef, marked by a buoy at its outer end well offshore, extends from the eastern point. Leave the buoy to port when entering the bay. Three marinas offer guest moorage.

The Makah Museum collection houses 300-500 year old artifacts recovered from the Ozette Archeological Site.

③ **Van Riper's Resort.** P.O. Box 246, 280 Front Street, Sekiu, WA 98381; (360) 963-2334; www.vanripersresort.com. Open summers, closed winters. Guest moorage on five docks with 450 feet each. Facilities include restrooms, showers, free Wi-Fi, campground, concrete launch ramp. No power. Boat and motor rentals, charter service, ice, groceries, charts, and books. Nearby post office, restaurant and bar, and marine supplies.

③ **Mason's Olson Resort.** P.O. Box 216, 444 Front St., Sekiu, WA 98381; (360) 963-2311. Open March through September. Gasoline and diesel at the fuel dock. Guest moorage in 300 slips behind a breakwater, 35-foot maximum boat length. No power. Services include restrooms, showers, laundry, 3-lane concrete launch ramp, and Wi-Fi near the office. Motel units available. Busy during salmon season. After 80 years of family ownership, the Olson family sold the resort in late 2014. The Mason family now owns and operates the resort.

③ **Curley's Resort.** P.O. Box 265, Sekiu, WA 98381; (360) 963-2281; (800) 542-9680; www.curleysresort.com. Open May through September, guest moorage while staying in one of the cabins. 750 feet of dock space, 30-foot maximum boat length. This is a private resort with moorage, motel rooms, and cabins for rent. Pets must remain on the boat.

NEAH BAY

The Makah Tribe town of Neah Bay is popular with sport fishermen, who trailer their boats in during the summer. It's also a good place to wait for a favorable weather window to round Cape Flattery and head down the Pacific Coast. Most boats bound to or from Barkley Sound, however, choose to stay along the Vancouver Island side of the Strait of Juan de Fuca. For cruising boats that do stop, moorage is at the Makah Marina docks, managed by Big Salmon Resort.

A long breakwater connects the mainland and Waadah Island, blocking ocean waves from getting in. Anchorage is good, sand bottom, throughout the bay. A second breakwater protects the Makah Marina. The Coast Guard station at the entrance to the bay serves the west end of the Strait of Juan de Fuca and the northern Pacific Ocean coast.

Neah Bay is not a U.S. Customs port of entry, although entrants with Nexus cards may be able to phone in for clearance. Those without Nexus must clear at a designated port of entry. Port Angeles is the nearest location.

The Makah Cultural & Research Center Museum features artifacts from the Ozette archaeological dig site. The museum is world-class—a must see. The Ozette dig unearthed a village site buried by a mudslide 500 years ago, before European contact. It is a time capsule of coastal Native life. The tools, clothing, furniture, weapons, and fishing implements are exquisitely preserved and displayed.

Neah Bay's general store is well-stocked, except for spirits. Neah Bay is dry.

④ **Makah Marina.** P.O. Box 137, Neah Bay, WA 98357; (360) 645-3015. www.makah.com/activities/marina; VHF 16 and 66. Open all year, guest moorage, 30 & 50 amp power, free Wi-Fi, potable water, restrooms, showers, laundry nearby, pumpout station, portapotty dump, 2-lane launch ramp with extended parking available for tow vehicles and trailers. Fuel dock with gas, diesel, and lubricants. Summertime visitor moorage is managed by Big Salmon Resort, see listing below. Slips vary from 30-70 feet; side-tie for vessels up to 100 feet. Shopping (on the rough and ready side) and lodging are nearby. The extraordinary Makah Museum is an easy walk.

The marina is spacious and well-built. The concrete docks are stable. The slips and the fairways between docks are wide. On shore, the administration building has restrooms and showers. Summertime moorage can be crowded with commercial boats and their gear, however, so don't expect a resort environment.

④ **Big Salmon Resort.** P.O. Box 140, 1251 Bay View Ave., Neah Bay, WA 98357; (360) 645-2374; (866) 787-1900; www.bigsalmonresort.net. Open April 1 to September 15. Gas and diesel at fuel dock. Pumpout. Haulout to 30 tons and 2-lane concrete launch ramp with long-term parking. Guest moorage at Makah Marina. A small store carries tackle, some groceries, local charts. Motels are nearby.

If the fuel dock is closed for the season, fuel is available at the Makah Mini Mart's commercial dock just beyond the commercial fish offloading pier.

⑤ **Snow Creek Resort.** P.O. Box 248, Mile Marker 691, Hwy 112, Neah Bay, WA 98357; (360) 645-2284; snowcreek@gmail.com. Open from April 15 to October 1. Guest moorage for up to 40 boats plus 25 buoys. Maximum boat size 26 feet. Restrooms, showers, campsites and RV parking, cabins, limited groceries, diving air, haulout, beach launch, and hoist launch.

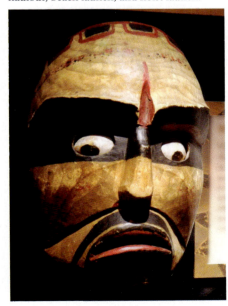

A tribal mask in the Makah Museum at Neah Bay

San Juan Islands

CHAPTER 6

SAN JUAN ISLAND
Friday Harbor • Roche Harbor • Garrison Bay

LOPEZ ISLAND
Fisherman Bay • Spencer Spit • Watmough Bay

ORCAS ISLAND
Eastsound • Deer Harbor • Rosario Resort

*Blakely Island • Sucia Island • Jones Island
Shaw Island • Stuart Island • James Island*

See Area Map Page 196 - Maps Not for Navigation

SAN JUAN ISLANDS

The well-known **San Juan Islands** are the dream destination for thousands of boaters each year. The scenery is stunning, the fishing is good, the anchorages are plentiful, and the amenities—marine resorts, settlements, villages and towns—are many and varied. The islands contain large flocks of bald eagles. Sailing in the company of porpoises and whales is almost commonplace.

The San Juans have a feel about them that is different from most other coastal cruising areas. In the San Juans we don't just head down the coast to another bay, or out to a little clutch of islets for the night. Instead, we are cruising among the peaks of a majestic sunken mountain range, and each island peak is different from the others. We've truly left the bustle of civilization behind and found a corner of paradise.

The San Juans have so much to see and do that a first-time visitor can be overwhelmed. We have a short list of stops that we recommend. They are not the only places to experience, but nothing like them exists anywhere else. Our short list is as follows: Rosario Resort, Roche Harbor, English Camp (Garrison Bay), Stuart Island (Prevost Harbor and Reid Harbor), Sucia Island, Friday Harbor. You will make many other stops as well. But these six are highly recommended, especially for the first-time visitor, or when you have guests.

Rosario Resort is a mansion and estate built in the early 1900s by Robert Moran, a turn-of-the-20th-century pioneer ship builder. The facilities include a luxury resort hotel and marina. Roche Harbor is another century-old monument, this one built around limestone quarrying. It's now a deluxe resort and a not to be missed experience. English Camp is at Garrison Bay, a short distance from Roche Harbor. This is where the British garrison was stationed during the historic 1859–1872 Pig War. The blockhouse, formal gardens, and several buildings remain. They are now a National Historical Park, with an interpretive center. You can anchor in the bay and visit by dinghy.

Stuart Island is a gem. In both Prevost Harbor and Reid Harbor you can anchor, tie to a mooring buoy, or moor on the coveted, but space-limited, State Park docks. Whichever you do, you will be surrounded by beauty. A hike along a well-marked, up-and-down trail leads to the dirt road that runs out to Turn Point Lighthouse. Along the way are the Stuart Island one-room school, library, and museum.

Sucia Island, with its weather- and water-sculpted sandstone, its fossils and fascinating shoreline, is the definitive anchorage of the San Juans. The problem will be choosing which of Sucia Island's five bays to stay in.

Friday Harbor is a lovely little town where you can browse the shops, or enjoy one of the many restaurants or pubs. Friday Harbor is the commercial hub of the San Juans, with more services than any other destination.

No, we've not mentioned the charming village of Eastsound on Orcas Island, or Lopez Village on Lopez Island, or the Shaw General Store at the Shaw Island ferry landing, or Spencer Spit, or a dozen other delightful places to see, although we certainly describe them in detail later in the chapter. This is the challenge with the San Juans. There are so many choices.

Watch for current running perpendicular to the dock at James Island State Park.

Although summertime tourism is a major industry in the San Juan Islands, the settlements have retained a small village atmosphere. Minutes out of town, you will be on winding roads in pastoral farm country. Island people are easygoing and friendly, and many of them are highly accomplished. Movie stars and industrialist families have estates there. The late author Ernest Gann lived on San Juan Island. One famous author's book bio says simply that he lives on an island. What it doesn't say is that the island is in the San Juans.

Drinking water is in short supply in the San Juan Islands. In almost every case you'll find no water for boat washing. Go to the San Juans with full water tanks, and conserve while you are there.

Personal Watercraft Restriction: Because some people were hot-dogging on their PWCs and harassing whales and other wildlife, San Juan County has banned PWC use in the San Juan Islands.

San Juan Islands National Wildlife Refuge: The San Juan Islands National Wildlife Refuge consists of 83 islands, islets, rocks and reefs. Boaters must remain 200 yards offshore from any refuge property.

No Discharge Zone: All of the inside waters of Washington State from Puget Sound to the Canadian Border, including all of the waters of the San Juan Islands, are a No Discharge Zone (NDZ). It is illegal to discharge any (treated and untreated) black water sewage. Gray water from showers and sinks is not covered by this restriction.

Getting to the San Juan Islands. If you are approaching from the east, you'll enter the San Juans through one of four passes: Lopez Pass, Thatcher Pass, Peavine Pass, or Obstruction Pass.

At times the waters outside these passes can be turbulent, dangerously so, the result of tidal current and wind opposing each other. Be sure you have a complete tide and current book, and are able to read it. You can't go wrong with the official government publications, but our preferred tide book is Ports and Passes, available at marine supply stores or www.WaggonerGuide.com. Ports and Passes uses a tabular format, covering the area from Olympia to the Alaska border and is corrected for Daylight Saving Time.

① **James Island Marine State Park**. (360) 376-2073; Open all year for day use, overnight mooring, and camping. James Island is a favorite spot, with trails to hike and wildlife to view. Visiting boats can use both sides of the 128-foot-long float located on the west side of the island. In the past, the float has been removed between October and March;

James Island Marine State Park

2020 waggoner CRUISING GUIDE

SAN JUAN ISLANDS — Reference Only – Not for Navigation

Sylvan Cove is a lovely anchorage, but the land ashore is all private.

Visitors enjoying the view from the end of Spencer Spit

the float is now available year-round. Beware that strong flood current can make docking challenging. Compost toilets located near the dock; no power or water. Strong currents and a rocky bottom make anchoring difficult in the west cove, use the float.

The east cove is exposed to wakes from passing traffic in Rosario Strait, but has 4 mooring buoys for boats 45 feet or less. Self-register and pay nightly mooring buoy fee on shore. The park has a picnic shelter and 13 primitive campsites, nearby pit toilets. A Cascadia Marine Trail campsite is at Pocket Cove (high bank gravel beach). Excellent hiking, picnicking, scuba diving. Pack out all garbage. If at the dock, raccoons will go aboard unattended boats if food or garbage is left in the open. Best to stow food well and close the boat tight.

LOCAL KNOWLEDGE

TIDE-RIP: At the eastern entrance to Thatcher Pass, watch for tide-rips on ebbing current and southerly winds.

Thatcher Pass. Thatcher Pass runs between Blakely Island and Decatur Island, and is one of the main entrances into the San Juan Islands. Currents can run strongly. Washington State Ferries use Thatcher Pass, so keep a sharp lookout.

Decatur Island. Decatur Island is east of Lopez Island and south of Blakely Island. Decatur Island has three vacation communities and about 70 full-time residents. Reads Bay, Brigantine Bay, Sylvan Cove, and the unnamed bay between Decatur Head and Fauntleroy Point are anchoring locations around Decatur Island. All of the island's uplands, docks, and mooring buoys are private. Kimball Preserve on the southern tip of the island is the only publicly accessible area. The island's year-round and seasonal residents come and go by water taxi service or by private aircraft.

Sylvan Cove. Sylvan Cove, at the northwest corner of Decatur Island, has good holding bottom in convenient depths. The bay is truly beautiful, with New England-style buildings ashore. All the land is private, as are the mooring buoys, the dock, and float that serve homeowners on the island.

Brigantine Bay. The area between Trump Island and Decatur Island is pretty, and has anchorage in 24 to 42 feet. The dock and all the land ashore are private. Center Island has good anchorage which can be found by simply cruising around Center Island into Reads Bay until you find an area out of the prevailing wind.

Reads Bay. Reads Bay is located between Center Island and the south end of Decatur Island and includes the channel connecting to Lopez Pass. A charted cable area, shallow areas, and hazards awash make the north portion unsuitable for anchoring. The connecting channel is better for anchoring; watch for several charted shallow areas. Good holding on a mud bottom. Be prepared for water taxi and supply barge traffic transiting between Center and Decatur Islands, and Lopez Pass.

Kimball Preserve. South of Reads Bay is the Kimball Preserve area, made up of two small

CAUTION IN ROSARIO STRAIT

Lopez Pass, Thatcher Pass, Peavine Pass and Obstruction Pass all connect with Rosario Strait. Especially on an ebb, when current in Thatcher Pass and Lopez Pass flows east into Rosario Strait, expect rougher water off their mouths. If a big southflowing ebb in Rosario Strait is opposed by a fresh southerly wind, expect severe turbulence. The tide-rips and heavy seas can persist completely across the strait.

We have seen some vicious rips at the south end of Rosario Strait. Walt Woodward *(How to Cruise to Alaska without Rocking the Boat Too Much)* recalls that a rip outside Lopez Pass was the worst he had ever encountered.

The waters between Guemes Channel and Thatcher Pass can be rough or even dangerous in these conditions (southflowing ebb in Rosario Strait opposed by fresh southerly wind). Guemes Channel enters Rosario Strait from the east, and Thatcher Pass enters from the west. Bellingham Channel angles in from the northeast. The conflict of the four currents, combined with the opposing wind, creates confused, high and steep beam seas as you cross. It seems that all experienced local yachting families (ourselves included) have their own horror stories of crossings in such conditions.

We have learned to treat Rosario Strait with great respect. Thus, one year when a 20-knot southerly was blowing, we left the San Juans for Seattle via Peavine Pass, at the north end of Blakely Island. As we suspected, Rosario Strait was rough, especially to the south. We angled northward and eastward across the top of Cypress Island, and looked down Bellingham Channel. It too was a mass of whitecaps.

So we continued eastward, and found calm water on the east side of Guemes Island. Our route plan back to Seattle then went past La Conner and south through Saratoga Passage. It was longer and slower than a fast run across the Strait of Juan de Fuca and down Admiralty Inlet, but it was unruffled.

– Robert Hale

SAN JUAN ISLANDS

See Area Map Page 196 - Maps Not for Navigation

Kimball Preserve, the only public access on Decatur Island, offers beautiful vistas to the south.

Fisherman Bay, Lopez Island

islands and the southern tip of Decatur Island. The southern tip of Decatur Island, the island to the southwest, and the isthmus connecting the two, are part of the San Juan Preservation Trust. The small rocky islet northwest of the isthmus is a Bureau of Land Management property, which joins the isthmus at low tide. The remains of a concrete structure are on the west side of the BLM island. The preserve is open all year, day use only, no facilities, no fires, no overnight camping, pack out all garbage. Anchor out. There is a dinghy or kayak beach landing area on the north shore of the isthmus. A half-mile trail along the south side of southern island continues across the isthmus and to the north end of the preserve property on Decatur Island. Excellent views in all directions can be found along the trail.

Lopez Pass. Lopez Pass connects Rosario Strait to Lopez Sound. Currents can flow strongly through Lopez Pass and the area calls for careful navigation.

Lopez Island. Lopez Island offers a variety of anchorages and moorages. On the northern end, sandy Spencer Spit is a favorite. Fisherman Bay, on the west side, has the village of Lopez, with marinas, a museum, a grocery store, and restaurants.

The southern end of Lopez Island is indented by several bays, and guarded by rocks and reefs. The geography is rugged and windblown, the result of the prevailing westerly winds from the Strait of Juan de Fuca. It's an interesting shore to explore when the wind is down.

Lopez Sound. Lopez Sound is the large body of water between Decatur Island and Lopez Island. This broad area has easy anchoring depths with few hazards. A selection of anchoring locations in Lopez Sound affords wind protection from a variety of directions. Among them are Hunter Bay and Mud Bay. Although Lopez Sound is surrounded by private homes and docks, it's very picturesque and feels special. A variety of scenery captures the mind's eye, everything from wind swept slopes and rocky beaches, to tree-covered hillsides and open pastures. Crabbing and clamming are popular local past-times.

Mud Bay. South end of Lopez Sound. This large bay has ample room for anchoring with good holding in 12 - 14 feet over a mud bottom. Watch your depths, charted shallow areas in the bay. Good protection except in strong northeast and southeast winds. Buoys in the bay are private. Tiny Mud Bay County Park (360) 378-8420, located along the southeast side of the bay, is open all year for daytime use. No shore side signage at the park. The park beach is a popular departure point for kayakers. Clamming on the mud flats is reported to be good; crabbing good at times.

Spencer Spit State Park

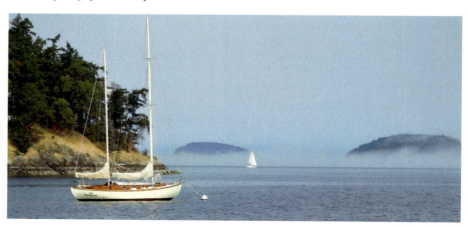

Large Mud Bay, on the south end of Lopez Sound, has ample room for many boats at anchor; mooring buoys in the bay are private.

SAN JUAN ISLANDS

Best to exit and enter the channel to Fisherman Bay on Lopez Island at mid to high tide.

Hunter Bay. Southwest corner of Lopez Sound. Hunter Bay is a good place to anchor, consistent depths of 15 feet over a mud bottom. The bay is surrounded by forest and protected from all but northeast winds. Located on the southeast side of the bay, just south of Crab Island, is a public launch ramp and public pier with a 45-foot float for day use, no overnight moorage. Crabbing is said to be good at times.

② **Spencer Spit Marine State Park.** 521 A. Bakerview Road, Lopez Island, WA 98261; (360) 468-2251; www.parks.wa.gov. On the northeastern shore of Lopez Island. Open all year, day use and overnight mooring and camping. The park has 12 mooring buoys; self-register and pay nightly mooring buoy fee on shore. The buoys, for boats 45 feet and under, typically fill up quickly during the summer, but anchoring is good. Restrooms are located upland, no showers. Restrooms are closed from the end of October to March. Water is available at the bottom of the trail to the uplands.

Spencer Spit is a popular park. A saltwater lagoon, fed from the north side, is in the middle of the spit. If you are on the north side, you must walk around the tip of the spit and back down the south side to get to the upland areas of the park. The park has standard and primitive campsites. To reserve a campsite call (888) 226-7688. Rabbits abound, and interpretive signs aid exploration. Spencer Spit is a Cascadia Marine Trail campsite.

Although the pass between Spencer Spit and Frost Island is narrow, it is deep and safe.

Swifts Bay. Swifts Bay, behind Flower Island and Leo Reef, is shallow, but a usable anchorage in settled weather. Anchor on a sand bottom in 10 to 20 feet.

Shoal Bay. Shoal Bay indents the northern tip of Lopez Island between Humphrey Head and Upright Head offering good, fairly protected anchorage. We think the best spot is behind the breakwater and off the private marina along the east shore. Numerous crab pot floats must be avoided in picking an anchorage.

LOCAL KNOWLEDGE

SHOAL ENTRY: The entrance to Fisherman Bay should not be attempted by deep draft boats at less than half tide.

③ **Fisherman Bay.** Fisherman Bay extends southward about 1.5 miles into the western shore of Lopez Island. The entrance is winding and shallow. About 200 yards off the entrance, a non-lateral sector light marks the center of the entrance channel; you can pass on either side, but stay close to remain in the

ISLANDS MARINE CENTER
YOUR HOME PORT IN THE SAN JUANS

P.O. Box 88 • Fisherman Bay • Lopez Island, WA 98261
Phone (360)468-3377 • Fax (360)468-2283 • VHF 69
E-mail imc@rockisland.com • www.islandsmarinecenter.com
Call or Radio for Reservations

- 100 Slip Modern Marina with Water, ATM Power, Ice, Pumpout, High Speed Internet
- Marine Parts • Napa Auto Supply
- Fishing Tackle & Bait
- Fully Stocked Chandlery
- Pursuit, Ocean Sport & Steiger Craft
- Volvo, Mercruiser, Yamaha
- Full Sales & Service
- Factory Trained Service Department
- Haulouts to 25 Tons
- Restaurants & Shopping Nearby

2020 WAGGONER CRUISING GUIDE

Rental kayaks and bicycles are available on the beach at the Lopez Islander Resort.

deepest water. Caution: watch for the charted rock awash approaching red Daybeacon 4. Leave this beacon to starboard, then follow the well-marked channel into the bay. Cutting any of the corners risks grounding.

The northernmost marina in Fisherman Bay belongs to Islands Marine Center. The docks next door belong to the Lopez Islander Resort. About one-half mile south of the Lopez Islander, the Galley Restaurant (360-468-2874) has two mooring buoys for restaurant patrons (marked with the number 23-077173); tie-up dinghies next to the ramp at the restaurant's dock.

Anchorage in Fisherman Bay is shallow, with a mud bottom. When entering or departing, resist the urge to cut inside any navigation marks. Departing, it's tempting to cut inside red nun Buoy 8, and there you are, aground. Remember: Red, Right, Returning, also means Red, *Left, Departing*.

Lopez Village is a little less than a mile away. You'll find excellent dining, well-stocked grocery stores, galleries, all the usual services, and the famous Holly B's Bakery. Another local favorite is Vita's Wildly Delicious, offering excellent deli foods and world-class wines.

The Lopez Historical Museum is open noon to 4:00 p.m., Wednesday to Sunday, May through September, with exhibits inside and on the field outside. A farmers market takes up an entire field at the village, 10:00 a.m. to 2:00 p.m. on Saturdays, May through September.

Keep one hand free to wave to passing vehicles as you walk or cycle the roads. It's the custom on Lopez Island. Everybody waves.

Note: Floatplanes typically use the northwest side of the bay for landing. This is also where local boat repair centers conduct on-water testing. Consider anchoring in other areas of the bay.

③ **Islands Marine Center.** 2793 Fisherman Bay Rd., Lopez, WA 98261; (360) 468-3377; imc@rockisland.com; www.islandsmarinecenter.com. Monitors VHF 69. Open all year, Monday through Saturday. Guest moorage along 1000 feet of dock space, 30 amp power, Wi-Fi, ATM, restrooms, showers, garbage, recycling, pumpout. Call ahead.

This is a well-run, full-service marina, with haulout to 25 tons, launch ramp, repairs, fishing supplies, and a fully stocked chandlery. One view guest room available for overnight lodging. Good depth at all docks.

③ **Lopez Islander Resort & Marina**. P.O. Box 459, 2864 Fisherman Bay Rd., Lopez, WA 98261; (360) 468-2233; (800) 736-3434; desk@lopezfun.com; www.lopezfun.com. Monitors VHF 78A. Open all year, gasoline & diesel at the fuel dock. Guest moorage in 64 slips plus 600-foot dock. Reservations recommended on busy weekends. Services include 30 & 50 amp power, restrooms and showers, laundry, swimming pool (heated June through September), year-round Jacuzzi, free Wi-Fi in the lodge. The seasonal dock store has ice, beer, wine, and bait, along with basics like milk, eggs, cheese, and snacks. Nearby bicycle and kayak rentals.

The resort has a good restaurant with an outdoor deck and sports lounge, a workout facility, a spa, massage, camping, and water-view lodging by reservation. Live music in the Tiki Bar most weekends June through September. The docks are solid, and the management is attentive. Shuttle service available for a fee.

Odlin San Juan Co. Park. (360) 378-8420; parks@sanjuanco.com. sanjuanco.com/495/Lopez-Island. West side of Lopez Island. Located between Flat Point and Upright Head. Open all year. Good bottom for anchoring, but exposed to northwest winds. Five mooring buoys are available, a nightly use fee is payable at the park office, located up the road past the baseball field. Small float for boats 30 feet and under with a 2-hour limit, or take your small craft ashore. Campsites, restrooms, beach area and sea wall, baseball diamond, picnic sites, cooking shelter, fire pits. Boat ramp and trailer parking.

Upright Channel Park. Northwest side of Lopez Island 1/4 mile east of Flat Point. Day use only. Restrooms, 4 picnic sites.

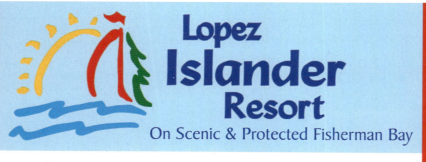

See Area Map Page 196 - Maps Not for Navigation   SAN JUAN ISLANDS

④ **Mackaye Harbor.** Mackaye Harbor and Barlow Bay at the south end of Lopez Island are a good overnight anchorage for boats planning an early morning crossing of the Strait of Juan de Fuca. Swells from a westerly wind can make their way into the harbor.

A county dock/boat launch is located at the northeast end of Mackaye Harbor. The Southend General Store & Restaurant (360) 468-2315 is located a half mile away. The restaurant is open for lunch and dinner, call ahead for hours. The well-stocked grocery includes a collection of local foods, art and jewelry. Docks and mooring buoys in Barlow Bay are private. Dinghy or kayak ashore at Mackaye Harbor.

Dangerous Wreck: A sunken boat is on the east side of the entry to Barlow Bay, approximately at the 2 fathoms, 5 feet sounding on Chart 18429. The wreck is visible at low tide. Mackaye Harbor is the site of a fish boat marina, and during the summer months a large fish boat fleet can be found in the harbor.

Iceberg Island. An undeveloped state park in outer Mackaye Harbor. Open all year, day use only. Anchor out. No facilities, no fires, no overnight camping. Pack out all garbage. Do not disturb wildlife or alter the surroundings.

Aleck Bay. Aleck Bay is big and easy to get into. Beaches are private. Anchor close to the head of the bay in 30 to 36 feet. Open to easterlies. Westerlies can make their way into the bay due to the low terrain.

Hughes Bay. Hughes Bay is well protected from winds except southerlies. High surrounding terrain provides protection from the northeast and northwest. A few homes along the shore with private mooring buoys. No public buoys. Good anchoring depths ranging in the teens to 30 feet.

McArdle Bay. McArdle Bay provides good anchorage in 20 to 30 feet, but is completely exposed to southerly winds coming off the Strait of Juan de Fuca. Beautiful homes are on the hills above the bay, with lovely beaches below. No private or public buoys in the bay. Just outside, the chart shows a rock in the passage between Blind Island and Lopez Island. The rock is actually a reef.

Castle Island. Castle Island is part of the San Juan Islands National Wildlife Refuge. Boats must stay 200 yards from shore to protect wildlife; no shore access.

Watmough Bay. A beautiful high sheer rock wall is on the north side of Watmough Bay. The chart shows the bottom as rocky, but we have found excellent holding in blue mud in 12 to 18 feet about halfway in. Three public mooring buoys are for boats 45 feet and under. They are ok to use for up to 72 hours. The bay is sheltered from southerly and westerly winds, but we've found waves work their way into the bay from freighters transiting Rosario Strait. Field Correspondent, Deane Hislop,

Stop at Blakely Island for a fresh donut and fuel. The self-pay fuel station is at the top of the ramp.

warns that if current in the bay is holding the boat in a north/south direction, a wake will be on the beam.

A pretty trail leads back through the woods from the head of the bay. A second, steep trail leads to the top of Chadwick Hill from the northwest side of the beach. The head of the bay and the trails are part of a San Juan County Land Bank preserve, made possible by donations from private citizens.

LOCAL KNOWLEDGE

TIDE-RIP: Nasty tide-rips can form off the eastern entrance to Peavine and Obstruction Passes when the wind is blowing from the south and the tide is ebbing.

Obstruction Pass and Peavine Pass. Obstruction Pass runs between Obstruction Island and Orcas Island. Peavine Pass runs between Obstruction Island and Blakely Island. Both passes connect the inner San Juan Islands to Rosario Strait. Currents run to 6.5 knots, and can make these passes challenging. Peavine Pass is preferred, but be alert for occasional ferry traffic. The ferries usually use Thatcher Pass. Peavine Pass is their storm route, although sometimes it is used in fair weather as well.

Blakely Island. Blakely Island is east of Lopez Island and Shaw Island. Both Blakely Island and tiny Armitage Island off the southeast corner of Blakely Island are privately owned, with no shore access. Anchorage is possible in Thatcher Bay, and, with care, behind Armitage Island. The Blakely Island Store & Marina, at the north end of Blakely Island, has guest moorage. Blakely Island is private, including the roads. Please confine your stays to the marina property.

⑤ **Blakely Island Store & Marina.** #1 Marina Dr., Blakely Island, WA 98222; (360) 375-6121; info@blakelyisland.com. Monitors VHF 66A. Moorage in 9 guest slips and in permanent slips as available; slips can accommodate boats to 70 feet; phone or email for reservations. Off-season guest moorage available; use the payment station located by the store. Fuel dock has gasoline and diesel, with a kiosk for self-serve credit card purchases from 6 a.m. to 8 p.m. during the summer months. Facilities include excellent concrete docks, 30 amp power, Wi-Fi, water, restrooms, showers, laundry and covered picnic area.

The store is open Memorial Day weekend through Labor Day. The store cafe serves dinner on Fridays until mid-August, and

Blakely Island Marina

2020 WAGGONER CRUISING GUIDE

SAN JUAN ISLANDS

breakfast and deli lunch daily. Fresh donuts, made on site, are available in the morning. Beer on tap and wine by the glass. They also carry a good selection of books and some gift items.

The channel leading to the boat basin is shallow, (5 feet of depth on zero tide) and may restrict deep draft vessels at the bottom of a very low tide. Other than those conditions, you should have plenty of water. If in doubt, call the marina office for guidance.

Shaw Island. The marina is adjacent to the Shaw Island ferry terminal. Resident boats occupy most of the dock space. Maximum length for short term guest moorage is 25 feet, call ahead at the Shaw General Store. It's better to anchor in Blind Bay and take the dinghy over. Tie up in a place that doesn't block a permanent boat. Wakes make their way into the moorage, either from the ferries or from boat traffic in the channel. Consider this when tying up to the dock.

Safety Note: Do not under any circumstances run the dinghy under the bow of a ferry tied up at the landing.

LOCAL KNOWLEDGE

Dangerous Rocks: Charted rocks obstruct the waters west of Blind Island. While it's possible to get through safely, our advice is do not pass west of Blind Island.

Blind Bay/Blind Island Marine State Park. Blind Bay, on the north side of Shaw Island, has good anchorage throughout the center portion. Blind Island is a minimally developed state park and Cascadia Marine Trail campsite, with 4 mooring buoys on its south side for boats 45 feet and under. Self-register and pay nightly mooring buoy fee on shore at Blind Island. Toilets are on the island. Pack out all garbage.

East of Blind Island a white daymark, installed and maintained by Bellingham Yacht Club since the 1950s, marks a rock that lies between Blind Island and the Shaw Island shore. Enter Blind Bay midway between that mark and Blind Island. The water shoals abruptly as you enter, but there's no danger unless you are close to the island. Several rocks are just under the surface on the west side of Blind Island. Transit should not be attempted on the west side without local knowledge. Crabbing can be good.

⑥ **Shaw General Store.** P.O. Box 455, Shaw Island, WA 98286; (360) 468-2288; www.shawgeneralstore.com. Open year-round. Very limited short-term day-use guest moorage, maximum 25 feet, call ahead. Pumpout at the end of the main dock. Groceries, beer and wine, ice, gift items, local organic produce, and bins with bulk foods. The back area of the store is a coffee and ice cream shop. Restrooms adjacent to the ferry dock.

Shaw General Store next to the Shaw Island ferry landing has an ice cream-coffee bar.

Blind Island and Shaw Island

Do your part to help protect these awe-inspiring Orca Whales, also known as Killer Whales, belonging to the dolphin family.

WHALE WISE - WASHINGTON STATE

Southern Resident Orca Whales.

In 2019, the State of Washington enacted new regulations governing whale watching and required safe distances from Southern Resident Orca whales in Washington waters. These new regulations are intended to help protect the endangered Southern Orca Whales. These new regulations include the following:

- It is illegal for vessels to get within 300 yards of a Southern Resident Orca whale.
- It is illegal for vessels to be within 400 yards of the path (behind and in front) of a Southern Resident Orca whale.
- There is a 7-knot speed limit within one-half nautical mile distance from a Southern Resident Orca whale.
- If a Southern Resident Orca whale comes within 300 yards of a vessel, the operator is required to disengage engine transmission(s) until the whale is a safe distance away.

While these new regulations apply to all vessels, they are mainly focused on commercial whale watch operators. In addition to increasing the separation between boats and Southern Resident Orca whales, Washington State law establishes licensing requirements for Commercial Whale Watching operators. The definition of Commercial Whale Watching operators is somewhat broadly defined to include kayak rental operators for whale watching purposes. Licenses are sold by Washington Department of Fish and Wildlife. This same department is tasked with creating and implementing rules for commercial operators that reduce the cumulative impacts on Southern Resident Orca whales and to consider the economic viability of licensed commercial operators.

Protecting Southern Resident Orca whales is a high priority in Washington State. The physical and social differences between Southern Resident Orca whales and Transient Orca whales may be hard for most recreational boaters to identify, so practically speaking, it is best to stay well clear of all Orca whales.

Marine Mammals & All Whales

Other whale species frequent Washington waters; and while these relatively new Washington State laws apply to Southern Resident Orca Whales, existing Federal and State regulations apply to other marine mammals in Washington waters. Give dolphins, porpoises, sea lions, seals, and other marine mammals the space they need. Coming too close can cause them stress and to abandon their young.

- Stay 100 yards from non-killer whales, dolphins, porpoises, and other marine mammals, and 200 yards if they are resting or with young.
- Turn off echo / depth sounders (voluntary) when not in use.
- Vessels are asked to avoid the Voluntary No-Go Zone on the West Side of San Juan Island, which extends ¼-mile offshore from Mitchell Bay to Cattle Point, and a ½-mile offshore at Lime Kiln Lighthouse.

SAN JUAN ISLANDS

See Area Map Page 196 - Maps Not for Navigation

North Bay on the east side of San Juan Island has room for many boats and the broad gravel beach at Jackson Park provides shore access.

You'll enjoy anchoring in Blind Bay and taking the dinghy over to meet Steve and Terri Mason, who have run the store for many years; their daughter now operates the business. The store was built in 1924. It's as charming as can be, with its straight-grain wood floors, old shelving and displays, and posters and signs from days gone by. The store is a local hangout for Shaw Island residents.

Parks Bay. An excellent anchorage in a southern blow; Parks Bay is a fine anchorage, but you can't go ashore. Except for three privately-owned parcels at the north end and a single parcel at the south end, the land surrounding Parks Bay is owned by the University of Washington as a biological preserve, and is off limits to visitors. Stub pilings are at the closed end, but there is plenty of anchoring room, mud bottom, throughout the bay. Parks Bay Island, at the mouth of the bay, is no longer a state park.

Hicks Bay. Hicks Bay has good anchorage, although it is exposed to southerlies. When entering, take care to avoid a reef extending from the southern shore.

Indian Cove. Indian Cove, a popular anchorage area has a big open feeling. Exposed to the south but well protected to the north. Watch for drying rocks between Canoe Island and Shaw Island, and a shoal 200 yards west of the southern point of Canoe Island. The Shaw Island County Park, with launch ramp, has an excellent beach. Anchor in 15 to 40 feet with good holding.

The County Park provides access to **Graham Preserve** and Reef Net Point County Park. Graham Preserve is a 99-acre San Juan Preservation Trust property with 1.2 miles of forested trails. The trailhead begins across the road from the entrance to Shaw Island County Park. After a short distance, the trail branches with a trail to the north leading to the Shaw Community Center, and a trail to the south leading to a trailhead opposite the entrance to Reef Net Point County Park. The half mile loop trail at Reef Net Point Park takes you along the shore of Reef Net Bay and past the remains of an historic log cabin. From Reef Net Point County Park, walk about 1/3 mile to the east on Squaw Bay Road to return to Shaw Island County Park.

Picnic Cove. Picnic Cove is immediately east of Indian Cove. It's a pretty little nook with room for a couple boats. A mid-channel entrance is best, to avoid reefs on each side of the cove. The head of the cove shoals to drying flats. Anchor in 20 to 25 feet. The mooring buoys in the cove are private.

SAN JUAN ISLAND

San Juan Island is the second largest of the San Juan Islands, and has the largest population. Friday Harbor, the only incorporated town, is the seat of county government.

Cattle Pass. Cattle Pass is the local name for the narrow channel between the south end of San Juan Island and Lopez Island. It is the only southern entrance to the San Juan Islands, and connects with San Juan Channel. Whale Rocks lie just south of Cattle Pass. It's easy to get close to them if you're not careful. When we enter Cattle Pass from the south, we try to favor gong Buoy 3, marking Salmon Bank, to port, and make a course for the middle of the entrance. This avoids Whale Rocks.

After we clear Cattle Pass northbound, we've felt a definite tendency to favor the Lopez Island shore. Maybe it's just us. In any case, this course leads dangerously close to *Shark Reef,* about one-half mile north of Cattle Pass. We recommend sagging west a little toward Griffin Bay until past Shark Reef.

Tidal currents can run strongly through Cattle Pass, and the waters can be turbulent with rips and eddies. Watch out for a big ebb current flowing out of San Juan Channel against a fresh westerly wind in the Strait of Juan de Fuca. We've seen this ebb current as much as a mile outside Cattle Pass. Against a fresh westerly it will create high, steep seas, the kind you definitely want to avoid. Current predictions are shown under San Juan Channel in the tide & current books. In Cattle Pass, it's possible to run behind Goose Island and avoid foul current, but local knowledge is called for.

Friday Harbor

204   www.WaggonerGuide.com

See Area Map Page 196 - Maps Not for Navigation

SAN JUAN ISLANDS

Friday Harbor Marine / Friday Harbor Yachts

Full Service Marine Repair
Indoor Shop, Parts, Supplies

REPAIR SERVICES
- After Hours & Weekends
- Mercury Authorized
- ABYC & NMEA Cert
- Diesel & Gasoline
- Cooling & Fuel
- Starting and Charging
- Diesel Fuel Polishing

PARTS- SUPPLIES
- Start/House Batteries
- Impellers & Pumps
- Inverters & Chargers
- Oil and Fuel Filters
- NMEA Networks

665 B Mullis St 360-378-6202 fridayharbormarine.com

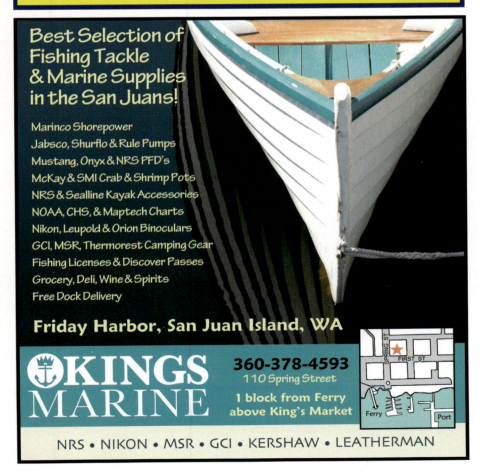

Best Selection of Fishing Tackle & Marine Supplies in the San Juans!

- Marinco Shorepower
- Jabsco, Shurflo & Rule Pumps
- Mustang, Onyx & NRS PFD's
- McKay & SMI Crab & Shrimp Pots
- NRS & Sealline Kayak Accessories
- NOAA, CHS, & Maptech Charts
- Nikon, Leupold & Orion Binoculars
- GCI, MSR, Thermorest Camping Gear
- Fishing Licenses & Discover Passes
- Grocery, Deli, Wine & Spirits
- Free Dock Delivery

Friday Harbor, San Juan Island, WA

KINGS MARINE
360-378-4593
110 Spring Street
1 block from Ferry above King's Market

NRS • NIKON • MSR • GCI • KERSHAW • LEATHERMAN

Fish Creek. Fish Creek is a tiny indentation near the southern tip of San Juan Island, lined with the docks and mooring buoys of the homes along its shores. Fish Creek has no public facilities, and swinging room is very restricted between the homeowners' floats.

Griffin Bay. You can anchor in several places in Griffin Bay. A stretch of beach inshore from Halftide Rocks is Griffin Bay Park, a public campground. American Camp, maintained by the U.S. Park Service as an historical monument to the 1859-72 Pig War, is a short walk from the campground. The Pig War resulted in setting the boundary between the U.S. and Canada in Haro Strait, keeping the San Juan Islands in the U.S.

Griffin Bay Park. Next to American Camp. Open all year. Toilets, no other facilities. Four campsites and a picnic area. Two inland campsites are exclusively for boaters arriving by human- or wind-powered watercraft. Vessels with motors are not allowed to moor at the park overnight. Watch for shallow water and pilings.

Unnamed Island #119. Griffin Bay, south of Dinner Island. This island is part of the San Juan Islands National Wildlife Refuge. Boats must stay 200 yards from shore; no shore access.

North Bay Anchorage. North Bay at the northern end of Griffin Bay, offers anchorage for many boats, with protection from northerly and westerly winds. Good anchorage on a mud bottom in 20 to 30 feet of water, located off the beach northeast of Little Island. The anchorage is exposed to southerlies and easterlies. The long beautiful driftwood beach, northeast of Little Island, is Jackson Beach Park. A free public boat launch is located on the lagoon side of the beach. This anchorage offers aviation enthusiasts the opportunity to watch airplanes land and depart from Friday Harbor Airport.

⑦ **Turn Island State Park.** (360) 376-2073; In San Juan Channel, at the southeast entrance to Friday Harbor. Turn Island is open all year for day use and overnight mooring. Boat access only; *land only on the west or southwest beach.* Pets are not permitted on shore. Outhouse and campsites. No fires. Pack out all garbage. Hiking, fishing, crabbing.

Turn Island is a beautiful park, completely wooded, with many trails. It's a popular stop for kayaks and beachable boats. Along the south side of the island the trees (madrona, cedar, hemlock, cypress) are bent and twisted, with much evidence of blowdown. The wind must howl though here in the winter.

Two mooring buoys, for boats 45 feet and under, are placed along the west side at the mouth of the pass, separating Turn Island from San Juan Island. Shoals quickly south of the southern most buoy. Currents can be quite strong in this pass, but these buoys are located safely out of the current. If you anchor

SAN JUAN ISLANDS

See Area Map Page 196 - Maps Not for Navigation

Fairweather Park overlooks the expansive marina in Friday Harbor.

to seaward of them, you will be in the current. We recommend the buoys. Self-register and pay nightly mooring buoy fee on shore.

Correspondents James and Jennifer Hamilton have anchored off the southwest tip of Turn Island in about 10 feet of depth at zero tide. Although the current ran noticeably, the anchor held perfectly. Other boats, anchored farther out and closer to the eastern mouth of the pass, appeared to have less current.

Turn Island is part of the San Juan Islands National Wildlife Refuge. Do not disturb animals in their natural habitat.

⑧ **Friday Harbor.** www.fridayharbor.org. Friday Harbor is the government and commercial center of the San Juan Islands. It is a U.S. Customs port of entry, and the terminal for ferries from Anacortes that also serve Sidney, B.C. The town swells with tourists during the summer months and has many boutiques, shops, galleries, restaurants and pubs to serve them. King's Market, a well stocked grocery store, is on the main street (Spring Street) two blocks up from the waterfront. Kings will drive you back to the marina with a sizable purchase.

Puget Sound Express (360-385-5288) has daily passenger only ferry service between Port Townsend and Friday Harbor; the boat, *Glacier Spirit,* operates early May to late September. Kenmore Air flies in from Lake Union and Boeing Field in Seattle, with a shuttle to Sea-Tac Airport. Friday Harbor Seaplanes flies in from their location on south Lake Washington in Renton. Check their websites for seasonal schedules.

Moor at the Port of Friday Harbor marina or anchor out. Anchorage is good in the cove north of the marina, and behind Brown (Friday) Island. Do not anchor in the cable-pipeline area between San Juan Island and Brown Island. Our friend John Mifflin cautions that the water close to Brown Island contains several sunken wrecks, "requiring diver assistance when raising anchor."

Enter Friday Harbor around either end of Brown Island. An unlighted daybeacon marks the end of a drying reef off the southwest corner of Brown Island. Brown Island is privately owned, and has its own dock and floats.

Take care to avoid interfering with the ferries and the large number of float planes taking off and landing in the harbor. The fuel dock is located between the Port marina and the ferry dock. The floats just south of the ferry dock are owned by the condominium apartments ashore. Jensen's Marina, in the southeast end of the harbor, can handle repairs. Jensen's is owned by the Port of Friday Harbor and managed by Marine Services Group; 35-ton Travelift. No transient moorage. The Port marina office can provide a list of repair people. Kings Marine carries marine supplies, fishing gear and apparel.

Bus Transportation: San Juan Transit, next to the ferry landing, has scheduled service

We Are Your San Juan Island Full Service Boat Yard

Albert Jensen & Sons SHIPYARD — FRIDAY HARBOR WA • SINCE 1910

OUR SERVICES

Repower • Rebuild • Bottom Paint • Electrical • Electronics • Plumbing • Fabrication
Inboard & Outboard • HVAC • Water Makers • Gensets • Bright Work • Mobile Services

WE SERVICE ALL BRANDS
BUT HERE ARE SOME OF OUR FAVORITES

YANMAR • SUZUKI • OXE DIESEL • KOHLER Marine • PCI Watermakers • LOWRANCE • SIMRAD
B&G • ICOM • SiriusXM Satellite Radio • Raymarine • GARMIN • FURUNO • vespermarine

Like us on Facebook • @albertjensenandsons

1293 TURN POINT ROAD - FRIDAY HARBOR, WA 98250 • **360.378.4343** • **JENSENSHIPYARD.COM**
A MEMBER OF MARINE SERVICES GROUP

206 www.WaggonerGuide.com

See Area Map Page 196 - Maps Not for Navigation

SAN JUAN ISLANDS

and tours all around San Juan Island; www.sanjuantransit.com; (360) 378-8887.

Taxi: Classic Cab, (360) 378-7519; Bob's Taxi, (360) 378-6777; Friday Harbor Taxi, (360) 298-4434; Rhodes Trips Taxi & Tours, (360) 298-6975; San Juan Taxi, (360) 378-8294.

Mopeds: Susie's Mopeds (800) 532-0087 (cars, mopeds, ScootCoupes).

Bicycles: Meat Machine Cycles (360) 370-5673.

Trolley: Friday Harbor Jolly Trolley Transportation (360) 298-8873. Offers guided rides to island attractions with hop on/hop off all-day passes.

Summer Concerts: Live music Saturdays at 2:00 p.m., July and August in the small park next to the marina.

Farmers Market: San Juan Farmers Market, Saturdays 10:00 a.m. to 1:00 p.m. mid-April through mid-October in the Brickhouse Plaza, 150 Nichols St., about 5 minutes from the marina.

THINGS TO DO

1. The Whale Museum. In Friday Harbor. Learn about orca whales that frequent the San Juan Islands.

2. Lime Kiln Point State Park. Watch for whales that often cruise by this park.

3. Tastings. San Juan Vineyards has a tasting room near Friday Harbor. San Juan Island Distillery, with a variety of apple-based spirits, has a tasting room within walking distance of Roche Harbor.

4. Westcott Bay Sculpture Park. More than 100 superb sculptures in iron, bronze, stone and wood displayed in a 20-acre park near Roche Harbor.

5. Pelindaba Lavender Farms. Walk through fields of purple lavender and shop for all things lavender.

6. Saturday Farmers Market. Fresh vegetables, flowers, plants, honey and more at the Brickworks in Friday Harbor.

7. English Camp. See the gardens, hike the trails, learn the history. In Garrison Bay near Roche Harbor.

8. American Camp. Located on the southern tip of San Juan Island, American soldiers lived here during the joint U.S./British occupation of the island in the mid-1800s.

9. Roche Harbor Mausoleum. Walk from Roche Harbor resort to this beautiful setting steeped in mythology.

10. Blackberries. In late summer they are everywhere, big, tasty, and free.

11. Krystal Acres Alpaca Farm. See alpacas and learn what they can be used for.

12. Susie's Mopeds. Rent mopeds or electric bicycles. Rental office in Friday Harbor 360-378-5244.

13. The "Retirement of the Colors" ceremony at Roche Harbor at sunset is unforgettable.

14. Friday Harbor Seafood. Fresh shrimp, oysters, crab, or fish for sale on the main dock.

15. Shuttle Bus Tour. Regular schedule in the summer. Ride the bus, getting on and off at locations such as the lavender farm, Lime Kiln Point, and English Camp.

⑧ **Port of Friday Harbor.** P.O. Box 889, 204 Front Street, Friday Harbor, WA 98250; (360) 378-2688; tamih@portfridayharbor.org; www.portfridayharbor.org. Monitors VHF 66A. Certified Clean Marina. Open all year, gasoline and diesel at the fuel dock. Side-tie guest moorage along 1500 feet of dock, plus moorage on the guest dock and in unoccupied slips. Reservations accepted. Only 30% of the guest moorage space is available for reservations; 70% is first-come, first-served. If reservations are full, space may be available on the day you arrive.

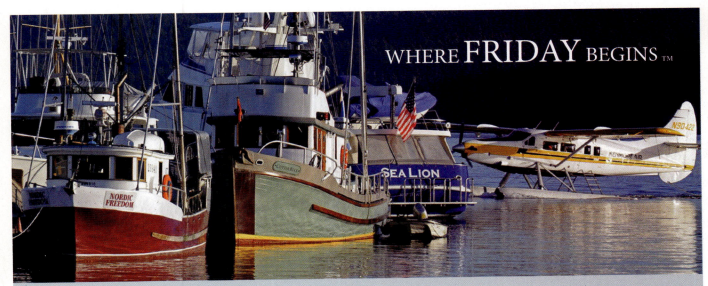

- Join us for Opening Day of Boating Season May 3rd
- Rock & Roll Regatta Saturday June 27th
- Book Your Cruising Club and Enjoy our new Activity Float
- Don't Forget to get a Stamp for Your 5th Night FREE

PORT OF FRIDAY HARBOR

Post Office Box 889 • Friday Harbor, WA 98250
VHF66A • 360-378-2688 • Fax: 360-378-6114
www.portfridayharbor.org

2020 WAGGONER CRUISING GUIDE

SAN JUAN ISLANDS

See Area Map Page 196 - Maps Not for Navigation

The slips handle boats up to 60 feet. Longer boats (to 200 feet) side-tie along the breakwaters (see marina diagram). Breakwater A has no power or water. Marina services include 120-volt 30 & 50 amp power, 240-volt 50 amp power, and three 240-volt 100 amp power. Guest docks G and H were upgraded in 2018, including new ELCI-protected shore power pedestals. Free excellent Wi-Fi. Restrooms and showers were refurbished in the fall of 2019. Excellent laundry. Recycle drop at the head of the pier; garbage drop located behind the office. Key required for used oil drop. The Pumpty Dumpty pumpout service is available seasonally to come to your boat for a small charge, or you can use the self-serve pumpout carts. A stationary pumpout is located on a float between C and M docks. At low tides, deep draft vessels should not venture shoreward of the pumpout. An ADA-compliant ramp connects the wharf above with the floats and slips below. A floating restroom is on the long float leading to guest moorage, dock G. A covered activity barge is available for groups or rendezvous. Ten or more vessels earn a group moorage discount. Individual boats staying four nights get a fifth night free from September 15 to June 15. Check the Port's website for seasonal specials and events.

If you do not have reservations, call on VHF 66A for a moorage assignment, but wait until you are within sight of the marina before

Roche Harbor Marina

- Marine Outboards
- Gas & Diesel Engines, Outdrives
- Electrical, Marine Heating Systems
- Watermakers, Marine Head Systems
- Yacht Care & Watch Programs
- Electronics
- Haul Out & Boat Storage
- Marine Parts Chandlery

360-378-6510
info@rocheharbormarine.com
www.rocheharbormarine.com

See Area Map Page 196 - Maps Not for Navigation

SAN JUAN ISLANDS

ROCHE HARBOR

Est. 1886 | San Juan Islands, Washington

Dining | Lodging | Marina | Air Strip
Grocery & Shopping | Pool & Tennis
Formal Gardens | Weddings | Spa | Hiking
Kayaking & Whale Watching

800-586-3590 Marina | 800-451-8910 Lodging
www.rocheharbor.com

calling. In the summer, a slip assignment station is staffed at the end of Breakwater B. A dinghy float and day moorage are available. Nearby haulout and repairs.

This is one of the busiest marinas in the Northwest, and the pressure on staff and facilities is enormous. To their credit, they maintain the docks, showers and restrooms quite well. Because they are so busy, when you depart it is courteous to call the marina on VHF 66A to let them know your slip is available.

Customs: U.S. Customs clearance is on Breakwater B. Tie up in the designated customs area and check in at the direct-phone kiosk on the dock. During the summer months the kiosk may be manned by a CBP agent. Occasionally customs officials will have you walk to the U.S. Customs office. The office has moved to the corner of Spring Street and First Street, about 3 blocks from the marina.

⑧ **Port of Friday Harbor Fuel Pier.** 10 Front Street, Port of Friday Harbor, Friday Harbor, WA 98250; (360) 378-3114; www.portfridayharbor.org. Between the Port of Friday Harbor marina and the ferry dock. Open 7 days a week, all year. Ethanol-free gasoline, diesel, oil, lubricants, propane, and ice.

Rocky Bay. Rocky Bay, close inshore from O'Neal Island, is a good anchorage and fairly well protected. Take care to avoid a drying shoal and a covered rock.

Lonesome Cove Resort. (360) 378-4477; located along the north shore of San Juan Island on Spieden Channel. Guest moorage for those staying in one of the on-shore accommodations. Five adorable cabins, Boat House, and Eagles Nest apartment; beautiful grounds and lovely views of Spieden Channel and Spieden Island. Maximum boat length 28 feet.

⑨ **Roche Harbor.** Roche Harbor, (pronounced Rohsh Harbor) on the northwest corner of San Juan Island, is popular, attractive, and has a number of interesting anchorages and moorages. From the north (Spieden Channel), enter Roche Harbor on the west side of Pearl Island. The passage east of Pearl Island is shallow, and is in line with dangerous rocks outside. From the south (Haro Strait), entry is through Mosquito Pass.

Roche Harbor is one of the busiest U.S. Customs ports of entry in the country for recreational boats. During the prime summer season, the floating customs office and the harbormaster's office are located on G-dock. The customs landing area on G-dock is noted with signs on the pilings. Moor between the signs only when clearing customs. On busy days, boats tend to create an informal line on the water, waiting for room on the customs dock. Be patient. It can be a challenge to maintain a place in line among boats at anchor, especially when a good breeze kicks up. Note that the

SAN JUAN ISLAND MARKETPLACE

RESTAURANTS, SHOPS & SERVICES

ACE HARDWARE
Ace Hardware is your locally owned and operated hardware store, specializing in marine hardware, stainless fasteners, electrical, tools, fishing licenses, tackle, bait, rain gear and all your hardware needs.
360-378-4622 • 340 Argyle Ave, Friday Harbor, WA 98250 www.AceAnacortes.com

THE GOURMET'S GALLEY
Since 1969 a favorite source of rare ingredients for the adventurous cook. Proper teas, teapots, and kettles. Quality tools for the serious chef. Whimsical gifts with food and marine themes. Monday-Saturday 10 - 5:30.
360-378-2251 • 21 Spring Street, PO Box 578

ALBERT JENSEN & SON'S SHIPYARD
Brings full services back to the original site that started it all. Since 1910 Jensen's has been providing superior mechanical, electrical, plumbing, finishing, and shipwright services to San Juan Island. Our boat yard, Travelift, and certified technicians operate year-round to keep you cruising. A Division of Marine Services Group
1293 Turn Point Road | Friday Harbor, WA 98250 | 360.378.4343 • www.jesnsenshipyard.com

KING'S MARINE CENTER
Best selection for your outdoor adventure gear. Everything from fishing gear, kayak accessories, marine supplies and camping gear to sportswear, shoes & boots, sunglasses, books and more.
360-378-4593 • 110 Spring St. W • Above King's Market • www.kings-market.com

LAVENDERA MASSAGE
Rest, renew, revitalize with a smoothing massage: Therapeutic, relaxation, combo, hot stone, couples, prenatal massage. Call for pricing. *Clothed massage and chair massage $1 per minute.* Body wrap, body exfoliation, foot therapy, and energy work also available. Call or email to book, go to our website for more info.
360-378-3637 • 285 Spring Street, Friday Harbor, WA 98250 • www.lavenderamassage.com

SUSIE'S MOPEDS
Explore San Juan Island at your leisure with an electric bike, moped, Scoot Coupe, or car. Let our professional and friendly staff help plan your island adventure which includes plenty of spectacular scenic stops. Hourly and daily rates. An island tradition since 1986. Reservations suggested.
360-378-5244 • 125 Nichols Street, Friday Harbor www.susiesmopeds.com

THE WHALE MUSEUM
Be Whale Wise! Founded in 1979, The *Whale Museum* in Friday Harbor is a natural history museum and is an easy walk from the docks. Our mission is to promote stewardship of whales and the Salish Sea ecosystem through education and research programs. Come learn about the endangered Southern Resident Orcas and other marine mammals. Browse the gift shop for that perfect Friday Harbor Whale Museum gift or souvenir. Our Orca Adoption Program is a great way to support us and makes a very unique gift.
360-378-4710 ext. 30 • 62 1st Street N., Friday Harbor

SAN JUAN ISLAND COMMUNITY EVENTS

May
Opening Day Boat Parade, Friday Harbor
Memorial Day Parade & Ceremony, Friday Harbor

June
San Juan Island Artists' Studio Tour
Three Lakes Triathlon & San Juan Island Marathon, Half Marathon & 10K Day
Orca Sing Annual Concert

July
July 4th Parade, Pig War Picnic, Friday Harbor
Rock the Dock dance, Fireworks, Port of Friday Harbor
Roche Harbor Old Fashioned Fourth - Games and Fireworks
San Juan Island Lavender Festival & Summer Arts Fair
San Juan Island National Historical Park Encampment
Summer Concert Series "Music in the Park" Port of Friday Harbor (July-Labor Day)
Music on the Lawn, July - August at the San Juan Historical Museum grounds

July – August
Shakespeare under the Stars

August
Shaw Island Classic Sail Boat Race, Jazz at the Labs
San Juan County Fair
Concours d'Elegance of the San Juan Islands

September
Friday Harbor Fly-In & Open House
San Juan Vineyards Harvest Festival
Savor the San Juans

October
Savor the San Juans
Friday Harbor Fall Farm Parade

November
Friday Harbor Film Festival
Artisans' Holiday Marketplace

December
Island Lights Festival – Friday Harbor
Lighted Boat Parade & Santa's Arrival – Friday Harbor
San Juan Historical Museum – Old Fashioned Christmas Celebration

www.visitsanjuans.com

See Area Map Page 196 - Maps Not for Navigation

SAN JUAN ISLANDS

seaplane dock is near the customs dock, and arriving seaplanes will need to cut through the line of boats. One summer we watched as one of the area's large wooden sailing schooners pulled up to the dock to clear customs. The space was much too small to lie alongside. The captain commanded her crew of high school students to drop the anchor at the right time, as she turned stern-to the dock. With an audience watching, she backed down and tied off, stern-to. She placed a 133-foot vessel into less than 20 feet of dock space, impressive.

Note: During fall, winter, and spring, the customs and harbor offices are floated inshore to the main float, just west of the fuel dock. Approach as though you are going to the fuel dock. The customs dock is to starboard, marked with signs, just below the ramp. Once tied to the dock, all crew must stay on the boat until cleared. The U.S. Customs agents are particular about procedures here.

Many boats anchor in Roche Harbor, but we've heard of anchors dragging in strong winds. Check your set and use ample scope. Anchorage is also possible in Open Bay on Henry Island, although it is exposed to southerly winds.

Bus Transportation: San Juan Transit has scheduled service to Friday Harbor and all around San Juan Island. The pick-up area is on the road across from the Roche Harbor Market. Call (360) 378-8887; www.sanjuantransit.com.

⑨ **Roche Harbor Marina**. P.O. Box 4001, Roche Harbor, WA 98250; (800) 586-3590; (360) 378-2155; marina@rocheharbor.com; www.rocheharbor.com. Monitors VHF 78A. Open all year, up to 250 guest slips, including moorage for boats to 150 feet. Call ahead for reservations. They work to fit everyone in, even on busy holidays. Last-minute holiday moorage may mean Med-tying stern-to on the cross docks. The dock crew provides plenty of help. Ethanol-free gasoline and diesel at the fuel dock, open 9:00 a.m. to 6:00 p.m. Services include 30, 50, and some 100 amp power (ELCI-protected power on some docks), restrooms, showers, laundry, portapotty dump, propane, and free Wi-Fi (best reception is in the hotel lobby). Pumpout is at the north end of the fuel dock, or call for the "Phecal Freak," for a courtesy pumpout at your slip. Their motto: "We take crap from anyone." Tips are appreciated. The moorage fee includes water, power, pumpout, trash disposal, and use of the pool and resort facilities. Excellent management. When we visited at the end of a busy day at the end of summer, we found all the facilities, including the showers, to be clean and in good condition.

This is one of the most popular spots in the islands, and in our opinion is a must-see destination. The historic Hotel de Haro, the heated swimming pool, formal gardens, tennis courts, Afterglow Spa, well-stocked grocery store, gift shops, and excellent restaurant and lounge are something apart from the usual tourist fare. An informal café also is available. Try the Roche Harbor donuts at the café, made fresh each morning.

Be sure to take a walk up to the Afterglow Vista Mausoleum. You've never seen anything like it. Another good walk is up the small mountain behind the resort, past the limestone quarries, to a lookout. The trail is easy and well-maintained, and the view is excellent. The entire loop took us approximately a half-hour. If we had stopped to smell the flowers it would have taken an hour. The hotel lobby has complimentary walking tour maps. For $1.00 they also have a pamphlet detailing the remarkable history of Roche Harbor. See the guest registry on display, and the pictures on the wall showing the history of Roche Harbor.

The Westcott Bay Sculpture Park is on the edge of the Roche Harbor property, across the road from the airstrip. The park is a display of outdoor sculpture—approximately 100 pieces —set in a large grassy field and along several trails through the woods. This description completely understates how impressive the display is. We spent an hour in the park and should have spent three more hours. It's magnificent. The pieces are first-rate and the setting works.

Major development continues on the hillside up from the hotel. Great effort has been made to design the new construction in keeping with the classic century-old style of the existing buildings. Many of the units are available for overnight or longer stays. Contact Roche Harbor Lodging at www.rocheharbor.com. The Afterglow Spa offers massage and other treatments for the crew. Advance reservations recommended.

Located just under a mile west of the Resort at 12 Anderson Lane, is San Juan Distillery (360-472-1532). Open for tastings on Saturdays from 1:00 p.m. to 4:00 p.m. Their specialties include gins, liqueurs, flavored brandies and small batch ciders.

A lovely bell concert rings out from the church at 9:00 a.m., noon, and late afternoon. At sundown each evening during the summer season the marina conducts a formal retirement of the colors. The Roche Harbor flag is lowered, followed by the British flag to "God Save the Queen," and the Canadian flag to "O Canada." Then the cannon fires—BOOM!—and the U.S. flag is lowered to "Taps."

Dinghy Docks: Dinghy docks are at the bottom of the ramp to the main wharf, or to port just past the fuel dock.

Bus transportation: San Juan Transit has scheduled service all around San Juan Island, with regular stops at Roche Harbor. Guests can take the shuttle from the ferry landing in Friday Harbor to Roche Harbor; www.sanjuantransit.com; (360) 378-8887.

Mopeds: Susie's Mopeds is near the airstrip; www.susiesmopeds.com; (360) 378-6262.

Posey Island Marine State Park. www.parks.wa.gov. North of Roche Harbor. Day use and overnight mooring and camping. Pit toilet, no other facilities. Cascadia Marine Trail campsite (primitive). The island is less

Henry Island and Mosquito Pass

SAN JUAN PRESERVATION TRUST PROPERTIES

Did you know that the San Juan Preservation Trust protects and preserves 300 properties on 20 different islands in the San Juan's? These properties offer miles of trails and shoreline, with public access. Many of these sites are accessed only by dinghy or kayak, where you will find trailheads with Preservation Trust signage. Some areas, like Vendovi Island, offer a day-use dock.

The Mission of the Preservation Trust is to purchase and conserve unique properties with natural beauty that are vital to the ecosystem and/or has significant historic and scenic value. Caring for these lands connects people to nature and provides the same opportunity for future generations. Visitors are asked to stay on designated trails to protect flowers, plants, and animal habitat.

The San Juan Preservation Trust is a 501(C)(3) charitable organization. Funds come from contributions provided by individuals, families, and private foundations that support research, maintenance, and purchases of island property. Making a contribution entitles you to membership, which includes "The Island Dispatch," a quarterly print newsletter, along with e-newsletters, and priority when registering for events and outings.

Vendovi Island is a favorite among boaters, but other locations are often overlooked because these island access points are not widely known to the boating public.

Kimball Preserve is one of those hidden gems with spectacular views from the ridge trail along the southern tip of Decatur Island. The unnamed Island along with the southern tip of Decatur Island and the isthmus that connects the two are part of the San Juan Preservation Trust. Boaters can anchor in the channel between Kimball Preserve and Center Island and take the dinghy to the northern shore of the isthmus. A "no-trespassing" sign painted on a rock is left over from an earlier time and no longer applies. A trail leads up the hillside with fabulous ocean views. Decatur property north of Kimball Preserve is private. The rocky islet between the unnamed island and Decatur Island in the Preserve is an undeveloped Bureau of Land Management property.

A portion of Henry Island near Roche Harbor is another special place to visit. Henry Island Preserve is made up of the isthmus forming the crossbar of the "H" on Henry Island along with some of the surrounding forest. Public access to a one-mile trail is available by dinghy on the beach at Open Bay or at the beach along Mosquito Pass east of the isthmus, depending on weather conditions. The beach along the isthmus of Open Bay is spectacular and is part of the Trust property. The cabin along the beach is private; the grave marker is in memory of Henry W. Perkins (1835-1887). A trail along the Mosquito Pass side of the isthmus heads northward through the forest. Other property on Henry Island is private.

To learn more about the San Juan Preservation Trust, or to make a donation, or to view the map of Trust Properties that you can visit, go to www.sjpt.org.

[Lorena Landon]

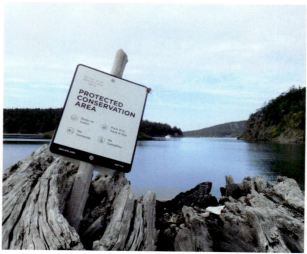

See Area Map Page 196 - Maps Not for Navigation

SAN JUAN ISLANDS

Wander the fields and tour the historic buildings at English Camp National Historic Park.

than 1 acre in size. Water surrounding the island is shallow. Motorized vessels are not permitted; anchor out and row in. Great sunset views on the west side.

Mosquito Pass. Mosquito Pass connects Roche Harbor to Haro Strait, and provides access to Westcott Bay and Garrison Bay. The flood current sets north in Mosquito Pass and the ebb sets south, out of Roche Harbor. Currents can be strong at times. The channel is narrow but well-marked. Navigate carefully. See Mosquito Pass Route map.

Westcott Bay. Westcott Bay is a large bay with good anchorage for many boats. Depths are consistently shallow throughout but adequate. Westcott is a quiet, scenic anchorage alternative to the often crowded Garrison Bay. Nearby English Camp National Historic Park, Westcott Bay Shellfish Co. (open to the public for sales), and Roche Harbor are all a dinghy ride away. Hiking trails connect English Camp Park with Westcott Bay Shellfish Co. The public beach near Bell Point reportedly has excellent clamming. Crabbing in the bay good at times.

Westcott Bay Shellfish Co. (360-378-2489). Located on the southeast shore of Westcott Bay, open six days a week (closed on Tuesdays) during the summer months from 11:00 a.m. to 5:00 p.m., Memorial Day weekend through Labor Day; open Saturdays during the off season. Retail shellfish sales. As time permits, staff will show you how to shuck your oysters. Local bakery bread, cheeses, and charcuterie are available for purchase from their deli to enjoy with your hand-shucked shellfish along with beer, wine, sodas or water. Picnic tables overlooking the bay complete this unique experience. Anchor in the bay; boaters are welcome to tie dinghies (bow-tie only) to the Shellfish Company's working docks to go ashore and make purchases. Barbequed oysters are available on select days. During the 1970's, Westcott Bay oysters were known in oyster bars around the world. This family-run aquaculture farm continues the legacy of providing quality oysters as well as clams and mussels.

Garrison Bay. Garrison Bay, the site of English Camp, is a popular and excellent anchorage, with room for a large number of boats.

English Camp National Historical Park. P.O. Box 429, 4668 Cattle Point Road, Friday Harbor, WA 98250; (360) 387-2240 ext. 2244; www.nps.gov. The grounds are open year-round until dusk. The Visitor Center, located in the old barracks, is open seasonally from 9:00 a.m. to 5:00 p.m. Anchor in the bay and dinghy to the park dock. British troops were garrisoned here during the 1859-72 Pig War, and the U.S. Park Service has restored the buildings and grounds as a historic site. You can tour the grounds, some of the buildings, and the cemetery, where several people from that era are buried. Rangers are on duty to provide information, and a film tells the history. It's a good stop for families with children. Restrooms, no other facilities. A steep trail leads to the top of 650-foot-high Young Hill, for a marvelous view.

Mitchell Bay. A shoal extends from the south shore almost to the middle of the entry. A rock is at the outer end of the shoal. Leave this rock to starboard when entering. Large scale Chart 18433 shows the entrance clearly.

⑩ **Snug Harbor Resort.** 1997 Mitchell Bay Road, Friday Harbor, WA 98250; (360) 378-4762; sneakaway@snugresort.com; www.snugresort.com. Monitors VHF 66A. Snug Harbor is open all year and welcomes visitors; no pets. Maximum boat length 60 feet. Depth at zero tide is 9 feet. Services include 30 amp power, Wi-Fi, restrooms, showers, garbage drop, recycling, barbecues, fire pits. Reservations recommended. The on-site convenience store has ice and limited groceries, gifts, propane, fishing and boating supplies. Mitchell Bay Coffee has free Wi-Fi, espresso, fresh pastries, waffles and soup.

Westcott Bay, Garrison Bay and English Camp

SAN JUAN ISLANDS

Canoes and kayaks available for guest use free of charge. Beautiful cabin accommodations.

Lime Kiln Point. Lime Kiln Point is a favorite place to watch for orcas, the so-called "killer whales," that often cruise within a few yards of shore. Anchorage offshore from this park would be very difficult and is not recommended. A small interpretive center with information about orca whales is in the park. Best visited by taking the San Juan Transit shuttle bus from Roche Harbor or Friday Harbor.

San Juan County Park. 4289 West Side Road N., Friday Harbor, WA 98250; (360) 378-2992; www.sanjuanco.com. Open all year. Facilities include launch ramp and restrooms. No power, no showers. A popular park for kayak campers who can pull up on the beach.

Henry Island. A Seattle Yacht Club outstation (no reciprocals) is in Nelson Bay. Nelson Bay is shallow, so use your depth sounder and tide table before anchoring.

Henry Island Preserve. The Henry Island isthmus and some of the surrounding forest is part of the San Juan Preservation Trust. The isthmus forms the crossbar of the "H" connecting Little Henry Island and Big Henry Island. Public access to a one-mile hiking trail is available by dinghy and kayak on the beach at **Open Bay** and the beach along Mosquito Pass (see *Henry Island and Mosquito Pass* map in this chapter). For more information go to sjpt.org. All property outside of the Preserve is private.

Unnamed Island #40. On the southwest side of San Juan Island, approximately 1 mile northwest of Pile Point. Open all year, day use only, no facilities. Anchor out at this undeveloped DNR (Dept. of Natural Resources) property. No fires or overnight camping. Pack out all garbage. Do not disturb wildlife or alter the surroundings.

Unnamed Island #38. On the southwest side of San Juan Island, near the center of Kanaka Bay. Open all year, day use only, no facilities. Anchor out at this undeveloped DNR property. No fires or overnight camping. Pack out garbage. Do not disturb wildlife or alter the surroundings.

LOCAL KNOWLEDGE

DANGEROUS REEFS: TowBoatU.S. reports the Wasp Islands are the number-one area for groundings in the San Juan Islands.

Wasp Islands. The Wasp Islands on the east side of San Juan Channel are a rock and reefstrewn area requiring careful navigation. The underwater hazards are charted but not all of them are marked, and the unwary can come to grief. Wasp Passage, however, is free of hazards, and the skipper who stays in the channel will have no problems.

All the major Wasp Islands are privately owned except Yellow Island, which is owned by The Nature Conservancy.

Yellow Island. (206) 343-4344; www.nature.org. Open all year, 10:00 a.m. to

Westcott Bay Oyster Farm

The Westcott Bay Oyster Farm, on San Juan Island, is conveniently accessible to boaters and is a foodie experience not to be missed. Anchor your vessel in Westcott Bay or Garrison Bay and take the dinghy to the guest dock at the Westcott Bay Oyster farm; tie-dinghies from the bow to save room for the farm's working vessel.

The oyster farm sells fresh mussels, clams, and oysters that you can hand-select from the farms tanks to take back to your boat and prepare for dinner, or shuck and slurp the oysters onsite. Farm staff are happy to show you how to shuck oysters as time allows. Better yet, place an order for barbecued oysters, prepared in a variety of tasty sauces, and enjoy a picnic lunch at one of the tables overlooking the bay. The store sells bread, cheeses, and drinks, including beer and ciders to accompany your barbecue.

The farm is open to the public 11 a.m. to 5 p.m. six days a week (closed on Tuesdays) during the summer months, and

open on Saturdays during the off-season. Erik and Andrea Anderson purchased the farm in 2013 and brought the property back to life, restoring its legacy as a quality oyster farm.

In the late 1970's the farm was widely known for its oysters, which appeared on menus around the country. The farm declined over the years and was put up for sale as a home site.

Thanks to the efforts of Erik and Andrea, and the San Juan Preservation Trust, the oyster farm has been returned to its former glory.

The depleted shellfish crops were replanted and the farm infrastructure replaced. There's even a large Net Shed for booking special events. It's not often that boaters have the opportunity to visit an oyster farm and see its operation firsthand, while enjoying fresh oysters off the grill.

4:00 p.m. Yellow Island is owned by The Nature Conservancy and administered as a wildlife preserve. No pets. Land dinghies on the southeast beach, below the wooden Dodd cabin. No landing permitted on the north side due to the sensitive ecosystem and wildlife. The Dodd cabin was built by Lew and Elizabeth Dodd between 1945 and 1947 with logs floated over from their Orcas Island property and windows from their chicken coop. Other materials consisted of scavenged driftwood from Yellow Island and pieces from decommissioned boats. The cabin remains virtually unchanged, and now serves as the caretaker's house for the island.

Northwest McConnell Rock. Northwest of McConnell Island. Part of the San Juan Islands National Wildlife Refuge. Boats must stay 200 yards from shore; no shore access.

⑪ **Jones Island Marine State Park.** (360) 376-2073; Open all year, day use and overnight mooring and camping. The bay at the north end of Jones Island is an excellent anchorage, but is exposed to northerlies. Boats anchoring near the beach run stern-ties ashore, leaving swinging room for boats anchored in the middle. Currents can swirl through the bay, so leave ample room when you anchor.

Four mooring buoys, for boats 45 feet and under, are in the north bay. A seasonal 160-foot-long mooring float connects to a wharf that leads to shore. A portion of the float is reserved for dinghies and the Park Ranger's boat. The float is removed between October and March. Self-register and pay mooring buoy fee at the head of the dock. Composting toilet facilities are ashore. A well provides drinking water, but may run dry in late summer. Use the water sparingly.

Three mooring buoys are in the small bay on the south side of the island. Self-register and pay mooring buoy fee on shore. No dock for shore access, kayak or dinghy ashore. In the middle of this bay, watch for a rock that lies awash at zero tide. The rock is shown on the charts, but the symbol is easy to overlook. Choose your anchorage based on which side of the island provides the best protection from the wind. We've had a pleasant night in the south anchorage when the wind was blowing from the north, while cruisers anchored in the north bay reported a difficult night.

The south bay is a Cascadia Marine Trail site, with 24 campsites and several camp shelters; toilet facilities at the campsite. Look for the fruit trees of a long-ago orchard, deer often go there. South bay is a popular kayak destination, with excellent views.

This is a wonderful park, popular for families with children. An easy trail connects the north and south moorages, with a 1.2-mile south loop trail branching off through forest and along rock headlands over the water. If you look carefully along this trail, you'll see low patches of prickly pear cactus growing along the way. At the north moorage especially, you probably will meet tame deer. If you dine at a picnic table they may try to join you. During the summer, mooring buoys and float space can be hard to get.

Caution: Raccoons will go aboard unattended boats at the dock if food is left in the open. Stow food well, and close the boat tightly.

Orcas Island. Orcas Island is the largest island in the San Juans, deeply indented by

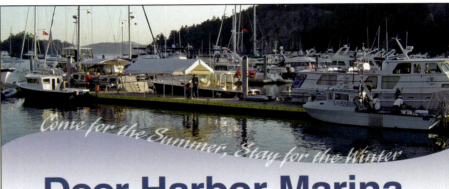

Deer Harbor Marina

Whether you're here for a vacation or are looking for permanent moorage in a Pacific Northwest paradise, Deer Harbor Marina should be a key waypoint on your journey. Come enjoy the beauty of Deer Harbor throughout the season.

- Winter Rates at $7 per foot
- Slips to 50'
- Guest side ties up to 150'
- 30 amp power/limited 50 amp
- New pool, showers & laundry
- Fuel dock (gas & diesel)
- Deli, groceries, beer, wine, ice cream, coffee, prep food, DVD rentals & ATM
- Whale watching, kayaks, bike & boat rentals, tours and charters
- Fresh water
- Pump-out
- Nearby restaurants
- Apparel, gifts, books, maps & charts

Deer Harbor Marina
Orcas Island, WA
Lat 48° 37' 135" • Lon 123° 00' 166"

CONTACT: 360.376.3037 • VHF 78A
EMAIL: mbroman@deerharbormarina.com
ONLINE: www.DeerHarborMarina.com

Deer Harbor Marina

SAN JUAN ISLANDS See Area Map Page 196 - Maps Not for Navigation

Deer Harbor Marina is a popular destination for families.

Pizza and wine await on the deck across the country road from Deer Harbor Marina.

Deer Harbor, West Sound and East Sound. Various locations around the island offer services ranging from float plane flights, to groceries, to luxurious spa experiences, to boat repairs. The island hosts several festivals and has a seasonal Saturday farmers market in Eastsound. See www.orcasislandchamber.com/orcas-island-events for more information.

Getting Around: Car rental delivery service is available through "Orcas Island Shuttle" (360-376-RIDE), offering a variety of interesting vehicles. We spotted a 2-seater Miata with the company logo; cars can be delivered anywhere on the Island. For taxi service, call (360) 376-TAXI. San Juan Transit has shuttle bus service around the island on Fridays, Saturdays, and Sundays.

⑫ **Deer Harbor.** Deer Harbor is a quiet, protected bay on the west end of Orcas Island that is home to two marinas. Deer Harbor Marina is the first marina entering the bay from the south with guest moorage space, guest services, and outstations for several yacht clubs. At the north end of the bay is Cayou Quay Marina with permanent moorage only and no transient services. The entire bay north of Fawn Island has good anchorage. A charted Cable Area surrounds Fawn Island and extends westward to the shore of Orcas Island. Waggoner reader, Roger Kutz, reports an uncharted derelict vessel submerged in 45 feet of water at 48°37.136' N /123°00.401'W in Deer Harbor; anchors have been caught on this submerged vessel.

⑫ **Deer Harbor Marina.** P.O. Box 344, 5164 Deer Harbor Road, Deer Harbor, WA 98243; (360) 376-3037; mbroman@deerharbormarina.com; www.deerharbormarina.com. Monitors VHF 78A. Certified Clean Marina. Open all year, reservations accepted; reservations also available through Dockwa.com. Facilities include ethanol-free gasoline and diesel at the fuel dock. Guest moorage for vessels up to 150 feet; 30 & some 50 amp power, water, free Wi-Fi; restrooms and showers, pumpout, laundry, and floating dock with BBQ for parties and rendezvous. Air service by Kenmore Air.

The docks are excellent, and the restrooms and showers are clean and spacious. A small store on the wharf offers groceries, beer, wine, espresso, Lopez Island Ice Cream cones, and has an ATM. A small cafe in the store offers breakfast items, grilled lunch items, and snacks during store hours. Fresh donuts made before your eyes on Saturdays and Sundays. A gift shop on the dock has books and beach toys, open morning hours, during July and August. Kayaks for rent from an operator on site; guided kayak tours available. Whale watching, boat charters, and fishing charters available. 12-passenger loaner van is available (weekdays only during summer), inquire at the office. We took the van to Turtleback Mountain for a hike with an impressive view of the area. We have also used it to pick up crew arriving by ferry at Orcas Landing.

A beautiful sand beach next to the wharf will entertain the little ones. At the north end of the beach, a small but lovely park has been built. The Resort at Deer Harbor is across the road. Marina guests have access to the resort's swimming pool. The Deer Harbor Inn Restaurant, a ten-minute walk north, is excellent. A gravel pathway runs parallel with the country road most of the way to the Inn; it's a pleasant half-mile hike. If you don't want to walk, you can ride the restaurant's courtesy "limousine." The entire area has an easy and relaxed "vacation" feeling. The marina purchased the restaurant building across the street from the marina. The Island Pie, with indoor and outdoor dining on the deck, serves pizza, beer, cider and wine. Try the seasonal squash pizza, topped with feta cheese and drizzled over with a balsamic reduction; it's delicious.

Cell Phones: Cell phone service is spotty at the marina. A free courtesy phone is available in the laundry room.

LOCAL KNOWLEDGE

SPEED LIMIT: A 7-knot zone marked by white cylindrical buoys extends from just west of Pole Pass eastward almost to Bell Island.

Pole Pass. Boats transiting between Harney Channel and Deer Harbor usually go through Pole Pass, a narrow notch

The pool at Deer Harbor is available for marina guests.

216 www.WaggonerGuide.com

See Area Map Page 196 - Maps Not for Navigation   SAN JUAN ISLANDS

West Sound Marina

A well-stocked country grocery store is steps away from the public county dock next to the ferry landing at Orcas Landing.

separating Crane Island from Orcas Island. Rocks obstruct the edges and approaches, and currents can run swiftly through the pass. A mid-channel course is safe. For most skippers, good sense dictates slow speeds. "No Wake" buoys are located along the Pass. Sometimes the sheriff is there, ticketing speeders.

⑬ **West Sound.** West Sound is the middle inlet of Orcas Island, where the Wareham family's West Sound Marina offers limited overnight moorage and complete service facilities. Next to the marina is the Orcas Island Yacht Club, with reciprocal moorage for visiting members. A day-use-only public dock is west of the Orcas Island Yacht Club dock. The Kingfish Inn is located upland from the public dock and is currently for sale; the cafe located in the Inn is closed until further notice.

Good anchorage is available at the head of the bay (stay well clear of Harbor Rock, marked by a daybeacon). Anchorage is also good off the village of West Sound, and behind Double Island.

⑬ **West Sound Marina.** P.O. Box 119, 525 Deer Harbor Road, Orcas Island, WA 98280; (360) 376-2314; info@westsoundmarina.com; www.westsoundmarina.net. Monitors VHF 16, switch to 09. Open all year, except closed Sundays in the winter. Facilities include ethanol-free gasoline and diesel at the fuel dock, propane, 400 feet of guest moorage, reservations 24 hours in advance, 30 amp power, restrooms, shower, pumpout. Recycling and used oil drop. Haulout to 30 tons with full service and repairs, including an enclosed area for major work. The chandlery has most boating supplies. When approaching, stay well off Picnic Island. A rock ledge extends into West Sound from the island. Once at the marina, stay close to the docks. The water shoals toward Picnic Island.

Victim Island. West side of West Sound. Open all year, day use only, no facilities. Anchor out at this undeveloped BLM property. No fires or overnight camping. Pack out all garbage. Do not disturb wildlife or alter the surroundings.

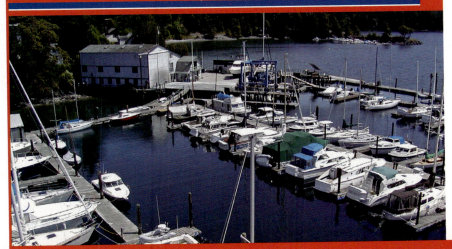

SAN JUAN ISLANDS

See Area Map Page 196 - Maps Not for Navigation

Unnamed Island #80 (Massacre Bay Rocks). West of Indian Point in West Sound. Open all year, day use only, no facilities. Anchor out at this undeveloped Bureau of Land Management (BLM) property. No fires or overnight camping. Pack out all garbage. Do not disturb wildlife or alter the surroundings.

Skull Island. North end of Massacre Bay. Open all year, day use only, no facilities. Anchor out at this undeveloped BLM property. No fires or overnight camping. Pack out all garbage. Do not disturb wildlife or alter the surroundings.

Unnamed Island #81 (Trinka Rock). South of West Sound Marina, north of Picnic Island. Open all year, day use only, no facilities. Anchor out at this undeveloped BLM property. No fires or overnight camping. Pack out all garbage. Do not disturb wildlife or alter the surroundings.

⑭ **Orcas Landing.** Orcas Landing has a float next to the ferry dock, but stays are limited to 30 minutes. The grocery store at the head of the ferry dock is well stocked, and has a good selection of wine and cheese, sandwiches to-go, and baked goods. Don't miss the cider garden just up the hill at the Cider Works shop. Be well-fendered and securely tied to the dock at Orcas Landing. Passing boat and ferry traffic in Harney Channel throw a lot of wake towards the dock.

Rosario Resort's new dock configuration accommodates more boats and improves access.

Grindstone Harbor. Grindstone Harbor is a small, shallow anchorage, with two major rocks in its entrance. One of these rocks became famous a number of years ago when the Washington State ferry *Elwha* ran aground on it while doing a bit of unauthorized sightseeing. Favor the east shore all the way in. Private mooring buoys take up much of the inner part of the bay, but there's room to anchor if you need to.

Guthrie Bay. Guthrie Bay indents Orcas Island between Grindstone Harbor and East Sound. It's a pleasant little spot with private mooring buoys around the perimeter and homes on the hillsides. Anchor in 24 to 42 feet.

East Sound. East Sound, the largest of Orcas Island's indentations, extends about 6 miles north from Foster Point. The shores on both sides are steep, and offer few anchorage possibilities. Rosario Resort is on the east side, a short distance up the sound past the village of Olga. The village of Eastsound is at the head. Fresh winds sometimes blow in East Sound, while outside the air is calm. Anchorage is also possible in Fishing Bay on the west Shore.

Eastsound. The village of Eastsound, at the head of East Sound, is the largest settlement on Orcas Island. A 40-foot seasonal county dock is on the eastern shore, small boats or dinghies only. A 10-minute walk leads to town. Eastsound has several very good restaurants, a large grocery store, an excellent museum, many interesting shops, and on Saturdays during the summer, a busy farmers market.

Anchoring Note: A sign on the county dock announces that the bottom inshore, from a line between the dock and the small islet off the town, is sensitive eelgrass habitat. It requests that you anchor to seaward of that line. Anchorage is possible in Fishing Bay on the west shore.

Fishing Bay & Judd Bay. West of Eastsound village and at the head of East Sound are Fishing Bay and adjacent, Judd Bay. Anchorage can be found in 20 to 45 feet of water. The bays are protected from all but southeasterly winds. The anchorage is semi-private with one or two cabins and homes along the shore. Judd Cove Preserve is accessible at the head of Judd Bay on a pebble beach. A restored stone lime kiln from the late 1800's marks the correct public beach access area; private lands are to the north and south.

⑮ **Rosario Resort & Spa.** 1400 Rosario Rd., Eastsound, WA 98245; (360) 376-2222; (800) 562-8820; harbormaster@rosarioresort.com; www.rosarioresort.com. Monitors VHF 78A. Radio contact is preferred rather than by phone; phone service is limited. Certified Clean Marina. Open all year, diesel and ethanol-free unleaded gasoline at the fuel dock (fuel dock by appointment October

TURTLEBACK MOUNTAIN PRESERVE ON ORCAS ISLAND

Turtleback Mountain Preserve is a San Juan County Land Bank property. The 1,578-acre property offers over 8 miles of hiking trails and scenic vistas. There are two trailhead access points with parking, one at the North Trail off of Crow Valley Road, and the other at the South Trail off of Deer Harbor Road. Boaters can use the shuttle van at Deer Harbor Marina to access the trails at Turtleback Mountain. Trails at the South Trailhead are for pedestrians only; the North Trailhead allows horses and mountain bikes on a rotation basis – bikes on even calendar days and horses on odd calendar days. Trails vary from forested pathways and open meadows, to moderately steep outcroppings and ridges. No garbage disposal or water available; pack it in, pack it out.

The 8-mile trail network spans the "turtle's back," connecting the preserve's north and south trailheads. An additional 1-mile trail leads to the "turtle's head," with jaw-dropping views. Thanks to a partnership between the San Juan County Land Bank and the San Juan Preservation Trust, the piece between Turtlehead and Turtleback was connected, now referred to as "Turtleneck." Through the efforts of the San Juan County Land Bank, the San Juan Preservation Trust, the Trust for Public Land, and more than 1,500 private donors, Turtleback Mountain Preserve was established in 2007.

As with all Preserve properties, hikers are asked to stay on the trails to protect plant and wildlife species. Habitats include rare Garry oak woodlands, grasslands, and scattered wetlands.

See Area Map Page 196 - Maps Not for Navigation   SAN JUAN ISLANDS

The Doe Island State Park dock and trail await visitors with smaller boats (all nearby buoys are private).

The public dock and pier at the charming village of Olga on Orcas Island

through April), 45-50 slips with unlimited water for filling tanks and boat washing, 30 & 50 amp ELCI-protected power, 8 mooring buoys, garbage drop with recycling, restrooms, showers, café, convenience store, swimming pools, excellent Wi-Fi, seaplane service to Seattle via Kenmore Air and NW Seaplanes. Reservations for moorage are strongly recommended. Buoys are for boats 50 feet and under, first-come, first-served. There's room to anchor, though the sound is exposed to southerlies. The outdoor swimming pool, nearest the docks, welcomes families as does the spa-pool inside the resort's Mansion; the Mansion's outdoor pool below the hotel is for adults only. For those wanting to explore Eastsound or the island, car rental delivery service is available through "Orcas Island Rental Car" (360-376-RIDE). "San Juan Transit" runs to Eastsound, Deer Harbor, Rosario and other locations on Orcas Island in the summer months on Fridays, Saturdays, and Sundays.

A 200-foot breakwater dock accommodates larger vessels up to 180 feet. The outer end of the breakwater is for seaplanes only. New docks in a U-shape configuration allow easy access into the marina through a center fairway. Moorage includes power, water, restrooms and showers. A pumpout cart is located on the dock. Boats on buoys pay a buoy fee and boats anchored out pay a landing fee for use of the marina pool, shower and restrooms; spa facilities are extra. Day use up to 2 hours is free on a space available basis, at the discretion of the Harbormaster, while dining and shopping at the resort. The Cascade Bay Grill and Store at the head of the dock is open from Memorial Day through mid-September and has snacks, sodas, beer and wine, gift items, and limited groceries. The Grill serves burgers, fish & chips, and casual fare, inside or out. Live entertainment scheduled periodically, check their website.

The centerpiece of the resort is the magnificent Moran Mansion, listed on the National Register of Historic Places. The mansion houses a restaurant, lounge and spa. Holiday buffets are an excellent way to spend your time while cruising the shoulder seasons. The mansion itself is a fascinating museum (open 8:00 a.m. to 9:00 p.m. daily), a chronicle of Robert Moran's history as a shipbuilder, the mayor of Seattle, then as the builder of Rosario. Christopher Peacock, longtime resident artist and musician and now resort manager, presents a slide presentation on the history of the resort, with musical accompaniment performed on the giant room-sized Wurlitzer pipe organ. The concert begins at 4:00 p.m. Tuesdays to Saturdays mid-June through mid-September, and Saturdays only through the winter. It's wonderful. Don't miss it. Moran State Park is about a 30-minute walk.

Figurehead: The beautiful figurehead above the marina is a replica from the wreck of the *America*, a wooden clipper ship converted to barge use. The ship went aground near False Bay on San Juan Island in 1914 while under tow from Seattle to Vancouver. During periods of small tides and slack water, the wreck's bones are still a dive site at False Bay (from *Northwest Dive News*).

⑯ **Olga.** Olga, a tiny pastoral village, is near the entrance to East Sound, on the east

Rosario Resort

Doe Bay

2020 WAGGONER CRUISING GUIDE

SAN JUAN ISLANDS   See Area Map Page 196 - Maps Not for Navigation

shore. Olga has a dock and 105-foot-long mooring float, but no power, restrooms, or showers. The float is removed in winter. A box for overnight moorage payment is at the bottom of the ramp. Three-day overnight limit. Day-use stay up to two hours. Limited anchorage offshore exposed to southeasterly winds. Numerous private mooring buoys and charted cable area limit the possible anchoring opportunities.

A sign above the dock lists local stores and locations. Up the road you will find the Artworks co-operative, the James Hardman Gallery, and the Catkin Café housed in the reconstructed barreling plant building.

Sucia Island State Marine Park invites exploration and discovery.

Twin Rocks. West of Olga. Open all year, day use only, no facilities. Anchor out at this undeveloped state park property. No fires or overnight camping. Pack out all garbage. Do not disturb wildlife or alter the surroundings.

Lieber Haven Resort. P.O. Box 127, Olga, WA 98279; (360) 376-2472; www.lieberhavenresort.com. In the middle of Obstruction Pass. Overnight moorage on the resort docks for cottage guests only. Two rental cottages along a nice sandy, light gravel shoreline. Store carries some groceries, beer and wine, and some marine supplies.

Obstruction Pass State Park. www.parks.wa.gov. Southeast tip of Orcas Island. Open all year, moorage at 3 buoys for boats 45 feet and under. Self-register and pay moorage buoy fee on shore. Toilets, no power or showers. Good anchoring on a gravel bottom. Campsites with fireplaces, picnic tables, hiking trails.

⑰ **Doe Island Marine State Park.** (360) 376-2073; On the southeast side of Orcas Island. Normally open all year with five camping sites. This is a beautiful tiny island with a rocky shoreline dotted with tidepools. A trail leads around the island, through dense forest and lush undergrowth. Compost toilet; no power, no water or showers. Pack out all garbage. Adjacent buoys are privately owned. A new 32-foot float was installed in 2019 at Doe Island. Moorage rates are payable 1:00 p.m. to 8:00 a.m.; use the self-registration payment station located upland. Currents run strongly between Doe Island and Orcas Island.

⑰ **Doe Bay Resort and Retreat.** 107 Doe Bay Road, Olga, WA 98279; (360) 376-2291; office@doebay.com; www.doebay.com. Doe Bay is an interesting off-the-beaten-path destination, with 2 guest buoys (call for reservations) and anchorage space for 3 to 6 boats. Dinghy ashore to the rocky beach to visit the café or use the creekside clothing-optional soaking tubs and cedar sauna. Buoy mooring fees include use of the soaking tubs and sauna for two; anchor guests can use the cafe, soaking tubs and sauna for $15 per person.

The café has an intriguing menu and is open for breakfast, lunch and dinner, with indoor and outdoor seating. A store has convenience groceries and items from local artisans. The resort has cabins, geodesic domes, yurts, a beautifully crafted treehouse, and campsites for rent. The waterfront Boat House, with hotel-style accommodations, opened in late-summer 2019. Doe Bay Fest, a popular music festival, is held in early August.

Smuggler's Villa Resort. P.O. Box 79, Eastsound, WA 98245; (360) 376-2297; smuggler@rockisland.com; www.smuggler.com. No transient moorage. Smuggler's Village has condos for rent, a swimming pool and hot tubs. Reservations required. Good base for trailer boaters who can rent a condo for overnights and explore the northern San Juans during the day.

⑱ **Barnes and Clark Islands.** These two beautiful islands lie parallel to each other in Rosario Strait, between Orcas Island and Lummi Island. Barnes Island is privately

Sucia, Patos, and Matia Islands

220   www.WaggonerGuide.com

See Area Map Page 196 - Maps Not for Navigation   SAN JUAN ISLANDS

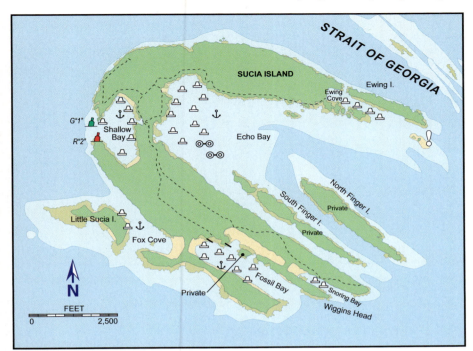

Sucia Island Marine State Park

owned, but Clark Island is a state park, with mooring buoys installed during the summer. Camping and picnicking sites are ashore, and trails meander along the island.

⑱ **Clark Island Marine State Park.** (360) 376-2073; Open all year, day use and overnight mooring and camping. Clark Island is exposed to Rosario Strait and the Strait of Georgia, and is best in settled weather. Mooring buoys are deployed between Clark Island and Barnes Island, and in the bay on the east side. The park has 9 mooring buoys for vessels 45 feet and under: 6 on the east side and 3 on the west side. Self-register and pay mooring buoy fee on shore. Toilets, picnic sites, fire rings, and primitive campsites. No power, no water. Pack out all garbage.

Note: A nasty rock is in the entrance to the bay.

Visitor Report: Correspondents Bruce and Margaret Evertz spent a night on a buoy on the east side of Clark Island and ". . .woke up three times in the middle of the night hanging onto the mattress as we rolled in the wake of something big. Next time we'll try one of the buoys on the west side." *No - current runs fast & swirly.*

⑲ **Matia Island.** (360) 376-2073; Open all year, day use and overnight mooring. Matia Island is part of the San Juan Islands National Wildlife Refuge. All access is restricted except the loop trail and the designated 5-acre moorage and picnicking area at Rolfe Cove. The rest of the island is off-limits to protect wildlife. Pets are not allowed on shore.

The favored Matia Island anchorage is in **Rolfe Cove**, which opens from the west. Strong currents can run through Rolfe Cove and the bottom is rocky. Be sure the anchor is well set and swinging room is adequate. Facilities include a 64-foot-long moorage float, 2 buoys (limit 45 feet), 6 campsites, toilet. No power, water or showers. The mooring float in past years was removed in winter. The new float, which was installed in 2019, is anticipated to be available year-round. Self-register and pay mooring fee at the head of the dock.

Those confident in their anchoring ability might try the little 1-boat notch between Rolfe Cove and Eagle Point, although you can't go inland from there. A stern-anchor will be required to keep the boat positioned. High cliffs surround this cove. It's very secluded and serene.

Anchorage is good in the bay indenting the southeast corner of the island. The remains of an old homestead are located at the head of that bay.

There is some disagreement about the pronunciation of Matia. Bruce Calhoun's book, *Cruising the San Juan Islands*, says it's pronounced "Mah-TEE-ah." We've been told, however, that a number of genuine old hands have always pronounced it "Mah-CIA," as in "inertia" or "militia." However the name is pronounced, Matia Island is a popular destination, beautiful and interesting.

LOCAL KNOWLEDGE

DANGEROUS REEFS: A reef extends westward from Little Sucia Island nearly to the shoal water near West Bank. Sucia Island is surrounded by such hazards. We strongly recommend that vessels in these waters carry and use Chart 18431.

⑳ **Sucia Island.** Open all year, day use and overnight mooring and camping. For information call (360) 902-8844; for campsite reservations call toll-free (888) 226-7688. Facilities include dock space, linear tie mooring systems, numerous mooring buoys, and toilets. Water, but no power, no showers. This probably is the most heavily used marine park in the system. As many as 500 boats can visit on one weekend in the high summer season.

Like Matia and Patos Islands, Sucia Island is made of sandstone carved by water and wind into dramatic shapes. Many fossils can be found in Sucia Island's sandstone. It is illegal to disturb or remove fossils.

The park has 55 primitive campsites and 2 group campsites, which can be reserved. Camping is permitted in designated areas only. A day use/picnic area, with picnic shelters, is on the neck of land separating Echo Bay and Shallow Bay, and can be reserved. The park has several miles of hiking trails and service roads. Fresh water is available at Fossil Bay and near Shallow Bay April through September. The most developed facilities are at Fossil Bay.

Sucia Island has several fingers that

Though small, Matia Island has a cove for anchoring, two mooring buoys, and a dock.

TURN POINT SPECIAL OPERATING AREA

The Turn Point Special Operating Area was created in 2001 to manage the high volume of commercial ship and recreational boat traffic around Turn Point. Ships longer than 100 meters (328 feet) must call in to Victoria Traffic on VHF channel 11 prior to entering the area and report their intended navigation movements and any other information necessary to comply with standards of care.

Recreational vessels should monitor VHF channel 11 in this vicinity so they can be aware of any ships. If ships are in the Special Operating Area, stay well clear until they are past. In a crossing situation, *cross behind the large ship*, not in front of it.

Turn Point is a blind corner. Be sure to check for AIS targets in the area. See *Chapter 1 - What Recreational Boaters Need to Know about VTS* for more information.

separate small bays. Facilities are as follows: Fox Cove: 4 mooring buoys; Fossil Bay: 2 docks, 13 mooring buoys; Snoring Bay: 2 mooring buoys; Echo Bay: 14 mooring buoys, 2 linear moorings; Ewing Cove: 4 mooring buoys; Shallow Bay: 8 mooring buoys. All mooring buoys are limited to boats 45 feet or less. Rafting allowed at the docks based on the size of boats. All docks and moorings are Washington State Parks facilities, self-register and pay a fee at the designated on-shore stations. The mooring buoy count can change based on winter weather and repairs.

Shallow Bay. Shallow Bay is an excellent, popular anchorage. Lots of room except on minus tides. Mooring buoys take most of the obvious good spots, so if they are taken you'll be looking at the south side of Shallow Bay. Check the tides before anchoring, and be sure you'll have enough water under the keel at low tide. Easy entry as long as you pass between the two buoys marking the entrance. The best place to beach the dinghy is on the narrow neck of land separating Shallow Bay from Echo Bay. Sunsets in Shallow Bay are beautiful.

Fox Cove. Enter Fox Cove from either side. Waters off the southern entry can be turbulent. At the west entry foul ground extends west farther than you expect. Tie to mooring buoys or anchor behind Little Sucia Island. A pretty spot with sandstone cliffs.

Fossil Bay. Fossil Bay is easy to enter, nicely protected, and beautiful. Anchor out, tie to one of the mooring buoys, or moor at the docks. In winter one of the docks is moved to a more protected area of the park. At the head of the outermost dock a plaque commemorates the yacht clubs that were members of the Interclub Boating Association of Washington, when Interclub worked to collect funds from ordinary citizens, then bought the island and gave it to the state as a state park. One of the points of land overlooking Fossil Bay is named for Ev Henry, the first president of Interclub, who conceived the idea and carried out the project.

Depths in Fossil Bay at zero tide are 6 feet at the outer end of the innermost dock, and they shoal rapidly toward the head of the bay. The park ranger told us depths are only 5 feet at zero tide near the outer dock. Be careful on low tides. A substantial day use shelter, excellent for group functions, has been built at the head of the dock. Call (360) 376-2073 for reservations.

Snoring Bay. Snoring Bay is easy to enter and has 2 mooring buoys. A good spot. As we understand the story, a park ranger was caught sleeping on duty in this bay, hence the name.

Echo Bay. Echo Bay is the largest of Sucia's bays. Although it is the most exposed, it is the most popular. Mooring buoys line the western shore, and 2 linear mooring systems are just outside the buoys. Picnic facilities are on the narrow neck of land separating Echo Bay from Shallow Bay.

The fine gravel beach at the head of Echo Bay is fairly steep, making dinghy landing much more convenient. We were able to step ashore without getting our feet wet.

The two long islands in Echo Bay (North Finger and South Finger Island) are privately owned. The south half of Justice Island (the small island off South Finger Island) is park-owned but closed to the public as a nature preserve.

Caution: A reader reported that he grounded his Cal 39 sailboat, which draws 6 feet 8 inches, on an uncharted rock in Echo Bay. The grounding occurred in the area marked 1 fathom, 5 feet extending from the small islet northwest of South Finger Islet, as shown on large scale Chart 18431. He sounded the area carefully after the grounding, and found the depths to be somewhat less than charted. The keel of his boat confirmed the soundings. On low tides especially, give the tip of this islet a good offing.

Despite occasional stories of anchor dragging in Echo Bay, we have found the bottom to be heavy, sticky clay, with excellent holding.

No-anchor Zone: A no-anchor zone is marked by buoys near the head of Echo Bay. They want to protect eelgrass from boat anchors and dragging chain rode. Mooring buoys in the bay use eco-friendly anchors that do not disturb eelgrass.

Active Cove on Patos Island is one of the most scenic anchorages in the San Juan Islands.

See Area Map Page 196 - Maps Not for Navigation   SAN JUAN ISLANDS

Ewing Cove. In our opinion, cozy little Ewing Cove, tucked in behind Ewing Island on the north side of Echo Bay, is the most charming of Sucia Island's bays. The cove has 4 mooring buoys and a lovely beach at the western end. We have reports of a rock in Ewing Cove's southern entrance, from Echo Bay. The rock is east of a white can that marks a fish haven, shown on large scale Chart 18431. We're told the rock is black and hard to see, and feeds on propellers at low tide. Be extra cautious. Reader Bruce Farwell sent lat/lon coordinates of 48°45.794'N/122°52.924'W. We've found the narrow pass at the northwest end of Ewing Cove to be deep and easily run as long as you pay attention. Danger Reef lies just outside.

㉑ **Patos Island.** (360) 376-2073; Open all year, day use and overnight mooring and camping. Facilities include 2 mooring buoys (limit 45 feet) in Active Cove; one buoy was reported to be submerged in 2019. Current can run strong in Active Cove, making mooring to a park buoy, or anchoring, difficult. Toilets and primitive campsites. Self-register and pay mooring buoy fee on shore. The remains of the dock that served the lighthouse on Alden Point are still there, but barely recognizable. A one-mile trail leads from the beach at the head of Active Cove to the lighthouse. Pack out all garbage. The island is a breeding area for birds.

㉑ **Active Cove.** The only possible Patos Island anchorage is in Active Cove, on the west tip of the island. The cove, with its sculpted sandstone walls, is one of the most scenic spots in the San Juans. Considerable current activity is outside the entrances. Inside the cove the currents are reduced, but it's tight. Use the mooring buoys when possible. In 2019, correspondents, Brent and Peggy Ann Bierbaum, reported that the buoy nearest shore was under water and in need of replacement. If the mooring buoys are taken, anchoring gets interesting. A stern-tie to shore probably will be called for.

Freeman Island. On President Channel. Open all year, day use only, no facilities. Anchor out at this undeveloped state park property. No fires or overnight camping. Pack out all garbage.

㉒ **West Beach Resort.** 190 Waterfront Way, Eastsound, WA 98245; (360) 376-2240; (877) 937-8224; vacation@westbeachresort.com; www.westbeachresort.com. Open all year, ethanol-free premium gasoline at the fuel dock, 10 mooring buoys in the summer and 3 in the winter, restrooms, showers. A new pumpout station was installed in 2018; the service is free and accomodates boats up to 60 feet. You can pick up a free pumpout kit, provided by Washington Sea Grant (WSG), at the marina office. Floats in deeper water accommodate larger boats. Larger powerboats and keel sailboats tie to mooring buoys. Most of the docks are removed from mid-September to late May, limited moorage in the winter. The fuel dock is open year round. The store has a little bit of everything, including groceries, ice, beer, wine, espresso, ice cream, and free Wi-Fi. Limited dock space in the off-season.

West Beach is a popular fishing resort with cabins, tent cabins, RV, camping, children's activities, food service, private launch ramp (free for guests, a fee is charged for non-guests) and parking. Be careful if you anchor out. The eelgrass bottom does not offer good holding in many places and you can drag.

One of the small, intimate marinas among the San Juan Islands; West Beach Resort has mooring buoys and seasonal dock moorage.

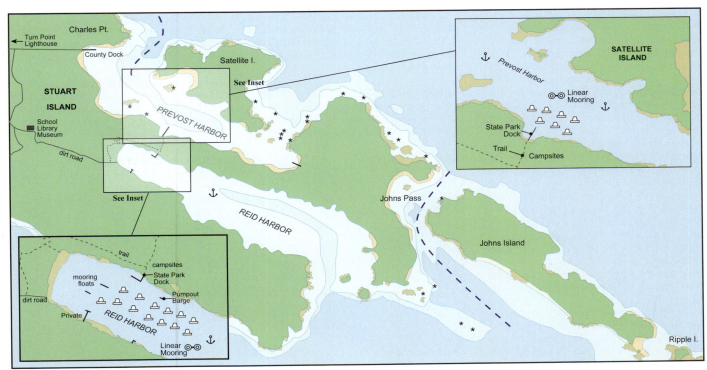
Stuart Island Marine State Park

2020 WAGGONER CRUISING GUIDE

SAN JUAN ISLANDS

㉓ Brandt's Landing. 340 Brandt-Landing Rd, Eastsound, WA 98245; (360) 376-4477; (360) 440-6297 harbormaster; sjharbormaster@gmail.com; brandtslandingmarina.net. Located on the north end of Orcas Island a mile north of the village of Eastsound, the marina's floats are in a long narrow canal entered between North Beach and Terrill Beach. Open all year, with limited guest moorage available for overnight and hourly stays for vessels up to 50 feet. Contact the marina for moorage. Reservations accepted. Guest moorage slips are located at the far south end of the channel. Water, 30 amp power, and garbage drop. Enter on mid to high tide level; entry channel at the break water is some of the shallowest area.

Waldron Island. In settled weather, anchorage is good in Cowlitz Bay and North Bay. Mail Bay, on the east shore, is rocky but usable. The mail boat from Bellingham used to arrive here, leaving the mail in a barrel hung over the water.

Cowlitz Bay. Cowlitz Bay has one of the loveliest sand beaches in the San Juan's. Three-quarters of a mile of shoreline and tidelands are part of the San Juan Preservation Trust and open to the public. The preserve begins about a half-mile west of the Waldron Island County Dock and continues to the low-bank and upland clearing areas, where you will find remnants of fallen cabins and fencing that once stood along the beach. In 2019, no upland trails were found. The remainder of Waldron Island is private with no public facilities.

㉔ Stuart Island. The center portion of Stuart Island, including Reid Harbor and Prevost Harbor, is a state park with campsites, potable water, and clean, spacious composting toilets. A trail and dirt road from Reid Harbor and Prevost Harbor lead out to the automated Turn Point lighthouse. The distance is about 3 miles, each way. It's an excellent walk, although the trail to the road goes over a mountain, and will have you puffing. The view down into Reid Harbor is excellent, however.

Once you get to the road, it's 0.7 mi. to the school house (1 room, K-8), library and museum, which in our opinion are on the must-see list. The school house is modern, but the library and museum buildings go back to earlier days. The museum is filled with information about island life, which, despite being close to big cities, is pretty primitive. There is no public electric power, for example. Every resident is responsible for his or her own electricity, and a few choose to do without. Ditto water and telephone, although cell phones have filled that void. Handmade postcards are for sale in the library on the honor system.

One island family, Ezra and Loie Benson and their children, have created a small business called Boundary Pass Traders. They operate the Treasure Chest, near the schoolhouse, and a second Treasure Chest along the road at Prevost Harbor. T-shirts and coloring books, with local scenes, are for sale. Strictly the honor system. Select the items you like and mail a check for your purchases, or you can pay online.

Prevost Harbor. Open all year, day use and overnight mooring and camping. Facilities include 256 feet of dock space, 7 mooring buoys (limit 45 feet), a linear mooring system, 18 primitive campsites, toilets. Self-register and pay dock moorage, mooring buoy, and linear mooring fee at the head of the state park dock. The favored entrance to Prevost Harbor is around the west end of Satellite Island. A county dock on the northwest end of Prevost Harbor, suitable for dinghies, shortens the walk to the Island school and Turn Point lighthouse. No overnight stays at the county dock.

Caution: Two reefs in the Prevost Harbor entrance cover at high tide. One is off the Stuart Island shore and dries at 6 feet. The other is off Satellite Island and dries at 4 feet. The reefs are clearly charted, but when they cover, the route to the dock looks to be wide open. If you're entering at higher tide when the reefs are covered, don't wrap tightly to port around the tip of Satellite Island. That's where one of the reefs is lying in wait. Proceed a short distance straight into the harbor (but not too far; that's where the other reef is located), then turn to port.

Except for the reefs noted above, anchoring is good throughout Prevost Harbor. After dinner we took a slow dinghy ride around the shoreline. A grass airstrip is at the east end of the harbor, beyond the docks. As we putt-putted along we found the houses, rock forms, and beaches fascinating. Crabbing reported to be good.

The passage to the east of Satellite Island is foul. It has been reported that, with care, these waters are passable at half tide or better, or by shallow draft boats; use caution. Shoreside facilities are shared with Reid Harbor, on the narrow but steep neck of land that separates them.

Satellite Island East Cove. "The little cove on the eastern shore of Satellite Island has good holding in mud in about 40 feet. Wonderful view across Boundary Pass. Inside, Prevost Harbor was packed with boats; we were alone." [Hamilton]

Reid Harbor. Open all year, day use and overnight mooring and camping. The entrance is straightforward. A 192-foot mooring dock is on the north shore. 13 mooring buoys (for boats 45 feet and under) dot the bay, and mooring floats (not connected to land) and a linear mooring system are within easy dinghy distance of the landing dock. Self-register and pay mooring fees at the head of the dock. Toilets, pumpout, and portapotty dump are located on a float along the north shore. Reid Harbor is long and narrow, and protected by high hills. The bottom is excellent for anchoring, and the harbor holds a great number of boats. It's a popular destination. The setting is beautiful. Shoreside facilities are shared with Prevost Harbor, on the narrow but steep neck of land separating them. The county dirt road leading to the Turn Point Lighthouse, with its museum (and the school house, museum and library along the way), begins at the head of Reid Harbor. No dock at the head of the bay, but if tides are favorable you could beach your dinghy there without having to carry it back through the mud.

Gossip Island. "Reid Harbor had too many boats for our taste. Preferring a view anyway, we dropped anchor just outside, in the cove formed by Gossip Island and the unnamed island immediately northwest of Gossip Island. It was very private, with two white sand beaches nearby. Good holding ground for the anchor. Southerly swells rocked us a couple times, but no worse than in the east cove of James Island. We had an excellent view through the islets to the Olympic Mountains, and of large ship traffic away off in Haro Strait." [Hamilton]

Johns Pass. Johns Pass separates Stuart Island and Johns Island, and is used regularly. At the south end of the pass foul ground, marked by kelp, extends about half of a mile southeast from Stuart Island. Boats heading southeast through Johns Pass should head for Gull Reef, then turn when well clear of the kelp. Anchorage is possible in Johns Pass and along the south side of Johns Island.

Departing Brandt's Landing on the north end of Orcas Island, with Sucia Island in the distance.

Gulf Islands

CHAPTER 7

GULF ISLANDS
*Victoria • Sidney • Butchart Gardens • Chemainus
Wallace Island • Pirates Cove • Nanaimo*

SALTSPRING ISLAND
Ganges • Vesuvius • Fulford Harbour

NORTH & SOUTH PENDER ISLAND
Bedwell Harbour • Port Browning • Otter Bay

GALIANO ISLAND
Sturdies Bay • Montague Harbour

GULF ISLANDS

See Area Map Page 227 - Maps Not for Navigation

Gulf Islands are comprised of eight or ten large islands and many smaller ones. For convenience, the Gulf Islands section of this book includes the southern tip and the east side of Vancouver Island as far up-island as Nanaimo. We divide this area into Northern and Southern sections with Active Pass and Houstoun Passage, the boundary between the two. The largest of the Gulf Islands is Saltspring Island (also written as Salt Spring Island), seventy square miles in area, and many smaller islands and islets. This is prime cruising territory with marine parks, anchorages, distinctive small towns and thriving cities. The first settlers arrived during the Fraser River gold rush and over the years the Islands' sunny climate and isolated proximity to civilization attracted many venturesome individuals including pioneers, artists, millionaires and refugees.

Geologically, the Gulf Islands are made of sandstone that has been folded and uplifted until it sticks out of the sea. Like the San Juan Islands, the Gulf Islands are in the lee of mountains. They receive much summertime sun and little summertime rainfall. Water can be in short supply and boat washing is often not allowed, at least in the islands themselves.

The Gulf Islands are blessed with dozens of anchorages, from one-boat notches to open bays that hold many boats. Marine parks provide anchorage, mooring and docking possibilities, with facilities ashore. Private marinas run the spectrum from rustic to deluxe, many with excellent dining on-site or nearby.

Victoria Harbour Authority's Causeway Floats are right in front of the Empress Hotel.

The largest town in the Gulf Islands proper is Ganges on Saltspring Island. If your definition of the islands expands (as ours does) to include southern and eastern Vancouver Island, then Victoria, Sidney, Ladysmith and Nanaimo are larger than Ganges. The best provisioning stops are Victoria, Sidney, Ganges, Ladysmith, Chemainus, and Nanaimo. Fuel is available throughout the islands.

Navigation is straightforward, but pay attention. It's easy to get confused, and the waters are dotted with rocks and reefs. Know where you are at all times. Canadian Hydrographic Services electronic chart packs RM-PAC02 Vancouver Island East and V-PAC-A Vancouver Island East include BSB-raster and ENC-vector charts respectively for the Gulf Islands. Chartbook 3313 is not inexpensive but is an excellent chartbook and has everything for the Gulf Islands

Customs – Entering Canada. Vessels entering Canada are required to clear Canadian Customs at their first stop in Canada. Most boats will clear customs at Bedwell Harbour on South Pender Island, Victoria (includes Victoria Inner Harbour, Oak Bay and Cadboro Bay), Sidney, or Nanaimo. Bedwell Harbour is just 4 miles north of Stuart Island in the San Juan Islands, but its station is open only from May 1 through September 30. See *Chapter 1 U.S. and Canadian Customs Information* for a more detailed explanation on the process of clearing Canadian Customs.

GULF ISLANDS

Southern Gulf Islands

GULF ISLANDS

See Area Map Page 227 - Maps Not for Navigation

Greater Victoria Harbour

See Area Map Page 227 - Maps Not for Navigation

GULF ISLANDS

Enjoy the views along Westsong/Songhees mile-long pathway served by foot ferry.

Gulf Islands National Park Reserve. The Gulf Islands National Park Reserve came into being in 2004. Many former provincial parks, and most of the uninhabited islands and islets south of Active Pass, were transferred to the new national park, plus a number of other properties that were purchased. Land continues to be purchased and added to the Reserve. Park lands have green and white location signs, or small yellow boundary signs bearing the stylized beaver symbol of Parks Canada. Dogs must be on leash. Camping is in designated areas only. Nominal usage fees are charged, often collected through honor boxes on shore.

For more information see www.pc.gc.ca/gulf; gulf.islands@pc.gc.ca; (250) 654-4000; (866) 944-1744. For emergencies or to report problems on park lands, call toll-free (877) 852-3100.

iOS and Android App: The Parks Canada Explora app, available free for iOS and Android, provides geo-tagged maps, photos, information, and quizzes about sites throughout the Gulf Islands National Park Reserve.

VICTORIA AREA

Esquimalt Harbour. Esquimalt Harbour is a wonderful but often overlooked anchorage, with excellent holding in thick mud southeast of Cole Island, with room to swing. Protection is reasonable, even with big winds blowing in the Strait of Juan de Fuca. With this bottom you're not going anywhere, anyway, but you might be rocking and rolling at times due to swell or wind waves. The Canadian Navy guards the entrance with a high speed inflatable and will advise you to keep 100 meters away from their ships and property. Anchor north of a line between the south end of Richards Island and the north end of Smart Island.

The British Navy once used Cole Island for munitions storage. The large brick buildings from the late 1800s on the island are still intact and make interesting exploration. Cole Island is a National Historic Site where visitors are welcome. A dinghy dock is located on the southwest side of Cole Island and boardwalk pathways connect all the buildings. For a map of the buildings on the island, go to www.coleisland.ca.

Security Zone: All vessels entering or departing Esquimalt Harbour are requested to contact QHM Operations on VHF channel 10 or by telephone (250) 363-2160. Give your vessel name, make, and direction of travel at Fisgard Lighthouse and Duntze Head. Fisgard Lighthouse was the first lighthouse on Canada's west coast (1860) and is still in operation.

You can anchor the dinghy off the beach at the lighthouse to tour Fisgard Light and the historic Fort Rodd Hill military site. Payment to enter the grounds should be made at the entrance gate to Fort Rodd Hill located above the lighthouse. The grounds are open from June through October. Gun emplacements, magazines, defensive walls and military houses from the late 1800's can be seen at Fort Rodd Hill; Fisgard Lighthouse contains archival photos and historical information about the lighthouse.

Fleming Beach at Macaulay Park. West of Victoria Harbour, in Esquimalt. Open all year. Facilities include launch ramp (fee charged) and washrooms. This is a charming little cove, protected by a rock breakwater, overlooked by most boating people. It is the home of Esquimalt Anglers' Association, a private sportfishing and fish enhancement group. The boarding floats at the launch ramp have room for temporary moorage while shopping nearby, or you can anchor out. Walkways and picnic areas have been built. Fleming Beach is adjacent to old coastal gun emplacements, which make for good exploring.

LOCAL KNOWLEDGE

Victoria Mandatory Traffic Lanes: All vessels 65 feet LOA and less must enter and depart Victoria's Inner Harbour between Shoal Point and Laurel Point along the south shore, as shown in the accompanying harbor map. Inbound vessels favor the docks; outbound vessels a little farther out. The traffic lanes are marked by buoys (keep the buoys to port when entering and exiting). The more open water in the middle of the harbor is used by the large number of float planes that land and take off constantly. Because of the volume of boat and float plane traffic, no sailing is allowed inside the breakwater. Sailboats under power must have sails lowered.

Visit the Waggoner Store

We carry one of the best collections of Northwest and Inside Passage books. If you are **in Anacortes** during the week, stop by and say hello.

WAGGONER CRUISING GUIDE

902 - 8th Street Anacortes • 360.299.8500 • www.WaggonerGuide.com

2020 Waggoner Cruising Guide   229

GULF ISLANDS

See Area Map Page 227 - Maps Not for Navigation

① **Victoria.** Victoria is the provincial capital of British Columbia, and the largest city on Vancouver Island. Vancouver Island is served by ferries from Port Angeles, WA to Victoria; from Tsawwassen to Sidney and Victoria through Swartz Bay; and from Vancouver (Horseshoe Bay) to Nanaimo. The fast-running Victoria Clipper passenger ferry connects Victoria and Seattle. Scheduled float planes also connect with Vancouver and Seattle, and other destinations.

Victoria is beautiful. The Empress Hotel, for which the word "majestic" could have been created, dominates the Inner Harbour. The Empress is flanked on the south by the B.C. provincial parliament buildings, themselves the embodiment of dignity, thoughtful deliberation, and orderly progress—the buildings, that is. Between the Empress and the parliament buildings stands the Royal British Columbia Museum, a must-see, especially for families. A giant ice-age mammoth dominates the entry, and the rest of the museum delights with a re-creation of Capt. Vancouver's ship, a Victorian town exhibit, a west coast seashore, a First Nations Big House and much, much more. Highly recommended.

The Maritime Museum of British Columbia (250) 385-4222 is located downtown in Nootka Court at 634 Humboldt Street, across from the Empress Hotel. This excellent museum is open 10:00 a.m. to 4:00 p.m. Tuesday through Saturday.

The Visitor Information Centre is on top of the causeway at the head of the Inner Harbour, across from the Empress Hotel. It's easy to find. The entire Victoria Inner Harbour is covered by Wi-Fi.

Inside Ogden Point, marinas and public wharves begin with Fisherman's Wharf and progress inward to the well-marked customs dock at Raymur Point. East of the customs dock is the Coast Victoria Harbourside Hotel & Marina. Next, in James Bay, comes the Causeway Marina, in front of the Empress Hotel. These docks are popular and fill first. Northward from the Causeway Marina comes Ship Point Marina. Continuing north are the Wharf Street Floats, and Johnson Street Marina. On the north shore of the Middle Harbour is the Victoria International Marina. With the exception of Harbourside Hotel & Marina and Victoria International Marina, all moorage facilities are managed by the Greater Victoria Harbour Authority. Details regarding these facilities are described below.

West Bay is home to three marinas, Westbay Marine Village, Sailors Cove, and Hidden Harbour, with permanent moorage and float homes. Two marinas in the Upper Harbour, Victoria Marina and Canoe Brewpub Marina & Restaurant, are permanent moorage only. The very substantial Point Hope Maritime Shipyard is located on the west side of Upper Harbour. **Johnson Street Bridge** separates Inner Harbour from the Upper Harbour, contact the bridge attendant on VHF 12.

For an interesting side trip, take the dinghy north under the Johnson Street Bridge, through Upper Harbour, Selkirk Water, and Gorge Waters to Portage Inlet. You'll travel through the industrial part of the city, then through park and residential areas. It's about a 3-mile trip; currents are a factor if you intend to row.

Harbor Master/Harbor Patrol: Contact Harbour Master/Patrol on VHF 18A or (250) 363-3578 office or (250) 380-8177 for 24-hour emergencies.

Customs: The customs dock is located at Raymur Point, just east of Fisherman's Wharf in front of the Harbourside Hotel & Marina. When arriving, check in using the dedicated phone at the customs dock.

Greater Victoria Harbour Authority: (GVHA) owns and operates several marine facilities, 3 of which have guest moorage: Causeway Marina, Ship Point Marina (large vessels), and Wharf Street Floats. Laundry, showers, and washrooms for all three guest facilities are located on the Broughton Street Pier–look for the gray building with a red roof. The Harbour Authority has a "meet and greet" program for visiting boats. When you enter the Inner Harbour, call on VHF 66A and they will direct you to available guest moorage.

Reservations: The Coast Victoria Harbourside Hotel & Marina, adjacent to the Fisherman's Wharf, accepts reservations. The Greater Victoria Harbour Authority accepts reservations and are recommended for larger vessels (60 feet and over), on special holidays, and during peak season months. Visit GVHA's website, gvha.ca, for more information about making reservations.

Symphony Splash: On the first weekend in August enjoy symphony music from a barge in the Inner Harbour, punctuated with cannons and fireworks. Over 40,000 people line the Inner Harbour for the evening event.

No Discharge Zone. Discharging raw sewage is prohibited in Victoria Inner Harbour, defined as beginning at the Ogden Point breakwater. This applies to "black water" only. "Gray water," such as from dishwashing or showers, is okay (if biodegradable).

Pumpout: A for fee pumpout station is located on B-dock of Fisherman's Wharf. Tokens to operate the pump are available at Victoria Marine Fuels and the Harbour Authority seasonal kiosk at the Causeway Marina.

Things to Do

1. Royal British Columbia Museum. An extraordinary museum covering the human and natural history of British Columbia is just above James Bay in Victoria.

2. B.C. Maritime Museum. Displays on B.C. marine history, the voyages of Captain George Vancouver, and other rotating exhibits.

3. Afternoon tea at the Empress Hotel. A special treat, high tea offers pastries and piano music in an elegant setting.

4. Victoria Inner Harbour. Watch street musicians, mimes, and artists. The waterfront comes alive in the summer.

① **Greater Victoria Harbour Authority - GVHA.** 100-1019 Wharf Street, Victoria, BC V8W 2Y9; (250) 383-8326; (800) 883-7079 after hours; gvha@gvha.ca; www.gvha.ca. Monitors VHF 66A. The Greater Victoria Harbour Authority owns, manages,

Victoria's parliament building competes with the Empress Hotel for the best view from Causeway Floats in the Inner Harbour.

and operates a number of recreational and commercial marine facilities throughout Victoria Harbour. Three of the popular GVHA guest moorage marinas in the Inner Harbour include Causeway Marina, Ship Point Marina, and Wharf Street Floats.

GVHA's most popular guest location is the Causeway Marina located in front of the Empress Hotel. Ship Point Marina is adjacent to Causeway Marina with amenities for larger boats. Moorage rates at all three of GVHA's guest marinas are the same and can be viewed on at gvha.ca. Washroom, shower, and laundry facilities for all of GVHA's guest facilities are located at Broughton Street Pier. GVHA's main office is located on the ground floor of an office building on Wharf Street, just above Wharf Street Floats. Seasonal guest registration kiosks are located at the bottom of ramp at Causeway Marina and Wharf Street.

GVHA commercial and permanent moorage facilities include **Johnson Street Marina** and **Hyack Terminal** in the Inner Harbour; **Fisherman's Wharf** and **Raymur Point Customs Dock** in the Middle Harbour; and the Cruise Ship Terminal and deep water facilities at Ogden Point. Fisherman's Wharf is reserved primarily for commercial and monthly moorage, no transient space. Johnson Street Marina is for monthly moorage only, primarily used by fish boats and commercial vessels. Hyack Terminal provides float plane services, permanent moorage, and facilities for marine adventure tour operators.

GVHA accepts reservations for guest moorage facilities, and are recommended for vessels 60 feet and over. Reservations are a must on special holidays, and during the peak season. Visit GVHA's website, gvha.ca, or call them for more information about making reservations.

Broughton Street Pier – GVHA. Showers, washrooms, and laundry facilities for GVHA moorage guests are located at this location. Garbage and recycle drop are also located here. No moorage at the Broughton Street Pier. Water taxis and tour boats arrive and depart from this facility.

Causeway Marina – GVHA. Open all year with 2000+ feet of side-tie dock space for vessels up to 60 feet. 30 amp power, potable water, free Wi-Fi, garbage and recycling drop. Limited guest moorage space October 1 through May 15. Docks are gated all hours through the year. The check-in kiosk, located beside the ramp to shore, is open June 15 through September 15. These are the picturesque and popular docks directly in front of the Empress Hotel. Downtown Victoria beckons with fabulous restaurants, shopping, hotels, museums, and sightseeing. Public washrooms (no showers) are located under the Visitors Centre building. Private,

The foot ferry will carry you between waterfront promenades that encircle the harbour.

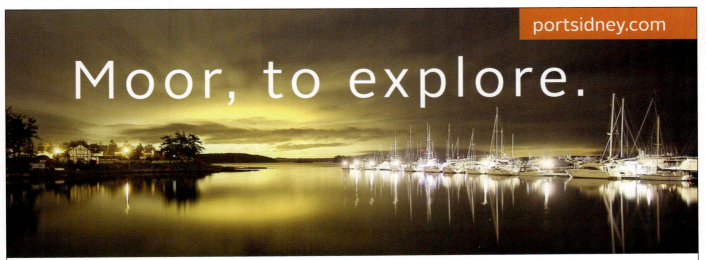

portsidney.com

Moor, to explore.

Come and visit the new Port Sidney marina, located at the best entrance to Beacon Ave. The marina now offers special group bookings, custom docks with a large covered tent, showers and laundry and wifi. So whether you stay for a night or a month it's the perfect location to Moor, and explore Sidney and the surrounding Gulf Islands.

MILL BAY MARINE GROUP

| **Bridgemans Bistro** Mill Bay BC | **Mill Bay Marina** Mill Bay BC | **Pacific Gateway Marina** Port Renfrew BC | **Port Browning Marina** Pender Island BC | **MK Bay Marina** Kitimat BC |

GULF ISLANDS   See Area Map Page 227 - Maps Not for Navigation

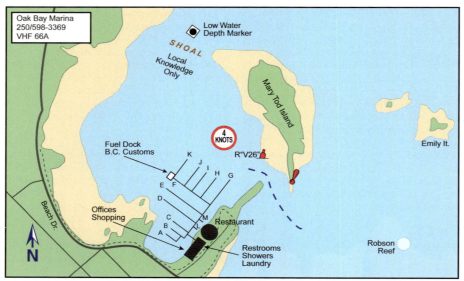
Oak Bay

clean Harbour Authority operated showers, laundry, and washrooms are at the Broughton Street Pier.

Ship Point Marina – GVHA. Open all year for larger vessels 60 feet to 280 feet; side-tie moorage. Docks are gated all-hours. Reservations highly recommended. Potable water, 30, 50, 100 amp single phase/208 & 3-phase/480 power. Free Wi-Fi, garbage and recycling drop. Public washrooms (no showers) are located under the Visitors Centre building. Private and clean Harbour Authority-operated showers, laundry and washrooms are at the Broughton Street Pier.

Wharf Street Floats – GVHA. Open all year for vessels to 375 feet, more than 1000 feet of side-tie visitor dock space. Limited guest moorage October 1 to the end of May. Potable water, 30, 50 & 100 amp power (single phase/208), garbage, free Wi-Fi. Power availability varies depending on location. Conveniently located downtown, just not quite as picturesque as the Causeway Floats in front of the Empress Hotel.

① **Victoria Marine Fuels Ltd.** (250) 381-5221; www.marinefuels.com. Fuel dock with gasoline and diesel, located at Erie Street Fisherman's Wharf at 1 Dallas Rd. Open all year, but with shorter winter hours, closed Christmas Day and New Year's Day. Store stocks snacks, food items, charts. This is the only fuel dock in the Inner Harbour.

① **Coast Victoria Harbourside Hotel & Marina.** 146 Kingston Street, Victoria, V8V 1V4; (250) 360-1211; coastvictoria@coasthotels.com; www.coasthotels.com. Guest moorage May through September, limited availability October through April; 30 & 50 amp power, potable water on the docks, washrooms and showers. Marina guests have full access to the dining room and lounge, indoor/outdoor pool, Jacuzzi, sauna, and fitness facilities. Reservations accepted.

Within walking distance of downtown.

① **Victoria International Marina.** 1 Cooperage Place, Victoria, BC V9A 7J9; (778) 432-0477; info@vimarina.ca; www.vimarina.ca. Monitors VHF 68A. On the north shore of Victoria Harbour, northeast of Pelly Island, two symmetrical one-story buildings sit on either side of this 28-slip marina designed to accommodate boats 65 to 175 feet in length. Six slips are leased for 40 years; seven slips are available for one-year renewable leases; seven slips for monthly leases with a 3-month minimum stay; and seven slips are reserved for guest moorage. This is a world-class marina with first-class marina services, a crew lounge, and event space. The marina is designed and built with luxury yachts in mind. Due to Victoria Harbour traffic restrictions imposed by Transport Canada, this marina is for yachts 65 feet and over; smaller boats by special permit only. The trendy Boom & Batten Restaurant and Cafe (250-940-5850) is located next to the marina. The beautiful Westsong/Songhees Walkway meanders along the shore offering outstanding views. Three water-taxi landings are located along the Walkway with departures to Victoria's downtown waterfront.

② **Oak Bay.** Oak Bay is on the east side of the south tip of Vancouver Island, west of the Chatham Islands. The channels between the various rocks and reefs are well marked. This is the route taken by many tugs with tows, and commercial fish boats of all sizes. The Oak Bay Marina and a separate small repair yard are located behind the breakwater.

② **Oak Bay Marina.** 1327 Beach Drive, Victoria, BC V8S 2N4; (250) 598-3369; (800) 663-7090 ext. 247; obm@obmg.com; www.oakbaymarina.com. VHF 66A. Open all year with gasoline and diesel. Customs clearance telephone at the fuel dock. Spectacular views of Mt. Baker. Guest moorage for boats to 70 feet; 15 & 30 amp power, washrooms, showers, laundry, Wi-Fi. Call ahead for availability or reserve through SwiftHarbour.com booking service.

The marina has excellent docks and a good licensed waterfront restaurant. Outdoor seating on the deck overlooking the marina. A coffee house for quick casual dining, and a gift shop with local products and sundry items. A small chandlery carries essential boating supplies. Repairs are at the Gartside Marine boatyard in a neighboring building, no haulout. The Oak Bay Beach Hotel is nearby for elegant dining. Complete shopping at quaint Oak Bay Village a short distance away. Regular bus service to downtown Victoria. Kayak tours and bike rentals available. Part of the Oak Bay Marine Group.

Discovery Island Marine Park. Open all year. An undeveloped park suitable for beachable boats only. The island was once the home of Capt. E.G. Beaumont, who donated the land as a park. The northern part of Discovery Island, adjacent Chatham Island, and some of the smaller islands nearby are Indian Reserve lands: no landing.

Cadboro Bay. Cadboro Bay is entirely residential except for the Royal Victoria Yacht Club, which has a breakwater-protected marina on the western shore. Moorage at Royal Victoria Yacht Club is for members of reciprocal clubs only. Customs clearance is available.

Anchorage in Cadboro Bay is excellent, mud and sand bottom. A 100-foot long

SPENCERS MARINE SUPPLY & CONSIGNMENT
Over 16 Years' Experience   Open 7 Days A Week
Good Quality New & Used Marine Gear
We Make Boating Fun & Affordable
10% Discount for Yacht Club Members
778-351-1400 ⚓ 2240 Harbour Rd, Sidney BC ⚓ www.spencersmarinesupply.com

concrete replica of Cadborosaurus, the elusive sea monster of Cadboro Bay, is prominent in the playground above the broad sandy beach at Cadboro-Gyro Park.

③ **D'Arcy Island (Gulf Islands National Park Reserve).** Open all year. This is an undeveloped island with no facilities other than some primitive campsites and a toilet. Dogs must be on leash. The island is surrounded by intimidating rocks, reefs, and shoals. Even if you study the chart carefully, kelp-covered rocks will pop up and surprise you. Approach with great caution. As far as we are concerned, there are no "good" anchorages at D'Arcy Island, only acceptable spots in the right weather. The cove on the east side of the island has depths of 10 to 25 feet with fair holding and some protection from, west and northwest winds. The single Parks staff mooring buoy is in this cove. This cove is closest to the island's campsites and pit toilets. If conditions allow, the cove on the west side of the island, south of the light, will work. Two coves on the northwest end look okay, but we didn't put the anchor down to confirm.

D'Arcy Island was B.C.'s first leper colony; from 1891 until 1925 it housed Chinese lepers. The colony was closed in 1925 and the island reverted to provincial jurisdiction. Ruins from the colony located just south of the west side light remain. A rustic shore side trail runs from the east cove campsites around the south end of the island to the west side light. A well-marked trail cuts across the island from just south of the campsites to the colony ruins. Plans for the island as a federal penitentiary were never realized. D'Arcy Island remained undeveloped, and was established as a marine park in 1961. *A Measure of Value*, by Chris Yorath, provides a good history of D'Arcy Island. To the east, Little D'Arcy Island is private property.

④ **Sidney Spit (Gulf Islands National Park Reserve).** The park, open all summer, occupies about one-third of Sidney Island, and all of the mile-long Sidney Spit with its white sand and shell beach extending northwest from the island. The island is closed to visitors from November through February to facilitate traditional hunting by First Nations to control the fallow deer population. Anchor or tie to one of 12 mooring buoys, or moor on the seasonal dock. Anchoring depths are shallow and the area has considerable eel grass. Self-registration and payment box located at the dock. Buoys are limited to vessels of 50 feet or less in winds up to 30 knots; 40 feet for winds up to 37 knots; no mooring in large waves. In the summers, a passenger ferry runs between Sidney Spit dock and Sidney Beacon Ave dock.

Picnic and camping areas are ashore. Dogs must be on leash. An easily walked 2-km loop trail winds around the park through a dense forest of cedar, hemlock, fir, big-leaf maple and vine maple. A herd of fallow deer is reported to be on the island. A large saltwater lagoon is habitat for many animal and plant species and is off limits; markers show its borders. The remains of a brick-making factory are near the lagoon, where a beach is covered with broken red bricks.

⑤ **Isle-de-Lis at Rum Island (Gulf Islands National Park Reserve).** Open all year, anchoring only, campsites and a pit toilet. This is a small, undeveloped, and very pretty park with a walking trail and beaches. Dogs must be on leash. Rum Island is located at the east end of Gooch Island (private), where Prevost Passage meets Haro Strait. Anchorage is on either side of the gravel spit connecting Rum Island and Gooch Island. The northern anchorage is preferred. Rum Island is said to have come by its name honestly during Prohibition. In 1995 the warship HMCS *Mackenzie* was sunk in approximately 100 feet just north of Gooch Island to create an artificial reef for divers. It is marked with 2 cautionary/information buoys.

Saanichton Bay. Just off Cordova Channel between James Island and the east shore of Saanich Peninsula is Saanichton Bay. This large bay is open to the north but protected from south and west winds. Good anchoring in 15 to 30 feet with room to swing. Along the shore to the southeast is Cordova Spit Park with nice sand and gravel beaches. Most boat traffic transits Sidney Channel farther to the east so there is minimal boat wake. A large barge is normally moored in the bay but is not a factor for anchoring.

Roberts Bay. Good anchorage, centrally located about a mile from both Sidney and Tsehum Harbour. Anchor in the center of the bay where the large shallow bay gives separation from the homes lining the shore. Good holding on a flat mud bottom, but exposed to north and northeast winds. Large wakes from boats entering and exiting Tsehum Harbour occasionally find their way into the anchorage but the bay becomes settled in the evening.

THINGS TO DO

1. Butchart Gardens in Brentwood Bay. A 55-acre display of flowers and gardens. Fireworks on Saturdays in the summer. Take the bus from Victoria or visit the area by boat.

2. Shaw Ocean Discovery Centre in Sidney. Learn more about the ecosystem of the B.C. coastal waters.

3. Bookstores. Downtown Sidney has numerous bookstores, everything from books for kids to collectors. Even a haunted bookstore. See why Sidney is called Booktown.

4. Lochside Regional Trail along the waterfront. Rent bikes for this flat and easy-to-ride trail from Victoria to Sidney.

⑥ **Sidney.** For boats crossing from Roche Harbor or the northern San Juan Islands, Sidney is a natural first stop to clear customs,

GULF ISLANDS — See Area Map Page 227 - Maps Not for Navigation

Delta Marine Service

2075 Tryon Rd Sidney BC Canada V8L 3X9
Tel: 250.656.2639   Fax: 250.656.2619
Westport Marina in Tsehum Harbour

tracy@delta-marine.com   www.delta-marine.com   brian@delta-marine.com

- Marine vinyl wrapping
- Custody & provisioning
- Bright work & detailing
- Professional paint & varnish facility
- Structural & cosmetic fiberglass repair
- Custom cabinet shop
- Interior yacht design
- Full mechanical & electrical service
- Stainless steel & aluminum fabrication
- 55 ton local travel lift & 100 ton option mid island

FLEMING

GB AUTHORIZED SERVICE CENTER

PHILBROOK'S BOATYARD LTD.

Experience a HIgher Standard

WE ...
- **Do It Once**
- **Do It Right**
- **Do It On Time**
- **Do It On Budget**
- **Do It All**

Haulouts
Canvas
Mechanical
Electrical
Paint
Composites
Wood
Metal Fabrication
Mobile Service

We Guarantee It

Toll Free 1-877-656-1157
Phone 250-656-1157
Sidney, B.C. Canada
philbrooks.com • yachts@philbrooks.com

CANADIAN SERVICE AND WARRANTY
PROVIDERS FOR NORDHAVN AND SELENE

234   www.WaggonerGuide.com

See Area Map Page 227 - Maps Not for Navigation

GULF ISLANDS

stroll around, and restock with fresh produce, meat, spirits, and more. Downtown Sidney and nearby Tsehum Harbour have much to attract boaters, including excellent bakeries just up Beacon Avenue (Sidney's main street). The town also has art galleries, interesting shops, liquor stores, several bookstores, several museums, and three supermarkets. Summer concerts are held on the lawn at the base of Beacon Street. A paved walkway stretches 2.5 km along the Sidney waterfront between Port Sidney Marina and south beyond the Washington State Ferries terminal. It is part of the 29 km multi-use Lochside Regional Trail stretching from Swartz Bay to Victoria.

The Sidney Historical Museum occupies the lower floor of the old Post Office Building, at the corner of 4th and Beacon. The museum has an excellent exhibit of early history in Sidney, admission by donation. Highly recommended, especially for families. Located at the nearby Sidney airport is the BC Aviation Museum, a short cab ride away.

The Shaw Ocean Discovery Centre in the Sidney Pier building has outstanding exhibits of marine life from local waters.

For an entirely different feeling from downtown Sidney, try Tsehum Harbour, a short distance north of downtown. The pace in Tsehum Harbour is much slower, and many of the moored boats are funkier. This is where the fishing fleet moors, and where the boat yards are. Van Isle Marina is the major marina.

Something about Tsehum Harbour attracts good restaurants, too. Tsehum Harbour's only disadvantage is the long walk to major shopping. Regular bus service runs into Sidney, or you could take a taxi or rent a car. Thrifty Foods charges $5 per order for delivery.

Market: The Sidney Street Market takes over the lower part of Beacon Avenue Thursday evenings May through September, 5:30 p.m. to 8:30 p.m.

Customs: Sidney is the western terminus of the Washington State Ferries that run from Anacortes and Friday Harbor, and is a Canada Customs port of entry. Customs can be cleared by telephone at Port Sidney Marina, Van Isle Marina or Canoe Cove Marina.

Wi-Fi: Free Wi-Fi throughout town. Select Sidney Wi-Fi network and accept terms to connect.

⑥ **Port Sidney Marina**. 9835 Seaport Place, P.O. Box 2338, Sidney, BC V8L 4X3; (250) 655-3711; admin@portsidney.com; www.portsidney.com. Monitors VHF 66A. Open all year. Facilities include 30, 50 & 100 amp power, water, excellent washrooms, showers, laundry, Shaw Go Wi-Fi on the docks and free Wi-Fi in the comfortable marina lounge. This is a popular marina, modern and well-maintained, adjacent to downtown Sidney. Reservations recommended. A for-fee pumpout, located between D and E docks, accommodates boats up to 40 feet. The marina is part of the Mill Bay Marine Group, a company that owns several marinas throughout B.C.

Call on VHF 66A low power before entering and exiting the breakwater. When approaching from the north, pass between the two buoys just outside the breakwater entrance. The easternmost of these buoys marks a reef. Do not try to enter between the north end of the breakwater and shore. If you are directed to the shore side of the long, main pier, do not stray outside the marked channel.

Port Sidney Marina

Tsehum Harbour

2020 Waggoner Cruising Guide

235

CANOE COVE MARKETPLACE

RESTAURANTS, SHOPS & SERVICES

ALL THINGS MARINE THRIFT STORE
The Maritime Museum of BC has opened the marine focused thrift store which will take in donated surplus marine equipment to be sold by volunteers of the Museum. This is a great way to reuse and recycle the many extra pieces of marine equipment that most boaters gather and see them go to a good use. The MMBC will be accepting donations of saleable marine equipment and tools at their location at Canoe Cove Marina on Fridays and Saturdays.
Open Fridays and Saturdays • 250-385-4222 ext. 102
www.mmbc.bc.ca

BLACKLINE MARINE INC.
Blackline delivers industry leading service in yacht rigging, composite repair, AwlGrip paint refinishing, custom metal fabrication, and seasonal maintenance. Canoe Cove Marina has been our home since 1980, and we are proud to be an active member of this service community.
Service & Haul Outs: 250-656-6616
www.blacklinemarine.com

CANOE COVE MARINA & BOATYARD
Canoe Cove Marina has been a preferred "one-stop" full service marina for over 75 years. Commitment to customer service, ongoing upgrading of technical skills, and regular expansion of facilities, has been the hallmark of the Marina's success.
250-656-5566 • 2300 Canoe Cove Rd.
www.canoecovemarina.com

NW EXPLORATIONS
NW Explorations is a premier charter, marine service and brokerage company offering first-class customer service in all areas. Whether you want to charter a yacht or need service for your existing boat, NW Explorations can help meet your needs.
236-237-6939 • Bldg. 6 • www.nwexplorations.com

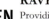

RAVEN MARINE
Providing professional yacht services to the Pacific Northwest for over 20 years. Our accredited technical teams are experienced with installations, maintenance, and repairs. Our professional brokers will provide the advice and expertise you need to make an informed decision.
250-655-3934 • info@ravenmarine.ca

See Area Map Page 227 - Maps Not for Navigation

GULF ISLANDS

The bottom has been dredged alongside the shoreside dock, but shoal water lies just a few feet inshore.

Customs: The customs check-in dock is on the end of G dock. Customs can be cleared by using the direct-line telephone on the dock. During summer months customs officers may be stationed there for inspections after calling in. Space at the dock is limited to one or two boats and once inside the breakwater maneuvering room is limited. The marina office has a video camera pointed at the dock and they can advise over the VHF if boats are waiting to clear customs.

⑥ **Sidney Beacon Ave. Public Wharf.** Sidney Beacon Avenue Public Wharf is used only for the summertime ferry to Sidney Spit Marine Park and does not have public dock space. A snack bar, café and a fresh fish market are at the end of the pier.

⑦ **Tsehum Harbour.** Tsehum Harbour (Tsehum is pronounced "See-um"), a shallow but navigable inlet about 1.5 miles north of downtown Sidney, contains a number of public, private, and yacht club moorages as well as chandleries. Enter favoring the Armstrong Point (south) side to avoid a marked rock. This is the working waterfront of Sidney, with several excellent boatyards. Van Isle Marina, the first marina on the south side, has a customs check-in telephone, fuel, and guest moorage. Westport Marina has guest moorage, and many services including haulout and free showers. Other moorages in Tsehum Harbour are North Saanich Marina, Capitol City and Sidney North Saanich yacht clubs, a Royal Victoria Yacht Club outstation, and private marinas. The main fuel dock is in Van Isle Marina. Fuel is also available at North Saanich Marina.

Speed limit: A speed limit of 4 knots is in force in Tsehum Harbour. Watch your wake.

Repairs: Haulout and complete repairs are available.

Van Isle Marina

LOCAL KNOWLEDGE

ROCKS: Stay close to the end of the dock when rounding the west end of the fuel and customs dock at Van Isle Marina. A substantial drying rock lies a short distance off, and each year a few boats manage to find it. The rock is marked by a beacon, but the rock extends toward the dock from the beacon.

⑦ **Van Isle Marina.** 2320 Harbour Road, Sidney, V8L 2P6; (250) 656-1138; info@vanislemarina.com; www.vanislemarina.com. Monitors VHF 66A. Open 7 days a week, all year. Gasoline and diesel at fuel dock, customs clearance with dedicated phones in the small shed at the end of the fuel dock, free Wi-Fi, 15, 30, 50 & 100 amp power, excellent washrooms, showers and laundry. Pumpout and launch ramp. A business center with computer connections, copy machine, fax machine, and conference room is available for marina guests. Complimentary bicycle rentals and taxi vouchers to nearby locations. Groceries can be delivered to the marina by Thrifty Foods.

A side-tie dock, 451 feet long and 15 feet wide, runs parallel to the breakwater on the east side of the marina. It is set up for yachts up to 200' and more, with 100 amp power, telephone, cable, and internet connections.

Excellence & Value in every Marina Experience.

CANADA CUSTOMS & FUEL DOCK

- 500 berths for annual, monthly or nightly moorage
- Service for boats 20' to 200'
- Fuel dock and marine store
- Canada Customs Port of Entry
- Haul outs and full repair facilities
- Yacht Park - 90 spaces for dry land storage and maintenance
- 15/30/50/100 amp shore power
- Casual dining at Sea Glass Grill
- Business centre and meeting room
- Laundry, showers and washrooms
- Yacht brokerage and sales
- Free WiFi

Situated in beautiful Tsehum Harbour by Sidney, British Columbia, Van Isle Marina is just 5 minutes from ferries, Victoria International Airport and shopping.

VAN ISLE MARINA
family owned & operated since 1955

Tsehum Harbour, Sidney, BC | 250.656.1138 | info@vanislemarina.com

vanislemarina.com

2020 Waggoner Cruising Guide

GULF ISLANDS

See Area Map Page 227 - Maps Not for Navigation

Large boat or small, it's best to call ahead for guest moorage availability.

Van Isle is a large and busy marina, about a mile from downtown. Full repair services, haulout to 45 tons, and dry storage are available. The Thrifty Foods in Sidney will deliver groceries to the marina. The Sea Glass Waterfront Grill is at the head of the dock, call (778) 351-3663 for reservations. The famous Latch Country Inn Restaurant is a short walk away. The marina offers bicycles at no charge to ride into Sidney or on the popular Lochside Trail, nearby.

Since 1955 Van Isle Marina has been owned and managed by three generations of the Dickinson family. The family's long-term commitment to doing things right is evident. The staff is excellent, and the facilities are top-notch.

⑦ **Tsehum Harbour Public Wharf.** (250) 655-4496. Open all year, 1043 feet of dock space, 20 & 30 amp power, washrooms, shower, Wi-Fi available at the office. This is a commercial fish boat harbor that accepts very limited guest moorage. Call in advance for availability. Fresh fish for sale.

⑦ **Westport Marina.** 2075 Tryon Road, Sidney, BC V8L 3X9; (250) 656-2832; westport@thunderbirdmarine.com; www.thunderbirdmarine.com. Open all year. 15, 20, 30 & 50 amp power, washrooms, free showers, Wi-Fi. Guest moorage in unoccupied slips, call ahead for availability. Haulout to 55 tons. Well stocked chandlery, charts, limited groceries.

⑦ **North Saanich Marina.** 1949 Marina Way, North Saanich, BC V8L 6B3; (250) 656-5558; nsm@obmg.com; www.northsaanichmarina.com. VHF 66A. Open all year. Gasoline and diesel at the fuel dock, not always attended. Wi-Fi. Washrooms at the main office. Permanent and guest moorage usually available for vessels to 70 feet; 15, 30 & 50 amp power. Recent dock refurbishments, and a large dog walking area. It's a short taxi ride to the nearby town of Sidney. Store carries sundries, fishing tackle, boat cleaning supplies, and ice. Call ahead for moorage availability. Home of the Sidney North Saanich Yacht Club, with reciprocal moorage. The marina is part of the Oak Bay Marine Group, a company that owns several marinas on Vancouver Island.

⑧ **Canoe Bay.** Canoe Bay, commonly called Canoe Cove, is tucked in behind a group of islands, only some of which have navigable passages between them. The clearest passage is **John Passage**, along the west side of Coal Island. From John Passage turn west into **Iroquois Passage**, and follow Iroquois Passage between Fernie Island and Goudge Island into Canoe Bay.

Page Passage should be run only with local knowledge or close study of large-scale Chart 3479. Tidal currents can run strongly, especially on spring tides.

⑧ **Canoe Cove Marina & Boatyard.** 2300 Canoe Cove Road, North Saanich, BC V8L 3X9; (250) 656-5566; (250) 656-5515; www.canoecovemarina.com. Monitors VHF 66A. Open all year, gasoline, diesel, propane at fuel dock, 30 & 50 amp power, washrooms, showers, laundry, 24-hour customs clearance at fuel dock, free Wi-Fi. This is a 450-berth marina with permanent and visitor moorage. Best to call ahead.

Navigate carefully on approach. A number of islands and rocks surround the entrance to Canoe Cove. They are well marked on the charts and easily avoided as long as you pay attention.

Porto Osteria Bakery & Cafe is in the center of the marina, and the excellent Stonehouse Restaurant is nearby. A short trail leads to the Swartz Bay ferry terminal for arriving or departing guests from Tsawwassen, on the B.C. mainland. A harbor taxi shuttle connects the marina with Sidney. Pacifica Paddle Sports (250) 665-7411 at Canoe Cove offers kayak, canoe, and paddleboard rentals along with lessons and tours.

Canoe Cove's major thrust is its environmentally friendly full repair facility, with an 83-ton Travelift, and extensive work areas. Two chandleries are nearby. The staff and management are friendly and competent. Together with Vector Marine, Blackline Marine, Raven Marine, Sea Power Marine Centre, Jespersen Boat Builders, Reyse Marine, and Lightship Marine Mobile, they can do anything.

Customs: The customs clearance dock is located on the fuel dock pier.

Swartz Bay Public Wharf. Open all year, adjacent to the ferry terminal, with 85 feet of dock space. No facilities. Watch for heavy ferry traffic near Swartz Bay.

Westport Marina

Canoe Cove Marina

www.WaggonerGuide.com

Piers Island Public Wharf. Open all year with 200 feet of dock space, no facilities.

⑨ Portland Island (Gulf Islands National Park Reserve). Formerly Princess Margaret Provincial Marine Park. Open all year, picnic and campsites, toilets, no other facilities. Dogs must be on leash and cleaned up after. In honor of her last visit to Victoria, Portland Island was donated to Her Royal Highness Princess Margaret, who later deeded the island to British Columbia. The park is now part of the Gulf Islands National Park Reserve.

Portland Island is wooded and hilly. Hiking trails follow the coastline. Easy-walking service roads and trails crisscross the center of the island. It would be easy to spend an entire day exploring. Reader Tyson Nevil says the coastline trail is easier to follow when walking in a counter-clockwise direction.

Anchor in Royal Cove (behind Chads Island) on the north side of the island, or in Princess Bay, behind Tortoise Island on the south side. The Royal Cove anchorage is exposed to the wakes of passing BC ferries, and Princess Bay also receives wakes. At Royal Cove you can have a quiet night if you can get well inside. Three red marked stern-tie rings are along the northeast shore in Royal Cove.

There's room for a couple of boats behind Brackman Island, off the southwest corner of Portland Island. Watch your depths at low tide. Brackman Island is a protected wildlife and bird sanctuary. No access is allowed above the high tide line and no pets are allowed.

Princess Bay is roomier and far more popular, but somewhat exposed to southerly winds. In summer it's usually fine. With its shallow depths, not much anchor rode need be paid out, and the boats squeeze in pretty tightly. Watch your depths as you approach the head of Princess Bay. The bottom shoals rapidly, farther from shore than you might expect. Dinghy docks in Royal Cove and Princess Bay provide shore access.

The host float in Princess Bay is staffed by yacht club volunteers during the summer. They answer questions and give out information.

The *G.B. Church*, a sunken freighter off the southwest shore of the island, is an artificial reef for divers. The freighter lies in 100 feet and is marked with bow and stern buoys.

PLUMPER SOUND AREA

Bedwell Harbour. Bedwell Harbour is home to Poets Cove, a luxury marina resort. North of the resort, anchorage is good (except in a southeasterly) off Beaumont Marine Park. Anchorage is also good in Peter Cove, on the west side of the harbour.

Anchorage is possible off Medicine Beach on the northwest side of Bedwell Harbour. A Nature Preserve is located next to the beach, and a short loop-trail on the bluff afords nice views. About 500 yards up the road from the beach is the adorable Slow Coast Coffee shop and Penderosa Pizza, along with a convenience store.

Customs clearance: The Canada Border Services Agency (Canada Customs) dock is adjacent to Poets Cove Marina and well marked. The customs dock was expanded in 2019 with ample side-tie moorage around a U-shape. The far end of the U is the seaplane dock. Open from May 1 to September 30. Except when landing your vessel, only the skipper can leave the boat until customs is cleared. The procedure is for the captain to go up the ramp to the direct-line telephones along the wall of the customs office. Have all of the vessel's paperwork and crew's passport information ready. Call in for clearance. In most cases the agent on the telephone will give you a clearance number, but you may be asked to standby for agents to inspect your

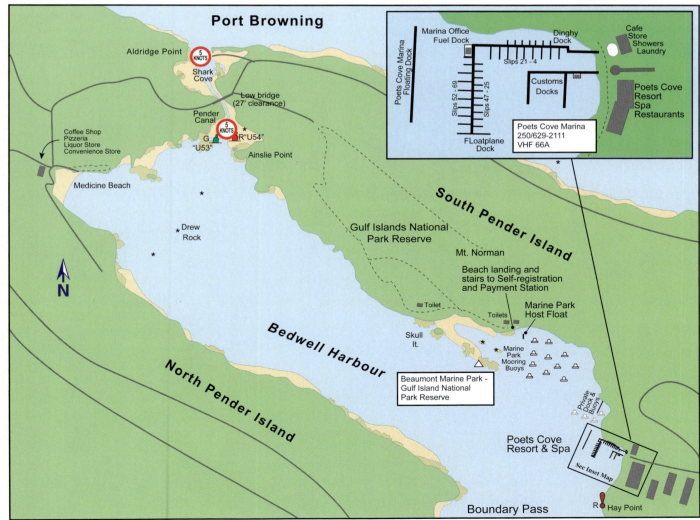

Bedwell Harbour

GULF ISLANDS　　　See Area Map Page 227 - Maps Not for Navigation

The large swimming pool at Port Browning is a hit with the kids.

vessel. Canpass or Nexus permits only from October 1 through April 30. See the U.S. and Canadian Customs Information section for more information on clearing Canadian Customs.

Peter Cove. Peter Cove is at the southern tip of North Pender Island. It is a well protected little anchorage, but permanently moored boats make anchoring a bit tight. A significant reef guards the mouth of the cove. Enter and depart north of the reef.

⑩ Poets Cove Marina. 9801 Spalding Road, RR #3, South Pender Island, BC V0N 2M3; (250) 629-2100; (250) 629-2111 marina; marina@poetscove.com; www.poetscove. com. Open all year, gasoline, diesel, and ice at the fuel dock. Guest moorage to 100 feet in 95 slips and side-tie; 30 amp power. Reservations recommended. If slips are filled, a floating dock is available at a reduced rate. Liquor store, cafe, pub with dining, heated pool, hot tub, spa, Eucalyptus Steam Cave, fitness center, and free Wi-Fi. Day passes for the pool are available for guests who anchor out. Coin-operated laundry machines are located adjacent to the pool.

The casual Moorings Cafe is located in the building adjacent to the pool and serves sandwiches, espresso, and baked goods. The cafe also sells liquor and convenience items. Syrens Bistro and Lounge, open April through October, serves lunch and dinner noon to 9:00 p.m. and has seating indoors or out on the patio. Aurora, a fine dining venue, serves breakfast and dinner, open seasonally.

Poets Cove has plenty of activities. Rent a bike, SUP, or kayak and explore the island; play a round of golf, or try out the disc golf course.

Beaumont Marine Park (Gulf Islands National Park Reserve). In Bedwell Harbour, west side of South Pender Island, in Bedwell Harbour. Open all year. Facilities include 15 mooring buoys. Pay buoy fees at the honor box above the staircase at the beach, northwest of the buoys, no charge before 3:00 p.m. Mooring buoys accommodate boats up to 50 feet, or 40 feet depending upon wind conditions. Signage for size limits are posted on the buoys. Toilets, no showers or fresh water. Walk-in campsites, picnicking, excellent walking and hiking trails. Hike to the top of Mount Norman, elevation 800 feet, for a memorable view. Dogs must be on leash.

Enter from Swanson Channel from the south, or from Plumper Sound and Port Browning through Pender Canal (27-foot clearance).

Pender Canal. Pender Canal is a man-made dogleg channel between North Pender Island and South Pender Island, connecting Bedwell Harbour and Port Browning. The canal is crossed by a bridge with 27 feet of vertical clearance. Pender Canal is narrow, shallow, and often has a swift current running

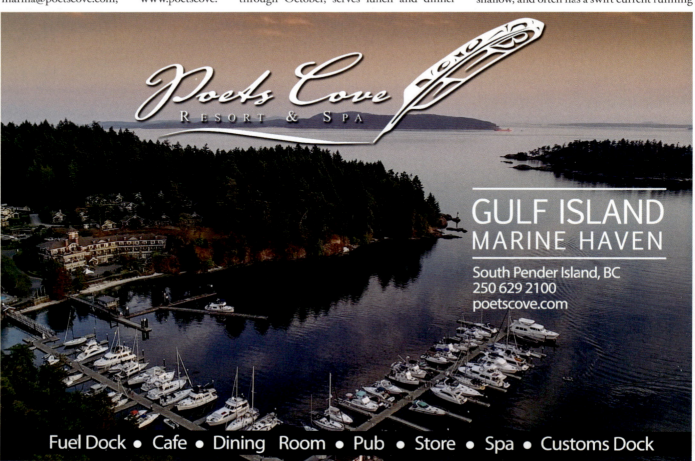

through it. Because of its dogleg shape, vessels approaching from opposite directions cannot see each other until they are in the narrowest section.

Before entering, broadcast your intentions on VHF 16, low power: *Securite, Securite, this is the 34-foot motor vessel Happy Days, northbound from Bedwell Harbour to Port Browning. Any concerned traffic please advise, channel one-six.*

⑪ **Port Browning.** Port Browning has a resort (Port Browning Marina) with moorage and other facilities. Anchorage is good throughout the harbor. The Driftwood Centre shopping area is about a half-mile walk from the marina or you can call the Pender Island Cab at (250) 629-2222. The Center has a well-stocked Tru-Value Foods, a bank, clothing shop, gift shop, book store, bakery, cafe, and liquor store. Tru-Value Foods will give you a ride back to the marina with purchases of $25 or more. The gas station at the Center carries marine supplies. Dog owners will love the outdoor complimentary dog wash facility at Driftwood Center.

The Nosy Point B&B, a grand old Victorian home, is just up the road from the marina. The award winning Sea Star Vineyards Winery (250-629-6960) is 1.4 miles (2.25 km) northeast of Port Browning Marina. Check the website at seastarvineyards.ca for wine tasting hours and special events. The marina provides transportation to the winery for a nominal fee during the peak season. The Twin Island Cider Co. is along the way, at the corner of Razor Point Rd. and Lupin Road; cider tastings are available Wednesday through Sunday during the sunmmner months, hours vary during the off-season.

⑪ **Port Browning Marina.** P.O. Box 126, North Pender Island, BC V0N 2M0; (250) 629-3493; contact@portbrowning.ca; www.portbrowning.ca. Monitors VHF 66A. Canpass/Nexus-only reporting station. Open all year, 3000 feet of guest moorage; 30 amp power, with 50 amp on the new 150-foot "hammerhead" end-tie dock. The main dock and several piers were replaced in 2019. A 300-foot wave-attenuator was added at the entrance to the marina, immediately west of red buoy U52, which marks shoaling and rocks; favor the wave-attenuator side of the channel when entering the marina. Free Wi-Fi, ATM, excellent washrooms, laundry, and launch ramp. Seasonal swimming pool; beer & wine sales. Kayak and SUP rentals through Pender Island Kayak Adventures (250-629-6939).

Port Browning Marina offers two dining venues: the licensed family Port Browning Pub (open daily, year-round), with large picture windows facing the bay; and the newly built Bridgemans Bistro, a multi-use space, that is open for all ages. Restaurant service is offered at Bridgemans on the weekends during the summer months. On other days of the week, the Bridgemans venue serves as The Kraken Theatre, showing classic movies as scheduled; see thekrakentheatre.com for the latest showings. The Bridgemans venue can be booked for rendezvous dinners for up to 100 people. Port Browning Marina is part of the Mill Bay Marine Group of properties.

Browning Harbour Public Wharf. Open all year, 89 feet of dock space, no facilities. Commercial fish boats have priority.

Shingle Bay (Gulf Islands National Park Reserve). This is a recent addition to the Gulf Islands National Park Reserve. Open all year, picnic tables, campsites, composting toilets. Dogs must be on leash and cleaned up after. See the remnants of the Shingle Bay fish reduction plant that operated intermittently between 1927 and 1959. It served as an important part of the local economy, employing 15 to 20 men at a time, mainly Pender Island residents.

Because the bay shoals rapidly, you must anchor well out, in line with the old reduction plant. Favor the north side, as a reef extends on the south. Anchorage is exposed to the southwest. The community park at the head of the bay is a welcome place to walk dogs, picnic, and access the island. A jungle gym is popular with children.

⑫ **Otter Bay Marina.** 2311 McKinnon Rd., North Pender Island, BC V0N 2M1; (250) 629-3579; info@otterbaymarina.ca; www.otterbaymarina.ca. Monitors VHF 66A. Online reservations highly recommended during the peak season. Side-tie and slip moorage open all year, full services May 15 to November 30. Four mooring buoys located in the bay south of the marina are used for guest moorage, contact the marina. Washrooms, showers, laundry; 15 & 30 amp power, 50 amp power on "A" dock. Launch ramp, gazebo, café, two heated pools, and free Wi-Fi. Scooters, kayaks and SUP rentals. This popular marina is on the west side of North Pender Island facing Swanson Channel; look for the tall flagpoles on the observation deck just past the ferry landing. The marina grounds are lovely and have a resort feel.

The upper family pool and lower adult pool are open mid-May through Labor Day. The small convenience store carries baked goods,

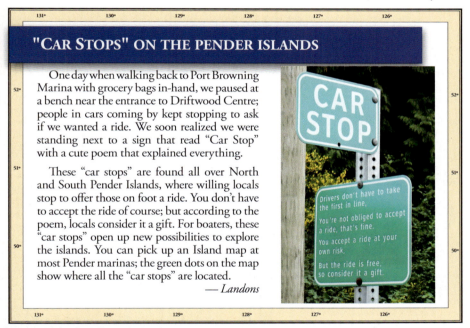

"CAR STOPS" ON THE PENDER ISLANDS

One day when walking back to Port Browning Marina with grocery bags in-hand, we paused at a bench near the entrance to Driftwood Centre; people in cars coming by kept stopping to ask if we wanted a ride. We soon realized we were standing next to a sign that read "Car Stop" with a cute poem that explained everything.

These "car stops" are found all over North and South Pender Islands, where willing locals stop to offer those on foot a ride. You don't have to accept the ride of course; but according to the poem, locals consider it a gift. For boaters, these "car stops" open up new possibilities to explore the islands. You can pick up an Island map at most Pender marinas; the green dots on the map show where all the "car stops" are located.

— Landons

Port Browning

GULF ISLANDS   See Area Map Page 227 - Maps Not for Navigation

Hope Bay Public Wharf

prepared foods, ice, and espresso. Daily breakfast specials are offered at the espresso bar; milkshakes, smoothies and lunch items in the afternoon. Two courtesy barbeques are available for small groups or social cooking. Many semi-private seating areas are located along the walkways among the colorful flower beds in the park-like grounds. A daily or weekly day camp is offered for children through Dog Mermaid Eco Excursions (250-222-0015).

An enclosed activity center, with a stone fireplace, is a nice venue for group events and rendezvous, even in the off-season. For a short excursion, take the dinghy across the bay to Roe Islet/Roesland National Park, a lovely spot to stretch the legs. The 9-hole Pender Island Golf Course is about a 15-minute walk from the marina. Tee times are recommended but not required. The marina provides a golf course shuttle service for a small fee. El Faro Restaurant (250-951-6224) is located at the golf course.

Caution: A green spar buoy is off the corner of the marina docks. Red, Right, Returning means you leave this buoy to port as you enter. Do not pass between the buoy and the dock. A rock 2 feet below the surface at zero tide lurks between the buoy and the dock.

Roesland/Roe Lake (Gulf Islands National Park Reserve). Located on North Pender Island, deep in Otter Bay. Field Correspondent Deane Hislop reports: "We set the anchor, good holding, and took the dinghy to the park's dinghy dock. We discovered a former 1908 farmhouse that now serves as the Pender Island Museum, offering a glimpse into the island's past. This is also the location of Parks Canada's field office. We took the short walk to the end of Roe Islet to take in an amazing view of Swanson Channel, Saltspring Island, and Vancouver Island. Then it was back along the islet and up Shingle Bay road to the Roe Lake trail head and through the forest to beautiful Roe Lake, making for a full day of hiking and exploring."

Port Washington Public Wharf. On North Pender Island. Open all year, 147 feet of dock space on two floats. The northwest float is for transient boats, the portion marked in yellow is a 15-minute load/unload area; eastern float appears to be assigned, permanent moorage. Floats are subject to boat wakes from Swanson Channel. No facilities ashore. Watch for a rock off the southeast dock. One float is designated for aircraft.

⑬ **Hope Bay Public Wharf.** (250) 813-3321 Wharfinger. East side of North Pender Island, facing Navy Channel. Open all year, 150 feet of dock space, and one or two day-use mooring buoys marked "Hope Bay Store." Transient moorage is limited to approximately 45 feet located on the outside, southeast end of the dock; other spaces are permanent moorage only. No power, no water. Restrooms available in the building on the pier during business hours. If the dock is full (it often is), tie to a mooring buoy or anchor in 30 to 35 feet with good holding over a mud bottom, and dinghy in. Wakes from passing ferries make rafting undesirable, and depths on the inside of the dock are shallow at low tide. Peter, at the upland Goldsmith & Clock shop, is the wharfinger.

Otter Bay Marina

242   www.WaggonerGuide.com

GULF ISLANDS

This historic landing has attractive buildings on the pier which house a number of small businesses, including the Gather Teahouse, the Pender Chocolates shop, the Pender Island Veterinary Clinic (250) 629-9909, Dockside Realty, and Blessings dress and gift shop. Gather Teahouse Eatery & Stage (250) 629-3923, which opened in Spring 2019, features farm-to-table dishes for lunch, along with specialty teas, coffee, and baked goods. In-house entertainment held on Thursdays, and outdoor concerts on Saturdays during the summer months. Tickets required for Saturday concerts.

Breezy Bay – Sea Star Vineyards. (250) 629-6960; www.seastarvineyards.ca. (Formerly the Saturna Winery.) At press time, new owners of the vineyards have not re-opened the winery or bistro. The dock is closed for repairs, and boaters are not to dock or walk the grounds. The owners are working towards re-opening the vineyard grounds, with a bistro, in the near future.

Irish Bay. Irish Bay, on the west side of Samuel Island, is a good anchorage with scenic rock walls, but the island is privately owned. If you venture above the foreshore, the caretaker will shoo you off.

Winter Cove. A Gulf Islands National Park Reserve. Winter Cove, between Samuel Island and Saturna Island, has an attractive park on the Saturna Island side, and shallow anchorage. We think the best anchorages are behind Winter Point, north of the cable line, or just off the National Park Reserve lands. The charts show shallow water in the middle of the cove, but you can patrol around—carefully—with the depth sounder and find anchoring sites away from the preferred spots. The mooring buoys in the southwest corner of the cove are private. A public dinghy dock is on the eastern shore. It has been reported that a sunken boat lies in the middle of Winter Cove.

Minx Reef partially blocks the Plumper Sound approach to Winter Cove. Entering, we have found the best way to avoid the reef is to point the bow at the northern shore of Irish Bay, and run well past Winter Point before turning south into the cove.

The annual Canada Day (July 1) Saturna Island Lamb Barbecue at Winter Cove is a big event. The cove is packed with boats; islanders shuttle visitors ashore and back. For more information go to www.saturnalambbarbeque.com.

The annual Saturna Lions Club Dog & Dogs Show is in early September. Prizes for best dog and owner look-alike, best puppy, best tail-wagger, and more. Bribes encouraged. Correspondents Bruce and Margaret Evertz happened upon the show and say it's wonderful. Bring your dog. For information see www.saturnalionsclub.net.

Boat Pass. Boat Pass connects Winter Cove with the Strait of Georgia. Currents in Boat Pass can run to 7 knots past several nasty rocks and reefs. Take this pass only at or near high water slack, preferably after seeing it at low water so you know where the rocks are.

⑭ **Lyall Harbour.** www.saturnatourism.com Lyall Harbour, on Saturna Island, is a large, well protected anchorage, with a ferry landing and store near the entrance. Nearby **Boot Cove** is a beautiful spot with anchorage in 12 to 18 feet, but it is crowded with resident boats on mooring buoys, and can be subject to williwaws blowing over a low swale on Saturna Island.

Lyall Harbour is off the beaten path for the Gulf Islands. It is quiet and gradually being discovered. Your choice, anchor in the bay or tie at the dock. Nothing fancy. This is not Ganges. The Lighthouse Pub, located upland, has very good food with fish and chips being their signature item, though some say their lamb burger is to die for. Lamb

---

Gather Teahouse Eatery & Stage

"Join us as we gather at the crossroads of hands and hearts," that is Matthew & Sherry Des Roches' motto, owners of the Gather Teahouse Eatery & Stage at Hope Bay. They have successfully created the right combination of entertainment and organic eats that draw locals and visitors alike to this unique venue.

Outdoor concerts in the courtyard are held on Saturdays during the summer months, advanced tickets required. Popular bands, playing a variety of genre, often draw 200 patrons from around the Gulf Islands. The Masimba Marimba band, which plays upbeat African music inspired by the culture of Zimbabwe, is just one example. Free live music is scheduled on Thursdays inside the Eatery and is a special treat, while enjoying the relaxed atmosphere over lunch.

Located at the Hope Bay Public Wharf, the Gather Teahouse Eatery is a perfect place for boaters to stop for lunch. Vessels can tie on the outside of the wharf as space allows, or anchor out in settled weather. A guest buoy, suitable for boats up to 38 feet, is available while visiting Hope Bay. The Gather Eatery is open from 11 a.m. to 3 p.m., Thursday through Monday, offering farm-to-table eats and specialty teas. A working relationship with local farms just down the road, supply this Eatery with the best local produce and seafood. There's nothing better than the taste of fresh lettuce and vegetables from the garden. The "Galaxy Bowl" is a

wonderful combination of seasonal vegetables and greens with organic brown rice topped with a nutritional yeast vinaigrette dressing; or try the Lightkeepers Seafood Chowder, a traditional 50's recipe from those who lived and tended west coast lighthouse stations. It's a grandfather's recipe from the staff at Gather and includes a cream base with pacific white shrimp, wild pacific cod, sole and local root vegetables served with local artisan bread and butter, ooh so good.

Don't forget to try their iced teas or warm tea lattes, perhaps the "Hope Bay Fog," an earl grey tea latte infused with loose-leaf tea, providing its own natural sweet flavor. Their small gift shop carries over 30 organic and fresh loose-leaf teas, along with packaged espresso coffee, and local craft beer and ciders that you can take back to the boat.

GULF ISLANDS

See Area Map Page 227 - Maps Not for Navigation

Great views of Plumper Sound from Lighthouse Pub at Lyall Harbour.

carries a special reverence on Saturna Island. Dine inside or out on the deck. The beer is cold and the drink menu is imaginative and available by the drink or by the pitcher. You get the idea. The people are very nice. They say hello. They like your business. The Pub is family friendly.

You can rent bicycles at Saturna Cycle (250-857-4102) upland from the wharf. For an interesting island ride, visit the Saturna General Store & Freight (250-539-2936), a 2.5km ride. Kayaks are for rent from the Saturna Paddle Shack (250-539-5553) located on the dock. An Outdoor Market is open seasonally on Saturdays in the store parking lot from 10:00 a.m. to 1:00 p.m.

⑭ **Lyall Harbour Public Wharf.** (250) 537-7293 wharfinger. Next to the ferry dock. Open all year, 200 feet of dock space. No power, no water. Showers and restrooms are located at the campground ¼ mile up the road from the wharf. Gasoline and diesel are available at the head of the wharf, and can be taken in 15-gallon jerry cans to the dock. Pay for fuel at the Saturna Cycle shop, just above the dock. Moorage is collected at the honor box at the top of the dock. Note, there are day rates and overnight rates.

Floatplanes arrive three times per day from the Vancouver airport for your guests. Two "glamping tents" are available for rent, which overlook the harbour in a beautiful treed setting. Check in at the Saturna Cycle shop.

Georgeson Passage. Georgeson Passage, between Mayne Island and Samuel Island, is short and pretty. Currents, based on Active Pass, are about half as strong as those in Active Pass, both flooding and ebbing. Still, they run vigorously. See the Georgeson Passage secondary station under Active Pass in the Tide & Current Tables Vol. 5, and Ports and Passes. If entering from the Strait of Georgia through the narrow pass between Campbell Point and Georgeson Island, be aware that a drying reef extends from Campbell Point into the pass. Favor the Georgeson Island side. Watch for rapids.

⑮ **Horton Bay.** The public wharf is a Canpass/Nexus-only customs reporting station, and has room for a dozen 30-foot boats, plus rafting. Entering the area between Mayne and Samuel Islands requires some care but is completely navigable.

From the Gulf Islands side, the best route is through Georgeson Passage, east of Lizard Island. Be careful of a kelp-covered rock in less than 6 feet, fairly close to Mayne Island. If entering west of Lizard Island, the rock is in the middle of your path into Horton Bay. A reef extends from Curlew Island into Robson Passage, which separates Curlew Island from Mayne Island. Use Plans Chart 3477 (larger scale, much recommended) or 3442. A study of Chart 3477 shows a mid-channel course is called for. The bay is filled with crab pots and private mooring buoys in the best part of

---

WHALE WISE - GULF ISLANDS

Southern Resident Killer Whales

In 2019, the Canadian government enacted new measures to protect Southern Resident Killer Whales (SRKW) in Critical Habitat areas of BC waters. Critical Habitat BC waters include the southern Strait of Georgia, the southeast portion of the Gulf Islands, Boundary Pass, Haro Strait, Strait of Juan de Fuca, and offshore from West Coast Vancouver Island up to Tofino. See the *Whale Wise* section in Chapter 1 for a map of these SRKW areas.

- Three (3) Interim Sanctuary Zones have been established where general vessel traffic is prohibited from June 1 – October 31. Vessel traffic is not allowed in these three areas: a) off the southwest shore of North Pender Island; b) off the southeast end of Saturna Island; and c) Swiftsure Bank at the east entrance to Strait of Juan de Fuca.
- A 400-meter approach distance has been established for recreational vessels and most commercial whale watching operators. Vessels must remain at least 400 meters from all killer whales when in Southern Resident Killer Whale Critical Habitat areas. Some exceptions will be permitted for commercial whale watch operators viewing Transient or Biggs killer whales.
- Three "Enhanced Management Areas" have been established (Frasier River mouth, waters around Pender Islands of the southern Gulf Islands, and Strait of Juan de Fuca) where all vessels are asked to reduce their speed to less than 7 knots when within 1 km of killer whales.

Yellow Areas are Interim Sanctuary Zones

- When safe to do so, vessel operators are asked to turn off their echo sounders and turn engines to neutral idle if a whale is within 400 meters.
- All vessels are being asked to voluntarily slow to reduce noise in Boundary Pass and Haro Strait. This applies to all classes of vessels, including large commercial ships.

Marine Mammals & All Whales

Existing Canada regulations protect all marine mammals in BC waters. Give dolphins, porpoises, sea lions, seals, and other marine mammals the space they need. Coming too close can cause them stress and to abandon their young.

- Stay 100 yards from non-killer whales, dolphins, porpoises, and other marine mammals, and 200 yards if they are resting or with young.

GULF ISLANDS

Busy Active Pass, connecting Trincomali Channel with Strait of Georgia, is aptly named.

ACTIVE PASS AREA

Active Pass. Active Pass separates Mayne Island and Galiano Island, and has long been one of the most popular fishing areas in the Gulf Islands. It also is the route taken by commercial traffic, including BC Ferries that run between Tsawwassen and Swartz Bay. Currents in Active Pass run to 7 knots on a spring tide. They flood eastward toward the Strait of Georgia. See the Tide and Current Tables Vol. 5, or Ports and Passes. Unless your boat is quite fast, slack water passage is recommended. If you are in the current, you can minimize turbulence by favoring Miners Bay.

Dinner Bay. Dinner Bay, between Crane Point and Dinner Point, looks to be a good anchorage, but is exposed to ferry wakes and northwest winds.

Village Bay. Village Bay is wide and deep, with convenient anchoring depths near the head. The bay is open to northwest winds and waves, but well protected from everything else. Village Bay has a ferry terminal.

⑱ **Miners Bay.** Capital Regional District (250) 539-3092 or (604) 765-3069; Neil Jensen is the wharfinger. The public wharf is located on the south side of Active Pass, and is subject to swirling tidal currents and wakes from passing ferries. A float is on each side of the wharf, best suited for smaller boats. Convenient anchoring depths are close to shore—most of the bay is quite deep.

A bakery, inn, pub, and two grocery stores are up the hill from the wharf. A small museum on Fernhill Road covers the history of this area with indoor and outdoor exhibits. Across from the museum, on Saturday mornings, from 10:00 a.m. - 1:00 p.m., the Mayne Island Farmers Market, has local produce, handicrafts, baked goods, and art work. Beginning in the 1800s, this was a popular stop for miners on their way to the gold mines. The Springwater Lodge (250-539-5521), built in 1892, overlooks the bay. It remains the oldest continuously operated hotel in British Columbia.

Customs: Miners Bay wharf is a Canpass/Nexus-only customs reporting station.

⑱ **Active Pass Auto & Marine.** (250) 539-5411. Open all year. Propane, stove alcohol, tackle, bait, ice, snacks, ice cream, marine supplies, haulout, 24-hour towing and moped and bicycle rentals. Located at the service station 200 yards from the dock.

⑲ **Sturdies Bay.** Sturdies Bay, on Galiano Island toward the eastern end of Active Pass, is a landing for ferries coming to and from Tsawwassen and continuing on to the other Gulf Islands. A public float is alongside the ferry dock. The community of Sturdies Bay, just up the road, has a grocery store and shops. Galiano Oceanfront Inn & Spa is south of the ferry landing with its own dock.

the bay. We have received reports of current running through the bay.

⑯ **Reef Harbour (Gulf Islands National Park Reserve).** Reef Harbour, along with nearby Cabbage Island and Tumbo Island constitute a marine park. The park is open all year, 10 mooring buoys, pit toilets, no water, no showers. Dogs must be on leash. Caution, some buoys are close together, watch swinging space. No rafting on the buoys. Maximum vessel size: 50 ft for winds 30 knots or less; and 40 ft for winds of 37 knots or less. This is a pretty anchorage between Cabbage Island and Tumbo Island, out on the edge of the Strait of Georgia. Caution for rocks and reefs on the approaches. From west northwest, approach between two long reefs. Approaching from south, cross the reef on the Tumbo Channel side, between two patches of kelp, a short distance from the north tip of Tumbo Island. This should show 30 feet under the keel all the way across. Chart 3441 shows good depths at that location. Field Correspondent Jim Norris noted a gentle swell in the anchorage in settled weather but notes that it might be a lumpy anchorage in northwest winds at high tide when the protective reefs around Cabbage Island are submerged.

Cabbage Island has picnic sites, campsites, and a wonderful sandy beach. Crabbing is reportedly good. Cabbage Island is interesting to explore. It isn't very big, so you can walk around the entire island in a reasonable time. Though tiny, the island is hardly dull. The beaches are different on every side, ranging from white sand, to sandstone reefs, to an aggregate of small rocks embedded in sandstone, to fine gravel. Inland, you'll find forests of Arbutus (madrona), Garry oak and western red cedar.

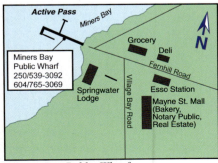
Miners Bay Public Wharf

Tumbo Island, privately owned until recently, is now part of the Gulf Islands National Park Reserve. Trails lead through the island where you will find remnants of the island's commercial past in the forests and fields. Coal mining was attempted in the early 1900s, but the shafts flooded and the effort was abandoned. In the 1920s and 1930s foxes were raised on the island. The original fox farm homestead, on the flatter northeast end of the island, can still be seen. Field Correspondent Jim Norris reports good access to the trailhead just opposite mooring buoys 3 and 4, where you will find an information kiosk, map, and a rope to help climb up the smooth rock face. The landowner who sold Tumbo Island to the reserve has a life tenancy for the house and a small area surrounding the house located on the northeast end of the island. If someone is in residence there, please respect their privacy.

⑰ **Narvaez Bay (Gulf Islands National Park Reserve).** Picnic tables and toilet, camping in 7 sites, ideal for kayakers. Dogs must be on leash. Beautiful Narvaez Bay indents the rock cliffs on the south shore of Saturna Island, and is open to southeasterly winds and the wakes of passing ship traffic in Boundary Pass. Parts of the bay's shoreline were added to the Gulf Islands National Park Reserve, including the small peninsula parallel to the western shore, a short distance in.

You can anchor in the little bight behind this peninsula and have shelter from wind and waves, although a reader wrote that in a northerly, they experienced williwaw winds of 20+ knots from the head of the bay. The wind in the Strait of Georgia was only 12 knots. The holding ground is not very good. It appears to be loose mud, the kind that washes off easily. It felt like a thin layer on top of rock—fine for a picnic in settled weather, but chancy for overnight.

The neck of land separating the peninsula from the rest of Saturna Island holds the ruins of an ambitious homestead. We didn't find any buildings, although fruit trees and the remnants of fences are there. A dirt service road runs the length of the peninsula and leads up the hill to a main Saturna Island road.

2020 Waggoner Cruising Guide

GULF ISLANDS

See Area Map Page 227 - Maps Not for Navigation

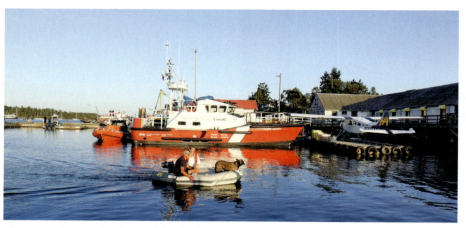

Ganges Harbour on Salt Spring Island is home to a contingent of the Coast Guard.

Sturdies Bay is a convenient stop to exchange crew arriving from or departing to the mainland on the BC Ferries. They can disembark the ferry, walk across to the provincial dock, and board the boat.

⑲ **Galiano Oceanfront Inn & Spa.** 134 Madrona Drive, Galiano Island, BC V0N 1P0; (250) 539-3388; info@galianoinn.com; www.galianoinn.com. Located in Sturdies Bay, north of the ferry landing. Open all year but dock in place May to October only, call for exact dates. Wi-Fi, but no power or water on the dock. The dock is subject to wakes from passing ferries in Active Pass. Set fenders accordingly. Reasonable dock rates; free if using spa, restaurant, or inn. Suites were renovated in late 2018.

This is a high-quality inn and spa, with casual fine dining, natural spa, and gardens. Pizza from a wood-fired oven is served for lunch and early dinner from a pizza terrace overlooking the bay (seasonal). Village shops are a block away with more choices for dining, shopping and liquor store. Smart cars are available for rental (inquire in advance). If you're in Montague Harbour and want to dine at Atrevida Restaurant at the Inn, or have spa treatments, call for pick-up and reservations, (250) 539-3388.

The Kunamokst Mural from the 2010 Olympic games is displayed in the lobby of the Inn. The mural is made from individual tiles, each independently illustrated by a different artist. Collectively they form an image of an orca whale and calf. It's quite striking.

Whaler Bay. Whaler Bay is on the east side of Galiano Island, just north of Active Pass. It is full of rocks and shoal water. Enter carefully through a rock-strewn passage from the south, or through a more open passage around the north end of Gossip Island. Whaler Bay has a public wharf. Good protection is near the wharf, but there's very little swinging room.

Whaler Bay Public Wharf. (250) 539-2264. Open all year, 350 feet of dock space, no facilities. Commercial fish boats have priority.

MAYNE ISLAND, CAMPBELL BAY TO HORTON BAY

Campbell Bay. Campbell Bay, on the northeast side of Mayne Island, is entered between Edith Point and Campbell Point. It is open to southeasterly winds, but has anchoring depths near the head, mud bottom.

Bennett Bay (Gulf Islands National Park Reserve). Bennett Bay, south of Campbell Point, has good anchorage but is exposed to southeast winds. Curlew Island and Samuel Island are privately owned.

Note: Campbell Point, a portion of the waters of Bennett Bay, Georgeson Island, and the Belle Chain Islets including Anniversary Island, are part of Gulf Islands National Park Reserve. To protect sensitive ecosystems, access to Georgeson Island and the islets is prohibited.

SALTSPRING ISLAND, FULFORD HARBOUR TO LONG HARBOUR

Russell Island (Gulf Islands National Park Reserve). Russell Island is just outside Fulford Harbour. Anchor on the northwest side of the island, fair to poor holding, with views of mountains above Fulford Harbour. A trail leads through open meadows and a forest of Douglas fir, Arbutus (madrona) and Garry oak. The original house dates back more than a century. Readerboards explain the history. The island casts a spell upon all those who visit.

Fulford Harbour. Fulford Harbour is wide and open. A public dock for locals only is located on the north side of the ferry terminal. On the south side of the ferry terminal is a public float with transient moorage that is exposed to wind and ferry wash. No services at the float. The charming village of Fulford has a restaurant, a good grocery store at the Salt Spring Mercantile, and an assortment of art galleries and stores specializing in crafts and country clothing. Everything feels very "island."

By all means take a 15-minute walk down the road to St. Paul's Catholic church (called the Stone Church), built in 1880. The graveyard, with island history chiseled into its headstones, is adjacent. On one visit we found the church's door unlocked, and stepped inside. It was lovely. "This is where God lives," we thought.

Bus Transportation: Regular bus service on Saltspring Island connects Fulford Village, Ganges, Long Harbour, Vesuvius and Fernwood. For schedule see www.busonline.ca; (250) 537-6758.

Fulford Outer Harbour - Harbour Authority of Salt Spring Island. (250) 537-5711 Open all year. www.saltspringharbours.com A public wharf and float is located immediately south of the BC Ferries terminal, managed by the Harbour Authority of Salt Spring Island. The 54-foot public float provides moorage on both sides. Overnight moorage permitted. No water, no power. Payment envelopes, moorage rates, and a self-pay box are located on the wharf. Locals tend to use this float primarily for loading and unloading purposes.

Fulford Inner Harbour - Harbour Authority of Salt Spring Island. Located just north of the BC Ferries terminal is a public dock filled with local boats; no space for transient boats.

Isabella Island (Gulf Islands National Park Reserve). A smallish anchorage is available behind Isabella Island, a short distance west of the mouth of Fulford Harbour. Although exposed to the west, it's a cozy little spot for one or two boats. Anchor in 24 feet.

Ruckle Park. Beaver Point on Saltspring Island. Open all year, day use and overnight camping. No mooring facilities, exposed anchorage on each side of Ruckle Point. Probably the best of these anchorages is in the first cove south of Ruckle Point. Swinging room is limited, and the cove is exposed to ferry wakes and southeast winds. The anchorage is pretty, though, and in settled weather could be a good day stop. This is an extensive park, with miles of shoreline and rocky headlands. Walk-in campsites. Great views of the southern Gulf Islands.

LOCAL KNOWLEDGE

DANGEROUS ROCKS & REEFS: Enter Ganges Harbour (5-knot speed limit), leaving all the Chain Islands to starboard; *do NOT* cut through any of the islands. No short cuts. There are rocks and reefs throughout. The entry channel itself can be a 'minefield' with crab pot floats, many in dark colors; considerable boat traffic, and a charted, busy floatplane operations area.

There are two similarly named dangers in Ganges Harbour. *Money Maker Reef* is northwest of Third Sister Island near the entrance to the Harbour; *Money Makers Rock* is 2 miles to the northwest and is one of at least two dangerous rocks in a shallow area

SALT SPRING ISLAND & GANGES HARBOUR MARKETPLACE

RESTAURANTS, SHOPS & SERVICES

BLACK SHEEP BOOKS
Get lost in a good bookstore. Explore two floors packed with volumes of enduring value, including familiar favorites, contemporary fiction, guides, and non-fiction titles covering everything from outer space to inner peace. Authorized dealer for CHS marine charts.
**250-538-0025 • 3101-115 Fulford Ganges Rd.
In Grace Point Square**
www.blacksheepbooks.ca

LI READ SEA TO SKY PREMIER PROPERTIES
You love boating among the Gulf Islands. See Li Read to find your new dream home port. Visit Li for what is for sale, an island map and market conditions. Office located across the street from Ganges Marina, Salt Spring Island. Welcome!
250-537-7647 • #4 - 105 Rainbow Road
LiRead33@Gmail.com
www.LiRead.com

MOBY'S PUB
Moby's Pub offers a comfortable atmosphere. The friendly staff, great food, legendary live entertainment, waterfront patio, and excellent location make Moby's the best place on Salt Spring Island to meet people.
250-537-5559 • 124 A Upper Ganges Rd.
mobyspub@gmail.com
www.mobyspub.ca

SALT SPRING ISLAND
Discover Yourself Here!

WHEN CAN YOU GET HERE?

BEAUTIFUL SALT SPRING ISLAND

ONE OF THE WORLD'S BEST PLACES TO VISIT, WORK AND PLAY

A GREAT PLACE TO VISIT YEAR ROUND

THERE IS SOMETHING ON SALT SPRING FOR EVERYONE

WWW.SALTSPRINGTOURISM.COM
250-537-4223

SALT SPRING INN
Come and Experience one of Salt Spring's finest restaurants. A wide variety of different dishes from all over the world. From seafood to pasta, the Salt Spring Inn has it all in a beautiful newly renovated building, which includes seven guest rooms in one of the most wonderful locations in British Columbia.
250-537-9339 • 132 Lower Ganges Rd.

HASTINGS HOUSE
Set amidst enchanting gardens, the distinctive old-world charm of our 18 well-appointed suites and cottages is reminiscent of a timeless era.
160 Upper Ganges Rd. 1-800-661-9255
www.hastingshouse.com

Salt Spring Island Community Calendar

Famous Saturday Market: April to October
Tuesday's Farmers Market: June to October
All Summer Long: Music under the Stars, ArtCraft, Salt Spring Studio Tours, ArtSpring Summer Performances, Live Music at Oystercatcher, Moby's Pub and Salt Spring Vineyards – and more!
January: Salt Spring Polar Bear Swim
February: February Festival • Family Day Concert • Seedy Saturday • Indoor Market
March: Documentary Film Festival • Salt Spring Home & Garden Show
April: Salt Spring Blooms in April • Easter Art Festival • Blossom Festival
May: Round Salt Spring Sailing Race • Ruckle Farm Day
June: Tour des Iles Festival Taste of Salt Spring • Solstice on Salt Spring
July: Canada Day Festivities • Classic Car Show • Lavender Festival
August: Firefly Lantern Festival • Movies in the Park
September: Pride Festival • Fall Fair Weekend • Working Boat Festival
October: Harvest Food and Drink Festival • Apple Festival • Sip & Savour Salt Spring • Harvest Grape Stomp • Halloween in Ganges Village
November: Remembrance Day Parade & Ceremonies • Christmas Light Up Events
December: Christmas on Salt Spring • WinterCraft at Mahon Hall
Christmas Craft Fairs • WinterCraft at Mahon Hall • Beaver Point Hall Fulford Hall ArtSpring Christmas Concerts • Annual Glowtini Contest Community Christmas Dinner • New Year's Eve Celebrations
Plus… Special Events during most Canadian Holiday Long-weekends!

GULF ISLANDS

See Area Map Page 227 - Maps Not for Navigation

Salt Spring Marina at the head of Ganges Harbour

Tree House Cafe, a one of a kind restaurant with great food and live entertainment.

between and southeast of Salt Spring Marina and Ganges Marina.

The dangerous shallow area, between Salt Spring and Ganges marinas, has two charted rocks; one lies off the end of Ganges Marina C dock and the other lies off the southeast end of Saltspring Marina. The rock off Ganges Marina's C dock is locally known as Zachary Rock, however, Canadian charts show its name as Money Makers Rock. The rock south of Salt Spring Marina is known locally as Money Makers Rock and is not named on Canadian charts. In 2018, locally known Money Makers Rock was in open water off the end of Salt Spring Marina and marked with two small buoys. Salt Spring Marina's new docks and breakwater now cover the locally named Money Makers Rock. The exact location and water depth of both these charted rocks and the surrounding shallow area remain uncertain. Use extreme caution when approaching Ganges Marina's north docks and Salt Spring Marina. The water depth at zero tide could be as shallow as 4 feet 3 inches.

㉑ **Ganges.** Ganges, at the head of Ganges Harbour, is a favorite destination. This bustling seaside village has marinas, good anchorage, shops, banks with ATM's, galleries, restaurants, and two large supermarkets with marina delivery. There is a dedicated centrally located dinghy dock. Thrifty Foods is the closest to the marinas. Above the store, entered from the street side, is "The Local," a liquor store associated with Thrifty Foods that also delivers to the marinas. Country Grocer (Liquor Agency in the store), at 374 Lower Ganges Road, has a "boaters van" (250-538-2398) with pick-up, drop-off services at any Ganges marina daily, from 10:00 a.m. to 6:00 p.m. Mouat's, a huge old hardware and household goods general store with a separate gift shop and apparel section, is a longstanding favorite. They also have fishing and marine supplies.

The sprawling Salt Spring Island Saturday Market, also called the Farmers Market, is held in Centennial Park at Grace Point on Saturdays 9:00 a.m. to 4:00 p.m., April through October. A Tuesday farmers market, no crafts, is held in the same location, 2:00 p.m. to 6:00 p.m. from June to the end of October. Although boats and tourists are important to summer trade, Ganges is not just a summer resort village. It's a bustling center of year-round local commerce.

Boats can anchor out in the bay. All buoys in the harbour are private. Moorage is available at Salt Spring Marina, Ganges Marina, or the town's Kanaka Wharf. Larger vessels might side-tie along the 240-foot-long floating breakwater that extends into the bay from the Coast Guard dock. An airplane float, pumpout station, and some power and water are on the breakwater. A ramp leads to shore. Because of the breakwater's high freeboard, it is best suited to larger boats. If the wind blows (especially a southeasterly), expect some movement.

The Saltspring Island Sailing Club's docks, to port as you approach Grace Point, have some space for reciprocal clubs. It's about a 1-mile walk to town. The Centennial Wharf public dock behind Grace Islet is permanent moorage only with some guest "hot berths" available if you call the Harbour Authority office. Off Mouat's store, the Kanaka Wharf is within close proximity to shopping; Kanaka dock moorage frequently opens up during the day as boats come and go.

More than 40 artists' studios are in Ganges and scattered around Saltspring Island. In addition to painters and sculptors, they include artisan cheese makers, bakers, wineries, distilleries, and now a microbrewery. Rental cars and vans are available at Saltspring Marina. A local map identifies stops and hours.

Artspring: Locally supported arts and theater, an easy walk from the village. See www.artspring.ca.

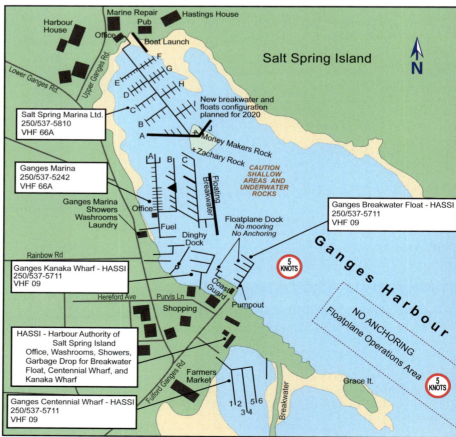
Ganges Harbour

248 www.WaggonerGuide.com

Foodie Heaven on Salt Spring Island

Salt Spring Island has been a foodie heaven since the late 1800s. Back then, fresh produce grown on the island was delivered to Hope Bay, where it was loaded on the ferry and shuttled to Vancouver.

Today, Salt Spring Island is home to brewers and vintners, farmers, cheesemakers, artisan bakers, and restaurateurs. If you love delicious food, Salt Spring Island is a fantastic destination.

FARMERS MARKET

Ganges hosts the best farmers market in the Gulf Islands. Each Saturday from March through October, the "Market in the Park" at Centennial Park is open for business. More than 100 vendors sell their wares, ranging from fresh produce to seafood to pastries and crafts. The variety is outstanding and everything is made locally.

Another, smaller, market is held Tuesday afternoons at the same location.

Both markets are perfect places for provisioning. We've found fresh seafood, unusual mushrooms, heirloom tomatoes, ripe melons, berries, a variety of sprouts, and more. Four artisan bakeries—ranging from Rendezvous French Patisserie (superb desserts) to the Salt Spring Island Bread Company and the Bread Lady—attend the market. Fair warning: it's best to go early, since many items sell out by closing time.

WINE AND BEER

Salt Spring has two wineries: Garry Oaks Estate Winery, and Salt Spring Vineyards. Each has a tasting room.

Both Garry Oaks and Salt Spring Vineyards require car transportation. Each winery hosts a variety of tasting events throughout the summer, some including food pairings or live music. Check their websites for a schedule of events.

The Sip and Savour festival in September celebrates Salt Spring Island's food and wine.

If beer is your preference, stop by one of B.C.'s smallest breweries: Salt Spring Island Ales, outside of Ganges. You can enjoy beer on tap, or pick up a bottle or growler for later. The beer is organic and made with locally grown ingredients—even the hops are from Salt Spring Island.

RESTAURANTS

Hastings House is one of the finest restaurants we've ever dined at. They've hosted movie stars and sports stars, royalty and heads of state. Almost everything, including bread and crackers, is prepared fresh in their kitchen. They grow many of their ingredients on site, and the garden is open to patrons. We recommend wandering through, either before or after your meal. It's not uncommon to see the chef gathering herbs, fruits, or vegetables.

Choose from a Bistro Dinner or Fine Dining menu, and we highly recommend the cocktail hour in the Manor House before dinner.

STILL HUNGRY?

If you're willing to travel beyond walking distance from Ganges, another world opens up. Salt Spring Auto Rentals (250 537-3122), located at Saltspring Marina, provides maps highlighting more than 40 destinations on Salt Spring Island. Many of these places are artisan food businesses, ranging from cheese makers to beekeepers.

One of our favorites is Salt Spring Island Cheese Company, near Fulford Harbour. A tour includes petting the goats and sampling some of their 20+ cheeses in a tasting room overlooking the production area. Afterword, customers can relax at outdoor tables and enjoy goat milk gelato.

Salt Spring Island's wide variety of food producers and restaurants, and their consistently high quality, make it the ideal destination for foodie boaters.

– Mark Bunzel

SALT SPRING MARINA

Your COMPLETE CRUISING Destination

HASTINGS HOUSE - exquisite Farm to Table Waterfront Dining and Luxury Hotel

MOBY'S - Great food and entertainment   **WELLSPRING SPA** - Facials & Massage

HARBOUR'S END for maintenance and emergency repairs - Rental Cars and Scooters

Shuttle to/from Country Grocer and Upper Ganges Liquor Store

Shuttle to Ganges Village for our boaters and hotel guests **BC Transit Bus** to all three Ferry Terminals

All New Docks 2019

SALTSPRING MARINA
at Moby's Pub
124 Upper Ganges Rd,
250.537.5810

124A Upper Ganges Rd,
250.537.5559

160 Upper Ganges Rd,
1 800-661-9255

The Hastings House gardens are outstanding.

Bird Sanctuary: While you can anchor a short distance south of the Sailing Club's docks, Walter Bay and the spit that creates it are a sanctuary for black oystercatchers. Please leave the sanctuary area alone.

Swimming Pool: The Rainbow Road Indoor Public Pool is an easy walk away. Call (250) 537-1402 for hours.

Bus Transportation: Regular bus service on Saltspring Island connects Fulford Harbour, Ganges, Long Harbour, Vesuvius and Fernwood. For schedule see www.busonline.ca; (250) 538-4282.

Shuttle: A free shuttle goes to upper Ganges shopping center, call (250) 538-2398.

Taxi: Silver Shadow Taxi (250) 537-3030; Amber Cab Co. (250) 537-3277

Car Rental: Salt Spring Car Rentals (250) 537-3122

THINGS TO DO

1. Studio Tour. Map available at the Visitor Centre. Rent a car, van, or moped at the Saltspring Marina and visit some of the 40 artist studios. Most are open every weekend.

2. Salt Spring Island Cheese Company. See the many steps needed to make artisan cheese. Then taste 20 different cheeses.

3. Wine Tasting. Two wineries are on Saltspring Island and they regularly have tastings. Wine and farm tours available at TourSaltSpring.com.

4. Salt Spring Island Saturday Market. The largest farmers market in the islands.

5. Hastings House. Reserve for an elegant dinner or a bistro lunch. Walk the grounds of this manor style resort.

6. Barb's Buns. Delicious coffee and fresh baked goods. Bring some back to the boat. Their breakfasts and lunches are also very good.

7. Embe Bakery. A "old style" full service bakery serving up freshly baked breads, pastries, dessert pies, and meat pies.

⑳ **Harbour Authority of Salt Spring Island.** 127 Fulford Ganges Road, Salt Spring Island, BC V8K 2T9; (250) 537-5711. Monitors VHF 09. www.saltspringharbours.com.

The Harbour Authority of Salt Spring Island manages eight marina facilities on Salt Spring Island: Ganges Centennial Wharf; Ganges Breakwater Float (which also includes the Wharfhead where the Coast Guard building is located); Ganges Kanaka Wharf; Vesuvius Bay; Fulford Inner Harbour; Fulford Outer Harbour; Burgoyne Bay; and Musgrave Landing. The Harbour Authority office and wharfinger are located at Ganges Centennial Wharf.

⑳ **Ganges Centennial Wharf - Harbour Authority of Salt Spring Island.** (250) 537-5711. Monitors VHF 09. www.saltspringharbours.com. This is the Grace Point facility. Mostly commercial and permanent moorage, but sometimes guest space is available, call the Harbour Authority Office.

⑳ **Ganges Breakwater Float - Harbour Authority of Salt Spring Island.** (250) 537-5711. Monitors VHF 09. www.saltspringharbours.com. This is the dock below the Coast Guard station. Moorage on the outside of the long floating breakwater or in several slips on the inside. Be sure to avoid the marked seaplane and Coast Guard areas. Limited 30 amp power and water. Pumpout at the dock. Washroom, shower and garbage drop at the Harbour Authority office at Centennial Wharf. Two hours free moorage before 4:00 p.m.

Wharfingers collect moorage daily, or pay in the drop box at the head of the docks or at the Harbour Authority office.

⑳ **Ganges Kanaka Wharf - Harbour Authority of Salt Spring Island.** (250) 537-5711. Monitors VHF 09. www.saltspringharbours.com. These docks are immediately north of the floating breakwater, with 1400 feet of visitor moorage, water, 30 amp power. Good free Wi-Fi on the docks or from nearby cafés. Three-day maximum stay from May 15 to September 15. Washroom, shower and garbage drop, with recycling, located at the Harbour Authority office at Centennial Wharf, about a block away. Free moorage for 2 hours. Boats come and go all day and moorage opens up after crews complete their shopping. The white bull rail area is not available for overnight moorage on specific days; check the posted signage.

Wharfingers collect check or cash for moorage daily, or pay in the drop box at the head of the docks, or at the Harbour Authority office.

LOCAL KNOWLEDGE

EXPLORING ISLANDS: Explore Third Sister Island by dinghy to see the midden shell beach and creative driftwood outhouse.

⑳ **Ganges Marina.** 161 Lower Ganges Road, Salt Spring Island, BC V8K 2L6; (250) 537-5242; gangesmarina@gmail.com; www.gangesmarina.com. Monitors VHF 66A. Moorage for vessels up to 120 feet. Open all year, gasoline, diesel and limited lubricants at fuel dock, ample guest moorage. Reservations recommended in summer. Facilities include 30 & 50 amp power, washrooms, showers, laundry, free Wi-Fi, garbage drop. On-site marine mechanic. Groceries, restaurants, propane, and other services nearby.

A floating breakwater, 500 feet long and 24 feet wide, can handle vessels to 400 feet.

⑳ **Salt Spring Marina.** 124 Upper Ganges Rd., Salt Spring Island, BC V8K 2S2; (250) 537- 5810; (800) 334-6629; info@saltspringmarina.com; www.saltspringmarina.com. Monitors VHF 66A. Work was underway in 2019 to replace all the docks with new and expanded floats, which were completed and installed in October. The new floats have guest moorage for a variety of boat sizes in a configuration that includes a floating breakwater covering Money Makers Rock. New electrical service is ELCI-protected, one of the first in BC. 30 & 50 amp power, washrooms, showers, laundry, water, ice, recycling, garbage drop, and mobile pump-out station. Shaw Go Wi-Fi and concrete launch ramp. No long term parking. At certain times of the year, when in short supply, water use at the docks may be restricted.

Adjacent Moby's Pub (take-out & off-sales) has a terrific menu, music and dancing. Check their website. Rendezvous French Bakery has fresh baked goods. Harbours End has full-service repairs with haulout to 40 feet (250-537-4202). Car, van, scooter, and bicycle rentals (250-537-3122).

Long Harbour. Long Harbour lies parallel to Ganges Harbour, but is much narrower. The BC ferry from Tsawwassen lands there. Good anchorage is beyond the ferry dock, taking care not to anchor over a charted cable

Woodstone Manor Restaurant & Patio
A new find on Galiano Island

The word spread during the middle of the 2019 cruising season about a new, not to be missed, restaurant on Galiano Island. While not within walking distance from the Montague Harbour Marina, Manor staff are happy to drive down to the marina, or the Park dock, to pick up boaters.

In short, the food and views are sensational! Located about 2 miles from the marina, the Woodstone Manor is nestled in a valley above a horse rescue farm, where former race horses go after retirement. The view from the patio, overlooking the valley, offers grand vistas, with the horses grazing off in the distance.

For more than 2 years, the Woodstone Manor has been open for overnight guests. In the summer of 2019, owners Roxanne and Stephan, along with general manager and sommelier, Anita, decided it was time to open fine dining service for lunch and dinner.

After being whisked up from the marina by the Manor's Mercedes, you arrive at the grand entrance feeling like a special guest. The tasteful decor features fine furnishings and artwork, with many tables near the windows that take advantage of the beautiful views of the valley. Enjoy a drink or glass of wine outside on the patio before dinner; and after your meal, savor dessert next to the patio's fireplace.

The key to any great restaurant is the chef, and Stephan and Roxanne brought in Katsuyuki Sekihata, the Japanese born chef with a three-star Michelin rating. Seki has worked in well-known restaurants around the world performing his culinary magic. He is truly an artist. His creative dishes are served with a beautiful presentation. I ordered the Roasted Venison in a Marchand du Vin red wine sauce, and Danielle ordered the Fresh Fish Duo, with fillets of sockeye salmon and sablefish in a beurre blanc sauce. The menu is featured on their website. Anita, the sommelier, recommended an excellent Malbec wine, a great choice and perfect pairing for our meal.

We elected to share a dessert served outside on the patio in front of the fireplace. The Fantasy Cheesecake, with a Black Forest Cake and fresh fruit was, again, presented in a most artistic fashion. The charming owners, Stephan and Roxanne, are often on site and may join you in front of the fireplace.

Galiano Island and Montague Harbour are becoming a destination for interesting dining. Woodstone Manor joins pilgrimme, the Crane and Robin, and the Galiano Inn (in Sturdies Bay) for fine dining, together with Babes in the Woods, and the Hummingbird Pub for additional well-rated choices in a more casual environment. Be sure to plan your trip to Galiano Island for several nights just to enjoy the excellent food. Advance reservations are highly recommended.

See Area Map Page 227 - Maps Not for Navigation   GULF ISLANDS

Montague Harbour

crossing. Royal Vancouver Yacht Club has an outstation in Long Harbour.

PREVOST ISLAND

㉑ **Prevost Island.** Prevost Island is a favorite of many. Annette Inlet and Glenthorne Passage, on the northwest end, are particularly attractive. The bays indenting from the southeast also look inviting, but with a southeaster always possible and with ferry traffic flying by in Swanson Channel, they might get a little lumpy.

Acland Islands. The passage between the Acland Islands and Prevost Island is a pleasant anchorage, with dramatic sheer rock walls on the Prevost Island side. Anchor in 25 to 35 feet with enough room to swing, or stern-tie to Acland Island.

Glenthorne Passage. Glenthorne Passage is the westernmost of the northern bays on Prevost Island. Well protected anchorage in 15 to 30 feet, good holding. Even though cabins line Secret Island, the surroundings are agreeable and the anchorage is popular. In summer months the sun sets in the narrow passage between Glenthorne Point and Secret Island.

Annette Inlet. Annette Inlet is a little wider than Glenthorne Passage, with few houses and a good sandy beach at the head. As you

MARINA & FUEL DOCK

Transient Moorage— May to September
30/15amp Power, Wifi & Garbage with Moorage
Ethanol Free Diesel and Gasoline
RESERVATIONS HIGHLY RECOMMENDED

GENERAL STORE & MARKET

Coffee Shop, Ice Cream, Produce, Meat, Seafood, Fishing
Gear, Bait, Ice, Books, Clothing & Gifts

FIVE DINING OPTIONS

GALIANO ISLAND, BC

250.539.5733
INFO@MONTAGUEHARBOUR.COM

VHF 66A
MONTAGUEHARBOUR.COM

2020 Waggoner Cruising Guide

GULF ISLANDS

See Area Map Page 227 - Maps Not for Navigation

approach, note the charted rock that dries at 0.9 meter, off the mouth of the inlet. A rock at the point is marked by a small, private beacon. Approach from the Glenthorne Passage side and wrap around the point, leaving the beacon to starboard. The head of the bay shoals to drying flats. Anchor in 8 feet (zero tide) anywhere, gray mud bottom. Southeast winds can blow across the low swale separating Annette Inlet from Ellen Bay on the other side of Prevost Island, but there isn't enough fetch to build waves.

Selby Cove & James Bay. A house and dock are on the right side as you enter Selby Cove. Anchor in 18 feet and be sure of your set. We found poor holding in one spot. James Bay is the most northeast bay, open to northwesterlies. It is a little deep for anchoring until close to the head. The lands surrounding James Bay and a portion of the north shore of Selby Cove are part of Gulf Islands National Park Reserve, as are the lands surrounding Richardson Bay and the Portlock Point light station at the southeast corner of Prevost Island. Ferries do not serve Prevost Island, thus it is less populated than the larger islands.

MONTAGUE HARBOUR

㉒ **Montague Harbour.** Montague Harbour is a popular stopping spot in the central Gulf Islands. It is well protected and has an outstanding marine park. Depending on wind direction, you can find good anchorages around the bay.

Entry is unobstructed, either from the southeast, past Phillimore Point, or from the northwest, between Parker Island and Gray Peninsula.

Caution: A shoal extends southeast from the tip of Gray Peninsula into Montague Harbour. We've seen a boat thoroughly grounded on that shoal, awaiting a rising tide. Continue well into the harbor before turning east to anchor or pick up a mooring.

Montague Harbour will hold a huge number of boats. We have anchored there during high season surrounded by more than 100 boats, yet no one was crowded. Anchor in about 40 feet over a mud bottom. The marina has a fuel dock, store, gift shop, scooter and kayak rentals, and restaurant. For-fee Wi-Fi is available throughout the harbor; cell phone reception is poor.

No Discharge Zone, Gray Water okay.

Customs: Montague Harbour is a Canpass/Nexus-only call-in customs clearance location.

Dining: A range of dining choices are available. Everybody enjoys the Hummingbird Inn Pub. A visit to Hummingbird Pub begins with a memorable ride on the Hummingbird Pub bus. Catch the bus on the road above the marina, about 300 yards to the right of the intersection. The bus also stops at the front gate of the marine park. Check the Hummingbird Pub website or signs at the marina and park entrance for the scheduled times for bus pick-up. The

Dinghies on one side of Butchart Gardens dock, the other side is reserved for floatplanes.

Hummingbird Pub serves food and is family friendly. The entertaining bus ride is worth the trip.

The Pilgrimme Restaurant (250-539-5392) operates in the former location of the French restaurant La Berengerie. It gets great reviews from visiting boaters. Reservations recommended. Walking distance from Montague Harbour Marina.

Located inland, at 743 Georgeson Bay Rd., is the impressive Woodstone Manor and Restaurant (250-539-2849). The Michelin Star chef prepares outstanding European cuisine. The hotel will pick up dinner guests from Montague Harbour.

㉒ **Montague Harbour Marine Park.** Montague Harbour Marine Park, at the north end of Montague Harbour, is beautiful, exceptionally well-maintained and very popular. The park is open all year. It has excellent white sand beaches on the south side and astonishing rock beaches on the north and west sides. If you walk along the beach on the north side, opposite the head of the lagoon, you'll find a midden beach with numerous shells. There's no hint of the midden on the trail above, but it's obvious from the beach. A tiny, secluded beach is on Gray Peninsula, facing Parker Island. The park has walk-in campsites, a picnic area and toilets. A dock with a 300-foot-long float is for dinghies and boats up to 11 meters (36 feet). Designated dinghy area is on the shore end of the float. There are approximately 39 mooring buoys off the dock. No boat size limitation is marked on the buoys but as a practical matter, be careful not to endanger other boats or damage buoy equipment. An honor box for paying moorage is at the top of the stairs. The Park Ranger will also accept VISA and MasterCard and will visit your boat in late afternoon/early evening to collect your payment. The park has anchorage for many boats on both sides of Gray Peninsula depending on wind direction. Garbage disposal for a fee is available, located up the stairs from the dock.

㉒ **Montague Harbour Marina.** 3451 Montague Rd, Galiano Island, BC V0N 1P0; (250) 539-5733; montagueharbourmarina@gmail.com; www.montagueharbour.com. Monitors VHF 66A. Open May 1 to September 30. Guest side-tie moorage, 15 & 30 amp power, no water at the docks, free Wi-Fi, and washrooms. Reservations strongly recommended during the high season. Garbage and recycle drop for overnight moorage guests. Dog friendly. Licensed restaurant, with daily specials. Groceries, marine supplies, and gift shop. Diesel and ethanol-free gasoline at the fuel dock. Fuel is available during the off-season on Saturdays from 10:00 a.m. to 2:00 p.m. or by arrangement. Moped, kayak, and motor boat rentals.

The store carries an expanded variety of goods, including smoked fish, meats, and local produce, fishing tackle, a good selection of books, souvenirs, and hand-dipped ice cream cones. Cappuccino bar service available. The licensed Crane & Robin is open for breakfast, lunch and dinner. Check their happy hour specials. Dinghy dock available for any boaters on anchor or mooring buoys who want to enjoy the marina's shopping and dining. Check in at the office, located across from the store, if you plan to leave the property. Limited Wi-Fi for anchored boats is available for a fee.

㉒ **Montague Harbour Public Wharf.** Open all year, 160 feet of dock space, no facilities. 2-hour complimentary tie-up for dingies and boats. Fee for additional stays, pay at self-registration payment box at head of the ramp. Video monitoring and the wharfinger enforce the 2-hour free limit. Surveillance ensures that everyone has an opportunity to use the dock. Wharfinger always greets you with a smile.

Walker Hook. Walker Hook, on the west side of Trincomali Channel, has a beautiful beach on its eastern shore, where it connects with Saltspring Island. Anchor in 24 feet. An approach between Atkins Reef and Saltspring Island takes the worry out of identifying just where the various rocks are.

Fernwood Public Wharf. Located on the Trincomali Channel side of Saltspring Island

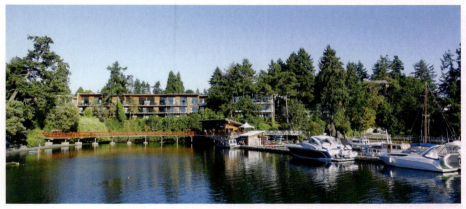
Elegant Brentwood Bay Resort near Butchart Gardens

north of Walker Hook, opposite Victoria Shoal and just south of Wallace Island. Open all year, 44 feet of dock space, no facilities. Correspondents Fred and Judy Triggs visited and say they'd stop again. They enjoyed the locals who came down to visit, and concluded, "A pleasant and unexpected surprise was the Fernwood Road Café, located at the head of the pier, 50 meters up the road. Well stocked, good bakery items, sandwiches and pizza – excellent food." We visited, and agree.

SAANICH INLET

Saanich Inlet extends south into Vancouver Island for about 12 miles. The northern part of the inlet is fairly civilized, especially along the Saanich Peninsula shore to Brentwood Bay, where Butchart Gardens is located. For a beautiful and often-overlooked trip, continue south through Squally Reach and Finlayson Arm. Boat traffic usually is minimal.

Holding Tank Pumpout Service: J.R. Pump Out, a mobile pumpout boat, serves the Brentwood Bay/Butchart Gardens area of Saanich Inlet. Because of a sill at the mouth of the inlet, Saanich Inlet does not exchange its water well and is growing increasingly lifeless along the bottom. Saanich Inlet is not a good place to pump overboard. J.R. Pump Out at (844) 507-3451 or VHF 88 (seasonally). During the summer season the pumpout boat goes out every evening. In winter, every two weeks.

Restricted Area: In Saanich Inlet, Area Whiskey Delta (WD) is restricted when the government is conducting certain operations. Before entering, listen to the continuous marine broadcast or call the Coast Guard on VHF 83 to ensure the area is not restricted before entering.

Deep Cove. Wain Rock, with good water on both sides, lies about 0.2 mile off Moses Point. The remains of a public wharf are in the south part of the cove. Deep Cove Marina is adjacent to this pier and is for permanent moorage; transient moorage available only when there is space available which is rare, call (250) 733-2991 Ext 300. Boaters can anchor in front of The Chalet restaurant on the north end of Deep Cove and land the dinghy on their private beach, while enjoying lunch or dinner. Call ahead for reservations (250) 656-3541, open Wednesday-Sunday. This is a unique venue overlooking Deep Cove and Saanich Inlet. The home was built as a teahouse for the B.C. Electric Rail Line in 1913 and has been a restaurant ever since. After coming ashore, leave your boots behind and slip on your nice shoes; this is a fine dining venue with prices to match. Remains of several pilings in front of The Chalet help locate the restaurant; see www.deepcovechalet.com for more details.

Patricia Bay. Patricia Bay, locally called Pat Bay, is open, but all the facilities are reserved for the Canadian Government's Institute of Ocean Sciences. It is here that the Canadian Hydrographic Service develops and maintains charts and related publications for western Canada and the Arctic.

Coles Bay. Coles Bay is east of Yarrow Point. It is good for temporary anchorage but open to southerly winds. If approaching from the north, the Canadian Small Craft Guide recommends that you give Dyer Rocks, off Yarrow Point, a 0.5-mile berth to avoid shoals extending south from the rocks.

LOCAL KNOWLEDGE

DANGEROUS ROCKS: A reef, marked by red nun Buoy U22, is a short distance off the Brentwood Bay ferry dock. Approach Brentwood Bay Resort & Marina from the north, leaving buoy U22 to starboard. Dangerous rocks lie on the other side of the buoy, and west and south of the resort's docks. Locals report that these rocks are hit frequently.

㉓ **Brentwood Bay.** Although Brentwood Bay can be entered on either side of Senanus Island, prawn trap floats often clog the water between the north end of the island and Henderson Point. Best to leave Senanus Island to port. The Mill Bay ferry departs a short distance south of Sluggett Point. The Seahorses Cafe, with a dinghy dock, is north of the ferry dock. Nearby Blue's Bayou Café to the south has Cajun/Creole style food. Open for lunch and dinner, reservations recommended (250) 544-1194. The Brentwood Bay Public Dock, next to the Cafe, is suitable for dinghies and small watercraft.

Pumpout is available monthly on the second Saturday throughout Brentwood Bay for free (donations appreciated) through J. R. Pumpout, (844) 507-3451 or VHF 88. This program is funded by Butchart Gardens. Butchart Gardens is one of the main attractions around Brentwood and is well worth a visit. Another popular attraction is the Victoria Butterfly Gardens (877) 722-0272 located about two miles from Brentwood Bay.

The village up at the highway has some shopping. Moorage is at Brentwood Bay Resort & Marina and limited moorage at Portside Marina and Angler's Anchorage Marina.

㉓ **Portside Marina.** 789 Saunders Ln., Brentwood Bay, BC V8M 1C5; (250) 652-2211; info@portsidemarina.net; portsidemarina.net. Open all year with limited guest moorage for boats up to 50 feet, reservations accepted. 30 amp power, water, washrooms, showers, and laundry. The marina is located in Brentwood Bay north of the BC Ferries terminal and next to the Seahorses Café. New owners took over the marina in 2017 and have been steadily making improvements. Guest moorage space was expanded in 2018. A small marine ways and boatyard that specializes in wooden boat

Brentwood Bay and Tod Inlet

GULF ISLANDS

See Area Map Page 227 - Maps Not for Navigation

building and repair is adjacent to the marina. Pacifica Paddle Sports (250-665-7411) is located at the marina and has rental kayaks, canoes, and SUPs.

㉓ **Brentwood Bay Resort & Marina.** 849 Verdier Ave., Brentwood Bay, BC V8W 1C5; (250) 652-3151; (888) 544-2079; marina@brentwoodbayresort.com; www.brentwoodbayresort.com. Monitors VHF 66A. The reservation-only marina has 22 slips of guest moorage and side-tie moorage for vessels to 125 feet, 15, 30 & 50 amp power, water, washrooms, laundry, garbage, recycling, showers, adult pool with drinks and pub food service, sushi and sake, cold beer & wine off-sales in the pub, free Wi-Fi. Live music and beer samplers on Sundays.

This is a highly rated resort and spa, with excellent views of Saanich Inlet, beautiful landscaping. A shuttle boat runs to Butchart Gardens for a fee (make reservations at the marina office), or it's a short dinghy ride away. Kayak and SUP rentals, bicycle rentals, and Paddle Sports eco-adventure tours available.

㉓ **Angler's Anchorage Marina.** (250) 652-3531; info@anglersanchorage.com; www.anglersanchoragemarina.com. Some guest moorage available in slips to 50 feet, call ahead, 30 & 50 amp power, washrooms, showers, laundry, garbage drop, pumpout. Reservations are accepted and recommended. Call or see their website for reservations. A new patio and ramp were added in 2017 to create a welcoming entrance to the refurbished marina office.

㉓ **Butchart Gardens.** 800 Benvenuto Avenue, Brentwood Bay, BC V8M 1J8; (250) 652-5256; (866) 652-4422; www.butchartgardens.com. Locally named **Butchart Cove** just outside the mouth of Tod Inlet is the back door to the celebrated and astonishing Butchart Gardens. The Gardens are a must-see attraction. They are lighted at night, creating an entirely different effect from the day. On Saturday evenings during the summer a fireworks display is held on a large field in the gardens. Many people arrive early and have a picnic dinner while waiting for darkness. A little known secret is — The Dining Room restaurant will prepare special picnic baskets to enjoy on the grounds during the summers — see their website for the menu. Bring blankets and cushions. Even for jaded viewers, it's worth the trip. The most interesting fireworks are done at ground level, accompanied by music — you have to be at the field for the full experience.

The Gardens' dinghy dock is in tiny Butchart Cove with 4 free mooring buoys for boats 40 feet and under (a fifth mooring ball for vessels 18 feet and under) that are first-come, first-served, maximum 24 hour stay. Eyes for stern-ties are set into the rock wall. Most visitors put the anchor down in adjacent Tod Inlet and go by dinghy to the dinghy dock. Dinghy dock is closed from December 1 to January 6.

Tod Inlet. *No Discharge Zone, Gray water okay.* Tod Inlet reaches back behind Butchart Gardens into Gowlland Tod Provincial Park, and has ample anchoring room. Anchor in water deeper than 20 feet to protect eelgrass. Green can Buoy U21 marks a rock. Leave the bouy to port when entering. The inlet is narrow when seen from Brentwood Bay, but opens somewhat after a bend. In the narrow sections you should plan to run a stern-tie to shore. Boats in the more open sections around the bend often can swing without a stern-tie. On Saturday nights the inlet is crowded with boats that come to see the fireworks display at the Gardens.

The dinghy dock on the southeastern shore of the inlet is provided by the Marine Conservation Society and BC Parks, look for the green Marine Ecology float building. A trail to the south leads to the main entrance of Butchart Gardens, about a 10 minute walk. Stay left at the 'Y' in the trail. It's also a short dinghy ride to Butchart Cove where you can tie to the shore side of the dinghy dock and pay admission to the gardens at the backdoor entrance. The dinghy dock in Tod Inlet serves as an access point for the Gowlland Tod Provincial Park with hiking trails connecting through the Gowlland Range. During the summer months, volunteers set up a float in Tod Inlet to provide information and answer questions. The float is staffed by members of the Capital City Yacht Club on behalf of BC Parks.

Finlayson Arm. Goldstream Boathouse is located at the head of Finlayson Arm, at the edge of drying flats off the mouth of the Goldstream River. The shoal water seems to be extending farther north, so come in close to the docks. If the approach is made from mid-channel, an unsuspecting skipper could run aground. Unique homes dot the hillsides and shoreline along Finlayson Arm. Look for the cute 'crooked little house' on a small point just before the power lines on the western shore at 48°31.14'N/123°32.5'W.

㉔ **Goldstream Boathouse.** 3540 Trans-Canada Hwy, Victoria, BC V9B 6H6; (250) 478-4407; www.goldstreamboathousemarina.com. Open all year, gasoline and diesel at fuel dock. Minimal guest moorage available, but even during the summer season they usually have room, call ahead. Complete repair facility and haulout by trailer up to 50 feet, small convenience store, 2-lane concrete launch ramp, 15, 30 & 50 amp power, washrooms, no showers. A new building for the store was constructed in 2019. Shower facilities are planned for the future.

㉕ **Mill Bay.** Mill Bay is a good anchorage. The west shore provides a lee from the usual summer west or northwest winds. The bay is, however, open to southeast winds. Just north of the Mill Bay Marina is a spar buoy zone marking a no-anchoring area. A charted pipeline extends from the northwest corner of the bay.

㉕ **Mill Bay Marina.** 740 Handy Road, Mill Bay, BC V0R 2P1; (250) 743-4303; contact@millbaymarina.ca; www.millbaymarina.ca. Monitors VHF 66A. 700 feet of guest moorage to accommodate boats to 300 feet; 30 & 50 amp power, water, gasoline, diesel, pumpout, laundry, showers, free Wi-Fi. Reservations recommended in season. Wide roomy slips and side-tie moorage on concrete docks. State-of-the-art marina with great views of Mt. Baker.

Picnic tables and propane barbeques for

Mill Bay

256   www.WaggonerGuide.com

guest use are on the docks. The Bridgemans Bistro restaurant, open for lunch and dinner, and brunch on weekends, is a hit. Soft drinks, ice cream. Live music on Sundays. Blue Dog Kayaking (250) 710-7693, located at Mill Bay Marina, offers kayak and SUP rentals, instruction, and expeditions.

The Mill Bay Shopping Centre is a short walk up the hill. The Center has a supermarket, drug store, liquor store, hardware store, bank and gift stores. Several restaurants and the Visitor Centre are also located there.

A public launch ramp is on the north side of the marina. Spar buoys north of the marina and boat launch, located in front of the Brentwood College School (a college prep boarding school), mark a no-anchoring area. The no-anchoring area protects an ocean loop geo-exchange system used for heating and cooling the school's buildings.

㉕ **Mill Bay Community Wharf.** Open all year, 50 feet of dock space, no facilities. Three hour maximum stay, no overnight moorage.

㉖ **Cowichan Bay.** www.cowichanbay.com. The waterfront village of Cowichan Bay is located near the southwest corner of Cowichan Bay. Docks at Fishermen's Wharf are behind a floating breakwater. The floating breakwater dock is not connected to land. A dinghy is needed for shore access. Two privately owned marinas are west of the public wharf and offer limited guest moorage. Mooring buoys for overnight stays are available from Classic Marine. Hecate Park, at the other end of town, has a launch ramp and ample trailer storage.

In settled weather anchorage is possible but not advised. We are told crabbing and prawning are good. The annual Cowichan Bay Regatta is held the first weekend in August, a popular event drawing many participants. The village is full of life. It has numerous shops and businesses, including liquor stores and good restaurants, not one of them part of a major chain. Interesting little shops are tucked away everywhere. The True Grain Bakery is superb as is Hilary's Cheese Shop. Udder Guys Ice Cream has some of the best ice cream on the coast. The Cowichan Bay Maritime Centre, built on a wharf extending from shore, has many interesting displays.

A grass tennis court, just like Wimbledon, is 3 miles west of town at 2290 Cowichan Bay Rd (250) 746-7282. Non-members can book a court online at info@lawntennis.ca during the season (May-Sept. 15); open daily. For winery and distillery tours of the area, see CheersCowichan.com (250) 710-7391.

㉖ **Cowichan Bay Fishermen's Wharf Association.** P.O. Box 52, Cowichan Bay, BC V0R 1N0; (250) 746-5911; cbfwa@shaw.ca. Monitors VHF 66A. Open all year, 900 feet of dock space for vessels to 100 feet, 30 amp power, free Wi-Fi, clean washrooms, laundry, showers, free pumpout, garbage and recycling drop, waste oil disposal. Short-term shopping stops are encouraged until 2:00 p.m.; check-in at the harbor office. Seafood sales available on the dock, Saturdays, June through the first week in September, 4:00 p.m. to 6:00 p.m. off the fish boat *Prawn Star*.

㉖ **Oceanfront Suites at Cowichan Bay.** 1681 Cowichan Bay Rd., Cowichan Bay, BC V0R 1N0; (250) 715-1000; info@oceanfrontcowichanbay.com; www.oceanfrontcowichanbay.com. Full service resort hotel. Moorage at the dock for hotel guests; no hourly stays. Dock suitable for shallow draft boats only. No power on the docks. The Oceanview restaurant overlooking the bay is open seasonally. Located immediately south of the Fishermen's Wharf dock. Watch your depths on very low tides.

㉖ **Classic Marine Transient Moorage.** 1725 Cowichan Bay Rd, Cowichan Bay, BC V0R 1N0; (250) 746-1093; info@classicmarine.ca; www.classicmarine.ca. Monitors VHF 66A. Classic Marine Store has eight (8) mooring buoys in Cowichan Bay for transient boats for a nightly fee. The buoys are marked "Classic Marine" and numbered. Buoy number "1" is for boats up to 55 feet; all other guest buoys are for boats up to 40 feet. Buoys are located north and west of the Fishermen's Wharf breakwater. Contact Classic Marine Store on VHF 66A for assignment and to arrange for payment (credit card or cash). A short-term dinghy

Cowichan Bay

Genoa Bay Marina

One of the new wider floats at Genoa Bay

GULF ISLANDS

See Area Map Page 227 - Maps Not for Navigation

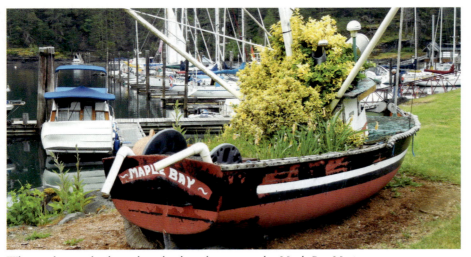

Whimsical artwork adorns the uplands at the ever popular Maple Bay Marina.

dock is located below the store, or tie your dinghy at Fishermen's Wharf.

Classic Marine Store is a well-stocked marine chandlery with marine parts, supplies, gifts, and fishing gear. Don't miss the Classic Café located in the store, offering delectable bites. Classic Marine also offers small boat rentals.

㉖ **Pier 65 (Dungeness Marina).** 1759 Cowichan Bay Rd., Box 51, Cowichan Bay, BC V0R 1N0; (250) 748-6789; info@dungenessmarina.com; www.dungenessmarina.com. Office hours 8:00 a.m. to 2:00 p.m. Tuesday through Saturday. 200 feet of transient moorage, maximum boat length 85 feet; 30 amp power in one box with 4 receptacles; water at the dock. First-come, first-served but may call ahead for available space.

㉖ **Bluenose Marina.** 1765 Cowichan Bay Rd., P.O. Box 40, Cowichan Bay, BC V0R 1N0; (250) 748-2222; deven@thebluenosemarina.com; www.thebluenosemarina.com. Open all year. Guest moorage available on a 100 foot dock, reservations accepted. 15 & 30 amp power, washrooms, showers, laundry. Nearby launch ramp, public playground, and kayak shop. The Cow Cafe & Cookhouse serves seafood and steaks. The Vine Restaurant and Creperie, and Udder Guys Ice Cream shop are nearby.

㉗ **Genoa Bay.** Genoa Bay indents the north shore of Cowichan Bay. Anchorage can be found off the marina docks. The Genoa Bay Marina has guest moorage.

Water Shuttle: The water taxi between Genoa Bay and Cowichan Bay ceased operation in 2018.

㉗ **Genoa Bay Marina.** 5000 Genoa Bay Rd., Duncan, BC V9L 5Y8; (250) 746-7621; (800) 572-6481; info@genoabaymarina.com; www.genoabaymarina.com. Monitors VHF 66A mid-May through end of October. Open all year, guest moorage along 1200 feet of dock space, call ahead. C Dock was widened in 2018, allowing more space for social gatherings. Excellent washrooms, showers and laundry; 15, 30 & 50 amp power. Potable water on the docks is locally produced; quantity of use may be limited. Launch ramp, covered picnic shelter, Wi-Fi.

This is a popular summer stop. The Genoa Bay Gallery has lovely paintings, prints, and sculptures. The Genoa Bay Café is often busy, reservations recommended. The "breakfast cabana" on the dock offers coffee, fresh baked goods, and other breakfast items daily, from the third weekend in June through Labor Day. The unusually good store carries convenience items, souvenirs, books, cruising guides, and snacks. Good crabbing in the bay. Ask at the office about the nearby "Mad Dog" trail that takes you to the top of Tzouhalem Mountain.

Musgrave Landing - Harbour Authority of Salt Spring Island. (250) 537-5711 saltspringharbours.com/musgrave-landing/. Musgrave Landing is on the southwest corner of Salt Spring Island, at the mouth of Sansum Narrows. It is managed by the Harbour Authority of Salt Spring Island. Musgrave Landing is a popular stopover, although it has only a small public float for visitor moorage, no facilities, and very restricted anchorage nearby. Upland you'll find good hiking along miles of logging roads. On a pleasant roadside walk we picked a bouquet of thistle, foxglove, dandelion, fern, salal, nicotiana and pearly everlasting for the galley table. A housing development, with private dock, is on Musgrave Point.

SANSUM NARROWS TO DUCK BAY

Sansum Narrows. Sansum Narrows connects Satellite Channel to the south with Stuart Channel to the north, and leads between high hills on Saltspring Island and Vancouver Island. The wind funnels down the axis of the narrows, turning at the bends. It also funnels down the valleys leading to the channel, so wind directions can be erratic. Currents seldom exceed 3 knots; usually they are less.

Burgoyne Bay - Harbour Authority of Salt Spring Island. saltspringharbours.com/burgoyne-bay/; Burgoyne Bay has ample anchorage in 18 to 30 feet at its inner end, but is subject to williwaws that blow across a low swale on Saltspring Island. Most of the bay is too deep for convenient anchoring. A 65-foot public float for visitor moorage is at the head of the bay, next to the anchorage, no facilities. One side of the float is available for guest moorage stays up to 48 hours. The other side is reserved for local use.

㉘ **Maple Bay.** Maple Bay is a major pleasure boat center, with public moorages and all necessary facilities and services. Birds Eye Cove, off the southwest corner of Maple Bay, is home to the Maple Bay Yacht Club, with reciprocal moorage, and the Maple Bay Marina and Birds Eye Cove Marina. Anchoring is good in Birds Eye Cove, but avoid anchoring on the east side of the cove, opposite the marina docks. Markers designate the no anchoring navigation channel.

Birds Eye Cove Farm, located a half-mile south of Maple Bay, is a favorite local attraction. The Farm raises beef, pork and chickens as well as farm-fresh produce. Visitors can purchase vegetables, eggs, pies and meat dishes from the "Gypsy Wagon" open daily from 9:00 a.m. to 5:00 p.m. Food items are created on their spit grill and wood-fired pizza oven. "Pizza Nights" are held from 4:00 p.m. to 8:00 p.m. on Mondays in May, and from June until Labor Day on Mondays and Wednesdays. It's a treat to join the social events among 300 acres of beautiful rolling fields. Gatherings are held in the large hand-cut timber frame barn and there are two timber frame cabins to rent. For more information go to www.birdseyecovefarm.com or call (250) 748-6379.

One of the best farmer's markets on Vancouver Island is held in downtown Duncan on Saturdays at the Market Square, look for the Clock Tower. The market is open year-round,

Birds Eye Cove and Maple Bay Marina

258   www.WaggonerGuide.com

Reference Only – Not for Navigation GULF ISLANDS

Northern Gulf Islands

spring/summer hours 9:00 a.m. to 2:00 p.m. Taxi service is available through Duncan Taxi (250) 746-4444 or make reservations for the shuttle service from Maple Bay Marina.

(28) **Maple Bay Marina.** 6145 Genoa Bay Rd., Duncan, BC V9L 5T7; (250) 746-8482; (866) 746-8482; info@maplebaymarina.com; www.maplebaymarina.com. Monitors VHF 66A. Open all year. Gasoline, diesel, lubricants, propane and pumpout service at the fuel dock. High-flow fuel pumps available. Mostly 15 & 30 amp power, some 50 amp, garbage, washrooms, showers, laundry, water, waste oil disposal, Shaw Go Wi-Fi, and free Wi-Fi. A lovely picnic shelter provides space for yacht club group functions. Mariners Market & Espresso Bar has coffee, hot breakfast items, muffins, sandwiches, convenience groceries and local art and crafts. The marina office is in the Mariners Market store. A chandlery has marine supplies and charts. Call ahead for slip assignment. Reservations recommended.

A 55-ton Travelift provides haulout for repairs. It is run by Lindstrom Marine, who has the small marine supply store at the marina.

The washrooms are spacious and clean, with good showers. The Shipyard Restaurant & Pub has good food, with daily specials and live music on Friday evenings. The pub offers off-sale beer and wine. Shuttle service is available to downtown Duncan twice a day on weekdays and on Saturdays for a fee. There is charter shuttle service to two different local golf courses. Ask for a schedule at the marina office. Hiking trail maps are available for Mount Tzouhalem and Mount Maple.

The marina offers float home and kayak rentals. Check the marina website for special events, including live music during the summer months.

Harbour Air has scheduled float plane service to Vancouver Harbour. Saltspring Air has scheduled service to Vancouver Airport and Vancouver Harbour.

(28) **Birds Eye Cove Marina.** 6271 Genoa Bay Rd., Duncan, BC V9L 5Y8; (250) 746-5686; info@birdseyecoveduncan.ca. Limited guest moorage with 15 & 30 amp power, washrooms. No showers. The fuel dock at Birds Eye Cove Marina is no longer operating. A 24-hour notice is required for transient space.

(28) **Maple Bay Public Wharf.** Open all year. Located in Maple Bay, not in Birds Eye Cove, which extends from the south side of Maple Bay. Moorage along 300 feet of dock space; no power. Self-register at kiosk. A nice beach is nearby. An underwater park is about 200 feet off the end of the dock. The wharf is managed by the Chemainus Harbour Authority and checked daily. The

2020 Waggoner Cruising Guide

GULF ISLANDS

See Area Map Page 259 - Maps Not for Navigation

Lion Rampant Pub (250-746-5422), with a 50-foot guest dock for patrons, is nearby.

Crofton Public Wharf. Open all year, 1000 feet of dock space, 20 & 30 amp power, washrooms, showers, laundry, garbage drop. Breakwater protected. The docks are usually full with local boats. Crofton is the pulp and paper mill town on the west side of Stuart Channel. The public dock is next to the terminal for the ferry to Vesuvius on Saltspring Island. Walking distance to all services including groceries, restaurants, fishing supplies and licenses. Playground two blocks away. Nearby outdoor swimming pool, tennis courts, hiking trails.

㉙ **Vesuvius.** Located on the northwest side of Saltspring Island, the village of Vesuvius is the terminus for the ferry to Crofton on Vancouver Island. Vesuvius has a public wharf, coffee shop with tasty lunch items, and a restaurant all within easy walking distance. The Seaside restaurant has its own private dock suitable for dinghies and small craft. Vesuvius Bay has anchorage that is open to the northwest with limited protection to the south and southeast. The bay is regularly rocked with wakes from the arriving ferry. More protected anchorage can be found nearby in Duck Bay.

㉙ **Vesuvius - Harbour Authority of Salt Spring Island.** (250) 537-5711 saltspringharbours.com/vesuvius-bay. The public wharf at Vesuvius, located behind the ferry landing, has side-tie visitor moorage on a 40 foot float; no power, no water. Self-registration, moorage rates and payment box are located at the wharfhead; first 2 hours stay at no charge 8:00 a.m. to 4:00 p.m. This is a popular well-used location.

Duck Bay. Just north of Vesuvius Bay, Duck Bay has good anchorage with steep, wooded cliffs rising on its east side. The bay is well-protected, except from northwest winds. A number of private docks, mooring buoys and homes surround the bay.

NORTHERN GULF ISLANDS

Stuart Channel. Stuart Channel runs from Sansum Narrows to Dodd Narrows. It is bordered on the west side by Vancouver Island, and on the east side by Saltspring, Kuper, Thetis and De Courcy Islands. Stuart Channel tends to be littered with drift because of extensive log towing to Crofton, Chemainus and Ladysmith. Keep a sharp watch ahead.

㉚ **Chemainus.** Chemainus is on the Vancouver Island side of Stuart Channel. It has a good public wharf, floats, and mooring buoys. Chemainus Bay, south of the Municipal Dock, is filled with commercial log boom operations and commercial maritime activities. The bay is not suitable for anchoring.

Chemainus is filled with boutiques, galleries, antique shops, and interesting-looking restaurants. More than 30 of the town's buildings have large, well-done murals, most of them depicting Chemainus' distant past as a Native seasonal campground and its more recent history as a mining, logging, and mill town. The mural project is now focused on celebrating Canadian artist Emily Carr's work. The first mural is a remarkable three-dimensional piece on the west side of the Chemainus Theatre Festival building.

Chemainus has grown so popular that a large parking area has been built for tour buses, and in they roll, filled with visitors from around the world. Horse-drawn tours are available. Two 49th Parallel grocery stores are located on Oak Street. The original historic general store is immediately above the municipal dock, and the new fully-stocked store is about half a mile up the road at 3055 Oak Street; call (250) 246-3551 for dock-side deliveries, a fee is charged. Also on Oak Street is the Chemainus Bakery with a good selection of fresh baked goods.

A ferry crosses between Chemainus and Thetis Island, about a 10-minute walk from either Thetis Island Marina or Telegraph Harbour Marina. This is a good way to visit Chemainus. If you take in an evening show in Chemainus, be sure you can get to the ferry before the last departure. Chemainus Water Taxi is another option (250) 246-7866 or (250) 246-9559.

Live Theater: The Chemainus Theatre Festival mounts live matinee and evening performances year-round (closed Mondays). Highly recommended. Call for tickets in advance: (250) 246-9820 or (800) 565-7738.

㉚ **Chemainus Municipal Wharf.** P.O. Box 193, Chemainus, BC V0R 1K0; (250) 715-8186; (250) 246- 4655; harmen.chemainus.munimarina@ gmail.com. Monitors VHF 66A. Day and overnight moorage; 30 & 50 amp power, water, washrooms, showers, garbage drop for overnight guests, pumpout and Wi-Fi. Make moorage reservations directly with the marina by phone or email; they have no relationship with third-party booking services. A nice laundromat is 1½ blocks away at 9870 Cross Street. This

Chemainus

See Area Map Page 259 - Maps Not for Navigation

GULF ISLANDS

Ladysmith Harbour

marina, with slips and side-tie, is next to the ferry terminal. Reservations recommended. Every two hours from morning to night, the ferry arrives and rolls things around a little. It's not bad, but first-time visitors should be aware of the wake.

Visitor boats will tie along 175 feet on the outside of the main dock or moor in slips on the inside of the main dock. Because Chemainus is a popular day stop, landing fees have been instituted—$6 under 40 feet; $12 over 40 feet. They found that the docks were full during the day then empty at night, and they need moorage income to maintain the facility. The irrepressible Harmen Bootsma is the manager.

Mooring Buoys: Eight mooring buoys are available off the park at the entrance to the bay. One boat per buoy, 45-foot maximum length. Cost is $10 per night if you pay at the Chemainus Municipal Dock office; $20 if they have to come out to collect. Private mooring buoys are also in the bay; look for the buoys labeled 'public.'

㉚ **Jones Marine Services Ltd.** Box 29, Chemainus, BC V0R 1K0; (250) 246-1100. Diesel and mid-grade gasoline. A fire in March of 2018 caused considerable damage to the building. New construction was underway in 2019. Fuel service is anticipated to be available for the 2020 boating season.

Evening Cove. Evening Cove, at the mouth of Ladysmith Harbour, is a possible anchorage. Correspondent Bruce Evertz reports: "We found good protection from northwest winds, but did have a few wakes from passing boats. There are several houses around the bay so it's not a good spot to take Fido ashore."

㉛ **Ladysmith Harbour.** Ladysmith is on Vancouver Island, approximately 6 miles north of Chemainus. Ladysmith is an active sawmill town. Logs are stored on the north side of the harbor and in front of the mill on the south side.

Ladysmith itself is about one-half mile from Ladysmith Community Marina and Fisherman's Wharf, up the hill and across the highway. It's a bit of a hike, but worthwhile. Before reaching the highway, the big blue building is the Ladysmith Waterfront Arts Centre, with interesting galleries and the Ladysmith Maritime Society's office and historical collection of outboard motors. The building used to be a railroad equipment repair facility. The tracks are still there. A train occasionally rumbles by.

The main street of Ladysmith looks as if time passed it by. Movie scenes have been filmed here. A large and friendly 49th Parallel Grocery is several blocks west from the main downtown area, and will deliver to the docks. A private liquor store is next door to the grocery.

The Old Town Bakery at 510 First Avenue (main street through town) is "to die for," with the widest variety of fresh-baked cinnamon buns we've ever seen. We had an excellent and reasonably priced deli lunch there, too. Buoma Meats, at 412 First Avenue,

2020 Waggoner Cruising Guide

GULF ISLANDS — See Area Map Page 259 - Maps Not for Navigation

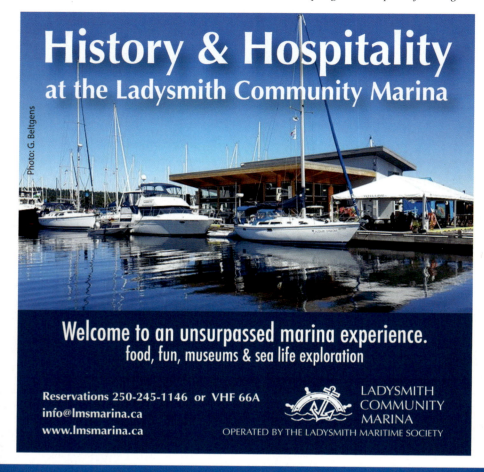

is an old-fashioned butcher shop, all weights in pounds and ounces. The Beantime Cafe serves fresh roasted coffee. A broad selection of restaurants are in town. Several restaurants will deliver to the marinas.

Ladysmith Community Marina, run by the Ladysmith Maritime Society, behind Slag Point on the south side of the harbor, is the first major set of docks. Ladysmith Fisherman's Wharf is adjacent, followed by Ladysmith Marina farther into the harbor. Page Point Marina, on the north shore, sometimes has transient moorage available. Ladysmith Yacht Club, located at Ladysmith Marina has reciprocal moorage. Near the mouth of Ladysmith Harbour, the long float in Sibell Bay on the north side of the Dunsmuir Islands is a Seattle Yacht Club outstation, member boats only; no reciprocal moorage.

Good anchoring is in Sibell Bay, at the head of Ladysmith Harbour, and in the small bay between north Dunsmuir Island and Bute Island. Sibell Bay is a bit more exposed then the other two possible anchorages. There is ample swinging room with good holding at the head of Ladysmith Harbour. The bay between North Dunsmuir Island and Bute Island is well protected with room for a few boats. A community dock on the west side of Bute Island has a 40-foot concrete float, which provides access to a loop trail on the island. Maxium 3-hour stay on the dock, no charge.

LADYSMITH MARKETPLACE

49th PARALLEL GROCERY AND CAFÉ
The 49th is a full-service grocery store, including fresh produce, meat, deli, bakery, café, and flower shop. We offer a delivery service back to your vessel – Check with the wharf for details. Located next to the Liquor Depot and a short hike from Ladysmith Marinas. Open 7 days a week!
250-245-3221 • 1020 First Ave. • www.the49th.com

FOX & HOUNDS
Our Tudor style British Pub offers 16 English, European and local craft beers on tap, and a full British menu with all your favourites. We are family-owned and family-friendly. Open seven days a week from 11:30am to 10pm. Look for the British red phone box on High Street.
250 924 1747 • 11 High Street
www.foxandhoundsladysmith.com

CHAMBER OF COMMERCE AND VISITOR CENTRE
The information hub of our community. Discover all the wonderful things there are to see and do in Ladysmith including some of the hidden hotspots. Find out where to dine, shop or what's going on around town. Visit us for all these questions and more.
250-245-2112 • 33 Roberts Street
www.ladysmithcofc.com or www.tourismladysmith.ca

For a Calendar of Events Visit
www.ladysmithcofc.com

LADYSMITH COMMUNITY MARINA
"The friendliest marina on the west coast"
Ladysmith Community Marina is all about community and making your stay enjoyable. Our 3000 sf floating Welcome Centre has beautiful amenities that will make you feel at home as you explore local islands, vineyards, forests and towns. Located 55 nautical miles north of Victoria, Ladysmith Community Marina is the first marina port side as you enter Ladysmith Harbour.
250-245-1146 • 610 Oyster Bay • www.lmsmarina.ca

LADYSMITH MARINA
Located on the protected east coast of Vancouver Island just outside of Nanaimo, BC, Ladysmith Marina is the perfect gateway to some of the most breathtaking boating grounds in British Columbia, including the Gulf Islands. With a waterfront picnic area and ample parking, this ocean paradise is easily accessed from nearby Nanaimo Airport and two BC Ferries terminals.
250-245-4521 • 901 Gladden Rd. • www.ladysmithmarina.com

PHARMASAVE LADYSMITH
Located at the top end of First Avenue, Pharmasave has been serving Ladysmith for over 35 years. More than a drug store, Pharmasave has a great selection of products & services ranging from full service pharmacy and cosmetic departments to beautiful giftware, greeting cards and a Post Office. Visit us today and "Live Well" with Pharmasave.
250-245-3113 • 441 1st Ave. • www.ladysmithpharmasave.com

SALAMANDER BOOKS
Visit our independent bookstore in historic downtown Ladysmith. Come in to our store, relax and browse. We have an interesting selection of both new and used books, including cookbooks, travel guides, local authors, and children's books. Open Monday to Friday from 9:30am to 5:30pm, and Saturdays from 10am to 5pm.
250-245-4726 • 535 1st Ave. • Find us on Facebook!

See Area Map Page 259 - Maps Not for Navigation   GULF ISLANDS

Ladysmith Community Marina is a great place to relax and meet other boaters.

Repairs: Saltair Marine Services offers marine repairs and haulout to 40 feet, (250) 714-6206. Sealegs Kayaking Adventures, located upland from Ladysmith Community Marina, offers equipment sales, tours and lessons. The office, located at 200 Transfer Beach Blvd., is a short hike up the hill, phone (250) 245-4096. Concerts are held in the park at Transfer Beach.

No-Discharge Zone. Gray water okay.

㉛ **Ladysmith Community Marina.** P.O. Box 1030, Ladysmith, BC V9G 1A7; (250) 245-1146; info@lmsmarina.ca; www.lmsmarina.ca. Monitors VHF 66A. Best to phone or email for availability. Open all year, 800 feet of guest moorage with 30 amp power, water, cube ice and block ice. Pumpout and free Wi-Fi. Garbage and recycling (donations are appreciated). Reservations recommended and can be made online. The impressive Ladysmith Maritime Society Welcome Centre, on a float at the docks, has a fireside lounge, washrooms, showers, laundry, and the seasonal Oyster Bay Cafe, which is open daily from mid-May to Labour Day. Adjacent to the Oyster Bay Cafe is the Sea Life Centre with interpretive displays and an underwater portal to view the marine life. It is a hit with the kids. The dinghy dock is on the cross dock by the Welcome Centre.

These are the first set of docks on the southwest side as you enter Ladysmith Harbour. The docks are very good and the historical displays, including restored museum boats and equipment, are fascinating. The Harbour Heritage Centre, an art gallery, and the Ladysmith Maritime Society with a naval display, are up the hill in the large blue building. The town of Ladysmith is a short walk farther up the hill.

The community is justifiably proud of this facility and its large meeting spaces. A large covered 40 X 20 foot picnic area with tables and grills, located on the docks, can accommodate up to 100 people. At the end of the day it is not unusual for a group to gather round, some grilling their dinners and some visiting others. Dine on the Dock programs are often held on Fridays during the summers and frequently sell out. Music and food on the Dock events are held in July and August. Their BBQ's and Open Mic Nights are popular. Check the website for more information. The Ladysmith Community Marina is run by the Ladysmith Maritime Society and is a true community marina, with over 250 volunteers. As guests, we could feel their enthusiasm.

㉛ **Ladysmith Fisherman's Wharf.** P.O. Box 130, Ladysmith, BC V9G 1A1; (250) 245-7511 or (250) 618-4720 after hours; office hours 10:00 a.m. to 1:00 p.m. Monday through Saturday. lfwa@telus.net; www.ladysmithfishermanswharf. com. Open all year, 1200 feet of dock space, 30 amp power, garbage drop, washrooms, showers, laundry services, waste oil disposal, trailer parking. Marine repairs, tidal grid and launch ramp.

2020 Waggoner Cruising Guide   263

GULF ISLANDS

See Area Map Page 259 - Maps Not for Navigation

Stern-tied in lovely Princess Cove on Wallace Island

Limited transient moorage. Commercial fish boats have priority during the winter months. Stairs lead up the hill toward the town of Ladysmith, about one-half mile away.

㉛ **Ladysmith Marina.** 901 Gladden Rd., Ladysmith, BC V9G 1K4; (250) 245-4521; ladysmithmarina@obmg.com; www.ladysmithmarina.com. Monitors VHF 66A. Open all year, washrooms, showers, and a public laundry. 30 & 50 amp power. Picnic area. This marina has permanent moorage, but guest moorage is often available in unoccupied slips, call ahead for availability; reservations accepted. Dock A on the east side of the marina is occupied by the Ladysmith Yacht Club, with reciprocal moorage. The marina is part of Oak Bay Marine Group, a company that owns several marinas.

㉜ **Page Point Marina Inc.** 4760 Brenton-Page Rd., Ladysmith, BC V9G 1L7; (250) 245-2312; (877) 860-6866; moorage@pagepointmarina.com; www.pagepointmarina.com. Monitors VHF 66A. Open all year. Permanent moorage to 66 feet, with limited guest moorage; 30 amp power, water, free Wi-Fi, garbage drop, compost & recycling. Free shuttle service to the airport. Pet-friendly. Reservations recommended. The dinghy dock is next to the ramp at the head of G dock.

Tent Island. Tent Island is off the south tip of Penelakut Island (formerly Kuper Island), at the junction of Houstoun Passage and Stuart Channel. The small bay on the west side of Tent Island is a popular anchorage in settled weather.

Preedy Harbour. Preedy Harbour indents the southwest corner of Thetis Island, due west of Telegraph Harbour. The ferry from Chemainus calls there. From the south, enter between Hudson Island and three long, thin reefs, marked with red (starboard hand) lights and day beacons. From Stuart Channel enter between Hudson Island and Dayman Island. Reefs, marked by green buoys on the Dayman Island side and a light on the Hudson Island side, extend from both these islands. Because the Hudson Island light is positioned upland from the toe of its reef, favor the Dayman Island buoys.

Entry from the north is clear as long as you stay mid-channel. For all three entries, check the chart carefully so you know where the reefs are, and how to avoid them.

A day-use-only community dock is in the northwest corner of Preedy Harbour, near the ferry landing. Anchorage is good in this area, keeping in mind the ferry comings and goings.

㉝ **Telegraph Harbour.** Telegraph Harbour is one of the Gulf Islands' most popular stops. It is located across Stuart Channel from Chemainus, between Thetis Island and Penelakut Island (formerly Kuper Island). Two marinas are in Telegraph Harbour: Thetis Island Resort and Telegraph Harbour Marina. Both marinas are walking distance to an inter-island ferry to Chemainus. While you're at Telegraph Harbour, you may enjoy walking the roads of Thetis Island. You'll find a number of interesting stops, including the Pot of Gold Coffee Roasting Co.

White Restricted Operations buoys mark the edges of the anchoring area. Note the shoal areas on the east side of the channel across from the Thetis Island Resort. Depths are shallower than charted.

Penelakut Island (formerly Kuper Island) is an Indian Reserve.

Farmers Market: A farmers market is held 10:00 a.m. to 2:00 p.m. on Saturdays, June through early September at Howling Wolf Farm at the corner of Marine Dr. and Pilkey Point Road.

LOCAL KNOWLEDGE

ENTRANCE CHANNEL: Channel markers indicate the channel between Thetis Island Resort and Telegraph Harbour Marina. Red to starboard when entering. On very low tides hug the breakwater outside the Thetis Island Resort's fuel dock as you enter Telegraph Harbour. The channel has about 9 feet of depth at zero tide.

㉝ **Thetis Island Resort.** 46 Harbour Rd., Thetis Island, BC ; (250) 246-1443; marina@thetisisland.com; www.thetisisland.com. Monitors VHF 66A; (250) 246-3464 (pub, year round). To port, this is the first marina as you enter Telegraph Harbour. Open all year, gasoline and diesel at the fuel dock, propane on shore, over 3000 feet of side-tie dock space, 15 & 30 amp power, washrooms, showers, laundry, ATM. New docks were added in 2017. Additional improvements were made in 2018, including a new patio area, a refurbished deck for the pub, and renewed finishes on the outside of the main building. New owner, Wayne Proctor, is planning for continued improvements. Music is held at the pub on most weekends during July and August. The marina has three rental suites, and they're quite nice. This is a full-service marina with a liquor store, convenience groceries, snacks, ice, and post office. Wi-Fi on the docks; get the password at the pub or the fuel dock. A cell phone booster covers the pub and deck areas. It's a 10- to 15-minute walk to the BC Ferries to Chemainus.

The fully-licensed pub has inside and outside dining and separate areas for families. The pub has good food and an excellent selection of beers, porters, stouts, and single-malt scotches.

The Resort has its own water desalination system, no water at the docks however. A covered picnic and barbecue area with seating is available for groups.

㉝ **Telegraph Harbour Marina.** Box 7-10, Thetis Island, BC V0R 2Y0; (250) 246-9511; (800) 246-6011; sunny@telegraphharbour.com; www.telegraphharbour.com. Monitors VHF 66A. This is the marina at the back of the bay. Although close to drying flats, the

Telegraph Harbour

264

GULF ISLANDS

Stern-ties are the rule at popular Pirates Cove Marine Park.

docks have at least 6 to 8 feet on all tides. Open 7 days a week, mid-June through mid-September, and weekends only from Easter through mid-June. In winter no facilities are available except moorage and electricity. Gasoline, diesel, and oil at the fuel dock. Moorage along 3000 feet of dock, 15 & 30 amp power, washrooms, showers, laundry, Wi-Fi, garbage drop, recycling, limited water.

The store carries convenience groceries including a variety of specialty meats, deli items to go, marine guides, books and gifts, and fresh-baked pies. The marina has pre-ordered homemade pizzas and fresh baguettes to go, and is the exclusive outlet for Thetis Island's Pot of Gold coffee. They have an old fashioned soda fountain where you can still get guilt-filled hard ice cream and milk shakes.

The marina is clean and well-maintained. Staff helps arriving boats land. They have a playground for kids, a dog run, a large covered area for group functions, and a picnic area with tables and barbecues. It's a 10 to 15 minute walk to the BC Ferries to Chemainus. Boaters are permitted to use the community trail system, accessible from the marina.

Rendezvous: Many rendezvous are held here in spring or early fall, best to call ahead for reservations on weekends and during the peak season. A few rendezvous fill the marina, but most do not. Moorage space is usually available.

The Cut. The Cut is a straight and uncomplicated drying pass connecting Telegraph Harbour with Clam Bay. Red, Right, Returning assumes you are returning from Clam Bay. Cruising boats should only try The Cut at or near high water, with local knowledge. Signs at each end purport to show the depth, but they read approximately 3 feet too deep. We took the dinghy through at the bottom of a 4.3-foot tide, sounding the shallow spots with a leadline. Although the two signs said 6 feet of water was in the channel, we found only 2 to 2.5 feet in the shallow spots near the Telegraph Harbour entrance and at a couple of narrow places on the Clam Bay side.

North Cove. North Cove indents the north end of Thetis Island and is a good anchorage, although it is open to northwesterly winds. A substantial rock breakwater protects a private float and boathouse at Fraser Point, the entrance to North Cove. Camp docks are in the southwest corner of the cove. Anchor in 24 to 36 feet (zero tide) along the south shore. High tide covers fingers of rock that extend from the south shore, but the rock reappears when the tide drops. Don't get too close. Stay clear of the rocks in the middle of the entry. The charts show them as ++, for dangerous rocks 6 feet or less beneath the surface.

Cufra Inlet. Cufra Inlet, about a mile long, extends into Thetis Island from the southeast corner of North Cove. Most of the inlet dries, but is good for dinghy exploring at higher water.

Clam Bay. Clam Bay is a large, relatively open bay with good anchoring in convenient depths. Reader Jerry Williams, who lived there, says his favorite spot is the little bight on the north shore, between Leech Island and Thetis Island. The mouth of the Clam Bay is partly blocked by Centre Reef. Rocket Shoal is in the middle of the bay. Lacking familiarity, the safest entry is south of Centre Reef, between Buoy U42 and Penelakut Spit, which extends from Penelakut Island (formerly Kuper Island). The charts show everything. Large scale Plans Chart 3477 is especially useful. Clam Bay is at one end of The Cut, the drying channel that separates Thetis Island from Penelakut Island.

Southey Bay. At the north tip of Saltspring Island, tucked in beside Southey Point, is a little notch that Tom Kincaid used as an anchorage in past years. An increasing number of private mooring buoys have restricted swinging room, but it's still a possible anchorage.

Secretary Islands. The Secretary Islands have several nice little anchorages, with the emphasis on *little*. One of the easiest is in the notch on the Trincomali Channel side between the two Secretary Islands.

Mowgli Island. Mowgli Island, off the northwest tip of the Secretary Islands, has good anchorage in a cozy bay between it and the first Secretary island. Swinging room is limited. We suggest a stern-tie across the gravel beach to driftwood ashore. The island is surrounded by reefs. They are easily seen at low tide, but be cautious at high tide.

㉞ **Wallace Island Marine Park.** www.env.gov.bc.ca/bcparks/explore/parkpgs/wallace/ Open all year. Wallace Island, a marine park purchased with the help of the local boating community, is a low and beautiful tree-covered island in Trincomali Channel. Enter from Houstoun Passage. You'll find sheltered anchorage and a dock at Conover Cove, anchorage for many boats in locally-named Princess Cove, and room for a couple of boats just inside Panther Point. The park has toilets, campsites and picnic areas, and trails crisscrossing the entire island. It's a fine place to walk through the forest and stretch the legs. Raccoons roam the area—especially at night, lock up all food items aboard and pack out refuse. Old cabins set in an orchard near Conover Cove are locked shut, awaiting funds for restoration. One cabin is festooned with carved name boards from visiting yachts. Please respect the two private properties on the island.

㉞ **Conover Cove.** A reef directly offshore from the entrance to Conover Cove on Wallace Island can be avoided by going around either end. Especially from the southeast, give the reef ample room. When you leave, remember the reef is there. We are told that each year boats depart at high tide and drive up on the rocks. A dock for boats 36 feet and under provides access to the island, a nominal fee is charged. An honor-system pay-box is located at the head of the ramp. Conover Cove is fairly shoal at the dock and shoals even more toward both ends of the bay. You can anchor and stern-tie to pins, with chain, set in the rocks on shore. Be sure to check your depths. The entrance to Conover Cove is shallow at low tide.

㉞ **Princess Cove.** Princess Cove is just northwest of Conover Cove, and has room for quite a few boats to anchor. 18 long chains, with large links for stern lines, are attached to existing pins set in the rock along the shoreline. If anchoring in the cove, set the anchor carefully in 18 to 24 feet (deeper toward the mouth of the cove), and maintain an anchor watch if the wind comes up. A dinghy dock is on the west side of the cove for convenient access to hiking.

㉞ **Panther Point.** Panther Point is the southeast tip of Wallace Island. There's room for one or perhaps two boats in 30 to 36 feet just inside the mouth of the cove. If you anchor any farther inside, a rock on the north side will restrict your swing. The anchorage is exposed to southeast winds but protected from other winds.

Retreat Cove. Retreat Cove, a small notch protected by off-lying Retreat Island, indents

2020 Waggoner Cruising Guide 265

GULF ISLANDS

See Area Map Page 259 - Maps Not for Navigation

Galiano Island across Trincomali Channel from the south tip of Wallace Island. The approach around the north side of Retreat Island is shallow and foul with rocks and reefs. Enter only from the south. The head of Retreat Cove shelves sharply. Anchor in 18 to 24 feet, but plan your swing to avoid the shelf. An 80-foot-long public dock, no facilities, is on the southern shore of the cove. Local boats take much of the space on the dock.

North Galiano. North Galiano is on the west side of Galiano Island. It lies to the northeast of Hall Island and has anchorage and a small public dock, no facilities.

Dionisio Point Park. Open all year, day use and overnight camping, toilets, no power, no showers. Anchor only. The park overlooks Porlier Pass. It has sandy beaches, rocky headlands and forested uplands.

Porlier Pass. Porlier Pass separates Galiano Island and Valdes Island. Several times a year, currents on large tides reach 9 knots. Current predictions are shown in the Tide and Current Tables Vol. 5, and Ports and Passes. The current floods north into the Strait of Georgia, and ebbs south into the Gulf Islands. The best time to transit is at slack water. A study of the chart shows it is safest to transit Porlier Pass on the south sides of Black Rock and Virago Rock, staying toward the Galiano Island side of the pass.

From the Strait of Georgia, begin your approach near Lighted Bell Buoy U41. South of the buoy, pick up the range on Race Point and Virago Point. Follow that range into Porlier Pass to clear the rocks extending from the northeast tip of Galiano Island. Once clear of the rocks, you can turn to follow a mid-channel course between Virago Rock and Galiano Island. Charts 3442 and 3443 show the range and the rocks to be avoided on both sides, but the larger scale Chart 3473 really helps understanding. Chartbook 3313 also shows the pass in excellent detail.

De Courcy Group. The De Courcy Group has several interesting small anchorages. **Whaleboat Island,** just off the southeast shore of Ruxton Island, is a relatively undeveloped provincial park. The preferred anchorage is south of the island, taking care to avoid a drying rock. The north end of **Ruxton Island** has **Herring Bay**, one of the more attractive small anchorages in the northern Gulf Islands, and frequently used when the anchorage at **Pirates Cove** on De Courcy Island is full (which it often is in the summer). Herring Bay has a white sand beach to enjoy. The De Courcy Group is named after Michael de Courcy, captain of the H.M.S. Pylades, who charted these waters from 1859 to 1861.

Whaleboat Island Marine Park. Just south of Ruxton Island. No facilities. Whaleboat Island is undeveloped, but provides an extremely limited alternate anchorage to Pirates Cove Marine Park. The preferred

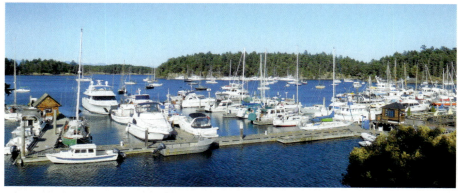

Silva Bay offers several moorage options.

anchorage is south of the island, taking care to avoid a drying rock.

Pylades Island. Reader Jerry Williams, who grew up on Pylades Island, tells us the little hole just north of the dot islet off the northeast corner of Pylades Island is "magical." Most of the land is private, please do not take dogs ashore. A drying shoal is between Pylades Island and the dot islet, so approach from the north. In Whaleboat Passage, between Pylades Island and Ruxton Island, note the drying rock off Pylades Island. Jerry Williams reports that the rock is farther from shore than one might think and recommends favoring the Ruxton Island side.

Herring Bay. Herring Bay indents the northwest end of Ruxton Island, off Ruxton Passage. The bay is bordered by weather-carved sandstone walls and has a beautiful sand beach on the southeast side. Good anchoring in 24 feet, much to explore.

A charted rock ledge that dries at 1 foot is in the west entrance to Herring Bay at 49°05.08'N/123°43.01'W. We use the north entrance exclusively.

LOCAL KNOWLEDGE

DANGEROUS REEFS: The entrance to Pirates Cove is guarded by a reef that extends parallel to the shoreline to a point a little beyond a concrete beacon. When entering, you must leave this beacon to port. A range, consisting of a white-painted arrow on the ground and a white × on a tree above, shows where to make your approach. Align the × on the tree above the arrow on the ground and proceed slowly until just past the concrete beacon to port. Turn sharply to port and leave the red Spar Buoy U38 to starboard. The entry is shallow. At lower tides deep-draft boats should be especially cautious.

㉟ **Pirates Cove Marine Park.** Pirates Cove is open all year, campsites, pit toilets, hand pump water (boil before use) on the south beach, no other facilities. It's a lovely little harbor, protected from seas but not all winds, with room for many boats (on a short scope). 24 stern-tie chains are set into the sandstone cliffs that encircle the bay; the boat's stern-tie line is run through a large link in the chain. Do not use trees for stern tie. Two dinghy docks are for shore access, one on the northeast and the other on the southwest side of the cove. Dinghies may go ashore at the south end beach. The small marina on the right as you enter is private.

Most of the land is a marvelous provincial park. The cove is surrounded by a forest of Douglas fir, Garry oak and Arbutus (madrona). Well-maintained trails lead through the forest and along the rock shoreline with its sculpted sandstone formations and tide pools. Be sure to stay on designated trails to avoid brushing against poison oak, a rash-causing plant species protected by the Provincial Marine Park. Pirates Cove has only a fair holding bottom of sticky mud. If the wind comes up during the night, you can expect a fire drill as boats drag anchor. It's best to stern-tie. When departure time arrives, be prepared to spend extra time cleaning the anchor as it comes aboard.

No Discharge Zone, No Gray Water Discharge.

On Ruxton Passage, the little notch at the south end of De Courcy Island is also part of the park, and you can anchor there. The beach is good for dinghy or kayak landing, and campsites are ashore. Additional anchorage is available at Whaleboat Island Marine Park, nearby. Another "Pirates Cove overflow" notch is just north of Pirates Cove off Link Island.

Boat Harbour. 2275 Kendall Road, Nanaimo, BC V9X 1W8; (250) 802-9963; marina.boatharbour@gmail.com; www.boatharbourmarina.ca; Joe, the wharfinger, is a delight. Located across Stuart Channel from De Courcy Island, Boat Harbour is home to **Boat Harbour Marina**. Open June-September, 9:00 a.m. to 5:00 p.m. Long-term moorage with transient space; max boat size, 100 feet. Two-day minimum stay on weekends. 30 & 50 amp power, water, garbage drop, Wi-Fi. Restrooms and showers. Call for reservations 48 hours in advance. Four mooring buoys also available by reservation. Floatplane service available through Vancouver via Pacific Coastal Airlines.

Boat Harbour Marina has substantial concrete floats and quality metal ramps and

GULF ISLANDS

pilings. The marina offers customized tours for groups of 8 or more. You can opt for hikes through the private upland trails, with a picnic at the lake, or you might choose cooking classes, catered parties or pig roasts. A pig and beef roast event is held on July 1, Canada Day. A gazebo for group gatherings is planned for the near future.

The anchorage area in Boat Harbour is within a private 'water lot' and is a no discharge zone. Anchorage allowed only with a permit by calling or texting (250) 802-9963 for application. The no-anchoring zone is marked with a line of spar buoys and posted signage. All of **Kenary Cove** dries on low tide.

The small community of Cedar on Yellow Point is two and a half miles (4 km) from Boat Harbour Marina. The popular English-style pub, Crow & Gate (250-722-3731), is located on Yellow Point Road. A Farmer's Market is held on Sundays at the Woodbank School.

GABRIOLA PASSAGE TO NANAIMO

Gabriola Passage. Gabriola Passage (Gabriola is pronounced "GAY-briola") is the northernmost entrance to the Gulf Islands from the Strait of Georgia. From Bowen Island on the east side of the strait, it is 14 miles to Gabriola Passage, the shortest crossing between the lower mainland and the islands.

Tidal currents on spring tides can run to

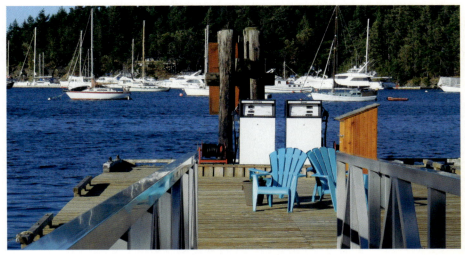
Page's Resort in Sliva Bay is a convenient stop for diesel and gasoline.

8 knots in Gabriola Passage, both flood and ebb. Typical maximum currents are around 4 knots. Transiting is best at slack. The current sets east on the flood and west on the ebb. Times of slack and maximum currents are given in the Tide & Current Tables, Vol. 5 and Ports and Passes.

Degnen Bay. Degnen Bay, on Gabriola Passage at the south end of Gabriola Island, is a good anchorage but a little crowded with boats on moorings. Entering Degnen Bay, favor the east side, close to Josef Point, to avoid rocks in the middle. A petroglyph of a killer whale is on a slab of rock near the head of the bay. Correspondents John and Lorraine Littlewood report additional petroglyphs on the United Church grounds. A public dock provides access to Gabriola Island. All other docks are private.

Degnen Bay Public Wharf. Has 190 feet of dock space, power, garbage drop, but no other facilities. Commercial fish boats have priority.

WATERFRONT SUITES & MARINA
NANAIMO'S NEW, PREMIERE MARINA

▸ Located in the heart of Nanaimo along Newcastle Channel (in front of buoy P-13)
▸ Brand new docks constructed of marine-grade aluminium
▸ 30 and 50 Amp Metered Power and Water service
▸ Comfortable, economical accommodations
▸ Annual and Transient Moorage available
▸ Marina Lounge for Moorage clients
▸ Waterfront Club Concierge Service
▸ Home of the Nanaimo Boat Show
▸ Washroom and Shower Facilities
▸ Laundry Facilities

1000 Stewart Avenue, Nanaimo, BC V9S 4C9 | 250-753-7111 | www.waterfrontnanaimo.com | moorage@waterfrontnanaimo.com

GULF ISLANDS

See Area Map Page 259 - Maps Not for Navigation

Nanaimo's 4 kilometer long Waterfront Promenade takes hikers to Departure Bay.

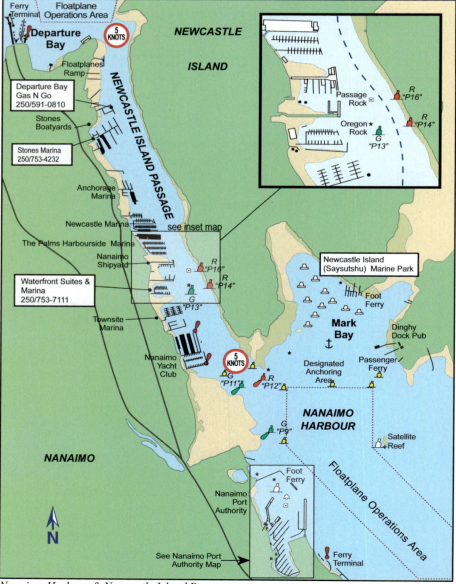

Nanaimo Harbour & Newcastle Island Passage

Wakes Cove. Wakes Cove, on Gabriola Passage at the north end of Valdes Island, has a beautiful provincial marine park occupying almost the entire north end of Valdes Island. The park has trails and historical interpretation information. It is served by a small dock, approximately 40 feet, for RCMP and BC Parks personnel. The park is accessible by dinghy and kayak. Anchorage is a little iffy.

Dogfish Bay. Kendrick Island, on the northeast side of Valdes Island, creates a narrow and shallow bay known locally as Dogfish Bay. Dogfish Bay is well protected and the holding ground is good. West Vancouver Yacht Club has an outstation on Kendrick Island, members only, no reciprocal moorage.

Drumbeg Provincial Park. South end of Gabriola Island, overlooking Gabriola Passage. Open all year, day use only. Toilets, no other facilities. Has shelving sandstone rocks and a small sandy beach.

Flat Top Islands. The Flat Top Islands are appropriately named, and from the north or east they're a little hard to tell apart. If approaching from the Strait of Georgia, pass north of Thrasher Rock Light. The light marks the northern end of Gabriola Reefs. All the Flat Top Islands are privately owned.

LOCAL KNOWLEDGE

DANGEROUS ROCK: When entering Silva Bay between Vance Island and Tugboat Island, leave the beacon marking Shipyard Rock to port. Do not turn at once for the Silva Bay floats or other facilities. Shipyard Rock is larger than it appears on the charts. Continue instead until about halfway to Law Point before making your turn. Give the rock plenty of room.

㉟ **Silva Bay.** Silva Bay is a popular destination in the Flat Top Islands area, well protected, with good holding bottom. From the north, enter through Commodore Passage between Gaviola Island and Vance Island; from the south enter through Commodore Passage between Acorn Island and Tugboat Island. From Commodore Passage, enter Silva Bay between Tugboat Island and Vance Island, leaving Shipyard Rock to port; notorious Shipyard Rock lies along the south side of this passage. Entering Silva Bay from the south through Sear Island Passage between Gabriola Island and Sear Island is possible only on high water tides.

Silva Bay Shipyard, with marine railway and 12-ton Travelift, is next to Silva Bay Resort & Marina.

Check the community bus schedule for pick up at Page's Inn for a visit to the Island's village core.

Anchoring: Anchoring is tight. Much of the bay is filled with private mooring buoys; a

GULF ISLANDS

designated float plane departure and landing area is located along the front of the docks, where anchoring is not allowed.

㊱ **Silva Bay Resort & Marina.** 3383 South Road, Gabriola Island, BC V0R 1X7; (250) 247-8662 ext. 8; info@silvabay.com; www.silvabay.com. Monitors VHF 66A. Open all year with guest moorage, 30 amp & limited 100 amp power, water on the fuel dock, garbage drop, washrooms, showers and laundry. Reservations recommended. Diesel and mid-grade gasoline at the fuel dock. Daily floatplane flights to Vancouver.

The Silva Bay Bar & Grill was destroyed by fire in October 2017. Dan Chen and family, new owners of the marina property, have plans to redevelop the uplands, including a restaurant and other resort amenities. Food trucks will be on the premises during the summer months until redevelopment begins.

㊱ **Page's Resort & Marina.** 3350 Coast Road, Gabriola Island, BC V0R 1X7; (250) 247-8931; info@pagesresort.com; www.pagesresortgroup.com. Monitors VHF 66A. Open all year. Visitor moorage accommodates vessels to 40 feet; two slips accommodate vessels up to 60 feet; one slip can accommodate a 75-foot vessel. Mid-grade marine gasoline and diesel at the fuel dock. 30 amp power, washrooms, showers, laundry, garbage, recycling, bicycle and scooter rentals, ice, free Wi-Fi. Cottages and tent sites for rent. Campers and RV guests share the one shower facility per gender with boaters. The grounds are well maintained.

Cab service and a community shuttle bus service can take you to Gabriola Island's shopping center, or you can rent bicycles or motor scooters at Page's.

For those interested in books, Page's carries a range of titles, especially books about local subjects by local authors. The refurbished office/store carries essential groceries, sundry items, bait, marine charts, and cruising guides. The store's freezer is stocked with ready-made dinners that can be prepared back at the boat or on the barbeque. Food includes items from Woodfire Restaurant; baked goods from Slow Rise Bakery; and coffee from a micro roaster on Gabriola Island. The Woodfired pizzas are designed to stay crisp when warmed up in the microwave. The cheeses at Page's "Lil Market" store are made by Paula Maddison, who teaches classes in cheese making on the island; see makecheesewithpaula.ca.

Page's Resort & Marina is friendly and well managed. Gloria Hatfield is the owner.

㊱ **Page's Inn on Silva Bay.** 3415 South Rd., Gabriola Island, BC V0R 1X7, (250) 247-9351; info@silvabayinn.ca; www.pagesresortgroup.com. This lovely Inn, formerly the Boatel, is now owned by Page's Resort & Marina. Meeting space is available on the top floor. Located west of Page's Marina, the docks at Page's Inn offer transient moorage for boaters staying ashore in one of the suites. A farmers' market, selling produce, food, and Gabriolan art, is held on the grounds on Sundays during the summer season.

Silva Bay Shipyard. 3445 South Road, Gabriola Island, BC V0R 1X7; (250) 247-9800; info@silvabayshipyard.com; www.silvabayshipyard.com. A do-it-yourself boatyard with a 12-ton travelift and 80-ton railway. Ships chandlery, mechanical & electrical repairs, stern drive mechanics, and wooden boat repair.

False Narrows. False Narrows is east of Dodd Narrows, and is an alternate connection between the Gulf Islands and Northumberland Channel. If you choose to make this passage, you will be traveling between reefs in a shallow channel that is best used at half tide or better. Local knowledge says if you strictly follow the two ranges shown on the chart you'll be okay. Go slowly to keep your wake down. Maximum currents in False Narrows are about half of those in Dodd Narrows. Watch for thick kelp beds.

㊲ **Dodd Narrows.** Currents in Dodd Narrows run to 9 knots as water swirls through the narrow deep passage between cliffs. The narrows are best taken at slack water. For the hour or so before the predicted turn, boats collect at each end waiting for the right time. These boats include commercial craft, even tugboats with log tows or large barges, so the period around slack water can get pretty interesting. Generally, the boats on the upstream side go first, catching the last of the dying fair current. When they are through, boats on the other end go through, picking up the beginnings of the new (for them) fair current. It all works well as long as no one gets impatient. Vessels will be transiting in both directions during and around slack periods. Check for traffic by viewing AIS targets on both sides of the narrows and listen on VHF 16 for Securité calls from traffic that might pose a safety concern for other vessels. Tugboats with log tows and large commercial vessels will typically announce their intentions on VHF 16. In recent years, VHF 16 has been flooded with Securité calls from boats that may not need to announce themselves, so if your boat does not pose a safety concern for others, there is no need to make a Securité call. If you do make a call, be sure to use 1-watt low power. Don't be in a hurry, and don't try to pass a slower boat. Dodd Narrows is short. Travel single-file and leave room between your boat and the boat ahead and share the channel with opposing direction traffic.

Northumberland Channel. Northumberland Channel is the passage from the Gulf Islands

Silva Bay

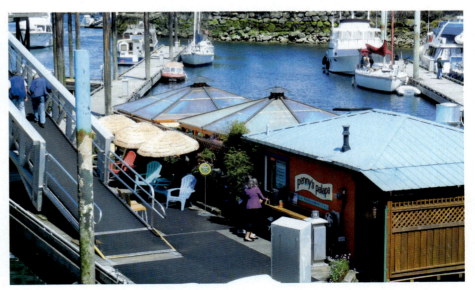

Below the Nanaimo marina office, you will find the popular Penny's Palapa floating restaurant.

2020 Waggoner Cruising Guide

GULF ISLANDS

to Nanaimo. It begins at False Narrows and runs northwest between Gabriola Island and Vancouver Island. Northumberland Channel exits in the Gulf of Georgia, or, at Jack Point, makes the turn to Nanaimo. Because of considerable log boom towing in the area, watch for floating debris. If you are not yet ready for civilization, you might lay over at Pilot Bay, on the north end of Gabriola Island.

Pilot Bay. Pilot Bay is on the north end of Gabriola Island. It's a good anchorage in a southeasterly, but is open to northwesterlies.

No discharge zone, gray water okay.

Gabriola Sands Park. North end of Gabriola Island. Open all year, day use only. Toilets, but no other facilities. This park fronts on Taylor Bay and Pilot Bay. It has a sandy swimming area and a playfield. Good for kids.

Sandwell Park. Northeast side of Gabriola Island. Open all year, day use only, toilets but no other facilities. This is a small seafront park with a sandy beach and forested uplands.

㊳ **Nanaimo.** As you pass Jack Point the city of Nanaimo opens up. Head for the prominent high rise condominium building, easily seen from Jack Point. The harbor is wide and sheltered from the Strait of Georgia by Protection Island and Newcastle Island.

The Nanaimo Port Authority public marina is at the south end of the business district near Nanaimo's famous Bastion (blockhouse), with access to downtown Nanaimo. The Bastion was built in 1853 by the Hudson's Bay Company, and is Nanaimo's oldest man-made landmark still standing. A Thrifty Foods supermarket, London Drug, ATM, B.C. liquor store, Starbucks and several fast-food and sandwich shops are in the Port Place shopping mall near the Port Authority marina. The Nanaimo Museum is in the Conference Centre, one block from the public marina.

The Canada Customs dock is marked at the head of E dock on the north side of the public docks, just behind the fuel dock area. Other moorages, including the Nanaimo Yacht Club, are in Newcastle Island Passage, the channel leading behind Newcastle Island to Departure Bay. The Nanaimo Yacht Club has guest moorage for visiting members of reciprocal clubs. Waterfront Suites & Marina has guest moorage and Stones Marina occasionally has room for transient boaters.

Satellite Reef caution: Buoy *PS* is west of Satellite Reef, approximately where boats entering from Northumberland Channel would plan to turn to anchor at Newcastle Island or continue through Newcastle Island Passage. Satellite Reef dries at zero tide and should be considered hazardous at all times. Stay west of Buoy *PS*.

Repair and haul-out facilities capable of handling any needed job are located along Newcastle Island Passage, known locally as Newcastle Channel.

Nanaimo is a natural point of departure for boats headed across the Strait of Georgia or north to Campbell River or Desolation Sound and beyond. It is the second largest city (behind Victoria) on Vancouver Island. Shops of all kinds line the narrow, winding streets of old town Nanaimo. We've prowled through several impressive bookstores—new and used—in downtown.

Nanaimo offers excellent dining, from casual to elegant. Several restaurants are on the water in the marina. A winding promenade takes walkers along the waterfront for 4 km (2.5 miles), from the marina to the B.C. Ferry Terminal in Departure Bay.

An 1853 cannon, intended in its day to protect the Bastion but used instead to welcome ships into the harbour, is fired at noon each day at the Bastion beginning in May. It's a ceremony complete with a piper in full regalia and a booming explosion with a cloud of white smoke. Beginning in June the Brigadoon Dance Academy's highland dancers perform from 11:15 a.m. to 11:45 a.m. Get there early and bring your camera.

Nanaimo is home to the Annual 'World Championship Bathtub Race' held during the third weekend in July. The event is preceded by a parade of bathtub race participants, games, food, and concerts. See www.bathtubbing.com.

Floatplane Activity: Beware of floatplane arrivals and departures when motoring in the

---

SILVA BAY · GABRIOLA ISLAND · BC

Located on Gabriola Island overlooking Silva Bay and the Flat Top Islands. Start Exploring Today!

VHF 66A 250-247-8931

250-247-9351

Open year round · Moorage · 30Amp · Fuel dock · WiFi · Shower & laundry
Marine chart dealer · Cottages · Suites · Campground · Mountain bike & kayak rentals

PAGESRESORTGROUP.COM

270 www.WaggonerGuide.com

See Area Map Page 259 - Maps Not for Navigation   GULF ISLANDS

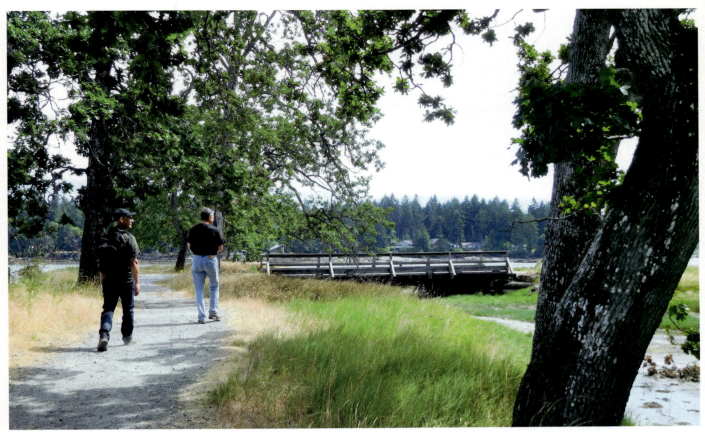

Hike the network of trails on Newcastle Island.

Nanaimo Port Authority

charted air operation area. A flashing white light, located on the Eco Barge pumpout dock, indicates air operation.

Chandlery: Harbour Chandler, south of the boat basin, is an excellent chandlery. At the north end is Stones Boatyard Marine Store.

Markets: Just north of the Bastion, a farmers market, often with entertainment, is open 9:00 a.m. to 2:00 p.m. on Saturdays, May to mid-September.

Taxi: AC Taxi, (250) 753-1231

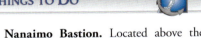

1. Nanaimo Bastion. Located above the marina, the Bastion is the oldest standing building in Nanaimo. You can explore it, or watch the cannon ceremony at noon.

2. Newcastle Island (Saysutshun). Hike to the sandstone quarry or rent a kayak, SUP, or bike. A foot ferry provides regular access to Newcastle Island from the Nanaimo waterfront or take your dinghy. A children's playground was recently added. Walking tours and a traditional tribal salmon bake are available on the island by reservation. See www.newcastleisland.ca for reservations information

3. Fresh seafood on the dock. Fishermen return to the Port Authority marina and sell their catch. You can prepare a fresh seafood dinner on your boat. Or, stop by Trollers for fish and chips.

4. Nanaimo Museum. Just up from the marina at 100 Museum Way. Learn the history of Nanaimo from its First Nations roots to the discovery of coal in the area.

5. Petroglyph Provincial Park. A taxi ride from the docks. See carvings of animals and sea creatures immortalized in the sandstone hundreds and thousands of years ago.

6. Dinghy Dock Pub. On Protection Island. Take your dinghy or the ferry ($9). Great sun deck, good food, and of course cold beer.

7. Walk or bike the multi-use Harbourfront Walkway trail along the downtown waterfront, and on north along the Newcastle Channel.

㊳ **Nanaimo Port Authority.** 100 Port Drive, P.O. Box 131, Nanaimo, -BC V9R 5K4; (250) 755-1216; (250) 754-5053; marina@npa.ca; www.npa.ca. During July and August call (250) 755-1216. Monitors VHF 67 (not 66A). Open year-round. Three hours of moorage complimentary, but call on VHF 67 for slip assignment. Fewer spaces have been reserved for guest moorage than in the past. Reservations recommended. Reservations must be made 48 hours in advance. Rafting is permitted. Dock assistants are available during the summer months to help you tie up. Numerous commercial fish boats are in the basin during the winter months, but pleasure craft moorage is available. Water at selected docks in the winter. Customs clearance available at the customs dock, just behind the fuel dock.

A floating breakwater dock is in the center of the harbour entrance, and the Eco Barge pumpout and portapotty dump is tied to the shore side of this dock. No charge for the Eco Barge. Arriving and departing vessels must pass south of the floating breakwater dock. The northern entrance is reserved for aircraft.

No Discharge Zone, Gray water okay.

The Port Authority harbour is actually two marina facilities: **Inner Boat Basin** and **W.E. Mills Landing & Marina** (formerly and locally known as Cameron Island Marina). We have used both and are happy either place.

㊳ **Inner Boat Basin** is mostly permanent moorage with some guest space. Facilities include extensive dock space, 20 & 30 amp power on all floats, some 50 & 100 amp power, water, free Wi-Fi, and waste oil disposal. Washrooms, showers with heated tile floors, and laundry are next to the wharfinger office.

㊳ **W.E. Mills Landing & Marina.** Larger vessels and ships will tie on the outside of the breakwater pier, smaller boats on the inside. Facilities include 20, 30, & 50 amp power and water. Free Wi-Fi. Washrooms, showers, and laundry are located in the Inner Boat Basin near the wharfinger office, a short dinghy ride but a long walk. Wakes from boats headed for the fuel dock or the Inner Boat Basin rock boats at W.E. Mills Landing & Marina. The docks have a security gate that is open 7:00 a.m. to 11:00 p.m. Between 11:00 p.m. and 7:00 a.m., you'll have to use the combination supplied by the dock help or call security to let you in. Watch the current when landing at W.E. Mills Landing & Marina. Usually there's no problem, but be aware.

Seasonally, fresh fish is sometimes sold at the Nanaimo Fisherman's Market dock at the entrance to the Inner Boat Basin. The dock is 250 feet long, 15 feet wide, and wheelchair accessible. With its flags and specially designed gazebos, you can't miss it. Fish & chips, Mexican food, and other delights are available at floating restaurants. Theaters, a waterfront promenade, and tennis courts are nearby. The seaplane terminal is north of the Inner Boat Basin. All of the Nanaimo commercial district is within a five-minute walk.

No Designated Dinghy Dock. If coming by dinghy, call the marina office on VHF 67 for tie-up instructions.

㊳ **Petro-Canada Coastal Mountain Fuels.** 10 Wharf St., Nanaimo, BC V9R IP2; (250) 754-7828. Open all year, gasoline and diesel at the fuel dock. Lubricants, accessories, ice, snacks. At the end of "E" dock. May to mid-September, 7:00 a.m. to 7:00 p.m.; October to May, 8:00 a.m. to 5:00 p.m.

㊳ **Waterfront Suites & Marina.** 1000 Stewart Ave., Nanaimo, BC V9S 4C9; (250) 753-7111; moorage@waterfrontnanaimo.com; www.waterfrontnanaimo.com. Open all year, moorage to 100 feet, 30 & 50 amp power, washrooms, showers, laundry, Wi-Fi available in the hotel lobby, 24-hour service and security. Reservations encouraged. The docks are modular and staff can configure a dock for odd sized boats. Often has space for transient boats when the other marinas are full.

㊳ **Stones Marina.** 1690 Stewart Ave., Nanaimo BC V9S 4E1; Marina (250) 753- 4232; www.stonesmarina.com. Open all year, 30 & 50 amp power, washrooms, showers, laundry, cable & internet. Limited transient overnight moorage by reservation only. The marina office is located in the white building up the driveway and along the main road. The marina complex has a pub and restaurant, liquor store, marine supplies store, boatyard, yacht charters, and day-use guest moorage dock. The 140 foot float in front of the pub restaurant has side-tie space for vessels visiting the Stones Marina complex. **Stones Boatyard & Marine Store** www.nanaimoboatyard.ca (250-716-9065) are located in the Stones Marina complex. The do-it-yourself or yacht services boatyard with 83-ton Travelift is available for scheduled and emergency repairs. Stones Boatyard & Marine Store is under separate ownership.

Caution: Waters are shallow around the day-use guest dock and Travelift; check your depth.

㊳ **Departure Bay Gas N Go.** 1840 Stewart Ave., Nanaimo, BC V9F 4E6; (250) 591-0810. Open all year. Fuel dock with gas and diesel at north end of Newcastle Channel. Small store carries snacks, tackle, some lubricants.

㊴ **Newcastle Island Marine Park (Saysutshun).** www.env.gov.bc.ca/bcparks/explore/parkpgs/newcastle/ Open all year, moorage with 1500 feet of dock space, excellent washrooms and showers. No power, no water. Anchoring is prohibited in Mark Bay; 43 mooring balls are available for vessels 40 feet and under (some are limited to 30 feet). A nightly mooring fee is paid onshore at the head of the dock. Extensive anchorage is still available just beyond Mark Bay and the docks. Several small bays, beaches, and playing fields. Many hiking trails. Walk-in campsites and picnic areas. Seasonal kayak, canoe, SUP and bicycle rentals. A passenger ferry connects the island with Nanaimo.

The 1931 pavilion houses a dance floor, snack bar, visitor center, and excellent interpretive displays on the natural and human history of the area.

This is an extraordinary park. The pulpstone quarry astonishes. The bays and beaches intrigue. Before European settlement, Newcastle Island was a summer campsite for First Nations people. Since European settlement, it has supported a shipyard and been mined for coal. In the early 1870s it was quarried for sandstone that built the San Francisco Mint. Between 1923 and 1932 its sandstone was quarried for pulpstones, giant cylinders that ground wood into pulp for making paper. Before WWII, Japanese fishermen ran herring salteries here. Through it all, Newcastle Island has been a popular holiday spot.

You might see rare albino raccoons, and dozens of bunny rabbits. If moored at the dock, raccoons will try to board vessels searching for food. Secure your boat well, and don't leave any food or garbage out. Arrive early enough to get literature from the visitor center. Try to spend the night. The lights of Nanaimo are beautiful. The Dinghy Dock pub is a short dinghy ride away.

Pulp stones from the sandstone quarry on Newcastle Island

Saturna Lamb Barbeque

Celebrating over 70 years of traditional Lamb Barbeques, the Island folk of Saturna invite all boaters, and those wishing to ride the BC Ferries, to join them for a family-style lamb barbeque with 1200 of your best new friends.

July 1st, Canada Day, is the date to anchor over in Winter Cove and take part in a bit of history. Saturna's 350 year-round residents have been celebrating this special event since 1950. Over 100 boats came last year to share the experience and flavor of island life, food, and fun.

Co-Chairs Peggy Warren and Joan Selby organize the event and guide island residents through the process of welcoming visitors to this special community picnic. Planning begins in September; "there are so many tasks and considerations to attend to, that it feels like a fulltime job," as noted by Peggy and Joan. The event is an all volunteer effort, and funds raised help support island services and programs. What does it take to put on this Barbeque? – 27 lambs, many cords of fire wood, a Fire Department crew to ensure a safe environment, and paramedics on-hand for any needed assistance. Making arrangements to have a Red Serge (Ceremonial Uniform) Royal Canadian Mounted Police in attendance is just one of the many tasks for the organizers. The officer often encourages selfies.

The bonfire pit crew starts early in the morning at 4 a.m. to prepare and light the fire for the barbeque. Once the fire has died down, the lamb is placed on stakes surrounding the fire pit, Argentinean style (a spectacle seen only by early morning risers). The lamb is then tended by Chefs lathering on a secret sauce, known only to a few on the island, to keep the meat moist, flavorful, and tender.

It's best to arrive early and purchase your tickets in order to have first-in-line privileges. Barbequed lamb, with all the fixings, is served around 1:30 p.m.; guests line up based on their ticket number. Lamb is not the only menu item. You can purchase other tasty treats like hamburgers, vegetarian dishes, ice cream and other delights offered by community groups like the Baseball team or perhaps the Library staff. Gathering with other boaters and locals in the Beverage Garden is another way to meet new friends. And what would a party be without those old-fashioned outdoor games, music, and artists sharing their crafts.

When making your plans for the cruising season, consider attending the Saturna Island Lamb Barbeque on July 1st. Put on your best Red and White for Canada Day and join in the fun. You'll find plenty of anchorage in Winter Cove, but be prepared for the crowds at this popular event. Tickets to partake in the lamb-bake feast are purchased ashore (cash only), beginning at 9 a.m. – $25 for adults and $12 for children under 12 years of age. A dinghy dock is provided and fills up quickly. Your best bet is to hail one of the courtesy shuttles for a ride to shore (life jackets required). For more details about the event, go to www.saturnalambbarbeque.ca. Each year's event is a truly unique experience.

By John Shepard
WG Field Correspondent.

Strait of Georgia

CHAPTER 8

CROSSING THE STRAIT OF GEORGIA

STRAIT OF GEORGIA
*Schooner Cove • French Creek • Denman Island •
Hornby Island • Comox Oyster River •
False Bay • Squitty Bay*

Crossing the Strait of Georgia. The Strait of Georgia is not to be trifled with. It's a big body of water, 110 miles long and 15 to 20 miles wide. Pleasure craft cross the strait all the time, but locals know better than to go out when the wind is blowing. They are especially careful when wind blows against strong currents.

When conditions are right, the strait need not be intimidating. The "typical" summertime fair weather wind pattern calls for calm mornings followed by a rising northwesterly sea breeze by early afternoon. By mid-afternoon the sea breeze can be 20 to 25 knots. In the evening the wind dies down. We have crossed early in the morning and in the evening and had no problems.

Frequently though, the typical pattern doesn't hold. If a weak frontal system passes over the area, the higher pressure behind the front will produce northwesterlies of 20 to 25 knots, sometimes reaching gale force. These winds can blow around the clock for three days or even longer, effectively closing the strait to small craft.

Summer afternoon southwesterly winds known as Qualicums can blow across the strait between Qualicum Beach and False Bay at the northern tip of Lasqueti Island. Qualicum winds resulting from the passage of a cold front can reach 40 knots but are short-lived.

When wind opposes current in Sabine Channel, between Lasqueti Island and Texada Island, 8-foot seas can result. Malaspina Strait can be rough, especially when wind is against

The Strait of Georgia on a calm day

current. Currents from Howe Sound and Burrard Inlet meet off Point Atkinson, and create rough seas. Wind makes them worse.

When the wind is up it produces a difficult 4- to 5-foot chop—sometimes higher—in the middle of the strait away from land influences. These aren't long, lazy ocean swells. Strait of Georgia seas are steep and close together. In southeasterly winds, the largest seas are found near Chrome Island and Cape Mudge, both locations with significant fetch. When the wind blows from the northwest, the largest waves are found in Sabine Channel and near Sand Heads. A well-handled boat might run with these seas, but taken on the bow or beam they are no fun at all.

Sometimes, the afternoon winds never materialize and the strait can be crossed all day. It's best to avoid being forced into crossing at a specific time or on a specific day. Wait for calm conditions and know that they don't always appear in the morning and evening. When the conditions are right, go. Be cautious yet decisive.

Even in calm conditions, you may find tide-rips off many of the points, and wherever passes or channels join the strait. When the current flows out of a pass or inlet into the strait, confusion results. Add wind, and big confusion results. While the ebb current flows from inlets into the strait, note that the flood current flows out of the Gulf Islands into the strait. At the eastern mouths of Active Pass, Porlier Pass, and Gabriola Pass, look for rough seas on the flood, especially when the wind is blowing.

We list these cautions not to frighten the reader but to inform. Weather patterns do exist and the bad spots are known. The skipper who monitors the VHF continuous marine broadcast will gather a sense of what is happening, where it is happening, and why it is happening. Go and no-go decisions get easier.

Here are a few tips for a safe and comfortable crossing:

- Monitor the buoy reports for Halibut Bank (Buoy 46146, off Gibsons) and Sentry Shoal (Buoy 46131, between Comox and Campbell River and below Mitlenatch Island). These reports provide frequent updates on sea state and wind conditions. They can be found online on Environment Canada's website, on the continuous marine broadcast, or by calling Dial-A-Buoy at (888) 701-8992 or (301) 713-9620.

- Monitor lightstation reports. Lightstations are at Chrome Island, Merry Island and Entrance Island. The lightkeepers provide information on visibility, wind speed and direction, and sea state, updated every three hours and broadcast on the VHF WX channels. Or call on VHF 82.

CROSSING STRAIT OF GEORGIA GO-NOGO CHECKLIST

Tides & Currents - See Ports & Passes; Canadian Tides & Current Tables Vol. 5
- ☐ Time your crossing to be near mid-Strait at slack
- ☐ Flood or ebb; avoid wind against current conditions
- ☐ Ebbing currents flow out of inlets into the Strait, except in Gulf Islands
- ☐ Flooding currents from both north and south directions meet at Mitlenach Island

Weather System Predictions – via Internet or satellite
- ☐ Check NOAA Ocean Prediction Center forecasts for any approaching significant weather systems
- ☐ Check Windy.com, Predictwind.com, SiriusXM Marine, or Sailflow.com
- ☐ See Environment Canada forecast for the Synopsis report for Strait of Georgia North of Nanaimo and Strait of Georgia South of Nanaimo

Weather & Seas Forecasts – via Internet, phone, or VHF
- ☐ See Environment Canada Forecasts for Strait of Georgia North of Nanaimo and South of Nanaimo; check for warnings and note forecast wind speed and direction

Observations & Present Conditions – via Internet, phone, or VHF
- ☐ Check Buoy Reports for Halibut Bank (46146) and Sentry Shoal (46131); note wind speed and direction
- ☐ Check Lighthouse and Station Reports from Chrome Island, Merry Island, and Entrance Island; note wind speed and direction
- ☐ Check the status of Restricted Area Whisky Golf north of Nanaimo

Go-NoGo Decision
- √ Check wind and wave direction in relation to direction of travel. Straight line crossing is the shortest distance, but may not be the most comfortable.
- √ Will the typical summer weather pattern with afternoon winds affect conditions?
- √ Is Restricted Area Whisky Golf active?

Fail-Safe Contingency Plans
- √ Duck-in locations along the route: lees may lie off Texada Island and Lasqueti Island

See *Chapter 1 Interpreting Northwest Weather* section for telephone numbers, website addresses, VHF channels, and buoy numbers.

STRAIT OF GEORGIA

Reference Only – Not for Navigation

Strait of Georgia

- Based on the wind direction and sea state, choose the best angle and direction for your crossing. The most direct course may not be the most comfortable. Don't be afraid to change your destination if the weather isn't cooperating.

- The north-flowing flood current from Strait of Juan de Fuca meets the south-flowing flood from Discovery Passage near Mitlenatch Island. When traveling the length of the strait, time your departure to take advantage of currents flowing in the same direction as the wind. When crossing, especially in the south, try to time your departure to hit slack in the middle of the strait. Both strategies will minimize the effect of wind against current.

- The area between Qualicum Beach and Lasqueti Island can be subject to southwesterly winds coming through the Alberni "notch" in the Vancouver Island mountains. Check Chrome Island for local southwesterly winds. Old salts also recommend checking winds at Cape Beale, on the west coast of Vancouver Island. If a strong southwesterly wind is blowing there, often it will flow right over Vancouver Island through the Alberni "notch," affecting the waters off Qualicum Beach.

- Take advantage of lees along the way. For example, you may choose to go up one side or the other of 27-mile Texada Island to stay in the lee of a southwesterly or northeasterly wind. Always be prepared to turn around and go back if things do not look right.

Whiskey Golf. Boats headed north from Nanaimo often must navigate through or around the restricted area "WG" (Whiskey Golf) when it is "live." Whiskey Golf is a deepwater range operated by the Canadian and U.S. Navies, and is used to test torpedoes and various ships' systems. Buoys and moorings may be laid anywhere within WG. Use extreme caution when transiting. The area consists of a network of underwater sensing devices joined by cables to a control site on Winchelsea Island. Torpedoes are fired from range vessels or aircraft along a predetermined course, and are tracked from the Winchelsea control center. No explosives are used; however, a hazard exists due to the possibility of the torpedo homing on vessels. After the run, the torpedoes are recovered either by helicopter or range vessels. Unauthorized craft are not permitted in the area while the range is in operation.

Typically, the range is active Mondays through Fridays, sometimes Saturdays, 7:00 a.m. to 5:30 p.m. For information on range

See Area Map Page 276 - Maps Not for Navigation

STRAIT OF GEORGIA

Tribune Bay on Hornby Island can accommodate many boats at anchor. The bay and its excellent beach is a popular stop in summer months.

area status, contact Winchelsea Control on VHF channel 10 or 16; or listen on VHF Weather 1 or 3. For next day planned range activity and status, call (250) 468-5080. The Coast Guard (VHF channel 83A) also knows if the range is active. If unsure, contact Winchelsea Control by phone or VHF, or the Canadian Coast Guard.

The Whiskey Golf restricted area is on the direct course across the Strait of Georgia from Nanaimo to Secret Cove, Smugglers Cove, Pender Harbour, and other destinations along the Sunshine Coast. We once saw an oblivious skipper cross right through the active range. Winchelsea Control made multiple calls to the offending vessel with no response. A patrol helicopter quickly flew over, hovered just in front of the offending vessel, and redirected it to safe water. Such encounters are best avoided.

The Canadian Navy established a safe transit route along the edges of the restricted area when the range is in use. After clearing Nanaimo Harbour or Departure Bay (being careful to avoid Hudson Rocks and Five Finger Island), head directly for the Winchelsea Islands. Pass east of Winchelsea Islands within 1000 yards. Turn to pass east of the Ballenas Islands within 1000 yards. Once well past the Ballenas Islands, steer a course for your destination on the mainland side of the strait, or northwest along the Vancouver Island side.

Nanoose Harbour. All of the waters and foreshore of Nanoose Harbour west of Wallis Pt. are a military Controlled Access Zone administered by the Department of National Defence. The harbour is open to the public within the limitations of the Controlled Access Zone regulations. All vessels entering the harbour are required to register their arrival, intended duration of stay, and departure from the harbor by contacting the Queen's Harbour Master at (250) 213-3325 or (250) 363-7584. Contact Winchelsea Island Control when south of Maude Island on VHF 10 or 16 before entering the harbour. Pleasure craft anchoring is only permitted south of a line west of Datum Rock and in the vicinity of Fleet Point. The docks and mooring buoys along the north shore are for Royal Canadian Navy and U.S. Navy vessels engaged in activity on the Winchelsea (Whiskey Golf) torpedo range and pleasure craft mooring and access is prohibited.

Schooner Cove. Schooner Cove is north of Nanoose Harbour. The cove is well-protected with a breakwater on the northwest entrance. The Fairwinds Marina fills most of the cove.

① **Fairwinds Marina.** 33521 Dolphin Dr., Nanoose Bay, BC V9P 9J7; (250) 468-5364; marina@fairwinds.ca; www.fairwinds.ca. Monitors VHF 66A. Fairwinds Marina, located at Schooner Cove, is open all year with gasoline and diesel at the fuel dock. Guest moorage for vessels up to 100 feet, 15, 30 & 50 amp power, washrooms, and showers. Reservations are a must. Proof of liability insurance coverage is required.

The pumpout system was being replaced in 2019, anticipated to be available for the 2020 season. Dock repairs were made in 2018, and renovation of the main upland building is ongoing, with plans to include a restaurant and pub on the second floor; marina office facilities on the first floor. Facilities are anticipated to be available for the 2020 boating season.

Easily accessed off of Ballenas Channel and Strait of Georgia, the marina has picturesque views of the Strait of Georgia and coastal mountains. Watch for a rock marked by a red buoy just inside the breakwater. Keep the buoy well to starboard when entering. The outstanding Fairwinds Golf club is part of the resort. A courtesy shuttle can take you there.

Schooner Reef. Schooner Reef is a short distance northward off the mouth of Schooner Cove and has caught a number of boats unaware. The light marking the reef is on the southernmost of its rocks. More rocks lie up-island from the light.

Nuttal Bay. Nuttal Bay is protected from southeasterly winds but exposed to northwesterlies. To enter Nuttal Bay, leave Dorcas Rock Buoy *P27* to port. Do not pass between Dorcas Rock Buoy *P27* and the land south of it. Buoy *P27* lies a good deal farther out than one might expect. If you are traveling up- or down-island, locate that buoy and pass to seaward of it.

Fairwinds Marina

2020 WAGGONER CRUISING GUIDE

STRAIT OF GEORGIA

See Area Map Page 276 - Maps Not for Navigation

Northwest Bay. Northwest Bay is home to a private moorage only marina with no services for transient boaters, and an active log dump and booming operation. The bay is protected from southerly winds but open to the north and northwesterly winds and seas. Suitable anchorage depths can be found at the head of the bay and in a bight along the west shore.

Mistaken Island. Privately owned and posted with "No Trespassing" signs.

Parksville. Parksville has a nice beach, but shoal water extends out some distance. No facilities are available for boaters.

② **French Creek Harbour Authority.** 1055 Lee Rd., Parksville, BC V9P 2E1; (250) 248-5051; hafc@frenchcreekharbour.ca. Monitors VHF 66A. Open all year with gasoline & diesel. Commercial vessels have priority for moorage, but room may be available for pleasure craft. No reservations; rafting is required. Washrooms and shower, 20 & 30 amp power. A key from the office is required for waste oil and garbage disposal. Office hours are 8:00 a.m. to 5:30 p.m. Restaurant, pub, marine supplies, nearby launch ramp and haulout. A fish market in the large white processing building sells fresh seafood. Groceries are at the mall, a 15-minute walk away.

French Creek is the only breakwater-protected harbor in the 25-mile stretch between Northwest Bay and Deep Bay. The breakwater has recently been extended. French Creek is the western terminus of the passenger ferry to Lasqueti Island.

Hornby Island. Hornby Island has anchorages in Tribune Bay, Ford Cove, and south of Shingle Spit (where a small ferry runs to Denman Island). Tribune Bay and Shingle Spit are exposed to southeast winds.

A seasonal dock for dinghies and shallow

French Creek Boat Harbour

draft water craft is located next to the ferry terminal. The dock is for guests dining at the Thatch Pub and Restaurant located above the dock. The fully licensed Pub and Restaurant has live entertainment, (250) 335-0136; thatchpub.com.

The annual Hornby Festival, held in early August, is a well-organized event drawing professional, award-winning musicians, song writers, and artists from around the country and across the border; see hornbyfestival.com.

Tribune Bay. Tribune Bay is a wonderful place to visit and justifiably popular. Anchor offshore in 18 to 30 feet and dinghy to a splendid sand beach. Visit Tribune Bay Provincial Park. Take the 3-mile hike to Helliwell Provincial Park, on St. John Point.

Caution: Tribune Bay has excellent protection from northwesterlies, but in a southeasterly the bay can get very rough. For a more private nook, try the little cove near St. John Point. Anchor in 20 to 30 feet.

③ **Ford Cove.** Located on Hornby Island, Ford Cove is a delightful community with ample guest moorage. A green spar buoy marks the southern end of Maude Reef. You'll see a rock breakwater and a floating breakwater. To enter, leave the rock breakwater to starboard. No fresh water on the dock. Good anchorage on rocky bottom.

A well-stocked grocery (250) 335-2169 is upland from the docks and sells fresh take-out pizza year-round. A seasonal fish & chips hut is adjacent. The store and eatery along with cottages, campsites, and RV parking make up a small resort called Ford's Cove Marina & Store.

There are numerous trails in the area. A well-traveled 1.5 mile trail leads northwest along the shore to Shingle Spit and the popular Thatch Pub.

③ **Ford Cove Harbour Authority.** 10800A Central Rd., Ford Cove, Hornby Island, BC V0R 1Z0; (250) 335-0003; VHF 66A; fordcoveharbour@gmail.com; www.fordcoveharbour.com. Open all year, guest moorage along 3000 feet of dock space and inside of the floating breakwater, 20 & 30 amp power, toilets, garbage drop, no water, no showers. Reservations accepted or call ahead for availability. Rafting allowed up to 20 feet deep. No rafting on the breakwater. Loading dock located near the ramp. Kayak and boat rentals.

Baynes Sound. Chart 3527 shows navigation aids not shown on Chart 3513. These aids are buoys marking extensive shoals off Gartley Point, Union Point, Denman Point and Base Flat (Buckley Bay); 2 buoys near Repulse Point; and 2 buoys marking the shoal off Mapleguard Point. Baynes Sound, a 12-mile-long refuge, is protected from the Strait of Georgia by Denman Island. A ferry to Denman Island crosses from Buckley Bay. Comox is at the north end of Baynes Sound and Deep Bay is at the south end. The northern entry to Baynes Sound is across the Comox Bar,

Ford Cove

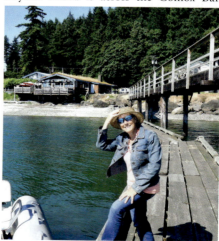

The dinghy dock at lively Thatch Pub is seasonal and dries on low tides.

STRAIT OF GEORGIA

See Area Map Page 276 - Maps Not for Navigation

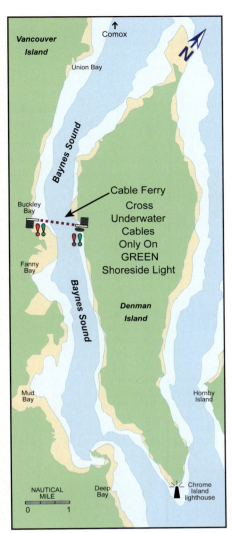

Denman Cable Ferry

marked by buoys and a lighted range on the Vancouver Island shore. The southern entry is past Chrome Island.

LOCAL KNOWLEDGE

NAVIGATION NOTE: A considerable shoal extends into the mouth of Baynes Sound outside Deep Bay. The shoal, and shoaling along the shoreline of Denman Island, opposite, are marked by buoys shown on Chart 3527, but not on Chart 3513.

④ **Deep Bay.** Anchorage is good in Deep Bay, though in deeper water than most boaters like. Derelict boats, which occupied a portion of the best space, have recently been removed. The Ship & Shore Cafe, which once sold convenience supplies, is now a full restaurant under new ownership. The restaurant is located near the head of the public wharf. Washroom and laundry facilities nearby.

④ **Deep Bay Harbour Authority.** 164 Burne Rd., Bowser, BC V0R 1G0; (250) 757-9331; deepbay-mgr@shawcable.com; www.dbha.ca. The government wharf and floats are open all year with moorage along 1130 feet of dock. Garbage drop, 20 & 30 amp power, free Wi-Fi, free pumpout, waste oil disposal, tidal grid, and guest dock. Washrooms and showers were upgraded in 2018. The pumpout is located at the loading zone on the main pier. Space is very limited and rafting is required, call ahead to see what is available.

Fanny Bay. Fanny Bay is primarily a camping area, with a small public float.

LOCAL KNOWLEDGE

CABLE FERRY: The *Baynes Sound Connector* cable ferry runs between Buckley Bay and Denman Island. Red and green lights are at each terminal. When the green lights are illuminated, vessels may cross the ferry lane. When red lights are illuminated, the ferry is in transit and vessels may not cross the ferry lane.

Denman Island. www.denmanisland.com. A public dock and 60-foot float are alongside the landing for the cable ferry that runs to Buckley Bay on Vancouver Island. Six hours of moorage is free, 2-day maximum stay. No power or water; 5 mooring buoys. Self-registration and payment box at the top of the ramp. Denman Village is a one-third mile walk up a steep hill. The Denman General Store with groceries, a post office, and liquor store is in Denman Village. A small museum, community center, bistro, and a craft shop are also in the Village.

The north end of Denman Island stretches out into a long spit, dotted with small islands and rocks. One of these islands, Sandy Island, is a provincial park. Off the south end of Denman Island is Chrome Island lighthouse, a dramatic landmark.

Sandy Island Marine Provincial Park. This park includes the Seal Islets, and is accessible only by boat. Anchor in Henry Bay, south of Longbeak Point. Picnic areas, swimming, fishing, hiking trails, and wilderness campsites. Sandy Island is a popular overnight stop for kayakers. At low tide it is possible to walk along the sandy spit all the way to its end—halfway to Comox.

LOCAL KNOWLEDGE

NAVIGATION TIP: If you follow the buoyed channel over the Comox Bar in a fresh southeasterly you will have 4- to 5-foot seas on your beam. In these conditions it's better to ignore buoys *P54* and *P52* and instead work

Boaters need to check the red/green light at each of the Denman-Buckley cable ferry terminals before crossing the ferry route in Baynes Sound.

The Denman-Buckley ferry runs on three underwater cables across Baynes Sound.

STRAIT OF GEORGIA

See Area Map Page 276 - Maps Not for Navigation

Comox Valley Harbour Authority

your way south until you can turn to fetch the inner Buoy *P50* while running with the seas. The chart indicates ample depths. Large scale Chart 3527 shows Buoy *P50*, but small scale Chart 3513 does not.

Comox Bar. The Comox Bar nearly joins Denman Island and Cape Lazo, with a shallow channel (least depth 15 feet) across the bar. A lighted range—white, with red vertical stripes—is on the Vancouver Island shore. The range's lights are visible in cloudy weather and at night, but in sunlight they are hard to see. Lighted red Bell Buoy *P54* marks the Strait of Georgia end of this channel. Red Buoys *P52* and *P50* show the course across the bar.

⑤ **Comox.** If you plan to go to Comox, we urge that you have Chart 3527 (1:40,000), with its 1:15,000 inset of Comox Harbour and the Courtenay River up to the Lewis Bridge. Chart 3527 shows the various ranges and other navigation aids in excellent detail, and could save you from much uncertainty.

Marine services at Comox include Desolation Sound Yacht Charters (250) 339-4919 offering cleaning, maintenance, hull inspection, and bright work (after-hours calls accepted); and Wills Marine Supply (250) 941-7373 offering electrical, mechanical, diving and repair services.

Comox is a busy little city, population 13,600, with breakwater-protected marina docks. HMCS Quadra, a Canada Sea Cadet camp, is on Goose Spit, across the bay from Comox.

The Comox Valley is a popular retirement area. Albertans from the oil patch can take daily flights to the Comox airport and enjoy golf and skiing within an hour of one another on Vancouver Island.

From Baynes Sound the entrance to Comox is well marked, but be careful of drying flats off Gartley Point and in the inner half of the bay. The breakwater in front of the town will be clearly visible. As the harbor map shows, the breakwater shelters four sets of docks: the Comox Bay Marina; the Gas N Go fuel dock and marina; the municipal marina; and one set of Comox Harbour Authority public docks used entirely by commercial fishing boats. A launch ramp and two tidal grids are behind the breakwater. The other set of Harbour Authority public docks, where pleasure craft are welcomed, is around the east end of the breakwater.

Showers and laundry are in the Harbour Authority's building at the head of its docks. A beautiful pavilion with meeting space overlooks the Comox Harbour Commercial Wharves and serves as a nice venue for club rendezvous. A Splash Park located behind the pavilion is a hit with the kids. Seasonal food trucks are located near the pavilion.

Comox has good shopping and a number of restaurants within walking distance of the marina. The downtown area includes a supermarket and chandlery. Regular bus service runs from the Comox Mall to the town of Courtenay with more shops, restaurants and a museum. You can also go by dinghy up the slough to Courtenay. See the Courtenay section for more information.

When you're in Comox, take the short walk to the Filberg Heritage Lodge & Park. It's a 9-acre estate built in the 1930s by logging baron R. J. Filberg, furnished and maintained in its original splendor. The heavy wood construction, fabulous gardens, and interesting outbuildings (root cellar, chicken coop, dairy barn, potting shed, and so forth) are must-see attractions. Weddings and art shows are held there. The seasonal Pavilion Kitchen, located on the grounds, is open Thursday through Sunday. See filberg.com for special events held at the park.

Float planes: A float plane landing and takeoff zone is southwest of the marina breakwaters, with regularly scheduled flights.

Cruise with New Friends

Join us for a fun-filled passage to Desolation Sound, The Broughtons, and to Ketchikan.

We organize activities along the way and teach you more about weather and how to cruise the area. Most of all, we have a lot of fun cruising and dining together. We take you to the best places along the way too.

Ask about our flotillas in the British Virgin Islands.

360.299.8500 • www.WaggonerGuide.com

See Area Map Page 276 - Maps Not for Navigation

STRAIT OF GEORGIA

The breakwater protects moorage and the fuel dock at Comox Harbour.

It does not affect anchoring behind Goose Spit or the approach to the marinas.

Festival: The Filberg Festival, an arts, crafts, food, and entertainment celebration, draws 20,000 to 25,000 visitors each year. It's held at Filberg Park, east of the public floats in Comox Harbour. Dates coincide with Comox Nautical Days and B.C. Day long weekend in early August. The park will be closed the week prior to the festival and the week following. Special events also can result in closures. Call first to confirm they are open (250) 941-0727. www.filbergfestival.com.

⑤ **Comox Valley Marina.** 1805 Beaufort, Box 20019, Comox, BC V9M 1R9; (250) 339-2930; manager@comoxvalleymarina.com; www.comoxvalleymarina.com. Side-tie moorage at a guest dock and in unoccupied slips. Water, 15, 30 & 50 amp power, shower, washroom, free Wi-Fi, 24-hour access to laundry, garbage, and nearby floatplane service. The amenities building and marina office are on the float at the base of the ramp.

⑤ **Gas N Go Marine Ltd.** 11 Port Augusta St., Comox, BC V9M 7Z8; (250) 339-4664; (888) 575-4664; gasngomarine@gmail.com; www.gasngomarine.com. Monitors VHF 66A. Open all year. Fuel dock with gasoline & diesel. Transient moorage when slips are available (call ahead), 15 & 30 amp power, washrooms, small store, Wi-Fi. As you approach, look for the Gas N Go sign.

⑤ **Comox Municipal Marina.** 1809 Beaufort Ave., Comox, BC V9M 1R9; (250) 339-3141. Permanent moorage only.

⑤ **Comox Valley Harbour Authority.** 121 Port Augusta St., Comox, BC V9M 3N8; (250) 339-6041; info@comoxharbour.com; www.comoxharbour.com. Monitors VHF 66A. Located at east end of the Comox breakwater. Guest moorage available on 2100 feet of docks, 20, 30 & 50 amp power. Holding tank pumpout, garbage drop, cardboard recycling, waste oil disposal, free Wi-Fi (get the password at the office). Clean washrooms, showers, laundry, and an air-conditioned lounge with a bucket of biscuits for visiting boat dogs.

This is a working waterfront facility, only two blocks from downtown Comox. In the summer, harbor staff move the fishing boats to one float and set aside the other docks for overnight pleasure craft. Fresh seafood may be available "off the boat," usually in the evening. The Harbour Authority staff works hard to make visiting pleasure boaters feel welcome and comfortable.

⑤ **Comox Harbour.** Anchorage can be found in Comox Harbour; with northerly winds, anchor south of the marina breakwater, taking care to avoid channel entrances on either end of the breakwater; in southerly winds, the favored anchorage is tucked into the cove north of Goose Spit. Mud bottom. The harbour is not as well protected as charts might suggest and can get uncomfortable in southerly winds.

⑥ **Courtenay.** For an adventurous outing, ask at the Harbour Authority office for local knowledge regarding taking the dinghy 3.3 nautical miles up the Courtenay River to the town of Courtenay. A drying river channel, marked by ranges, leads through the delta to the river mouth. The mouth is blocked by a weir that dries at 7 feet; without the weir the slough would empty completely at low tide. A small private marina is on the left (southwest shore) just after passing the weir. Next is an opening bridge with a vertical clearance of 6.9 feet. Just before you reach the fixed Lewis Bridge, Courtenay Slough leads off to the right. Inside, an extensive Comox Valley Harbour Authority float parallels the shore, and a city float is at the head. Enter the slough at high tide only. The slough's Harbour Authority dock is gated and locked. Harbour Authority registered guests may pick up a re-entry key at the Harbour Authority office in Comox. An imposing restaurant dominates the view at the head of the slough. Excellent shopping and several restaurants are within easy walking

2020 Waggoner CRUISING GUIDE

STRAIT OF GEORGIA

distance. If the tides aren't cooperating, you can take the bus (250-339-5433) or taxi (250-339-7955) into Courtenay.

Museum: We highly recommend a visit to the Courtenay & District Museum (250-334-0686), a 4-block walk from the slough. There, hung from the ceiling, is the 40-foot-long skeletal reconstruction of an 80-million-year-old elasmosaur, excavated from the banks of the nearby Puntledge River. This is the most dramatic exhibit in an outstanding paleontological display. Other things you will see are dinosaur footprints, an extinct marine reptile that resembles a 15-foot-long alligator, and an ancient fish they call a "sabre-toothed salmon." We toured the museum and were impressed. Families with inquisitive children will be rewarded. There's much more than we can cover here. The museum is in the old brick post office building at 4th St. and Cliffe Avenue.

Cape Lazo. Cape Lazo is marked by a high cliff. *Be sure to stay to seaward of Buoys PJ and PB.* The buoys are well offshore, but shoals studded with boulders reach almost all the way out to them.

Somewhere just north of Cape Lazo is the point at which the tidal currents change direction and begin flooding south from the north end of Vancouver Island, rather than north from Victoria.

Little River. Little River, 3 miles up-island from Cape Lazo, is the western terminus for the ferry to Westview/Powell River. Marginal moorage for a few small craft can be found behind the ferry dock.

Oyster River. A channel, dredged annually and marked by pilings, leads to the protected Pacific Playgrounds Marina next to the mouth of the Oyster River.

⑦ **Pacific Playgrounds Resort & Marina.** (250) 337-5600; info@PacificPlaygrounds.com; www.PacificPlaygrounds.com; open year-round, secure marina with transient and permanent moorage up to 40 feet, a few 46-foot spaces; 15 amp power, water at the docks, restrooms, showers; reservations accepted. Payment made at the upland office open 9:00 a.m.-8:00 p.m. summer months. Payment can also be made at the dockside "fishing shack" summer hours 6:00 a.m.-8:00 p.m.; hours vary off-season. Located 16 miles south of Campbell River (49° 52' N / 125° 7' W), Pacific Playgrounds is accessed through a channel alongside, and south of Oyster River. This is a challenging entrance, check the tide tables; marina personnel advise that a minimum tide of 7 feet is needed for a boat with a 4.5 foot draft; the depth is shallowest at the outermost channel marker; access is not advised during high winds and swells Oyster River Plaza is a short walk from the marina, with shops, cafes, a supermarket, and other services. A beautiful trail from the marina leads to a one-lane timber truss bridge over Oyster River, where you will find the Fishermen's Lodge Pub.

⑦ **Salmon Point Resort.** (250) 923-6605; sales@salmonpoint.com; www.salmonpoint.com. Gas, propane, launch ramp, store, laundry, pool, jacuzzi and kids' activity areas. Located 15 miles south of Campbell River on the western shore of Discovery Passage, this marina, built behind a riprap breakwater, has room for powerboats up to 32 feet. The entrance is very shallow and dries at low tide. "Stay-aboards" (overnighting on boat) not permitted. The resort is an RV park primarily serving recreational fishermen, with 1 to 2 bedroom cottages, rental RVs, and a licensed restaurant and pub on site.

LASQUETI ISLAND

Lasqueti Island is often overlooked by pleasure craft as they hurry across the strait between Nanaimo and the Sunshine Coast, or run along the Vancouver Island shore between Nanaimo and Campbell River. The island has a number of good anchorages. A convenience store is at the village of False Bay, located upland from the ferry landing on the left. The shores of Lasqueti Island are indented by a number of bays that invite anchorage. Along the south shore are Boat Cove, Old House Bay, Richardson Cove and Jenkins Cove, all of which are somewhat open to southerlies, but offer good protection from northerlies or in settled weather. This part of the Lasqueti shoreline is rugged and beautiful. Squitty Bay is at the southeast end of Lasqueti Island—tiny, but with a public float. Several little dogholes for anchoring can be found in Bull Passage. Little Bull Passage, between Jedediah Island and Bull Island, has a number of good anchorages in both ends, and is passable for most boats. Other anchorages are Boho Bay, Tucker Bay and Scottie Bay. Spring Bay is only partially protected from the north by a group of small islands offshore.

⑧ **False Bay.** False Bay is the primary settlement on Lasqueti Island with a public float offering limited dock space and a float plane tie-up. A passenger-only ferry runs between False Bay and French Creek on Vancouver Island. Island residents transport not only themselves by ferry but also bring a large quantity of supplies, everything from food and clothing to appliances. It's quite a scene when the ferry arrives at False Bay. An open-air market is held at the arts center, a quarter mile up the road from the ferry landing, from mid-June to September.

Buoys adjacent to the ferry landing are private and fill most of the anchoring area near the public float. The preferred anchorage is the north shore of the bay, an easy dinghy ride to the public float. On warm summer afternoons strong winds, called Qualicums, can blow through False Bay; waves break at the dock, making tie-up difficult. If you must tie in these conditions, make sure you have robust dock lines and fenders. Kevin Monahan, a long-time resident of Lasqueti Island, reports that southwest gale force winds at Cape Beale often serve as a presage of Qualicum winds arriving at False Bay.

⑨ **Squitty Bay.** Squitty Bay is a tiny, narrow and shallow notch at the southeast corner of Lasqueti Island. It would be harrowing to enter Squitty Bay in a roaring southeasterly, but at other times entry should be easy. Rocks border the north side of the entrance; favor the south side. The unnamed point on the south side of Squitty Bay is an ecological reserve, noted for prickly pear cacti and Rocky Mountain juniper. The public dock, 150 feet long, may be largely occupied by local boats. Rafting is permitted. Ashore, the trees in this

The public dock at False Bay on Lasqueti Island is a hub of activity when the foot-ferry arrives.

Texada Boat Club in Sturt Bay on Texada Island has guest moorage for visiting boats.

area are bent and broken, obviously by strong winds. Tall trees are rare. A walk along the road is fascinating.

Bull Passage. Bull Passage and the islands that lie off the south end of Jedediah Island are rugged and scenic.

Little Bull Passage. Between high rock cliffs, Little Bull Passage is narrow and beautiful. Watch for the charted rock on the Jedediah Island side. It hides at high tide. Our notes say, "The east end of Little Bull Passage is absolutely fabulous. So much variety and strength in the rock walls and islands. Worth a side trip just to see the sights."

Jedediah Island. Jedediah Island is a marine park. Although good anchorages are scarce and tight, Jedediah Island is increasingly popular. One of the best anchorages is in the little notch, called Deep Bay, opposite the south end of Paul Island, where chains have been installed around this small bay to facilitate stern-ties. It is impractical that all these stern-ties could be used at the same time in this tiny, v-shaped bay, except for the smallest of boats. The large number of stern-ties are provided to allow different options for boaters. Long Bay just south of Deep Bay is usable, too. Long Bay goes dry a short distance inside the mouth. Codfish Bay on the southeast side of Jedediah Island has room for two or three boats to stern-tie. If nothing looks good at Jedediah Island itself, Boho Bay at Lasqueti Island, about 1 mile away, is an alternative.

One interesting spot is the narrow and protected steep-sided notch at the southeast end of Jedediah Island. Although its sheer walls might discourage much on-shore exploration, it is possible to scramble from the head of the notch up the bluffs on the north side. You will be rewarded not only with access to the rest of the island but also an excellent view toward Texada Island. [*Hamilton*]

For easy access to the island, take the dinghy ashore at Deep Bay and hike the short, well-marked trail across the island. A map of the island is posted at the head of the trail from both Deep Bay and Long Bay. A trail also leads from Codfish Bay. A visit to the old homestead on the east side of Jedediah Island is an exciting adventure and should not be missed. The homestead is frozen in time and left undisturbed. Please respect the property and leave things as found for others to enjoy. The island was owned by several families over the years. The Foote Family first purchased the island in 1890. Alan and Mary Palmer, the last owners, didn't want this island paradise to be developed so sold Jedediah Island to the Provincial Government in 1994 to be used as a Marine Park. A plaque on the island commemorates their generous forethought. You can learn more about the history of Jedediah Island in the book - *Jedediah Days, One Woman's Island Paradise*, by Mary Palmer.

TEXADA ISLAND

Texada (pronounced "Tex-AY-da") Island has three main anchorages: Anderson Bay on Malaspina Strait at the south end; Blubber Bay at the northern tip; and Sturt Bay, a couple miles south along the Malaspina Strait (eastern) side. Although it has a ferry landing and public float, **Blubber Bay** is dominated by an enormous quarry and is not inviting, but anchorage is possible if needed. Texada Island has a long history of mining including iron, copper, silver and gold. In more recent years, Texada has been a continuous source of high quality limestone.

The Texada Blues & Roots Festival is held in late July at Gillies Bay Ball Park. Also held at Gillies Bay is the popular Sandcastle Weekend, the first weekend in August.

Anderson Bay. Anderson Bay is at the south end of Texada Island on Malaspina Strait. It is a beautiful spot, lined with sheer rock walls. Anchor in 24 feet near the head.

The safest approach is from the southeast. In our opinion, the pass between Texada Island and the unnamed 20-meter island is not as open as the charts suggest. We explored this pass at the bottom of a 1.6-foot low tide and found rock shelves extending from the Texada Island side well into the pass. Be especially careful of the reef that extends from the southwest point of Texada Island. The reef dries at low tide, but at higher stages of tide it could be a nasty surprise.

⑩ **Sturt Bay.** Locally called Marble Bay, on Malaspina Strait near the north end of Texada Island; it has the best anchorage and moorage on Texada Island. Anchorage is in the bay, but beware of forest and mining equipment said to be lying on the bottom.

The full service grocery store has liquor, good meats and produce. A farmers market is held Sundays at Gillies Bay Ballpark. The Texada Island Museum, housed in a wing of the local school at 2003 Waterman Ave., covers the history of Texada mining and quarrying; open Wednesdays from 10:00 a.m. to noon.

Caution: Sturt Bay is a welcome haven if a northwesterly is kicking up Malaspina Strait, but not suitable in a fresh southeasterly. Blubber Bay provides better anchorage in a southeasterly.

Texada Boat Club. (604) 414-5897; texadaboatingclub.ca; VHF 66A. Located in the SE corner of Sturt Bay, behind a breakwater, the Texada Boat Club has extensive floats for members and visitors. The first three floats (docks 1, 2, 3) as you enter the bay are marked for members only; the last float (dock 4) is marked for visitors and has first-come first-serve side-tie space on both sides. Water, 15-amp power, and garbage drop for a per bag fee. Self-register and make payment (cash only) at the harbormasters office, lower level of the first house on the left about 130 yards/meters up the road. Bob Timms is the harbormaster, (604) 414-5897.

Van Anda (Vananda). A 50-foot public dock is located in Van Anda Cove. Guest moorage at the dock can be lumpy in northwesterlies. Nearby Sturt Bay is preferred.

Harwood Point Regional Park. Gillies Bay, Texada Island. Anchor out only and dinghy in to a 40-acre park. Grass fields, picnic tables, campsites, pit toilets.

Vancouver, Mainland B.C. & The Sunshine Coast

CHAPTER 9

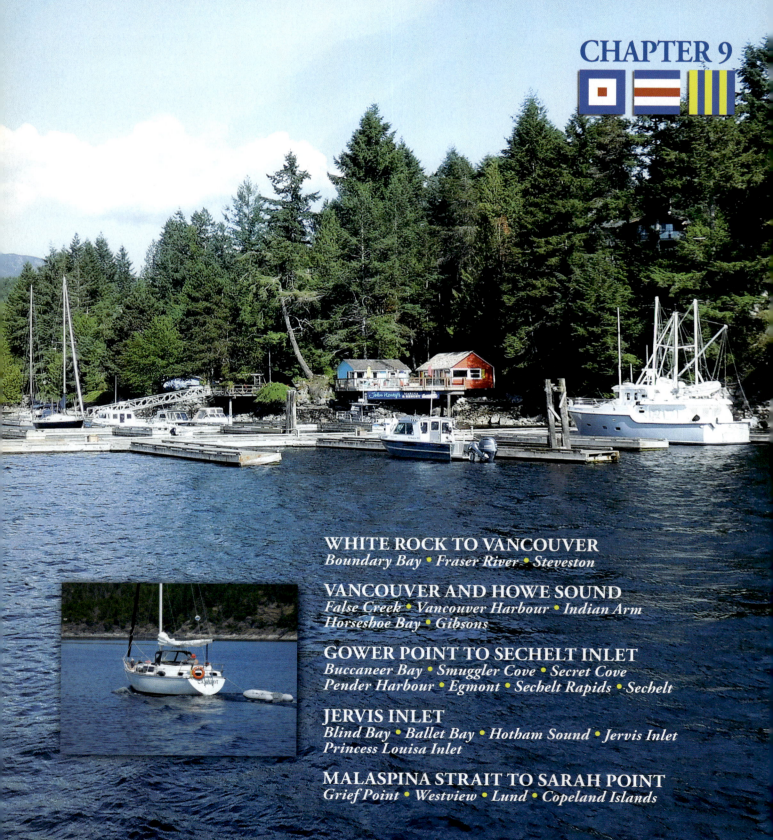

WHITE ROCK TO VANCOUVER
Boundary Bay • Fraser River • Steveston

VANCOUVER AND HOWE SOUND
*False Creek • Vancouver Harbour • Indian Arm
Horseshoe Bay • Gibsons*

GOWER POINT TO SECHELT INLET
*Buccaneer Bay • Smuggler Cove • Secret Cove
Pender Harbour • Egmont • Sechelt Rapids • Sechelt*

JERVIS INLET
*Blind Bay • Ballet Bay • Hotham Sound • Jervis Inlet
Princess Louisa Inlet*

MALASPINA STRAIT TO SARAH POINT
Grief Point • Westview • Lund • Copeland Islands

VANCOUVER, MAINLAND B.C. & THE SUNSHINE COAST

WHITE ROCK TO VANCOUVER

The coastline between Boundary Bay and Vancouver is an uninteresting river delta and the waters are often rough. Fraser River sediment, locally known as Sand Heads, has created shoal depths for some distance offshore. The prevailing winds tend to blow against the river current in the shallow water, and steep seas build quickly. Stay well off in deeper water, but even there, a 20-knot wind can make for a rough ride.

We listened to the VHF one day when a storm front blew through, and we sympathized with a terrified woman aboard a chartered 45-foot powerboat caught in steep seas near Roberts Bank. She kept repeating their lat/lon coordinates from the GPS and begging for help. The boat wasn't taking on water and no one was injured, but conditions were awful and they were scared. There was nothing another boat could do.

A few weeks earlier we spoke with a couple who had gone up that shore to Vancouver and had a very rough ride, the kind of ride they never wanted to repeat—period. We have run that coast in calm conditions and had no problems. [*Hale*]

Most pleasure craft choose to go north through the Gulf Islands, then pick a patch of good weather to cross the Strait of Georgia to Vancouver or Howe Sound. The shortest distance across the strait, from Gabriola Pass to Howe Sound, is 14 miles. Even slow boats can make the crossing in two or three hours; faster boats can cross in an hour or less. Listen for the weather report for the Halibut Bank buoy, or call Dial-a-Buoy at (888) 701-8992 or (301) 713-9620 and enter 46146 for the wind and wave conditions in the Strait of Georgia, off Sechelt.

Boundary Bay. The U.S./Canada border runs through Boundary Bay. Delta, B.C. is located on the northwest shore. Point Roberts, Washington, is to the southwest. White Rock and the Semiahmoo First Nation's reserve are on the southeast shore. The southeastern section of Boundary Bay, straddling the U.S./Canada border is known as Semiahmoo Bay. The northern tip of Boundary Bay is known as Mud Bay.

① **White Rock.** White Rock, in Canada, is almost due north of Blaine, in Boundary Bay. A long pier, with floats at the outer end, crosses tide flats. The waterfront village has interesting restaurants, shops, and galleries.

① **City of White Rock Pier.** (604) 626-5330. White Rock is a Canada Customs port of entry; call (888) 226-7277. The south side of the eastern float has about 50 feet of space reserved for transient moorage, 2 hours maximum stay, no power or water. Repairs were made to the pier in 2019.

② **Crescent Beach.** North of White Rock, the Nicomekl River empties into Boundary Bay, creating a channel that leads to the village of Crescent Beach and the Crescent Beach Marina. The channel is marked by port and starboard daymarks. The marina is located just beyond the Burlington Northern Railway swing bridge that crosses the river to Blackie Spit. Depending on tide, bridge clearance ranges from 9 to 20 feet. The bridge is manned 7 days a week, from 6:30 a.m. until 10:30 p.m., and will open to 3 horn blasts. Call the bridge at (604) 538-3233 or call the Crescent Beach Marina at (604) 538-9666, and they will contact the bridge tender.

② **Crescent Beach Marina Ltd.** 12555 Crescent Road, Surrey, BC V4A 2V4; (604) 538-9666; info@crescentbeachmarina.com; www.crescentbeachmarina.com. Open all year, hours vary in the off-season. Gasoline & diesel at the fuel dock. Guest moorage for boats to 60 feet; call first. Haulout on hydraulic trailers to 30 tons, 15, 20 & 30 amp power, washrooms, ice, repairs, chandlery, launch ramp, showers, laundry, pumpout, dry storage. Used oil drop.

Canoe Passage. Canoe Passage is the southernmost mouth of the Fraser River. The seaward entrance is marked by a government buoy, but private dolphins mark its winding path through Roberts Bank. Although mainly used by commercial boats with local knowledge, Canoe Passage can be used by small craft, especially at half tide or better on a rising tide. The swing bridge connecting Westham Island with the mainland is manned 24 hours a day, and opens to 3 whistle blasts. Contact the bridge tender on VHF 74 or by telephone at (604) 946-2121. In 1997 the Canadian Hydrographic Service published large scale Chart 3492 (1:20,000) showing Canoe Passage, but we are skeptical. Locals who use the passage re-mark the channel yearly, after major runoff has moved the sand bars.

South Arm Fraser River. Sand Heads marks the mouth of the South Arm (also called the **Main Arm**) of the Fraser River. The South Arm is the Fraser's major entry, and is protected on its north side by the Steveston Jetty. Currents in the Fraser River can run to 5 knots, depending on the volume of water in the river, which in turn depends on rain and snow melt upstream. Large flood tides will at times slow or reverse the current.

Caution: An on-shore wind meeting an ebb current, combined with heavy outflow from the river, will create dangerously steep and high seas in the river mouth. Friends who keep their boats on the river tell of their entire boat being airborne in these conditions.

The lower part of the Fraser River is delta country, low and flat. The marshlands are havens for wildlife, and you'll see many eagles. The river itself contains much drift. The river is used heavily by fish boats, tugs towing barges or log booms, Coast Guard boats, work boats of all description, and freighters.

White Rock to Vancouver

2020 Waggoner Cruising Guide

VANCOUVER, MAINLAND B.C. & THE SUNSHINE COAST

See Area Map Page 285 - Maps Not for Navigation

Steveston Harbour

Water-oriented industrial companies are located along the shores.

Relatively few cruising boats go up the Fraser River, in part because the entire coast between Point Grey and Point Roberts is uninteresting to view, and hostile in any kind of wind. Most of the marinas on the Fraser River exist primarily for permanent moorage tenants, with few facilities for visitors.

③ **Steveston.** The first stop on the Fraser River is Steveston, a long, slender harbor on the north side of Cannery Channel, protected by a sand island (Steveston Island). Although Steveston is primarily a fishing town with moorage and other services for commercial fishermen, it has become a lively tourist destination as well. Transient moorage is available at the Steveston Wharf and at Imperial Landing located a third of a mile east of the wharf. Steveston has a fuel dock. Antique shops, bookstores, plenty of dining and all the other facilities of a small city are ashore. The streets of Steveston are quaint; the local movie industry sometimes films scenes there. Steveston has much to offer above and beyond its attractive shops and cafes. The excellent Gulf of Georgia Cannery Museum on the west end of the Public Wharf is a must see, as is the Britannia Shipyards National Historic Site on the east end of the village, reached by a beautiful promenade along the shoreline. Hikers and bicyclists make use of the extensive trail system that leads to the North Arm of the Fraser River and to the City of Richmond. For a short hike, walk the trail west of town to Garry Point Park with beach access and great views over the South Arm and the Gulf Islands.

③ **Steveston Harbour Authority Wharf.** 12740 Trites Rd., Richmond, BC V7E 3R8; (604) 272-5539; www.stevestonharbour.com. Open all year, 30 amp power, water, washrooms, and showers. No Wi-Fi. Side-tie transient moorage is available by reservation only on the east side of the unlabeled float, east of the fish sales float (the eastern most Wharf float.) Additional side-tie transient moorage is available on the shore side of A-dock on a first-come, first-serve basis. All transient guests must register and make payment by phone; the Harbour Authority office is located more than a mile away, at their Paramount Basin site. A key to the showers is provided upon request. Showers and public washrooms are located next to the Gulf of Georgia Cannery Museum.

③ **Steveston Chevron.** (604) 277-4712. Fuel dock with ethanol-free gasoline, diesel, washrooms. Limited marine supplies, lubricants, snacks.

③ **City of Richmond Imperial Landing.** Located a third of a mile east of the Steveston Harbour Authority docks; parksprograms@richmond.ca; www.richmond.ca/parks. A Richmond City Parks Department facility (604) 244-1208. Transient side-tie moorage on this substantial 600-foot concrete dock, first-come, first-served; 30 amp power, no water, no washrooms, or showers. First three hours are free. Rates for stays over three hours are posted at the automated pay-station at the head of the ramp. Maximum stay is three consecutive days. This dock offers a more secluded moorage option when visiting the community of Steveston. Charted depths are deeper off the west end of this dock than around the Steveston Harbour docks.

Caution: Hazardous submerged piles are reported near the inside (shore side) of the east half of the dock.

④ **Ladner.** Ladner is a pretty town. Leave the main branch of the Fraser River and take Sea Reach to Ladner Harbour, fronted by float homes. Moorage for fish boats is on the port side, and pleasure craft are welcome when the

286   www.WaggonerGuide.com

VANCOUVER, MAINLAND B.C. & THE SUNSHINE COAST

fleet is out. Strongly favor the south shore as you enter Ladner Harbour, skirting the docks of marinas and businesses located along River Road. A drying mud bank, studded with deadheads, extends a considerable distance from the north side of the harbor.

④ **Ladner Yacht Club.** (604) 946-4056; www.ladneryachtclub.ca. Reciprocal boats only if space is available. Water, restrooms, 30 amp power, secured marina.

Deas Slough. A little farther up the river from Ladner, Deas Slough is home to Captain's Cove, located behind Deas Island. A low bridge (Hwy. 99) blocks passage any farther up Deas Slough, except for small boats with no masts.

⑤ **Captain's Cove Marina.** 6100 Ferry Rd., Ladner, BC V4K 3M9; (604) 946-1244; info@captainscovemarina.ca; www.captainscovemarina.ca. Permanent moorage only. Haulout to 60 tons, and a do-it-yourself yard for repairs.

⑥ **Shelter Island Marina Inc.** 6911 Graybar Rd., Richmond, BC V6W 1H3; (604) 270-6272; infodesk@shelterislandmarina.com; www.shelterislandmarina.com. Open all year, some guest moorage, call ahead. Washrooms, showers, laundry, water, 15, 30, & 50 amp power, several Travelifts for boats up to 220 tons, chandlery with hardware section in the marina office and a full-service chandlery across the parking lot. Restaurant and pub with free Wi-Fi, beer and wine store, and a full liquor store two blocks away.

Shelter Island Marina is behind Don Island at the south entrance to Annacis Channel. It is a busy facility with a number of boat repair companies.

New Westminster. New Westminster is located at the confluence of the North and South Arms of the Fraser River, and is heavily industrialized along the waterfront.

Tom Kincaid has run the river past New Westminster to the Pitt River, where he spent the night at the Pitt Meadows Marina. A few friends have continued to the Harrison River, running up the Harrison River to Harrison Lake and Harrison Hot Springs. All recommend having a fast boat and a knowledgeable pilot aboard before attempting to run either of these rivers. The Fraser River beyond Richmond is poorly marked, and sand bars are constantly changing. The river is navigable as far as Hope during high water stages, but mariners should rely on local knowledge before attempting this run.

North Arm Fraser River. The North Arm of the Fraser River is lined with boatbuilding and repair yards and other businesses that serve the marine community. A jetty runs through Sturgeon Bank along the south side of the North Arm, parallel to the Point Grey shoreline. A dredged basin, known locally as "Coward's Cove" or the "Chicken Hole," is on the north side of the channel, just before the North Arm enters the Strait of Georgia. The basin gives good protection to skippers while they assess conditions out on the strait.

⑦ **Richmond Chevron.** 7891 Grauer Rd., Richmond, BC V7B 1N4; (604) 278-2181. Beneath Arthur Laing Bridge. Open all year, gasoline, diesel, lubricants and waste oil disposal.

Middle Arm Fraser River. The Middle Arm of the Fraser River runs along the south side of Sea Island, which is almost entirely taken up by Vancouver International Airport. The west entrance is blocked by Sturgeon Bank with no marked channels. We have seen a small, fast cruiser enter the Middle Arm, but the tide was high and perhaps the skipper had local knowledge (or maybe was just lucky). Prudence dictates entry from the North Arm only. The Delta River Inn Marina and Vancouver Marina are on the Middle Arm near a low swing bridge connecting the city of Richmond with the airport.

⑦ **Pier 73 Marina & Yacht Club.** 3500 Cessna Drive, Richmond, BC V7B 1C7; (604) 970-4882; info@pier73marina.com; pier73marina.com. Located 8 miles up the North Arm of the Fraser River in Moray Channel at the Pacific Gateway Hotel Vancouver Airport. Open all year, limited guest moorage, call ahead. This fully refurbished marina has slips from 30 to 80 feet, 30 & 50 amp power, water. The hotel has several restaurants, a bar, and a pool. They run a bus to the airport.

⑦ **Vancouver Marina.** #200-8211 River Road, Richmond, BC V6X 1X8; (604) 278-9787; (604) 278-3300 fuel dock; mooring@vancouvermarina.com; www.vancouvermarina.com. Monitors VHF 66A. Open all year, call ahead for guest moorage. Gasoline & diesel at the fuel dock, 15, 20 & 30 amp power, garbage, pumpout, recycling and waste oil disposal, washrooms, no showers. They carry marine supplies, snacks, bait, and ice. Restaurant, mechanic and parts department, haulout to 30 feet, 24-hour security. Located in the heart of Richmond on the Middle Arm of the Fraser River.

⑦ **Skyline Marina.** 8031 River Road, Richmond, BC V6X 1X8; (604) 273-3977; www.skylinemarina.ca. Open all year, no transient moorage. The marina has a boatyard and 30 ton Travelift.

⑦ **Milltown Marina.** 9191 Bently Street, Vancouver, BC V6P 0B9; (604) 697-9191; admin@milltownmarina.com; www.milltownmarina.ca. Office open Tuesday through Saturday. Permanent and transient moorage for vessels up to 80 feet, 30 & 50 amp power, water, restrooms, showers, garbage, and recycle drop. Propane refills. This is one of Vancouver's newest marinas located on the Fraser River near the Vancouver International Airport.

A restaurant is located upland. Milltown Marine Services (604-264-8020) is next door near the marina.

VANCOUVER

Vancouver is the largest city in British Columbia, and the major deepwater port on the west coast of Canada, handling cargo from across Canada and around the world. The city is clean, safe, and thoroughly cosmopolitan. Its architecture is exciting. Vancouver's parks, museums, hotels, and dining are wonderful.

If you are approaching Vancouver from the south, you could go up the North Arm of the Fraser River to a number of marinas in the Richmond area, and take a bus into the city. If you are approaching from the north, you could tie up at Horseshoe Bay on the north shore of West Vancouver, or at Snug Cove on the south side of Bowen Island. A private foot ferry runs between Snug Cove and Granville Island during the summer months. Or take the BC Ferries from Snug Cove to Horseshoe Bay, then board a bus for the trip into Vancouver—or as far south as White Rock if that's where you wanted to go. The Vancouver

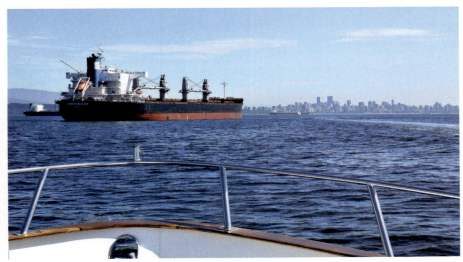
Negotiating around the ships at anchor in English Bay on the way to False Creek

VANCOUVER, MAINLAND B.C. & THE SUNSHINE COAST

transit system is excellent and affordable.

For moorage in Vancouver proper, choose either the Vancouver Harbour area or the False Creek area. Each has advantages, and each is good. Once you're settled, Vancouver's bus system allows you to get around the entire area with minimum delay. A Costco store is located near the northeast end of False Creek at 605 Expo Blvd. (604) 622-5050.

Anchoring restriction: A permit, at no cost, is required for all vessels anchoring in False Creek (see False Creek area description for details).

Point Grey. Point Grey marks the southern entrance to Burrard Inlet. When approaching from the south, cutting too close to Point Grey risks grounding on Spanish Bank. Leave the buoys to starboard when entering.

Spanish Bank. Spanish Bank is an extensive drying bank off the north shore of Point Grey. The outer edge of the bank is marked with buoys. Royal Vancouver Yacht Club has its main clubhouse and sailboat moorage about 3 miles from Point Grey along the south shore of English Bay. A launch ramp is close to the former Kitsilano Coast Guard station near the entrance to False Creek.

FALSE CREEK

False Creek is an ideal centrally located bay with a number of marina moorage options, well-protected anchorage and a full service boatyard with Travelift. A well-monitored anchoring permit system helps to keep anchoring space available and prevents permanent anchorage abuses. Anchoring permits (free) are required for day anchoring longer than 8 hours and overnight anchoring. Permits can be picked up at Heather Civic Marina or online at http://vancouver.ca/streets-transportation/anchoring.aspx. Boats without permits are subject to ticketing and fines up to $500.

False Creek Yacht Club, on the north shore of False Creek, usually has guest slips available. Quayside Marina, also on the north shore, has excellent facilities with guest slip and side-tie moorage. Foot ferries stop at Quayside. On the south shore, the Fishermen's Wharf marina, managed by the False Creek Harbour Authority, has transient moorage and good facilities. It is a short walk from the marina to the Granville Island Market, shops, and restaurants. False Creek is covered by Wi-Fi.

Blue Pacific Charters, on the west side of Granville Island near the Granville Market, sometimes has moorage available in unoccupied slips, reservations required. To reach these docks turn just before the Bridge Restaurant, on the south side when you enter False Creek, and work your way towards the docks. On the east side of Granville Island the Pelican Bay Marina, next to the Granville Island Hotel, has some guest moorage.

Granville Island is an active and vibrant place, full of people. You'll find a busy food market (similar in many ways to Seattle's Pike Place Market), many restaurants, galleries, shops, and a variety of marine supplies, both on the island and a short walk away. Docks face the waterway, and are posted for 3-hour maximum stay.

Two harbor foot ferry franchises serve False Creek, it's a great way to tour the harbour. These foot ferries no longer stop to pick up passengers from boats anchored in the bay.

Fuel: Fuel is available at the False Creek Fuels.

Pumpouts: Pumpouts are located at Burrard Bridge Civic Marina, False Creek Harbour Authority Fishermen's Wharf, Heather Civic Marina (under the large "Monk's" sign), and Quayside Marina. The City of Vancouver and the Vancouver Park Board started a free mobile pumpout service pilot project in 2017, which has been ongoing to provide service during the summer months. To schedule the service, contact Skookum Yacht Services at (778) 683-7867 or email at pumpout@skookumyachtservices.com. At press time, it was not known if the city's contract with Skookum Yacht Services would be renewed for the 2020 season.

No Discharge Zone. Gray Water Okay.

First Narrows under Lions Gate Bridge

Things to Do

1. Granville Market. On Granville Island, a delight to the senses with flowers, spices, teas, fruit and other food markets, restaurants and crafts.

2. Foot Ferries. Crisscross the water from False Creek. Travel to different attractions or stay aboard to tour the entire harbor area. Some ferries allow bicycles.

3. Vancouver Maritime Museum. Learn more about B.C. maritime history from Vancouver to the Arctic. See tugboats, fireboats and even pirates. Easily reached by foot ferry.

4. Stanley Park. Several bike rental shops are on Denman Street, near Coal Harbour. Rent a bike and ride the trail along the seawall. Or, take a walk around the park. While in Stanley Park, learn more about B.C.'s First Nations people in Klahowya Village.

5. Vancouver Aquarium. Located in Stanley Park. Excellent. Don't miss the white Beluga whales.

6. Spirit Catcher Miniature Train. Take a ride and see the story of Sasquatch.

7. Science World. The distinctive domed glass building on False Creek with imaginative exhibits and hands-on experiments for young and old.

8. Bloedel Floral Conservatory. In Queen Elizabeth Park. Tropical plants; colorful birds flying about.

9. Museum of Anthropology. On the University of British Columbia campus. Study of First Nations people and other B.C. cultures.

10. Deeley Motorcycle Exhibition. Over 250 motorcycles on exhibit, spanning 115 years and 59 different manufacturers.

11. Yaletown or Gastown. Key shopping areas with many shops and boutiques.

Vancouver Maritime Museum. 1905 Ogden Avenue in Vanier Park, Vancouver, BC V6J 1A3; (604) 257-8300; www.vancouvermaritimemuseum.com. Vancouver Maritime Museum is on the south shore of English Bay at the entrance to False Creek. The museum's docks are for display boats only. The vessel St. Roch, which explored the Northwest Passage, is on display in its own building. The False Creek Ferry stops at the museum docks.

VANCOUVER, MAINLAND B.C. & THE SUNSHINE COAST

Reference Only – Not for Navigation

Vancouver and Howe Sound

⑧ **Vancouver Boating Welcome Centre.** 1661 Granville St., Vancouver, BC V6Z 1N3; (604) 648-2628; welcome@fcyc.com. Hours 9:00 a.m to 5:00 p.m. Located in a boat at False Creek Yacht Club. The Welcome Center is a good resource to help with boating related matters. Anchor permits for False Creek are no longer available through the Welcome Centre. The Yacht Club is phasing out of their participation in the Welcome Centre over the next two years, but still currently under contract with the city of Vancouver to provide this service.

⑧ **False Creek Yacht Club.** 1661 Granville St., Vancouver, BC V6Z 1N3; (604) 648-2628 dockmaster; (604) 682-3292 administration & event scheduling; www.fcyc.com; welcome@fcyc.com. Washrooms, showers, laundry, pumpout, free Wi-Fi, 30 amp power, and lounge. Open all year on the north side of False Creek, directly under the Granville Street Bridge. Reciprocal and public guest moorage in unoccupied slips. Limited moorage for boats over 50 feet. Call the dockmaster upon arrival. A passenger foot ferry runs regularly to Granville Island.

⑧ **Quayside Marina.** 1088 Marinaside Crescent, Vancouver, BC V6Z 3C4; (604) 681-9115; (604) 209-6456; qsmarina@ranchogroup.com; www.ranchovan.com/marina. Monitors VHF 66A. Open all year for vessels to 135 feet, 30, 50 & 100 amp power, water on the docks, washrooms, showers, laundry, pay telephone, pumpout, garbage and recycling, ice, security. Wheelchair accessible. Online Reservations are available on their website. Slip sales and long-term lease information also found on their website.

The Quayside (pronounced "Keyside") Marina is on the north shore of False Creek, in the middle of Vancouver's cosmopolitan Yaletown district. Most of the slips are for permanent moorage, but guest moorage is available on a 500-foot-long float extending from shore, or in vacant slips. Colorful Aquabus foot ferry boats come and go from their spot near the head of that float as do the small passenger False Creek Ferries. Moorage reservations are essential during high season and requested year-round. Although it's a bit of a walk from the guest dock to the office, check in promptly after you arrive. For provisioning, visit the Urban Fare Market, a block away, at 1688 Salt Street. Costco, located at 605 Expo Blvd., is a short walk or taxi ride away.

⑧ **Pacific Boulevard Marina.** Box 26, 750 Pacific Blvd., Vancouver, BC V6B 5E7; (604) 683-7035; info@pacblvdmarina.com; www.pacblvdmarina.com. Permanent moorage marina with transient space when available for vessels up to 40 feet; 30 amp power, water, security gates. Located at the northeast end of False Creek. Reservations requested no more than one week in advance. Transient space is most likely available during March and April. Sea-Doo and pontoon boat rentals.

2020 Waggoner Cruising Guide   289

VANCOUVER, MAINLAND B.C. & THE SUNSHINE COAST

See Area Map Page 289 - Maps Not for Navigation

⑨ **Burrard Civic Marina.** 1655 Whyte Ave., Vancouver, BC V6J 1A9; (604) 733-5833 (604) 505-5833 cell; burrard.marina@vancouver.ca. The first marina in False Creek, with over 420 berths. Open 7 days a week all year. Operated by the City of Vancouver. Permanent moorage with some space for transient boats in vacant slips to 36 feet (occasionally up to 45 feet). Call for availability. Water, 15 amp power, washrooms, showers, pumpout, waste oil disposal, security gate with key-card, free Wi-Fi. The marina is convenient to the Vancouver Maritime Museum, walking and bike paths, and the False Creek foot ferries.

⑨ **False Creek Fuels.** 1655 Whyte Avenue, Vancouver, BC V6J 1A9; (604) 638-0209; fillup@falsecreekfuels.com; www.falsecreekfuels.com. Monitors 66A. Just west of the Burrard Street Bridge, the fuel float carries gas, diesel, oil, lubricants. Open 7 days a week. Waste oil and fuel disposal. Accommodates vessels to 165 feet. The store has drinks, snacks, ice cream, sandwiches (seasonal), and a coffee bar. It also has ice, bait, tackle, marine supplies, guidebooks.

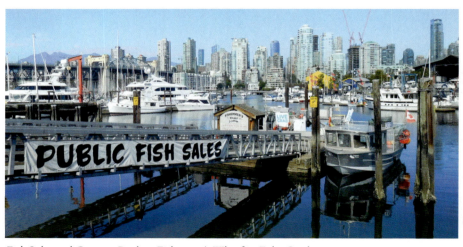

Fish Sales and Customs Dock at Fishermen's Wharf in False Creek

⑨ **False Creek Harbour Authority Fishermen's Wharf.** Fishermen's Wharf. 1505 W. 1st Ave., Vancouver, BC V6J 1E8; (604) 733-3625; info@falsecreek.com; www.falsecreek.com. Monitors VHF 66A. This is a 5-Anchor Clean Marina rated facility. Open 24 hours a day year-round. Located on the south shore of False Creek, west of Granville Island. Contact the Harbour Authority office for docking instructions prior to arrival. 20 & 30 amp power on all docks; 50 & 100 amp power on some. Contact the Harbour office for access to locked power connection boxes. Water, washrooms, showers, laundry, ice, pumpout, recycling, waste oil disposal, free Wi-Fi, and 24-hour security. Ramps between shore and the floats are wide, long and compliant with Canadian Disability Policy Alliance. A fish sales dock is just east of the Harbour Authority office, where you may purchase fresh seafood directly from the fish boats. The upland Go Fish Seafood Shack's fish & chips are not to be missed, take-out or enjoy at the outdoor bar and picnic tables. Expect long lines around noon time.

The Vancouver Maritime Museum in Vanier Park is a short walk away. The popular Shakespeare Festival, under the tents in Vanier Park, is held early June through mid-September. Granville Island, with its excellent market, shops, cafes and theaters is within easy walking distance from Fishermen's Wharf.

Customs Clearance. A courtesy customs clearance area is located in the yellow painted

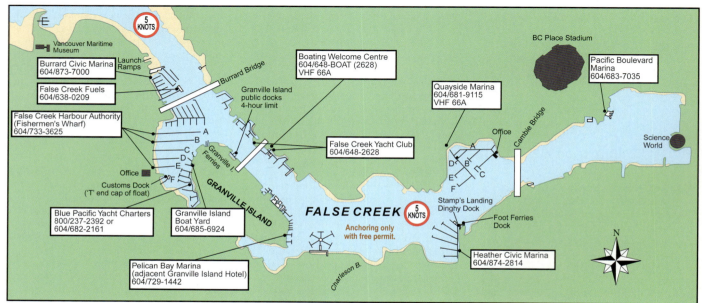

False Creek, Vancouver

See Area Map Page 289 - Maps Not for Navigation

VANCOUVER, MAINLAND B.C. & THE SUNSHINE COAST

Coal Harbour Marina is in the middle of downtown Vancouver and the most centrally located.

bull-rail area on the 'T' end of F-dock. There is no dedicated phone, you will need to use your cell phone.

⑨ **Blue Pacific Yacht Charters.** 1519 Foreshore Walk, Vancouver, BC V6H 3X3; (604) 682-2161; info@bluepacificcharters.ca; www.bluepacificcharters.ca. Open all year, moorage in unoccupied slips as available, 30 & 50 amp power, washrooms, and showers. Located on the west side of Granville Island.

⑨ **Granville Island Boat Yard.** (604) 685-6924; www.granvilleislandboatyard.com. A full service boatyard with 55 ton Travelift is located on the west side of Granville Island. The boatyard has repair service trades people available and welcomes do-it-yourself.

⑨ **Pelican Bay Marina.** 1708 W. 6th Ave., Vancouver, BC V6J 5E8; (604) 729-1442; pelicanbaymarina@gmail.com. Open all year, adjacent to the Granville Island Hotel on the east end of Granville Island. Moorage in unoccupied slips when available, call ahead. Water, 15, 30 & 50 amp power, washroom, ice.

⑨ **Heather Civic Marina.** 600 Stamps Landing, Vancouver, BC V5Z 3Z1; (604) 874-2814; heather.marina@vancouver.ca; www.vancouver.ca/streets-transportation/heather-civic-marina.aspx. Open all year with guest moorage to 42 feet in unoccupied slips, call for availability. Washrooms, showers, pumpout, 15, 30 & 50 amp power. Restaurants and pub nearby. A passenger foot ferry runs to both sides of False Creek. The Heather Civic Marina office issues anchoring permits for False Creek.

LOCAL KNOWLEDGE

STRONG CURRENTS: Currents run strongly in both First and Second Narrows. Use caution, especially because of the heavy traffic that frequents the area.

Vancouver Harbour (South). Vancouver Harbour is entered under the Lions Gate Bridge through First Narrows, in the northeast corner of Burrard Inlet. Because of heavy commercial traffic, strong currents and narrow channels, sailing craft must be under power from westward of First Narrows until well into Vancouver Harbour. No sailing is permitted through Second Narrows, either. In First Narrows, a strong ebb current meeting a fresh onshore breeze can create high, steep seas. Current predictions are shown in the Tide and Current Tables Vol. 5, and Ports and Passes. Monitor VHF 12 for Vessel Traffic Services (VTS) information.

Watch for drifting logs, float plane traffic, and Vancouver Rowing Club rowers in Vancouver Harbour. Approaching Coal Harbour, leave Burnaby Shoal and the Chevron fuel barge to starboard. Observe a 5-knot speed limit.

Once into Vancouver Harbour, your best bet for moorage is along the southern shoreline in the Coal Harbour area. Vancouver Rowing Club, located adjacent to Stanley Park, has moorage for members of reciprocal yacht clubs. Stanley Park is nearby.

Bayshore West Marina, next to the Harbour Ferries docks, offers some guest moorage.

Coal Harbour Marina, just east of the Bayshore Hotel, makes a visit to Vancouver a real pleasure. It is first class in every way, and is an excellent base for a few days in town.

These marinas are close to downtown Vancouver, a pleasant walk or short cab ride away. Wright Mariner Supply, occupying a floating structure in the Coal Harbour Marina, sells a complete range of marine supplies, clothing, charts, and books.

Robson Street's shops, galleries and wide range of restaurants are just a few blocks away.

Anchoring restriction: Pleasure craft may not anchor in Vancouver Harbour between First Narrows and Second Narrows.

Customs dock: (888) 226-7277. The customs dock is a Parks Board dock called "Harbour Green," located east of Coal Harbour Marina. Day moorage up to 3 hours, no overnight. The dock has been closed and removed for redesign and permitting; construction anticipated to start in early 2021. For updates, go to vancouver.ca website and search for harbour-green.

⑩ **Coal Harbour Chevron.** (604) 681-7725. Fuel barge in Coal Harbour open 7 days a week 7:00 a.m. to 11:00 p.m., gasoline & diesel, washrooms, showers. They do oil changes and have waste oil disposal.

⑩ **Coal Harbour Marina.** 1525 Coal Harbour Quay, Vancouver, BC V6G 3E7; (604) 681-

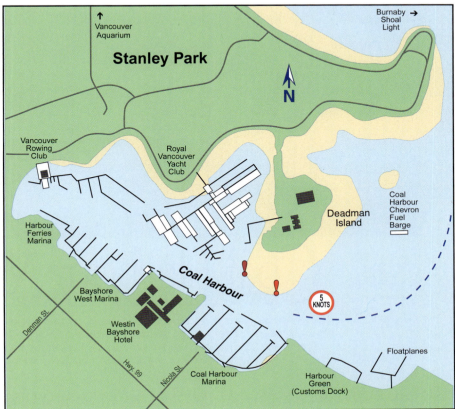
Coal Harbour

2020 Waggoner Cruising Guide

VANCOUVER, MAINLAND B.C. & THE SUNSHINE COAST

See Area Map Page 289 - Maps Not for Navigation

Coal Harbour Marina

Bayshore West Marina

Mosquito Creek Marina

2628; guestservices@coalharbourmarina.com; www.coalharbourmarina.com. Monitors VHF 66A. Open all year, guest moorage for boats to 330 feet, reservations recommended. Facilities include 30, 50 & 100 amp single/3-phase power, Wi-Fi, pumpout, washrooms, showers, laundry. This is a first-class marina with wide concrete docks, 24-hour staff, security gates, a restaurant, marine supply store, and easy access to downtown Vancouver. Reservations in season highly recommended.

⑩ **Bayshore West Marina.** 450 Denman St., Vancouver, BC V6G 3J1; (604) 689-5331; info@bayshorewestmarina.com; www.bayshorewestmarina.com. Open all year, mostly permanent moorage with limited guest moorage to 80 feet; 30, & 50 amp power, garbage, recycling Wi-Fi, washrooms, and pumpout. Located in Coal Harbour between Stanley Park and the Westin Bayshore Resort. Restaurants and shopping within easy walking distance. The slips and fairways are wide for easy maneuvering.

Vancouver Harbour (North). With the exception of the re-developed Lonsdale area, the north shore of Vancouver Harbour is mostly heavy commercial. Transient moorage is available at Mosquito Creek Marina and at the City of North Vancouver's St. Roch dock. Both are near the Lonsdale area which has a selection of restaurants and pubs, grocery, and shopping. SeaBus foot ferry service at Lonsdale Quay in North Vancouver runs to downtown Vancouver. The crossing takes 12 minutes and connects with other transportation options in downtown Vancouver. More info at: Vancouver transit planning at www.translink.ca.

A number of good marine repair shops are in Mosquito Creek Marina and at Lynnwood

Vancouver's Premier Marina
Convenient location in the Heart of Vancouver's Waterfront

◊ Guest Moorage available 30' to 330'
◊ 30, 50 & 100 AMP power
◊ Dockside assistance 24 hrs
◊ GUEST services 8:30 am – 5:00 pm
◊ Security gates & video cameras

Coal Harbour Marina
LOCATION • QUALITY • SERVICE

◊ Laundry, washrooms & showers
◊ Chandlery & shipwright service
◊ Marine pub & restaurant
◊ Adjacent Fueling Station

Coal Harbour Marina is Vancouver's premier provider of salt-water moorage offering a range of amenities in one of the most spectacular harbours in the world. Shopping, restaurants, sporting events, live theatre, museums and Stanley Park are just a short jaunt away. Follow the Seawall Trail on foot, bike or blades! Find us on Facebook and Twitter.

Telephone 604.681.2628 • Fax 604.681.4666 • VHF 66A (24 hrs) • WWW.COALHARBOURMARINA.COM
1525 Coal Harbour Quay Vancouver, BC V6G 3E7 • 49°17.500'N 123°07.600'W • guestservices@coalharbourmarina.com

VANCOUVER, MAINLAND B.C. & THE SUNSHINE COAST

Marina, just west of Second Narrows.

Saturday Summer Concerts: July through August at Shipbuilders' Square at the foot of Lonsdale. Shipyards Night Market: May through September from 5 to 10 p.m. on Fridays. Live music, fresh food and locally made products.

Caution: The SeaBus north terminus is just west of Lonsdale Quay with frequent arrivals and departures of two foot-passenger catamaran SeaBus ferries.

St. Roch Dock. (604) 982-3910; www.cnv.org/piers. 80 feet of floating dock for short-term and overnight moorage. Located east of Lonsdale Quay with its "Q" on top of the tower, just below the historic yellow crane and next to the re-developed 700x50 feet Burrard Dry Dock. This pleasure craft float is conveniently located but exposed to Vancouver Harbour on the south. No charge for the first 3 hours of stay. Thereafter, call the City of North Vancouver (604) 982-3910 to make payment.

The City of North Vancouver has two other docks nearby. The Goldsworthy Pier float has 36 feet of day-use only space with stays limited to 3 hours at no charge. The Burrard Dry Dock is for large vessels and requires prior arrangement scheduling and a signed agreement.

⑪ **Mosquito Creek Marina.** 415 West Esplanade, North Vancouver, BC V7M 1A6; (604) 987-4113; (604) 980-8370 fuel bar; mcmb_dockmaster@squamish.net; www.mosquitocreekmarina.com. Open all year with guest moorage in unoccupied slips, reservations recommended. 15, 30 & 50 amp power (100 amp on Dock A), washrooms and laundry, Wi-Fi, 50-ton Travelift, water, pumpout, marine repairs, security gates, 24-hour security. Fuel dock with mid-grade gasoline, high-speed diesel, ice, bait and fishing supplies. On-site cafe located in a double-wide trailer near the office.

The marina is operated by the Squamish Nation. A mixture of open moorage and covered moorage with a variety of slip sizes. Know your assigned slip and study the Mosquito Creek Marina dock diagram before entering the marina as dock and slip signage is lacking. Replacement of finger piers and decking is ongoing.

A foot path connects the marina with Lonsdale Quay shopping, with restaurants and a farmers market. Several boat repair companies with complete services are on-site. It's a 10-minute walk to the SeaBus foot ferries to downtown Vancouver.

⑪ **Lynnwood Marina.** 1681 Columbia St., North Vancouver, BC V7J 1A5; (604) 985-1533; info@lynnwoodmarina.com; www.lynnwoodmarina.com. Moorage for repair customers only. The marina has 15 & 30 amp power, complete repairs, and haulout to 60 tons. Shopping is about a 10-minute walk away.

BURNABY, PORT MOODY, INDIAN ARM

Second Narrows. To proceed eastward from Vancouver Harbour to Burnaby and Port Moody, you first must go through Second Narrows. On spring tides, flood currents can reach 6.5 knots and ebb currents 5.5 knots. The narrows are not to be treated lightly. Wind and current opposing each other can create standing waves and difficult seas. The best advice is to go through near times of slack, although on small tides the current should present few problems for boats with adequate power. Current predictions are shown as a secondary station in the Tide and Current Tables Vol. 5, and Ports and Passes. Due to extensive heavy displacement commercial traffic, monitor Vessel Traffic Service on VHF channel 12. Sailing is not permitted in Second Narrows.

Cates Park. Cates Park is at Roche Point, near the entrance to Indian Arm. The park has a paved launch ramp, beach, trails, playground, changing room, and picnic shelter. Temporary anchorage only.

Burnaby. The park at Burnaby is the site of an old sawmill. The park has no public float, but anchorage is good just east of the fishing pier.

Port Moody. Port Moody ends in drying flats, but a dredged channel on the south shore leads through the flats to Rocky Point Park. The park has a launch ramp, swimming pool and picnic areas, and is the location of the Port Moody Museum. A large designated anchorage area is located at the head of the bay with protection from all except northwesterly winds. This is an industrial area with commercial traffic.

⑫ **Reed Point Marina.** 850 Barnet Highway, Bldg. #1, Port Moody, BC V6H 1V6; (604) 937-1600; office@reedpoint.com; www.reedpoint.com. Open all year, mid-grade gasoline and diesel. Washrooms, showers, pumpout, haulout to 55 tons, chandlery, sundries, restaurant, marine supplies and service. Permanent moorage only.

INDIAN ARM

Indian Arm extends 11 miles into Coast Range mountains soaring to 5000 feet. Indian Arm is largely unpopulated beyond Deep Cove, because Deep Cove is the end of the road from North Vancouver. The waters in Indian Arm generally are calm, but can be ruffled by local downdraft winds off the mountains. Indian Arm is a little secret that Vancouver boaters cherish. It feels remote, yet it is close to the city.

Indian Arm Marine Park. In 1996 the Indian Arm Marine Park was expanded from the Twin Islands and Racoon Island to include most of the fjord. Croker Island and Granite Falls are part of the park.

Belcarra. Belcarra Regional Park is located on the east shore of Indian Arm, near the entrance. The public float is for loading and unloading only. Anchorage is good. The park has 2 lakes, 4 miles of shoreline, and complete facilities. It's a popular stop.

Strathcona. The small Strathcona municipal float is at the mouth of Indian Arm across from Belcarra, behind White Rock and the Grey Rocks Islands. The float dries at low tide.

⑬ **Deep Cove.** Deep Cove is a city of about 5,000 people. The public float provides access to shopping in the town of Deep Cove for vessels up to 36 feet, no overnight moorage. The commercial village, adjacent to the public float, is upscale. Deep Cove is the location of the Deep Cove Yacht Club. Deep Cove Northshore Marina has moorage, fuel, and other amenities. Speed limit in Deep Cove is 5 knots.

⑬ **Deep Cove Public Wharf.** The dock is 145 feet long, and is within walking distance of grocery stores, restaurants, live theater, and other facilities. Day use only, for boats up to 36 feet, no overnight moorage.

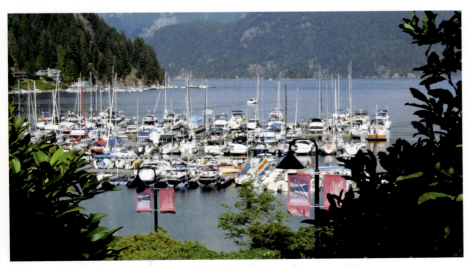

Remote and scenic Deep Cove is a surprisingly short distance from metro-Vancouver.

VANCOUVER, MAINLAND B.C. & THE SUNSHINE COAST

See Area Map Page 289 - Maps Not for Navigation

⑬ **Deep Cove North Shore Marina.** 2890 Panorama Drive, North Vancouver, BC V7G 1V6; (604) 929-1251; info@deepcovemarina.com; www.deepcovemarina.com. Open all year, gasoline and diesel at the fuel dock, limited guest moorage in unoccupied slips and side-tie. Call ahead. Facilities include washrooms, showers, laundry, and convenience store. Deep Cove Village with restaurants and shopping is located a mile to the west.

Bedwell Bay. Bedwell Bay has the best anchorage in Indian Arm. The bay is sheltered from southerly winds. The anchorage can be crowded during peak season. Speed limit 5 knots.

Twin Islands and Racoon Island. The larger of the Twin Islands has a dinghy float on its east side, and picnic and sanitary facilities ashore. Anchorage offshore is quite deep (between 80 and 150 feet). Twin Islands and Racoon Island are used by kayakers and canoeists who pull their craft ashore.

Granite Falls. Granite Falls, the largest of the falls entering Indian Arm, tumbles off a cliff along the east bank. A small day dock makes access easy and serves campsites ashore. Anchorage is fair just offshore. The climb up the cliff is good exercise for cramped muscles. Because of the questionable anchoring bottom, overnight anchoring is not recommended if outflow winds are expected.

Wigwam Inn. The Wigwam Inn, at the head of Indian Arm, was a luxury resort whose rich history goes back to 1906. Today it is a Royal Vancouver Yacht Club outstation. RVYC members only. Burrard Yacht Club and Deep Cove Yacht Club have outstations nearby—members only, no reciprocals.

POINT ATKINSON TO HORSESHOE BAY

Caulfeild Cove. Caulfeild Cove is a tiny bight, protected from nearly all winds and seas, tucked into the shoreline just east of Point Atkinson. A 52-foot public float lies along the east side of the cove with 6 feet of depth alongside.

Point Atkinson. Point Atkinson is the north entrance to Burrard Inlet.

LOCAL KNOWLEDGE

TIDE-RIPS: The waters just off Point Atkinson can be very rough, especially on a large ebb flowing against a fresh onshore wind. Often, a course well to seaward is called for, and even that can be heavy going. Point Atkinson is well known to Vancouver boaters, who give this area great respect.

Eagle Harbour. Eagle Harbour is the home of the Eagle Harbour Yacht Club. No guest moorage.

Fishermans Cove. Fishermans Cove, the home of West Vancouver Yacht Club, is filled with Thunderbird Marina. West Vancouver Yacht Club has some guest moorage for members of reciprocal clubs.

Important: Enter on the northwest side of the 39-meter island and Eagle Island, leaving the flashing red light to starboard. A "false entrance" between the 39-meter island and Eagle Island could put you in real trouble.

The passage from Eagle Harbour east of Eagle Island is shown clearly on Plans Chart 3534 but not on smaller scale Chart 3481.

The daymark in the northern mouth of the passage east of Eagle Island has been changed from port hand to starboard hand. This daymark relates to craft approaching from the north side of Eagle Island. Those craft should leave that daymark to starboard, to stay between the daymark and the docks on the north side of Fishermans Cove. Vessels northbound from Eagle Harbour should leave the daymark to port.

⑭ **Thunderbird Marina.** 5776 Marine Drive, West Vancouver, BC V7W 2S2; (604) 921-7484; thunderbird@thunderbirdmarine.com; www.thunderbirdmarine.com. Permanent moorage with limited transient moorage, reservations required. Haulout to 25 tons for boats to 50 feet. Do-it-yourself or use trades people boatyard. Thunderbird Marine Supplies carries marine supplies and hardware, open Tuesday through Sunday. Marine electrical, electronics, and other marine services onsite.

⑭ **Fishermans Cove Marine Fuels.** 5908 Marine Drive, West Vancouver, BC V7W 2S2; (604) 921-7333; Gas and diesel. Convenience store with supplies, snacks, and ice cream. They also provide water taxi services to surrounding islands.

HOWE SOUND

Howe Sound is a 23-mile long, deep-water inlet off the Strait of Georgia, with Squamish at its head. About 12 miles from Vancouver, Howe Sound is the "backyard" for Vancouver area boaters. Stunning Coast Range mountains surround Howe Sound.

Most boaters visit the communities and anchorages in the southern portion of Howe Sound. The town of Gibsons, on the west shore, is served by ferry from Horseshoe Bay, and offers two marinas and a fuel dock. Good restaurants, fun gift shops, a grocery and farmers market are available in Gibsons. The village of Snug Cove on Bowen Island is another delightful destination with boutiques, pubs and cafes, two grocery stores and hiking opportunities. Bowen Island is served by ferry at Snug Cove. Smaller marinas dot the eastern shore of Howe Sound, frequented by runabouts and sport fish boats. The south end of Gambier Island has several anchorages, including Port Graves, with room for a large number of boats. Two yacht club outstations are on the north side of Gambier Island. Keats Island, near Gibsons, offers anchorage and moorage at Plumber Cove Marine Park,

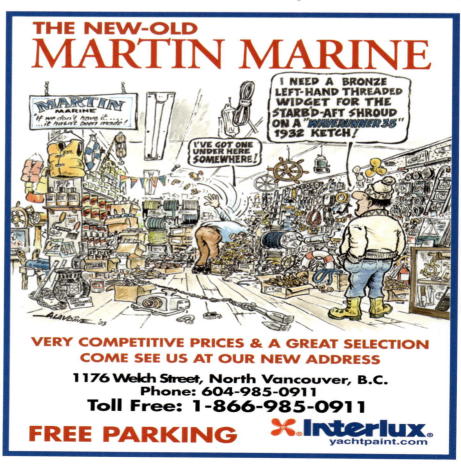

See Area Map Page 289 - Maps Not for Navigation

VANCOUVER, MAINLAND B.C. & THE SUNSHINE COAST

with upland park areas. On the eastern shore of Howe Sound, Porteau Cove has a lovely beach and detached 60-foot Park float and one mooring buoy.

Continuing north, the population becomes sparse in a wilderness setting with few anchorages. The water turns emerald green north of Anvil Island with stunning views of the Coast Range mountains. Glimpse views of the Sea-to-Sky highway, carved into the granite outcroppings, gives testament to this wilderness environment. "**Mariners Rest**," an islet off Mariners Rest Point, is a Provincially designated burial site for ashes at sea, look for the silver cross and anchor on the islet. Ashes are not buried on the islet, but rather at sea nearby, going ashore is not permitted.

In the distant northwest shore of Howe Sound are several large pulp and paper operations. Log booming areas fill the waters in front of these operations. Watch for considerable drift that may be present in Howe Sound. The town of Squamish is at the head of Howe Sound. Squamish is a vibrant town that has attracted young families, and brings in tourists seeking hiking opportunities and special attractions like the Sea to Sky Gondola near town, and Whistler Blackcomb, a world-class ski resort, located farther north. Moorage is available at the Squamish Port Authority docks and at the adjacent Squamish Yacht Club docks, where guests are welcome from just about any yacht club. Squamish has excellent pubs and cafes; groceries, hardware and other necessities.

⑮ **Horseshoe Bay.** Horseshoe Bay is the eastern terminus of ferries serving the Gulf Islands, Sunshine Coast, and Vancouver Island. Sewell's Marina, a large breakwater-protected public marina, is located to the west of the ferry docks. Boaters transiting this area are urged to use caution because of the steady procession of large ferry boats.

⑮ **Sewell's Marina Ltd.** 6409 Bay St., West Vancouver, BC V7W 3H5; (604) 921-3474; info@sewellsmarina.com; www.sewellsmarina.com. Open all year, gasoline and diesel fuel, ice, limited 15 & 30 amp power, concrete launch ramp, frozen bait. Limited guest moorage, mostly for boats 45 feet and under, call ahead. Fishing charters. Restaurants, groceries, and a post office nearby.

⑮ **Horseshoe Bay Public Wharf.** (604) 925-7129. Guest float, approximately 100 feet, on the south side of the wharf for short-term tie-up, maximum 4 hour stay. A float on the east end of the wharf is a 10-minute pick-up, drop-off area.

⑯ **Sunset Marina Ltd.** 34 Sunset Beach, West Vancouver, BC V7W 2T7; (604) 921-7476; sunsetmarina@shawlink.ca; www.sunsetmarinaltd.com. Open from March 1 to October 15. Gasoline, guest moorage to 24 feet, haulouts to 25 feet (power boats only), repairs, launch ramp with long term parking, washrooms. They carry marine supplies, tackle, and bait.

Bowen Island. Bowen Island is served by ferry from Horseshoe Bay. Snug Cove has a public wharf and two marinas. It's a wonderful destination with shops, a number of good restaurants, and a 600-acre park. A co-op store up the hill from the harbor has provisions. On the northeast corner of Bowen Island, Columbine Bay and Smugglers Cove offer good anchorage. Galbraith Bay has a public float. Anchorage is in Bowen Bay and Tunstall Bay.

⑰ **Snug Cove.** Snug Cove on Bowen Island is a favorite stop. It has a public dock and two marinas, and is served by ferry from Horseshoe Bay. From there you can take a bus to downtown Vancouver. Or take the seasonal foot ferry that runs directly to Granville Island.

The commercial village at Bowen Island has several boutiques, restaurants, grocery store, bakery/coffee house, pharmacy, wine store and liquor agency, and a couple of pubs. Bowen Island residents are artistic, interesting, and eclectic, and the local shopping reflects the character of the population.

Pubs: Visit Bowen Island Pub located in an impressive building up the hill; new for 2019 is the Copper Spirit Distillery with a selection of locally crafted vodka, gin and whisky.

Dock Dance: The annual Dock Dance, a benefit dance for the local volunteer firefighters, is held in early August. Participants take over the dock at Snug Cove for a party that literally rocks the dock with music and dancing.

Golf: The 9-hole par 35 Bowen Island Golf Club is challenging and beautiful, with greens that are devilishly hard to read. Call (604) 947-4653. Union Steamship Co. provides transportation for its guests.

Ferry Noise: Ferry propellers make underwater noise that can sometimes be heard throughout Snug Cove. If you hear what you think is an onboard pump cycling ON whenever a ferry is at the dock, realize that it may actually be noise transmitted from the ferry's props to your hull.

⑰ **Bowen Island Marina.** 375 Cardena Dr., RR 1 A-1, Bowen Island, BC V0N 1G0; (604) 947-9710; www.bowen-island.com. Moorage for boats on an annual basis. No overnight transient moorage. Located on the starboard side when entering Snug Cove. Shops with ice cream, pies, pastries, tacos, gifts and kayak rentals.

⑰ **Snug Cove Public Wharf.** (604) 328-5499. This wide concrete dock, with 350 feet of space, is next to the ferry landing in Snug Cove and exposed to ferry wash. No water or electricity. First-come, first-served in areas that are not reserved for load/unload and water taxis. Some areas are reserved for monthly moorage from mid-September to mid-June. Self-registration and payment at the top of the ramp on the pier.

⑰ **Union Steamship Co. Marina.** P.O. Box 250, Bowen Island, BC V0N 1G0; (604) 947-0707; marina@ussc.ca; www.unionsteamshipmarina.com. Monitors VHF 66A. Open all year, ample guest moorage, pumpout, 30 & 50 amp power, a boaters lounge with washrooms and showers, laundry, free Wi-Fi. The washroom and shower building, one of the finest on the coast, also includes a comfortable lounge with

Snug Cove

2020 Waggoner Cruising Guide

VANCOUVER, MAINLAND B.C. & THE SUNSHINE COAST

big screen TV and a computer station, all near the showers and laundry.

This is an excellent place to stop. Rondy Dike, an architect by training, and his wife Dorothy have restored the Union Steamship Co. landing into a wonderful destination resort. Their daughter, Oydis Dike Nickle, now manages the resort and marina. The staff is attentive and standing by to help. A lovely boardwalk leads from the marina, connecting several shops, cafes, and Doc Morgan's Pub & Restaurant. Easy walking trails are found through the adjacent 600-acre park. It seems that everyone who stays at Union Steamship has a good report. Reservations recommended.

The marina has 8 cottages available on the hillside.

Mount Gardner Park Public Dock. Galbraith Bay, northwest side of Bowen Island. Has 110 feet of space.

Gambier Island. Gambier Island has three significant inlets, all opening from the south: West Bay, Centre Bay, and Port Graves. A smaller inlet, Halkett Bay, is at the southeast corner of the island. Thornbrough Bay, on the west side of the island, has a public dock. We are told that boats often tie to log booms on the western (Port Mellon) side of the island. In the summertime the water around Gambier Island warms to swimming temperatures. We know, we tried it.

Gambier Harbour Public Wharf has 100 feet of dock space.

Burrard Yacht Club and Thunderbird Yacht Club have outstations at Eakins Point at the north end of Gambier Island. Members only, no reciprocals.

West Bay. Favor the west shore when entering West Bay to avoid the reef extending from the eastern shore. West Bay once was a major log booming site and the bottom is apt to be foul with old cable and equipment.

Anchorage in West Bay is in at least two places. The first is on the north side of the reef, close to the reef. The second is in the bight at the northeast corner of the bay. Easy anchoring depths are close to shore in this bight, but because of real estate development, you probably shouldn't run a stern-tie to shore.

Centre Bay. Most of Centre Bay is deep, but the little bight on the west side, just inside the entrance, has 18- to 24-foot anchoring depths, and is delightful. Royal Vancouver and West Vancouver yacht clubs have outstations in Centre Bay. The docks belonging to the Centre Bay Yacht Station are at the head of the bay.

Port Graves. Port Graves is definitely the most scenic of Gambier Island's inlets and has good anchoring depths at the head. Because of real estate development in West Bay and Centre Bay, Port Graves is the best anchoring spot on the island. A small float at the public wharf, located at the head of the bay, is used for dinghy tie-up. The marked yellow side-tie is reserved for a water taxi. The adjacent floats belong to a Christian camp and are private. The wharf is under the auspices of the Sunshine Coast Regional District (604) 885-6802. A 2.5-mile trail near the head of the wharf leads to Lost Lake.

Halkett Bay. Halkett Bay at the southeast corner of Gambier Island has one mooring buoy, labeled B.C. Parks, and has room for 4 to 5 boats to anchor; beware that chop can be somewhat active in southerly winds. In 2018, 5 stern-tie pins, with chain, were installed

Plumper Cove Marine Park has an excellent dock, but no power or water. The yellow buoy pictured in the upper right marks a rock.

along the western shoreline within the park boundary by BC Parks and the BC Parks Forever Society. Approach along the east shoreline as rocks lie on the west side of the bay. A dinghy dock provides access to Halkett Bay Marine Park with pit toilets, primitive campsites, and trails.

Halkett Bay Fircom Dock. A Sunshine Coast Regional District dock (604) 885-6800. Fircom dock is located on the southeast side of Gambier Island, along the west shore south of Halkett Bay. The 52-foot float is available on a first-come, first-serve basis for 24 hours at no charge. No water, no

UNION STEAMSHIP COMPANY MARINA & RESORT
SNUG COVE, BOWEN ISLAND, B.C.
A first-class marina & resort just eight nautical miles from Vancouver.
Guest moorage to 210', Doc Morgan's Restaurant, Chandlery & Gift Shop.
www.ussc.ca 604.947.0707 VHF 66A marina@ussc.ca

VANCOUVER, MAINLAND B.C. & THE SUNSHINE COAST

power. The Fircom Market, located upland, sells fresh produce on Friday evenings and Saturday mornings, seasonally.

Brigade Bay. Brigade Bay is on the eastern shore of Gambier Island. Anne Vipond, reporting in Pacific Yachting, suggests that because of deep water fairly close to shore, a stern anchor be set toward the beach and the main anchor set offshore.

Thornbrough Bay. The New Brighton Public Wharf in Thornbrough Bay has 390 feet of dock space.

⑱ **Plumper Cove Marine Park.** Plumper Cove Marine Park is in a cove formed by Keats Island and two small nearby islands. The park has 400 feet of dock space and approximately 9 mooring buoys. Field Correspondent Jim Norris reports wave action at the dock. The bay has anchorage for several boats. A rock, marked by a yellow buoy, lies a dozen yards off the dock.

Porteau Cove. Porteau Cove is on the east shore of Howe Sound in Montagu Channel at latitude 49°33'N. The park is open all year; toilets, launch ramp, walk-in campsites, hiking trails and a picnic area. Tiny Porteau Cove itself has a 60-foot mooring float, not connected to land, and 1 mooring buoy. Two shallow-water buoys near the float mark shallow areas and are not mooring buoys. Sunken ships and man-made reefs provide excellent scuba diving. White caution buoys mark the yellow-buoyed diving area. Watch your depths; some of the cove dries at low tide. Anchoring within the park is prohibited.

⑲ **Lions Bay Marine Ltd.** 60 Lions Bay Ave., P.O. Box 262, Lions Bay, BC V0N 2E0; (604) 921-7510; www.lionsbaymarina.com. Open all year, except closed December 15 to January 15. In winter, closed on Tuesday and Wednesday. Gasoline, diesel and propane available. In summer they have transient moorage for boats up to 32 feet on 400 feet

of dock space. Haulout to 30 feet (powerboats only) with repairs on site. Groceries and a post office are nearby.

⑳ **Squamish.** www.squamish.ca. The town of Squamish, pop. 20,000, is nestled against the Coast Range mountains at the north end of Howe Sound, between Vancouver and Whistler. Since the 2010 Winter Olympics at nearby Whistler, Squamish has become a vibrant town with young families and outdoor enthusiasts. A bus transit service (604-892-3567) runs to Whistler and the Sea to Sky Gondola, or you can rent a car. The Sea to Sky Gondola is about 2.5 miles from the docks and the views from the top are outstanding. At the top, a suspension bridge leads over a canyon to a trail with scenic overviews. There are many hiking and rock climbing opportunities near and around the gondola base station. The Squamish shopping district is about one-quarter mile from the docks where you will find excellent pubs and restaurants. There are two grocery stores within a half-mile walk of the docks. A Saturday Market is held in a parking lot at the north end of Junction Park, April through October.

Summertime inflow winds usually begin between 11:00 a.m. and noon. By 2:00 p.m., the wind can make landing tricky. Best to go to Squamish in the early morning. The Harbour Authority docks are your best bet for moorage or the adjacent yacht club for reciprocal moorage from any yacht club. The Blue Heron Marina (604-898-3733) and Sea To Sky Marina (604-892-9282) are private permanent moorage marinas located farther up the channel beyond the Harbour Authority and yacht club. On a recent visit, we saw a sailboat anchored in the channel just north of the yacht club docks.

Transit Mamquam Blind Channel between the head of Howe Sound and the Squamish marinas with caution on a mid or high tide. The channel has a lighted range. On entry, follow the range, favoring the starboard side until abeam Stawamus River, then favor the port (west) side of the channel through the charted quarter mile shallow area. Stay close to the piling painted green/white/green at the charted shallowest area. The channel in front of the public dock and yacht club is marked with private red and green spar buoys

⑳ **Harbour Authority of Squamish Boat Harbour.** P.O. Box 97, Squamish, BC V8B 0A1; (604) 892-3725 or (604) 815-9658 Harbourmaster. VHF 69. Open all year. Located near downtown Squamish next to the Squamish Yacht Club. 80 feet of summer transient moorage; maximum boat length 55 feet. Pumpout, 15 and 30 amp power, washrooms, showers, garbage, boat launch. First-come, first-served; call ahead to check availability. Plans are in the works to add floats in the near future. Expect a relaxed, informal experience. They don't get many visitor boats.

⑳ **Squamish Yacht Club.** 37778 Logger's Lane, P.O. Box 1681, Squamish BC V8B 0B2; (604) 815-9533, yacht club port captain; reciprocals are available for just about any yacht club, must display yacht club burgee. Guest moorage on docks D17-19 (the yellow zone) on a first-come, first-serve basis; call ahead to check available space. Maximum boat length 45 feet. 15, 20 and 30 amp power, water, restrooms, showers and garbage. Guest key assigned. Docks are within walking distance to downtown.

Shoal Channel (The Gap). The Gap is a sandy shoal with a least depth of approximately 5 feet at zero tide, between Keats Island and Steep Bluff, at the mouth of Howe Sound. Although waves off the Strait of Georgia tend to break on this shoal, if you know your draft and the state of the tide you can approach Gibsons from the strait via The Gap and have no problems—unless it's rough, and then you should go around Keats Island. Stay mid-channel. Boulders line the edges of the passage. The distance to Thrasher Rock, outside Gabriola Pass in the Gulf Islands, is approximately 16 miles. Use Chart 3463 for the crossing, changing to Chart 3526 as you approach Popham Island. This approach, with Howe Sound islands backed up by the Coast Range mountains, is magnificent.

Correspondent Pat Shera says you can cross Shoal Channel at anything but low tides using a natural range. Keep the FlG (flashing green) light located east of the Gibsons Harbour entrance just barely visible in line with the base of Steep Bluff in the foreground. This transit takes you across the shoals with a minimum depth of 7 feet at zero tide. Travel along the 20- to 30-foot depth contour from either side until this natural range lines up, then stay on the range until you reach 20- to 30-foot depths on the other side. Not recommended when a strong southerly is blowing.

㉑ **Gibsons.** Gibsons is a charming seaside village, a good place to take the day off and stretch your legs. The lower Gibsons downtown area is filled with shops, restaurants, and pubs ranging from elegant to funky. The Sunshine Coast Museum & Archives is excellent. Hours are 10:30 a.m. to 4:30 p.m., Tuesday through Saturday.

The nearest supermarket is SuperValu in upper Gibsons. You'll need a ride. Be sure to see Fong's Market & Gifts in lower Gibsons, one of the more unexpected places on the coast. They have many of the essential grocery items, a good selection of Asian foods and a broad array of bowls, tea pots and other imported items. The Gibsons Market is just up from the Gibsons Marina. Some may remember the Market from earlier visits. In 2016 they expanded (rebuilt) the Gibsons market to be a two-story building with more local produce, meats, cheese and local crafts; an aquarium is located upstairs. They re-used the cupola from the old building by lifting it up to the top of the new building by crane.

As you enter the marina complex at Gibsons, you will see The Gibsons Landing Harbour Authority public dock to the north. Gibsons

Squamish

2020 Waggoner Cruising Guide

Sunshine Coast and Jervis Inlet

See Area Map Page 289 - Maps Not for Navigation

VANCOUVER, MAINLAND B.C. & THE SUNSHINE COAST

Marina and Fuel Dock are ahead and to the south. There are several private docks and a private marina behind the breakwater at Gibsons. A shoal extends from the shore between the public dock and the fuel dock. Approach each moorage directly from seaward.

Some boats anchor outside the breakwater and to the east of the pier, in front of the townsite. This is unprotected and suitable only in settled weather.

Sea Cavalcade: The Sea Cavalcade festival, featuring food, dancing, fireworks and other events, is held each July. See www.seacavalcade.ca.

㉑ **Gibsons Landing Harbour Authority.** P.O. Box 527, Gibsons, BC V0N 1V0; (604) 886-8017; glha@telus.net; www.gibsonsha.org. Monitors VHF 66A. Open all year, guest moorage, 15, 30, 50 and 100 amp power but mostly 15 amp with 20 amp receptacles, 3-ton crane, washrooms and showers, laundry, pumpout, garbage dumpster. Docks inside the breakwater are first-come, first-served; call ahead to check on available space. The public wharf has been upgraded with beautiful offices, improved shoreside amenities, and surveillance television security. Much of the moorage space is taken by permanent tenants, but they work to fit visitors in. Reservations accepted for vessels over 45 feet, which are assigned to the concrete float outside the harbour breakwater, located on the northeast side of the pier. No water on the float. Plans are in the works to add water and an additional concrete float for large vessel moorage in the near future. A year-round 80-foot long float for short-term stays up to 4 hours is on the shore side of the wharf outside the breakwater protected harbour, adjacent to the large vessel reserved moorage. Register and pay at the Harbour Authority Office.

㉑ **Gibsons Marina and Fuel Dock**. P.O. Box 1520, Gibsons, BC V0N 1V0; (604) 886-8686 (marina), (604) 886-9011 (fuel dock). Monitors VHF 66A. Open all year except Christmas Day. Reservations accepted. 15 and some 30 amp power, free Wi-Fi, washrooms, showers, well-stocked chandlery, laundry, pumpout, garbage, recycling, concrete launch ramp. The fuel dock has gasoline and diesel. The store on the fuel dock has lubricants, snacks, and ice cream.

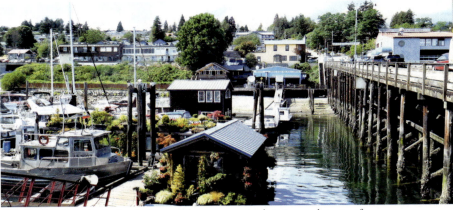
Gibsons Harbour Authority docks provide easy access to shopping and great cafes.

GOWER POINT TO SECHELT INLET

From Howe Sound to Pender Harbour the coast is largely a barren run. The exceptions are Buccaneer Bay, Secret Cove, Smuggler Cove, and to a lesser extent, Halfmoon Bay. When the weather gets up, the going can be wet and slow; but with a weather eye, the passages can be easy.

Trail Bay. A rock breakwater protects a small moorage at **Selma Park** on the south shore of Trail Bay. We once waited out a nasty southeasterly, riding on the hook in this hideout.

LOCAL KNOWLEDGE

STRONG CURRENTS: Currents run to 3 knots at the north end of Welcome Passage and 2 knots off Merry Island at the south end. When wind and current oppose each other, the waters can be rough and uncomfortable. Watch for drift.

Welcome Passage. Welcome Passage separates South Thormanby Island from Sechelt Peninsula and is used by boats of all types bound up or down the Sunshine Coast. The passage west of Merry Island is deep and easily navigated.

Halfmoon Bay. Sunshine Coast Regional District facility (604) 885-2261. A public pier, with a 75-foot float, is at the head of Halfmoon Bay. It is very shallow on the land end of the mooring float. Side-tie available on the outside of the float. Onshore, you can walk about a half block through a residential neighborhood to an area with a store (a longtime landmark) and a cafe with fresh bakery goods. Henry Hightower, a resident of Halfmoon Bay, provided us with the following insider's view of the facilities and anchorage possibilities. He writes:

"The store at the Halfmoon Bay government wharf is well stocked, and has the best bacon and free-range eggs, as well as fresh and packaged meat, fruit, vegetables and staples, fishing gear, beer, wine and liquor,

Gibsons Landing

2020 Waggoner Cruising Guide

VANCOUVER, MAINLAND B.C. & THE SUNSHINE COAST

See Area Map Page 298 - Maps Not for Navigation

Secret Cove

Priestland Cove is southeast of the government dock.

㉒ **Smuggler Cove.** Smuggler Cove has a narrow entrance through the rocks, but opens to a beautiful anchorage that is protected from most weather. We have received reports that the cove is not protected from northwesterlies. First-timers should study the charts carefully before entering the cove to avoid rocky shoals extending from the south shore. Inside is Smuggler Cove Marine Park, which has no facilities for boaters or campers, but does have trails through the park's 457 acres of woodlands. A favorite activity is paddling a kayak or dinghy among the little islets and coves. Reduce swinging room by taking one of many stern-ties (38), with lengths of chain, set in the rock ashore. New stern-ties were added in 2018 and old-stern-tie installations upgraded by BC Parks and the BC Parks Forever Society.

Story has it that Larry Kelly, "King of the Smugglers," hid unemployed Chinese workers in the late 1800's and transported them into the U.S. for a fee. Official entry was forbidden at that time. During Prohibition (1920-1933) the cove was used by rum runners.

No Discharge Zone. Gray water okay.

Buccaneer Bay. Buccaneer Bay is between North Thormanby and South Thormanby Islands, and has a beautiful white sand beach at the south end and west side.

Be careful to enter Buccaneer Bay by leaving the Tattenham Ledge Light Buoy Q51 to port. The buoy is well north of South Thormanby Island, but it marks the end of Tattenham Ledge and should be respected.

Once in Buccaneer Bay, anchor in 30 to 40 feet behind the Surrey Islands or in 20 to 30 feet in Water Bay. The Surrey Islands anchorage is particularly cozy and attractive.

A private moorage is in Water Bay. During the day small boat traffic to and from the dock will rock you some, but it dies down at night. The dock is posted for loading/unloading.

Watching your depths, you can also snug up to the shoaling waters off Gill Beach at the south end of the bay. In a southeasterly, you'll get some wind but no seas. There's no protection from a northwesterly, however. One year, we anchored in calm conditions only to have a northwesterly come in around midnight and ruin our night's sleep. It was pretty bouncy.

Secret Cove. Secret Cove has three branches, each with excellent weather protection and easy anchoring depths. Unfortunately, the Secret Cove bottom is notorious for anchor dragging in strong winds, so be sure you are well set if you do anchor.

Enter Secret Cove north of a light on a small rock in the middle of the entrance. Inside are the three arms. The southern arm has a very narrow entrance but adequate depths inside. This arm is lined with private docks that restrict swinging room in the middle. You can find room, however, off the Royal Vancouver

convenience store stuff, and a gift shop." After visiting, we agree.

If a strong wind is blowing or forecast, there will almost certainly be at least one tug with a log boom waiting for favorable weather, positioned across the open south side of Priestland Cove between the shore and the charted rocks. There is quite a bit of room to anchor behind its shelter.

secretcove MARINA

The sunshine coast's best kept secret for moorage, fuel, dining & supplies . . .

marina
visitor moorage
up to 150', with
water, power

fuel dock

services
showers, recycling
BroadbandXpress Wireless

store
B.C. liquor agency
groceries, meats & produce
marine supplies & hardware
tackle, fishing licences
baked goods, organic coffee
books, magazines
charts & clothing
giftware, cuban cigars

close to Smugglers Cove & the beaches of Thornamby Island

+ the upper deck restaurant

monitoring VHF channel **66A**
www.secretcovemarina.com
1-866-885-3533
5411 Secret Cove Road, Box 1118 Sechelt B.C. V0N 3A0
reservations recommended in summer months

the upper deck restaurant
fully licenced
gourmet dinners
weekend brunch
casual breakfasts & lunches

See Area Map Page 298 - Maps Not for Navigation

VANCOUVER, MAINLAND B.C. & THE SUNSHINE COAST

John Henry's
MARINA & RESORT
johnhenrysresortmarina.com

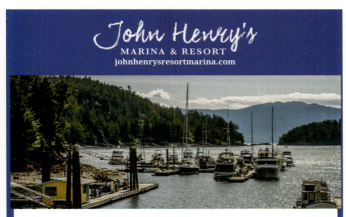

YOUR FULL-SERVICE STOP IN PENDER HARBOUR

Boating Amenities:
- Transient moorage for vessels up to 70ft, 30 & 50 AMP power available, reservations strongly recommended
- Fuel dock - ethanol-free mid-grade gas & diesel, discount offered to overnight guests
- Showers
- Laundry facilities
- Ice - cubes & blocks
- Well-provisioned General Store
- Marine supplies - charts & guides, basic parts, engine oils, fishing tackle & bait

Café:
- Open from May to September
- Indoor & outdoor seating, ocean view

General Store:
- Open daily year round
- Groceries, produce, dairy, meat
- Specialty foods
- Fully-stocked liquor store
- Personal care & household products
- Eclectic gift selection
- John Henry's famous ice cream & candy bars, now serving milkshakes
- Propane
- ATM
- Post Office next door

Accommodation:
- All accommodation is oceanfront
- 4 bright, comfortable cottages (sleep 2-4)
- 4-bed vacation home (sleeps 8)
- 4 RV sites
- 1 campsite

"Great resort on the Sunshine Coast. Full service Marina; fuel, water, showers, grocery, ice cream!"

"Fantastic Marina... with top notch management. Excellent experience. Thank you John Henry's!"

"We returned, after a great stay last year, to dock staff with the same helpful and attentive attitude as before. We'll be back!"

Tel: 604-883-2336 | 49° 37' 51.627" N / 124° 1' 56.273" W | VHF 66A
info@johnhenrysresortmarina.com

Yacht Club outstation docks about halfway in. Correspondents James and Jennifer Hamilton have anchored there and report the holding ground is excellent. The center arm has Buccaneer Marina. The north arm is occupied almost entirely by Secret Cove Marina, but there is still plenty of room for anchoring, using stern-ties to shore if needed; a few chains and ropes are found along the west shore. A public float is adjacent to Secret Cove Marina.

㉓ **Secret Cove Public Wharf.** Managed by the Harbour Authority of Pender Harbour (604) 883-2234. Dock has 144 feet of moorage with 20 amp power, no water. Self-registration, payment box located on the wharf. Primarily used by local commercial fish boats and the Thormanby water taxi.

㉓ **Secret Cove Marina.** 511 Secret Cove Road, Sechelt, BC V0N 3A0; (604) 885-3533; info@secretcovemarina.com; www.secretcovemarina.com. Monitors VHF 66A. Reservations requested. Open April 1 through Canadian Thanksgiving. This is a full service marina in the north arm of Secret Cove, with gasoline and diesel fuel, guest moorage, 15 & 30 amp power, washrooms, clean showers, liquor agency, restaurant, store with groceries, gift items, clothing, block and cube ice, boating and fishing supplies, Wi-Fi. Fishing charters, kayak and paddleboard rentals. This marina resort is well managed and continues to receive excellent reviews.

The "Upper Deck," a first-class restaurant, re-opened in 2019. Dinners begin at 5:00 p.m. and run late into the evening (closed Mondays), beginning late June till Labour Day; reservations strongly recommended. Happy Hours begin at 3:00 p.m.

㉔ **Buccaneer Marina & Resort Ltd.** 5535 Sans Souci Rd., Halfmoon Bay, BC V0N 1Y2; (604) 885-7888; buccaneermarina@telus.net; www.buccaneermarina.com. Open all year, gasoline and diesel fuel, limited guest moorage with 15 amp power, chandlery, engine and outboard repairs (weekdays), propane, haulout to 40 feet, paved launch ramp with long term parking. Fishing tackle and one of the few places with live herring bait. Water taxi to Thormanby

FIRST-AID SUPPLIES & PREPAREDNESS

A good first-aid kit is critical when cruising in some of the more remote places. Medical help could be a day or more away. Consider adding a few additions not always included in First Aid kits that fit your lifestyle. We try to cover a reasonable range of potential medical emergencies or discomfort.

Dressings:
- Hydrogen Peroxide
- Adhesive bandages
- Band-Aids (various sizes)
- Gauze pads, rolls, tape
- Blister pads (Moleskins)

Equipment:
- Surgical gloves
- Tweezers and scissors
- Splinting material
- Thermometer
- Gel packs (heat/cold)

Ointments:
- Antibacterial ointment
- Aquaphor for cracks and dry skin
- Insect sting relief
- Medicated pads

Medications:
- Pain relivers
- Prescriptions
- Anti-acids
- Allergy medication
- Sea Sickness medication
- Cold & Flu medications

2020 Waggoner Cruising Guide

VANCOUVER, MAINLAND B.C. & THE SUNSHINE COAST

See Area Map Page 298 - Maps Not for Navigation

Islands. Located in the center arm of Secret Cove. Owned and operated by the Mercer family since 1968.

Bargain Bay. Although its entry is actually off the Strait of Georgia, Bargain Bay is properly a part of the complex of bays that make up Pender Harbour. Enter between Edgecomb Island to the east and Francis Peninsula to the west. The entry is easy and open until you are part way inside, where a drying reef and an underwater rock extend from the west shore to the middle of the channel. Another underwater rock lies off the east shore. Pass between the two rocks and proceed into the bay.

Bargain Narrows, called Canoe Pass, is a drying channel spanned by a bridge with 4 meters (13.12 feet) vertical clearance. The pass runs between Bargain Bay and Gerrans Bay inside Pender Harbour.

PENDER HARBOUR

Pender Harbour is a natural stopover for boats heading north or south in the Strait of Georgia. For northbound boats, it's just the right distance for a day's run from Nanaimo, Silva Bay, or Howe Sound. For boats southbound from Desolation Sound, it's a good place to prepare for the long, exposed legs across the Strait of Georgia or down the Sunshine Coast. Boats bound to or from Princess Louisa Inlet often use Pender Harbour both going and coming.

Pender Harbour has good marinas, good anchorages, good eating, and good shopping. It has fuel and a haulout and repair facility. Diving services available through Wet Dock Divers (604-740-5969). The harbor is nestled against steep mountains; the scenery is beautiful. It's a good place for walking and hiking. If you carry trail bikes, the Madeira Park Public Wharf has a map of the nearby Suncoaster Trail, built and maintained by volunteers.

Pender Harbour is not a single large bay. It is a complex of coves, each with its own personality. Duncan Cove has a marina resort along the north shore. Gerrans Bay has marinas and anchorage. Hospital Bay and Garden Bay have marinas, fuel, shopping and dining. The best anchorages are in Garden Bay and Gerrans Bay, and in the bay between Garden Peninsula and Madeira Park. John Henry's Resort & Marina is the only place for fuel in Pender Harbour. Madeira Park, in the southeast corner of Pender Harbour, has moorage, haulout and repairs. A shopping center is a short walk from the Madeira Park dock.

Pender Harbour has several drying and underwater rocks throughout, but most of them are marked. With Chart 3535 (or good electronic charts) and a little care, you should have no problems.

Pender Harbour Music Festivals: The Pender Harbour Music Society sponsors a concert series throughout most of the year; check their website for dates and tickets at www.penderharbourmusic.ca or call (604) 989-3995.

Transportation: There's no bus or taxi service. Use your dinghy, or try the **Slo-Cat Harbour Ferry**, based in Madeira Park, (604-741-3796) or VHF 66A, for excursions or shopping trips.

Irvines Landing Marina & Pub. Closed.

㉕ **Pender Harbour Resort and Marina.** 4686 Sinclair Bay Road, Garden Bay, BC V0N 1S1; (877) 883-2424; (604) 551-2742 (phone or text); info@phrm.ca; www.phrm.ca. Open all year with moorage to 50 feet. New docks, with a new configuration, were installed in 2018. Transient moorage is in unoccupied slips. Reservations accepted through "Swift Harbour" online booking. No VHF monitoring; call the marina a day ahead for slip assignment. Water, 15 & 30 amp power, Wi-Fi, showers, laundry, launch ramp, garbage and recycling drop. Marina guests have access to all resort amenities, including heated seasonal swimming pool, fire pit, gazebo, and sports field. Cottages, motel rooms, yurts, campsite, small boats, stand-up paddleboards, and kayaks are available to rent. There is a small store in the office with snacks, essentials, bait and gifts.

Hospital Bay. Hospital Bay is on the west side of Garden Peninsula, facing the mouth of Pender Harbour. The harbor is home to the former Fisherman's Resort and Marina (now part of John Henry's), John Henry's store and fuel dock. Hospital Bay Public Wharf is next door. Hospital Bay is also the site of the St. Mary's Columbia Coast Mission Hospital building, built in 1929.

A narrow isthmus divides Hospital Bay from Garden Bay with a walkway between the two. Dan's Grill, an old-fashioned diner (previously LaVerne's) is located here. Dan's, which opened in July 2018, carries on the tradition of tasty burgers, milkshakes, fish n' chips, and offers breakfast all day.

㉖ **Fisherman's Resort & Marina.** Fisherman's Resort and Marina was purchased in 2015 and is now part of John Henry's. See the listing below.

㉖ **John Henry's Resort & Marina.** P.O. Box 40, 4907 Pool Lane, Garden Bay, BC V0N 1S0; Moorage: (604) 883-2336 Store: (604) 883-2253; info@johnhenrysresortmarina.com; www.johnhenrysresortmarina.com. Monitors VHF 66A. Call for reservations. John Henry's and Fisherman's Resort are now operated as a single entity. Open all year with 2300 feet of moorage, water, 20, 30 & 50 amp power, washrooms, showers, laundry, Wi-Fi, garbage, recycling, ice, launch ramp. Gasoline, diesel, 50:1 pre-mix, and propane at the fuel dock. Moorage guests receive a fuel discount. Kayak, SUPs, powerboat, cottage, and RV site rentals available. Kenmore Air and Harbour Air provide float plane service from Seattle and Vancouver.

This is a quiet, well-cared-for marina and resort with beautiful lawns and flower gardens. The well-stocked store above the fuel dock has fresh produce, meats, sandwiches, charts, cruising guides, books, liquor agency, post office, and an ATM. The store also carries tackle, bait, ice, gift items and hand-scooped ice cream. The store at the fuel dock carries snack items, fishing tackle, and boat supplies.

The nice restaurant has indoor and outdoor seating.

Hospital Bay Public Wharf. P.O. Box 118, Madeira Park, BC V0N 2H0; Harbour Authority of Pender Harbour; (604) 883-2234; penderauthority@telus.net. Across from the fuel dock in Hospital Bay, 400 feet of first-come, first-served side-tie transient moorage on the south side of the middle float and both sides of the southern-most float. 20 & 30 amp power, water, garbage drop for fee, at the top of the dock. Portapotties are in the pocket park 200 feet up the road. Close to John Henry's and the pub in Garden Bay.

Garden Bay. Garden Bay is at the northeast corner of Pender Harbour. The Garden Bay Hotel hasn't been a hotel for a long time, so don't look for rooms to rent.

Seattle Yacht Club, Burrard Yacht Club and Royal Vancouver Yacht Club have

Pender Harbour has ample anchorage and many marinas with transient moorage.

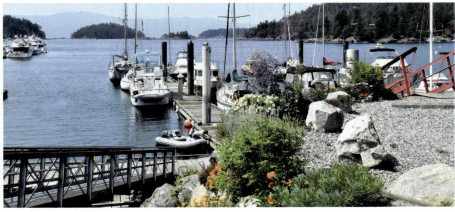
Hospital Bay Public Wharf in Pender Harbour has transient moorage on two docks.

outstations in Garden Bay—members only, no reciprocals. Many boats anchor out in Garden Bay and dinghy either to the marinas, John Henry's, or to Madeira Park. The Garden Bay holding ground is good and protection is excellent in most weather.

Garden Bay Provincial Park has about 50 feet of frontage on the north shore. The park has a dinghy dock, toilets, and a network of excellent walking trails, but no other facilities for boaters. Garden Bay Lake, a popular swimming destination, is within walking distance of the Provincial Park.

㉗ **Garden Bay Hotel Marina & Pub.** P.O. Box 90, Garden Bay, BC V0N 1S0; (604) 883-2674; gbhm@dccnet.com; www.gardenbaypub.com. Call ahead for space. Open all year, 1200 feet of side-tie moorage, 15 & 30 amp power, washrooms, showers on shore across from the pub entrance, Wi-Fi. This is a good-sized marina with a pub, including an outdoor seating area. The pub is open 7 days a week.

On a beautiful day, the deck overlooking Garden Bay is quite pleasant. A road leads from the pub to Hospital Bay and John Henry's store. A separate walking trail leads along the shore to the Royal Van outstation, and connects with the road to John Henry's.

Gunboat Bay. Gunboat Bay, surrounded by high, steep mountains, is entered through a narrow channel with a least depth of 4 feet. An underwater rock lies just to the north of the centerline of the entry channel. Currents in the entry channel are quite strong except at slack water. Although the bay is open and good for anchorage before it peters out into drying flats, few boats anchor there because Garden Bay is so much easier.

㉘ **Sunshine Coast Resort & Marina.** P.O. Box 213, Madeira Park, BC V0N 2H0; (604) 883-9177; (888) 883-9177; vacation@sunshinecoast-resort.com; www.sunshinecoast-resort.com. Monitors VHF 66A. Open all year with moorage for boats to 100 feet, call for reservations, 15 & 30 amp power, water, washrooms, showers, free Wi-Fi, hot tub on the deck, laundry, bait, small boat and kayak rentals, and a hillside lodge with 16 truly outstanding rooms.

The entire property is tidy and well-maintained. Manager Ralph Linnmann is committed to providing attentive customer service.

A steep mountainside rises above the docks. The laundry, showers, and road to town are a considerable climb up the hill, although the office and additional showers are in the lodge about halfway up. The marina is in the small bay to the right as you approach Gunboat Bay, about a half-mile north of Madeira Park shopping. You can walk to Madeira Park down the hill (and back up to return) or take the dinghy (we'd take the dinghy). Free transportation to the challenging Pender Harbour Golf Club.

㉙ **Madiera Park.** If you want to provision, Madeira Park is where you'll do it. The Harbour Authority Public Wharf is close to two grocery stores (the well-stocked IGA, and the Oak Tree Market with excellent meats and cheeses). The IGA is open 7 days a week 8:30 a.m. to 7:00 p.m., and 8:30 a.m. to 8:00 p.m. in July and August; delivery to the wharf by request. A drugstore, liquor store, bank with ATM, book store, and veterinarian are close by. No laundromat. Madeira Park has a full-service medical clinic. The Grasshopper Pub has been rebuilt and has temporary moorage at their dock while dining or shopping at their liquor store.

㉙ **Madeira Park Public Wharf.** P.O. Box 118, Madeira Park, BC V0N 2H0; (604) 883-2234; Harbour Authority of Pender Harbour; penderauthority@telus.net. Monitors VHF 66A. Open all year, 600 feet of first-come, first-served transient moorage space located on both sides of B-dock. 15, 20, 30 and 50 amp power, water, washrooms, showers, garbage drop for fee, recycling, pumpout, floatplane dock, free Wi-Fi. The dinghy dock (south side of A-dock) faces shore, adjacent to the launch ramp. No dinghy check-in is needed and no charge for daytime dinghy tie-up for the first hour. Marine repair, chandlery, and mechanics nearby.

Madeira Park Public Wharf is a destination in its own right. A small park with a gazebo and benches overlooking the marina is ideal for relaxation or a picnic. Two well-stocked grocery stores and a liquor store within walking distance make this a great place to provision. Stores allow customers to use their shopping carts to haul items to the Wharf, where the carts may be left. This well-managed facility is a popular destination.

㉙ **Madeira Marina.** P.O. Box 189, Madeira Park, BC V0N 2H0; (604) 883-2266; madeiramarine@telus.net. Open all year. Marine railway with haulout to 40 tons, complete marine repairs, parts, indoor painting facility for boats up to 30 feet, and chandlery. Prompt, competent repair service.

Pender Harbour Hotel & Grasshopper Pub. 12671 Sunshine Coast Hwy, Madeira Park, BC V0N 2H0; (604) 883-9013; penderharbourhotel.com. Located in Madeira Park high above Welbourn Cove. The Hotel's private dock has space for temporary moorage while visiting the Grasshopper Pub or shopping at their liquor store. Call for moorage and courtesy pickup at the dock; it's a short but steep walk up the driveway to the Hotel and Pub. Good food and drink with outstanding views.

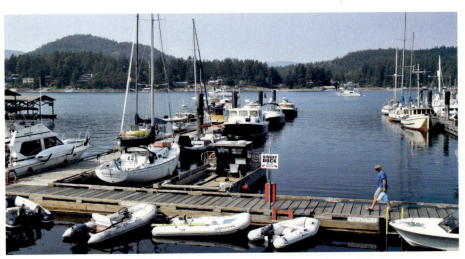
Dinghy dock at Madiera Park Public Wharf, with access to shops and grocery stores.

VANCOUVER, MAINLAND B.C. & THE SUNSHINE COAST

See Area Map Page 298 - Maps Not for Navigation

Gerrans Bay. Gerrans Bay is one of the larger bays in Pender Harbour with suitable anchoring depths. It is quieter and less traveled than other areas of Pender Harbour. The bay is dotted with rocks that are charted and or marked. It is mostly residential, with some of the homes obviously in the commercial fishing business. Two marinas, Coho Marina and Painted Boat Resort & Marina, and the Whisky Slough Public Wharf, have moorage for transient boaters. A private marina with no transient moorage is located on the west shore near the southwest head of the bay. Anchoring can be found in the southwest head of the bay or in the northeastern half of the bay over a mud bottom with good holding.

㉚ **Coho Marina and RV Resort.** 12907 Shark Lane, Madeira Park, BC V0N 2H0; (604) 883-2238; (604) 396- 3353 cell; info@cohomarina.com; www. cohomarina.com. Open all year with guest moorage for boats to 40 feet in unoccupied slips, reservations accepted. Located on the east side of Gerrans Bay, the marina approach is through marked and charted rocks and reefs. 15 & 30 amp power, water, restrooms, and showers; 5-minute walk to Madeira Park shopping center with grocery and liquor. The docks were re-configured in 2018, making this a 100-slip marina.

㉚ **Painted Boat Resort Spa & Marina.** P.O. Box 153, 12849 Lagoon Rd., Madeira Park, BC V0N 2H0; (604) 883-2456; (866) 902-3955; reservations@paintedboat.com; www.paintedboat.com. Open all year with guest moorage to 70 feet, moorage reservations needed. The approach from east Gerrans Bay winds through rocks and reefs. We suggest entering carefully with a bow watch. The docks have 15, 30 & 50 amp power and water, no washrooms, no showers, no laundry. This is a first-class resort. The upscale but relaxed Lagoon Restaurant at Painted Boat is open seasonally for dinner, with 58-feet of short term moorage and 92-feet of dinghy tie-up (near shore) for restaurant patrons. Restaurant reservations required. It is elegant with a great view. The full-service spa is available for an additional charge; swimming pool is for lodge guests only.

㉛ **Whiskey Slough Public Wharf.** P.O. Box 118, Madeira Park, BC V0N 2H0; (604) 883-2234; penderauthority@telus.net. Limited first-come, first-served side-tie transient moorage is available on two floats, with the best chance to find open space on the eastern most float. 20 & 30 amp power, limited access to potable water, no facilities or services. Mostly commercial fish boats here.

Agamemnon Channel. Agamemnon Channel runs northeast between Nelson Island and the mainland, and is the shortest route for those heading for Princess Louisa Inlet, Egmont, or Sechelt Inlet. The only

Pender Harbour

304 www.WaggonerGuide.com

reasonable anchorage is at Green Bay. A private marina is in Agamemnon Bay.

Green Bay. Green Bay is a well-protected small bay on the northwest side of Agamemnon Channel. Prime anchorage is at 30 feet in the cove on the west side of Green Bay in front of the lake shown on the chart. A stream with a waterfall runs from the lake to the cove. A drying reef nearly closes the pass to the back cove to the north of the prime anchoring area. Holding is fair on a hard mud bottom. Use caution approaching and within Green Bay as it is not well charted. Sailing Directions warns of rocks on the east side of the entry to Green Bay which are not shown on the chart. A large uncharted rock/pinnacle with 6 feet of water at zero tide is located mid-channel off a cabin with a small float, on the northeast side of Green Bay, east of the prime anchoring area. We entered favoring the west side of Green Bay. Several cabins, some with private docks, cling to the shore. The gentle sound of the waterfall makes for a restful anchorage.

SECHELT INLET

Egmont. Egmont, on the Sechelt Peninsula, is near the entrance to Skookumchuck Narrows and Sechelt Rapids. Sechelt Inlet lies beyond the rapids. Backeddy Resort & Marina and Bathgate General Store & Marina both have fuel. Backeddy Resort & Marina fronts on Skookumchuck Narrows; Bathgate is closer to the rapids, behind a well-marked reef in Secret Bay. The public dock is adjacent. Beautiful West Coast Wilderness Lodge, with fine dining, is immediately south and up the hill from Backeddy Resort & Marina. It's an easy walk between the two, and the view from the dining room and deck at West Coast Wilderness Lodge is a knockout. One of our correspondents reports that their dinner was as good as the view—world class, they said. We agree.

The Egmont Heritage Centre is a short walk up the main road from the marinas.

LOCAL KNOWLEDGE

STRONG CURRENTS: Strong currents can whip through Backeddy Marina. Use caution when docking. Sechelt Rapids currents in the Tide and Current guides will give you an idea of the current direction and force.

DANGEROUS ROCKS: The red triangle day beacon off Backeddy Marina's south docks means Red, Right, Returning for the channel outside. Approaching the docks, leave the beacon to port or you will run up on a rock shelf that extends from shore.

㉜ **Backeddy Resort & Marina.** 16660 Backeddy Rd., Egmont, BC V0N 1N0; (604) 883-2298; (800) 626-0599; info@backeddy.ca; www.backeddy.ca. Monitors VHF 66A. Open all year with guest moorage and services, reservations recommended. Gasoline and diesel fuel, 400 feet of moorage for vessels up to 120 feet. 15 & 30 amp power, washrooms, showers, laundry, garbage drop with fee, Wi-Fi, water at the fuel dock. Cabins, 5 geodesic domes for luxury camping, concrete launch ramp. Float plane access for Kenmore Air and West Coast Air. Small convenience store on site with ice. Backeddy Pub open for lunch and dinner, hours vary between October and April, call ahead.

The marina is opposite the Sutton Islets. This is a well-run marina, its rustic exterior hides the well-appointed pub and accommodations. Kayak and bicycle rentals available at the marina. Tours for Princess Louisa Inlet leave from the Backeddy dock. Water taxi service available. The Backeddy fuel dock is the first and last on the way to and from Princess Louisa Inlet.

㉜ **West Coast Wilderness Lodge.** 6649 Maple Road, Egmont, BC V0N 1N0; (604) 883-3667; lodge@wcwl.com; www.wcwl.com. This beautiful luxury lodge is located within easy walking distance from Backeddy Marina and offers a fine dining venue for boaters and lodge guests. Open for breakfast and dinner during the shoulder seasons; breakfast, lunch, and dinner during the summer. Reservations highly recommended during peak season, July and August. The float below the lodge is for seaplanes; however, dingies may tie-up while dining at

VANCOUVER, MAINLAND B.C. & THE SUNSHINE COAST

See Area Map Page 298 - Maps Not for Navigation

Backeddy Resort & Marina on Sechelt Inlet is your last stop on the way to Princess Louisa Inlet.

the lodge, contact on VHF 68A. A steep trail leads from the dock to the lodge. Adventure tours can be booked through the Egmont Adventure Centre located below the Lodge (778-280-8619). Moorage can be found near the Lodge at Backeddy Marina or at Egmont Public Wharf.

㉝ **Bathgate General Store, Resort & Marina.** 6781 Bathgate Rd., Egmont, BC V0N 1N0; (604) 883-2222; info@bathgate.com; www.bathgate.com. Contact on VHF 16. Open all year, gasoline and diesel at the fuel dock, limited guest moorage, 15, 20 & 30 amp power, showers, washrooms, laundry. Reservations recommended. Shallow depths at the fuel dock restrict access. The store has fresh produce and a good selection of groceries, propane, marine supplies, liquor agency, bait and tackle, block and cube ice. It's the only well-stocked store for miles. Deluxe wheelchair-accessible waterfront motel unit available. Short and long term parking.

The reef in Secret Bay can confuse a first-time visitor, especially one who isn't that familiar with navigation aids. Remember: Red, Right, Returning. When entering, leave the red daymark well to starboard and you'll have no problems. If you still aren't sure, just remember to go around the ends, not between the two beacons.

㉝ **Egmont Public Wharf.** Managed by the Egmont Harbour Authority, 604-883-9652 or 604-883-9463, two public floats and one private float are accessed from the public wharf. The small float northwest of the wharf is private with no public access. The two large floats south of the wharf are public with permanent moorage on the southerly of these two floats and 150 feet of transient moorage for up to 48 hours on the northerly side of the north float. Self-registration and payment is at the head of the ramp. 20 & 30 amp shore power.

Sechelt Inlet. Beautiful Sechelt Inlet, with few anchorages and limited facilities for pleasure craft, is often passed by—especially with Princess Louisa Inlet at the end of nearby Jervis Inlet. Sechelt Rapids also serve as a gate to keep out all but the determined.

To explore Sechelt Inlet and its arms, use Chart 3512 (1:80:000) or Chartbook 3312. The inlet is shown at 1:40,000 in Chartbook 3312. Sechelt Inlet extends about 15 miles south of Sechelt Rapids. It ends at Porpoise Bay, the back door to the village of Sechelt, where there is a public float and easy anchorage. Two arms, Salmon Inlet and Narrows Inlet, run from the eastern side of Sechelt Inlet into the heart of the Earle Mountain Range. A number of provincial park sites are in Sechelt Inlet, most of them best suited to small boats that can be pulled up on the beach.

Inflow winds can blow from south to north in Sechelt Inlet and up Salmon Inlet and Narrows Inlet. Even when the northern part of Sechelt Inlet is near calm, the southern part can be increasingly windy. In Salmon Inlet and Narrows Inlet, the inflow winds will grow stronger as the inlets deepen and narrow. Outflow winds can develop at night, but in the summer they often don't unless a strong southeasterly is blowing out on the strait.

The tidal range does not exceed 10 feet in Sechelt Inlet, and the times of high and low tide are 2 to 3 hours after Point Atkinson. Two secondary ports, Porpoise Bay and Storm Bay, are shown in Tide & Current Tables, Vol. 5. Current predictions for Tzoonie Narrows, in Narrows Inlet, are shown under Secondary Stations in Tide & Current Tables, Vol. 5 and Ports and Passes. Depths at the head of the Inlet are shallow enough for easy anchoring over a mud bottom. Usually there are other boats at anchor and a number of private buoys, but it's a large area with ample space.

For a complete description of Sechelt Inlet cruising, including excellent hiking trails, see our sister publication, *Cruising the Secret Coast*, by Jennifer and James Hamilton.

LOCAL KNOWLEDGE

DANGEROUS CURRENTS AND INCORRECT TIDE DATA: We've had reports that some current tables contained in electronic navigation programs don't agree with the printed tables for Sechelt Rapids. Use the Canadian Hydrographic Service or Ports and Passes tables.

Sechelt Rapids. On large tidal exchanges, Sechelt Rapids can run 16.5 knots, the world record holder. Sechelt Rapids, also known as the Skookumchuck Rapids (Sechelt is pronounced "SEE-shelt"; skookum means "big" or "strong," and chuck means "body of water"), provide the only water access to Sechelt Inlet.

Times of turn and maximum current are shown in the Tide and Current Tables, Vol. 5 and in Ports and Passes. Sechelt Rapids can be extremely dangerous except at or near slack water. At full flow the rapids are boiling

Egmont (Backeddy, Bathgate, Egmont Marinas & Wilderness Lodge)

VANCOUVER, MAINLAND B.C. & THE SUNSHINE COAST

cauldrons with 8-foot overfalls and 12- to 16-knot currents. Even an hour before slack, when many other rapids may have calmed down, the Sechelt Rapids can be menacing. Traverse the rapids only at slack water. Be aware of where you are time-wise in the lunar cycle. When close or on a full moon or a new moon, the period of slack water is short. When the rapids are running at full strength this area is deadly.

Lacking prior experience, do not go through without accurate charts for Sechelt Rapids and Secret Bay. Sailing Directions says the best route through the rapids is west of Boom Islet (choked with kelp, but safe) and west of the Sechelt Islets light.

We, however, have run a dogleg course without discomfort through the middle of the channel, between the Sechelt Islets and the unnamed islet directly north of the Sechelt Islets. This area is where dangerous whirlpools can develop on ebbs, so be careful. Give Roland Point a wide berth, especially on a flood.

Either direction, Sechelt Rapids are just fine at slack, and if you time it well (easily done) you'll slide through with no problems at all. But when the rapids are running, their roar can be heard for miles. Lives have been lost there.

Before making your own entrance it can be instructive to walk to the rapids from the public dock in Egmont to watch the channel in full boil.

Sechelt Rapids Viewing. On flood current watch standing waves and kayakers surfing the waves from Rowland Point Viewing Area; on ebb current watch whirlpools from the North Viewing Area. Viewing times are 30 minutes of max current. The 4km long trail is an easy walk from Bathgate, with minimal elevation gain; walking time is about 1 hour each way.

㉞ **Poise Cove Marina.** 5991 Sechelt Inlet Rd., Sechelt, BC V0N 3A3; (604) 885-2895. Open all year with limited guest moorage for boats to 25 feet, limited 15 amp power, concrete launch ramp for boats 25 feet or less. No long term parking. Located on the east side of Sechelt Inlet near Porpoise Bay Marine Park.

㉞ **Choquer & Sons Ltd.** 5977 Sechelt Inlet Rd., Sechelt, BC V0N 3A0; (604) 885-9244; choquerandsons@telus.net. Good docks with guest moorage for boats to 75 feet, deep enough for sailboats, 15 & 30 amp power, bathroom, showers. Launch ramp and trailer lift. Full marine repair. Their primary business is a machine and metal fabrication shop upland.

㉟ **Lighthouse Pub & Marina.** 5764 Wharf Rd., Sechelt, BC V0N 3A0; (604) 885-9494; info@lighthousepub.ca; www.lighthousepub.ca. Located at the south end of Sechelt Inlet with easy access to Sechelt village. Docks with slips from 16 to 40 feet plus side-tie moorage, 30 amp power, showers, laundry, washrooms. Call ahead for moorage, make

Sechelt (Skookumchuck) Rapids running at a 12 knot flood, less than full boil at almost 16 knots

payment at the pub. The long and often empty dock extending from the pub is reserved for Harbour Air floatplanes. The dock to the east, marked 'Day Use' is used for transient side-tie. Dinghies may tie-up on the fuel dock, near shore, when dining at the pub or visiting in town. For taxi service call (604-885-3666). Gasoline and diesel at the fuel dock. Lighthouse Marine Store (778-458-3625) carries marine hardware, charts, fishing supplies, snacks, ice. Look for the lighthouse on top of the pub. We've heard the food at the pub is excellent. Three 2-bedroom "Bed & Boat" cottages are available for rent, reservations at bedandboatcottages.com.

㉟ **Royal Reach Marina & Hotel.** 5758 Wharf Rd., Sechelt, BC V0N 3A0; (604) 885-7844. Open all year, moorage to 30 feet is for hotel guests only, limited 15 amp power, must call ahead. Located at the head of Sechelt Inlet. Watch your depths at low water.

㉟ **Porpoise Bay Government Wharf.** 5770 Wharf Street, Sechelt, BC V0N 3A0; (604) 740-7528. Next to the Lighthouse Pub & Marina. This dock usually is completely taken by local boats, but space does become available from time to time. Call Les, the Wharfinger, regarding available space. Docks accommodate boats up to 30 feet; 20 & 30 amp power, water, pumpout, and grid. Self-registration and payment box at the head of A-dock. Dinghies may tie-up in available space at the dock.

Narrows Inlet. Narrows Inlet is mostly 150 to 180 feet deep except at the head, where the Tzoonie River makes a delta. Tzoonie Narrows, about a third of the way along, is a spectacular cleft in the high mountains that surround the inlet. Tidal currents run to a maximum of 4 knots through Tzoonie Narrows, but the passage is free of hazards. All but the slowest or lowest-powered boats could run them at any time. Arguably the best anchorage in this area is in Storm Bay at the mouth of Narrows Inlet. Storm Bay is very pretty with a dramatic rock wall on its eastern shore. Anchor behind the little islets at the entrance or near the head of the bay.

Tzoonie Narrows Park. This park takes in both sides of the narrows and is good for swimming, fishing, diving, and picnicking. Walk-in campsites. The 1-meter islet shown on the chart is a long, narrow reef with large extensions under the surface. You can anchor inside the reef, or in the deep bight on the other side of Narrows Inlet.

Salmon Inlet. Salmon Inlet is very deep, although anchorage is good in Misery Bay, where the water is warm enough for swimming. A drying shoal almost blocks the passage across the inlet at Sechelt Creek. The shoal can be passed safely by staying close to the north shore.

MALASPINA STRAIT TO JERVIS INLET

Quarry Bay. Quarry Bay faces the Strait of Georgia and is too deep and exposed to be a destination of first choice. If you must anchor there, you could work your way in among the rocks in the southeast corner of the bay. It would be a good idea to run a stern-tie to keep from swinging onto a rock. At the north end of Quarry Bay a little cove, surrounded by homes, is well protected and has good anchoring depths. It would be a good hideout. Chart 3512 (1:80,000) and Chartbook 3312 (1:40,000) show a stream connecting this cove with Quarry Lake. Three rocks in this cove are shown in Chartbook 3312.

Cape Cockburn. An unmarked drying rock is a short distance off Cape Cockburn. Give the cape a good offing.

Cockburn Bay. Cockburn Bay is completely plugged by drying rocks and is accessible only by small craft at or near high water.

Hidden Basin. Hidden Basin is blocked by drying shoals and rocks, and currents run strongly through the restricted entrance. Chartbook 3312 (1:40,000) shows Hidden Basin better than Chart 3512 (1:80,000). Entrance to Hidden Basin should be made—carefully—at high water slack. Secure anchorage is available once inside.

2020 Waggoner Cruising Guide

VANCOUVER, MAINLAND B.C. & THE SUNSHINE COAST

See Area Map Page 298 - Maps Not for Navigation

Ballet Bay on Nelson Island is a popular anchoring spot on the Sunshine Coast.

㊱ **Blind Bay.** Blind Bay once had a number of good anchorages, especially along the Hardy Island side. Most of them now are taken with private homes and their docks, so the choices are fewer. One good spot on the south side is popular Ballet Bay. On the north side, Hardy Island Marine Park (formerly Musket Island Marine Park) has anchoring. Nearly all anchorages require a stern-tie. Use your chart and depth sounder, watch for rocks, and go slowly.

㊱ **Ballet Bay.** Ballet Bay, on Nelson Island, is a popular, well-protected anchorage in Blind Bay.

Ballet Bay can be entered from the north, but many rocks obstruct the path and close attention is called for. The easier entry is from the west, between Nelson Island and Clio Island. If you do enter from the west, the rock shown at the point before you turn into Ballet Bay truly is there, and farther offshore than you might expect. Give it a wide berth. Some of the many rocks around Ballet Bay are marked with sticks or cairns, but don't count on all of the rocks being marked. Not all the rocks are charted. Go slowly and pay attention.

The center of Ballet Bay is good-holding mud, but the bottom grows rockier toward shore. It has been reported that cables and debris lie on the bottom. Note the charted cable crossing areas.

Hardy Island Marine Park. Formerly Musket Island Marine Park. Located behind Fox Island, near the western entrance to Blind Bay. The upland area of the park is on Hardy Island. A beautiful spot. Anchor behind the tiny islet, or in the bay that opens up to the north of the islet. In most cases you'll stern-tie to shore. The bottom can be rocky, so be sure you have a satisfactory set. You also can anchor in the narrow, vertically sided, almost landlocked cove indenting Hardy Island immediately northwest of the park itself. Rock has been quarried on the peninsula high above the cove. It's quite dramatic. The area is poorly charted and some of the depths are deeper than charts show.

Telescope Passage. Telescope Passage connects Blind Bay with Jervis Inlet, but is partly blocked by underwater rocks that extend from the 70-meter island at the north entrance. Strongly favor the Nelson Island side until past the 70-meter island. Then, trend toward the middle of the passage to avoid charted and uncharted rocks along the Nelson Island side. When approaching Telescope Passage from Jervis Inlet, you might be confused (we were) by the presence of a tiny islet almost 100 feet high just outside the entrance. Check the chart closely; the islet is shown as the smallest oval imaginable with (26), for 26 meters high, directly beside it.

JERVIS INLET

Jervis Inlet extends 46 miles into Coast Range mountains and is the route to fabled Princess Louisa Inlet. Jervis Inlet is 1 to 1.5 miles wide and often more than 600 feet deep. Steep-to shores, with mountains rising directly above, make for few good anchorages. Currents in Jervis Inlet are light, and are often affected by winds. Watch for drift. Heading up-inlet, Backeddy Resort & Marina and Bathgate Marina in Egmont are the last fuel stops.

Once beyond Foley Head and Egmont Point, you'll find only indifferent anchorages at Vancouver Bay, Deserted Bay, and Killam Bay. The 30 miles of Princess Royal Reach, Prince of Wales Reach, and Queen's Reach do not have useable anchorages. Unlike the other deep fjords that penetrate from the sea, however, Jervis Inlet has a spectacular prize at the end: Princess Louisa Inlet.

Pictograph: Correspondent Pat Shera reports a good pictograph of what appear to be a group of salmon and other figures on the north side of Princess Royal Reach, midway between Osgood Creek and Patrick Point.

McRae Cove. Indenting the south end of the peninsula to the east of McRae Islet where Jervis Inlet joins Malaspina Strait, this small cove can be a day or overnight stop. The bay has consistent depths that are shallow for deep draft vessels. Watch for charted rocks at the entry and drying area at the head of the cove. The cove is scenic with windows to Malaspina Strait. A couple of homes occupy the north shore. This is a well-protected cove that is larger than it appears on the charts and has room for two or three boats.

Thunder Bay. Thunder Bay, immediately inside the north entrance to Jervis Inlet, has anchorage in the protected cove on the south shore, and in the open cove at the northwest corner. Correspondent Capt. Fred Triggs reports that in the southern cove, the rock drying at 2.1 meters appears to be farther offshore than charted. The cove looks a little small on the chart, but Capt. Triggs says it has room for several boats and good holding. The shores are lined with vacation cabins. Mooring floats restrict anchoring room. Rocks extend from the point as you approach. Give the point a good offing. At low tide the charted rock looks like a small haystack. If you stay off the west shore you'll be fine.

Saltery Bay. Saltery Bay has a public float, picnic sites and a seasonal take-out eatery. It is the ferry landing for road travel along the Sunshine Coast. The Saltery Bay Provincial Park, with beach access, is about half a mile to the west. A log booming operation, with signs warning boaters of cables, fills most of the possible anchoring area in the bay, and what remains has several private mooring buoys. An underwater cable area is to the west of the ferry landing.

Saltery Bay Harbour. (604) 487-0196. Public floats are located adjacent and east of the ferry landing. Visitor moorage is available along 650 feet of space on three floats on a first-come, first-serve basis. The western most float is 240 feet long with stays limited to 48 hours on the outer western portion of the float. No power, no water. Most of the space is taken by local boats. Space for smaller boats can usually be found. Commercial vessels have priority.

Saltery Bay Provincial Park. Open all year, anchor only or moor at the public dock, a 1-km walk from the park entrance. Picnic facilities and a dive rinse station are

Blind Bay

located above the small sandy beach. Most of the shoreline is rock, however, and very impressive. In Mermaid Cove, scuba divers can look for the underwater statue of the mermaid. The dive reef is marked by white buoys. A launch ramp is a short distance west of Mermaid Cove.

St. Vincent Bay. Much oyster culture activity. Sykes Island and Junction Island may have anchorage.

Hotham Sound. Hotham Sound is a beautiful 6-mile-long body of water surrounded by high, rugged mountains that rivals Princess Louisa Inlet for beauty, but with far fewer boaters. Friel Lake Falls tumbles 1,400 feet down a sheer mountainside near Harmony Islands. The Sound is generally sheltered from most strong winds; however, williwaws can blow down from the mountains. Good anchorages in Hotham Sound are few. Suitable anchorage is found in Harmony Islands Marine Park, Baker Bay, and at the head of Hotham Sound.

Harmony Islands Marine Park. The Harmony Islands in Hotham Sound are lovely. Four islands comprise the Harmony Islands Group. Three of the islands, the southern-most and the two northern-most, are part of the Marine Park. The middle island is private property and is not part of the park. The northwestern-most island was acquired by BC Parks (with substantial help from BC Marine Parks Forever Society) in 2018.

The middle island is privately owned with a house and private dock that is posted with "Private" signs. Please respect the private property and do not access or land on the middle island (including stern-ties).

Anchorage is possible in the south half of the channel east of the islands, where you can find depths of 40 to 60 feet to drop the anchor and then stern-tie to the mainland side of the channel (don't tie to the private middle island.) If you are setup for deeper anchoring, it is possible to anchor in the northern part of the channel and stern-tie. Anchorage for smaller vessels may be found in locally-named Kipling Cove, a nook surrounded by the two northern islands and the middle island. The bottom is rocky and a private dock occupies the south portion of the cove. Stern-tie to shore on either of the northern islands, which are owned by BC Parks.

In settled weather it is possible to anchor in the rocky and exposed nook on the west side of the islands – watch for reefs and rocks. Rings for stern ties might be found along the high tide line. We have been told that williwaws can make anchoring interesting.

Dark Cove. Dark Cove is a little notch between Foley Head and Goliath Bay, and was recommended to us by an experienced sailboater we met at Princess Louisa Inlet. We motored through Dark Cove the next day but didn't stop. At 90 feet deep, Dark Cove isn't ideal for anchoring, although protection behind Sydney Island is excellent.

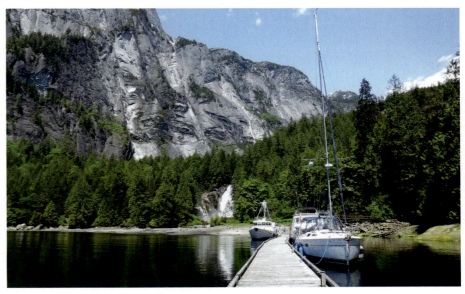

A trail leads from the head of the dock to Chatterbox Falls at Princess Louisa Marine Park.

Malibu Rapids. Malibu Rapids mark the entrance to Princess Louisa Inlet. The rapids are narrow and dogleg-shaped, and boats at one end cannot see boats at the other end. It is courteous—and wise—to warn other vessels via VHF Channel 16 that you are about to enter the rapids, and the direction you are traveling. First, be sure to set your VHF radio to LOW POWER. The transmission can be brief: *"Securité, Securité. This is the 34-foot motor vessel Happy Days, inbound to Princess Louisa Inlet. Any concerned traffic please respond on channel one-six."*

A VHF securite call is a notice of safety to boaters. When making a securite call at Malibu Rapids, it is for safety reasons and not for any right-of-way statement. Rules of the road for vessels operating in current flow are determined by current flow direction. Vessels traveling with the current are the 'stand-on' and vessels traveling against the current flow are the 'give-way.' The path through Malibu Rapids is 'S' shaped. While it might be tempting to 'cross over' the opposing traffic path to get a look at the rapids, this may create a conflict with boats coming in the opposite direction.

Currents in Malibu Rapids run to 9 knots and create large overfalls. Run this passage at slack water. High water slack occurs about 25 minutes after high water at Point Atkinson, and low water slack about 35 minutes after low water at Point Atkinson. High water slack is preferred because it widens the available channel somewhat. High slack or low, before entering or leaving Malibu Rapids, local knowledge says to wait until the surf created by the overfall subsides entirely.

Important: Use the Volume 5 Canadian Hydrographic Service or Ports and Passes tide tables for Point Atkinson tides.

Princess Louisa Inlet. Princess Louisa Inlet, 4 miles long, is the "holy grail" for cruising people from all over the world. Entered through Malibu Rapids, the inlet is surrounded by 3000-foot-high mountains that plunge almost vertically into 600-foot depths below. Entering Princess Louisa Inlet is like entering a great cathedral. The author Earle Stanley Gardner wrote that no one could see Princess Louisa Inlet and remain an atheist. It is one of the most awesome destinations on the coast. What words can describe this place? All the superlatives have been used up on lesser subjects.

Please observe a no-wake speed limit. Larger wakes bounce off the sides of the inlet.

Malibu Club, a Young Life Christian summer camp for teenagers, is at the entrance to the inlet, just inside Malibu Rapids. The kids and staff are welcoming and polite. Tours are possible. It's probably best to visit by dinghy after your boat is settled at Macdonald Island or the park dock at Chatterbox Falls.

As you clear Malibu Rapids and motor up Princess Louisa Inlet, you will be treated to waterfalls streaming down the mountainsides. About halfway along, 5 mooring buoys are behind Macdonald Island.

Princess Louisa Park is at the head of the inlet, surrounded by a bowl of high sheer cliffs that astonish even repeat visitors. The 650-foot-long park dock will hold a large number of boats. The dock is available at no charge; maximum boat length is 55 feet and stays are limited to 72 hours. Snug up close to the boat in front to leave room for others. The float at the end of dock is for floatplanes. Five mooring buoys were recently installed just south of the dock along the eastern shore.

If the dock is full, you will need to make use of one of these five buoys, or one of the four mooring buoys at Macdonald Island. Buoys can accommodate boats up to 70 feet; buoys are marked. Anchorage is possible at Macdonald Island but may not be practical due to depths and lack of swinging space. A dinghy dock

VANCOUVER, MAINLAND B.C. & THE SUNSHINE COAST

See Area Map Page 298 - Maps Not for Navigation

Princess Louisa Inlet on a high-speed tour boat

is provided on the mainland shore opposite Macdonald Island for visitors to access a 1 km loop trail. Trail map at the Kiosk.

Since most people don't stay longer than a day or two, there's good turnover. A boat at anchor or on a mooring buoy need only wait for the twice-daily departure of boats from the dock running for slack at Malibu Rapids. Space then can be found before the next fleet arrives from the rapids. Water (not potable) is available all the way out the dock (May 1 - Oct 30) but no power. Up-inlet thermal winds can develop on warm afternoons. Be aware if you're out in the dinghy.

The park is beautifully developed and maintained. Use the shoreside toilets. Limit generator use to 9:00 a.m. to 11:00 a.m. in the morning and 6:00 p.m. to 8:00 p.m. in the evening. Quiet hours are 11:00 p.m. to 7:00 a.m. The water is warm enough for swimming, even by adults who usually don't go in anymore. Field Correspondents Dan and Karin Leach report that a "Do Not Swim During Lion Mane Jellyfish Season" sign is posted at the dock,

No discharge zone. Gray water okay.

There's a covered fire pit for group get-togethers. For those who wish, a short walk to the pools near the base of Chatterbox Falls will yield a bracing bath/shower followed by a power rinse.

A delightful waterfall-fed pool is hidden in the forest on the north side of the inlet. From the dock you can see a large boulder that marks the spot. Land the dinghy on the small beach just beyond the boulder and walk a few steps to the pool. A bather we met yelped when he jumped in, but a moment later said the water was fine.

No hook-and-line fishing. Princess Louisa Inlet is a rockfish conservation area.

Trapper's Cabin is about a 2-hour very demanding hike from the dock area. The cabin is now completely collapsed. The trail is steep, and often muddy and slippery. We're not kidding about the hike being demanding, serious injuries have occurred.

With a fast boat, Princess Louisa Inlet could be seen in one day. Zoom up for the morning slack at Malibu Rapids, see the sights for a few hours, and zoom out on the afternoon slack. That, however, would be seeing Princess Louisa Inlet but not experiencing it. Something good happens to people when they're at Princess Louisa Inlet. We suggest at least three days for the trip: one day up 46-mile-long Jervis Inlet; the next day at the park; and the third day back down Jervis Inlet on the morning slack.

Princess Louisa Society. The Princess Louisa Society was formed to buy and preserve the area around Chatterbox Falls for perpetuity. The Society gave the property to B.C. Parks, but maintains an active role in the care of the facilities. Fundraising continues to maintain and develop the facilities at docks and in the area. Annual memberships are $40 U.S or Cdn.; life memberships are $200 U.S. or Cdn. The Society website is www.princesslouisa.bc.ca.

MALASPINA STRAIT TO SARAH POINT

Malaspina Strait, 36 miles long, separates Texada Island from the mainland. Although the strait looks protected from the open water of the Strait of Georgia, storms can create high seas. Especially on an ebb tide, confused seas often build up off the mouth of Jervis Inlet and extend almost to Texada Island. Grief Point, at the north end of Malaspina Strait, is another bad spot in a southeasterly. Other than the mouth of Jervis Inlet, however, Malaspina Strait poses no threat in settled weather.

McRae Cove faces Malaspina Strait, just west of Scotch Fir Point at the mouth of Jervis Inlet. The cove is well protected but shallow. The charts show a straightforward entry between the 27- and 29-meter islands, then along a 36-meter island. Anchoring is in the vicinity of the 36-meter island in 6 feet at zero tide. Don't go much farther in—the bottom shoals quickly.

㊲ **Beach Gardens Resort & Marina.** 7074 Westminster St., Powell River, BC V8A 1C5; (604) 485-6267; (800) 663-7070; beachgardens@shaw.ca; www.beachgardens.com. Monitors VHF 66A July & August. Reservations accepted. Open all year, moorage, 15 & 30 amp power, water, free Wi-Fi, washrooms, showers, coin laundry, fitness center, indoor pool, ice, well-stocked beer and wine sales store. Gasoline, diesel and lube oil at the fuel dock, seasonal only. This is a breakwater-protected marina with good docks, just south of Grief Point. Deluxe

Princess Louisa Marine Park

Reference Only – Not for Navigation

VANCOUVER, MAINLAND B.C. & THE SUNSHINE COAST

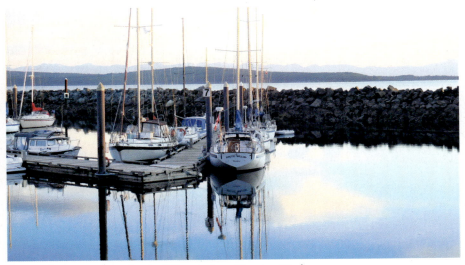

Spectacular sunsets across Strait of Georgia from Westview Harbour

waterfront rooms are available. Kayak and paddle board rentals available.

Beach Gardens Resort features a new building overlooking the marina and fronting the older buildings of the resort. The laundry, beer and wine store, and the excellent Seasider Bistro, (604) 485-0996, are on the bottom level with beautiful views of Malaspina Strait. Check www.theseasider.ca for hours of operation. A market with a coffee bar is within walking distance of the marina. Free shuttle service from the marina to Powell River Town Centre Mall is available in July and August. The city bus stop is a short walk away.

Grief Point. Grief Point marks the northern end of Malaspina Strait on the mainland side. The seas around Grief Point get particularly rough when the wind blows.

㊳ **Westview/Powell River.** There are two main moorage areas at Powell River's Westview area: the North Harbour for permanent moorage located north of the ferry landing with its own entrance; and the working harbour and transient guest moorage facility with an entrance located south of the ferry landing. The guest moorage facility consists of two basins referred to as Westview and South Harbour; these two basins are accessed through the shared south entrance and the floats are used by working vessels and transient pleasure craft. Fuel, water and power are available at the Westview and South Harbour basins; nearby stores have marine supplies. Grocery stores and a major shopping center are a taxi or a free seasonal shuttle from the marina.

The section adjacent to the ferry loading area between the two main moorage areas, north and south, has been redeveloped and now houses the harbor office, new washrooms, showers, and laundry. Access to excellent restaurants, the Willingdon Beach Trail, and the historic "Townsite" district makes Powell River a destination worth visiting.

An excellent stock of marine and fishing supplies is available at nearby Marine Traders chandlery. Shops and a range of restaurants are on the main commercial streets, a short walk away. The Chopping Block, an old-fashioned butcher shop, is at the north end of Marine Avenue. Their meats, seafood, homemade smoked sausage, and cheese are delicious. The Town Centre Mall, with Save-On Foods, Safeway, Shoppers Drug Mart, Walmart, liquor store and other shops, is located some distance away, up a steep hill on Courtenay Street (they call it Cardiac Hill). It's a hike. Another shopping center has a QF grocery store that will deliver to the marina.

The original Powell River townsite is a couple of miles up the road from Westview. Visitors can walk or bicycle along the shoreline through a beautiful forested trail starting at Willingdon Beach on the north end of downtown Powell River. Numerous pieces of historic logging equipment are on display along the Willingdon Beach Trail, serving as a fascinating outdoor museum complete with interpretive signage. For energetic hikers, you can access the old "Townsite" district above the Mill off the end of the trail. Take a taxi for the return trip to Powell River. "Townsite" is the original settlement of Powell River and is a designated National Historic District. Four hundred of the original buildings from the early 1900s remain. Many have been refurbished and are still in use. A row of large oak trees and grand homes from the era stand proudly overlooking the mill and Malaspina Strait. Several cafes are found in "Townsite" and a brewery offering craft beer samplers.

In Powell River, history buffs may want to visit the small history museum adjacent to Willingdon Beach. The Blackberry Festival is in early August. Check the town's website (www.discoverpowellriver.com) for a schedule of activities.

㊳ **Westview Harbour.** 6790 Wharf Street, Powell River, BC V8A 1T9; (604) 485-5244; jkinahan@powellriver.ca. Monitors VHF 66A. Open all year, potable water, 30 &

Beach Gardens Resort & Marina

Powell River & Lund

2020 Waggoner Cruising Guide   311

VANCOUVER, MAINLAND B.C. & THE SUNSHINE COAST

See Area Map Page 311 - Maps Not for Navigation

Willingdon Beach in Powell River

50 amp power, washrooms, large showers, laundry. Waste oil disposal, recycling, no garbage drop. Free Wi-Fi and pumpout. Leave the daymark inside the harbor entry to port when entering. Guest moorage is available at both Westview Harbour and South Harbour basins, which share the same south entrance. Westview Fuels is the demarcation between the two moorage areas. First-come, first-served; call ahead for available space.

Rafting may be required or stern-tie to the main dock. South Harbour (floats 7-11) can accommodate vessels up to 150 feet (20-foot draft at zero tide). A short trail connects the South Harbour basin and the Westview Harbour basin.

Washrooms, showers, and garbage drop are available at both Westview and South Harbour; the newest facilities are located at Westview with the older more basic facilities at South Harbour basin.

Two-hour complimentary moorage, call ahead. Free scheduled shuttle to the mall picks up outside the harbor office four times per day during the ten-week season. Schedule is posted at the marina office.

㊳ **Westview Fuels**. P.O. Box 171, Powell River, BC V8A 4Z6; (604) 485-2867. Monitors VHF 66A. Gasoline, diesel, lubricants, washrooms, and ice. Located between Westview Harbour and South Harbour. Joe and Debbie Hooper are the owners and they're great.

Dinner Rock. Dinner Rock, exposed at all tides, is approximately 0.2 mile off the mainland shore, slightly southeast of Savary Island. In 1998 a 1000-lb. cross was erected on the rock. It is a memorial to the five people who died there in October 1947, when the vessel *Gulf Stream*, proceeding in darkness with rain falling, struck the rock and sank.

Savary Island. Savary Island is a 4-mile-long sandy island that lies approximately east and west, and is served by water taxi from Lund. The island is a favorite destination for Vancouverites. The small public dock on the north shore is for loading and unloading only. Anchorage is good, sand bottom, within easy dinghy distance of shore. Savary Island has no real protected harbor, but the beaches are some of the best in B.C.

In summer months Riggers, a licensed pub-style restaurant, and a small general store are open. From the public dock turn right and follow the road for about one-half mile. Bicycles can be rented nearby. A number of years ago Bob Hale anchored off the north shore for the night and "got away with it." By contrast, Tom Kincaid once anchored overnight in the same area, but by morning the wind had come in from the north and he was on a lee shore. We visited Savary Island recently and anchored in 50-70 feet just off the dock and mooring field. We took the dinghy to shore and explored the island. The gently sloping beach makes landing and mooring the dinghy a challenge. Visiting by water taxi from Lund might be a better idea if you plan to spend the day there.

Nearby **Hernando Island** is surrounded by rocky shallows, and is seldom visited by cruising boats. Renowned authors Lin and Larry Pardey, however, report excellent anchorage with protection from southeast winds in **Stag Bay**, northwest of the pier. Anchor in 18 to 24 feet on a firm sand bottom.

Mitlenatch Island. Roughly west of Hernando Island, Mitlenatch Island appears to be an uninviting rock out in the middle of the Strait of Georgia. It is in fact a thriving and ruggedly beautiful wildlife refuge, with a small, protected anchorage on its east side. Park volunteers spend a week in turn each year on the island doing trail maintenance and guiding tours. Visitors are asked to stay on the trails to avoid disturbing birds. Those who visit will be rewarded, as this note from Correspondents John and Lorraine Littlewood suggests:

"If you can get there on a calm clear day in September, you'll see an incredible variety of wildlife, from Goshawks to huge sea lions. An additional benefit is water so clear that we could actually watch our Bruce anchor deploy. It hit the bottom in about 20 feet,

Westview Harbour

Lund Harbour

See Area Map Page 311 - Maps Not for Navigation

VANCOUVER, MAINLAND B.C. & THE SUNSHINE COAST

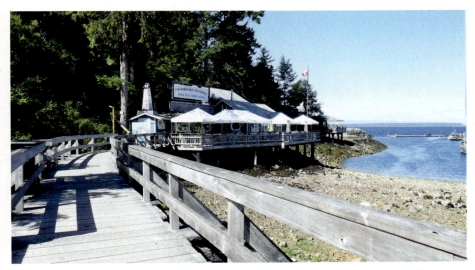
Enjoy great food, great company, and great views from the Boardwalk Restaurant at Lund

flipped over, bit, and buried itself. This was on only 2:1 scope, although we later paid out to our normal 3:1."

We thank reader Sharl Heller for increasing our awareness of Mitlenatch Island.

㊴ **Lund**. Lund is the north end of the Pacific Coastal Highway, the road that leads all the way to the tip of South America. Lund is a busy place in the summer, a jumping-off point for Desolation Sound with fuel, provisions, and pumpout.

The historic Lund Resort, with restaurant and pub, is at the head of the fuel dock. The small but well-stocked store, in the same building as the resort, has a good deli, fresh (often local) vegetables, ice cream, frozen meats, liquor agency with good wine and beer selection, pet supplies, prawn bait, frozen herring, camping and picnic supplies, and more.

Lund is the mainland's closest launch site to Desolation Sound. Long-term auto, trailer and tow vehicle parking available. Lund Auto & Outboard is a few blocks away. Nancy's Bakery is in the modern, larger building overlooking the public docks. Nancy's pastries, pizzas, and other specialties are famous. Nancy's also has good Wi-Fi. Upstairs from Nancy's is Pollen Sweaters, specializing in locally made sweaters, and Terracentric Adventures, a kayak tour operator.

The town assumed operation of the public docks following divestiture by the federal government several years ago. With commercial fishing in decline, the docks and shoreside facilities were upgraded to make them more inviting to visiting pleasure craft. Rafting may be required. When the docks are full, you can moor along the inside of the breakwater and dinghy to the dinghy dock. There's a good launch ramp, and modern public washrooms with excellent showers.

Over on the north side of the bay a public float, with no access to shore, is in the middle of Finn Cove.

Fuel: The busy Lund Resort fuel dock has gasoline and diesel.

Garbage: During the season a truck at the top of the boat launch will take your garbage for a fee. Recycling is available behind the hotel.

Haulout: Jack's Boatyard in Finn Cove has a repair yard, haulout to 50 tons and boat storage.

About Finn Cove: Sailing Directions and the charts call it Finn Cove, but the locals call it Finn Bay. The road that leads from the village to the cove is named Finn Bay Road. The Waggoner will call it Finn Cove, however, to be consistent with the charts. No anchoring in Finn Cove.

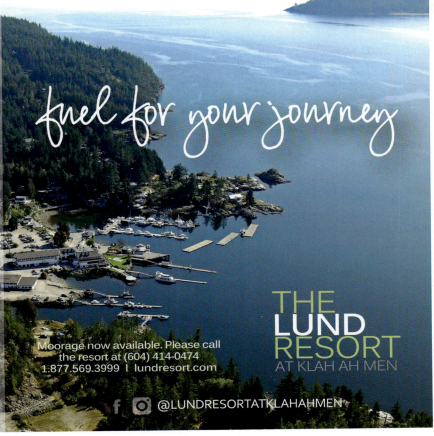

2020 Waggoner Cruising Guide

VANCOUVER, MAINLAND B.C. & THE SUNSHINE COAST

See Area Map Page 311 - Maps Not for Navigation

㊴ **Lund Small Craft Harbour.** P.O. Box 78, Lund, BC V0N 2G0; (604) 483-4711 or (604) 414-0474; lundharbour-wharfinger@ twincomm.ca; www.lundharbourbc. wordpress.com. Monitors VHF 73. Open all year, 1500 to 1700 feet of breakwater-protected dock space, 20, 30 & some 50 amp power. Water at the docks for overnight guests. The harbor has one of the only pumpout stations in the area. Garbage drop, with a fee per bag, is above the fuel dock; off-season, use the garbage drop at the general store. No oil disposal. Excellent washrooms and showers. Wide concrete launch ramp with 4 lanes, good for most launchings down to about 5 feet above zero tide, some say 3 feet.

Enter north of the floating breakwaters. The northern dock located inside the breakwater is reserved for pleasure craft, rafting required. Don't give up if the docks appear full. Office hours are 8:00 a.m. to 11:00 a.m. and 3:00 p.m. to 5:00 p.m. October to May, 8:00 a.m. to 5:00 p.m. June and September, 8:00 a.m. to 8:00 p.m. July 1 to Labour Day. Moorage is free for the first hour, 1 to 3 hours are charged at the half-day rate. Radio ahead for a slip assignment when near the entrance, even for short stays.

The floating concrete breakwater noted above (no power or water) protects the inner docks. You can tie inside of these floats and dinghy to the marked dinghy dock area below the ramp. Overnight moorage is charged on the breakwater.

The area near the launch ramps had a green buoy to mark a shallow spot for years. It has been removed. Local knowledge says to be aware of a high spot there, about 4 feet at its shallowest.

㊴ **The Lund Resort & 13 Moons Marina (formerly the Lund Hotel & Marina).** 1436 Highway 101, Lund, BC V0N 2G0; (604) 414-0474; (877) 569- 3999; info@lundhotel. com; www.lundhotel.com. Open year-round; An 80-foot dock provides limited overnight moorage on a first-come, first-serve basis. Free moorage for hotel guests. Free Wi-Fi. The laundry facility is clean, with good machines. The store and deli are well stocked. The fuel dock has gasoline, diesel, and lubricants. Water for a fee.

The historic hotel, which dates back to 1905, has been restored and remodeled with a pub and separate dining area. The hotel has 31 rooms, all renovated in 2018, ranging from budget-sensitive to four "boutique superior oceanfront" rooms overlooking the water. Rooms feature unique hand-painted murals. The hotel, pub, general store, and fuel dock are under the ownership of the Tla'amin Nation. Tug Guhm Gallery & Studio, well known for lifelike seal heads carved from a single block of stone, is in the lower part of the hotel.

㊴ **Lund Water Taxi.** (604) 483-9749. Scheduled service to Savary Island. Can deliver parts or people to Desolation Sound and surrounding areas.

㊴ **End Of The Road Parking.** P.O. Box 94, 1440 Lund Rd., Lund BC V0N 2G0; (604) 483-3667. Daily and long-term vehicle and trailer parking in secure lots off-site.

㊴ **Lund Automotive & Outboard Ltd.** 1520 Lund Hwy, Lund, BC V0N 2G0; (604) 483-4612. Long-term tow vehicle and trailer parking in secure lots. Call ahead for reservations. Mechanics are on staff for mechanical and electrical repairs and they are an authorized service facility for several engine brands. Haulout to 30 feet.

㊴ **Jack's Boatyard (Finn Cove).** 9907 Finn Bay Road, P.O. Box 198, Lund, BC V0N 2G0; (604) 483-3566; info@jacksboatyard. ca; www.jacksboatyard.ca. Located 1/3 of a mile northwest of Lund in Finn Cove, owner Jack Elsworth created this do-it-yourself boatyard. The yard is equipped with a 50-ton Travelift and a custom-made 30-ton lift. The large upland boatyard and storage area is accessed by the 30-ton lift, while the 50-ton lift services the lower and smaller yard area with limited space for larger boats. The larger upland boatyard has plenty of room that allows you to work at your own pace. The boatyard has a list of local marine specialists.

You can stay on your boat while working on it; water, power, washrooms, showers, laundry, garbage and recycling drop are available. Wi-Fi is available in the upland boatyard.

Jack's haulout lifts and those in Campbell River are the only haulout lifts until Sointula's marine ways near Port McNeill, and Shearwater's Travelift some 200 miles north.

Copeland Islands. The Copeland Islands (locally known as the Ragged Islands) are a provincial park. Anchorage is possible in several nooks and coves among the islands, although some of the coves are exposed to wakes from boats transiting Thulin Passage. Because of remnants of booming cable on the bottom, a buoyed trip line to the anchor crown is a good idea. Check your swing when you anchor. 19 stern-tie pins, with chains, were installed by BC Parks and the BC Marine Parks Forever Society in 2018, making it easier for boaters to visit the Copeland Islands. Please watch your wake in Thulin Passage. There are environmentally sensitive areas in the Copeland Islands.

Sharpe's Landing. A private marina with no facilities for transient boaters is in a small bay on the north end and east side of Thulin Passage. Please watch your wake as you go by.

㊵ **Bliss Landing Estates.** (604) 414-9417; (604) 483-8098; bliss@twincomm. ca. Located in Turner Bay, north of Lund. Open May through October. First-come, first-served guest moorage for boats under 60 feet. The docks belong to the development. Transient moorage is in unoccupied slips or side-tie at the south side of the southerly docks. Washrooms, showers, laundry, 30 & 50 amp power, water, free Wi-Fi. Docks are exposed to westerly winds; moor bow-out. It's about a 15-minute dinghy ride to Lund.

Copeland Islands Stern-tie Anchor Pins

Secret Cove - The Upper Deck

There's something intriguing about sailing into the protected harbour of Secret Cove, situated about halfway between Pender Harbour and Sechelt along the Sunshine Coast.

Secret Cove Marina has an intimate feel, and the delightful marina store is overflowing with gifts, jewelry and groceries, offering some unique finds. It is amazing they fit so much into the store along with all of the grocery essentials. The recently re-opened Upper Deck restaurant, located above the store, is where you can indulge in great food and wonderful views of the cove and the harbour entrance. Guests have a front-row seat to view all the boating activity from the outdoor deck. If the weather is iffy, there is an indoor seating area too. You'll want to make reservations for this special venue, which has quickly returned to its former reputation as a boater's favorite stop for good eats.

The cuisine at The Upper Deck is flavorful and creative, with daily features and house-made desserts. While making our rounds for Waggoner Guide research, we stopped for Happy Hour, which runs from 3-5 p.m. and enjoyed the opportunity to relax and take in some tasty, hearty dishes. The bowl of large prawns with pasta and slices of green peppers in a seasoned tomato sauce, satisfied our cravings as did the wonderful crab cakes in a red pepper yogurt sauce served as an appetizer. We couldn't pass up the desserts, of course, which included berry flan; rich chocolate cake with berry fraiche; and ice cream sundaes. Definitely, save room for the desserts.

Dinners at The Upper Deck begin at 5 p.m. and run late into the evening (closed Mondays) beginning late June till Labour Day. Dinner starters include Fried Squid with celery remoulade and edible flowers, or try the Pacific Scallop Ceviche with sweet pea velouté and shoots. Mains include Duck Breast with rutabaga & carrot mash, braised greens, and blackberry caramelized sauce. Or you might want to try the Braised Beef Flat in natural jus, served with potato terrine and young vegetables and greens.

When cruising the Sunshine Coast, we can recommend a stop at Secret Cove to take in the delightful eatery and charming marina. It's a favorite with the locals too, which says a lot. To book dinner reservations, call 604-885-3533.

Desolation Sound & Discovery Passage

CHAPTER 10

DESOLATION SOUND
Prideaux Haven • Homfray Lodge
Pendrell Sound • Refuge Cove • Teakerne Arm
Toba Inlet

CORTES ISLAND
Squirrel Cove • Cortes Bay • Von Donop Inlet
Gorge Harbour

QUADRA ISLAND
Rebecca Spit • Heriot Bay • Octopus Islands
Okisollo Channel

DISCOVERY PASSAGE
Campbell River • April Point • Brown Bay
Small Inlet

Captain George Vancouver had it all wrong when he explored and wrote about this area during his cruise in 1792. He named it **Desolation Sound**, saying, "there was not a single prospect that was pleasing to the eye." Granted, his crew did have a challenging time with weather, fleas, and even shellfish poisoning. In reality, Desolation Sound, located today literally just beyond the end of the road, is a place of extraordinary beauty. It's one of the Northwest's most dreamed-about and sought-after cruising destinations.

Officially, Desolation Sound is the body of water north of Sarah Point and Mary Point, and south of West Redonda Island. When most people think of cruising these waters they consider Desolation Sound to include the entire area north of Cape Mudge and Sarah Point, and south of Yuculta Rapids and Chatham Point, including Discovery Passage (Campbell River).

For those departing from the Seattle or Vancouver areas, the trip to or from Desolation Sound might take as long as a week, depending on boat speed, weather, and stops along the way.

Desolation Sound is not a huge area. Even slow boats can go from one end to another in a day. But Desolation Sound offers a wilderness setting, generally easy waters, many bays and coves to explore and anchor in, and marinas where fuel and supplies are available. On the west side of these cruising grounds, Campbell River on Vancouver Island is a vibrant small city. Campbell River has complete supplies and even a boatyard for haulout and repairs. Lund, on the B.C. mainland, is at the eastern entry to Desolation Sound. Lund is a quaint, small village that has several services vacationing boaters are apt to need, including a nearby boatyard and lift. Lund also is the northern terminus of Highway 99, a road that extends to Tierra del Fuego on the tip of South America. Small marinas scattered throughout Desolation Sound offer fuel, water, and limited supplies.

Since it is close to the point where the tidal currents meet on the inside of Vancouver Island, the water in Desolation Sound is not regularly exchanged with cold ocean water. During the summer, water temperatures of 70° to 80°F are not unusual in some of the bays, making for comfortable swimming.

Okeover Harbour Authority docks

Navigation is straightforward, with few hazards in the major channels. Closer to shore it's a different story, but the rocks and reefs are charted.

The most popular time to cruise Desolation Sound is from mid-July through the end of August, when the prospects for sunny, warm weather are best. It's also when the anchorages and facilities are most crowded. June weather can be cool and rainy, but crowds are not a problem. It's then that the waterfalls are most awesome and the resorts and businesses, while open and stocked, are the least harried.

If your calendar permits, the very best time to cruise Desolation Sound might be early- to mid-September. By then the high-season crowds have departed, yet summer usually hangs on for a last and glorious finale. Stock in the stores may be thin and the young summertime help has headed back to school, but the low slanting sunlight paints the hills and mountains with new drama, and the first colors of autumn make each day a fresh experience. Watch the weather closely. Leave before the fall storm pattern begins, although usually that's not before October.

Navigation Note: Tide information for locations in Desolation Sound is shown in Ports and Passes and Canadian Tide and Current Tables, Vol. 5 (they are shown as secondary ports based on Point Atkinson Tides). Currents for Beazley Passage, Hole in the Wall, and Discovery Passage are shown in Vol. 6 and Ports and Passes as are corrections for Upper Rapids and Lower Rapids in Okisollo Channel. Owen Bay tides and Okisollo Channel secondary port tide corrections also are in Vol. 6 and Ports and Passes.

Sarah Point. For boats running north through Thulin Passage, Sarah Point, at the tip of the Malaspina Peninsula, is the dramatic entrance to Desolation Sound. The high hills of the Malaspina Peninsula hide the Coast Range mountains. But on a clear day, once Sarah Point is cleared, the mountains come into magnificent view.

MALASPINA INLET

Malaspina Inlet, Okeover Inlet, Lancelot Inlet and Theodosia Inlet all are entered between Zephine Head and Myrmidon Point. On a spring flood tide you will most likely find current at the mouth of Malaspina Inlet, all the way to Grace Harbour. Much of Gifford Peninsula, to the east of Malaspina Inlet, is Desolation Sound Marine Park. Several good anchorages are in this area. You'll also find rocks and reefs, most of them covered in kelp in summer and easily identified. They'll keep you alert, though.

Aquaculture occupies several otherwise inviting anchorages, but there are still plenty of choices in this area. Malaspina Inlet is popular with kayakers. Be mindful of your wake.

① **Grace Harbour.** Grace Harbour is a popular anchorage. The inner bay is surrounded by forest and almost completely landlocked, with anchorage for quite a few boats. Many of the anchorages are along the shore, so be prepared to run a stern-tie. In 2018 BC Parks and the BC Parks Forever Society added 10 stern-tie pins, with chains, for a total of 16 stern-ties in the harbour. A fire pit is in a little park-like area at the north end. A rock, shown on the charts, is in the middle of this innermost bay. The anchor just skids across the rock before finding holding ground on the other side. On a crowded summer weekend, the empty spot in the middle is there for a reason.

Cochrane Bay. Located on the west side of Malaspina Inlet, Cochrane Bay along with the two small islands in front of the bay, are within the Desolation Sound Marine Park. The only safe entrance into the bay is from the south. Field Correspondent Deane Hislop reports that there appears to be an entrance on the north side, but it's not safe due to uncharted rocks that lie below the surface. Set

DESOLATION SOUND & DISCOVERY PASSAGE Reference Only – Not for Navigation

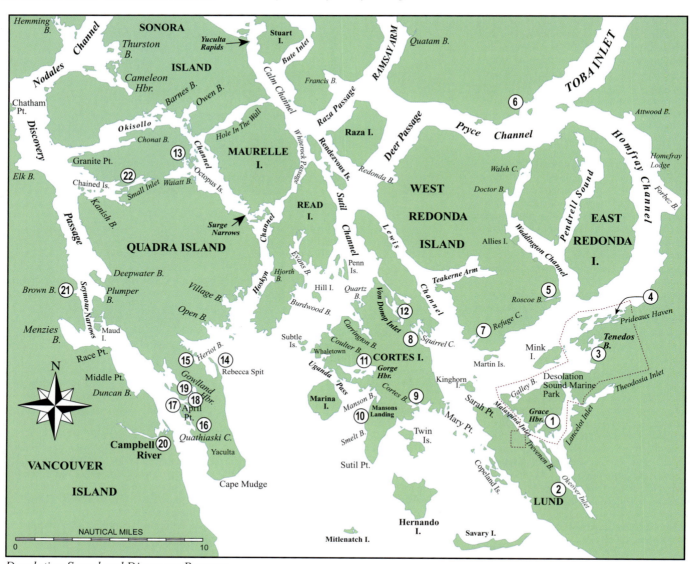

Desolation Sound and Discovery Passage

the hook in 35 feet of water over a sand and gravel bottom. A short trail on the western shore of the bay leads to the Sunshine Coast Trail system.

Trevenen Bay. The head of Trevenen Bay looks like a good anchorage on the chart, but the bay is largely taken by aquaculture.

Penrose Bay. Anchorage at the head of the bay. The Okeover Harbour Authority docks are on the west shore to the south.

② Okeover Harbour Authority. Okeover Inlet borders the Desolation Sound Marine Park area. The Okeover Harbour Authority docks are located on the western shore of Okeover Inlet a short distance south of Penrose Bay with road access to Lund. Oysters and other seafoods are grown in several places along beautiful Okeover Inlet.

The docks at Okeover are managed by the Okeover Harbour Authority (604) 483-3258, contact via VHF 66A. Docks located behind the L-shaped breakwater are for local working boats. The large outer breakwater (440 feet each side) provides plenty of space for transient moorage, no power, no water; the seaward side of the breakwater is exposed to northerly winds. Moorage is on a first-come, first-serve basis; payment made to wharfinger or fill out the self-registration envelope and deposit at the office door-drop. Office located on the wharf is open 12:30 p.m.-6:30 p.m. daily during the summer months, hours vary during the off-season. Launch ramp on-site.

The Laughing Oyster Restaurant (604) 483-9775 is located above the docks. It is an excellent restaurant with outstanding cuisine, lovely surroundings and a stunning view. Reservations recommended. It's one of those gems not to be missed.

Lancelot Inlet. Isabel Bay in Lancelot Inlet is popular. The best anchorage is behind Madge Islands, with a beautiful view and room for one or two boats among the large rock formations. Good anchorage is also in Thors Cove. The bay is deep, except in nooks or close to shore.

Correspondent Pat Shera, from Victoria, wrote to tell us that in Isabel Bay he fouled his anchor on a section of bulldozer track at the head of the anchorage, just west of the north tip of Madge Island. If you have Chartbook 3312, it's where the 4.2-meter sounding is shown. He says another section of track was high and dry on a nearby rock.

Theodosia Inlet. Theodosia Inlet has a narrow, shallow, and kelp-choked entrance, but is navigable by most boats at all stages of the tide. Once inside, the bay opens up. Logging activity takes away from the remote feeling of the bay. Boomed logs can occupy much of the shoreline. Anchorage is in a number of gunkholes along the shoreline.

Wootton Bay. At the head of Lancelot Inlet is Wootton Bay. Good anchorage is located in the cove at the north end of Wootton Bay near the neck of land separating Wootton Bay from Portage Bay. The anchoring cove has swing room for 2 to 3 boats in 40 to 55 feet of water with good holding. The neck of land to Portage Bay, along with land about ¼ mile to either side is private property and is not part of the park. Stern tie is not possible in the anchoring cove, because the shore and

DESOLATION SOUND & DISCOVERY PASSAGE See Area Map Page 318 - Maps Not for Navigation

Galley Bay Stern-tie Anchor Pins

Prideaux Haven and Laura Cove have some spectacular mountain views.

uplands to the north are private. The shore to the east is part of the Desolation Sound Marine Park. However, drying shoals prevent stern ties. Water temperatures in Wootton Bay on Memorial weekend can be in the high sixties.

MINK ISLAND AREA

Galley Bay. Galley Bay is just east of Zephine Head. It is a good anchorage, particularly in the eastern end. In 2018, 9 stern-tie pins, with chain, were installed in the area by BC Parks and the BC Parks Forever Society.

Mink Island. Mink Island is private property, but you'll find excellent anchorage in the bay that indents the southeast shore, particularly if you work in behind the little island in the center of the bay. You'll probably run a stern-tie to shore.

Curme Islands. Wolferstan describes navigation in the Curme Islands, east of Mink Island, as "challenging." The Curme Islands are extremely tight with shallow waterways, but with anchoring possibilities if the boat uses 4-way ties to hold position. For most people, dinghies and kayaks are probably the way to go.

③ **Tenedos Bay.** Tenedos Bay (also called Deep Bay) is a favorite, for a couple of reasons. First, it's a good, protected anchorage, with a landlocked basin behind Bold Head. Second, it's just a short dinghy ride to a 1/4 mile trail that leads to Unwin Lake, a popular freshwater swimming hole. The trail continues beyond Unwin Lake to two smaller lakes and all the way to Melanie Cove and Prideaux Haven, a 1 to 2 hour journey.

In addition to the landlocked basin noted above, you'll find anchorages in coves along the shore of Tenedos Bay. 14 stern-tie pins, with chain, are located around the bay; installed by BC Parks and the BC Parks Forever Society. The center of Tenedos Bay is too deep (300 to 600 feet) for anchoring.

Caution: As you enter Tenedos Bay, a nasty rock lies submerged off the south side of Bold Head. Especially if you are headed to or from Refuge Cove, Mink Island, or around Bold Head to Prideaux Haven, this rock is right on your probable course. The rock lies farther offshore than you might expect. Give it an extra wide berth, just to be sure. A number of rocks are charted. All are easy to avoid if you are aware of them.

Otter Island. A very narrow but navigable channel runs between Otter Island and the mainland. Ample space for a few boats to anchor on the north side, using stern-ties to shore.

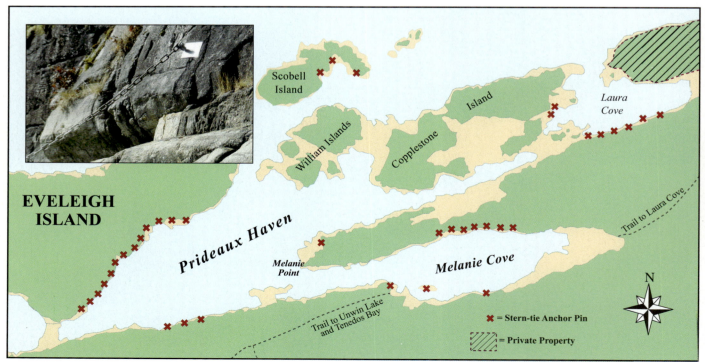
Prideaux Haven Area

320 www.WaggonerGuide.com

PRIDEAUX HAVEN AREA

The coves that make up the area generally known as Prideaux Haven are the most popular spots in Desolation Sound, with several requiring stern-ties to increase the number of boats accommodated. The area is described in great detail by M. Wylie Blanchet in her classic book, *The Curve of Time*.

At the head of Melanie Cove you can find the remains of Mike's place, and in Laura Cove traces of old Phil Lavine's cabin site are visible (both from *The Curve of Time*). The evidence, however, is getting pretty faint.

The entire clutch of islands and shallow waterways invites exploration by dinghy or kayak. The narrow pass between Scobell Island and the William Islands, for instance, is beautiful. During high season, the only thing missing is solitude. You'll have lots of company. There is some cell phone reception in the area, including Prideaux Haven.

No Discharge Zone. Gray water okay.

Eveleigh Island. Anchorage is in Eveleigh Anchorage, the western cove behind Eveleigh Island. A drying reef connects Eveleigh Island with the mainland. Entry to the other Prideaux Haven anchorages is around the east end of Eveleigh Island. A reef almost, but not quite, closes this entrance. Use Chart 3555 (recommended) or Chartbook 3312. Smaller scale Chart 3538 (1:40,000) shows the entry but with too little detail to inspire confidence. After rounding Lucy Point, strongly favor the Eveleigh Island side of the passage to clear the reef.

④ **Prideaux Haven.** Boaters will find numerous stern-tie installations throughout the Prideaux Haven area including: along the southeast shore of Eveleigh Island; along the southeast shore of Scobell Island; on the north and south shores of Melanie Cove; and on the south and west shores of Laura Cove.

No Discharge Zone. Gray water okay.

④ **Melanie Cove.** Melanie Cove is perfectly protected, with ample room along both shores for boats to anchor and stern-tie. 7 stern-ties were installed along the north shore in 2017 and 3 stern-ties installed along the south shore in 2018 as part of the BC Parks and BC Parks Forever Society stern-tie project. A few boats can anchor in the middle without a stern-tie.

Mike's cabin once stood at the head of the cove as described in *The Curve of Time* by M. Blanchet. A half-mile trail, starting on the north side at the head of Melanie Cove, leads to Laura Cove. The trail is well-worn, but a number of trees have fallen across the trail requiring some scrambling.

Another trail from Melanie Cove leads to Unwin Lake at Tenedos Bay. The trailhead begins on the south shore of Melanie Cove, look for the small wooden trail sign on the point near the cove entrance. The trail is steep in places and takes 1-2 hours to reach Tenedos Bay. For a shorter hike, take the left fork in the trail to a small lake overlook, a trail sign points the way.

④ **Laura Cove.** Laura Cove has a fairly narrow entrance, with a least depth of approximately 10 feet at zero tide. Rocks extend from both sides. Enter cautiously. Once you're inside, the bay is beautiful. A few cherry trees and English Ivy mark Old Phil, the Frenchman's cabin site mentioned in *The Curve of Time*, at the head of this bay. Anchorage is to the east of Copplestone Point. The west end of the cove is a maze of rocks and reefs. In 2018, 6 stern-tie pins were installed along the south shore and 2 stern-tie pins on the northwest end of the cove by BC Parks and the BC Parks Forever Society.

Roffey Island. If you can't find a place at Prideaux Haven, Melanie Cove, or Laura Cove, try the little bay behind Roffey Island. Room for one or more boats away from the crowd.

Homfray Channel. Homfray Channel curves from the south end of West Redonda Island and around East Redonda Island, until it merges with Toba Inlet. The only bays of consequence are Forbes Bay and Atwood Bay. The center of Atwood Bay is too deep for convenient anchoring, though we've successfully anchored in the nook indenting the north shore. Bob Stephenson, the former owner of Desolation Sound Yacht Charters, says Forbes Bay can be good for anchoring.

In Bill Wolferstan's book, *Desolation Sound and the Discovery Islands*, he tells of two Native pictographs on the west shore of Homfray Channel—one of a single fish, the other unidentified. Actually, there are several pictographs located about 10 feet above the high water line located across the channel from Lloyd Point.

Homfray Lodge. (604) 566-8026 or (844) 504-1391; info@homfraylodge.com; www.homfraylodge.com; VHF 66A. Office hours 9:00 a.m. to 5:00 p.m. Monday-Friday. Located just north of Forbes Bay. Beautiful and remote location with 250 feet of moorage and two mooring buoys. Moorage is for guests who have booked overnight stays at the lodge or in one of the cabins. Potable water, showers; Wi-Fi at the lodge. No power or food service. Guests can sit on the covered porch and enjoy a beautiful view up the channel. Fishing and sightseeing charters can be arranged. Reservations recommended during the high season.

WADDINGTON CHANNEL

⑤ **Roscoe Bay/Roscoe Bay Marine Park.** Roscoe Bay, on West Redonda Island where Waddington Channel meets Homfray Channel, is an excellent, protected, and popular anchorage. The bay is divided into an inner cove and an outer cove, separated by a drying shoal easily crossed by shallow draft boats at half tide or better. If in doubt, go in on a rising tide. At high tide most sailboats can get in. 12 stern-tie pins, with chains, were added in 2018 by BC Parks and the BC Parks Forever Society for a total of 22 stern-ties in Roscoe Bay.

The inner cove is pretty, and except for the other boats enjoying the bay with you, it's a good example of what cruising in these waters is all about. Dinghy ashore and take the short hike up to the knob dividing the two bays.

At the head of the inner cove an old logging road with a short stream beside it connects with Black Lake. During summer months, the water in Black Lake is warm and excellent for swimming or bathing. Trout fishing is reportedly good. If you carry your dinghy up the road, you can launch it along the lake's shoreline.

On the west side of Roscoe Bay a large red float (a "scotsman") hangs in a tree marking the beginning of a trail to the top of a 2200-foot-high mountain. A rock cairn has been built at the summit, and on the cairn is a bottle with pencil and paper inside. Write your name on

Roscoe Bay is a scenic and popular anchorage. A lake is a short walk from the head of the bay.

DESOLATION SOUND & DISCOVERY PASSAGE

See Area Map Page 318 - Maps Not for Navigation

Walsh Cove Stern-tie Anchor Pins

the paper and add it to the collection. The hike is demanding and a round trip takes several hours, so use your judgment.

No Discharge Zone. Gray water okay.

Pendrell Sound. With summer water temperatures dependably in excess of 68°F, Pendrell Sound has been called the "warmest saltwater north of Mexico." Major oyster culture operations are in the sound, providing seed oysters to growers all along the coast.

Strings of cultch material (often empty oyster shells) are suspended from floats in the bay until the oyster spat adheres to them, at which point they are shipped.

The favored anchorage is at the head of Pendrell Sound, probably stern-tied to trees ashore. Wear good shoes and sturdy gloves when you're clambering around on the rocks.

Another anchorage is on the western shore, about three-quarters of the way up the sound, tucked in behind a small islet at the outfall from a saltwater lagoon.

Speed Limit Zone: A 4-knot speed limit is in effect throughout the north half of Pendrell Sound to protect seed oyster growing operations

Elworthy Island. A delightful cozy anchorage lies behind Elworthy Island, a mile north of Church Point, roughly across Waddington Channel from the entrance to Pendrell Sound. The aquaculture noted on charts no longer is present. The island is called Alfred Island by Wolferstan, but in 1992 it was renamed Elworthy Island for seaman Richard Elworthy, who died serving freedom in 1942. A handsome plaque is set into rock on the northeast corner of the island. Enter the anchorage from either end, but watch for a drying rock near the north entrance. The south entrance shallows to about 12 feet. The island's shoreline is covered with oysters.

Allies Island. Allies Island is connected to West Redonda Island by a drying reef. The north cove is pretty well choked with aquaculture; anchorage is possible in the south cove. The south cove offers a secluded anchorage for 1 to 3 boats and is exposed to the southeast. The rocks around the cove are full of oysters.

Doctor Bay. Doctor Bay is mostly filled with aquaculture. Correspondent Fred Triggs reports good anchorage in 35-40 feet north of the aquaculture operation. We've also heard reports that the aquaculture operation allows pleasure boats to tie up to some floats; check with an employee for instructions.

Walsh Cove Marine Park. Walsh Cove Marine Park is a beautiful little spot with room for several boats to stern-tie along the rocky shore. 15 stern-tie pins, with chain, were installed in 2018 by BC Parks and the BC Parks Forever Society. See Walsh Cove reference map for locations. Enter Walsh Cove from the south. At the north end of the cove, a rock-strewn reef connects Gorges Island to West Redonda Island. The middle of the cove is deep. The cove is well protected from down-channel winds but open to up-channel winds from the south. Two sets of Native pictographs are at Butler Point.

⑥ **Toba Wilderness Marina.** (250) 330-2269; inquiries@tobawilderness.com; www.tobawilderness.com. Contact VHF 66A ahead of time for tie-up instructions upon approach. Reservations highly recommended

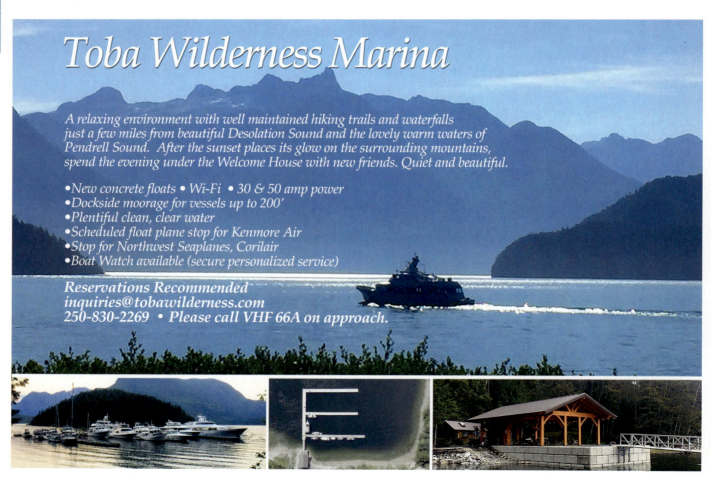

Toba Wilderness Marina

A relaxing environment with well maintained hiking trails and waterfalls just a few miles from beautiful Desolation Sound and the lovely warm waters of Pendrell Sound. After the sunset places its glow on the surrounding mountains, spend the evening under the Welcome House with new friends. Quiet and beautiful.

- New concrete floats • Wi-Fi • 30 & 50 amp power
- Dockside moorage for vessels up to 200'
- Plentiful clean, clear water
- Scheduled float plane stop for Kenmore Air
- Stop for Northwest Seaplanes, Corilair
- Boat Watch available (secure personalized service)

Reservations Recommended
inquiries@tobawilderness.com
250-830-2269 • Please call VHF 66A on approach.

See Area Map Page 318 - Maps Not for Navigation

DESOLATION SOUND & DISCOVERY PASSAGE

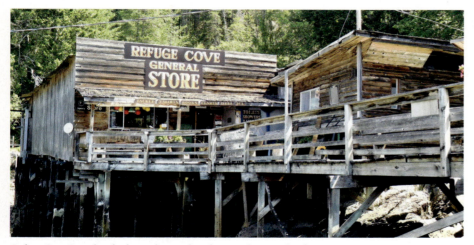

Refuge Cove Store has food, supplies, and a selection of marine hardware.

during July and August. This is a quiet marina, located behind Double Island at the mouth of Toba Inlet. The views up Toba Inlet are breathtaking. The marina has 1400 feet of moorage, on concrete floats, for vessels up to 200 feet. No requirement for rafting. Enjoy the attractive Welcome House located upland for afternoon and evening get-togethers. 5 km of hiking trails, Wi-Fi, free ice, washroom, showers, and garbage drop-off (1 bag only per day with overnight moorage). Abundant clean clear water is available on the dock, with 30 and 50 amp power. Scheduled float plane service available through Kenmore Air, NW Seaplanes, and Corilair. Secure long-term moorage and boat watch available. Please do not go into the water while hiking to the base of the falls, as this is the source of the marina's drinking water. This marina is not setup for day visits or tours. Overnight guests only please. Anchoring in the bay adjacent to the dock is not recommended.

Toba Inlet. Toba Inlet extends 20 miles into the 8,000-foot-high Coast Range mountains until it ends in drying flats at the mouth of the Toba River. The water is very deep right up to the rock wall shores. Look for two Native pictographs in Toba Inlet: one along the west shore 1 mile south of Brem Bay and another on the north shore 3.6 miles east of Brem Bay. Magnificent waterfalls crash into the sea, especially early in the season when the snowpack is rapidly melting. Toba Inlet reminds us of the inlets north of Cape Caution. Limited anchorage is possible at the head of the inlet, and in Brem Bay off the mouth of the Brem River. We observed a boat stern-tied in a small bight off the north shore near a river inlet at approximately 50°26'N/124°32'W.

Correspondent Gil Flanagan reported that he has anchored, stern-tied, on the northeast side of Brem Bay, at the mouth of a cove created by a rock breakwater not shown on the chart. The views were beautiful.

Toba Inlet's most dramatic waterfalls are on the south side of the inlet, about 3 miles past Snout Point, which is located opposite Brem Bay.

LEWIS CHANNEL

Lewis Channel runs between West Redonda Island and Cortes Island.

⑦ **Refuge Cove.** Refuge Cove, with a public marina, fuel dock, shops and well-stocked store, is a good resupply stop in the heart of Desolation Sound. The busiest times are between 11:00 a.m. and 3:00 p.m. For easiest moorage and fuel dock use, early morning and late afternoon are recommended. Several homes, joined by boardwalks, surround the cove. Ample moorage is available. A floating dock, just off the fuel dock, is for overflow moorage, with no power or water. Dogs should be on a leash. A pet path is beside the used-book stand. Anchorage is possible toward the head of the bay.

Traffic can be heavy during high season. Approach slowly, and wait your turn for dock space or fuel. Turnover is rapid; you shouldn't have to wait long. Refuge Cove is a scheduled stop for float plane service.

Garbage Barge: Around mid-June, an enterprising chap named Dave Cartwright moors a barge near the mouth of Refuge Cove. For a reasonable fee charged by the pound, he accepts bagged garbage and responsibly takes it away. If you have accumulated garbage from several days in Desolation Sound, this is one of the few places to dispose of it.

⑦ **Refuge Cove General Store.** General Delivery, Refuge Cove, BC V0P 1P0; (250) 935-6659; refcov@twincomm.ca; www.refugecove.com. Guest moorage along 2000 feet of side-tie dock space. No reservations; first-come, first-served. The fuel dock has gasoline, diesel, and propane. Washrooms, showers and laundry are up by the store. Free purified water, 15 amp power available during store hours, fee-based Wi-Fi.

The store carries groceries, fresh produce, deli items including cheeses and meats, hand-dipped ice cream, a complete liquor agency with interesting wine selections, some marine supplies and fishing gear, charts, cube and block ice, a good selection of books and magazines. It is also a post office. If Judith

Refuge Cove

Replenish
Refuel
Refresh
in the Heart of Desolation Sound

- Complete Groceries including Fresh Produce, Meats, Dairy Products, Deli
- Gas, Diesel, Oil, Propane
- Large Liquor & Wine Selection
- Block & Party Ice
- Showers, Laundry, Post Office
- Gifts, Books & Charts
- Fishing Tackle & Bait
- Espresso, Desserts, Burgers
- Wireless Internet
- Float Plane Service
- Moorage year-round & overnight
  – no reservations necessary
  – 4hr courtesy stopover

Seasonal Hours
June: 9am-5pm
July & Aug: 9am-6pm
Sept. 1-15: 9am-5pm

Winter Hours
Sept. 16 - May 31
1pm - 3pm M,W,F

Famous Friendly Service
250-935-6659
refcov@twincomm.ca

DESOLATION SOUND & DISCOVERY PASSAGE

See Area Map Page 318 - Maps Not for Navigation

Williams' delightful book, *Dynamite Stories*, is in stock, pick up a copy. The stories are a blast, literally. The store has limited operating hours in the fall.

Most businesses, including the art gallery and gift shop, are open June through August. The cafe has fresh bakery items; open for breakfast, lunch and dinner. Licensed for wine and beer with Happy Hour specials.

Teakerne Arm. Teakerne Arm is a deep inlet extending from Lewis Channel into West Redonda Island. Anchorage is just inside the entrance in Talbot Cove, or in front of the waterfall from Cassel Lake at the head of the north arm, or in the south arm. Both arms are deep, except very close to shore.

The area near the waterfall is a provincial park, with a dinghy float connected to shore by an aluminum ramp. Anchorage is in 90 to 150 feet. A cable in fair but serviceable condition hangs down the rock wall west of the waterfall for stern-ties. Several rings are set in the rock just above the high tide line and on either side of the dinghy dock. The waterfall is stunning, about 2½ stories high. Taking the short, vigorous hike from the dinghy float to Cassel Lake for a swim is a popular pastime. The water warms in the summer.

Talbot Cove. Talbot Cove is near the entrance to Teakerne Arm, on the south shore. The cove is marked with large yellow propane floats for a commercial operation. Anchor with a stern-tie in the southeast corner.

Gorge Harbour

CORTES ISLAND

Recommended book: Destination Cortez Island, by June Cameron, describes the early days on Cortes Island. In our opinion this book joins *The Curve of Time* as entertaining background reading about the B.C. coast. After reading *Destination Cortez Island* you will have an entirely different outlook about your explorations of Cortes Bay, Squirrel Cove, Von Donop Inlet, Whaletown, Gorge Harbour, Mansons Landing, and the entire Desolation Sound area.

Published in Canada by Heritage House and in the U.S. by Fine Edge Nautical Publishing.

⑧ **Squirrel Cove.** Squirrel Cove is made up of an outer bay and an inner bay. The outer bay provides access to the public wharf and the Squirrel Cove Trading Co. general store dock. The inner bay, consisting of two anchorage areas, has better protection and during the summer is often full of anchored boats. A saltwater lagoon is at the head of the inner bay. A connecting rapids runs into the lagoon at high tide and out of the lagoon at

HOW FRESH TOMATOES GET TO REFUGE COVE

Have you ever thought about how a remote marina like Refuge Cove can have such a well-stocked store with fresh produce? Boaters who come to cruise the Desolation Sound region know that the store at Refuge Cove will be ready for them, stocked with all the basics and even fresh produce. But how is it done? We discovered how on a recent visit to this cove of refuge, tucked along the western shore of West Redonda Island.

We stopped at the store in late May, hoping to resupply our galley with tomatoes and other fresh fruit. The storekeeper informed us that a shipment would be arriving that afternoon. Loading boxes of canned goods, along with breads and fresh produce can be a day-long task, especially with the added logistics of transporting supplies to an island. This realization prompted our questions — "Where do the supplies come from and how do you get them here?"

We got the full story that went something like this — We must first motor our barge across Lewis Channel to the public wharf at Squirrel Cove on Cortes Island, where a truck with a load of fresh supplies will be ready to meet us. The truck, of course, had to take the ferry from Campbell River on Vancouver Island to Quathiaski Cove on Quadra Island, then drive across Quadra Island to Heriot Bay to get on another ferry to Whaletown on Cortes Island, and then drive across Cortes Island to Squirrel Cove. Once we arrive at the public wharf at Squirrel Cove, we unload the truck and start stacking a makeshift sled with a yoke and rope that is used to carefully lower the sled, as it slides down the ramp to the dock below. We then start loading the barge, carefully stacking the boxes onto pallets for weight and balance. The process is repeated over and over again until all the boxes and produce have been unloaded from the truck. Then we are off once again, motoring across Lewis Channel in the hopes that the weather will hold for a safe crossing. Back at Refuge Cove, we pull the barge alongside the dock underneath a hoist, where the pallets of supplies are lifted up to the storefront. But we're not done yet, everything must be stacked neatly on the store shelves and arranged in baskets for that added customer appeal.

After hearing their story, we came to more fully appreciate the effort it takes to keep a remote island store stocked with goods throughout the busy cruising season. So next time you bite into that perfectly ripe tomato at Refuge Cove, think about how far that tomato traveled to get there – then slice, dice and enjoy.

[Lorena Landon]

low tide. Be sure to plan an exit strategy if you enter the lagoon by dinghy.

The Cove Restaurant, with a take-out menu, is located upland; open daily beginning the second weekend in June. Seating is available in the licensed restaurant, or sit out on the deck and enjoy the lovely view.

A farmers market is held Sundays from 11:00 a.m. to 3:00 p.m.

At one time the inner bay was used for log booming. The late June Cameron wrote an article in Pacific Yachting telling of a tangle of sunken logs on the bottom. Our side-scan sounder showed the bay filled with logs scattered like matchsticks.

In 2019, a Waggoner reader reported fouling their anchor in fish-farm debris at position 50°8.0467'N/124°55.5680'W, about where Chart 3554 shows a fish-farm.

A trail leads from the northwest corner of Squirrel Cove to Von Donop Inlet.

The large building on the west shore is a Native Cultural Centre and offices.

No Discharge Zone. Gray water okay.

⑧ **Squirrel Cove Public Dock.** (Harbour Authority of Cortes Island), Box 329, Manson's Landing, B.C., V0P 1K0; (250) 293-0007; www.cortesharbours.ca; hacimgr@gmail.com. Open all year with 200 feet of floating dock that is often filled with local boats. First-come, first-served; commercial vessels have priority. There's always room for the dinghy. Rafting is encouraged. 15, 20, & 30 amp power. Self-registration and payment at the honor box located at the head of the ramp or pay with credit card, or Paypal at the Harbour Authority website. Garbage drop for a fee (cash).

The dock is close to the Squirrel Cove Trading Co. store and The Cove Restaurant. A full-time diver is nearby for maintenance and recovery, phone number posted at the dock.

At very low tides the ramps from the wharf to the floats are quite steep. Local boats often take much of the dock space, although by being patient we've found room. A public mooring ball is available in front of the store.

⑧ **Squirrel Cove Trading Co. Ltd.** P.O. Box 1, Squirrel Cove, BC V0P 1T0; (250) 935-6327; squirrelcovetrading@yahoo.ca; www.squirrelcove.com. Open all year. Washrooms, showers and laundry are in a separate building just west of the store. Potable water at the dock. Gasoline, diesel, propane and kerosene available upland. Gas and diesel available at the dock via hoses from the upland pumps. The dock is 6 feet below the local tide chart and only accessible at high tides, plan accordingly. Plans are in the works to extend the guest fuel dock beginning in 2020. Picnic tables available.

Liquor, ice and an assortment of groceries; limited selection of fresh items. Books, marine hardware, post office, pay phone, Wi-Fi, ATM. The expanded hardware section downstairs has just about anything a person might need.

A crafts shop and gallery is next to the store, stocked with island-made (or designed) goods and clothing. Artists take turns staffing the shop. A Sunday market, with crafts, local produce, baked goods and musicians, runs from 11:00 a.m. to 3:00 p.m., summers only.

⑨ **Cortes Bay.** Cortes Bay is well protected, but in some places the soft mud bottom doesn't hold well. Use Chart 3538 when approaching. Several charted rocks and reefs near the entrance have claimed the inattentive. These include Central Rock, north of Twin Islands, several rocks around Three Islets, and a rock off the headland midway between Mary Point and the entrance to Cortes Bay. To be safe, we always pass south of Three Islets.

Pay close attention to the beacon in the middle of the narrow entry to Cortes Bay. This beacon, with its red triangle dayboard, marks the south end of a nasty reef. Leave the beacon to starboard (Red, Right, Returning) as you enter. If you doubt the existence of this reef, one look at low tide will convince you. A small public wharf is at the head of Cortes Bay. It is usually full during the summer. Rafting is required.

Seattle Yacht Club has an outstation on the south shore of Cortes Bay, at the location of a former marina. Royal Vancouver Yacht Club has an outstation on the north shore. No reciprocals at either outstation.

Local knowledge says good holding ground is east of the Royal Van outstation, off the mouth of a small drying cove. During a 30- to 40-knot southeasterly blow, we saw several boats anchored successfully off the SYC outstation as well.

No Discharge Zone. Gray water okay.

Twin Islands. Twin Islands, located off the southeast side of Cortes Island, are really a single island divided by a drying spit. Anchorage is possible close to the drying spit on either side.

Sutil Point. Sutil Point is the south end of Cortes Island. A long, drying spit dotted with boulders extends south from the point, almost to buoy Q20. Give this buoy plenty of sea room.

A fresh southeast wind, especially if it is blowing against an ebb current (see Point Atkinson tides), will set up high steep seas south of Sutil Point and east past Mitlenatch Island. Sutil Point can be dangerous in a southeasterly.

Smelt Bay Provincial Park. One mile north of Sutil Point on the west side of the peninsula. Good temporary anchorage is close to shore. The park has 23 campsites, picnic tables, and a white sand beach.

⑩ **Mansons Landing.** Mansons Landing on Manson Bay, located on the south side of Cortes Island has good anchorage, a public dock, a marine park, a lagoon, and a community village one mile from the public dock. The east shore of Manson Bay, the uplands and the lagoon to the east, are all part of the Mansons Landing Marine Park. The public dock also on the east shore provides access to the park and the road to the village. Anchorage is good north of the public dock. The entire area is exposed to the south.

The one mile walk to the village is uphill on a very lightly traveled road. The village has a well stocked co-op grocery store with a wide selection of organic foods and a café with Wi-Fi. The post office, community center, and take-out restaurant with outdoor seating, and a small store are across from the co-op. A small museum and visitor information center, housed in the historic Mansons Landing store building, are beyond the community center on the road to the west. A farmers market is held Fridays from 12:00 p.m. to 3:00 p.m at Mansons Hall Community Center (250-935-

Uganda Passage

DESOLATION SOUND & DISCOVERY PASSAGE

See Area Map Page 318 - Maps Not for Navigation

Explore the coves and lagoon in Von Donop Inlet on Cortes Island.

0015). Don't miss the homemade pies and rootbeer floats at the community center cafe.
No Discharge Zone. Gray water okay.

⑩ **Mansons Landing Marine Park.** Open all year, 117 acres. The park has no dock of its own, but can be reached from the Mansons Landing public dock, or you can anchor out. Hague Lake, with warm water and swimming beaches safe for small children, is a 10-minute walk from the public dock. The lagoon reportedly has clams and oysters.

⑩ **Mansons Landing Public Dock.** (Harbour Authority of Cortes Island), Box 329, Manson's Landing, B.C., V0P 1K0; (250) 293-0007; www.cortesharbours.ca; hacimgr@gmail.com. Open all year with a 240 foot float that is often filled with local boats. First-come, first-served; commercial vessels have priority. 20 & 30 amp power. First hour is free; up to 4 hours are at half-rate; thereafter, full-rate; rates apply to dinghies. Self-registration and payment in the honor box at the head of the ramp, or pay by credit card on their website. Garbage drop for a fee (cash). North end of the float is reserved for floatplane and load/unload.

⑪ **Gorge Harbour** is a large bay with many good spots to put the hook down. The entry is through a narrow cleft in the rock cliff. Orange-colored Native pictographs, including a stick figure man, a man on what appears to be a turtle or fish, and several vertical lines, are on the rock wall to port as you enter. You have to look closely to identify them. Current runs through the entrance, but boats go through at any time. Inside you'll find good, protected anchorage. Several aquaculture operations are in the harbour. A field of private buoys is to port. The Gorge Harbour Marina Resort, on the northwest shore, has many amenities, including a restaurant. If the marina is full, anchor in the protected bay in 55 to 60 feet.
No Discharge Zone. Gray water okay.

⑪ **Gorge Harbour Marina Resort.** P.O. Box 89, Whaletown, BC V0P 1Z0; (250) 935-6433 ext. 4; moorage@gorgeharbour.com; www.gorgeharbour.com. Monitors VHF 66A. Open all year, gasoline and diesel at the fuel dock, guest moorage along 1800 feet of dock. Reservations are recommended May 15 to September 15; held-back moorage space is released daily at 4:00 p.m., first-come, first-served. Facilities include 30 & 50 amp power, water, swimming pool, hot tub, barbecue areas, washrooms, showers, laundry, Wi-Fi, pay phones. A well-stocked convenience store has fresh vegetables, meats, dairy products, liquor, ice, propane, DVD movie rentals. Four lodge rooms and a poolside cottage for rent. Garbage disposal is available for marina guests for a fee, no charge for recycling. Complete recycling instructions available. Dock staff will pick up garbage by your boat twice a day for a fee. The resort has an RV park, 2 trailer rentals, campground, lodge accommodations, and float plane service. Boats, kayaks, stand-up paddleboards, and cars for rent.

The resort features a pool and hot tub surrounded by attractive landscaping. A patio with a fireplace and barbecue area are available for guest use. Both overlook the harbor. Live music is often performed in the evening on the patio. There is an elaborate children's play area. Many boaters consider Gorge Harbour Marina & Resort to be on the list of special destinations. The Gorge Harbour Marina farmer's market is open from 10 a.m. to 1:00 p.m. on Saturdays during summer. Anchored guests are welcome to use the resort facilities; passes for use of the pool are available at the store for a fee.

The Floathouse Restaurant always gets excellent reviews. The atmosphere is cozy and conducive to multi-table conversations. Open from May through September, with reduced hours in winter. During peak season the restaurant offers breakfast, lunch, tapas (3:00p.m. to 5:00p.m.), dinner and a Sunday brunch. Espresso and pastries at the bar all day long. Year after year, they have a great chef. The restaurant has two areas, one part is covered with a bar and cocktail area; the other part is open with seating overlooking the harbor. Restaurant reservations recommended in the high season, outdoor seating can be requested.

⑪ **Gorge Harbour Public Dock.** (Harbour Authority of Cortes Island), Box 329, Manson's Landing, B.C., V0P 1K0; (250) 293-0007; www.cortesharbours.ca; hacimgr@gmail.com. Located a short distance east of the Gorge Harbour Marina. Open all year with a 100 foot float that is often filled with local boats. First-come, first-served; commercial vessels have priority. Self-registration and payment honor box at the head of the ramp, or pay by credit card on their website. Garbage drop for a fee (cash). Boat launch ramp located adjacent to the dock.

Uganda Passage. Uganda Passage separates Cortes Island from Marina Island. The pass is narrow and winding, but well marked and easy to navigate as long as you pay attention. Red, Right, Returning assumes you are returning from the south. See the Uganda Passage map showing the route through the passage. Shark Spit is long and low, with a superb sand beach. Swimming is good. Anchorage is south of the pass, on either the Cortes Island side or the Marina Island side.

Whaletown. Whaletown is the terminus of the ferry between Cortes Island and Quadra Island. The ferry dock is on the north side of the bay, and a 200-foot public float is on the south side. Watch for several marked and unmarked rocks, normally covered by kelp. The public float is mostly taken up by local boats. First hour free; stays up to 4 hours at half rate; stays over 4 hours at full day rate. Self-registration and payment box located on the wharf at the head of the ramp.

Subtle Islands. The two Subtle Islands are separated by a drying shoal. Good anchorage is off this shoal on the east side, particularly in settled weather. The little bay on the north side is very deep except at the head. It has a lovely (and exposed) view to the north. The islands are privately owned and marked with "stay off" and "keep away" signs.

Coulter Bay. Coulter Bay is pretty, but as the chart indicates, much of the bay is too shallow for anchoring. Most of the good spots are taken by local boats. You could anchor in the tiny nook behind Coulter Island, beside a little unnamed islet to the west. Some cabins are nearby, but they are screened from view.

Carrington Bay. Carrington Bay is pretty, and well protected except from the north. The bottom is rocky so be sure your anchor is properly set before turning in for the night. Carrington Lagoon, at the head of the bay, is interesting to explore. You can portage a kayak across the logs that choke the entrance to the lagoon. The late June Cameron, in *Destination Cortez*, says the lagoon entrance was blasted out of rock. A foot-bridge now crosses the entrance.

A good anchorage is to the right, near the

entrance to the lagoon, with a stern-tie ashore. We've seen other boats anchored in the little bight a short distance to the left of the lagoon entrance and behind the tiny island just off the eastern shore of the bay. The best anchorage is in the lee of Jane Islet or in the lee of the 58-meter islet.

No Discharge Zone. Gray water okay.

Quartz Bay. Quartz Bay is unusually pretty, with good holding bottom. The eastern cove of the bay has several homes and a few private docks along the shoreline. You can anchor with swinging room in 30 to 42 feet near the head, but you're in their front yards. The western cove has some aquaculture, one cabin on the shore, and anchoring depths near the south and west shores. You may have to run a stern-tie to shore. It is exposed to north winds, but it's a nice spot.

LOCAL KNOWLEDGE

DANGEROUS ROCK: About halfway into Von Donop Inlet, a rock lies in the narrowest part of the channel. Look for two prominent rock outcroppings covered with lichen, moss and grass on the left side of the channel. The rock is opposite the second, or inner, of these outcroppings. Hug the right side and keep that rock to port, even if tree branches try to brush the starboard side of the boat or rigging.

⑫ **Von Donop Inlet.** Von Donop Inlet, on the northwest tip of Cortes Island, is a 3 mile long landlocked inlet entirely within the Hathayim Provincial Marine Park. The inlet is entered through a 2-mile long channel with a narrow neck mid-way along the channel. Caution at the neck for rocks in the middle of the channel; hug the south side of the channel. Best entry and exit is at high-water slack. Once inside, several coves provide protected anchorage. The largest of these coves takes up the entire head of the inlet and has room for many boats. The bottom in this area is sticky mud. It is ideal for holding, but requires extra cleaning time when departing. The lagoon at the northeast end of the inlet can be explored by dinghy at high-water slack. The outlet of this lagoon has reversing tidal overfalls. All of the uplands are park lands. Several maintained trails lead from the head of the Inlet to the lagoon, lakes, Squirrel Cove, and a longer trail leads to the road to Squirrel Cove Store and Gorge Harbour. The trailhead is on the southeast shore at the head of the inlet.

See Area Map Page 318 - Maps Not for Navigation

⑫ **Háthayim Provincial Marine Park (Von Donop).** This 3155-acre park includes Von Donop Inlet, Robertson Lake and Wiley Lake.

Read Island. The east side of Read Island is indented from the south by **Evans Bay**, where several little notches are worth exploring as anchorages. Most have drying flats at their heads. **Bird Cove** is probably the best protected, although Tom Kincaid has spent a quiet night behind the little islets in the bay just to the north of Bird Cove. A small public float is near the entrance to Evans Bay.

Hill Island. Hill Island is privately owned. According to Sailing Directions, a private lodge with a floating breakwater is in Totem Bay. The island is not open to the public.

Burdwood Bay. Burdwood Bay has several possible anchorages, particularly on the lee side of the little islands that extend from the south side of the bay, and in a notch in the north end. Burdwood Bay is not particularly pretty, but could be a hideout in a storm.

Hoskyn Channel. Hoskyn Channel runs between Read Island and Quadra Island and connects at the north with Whiterock Passage and Surge Narrows.

Bold Island Anchorage. Bold Island is just north of Village Bay on the west side of Hoskyn Channel. Enter through Crescent Channel. Anchorage is in the basin at the northwest corner of Bold Island, approximately between the two drying reefs. Two oyster farms are in the area with one along the northwest shore of Bold Island. The bay opens to the south with views across Read Island. The anchorage might be exposed to southerlies.

Hjorth Bay. Hjorth Bay, on Hoskyn Channel along the west side of Read Island, is a good anchorage except in a strong southerly. Anchor in 50 to 60 feet, probably with a stern-tie to shore. A small cabin is on shore behind the island.

DESOLATION SOUND & DISCOVERY PASSAGE

Whiterock Passage. Whiterock Passage is narrow, and the dredged channel is bounded on both sides by drying shoals studded with angry boulders. Least depth at zero tide is 5 feet. Maximum currents are 2 knots. Running Whiterock Passage at half tide is a good idea—it exposes the shoals on both sides but provides a little extra depth. The uninitiated tend to avoid Whiterock Passage, but it's easy to run if you pay attention and know how. Here's how:

Carefully study Plans Chart 3537 or Chartbook 3312, both of which detail Whiterock Passage at a scale of 1:10,000. As the charts show, two ranges are on the Read Island side of the passage. Going either direction, one will be a leading range as you enter, and the other a back range as you depart. Approaching, find the leading range and stay exactly on it. Proceed slowly and watch astern as the back range comes into view. When the back range lines up, turn the appropriate direction and let the back range keep you on course as you complete your transit.

Remember that the course lines on the charts are true, not magnetic. You must subtract the magnetic variation from the true heading to get the magnetic course. Before entering, make sure you have a clear view astern from the helm to view the back range markers.

Rendezvous Islands. The Rendezvous Islands have a number of homes along their shores. Anchorage may be possible in a bight between the southern and middle islands, but a private float and dolphins restrict the room available.

CALM CHANNEL

Calm Channel connects Lewis Channel and Sutil Channel to the south, and with Bute Inlet and the Yuculta Rapids to the north. It is appropriately named, often being wind-free when areas nearby are breezy.

Frances Bay. A logging road and logging dump area are located on the westerly side at the head of the bay, indicating past logging operations. In 2017, no logging operations were observed and boats were seen anchored at the head of the bay in the eastern portion. It has been reported that the bottom is rocky throughout the rest of the bay and an anchor fouling cable is near the log dump.

Church House. Church House is an abandoned Indian Reserve opposite the entrance to Hole in the Wall on Calm Channel, and near the mouth of Bute Inlet. The white-painted church, an often-photographed landmark, has collapsed in a heap.

Redonda Bay. Redonda Bay has the ruins of an old wharf left over from logging days, but otherwise is not a good anchorage. The wharf is no longer usable and the ramp leading from the float to the wharf is gone. Several rocks in the bay are charted.

Bute Inlet. Bute Inlet, approximately 35 miles long, is very deep. Except in small areas near the

Quiet anchorage in Octopus Islands Marine Park, northwest of the northerly narrow entrance channel

2020 WAGGONER CRUISING GUIDE

DESOLATION SOUND & DISCOVERY PASSAGE

See Area Map Page 318 - Maps Not for Navigation

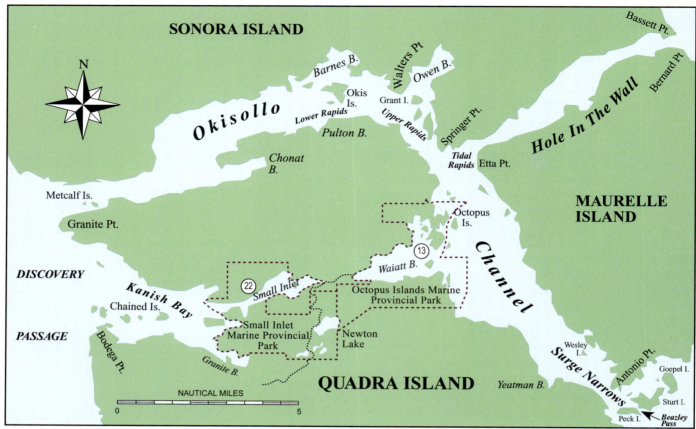

Okisollo Channel

mouths of rivers and at the head of the inlet, it is not good for anchorage. Usually, the bottom drops away steeply, making a stern-tie to shore necessary. Anchorages should be chosen with an eye to strong inflow winds during the afternoon, followed by calm, then by icy outflow winds in the morning. Correspondents Gil and Karen Flanagan explain:

"The glaciers around Bute Inlet were melting and there are a lot of them. The water was milky by Stuart Island, and got darker and darker the farther up we went, turning from light green to gray to brownish. We saw considerable drift, including complete trees with roots sticking 8 feet or so into the air. At times we had to slow to idle, shift to neutral and coast through bands of drift. Jack Mold, the caretaker at Southgate Camp, said what we experienced was normal. Waddington Harbour, at the head of Bute Inlet, has a lot of good anchoring spots in 10 to 50 foot depths. We anchored as close to the northeast shore as we could get, and still were at least 100 yards from the beach (don't bother trying to stern-tie). There is no protection from wind, but we had no wind. We didn't see much driftwood on the beach, either. We doubt if inflow winds blow hard or long, probably because even on hot days the massive ice fields in the mountains above preclude high land temperatures.

Because of the ice fields, we had an overnight low in the upper 40s on September 1. It was 10 to 20 degrees lower than temperatures we had been experiencing in Desolation Sound. The morning air was cold enough that we needed heavy coats, even in the sun.

Mountains 6,000 to 7,000 feet high rise directly from the head of the inlet. They have snowfields, and are spectacular.

The milky water, drifting logs, huge harbor and high mountains create an environment that felt wild and different from anywhere we have been on the coast. We spent only 19 hours in Waddington Harbour, which wasn't long enough to take the dinghy up either river. We did see a grizzly bear on the beach near our anchorage. We definitely will go back." [*Flanagan*]

Reader Richard McBride sent a note about a tiny anchorage he calls "The Nook," just outside Orford Bay:

"It is a small crack in the mountain wall about 100 feet wide at the opening and about 150 feet deep, with a little waterfall at the head. This is a terrific spot for a couple of small boats to tuck in. Lat/lon 50°34.368'N/124°52.439'W."

OKISOLLO CHANNEL/ SURGE NARROWS

Owen Bay tides and Okisollo Channel Secondary Port tide corrections are contained in Canadian Tide and Current Tables Vol. 6, and Ports and Passes. Okisollo Channel runs along the east and north sides of Quadra Island, from Surge Narrows to Discovery Passage.

Surge Narrows & Beazley Passage. Surge Narrows and Beazley Passage should be run at or near slack water. Spring floods set eastward to 12 knots and ebbs set westward

Middle entrance to Waiatt Bay in Octopus Islands Marine Park

See Area Map Page 318 - Maps Not for Navigation **DESOLATION SOUND & DISCOVERY PASSAGE**

Anchorage can be found on the Drew Harbour side of Rebecca Spit Provincial Marine Park, with dinghy access to the long beaches.

to 10 knots. Current predictions are shown under Beazley Passage in the Canadian Tide and Current Tables Vol. 6, and Ports and Passes.

Although Beazley Passage, between Peck Island and Sturt Island, has the strongest currents in the Surge Narrows area, it is the preferred route between Hoskyn Channel and Okisollo Channel. Especially on an ebb current in Beazley Passage, watch for Tusko Rock, which dries at 5 feet, on the east side of the pass at the north end. Stay well clear of Tusko Rock.

Sailing Directions says the duration of slack at Surge Narrows varies between 5 and 11 minutes. The passage north of the Settler's Group is useable following the deeper channel, avoiding the charted rocks and shoals.

⑬ **Octopus Islands Marine Park.** This is a beautiful, popular anchorage and exploration area, wonderfully protected. The park includes all of Waiatt Bay, the uplands south of Waiatt Bay, and all but the two large islands in the Octopus Islands group. The two islands charted on Chart 3539 as 50 meter and 71 meter islands are private and not part of the park. Octopus Islands Marine Park was expanded and Chart 3539 shows its present boundaries. Much of the upland areas to the north of Waiatt Bay are not part of the park and are private property.

You can enter Waiatt Bay from Okisollo Channel with care for the rocks, but the usual entry is by a narrow channel from the north. Anchor in Waiatt Bay or any of several coves in the Octopus Islands group and run a stern-tie to shore. At the end of the narrow channel as you enter from the north, a rock, clearly shown on Plans Chart 3537, obstructs part of the entry to the first cove on the right. This rock is easily seen as a white smear under the water.

Waiatt Bay. Waiatt Bay is broad and protected, with convenient anchoring depths throughout. The entire bay is part of the Octopus Islands Marine Park. The bay's entrance is choked with islets and rocks, and Sailing Directions (written for large vessels) warns against entering. With the aid of large scale Plans Chart 3537, however, a small boat can pick its way in along the south shore, or in the middle of the islets, or along the north shore. The chart shows the possibilities. You might anchor in a notch along the shore, or at the head of the bay.

A half-mile easy trail connects the head of Waiatt Bay with Small Inlet. About half way between Waiatt Bay and Small Inlet, a sign points the way to Newton Lake with a less traveled trail branching to the northwest. Follow the Newton Lake sign direction, which also takes you to Small Inlet. A trail sign at the head of the cove in Small Inlet marks the end of the trail between Waiatt Bay and Small Inlet. From here, the trail to Newton Lake follows the south shore of Small Inlet cove before becoming difficult and steep. It is one mile from the trail head at Small Inlet cove to Newton Lake. Don't confuse a small pond, a short distance before Newton Lake, for the real thing. The crystal clear waters of Newton Lake invite a fresh water swim. From Newton Lake a two-mile trail continues to Granite Bay Road and Granite Bay.

Hole in the Wall. Hole in the Wall connects Okisollo Channel with Calm Channel to the east. Boats accumulate on each side of the rapids at the western entrance to Hole in the Wall, waiting for slack water. In general, boats on the upstream side will catch the last of the fair current when the rapids calm down, leaving room for the boats on the other side to pick up the new fair current in the opposite direction. Slacks occur 50 to 55 minutes before Seymour Narrows, and last about 4 minutes (Seymour Narrows currents are shown in Canadian Tide and Current Tables Vol. 6, and Ports and Passes). The flood current sets northeast. Maximum currents run to 12 knots on the flood and 10 knots on the ebb.

LOCAL KNOWLEDGE

DANGEROUS CURRENTS: Upper Rapids and Lower Rapids in Okisollo Channel can be dangerous and should be run at or near slack. Slacks occur 50 to 55 minutes before slack at Seymour Narrows.

Upper Rapids. These are the first rapids in Okisollo Channel north of Hole in the Wall, and they are dangerous unless run at or near slack water. Slack occurs 55 minutes before Seymour Narrows (Seymour Narrows currents are shown in Canadian Tide and Current Tables Vol. 6, and Ports and Passes). At full rush on a spring tide, the rapids running at 9 knots are frightening to watch. A wall of white water stretches nearly across the channel almost until slack. When it's time to go through, steer a little east of mid-channel to avoid Bentley Rock. Chart 3537 makes the course clear.

Barnes Bay and several small indents in this part of Okisollo Channel could be good anchorages, except for the large amount of log booming and aquaculture. Owen Bay is the preferred anchorage.

LOCAL KNOWLEDGE

STRONG CURRENTS: Currents run strong through the islands that separate Owen Bay from Upper Rapids. If you explore these islands, exercise caution to avoid getting sucked into the rapids.

Heriot Bay

2020 WAGGONER CRUISING GUIDE

DESOLATION SOUND & DISCOVERY PASSAGE   *See Area Map Page 318 - Maps Not for Navigation*

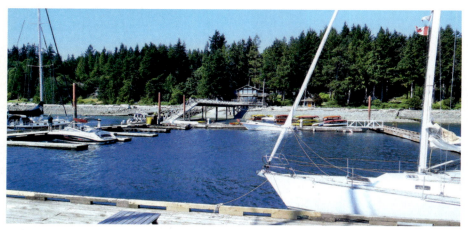
Taku Resort and Marina has nice views of Rebecca Spit Marine Park.

Owen Bay. Owen Bay is large and pretty. Our recommended anchorage is in the second little notch on the west side of the bay. This notch is quite protected, and has room for about 5 boats if the spots are well chosen and stern-ties are used. Enter Owen Bay through a narrow channel between Walters Point and Grant Island. A reef, marked by kelp, extends from Walters Point nearly halfway across this channel. It will inspire you to hug the Grant Island side. Correspondent Pat Shera adds that there is good holding and shelter near the small public float on the east side of the bay. Shera also says that the northeastern head of Owen Bay has "acres of good holding on a flat bottom." That area, however, is subject to being hit by strong (and cold) outflow winds from Bute Inlet. He was "kissed by the Bute" one sleepless night and knows what he's talking about.

Lower Rapids. Lower Rapids turns at virtually the same time as Upper Rapids—55 minutes before Seymour Narrows (Seymour Narrows currents are shown in Canadian Tide and Current Tables Vol. 6, and Ports and Passes). Currents run to 9 knots on spring tides, and you must steer a course to avoid Gypsy Shoal, which lies nearly in the middle. Transit at slack water only.

We recommend avoiding Lower Rapids altogether by going through Barnes Bay, north of the Okis Islands. At times other than slack you will still see considerable current, but you will avoid the hazards of Lower Rapids.

Barnes Bay. Barnes Bay and several small indents in this part of Okisollo Channel could be good anchorages, except for the fair amount of aquaculture. Anchorage may be possible to the west in **Chonat Bay** and in the notch behind **Metcalf Island**.

QUADRA ISLAND, SOUTH

⑭ **Drew Harbour/Rebecca Spit Marine Park.** Drew Harbour is large, and in the right winds the open harbor can be lumpy. The preferred anchorage is in the bight immediately inside the north tip of Rebecca Spit. A drying shoal defines the south side of this bight. The shoal extends a considerable distance from shore, and it could fool you at high tide.

If the preferred bight is full, anchor south of the drying shoal in 24 to 36 feet, although it isn't as protected. Rebecca Spit Marine Park is popular. The Drew Harbour side of the spit has a lovely sand beach. Trails with picnic tables run the length of the spit. The exposed Sutil Channel side has a beach of remarkable small round boulders.

Bill Wolferstan's cruising guide to Desolation Sound contains an excellent section describing silvered tree snags on the spit, the result of subsidence during a 1946 earthquake. Wolferstan also describes the mounded fortifications, thought to be defenses built 200 to 400 years ago by the local Salish tribe against attacks from the Native Kwakiutl.

⑮ **Heriot Bay.** Heriot Bay has a public wharf, a supermarket, the Heriot Bay Inn & Marina, and the Taku Resort. During the summer high season the public dock usually is full with boats rafted several deep. Anchorage area north of the public wharf is filled with private mooring balls. Transient anchorage is found further east in 50 to 60 feet of water. The Heriot Bay Inn & Marina is between the ferry dock and the public dock. Just south of Heriot Bay, in Drew Harbour proper, Taku Resort has excellent docks and facilities. Heriot Bay Tru-Value Foods, a short walk from the Heriot Bay or Taku resorts, is the best-stocked grocery store in Desolation Sound, with complete groceries, including fresh vegetables and meats, a post office, gift shop, and liquor store; Java Bay Cafe is located in the same building. Free grocery delivery to the docks from Tru-Value Grocery (250) 285-2436. Bicycles can be rented from a shop on the road above Taku Resort. The Quadra Island Golf Course is a short ride away.

⑮ **Heriot Bay Public Wharf.** (250) 285-3622; www.qiha.ca. Open all year, 670 feet of dock space, power, water, portable toilets, Wi-Fi, garbage drop, launch ramp. The docks have recently been rebuilt. Watch for ferry wash on the outer face. Heriot Bay Inn and shopping nearby. The dock is managed by the Quadra Island Harbour Authority.

⑮ **Heriot Bay Inn & Marina.** P.O. Box 100, Heriot Bay, BC V0P 1H0; (250) 285-3322; (888) 605-4545; info@heriotbayinn.com; www.heriotbayinn.com. Monitors VHF 66A. Open all year, gasoline, diesel, propane, ice and fishing tackle. Guest moorage available on 1800 feet of side-tie dock, mostly 15 amp power with some 30 amp, washrooms, showers, laundry, limited Wi-Fi. Reservations recommended June through September. Fairways between the finger floats are narrow, larger vessels should 'starboard-tie' on the outside of Float 1. The outer docks and fuel dock are subject to wakes from passing ferries.

The hotel is delightful. This 1913 historic hotel has ten rooms, three cabins, and a suite. The restaurant has outdoor seating overlooking the bay, and the pub has live music on many nights. The gift store off the lobby has local guidebooks, local artisan jewelry, crafts, and souvenirs. The office can provide contact information for local tours and fishing guides. Heriot Bay Tru-Value Foods is a short walk up the hill. Bicycle and kayak rentals nearby.

In 2008 a group of 20 Quadra Island residents ("old hippies," one of them said) bought the property and set about making improvements. Among them they had all the needed skills: carpentry, electrical, painting, administrative, whatever else was required. In recent years the Heriot Bay Inn's public

See Area Map Page 318 - Maps Not for Navigation   **DESOLATION SOUND & DISCOVERY PASSAGE**

April Point marina, with ample side-tie moorage, is a short dinghy ride to the Resort Lodge and Spa.

areas have been upgraded with lovely flower beds and walkways. The goal of this working community is to maintain the property with the spirit of welcoming the traveling public.

⑮ **Taku Resort & Marina.** P.O. Box 1, Heriot Bay, BC V0P 1H0; (250) 285-3031; info@takuresort.com; www.takuresort.com. Monitors VHF 66A. Open all year. The docks have 30 & 50 amp power, potable water and Wi-Fi. Washrooms, coin showers, laundry and a 14-room resort are ashore, as are RV sites, tennis, volleyball, badminton and horseshoes. The docks are exposed to southeast winds across the bay, but the inside moorage is protected. The views and proximity to Rebecca Spit Marine Park make this a popular marina. A shopping center and Tru-Value Foods grocery store is a short walk away. A kayak tour operator is on site and a bicycle rental store is just up the road. The resort offers kayak, paddleboard rentals, and cooking classes. The facilities and service are high quality. Lynden McMartin is the manager.

DISCOVERY PASSAGE

Discovery Passage is approximately 20 miles long, and separates Quadra Island and Sonora Island from Vancouver Island. It is the main route for commercial traffic north and south along the east side of Vancouver Island. Cape Mudge is the south entrance to Discovery Passage. At the north end, Discovery Passage connects with Johnstone Strait at Chatham Point. An enormous amount of water flows through Discovery Passage, flooding south and ebbing north. Tide-rips are frequent.

Cape Mudge. The area around Cape Mudge and Wilby Shoals is a famous hot spot for salmon fishing and often full of small fishing craft during the summer months. Several resorts in the area cater to sport fishermen. Guides are available for hire in Campbell River.

On a flood tide, a backeddy often sets up at Cape Mudge running north along the western edge of Wilby Shoals all the way to the Cape Mudge Lighthouse.

LOCAL KNOWLEDGE

TIDE-RIPS: A strong southeasterly wind blowing against a large, south-flowing flood tide can set up high and dangerous seas. Lives have been lost off Cape Mudge in such conditions. Cape Mudge, at the south end of Quadra Island, has been a graveyard for vessels of all sizes, particularly in the winter months. If a southeaster is blowing, Sailing Directions recommends entering at or after high water slack. Good advice.

Yaculta. The First Nations settlement of Yaculta, located on Quadra Island, is the site of the Nuyumbalees Cultural Centre, with its splendid collection of potlatch regalia and historical artifacts and photos. Open 7 days

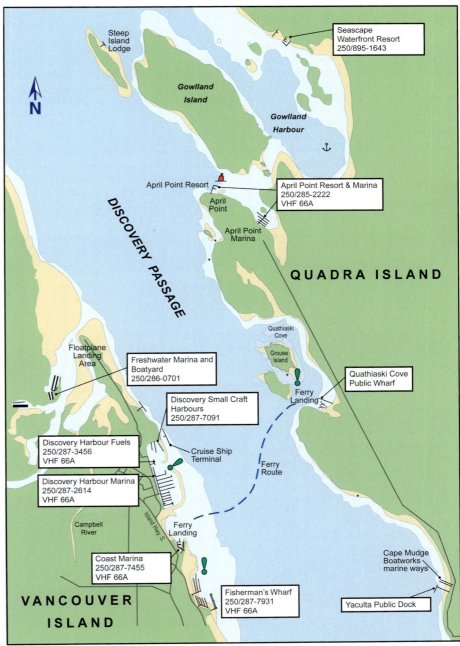
Campbell River

2020 WAGGONER CRUISING GUIDE   331

DESOLATION SOUND & DISCOVERY PASSAGE

See Area Map Page 318 - Maps Not for Navigation

a week, May to September. The Centre is a 3-block walk south from the public dock. We urge a visit. **Cape Mudge Boatworks** (250) 285-2155 is located here. They have a large marine ways and often work on recreational boats.

Yaculta Public Dock. Located at 50°01.4'N on the east side of Discovery Passage, next to the Cape Mudge Boatworks marine ways. Public dock with 220 feet of float; 30 amp power and water. No charge. Not recommended for overnight stays, exposed to winds and boat wakes, use at your own risk. Near the Yaculta village and the Nuyumbalees Cultural Centre. Moorage space on the more protected inside of the floats is normally occupied by local boats.

⑯ **Quathiaski Cove.** Quathiaski Cove (known locally as Q-Cove) is the Quadra Island landing for the ferry to Campbell River. A public dock is next to the ferry landing and may be rolly from ferry wakes and passing vessels. A seasonal snack stand is in the ferry parking lot; a pub and restaurant are a short walk away. A shopping center with a good grocery store, a tasty informal café, pizza restaurant, bank with an ATM, and a variety of stores to peruse are a few blocks up the hill from the ferry landing. The grocery store will deliver to the dock. The Visitor Centre is next to the bank. A farmers market adjacent to the Visitor Centre is open Saturday mornings during the summer months.

Because of ferry traffic, the best anchorage is farther north in the cove behind Grouse Island. Fingers of current from Discovery Passage work into Quathiaski Cove at some stages of the tide, so be sure the anchor is well set.

⑯ **Quathiaski Cove Public Wharf.** (250) 285-3622; www.qiha.ca. Adjacent to the ferry landing. The dock has 20, 30 & 50 amp power, water, Wi-Fi, pay telephone, and launch ramp. Above the dock are washrooms and shower facilities, with a number to call for the keycode after hours. The dock has considerable mooring space, but we often find it crowded with local and commercial fish boats. Commercial fish boats have priority. South side of the south float is for seine fishing vessels. Managed by the Quadra Island Harbour Authority.

⑰ **April Point Resort, Spa & Marina**. P.O. Box 381 Quathiaski Cove, BC V0P 1N0; (250) 285-2222 x264; marina@northcoasthotelresort.com; www.aprilpoint.com. Monitors VHF 66A. Resort and spa open mid-May to October, moorage open all year. The resort lodge and spa are located at April Point and the marina is located in the cove a half mile southeast. The marina has moorage for vessels up to 200 feet, Wi-Fi, water, garbage, and 30, 50, & 100 amp power. Laundry, showers, and a picnic area are available at the resort lodge along with kayak and bike rentals. The resort lodge is a 10-minute walk from the marina or an easy commute by dinghy. In 2017 the G/H dock at the marina was replaced for an additional 600 feet of moorage.

Approaching, you will see a red spar buoy at the entrance to the bay. The buoy marks a shoal, keep the buoy to starboard as you enter (Red, Right, Returning). The proper channel will appear narrow, especially at low tide. You will be strongly tempted to leave the buoy to port, which might put you aground. The docks in front of the lodge are for resort boats and dinghies only; however, boats under 25 feet may be allowed to tie-up while dining at the lodge.

April Point Resort & Spa is a deluxe destination vacation resort. Notable stars from previous generations, like Bob Hope and John Wayne, vacationed here. It has everything for the most demanding guest, including excellent rooms, a beautiful spa, fishing guides, renowned dining, and scheduled air service by Kenmore Air. The marina and resort are owned by North Coast Hotel Resort Ltd, which operates a number of high-quality resorts. Painter's Lodge, north of Campbell River on the west side of Discovery Passage, is a North Coast Hotel resort and is accessible by the resort water taxi from April Point. April Point moorage guests have full access to the amenities at Painter's Lodge, including dining, swimming pool, hot tub and tennis courts.

Limited anchorage can be found in the cove near the marina. A rock-strewn passage, suitable

DESOLATION SOUND MARINE PARK TRAILS

Melanie Cove to Laura Cove – 0.6 miles each way with an elevation gain of 287 feet. Approximate travel time of 45 minutes one way to Laura Cove. Two cairns on a large flat rock near the head of Melanie Cove indicate where you can tie-off the dinghy and access the trailhead. There is a pit toilet at the trailhead and a rustic campsite. The trail is easy to follow with red surveyor's tape at a few spots along the way. The hike is moderate to difficult, with a number of fallen trees across the trail that require climbing over or under. The hike takes you past an established second growth forest with carpets of moss.

Melanie Cove to Lake Overlook – a half-mile trail leads from Melanie Cove up 360 feet to an overlook at one of two small lakes north of Unwin Lake. Melanie Cove Trailhead is at 50°08.44N 124°40.67W and is marked with a small rustic wooden "Trail" sign. A stern-tie installation is along the south shore of Melanie Cove near the trail sign where you can tie-off the dinghy. The trail is moderately difficult with some downed trees and limbs across the trail. About .4 miles from Melanie Cove, the trail branches with signs that mark the way to "Lake Overlook" and mark the way to "Unwin Lake."

Melanie Cove to Tenedos Bay via Unwin Lake – a two-mile trail goes between Melanie Cove and Tenedos Bay and passes along the northwest shore of Unwin Lake. This trail joins the Melanie Cove to Lake Overlook trail as described above, along with the Tenedos Bay to Unwin Lake trail described below. The trail passes two small lakes just north of Unwin Lake.

Tenedos Bay to Unwin Lake – an easy, less than a quarter-mile trail begins at the northeast corner of Tenedos Bay at 50°07.42N 124°41.38W with an elevation gain of 130 feet. The trail is moderate with an easy section from Tenedos Bay to a bridge at Unwin Lake. After the bridge, the trail north along Unwin Lake shore is moderate. There are several spots to access the Lake for a warm-water swim. The main trail from Tenedos to the bridge is short enough and wide enough to portage a light weight kayak or canoe to explore large Unwin Lake.

Grace Harbour to Isabel Bay – a one-half mile trail is reported to lead from the east cove in Grace Harbour to Isabel Bay.

Grace Harbour to a small lake – a one-third mile trail is reported to lead from the north cove in Grace Harbour to a small lake northward.

See Area Map Page 318 - Maps Not for Navigation **DESOLATION SOUND & DISCOVERY PASSAGE**

for kayaks and dinghies only, leads between the cove and adjacent Gowlland Harbour.

Steep Island Lodge. P.O. Box 699, Campbell River, BC V9W 6J3; (250) 830-8179; info@steepisland.com; www.steepisland.com. Open May 15 to September 30. Guest moorage for those staying in lodge accommodations. Water at the dock, no power. This is a beautiful resort with private cabins. It is on the east side of Steep Island, off the northwest corner of Gowlland Island. Fishing and kayak charters available. Float plane service. Jacuzzi. Dinner is all-inclusive and by reservation only.

⑱ **Gowlland Harbour.** Gowlland Harbour is a large, protected bay behind Gowlland Island, with considerable log booming activity along the shoreline. Before entering, study the chart so you can avoid Entrance Rock, north of Gowlland Island.

You'll find good anchoring depths at the north end of the bay, but it's much prettier at the south end, especially behind Stag Island. Although homes and docks are on the shores, we didn't feel closed-in-upon. Good anchoring is also behind Wren Islet, Crow Islet, and the Mouse Islets, all of them a little to the north of Stag Island. These islets, which are protected as provincial park preserves, make good picnic spots.

⑲ **Seascape Waterfront Resort.** P.O. Box 566, Quadra Island, BC V0P 1N0; (250) 895-1643; theseascaperesort@gmail.com; www.seascapewaterfrontresortandmarina.com. Located north of Stag Island in Gowland Harbour; 50°04.9'N 125°13.4'W Open all year, 1000 feet of guest moorage, 15 & 30 amp power, washrooms, showers, laundry, and free loaner kayaks. Docks and cabins were refurbished in 2018. The large upland octagon building serves as a venue for rendezvous and special events; the interior has beautiful wood finishes and sculptures, a nautical-themed bar, large stone fireplace and comfortable furnishings; wonderful views of the harbour. New owners of the resort continue to make plans for additional improvements.

CAMPBELL RIVER

Campbell River calls itself the "Salmon Capital of the World," and is working to become an important tourist destination. While dozens of guideboats take sportfishermen to prime fishing areas in Discovery Passage and off Cape Mudge, lunker-size salmon are still caught from marina breakwaters and the public fishing pier.

Campbell River has complete shopping, dining, and marine facilities, all close to the waterfront. Fisherman's Wharf and the Coast Marina are close to Tyee Plaza with

Seascape Waterfront Resort

Coast Marina

Fisherman's Wharf, Campbell River

2020 WAGGONER CRUISING GUIDE

SEYMOUR NARROWS

Note how the current is pushing the barge to one side in Seymour Narrows.

Seymour Narrows is a wide pass, clear of hazards, and offers a direct route north past the important provisioning town of Campbell River. It is the easiest connection from the Strait of Georgia to Johnstone Strait or Cordero Channel.

Most commercial vessels stay clear of Seymour Narrows except at slack. A ship or barge-towing tug cannot afford to go sideways for even a few seconds. Small fishboats and recreational vessels, however, often transit Seymour Narrows within an hour of the turn, especially if going with the current. We always take Seymour Narrows going with the current and we've rarely had an anxious moment.

Smaller tides, where maximum current is predicted at six knots or less, can be taken at any time for most boats (again, going with the current). Larger tides should be taken within a half-hour of the turn. If it's a strong current cycle, in the 14- to 16-knot range, arrive at the pass within 15 minutes of slack water and the current will be manageable. The strongest current doesn't extend very far in either direction, so the transit past whirlpools lasts only a few minutes.

Hydrographers say the strongest currents at the Narrows are in the vicinity of Ripple Rock (slightly west of mid-channel, directly beneath the hydro lines strung between Vancouver Island and Maud Island). On a flood, the strongest turbulence will be along the west wall and in the area south of Ripple Rock. On an ebb, the turbulence and the set starts between Maud Island and Ripple Rock. The ebb current sets northwest to the west wall.

Northbound vessels: On small tides, northbound vessels should arrive off the Maud Island light an hour before the end of the ebb, or an hour prior to high water slack, before the ebb begins. Once into the narrows, steer toward the tongue of the current stream (east of mid-channel) to avoid the whirlpools and eddies north of Maud Island up to North Bluff. On big tides, low-powered vessels will find it prudent to be at the Maud Island light at high water slack, or just a few minutes into the north flowing ebb.

If the slack is at low water, arrive at the pass before the end of the ebb. Slack on large tides is not very long, five to ten minutes at most. You'll want to be past Brown Bay before the southflowing flood gets underway. It can be brutal in a slow-moving boat. You may find a back eddy along the eastern shore. On a large flood, Seymour Narrows can reach 16 knots, no place to be in any kind of boat.

Southbound vessels: Southbound boats should be opposite Brown Bay within an hour of the beginning or end of a neap (small) flood. On a large spring flood, it would be wise to be opposite Brown Bay within a half-hour of its end or beginning. Keep well off the sheer rock wall on the west shore of the narrows. Current turbulence can set a vessel onto that wall. The worst turbulence is usually south of Ripple Rock, especially if wind is against current. Stay on your side of the channel (i.e. to starboard) to be clear of any tugs or large ships headed the other way. The good news about Seymour Narrows is that there are no obstructions and just one strong, main stream.

[Bill Kelly]

OCEAN PACIFIC
MARINE STORE & BOATYARD

The North Island's Largest Marine Supply Store & Boatyard
LOCATED IN DISCOVERY HARBOUR MARINA & SHOPPING CENTRE

www.oceanpacificmarine.com

Our Full-Service Boatyard Offers:
- 110 Ton Travelift
- ABYC Certified Marine Technicians & Electricians
- CWB Certified Welders
- Certified Diesel Mechanic,
- Fibreglassers, Painting and Detailing
- Shipwrights & Fine Wood Workers
- Emergency Services Available

Toll-Free: 800-663-2294
Local Phone: 250-286-1011
Fax: 250-286-6254
102-1370 Island Highway
Campbell River, B.C. V9W 8C9

See Area Map Page 318 - Maps Not for Navigation

DESOLATION SOUND & DISCOVERY PASSAGE

Coast Marina is a personable, friendly marina, with Dockside Fish & Chips.

drugstore, liquor store, excellent laundromat, and more. Discovery Harbour Marina is part of the extensive Discovery Harbour Centre with grocery and big-box general merchandise stores, liquor store, fast food, restaurants, and pubs. Buses leave hourly from a shelter at the mall, providing a convenient way to visit other areas of town.

An attractive promenade runs the length of the shoreline from Fisherman's Wharf to Discovery Harbour Marina. The recently extended promenade now connects the two shopping areas.

As you approach Campbell River from the south you will find four marinas, with transient moorage, each protected by a breakwater. The southernmost marina is Fisherman's Wharf (formerly the Government Dock, now Campbell River Harbour Authority).

Coast Marina is the second breakwater protected marina, offering guest moorage as you progress northward. The BC ferry run between Quathiaski Cove on Quadra Island and Campbell River lands adjacent to Coast Marina. Coast Marina is closest to downtown Campbell River.

The third marina is Discovery Harbour Marina with considerable moorage, including slips and side-tie. The 52-acre Discovery Harbour Centre adjoins the marina for convenient shopping, including Ocean Pacific Marine Supply, a well-stocked chandlery. Adjacent to the shopping center is a repair yard with 110-ton Travelift haulout.

The fourth marina (north side of Discovery Harbour) named Discovery Harbour Authority Small Craft Harbours is located behind the same breakwater that protects Discovery Harbour Marina. This fourth marina is located on the north side of Discovery Harbour Fuels sales dock and provides transient moorage and a boat ramp. All four marinas monitor VHF 66A.

Located one half-mile up the Campbell River is Freshwater Marina and Boatyard, offering permanent moorage, repair services and a 50 ton Travelift.

Marine Parts & Supplies: Well-stocked Ocean Pacific (250-286-1011) has overnight delivery from major suppliers in Vancouver for just about anything.

Museums: The Campbell River Museum & Archives, at 470 Island Hwy, is in the "don't miss" category. The care and imagination of the exhibits remind us of the Royal British Columbia Museum in Victoria, only smaller, and without the giant ice age mammoth.

The Maritime Heritage Centre, a short walk south from Fisherman's Wharf, features a number of fishing and maritime exhibits.

The Discovery Passage Aquarium is just above the docks at Fisherman's Wharf. It is small, but the exhibits are well done. Younger crew will enjoy it.

Farmers market: Sundays, May through September, 10:00 a.m. to 2:30 p.m. in the fishing pier parking lot at the Fisherman's Wharf docks. Fresh farm produce, baked goods, fresh fish, all the things you'd expect.

㉚ **Fisherman's Wharf (Campbell River Harbour Authority).** 705 Island Highway, Campbell River, BC V9W 2C2; (250) 287-7931; fishermans@telus.net; www.fishermanswharfcampbellriver.com. Monitors VHF 66A. Open all year, water on docks, 20, 30, limited 50 & one 100 amp power, pumpout, ample dock space, washrooms, showers, tidal grid, Wi-Fi, garbage, recycling. Reservations accepted. All but one of the docks are side-tie only, rafting permitted. Docks A, B, and C are in the North Basin and docks 1-6 are in the South Basin. Docks A,B,1,2 and the west side of 3 are reserved. Transient space is located on dock 5, the east side of 3, and the east side of C. The pumpout is on dock C in the north basin in the area marked "Loading Zone."

This was almost entirely a commercial fish boat moorage basin until the harbor authority took over operation. Several improvements have been made to attract pleasure craft. All the docks have been recently re-decked, and a new building completed with washrooms, showers, and the harbor office. The well known Dick's Fish and Chips moved from the Coast Marina to a new storefront across from the Wharf. Crabby Bob's on finger 6 on the south wharf has fresh and frozen seafood on the dock. Other boats sell fresh fish on the floats between fingers 2 & 3. Call the office for a heads-up on what's available. Office hours are 8:00 a.m. to 5:00 p.m., 7 days a week. If the office is closed, take an empty space and register in the morning.

㉚ **Coast Marina.** 1003 Island Highway, Campbell River, BC V9W 2C4; (250) 287-7455, or (250) 204-3900; coastmarina@gmail.com; www.coastmarina.ca. Monitors VHF 66A. The Coast Marina is located behind the middle of Campbell River's three breakwaters, and has facilities for boats to 180 feet in length. Open all year, guest moorage, 30, 50 & 100 amp power, washrooms, showers, excellent laundry across the street in the plaza, garbage, recycling, water, and free Wi-Fi. Charismatic owner and manager, Derik Pallan, is a delight and always makes

2020 WAGGONER CRUISING GUIDE

"Everything a boater needs is here."

- 24 Hr Video Surveillance
- Washrooms & Showers
- Power & Water
- Modern Guest Docks
- Fresh Water Filling
- Fish Cleaning Facilities
- Fishing Guide Services
- Internet Available
- Laundry Facilities
- Block & Cubed Ice
- Garbage Disposal

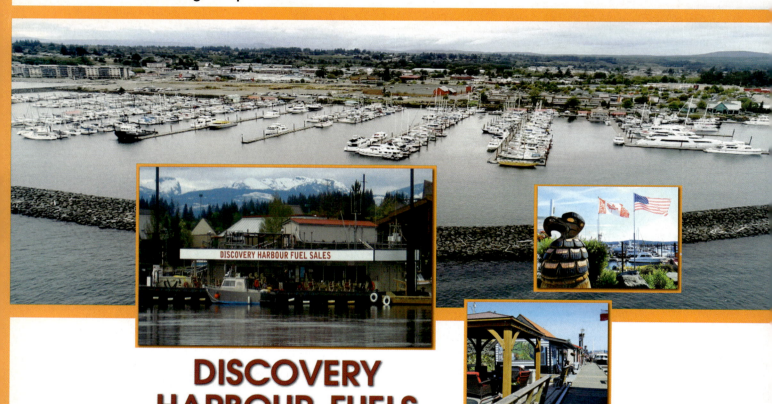

DISCOVERY HARBOUR FUELS
NO RESERVATIONS REQUIRED OR WAIT TIMES TO REFUEL

- Check For Our Low Fuel Prices
- 14 Fuel Filling Pump Dispensers
- Current Navigation Charts
- Ice & Convenience Store Items
- Full Line of Marine Parts, Oil & Filters
- Propane Bottle Exchange
- Fishing Gear

Discovery Harbour Marina: phone 250.287.2614 ~ fax 250.287.8939
www.discoveryharbourmarina.com ~ email info@discoveryharbourmarina.com

Discovery Harbour Fuels: phone 250.287.3456 ~ fax 250.287.3442
www.discoveryharbourfuel.com ~ email info@discoveryharbourfuel.com

The Laughing Oyster - Okeover Inlet

Where can you get great food, fabulous views, and unwind in casual elegance? The Laughing Oyster Restaurant, located in Okeover Inlet, consistently delivers great food in a relaxed atmosphere. Boaters who spend time in Desolation Sound, can head down Okeover Inlet and tie-up at the Okeover Harbour Authority docks, conveniently located near the Laughing Oyster. It's a short walk up the road to the restaurant, located in a home overlooking the Inlet, backed by forested mountains of the Coast Range. Reservations are a must at this popular restaurant frequented by tourists, locals, and boaters in the know.

At the Laughing Oyster, Chef Dave takes pride in his culinary presentation, taste, and texture. Many of the herbs, vegetables and berries are grown on the property, other foods are brought in from quality local growers. On our first visit to the Laughing Oyster, we chose a seafood dish with fresh mussels, scallops, and salmon in a delicious herb red sauce; along with a roasted vegetable, salmon dish; and a wonderful seafood pasta. The ambience, views, and gracious service make for a nice evening out, and the white linen tablecloths add to the special appeal without being pretentious. The Laughing Oyster has perfected the balance of casual with the right touch of relaxed elegance. Guests can sit outside on the large covered deck, or inside; both areas offer the same great views.

On another visit to the Laughing Oyster, we happened upon Sunday Family Buffet night, which proved to be an excellent value for the opportunity to taste a variety of food creations. Live music from a pianist-vocalist created an atmosphere of quality family time, while guests enjoyed a selection of seafood dishes, meat roasts, and various fruits and salads, all offered buffet style. Wednesday is Seafood Buffet night with added barbecued pork and angus beef selections, or you can opt for the "Only Tapas" menu. During the spring and fall, Dave offers the "Beggar's Banquet" on Fridays with musical guests, which he often joins, being a musician himself.

The Laughing Oyster is open seasonally (closed from January to early April), so be sure to visit this special venue next time you're cruising Desolation Sound, it's a treat not to be missed. For a schedule of events or to make reservations, go to www.laughingoyster.ca or call 604-483-9775.

DESOLATION SOUND & DISCOVERY PASSAGE

See Area Map Page 318 - Maps Not for Navigation

you feel right at home.

The marina has wide concrete docks with power and water to each slip. Docks C and D were extended in 2018. The marina is just steps away from Foreshore Park and downtown Tyee Plaza shopping. Dockside Fish & Chips is a fully licensed restaurant with indoor and outdoor seating right on the docks. CR Whale & Bear Excursions office on site, available for bookings.

⑳ **Discovery Harbour Marina.** Suite 392-1434 Ironwood St., Campbell River, BC V9W 5T5; (250) 287-2614; info@discoveryharbourmarina.com; www.discoveryharbourmarina.com. Monitors VHF 66A. Open all year, with a mixture of slips and side-tie. Washrooms, showers, laundry, garbage drop, ample guest moorage, 20, 30, 50 & 100 amp single/3- phase power, Wi-Fi. In-slip pumpout service. The G, H, I and J floats have side-tie moorage that can handle mega-yachts, additional side-tie on docks C and D. Finger piers have recently been added to docks A and C for 30, 40 and 50-foot slips. Customs clearance available. This is the largest of Campbell River's four breakwater-protected marinas. The marina has excellent docks, landing assistance and friendly people.

The marina office, with showers, washrooms, and laundry, is in a two-story floating facility at the foot of the north ramp on K dock. Floating washrooms are also near E dock to save the long walk to the main washrooms. The docks can be busy with whale and bear tour operators. Water taxi located on the main dock.

The extensive Discovery Harbour Centre shopping plaza is adjacent to the marina, with everything you would expect to find in a major center.

⑳ **Discovery Harbour Fuels.** Box 512, Campbell River, BC V9W 5C1; (250) 287-3456; dhfs@telus.net; www.discoveryharbourfuel.com. Monitors VHF 66A. Located straight ahead as you enter the Discovery Harbour breakwater. Fuel dock open all year; gasoline, diesel, propane-exchange, self-service oil change system, and sani-pump station. Fresh water fill, water is excellent. A full line of cruising guides, maps, extensive charts, fishing gear, marine parts, ice, kerosene and convenience supplies.

⑳ **Discovery Harbour Authority Small Craft Harbours.** (250) 287-7091. Monitors VHF 66A. This marina was formerly for commercial boats only but is now open to recreational vessels; the marina is managed by the Discovery Harbour Authority. Open all year with 4000 feet of dock space located north of the fuel sales just inside the Discovery Harbour breakwater. Transient moorage with mandatory rafting; permanent slips for commercial vessels; launch ramp on site. 30 & 50 amp power and two 100-amp stations; no reservations, may call ahead for availability. Washrooms, showers, laundry, garbage drop with recycling and waste oil disposal; no Wi-Fi. Payment made at wharfinger office on site open 8 a.m.-4 p.m. daily; after hours use envelope payment drop at office door. Marina has a night watchman and camera surveillance.

Freshwater Marina and Boatyard. 2705 N Island Hwy, Campbell River, BC V9W 2H4; (250) 286-0701 Marina; (250) 203-2635 Boatyard; jwtimber@uniserve.com Marina; darcybain@gmail.com Boatyard; www.freshwatermarina.ca. Open all year Monday – Friday. Freshwater Marina is located about half a mile up the Campbell River from Discovery Passage; the Marina and Boatyard are accessible on a 6 foot tide or better for small craft and higher tides for larger vessels. River pilots are available, contact Freshwater Marina. Permanent moorage is available for vessels up to 65 feet, dryland storage for smaller craft. Tide dependent launch ramp. No transient moorage. Freshwater Boatyard has a 50 ton Travelift and do-it-yourself boatyard that also welcomes trades contractors.

Seymour Narrows. Currents in Seymour Narrows run to 16 knots on the flood and 14 knots on the ebb, flooding south and ebbing north.

Northbound, you can wait for slack either in Menzies Bay on the Vancouver Island side, or in the good-size unnamed bay behind Maud Island on the Quadra Island side. South of Maud Island the flood forms a backeddy along Quadra Island, easily sweeping northbound boats toward Maud Island. Southbound, Plumper Bay is a good waiting spot on the east side, as is Brown Bay on the west side. Brown Bay has a floating breakwater, and a marina with a fuel dock and restaurant.

Both **Deepwater Bay** and **Plumper Bay** are too exposed and deep to be attractive as anchorages. **Menzies Bay** may have good anchorage, being careful to go around either end of a drying shoal which almost blocks the entrance. This area is used as a booming ground for the pulp mill in Campbell River.

Seymour Narrows is the principal route for northbound and southbound commercial traffic, including cruise ships. Give large vessels ample room to maneuver. Before going through, we urge you to read the Sailing

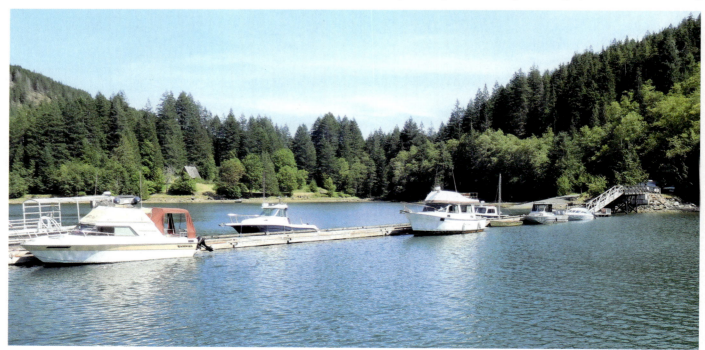

The Strathcona Regional Public Dock is tucked in the south end of Granite Bay, a locals favorite.

Directions section on Seymour Narrows. Especially on a flood, Sailing Directions counsels against the west side because of rough water. Monitor the passage times of commercial traffic on VHF 71, the area Vessel Traffic Services (VTS) frequency.

The warship HMCS *Columbia* was sunk off Maud Island to create an artificial reef.

㉑ **Brown's Bay Marina & RV Park.** 15021 Brown's Bay Road, Campbell River, BC V9H 1N9; (250) 286-3135; marina@brownsbayresort.com; www.brownsbayresort.com. Monitors VHF 12 & 66A. Open all year, gasoline and diesel, side-tie moorage to 100 feet along 2000 feet of dock, 50 slips for boats to 24 feet, 15, 30 & 50 amp power, free Wi-Fi, washrooms, showers, laundry, ice, cable television, phone, garbage drop, marine & RV store, boat launch. Four rental cabins and tent cabins for camping available.

This marina is on Vancouver Island, at the north end of Seymour Narrows. Enter around the north end of the breakwater. Strong currents can sweep through the marina; be sure to take the current into account when maneuvering, and tie your boat to the dock securely.

The store has a variety of snack items, clothing, and fishing gear. The seasonal floating restaurant offers all-you-can-eat crab on Thursdays and Fridays, when available, along with their annual Luau. Call or check their website for the schedule.

Kanish Bay. Kanish Bay has several good anchorages. You could sneak behind the **Chained Islands**, and with some thought and planning find a number of delightful spots, especially in settled weather. A charted large aquaculture, or at least the buoyed anchor points for same, lies mid-channel between 61-meter island and the entrance to Granite Bay. The small bay between Granite Bay and Small Inlet offers protection from westerlies. An aquaculture operation is in the mouth of this bay.

Correspondents James & Jennifer Hamilton anchored in the cove behind Bodega Point, just south of the 2-meter rock. "Really beautiful. Birds calling. Good holding in sticky mud."

Granite Bay. Granite Bay is well protected with a good bottom and room for several boats to anchor. The shore to the north is part of Small Inlet Marine Park and the shore on the south has a few houses. The Strathcona Regional District (250-830-6700) public dock has a 230 foot float with side-tie space that is mostly occupied by local boats. Self-registration and payment box at the head of the dock. Two 15 amp shore power receptacles located at the base of the ramp offer power during limited hours. No other services at the dock. A launch ramp (limited to boats 20 feet or less) and trailer parking are located at the park.

㉒ **Small Inlet.** A narrow but easily-run channel with a least depth of 8 feet leads from the northeast corner of Kanish Bay to Small Inlet. This inlet, surrounded by steep, wooded mountains, is beautiful, although we can confirm that a strong westerly from Johnstone Strait can get in and test your anchoring. Once through the kelp-filled entrance channel, a number of good anchorages can be found along the north shore. A couple of boats can fit behind a little knob of land near the southeast corner. The chart shows 3 rocks in this anchorage—actually, it's a reef with 3 high points. You also can anchor in the cove at the head of Small Inlet, behind two small islands.

A half-mile easy trail connects the cove at the head of Small Inlet with Waiatt Bay. The trail head is at the head of the cove in Small Inlet with a trail sign pointing east to Waiatt Bay. To the west, a trail to Newton Lake follows the south shore of Small Inlet cove with two dinghy landing sites, one at the rock outcropping across from the two islands forming the cove, and the other at a rocky shore midway between the previous rock outcropping and the head of the cove. The trail to Newton Lake is a one-mile steep and sometimes difficult forest trail. Don't confuse a small pond, a short distance before Newton Lake, for the real thing. The crystal clear waters of Newton Lake invite a fresh water swim. From Newton Lake a two-mile trail continues to Granite Bay Road and Granite Bay

㉑ **Small Inlet Marine Park.** Located on the west side of Quadra Island bordering Octopus Islands Marine Park on the east, Small Inlet Marine Park has good anchoring opportunities in Small Inlet itself and in nearby Granite Bay and Kanish Bay. The marine park includes upland areas and trails. See *Okisollo Channel* map in this chapter.

Granite Point. If you are traveling between Discovery Passage and Okisollo Channel, you can safely steer inside Min Rock, north of Granite Point, and run close to Granite Point itself. You will be treated to the sight of some extraordinary rock formations on Granite Point.

Rock Bay Marine Park (Otter Cove). Otter Cove is just inside Chatham Point. It's a useful little anchorage, with convenient depths and protection from seas rolling down Johnstone Strait. If you need a place to hide until the wind or seas subside, it's a good spot.

MARINA
- Campbell River's only Fresh Water Marina
- Holds up to 162 boats overall
- All covered boathouses with hydro & water
- Boats up to 55ft long
- Dryland Storage
- Boat launch available

TRAVEL LIFT
- 50 Ton Travel Lift
- Do it yourself boatyard
- Contractors Welcome
- River Pilot available
- Hydro & water available upon request
- (2) 60ft covered sheds available

2705 N. Island Hwy, Campbell River, BC V9W 2H4   250.286.0701

GET YOUR WAGGONER GUIDE UPDATES AT www.WaggonerGuide.com

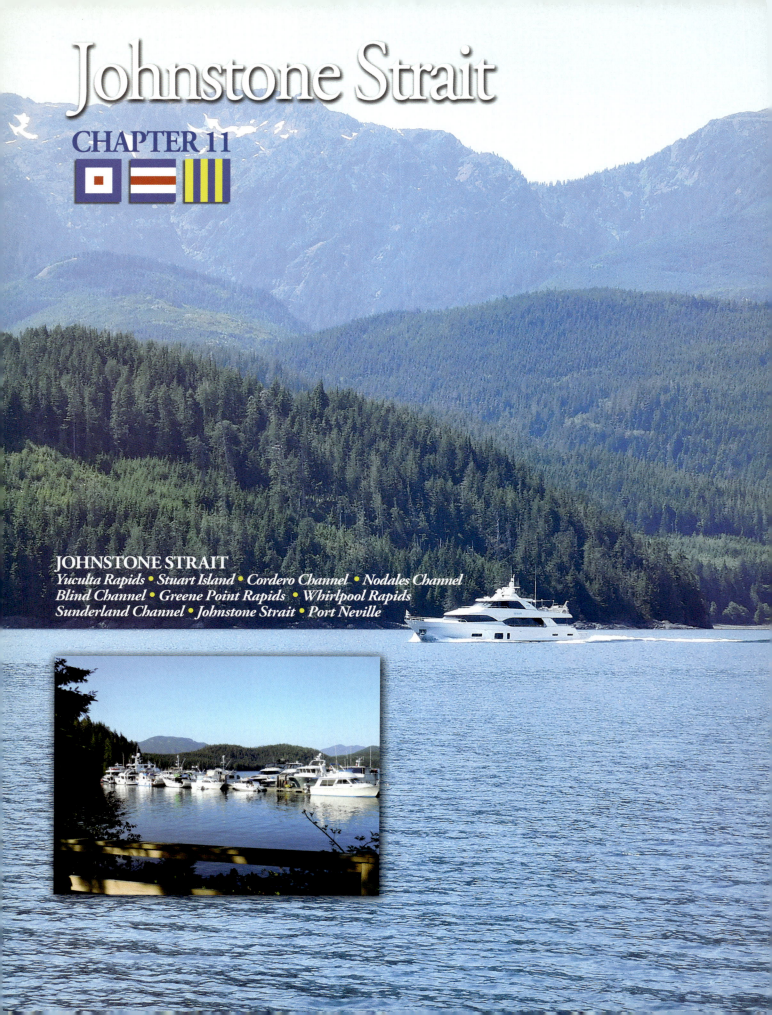

Johnstone Strait

CHAPTER 11

JOHNSTONE STRAIT
*Yuculta Rapids • Stuart Island • Cordero Channel • Nodales Channel
Blind Channel • Greene Point Rapids • Whirlpool Rapids
Sunderland Channel • Johnstone Strait • Port Neville*

JOHNSTONE STRAIT

See Area Map Page 342 - Maps Not for Navigation

The southern tip of Stuart Island marks the northern boundary of Desolation Sound. North of Desolation Sound, you'll find colder water, harsher weather, fewer services, and a greater number of rocks, reefs and tidal rapids. You should have good ground tackle and know how to use it.

Fewer boats venture north of Desolation Sound. Many stay out for four to eight weeks or more, and the larger boats provide more comfortable accommodations. On average the occupants are older, too. The farther north you go, the more remote conditions become, all the way to Alaska.

It is possible to do a quick two- to three-week trip from Seattle to this area, although it might require long days on the water to get there. The reward is experiencing beautiful cruising grounds few others will see.

Garbage Drops. While occasionally you will find a lack of garbage drops in Desolation Sound and south, garbage becomes a much greater problem farther north. Garbage must be hauled from marinas and settlements to authorized dumps, usually on Vancouver Island. Since marinas must pay for hauling and disposal, most charge a fee for garbage, if they accept it at all. Those that do will sometimes take recyclables at no charge. Use as little glass as possible, wash and flatten cans, and pack paper out.

Fresh Water. Fresh water can be a problem even in Desolation Sound, and northward the supplies are fewer. Many marinas prohibit boat washing. Some marinas limit the amount of water for filling tanks. Check with marina staff before washing the boat or filling the tanks.

Some stops, such as Lagoon Cove or Blind Channel, have sweet spring water from deep wells. In some places, the potable water has a brown cast from cedar bark tannin. We don't know of anybody who has had a bad experience from it. As an added protection, water can be filtered with a 3-stage filter system available at most marine supply stores and online.

Prices. The season is short and the costs are high. Everything must be brought in by water taxi, barge, or air. Don't be upset when prices are higher than at home. Remember, too, that during the season the marina personnel's workday starts early and ends late, and calls for a smile at all times.

Provisions. Going north there are major shopping centers and large grocery stores in Campbell River, Port McNeill and Port Hardy. There are small stores with many items and the essentials in Telegraph Harbour, Pierre's Echo Bay, Sullivan Bay, Sointula, and Alert Bay. You will not starve, though you may not always find those special ingredients for a unique recipe, like Old Bay for a prawn boil.

Recommended books. Peter Vassilopoulos' cruising guide, *Broughton Islands Cruising*

Chatham Point marks the Southern end of Johnstone Strait.

Guide, is excellent. The book covers the waters from Yuculta Rapids to Port Hardy, and is packed with maps, history, and hundreds of aerial color photos.

Exploring the South Coast of British Columbia, by Don Douglass and Réanne Hemingway-Douglass, is another excellent book covering this area.

Local Knowledge: The Skipper's Reference, Tacoma to Ketchikan by Kevin Monahan, is a compilation of useful navigation and trip-planning information, including mileage and conversion tables. It has a comprehensive section on tidal rapids, recommended strategies, and how to calculate timing for transit. We use the mileage charts regularly. Monahan's excellent Johnstone Strait diagrams are included in this chapter.

THE INSIDE ROUTE TO THE BROUGHTONS

Most cruisers heading north choose the sheltered inside route through Cordero Channel, Chancellor Channel, Wellbore Channel and Sunderland Channel rather than face a long, possibly rough passage in Johnstone Strait against the prevailing northwest winds. Often the Johnstone Strait route is taken on the way home with the winds from astern and ideally on a flood tide. The inside route runs from the north end of Calm Channel (the south tip of Stuart Island), through five sets of rapids: Yuculta Rapids, Gillard Passage, Dent Rapids, Greene Point Rapids and Whirlpool Rapids. The route includes an open stretch of approximately 13 miles in Johnstone Strait (which cannot be avoided) between Sunderland Channel and Havannah Channel, after which the currents of Chatham Channel must be negotiated. Careful planning is paramount. You need to know the times of slack water at each rapids, and you need to know how long it will take to get to each rapids.

Up-to-date charts and a copy of the Canadian Tide and Current Tables Vol. 6 or Ports and Passes are critical for safe navigation.

Using the corrections shown in the Reference and Secondary Current Stations in the front part of the Tide and Current Tables (back of Ports and Passes), you must be comfortable calculating the times of slack water at the various rapids. For anchoring or transiting shallow channels, use the corrections in the Reference and Secondary Ports pages to calculate times and heights of tides.

The calculations can be daunting at first, but an evening spent reading the excellent instructions will clear matters considerably. For clarifications, don't be shy about asking a few old salts on the docks. They (we) love to help.

Since the waters north of Desolation Sound flood southward from the top of Vancouver Island and ebb northward, the northbound boat (if it wishes to clear a number of rapids in one run) has a timing problem. Assuming a start with Yuculta Rapids, all the rapids to the north will already have turned before slack water occurs at the Yucultas. It is best to approach Yuculta Rapids before the southbound flood turns to the northbound ebb, and utilize two backeddies (described below) to help your way against the flood for the two or so miles to Gillard Passage and Dent Rapids. Done correctly, you'll go through Dent Rapids against the last of the flood current, and let the new ebb current flush you out Cordero Channel.

The ebb will already have been running 13 miles away at Greene Point Rapids, which turned earlier. Depending on your boat's speed, the ebb could be at full force when you arrive. Rather than go through in these conditions, many choose to overnight at Blind Channel Resort. Shoal Bay and the Cordero Islands are other good places to wait for Greene Point Rapids to turn to slack.

The next day you can depart before high water slack and push through Greene Point Rapids in the dying flood current. Then you'll hurry to Wellbore Channel, to take Whirlpool Rapids early in the favorable ebb current. If this is done early in the morning, it is possible the wind will not have started building for the stretch in Johnstone Strait. With luck it can

JOHNSTONE STRAIT

Reference Only – Not for Navigation

Distances (nm)
(Approximate, for planning. Distances from end of one rapids to beginning of next rapids will be less.)

- Harbott Pt. (south tip of Stuart Is.) to Gillard Passage—2.0
- Gillard Passage to Dent Rapids (Devils Hole)—2.0
- Dent Rapids (Devils Hole) to Shoal Bay—7.4
- Shoal Bay to Greene Pt. Rapids (Griffiths Islet Lt.)—6.0
- Greene Pt. Rapids (Griffiths Islet Lt.) to Whirlpool Rapids—11.0
- Whirlpool Rapids to Port Neville—13.0
- Port Neville to Havannah Channel—9.0
- Havannah Channel entrance to Chatham Channel E entrance—6.6
- Chatham Channel E entrance to Minstrel Is (Blow Hole)—4.5

Johnstone Strait

be a pleasant run down Sunderland Channel and into Johnstone Strait for the 13-mile run to Havannah Channel. How well this works depends on the speed of your boat, the time of day, the conditions, and the flexibility of your schedule.

Southbound the options are greater. Take your first rapids against the last of the dying ebb, and let the new flood current flush you south. Each rapids in succession turns at a later time. Given the right conditions even a slow boat can take all the rapids on one tide, with only a few hours' wait if the boat arrives at any given rapids when they are running too hard to risk transit.

Note: Canadian Tide and Current Tables *do not adjust* for Daylight Saving Time. Ports and Passes tide and current times are adjusted for Daylight Saving Time.

Caution: A tight schedule is not justification for taking a chance with bad conditions. The dangers are real.

① **Yuculta Rapids.** The Yuculta (pronounced "YEW-cla-ta") Rapids separate Stuart Island and Sonora Island. Taken at slack they are benign, but at full force on a spring tide, especially against an opposing wind, they can be extremely dangerous. Northbound, Sailing Directions recommends that slow and low-powered boats arrive at the rapids an hour before high water slack, and use a backeddy along the Stuart Island shore until off Kellsey Point. Then cross to the Sonora Island shore to use a prevailing northerly current. This should position the boat to go through Gillard Passage and Dent Rapids satisfactorily. If you are late and unsure about transiting Dent Rapids, wait in Big Bay for the next slack.

② **Big Bay (Stuart Island).** For decades, Big Bay on Stuart Island has been a major fishing resort center. The public floats are behind a plank and piling breakwater at the head of Big Bay. The former Big Bay Marina is now a private fishing resort with no services for cruising boats. The Stuart Island Community dock has moorage and a store. Big Bay has seen an increase in development of exclusive, high-end fishing resorts and lodges over the past few years. Many boats criss-cross the bay during the summer and peak fishing seasons.

② **Stuart Island Community Dock.** P.O. Box 5-6, Stuart Island, BC V0P 1V0; (250) 202-3625; postmaster@stuartisland.info; www.stuartislandca.info. Monitors VHF 66A. Moorage, water, liquor, laundry, post office, store, ice, fishing guides, good cell phone coverage, free Wi-Fi. No power, no fuel. Staff is on call 24 hours a day in season.

The docks were rebuilt and expanded to accommodate boats to 100+ feet. The store carries convenience items, liquor, locally made goods. Store hours are 8:00 a.m. to 5:00 p.m. seven days a week in season. A large deck with a covered picnic area connects to the store.

A well-marked road and trail lead to Eagle Lake, where a skiff is kept. It's a good walk, through beautiful forest.

Shoal: An important shoal lies a short distance off the dock. Approach from the south.

Gillard Passage. Currents run to 13 knots on the flood and 10 knots on the ebb. Transit near slack water. Times of slack are shown in Canadian Tide and Current Tables Vol. 6 and Ports and Passes. Pass south of Jimmy Judd Island. Big Bay is a good place to wait if the current is too strong.

If you're lucky, you might find the trees on and near Jimmy Judd Island filled with eagles that swoop down to the swirling waters to feed on hake, whose air bladders have brought them to the surface. It's a real sight.

③ **Fisherman's Landing & Lodge.** P.O. Box 5-3, Stuart Island, BC V0P 1V0; (250) 202-0187; fishermanslandingandlodge@hotmail.com. Monitors VHF 66A (previously known as Morgans Landing). All new concrete docks were installed by the new owners in 2018. 350 feet of guest moorage, with 30, 50 and 100 amp power. Some 200 amp power. Wi-Fi, water, washrooms, showers, laundry and ice. Reservations recommended. The 50-foot float on the west end is for float planes. Happy Hours are held on weekends. The dining room is expected to be open by 2020. Meals are by reservation. Plans are underway for additional moorage floats and a fuel dock in the near future. Facilities include accommodations,

RUNNING THE RAPIDS

The cautious advice—the first rule of thumb—for transiting tidal current rapids is to wait for slack water and go through then. This rule of thumb is fine but imperfect. There you sit, watching other boats go through before slack and after slack.

A second rule of thumb is a corollary of the first. It says that boats should arrive at a rapids an hour before predicted slack, so they're ready to go through as soon as the rapids grow quiet. Like most rules of thumb, this one doesn't always work either. Sometimes it appears as if the rapids would be safe much longer than an hour before or after. Sometimes one look tells you it's smarter to wait. With a little study, however, it's possible to predict when the window of opportunity will be wider or narrower.

Before going further, two definitions:

Slack water. Slack water is the time when rapids cease flowing one direction but haven't begun flowing the opposite direction. Another word for slack is turn, meaning the time when the water's flow turns from one direction to the other.

Window, or window of opportunity. For purposes of this article, window means a time when most boats can transit a rapids safely, without too much excitement.

This article gelled with me in Malibu Rapids at the mouth of Princess Louisa Inlet. It has its origins in the successful running of the Pacific Northwest's tidal current rapids over a span of nearly four decades.

Understand that my wife and I are the original cautious and conservative boaters when it comes to rapids. Several years ago we hiked from Big Bay, on B.C.'s Stuart Island, to Arran Rapids, one of the most deadly rapids on the coast. We arrived in what must have been the middle of a large tide exchange, with its frightening whitewater overfalls, upwellings and whirlpools that no sensible boat could be expected to survive. White water is full of air, and less buoyant than green water. Boats float lower, with less freeboard. Rudders lose effectiveness and propellers lose their bite. We got the message: Rapids are not to be trifled with.

With experience, we have developed a loose sense of when a rapids could be run at times other than slack. Until our transits of Malibu Rapids, however, this sense was not refined to any kind of structure.

For what it's worth, here's our thinking. But first,

Caution: Every rapids has its own personality and characteristics. What follows is general in nature, and may not apply to any given rapids. It is a way of looking at things, an approach to the problem. It is not a guarantee.

The determining factors are 1) high water slack vs. low water slack; 2) neap tides vs. spring tides; 3) the size of the exchange on each side of slack.

High water slack vs. low water slack. We entered Princess Louisa Inlet through Malibu Rapids without drama nearly two hours before high water slack. When we departed two days later we found definite swirls, overfalls and whirlpools only 20 minutes before low water slack. The two transits were entirely different.

Our entry to Princess Louisa Inlet was at high water, when the narrow, shallow channel was full. Our departure was at low water, when the channel was much less full and much narrower. The less water in the channel, the faster the current must run.

General Rule: The window of opportunity is wider at high water slack. The narrower and shallower the channel, the more this is true.

Neap tides vs. spring tides. Neap tides are small tides that occur around the times of half moon. Neaps often show only a small dip from one high water to the next. The widest windows of opportunity occur on that small dip.

Spring tides occur around the times of full moon or no moon. Low tides can be very low and high tides very high. On springs even the dip between two high tides can be significant. The

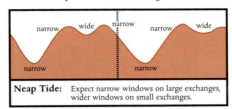

Neap Tide: Expect narrow windows on large exchanges, wider windows on small exchanges.

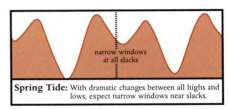

Spring Tide: With dramatic changes between all highs and lows, expect narrow windows near slacks.

windows of opportunity are narrower on spring tides than on neap tides.

Since it takes only a week to go from neap tide to spring tide (and another week to go from spring tide to neap tide), the experience from just a few days earlier has no bearing on the day you're going through. Each day, each transit, must be evaluated on its own.

Size of the exchange. Imagine this exercise. Using a garden hose, fill a five-gallon container in a minute. Then fill a one-gallon container in a minute. You had to turn the flow of water way down for the one-gallon can. Our neap tide entry through Malibu Rapids was near the top of a fairly small rise from lower low water to high water. The smaller the rise or fall, the less the current.

Conclusions

1. The window is narrowest at lower low water slack. The tide has dropped a long way and will be rising a long way. The farther the tide has dropped and the farther it is to rise, the narrower the window. Also, the shallower and narrower the rapids, the narrower the window at lower low water. At lower low water, plan to go through fairly close to slack.

2. The window at high water slack is wider on neap tides than on spring tides. The window is widest in the "dip" between the two high waters on neap tides.

3. At high water slack, the window is narrower on the rise from lower low water. The window is wider between the next two high waters.

Disclaimer. Skippers are responsible for the welfare and safety of their vessels and passengers. The purpose of this article is to provide tools for evaluating situations. It is not the purpose of this article to tell a skipper when to transit a rapids. When in doubt, the safest course is to transit at slack water, regardless of what other boats are doing.

– Robert Hale

JOHNSTONE STRAIT

See Area Map Page 342 - Maps Not for Navigation

MONAHAN'S LOCAL KNOWLEDGE

LEGEND
Boils (upwelling)   Whirlpool   Turbulence (Tide Rip)
← Direction of ebb current   ⇒ Direction of flood current

LOCAL EFFECTS – EBB

West of Port Neville, the ebb begins along the mainland shore and takes almost two hours to completely cover the strait from one side to the other.

Turn to flood occurs in Sunderland Channel 1h 40m before Johnstone Strait Central and 1h 20m before Camp Point.

To avoid heavy weather in Johnstone Strait (especially when wind opposes currents) Sunderland, Wellbore and Cordero Channels offer calmer conditions.

Current Passage turns to ebb 50m after Johnstone Strait Central, but 1h 15m before Camp Point.

Turn to ebb at Vansittart Point occurs up to 30m before Current Passage, almost two hours before Camp Point.

Freshet conditions in mainland rivers may encourage a premature turn to ebb in the vicinity of Mayne Passage.

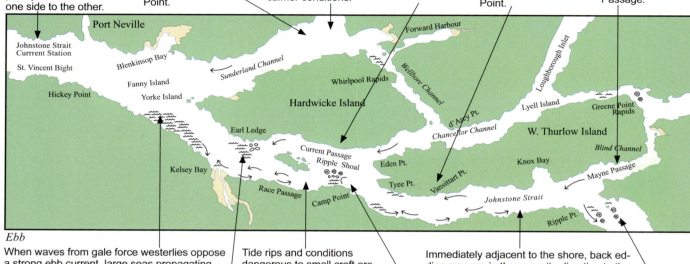
Ebb

When waves from gale force westerlies oppose a strong ebb current, large seas propagating southward are generated in this area. In this case, smaller boats should seek shelter at Port Neville or enter the harbour at Kelsey Bay and wait for the contrary current to moderate.

Tide rips and conditions dangerous to small craft are generated in this area during large tides, especially when strong westerlies oppose the ebb current.

A steep underwater ridge extends southward from Earl Ledge across the channel to the Vancouver Island shore. Deep tidal currents meet this steep topography and are deflected to the surface, causing extreme turbulence west of Helmcken Island during large tides.

Stay clear of Ripple Shoal. Dangerous whirlpools form to the west of the shoal during the ebb.

Immediately adjacent to the shore, back eddies may run in the opposite direction to the main flow. However, at headlands between back eddies, the ebb current is strong right up to the shore.

Tide rips and turbulent conditions are generated in this area during large tides, especially when strong westerly winds oppose the ebb current.

LOCAL EFFECTS – FLOOD

Near Port Neville, the mainland and Vancouver Island shores turn to flood up to one hour before the center of the channel.

In Current Passage, turbulence is weaker near the north shore.

To avoid heavy weather in Johnstone Strait (especially when wind opposes currents) Sunderland, Wellbore and Cordero Channels offer calmer conditions.

Stay clear of Ripple Shoal. Dangerous whirlpools form to the east of the shoal during the flood.

First ebb current in eastern Johnstone Strait begins between Mayne Passage and Vansittart Point, up to two hours before turn to ebb at Camp Point.

Flood

Tide rips and conditions dangerous to small craft are generated in this area during large tides, especially when strong southeasterlies oppose the flood current.

The ebb current in Current and Race Passages persists approximately 1h 20m longer than in Sunderland Channel.

Immediately adjacent to the shore, back eddies may run in the opposite direction to the main flow. However, at headlands between back eddies, the flood current is strong right up to the shore.

Tide rips and turbulent conditions are generated in this area during large tides, especially when strong southeasterlies oppose the flood current.

Copyright © Kevin Monahan, Local Knowledge: A Skipper's Reference, Tacoma to Ketchikan eco tours and guided fishing charters. This is an upscale fishing lodge located at the mouth of the little bay that separates Dent Island from the mainland. Floatplane and water taxi service available.

③ **Dent Island Lodge.** P.O. Box 8, Stuart Island, BC V0P 1V0; (250) 203-2553; info@dentisland.com; www.dentisland.com. Monitors VHF 66A. Open late May to mid-September, guest moorage for boats to 200 feet on wide, stable concrete docks, 30 & 50 amp power at every dock pedestal, plus single-phase 100 amp power upon request. Potable water on the docks, Wi-Fi, good cell phone service, fishing guides, restaurants, gift shop, sauna, showers, exercise room, hot tub.

The service at Dent Island Lodge is first class, with moorage and dinner prices to match. The main lodge was removed in 2017 for the construction of a new bigger and better lodge that opened in late June of 2018. The new lodge takes advantage of the gorgeous views. The enlarged dining room and other spaces flow out to the rapids of Canoe Passage.

The professional staff treats you like a special guest in a small, quiet, private retreat. At the end of the day after the guide boats have returned from fishing, an elegant appetizer table is set out. The dinner menu in the main dining room offers a wide menu selection. The less formal Rapids Outdoor Grill is a small-plate-style dining area with a view of Canoe Pass rapids. Tables surround the kitchen and the chef personally prepares each dish directly in front of you. Both dining options are popular; reservations highly recommended.

Food is prepared right in front of you at Dent Rapids Outdoor Grill.

A hiking trail, rough in places, is a good place to work off some of the calories.

The lodge is at the back of a little bay separating Dent Island from the mainland, next to Canoe Pass rapids, where 10- to 12-knot whitewater tidal currents churn. A spacious deck overlooks the pass. Another deck, screened by forest, holds a hot tub.

The lodge has a fast jet boat for eco-explorations and thrilling rides in the rapids. They offer tours to the head of Bute Inlet, including runs up the rivers in the inlet. Resort manager Justin Farr is an experienced fishing guide in these waters, and he knows every swirl, overfall and calm spot. The boat turns in its own length and dances through rough waters. The tour will make you respect the waters around Dent and Arran Rapids. Salmon charters can be arranged by the resort.

Schedule arrivals and departures to coincide with slack water in Gillard Passage,

JOHNSTONE STRAIT

and approach from the southeast. Chart 3543 shows the lodge location, including the dock. Watch for a shoal area 0.9 meter deep at zero tide on the east side of the entry. Stay mid-channel. It is best to make reservations, even in the less-busy weeks of the season. Reservations are just about essential during high season.

④ **Dent Rapids.** Currents run to 9 knots on floods and 8 knots on ebbs. Time corrections are shown under Reference and Secondary Current Stations in Tide and Current Tables Vol. 6 and Ports and Passes. Per Sailing Directions, "In Devils Hole, violent eddies and whirlpools form between 2 hours after turn to flood and 1 hour before turn to ebb." People who have looked into Devils Hole vow never to run that risk again. Favor the Sonora Island shore of Dent Rapids.

Tugboat Passage, between Dent Island and Little Dent Island, avoids the potential problems of Devils Hole, and the current is less. Use the large-scale inset on Chart 3543, and favor the Little Dent Island side.

Arran Rapids. Arran Rapids separate the north side of Stuart Island and the mainland, and connect Bute Inlet with Cordero Channel. Current predictions for Arran Rapids are shown in Canadian Tide and Current Tables Vol. 6, and Ports and Passes. Arran Rapids are unobstructed, but tidal streams run to 13+ knots. These rapids have a long history of killing the unknowing or foolhardy. Run Arran Rapids at slack water only, if at all. We have hiked from Big Bay to Arran Rapids and watched the water during a spring tide. The enormous upwellings, whirlpools, and overfalls were frightening.

⑤ **Denham Bay.** (250) 703-6978 (Peter); (250) 218-8538 (Sarah); denhamdocks@gmail.com; www.denhambay.com. Monitors VHF 66A. Denham Bay is located in a lovely setting with park-like grounds offering several well-appointed vacation cabins. Be sure to stay clear of Secord Rock located approximately 400 yards offshore lying northwest of Horn Point; there is currently no buoy marking this rock. Open May 15 to October 15, water, Wi-Fi, no power.

Owners Peter Geneau and Sarah Askwith are friendly and welcoming. Peter has worked in salmon enhancement and as a fishing guide in the area. Sarah worked as a high-end pastry chef for some of the local resorts.

A dock was added in 2017, increasing moorage space to approximately 500 feet. Reservations are taken for group events, priority is given to boats making use of the cabins. Denham Bay primarily caters to smaller boats but can accommodate boats up to 95 feet as space allows, call ahead for availability. A beautiful outdoor kitchen area with granite countertops is available for cabin guests, and boaters moored at the marina can make use of a separate shore-side kitchen area and the wood-fired pizza oven. The grounds are a delight, with lovely walkways and a shore-side boardwalk. Hiking trails in the area. Salmon charters can be arranged with prior notification.

Frederick Arm. Frederick Arm is deep, with almost no good places to anchor. You can anchor in several nooks along the eastern shoreline, or near the head, where the bottom shoals rapidly.

Estero Basin. If the crowds are getting to you, uncharted Estero Basin, at the head of Frederick Arm, is where you can avoid them. The narrow passage into the basin, called "The Gut," is passable only at high water slack (very high water slack, we now are told), and slack doesn't last long. A dinghy with outboard motor is a good way to go, and you may have to drag it part of the way. We have not been in Estero Basin, but Wolferstan has. He writes convincingly about the strong currents in The Gut and the eerie stillness of the 5-mile-long basin with its uncharted rocks. Friends tell us that Estero Basin is absolutely beautiful, usually deserted, with small islands, sheer cliffs, and water that grows fresher the farther you go. "Bring your lunch and shampoo," we're advised.

Waggoner reader Patrick Freeny reported that he had just enough water for his inflatable dinghy on a 13-foot tide. On a 10-foot tide the dinghy had to be dragged in. Dinghies or skiffs only, no larger boats.

NODALES CHANNEL

Thurston Bay Marine Park. Thurston Bay Marine Park is large enough to hold many boats without feeling too crowded. We've had good overnight anchorages in Handfield Bay, and in 36 feet behind Block Island.

The landlocked inlet behind Wilson Point, on the south side of Thurston Bay, is best entered at half tide or higher. Wolferstan calls this inlet Anchorage Lagoon. At the entrance, least depth at zero tide is 2 feet or less. We tiptoed in near the bottom of a 2.9-foot low tide with the depth sounder showing 6 feet (our boat drew 3 feet). Inside we found four boats at anchor in a pretty setting, with 9 to 10 feet of depth. This is a good place to know your vessel's draft and the tidal range during your stay.

Be bear aware when ashore.

LOCAL KNOWLEDGE

Dangerous Rocks: Note that in the entrance to Cameleon Harbour, Douglas Rock, which dries at 1.5 meters, is detached from Bruce Point. Give Bruce Point ample room.

Handfield Bay. Enter via Young or Burgess Passages, located to port as you enter Cameleon Harbour. Chart 3543 (1:40,000) makes it clear that you should enter Handfield Bay leaving Tully Island to port. Once inside you'll find excellent protection, good anchoring depths, and shore access. The rock north of Tully Island is usually easy to spot at half tide. Handfield Bay is a favorite stop for many cruisers.

Cameleon Harbour. Cameleon Harbour is a big, open bay with ample protected anchorage, depending on where you need the shelter.

Hemming Bay. Enter leaving the Lee Islands well to starboard to avoid Menace Rock in the middle of the bay. Most of Hemming Bay is deep, but you can find anchoring depths near the head. Field Correspondent Deane Hislop reports a large booming operation on the north shore with signage warning of cables across the bottom; anchorage is possible at the southwest side of the bay, but the beauty of the bay is spoiled by the logging operation.

⑥ **Shoal Bay.** Shoal Bay has a public float with good anchorage off the outboard end. The water shallows dramatically at the head of the bay. Shoal Bay is protected from most winds blowing down Cordero Channel, but is open to wakes from passing boats. It has a beautiful view up Phillips Arm. It's a good place to wait for slack water at the rapids north

Denham Bay docks just above Dent Rapids overlooking Cordero Channel

or south. Rafting is mandatory; set out fenders on both sides. The docks fill quickly during the summer, so arrive early or be prepared to anchor out. No power or water at the docks. Mark MacDonald is the wharfinger, and moorage fees are collected at the Shoal Bay Pub, just up from the head of the wharf.

⑥ **Shoal Bay Pub.** General Delivery, Blind Channel, BC V0P 1B0; (250) 287-6818; shoalbay@mac.com; www.shoalbay.ca. Open May 1 to October 1, cash payments. Free Wi-Fi at the pub, washrooms, showers and laundry. Guest cabins through Airbnb. The pub has cold beer and other beverages, indoor seating, and a deck with breathtaking views up Phillips Arm.

A large vegetable patch, adorned with sculpture, is available for garden-deprived cruisers who like to get their hands dirty. All tools are provided. Pay by donation for what you pick. Mark's wife Cynthia is a talented potter, and her locally thrown and fired pottery is available for sale. Her work adorns the property.

For exercise, take the sometimes challenging hike up the mountain to the abandoned gold mine. Be bear aware.

The Shoal Bay International Blues Festival is held in early August, check their website for dates. What started out as a bunch of friendly folks jamming now has a stage with a schedule of acts. The dock and anchorage fill quickly, so arrive early. The music goes on into the wee hours and echoes across the bay.

Phillips Arm. Phillips Arm is deep, with little protection along the shores. Fanny Bay looks good on the chart, but has log booming activity. A northwest wind can blow through a saddle in the mountains at the head of **Fanny Bay**. On an earlier visit we found a stiff breeze in the bay; in Phillips Arm the air was calm. Large logging operations are located near the head of the inlet. A friend, much experienced, tells us not to anchor in the area of Dyer Point. The bottom there is foul with a tangle of sunken logs. *[Hale]*

Bickley Bay. Bickley Bay on Cordero Channel has anchoring depths toward the head of the bay. Favor the east shore to avoid a shoal area. Friends who have cruised in the area extensively warn of poor holding ground and won't go in anymore. Phil Richter at Blind Channel Resort also warns of poor holding. Caution advised.

⑦ **Cordero Lodge.** Cordero Lodge, General Delivery, Blind Channel, BC V0P 1B0; currently no phone number; corderolodge@gmail.com; www.corderolodge.com. The Lodge and restaurant closed in 2017 due to the death of the previous owner. New owners have not taken any steps to-date to refurbish the facility.

Please slow down. Passing boat traffic in Cordero Channel can put out wakes that damage the remaining docks.

Crawford Anchorage. Crawford Anchorage, between Erasmus Island and East Thurlow Island, is chancy at best, with a rocky and poor holding bottom. Friends report they have anchored in Crawford Anchorage successfully, using a Bruce anchor and a stern-tie to Erasmus Island. We tried anchoring with indifferent results. Enter Crawford Anchorage from the west—rocks lie in the eastern entrance. Rocks also lie southeast of Mink Island.

Mayne Passage (Blind Channel). Mayne Passage connects Cordero Channel with Johnstone Strait. From Johnstone Strait, the entrance can be hard to spot, hence the local name "Blind Channel." The current in Mayne Passage reaches 5 knots at springs, flooding north and ebbing south. Chart 3543 (1:40,000) shows rips in the northern part of Mayne Passage, and Sailing Directions warns of whirlpools and overfalls. Passages near slack are recommended. Blind Channel Resort, on the west shore of Mayne Passage, is popular. On the east side of Mayne Passage, Charles Bay is a good anchorage.

Charles Bay. On the east side of Mayne Passage, Charles Bay has convenient anchoring depths around Eclipse Islet in the center of the bay. Just east of Eclipse Islet, however, the bay shoals to drying flats.

LOCAL KNOWLEDGE

STRONG CURRENTS: Current runs across the face of the floats at Blind Channel Resort and landing can be a little tricky. At the fingers themselves, the current runs from north to south about 90 percent of the time, regardless of the current in the middle of the channel. A short distance off the fingers, however, the current usually runs from south to north. You can verify the current direction at the docks by observing which way the fingers press against the pilings at the outer ends. Call on the VHF for docking instructions. One of the staff always comes down to help with landings. They know what to do.

⑧ **Blind Channel Resort.** Blind Channel, BC V0P 1B0; (888) 329-0475; info@blindchannel.com; www.blindchannel.com. Monitors VHF 66A. Open all year, gasoline, diesel, propane. Ample moorage on 2000 feet of dock, 15, 30 & some 50 amp power, washrooms, showers, laundry, UV-treated spring water, free Wi-Fi. Garbage drop for a fee, no charge for glass and cans. Floatplanes stop here. This is a

The view of Phillips Arm and Shoal Bay public floats from the Shoal Bay Pub

JOHNSTONE STRAIT

See Area Map Page 342 - Maps Not for Navigation

Blind Channel Resort's Cedar Post Restaurant features menu items with a focus on German cuisine. Reservations are recommended.

complete, well-run, and popular marina and resort, with water taxi, adventure tours, accommodations, well-stocked store, fresh-baked goods during the high season, post office, liquor agency, gift items. The nice gazebo overlooking the marina is a welcome addition in rainy weather. Several events are held throughout the summer months, check their website for the season's schedule.

The resort is surrounded by hiking trails, developed and maintained by Interfor. One trail leads to an 900-year-old cedar, 16 feet in diameter. It's a good hike and a splendid old tree. Recommended.

The fully-licensed Cedar Post Restaurant (open June-Labour Day) is excellent. Alex Barton, who grew up with German cuisine, is head chef and has a passion for fresh local ingredients. Breakfast, lunch and dinner are offered daily during the peak season. The Grill Shack on the seaside patio is open for Happy Hour in July and August, starting at 5:00 p.m. Don't miss the home-made pretzels.

This is a real family enterprise, now spanning four generations. Edgar and the late Annemarie Richter bought Blind Channel in the early 1970s. Edgar designed and built all the buildings, and Annemarie's distinctive and lovely artwork decorates the dock and the restaurant. What they built, with long hours and hard labor, is a long way from what they bought 40 years ago.

Their son Phil Richter is general manager. Phil and Jennifer's sons Eliot and William grew up working on the docks and in the dining room. Eliot is now a partner in the business and lives on-site. You will most likely see Eliot's children running around the property, learning and having fun.

LOCAL KNOWLEDGE

Tidal Current Turbine Generator: July 2017, Blind Channel Resort added a tidal current turbine generator anchored in Mayne Passage less than 1/4 mile north of the resort and 400 feet from the West Thurlow Island shore. Most of the turbine generator is below the water's surface with part of the frame floating above. The turbine supplies electrical power to the resort.

⑨ **Greene Point Rapids.** Currents in Greene Point Rapids can run to 7 knots on spring tides. On small tides currents are much less. Sailing Directions warns of "considerable overfalls, whirlpools and eddies," and recommends transiting near slack. Slack water occurs about 1 hour and 30 minutes before slack water at Seymour Narrows. Current corrections are shown under Seymour Narrows in the Secondary Stations section in Tide and Current Tables Vol. 6, and in Ports and Passes. When eastbound on flood tides, low-powered boats, and boats with tows, are cautioned against being set against Erasmus Island.

Loughborough Inlet. Loughborough (pronounced "Loch-brough") Inlet, off Chancellor Channel, is deep, with steep-to sides and few good anchorages. The best anchorage used to be in Beaver Inlet, a short distance from the mouth on the western shore. Beaver Inlet is now a log booming ground with significant commercial activity, making it ill-suited to pleasure boats. Edith Cove in Beaver Inlet is occupied by a float home and log raft, so it's not an anchorage.

Sidney Bay. Sidney Bay indents the western shore of Loughborough Inlet, where resident homesteaders Dane Campbell and Helen Piddington operate a rustic 200-foot float for visiting boats, located on the south side of the bay 50°30.88'N/125°36.06'W. Payment can be made at the float shed, or across the bay at their home on the north shore. A picnic table and book exchange are in the float shed. Dane most likely will be ready to receive your painter line and provide good conversation. Field Correspondent Deane Hislop writes, "It's well protected from the wind and a beautiful location. We've stayed many times." Dane is a soft spoken commercial fisherman that we have found quite interesting to talk to. In 1975 he and his wife moved to Sidney Bay, where they raised their two children. Helen's book, *The Inlet*, describes life and their experiences in Loughborough Inlet." Her other book, *The Rumble Seat*, describes growing up in the 1930's near Victoria BC. The Landons report that Helen's health is failing; boaters may wish to visit this pioneer out-station, one of the last remaining from a bygone era, before it too passes with time.

WELLBORE CHANNEL

⑩ **Whirlpool Rapids.** Whirlpool Rapids on **Wellbore Channel** has currents to 7 knots. The time of turn is based on Seymour Narrows, and corrections are shown under Secondary Current Stations in the Tide and Current Tables Vol. 6, and Ports and Passes. The flood sets southeast and the ebb sets northwest. When the current is running, expect strong whirlpools, upwellings and back eddies on the downstream side. The turbulence occurs south of Carterer Point on the flood, and north of Carterer Point on the ebb. It is best to transit within a half-hour of slack, although on small tides boats seem to go through anytime. At low tide you might see bears on the beach near the south entrance to Wellbore Channel.

Forward Harbour. The entrance to Forward Harbour is narrow but unobstructed. Most of the harbor is 60 to 90 feet deep. Douglas Bay is a pretty anchorage, sheltered from Johnstone Strait westerlies that turn and blow through Sunderland Channel. The bottom of Douglas Bay drops off quickly, and you may find yourself anchored in 60 feet of water instead of 30 feet—a good reason to carry at least 300 feet of anchor rode. We've had a report that a southeast wind can make for a rough time for boats anchored along the northern shore. Field Correspondent Jim Norris reports cell reception outside and east of Douglas Bay, along the north shore.

A trail leads from Douglas Bay to a white sand beach at Bessborough Bay. The trail is reportedly well-marked and easy to walk with blue rope marking the trailhead at each end.

If Forward Harbour is too full, good anchorage can be found in the little bay on Hardwicke Island, directly across from the mouth of Forward Harbour.

Bessborough Bay. Although you can find anchoring depths in the southeast corner, the entire bay is open to strong westerlies blowing up Sunderland Channel.

Topaze Harbour. Big and pretty enough, but little shelter for small boats.

Sunderland Channel. Sunderland Channel connects Wellbore Channel with Johnstone Strait. If the westerly is blowing and whitecaps are in Sunderland Channel, it will likely be worse in Johnstone Strait. Many boats wait out these conditions in Forward Harbour.

All of the channels northwest of Yuculta Rapids—Nodales Channel, Mayne Passage, Chancellor Channel, and Sunderland Channel—lead to Johnstone Strait. Each provides some protection and a chance to observe conditions on Johnstone Strait before venturing out. A strong westerly wind opposed by an ebb current can make Johnstone Strait difficult.

JOHNSTONE STRAIT

Johnstone Strait is a seductive and difficult body of water. The strait begins at Chatham Point in the east, and stretches 54 miles along the northeast side of Vancouver Island to Blinkhorn Peninsula. It is the shortest route up- or down-island. Especially on the Vancouver Island side, Johnstone Strait is bounded by steep, high and beautiful mountains. On a clear day the scenery is awesome.

That is the seductive part. The difficult part is what the wind and current in Johnstone Strait do to each other. The flood current flows eastward, down-island, toward Discovery Passage and Campbell River. The ebb current flows westward, up-island, toward Queen Charlotte Strait and the North Pacific Ocean. A residual ebb surface current exists in Johnstone Strait, increasing the west-flowing ebb current's strength and duration. In the summer, the prevailing wind in Johnstone Strait is a westerly, often a gale-force westerly, funneled by the mountains. The result is a classic wind-against-current heaping up of the seas.

Conditions are worst where the meeting of currents creates tide-rips, even in calm conditions. This stretch begins at Ripple Shoal, east of Kelsey Bay. It extends westward past Kelsey Bay, through Race Passage and Current Passage, and across the mouth of Sunderland Channel. Especially on an ebb, when the westerly is blowing you don't want to be there—period. Leave the heroics to others. Johnstone Strait can take all the pleasure out of a pleasure boat. Monahan's Local Knowledge diagrams, earlier in this chapter, illustrate Johnstone Strait's trouble spots.

Despite the potential problems, we have run the length of Johnstone Strait, both directions, many times, and often had an excellent ride. But we listened to the weather and went when conditions were calm or near-calm. If the wind had come up, we were prepared to run for cover in a bay or seek out a friendly point to hide behind until conditions improved. We always keep a bail-out point in mind. Conditions can change quickly.

Watch for drift in Johnstone Strait. There's considerable current activity, and many shear lines where scrap wood, tree limbs, logs, and even entire floating trees accumulate.

Turn Island. Turn Island is off the southern tip of East Thurlow Island, at the intersection of Johnstone Strait and Discovery Passage. Anchor behind Turn Island, about where the 5.8-meter sounding is shown on the chart across from Turn Bay, with good holding and room to swing. The anchorage has nice views to Johnstone Strait and the mountains on Vancouver Island. *[Hamilton]* Charts show a log dump north of this anchorage. Reader Kelly Calvert reports snagging a logging cable when they anchored in small Turn Bay behind Turn Island.

Knox Bay. Knox Bay is located on the north side of Johnstone Strait, near the mouth of Mayne Passage. Knox Bay would be a poor choice for an anchorage, but a good hideout to escape a strong westerly in the strait. The northwest corner of the bay is best protected. Unfortunately, it is deep and occasionally has log booming.

Fanny Island. When the Environment Canada weather station was moved from Helmcken Island to Fanny Island a few years ago, Johnstone Strait weather reports improved dramatically (Helmcken Island could report 8 knots of wind when it was blowing 30). We're told, however, that while Fanny Island reports of northwest winds are fairly accurate, south and east winds can be reported less than what's actually going on.

Helmcken Island. Helmcken Island has protected anchorage on its north side in Billygoat Bay. Currents in this part of the strait run at 5 knots. When opposed by wind from the opposite direction large, dangerous seas can build rapidly. Billygoat Bay is a good place to hide out. Anchor in approximately 30 feet, although Correspondents James and Jennifer Hamilton found only poor holding over rock. Instead, they recommend the cove northwest of Billygoat Bay. They go up to the head of the cove, where they have found calm water, with an "awesome" view eastward. The cove is unnamed in Sailing Directions or on the chart. The Hamiltons call it Helmcken Cove.

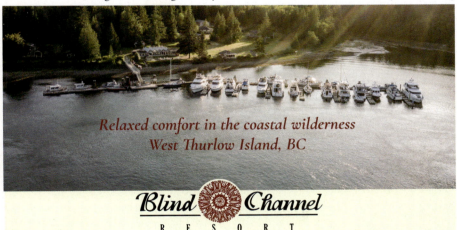

Relaxed comfort in the coastal wilderness
West Thurlow Island, BC

Blind Channel RESORT

Full Service Marina & Fuel Dock with power, potable water, gas, diesel & propane.

Dine at the Cedar Post Inn: Seasonal breakfast, grilled lunch, happy hour & dinner.

Well stocked store: groceries, liquor, ice & fresh baked goods

Amenities: WIFI, showers, laundromat, tours, water taxi & post office.

Versatile rental cottages.

Enjoy the ambiance.
Marina • Hiking Trails • Tours • Water Taxi • Cottages

info@blindchannel.com | 1-888-329-0475 | www.blindchannel.com

JOHNSTONE STRAIT

⑪ **Kelsey Bay.** (250) 282-3623. Kelsey Bay, on the north side of Vancouver Island, has a breakwater southeast of the harbor, made of old ship hulks—the Union Steamship *Cardena* and three WWII frigates: *HMCS Runnymede, HMCS Lasalle,* and *HMCS Longueil*. Enter leaving the light green breakwater to starboard and the old ships to port. Watch for current entering the breakwater. Transient moorage is on A, B, and C docks, maximum length 60 feet. Water, 20 and 30 amp power, garbage drop, recycling, oil disposal. Most of the moorage is occupied by commercial fish boats. Rafting may be required. Moorage is paid at the honor box at the top of the ramp, an attendant is on site during the summer months. We found the docks to be clean and well maintained The Straits View Cafe, located behind the breakwater, welcomes boaters at their 100-foot dock while enjoying lunch or dinner. The cafe is open Thursday and Friday starting at 11:00 a.m., and Saturday and Sunday starting at 9:00 a.m., operating until 7:30 p.m. Overnight stays are permitted on the Cafe dock, moorage charged, 20-amp power, reservations accepted, call (250) 282-0118.

A small gift shop that doubles as a tourist office is located on the wharf at the north end of the marina. The small village of Sayward is approximately one mile south, some services but the grocery store is no longer open.

Yorke Island. Located in the middle of Johnstone Strait, west of Hardwicke Island, Yorke Island is the site of several gun emplacements which were installed in 1937. These ruins from WWII were originally intended to block enemy backdoor approach to the Strait of Georgia and the cities of Vancouver and Victoria. Well maintained trails by BC Parks lead from the south cove on the island to various gun and battery sites. The main gun emplacement is at the highest point on the island with great views of the Strait and is visible from passing boats. Yorke Island is a haunting place to visit and worth the stop in the right conditions. Maps of the island and more historical information can be found at www.wikipedia.org/wiki/Yorke_Island_(Canada). Temporary anchorage can be found in 30 to 45 feet of water, east of the unnamed cove on the south side of the island. The cove is often covered with kelp and the bottom is rocky with poor holding. Wind and current are a consideration. Leaving the boat unattended is not recommended. Charted rocks lie south of the cove.

Blenkinsop Bay. Blenkinsop Bay has reasonably protected anchorage along the north shore of Johnstone Strait, but swells from westerly winds work into the bay. The chart shows tide-rips off Blenkinsop Bay. The chart isn't kidding. McLeod Bay and an unnamed bay inside Tuna Point are possible temporary anchorages.

⑫ **Port Neville.** Port Neville is an 8-mile-long inlet, a popular hideout for the fishing fleet, and an excellent spot to duck into if the weather in Johnstone Strait deteriorates. The inlet is a good anchorage. A government dock and float are a short distance inside, along the eastern shore. Boomed logs are stored in several places toward the inner end of the inlet. No public facilities or services are in the vicinity. The current can run swiftly past the government float, so plan your approach carefully. Remember, there's no shame in making several attempts before you get your landing right.

For years Olaf "Oly" Hansen, at the government dock post office, could be reached by radio for a report on conditions on Johnstone Strait. Oly died in January, 1997 at age 87, another legend gone from the coast. Oly's widow Lilly lived on in the family house for a few years, but finally had to move down-island. In 2003, shortly after her 90th birthday, she too left us. Their daughter Lorna (Hansen) Chesluk raised her daughter Erica in the house at the head of the wharf. Lorna was the postmaster, and she happily looked out on the strait and gave a report if you called on the radio.

The post office was closed in 2010, and Lorna moved to Campbell River to be closer to family. The Hansen family had lived at Port Neville since 1891. Until it closed, the Port Neville post office was the longest continuously-operating post office in the province. Yet another page of coastal history is turned. A caretaker now looks after the property. The wonderful old store building is at the head of the wharf. Occasionally tour and whale watching groups stop by to see the old post office, still frozen in time.

If you go ashore, keep pets on a leash. Wild animals (grizzly bears and black bears) and protective mother deer are in the area.

On the west side of Robbers Nob, near the tip, several petroglyphs can be seen below the high tide line. The property above the high tide line is private.

Anchoring: Correspondents Elsi and Steve Hulsizer report after trying several anchoring locations in Port Neville, their preferred spot is across the inlet from the public dock where the water is protected from northwest winds by hills. Correspondents James and Jennifer Hamilton recommend anchoring in Baresides Bay, directly south of the MSh symbol on Charts 3545 and 3564 where you will be in 15 feet of water at zero tide, about 200 feet from shore. Excellent holding. Not the most protected but out of the worst of westerly winds.

LOCAL KNOWLEDGE

RESTRICTED AREA: Robson Bight, on the Vancouver Island side near the north end of Johnstone Strait, is an Ecological Reserve, a gathering place for Orcas. Unauthorized vessels (meaning yours and ours) are not allowed. Stay outside of the Reserve's boundary lines noted on the charts.

Robson Bight. The Robson Bight Ecological Reserve is a restricted area that runs 0.5 mile offshore and for 5 miles off Robson Bight. It is part of a reserve for Orca whales. The Reserve is not centered on the Bight and extends more to the east. The Reserve is shown on most charts but may be hard to see. If you stray into the restricted area, wardens will intercept your boat and instruct you to leave immediately.

Views of Johnstone Strait from Yorke Island's WWII gun emplacements

The view from the Straits Bay Cafe at Kelsey Bay

Dent Island Lodge

Dent Island Lodge is one of the premier yachting destinations of the Pacific Northwest. Uniformed dock attendants meet arrivals with cheerful greetings and a helpful hand; every guest is made to feel personally welcomed and remembered. Meals are exceptional, both at the main restaurant and at the outdoor Rapids Grill. Advanced reservations are a must for both dining venues, especially during the peak season.

While the prices reflect the high quality of fine dining, the experience is worth the splurge. Waggoner readers Peter Brown and Janet McKinnon reported their favorable experience at Dent Island Lodge with the Waggoner Team. They found the new lodge and expanded chef's kitchen impressive. A five-course evening meal is served in the dining room, with menu items ranging from wild salmon, local Dungeness crab, and halibut, to duck, lamb, and the finest cuts of beef. The outdoor Rapids Grill offers a casual, relaxed setting overlooking Canoe Pass rapids, or you can sit around the Rapids Grill bar where meals are prepared right in front of you. It's a one-of-a-kind venue for enjoying fine wines, great food, and good conversation.

Peter chose the Organic Cranberry, vegetable & Goat Cheese Stuffed Pork Tenderloin with wild mushroom risotto in a house bourdelaise, and Janet chose the Porcini Mushroom Crusted Beef Tenderloin with sautéed spot prawns, served with herb & garlic whipped potatoes and Pattison farm vegetables. Other choices included the Pan Seared Halibut and the House Dijon Crusted Rack of Lamb. Breakfast and lunch are other options available to boaters, who want to experience the unique, natural setting found on little Dent Island.

The Broughtons

CHAPTER 12

THE BROUGHTONS
*Port Harvey • Lagoon Cove
Minstrel Island Harbour
Kwatsi Bay • Echo Bay
Sullivan Bay • Jennis Bay*

THE BROUGHTONS

Beautiful Lacy Falls in Tribune Channel near Watson Cove and Kwatsi Bay

"**The Broughtons**" is an all-encompassing term for the inlets, islands and waterways on the mainland side of Queen Charlotte Strait, north of Johnstone Strait. This area includes the islands adjoining Blackfish Sound and Fife Sound. It also includes Knight Inlet, Kingcome Inlet, Tribune Channel, Drury Inlet, and Mackenzie Sound. For convenience we include Havannah Channel and Chatham Channel. Locals call this area the Mainland, to distinguish it from the Vancouver Island side from Sayward (Kelsey Bay) to the top of Vancouver Island, which they call North Island.

The Broughtons, or the Mainland, is one large, complex cruising ground. It offers anchorages from raw and wind-swept Fife Sound and Blackfish Sound, to the gentler waters of Simoom Sound, Greenway Sound and Drury Inlet. A few small, family-owned resorts—no two of them alike—are found throughout the Broughtons. Most cruisers anchor out some of the time and enjoy the social side of marina life the rest of the time. During the course of a cruising holiday, most cruisers either stop at or overnight at all the marinas: Lagoon Cove, Kwatsi Bay, Pierre's at Echo Bay, Sullivan Bay, and Jennis Bay, along with docks at Port Harvey and Minstrel Island.

Resupply and repairs are on the North Island side, at Port McNeill, Alert Bay, Sointula, and Port Hardy. North Island is described in the next chapter.

The rich history of the Broughtons begins with Native habitation dating back thousands of years. On Mound Island, 14 depressions in the earth are evidence of Native Bighouses and Longhouses, each of which held extended families. We're told that trading beads, the colorful glass beads exchanged for valuable pelts by early traders, can sometimes be found on beaches throughout the Broughtons. The ruins of two uninhabited native village sites in the Broughtons can be visited, one at Karlukwees on Turnour Island and Mimkwamlis on Village Island. Pictographs can be found in several locations in the Broughtons and their locations are noted in this chapter. The village of New Vancouver on the north tip of Harbledown Island is home to native peoples with settlements along Knight Inlet. At New Vancouver you will find a dock with guest moorage; ask about a tour of the longhouse.

The Broughtons were homesteaded in the late 1800s and early 1900s. Families were raised on rude farms. The men rowed across Queen Charlotte Strait to Alert Bay, or rowed—*rowed*—200 miles south to Vancouver or Victoria to conduct business and bring back supplies.

In most cases, the forest has erased all traces of the homesteaders' now-abandoned efforts. One notable exception is remarkable "Monks' Wall," at the north end of Beware Passage. There, hidden in the trees, are the remains of rock walls from William and Mary Anne Galley's wilderness trading post that was active from the late 1800s until after the First World War.

The Broughtons are a destination. Take your time and don't hurry through. See Billy Proctor's museum in Proctor Bay. Marvel at Lacy Falls on Tribune Channel. Anchor out in the coves and lagoons. Visit the marinas and meet the families who run them.

Ask questions, read the history, and take time to explore. If you spend your entire cruise in the Broughtons, you might—you just might—scratch the surface.

Marinas: Marinas in the Broughtons are different from marinas elsewhere on the coast. They're small and often family run; each marina has its own character and charm. Some cruisers develop friendships with the owners, and come back year after year to catch up. Owners of these wilderness marinas make do with what they have in regards to power and water. Power is normally an additional charge and can be more expensive than elsewhere. Most of the power is generated on site using expensive fuel powered generators managed by the marina.

Wi-Fi: Internet in the Broughtons is provided by satellite, and bandwidth is limited. Marina owners request that visitors refrain from downloading videos, sending large email attachments, using Skype, or engaging in other high bandwidth activities.

Potluck Hour: Several of the marinas in the Broughtons have a potluck hors d'oeuvre—or even a potluck dinner—gathering around 5:00 p.m. Bring your own beverages, leaded or unleaded and your own plate with utensils. It's an ideal time to meet other boaters and exchange information. Kids usually are more than welcome, although if they're the only ones they might get bored with grownups' chit-chat. You'll want to carry a stock of suitable fixings for your hors d'oeuvre or

Small intimate marinas are found among the Broughtons Archipelago.

THE BROUGHTONS — Reference Only – Not for Navigation

The Broughtons - East

See Area Map Page 354 - Maps Not for Navigation

THE BROUGHTONS

Range markers in Chatham Channel guide you safely through.

potluck contribution. The fixings don't have to be fancy. If you're down to Doritos and salsa, they'll be hoovered into mouths in short order. If you enjoy preparing something special, this is a good time to show your stuff.

Good Books: Tide Rips and Back Eddies; and Full Moon, Flood Tide. Both by Bill Proctor, edited and illustrated by Yvonne Maximchuk. Published by Harbour Publishing. These books are highly recommended reading before or during a cruise to the Broughtons. If you are hungry for a little more, consider Yvonne's book, *Drawn to Sea*, for more insights on life and the people of this area.

HAVANNAH CHANNEL

Havannah Channel leads northward to Call Inlet, Chatham Channel and Knight Inlet.

① **Port Harvey.** Port Harvey is large, and although it is open to westerlies from Johnstone Strait, it is an excellent anchorage. If you're planning an early morning run on Johnstone Strait, it's a good place to overnight. You'll find anchorage in several notches along the east side before you reach the head of the bay, and ample anchorage at the head.

A big logging operation is on the west side of Port Harvey. A permanent house with private mooring floats is on the shore. The wind blows through Cracroft Inlet, and a gentle, low surge can come in if the wind is blowing on Johnstone Strait.

Caution: Do not attempt the narrow channel that leads between Port Harvey and Cracroft Inlet that dries and is studded with boulders.

Port Harvey Marine Resort is located at the head of Port Harvey. They charge a fee for landing the dinghy on their docks.

① **Port Harvey Marine Resort.** St. 108, 1434 Ironwood St., Campbell River, BC V9W 5T5; (250) 902-9003; portharveymarine@gmail.com; www.portharvey.blogspot.com. Monitors VHF 66A. Guests welcomed with ample 1000 feet of side-tie moorage on good docks. Easy access to shore for walking the dog or walking the trail through the forest.

George Cambridge, who had the vision and created this special marina, passed away unexpectedly in July 2018. George was industrious and hard-working, he will be missed. The docks are open for moorage at your own risk on a first-come, first-serve basis. No power, no water or Wi-Fi. In 2019, a wharfinger was on site during the months of July and August to collect moorage, cash only.

The marina isn't visible until you get all the way to the head of Port Harvey beyond Range Island. You will see the industrial operation on the shore first. Port Harvey Marina is just across the bay.

Bockett Islets. Tom Kincaid has anchored for a few hours among the Bockett Islets awaiting favorable current in Chatham Channel.

Boughey Bay. Anchorage is toward the south end of Boughey (pronounced "boogie") Bay. John Chappell (*Cruising Beyond Desolation Sound*) says easterly winds can spring up suddenly in the bay.

Matilpi. Matilpi (pronounced MAT-il-pi) is a former Indian village site. It is beautiful, with a white shell beach backed by dense forest. Anchor behind the northern of the two islands, or between the islands. Protection is excellent.

Burial Cove. Burial Cove is pretty, though open to most winds. It is well-protected from seas and has good holding in 25 feet. A few houses are on shore. We've anchored there twice. A large set of private docks are along the northeast shore.

Call Inlet. Call Inlet is approximately 10 miles long, and runs through beautiful, steep-sided mountains. You can find anchoring depths in the **Warren Islands**, near the mouth of the inlet. Anchorages are open to views up Call Inlet; and open to westerly and easterly winds. Holding is fair; preferred locations are on the east and west ends of the island chain away from upland buildings and a work barge with heavy equipment. The Islands are a pretty stop, where you can wait for the current to change in Chatham Channel, or for an overnight stay in settled weather. Field Correspondent Deane Hislop reports "two wonderful nights anchored in a depth of 35 feet; views of the islands and Call Inlet are outstanding."

Chatham Channel. Chatham Channel is easier to run than it appears from the chart. The southern section is the narrowest, with the least room in the channel, and requires the greatest attention. The current floods east and ebbs west. Near slack water is the most pleasant time to transit this southern section.

Slacks are based on Seymour Narrows predictions. Correction factors for the times of slack water are found under Secondary Stations in the Tide and Current Tables, Vol. 6, and Ports and Passes. Chart 3545 (1:40,000) shows the area, including the range locations. Chart 3564 (1:20,000), with its 1:10,000 insert of the southern section, really helps understanding. We highly recommend Chart 3564.

If you are running compass courses through the southern section, remember that the headings shown on the chart are true, and must be corrected to magnetic. We have found that in some lighting conditions, or if the trees are not trimmed, the ranges are hard to locate from the far ends of the lower channel. Going either direction, a sharp-eyed crew should sight astern at the back range until it grows difficult to see. By then the leading range should be visible. Maximum currents in the southern section run to 5 knots on a spring tide, with no significant swirls or overfalls. In our experience, the current usually is much less than shown (but not always; twice, we have found considerable current). Chatham Channel can be taken at times other than slack water, but you should know what you are doing, and in the southern section *keep your boat lined up on the range*. Keep your eyes open. We encountered a bear swimming across Chatham Channel one morning.

Cutter Cove. Cutter Cove, located across from Minstrel Island Resort (now closed) at the north end of Chatham Channel, is very pretty and a good anchorage. A fresh west or northwest wind can enter the cove. No swells, but aggressive little whitecaps. The bottom looks flat, as if it's pure mud. "At least one noisy old rock is down there, though, because the anchor chain dragged across it all night long." *[Hale]* Anchor in 24 feet (zero tide).

Minstrel Island Harbour. Minstrel Island Harbour is well protected from all winds and offers anchorage for a number of boats. A new 160-foot dock, along with a re-purposed 90-foot dock, are available for guest moorage at no charge; both docks are detached from land. No power, no water, and no garbage drop. There are no upland services. Boaters may go ashore by dinghy or kayak to the pubic uplands; other surrounding property is private.

This site has a long and varied history. Its name comes from the late 19th century when

2020 WAGGONER CRUISING GUIDE

THE BROUGHTONS

See Area Map Page 354 - Maps Not for Navigation

Lagoon Cove docks and office with Clio Channel in the distance

Popular Happy Hour at Lagoon Cove is held at the historic workshop.

a survey ship visited the area with a minstrel troupe onboard, who provided musical entertainment. During the early 1900's, Minstrel Island had a hotel, dance hall, store, and school along with a machine shop and boat repair services. An old pier was once the center for freight deliveries, including mail for residents of The Broughtons. In later years, the docks served as a popular destination for motor yachts, with a floatplane base.

The pier, floats, and upland buildings deteriorated for over a decade. In 2019 the pier and old docks were removed by Small Craft Harbours, part of the Fisheries & Oceans Department. Boaters can now make use of the two detached floats for guest moorage.

LOCAL KNOWLEDGE

CAUTION: When entering Lagoon Cove from Blow Hole, give the Islet and shoal across the channel from Perley Island a wide berth as the shoal extends further west than chart 3564 indicates. Look for a private orange and/or green round plastic float which should pass to your port side entering Lagoon Cove.

The Blow Hole. The Blow Hole is a short, shallow, easily-navigated channel between Minstrel Island and East Cracroft Island. The channel gets its name from strong westerly winds that sometimes blow through. Near the west end a reef, shown clearly on Chart 3564, extends from East Cracroft Island on the south side of the channel. Brave the kelp and favor the north side of the channel and you'll have no problems.

② **Lagoon Cove.** Lagoon Cove has good anchorage along the shorelines, although the middle of the bay is a little deep for most boats. Lagoon Cove Marina is on the east side of the bay. Locals recommend against anchoring on the west side of the bay, which they say is foul with logging cable. We got a note from a reader who said at least one cable can be found on the east side as well.

② **Lagoon Cove Marina.** c/o Minstrel Island P.O., Minstrel Island, BC V0P 1L0; (778) 819-6962; info@lagooncovemarina.com; www.lagooncovemarina.com. Monitors VHF 66A. Open all year. Reservations accepted; a portion of the docks are held open for drop-ins. Lagoon Cove has gasoline, diesel; 15, 30, & 2×30 amp power, water, washroom & showers, gift shop. Wi-Fi has been extended to the docks with repeaters. A cell phone booster is located in the book exchange. Kenmore Air, Corilair, and NW Seaplanes service to Seattle.

A do-it-yourself burn barrel is available for burnable garbage (no fair just dropping a bag of garbage in, for someone else to deal with). The fuel dock office carries fishing tackle, prawn and crab traps, ice, and ice cream. Pick up a jar of their Lagoon Cove prawn sauce or Lagoon Cove coffee. Complimentary coffee service is available on the dock each morning. A separate store with the grand name "Edgewater Emporium" carries Lagoon Cove branded clothing.

Lagoon Cove Marina
Easy to find, hard to leave

www.lagooncovemarina.com
778-819-6962 (text or call)
info@lagooncovemarina.com

- Moorage for boats large & small • Daily potluck happy hour
- Wi-Fi on the docks • 24 hour 15, 30, & 2×30 power
- Clear spring water • Diesel & gas • Hiking trails
- Fishing tackle • Washrooms & showers • Book exchange
- Clothing & gift shop • Friendly, relaxed atmosphere

The entire property has a whimsical quality about it. The workshop is a "historic" workshop full of old tools. A totem pole is made from pieces of outboard motors and all sorts of other junk. Two "exercise stations," one of them a pile of wood with an axe, the other a brightly painted lawnmower, invite the eager. Several hiking trails are maintained. A pet path is available for the four-legged crew. Be bear aware.

Lagoon Cove Marina is one of the most popular stops on the coast and fills during the summer months. Happy hour appetizer potlucks for marina guests are held almost every day in the "historic" workshop. Guests bring treats from their boats. Happy hour often morphs into a casual potluck dinner. Ping-Pong under the fruit trees is also a popular passtime.

Current owners, Jim and Lou Ryan, purchased the property in 2016 and began their first season in 2017 with lots of energy, making improvements to the marina while maintaining the beloved character and charm of Lagoon Cove. Their daughter Kelley and son-in-law Dan round out the family team. The Ryans are committed to "enhancing but not changing" this popular destination, as evidenced by dock repairs in 2018 and 2019 along with other upgrades.

Knight Inlet. Knight Inlet (locally called Knight's Inlet) extends from its mouth at Midsummer Island to its head, at the mouth of the Klinaklini River. The inlet is about 70 miles long and 2 miles wide, the longest of the fjords indenting the B.C. coast. Along most of its length, the shores rise steeply to 6,000-foot-high mountains. Anchorage is iffy at best, so for many, the inlet's upper reaches are explored mainly by fast boats able to make the round trip in a single day. Boats with limited fuel capacity should top off at Lagoon Cove before making the trip. Extensive logging activity has put considerable debris in the water. Watch carefully.

The section above Glendale Cove is reported to be more dramatic than Jervis or Bute inlets. Reader John Tyler reports, "Even with the distances involved, it's well worth the time to cruise up there."

Tsakonu Cove is a pretty anchorage with open views to the west and up Knight Inlet. It is protected from westerly inflow, but exposed to the east. It can be blowing summertime inflow outside the cove while much calmer inside. Anchor near the head of the cove in 50 to 70 feet with good holding. Driftwood logs on the shore suggest that outflow winds in Knight Inlet probably roar into Tsakonu Cove, accompanied by substantial seas. In 2019, the log dump on the south shore was not active. "Late one August afternoon we were pushing against 20 to 30 knot westerly winds on Knight Inlet when we pulled in to Tsakonu Cove for the night and found 5 to 8 knot winds inside the cove." [Landons].

Hoeya Sound. Hoeya Sound is pretty, but deep and completely exposed to the westerly winds that are prevalent in the summer.

Glendale Cove. Glendale Cove on Knight Inlet is a popular destination for recreational boaters and commercial tour operators. It has one of the highest concentrations of Grizzly Bears, also referred to as Brown Bears, on the west coast of British Columbia. Bears feed on tidal area sedge in the spring; and by mid-August, feed on salmon.

In May of 2017, the DAFN Glendale Cove Water-Based Grizzly Bear Viewing Management Plan was put into effect to create a sanctuary for bears by strictly managing the number of people accessing the bear viewing areas, and to limit boat traffic in Glendale Cove. Too many boats can easily crowd and displace the bear population. The Da'naxda'xw/Awaetlatla First Nations Band (DAFN) serve as Guardians and closely monitor all activities in the Cove, their traditional native territory. All of Glendale Cove waters and uplands are included in the managed area. The DAFN Keogh Indian Reserve (I.R.) #2 area is in the southeast corner of the Glendale Cove and is a Do Not Enter Zone.

When entering Glendale Cove, boaters should contact the "Glendale Cove Guardians" on VHF 68 to receive a copy of the Bear Viewing Guidelines brochure and map. All bear viewing is done from your vessel, kayak, or dinghy. No shore access at any time; dogs should not be taken on shore in Glendale Cove. The nearest beach access is at Duncan Bight to the northeast and Siwash Bay to the west.

There is a 5-knot speed limit throughout the cove (including dinghies). Boaters should be respectful of boat speed, noise, distance, and viewing time. Viewing is limited to 6 small craft at a time, maintaining a distance of 50 meters (164 feet) from shore. Commercial tour operators have prescribed time slots for viewing. Recreational boaters

Glendale Cove

Glendale Cove, up Knight Inlet, has one of the highest concentrations of Grizzly Bears on the Northern BC Coast.

THE BROUGHTONS

See Area Map Page 354 - Maps Not for Navigation

Nearby waterfalls gently interrupt the solitude of Kwatsi Bay Marina's remote setting, surrounded by towering mountains.

should contact "Glendale Cove Guardians" prior to viewing bears. Being good stewards and respectful boaters is important for the future preservation of Grizzly Bears.

Knight Inlet Lodge, located on the east side of Glendale Cove, is a private resort providing Grizzly Bear tours for their guests, seventy percent of whom visit from Europe and twenty percent come from Australia. Reservations are booked well in advance for this distinctive lodge. The Lodge does not provide transient moorage and does not offer any services for boaters visiting the area. A couple of small tour operations also operate in the area. Tour operators and private boaters alike all abide by the same bear-viewing regulations.

Anchorage is available in two small bights along the western shore of Glendale Cove. Anchor at least 200 meters (656 feet) from the waterline so as not to disturb bears that come to feed along the shore. Anchorages are protected from inflow westerly winds but are exposed to northeast outflow wind. Holding is good. About 4 nautical miles west of Glendale Cove is a small bay with possible anchoring behind Tomakstum Island on the south shore of Knight Inlet.

Wahshihlas Bay. Located at the mouth of the Sim River, Wahshihlas Bay is a possible anchorage. Although we've never tried it, Correspondents Bruce and Margaret Evertz have. "It was settled weather and we anchored in the northwest corner, just off the shoal. There were some snags to avoid. If we expected any winds we could have moved away from the shoal a little and anchored with a stern tie to shore or to some old pilings. The bay is far from 'bomb proof,' but we felt secure with the weather we had." [Evertz]

Port Elizabeth. Port Elizabeth is a great big bay bounded on the west by low hills that let westerlies in. A substantial log booming operation is in the cove in the northwest corner. You can find good anchorage near the booming site and along the western shore, west of the largest of the three islands. The two smaller islands are joined on the west by drying flats.

Correspondents John and Lorraine Littlewood provided us with the following extra information:

"The unexpected difficulty with the anchorage in Duck Cove at the west end of Port Elizabeth is that in any winds from 0 to 180 degrees you will feel the full force. We were getting gusts to 30 knots in a southeaster, supposedly sheltered. The only real shelter is in the extreme southeastern end of Port Elizabeth, except in a northwest blow." [Littlewood]

Sargeaunt Passage. Sargeaunt Passage connects Knight Inlet and Tribune Channel. The passage runs between steep-sided mountains with a shallow narrow neck near the middle. Some current is noticeable at the narrows. The shoal at the narrows extends from the east shore across much of the passage. Favor the west shore. The shallowest point is at the south end of the narrows with a minimum depth of approximately 9 feet at zero tide; much less than charts indicate. Anchorage is possible at either end of the narrows, although one cruiser warned of logging cables fouling their anchor and a deadhead marked with a red float was sighted on the southeast side.

Tribune Channel. Tribune Channel borders the east and north sides of Gilford Island. Several anchoring locations can be found along Tribune Channel but most are deep or best in settled weather. The only marina on Tribune Channel is at Kwatsi Bay. Lacy Falls on the north shore of Tribune Channel can be stunning. Two small native pictographs are clearly seen on a rock face about 20 to 30 feet above the high waterline on the east side of Miller Point.

Kumlah Island Anchorage. Kumlah Island is in Tribune Channel, roughly across from the mouth of Thompson Sound. Waggoner reader Joel Erickson found suitable anchorage in 16 to 24 feet behind Kumlah Island, between it and Gilford Island. We haven't spent the night, but would consider anchoring there in settled weather. The view is beautiful.

Thompson Sound. Thompson Sound is surrounded by forested mountains so steep that the hillsides are scarred by many landslides. Earlier editions of the Waggoner said Thompson Sound has no good anchorages, but Correspondents John and Lorraine Littlewood set us straight with this email: "There is excellent anchorage at the head of Thompson Sound, on the shelf between the mudflats at the mouth of the Kakweiken River. You can explore the river for a couple miles at high tide; there is lots of bear sign, and we don't mean black bears, either!"

A reader reported that when they tried to anchor, they found the shelf dotted with crab trap buoys, leaving no room. They anchored briefly in the lee of Sackville Island, with a stern-tie to shore.

Bond Sound. In the past, we reported that Bond Sound had no good anchorages. But inspired by Bill Proctor's wonderful book, *Full Moon, Flood Tide*, readers Jim and Marsha Peters anchored their Grand Banks 42 *Dev's Courage* at the head of the sound in settled weather and took the dinghy some distance up the Ahta River. They said it was beautiful. Correspondents Steve and Elsie Hulsizer say to go up about two hours before high water. Another reader, Bill Cooke, told us that cutthroat trout fishing is good at the head of the sound. Correspondents John and Lorraine Littlewood add this note from an early September cruise:

"Bill Proctor's book, *Full Moon, Flood Tide*, led us to the Ahta River at the head of Bond Sound, an absolutely pristine salmon spawning river teeming with every sort of wildlife, from very large, dead salmon that have just completed their life cycle, to much larger hairy brown mammals that feed on them (and just about anything else they want to). The place is like something from a fairy tale. It is not all that easy to find and explore, but very much worth it. Anchorage is tricky just off the drying bar at the mouth of the rivers (there are two: Ahta Creek on the left

A short rustic trail leads to the 1,000-year-old cedar tree at Watson Cove.

Reserve your space at Echo Bay's popular marina docks or try their Cliffside option on the other side of the bay.

as you face the estuary and the Ahta River on the right). The Ahta River, with a smaller opening, is deep, fast and clear. Don't tell a soul."

Note: Strong winds can funnel through Bond Sound, making it mostly unsuitable for overnight anchorage.

③ **Kwatsi Bay.** The inner cove of Tribune Channel's Kwatsi Bay is a stunning anchorage. This serene cove is surrounded by a high bowl of granite rock faces, waterfalls, and forested steps, one of the most impressive in the Broughtons. Sunrises and sunsets are magnificent. Rain will bring a number of waterfalls to life and will turn the waters darker with tannin. The bay is deep, over 100 feet in much of the inner cove. The favorite area for anchoring is in the northeast corner of the cove in 50 to 80 feet of water.

③ **Kwatsi Bay Marina.** Simoom Sound P.O., Simoom Sound, V0P 1S0; (250) 949-1384; kwatsibay@kwatsibay.com; www.kwatsibay.com. Monitors VHF 66A. Moorage, water, small gift store, Wi-Fi during set hours. No shore power. Visa and Mastercard accepted. Reservations are recommended for July and August, email is best.

Max Knierim and his wife Anca Fraser opened Kwatsi Bay Marina in 1998. Together with their daughter Marieke and son Russell, they carved out a place to live in the bush. Marieke and Russell have grown up and are pursuing their own careers. Max and Anca are empty nesters, except for the many friends and guests who visit Kwatsi Bay during the summer.

The store is small but classy, with a selection of local arts and crafts ranging from pottery and jewelry to woodwork. It also carries souvenir T-shirts, caps and sweatshirts. Short hiking trails are nearby, reached by dinghy. One leads to a beautiful waterfall. Max or Anca can provide directions. Kwatsi Bay often hosts a potluck happy hour on the dock in the evening. This is not a luxury resort; this is the wilderness, at its gentle but hardworking best.

Watson Cove. Watch for a charted rock in the entrance, and favor the north shore when entering. A 30 to 40 foot shallow shelf is just outside the entrance. Watson Cove is surrounded by shear rock walls, dense forest, and beautiful waterfalls on the north side. Although open to westerly winds and reportedly foul with logging debris, the cove is accessible for anchoring in 50 to 60 feet.

Land your dinghy at the rock slab about 200 feet before the head of the cove on the south shore, where you will find a large rusty anchor pin set into the rocky shoreline. Immediately above this landing, you will find a very rustic trail (bring boots) leading to the 1000-year-old cedar tree mentioned in Billy Proctor's *Full Moon, Flood Tide*. The tree is a memorable sight.

Lacy Falls. Just west of Watson Cove, Lacy Falls washes down an expanse of smooth black rock and tumbles into the sea. The boat can be brought up close, but not too close. The bottom at the base of the falls is rocky. Note: During dry periods, water does not fan across the rocks.

Wahkana Bay. The inner cove of Wahkana Bay is attractive, but 120 feet deep except near shore. The south shore has spots where you can anchor in 48 to 72 feet with swinging room, however. Parts of the east shore are reported to be foul with logging debris and old pilings beneath the surface. The head of the inner cove shoals rapidly so watch out. Wind can blow through the saddle that reaches to Viner Sound.

Viner Sound. Three-mile long Viner Sound is a fjord-like inlet. The entrance is wide and deep and the head of the inlet is a ¾ mile long drying area. The middle ¾ mile section is narrow and shallow with a few anchoring options and two sets of mooring buoys.

The indent on the north side, a short distance down the narrow channel, will hold one boat near the opening. Just inside that indent the water shoals immediately. Further up the narrow channel, two public mooring buoys are in the little cove on the north side and two older mooring buoys are in the indent immediately to the south of the cove. One of the two older buoys is half submerged.

The long shoaling area shown on the chart at the head of Viner Sound is real. Watch your depths as you explore. A trail reportedly goes from the north cove to a lake.

Scott Cove. Scott Cove once was a busy logging camp, but the camp is now closed. This was the location of Pierre's Bay Marina, which moved to Echo Bay in 2008. We're told a surprising number of people still show up every summer mistakenly looking for Pierre's Bay Marina in Scott Cove.

LOCAL KNOWLEDGE

POWELL ROCK WARNING: A nasty drying rock lies off Powell Point, the southwest corner of Scott Cove. A boat running between Tribune Channel and Echo Bay or Cramer Passage could easily run up on this rock. Give Powell Point (and the rock) a big, wide offing.

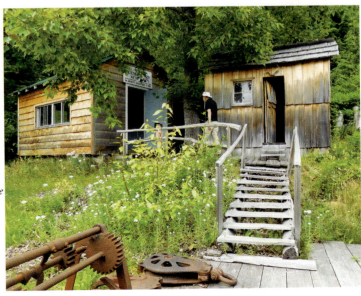
Children and adults alike enjoy visiting Billy Proctor's museum, including an old-fashioned school house and logger's cabin. It's a short hike from Echo Bay, or you can arrive by dinghy.

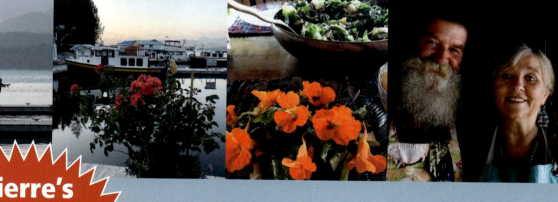

See Area Map Page 354 - Maps Not for Navigation   **THE BROUGHTONS**

Dinner events at Pierre's Echo Bay are very popular, reserve your place early.

④ **Echo Bay.** Echo Bay has been a gathering place for thousands of years, and for more than 100 years it has been a center for loggers, fishermen, and now summertime boaters. In 2008 Pierre and Tove (pronounced "Tova") Landry bought the Echo Bay Resort and moved Pierre's Bay Marina from nearby Scott Cove to Echo Bay. The Echo Bay Resort docks were scrapped and new docks, with upgraded power, were installed. The store was refurbished and restocked. A new fuel dock was built. In a span of about three months the resort was transformed—a remarkable achievement in a remote location where help is scarce and everything must be barged in. Since then Pierre has continued expanding and improving the facilities.

Echo Bay has much to offer. Visit Billy Proctor's museum of local artifacts. A short but steep trail leads from Pierre's to the museum. An easier trail begins at the Cliffside docks. Or take the dinghy over to Shoal Harbour and see local author and artist Yvonne Maximchuk's SeaRose Studio www.yvonnemaximchuk.com.

A deep midden at the head of Echo Bay is easily investigated from the beach. A schoolhouse once stood on shore, but the school-age population of the area has fallen below the threshold needed to keep the school open. The school closed in 2008, and was removed in fall 2014. A good hike begins behind where the former schoolhouse stood, and leads back into the hills past two dams, across a couple of bridges, and onto a logging road. The logging road is heavily overgrown with alder; however, and you probably won't go much farther. Be bear aware and make noise when hiking the area.

Slow down: The wakes from passing vessels and the following wake from approaching vessels can get inside the bay and set things a-rocking. Please slow down well outside the marina when approaching.

Caution: See Pym Rocks warning.

④ **Pierre's Echo Bay Lodge & Marina.** c/o General Delivery, Simoom Sound PO, BC V0P 1S0; (250) 713-6415; info@pierresbay.com; www.pierresbay.com. Monitors VHF 66A. Phone coverage is spotty in the area. Best to contact the marina by email. Open all year, gasoline, diesel, propane, 15, 30 & 50 amp power, rental cabins, store, ice, water, washrooms, showers, laundry, limited Wi-Fi; a cell phone booster is located in the dining hall. Ample guest moorage, reservations recommended mid-July through mid-August. Floatplane service by Kenmore Air and NW Seaplanes.

This is a busy destination in the Broughtons, with wide, sturdy docks, ample electric power, fuel dock and a well-stocked store with fresh fruits and vegetables; some supplies may be in storage, so ask. The protected bay, with dramatic sheer rock faces, is beautiful. Caution, beware of current that can run swiftly around the floats.

Pierre's is a social place. Happy hour gatherings are common and sometimes lead to potluck dinners. Visitors enjoy sitting around a cozy fire pit located onshore above the docks and on the colorful Adirondack Chairs at the bottom of the ramp. During summer, Pierre and Tove host several weekly food events, such as fish n' chips night and prime rib night. Saturday night pig roasts, their signature event, run from the last weekend in June to the first weekend in September. Many visitors arrive on Fridays to get a good spot on the dock. Check their website for the schedule.

After many years of providing great service and events for boaters, Pierre and Tove have made the decision to retire and have put the marina up for sale. They will continue to be involved with the marina until a suitable buyer is found; boaters can expect the same fun atmosphere.

④ **Pierre's Echo Bay - The Cliffside.** Formerly Windsong Sea Village, acquired by Pierre's at Echo Bay in 2013. The Cliffside offers overflow moorage for Pierre's at Echo Bay. Water, no power. For cruisers who prefer less hustle-and-bustle, The Cliffside is a good alternative to the main docks at Pierre's. A ramp to shore leads to a trail through the woods to Billy Proctor's Museum. Use the dinghy to cross over to the main dock to visit the store, pay moorage, and attend activities.

④ **Echo Bay Marine Park.** The dock has been condemned and is now closed. The holding bottom can be poor; anchor with care. The park has walk-in campsites and picnicking. A nice beach is often used as a landing for kayakers.

Shoal Harbour. Shoal Harbour has good, protected anchorage, mud bottom. We would anchor just to the right, inside the entrance. Study the charts and use caution when transiting the narrow entrance. Watch the depths; the main head and northern arm shoal quickly.

Billy Proctor's Museum. Open 9:00 a.m. to 5:00 p.m. A trail, rough in places, leads from Pierre's to Echo Bay. An easier trail begins at The Cliffside. By boat, if you leave Echo Bay and turn left toward Shoal Harbour, you can follow the shoreline around the peninsula and into a cozy bay with a home, small dock and marine railway haulout. This is where legendary Billy Proctor, who has logged, trapped and fished on the coast all of his many years, lives and has his museum.

Over a lifetime, Billy Proctor has collected a treasure of Chinese opium bottles, Chinese and Japanese beer bottles, engine plates, tools, arrowheads, bone fish hooks, a 1910

Two coves at the east end of Viner Sound have public mooring buoys and space to anchor.

THE BROUGHTONS See Area Map Page 354 - Maps Not for Navigation

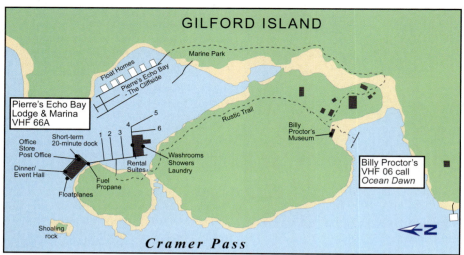
Echo Bay

SURPRISE ON KNIGHT INLET

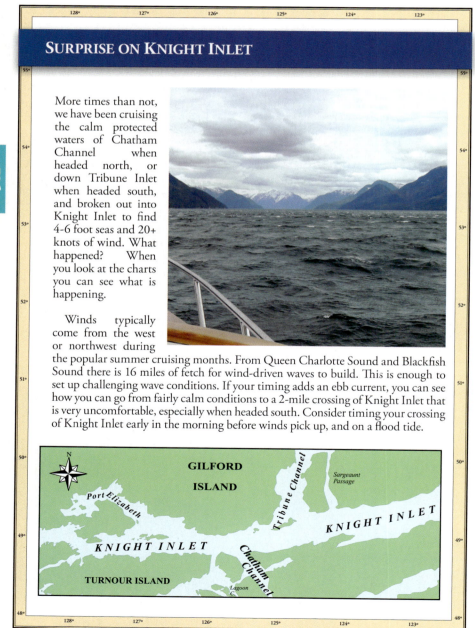

More times than not, we have been cruising the calm protected waters of Chatham Channel when headed north, or down Tribune Inlet when headed south, and broken out into Knight Inlet to find 4-6 foot seas and 20+ knots of wind. What happened? When you look at the charts you can see what is happening.

Winds typically come from the west or northwest during the popular summer cruising months. From Queen Charlotte Sound and Blackfish Sound there is 16 miles of fetch for wind-driven waves to build. This is enough to set up challenging wave conditions. If your timing adds an ebb current, you can see how you can go from fairly calm conditions to a 2-mile crossing of Knight Inlet that is very uncomfortable, especially when headed south. Consider timing your crossing of Knight Inlet early in the morning before winds pick up, and on a flood tide.

mimeograph machine from Minstrel Island, a crank telephone, a scale from the old Simoom Sound post office, and thousands of other artifacts of the coast's past.

Finally, in a structure he built from lumber he milled himself, the remarkable collection is displayed. Out the back door is a fish pond. Out the front door is another building he put up himself, housing a small book and gift shop, and more treasures. Everything has a story, even the windows and doors.

Billy built a replica of a hand logger's cabin, circa 1900. All the wood came from a single cedar log he found floating. Recently, he built a small schoolhouse and filled it with items from the old Echo Bay schoolhouse. Visitors can write on the old blackboards and look through old pictures. The kids love it.

No admission charge for the museum or schoolhouse, but a box marked "donations," which go to salmon enhancement, is next to the door. Billy also has an excellent selection of books on the area, including his own.

If you want to call ahead, try *Ocean Dawn* on VHF 16 or 06. Hike the occasionally challenging trail from Pierre's. Meet Billy and go have a look. We think you'll be glad you did.

Pym Rocks. *Caution*: When crossing from the vicinity of Echo Bay bound for Simoom Sound, Shawl Bay, Greenway Sound and so forth, Pym Rocks, off the northeast tip of Baker Island, lie very close to your probable course. We know of one experienced skipper whose attention wandered briefly and he went right up on the rocks. We had a close call with the rocks ourselves, but steered clear in time. The rocks are farther out than they ought to be, and unless you're on autopilot they keep drawing the boat toward them. *[Hale]*

Burdwood Group. The Burdwood Group is a beautiful little clutch of islands, a gunkholer's dream. The group is dotted with rocks and reefs, and Chart 3515 (1:80,000) doesn't show a lot of detail. With a sharp lookout, however, small boats can slowly maneuver among the islands. Anchorages are scarce, deep and rocky, and recommended in settled weather only. Given the opportunity, the cruising boat should at least patrol through these islands.

Simoom Sound. Simoom Sound is a dogleg inlet, very scenic, but most of it is too deep for convenient anchoring. The best anchorages are in **O'Brien Bay** at the head of Simoom Sound, and in **McIntosh Bay** and the bays adjacent, along the north shore. You'll be in 48 to 60+ feet in O'Brien Bay, and 18 to 36 feet in the McIntosh Bay area. We spent a quiet night in McIntosh Bay behind the small island. The views took our breath away. In an emergency you could find anchorage off the northeast corner of Louisa Islet, and near the mouth of a creek on the Wishart Peninsula side.

⑤ **Laura Bay.** Laura Bay is a pretty and popular anchorage. Anchorage is in two

THE BROUGHTONS

Reference Only – Not for Navigation

The Broughtons - West

2020 WAGGONER CRUISING GUIDE 363

THE BROUGHTONS

See Area Map Page 363 - Maps Not for Navigation

Laura Bay

sections: one, with a challenging entry, is in the long neck that extends westward behind the outer anchorage; the other is the outer anchorage in the cove between Trivett Island and Broughton Island. The cove behind Trivett Island is lovely. A little islet is in the cove, but the chart incorrectly shows good water all around. A rock is in the narrow passage to the east of the islet. Entering the cove, leave the islet to starboard.

Caution: A major drying reef lies a short distance inside the entry to the neck of the bay that extends westward from the outer anchorage. This reef is shown on small scale Chart 3515, but without enough detail to indicate how to get around it. Our observations indicate that the reef extends from the south shore until somewhat past the middle of the channel. Approaching the reef, favor the north side at dead slow with an alert bow watch.

Field Correspondent Deane Hislop reports that Laura Bay and Laura Cove are favorite locations for commercial crabbers. Recreation boaters have been known to snag pot lines that stretch under water over a hundred feet.

Sir Edmund Bay. Sir Edmund Bay should be entered east of Nicholls Island to avoid a rock west of the island. This rock is farther offshore than you might expect. Fish farms take up considerable space, but anchorage is possible in a cove at the northwest corner of the bay, and in another cove at the south corner.

The northwest cove is 48 to 60 feet deep until well in. Then it shoals to 30 feet before the shelf is reached. An all-chain anchor rode would yield a small enough swinging circle; boats with combination chain and rope may need to stern-tie to a tree. The cove is not very pretty and wouldn't be our first choice.

The southern cove has anchorage behind a charted drying rock. Some years ago, we visited near the bottom of a 7-foot low tide and failed to locate the rock. Others who have anchored there say the cove is a good spot, however. Until we know more we neither recommend nor discourage anchoring.

⑥ Shawl Bay & Moore Bay. Shawl Bay and Moore Bay are a short distance inside the entrance to Kingcome Inlet on the east side. The bays are connected by a narrow channel that reportedly is navigable at half tide or better. Moore Bay has no marinas. Anchorage is behind Thief Island in the south part of Moore Bay, or in 36 feet close behind the 55-meter island near the north shore. Two other nooks along the east shore might also be workable anchorages, depending on the weather. Along the north shore, near where a stream from Mt. Plumridge enters the bay, the Ministry of Forests installed a dinghy dock and four campsites with picnic tables and an outhouse.

Shawl Bay Marina. c/o General Delivery, Simoom Sound, BC V0P 1S0; (250) 483-4022; shawlbaymarina@gmail.com; www.shawlbaymarina.com. New owners purchased Shawl Bay Marina in 2016 and closed the marina for renovations, which began in 2017. Construction continued through 2018 and 2019. At press time, it was not known if Shawl Bay Marina will become available for public transient moorage in the future.

Reid Bay. Reid Bay, on the western shore just inside the entrance to Kingcome Inlet, is open, deep, and uninteresting. It is no place to anchor. Just south of Reid Bay, however, an unnamed cove has possibilities. It is rather pretty and has good protection from westerlies. The chart indicates depths of approximately 6 fathoms throughout the bay, but our depth sounder showed 60 to 80 feet, except about 36 feet close to the head. If you go into this cove, give a wide berth to the point at the south entrance. We saw one uncharted rock just off the point; Chappell's guidebook says there are two.

KINGCOME INLET

Kingcome Inlet extends 17 miles inland between high and beautiful mountains, terminating at the delta of the Kingcome River. The water is milky from glacier runoff and the surface body of water can be surprisingly fresh. Just beyond Petley Point at the head of the inlet, a magnificent new pictograph, a real work of art, is painted high on a rock cliff on the north shore. It is the work of Native artist Marianne Nicolson. The pictograph is brilliant red in color, and measures 28 feet wide and 38 feet high. A half mile south of the new pictograph, there is a much older Native pictograph. The book, *Two Wolves at the Dawn of Time*, by Judith Williams, describes the project. The book's prose is a bit rich, but the story is interesting.

Kingcome Inlet's great depths and sheer rock walls allow virtually no suitable anchorages in the upper portions, except in settled weather.

Wakeman Sound. Wakeman Sound branches off Kingcome Inlet and extends about 7 miles north into the mountains. Although it has no good anchorages, on a clear day the scenery is beautiful. Wakeman Sound is a center for logging activity. Watch for drift in the water.

Belleisle Sound. Belleisle Sound branches off Kingcome Inlet to the south. Entry is between two high green mountains—the kind that make you feel small. Belleisle Sound is beautiful and remote-feeling, but generally too deep for easy anchoring. Only a small area just inside the entrance is usable. Chappell and Sailing Directions warn that strong westerlies can blow through. On the day of our visit the surface was mirror-calm. The water was warm and people on another boat took a swim, right out in the middle. We spent the night in Belleisle Sound without difficulty, anchored and stern-tied to the little islet across from the entrance. [Hale]

SUTLEJ CHANNEL

Cypress Harbour. Cypress Harbour is a pretty spot, but a large fish farm occupies part of Miller Bay, and two log booms are present in Berry Cove farther in. Good anchorage, removed from the fish farm and log boom, is in lovely Stopford Bay in the southeast corner of Cypress Harbour. Be sure to avoid the charted rock. We've had a report of a stretch of logging cable lying on the bottom a short distance before the rock is reached. Watch the depths in Stopford Bay; the bottom grows increasingly shoal until it becomes drying flats. Recommended if you want a quiet, tucked-away anchorage.

Field Correspondent Deane Hislop reports that the Forest Service Recreation site on Clawston Point offers 5 camp sites with picnic tables, fire pits, and a pit toilet.

Broughton Lagoon. "The entrance to Broughton Lagoon is a reversing tidal rapids. At Alert Bay high slack, water pours in through the narrow passage, trying to fill the lagoon. At Alert Bay low slack, water pours out at a ferocious rate. The calmest time to enter Broughton Lagoon is about 1 hour 15 minutes after Alert Bay high slack. For about 30 minutes around that time the rapids are at their least flow. Use the north entry channel only. The other channel often dries. This is a beautiful lagoon. It has plenty of width and depth for powerful dinghies. Not recommended for larger craft without local knowledge." [Tom Taylor]

See Area Map Page 363 - Maps Not for Navigation

THE BROUGHTONS

Greenway Sound. Greenway Sound has several good anchorages. The bay behind Broughton Point, at the east end of Carter Passage, is nice.

Depending on conditions, anchorage is in a number of little nooks on both sides of Greenway Sound and behind Simpson Island, near the head of the sound. Leave Simpson Island to starboard when approaching the head of Greenway Sound. For exercise, Broughton Lakes Park, with access from a dinghy dock on the west shore of the bay due east of Greenway Point, received much work in recent years and has excellent hiking. The bay itself is a little deep for anchoring, so anchor elsewhere and take the dinghy over. Good trout fishing at the lakes (fresh water license required), beautiful views.

Cartwright Bay. This bay is open to the wakes from passing traffic in Sutlej Channel, but offers easy anchorage at its inner end.

⑦ **Sullivan Bay Marina Resort.** Box 6000, Port McNeill, BC V0N 2R0; (604) 484-9193; sullivanbaymarina@gmail.com; www.sullivanbay.com. Monitors VHF 66A. Fuel open year-round, store, and seasonal moorage. No garbage drop, but recycling is accepted at the store between 3:00 p.m. and 4:00 p.m. Services include gasoline, diesel, propane, 15, 30 & 50 amp power, water, washroom, showers, laundry, exercise room, and limited Wi-Fi at the Happy Hour Internet Cafe tent for moored guests. Happy Hour starts at 5:00 p.m.

Everything except the fuel storage tanks is on floats, in cozy float houses that date from the mid-20th century. Guests often gather around 5:00 p.m. for drinks and appys at the "Sullivan Square" area. Golfers can try their hands on the 1-hole golf course. Depending on tide and wind, the floating target is 100 to 140 yards out. Last year, there were two holes in one.

Sullivan Bay is legendary among cruising boaters. It has ample moorage (3000 feet), a

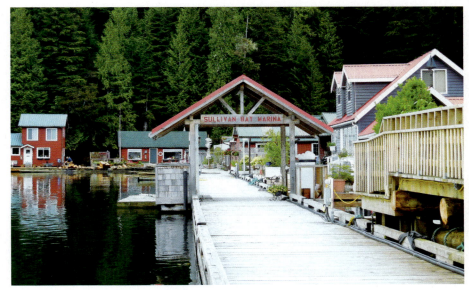
The small community at Sullivan Bay is entirely on floats; even the one-hole golf feature.

SULLIVAN BAY • MARINA RESORT

WELCOME TO OUR UNIQUE FLOATING VILLAGE!

Sullivan Bay Marina Resort is located off Wells Passage on North Broughton Island, in the midst of mountains and channels. Sitting at the edge of the Broughton Archipelago, Sullivan Bay Marina Resort enjoys the many wonders of this magical area. With the beauty of nature at every turn, visitors are bound to see whales, dolphins, eagles and many more wonders.

The Marina Offers:
- Gasoline, Diesel, Propane
- Showers & Laundry
- 15, 30 and 50 Amp Power
- Free Internet with Moorage
- Fishing Tackle
- Boat Babysitting Our Specialty
- Exercise Room

- Liquor Agency
- Well-stocked Store with Fresh Baked Goods Daily
- Regular International & Local Float Plane Service
- Buffet Style Restaurant 3 nights for dinner & 3 afternoons for lunch.

Cruise on over and enjoy the marina and hospitality.

SullivanBayMarina@gmail.com
WWW.SULLIVANBAY.COM

604.484.9193
VHF CH. 66A

SULLIVAN BAY MARINA
BOX 6000
PORT MCNEILL, B.C. V0N 2R0

2020 WAGGONER CRUISING GUIDE

THE BROUGHTONS

See Area Map Page 363 - Maps Not for Navigation

Sullivan Bay Marina Resort

well-stocked grocery store with liquor agency, bait and tackle; open 9:00 am to 5:00 p.m. and on demand 7:00 p.m. to 8:00 p.m. They also offer fresh-baked pastries and cinnamon buns. The Town Hall Restaurant is open Monday, Wednesday, and Friday with a fixed price, buffet-style dinner; we have received rave reviews, especially over the prime rib dinner, call for reservations. Limited menu lunch service is available Tuesdays, Thursdays, and Sundays.

This is a popular turnaround point for Broughtons cruisers. Daily floatplane service to Seattle and elsewhere. Boat sitting available.

The annual July 4th celebration and parade on the docks is hugely popular. Reservations recommended.

A community of handsome vacation float homes occupies a portion of the Sullivan Bay moorage. Improvements continue every year.

Debbie Holt is the attentive manager. Tucker, the four-legged assistant manager, is an enthusiastic member of the community. He is happy to show other dogs the 'poop deck' located behind the fuel dock.

Atkinson Island. Find anchorage in either end of the passage south of Atkinson Island.

GRAPPLER SOUND

Grappler Sound, north of Sutlej Channel and Wells Passage, has several good anchorages.

Kinnaird Island. The bay in the northeast corner of the island is reported to be good in settled weather.

Hoy Bay. Some anchorage is possible in Hoy Bay, behind Hopetown Point, west of Hopetown Passage.

DANGEROUS CURRENTS: If Hopetown Passage is attempted at all, it should be done cautiously, at high water slack in a shallow draft boat.

Hopetown Passage. The eastern entrance to Hopetown Passage is blocked by a drying reef. Strong currents, tidal overfalls and shallow depths make this a challenge. Explore by dinghy first.

⑧ **Carriden Bay.** Carriden Bay is located just inside Pandora Head, at the entrance to Grappler Sound. The holding is reportedly good, if a little deep when away from the shoreline. One reader calls Carriden Bay "a special spot." As you look in, the spectacular knob of Pandora Head rises on the left, and when you're in, you see a beautiful vista of mountains out the mouth of the bay. This vista makes Carriden Bay exposed to east winds, however. It could be an uncomfortable anchorage in such winds.

⑨ **Claydon Bay.** This is a popular anchorage. Entering or leaving, favor the Morton Point side. Foul ground, shown on the chart, extends from the opposite side of the entry. In Claydon Bay you can pick the north arm or south arm, depending on which way the wind is blowing. An islet is in the entry to the north arm. Leave this islet to starboard when entering. Note also that the drying reef surrounding the islet extends a considerable distance southeast of the islet. The northern arm has room for about a dozen boats; holding is good with a thick mud bottom. Crabbing is reportedly good.

Woods Bay. Woods Bay is deep until close to shore, and exposed to westerly winds. This bay has been reported to be a good spot in settled weather, but we think other anchorages in the area are more appealing.

Embley Lagoon. Too shallow for anything but dinghies, but an interesting exploration.

⑩ **Turnbull Cove.** Turnbull Cove is a large, popular, and beautiful bay, with lots of room and good anchoring in 30 to 50 feet. Avoid the areas in front of recent slides. The bottom there probably is foul with debris. Chappell warns that an easterly gale can turn the entire bay into a lee shore, so be aware if such winds are forecast.

The Ministry of Forests built a trail from Turnbull Cove over the mountain to Huaskin Lake. Field Correspondents Brett and Sue Oemichen report that an old steam donkey, somewhat hidden by trees, is to the right of the dinghy landing near the trailhead to the lake. A large float for swimming, a picnic table, a tent platform, and a fire pit are at the lake. It's really nice. The trail goes straight up and straight back down, and it's muddy in places. Steps and even a handrail are on the lake side. They make a big difference. The lake is scenic and looks as if it goes forever.

Approach: Currents of 2+ knots flow through the channel leading to the entry. The currents are not hazardous, but they can come as a surprise. The west side of the entry to Turnbull Cove is charted as clear, but lots of kelp is growing there. A mid-channel course is recommended.

Nepah Lagoon. The adventuresome might want to try Roaringhole Rapids into Nepah Lagoon. Transit, by dinghy with an outboard motor, should be attempted only at high water slack, which lasts 5 minutes and occurs 2 hours after the corresponding high water at Alert Bay. The channel is only 3 feet deep at low water. Nepah Lagoon doesn't appear to have any useable anchorages, except possibly a little notch about a mile from the rapids.

Turnbull Cove

MACKENZIE SOUND

Kenneth Passage. Kenneth Passage has sufficient depths at all stages of tide, however be careful of a covered rock off Jessie Point. Currents can be quite strong and whirlpools sometimes appear. Slack water entry is advised, especially on spring tides. The best advice is to take a look and decide if conditions suit you and your boat.

Steamboat Bay. Steamboat Bay is a good anchorage, with room for a few boats. The bay shoals to drying flats all around. Watch for the drying rocks along the east shore at the entrance.

Burly Bay. Burly Bay is a good anchorage, mud bottom, but the muddy shoreline makes going ashore difficult. The little notch just to the west of Blair Islet is better. Blair Islet has ample room for two boats to swing at anchor in 20-30 feet, mud bottom. At low tide, a drying, rocky bar separates Blair Islet from Burly Bay. At high tide, you can take the dinghy across the rapids just around the corner to explore the east end of Hopetown Passage. From the open water on the north side, the views of Mt. Stephens are stunning.

Little Nimmo Bay and Nimmo Bay. Little Nimmo Bay is a pretty anchorage, and the rock-strewn entrance is not as difficult as it appears on the chart—except on a low tide. The Nimmo Bay Wilderness Resort is located there. Anchor in 24 feet, mud bottom. Several small waterfalls tumble through the forest. With care it is possible to go through to Nimmo Bay, which has roomy anchorage offering 15-40 foot depths, with a sticky, mud bottom. At low tide, an extensive, drying flat forms from the head of the bay. In late summer, the bear watching here is excellent with numerous bears roaming the beaches at low tide.

⑪ **Nimmo Bay Wilderness Resort.** Box 696, Port McNeill, BC V0N 2R0; (800) 837-4354; heli@nimmobay.com; www.nimmobay.com. VHF 10. Nimmo Bay Wilderness Resort is a luxury destination resort.

Resort services are available by advance reservation from May through August with reservations accepted beginning April 15th. Visiting boaters with advance reservations may enjoy a gourmet dining experience and spa treatments at the lodge. Moorage is only for guests with reservations for resort services. Anchoring out is also an option in Nimmo Bay or Mackenzie Sound. Floatplane service available from Kenmore Air and NW Seaplanes.

DRURY INLET

Drury Inlet is much less visited than other waters in the area. The entrance, off Wells Passage, is clearly marked on the charts, as is Stuart Narrows, 1.5 miles inside the entrance. Good anchorage is in two arms of Richmond Bay (choose the one that protects from the prevailing wind); near Stuart Narrows; in Jennis Bay; and in Sutherland Bay, at the head of Drury Inlet. Approach Sutherland Bay around the north side of the Muirhead Islands, after which the bay is open and protected.

Our sister publication, *Cruising the Secret Coast,* available at WaggonerGuide.com, by Jennifer and James Hamilton, devotes an entire chapter to exploring Drury Inlet and Actaeon Sound, with details about interesting hikes.

Helen Bay. Helen Bay is just east of Stuart Narrows. It is reportedly a good anchorage. Halibut are said to be caught in the area.

Stuart Narrows. Currents in Stuart Narrows run to a maximum of 7 knots, although on small tides they are much less. Times of slack are listed under Alert Bay, Secondary Current Stations, in the Tide & Current Tables Vol. 6, and Ports and Passes. The skipper of a tug

Nimmo Bay Wilderness Resort - A Gourmet Treat in the Wild

There is a feeling of remote elegance when you go through the narrow entrance to Little Nimmo Bay and see Nimmo Resort with its colorful cabins, kayaks, and the main buildings and docks. Anchor in about 40 feet in the bay to enjoy this scenic location. If you made reservations for dinner at the Resort, you are in for a real treat.

Around 6:30 p.m., take your dinghy to the guest dock and gather with others for the social hour around the fire pit at "the fire dock." Briana will greet you and bring you your favorite welcome cocktail drink. Cocktail hour at Nimmo Bay is a very social affair. Guests staying in the resort could be from anywhere in the world. Some are there to relax, others come for the heli-fishing, or a heli-tour of the glaciers. While enjoying tasty appetizers from the kitchen, conversations flow among new found friends. Everything is prepared on site, even the crackers. Soon, dinner is announced and guests work their way inside the lodge to the big round tables. One evening, I sat next to the president of Manitowoc Ice Company, who shared the science and marketing of ice. To my left was a travel journalist from the Sydney Morning Herald, he was on assignment to write about the Top 100 Places to Visit Before You Die; Nimmo Bay was one of them.

Next, three courses start to stream out from the kitchen. The chef and kitchen present some of the best food in all of BC. The menu changes daily with fresh locally caught salmon, foraged plants, the best pasture-raised BC beef, and locally sourced vegetables and fruit. The seafood might also be local spot prawns, halibut, Dungeness Crab or Albacore Tuna. Dishes may include shoots, berries, leaves, and roots from the same plant, used at various times throughout the season. At Nimmo Bay, the food is truly an art. Desserts are naturally to die for. After dinner the group moves back outside, where a roaring fire awaits. The comfortable Adirondack chairs are donned with blankets for a cozy evening. Time it right with a full moon, and you are in heaven.

Dinner at Nimmo Bay is $185CDN including one drink. Taxes and gratuities are extra. Reservations are required. While high priced, we feel it's worth the special experience and excellent cuisine.

THE BROUGHTONS

See Area Map Page 363 - Maps Not for Navigation

towing a log boom through Stuart Narrows advised us that he times slack for 10 minutes after both high and low tides at Alert Bay, which is in line with the tide and current tables information. The only hazard is Welde Rock. You will most likely see the kelp. Get way over to the south side of the channel. The current flows faster south of Welde rock, although passage can be made north of the rock as well. Leche Islet should be passed to the north. A study of the chart shows a rock patch to the south.

Note that Stuart Narrows is well inside the mouth of Drury Inlet.

Richmond Bay. Located just south of the west entrance to Stuart Narrows, Richmond Bay contains three coves. The southwest inner cove is filled with a float house and a large work float. The best anchorage is in 50 feet just off the work float.

⑫ **Jennis Bay.** Jennis Bay is the site of a logging camp and booming ground, with good anchorage in the cove northwest of Jennis Bay Marina.

⑫ **Jennis Bay Marina.** P.O. Box 456, Port McNeill, BC V0N 2R0; (778) 762-3037, jennismarina@gmail.com; www.jennisbay.com. Limited monitoring of VHF 66A; "preference is to just come on in." Jennis Bay Marina is a historic logging camp with a quaint, rustic feel. Moorage available year-round, 300 feet of transient moorage space for up to 11 boats depending upon size and rafting options. An additional 150-foot float was added in 2019. Free Wi-Fi; reader Joanne Wilshin reports good, reliable internet. No power at the docks. One hose tap for spring water, and one hose tap for cedar water for boat washing. Burn barrel for trash. Washroom and shower. Four cabin rentals. Kayaking, mountain biking, hiking, and miles of logging roads and trails for exploring. Happy Hour potlucks are ad-hoc, organized by visiting pleasure boaters at the covered barbecue area.

From Drury Inlet, enter Jennis Bay around either end of Hooper Island. If entering during limited visibility, the west end may be safest. Keep to a mid-channel course to avoid rocks along the shores. Leave the floating log breakwater and yellow buoys to starboard entering the marina.

Caution: Obstructions in the water lie about 500 feet southeast of the marina's log boom breakwater, consisting of a float plus a separate standing boom, neither of which are lit.

Davis Bay. Davis Bay looks inviting on the chart, but is not very pretty and is open to westerlies. Enter on the south side of Davis Islet, strongly favoring the Davis Islet shore. Anchoring depths of 24-30 feet.

Muirhead Islands. The Muirhead Islands, near the head of Drury Inlet, are rock-strewn but beautiful. They invite exploring in a small boat or kayak. The cove on the northeast side, behind the dot island, is a suitable anchorage, as is the cove on the south side, immediately west of the 59-meter island.

Actress Passage and Actaeon Sound. Actress Passage, connecting Drury Inlet with Actaeon Sound, is rock- and reef-strewn, narrow and twisting. Careful navigation is required. There are two theories: some feel high water slack is best to have more water; others feel low water slack is best to allow a better chance of seeing the rocks and hazards in the water. One approach is to enter Actress Passage between Dove Island and the mainland to the north, avoiding the charted rock. Tugs and tows and other commercial traffic, however, use the shorter channel east of Dove Island, splitting rocks marked with sticks at the entrance to Drury Inlet.

Once into Actress Passage, the overriding navigation problem is the area between Skene Point and Bond Peninsula, where a careful S-shaped course around the rocks is required, hence the local name Snake Passage. Another choice is to follow Chappell's suggestion of crossing from Skene Point to Bond Peninsula, and working past the charted hazards around the corner.

In our sister publication, *Cruising the Secret Coast*, the Hamiltons have extensively explored this area and present specific directions for this passage and the area.

WELLS PASSAGE

Tracey Harbour. Tracey Harbour indents North Broughton Island from Wells Passage. It is pretty and protected. No anchorage is viable, however, until near the head of the bay. There, you can find anchorage on mud bottom in Napier Bay, or on rocky bottom in the bay behind Carter Point. You're apt to find log booms in Napier Bay, and leftover buildings from an old logging operation. Anchor near the head of the cove behind Carter Point. The cove is beautiful and cozy-feeling, but the bottom feels like a thin layer of mud on top of rock and it wouldn't take much to drag the anchor.

Carter Passage. Since Carter Passage is blocked in the middle by a boulder-strewn drying shoal, it is actually two harbors, one off Wells Passage and one off Greenway Sound, with good anchorages in each end. The west entrance has tidal currents to 7 knots, and should be taken at or near high water slack. A reef extends from the south shore, so keep north of mid-channel. Two pleasant anchorages are in this west end.

The east entrance, off Greenway Sound, is somewhat easier, in terms of both tidal currents and obstructions.

Dickson Island. Dickson Island is near the mouth of Wells Passage. The small anchorage on the east end of the island provides good protection from seas, but the low land allows westerly winds to blow across the bay. Two other bays along the west side of Broughton Island are too exposed to westerly weather to be good anchorages.

Polkinghorne Islands. The Polkinghorne Islands are outside the mouth of Wells Passage. A channel among the islands is fun, particularly on the nice day. The anchoring bottom we've found is not too secure, so an overnight stay is not recommended. *[Kincaid]*

FIFE SOUND

Cullen Harbour. Cullen Harbour is on the south side of Broughton Island, at the entrance to Booker Lagoon. It is an excellent anchorage, with plenty of room for everyone. You might rock a little if the wind is blowing from northwest. The bottom is mud, and depths range from 24 to 50 feet.

UNCHARTED ROCK: Correspondents John and Lorraine Littlewood did some independent chart work surveying Booker Lagoon, and found a ledge of rock not shown on the charts (see Booker Lagoon map). Its

Wells Passage connects western Broughtons with Queen Charlotte Strait.

presence was confirmed by two bent props, one bent skeg and one bent rudder — "a real boat-eater," according to John.

Booker Lagoon. The entrance to Booker Lagoon is from Cullen Harbour through Booker Passage, a narrow channel bounded by reefs on both sides. The channel is about 50 feet wide and has ample depths. Best to transit at slack water. Use the Sunday Harbour secondary station in Canadian Tide and Current Tables Vol. 6, or Ports and Passes. On big tides the duration of slack water is about 10 minutes, and the stream can build to 7 knots or more. The aquaculture pens that once occupied the four arms of Booker Lagoon have been removed, so it's a good anchorage again on a sticky mud bottom. Don't enter Booker Lagoon through the passage on the west side of Long Island. The passage is shoal and choked with kelp.

Once in Booker Lagoon you'll be in a secluded coastal paradise. The lagoon is quite large, and deep in the middle. Watch for a couple of hazards near the entrance to the west arm, they appear to be low floating buoys, which are difficult to see. Explore around, then anchor in one of the arms, perhaps away from other anchored boats; it's that kind of place.

Deep Harbour. In the past the inner part of Deep Harbour was blocked by boomed logs and the center of the bay taken over by aquaculture pens. It is now clear and there are little nooks around the edges with room for one boat.

BROUGHTON ARCHIPELAGO

Much of the Broughton Archipelago is now a marine park. Some of the islands are private, however, so use discretion when going ashore.

Our journal, written while at anchor after a day of exploring, reads, "A marvelous group of islands and passages, but few good anchorages. We navigated around Insect Island and through Indian Passage. Very pretty—many white shell beaches. Rocks marked by kelp. A different appearance from Kingcome Inlet or Simoom Sound. The trees are shorter and more windblown. The west wind is noticeably colder than farther east. Fog lay at the mouth of Fife Sound; a few wisps blew up toward us. Great kayaking, gunkholing country." [*Hale*]

This large group of islands west of Gilford Island does have anchorages, including Sunday Harbour, Monday Anchorage, and Joe Cove. The area is dotted with rocks, reefs, and little islands, which in total provide good protection, but also call for careful navigation.

M. Wylie Blanchet (*The Curve of Time*) was blown out of Sunday Harbour, and we've heard mixed reports about Monday Anchorage. Chappell wasn't impressed with either one. Joe Cove is considered to be a good anchorage. Chart 3546 (1:40:000) should be studied carefully before going into these waters, and kept close at hand while there. Currents run strongly at times through the various passages.

⑬ **Sunday Harbour.** Sunday Harbour is formed by Crib Island and Angular Island, north of the mouth of Arrow Passage. The bay is very pretty, although exposed to westerly winds. We would anchor in the middle for a relaxing lunch on a quiet day. The little cove in the northeast corner looks attractive but is full of rocks.

⑭ **Monday Anchorage.** Monday is a large and fairly open anchorage between Tracey Island and Mars Island. There are a number of bays, bights and coves with varying depths. Field Correspondent Deane Hislop set the hook between the most eastern islet and Tracey Island in 30 feet of water and spent time exploring tide pools and a large midden on Tracey Island. When entering the anchorage from the south, beware of the foul ground shown on the chart, extending from Tracey Island to starboard.

⑮ **Joe Cove.** Joe Cove, perfectly protected and private feeling, indents the south side of Eden Island. The best anchorage is near the head. A little thumb of water extends southeast near the head of the cove, but access is partially blocked by several rocks. It is possible, however, to feel your way in by hugging the shore to starboard as you enter. The passage is narrow but clear. The float in the cove has deteriorated to the point where it is no longer safe to use; a sign warning not to use the float has been posted.

East of Eden (Lady Boot Cove). Lady Boot Cove is what Don and Reanne Douglass call this nice little anchorage in *Exploring the South Coast of British Columbia*. Locals tell us the correct name is East of Eden. The cove indents the northeast corner of Eden Island, with Fly Island directly off the mouth. As the chart shows, the southern indent is shoal and foul with a drying reef. The northern indent is beautifully protected with room for 3-4 boats; room to swing is limited so a stern-tie is best.

RETREAT PASSAGE

Seabreeze Cove. This otherwise unnamed lovely little anchorage in Gilford Island was suggested by Correspondents James and Jennifer Hamilton. It lies behind the 70-meter island due east of Seabreeze Island, at the western entrance to Retreat Passage. Their report: "We anchored in 18 feet south of the 70-meter island and held very well in sticky mud. Some southwest winds did blow through, but nothing major. The water was barely rippled. Caught three big Dungeness crabs overnight."

Be aware that the bottom shoals rapidly once past the 70-meter island.

Bootleg Bay. South of False Cove, a thumb-like island protrudes northwest from Gilford Island. The cove south of that island has about 30 feet at the entrance, shoaling gently toward the head. No name appears on the charts. According to Chappell it is known locally as Bootleg Bay. A wrecked fish boat has been reported at the head of the bay. Anchoring depths 20-40 feet.

Booker Lagoon

THE BROUGHTONS

⑯ **Waddington Bay.** Waddington Bay indents the northeast corner of Bonwick Island. The bay is popular, with room for several boats. It has good holding in 18 to 30 feet. The approach is off the little pass that connects Retreat Passage and Arrow Passage. Turn to leave the 46-meter island to starboard, and go on in. Be sure you have the right island; they all look alike. The approach is wide enough, but rocks are all around and careful piloting is called for. Know your position at all times. Waddington Bay shoals at the head. The wind direction and your depth sounder will tell you where to put the hook down. Wind will get in when the westerly is blowing, but there's no fetch for seas to build. This is a tranquil anchorage—a good place to hide out for a few days.

Grebe Cove. Grebe Cove indents the east side of Bonwick Island off Retreat Passage. The cove shallows to 40 to 50 feet about 200 yards from the head, and 30 to 40 feet near the head, mud bottom, with good depths side to side. A saddle in the hills at the head might let westerlies in, but the seas would have no fetch. On one visit, a couple in a 20-foot pocket cruiser called out, "Great anchorage! The otters will entertain you!"

Carrie Bay. Carrie Bay indents Bonwick Island across Retreat Passage from Health Bay. The head of the bay is pretty and protected from westerly winds. The bottom shoals rapidly from 40 to 50 feet in much of the bay to around 20 feet at the head. Good holding in sand and shell bottom.

Health Bay. The Health Bay Indian Reserve, with a small dock offering overnight moorage with power, fronts on Retreat Passage, ask for Charlie. Health Bay itself is strewn with rocks. Anchorage is best fairly close to the head of the bay, short of the first of the rocks. Field Correspondents Brett and Sue Oemichen report reliable cell signal in Retreat Passage in front of the Health Bay community.

BLACKFISH ARCHIPELAGO

The name Blackfish Archipelago does not appear on the charts or in Sailing Directions, but generally refers to the myriad islands and their waterways adjacent to Blackfish Sound.

Goat Island Anchorage. You'll find a good anchorage in the cove that lies off the southeast corner of Crease Island.

Enter Goat Island Anchorage between Crease Island and Goat Island, leaving Goat Island to port and Crease Island to starboard. The chart makes the preferred entry clear. Caution for the charted shoals northeast of Goat Island as you approach the preferred entrance. Chart 3546 in raster mode appears to mislabel a smaller island to the south of Goat Island, along Village Channel, as Goat Island. Vector mode charts correctly show Goat Island as the small island immediately southeast of a short peninsula on Crease Island.

Anchor in 12 to 18 feet on a sometimes rocky bottom, wherever it looks good. The cove is excellent for crabbing. Weed on the bottom might foul some anchors. A reader reported that their anchor found a large diameter line on the bottom, probably left over from earlier logging. Where there's one cable there might be more. It would be a good idea to rig a trip line to the crown of the anchor. The view to the southeast is very pretty.

Leone Island. A bay lies between Leone Island and Madrona Island. Tom Kincaid has anchored there and recommends it. "'Friends, with extensive experience, also recommend it. We, however, tried to set our anchor four times over a 2-day period, and failed each time. Twice the anchor did not penetrate large, leafy kelp. Once it refused to set in thin sand and reedy weed. On the last try the anchor seemed to set, but it dragged with only moderate power in reverse." [*Hale*]

Mound Island. The cove behind Mound Island is a good anchorage, paying mind to the rocks (shown on the chart) that line the shores. Tom Sewid at Village Island told us that 14 depressions in the earth were once the sites of big houses. Correspondent Pat Shera reports that the depressions are obvious, just inland from the beach at the western end of the island.

⑰ **New Vancouver. (Tsatsisnukwomi)** (250) 974-2703. VHF 78. Moorage, with 30 amp power (15 amp breakers). Cash only payment. Washrooms, showers and laundry are located in a new building upland from the pier. Three rooms for overnight accommodations are located in the same building.

New Vancouver, traditionally known as Tsatsisnukwomi Village, is on the north side of Harbledown Island, a short distance west of Dead Point, the entrance to Beware Passage. The location is marked IR on the chart, for Indian Reserve. It is the ancestral home of the Da'naxda'xw Native Band, who moved from Knight Inlet in the 1960s. Efforts are underway to protect eelgrass in the area, anchor in deeper water. The band is welcoming and offers cultural tours of the village and Bighouse for a fee; the tour is very interesting and inspiring.

Farewell Harbour. You'll find good anchorage in Farewell Harbour close to the Berry Island side. The Farewell Harbour Marine Resort, shown on the chart, is actually a luxury fishing resort and doesn't cater to visiting yachties.

Chiefs Bathtub. The Chiefs Bathtub is located on Village Channel on the north side

Da'naxda'xw Tribal Band members lead guided tours of their Bighouse at New Vancouver.

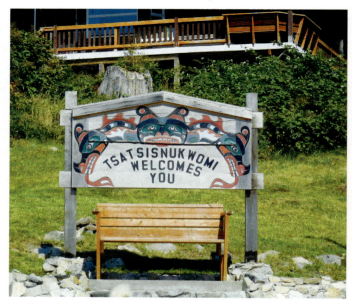

The village of New Vancouver (Tsatsisnukwomi) and their docks with guest moorage are located on the north tip of Harbledown Island.

www.WaggonerGuide.com

See Area Map Page 363 - Maps Not for Navigation   THE BROUGHTONS

Use of the Mimkwamlis private dock and access to the uplands at Village Island is by permission only.

The native village ruins at Village Island are accessible with prior permission; a donation to the Native Band is requested.

of Berry Island, at approximately 50°36.45'N /126°39.56'W (NAD 83). It's a sculpted-out depression in a rock cliff, a little below the high water line. According to Tom Sewid, up-and-coming chiefs had to sit in this bathtub four times a day for four days as the cold waters of the tide washed in. If you take the dinghy to see the tub more closely, don't touch the pictographs on the rock. Skin oils deteriorate the paint.

⑱ **Village Island.** Mamalilikulla First Nation, 1441B 16th Ave Campbell River, BC V9W 2E4; (250) 287-2955; viband@mamalilikulla.ca; Mamalilikulla.ca.

A site on the western shore of Village Island is often known incorrectly as Mamalilaculla. It is the uninhabited village of Mimkwamlis and the ancestral home of the Mamalilikulla First Nation. Uplands are protected Indian Reserve property and access is by permission of the Mamalilikulla First Nation Band office. The Band requests a donation of $20 per person to tour the village site, with its empty school building, collapsing houses, fallen totem poles and Bighouse remains. All fees go to the clean up of the village site and support the Band's guardian watchmen program.

Anchor in the bay north of the village site; be sure of your set. A 160-foot private dock is located in the bay north of the village to provide improved access for band members, and visitors with permission to go ashore. Tie-up is allowed only by permission from the Mamalilikulla First Nation. The moorage fee of $1 per foot is payable at the dropbox located upland from the ramp; short-term stays, no overnight moorage.

Mimkwamlis is protected under the Heritage Conservation Act; respect the village property; leave all artifacts and remains as they lie; and do not enter any of the buildings. No camping or fires ashore; leave only footprints.

Native Anchorage. Native Anchorage is located at the southwest corner of Village Island. It's no place to be in a southerly storm, but in all other winds it's a fine anchorage. Put the hook down in 18 to 24 feet. Excellent mud bottom.

Canoe Passage. Canoe Passage runs east-west between Turnour Island and Village Island. The waterway dries at low tide, but can be transited at higher tides, depending on a vessel's draft.

CLIO CHANNEL

Cracroft Inlet. Cracroft Inlet is on the south side of Dorman and Farquharson Islands. While we have not anchored there (yet), it is reportedly well protected, with good holding bottom on either side of the large charted rock. Lagoon Cove, on the other side of Farquharson Island, can be reached by taking the dinghy around the east end of the island. The passage is shallow, so check the tides and be sure of your depths.

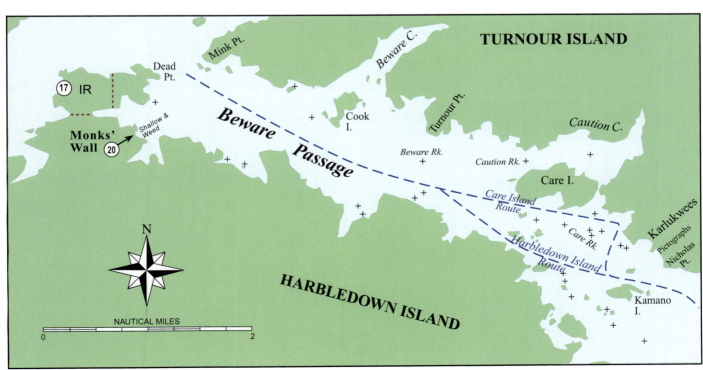

Beware Passage

2020 WAGGONER CRUISING GUIDE

THE BROUGHTONS

Bones Bay. The entire bay is fairly open, although you may find temporary anchorage behind the islets along the south shore. Watch for rocks around the islets. A floating fishing lodge is moored behind these islets.

Bend Island. Bend Island is connected to West Cracroft Island by a drying ledge, but good anchorage is in either end. Friends have anchored in the tiny nook just east of Bend Island, with a stern-tie to shore.

⑲ **Potts Lagoon.** The outer bay behind Klaoitsis Island and the 119-meter headland is open for anchorage; the previous log booming operation has been removed, only the landing site remains. A small float at the landing site serves as a good dinghy dock to access the logging roads for hiking. Two inner bays provide good protection from all winds. The inner bay to the southeast of the 41-meter island is the more popular and spacious with anchoring depths of 18 to 24 feet. Ruins from an old pier along with a few float homes add to the character of this hidden scenic anchorage. A smaller but more private cove is found to the northeast of the outer cove.

Klaoitsis Island. Anchorage might be found in the bay northwest of Klaoitsis Island, and in a notch on the south shore of Jamieson Island. Currents can run through these anchorages. For most boats, Potts Lagoon is a better choice.

Beware Passage. Place names from Chart 3545 for Beware Passage might scare you away; Beware Passage, Caution Rock, Caution Cove, Beware Rock, Beware Cove, and Dead Point. Beware Passage is aptly named, but you can get through safely. Sailing Directions recommends transiting at low water when rocks are visible.

There are two routes through Beware Passage; Care Island route and Harbledown Island route. Both routes are shown on the Beware Passage map. Locals suggest using either route at low water slack, when rocks can be seen and current isn't making course changes difficult. We recommend proceeding dead slow with a careful watch on depth sounder and a bow watch for both routes. Assuming a passage from east to west, both routes start by entering just off Nicholas Point on Turnour (pronounced "Turner") Island.

There are several Native pictographs on a rock face 300 yards west of Nicholas Point. North of the pictographs is a midden beach, which is the site of the early native village of Karlukwees. Boaters can anchor off the beach and come ashore by dinghy or kayak to visit the site; please respect the land and leave things as found. Watchmen are present on occasion. Around 1850, the Tlawitsis Band moved here from Klaoitsis Island located just south of Beware Passage. The Tlawitsis lived here until the 1960's and were active in the fishing industry.

After Nicholas Point and the pictographs, both routes follow mid-channel between Kamano Island and the unnamed islet north of Kamano Island. At the west end of Kamano Island, the two routes separate.

For Harbledown Island route, turn to heading 275° magnetic when the west end of Kamano Island is abeam your port side. Proceed to the Harbledown Island side of Beware Passage and a narrow channel between Harbledown Island and a pair of small islands that lie just offshore from Harbledown Island. This narrow channel has kelp, and a charted shoal on the Harbledown Island side. Exit this narrow channel on a heading of 305° magnetic. Turn to port and continue northwest on Beware Passage when Dead Point is on a course of 273° magnetic.

For Care Island route, when the west end of Kamano Island is abeam your port side, turn to a heading of approximately 346° magnetic. Turn to a heading of approximately 266° magnetic when you see a forested rock outcropping on Turnour Island shore to your starboard. Check your GPS chartplotter to confirm this critical turn to the west making sure you avoid the rock awash to port and the charted rock that dries at 1.2 meters. Proceed, favoring the Care Island side until past Care Island. Then turn to heading 271° magnetic. For both routes, pass between Beware Rock and the charted rock that dries at 0.9 meters and proceed to Dead Point.

Caution Cove. Caution Cove is open to prevailing winds, but the bottom is good. Caution Rock, drying at 4 feet, is in the center of the entrance. The rock is clearly shown on Chart 3545, as are the rocks just off the drying flats at the head of the cove. An extensive logging operation may be operating in the cove. Beware Cove might be a better option.

Beware Cove. Beware Cove is a good anchorage, very pretty, with protection from westerlies but not southeasterlies. Easiest entry is to the west of Cook Island, leaving Cook Island to starboard.

⑳ **Monks' Wall.** The ruins of a once massive and mysterious rock wall lies hidden just inside the treeline on Harbledown Island, at the north end of Beware Passage. Chinese Buddhist monks are reported to have been on the island more than a century ago, and some have speculated that they are the ones who built the wall. It makes an intriguing story: far from their homeland, devout Buddhists in their robes carrying and positioning huge stones for what?—a temple, perhaps.

The real story is not as intriguing, but it is at least as inspiring. The wall was not built by monks. It was built by white settlers, William Herbert Galley and his wife Mary Anne Galley. In the late 1800s, Galley acquired 160 acres on Harbledown Island and built a trading post there. According to Galley's great-granddaughter, great-grandfather Galley married Mary Anne Wharton in 1889. Together they cleared the land, planted 125 fruit trees, and kept cows, pigs, chickens, ducks and sheep. The homestead was defined by carefully-built rock walls, straight and solid. An archway marked the entrance to the trading post. It is said that Mary Anne Galley carried rocks in her apron. Those rocks are big. Some apron. Some great-grandmother.

The Monks' Wall is located on the west side of Beware Passage, a short distance south of

The village of Karlukwees, located along Beware Passage, is the traditional territory of the Tlowitsis First Nation.

Nature is slowly reclaiming the once massive but still intriguing Monks' Wall.

See Area Map Page 363 - Maps Not for Navigation

THE BROUGHTONS

Dead Point. It is on the point of land separating two large, shallow bays, at lat. 50°35.40'N. (This latitude was measured on the chart, and is approximate.) Anchor in the bay north of that point of land and row the dinghy in. The bottom shoals when approaching the cove, and is dense with weeds that could foul a propeller. Working from north to south, identify the third little nook on the point of land. It's a definite indent. The ruins of the magnificent walls are just inside.

If you hike through the woods around the area you'll find more walls; taken together they're impressive. All built by hand. Straight and true. Enveloped now by the relentless forest. The archway has since collapsed.

Although Monks' Wall is a misnomer, it looks like the name will stick. Our thanks to Galley great-granddaughter Kathy Young for her historical background, and to Billy Proctor for his quickly-drawn map that showed us where to find the site.

Request: The wall and the lesser walls in the surrounding forest are a treasure. Please, no souvenirs, no destruction, no litter.

Dead Point. The unnamed cove just inside Dead Point offers protection from westerlies.

LOCAL KNOWLEDGE

CURRENT DIRECTIONS: Current in Baronet Passage floods west and ebbs east, the opposite of the flows in Johnstone Strait a mile south, and in Knight Inlet 4 miles north.

Baronet Passage. Baronet Passage is very pretty. It's partially obstructed by Walden Island, with the preferred passage in the deeper channel to the north of Walden Island. This is a well-used passage for boats heading to and from Blackfish Sound.

㉑ **Growler Cove.** Growler Cove, on the west end of West Cracroft Island, is an excellent anchorage, with ample room and good protection from westerlies and easterlies. It is popular with commercial fishermen who work Johnstone Strait and Queen Charlotte Strait. During prime commercial fishing months of July and August, Growler Cove is apt to be full of commercial boats, with little room for pleasure craft.

If you're approaching from the east, enter along West Cracroft Island, favoring the island as you work your way in. We saw an extensive kelp bed, not shown on the chart, off the point that leads to the entrance. We would keep clear of that kelp. If you're approaching from the west, enter between Sophia Islands and Baron Reef, both shown on the chart. Inside, keep a mid-channel course, favoring the north side to avoid a charted rock about halfway in. Good anchoring near the head in 18 to 24 feet.

Hanson Island. The rugged and beautiful north shore of Hanson Island is indented by a number of bays and coves that are a gunkholer's paradise. The most popular anchorage is in Double Bay, also the location of the Pacific Outback Resort, a private fishing lodge. Enter only along the west side of the bay. The bay behind Spout Islet, to the east of Double Bay, is also a good anchorage. Field Correspondent Deane Hislop writes: "We spent a night in the beautiful bay to the east of Spout Islet. The holding was good and provided protection from the summer afternoon westerlies. The view of the whales in Blackfish Sound, the Miriam Range, and 1238-meter Mt. Mathison were spectacular."

PLANNING FOR HAPPY HOUR

Happy Hour is the primary social gathering when cruising the Broughtons. This ritual typically begins around 4:00 to 5:00 p.m. and can extend well past dinnertime. I am told a movement is underway at some marinas to move the start of happy hour to 3:00 p.m., or maybe sometime after lunch. If a Happy Hour is not scheduled it could happen spontaneously when a group is hanging around the dock with nothing to do. All of a sudden someone gasps, "Hey, we ought to have a Happy Hour!" The drinks start flowing and food emerges.

During our early years of cruising the Inside Passage, we never seemed to have the right provisions for a proper Happy Hour contribution. We once showed up at an impromptu Happy Hour with a plate of store bought Oreo cookies (oh, the horror!), though the Oreos always disappeared. No one had briefed us on Happy Hour etiquette, and our cruising guides lacked this critical information.

With a few seasons under my belt I now begin preparing for Happy Hour at the beginning of the cruising season. In addition to making sure we have an adequate supply of oil, filters, and belts, I make sure we have plenty of items for whipping up a jaw-droppingly impressive Happy Hour hors d'oeuvre, preferably something that will stack or mound to 8-12 inches high or more.

What is my secret? A good supply of cream cheese and crackers!

At the beginning of the season I make a special trip to my local warehouse store for bricks of cream cheese. In order to carry sufficient quantities, I purchased and installed a dedicated refrigerator. I also buy a variety of crackers, boxes of them. I stock onion soup mix, different spice combinations, canned smoked salmon, canned crab, and even canned shrimp. Just in case I end up cruising to multiple locations with the same people, I also have a number of sweet mixes for cream cheese to change things up. Dried cherries, cran-raisins, dried apricots, and a few syrups to add color and flavor.

Now, cream cheese adaptations go over well, but I have noticed some captain and first mate teams look for extra points in the unspoken Happy Hour competition. They bring a dip with fresh caught crab (sometimes even artfully arranged in the shell) with chunks of crabmeat. Or, they show up with a bowl of fresh prawns caught that morning, still warm from a spiced boil. I really hate the guy who shows up with his salmon caught that morning and smoked on the dock next to his boat. How does he do this? He is one competitive Happy Hour cruiser!

Other Happy Hour recipes show up too. I long for the pea salad like my mother used to make, or the spicy coleslaw someone brings in an antique bowl. Sometimes someone will bring a simple green salad with fresh tomatoes and basil brought over from Vancouver Island that morning, garnished with pine nuts. Fresh brownies are a wonderful contribution, and yes, I might even sneak an Oreo cookie or two when one of the first-timers joins the party on the dock.

Our best galley advice for cruising in the Broughtons? Be ready and go bold for Happy Hour. Mix it up, mound it high, and watch it fly. Fellow cruisers will love the end result!

2020 WAGGONER CRUISING GUIDE

Pierre's Pig Roast at Echo Bay and the Art of the Potluck Dinner

Throughout the Broughtons, meals are often a marina potluck event. Nowhere is the art of the Potluck practiced to a higher level than the Saturday night Pig Roast and Potluck Dinner at Pierre's Echo Bay Lodge and Marina. The Pig Roast day starts at 4:30 a.m. with a succulent pig placed in the grill by pig roast master Pierre Landry. Throughout the day, the pig "slow roasts" on a custom grill that was designed and provided years ago by the Des Moines Yacht Club. Pierre has made the pig roast a must-see event, and his 120-seat dining hall quickly fills with a bunch of happy boaters and their guests. Reservations are a must. Around 4:00 p.m., an hour before the potluck, the precession of diners makes their way to the dining hall, bringing their food dish to share with others. The wines brought by some of the guests, don't look too shabby either. Boaters are to bring their own place settings, and some folks go all out with fine china, glassware and silverware.

Next, incredible salads, side dishes and desserts stream out of the galleys of the visiting boats, and are laid out buffet style in the dining hall. And what a selection! Pierre's wife, Tova, starts the dinner at 5:00 p.m. with a cheer and a prayer, then tables are called one by one for folks to fill their plates. The potluck "professionals" are evident in their skill at stacking delicious food on their plates, leaving just enough room for a generous portion of the freshly barbecued pig.

When you visit these small, family run marinas that host potlucks, what should you bring? It is rumored that there is an unsaid competition with the different dishes that show up at a potluck. Special fruit salads, appetizers, and tasty pasta dishes are all there to tempt you. Special points are given to those who bring smoked salmon, or freshly caught and cooked prawns. For dessert – bowls of fruit and special cakes, cookies and brownies. One competitive cruising guide writer is said to bake delicious cheesecakes on his boat for his potluck offering.

It is all about fun with friends and making new friends, while enjoying delicious food at Pierre's Echo Bay Lodge and Marina. Check their website for other food events during the week. Some are potlucks and some events include the full meal provided by the marina. While we joke about the unsaid "potluck competition," some boat crews have told stories about how a plate of Girl Scout cookies, or a package of Oreo cookies, artfully arranged on a plate, disappeared before the end of the evening. The point is to have fun, and enjoy the variety of foods others bring.

Many other family run resorts in the Broughtons also feature a potluck dinner or happy hour. Lagoon Cove is known for providing prawns; guests at Kwatsi Bay meet daily on the covered dock; and boaters at Sullivan Bay Marina meet at Happy Hour Square for appetizers. Jennis Bay is very informal, boaters spontaneously meet for potluck around the picnic table. North Island Marina, at Port McNeill, has a large sheltered enclosure with several barbecues for informal gatherings.

North Vancouver Island

CHAPTER 13

WEYNTON PASSAGE
Bauza Cove • Telegraph Cove
Beaver Cove • Pearse Islands

BROUGHTON STRAIT
Port McNeill • Alert Bay • Sointula

QUEEN CHARLOTTE STRAIT
Beaver Harbour • Port Hardy • Bear Cove

NORTH VANCOUVER ISLAND

See Area Map Page 377 - Maps Not for Navigation

North Island refers to the eastern side of Vancouver Island from Sayward (Kelsey Bay) to the top of the island. North Island is served by Highway 19 and is the center of commerce for both sides of the Inside Passage in this area. Port McNeill and Port Hardy are the principal towns. Alert Bay on Cormorant Island and Sointula on Malcolm Island also have facilities.

Boats cruising the Broughtons or continuing farther up the coast usually stop at one or more of the North Island towns for supplies, repairs, fuel, and water. For this reason, the North Island chapter opens with comments about crossing Queen Charlotte Strait.

Kelsey Bay and Robson Bight are covered in the Johnstone Strait section.

Hospitals: Port McNeill and Port Hardy have fully-staffed hospitals. The Cormorant Island Community Health Centre in Alert Bay is in a new building, behind the U'mista Cultural Centre. It has a doctor on duty every day.

Queen Charlotte Strait. Queen Charlotte Strait is about 15 miles wide. The prevailing winds are from the northwest in the summer and the southeast in the winter. In the summer, winds are often lighter in the morning.

Typically, by late morning or early afternoon a sea breeze will begin, and by mid-afternoon it can increase to 30 knots with very rough seas. The sea breeze usually quiets at sundown.

Tom Taylor, owner of the now-closed Greenway Sound Marina Resort, has crossed the strait between Wells Passage and Port McNeill hundreds of times, and tells us that in good weather he could go (in a fast boat) as late as 2:00 p.m. Any given day can go against the norm, however. Skippers should treat Queen Charlotte Strait with great respect.

Weather information: The wind report from Herbert Island, in the Buckle Group, can be a good reference for approaching northwesterly winds. If it's not blowing at Herbert Island, there's a good chance Queen Charlotte Strait will be okay. If Herbert Island is windy, however, Queen Charlotte Strait probably will be next.

Bauza Cove. Bauza Cove is an attractive but deep bay with good protection from westerly swells. It is open to the wakes of passing traffic in Johnstone Strait.

① **Telegraph Cove.** Telegraph Cove is postcard picturesque. The boardwalk is lined with old, brightly painted buildings on pilings, including a good restaurant and pub. The old homes are now cottages for resort guests. The place is the embodiment of the word "charming." A whale museum is located at the end of the docks and a whale watch excursion boat leaves several times each day. Tide Rip Grizzly Tours takes groups up Knight Inlet by fast boat to see grizzly bears. Charter fishing boats head out to fish for salmon, and a kayak operator takes groups out to the islands and Johnstone Strait.

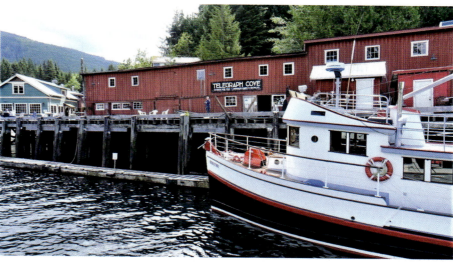

This historic building at the entrance to Telegraph Cove houses the Whale Interpretive Centre.

The Telegraph Cove Resort moorage is to starboard as you enter. Moorage is primarily for small boats, but some room is available for larger boats at the dock near the entrance. To port as you enter, Telegraph Cove Marina has some side-tie guest moorage for larger boats, and a considerable number of guest slips for boats to 30 feet.

Be advised, though, that Telegraph Cove isn't very big. There's room to maneuver, but "spacious" is not the word that comes to mind, especially when the wind picks up.

① **Telegraph Cove Marina.** Box 1-8, 1642B, Telegraph Cove, BC V0N 3J0; (250) 928-3163; (877) 835-2683; reservations@telegraphcove.ca; www.telegraphcove.ca. Monitors VHF 66A. Open all year, 130 slips to 30 feet, limited side-tie moorage to 65 feet. Mostly permanent moorage, limited transient space. Potable water, some slips have 15, 30 & 50 amp power. Concrete launch ramp. Showers, laundry, and washrooms. Wi-Fi available for a fee. Reservations requested.

It's an easy walk around the cove to

Telegraph Cove

NORTH VANCOUVER ISLAND

North Vancouver Island

amenities and tour operators, such as whale watching, grizzly bear viewing, and kayak tours. The Seahorse Cafe has good food and a great view over the marina.

① **Telegraph Cove Resort.** Box 1, Telegraph Cove, BC V0N 3J0; (250) 928-3131; (800) 200-4665; info@TelegraphCoveResort.com; www.telegraphcoveresort.com. Open seasonally with gasoline (no diesel), launch ramp, restaurant, pub, two coffee shops, general store with gifts and fishing tackle. Slips for boats to 25 feet. Larger boats may be able to overnight on the fuel dock, check with management. No power or water. Cabins and campsites available for rent. The resort maintains the historic boardwalk, with cottages and buildings from when this was a telegraph station during the early 1900s. Attractions include fishing charters, whale and bear watching tours, and the Whale Interpretive Centre. The restaurant and pub are good.

Beaver Cove. Fairly deep anchorage can be found along the shores of Beaver Cove, the site of an old sawmill. Logs may be boomed in the bay, and the bottom is almost certainly foul with sunken logs and debris.

Pearse Islands (Cormorant Channel Marine Park). Careful piloting is called for when exploring this area because of rocks, reefs, and strong currents in the narrow channels between the islands. Correspondents James and Jennifer Hamilton report:

"We anchored in 30 feet (zero tide) just north of the 72-meter islet, about where the 9.8-meter sounding is on Chart 3546. A little wind blew through from the northwest, but we saw very little boat traffic. It was a lovely spot with an excellent view down Broughton Strait. Good holding—the anchor set instantly with 150 feet of rode out. It looks like excellent dinghy-exploring country, but it had been a long day and we didn't have the strength.

The next morning the current was really whipping through the passage, but we held just fine. When we left, we found the current very strong off the tip of the 88-meter island, with whirlpools and upwellings." [Hamilton]

Correspondent Pat Shera reports that when the current is flooding east in Broughton Strait, a strong westward countercurrent is present when approaching the Pearse Islands from the south.

② **Alert Bay.** One can learn more about native culture here, in less time, than anywhere on this part of the coast.

Chart 3546 shows Alert Bay in good detail and shows where current runs up to 4 knots.

2020 Waggoner Cruising Guide

Alert Bay
Discover our World

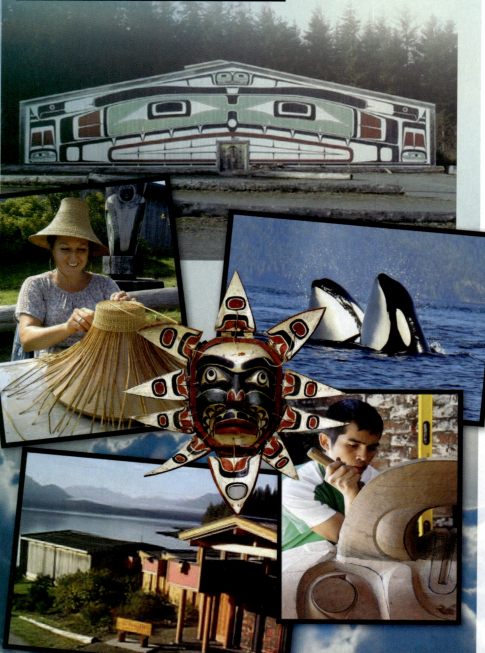

Arts | Culture | Heritage

U'mista Cultural Centre
Alert Bay Visitor Centre
and Art Gallery
Alert Bay Museum
Big House & World's
Tallest Totem Pole
'Namgis Burial Ground with
stand of totems
Traditional dance performances
in Big House

Activities

Whale watching
Fishing
Nature Trails
Traditional Canoes
Skate Park
Cultural Playground

Health

Hospital and Health Centre
Dental Clinic

Business

Full service Marina
Accommodations -
Hotels, B&B's Cabins
Campground
Grocery Store | Pharmacy
Restaurants | Pubs
Liquor Store | Post Office
Churches | Banking | Hair Salon

For general inquiries and cultural planning:
Alert Bay Visitor Centre

Phone: (250) 974-5024
Fax: (250) 974-5026
E-mail: info@alertbay.ca
www.alertbay.ca

U'mista Cultural Centre
For events and cultural activities check here
www.facebook.com/Umista.Cultural.Society
(250) 974-5403 or 1-800-690-8222 | www.umista.ca

Living Tradition
online museum:
umistapotlatch.ca

Alert Bay — The Spirit of U'mista

The heritage of the Inside Passage is a rich tapestry of man's life on the land and his utilization of its waters for both transportation and sustenance. Today we enjoy the beauty of the islands and animals, the fjords and waterfalls. And, occasionally, nature's bounty, hauled to the surface in a crab pot or caught on the end of a fishing line. But for thousands of years, since long before Europeans arrived, the area was carefully occupied by First Nations people.

The First Nations people depended on the environment around them in ways often lost in modern life. Their beliefs and customs are inextricably linked to the Inside Passage. A glimpse into their culture reveals a belief in family and clan and an interest in preserving life and land. They believe in sustaining their people by maintaining nature's balance.

They are also a giving people, always ready to share. Perhaps there is no better example of their culture of sharing than their potlatch ceremonies.

Potlatches bring together neighboring families and nearby tribes. Cultural traditions, like songs and dances, are performed and ceremonial regalia, like coppers, masks and robes, are shown off. Feasts are prepared. Gifts, ranging from blankets to berries, are given. Successful potlatches can be reminisced about for years. Potlatches may celebrate marriage, birth, death or other rites of passage. Regardless of the reason for celebration, potlatches are a vehicle for giving. The more a family shares, the better the event is remembered.

In 1885, the government of Canada banned potlatches. Unwilling to give up centuries old traditions, the celebrations secretly continued. But in the early 1920s, a new Director of Indian Affairs gave orders to enforce the potlatch laws. First Nations members were arrested and some were jailed for up to two months. Regalia was confiscated, packed and shipped to Ottawa for storage. Some masks were kept for the personal collection of the Superintendent General of Indian Affairs.

Beginning in the 1960s, the Canadian government slowly repatriated the items they had taken. They reached an agreement where the regalia would be returned and placed on display in two museums, the Nuyumbalees Cultural Centre near Cape Mudge, and the U'mista Cultural Centre in Alert Bay. When a person returns from a restricted life, they are said to have "u'mista," and the same can be said for the potlatch regalia that has now been returned to the First Nations people.

Today, the spirit of u'mista is alive in the coppers, robes and masks on display in the U'mista Cultural Centre.

NORTH VANCOUVER ISLAND

See Area Map Page 377 - Maps Not for Navigation

Welcoming office and docks at Sointula on Malcolm Island

A short (uphill) walk from Alert Bay Harbour, you will find this boardwalk through the Alert Bay Ecological Park.

Protected moorage is available in the Boat Harbour basin at the head of the bay.

A small public float is in front of the main part of town. The float is exposed to all winds, and currents can run swiftly, but it is convenient when provisioning at the nearby grocery. Deeper in the bay, the breakwater-protected Boat Harbour basin, northwest of the ferry landing, has moorage. Anchorage is available in the bay; be sure to anchor clear of the ferry dock and its approach.

The Alert Bay village is about a half-mile walk from the Boat Harbour. At the top of the dock, take a right and walk along the waterfront. The village has a grocery store, pharmacy, pub, liquor store, restaurants, salon and spa, ATM, post office, and walk-in emergency clinic. An excellent Visitor Centre is on the water side of the road, about midway into the commercial area. It's open 7 days a week during the season. You will get good information about the attractions in Alert Bay: the world's tallest totem pole (whose top blew off in a 2007 winter storm); the U'mista Cultural Centre and gift shop; the Ecological Park, where you can see culturally modified cedar trees (trees partly stripped of bark to make baskets, regalia, and clothing); the burial grounds; and the Anglican church that dates back to 1879. Brochures give information and map routes for self-guided tours. Interpretive displays have been installed. U'mista Cultural Centre is about a one-mile walk to the left from the Boat Harbour docks. Five awakwas (places to meet) along the way represent the five clans of the 'Namgis First Nation.

Cruisers moored at Port McNeill can walk-on the BC ferry to Alert Bay. Catch the 8:40 a.m. ferry from Port McNeill and return on the 5:55 p.m. or 8:25 p.m. ferry from Alert Bay. Bring your camera. The entire town of Alert Bay is walkable and photogenic.

Hiking trails: Cormorant Island has an extensive system of predator-free hiking trails. Ask for a map in the Visitor Centre or harbor office.

Seafest: Fourth weekend in July along the boardwalk. Table vendors, music, fun contests, and Artfest.

Alert Bay 360: B.C. Day is the first Monday of August. Observe or take part in the paddling race around Cormorant Island.

② **Alert Bay Boat Harbour.** 20 Fir Street, Bag 2800, Alert Bay, BC V0N 1A0; (250) 974-5727; boatharbour@alertbay.ca; www.alertbay.ca. Monitors VHF 66A. Excellent docks, 30 amp power, water, pumpout. This is the breakwater-protected public wharf and floats in Alert Bay, located next to the ferry landing. The harbor manager's office features showers and flat-rate laundry with nice machines.

② **U'mista Cultural Centre.** P.O. Box 253, Alert Bay, BC V0N 1A0; (250) 974-5403; (800) 690-8222; info@umista.ca; www.umista.ca; www.facebook.com/umista.cultural.society. We doubt that anyone could see this collection of historical coppers, masks and other ceremonial regalia without being affected. Open daily 9:00 a.m. to 5:00 p.m. from Canada Day to Labor Day, and Tuesday through Saturday, 9:00 a.m. to 5:00 p.m. in winter.

The displays portray the history of the area and the significance of the potlatch. In 1885 the government attempted to outlaw potlatch ceremonies, but the law was generally ignored and unenforced. In 1921, however, 45 people in the village were charged with violating a revised version of the law. Twenty-two people received suspended sentences, in an agreement where potlatch paraphernalia and ceremonial regalia, including masks and coppers, were turned over to the Indian Agent at Alert Bay. The items were sent to museums; some ended up in the personal collection of a government official. The people of Alert Bay successfully negotiated the return of their property in the 1960s, with the stipulation that museums be constructed for their display in Alert Bay and in Yaculta, near Cape Mudge. The result in Alert Bay is the U'mista Cultural Centre.

If you can, schedule your visit to see the T'sasala Cultural Group dance performance, Thursdays through Saturdays at 1:15 p.m. in the 'Namgis Bighouse: $20 adults, $10 for 4-12 year olds; no charge for children under 4. They explain and perform traditional dances, complete with regalia and masks. The audience joins in a dance at the end. Afterward, a visit to the U'mista Cultural Centre takes on greater importance. The artifacts on display are extraordinary. You can participate in a variety of free drop-in programs such as cedar bark weaving, traditional medicine, and story telling, to name a few. Check their Facebook page for free events and classes during the summer. The children's play area is a natural playground of trees and rocks that kids can climb. Future plans include an open-air Longhouse.

③ **Sointula.** Sointula is a pleasant stop with amenities including an Info Centre, Co-op grocery store and bakeries. The Malcolm Island Lions Harbour Authority marina has space in the summer for visiting boats in both the north and south sections. The Sointula Co-op, across the road from the south docks, carries charts and a good selection of marine hardware. A Co-op grocery store in the village, closed on Sundays and Mondays, has a small liquor agency. The Co-op does not use plastic

Alert Bay Boat Harbour

See Area Map Page 377 - Maps Not for Navigation

NORTH VANCOUVER ISLAND

Malcolm Island (Sointula)

bags. Bring your own bags for purchases. A farmer's stand, actually a box on the side of the Info Centre, carries local items including eggs and breads and uses an honor box for payment. An ATM is in the co-op store in the village and at the hotel, which also has a restaurant and gift shop featuring local artisans.

Sointula means "place of harmony" in Finnish, and was settled by Finnish immigrants as a utopian cooperative shortly after the turn of the 20th century. Utopia didn't last, but the Co-op store is a reminder of earlier days. There's no doubting the Finnish influence as you walk around—the town is clean, well-maintained and orderly. You'll find well-tended lawns and gardens, with unique wood fencing.

Schedule time to see the museum. It's nicely done, and volunteers on duty love to share the town's history.

Sointula is a place where drivers wave as they go by, and are apt to stop and ask if you'd like a ride. It's a place where people put down what they are doing to chat briefly and exchange a small joke or two.

You can also visit Sointula by walking on the BC ferries from Port McNeill.

Note: the concrete float that used to be next to the BC Ferries dock in front of the town center has been removed.

③ **Malcolm Island Lions Harbour Authority**. P.O. Box 202, Sointula, BC V0N 3E0; (250) 973-6544; milha@cablerocket.com; www.sointulaharbour.com. Monitors VHF 66A. Excellent docks with 20 & 30 amp power, some 50 amp; water, laundry, showers, garbage drop, Wi-Fi. Office hours are 8:30 a.m. to 4:30 p.m. in summer, 8:30 a.m. to 12:30 p.m. in winter. Downtown Sointula is an easy bike ride away, loaner bicycles are available at the Harbour Office.

Sointula's extensive public docks are behind a rock breakwater at the head of Rough Bay, 1 mile north of the ferry landing. The docks are divided into north and south sections. Both sections are available to visiting boats and it's an easy walk on the road between the two. Each set of docks has a garbage drop and pay phone. The north docks also have washrooms, showers, and laundry, built and maintained by the Malcolm Island Lions Club. Solar panels on the roof provide the hot water. Both sections have potable water on the docks. All moorage is first-come, first-served, side-tie only, no reservations, rafting allowed. Moor where it makes sense. Pay at the office in the north section. Lorraine Williams is the manager. The office staff is happy to provide you with more information on the town.

The Burger Barn, a local favorite, with good hamburgers, wraps, and fish & chips, is in the bright red building in the parking lot.

Tarkanen Marine Ways (250) 973-6710, capable of major and emergency work, is located near the boat basin. Tarkanen has three marine ways with varying size cradles that can accommodate vessels up to 60 feet. With the closing of the Quarterdeck Boatyard in Port Hardy, this is the only marine ways between Campbell River or Lund and Shearwater. It is often busy serving commercial fishing boats. Tarkanen Marine Ways was completely rebuilt after a fire in 2016 and re-opened for business in 2017.

Mitchell Bay. Mitchell Bay, near the east end of Malcolm Island, is a good summertime anchorage, protected from easterlies and northwest winds. Not suitable in south or southwest winds. A public dock managed by the Malcolm Island Lions Harbour Authority is located on the east side of the bay; first-come, first-served. The L-shaped public dock has approximately 150 feet of moorage on the outside. Inside portion of the docks are usually occupied by smaller, local boats. Self-registration and payment box located at the head of the ramp. Don't miss visiting the bright 'Red Net Shed' at the head of the pier, where you can purchase antiques and other collectibles. A log boom area is north of the public dock.

④ **Port McNeill.** Port McNeill is a modern small city on Highway 19, which runs the length of Vancouver Island. It has banks, stores, hotels, restaurants, marine supplies, marine repairs services, and transportation to the rest of Vancouver Island. With most services located within easy walking distance

FLAG ETIQUETTE

The National Flag. Vessels should fly the National Flag in which they are registered. As a general rule, the ship's National Flag should be 1 inch for each foot of the vessel's overall length; be sure this flag is not too small in proportion to your vessel. The National Flag is properly flown from a staff pole at the stern of a power boat, and from the leech of the most aftersail of a sailboat. The Flag should be flown from 0800 to sunset, and at half-staff on Memorial Day until 12:00.

Courtesy Flag. As a courtesy, vessels should fly the National Flag of a foreign nation when cruising in their waters. Proper placement is on the mast of a power boat, or on the end of the starboard spreader for sailboats. For sailboats with more than one mast, the Courtesy Flag is flown from the starboard spreader of the forward mast. A power vessel without a mast, may fly the Courtesy Flag from the bow in lieu of a burgee; or preferably, on the starboard antenna strong enough to support it. For sizing purposes, use one-half inch for each foot of the vessel's overall length. The Courtesy Flag is raised after clearing customs.

Burgee. A burgee is a small flag with a symbol indicating membership in a yacht club or boat club. The burgee is flown from the bow on power boats and usually at the end of the lowest starboard spreader on sailboats. Only one burgee should be flown at a time, indicating the group or activity in which you are participating. Burgees can be sized to one-half inch for each foot of the vessel's overall length.

Quarantine Flag. A yellow flag signals that a vessel has not yet cleared customs and is awaiting inspection. Boaters should fly the yellow Quarantine Flag from the mast just prior to reaching a customs dock or assigned slip, and then remove the flag after clearing customs.

2020 Waggoner Cruising Guide

NORTH ISLAND MARINA
PORT McNEILL
BRITISH COLUMBIA

Gateway to the Broughtons and Northern BC

Friendly Service

- *Transient and Guest Moorage for yachts up to 285'*
- *In berth fueling for Marine Diesel, Marine Gas, Avgas and Jet Fuel*
- *Propane*
- *Laundromat, Chandlery and Parts Store*
- *BBQ and Patio Area*
- *Free WiFi*

Marina: 250-956-4044 • Winter: 250-956-3336 • VHF 66a

For reservations visit www.NorthIslandMarina.com

See Area Map Page 377 - Maps Not for Navigation   NORTH VANCOUVER ISLAND

Port NcNeill

history of logging in the area. It is a short walk from the docks. Nearby, the world's largest burl is on display. BC Ferries operates a ferry from Port McNeill with service to Sointula and Alert Bay. Many visitors moor their boat in Port McNeill and walk-on the ferry to Sointula and Alert Bay.

④ **Port McNeill Harbour.** 1594 Beach Drive, P.O. Box 1389, Port McNeill, BC V0N 2R0; (250) 956-3881; info@portmcneillharbour.ca; town.portmcneill.bc.ca/harbour. Monitors VHF 66A. When approaching, call on the VHF for a slip assignment. Open all year, guest moorage, 20, 30, 50 & 100 amp power, water, washrooms, showers, pumpout, waste oil disposal, garbage drop. This is a well-managed, friendly, and inviting marina with guest moorage room for all sizes of boats. No reservations; first-come, first-served. The marina office works to get everyone in when calling upon arrival.

The marina office is in the Visitor Centre building, above the marina. The BC Ferries landing, with service to Alert Bay and Sointula, is east of the marina. The Harbour showers are located above the BC Ferries landing and are $5 per day, payable at the Harbour Office. A passcode for the combination lock to the showers is provided with payment. Carts are available at the head of the dock for the short trip to the nearby grocery and liquor store.

A 28-foot loading dock is available for short-term stays of up to 1-hour. Contact the Harbour Office on VHF 66A for permission to use the dock. Water is available at this dock along with a for-fee pumpout. Vessel captains must remain with the boat while on this dock.

④ **Port McNeill Federal Docks.** (250) 956-3881; info@portmcneillharbour.ca; town.portmcneill.bc.ca/harbour. Located behind the breakwater within Port McNeill Harbour. These are working docks, mostly taken by government and commercial vessels. Managed by Port McNeill Harbour Office with guest moorage first-come, first-served, subject to rafting.

④ **North Island Marina.** 1488 Beach Dr., Port McNeill, BC V0N 2R0; (250) 956-4044; (855) 767-8622 Reservations; www.northislandmarina.com. Monitors VHF 66A. Formerly Port McNeill Fuel Dock and Marina. Open all year with 2100 feet of guest moorage for vessels to 280 feet. 30, 50 (120/208 volt) and 100 amp (single and three phase) power, water, Wi-Fi. Garbage, and recycling at the head of the dock. The main dock has a security gate; get the passcode from the marina office. Reservations highly recommended. The fuel dock has gasoline, diesel, 100 LL and Jet A aviation fuel, propane. A long fuel hose and reel allows for in-berth fueling.

The dock store has ice, lubricants and some marine parts. This is a well-staffed marina located adjacent to the municipal marina. You can't miss the large "Happy Hour" float with

---

of the boat harbor, Port McNeill is an excellent resupply point for boats headed north, south, or into the Broughton Islands. A Saturday Market is held from 9:00 a.m. to 1:00 p.m. on the lawn in front of the Port Authority and Visitor Center building.

Port McNeill has three marinas: the North Island Marina, Federal Docks, and the Town of Port McNeill Harbour Municipal floats. All are protected by an extensive breakwater. The Port Harbour docks are the first, to port as you round the end of the breakwater. North Island Marina and fuel dock is to starboard. Federal Marina is tucked between the Port Municipal floats and the breakwater, and managed by the Port McNeill Municipal office. All three facilities are close to shopping, restaurants and a modern laundromat with free Wi-Fi. The well-stocked IGA is in a shopping center a few blocks from the docks. The IGA has a van and will make deliveries or you can wheel grocery carts to the marinas. Fishing tackle, post office, large liquor stores, drug store and more are within a few minutes' walk. An auto parts store is just beyond the head of the North Island Marina docks and carries marine parts, batteries and lubricants. A short distance from the harbor is Progressive Diesel with factory trained service representatives and access to parts for several major brand marine engines. Parts that are not available locally can be ordered and often flown in the next day. While there is no boat yard in Port McNeill, there are a number of resources for marine services and repairs. Both marina offices can provide a list of boat service providers. The Shop-Rite marine and logging store handles outboard repairs.

Regular floatplane service connects downisland. Kenmore Air and NW Seaplanes fly to Seattle from North Island Marina. The Port Hardy International Airport, with air service north and south, is a 30-minute taxi ride from Port McNeill. Taxi service available through Wavin' Flags Taxi (250-230-7655). During prime season, moorage can be tight, anchorage is possible across the bay from the marinas with good holding in thick, sticky mud. Be sure to see the Port McNeill & District Museum, which showcases the

HARBOUR OFFICE & INFORMATION CENTRE
Call on 66A for a slip assignment
Pumpout - Wi-Fi - Showers

Phone: 250-956-3881 • Fax: 250-956-2897 • info@portmcneillharbour.ca • www.portmcneill.ca

2020 Waggoner Cruising Guide

NORTH VANCOUVER ISLAND

See Area Map Page 377 - Maps Not for Navigation

Beaver Harbour is the ancestral home of the Kwakiutl First Nations people and the location of historic Hudson's Bay Company at Fort Rupert.

wind-break and awning cover, which has become the gathering place for special events. The 10-foot long custom made charcoal grill is started each evening during the summer season for your steak, burgers, or just-caught salmon. The custom-made tables have built-in stainless tubs for ice to keep beverages chilled. North Island Marina offers many services, including a courtesy car, and pick-up and drop-off at the Port Hardy airport, about 24 miles away.

The marina staff can arrange for other services, including boat watch. For those who need to return home, North Island Marina is a good spot to leave your boat. Kenmore Air and Northwest Seaplanes leave directly from the North Island Marina floatplane dock with flights to Seattle. Bruce and Nancy Jackman have owned and operated the marina for many years. Their son Allan and other family members continue to be involved with the management and care of the marina.

Beaver Harbour. The islands in Beaver Harbour are picturesque. The west side of the Cattle Islands is protected; anchor on a mud bottom in 30 to 45 feet. Patrician Cove has been recommended to us. Several white shell midden beaches are located throughout the islands. Reader Jack Tallman reports fresh northwesterly winds get in and can make for a "troublesome night."

Our sister publication, *Cruising the Secret Coast* by Jennifer and James Hamilton, devotes a chapter to Beaver Harbour and the Native village of Fort Rupert.

Fort Rupert. Located in Beaver Harbour past Thomas Point. Exposed to north and east winds, but with several areas that serve well for day anchorage or overnight in settled weather. The town of Fort Rupert consists of two distinct areas, the newer town on the southwest shore of Beaver Harbour and the Native Reserve on the southernmost shore. Both areas are accessible by dinghy or kayak. Storey's Beach Park on the southwest offers a sandy beach and picnic tables. The south shore is the site of the Kwakiutl Band Longhouse and cemetery with exceptional carvings and paintings by Calvin Hunt, a well-known Master Carver and local resident. Visitors are welcome at the community carving shed located near the Longhouse and at Calvin Hunt's art gallery located on Copper Way.

Anchor off the south beach in 16 to 30 feet of water and dinghy to shore, look for the public gazebo for a landing spot. Position the dinghy appropriately for the charted extensive drying beach. A short trail leads to the cemetery and Longhouse; the small Fort Rupert General Store is nearby.

This area was once the site of a Hudson's Bay Company fort, built in 1849, first commanded by William Henry McNeill. The fort burned down in 1889. One of the remaining eight-pound cannons is displayed in front of the Longhouse.

⑤ **Port Hardy.** Port Hardy is the northernmost community on Vancouver Island. Moorage is at the seasonal Seagate T-Floats, formerly called the City Dock (summer only), Quarterdeck Marina, and Port Hardy Harbour Authority.

The seasonal Seagate T-Floats are adjacent to the Coast Guard wharf, and have the closest access to town and shopping. If the floats are full, you can anchor out and take the dinghy in.

The Quarterdeck Marina and the Harbour Authority floats are a mile or so farther into Hardy Bay, past a narrow entry channel. It's a one-mile walk from this inner bay to downtown. Stryker Electronics Ltd. (250) 949-8022, with marine electronics, repairs and a chandlery is across the street.

A large Save-on Foods supermarket is at Thunderbird Mall. For items with "Regular price/Member price" shelf tags, we found that non-members can get the Member price by asking the checker for a tourist card. The store will pay the cab fare to deliver large orders to the Seagate Summer Floats, Harbour Authority floats, and Quarterdeck Marina. They didn't give us an exact amount, but something around $100 probably would qualify.

Port Hardy is clean and friendly. A park is

Port Hardy

along the shore with a seaside promenade past tidy waterfront homes. The Visitor Centre is next to the park. Be sure to read the sign commemorating completion of the Carrot Highway. A nearby library houses a small but excellent museum. Taxi transportation is available in the area; Town Taxi (250) 949-7877; Waivin Flags Taxi (250) 230-7655.

Port Hardy has city amenities, including a hospital and airport with scheduled flights to and from Vancouver. Nearby Bear Cove is the terminus for the BC Ferry that runs to Prince Rupert during the summer. Coastal Mountain Fuels is in Bear Cove. There is a recreational boat marina in Bear Cove with portapotties and two lane boat ramp.

Dining: Port Hardy has several restaurants. We've had a good lunch and dinner at the Quarterdeck Pub at the Quarterdeck Marina. In town, breakfast at Captain Hardy's is a local favorite, complete with oversized portions. Cafe Guido has excellent coffee, sandwiches and baked goods. The Book Nook, the West Coast Community Craft Shop and The Drift are co-located with Cafe Guido. A local favorite, The Sporty Bar & Grille is down the street. A recent addition to Port Hardy is the beautiful Kwa'LiLas Hotel, formerly the Port Hardy Inn. Three Native tribes; Nakwaxda'xw People, Gwa'sala People, and Kwakiutle People came together to completely rebuild the structure, making extensive use of local cedar as an expression of native culture. The Kwa'LiLas Hotel houses the fine dining Ha'me' Restaurant with an excellent menu. Ha'me' is open for lunch and dinner; (250) 949-8884 for reservations.

Museum: The museum on the main street in town is small but superb. It also houses the finest collection of local history and local interest books we've seen. We recommend it.

Fuel: Fuel is available on the east side of Hardy Bay at Coastal Mountain Fuels in Bear Cove, and at Quarterdeck Marina farther in the bay.

Walkway & Nature Trail: A walking trail with picnic tables and viewpoints starts near the Quarterdeck Marina, leads past the Glen Lyon Inn, and continues along the edge of Hardy Bay. At the head, you can turn north and walk to the Quatse River estuary, or take the Quatse River loop through the woods to the Quatse River Salmon Hatchery (www.quatsehatchery.ca or call (250) 949-9022 to arrange a tour). The trail is very easy, and much of it is wheelchair-accessible. It's a great side-trip that offers a different perspective of Port Hardy. [*Hamilton*]

LOCAL KNOWLEDGE

FLOATPLANE OPERATIONS FLASHING LIGHTS: Two floatplane pilot-activated white flashing lights in Port Hardy's inner harbour, when flashing, indicate floatplane aircraft take-off and landing activity. Both lights are charted, one is located on the east shore 300 yards south of red and green inner harbour entrance markers, and the other is located on the tip of the south shore breakwater.

DANGEROUS REEF: South of the Port Hardy Seagate T-Floats in the outer bay, yellow buoys mark a large drying reef. If proceeding to the inner bay, pass well east of the reef.

⑤ **Fisherman's Wharf** - Port Hardy Harbour Authority. 6600 Hardy Bay Rd., Port Hardy, BC V0N 2P0; (250) 949-6332; (250) 949-0336 cell; porthardyharbour@gmail.com; www.porthardy.ca. Monitors VHF 66A. The finger floats have mostly 20 amp power, some 30 amp. The main float has increased the number of 30 and 50 amp outlets. Although this basin is primarily for commercial fishing vessels, there is limited room for pleasure craft in the summer when the fleet is out. The facility has washrooms, pumpout, and launch ramp; no showers or laundry.

⑤ **Quarterdeck Inn & Marina Resort.** 6555 Hardy Bay Rd., P.O. Box 910, Port Hardy, BC V0N 2P0; (250) 949-6551; (250) 902-0455; marina@quarterdeckresort.net; www.quarterdeckresort.net. Monitors VHF 66A. Open all year, gasoline, diesel, propane, guest moorage, 15, 30 & 50 amp power, washrooms, showers, laundry, Wi-Fi access, liquor store. During winter the fuel dock and marina office are closed on Sundays. The Quarterdeck Pub & Restaurant is on the same property.

Quarterdeck's 40-room hotel is attractive and well-appointed. It has full wheelchair access, ocean views, and a covered walkway to the pub, with a nice area for families.

The boatyard and Travelift are no longer operating.

⑤ **Seagate T-Floats** - Port Hardy Harbour Authority. (250) 949-6332; (250) 949-0336 cell; porthardyharbour@gmail.com; www.porthardy.ca. Monitors 66A. Seasonal floats with 30 amp power, water, and garbage drop. Close to town and shopping. Side-tie for boats up to 60 feet. Docks are best used in settled weather as the area is exposed to the north. Docks are managed by Port Hardy Harbour Authority; moorage payment can be made with credit card by telephone or to Harbour Authority staff who come to the floats twice daily. This is a convenient place to stop and fill water tanks before heading around Cape Caution or into the Broughtons.

⑥ **Coastal Mountain Fuels** (Bear Cove). 6720 Bear Cove, Port Hardy, BC V0N 2P0; (250) 949-9988. Monitors VHF 16. Open all year, gasoline, diesel, kerosene, propane. Despite commercial appearance, they welcome pleasure boats. Washrooms, bait, ice, waste oil pump and disposal. Located near the BC Ferries terminal. Launch ramp and convenience store.

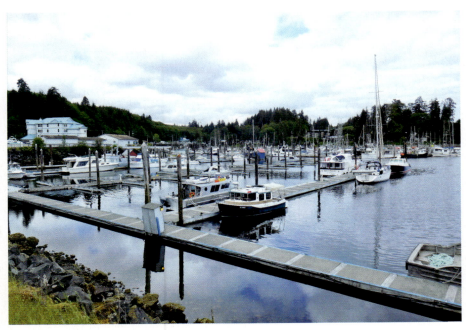

Port Hardy's Quarterdeck Marina has side-tie transient moorage.

Cluxewe Waterfront Bistro

This waterfront bistro, almost literally at the end of the road, is a real find, an excellent dining experience, but a little out of the way – making it a bit more special. Only 12 kilometers north of Port McNeill, it's worth it to take a cab, or borrow the van at North Island Marina if you're a guest. Some trepid anticipation may be involved as you travel down the gravel road, past a logging road, and into an RV park. Look for the building facing the water, with views of Broughton Strait and the Pulteney Lighthouse. If you have cruised north to Port Hardy or Cape Caution, you have passed this special waterfront restaurant. This is where Chef Chris Pankratz and Julie Pankratz have created a special dining experience. "We were looking for a special location," said Chef Chris; "we drove down the road and could not believe the view. Being out of the way is part of its charm." Chris has worked as a chef in many BC restaurants and is well known in the restaurant business as a consultant and turn-around expert. Needless to say, Cluxewe is first class, with both Chris and Julie spending time in the dining room with their customers.

Cluxewe, now in its fifth year of operation, has gained the reputation as the "go-to place" for fine dining in a relaxed atmosphere in the north Vancouver Island area.

Chef Pankratz says braising his meats is one of his secrets in creating tasty, succulent dishes. Yellowfin Tuna, Lamb Shank, Chicken & Fig Linguini, and Trout are just a few of his delectable creations. The seasonal fare, with locally sourced flowers and herbs, changes from time to time depending on local produce and the latest products. Be sure to make reservations, as tables fill quickly at this popular bistro.

The Waggoner team of Editor/Publisher Mark Bunzel with Danielle Bernardo, and Managing Editors Leonard and Lorena Landon had the pleasure of experiencing the Cluxewe Waterfront Bistro during the cruising season. Our evening meal started off with bruschetta, a grilled focaccia topped with fresh mozzarella, tomatoes, basil, shallots and balsamic; and the Yellowfin Tuna, slices of fresh tuna in a sweet sauce with mango. Other starters included the Poached Pear Salad, Fry Bread & Beet Hummus, and the New Orleans Shrimp.

For the main, Danielle and Lorena chose the Chicken and Fig Linguini with tender chicken breast, black mission figs and garlic in a gorgonzola cream sauce; an incredible combination to delight the palate. Leonard chose the Pan Seared Trout, a stack of local BC Trout filets, new potatoes, and mushrooms in a truffle spring pea puree. Mark went with the oversized Lamb Shank in a delicious red wine sauce over a bed of mashed potatoes and fresh steamed broccoli. Other seasonal mains offered that night included the Pan Seared Halibut in a squash puree; the Roasted Beet Salad with Asian greens; and the plate of PEI Mussels and Fries.

For a finale, we enjoyed the view across the water, watched a bald eagle soar over the beach, and shared the rich Black Pudding Cake in caramel sauce with a side of whipped cream. Needless to say, we enjoyed the full experience at Cluxewe and departed as satisfied, happy food enthusiasts. Cluxewe Waterfront Bistro (250-230-1006) is open seasonally from June 1 through September 30, serving dinner

Wednesday-Sunday from 5:00 p.m. to 9:00 p.m. Reservations are highly recommended. Though off the beaten path, Cluxewe Waterfront Bistro has been discovered.

West Coast of Vancouver Island

CHAPTER 14

HARDY BAY TO QUATSINO SOUND
*God's Pocket • Goletas Channel • Nahwitti Bar
Cape Scott • Sea Otter Cove*

QUATSINO SOUND TO KYOQUOT
*Winter Harbour • Quatsino Narrows • Coal Harbour
Brooks Peninsula • Bunsby Islands*

KYUQUOT SOUND TO ESPERANZA INLET
Clear Passage • Zeballos • Esperanza • Tahsis Narrows

NOOTKA SOUND TO HOT SPRINGS COVE
Tahsis • Critter Cove • Friendly Cove • Estevan Point

CLAYOQUOT SOUND
Bacchante Bay • Ahousat • Lemmens Inlet • Tofino

BARKLEY SOUND
Ucluelet • Broken Group • Port Alberni • Bamfield

WEST COAST OF VANCOUVER ISLAND

Cruising West Coast Vancouver Island. For many, the area from Port Hardy, at the top of the east coast of Vancouver Island, down the west coast of Vancouver Island to the mouth of the Strait of Juan de Fuca, is the finest cruising ground in the Northwest—except, perhaps, Alaska. Little can compare with the variety, beauty, ruggedness, remoteness, and sheer satisfaction of this voyage. Please allow enough time when you make the trip. Plan for three weeks, two weeks at a minimum. This is a large cruising area to cover and you may have to allow for being weathered in.

The West Coast is broken into five inlets and sounds that snake their way into the heart of Vancouver Island. Mountains rise all around. Rocks lurk in the waters. Fish and wildlife abound. Only the hardy (and occasionally the foolhardy) are out there with you. This is Northwest cruising writ large.

Except for the rounding of Cape Scott and the long run down the Strait of Juan de Fuca, the distance between inlets and sounds is in the 20- to 30-mile range. Wait for good weather and dash around. Once inside, let the wind outside blow. You're safe.

Clockwise or counter-clockwise? Most boats travel the west coast of Vancouver Island traveling counter-clockwise. For sailboats, the prevailing summertime westerly winds combine with the westerly swells of the Pacific Ocean, and create some splendid downwind offshore sailing. Most powerboats have an easier time running with the seas than into them, so they prefer the prevailing conditions. "Prevailing," though, does not mean guaranteed, and the wind can blow from the south.

The difficulty with a counter-clockwise trip is the time it takes. To go down-island on the outside, you first must go up-island on the inside, and the weeks go by. Those who do not have the luxury of time to circumnavigate Vancouver Island can cruise the West Coast by running out the Strait of Juan de Fuca to Barkley Sound. They begin their explorations from Barkley Sound, traveling clockwise up the coast, perhaps only as far as Nootka Sound and then back down the coast. They must pick their weather for outside passages up-island into the prevailing swells, but that can be done. And if weather delays a passage for a day or even a few days, at least the time is spent on the West Coast, not in traveling up the Inside Passage.

Strait of Juan de Fuca. For boats coming from Puget Sound or Vancouver/Victoria, the Strait of Juan de Fuca can be a difficult body of water. The typical summer weather pattern calls for calm conditions in the early morning, with a sea breeze building by afternoon, often to 30+ knots. When wind and tidal current oppose, large, steep seas result.

On the American side, boats can leave Port Townsend at first light and get to Sequim Bay, Port Angeles, Pillar Point or even Neah Bay before the wind builds. From there they can cross to the Canadian side for the run to Ucluelet Customs the next day. Weather permitting, a fast boat can make it in one day.

On the Canadian side, boats can depart Victoria or Sooke at first light, and reach Port San Juan or even Barkley Sound, conditions and boat speed permitting. The distance from Victoria to Bamfield is approximately 92 nautical miles.

These thoughts are for typical conditions.

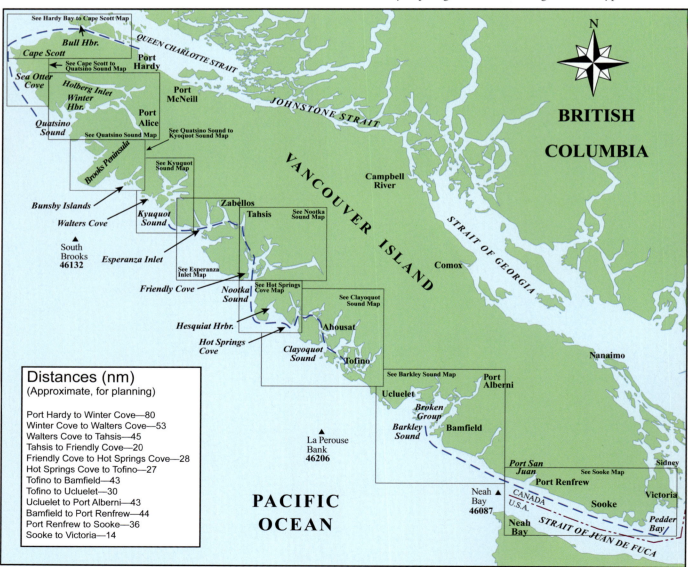

West Coast Vancouver Island

See Area Map Page 388 - Maps Not for Navigation

WEST COAST OF VANCOUVER ISLAND

Variations often change typical conditions. We have seen the strait windy all day and calm all day. Listen to the weather broadcasts, watch the barometer and sky, and be cautious.

The boat. Large or small, a boat for the West Coast should be seaworthy, strong, and well-equipped. The seas encountered on the offshore passages will be a test, especially at Cape Scott, Brooks Peninsula, Tatchu Point, Estevan Point, the entrance to Ucluelet, Cape Beale, and in the Strait of Juan de Fuca.

The wind accelerates as it is diverted at the capes and points, and the ocean's currents grow confused. Between wind and current, the seas grow noticeably higher and steeper. Even on moderate days, a boat can suddenly be surrounded by whitecaps. At Cape Scott and off Brooks Peninsula, pyramid-shaped waves can appear, break (or crumble into foam), and sweep past.

These 'rogue' waves can come from directions different from the prevailing seas. Assuming a summertime westerly wind and a course in following seas, they can grab the broad sterns of many powerboats and make broaching a hazard. A double-ender, especially a double-ended sailboat with a large rudder, will not be affected as much. In fact, sailing in these seas with a 25-knot breeze from astern could be high points of the trip. But a planing-hull powerboat skipper will pay close attention to the waves and their effect.

It is at times such as these that the skipper and crew know they are in serious water, and that their boat and equipment must be dependable. It is no place for old rigging, uncertain engines, sticky steering, intermittent electrical power, broken antennas, small anchors, unswung compasses, or clogged pumps. For a lifelong city-dweller, the West Coast is a wild coast with open seas and rocks a mile offshore. It pays to be prepared.

There are essentially no repair services between Port McNeill/Port Hardy and Ucluelet. Where service is available, it is oriented towards sport fishing vessels, with limited capabilities and parts to service inboard engines, onboard auxiliary systems and electronics. Even if you have the parts, the shop will very likely not have the time to help you since their bread and butter is the sport and commercial fishery.

You, the owner and operator of the boat, must decide which systems are critical to continuing the voyage and carry your own spares and learn how to install them. Parts not common to sport fishing vessels may be available from Campbell River, the nearest large town with an industrial base. Make sure that you have the maintenance and parts books available and the tools needed. With the right parts and tools, another cruiser may be able to help.

Most consider radar all but essential. The local boats, even the little ones, have radar. A GPS chartplotter will add to your navigational peace of mind. Even on clear days in mild conditions, GPS can identify turning points and confirm visual navigation. A chartplotter can take the anxiety out of navigating among ugly black rocks. In thick weather or fog, radar and electronic navigation will raise the comfort level aboard dramatically.

Weather. Winter on the West Coast is stormy, and not a place for pleasure craft. In early spring, conditions begin to improve, and by June or July the pattern of calm early mornings followed by rising westerly winds establishes itself. In the evening, the winds subside. That said, even in summer, serious storms can hit the West Coast.

Northwest winds coming down the coast tend to turn inland at the entrances to sounds and inlets. Sailors making a downwind run along the coast will often be able to carry that wind into the sounds, ending their day with a glorious sail on smooth water.

Fog can be a problem, particularly in August and September. We've heard the month of August referred to as "Foggust." The typical fog forms in early morning and burns off in late morning or early afternoon—just as the westerly fills in. If an outside passage is planned but the morning is blanketed in fog, the skipper will appreciate having radar and a chartplotter. It is also important to have your day's route layed out and saved on your chartplotter, complete with waypoints.

Plan for rain and cool temperatures as well as sunshine during a visit of two to four weeks or more.

The Coast Guard broadcasts continuous weather information from several locations along the way. The reports are limited in scope to weather that affects the West Coast, and include wind and sea state reports from lighthouses and weather-monitoring stations. In surprisingly short time, a visitor who's paying attention learns how to interpret the weather broadcasts and decide whether the time is right for an outside passage.

Lighthouse weather reports are particularly valuable. These reports include visibility, wind speed and direction, human-observed sea state, and swell height and direction. Reports are issued every three hours, but light keepers can often be reached on VHF 82 for up-to-the-minute weather information.

Fuel. Although the West Coast is a wilderness, it is a wilderness with fuel. Gasoline and diesel are available all along the way, within workable ranges for virtually any boat capable of safely being out there. The fuel stations exist to serve the fishing fleet, logging camps, and the pockets of permanent residents, especially Native communities. Fuel can be found at Winter Harbour, Coal Harbour, Fair Harbour, Zeballos, Esperanza, Tahsis, Critter Cove (gasoline only), Moutcha Bay, Ahousat, Tofino (gasoline and biodiesel), Ucluelet, Bamfield, Poett Nook (gasoline only), Port Alberni, Port San Juan, Sooke, and Victoria.

Ice. Although finding block ice can be a challenge, it is becoming more common on the west coast. Where commercial fishing is allowed, the fish processing plants may have flaked ice for the fish boats, which take it on by the ton. A polite inquiry usually will yield enough ice for the icebox or cooler—sometimes for a charge, often not. Fish ice is "salt ice," and not recommended for the cocktail hour.

Water. Ask locals before filling the tank.

Fresh vegetables. Uneven quality. Best to plan ahead and stock accordingly. Port Alice, Port Alberni, Tofino and Ucluelet are the only towns with real supermarkets.

Public docks. Every community has a public dock with moorage fees collected by a local resident. At some of the docks the local resident isn't around, or doesn't bother to come collecting. Accept the no-charge tie-ups where you find them, pay gladly where the charge is collected.

Reference books and guidebooks. The Canadian Tide and Current Tables, Vol. 6 (blue cover) gives tides and currents south to Port San Juan. Vol. 5 (green cover) covers the Strait of Juan de Fuca and inland waters of Strait of Georgia and Puget Sound. Ports and Passes covers the entire west coast and Strait of Juan de Fuca. Sailing Directions, B.C. Coast, South Portion, is the official government publication and should be considered essential. Note that Sailing Directions is intended for large vessels. A cove listed as good for anchoring may be too deep or exposed for small craft, but a passage listed as tortuous may be easily run by small craft.

For guidebooks, we recommend carrying the the most current edition of the *Waggoner Cruising Guide* for updated information on facilities (only the Waggoner is updated each year). Three other good guidebooks exist, and all three are carried in the Waggoner Store. The three are very different. Look for the one that most matches your cruising style.

The first is Don and Reanne Douglass' *Exploring Vancouver Island's West Coast*, 2nd ed., published in 1999. The book is clear, easy to understand, and describes a large percentage of bays and coves along the West Coast. Not every bay described is a desirable anchorage, but the Douglasses tell the reader what to expect if forced to enter.

The second is Anne and Laurence Yeadon-Jones' *Dreamspeaker Cruising Guide, Vol. 6: The West Coast of Vancouver Island*, 2nd edition published in 2017 by Fine Edge in the U.S. and Harbour Publishing in Canada. They favor stern-tieing and tight anchorages which some boaters may not care for, particularly since stern-tieing is rarely necessary on the west coast.

The third is Don Watmough's *Cruising Guide to the West Coast of Vancouver Island*, published in 1984 as part of the Pacific Yachting series on British Columbia cruising, and republished (unrevised) in 1993 by Evergreen Pacific Publishing Co. The rocks have not moved since 1984, and the excellent aerial photos by George McNutt

2020 Waggoner Cruising Guide

WEST COAST OF VANCOUVER ISLAND

Reference Only – Not for Navigation

Hardy Bay to Cape Scott

will help with navigation. The book was written before boats had GPS and radar. The author's dependence on traditional coastal navigation skills is instructive. Watmough gives a good picture of what the coast was like in the 1980s. Keep in mind that the coastal towns have gone through dramatic economic changes with declines in both fishing and logging and the closing of pulp and sawmills.

Supplemental Reading: *Voyages to Windward* by Elsie Hulsizer, paperback edition, 2015. Well-told stories of West Coast adventures packed with information about the coast's history, people, and natural history. Excellent photos. Provides a good sense of what it's like to cruise this challenging and interesting coast.

Charts. The Canadian Hydrographic Service electronic raster charts are available for all of West Coast Vancouver Island and Haida Gwaii as a package, PAC-01, for $175. Canadian Hydrographic Service has more than 30 charts that cover the coast between Port Hardy and Trial Island. Buy them all. Let the few that you don't use be insurance that you will have the chart you need, regardless of where you are. The charts are of excellent quality and easy to read. The West Coast is no place for approximate navigation.

Coast Guard. The Canadian Coast Guard stationed along the West Coast is simply incredible. They watch like mother hens over the fleets of fish boats, pleasure boats and work boats, ready to deploy helicopters and rescue craft instantly. They know what the weather is doing and where the traffic is. They know where to find help. A call to the Coast Guard brings action.

Local communities can often respond even faster than the Coast Guard. In the area off Kyuquot Sound, for example, we were told that a call to Walters Cove on VHF 06 or 14 would bring help a-running. Be sure to call the Coast Guard on channel 16, too.

Insurance. Insurance policies for most inshore boats do not cover the west coast of Vancouver Island. Read your policy and check with your agent about extending the coverage for the period of your trip.

Communications. Cell phone service is found in Ucluelet, Bamfield, Tofino, Hot Springs Cove, many locations in Clayoquot Sound, most locations in Barkley Sound and in many locations in Quatsino Sound. Wi-Fi services that might be found at marinas, coffee shops, and restaurants are usually satellite based, which is slower than you may be used to.

Oregon's Secret. Many of the boats cruising the West Coast come from Oregon. For years it's been their playground, their little secret. The reason is obvious. After the trip along the Washington coast, their first stop is the west coast of Vancouver Island. In good weather it's a long but easy run. Boats from the population centers of Puget Sound or Vancouver/Victoria must fight the Strait of Juan de Fuca or go around the top of Vancouver Island. Often, it is easier for them to enjoy cruising in the protected waters inside Vancouver Island.

Trailer Boats. Launch ramps are available on each of Vancouver Island's sounds and inlets. Many kayakers choose whatever part of the West Coast they wish without making a summer of it. The West Coast truly is kayak country, with kayak delivery services from small speedboats with kayak racks, to the coastal the freighters *Frances Barkley* and *Uchuck III*.

HARDY BAY TO CAPE SCOTT

We will start from the north as though leaving from Port McNeill or Port Hardy, both excellent ports with provisioning and other services. Most importantly, you can watch the internet for the right weather window. Many cruisers like to watch for a 1-3 day settled weather window for the trip leg from the top of Vancouver Island south past Brooks Peninsula.

Goletas Channel stretches west-northwest 23 miles between Duval Point (entrance to Hardy Bay) and the western tip of Hope Island. At the west entrance of Goletas Channel the notorious Nahwitti Bar blocks westerly swells from entering. Goletas Channel's shorelines are steep-to. Winds can funnel between them and grow stronger, but in usual summer conditions the channel, while it can get pretty choppy, is not known for dangerous seas. Be alert, however, for

Rounding remote Cape Scott is a part of the West Coast Vancouver Island experience.

When the wind and current are calm, Nahwitti Bar can be easily negotiated.

turbulence and debris in the water where Christie Passage, Browning Passage and Bate Passage join Goletas Channel. The mouth of Hardy Bay can be slow going as you pick your way through drift. Bull Harbour indents Hope Island at the west entrance to Goletas Channel. It is the usual waiting point for slack water on Nahwitti Bar.

God's Pocket is a favorite layover in Christie Passage on the west side of Hurst Island, just off Goletas Channel. Boats bound around Vancouver Island probably will not see God's Pocket unless to escape a chop in Goletas Channel. But boats planning a direct crossing of Queen Charlotte Sound to Haida Gwaii (Queen Charlotte Islands), or boats bound past Cape Caution, find God's Pocket to be a good departure spot. God's Pocket is a local name, not shown on the chart.

God's Pocket Resort. P.O. Box 130, Port Hardy, BC V0N 2P0; (250) 949-1755; info@godspocket.com; www.godspocket.com. This is primarily a diving resort with friendly people. Room for three to four boats at the dock, or anchor out. No power or water on the docks. No washrooms and no showers. Breakfast, lunch and dinner are available for the resort's diving guests; others can be accommodated on an as-available basis, with reservations.

Port Alexander. Port Alexander, indenting Nigei Island west of Browning Passage, is a good anchorage for boats bound for Cape Scott or around Cape Caution. Anchor near the head in 50 to 60 feet. The beach is good for dog walking. The westerly wind blows in across the island, but has no fetch for seas to build. The west side of the bay seems more protected than the east. The accumulation of large logs on the beach indicates that this is no place to be in a southerly storm.

Clam Cove. Clam Cove is a local name, not shown on the chart, for an anchorage on the Gordon Channel side of Nigei Island, where Browning Passage meets Gordon Channel. The entrance is approximately 0.7 miles southeast of Hougestal Point. The entrance is guarded by rocks, but Correspondent Bruce Evertz reports that, with attention, entry isn't a problem. Correspondents Carol-Ann Giroday and Rick LeBlanc tell us the entry is wider than it appears on the chart and kelp marks the shallow spots. The basin has room for several boats, with protection from all winds. An easily-walked trail leads from the south end of Clam Cove to Port Alexander. A cluster of float homes is located at the north end of the inner-most part of the cove.

Shushartie Bay. "We stopped for breakfast in Shushartie Bay after rounding the top end of Vancouver Island (clockwise circumnavigation). A 30-knot southeasterly wind was blowing against a strong flood current, making Goletas Channel very rough. We went deep into the bay and dropped the hook in 50 feet just inside the 30-meter line, west of some dolphins marked 'Dns' on the chart. Holding was good in thick mud. This is no Prideaux Haven, but considering the conditions outside, the swell that came in wasn't too bad. The Douglasses description of Shushartie Bay is fairly negative, and we don't know how it would be in a westerly. But it worked for us that day." [*Hamilton*]

Bull Harbour. Bull Harbour is a lovely bay almost landlocked in Hope Island. It is the place to wait for weather and for slack water on Nahwitti Bar.

Enter Bull Harbour around the east side of Norman Island, which blocks the southern entrance. A light marks the entrance. 3-knot speed limit inside the harbour. Parts of Bull Harbour grow quite shoal on a low tide. Check the depths and tide tables before anchoring for the night. The bottom is mud and holding is excellent. Sailing Directions says the southern portion of the harbor is reported to be foul with old chain and cable. During the fishing season, commercial fish boats often crowd the harbor. The entrance should be kept clear for floatplane landings and departures. The Coast Guard station, once active here, has been decommissioned.

All of Hope Island, including Bull Harbour, at the west end of Goletas Channel, is the property of the Tlatlasikwala Native Band. Boaters may tie-up at the Band's dock in mid-harbour but may not go ashore on Hope Island, all of which is private Indian Reserve land. Moorage is first-come, first-served. The northern most section of the dock is reserved for floatplanes. A detached float just past Norman Island near the harbour entrance is also available for moorage. Payment for moorage can be mailed to the Band at Tlatlasikwala First Nation, PO Box 339, Port Hardy, BC V0N 2P0. See their website at www.tlatlasikwala.com.

Westerly winds can enter Bull Harbour, as can southeast gales. If you are anchored, be sure the anchor is well set with adequate scope.

Nahwitti Bar. Nahwitti Bar should be attempted only at or near slack. Slack water and current predictions are shown in Tide and Current Tables, Vol. 6. Maximum tidal currents over the bar reach 5.5 knots. From seaward, the bar shoals gradually to a least depth of approximately 35 feet. When ocean swells from deep water hit the bar, friction from the shallowing bottom slows the water there, while the top of the swell continues its pace. As a result the waves grow high and steep. If a strong ebb current opposes westerly winds, dangerous and heavy breaking seas will develop.

It is often said that the ideal time to cross Nahwitti bar is at high slack water, when the typical westerly wind blows with the flood current. This tends to keep seas down and permits crossing a few minutes before the slack. The subsequent ebb current flows to 3 knots along the coast all the way to Cape Scott.

A crossing at high slack is not without its disadvantages, though. First, the ebb that follows will oppose the prevailing westerly wind, and could build a steep chop along the run to Cape Scott. Second, if you cross Nahwitti Bar at slack, you are almost guaranteed to arrive at Cape Scott around mid-tide, when currents there could be kicking up the seas. One alternative is to take the inner route around Nahwitti Bar prior to high or low slack at the bar, timing your arrival at Cape Scott for high or low water.

Thus the wise skipper considers all factors before crossing Nahwitti Bar: current direction and speed, weather, time of day, and vessel speed. At least 30 minutes should be allowed to get through the swells on the bar. Even fast boats usually must proceed slowly. At slack water in windless conditions, we found impressive swells extending 2.5 miles out to Whistle Buoy *MA* before they died down.

Nahwitti Bar Inner Route. A September 1992 *Pacific Yachting* article by June Cameron describes a quieter inner route that avoids Nahwitti Bar altogether. While in Bull Harbour, an old and grizzled commercial fisherman told us he hadn't gone across the

WEST COAST OF VANCOUVER ISLAND

Reference Only – Not for Navigation

bar in years, and we were nuts if we didn't take the inner route. Cross to the bay on the south shore of Goletas Channel and work in behind Tatnall Reefs. Follow the Vancouver Island shoreline around the bay, passing on either side of Weser Island. If the westerly is blowing, you can hide in the little nook behind Cape Sutil. We did it and it works. We don't plan to cross Nahwitti Bar again. [*Hale*]

Cape Sutil to Cape Scott. Sailing Directions says the distance from Cape Sutil to Cape Scott is 15 miles, but this understates the actual running distance after crossing Nahwitti Bar. A more realistic distance would be measured from Whistle Buoy *MA*, and would be approximately 16.5 miles. Although the run across the bottom of Queen Charlotte Sound is exposed to westerlies, except for the relentless Pacific swell the early morning conditions are often quiet. Rocks extend as much as a mile offshore all along the way. Stay well off.

According to Sailing Directions, temporary anchorage can be found in Shuttleworth Bight, Nissen Bight, Fisherman Bay (southwest corner of Nissen Bight), Nels Bight, and Experiment Bight. Study the chart before entering, and watch the weather.

Cape Scott is the westernmost point of Vancouver Island. Dangerous rocks extend 0.5 mile offshore, northward and westward. The cape itself is a low piece of land connected by a narrow neck with the main body of Vancouver Island. The Cape Scott Light, on a square tower 13 feet high, is on higher ground about a quarter-mile inland from Cape Scott.

Currents flowing on both sides of the cape meet at Cape Scott. Especially when opposed by wind, the currents can produce heavy seas and overfalls, dangerous to small craft. Even in calm conditions, seas can emerge seemingly from nowhere, the result of colliding currents. With its seas, rocks, and shortage of convenient hidey-holes, Cape Scott is not a place to treat lightly. A vessel in trouble at Cape Scott could be in serious distress, and quickly.

It is with good reason that guidebooks (including this one) and magazine articles emphasize the dangers and cautions at Cape Scott. The waters can be treacherous. Yet in settled summer conditions, a well-managed seaworthy vessel, with a good weather eye, can make a safe and satisfying rounding. The standard advice is to round Cape Scott at slack. Other factors may persuade a skipper to round at times other than slack. Each situation, each boat, is different. What worked yesterday may not work today. A careful skipper, fully aware that safety of the vessel and crew truly are at risk at Cape Scott, must judge conditions and make the right choices.

Weather information: The Cape Scott lighthouse weather report is regularly updated with wind speed and direction, sea conditions, and visibility information. The automated weather station on Sartine Island provides wind speed and direction. Listen to the continuous marine broadcast for the latest weather information.

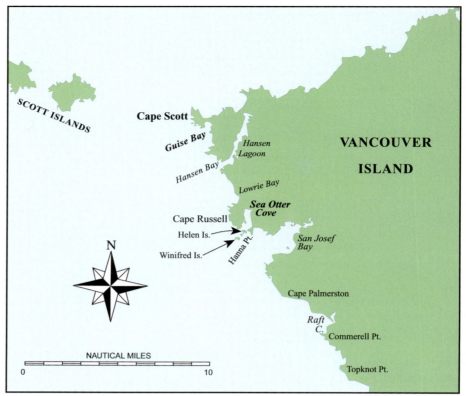

Cape Scott to Quatsino Sound

CAPE SCOTT TO QUATSINO SOUND

Depending on the courses chosen, the run from Cape Scott to the entrance of Quatsino Sound is approximately 28.5 miles. To stay clear of off-lying rocks and reefs, the general advice is to follow the 20-fathom curve all the way down the coast. Douglass says he prefers the 30-fathom curve for an extra margin of safety. We are inclined toward Douglass' 30-fathom standard. In moderate conditions with excellent visibility, we felt comfortable in 25 to 30 fathoms. Had conditions worsened, we would have moved out.

With the summer westerly in place, the run between Cape Scott and Quatsino Sound is a downhill sleigh ride. Powerboaters, especially those with planing hulls, will have to saw away at the helm and play with the throttle to stay in harmony with the relentless procession of rollers. They will arrive tired. The sailboaters will have all the fun, especially if the boat and crew can handle a spinnaker. They too will arrive tired, but exhilarated.

Given the conditions, many boats make a direct passage between Cape Scott and Quatsino Sound, and leave the bays between for another day. Sailboats, after a long passage at 6 knots, will be apt to put into one of those bays, particularly Sea Otter Cove. Boats heading clockwise, toward Cape Scott, might also be more apt to investigate the shoreline, choosing to spend the night in Sea Otter Cove. They could make an early departure the next morning and round Cape Scott before the westerly fills in.

Weather information: At the north end, the

God's Pocket Resort has space for a few boats and is a good jumping-off point when rounding Cape Scott.

WEST COAST OF VANCOUVER ISLAND

Cape Scott lighthouse weather report informs mariners of wind and sea conditions. At the south end, the Quatsino lighthouse report does the same. Listen to the continuous marine broadcast for the latest weather information.

Guise Bay. Guise Bay is just south of Cape Scott. Sailing Directions says the entrance to Guise Bay is encumbered with rocks, and local knowledge is called for. The chart suggests that entrance is possible, but Douglass says that the rocks are often covered with foam and a strong heart is needed. Correspondents Gil and Karen Flanagan, however, put in to Guise Bay, and here is their report:

"Guise Bay is a great anchorage. The shore is so interesting we would consider overnighting there. The walk to the lighthouse is well used, and pretty easy. The anchorage area is about 600 yards long by 600 yards wide. The swell that day was only a few inches. Behind the island, the main south entrance channel is 1000 feet wide and 42 feet deep. If it is a reasonably nice day, don't pass it by." [Flanagan]

A community boardwalk skirts the shoreline at Winter Harbour.

Hansen Bay. Hansen Bay was the location of a Danish settlement around 1900. Supply vessels could anchor in good weather only. The settlement failed. Sailing Directions says Hansen Bay "affords no shelter," although commercial fish boats do hole up there.

Sea Otter Cove. Sea Otter Cove, south of Cape Scott, is described in Sailing Directions as "indifferent shelter." Nevertheless, Sea Otter Cove is a favorite of fish boats, and well-known to yachtsmen. The rocks and islets outside the entrance are awesome in their ruggedness. Inside, you feel safe but surrounded by hostile ground. Sea Otter Cove is an exciting place to be. We recommend it.

Enter from the south, between Hanna Point and the Helen Islands. Watmough's book shows swells breaking almost across the entrance, but careful attention to the chart will bring you through. The channel is narrow, and grows shallower as you go in. Deep draft vessels should be careful if they anchor there due to the shallow depths. Four storm mooring buoys were in place in 2015; least depth was about 8 feet at zero tide.

San Josef Bay. San Josef Bay is protected from northerly winds, but open to westerly and southerly winds. Anchor in settled weather.

QUATSINO SOUND

Quatsino Sound is the northernmost of the five sounds that indent the west coast of Vancouver Island. Despite fish farms and logging operations, Quatsino Sound still provides scenic coves and interesting anchorages. With the exception of North Harbour and Winter Harbour on the north side near the entrance, Quatsino Sound is probably the sound least explored by cruising yachts.

Quatsino Sound is the first quiet anchorage after the 50-mile run from Bull Harbour, and a welcome sight it is after anxiety at Cape Scott and hours of rolling seas. The entrance is straightforward. Using large-scale Chart 3686, identify South Danger Rock and Robson Rock (both of them well away from land), stay close to Kains Island, and proceed into Forward Inlet. North Harbour and Browning Inlet are good anchorages, or you can continue to Winter Harbour.

For those coming from Haida Gwaii or the Central Coast, Quatsino Sound offers the opportunity to do major provisioning, either at Port Alice or by taking a bus to Port Hardy from Coal Harbour.

VHF: We are told the fishermen work on channels 73, 84, and 86.

Cell phones: There is Telus service throughout most of Quatsino Sound except Forward Inlet north of Montgomery Point.

① **Winter Harbour.** Winter Harbour once was a commercial fishing outpost, and B.C. Packers owned the first major set of docks as you enter, including the fuel dock. With the closing of fishing, their docks and fuel facility have been taken over by the company that owns and runs the Outpost store. Today Winter Harbour has 12 full time residents and about 70 summer residents.

Beyond the Outpost and its facilities is the campground of the Winter Harbour Lodge, followed by the Qualicum Rivers Fishing Resort (the large white building), and finally, the Winter Harbour Authority public dock.

The library, located above the public dock, has irregular hours. Pay phones are on the far side of this building. A post office and book exchange is located in a small building to the right of the public wharf. For-fee Wi-Fi is available in Winter Harbour.

Van Isle 360: The Van Isle 360 sailboat race, held in odd-numbered years, visits Winter Harbour. They fill the docks when they arrive.

① **Outpost at Winter Harbour, Grant Sales Ltd.** 108 Winter Harbour Rd., Winter Harbour, BC V0N 3L0; (250) 969-4333; winterharbour@telus.net; www.winterharbour.ca. Monitors VHF 19. Open all year, moorage for boats to 75 feet, gasoline, diesel, oil, laundry, washrooms & showers, general store, water at fuel dock, campsites. The showers are in a small building on a dock near the Outpost. The general store has frozen foods including some frozen meat, canned goods, packaged foods and ice. Produce is

SEA OTTER COVE

For boats rounding Cape Scott heading down the West Coast, the first fully protected harbor is Sea Otter Cove. Kayakers and rowers sometimes stop in Hansen Lagoon, where they can more easily pull their boats up on the beach. But for boats that need to anchor, Sea Otter Cove is a welcome retreat, safe from whatever might be going on out on the ocean.

Boats can enter and leave Sea Otter Cove from either the north or south. The south entrance to Sea Otter Cove is protected by a group of small islands, each one of which is surrounded by a reef. Using care, entry can be made on either side of these islands. If you choose the southernmost route, a single red light kept to starboard (Red, Right, Returning) provides a reference point for the very narrow channel between the reefs. The northern-most route is broader and deeper, but more exposed to the ocean swells until you're well into the bay.

Once inside, you'll note that the entire bay is quite shallow, in many places less than 5 feet at zero tide. Be very careful during extreme low tides.

2020 Waggoner Cruising Guide

WEST COAST OF VANCOUVER ISLAND

limited. Grocery availability may depend on delivery schedules. The Outpost also carries liquor, clothing, charts, fishing equipment, and miscellaneous tools. The liquor agency has a decent wine selection. Wi-Fi can be purchased and used at an attractive patio area overlooking the harbor. Greg Vance is the owner.

① **Winter Harbour Authority.** (800) 960-2646 rob@qualicumrivers.com; Moorage on 450 feet of dock, water, waste oil disposal, garbage drop, recycling, 15, 20, & 30 amp power. Power is run to the dock by extension cord; quality varies. A pay phone is at the top of the dock. Cruisers may need to go to the Outpost to use the for-fee Wi-Fi. A tidal grid is available. Qualicum Rivers, the fishing lodge next door, operates June through September and sells flaked ice to cruisers and has a restaurant. Reservations required at the seasonal restaurant.

A sign on the dock asks shallow draft boats to allow deeper draft boats priority on the outer side. Larger boats also anchor to the north of the public dock and at the head of Winter Harbour.

North Harbour. North Harbour, north of Matthews Island in Forward Inlet, is an excellent anchorage, popular with boats planning a morning departure from Quatsino Sound. A small float house is moored close to shore and does not significantly interfere with anchorage. North Harbour is sheltered and quiet, yet close to the mouth of Quatsino Sound.

Browning Inlet. Browning Inlet is narrow and sheltered from seas and swells, with good holding in 18 to 30 feet. Crabbing is reportedly good. In strong northwesterlies, winds blow from the valley to the north. In those conditions North Harbour or Winter Harbour are preferable.

Koskimo Bay. Koskimo Bay has a couple of anchorages, one behind Mabbott Island and one at Mahatta Creek. The Koskimo Islands are at the east end of Koskimo Bay.

Mabbott Island. The little area behind Mabbott Island would be a cozy spot to drop the hook if the large fish farm and float house didn't take much of the anchorage.

Mahatta Creek. In Koskimo Bay. Work your way east of the mouth of the creek, anchor in 30 to 45 feet. At high tide you can explore the creek. Waves can build across the sound in strong northwesterlies. On those days it's best to move north to East Cove.

Koskimo Islands. Explore by dinghy. The narrow passage between the largest of the islands and Vancouver Island can be run (carefully), but with safe water just outside the islands we see no need to.

Koprino Harbour. Most of Koprino Harbour is too deep for pleasure craft to anchor, but the area of East Cove, near the northeast corner of Koprino Harbour, is excellent.

East Cove. East Cove is tranquil, snug and tree-lined, with good dinghy access to shore—cruising as it should be. If East Cove were in Desolation Sound instead of Koprino Harbour, it would be filled with 25 boats every night, all stern-tied to shore. But because East Cove is on the west coast of Vancouver Island, you will probably be the only boat at anchor and won't need a stern-tie. Another cove, almost as delightful, is just to the north, behind a group of little islets. The largest of these islets is identified on the chart as Linthlop Islet.

Pamphlet Cove. Pamphlet Cove, part of a provincial recreation reserve, is located on the north side of Drake Island, about 3.5 miles west of Quatsino Narrows. Pamphlet Cove is scenic and protected, an ideal anchorage. You can go ashore and enjoy the reserve. At high tide several small lagoons make for good exploring by dinghy or kayak.

Julian Cove. Southeast of Drake Island and east of Kultus Cove. Protection is excellent and holding is good. Probably the most pristine cove in Quatsino Sound, Julian Cove has room for four or five boats. Beautiful forested hills surround it without a clearcut in sight. At the head of the bay a stream crosses a marsh and salmonberries grow along the shore. Watch for bears. Entry is direct and easy.

Smith Cove. It's been reported that a large float and separate float house, with cables running to shore, occupies much of Smith Cove. Nearby Julian Cove is a better choice.

Atkins Cove. Atkins Cove is well protected except south. Good holding over a mud bottom.

"Early Bird Cove," Douglass' name for the almost-landlocked cove accessed through the narrows on the north side of Atkins Cove, is also a good anchorage. We went through the narrow, shallow entrance strongly favoring the west shore. On an 8.5-foot high tide we saw depths of 6.5 feet.

Neroutsos Inlet. "The wind blows hard every afternoon in Neroutsos Inlet," one knowledgeable local told us. Neroutsos Inlet is long and straight-sided, with little diversion along the way. A former pulp mill is at Port Alice near the south end.

② **Port Alice.** Port Alice, properly Rumble Beach, but locally called Port Alice, is a friendly, former cellulose-mill town struggling to adjust to the recent sale and subsequent closure of the mill. Amenities include a liquor store, and a grocery market that almost qualifies as a supermarket (and the best grocery shopping between Port Hardy and Tofino). Restaurants are scarce. Fuel is available from a service station near the public dock at the north end of town for a $20 fee. A tricky 9-hole golf course is located at the site of the former mill, the real Port Alice, about a mile south of the town. Showers and laundry are available at the campground half a mile south of the yacht club and Rumble Beach Marina.

Visitors are warmly welcomed in Port Alice. It is a delightful stop and a good alternative to a bus ride into Port Hardy from Coal Harbour for provisioning.

② **Rumble Beach Marina.** (250) 209-2665; (250) 284-3391. Open all year with moorage to 100 feet. This marina, just south of the Port Alice Yacht Club, is the best moorage prospect in Port Alice. Potable water and garbage drop. No power, laundry or showers.

The marina is operated by the city and is within walking distance of all Port Alice amenities.

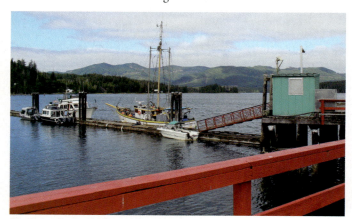

Harbour Authority float at Winter Harbour

Julian Cove is an outstanding anchorage.

Reference Only – Not for Navigation   **WEST COAST OF VANCOUVER ISLAND**

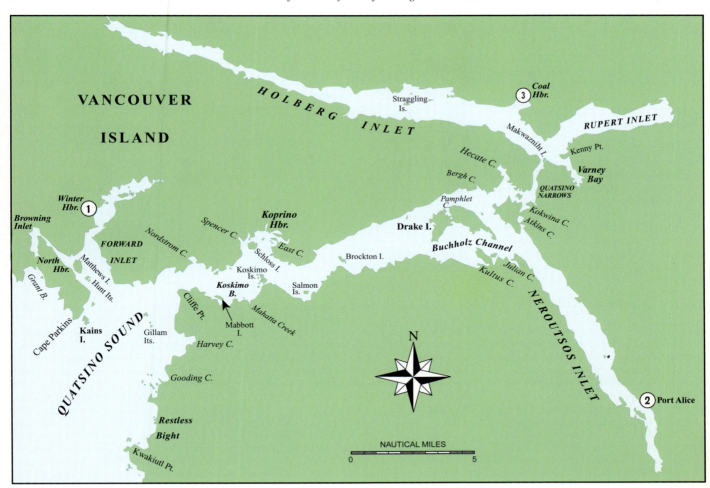

Quatsino Sound

② **Port Alice Yacht Club.** You must belong to a yacht club with reciprocal privileges to tie up here. A log breakwater protects the yacht club and the public dock/launch ramp to the south. Moorage is available in members' vacant slips. Slips are generally not available in July and August. Boats that have been trailered to Port Alice cannot stay at the yacht club.

Although the yacht club is designed primarily for smaller boats, it may have room for larger boats if two adjacent moorage spaces are open. A volunteer worker may point you to your slip, help you tie up, then show you around town. Good water and 20 amp power on the docks. If you come in after hours, the gate is locked but the phone numbers of volunteers are posted. A public park with picnic tables and playground equipment is immediately to the north. We were told that boats can anchor south of the Frigon Islets.

Quatsino Narrows. Quatsino Narrows connects with Rupert Inlet and Holberg Inlet, and the village of Coal Harbour. With tidal streams near Makwazniht Island running to 9 knots on the flood and 8 knots on the ebb, it is best to take the narrows near slack. Predictions for Quatsino Narrows are shown as a secondary station based on Tofino in Canadian Tide & Current Tables Vol. 6, and Ports and Passes. You'll find considerable turbulence near Makwazniht Island. The range on the eastern shore of the narrows is for large ships with 30-foot drafts; small boats need not stay on the range. Turbulence, though less than that found near Makwazniht Island, is present near the south entrance to Quatsino Narrows. At slack water, watch for tugs with log boom tows.

Varney Bay. Varney Bay, at the mouth of the Marble River and east of the north entrance to Quatsino Narrows, is scenic, tranquil and protected. A dinghy ride up the Marble River is worth a trip through Quatsino Narrows. Anchor inside Kenny Point behind the 3-meter island, and watch for rocks and deadheads as you enter. Varney Bay is a fish preserve. No fishing. Correspondents Gil and Karen Flanagan add this report: "After you cross the rather large delta, the Marble River flows through a canyon. The river has undercut some of the canyon walls, forming fantastic caverns. We went up the river about 2.7 miles to a rapids, where we found a huge cavern, measuring at least 30 feet by 30 feet. A must-see." To ensure enough water to safely cross the delta and reach the cavern, plan to be at the rapids as close to high tide as possible.

Rupert Inlet. Rupert Inlet is the site of the giant Utah Mines open pit copper mine, now closed and flooded.

③ **Coal Harbour.** Coal Harbour has a small village with launch ramp, marina, and museum. It is 8 miles by road from Port Hardy.

Thrice-daily bus service to Port Hardy, with connections to Port McNeill, leaves from the village.

During World War II, Coal Harbour was a Royal Canadian Air Force seaplane base. The large building on the waterfront was the hangar. The Coal Harbour Whaling Station, the last whale-processing site on the West Coast, later operated out of these same facilities. Whaling operations ceased in 1967. The hangar and adjacent land now serve as seaplane storage, launching facilities, and water taxi service.

Three rooms in the hangar make up a museum, with artifacts, newspaper clippings and photographs from Coal Harbour's years as an RCAF base and a whaling station. Ask at the desk to see it. If you're lucky you'll get a guided tour. No charge. The large whale jawbone shown in photos of Coal Harbour has been repaired and is on display in the hanger. Recommended.

③ **Quatsino First Nations Dock.** 322 Quattishe Road, Coal Harbour, BC V0N 1K0; (250) 949-6870; Moorage, gas, diesel, water, some 20 amp power. Showers and laundry facilities available beyond the wharfinger office. The floats can be busy with

2020 Waggoner Cruising Guide   395

WEST COAST OF VANCOUVER ISLAND
See Area Map Page 397 - Maps Not for Navigation

commercial boats. Floats can accommodate vessels up to 60 feet.

Holberg Inlet is 18 miles long, narrow and deep, a classic fjord. It has few places to anchor, and not much for the cruising yachtsman. With its 36-mile round trip and no facilities or attractions, it is seldom traveled by cruising yachts.

Quatsino Village. The public dock at Quatsino Village is mostly for smaller boats and loading/unloading. We tucked into the only larger space available only to be shouted at by a taxi boat operator who appeared to have plenty of space to maneuver. We walked into the village and to the 1898 Anglican church, open for visitors. A small museum and snack shop are open one hour per day, several days a week. Chart 3681 shows the details for entry. Room to anchor off the dock if necessary.

BROOKS BAY

Brooks Bay is between Quatsino Sound and Brooks Peninsula. It's about 19 miles from a departure point south of Kains Island (at the entrance to Quatsino Sound) to a point about 2 miles west of Solander Island. Depending on the course chosen, it's another 22 to 25 miles from Solander Island to Walters Cove—a total of at least 40 miles in the open sea. If wind and seas are favorable, those heading south will want to seize the opportunity to round Brooks Peninsula. They can be excused for not exploring Brooks Bay. If the weather is unfavorable, Brooks Bay is a good place to explore while waiting for a weather window. If you have the time, it is recommended.

Two inlets, Klaskino Inlet and Klaskish Inlet, are beautiful and have good anchorage, although portions of Klaskino Inlet have been logged. Brooks Bay is dotted with unmarked (but charted) rocks and reefs that make navigation exciting. Plot courses carefully.

The entrance to Klaskish Basin is narrow.

④ **Klaskino Inlet.** Assuming an approach from the north, leave Lawn Point approximately 2 miles to port. (Lawn Point's grassy-looking slopes are in fact covered with low bushes). Continue, leaving Scarf Reef to port. Then turn to leave Rugged Islets to starboard. Turn to pass midway between Buoys *M17* and *M18*, then turn to enter Klaskino Inlet.

For a quick anchorage, skirt around Anchorage Island into Klaskino Anchorage or into the small bight north of Klaskino Anchorage.

If you'd like to explore further, go through Scouler Pass. Use the more open northern channel, leaving Buoy *M23* to port. The kelp will be close enough to hold your attention. Anchor in the bight between the 67- and 53-meter islands, in the area shown as 7 meters at zero tide. The drying flats of the river mouth come up sharply. Be sure you don't swing onto them.

Correspondent Gil Flanagan went all the way to the head of Klaskino Inlet (about 4 miles from Scouler Pass), and recommends the anchorage behind the little island near the head. He says shore access is excellent, with logging roads for walking. Make noise; bears frequent the woods.

Leaving Klaskino Inlet, the safest route is back between Buoys *M17* and *M18*. Although it's possible to take a route westward through Steele Reefs, we're not sure we'd do it again. Our course took us directly over the word "Steele" on the chart. We had good depths, but even on a quiet day the surf crashing on the rocks seemed closer than we expected. [*Hale*]

⑤ **Klaskish Inlet**. If you run from Quatsino Sound directly to Klaskish Inlet, your probable course will take you very near to Hughes Rock, which dries 5 feet. Hughes Rock is clearly shown on the chart. Don't run over it.

Consider anchoring in magnificent Klaskish Basin, reached through a knockout, must-see narrow gorge with vertical rock sides overhung with dense forest. Once through, you are separated from the rest of the world. All the mooring buoys shown on the chart have been removed.

Brooks Peninsula. Brooks Peninsula and the waters off Cape Cook are, together with Cape Scott, the most hostile on the west coast of Vancouver Island. Like rounding Cape Scott, rounding the Brooks is a milestone in a circumnavigation. The peninsula itself is a mountainous, rectangular promontory that extends 6 miles out from Vancouver Island, like a growth on the side of an otherwise handsome face. Rocks and reefs guard much of the shoreline. Tangles of driftwood make beaches impassable. Cliffs rise from the beaches. At the tops of the cliffs, wilderness. Much of the peninsula is a provincial park, preserved for its wildness. Twenty thousand years ago, when glaciers covered most of Vancouver Island, the Brooks Peninsula remained ice-free. Plant species wiped out

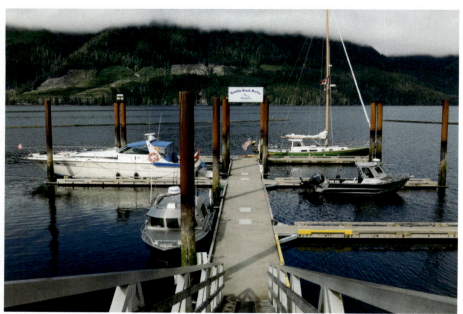
Docks at Rumble Beach Marina are within walking distance to Port Alice.

Reference Only – Not for Navigation   **WEST COAST OF VANCOUVER ISLAND**

Brooks Peninsula

in glaciated areas are still found here. Park status helps preserve those species.

Cap on the Cape: When a cloud forms on top of Brooks Peninsula over Cape Cook, it often means that strong northwesterly winds will follow.

Cape Cook & Solander Island. Cape Cook is the northwestern tip of Brooks Peninsula. Rocks and shoals extend offshore from Cape Cook nearly to Solander Island.

The Cape Cook/Solander Island area can be a dangerous patch of water. When conflicting currents meet accelerating winds, conditions can sink a boat. Cape Cook has driven back large ships. The marine weather broadcasts often talk of "local winds off the headlands" of 35 knots. The headland they have in mind is Cape Cook. While no headland on the West Coast should be taken lightly, Cape Cook (and Cape Scott) should be given the greatest respect. Listen to the weather broadcasts. If conditions sound questionable, wait. When your opportunity comes, seize it.

On all but the quietest days, the safe route past Cape Cook is well offshore from Solander Island. If you are one of the rare lucky ones to round the Brooks on a quiet day and can approach Solander Island more closely, you'll see Steller sea lions hauled out on the base of the island and puffins swimming near your boat.

Weather information: An automated weather station on Solander Island provides wind speed and direction, updated hourly. Listen to the continuous marine broadcast for the latest weather information.

Clerke Point. Clerke Point marks the southeast corner of Brooks Peninsula. Shoals extend at least 0.5 mile offshore. Following the 20-fathom curve will leave ample room for safety. The pyramid-shaped seas we had battled at Solander Island disappeared completely by Clerke Point.

Once past Brooks Peninsula, the winds slacken, the weather warms and conditions improve.

CHECLESET BAY

Checleset Bay has a number of anchorages, including the Shelter Sheds, Columbia Cove, and the Bunsby Islands. If you have just rounded Brooks Peninsula, Shelter Sheds or Columbia Cove are good stops. Columbia Cove is exceptional.

Shelter Sheds. The Shelter Sheds are lines of reef extending from Brooks Peninsula into Checleset Bay. Fishermen have found shelter in their lee, hence the name. Correspondent Gil Flanagan reports that Shed 4 has by far the finest beach his family has found—better even than West Beach at Hakai. The water was near 70° F. A trail leads to Columbia Cove, but Correspondents Steve and Elsie Hulsizer report that windfall has made the trail difficult, especially the first 200 yards.

⑥ **Columbia Cove.** Beautiful Columbia Cove is known locally as Peddlers Cove.

2020 Waggoner Cruising Guide   397

WEST COAST OF VANCOUVER ISLAND
See Area Map Page 397 - Maps Not for Navigation

Neither name is on the chart. The cove is immediately north of Jackobson Point, snugged up against the base of Brooks Peninsula. Depths in Columbia Cove are shallower than charted.

Be sure to enter between Jackobson Point and the 215-foot island. Columbia Cove has experienced some silting over the years and anchoring room has become limited. The mouth of the cove, between Jackobson Point and the 215-foot island, is safe in a northwesterly. In southerlies, winds and waves make this area uncomfortable, leaving room for only about three boats in the cove itself. Columbia Cove is a voluntary no-discharge zone. Please volunteer.

The name Columbia Cove comes from Captain Robert Gray's ship Columbia, which overnighted here twice. If you think Columbia Cove is crowded with three boats, now imagine it with the Columbia, the schooner Adventure, and the ship Margaret, of Boston, all at the same time. A sometimes muddy trail across the small peninsula formed by Jackobson Point leads to a beautiful sandy ocean beach. Great beachcombing. Take the dinghy up the stream to the trailhead, but watch the tide. You can be stranded, with a long walk across tideflats dragging your dinghy or kayak.

Weather Note: When strong winds from the northwest are forecast south of Brooks Peninsula, the Brooks provides a lee for Columbia Cove and adjacent waters. Winds may be strong but seas will be quiet. It's a good place to wait out a northwest gale. It's not a good place to wait out a southeast gale.

⑦ **Battle Bay.** Battle Bay, north of the Bunsby Islands, has acceptable anchorages roughly off the Indian reserve, and in the nook that makes up the northeast shore. Approach the Longback Islands before making your turn into Battle Bay. One interesting anchorage is immediately west of Battle Bay, against the east shore of Acous Peninsula. To reach that anchorage, leave the Skirmish Islands to starboard as you approach. From there you'll look across a sea of islands and rocks to the Bunsbys.

Brooks Peninsula is famous for high winds and rough water. It demands respect.

The Indian Reserve on the Acous Peninsula is the former home of the Checleset Band, now located in Walters Cove. You can find fallen totem poles serving as nurse logs, and the depressions of old Longhouses.

⑧ **Bunsby Islands.** "Did you get to the Bunsbys?" That's what people ask when they learn you've been down the west coast of Vancouver Island. Don't disappoint them by saying no. The Bunsby Islands are rocky, rugged, and beautiful. They were named for a character in the Charles Dickens novel *Dombey and Son*. A number of other features in the area also carry names from that novel.

Study the chart and know your location at all times. Enter the Bunsby Islands only through Gay Passage. Two anchorages are off this passage: either the cove in the southern island or the slightly larger bay in the northern island. Enter the northern island's bay favoring the north shore to avoid a shoal extending from the south side. In this larger bay, note the rock directly beneath the 6-fathom sounding. The lagoon adjacent to this bay may be fine for an adventuresome trailerable boat.

The cove on the west side of Gay Passage is guarded by two rocks that dry 4 feet. The rocks are easy to identify and avoid if you're paying attention. The cove has room for several boats.

Checleset Bay has a large population of sea otters, the successful result of a 1969 effort to re-establish these delightful creatures. From the Bunsbys, where they were first reintroduced, the sea otters have spread up and down the coast, as far south as Barkley Sound and as far north as the Cape Caution area on the mainland. You'll sometimes see them in "rafts," groups of otters hanging together, in kelp beds.

If weather allows, take the dinghy or kayak around the islands. The rugged, windswept rocks and islets are too stunning to try to describe. It's easy to get disoriented. Carry a chart, compass, handheld GPS and handheld VHF radio.

KYUQUOT SOUND

With the exception of the outer islands and Rugged Point, Kyuquot (pronounced "Ki-YU-kit") Sound is protected and pretty, surrounded by high mountains, with easy waters. On the inside, Dixie Cove and Don Douglass' "Petroglyph Cove" (known locally as Blue Lips Cove) are excellent anchorages, and several others are attractive. The settlement of Walters Cove is a favorite.

From the south, enter Kyuquot Sound past Whistle Buoy M38. Leave the buoy to starboard, and proceed through Kyuquot Channel. Most visiting pleasure craft, however, will approach from the north and stop at Walters Cove before entering Kyuquot Sound proper.

⑨ **Walters Cove.** For communication, call on VHF channels 06 or 14. The little settlement of Walters Cove has almost everything you might need after a week or two of working your way along the coast: outpost hospital, ice, charts, a small general store, pay phone, a restaurant and coffee shop, relaxed and friendly people, happy kids and lazy dogs. The store at the public dock, on the south side, is open Monday, Wednesday and Friday; and the store above the dock, on the Kyuquot side, is open evenings only. The

Solander Island off Cape Cook, the Cape of Storms, on a rare calm summer afternoon.

WEST COAST OF VANCOUVER ISLAND

The Bunsby Islands are not to be missed. The rugged scenery and sandy beaches are a highlight of the west coast of Vancouver Island.

Kyuquot Inn Restaurant, also known as Java The Hutt, is open daily with free Wi-Fi for customers; cash only.

One thing Walters Cove does not have is liquor. Walters Cove is dry, by vote of the Kyuquot Native community, and there's not a drop to be bought. Nor is liquor in evidence, even on the dock.

Another thing you won't find is fuel. Be sure you have enough fuel in your tanks. The nearest fuel is in Fair Harbour.

From seaward, the safest approach to Walters Cove in all weather is from Whistle Buoy *MC*, at the entrance to Brown Channel. Use Chart 3683. Go through Brown Channel and turn to starboard on a course to leave Gayward Rock to starboard. At Gayward Rock go to large scale Chart 3651 to work your way past the east side of Walters Island and into Walters Cove.

Boats coming down from the Bunsby Islands probably will follow Chart 3683's rather obvious passage along the Vancouver Island shoreline, leaving Cole Rock to starboard, and McLean Island and Chief Rock Buoy *M29* to port. At Gayward Rock they would move to large-scale Chart 3651.

On Charts 3623 and 3683, take note of the charted rock awash at 10 ft (50°03'06"N/127°27'07"W). This rock is along your probable shoreline passage course. At a depth of 10 feet at zero tide the rock is not a concern for most boats, but you should know it's there.

Without Chart 3651, entry to Walters Cove would be a tricky matter. Although it is marked by buoys and a daybeacon, the channel past the east side of Walters Island is easy to misread, and the unwary skipper could be on a rock. With Chart 3651 the channel is apparent, and following the rule of Red, Right, Returning, entry is safe. The one daybeacon along the way marks the narrow passage that leads directly into Walters Cove. Don't cut it close. Remember that beacons are attached to the earth; rock extends well into the passage from the beacon. Use a mid-channel course favoring the north side between the beacon and the 51-meter island opposite. The chart makes the route clear.

Several locals insist, "Don't anchor in Walters Cove!" The bottom, they say, is foul with debris. Furthermore, the floor of the bay is crisscrossed by high voltage submarine electrical cables, a Telus phone line, and the water lines serving the community.

Instead of anchoring, tie up at the public wharf to port as you enter. Long mooring floats are on each side of the public wharf. The general store and post office is at the head of the wharf. Open Monday, Wednesday, and Friday 1:00 p.m. to 5:00 p.m. Stock arrives once per week.

Java the Hutt Coffee Shop, which began its life as a "boat-through" rather than "drive-through" coffee shop on the Kyuquot Inn dock, is now located in the renovated school house at the inn with an expanded menu. They serve coffee, pastries and a variety of burgers and salads. Free Wi-Fi is provided. Showers are available at the inn. Owner Eric Gorbman is among one of the friendliest people on the coast.

The best time to arrive at Walters Cove is Thursday afternoon. The *Uchuck III* arrives that day, sometime around 5:00 p.m., depending on the other stops they have scheduled. Walters Cove becomes a bustle of activity when the ship lands, with skiffs arriving from all over the cove and outlying areas. Watching the *Uchuck III* unload its cargo is a slice of West Coast life you won't want to miss. Everyone pitches in. Fuel barrels, boxes, even washers and dryers are loaded off the boat's starboard side into waiting skiffs. Pallets of groceries are loaded off the port side onto carts on the dock.

Because the ship overnights at Walters Cove, passengers spend the night at lodges and B&Bs. For dinner, passengers eat at the Java The Hutt Coffee Shop. When there is space, the Java The Hutt also feeds boaters, guests at the lodges, and anyone else who asks by mid-afternoon. Dinner is delicious. Guests eat family-style at a long table.

For medical matters, contact the VIHA (Vancouver Island Health Authority) outpost hospital at Walters Cove, (250) 332-5289.

Good water is available at the store for a small fee.

The Kyuquot Band Native community of approximately 200 is across the bay, served by its own public dock. We met a resident of the Native community who told us that she operates a small store near the head of the dock selling snacks, soft drinks, some groceries and native crafts.

All transport is by boat in Walters Cove, and from an early age the Kyuquot children (and Native children all along the coast) are accomplished boat handlers. Their outboard-powered craft seem to have but two directions: forward and reverse; and two throttle settings: full-power and off.

Walters Cove has been a popular gathering place for decades. Years ago it was home to five fish camps in the summer. When people were stuck in port waiting for the weather to break, the talk flowed. Long ago Walters Cove got its local name of Bull--t Bay, BS Bay in polite company. A cafe in Walters Cove was called the BS Cafe. (The BS Cafe, with its memorabilia-laden walls, burned in 1998.)

⑨ **Walters Cove Resort.** (250) 332-5274; (250) 287-2223; gofishing@walterscoveresort.com; www.walterscoveresort.com. Monitors VHF 78A. Open in summer with moorage for those staying at the lodge; water, ice, Wi-Fi. No power. Reservations required. This is a first class fishing lodge. Fishing charters and fish packing available.

The public dock at Walters Cove. The building at the head of the dock is a post office and well-stocked store.

2020 Waggoner Cruising Guide

WEST COAST OF VANCOUVER ISLAND *Reference Only – Not for Navigation*

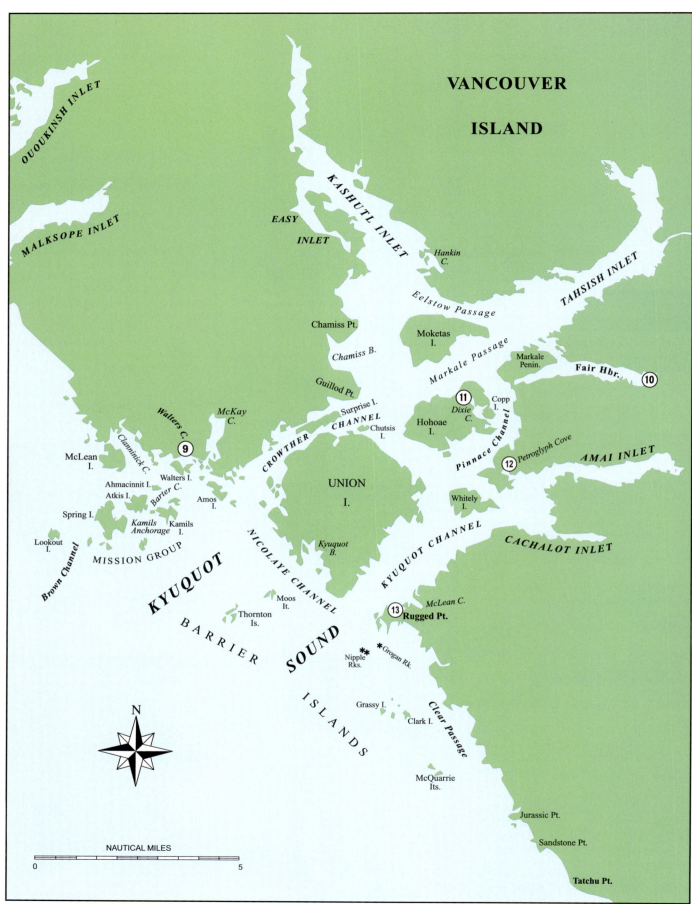

Kyuquot Sound

Barter Cove. Barter Cove, in the Mission Group islands outside Walters Cove, is open, unprotected and not as interesting as anchorages inside Kyuquot Sound. Leave Ahmacinnit Island and the tiny islet east of Ahmacinnit Island to starboard, and feel your way in.

Kamils Anchorage. Kamils Anchorage in the Mission Group islands is more exposed than Barter Cove. Enter, very carefully, through Favourite Entrance.

Amos Island. From Walters Cove, the easiest entrance to Kyuquot Sound is around the east side of Amos Island into Crowther Channel. Use Chart 3651 to identify the channel between Walters Cove and Nicolaye Channel, then Chart 3682 to find the route past Amos Island. The passage east of Amos Island is deep but narrow, and bounded by rocks. The first time through can be unsettling, but after you've done it once, it's easy.

Surprise Island. Surprise Island, steep, round, and logged off to stumps, is located in Crowther Channel. On the south side of Surprise Island, Crowther Channel is deep and open, but on the north side a narrow passage is interesting. At zero tide least depths in this passage are approximately 18 feet. A ledge of rock, shown on the chart, extends from the north shore. Favor the Surprise Island side all the way through.

Hankin Cove. Hankin Cove is located near the mouth of Kashutl Inlet, on the east side. It is a beautiful little cove with good holding and completely protected. Stands of small trees covering the hillsides show evidence of past logging. Correspondents Gil and Karen Flanagan anchored in the southeast cove, and add, "Chart 3682 is way off on the shoal in this cove. The shoal extends only halfway across from the east shore. Depths are 12 to 18 feet along the west shore, almost to the south end of the cove."

⑩ **Fair Harbour.** Enter Fair Harbour south of Karouk Island, leaving the two lighted beacons to port. The passage north of the island has two reported rocks, not shown on the chart.

Fair Harbour has a wide launch ramp at the head, with a small campground and ample parking. A dirt road leads from Zeballos to Fair Harbour, the only road access to Kyuquot Sound. This is a popular trailer boat launch point. A good-sized public wharf, with a long float, is at the head. If the float is full, anchor in approximately 60 feet.

⑩ **Fair Harbour Marina & Campground.** (250) 483-3382; fairharbourmarina@gmail.com; www.gatewaytokyuquot.com. Open all year. Limited moorage, gas, diesel, propane, water, garbage drop, boat launch. No power on the docks. This is the only fuel in Kyuquot Sound. A small store carries fishing tackle, ice, convenience food. For-fee Wi-Fi; complimentary for paying customers.

⑪ **Dixie Cove.** Dixie Cove indents the east side of Hohoae Island, and is a wonderful anchorage. Enter south of Copp Island, through a narrow but deep passage to the first of two anchorages. The outer anchorage is approximately 30 feet deep, with good holding. Another narrow passage leads to the inner cove, completely secluded, with rock cliffs on one side. Depths here are approximately 18 feet, mud bottom with excellent holding. Landing on shore is a problem, so you're restricted to the boat. As a place to put the hook down, though, Dixie Cove is highly recommended.

⑫ **Petroglyph Cove** (Blue Lips Cove). In his excellent book, *Exploring Vancouver Island's West Coast*, Don Douglass describes this previously-unnamed anchorage and calls it "Petroglyph Cove." In the second edition of his book, Douglass acknowledged that others had not been able to find the petroglyphs. Hulsizer reported finding what looked like a faded pictograph (red ochre painting) and noted that the local name for the cove is Blue Lips Cove—because when residents went swimming the water was so cold their lips turned blue. Petroglyph, Pictograph or Blue Lips, the cove is located near the mouth of Amai Inlet, roughly due west of Amai Point. The narrow entry is hidden until you're right on it. The channel shallows to a least depth of 12 to 18 feet, but has no hazards. Once inside you are protected. While in our opinion Petroglyph Cove is not as pretty as Dixie Cove, it is an excellent spot.

Volcanic Cove. Exposed to the north, small, no room to swing. Temporary only for small boats, in our view.

⑬ **Rugged Point Marine Park.** Rugged Point marks the southern entrance to Kyuquot Sound. Our notes read, "Wow!" The beaches on the ocean side are spectacular, and deserve a visit. Anchor along the inside beaches in 18 feet on a kelp-covered hard sand bottom, and dinghy ashore. The Pacific swell, though diminished, can get into the anchorage. The anchorage is protected from southeasterlies and westerlies but is subject to occasional nighttime outflow winds. Be sure you anchor far enough offshore to avoid swinging onto shallows if outflow winds develop.

A trail, now upgraded with a boardwalk, leads through the park to the ocean beaches. Bear and cougar prints have been sighted, so be noisy. Once on the ocean beach, you will find a series of paths leading around headlands all the way to the Kapoose Creek. Some of the paths are steep and involve climbing ladders or using ropes for assistance.

Cachalot. Cachalot, the site of a former industrial whaling center, makes an interesting lunch stop or afternoon exploration. Locate it by finding the abandoned pilings between Cachalot Inlet to the east and Cachalot Creek to the west. Although pronounced locally as "catch a lot," the name means sperm whale in French (and in French would be pronounced "caa-shaa-low"). The whaling center operated between 1907 and 1926, then served as a pilchard reduction plant until the 1940s.

Anchor off the old pilings in 30 to 60 feet of water and take the dinghy ashore. You'll find old whale bones, crockery, and miscellaneous hardware on the beach, and rusty equipment in the forest. Next to the creek, a ferrocement statue of a sperm whale serves as a memorial to the whales that were processed at this site. The statue was placed there by Vancouver Island artist Wayne Adams in the 1970s. Hulsizer gives the history of the site in her book *Voyages to Windward*.

When anchoring, avoid the drying shoal on the north end of the site near the river and be sure to anchor in at least 30 feet of water to avoid your anchor being entangled in kelp.

Kyuquot Sound to Esperanza Inlet. Depending on the course chosen, it is approximately 13.5 miles between Rugged Point and the entrance to Gillam Channel, which leads into Esperanza Inlet. In good visibility the route through Clear Passage is smooth and interesting. In poor visibility, we would head seaward from Rugged Point to entrance Buoy M38, then turn southeastward toward Gillam Channel.

Clear Passage to Tatchu Point. Clear Passage takes you about 4 miles along the coast in

Fair Harbour, home to Fair Harbour Marina with the only fuel in Kyuquot Sound.

WEST COAST OF VANCOUVER ISLAND

See Area Map Page 403 - Maps Not for Navigation

waters protected by the Barrier Islands, past a steady display of rugged rocks and rock islets. The channel is free of hazards. To enter Clear Passage, leave Grogan Rock to starboard, watching carefully for the rock to port, marked by kelp, that dries at 4 feet. Heading down-island, we got a little close to Grogan Rock, and the depths came up sharply. We moved off to port and they went back down. You will have no trouble identifying Grogan Rock. It is an awful 23-foot-high black pinnacle and it commands attention. Lay a course to take you north of McQuarrie Islets, and exit Clear Passage leaving McQuarrie Islets to starboard. The rocks and islets along Clear Passage all look alike. It helps to plot a waypoint at the spot where you intend to turn to exit past McQuarrie Islets. Clear Passage is also a good route when heading north. Leave McQuarrie Islets and Grogan Rock to port.

The island just south of Grassy Isle is a good place to hunt fossils. "We anchored south of Clark Island and took the dinghy ashore to a shell beach on the southeast corner of the island. The fossils were just lying on the beach. We recommend doing this on a calm day only. With a more detailed metric chart, it might be possible to find anchorage between Grassy Isle and Clark." [*Hulsizer*]

Local fishermen say the waters from Jurassic Point past Tatchu Point can be an "ugly patch of water." Use caution and careful judgment.

⑭ **Rolling Roadstead** (Catala Island Provincial Park). Rolling Roadstead offers acceptable anchorage in fair weather. From the west the approach can be tricky. Douglass and Watmough describe the approach in their books. Careful navigation is called for, including the finding and identifying of the various rocks and reefs in the entrance. The hazards are easily identified, either by the breaking surf or kelp growing in the shallows. With the hazards accounted for, the entry is reported to be safe. All agree that it should be run in fair weather only, with good visibility.

If you're coming down from Tatchu Point, especially in a fresh westerly, it's easier to enter via Gillam Channel, leaving Black Rock and Entrance Reef to port and approach Rolling Roadstead from the southwest. Anchor in the lee of the point of land that juts abruptly from Catala Island.

Catala Island, which protects Rolling Roadstead, is a provincial marine park. The beach on Catala Island is beautiful. Several sea caves are accessible.

Gillam Channel. Gillam Channel, more than one-half mile wide and well-buoyed, is the safe entrance to Esperanza Inlet. Approaching, leave the entrance buoy *M40* and buoy *M42*, which marks the west end of Blind Reef, to starboard. Leave buoy *M41* to port, and continue into Esperanza Inlet.

ESPERANZA INLET

Esperanza Inlet is on the west side of Nootka Island, and ultimately connects with Nootka

At anchor in lovely Hankin Cove

Sound. The inlet is part of the "inside route" through this portion of the coast. This route is served by three communities—Zeballos, Tahsis, and Gold River—and by the Esperanza Mission, with its fuel dock and excellent water. The waterways are beautiful, and contain several good stopping places. Tahsis Narrows connects Esperanza Inlet with Tahsis Inlet on the Nootka Sound side, and is not difficult to run.

Nuchatlitz Inlet. Reader Don Thain reports that Mary Basin is a delightful and protected anchorage with good holding in mud. A pretty waterfall on Laurie Creek is reachable by dinghy on a 7-foot tide. The inner basin is a tidal lagoon.

⑮ **Nuchatlitz Provincial Park.** Nuchatlitz Provincial Park is a beautiful and interesting stop with a well-protected anchorage. It's a favorite among kayakers and campers. The area contains a number of archeological treasures, including burial canoes on land and burial caves on the outer islands.

The entry to Nuchatlitz is very complex with numerous rocks and reefs; a careful study of the charts is warranted. Inside, a large bay has a uniform bottom with approximately 30- to 40-foot anchoring depths. In good weather, if you choose an anchoring spot where you can see over the islands towards the northwest, you may be rewarded with a magnificent sunset. The anchorage can be absolutely calm when the wind dies in the evening, but you can hear the surf breaking on the outer islands.

The abandoned Indian village of Nuchatlitz is on the shore of a 44-meter island marked Indian Reserve, above a marvelous beach. At low tide you can walk the drying sand bar from the reserve island to a second 44-meter island to the west. Although the village was moved from this site to Espinosa in the 1980s, the site is still visited by the band. Local kayak tours use it as a landing site.

A number of private homes dot the shores of a privately-owned unmarked island on the south side of the anchorage. Private buoys mark the route past submerged rocks to homes on the island's back side and to a shallow lagoon. Use Chart 3676, which reflects hydrographic survey work performed between 1992 and 1996 at the cost of many survey launch propellers.

The easy but long entry to Nuchatlitz is from the northeast, passing east of Rosa Island. From there the chart makes the course clear: Follow the winding channel east of the 37-meter and 34-meter islands, and east of the two red spar buoys *M46* and *M48* (Red, Right, Returning). At Buoy *M48* the bay opens up. Both Douglass and Yeadon-Jones describe a second, more direct entrance, leaving the light on the 37-meter island (known locally as Entrance Island) to starboard as you enter.

⑯ **Queen Cove.** Queen Cove is a short distance inside the entrance to Port Eliza, the first inlet to port as you enter Esperanza Inlet. It is a safe and satisfying spot to put the hook down and go exploring, although not as beautiful as Nuchatlitz on the east side of Gillam Channel. Queen Cove is a popular anchorage among island circumnavigators. Anchor here and you'll soon have company. The cove is well protected, and has excellent holding in 20 to 40 feet. It is large enough for several boats to swing. We have received reports that the Queen Cove Band collects a fee for anchorage. A cabin with a dock is at the north end of Queen Cove. The Park River enters at the north end, and makes for good dinghy exploration.

The most protected anchorage is the nook at the south end of Queen Cove, between the little island and the rock that dries at 3.4 meters (11 feet). Swinging room is a little restricted, but the anchorage is workable. We overnighted in Queen Cove, anchored in the wider and much more exposed northern area. At 5:00 p.m. the wind came in, and built to about 25 knots before dying at sundown. We sailed back and forth on our anchor, but we didn't budge. [*Hale*]

Espinosa Inlet. Espinosa Inlet is deep and high-walled. No place to anchor. The Native village of Ocluje is located at its head.

Newton Cove Resort. (877) 337-5464; info@nootkamarineadventures.com; www.

Esperanza Inlet

WEST COAST OF VANCOUVER ISLAND

See Area Map Page 403 - Maps Not for Navigation

Zeballos is bounded by impressive mountains.

nootkamarineadventures.com. Monitors VHF 06. Call for advance reservations. Newton Cove Resoert near the mouth of Espinosa Inlet is a fishing resort with services and facilities for resort guests only.

⑰ **Zeballos.** www.zeballos.com. Zeballos (pronounced "Ze-BAH-los") is the most unexpected town on the west coast of Vancouver Island. While other settlements range from fishing camp (Winter Harbour) to bustling town (Tofino), Zeballos stands alone.

The trip up Zeballos Inlet is an especially scenic one, with bulbous-topped odd-shaped mountains, and sheer rock faces rising above the shores. Zeballos is a mining town that looks like Cicily, Alaska, the fictional town made famous by the television show *Northern Exposure*, with wandering streets, false-fronted buildings, and a museum. The town is built at the mouth of the Zeballos River, next to mountains that go *straight up*.

The museum, located on the main road heading out of town, is one of the town's main attractions. It's small but fascinating, with mining paraphernalia, photographs, and a full-scale model of a mine entrance. In 2016 it was staffed by a full-time curator, but in previous years has not always been open regularly. If you arrive at the museum during the workweek and no one is there, inquire at the municipal hall and someone will give you a tour.

The town recently constructed a boardwalk trail through the Zeballos River estuary. It's a beautiful walk along the river.

Much gold has been taken out of the highly mineralized mountains around Zeballos. Over dinner at the hotel on our first visit, we talked with a wildcat prospector whose eyes burned bright as he told of pockets of gold still waiting to be taken. He insisted that he didn't have gold fever, *but he knew where the gold was.* [*Hale*]

Tie up at the public dock, to the right of the fuel dock as you approach. Pay telephones are at the head of the dock and on the seaplane dock. The village has a wharf to the left of the fuel dock, but it is for large vessels, loading and unloading only. The small float next to the wharf is for short-term (a few hours) tie-up. A bird-viewing platform overlooks the estuary.

A fish-processing plant is shoreward of the fuel dock and is one of the town's economic mainstays. It's a good place to purchase chipped ice.

Provisioning: Cruising boaters often ask whether they should stop at Zeballos or Tahsis for provisioning. The answer is you may need to stop at both for everything you need. At present, no good store exists in Zeballos. The store near the fuel dock carries ice cream and convenience foods, as well as frozen meat and bread, and liquor. The Rosa Island General Store also offers limited items including staples, snacks, and cigarettes. Fruits and vegetables were in short supply at both stores. Zeballos is a good place to spend the night. The inlet leading to the town is long and beautiful. There's no point going both ways in one day.

⑰ **Zeballos Fuel Dock Inc.** P.O. Box 100, Zeballos, BC V0P 2A0; (250) 761-4201. Open all year. Gasoline, diesel, propane, kerosene, petroleum products, some marine supplies. Candace Saulkner is the owner.

⑰ **Village of Zeballos Municipal Wharf.** (250) 761-4229. Open all year. For large vessels, loading and unloading only. The small float next to the wharf is for short-term (a few hours) tie-up. Some overnight moorage with permission. Access to power and water if absolutely necessary.

⑰ **Zeballos Small Craft Harbour.** P.O. Box 99, Zeballos, BC V0P 2A0; (250) 761-4991. Monitors VHF 06. Open all year with 400 feet of moorage, 30 amp power, year-round washrooms & showers, water, waste oil collection, all tide launch ramp, long term parking (launch ramp is run by the village). A sign on the east side of the easternmost dock warns of shallow water, but the Hulsizers report finding 2.7 meters when sounding the depth with a lead line at low tide.

⑱ **Esperanza (Nootka Mission).** P.O. Box 368, Tahsis, BC V0P 1X0; (250) 483-4162; www.esperanza.ca. info@esperanza.ca Monitors VHF 06. Fuel dock open all year from 7:00 a.m. to 9:00 p.m. with gasoline, diesel, lube oil. Excellent water, phone service and free Wi-Fi for one hour for customers. A small store, with fishing gear and limited groceries, is on the fuel dock; no alcohol or

Zeballos

The floats at Zeballos are well maintained, with power and water.

WEST COAST OF VANCOUVER ISLAND

See Area Map Page 405 - Maps Not for Navigation

tobacco. Moorage is available at the dock for boats up to 120 feet in front of the old boathouse, except during the month of July; call ahead. The mission runs camps for local children. When a camp is in session, facilities may not be available.

Esperanza is the home of the Nootka Mission. Its story goes back to 1937, when the Shantyman Mission began a hospital at Esperanza. This was in the tradition of the Mission, founded in northern Ontario in 1907 to serve shanty dwellers in outlying areas. The Esperanza hospital no longer operates and the property is now owned by the Esperanza Ministries Association, serving people of the west coast of Vancouver Island. The property is immaculately kept. The fuel dock is an important source of revenue.

Inquire about availability for visiting boaters. Showers, washrooms, some 15 amp power, water, ice, and laundry are available. Sometimes, fresh Esperanza-grown produce and canned cheesecake are available for purchase.

Tahsis Narrows. Tahsis Narrows connects the Esperanza Inlet side of Nootka Island with the Nootka Sound side. From the chart, one would think reversing tidal currents rage through the narrows four times a day, but they do not. The narrows are deep and free of hazards, with little tidal current activity. Passage can be made at any time.

TAHSIS INLET

Tahsis Inlet (Tahsis is pronounced with a short-a, as in cat) is long and narrow, and bounded by mountains. The wind funnels and blows up-inlet or down, depending on conditions. The normal situation in prevailing westerly winds is for light or outflow winds in the morning and strong inflow winds in the afternoon, building stronger as you approach the town. But during extended periods of warm weather, strong outflow winds can also develop, especially at night and early morning. Gale-force easterlies rarely reach upper Tahsis Inlet, making it a good place to wait out a storm.

⑲ **Tahsis.** At the head of the inlet the sawmill town of Tahsis once had full facilities, but the mills closed and have been dismantled. The loss of the mills just about killed the town. Now, Tahsis is struggling but surviving. Outsiders bought the houses at bargain prices, which, at least initially, gave the economy a small boost. Through it all, the Westview Marina has remained an outstanding operation.

In town, the Tahsis Supermarket has consolidated many of the operations previously run by others. The Supermarket sells groceries, liquor and fuel. It also has a small cafe. This is a small town, and grocery selection is limited. Tahsis Building Centre, a hardware store, is just north of the Supermarket. A post office is located at the other end of town, near the seaplane dock.

The Tahsis library, in the municipal building, has free Wi-Fi and an excellent view. It's a wonderful place to while away a stormy afternoon.

⑲ **Westview Marina & Lodge.** P.O. Box 248, Tahsis, BC V0P 1X0; (250) 934-7672; (800) 992-3252; info@westviewmarina.com; www.westviewmarina.com. Monitors VHF 06. The fuel dock has gasoline, diesel, lubricants, and marine parts. Mechanic available 24/7. Washrooms, showers, laundry, free Wi-Fi, small store with ice and good gift selection, licensed restaurant with patio, and the Island Attitude Coffee Café. The Café opens at 5:00 a.m. during the summer. Moorage with 15, 30 & 50 amp power and potable water. Kayak rentals and eco tours. Courtesy car available. Email your provisioning list a week ahead and they'll have it ready for you.

This marina, at the head of Tahsis Inlet, is set up to serve the summer flotilla of small sportfishing boats. Cruisers are welcome, too, and the marina has just about anything a cruising boater might need. Reservations recommended May to September, but the marina will always try to fit you in. The restaurant has live music and steak dinners on Friday nights, June through September. Each year, we hear good things from readers, praising the facilities and the treatment they receive. The marina is neat and attractive, the people helpful, and the fuel dock easy to approach.

Tsowwin Narrows. The major navigation danger in Tahsis Inlet is Tsowwin Narrows, created by the outfall from the Tsowwin River. A beacon marks the edge of the shoal. Pass between that beacon and another beacon on the west shore of the inlet. Remember that beacons are attached to the earth, and shoal water can extend into a channel from a beacon. Give each beacon a good offing. While we did not see much debris, Tahsis Inlet is reported to have considerable drift and deadheads, depending on logging activity. Keep a close watch on the water ahead.

Princesa Channel. Princesa Channel runs between Bodega Island and Strange Island, and connects Tahsis and Kendrick inlets. A route through Princesa Channel gets a boat out of the Tahsis Inlet chop and cuts some distance off a passage for southbound boats heading to Friendly Cove, but the Tahsis Inlet entrance to Princesa Channel is narrow and partly guarded by underwater rocks.

From Tahsis Inlet to Kendrick Inlet (east to west) the problem is the flood tide. The flood current flows northward into Tahsis Inlet, and a boat entering Princesa Channel will find a definite northward set to its course. This northward set will tend to put the boat onto a submerged rock charted about 200 feet north of the Princesa Channel light, at the east entrance to Princesa Channel. Don and Reanne Douglass, in their book *Exploring Vancouver Island's West Coast*, believe the rock is closer to 100 feet from the light. Whether 100 feet or 200 feet, the rock is not far away. The goal is to wrap around the Princesa Channel light but avoid yet another charted rock south of the light, while not being set onto the rock 100 to 200 feet north of the light. Chart 3675 shows the rocks clearly. Study the chart and you will understand not only the challenge but the decisions required to meet the challenge.

We ran Princesa Channel in a stout flood current and had no problems. In our case, we ran south in Tahsis Inlet until the Princesa Channel light bore 235° magnetic, then turned toward the light. We kept the light on our nose (we had to crab to make good our course) until the light was close aboard, then laid off to starboard to give the light 50 feet of clearance, and entered the channel. The key was to be aware of the rock 100 to 200 feet north of the light and keep our course south of that rock. Once past the light we held a mid-channel course and waltzed on through. [*Hale*]

Bodega Cove. Douglass calls this previously unnamed anchorage "Bodega Cove" and we see no reason to argue. Bodega Cove lies at the head of Kendrick Inlet, between Nootka Island and Bodega Island. The area has been logged, so the scenery is not that of primeval forest. Protection is excellent, however, and the shores are accessible. A reef extends from the Nootka Island side of the entrance. Favor the eastern, Bodega Island, side. The recommended approach

Tahsis Inlet

406   www.WaggonerGuide.com

WEST COAST OF VANCOUVER ISLAND

is to divide the entry channel in half, then split the eastern, Bodega Island, portion in half again (in other words, three-quarters of the way toward the eastern shore), and run down that line.

A large log dump and booming ground is on Nootka Island near the head of Kendrick Inlet. When it's in operation, you can watch huge machines dumping piles of logs into the water.

NOOTKA SOUND

Nootka Sound is where European influence in the Northwest began. Although Captain Cook first landed at Resolution Cove in 1778, it was at Friendly Cove that Captain Meares built the *Northwest America*, 48 feet on deck, the first ship ever built on the west coast, and launched it in 1788.

The long arms (Muchalat Inlet and Tlupana Inlet) that reach out from Nootka Sound have few anchorages, and they tend to be deep. The Port of Gold River is at the head of Muchalat Inlet. The town of Gold River is 9 miles from the dock. Trailerable boats, most of them here for salmon fishing in Nootka Sound, are launched at Gold River.

㉔ **Critter Cove.** Critter Cove is the name given by Cameron Forbes to this previously unnamed spot about 1 mile south of Argonaut Point on Tlupana Inlet. Cameron has established a sportfishing resort in the cove and named it after his nickname of "Critter," when he played hockey. The inner cove is no longer suitable for anchoring.

㉔ **Critter Cove Marina.** P.O. Box 1118, Gold River, BC V0P 1G0; (250) 412-6029; info@crittercove.com; www.crittercove.com. Fuel dock carries mid-grade gasoline, oil, ice, bait, coffee, convenience food, fishing tackle,

The Island Attitude Coffee Café at Westview Marina.

and ocean-themed pottery. Fuel dock hours are 10:00 a.m. to 6:00 p.m. in June, and 8:00 a.m. to 9:00 p.m. in July and August. Moorage, cabins, lodge rooms, suites, restaurant, showers, washrooms. No power or water on the docks. Showers are for overnight guests only.

Cameron Forbes, one of the nicest guys you'll meet, has quite a sportfishing camp here. Most of Critter Cove is on floats, including the licensed restaurant and some of the accommodations. The Critter Cove Cafe is open for breakfast, lunch and dinner. Boaters who are not overnight guests are welcome at the cafe. There are also self-contained beach cottages on the land adjacent to and behind the floating portion of the resort. Most of the boats at Critter Cove are trailered into Gold River, where they are launched. They do have room for a few visiting cruisers.

Nootka Sound Resort. (877) 337-5464; VHF 06 info@nootkamarineadventures.com; www.nootkamarineadventures.com. Nootka Sound Resort is fishing resort; facilities and services are for resort guests only.

Hisnit Inlet. Hisnit Inlet extends north from Tlupana Inlet. Hisnit is one of the few anchorages in Nootka Sound that is well-protected, shallow enough for convenient anchoring, and large enough for a number of boats. Two submerged rocks lie almost mid-channel a short distance into Hisnit Inlet. Do not be deceived by the open and safe appearance of the inlet as you arrive or depart. Favor the south shore.

The view of mountains up the stream at the head of the inlet is stunning. A marble quarry once operated on the east shore. Piles of white marble are visible on the beach and in the nearby forest. The quarry itself is buried under fallen trees and is difficult (and dangerous) to locate. Near the head of the inlet on the same east shore is a large rock shaped like a human head.

Anchorage at the head of the inlet is in 40 to 60 feet. It is open but protected. The shoreline is accessible.

㉑ **Moutcha Bay Resort.** (877) 337-5464; info@nootkamarineadventures.com; www.moutchabay.com. Moutcha Bay Resort is a full service marina, with moorage to 150 feet, fuel dock with gasoline, diesel and propane, water, 15 & 30 amp power, pumpout, Wi-Fi, and a concrete launch ramp. Washrooms and showers are at the top of the docks. The docks are beautifully built, wide and stable. A small store carries limited groceries, gift items, and ice.

The restaurant is good and features local seafood, meat, and produce. Fishing charters, guided and unguided, are available on a fleet of rental boats. Fish processing and packing is offered. Yurts, chalets, and campsites can be rented. The staff is helpful and courteous. This is a luxury resort with facilities to match.

Ewin Inlet. Ewin Inlet indents the south side of Bligh Island some 3 miles, with no anchorages

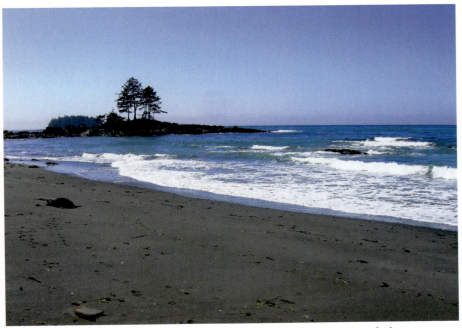

It is a short walk from Friendly Cove to this beautiful beach looking west towards the ocean.

2020 Waggoner Cruising Guide

WEST COAST OF VANCOUVER ISLAND

until the head is reached. The cove to the west at the head of the inlet is quite protected and has depths of 30 to 40 feet. "We rounded the little islet in the cove at low tide, about 100 feet off, and the depth sounder abruptly but briefly showed a depth of 15 feet. We suspect it found an uncharted rock." [*Hale*]

Resolution Cove. Historic Resolution Cove is on Bligh Island, near the south end of Clerke Peninsula. In March, 1778, Captain Cook anchored his two ships there and found and fitted a new foremast for the *Resolution*. A flagpole and plaques commemorating Cook's visit have been placed on a knoll above the cove. Anchor in 40 to 50 feet, either with a stern-tie to shore or enough room to swing. You'll probably make your visit a short one. Swells from the ocean wrap around the Clerke Peninsula into the cove.

Santa Gertrudis Cove. The western cove in Santa Gertrudis Cove is an excellent anchorage: cozy, good holding, protected. As you enter you will see an island in the northern cove. A submerged rock extends from that island a considerable distance toward the south shore, farther than we expected. Be sure to identify this rock and give it room as you favor the south shore. There is sufficient room to pass between this rock and the drying rock shown off the south shore on the chart. The north cove of Santa Gertrudis Cove, around the island, is foul and tight.

㉒ **Friendly Cove.** Friendly Cove is where Captains Vancouver and Quadra met in 1792 and attempted to negotiate the final details of the Nootka Convention of 1790, in which Spain relinquished to England all its claims to Northwest lands. Hulsizer, in her book *Voyages to Windward*, gives an interesting and succinct explanation of the complicated events in Friendly Cove that brought Spain and Great Britain to the brink of war before they worked out their differences in the Nootka Convention.

Friendly Cove is shallow and fairly protected from typical summertime winds, with good anchoring for four or five boats on a sand bottom. Outflow winds can make Friendly Cove bumpy. Nearly all the land ashore belongs to the Mowachaht Band, and a fee (cash only) must be paid for landing. The band has summertime staff on hand who monitor VHF 66A and collect the fee. The landing fee is the same, whether you dinghy in from an anchored boat or tie up at the wharf and floats on the west side of the bay.

When you anchor, be aware that the *Uchuck III* delivers tourists and freight to the dock regularly. To watch the *Uchuck III* wind its way through anchored boats is awe-inspiring—and terrifying if you're on one of the boats.

A trail runs through campgrounds and above the ocean beach. It passes the Native graveyard and leads to a lake that's good for swimming. Six rental cabins, small and rustic, are just beyond the lake. The spired Catholic church is filled with Native carvings, and has two marvelous stained glass windows. They depict the transfer of authority over the area from Spain to England in 1792, and were a gift from the government of Spain. A carved welcome figure stands on the far shore of the cove, facing the open sea.

㉒ **Nootka Light Station.** You can walk from the Friendly Cove beach to the Nootka Light Station on San Rafael Island. A well-maintained series of stairs leads up from the beach to the light station. Once at the station, be sure to sign the guest book.

Nootka is a repeater station for Prince Rupert Coast Guard radio, and has considerable radio equipment. Every three hours from early morning until nightfall, the Nootka station reports weather conditions for the marine weather broadcast, including estimated wind strength and sea conditions offshore.

Thanks to the miracle of the Fresnel lens, the light uses only a 35-watt LED bulb to cast a beam that can be seen for 15 miles.

The Nootka Light Station and its light keepers are powerful arguments for retaining manned light stations along the coast. They are invaluable for timely and accurate weather information, and for communication in areas that may not have good cell phone coverage. The lightkeepers monitor VHF channel 82. We are told that many of the lightkeepers maintain an open Wi-Fi signal for visiting boaters.

Estevan Point. Estevan Point is the southwest corner of Hesquiat Peninsula, another of the headlands where winds and seas build and become confused. Estevan Point can be ugly in a storm, but in more settled conditions does not present the challenge found at Cape Cook or Cape Scott. In fog, the problem with Estevan Point is its low, flat terrain, which makes its shoreline a poor target for radar. The rocks more than a mile offshore make Estevan Point unforgiving for the navigator who is off-course.

From Nootka Sound, a rounding of Estevan Point first must clear Escalante Rocks and Perez Rocks, both of them on the west side of Hesquiat Peninsula. Unfortunately for the navigator, no single chart shows all of Estevan Point from Nootka Sound to Hesquiat Bay in large scale. You will be forced to plot your course on small scale Chart 3603, which doesn't give much close-in detail. Once at Estevan Point, you can use Chart 3674 to continue to Hot Springs Cove.

Especially with the lack of a single good large scale chart for the west side of Hesquiat Peninsula, the general advice is to give Estevan Point "lots of room." Give Escalante Rocks and Perez Rocks lots of room, too. This applies when heading north as well.

Weather Information: The Estevan Point lighthouse provides updated wind, sea, and atmospheric conditions every three hours. Listen to the continuous marine broadcast for the latest weather information.

Hesquiat Harbour. Hesquiat Harbour is protected from westerly winds, and Hesquiat Bar (24 feet deep) knocks down the Pacific swell. Crossing the bar may be unsafe in a southeasterly; storm seas can break over it. Anchorage depths can be found in **Boat Basin** located at the northeast end of Hesquiat Harbour; but Rae Basin provides better protection since Boat Basin is open to the south. Most of the upland areas around Hesquiat Harbour and Boat Basin are included within the Hesquiat Peninsula Provincial Park. **Rae Basin** is a well-protected anchorage in the northeast corner of Boat Basin and offers bear viewing opportunities at low tide. Rae Basin consists of an outer basin anchorage and an inner basin anchorage.

Climb the stairs to the Nootka Light Station for a view of Friendly Cove.

COUGAR ANNIE'S GARDEN IN HESQUIAT HARBOUR

Cougar Annie
In 1915, the wily pioneer Cougar Annie set foot on the beach at Boat Basin in Hesquiat Harbour with her husband and three children. For seventy years, while bearing 8 more children and outliving three more husbands, she cleared and cultivated land, trapped small animals, and defended her turf and family from cougar and bear. Ada Anne (Cougar Annie) was successful in creating a mail-order garden nursery in addition to her other endeavors. As she grew old, her extensive gardens became overgrown until visionary Peter Buckland established the Boat Basin Foundation, which provided needed funding to restore the expansive gardens. His creativity has infused over 33,000 hours of labor to build more than a mile (2,100 meters) of cedar boardwalk and over 20 structures, built entirely from cedar windfall on the property.

Touring The Gardens
A tour of the property will take the better part of an afternoon or morning, winding past magnificent 500- to 1,000- year old cedars, Cougar Annie's gradually fading home, and Peter's structural sculptures. This is a real highlight of West Coast Vancouver Island. To arrange a visit, contact boatbasinfoundation@gmail.com with an estimate of your arrival dates. You can confirm or adjust your arrival date with Peter by email, using cell service with data via a nearby cell tower in Hot Springs Cove.

Tour Guide
You will find Peter's house at the head of Hesquiat Harbour in Boat Basin. Peter will welcome you ashore and accompany you to Cougar Annie's Garden and the Boat Basin Foundation, which provides education in temperate rainforest ecology. The tour fee is $30, payable only by credit card, or you may be able to make payment by engaging in 2-hours of volunteer work on the property.

Where To Anchor
Anchorage can be taken in Boat Basin, or you can duck into the front portion of Rae Basin. At higher tides, it is even possible to enter the furthest reach of Rae Basin, but this maneuver is only for skippers who are confident of their ability to navigate by depth sounder. Bear wander the shores at low tide; and at a tide greater than 11 feet, you can dinghy up the creek to Hesquiat Lake.

Entering Hesquiat Harbour
Boaters should use caution when entering Hesquiat Harbour, seas can break over the 24-foot deep Hesquiat Bar; check weather and consult charts before heading to this very special place. Cougar Annie's Garden is a short distance northwest of popular Hot Springs Cove at Maquinna Marine Provincial Park.

- Mary Campbell, WG Field Correspondent

Hot Springs Cove

Most boats will prefer anchoring in the outer area of Rae Basin. Anchorage is possible for shallow draft vessels in Rae Basin's inner area. At a tide of 11 feet or higher, you can dinghy into Hesquiat Lake from Rae Basin.

From Boat Basin or Rae Basin, you can take the dinghy to **Cougar Annie's Garden** for an interesting educational tour. Pioneers Ada Anne (Cougar Annie), and husband William Rae-Arthur, cleared land for a homestead in 1915 at Boat Basin where they raised their three children and established a large garden. Today, the garden is maintained as a heritage site with research studies in temperate rainforest ecology. Tours are arranged through the Boat Basin Foundation (www.boatbasin.org); email boatbasinfoundation@gmail.com or call (250) 726-5096 a couple of days before your arrival. Admission is charged to help pay for the restoration and ongoing research there; credit card payment preferred. Field Correspondent Mary Campbell reports that the visit is well worth the $30 donation fee. Land or anchor your dinghy off the beach in front of Peter's house and cabin located along the north shore of Boat Basin. Peter, who acts as guide, will accompany you along the trail to Cougar Annie's Garden.

Hot Springs Cove Area. Hot Springs Cove is adjacent to Sydney Inlet, the northern entrance to Clayoquot Sound. Depending on the points of departure and arrival and the exact course chosen, the distance from Nootka Sound around Estevan Point, past Hesquiat Peninsula, and east to Hot Springs Cove, is approximately 30 to 31 miles. When traveling south, once you are past Chief Matlahaw Point, you can duck into the lee of Hesquiat Peninsula to avoid the worst of the ocean swells.

㉓ **Hot Springs Cove.** www.env.gov.bc.ca/bcparks/. Hot Springs Cove is home to **Maquinna Marine Provincial Park** and Protected Area, and **Ramsay Hot Springs**. The park and hot springs are reasons why cruising boats do the West Coast. The challenge of getting to Hot Springs Cove is sufficient to make the reward—a soothing bath in comforting water (no soap, please)—worth the entire trip. In earlier times, most visitors came the hard way, up from Barkley Sound or down from Cape Scott. Now tour boats, floatplanes, and even helicopters carrying visitors who have arrived without effort at Tofino, visit Hot Springs Cove many

WEST COAST OF VANCOUVER ISLAND

Reference Only – Not for Navigation

Hot Springs Cove

times a day. An hour by high-speed boat, and they are there.

The cove is easy to enter. Chart 3674 shows that the mouth is open and the channel free of dangers. The marine park public dock is approximately 1.7 miles farther into the cove from the hot springs themselves. You can anchor in 24 feet, or boats less than 12 meters (40 feet) can tie to the Park dock; self-registration and fee payment box on shore at the Park Information Shelter. Hot Springs Cove is within the Ahousat First Nation territory; the Ahousaht Stewardship Program may collect donation fees for anchorage, look for the yellow *Ahous Hakoon* vessel; they can answer questions and will provide you with a receipt.

A 1.2-mile walk along a well-maintained boardwalk leads to the hot springs. A $3 per person park fee is payable at a drop box near the head of the dock. In the past, visiting craft had a tradition of bringing a plank to add to the boardwalk. On the plank would be carved the name of the boat and the year of the visit. Many of the planks showed remarkable artistic talent. This practice has been discontinued by the parks department. A multi-year project to replace and widen the boardwalk from the dock to the hot springs was started in 2018. Access to the hot springs is open during construction. The hike through the rainforest to the hot springs is easy and beautiful. Toilets are available at the end. The modest will find a pleasant changing room in which clothes may be doffed and a bathing suit put on. Traditionalists will lament that the hot springs no longer can be enjoyed in the old way, sans bathing suit. The place is popular. Although a constant stream of bathers hike the trail and soak in the springs during the day, savvy boaters know that if they come before 9:00 a.m. or after 6:00 p.m., they will share the springs only with other boaters. Note: pets not permitted beyond the start of the boardwalk; alcoholic beverages not permitted within the park.

The B&B boat *InnChanter*, with attached dinghy floats, is normally anchored nearby and may have space for visiting boaters for dinner or breakfast. Call Shaun on the *InnChanter* at (250) 670-1149. Hot Springs

Dine at InnChanter In Hot Springs Cove

Shaun, chef and captain of the InnChanter, looks forward each season to welcoming guests aboard his ship, moored in Hot Springs Cove on the west side of Vancouver Island, north of Tofino. The InnChanter is a heritage vessel built in the 1920's and refitted to host overnight guests and provide gourmet meals. Boaters anchored in Hot Springs Cove may join B&B guests of the InnChanter for meals, as space and supplies allow. Call ahead at 250-670-1149 or email innchanterbb@gmail.com to check availability.

This unique vessel and dining venue in the wilderness require advanced planning for hosting guests; keeping supplies on-hand can be a challenge, with re-stocking goods on a regular basis. Shaun appreciates boaters calling the InnChanter to join others for a unique dining experience and the opportunity to see this heritage vessel. The menu varies and the meals are always creative and expertly prepared; fresh fish is often part of the fare.

If you want to avoid extra time motoring or sailing your own boat to Hot Springs Cove, you can arrive by sea plane, tour boat, or water taxi from Tofino for a short day, weather permitting. Be sure to book space with the InnChanter for either breakfast, lunch, or dinner. Shaun always gives a warm welcome and loves sharing local history and insightful tips about visiting the Cove. You may want to book a B&B overnight stay to spend more time in this beautiful area.

During your visit, you won't want to miss walking the 1.2-mile boardwalk at Maquinna Marine Provincial Park, which leads to Ramsay Hot Springs, a series of natural pools found among the rock walls. Changing rooms are available at the head of the boardwalk. You can access the trailhead from the park dock in the Cove, available to boats under 40 feet for a fee, payable at the self-registration payment box ashore. A $3 park fee per person is also payable ashore.

WEST COAST OF VANCOUVER ISLAND

See Area Map Page 413 - Maps Not for Navigation

has campsites, often used by kayakers. A cell phone tower in the Native village across from the Park now provides four to five bars of cell phone service (Bell).

CLAYOQUOT SOUND

Clayoquot Sound is a series of inlets and passages with entrances at both its north and south ends. By traveling inside Clayoquot Sound you can explore many coves and anchorages, and avoid 20 miles of ocean swells. Tofino is the only major town, although fuel and some groceries are available at Ahousat. There is cell coverage around Tofino and Hot Springs Cove, but coverage is spotty in outlying areas and inlets.

Much of Clayoquot Sound is within the traditional territory of the Ahousaht First Nation, who have established a Stewardship Guardian Program. First Nation representatives of the **Ahousaht Stewardship Program** collect donation fees at various anchorages within the Clayoquot Sound in support of their programs which include care for beaches and trails, search and rescue support, management and cultural interpretation for visitor access, and training in first aid. Receipts for payment are provided via a representative aboard the *Ahous Hakoon* vessel. Guardians monitor VHF channel 65A and may be contacted if you are in need of support. For more information call Ahousaht Stewardship Operations at (250) 731-6957.

Sydney Inlet. Sydney Inlet is the northern entrance to Clayoquot Sound. It is adjacent to Hot Springs Cove and leads approximately 11 miles into the mountains of Vancouver Island, with several good anchorages. Rounding Sharp Point after leaving Hot Springs Cove, be aware of two charted but unmarked off-lying rocks. The first is fairly close to Sharp Point and easy to avoid. The second is about 0.2 mile off. Most boats will choose to pass between the two rocks. Be sure you know where you are. Once in Sydney Inlet, the fairway is open and unencumbered. Reader Don Thain reports that sea otters are now well established in Sydney Inlet and that crabbing is poorer where the sea otters have colonized.

Sydney Inlet Unnamed Cove. This is the cove that lies behind the 65-meter island about 0.5 mile south of Hootla-Kootla Bay, at latitude 49°21.85'N on the east shore of Sydney Inlet. (Douglass, in both editions of *Exploring Vancouver Island's West Coast*, mistakenly calls this cove Hootla-Kootla, but the chart leaves it unnamed and calls the next cove to the north Hootla-Kootla.) Enter from the south. You'll see a beautiful white beach. Although the water is a little shallow near the beach, it's the prettiest spot in the cove. You could also anchor at the north end of the cove, behind the 65-meter-high island. Do not attempt to enter the cove at the north end. It is foul.

Young Bay. Young Bay, on the east side of Sydney Inlet, is a lovely place to anchor, although a little deep until you get close to shore. The middle is 50 to 60 feet deep, but along the shore it's easy to find 35- to 40-foot depths. On the south shore a stream connects with Cecilia Lake, one-half mile away. A rough trail leads up the stream to the lake. Trout fishing at the lake is reported to be good. A copper mine and a pilchard reduction plant both operated here in the past. Only a few concrete platforms and pieces of machinery remain.

Enter Young Bay right down the middle, to avoid shoals that extend from either side. Once inside you will see a small islet with trees on it. Pass to the south of that islet.

Bottleneck Bay (Coyote Cove). This is an otherwise unnamed bay that cruising guide author Don Watmough fell in love with. Bottleneck Bay is located just north of Young Bay, east of Adventure Point. The entrance is narrow but deep. Inside, the high, treed hills make the feeling of seclusion complete. Easy anchoring in 30 feet.

Holmes Inlet Nook. An intimate back cove in Holmes Inlet, with room for 2 to 3 boats over a mud bottom; anchoring depths of 20 feet. Swinging room is tight so you may want to stern-tie.

Hootla-Kootla Bay. Hootla-Kootla Bay is located about 0.25 mile north of the 65-meter-high island on the east shore of Sydney Inlet, approximately 1.6 miles from the mouth of the inlet. This cove is known locally as Baseball Bay, but the chart shows it as Hootla-Kootla Bay. The entrance is shallow, and is partly blocked by a charted rock just south of mid-channel. Divide the channel north of the rock in half, and enter the northern half "mid-channel." "Least depth on the depth sounder was 12.5 feet near the bottom of a 3.6-foot low tide at Tofino. Anchorage is good once inside." [*Hale*]

Riley Cove. Riley Cove is just east of Starling Point, on the northwest tip of Flores Island. It may not be the best choice for an anchorage. The cove is open and uninteresting, and a little deep for anchoring until close to the head. At the head, Riley Cove is divided into two smaller coves; the cove to the west has a sandy beach. A rock, not shown on the chart, is just off the point that separates the two coves. A shoal extends from the east shore near the entrance of Riley Cove. Favor the west shore.

Steamer Cove. Steamer Cove is on the north side of Flores Island, behind George Island. The small cove at the southwest corner of Steamer Cove is well protected and has easy anchoring depths.

㉔ **Bacchante Bay.** Bacchante Bay, at the east end of Shelter Inlet, is a dramatic anchorage, with steep cliffs on both sides, an inviting grassy meadow at the head and a snow-capped mountain beyond. The narrow, shallow entrance is hidden until you are close. Bacchante Bay is part of Strathcona Provincial Park. Minimum depth at entry is 18 feet; a shallowing bar, just outside the entrance, has a minimum depth of 16 feet.

Bacchante Bay has ample room to anchor in 40 to 50 feet. Holding is excellent. If you run to the head of the bay, watch for abrupt shoaling off the meadow. At high tide explore Watta Creek by dinghy.

Readers Mike and Sandy Cecka report fouling their anchor in Bacchante Bay. They anchored on the west side of the bay, below steep cliffs. We've had no problem anchoring in the middle of the bay.

Hayden Passage. Hayden Passage is on the west side of Obstruction Island, and connects Shelter Inlet with Millar Channel. Tidal current predictions are shown with Hayden Passage as a secondary station based on Tofino in the Tide and Current Tables, Vol. 6 and Ports and Passes. The flood sets southeast; the ebb, northwest. Be sure to pass west of the red daymarker beacons (Red, Right, Returning).

Because the flood currents meet at Hayden Passage, you may find that the currents don't behave as predicted. The cautious passage would be at slack water. If transiting sometime other than slack water, maintain a constant watch for current set, and crab as needed to stay in the channel.

Lennard Island Lighthouse along the west coast of Vancouver Island. Photo by John Forde, The Whale Centre.

Reference Only – Not for Navigation **WEST COAST OF VANCOUVER ISLAND**

Clayoquot Sound

Sulphur Passage. Sulphur Passage connects Shelter Inlet and Millar Channel on the east side of Obstruction Island and is far more tortuous than Hayden Passage. The northern portion of Sulphur Passage is the tricky part. There, the channels twist and turn and are bounded by submerged rocks. Don Douglass ran Sulphur Passage along the east side of the 38-meter island in the northern portion, and reported it to be a period of "high anxiety." Locals favor passing on the west side of 38-meter island, where the Landons found a minimum depth of 35 feet on the south end of the narrow channel, between 38-meter island and Obstruction Island. Tidal current predictions are in Tides & Currents Vol 6 and Ports & Passes as a secondary station based upon Tofino.

Friendly Dolphin Cove. Friendly Dolphin is Douglass' name for the cove that indents Obstruction Island, just inside the south entrance to Sulphur Passage. The cove is pretty, private and appealing. Well protected from wind and current. Anchor near the head in 40 to 50 feet, probably with a stern-tie ashore to control swinging, or in 50 to 60 feet with room to swing. Space for 3 or 4 boats. The Landons reported a pleasant stay early in the season.

Shark Creek. 49°23.95'N/126°04.00'W. "This is a kayakers' secret: a beautiful 70-foot-high waterfall in a chimney, accessible at high tide by dinghy only. It is located in Millar Channel, just north of Atleo River. Anchor north of the small island and dinghy in. Best in late afternoon when sunlight makes a rainbow on the rocks behind the falls." [*Hulsizer*]

Matilda Inlet indents the southeast corner of Flores Island and is bordered on the east by McNeil Peninsula. Anchorage is possible near the head of Matilda Inlet. From the anchorage, a warm springs in Gibson Marine Park can be visited (best at high tide; at low tide it's a muddy hike) or a trek made to the beach. Don Watmough describes the area in fond detail. The Native community of Marktosis is on McNeil Peninsula. Across the inlet and a short distance north are the store and fuel dock of Ahousat.

㉕ **Ahousat.** General Delivery, Ahousat, BC V0R 1A0; (250) 670-9575. Ahousat, with its general store, fuel dock and marine ways, is on the west shore of Matilda Inlet, at the southeast corner of Flores Island. Ample moorage for transient boaters; high dock with metal facia, may need to adjust fenders. Gasoline and diesel at the fuel dock, washrooms, 15 amp power, showers and laundry, haulout to 30 feet. Potable water, pay phone, post office, and motel rooms are available. The store is a rough-and-ready place, with a cougar head on the wall, but with luck, it may have what you need: groceries, miscellaneous hardware and marine supplies. No charts or liquor.

Marktosis. Marktosis is the Native village across Matilda Inlet from Ahousat. Carved Native canoes can be seen on the beach and at the shed by the Government Wharf. Docks at the wharf are filled with commercial fish boats and sport fish boats; transient moorage is limited. Permits for the Wild Side Trail can be purchased at the fuel dock; the trail is mostly boardwalk to White Sand Cove (www.wildsidetrail.com). You can anchor south of Ahousat in the bay near the "slightly warm" springs, and take the dinghy back to the village. Leave the dinghy at the Government Wharf and touch base with the band office before exploring further. The fuel dock (250-670-6803) was completed in 2017; rocks make the approach hazardous; larger boats should enter only at high tide.

2020 Waggoner Cruising Guide

WEST COAST OF VANCOUVER ISLAND
See Area Map Page 413 - Maps Not for Navigation

Well-protected Quait Bay, just inside this narrow entrance, has anchorage for many boats.

Gibson Marine Park. Gibson Marine Park is at the head of Matilda Inlet, past Ahousat. At one time, Hugh Clarke, at the Ahousat General Store, hacked out a trail from the head of the inlet to the hot springs. Boots are necessary on the trail, which transits some boggy areas. Clarke recommends going in at half tide on a rising tide, to avoid tramping across the mud flats. Correspondent Gil Flanagan tells us that you can hike for many miles on the ocean beach to the west. The only problem, Flanagan says, are bands of gravel that make barefoot walking uncomfortable. He adds that the beach is popular with kayakers and tourists from Tofino. The park requests that dogs are kept out of the park as there have been incidents of wolves killing the dogs.

Herbert Inlet. The run up Herbert Inlet is even more spectacular than many other inlets along the coast. High mountains and rock walls line the shores. Deep alpine river valleys lead away into the mountains. Snowcapped peaks can be seen in the distance.

West Whitepine Cove. Although unnamed, both Watmough and Douglass call this delightful anchorage West Whitepine Cove, and we shall do the same. West Whitepine Cove lies to the west of Whitepine Cove, near the mouth of Herbert Inlet. Entry to the inner bay is along the south side of the 67-meter island. We entered slowly, strongly favoring this island. Rocks were visible underwater and easily skirted. Once inside, the cove is lovely and protected. Bears are reported to frequent the south shore.

A charted rock is in the cove, off the tip of the little peninsula that extends southeast from the 94-meter island. When anchoring, stay away from it.

Gibson Cove. Gibson Cove indents the west side of Herbert Inlet, about 5 miles north of Whitepine Cove. Since Gibson Cove is not on the way to anyplace else, we suspect it sees few visitors. Those who do visit are in for a treat. Gibson Cove is beautiful, but a little deep for anchoring. Although it appears protected, strong afternoon westerlies can bring wind and waves.

Quait Bay. The entrance to nearly landlocked Quait Bay is located on the northeast side of Cypress Bay. Watch for the numerous crab pot buoys in Cypress Bay. From Cypress Bay, enter Quait Bay passing 45-meter island off your starboard side, favoring the port-side of the channel. The chart makes the course clear. A large floating lodge, with no services for boaters, is just inside the entrance on the left. Quait Bay has room for many boats. Anchor nearly anywhere in 20-40 feet of water. Southwesterly winds do find their way into the bay.

The most popular spot is in the little cove in the east corner in about 10 feet. A submerged concrete structure (49° 16.603N 125° 50.843W) lies in the mouth of the two nooks at the back of this cove. The structure dries at 2 feet. A private 40-foot float is located on the north shore.

For a peek at what life is like for Clayoquot Sound's year-round floating home residents, take your dinghy out the entrance of Quait Bay, enter the unnamed cove south of Quait Bay (49° 15.86N 125° 51.57W) and continue all the way to the head of the cove to visit Wayne Adams and Catherine King in their floating garden on their magenta and turquoise floating home. Wayne and Catherine must hold the record for interviews and feature articles about Clayoquot Sound residents.

Matlset Narrows. Matlset Narrows runs to a maximum of 4 knots on spring tides. The flood sets east. Sailing Directions warns of strong tide-rips in the vicinity of the Maltby Islets at the east end of the narrows. We ran the narrows against a west-flowing ebb. We saw definite current activity, but had no problem. We suspect any tide-rips would be on a flood.

Calmus Passage to Heynen Channel. The route from Millar Channel to Heynen Channel via Calmus Passage and Maurus Channel is the beginning of shallower water. The channels are well marked by buoys and beacons but the navigator must stay alert, keep an eye on the depth sounder, and know the vessel's position at all times. Large-scale Chart 3685 is extremely helpful.

Lemmens Inlet. Lemmens Inlet indents Meares Island, just a few miles from the town of Tofino. Be sure to use large scale Chart 3685 while navigating around Tofino and into Lemmens Inlet. The entry channel to the inlet is amply deep, but bordered by drying flats. Once inside, you have your choice of three possible anchorages—although float homes now are moored in all of Lemmens Inlet's coves, so anchoring may be a challenge. Watch for numerous crab pot bouys throughout the Inlet.

Adventure Cove. Adventure Cove, where Capt. Robert Gray built the small schooner *Adventure* in 1792, is filled with history. The beach is easy to land on. While walking in the woods we could almost feel the presence of Gray's Fort Defiance and the shipbuilding activity. Though the area is now overgrown with large trees, some say you can feel as though *something went on here*. Watmough and Douglass describe the history well. Hulsizer discusses it more thoroughly in *Voyages to Windward*. Unfortunately, a floathouse and a fish farm take up most of the cove, leaving little room for anchoring. Discarded fish farming equipment on the beach makes beach access challenging. A reader tells us an uncharted rock lies SSW of the island in the mouth of Adventure Cove.

Lemmens Northwest Cove. Lemmens Northwest Cove is Douglass' name for this anchorage in the northwest corner of Lemmens Inlet. It is identified on the chart by the 39-meter island. Two charted drying rocks east of 39-meter island and a large oyster farm obstruct entrance to the cove. Rows of oyster aquaculture farming fill the area on both sides of these two drying rocks to the shoreline to the northwest. Enter the cove with 39-meter island on your port side and the oyster farm very close on your starboard side. Caution for the charted shoals on the northeast side and north tip of 39-meter island. Bow watch is recommended. Once inside, you'll find good anchoring depths and adequate protection; caution for the charted shallow spot. Several float homes are tucked into various areas of the cove.

Gods Pocket. Gods Pocket is the cove northwest of Lagoon Island, on the west side of Lemmens Inlet. Protection is good, with anchorage in 25 to 30 feet. Aquaculture is in the cove with buoys set in half of Gods Pocket. Three or four float homes are tucked into bights along the northern shore.

Fortune Channel. Fortune Channel connects Tofino Channel with Matlset Narrows, which in turn connects with the waters of upper and western Clayoquot Sound. In Fortune Channel you can choose from three good anchorages: Windy Bay, Heelboom Bay and Mosquito Harbour. Chances are, you won't see much boat traffic in this area.

Mosquito Harbour. Although not as scenic and cozy as Heelboom Bay, Mosquito Harbour is big and open and easily entered. Anchor in 20 feet behind the Blackberry Islets. Approach on either side of the Wood Islets, but from Fortune Channel you'll probably approach by way of Plover Point or Dark Island. Kelp marks the rocks off the north end of Dark Island. Note the location of Hankin Rock. We would trend toward Plover Point before turning to enter Mosquito Harbour.

Heelboom Bay. Heelboom Bay, located near the south end of Fortune Channel, is a good anchorage, surrounded by lush evergreen forests. Room for 3-4 boats. We found outstanding holding in 35 feet. This Bay was the site of a major protest against logging in Clayoquot Sound and is considered almost sacred by some residents. Approaching, favor the east shore and stay well clear of rocks off the western shore. One of these rocks is considerably detached from the shoreline. Chart 3685 helps understanding.

Windy Bay. Windy Bay is beautiful. The south shore is heavily forested, and the north shore is sheer rock wall. Westerly winds accelerate over the saddle at the head of the bay, but they have no fetch to build up seas. With 15 knots of wind outside Windy Bay, we had gusts to 30 knots inside. Anchor in 30 to 35 feet with excellent holding.

Browning Passage and Tsapee Narrows. Rocks abound and shoals threaten. The larger scale Chart 3685 will show you the way. If you are coming from Heynen Channel or Lemmens Inlet, the course will be clear: Pass west of Morpheus Island and east of Buoy Y35, and continue down Browning Passage and through Tsapee Narrows. Note that currents on springs can run to 5 knots near Morpheus Island and 4 knots at the narrows. Go slowly. Look ahead and identify all buoys, islands and visible rocks well in advance. Keep a close reference between your charts and your navigation electronics. Done this way, the passage should not be difficult.

If you are departing Tofino, leave Buoy Y29, opposite the 4th Street dock, to starboard, and run toward Arnet Island until you can safely turn to run south, along the west side of Riley Island. Favor Riley Island to pass clear of the rocks shown on the chart. Once south of Riley Island you are in Browning Passage.

TOFINO INLET

Island Cove. Island Cove is easy to enter around either side of Ocayu Island. Study the chart to avoid the rocks that lie off the southwest shore of the approach. Unfortunately, the hillsides surrounding Island Cove have been logged down to the water's edge and the cove isn't very pretty. Anchor in 40 to 50 feet, close to the west shore.

Gunner Inlet. It's tricky to get into the inlet and not very scenic when you make it. Approach favoring the east shore and use a small low islet with a distinctive white top as your leading mark. Make an S-turn around the islet and follow the chart in. Anchoring depths vary, 20-60 feet.

Tranquilito Cove. Tranquilito Cove is the name Douglass gave this unnamed cove on the east side of Tranquil Inlet, near the head. This cove is secluded and beautiful. The rock wall on the north side has been strikingly sculpted by glaciers. Favor the northern side of the entry to avoid a shoal that extends from the point of land on the south side. Anchor in 20 feet.

Cannery Bay. Cannery Bay, at the mouth of the Kennedy River, provides good protection and is easy to get in. Despite its flat terrain, it's rather pretty. Consider the nook just to port as you enter. Anchor in 15 to 20 feet over mixed mud and sand with excellent holding.

Kennedy Cove. Kennedy Cove is easy to enter by favoring the 68-meter island. Anchor wherever you like in 15 to 30 feet. It's a pretty spot. A private dock and water slide is on the north shore, labeled "ruin" on some charts. Farther in the bay is a private gazebo overlooking the cove from IR Land.

㉖ **Tofino.** If you come from up-island, Tofino will be your first major town since Port McNeill or Port Hardy, and it's more vibrant than either of them. During the summer season, Tofino's bustle and busyness may surprise you. After growing accustomed to the slower life up-island, Tofino, with its commerce, tourists, fast traffic and loud engines, can cause culture shock. Welcome to the city.

As long as you're in the city you might as well spend some money. You can choose from several good restaurants, the kind that serve meals without french fries. Gift shops and galleries—at last!—are available for mementos and presents. The Co-op store, close to the waterfront, is a complete supermarket and will deliver if asked. The Co-op also carries clothes. Showers are available at the 4th Street Dock and at the laundromat at 4th & Campbell. Set expectations for the laundromat by first checking the online customer reviews. Common Loaf is all-organic and features a local favorite: peasant bread. SoBo, open for lunch and dinner, uses locally grown ingredients in their dishes; reservations recommended (250) 725-2341. The "1909 Restaurant" at Tofino Resort & Marina is also excellent. For a guided food tour, contact Tofino Food Tours at (800) 656-0713.

Be sure to allow enough time to see all the sights that Tofino has to offer. The Tofino Botanical Gardens (250) 725-1220 located 1.5 miles out of town, is worth a visit and is open daily. A network of paths and boardwalks are contained within the 12 acres of gardens, forest, and shoreline. Tofino is known for its beautiful beaches and has several surf shops in town. You often see surfboards strapped to bicycles, as surfers make their way to the beaches. Surf reports are given for North & South Chesterman Beach and Cox Beach. Other beaches include Mackenzie, Middle, and Tonquin Beaches, with Tonquin being the closest to Tofino.

The Tofino Transit Shuttle (250-725-2871) on Campbell Street can take you out to the beaches, or call the Tofino Water Taxi (250-725-8844). Bike rentals are available next to the Tofino Bus station. A dedicated bike path follows the highway south of town; plans include extending the bike path to Ucluelet junction. Bus service was recently extended to Ucluelet.

The Big Tree Trail on nearby Mears Island is another worthwhile excursion. A dinghy dock on the west side of the island is available while hiking the 3 km loop trail, which takes

Tofino

WEST COAST OF VANCOUVER ISLAND

See Area Map Page 413 - Maps Not for Navigation

about 2 hours. A small fee to hike the trail is collected by a guard on duty, or you can use the on-site payment box. Some of the largest trees in B.C. are found here, ranging in age from 1,000 years to 1,500 years old. The largest tree is known as "the hanging garden." The Tofino Water Taxi makes stops at the Big Tree Trail.

Opitsaht First Nations Village, located on the southwest end of Mears Island, is the oldest, continuously run Native settlement. A campground/hostel above the beach is a starting point for the popular Lone Cone Trail to the summit of Lone Mountain, contact (250) 725-2169 or go to www.LoneConeTrail.ca for more information. The Water Taxi from Tofino can take you to the Opitsaht Dock.

Hot Springs Cove, located 28 nautical miles northwest of Tofino, is a popular destination. The high-speed Tofino Water Taxi makes runs to Hot Springs Cove and is a nice option for visitors arriving in Tofino by private boat or by car.

From seaward, enter Tofino via Templar Channel. While Chart 3673 gives a good overall view for the close navigation needed, we strongly recommend large scale Chart 3685. Note how the buoyed fairway twists and turns to avoid shallows. Identify each buoy as you proceed, and leave the buoys off the proper hand.

From the north, enter Tofino via Deadman Pass, narrow and bordered on both sides by drying flats. Be sure to use large scale Chart 3685. Note that while you may be returning to Tofino, the buoyage system in Deadman Pass is not. As you head south in Deadman Pass you will leave the red buoys to port.

The approach to Tofino, whether through Templar Channel or Deadman Pass, is one of the few places on this coast where you need to carefully watch the currents. Time your arrival for slack water to avoid the strong currents that swirl around the docks.

Stay close to the docks once at Tofino. A serious drying reef lies a short distance off.

Anchoring can be a challenge because of strong currents that sweep through the harbor. Although Tofino has several public docks, moorage for visiting boats is limited. The District of Tofino Dock (called the Whiskey Dock) near Grice Point is closest to the Co-op and the liquor store, but is busy day and night with water taxis and locals. Moorage may be available at the Method Marine Supply fuel dock. It tends to be full during the busy season, but you can check.

The most popular moorage is the Tofino Harbour Authority 4th Street Public Dock. Farther east, the Tofino Resort & Marina may have space, but without advance reservations the docks often are taken by their sport fishing guests. The easternmost public dock is called the Crab Dock. The Crab Dock is a longer walk from the commercial district, however. Currents can make landing on a flood tide tricky. Do not proceed eastward past the Crab Dock. A major rock blocks the channel.

㉖ **Tofino Harbour Authority 4th Street Public Dock.** P.O. Box 826, Tofino, BC V0R 2Z0; (250) 725-4441; info@tofinoharbour.ca; www.tofinoharbour.ca; Monitors VHF 66A. Open all year, 20 & 30 amp power, water, for fee pumpout, washrooms, showers, laundry, for fee Wi-Fi. This is the closest moorage to Tofino, convenient to the commercial district. Watch the current. Office open daily 11:00 a.m. to 1:00 p.m. in summers; open Tuesday, Wednesday and Thursday during the off season.

A shoal extends into the channel from a piling east of the easternmost dock, and leads across the ends of B, C and D docks. Dredging was completed in 2017. Minimum depth is 8 feet at 0 tide.

This is a commercial fishing harbour with some recreational and transient moorage. The "L" end of E-dock is designated for transient vessels. The remainder of E-dock is for recreational boats over 25 feet and includes both transient and long-term moorage. The shore side of the main spine float connecting all the labeled floats is for recreational vessels less than 25 feet. Approximately 50 feet of transient moorage is located on the east side of the deep-water end of A-dock. Sixty feet of active loading/unloading space is located on the west side of the shore-end of A-dock, just below the ramp. All transient moorage is first-come, first-served. Rafting encouraged up to two deep. Permanent spaces used for guest moorage as assigned by the harbourmaster. The Harbour Authority tries to fit everyone in.

The dock water system operates by a 'loonie' timer, similar to pay showers. Make sure all the other faucets are closed, then feed a loonie into the timer, which pressurizes the dock system for about 15 minutes. Water pressure is good and one dollar should get you about 100 U.S. gallons of water. Be all set up before you start the system. Car day parking available for purchase.

㉖ **Method Marine Supply.** Box 219, 380 Main Street, Tofino, BC V0R 2Z0; (250) 725-3251; sbernard@methodmarine.ca; www.methodmarine.ca. Open all year. Gasoline, bio-diesel, lube oils, propane, water, ice, divers' air, vacuum waste oil disposal. Moorage has electrical hookup, but moorage often is fully reserved in the busy season. This is a modern, well-run facility, with a good chandlery that carries a wide range of equipment and supplies, including sport fishing gear, fishing licenses, bait, snacks, foul weather wear, and charts. Storm Light Outfitters, a well-stocked outdoor gear store, is right behind, up on the street.

㉖ **Tofino Resort & Marina.** 634 Campbell St, Tofino, BC V0R 2Z0; (844) 680-4184

WHALE WISE - BC JUAN DE FUCA

Southern Resident Killer Whales

In 2019, the Canadian government enacted new measures to protect Southern Resident Killer Whales in Critical Habitat areas of BC waters. Critical Habitat BC waters include the southern Strait of Georgia, the southeast portion of the Gulf Islands, Boundary Pass, Haro Strait, Strait of Juan de Fuca, and offshore from West Coast Vancouver Island up to Tofino. See the *Whale Wise* section in Chapter 1 for a map of these SRKW areas.

Yellow Interim Sanctuary Zone

- Three (3) Interim Sanctuary Zones have been established where general vessel traffic is prohibited from June 1 – October 31. Two are in the Gulf Islands and the third is Swiftsure Bank at the east entrance to Strait of Juan de Fuca.

- A 400-meter approach distance has been established for recreational vessels and most commercial whale watching operators. Vessels must remain at least 400 meters from all killer whales when in Southern Resident Killer Whale Critical Habitat areas.

- Three "Enhanced Management Areas" have been established (Strait of Juan de Fuca, Frasier River mouth, southern Gulf Islands) where all vessels are asked to reduce their speed to less than 7 knots when within 1 km of killer whales.

- When safe to do so, vessel operators are asked to turn off echo sounders and turn engines to neutral idle if a whale is within 400 meters.

Marine Mammals & All Whales

Existing Canada regulations protect all marine mammals in BC waters. Give dolphins, porpoises, sea lions, seals, and other marine mammals the space they need. Coming too close can cause them stress and to abandon their young.

- Stay 100 yards from non-killer whales, dolphins, porpoises, and other marine mammals, and 200 yards if they are resting or with young.

ext. 002; (778) 841-0186; marina@tofinoresortandmarina.com; www.tofinoresortandmarina.com. Monitors VHF 66A. This is a high-end resort with secure gated docks, open all year. 15 & 30 amp power, water, showers, laundry, Wi-Fi and fitness room. Most of the slips and side-tie are for smaller boats with limited side-tie moorage for medium sized boats on the 'T' ends of several docks. There is a side-tie area for yachts up to 130 feet with 100 amp power. Reservations requested. The fuel dock has marine gasoline, no diesel. Harbour Air Service available from the dock. The upland '1909 Restaurant' offers fine dining, with casual eats available at the adjacent 'Hatch Pub'. Adventure tours to Hot Springs Cove, hiking excursions through National Parks, and whale/bear watching are offered through the upland resort/marina office.

㉖ **Tofino Harbour Authority Crab Dock.** P.O. Box 826, Tofino, BC V0R 2Z0; (250) 725-4441; tofharbour@gmail.com Monitors VHF 66A. Maddy Prince is the harbormaster. This is the easternmost dock on the Tofino waterfront. Some transient recreational moorage for vessels up to 40 feet, 20 & 30 amp power, water, Wi-Fi. First-come, first-served. Use caution upon approach as there are rocks off the northeast end of the docks and a shoal located just north of the dock; check your charts.

CLAYOQUOT SOUND TO UCLUELET

It is approximately 19 miles from Lennard Island, at the southern entrance to Clayoquot Sound, to Whistle Buoy *Y42* offshore from Ucluelet Inlet. These 19 miles cross the ocean face of the Pacific Rim National Park; but since you'll probably be about 3 miles out, you won't see much of the park. Sailing Directions says to stay 2 miles off the coast; Watmough likes 3 miles. So do we. Plot a waypoint for Whistle Buoy *Y42*, go 3 miles offshore from Lennard Island, turn left, and make for the buoy. In fog, radar is a big help in avoiding the many fish boats that work these waters. Sport fishing boats that travel full speed even in thick fog are especially worrisome. Absent a GPS and radar, in fog we would go out to at least 30 fathoms deep and follow the 30 to 40 fathom curve to Buoy *Y42*.

Weather Information: The Lennard Island lighthouse, just outside of Clayoquot Sound, and the Amphitrite Point lighthouse, just outside of Barkley Sound, provide a picture of outside weather conditions. Listen to the continuous marine broadcast for the latest weather information or you can attempt to call the lighthouse keepers on VHF 82.

Amphitrite Point. Amphitrite Point, at the end of the Ucluth Peninsula, can present a challenge. The essential navigation problem is to get around Amphitrite Point while staying well clear of Jenny Reef, shown on the chart, yet staying off the Amphitrite Point shoreline. The problem is made more difficult in fog, when the radar may lose Buoy *Y43* against the shoreline.

Carolina Channel is the entry suggested by Sailing Directions, except in thick weather, when Carolina Channel can be too rough for safe navigation. The outer entrance to Carolina Channel is marked by Whistle Buoy *Y42*, about 0.5 mile offshore. The channel leads past Bell Buoy *Y43*, which lies but 300 meters off the rocky shore. In reduced visibility, life can get interesting when you're trying to raise Buoy *Y43*. If you have trouble seeing the buoy against the rocky shoreline, the light structure on the east side of Francis Island could serve as a leading mark.

As you approach Carolina Channel, leave Whistle Buoy *Y42* close to starboard, and turn to a course of 037° magnetic to raise Buoy *Y43*. After passing close south of Buoy *Y43*, Sailing Directions suggests using the summit of South Beg Island as a leading mark. It should bear approximately 075° magnetic. Run approximately 0.2 mile until the eastern extremity of Francis Island is abeam, then round Francis Island and enter Ucluelet Inlet.

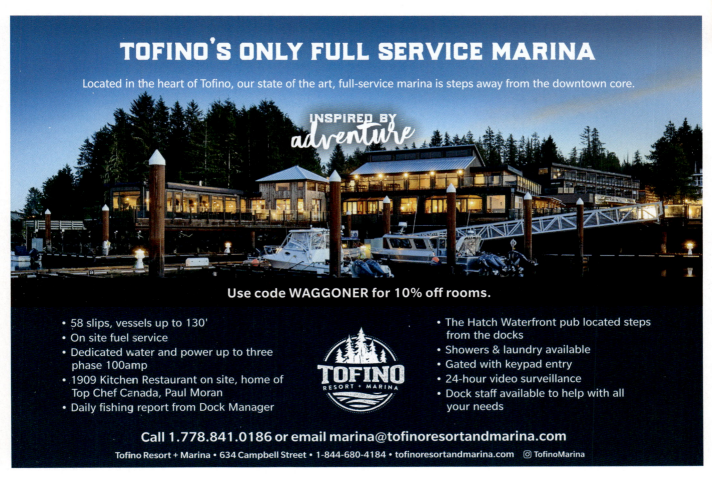

WEST COAST OF VANCOUVER ISLAND   See Area Map Page 419 - Maps Not for Navigation

The 1909 Restaurant at Tofino Resort & Marina has nice views and great food.

BARKLEY SOUND

Depending on your direction, Barkley Sound is the first sound on the way north or the last sound on the way south. Barkley Sound is named after English Capt. Charles William Barkley, who in 1787 sailed into the sound on his ship *Loudoun*, which he had illegally renamed *Imperial Eagle* (Austrian registry) to avoid paying a license fee to the East India Company. With Capt. Barkley was his 17-year-old bride, Frances Trevor Barkley. Capt. Barkley came to trade with the Indians for furs. You'll find reminders of the Barkleys in many names around Barkley Sound, including Imperial Eagle, Loudon and Trevor Channels.

Barkley Sound is roughly square in shape, measuring 15 miles across its mouth and approximately 12 miles deep, not counting the 20-mile-long canal to Port Alberni. The sound is dotted with rocks and islands, and the waters are famous for their excellent fishing. A cruising boat could spend weeks in Barkley Sound, fishing, exploring, and moving from one nook to another. In fact, many boats do just that, coming directly from Puget Sound, Oregon, or the Strait of Georgia region.

During the summer months, fog often forms just offshore. In minutes, it can sweep in, even with no wind. It is essential, therefore, that the navigator know the vessel's position at all times. GPS and electronic navigation will prove useful in foggy conditions. Radar is a big help. Most boats cruising Barkley Sound, large and small, have radar. Even with electronic help, the navigator must remain alert and aware.

If approaching from up-island, you will probably enter Barkley Sound from Ucluelet. Note that a course across Sargison Bank from Ucluelet to the Broken Group takes you very close to a rock that lies approximately 0.7 miles east of Chrow Island. The rock is shown on the chart not with a rock symbol, but by a depth of 0.5 meters. It is easy to overlook while scanning the chart for hazards.

If approaching from the Strait of Juan de Fuca or Oregon, leave Cape Beale at least one-half mile to starboard, which will leave the offshore rocks a safe distance off. If the boat is coming from the United States, it must go directly to Ucluelet for Canadian Customs, although it may duck into Barkely Sound to get out of the ocean swells. A good option is to enter Imperial Eagle Channel, leave Effingham Island to port, and proceed west between Clarke and Benson Islands to Loudoun Channel and Ucluelet.

In Barkley Sound you will find superb exploring everywhere: Pipestem Inlet, the Pinkerton Islands, Julia Passage, the Chain Group, the Deer Group and the famous Broken Group. Settled summer weather makes it possible to anchor in any of hundreds of coves or nooks and explore by dinghy.

We do not cover all the areas mentioned above, an unfortunate consequence of limited exploration time. Other references—especially Douglass' *Exploring Vancouver Island's West Coast* are excellent resources. In the end, your own inquisitiveness and derring-do will determine the range of your exploring.

Ucluelet. Ucluelet is pronounced "You-CLOO-let." With moorage, fuel, provisions, repairs and good dining, the village of Ucluelet (pop. approx. 1800) is the commercial center of Barkley Sound. The channel leading into Ucluelet is well buoyed. Following the rule of Red, Right, Returning, you will have no problems. Spring Cove, to port a short distance inside the channel, is where fish boats used to discharge their catches. The plant deep in the cove is closed and the docks are posted with No Trespassing signs. Spring Cove is a good anchorage.

Ucluelet has one fuel dock, located on the town side. Several fish processing plants and public docks used by large commercial boats are also on the town side of the inlet. Small public docks used by the Ucluelet Native Band are on the east side of the inlet, across from town.

West of the north tip of Lyche Island, the Ucluelet Small Craft Harbour is the principal marina, and the one we recommend. Another marina to consider is Island West Resort, on the west side of the inlet just before the turn to the small craft harbor. The docks are built almost entirely for trailerable boats. They have no designated guest dock, so call ahead by phone.

In town, halfway up Ucluelet Inlet, Pioneer Boat Works (250-726-4382) has a marine railway for haulout and repairs. Their chandlery, next to the ways, has a good stock of marine supplies, commercial and sportfishing tackle, and charts. Cruisers will find what they need there. For engine repairs and electrical services, contact Erik Larsen, LLC (250-726-7011). They are the only shop on the Vancouver West Coast that deals with diesel engines.

Around the winding streets of Ucluelet you will find gift shops, art galleries, including an excellent Native Gallery, the Ucluelet Aquarium, dining from casual to quite nice, a large co-op grocery, an excellent bakery, general merchandise store and other essential services.

It's a pleasant hike or bike ride out the road to the Coast Guard Station at Amphitrite Point Lighthouse. The Wild Pacific Trail begins just beyond He-Tin-Kis Park, near the Coast Guard Station.

In Ucluelet Inlet, Lyche Island can be passed on either side. If passing on the west side (the town side), check Chart 3646 and leave the buoys and beacons off the proper hands.

Customs: Ucluelet is the only customs reporting station on the west coast of Vancouver Island. Open all year. The 52 Steps Dock in Ucluelet Inlet, a short distance beyond buoy Y44, is the official Customs dock. Call (888) 226-7277 by cell or at the on-dock payphone.

㉗ **Eagle Marine, Ltd./Columbia Fuels.** 1231 Eber Road, Ucluelet, BC V0R 3A0; (250) 726-4262; www.columbiafuels.com. Open 7 days a week all year, summer 7:30 a.m. to 6:00 p.m., winter 8:00 a.m. to 5:00 p.m. Gasoline, diesel, lubricants, water, ice, bait, tackle, convenience items, garbage drop.

Whiskey Landing. 1645 Cedar Rd, Ucluelet, BC V0R 3A0, Canada; (250) 726-2270; www.whiskeylanding.com; info@whiskeylanding.com. Guest moorage for hotel guests.

㉘ **Ucluelet Small Craft Harbour.** 200 Hemlock St., Ucluelet, BC V0R 3A0; (250) 726-4241; (250) 725-8190; kcortes@ucluelet.

Barkley Sound

WEST COAST OF VANCOUVER ISLAND

See Area Map Page 419 - Maps Not for Navigation

Ucluelet Harbour

ca. The marina has 30 amp and some 50 amp power, water, washrooms, tidy showers and laundry, pumpout, garbage drop, recycle, waste oil disposal, and for-fee Wi-Fi. The outside basin, before entering the large main basin, has three floats that are usually for commercial boats, with a pumpout at the bottom of the ramp. Docks B & C in the main basin are marked for commercial boats only; docks D, E & F are for recreational and commercial boats. The facility is completely protected, well maintained, and quiet. It's where most cruising boats tie up. The staff is attentive and helpful. Kevin Cortes is the wharfinger.

㉘ **Island West Resort.** Box 879, 1990 Bay St., Ucluelet, BC V0R 3A0; (250) 726-7515; fish@islandwestresort.com; www.islandwestresort.com. Open all year, reservations accepted. Limited moorage for larger boats up to 40 feet, call ahead. A busy sportfishing resort, often fully reserved a year ahead for July and August. Limited 15 amp power, washrooms, seasonal showers and laundry, free Wi-Fi, portapotty dump, launch ramp, marine supplies, ice, convenience groceries, excellent pub. Fishing charters.

㉙ **52 Steps Dock.** (250) 726-4241; (250) 725-8190; kcortes@ucluelet.ca. Located on the west side, north of the fuel dock and south of town, open all year with moorage on both sides of a 450 foot float. Water, no power, no restrooms or showers. This facility is managed by the Small Craft Harbour wharfinger. Pay by phone or when the wharfinger makes his rounds at the dock, twice daily. 52 Steps dock is a designated customs dock.

WESTERN BARKLEY SOUND

The western part of Barkley Sound, from Ucluelet to Pipestem Inlet and over to the Pinkerton Islands, is relatively open and easily run. As long as you stay in the middle, Newcombe Channel and Macoah Passage present no problems. They lead to the Stopper Islands and, beyond them, to Pipestem Inlet. Pipestem Inlet is where the magical falls at Lucky Creek await.

Stopper Islands. The Stopper Islands are quite pretty and beg exploration by dinghy or kayak. Anchor between Larkins Island and the large island.

Toquaht Bay Marina. www.secretbeachcampground.com. On the west side of Toquaht Bay behind a breakwater constructed of orange railroad tankers. Boat launch and moorage for trailerable boats.

Pipestem Inlet. Pipestem Inlet is long, beautiful and bordered by high mountains. Most of the inlet is too deep for anchoring, but there are several good anchorages near the mouth and at the head of the inlet. Anchorages near the mouth are behind **Bazett Island** in the southwest cove and southeast cove. The southwest cove has a fish farm work float and a number of large yellow buoys. The southeast cove is in the little thumb-shaped inlet; an adjacent shore provides stern-tie opportunities. A third anchorage option at the mouth of the inlet is on the north side of **Refuge Island**, a bit east of the 16-meter island. These anchorages are within easy dinghy commute to Lucky Creek. At the head of the inlet, you can tuck behind 32-meter island, or continue to the very end to anchor in a basin formed by a shoaling area.

㉚ **Lucky Creek.** The late John Schlagel, fearless longtime explorer, did not suggest that we see Lucky Creek, he instructed us to see Lucky Creek, and he was right. This is a window-of-opportunity trip and the window corresponds with high tide.

We suggest taking the outboard-powered dinghy up to the falls an hour before high water and coming out an hour after. Former Managing Editor Sam Landsman took a shallow-draft, outboard powered 22' C-Dory in, and wouldn't want to go in anything much bigger.

The entrance is directly across Pipestem Inlet from Bazett Island. After crossing the shallow entry (bordered by meadow grass and wildflowers), the channel winds through marvelous mature forest, with overhanging cedars. The deeper part of the channel tends to follow the outside of the bends, river-style. The water is clear. We kept our eye on the bottom. Close to the falls the bottom shoals and we sought out the narrow, U-shaped channel to follow.

Suddenly, before our eyes was a storybook waterfall directly out of Walt Disney's imagination. Seeing that waterfall, we knew Tinker Bell was around; she was just too quick for us to see. When you go, tie the dinghy off to the side and climb up to a series of bathing pools. Be careful, the rocks can be slippery. And remember, just as Cinderella had to run when the clock tolled twelve, you cannot stay. If you tarry too long the falling tide will close you in.

You probably won't be alone at Lucky Creek. The lodges and resorts in the area are fully familiar with Lucky Creek and the boat drivers know the channel well. We got to Lucky Creek a half-hour after high tide, and the guests were all leaving—at top speed in the narrow waterway that was unfamiliar to us. They came right at us and swooped past, all smiles and happiness as we splashed through their wakes. No matter, the trip was worth it. [*Hale*]

Entrance Inlet. Entrance Inlet indents Vancouver Island at the northeast corner of Mayne Bay. Anchor in the outer basin in 40 feet. During the day you will have boat traffic from the fishing resort in Cigarette Cove.

Cigarette Cove. You can anchor in Cigarette Cove, but the resort takes up much of the space.

See Area Map Page 419 - Maps Not for Navigation

WEST COAST OF VANCOUVER ISLAND

Take the train to visit Historic McLean Mill, a working steam-powered mill.

The entry is narrow and bounded by rocks. If you pay attention, you will have no problems.

Southeast Cove. This cove is open to the west, but is good in settled weather. Anchor in 35 to 40 feet.

Pinkerton Islands. Far from the wildness of the outer islands, the Pinkerton Islands are north of the Broken Group, next to Vancouver Island. The Pinkertons are small and protected, with narrow channels, and are ideal for gunkholing. Watch for rocks. The easiest anchorage is in the cove northwest of Williams Island. Unless several boats want to share the cove, no stern-tie is required. A study of the chart will suggest a number of other possibilities, most of which will require a stern-tie to shore.

UPPER BARKLEY SOUND

Effingham Inlet. Sailing Directions says Effingham Inlet is high, steep and deep, with few if any anchoring possibilities. Correspondents Bruce and Margaret Evertz explored Effingham Inlet and here is their report:

"We found anchorage in the bay on the west side of Effingham Inlet about one-quarter of the way in. The center of the bay is fairly flat and approximately 75 feet deep. Our anchor set well at 49°00.959'N/125°10.659'W. Another secure spot would be at the south corner of the bay in 30 to 40 feet with a stern-tie. We were told that boats often anchor on the north side of the small peninsula near John Islet, at the entrance."

"While several oyster farms are in the lower part of Effingham Inlet, we saw few signs of man farther in. It isn't Princess Louisa, but like Pipestem Inlet it's still pretty. The sides are high, steep and forested, with many interesting cliffs. We saw only two waterfalls. We didn't see many anchoring opportunities unless you want to stern-tie, and there were many small bights for that. We were told that afternoons can be windy, but the trees grow right to the high water line so we don't think the winds amount to much." [*Evertz*]

㉛ **Jane Bay/Franks Bay.** This bay, known locally both as Jane Bay and Franks Bay, is not named on the chart. It is located at the back of Barkley Sound, connected by a narrow but safe passage with Vernon Bay at 48°59.80'N/125°08.80'W. Anchor, carefully, near the head before the flats shoal too much. A water line is clearly marked with yellow buoys. Or tie up at Eagle Nook Lodge.

㉛ **Eagle Nook Resort (Vernon Bay).** P.O. Box 289, Ucluelet, BC V0R 3A0; (800) 760-2777; (604) 357-3361; samantha@eaglenook.com, www.eaglenook.com. Monitors VHF 73. Marina is immediately to starboard as you enter the bay. Moorage to 100 feet, 30 & 50 amp power, water, Wi-Fi, washrooms and showers. Reservations recommended, especially for larger boats. Open June to mid-September. An elite high-end restaurant. Guided fishing and kayak tours are available to visiting boaters. Stay in one of the luxurious water-view rooms for waived moorage. Well-maintained walking trails lead through the forest. Corporate retreat packages.

Useless Inlet. Useless Inlet contains a number of aquaculture leases and recreational float homes. Entry to the inlet is made interesting by a series of large rocks that are covered except at lower stages of the tide. The rocks were covered when we were there and the wind rippled the water, making them hard to see. The obvious safe entry is along the north shore, to avoid the rocks in the middle. We attempted that route twice but didn't feel comfortable. We did see several trailerable sport fishing boats roar in and out of Useless Inlet, running between the rocks in the middle. They knew where the channel was; we didn't.

Correspondents Bruce and Margaret Evertz went into Useless Inlet. They report that "Useless Nook," described in the Douglass book, has an oyster farm in it, and a sign on shore that says, "No anchorage or trespassing in bay—oyster farm."

Rainy Bay Cove. Located on the north side of Junction Passage on Seddall Island. Tucked behind the smaller Boyson Islands, a narrow passage leads into Rainy Bay Cove, home to a quiet community of float cabins along the western shore. Good anchorage at the north end of the cove to the west of the shoaling nook; anchoring depths of 30 feet over a mud bottom.

ALBERNI INLET

Alberni Inlet begins between Chup Point and Mutine Point, where it meets with Trevor Channel and Junction Passage. The inlet continues some 21 miles into the heart of Vancouver Island to the town of Port Alberni. Alberni Inlet is narrow and high-sided. A well-protected detached public float is in San Mateo Bay, near the mouth of the inlet, and in Hook Bay about half way up the inlet. China Creek Marina, about 6 miles down-inlet from Port Alberni, has limited guest moorage for larger vessels. Tidal current flows are less than 1 knot both directions, but the surface current can flow as fast as 3 knots when wind and current direction are the same.

In the summer, an up-inlet thermal wind develops at 1:00 p.m. ("You can set your clock by it," says a friend in Port Alberni), and will increase to 25 to 30 knots by mid-afternoon. The wind produces a short, uncomfortable chop. We would run Alberni Inlet in the morning.

Port Alberni. In our opinion, the McLean Mill National Historic Site, accessed via a 1954 diesel locomotive train, is the highlight and reason to visit Port Alberni. Port Alberni offers several moorage options for pleasure boaters. Port Alberni is also very popular as a saltwater trailer boat destination, giving. trailer boaters safe and easy access to Barkley Sound, one of the most diverse

Port Alberni

2020 Waggoner Cruising Guide

WEST COAST OF VANCOUVER ISLAND

See Area Map Page 419 - Maps Not for Navigation

and interesting cruising grounds in the Northwest. It's a 21-mile run down the Alberni Inlet to Barkley Sound.

To get to Port Alberni from the mainland, trailer the boat to the BC Ferries terminal at Tsawwassen, near the U.S. border, or to the Horseshoe Bay terminal, north of Vancouver. Large, comfortable ferries will take you to Nanaimo's Duke Point or Departure Bay terminals. (Or, if you are coming from the south, take the private ferry Coho from Port Angeles, Wash. to Victoria.) Our trailer boat friends tell us the fares for trailered boats are not inexpensive, so be prepared. From the Duke Point ferry terminal at Nanaimo, an easy and often beautiful 1½- to 2-hour drive on paved highway will take you to Port Alberni.

Along the way, be sure to stop at Cathedral Grove for a walk through a towering forest of 1000-year-old cedar, hemlock and Douglas fir. The trail is easy and well-maintained. If you hurry along, you can walk it in 20 minutes. If you linger to absorb more of the majesty, it could take about an hour. Interpretive signs explain everything.

To reach Port Alberni you do have to go over a 1230-foot-high mountain pass, with an 8 percent grade on the east side and a 6 percent grade on the west. Be sure your rig has enough power and brakes.

Once at Port Alberni, you'll find good launch ramps at Clutesi Haven Marina at the mouth of the Somass River, and at China Creek, located 6 miles down the Alberni Inlet. Long-term parking is available at both locations. All the marinas are operated by the Port Alberni Port Authority; www.portalberniportauthority.ca.

In Port Alberni you'll find complete services including hospital, shopping, marine supplies and a boatyard. The "Port Boat House" (250-724-5754) provides service for trailerable boats.

A 1954 diesel locomotive pulls a train that runs from downtown Port Alberni to the McLean Mill National Historic Site, the only working steam-operated sawmill in Canada. It takes about 35 minutes each way. The McLean Mill is a fascinating tour, with interpretive signs to explain what you are looking at. The cookhouse, blacksmith shop, workers' housing and other buildings have been restored. Mill demonstrations and a guided theatrical experience are offered as scheduled. Logs are in the mill pond. A trip to the McLean Mill is a step back in time. The entire family will enjoy it. Call (250) 723-1376. Better yet, for latest information and schedules see www.alberniheritage.com.

For information on other attractions and events, contact the Alberni Valley Chamber of Commerce, (250) 724-6535.

Salmon Festival: Port Alberni's Salmon Festival & Derby (www.salmonfestival.ca) is held Labour Day weekend each year at Clutesi Haven Marina. We are told that the Somass River is the third largest salmon stream in B.C. Only the Fraser River and the Skeena River have larger returns.

Haulout: Alberni Engineering and Shipyard has haulout and complete repairs for boats to 100 feet. Call (250) 723-0111.

Fuel: Marine gasoline and diesel are available at Tyee Landing in Port Alberni and in China Creek.

San Mateo Bay. Located at the junction of Trevor Passage and Junction Passage on the east side. A 70-foot public float, managed by Port of Alberni Port Authority, offers overnight side-tie moorage at no charge. Moorage available on both sides of the float, which is detached from shore. The float, tucked behind Bernard Point, provides shelter from most winds. Depths in the bay are too deep for anchoring.

Uchucklesit Inlet. A branch near the entrance of Port Alberni Inlet, Uchucklesit leads northwest to Snug Basin. The east shore of this deep inlet is lined with float homes, summer cabins and year-round residences; watch your speed and wake. The variety of homes makes for an interesting cruise. About half way up the inlet on the east shore near Case Creek is the small community post office on floats; this is also the landing for the *M/V Barkley Sound* passenger vessel. No services for pleasure boaters. Anchorage can be found in **Snug Basin**, with good protection in depths of 50-60 feet over a flat mud bottom.

Green Cove. Located east of Cheeyah Island at the entrance to Uchucklesit Inlet, Green Cove offers protected anchorage from all except northwesterly winds which have fetch. Anchorage depths are as charted, with a flat mud and sand bottom. Upland homes and cabins dot the shoreline, some with fanciful names. In 2018 the Landons noted a non-operational fuel dock just inside the cove entrance on the north shore of Strawberry Point peninsula. No log booms were observed in the cove in 2018.

Limestone Bay. Located on the west side of Alberni Inlet, just north of the entrance to Uchucklesit Inlet. Use only the southwest entrance into the bay. The small bay has space for one or two boats to anchor at the northwest head of the bay. Two float cabins, both with log breakwaters, are not a factor for anchoring. Anchoring depths of 12 feet over mixed mud and sand, protection from northerlies but open to south westerlies.

㉜ **China Creek Marina & Campground.** (250) 723-9812; www.campchinacreek.com; chinacreek@alberniport.ca. Open April through September, 88 slips and 2300 feet of side-tie moorage, 4-lane launch ramp. Gasoline, diesel, propane, 15, 20 & 30 amp power, washrooms, showers, laundry, ice, garbage drop, fish cleaning stations, playground. Campsites and RV sites are adjacent. Shallow depths with shifting sandbars make the marina entrance challenging.

Hook Bay. Located about half way up Port Alberni Inlet on the west shore, Hook Bay provides protection from up-inlet winds. Anchor in 30-40 feet over a flat bottom. A 50-foot public float, managed by the Port Alberni Port Authority, is available for overnight moorage at no charge; side-tie on both sides of the float, which is not connected to shore.

㉝ **Harbour Quay.** 2900 Harbour Rd., Port Alberni, BC V9Y 7X2; (250) 723-1413; www.portalberniportauthority.ca; harbourquay@alberniport.ca. Harbour Quay has 15 slips and 2000 lineal feet of side-tie moorage, 20 & 30 amp power, washrooms, showers, laundry, potable water on the floats, garbage drop and secured gate access. This is a breakwater-protected marina close to downtown. The docks have been reconfigured to create more side-tie moorage, making it attractive for larger boats. Check ahead for availability. Adjacent to the Maritime Heritage Discovery Centre, located in a genuine west coast lighthouse.

㉝ **Fishermen's Harbour.** 3140 Harbour Rd., Port Alberni, BC V9Y 7X2; (250) 723-2533; www.portalberniportauthority.ca; fishermensharbour@alberniport.ca. Open all year, 7600 feet of moorage, 20, 30 and some 50 amp power, water, washrooms & showers, garbage drop and pumpout. Shipyard, marine ways and a two-ton electric winch on site. Fishermen's Harbur is adjacent to downtown Port Alberni, with all the services of downtown

Harbour Quay provides moorage for pleasure boaters visiting Port Alberni.

close by. They never turn anyone away, but be prepared to raft. June is the busiest month.

㉝ **Tyee Landing.** 3140 Harbour Rd., Port Alberni, BC V9Y 7X2; (250) 723-2533; www.portalberniportauthority.ca; fishermensharbour@alberniport.ca. 160 feet of side-tie moorage is located north of Fishermen's Harbour and to the shore side of the fuel dock. Contact the Port Authority for availability.

㉝ **Port Alberni Marine Fuels & Services.** 990-3300 Harbour Rd., Port Alberni, BC V9Y 7X2; (250) 730-3835; At the end of the Tyee Landing dock, located just north of Fishermen's Harbour, this fuel facility opened in 2016. Marine gasoline and diesel including high-speed diesel. Convenience store. Open Monday through Friday 9:00 a.m. to 5:00 p.m.; Saturday, Sunday, and holidays 9:00 a.m. to 3:00 p.m.

㉞ **Clutesi Haven.** (250) 724-6837; www.portalberniportauthority.ca; clutesihaven@alberniport.ca. Open all year. Moorage sometimes available, call ahead. Water, 15, 20 & 30 amp power, washrooms, garbage drop, 4-lane launch ramp. Clutesi Haven is located behind a breakwater near the mouth of the Somass River. Best suited to boats 40 feet or less. This is a popular launching spot for trailerable boats. Hotels, pubs, and liquor store are nearby. Groceries are 5 blocks away.

BROKEN GROUP

The Broken Group extends from the wind-and-wave-lashed outer islands to peaceful islands deep inside Barkley Sound. The Broken Group is part of the Pacific Rim National Park, to be preserved in its natural state in perpetuity. For many Northwest boaters, a holiday spent in the Broken Group is the fulfillment of a lifelong dream.

Boats visiting the Broken Group will find dozens of little nooks and bights to put the hook down, depending on weather and the mood on board. Don Watmough, Don Douglass, and the Yeadon-Joneses all describe a number of them in their guides. The major anchorages are Effingham Bay, Turtle Bay and Nettle Island.

Pets: The Broken Group is part of Pacific Rim National Park. In order to protect native flora and fauna, pets are not permitted on shore anywhere in the Broken Group.

Effingham Bay. Effingham Bay is large, pretty, and protected. On the nights of our visits we have shared the bay with 10 to 20 other boats, yet everyone had room to swing and we didn't feel crowded. The chart shows the entrance. Anchor in 30 to 50 feet, good holding. Sunsets, seen out the mouth of the bay, can be dramatic. Because Effingham Bay is open to the west, westerly winds can make the anchorage a bit bumpy.

Take the time to dinghy ashore and hike to the ancient Native village site on the east side of Effingham (Village) Island. The trail begins on the right side (as you face the land from the water) of the little thumb of water at the head of Effingham Bay and leads through lush and mature forest. Take care to turn right, the left side leads in the wrong direction. Don't be fooled; the wrong trail leads to mud, fallen trees and other obstacles. The sign warns of wolves on the island. Do pay attention to what it says:

"When in a group, act in unison to send a clear message to the wolves they are not welcome. Back away slowly, do not turn your back on the wolf. Make noise, throw sticks, rocks and sand at the wolf."

The trail across the island is generally easy, but a little primitive and challenging in places. The village site, on the eastern shore, is mystical. Widely-spaced trees suggest the location of the main village. The large midden, with shells poking out of it, indicates a long and populous habitation. Near the beach you can find an old Longhouse beam that now serves as a nurse log. A sea cave is located there, but is inaccessible at high tide. Late in the day the view eastward from the beach—the sea, with the mountains of Vancouver Island painted in low reddish light—is inspiring.

Benson Island. In settled weather you can take anchorage off the east shore of Benson Island, in the cove opposite the water faucet icon on the chart. A trail leads across the island to a scenic rocky beach with a blowhole that sounds just like a whale blowing.

Clarke Island. Temporary or settled weather anchorage can be found on the east side of Clarke Island.

Turret Island. The cove formed by the 36-meter island on the southwest side of Turret Island is okay for anchoring, though the bottom is thick with kelp. The surrounding area has interesting rock formations and is good for exploring by dinghy or kayak.

㉟ **Turtle Bay.** Turtle Bay is a local name for the bay formed by Turtle Island, Willis Island, and Dodd Island. Joes Bay, an appendage of Turtle Bay, indents Turtle Island. It is the little nook where Salal Joe, the Hermit of Barkley Sound, made his home.

The best entrance to Turtle Bay is from the north, off Peacock Channel, between Dodd Island and Chalk Island. A study of the chart shows the entrance channel bounded by rocks and drying rock outcroppings along the way. A careful entry, proceeding slowly and identifying the hazards, will bring you in safely. Those who have been in a few times know where the rocks are and roar right in.

Anchor in 25 to 30 feet on a mud bottom, good holding.

Nettle Island. Nettle Island has three good anchorages—one in the large bay that indents the southern shore, and the other two in the channel between Nettle Island and Reeks Island to the east. In Nettle Island's large bay we prefer the eastern portion, off the park ranger's float cabin. The center of the bay is a little deep (50 to 60 feet, depending on state of tide), but you can find depths of 20 to 30 feet near the shore north of the ranger's cabin. Reader Dick Drinkow reports that the park ranger warns that boats have grounded on the shelf, and recommends anchoring in the center of the bay.

Watmough describes two other anchorages along the east side of Nettle Island, opposite Reeks Island. These nooks will hold a couple of boats each, and Watmough says they are delightful. The charted rocks are easy to identify and avoid.

Outer Islands. The outer islands of the Broken Group are marked by twisted trees, the result of relentless onshore winds, especially in the winter. If your needs include the desire to navigate "at the edge," the outer islands can satisfy that need. Here, you'll have your opportunity to run in wind and fog, with the Pacific Ocean swells beating against the rocks. Navigate carefully. The low islands are easy to get mixed up. Rocks and reefs are charted, but they're everywhere. This is beautiful, raw country. The kayakers have it best. The favored anchorage is at Wouwer Island.

A variety of float homes and vacation homes line the north shore in Uchucklesit Inlet.

WEST COAST OF VANCOUVER ISLAND

Wouwer Island. Wouwer Island is breathtaking, both in its scenery and gunkholing. At half tide or higher, most boats can make it through the slit between Batley Island and Wouwer Island. A bow watch will only scare you.

We anchored temporarily in a nook south of two islets, west of the slit between Batley and Wouwer Islands. A trail leads across the island to a lovely beach with great beachcombing.

EASTERN BARKLEY SOUND

㊱ **Poett Nook.** Poett Nook is on the eastern shore, at lat 48°53'N. It doesn't look like a nook when you see it. It is a spacious, rather pretty bay, with good anchoring in 25 to 35 feet. The entry is narrow but deep. The Poett Nook Marina, a large sport fishing resort, is on the eastern side of the bay.

㊱ **Poett Nook Marina & Campground.** Mailing: P.O. Box 1083, Port Alberni, BC V9Y 7L9; (250) 758-4440; (250) 720-9572; poettnookmarina@gmail.com; www.poettnook.com. Gasoline at the fuel dock, washrooms, showers. No power, non-potable water. A small store carries convenience food, ice, and tackle. Fee-based garbage drop. This is a busy small-boat sportfishing resort, with 123 RV/camping sites and berths for 174 boats. Maximum length 36 feet. Most boats launch at Port Alberni or China Creek.

Robbers Passage. Robbers Passage leads between Fleming Island and Tzartus Island in the Deer Group, and is a likely route for boats bound between points near the head of Barkely Sound and Bamfield. A rock that dries 1 meter is in the western approach to Robbers Passage. Although the rock is clearly charted, people at the Port Alberni Yacht Club swear this is one rock that moves. Give the rock a wide berth. The S-shaped channel leading into Robbers Passage requires close attention, but with attention it is safe. A study of large-scale chart 3668 will make the route clear. Inside the passage, the Port Alberni Yacht Club has its floating clubhouse and docks. Several large buoys might be mistaken for mooring buoys. These buoys are not designed for mooring and have dragged when boats tied to them.

Port Alberni Yacht Club. Consider spending at least one night at the Port Alberni Yacht Club. The facility is clean and well-maintained, and the folks are friendly and helpful. They have a wealth of local knowledge to share. Be sure to walk the beautiful trails around the peninsula behind the yacht club. The moorage charge is modest and goes back into the facility. All are welcome; no yacht club membership needed. Washrooms, showers, and non-potable water available. Note that upland trails and facilities are private property and are for yacht club members and paying overnight guests. If you anchor out, do not come ashore.

Fleming Island. The day was sunny with only a gentle breeze, so we left the boat at the yacht club and motored the dinghy around Fleming Island. The impossibly rugged shoreline is dotted with sea caves. We were told that some of the caves extend far into the rock. For thousands of years the First Nations people in Barkley Sound put some of their dead in bentwood boxes and hid them in sea caves. We were fascinated by the stories.

We did, however, ease the dinghy through a narrow cleft in the rock and up to the mouth of one cave. The opening loomed above us, and we could see the floor of small boulders rise and disappear in darkness. The rock walls of the cleft were covered with orange and purple sea stars. Other neon-hued sea life waved in the surge. The word impressed does not begin to describe the effect on us. [Hale]

Tzartus Cove. Tzartus Cove (our preferred anchorage on Tzartus Island) is the name Douglass gives to this excellent anchorage about 0.5 mile north of Marble Cove. Rocks extend from both shores, so go right down the middle when you enter. Anchor near the head in 25 to 30 feet. Sea caves are nearby. Reader Dick Drinkow reports that a bit of northwest swell can get into the cove and that kelp fouled their anchor.

Marble Cove. Marble Cove is on the west side of Tzartus Island, and often is mentioned as a good anchorage (we would choose instead the cove one-half mile north). A rock stack between two islands and reddish rocks on the shore add to the scenic nature of the cove. A float house is on the north side of Marble Cove. Anchor in 25 to 30 feet off the gravel beach on the island opposite the float house. This is a good place to explore tidepools at low tide.

Grappler Inlet. Grappler Inlet joins near the mouth of Bamfield Inlet and leads to Port Désiré, a protected anchorage with a launch ramp and a public dock. Although Grappler Inlet is beautiful, it is surrounded by homes.

㊲ **Bamfield Inlet.** Bamfield Inlet is open and easy to enter. The village of Bamfield is along the shores of the inlet. Several docks open to the public are located on each side. Moorage is limited, but space usually can be found for pleasure craft. West Bamfield public dock has the most moorage space. East Bamfield public dock has limited space available. At the head of the inlet, past Rance Island, is a quiet basin where boats can anchor, although an overhead power cable limits mast height to 17 meters (55 feet). Larger boats anchor off the East Bamfield public dock. There are no mooring buoys open to the public.

㊲ **Bamfield.** They call the inlet "Main Street." The village of Bamfield covers both sides of the inlet, and the west side is not connected by road with the east side. You cross by dinghy or water taxi (250-728-1212). The Bamfield General Store, with liquor agency, is on the west side of the inlet. A boardwalk runs along the homes and businesses on the west side, and folks get around by walking. The seasonal Boardwalk Bistro located near the West Bamfield public dock serves espresso drinks and delicious salmon burgers.

The east side has roads that tie its businesses and homes together. They connect with the 60-mile-long dirt logging road that leads to Port Alberni. The east side has a hardware store and a marine store, motel with a pub, and a convenience grocery store with a cafe. The trail to Cape Beale begins on the east side of the inlet. Anchorage and a launch ramp are at nearby Port Désiré.

A small Outpost Hospital is located on the east side. It is set up to treat illness or injury, deliver babies, and dispense medication. The hospital is operated by registered nurses, and a visiting physician calls on a regular schedule. They work closely with the Coast Guard for emergency helicopter transport when needed. A fee schedule accommodates non-Canadians who need medical attention.

Fiber optic cables were installed at Bamfield in 2018. Some docks and lodges may now offer Wi-Fi.

The large building on the east side of the inlet near the entrance houses the Bamfield Marine Research Station. The station is owned

The Port Alberni Yacht Club docks are in Robbers Passage.

by five universities in British Columbia and Alberta, and began operation in 1971. Visitors are welcome and tours are offered during the summer, 1:00 p.m. to 2:30 p.m. Wednesdays, Fridays and Sundays, no charge, donations appreciated. This facility once was the eastern terminus of the transpacific cable that connected North America with Australia. Its first message was sent on November 1, 1902; its last message was sent in 1959. See their website at www.bms.bc.ca.

Bamfield offers several events during the year, including the Music by the Sea Festival (250-728-3887), with classical and jazz musicians from all over. Lodging is at a premium, but boaters can stay on board. See www.bamfieldchamber.com/events.html for events and dates or call (250) 728-3006. The festival welcomes boaters. The first time you attend, they will award you a festival burgee to fly from your boat. Come a subsequent year, and they'll give you a second burgee with two stars on it. Repeat as many times as you want and get as many burgees as your number of visits, each with more stars. The experience of sitting in the Bamfield Marine Research Station's modern auditorium and watching the sun set over Barkley Sound through floor to ceiling glass windows while listening to wonderful music is well worth repeating.

While in Bamfield, don't miss the Kiixin Tour (pronounced Keein). The Native village of Kiixin, located near Pachena Bay, is a National Historic Site with remains of a traditional First Nations village and is the most complete known on the southern B.C. coast. Call or book online with the Huu-ay-aht First Nation to reserve a tour of the village. A tour bus leaves from the East Bamfield Public Dock to the trail head, scheduled from June 15 through September 15, daily. Contact Kiixintours@huuayaht.org or call (250) 735-3432. Advance reservations recommended.

For a fine dining experience, book reservations at Pacific Wilderness Gateway Lodge (888-493-8933) located at the north tip of West Bamfield. Dinner guests can tie their dinghy at the dock belonging to the lodge. Dinners are available seasonally, beginning June 1st.

㊲ **East Bamfield Public Dock**. (250) 728-3231; hfnmarket@gmail.com hfndevelopmentlp.org; Located on the east side at the south end, 100 feet of guest moorage on the outside of the western-most float for vessels up to 15 meters (50 feet); water, for-fee garbage drop, 20 & 30 amp power at one stanchion located under the ramp. No washrooms. Dinghy landing space can usually be found. Preferred method to register and pay is at nearby upland "The Motel - Bamfield" (250-728-3231) or self-registration and pay with cash at the box located at the top of the ramp. Managed by the Huu-ay-aht Development Limited Partnership which also manages the nearby convenience store and "The Motel - Bamfield."

West Bamfield Public dock, your best option for moorage

㊲ **Kingfisher Marina.** 211 Nuthatch Rd., Bamfield, BC V0R 1B0; (250) 728-3231; frontdesk@hunayaht.com. Located on the east side of the inlet opposite the "Y54" red spar buoy. Open all year, limited side-tie guest moorage behind the fuel dock. Gas and diesel at the fuel dock. Laundry service, Wi-Fi, and ice. No power, no water. Waterfront suites are available upland.

㊲ **West Bamfield Public Dock.** (250) 720-7548; bhadockmanager@gmail.com. Side-tie moorage on both sides of 500 feet of floats, 20 & 30 amp power, water. No washrooms, no garbage drop. Reservations recommended during July and August. Self-registration and payment box located at the head of the ramp. If the public docks are full, contact Bamfield Lodge (250-728-3419) located directly behind the public docks. **Bamfield Lodge** accepts overflow moorage at their dock as space allows.

㊲ **Harbourside Lodge.** (250) 728-3330; (604) 328-1656; requests@harboursidelodge.com; www.harboursidelodge.com. VHF 06 & 72. Open June to mid-September with guest moorage, 30 & 50 amp power, water, washroom, and showers. Gasoline and diesel. Located on the west side of the inlet, just past the public dock. Convenience store has ice, bait, tackle.

㊲ **McKay Bay Lodge.** (250) 728-3323; mckaybay@island.net; www.mckaybaylodge.com. Located on the west side of the inlet at the south end. Transient moorage as space available; lodging guests have priority; call ahead. They usually have space early and late in the season but are often full in July and August. Gasoline, limited quantity of diesel, tackle, ice. Reservations are taken for dinner at the lodge. Washroom, guest rooms.

Dodger Channel. A small basin on the south portion of the channel, just east of Haines Island off the southwest corner of Diana Island, provides anchorage in settled weather; anchorage is open to the northwest and southwest. A drying rock lies on the west side of the north entrance to Dodger Channel. The south entrance from Trevor Channel is shallow, with rocks on both sides. Field Correspondent Mary Campbell reports that the south basin anchorage serves well as an early morning departure point from Barkley Sound. "It's the perfect anchorage for a good night's sleep before the run down the Strait of Juan de Fuca and has shallow depths, good crabbing and good views of the open sea. Diana Island is reminiscent of beaches in the South Pacific."

BARKLEY SOUND TO BECHER BAY

The final leg of a counter-clockwise circumnavigation of Vancouver Island is from Barkley Sound into the Strait of Juan de Fuca. On the Canadian side, Port Renfrew is the only protection between Barkley Sound and Sooke.

The typical summer weather pattern calls for calm conditions in the early morning, with a westerly sea breeze building by afternoon, often to 30+ knots.

Currents in the Strait of Juan de Fuca can be strong. This can speed up the passage, especially for sailboats. Or, they can substantially slow the trip. When the wind blows against the current, steep, sometimes-dangerous seas result. Pay attention to the current when planning to transit the Strait of Juan de Fuca.

Several weather resources make the trip less nerve-racking. Lighthouses at Cape Beale, Pachena Point and Carmanah Point provide regular weather updates. Automated stations at Shearingham Point and Race Rocks report hourly wind speed and direction. The Neah Bay weather buoy (46087) provides regular wind speed updates, and the New Dungeness buoy (46088) provides wind speed, direction, and sea state. Put together, you can get a picture of conditions on the Strait before venturing out.

Cape Beale. Cape Beale, surrounded by off-lying rocks, marks the eastern entrance to Barkley Sound. Trevor Channel exits at Cape Beale, and is the safest entry to, or exit from, Barkley Sound in thick weather or poor visibility. Seas can be difficult off Cape Beale when an outflowing current from Barkley Sound meets the longshore current outside.

WEST COAST OF VANCOUVER ISLAND

See Area Map Page 427 - Maps Not for Navigation

Pacific Gateway Marina, the only protected marina between Sooke and Bamfield

The collision of currents, combined with wind and shallow depths around the cape, can make for heavy going.

The usual advice is to round Cape Beale in early morning, before the summertime westerly wind gets up.

The local lightkeepers have provided this bit of local knowledge: A nasty reef is one-quarter of a mile in front of the lightstation. Beware of coming in close to take photos. Lightkeepers have had to summon the Bamfield Lifeboat crew a good many times to rescue overturned sports-fishing and pleasure craft occupants.

Nitinat Narrows. Nitinat Narrows connects Nitinat Lake with the Pacific Ocean. Entrance to the narrows is obstructed by rocks and a shallow bar. An onshore wind can cause breaking seas. A crossing of this bar and negotiation of the narrows to Nitinat Lake is considered a supreme Northwest navigation challenge by a small number of adventurers. Each year a few boats do make it through.

Many years ago Don Douglass took his 32 Nordic Tug across the bar, through the narrows, and into Nitinat Lake. His guidebook, *Exploring Vancouver Island's West Coast, 2nd Ed.* describes the experience, including the comment that his crew refused to ever try it again.

㊳ **Port San Juan.** For shelter off the Strait on the Canadian side consider Port San Juan, about halfway between Victoria and Barkley Sound. Port San Juan is a rectangular notch in Vancouver Island, with Port Renfrew on the eastern shore near the head of the bay. The breakwater protected marina at Port Renfrew offers year-round moorage and services. A public dock at Port Renfrew has limited moorage for smaller boats. The village and surrounding area has a grocery, pub, and several cafes.

The historic hotel and pub, at the head of the public dock, is a great place to relax over drinks. Port Renfrew is at the end of the road; hundreds of hikers, kayakers and sight-seers pour through town during the summer months.

Thrashers Cove. About one-third of a mile north of Quartertide Rocks, just off Hobbs Creek along the west shore of Port San Juan is a small bight with good anchoring depths and fair protection from northwesterly winds. Upland areas are part of the Pacific Rim National Park Reserve and the West Coast Trail. On shore you will see trail hikers camped for the night. A permit is required to visit the Park Reserve and hike the trail.

Woods Nose. Anchorage can be found close to shore behind Woods Nose on the south shore of Port San Juan. Woods Nose head breaks up the swell. Trees ashore block southerly winds, but the anchorage is open to northerly and westerly winds. In 2018, Landons reported that a private float and crab trap buoys occupied much of the desirable anchoring area.

㊳ **Port Renfrew Community Dock.** 17280 Parkinson Rd., Port Renfrew, BC V0S 1K0; (250) 647-5431. VHF 06 & 68 "Medd-O Base." Floats with room for 20 boats are installed from mid-May through mid-September. All are taken by charter boats. No electrical power; water is on the wharf but not on the floats. Best to call ahead for availability and reservations. Stan Medd is the harbormaster.

㊳ **Pacific Gateway Marina.** (250) 412-5509; contact@pacificgatewaymarina.ca; www.pacificgatewaymarina.ca. VHF 66A. Open year round. 60 slips designed for sport fishing boats and 200 feet of side-tie for larger vessels. Larger vessels should call ahead for availability. Reservations highly recommended. Water and 30 amp power are available on A and B docks. Washrooms with toilets; showers planned for the future. Ice and free Wi-Fi. Gasoline and diesel on the fuel dock. Launch ramp. This marina is owned and managed by the Mill Bay Marine Group. Repairs to the breakwater and docks have been completed following storm damage from January 2018. Bridgemans West Coast Eatery is open year-round, overlooking the marina with views of Port San Juan. SUP and sea kayak tours and rentals available nearby. A general store with groceries is within walking distance of the marina. The Botanical Beach Provincial Park is 3 km away; the marina may be able to help with transportation.

Renfrew Marina and RV Park. 7505 Gordon River Rd., Port Renfrew, BC V0S 1K0; (250) 483-1878; info@portrenfrewmarina.com; www.portrenfrewmarina.com. Open seasonally May through September. Monthly and daily moorage for small craft when available. First-come, first-served. Marine gasoline and launch ramp. Renfrew Marina is located at the head of Port San Juan, 1-mile up the Gordon River. River bar access is only navigable by shallow draft smaller vessels at mid to high tide (3 foot plus) with local knowledge; check tides.

SOOKE AND BECHER BAY

㊴ **Sooke Harbour.** Enter between Company Point and Parsons Point. The harbor is protected by Whiffen Spit, which nearly blocks the passage. Enter by keeping Whiffen Spit close to port. Two intersecting ranges mark the entrance channel. Follow the marked channel to town on the west bank. An area just inside Whiffen Spit, with charted depths of 7 meters (3 ¾ fathoms), has good anchorage, although wakes from passing boats make it rolly. Sooke Harbour Marina is the first set of docks. Just north of that is Jock's Docks, then Prestige Resort and a little farther up is Sooke Harbour Authority wharf with guest moorage. Sooke Harbour Marina and Jock's Docks have moorage for smaller vessels. Two day-use floats are located at the north end of the city boardwalk north of the of Harbour Authority city floats. Currents run quite strongly along the city waterfront, take care when landing.

Sooke Basin, the innermost harbor, is seldom visited by pleasure craft. The shallow channel follows the curve of the shoreline east of Middle Ground, between Eliza Point and Trollope Point. Notices to Mariners advises that entry to Sooke Basin be made after low water during daylight hours, when the drying banks are visible. Sooke is 15 miles closer to Barkley Sound than downtown Victoria, and often used as a departure point for boats heading up the west coast of Vancouver Island.

Sooke has a wide variety of services close to the Harbour Authority city floats, including a marine railway and machine shop, groceries, fuel, and restaurants. Just south of the Harbour Authority docks is the beautiful Prestige Oceanfront Resort, which

Reference Only – Not for Navigation

WEST COAST OF VANCOUVER ISLAND

Sooke

houses the West Coast Grill. Shops, grocery, and restaurants are in town about half a mile north from the Harbour Authority docks. Follow the road the full half-mile distance or take the trail to the boardwalk for the last quarter-mile. The trail to the boardwalk starts in McGregor Park and follows the shoreline before climbing a hill into town.

No customs clearance is available in Sooke. The nearest Canadian Port of Entry is Victoria.

㊴ **Sooke Harbour Resort & Marina**. 6971 West Coast Road, Sooke, BC V9Z 0V1; (250) 642-3236; reservations@sookeharbourmarina.ca; www.sookeharbourmarina.ca. Open all year with side-tie guest moorage to 50 feet along outside breakwater. Inside docks are for boats up to 25 feet. First-come, first-served. Services include washrooms, showers, 30 & 50 amp power, Wi-Fi on shore, and 2-lane concrete launch ramp. This is the first marina as you come into the harbor.

㊴ **Jock's Dock**. 6947 West Coast Rd., Sooke, BC V9Z 0V1 (778) 425-2703. Open all year; 60 slips for small sport fishing boats and runabouts; occasional guest moorage when available; first-come, first-served, call ahead. Water at the docks; two launch ramps, fishing charters. The upland Crab Shack (250-642-4410), open May to October, sells smoked fish, prawns and live crab.

㊴ **Sooke Harbour Authority.** 1800 Maple, Sooke, BC V9Z 1H5; (250) 642-4431; (250) 893-6578 cell; sookeharbour@telus.net. Open all year, first-come, first-served guest moorage along both sides of 400 foot A-dock, 20 & 30 amp power, water, garbage drop, used oil disposal; no washrooms or showers. Rafting required. Gate-secured floats are well maintained. Watch for current when approaching the floats. Walking distance to town via the park boardwalk.

Sunny Shores Resort & Marina. 5621Sooke Rd., RR 1, Sooke, BC V9Z 0C6; (250) 642-5731; www.sunnyshoresresort.com. Gasoline and diesel at fuel dock. Guest moorage for 6 to 10 smaller boats, call ahead for availability. Docks are in an advanced stage of deterioration. Washrooms, showers, laundry, 15 amp power, haulout. Motel accommodations and campground. Store carries ice, fishing tackle, limited groceries. Taxi to town 3 miles away.

Becher Bay. Becher Bay is a good alternative to Sooke for boaters wishing to avoid a difficult entry in fog. Although Becher Bay is farther east than Sooke, the time not spent winding your way past Whiffen Spit makes up for it. Campbell Cove on the west side of Becher Bay is a pleasant anchorage, but be careful of a drying rock near the south end. It's a good departure point for the run to Barkley Sound. Kelp is on the bottom; be sure of your set. Murder Bay, at the north end, is another recommended anchorage, also with kelp, though. Another pleasant anchorage lies to the east of Wolf Island. For a bit of gunkholing, enter between Wolf and Lamb Islands. Be sure to avoid the submerged power cable when anchoring.

㊵ **Becher Bay Marina & Campground**. 241 Becher Bay Rd., Sooke, BC V9Z 1B7; (250) 642-3816. Open May 1 to September 30. Limited guest moorage by reservation only, maximum boat length 30 feet. Services include washrooms, no showers, 2-lane concrete launch ramp, no power. Smokin' Tuna Cafe on site. RV parking.

Pedder Bay. Pedder Bay is a mile-long inlet, shallow and narrow, just south of William Head. No anchoring in bay due to submerged utility pipes. A launch ramp with floats is at the head.

㊶ **Pedder Bay Marina.** 925 Pedder Bay Drive, Victoria, BC V9C 4H1; (250) 478-1771; pbm@obmg.com; www.pedderbay.com. Monitors VHF 66A. Open all year, gasoline only at fuel dock. Permanent and visitor moorage available for vessels up to 50', call ahead for larger boats. Washrooms, showers, laundry, 30 amp power, free Wi-Fi, 3-lane concrete launch ramp, year-round RV resort, camping, coffee shop, chandlery with bait, tackle, and ice. Approaching, use Chart 3410; watch the wind. Located between Pearson College and Dept. of National Defence (don't stop there; it's a prison). The marina is part of Oak Bay Marina Group, a company that owns several marinas on Vancouver Island.

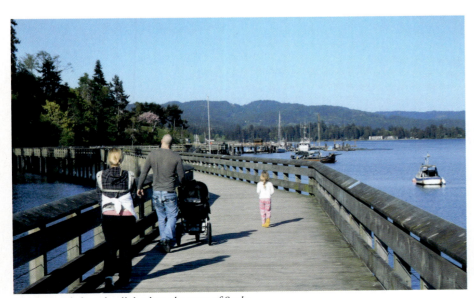

Harbour-side boardwalk leads to the town of Sooke.

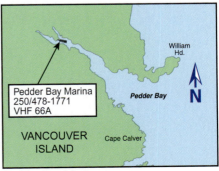

Pedder Bay Marina

2020 Waggoner Cruising Guide

Rounding Cape Caution

CHAPTER 15

PINE ISLAND ROUTE
Pine Island • Egg Island

WALKER ISLAND GROUP ANCHORAGE
Kent Island • Staples Island

PULTENEY POINT–JEANETTE ISLAND ROUTE
Malcolm Island • Jeanette Islands • Harris Island
Hot Spring Island • Richards Channel • Allison Harbour

MAINLAND ROUTE
Blunden Harbour • Allison Harbour • Miles Inlet
Nakwakto Rapids • Southgate Group

See Area Map Page 430 - Maps Not for Navigation

CAPE CAUTION

Cape Caution, for some, is a fearsome barrier to exploring the remote and beautiful northern areas of British Columbia and on to Southeast Alaska. Like many of the challenging cruising areas of the Inside Passage, careful planning, attention to the weather reports, patience and time can lead to a smooth and uneventful crossing. We have met cruisers who may wait for days for the right settled conditions. Good weather for a crossing happens more often than you might think.

To get to the central and northern B.C. Coast you first must round Cape Caution. Although the distance in open water is only about 40 miles, the seas can be high and steep. The bottom shoals from 100+ fathoms off the continental shelf to 20-70 fathoms in Queen Charlotte Sound itself, causing seas to heap up. The problem is made worse when these seas are met by the outflowing ebb currents from Queen Charlotte Strait, Smith Sound, Rivers Inlet and Fitz Hugh Sound.

We've refined our "go, no-go" decisions to six factors: weather forecast; time of day; lighthouse wind and sea reports; flood or ebb tide; size of tidal exchange (spring tide or neap tide); and the automated combined wave (wave and swell) height reports from the West Sea Otter Buoy. We have learned that our tolerances are different for head seas versus following seas. Generally, we can tolerate higher wave conditions with following seas than head seas with waves over the bow.

Weather Forecast. Regardless of other factors, we want a favorable forecast or we're not going. Fog, while limiting visibility, often indicates little to no wind, favorable for a crossing if you are skilled at operating your radar. Radar is very helpful as it is not unusual to have opposing traffic in this area during periods of settled conditions.

Time Of Day. The typical summertime weather pattern calls for calm early mornings, followed in late morning or early afternoon by a rising westerly sea breeze, sometimes to gale force. "Typical," however, does not mean every day. We've seen windy mornings and flat-calm late afternoons.

Lighthouse Wind And Sea Reports. From south to north, lighthouses, and automated stations, at Scarlett Point, Herbert Island, Pine Island, Egg Island, and Addenbroke Island report conditions approximately every four hours, posted on the Continuous Marine Broadcast. Pine Island and Egg Island are the most relevant. Addenbroke Island, inside the mouth of Fitz Hugh Sound, often reports quiet conditions when Pine Island and Egg Island are much rougher. Scarlett Point, just off the north part of Vancouver Island, usually is quieter than Pine Island and Egg Island.

Flood Or Ebb Tide. Flood tide is preferred. On a flood, the incoming swells and prevailing westerly wind are aligned and the seas are flattened. The ebb is the reverse: outflowing ebb currents meet the westerly swells, making them higher and steeper. One year we made the mistake of crossing the mouth of Rivers Inlet in a mounting sea breeze that was blowing against a strong outflowing ebb, and we took a beating. We *will not* do that again.

Size Of Tidal Exchange. If possible, cross during a time of neap tides (half moon). If that can't be done, try to cross on a flood. If that can't be done, try to cross at the end of one tide, when currents are growing less, and the beginning of the next tide, while currents are still low. Avoid crossing the mouth of Rivers Inlet on an ebb.

West Sea Otter Buoy. When West Sea Otter Buoy reports seas 1.3 meters or less, with a dominant wave period greater than 8 seconds, crossing is likely to be pleasant. Combine this information with the weather forecast, lighthouse reports, and flood and ebb tides.

VTS Radio Note. South of Cape Caution, Victoria VTS, channel 71, controls large vessel traffic. North of Cape Caution, traffic is controlled by Prince Rupert VTS, channel 11. Especially in reduced visibility, one radio should be monitoring VHF 16 and a second radio should be scanning channels 11 and 71.

Pine Island Route. This is the most popular route from Vancouver Island. It begins at Scarlett Point at the mouth of Christie Passage on Gordon Channel, and ends at Fury Cove, at the north end of Rivers Inlet. The distance is approximately 40 miles. Boats often provision and refuel in Port McNeill or Port Hardy, and move to a departure point near Christie Passage for a crossing the next morning. God's Pocket in Christie Passage, Port Alexander in Browning Passage, or Clam Cove in Gordon Channel just west of Browning Passage, are often used. Another good spot is the cove between Staples Island and Kent Island in the **Walker Group**.

The Pine Island route leads westward in Gordon Channel to Pine Island, then northward past the tip of the Storm Islands, past Egg Island, and on to Smith Sound, Rivers Inlet or Cape Calvert. This route will give Cape Caution an offing of 1.5 to 2.5 miles.

Gordon Channel is a principal passage for commercial vessels. In thick weather or fog, having radar, GPS and AIS is extremely helpful. Especially in low visibility or fog, most commercial traffic can be avoided by crossing Gordon Channel to the Redfern Island/Buckle Group side, and favoring that side to Pine Island.

Pulteney Point to Jeanette Islands Route. If Queen Charlotte Strait is behaving, this can be a good route from Port McNeill, on Vancouver Island, to the mainland side. From Pulteney Point at the west tip of Malcolm Island, turn to a course of 309° magnetic. This will leave the charted kelp patch to port. Twenty miles later you will arrive at the Jeanette Islands on the mainland side of Queen Charlotte Strait. Proceed through Richards Channel until Buoy N31 is abeam to port. Alter course slightly to leave Harris Island to starboard and Allen Rocks Lighted Whistle Buoy N33 to port. A course of approximately 293° magnetic will take you to a common intersection point west of Cape Caution.

Caution in Richards Channel. On an ebb, especially a big ebb, Richards Channel can

ROUNDING CAPE CAUTION GO-NOGO CHECKLIST

Tides & Currents - See Ports & Passes; Canadian Tides & Current Tables Vol. 7
- ❏ Phase of the moon – Spring or Neap Tide: Neap Tides are preferred
- ❏ Check for Slack Water time at Slingsby Channel
- ❏ Flood or Ebb; Flood is preferred

Weather System Predictions – via Internet or satellite
- ❏ Check NOAA Ocean Prediction Center forecasts for any approaching significant weather systems
- ❏ Check Windy.com, Predictwind.com, SiriusXM Marine, or Sailflow.com
- ❏ See Environment Canada forecast for the Synopsis report for Central Coast From McInnes Island To Pine Island

Weather & Seas Forecasts – via Internet, phone, or VHF
- ❏ See Environment Canada Forecast for Central Coast; Check for warnings, note wind speed and direction, wave height and interval, and trends of forecast conditions
- ❏ Check Environment Canada Forecasts for Queen Charlotte Sound, and West Coast Vancouver Island North; forecast conditions that are much different than the forecast for Central Coast may signal changing conditions

Observations & Present Conditions – via Internet, phone, or VHF
- ❏ Check Buoy Report for West Sea Otter (46204); note wind and sea conditions
- ❏ Check Lighthouse Reports from Scarlett Point, Herbert Island, Pine Island, Egg Island, and Addenbroke Island; note wind speed, wind direction, and sea conditions

Go-NoGo Decision
- √ Check wind and wave direction in relation to direction of travel.
- √ Is there a northwest wind against an ebb current situation?
- √ Do the wind and wave conditions exceed your limits?

Fail-Safe Contingency Plans
- √ Duck-in locations along the route: Allison Harbour, and Millbrook Cove

See *Chapter 1 Interpreting Northwest Weather* section for telephone numbers, website addresses, VHF channels, and buoy numbers.

2020 Waggoner Cruising Guide

CAPE CAUTION

Reference Only – Not for Navigation

Cape Caution

be difficult. One year, although the wind was calm, a big ebb set up a 2.5-knot outflowing current that opposed the incoming swells, creating larger and more threatening seas. We aborted our crossing and anchored instead in Allison Harbour.

Mainland Route. The mainland route offers more shelter in case of a blow and lets you visit Blunden Harbour, Allison Harbour, Miles Inlet, and Milbrook Cove in Smith Sound. You could even take a major side trip through famed Nakwakto Rapids (at slack) and spend time in Seymour Inlet and Belize Inlet. Many boats prefer the mainland route for its greater interest and possibility of shelter. The major cautions are Richards Channel on an ebb (above) and the waters off Slingsby Channel on an ebb.

Slingsby Channel Caution. Slingsby Channel is the primary drain for the hundreds of miles of inlets behind Nakwakto Rapids. What Slingsby Channel does to Queen Charlotte Strait on a big ebb can be terrifying. Outer Narrows at the mouth of Slingsby Channel runs to 9 knots on an ebb. The water fire-hoses into Queen Charlotte Strait, where it collides with the Pacific Ocean's incoming swells. If a westerly is blowing against this vast outpouring, conditions can be as bad as the worst at Cape Mudge.

Outer Narrows currents turn 10 minutes before Nakwakto Rapids, both flood and ebb. We departed our anchorage in Allison Harbour at 8:00 a.m., not realizing that two hours earlier the maximum ebb at Nakwakto Rapids was 11.4 knots. Shortly after 8:00 a.m. Slingsby Channel was still roaring. Although not a breath of wind was stirring, we found ourselves in large, steep seas that lifted the bow high, then crashed us down into the troughs. We pressed on, hoping not to meet a log in the bottom of a trough, and got through without injury or damage. The turbulence diminished but persisted all the way to Cape Caution, which we rounded at 10:10 a.m., a half-hour after the turn to flood in Slingsby Channel.

Summing up. Rounding Cape Caution is more than simply rounding the Cape itself. From the departure points to arriving in Fitz Hugh Sound, you will transit different areas with varying weather and sea conditions. The total experience involves planning for and choosing a route through the various sections. These sections include: staging and anchoring the night before; transiting of Queen Charlotte Strait; avoiding conditions off Slingsby Channel; rounding the Cape itself; and passing outside or inside Egg Island. You might include in your plan a stop in Smith Sound. You will need to choose the day's stopping point: Millbrook Cove, Fury Cove, Goose Bay, or go all the way to Pruth Bay. Patience and diligence in planning is the key. Start the planning process well ahead of time; start watching the forecast weather and the subsequent buoy and lighthouse observations a week ahead to familiarize yourself with conditions and place names.

Northern B.C. Coast

CHAPTER 16

BLUNDEN HARBOUR TO SLINGSBY CHANNEL
Allison Harbour • Miles Inlet • Nakwakto Rapids

SMITH SOUND
Table Island • Millbrook Cove • Ahclakerho Channel

RIVERS INLET & FISH EGG INLET
Dawsons Landing • Fury Cove

FITZ HUGH SOUND & FISHER CHANNEL
Pruth Bay • Ocean Falls • Shearwater

BURKE & DEAN CHANNELS, BELLA COOLA
Eucott Hot Springs • Elcho Harbour

SEAFORTH CHANNEL & MILBANKE SOUND
Roscoe Inlet • Reid & Jackson Passages • Fiordland

FINLAYSON CHANNEL TO PRINCE RUPERT
Klemtu • Butedale • Bishop Bay • Hartley Bay

NORTHERN B.C. COAST

Planning a Trip to the Northern B.C. Coast. Most cruisers limit their voyages to the waters south of a line that runs between Wells Passage on the mainland to Port Hardy on Vancouver Island. North of this line the northern part of Queen Charlotte Strait is a natural barrier. It takes time, a strong boat, and good navigation skills to proceed farther up the coast. To be fair, a lifetime of cruising could be spent south of that line with complete satisfaction.

But—to those with the time and inclination—the coast north of Wells Passage is a special experience. The scenery is magnificent, the population is small and self-sufficient, the fishing can be exceptional and you can even take a warm soak at one of several hot springs. You can anchor in bays with no other boats and take in the scenery all by yourself.

This is the part of the coast where you'll find the famous names: Nakwakto Rapids, Rivers Inlet, Fish Egg Inlet, Hakai, Bella Bella, Ocean Falls, Ivory Island, Fiordland, Butedale, Grenville Channel, Prince Rupert. It's a coast filled with history and possibilities. If it's wilderness you seek, you can find it here.

Be self-reliant. Between Port Hardy and Prince Rupert, there are few marinas with services for pleasure boats. Be glad the facilities are there, and don't complain if they're a little rough and maybe a bit more expensive. Don't expect marina help to come down to take your lines as you land.

Most facilities and businesses are set up to take credit cards. ATMs are limited except for a machine at Shearwater and sometimes in Klemtu, and you have full banking in Prince Rupert. Cell phone coverage is spotty. To determine whether you have cell phone coverage or roaming in this area, check with your provider. There are several areas with cell phone coverage between Port Hardy and Prince Rupert. Generally speaking you will find coverage at Shearwater/New Bella Bella, Klemtu, Hartley Bay, Kitimat, and Bella Coola. Some boats rent or purchase satellite phones when cruising this area. Satellite based messaging devices, such as the Garmin InReach system, with weather forecast delivery options, are useful in isolated areas with no VHF radio reception. Land line pay phones are in Bella Coola, Shearwater, New Bella Bella, Ocean Falls, and Klemtu.

Insurance. Some vessel insurance policies don't cover these waters without a special rider. Check with your marine insurance broker before you leave.

The boat. Not many small boats cruise the northern coast. You'll sometimes see jerry cans filled with extra fuel or water lashed to the rails or in the cockpits. Radar and GPS should be considered standard equipment. This is remote country. The boat should be in top mechanical condition. Complete spares should be carried.

Many anchorages along this coast are 60 to 90 feet deep, with shallower water too close to

Dall's Porpoise love to accompany boats.

shore to swing in comfort. You'll need ample anchor rode—300 feet should be considered the minimum.

Bottoms often are rocky. Because of its resistance to bending and its ability to set and hold in nearly any bottom, including rock, Bruce is a popular anchor. Manson Supreme, Rocna, CQR, Ultra and Delta anchors also are popular. You don't see as many Danforth style anchors. Danforth style anchors are good in sand and mud, but they have trouble setting in rock, and once wedged they are easily bent.

Be sure to carry at least two anchors. Whatever the style of anchors chosen, they should be big, strong, and ready to deploy.

Fuel and water. Fuel is plentiful, both gasoline and diesel, all the way up the coast. Rivers Inlet has gasoline and diesel at Dawsons Landing. You can get gasoline and diesel at Bella Coola, Shearwater, New Bella Bella, Klemtu, Kitimat, Hartley Bay, and Prince Rupert. The longest distance between fuel stops is roughly 70 miles.

Water is available all along the way. Some of it may be tinged brown from cedar bark tannin, but people have been drinking cedar water for decades with no ill effects. The dock at Ocean Falls has sparkling clear, purified water. New Bella Bella, Klemtu and Hartley Bay have multi-million-dollar water treatment plants that deliver clear, pure water.

Weather. Bring clothes for all conditions, from cold and rainy to hot and sunny. Expect wet weather at least part of the time. The residents of Ocean Falls call themselves "The Rainpeople" for good reason. Some years have been so wet that a few boats quit their cruise.

Plan for clouds down on the deck, for fog, for rain (both vertical and horizontal), and for storms. Leave enough flexibility in the schedule to anchor through serious foul weather. Be sure the boat is well-provisioned and equipped with generator or battery power to spend several days at anchor in one location.

Plan on sunshine, too, maybe a lot of sunshine. It can get *hot*. Bring bug spray, and equip the boat with screens on doors, hatches, opening ports, and windows.

You should have a heat source while underway and a heat source to be used at anchor. A hydronic system, with heat exchanger and furnace, can be used for both. There are various combinations of different heaters that can provide warmth.

Sailboaters will want some sort of cockpit protection, from a companionway dodger to full cockpit enclosure. Keep the cabin warm and dry, or you'll be miserable.

Marinas. There aren't many marinas on this coast. In Rivers Inlet, Dawsons Landing has moorage, fuel and supplies. The Native band stores at New Bella Bella and Klemtu have a good grocery selection. Shearwater, near New Bella Bella, has moorage, a restaurant and pub, groceries, chandlery, fuel, water, haulout and repairs. Ocean Falls has moorage, power, water, Wi-Fi and a pub in nearby Martin Valley. Farther north, Hartley Bay has fuel, water, and limited moorage. Prince Rupert has just about everything.

If you're in a jam, you could seek help at one of the sportfishing lodges along the coast, but remember that their business is serving their fly-in fishing guests, not recreational boats.

Dogs and hiking. Shorelines often are steep and rocky along this part of the coast, with few good places to walk the dog or take a walk yourself. Although we have seen many pets on board, we've met a number of cruisers who feel it's just too difficult to get a dog ashore. People who enjoy regular walks and hikes will find their options limited. All agree that the coast is beautiful, but some would welcome more opportunity for exercise.

Repairs. While it's best to carry complete spares and know how to fix whatever goes wrong, nobody can be ready for everything. Parts and mechanics can be flown in anyplace along the coast between Port Hardy and Prince Rupert. The only full-service shipyard

NORTHERN B.C. COAST

See Area Map Page 433 - Maps Not for Navigation

is at Shearwater. Parts can be easily flown in to New Bella Bella. Kitimat has facilities and a yard for repairs. Prince Rupert has full services, though they primarily serve the fishing fleet.

Charts and reference books. Canadian Hydrographic Service (CHS) has more than 65 charts that cover the coast from Wells Passage to Prince Rupert. Vector (ENC) digital charts for Northern BC Coast are available from CHS individually or in chart pack PAC-B. This chart pack includes the west side of Vancouver Island, Northern BC Coast, and Haida Gwaii. Raster (BSB) digital charts for Northern BC Coast are available from CHS individually or in chart pack PAC03, which includes Queen Charlotte Sound, Hecate Strait to Portland Canal. Navionics includes Northern BC vector charts with their Canada coverage. Coastal Explorer users may purchase the CHS west coast vector and raster chart packs from Coastal Explorer.

Boaters who carry paper charts will make the passage with fewer than 65 charts, but the number of charts on board likely will be closer to 65 than 35. It takes a capital investment to cruise this coast safely and enjoyably.

Tides and currents are shown in Ports and Passes and Canadian Tide and Current Tables, Vol. 7, (the purple book). North of Cape Caution you may want to consider getting the 3-volume set of Sailing Directions for the North Coast, PAC 200, 205, and 206.

An indepth guidebook is *Exploring the North Coast of British Columbia, 3rd Ed.*, by Don Douglass and Réanne Hemingway- Douglass, published and updated in 2017. Check www. WaggonerGuide.com/store for information on the updated edition. *Cruising the Secret Coast*, by Jennifer and James Hamilton, includes anchorages in some of the most scenic, out-of-the-way locations for this area.

For the latest news, sign up for WaggonerGuide.com email alerts. Under "Cruising Tweets" on our web site you can read the latest updates regarding marinas and anchorages.

BLUNDEN HARBOUR TO SLINGSBY CHANNEL

The entrance to Blunden Harbour is approximately 11 miles northwest from the mouth of Wells Passage.

Blunden Harbour. Blunden Harbour is a lovely, well-protected bay, with excellent holding ground. As you approach the entrance it is important to identify Siwiti Rock and leave it to starboard. Study the 1:15,000 Blunden Harbour inset on Chart 3548 or your chartplotter. Note the several rocks along both sides of the passage into Blunden Harbour. These rocks make a somewhat serpentine route necessary as you go in.

Anchor anywhere in the large basin, or between Moore Rock and Byrnes Island. We feel that Moore Rock is closer to Byrnes Island than the chart suggests. An abandoned Indian village is on the north shore, and the beach is littered with relics. A large "no trespassing" sign warns against exploring the uplands, however.

You can explore Bradley Lagoon in the northeast corner of Blunden Harbour. Those who have say it's interesting. Take the dinghy through the rapids at high water slack.

Southgate Group. The Southgate Group is a cluster of islands at the corner of the route between Blunden Harbour and Allison Harbour. A passage between Southgate Island and Knight Island makes for a scenic, sheltered shortcut. Basins on either side of the narrows appear just right for anchoring. Chart 3921 shows the passage in large detail.

Allison Harbour. Allison Harbour is large, long and nicely protected, with room for many boats. Log booms may be tied to shore. Crabbing is said to be good. The best holding ground is toward the head, in 20 to 25 feet. *Favor the western shore as you enter and leave, to avoid a rock that lies almost mid-channel, about halfway in.*

Murray Labyrinth. This one is for the brave, who will be rewarded. *Exploring the North Coast of British Columbia* has a good description of Murray Labyrinth, and *Best Anchorages of the Inside Passage,* authors Kelly and Vipond describe Murray Labyrinth in glowing terms. Waggoner Correspondents Lorraine and John Littlewood report:

"The inner cove is a special place to us and nearly a perfect anchorage. It's guarded by what looks to be an impossibly tortuous, kelp-choked entrance, so most boats pass on by (in 10 years, we've not seen another boat there). It's not that hard, though, and the reward is that extreme rarity on the coast: a landlocked, completely protected anchorage with access at any tide and endless exploration potential by kayak or dinghy.

We took our 43-foot Ocean Alexander in twice, and other boats before. It was a piece of cake each time—just keep a bow watch and go dead slow, in and out of gear as necessary to give yourself plenty of time to react. All obstacles are plainly visible or charted. Use the south entry only. Do not attempt to enter or leave through the northern passage in anything other than a kayak or dinghy. It's foul, and what appear to be two rocks are really one rock with the middle part awash at low tide." [*Littlewood*]

Skull Cove. Skull Cove is on Bramham Island, roughly opposite Murray Labyrinth. It is one of the prettier anchorages you will find. If approaching from the south, we would pass behind Southgate Island and follow the eastern mainland shore almost to City Point. Then we would turn northwest, leaving Town Rock to port, and go through the passage between the Deloraine Islands and Murray Labyrinth, thus avoiding all the rocks and reefs that lie offshore. If approaching from the north, follow the Bramham Island shore.

Enter Skull Cove on the east side of the unnamed island and take anchorage in the cove immediately to port, in 20 to 25 feet. The view on the west side of the island is superb.

Miles Inlet. Miles Inlet indents the west shore of Bramham Island and is beautiful. The narrow passage is lined with silver snags. The trees are not tall, suggesting wind from winter storms blows strongly in the inlet. The entrance is narrow, but using McEwan Rock as a reference, the entrance is easy to locate. Offlying rocks are on each side of the entrance. Go directly down the middle. Once inside, anchor in a little nook on the north side of the entrance channel or at the T intersection. The two arms of the T shoal rapidly, but the north arm has more room.

Schooner Channel. Schooner Channel, along the east side of Bramham Island, is narrow and requires constant attention to avoid rocks and reefs. With attention, however, the channel is not difficult to run. Watch tidal currents closely. The flood runs to 5 knots and the ebb to 6 knots. Schooner Channel currents are shown in Ports and Passes and Canadian Tide and Current Tables, Vol. 6, as a secondary station based on

Blunden Harbour is a beautiful anchorage, with room for many boats. It's a good starting point for an early morning rounding of Cape Caution.

Reference Only – Not for Navigation   NORTHERN B.C. COAST

Boat name signs attached to trees on Turret Rock in Nakwakto Rapids

Nakwakto Rapids.

An unnamed bay opposite Goose Point at the north end of Schooner Channel is mentioned in Sailing Directions as a good anchorage for small craft.

 LOCAL KNOWLEDGE

Tide-Rip: Mike Guns, a commercial fisherman with much experience in these waters, reports that when an ebb current opposes a westerly wind, the entrance to Outer Narrows and Slingsby Channel is on par with the worst conditions that Nahwitti Bar or Cape Mudge can produce. He has seen "noticeable turbulence" as long as 3 hours after maximum ebb at Nakwakto Rapids. Take this patch of water seriously.

Slingsby Channel. Slingsby Channel runs between the mainland and the north side of Bramham Island. Currents in Outer Narrows, between the Fox Islands and Vigilance Point, run to 7 knots on the flood and 9 knots on the ebb. Outer Narrows is shown as a secondary station based on Nakwakto Rapids in Canadian Tide and Current Tables, Vol. 6 or Ports and Passes.

Enter Slingsby Channel via a narrow, scenic channel that runs between Fox Islands and Bramham Island, thus avoiding Outer Narrows entirely. The channel is easy to run, and deeper than the chart shows.

Treadwell Bay. Treadwell Bay is a good, protected anchorage at the east end of Slingsby Channel. It is often used by boats awaiting slack water at Nakwakto Rapids. Favor the east shore as you enter to avoid rocks off the Anchor Islands. The rocks are shown clearly on the charts. Inside, beware of rocks shown on the chart off the south shore of the bay.

Nakwakto Rapids. Nakwakto Rapids is among the world's fastest. Especially on spring tides, they must be transited at slack water only. At neap tides the window of safety opens a little wider. We have been told that high water slack is much preferred over low water slack. On big tides in particular, take this advice very, very seriously.

During the full rush of a maximum tidal current, the sound and action of the rushing water give the impression that Turret Rock actually trembles. Brave mariners have nailed boards with their boat names to trees on Turret Rock. Favored passage is on the west side.

Behind Nakwakto Rapids lie the extensive waterways of Seymour Inlet, Belize Inlet, Nugent Sound, and Alison Sound.

Note: Our sister publication *Cruising the Secret Coast*, by Jennifer and James Hamilton, devotes three chapters to the approaches to Nakwakto Rapids and the extensive waters of Seymour Inlet and Belize Inlet. Highly recommended.

SMITH SOUND

Smith Sound doesn't see many pleasure boats, but it's reputed to be full of fish. We visited during an opening for gillnet commercial salmon fishing, and the boats turned out in force. Picking our way among the nets required close attention, but all went well.

You're on your own in Smith Sound itself. There are no resorts or settlements. Several bays are good for anchoring, although only one, Millbrook Cove, really appeals to us.

From the south, enter Smith Sound

Blunden Harbour to Slingsby Channel

2020 Waggoner Cruising Guide   435

NAKWAKTO RAPIDS AND BELIZE INLET

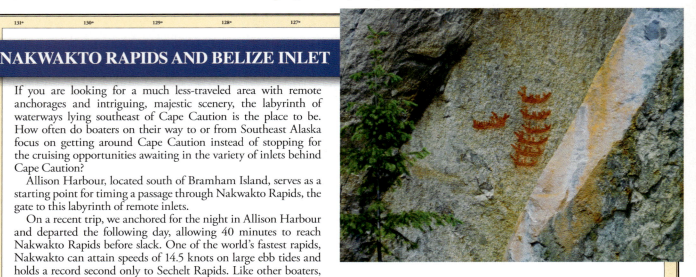

If you are looking for a much less-traveled area with remote anchorages and intriguing, majestic scenery, the labyrinth of waterways lying southeast of Cape Caution is the place to be. How often do boaters on their way to or from Southeast Alaska focus on getting around Cape Caution instead of stopping for the cruising opportunities awaiting in the variety of inlets behind Cape Caution?

Allison Harbour, located south of Bramham Island, serves as a starting point for timing a passage through Nakwakto Rapids, the gate to this labyrinth of remote inlets.

On a recent trip, we anchored for the night in Allison Harbour and departed the following day, allowing 40 minutes to reach Nakwakto Rapids before slack. One of the world's fastest rapids, Nakwakto can attain speeds of 14.5 knots on large ebb tides and holds a record second only to Sechelt Rapids. Like other boaters, we had heard about these rapids and had seen photographs which tend to deter boaters from taking this passage. As we discovered, however, transiting the rapids at slack is a non-event; admittedly, timing the rapids is crucial. Not only is it the speed that makes Nakwakto treacherous, but also the whirlpools and eddies. Nakwakto Rapids is not one to challenge in anything but slack; within 15 minutes of slack, you can see turbulence and eddies. While transiting the rapids at slack is easily done, it's not uncommon to meet a tug pulling a raft of logs. As we neared the entrance to Nakwakto Rapids, we saw a tug approaching from the opposite direction and circled around a small islet to wait for the tug to be well clear before continuing into the passageway. Normally, seeing tugs at rapids is often a concern; but in this case, they serve as a confirmation that it's time to go through. Turret Rock, known locally as 'Tremble Island,' lies in the middle of the narrow Nakwakto Rapids. Boaters can pass around either side of Turret Rock; the west side is considered the preferred side. On our return trip, however, we passed on the east side with equal ease. Transiting each side allowed us to see all of the boat names attached to trees on this tiny rock island, a long-standing tradition.

Once through Nakwakto Rapids, boaters have three main headings to explore: east into Nugent Sound; southeast into Seymour Inlet which includes Frederick Sound; or northeast into Belize Inlet which includes Mereworth Sound and Alison Sound. Seldom visited by pleasure boaters, we found ourselves completely alone among these isolated scenic inlets, hidden from the outside world. With limited time, we chose the beautiful Belize Inlet route, a fjord-like channel with steep mountains and numerous waterfalls. Putting the nose of Got d' Fever up close to one of the falls, we took in the quiet, undisturbed majesty of this remote backcountry.

While traversing through the bends and turns admiring the variety of geological formations and vegetation, we couldn't help but marvel that this area was once home to the Nakwaktok people. Pictographs in the area give evidence of their previous life here. A pictograph on the northern shore of Belize Inlet (near the entrance to Alison Sound) depicts a sailing ship and some canoes, men in the canoes appear to be holding what looks like rifles. As we turned up Alison Sound following the narrow, twisting channel lined with more mountain peaks and cascading waterfalls, we found a second pictograph on the north shore showing a row of canoes with one lone canoe approaching. It is reported that a Native Nakwaktok camp in Village Cove of Mereworth Sound was fired upon in 1868 in retaliation for an assault on a trading vessel named Thorton; perhaps these pictographs record this incident. History indicates that a main village, as well as summer camps, were established throughout these inlets.

For us, our journey took us to the head of Belize Inlet ending at a delta. Backtracking a short distance, we found anchorage at Summers Bay over an irregular bottom in about 60 feet of water. The still quiet evening was interrupted only by the sound of a nearby waterfall and the chirping of birds as the sun went behind the peaks above Chief Nollis Bay at the western end of Alison Sound.

– Lorena Landon

One of many scenic stops on Belize Inlet on the way to Alison Sound

Dramatic scenery on Belize Inlet where very few boaters venture

NORTHERN B.C. COAST

Reference Only – Not for Navigation

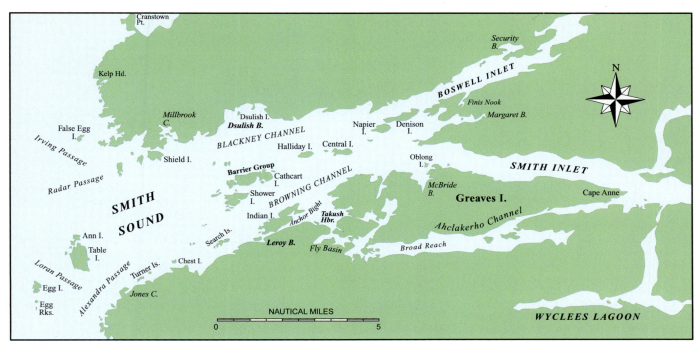

Smith Sound

through Alexandra Passage, between North Iron Rock and Egg Rocks. From the west, enter through Radar Passage. From the north, enter through Irving Passage. We suggest that you plot waypoints to keep clear of rocks. This is especially true in reduced visibility.

Table Island. Table Island is in the mouth of Smith Sound, and the casual visitor would not think of it as an anchorage. But fish boats anchor there and have no problems. A boat waiting to make a southerly dash around Cape Caution could find this anchorage useful, as could a boat seeking shelter from a westerly in Queen Charlotte Sound. The Hulsizers report spending a rolly night at this anchorage.

Jones Cove. Jones Cove is on the south shore of Smith Sound, near the mouth. The cove is cozy and well protected and often used by commercial fish boats. Anchor in 20 feet with limited swinging room. Depending on the rise and fall of the tide and the presence of other boats, you may choose to run a stern-tie to shore.

Fly Basin. Fly Basin is on the south side of Smith Sound at 51°16.35'N/127°36.20'W. "It is very private and protected, but entry requires care. Study of the chart will show that you should favor the western shore until opposite the point of land extending from the eastern shore. Then swing to the east side of the channel. The charted rocks can be difficult to see except at low water. Once in, anchor in 15 to 25 feet (zero tide) in the eastern section of the bay, excellent holding in mud." [*Hamilton*]

Correspondents John and Lorraine Littlewood report the western basin is also good. Work your way in past the rocks, and anchor in pristine surroundings on a good mud bottom. They begged us to not tell a soul about this anchorage, but since we are friends we feel safe letting you in on it.

McBride Bay. This bay is on the north side of Greaves Island, at the east end of Browning Channel. It is deep until near the head, which has 30 to 40 foot anchoring depths. Protection is excellent, but swinging room is a little limited.

Ahclakerho Channel. Ahclakerho Channel leads along the south side of Greaves Island. The current runs hard in the channel. Transit at slack water, especially on big tides. Slack appears to be around the time of high and low water at Bella Bella. Correspondent Gil Flanagan reports: "This is an overlooked gem. The narrow part of the channel is probably 200 feet wide. The anchorage on the east side of the 78-meter east Ahclakerho Island gives good protection from west winds in Smith Sound. We stern-tied among numerous rocks and small islands. It was beautiful."

Margaret Bay. Margaret Bay is at the head of Smith Sound, on the point of land that separates Boswell Inlet and Smith Inlet. Chambers Island, rather small, is in the middle of the bay, about halfway in. West of Chambers Island depths are too great for anchoring. East of the island they shallow to 50 to 55 feet. The head shoals sharply, and old pilings take up much of the room at the head. Protection is excellent.

Ethel Cove. Ethel Cove is just outside the mouth of Margaret Bay. It looks right out to sea, however, and we found a very low surge coming in. Get close to shore or anchor in 50 to 60 feet farther out.

Crossing Smith Sound at Blackney Channel for a night's anchorage in Millbrook Cove.

2020 Waggoner Cruising Guide   437

NORTHERN B.C. COAST

See Area Map Page 439 - Maps Not for Navigation

Millbrook Cove is a quiet, protected anchorage at the entrance of Smith Sound.

Finis Nook. Finis Nook is located near the mouth of Boswell Inlet, on the south shore, sort of "around the corner" from Margaret Bay. It is nearly landlocked and completely protected; it seems a perfect anchorage. A log boom blocks the back bay, however, and a float house is on the east side, with the wreck of a fish boat. Anchoring depths in the area not already taken are approximately 35 feet. We were disappointed, and went back to Millbrook Cove to overnight. (In *Cruising the Secret Coast,* the Hamiltons like Finis Nook).

Dsulish Bay. Dsulish Bay, with beautiful white sand beaches, is on the north shore of Smith Sound. A trail reportedly leads to Goose Bay to the north. The best anchorage is behind the 46-meter island, deep inside the bay. It is a little open but workable. We have seen fish boats anchored along the west side of Dsulish Bay. In the right conditions it would be a good lunch stop, though we're not so sure about overnight.

Millbrook Cove. This is the outermost anchorage on the north side of Smith Sound. To us it is the favored anchorage. The cove is completely landlocked, with 25 to 35 foot depths, good holding ground, and ample room.

Getting in will hold your attention, at least the first time. Find the red spar buoy E6 marking Millbrook Rocks. The buoy has a small radar reflector on top. Leave this buoy to starboard (Red, Right, Returning), and aim the boat toward the 30-meter island. Keep a sharp lookout for rocks on both sides, especially the west side, as shown on the chart. The 30-meter island can be passed on either side, although the east side is a little deeper.

Once in, watch for a drying rock a short distance off the northeast corner of the 30-meter island. Minding your depths, anchor anywhere.

RIVERS INLET

Note: Cruising the Secret Coast, by Jennifer and James Hamilton, contains an entire chapter devoted to cruising the parts of Rivers Inlet not covered here, with a little overlap.

Rivers Inlet is a famed salmon fishing area and, at one time, had 18 salmon canneries. All the canneries are closed now and most are sinking into ruin. Absent its commerce of former years, Rivers Inlet is prime cruising ground. The scenery is beautiful and the anchorages excellent. The area is served by Dawsons Landing and private fishing lodges. In Goose Bay, a substantial concrete dock provides access to the Goose Bay Cannery, but no amenities.

Open Bight. Open Bight, well named, is just inside Cranstown Point at the entrance to Rivers Inlet. Anchorage, with protection from westerlies but not easterlies or northerlies, is along the south and west shores. The west shore is preferred. We would put the hook down outside the kelp line in 25 to 30 feet, within view of a stunning white shell midden beach. Gentle swells will rock the boat.

Home Bay. Home Bay, on the south shore a short distance inside the mouth of Rivers Inlet, is a pretty spot.

Just west of Home Bay is another nook, which Douglass calls West Home Bay in *Exploring the North Coast of British Columbia*. The bay has anchorage behind the first of two islets inside. Contrary to Douglass' illustration, however, low tide reveals rocks that foul the western side of that first islet. We would pass the islet only to the east.

Other anchoring possibilities lie in the unnamed group of islands just west of Duncanby Lodge. Larger boats will find good anchoring in deep water in the unnamed cove marked with 29-meter and 35-meter soundings. The large island with the 105-meter hill is at the north end of this cove. Smaller boats can creep into the unnamed cove east of the deep water cove. This cove is marked with a 9-meter sounding in the mouth and a 16-meter sounding inside. A fishing resort outpost is moored on the eastern shore. The little nook at the northeast end of the cove offers quiet anchorage in 60 to 120 feet, but be careful when you enter this nook. A reef extends northward nearly halfway across the entrance, much farther than the chart suggests. Favor the north side.

Duncanby Lodge. (604) 628-9822; (877) 846-6548; www.duncanby.com. Duncanby is a high-quality fly-in fishing resort. Meals, lodging and charter boats are all inclusive as a guest package. The restaurant and docks are no longer open to the general boating public. No fuel service.

Goose Bay. Anchorage is good in 20 to 50 feet on a sticky bottom across the bay from the cannery buildings. Crabbing is reported to be good.

Goose Bay Cannery Dock. (778) 373-6346; Monitors VHF 06. Open during peak summer season. This is a private facility which is at the discretion of the owners to permit visitors to come ashore. The historic cannery in Goose Bay, built in 1926, processed and canned salmon from 1927-1957; 350 people once worked and lived at the cannery. A clean, sturdy 175-foot concrete dock is available for short-term and overnight stays on a first-come, first-serve basis; no power; no water. Leave space on the dock for floatplanes. A self-registration payment box is located at the end of the dock ramp, expect a donation fee of $1 per foot. Fees collected go towards making improvements on the cannery buildings. Projects are ongoing and

Visitor moorage at Goose Bay Cannery. Sign in at the head of the dock.

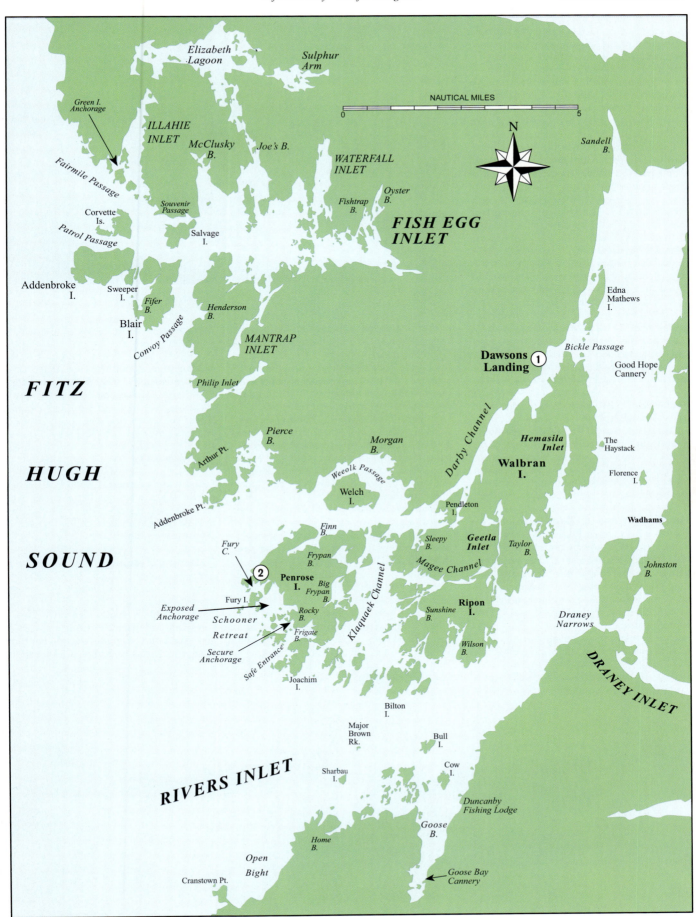

Rivers Inlet & Fish Egg Inlet

shared among the multiple owners of the property. A two-bedroom cabin is available for rent. Depending on which owner you meet and the work scheduled for that day, you might be able to finesse an invitation for a brief tour of the grounds and cannery. With permission, hiking the 1 mile trail to a dam located above the cannery may be of interest, but be "bear aware" and take appropriate precautions. A waterfall, and a suspension bridge built in the 1940's can be seen near the dam. Correspondents Knut and Christine Hildebrand report that the trail is challenging. Use at your own risk.

Hemasila Inlet. "Entry to the inner basin looks impossible on the chart, but isn't. The charted rock is central in a 200-foot-wide channel and is visible except at very high tides. Favor the east side—it has slightly more room and the shore is steep. We anchored in 35 feet just north of the 9.1-meter sounding with plenty of room to swing. Holding was excellent in thick mud. It was sheltered and pretty, with a small creek at one side and a small waterfall at the other side. Watch for a rock 2.5 meters deep at zero tide in the mouth of the inlet where the R symbol and 24 meter sounding are located." [*Hamilton*]

Taylor Bay. Taylor Bay indents the east shore of Walbran Island and has tranquil, lovely anchorage in 35 to 50 feet, although swinging room is limited. Anchor all the way in or try the nook behind the north end of the inner island, between the inner island and Walbran Island. Protected from most winds except east and southeast.

Draney Narrows & Draney Inlet. The current runs hard in Draney Narrows. We looked in 1½ hours before the predicted turn and decided against it. Fifteen minutes before the turn the narrows were flat. Predictions are shown in Canadian Tide & Current Tables, Vol. 7 and Ports and Passes as a secondary station based on Prince Rupert Tides.

Draney Inlet, approximately 24 miles long, is surrounded by high, steep mountains. It's

The floating village of Dawsons Landing with guest moorage and a store.

beautiful. Because it is not on the way to anyplace else, it sees little pleasure craft traffic. Good anchorage in 30 to 35 feet is available in Fish Hook Bay, a short distance inside the narrows. When we visited, a float home with two floating outbuildings was on the south shore of Fish Hook Bay, near the entrance. A large sign read, "Warning, Private Property, No Trespassing." A convincing watchdog greeted our boat with don't-mess-with-me barks and growls. We didn't argue.

Note: Our sister publication, *Cruising the Secret Coast*, by Jennifer and James Hamilton, devotes a chapter to Draney Inlet, with much information about anchorages and what to see.

Johnston Bay. Johnston Bay, on the east shore of Rivers Inlet just south of Wadhams, is a former cannery site. The bay is quiet and beautiful, but deep until very near the head. As the chart shows, a reef lies in the center of the outer part of Johnston Bay, and a rock is close to the eastern shore at the entrance. Favor the western shore all the way in and you'll have ample depths of 30-50 feet.

Sandell Bay. "North shore of Rivers Inlet, where the inlet takes that east bend. Anchor well into the bay in 25 feet, zero tide. Excellent holding in mud/sand/rock/shell. Kind of like a cement mix, and held like it, too. Sandell Bay looks exposed on the chart, but is actually protected. It was blowing 30 knots in Rivers Inlet when we came in, and from the anchorage we could see a line of whitecaps out there. But hardly any wind or fetch reached us." [*Hamilton*]

Good Hope Cannery. Good Hope Cannery is the large, white building visible when cruising past Draney Inlet. The facility is a high-end fly-in sport fishing resort. No services for cruising boats.

① **Dawsons Landing** (Dawsons Landing General Store). (604) 629-9897; dawsonslanding@gmail.com; www.dawsonslanding.ca. Monitors VHF 06. Phone service is spotty; it's often best to communicate by email. Open all year, gasoline and diesel fuel. Guest moorage, hardware, groceries, charts, ice, fishing licenses, fishing

Informal owner-conducted tours of the Goose Bay Cannery might be available as owner's time permits.

The short, narrow entrance to Big Frypan Bay is straight-forward and easy to transit.

NORTHERN B.C. COAST

Supplies, mail, and guests arrive and depart remote Dawsons Landing on the historic Grumman Goose.

and hunting gear, liquor, washroom, showers, laundry, post office, two rental cabins with kitchenettes. Satellite based Wi-Fi available for a fee, pay at the general store. Locally produced water available on the dock. A helipad takes up part of the south end dock. They have scheduled air service from Wilderness Seaplanes and NW Seaplanes.

Dawsons Landing is owned by Rob and Nola Bachen, and has been in the family since 1954. This is a real general store, with an excellent stock of standard grocery items and an astonishing accumulation of tools and hardware. One year, for example, we needed an in-line fuse holder to replace a spare we had used. Dawsons had it.

Note that instead of cleats, you'll tie to loops of rope set into the planks. Absent bull rails, it's easier and safer to clear the docks of snow in the winter. The one dock with bull rails is used by float planes.

Smoked salmon: It's almost worth a trip to Dawsons Landing simply to stock up on the Bella Coola Valley Seafoods smoked wild Pacific salmon that Nola carries in the store. Several smoke flavors to choose from; time of year varies depending on the commercial fishing season.

Darby Channel (Schooner Pass). Darby Channel, locally called Schooner Pass, borders the west side of Walbran Island, and is easily run. Southbound boats should favor the west shore of the channel to avoid being lured into foul ground behind Pendleton Island. The rock off the southwest corner of Pendleton Island is clearly marked by a beacon and easily avoided.

Pierce Bay. Exercise caution, because Pierce Bay contains dangerous rocks not necessarily shown on the chart. One of the rocks is east of the south tip of the largest island, at 51°31.665'N/127°45.667'W. This rock is in relatively open water, and could surprise a person. Another is off the northwest point of the large island, where the anchorage opens up.

Frypan Bay. Frypan Bay, spacious, scenic and well protected, is at the northeast corner of Penrose Island. Anchoring depths, along the south shore, are 25 to 40 feet and, in the middle, 50 to 85 feet with good holding. This anchorage is a favorite of many cruisers. The narrow entrance has an uncharted shoal on the port side shore as you enter.

Big Frypan Bay. Located on the east side of Penrose Island, this large bay has ample room for numerous boats; anchoring depths of 68 feet on a sand-mud bottom. Shallower depths can be found in a couple of coves within the bay. The short, narrow entrance to Big Frypan is straight-forward and easy to transit.

Finn Bay. Finn Bay, on the north side of Penrose Island, is well protected. An abandoned sport fishing camp is in the bay. Anchoring depths of 36-66 feet can be found in the bay.

Sunshine Bay. Tucked in the middle of Ripon Island, the bay is entered through a narrow channel off of Klaquaek Channel. The charted shoal on the south shore at the neck of the entrance is not as extensive as depicted on the charts. Anchoring depths are 25 to 30 feet over a flat mud bottom. This intriguing bay is home to a hidden community of float-homes. During the off-season, this bay is the parking location for several fishing lodge buildings.

② **Fury Cove.** The cove behind Fury Island is a beautiful and a popular anchorage, with a perfect white shell beach. Fury Cove, as it is commonly called, is entered by leaving Cleve

DAWSONS LANDING
GENERAL STORE LTD.

Supplying Rivers Inlet for Over 65 Years

A GENUINE OLD-TIME GENERAL STORE

Fuel • Complete Grocery
Well-Stocked Liquor Agency
Block & Cube Ice
Bottled Water • Water on Dock
Internet Hookup
Bait • Souvenirs
Moorage • Post Office
Showers & Laundry
Rental Cabins
Scheduled Air Service
We Freeze Fish

IN THE MIDDLE of the **WORLD-FAMOUS RIVERS INLET FISHING GROUNDS**

WWW.DAWSONSLANDING.CA
dawsonslanding@gmail.com • Phone 604/629-9897
Proprietors Rob & Nola Bachen • Dawsons Landing, BC V0N 1M0 • VHF 06

2020 Waggoner Cruising Guide

NORTHERN B.C. COAST

See Area Map Page 439 - Maps Not for Navigation

Island to port, then turning to port towards the narrow entrance.

Fury Cove is a good place to spend the night before a southbound rounding of Cape Caution, or when headed north after crossing Cape Caution. It is popular and occasionally fills up; consider Big Frypan Bay as an alternative. While at anchor, you can look across the beach and see the conditions on Fitz Hugh Sound. Inside, avoid the charted rock that dries at 10 feet close to Fury Island. Consider taking the dinghy to shore to explore the beach and tide pools. A cabin used by kayakers is nestled in the woods on the north shore of Fury Island.

Cleve Island is mentioned in Sailing Directions, but shown on the chart only as a 61-meter island—no name. **Breaker Pass** separates Fury Island from Cleve Island. We have run through the pass in calm weather, but we could tell it wouldn't take much of a southwesterly for Breaker Pass to live up to its name.

No Discharge Zone: No black water overboard discharge, please. Fury Cove does not flush well.

Philip Inlet. Philip Inlet indents the mainland side of Fitz Hugh Sound approximately 3 miles south of Addenbroke Island. The entrance can be hard to identify. Use caution when entering: ledges of rock extend from each side of the inlet near the mouth. About halfway in, a small island creates a rock-strewn, tight and tricky narrows. A bow watch is recommended. Field Correspondents Jim Norris and Anita Fraser report: "We came here to hide from an approaching southeast gale. We entered midway on the flood and found the entrance narrow in one spot, but well charted on Chart 3934. Least depth was 18 feet at half tide with very slight current. We anchored in 55 feet in the middle of the bay with good holding. The next morning Addenbrook Island lighthouse reported southeast 15 knot winds; we had northwest 3 knots."

Fifer Bay. Fifer Bay indents the western side of Blair Island, with lovely 6- to 12-foot anchorage for small craft at the head of the southernmost cove. There's room for one boat if it swings, more if all stern-tie to shore. When entering, favor Sweeper Island to avoid the rocks lying off the southern side of the entrance. When clear of the rocks, turn south and work your way into the anchorage.

FISH EGG INLET

Fish Egg Inlet indents the east side of Fitz Hugh Sound, behind Addenbroke Island. This is beautiful cruising country, and is becoming one of the popular spots on the coast. Those who say you'll be all alone are wrong. The gunkholing possibilities are many, but here are notes on some of the better-known anchorages.

Mantrap Inlet. Once you're inside, Mantrap Inlet offers good anchorage. The entrance,

Fury Cove is well protected with sandy beaches and windows to Fitz Hugh Sound.

however, is narrow, made narrower by an uncharted ledge of rock that extends from the west shore. Consider going through at half tide or higher, dead slow, with a lookout.

Oyster Bay. Oyster Bay, next to Fish Trap Bay at the head of Fish Egg Inlet, is a nice anchorage with a remote feel to it. We had a late and relaxed lunch there, anchored in 20 feet near the head of the bay. Recommended. [*Hale*]

Fish Trap Bay. Awfully tight, but room for one boat, stern-tied. At lower water levels the Native fish trap is clearly visible.

Waterfall Inlet. Pretty spot, but we couldn't find any comfortable anchorages. We felt that the west entry, leaving the 99-meter island to starboard, was safest. Go slowly and watch for rock ledges that extend from each side of the narrow pass.

Joe's Bay. Joe's Bay has become quite popular. When we visited in early July one year, five other boats were already anchored. Joe's Bay is worth the crowds, though. It's tranquil, tree-lined and snug. Anchoring is straightforward in the southern basin; rocks and reefs make the northern portion somewhat trickier. A stern-tie to shore might be called for to keep the boat from swinging onto a rock. Once anchored, the tidal rapids leading to Elizabeth Lagoon and Sulphur Arm are worth exploring with the dinghy.

Souvenir Passage. Sailing Directions says that Souvenir Passage is very narrow at its eastern end and the chart shows a rock on the north shore. We have found good water all the way by favoring the south side of the passage.

Illahie Inlet. The head of Illahie Inlet would be a delightful anchorage in 30 to 40 feet, mud bottom, with good protection. Favor one shore or the other as you enter Illahie Inlet. Rocks lie in the middle of the channel, partway in.

Green Island Anchorage. Green Island Anchorage, just off Fitz Hugh Sound at the mouth of Illahie Inlet, is about as cozy as an anchorage needs to be. Excellent holding in 35 to 40 feet. From seaward, wrap around the 70-meter island and follow the shoreline in. This is a good spot to rest after crossing Queen Charlotte Sound.

Entrance to the very well-protected Sunshine Bay on Ripon Island

Fitz Hugh Sound to Burke Channel

NORTHERN B.C. COAST　　　See Area Map Page 443 - Maps Not for Navigation

FITZ HUGH SOUND

Fitz Hugh Sound begins at Cape Calvert and continues north to Fisher Channel. Boats crossing Queen Charlotte Sound from the south will find the ocean swells quickly vanish once Cape Calvert is behind them. A southwesterly can still make things nasty, especially in a south flowing ebb current. Even in settled conditions, expect to find rougher water where Hakai Passage joins Fitz Hugh Sound.

Northbound boats that don't stop at Rivers Inlet probably will stop in Fifer Bay, Safety Cove, or Pruth Bay. Green Island Anchorage is another good choice for passing traffic.

Safety Cove. Safety Cove is a steep-walled, uninteresting bay that indents Calvert Island approximately 7 miles north of Cape Calvert. The bottom shoals sharply a fair distance from the head of the bay. Sailing Directions recommends anchoring immediately when the depth reaches 100 feet. If you press in to find shallower water, watch your swing or you could find yourself aground on the shelf at low tide. Despite its name and regular use, Safety Cove is not our first choice of anchorages in the area.

③ **Pruth Bay.** Pruth Bay is at the head of **Kwakshua Channel,** some 7 miles north of Safety Cove. Pruth Bay has long been a favorite stopover point. It offers ample room, 40- to 50-foot anchoring depths, and a flat bottom with good holding. Storms coming off the ocean can make the bay quite windy.

This entire area is part of the **Hakai Luxvbalis Conservancy Area**, a huge provincial park that includes the northern half of Calvert Island, the southern two-thirds of Hunter Island, and Goose Island.

Correspondents James and Jennifer Hamilton have anchored in about 50 feet with good holding in the unnamed cove west of Keith Anchorage, on the south shore of Kwakshua Channel, a short distance east of Pruth Bay. Anchor in this cove or one of the others that indent that shore, in Pruth Bay itself, or in the bay north of the thumb of land marked by Whittaker Point.

Southbound, we often overnight at Pruth Bay before rounding Cape Caution. Hakai Beach Institute provides free Wi-Fi in the bay, handy for downloading weather information.

Note: Our sister publication, *Cruising the Secret Coast*, by Jennifer and James Hamilton, devotes a chapter to this area. It describes anchorages not included in the Waggoner, and includes coverage of anchorages at the mouth of Hakai Passage.

③ **Hakai Beach Institute.** In 2010 the luxury fly-in fishing resort at the head of Pruth Bay was purchased by the Tula Foundation and became the Hakai Beach Institute. The facility is now used for research and as a conference center. Visitors are welcome to moor their dinghies and use the marked walk-way and trail to the Pacific side of the Institute's grounds.

No fuel or commercial services are available at Hakai Beach Institute. When arriving by dinghy, moor only at the clearly marked "dinghy dock" section of the float. The Institute requests that visitors sign the guest log at the Welcome Centre, at the head of the dock. A public washroom is adjacent.

The grounds are immaculate. Follow the signs for the trail to West Beach, one of the finest beaches on the coast. The trail is substantially covered with a boardwalk, but unfinished and muddy in some places. Carry bug spray. After a pleasant and flat hike of almost a half-mile, you hear the ocean and

West Beach near Pruth Bay is arguably the best beach anywhere on the west coast.

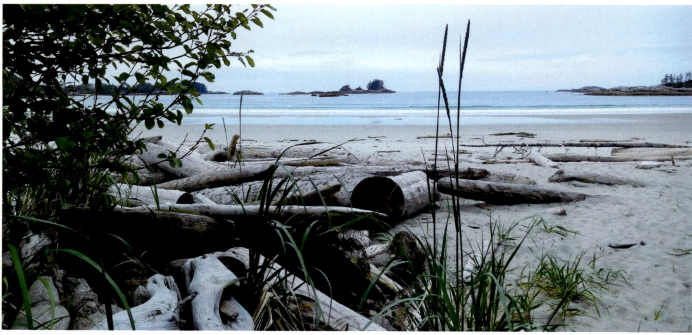

Easy trail from Pruth Bay brings you to West Beach.

Hakai Beach Institute – Pruth Bay

Pruth Bay has always been a good overnight stop along the Inside Passage. The bay, at the head of Kwakshua Channel, is well protected and scenic. But the real attractions are West Beach and North Beach, two of the most beautiful sand beaches in the Northwest.

Access to the beach areas, however, has not always been easy. As the owners of the property have changed, the state of the trail leading across Calvert Island has ranged from poor to acceptable.

A few years back the property, formerly a fishing lodge, was acquired by the Tula Foundation and rechristened as the Hakai Beach Institute. Eric Peterson and Christina Munck, the principals of the Tula Foundation, have since transformed the property into a world-class conference and research center.

The improvements are apparent as soon as you arrive. Beautiful new docks have been installed, welcoming signage posted, and top-notch facilities constructed. Signs direct visitors to the West Beach trail, a well-maintained boardwalk and gravel pathway.

Researchers and educators use the facilities to investigate and collaborate. Areas of research include local archaeology, ecology, and First Nations culture. The institute has a fleet of boats available to transport personnel and equipment throughout the area and scientific labs to support research activities.

Due to its location, the Hakai Beach Institute is totally off the grid. Electricity is generated by a 50 kw solar farm feeding into a nearly 10,000 amp hour battery bank. Water is collected on site. Sewage is heavily treated before being released. And perhaps most welcome for visiting boaters, internet is piped in through nine satellite links and distributed wirelessly throughout the property and anchorage (please, no streaming video or other bandwidth intensive tasks).

We are fortunate to have people like Eric and Christina, focused on understanding our environment and sharing the beauty of this area with visiting boaters.

You can learn more about the Hakai Beach Institute and the work of the Tula Foundation on their blog and website, www.hakai.org.

– *Mark Bunzel*

break out of the forest to a beautiful beach, with white sand extending in both directions. On a sunny day it seems almost tropical. On an overcast day, with crashing waves, it carries the beauty and furor of the wild Pacific Ocean. A less-developed trail leads north to North Beach, a sandy beach facing Hakai Pass; and a longer more challenging trail leads south to nine scenic west facing beaches.

Visiting boats are welcome to anchor in Pruth Bay, as long as they stay 100 meters from the dock so seaplanes have room to maneuver. Free Wi-Fi covers the entire bay. Wi-Fi internet use is limited to 300mb of data per device per day. The best reception is close to the head of the bay.

Meay Inlet. Meay Inlet leads north from Kwakshua Channel to Hakai Pass. Immediately after the turn past Whittaker Point is a small scenic cove with room for 4 or 5 boats. The Hamiltons, in *Cruising the Secret Coast*, named this cove Whitaker Point Cove and report anchorage in 40 to 60 feet, with good holding in mud mixed with shell.

The Hakai Lodge (hakai-lodge.com) fly-in fishing resort, owned by the principals of NW Seaplanes, is in a nearby cove from late June until September. The resort has almost daily floatplane service to the Renton/Seattle area, making this a good place to drop off or pick up crew or parts. The lodge serves meals to visiting boaters, reservations required 24-hours in advance for breakfast, lunch, and dinner. Reservations also accepted for guided fishing tours. Email ccarlson@hakailodge.com or hail on VHF 16 for meal reservations. This is a seasonal resort, floats are removed in the off-season.

Hakai Passage. Hakai Passage is one of the great fishing spots, yielding 50- to 60-pound salmon and large bottom fish. Since Hakai Passage opens to the Pacific Ocean, it can get rough. Treat it with respect. On an otherwise pleasant afternoon we overheard two well-managed boats discussing on the radio whether the swells they were facing in Hakai Passage began in Japan or just Hawaii.

Goldstream Harbour. Goldstream Harbour is a lovely little anchorage at the north end of Hecate Island. Enter from the east favoring Hat Island, which extends from the south shore about 0.2 mile inside. Don't favor Hat Island too closely, though; rocks extend out from it. Hat Island is not named on the chart, but its height (39 meters) is shown. Once past Hat Island, pass Evening Rock, which dries at 1.2 meters, leaving it to starboard. Evening Rock lies about 300 feet off the northwest corner of Hat Island (it helps to refer to the chart as you read these instructions). Inside, the middle of Goldstream Harbour is about 30 feet deep. Rocks extend out from the shore, so pick your anchoring spot carefully to swing safely. This is a nice protected spot with an opening in rocks to look out at the conditions in Hakai Pass.

Ward Channel. Ward Channel connects Hakai Passage with Nalau Passage. Running it is straightforward as long as you follow the chart to keep track of the rocks.

Edward Channel. Edward Channel, west of Ward Channel, also connects Hakai Passage with Nalau Passage, but the southern entry is much tighter than Ward Channel. Pass between the 27-meter and 31-meter islets, staying well clear of the detached rock that dries at 1.6 meters off the south tip of the 27-meter islet. Chart 3935 (1:40,000) is quite clear. Don't try the south entry

NORTHERN B.C. COAST

See Area Map Page 443 - Maps Not for Navigation

with the older Chart 3727 (1:73,584). It doesn't show enough detail where you need it. The primary reason to be in Edward Channel is the lovely anchorage of Lewall Inlet.

Lewall Inlet. Lewall Inlet indents the east shore of Stirling Island and is a delightful anchorage. Run all the way to the bend and anchor in 10 to 20 feet, north of the north shore of the entry channel. Stay well off the little treed islet near the south shore. A ledge of drying rock reaches out from that islet.

Uncharted rock: An uncharted rock lies mid-channel just north of the anchorage bend at approximately 51°46.150'N/128°06.266'W. The rock dries on a +2 foot tide. Use extreme caution if going north of the bend at the anchorage.

Nalau Passage. Nalau Passage, scenic and open, separates Hunter Island and Stirling Island, and connects Fitz Hugh Sound with Kildidt Sound. A conservative, mid-channel course has no hazards. The western entrance, however, is made interesting by drying rocks offshore from the north side of the passage. Eastbound boats crossing Kildidt Sound may have anxious moments finding the exact entrance. We used the following waypoint for the western entrance successfully: 51°47.10'N/128°07.20'W.

SPIDER ISLAND AREA

Note: Our sister publication, *Cruising the Secret Coast*, by Jennifer and James Hamilton, contains extensive coverage of these cruising grounds, including Kildidt Sound, Kildidt Inlet, the Goose Group, the McNaughton Group, and other wild areas between Hakai Passage and Seaforth Channel.

Kildidt Sound. Kildidt Sound is remote and beautiful with many anchorage possibilities. Consult *Cruising the Secret Coast* for more information on the numerous islets and anchorages in this area.

Serpent Group. Correspondents James and Jennifer Hamilton have anchored successfully in the cove on the easternmost side of the 57-meter island, southwest of the 31-meter island. Their anchorage was tranquil, but when they dinghied ashore and climbed to the seaward side they found windblown trees barely holding to the shore.

Kildidt Narrows. Kildidt Narrows is the reversing tidal rapids at the entrance to Kildidt Inlet, which the Waggoner does not yet cover. We include it here only because observations by Waggoner Correspondents James and Jennifer Hamilton, and confirmed by Canadian Hydrographic Service, indicate that the Sailing Directions times are incorrect. High water slack occurs approximately 1.5 hours after high water at *Bella Bella*. The time difference for low water slack varies with the height of the tide. For a low water of 0.4 meter, slack occurs approximately 2 hours after low water at *Bella Bella*; for a low water of 2.5 meters, slack occurs approximately 1 hour after low water at *Bella Bella*. Bella Bella is italicized because Sailing Directions calls for Prince Rupert tides.

For complete coverage of Kildidt Narrows and Kildidt Inlet, see *Cruising the Secret Coast*.

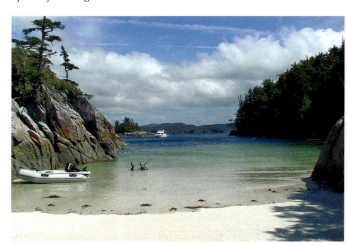

James & Jennifer Hamilton found this perfect anchorage in Kildidt Sound's Serpent Group. Photo by James Hamilton.

Brydon Channel. Brydon Channel connects Kildidt Sound and Spider Anchorage. Westbound across Kildidt Sound, lay a course well south of Lancaster Reef, then turn north toward the Brydon Channel entrance. When studying the chart, you will see the easternmost dogleg in Brydon Channel is foul with rocks. Mike Guns, a commercial fisherman with much experience in these waters, told us the

Brydon Channel

safe route through is to hug the northwest end of the 72-meter island at the eastern end of the channel. This keeps you clear of the rocks farther out. See the reference map.

Brydon Anchorage. Brydon Anchorage extends northward into Hurricane Island at the west end of Brydon Channel at 51°50.25'N/128°12.25'W (NAD 83). Correspondents James and Jennifer Hamilton anchored in 30 feet near the very head. They report, "An amazing view to the south, not a soul around. It was an astonishingly quiet and beautiful anchorage—like no other. Most places remind us of somewhere else. This one stands alone." [*Hamilton*]

Spider Island area. This area is beautiful, raw, remote feeling, and little visited. The waters are also full of rocks. This is perfect gunkholing country, a paradise for kayakers.

You have a choice of two ways to get there, outside or inside. The outside route goes out the mouth of Hakai Passage into Queens Sound, then bends northwest toward the west side of Spider Island. Breadner Point, on the west side of Spider Island, is a famous hot spot for spring salmon. South of Spider Island, enter through Fulton Passage, or north of Spider Island through Spider Channel.

The inside route goes through Nalau Passage, across Kildidt Sound, and through rock-choked Brydon Channel into Spider Anchorage. An alternate to the Brydon Channel portion is Spitfire Channel, along the north side of Hurricane Island. Spitfire Channel has one spot so tight, however, we recommend you explore by dinghy before committing the mother ship. Near high tide, and with a lookout on the bow, we squeezed through in a 52-foot Grand Banks.

The following information is an overview of the main places. It would take several days to poke around all the delights of this area.

Southbound in Spider Channel, approaching the Stopper Group islands on the way to Spider Anchorage

Passage between Spider Anchorage and Spitfire Channel. This passage separates Spitfire Island and Hurricane Island. The passage is clear until the north end, where rocks extend from Spitfire Island. This area is fairly well covered with bull kelp floating on the surface and thick leaf kelp below. We went in near the top of a high tide without difficulty. Next morning we departed 1½ hours after a 3.3-foot low tide and gathered a heavy glop of leaf kelp on our props and rudders. A low-powered fin keel sailboat could have been stopped dead. This passage is best run near high water.

Hurricane Anchorage. "Hurricane Anchorage" is Douglass' name for the otherwise unnamed cove in the hook formed by the south end of Hurricane Island. As shown on the reference map, enter north of the group of islets that make up the hook. Well protected and scenic.

Spitfire West Anchorage. This is Douglass' name for the otherwise unnamed cove that indents Hurricane Island, immediately west of the Spitfire Channel narrows. Several people have recommended it to us. Douglass says the bottom offers only fair to poor holding, however.

Spitfire North Anchorage. This is our name for the otherwise unnamed cove that indents Hunter Island, west of the Spitfire Channel narrows. Mike Guns recommended it to us. We would anchor in the outer part only. At low water the mouth leading to the inner lagoon appeared to be impassable or nearly so. The east side of the outer cove had a bottom that felt like a thin layer of mud on top of rock, and we dragged easily. The west side of the cove yielded good holding in 50 to 55 feet.

Spitfire Channel. Spitfire Channel separates Hurricane Island and Hunter Island, and except for the narrows at the west end, is easily run. The narrows are another matter. A medium-size cruiser can go through these narrows without difficulty, but with great caution and a sharp lookout. Underwater rocks extend into the channel, especially from the north side. Plan your transit at high water slack—high water, to get the greatest width possible; slack because we wouldn't want current pushing us where we didn't want to go. Least depth is 1.9 meters (approximately 6 feet) at zero tide.

Bonsai tree on wind-swept island near Spider Anchorage and Spitfire Channel

NORTHERN B.C. COAST

FITZ HUGH SOUND, CONTINUED

Kwakume Inlet. Kwakume Inlet is a beautiful and roomy anchorage, but study your chart closely before entering. A rock awash at zero tide is shown outside the entrance, and you'll want to steer a course to avoid it. Mike Guns, a commercial fisherman with 35 years' experience in these waters, says the preferred approach is from the north. He recommends favoring the mainland shore, to pass between the rock and the shore.

Once past the rock, pass between the larger islet in the entrance and the little dot islet south of the larger islet. Inside, two rocks are shown a short distance along the north shore, one of them dries at 1.5 meters. Near the head of the main basin and south of its islet, another rock is shown, this one dries at 1.8 meters.

The south cove immediately inside the entrance has been recommended as an anchorage, but might be filled with aquaculture. Other aquaculture is located along the north side of Kwakume Inlet. Fortunately, it doesn't occupy any favored anchorages.

With the south cove taken, the best anchorage is in 25 to 30 feet (zero tide) at the head of the inlet, between the shore and a rock shown as drying at 1.8 meters. Anchor either there or in the inner basin.

If you can get into it, the inner basin is unusually secluded and snug feeling. Be aware, however, that the short fairway leading to the inner basin is narrow, and that a substantial drying rock lies in the middle, with more rocks on each side. *High water only, this little pass, dead slow bell, with alert lookouts.* We favored the north side.

Having a high tide when we arrived in early evening, we felt our way into the inner basin for the night. We were treated to glass-smooth water and the most plaintive loon's call we've ever heard. As we slipped out at high water early the next morning we were stopped cold by a wolf's cry—a long lonesome troubled howl, repeated just once. *[Hale]*

Koeye River. A charted rock lies north of Koeye Point. Enter north of that rock and wrap around into the cove behind the point. A lodge is near the point.

A few years ago we talked with the lodge caretaker, who told us that an onshore wind blowing out of Hakai Passage creates large seas that roll into the bay. He also said this is grizzly bear country. Later, we talked with a boat that experienced the seas mentioned above. The skipper said the seas were awful. They had come back from the mine and had much trouble getting from the dinghy to the boat. Stay away in a westerly.

Although in our opinion Koeye (pronounced "Kway") River is not a good spot for overnight anchoring, several people have told us a dinghy trip up the river to the mine ruins is beautiful. At the mine you'll find two open pits connected by a tunnel. The remains of a shop are there, and a huge old 1-cylinder steam engine. The buildings on the point at the mouth of the river are a Bella Bella Native band summer camp. *[Hale]*

Sea Otter Inlet & Crab Cove. Sea Otter Inlet, on Hunter Island, has two arms that form a "T" at the entrance. Crab Cove, the northern arm, was recommended by a park ranger at Pruth Bay. Anchor near the head in 30 to 35 feet. The south arm is prettier than Crab Cove and more private feeling. Anchor near the head of the south cove in 35 to 40 feet.

Kiltik Cove. Mouth of cove at 51°53.80'N /128°00.05'W. Kiltik Cove indents the east side of Hunter Island, approximately across from Namu. It is extremely well protected. The bottom shoals abruptly just past the tiny rock islet on the east shore of the arm. We would anchor in 35 to 40 feet a short distance north of that rock.

Warrior Cove. Warrior Cove is on the mainland (east) side of Fitz Hugh Sound, approximately 1.5 miles south of Namu. With a typical westerly wind, a following sea will chase you into the cove, but the seas subside when you pass the 82-meter island (in a southeast gale a lump may get in). The inner cove is pretty and protected. Scout around for just the right spot, and put the hook down in 20 to 25 feet, good holding.

Namu. The falling-down cannery at Namu went through a transition. For many years caretakers Pete and Rene (pronounced "Reenie") Darwin, and Rene's longtime friend Theresa, managed the facility. They created a unique destination on a collection of floats, complete with a covered common area, gift store, workshop, greenhouse, and docks. They transformed the uplands of the old cannery with art and and creative landscaping. Pete and Rene have moved on, physically moving their floats to Lizzie Cove on Lama Passage. See Lizzie Cove entry for more information.

Anchorage is still available at Namu or in nearby Rock Inlet.

Navigation note: The beacon is gone from Loo Rock, between the Namu floats and the entrance to Rock Inlet, but Loo Rock still exists. The Namu Harbour inset on Chart 3936 shows the rock's location. Watch for another rock located in front of the abandoned cafe building and for other possible obstacles in the area.

Rock Inlet. Rock Inlet extends northeast from Whirlwind Bay (Namu), and it's a good, protected spot. Entering or departing, be sure to identify Verdant Island, near the mouth, and pass east of it. Keep a mid-channel course and watch for rocks. The chart shows the way. Inside, anchor in 25 to 40 feet. The bottom is rocky, and our anchor skipped across for some distance before setting.

FISHER CHANNEL

The north end of Fitz Hugh Sound divides into Burke Channel and Fisher Channel. Burke Channel leads eastward to Bella Coola, which is connected by road to Williams Lake and the highways inland. Bella Coola has facilities and is mentioned often by the few residents on this part of the coast, but is little visited by pleasure craft.

Fisher Channel is a continuation of the Inside Passage route, although the Inside Passage soon leads west and north, via Lama Passage or Gunboat Passage, to Bella Bella and Shearwater. If you remain in Fisher Channel you will reach Cousins Inlet. Ocean Falls, at the head of Cousins Inlet, is the most complete and interesting ghost town on the coast.

Humchitt Island. Humchitt Island is immediately off the south tip of King Island, at the intersection of Fitz Hugh Sound, Burke Channel and Fisher Channel. "With 15-knot southeasterlies blowing up Fitz Hugh Sound, we overnighted in the cove on the northeast shore of Humchitt Island. The seas were 2 to 3 feet outside, but our anchorage was tranquil and calm, with an amazing view up Fisher Channel. Anchor in 10 to 20 feet, moderate to good holding over rock, with a 150-foot swing radius." *[Hamilton]*

Kisameet Bay. Kisameet Bay is on King Island, about 3.5 miles north of the mouth

The Kisameet Bay anchorage is somewhat smaller than this photo suggests. Work your way in around rocks, all of them charted.

See Area Map Page 443 - Maps Not for Navigation

NORTHERN B.C. COAST

This sandy beach at Sagar Lake is reached by trail from Codville Lagoon.

of Burke Channel, roughly east of Fog Rocks. Correspondents John and Lorraine Littlewood report: "A splendid anchorage. The northernmost part of the bay, behind the island, is the place to be. It's quiet and fully protected from wind and sea, with a 'window' out into Fisher Channel to observe conditions." This is a very pleasant place to hide out. Anchor in 30 to 40 feet. We overnighted in this anchorage three seasons ago before heading south to cross Cape Caution. We found it to be just as the Littlewoods described and recommend it.

Codville Lagoon. Codville Lagoon is a provincial park on the east side of Fisher Channel. It is a popular anchorage, protected and pretty. Readers John and Deb Marshall reported that strong winds will work their way to the back cove. The narrow entrance is hard to locate, but Codville Hill, its moonscape of three peaks and barren rock slopes, is a good landmark. Favor the south side of the entrance to avoid a rock off the north shore. Anchor in 40 to 50 feet at the eastern head of the inlet. A trail runs from the northeastern shore of the anchorage to sandy beaches at beautiful Sagar Lake. Field Correspondent Jim Norris warns of vicious sand fleas. This is bear country. Make noise as you walk.

The Trap. The Trap is located behind Clayton Island on the west side of Fisher Channel, about 2 miles south of Lama Passage. North entrance at 52°02.35'N/127°56.80'W. South entrance at 52°01.05'N/127°56.80'W. We read about this spot in Iain Lawrence's *Far Away Places* (now out of print). Southbound on a windy, rainy afternoon we decided to tuck in for a look. The passage behind Clayton Island is as Lawrence describes it: deep, but protected from the wind. Lawrence says the bottom is rocky and requires a stern-tie to shore to prevent swinging. The Trap itself is the bay at the very south end of the passage. Lawrence says this bay empties at low tide, revealing a labyrinth of ancient fish traps.

Long Point Cove. Long Point Cove is located on the west side of Fisher Channel, approximately 1 mile south of Lama Passage. Although Sailing Directions mentions Long Point Cove as a good anchorage for small craft, it isn't as scenic or interesting as other anchorages in the area. On entering, favor the west shore to avoid a rock that dries some 250 to 300 yards north of Long Point. The rock is shown on the chart.

④ **Ocean Falls (Cousins Inlet).** Ocean Falls is a favorite destination. Although a ghost town, Ocean Falls is a busy ghost town. The winter population of 25 swells to 100 in the summer, but services are limited. Two bed and board inns offer services to their guests. Saggo's Saloon in nearby Martin Valley is usually open Mondays, Wednesdays, and Fridays from 4:00 p.m. to 7:00 p.m.; check the bulletin board at the top of the dock.

A right turn at the top of the ramp from the Small Craft Harbour leads to Ocean Falls proper. Other than the small gift store in the corner of the marine ways building, Ocean Falls Lodge (formerly Darke Waters), and the Old Bank Inn (formerly the Ocean Falls Fishing Lodge) are the only operating businesses.

The dam dominates the head of the inlet and supplies electrical power for Ocean Falls, Shearwater, and New Bella Bella. The dam also provides water and power for the town's multi-million dollar hatchery and rearing pen facility for Atlantic salmon smolt for fish farms. Some 30 large green fiberglass rearing pens have been installed beside the former Crown Zellerbach mill site. Mixing ponds, where freshwater and saltwater are blended in exact proportions for the developing smolt, have been blasted out of the rocky mountainside leading to the dam. High tech has arrived in Ocean Falls. In early 2018, a computer-based cryptocurrency "mining" entity leased a building with a computer processing facility, which requires large amounts of electrical power.

A trip to Ocean Falls is not complete without a hike to the dam with vistas of Link Lake and views of the once busy mill town below. A walk through this "ghost town" can't help but stir the imagination. Make noise— you might meet a bear. Trout fishing in Link Lake is said to be excellent.

A left turn at the top of the dock leads visitors on a 1.5-mile road to Martin Valley. It's an easy, scenic stroll. The first house you come to is Saggo's Saloon. A little farther along, a concrete launch ramp serves amphibious planes.

The houses in Martin Valley were taken over by the province when Ocean Falls was abandoned. They have since been sold to people who enjoy the beauty and solitude of the area. Visitors as well as locals arrive at Ocean Falls by ferry service from Bella

The view of Ocean Falls from the Small Craft Harbour.

2020 Waggoner Cruising Guide

449

NORTHERN B.C. COAST   See Area Map Page 443 - Maps Not for Navigation

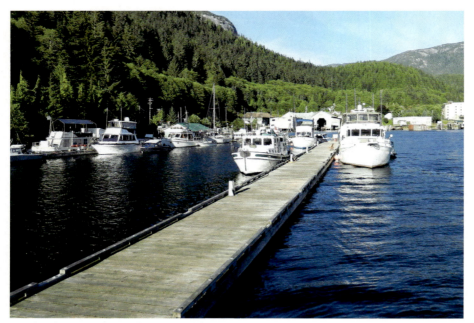
Ample side-tie at Ocean Falls Small Craft Harbour

Bella, Shearwater, and Bella Coola (check BC Ferries for the scheduled service). A water taxi based in Ocean Falls takes passengers to various destinations on the central coast, call (250) 289-3396.

Crabbing is excellent off the old mill site. Halibut and salmon can be caught in Cousins Inlet. Consider dropping a prawn trap in Wallace Bay on your way up the inlet. We think Ocean Falls is a "don't miss" stop for its unique charm and beauty.

Lodging can be found in Ocean Falls at Old Bank Inn. Martin River Lodge, in nearby Martin Valley, offers fishing charters and B&B guest rooms. Don't miss the "Little Licker" ice cream shop next to the Old Bank Inn. Air service to and from Ocean Falls is available through Wilderness Seaplanes.

④ **Ocean Falls Small Craft Harbour.** General Delivery, Ocean Falls, BC V0T 1P0; (250) 289-3859; www.oceanfalls.ca/blog/ofha. Open all year, public dock with ice, potable water, free Wi-Fi, 20 & 30 amp power, no fuel.

Ample dock space with reasonable rates and all the Link Lake water you need. The water is sweet and pure and has gone through a further purification process.

"The Shack," a yellow float house next to the ramp, has a book exchange, computer with internet, and tables and chairs. Pay moorage in The Shack, or wait for the wharfinger to come down the docks in the morning or late afternoon. Visa and MasterCard accepted.

Harbor owner Herb Carpenter runs the marine ways. Herb built Melissa, the gold-colored mermaid who welcomes boats to the docks. In the downstairs corner of the marine ways building, Herb's wife Lena has set up a little gift shop called C' shores Gift Shop.

Upstairs is Nearly Normal Norman's Ocean Falls Museum, filled with items left behind by former residents of Ocean Falls. Those of us over 50 will recognize many of the objects. If the door is not open, ask around. Norman will open up for visitors. Donations accepted. Children will love visiting the "Fairy Rock" located a short distance from the docks on the road to Martin. Children take great delight in finding coins hidden in the Rock. Be sure to let the wharfinger know if you plan to visit Fairy Rock so the fairies can be alerted; you can contribute coins at The Shack in support of this long-standing tradition at Ocean Falls. Another fun tradition is the Annual Salmon Derby Barbecue weekend held in late August, a popular event drawing participants from other nearby communities. Tickets for the barbeque can be purchased at The Shack.

No garbage drop: Recycling bins for plastic, glass, tin, aluminum and burnables are located at The Shack. Take everything else with you.

Weather radio channel WX 1: The signal is spotty. If necessary, walk along the dock with a handheld VHF until you find reception, or use the computer in The Shack to check the forecast online.

④ **Ocean Falls Lodge.** oceanfallslodge@gmail.com. New owners purchased the former Darke Waters Inn, the historic hospital building across from the marine ways. The lodge now serves as a hostel; boaters may use the laundry and shower facilities. The building is in need of repairs, which the owner tells us are ongoing.

④ **Old Bank Inn.** (250) 289-9624; info@lemarston.com. Les and Toni LeMarston purchased the former fishing lodge near the historic Ocean Falls Hotel and converted the lodge into a cozy bed and board guesthouse offering comfortable, nicely-appointed rooms with breakfast, lunch and dinner included in the daily rate. You guessed it, the building was originally the bank in Ocean Falls.

Lama Passage. Lama Passage leads westward and northward from Fisher Channel to New Bella Bella and Shearwater. Cruise ships and BC Ferries use this passage regularly. Keep a sharp lookout ahead and astern.

Fancy Cove. Fancy Cove is on the south shore of Lama Passage and is a delightful little anchorage. Don and Reanne Douglass write about the cove in their book *Exploring the North Coast of British Columbia*. This nearly landlocked cove is well protected. Anchor in 10 to 25 feet.

Fannie Cove. Fannie Cove is in Cooper Inlet on the south shore of Lama Passage.

The once charming homes of Ocean Falls are now in disrepair.

Children love visiting the Fairy Rock for hidden coins at Ocean Falls, a long-standing tradition from years past.

See Area Map Page 443 - Maps Not for Navigation   NORTHERN B.C. COAST

Visit Lizzie Cove for a genuine taste of island living.

It's a beautiful little spot, with an obvious anchoring nook on its eastern shore just inside the entrance. Unfortunately, the holding ground is only fair. We tried twice to get a good set in the little nook and once farther out, but each time we dragged without much effort. We would overnight in settled weather only. Study the chart before entering. Leave Gus Island and the little dot islet west of Gus Island to port as you approach.

Lizzie Cove. Monitors VHF 10. Their hospitality has been a favorite of cruisers for many years. Pete and Rene Darwin moved their floats, BBQ shelter, and gift shop from Namu to Lizzie Cove. Tucked inside the southeast end of Lizzie Cove, there is 100 feet of side-tie moorage for visitors and overnight guests. Cash only. No power or water. Don't miss the gift shop filled with custom-made wood working items and other crafts. Their self-sufficient gardens are impressive and include a hothouse with fruit trees.

Two routes, Hogan Rock Route and Gus Island Route bring you into Lizzie Cove from Lama Passage. Two privately maintained buoys mark the channel for red right returning to Lizzie Cove from Lama Passage. Buoys are privately maintained and may not be in place; red and green markings may be faded or obscured by marine growth. Bow watch is recommended.

Hogan Rock Route - leave Hogan Rock and the awash rock northwest of Hogan Rock to port; then proceed south-southwest passing the reef that dries at 3-meters to port and the private red buoy marker to starboard; then turn west-northwest passing the private green marker buoy, which marks the 41-meter island shoal, to port; and wrap around the 41-meter island. Give the northwest end of 41-meter island shoal a wide berth. Gus Island Route – leave Gus Island to port; proceed south-southwest; then turn northwest, passing 41-meter island to port and the reef that dries at 2.1-meters to starboard; and wrap around the 41-meter island, passing the private green marker buoy to port and the private red buoy marker to starboard. Give the northwest end of 41-meter island shoal a wide berth.

Jane Cove. Jane Cove, on the south shore of Lama Passage in Cooper Inlet, offers shelter but lacks scenic quality. Study the chart carefully before entering to avoid shoals and rocks. Fannie Cove, despite its marginal holding, or Fancy Cove, which is spectacular by comparison, are preferred.

⑤ **New Bella Bella.** New Bella Bella (Waglisla) is a major Native village, with fuel, potable water, garbage drop, and a grocery store and nice cafe; cell phone service is good. The village has a hospital. The closest laundromat is at Shearwater. The BC Ferries terminal is located south of town.

The main pier and floats are busy with water taxis and local boat traffic. Moorage is filled with commercial and local boats; there is no transient moorage but always room for a dinghy. The fuel dock (250-957-2440) has gas and diesel, call ahead for service. The attendants are courteous, but religious about closing during their lunch hour. You may have to be patient. New Bella Bella's water treatment plant provides a steady stream of clear, potable water at the fuel dock.

A new, large grocery store opened in 2018 and includes a bakery and meat department. This is a fun place to shop for gifts and food items to re-stock your galley. The supply barge arrives weekly on Sundays. Just north of this store is the Waglisla Senior Centre, with native artwork. The locals are friendly and eager to share their stories. Visitors are also welcome to tour the K-12 Bella Bella Community School.

Guests at Shearwater can take the water taxi to New Bella Bella to shop at the band store or to drop off or pick up passengers or parts from the airport. Scheduled airline service runs throughout the day.

The New Bella Bella airport is about 2 miles from the village. You can walk along the road or take a taxi. The taxi is often standing by before or after a flight or call (250) 957-2582 or on VHF channel 14. They know the schedules. Wilderness Seaplanes serves New Bella Bella with multiple flights per day.

Bella Bella. Bella Bella (Old Bella Bella) is on Denny Island on the northeastern shore of Lama Passage. The excellent docks and lovely buildings ("Whistler North") house the Coast Guard Search and Rescue vessel *Cape Farewell*, its crew and support staff, and Fisheries and Oceans personnel. No transient moorage.

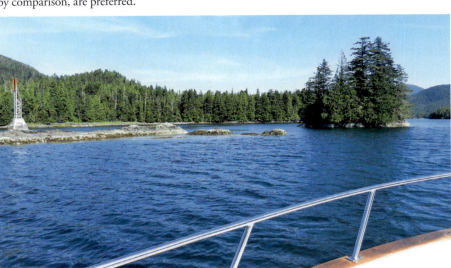

Lizzie Cove

Range markers in Gunboat Passage guide you through the channel.

NORTHERN B.C. COAST   See Area Map Page 443 - Maps Not for Navigation

The sculptures at Shearwater commemorate the area's war veterans.   *Shearwater Marina docks are the crossroads of the Northern BC Coast.*

Kliktsoatli Harbour. Shearwater Resort & Marina is located in Kliktsoatli Harbour, 2 miles east of New Bella Bella on the north side of Denny Island. Good anchorage can be found on the eastern shore.

⑥ **Shearwater Resort & Marina.** (250) 957-2666; moorage@shearwater.ca; hotel@shearwater.ca; www.shearwater.ca. Monitors VHF 66A, the fuel dock monitors VHF 08. Open all year, 1700 feet of guest moorage (200 feet added in 2019), 15, 30 & 50 amp power on the main spine float and on part of the T-ends. Free Wi-Fi and for-fee premium Wi-Fi. Potable water is available on the guest dock. Seasonally, there are two waterlines for different uses; one carries potable water, and the other is for washdown. White hoses carry potable water, and the green hoses are for washdown. Please be sparing and sharing with the potable water. During prime season, register and pay for moorage at the dockside harbourmaster's office, or at the hotel during shoulder season. Moorage reservations are highly recommended during the busy summer months. If the main docks are full, you can moor on the inside of the breakwater docks, no power or water. Cellular service is good.

The fuel dock has diesel, gasoline, lubricants, propane, Avgas and Jet A. On shore you'll find an ATM, washrooms, showers, laundry, ice, restaurant, pub, haulout, launch ramp, facilities for waste oil dump, garbage drop and recycling center. There is a small fee for recycling to cover the costs of barging the material to Richmond B.C. A well-stocked grocery store, liquor store, and marine supply store are on site along with a post office, coffee pastry bar, and gift shop. The showers and laundry room, in the building across from the store, are excellent.

The popular pub, with live entertainment, has a nice deck for outdoor dining. It's a great place to meet other boaters and locals, who often share a table.

Shearwater is the most complete marine facility between Campbell River and Prince Rupert. The shipyard can haul boats to 70

See Area Map Page 443 - Maps Not for Navigation

NORTHERN B.C. COAST

tons and handle almost anything, from toilet repairs to electronics to repowers. They can order parts for you and coordinate their arrival by air if needed. Shearwater has its own 3,000-foot airstrip for private aircraft. Scheduled airline service to Port Hardy and Vancouver is available at New Bella Bella. Shearwater is also a stop for the BC Ferries system. Hunter Helicopter Tours (778-899-0513 or 604-533-9733) can provide airport transfers and sightseeing excursions. The Sea-Bus water taxi connects Shearwater and New Bella Bella (Waglisla) with a 10-minute, 2.5-mile ride. In calm weather you can scoot over in a dinghy. Shearwater is the crossroads of the northern coast and gets a full range of visitors.

The marina was the site of a WWII Royal Canadian Air Force seaplane base. The large historic hangar now serves as the shop. In 2013, Craig Widsten, the principal owner of this family-owned resort, created two special tributes to the heritage of Shearwater and the surrounding area. When a wall of the shop needed replacement, Craig had it rebuilt and commissioned muralist Paul Gartua to paint the images of seventeen people who had an impact on the growth and development of Shearwater. They include tribal leaders, medical professionals, the original manager of the Hudson's Bay Co. outpost, and even Craig's father, Andrew, the founder of Shearwater. Measuring 120 feet wide and 22 feet tall, the mural is quite striking.

Craig also installed a cenotaph to commemorate Shearwater and New Bella Bella residents' war service. He commissioned the casting of a 17-foot scale replica of the Stranraer flying boat that was based at Bella Bella during WWII. Nearby, a carved Eagle pole commemorates First Nations veterans, and an obelisk commemorates other veterans from the area.

Kakushdish Harbour. Kakushdish Harbour, long and narrow, extends into Denny Island immediately east of Kliktsoatli Harbour (Shearwater). An overhead power cable with 23 meters (75 feet) vertical clearance crosses the entrance. "We favored the north shore through the entrance bar and saw a minimum depth of 11 feet, zero tide. Anchor in 20 to 25 feet, good holding in mud. The anchorage was surprisingly deserted and tranquil." [*Hamilton*]

LOCAL KNOWLEDGE

NAVIGATION NOTES: The trickiest spot in Gunboat Passage is the narrow fairway between Denny Point and Maria Island. Use caution to navigate away from the rocks. A second tricky spot is the reef that extends from the southern shore toward Dingle Island. Watch the currents in this area. A red nun buoy marks the outer end of this reef. Red, Right, Returning assumes you are returning eastbound, from the sea. The third tricky spot is the range at the west end of Gunboat Passage. Entering or departing, stay on the range.

Gunboat Passage. Gunboat Passage connects Seaforth Channel with Fisher Channel and is a scenic route between Ocean Falls and New Bella Bella/Shearwater. The passage is littered with reefs and rocks, but all marked with new, upgraded aids to navigation installed by the Canadian Coast Guard in 2019.

Beales Bay. The entrance looks tricky on the chart, but if you leave the small islet to port as you enter, you'll have good water. Anchor inside in 30 to 40 feet. Stay well clear of the mouth of Beales Lagoon. At least two detached drying rocks lie in the cove off the lagoon's mouth. Excellent protection.

Gosse Bay. Gosse Bay is west of Maria Island, a good anchorage on the west side of the westernmost cove.

Forit Bay. Forit Bay, on the eastern approach to Gunboat Passage, is an excellent, protected anchorage in 15 to 25 feet. The entrance, however, is encumbered by a large rock between Flirt Island and the point of land that marks the inner part of the bay. The rock is not visible at high tide, but is visible through the water at a little less than half tide.

Enter Forit Bay by wrapping around the north tip of Flirt Island, leaving the island to port.

BURKE CHANNEL, DEAN CHANNEL, BELLA COOLA

Burke Channel and Dean Channel border the south and north sides of King Island and plunge deep into the Coast Range mountains. This is some of the most beautiful and awe-inspiring country imaginable, but after seeing so much beautiful country all along the B.C. coast, we expected it to be just more of the same. We were wrong. A circumnavigation of King Island will astonish you. Gone is the raw coast with its low, wave-pounded islands. A short distance up either channel puts you inland, bounded on each side by high mountains. If you're going to spend some time on this coast, see these waters.

LOCAL KNOWLEDGE

EBB CURRENT: On warm summer days, heating of inland air produces an up-channel sea breeze in Burke Channel that can begin as early as 10:00 a.m. and blow strongly until sundown. Make your runs early and find shelter before the wind starts blowing.

TIDE-RIPS: The surface water in Burke Channel is often in an almost constant ebb, the result of fresh water flowing toward the sea. When this surface ebb meets a spring flood, tide-rips, whirlpools, and general confusion results.

Burke Channel. Burke Channel leads 38 miles inland, beginning at Edmund Point, just north of Namu. From Edmund Point to Restoration Bay, the lower reaches of Burke Channel are subject to strong tidal currents and heavy tide-rips, but in the upper reaches the tidal streams are weak.

The north end of Burke Channel divides into South Bentinck Arm and North Bentinck Arm (Bella Coola is at the head of North Bentinck Arm), and Labouchere Passage, which leads to Dean Channel. When the ebb current is flowing and the up-channel sea breeze is blowing, expect rough seas at the confluence of these channels. Early morning, before the B.C. interior heats up, is often the calmest time of day.

All these cautions make Burke Channel sound impenetrable, which isn't the case. The

Shearwater Marine Resort

2020 Waggoner Cruising Guide 453

NORTHERN B.C. COAST

See Area Map Page 443 - Maps Not for Navigation

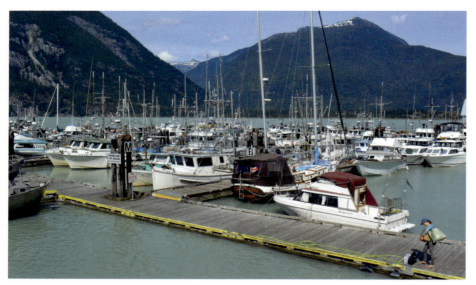

The Bella Coola docks look more spacious in this photo than when we were trying to raft off in 20-knot winds.

prudent skipper simply will avoid being out there in the wrong conditions.

The best anchorage along Burke Channel is at the head of Kwatna Inlet, with a second-best choice being the small cove just north of Cathedral Point.

Fougner Bay. Fougner Bay is near the mouth of Burke Channel on the south side, just east of Edmund Point. The outer part of the bay is somewhat protected, with anchorage in 40 to 60 feet. To us it feels uninviting. An inner cove, however, is a perfect spot.

Find the 4.1-meter sounding back in the bay. That's the cove. To get in, the chart shows good water by leaving the + symbol (indicating a dangerous underwater rock 2 meters or less at zero tide) to starboard. Once clear of the rock, loop into the back cove. Very cozy and protected. Study the chart carefully before entering Fougner Bay. The rocks off the entry are easy to avoid, but you want to know where they are and where you are.

Kwatna Inlet. Kwatna Inlet extends some 12 miles into the mainland and is too deep for anchoring until near the head. Watch carefully for the drying flats at the head. We are told by several people that it is an excellent place to put the hook down.

Cathedral Point. Cathedral Point, a weather reporting station, marks the north entrance to Kwatna Inlet, and is easily identified by its white building and tower. Just north of the point, a tiny cove with dramatic granite walls makes a good anchorage in 25 feet. The cove has excellent protection from up-channel winds, but the mass of large logs on the south beach suggests that down-channel winds and seas blow right in. We patrolled the cove but did not stay. Early Correspondent Bill Hales, from Victoria, anchored for the night and reported a pleasant experience.

South Bentinck Arm. South Bentinck Arm, 25 miles long, lies between high mountains. The relatively few cruisers who have gone all the way up the arm say it is beautiful. We have gone as far as Larso Bay, which has good anchorage in 35 to 70 feet. The mountains across from Larso Bay are beautiful. Correspondent Gil Flanagan found one of the largest red cedars in B.C. by walking about 1 km up a logging road that begins in the north part of the bay. The tree is on the right side of the road, marked with a plaque.

Tallheo Hot Springs. Tallheo Hot Springs is about one-quarter mile north of the mouth of Hotsprings Creek on the west shore of South Bentinck Arm, a short distance south of Bensins Island. Anchorage is exposed.

North Bentinck Arm. The water in North Bentinck Arm is green and milky, the result of the Bella Coola River emptying into the head of the arm. We found no good anchorages, so you have to hope for room at the Bella Coola docks. Watch for drift. Windy Bay is on the south side of North Bentinck Arm, near the junction with Burke Channel. When we crossed the mouth of Windy Bay in early afternoon we learned how it got its name. Whew!

LOCAL KNOWLEDGE

WEATHER TIP: The wind can blow almost constantly at Bella Coola, making for rough seas going in or out. There aren't many places to hide from the weather, either. Be aware of the tendency for strong inflow and outflow winds before deciding to go to Bella Coola.

⑦ **Bella Coola.** Bella Coola is seldom visited by yachts but interesting nonetheless. The government floats are run by the Bella Coola Harbour Authority, and they are making improvements. Water is available on the docks, shore power, washrooms, and showers are available as well.

The Columbia Fuels fuel dock is adjacent to the public floats.

Correspondent Gil Flanagan says the best way to visit is to overnight in Larso Bay in South Bentinck Arm or Eucott Bay on Dean Channel, and come over in the morning. A visitor at the Seattle Boat Show recommended anchoring in Bryneldsen Bay, near the north end of Labouchere Channel, and going to Bella Coola early the next morning. Use Chart 3974. Bryneldsen Bay is behind the thumb of land that extends southeast, approximately 0.8 miles from Ram Bluff. The bay is not labeled, but Chart 3974 does show an anchor symbol beside it.

The town of Bella Coola is 3 kilometers (about 2 miles) from the dock. Taxis may be available. The Bella Coola Estuary makes for a beautiful stroll. Stay on the water side of the road, since it's wider and safer for walking.

We urge you to see the Bella Coola Museum, housed in buildings dating from 1892 and 1898. It is on the edge of town along the road from the marina. Bella Coola is where, in 1793, Alexander Mackenzie touched saltwater on his transcontinental crossing of Canada. Much of the museum's display

Bella Coola

454   www.WaggonerGuide.com

is about Mackenzie. We bought a booklet of Mackenzie's journal entries (including comment about the unrelenting wind) in the Bella Coola and Dean Channel area.

The town has provincial and federal government offices, a post office, hospital, motel, liquor store, laundromat, showers, and a well-stocked co-op grocery store and Moore's Organic Market. Take a tour of the area on the Bella Coola Valley Bus for $2.50; call (250) 799-0079 before 8:00 p.m. the day before you want to ride the bus.

Correspondents Bruce and Margaret Evertz add the following: "A worthwhile attraction in this area are the petroglyphs. The Native band wants them preserved, so they are not marked on any maps. Guides may be available. You can get information about them at the museum."

Correspondents Gil and Karen Flanagan report that rental cars are available (Bella Coola Vehicle Rentals 250-957-7072). "We put about 150 miles on a Dodge Caravan, all on good paved roads. The spectacular drive to Tweedsmuir Park inland is rated as one of the 10 most scenic drives in Canada."

Bella Coola is the B.C. Interior's window on the coast. Each year, a remarkable number of boats are trailered from the Interior to Bella Coola, where they stay the summer, either tied to the dock or on trailers.

⑦ **Bella Coola Harbour Authority.** P.O. Box 751, Bella Coola, BC V0T 1C0; (250) 799-5633; bellacoolaharbour@gmail.com. They try to monitor VHF channels 06 & 16. Open all year with guest moorage. Facilities include 20 & 30 amp power (20 amp shore power breakers have 20 amp receptacles—bring adaptor), water, washrooms, laundry and showers (showers closed November through March), tidal grid, garbage drop, waste oil drop, pumpout, launch ramp, pay phones, Wi-Fi. Fuel dock adjacent. The harbor office is at the head of the pier. Office hours June through September 8:00 a.m. to 6:00 p.m. and off season Monday through Saturday 8:00 a.m. to 12:00 p.m.

Float "A" is dedicated for visiting pleasure craft 14 meters and longer. The float is exposed to westerly winds. Smaller boats can tie up there, but if a boat 14 meters or longer arrives, the smaller boats will have to move.

Bella Coola is a popular launch point for trailerable boats. The Harbour Authority has added additional boat launch floats to make launching and retrieving easier.

The marina is tight and the wind can blow almost constantly. Rafting is required. If necessary, take temporary moorage at the loading zone. Put out lots of fenders, both sides. Of all the places we have landed, Bella Coola is one of the most challenging.

The floats are located south of a rock breakwater, behind a floating log breakwater. They are home port to a large number of commercial fish boats. All of A dock and the south side of B dock are reserved for pleasure craft, however. You may have to raft to a permanent boat. The channel on the land side of A dock is narrow, especially at low tide. Feel your way in and find a spot.

Now that the local Harbour Authority is running the facility, more interest is devoted to visiting boaters. Even so, Bella Coola is not a "resort marina." Self-reliance is the key.

Columbia Fuels Fuel Dock. (250) 799-5580. Open Monday through Friday 9:00 a.m. to 4:00 p.m. all year. Call (250) 305-8333 for off-hours service. Gasoline, diesel, lubricants. Dwayne Saugstad is the manager. Dwayne's great-great-grandfather led the original band of Norwegian settlers to Bella Coola. Dwayne's great-grandfather remained, as did Dwayne's grandfather, Dwayne's father, and now Dwayne and his two children. All have called or presently call Bella Coola their home. Six generations.

Labouchere Channel. Labouchere Channel connects the north end of Burke Channel with Dean Channel. **Mesachie Nose**, at the confluence of the two channels, is a magnificent glacier-smoothed rock prominence on the north shore. Tidal currents combined with winds and surface water runoff can create very difficult seas in this area. If the water is flat, see Mesachie Nose, up close.

The waters of Labouchere Channel itself are generally smooth and wind-free. The scenery, with waterfalls spilling from high mountains, is fabulous. Our notes say, "So many waterfalls!"

LOCAL KNOWLEDGE

WEATHER TIP: Strong up-channel sea breezes can develop when warm temperatures in the Interior heat the air and suck cold ocean air up the various inlets. This sea breeze can begin as early as 10:00 a.m. and last until sundown. Because summertime freshets often create a nearly permanent ebb surface current, an ugly chop can develop when the wind blows against the current.

This monument marks Sir Alexander Mackenzie Rock, where Mackenzie ended his overland westward explorations in 1793.

Dean Channel. Dean Channel connects with Fisher Channel at the mouth of Cousins Inlet (Ocean Falls) and continues 53 miles northward. It is bordered on both sides by high mountains; Burke Channel offers some of the finest scenery along the coast. In Dean Channel we felt as if we were high up in the mountains on a huge lake, like we should be chewing gum to clear our ears. The concept of being at sea level in these surroundings was hard to grasp.

The principal points of interest on Dean Channel are Elcho Harbour, Sir Alexander Mackenzie Rock, and Eucott Bay and hot springs. Cascade Inlet is stunning, but not a good place to anchor.

Jenny Inlet. If Jenny Inlet were someplace else it might be interesting. But we found it ordinary, too deep for anchoring, with a logging camp near the head. Elcho Harbour, 8 miles farther up Dean Channel, or Cousins Inlet (Ocean Falls), 5 miles down-channel, are better choices.

Elcho Harbour. If you are looking for a scenic spot, Elcho Harbour qualifies. It's stunning. The inlet reaches a little more than 2 miles back between steep high mountains, and appears perfectly protected from all winds. Waterfalls plummet from the sides. A lovely bowl is at the head of the inlet, with the obligatory stream that creates an estuary and mudflat. Anchor in 90 to 110 feet off a delightful waterfall on the west side, about one-third of the way in. Or anchor at the head in 90 feet before it shelves up to mudflat. Take the dinghy back out to Sir Alexander Mackenzie Rock for a little history.

Sir Alexander Mackenzie Rock. Sir Alexander Mackenzie Rock is marked by a cairn at the mouth to Elcho Harbour. On 22 July 1793 Mackenzie completed his overland journey across Canada to the Pacific Ocean, and marked his accomplishment with ochre paint on the rock. Later, the inscription was

NORTHERN B.C. COAST

See Area Map Page 443 - Maps Not for Navigation

carved into the stone. You can bring the boat right up to the monument, watching for underwater rocks close to shore, and take your own picture of it. Or you can anchor out and dinghy ashore, leaving somebody aboard in case the wind kicks up.

Apparently, Mackenzie ended his westward trek here because the waters beyond were Bella Bella Indian country, and his Bella Coola Indian guides could not guarantee safety. A few miles west on the north side of Dean Channel, ochre pictographs on white cliffs are thought to be boundary markers. They are a short distance east of Frenchman Creek. We found the pictographs about 0.6 nautical miles south of the daymark near Hokonson Point.

Eucott Bay. Eucott Bay is a gorgeous spot, about as pretty as any we have anchored in. The mountains along the eastern and northeastern sides remind us of Yosemite. Photographers, bring your camera—Half Dome exists in Eucott Bay. Eucott Hot Springs is near the head of the bay, inshore of a line of pilings. The hot springs have been improved with concrete to make an excellent soaking basin. The water used to be too hot for soaking, but now the temperature can be adjusted.

Craig Widsten, principal owner of Shearwater Marine Resort, told us that in 1948 his father and he journeyed to Eucott Bay to pack mud and hot spring water for sale to health and beauty fanatics in Europe. We're sure it was elegant—hot spring water and mud from the remote Canadian coast, to smooth away the wrinkles and cure what ails you.

Enter Eucott Bay along the east (starboard) side. We are told the entrance has silted up, and is much shallower than charted. Once inside, a large basin unfolds. Find a good spot in the middle and put the hook down. Take the dinghy up to the hot springs. Insect repellant might be needed to protect against deer flies ("those man-eating winged demons," one reader wrote). At low tide wear boots. The beach is muddy.

Nascall Bay. Nascall Hot Springs is near the mouth of Nascall Bay. You'll recognize the buildings by their blue roofs. Previous owners had ambitious development plans, but they didn't work out. The facility is private with posted No Trespassing signs.

SEAFORTH CHANNEL, MILBANKE SOUND, FINLAYSON CHANNEL

Navigation Note: Although Seaforth Channel is connected with the sea, west of Lama Passage the buoyage system defines "returning from the sea" as returning from south to north, not west to east. If you are outbound in Seaforth Channel, west of Lama Passage you will leave red aids to navigation (buoys, beacons, lights) to starboard (Red, Right, Returning from the south). If you are inbound in Seaforth Channel, west of Lama Passage, leave red aids-to-navigation to port.

"Returning from the sea" changes at Lama Passage. East of Lama Passage, inbound vessels will leave red buoys, beacons and lights to starboard.

Seaforth Channel. Seaforth Channel connects the New Bella Bella/Shearwater area with Milbanke Sound to the west and is part of the Inside Passage route. Ivory Island is at the western entrance.

Troup Passage. Troup Passage runs between Chatfield Island and Cunningham Island, and leads to Roscoe Inlet. Troup Narrows is at the northern end. Near the southern end of Troup Passage an unnamed bay sometimes called Discovery Cove is an excellent anchorage.

Discovery Cove. Discovery Cove at lat 52°13.50'N, unnamed on the charts, is the only major indent of Cunningham Island from Troup Passage. It was first recommended to us by John and Evonne MacPherson, who spent many summers cruising the coast in their perfectly-maintained 45-foot Grenfell, *Malacandra*. The chart shows rocks on the southwest shore of the entry, but if you go in along the northeast shore you'll have no problems. This is one of the most beautiful coves on the coast. It is surrounded by mountains and seemingly immune to any storm winds that might be about. Anchor in either of the two nooks along the north shore or the area to the east.

Troup Narrows. Troup Narrows, with maximum tidal currents of only about 2 knots, is easily run. Assuming a passage from south to north, identify the reef that dries 15 feet near the south entrance to the narrows. Leave the reef to port, and slide west to the beautiful rock cliffs of Chatfield Island. Stay on the Chatfield Island side until the point of land on Cunningham Island is abeam, then trend east to the far shore of Cunningham Island to avoid the reef that extends from the 65-meter island. Study the chart to find the rocks you must avoid.

Roscoe Inlet. Roscoe Inlet is drop-dead beautiful. Beginning where Johnson Channel meets Return Channel, Roscoe Inlet winds some 21 miles back through high mountains that plunge straight down into the sea. Exquisite bowls and valleys lead into the mountains. Sheer cliffs tower overhead. In some places you can bring the boat alongside a vertical granite wall that rises to a mountain peak 3600 feet above and still have more than 450 feet of water below. Dramatic.

Good anchorages are scarce. For a day trip, we suggest motoring up in the morning, dropping the hook for lunch at the head of the inlet, and motoring back in the afternoon. You can overnight, of course.

Other than the head of the inlet, in our opinion **Boukind Bay** is the easiest anchorage along the way. A large, 25- to 30-foot-deep area allows plenty of room to swing. If an inflow wind is blowing, however, it might be a little bouncy. **Quartcha Bay** is a visually stunning anchorage, although deep until close to the sides or the mud flats at the head. Waterfalls tumble down the mountain sides. From near the head you can look back into two glacier-polished bowls of rock (called cirques) and extensive meadows. Correspondent Gil Flanagan reports that

Roscoe Inlet has some of the most awe-inspiring scenery on the coast.

Ivory Island Lighthouse marks the decision point, a northeast turn to protected Reid Passage, or continue west up Milbanke Sound.

evidence of ancient fish traps can be found on the large tide flats. **Shack Bay** and **Ripley Bay** are exposed to inflow winds, and deep until very close to shore. We didn't like them. **Clatse Bay**, at the south end of Roscoe Inlet, is a good anchorage. Go all the way to the head and anchor in 40 to 50 feet.

Bugs: Several readers have warned about ravenous deer flies. Bring insect repellant.

Morehouse Bay. Morehouse Bay, indenting Chatfield Island off Return Channel, has a lovely one-boat anchorage (more, if all are stern-tied to shore) in a cove at the very back, or room for more boats in 60-foot depths outside the back cove. To enter the outer anchorage, leave the 53-meter island to port and the 44- and 59-meter islands to starboard. The more secluded back cove is in the south part of the bay, behind the 59-meter island. Leave a large rock, shown as a 1.2-meter depth, to starboard as you enter. The entry is easy—just be sure you know where that rock is. Anchor in 25 to 35 feet.

Wigham Cove. Wigham Cove, on the south shore of Yeo Island, is a popular anchorage and an excellent place to overnight before transiting Seaforth Channel. Favor the west shore as you enter, until abeam the islets in the middle of the bay. Then turn to pass north of the islets to the favored anchorage in the northeast nook of the cove, which has room for several boats. We have shared this anchorage with a 60-footer and a 43-footer with no crowding at all.

Dangerous rock: Be careful if you enter the southernmost nook of Wigham Cove. A dangerous underwater rock with a depth of 0.5 meters at zero tide is reported lying close to and just east of the northernmost of the three drying rocks that extend from the eastern shore of the entrance to Wigham Cove. When entering this nook, favor the islets to the east.

Spiller Channel. Spiller Channel and Bullock Channel run north from Seaforth Channel on either side of Yeo Island and lead to famed Ellerslie Lagoon, whose entrance rocks have bumped many a boat. Neither run is particularly scenic. Compared with other areas, the hillsides are low.

Neekas Cove, across the channel from the north tip of Yeo Island, is the only easy anchorage in the southern part of Spiller Channel. Yeo Cove, near the south entrance to Spiller Channel, has a rock-studded entry and only limited anchorage deep in the southeast corner. Tate Lagoon, which leads into Don Peninsula, has a treacherous entrance. This lagoon is shown as unnamed on Chart 3940. Douglass describes both places.

The top of Spiller Channel is a little better. The hidden anchorage Douglass calls "Nash Narrows Cove" is lovely. Decent anchorage can be found in the bay immediately south of Ellerslie Lagoon.

Neekas Cove. Neekas Cove is opposite the north tip of Yeo Island in Spiller Channel. The cove is narrow and pretty, but deep until close to the head, where the bottom shelves rapidly. Anchor in 50 feet (zero tide) if cautious; 35 feet if braver; less, at your peril. Watch for bears on the shore here.

Nash Passage. Nash Passage (Douglass' name for this otherwise unnamed winding channel), separates Coldwell Peninsula from a good-sized unnamed island on the approach to Ellerslie Bay, just before Spiller Inlet. The chart shows rocks, but the ones to watch out for dry at 4.3 meters, so they should be visible much of the time.

Nash Narrows Cove (Douglass' name again), is the little cove at the turn of Nash Passage. It is beautiful, and would be a good spot to put the hook down.

A peninsula separates Ellerslie Lagoon from a substantial bay immediately to the south. Anchorage is in the inner bay, east of an islet in the middle of the fairway. Pass either side of the islet. Our preferred spot is in 60 feet (zero tide) on the south side, under a towering cliff. The north side of the bay might get down to 40-foot depths, but isn't as protected or cozy feeling.

Ellerslie Lagoon. Because of dangerous rocks, a spring tide high water entry is called for. Two sets of narrows lead in. Ellerslie Lake pours a lot of water into the lagoon; expect the outflowing current through the narrows to last longer than usual.

Spiller Inlet. Spiller Inlet extends northward from the top of Spiller Channel. The sides are steep and the water is deep until near the head, where the depths shoal rapidly to a shelf. Near the head of the inlet, the granite cliff on the east side has fractured and fallen away to create Weeping Woman, a Picasso-like natural sculpture on the mountainside. It's quite dramatic.

Bullock Channel. Bullock Channel is a straight run between Return Channel and the top of Yeo Island. Study the chart and favor the Coldwell Peninsula side of the channel. The shoal areas on the Yeo Island side have a tendency to be right where you think you should be going.

The only good Bullock Channel anchorages are on the Coldwell Peninsula side—one at the south end, the other at the north end (where we overnighted). We checked the purported anchorages on the Yeo Island side, but they weren't satisfactory. We found poor holding in the northernmost anchorage, and rock, rock, rock in the bight a little south of the north anchorage.

The water is warm near the top of both channels. In colder waters we like our cabin heat in the morning, but we had no need for it there. [Hale]

Bullock Channel North Cove. This is Douglass' name for the otherwise unnamed anchorage behind the 39-meter island at the north end of Bullock Channel, on the Coldwell Peninsula side. We found excellent overnight holding in 50 feet (zero tide) opposite the west opening to the cove. The chart shows a rock awash at zero tide in this west opening. Enter and depart this cove from the north.

Bullock Spit Cove. Again, Douglass' name for this unnamed anchorage located inside the 70-meter island on the Coldwell Peninsula side, near the south entrance to Bullock Channel. As the chart shows, you don't want to go very far in or you'll run aground. We found good holding in 35 feet just south of the tip of the island.

Kynumpt Harbour. Kynumpt Harbour indents the north tip of Campbell Island, east of Raymond Passage. Sailing Directions says the local name is Strom Bay. The entrance is

NORTHERN B.C. COAST   See Area Map Page 443 - Maps Not for Navigation

The marker and its concrete base in Reid Passage was replaced in 2019.

open and easy, but study the chart carefully to identify and avoid rocks on the western and southern shores. The northernmost indent on the eastern shore is reported to be a good anchorage, as is Strom Cove, the arm that extends to the southeast. We poked around Strom Cove to find a good lunch stop, but saw mostly 55 to 75 feet on the sounder. At those depths, even a 3:1 scope would swing us too close to rocks near shore, so we anchored in the outer bay, 40 feet, west of Spratt Point.

Dundivan Inlet. Dundivan Inlet indents Dufferin Island west of Raymond Passage. It's a pretty spot with several islets to break up the scenery, but the water is deep except near hazards. Two arms make up Lockhart Bay, near the head. The western arm is the more attractive anchorage. For overnight we would run a stern-tie to a tree. The eastern arm is deep (60 feet) until very near the head and requires a stern-tie. Dundivan Inlet would not be our first choice unless weather was ugly and we were looking for a place to hole up.

Raymond Passage. Raymond Passage connects Seaforth Channel with Queens Sound and sees few pleasure craft. The passage is open, free of hazards, and connects with Codfish Passage at the south end. If you're looking for a raw and exposed wilderness experience and have the boat and navigation skills to manage it, Raymond Passage is a good choice.

Thompson Bay. Thompson Bay is on the west side of Potts Island. Examine the area on your chartplotter or study Chart 3938. This entire area is beautiful and seldom visited. At the northeast corner of Thompson Bay an excellent, protected cove indents Potts Island. Enter the cove from the north, at 52°09.75'N/128°20.75'W.

To get from Raymond Passage to Thompson Bay, run a course of approximately 239° magnetic from the southern tip of Alleyne Island to the 45-meter island, then turn to a course of approximately 292° magnetic to Agnew Islet. You will leave Seen Island approximately one-quarter mile to the south. Rocks will be all around you, but stay in the pass and you will have water.

St. John Harbour. Enter from the north, leaving red buoy *E46*, marking Rage Reefs, to starboard. Several floating fishing resorts are around Dyer Cove. We prefer the back cove; be sure to avoid the drying shoal. The shallowest point of the channel is at least 7 feet deep. Holding is good.

Milbanke Sound. Milbanke Sound is the shortest route north or south for boats trying to make time along the Inside Passage. In quiet conditions Milbanke Sound is easy. But if the wind is blowing the crossing can be brutal.

From Seaforth Channel to Finlayson Channel, leave Ivory Island to starboard and lay a course that passes north of Susan Rock and west of Vancouver Rock Buoy *E54*. From there, lay a course to the mouth of Finlayson Channel. Our course took us fairly close to Jorkins Point and the east side of Swindle Island. Total distance was about 12 miles. We've seen boats pass east of Vancouver Rock and take Merilia Passage. This saves about a mile.

Tuno Creek Anchorage. "At the south end of Reid Passage, Blair Inlet extends nearly 2 miles eastward into the Don Peninsula. Tuno Creek empties into the head of Blair Inlet. Anchor south of the creek in 25 to 30 feet, good holding over mud. Strong westerly winds probably will reach the anchorage, but wind protection is good from other directions." [*Hamilton*]

Reid Passage & Port Blackney. If there's much wind at all, most pleasure craft headed north or south will avoid Milbanke Sound and use the Reid Passage route east of Ivory Island. Chart 3910 makes navigation straightforward. At the south end, be sure to identify all the rocks and islets, and Buoy *E50*. In the middle of Reid Passage, pass to the east of Carne Rock. Port Blackney, at the north end of Reid Passage, has two anchorages, Boat Inlet and Oliver Cove, that can be used before crossing to Perceval Narrows.

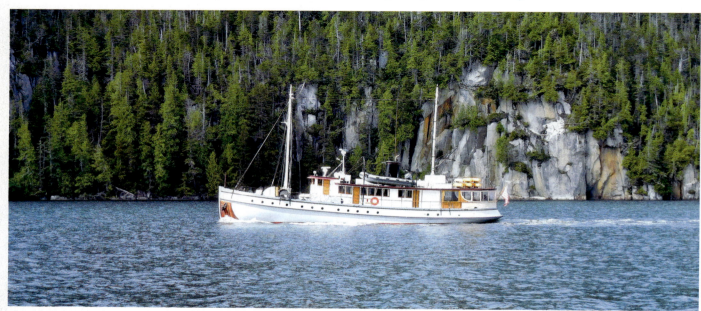

Majestic motor vessel on her way into Pruth Bay in Kwakshua Channel

NORTHERN B.C. COAST

Boat Inlet. Boat Inlet, at the southwest corner of Port Blackney, has a delightful basin for anchorage, with an untouched feeling. The passage that leads to the basin is shallow, however, and rocks encumber the south shore and middle of the channel. Favor the north shore all the way in, with an alert lookout for underwater rocks. The little bay on the north shore at the east end of the passage is shallow and rocky. Stay out. Depending on your vessel's draft, wait for half tide or higher before running Boat Inlet.

Oliver Cove. Oliver Cove Marine Provincial Park, on the east side of Port Blackney, is a safe and pretty anchorage. Enter carefully, avoiding a charted rock in the middle of the fairway and another on the south side. Put the hook down in 35 feet. A few years ago we saw a bear and her cubs on the rocky shore.

Perceval Narrows. The Inside Passage route leads across Mathieson Channel between Port Blackney and Perceval Narrows. Tidal current predictions are found as a secondary station under Prince Rupert in Tide and Current Tables, Vol. 7 and Ports and Passes. From south to north, lay a course that gives Cod Reefs a good offing to port as you leave Port Blackney. Then turn to approximately 270° magnetic and cross Mathieson Channel toward Martha Island, leaving Lizzie Rocks to starboard. We found turbulence in Mathieson Channel off Lizzie Rocks on an ebb tide.

Cockle Bay/Lady Douglas Island. Cockle Bay, a short distance north of Perceval Narrows, has a beautiful beach and good protection from westerlies. You can find 30- to 35-foot depths along the south shore and 60 to 90 feet in the middle, as shown on the chart.

Tom Bay. Tom Bay is on the east side of Mathieson Channel at lat 52°24.20'N. It's a good anchorage, though scarred by recent logging. As with most bays on this coast, Tom Bay shoals at the head. Anchor in 60 to 70 feet.

Dowager Island & Arthur Island. The coves north of Arthur Island, approximately 1.5 miles south of Oscar Passage on the west side of Mathieson Channel, are mentioned in Sailing Directions as a small boat anchorage. Neither cove is very scenic and driftwood clogs the eastern cove. We would choose Rescue Bay on Susan Island, Salmon Bay to the north, or Tom Bay to the south.

Salmon Bay. Salmon Bay is on the east side of Mathieson Channel, opposite the mouth of Oscar Passage. It is deep until the very head, where the bottom comes up to 50 to 60 feet. The bay is cozy and we heard a loon—always a soothing sound.

Oscar Passage. Oscar Passage is the wide-open Inside Passage route between Mathieson Channel and Finlayson Channel. On an ebb, however, the seas can heap up where Oscar

The view while anchored in Rescue Bay on the east end of Jackson Passage

Passage joins Finlayson Channel, the result of swells from Milbanke Sound meeting outflowing current. Larger vessels often use Oscar Passage rather than Jackson Passage.

Rescue Bay. Rescue Bay is the most popular anchorage in this area. It is well protected with good holding, and has room for many boats. Study the chart carefully before entering, and steer a determined mid-channel course between the two islands and their reefs that mark the entrance. Once inside Rescue Bay, scout around with the depth sounder and pick your spot carefully. We saw one boat on the western side find the bottom at low tide, after being too eager to get the anchor down.

Note the drying rock in the southeast corner of the bay. Note also the drying reef that extends from the east side of the bay, south of the round islet. The reef covers at high water, and we anchored a little close to it. After checking things out by dinghy and seeing how near the reef was, we re-anchored farther out. At low water the reef showed itself. We were glad we had moved.

Jackson Passage. Jackson Passage is the scenic route between Mathieson Channel and Finlayson Channel. The passage is easily navigated, except for a tight spot at Jackson Narrows at the eastern end, where the depth shows as low as 12 feet on the charts. The fairway through the eastern end of Jackson Narrows is quite narrow and shallow; kelp marks the rocks. Larger vessels may prefer Oscar Passage to the south. While neither the chart nor Sailing Directions shows the current directions, our observations from several transits indicate the flood current sets east and the ebb current sets west.

Jackson Narrows is blind. Before entering, either direction, it's a good idea to call ahead on VHF channel 16, low power, to announce your intentions *(Securité, securité, this is the 34-foot motor vessel Happy Days, about to enter Jackson Narrows westbound. Any eastbound traffic please advise, channel one-six).* One year, to our astonishment, a boat approaching from the other end called back on channel 16. Since we were about to enter, the other boat waited until we got through. Strongly favor the south shore all the way through the narrows, and keep a sharp lookout. A transit near high water slack would be the least anxious, although we have gone through at low water slack with no difficulty.

James Bay. James Bay, on the west side of Mathieson Channel, is open to southerly winds, but gets you out of the chop in the channel. It is a pretty spot, but the bottom shoals abruptly in the northwest corner. Anchor in 75 feet, where the little anchor symbol is on the chart.

FIORDLAND RECREATION AREA

The Fiordland Recreation Area was established in 1987, and is some of the most striking country on the coast. The mountains are sheer and beautiful and the wildlife abundant, but anchorages are just about nonexistent. Fortunately, good anchorage can be found in Windy Bay, only a short distance away.

Fiordland begins just east of Bolin Bay at the north end of Sheep Passage, and includes Mussel Inlet and Kynoch Inlet. We include Bolin Bay in this section because it is so pretty, and Windy Bay because it is the best anchorage near Fiordland.

Windy Bay. Windy Bay is on the south shore of Sheep Passage, near the eastern end. The chart shows anchorage in the middle, but more protected anchorage is in 60 feet in what we call Cookie Cove, just east of the little island at the northeast corner of the bay. Excellent holding.

2020 Waggoner Cruising Guide

NORTHERN B.C. COAST

See Area Map Page 443 - Maps Not for Navigation

The size, scale and grandeur of Fiordland are awe inspiring.

Waterfalls abound in Kynoch Inlet.

Bolin Bay. Bolin Bay is set in a bowl of sheer rock mountains with a beautiful drying flat at the head. We didn't anchor, but we did find a few spots with depths of 35 to 60 feet near the head of the bay. With care you might get a safe amount of scope out and stay off the flats. Windy Bay is a better choice.

Oatwish Bay. Oatwish Bay is at the north end of Mussel Inlet. Amazing Lizette Falls will have you reaching for the camera. The bay is too deep for anchoring. We enjoyed lunch there, drifting, engines off.

Poison Cove. At the northeast end of Mussel Inlet lies Poison Cove and Mussel Cove/Mussel River. This is a protected wildlife area for bears and mountain goats which is jointly monitored by BC Parks and the Mussel River Watchmen program. When arriving at the area, boaters should contact the Watchmen on VHF Channel 06. A maximum number of people/boats are allowed in the area at one time. For more information go to www.env.gov.bc.ca/bcparks/explore/parkpgs/fiordland/. The run to the east of Mussel Inlet to Poison Cove left us awestruck. Our notes say, "Poison Cove dwarfed us. I ran out of superlatives."

Kynoch Inlet. Located off Mathieson Channel, Kynoch Inlet is a spectacular deep water fiord with unsurpassed beauty. Words such as amazing, awesome, incomparable and magnificent suggest but do not capture the grandeur of this inlet. Black rock mountains rise straight up and waterfalls spill down the mountain faces. The inlet is so narrow and the sides are so steep that our GPS lost its satellites. The only anchoring in the Inlet is in deeper water off the drying flats of Kainet Creek. Correspondents Elsie and Steve Hulsizer reported in 2018 that waters off Kainet Creek have silted, and they touched bottom with a 6 foot keel where the chart showed 10 meters. They also reported strong inflow afternoon winds blow up Kynoch Inlet; and suggested planning a visit to Culpepper Lagoon during neap tides to provide longer slack water intervals for entering and exiting.

Culpepper Lagoon. Enter or depart Culpepper Lagoon around high water slack. Captain Brian Pemberton, who has been in and out many times, reports that current in the entrance turns at high water for nearby secondary tide station Tom Bay.

Correspondent Bill Hales reports a least depth of 10 to 15 feet at the entrance.

FINLAYSON CHANNEL TO PRINCE RUPERT

Nowish Cove. Nowish Cove is on the east side of Finlayson Channel, south of Jackson Passage, at the entrance to Nowish Inlet. Despite being shown as an anchorage, we weren't impressed. The bottom is 85 feet deep and currents from Nowish Narrows swirl through the bay. If protection is needed from a southerly storm, we would consider this cove. Otherwise, if we were looking for a place to hide and had the time, Bottleneck Inlet, 11 miles farther north, is a better choice.

⑧ **Klemtu.** The fuel dock (250-839-1233) and Kitasoo band store are at the north end of town. Both are open Monday through Saturday, closed for lunch 12:00 p.m. to 1:00 p.m., limited hours Sundays. Boaters may tie-up at the fuel dock when shopping for groceries at the band store as space permits. The band store has an ATM. You'll find gasoline, diesel, propane, stove oil, and ample clear water from the village's water treatment system. The fuel dock faces the channel and wakes from passing boat traffic are apt to bounce you against the dock. Be sure you are well-tied and well-fendered. If the attendant is not in the office shack on the pier, try calling First Nations Fuel on VHF 06 or ask someone in town what the fuel situation is. The fuel dock is closed Sundays, but someone might be available to turn on the pumps.

Klemtu is the last fuel stop until Hartley Bay, approximately 65 miles north. In several recent instances, Hartley Bay has temporarily run out of fuel. Choose fuel stops accordingly.

BC Ferries and Wilderness Seaplanes have scheduled service into Klemtu.

An 11-foot-wide, 210-foot-long concrete dock has been installed in the bay near the village. The dock has no power. The docks can get crowded with local fishing boats and nets are often stacked on the floats. Be prepared to anchor, being mindful of large drying shoals on the south and west sides of the bay.

The village has a K-12 school, good cell

Deep water anchorage at the head of Kynoch Inlet near the entrance to Culpepper Lagoon

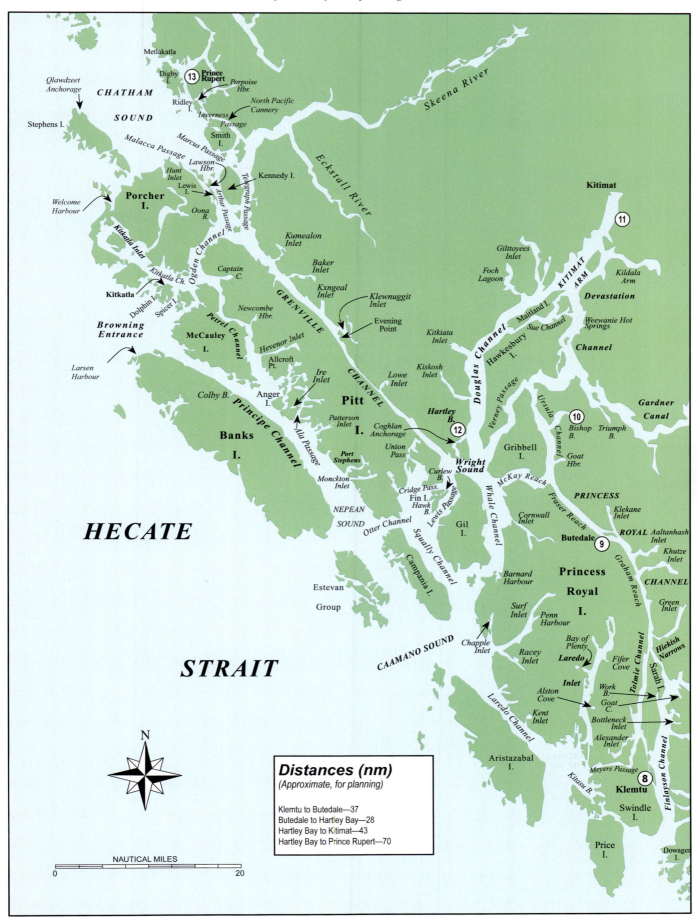

Finlayson Channel to Prince Rupert

NORTHERN B.C. COAST

See Area Map Page 461 - Maps Not for Navigation

The Native village of Klemtu has the Kitasoo Band Store with groceries and fuel.

phone coverage, two nurses, a post office and three stores. We have shopped in two of the stores: the band store at the fuel dock, and Robinson-Mason General Store in the village.

The band store at the head of the fuel dock pier carries a good selection of groceries and other essentials (no liquor), but the stock can thin a few days after scheduled ferry deliveries. On our last visit, we watched the last gallon of milk get snatched up. The store receives supplies only once every two weeks. A small restaurant with breakfast, burgers, and Chinese food is in the entry to the store. You can dine in or order takeout. A pay telephone is just outside the store.

If you'd like to see the extraordinary Bighouse overlooking the harbor, contact the band. Tours are $10 per person. A boardwalk runs around the harbor from the fuel dock to the Bighouse. In 2017 we were surprised to see a medium sized cruise ship stopped at Klemtu. It waited near the ferry landing while its tender shuttled passengers to the Bighouse and Cultural Center.

Clothes Bay. Clothes Bay is south of Klemtu on the west side of the channel between Swindle Island and Cone Island. The bay is well protected except from southeasterly winds. We anchored for the night behind the north tip of Star Island at the mouth of the bay. At low tide, we discovered that the charted "something," extending from Base Point north of us, was a substantial drying reef. The bay has good holding but limited room for only a couple of boats. Being near Klemtu, there is cell phone service in the bay.

Alexander Inlet. Alexander Inlet extends 5 miles into Princess Royal Island, beginning where Meyers Passage and Tolmie Channel meet. If you're fed up with the throngs of boaters and crowded anchorages on this part of the coast (we're joking), here is where you can escape. The early sections of Alexander Inlet are bordered by steep mountains, and are beautiful. The head, however, is surrounded by low hills and is rather ordinary. But, being 5 miles off the beaten path, chances are you'll be the only boat.

The chart shows the inlet well. The only tricky part is near Bingham Narrows. After clearing the drying reef before you reach Bingham Narrows, sag to the west shore to avoid the drying rocks, marked by kelp, just before the narrows themselves.

The head of the inlet is wide open, with ample room to avoid the rock that dries at 2.4 meters lying off the west shore. Anchor in 30 to 35 feet with outstanding holding.

One of the hilltops looks like the profile of a woman lying on her side, and we called it Sleeping Woman. See if you agree. We saw a pair of birds that our field guide identified as red-throated loons, not seen as often as common loons. A lagoon pours into the very head of the inlet, making fluffs of white foam on the water's surface. We rowed over and took pictures, but didn't take the time to explore further. It's very pretty.

The next morning our final note, written after the previous day's notes called the head of Alexander Inlet rather ordinary, reads, "This is a neat spot." [Hale]

OUTSIDE ROUTE – PRINCESS ROYAL ISLAND & PITT ISLAND

At this point we step away from the main Inside Passage route to describe the routes west of Princess Royal and Pitt Islands. Those continuing through Finlayson or Tolmie Channels, past Butedale, and through Grenville Channel will find that information resuming on page 449.

Without question, the preferred Inside Passage route to Prince Rupert and beyond is through Finlayson or Tolmie Channels (past Klemtu), past Butedale, and up through Grenville Channel. The waters are protected, the scenery is outstanding, and there's enough boat traffic that if you have a problem, somebody will be along to help out.

An alternate route is on the outside of Princess Royal and Pitt Islands. This route is popular with sailors and adventuresome power boaters. It's as beautiful as the traditional route, but wilder and much less traveled, with more islands and anchorages but fewer waterfalls. Sailors will find more consistent and stronger winds due to the wider channels and lower hills. There's even room for tacking. Because of their remoteness, we recommend these passages for more experienced cruisers only.

From south to north, the outside route first leads up the west side of Princess Royal Island. It begins by running west through Meyers Passage (near Klemtu), then through Laredo Channel and Whale Channel, and rejoins the Inside Passage at Wright Sound. To cruise the outside of Pitt Island, the route runs west from Wright Sound (south end of Grenville Channel), and north through Principe Channel and Petrel Channel, then east through Ogden Channel to rejoin the Inside Passage.

On the outside of either island you could travel all day and only see one or two other pleasure boats, although you're sure to see a few fish boats, perhaps a tug and barge or even a cruise ship. You'll find good anchorages on the outside. In many cases you'll be the only boat.

Weather permitting, you could travel the traditional Inside Passage going one way and all or part of the outside route going the other. The inside and outside routes are roughly the same distance. However, if you take only part of the outside route, going back and forth between the inside and the outside, your total trip will be longer. If you are considering the outside route, carry Sailing Directions PAC 206, and *Exploring the North Coast of B.C.*, by Don Douglass and Réanne Hemmingway-Douglass. The Waggoner Guide describes only the most direct outside routes and focuses on good anchorages. The other books cover a wider area and describe places that require caution and may be more challenging than some skippers would like. If you have the desire for a coastal cruising challenge, with the boat and skills to meet that challenge, the west coast of Princess Royal Island and Pitt Island are excellent cruising areas.

If winds are favorable, sailboats (or slower powerboats) can cut almost a day off their time on the outside route with an open water passage that avoids Klemtu and Meyers Passage. Northbound exit Seaforth Channel, cross Milbanke Sound, and transit Catala Passage. Or, go around McInnes Island, then north up Laredo Sound to Laredo Inlet. This open water route has no stops until you reach Higgins Passage, so pick your weather window carefully. Pay careful attention to your navigation in Catala Passage. The islands and rocks are easily confused, especially in fog. Watch for cruise ships and freighters that occasionally use Laredo Sound.

WEST SIDE OF SWINDLE ISLAND

Higgins Passage. Higgins Passage connects the north end of Milbanke Sound to Laredo Sound, between Swindle and Price Islands. The middle section of the passage, however, has strong currents, many turns, and dries on a six foot tide.

Anchorage can be found in the western end of Higgins Passage. From Laredo Sound, enter Higgins Passage south of Kipp Islet. **Grant Anchorage** is deep and not well protected from southeast winds. Proceed through the anchorage and anchor in 30 to 40 feet on the west side of **Lohbrunner Island.** This anchorage is well protected from all winds, mud bottom.

Kitasu Bay. Kitasu Bay is between Wilby Point and Meyers Passage. Several anchorages are available, ranging from good to excellent. The bay itself is exposed to northwesterly winds, which blow straight down Laredo Channel into **Parson's Anchorage.** In southeasterly or southwesterly weather, however, Parson's Anchorage provides good holding.

The **Marvin Islands** provide shelter from northwest winds. Anchor on the southeast side of the islands in about 50 feet. Several boats can anchor in this location and be protected from moderate winds. Gale force northwesterly winds can make this anchorage uncomfortable.

Jamieson Point Anchorage (also known as Coward's Cove) is just east of Jamieson Point and provides total protection from all winds. Stay mid-channel when entering to avoid a rock on the west side of the entrance. This rock is usually marked by kelp. Once inside, anchor in 30 to 40 feet over a sticky mud bottom.

The eastern basin of **Osment Inlet** provides good anchorage in most weather but the bottom is rocky and irregular.

WEST SIDE OF PRINCESS ROYAL ISLAND

Meyers Passage. Meyers Passage separates Swindle Island and Princess Royal Island and is the low-anxiety way to travel between Finlayson Channel and Laredo Sound. The only tricky spot is kelp-choked Meyers Narrows. Although the narrows are not difficult to run, kelp may be present. Current can run to 3 knots in the narrows.

See Area Map Page 461 - Maps Not for Navigation

We went through slowly, avoiding the kelp as best we could. When we got through we said, "Piece of cake."

Field Correspondents Jim Norris and Anita Fraser confirmed that there's good anchorage in 45 feet in the bay on the south shore of the passage.

LOCAL KNOWLEDGE

NAVIGATION NOTE: Red spar Buoy *E70* is in the middle of the tight spot in Meyers Passage. Pass north of the buoy, midway between the buoy and the north shore. Currents to 3 knots flood east and ebb west. Sailing Directions says least depth at zero tide is 4 feet. Kelp shows the places to avoid.

Laredo Channel. Laredo Channel separates Princess Royal Island and Aristazabal Island, and connects Laredo Sound at the south end with Caamaño Sound and Campania Sound at the north end. Aristazabal Island, on the west side of Laredo Channel, is incompletely charted and considered extremely challenging.

While several inlets lead off Laredo Channel into Princess Royal Island, Laredo Inlet at the south end and Surf Inlet at the north end are the major indents.

LOCAL KNOWLEDGE

INACCURATE CHART: We've heard reports that Chart 3737 is based on an unknown datum, resulting in significant inaccuracies. Electronic charts based on Chart 3737 have similar inaccuracies.

Laredo Inlet. Laredo Inlet is about 10 miles long, and is well protected from westerly storms. If you're approaching from the south, such as from Meyers Passage, the closest entry is through Thistle Passage. Rocks extend first from the east side of the narrows, then from the west side. They aren't shown well on the chart. We went through at the top of a 12.8-foot tide. We didn't see any sign of the rocks and they were not marked by kelp. Caution advised. The chart shows 4½ fathoms least depth at the north end of the narrows.

Palmer Anchorage. Fisherman Mike Guns suggests Palmer Anchorage at the south end of Thistle Passage as a good wait-and-see temporary anchorage in a northwest gale, but it's deep, and not what we'd select as the best overnight cruising anchorage.

While several overnight anchorages are available in Laredo Inlet, we think you'll be choosing between Quickly Creek Cove, Alston Cove, Bay of Plenty, and perhaps Fifer Cove. We spent the night in Alston Cove and explored Fifer Cove and Bay of Plenty.

NORTHERN B.C. COAST

Quigley Creek Cove. From the top of Thistle Passage, turn east just beyond the first small island, leaving the remaining islands to port, then follow the shore into a landlocked basin at the mouth of Quigley Creek. The basin has a depth of about 60 feet at zero tide. A beautiful spot, protected by surrounding islands from wind and waves. This is one of the few outer channel anchorages that you might share with another boat.

Alston Cove. Mouth 52°45.10'N/128°45.75'W. Lovely Alston Cove is easy to enter and is surrounded by mountain peaks. We put the hook down in sticky brown mud just onto the 6½-fathom area on the north side of the cove, near the flats. When we departed the next morning we were glad to have the anchor washdown system. It took a long time to hose the chain and anchor clean.

Fifer Cove. Mouth 52°52.15'N/128°45.15'W. Fifer Cove is surrounded by mountain peaks and is very scenic, but most of the cove is too deep for easy anchoring. To enter, wrap around Tuite Point, leaving it to starboard. We found 40- to 50-foot depths near the head of the cove, off the stream mouth. Correspondents James and Jennifer Hamilton report the creek shoals out much farther than the chart indicates or they expected, and holding was poor.

Kohl Island Anchorage. "Kohl Island is in Weld Cove, directly south of Bay of Plenty. The bight at the northwest tip of Kohl Island is a sheltered anchorage with mountain views. Approach between Kohl and Pocock Islands and turn west when clear of the rocks off the north tip of Kohl Island. The anchorage is at 52°49.00'N/128°46.09'W between two uncharted rocks. One rock rarely covers and the other is awash at 12 feet. We dropped the anchor between the rocks and pulled back 150 feet to stern-tie onto Kohl Island. Holding was good in 10 to 20 feet over mud and shell." [*Hamilton*]

Bay of Plenty. Bay of Plenty was recommended to us by Correspondents Mike Guns and Laurie and Anita Dowsett. On our chart, Guns drew the entrance channel south of the 120-foot island, and north of the little islet in the middle of the Bay. Anchor in 30 feet, short of the flats. Those flats, by the way, come out a long way. The bay is open to southwest storms.

Field Correspondent Jim Norris reports good anchorage, but his empty crab pot had him renaming this spot "Bay of Not so Much."

Buie Creek. "A spectacular two-level waterfall is a short distance up Buie Creek at the head of Laredo Inlet. To visit, anchor temporarily off the head of Laredo Inlet at 52°58.128'N/128°39.763'W in 90 feet with a 250-foot swing radius, moderate holding." [*Hamilton*]

NORTHERN B.C. COAST   See Area Map Page 461 - Maps Not for Navigation

The ruins of a power house at the head of Surf Inlet

Kent Inlet. Kent Inlet is on the east side of Laredo Channel. Once inside, Kent Inlet is scenic and appears to be well protected. To get inside, however, you must go through Philip Narrows, which is guarded by rocks. Sailing Directions says currents through Philip Narrows run to 8 knots at spring tides, and recommends a transit at slack water only.

We arrived at Kent Inlet near high water slack, so we went in. Kelp marked the rocks at the entrance, off Laredo Channel, and they were not a problem. Kelp did *not* mark the rocks a short distance east of Loap Point. Rocks are out in the middle, exactly where you think you want to be. Stay south of those rocks. Give them room.

At slack water Philip Narrows was easy. Correspondents Laurie and Anita Dowsett recommended anchoring either near the west shore immediately inside Phllip Narrows, or in the back basin off the tidal waterfall. Favor the north shore to get to the back basin. Note the rocks on the south side when entering the back basin. The water in Kent Inlet was dark with rain runoff when we visited; we couldn't see more than a foot or two into it. We had good depths all around the point that defines the back basin. This anchorage is beautiful, marred only by many diseased trees.

LOCAL KNOWLEDGE

CHARTPLOTTER ERRORS: In Surf Inlet, one of our chartplotters placed our boat several hundred feet from where it actually was. Navigate cautiously in this area.

Surf Inlet. Beautiful Surf Inlet stretches 13 miles into Princess Royal Island at the north end of Laredo Channel, ending at a stunning waterfall over a dam that separates Bear Lake from the inlet.

An abandoned concrete power house is on a point below the dam at the head of Surf Inlet. A road leads to a point below the falls. We've been told that if you can get a dinghy or kayak up to the dam (the road looks like the way to go), you can go up Bear Lake to an old mining camp that is surprisingly intact.

Chapple Inlet, at the mouth of Surf Inlet, has a few anchorage possibilities, but Surf Inlet itself has only one, Penn Harbour.

Penn Harbour. Penn Harbour is beautiful and spacious, with a straightforward entry and ample anchoring room in 40 to 50 feet near the head. A stream cascades into the east end and makes little white icebergs of foam on the surface—except that on the night of our visit the icebergs weren't white, they were tan. The water was brown and the anchor turned brown as it penetrated the surface. It disappeared altogether within a foot or two.

Chapple Inlet. Chapple Inlet leads north from the mouth of Surf Inlet, and has anchorage possibilities. These include a little nook on the west shore at Doig Anchorage, another nook behind Chettleburgh Point, and in Kiln Bay. Entry to Chapple Inlet is easy at Mallandaine Point. Follow a midchannel course along the east shore.

At **Doig Anchorage**, try the area just north of the point at 52°55.10'N/ 129°07.80'W. We didn't verify the depths, but we saw three rafted powerboats anchored and stern-tied to shore.

Behind **Chettleburgh Point**, we would anchor in 60 feet, with ample swinging room. This is where you will appreciate an all-chain anchor rode so you can swing in a smaller circle on shorter scope. If you move closer in for shallower water, you'll probably want to run a stern-tie to shore.

In **Kiln Bay**, anchor in 60 feet, north of the little island.

LOCAL KNOWLEDGE

CHARTPLOTTER ERRORS: In Emily Carr Inlet, one of our chartplotters placed our boat several hundred feet from where it actually was. Navigate cautiously in this area.

Emily Carr Inlet. Emily Carr Inlet is on the north side of Surf Inlet, right at the mouth. The inlet is beautiful, and the main body of the inlet is open. With close attention it should present no problems. A reef, however, extends from Webber Island nearly across Holgate Passage, making the entry from Chapple Inlet a little tricky.

We went through Emily Carr Inlet from north to south, then turned northeast to complete our circumnavigation of Princess Royal Island. Although the winds were light, we got into a nasty tide-rip off the 207-foot island south of Duckers Island and wet the boat down pretty thoroughly. It wasn't fun. We crowded over close to Duckers Island and found calmer water. [*Hale*]

Barnard Harbour. Mouth, west side of Borde Island, 53°04.90'N/129°07.75'W; east side of Borde Island, 53°05.20'N/129°06.65'W. Barnard Harbour is shown on planning Charts 3737 and 3742, see Chart 3911 for detail.

Barnard Harbour is big, open, and beautiful. It was a center for fly-in sport fishing lodges, but these lodges have since moved. Anchor in Cameron Cove along the

Whales are a welcome sight; keep your camera ready.

www.WaggonerGuide.com

See Area Map Page 461 - Maps Not for Navigation

NORTHERN B.C. COAST

Campania Island on what Douglass terms the "Outside Passage."

west shore in 30 to 35 feet or in 40 to 60 feet off the mouth of Barnard Creek.

Campania Island. Campania Island, with its bald, knobby mountaintops, is recognizable from miles away. Several inlets on Campania Island's west shore provide sheltered anchorages, interesting views, and opportunities for exploration by kayaks and dinghies. All are well charted; use Charts 3724 and 3912.

McMicking Inlet. McMicking Inlet, in Estevan Sound on the west side of Campania Island, is one of the few places in the outer channels where, at least in July and August, you might have competition for the best anchoring spots. The looming granite mass of Pender Mountain makes for a dramatic anchorage, and twisted cedars growing among the rocks add to the scenic character. Use Charts 3724 and 3912. Although the entrance to McMicking Inlet is open to the south, islets, rocks and reefs diminish any swells. Enter south and east of a chain of islets and drying reefs extending from the south end of Jewsbury Peninsula. Anchor north of the narrows.

Weinburg Inlet. Located off Estevan Sound on the west side of Campania Island, Weinburg Inlet is the maze of islets and lagoons that include Anderson Passage and Dunn Passage, and related bays, coves, and basins. Approximately 3 miles of passage ways lead from Estevan Sound to the head of Weinburg Inlet.

At the head of **Anderson Passage** is a large basin where there is good anchorage with swinging room for several boats. This is the easiest way to enter Weinburg Inlet in limited visibility. Larger boats can anchor in the center of the basin in about 13 fathoms. Small boats can anchor in the more scenic and intimate southeast nook.

The head of **Dunn Passage** provides good anchorage among a labyrinth of rocks and islets. There is room for one or two boats, but swinging room is limited. Field Correspondent Jim Norris reports spending three nights anchored here in 2016, waiting out a southeast gale, with good holding but limited swinging room on a 5 to 1 scope.

WEST SIDE OF PITT ISLAND

This route leads from the south end of Grenville Channel.

Otter Channel. Two possible anchorages appear to be available on the south tip of Pitt Island (the north side of Otter Channel). The first is Dillon Bay, where we saw a sailboat anchored. The second is Saycuritay Cove.

Saycuritay Cove. The small cove east of Fleishman Point on the southwest corner of Pitt Island. Approach from 53°12.67'N/129°33.54'W, heading north. Favor the Pitt Island shore beyond the islet at the entrance, and wrap around the north side of the first of the three small islets inside. Minimum depth on entry is 10 feet. Anchor in 25 feet with room to swing between the first and second of the three small islets. Holding is good over a soft bottom, with reasonable wind protection and views out between the islets. Good anchoring depths also are at the 6-fathom sounding on the chart. The ruins of an old settlement, now a kayaker camp, are on the east shore of the bight in the north side of the large islet that makes up the south shore of the cove." [*Hamilton*]

Monckton Inlet. Monckton Inlet indents Pitt Island at lat 53°18.65'N. The inlet is well protected, with three anchorage possibilities. The first is in 60 feet on the back side of Monckton Point, a short distance inside the inlet on the north side. If you can get in and out near high water, this would be a marvelous, snug anchorage. With propellers and rudders hanging down, however, low water access is scary.

The second anchorage is about three-quarters of the way into the inlet in the bay that extends north almost a mile behind Roy Island. Go up near the head, past the two rocks marked with a + on the chart. Anchor with lots of room in 40 to 50 feet, mud bottom. We tried to find the two rocks mentioned above, but didn't see them. They were not marked by kelp. Be aware.

The third anchorage is at the very head of Monckton Inlet in 50 to 60 feet, mud bottom. It's not very interesting.[*Hale*]

Kooryet Bay. Kooryet Bay, on Banks Island, roughly across Principe Channel from Monkton Inlet, can provide a convenient escape when fog sets in or winds kick up in Principe Channel. Inside the bay you'll have a good vantage point for watching changing conditions in the channel. In southerly winds, anchor in the south cove. In northerly winds, anchor off the creek bed or northwest of Kooryet Island.

Patterson Inlet/Princess Diana Cove. Patterson Inlet is narrow, beautiful, and appears well protected. The head of the inlet divides into a north arm and a south arm. The south arm is very pretty, with a stunning rock wall on the north side near the entry. The bottom is 90 feet deep, though, and a grown-over log booming ground is near the head. We see no need to anchor in the south arm.

The north arm is known as Princess Diana Cove. We overnighted there. It was a perfect anchorage, 25 to 30 feet deep, thick mud bottom. Anchor in the middle. Rocks and reefs sneak up along the shores.

Note: A reader tells us this bay was not good in a southeast gale.

Ire Inlet. Ire Inlet is entered from Ala Passage at latitude 53°30'N. The entry is narrow and quite dramatic, but the fairway is clear. The hillsides are covered with remarkable trees, tall and straight with very short limbs. They look like green pipe cleaners. The trees on top of the rock mountain on the north side of Ire Inlet are twisted and have few limbs. From our distance they looked like bonsai trees.

The little cove on the south shore has rocks as shown on Chart 3984 but not on 3741. Not a good spot. A much better anchorage is between the little islet and the head of the inlet in 20 to 25 feet. Pass north of the little islet. Rocks lie off the south side, and a large drying shoal extends from the south shore of the inlet.

If you visit Ire Inlet (recommended), study the chart carefully before entering Ala Passage. A number of islets and drying rocks must be identified and located. Know where you are at all times and check for fallen trees before entering.

Azimuth Island. Mike Guns put us onto this one. A small unnamed island lies southwest of Azimuth Island, and a convenient anchorage is behind that island at 53°31.45'N/129°59.50'W on the chart. Anchor in 60 to 65 feet. Be sure to enter this anchorage from the north. The southern entry is foul with rocks.

Tangent Island. Tangent Island lies in a cluster of islands located north of Anger

2020 Waggoner Cruising Guide   465

NORTHERN B.C. COAST   See Area Map Page 461 - Maps Not for Navigation

Signs like this one at Newcombe Harbour mark several anchorages.

The public dock in Kitkatla. When maneuvering, stay close to the dock.

Island, near the intersection of Petrel and Principe Channels. The cove on the east side of Tangent Island provides good protection, with a view to the mountains of Pitt Island to the east. Although the anchorage is 100 feet deep, it has good holding and is well protected. Tangent Island also provides an opportunity to refresh your geometry. Enter via Markle Passage, passing between Sine Point to the west, Tangent Point to the east and Logarithm Point to the south.

Colby Bay. Colby Bay is on Banks Island, the west side of Principe Channel, at latitude 53°32.10'N. Go down the middle and anchor in 30 feet where the bay opens up. You'll be surrounded by mountains and protected from northwest or southeast gale winds in Principe Channel. Mike Guns, who first recommended Colby Bay to us, called this spot "a joy."

Petrel Channel. Petrel Channel begins at the south tip of McCauley Island and winds along the west side of Pitt Island to Captain Cove. It has four anchorages, all on the Pitt Island side.

Allcroft Point. Just south of Allcroft Point, at lat 53°35.65'N, is an unnamed bay that gets you off Petrel Channel. Anchor in 75 to 90 feet when you get to the wide spot. The chart shows a rock awash at zero tide obstructing access to the back cove. You may prefer Hevenor Inlet.

Hevenor Inlet. Hevenor Inlet stretches 5 miles into Pitt Island's mountains and you have to go all the way to the head of the inlet for suitable anchorage. The hills on both sides have been clearcut, but already are green again. Anchor in 35 to 60 feet off the falls (you'll see them) or off the mouth of the lagoon.

Newcombe Harbour. Newcombe Harbour is a fine, well-protected anchorage. Motor straight in and anchor off the drying flats in 40 to 50 feet. We wouldn't bother with the little nook on the east shore, a short distance inside the entrance. It is rather tight and not that exciting. With such good, easy anchorage only a little farther in, it's not worth the effort. The log booms reported in the Douglass *Exploring the North Coast of British Columbia* were not there when we visited.

Captain Cove. Captain Cove is a cozy, protected anchorage at the northwest corner of Pitt Island, near the south entrance to Ogden Channel. Anchor in 60 to 80 feet in the large basin behind the 84-foot island, or in the 5-fathom basin along the south shore, behind the little dot islet. We have anchored twice in the 5-fathom basin and once behind the 84-foot island. If you don't mind 70 to 80 feet, the anchorage behind the island is excellent.

Kitkatla. (250) 848-2214. Kitkatla is a Native village on the north end of Dolphin Island, west of Ogden Channel. The dock has 20 & 30 amp power but no other amenities. Most of the dock is taken by local boats. Fuel is available by jerry jug; pay in advance at the band office.

Kitkatla is a pleasant community. Ann's B&B has a nice display of small baskets and conical hats, which Ann wove in years past. Several small convenience stores operate out of homes.

Don't plan to stop at Kitkatla on weekends. Most of the village goes shopping in Prince Rupert.

We left Bully Island to port and went up Kitkatla Channel, leaving the Kitkatla Islands to starboard. Sailing Directions says a church spire is a significant Kitkatla landmark from the water, but new construction makes the spire less significant. Green Buoy E95 marks the end of a rocky shoal when you get close to the moorage area, and a little island lies beyond. Leave Buoy E95 to port and turn toward shore. Head for the large loading dock, leaving the little island to starboard. Go slowly. Kelp marks the shallow spots. Once past the island, run right along the public dock or as close as the rafted boats allow. Rocks lie along the island.

Deep draft boats beware: Depth alongside the dock is approximately 6.5 feet at zero tide.

Spicer Islands. Located off Beaver Passage, between Spicer Island and South Spicer Island. Follow the channel to the well-protected, roomy basin. Anchor in 25 feet, good holding. The Spicer Islands are used by many as an overnight jumping off point for crossing Hecate Strait for Haida Gwaii.

Larsen Harbour. Larsen Harbour, at the northwest corner of Banks Island, is a scenic anchorage. Low-lying rocks surround the anchorage and storm-battered trees line the shore. Field Correspondent Jim Norris reports that there is no significant kelp blocking the entrance and that the anchorage is well-protected from swells originating in Hecate Strait but not from northwest winds which can build steep waves at the entrance. Jim also reports that there are no buoys in the harbour,

The view out the mouth of Bottleneck Inlet the morning after a storm. At high tide the entry looks wide, but a rock ledge extends from the south shore.

contrary to some other guidebooks.

Conditions on Hecate Strait are visible from within the anchorage, making it a good place to stage a trip across the strait to Haida Gwaii. Anchor in 15-25 feet, with fair holding on a rocky bottom with patchy kelp.

Welcome Harbour. Welcome Harbour is on the east side of Henry Island. A maze of rocks and islets guard the entrance; navigate carefully. The channel on the west side of Dancey Island leads to Secret Cove. Welcome Harbour is a favorite of many Prince Rupert boaters.

INSIDE PASSAGE ROUTE, CONTINUED

Mary Cove. Mary Cove is on the east side of Finlayson Channel across from Klemtu. It is a pleasant little cove, but it appears open to southwest winds. Anchor in 50 to 55 feet inside. A salmon stream empties into Mary Cove.

Bottleneck Inlet. Bottleneck Inlet, at latitude 52°42.8'N on the east side of Finlayson Channel, is an outstanding anchorage. It is protected and beautiful, and large enough for a number of boats. The north side of the inlet has superb rock walls. The chart shows a least depth of just over a fathom in the narrow entry, and a rock shelf extends from the south shore at the narrow part. Favor the north shore. Deeper draft vessels should enter cautiously at low tide. The chart fails to show a 13-15 fathom hole a short distance inside the entry sill. The bottom then comes up to 25-30 feet.

Although we have anchored in Bottleneck Inlet several times now, one night in particular was memorable. That was the night a forewarned on-shore gale struck the coast. At 1:30 a.m. the winds hit. We could see clouds racing overhead and hear the wind roaring in the trees above us, but except for four tongues of strong wind that slammed into our boat between 1:30 a.m. and 4:00 a.m., the air around us was almost calm. [*Hale*]

Goat Cove. Goat Cove indents the eastern shore near the north end of Finlayson Channel. An inner basin is reached by running through a narrow neck. Inside, Sailing Directions says good anchorage can be had in 17 fathoms, which is pretty deep. Don Douglass likes this inner basin, too, and would anchor near the head in 36 feet. We don't like it at all. We went in during a gathering storm, and wind gusts found their way to us with nothing to stop them. The bottom shoaled too quickly for us to anchor in 36 feet and pay out scope to stand up to the wind. "Oversold!" we decided, and left. We must add that since then, we have met other cruisers who like Goat Cove, so perhaps it comes down to what the weather is doing. [*Hale*]

Work Bay. Work Bay is on the west side of Finlayson Channel near the north end. The bay appears open to southerly winds, but we anchored there in the southerly storm that chased us out of Goat Cove, and found no wind and only remnants of a few rollers from Finlayson Channel. In our opinion Work Bay has room for just one boat at anchor unless all boats stern-tie. The bay is 40 to 50 feet deep. With only a 3:1 scope (150 feet) of anchor rode out, you must be in the center or you will swing onto shore or onto the drying shelf at the head of the bay.

Lime Point Cove. Lime Point Cove, on Griffin Passage, is an indentation just south of the north end of Pooley Island. For years it has been passed by after the area above the cove was logged. New growth has filled in and once again it is a quiet, scenic anchorage, although exposed to southerlies passing up through Griffin Passage. Anchor in the shallow areas of the cove in 36 to 70 feet.

Carter Bay. Carter Bay is on the north side of Sheep Passage at the east entry to Hiekish Narrows. The bones of the steamship Ohio, which ran up on Ohio Rock in 1909, are there. Knowing he was sinking, the captain of the Ohio made it across the mouth of the narrows and into Carter Bay, where he grounded the ship. Of the 135 passengers and crew, only four were lost. Anchoring depths of 54 feet near the head of the bay. The anchorage is exposed to southwest winds.

Hiekish Narrows. Hiekish Narrows connects with Sheep Passage and Finlayson Channel at the south end, and Graham Reach, the continuation of the Inside Passage, at the north end. Current predictions are given under Hiekish Narrows in Ports and Passes and Canadian Tide and Current Tables, Vol. 7. Currents run to 4.5 knots on the flood, 4 knots on the ebb. The flood sets north. The water behind Hewitt Island appears to be a possible anchorage, but the current runs strongly through it.

Graham Reach & Fraser Reach. Graham Reach and Fraser Reach are wide, straight and deep, and lined with beautiful waterfalls. Cruise ships make this their highway. The principal stopping point for pleasure craft is Butedale.

Horsefly Cove. Horsefly Cove is a short distance inside the mouth of Green Inlet on the east side of Graham Reach. The cove is cozy and protected, but 80 to 90 feet deep. You may have to stern-tie to shore to restrict your swing.

Swanson Bay. Swanson Bay is on the east side of Graham Reach. This bay is exposed, but interesting. Ruins of an old sawmill and pulp mill are on the beach and back in the trees. A 3-story concrete building is just inside the treeline. Farther back, a tall red brick chimney is hidden in the trees. Although the chart shows the chimney as a landmark, summer foliage has almost obscured it from view.

We had trouble finding a comfortable place to anchor at Swanson Bay, settling finally for the shallower water off the creek mouth. Current from the creek kept the boat from swinging. Ashore are the ruins of what once was a formidable shipping center. We have seen a photo of a long wharf at Swanson Bay, with a large square-rigger tied alongside. The wharf is gone, and only a few pilings remain. Unfortunately, the dense forest inhibited our exploration on land.

Our notes say that Swanson Bay shipped its first load of pulp in 1909, and in the 1920s had a population of 500. Its last shipment was in 1934. For some reason the notes don't show the source of this information, so no guarantees as to accuracy.

A few years ago we saw a black-colored wolf on the south shore of Swanson Bay. It watched as our boat slowly approached. Then, with a dismissive air it ambled back into the forest. [*Hale*]

Khutze Inlet. Khutze Inlet stretches eastward from Graham Reach nearly 5 miles and rewards visitors with a stunning anchorage near the head. From there you can look across the drying flats of the Khutze River into a broad valley with mountains on both sides. Don't get too close to the flats. The water can be murky and the bottom comes up sharply. A long and beautiful waterfall tumbles down the mountain to your right. The outfall stream forms an alluvial fan off its mouth. We've seen boats anchored there, and earlier editions suggested that you could find a good spot on that fan to put the hook down. A few years ago, however, a 42-foot boat anchored in that location, but swung too close to shore and went aground.

We have anchored toward the river mouth

Personalized decorations adorn the shelter at Bishop Bay Hot Springs.

NORTHERN B.C. COAST

See Area Map Page 461 - Maps Not for Navigation

in 90 to 100 feet, and between the river mouth and the waterfall in 60 feet. Approach the drying flats slowly until you reach your depth, and put the anchor down. Note that a drying spit extends from the south shore of the Khutze River into the bay. You want to anchor on the south side of that spit.

You can also anchor behind Green Spit near the mouth of the inlet. One good spot is along the south shore, just west of the stream mouth. The chart shows the right spot.

⑨ **Butedale.** Inside Passage Marine Corporation; skennedyau@gmail.com. Located on Princess Royal Island, at the south end of Fraser Reach, Butedale is the site of an historic cannery. Only a few original buildings of the former large cannery remain.

The Butedale property was puchased in 2013 and plans to re-develop the property have been ongoing. The uplands are a construction site and remain closed to visitors. We don't know what the future holds for this boater stop; additional investors are currently being sought. Clearing of the uplands was underway in 2018 and in 2019.

New floats were installed in 2019 for moorage of 4 to 5 vessels. Site construction vessels have priority; guest moorage is as available. Registered visitors of the Inside Passage Marine Corporation may tie up at the floats, at their own risk, and take on untreated water. A caretaker may be onsite with visitor registration paperwork. At this time, there are no other facilities at Butedale.

Anchorage is possible, though the bottom near the dock may be foul with cable. The nearby waterfall is lovely. Spirit Bears are sometimes seen in the area.

⑩ **Bishop Bay Hot Springs.** Bishop Bay Hot Springs is located at the head of Bishop Bay, on the east side of Ursula Channel. This is one of the don't-miss stops along the northern B.C. coast. Local residents have done an outstanding job building and maintaining the bathhouse and boardwalk. A voluntary use fee was initiated in 2017 with an honor box upland on the way to the hot springs. At the bathhouse, the hot spring water is an agreeable temperature and odor-free. The boardwalk parallels the shoreline through fabulous, moss-covered and moss-hung forest. In 2019, work was underway on trail maintenance and rebuilding the boardwalk to the hot springs.

The dock is small, maximum boat size is 36 feet, plan on rafting. Fish boats sometimes raft-up at this dock. Anchoring is only fair to poor, because the bottom slopes quickly to deep water. A stern-tie would make anchoring more comfortable. A short distance south of the dock a shoal, not shown on the charts, extends into the bay from the shoreline. Be aware of that shoal and plan your swing to stay well off it. The three mooring buoys marked "Private" actually are for public use, use at your own risk. We have seen some boats drag on the mooring balls.

Verney Passage. Verney Passage, along the west side of Gribbell Island, must be one of the more beautiful places on earth. It is lined, both sides, with raw, polished rock mountains, 3500 feet high. Great glacier-carved bowls, called cirques, are hollowed into the mountains. From the water you can see their forested floors and sheer rock walls. Especially on a sunny day, a visit to Bishop Bay Hot Springs should include a circumnavigation of Gribbell Island, to see Verney Passage.

Weewanie Hot Springs. Midway up Devastation Channel, Weewanie Hot Springs is a beautiful small bay, surrounded by sheer rock walls and forest. One mooring buoy was available in 2015.

Though the anchorage is beautiful, the hot springs on shore are the primary attraction. The Kitimat Aquanauts Scuba Club built a rustic bathhouse and soaking tubs. Land a dinghy on the rocky beach and follow the trail past a campsite to the bathhouse. Or, land the dinghy on the rocks just below the bathhouse, tie to a log ashore, and climb up to the bathhouse. We've found Weewanie Hot Springs quiet and tranquil, less crowded than popular Bishop Bay.

Proper hot spring etiquette is to pull the plug on the lower tub, drain, then replug. The tub will fill again from the hose connected to the underground hot springs.

⑪ **Kitimat.** Kitimat, pop. 10,000, is a small city located at the head of Douglas Channel. While it has shopping for nearly everything one might need, the town itself is located about 5 miles from the nearest marina, MK Bay Marina. Taxi service (Coastal Taxis, 250-632-7250), if available, is about $25 each way. We suspect a person needing to get to town for shopping could find a ride.

Kitimat is a classic company town, built by Alcan in the 1950s to make aluminum. In the middle of the shopping area, the small Kitimat Museum and Archives has several exhibits that show how the town was built, including the massive tunnels and hydroelectric power dam for the smelting plant. The Alcan plant was one of the largest non-defense construction projects of the 1950s. Today, new owners continue updating and operating the plant.

Just a few miles west on Douglas Channel you can see the clearing and construction for a Liquid Natural Gas plant planned for sometime in the future. When completed, this will be the terminus for an LNG pipeline beginning in the Interior. The gas will be processed, chilled into liquid form, and loaded on ships for distribution.

⑪ **MK Bay Marina.** 4935 Kitimat Village Rd, Kitimat, BC V8C 2G7; (250) 632-6401; contact@mkbay.ca; www.mkbaymarina.ca. Monitors VHF 68. Open all year, 420 feet of guest side-tie moorage on D-dock and occasional slip moorage. 20, 30 & 50 amp power, water, washrooms, showers, laundry, and free Wi-Fi. Call ahead to reserve space; guest moorage space can be tight during the peak season. The convenience store has deli items, fishing supplies, and ice. Gas and

Hartley Bay

Hartley Bay is a pleasant boardwalk community with a government dock behind the breakwater.

diesel fuel, haulout to 20 tons, and launch ramp on site.

The marina is on the east side of Kitimat Arm. Boats on the seaward side of the dock should consider extra fenders. Inflow winds, common in the afternoon, produce significant chop. Walkways were upgraded and new washing machines installed in 2018. A full-service campground opened in August 2019. The marina added approximately 100 new slips in 2019. An overnight guest house is available at the marina. The marina is co-owned by The Mill Bay Marine Group and Haisla Nation.

LOCAL KNOWLEDGE

WEATHER TIP: When crossing Wright Sound in an outflow wind in Douglas Channel, it is better to lay a course to Juan Point, at the north end of Gil Island. We tried this route in an outflow wind, and found it much smoother than our previous crossing, in which we tried a direct (and wet) route between Point Cumming and Cape Farewell.

Wright Sound. Wright Sound is at the junction of Grenville Channel, Douglas Channel, Verney Passage and McKay Reach. All these passages pour their currents into Wright Sound, where the waters collide and mix. Especially on an ebb, not much wind is needed to make conditions ugly.

Coghlan Anchorage. Coghlan Anchorage is behind Promise Island, and is connected by Stewart Narrows with Hartley Bay. The anchorage is open to the south, but still decently protected. There are no mooring buoys in the anchorage. One year we anchored briefly in 35 to 40 feet just north of Brodie Point. The protection and holding ground were excellent, if not scenic. Anchorage is also possible on the shore opposite Brodie Point, off Otter Shoal. [*Hale*]

 Hartley Bay. Band Office, 320 Hayimiisaxaa Way, Hartley Bay, BC V0V 1A0; (250) 841-2500; hbvc@gitgaat.ca. Open all year. Gasoline and diesel, pure water (from the water treatment plant) at the fuel dock, 30 amp power on the floats. Garbage drop, but only separated recycling accepted. Major credit cards accepted.

Hartley Bay, near the south end of Douglas Channel, is a friendly and modern-looking village that is home to the Gitga'at First Nations people; population 130. A no-charge government dock behind a rock breakwater has limited transient moorage. The Cultural Centre is upland near the fuel dock. No liquor. No pay phone, but cell phones work.

Fuel dock hours are Monday through Thursday 8:00 a.m. to 12:00 p.m., and 1:00 p.m. to 5:00 p.m.; Friday through Sunday on call, VHF 06, Hartley Bay Fuel. Hartley Bay has run out of fuel several times in recent years. Boats that must take on fuel at Hartley Bay should call ahead to ensure availability.

It is a pleasure to walk the Native village of Hartley Bay where homes and public buildings are all connected by a series of wide, substantial boardwalks. There are no roads in town except for the wide boardwalks used occasionally by ATV's and Smart Cars; residents generally get around by bicycle or on foot. For supplies and groceries locals must ride the foot ferry to Prince Rupert, an 80-mile journey one way. This interesting community has a small fishing fleet and a fish hatchery. A trail along Kukayu River leads to the fish hatchery, where visitors are welcome. Continuing farther along the trail we discovered the "local swimming hole" where you can hike down the stairs to enjoy a natural pool. Rumor has it that locals know where you might see a "Spirit Bear," stop by the Band Office for more information.

Fin Island. Fin Island lies between Lewis Passage and Cridge Passage, immediately west of Gil Island. Fin Island is fairly low and not particularly interesting, but it has two workable anchorages, Curlew Bay and Hawk Bay. Hawk Bay is the better of the two.

Curlew Bay. Curlew Bay indents the northeast corner of Fin Island. It isn't a destination anchorage by any means, but it will do in settled weather or a southerly. The bay appears open to a northerly and to outflow winds from Douglas Channel. The chart shows shoaling a short distance west of the narrows. We anchored in 20 feet at the east end of the narrows. The anchor bumped twice on what felt like rock, then set solidly. [*Hale*]

Hawk Bay. Hawk Bay, on the west side of Fin Island, is more scenic and has more room than Curlew Bay. The anchorage is somewhat open to westerly winds and you'll swing around if it's blowing. Anchor in the middle in 60 feet.

Grenville Channel. Sometimes called "The Ditch," Grenville Channel is a straight and unobstructed 45-mile-long channel running between Wright Sound in the south and Arthur Passage in the north. The Sailing Directions indicate that currents in Grenville Channel reach a maximum of 2 knots, but between Lowe Inlet and Evening Point, in the narrowest portion of the channel, we've seen as much as 3 to 4 knots on the flood and up to 6 knots on the ebb, especially near Lowe Inlet. Canadian Hydrographic Service does not provide current predictions for Grenville Channel but does provide corrections for high and low water at Lowe Inlet, based on Bella Bella. These corrections can be found in Ports and Passes and the Canadian Tide and Current Tables, Vol. 7. NOAA provides secondary corrections for Grenville Channel, but they are based on Wrangell Narrows and are suspect. Virtually all software predictions for currents in Grenville Channel are based on the NOAA data, and are equally suspect.

Tidal currents flow in and out of each end of Grenville Channel. According to Sailing Directions, flood currents meet near Evening Point, about 25 miles from the south entrance, and ebb currents separate about one mile further to the northwest. This advice is misleading because it is true only in certain circumstances.

Height of the tide at each end of the channel is what drives the flood current to the central parts of the channel. The timing and strength of these currents would be reasonably predictable if that was all there was to it. But many other factors combine to make the currents in Grenville Channel very difficult to predict. High water occurs at different times and reaches different heights in Wright Sound and Chatham Sound. Depending on which end has the higher tide, the strength of the current, and even its direction, may change significantly.

The meeting and separating points of flood and ebb are also variable. The wind regime in Chatham Sound and Wright Sound may be considerably different and may have a strong influence on tidal heights. When onshore winds pile up water in Chatham Sound, Wright Sound may be under the influence of outflow winds from Douglas Channel, diminishing the height of the tide. This scenario forces the meeting point of the currents to the southeast.

When the Skeena River is in flood, vast amounts of fresh water are deposited into the northern end of Grenville Channel. This

NORTHERN B.C. COAST

forces the meeting point of the currents far to the southeast, and when combined with certain wind conditions, pushes it nearly all the way to Wright Sound.

Finally, though Grenville Channel appears to be well protected, when strong currents in the northern, more open part of Grenville Channel oppose strong winds from the NW or SE, a heavy chop develops, making travel very uncomfortable. At those times, conditions in the northern end of Grenville Channel may actually be worse than in the open waters of Chatham Sound.

Be sure to give Morning Reef, north of Evening Point, a wide berth.

Grenville Channel is a major waterway on the Inside Passage. You may see tugs with tows, all types of fish boats and large commercial vessels, the BC Ferries, and cruise ships. In limited visibility, radar is essential and AIS is helpful. We monitor Prince Rupert Vessel Traffic Service on VHF 71 when approaching Prince Rupert Harbour. Large vessels have Call-in Points shown on the charts. Their check-ins with VTS will help you develop a mental picture of the large vessels that may be a factor on your passage, especially those approaching from ahead or overtaking from astern.

Union Passage. Union Passage, on the west side of Grenville Channel, is served by Hawkins Narrows from Grenville Channel, and Peters Narrows from the south. It is one of those places people talk about but not many visit. The problem is the two sets of narrows. The chart shows 8-knot currents in Hawkins Narrows and 7-knot currents in Peters Narrows. Hawkins Narrows slack is shown as 5 minutes in duration. Neither the chart nor Sailing Directions say much about Peters Narrows. Once inside, the scenery is not remarkable.

The currents often are much less than shown, and the window of least current much wider than 5 minutes. We entered Union Passage through Hawkins Narrows at low water slack, poked around for a few minutes, then departed the way we came. The day was windy, rainy and cold. Our spirit was with the great explorers, but our resolve that day was weak. [Hale].

The entrance to Hawkins Narrows is at latitude 53°22'N. The channel is open until the inner end is approached. There, a rock awash at zero tide lies off the eastern shore. Favor the western shore to avoid it.

Lowe Inlet (Verney Falls). Lowe Inlet, a provincial park 14.5 miles from the southern entrance to Grenville Channel, is an excellent spot to overnight. You can anchor either in the outer basin or in Nettle Basin, the cozier inner cove. Walt Woodward, in his book *How to Cruise to Alaska Without Rocking the Boat Too Much*, recommends anchoring directly in front of Verney Falls where they pour into Nettle Basin. Current holds the boat in place, and you are treated to a wonderful view of the falls. Depending on the time of year, you may see bears fishing in the falls. Holding ground is only fair, so be sure the anchor is well set and you have ample scope for high tide. An alternative is to anchor far enough from the falls that the current, while still enough to hold the boat steady, is not very strong.

Douglass, in *Exploring the North Coast of British Columbia*, likes the Verney Falls anchorage, but also suggests an anchorage along the south shore of Nettle Basin, off the shelf formed by a creek that empties into that area. We tried to put the hook down in 60 feet off that shore, but found that we would swing too close to the shelf. After two tries in wind squalls and heavy rain showers, we moved out to the middle and anchored in 100 feet with 300 feet of rode out. Shortly after we were settled another boat came in, tried to anchor as we earlier tried, then moved out to the middle as we had. Our holding ground was excellent. We had trouble tripping the anchor the next morning.

Lowe Inlet is beautiful. Our notes read, "If you're looking for a scenic spot, this is it." [Hale]

Klewnuggit Inlet. At approximately 120 feet, Klewnuggit Inlet is too deep for most boats to anchor. We talked with some folks, however, who found excellent crabbing near the head of the inlet.

East Inlet. East Inlet is adjacent to Klewnuggit Inlet. The inner cove of East Inlet is a superb anchorage, surrounded by high mountains and protected from seas. In a storm, however, winds might swirl through. Anchor near the head of the inner basin in 50 to 55 feet. You can also find anchorage in the little cove on the south shore, just inside the entrance to the inner basin.

We anchored at the head of East Inlet, a perfect night in a perfect place. Mountains reflected in the calm water. A small stream drained from a lake into the head of the inlet, and waterfalls poured down from the sides. We found an inukshuk, a small, stonehenge-like marker, next to the stream mouth. [Hale]

Kxngeal Inlet. Kxngeal Inlet, on the north side of Grenville Channel approximately 4 miles northwest of Klewnuggit Inlet, is a beautiful bowl in the mountains. Favor either shore as you enter to avoid a nasty rock that dries 16 feet in the entrance. The inlet is at least 130 feet deep until it shelves at the head, and when it shelves, it shelves right now. Trees are at the head of the inlet, with logged areas on each side. The shelf is on a line with the points where the trees begin. Anchor in 90 feet.

Watts Narrows. Watts Narrows is a short passage that connects Baker Inlet with Grenville Channel. A dogleg turn near the inner entrance makes the passage blind. Before entering, either direction, announce your intentions on VHF 16, low power. Sound the ship's horn as you approach the turn. The current runs swiftly through the narrows, but people tell us they have gone through in the presence of current without trouble. We have waited for slack water, which occurs about the times of high and low water at Prince Rupert. As the chart shows, the narrows are narrow, but they are deep. A mid-channel course will get you through safely.

Baker Inlet. Baker Inlet, entered through Watts Narrows, is wonderful. The best overnights are at the head of the inlet, 60 feet, good bottom, mountains all around. Remote and beautiful.

Kumealon Island/Kumealon Inlet. The little cove behind Kumealon Island is a good anchorage for a small number of boats. The much larger Kumealon Inlet, immediately

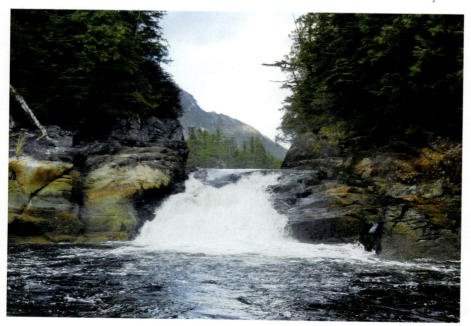

Small boats can anchor just beneath Verney Falls where the current prevents you from swinging into the rocks. If the salmon are running, the bear viewing is fantastic.

south, also is good. Behind Kumealon Island, anchor in 15 to 25 feet north of the island, near the head.

Kumealon Inlet is well protected and has beautiful scenery. Anchor in the inner basin, behind the little island. Find a good spot and put the hook down in 50 to 70 feet. A reader reported that two uncharted rocks lie close to shore near the southeast corner.

Oona River. The village of Oona River, a tiny Swedish fishing and boatbuilding community, indents Porcher Island at the east end of Ogden Channel. A public dock is behind a stone breakwater, and is served by a narrow channel through drying mudflats. From the white buoy, line up on the private range markers on the rock jetty and proceed along the markers set in the entrance. Use caution, but depths should be adequate for most pleasure vessels. Call "Oona River" on VHF channel 06 for additional information, though you may not always get an answer. Cell phones work near Oona River.

Arthur Passage to Chatham Sound. Assuming a northbound route, begin your run west of Watson Rock (west of Gibson Island) at the northern entrance to Grenville Channel. Continue north to a waypoint off the flashing light on the southwest shore of Kennedy Island. Then turn westward slightly to run past the southwest corner of Hanmer Island and leave Bell Buoy *D9*, marking Cecil Patch, to port. Continue to a waypoint in the passage west of Genn Island, then to a waypoint east of Holland Rock.

From Holland Rock, run to a waypoint west of Barrett Rock at the entrance to Prince Rupert Harbour. The entire area is well-buoyed, but it is easy to get the buoys confused.

LOCAL KNOWLEDGE

WEATHER TIP: Chatham Sound can be downright ugly when the wind blows. Especially on an ebb, when the onshore wind meets the combined ebb current and Skeena River runoff, seas can get high, steep and close together. On the VHF weather channel, listen to the hourly updates for Holland Rock. If it's blowing at Holland Rock, conditions can be rough when you try to cross.

Lawson Harbour/Kelp Passage. Kelp Passage is on the west side of Lewis Island, across Arthur Passage from Kennedy Island.

Lawson Harbour indents the top of Lewis Island. Neither would be our first choice for scenery, but each serves as an anchorage if needed. A reef extends from the western shore inside Lawson Harbour. Anchor near the south end of the reef in 35 to 40 feet.

In Kelp Passage, anchor in the area marked 8.8 meters on Chart 3947, mud bottom. The small basin at the south end of Kelp Passage provides good protection in a northerly wind.

Qlawdzeet Anchorage. A large bay on the north end of Stephens Island, well protected from all but northerly winds. This anchorage is often used by fishing vessels and has plenty of room for a number of boats. Anchorage can be found in the main bay or tucked into small bights. Use Chart 3909.

Porpoise Harbour. (250) 628-9220; info@peharbour.ca. Located at Port Edward, Porpoise Harbour gives priority to long-term, year-round customers. Transient moorage available on a first-come, first-serve basis, best to call ahead, 15 & 30 amp power, water,

NORTH PACIFIC CANNERY
A CENTURY OF SALMON

Imagine a century ago, when hundreds of fishing boats would be out on the Skeena and Nass Rivers for 4-5 days per week, 24 hours per day during the salmon runs, in all kinds of weather and sea conditions. Tender boats would shuttle the salmon catch back to the docks of the North Pacific Cannery. Picture a dock with thousands of silvery salmon being cued up for processing. It was tough work done by specialists of different ethnic backgrounds. In the beginning the work was all manual, even the cans were made by hand. As time went on, new machines and processes improved the efficiency and ability to can more salmon.

The North Pacific Cannery was more than just a cannery. It was a small town, processing salmon for over 90 continuous years from 1889 to 1968, and remains the oldest standing cannery on the West Coast. A tour of the North Pacific Cannery is a glimpse back in time, where you get a sense of how these hardy people fished, processed the salmon, and lived in different housing areas onsite. As you tour the buildings and grounds, you can almost hear and feel what it must have been like.

The North Pacific Cannery museum captures what cannery life was like for the Japanese, Chinese, First Nations, and Europeans working in this plant. You can walk from building to building and see how a cannery worked, see the company store, office building, and rows of houses. You can tour the cannery on your own, or take one of the group tours to learn more about the canning process and the social aspects of life here.

The North Pacific Cannery is located 22 km south of Prince Rupert. You can rent a car in town or take the local bus which stops right in front of the cannery. Allow about 3 hours for a docent's tour of the facility. The Crew Kitchen, a small café at the cannery, sells baked goods and is open for lunch. Don't forget to stop by the gift shop.

The North Pacific Cannery is accessible by boat, 5 miles up Inverness Passage from Chatham Sound. The cannery has a 45-foot guest dock for stays up to 4 hours on a first-come, first-serve basis. It's best to time your visit around high tide to minimize the effects of river flow from the Skeena River.

NORTHERN B.C. COAST

garbage drop, washrooms, showers, laundry. Approach using the range south of Ridley Island marked with a buoy for Porpoise Channel.

The harbor is close to the North Pacific Cannery, a museum showing what cannery life was all about. Bus service to Prince Rupert is available.

North Pacific Cannery Dock. (250) 628-3538; www.northpacificcannery.ca info@northpacificcannery.ca. Hours: 10:00 a.m. to 5:00 p.m., May-September, max. 4-hour stay. Located on the north shore of Inverness Passage, the North Pacific Cannery National Historic Site/Museum has a concrete 45-foot day-use dock available for boaters visiting this interesting, picturesque historic cannery. Available on a first-come, first-serve basis, no charge for use of the dock. Located about 5 miles up the Inverness Passage from Chatham Sound, a short side-trip on your way to or from Prince Rupert. Inverness Passage is well charted but open to river flow from the Skeena River which can carry wood debris. To minimize river flow influence, time your visit around high tide. Follow the west side of Smith Island to enter Inverness Passage, use Charts 3947 and 3958. Fender and secure well as current runs past the dock. A boomstick was recently attached to the up-river corner of the dock to deflect some of the windfall debris coming down the Skeena River.

The North Pacific Cannery is the oldest standing cannery on the West Coast and is a National Historic Site. The cannery operated from 1889 to 1968. Visitors can tour the cannery buildings including the processing plant, check in at the museum entrance. Guided tours are available three times daily, July through September; and Tuesday through Sunday during May and June. Tour boats occasionally reserve the dock, call ahead for availability.

LOCAL KNOWLEDGE

SPEED LIMIT: A 5-knot speed zone in Prince Rupert Harbour is enforced within 600 yards of the Prince Rupert shore. It is up to you to gauge the distance as there are no speed limit buoys.

⑬ **Prince Rupert.** As you approach Prince Rupert, it's a good idea to monitor Prince Rupert Traffic (VTS) on VHF 71 in case a large ship decides to depart while you're coming in. The fairway gets narrow in places. This is especially important in poor visibility.

As you approach, the large coal and grain loading areas are part of the Port of Prince Rupert's Ridley Terminals. From Barrett Rock at the entrance to Prince Rupert Harbour, it is another 5.5 miles of slow speed travel to town. Four marinas serve Prince Rupert: Fairview at the south end, the Cow Bay Marina in front of Atlin Terminal, Prince Rupert Rowing and Yacht Club in the middle, and Rushbrooke at the north end.

Rushbrooke Floats, Fairview Small Craft Docks, and Porpoise Harbour are all managed by the Port Edward Harbour Authority, (250) 628-9220.

Fairview is primarily a commercial boat moorage, although some pleasure boats do tie up there. It is fairly far from downtown, with limited bus service. Rushbrooke, at the north end, has better facilities for pleasure boats, but during the commercial fishing months many fish boats occupy the slips. The walk from Rushbrooke to town is long but manageable. Most pleasure boats go directly to the Cow Bay Marina and the Prince Rupert Rowing and Yacht Club, located at Cow Bay. In the past, the Prince Rupert Rowing and Yacht Club would quickly fill during the summer months. Cow Bay Marina is a welcome addition to the Cow Bay area, offering ample moorage which fills quickly during the busy summer months, reservations are recommended. This is a secure marina with key cards issued to overnight guests. Demand for moorage at Prince Rupert continues to be high. Discussion is underway to open a new marina west of Cow Bay Marina in the foreseeable future. Good anchorage is in Pillsbury Cove, across the harbor. Northwest Fuels operates a large fuel dock in Cow Bay, just past the Prince Rupert Rowing & Yacht Club.

Prince Rupert ("Rainy Rupert"), population 12,500, is a complete city. With a large fishing fleet to support, you can find anything you need for your boat. What isn't there can be flown in. Fuel and waste oil disposal are available at Northwest Fuels in Cow Bay.

Restaurants, a pub, and fish market are near the marinas. A shopping mall is a pleasant walk uptown, or you can take a cab. A Walmart is now located in the mall. A large Safeway is located between Cow Bay and the mall. The Save-On-Foods market, farther uptown, is another option for provisions, and will deliver to the docks for a fee. The provincial liquor store is close to the Safeway parking lot. A smaller, private liquor store is at Cow Bay.

The Museum of Northern British Columbia is excellent, and sponsors a variety of informative day and evening programs during the summer. Highly recommended. Several restaurants are in town and in the Cow Bay area, some of them quite good. The Port Interpretive Centre, located on street level in Atlin Terminal, gives free tours about the past, present and future of the Port of Prince Rupert. Recommended.

Located above Cow Bay, Sea Sport

Prince Rupert Harbour

Prince Rupert Waterfront

PRINCE RUPERT MARKETPLACE

RESTAURANTS & SHOPS

MUSEUM OF NORTHERN BC
Explore the Museum of Northern BC's collection of art and artifacts and discover the wealth of history and culture on BC's Northwest Coast. Witness the legacy of oral history, archaeological discoveries and unique artifacts that depict ten thousand years of ancient history.
250.624.3207 • 100 First Avenue West
www.museumofnorthernbc.com

NORTH PACIFIC CANNERY
Experience the history of BC's oldest surviving salmon cannery. Built in 1889, North Pacific Cannery is now a designated national historic site and museum.
Exhibits, guided tours, original architecture, historically-inspired cuisine and the pristine wilderness surroundings tell the story of an industry that played an integral role in BC's economic, cultural and natural development over the last century.
250-628-3538 • 1889 Skeena Drive • Port Edward
www.northpacificcannery.ca

ICE HOUSE GALLERY
The Ice House Gallery is the the Northwest Coast Artists' Cooperative, where you'll find a wide range of high quality, original artwork created by Northwest Coast artists.
The artists share their art, skills, information, vision and culture, providing a high quality display of regionally produced art including cards, carvings, knitting, paintings, glass and jewelry.
250-624-4546 • Suite 190-215 Cow Bay Road
www.icehousegallery.ca

THE PORT INTERPRETIVE CENTRE
The Port Interpretive Centre is where Prince Rupert goes to find out what's happening at the Port. Our ambassadors answer your questions with the assistance of interactive exhibits, video experiences and children's activities to explore the port's world. Learn about the products, vessels and vehicles moving through the Port of Prince Rupert, the communities and countries that we connect to, and the types of people and partners who make it all possible.
250-624-4559 • 215 Cow Bay Road • www.rupertport.com

COWBAY CAFÉ
We offer big and bold rustic Italian flavours with our fresh house pastas, bright salads and traditional stone oven pizzas. Perfect alone or for sharing di famiglia. These classics are paired with our own take on modern westcoast cuisine through our chef-inspired menu board, featuring seasonally harvested ingredients and locally sourced seafood. An integral part to dining with us is wine and we take it just as seriously. We have chosen select award-winning British Columbian, Italian and International wines to enhance our cuisine.
250-627-1212 • 205 Cow Bay Road
www.cowbaycafe.com

WHEELHOUSE BREWING COMPANY
Wheelhouse Brewing Company is the vision of three friends who fell in love with a remote North Coast town. Established in 2013, the Wheelhouse Brewing Company was created to satisfy the demand for great quality, great tasting beer on British Columbia's North Coast. But more than that, the partners simply love making and sampling varieties of beer and want to share that love with the people they live with.
A typical visit to Wheelhouse is a lively affair and a great opportunity to mix with the locals! Also look for wheelhouse on tap and in bottles while visiting the restaurants around Prince Rupert
250-624-2739 • 217 1st Ave East
www.wheelhousebrewing.com

Visit Here To Learn About Annual Events
www.visitprincerupert.com/see-and-do/annual-events

NORTHERN B.C. COAST

See Area Map Page 461 - Maps Not for Navigation

The green "Lightering Dock" is for Customs check-in and clearance.

Outboard Marine and Clothing has an excellent selection of clothing, fishing equipment, safety gear, and marine parts. They also have a machine shop on site.

The King Coin laundry in the center of town is self-serve laundromat, or use their drop-off/pickup service. Rupert Cleaners, located 1.5 blocks from Safeway, also has drop-off laundry service in addition to pickup and delivery service at your boat.

Just beyond the mall, at 617 2nd Ave. is Gary's Lock and Security Shop. Gary Weick, the longtime owner, collects things. His shop is a museum. In the window are wonderful toys from the 1930s and 40s, Canadian Pacific Railroad conductors' caps, old photos—and a stuffed and rare, mounted fur-bearing trout. It was caught in Lake Superior, from depths so great trout grow fur to keep warm. This trout's fur is white. Everything is explained on the sign next to the specimen. You have to see it.

For a glimpse back in time take the bus to Port Edward for a tour of the North Pacific Cannery, now a museum. You'll see how the workers lived during the late 1800s and early 1900s. The cannery has a 45 foot dock for stays up to 4 hours. It's best to time your visit around high tide to minimize the effects of river current flow on Inverness Passage; call ahead for available space.

For an exciting tour to the Khutzeymateen Grizzly Bear Sanctuary at the head of Khutzeymateen Inlet, contact Prince Rupert Adventure Tours at (250) 627-9166.

Prince Rupert was hurt by the decline of the commercial fishing and forest industries, and then the pulp mill closed. The town lost about one-third of its population. In the last twelve years it has become a major deepwater seaport, in heavy competition with Vancouver, Puget Sound, and California. Prince Rupert is closer to Asia than any other west coast port, and CN Rail owns tracks from Prince Rupert to Memphis, Tennessee. Transit time from Asia to the heartland of the U.S. is cut by at least two days. Prince Rupert can handle the largest container ships now afloat.

Prince Rupert is the last major city in British Columbia before transiting Dixon Entrance on the way to Ketchikan and Southeast Alaska. While there is good shopping and liquor stores in Prince Rupert, vessels bound for Alaska may want to wait to provision until Ketchikan to avoid customs issues with liquor, produce, and meat. On the way south from Alaska, Prince Rupert is the best place to stock up on produce, meat and liquor.

Customs clearance: Tie up at the 100-foot-long green-painted "Lightering Dock," where a dedicated toll-free phone for customs clearance is installed. The dock is located beneath the large shopping mall building at the top of the hill. The railroad museum building is near the shore, and a whale sculpture. Lat/Lon 54°18.827'N/130°19.930'W. Touch-and-go for customs clearance only. A locked gate prevents shore access.

Most southbound boaters clear customs by calling from their slip at Rushbrooke, the Prince Rupert Rowing and Yacht Club, Cow Bay Marina and Fairview Government Dock; call 888-226-7277, or call on a dedicated phone at each of the four marinas. Customs agents have the option of calling out a local officer for an inspection.

Airport: The Prince Rupert airport is located on a separate island from the city and all passengers use an airport shuttle. The shuttle center is located downtown in the Prestige Hotel Building. There is only one shuttle trip for each flight. Shuttle service is included in the airline ticket fare. Shuttle schedule and more information can be found on the airport website www.ypr.ca.

Trailer and Vehicle Storage: For those trailering boats to Prince Rupert and looking for places to store their tow vehicle and boat trailer, contact: Coastal Propane (250) 624-5011; Bandstra Transport (250) 624-6826; Bridgeview Marine (250) 624-5809.

Car Rentals: National, (250) 624-5318. Located on the west end of town in the Highline Hotel.

Cruise Ships: A cruise ship will call once or twice a week during the summer. When a ship is in town, the streets and stores are apt to be crowded.

Fairview Small Craft Harbour. (250) 624-3127; info@peharbour.ca. Open 7 days a week 5:00 a.m. to 8:00 p.m. during the summer; 8:30 a.m. to 5:00 p.m. Monday through Friday the rest of the year. This is the first set of docks as you approach Prince Rupert. Commercial vessels primarily, but sometimes room for a few pleasure boats. Water, 15 & 30 amp power, garbage drop, washrooms. First-come, first-served.

⑬ **Cow Bay Marina.** (250) 622-2628; www.cowbaymarina.ca. Monitors VHF 66A. Open all year with moorage for boats up to 80 feet and can accommodate larger yachts up to 140 feet on the breakwater docks; 30, 50 & 100 amp power, washrooms, showers, laundry, water, garbage drop, recycling, and free Wi-Fi. The showers and laundry facilities for marina guests are located in the white building at the bottom of the ramp near docks A and B. Reservations recommended. This 51-slip marina is located in Cow Bay in front of the Atlin Terminal building. Be sure to fender well as wakes from passing boats

See Area Map Page 461 - Maps Not for Navigation

NORTHERN B.C. COAST

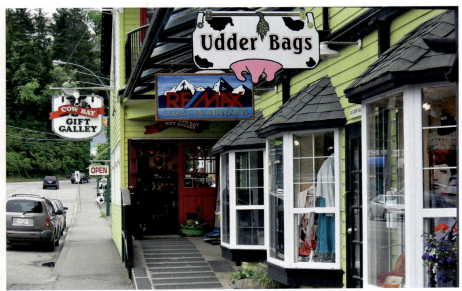
Cow Bay shops and restaurants near Cow Bay Marina and Rowing Club

How to Prepare Sea Asparagus

Sea asparagus, although quite salty, is actually good for you; it's loaded with minerals including calcium, iron, Vitamin B and C and high in Vitamin A. Sea asparagus is abundant on the western and eastern coasts of Canada, found growing along saltwater beaches in protected coves during mid-summer. You can also look for sea asparagus at farmers' markets like the Victoria Public Market and at the Granville Island Market in Vancouver. We happened to find sea asparagus at a summer outdoor market during a stay in Sitka, Alaska.

Yes, sea asparagus is a vegetable and looks like the garden variety of which we are all familiar. Due

to the crunch and briny taste, sea asparagus is a natural fit with most types of seafood. You can use it cooked or blanched to sprinkle atop shucked oysters or over smoked salmon, minced or chopped. You can also steam or boil sea asparagus, like green beans, and use in salads, soups, and omelets. Because of its high salty content, a little bit goes a long way. Pickled sea asparagus can be purchased at some health food stores; try blending it with basil, parmesan cheese and pine nuts for a pesto, or mix pickled sea asparagus with tuna for sandwiches.

find their way into the marina despite the posted "no wake" sign. The marina is close to the center of town and is a welcome addition to the tight moorage options at Prince Rupert.

⑬ **Prince Rupert Rowing and Yacht Club.** P.O. Box 981, 121 George Hills Way, Prince Rupert, BC V8J 1A3; (250) 624-4317; info@prryc.com. Monitors VHF 73. Open all year, 30 & 50 amp power, new washroom and shower, recycling, water, pay phone, garbage drop, Wi-Fi, fish cleaning station. Waste oil dump at the Northwest Fuels facility next door.

This is more of a marina than a traditional yacht club. There is no reciprocal moorage. Although reservations are not accepted, visitors are encouraged to call at least 24 hours ahead to get on a wait list for moorage. Cell phones work for calling the Yacht Club from Hartley Bay and Oona River. As you approach, call on VHF 73. The dock staff can be busy.

The yacht club docks are strong and safe, but well used. The main dock has been replaced, and more replacements are planned. New docks or old, be aware that you will be squeezed in more tightly than at most marinas. If the commercial salmon fishing fleet is in the midst of an opening, the boats will come and go all night, and moorage at the outermost docks can be pretty bouncy. Put out lots of fenders.

A new club house, with a bright red roof, was completed in 2018. The yacht club is close to good dining in Cow Bay or you can walk or take a cab uptown for more restaurants and shopping.

⑬ **Northwest Fuels Ltd.** (250) 624-4106. Located in Cow Bay next to the Yacht Club. Monitors VHF 71. Open every day, extended hours in summer. Petro Canada gasoline, diesel, lubricants, washrooms and showers. Block, cube and salt ice. Small convenience store on the pier with a surprising number of marine and fishing tackle items. Garbage drop, waste oil disposal. Propane is available a few blocks away. This fuel dock is often busy; be prepared to wait for a space to clear.

⑬ **Rushbrooke Floats Small Craft Harbour.** (250) 624-9400; info@peharbour.ca. Open all year, water, 15 amp power, washrooms, and single pay shower. Commercial vessels have priority in the summer, but there may be room for pleasure craft. Rafting required. Located about a mile north of town. Rushbrooke has the only launch ramp in Prince Rupert. First-come, first-served. The office upland is open Monday through Friday, and open daily during the fishing season.

Pillsbury Cove. Pillsbury Cove, on the west side of Prince Rupert Harbour, is an excellent anchorage: level bottom, great holding, beaches and tide pools, and lots of crab. If the marinas in Prince Rupert are all full or you prefer anchoring, this is

NORTHERN B.C. COAST   See Area Map Page 461 - Maps Not for Navigation

Cow Bay

Cow Bay Marina is just one block from shops and restaurants and three blocks from town.

a good choice. Prince Rupert is a 3-mile dinghy ride away. Field Correspondent Jim Norris notes that entering Pillsbury Cove can be intimidating due to the extensive aquaculture floats crowding the east side of the entrance channel; hug close to these floats on your starboard side as you enter.

Things to Do

1. Cow Bay. Several good restaurants and shops. One casual favorite is Cowpuccino's for coffee, fresh baked goods and excellent Wi-Fi.

2. Khutzeymateen Sanctuary. Also called "Valley of the Grizzly," this is the only park of its kind in Canada. It contains one of the largest populations of grizzly bears–about 50 –in British Columbia. Located 45 km NE of Prince Rupert.

3. North Pacific Cannery. The oldest, most completely preserved cannery remaining of 200-or-so that once dotted B.C.'s northwest coast. A bus or car ride away from town.

4. Museum of Northern British Columbia. An impressive collection about the northwest coast. A First Nations Longhouse describes the history of the people and area going back to the last ice age. It contains well-preserved, historical Tsimshian and other First Nations works of art, clothing, baskets and more. A short walk from the marinas.

5. Firehall Museum. Focused on the history of the local fire department since 1908. A rebuilt red fire truck from 1925 sits in the middle of the museum.

6. Kwinitsa Railway Museum. Authentic railway station with artifacts from the early 1900s, the heyday of the Grand Trunk Pacific Railway. On the waterfront, near the Lightering Dock.

7. Farmer's Market. In town on Sunday afternoons during the summer season.

8. Earl Mah Aquatic Center. A short walk from Cow Bay.

9. Seafest. The town's biggest annual festival, held each June.

10. Port Interpretive Centre. Hands-on activities let visitors explore the growth of Prince Rupert's commerce including, containers, coal and grain.

476   www.WaggonerGuide.com

Haida Gwaii

CHAPTER 17

GRAHAM ISLAND
Masset • Port Clements • Skidegate • Queen Charlotte

MORESBY ISLAND, HEADING SOUTH
Sandspit Harbour • Louise Narrows • Skedans Bay • Dana Passage • Hoya Bay

GWAII HAANAS NATIONAL PARK RESERVE
Tanu Island • Louise Narrows • Hotspring Island • Rose Inlet

ANTHONY ISLAND (SGANG GWAAY)
Nan Sdins • Grays Cove

HAIDA GWAII

See Area Map Page 479 - Maps Not for Navigation

Haida Gwaii. Located 130 miles north of Vancouver Island and 65 miles west of the B.C. coast's mainland islands, Haida Gwaii offers some of the Northwest's most spectacular cruising. Haida Gwaii, formerly called the Queen Charlotte Islands, is an archipelago of over 150 islands, best explored by boat. It is remote and pristine with a unique geological history. Glaciers once covered this area and receded 2,000 years before the rest of British Columbia, resulting in an ecosystem with some species of plants and animals not seen anywhere else. It has been referred to as the "Galapagos of the Northwest" with hundreds of species of birds, unique species of bears and many trees and plants growing in areas from the rain forests of the western coast to the dry forests on the eastern coast.

Buddy-boating helps with difficult anchorages at Gwaii Haanas Watchmen Sites.

Haida Gwaii means "Islands of the People" in the language of the first people to settle here. The Haida were revered and respected along the coast as ambassadors and warriors, with a unique culture. The islands had a population of more than 10,000 until the 1800s when many succumbed to smallpox and other diseases from Europe. By 1900, only 350 remained. A visit to Haida Gwaii and the Gwaii Haanas National Park will take you to a place where you can see what remains of this once great culture. As you walk the trails through the rain forest and moss-covered rock canyons around the old villages you may even feel the presence of the people who inhabited this rugged and beautiful area.

Haida Gwaii experienced the impact of an imbalance caused by western man. In the 1800s sea otters were hunted almost to extinction. Their pelts were highly valued around the world and greed took over. In time the sea urchin population grew out of control without the sea otters to keep them in check. Later, the health of the kelp beds was affected by the overabundance of sea urchins. Nature's balance was thrown off. Today the symbol of Haida Gwaii is the sea otter and the sea urchin, a reminder to keep the ecosystem in balance.

Fishing and crabbing are allowed within the Gwaii Haanas Reserve except in designated closed areas, which are described at orientation. Appropriate fishing licenses required.

Permits. The Gwaii Haanas National Park Reserve, a Protected Area, was created in 1987 and encompasses the southern third of the Haida Gwaii archipelago. The Reserve is jointly managed by the Haida and the government of Canada. It is unique in Canada, covering both land and sea. A visit to Gwaii Haanas requires a permit for the time you will be in the Reserve. The daily fee is $49.00 for families (up to 7 people, max of 2 people over 18), $19.60 for adults, $16.60 for seniors (65 and over), and $9.80 for youths (6 to 16 years). No limit on the number of days you may stay within the Reserve; however, after six days, it is more cost effective to purchase a Season Pass.

Only 100 people are permitted in Gwaii Haanas National Park Reserve at once. Advance reservations are recommended to ensure you'll get a permit. An orientation is required for all visitors, either in advance by DVD or at the **Haida Heritage Centre** in Skidegate. The Heritage Centre has a gift shop. Orientation sessions are typically at 9:00 a.m. Monday-Friday in June and after mid-August, and Monday-Saturday July to mid-August. Orientation sessions can be scheduled by appointment if staff is available. Reserving space for scheduled orientations is not required. A permit tag is issued at the time of orientation and must be carried ashore within the Park Reserve. The excellent orientation covers the history of Gwaii Haanas as well as the procedures to visit the different sites within the park. All protected sites are managed by Haida Watchmen. They can be reached on VHF 06 prior to going ashore at each site. They manage the number of people on shore at a time. They also provide interpretive talks about the site and are very welcoming.

A fee is not required between October 1st and April 30th, but visitors must register and attend an orientation session. Check the Parks Canada Gwaii Haanas website for more information. Call (877) 559-8818 (8:30 a.m. to 4:30 p.m. Monday through Friday after April 2nd) for more information or to arrange for a permit (www.pc.gc.ca/gwaiihaanas). As a convenience, orientation sessions are generally offered in early March in Vancouver BC, Victoria, or Sidney; check their website for the year's schedule. If planning to enter Gwaii Haanas from the south, it may be possible to get an orientation package by mail for a fee; contact the Haida Heritage Centre.

Getting to and from Haida Gwaii. Separated from mainland British Columbia by Hecate Strait; from Vancouver Island by Queen Charlotte Sound; and from Alaska by Dixon Entrance, getting to Haida Gwaii by boat requires crossing some of the Northwest's most feared bodies of water. Hecate Strait is notorious for rough water. With shallow depths in the northern portion, ranging from 50 to 115 feet, winds can quickly whip up big, uncomfortable seas. Tides move large volumes of water through Hecate Strait and Dixon Entrance. When wind blows against current, dangerous conditions can result. Particularly during spring tides, be mindful of possible wind-against-current situations. Nevertheless, we have had several smooth passages by timing the transit to the correct conditions and forecast.

Orientations for Gwaii Haanas National Park are held at the Haida Heritage Center in Skidegate.

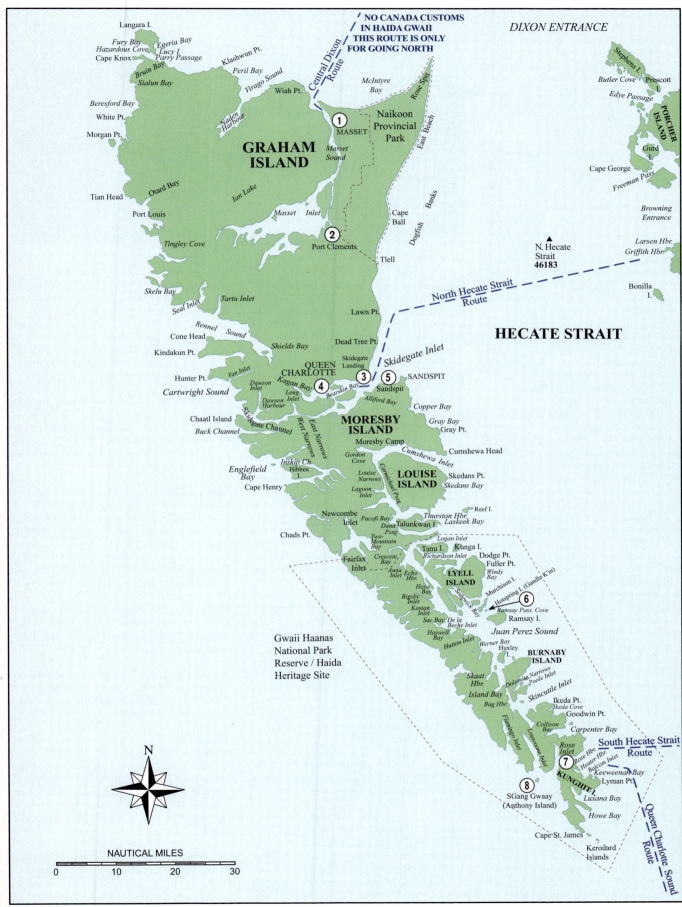

HAIDA GWAII

See Area Map Page 479 - Maps Not for Navigation

There are basically three options for getting to and from Haida Gwaii; Crossing Hecate Strait from mainland BC Coast is the shortest open water route and the most common; Crossing Queen Charlotte Sound from Vancouver Island is the most direct but the longest open water route; Crossing Central Dixon Entrance to the north is only possible when departing Haida Gwaii as there are no Canada customs clearance locations in Haida Gwaii.

Crossing Hecate Strait. Shearwater, Bella Bella, and Klemtu in the south, and Prince Rupert in the north, are the popular starting points. There are a number of anchorages on the islands between Hecate Strait and BC mainland's Inside Passage. Routes from these anchorages offer the shortest open water crossings, ranging from 85 miles for southerly departure points and 65 miles from the northerly departure points. Many boats depart for Haida Gwaii from Prince Rupert. This route offers the shortest crossing (roughly 60 to 65 miles of open water), allowing boaters to minimize their exposure to potentially hazardous weather. Prince Rupert is a major city, and has anything a cruising boater might need before heading out to explore Haida Gwaii. With fuel, provisions, and internet access for weather information, Prince Rupert makes a logical starting point. After leaving Prince Rupert, several anchorages provide a place to spend the night and wait for better weather before crossing Hecate Strait. Larsen Harbour, anchorages in the Spicer Islands, and Welcome Harbour are good choices. In the past we have been warned of extreme kelp in Larsen Harbour. More recently we have been told that Larsen Harbour is easily navigable. It is the shortest point of crossing to Lawn Point on Graham Island. During our recent trip, we anchored in the Spicer Islands. For our early morning departure we listened for the wind and wave report from the North Hecate Strait weather buoy Station 46183 and navigated directly across Hecate Strait, passing the buoy on the way to Lawn Point. Note the shoal area leading north from the entrance to Skidegate Inlet. If headed to Sandspit Harbour or Queen Charlotte, follow the deeper channel to Skidegate Inlet or Shingle Bay. In settled conditions and higher tides, we have crossed just north or south of Bar Rocks near the green can buoy.

Shearwater, Bella Bella, and Klemtu have provisions, fuel, water, and internet access and are good southern starting locations. Departing from Shearwater, Bella Bella, or Klemtu, boaters can take one of several routes from the Inside Passage to what Douglass terms the Outer Passage, where you will find several anchorages on Aristazabal Island before crossing Hecate Strait to Rose Harbour on Moresby Island. Because Rose Harbour is within the Gwaii Haanas National Park Reserve, you will be required to have a permit and have already completed the required Park orientation. This 85 mile crossing can be done in one long summer daylight day. This route crosses the southern area of Hecate Strait, which is not as shallow as the northern portion. There are no services at Rose Harbour, so boaters landing in Rose Harbour need to have fuel, provisions, and water until arriving in Queen Charlotte or Sandspit. Field Correspondent Mary Campbell has had four smooth crossings along this route. She suggests Borrowman Bay or Weeteeam Harbour for overnight anchorages. This route is also a good option when returning from Haida Gwaii after your stay in Gwaii Haanas Park.

Protected moorage at Sandspit Harbour, northeast end of Moresby Island

Crossing Queen Charlotte Sound. Haida Gwaii can also be accessed from Vancouver Island to the south. The trip is long— about 160 nautical miles—and exposed to the full brunt of the open Pacific Ocean. Sailboats and slow powerboats will have to make an overnight passage. For faster boats in settled weather, the trip can be completed in a very long day. Keep in mind, however, that sea conditions may not be conducive to high-speed operation. Also remember that fuel is not available anywhere south of Sandspit. You will need a Gwaii Haanas National Park Reserve permit and have completed the required orientation. From the south, plot a route from the area north of Vancouver Island to Houston Stewart Channel and Rose Harbour. Use West Sea Otter weather buoy, Station 46204, and the South Hecate Strait weather buoy Station 46185 for wind and wave reports for the area. This might also be your return route when leaving Haida Gwaii for points south.

Crossing Central Dixon Entrance. Boats returning to British Columbia from Alaska may be tempted to cross Dixon Entrance to Masset instead of Prince Rupert. Unfortunately, there are no Canadian Government customs offices anywhere in Haida Gwaii. Boats southbound from Alaska must first clear customs in Prince Rupert. Boaters going north from Haida Gwaii and into Alaska may cross Dixon Entrance and proceed to Ketchikan for required U.S. Customs clearance. Keep in mind that you may not anchor or make landfall anywhere in U.S. waters before clearing customs in Ketchikan. From Masset to Ketchikan is approximately 85 miles, which can be done in one long day. Check weather, current, and conditions in Dixon Entrance carefully. Use Central Dixon Entrance weather buoy, Station 46145 for wind and wave reports.

Fuel. Fuel is available at Masset on the north end of Graham Island, at Sandspit, and in the town of Queen Charlotte in Skidegate inlet. Cruising in Haida Gwaii is wilderness cruising with no major repair services or boatyards.

Water. Masset, Port Clements, Sandspit, and Queen Charlotte have potable water. Parks Canada maintains fresh water hoses at Hoya Bay and at Louscoone Inlet; water at both locations is untreated.

Garbage Drops. In the remote and protected areas all trash must be carried out with you.

Insurance. Not all vessel insurance policies cover Haida Gwaii, check with your insurance agent to ensure that you have coverage for this area.

Provisioning. Groceries are available in Masset, Skidegate, Queen Charlotte, and Sandspit. Deliveries are usually once a week. Selection may be limited.

Trailering. BC Ferries serve Masset, Skidegate, Sandspit, and Alliford Bay. Check www.bcferries.com for schedules and rates. Boat launches are located at Alliford Bay, Sandspit, Masset, and Copper Bay. Trailering small boats to Haida Gwaii may save time and money and can minimize weather delays.

Resources. Don and Reanne Douglass *Exploring the North Coast of British Columbia* is a helpful cruising guide for Haida Gwaii. It was updated in 2017.

HAIDA GWAII

Queen Charlotte Harbour Authority floats, with Bearskin Bay anchorage in the background

GRAHAM ISLAND

① **Masset.** During the summer months, Masset, the northernmost community on Haida Gwaii, is a hub of sport fishing operations. The local airport offers regular flights to Vancouver, and floatplanes run regularly from Prince Rupert. You'll find restaurants, a liquor store, three grocery stores, a hardware store, pubs, car rentals and an internet cafe.

Local businesses cater to tourists, with sightseeing trips and fishing charters. Hikes give boaters the opportunity to stretch their legs and see a different side of Haida Gwaii. The 9-hole Dixon Entrance Golf Club is 5 kilometers outside of town. The Dixon Entrance Maritime Museum showcases the maritime history of the area.

① **North Arm Transportation.** (250) 626-3328; nat@northarm.bc.ca; www.northarm.bc.ca. Open all year. Located at the government dock. Gas, diesel, and lubricants available.

① **Delkatla Slough Harbour Authority.** (250) 626-5487. Open all year, first-come, first-served, primarily a commercial boat facility. Power and water on the docks, garbage drop, tidal grid. Rafting required.

Refuge Cove. Known locally as 7-mile Cove, Refuge Cove provides good protection from weather and has 600 feet of dock space. This is a good place to wait out a storm, or to wait for favorable currents to enter Masset. Use caution entering Refuge Cove. The fairway is narrow, about 100 feet wide, with 6-foot depths at zero tide. In stormy conditions, swells can break across the entrance channel, making it impassable. Fishing outside Refuge Cove is reportedly excellent.

Langara Island. Langara Island, the northernmost island in the archipelago, is known for its exceptional salmon fishing. Sport fishing lodges on the island cater to fly-in guests. Several anchorages are available, although they are typically busy with sport fishing boats.

Skidegate Inlet

2020 Waggoner Cruising Guide

HAIDA GWAII

See Area Map Page 479 - Maps Not for Navigation

Dining with the Kings

When planning a trip to Haida Gwaii, located 65-85 miles off the coast of British Columbia, first-class dining is not the immediate thing that comes to mind. In fact, the population might be considered sparse with only a few main villages on northern Graham Island, namely, Queen Charlotte, Skidegate, Port Clements, and Masset; Sandspit is the only village on Moresby Island to the south. The rest of the southern portion of Haida Gwaii consists of the Gwaii Haanas National Park Reserve with several Haida Heritage sites. So how did "Dining with the Kings" restaurant evolve on the islands of Haida Gwaii? After thirty years in the newspaper business, Dianne and Jeff King decided to open their home during the summer months to host locals and visitors to the islands, providing exceptional creative dishes that one would find in a big city like Vancouver or Victoria. Dining with the Kings not only offers exceptional cuisine, but also an exceptional experience

Guests for the evening are warmly greeted at the door with complimentary sparkling wine and a side-table set with an exquisite variety of appetizers like Salmon Mousse with crème fraiche, Antipasti, Smoked Tuna Loin with minted pea puree, and the Polpette Wontons with red pepper puree canapes and handmade flatbread, to name a few. While dinner is being prepared, guests can mingle on the patio and admire the fabulous views, sharing stories of how they came to Haida Gwaii. After being seated among new friends, the next course is a choice of soup or a pasta dish, followed by a choice of two mains like Local Wild Halibut with caper sauce, or the Porchetta-style Pork Tenderloin, which are served with a market vegetable. Scrumptious desserts like the Pistachio Semifreddo, or the Raspberry Sorbet with chocolate wafers, or perhaps the Chocolate Tart is presented as a finale. Yes, it's a four-course meal that's fit for a king. The menu varies and is posted every Thursday on their Facebook page (facebook.com/diningwiththekings/).

Dining with the Kings is located at 4307 Husband Road, just off Oceanview Drive, between Queen Charlotte and Skidegate. Reservations are accepted for up to 18 guests per night, hosted at 7 p.m. from mid-June to mid-September, Friday through Monday. Contact diningwiththekings@gmail.com for reservations or call 250-637-1976.

Boaters staying at the Queen Charlotte Harbour Authority docks on Graham Island will find it convenient to reach Dining with the Kings by taxi — call 250-637-1162 for taxi service, or car rental, offered by Gwaii Taxi and Tours.

Masset Sound. Masset Sound connects Masset to Port Clements and Masset Inlet. Currents run to 5.5 knots, although the Douglasses report little turbulence. Boats, particularly slow boats, should use caution when transiting the area. Vessels entering Masset Sound should do so on a flood, and exit on an ebb.

② **Port Clements.** Port Clements is a small town south of Masset. It has a grocery store, post office, health clinic, liquor store, restaurants, and a pub. A museum showcases the history of logging on Haida Gwaii. Local businesses offer sightseeing tours and fishing trips.

Several miles from town, a hiking trail leads to the Golden Spruce heritage site, where a sacred, golden-colored Sitka Spruce tree stood until a logger-turned-conservationist famously cut it down to protest logging. John Vaillant's book, *The Golden Spruce*, tells this story with a lot of interesting facts about Haida Gwaii.

② **Port Clements Small Craft Harbour.** P.O. Box 198, Port Clements, BC V0T 1R0; (250) 557-4295; www.portclements.ca. Open all year. Transient moorage, 20 & 30 amp power, garbage drop, unpaved boat launch. First-come, first-served, rafting required. Register at office three blocks away. Ice, a pay phone and groceries are available at the nearby Bayview Market.

SKIDEGATE, QUEEN CHARLOTTE, AND SANDSPIT

③ **Skidegate.** Skidegate offers lodging, restaurants, groceries, and shops with local crafts. In fair weather boats can anchor offshore and dinghy in. Visiting cruisers may want to visit Skidegate by road from Queen Charlotte.

④ **Queen Charlotte.** Queen Charlotte, on the south end of Graham Island, has many services and supplies. Groceries, restaurants, pubs, a liquor store, ATM, marine supplies, a hardware store, rental cars, lodging, a post office, and an internet café are available. Local outfitters offer guided tours which can be an option to see the protected areas.

A visitor center is just east of the Harbour Authority floats. The staff is friendly and can answer most questions about the area. Many summer events are hosted at a "square" just below the visitor center.

The grocery store is located approximately ½ mile west of the Harbour Authority. It is restocked each Monday. The post office, laundromat, and liquor store are in the same complex. A farmers market is held each Saturday near the community center and library.

Anchorage, in 20-35 feet, is good in Bearskin Bay, although it is open to wind and chop from the east.

④ **Queen Charlotte Harbour Authority.** P.O. Box 68, Queen Charlotte, BC V0T

HAIDA GWAII

1S0; (250) 559-4650; harbour@qcislands.net. Open all year with moorage, 15 & 30 amp power, and garbage drop. A tidal grid is available for haulouts, and nearby there is a boat launch for trailerable boats. Water is available, but not on all docks.

④ **Fast Fuel LP.** (250) 559-4611; sales@fastfuel.ca; www.fastfuel.ca. Located at the Inland Air pier. Open 9:00 a.m. - 5:00 p.m. mid-June to late August, open all year for call outs. Gas and diesel. Call ahead for lubricants.

Skidegate Channel. Skidegate Channel is the narrow, shallow, and winding channel between Graham and Moresby Islands, connecting Hecate Strait with the Pacific Ocean. East and West Narrows are particularly challenging, though daybeacons make transiting easier than in the past. Because of the difference in tidal swings on the Pacific and Hecate Strait sides of Haida Gwaii, tides and currents in Skidegate Channel are complex and difficult to predict. It's best to plan on arriving at McLellan Point roughly three hours after low water in Queen Charlotte.

Alliford Bay-Skidegate Ferry. Graham Island and Moresby Island are separated by Skidegate Inlet and Skidegate Channel. A small ferry runs daily from Alliford Bay near Sandspit on Moresby Island, to Skidegate Landing on Graham Island. Boaters visiting the two main islands by rental car should be aware of the last ferry sailing of the day. The last sailing from Moresby Island is normally 5:35 p.m., and the last sailing from Graham Island at Skidegate is normally 6:10 p.m. For the current ferry schedule, go to bcferries.com.

⑤ **Sandspit.** Sandspit, on the northeast end of Moresby Island, is a settlement with a launch ramp and well-protected marina, restaurants, pubs, liquor store, lodging, post office, and laundromat. The grocery store, about 4 km northeast from the marina, is restocked each Monday and Friday.

Sandspit has hiking and biking trails, the Willows Golf Course, (Haida Gwaii's only 18-hole golf course), and an airport with scheduled commercial service to Vancouver. Airport shuttle service and freight delivery is provided through Eagle Transit (250) 559-4461.

⑤ **Sandspit Harbour.** P.O. Box 477, Sandspit, BC V0T 1T0; (250) 637-5700; sandspitharbour2@outlook.com; www.sandspitharbour.com. Monitors VHF 06, 08, 09, 73. Open all year with guest moorage to 100 feet, 15, 30, 50 & 100 amp power, seasonal water, pumpout, pay phone, showers, washroom, garbage drop, launch ramp and free Wi-Fi. Marina office hours are the same as the Fuel Dock hours listed below. This is the most modern marina in Haida Gwaii. Reservations strongly recommended in the summer for vessels over 45 feet. Bridgeview Marine for repairs is located across the road.

⑤ **Sandspit Harbour Fuel Dock.** Operated by and located at Sandspit Harbour. Open June through August 7:00 a.m. to 9:00 a.m. and 6:00 p.m. to 9:00 p.m. Open September, through May 9:00 a.m. to 12:00 p.m. Gas and diesel available.

⑤ **Bridgeview Marine.** 537 Beach Road, Sandspit, BC V0T 1T0; (250) 637-5432; www.bridgeviewmarine.com. Open all year 8:00 a.m. to 5:00 p.m., Monday to Friday. Haulout to 36 feet. Marine supplies, mechanics with extensive outboard and stern drive experience, limited diesel and inboard experience.

Moresby Camp. Moresby Camp has road access to Sandspit, a public float, and a boat launch.

Gordon Cove. Gordon Cove, just south of Moresby Camp, is a an excellent anchorage. Good holding in 15-30 feet.

Louise Narrows. The small boat passage at Louise Narrows is scenic, shallow and narrow, only 30 feet across in some places. It is best to travel through the passage before high water and while the gravel banks are still visible. This way, you can see the channel, and if you inadvertently run aground, the rising tide will float you off.

When we transited we saw depths of less than five feet under the keel. It was manageable, but added a bit of excitement to the passage. Given the limited space for maneuvering within the narrows, boats transiting Louise Narrows should make a sécurité call on VHF 16 low power before entering.

Skedans Bay. Skedans (or K'uuna Llnagaay) is situated on the the eastern tip of Louise Island. It faces south onto Skedans Bay from a crescent beach that forms the neck of a small peninsula. As the furthest north of all the Watchmen sites, its relative accessibility makes it one of the most often visited. Skedans Bay is not within the protected area of the Gwaii Haanas National Park Reserve but visitors

Louise Narrows

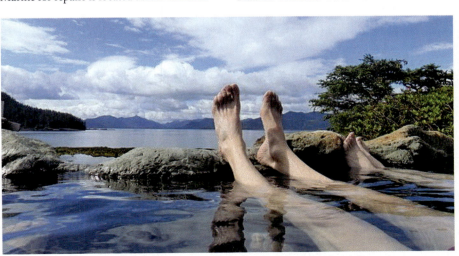

Hot spring pools on Hotspring Island have refilled after earthquake-induced disruption.

HAIDA GWAII

are still required to have had an orientation and to pay the day visit fee. The procedure for visiting all Watchmen sites is to contact the Haida Watchmen on VHF 06 before coming ashore. If the site already has visitors, the Watchmen may ask you to stand by on board until the next group can come ashore. K'uuna Llnagaay means Village at the Edge, but it was also known by the Haida as Grizzly-Bear-Town because of the large number of grizzly bear carvings found there. Visiting traders named it Skedans, a corruption of the name of its chief, Gida'nsta.

In the mid-1800s, almost 450 Haida lived here in about 26 Longhouses. Records show there were 56 monumental cedar sculptures, including frontal poles, single and double mortuary poles, memorial poles and mortuary figures.

K'uuna Llnagaay is one of the few remaining village sites with some standing poles and remnants of large Longhouses. Crests featured on the poles, such as rainbow, frog, eagle, beaver, and two-finned killer whale, signify which families lived there. A path winding through the old village allows you to appreciate the artistry of the poles, now in varying stages of decay, and provides a glimpse of what Haida life might have been like many years ago.

We anchored in 45 feet, about one mile southeast of the Watchmen site, and took the dinghy to shore. The anchorage immediately south of the Watchmen site was smaller and more exposed to northerly wind than we liked.

Thurston Harbour. Thurston Harbour on Talunkwan Island is a well-protected anchorage conveniently located between Skedans Watchmen site to the north and Tanu Watchmen site to the south. Anchor here following an afternoon visit to Skedans and get an early morning start to visit Tanu. There is plenty of room and good holding. While located near Gwaii Haanas Park, this anchorage is outside the park boundary and does not require a reservation or daily fee.

Dana Passage. Dana Passage is a narrow and scenic route between Talunkwan and Moresby Islands. At the narrowest section, the passage is only about 100 feet wide, but depths are at least 30 feet throughout.

GWAII HAANAS NATIONAL PARK RESERVE

Tanu Island. The beautiful and haunting village of T'aanuu Llnagaay is located on the east shore of Tanu Island, on Laskeek Bay. T'aanuu means eelgrass, which commonly grows in shallow water around the village. T'aanuu Llnagaay follows the shoreline of two beaches divided by a rocky shoal. In the mid-1800s, the village population was about 550, with 25 Longhouses, 31 mortuary columns, and 15 mortuary houses. Present-day visitors notice the many logs on the ground and may mistake them for windfalls; these, however,

are the posts and beams of old Longhouses. The Longhouses faced the shoreline, and were dug into the ground for protection from the weather. Large, rectangular pits mark their locations. Though there are no standing poles here, on close inspection you can see ancient carvings made smooth by time and furred by moss. Walking amidst the ruins, surrounded by the protective rainforest, one gets a strong sense of the people who lived there. Contact the Haida Watchmen on VHF 06 for permission before coming ashore.

Fair weather anchorage can be found just off the landing beach, in 35-50 feet. Holding is marginal and currents run strongly. When the wind is blowing from the north, swells roll in from Hecate Strait.

Crescent Inlet. The head of secluded Crescent Inlet has sheltered anchorage with good holding. The inlet has beautiful views of mountains and old growth forest. Bears frequent the meadow at the head of the inlet. Moresby Explorers, a tour company, maintains a small floating lodge in Crescent Inlet. The inlet is outside the protected area, anchorage here does not require a reservation or payment.

Anna Inlet. Beautiful, knobby mountains surround Anna Inlet. The narrow entrance is difficult to see but easily navigated. Steering a mid-channel course, we never saw depths less than 35 feet at zero tide. Anchor in 50-60 feet at the head of the inlet.

Echo Harbour. Picturesque and well protected, Echo Harbour just off Darwin Sound offers good anchorage. Take your dinghy around the corner to the head of the cove where you will find a waterfall and wildlife viewing. Field Correspondent Mary Campbell reports seeing kingfishers standing watch over the stream outflow and bears roaming the beach looking for clams. Douglass reports finding evidence of an old homestead and apple trees on shore. Watch for bears.

Hoya Passage. Currents run to 2 knots, flooding north and ebbing south.

Hoya Bay. Hoya Bay, also known as Freshwater Cove, located off Hoya Passage, has a public float with untreated fresh water available. For overnight stays, anchor out or use one of the two public mooring buoys.

De la Beche Inlet. According to Douglass, De la Beche Inlet has two interesting anchorages, De la Beche Cove and Sac Bay. De la Beche Cove is a small nook on the south shore of De la Beche Inlet, landlocked by an island. Douglass reports adequate holding at the head of the bay.

Sac Bay. Sac Bay juts out to the south from De la Beche Inlet, good holding and spectacular mountain scenery.

Standing mortuary poles on Anthony Island

⑥ **Hotspring Island.** Hotspring Island is one of the most popular stops in Haida Gwaii. The hot springs, located on the south side of the island, were struck by a magnitude 7.7 earthquake that shook the area in October of 2012 and changed mother nature's plumbing. For several years, the flow of hot water ceased entirely. In 2015, pools of hot water appeared below the high tide line, and in 2016 some of the pools began filling again. By 2017, three pools were full, with the hottest one near the Watchmen dwelling, and the other two nearby pools linked by a new boardwalk. In addition to the attractive boardwalk, changing facilities and a bathhouse were added at the site. 2018 saw the return of more boaters to once again enjoy this fabulous destination.

Haida Watchmen are on site and require boaters to call on VHF channel 06 before coming ashore. The anchorage directly off the hot springs is exposed, with marginal holding on a rocky bottom. A better anchorage is between Hotspring and House islands.

Ramsay Passage Cove. Fairly well-protected alternative to Hotspring Island anchorages, but requires a 1.5-mile dinghy ride.

Hotspring Island

Dolomite Narrows. Dolomite Narrows is the narrow, shallow neck within Burnaby Strait and is poorly charted. One section dries completely on a 2-foot tide. Currents run to several knots. Small, privately maintained range markers show the route the locals take, but the markers are often missing or hard to locate.

The Narrows are famous for the fabulous assortment of tidal life to be seen. Bat stars in a rainbow of colors, blood stars, and other amazing creatures rarely seen in the Pacific Northwest carpet the shallows. Field Correspondent Mary Campbell suggests anchoring in Bag Harbour to the south, or pick up the buoy just north of the narrows, and transit the narrows at low tide in your dinghy or kayak. This allows you to see how you feel about bringing your big boat through at high water slack, depending on the condition of the range markers and the expected depths. Alternatively, you can take the longer, more exposed route around Burnaby Island rather than chance grounding.

Bag Harbour. Bag Harbour is a secure anchorage at the south end of Dolomite Narrows. It's a good place to wait for appropriate conditions for a northbound transit of Dolomite Narrows, or relax after a transit.

Ikeda Cove. Ikeda Cove is a lovely, protected anchorage with excellent holding. A grassy meadow is a haven for wildlife. We spotted deer, a bear and cub, and a pair of sandhill cranes. Remains of cabins, wharves and machinery can be found on shore.

Collison Bay. Good protection but some swell can find its way into the bay. Anchor behind the islet on your starboard when entering the inner part of the bay. Holding and anchoring depths are good. The Landons waited-out a strong southeasterly for two days and watched a spectacular whale show at the entrance to the inner bay.

Windy Bay. Windy Bay, or Hlk'yah GaawGa, is a fair weather anchorage used to visit the historic fishing village called Hlk'yah Llnagaay (Falcon Town). Near here in 1985, the Haida blocked logging roads in their protest to put an end to logging on Lyell Island and protect the area that became Gwaii Haanas. The Longhouse is named "Looking Around and Blinking House" to honor this victory. An old growth forest contains trees over 1000 years old and more than 200 feet tall. A trail leads through huge Sitka spruce and western red cedar trees, draped with mosses and lichens. The Haida Watchmen can point out culturally modified trees where the bark was stripped for making baskets or hats. Some of these trees show where test holes were cut in them to check their suitability for making a canoe or carving a pole.

In August 2013, the Legacy Pole, the first new monumental pole in 130 years, was raised in Windy Bay. This pole was carved to celebrate the 20 years of co-management of the Reserve by the Haida Nation and the government of Canada. It is visible from the water.

We anchored just offshore from the Watchmen cabin, on the 3.7 meter sounding, in 20-30 feet, fair holding on a rocky bottom. Contact the Haida Watchmen on VHF 06 before coming ashore.

Heater Harbour. Located on the east side of Kunghit Island, Heater Harbour offers reasonable protection in settled weather with plenty of swinging room. The north and northwest arms are kelp gardens and you may need to spend time de-kelping your anchor; holding is good. Field Correspondent Mary Campbell reports that on a kayak trip up the northwest arm she spotted sandhill cranes and black-tailed deer.

⑦ **Rose Harbour.** Once a bustling whaling station, Rose Harbour is now a small, quiet community and the only piece of privately owned land within Gwaii Haanas. Remnants of the old whale rendering facilities can still be seen on the shoreline. Local residents provide bed and breakfast style lodging, tours, and meals; try contacting Frances on VHF 06. No fuel, water, or services available. This is a favorite stop for kayakers.

Rose Inlet. Open to the south, this large inlet with suitable anchoring depths is protected from most conditions except southerly weather. Field Correspondent Mary Campbell suggests good anchoring can be found at the head of the inlet or east of Denny Rocks; beachcombing and crabbing are good.

Louscoone Inlet. Louscoone Inlet at the south end of Moresby Island has several possible anchorages. Small Cove, east of Crooked Point, is reportedly rocky and filled with kelp. Etches Point Cove, between two unnamed islands northwest of Etches Point, is the best anchorage. The Douglasses report another small and unnamed cove with limited swinging room 1 mile northwest of Etches Point Cove and 0.4 mile north of Cadman Point.

Untreated fresh water is available from a hose on a buoy (52° 11.70N 131° 15.40W) shown on Chart 3857; boil before consuming.

⑧ **Anthony Island.** Anthony Island or SGang Gwaay, on the northwest side of Kunghit Island, is recognized worldwide as a historic UNESCO World Heritage Site. Nan Sdins (also known as Ninstints) is a former Haida village and the major attraction. Filled with the largest collection of original Haida heraldic and mortuary poles, Nan Sdins offers a remarkable look into the Haida culture. The poles at Nan Sdins have been reset upright for the last time. Going forward, when a pole naturally falls it will be left to decay, following the tradition of the memory fading for the chief or family depicted by the pole, and for whom it was created.

Anchorage is not permitted directly off the totem park. Instead, anchor in Grays Cove, or in the cove on the northwest corner of the island. Vessels with deeper draft will prefer anchoring in Grays Cove. If anchored in the northwest cove, look for the bright orange fishing floats on the beach. These floats mark the boardwalk trail through the woods to the Watchman cabin for check-in. Call the Haida Watchmen on VHF 06 for permission to come ashore.

SGang Gwaay and the Nan Sdins Village Site is one of the top 10 places to visit on the entire coast. You might feel the spirits of the Haida as you walk through the woods to Nan Sdins. You emerge from the wood into a grove of carved poles. From the beach you can see what it must have been like when the Haida pulled their long war canoes up in front of the village. Nan Sdins should not be missed.

⑧ **Grays Cove.** Grays Cove, on the eastern shore of SGang Gwaay, is about a quarter-mile south of Nan Sdins, with a good dinghy landing beach and trail to the site. While well-protected from west and northwest weather, it is open to the south and east. The bottom is rocky and notorious for poor holding. Set well and check your set; anchor watch is advised.

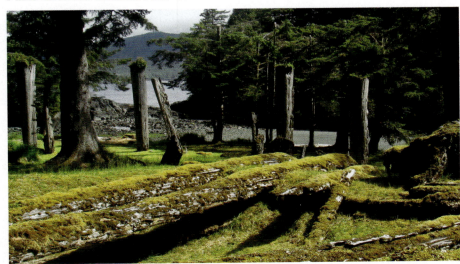

Mortuary Poles on SGang Gwaay (Anthony Island)

Haida Gwaii, Cape St. James

Crossing Dixon Entrance

CHAPTER 18

VENN PASSAGE TO METLAKATLA BAY
Du Vernet Pt. • Metlakatla

PORTLAND INLET AND TONGASS PASSAGE ROUTE
Port Simpson • Tongass Passage • Lincoln Channel

NORTH DUNDAS ISLAND ROUTE
Green Island • Holliday Passage • Danger Passage

FOGGY BAY OR MARY ISLAND TO KETCHIKAN
Revillagigedo Channel • Tongass Narrows

CROSSING DIXON ENTRANCE

See Area Map Page 489 - Maps Not for Navigation

On to Southeast Alaska! This chapter covers the departure routes from Prince Rupert and Chatham Sound, the options for the open water crossing of Dixon Entrance, and the approach to Ketchikan.

The distance from Prince Rupert to Ketchikan (via Venn Passage) is 82 nautical miles. Depending on the speed of your vessel, the weather and sea conditions, a stop in Prince Rupert before crossing Dixon Entrance might be required. Foggy Bay is 50 miles from Prince Rupert and could be an option for an overnight stop. It's a beautiful anchorage with good protection.

Vessels must report arrival into U.S. waters in Alaska to U.S. Customs and Border Protection (CBP) by one of three means: CBP ROAM App; telephone call to CBP Small Boat Reporting Office if all aboard are enrolled in a Trusted Traveler Program such as Nexus, Global Entry, or I-68; or by reporting in-person to a CBP Officer in Ketchikan. Cellular coverage is usually found near Cape Fox where arrival reporting to CBP may be possible with the ROAM App or call to Small Boat Reporting Office. Vessels that have reported arrival, completed clearance, and have a clearance number from CBP by ROAM may proceed to their destination. Those that need to report in-person in Ketchikan and need more than one day to reach Ketchikan will need to contact CBP in Ketchikan in advance for permission to anchor one night in Foggy Bay. Vessels planning to overnight in Foggy Bay before clearing customs must call CBP in Ketchikan (907-225-2254) for permission. See *Chapter 19 Arriving In Ketchikan* and *Chapter 1 U.S. And Canadian Customs Information* for more about clearing customs.

Before leaving British Columbia, however, consider some of the excellent cruising in Portland Inlet and Portland Canal, just north of Prince Rupert. Portland Canal is one of the longest fjords in North America and defines the border between the U.S. and Canada. It is beautiful and remote. Farther up the canal, the water becomes increasingly opaque, almost milky, the result of glacial run-off. The outpost of Stewart, B.C., with Bear Glacier just above town, has a public dock, a "yacht club," and other services. Stewart, B.C. is so remote that there is no VHF weather radio reception.

Hyder, Alaska is on the other side of the canal, less than a mile from Stewart. Hyder does not have a U.S. Customs office for clearance. Ketchikan is the closest CBP office. The typical strategy is to explore British Columbia on the way north, then go to Ketchikan for customs clearance. When headed home from Southeast Alaska, explore the areas south of Ketchikan, such as Misty Fjord or Hyder. Then go to Prince Rupert for customs clearance into Canada.

Both the United States and Canada require vessels to check in with customs authorities prior to anchoring, mooring, or going ashore.

In addition to Portland Canal, Observatory Inlet has a number of good anchorages. This area was the base camp for Captain George Vancouver when his expedition explored this area in 1793.

Cruising in Portland Canal is covered in detail by Don and Reanne Douglass in their cruising guide, *Exploring the North Coast of British Columbia,* published by FineEdge.com.

Crossing Dixon Entrance: Heading North. Several options exist for transiting Chatham Sound and crossing the open water of Dixon Entrance.

Understanding how to read the weather, sea conditions, and currents is critical to planning a safe and comfortable passage. Good planning for the crossing starts with examining the weather forecast and course options.

A stop at Prince Rupert can be a welcome break after the long passage up Grenville Channel and through northern British Columbia. Prince Rupert is the last fuel stop in Canada, and some boats may need to take on fuel before proceeding the 82 miles to Ketchikan.

If conditions are favorable, many boats bypass Prince Rupert entirely on their way north. This saves several hours of transit time. Anchorages are available in the Moffatt Islands, Qlawdzeet Anchorage on Stephens Island, and Brundige Inlet on Dundas, or in Foggy Bay after crossing Dixon Entrance (with a call to U.S. Customs and Border Protection in Ketchikan, (907) 225-2254).

The first route option is the shortest but the most exposed. From Venn Passage steer towards the northeast tip of Dundas Island. Then set a course past Cape Fox (leave plenty of sea room) to Mary Island and up Revillagigedo Channel.

A second route is a variation on the first: Cross Chatham Sound on a northwest heading and pass through the Moffatt Islands. They're beautiful and protected, but require good situational awareness to navigate among the many small islands, islets, and rocks. Several anchorages are tucked among the islands, pleasant enough for an overnight at anchor. At Dundas Island cross to Cape Fox and follow the coastline to Foggy Bay to overnight. The next morning continue up Revillagigedo Channel to Ketchikan.

The third choice is a longer route. First travel along the east side of Chatham Sound, then cross Portland Inlet. Sometimes referred to as the "mainland route," it offers some protection, and minimizes the open water crossing by harbor hopping along the shoreline. Attention needs to be focused on the effect of outflow wind and current from Portland Inlet.

The longer routes offer more shelter and duck-in points. The best choice depends on weather and current conditions. It is critical to develop a good picture of the currents, wind speed and direction, and ocean swells from the Environment Canada and NOAA weather forecasts, buoy reports, and lightstation reports. Monitoring these

---

DIXON ENTRANCE GO-NOGO CHECKLIST

Tides & Currents - See Ports & Passes; Canadian Tides & Current Tables Vol. 7
- ❏ Phase of the moon – Spring or Neap Tide; Neap Tides preferred
- ❏ Check for slack water time at Kelp Island Passage, Duke Island and Port Simpson

Weather System Predictions – via Internet or satellite
- ❏ Check NOAA Ocean Prediction Center forecasts for any approaching significant weather systems
- ❏ Check Windy.com, Predictwind.com, SiriusXM Marine, or Sailflow.com
- ❏ See Environment Canada and NWS NOAA forecasts for the Synopsis for Dixon Entrance East

Weather & Seas Forecasts – via Internet, phone, or VHF
- ❏ See Environment Canada Forecast for Dixon Entrance East; Check for warnings, note wind speed and direction, wave height and interval, and trends
- ❏ See NOAA NWS Forecast for Clarence Strait; check for warnings; note wind speed, direction and sea conditions

Observations & Present Conditions – via Internet, phone, or VHF
- ❏ Check Buoy Reports for West Dixon Entrance (46205), and Central Dixon Entrance (46145); note wind speed and direction, wave height and interval, and sea conditions.
- ❏ Check Lighthouse and Station Reports for Rose Point, Triple Island, Green Point, and Dundas Island; note wind speed, direction, and sea condition

Go-NoGo Decision
- √ Check wind direction in relation to direction of travel.
- √ Do the wind and wave conditions exceed your limit?
- √ Is there a wind against wave or current situation?

Fail-Safe Contingency Plans
- √ Duck-in locations along the route: Moffett Islands, Simpson Bay, Tongass Passage, Brundige Inlet, Dundas Island, Foggy Bay

See *Chapter 1 Interpreting Northwest Weather* sections for telephone numbers, website addresses, VHF channels, and buoy numbers.

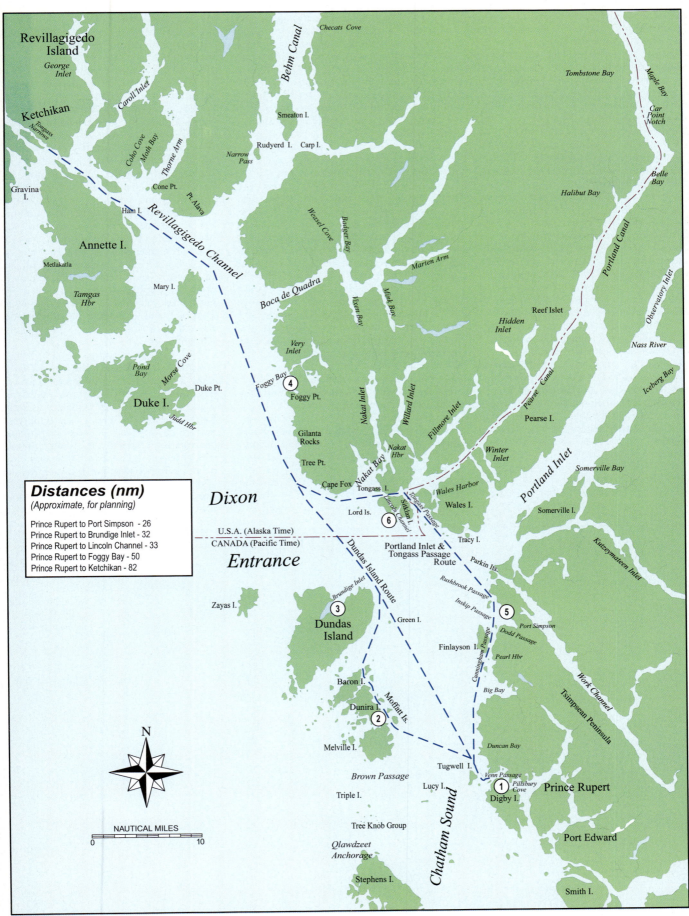

Dixon Entrance

CROSSING DIXON ENTRANCE

2020 Waggoner Cruising Guide

CROSSING DIXON ENTRANCE

See Area Map Page 489 - Maps Not for Navigation

resources for several days prior to crossing Dixon Entrance can give a skipper a good understanding of what to expect during a crossing. Once headed up Revillagigedo Channel, instructions for clearing U.S. Customs and arriving in Ketchikan are covered in the Ketchikan chapter.

Weather planning. Planning a Dixon Entrance crossing starts with NOAA and Environment Canada forecasts. Use NOAA's "Dixon Entrance to Cape Decision" forecast and Environment Canada's "Dixon Entrance East" forecast.

Given a favorable forecast, several weather reporting stations are useful in determining if conditions are acceptable. The Central Dixon Entrance Buoy (Buoy 46145) provides regularly updated wind speed, direction and sea state information. This information can be accessed by listening to the continuous marine broadcast, using the Dial-a-Buoy service (888-701-8992), or (301) 713-9620, or checking online at www.ndbc.noaa.gov.

Automated, land-based weather stations at Lucy Island, Grey Islet, and Rose Spit provide wind speed and direction, updated hourly. The Green Island and Triple Island lightstations are staffed with lightkeepers year round. These lightkeepers provide updated weather observations every three hours, including wind and sea conditions. Listen for their reports on the continuous marine broadcast, or visit www.weather.gc.ca. You may also be able to call them directly on VHF 82.

The NOAA Ocean Prediction Center, Pacific Marine section website has extensive forecast information (www.opc.ncep.noaa.gov/Pac_tab.shtml). The Current, 24, 48, 72, and 96 hour surface wind and wave forecast charts are valuable resources for a graphical look at upcoming weather systems and conditions. Mariners are also using Apps like PredictWind.com, SailFlow.com, and Windy.com which give visual representations of forecast winds and sea conditions to judge the open ocean crossing. These Apps require a good internet connection.

Consider reading a weather book or taking a weather course to help understand and interpret weather data. Much data is available, even if the only source is the VHF continuous marine broadcast. The key is to understand the information as it streams by, and to use reports from multiple stations to paint a complete picture for the area you are interested in. An outflow wind from Portland Inlet blowing against a flood current, for example, will make for rough conditions as far away as Dundas Island. Even with the best preparations, conditions can change. Have a backup plan, such as using Brundige Inlet as a duck-in point before crossing. Be sure your vessel and crew are ready for changing weather conditions.

① **Venn Passage to Metlakatla Bay.** Venn Passage and the route through Metlakatla Bay is suitable for recreational boats of 75 feet or less. The route through Venn Passage is narrow and twisting, with shoals on each side. Buoys and range markers help navigation. Depths can be less than 10 feet, so some skippers time their passage for mid- or high-tide.

This route saves about 12 miles, compared with going south from Prince Rupert Harbour and rounding Digby Island. It's the channel favored by the fishing fleet, and it can be busy with fish boats. The route requires careful situational awareness and attention to the depth sounder and chartplotter. Even the buoys are suspect. In the past some have been dragged hundreds of yards out of position by log tows. Use caution when passing the landing for the ferry to the airport at Du Vernay Point. It is a regularly enforced no-wake zone. A no-wake zone in front of the village of Metlakatla is also enforced. Spend time studying the charts or your chartplotter to understand this route before attempting.

From Prince Rupert, head west to Grindstone Point and enter the channel. Follow the buoys and range markers. Note when heading west through Venn Passage, the range markers will be astern (back ranges). You will need either a clear view astern, or a stern watch with clear communication to the helm. At Tugwell Island, a turn to the north takes you into Chatham Sound toward Dundas Island, or along a route that follows the shoreline toward Port Simpson and Portland Inlet.

Dundas Island Route. The shortest route across Dixon Entrance is to depart Metlakatla Bay, take a direct course towards Green Island, then head up Holliday Passage. Round the top of Dundas Island and turn toward Mary Island. Proceed via Tongass Narrows to Ketchikan. If Dixon Entrance is too rough, you can anchor in protected Brundige Inlet on the north end of Dundas Island and remain in Canadian waters. If conditions allow a crossing of Dixon Entrance late in the day you can proceed to Foggy Bay

Venn Passage

CROSSING DIXON ENTRANCE

for the night. The next day go from Foggy Bay to Ketchikan via Revillagigedo Channel and Tongass Narrows.

For planning purposes, it's about 26 miles from Metlakatla to Brundige Inlet. It's an additional 22 miles from Brundige Inlet to Foggy Bay through mainly open water. Foggy Bay to Ketchikan is 32 miles. The total distance from Prince Rupert to Ketchikan is 82 miles—a long day for a displacement-speed cruising boat. There are no services along this route.

② **Moffatt Islands.** For an interesting and scenic passage, depart Metlakatla Bay and head west to Melville Island. Carefully pick your way through the channel between Dunira Island and the Moffatt Islands. Cross to Dundas Island and Holliday Passage and proceed to the north end of Dundas Island. Several small anchorages are along the way in the Moffatt Islands. Canadian Sailing Directions cautions against this route without local knowledge. We found it easy enough to follow with good charts or a chartplotter.

③ **Brundige Inlet.** Brundige Inlet extends for about 2.5 miles. Enter at Prospector Point. The inlet is well protected, though windblown and barren in areas. Some have advised of vicious black flies on the island. Not the prettiest anchorage, but a good protected departure point to cross Dixon Entrance.

④ **Foggy Bay.** Foggy Bay is a well-protected stopping place between Prince Rupert and Ketchikan. For those headed north, it can provide an escape from rough conditions in Dixon Entrance. Headed south, it is a good overnight anchorage to shorten the leg to Prince Rupert and allows for an early morning departure to cross Dixon Entrance. Most boats anchor in the "inner cove," which provides a view of the conditions in Foggy Bay and Dixon Entrance. Uncharted rock awash reported at 54° 57.518'N , 130° 57.280' W. If you want privacy in a remote environment,

cruise deep into Very Inlet to the "north basin." Use the Douglass' *Exploring Southeast Alaska* for detailed information on the anchorage in Foggy Bay and other interesting anchorages in the area.

LOCAL KNOWLEDGE

Fishing Nets: From Cape Fox to Tree Point, you may encounter many gillnet fish boats. Gillnets can extend up to 1800 feet from the boat (mostly from the stern, but sometimes from the bow) and show hard-to-see small white floats along the top of the net. The end is marked by an orange float, which is often difficult to see in choppy seas. They sometimes monitor VHF 16 when their nets are set.

Foggy Bay or Mary Island to Ketchikan. This route appears to be a straight shot up Revillagigedo Channel to Ketchikan, although weather conditions can vary from one side of the channel to the other. You might also encounter changing conditions as you pass Behm Canal, Thorne Arm or other inlets, depending on the wind direction and speed. Expect to see more recreational vessels, fish boats, tugs with tows and even large cruise ships maneuvering in Tongass Narrows as you approach Ketchikan.

Note the location of Behm Canal as you pass. Later in the trip you might want to visit some of the majestic cruising areas in Misty Fjords.

Danger Pass. At the south end of Mary Island and off Edge Point, this narrow passage will allow you to move out of the main channel and along the back side of Mary Island. Depending on the wind direction, this route allows you to travel in the lee of Mary Island.

Portland Inlet & Tongass Passage Route. This route is preferred when northern outflow winds from Portland Inlet create a sharp chop in Chatham Sound. It reduces the open water across Portland Inlet to less than 5 miles. The total distance from Metlakatla Bay to Foggy Bay is about 50 miles.

If planning to overnight in Foggy Bay, the skipper must call U.S. Customs and Border Protection (907) 225-2254 in Ketchikan and inform them.

⑤ **Port Simpson.** North of Metlakatla Bay, Port Simpson can be used as a jumping-off point for crossing Portland Inlet. Port Simpson is a tribal village protected behind Rose Island. There are several floats, though they're often filled with commercial and fishing vessels, requiring rafting. A small store is in the village.

⑥ **Lincoln Channel.** Lincoln Channel, between Tongass Island and Kanagunut Island on the west and Sitklan Island and the mainland on the east, provides an interesting stop with easy access for boats coming from either Ketchikan, or Nichols Bay on Prince of Wales Island. The south end of Lincoln Channel is only two miles from the Canadian border and 38 miles from Prince Rupert, making it a good departure point for vessels heading south.

This is a popular anchorage for fish boats during the gillnet season. Several fishermen keep float houses here. Tongass Island was the site of Fort Tongass, the first U.S. Customs office in Alaska, and a major Tlingit village. The rocky shores of Kanagunut Island contain interesting rock formations. You may even find garnets near Garnet Point on the south tip of the island.

Enter at either the north or south end of the channel, or between Tongass Island on the north and Kanagunut Island on the south. If entering between Tongass and Kanagunut, follow Chart 17437 or your chartplotter carefully and watch for rocks. The best anchorage is north of a small unnamed island in 80-100 feet. Anchorage can also be found off Tongass Island or, in northerly winds, south of the unnamed island.

Crossing Dixon Entrance: Heading South. Southbound vessels coming from Southeast Alaska must clear Canadian Customs if they intend to stop or anchor in British Columbia. If transiting non-stop between Ketchikan and the U.S., as delivery captains or fish boats often do, customs clearance is not required. Most recreational boats will stop along the way and thus require clearance into Canada in Prince Rupert.

Approach Prince Rupert through Metlakatla Bay and Venn Passage, or continue down the west side of Digby Island and enter through Prince Rupert Harbour.

Once in the harbor, proceed to the designated customs dock or one of the four marinas where customs reporting is allowed by telephone: Fairview Terminal, the new Cow Bay Marina at Atlin Terminal, Prince Rupert Rowing & Yacht Club, or Rushbrooke Floats.

The customs dock, or "lightering dock," is painted green and located west of the Cow Bay area and below a shopping mall on shore. Call customs from the dedicated phone on the dock. The gate to the street is locked.

If clearing customs at another facility, call by cell phone (888) 226-7277.

Until cleared, all crew must remain on the boat. Canadian Customs may send agents to your boat for an inspection. Once cleared, you will be given a clearance number to post on the dockside window of your vessel and record in the ship's log.

If the weather deteriorates and you must anchor in Canadian waters before clearing customs in Prince Rupert, call Canadian Customs by phone, or notify the Canadian Coast Guard on VHF 16.

Note: All calls to Canadian Customs are directed to a call center in Hamilton, Ontario. While the customs agents on the phone are not located in Prince Rupert, they can still call out local agents if a clearance requires an inspection.

2020 Waggoner Cruising Guide 491

Arriving in Ketchikan

CHAPTER 19

KETCHIKAN
Thomas Basin • Casey Moran •
Bar Harbor North & South

KETCHIKAN

Ketchikan is Alaska's first shopping and dining destination.

Ketchikan. Tongass Narrows is the transition from crossing Dixon Entrance to arrival in a bustling maritime city. The transition begins at Mountain Point, and the closer you get to the city, the more signs of humanity you see. Overhead, float planes take summer tourists to Misty Fjords and other sites. The shoreline changes from remote and pristine to a few homes, then a few more, and eventually a developed roadway. Soon, cars are whizzing by. Off in the distance, up Tongass Narrows, the shapes of what seems to be a major city appear. In reality, they are the profiles of cruise ships lined up at the docks, towering 10 stories high, dwarfing the buildings below.

We enjoy visiting Ketchikan. Shopping is good. Several restaurants serve excellent food. The airport is convenient for exchanging crew or flying home. Boat repairs can be arranged, although the local mechanics cater mostly to the fishing fleet. The Fourth of July parade and fireworks are a favorite.

Cruise ships frequent Ketchikan. Three to four cruise ships are typically moored in Ketchikan during the day, their passengers touring the city, shopping, or just hanging out and absorbing their first (or last) stop in Alaska. You may encounter one of the cruise ships headed towards you, an imposing sight. Remember that federal law requires boats stay at least 100 yards from cruise ships. Occasionally the Coast Guard will escort cruise ships in and out of town and require 200 yards of separation. Listen to VHF channel 16 or 13 for Securité calls from cruise ships (and other commercial ships) as they prepare to get underway, and be prepared to alter course to maintain adequate separation.

Ketchikan calls itself "Alaska's First City"—the first city visitors see when they arrive in Southeast Alaska by boat. The cruise ships typically arrive early in the morning and depart by mid-afternoon or early evening. During the day the town can be bursting with 10,000 visitors if several cruise ships are docked. When the ships leave, usually in late afternoon or early evening, the tourist shops close and Ketchikan returns to a sleepy little Alaskan town.

Ketchikan has three public marinas and two private marinas for transient moorage, each with its own advantages, disadvantages, and personality.

A Walmart north of town runs a free shuttle between their store and the cruise ship docks. Ketchikan has several options for provisioning and picking up parts and marine hardware.

Ketchikan also has a number of local attractions and museums, including the Totem Heritage Center, the Southeast Alaska Discovery Center, and the Tongass Historical Museum. All are within walking distance of the marinas. Totem Bight State Park and Saxman Native Village are accessible by bus. The buses run every 30-45 minutes.

Ketchikan has a good public bus system, the Ketchikan Gateway Borough Bus, that shuttles passengers to the main attractions, or from the airport ferry to downtown. Individual rides are $2; a day pass is $5, please have exact change. The bus also runs to several places you may want to visit, such as Totem Bight State Park, Saxman Native Village, and additional shopping farther

KETCHIKAN

from the waterfront. Taxis are also available, though they seem to use "cruise ship flat rate pricing" to some destinations. The bus is convenient and low cost, with stops near the three marinas. Schedule posted at bus stops.

Customs Clearance. Vessels entering Alaska from B.C. are required to clear customs in Ketchikan. There are three methods to report arrival to U.S. Customs and Border Protection (CBP). New for 2019, boaters may use the CBP ROAM App on their Android or iOS mobile phone or tablet to report their arrival. Cellular phone service, which usually begins near Cape Fox, is required in order to use this option. The ROAM App satisfies U.S. CBP requirements to report your arrival. See *Chapter 1 - U.S. and Canadian Customs Information* for more about CBP ROAM. If all aboard are enrolled in a Trusted Traveler Program such as Nexus, Global Entry, or I-68, then you can report arrival by calling the CBP Small Boat Reporting Office (800) 562-5943 by cellular or satellite phone upon entering U.S. waters in Dixon Entrance. The third option remains, reporting in-person to a CBP Officer upon arrival in Ketchikan by calling Ketchikan CBP at (907) 225-2254.

Vessels are not allowed to drop anchor or land in Alaska until they have reported their arrival and obtained a CBP clearance. With prior approval, Ketchikan CBP typically allows vessels that need more than one day to arrive in Ketchikan for in-person customs clearance to stay one night in Foggy Bay before proceeding to Ketchikan for customs clearance. The procedure is to call (907) 225-2254 and advise CBP of your plans. Many crews will call from Prince Rupert. U.S. cell phone coverage usually begins at Cape Fox with fairly good coverage in Dixon Entrance. To date, we haven't found cell coverage in Foggy Bay.

Assuming a good phone connection, a CBP agent will take all of the necessary information about your vessel and crew. Be ready with your information when you call. The next day when you arrive in Ketchikan, the agent will have this information when he or she comes to your boat. At this point, all they need to do is verify ID with your passport photo. If weather or other unforeseen circumstances cause you to anchor in U.S. territory before reporting to CBP and you can't make telephone contact, hail U.S. Coast Guard on VHF and report your circumstance.

If you will be reporting arrival in-person in Ketchikan and you will be arriving after normal office hours, call ahead. CBP officers do check the marinas to confirm that all vessels have checked in.

You'll pass two fuel docks as you approach Ketchikan. Upon request, and if workload allows, CBP may meet you at the fuel dock for clearance, allowing you to refuel and clear customs at the same time. Call first to see if this is possible.

In our experience, we have found that CBP agents often take a common sense approach to bringing fruits and vegetables into Alaska. They may request that you commit to consuming the items. Declare all items.

Non-U.S. flagged vessels that don't already have a Cruising License (including Canadian vessels), may request a Cruising License upon clearing customs; a Cruising License reduces the cost and complexity for foreign-flagged vessels. See Chapter 1 Cruising License section under U.S./Canada Border Crossings. Cruising Licenses do not affect customs reporting requirements.

Note: U.S. flagged vessels that have departed from a U.S. port without stopping or clearing Canada customs do not need to clear customs in Ketchikan.

Guidebook. For cruising in Alaska we recommend Don and Reanne Douglass' excellent guide, *Exploring Southeast Alaska*, 3rd Ed. Full disclosure: our sister company, Fine Edge, is the publisher. For 2018, the Southeast Alaska book was extensively updated by Reanne Douglass and her staff. It is the only comprehensive cruising guide for Southeast Alaska and includes additional tips for crossing Dixon Entrance and arriving in Ketchikan.

Time change. Ketchikan is in Alaska Time Zone, one hour earlier than Seattle and British Columbia. Set clocks back one hour when you arrive.

Alaska Pilotage Requirements. Non-U.S. flagged vessels longer than 65 feet must employ an Alaska Marine Pilot when operating in Alaskan waters or apply for and receive an exemption. The State of Aklaska offers a downloadable Yacht Navigation Package with useful information; visit www.commerce.alaska.gov.

Moorage. City of Ketchikan's Port & Harbors department manages three marinas on the Ketchikan waterfront, Thomas Basin, Bar Harbor, and Casey Moran. Thomas Basin and Bar Harbor basins slips are permanently assigned, with waiting lists for vacancies.

Tongass Narrows

KETCHIKAN

Visiting boats are hot-berthed into one of these slips when the local boat is gone. First-come, first-served open moorage can be found at Casey Moran, and in designated areas of Thomas Basin and Bar Harbor Basins. Two private marinas, Doyon's Landing and Ketchikan Moorage (Ellis Floats), cater primarily to larger yachts with limited moorage for other boats.

The City Port & Harbors office does not take reservations. Things change by the hour; the office will work with you to find moorage. For many first-time visitors, especially with larger boats, not having a reservation is disconcerting. The staff is good at fitting everyone in. For a slip assignment, call "Ketchikan Harbormaster" on VHF 73 (preferred), VHF 16, or phone (907) 228-5632. Harbormasters are on duty 7-days a week 6:00 a.m. to 10:00 p.m. May through September, and 8:00 a.m. to 5:00 p.m. October through April. The office is open 8:00 a.m. to 5:00 p.m. 7-days a week during summer months and Monday through Friday during winter. For moorage at one of the first-come, first-served areas, take an unoccupied space and then register and pay at the office. See maps in this section or www.ktn-ak.us/harbors for designated open moorage. There are limited options for unattended long-term moorage when leaving your boat for an extended period.

All vessels must register with the Harbormaster's office at Bar Harbor North by visiting the office or by phone; or by emailing an electronically completed registration form to the email address indicated on the form which can be downloaded from the City website at www.ktn-ak.us/harbors. Moorage fees are paid by calling the harbor office with credit card information, or in person at the harbor office with credit card, cash, or check.

Hot-berthing usually works well; harbor staffers are on the docks often checking the status of slips matching visiting boaters' planned stays with permanent tenant vacancies. Sometimes, though, a permanent tenant returns to their slip sooner than planned. If this happens, the office will re-assign the visiting boat to a new slip and you must be available to move your boat. The Harbormaster's office will contact you with instructions to move to another slip, sometimes between marinas, from Thomas Basin to Bar Harbor for example. When your crew goes out touring or shopping, they could come back to find the boat has moved to a new moorage a mile away. It helps to have a communication plan in case things change. The Harbormaster works hard to accommodate everyone.

Shore power may not be available at all hot-berthed slips. Specify your power requirements when requesting a slip at Thomas Basin or Bar Harbor basins. Most shore power hookups, whether locked or not, are privately owned by the permanent tenant; do not plug into power without permission from the Harbormaster. At Casey Moran, all shore power hookups are available for use. In Thomas Basin and Bar Harbor basins, power hookups marked with a red "HP" (Harbor Power) sticker near the electric meter face are available for use. There is a separate charge for shore power. Shore power has been upgraded to ELCI-protected circuits at Thomas Basin and Float 9 at Bar Harbor.

Thomas Basin, the first major marina you'll see when approaching from the south, is at the foot of Creek Street in the heart of the tourist district. It's an easy walk to groceries, local shops, and attractions. Ketchikan Yacht Club is in the red building on float 2, with some transient (no reciprocal) moorage available. The members are friendly, helpful, and a good source of local knowledge.

Casey Moran Harbor, formerly known as (and still often called) "City Floats," is next. It's small and in the middle of downtown, right in the shadow of the cruise ships. Moorage is first-come, first-served anywhere with unpainted bull rails.

Bar Harbor North and South are about a mile north of the center of Ketchikan. A Safeway, shopping mall, and chandlery are a short walk away.

Weather. Ketchikan gets more than 150 inches of rain each year. Its driest month

KETCHIKAN MARKETPLACE

ALASKA EAGLE ARTS
Alaska Eagle Arts Gallery features contemporary Native artist Marvin Oliver. Established in 1991 by Brigette Ellis (granddaughter of legendary aviator Bob Ellis of Ellis Airlines). This fine art gallery features Marvin's work in glass, bronze, steel, wood, paper and more!
907-225-8365 • #5 Creek Street • www.alaskaeaglearts.com

ALASKA FISH HOUSE
Come and visit us, in the heart of downtown Ketchikan, for a taste of fresh, locally caught, Alaskan seafood. Cozy up around the fireplace and enjoy the view overlooking our private marina. If you prefer a more exclusive dining experience, call us to reserve our captain's room and customize your menu.
907-225-4055 • #3 Salmon Landing • www.alaskafishhouse.com

BARANOF FISHING EXCURSIONS
Let Baranof introduce you to Ketchikan's world renowned fishing waters. Enjoy halibut and salmon fishing, bottom fishing, dungeness crabbing and seafood dining at our remote wilderness campsite. We are happy to help create the perfect Alaska Fishing adventure for you and your group.
907-225-4055 • #3 Salmon Landing (below the Alaska Fish House) • www.exclusivealaska.com

CRAZY WOLF STUDIO
Authentic, traditional NW Coast Native art by Ketchikan Tsimshian Ken Decker and other regional artists. Local native owned and operated store. Masks, paddles, bentwood boxes, drums, prints, ivory, argillite, apparel, and handcarved native jewelry.
907-225-9653 • 633 Mission St. • www.crazywolfstudio.com

PACIFIC PRIDE OF ALASKA
Locally owned commercial and sport fishing gear store. We pride ourselves in a large inventory to keep you on the water catching fish. Stop in and see why we're the name fish fear most.
907-225-3135 • 1050 Water Street

PARNASSUS BOOKS AND GIFTS
For three decades, Parnassus Books and Gifts has specialized in books about Alaska from around the world. We also have an outstanding handpicked selection of general stock, best-sellers, gift items, chocolate and local handcrafted arts and crafts.
907-225-0870 • 105 Stedman St. • parnassusak@gmail.com

SOHO COHO
A contemporary art and craft gallery featuring local artists and natural history items. Located on Creek Street, the Soho Coho is also a planetary headquarters of Ketchikan artist Ray Troll.
907-225-5954 • 5 Creek Street • www.trollart.com

TIMBER & MARINE SUPPLY INC.
Located in the heart of Bar Harbor for over 40 years. We are a marine hardware retail store. We sell and service Honda and Suzuki outboard motors, and are a Lund Boat and Achilles Inflatable dealer.
907-225-6644 • 2547 Tongass Ave. • www.timberandmarine.com

Visit www.visit-ketchikan.com for list of community events

KETCHIKAN

See Area Map Page 494 - Maps Not for Navigation

(July) is wetter than Seattle's wettest month (November). Daytime summer temperatures typically range from the high 40s to the mid 60s, but occasionally reach into the 80s. Rain boots, better known as "Alaska Sneakers," are readily available in local stores. Locals swear by the brown XtraTuf brand.

Fuel. Diesel, gasoline, and propane are available at three locations. Petro Marine Services and Crowley Fuels are located south of town and north of the Coast Guard station. North of town, near the airport ferry landing, is Crowley Fuels, with attendant service during business hours and credit card self-serve on off-hours.

Airport. The Ketchikan Airport is convenient for visitors and crew. Alaska Airlines and Delta Airlines each have several daily flights to Seattle. The airport is located across Tongass Narrows on Gravina Island, and connects with Ketchikan by a ferry that departs and arrives just north of Bar Harbor Marina. The ferry leaves the airport terminal every hour and half-hour, daily. The ferry leaves the Ketchikan side on the quarter hours. Crossing time is approximately 10 minutes. If flying out, allow time for the ferry schedule and walk to the airport.

Stairs and ramps connect the airport terminal with the ferry. If you have considerable luggage, it's best to take an airport shuttle van that will deliver you and your luggage door-to-door. On the airport side of the narrows, a small dock, north of the ferry dock and connected to the float plane dock, is below the covered stairway. Dinghies and boats under 35 feet can tie-up to drop off or pick up guests and luggage. The modest

THE OFFSHORE DRILLING BUSINESS

This offshore drilling has nothing to do with petroleum but rather the kind of drilling service practiced by dentists. It's the story about Dr. Vic Stime and how he combined his passion for boating with a retirement dental practice that brings dental services to remote villages in Southeast Alaska.

Dr. Stime sold his Spokane, Washington dental practice of 30 years when he was diagnosed with a deteriorating heart valve. After a successful operation which replaced the failing heart valve, he wanted to use his skills as a dentist and find a way to give back. Dr. Stime decided to combine business with pleasure and outfit his newly acquired Ranger Tug as a dental office. Providing his services to those who lived in the remote villages of Southeast Alaska was a perfect fit.

Dr. Stime seasonally tours eight communities in Southeast Alaska. He usually departs Bellingham in July on his Ranger Tug 31 to start the cruise to Ketchikan, where he begins his schedule of appointments. His website and Facebook page include his schedule and invite patients to make their appointments based on his scheduled destinations. In the 2018 season, his route included stops at the villages and towns of Ketchikan, Myers Chuck, Wrangle, Thoms Place, Thorne Bay, Metlakatla, and Coffman Cove. Destinations on his circuit range in size from Thoms Place with 10 people, to Ketchikan with 13,000.

Dr. Stime's Ranger Tug is a fairly standard production model Ranger 31 that has been outfitted with state-of-the-art dental equipment, including a digital x-ray machine. A mini-compressor provides power for the dental equipment, and an autoclave is used for sterilizing instruments. A dental chair has been installed in a canvas-enclosed area on the Tug's aft cockpit; patients can expect the extra benefit of a gentle rocking motion. Electrical power comes from an onboard generator, or shore power (when available). Sorry, there is no waiting room with out-of-date magazines; appointments are scheduled ahead of time and there's no waiting.

Patients include both children and adults. Dr. Stime's services include exams, x-rays, cleanings, fillings, fluoride treatment, sealants, and extractions. He accepts patients with insurance and Medicaid. For patients without insurance, he accepts cash and credit card. Sorry, no fish as payment.

2018 was Dr. Stime's second season in Southeast Alaska. His startup of Offshore Drilling in 2017 came at the right time. For the past 38 years, Dr. Fred Bache has been bringing his dental services to Southeast Alaska on his vessel/dental office and reportedly will be retiring soon. Dr. Stime now carries on the tradition and much needed service.

Dr. Stime was inspired to start Offshore Drilling Dentistry by Dr. Fred Bache, an Aberdeen, Washington dentist who has been visiting rural Alaskan communities on his boat the JENNY-B. Fred and Jenny Bache have been touring Southeast Alaska since 1969 in their purpose-built boat and dental office from a generation ago.

Dr. Victor Stime DDS is a graduate of the University of Washington. His private practice in Spokane of 30 years provided him the necessary experience, having filled more than 50,000 teeth and extracted more than 10,000 teeth. Dr. Stime's nephew, Luke Stime, travels with him and serves as dental assistant. Luke helps keep all the mechanical systems running smoothly on the Ranger Tug. Luke is also connected to the maritime industry; you can find him most of the year in Tofino, BC where he is the Assistant Manager at the Tofino Harbour Authority docks.

Dentistry and boating may seem like an unusual mix, but it works. When not treating patients, Dr. Stime is out in Alaskan waters with his Ranger Tug fishing for salmon or halibut.

To learn more, go to their website at OffshoreDrillingLLC.com and their Facebook page @OffshoreDrillingDentistry

~ Leonard & Lorena Landon

KETCHIKAN

See Area Map Page 494 - Maps Not for Navigation

short-term moorage fee is paid in an honor box on the dock.

Doyon's Landing. 1716 South Tongass Highway, Ketchikan, AK 99901; (907) 225-5155; moorage@mistyfjords.com; www.doyonslanding.com. Open May through September. Power, water, 24-hour security, internet. Reservations encouraged. This is a full service marina that caters to large yachts. Located south of town near the Coast Guard station.

Petro Marine Services. 1100 Stedman St., P.O. Box 7398, Ketchikan, 99901; (800) 478-7277; (907) 225-2106; www.petromarineservices.com. Monitors VHF 16. Located on Tongass Narrows next to the U.S. Coast Guard station (buildings with red roofs). In summer, open 7 days a week from 7:00 a.m. to 7:00 p.m. In winter, Monday through Saturday, 8:00 a.m. to 5:00 p.m. and Sunday 9:00 a.m. to 5:00 p.m. Gasoline, diesel, propane, lubricants, restrooms, showers, garbage, and waste oil disposal.

Crowley Fuels. 900 Stedman St., P.O. Box 5858, Ketchikan, AK 99901; (907) 225-2163; www.anderesoil.com. Monitors VHF 16. Open summers: Monday through Friday 7:00 a.m. to 7:00 p.m., Saturday 7:00 a.m. to 6:00 p.m., and Sunday 8:00 a.m. to 5:00 p.m. Winter hours vary. Located on Tongass Narrows. Gasoline, diesel, propane, lubricants.

Thomas Basin, as seen from a cruise ship, has guest moorage near restaurants and shops.

Thomas Basin - Ketchikan Harbors. (907) 228-5632; www.city.ketchikan.ak.us. Monitors VHF 73. Moorage for boats to 60 feet, call ahead for a slip assignment, or find an unoccupied space in first-come, first-served areas. Water, pumpout, garbage and waste oil disposal, tidal grid to 100 tons (reservations required for grid). Power varies from slip to slip, check with the harbor office and inform them of power requirements when requesting a slip. All power is ELCI-protected. A hot berth system is maintained. You may be asked to move if the owner of a slip returns sooner than scheduled. Supermarket, restaurants, shops, and bars nearby. Located at the foot of Creek Street. Many attractions within

Port of Ketchikan, Thomas Basin

DON'T MISS MISTY FJORDS NATIONAL MONUMENT

Misty Fjords National Monument is among the most breathtaking places on the coast. Sheer granite walls plunge into the water from thousands of feet above and waterfalls gush from the snowcapped peaks. It's like Princess Louisa Inlet, only bigger and seldom visited by cruising boats.

Misty Fjords is on the west side of Behm Canal, which winds around Revillagigedo Island, and is entered either south or north of Ketchikan. Boats arriving from British Columbia typically pass the southern entrance, but because they have not yet cleared customs they are not allowed to visit. Thus, visiting Misty Fjords National Monument requires a bit of backtracking from Ketchikan.

Due to this backtracking, many save Misty Fjords for the end of their Southeast Alaska cruise. Upon exiting Behm Canal, they can overnight in Foggy Bay or clear Canadian Customs.

Some cruisers visit Misty Fjords by circumnavigating Revillagigedo Island. The downside is the relatively boring western section. An alternative is to head southeast from Ketchikan for about 20 miles. Then turn north into Behm Canal.

Smeaton Bay is the first bay and is not visited often. Rudyerd Bay is the next bay, just past New Eddystone Rock. New Eddystone has a sandy beach and a remarkable tree covered spire of rock jutting 200 feet into the air. Rudyerd Bay is probably the most visited area of Misty Fjords National Monument. Punchbowl Cove, the first anchorage, juts off to the south. It's deep and astoundingly beautiful. Think Yosemite, multiply by 3 or 4, and fill the valleys with water. A steep muddy trail leads to a lake about 1000 feet above sea level.

Don't expect to be alone in Punchbowl Cove. Tour boats and floatplanes bring cruise ship passengers from Ketchikan to Misty Fjords. We were shocked at how many camera flashes we saw going off as they passed our boat!

– Mark Bunzel

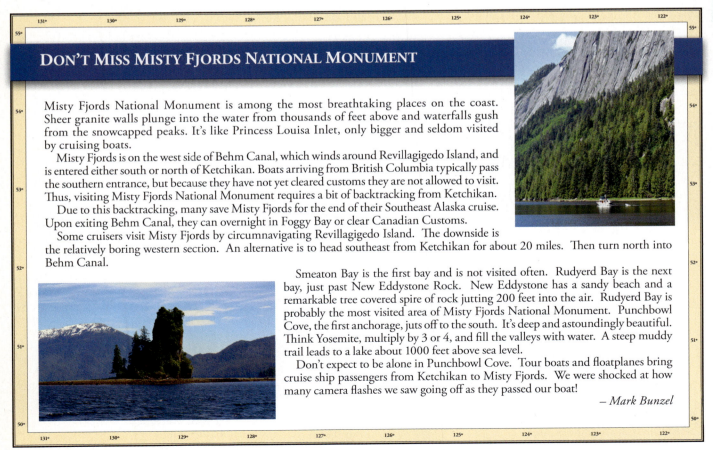

2020 Waggoner Cruising Guide

KETCHIKAN

See Area Map Page 494 - Maps Not for Navigation

walking distance. Local bus and taxi available on nearby Steadman Street.

Ketchikan Yacht Club. Clubhouse phone (907) 225-3262 relays the Port Captain's number; info@ketchikanyachtclub.com; ketchikanyachtclub.org/blog. On float 2 in Thomas Basin, with guest moorage when a member's slip is not being used. Pick an empty slip that fits your boat and check the whiteboard at the head of the slip for the return date of the slip holder. South side: boats 36-45 feet. North side: boats 24-39 feet. Slips cannot be reserved. Moorage is paid in the honor box at the yacht club. Power is 30 & limited 50 amp. A keycode to the clubhouse is available for guest boats. The clubhouse has Wi-Fi, restrooms, showers, laundry, kitchen, barbecue and social area. Guests are welcome to use the facility.

Casey Moran - Ketchikan Harbors. (907) 228-5632; www.city.ketchikan.ak.us. Monitors VHF 73. First-come, first-served moorage for boats to 90 feet, 30 & 50 amp power, water, garbage drop, pumpout, and waste oil disposal. White bull rails designate loading, blue designates handicap access. Unpainted bull rails show open moorage area, rafting is allowed. Close to all downtown attractions and in the shadow of cruise ships during the day. Restaurants, bars, and marine supplies nearby. Bus and taxi service are on the busy street above the marina.

Ketchikan Moorage (Locally known as Ellis Floats). (907) 225-8285; info@ketchikanmoorage.com; www.ketchikanmoorage.com. Open May through September. Moorage for boats to 170 feet, 30, 50 & 100 amp (single and 3-phase) power, water, garbage drop, free Wi-Fi and secure gate. Reservations encouraged. This is a full service marina that caters to larger yachts with a limited number of slips. Located north of Casey Moran and south of Bar Harbor.

Bar Harbor North and South - Ketchikan Harbors. (907) 228-5632; www.city.ketchikan.ak.us. Monitors VHF 73A. First-come, first-served moorage available on the ends of floats 3 - 5; 9 - 15; and the north side of float 7. All other slips reserved. Do not moor in a slip without authorization from harbormaster. Limited power (some of the docks are old). Power on dock 9 has been upgraded to ELCI-protected. Pumpout, water, restrooms, showers (8 minutes for $2 in quarters, change available in harbor office), garbage and waste oil disposal at the head of the dock. Tidal grid available by reservation. Restaurants, groceries, laundry, chandlery and shopping mall nearby. The marina is walking distance to the Alaska Marine Highway ferry terminal and the local ferry to the airport. The downtown area is about a 1.5 mile walk. Bus and taxi service available. The harbor office, with restrooms and showers, is in the green building between the north and south areas of the harbor.

Crowley Fuels. 4161 Tongass Avenue, Ketchikan, AK 99901; (907) 225-1985; www.anderesoil.com. Located on Tongass Narrows just south of the airport ferry. Gasoline, diesel, and lubricants. In summer, staffed 7 days a week, 8:00 a.m. to 6:00 p.m. In winter, Monday through Friday, 8:00 a.m. to 5:00 p.m. A card lock/credit card payment system is on the dock for after hours payment. It stops at $150, but can be used three times.

Ketchikan's popular lumberjack show engages the audience.

THINGS TO DO

1. **Totem Heritage Center.** Located Northeast of Thomas Basin and within walking distance. Great display of historic old totems.

2. **Saxman Native Village and Totem Bight State Park.** A glimpse into the traditions of the Tlingit culture. Both can be reached by bus. Saxman has tours and ceremonial dances, Totem Bight has 14 poles and a Longhouse.

3. **Southeast Alaska Discovery Center.** Located just above Thomas Basin. This National Park Service museum includes exhibits and interactive displays about the land, people, and culture of Southeast Alaska.

4. **Creek Street.** Just above Thomas Basin. Cute shops and galleries, though a little touristy. Still fun to stroll.

5. **Tongass Historical Museum.** Located at the top of Creek Street. This is the town museum; small and well done, covering the history of Ketchikan.

6. **Float Plane to Misty Fjords.** A number of operators along the waterfront offer breathtaking tours of Behm Canal and Misty Fjords. Tip: Ask for the "local rate."

7. **Rent a Car.** You can tour the area in a standard rental car, or a classic 1950s rental car. You won't be going far, though, since there aren't many roads around Ketchikan.

8. **Tongass Trading Company.** Above the Casey Moran Floats. A large store with souvenirs and gifts on two floors. The second floor has a good selection of outdoor clothing and boots.

9. **Catch a Salmon.** Charter a fishing boat from one of the many outfits in town. Local guides know the waters and can take care of your license.

10. **Bear watching** at Herring Bay in August and September

Port of Ketchikan, Bar Harbor Basin

Port of Ketchikan, Casey Moran

498   www.WaggonerGuide.com

Index

1st Avenue South Bridge 120
13 Moons Marina 314
24th Avenue Landing 122
52 Steps Dock 420

A

Acland Islands 253
Actaeon Sound 368
Active Cove 223
Active Pass 245
Active Pass Auto & Marine 245
Actress Passage 368
Admiralty Inlet 148
Adventure Cove 414
Agamemnon Channel 304
Agate Passage 135
Ahclakerho Channel 437
Ahousat 413
AIS Prevention Permit 90
Alderbrook Resort & Spa 144
Aleck Bay 201
Alert Bay 377, 380
Alert Bay Boat Harbour 380
Alexander Inlet 462
Alice Bight 179
Allan Island 179
Allcroft Point 466
Allies Island 322
Alliford Bay Ferry 483
Allison Harbour 434, 436
Allyn Waterfront Park Marina 100
Alston Cove 463
Amos Island 401
Amphitrite Point 417
Amsterdam Bay 101
Anacortes 170
Anacortes Marina 178
Anchoring 58
Anderson Bay 283
Anderson Passage 465
Andrews Bay 130
Angler's Anchorage Marina 256
Anna Inlet 484
Annette Inlet 253
Anthony Island 485
April Point Resort, Spa & Marina 332
Arabella's Landing 104
Arran Rapids 346
Arthur Island 459
Arthur Passage 471
Atkins Cove 394
Atkinson Island 366
Azimuth Island 465

B

Bacchante Bay 412
Backeddy Resort & Marina 305
Bag Harbour 485

Baker Inlet 470
Ballard Locks 121
Ballard Mill Marina 124
Ballard Oil Co. 122
Ballet Bay 308
Bamfield 424
Bamfield Inlet 424
Bamfield Lodge 425
Bargain Bay 302
Bar Harbor North and South 498
Barkley Sound 418
Barnard Harbour 464
Barnes Bay 330
Barnes Island 220
Baronet Passage 373
Barter Cove 401
Bathgate General Store,
    Resort & Marina 306
Battle Bay 398
Bauza Cove 376
Baynes Sound 278
Bay of Plenty 463
Bayshore West Marina 292
Bazett Island 420
B.C. Points of Entry 27
B.C. Towing Phone Numbers 92
Beach Gardens Resort & Marina 310
Beales Bay 453
Beaumont Marine Park 240
Beaver Cove 377
Beaver Harbour 384
Beazley Passage 328
Becher Bay Marina & Campground 427
Bedwell Bay 294
Bedwell Harbour 239
Belcarra 293
Belfair State Park 144
Belize Inlet 436
Bella Bella 451
Bella Coola 454
Bella Coola Harbour Authority 455
Belleisle Sound 364
Bellevue Marina 129
Bell Harbor Marina 119
Bellingham 183
Bend Island 372
Bennett Bay 246
Benson Island 423
Bessborough Bay 349
Beware Passage 372
Bickley Bay 347
Big Bay 342
Big Frypan Bay 441
Big Salmon Resort 193
Billy Proctor's Museum 361
Birch Bay 185
Birds Eye Cove Marina 259
Bishop Bay Hot Springs 468
Blackfish Archipelago 370

Blaine 185
Blaine Harbor 185
Blake Island Marine State Park 116
Blakely Harbor 137
Blakely Island 201
Blakely Island Store & Marina 201
Blenkinsop Bay 350
Blind Bay 202, 308
Blind Channel Resort 347
Blind Island Marine State Park 202
Bliss Landing Estates 314
Blubber Bay 283
Bluenose Marina 258
Blue Pacific Yacht Charters 291
Blunden Harbour 434
Boat Basin 408
Boat Harbour 266
Boat Harbour Marina 266
Boat Haven 154
Boat Inlet 459
Boat Pass 243
Bockett Islets 355
Bodega Cove 406
Bold Island Anchorage 327
Bolin Bay 460
Bond Sound 358
Bones Bay 372
Booker Lagoon 369
Boot Cove 243
Bootleg Bay 369
Boston Harbor 98
Boston Harbor Marina 98
Bottleneck Bay 412
Boughey Bay 355
Boukind Bay 456
Boundary Bay 285
Bowen Island 295
Bowen Island Marina 295
Bowman Bay 167
Brandt's Landing 224
Breaker Pass 442
Breakwater Marina 108
Breezy Bay 243
Bremerton Marina 131
Brentwood Bay 255
Brentwood Bay Resort & Marina 256
Bridgeview Marina 132
Bridgeview Marine 483
Brigade Bay 297
Brigantine Bay 197
Broad Spit Park 141
Broken Group 423
Brooks Bay 396
Brooks Peninsula 396
Broughton Archipelago 369
Broughton Lagoon 364
Broughton Street Pier 231
Browning Harbour Public Wharf 241
Browning Inlet 394

2020 WAGGONER CRUISING GUIDE

INDEX

Browning Passage 415
Brown's Bay Marina & RV Park 339
Browns Point Park 115
Brundige Inlet 491
Brydon Anchorage 447
Brydon Channel 446
Buccaneer Bay 300
Buccaneer Marina & Resort Ltd. 301
Budd Inlet 95
Buie Creek 463
Bull Harbour 391
Bullock Channel 457
Bullock Spit Cove 457
Bull Passage 283
Bunsby Islands 398
Burdwood Bay 327
Burdwood Group 362
Burfoot County Park 98
Burgoyne Bay 258
Burial Cove 355
Burke Channel 453
Burly Bay 367
Burnaby 293
Burnaby Strait 485
Burrard Civic Marina 290
Burrows Island State Park 179
Butchart Cove 256
Butchart Gardens 256
Butedale 468
Bute Inlet 327
Bywater Bay 139

C

Cabbage Island 245
Cachalot 401
Cadboro Bay 232
Call Inlet 355
Calm Channel 327
Calmus Passage 414
Cama Beach State Park 162
Camano Island State Park 162
Cameleon Harbour 346
Cameron Island Marina 272
Campania Island 465
Campbell Bay 246
Campbell River 333
Canoe Bay 238
Canoe Cove Marina 238
Canoe Passage 285, 371
Cape Beale 425
Cape Caution 429
Cape Cockburn 307
Cape Cook 397
Cape Lazo 282
Cape Scott 392
Cape Sutil 392
Cap Sante Marina 176
Captain Coupe Park 163

Captain's Cove Marina 287
Carillon Point Marina 128
Carriden Bay 366
Carrie Bay 370
Carrington Bay 326
Carter Bay 467
Carter Passage 368
Cartwright Bay 365
Casey Moran 498
Castle Island 201
Cates Park 293
Cathedral Point 454
Cattle Pass 204
Caulfeild Cove 294
Causeway Marina 231
Caution Cove 372
Centre Bay 296
Chained Islands 339
Chandler's Cove 126
Chapple Inlet 464
Charles Bay 347
Chatham Channel 355
Chatham Sound 471
Checleset Bay 397
Chemainus 260
Chemainus Municipal Wharf 260
Chettleburgh Point 464
Chiefs Bathtub 370
China Creek Marina & Campground 422
Chinook Landing Marina 115
Chonat Bay 330
Choquer & Sons Ltd. 307
Chuckanut Bay 182
Church House 327
Cigarette Cove 420
City of Des Moines Marina 116
City of Richmond Imperial Landing 286
City of White Rock Pier 285
Clallam Bay 192
Clam Bay 265
Clam Cove 391
Clarke Island 423
Clark Island Marine State Park 221
Classic Marine Transient Moorage 257
Clatse Bay 457
Claydon Bay 366
Clayoquot Sound 412
Clear Passage 401
Clerke Point 397
Clio Channel 371
Clothes Bay 462
Clutesi Haven 423
Coal Harbour 395
Coal Harbour Chevron 291
Coal Harbour Marina 291
Coastal Mountain Fuels 272, 385
Coast Marina 335
Coast Victoria Harbourside
    Hotel & Marina 232

Cochrane Bay 317
Cockburn Bay 307
Cockle Bay 459
Codville Lagoon 449
Coghlan Anchorage 469
Coho Marina and RV Resort 304
Colby Bay 466
Coles Bay 255
Collison Bay 485
Columbia Cove 397
Columbia Fuels Fuel Dock 455
Colvos Passage 115
Commencement Bay 108
Comox 280
Comox Bar 280
Comox Harbour 281
Comox Municipal Marina 281
Comox Valley Harbour Authority 281
Comox Valley Marina 281
Conover Cove 265
Conversion Tables 93
Copeland Islands 314
Cordero Lodge 347
Cornet Bay 167
Cortes Bay 325
Cortes Island 324
Cougar Annie's Garden 409
Coulter Bay 326
Coupeville 163
Coupeville Wharf 163
Courtenay 281
Cousins Inlet 449
Covich-Williams Chevron 124
Coward's Cove 463
Cow Bay Marina 474
Cowichan Bay 257
Cowichan Bay Fishermen's Wharf
    Association 257
Cowlitz Bay 224
Coyote Cove 412
Cozy Cove and Fairweather Bay 129
Crab Cove 448
Cracroft Inlet 371
Crawford Anchorage 347
Crescent Bay 192
Crescent Beach 285
Crescent Beach Marina Ltd. 285
Crescent Harbor 166
Crescent Inlet 484
Critter Cove 407
Critter Cove Marina 407
Crofton Public Wharf 260
Crowley Fuels 497, 498
Cufra Inlet 265
Cullen Harbour 368
Culpepper Lagoon. 460
Curlew Bay 469
Curley's Resort 193
Curme Islands 320

INDEX

Cutter Cove 355
Cutts Island Marine State Park 102
Cypress Harbour 364
Cypress Head 180
Cypress Island 179

D

Dabob Bay 141
Dana Passage 484
Danger Pass 491
Darby Channel 441
D'Arcy Island 233
Dark Cove 309
Dash Point State Park 115
Davis Bay 368
Dawsons Landing 440
Days Island 103
Dead Point 373
Dean Channel 455
Deas Slough 287
Decatur Island 197
Deception Pass 167, 189
Deception Pass Marina 167
Deception Pass Marine State Park 167
De Courcy Group 266
Deep Bay 279
Deep Bay Harbour Authority 279
Deep Cove 255, 293
Deep Cove North Shore Marina 294
Deep Cove Public Wharf 293
Deep Harbour 369
Deepwater Bay 180, 338
Deer Harbor 216
Deer Harbor Marina 216
Degnen Bay 267
Degnen Bay Public Wharf 267
De la Beche Inlet 484
Delin Docks 113
Delkatla Slough Harbour Authority 481
Denham Bay 346
Denman Island 279
Dent Island Lodge 345
Dent Rapids 346
Departure Bay Gas N Go 272
Des Moines 116
Desolation Sound 317
Dickson Island 368
Dinner Bay 245
Dinner Rock 312
Dionisio Point Park 266
Discovery Bay 190
Discovery Cove 456
Discovery Harbour Authority Small Craft Harbours 338
Discovery Harbour Fuels 338
Discovery Harbour Marina 338
Discovery Island Marine Park 232
Discovery Passage 331

Dixie Cove 401
Dixon Entrance Heading North 488
Dixon Entrance Heading South 491
Dock Street Marina 113
Dock Street North Pier 113
Dockton Park 115
Doctor Bay 322
Dodd Narrows 269
Dodger Channel 425
Doe Bay Resort and Retreat 220
Doe Island Marine State Park 220
Dogfish Bay 268
Doig Anchorage 464
Dolomite Narrows 485
Dosewallips State Park 142
Dowager Island 459
Doyon's Landing 497
Draney Narrows & Draney Inlet 440
Drew Harbour 330
Drumbeg Provincial Park 268
Dsulish Bay 438
Duck Bay 260
Duncanby Lodge 438
Dundas Island Route 490
Dundivan Inlet 458
Dungeness Spit 191
Dunn Passage 465
Duwamish Bridge 120
Dyes Inlet 132

E

Eagle Harbor 180
Eagle Harbor (Bainbridge Island) 136
Eagle Harbor Marina 137
Eagle Harbor Waterfront Park & City Dock 136
Eagle Harbour 294
Eagle Island Marine State Park 101
Eagle Marine, Ltd./Columbia Fuels 418
Eagle Nook Resort 421
East Bamfield Public Dock 425
East Channel Bridge 129
East Cove 394
East of Eden 369
East Passage 115
Eastsound 218
East Sound 218
East Waterway 120
Echo Bay 222, 361
Echo Bay Marine Park 361
Echo Harbour 484
Edmonds 157
Edward Channel 445
Effingham Bay 423
Effingham Inlet 421
Egmont 305
Egmont Public Wharf 306
Elcho Harbour 455

ELCI Protected Shore Power 60
Eld Inlet 99
Elger Bay 162
Ellerslie Lagoon 457
Elliott Bay 117
Elliott Bay Marina 119
Elworthy Island 322
Embley Lagoon 366
Emily Carr Inlet 464
End Of The Road Parking 314
English Camp National Historical Park 213
Entrance Inlet 420
Esperanza 404
Esperanza Inlet 402
Espinosa Inlet 402
Esquimalt Harbour 229
Estero Basin 346
Estevan Point 408
Ethel Cove 437
Eucott Bay 456
Eveleigh Island 321
Evening Cove 261
Everett 160
Everett Marine Park 161
Ewing Cove 223
Ewin Inlet 407

F

Fair Harbor Marina 100
Fair Harbour 401
Fair Harbour Marina & Campground 401
Fairhaven Moorage 183
Fairview Small Craft Harbour 474
Fairwinds Marina 277
False Bay 282
False Creek 288
False Creek Fuels 290
False Creek Harbour Authority 290
False Creek Yacht Club 289
False Narrows 269
Fancy Cove 450
Fannie Cove 450
Fanny Bay 279, 347
Fanny Island 349
Farewell Harbour 370
Fast Fuel LP 483
Fay Bainbridge Park 135
Fernwood Public Wharf 254
Fidalgo Marina 178
Fifer Bay 442
Fife Sound 368
Filucy Bay 101
Fin Island 469
Finis Nook 438
Finlayson Arm 256
Finlayson Channel 460

INDEX

Finn Bay 441
Finn Cove 314
Fiordland Recreation Area 459
Fish Creek 205
Fisher Channel 448
Fisherman Bay(San Juan Islands) 199
Fisherman Harbor(Hood Canal) 141
Fishermans Cove Marine Fuels 294
Fisherman's Landing & Lodge 342
Fisherman's Resort & Marina 302
Fisherman's Wharf/Campbell R. 335
Fisherman's Wharf/Port Hardy 385
Fisherman's Wharf/Victoria 231
Fishermen's Harbour/Port Alberni 422
Fishermen's Terminal/Port of Seattle 124
Fishermen's Wharf/False Creek 290
Fishing Bay & Judd Bay 218
Fish Trap Bay 442
Flat Top Islands 268
Fleming Beach 229
Fleming Island 424
Fletcher Bay 134
Flounder Bay 179
Fly Basin 437
Foggy Bay 491
Ford Cove 278
Ford Cove Harbour Authority 278
Forit Bay 453
Fort Ebey State Park 157
Fort Flagler Marine State Park 154
Fort Rupert 384
Fort Townsend Marine State Park 153
Fortune Channel 414
Fort Ward Park 130
Fort Worden Marine State Park 155
Forward Harbour 348
Foss Harbor Marina 113
Fossil Bay 222
Foss Waterway Seaport 110
Fougner Bay 454
Fox Cove 222
Fox Island 102
Frances Bay 327
Fraser Reach 467
Frederick Arm 346
Freeman Island 223
French Creek Harbour Authority 278
Freshwater Marina and Boatyard 338
Friday Harbor 206
Friendly Cove 408
Friendly Dolphin Cove 413
Frye Cove County Park 99
Frypan Bay 441
Fulford Harbour 246
Fulford Inner Harbour 246
Fulford Outer Harbour 246
Fury Cove 441

G

Gabriola Passage 267
Gabriola Sands Park 270
Galiano Oceanfront Inn & Spa 246
Galley Bay 320
Ganges 248
Ganges Breakwater Float 251
Ganges Centennial Wharf 251
Ganges Kanaka Wharf 251
Ganges Marina 251
Garden Bay 302
Garden Bay Hotel Marina & Pub 303
Garrison Bay 213
Gas N Go Marine Ltd. 281
Gedney Island 158
Gene Coulon Memorial Beach Park 130
Genoa Bay 258
Genoa Bay Marina 258
Georgeson Passage 244
Gerrans Bay 304
Gibson Cove 414
Gibson Marine Park 414
Gibsons 297
Gibsons Landing Harbour Authority 299
Gibsons Marina and Fuel Dock 299
Gig Harbor 104
Gig Harbor Marina and Boatyard 104
Gillam Channel 402
Gillard Passage 342
Glen Ayr Resort 142
Glen Cove 102
Glendale Cove 357
Glenthorne Passage 253
Goat Cove 467
Goat Island Anchorage 370
God's Pocket 391
Gods Pocket 414
God's Pocket Resort 391
Goldstream Boathouse 256
Goldstream Harbour 445
Goletas Channel 390
Good Hope Cannery 440
Goose Bay 438
Goose Bay Cannery Dock 438
Gordon Cove 483
Gorge Harbour 326
Gorge Harbour Marina Resort 326
Gorge Harbour Public Dock 326
Gosse Bay 453
Gossip Island 224
Gowlland Harbour 333
Grace Harbour 317
Graham Island 481
Graham Preserve 204
Graham Reach 467
Granite Bay 339
Granite Falls 294
Granite Point 339

Grant Anchorage 463
Granville Island 288
Granville Island Boat Yard 291
Grappler Inlet 424
Grappler Sound 366
Grasshopper Pub 303
Grays Cove 485
Greater Victoria Harbour Authority 230
Grebe Cove 370
Green Bay 305
Green Cove 422
Greene Point Rapids 348
Green Island Anchorage 442
Grenville Channel 469
Grief Point 311
Griffin Bay 205
Griffin Bay Park 205
Grindstone Harbor 218
Growler Cove 373
Guemes Channel 178
Guise Bay 393
Gulf Islands 226
Gulf Islands National Park Reserve 229
Gunboat Bay 303
Gunner Inlet 415
Guthrie Bay 218
GVHA - Greater Victoria
        Harbour Authority 230
Gwaii Haanas National Park Reserve 478

H

Hadlock Public Dock 153
Haida Gwaii 478
Haida Heritage Centre 478
Hakai Beach Institute 444
Hakai Luxvbalis Conservancy 444
Hakai Passage 445
Hale Passage 102
Halfmoon Bay 299
Halkett Bay 296
Halkett Bay Fircom Dock 296
Hammersley Inlet 99
Handfield Bay 346
Hankin Cove 401
Hansen Bay 393
Hanson Island 373
Harbor Island Marina 120
Harbor Marine Fuel 184
Harbour Authority of
        Salt Spring Island 251
Harbour Authority of
        Squamish Boat Harbour 297
Harbour Marina 137
Harbour Quay 422
Harbourside Lodge 425
Harbour Village Marina 127
Hardy Bay 390
Hardy Island Marine Park 308

INDEX

Harmony Islands Marine Park 309
Haro Strait 189
Harper State Park 115
Harstine Island 99
Harstine Island State Park 101
Hartley Bay 469
Harwood Point Regional Park 283
Háthayim Provincial Marine Park 327
Havannah Channel 355
Hawk Bay 469
Hayden Passage 412
Hayle Bay 362
H.C. Henry Marina 126
Health Bay 370
Heater Harbour 485
Heather Civic Marina 291
Heelboom Bay 415
Helen Bay 367
Helmcken Island 349
Hemasila Inlet 440
Hemming Bay 346
Henderson Inlet 103
Henry Island 214
Henry Island Preserve 214
Herb Beck Marina 141
Herbert Inlet 414
Heriot Bay 330
Heriot Bay Inn & Marina 330
Heriot Bay Public Wharf 330
Hernando Island 312
Herring Bay 266
Herron Island 101
Hesquiat Harbour 408
Hevenor Inlet 466
Heynen Channel 414
Hicks Bay 204
Hidden Basin 307
Hiekish Narrows 467
Higgins Passage 463
Hill Island 327
Hilton Harbor Marina 184
Hiram M. Chittenden Locks 123
Hisnit Inlet 407
Hjorth Bay 327
Hoeya Sound 357
Holberg Inlet 396
Holmes Harbor 162
Holmes Inlet Nook 412
Home Bay 438
Homfray Channel 321
Homfray Lodge 321
Honeymoon Bay 162, 163
Hood Canal 139
Hood Canal Floating Bridge 139
Hood Canal Marina 142
Hood Head 139
Hoodsport 142
Hook Bay 422
Hootla-Kootla Bay 412

Hope Bay Public Wharf 242
Hope Island 167
Hope Island Marine State Park 99
Hopetown Passage 366
Hornby Island 278
Horsefly Cove 467
Horsehead Bay 102
Horseshoe Bay 295
Horseshoe Bay Public Wharf 295
Horton Bay 244, 246
Hoskyn Channel 327
Hospital Bay 302
Hospital Bay Public Wharf 302
Hotel Bellwether 184
Hotham Sound 309
Hotspring Island 484
Hot Springs Cove 409
Howe Sound 294
Hoya Bay 484
Hoya Passage 484
Hoy Bay 366
Huckleberry Island 170
Hughes Bay 201
Humchitt Island 448
Hunter Bay 199
Hurricane Anchorage 447
Hyack Terminal 231
Hylebos Waterway 115

I

Iceberg Island 201
Ikeda Cove 485
Illahee Marine State Park 133
Illahie Inlet 442
Inati Bay 184
Indian Arm Marine Park 293
Indian Cove 204
Indianola 135
Inner Boat Basin 272
Inner Port Madison 135
Ire Inlet 465
Irish Bay 243
Irondale 150
Iroquois Passage 238
Irvines Landing 302
Isabella Island 246
Island Cove 415
Islands Marine Center 200
Island West Resort 420
Isle-de-Lis at Rum Island 233

J

Jack's Boatyard 314
Jackson Passage 459
James Bay 254, 459
James Island Marine State Park 195

Jamieson Point Anchorage 463
Jane Bay/Franks Bay 421
Jane Cove 451
Jarrell Cove 99
Jarrell Cove Marine State Park 99
Jarrell's Cove Marina 99
Jedediah Island 283
Jennis Bay 368
Jennis Bay Marina 368
Jenny Inlet 455
Jerisich Dock 106
Jervis Inlet 308
Jetty Island 161
Jock's Dock 427
Joe Cove 369
Joemma Beach State Park 101
Joe's Bay 442
John Henry's Resort & Marina 302
Johnny's Dock 113
John Passage 238
Johnson Street Marina 231
Johns Pass 224
Johnston Bay 440
Johnstone Strait 349
John Wayne Marina 190
Jones Island Marine State Park 215
Jones Marine Services Ltd 261
Joseph Whidbey State Park 157
Juanita Bay 128
Julian Cove 394

K

Kakushdish Harbour 453
Kamils Anchorage 401
Kanish Bay 339
Kayak Point County Park 161
Kelp Passage 471
Kelsey Bay 350
Kenary Cove 267
Kenmore 127
Kennedy Cove 415
Kenneth Passage 367
Kent Inlet 464
Ketchikan 493
Ketchikan Moorage 498
Ketchikan Yacht Club 498
Ketron Island 102
Khutze Inlet 467
Kiixin Tour 425
Kiket Island 167
Kildidt Narrows 446
Kildidt Sound 446
Kilisut Harbor 153
Kiln Bay 464
Kiltik Cove 448
Kimball Preserve 197
Kingcome Inlet 364
Kingfisher Marina 425

2020 WAGGONER CRUISING GUIDE   503

INDEX

Kingston 146
Kinnaird Island 366
Kirkland 128
Kisameet Bay 448
Kitasu Bay 463
Kitimat 468
Kitkatla 466
Kitsap Memorial Marine State Park 139
Klaoitsis Island 372
Klaskino Inlet 396
Klaskish Inlet 396
Klemtu 460
Klewnuggit Inlet 470
Kliktsoatli Harbour 452
Knight Inlet 357
Knox Bay 349
Koeye River 448
Kohl Island Anchorage 463
Kooryet Bay 465
Kopachuck Marine State Park 102
Koprino Harbour 394
Koskimo Bay 394
Koskimo Islands 394
Kukutali Preserve 167
Kumealon Island 470
Kumlah Island Anchorage 358
K'uuna Llnagaay 483
Kwakshua Channel 444
Kwakume Inlet 448
Kwatna Inlet 454
Kwatsi Bay 359
Kwatsi Bay Marina 359
Kxngeal Inlet 470
Kynoch Inlet 460
Kynumpt Harbour 457
Kyuquot Sound 398

L ▪▪

Labouchere Channel 455
La Conner 167
La Conner Landing Fuel Dock 170
La Conner Marina 170
Lacy Falls 359
Ladner 286
Ladner Yacht Club 287
Lady Boot Cove 369
Lady Douglas Island 459
Ladysmith Community Marina 263
Ladysmith Fisherman's Wharf 263
Ladysmith Harbour 261
Ladysmith Marina 264
Lagoon Cove 356
Lagoon Cove Marina 356
Lakebay Marina & Resort 102
Lake Union 124
Lake Washington 126
Lakewood Moorage 130
Lama Passage 450

Lancelot Inlet 318
Langara Island 481
Langley Boat Harbor 162
Langus Waterfront Park 161
Laredo Inlet 463
Larrabee State Park 182
Larsen Harbour 466
Lasqueti Island 282
Laura Bay 362
Laura Cove 321
Lawson Harbour 471
Lemmens Inlet 414
Lemmens Northwest Cove 414
Leone Island 370
Lewis Channel 323
Liberty Bay 134
Lieber Haven Resort 220
Lighthouse Marine County Park 187
Lighthouse Pub & Marina 307
Lime Kiln Point 214
Lime Point Cove 467
Lincoln Channel 491
Lions Bay Marine Ltd. 297
Little Bull Passage 283
Little Nimmo Bay 367
Little River 282
Lizzie Cove 451
Logboom Park 128
Lohbrunner Island 463
Lonesome Cove Resort 209
Longbranch Improvement
    Club Marina 101
Long Harbour 251
Long Point Cove 449
Lopez Island 198
Lopez Islander Resort & Marina 200
Lopez Pass 198
Lopez Sound 198
Louise Narrows 483
Louscoone Inlet 485
Lowe Inlet 470
Lower Rapids 330
Lucky Creek 420
Lummi Island 184
Lummi Island Recreation Site 185
Lund 313
Lund Automotive & Outboard Ltd. 314
Lund Resort 314
Lund Small Craft Harbour 314
Lund Water Taxi 314
Lyall Harbour 243
Lyall Harbour Public Wharf 244
Lynnwood Marina 293

M ⚑

Macaulay Park 229
Mackaye Harbor 201
Mackenzie Sound 367

Madeira Marina 303
Madeira Park Public Wharf 303
Madiera Park 303
Mahatta Creek 394
Makah Marina 193
Malaspina Inlet 317
Malaspina Strait 310
Malcolm Island Lions
    Harbour Authority 381
Malibu Rapids 309
Manchester State Park 130
Mansons Landing 325
Mansons Landing Marine Park 326
Mansons Landing Public Dock 326
Mantrap Inlet 442
Manzanita Bay 134
Maple Bay 258
Maple Bay Marina 259
Maple Bay Public Wharf 259
Maquinna Marine Provincial Park 409
Marble Cove 424
Margaret Bay 437
Marina Mart 126
Marina Park 128
Mariners Rest 295
Marine Servicenter 178
Marktosis 413
Marvin Islands 463
Mary Cove 467
Mary Island 491
Mason's Olson Resort 193
Massacre Bay Rocks 218
Masset 481
Masset Sound 482
Matia Island 221
Matilda Inlet 413
Matilpi 355
Matlset Narrows 414
Mats Mats Bay 148
Mattson's Bay Marine 135
Maury Island Marine Park 115
Mayne Passage 347
Mayo Cove 102
McArdle Bay 201
McBride Bay 437
McIntosh Bay 362
McKay Bay Lodge 425
McLane Cove 100
McMicken Island Marine State Park 101
McMicking Inlet 465
McRae Cove 308
Meay Inlet 445
Melanie Cove 321
Menzies Bay 338
Mesachie Nose 455
Metcalf Island 330
Method Marine Supply 416
Metlakatla Bay 490
Meydenbauer Bay 129

504

www.WaggonerGuide.com

INDEX

Meyers Passage 463
Middle Arm Fraser River 287
Milbanke Sound 458
Miles Inlet 434
Mill Bay 256
Mill Bay Community Wharf 257
Mill Bay Marina 256
Millbrook Cove 438
Miller Bay 135
Milltown Marina 287
Miners Bay 245
Mink Island 320
Minstrel Island Harbour 355
Mistaken Island 278
Mitchell Bay 213, 381
Mitlenatch Island 312
MK Bay Marina 468
Moffatt Islands 491
MOHAI Docks 126
Monckton Inlet 465
Monday Anchorage 369
Monks' Wall 372
Montague Harbour 254
Montague Harbour Marina 254
Montague Harbour Marine Park 254
Montague Harbour Public Wharf 254
Montlake Cut 126
Morehouse Bay 457
Moresby Camp 483
Morrison's North Star Marine 126
Mosquito Creek Marina 293
Mosquito Harbour 415
Mosquito Pass 213
Mound Island 370
Mount Gardner Park Public Dock 296
Moutcha Bay Resort 407
Mowgli Island 265
Mud Bay 198
Muirhead Islands 368
Mukilteo 158
Murden Cove 136
Murray Labyrinth 434
Musgrave Landing 258
Mystery Bay Marine State Park 154

N

Nahwitti Bar 391
Nahwitti Bar Inner Route 391
Nakwakto Rapids 435, 436
Namu 448
Nanaimo 270
Nanaimo Port Authority 271
Nanoose Harbour 277
Nan Sdins Village Site 485
Narrows Inlet 307
Narrows Marina 103
Narvaez Bay 245
Nascall Bay 456

Nash Narrows Cove 457
Nash Passage 457
Native Anchorage 371
Nautical Landing Marina 126
Naval Base Kitsap (Bangor) 141
Neah Bay 193
Neekas Cove 457
Nepah Lagoon 366
Neroutsos Inlet 394
Nettle Island 423
New Bella Bella 451
Newcastle Island Marine Park 272
Newcombe Harbour 466
Newport Shores 129
Newton Cove Resort 402
New Vancouver 370
Nimmo Bay Wilderness Resort 367
Nisqually Reach 103
Nitinat Narrows 426
Nodales Channel 346
Nootka Light Station 408
Nootka Mission 404
Nootka Sound 407
North Arm Fraser River 287
North Arm Transportation 481
North Bay Anchorage 205
North Bentinck Arm 454
North Cove 265
Northern Gulf Islands 260
North Galiano 266
North Harbour 394
North Island Marina 383
North Lake Marina 127
North Pacific Cannery Dock 472
NorthPoint Landing 97
North Saanich Marina 238
North Shore Dock 144
Northumberland Channel 269
Northwest Bay 278
Northwest Fuels Ltd. 475
Northwest McConnell Rock 215
Nowish Cove 460
Nuchatlitz Inlet 402
Nuchatlitz Provincial Park 402
Nuttal Bay 277

O

Oak Bay 150, 232
Oak Bay County Park 150
Oak Bay Marina 232
Oak Harbor 163
Oak Harbor Marina 163
Oakland Bay Marina 99
Oatwish Bay 460
O'Brien Bay 362
Obstruction Pass 201
Obstruction Pass State Park 220
Ocean Falls 449

Ocean Falls Lodge 450
Ocean Falls Small Craft Harbour 450
Oceanfront Suites at Cowichan Bay 257
Octopus Islands Marine Park 329
Odlin San Juan Co. Park 200
Okeover Harbour Authority 318
Okisollo Channel 328
Old Bank Inn 450
Old Town Dock 108
Olga 219
Olympia 95
Oona River 471
Open Bay 214
Open Bight 438
Orcas Island 215
Orcas Landing 218
Oscar Passage 459
Osment Inlet 463
Ostrich Bay 132
Otter Bay Marina 241
Otter Channel 465
Otter Cove 339
Otter Island 320
Outer Islands 423
Outpost at Winter Harbour,
    Grant Sales Ltd. 393
Owen Bay 328, 330
Oyster Bay 132, 442

P

Pacific Boulevard Marina 289
Pacific Gateway Marina 426
Pacific Playgrounds Resort & Marina
    282
Padilla Bay 170
Page Passage 238
Page Point Marina Inc. 264
Page's Inn on Silva Bay 269
Page's Resort & Marina 269
Painted Boat Resort Spa & Marina 304
Palmer Anchorage 463
Pamphlet Cove 394
Panther Point 265
Parks Bay 204
Parksville 278
Parson's Anchorage 463
Patos Island 223
Patricia Bay 255
Peale Passage 99
Pearse Islands 377
Peavine Pass 201
Pedder Bay 427
Pedder Bay Marina 427
Pelican Bay Marina 291
Pelican Beach 180
Pender Canal 240
Pender Harbour 302
Pender Harbour Hotel 303
Pender Harbour Resort and Marina 302

2020 WAGGONER CRUISING GUIDE 505

Index

Pendrell Sound 322
Penelakut Island 264
Peninsula Yacht Basin 106
Penn Cove 163
Penn Harbour 464
Penrose Bay 318
Penrose Point Marine State Park 102
Perceval Narrows 459
Percival Landing 97
Peter Cove 240
Petrel Channel 466
Petroglyph Cove 401
Petro Marine Services 497
Philip Inlet 442
Phillips Arm 347
Phinney Bay 132
Pickering Passage 99
Picnic Cove 204
Pier 65 (Dungeness Marina) 258
Pier 73 Marina & Yacht Club 287
Pierce Bay 441
Pierre's Echo Bay 361
Pierre's Echo Bay Lodge & Marina 361
Piers Island Public Wharf 239
Pillar Point 192
Pillsbury Cove 475
Pilot Bay 270
Pinkerton Islands 421
Pipestem Inlet 420
Pirates Cove Marine Park 266
Pitt Island 462, 465
Pitt Passage 102
Pleasant Harbor 142
Pleasant Harbor Marina 142
Pleasant Harbor Marine State Park 142
Plumper Bay 338
Plumper Cove Marine Park 297
Plumper Sound Area 239
Poets Cove Marina 240
Poett Nook 424
Poett Nook Marina & Campground 424
Point Atkinson 294
Point Defiance 108
Point Defiance Boathouse Marina 108
Point Grey 288
Point Hudson Marina 155
Point No Point 148
Point Roberts 186
Point Roberts Marina Resort 186
Point Robinson 116
Point Wilson 157
Point Wilson Tide-Rip 189
Poise Cove Marina 307
Poison Cove 460
Pole Pass 216
Polkinghorne Islands 368
Porlier Pass 266
Porpoise Bay Government Wharf 307
Porpoise Harbour 471

Portage Bay 126
Port Alberni 421
Port Alberni Marine
    Fuels & Services 423
Port Alberni Yacht Club 424
Port Alexander 391
Port Alice 394
Port Alice Yacht Club 395
Port Angeles Boat Haven 192
Port Angeles City Pier 192
Port Blackney 458
Port Browning 241
Port Browning Marina 241
Port Clements 482
Port Clements Small Craft Harbour 482
Porteau Cove 297
Port Elizabeth 358
Port Gamble 139
Port Graves 296
Port Hadlock 150
Port Hadlock Marina 150
Port Hardy 384
Port Harvey 355
Port Harvey Marine Resort 355
Portland Inlet 491
Portland Island 239
Port Ludlow 148
Port Ludlow Resort and Marina 148
Port McNeill 381
Port McNeill Federal Docks 383
Port McNeill Harbour 383
Port Moody 293
Port Neville 350
Port of Allyn North Shore Dock 144
Port of Anacortes 176
Port of Bellingham 184, 185
Port of Brownsville 133
Port of Edmonds 158
Port of Everett Marina 160
Port of Friday Harbor 207
Port of Friday Harbor Fuel Pier 209
Port of Hoodsport 142
Port of Keyport Marina 134
Port of Kingston 146
Port of Manchester 130
Port of Port Townsend Boat Haven 154
Port of South Whidbey 162
Port Orchard 131
Port Orchard Marina 131
Port Plaza Dock 97
Port Renfrew Community Dock 426
Port San Juan 426
Portside Marina 255
Port Sidney Marina 235
Port Simpson 491
Port Susan 161
Port Townsend 154
Port Townsend Boat Haven 154
Port Townsend Canal 150

Port Washington Public Wharf 242
Posey Island Marine State Park 211
Possession Sound 158
Potlatch Marine State Park 142
Potts Lagoon 372
Poulsbo 134
Poulsbo Marina / Port of Poulsbo 135
Powell River 311
Preedy Harbour 264
Prevost Harbor 224
Prevost Island 253
Prideaux Haven 321
Prince Rupert 472
Prince Rupert Rowing
    and Yacht Club 475
Princesa Channel 406
Princess Cove 265
Princess Louisa Inlet 309
Princess Louisa Society 310
Princess Royal Island 462
Pruth Bay 444
Pylades Island 266
Pym Rocks 362

Q

Qlawdzeet Anchorage 471
Quadra Island 330
Quait Bay 414
Quarry Bay 307
Quartcha Bay 456
Quarterdeck Inn & Marina Resort 385
Quartermaster Marina 115
Quartz Bay 327
Quathiaski Cove 332
Quathiaski Cove Public Wharf 332
Quatsino First Nations Dock 395
Quatsino Narrows 395
Quatsino Sound 393
Quatsino Village 396
Quayside Marina 289
Queen Charlotte 482
Queen Charlotte Harbour Authority 482
Queen Charlotte Strait 376
Queen Cove 402
Quigley Creek Cove 463
Quilcene Bay 141

R

Racoon Island 294
Radio Emergency Signals 91
Rae Basin 408
Rainier Beach 130
Rainy Bay Cove 421
Ramsay Hot Springs 409
Ramsay Passage Cove 484
Raymond Passage 458

INDEX

Raymur Point Customs Dock 231
Reach Island 100
Read Island 327
Reads Bay 197
Rebecca Spit Marine Park 330
Redonda Bay 327
Redondo 115
Reef Harboiur 245
Refuge Cove 323, 481
Refuge Cove General Store 323
Refuge Island 420
Reid Bay 364
Reid Harbor 224
Reid Passage 458
Rendezvous Islands 327
Rescue Bay 459
Resolution Cove 408
Retreat Cove 265
Retreat Passage 369
Richards Channel 429
Richmond Bay 368
Richmond Chevron 287
Rich Passage 130
Riley Cove 412
Ripley Bay 457
Rivers Inlet 438
ROAM App 31
Robbers Passage 424
Roberts Bay 233
Robson Bight 350
Roche Harbor 189, 209
Roche Harbor Marina 211
Rock Bay Marine Park 339
Rock Inlet 448
Rocky Bay 100, 209
Rocky Point 166
Roesland/Roe Lake 242
Roffey Island 321
Rolfe Cove 221
Rolling Roadstead 402
Rosario Resort & Spa 218
Rosario Strait 189
Roscoe Bay/Roscoe Bay Marine Park 321
Roscoe Inlet 456
Rosedale 102
Rose Harbour 485
Rose Inlet 485
Royal Reach Marina & Hotel 307
Ruckle Park 246
Rugged Point Marine Park 401
Rumble Beach Marina 394
Rupert Inlet 395
Rushbrooke Floats
     Small Craft Harbour 475
Russell Island 246
Ruston 108
Ruxton Island 266

S

Saanich Inlet 255
Saanichton Bay 233
Sac Bay 484
Saddlebag Island Marine State Park 170
Safety Cove 444
Saint Edward State Park 128
Salmon Bay 122, 459
Salmon Bay Marina/Port of Seattle 122
Salmon Bay Marine Center 122
Salmon Inlet 307
Salmon Point Resort 282
Salsbury Point County Park 139
Saltery Bay 308
Saltery Bay Harbour 308
Saltery Bay Provincial Park 308
Salt Spring Marina 251
Saltwater Marine State Park 115
Sand Heads 285
Sand Point 127
Sandspit 483
Sandspit Harbour 483
Sandspit Harbour Fuel Dock 483
Sandwell Park 270
Sandy Island Marine Provincial Park 279
Sandy Point 185
San Josef Bay 393
San Juan County Park 214
San Juan Island 204
San Juan Islands 195
San Mateo Bay 422
Sansum Narrows 258
Santa Gertrudis Cove 408
Sarah Point 317
Saratoga Passage 161
Sargeaunt Passage 358
Satellite Island 224
Savary Island 312
Scenic Beach State Park 141
Schooner Channel 434
Schooner Cove 277
Schooner Reef 277
Scott Cove 359
Seabeck Bay 141
Seabreeze Cove 369
Seaforth Channel 456
Seagate T-Floats 385
Sea Otter Cove 393
Sea Otter Inlet 448
Seascape Waterfront Resort 333
Sea Star Vineyards 243
Sechelt Inlet 305, 306
Sechelt Rapids 306
Second Narrow 293
Secretary Islands 265
Secret Cove 300
Secret Cove Marina 301
Secret Cove Public Wharf 301

Secret Harbor 182
Selby Cove 254
Selma Park 299
Semiahmoo Marina 186
Sequim Bay 190
Sequim Bay Marine State Park 190
Serpent Group 446
Sewell's Marina Ltd. 295
Seymour Narrows 338
SGang Gwaay 485
Shack Bay 457
Shallow Bay 222
Shark Creek 413
Sharpe Cove 167
Sharpe's Landing 314
Shaw General Store 202
Shaw Island 202
Shawl Bay Marina 364
Shawl Bay & Moore Bay 364
Shearwater Resort & Marina 452
Shelter Bay Marina 167
Shelter Island Marina Inc. 287
Shelter Sheds 397
Shelton 99
Shilshole Bay Fuel Dock 121
Shilshole Bay Marina 121
Shine Tidelands State Park 139
Shingle Bay 241
Ship Canal Bridge 121
Ship Point Marina 232
Shoal Bay 199, 346
Shoal Bay Pub 347
Shoal Channel 297
Shoal Harbour 361
Shushartie Bay 391
Sidney Bay 348
Sidney Beacon Ave 237
Sidney Spit 233
Silva Bay 268
Silva Bay Resort & Marina 269
Silva Bay Shipyard 269
Silverdale Marina 132
Similk Bay 167
Simoom Sound 362
Sinclair and Eliza Islands 182
Sir Alexander Mackenzie Rock 455
Sir Edmund Bay 364
Skagit Bay 166
Skagit Island 167
Skedans Bay 483
Skidegate 482
Skidegate Channel 483
Skidegate Ferry 483
Skookum Inlet 99
Skull Cove 434
Skull Island 218
Skyline Marina 179, 287
Slingsby Channel 430, 435
Small Inlet 339

2020 WAGGONER CRUISING GUIDE

INDEX

Small Inlet Marine Park 339
Smartphone Apps for Cruisers 55
Smelt Bay Provincial Park 325
Smith Cove 394
Smith Sound 435
Smuggler Cove 300
Smuggler's Villa Resort 220
Snohomish River Delta 161
Snoring Bay 222
Snow Creek Resort 193
Snug Basin 422
Snug Cove 295
Snug Cove Public Wharf 295
Snug Harbor Resort 213
Sointula 380
Solander Island 397
Sooke Harbour 426
Sooke Harbour Authority 427
Sooke Harbour Resort & Marina 427
South Arm Fraser River 285
South Bentinck Arm 454
Southeast Cove 421
Southey Bay 265
Southgate Group 434
South Park Marina 120
South Puget Sound 95
South Whidbey State Park 157
Souvenir Passage 442
Spanish Bank 288
Spencer Spit Marine State Park 199
Spicer Islands 466
Spider Anchorage 447
Spider Island area 447
Spiller Channel 457
Spiller Inlet 457
Spitfire Channel 447
Spitfire North Anchorage 447
Squalicum Harbor 184
Squamish 297
Squamish Harbor 139
Squamish Yacht Club 297
Squirrel Cove 324
Squirrel Cove Public Dock 325
Squirrel Cove Trading Co. Ltd. 325
Squitty Bay 282
Stag Bay 312
Stan Sayers Memorial Park 130
Steamer Cove 412
Steep Island Lodge 333
Steilacoom 103
Stern Tie 59
Steveston 286
Steveston Chevron 286
Steveston Harbour Authority Wharf 286
St. John Harbour 458
Stones Marina 272
Stopper Islands 420
Strait of Georgia 275
Strait of Juan de Fuca 189, 388

Strathcona 293
Strawberry Island - Cypress Island 182
Strawberry Island - Deception Pass 167
Stretch Island 100
Stretch Point Marine State Park 100
St. Roch Dock 293
Stuart Channel 260
Stuart Island 224
Stuart Island Community Dock 342
Stuart Island (Johnstone Strait) 340, 342
Stuart Narrows 367
Sturdies Bay 245
Sturt Bay 283
St. Vincent Bay 309
Subtle Islands 326
Sucia Island 221
Sullivan Bay Marina Resort 365
Sulphur Passage 413
Summertide Resort & Marina 144
Sunday Harbour 369
Sunderland Channel 349
Sunny Shores Resort & Marina 427
Sunrise Motel & Resort 142
Sunset Marina Ltd. 295
Sunshine Bay 441
Sunshine Coast Resort & Marina 303
Suquamish 135
Surf Inlet 464
Surprise Island 401
Sutil Point 325
Sutlej Channel 364
Swanson Bay 467
Swantown Marina 97
Swartz Bay Public Wharf 238
Swifts Bay 199
Swindle Island 463
Sydney Inlet 412
Sydney Inlet Unnamed Cove 412
Sylvan Cove 197

T ▮▮

Table Island 437
Tacoma Fuel Dock 113
Tacoma Narrows 103
Tahsis 406
Tahsis Narrows 406
Taku Resort & Marina 331
Talbot Cove 324
Tallheo Hot Springs 454
Tangent Island 465
Tanu Island 484
Tatchu Point 401
Taylor Bay 101, 440
Teakerne Arm 324
Telegraph Cove 376
Telegraph Cove Marina 376
Telegraph Cove Resort 377
Telegraph Harbour 264
Telegraph Harbour Marina 264

Telephone Numbers 92
Telescope Passage 308
Tenedos Bay 320
Tent Island 264
Texada Boat Club 283
Texada Island 283
Thatcher Pass 197
Thea Foss Waterway 108
The Blow Hole 356
The Cliffside 361
The Cut 265
The Fish 'N' Hole 155
The Gap 297
Theodosia Inlet 318
Thetis Island Resort 264
The Trap 449
Thompson Bay 458
Thompson Sound 358
Thornbrough Bay 297
Thorndyke Bay 139
Thrashers Cove 426
Thunder Bay 308
Thunderbird Marina 294
Thurston Bay Marine Park 346
Thurston Harbour 484
Titlow Park 103
Toba Inlet 323
Toba Wilderness Marina 322
Tod Inlet 256
Tofino 415
Tofino Harbour Authority 4th Street
    Public Dock 416
Tofino Harbour Authority
    Crab Dock 417
Tofino Resort & Marina 416
Tolmie Marine State Park 103
Tom Bay 459
Topaze Harbour 349
Toquaht Bay Marina 420
Totten Inlet 99
Town of La Conner Public Floats 170
Tracey Harbour 368
Trail Bay 299
Tramp Harbor 116
Tranquilito Cove 415
Trevenen Bay 318
Tribune Bay 278
Tribune Channel 358
Triton Cove State Park 142
Triton Head 142
Troup Narrows 456
Troup Passage 456
Tsakonu Cove 357
Tsapee Narrows 415
Tsehum Harbour 237, 238
Tsowwin Narrows 406
Tugboat Passage 346
Tumbo Island 245
Tuno Creek Anchorage 458

508

www.WaggonerGuide.com

INDEX

Turnbull Cove 366
Turn Island 349
Turn Island State Park 205
Turret Island 423
Turtle Bay 423
Twanoh Marine State Park 144
Twin Islands 325
Twin Rocks 220
Tyee Landing 423
Tyee Marina 115
Tzartus Cove 424
Tzoonie Narrows Park 307

U

Uchucklesit Inlet 422
Ucluelet 418
Ucluelet Small Craft Harbour 418
Uganda Passage 326
U'mista 379
U'mista Cultural Centre 380
Union Bay 126
Union Passage 470
Union Steamship Co. Marina 295
Upper Barkley Sound 421
Upper Rapids 329
Upright Channel Park 200
U.S. and Canadian Customs
        Information 26, 27, 29
U.S. Coast Guard 92
U.S. Customs Clearance Numbers 92
Useless Inlet 421
U.S. Points of Entry 30
U.S. Towing 92
U.S. Towing and Emergency Numbers 92

V

Vananda 283
Van Anda 283
Vancouver Boating Welcome Centre 289
Vancouver Harbour (North) 292
Vancouver Harbour (South) 291
Vancouver Marina 287
Van Isle Marina 237
Van Riper's Resort 193
Varney Bay 395
Vaughn Bay 100
Vendovi Island 182
Venn Passage 490
Verney Falls 470
Verney Passage 468
Vernon Bay 421
Vessel Traffic Service 49
Vesuvius 260
VHF Channels for Pleasure Craft 91
Victim Island 217
Victoria 230

Victoria Area 229
Victoria International Marina 232
Victoria Mandatory Traffic Lanes 229
Victoria Marine Fuels Ltd 232
Village Bay 245
Village Island 371
Viner Sound 359
Volcanic Cove 401
Von Donop Inlet 327
Von Geldern Cove 102
VTS Radio Channels 50, 51

W

Waddington Bay 370
Waddington Channel 321
Waddington Harbour 328
Wahkana Bay 359
Wahshihlas Bay 358
Waiatt Bay 329
Wakeman Sound 364
Wakes Cove 268
Waldron Island 224
Walker Group 429
Walker Hook 254
Walker Island Group 428
Wallace Island Marine Park 265
Walsh Cove Marine Park 322
Walters Cove 398
Walters Cove Resort 399
Warren Islands 355
Warrior Cove 448
Washington Park 179
Wasp Islands 214
Waterfall Inlet 442
Waterfront Suites & Marina 272
Watmough Bay 201
Watson Cove 359
Watts Narrows 470
Weather 34
Weinburg Inlet 465
Welcome Harbour 467
Welcome Passage 299
Wellbore Channel 348
Wells Passage 368
W.E. Mills Landing & Marina 272
West Bamfield Public Dock 425
West Bay 296
West Bay Marina 97
West Beach Resort 223
West Coast Wilderness Lodge 305
Westcott Bay 213
Westcott Bay Shellfish Co 213
Westport Marina 238
West Sound 217
West Sound Marina 217
Westview Fuels 312
Westview Harbour 311
Westview Marina & Lodge 406

Westview/Powell River 311
West Waterway 120
West Whitepine Cove 414
Whaleboat Island Marine Park 266
Whaler Bay 246
Whaler Bay Public Wharf 246
Whaletown 326
Wharf Street Floats 232
Whirlpool Rapids 348
Whiskey Golf 276
Whiskey Landing 418
Whiskey Slough Public Wharf 304
White Rock 285
Whiterock Passage 327
Wigham Cove 457
Wigwam Inn 294
Windy Bay 415, 459, 485
Winslow Wharf Marina 137
Winter Harbour 393
Winter Harbour Authority 394
Wollochet Bay 102
Woods Bay 366
Woods Nose 426
Wootton Bay 318
Work Bay 467
Wouwer Island 424
Wright Sound 469

Y

Yaculta 331
Yaculta Public Dock 332
Yarrow Bay Marina 129
Yellow Island 214
Yorke Island 350
Young Bay 412
Yuculta Rapids 342
Yukon Harbor 116

Z

Zeballos 404
Zeballos Fuel Dock Inc. 404
Zeballos Municipal Wharf 404
Zeballos Small Craft Harbour 404
Zittel's Marina Inc. 103

GET YOUR WAGGONER GUIDE UPDATES AT www.WaggonerGuide.com

2020 WAGGONER CRUISING GUIDE   509

ADVERTISER INDEX

13 Moons Marina 313
3C Canvas 171, 174
49th Parallel Grocery and Cafe 262

A
AAA Yachtfinders 18
Ace Hardware Anacortes and
  Friday Harbor 172, 210
Alaska Eagle Arts 495
Alaska Fish House 493, 495
Albert Jensen & Sons
  Boatyard 206, 171, 210,
Alderbrook Spa and Resort 33
Alert Bay Visitor Centre 378
All Bay Marine Ltd. 233
All Things Marine Thrift Store 236
ALT Insurance Group 172
American Tug 67
Anacortes Chamber of Commerce 173
Anacortes Marine Electronics 171, 174
Anacortes Marine Insurance 172
Anthony's at Cap Sante Marina 172, 178
Anthony's at Gig Harbor 107, 108
Anthony's at Point Defiance 108
Anthony's at Sinclair Inlet 132
Anthony's at Squalicum 184
Anthony's Beach Cafe - Edmonds 158
Anthony's Cabana - Anacortes 172, 178
Anthony's Chinook's - Salmon Bay 124
Anthony's Hearthfire Grill -
  Bellingham 181, 184
Anthony's Hearthfire Grill - Olympia 97
Anthony's Home Port - Bellingham 181
Anthony's Home Port - Des Moines 116
Anthony's Home Port - Edmonds 158
Anthony's Home Port - Everett 159, 161
Anthony's Home Port - Kirkland 128
Anthony's Home Port - Olympia 97
Anthony's Pier 66 & Bell Street 119
Anthony's Restaurants 69
Anthony's Woodfire Grill -
  Everett 159, 161
Aspen Power Catamarans -
  Inside Front Cover

B
Baranof Fishing Excursions 493, 495
Bayside Marine and Dry Stack 159
Beach Gardens Resort & Marina 310
Bell Harbor Marina 120
Black Sheep Books 247
Blackline Marine Inc. 236
Blaine Harbor 186
Blind Channel Resort 349
Bremerton Marina 132
Brown Lantern Ale House 172
Butchart Gardens 13

C
Canoe Cove Marina & Boatyard 236
Cap Sante Marina 177
Captain's Supplies 41
Children's Museum of Tacoma 114
Chinook's at Salmon Bay 124
Classic Marine Ltd 256
Coal Harbour Marina 292
Cow Bay CafE 473
Cow Bay Marina 476
Cowichan Bay Fishermen's Wharf
  Association 257
Crazy Wolf Studio 495

Crows Nest Yacht Sales 60
Cruisers College/NW Center for
  Excellence 46, 158
CSR Marine 120
Cutwater Boats 512

D
Dawsons Landing General Store 441
Deer Harbor Marina 215
Delta Marine Service 234
Dent Island Lodge 345
Des Moines Marina, 116
Desolation Sound Yacht Charters 281, 317
Devlin Designing Boat Builders 49
Discovery Harbour Marina & Fuels 336
Doc's Marina Grill 150
Dock Street Marina 114

E
Edmonds Marina 157
Elevated Ice Cream & Candy Shop 152
Elliott Bay Marina 119
Emerald Harbor Marine 15, 71

F
False Creek Harbour Authority 290
Fisheries Supply 53, 70, 78, 79
Fisherman's Wharf (Campbell River) 335
Flagship Maritime Training 61
Foss Waterway Seaport 114
Fountain Cafe 152
Fox & Hounds 262
Fraser Fibreglass 2
Fresh Water Marina 339
Friday Harbor Marina (Port of Friday
  Harbor) 207
Friday Harbor Marine 205
Furuno 15

G
Garmin 78
Gourmet's Galley 210
Grundens 86

H
Hampton Yachts 1
Harbor History Museum 107
Harbour's End 250
Hasse & Company/Port Townsend
  Sails 150
Hastings House 250
Heritage Distilling 107

I
Ice House Gallery 473
IGA (Madeira Park Pender Harbour) 305
Irwin Yacht Sales 28
Islands Marine Center 199
Isotherm Marine Refrigeration 79

J
J & G Marine Supply 113
Jarrell's Cove Marina 100
Jensen's Boatyard (Albert Jensens &
  Sons) 206, 171, 210
John Henry's Marina & Resort 301
JW Timber Company (Fresh Water
  Marina) 339

K
Kenmore Air 25
Kings Marine Center 205, 210
Kingston Marina 146

L
La Conner Brewing Company 168
La Conner Chamber of Commerce 168
La Conner Landing Fuel Dock 168
La Conner Marina 169
La Conner Maritime Service 51, 168, 169
Ladysmith Chamber of Commerce
  and Visitor Centre 262
Ladysmith Community Marina 262
Ladysmith Marina 261, 262
Lagoon Cove Marina 356
Lavendera Massage 210
LeMay - America's Car Museum 114
Lewmar 53
LFS Marine 84, 85, 86, 180
Li Read Sea to Sky Premier Properties 247
Lopez Islander Resort 200
Lund Resort & 13 Moons Marina 313

M
Madeira Marina 305
Marine Services Group 171, 174
Marine Thrift Store 152
Martin Marine 294
Milltech Marine 64
Moby's Pub 247, 250
Monkey Fist Marine 126
Montague Harbour Marina 253
Museum of Glass 114
Museum of Northern BC 473

CULINARY DESTINATIONS INDEX

Ajax Cafe 151
Anthony's Family of Restaurants 118
Bakeries of the Inside Passage 12
Cluxewe Waterfront Bistro 386
Dent Island Lodge 351
Dine at InnChanter-Hot Springs Cove 411
Dining with the Kings 482
Edible Flowers 83
Farmers Markets 14
Foodie Heaven on Salt Spring Island 249
Gather Teahouse Eatery & Stage 243

How to Prepare Sea Asparagus 475
Nimmo Bay Wilderness Resort 367
Ocean-Aged Rum and Bourbon 156
Pierre's Pig Roast at Echo Bay 374
Saturna Lamb Barbeque 273
Secret Cove-The Upper Deck 315
The Laughing Oyster-Okeover Inlet 337
Theme Recipe First Prize 17
Theme Recipe Grand First Prize 16
Westcott Bay Oyster Farm 214
Woodstone Manor Restaurant & Patio 252

www.WaggonerGuide.com

ADVERTISER INDEX

N
Nordhavn Yachts Northwest 82
Nordic Tugs 44
North Harbor Diesel & Yacht Service 174, 175
North Island Boat Company 171, 174
North Island Marina 382
North Pacific Cannery 473
North Saanich Marina 238
Northwest Maritime Center 150
Northwest Rigging 54
Northwest Yachtnet Brokerage 114
NW Explorations 74, 181, 236
NW Explorations - Brokerage 75
NW Explorations - Chartering 65
Northwest Seaplanes 24

O
Oak Bay Marina 233
Oak Bay Marine Group Marinas 226
Ocean Falls 449
Ocean Pacific Marine Store & Boatyard 334
Ocens 45
Otter Bay Marina 242

P
Pacific Fiberglass 128
Pacific Pride of Alaska 495
Page's Resort & Marina 270
Page's Inn 270
Page's Resort Group 270
Parnassus Books and Gifts 495
Pharmasave Ladysmith 262
Philbrook's Boatyard 234
Pierre's Echo Bay Lodge & Marina 360
Pleasant Harbor Marina Resort 143
Poets Cove Resort & Spa 240
Point Hudson Marina and RV Park 155
Point Roberts Marina Resort 187
Port Angeles Boat Haven 192
Port Interpretive Centre 473
Port Ludlow Resort & Marina 149
Port McNeill Harbour Authority 383
Port of Anacortes 177

Port of Bellingham-Blaine Harbor 186
Port of Bellingham-Squalicum Harbor 182
Port of Bremerton-Bremerton Marina 132
Port of Bremerton-Port Orchard Marina 131
Port of Edmonds Marina 157
Port of Friday Harbor Marina 207
Port of Kingston Marina 146
Port of Olympia - Swantown Marina 98
Port of Port Townsend - Boat Haven Marina 154
Port of Port Townsend - Point Hudson Marina 155
Port of Seattle - Bell Harbor Marina 120
Port of Seattle - Shilshole Bay Marina 121
Port of Silverdale - Silverdale Marina 133
Port of Skagit - La Conner Marina 169
Port Orchard Marina 131
Port Sidney 231

R
Ranger Tugs - Inside Back Cover
Raven Marine 236
Refuge Cove 323
Roche Harbor Marine Services 208
Roche Harbor Resort & Marina 209
Rock The Dock 114
Rockfish Grill & Anacortes Brewery 174

S
Salamander Books 262
Samlex America 84
Salish Marine 174
Salt Spring Island Chamber of Commerce 247
Salt Spring Marina 250;
San Juan Sailing 181
Scan Marine 63
Sea Grant 19
Sea Sport Outboard Marine & Clothing 474
Sea-Dog 85, 180
Seattle Yachts Brokerage 23, 174
Secret Cove Marina 300
Shaw General Store 202

Shearwater Resort & Marina 452
Shilshole Bay Marina 121
Silverdale Marina 133
Skyline Marine Center & Marina 178
Soho Coho 495
Sound Marine Services 281
Spectra Water Makers 71
Spencers Marine Supply & Consignment 232
Squalicum Harbor 182
Squirrel Cove Store 325
Steveston Marine & Hardware 286
Sullivan Bay Marina Resort 365
Susie's Mopeds 210
Swan Hotel and Cottages 152
Swantown Marina & Boatworks 98

T
Tacoma Art Museum 114
Taku Resort & Marina 330
Thetis Island Resort 263
Timber & Marine Supply 495
Toba Wilderness Marina 322
Tofino Resort & Marina 417
Tri-County Diesel Marine 181

U
Union City Market/Alderbrook 33
Union Steamship Co. Marina & Resort - Back Cover, 296

V
Van Isle Marina 237
Victoria International Marina 87

W
Washington State Historical Society 114
Waterfront Suites & Marina 267
Wellspring Spa 250
West Sound Marina 217
Westview Fuels 312
Whale Museum 210
Wheelhouse Brewing Company 473
Wine Seller 152
Wooden Boat Chandlery 152

SIDEBAR INDEX

"Car Stops" on Pender Islands 241
A Tribute to the Douglasses 55
Alert Bay - The Spirit of U'mista 379
Aquatic Invasive Species (AIS) Prevention Permit 90
Caution In Rosario Strait 197
Cougar Annie's Garden In Hesquiat Harbour 409
Cruising the Shoulders 106
Derelict Vessel Reporting 62
Desolation Sound Marine Park Trails 332
Dogs Onboard 149
Don't Miss Misty Fjords National Monument 497
First-Aid Supplies & Preparedness 301
Flag Etiquette 381
Hakai Beach Institute - Pruth Bay 445
Hiram M. Chittenden Locks 123

How Fresh Tomatoes Get To Refuge Cove 324
It Will Never Happen To Me 87
Large Scale, Large Detail 41
Nakwakto Rapids And Belize Inlet 436
Nautical Slang - Common Expressions 231
No Discharge Zones 48
North Pacific Cannery - A Century of Salmon 471
Olympic Discovery Trail 191
Planning For Happy Hour 373
Puget Sound No Discharge Zone 40
Radio Check 45
Running in The Fog 42
Running The Rapids 343
San Juan Preservation Trust Properties 212
Scolding On The Radio 47
Sea Otter Cove 393
Seattle Aquarium 127

Securite Call Instead of Big Wake Scold 47
Seymour Narrows 334
Stern Ties 59
Swinomish Channel 165
Tacoma Foss Waterway 112
Tacoma Museums 111
The Offshore Drilling Business 496
The Surprise On Knight Inlet 362
Third-party Moorage Reservation Services 72
Turn Point Special Operating Area 222
Turtleback Mountain Preserve On Orcas Island 218
U.S. Customs CBP ROAM App 31
We Bought a Marina 105
Whale Wise - BC Juan de Fuca 416
Whale Wise - Gulf Islands 244
Whale Wise - Washington State 203

2020 WAGGONER CRUISING GUIDE

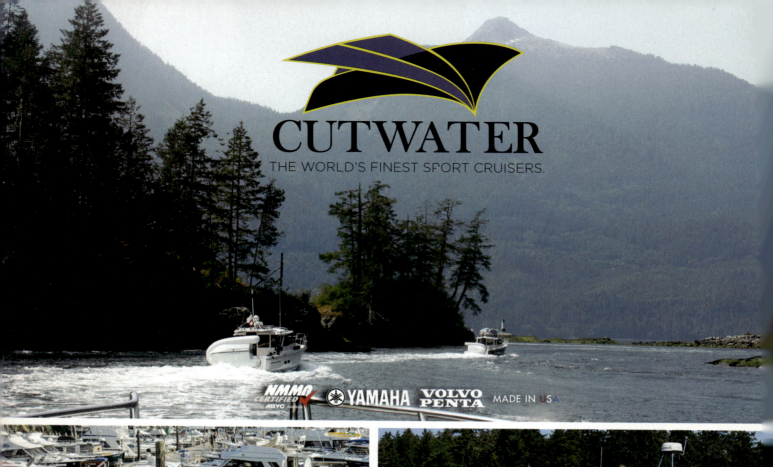

CUTWATER
THE WORLD'S FINEST SPORT CRUISERS.

CUTWATER
Cutwater Cruise
Canadian Gulf Islands

CutwaterBoats.com

Photos courtesy of: The Walker Family & Cutwater Boats

Waggoner Cruising Guide 2018

The Ranger Tug fleet now numbers in the hundreds of these beautiful boats between the U.S. and Canada. Every season the "Tugnuts" are seen cruising around and having fun. For this year's cover, Captain Sue Peterson was photographed in Northern B.C. headed home with her Ranger Tug 31 from her summer cruise in Southeast Alaska. Photo by Mark Bunzel.

PREPARING AND PLANNING FOR THE CRUISE

- 4 Locator Maps
- 8 About the Waggoner Cruising Guide
- 11 How to Cruise the Pacific Northwest
- 18 Floatplane Travel
- 20 U.S. and Canadian Customs Information
- 26 Differences between U.S. and Canadian Charts
- 28 About Anchoring
- 30 ELCI Shore Power
- 34 Chartering
- 36 Maintaining Your Boat Like A Pro
- 39 VHF Radio Procedures
- 42 Cellular, Internet and Satellite Communications
- 48 Boating from Inn to Inn
- 50 Developing an Itinerary to Delight the Entire Crew
- 52 Provisioning
- 55 Potable Water
- 56 Interpreting Northwest Weather
- 61 Buoys, Beacons, and Ranges
- 62 Boardings
- 63 Homeland Security
- 64 State and Provincial Parks and Public Wharves
- 65 What Recreational Boaters Need to Know About VTS
- 66 VTS Radio Channels
- 69 Contact Phone Numbers
- 70 VHF Channels
- 71 Reference Pages - Conversion Tables

INDEXES

- 467 Index to Places, Parks, Marinas and Anchorages
- 477 Advertiser Index
- 478 Local Knowledge Index
- 479 Sidebar Features Indexes
- 479 Early Maritime Explorers

CRUISING AREAS

- 73 South and Central Puget Sound
- 117 Hood Canal
- 125 North Puget Sound
- 167 Strait of Juan de Fuca
- 174 San Juan Islands
- 203 Gulf Islands
- 249 Strait of Georgia
- 259 Vancouver, Mainland B.C. and the Sunshine Coast
- 291 Desolation Sound and Discovery Passage
- 312 Johnstone Strait
- 323 The Broughtons
- 345 North Vancouver Island
- 356 West Coast of Vancouver Island
- 397 Rounding Cape Caution
- 400 Northern B.C. Coast
- 446 Haida Gwaii
- 456 Crossing Dixon Entrance
- 461 Arriving in Ketchikan

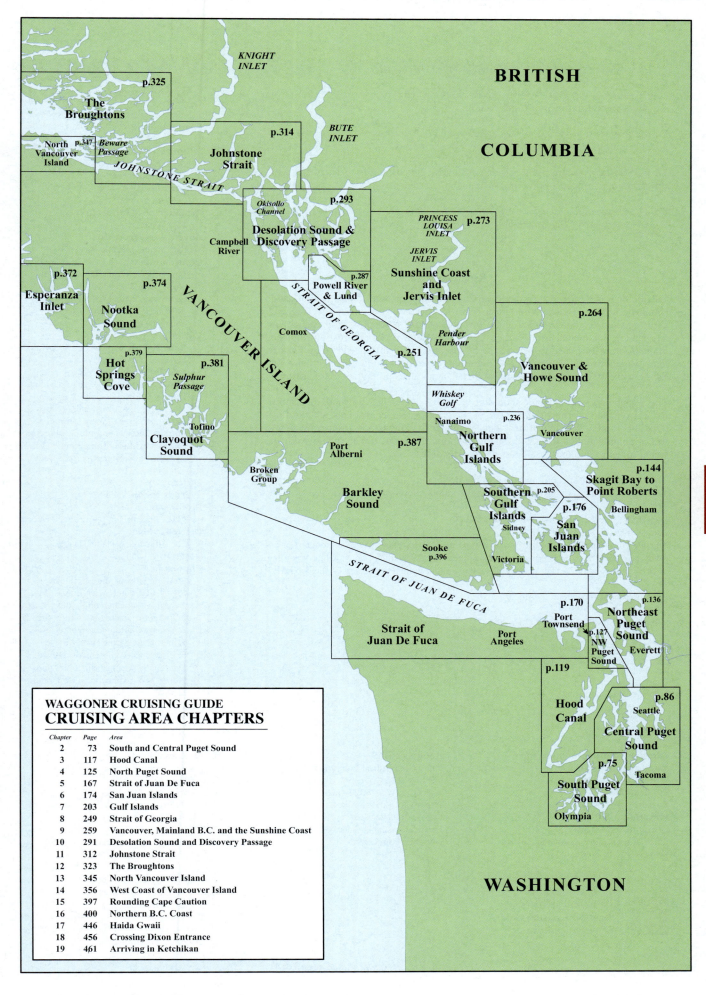

ABOUT WAGGONER CRUISING GUIDE

We want to hear from you!

Your comments, suggestions and corrections are invited. We appreciate hearing from anyone who finds errors in this publication.

We are interested in ideas about what you would like in future editions of the Waggoner Cruising Guide. There are a number of members of the Waggoner community who contribute to our website. Our readers are interested in your experiences and tips. We post cruising reports, pictures, video, updates about changes in specified areas, and tips that range from anchoring to restaurants to technical issues.

Contact us through our website www.WaggonerGuide.com, or by telephone, mail, or e-mail at waggtalk@WaggonerGuide.com.

CAUTION

This book was designed to provide experienced skippers with cruising information about the waters covered. While great effort has been taken to make the Waggoner Cruising Guide complete and accurate, it is possible that oversights, differences of interpretation, and factual errors will be found. Thus none of the information contained in the book is warranted to be accurate or appropriate for any specific need. Furthermore, variations in weather and sea conditions, a mariner's skills and experience, and the presence of luck (good or bad) can dictate a mariner's proper course of action.

The Waggoner Cruising Guide should be viewed as a reference only and not a substitute for official government charts, tide and current tables, coast pilots, sailing directions, and local notices to mariners. The Waggoner Cruising Guide assumes the user to be law-abiding and of good will. The suggestions offered are not all-inclusive, but are meant to help avoid unpleasantness or needless delay.

The publisher, editors, and authors assume no liability for errors or omissions, or for any loss or damages incurred from using this publication.

Copyright © 2018 by Burrows Bay Associates LLC

All rights reserved. Except for use in a review, no part of this book may be reproduced or utilized in any form or by any means, electronic or mechanical, including photocopying, recording, or by any information storage or retrieval system without written permission of the publisher.

Printed in the United States of America
ISBN: 978-0-9969799-9-3
Spiral Edition ISBN: 978-0-9993560-0-5

Library of Congress information available upon request.

WAGGONER CRUISING GUIDE

Founding Editor
Robert Hale
Editor/Publisher
Mark Bunzel
Managing Editors
Lorena Landon
Leonard Landon
Art Director & Production
Sara White
Advertising Production
Sara White, Melanie Haage
Contributors
Jim Bathurst, Deane Hislop, David Hoar, Steve & Elsie Hulsizer, Sam Landsman, Lydia McKenzie, Kevin Monahan, Duart Snow, Sadie Youngstrom
Correspondents
Bruce & Margaret Evertz, Gil & Karen Flanagan, Carol-Ann Giroday & Rick LeBlanc, Stephen & Debbie Gratton, Mike Guns, Jennifer & James Hamilton, Knut & Christine Hildebrand, Dean Hislop, Steve & Elsie Hulsizer, Sam Landsman, Linda Lewis, John & Lorraine Littlewood, John Mifflin, Jim Norris, Pat Shera, Bob & Shino Posey, Al & Becca Szymanski, Fred & Judy Triggs
Office
Karla Locke, Linda Matson
Proofreading
Linda Matson, Jim Norris, Sue Peterson
Reference Maps
Sue Athmann, Melanie Haage, Leonard Landon
Photography
Steve Berentson, Sheri Berkman, Michael Bertrand, Mark Bunzel, M.J. Bunzel, Susan Churchhill, JoJo Gagner, Jeff George, Stacia A.M. Green, Stephen & Debbie Gratton, Marilynn Hale, Robert Hale, Deane Hislop, Steve & Elsie Hulsizer, Lorena & Leonard Landon, Sam Landsman, John Lund, Jim Norris, NW Explorations, Don Odegard, Sara White
Historical Data
Wikimedia

Direct advertising inquiries to:
Waggoner Cruising Guide
Burrows Bay Associates
PO Box 726
Anacortes, WA 98221 USA
Phone (425) 780-5015
Fax (360) 299-0535
Email: waggtalk@WaggonerGuide.com
www.WaggonerGuide.com

Like us on Facebook
Waggoner Cruising Guide
WaggonerGuide.com

Book Sales U.S.
Fine Edge Nautical Publishing
PO Box 726
Anacortes, WA 98221 USA
Phone (360) 299-8500
Fax (360) 299-0535
Email: orders@FineEdge.com
www.FineEdge.com

Book Sales Canada
Chyna Sea Ventures, Ltd.
Unit 4, 147 E. Fern Rd.
Qualicum Beach, BC, V9K 1T2
Phone: (250) 740-1184
Fax: (250) 740-1185
Toll Free: 866-627-8324
Email: orders@ChynaSea.com
www.ChynaSea.com

Heritage Group Distribution
Suite 8, 19272 - 96th Avenue,
Surrey, BC V4N 4C1
Phone: (604) 881-7067 or (800) 665-3302
Fax: (604) 881-7068 or (800) 566-3336
orders@hgdistribution.com

WE ARE ALL EXPLORERS

In this 2018 Edition of the Waggoner Cruising Guide, we celebrate the early explorers. Throughout the book you will find stories about the brave captains and crews that sailed this area as early as the 1500's. We are all explorers too, though we have the advantage of guidebooks, charts, and chart plotters. What hasn't changed is the excitement we feel when traveling in unknown waters for the first time. It's intriguing to think what it must have been like to travel the passages and fjords of the Inside Passage years ago. Imagine what Deception Pass, Dodd Narrows, or even Seymour Narrows must have been like before they were charted and the local tides and currents understood. Or, what it must have been like to hit an uncharted rock with a jolt, and hear the ship's timbers cracking. It was then off to a careening spot to unload the entire vessel and row the cargo ashore to allow the shipwrights to replace a plank, or two or three.

We encourage you to explore further. We offer classes and a full range of books to increase your nautical knowledge beyond this book.

In the Waggoner Guide we share many of our secrets to cruising this beautiful area. Each year we add more to the front section of this book. Read it carefully for safe and comfortable cruising.

We also share many of our secret spots including beautiful anchorages you may have passed many times; or places with hot springs, or a drop dead gorgeous view. Where are your secret spots? Over the next year, we are offering a prize for the best secret spot. Send us a photo and your comments on why your spot is so special. You can even ask us to keep it a secret and not publish its location. See WaggonerGuide.com

for more details.

We look forward to seeing you out on the water, exploring the beautiful Pacific Northwest.

Mark Bunzel, Editor & Publisher

WHAT'S NEW IN THE 2018 WAGGONER CRUISING GUIDE?

Managing Editors Lorena and Leonard Landon, along with Editor Mark Bunzel, spent an extended summer season gathering new information for marinas and anchorages for this 2018 Waggoner. In addition to updating guidebook content from this season's cruising discoveries, we embarked on an ambitious list of enhancements and upgrades to the guide's usability. With each update, we found opportunities to re-write and improve how information is shared with our readers. Boaters can look forward to new docks at Eagle Harbor Waterfront Park, Eagle Harbor Marina, Rosario Resort, Saltspring Marina, Port Browning, and Shearwater along with improved services and facilities at other frequented destinations. In addition to the countless text updates, more than half of the 225 reference maps have been revised, and an additional 16 new detailed reference maps have been added to this year's edition. As reported by our readers, detailed reference maps and dock diagrams are an indispensable help when planning a trip and identifying assigned moorage at new destinations.

Perhaps you've noticed the new look for the Waggoner Cruising Guide this year. Colored tabs for each chapter are now found along the outside edge of the pages, a different color identifies each section or chapter. While readers can find specific names and places in the index, you can now quickly turn to the desired chapter identified by a specific colored tab. The front section of the book, containing reference material such as navigation, weather, anchoring, and communications can quickly be identified by its own unique color. You will also find helpful information in the front section

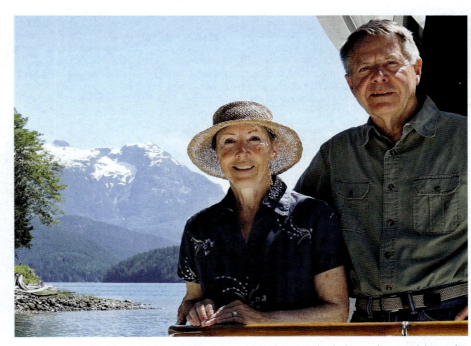

regarding ELCI-protected shore power, newly installed at a number of northwest marinas. The list of marinas with ELCI-protected power will continue to grow; find out why ELCI is required, and how you can make a successful connection.

Beginning with the 2018 edition, the Waggoner Team has embarked on creating theme-based editions of the Waggoner Cruising Guide. 'Early Maritime Explorers of the Pacific Northwest,' our theme for 2018, includes 17 sidebars describing the explorations of early maritime captains who sailed the Pacific Northwest. Check the Explorers Sidebar Index to find these fascinating snapshots of history. Topics in the front section have also been enhanced, including additional information for weather strategies and tips for maintaining your boat. These strategies and maintenance tips help ensure a more enjoyable boating season. The Waggoner Cruising Guide continues to provide important information for planning and preparing one's personal voyage of adventure.

- Lorena and Leonard Landon, Managing Editors

ABOUT THE WAGGONER CRUISING GUIDE

Waggoner Guide (pronounced [wagənər] not [wagənir]) has been guiding boaters to the spectacular Northwest destinations since 1994. It provides the reader with information about marinas, anchorages, passages, and attractions from Olympia, Washington to Ketchikan, Alaska. It is referred to by boaters as *The bible for northwest cruising*. This all-inclusive guidebook is updated annually.

Waggoner Guide strives to be the most up-to-date cruising guidebook with the most accurate information. The writing style is intended to be as concise, factual, and informative as possible.

How the book is organized. The first section of the book, referred to as 'Front Matter,' contains valuable information that helps boaters plan and execute a successful trip. This Chapter 1, Front Matter, has instructional material regarding customs, weather, anchoring, communications and other pertinent 'how-to' information.

The body of the book is divided into chapters by geographic cruising area, starting in the south at Olympia Washington and progressing north to Ketchikan, Alaska. Keeping with the south to north organization, material within each chapter generally progresses northward. Each chapter begins with an overview of the area followed by detailed information for each marina along with passages and designated anchorages. Ports, harbors, and cities with multiple boating facilities also begin with an overview description to help the reader become familiar with the area.

Reference maps for the chapter's coverage area are located at the beginning of the chapter with additional reference maps found throughout the chapter. A Legend of symbols used on Waggoner Guide reference maps can be found in this section. Area reference maps indicate destinations with numbers, which correspond to the numbered text for marinas and significant anchorages. Reference maps are not for navigation and do not show all navigation aids, beacons, marks, lights, and hazards. Maps are not to scale and are for reference purposes only. Boaters should carry up-to-date electronic charts and/or paper charts. For those who carry paper charts, a list of area charts is provided in each chapter.

You will also find 'Local Knowledge' and 'Sidebars' within many of the chapters. Local Knowledge provides helpful tips and warnings regarding shoals, rocks, tides and current for specific locations, which may not be depicted on navigational charts. Short articles, called Sidebars, relate personal experiences that are informative and helpful to the reader. Sidebars also provide historical background for a number of destinations, enlightening the imagination and purpose of why we go there in the first place.

The Year's Theme. Many of the Sidebars in the Waggoner Guide focus on a chosen theme for each year. 'Early Maritime Explorers of the Pacific Northwest' was chosen as this year's theme. How many of us have marveled over the accomplishments and challenges these early explorers faced without the benefit of modern technology? They didn't have chart plotters, GPS, and communications for weather reports; nor did they have the modern conveniences for food preservation and preparation. Equally intriguing is the fact that these explorers from the 1700's and earlier, sailed the very waters we enjoy today. This year's edition includes sidebars for 17 different explorers who sailed the Pacific Northwest, whose names are attributed to our islands and waterways. A timeline of these early explorers is included here.

How the Book is Made. The Waggoner Guide Team of Northwest boaters, cruise Northwest waters and the Inside Passage to Alaska each year, gathering updates for marinas, anchorages,

1492	1500s		1643	1770s	
Christopher Columbus reaches the New World	The first *Waggoners* Published (see history opposite-top right)	Juan de Fuca discovers strait of his namesake	Invention of the Sextant & Chronometer	Juan Perez discovers Haida Gwaii	James Cook's Third Voyage
	Francis Drake explores the Pacific NW Coast	Gerard Mercator invents Mercator Map Projection	Invention of the Barometer	U.S. Declartion of Independence 1776	Bodega Y Guarda searches for the NW Passage

and passages found in the Waggoner Guide. The Waggoner Team along with experienced, knowledgeable contributors and correspondents, provide the many hundreds of updates included in each year's edition of the Waggoner Cruising Guide. While it is not possible to physically go to every anchorage or marina each year, every effort is made to get the latest information directly from marinas by phone or other means. Editorial work begins in September to incorporate these changes and updates, including new reference maps and photos. Editors, proof readers, and designers of maps, ads, and page layout spend untold hours preparing copy for final proofs, while meeting our print deadline. The much-anticipated announcement of the current edition of the Waggoner Guide is provided in our 'eNews.' Copies of the Waggoner Cruising Guide are made available at the Seattle Boat Show, where boaters enthusiastically purchase the new edition and begin making plans for their next adventure. Copies are also available at retailers throughout Washington, B.C., and Alaska.

How to send us Comments and Feedback. The Waggoner Team invites your comments, suggestions and corrections. We appreciate hearing from our readers regarding ways we can improve our publication. Your ideas for future editions are always welcome along with your experiences and tips, which inform and help other boaters.

Contact us through our website www.WaggonerGuide.com, or by telephone, mail, or e-mail at waggtalk@WaggonerGuide.com; you can also find us on Facebook.

WaggonerGuide.com and eNews. At WaggonerGuide.com, we have a dedicated team of experienced boaters and travel experts who share a variety of articles each month about boating in Washington, British Columbia, and Southeast Alaska. Some of the topics include maintenance tips, cruising destinations, boat reviews, and on-the-water reporting. You'll also find boating seminar announcements, guidebook updates, access to free downloads, and our collection of boating and nautical-themed books in the Waggoner Store.

A great way to stay tuned into WaggonerGuide.com is to subscribe to Waggoner eNews. This newsletter is sent out twice a month and contains our latest boating related articles. It also gives you access to our eNews subscriber-only downloads. All of our content is geared toward you, our reader, who lives and breathes boating in the Pacific Northwest.

To enroll in the Waggoner eNews visit WaggonerGuide.com. You'll find the subscribe button on the right column. Or, visit our Facebook page at https://www.facebook.com/WaggonerCruisingGuide and in the left-hand column, you'll find the Subscribe to eNews tab.

Advertisers. Advertising helps provide the best cruising information at the best price to you the cruising public; advertisements often provide more extensive information about the facility that is not part of the mission of the Waggoner Guide. Advertising helps us keep in touch with the marinas and service providers, who provide information about what is coming for the next cruising season. This symbiotic relationship helps the Waggoner Team stay in communication with the Marine Trade Industry and provide guidance regarding cruisers' needs. Combined ads, called Community Market Place, inform our readers of local events, farmers' markets, and other local points of interest.

Let our advertisers know that you saw them in the Waggoner Cruising Guide.

A History of the Waggoner

About 1584 the Dutch pilot Lucas Janszoon Waghenaer published a volume of navigational principles, tables, charts, and sailing directions, which served as a guide for other such books for the next 200 years.

These "*Waggoners*," as they came to be known, met with great success, and in 1588 an English translation of the original book was made. During the next 30 years, 24 editions of the book were published in Dutch, German, Latin, and English. Other authors followed the profitable example set by Waghenaer. Soon, American, British, and French navigators had Waggoners for most of the waters they sailed.

The success of these books and the resulting competition led to their eventual demise. Each writer attempted to make his work more inclusive than any other; the result was a tremendous book difficult to handle. In 1795 the British Hydrographic Department was established, and charts and sailing directions were issued separately. Within a few years the Waggoners disappeared.

We hope you find this new Waggoner to be as useful as the Waggoners of old, but without their excess bulk or needless detail. *Waggoner* is an ancient name with a proud history. Use and enjoy!

| George Dixon sails the Pacific NW Coast | Jose Narvaez explores Pacific NW Coast | Martinez & Eliza at Nootka Sound | George Vancouver surveys Pacific NW Coast | Puget & Whidbey explore Puget Sound | Alexander Mackenzie reaches West Coast overland |

1780s — **1790s** — — — **1793** **1805**

| Charles Barkley sails Pacific NW Coast | Malaspina's scientific voyage | Fidalgo explores Pacific NW Coast | Broughton explores Broughton Archipelago | Galiano & Valdes explore Pacific NW Coast | Lewis & Clark reach West Coast overland |

HOW TO CRUISE THE PACIFIC NORTHWEST

HOW TO CRUISE TOPICS
"Gates" and their effect
Chartering.
Trailering a Boat.
Anchoring vs. marinas.
Moorage Reservations
Have flexible expectations
About the boat
Be self-reliant
Best months
GPS chartplotters, charts and books
It Takes Teamwork
Use FRS radios
Don't be cheap
What to Bring & How to Equip the Boat
Cruising Tips & Techniques

Inside Passage. The Inside Passage is one of the best cruising grounds in the world. The distance from Olympia, Washington to Ketchikan, Alaska is about 600 miles as the crow flies. On a boat, meandering through fjords and between islands, the distance multiplies. Most of these waters are protected; open water passages are relatively short, and anchorages are plentiful.

Wildlife is outstanding. Whales—orcas, humpbacks, grays, and more—are regularly spotted. Bald eagles are everywhere. Bears snatch salmon from seaside rivers or forage on the beach. Porpoises, seals, sea lions, sea otters, and myriad other life call the Inside Passage home.

Natural beauty overwhelms. The great volcanoes of the Cascade mountains are visible throughout Puget Sound and the San Juan Islands. Sandstone in the Gulf Islands, eroded by wind and water, forms fascinating patterns and shapes. Magnificent, glacier carved fjords run deep into British Columbia's interior. Waterfalls plunge thousands of feet from snow-covered peaks all the way to the waters' edge.

We have impressive cities, too. Seattle, Victoria, and Vancouver are easily visited by boat and have every amenity imaginable. Smaller cities like La Conner, Anacortes, Sidney, Cowichan Bay, Ladysmith—even Port McNeill, Port Hardy, Prince Rupert, and Ketchikan farther north—roll out the red carpet for visiting boats. They have restaurants, shops, and museums to explore or enjoy.

Small resorts and marinas, many family run, dot the coast. Some are as simple as local logs felled, milled, and lashed together to form a dock. Others have spas and high-end restaurants. Potluck dinners and happy hours are common at the smaller marinas.

You won't go hungry cruising this area. Bigger towns have grocery stores. Many marinas stock the essentials for their guests. Farmers markets, local bakers, artisan cheese makers, and craft wineries, breweries and now a few distilleries operate along the Inside Passage. Seafood, of course, is plentiful. Cruisers catch salmon, halibut, lingcod, prawns, and crab. They pick oysters and harvest sea asparagus.

The history is rich. Yaculta and Alert Bay have superb museums detailing the history of Native cultures. In Ketchikan, Totem Bight State Park has a remarkable collection of totems. Cruisers can follow in the footsteps of Capt. George Vancouver's 1790s expedition and the early expeditions of the Spanish explorers, during which many of the waterways and land masses in this area were named. Opportunities to enjoy the arts are readily available; in this book we describe the full range of museums at destinations along the way. Tacoma alone has six museums and a zoo, all within easy walking distance from the docks.

The variety of experiences, the majesty of the vistas, and the splendor of the wildlife and the variety of attractions in our towns and cities on the water keep us cruising.

"Gates" and their effect. The Pacific Northwest is a series of cruising areas separated by what we call "gates"— significant bodies of water that must be crossed. Although gates define our experience and abilities, they also serve as natural stopping points. Some cruisers stay in Puget Sound because the Strait of Juan de Fuca and San Juan Channel is a gate. Some stay in the Gulf Islands because the Strait of Georgia and Dodd Narrows crossing is a gate bringing concerns about the sea state conditions. Some go no farther than Desolation Sound because Johnstone Strait and the reversing tidal rapids north of Desolation Sound are gates. And some stay south of Cape Caution because the ocean swells of Queen Charlotte Sound can be looked at as a gate. Gates exist all the way up the coast, all the way to Alaska.

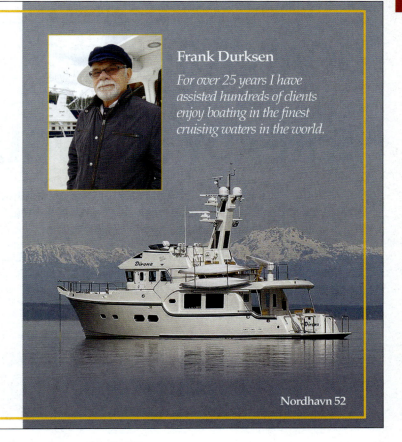

"Making your boating dreams come true."
—Frank Durksen

At Yacht Finders International we specialize in Passage-Making Trawlers, and quality power yachts.

We list only the best.

AAA YACHT FINDERS *International*

1.800.704.2628 • www.findyachts.com

Frank Durksen
For over 25 years I have assisted hundreds of clients enjoy boating in the finest cruising waters in the world.

Nordhavn 52

2018 WAGGONER CRUISING GUIDE

HOW TO CRUISE THE PACIFIC NORTHWEST

Once beyond a gate and in a given cruising area, the waters are protected. Fortunately, summer weather usually is agreeable. With a study of the tide and current books, a close eye on the winds, an understanding of the weather, and a properly-equipped boat, the gates can be negotiated in safety, and often in comfort. The farther one decides to explore, the more time is needed. For the dedicated summertime Northwest cruiser, time is the principal element limiting cruising choices.

Chartering. The most popular charter boat waters run from the San Juan Islands to Desolation Sound, a distance of approximately 160 miles. These waters include the San Juan Islands, the Canadian Gulf Islands, the cities of Victoria and Vancouver, Howe Sound, Princess Louisa Inlet and the ever popular Desolation Sound. Most charters are for a week or two. It would take years of careful planning and repeat visits for a regular charter cruiser to see all there is to see in this area. For more information see Chartering in Chapter 1.

Trailering a Boat. Trailering is faster and more affordable than running a boat on its own bottom, and it avoids difficult passages across open water—the "gates" described earlier. Trailer boats can be towed to all the cruising grounds from Puget Sound to the far end of Vancouver Island. Even the sounds and inlets of the west coast of Vancouver Island can be seen easily and safely. Some people trailer all the way up Vancouver Island, launch at Port Hardy, and—watching the weather carefully—cruise north past Cape Caution to Rivers Inlet and beyond.

Many boats are trailered from the B.C. Interior to launch at Bella Coola or Prince Rupert. It's a long drive, but the waters they get to are some of the finest in the world. From Prince Rupert, you can cruise north into Southeast Alaska, which is not accessible by road. Another option is to tow the boat and trailer onto the ferry. Although expensive, both the BC Ferries and the Alaska Marine Highway ferries allow trailered boats.

Anchoring vs. marinas. Compared with the waters farther north, Puget Sound has relatively few good anchorages. Most Puget Sound cruising is from marina to marina, or hanging off state park buoys. The San Juan Islands and Canadian Gulf Islands have many marinas and many anchorages. Desolation Sound is mostly anchorages with a few marinas. State and provincial marine parks dot the waterways from Puget Sound to Desolation Sound, many but not all with mooring buoys. The Broughtons have a wide variety of marinas and many, many anchorages. The west coast of Vancouver Island and the waters north of Cape Caution have a few marinas but mostly anchorages. It is possible to cruise all the way to the top of Vancouver Island and stay only at the dock in a marina. For more information see 'About Anchoring' in the front section.

Moorage Reservations. Many marinas accept advance reservations for transient moorage. Reserving moorage in advance is always a good idea and highly recommended during the busy summer season. A telephone call is the most universally accepted means for making reservations. Increasingly, some marinas have web-based reservation systems and a few accept email requests.

Some marinas don't require any credit card information but others do. Ask about their policy for charging your credit card and about their cancelation policy in case weather or unexpected delays cause a change in plans. Some marinas charge for no-shows. Ask about your slip assignment; a few marinas assign a slip at the time of reservation, while others request you contact them by radio upon arrival.

It's best to contact the marina directly for slip reservations. There are a few third-party centralized marina slip reservation providers, which began on the U.S. East Coast and have a very limited number of west coast marinas under contract. There are some websites that purport to have relationships with local marinas but do not. Check with the marina first before contacting any third-party web provider.

Have flexible expectations. Marina facilities run the range from elegant to, shall

---

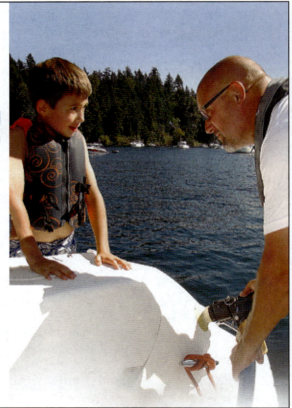

BOATERS: THE PUMPOUT GUY IS READY FOR YOU!

Get your onboard holding tank emptied for free on Lake Washington, Portage Bay, Duwamish River and at select marinas at Gig Harbor, Liberty Bay and Eagle Harbor.

This service is provided courtesy of Washington State Parks, Washington Sea Grant and the Pumpout Guy. **Let's work together to protect the waters we love!**

To arrange: pumpoutguy.com, 206.437.6764 or radio, VHF Ch 68

For more information see
pumpoutwashington.org

we say, rustic. Managements span the same range. A person who expects 5-star facilities and service at every stop will be disappointed. Especially in the remote areas, the docks and other facilities can be rather on the rough side. Service at the Native villages up the coast, for example, is provided on their terms, in their way, and that's different from the city approach most Waggoner readers are accustomed to. When we're out cruising we have found it helpful to relax and take things as they come. We appreciate the places that do things our way, but we get along with the places that don't.

The one area we have less patience with is cleanliness. We think public washrooms, showers and laundry areas should be clean and in good condition, always. If we could have one message for marina operators, it would be, *keep those areas sparkling.*

About the boat. Northwest cruising is coastal cruising in generally protected waters, so blue-water ocean voyaging vessels are not required. But the waters can get rough. Whether power or sail, good Northwest cruising boats are strongly built and seaworthy. Lightweight pontoon boats or open ski boats that are so popular on inland lakes are not well suited to these waters.

The weather can be cool and often wet. Northwest cruising powerboats tend to have large cabins and ample window area. Northwest cruising sailboats tend to have dodgers across the fronts of the cockpits or even full cockpit enclosures. Winds often are light and on the nose—"noserlies"—so sailboats should have good power.

Most Northwest cruising boats are equipped with cabin heat. It could be heat generated while the engine is running, a diesel heater or diesel furnace, or electric space heaters on the dock's shore power. Heat can add comfort when it is raining, on a cool night, or when cruising in the off-season.

GPS has become so affordable that no Northwest cruising boat should be without a GPS system. A chartplotter, whether a dedicated marine unit or computer software on a PC or pad/tablet device, makes it easy to always know your position. There is even chartplotter software that runs on your smartphone.

AIS (Automatic Identification System) is increasingly popular. AIS receivers display vessel name, course, speed, and closest point of approach for nearby boats equipped with an AIS transponder, which broadcasts the vessel's boat information, course, and speed. Large commercial craft, such as ferries, cruise ships, and freighters, all broadcast AIS signals.

Radar has grown better and prices are trending down. In the last two years new digital radar systems now require less power, are lighter and often plug right into a chartplotter. Most important the new digital radar units are very sensitive and provide a better resolution and presentation in color. Since fog and rain clouds can lower visibility to near-zero any time of the year, cruising boats in the Northwest often end up with radar. Autopilots take the uncertainty out of steering in fog and make long passages less tiring. They too are quickly added.

Dinghies and tenders and convenient dinghy launching/ recovery systems are important. When anchored or tied to a mooring buoy, the dinghy will be used to travel to shore. Some cruisers use their dinghies extensively for exploring and fishing.

Substantial anchoring systems are important. See the *Anchoring* section of Chapter 1 for more information about anchoring.

The minimum size for a cruising boat probably is in the 18- to 20-foot range, and that's pretty minimum. Most mom-and-pop cruising boats fall into the 25- to 50-foot size range, with the majority in the 32- to 50-foot range—large enough to be comfortable, small enough to be handled by two people.

Be self-reliant. Don't venture out with the idea that if things go wrong, you can always call the Coast Guard. An important part of good seamanship is being able to handle whatever's thrown at you. Calling the Coast Guard is for true emergencies.

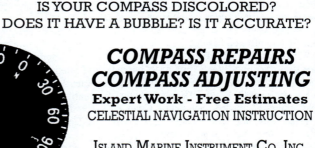

HOW TO CRUISE THE PACIFIC NORTHWEST

Best months. The prime cruising months begin in April and end by October, with July-August the most popular. Boats are used yearround in Puget Sound. On winter weekends Puget Sound's popular ports are surprisingly busy. Cabin heat is a must in the winter. As mentioned above, cabin heat is almost a must the rest of the year.

North of Puget Sound, pleasure boating is best done between early May and late September. Really dependable summer weather (little rain, long days of glorious sunshine) normally doesn't arrive in the Northwest until July. September can be an outstanding cruising month. The crowds are gone and the weather can be perfect.

Use caution with winter cruising north of Puget Sound. (Be careful in Puget Sound, too.) Storms lash the British Columbia coast. A Northwest boat with a warm and dry pilothouse is the way to enjoy winter cruising. Some, with flexible schedules, cruise yearround. It takes a good understanding of the weather, and a warm, dry boat. There are many resources available to understand the weather and help keep you from an unexpected surprise. See the Interpreting Northwest Weather section for our approach to understanding the weather.

About GPS chartplotters, charts and other publications. To keep this book informative and up-to-date, we have stuck our nose into many ports, bays, and coves along the coast. In the process we have become unyielding advocates of chartplotters, charts, and navigation publications. Properly used, charts not only keep a boat out of trouble, they allow one to enter areas you wouldn't want to try without the chart. With advancements in electronic charting in recent years, more mariners are asking whether carrying paper charts is still worthwhile. For years, we would not leave the dock without a set of paper charts. Even with computer navigation and a complete selection of electronic charts, it seemed wise to have paper charts as a backup.

But times are changing. Tablets and smartphones, with built-in GPS receiver systems and robust batteries, provide excellent redundancy. Low cost, highly effective chartplotting software is available for most tablet platforms. Many of these "apps" make updating charts easy. If relying on a tablet or smartphone as a backup, consider carrying an extra battery pack. They're inexpensive and greatly extend battery life. When using electronic charts, be aware that hazards can disappear at certain zoom levels. We always examine our route at several zoom levels to ensure that it is free of hazards.

Whatever form of charts you decide to carry, keep them updated. While rocks haven't changed location, navigation aids do change. Several years ago, for example, significant buoyage changes were made in Swinomish Channel. In British Columbia, some buoys were determined as unnecessary or redundant and were removed to meet budget goals. New charts reflect the change whether on paper or on new electronic updates. A five year old (or older) chartplotter may have very old charts and not reflect navigational updates.

Many cruising guides cover the Inside Passage and each offers a different point of view. We carry as many as we can fit, and keep several open at the helm. The U.S. Coast Pilot and Canadian Sailing Directions are good resources to have aboard, but they are focused on large commercial craft navigation.

Accurate tide and current tables are essential. Many electronic charting packages include tide and current data. However, we've found these are often inaccurate because they are based on old or estimated data. Note: Both U.S. and Canadian government tide tables are not corrected for Daylight Saving Time, so you'll have to make the corrections manually. Capt'n Jack's, covering Puget Sound, and Ports and Passes, covering Olympia to Prince Rupert and Southeast Alaska, are excellent and inexpensive, and times are corrected for Daylight Saving Time. Ports and Passes is updated each year with official government data. We have found some chartplotter tides and currents information to be off by as much as 45 minutes. Full disclosure: We are also the publishers of Ports and Passes.

U.S. Coast Guard Local Notices to Mariners, Canadian Notices to Shipping, and Canadian Notices to Mariners provide updated information on navaids and regulatory changes. U.S. and Canadian light lists are useful, too. The links to these sites are available in the "cruise planning" section of the Waggoner website.

We do not understand the mentality of the owner that will make a major investment in a boat and fuel, then hold back on charts and other navigation information. At the other extreme is the person who has very little invested, and won't buy navigation information because it costs too much compared to the value of the vessel. *Remember:* the rocks, tides and weather are indifferent to how much the boat cost. They treat all boats equally.

It Takes Teamwork. Like many boating couples, we work together as a team, checking and doublechecking routes, depths, and charted hazards along a chosen course. If we question or doubt our path, we come to a stop until the safest course can be verified before continuing on. This is not the time for wounded pride or "I told you so's," it's a matter of successfully accomplishing the task at hand, and the opportunity to learn and grow as a team. Everything looks different on the water, so it's easy to mistake land marks and aids to navigation. The more experienced you are as a team, the better off you will be when the going gets tuff, or when you are faced with a true emergency. Both partners should know how to use the radio, handle the helm, navigate, and manage sea conditions for a safe arrival into port. Docking and line-handling should be shared responsibilities, it's a good idea to schedule time for practice as well as a shakedown cruise for boat maintenance checks. The more comfortable you become with our own skills and know what your boat can handle, the more fun you will have. On a power vessel, it is imperative to conduct engine room checks, requiring a confident partner to take over the helm. Extended excursions or overnight passages for both power and sail, require taking turns at the helm so your partner can get some rest. The more you learn, the more opportunities you will have for new adventures further afield.

Use FRS radios. Inexpensive, handy, no license required. Excellent for replacing shouts or if you get separated at the county fair or at Costco. If cruising with other boats, they keep needless chatter off VHF channels.

Don't be cheap. It's bad form to use a private marina's facilities and not pay for the privilege. Even if a direct charge is not made, usually something can be purchased. When we overnight at a marina, we pay the moorage, just as our readers do. We're glad the marina is there, and we want it to be there for the future. We are pleased to do our part.

WHAT TO BRING AND HOW TO EQUIP THE BOAT.

Carry tools and spares. Our tool box is in the main cabin, available for immediate access. It seems like we are in that box at least once a day, usually for something minor, but it has to be fixed. Carry all owner's manuals, extra engine oil, transmission fluid, hydraulic fluid, coolant, and distilled water (for the batteries), spare V-belts, ignition parts, impellers and filters. Carry a spare raw water pump. The list of tools and spares has no end. You can't prepare for everything, but you can prepare for likely problems.

Carry and use all appropriate publications, paper and electronic. Charts! Tide and current tables. Local cruising guides. Good information adds to the enjoyment of the trip.

Carry self-amalgamating tape. This is stretchy tape that sticks to itself but not to what it's

wrapped around. Usually it is available in black or white. The black is stronger. We have used self-amalgamating tape to repair a leaking high pressure fuel line, and to repair a broken oven door handle. The stuff is magic. We wouldn't cruise without it.

Carry shore power adapters for every electrical combination. If your boat has 30 amp shore power, you will need adapters for 15 amp, 20 amp and 50 amp outlets.

Carry a second shore power cord. It hasn't happened often, but there have been times when the nearest power receptacle was more than 50 feet away. We carry a second 50-foot shore power cord.

First aid is important. Nobody knows when an accident might occur (that's what makes it an accident). In many areas you will need to be self-reliant. It could be hours or even the next day before medical aid might be available at your location. Carry a comprehensive medical kit and know how to use it. Carry spare medication for many of the common ailments. Call the Coast Guard if you do have a medical emergency. The U.S. Coast Guard has a medical professional on duty somewhere (it might be Kodiak, AK); they can be patched through for medical advice if needed. If you have guests onboard, ask if there are any medical issues or allergies. While your cruising may be recreational boating, the captain has responsibility for crew and guests.

Clothing. Except for some areas of Desolation Sound in the summer, most of the waters of the Northwest are cold. Even during warm weather you may welcome a sweater or jacket. Layering clothing works well. Rain gear is essential on sailboats.

On an enclosed powerboat, rain gear makes exploring shoreside attractions more pleasant when it is raining. Rubber boots are useful. Shoreside attire can be as nice as you want; most people do fine with comfortable sports clothes.

CRUISING TIPS & TECHNIQUES.

Turn off shore power before plugging in or unplugging. Since not all docks have breakers to turn off individual outlets, we turn the boat's 110-volt switch to OFF before we hook up or unplug shore power. If the dock power has its own breaker, we turn it to OFF, too. When everything is hooked up, we turn the dock switch to ON, and then the boat switch.

Update credit cards. Credit and debit cards seem to be the preferred form of payment on both sides of the border. Even the remote areas have some means of accepting credit or debit cards. Some credit card companies have a very favorable exchange rate and withdrawing cash at ATMs may be cheaper than exchanging money beforehand. Before traveling out of the country call your credit card companies to tell them where you will be and the dates of your trip. Otherwise they might (will) refuse a charge, usually at the most awkward moment. Getting it straightened out is exasperating. We speak from experience.

Turn everything off. When you leave the boat or turn in for the night, be sure that appliances, stoves and heaters are turned off.

Take your own paper to public toilets. Especially outhouses at parks and campgrounds. We speak from experience.

Keep pets on leash, and clean up after them. Marina owners would prefer that pets didn't exist, but since so many people do cruise with pets the marinas accommodate them. Use the designated pet-walking areas. Don't let the dog lift his leg against the water faucet or power box. Carry plastic bags and clean up if the pet doesn't make it to the potty area.

HOW TO CRUISE THE PACIFIC NORTHWEST

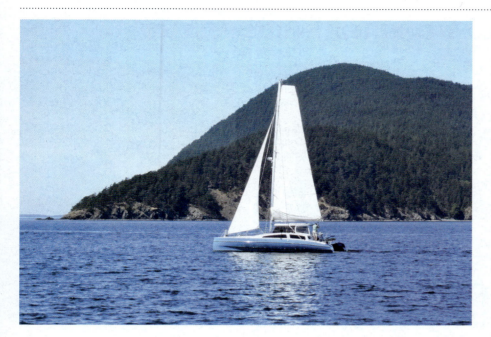

When helping arriving boats, follow the skipper's instructions. When we take a line we hold it loosely, awaiting instructions. Most skippers have a plan that will stop the boat and lay it alongside the dock. A bow line pulled tight at the wrong time can ruin the plan: the bow swings toward the dock and the stern swings away. Obviously, if the landing plan has failed and the boat is being swept off, the dock crew goes into action. Even then it's a good idea to confirm with the skipper rather than acting on one's own.

Pick up mooring buoys from the stern, not the bow. If the bow of the boat is very high off the water it may be impossible to loop a line through a mooring buoy ring. Carry a line aft to a low point of the hull (it may be the swim step), loop it through the ring on the buoy, then carry the line back to the bow. You may want to cleat or tie off one end of the line amidships to keep control of it throughout the process.

De-squeak fenders with dishwashing soap. Joy, Ivory Liquid, whatever is handy seems to work. Slather it on. One application lasts for hours.

Use Scoot-Gard. This is the bumpy, rubbery material carried on big rolls at the marine store. It keeps things from sliding around. We use it for drawer and shelf liners. The microwave oven and the laptop computer with our charting and navigation program sits on it. Whenever we want something to stay where we put it but don't want to bolt or tie it into place, we use Scoot-Gard. It's inexpensive and it works.

Consider making a boat card. One of the joys of cruising is the people you meet along the way. Boat cards are like business cards for your boat, and make it easy to stay in touch with people you meet.

Pack finger food for happy hour gatherings, potlucks, and entertaining on board. Impromptu gatherings are common.

CRUISERS COLLEGE
INCREASE YOUR NAUTICAL KNOWLEDGE AND DIY CLASSES

WATCH FOR OUR SEMINAR COURSES ON:
- Hands-on Diesel Engine Troubleshooting
- Troubleshooting Electrical Problems on Your Boat
- Taking Care of the Fiberglass Boat
- Troubleshooting Outboard Motors
- Troubleshooting Vessel Systems
- Marine Weather
- Cruising Essentials for Women
- Using New Technology for Navigation and Communications

To see a schedule of our up coming classes go to www.WaggonerGuide.com/CruisersCollege Or call the Waggoner Guide office to register at 425.780.5015

Cruisers College is brought to you by

2018 WAGGONER CRUISING GUIDE

FLOATPLANE TRAVEL ALONG THE INSIDE PASSAGE

For cruisers who need to travel home during a cruise, need parts shipped to them, or want to have guests join them in remote areas, floatplane travel can be a good option.

Floatplane flying provides a new perspective for boaters. If you can, sit in a window seat, or even the co-pilot seat up front. Take a small map, or this book, and pick out the islands as you fly by. The view is unforgettable—especially on a sunny day, the islands unfold dramatically. Currents are visible. Sometimes whales are spotted, and the pilot may even spend a few moments circling for a better view. On cloudy days you'll fly low—300 to 500 feet above the water.

Be prepared for a flight to have several stops along the route. If transiting from one country to the other, there will be a stop for customs clearance.

Many marinas offer boat watching service, perfect for when owners fly home. Some can even clean, fuel, and provision boats. For time-strapped cruisers, these services can be useful.

Floatplane operators are accommodating. We've seen floatplanes deliver parts and people to boats in remote anchorages.

The cost to use a floatplane service may

initially appear high, but the time savings and convenience are huge. Consider that it's only a 3-hour flight from Port McNeill, near the north end of Vancouver Island, to Vancouver or Seattle.

THE BEAVER

For airplane buffs, a floatplane ride can be particularly thrilling. The venerable de Havilland DHC-2 Beaver is among the most widely used floatplanes in the northwest. De Havilland began producing the Beaver in 1948, and built nearly 1700 of them during a 19-year production run. Although the last Beaver was produced in 1967, operators and enthusiasts alike still appreciate its unparalleled combination of short field performance, durability, and versatility. Kenmore Air, Pacific Coastal, NW Seaplanes, Seair, Inland Air, and Tofino Air all operate Beavers. Pilots rave about flying them.

Equipped with a powerful engine (450 h.p. for piston Beavers) and a large wing optimized for short takeoff and landing distances, Beavers can reach places other planes can't. They can carry things other planes can't, too. De Havilland engineers designed the Beaver with doors wide enough to accommodate a 45-gallon drum and the ability to carry 2100 pounds of payload. Piston Beavers cruise at about 100 knots burning about 23 gallons of fuel per hour—enviable economy compared to many powerboats. Some operators have upgraded the original piston power plant to

NORTHWEST SEAPLANES

SCHEDULED AND CHARTER FLIGHTS
from Seattle to British Columbia's Inside Passage

Campbell River • April Point • Desolation Sound • Toba Wilderness Marina
Discovery Islands • Blind Channel • Lagoon Cove • Echo Bay Sullivan Bay
Port McNeill • Rivers Inlet • Hakai Pass • Shearwater

FRIDAY HARBOR SEAPLANES

SCHEDULED FLIGHTS FROM SEATTLE TO THE SAN JUAN ISLNANDS

Convenient departures from South Lake Washington, just minutes from Seattle's Sea-Tac Airport and downtown Seattle. Complimentary shuttle service to and from Sea-Tac.

For reservations and information call:
425-277-1590
U.S. and Canada 1-800-690-0086
or online at **www.nwseaplanes.com**
or at **www.fridayharborseaplanes.com**

FLOAT PLANE TRAVEL ALONG THE INSIDE PASSAGE

a newer turbine engine, increasing speed, payload capacity, and range.

The Beaver is so popular that well maintained examples have actually appreciated in value. When new, Beavers sold for about $50,000. Today, they can fetch more than $500,000.

KENMORE AIR
(866) 435-9524
Seattle (Lake Union or Kenmore)
to Sullivan Bay and Port McNeill

NW SEAPLANES
(425) 277-1590
Seattle (Renton) to Hakai Pass and many points in between

FRIDAY HARBOR SEAPLANES
(425) 277-1590
Friday Harbor and San Juan Islands

PACIFIC COASTAL AIRLINES
(800) 663-2872
Victoria, Vancouver, Comox, Campbell River, Powell River, Port Hardy, Bella Bella, Masset

HARBOUR AIR VANCOUVER
(800) 665-0212
Victoria to Gulf Islands and Sunshine Coast

SEAIR SEAPLANES
(800) 447-3247
or
(866) 692-6440
Vancouver to Gulf Islands and Nanaimo

INLAND AIR
(888) 624-2577
Prince Rupert, North B.C., Haida Gwaii

TOFINO AIR
(866) 486-3249

WILDERNESS SEAPLANES
(800) 343-5963
B.C. Central Coast

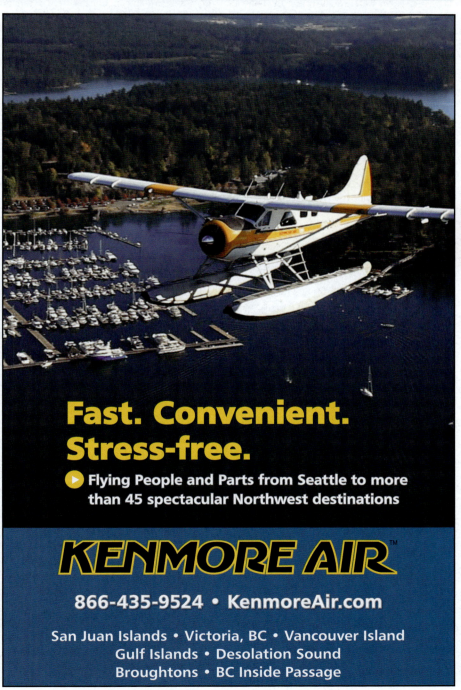

Fast. Convenient. Stress-free.

▶ Flying People and Parts from Seattle to more than 45 spectacular Northwest destinations

KENMORE AIR™

866-435-9524 • KenmoreAir.com

San Juan Islands • Victoria, BC • Vancouver Island
Gulf Islands • Desolation Sound
Broughtons • BC Inside Passage

U.S. AND CANADIAN CUSTOMS INFORMATION

U.S. / CANADA BORDER CROSSING

Customs must be cleared whenever the U.S.-Canada border is crossed, in either direction. Generally the process is quick and straightforward; but if the skipper isn't prepared with the proper information, it can be time consuming. It is extremely important to follow all the rules and be polite. While customs officers are trained in courtesy and usually are cordial, they have at their disposal regulations that can ruin your day.

All vessels are required to clear with Customs when arriving in either the U.S. or Canada from a foreign port. Canadian and U.S. vessels do not need to clear out when leaving Canada. U.S. vessels do not need to clear out when leaving U.S., except if the vessel is being exported. Canadian vessels with a U.S. Cruising License do not need to clear out when leaving U.S. waters. Canadian vessels without a U.S. Cruising License are required to check-out when leaving U.S. waters.

Customs hours, rules, and requirements can and do change with short notice throughout the year. We urge readers to check the U.S. Customs and Border Protection website and Canada Border Services Agency (CBSA) website for the latest. Check the Waggoner Guide website www.WaggonerGuide.com for border crossing updates.

PASSPORTS

If you don't have passports, get them. Lacking a passport, carry proof of citizenship such as an enhanced driver's license, enhanced identification, birth certificate, certificate of citizenship or naturalization, and photo ID. Standard (non-enhanced) drivers licenses are not proof of citizenship and are not accepted for border crossing. Citizens of some countries need visas as well. Carry birth certificates for all minors aboard—you may be asked for them.

CANADA BORDER SERVICES AGENCY

All vessels arriving in Canada from a foreign country must clear Border Services immediately after the vessel comes to rest. The master, or the master's designated representative, must report to Border Services in-person, or by telephone from a Border Services direct land line phone, or by calling (888) 226-7277. No one else may leave the vessel, and no baggage or merchandise may be removed from the vessel.

Proof of citizenship and identification is required of all on board when entering Canada. If you are bringing a child other than your own into Canada, carry a notarized statement authorizing you to take the child into Canada, and proof that the person signing the statement has custody of the child. The letter should include parents' or guardians' addresses and phone numbers. Canada Border Services Agency website has a sample letter.

You must report at a designated port of entry unless you have Canpass or Nexus. At some locations Border Services officers will be present; at others you will report by telephone. Even if you report by telephone, your boat may be subject to inspection.

To avoid delays, have the following ready when you report:

- Vessel name and length

- Names, addresses, citizenship, birth dates and passport numbers of all passengers

- Length of absence from Canada (Canadian boats); Length and purpose of stay in Canada (U.S. boats)

- Declare all goods being imported, including firearms

Once cleared, either by phone or by an officer, you will be given a clearance number. Post your clearance number in both side windows. Log this number with the date, time, and place of clearance. Vessels are subject to re-inspection while in Canadian waters, usually by RCMP officers when their patrol boat reaches a marina.

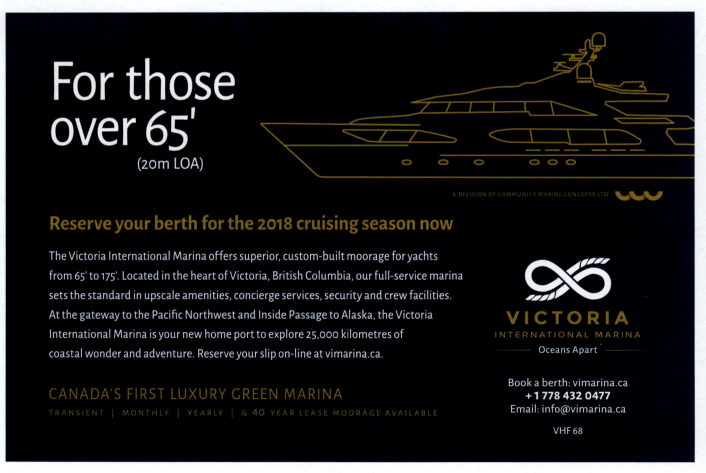

U.S. AND CANADIAN CUSTOMS INFORMATION

The officers are well trained and polite, but be sure you don't have anything on board you shouldn't have.

Nexus. If all passengers aboard a boat have a Nexus permit, a vessel can clear Canada Border Services Agency by calling, toll-free, (866) 996-3987 at least 30 minutes and up to 4 hours before arriving at a designated CBSA or Nexus reporting station. The vessel *must* physically check in at a designated CBSA or Nexus reporting station.

At the time of Nexus call-in, the Border Services officer will ask for the vessel's identification number, vessel's intended reporting station, estimated time of arrival, purpose of the trip, and length of stay. If no officer is present at the reporting station at that time, the vessel may continue on its way without further action. In the accompanying list of designated reporting stations, *note that some are for Nexus/Canpass vessels only* (see below). Non-Nexus/ Canpass vessels may not clear at those stations.

See additional Nexus instructions in the U.S. Customs and Border Protection section.

Canpass-Private Boats. If you have Nexus, you don't need Canpass. Reporting requirements are the same as Nexus, above.

The Canpass application comes with four pages of instructions. Briefly, the program is limited to citizens or permanent residents of Canada or the U.S. with no criminal records and no customs or immigration violations. The approval process takes several weeks. Each person must complete and sign an application. The cost for Canpass is $40 (Cdn.) and is good for five years (no charge for dependents under 18). Visa and Mastercard accepted.

For more information and an application call 604-538- 3689 or 1-866-496-3987. Applications can be downloaded from their website at www.cbsa-asfc.gc.ca/prog/canpass/canpassprivateboat-eng.html

Firearms restrictions. You may not bring switchblades, most handguns, automatic weapons, anti-personnel pepper spray or mace into Canada. Under certain circumstances some long guns are allowed. Bear spray, if labeled as such, is permitted if declared. A Non-Resident Firearm Declaration Form is needed to bring firearms into Canada. Call the Canadian Firearms Centre at (800) 731-4000 for a copy of the form, or download one from www.cfc-cafc.gc.ca. The cost is $25 (Cdn.) and it is good for 60 days. All weapons and firearms must be declared to CBSA. See www.WaggonerGuide.com for links for more information and the application form.

Liquor & tobacco restrictions. Not more than 1.14 liters (38.5 oz.) of hard liquor, or 1.5 liters of wine, or a total of 1.14 liters of wine and liquor, or 24 12-ounce bottles of beer or ale per person of legal drinking age (19 years old in B.C.). Not more than 1 carton of cigarettes and 2 cans (200 grams) of tobacco and 50 cigars or cigarillos, and 200 tobacco sticks per person 19 or older without paying duty and taxes on the excess amount.

Food restrictions. Other than restricted foods, you can carry quantities of food appropriate for your stay. Because of possible restrictions, don't bring houseplants (including potted herbs).

CBSA customs dock at Port Sidney

- No apples
- No pitted fruit (apricots, plums, peaches, nectarines)
- Cherries are sometimes okay
- No potatoes
- No fresh corn

If in doubt, call (204) 983-3500 for inspection.

Pets. Owners of dogs and cats must bring a certificate issued by a licensed U.S. or Canadian veterinarian clearly identifying the pet and certifying that it has been vaccinated against rabies during the previous 36 months.

Currency. Cash or other monetary instruments in excess of $10,000 Cdn. per boat must be reported. For current rules and regulations check out the Canada Border Services Agency website www.cbsa-asfc.gc.ca.

Boat Stay Limits. The maximum stay for a recreational vessel in Canada without importing the vessel and paying taxes is 12 months.

B.C. POINTS OF ENTRY

Designated B.C. Points of Entry for Pleasure Craft Reporting
All locations contact Canada Border Services Agency
Toll-free (888) 226-7277 (7 days a week, 24 hours a day)

Bedwell Harbour:	May 1–Friday before Victoria Day 9:00 a.m. to 5:00 p.m. Friday before Victoria Day–Labour Day 8:00 a.m. to 8:00 p.m. Labour Day–Sept. 30 9:00 a.m. to 5:00 p.m. Oct. 1–Apr. 30 (Canpass/Nexus only)
Cabbage Island:	(Canpass/Nexus only)
Campbell River:	Coast Marina; Discovery Harbour Marina
Galiano Island:	Montague Harbour Marina (Canpass/Nexus only)
Mayne Island:	Horton Bay (Canpass/Nexus only) Miners Bay (Canpass/Nexus only)
Nanaimo:	Nanaimo Port Authority Basin–E Dock Summer 8:00 a.m. to 5:00 p.m. Winter 8:00 a.m. to 4:30 p.m. Townsite Marina (Canpass/Nexus only)
North Pender Is.:	Port Browning Marina (Canpass/Nexus only)
Prince Rupert:	Lightering Dock Prince Rupert–Cow Bay Marina Prince Rupert–Fairview Govt. Dock Prince Rupert Rowing and Yacht Club Rushbrooke Government Dock
Saltspring Is.:	Ganges Harbour Seaplane Dock– First floating breakwater (Canpass/Nexus only)
Sidney:	Canoe Cove Marina Port Sidney Marina Royal Victoria YC Outstation Tsehum Marina Van Isle Marina
Ucluelet:	52 Steps Dock June 1–Sept 30 only 8:00 a.m. to 10:00 p.m. Oct. 1–May 31 (Canpass/Nexus only)
Vancouver:	False Creek Public Dock Delta Marina Steveston Harbour Authority Dock Burrard Inlet/Coal Harbour All marinas until further notice
Victoria:	Oak Bay Marina Royal Victoria YC (Cadboro Bay) Inner Harbour Border Services Dock
White Rock:	White Rock Public Dock Crescent Beach Marina

2018 WAGGONER CRUISING GUIDE

U.S. AND CANADIAN CUSTOMS INFORMATION

U.S. CUSTOMS AND BORDER PROTECTION (CBP)

Effective June 1, 2009 the Western Hemisphere Travel Initiative (WHTI) requires approved identification, such as U.S. or Canadian passport, U.S. Passport card, Trusted Traveler Program cards (Nexus, FAST and Sentri), I-68, State or Provincial issued enhanced driver's license, and others, for entry to the U.S. We recommend that everyone aboard have a passport.

Reporting to U.S. Customs. You must clear U.S. CBP at a designated point of entry; or if you are a participant in the I-68 or Nexus program, clearance may be conducted by calling (800) 562-5943. Whether in person or by phone, to avoid delays have the following information available when you report your arrival:

- Name, date of birth and citizenship of all persons on board (including passport number or WHTI identification)
- Name of the boat and/or BR number, vessel registration or documentation number
- Vessel name, builder and length
- CBP user fee decal number (if over 30 feet in length)
- Canadian clearance number. Required for U.S. moored boats.
- Estimated length of stay in U.S. (Canadian vessels); date you departed U.S./ length of stay in Canada (U.S. vessels).

Designated U.S. Ports of Entry. Arrivals requiring an in-person report may be made at any of the following Ports of Entry: Friday Harbor, Roche Harbor, Port Angeles, Point Roberts, and Anacortes. *All other ports require appointments to be made in advance for face-to-face inspections* (during regular business hours only). Don't assume that if you call for an appointment you will get one. To save time and avoid problems, clear U.S. Customs at one of the five designated Ports of Entry. If you arrive after normal business hours, call (800) 562-5943 for further instructions. Local customs office numbers are listed on page 24. I-68s are available at all locations listed.

Clearing by telephone. Boaters with nothing to declare normally can clear U.S. Customs by telephone *if all on board have I-68s or Nexus*. Otherwise, the vessel must report at a designated port of entry for physical inspection.

With I-68 or Nexus, after entering U.S. waters you can call the Small Boat Reporting Office at (800) 562-5943 and be cleared. If you call by cell phone while underway, call from an area with good reception. While you report, slow to idle speed to reduce background noise and remain in the good reception area. The Small Boat Reporting Office operates from 8:00 a.m. to 10:00 p.m. from the second week in May through September, and from 8:00 a.m. to 5:00 p.m. the balance of the year. If you enter the U.S. outside these hours, you must remain aboard your boat until you can clear.

Direct connect CBSA Customs telephone at Port Sidney

I-68. The I-68 Permit is valid for 1 year from the date of issue. U.S. citizens, Lawful Permanent Residents, Canadian citizens and Landed Immigrants of Canada who are nationals of Visa Waiver Program countries are eligible to apply. The cost is $16 per person, $32 for families. Apply at CBP offices within the Puget Sound area. Bring proof of citizenship, such as a passport, certified copy of your birth certificate, and photo ID. Vessel information also helps. Each person applying must appear. Children under 14 can be listed on parents' I-68.

Nexus. With Nexus, each person applies online and then contacted to set an appointment for an interview by both Canadian and U.S. customs agents at the Vancouver, B.C., Blaine, or Seattle CBP offices. The card is good for 5 years, and

PLAN YOUR NEXT TRIP

The Inside Passage Planning maps, North and South, present a birds-eye view of the entire Inside Passage. Trip planning is easier than trying to review 60 or more nautical charts of different scales or a computer screen. All significant destinations are called out on the map with a Lat/Long listing on the back of the map for easy reference. The folded map works well on the boat. The laminated and rolled map works best for hanging on the wall or marking with an erasable marker. Both maps are 24" wide and 60" long. See our website for sample views of these interesting and colorful planning maps.

FINE EDGE
Nautical & Recreational Publishing

Planning Maps
Inside Passage - South
Inside Passage - North
Folded - $19.95 each
Laminated & rolled - $29.95 each

Start planning your next cruise today! • www.FineEdge.com • 360-299-8500

U.S. AND CANADIAN CUSTOMS INFORMATION

the cost is $50 U.S. or Cdn. per person. From start to finish, the entire process takes several months. If you cross the border by car once you have your card, you'll have the additional benefit of using the Nexus lanes at the border. For general information or to begin the application process, U.S. citizens go to www.cbp.gov/travel/trusted-traveler-programs/nexus and Canadians, go to http://www.cbsa-asfc.gc.ca/prog/nexus/application-demande-eng.html.

Local Boater Option (LBO)/Small Vessel Reporting System (SVRS). The Small Vessel Reporting System is a web-based, automated, online reporting program. Once enrolled in the system, an SVRS float plan can be filed online well in advance of a scheduled trip. It is then activated within no more than 24 hours of departure from the U.S. or from Canada. Activation is online only. The program allows for expedited arrival back in the U.S. Upon phoning U.S. Customs, you will be asked a series of questions. Based on your responses, you may be given a clearance number or asked to present your vessel to an agent at a port of entry. You can learn more at svrs.cbp.dhs.gov/Default.aspx.

Entering Alaska. All vessels entering Southeast Alaska from a foreign country must clear U.S. Customs. U.S. Customs in Alaska officially has a 100 percent boarding policy. However, based on workload, CBP may allow boaters with I-68 or Nexus to clear by telephone. For detailed instructions on clearing U.S. Customs in Alaska, see *Chapter 19 – Arriving in Ketchikan*.

Processing fee. Pleasure vessels 30 feet in length or more must pay an annual processing (user) fee of $27.50 (slated to increase January 1, 2018) to enter or re-enter the United States. U.S. vessels less than 30 feet are not subject to the fee, provided they have nothing to declare. Payment is required at or before the vessel's first arrival each calendar year. If you report by telephone, they charge your credit card. A non-transferable decal will be issued upon payment. Renewal notices for the next year's decal are mailed or emailed in the autumn. Vessels with a valid Cruising License do not have to pay this fee and do not require a decal.

Order your sticker before you need to enter the U.S. Even if you have Nexus or I-68 preclearance, lack of a current-year sticker may direct you to a designated port of entry for inspection.

User Fee stickers are not sold at CBP offices, but can be ordered online at https://dtops.cbp.dhs.gov or by phone (317) 298-1245, or email decals@cbp.dhs.gov.

Cruising License. A Cruising License is available to Canadian and most, but not all, foreign flagged vessels. A Cruising License saves time and money for boaters frequenting U.S. waters. Foreign vessels without a Cruising License must complete form CBP-1300 and pay a $19.00 Navigation fee upon entering U.S. waters, with each movement within U.S. waters, and upon exiting U.S. waters. With a Cruising License, form CBP-1300 and the Navigation fee are only required at the vessel's initial reporting and clearance with CBP.

To get a Cruising License, foreign vessels from certain countries (Canada is included) upon entering U.S. waters, must report to one of the designated CBP Ports of Entry where they submit form CBP-1300 and pay the $19.00 fee. CBP will inspect the vessel and process CBP-1300. A Cruising License can then be requested. There is no charge for the Cruising License. Cruising Licenses are good for one calendar year. Vessels with a Cruising License do not need the $27.50 decal. Cruising Licenses cannot be extended. Cruising Licenses are available only when the vessel reports in and clears at one of the CBP Ports of Entry. Foreign flagged vessels made outside of the U.S. must wait 15 days after expiration of their Cruising License before requesting a new Cruising License. During this 15-day period, the vessel may enter and depart U.S. waters by submitting a CBP-1300 and paying $19.00 upon entry, exit and movement. Vessels made in U.S. are exempt from this 15-day waiting period.

Cruising Licenses do not affect customs reporting requirements. Vessels must report and clear in with CBP upon entry to U.S. waters by reporting to a Port of Entry or by one of the trusted traveler programs like Nexus. You will need your Cruising License number when reporting in with CBP.

Food restrictions. Food restrictions are subject to change without notice. See www.WaggonerGuide.com for updates and for a downloadable copy of CBP information regarding food products that may not be

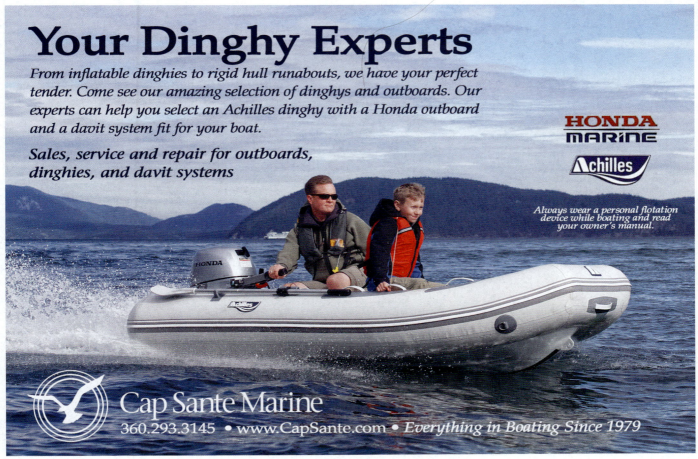

U.S. AND CANADIAN CUSTOMS INFORMATION

brought in to the U.S. For specific food related questions, contact an Agricultural Specialist at (360) 332-8661 or (360) 988-2971.

As a general guideline, any food you bring into the U.S. must be made or grown in Canada or the U.S., and labeled as such. Don't bring fresh tropical fruits or vegetables in, even if you bought them in the U.S. CBP recommends declaring all meat and produce when entering the U.S. If declared, prohibited goods will be seized but no fine will be levied. Subject to change without notice, use the following list to minimize problems:

- No sheep lamb or goat in any form. This includes pet food.

- Meat (beef, pork, chicken, turkey) and meat products from Canada are allowed.

- Keep pet food in original packaging.

- No fresh citrus, regardless of where you bought it.

- No fresh produce (vegetables or fruit) grown outside the U.S. and Canada. Canned fruits and vegetables, however, are unrestricted regardless of origin. Leave labels/stickers on produce.

- No tomatoes

- No garlic, chives, green onions, leeks, and other green Allium vegetables from Canada

- No potatoes

- No cut flowers or potted plants (they are subject to so many restrictions that it's better to leave them in Canada and avoid the hassle).

- Seafood is okay.

- Dairy products are okay.

- Eggs are usually okay.

- All firewood is prohibited; boaters with firewood may be required to return to Canada to dispose of it.

Pets. Dogs and cats must be healthy, and dogs require current rabies certificates. Birds are subject to USDA Veterinarian inspection to enter or re-enter. Usually not advisable to bring birds across the border.

Currency. Cash or other monetary instruments in excess of $10,000 U.S. per boat must be reported.

Duty-free limits. U.S. residents outside of the U.S. less than 48 hours can import merchandise up to $200 in value per person without duty. If the stay is more than 48 hours, the limit is $800 per person. For ease and simplicity, try to restrict what you bring back home to products made or grown in Canada (see below: sometimes even that isn't sufficient). For the latest customs information, go to the U.S. Customs and Border Protection website pages for pleasure boats at www.cbp.gov/travel/pleasure-boats-private-flyers/pleasure-boat-overview.

Declare All Items. If in doubt, declare it to CBP. This is especially true for food items. If you are not sure, simply declare it and let the CBP officer make the decision. It is always best to inform CBP agents of items that you have on board. Failure to declare items can result in fines and penalties.

Pilotage Exemption for Foreign Flagged (other than U.S. or Canadian) Vessels. Foreign flagged vessels (other than Canadian) in Washington waters are required by Washington State law to have an exemption in order to operate without a professional Pilot. To request an exemption, download and submit an application from the www.pilotagewa.gov website or call the Washington Board of Pilotage Commissioners at (206) 215-3904.

U.S. POINTS OF ENTRY

Anacortes (360) 293-2331
Office at Cap Sante Marina
8:00 a.m. to 8:00 p.m. Summer
8:00 a.m. to 5:00 p.m. Off-season
(closed 1 ½ hours mid-afternoon)

Friday Harbor (360) 378-2080
Customs booth at the dock with phone
Office at Spring & First Streets
8:00 a.m. to 8:00 p.m. Summer
8:00 a.m. to 5:00 p.m. Off-season

Point Roberts (360) 945-5211
or (360) 945-2314
Customs Dock near Fuel Dock
8:00 a.m. to 8:00 p.m. Summer
8:00 a.m. to 5:00 p.m. Off-season

Port Angeles (360) 457-4311
Office Boat Haven
8:00 a.m. to 9:00 p.m. Summer
8:00 a.m. to 5:30 p.m. Off-season

Roche Harbor (360) 378-2080
Customs dock at Roche Harbor Marina
8:00 a.m. to 8:00 p.m. Summer
8:00 a.m. to 5:00 p.m. Off-season

Ketchikan (907) 225-2254
Call and wait for agent at assigned slip
6:00 a.m. to 6:00 p.m. Summer

Other Customs Offices
(by appointment only, call 24 hours ahead for availability and instructions):

Aberdeen (360) 532-2030
or (360) 310-0109

Bellingham (360) 734-5463

Blaine (360) 332-6318

Everett (425) 259-0246

Port Townsend (360) 385-3777

Seattle (Boeing Field) (206) 553-0667

Tacoma/Olympia (253) 593-6338

OUTER REEF YACHT ARGO ROUNDS CAPE HORN

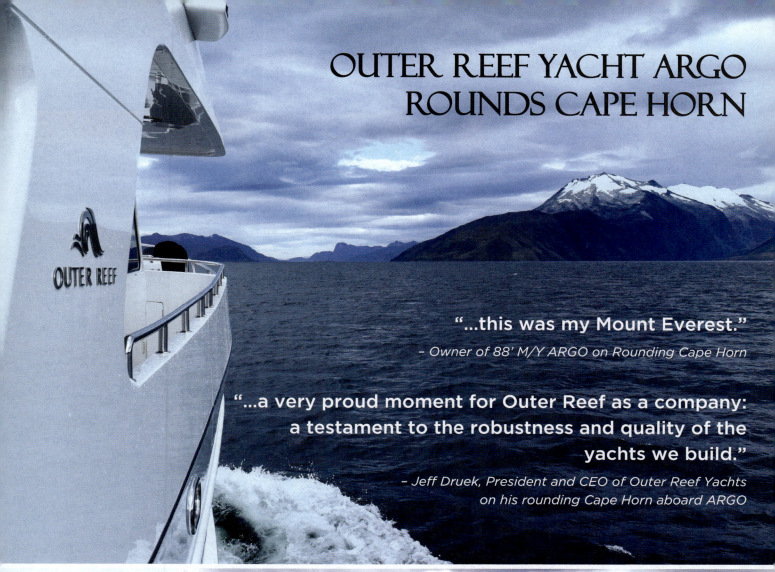

"...this was my Mount Everest."
— *Owner of 88' M/Y ARGO on Rounding Cape Horn*

"...a very proud moment for Outer Reef as a company: a testament to the robustness and quality of the yachts we build."
— *Jeff Druek, President and CEO of Outer Reef Yachts on his rounding Cape Horn aboard ARGO*

Photo by Andrew Ulitsky

After extensive research, Bainbridge Island resident Paul Hawran chose Outer Reef Yachts to build his yacht ARGO for his life-changing journey. Starting with a shakedown cruise to Alaska, Paul proceeded south to round Cape Horn. Learn more about this bucket-list cruising expedition, and why the yacht chosen for this unforgettable journey was an Outer Reef.

580   610   630   650   700   720   730   800   820   860   880

OuterReefYachts.com ▪ info@outerreefyachts.com

DIFFERENCES BETWEEN U.S. & CANADIAN CHARTS

Canada and the United States are two separate nations, and their charts, while similar in many ways, have important differences.

U.S. charts are in fathoms and feet; most Canadian charts are metric. *With all charts, read the chart title and margin information to see if the chart is metric, fathoms and feet, or feet.* Metric charts show soundings and heights in meters. A meter (spelled metre in Canada) equals 39.37 inches, or 3.28 feet. Two meters equals 6 feet 7 inches, or just over one fathom. The difference is significant. Don't confuse fathoms with meters.

Waters appear to be deeper on U.S. charts of Pacific Northwest waters. This difference is important wherever the water is shallow, and is the result of the two countries using different *chart datums.*

Depths on a chart are measured from the chart datum, also called the reference plane or **tidal datum.** On Canadian charts, the chart datum is either Lowest Normal Tides, or Lower Low Water, Large Tide. For that reason, you don't find many "minus tides" in Canadian tide tables.

On U.S. charts of Pacific Northwest waters, however, the chart datum is Mean Lower Low Water. Mean Lower Low Water is the mean, or average, level of the lower of the two low tides each day. Since the U.S. chart datum has half the lower waters above it and half below it, U.S. tide books show minus tides.

It's not a question of whether the tide drops lower in Canada or the U.S. It's a question of where the depth is measured from. U.S. charts start their measurements from a point higher than Canadian charts. The difference can be as much as 1.5 meters, or almost 5 feet.

Example: Assume that you are in the U.S., skippering a sailboat. The sailboat's keel draws 5 feet, and you want to anchor overnight in a bay with a charted depth of one fathom (6 feet). According to the tide table, low tide will be minus 1.5 feet at 0700. Knowing that your boat, with its 5 feet of draft, would be aground in 4.5 feet of water, you would look for a more suitable anchorage.

If this bay were in Canada, the chart would show a depth of perhaps just 1 meter (assuming a Lowest Normal Tide lower than the tide at 0700). The tide table would show a low tide at 0700 of perhaps .4 meters. You would add the 1 meter depth from the chart to the .4 meter low tide from the tide table, and get 1.4 meters of water at 0700. Since you draw more than 1.4 meters (55 inches), you would not anchor in the bay that night.

Important exception: Both Canadian and U.S. charts show soundings in the other country's system when the charts cover both sides of the border. The U.S. chart would convert Canadian meters to U.S. fathoms, but would adopt the Canadian chart datum in Canadian waters. The Canadian metric chart would convert U.S. fathoms to meters, but would adopt the U.S. chart datum in U.S. waters. This is explained in the chart legends.

Clearances appear to be greater on U.S. charts. U.S. charts for Northwest waters measure clearances from Mean High Water. One-half the high waters are above the mean. Canadian charts measure clearances from Higher High Water, Large Tides. The same bridge, over the same waterway, would show less vertical clearance on a Canadian chart than on a U.S. chart. Metric Canadian charts show heights and depths in meters; Canadian charts in fathoms and feet show heights in feet and depths in fathoms. A Canadian metric chart might show a bridge clearance as "3," meaning 3 meters above Higher High

---

THE END OF PAPER CHARTS?

April 13, 2014 was the last day NOAA printed paper charts. Charts are still updated, though. Now they are released on a daily basis for download and for Print on Demand services. Printed charts can now be purchased through Print on Demand (POD) map vendors. Print on Demand charts have the additional advantage that they always have the most up-to-date information.

CANADA – U.S. BORDER DISPUTE AT DIXON ENTRANCE

When crossing Dixon Entrance from Canada into Alaska, exactly where you enter the U.S. is not clear. Canadian Hydrographic Services (CHS) chart 3002 clearly shows an international boundary line near 54° 40' latitude extending from Cape Muzon, on the west, to a point immediately south of Haystack Island off Tongass Passage on the east. However, NOAA chart 16016 shows no international boundary line in Dixon Entrance west of Haystack Island. Chart 16016 shows an international boundary in Tongass Passage that ends just north of Haystack Island.

To this day, the exact boundary between Canada and U.S. in Dixon Entrance is disputed. A court of arbitration in 1903 attempted to resolve the disputed boundary with their determination, which is approximately the line depicted on CHS chart 3002. However, the U.S. does not agree with Canada's interpretation of the 1903 determination and claims a boundary line that is south of the line claimed by Canada. The only land mass in the disputed area is Nunez Rocks, off of Nunez Point on Prince of Wales Island. Nunez Rocks is dry half the time and submerged the other half. By virtue of another maritime law, and the ongoing border dispute, Nunez Island is U.S. for half the time and Canadian the other half.

Canada Chart 3002 shows international border, but U.S. chart 16016 shows none.

DIFFERENCES BETWEEN U.S. & CANADIAN CHARTS

Water, Large Tides. A U.S. chart would show a bridge clearance as "12" or more, meaning 12 feet or more above Mean High Water.

Canadian charts use more symbols to show buoys and tide rips. Canadian charts use symbols that approximate the shapes of buoys, with letters to indicate the buoy's characteristics. U.S. charts use a single diamond-shaped symbol for nearly all navigation buoys, with descriptive letters to indicate the buoy's characteristics.

For example, U.S. Chart 18421, Strait of Juan de Fuca to Strait of Georgia (1:80,000), shows the bell buoy marking Buckeye Shoal, north of Cypress Island, as:

But on Canadian Chart 3462, Juan de Fuca Strait to Strait of Georgia (1:80,000), the buoy is shown as:

Canadian charts may use arrows to show the location of the buoy or beacon. If other detail on the chart makes precise location difficult, the Canadian chart will offset the symbol slightly, in the direction of the preferred navigable water. The offset is indicated by an arrow pointing to the actual location of the buoy or beacon. Sometimes the arrow is easy to overlook.

U.S. Chart 18421

Canadian Chart 3462

Chart No. 1 cracks the code. Nautical charts are filled with important navigation information. Unfortunately, so much of the information is in the form of symbols, abbreviations and undefined terms that it can be confusing. Each country has published a book that shows each symbol and defines each term used on its charts. The U.S. book is titled *Chart No. 1*; and the Canadian book is titled *Chart 1*. The Canadian book is available from Canadian Hydrographic chart agencies. The U.S. book is produced by several private publishers. Copies are available at marine supply outlets.

The Canadian Coast Guard publication *The Canadian Aids to Navigation System* explains the Canadian buoyage and light system, and is highly recommended. A PDF version is available on the Canadian Coast Guard website. The cost for the print version is $7.50 (Cdn) from Canadian Hydrographic chart agents, nautical bookstores and chandleries.

The introduction pages of both these books are filled with essential information. Don't overlook them.

LARGE SCALE, LARGE DETAIL

Large scale, large detail, that's the easy way to remember the difference between small scale and large scale charts. A small scale chart shows a large part of the earth's surface, but in small detail. Conversely, a large scale chart shows a small part of the earth's surface, but of course in great detail. Yes, it's counter-intuitive and confusing, but that's how it is. In the Northwest, large scale harbor charts typically have scales of 1:6,000, 1:12,000, 1:24,000. Medium scale charts have a scale of 1:40,000. Small scale charts have scales of 1:73,000 or 1:80,000.

At a scale of 1:12,000, 1 inch on the chart equals 12,000 inches (1,000 feet) on the earth. At a scale of 1:80,000, 1 inch on the chart equals 80,000 inches (6,667 feet) on the earth. When you are looking for the rock or picking your way through a narrow channel, the larger the scale of your chart, the easier your task will be.

If the Waggoner Cruising Guide is obsessed with anything, it is with safe navigation and the tools needed to accomplish safe navigation. *Large scale, large detail.* It works.

About Anchoring

Learning to stern-tie can provide additional mooring options.

One of the unique features of boating is the freedom of movement and independence to make any protected body of water home for a quick lunch stop or for an overnight. Some people look forward to dropping anchor in an unfamiliar cove or bay. Many people do not share this enthusiasm. There are a few general principles that will help everyone anchor successfully. Cruising from dock to dock is fun, and no one can fault the conveniences. But a world of possibilities opens to those who have good anchoring gear and know how to use it.

Use good gear. Big, strong anchors work; small, cheap anchors don't. The most experienced cruisers seem to carry the biggest anchors. Well-equipped, wide-ranging boats carry all of the common designs: Bruce, CQR (plow), Danforth, Delta, Northhill, Rocna, Manson Supreme, and Ultra. Make sure your anchor is made of high quality steel. If it's wedged in a rock, you don't want it to bend. While Danforth style anchors are easiest to bend, within the limits of their design they can be made strong and expensive or weak and cheap. There are no strong, cheap Danforth style anchors. Read the sizing charts carefully, and size your anchor for storm conditions. Some sizing charts are written for 20-knot winds. Others are written for 30 knots. The Bruce chart is written for 42 knots and Rocna sizing is based upon 50 knots. When the wind comes on to blow hard at 3:00 a.m., you don't want a 20-knot anchor out there.

Pick your spot. Unless you're setting out a stern anchor or running a stern-tie ashore, plan on your boat swinging through an entire 360-degree circle. You don't want to bump up against a rock, a dock or another boat. Be sure to account for tidal changes. We've seen anchored boats aground at low tide because they didn't allow for drying flats or a sand bar in their swing circle. Other anchored boats will tend to swing as your boat swings, but not always. One night at Jones Island in the San Juans, swirling tidal currents had anchored boats swooping toward one another in a "dance of death."

Carry ample rode. For an anchor to bury and hold properly, you should pay out anchor rode at least five times the water depth. In 20 feet of water you would want 100 feet of rode out. In 60 feet of water you would want 300 feet out. Often, especially in crowded anchorages during high summer season, it will not be possible to anchor on 5:1 scope (five times the depth of the water). That is understood. In fact, the norm for most Northwest anchorages seems to be 3:1. But I've watched people put out 30 feet of rode in 20 feet of water, and wonder why the anchor wouldn't bite. For the deep waters of the Pacific Northwest, carry at least 300 feet of anchor rode, whether all-chain or combination chain and rope. Opinions vary about how much chain a combination rode should include, but no one would criticize you for having at least a foot of chain for every foot of boat length. Mark your rode well with something that is easily seen and clearly indicates the length. We have seen people with all chain that have no markers and therefore no way to know how much rode is out.

Rope or chain? For years we used a combination anchor rode—a length of chain backed up with 300 feet of top-quality nylon rope—and we anchored successfully. On a smaller boat with no anchor windlass, a combination rode is the way to go. When we moved to the 37-footer we found a new religion: *all-chain*. With all-chain, if we let out 100 feet of chain in 30 feet of water, 70 feet of chain will be lying on the bottom after the anchor is set. At a pound a foot, that's 70 pounds of chain that must be lifted off the bottom before we get to the anchor. During settled conditions we now get by with less scope, and our swinging circle is smaller. In storm conditions, of course, we're back to 5:1, or as close to 5:1 as we can manage.

Read the tide tables. If the overnight low tide isn't very low, a shallow anchorage can be just right. On the other hand, if the moon is either new or full (the two times during the month when the tidal range is the greatest) the shallow anchorage might go dry at low tide. You also want to know the maximum height of the tide during your stay. Set your scope for five times the water depth at high tide, or if you can't get five times, as much as you can get away with.

Set the anchor well. To get the best bury in the bottom, you want the angle between the anchor and the boat to be as flat as possible. After lowering the anchor, back well down before you

Stern Ties

Stern-ties are desirable and often necessary when a boat anchors in the Northwest. In crowded anchorages, stern-ties keep boats from swinging into one another. Often they are essential if a boat is to remain safely at anchor between two rocks, rather than swing onto them. We have seen stern-tie tackle of varying lengths and appropriateness, from sailboat spinnaker sheets tied together, to reels of rope cleverly mounted, ready for use. While rope of any kind will serve in a pinch, we think the best choice is polypropylene. It's strong, it floats, and it's cheap. We also think it's better to have too much line, not too little. A 600-foot reel of ½-inch polypropylene rope will meet almost any need, yet stow nicely on nearly any size boat. With 600 feet available, a stern-tie can be run around a tree and back to the boat. A dead tree is best, to prevent damage to the bark. When it's time to depart the tie can be recovered without rowing ashore. The trick is to mount the reel of rope so it can pay out and be recovered quickly, easily, and without tangling. The pictures here show some alternatives.

A beautiful Pro-Tech Yacht Services reel mounted on rails.

This custom-built stainless steel reel probably cost a fortune, but it fits perfectly and holds a lot of line.

Rough and ready, but this reel on the back of a converted fishing boat is just right.

An elegant semi-custom assembly by Clear Marine sends a messenger line with the stern-tie line. Photo courtesy of Clear Marine.

An off-the-shelf plastic hose reel serves well on the back of a powerboat.

ABOUT ANCHORING

set the hook. As you set, the rode should seem to stretch almost straight out from the bow. If the rode angles downward very much, you don't have enough scope out. When the anchor is set, you can shorten up to avoid swinging into other boats or onto a sandbar. You'll know, by the way, when the anchor is set. The anchor rode pulls straight and the boat *stops*. If you have any doubt as to whether the anchor is set, then it probably isn't. Weeds can foul an anchor, especially a Danforth style anchor, and many bottoms have weeds. I've heard of anchors grabbing a sunken tire and dragging it across the bottom. Once the anchor is set, you don't have to pour on all 600 horsepower to prove your point. Anchors gain holding power through pulling and relaxing over time, a process called *soaking*. An anchor put down for lunch might be recovered with little effort. Left overnight it might feel as if it had headed for China.

Look at your chart. For happy anchoring you want a good holding bottom, appropriate depths, and protection. The nautical chart can help with all these needs. If the chart says *Foul*, don't anchor there. If the chart shows submerged pilings at the head of the bay, avoid the head of the bay. If the chart shows 200-foot depths right up to the shoreline, that's a bad spot. If it shows the bay open to the full sweep of the prevailing wind and seas, find another bay or you could be in for a rough night. I find the easiest anchorages to be in 20 to 50 feet of water, with a decided preference for the 20- to 30-foot depths. Approach slowly, take a turn around the entire area to check the depths, and decide where you want the boat to lie after the anchor is set. Then go out to a spot that will give you sufficient scope and lower the anchor. Back way down, set the hook, and shorten up to the desired location.

Anchor in the right places. Don't anchor in cable crossing areas or near charted underwater pipeline areas. Increasingly, some communities and locales are discouraging anchoring in or near eelgrass. Anchoring gear, especially anchor chain, can be harmful to eelgrass. Eelgrass areas are not generally charted so check the Waggoner Cruising Guide or check for signage on spar buoys in the area marked, "no anchoring."

Use an anchor watch. There are a number of GPS based anchor watch systems that monitor your boats position and signal an alarm if the boat moves outside of a predetermined boundary circle. There are a number of Android and IOS smartphone Apps available with anchor watch features. Some chartplotters and chartplotter PC software have boundary circle features. For these anchor watch systems to work well, place the center of the boundary circle at the spot where you drop the anchor. This may mean taking the anchor watch system to the bow when you center the circle. After centering the boundary circle, set the radius of the circle equal to the scope, plus the distance from the bow roller to the place on the boat where the anchor watch will rest while anchored, plus an appropriate GPS error factor, plus any significant tidal exchange that increases your swing. Anchor watch systems monitor the boats current location and sound an alarm if outside of the boundary circle. Some smartphone apps can also SMS text or email an alarm to another phone that goes ashore with you.

Carry a stern-tie. In some locations you will set the anchor offshore, back toward shore to set, and take the dinghy in with a line from a stern cleat to tie around a rock or tree. Boats line Tod Inlet, near Butchart Gardens, tied this way. In many small bays it's the only way you can anchor. Sometimes you'll find a little niche that will hold just your boat—if the stern is tied to shore. We carry 600 feet of inexpensive polypropylene rope for stern ties. Some popular anchorages necessitating stern-tie have metal rings secured to shore through which you can pass your stern-tie line. After passing the end through the ring, bring the end back to the boat. That way, when you are ready to depart, you can release and recover the stern-tie line without leaving the boat. When there are no steel ring anchor points, find something secure on shore to anchor your stern-tie line. Carry a disposable short length of rope, about 5 feet long, that can be looped around something solid on shore like a rock outcropping. As a last resort loop your stern-tie around a dead tree. Many parks in BC and Washington not only frown on using live trees, but some have made it illegal.

How to use a trip line. If you have any indication that the area you will be anchoring in is prone to fouling or snagging your anchor, use a trip line to help you recover the anchor. Anchors prepared for trip lines will have a small hole on the nose of the anchor (somewhere near the top and far forward. Before deploying the anchor, attach a length of line that is slightly longer than the maximum tidal water depth at your intended anchoring location. To the other end of the line attach a small float or buoy. Later when you go to weigh anchor and it is caught, you can use the trip line to help free it. The float or buoy also alerts other boaters of your anchor location.

Up-slope anchoring. Up-slope anchoring is used when the only convenient anchoring depths are near to shore. Up-slope anchoring involves dropping the anchor on the up-sloping sea bottom as it shallows. Once the anchor is set, back-down toward the nearby shore and stern-tie to shore. The stern-tie holds the boat in a position where it is always pulling the main anchor up the slope and keeps the anchor set.

Secure the anchor rode to the boat. We have all heard stories about boaters losing their all chain anchor, when they discover that the end, buried under hundreds of pounds of rode in the anchor locker, was not attached to the boat. Be sure the end of your anchor chain is attached to the boat – but not hard attached. The anchor should be attached to a length of nylon rope that is secured to the boat. In the event the anchor is stuck or if you need to get away from the anchor quickly, the rope can be cut. Secure a floating buoy to the end of the nylon rope so that you can retrieve the anchor and chain later.

2018 WAGGONER CRUISING GUIDE

ELCI Protected Shore Power

ELCI Breaker with Test/Reset on Eaton Pedestal

Shore Power Changes Are Coming
Since 2011, efforts have been underway from both the building code side and from the boat building side to address safety issues due to stray electrical current in and around docks and marinas. The National Electrical Code Article 555 addresses electrical shock drownings caused by leakage of electrical current from A/C shore power facilities on docks and marinas. Concurrently, the American Boat & Yacht Council (ABYC) section E-11.11 has made changes to address A/C power leakage from boats into surrounding waters that endanger people.

As marinas upgrade their facilities, they will be required by building code to add Equipment Leakage Circuit Interrupter (ELCI) ground fault protection breakers to shore power receptacles. ELCI-protected breakers are designed to 'trip' and turn-off power if an imbalance is detected between the power (amperage) going to the boat and returning back to the shore power receptacle. In the past, marina shore power receptacle breakers only protected wiring and cables from over-amperage. The new ELCI-protected breakers will trip, turning off power, if the boat incorrectly leaks amperage or too much amperage is consumed.

Newly built boats and older boats upgraded to current ABYC standards include ground fault protection with an onboard ELCI (sometimes known as an RCD – Residual Current Detector). In the past, a boat's A/C breakers only protected wiring and cables from over-amperage problems. Onboard ELCI breakers now add electrical leakage protection to the boat.

How ELCI-Protected Power Might Affect You
Your first visit to a marina with upgraded shore power may require some extra time and effort. Fortunately, this is a one-time process, so once you have successfully connected to ELCI-protected shore power you can rest assured that your boat is ready for the next one.

Before attempting your first-time connection to ELCI-protect power, make sure you know how to reset the ELCI feature on the shore power receptacle. There are a variety of different ELCI-protected breaker configurations and the ELCI reset isn't always easy to find make sure it's the ELCI reset as differentiated from the over-amperage reset.

Some breakers have a single "reset" position on the breaker toggle switch for resetting both the ELCI trip and the over-amperage trip. Others have two separate reset positions. Some ELCI-protected shore power installations have no ELCI reset at each power receptacle. Instead, they have one ELCI-protected breaker located at the power distribution panel providing power for a section of the marina. Any boat leaking excessive amperage within that section of the marina will trip the single ELCI-protected breaker, turning off power to all of the boats in that section of the marina, and marina staff will need to be notified to correct the problem.

First, try your usual connect and power-up sequence for shore power. If this works, great

Under local ownership since 2010

Crow's Nest Yachts Seattle, featuring a robust brokerage yacht sales business, has been under the ownership of three local yacht brokers since 2010. With more than 80 years combined experience in the industry, Dan Wood, Vic Parcells, and Dale Partna became the new principals, "...giving us more autonomy and the ability to better serve yacht owners here in the Northwest," said Partna in 2010. "With our long time experience on the water, we're in tune with local cruising grounds and how people boat in this area." — *Read more on our Facebook page!*

   For instant listing updates, follow us on social media!

CROW'S NEST YACHTS SEATTLE
(206) 625-1580 • seattle@crowsnestyachts.com

WWW.CROWSNESTYACHTS.COM

kick back and enjoy your now safer stay, knowing that your boat doesn't have A/C power leakage issues.

If the ELCI breaker trips as soon as you bring shore power to your panel, then try some alternate sequences of turning switches and flipping breakers on your boat's A/C power panel.

1. Turn off Shore power on your breaker panel.

2. Turn off all A/C panel breakers on your boat, including A/C breakers on the separate inverter panel if equipped. Also, turn off all main A/C and Inverter breakers (double-pole breakers – the ones where two breaker switches are tied together).

3. Reset the dockside ELCI breaker and then turn the breaker to ON.

4. If the ELCI-protected breaker trips again, you likely have a boat wiring issue that will need to be addressed by a marine electrician. You will need to find shore power without ELCI-protection or go without shore power until the problem is fixed.

5. If the ELCI-breaker has not tripped, then return to your boat's breaker panel.

6. Switch the power source to Shore Power.

7. Try different sequences of turning main-double pole breakers on and individual circuit breakers on to discover what is causing the ELCI Breaker to trip. This may take some time as you will need to restart the process by resetting the on-shore ELCI breaker with each attempt. Having someone on the dock resetting the ELCI breaker helps to facilitate this trial and error process.

What is causing the ELCI Breaker to Trip?
Reverse Y-splitters (adapters that combine two 30 amp receptacles into one 50 amp or two 50 amp into one 100 amp) are a known source of ELCI-protected breaker problems and unless specifically designed for ELCI-protected power, will likely not work.

Marine inverters appear to be a possible source of inadvertent ELCI breaker issues. Properly installed marine inverters may trip the ELCI breaker if other onboard A/C breakers are switched on before the inverter completes its process of synchronizing with shore power. Marine inverters correctly tie or connect the boat's neutral (white) A/C wire with the ground (green) wire when the inverter is creating A/C from DC battery power. When the inverter senses A/C shore power it begins a process of synchronizing and switching to pass-thru mode.

Once the syncing and switching process is complete, the inverter breaks its neutral to ground connection and correctly leaves the boat's ground and neutral connected to shore power ground and neutral. If other main double-pole A/C breakers are ON during this syncing process, amperage on the neutral wire is conducted to the ground wire through the inverter's neutral to ground bonding and may trip the ELCI breaker.

Wait for about 30 seconds after supplying shore power to the inverter before turning other main and individual breakers on.
Marine battery chargers are another potential cause of ELCI breaker issues. Try turning off or lower the amperage setting to provide a temporary solution.

Self-testing galvanic isolators may also be a cause of ELCI breaker problems. Replace with a newer galvanic isolator.

A possible source of an unwanted, problematic, neutral-to-ground connection occurs when home-store (non-marine) appliances are installed on boats.

Inverter installation may be a source of incorrect neutral-to-ground connection when the neutral conductors are not separated into two busses; inverted and non-inverted. ABYC recommendations call for separating all neutral and ground wires for inverter loads from non-inverted. A neutral/ground connection should only be present at a source of power.

If you experience problems with these new ground fault systems, have a qualified electrician check your boat's wiring.

Do I Need an Isolation Transformer?
An isolation transformer is not required in order to use ELCI-protected power sources. If your boat is properly wired and powered up correctly, there is no requirement for an isolation transformer.

Start here, start now!
FLAGSHIP MARITIME
VA Approved – Mariner Proven

U.S. Coast Guard
Captain's License Training

OUPV / 6-Pack • Upgrade OUPV to Master 100 Tons
Commercial Assistance Towing • Auxiliary Sail Endorsement
FCC Marine Radio Operator Permit • License Renewals
Maritime Licensing and Consulting Services

Experience the Flagship difference for yourself!
Enroll today!
(253) 905-5972
www.flagshipmaritimellc.com

ELCI PROTECTED SHORE POWER

Isolation transformers all but eliminate the possibility of tripping dock ELCI breakers. They also bring other benefits and are generally a good addition to the boat. Transformers are available in a variety of different voltages and amperages ranging in price from $1,000 to $4,000.

If an isolation transformer is installed within 10 feet of the boat's shore power inlet, an onboard ELCI breaker is not required in order to be ABYC compliant.

Why ELCI Breakers?
ELCI Breakers are safety devices to prevent Electric Shock Drownings. While more dangerous in fresh water, drownings happen in both fresh and saltwater when people become better electrical conductors of leakage A/C current than the surrounding water. Faulty dock or boat wiring is a common cause of dangerous electrical power in waters around docks and marinas. The danger only becomes known when someone enters the water and is immobilized by the electrical shock. These tragedies grow when rescuers enter the same dangerous waters in an attempt to help, and become victims as well.

ELCI Breakers detect amperage difference (imbalance) between the hot (black) wire and the neutral (white) wire and trip if there is a significant difference (leakage) between power going to the boat (hot wire) and that coming back (neutral wire) from the boat to shore power.

ELCI, RCD, GFCI, GFI Different or Same?
All of these devices perform the same function of detecting an amperage imbalance. The difference is in the level of imbalance, or leaking amperage (actually milliamps), that trips the breaker. In-home GFI and GFCI breakers trip at very low imbalance levels while ELCI breakers trip at much higher imbalance levels. RCD's trip at imbalance levels between GFI and ELCI.

Marinas with ELCI-protected Shore Power?
ELCI-protected breakers first appeared at new or rebuilt marinas in Southeast Alaska; North Harbor in Petersburg, Thomas Basin in Ketchikan, and some docks at Bar Harbor South in Ketchikan.

In Washington State, Rosario Resort, Poulsbo Marina, Eagle Harbor Marina, and Eagle Harbor Waterfront Park dock, have upgraded all their docks to ELCI-protected power. Roche Harbor, Point Roberts Marina, and Skyline Marina in Anacortes, have upgraded some of their docks. We are not aware of any ELCI-protected power in British Columbia marinas at this time.

In the 2018 Waggoner Cruising Guide, marinas that have upgraded their shore power are identified with the label "ELCI-protected power."

It's Not the Marina's Shore Power
If you are having problems with upgraded shore power, the first place to look is your boat. Ground fault monitoring and interrupt technology has been protecting us in our homes for many decades with GFCI outlets

One way to prepare your boat is to install an ELCI or RCD breaker on your boat. Installing an ELCI breaker on your boat now, will not only help ensure that you won't have unexpected problems while cruising, but will also make for safer boating. If there are any electrical leakage issues on your boat, an ELCI will bring them to your attention and will do so at your schedule.

ELCI breakers cost about $500 or less and can be added to your existing panel or in a separate enclosure near your boat's shore power inlet.

~Leonard Landon, Co-Managing Editor, Waggoner Cruising Guide

Onboard Blue Sea Systems ELCI and Over-amperage breaker

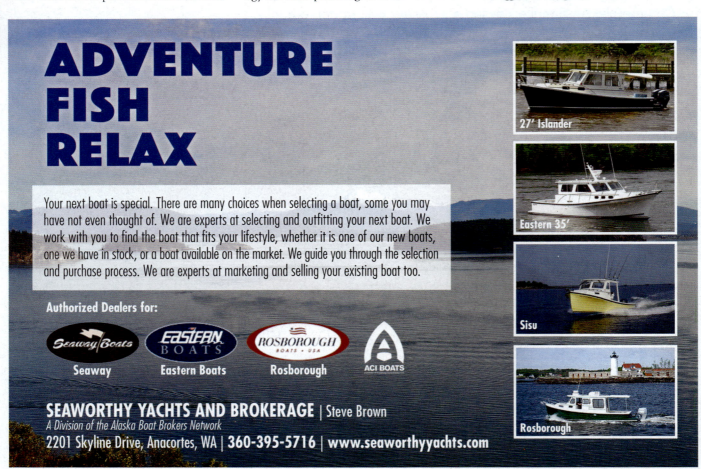

TWO IN ONE!
THE ULTIMATE COMPACT SOLUTION FOR ONBOARD HEATING AND COOKING.

LID UP: COOKING

LID DOWN: CABIN HEATING

VARIABLE POWER FROM 2,000 TO 6,650 BTU

wallas®
Nordic Dt
DIESEL
Stove/Heater

- AUTOMATIC OR MANUAL POWER CONTROL
- UNMATCHED FUEL AND POWER EFFICIENCY
- HIGH TEMPERATURE, RESPONSIVE COOKING POWER
- KEEPS CABIN WARM AND DRY WITH QUIET OPERATION

CE

Let the WALLAS Nordic Dt give back those boating days lost to changeable weather. Safe, efficient diesel heat and a high temp cooking surface means the best use of valuable galley space. Perfect for new build or retrofit, great for DIY installations.

Also check out our WALLAS GB Series variable power marine diesel heaters for the ultimate in clean, efficient heat!

imported & distributed by:

ScanMarine EQUIPMENT

2144 Westlake Ave N, Suite D - Seattle, WA 98109
206-285-3675   fax 206-285-9532
Toll free: 1-888-606-6665   email: info@scanmarineusa.com
Please visit our web site: www.scanmarineusa.com

CHARTERING

Bareboat or crewed; sail or power; small and intimate or large and luxurious; one week or one month; on your own or with a group; chartering is an excellent way to not only cruise the Northwest waters and the Inside Passage, but it's a great way to try different styles of cruising. It's also an option for those who routinely cruise Puget Sound and San Juan Islands, but have always wanted to cruise further north. You could charter a boat in Comox B.C. and cruise Desolation Sound or The Broughton Archipelago. Or charter a smaller, faster boat and use onshore accommodations for overnighting, see the Cruising Inn to Inn section for more information on this option.

Charter cruising is really all about flexibility. If you do not own a boat, you can rent one and cruise some of the most beautiful destinations in the world. Already have a boat but need a larger boat with extra staterooms for family and friends? You can rent one. Or, do you want to try cruising with a different design before you consider purchasing. No experience is required. The charter company can provide an instructor-skipper to teach you how to handle a boat, or you can hire the captain to guide you to the most beautiful places. First mates, chefs and naturalists are available too. The surprising thing is that chartering a boat is relatively inexpensive compared to staying at luxury inns and hotels. Your destination can change every day without having to pack and unpack your luggage between destinations. The trips are memorable for all the wildlife experiences, secluded anchorages, and the choice of fine dining destinations – right on the water.

Flexibility includes the type of boats from which to choose, everything from sailboats and power trawlers, to large yachts. Take a look at the different companies' websites and the variety of boats they offer. Often the search starts with selecting power or sail. Then how many people will be on the boat. How many staterooms will you need? Do your guests mind sharing a head (bathroom), or do you need individual en-suite heads for all cabins? The age of the boat may vary the price. Next, how much do you want to spend versus how much room do you need or want? The range can go from about 26 feet up to 65-foot yachts.

Some charter operators offer a stay-the-night-before option so you can get an early start cruising on the first day of your charter. This option allows you to get onboard, load your personal items, equipment, and provisions. You can sleep aboard the boat but may not leave the dock until the morning of your planned charter. This option is usually charged at half the daily charter rate.

You might consider an organized flotilla where you can travel with a group of like-minded mariners guided by a professional that knows the area. Often activities are arranged every day and you meet some of the greatest people in the world.

At the end of your charter you will be expected to do some basic cleaning to return the boat in good order. Wash the dishes and put things away in the galley; re-fill the fuel and wa-

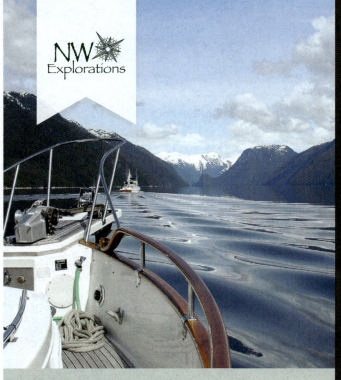

Charter a world-class yacht and book a flotilla today.
Contact charters@nwexplorations.com
or (360) 676-1248 or visit nwexplorations.com

Your ADVENTURE AWAITS

❝ *I can say, without exception, we have never had an experience that came close to matching our adventure.*

—Jeremy, returning client for 8 years

Explore the most spectacular cruising area in the world on a flotilla in a luxury charter yacht.

- Get a front row seat to towering glaciers, quaint marinas, and stunning wildlife

- Go off the beaten path—explore secluded boating spots, hand-picked by experts

- Benefit from a lead boat captain, naturalist, and mechanic on your trip

CHARTERING

ter tanks; empty holding tank(s); and hose down the exterior of the boat.

Some charter operators offer concierge services where they will provision the boat for you, set an itinerary and help with trip planning, and cleanup the boat afterwards.

You can plan and take your dream trip without the cost of owning a boat. Or, if you live and boat in a different area of the world, charter a boat and enjoy Pacific Northwest and Inside Passage cruising.

For a list of charter companies and further tips for charter cruising see our website at WaggonerGuide.com/Charter.

WHAT DO I NEED TO BRING/GET?

Insurance – review the insurance provided by the charterer. Consider not only insurance on the rented boat but also liability insurance. If you are relying on your umbrella liability coverage, make sure that the coverage is good for boat operation and provides coverage in all your planned cruising areas (foreign countries).

Fishing License – in all Northwest and Inside Passage waters, recreational fishing licenses are issued to the person and not to the boat. Everyone in your party will need to get and carry the appropriate fishing licenses, permits, and tags for your planned fishing. Collecting other seafood such as crab, prawns, shrimp, clams, oysters, mussels, and geoduck require a license or permit. Check the with the appropriate fish and game department for open and closed seasons. Also with fish and game for any red-tide warnings for bivalve seafood. Check the rules and regulations for seafood collection – websites are good resources for Washington, B.C., and Alaska waters.

Crab and prawn traps are often onboard and provided as part of the charter boat's equipment.

Fishing gear is occasionally part of the charter boat's equipment. Check with the charter operator.

Navigation Charts and Guidebooks – charts are almost always part of the chartered vessel. Guidebooks are often onboard the vessel but may not be up-to-date. We recommend purchasing your own guidebooks for advance planning and to have onboard that you can markup for future use.

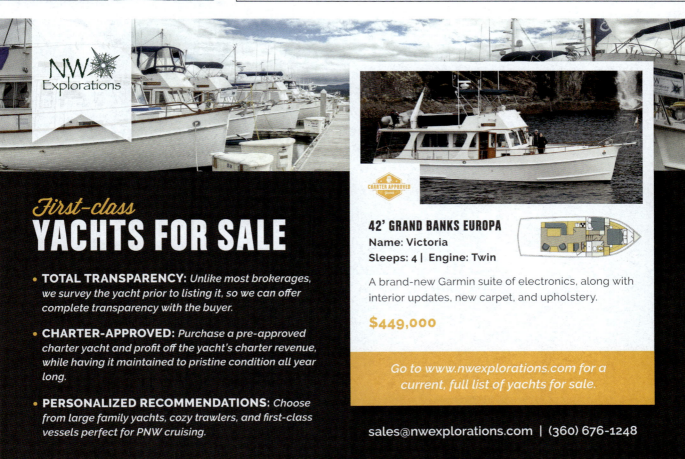

NW Explorations

First-class YACHTS FOR SALE

- **TOTAL TRANSPARENCY:** Unlike most brokerages, we survey the yacht prior to listing it, so we can offer complete transparency with the buyer.

- **CHARTER-APPROVED:** Purchase a pre-approved charter yacht and profit off the yacht's charter revenue, while having it maintained to pristine condition all year long.

- **PERSONALIZED RECOMMENDATIONS:** Choose from large family yachts, cozy trawlers, and first-class vessels perfect for PNW cruising.

42' GRAND BANKS EUROPA
Name: Victoria
Sleeps: 4 | Engine: Twin

A brand-new Garmin suite of electronics, along with interior updates, new carpet, and upholstery.

$449,000

Go to www.nwexplorations.com for a current, full list of yachts for sale.

sales@nwexplorations.com | (360) 676-1248

2018 WAGGONER CRUISING GUIDE

Maintaining Your Boat Like A Pro

The Waggoner Cruising Guide team takes boat maintenance very seriously. A breakdown can ruin your day, or even a week. For us and the boats in our flotilla trips, or when we are out researching for the Waggoner Guide, we cannot afford to breakdown. We certainly don't want a breakdown while underway in the remote areas of Northern B.C. or while crossing an open body of water like Dixon Entrance or rounding Cape Caution. You do not want to breakdown either. Time for summer cruising is a valuable commodity. The worst thing that can happen is when you have a breakdown and your family and friends are stuck waiting for repairs or parts. It is important to develop a maintenance program that is pro-active and preventative.

We have established a maintenance program that starts in the fall just after the cruising season ends. We begin by updating the list of our normal maintenance items such as taking an oil sample before changing the oil and filters. Coolant is inspected and changed. We inspect all systems to see what has broken or needs repair; we like to take care of this in the fall before the boat is laid up for the winter. Corrosives in used oil sitting over the winter can add to the wear on an engine.

It all starts with a checklist specifically tailored for our boat, identifying work to be done. After completing annual maintenance items, we start on upgrade items or refit. Scheduling work in the fall allows us to order needed parts that are often on sale during the winter months or available at boat show prices.

We also inspect our spares. When we purchase spares, the new spare is installed and the old part becomes the spare. This way we know the spare works and has all of the hardware it needs for installation. We carry a spare water pump – the old one stands by and ready to be installed. Parts stores are typically hard to find in our cruising areas. The old part probably has plenty of life in it for a temporary fix. We pack more spares for a single engine boat than we do for a twin-engine boat, where our second engine is our spare.

Look at spares as systems. For example, we do not believe in carrying a rebuild kit for the head. We do carry a complete, working pump assembly ready to be installed and carry spare duckbill valves. Rebuilding a pump for the head is not a pleasant task, nor would it go over well with the rest of the crew.

Our inspection checklist includes due dates for many items like hoses and belts.

BOAT SYSTEMS FOR INSPECTION AND SERVICE

- Engine Systems
- Control Systems
- Heat and water heater
- Electrical
  batteries, inverters and power cables
- Fuel System - all filters and tanks
- Water - filters, pumps and tanks
- Heads and Waste systems
- Lighting - external and internal
- Fire Suppression - all extinguishers
- Emergency Kits
  includes flares and first aid
- Electronics and Communications
  including charts and cruising guides
- Anchor Systems
- Galley and Refrigeration
- Dinghy
- Bedding and all soft goods
- Accessories and Recreational Gear

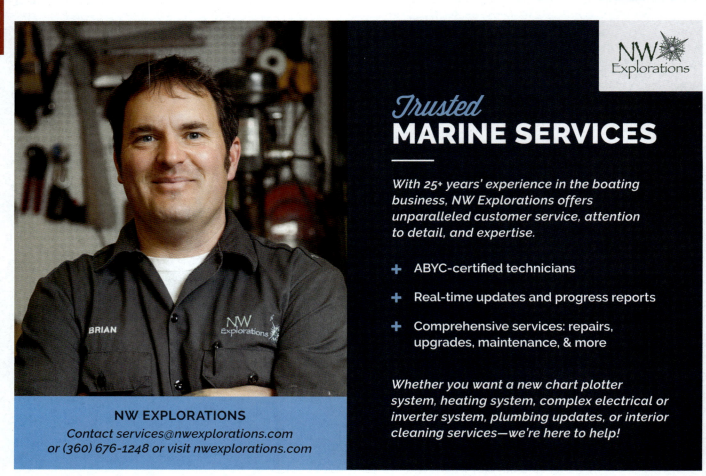

NW EXPLORATIONS
Contact services@nwexplorations.com
or (360) 676-1248 or visit nwexplorations.com

Trusted MARINE SERVICES

With 25+ years' experience in the boating business, NW Explorations offers unparalleled customer service, attention to detail, and expertise.

+ ABYC-certified technicians
+ Real-time updates and progress reports
+ Comprehensive services: repairs, upgrades, maintenance, & more

Whether you want a new chart plotter system, heating system, complex electrical or inverter system, plumbing updates, or interior cleaning services—we're here to help!

MAINTAINING YOUR BOAT

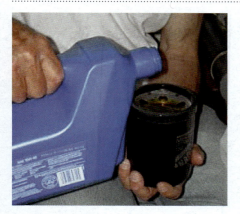

Prefill new filter with clean oil when changing engine oil.

Dates are also set for various systems: the cooling system on the engine is sent out for flushing at a radiator shop every 5 years; the exhaust system is removed and inspected annually. If you have a stainless steel or ceramic coated exhaust system, the interval can be much longer. For gensets and small diesel auxiliaries, the exhaust systems may be very hard to remove and inspect. It may be cheaper to just replace the exhaust system at a cost for parts of about $200. The transmission oil cooler is replaced every 5 years. Some transmission coolers can be sent to a radiator shop to flush, pressure test and service. Soft goods such as dripless seals, sail drive boots, hoses, belts etc. are inspected every year; after 10 years they are all replaced. We service the windlass system with an inspection and lubrication annually. Every 5 years the windlass gets a major inspection, and every 10 years the windlass motor is sent out to a motor shop to be rebuilt. An anchor windlass is a single point of failure, keeping the windlass in great shape can save you from a real headache on the summer cruise.

Our maintenance checklist is divided among the boat's systems. The engine and propulsion systems are well understood, but we also breakdown our checklist into the other systems, such as the anchoring system, refrigeration, furnaces and heat, including the water heater. Electrical systems are checked – both 12V and 120/240V. Start and House Batteries are serviced and possibly replaced. We plan to replace batteries every 7-10 years for sealed batteries, and every 4-7 years for lead acid batteries if they were properly maintained. And, remember when you replace battery banks, you need to replace all the batteries in the bank even if just one is not performing to specifications. We even view the dinghy as a system and make sure the outboard is serviced and the fuel replaced annually. We check the dinghy's steering system, anchor system and the gear bag for first aid supplies and other safety items.

You do not have to do all the work, but often you do have to manage the work to make sure it gets done. If you elect not to do some things on your checklist, have your shop update your checklist and ask them to sign off on the inspection and service items to ABYC standards.

Determine what items on your checklist you want to work on and those you would prefer a marine professional handle. For example, inspecting and remarking your anchor chain may be a day project you want to do. A boat is a complex series of systems, all working in a corrosive environment. Your boat's systems are in standby through most of the year, ready for those good months when you go boating. It is best for boats to be used on a regular basis; you may want to use your boat more often and go boating once or twice every other month, but with our busy lives that may not be practical. The key is to have a process for good routine maintenance built into your boat ownership to maximize fun with family and friends for an enjoyable cruise.

For more information on the Checklist Approach, see our Maintaining Your Boat Like a Pro checklist in the WaggonerGuide.com Free Downloads section. The list is in MS-Word format and you can modify it for your boat. A course is offered at the Seattle Boat Show University and Cruisers College programs.

We Don't Fix Boats
We MAINTAIN Boats

We don't like to fix boats, we prefer to maintain boats, so they don't break down. A well maintained boat breaks down less. Sounds simple. We will design a maintenance program for your vessel. We will make sure you have the right spare parts so if something does break, we can get you back out on the water as quickly as possible.

We take the same approach with special projects — like new electronics, watermaker, bow and stern thruster, or even a whole new galley. We know our craft and pride ourselves on our professional approach to engineer and install innovative solutions.

Let us work with you to maintain and improve your boat.

www.S3Maritime.com | (206) 420-4952

2018 WAGGONER CRUISING GUIDE

Find the Boat of Your Dreams

The Northwest is one of the most beautiful cruising grounds in the world. Every day presents beautiful vistas and wildlife including eagles, whales, porpoises and bears. Or, consider catching salmon, halibut, prawns or crab all accessible when cruising with a Nordic Tug. Thousands of people do.

We can help you find a new Nordic Tug that will best meet your cruising lifestyle. Or, we can find the passage making yacht to meet your budget and boating needs. Let Nordic Yachts Northwest help you find the boat of your dreams.

NORDIC YACHTS
Northwest

1019 Q Ave., Anacortes, Washington, (360) 293-9411 • www.nordicyachtsnw.com

VHF Radio Procedures

The VHF radio is an important piece of safety equipment, and VHF 16 should be monitored when the boat is underway. While monitoring, you will hear weather and safety warnings, and be aware of what's happening around you. A boat close by, for example, may be having problems and call for help. By monitoring your radio, you can respond.

Station licenses, U.S. Vessels. Until 1996, U.S. pleasure craft were required to have station licenses for their marine VHF radios. In 1996, however, the requirement was dropped for pleasure craft under 20 meters (65 feet), operating inside the U.S. only. All U.S. vessels operating in foreign waters, including Canada, still need a U.S. station license. With the 1999 dropping of station licenses in Canada (see below), it was hoped that pleasure craft exempted from station licenses in the U.S. no longer would need a station license to travel in Canadian waters. It now appears that it would require an act of Congress—literally!—to exempt U.S. pleasure craft from needing a station license for Canadian travel, and that's not likely. As a practical matter, Canadian authorities do not enforce U.S. radio license laws, and U.S. authorities are not going to follow a boat into Canada. In other words, there's no enforcement. We have our station license, however, and would not be without it, enforcement or no enforcement. We recommend that our readers do the same. Apply for your station license at the same time you register for your Maritime Mobile Service Identity (MMSI) number. You will need this number to use the Digital Selective Calling (DSC) and emergency calling features all VHF radios have. You can register online at www.fcc.gov, using the Universal Licensing System (ULS). The online process is cumbersome, but the processing time is short. The forms are also available from the FCC at (888) 225-5322 (Monday through Friday) if you apply by mail. If you call, choose menu option 2, Licensing. The woman who took our call was well-informed and helpful. A station license serves the entire vessel, regardless of the number of VHF radios the vessel has. The station license also covers the use of a tender's VHF radio (such as a handheld model) as long as the radio is used in tender service, and as long as it is not used on land. It's all right for two or more radios from the same vessel with the same call sign to talk to each other via handheld VHF radio. U.S. pleasure craft longer than 20 meters, and all U.S. commercial vessels, are required to have an FCC station licenses.

Station licenses, Canadian Vessels. Beginning in March 1999, station licenses no longer were issued to Canadian vessels so long as 1) the vessel is not operated in the sovereign waters of a country other than Canada or the U.S.; 2) the radio equipment on board the vessel is capable of operating only on frequencies that are allocated for maritime mobile communications or marine radio navigation. Canadian vessels not meeting those two requirements must have station licenses.

Operator's Permit, U.S. The U.S. does not require operator's permits for VHF radio use within the U.S. For foreign travel, however, a Restricted Radio Operator's permit is required. The U.S. individual permit is issued for life, and costs $60. If you are from the U.S. and take a boat to Canada, you will need a Restricted Radio Operator permit. Use Schedule E of FCC Form 605 to apply, and Form 159 to remit payment. If you are applying for both a station license and a Restricted Radio Operator permit you will need a separate Form 159 for each application. The forms can be downloaded from www.fcc.gov, or you can apply electronically on the FCC website.

Operator's Permit, Canada. Canada requires each person operating a VHF radio to have a Restricted Operator's Certificate. For Canadian residents a test must be passed, but the certificate is free and issued for life. Training for the test and the issuing of certificates is handled by the Canadian Power and Sail Squadrons.

VHF RADIO TOPICS

Station licenses, U.S. Vessels
Station licenses, Canadian Vessels
Operator's Permit, U.S.
Operator's Permit, Canada
How to use the VHF radio
The low power switch
When not to call on channel 16
DSC & GMDSS
Mayday hoaxes
Reach the Coast Guard by Cell
Automatic Information System

Radio Check

U.S. and Canadian Coast Guard ask that VHF Radio Check requests be made on a working channel. In U.S. waters that would be channel 22A and in Canadian waters that would be 83A. Requests for radio check should never be made on channel 16.

Reliable voice, email and **messaging** communications for the **Inside Passage** to Alaska and beyond.

Enjoy the piece of mind that a satellite phone system can bring you on your next trip and stay in contact with those back home, for less than cellular roaming in many cases.

Satellite Communications Sales, Support, & Rentals

206.878.8270
www.ocens.com

2018 WAGGONER CRUISING GUIDE

VHF RADIO PROCEDURES

AIS display shows nearby vessels and potential conflicts.

SCOLDING ON THE RADIO

When a fellow boater does something that is dangerous or inconsiderate, proper VHF radio protocol does not allow the injured party to start yelling at "the boat that just went by" without identifying themselves – especially not on high power. If it's necessary to talk to the other boater – first switch to LOW POWER – then try to hail the boat by name and switch to a working channel.

Most people don't realize they're doing something wrong, so start by explaining the situation. Make sure it's a conversation and not a lecture. Explain the situation and listen to the response. A civil conversation is more likely to get results than an angry lecture. Make sure you are on a working channel and on low power.

GLACIERS, BEARS AND TOTEMS
Sailing in Search of the Real Southeast Alaska

BY ELSIE HULSIZER

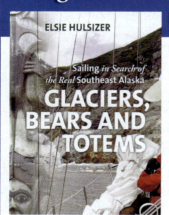

Marine writer Elsie Hulsizer, whose *Voyages to Windward* unlocked the mysteries of cruising Vancouver Island's west coast, now does the same for Southeastern Alaska. Elsie and her husband Steve spent three summers sailing, writing and photographing the towering fjords, immaculate glaciers, throwback fishing villages and overexposed tourist traps of America's largest state. *Glaciers, Bears and Totems* is a rich book of adventure travel.

FINE EDGE
Nautical & Recreational Publishing

To order, visit **www.waggonerguide.com** or call 360-299-8500.

How to use the VHF radio. The easiest way to get a general sense of radio use is to monitor VHF 16, the hailing and distress channel; VHF 22A, the U.S. Coast Guard channel; VHF 83A, the Canadian Coast Guard channel, and the working channels. The VTS channels are good, too, because you'll be listening to professional mariners at work. VTS transmissions are brief and often informal, but you'll be listening to experienced people in action. On VHF 16 and the ship-to-ship working channels, you'll also hear inexperienced people. The difference will be obvious. To use the radio, call on the calling channel, VHF 16. When communication is established, switch to a working channel for your conversation. Except instances of distress, you may not have a conversation on VHF 16. VHF 09 may be used for conversations; but because it is an alternate calling channel in the U.S., the conversations should be brief.

The low power switch. VHF radios can transmit at 25 watts, their highest power rating, or at 1 watt, the low power mode. Handheld VHF radios usually have a maximum power of 5 watts and low power of 1 watt. Whenever practical, use the low-power mode. Other vessels a few miles away can then use the same channel without interference from you. The difference between high power and low power affects transmission distance only. Reception ability is unaffected. Handheld radios should use low power whenever possible. The battery lasts longer. When making a securite call, such

SECURITÉ CALL INSTEAD OF BIG WAKE SCOLD

When a nearby boat is creating a large and potentially dangerous wake, instead of getting on the VHF radio and blindly scolding – do everyone a favor and issue a Securité call to alert other boats in the area. First switch to LOW POWER, then call: "Securité, Securité, this is the 34-foot sailing vessel WINDY– caution for a potentially dangerous wake from a fast-moving large black-on-white power boat in Mosquito Pass."

"SECURITÉ"

"SECURITÉ"

"SECURITÉ"

as transiting Dodd Narrows or Malibu Rapids, be sure to have your VHF radio set on low power (1 watt). A securite call is for traffic safety purposes only and is not a call for right-of-way. Vessels traveling with the current are the 'stand-on' and vessels traveling against the current flow are the 'give-way.'

When not to call on channel 16. Large vessels in the VTS traffic lanes usually do not monitor VHF 16. They monitor the VTS channel for their area. In Puget Sound waters covered by Seattle VTS Traffic, large vessels also must monitor VHF 13, the bridge-to-bridge communications channel. Seattle Traffic covers all U.S. waters and the entire Strait of Juan de Fuca, including the Canadian side. If you are disabled in a traffic lane and a large vessel is bearing down on you, call the vessel on the appropriate VTS channel (see VTS Radio Channels chart in the What Recreational Boaters Need to Know About VTS section in this chapter). If you are still unsure about what to do, call the Coast Guard on VHF 16 and ask them to contact the vessel for you, or to provide you with the correct channel.

DSC & GMDSS. DSC stands for Digital Selective Calling, and is part of the Global Maritime Distress and Safety System (GMDSS). Basically, if you have a DSC radio with a valid MMSI (Maritime Mobile Service Identity) number in its memory and push the covered red button, the radio will send an automatic digital distress message on VHF 70. This message contains the MMSI number, which is linked to a database that includes your name, vessel information, emergency contacts, and other information. If the vessel's GPS is connected to the VHF, or the radio is equipped with a GPS receiver, the radio also transmits GPS coordinates. For this to work, the radio must have the vessel's MMSI number stored in its memory. MMSI numbers are issued in the United States by the FCC or Boat U.S., and in Canada by Transport Canada and Industry Canada. Important for U.S. vessels traveling to Canada: Officially, MMSI numbers issued by Boat U.S. are only for use in the United States. However, a Boat U.S. MMSI number will work in Canada., but the database information may not be available to Canadian authorities. The distress signal and your location, if your radio is connected to a GPS signal, will be transmitted to authorities and other DSC equipped vessels to alert other boats. Brief your crew before heading out on a passage on how to summon help using the red DISTRESS button on your VHF radio. Consider preparing a check-list for emergencies for your crew that includes summoning help on the VHF radio and even the location of your safety equipment. For more information on this critical topic, see WaggonerGuide.com and search for the article on What to do when the Captain drops dead - or is incapacitated. While it is a catchy title, the article has many useful tips on how to prepare an emergency manual for use by your crew in case of an emergency.

Mayday hoaxes. Each year, hoax Mayday calls cost the U.S. and Canadian Coast Guards millions of dollars ($2 million in Seattle alone) and in some cases put lives at risk. Sometimes the hoax is Junior playing with Grandpa's radio, sometimes it is the result of things getting too festive, sometimes the caller has a mental problem. Now that direction-finding equipment can locate the sources of radio calls, arrests can be made and penalties assessed. Radios are not toys, and hoax Mayday calls are not jokes. Large fines and even jail terms are the penalties.

LOCAL KNOWLEDGE

To Reach the Coast Guard by Cell or Smart Phone
U.S. Coast Guard Rescue Center Seattle
911 or (206) 220-7001

U.S. Coast Guard Rescue Center Juneau
(for all of southeast Alaska) 911
or (907) 463-2000

Canadian Coast Guard 911
or *16 or (250) 413-8933

Android and IOS smartphones can access and hail U.S. Coast Guard with their free official USCG App. The App has an emergency button as well as access to other helpful information.

Automatic Information System (AIS). AIS is a VHF-based radio tracking system for commercial and recreational vessels. Vessels equipped with AIS transponders transmit their name, course, speed, MMSI number, vessel size, and destination. Vessels equipped with AIS receivers display information from surrounding vessels and warn of potential conflicts. Large commercial vessels are required to have Class-A transponders while recreational vessels optionally have Class-B transponders. In the past, the high cost limited AIS transponders to only larger recreational vessels and AIS receivers to some recreational boats. The cost to equip your boat with both transmit and receive continues to get more affordable all the time. In 2017 Standard Horizon came out with a VHF radio that includes both transponder and receiver built-in to a single box. Simply replace your VHF radio to show boats your information and receive their AIS information. AIS is particularly valuable in low visibility situations and when operating near large commercial traffic. Vessel name and MMSI AIS information makes it much easier to call a nearby vessel regarding potential conflicts. The price to equip your vessel with an AIS receiver is very affordable and well worth the expense.

New AIS applications show up each season. Small AIS man-overboard devices that attach to lifejackets are available; when activated, show a MOB alert on all AIS equipped vessels nearby. AIS system design provides for a number of different message types that include virtual navigation aids, observed weather information, and local harbor/port information.

RESOURCES FOR CRUISING HAMS

Lydia and Patrick McKenzie, longtime northwest cruisers and active ham radio users sent us the following information on using a ham radio while cruising.

Ham radio enthusiasts have some excellent resources available in the Pacific Northwest. Dedicated individuals run morning and evening networks where boaters can check in and stay in touch with each other and learn about what is happening along the coast. Cruisers can report where they are, where they are headed, weather conditions and other information. We have met new friends and learned about everything from interesting new anchorages to up-to-the-minute weather conditions in a particular area.

The *Great Northern Boaters Network* meets each morning with a northern and a southern section. Tune your single sideband radio to frequency 3870 KiloHertz at 7:30 a.m. Pacific Daylight Time to hear the cheerful voice of Darlene (KL0YC) in Dora Bay, AK, greeting the day. From April through early September, she runs the northern half of the network until 8:00 a.m. when Barbara (VE7KLU) in Sidney, B.C. takes over and runs the southern portion of the net. The southern portion of the net runs year-round.

The *West Coast Boaters Network*, run by Bill (VE7WSM) in Tofino, meets each evening from late spring or early summer until the last boater checks in safely in the fall. It covers from San Francisco to northern Alaska. Starting at 6:00 p.m. PDT, tune to frequency 3860 KHz.

The Great Northern and West Coast Networks pass traffic (messages) between them, a great help to boaters who are trying to get in touch with each other or even receive important messages from home. These cruising nets can be both fun and helpful to cruisers.

Cellular, Internet and Satellite Communications

Voice and data communications remain one of the priorities when cruising. Lately, with a multitude of smart and connected devices onboard, data communications have become a top priority for cruisers. Email, social media, weather information, financial transactions, marina slip reservations, and web browsing have all become essential elements of today's cruising. Cellular is the most cost effective solution for voice, messaging, and data communications in much of the Northwest cruising area. Satellite service provides the best geographic coverage but at a higher cost. Wi-Fi internet service is available from a number of different free and for-fee providers. In more remote areas, service is not always available or the service is slow and unreliable.

Cellular. In Washington waters, cruisers have a number of cellular providers to choose from, all with excellent voice, messaging, and data service. All of the Washington waters, except the western half of Strait of Juan de Fuca, have excellent cellular coverage. U.S. based cellular providers have a range of plans at reasonable rates. In 2017, reasonably priced plans were introduced with unlimited voice and data that include roaming in Canada. Today's cellular data speeds are good and service is very reliable. If you are on one of the newer rate plans, cellular is a cost effective way to handle your voice, messaging, and internet needs while cruising all of the Northwest waters. Be sure you have a voice, messaging, and data plan which includes roaming in Canada; if you don't, you may be shocked when you get the bill.

Three major cellular providers: Telus, Rogers, and Bell, operate in B.C. with voice, messaging, and data coverage. Voice, messaging, and data coverage is complete from the U.S. border on the south, to Campbell River/Desolation Sound on the north. There is no coverage in Jervis Inlet and spotty in mountainous areas. The west coast of Vancouver Island has coverage from Hot Springs south to Barkley Sound. There is coverage in Quatsino Sound in the north. From Campbell River/Desolation Sound to Port McNeill, cellular coverage is spotty. Johnston Strait has the better coverage, with little if any coverage in the passages and inlets off of the Strait. Cellular towers high atop mountains near Port McNeill and Port Hardy provide coverage in much of Queen Charlotte Strait, and the edge of the Broughtons. Between Port Hardy and Prince Rupert, cell coverage is limited to the area around the towns of Bella Bella/Shearwater, Klemtu, Hartley Bay, Kitimat, and Bella Coola. The area around Prince Rupert has good cell coverage that continues north to the U.S. border in Dixon Entrance. Haida Gwaii has cell coverage in and around the city of Queen Charlotte, Sandspit, and Masset. Cellular service keeps getting better every season with more and better coverage in remote areas. Coverage between Campbell River and Port McNeill keeps getting better each season.

Southeast Alaska coverage begins in Dixon entrance near Cape Fox but is spotty until you pass the entrance to Behm Canal on your way to Ketchikan. Four major U.S. cellular carriers provide voice, data, and messaging coverage in and around populated areas in Southeast Alaska.

Cellular Amplifiers. Cellular amplifiers are a good addition when cruising north of

COMMUNICATIONS TOPICS
Cellular
Cellular Amplifiers
Satellite Communications
Satellite Messengers
Wi-Fi Internet
Being a Good Wi-Fi Citizen
Wi-Fi Amplifiers

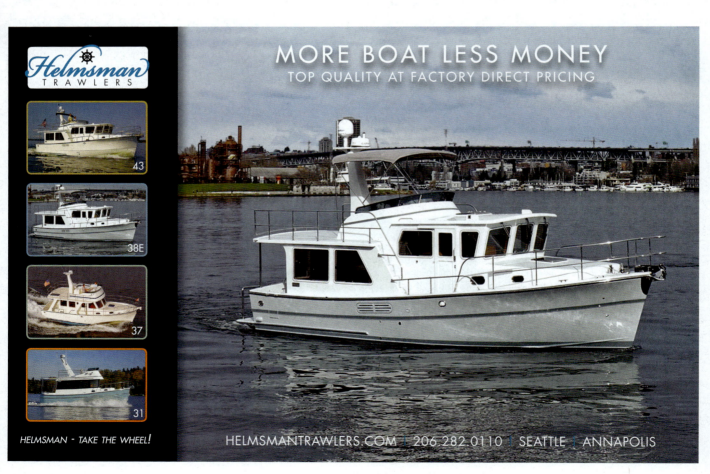

CELLULAR, INTERNET AND SATELLITE COMMUNICATIONS

The InReach system now offers weather information from Ocens.

Campbell River and Desolation Sound. From Campbell River north, there are fewer cell towers and the distances between them are much greater. Cellular signals emitting from the towers are powerful, but the return signals from your phone are relatively weak. A cell amplifier's main advantage is in boosting the signal from your phone so that the distant cell tower can "hear" your phone. The best amplifiers have an external antenna. Be sure and match the amplifier's frequencies to your phone, and the carriers for your planned cruising area.

Cruise ships have a predictable effect on cell service. In remote areas north of Campbell River and especially in southeast Alaska, cell phone service is noticeably degraded when a cruise ship or two are in the cell tower area. These remote systems, sized to limited cellular demand, are often swamped by the thousands of devices in the hands of cruise ship passengers.

Important: For emergency, distress, and rescue operations, cellular telephones are not substitutes for VHF radios. If you have a problem and need help, get on channel 16 and start calling. The Coast Guard and neighboring vessels will hear you and may be your closest and fastest aid.

Satellite Communications. Satellite today is more than just phones. Two satellite providers, Iridium and Globalstar, offer a number of equipment and service plans with voice, message, and data communication services. Satellite phones give you voice communication nearly everywhere. Prices of satellite phones have come down, but airtime is still more expensive than cellular. Satellite messaging and data services have recently become much easier to use with the introduction of Iridium Go and Globalstar Sat-Fi devices. These devices bring satellite communications to your smartphone, tablet, and PC. Both Iridium Go and Sat-Fi connect your smartphone, or any Wi-Fi enabled device, to the respective satellite system for voice, data, and messaging. The devices are easy to use and allow multiple devices to connect to the satellite service. Data speeds are slow to very slow, with bandwidth for simple email and light browsing. Some weather information services are available, designed for transmission over satellite service. Satellite phone rentals are available. See www.WaggonerGuidecom for more information about satellite phones.

Satellite messengers. Satellite messengers like those from SPOT and Garmin offer an inexpensive way for cruisers to track and check in. Depending on the device and service plan selected, satellite messengers can send automated position reports, link to smartphones to send and receive text messages via satellite, or send a distress signal. Basic weather forecasts and marine weather forecasts are now available on the Garmin's InReach device. Satellite messengers rely on private satellite constellations, not the internationally organized Cospas-Sarsat network that EPIRBs and PLBs use. SOS messages go through a private emergency center that passes on the message to government emergency services. Satellite messengers are not EPIRBs and should not take the place of an EPIRB, but they can provide low-cost communications far beyond cell phone service. Satellite messengers offer the coverage of satellite service at a lower cost.

WiFi Internet. Wi-Fi may be one of the most universal and inexpensive means

2018 WAGGONER CRUISING GUIDE

CELLULAR, INTERNET AND SATELLITE COMMUNICATIONS

of accessing the internet when cruising. However, availability, speed, and reliability are often problematic. Most marinas have Wi-Fi available for their guests. How the marina provides this Wi-Fi service varies from marina to marina. The larger, popular marinas have in-house installed commercial grade Wi-Fi systems that are accessible, and reliable with bandwidth for most internet needs. Other marinas have contracted with commercial Wi-Fi providers such as Shaw-Go and Beacon (formerly BBX) for commercial grade Wi-Fi service. A few marinas with commercial grade Wi-Fi systems offer high bandwidth, for a fee, as an alternative to their lower bandwidth free Wi-Fi. A number of marinas have in-house installed Wi-Fi, built from home-grade equipment connected to residential bandwidth internet service. In remote areas of B.C., where there are no landlines, marina Wi-Fi is via limited bandwidth Dish Satellite Internet providers. Satellite internet service is much slower and at a much higher cost than landline data service. Marina operators provide this service to guests at a high price; and it is metered. Every bit (pun intended) of data is a cost to the marina operator.

A decade ago, when a boat pulled into a marina moorage space, the boat might use one or possibly two Wi-Fi connection ports, and their usage consisted of simple emails and some limited bandwidth web browsing. But today, every person onboard has a smartphone that they want to connect to Wi-Fi, and they may have a tablet or PC. In addition, the boat has its own devices, including a chartplotter, wanting to connect. Young people onbard may have gaming devices as well. Then there's Fire TV that attemps to connect for streaming video or movies. Every piece of electronics today is Wi-Fi enabled. The demand for internet bandwidth has increased tenfold, putting an enormous strain on Wi-Fi systems.

Wi-Fi user expectations have changed dramatically, at home the average internet user has grown accustomed to large bandwidth internet connections with almost limitless amounts of data transfer. We all assume that any internet connection will be fast, available, and constant.

Marinas are challenged to keep up with this increasing demand. Remotely located marinas, where landline internet is not available, have an almost impossible task trying to meet demand with very limited bandwidth satellite internet connections.

How to be a Good Wi-Fi citizen. Adjust your expectations and your internet usage for Wi-Fi. Be prepared for internet access slower than you might be accustomed to; allow extra time for the online task and have an alternate plan. Most importantly, adjust your internet usage to minimize data transfer. Be especially aware of data upload, as upload speeds are the slowest on nearly every type of connection.

1. Turn off automatic updates. Not always as simple and straight-forward as it sounds.

2. On smartphones, tablets, and PC's, turn off automatic photo backup to cloud storage. Do you really need all 200 images uploaded to the cloud right now?

3. Smartphones – almost all of the Apps on our smartphones are searching for App updates. This constant 'pinging' to check for updates is largely unnecessary internet traffic when we are out boating. So go through your Apps one-by-one and turn off updates. Each App is different.

4. Don't even think of using Apps like Facetime, Netflix, Amazon Video, and gaming apps.

5. Limit your use: email with no attachments; Facebook, scrolling slowly and no video viewing; voice only skype, no video; and limit smartphone usage when Wi-Fi is the only signal available.

Wi-Fi Amplifiers. When your assigned slip is far out on the end of the most distant dock, the marina's free Wi-Fi may not help you much if you don't have an amplifier onboard. Relatively inexpensive, Wi-Fi amplifiers boost the often weak marina signal. Amplifiers allow you to reach otherwise unusable Wi-Fi signals from the surrounding area. These include Wi-Fi from providers like Shaw and Xfinity. Wi-Fi amplifiers connect to an onboard Wi-Fi router to bring the amplified signal throughout your boat. Wi-Fi amplifiers often allow boats at anchor to use nearby Wi-Fi.

44 www.WaggonerGuide.com

Fisheries Supply
Marine Supplies Since 1928

Don't let a broken pump, clogged fuel filter or lost anchor ruin your vacation. Fisheries Supply has a full range of shipping options throughout the Pacific NW and Alaska, including custom solutions via Kenmore Air to almost anywhere in the San Juans, BC and the Inside Passage.

LARGEST SELECTION
of Marine Supplies in the Pacific Northwest

SAME-DAY SHIPPING
for Orders Placed by 2pm

CUSTOM SHIPPING
to the San Juans, BC and Inside Passage*

*via Kenmore Air, certain restrictions apply

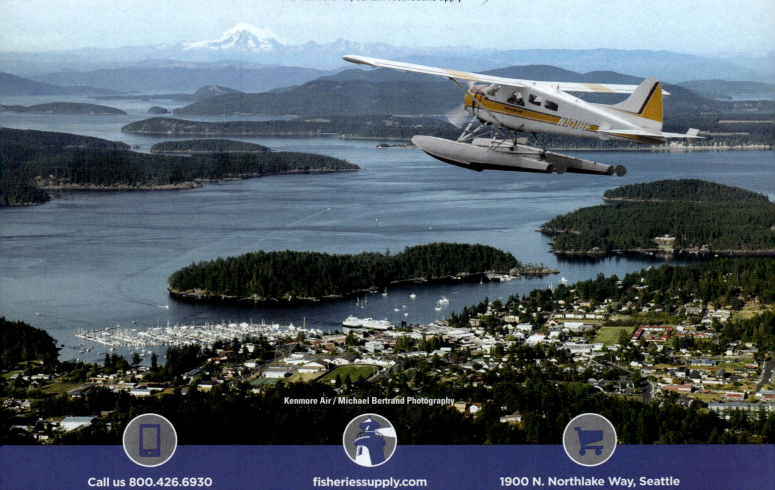

Kenmore Air / Michael Bertrand Photography

Call us 800.426.6930   fisheriessupply.com   1900 N. Northlake Way, Seattle

Safe, Comfortable and Stylish by Design

NORTHWEST YACHTS

ARTIST RENDERING

Choose a model, pilothouse style and let's build your Northwest!

NW 48 **NW 52** **NW 62** **NW 70** **NW 75**

Why a Northwest? Northwest motor yachts are built to go places in safety, comfort and style. Every effort is made in concept, design and construction to deliver the safest possible vessel. High bulwarks, beefy railings, dock level (or near dock level) main decks make for safety at sea, as well as at the dock.

We believe your yacht is your home underway. You should be as comfortable aboard your Northwest as you would be at home. Design elements include: wider passageways, less steep stairs, room to move about, ergonomically comfortable settees, easy access and plentiful storage. Naval designer Steven R. Seaton and Peter Whiting have worked to meld style and function together in all the Northwest designs.

Motor Yachts with a Trawler Pedigree.

7001 Seaview Ave NW, Ste 150
Seattle WA 98117

844.692.2487
www.northwestyachts.com

2415 T Ave, Ste 112
Anacortes WA 98221

SEATTLE YACHTS
Power & Sail

Our Business is "Fun!"

Visit us today and join in the fun of owning a yacht!

Nimbus | Elan | DeFever | Tartan
Legacy | Northwest | Alaskan

We know the fun of boating. We can help you find the right boat for maximum enjoyment! We have thrilling sailboats and comfortable passagemaking yachts to explore the islands or take you to Southeast Alaska. Do you need to sell your existing boat? We can even make listing and selling your boat fun too! Go on our website for more information and to see all of our brokerage listings.

Shilshole Bay Marina
(206) 789-8044
7001 Seaview Ave NW Suite 150 Seattle, WA 98117

Anacortes Marina
(360) 299-0777
2415 T Ave. Suite 112 Anacortes, WA 98221

www.SeattleYachts.com

BOATING FROM INN TO INN

Boating from Inn to Inn

There is a new trend in boating where you can plan to use shore-side inns, hotels or cabins as extra staterooms. Many of them are designed for visiting boating guests and are very cool. You can boat with friends or family and give them the option of staying onshore. Handy if your boat does not have that second or third stateroom. This is also handy if you would like a night ashore and some of the options like yurts or bubble homes are very interesting. If you have a fast speedboat with a cuddy cabin, you can run up the Inside Passage to Alaska in two long days or less. There are lots of options.

When we started seeing this trend, we recognized the opportunity for guests aboard a boat to enjoy the day's cruise with the option to stay overnight onshore at an inn, cabin, or hotel room. There are even boats and houseboats in marinas that you can rent for the overnight stay. Some of these options can be booked through the marina or even on Airbnb. Grandparents can now join the fun of a day's cruise with the family and spend the night ashore in a comfortable bed with a normal sized bathroom facility. With a little creative planning and the Waggoner Cruising Guide in hand, you can create a cruising itinerary with stays in marinas that have nearby shore-side overnight accommodations that range from luxury inns and hotel rooms to other boats in the marina, yurts, and even camp sites where the kids can stay in a tent.

Downsize your boat. We also see a trend where some cruising couples are downsizing their boat. They have owned a 45 foot to 60 foot displacement trawler, allowing them to cruise for weeks or

The Union Steamship Co. in Snug Cove on Bowen Island has beautiful cabins to rent above the marina.

Camp in luxury in Back Eddy Resort & Marina.

The cottage at Westbay Marine Village in Victoria

BOATING FROM INN TO INN

months at a time. They have done the long trips and now want to downsize to reduce their boating costs, allowing them to experience other types of travel. Rather than letting go of the boating scene, they change their boating style and purchase a smaller vessel with basic overnight accommodations for two. They buy a faster boat and plan their trips to quickly dash to different places and stay ashore for most of the time during their trip. One owner who downsized from a 45-foot semi-displacement trawler to a new 28-foot Sea Sport with twin outboards, is planning a four-day passage from Anacortes to Ketchikan. He and his wife will be staying in cabins at Blind Channel and Echo Bay and then hotel rooms at Shearwater and Prince Rupert before arriving in Ketchikan. While their new 28-foot boat was not inexpensive, they save on moorage, insurance, and general maintenance with a smaller boat.

A growing family or bringing grandchildren along. If your cute young children are growing into gangly teenagers, and a new larger boat with cabins for all is not in your future, consider putting them off the boat ashore. There are many anchorages and marinas with camping areas and tent sites. It can be an adventure to arrive by boat and take the dingy to shore and set up camp. Some marina resorts have swimming pools, kayak rentals, and many recreational activities. Involve the kids in the planning. Let them research and make some of the choices on where to stay. This works for grandchildren too. The added benefit - with the kids ashore - you get your privacy back at the boat. See our updated list for 2018 of onshore accommodations in the Free Downloads section at WaggonerGuide.com.

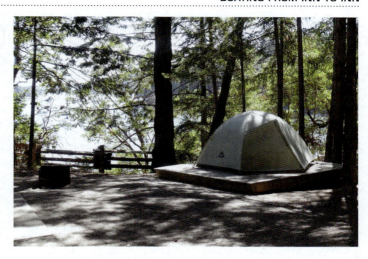

The tent sites are just up from the Provincial dock at Montague Harbour Marine Park

Hastings House has beautiful classic cottages overlooking Ganges Harbour on Salt Spring Island.

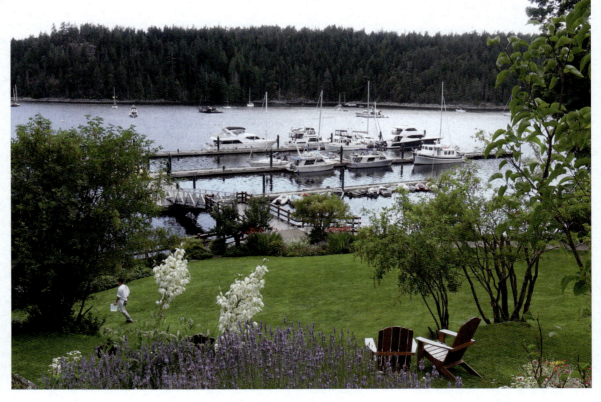

In the Desolation Sound area, Gorge Harbour offers cabins, camp sites and a pool overlooking the harbor.

2018 WAGGONER CRUISING GUIDE

Developing an Itinerary to Delight the Entire Crew

Planning an itinerary for you and your crew generates enthusiasm for the trip and establishes team effort. For many, trip planning is part of the fun, starting months before the actual trip. You can dream about what your cruise will be like through the islands or Desolation Sound.

Involving the crew. You can start by involving the crew with pre-trip research, or you create the first draft as Captain. Look through the many cruising guides available (we stock most in the WaggonerGuide.com store). Also look through past issues of magazines that cover the Northwest like Pacific Yachting, Northwest Yachting Magazine, 48 North and SEA magazine to name a few. Start that short list of places you want to visit for the first time, re-visit, or see from a different point of view and share with guests who have previously never seen this beautiful area.

Everyone can prioritize activities and destinations based on their interests and work together to finalize the itinerary. Depending on how much time you have for the trip and knowing the distances involved, you can create an itinerary with reasonable expectations. Time should be factored in for provisioning, fuel stops, weather delays, and transiting any rapids along your route. Consider time for relaxing too. Those on a tight schedule might move to a different destination every day to see as much as possible. Others plan for a day or two, or plan short cruising legs to allow plenty of time to fully enjoy a destination.

A few questions to start. Asking a few basic questions will help you develop an itinerary. Many boaters have preconceived ideas about their anticipated cruise, or expect to see and do certain things they have in mind. A pre-planned itinerary, with some specifics, helps set the expectations for a pleasant and rewarding cruise. Consider:

How much time do you have, including the trip back? What speed do you expect to cruise at?

What do you want to see? This list could include wildlife, quaint villages, cannery ruins, museums, or simply relax at remote anchorages.

What activities do you want to do? Perhaps go fishing, swimming, or kayaking. Or you may prefer attending happy hours at the smaller marinas, or souvenir shopping when in town. Walking the beaches and hiking the trails found on many of the islands is always a favorite. You may have a crew that is split where some will want to see the local museum while others rummage through the shops in town. There are many locations that fit this criteria.

Are friends and family flying in to meet you? Options may include commercial airports, smaller community airports, or perhaps arriving by seaplane at more remote areas. You may want to factor in extra time for missed connections if you have guests arriving by plane.

Is this your first time cruising the Northwest? Are you planning a 1-week or 2-week bareboat charter? There are so many places to go and enjoy both near and far. Most people who are new to the area start by cruising among the San Juan Islands on a 1-week to 2-week itinerary, leaving from the charter bases in Anacortes or Bellingham. If you want to focus on the islands of British Columbia, there are bareboat charter companies in Sidney, Nanaimo and Vancouver. If you really just want to cruise Desolation Sound and the Broughton Islands area, there is a reputable charter company in Comox, BC where you can save a day or two by starting your cruise much closer to these areas.

Begin with the basics. With the basic information, we like to create an itinerary in a spreadsheet, or on a pad of paper. For those who like to work with spreadsheets, we have posted a few sample itineraries at www.WaggonerGuide.com/Itineraries. Start laying out a day on each line with a few notes. There may be some special events such as the Saturday Market in Ganges, or the world-famous fireworks at Butchart Gardens. Your schedule may shift, so remain flexible. A 90-mile day of cruising may be too much, or a passage may miss slack at one of the tidal rapids.

At the Waggoner Guide, we like to start our itinerary with the "knowns" in place. For example, if we were planning a trip north to Desolation Sound, the Broughtons or Southeast Alaska and leaving from Anacortes, we know to plan for clearing Canadian Customs. We have three basic choices for clearance, heading north to Sidney, Bedwell Harbour, or Nanaimo. Nexus, i68 and Canpass holders will have many more options to clear customs if the entire crew is registered in the programs.

Timing Dependencies. Typically we cross over to the Canadian Gulf Islands and work our way north through the protected waters of the islands. We then look at the times of slack water for Dodd Narrows, near Nanaimo. We record the time of morning and afternoon slack in our itinerary and then determine the approximate time and point of departure. It is a long day's cruise from Anacortes to Nanaimo at a cruise speed of 7-9 knots. If slack at Dodd Narrows is at noon, we probably will not be able to get there in time, especially if we need to allow nearly an hour to clear Canadian Customs in Bedwell Harbour. Instead we may elect to stay a day in the Gulf Islands and catch the morning slack at Dodd Narrows the following day, or plan for the evening slack and get to Nanaimo at around 7:00 p.m. This is where the different choices come into play. If you cannot get to Dodd Narrows in time, you can save an hour by planning to clear Canadian Customs in Nanaimo. This option would eliminate the stop at Bedwell Harbour (Poets Cove) and require an arrival at the Nanaimo Canadian Customs dock well before the closing time of 5:00 p.m. in the summers (4:30 p.m. in the off-season).

Why stop in Nanaimo? It is a good jumping off point for heading north to Campbell River or crossing over to the Sunshine Coast. The weather is typically better in the early morning when winds should be lighter. You can make the open water crossing before afternoon winds kick up. Nanaimo is also a good provisioning point. Markets and liquor stores near the marina allow you to stock up on food items that may have been restricted when clearing Canadian Customs.

There are other options you can build into the plan. When leaving from Seattle, you may need to allow a day to reach the Anacortes area or the San Juan Islands. Stopping in historic Roche Harbor or Friday Harbor may be a crew member's request. However, it may make more sense to save this stop for the return trip from Canada since both locations are a U.S. Customs Port of Entry.

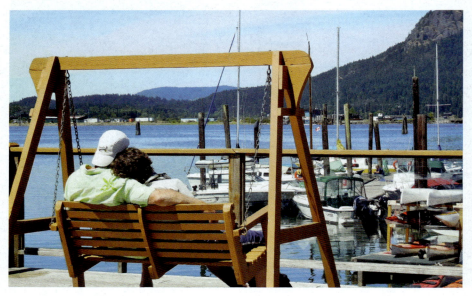

NORDHAVN
Oceans Apart from the Rest

After almost six million documented ocean miles, no production motor yacht or any other builders' motoryachts combined can come close to matching the incredible accomplishments of our Nordhavns. Consider the following facts;

- Over 150 Nordhavns have successfully crossed the Atlantic, Pacific and/or the Indian Ocean
- Ten Nordhavns have successfully circumnavigated the world
- Four Nordhavns have rounded Cape Horn – multiple times
- A Nordhavn 40 holds the world record for the fastest circumnavigation by a production power boat of any size
- A Nordhavn 68 has traveled further North than any private production motoryacht – to 81 degrees - 27 minutes north
- A Nordhavn 57 has transited the Northwest Passage from East to West
- South Georgia Island has been visited by only one production powerboat – a Nordhavn 63

- *RELIANCE*, a Nordhavn 76, has visited the continent of Antarctica
- The largest fleet of production power boats to cross the Atlantic in convoy – not once or twice but three times
- Dozens of north - south transits of the South China sea
- Dozens of east - west Mediterranean transits
- At least three Australian circumnavigations

If you dream of safe and comfortable worldwide Adventure Cruising without limitation, you will conclude, as have the world's most accomplished cruisers, there simply is no better choice than a Nordhavn.

Please visit Nordhavn.com for a detailed overview of why Nordhavn is "Oceans Apart from the Rest".

For information, visit nordhavn.com or contact us at info@nordhavn.com

Visit Nordhavn Yachts in Seattle at 2601 W. Marina Place, Suite S, or call 206-223-3624.

Provisioning Your Boat for a Well Fed and Happy Crew

Good food on board is a big part of the cruising experience. Having that perfect meal surrounded by magnificent scenery is part of what makes our boating lifestyle with significant others, family and friends so special. It is a fine balance between meals that are fun to prepare and keeping life and chores on board simple.

A few questions to start. How long is your cruise plan? Looking at an itinerary roughly how many nights will you be dining on board versus eating at many of the very good restaurants along the way? Do you have anyone on your crew who has special food needs, is a vegetarian, needs glutenfree or likes milk in their coffee? Fat-free milk or whole milk? Does anyone on the crew have any allergies, or food items they like everyday. You can see where this is going. If you are doing the cooking - how much work do you want to do? Pancakes in the morning or frozen waffles? It begs the question - do you have maple syrup on board? Or, do you like to sleep in and leave breakfast items out for crew and guests to help themselves.

Are you headed to Canada, or from Canada into the U.S.? Will you need to purchase some items once you get into Canada due to border restrictions.

How much space do you have in your refrigerator or on-board freezer? Do you have a refrigerator or are you working from a cooler with ice. Your menu planning will change based on what foods you can store safely.

Headed up to the Broughtons? Be prepared to have your favorite dish to share for pot luck Happy Hours. Sometimes they are full meals and sometimes they are appetizer Happy Hours with finger foods. Hopefully you have a few recipes that are quick and easy to prepare. My favorite item is a supersize box with six packages of rich brownie mix. I make it more indulgent with chocolate chips, cream cheese and butter. It is quick, easy and I have never come back to the boat with anything left on the plate. Not even a crumb. I carry lots of cream cheese on the boat and can quickly mix in smoked salmon or a spice mix to make a quick dip for crackers or chips.

Wine, beer, spirits for mixed drinks - don't forget the mixers. A warm day in the islands on Taco Tuesday begs for a margarita or a cold Corona. Stock what you need, being mindful of the limits imposed by Customs on either side of the border.

Make up your list. Indicate whether you should buy items in Canada or the U.S. depending on which direction you are headed across the border. Depending on the exchange rate, prices may appear lower in Canada but sometimes the price with tax is equal or more. Liquor is generally more expensive in Canada due to the taxes imposed. The selection of wines at retail is better in the U.S. and maybe you should just pay the duty of 90% of the value for a selection of good wines for your vacation cruise – that's right - almost double. Luckily many customs agents will average the value of your wine low when calculating the duty. Let them come up with a value. You can have a list of what is on board; but in reality, it is very hard to value liquor coming into the country. You will be surprised that an agent's estimate is probably lower than you might think.

Do not try to sneak extra alcohol into either country. We have seen too many bottles of very good liquor confiscated because the boater was not honest. Agents seem to be looking for liquor more than anything else. The irony is the laws go back to a period where the thinking was that one might be smuggling liquor into the country to sell for income, denying the country of duty and tax.

Don't forget the incidentals. A charcoal grill - needs charcoal and lighter fluid. Is your grill gas, do you need a supply of propane tanks? When cruising, you need to be self-sufficient. You do not have the ability to jump in the car and head to the store to purchase that missing ingredient or favorite food item. You could be a week or ten days between major grocery markets.

Pre-packaged Portions. One of our instructors and an excellent cook, Lynette Brower, likes to pre-prepare foods and place them into plastic bags for a complete meal. She keeps freezer bags filled with chicken or steaks broken down into portions for dinners. When she has guests, out come two bags. Often she will store the spices inside the bag along with the food item. By planning ahead with pre-packaged meals, time is saved and entertaining becomes more enjoyable.

Get rid of un-necessary packaging. Is your boat limited on storage space for food or perishables? Consider removing food from boxes and bulky packaging. Mark the inner bag with a Sharpie. If it is a mix for preparation, cut the cooking directions from the box and tape it to the bag. Getting rid of the packaging before items are stored on your boat carries an additional benefit. Once north of Desolation Sound, getting rid of trash is a challenge and an expense. Many resorts charge by the bag or the pound to take your trash. Sometimes the trash needs to be stored for several days in a warm lazerette before it can be responsibly disposed. Getting rid of un-necessary packaging helps reduce trash.

Use plastic bins. A good system is to store dry food items in plastic bins sized to fit into the cabinets in the galley. They can be segmented for how they are used. I have a bin for baking ingredients such as flour, sugar, baking soda and baking powder. The bin keeps the mess contained and supplies at-hand when doing a baking project. Bins keep canned goods from sliding around in rough seas and can be safely stowed.

Don't overstock. In our experience, most people over stock their boats with food. It must be a comfort factor. There are plenty of places to purchase food items on the Inside Passage. Even the smallest marina markets try to support their guests with a means of purchasing food items and sometimes even fresh produce. We have not heard of anyone starving while out on a summer cruise. If anything, they come back refreshed and maybe even a pound or two content.

Keep it fun. Lastly, consider who is doing the cooking and cleaning up on your boat. It should not be the same person. This is a vacation in northwest paradise. Keep it light, keep it fun - and no galley slaves.

How To Catch Dinner

If you love to eat salmon, halibut, rockfish, crab or prawns - you are boating in the right place.

Crabbing is inexpensive and fun for even an inexperienced crew. Crabbing gear is relatively easy to purchase at a few hundred dollars, but the costs go up from there. Catching prawns can be more costly if you purchase a pot puller to pull the weighted traps up from 250-300 feet deep. A license is required in both the State of Washington and British Columbia for fish, prawns and crab. Sporting goods stores in the U.S. sell fishing licenses. You can purchase the different levels of fishing licenses for B.C. online and print out your own fishing license. See http://www.fishing.gov.bc.ca/ for more information.

Investing in Gear. Many have outfitted their boats or dinghies to target salmon with all the best equipment, spending thousands of dollars for down riggers, trolling motors, special rods, reels, lures and a fishfinder. Some salmon fishing fanatics even tow a special boat set up to catch salmon. There is a lot of money invested and don't dare ask how much the investment totals compared to the cost of buying quality salmon at the market.

Charter fishing. At the Waggoner Guide, we love to fish, or to put it more directly, we love to "catch" fish. Rather than investing a fortune "gearing up" to fish, we have gotten into the practice of hiring an expert with all the right equipment and going charter fishing for salmon or halibut once or twice a summer. The experts know their local waters, where the fish are and how to fish. We nearly always fill our freezer with as much fish as we can handle and have a lot of fun.

Guests. We typically treat our guests to a fishing expedition in the Johnstone Strait areas, the Broughtons, Northern B.C. or in Southeast Alaska. A half-day charter will often do it; and with a good guide and good conditions, we limit out within the half-day charter and fill the freezer. We have also found it is best to ask the charter captain when to fish. Many start out the day early in the morning. We have also had excellent results when our charter captain suggested fishing on the evening change of tide.

Fishing licenses and gear. Your charter captain can conveniently issue fishing licenses for the charter. He or she, has all the gear and fresh bait. They know what they are doing and where the fish are biting. You just show up and pay - much less than if you invested in all of the gear yourself. Depending on the location, the charter captain also knows where to take the fish to be processed, flash frozen and stored in the freezer to be shipped home, where you can accept the shipment even a few weeks later. For guests this is critical. The shipping is not inexpensive and is guaranteed. The overall cost per pound is still under the cost of good quality salmon.

Finding a good charter. Ask around at the marinas you will be visiting. They know the good local fishing guides. You may want to book a charter well in advance of your stay at a marina. When the bite is on, reservations with the best charter captains fill up quickly. The charter captains will often pick you up at your marina or even at your boat on the hook at an anchorage with a fast boat to quickly get you to the best fishing spots in the area. Most charter captains I have fished with take real pride in finding fish and helping you land them on the boat. They want you to catch fish, take them home, and tell your friends!

Catching fish without fishing. There is another technique we have found to catch fish without even dropping a hook in the water. It all starts with being nice to people. Most fisherman catch more fish than they can use. We have seen some excellent techniques among

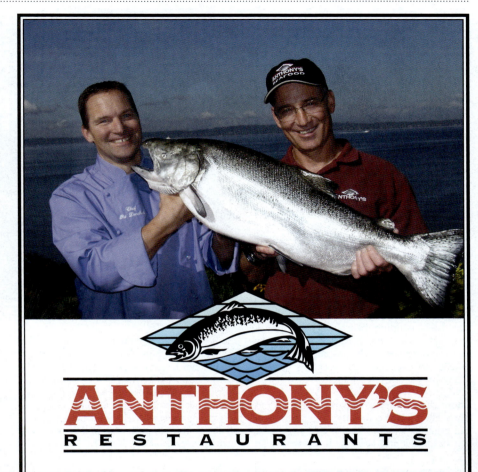

ANTHONY'S RESTAURANTS

You're on the Water, and so is Anthony's!

Waterfront dining on the Puget Sound from Olympia to Bellingham and throughout the Northwest!

Anthony's opened our own seafood company in 1984 for the sole purpose of ensuring our guests only the highest quality northwest seafood. Complementing our seafood, Anthony's family-owned restaurants offer fresh seasonal produce from local farms, local microbrews and Northwest wines, enhanced with backdrops of scenic Puget Sound locations.

If you're cruising in Puget Sound, bring the crew ashore at your nearest Anthony's. Visit our website for guest moorage information and reservations.

www.anthonys.com

PROVISIONING YOUR BOAT FOR A WELL FED AND HAPPY CREW

pleasure boaters to catch fish with fresh baked bread, cookies and pies carried down a dock full of commercial fishing boats during the season, offering a trade. Many guys use the traditional technique of walking down the dock with a six pack of beer or a 20 dollar bill which usually lands a catch. The fresh bakery technique seems to work equally well if not better.

Be nice. One late afternoon, we saw a tribal fishing boat and crew headed towards the fuel dock in Shearwater B.C. about to pass by. We waved and let them go first, acknowledging that they were working. When we reached the fuel dock, one of the crew walked over to say hello and asked us if we would like to have a salmon. You bet. Conversely, one day we could not get our last salmon from a charter into the freezer. We had passed some friends who had just arrived on their boat. We walked back and asked if they wanted a fresh fillet for dinner. They looked at the large deep orange fillet from a 24 pound King salmon and were flabbergasted, almost speechless, nodding their heads. The offer of fresh salmon can do that to you. They have never forgotten the gesture and mention it whenever we see them. It feels pretty good to share the gift of fresh salmon.

Share the bounty or freeze It. It is easy to catch a trap full of crab and giving away a few can bring new found friends. Otherwise crab can be frozen and keeps well, up to a year.

Local markets are great places to pick up fresh fruit and vegetables after crossing the border.

Some folks will cook their crab, clean the meat out of the shell, and then pack it in freezer bags or vacuum bags with clean seawater or milk. This method saves room in the freezer. When you are ready, defrost and squeeze the excess liquid out of the meat. Freezing in milk or seawater also works well for uncooked prawns. It keeps the meat from breaking down and getting freezer burn.

Fishing, catching and fresh seafood are part of the northwest cruising experience. While much of your catch may end up frozen for later, fresh fish, prawns and crab, consumed just an hour or two after coming out of the water is about as good as it gets. You don't have to have all of the expensive gear and licenses. You can catch fish in a variety of innovative ways with just a little imagination and respect.

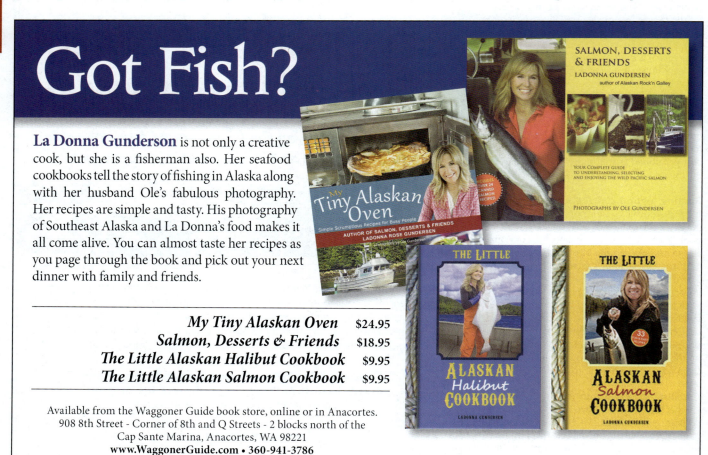

Got Fish?

La Donna Gunderson is not only a creative cook, but she is a fisherman also. Her seafood cookbooks tell the story of fishing in Alaska along with her husband Ole's fabulous photography. Her recipes are simple and tasty. His photography of Southeast Alaska and La Donna's food makes it all come alive. You can almost taste her recipes as you page through the book and pick out your next dinner with family and friends.

My Tiny Alaskan Oven	$24.95
Salmon, Desserts & Friends	$18.95
The Little Alaskan Halibut Cookbook	$9.95
The Little Alaskan Salmon Cookbook	$9.95

Available from the Waggoner Guide book store, online or in Anacortes.
908 8th Street - Corner of 8th and Q Streets - 2 blocks north of the
Cap Sante Marina, Anacortes, WA 98221
www.WaggonerGuide.com • 360-941-3786

POTABLE WATER, CAN I DRINK IT?

"Is your water potable?" That's often one of the first questions boaters ask marinas when cruising Northern BC Coast, the Broughton Archipelago and sometimes even in the Gulf Islands. Boaters often find a 'boil water' notice or 'not-potable' sign at water spigots and hose-bibs on the docks. But what does this mean to boaters and why has this sign been posted?

What is not-potable water?
These notices indicate that the marina's private water system has not been certified by the Health Department as a public water system. Establishing a water system as a certified public water supply is an extensive and costly process, often not justifiable at remote, small marinas. Sometimes it requires a process for purification and exposure to UV light to kill certain bacteria. Sometimes the water is good and just needs to be tested regularly and sent in for certification. Water from private water systems may or may not be tested regularly but is used routinely, and may have been used for years with no ill effects. Remote resort locations like Pierre's Echo Bay Resort & Marina have been using the same well water for years with no ill effects. The hose bibs are marked non-potable and boil first, the water does have a slight brown tinge, but no one has reported problems with the water.

If other than owners are using or consuming water from a non-certified water system, the Government requires that a non-potable or boil notice be posted. The sign doesn't mean that the water is bad, but rather serves to inform guest users of the water source and allow the guest user to make a choice or further inquiries.

As boaters, what do we do with this information?
Depending on your comfort level, there are several options for non-potable water:

Simply don't use the marina water, use only the water from your onboard tank.

Do your own checking – ask locals if they regularly use the water for household needs. After your evaluation, you may choose to use the local source.

Before your trip, you may wish to purchase a 3-stage water filter (the third stage needs to be a ceramic filter) and use this filter system to filter the marina water when filling your tank.

If you have a watermaker onboard, you may wish to use your own established procedures for making water and filling or re-filling your onboard tank.

Another option is to sanitize the marina water put in your tank with a chemical additive. You will need to research and purchase these additives before your trip.

Lastly, installing filters and a UV light sanitizing system to your onboard water system will ensure you have safe water no matter where you fill your water tank.

What is the brown color in the water?
Additionally, boaters may have discovered that a few water sources on Northern BC Coast and in the Broughtons have a slight tannin or brown color to the water. While the water may be potable and not harmful, it certainly can be unappealing. Nature has its own filtration system that sometimes picks up coloring from cedar roots which result in the weak tea appearance to the water. This is an isolated issue, and nearly all of the marinas and water sources in the area have clear water.

In summary, small outlying marinas provide a surprising number of amenities for boaters, including acceptable sources of water. During their short business season, it's amazing what they can and do provide for the boating community. We encourage boaters to let them know how much we appreciate their facilities.
~*The Waggoner Cruising Guide Team*

Unmatched...

Availability - Each unit is backed by our Global Network of more than 300 Dealers and Distributors

Reliability - Produced with Highest Quality of Parts, coupled with Manufacturing Excellence

Serviceability - Delivered from Intuitive Controller with Remote Mountable 7" Color Screen

Maintainability - Achieved with Ease and Speed, allowing you to Conquer the Ocean or your next adventure with carefree, endless source of safe water on board.

Visit us at: www.SeaRecovery.com

INTERPRETING NORTHWEST WEATHER

Weather is one of the biggest fears of many boat crews. There is a lot of information available if you know how to understand it and make effective go or no-go decisions.

Weather on the Internet, Cell Phone and VHF WX. At the Waggoner Guide we have developed a means of using all of the weather information available to avoid getting into an uncomfortable situation. Many don't realize how you can use the internet to gather a good picture of the weather. No internet available? If you have cell phone coverage you can use a cell phone to call for weather and buoy reports. Out in a very remote area? If you have VHF WX coverage, you can gather the right information you need over the radio, it just takes a little bit more effort. In remote areas of Haida Gwaii and Northern B.C., you can use satellite based systems such as Garmin InReach, Iridium Go, and Globalstar Sat-Fi to access weather information. There is a description of this system in the Cellular Internet and Satellite Communications section of this chapter.

Weather Overview. First, we start using the internet to view weather information days before our intended departure. We use the internet to look at the weather patterns as they develop and cross the Pacific Ocean. We use the NOAA Ocean Prediction Center, Pacific Region, Current Surface Analysis and then the 24, 48, and 96 hour forecast. We look at the High and Low pressure systems and how they are forecast to move typically from west to east. While this is offshore weather, it provides an indication of the weather systems that will pass over Puget Sound and the Inside Passage. Often in July and leading into August a large high pressure system will sit offshore resulting in very good weather for an extended period of time. This is called the Pacific High and typically offers favorable conditions.

Next, we look at the isobar lines over the coastal areas where we will be cruising. The isobar lines show the change in barometric pressure over a distance. Tighter isobar

56 www.WaggonerGuide.com

INTERPRETING NORTHWEST WEATHER

patterns show areas of wind and its counter-clockwise direction around a low. We look for areas of big lazy (widely separated) isobars around a high indicating limited wind. Looking at the weather charts gives us a visual overview of the weather and which systems will be affecting our route over the next couple of days. Even if we do not have access to the internet while enroute for a few days, we have the overview.

To add to the overview, we look at one of the new visual services on the internet at www.windy.com. This web site puts the weather prediction models into motion where you can see the wind patterns circulating and how they flow across the Pacific. You can also see a visual of the offshore wind conditions. Another popular weather app for mariners is Predict Wind. It too presents a lot of visual information when an internet connection is available.

The Forecast. We then look at the NOAA Marine Forecasts for US waters, and when traveling north into British Columbia we look at the Environment Canada reports and forecasts. We compare the forecast in text format with the NOAA Surface Analysis charts. They should coincide. Even the 48-hour forecast should coincide with the forecast results. We take notes and start worksheets for the upcoming days.

We have developed a weather worksheet we use for recording the information from the internet, phone, and VHF broadcasts while underway. You can download this worksheet at www.WaggonerGuide.com/weatherworksheet. Modify it as you see fit.

Weather Reporting Stations. We note the four weather reporting stations from the maps on page 56-57 along our route for a day and record them on our worksheet. Next, we gather the weather reports for those points from either the internet, by calling on a cell phone to the numbers shown on the weather maps, or by listening on the WX VHF. The list of weather reporting stations we need, keeps us focused on what stations we care to record when it is in a continuous audio format on either the phone or VHF WX. When we listen to the WX channels for our area, we listen for those places along our route. On the back of the weather sheet is the outline of the Continuous Marine Broadcasts for the U.S. and Canada. They are different. You can use this to determine where you are in the sequence of a WX broadcast.

We write down the synopsis for the area. Next, we record the relevant station reports and then the lighthouse and buoy reports for our route with particular attention to the reported wind direction, speed and sea condition.

Check the Tides and Currents. Next, we look up in a Tide and Current Guide to determine whether we will be cruising with a Flood or an Ebb current, and the time of slack. This will be useful to understanding the sea state as the day continues over our route. We are looking to be aware or avoid wind

Current Surface Analysis Chart for September 16, 2016 shows High Pressure over the area from Seattle up through the Strait of Georgia. The big lazy isobar lines indicate light wind. Note how this lines up with both the U.S. and Canadian text forecasts on the next page.

On the 24-Hour Surface Forecast we can see the low moving in from offshore and the isobars bunching up tighter. The text forecast shows the wind and waves picking up as the low comes ashore on Saturday through Saturday night. You can use this to make a go or no-go decision. From this you can see that it would be best to go north on Friday. If you cannot leave then you should most likely wait until Sunday.

For the 48-Hour Surface Forecast you can see how another low is coming in for a forecast of 2 ft. seas. Tuesday's forecast returns to about 1 ft. seas.

INTERPRETING NORTHWEST WEATHER

```
National Weather Service Marine Forecast FZUS56 KSEW

FZUS56 KSEW 160957
CWFSEW

COASTAL WATERS FORECAST FOR WASHINGTON
NATIONAL WEATHER SERVICE SEATTLE WA
300 AM PDT FRI SEP 16 2016

INLAND WATERS OF WESTERN WASHINGTON AND THE NORTHERN AND CENTRAL
WASHINGTON COASTAL WATERS INCLUDING THE OLYMPIC COAST NATIONAL
MARINE SANCTUARY

PZZ100-161615-
300 AM PDT FRI SEP 16 2016

.SYNOPSIS FOR THE NORTHERN AND CENTRAL WASHINGTON COASTAL AND INLAND
WATERS...LIGHT ONSHORE FLOW CONTINUING TODAY. A COLD FRONT WILL
APPROACH THE WASHINGTON COASTAL WATERS FROM THE NW TONIGHT AND MOVE
THROUGH THE AREA DURING THE DAY SATURDAY FOR INCREASED ONSHORE FLOW.
A SURFACE TROUGH WILL MOVE ACROSS THE AREA ON SUNDAY. WEAK ONSHORE
FLOW WILL DEVELOP ON MONDAY AND CONTINUE INTO TUESDAY.
```

```
PZZ150-161615-
COASTAL WATERS FROM CAPE FLATTERY TO JAMES ISLAND OUT 10 NM-
300 AM PDT FRI SEP 16 2016

TODAY
N WIND TO 10 KT...BECOMING SW IN THE AFTERNOON. WIND WAVES
1 FT. W SWELL 3 FT AT 10 SECONDS.

TONIGHT
SW WIND 5 TO 15 KT...BECOMING S 10 TO 20 KT AFTER
MIDNIGHT. WIND WAVES 1 TO 3 FT. W SWELL 4 FT AT 9 SECONDS. RAIN
LIKELY IN THE EVENING...THEN RAIN AFTER MIDNIGHT.

SAT
S WIND 15 TO 25 KT...BECOMING SW 5 TO 15 KT IN THE
AFTERNOON. WIND WAVES 2 TO 4 FT. W SWELL 5 FT AT 8 SECONDS. RAIN
LIKELY IN THE MORNING...THEN A CHANCE OF RAIN IN THE AFTERNOON.
```

National Weather Service Forecast Synopsis for Northern Waters

```
PZZ133-161615-
NORTHERN INLAND WATERS INCLUDING THE SAN JUAN ISLANDS-
300 AM PDT FRI SEP 16 2016

TODAY
LIGHT WIND...BECOMING S 10 TO 15 KT IN THE AFTERNOON. WIND
WAVES 1 FT OR LESS.

TONIGHT
S WIND 5 TO 15 KT. WIND WAVES 2 FT OR LESS. A CHANCE OF
RAIN IN THE EVENING...THEN RAIN AFTER MIDNIGHT.

SAT
SE WIND 10 TO 20 KT...RISING TO 15 TO 25 KT IN THE
AFTERNOON. WIND WAVES 2 TO 4 FT. RAIN IN THE MORNING...THEN RAIN
LIKELY IN THE AFTERNOON.

SAT NIGHT
S WIND 5 TO 15 KT. WIND WAVES 2 FT OR LESS.

SUN
SW WIND TO 10 KT. WIND WAVES 1 FT OR LESS.

SUN NIGHT
SW WIND 5 TO 15 KT...BECOMING S AFTER MIDNIGHT. WIND
WAVES 2 FT OR LESS.

MON
SE WIND 5 TO 15 KT...BECOMING SW. WIND WAVES 2 FT OR LESS.

TUE
SW WIND TO 10 KT. WIND WAVES 1 FT OR LESS.
```

National Weather Service Summary Forecast for Northern Waters

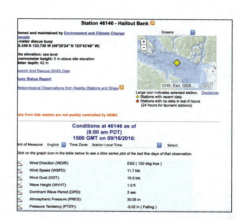

The Halibut Bank - Buoy Report shows actual conditions on Friday, September 16th with wave heights of 1 foot or less. A DPD of 3 seconds gives you a warning of a light chop.

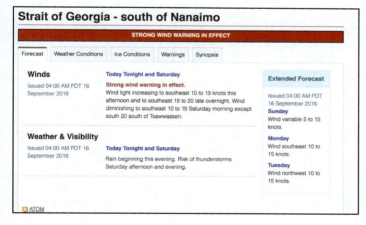

Environment Canada Forecast for the Strait of Georgia - South of Nanaimo

opposing wave situations. This information is not included in a weather forecast and must be understood by the mariner using a tide and current guide or software to understand the sea state. Rather than just a go or no-go situation, we may see that it is best to delay a departure for a couple of hours to experience a different current situation. Lastly, we can see where we are in the lunar cycle by looking up the phase of the moon in the Tide and Current guide. A full moon or a new moon means tides and currents will be at their strongest, and slack will be very short for tidal rapids.

Once all this information is gathered, you have the information to develop a pretty good picture of the weather for your departure and route for the day. You will understand where the weather systems are and the resulting conditions for your route.

You will know areas of wind, you can check to see if there will be wind opposing a current and determine your strategy. You can see if the forecast matches the conditions reported in a lighthouse or buoy report. If the forecast does not match, beware.

Your Tolerances. Next is comparing the weather conditions to your tolerances for your vessel and especially for your crew. For crossing the Strait of Georgia or Cape Caution, you can look to see if you have an opposing, beam-to, or following sea. This may change your go or no-go tolerances or the direction on your route.

Gather the information described above and there should not be too many surprises while underway, though mother nature is known to shift plans. Having a Plan B or duck-in point if things change is a good idea.

Logging Actual Conditions. At regular intervals along your planned route, make log entries noting the winds and sea conditions you encounter. Record how your boat handled the different seas. Reviewing these log entries over time will help develop your personal go or no-go thresholds for future planning.

Planned vs Actual. After arriving at your destination, review your log of actual conditions encountered along your route to help develop experience with the forecasting tools. This will help with future planning, for example, what a forecast of 15 to 20 knot winds felt like and how your vessel handled in five to six foot seas with a Dominant Wave Period (interval) of 12-15 seconds, most likely a rolling swell.

For a better understanding of weather. Consider learning more and taking a weather course. The Waggoner Guide and our Seattle Boat Show University or Cruisers College programs offer a few different courses with weather experts, from 3-hour seminars to multi-day courses. Understanding the weather is a fascinating part of boating. The rewards when you do it right are substantial for you and your crew.

Running in Fog

Fog is an unavoidable reality of summer weather in the Northwest and on the British Columbia coast. On the Strait of Juan de Fuca, Vancouver Island's west coast, Johnstone Strait, Queen Charlotte Strait and Sound, and the Central Coast, you can pretty much depend on encountering fog almost daily from mid-July through September and sometimes much later in the season. So learning to navigate safely in "low viz" is critical.

The American Meteorological Society's *Glossary of Meteorology* defines fog as a collection of water droplets suspended in the atmosphere near the earth's surface that affects visibility. In temperate coastal areas like ours, fog results when warm air cools as it passes over cold water, which causes water vapor to condense and saturate the air. Fog may form in the evening, overnight or early-morning hours, then dissipate as the day warms. It may start sneaking over the trees into your anchorage near the end of cocktail hour – and you know you will wake up to pea soup.

When you do – and you will if you venture far from Puget Sound or the Strait of Georgia – here are some thoughts to help you prepare for your next "low-viz" passage.

Go or no-go? Should you set out in poor visibility in the first place? If you don't really have to go, don't. Running in fog is a stress-inducing business that can take the fun out of cruising and it can be dangerous. The wisest course may be to wait for the fog to burn off, as it always does sooner or later.

In weighing a decision to run in fog, consider how well you know the waters you'll be navigating – a run through home water is a completely different challenge from transiting an area for the first time. Are the waters you'll navigate unobstructed – or encumbered with hazards that radar may not help you avoid? How much vessel traffic – big and small – might you encounter? High-traffic areas of Puget Sound, the Strait of Georgia and the Inside Passage are subject to vessel traffic management systems. Do you know how to listen for VTS operators' instructions to mariners around you and call them for guidance?

Make a Plan B. Where will you go if it becomes too risky to continue…or your nerves fail you? Is there a harbor en route that is clear enough to enter safely even if you can't see a thing?

And consider this: if you cruise long enough and seriously enough you will probably have to run in fog someday. If you can do it safely, why not try? It can be a tremendous learning opportunity and confidence-booster.

Slow down. This sounds obvious – but some boaters have trouble doing this under any conditions. Reducing your speed increases the amount of time you have to spot obstacles, hazards or vessels and take evasive action. If you hit something at reduced speed it will do less damage and hopefully you will avoid catastrophic damage.

Trust your equipment. It goes without saying that you should have complete confidence in your navigation suite – plotter, sounder, radar, AIS and, yes, paper charts – you should know how to use them and know their limitations. We rely on sight to orient ourselves in space and find our way. Deprive us of visual cues and we veer off course or ramble in circles, still convinced we're on course. But magnetic compasses have helped mariners for centuries, so trust yours. Better yet, the electronic compass built into your vessel's autopilot is even more accurate and enables your pilot to steer a precise course for hours or days, freeing you to keep a closer watch.

Radar paints a clear picture of your surroundings, *as long you know how to read it*. It's a good habit to run with radar even in clear conditions so you can see how blips and images appear on screen in relation to vessels and objects around you while you can still see them. Add an AIS receiver/transceiver and you'll have a clear, precise reading of the course, speed and size of vessels you may not be able to see, especially the big, fast-moving ones.

However, it is the modern chartplotter running reliable electronic charts that brings safe passages in low visibility within reach of recreational mariners. Zoomed in to an appropriate level, a good plotter enables you to accurately pinpoint hazards you can't see and find safe water through them. (Remember: not all obstacles on all charts are depicted precisely, so a margin of error is prudent!). Set your radar range to the same scale as your plotter – or overlay it on the plotter if you can – so you can match charted features with radar for a clearer picture of your surroundings. Three-dimensional charts that show bathymetric data are better still. Use your plotter's predicted track feature to point your way past hazards.

Finally, use your VHF radio. Commercial vessels routinely broadcast their approach to points or channels which may bring them close to other traffic, so monitor Channel 16 and VTS channels. Follow their example and announce your intentions when you enter waters where you may meet other vessels; invite concerned craft to respond. If you spot a converging target on radar, call them to determine their intentions and discuss how to pass or cross safely.

Listen and look carefully. There is still a place for our own sharpened senses when we think we can't see diddly. In steamship days, skippers and pilots used to blow a whistle and listen for the time it took for echoes to return in order to determine their distance from shore. It makes sense to throttle back from time to time. Step on deck and listen for whatever you might hear: a horn, voices, a nearby outboard, birds calling, the lap of waves against the shoreline, the low thrum of really big engines…or nothing at all.

In restricted visibility, Collision Regulations require you to sound a single prolonged (four to six seconds) horn blast every two minutes if you are under way, and two prolonged blasts if you are stopped. Sound carries well across still water and in fog and sends a clear message to anyone around. Don't forget to use your nose, as well. Water smells different than land, the odor of guano may tip you off to a seabird colony on an isolated rock, a whiff of engine exhaust may warn you of vessels nearby.

Even when you're sure you can't see a thing, you often still can – if you look hard enough. Have your crew keep an intent bow watch for *anything* you may not see from the helm. Step outside and look around carefully yourself. The white hull of that lone sport fisher rolling in the chop may appear so faintly you aren't sure it's there. Or the superstructure of a container ship or ferry may float serenely through the top layer of the mist…and, hopefully, it won't be too close.

– *Duart Snow*

Buoys, Beacons and Ranges

Red, Right, Returning means leave **Red** navigation aids off your **Right** hand when you're **Returning** from seaward. If the navigation mark is not red, leave it off your left hand when you're returning from seaward.

This is the general rule in U.S. and Canadian waters, with three subtle refinements:

- Safe water mark. A buoy with red and white vertical stripes that marks an approach or mid-channel. Unobstructed water surrounds this mark. Both inbound and outbound, it is good practice to leave this buoy to port.
- Preferred channel mark. A buoy or a beacon with red and green horizontal bands. This aid marks a channel junction or an obstruction. While the aid can be passed on either side, the color of the top band indicates the preferred or main channel.
- Isolated danger mark. An aid—either a buoy or a beacon—with black and red horizontal bands that marks an isolated danger (an example would be the Blakely Island Shoal Isolated Danger Buoy DS, west of Blakely Island in the San Juan Islands). These marks have navigable water all around, but should not be approached closely without caution.

Nuns. All red buoys marking channels are shaped as cones, and are called nuns. Most nun buoys are painted solid red. If the nun buoy has a green horizontal band painted on it, the buoy marks the meeting of two channels, with the left channel being the preferred, or main, channel. (If you leave the buoy to starboard, you will be in the left channel.) If lighted, the light will be red.

Cans. All green buoys marking channels are called cans. They are shaped like, well, *cans*. Most can buoys are painted solid green. If the can buoy has a horizontal red band painted on it, the buoy marks the meeting of two channels, with the right channel the preferred, or main channel. If lighted, the light will be green.

Beacons. Buoys float, and are held in place by heavy anchoring systems, but beacons are permanent navigation aids attached to the earth. Beacons can be located on land, installed on docks or breakwaters, or mounted on pilings. A lighthouse is a beacon. A beacon not on land will be placed in shallow water outside a channel. *Do not pass a beacon close aboard.* Give it considerable room.

An unlighted beacon is called a **daybeacon.** A lighted beacon is called a **minor light.** A minor light marking the right side of a channel will carry a red light (Red, Right, Returning). A minor light marking the left side of a channel will carry a green light. If a minor light marks the meeting of two channels, it will be red if the left channel is preferred; green if the right channel is preferred.

Daymarks are the colored panels mounted on beacons. Red panels are triangle shaped; green panels are square. A triangle shaped red panel with a green horizontal stripe indicates the meeting of two channels, with the left channel the preferred, or main channel. A square panel painted green with a red horizontal stripe indicates the meeting of two channels, with the right channel the preferred channel.

Whenever a navigation aid is marked with a horizontal stripe of contrasting color, the color at the top of the aid indicates the preferred, or main channel.

Approaching a channel from seaward, buoys and beacons are numbered, beginning with the marks to seaward. Red buoys, daybeacons, and minor lights carry even numbers, such as 2, 4, 6, and so on. Green buoys, daybeacons, and minor lights carry odd numbers, such as 1, 3, 5, and so on. Depending on the channel, it might be appropriate to skip some numbers, so that buoy 6 is roughly opposite buoy 5, even if no buoy 4 exists.

Ranges. Ranges are used to help a boat stay in the middle of a narrow channel.

Ranges are rectangular panels stood vertically, each with a wide stripe running from top to bottom down the middle of the panel. Ranges are attached to the earth and arranged in pairs, one behind the other. The rear range board stands taller than the front range board. To use a range, steer until the rear range board appears to be on top of the front board. You can steer toward a range, looking ahead (leading range), or away from a range, sighting astern (back range).

Buoys and beacons are not selected and placed at random. They follow a plan, although to a newcomer the plan may at times seem obscure.

Despite the complexity of the buoyage and light system, you will find that as you understand it better your enjoyment afloat will increase. At some point you will want a thorough explanation of the entire system. For U.S. waters it will be found in the introduction to the Coast Guard Light List. For Canadian waters it will be found partly in the introduction to the Canadian Coast Guard List of Lights, Buoys and Fog Signals, and completely in the Canadian Coast Guard publication, The Canadian Aids to Navigation System. Latest editions of these publications should be aboard every boat. They are available at chart agencies and chandleries.

Red, Right Returning

Red, Right, Returning from the sea means the conical red nun buoy marks the right side of the channel. Vessels returning from the sea upstream will leave red navigation aids to starboard. Red aids are assigned even numbers, beginning with No. 2 at the seaward end of the channel.

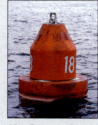

Nun Buoy

A green can buoy marks the left side of the channel. Vessels returning from the sea or upstream will leave green navigation aids to port. Green aids are assigned odd numbers, beginning with No. 1 at the seaward end of the channel. Buoys and beacons can be lighted or unlighted.

Can Buoy

A beacon, such as this light at Webster Point in Lake Washington, is attached to the earth, and should be given a good offing. Port-hand beacons carry square green dayboards; starboard-hand beacons carry red triangular dayboards.

Lighted Beacon

Cylindrical white restricted operations buoys, such as this one, mark speed zones, restricted anchoring areas, fish habitats and other important information.

Restricted Operation Buoy

2018 WAGGONER CRUISING GUIDE

Boardings

"Welcome Aboard" – may not be the first thing that comes to mind when someone in uniform steps aboard your vessel. However, if we are prepared, it's more likely that we will be ready to welcome these agents of safety and law enforcement when we are out cruising. There are a number of different agencies and agents that may board recreational vessels.

U.S. Agencies. On the U.S. side of the border, the Coast Guard (USCG) routinely boards vessels to check for compliance with required devices and safety equipment. If underway and approached by a USCG patrol vessel for boarding, the officer may want you to slow down but continue underway. They will come alongside and board while underway; however, you may choose to come to a stop. An officer will board and conduct a standard safety inspection. Their inspection includes checking for proper vessel documentation, personal floatation devices, and vessel safety equipment. The inspection takes about 15 to 30 minutes and includes a 'results form' with any deficiencies noted on the signed form. Any deficiencies noted on the form must be addressed and acknowledged by the Coast Guard. If there are no deficiencies, you will receive the same signed form noting the successful inspection. Keep this form on the vessel as it serves to waive any subsequent inspection boarding within the next 12 months.

State police, county Sheriff, city police, and port authorities have on-the-water patrol boats for safety, search and rescue, and law enforcement. Agents of these departments can and do board recreational vessels. Unlike the U.S. Coast Guard's once-a-year limit on vessel boarding, there is no limit for these other law enforcement agencies.

Retain the paperwork from a boarding, it will save you from future boardings for one year.

Canada Agencies. On the Canadian side of the border, Canadian Coast Guard does not have maritime or law enforcement responsibilities and does not perform vessel inspections. Royal Canadian Mounted Police (RCMP) and city police have law enforcement responsibilities. RCMP does not routinely board vessels for marine safety inspections.

When cruising near the U.S. and Canada international border, you may be stopped and boarded by agents of the respective border patrol (U.S. Customs and Border Patrol, and Canadian Border Services Agency). They patrol the border crossings with their high-speed boats.

While fishing, crabbing, or prawning, agents from wildlife departments from Washington, Alaska, or British Columbia may board your vessel to check for compliance with seafood-collection rules and laws.

Preparation. While there are no guarantees, responsible cruisers can reduce their chances of boarding by keeping their boats clean, orderly, and in good condition; running the boat cautiously and competently, consistent with weather and sea conditions; doing nothing that would invite closer scrutiny. A current Coast Guard Auxiliary voluntary safety inspection sticker in the window might be a help. Consider doing your own inspection before the boating season to make sure you have all of your documentation, flares and approved life jackets or PFDs, placards and other items in order. For the complete list, you can search USCG Vessel Safety Checklist on the internet and find the same list used by the Coast Guard. Expect more checks by small boats. We watched armed USCG personnel in a mid-20-foot inflatable check the boats on moorings in Fossil Bay (Sucia Island) and board one of them.

Have all required boat documentation, licenses, and other paperwork ready in the event you are boarded. It is helpful to have a folder with the most current official documents. Keep a second folder for copies of original documents in the event you need to leave a copy with an official. Record each boarding event in your log, including the agent's name and authority. These agents help keep our cruising waters safe, thank them with a smile.

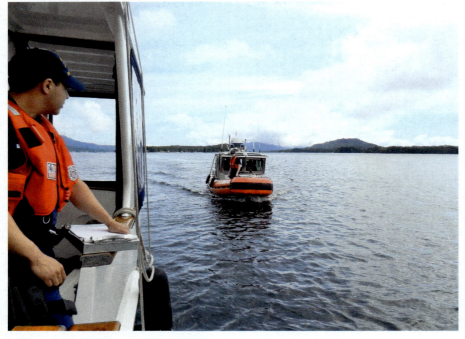

U.S. Coast Guard may want to board your vessel while remaining underway.

HOMELAND SECURITY

Here are some do's and don't's, drawn from material published by the U.S. Coast Guard and expanded upon by our own experiences.

Keep your distance from all military, cruise line or commercial shipping. For U.S. naval vessels, slow to minimum speed within 500 yards, and do not approach any U.S. naval vessel within 100 yards. Violation of the Naval Vessel Protection Zone is a felony offense. If you must pass within 100 yards of a U.S. naval vessel, you must contact the vessel or its Coast Guard escort vessel on VHF 16. The only exceptions to these requirements would be in a congested area, where there is no way to give this kind of room, or in a narrow channel, such as the mouth of the Snohomish River in Everett, which fronts on the Navy base there. In such cases, navigate slowly, predictably, and obey all instructions.

Observe and avoid all security zones. Also avoid commercial port operation areas, especially those that involve military, cruise line, or petroleum facilities. Observe and avoid other restricted areas near dams, power plants etc. Violators will face a quick, determined, and severe response. Translation: You risk being blown out of the water. The buoyed security zone protecting the Trident submarine base at Bangor, in Hood Canal, is a good example. The restricted area is patrolled by four high-speed small craft, at least two of them with impressive guns mounted on the decks. Although we give the security zone a wide berth as we go by, it is obvious that we are being watched. When we increase our speed from 8.5 knots to 16 knots one of the patrol craft will turn abruptly and run on a parallel course at our speed until we pass the far boundary. We thought about taking photos of the base with at least one of the patrol boats in view, but decided it would be prudent to motor along as predictably and innocently as possible.

Don't stop or anchor beneath bridges or in the channel. If you do, you can expect to be boarded by law enforcement officials.
Be alert for anything that looks peculiar or out of the ordinary. Report suspicious activities to local authorities, the Coast Guard, or port or marina security. Do not approach or challenge those acting in a suspicious manner. Suspicious behavior includes:

- Suspicious persons conducting unusual activities near bridges, refineries, or around high security areas on or near the water

- Individuals establishing roadside stands near marinas or other waterfront facilities

- Persons photographing or making diagrams of things such as the underside of a bridge, the area around nuclear power plants, and waterfront facilities near what might be high-risk vessels

- Unknown or suspicious persons loitering for long periods of time in waterfront areas

- Suspicious persons renting or attempting to procure or "borrow" watercraft

- Suspicious vendors attempting to sell or deliver merchandise or drop off packages in waterfront areas

Always secure and lock your boat when not on board. Do not leave your boat accessible to others. Always take the keys with you.
When storing your boat, make sure it is secure and its engine is disabled. If the boat is on a trailer, make the trailer as immovable as possible.

Be Prepared for a Vessel Boarding. Expect to see U.S. Coast Guard surveillance and vessel boardings. The physical size and geographic complexity of Northwest waters make these waters difficult to patrol and quite "porous" for vessels doing illegal things. More "assets," as the military calls them, are being deployed here.

2018 WAGGONER CRUISING GUIDE

STATE AND PROVINCIAL PARKS AND PUBLIC WHARVES

The waters from Puget Sound north into B.C. are dotted with more than 200 state, provincial, and national parks, and in B.C., more than 220 public wharves.

Washington Parks. At the state level, parks are administered by the Washington State Parks and Recreation Commission and by the Department of Natural Resources (DNR). Usually, DNR sites are on the primitive side. State parks, which tend to be more developed, charge for moorage at buoys and docks. For docks and floats, expect to pay $.70 per foot, $14 minimum. Mooring buoys are $15. The dock or buoy fee applies after 1:00 p.m., payable for even a stop-and-go visit, such as walking the dog. *Unless otherwise marked, buoys are for boats 45 feet and less; boats longer than 45 feet are not allowed.* Rafting is allowed for boats 36 feet and less. Each rafted boat must pay a moorage fee.

State parks charge moorage fees year-round. Annual moorage permits are available and valid from January 1 to December 31, $5 per foot, $60 minimum. Contact Washington State Parks Information, (360) 902-8844 (Monday through Friday), or infocent@parks.wa.gov. Or check their informative website at parks.state.wa.us/435/Boating.

Campsite fees are paid in addition to dock or mooring buoy fees. Self-register ashore for moorage or campsites.

Boat launch sites. State parks with boat launches charge fees of $7. The launch fee includes the daily parking fee. Annual launch permits cost $80 and are valid for a year from date of purchase. Contact Washington State Parks, (360) 902-8844, or from www.parks.wa.gov/boating/launch/.

Reservations. Moorage is unreserved. Leaving a dinghy or other personal property at a buoy or dock does not reserve moorage. Rafting is permitted but not mandatory. Rafting is allowed on buoys, within specified limits. Reservations (for campsites only) in all state parks are accepted. Call toll-free (888) 226-7688.

Department of Natural Resources parks generally are primitive or have few facilities, and most do not charge fees.

Washington Boater Education Card. All operators of boats with motors of 15 horsepower or more born after January 1, 1955 are required to have their Washington State Boater Education Card. Washington State Parks administers this program. See their website at http://boat.wa.gov/ or call (360) 902-8555.

If you are boating in Canadian waters for longer than 44 days a Canadian Operator Card or the equivalent issued by a state in the U.S. is required. The Washington Boater Education Card qualifies for cruising more than 44 days, as do U.S. Coast Guard licenses such as Captain's or Mate's license.

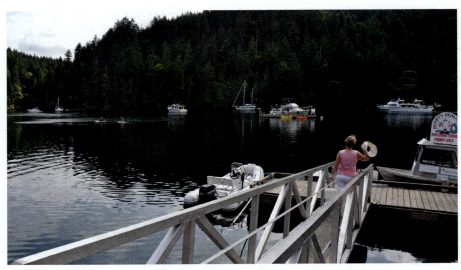
Public docks provide access to parks and islands.

Canadian Boater Pleasure Craft Operator Card (PCOC). Canada has a similar program for its boaters, requiring boater education and certification. In B.C., several firms offer classes and testing services to prove competency. A special program called "Rental Boating Safety Checklist" is for power-driven rental boats and bareboat charter boats. Consult your Canadian charter company for more information and requirements.

B.C. Parks, Including Gulf Islands National Park Reserve Parks. Most B.C. marine parks have floats or mooring buoys, and safe, all-weather anchorages. Marine parks are open year-round. Some have no on-shore facilities, others have day-use facilities, picnic areas, developed campsites. Most parks have drinking water. Overnight moorage fees ($12 for a buoy; $2/meter for dock moorage) are charged at a number of the more developed parks. No rafting is permitted on mooring buoys. No charge for anchoring, even with a stern-tie to shore. Tent sites are extra. Contact B.C. Parks General Information at www.env.gov.bc.ca/bcparks. For more information on the Gulf Islands National Park Reserve, contact (866) 944-1744 or see their website at www.pc.gc.ca. On the homepage select "Find a National Park" and select "Gulf Islands National Park Reserve."

Public Wharves. In British Columbia, public wharves provide moorage for commercial vessels (primarily the fishing fleet) and pleasure craft. Especially in the off-season, public wharves are filled with fish boats, leaving little or no moorage for pleasure craft. Facilities vary, from a dock only, to fully-serviced marinas. Most of the public wharves now are operated by local harbor authorities or their equivalents. Locally-run public wharves charge market rates, and may reserve space for pleasure craft. Moorage fees vary. Public wharves are easily identified by their red-painted railings.

NO DISCHARGE ZONES IN B.C.

Approved holding tanks are required in these areas. Macerator treatment systems, even if approved in the U.S., do not qualify. "Gray water" is not included in the regulations. It's okay to take a shower and wash dishes.

- Carrington Bay
- Cortes Bay
- Gorge Harbour
- Ladysmith Harbour
- Mansons Landing
- Montague Harbour
- Pilot Bay
- Pirates Cove (no gray)
- Prideaux Haven
- Roscoe Bay
- Smuggler Cove
- Squirrel Cove
- Tod Inlet
- Victoria Harbour

WHAT RECREATIONAL BOATERS NEED TO KNOW ABOUT VTS

Much of the information below is general in nature. It is intended to give recreational boaters a broad understanding of the Vessel Traffic Service (VTS) and how VTS can improve safety for all boats.

VTS is primarily for commercial vessels, although all power driven vessels 40 meters (131 feet) or longer, commercial or recreational, must be active participants. Active VTS participants are required to maintain radio watch on the assigned VTS channel for the waters they are in, and to call in at designated points with their location, course, speed, and estimated time of arrival (ETA) at the next call-in point. The VTS centers keep track of all active participant vessels and advise of any traffic that might interfere.

All power driven vessels between 20 meters (66 feet) and 40 meters (131 feet) must be passive participants, meaning they must keep a radio watch on the appropriate VTS radio channels.

Pleasure craft should monitor VTS. Although recreational vessels shorter than 20 meters are exempt from being active or passive participants in VTS, they must know how to keep out of the way of large, slow-maneuvering vessels. We keep our radio set on the VTS channel for the area we are cruising to hear where the large commercial vessels are operating.

Turn Point Special Operating Area. Turn Point is the northwest corner of the San Juan Islands' Stuart Island, where Haro Strait joins Boundary Pass. Turn Point is a blind corner. A recreational vessel could be completely unaware of a fast approaching ship on the other side. Monitor channel 11.

Separation Zones. The VTS lanes in Puget Sound, the Strait of Juan de Fuca, and the approaches to Haro Strait and Rosario Strait are divided into inbound and outbound lanes, with a separation zone between the two. The separation zones vary in width and are shown in magenta on the charts.

With the following precautions, pleasure craft are free to operate in the Puget Sound VTS lanes:

Pleasure craft, even vessels under sail, do not have right-of-way over VTS participant vessels and must not impede them in any way.

Wherever practical, pleasure craft should stay out of the VTS lanes, or at least minimize the length of time spent in the lanes. Large commercial vessels are required to remain in the VTS lanes unless cleared to do otherwise. It makes no sense to compete for that space.

If inbound in the VTS lanes, run in the inbound lane; if outbound, run in the outbound lane. Keep a lookout astern for overtaking vessels.

If crossing the VTS lane(s), try to cross at right angles to minimize the time spent in the traffic lanes. This is not always possible or practical, but it should be the objective.

Do not loiter or fish in the VTS separation zones.

Be aware of what is going on—ahead, astern, and to the sides. In the jargon this is called "situational awareness." Give large vessels lots of room. Make early and substantial course adjustments. Show them some side, meaning the side of your boat. (This is good practice whenever two vessels meet, regardless of size.)

If there's any doubt at all, cross behind a large vessel, not in front of it. A container ship traveling at only 11 knots needs more than a mile to come to a complete stop. Many container ships travel at 20 knots or more, which lengthens their stopping distance.

If you see a tug, look for a tow. Never, ever, pass between a tug and its tow. Leave ample room when crossing behind a tow.

Radio communication. While active VTS participants (large vessels and tugs with tows) are required to maintain radio watch on the appropriate VTS radio channel, such as VHF 14 in Puget Sound south of Bush Point, they are not required to monitor VHF 16, and many do not. Participants in Seattle Traffic waters also are required to monitor VHF 13, the U.S. bridge-to-bridge channel. Canada does not use VHF 13.

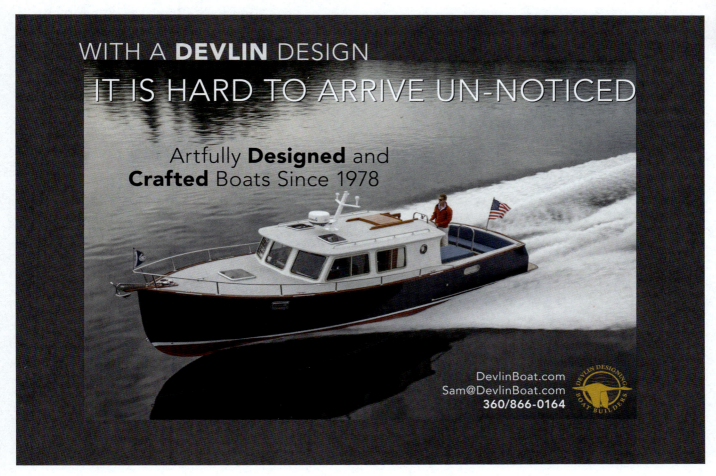

VTS RADIO CHANNELS - PUGET SOUND TO DIXON ENTRANCE

WHAT RECREATIONAL BOATERS NEED TO KNOW ABOUT VTS

VTS RADIO CHANNELS

TRAFFIC AREA	AREA DESCRIPTION	VHF CHANNEL
Seattle Traffic	Puget Sound west of Whidbey Island and south of Bush Point.	14
Seattle Traffic	Strait of Juan de Fuca (including Canadian waters), and Puget Sound north of Bush Point on the west side of Whidbey Island, including the San Juan Islands and Rosario Strait. Also the entire east side of Whidbey Island.	05A
Prince Rupert Traffic – South	West Coast of Vancouver Island & approaches to the Strait of Juan de Fuca.	74
Victoria Traffic – Sector One	Southern Area, Race Rocks (Victoria) to Ballenas Island/ Merry Island. This includes Haro Strait, Boundary Pass, the Gulf Islands, and the southern part of the Strait of Georgia, except for Vancouver Harbour and the Fraser River.	11
Turn Point Special Operating Area	Haro Strait/Boundary Pass. See map and text.	11
Victoria Traffic – Sector Two	Fraser River, Sand Heads to Shoal Point, New Westminster.	74
Victoria Traffic – Sector Three	Vancouver Harbour and approaches.	12
Victora Traffic – Sector Four	Ballenas Island/Merry Island north to Cape Caution. This includes the northern part of the Strait of Georgia and Inside Passage waters north to Cape Caution.	71
Prince Rupert Traffic – Sector One	Prince Rupert Harbour & approaches, including the north end of Grenville Channel, Chatham Sound, and all of Dixon Entrance to Langara Island.	71
Prince Rupert Traffic – Sector Two	Remainder of Zone. Hecate Strait, Cape Caution north to Alaska on the west side of Haida Gwaii.	11

To contact a large vessel, in Seattle Traffic waters call on VHF 13. In Canada VTS waters call on the appropriate VTS channel, such as VHF 11 in southern Strait of Georgia waters.

We have made such calls a few times with excellent results. Twice in narrow channels, the large vessel voluntarily reduced speed to lower its wake. One time it was a cruise ship in northern B.C.; the other time it was a deadly-looking U.S. warship at the mouth of Admiralty Inlet.

Consolidation of Canadian Marine Communications and Traffic Services (MCTS) Centres.
The following stations consolidated in 2016 were:

- Vancouver Coast Guard Radio consolidated to Victoria Coast Guard Radio
- Comox Coast Guard Radio consolidated to Victoria Coast Guard Radio
- Tofino Coast Guard Radio consolidated to Prince Rupert Coast Guard Radio

Monitor VTS channels. This is called being a passive VTS participant. Many of the transmissions are extremely brief: a vessel calls in and is off the air almost before you realize it. But by monitoring you'll learn that a ferry is departing the dock, or that a large vessel is about to emerge from a channel just around the next point, or that a container ship is calling in from 5 miles behind you, traveling at 22 knots.

These are good things to know, even in clear weather. In thick weather, at night or in fog, the information is invaluable. We have even called the VTS center ourselves, such as prior to a fog-bound crossing of Puget Sound. We kept our transmission brief, and made sure we weren't a pest. Their response advised us of any potentially conflicting traffic and was always was helpful, polite, and professional.

VESSEL TRAFFIC SERVICE PHONE NUMBERS

WASHINGTON:
USCG Puget Sound Vessel Traffic Center
(206) 217-6040

B.C.:
Prince Rupert MCTS Centre
(250) 627-3074 or (250) 627-3075

Victoria MCTS Centre
(250) 363-6333

Explore the Inside Passage
Cruising and Planning Information
See WaggonerGuide.com

Exploring Southeast Alaska

Exploring the North Coast of British Columbia

Exploring the South Coast of British Columbia

Exploring the Pacific Coast

Exploring the San Juan and Gulf Islands

FINE EDGE
Nautical & Recreational Publishing

The complete Exploring series by Don Douglass and Reanne Hemingway-Douglass is available at your local nautical bookstore, and WaggonerGuide.com or at 360-299-8500. In Canada available through Chynasea at 250-594-1184 and portsandpasses.com. Also on Amazon.

Exploring Vancouver Island's West Coast

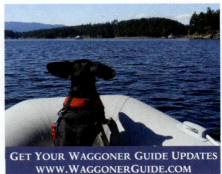
GET YOUR WAGGONER GUIDE UPDATES
WWW.WAGGONERGUIDE.COM

CONTACT PHONE NUMBERS & WEB ADDRESSES

U.S. COAST GUARD

U.S. Coast Guard Emergencies	**VHF CH 16 or call 911**
	(206) 217-6001 or (206) 220-7001
U.S. Coast Guard Emergency Juneau	**911 or (907)463-2000**

Cellular Phones Only	**911**
U.S. Coast Guard District Office: Seattle	(206) 220-7000
U.S. Coast Guard Smart phone App	

U.S. TOWING

Fremont Tugboat Co.	(206) 632-0151
Towboat U.S. all locations 24-hour dispatch	(800) 888-4869
Towboat U.S. Anacortes	(360) 675-7900
Towboat U.S. Everett	(425) 344-3056
Towboat U.S. San Juan	(360) 378-1111
(Friday Harbor & Roche Harbor)	
Towboat U.S. Lake Washington	(206) 793-7375
Towboat U.S. Oak Harbor	(360) 675-7900
Towboat U.S. Olympia	(360) 790-9008
Towboat U.S. Port Townsend	(360) 531-4837 or (360) 301-9764
Towboat U.S. Port Hadlock	(360) 301-9764
Towboat U.S. Seattle	(253) 312-2927
Towboat U.S. Tacoma	(253) 312-2927
Marine Services Whidbey (Deception Pass)	(360) 675-7900

U.S. WEATHER INFORMATION NUMBERS

Seattle	(206) 526-6087
Dial-A-Buoy	(888) 701-8992

U.S. CUSTOMS CLEARANCE NUMBERS

For customs entry call:	(800) 562-5943

The office numbers below are for weekdays only.

Anacortes	(360) 293-2331
Friday Harbor/Roche Harbor	(360) 378-2080
Point Roberts	(360) 945-5211 or (360) 945-2314
Port Angeles	(360) 457-4311
Aberdeen	(360) 310-0109 or (360) 532-2030
Bellingham	(360) 734-5463
Blaine	(360) 332-8511
Everett	(425) 259-0246
Port Townsend	(360) 385-3777
Seattle	(206) 553-0770
Tacoma/Olympia	(253) 593-6338
Ketchikan	(907) 225-2254

WA PARKS INFORMATION NUMBERS

Wash. State Parks Launch & Moorage Permit Program	(360) 902-8500
San Juan County Parks	(360) 378-8420

CANADIAN COAST GUARD

Canadian Coast Guard Emergency Numbers	**VHF CH 16**
Cellphone	*16
Search and Rescue: Vancouver	VHF CH 16 or (800) 567-5111
Search and Rescue: Victoria	(250) 413-8933 or (800) 567-5111
Search and Rescue: Other areas	(800) 567-5111
Canadian Coast Guard District Office: Victoria	(250) 480-2600

B.C. TOWING

Vessel Assist Gulf Islands	(800) 413-8222
C-Tow	VHF CH. 07A or (888) 419-2869

Covers Victoria to the north end of Vancouver Island & the Tofino area

Port McNeil	(250) 974-5305

CANADIAN WEATHER INFORMATION NUMBER

Vancouver	(604) 666-3655
Victoria	

CANADIAN BORDER SERVICES CLEARANCE NUMBER

All locations & CANPASS	
contact Canada Border Services Agency toll-free:	(888) 226-7277

CANADIAN PARKS INFORMATION NUMBERS

B. C. Parks General Information	(604) 582-5200
Gwaii Haanas National Park Reserve	(250) 559-8818
Gulf Islands National Park Reserve	(250) 654-4000 or (866) 944-1744

MARINE MAMMAL RESOURCES

San Juan County Marine Mammal Stranding Network is a collaborative program of the Whale Museum (Friday Harbor) and the National Marine Fisheries. To Report a Stranding in San Juan County
Call 1-800-562-8832 or email hotline@whalemuseum.org
This hotline is a voicemail system that is checked frequently throughout the day. Leave your name and phone number.

NOAA Marine Mammal Disentanglement Network is a program for boaters to help entangled marine mammals in U.S. waters.
To report entangled whales call NOAA Fisheries hotline at (877) 767-9425.
NOAA 24/7 Hotline - To report injured or stranded whales, dolphins, porpoises, seals and sea lions, or to report incidents of marine mammal harassment:
Call NOAA's 24/7 hotline at (800) 853-1964.

BC Marine Mammal Response Network – handles marine mammal matters in B.C. waters, they ask that boaters report all injured, distressed and dead marine mammals and sea turtles.
Call their 24/7 hotline (800) 465-4336

FISHERIES & FISHERIES MANAGEMENT

Paralytic Shellfish Poisoning PSP shellfish closures can be expected without warning at any time during the season.

For PSP closures in Washington, phone (800) 562-5632. Washington State Dept. of Health Paralytic Shellfish Poisoning page: www.doh.wa.gov and search PSP. The website has a PSP fact sheet and links to PSP toxin closed areas of Puget Sound and San Juan Islands.

Washington State Dept. Fish and Wildlife information on fish and wildlife action plans: wdfw.wa.gov/conservation/cwcs/

Washington State Dept. Fish and Wildlife information fishing and shellfishing: wdfw.wa.gov/fishing/

U.S. Fish and Wildlife Service Fisheries and Habitat Conservation: www.fws.gov/fisheries/

For PSP closures in B.C., phone the Openings and Closures Toll Free Line: (866) 431-3474 or (604) 666-2828 in the Lower Mainland, or go to: www.pac.dfo-mpo.gc.ca/fm-gp/contamination/biotox/index-eng.htm

Fisheries Management Areas. Download map of Fisheries Management Areas to enable you to decipher closure areas at: www.pac.dfo-mpo.gc.ca

Rockfish Conservation Areas booklet contains chartlets of all conservation areas. Many people do not realize that RCA's prohibit ALL hook and line fishing, not just fishing for rockfish. To view or download a copy of the booklet, go to: www.pac.dfo-mpo.gc.ca

2018 WAGGONER CRUISING GUIDE

VHF CHANNELS FOR PLEASURE CRAFT

WASHINGTON WATERS

05A VESSEL TRAFFIC SERVICE SEATTLE—Northern Puget Sound and Strait of Juan de Fuca. Vessels not required to participate are highly encouraged to maintain a listening watch. Contact with VTS is encouraged if essential to navigational safety.

06 INTERSHIP SAFETY. Only for ship-to-ship use for safety communications. For Search and Rescue (SAR) liaison with Coast Guard vessels and aircraft.

09 INTERSHIP AND SHIP-SHORE ALL VESSELS and CALLING & REPLY FOR PLEASURE VESSELS (optional, U.S. only). Working channel.

13 Vessel BRIDGE to Vessel BRIDGE, large vessels. Low power only. May also be used to contact locks and bridges BUT use sound signals in the Seattle area to avoid dangerous interference to collision avoidance communications between large vessels. Call on Channel 13 or by phone at 206/386-4251 for nighttime bridge openings (after 2300) in the Lake Washington Ship Canal, Seattle.

14 VESSEL TRAFFIC SERVICE SEATTLE—Southern Puget Sound. Vessels not required to participate are highly encouraged to maintain a listening watch. Contact with VTS is encouraged if essential to navigational safety.

16 INTERNATIONAL DISTRESS AND CALLING. Calling channel. Used only for distress and urgent traffic, for safety calls and contacting other stations. Listen first to make sure no distress traffic is in progress; do not transmit if a SEELONCE MAYDAY is declared. Keep all communications to a minimum. Do not repeat a call to the same station more than once every two minutes. After three attempts, wait 15 minutes before calling the same station. Pleasure vessels may also use Channel 09 for calling.

22A COAST GUARD LIAISON. A government channel used for Safety and Liason communications with the Coast Guard. Also known as Channel 22 US. The U.S. Coast Guard does not normally monitor 22A so you must first establish communications on Channel 16.

66A PORT OPERATIONS. Marinas in Puget Sound are being encouraged to use this common frequency for arranging moorage.

67 INTERSHIP ONLY FOR ALL VESSELS (U.S. only, Puget Sound.) Working channel.

68 INTERSHIP and SHIP-SHORE FOR PLEASURE VESSELS ONLY. Working channel.

69 INTERSHIP and SHIP-SHORE FOR PLEASURE VESSELS ONLY. Working channel.

70 DIGITAL SELECTIVE CALLING ONLY (No Voice) FOR DISTRESS AND CALLING.

72 INTERSHIP ONLY FOR ALL VESSELS (U.S. only, Puget Sound.) Working channel.

78A INTERSHIP and SHIP-SHORE FOR PLEASURE VESSELS ONLY (Not available in Canada). Working channel. Marinas in Puget Sound are being encouraged to use this as a secondary working channel.

BRITISH COLUMBIA WATERS

05A VESSEL TRAFFIC SERVICE SEATTLE—Strait of Juan de Fuca west of Victoria.

06 INTERSHIP SAFETY. Only for ship-to-ship use for safety communications.

09 INTERSHIP AND SHIP-SHORE. All vessels. Working channel.

11 VESSEL TRAFFIC SERVICE VICTORIA—Strait of Juan de Fuca east of Victoria; Haro Strait; Boundary Passage; Gulf Islands; Southern Strait of Georgia.

VESSEL TRAFFIC SERVICE PRINCE RUPERT—North of Cape Caution.

12 VESSEL TRAFFIC SERVICE VANCOUVER—Vancouver and Howe Sound.

16 INTERNATIONAL DISTRESS AND CALLING. Calling channel. Used only for distress and urgent traffic, for safety calls and contacting other stations. Listen first to make sure no distress traffic is in progress. Do not transmit if a SEELONCE MAYDAY is declared. Keep all communications to a minimum. Do not repeat a call to the same station more than once every two minutes. After three attempts, wait 15 minutes before calling the same station.

66A PORT OPERATIONS. Most marinas in southern B.C. will use this channel.

67 INTERSHIP AND SHIP-SHORE. All vessels. Working channel.

68 INTERSHIP AND SHIP-SHORE. Pleasure vessels. Working channel.

69 INTERSHIP AND SHIP-SHORE. Pleasure vessels. Working channel.

70 DIGITAL SELECTIVE CALLING ONLY (No Voice) FOR DISTRESS AND CALLING.

71 VESSEL TRAFFIC SERVICE COMOX—Northern Strait of Georgia to Cape Caution.

VESSEL TRAFFIC SERVICE—Prince Rupert, Dixon Entrance and Chatham Sound.

72 INTERSHIP. All vessels. Working channel.

73 INTERSHIP AND SHIP-SHORE. All vessels. Working channel.

74 VESSEL TRAFFIC SERVICE VICTORIA—Victoria-Fraser River.

VESSEL TRAFFIC SERVICE TOFINO—West of Vancouver Island.

83A COAST GUARD LIAISON. Primary Canadian Coast Guard Safety and Communications Channel. Also known as Channel 83 U.S. mode.

RADIO EMERGENCY SIGNALS

MAYDAY	Vessel threatened by grave and imminent danger and requests immediate assistance.
PAN PAN	Urgent message concerning safety of vessel or person on board or in sight.
SECURITÉ	Message concerning safety of navigation or meteorological warning.
SEELONCE MAYDAY	Mayday in progress, do not transmit normal communications.
SEELONCE FEENE	Resume normal communications.

To contact the Canadian Coast Guard, use Channel 16 to call the station nearest you: Victoria, Vancouver, Comox, Prince Rupert or Tofino.

Even though you may use alternate communication means such as cellular phone, MONITOR VHF 16. The safety of yourself, your family and your friends is enhanced by a watch on 16 by all vessels.

Conversion Tables

TEMPERATURE (FORMULAS)

FAHRENHEIT TO CELSIUS
To convert temperature from Fahrenheit to Celsius:

(F° - 32) × .555 = C°

Example: Convert 40° F to C:
(40 - 32) = 8; 8 × .555 = 4;
thus 40° F = 4° C

CELSIUS TO FAHRENHEIT
To convert temperature from Celsius to Fahrenheit:

(C° × 1.8) + 32 = F°

Example: Convert 4° C to F:
(4 × 1.8) = 7.2; 7.2 + 32 = 39.2 (round to 40); thus 4° C = 40° F

QUICK REFERENCE

32° Fahrenheit = 0° Celsius
0° Fahrenheit = -17.8° Celsius

VOLUME

U.S. GALLONS TO LITERS
1 U.S gallon = 3.7854 liters

To convert U.S. gallons to liters, multiply U.S. gallons × 3.785.
Example: 40 U.S. gallons × 3.785 = 151 liters

To convert liters to U.S. gallons, divide by 3.785.
Example: 151 liters ÷ 3.785 = 39.89 U.S. gallons (round to 40)

IMPERIAL GALLONS TO LITERS
1 Imperial gallon = 4.546 liters

To convert Imperial gallons to liters, multiply Imperial gallons × 4.546.
Example: 40 Imperial gallons × 4.546 = 182 liters

To convert liters to Imperial gallons, divide by 4.546.
Example: 182 liters ÷ 4.546 = 40.035 (round to 40)

U.S. GALLONS TO IMPERIAL GALLONS
1 U.S. gallon = .833 Imperial gallons

To convert U.S. gallons to Imperial gallons, multiply U.S. gallons × .833.

Example: 40 U.S. gallons × .833 = 33.32 Imperial gallons

To convert Imperial gallons to U.S. gallons, multiply Imperial gallons × 1.20.

Example: 33 Imperial gallons × 1.20 = 39.6 U.S. gallons

LITERS AND QUARTS
1 liter = 1.0567 quarts, or 33.8 ounces
1 quart = .9467 liters, or 947 ml

SPEED

Convert knots to miles per hour: Knots × 1.15
Convert miles per hour to knots: MPH × .868

WEIGHT

1 kilogram (kg) = 2.2 pounds (lbs.)

1 pound = .4545 kilograms (454 grams)

1 U.S. gallon of fresh water weighs 8.333 lbs. or 3.787 kg

1 Imperial gallon of fresh water weighs 10 lbs. or 4.545 kg

1 liter of fresh water weighs 2.2 pounds or 1 kg

1 U. S. gallon of gasoline weighs 6.2 lbs. or 2.82 kg

1 Imperial gallon of gasoline weighs 7.44 lbs. or 3.38 kg

1 liter of gasoline weighs 1.64 lbs. or 0.744 kg

1 U.S. gallon of No. 2 diesel fuel weighs 6.7 pounds or 3.05 kg

1 Imperial gallon of No. 2 diesel fuel weighs 8.04 pounds or 3.66 kg

1 liter of No. 2 diesel fuel weighs 1.77 pounds or 0.8 kg

DISTANCE

1 inch = 2.54 centimeters

1 foot = .3048 meters

1 meter = 3.28 feet

1 fathom = 6 feet

1 fathom = 1.83 meters

1 cable = 120 fathoms

1 cable (British) = 0.1 nautical mile

1 statute mile = 5280 feet; 7.4 cables; 1.609 kilometers

1 nautical mile = 6076 feet; 8.5 cables; 1.852 kilometers

1 statute mile = 0.868 nautical mile

1 nautical mile = 1.15 statute mile

BAROMETRIC PRESSURE

2018 WAGGONER CRUISING GUIDE

CONVERSION TABLES

CURRENCY

Generally, the most favorable exchange rates are on credit card transactions. Banks give slightly less favorable rates, and merchants tend to be the least favorable. Expect to pay more than the exchange rate when you buy currency, and receive less when you sell.

Examples:
Assume an exchange rate of $1.05 U.S./$.952 Cdn. (Exchange rates change constantly.)

To convert $100 Canadian to U.S. $,
multiply Canadian $ by 1.05 or divide by .952:
$100 Cdn × 1.05 = $105.00 U.S.
$100 Cdn ÷ .952 = $105.00 U.S.

To convert $105 U.S. to Canadian $,
multiply U.S. $ by .952 or divide by 1.05:
$105 U.S. × .952 = $100 Cdn.
$105 U.S. ÷ 1.05 = $100 Cdn.

INTERNATIONAL MORSE CODE & PHONETIC ALPHABET

A	ALPHA	•—	N	NOVEMBER	—•	1	ONE	•————
B	BRAVO	—•••	O	OSCAR	———	2	TWO	••———
C	CHARLIE	—•—•	P	PAPA	•——•	3	THREE	•••——
D	DELTA	—••	Q	QUEBEC	——•—	4	FOUR	••••—
E	ECHO	•	R	ROMEO	•—•	5	FIVE	•••••
F	FOXTROT	••—•	S	SIERRA	•••	6	SIX	—••••
G	GOLF	——•	T	TANGO	—	7	SEVEN	——•••
H	HOTEL	••••	U	UNIFORM	••—	8	EIGHT	———••
I	INDIA	••	V	VICTOR	•••—	9	NINE	————•
J	JULIET	•———	W	WHISKEY	•——	0	ZERO	—————
K	KILO	—•—	X	X-RAY	—••—			
L	LIMA	•—••	Y	YANKEE	—•——	DISTRESS/		•••———•••
M	MIKE	——	Z	ZULU	——••	SOS		

WEATHER WARNINGS

Light winds:	Less than 15 knots	Gale Warning:	34–47 knots
Moderate winds:	16–19 knots	Storm Warning:	48–63 knots
Small Craft/Strong Wind Warning:	20–33 knots		

BEAUFORT WIND SCALE

Scale Number	Wind Speed		Effects
	Knots	MPH	
0	under 1	under 1	Calm
1	1-3	1-3	Ripples
2	4-6	4-7	Small wavelets
3	7-10	8-12	Large wavelets; small crests
4	11-16	13-18	Small waves; some whitecaps
5	17-21	19-24	Moderate waves; some spray; many whitecaps
6	22-27	25-31	Larger waves; whitecaps everywhere
7	28-33	32-38	Sea heaps up; white foam from breaking waves
8	34-40	39-46	Moderately high; waves of greater length; foam blown in well-marked streaks
9	41-47	47-54	High waves; sea begins to roll; dense streaks of foam; spray reduces visibility
10	48-55	55-63	Very high waves with overhanging crests; sea takes on a white appearance; rolling is heavy
11	56-63	64-72	Exceptionally high waves; sea covered with white foam patches; visibility still more reduced
12	64 & over	73 & over	Air filled with foam; sea completely white with driving spray; visibility greatly reduced

South & Central Puget Sound

CHAPTER 2

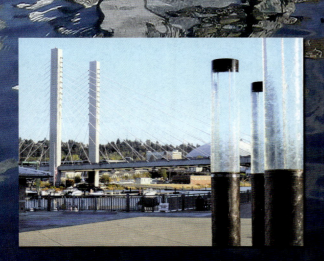

SOUTH PUGET SOUND
Olympia • Case Inlet • Carr Inlet • Tacoma Narrows

CENTRAL PUGET SOUND
*Gig Harbor • Tacoma • Vashon Island • Seattle
Bremerton • Poulsbo • Bainbridge Island*

SOUTH AND CENTRAL PUGET SOUND   See Area Map Page 75 - Maps Not for Navigation

South Puget Sound begins at Olympia and ends at Tacoma Narrows. For scenic quality, relatively calm seas and solitude, South Puget Sound is an excellent region to explore. For some reason, Seattle boats that voyage hundreds of miles north often do not consider venturing just a few miles south. Yet South Sound is dotted with marine parks and served by enough marinas to meet most needs. We like South Sound and recommend it.

The waters are generally flatter in South Sound, good for cruising year-round. The channels are relatively narrow and have enough bends to minimize fetch and prevent most wind from creating large seas. Tide-rips, of course, still form where channels meet, and skippers must be aware of them.

Olympia is South Sound's only significant city. Getting away from civilization is easy, yet it is always close by. First-time visitors usually are surprised at the beauty of this area. Mt. Rainier, an inactive volcano 14,410 feet high, dominates many vistas. The islands and peninsulas tend to be either tree-covered or pastoral, with pockets of homes or commercial enterprise. Most marine parks have docks, buoys, and anchoring. The marinas are friendly and well-kept.

BUDD, ELD, TOTTEN INLETS

Budd Inlet. The mile-wide entrance to Budd Inlet is between Dofflemyer Point and Cooper Point. Approaching from the north, simply round Dofflemyer Point, where a white-painted light blinks every 4 seconds, and head for the Capitol dome.

Anchorage in Budd Inlet is along both shores in 10 to 20 feet, mud bottom, with Butler Cove and Tykle Cove preferred. Private mooring buoys line the shores, so consider your swinging room when anchoring.

Launch Ramps: Swantown Marina has a 2-lane launch ramp. Another launch ramp is at the Thurston County park just south of Boston Harbor near Dofflemyer Point. Boston Harbor also has a launch ramp and parking for tow vehicles and trailers.

The City of Olympia's Priest Point Park, on the east side of Budd Inlet, has one of the finest sand beaches in southern Puget Sound.

Olympia. Olympia is one of the most charming stops in Puget Sound, the more so because so few boats from central and northern Puget Sound ever visit. Olympia is an undiscovered treat for many northern boaters.

Moorage in Olympia is at five marinas: NorthPoint Landing, Port Plaza Dock, Percival Landing Park, West Bay Marina, and Swantown Marina. Fuel is available at Boston Harbor Marina and Swantown Marina.

To get to the marinas, continue past Olympia Shoal, marked by lighted beacons on the shoal's east and west sides. From Olympia Shoal pick up the 28-foot-deep dredged and buoyed channel leading to the harbor. A spoils bank from channel dredging is east of the channel. The spoils area is quite shoal and parts of it dry. Stay in the channel.

The channel branches at a piling intersection marker south of the privately-owned West Bay Marina. The dayboard on the marker is green on top, red on the bottom. The green top-color marks the main channel. If you leave the marker to port you'll proceed down the western leg past the Port of Olympia large ship docks, to the new docks at Percival Landing, and to the Olympia Yacht Club at the head of the inlet. If you leave the marker to starboard, you'll take the eastern leg to the Port of Olympia's Swantown Marina and Boatworks. On both sides of each channel the water shoals rapidly to drying flats. The Olympia harbor has a no-wake rule.

West Bay Marina has a few guest slips and a restaurant, but no fuel dock. The Olympia Yacht Club has guest moorage for members of reciprocal clubs only. In the western channel, Percival Landing has guest moorage. In the eastern channel, the Port of Olympia's Swantown Marina has guest moorage.

Port of Olympia

CHARTS	
18448	Puget Sound, Southern Part (1:80,000)
18456	Olympia Harbor and Budd Inlet (1:20,000)
18457	Puget Sound – Hammersly Inlet to Shelton (1:10,000)
18474	Puget Sound – Shilshole Bay to Commencement Bay (1:40,000)

Reference Only – Not for Navigation　　　**SOUTH AND CENTRAL PUGET SOUND**

South Puget Sound

A beautifully landscaped walkway surrounds the Percival Landing area. It's a popular place for strolling, with an excellent view of harbor activities. Good restaurants, a supermarket, a fish market, and wine shop are nearby. Some boaters find the number of people walking just above their boats disconcerting, although we have found nights to be quiet. Swantown Marina, in East Bay, does not have the crowds walking by the boats.

Deschutes Basin, the southernmost tip of Puget Sound, and Capitol Lake are blocked by a dam and crossed by city streets. They are used by small boats launched from the city park just across the road from Percival Landing and the yacht club.

Olympia is the state capital, and we urge a tour of the Capitol Campus and its buildings. Besides housing the largest chandelier ever made by Louis Comfort Tiffany, the Capitol dome, at 287 feet tall, is one of the tallest masonry domes in North America. The grounds are beautiful and the buildings are magnificent. Informative tours are conducted on the hour, 10:00 a.m. to 3:00 p.m. on weekdays, 11:00 a.m. to 3:00 p.m. on weekends. No charge for these tours. The free Dash shuttle bus runs regularly from the farmers market to the campus and back.

Downtown Olympia has its own charm. Parts of it got stuck in the '50s. If you've seen the film "Pleasantville," you'll recognize the storefronts. The State Theater's tall art deco sign is not a bit out of place in Olympia's downtown. The Eastside Club Tavern was the inspiration for Moe's Tavern on "The Simpsons" TV show. Some of the restaurants have employees who have been there 20 to 40 years, and they're open every day of the year so regular customers have somewhere to go, even at Christmas.

Take the self-guided Historical District Walking Tour to learn local history: www.olympiawa.gov/city-services/history-preservation/walking-tours-of-historic-olympia.

About 20 antiques stores are located in the downtown area and out past Percival Landing. Art galleries are springing up. If you need a jolt of caffeine, coffee roaster Batdorf & Bronson is just east of the farmers market. They have a tasting room, just like a winery, only with coffee. Samples are free, but we always buy at least a couple bags of coffee. We enjoy it.

Olympia Farmers Market. The Olympia Farmers market is located between Percival Landing and the Port of Olympia's Swantown Marina. The market is open Thursdays through Sundays from April through October. Hours are 10:00 a.m. to 3:00 p.m. The market is open weekends in November and December, and and Saturdays only January through March Everything sold is

2018 waggoner CRUISING GUIDE 　　75

SOUTH AND CENTRAL PUGET SOUND See Area Map Page 75 - Maps Not for Navigation

The marinas in Olympia are in the shadow of the Capitol building.

grown or made locally, except for a few fruits that come from Yakima. Musicians perform on a covered stage, and take-out food is available from several outlets. No pets allowed. The market's roof is topped by a weathervane in the shape of a traditional flying pig.

Olympia hosts several festivals each year. For additional information visit: www.downtownolympia.com or www.visitolympia.com.

Fuel. New for 2017–Olympia now has a fuel dock at the Swantown Marina with marine gas and diesel.

With all the services and shopping opportunities of a major city, combined with beauty and the friendliness of a small town, Olympia makes a truly pleasant destination for boaters exploring south Puget Sound.

THINGS TO DO

1. **Washington State Capitol**. Take a short walk from the marinas for a free 60-minute tour of the architecturally magnificent legislative building.

2. **Washington State Capital Museum**. Good exhibits on the history of Washington State. Seven blocks from the Capitol.

3. **Hands On Children's Museum**. This children's museum has exhibits and an outdoor discovery center. A must-see for kids. Adjacent to Swantown Marina.

4. **Olympia Farmers Market**. One of the largest farmers markets in all of Puget Sound. It is open Thursday through Sunday, April to October, and limited days during the off-season. Located between Swantown Marina and Percival Landing.

5. **Percival Landing Park**. See classic boats, sculptures, and views of the Capitol on this landscaped walkway around the harbor.

6. **Antique and specialty shops**. More than 20 in the downtown area, a short walk from the waterfront.

7. **Batdorf & Bronson Coffee Roasters**. Taste the difference and learn the finer points of coffee.

① **Percival Landing Park.** 217 Thurston Ave., Olympia, WA 98501; (360) 753-8380; www.olympiawa.gov. Newly renovated Percival Landing Park has improved showers and restrooms. The park, with moorage, is adjacent to downtown Olympia near shopping, restaurants, and other facilities. Four hours day moorage, no charge. Guest moorage is along E float on the east side of the waterway. Water, 30 & 50 amp power are available on E float. Pumpout is on F float. D float, below the Olympia Oyster House restaurant on the west side, has limited space, no power or water. Register at The Olympia Center. Group reservations available from October 1 to April 30.

The floats have access to toilets, showers, and portapotty dump. After-hours or weekends, self-register at the kiosk next to the parking lot. Cash or checks only at the kiosk, no credit cards. First-come, first-served. Maximum 7 days in a 30-day period. No manager is on site, so you may have to search for everything, including the registration kiosk. Good grocery shopping at Bayview Thriftway, west of the yacht club. The Harbor House meeting center was built as part of the Percival Landing renovation and is available for group gatherings to 30 people. Call (360) 753-8380. There are also two outdoor pavilions.

Limited guest moorage during the Wooden Boat Show in May, and Harbor Days, with its tugboat races, early September.

① **Port Plaza Dock.** 701 Columbia St. NW, Olympia, WA 98501; (360) 528-8049; marina@portolympia.com; www.swantownmarina.com. Monitors VHF 65A. This is a modern, all-concrete set of floats on the east side of the waterway leading to Percival Landing and Olympia Yacht Club. The docks are intended for day use but are available for overnight. Location is convenient to dining and shopping, 4 hours no charge. No water, no power. Self-register at kiosk at the head of the ramp. Reservations accepted for $5 non-refundable fee.

The Port Plaza itself is a work of art. The sculpted concrete work suggests waves. It's completely flat but very effective. Bronze shells, golf balls, drafting tools—all sorts of things are set into the cement. The more you look, the more you see.

① **NorthPoint Landing.** 1675 Marine Drive NW, Olympia, WA 98501; (360) 528-8000; www.portolympia.com. Small dock operated by the Port of Olympia, at the north end of the waterway leading to Percival Landing and Olympia Yacht Club. Day use only. Max 4 hour stay. No power or water and 4 feet of depth at zero tide. Anthony's Hearthfire Grill is adjacent to the dock.

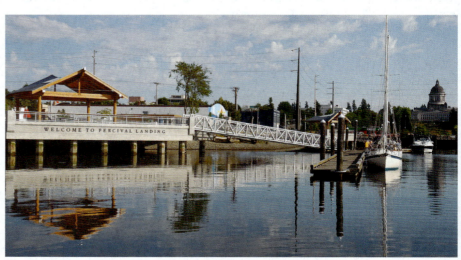

The docks at Percival Landing Park

See Area Map Page 75 - Maps Not for Navigation   SOUTH AND CENTRAL PUGET SOUND

1675 Marine Drive NE
(360) 705-3473

② **West Bay Marina.** 2100 Westbay Drive NW, Olympia, WA 98502; (360) 943-2022; westbaymarina@hotmail.com; www.westbaymarina.com. On the west side of Budd Inlet. Guest moorage to 40 feet; call ahead for availability. Facilities include 30 amp power, restrooms, showers, coin-operated laundry, pumpout. Tugboat Annie's restaurant and pub, a longtime favorite, is on site.

③ **Swantown Marina.** 1022 Marine Drive NE, Olympia, WA 98501; (360) 528-8049; marina@portolympia.com; www.swantownmarina.com. Certified Clean Marina. Monitors VHF 65A. This is the Port of Olympia small boat moorage. Open all year, 50+ guest moorage slips for vessels to 100 feet. In 2017 a fuel dock was added to A Dock with diesel and ethanol-free gasoline. Outstanding restrooms, showers and laundry. Pumpout, portapotty dump, 30 & 50 amp power, garbage drop, waste oil dump, security patrols, well-tended grounds, free Wi-Fi, ice. Reservations accepted for $5. Dry boat storage, 2-lane launch ramp. Block and crushed ice at Harbor Office. Groceries are a 15-minute walk away. The Olympia Farmers

The busy farmers market is a popular attraction in Olympia.

Market and a seafood market are in the marina area. Downtown Olympia attractions and a children's museum are within walking distance.

The channel leading from the intersection beacon with its green and red dayboard can be confusing. If the weather is clear, you'll see a long, low 2-story condominium block on the eastern shore. Aim for those condominiums. At the approach to Swantown Marina, Beacon 1 will be at the north end of the condominiums; Beacon 2 will be at the south end.

Guest moorage is on A-dock a short distance inside the entry, next to the launch ramp. Register and pay moorage at the kiosk at the head of the ramp, or in the office at the head of I-Dock. Swantown Marina is parklike: clean, quiet, spacious and well-maintained.

Swantown Boatworks, (360) 528-8059, with 82-ton Travelift, is at the south end of the marina. Pettite Marine chandlery is located in the same building.

Burfoot County Park. 6927 Boston Harbor Rd. NE, Olympia, WA 98506. Located a half-mile south of Dofflemyer Point. This is a 60-acre county park, open all year, day use only. Restrooms, picnic tables, trails, and play area. Anchoring or beaching only. Buoys mark an artificial diving reef.

④ **Boston Harbor.** Boston Harbor is a halfmoon-shaped bay between Dofflemyer Point and Dover

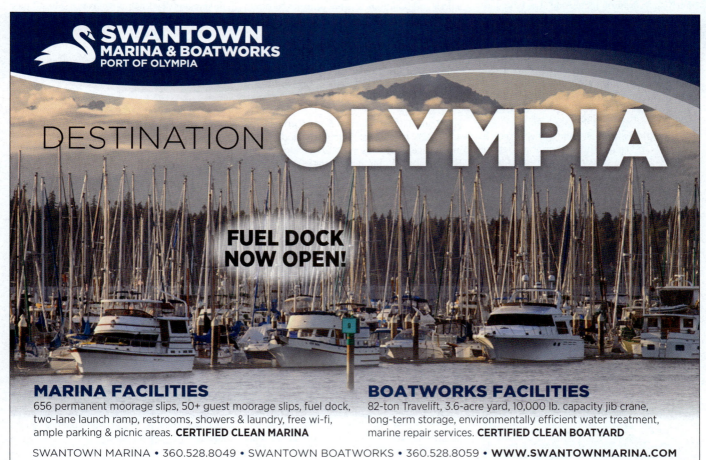

2018 WAGGONER CRUISING GUIDE   77

SOUTH AND CENTRAL PUGET SOUND   See Area Map Page 75 - Maps Not for Navigation

The large deck adjacent to the Boston Harbor Store is popular.

Kayak and stand-up paddleboards for rent at Boston Harbor

Point. Anchorage is limited but possible. Much of the bay is taken up by the Boston Harbor Marina.

④ **Boston Harbor Marina.** 312 - 73rd Ave. NE, Olympia, WA 98506; (360) 357-5670; www.bostonharbormarina.com. Phone ahead for slip assignment. Open all year with very limited guest moorage. Guest moorage is located in front of the store on the west side of the 600 Dock and in unoccupied slips. Caution: the south end of the 600 Dock dries at low tide. The north docks, which were damaged in recent storms, will be under repair for the next few years. 20 amp power, picnic area, beach access, free Wi-Fi, restrooms, but no showers. The launch ramp dries on minus tide. The store has groceries, ice, beer, wine, fresh seafood, some marine supplies, gifts, clothing, and books. Sandwiches, soups, and soft-serve ice cream at the store. Rental kayaks and SUPs available.

This is a real neighborhood place, a throwback to when small marinas up and down Puget Sound served surrounding communities. The quaint old store is built on pilings, and there's not a level floor to be found. The store and docks are gathering places for locals, and a cheery bunch they are. On Fridays, from Memorial Day to Labor Day, live music with beer tasting is held on the pier. Breakfast is served on the pier Sunday mornings from 10:00 a.m. to 1:00 p.m., summer season only. If you relax and just let it happen, you'll think Boston Harbor is a delight.

Boston Harbor Marina

No-wake zone. Several white warning buoys off the mouth of Boston Harbor mark a no-wake zone. Please slow down. Wakes from passing craft play havoc with the moored boats.

Eld Inlet. Eld Inlet is immediately west of Budd Inlet, and extends about 5 miles south from Cooper Point before it becomes aptly-named Mud Bay. Hold to a mid-channel course past Cooper Point, which has an extensive drying shoal northward from the point.

Eld Inlet has no marinas, but anchorage is good, mud bottom along both shores. Directly across the inlet is the waterfront activities center for The Evergreen State College. The center has a float and buildings to store canoes and other small craft used by students.

Frye Cove County Park. 4000 NW 61st Ave., Olympia, WA 98502. Just north of Flapjack Point in Eld Inlet. Open all year, day use only. Toilets, no other services. Anchoring or beaching only. Picnic shelters, barbecues, hiking trails.

⑤ **Hope Island Marine State Park.** (360) 426-9226. Junction of Totten Inlet and Pickering Passage. Boat access only. Undeveloped Hope Island is one of the newest parks in the state system. Trails crisscrossing the island lead through forest, meadows, and old orchards. Interpretive signs explain the island's history and ecology. Visitors rave about this park. A Park Aide lives on the island during the summer. The park has 3 mooring buoys on the west shore, 2 mooring buoys off the south shore and decent anchorage in 30 feet or less on the east side. Campsites, pit toilets, no fires, no pets. Pack out all garbage.

Totten Inlet. Enter Totten Inlet past Steamboat Island, connected to the the mainland by a causeway from Carlyon Beach. Homes and a private marina are on the island and mainland beach. The beach is marked by a quick flashing light. All of Totten Inlet is less than 60 feet deep. The inlet shoals to drying mud flats toward its south end, called Oyster Bay.

The entrance to Skookum Inlet is on the west side of Totten Inlet, about 3 miles southwest of Steamboat Island. Skookum Inlet is called "Little Skookum" by locals, to differentiate it from nearby Hammersley Inlet, which they call "Big Skookum." Little Skookum is a pleasant exploration, but not navigable beyond Wildcat Harbor except by dinghy. Little Skookum is one of south Puget Sound's major oyster growing areas.

HAMMERSLEY INLET AND SHELTON

Hammersley Inlet extends westward about 6 miles to **Oakland Bay** and the city of **Shelton**. Note the shoal area that blocks the entire south side of the entrance to Hammersley Inlet. Enter Hammersley Inlet on the north shore past Point Hungerford, marked by a beacon with a flashing red light. As Chart 18457 shows, depths in Hammersley Inlet range from 10 to 30 feet. Currents to 4 knots flood in and ebb out. The strongest currents occur around Cape Horn, a sharp, constricted bend just inside the entrance. Be mindful of tugs with tows. Moorage is at the Port of Shelton's Oakland Bay Marina, about a mile from Shelton.

Shelton. Shelton is the site of a major lumber mill, with rafted logs in storage in front of the town. Oakland Bay grows shallow north of Shelton, but is navigable at other than extreme low tide, and could offer anchorage on a mud bottom.

⑥ **Oakland Bay Marina (Port of Shelton).** 21 W. Sanderson Way, Shelton, WA 98584; (360) 426-1425; www.portofshelton.com. Open all year, 120 feet of guest moorage, 30 amp power. No fuel. The visitor dock is between the boat houses. Least depth 10 feet. Pumpout, portable toilet above the dock. Home to the friendly Shelton Yacht Club. Groceries, restaurants, and services are in town, about a mile away. The Port continues making improvements to the pier and uplands. Visitors welcome.

PEALE AND PICKERING PASSAGES AND CASE INLET

Pickering Passage extends northward from Totten Inlet past the west sides of Squaxin Island and Harstine Island. Mid-channel courses encounter no obstructions.

Peale Passage runs along the east side of

Squaxin Island. Shallow but passable depths.

Harstine Island is connected to the mainland at Graham Point by a bridge with a mean high water vertical clearance of 31 feet.

The small marina between Jarrell Cove and Dougall Point is private.

Jarrell Cove. Jarrell Cove is off Pickering Passage near the northwest corner of Harstine Island. Jarrell's Cove Marina and 43-acre Jarrell Cove State Marine Park occupy this pleasant, sheltered cove.

LOCAL KNOWLEDGE

Shallow Area: A shallow spit at Jarrell Cove State Park extends from the point that protects the second park dock, the dock deeper in the cove. Boats sometimes cut the point too closely on low tides and go aground.

⑦ **Jarrell's Cove Marina.** 220 E. Wilson Rd., Shelton, WA 98584; (360) 426-8823. Open 7 days a week Memorial Day to Labor Day. The fuel dock has diesel and gasoline. In the winter, the store is closed and fuel is by appointment. Facilities include 3 RV sites, 30 amp power, restrooms, showers, laundry, pumpout, limited guest moorage. Get a slip assignment from the fuel dock before landing, even for a short stay. The store has groceries, beer, ice, some marine hardware, books, propane. The piña colada shaved ice sno-cones are popular with adults who might add a little something when they get back to the boat. Lots of other flavors available, too. Gary and Lorna Hink are the owners.

⑦ **Jarrell Cove Marine State Park.** 391 E. Wingert Road, Shelton, WA 98584; (360) 426-9226. Northwest end of Harstine Island. Open all year. This is a large, attractive park, with 650 feet of dock space on two docks, 14 mooring buoys (boats 45 feet and under), clean and well-maintained restrooms and showers, picnic shelters, RV sites and standard campsites. Except for the single buoy between the inner dock and shore, mooring buoys

Jarrell's Cove

have minimum 10 feet of water at all tides. The inner end of the outer dock can rest on mud bottom on minus tides. The inner dock has 6 feet of water on zero tide. The outer end has sufficient depths for most drafts on all tides. Fishing, clamming, hiking, and bird watching.

During the fall of 2016, the inner dock was replaced with an eco-friendly float and 30 amp power for 16 hookups, making this park a wonderful off-season destination.

McLane Cove. Across Pickering Passage from Jarrell Cove. Protected, quiet, lined with forest. Anchorage in 10 to 20 feet.

⑧ **Stretch Island** has good anchorage in the bay south of the bridge to the mainland. The bridge has a mean high water clearance of 14 feet. The channel under the bridge dries at low tide.

⑧ **Stretch Point Marine State Park.** On Stretch Island. Open all year, accessible only by boat. No power, water, restrooms or showers. Day use only, 5 overnight mooring buoys for boats 45 feet and under. Buoys are close to shore because of a steep dropoff. Swimming and diving, oysters and mussels, and a smooth sand beach. The park has no garbage drop and a "pack it in–pack it out" policy. The rustic shelters built behind the beach are on private land and not part of the park.

Reach Island. At the southern end of Reach Island is **Fair Harbor**, the location of Fair

Jarrell's Cove Marina has great snow cones. It's a popular stop.

SOUTH AND CENTRAL PUGET SOUND

See Area Map Page 75 - Maps Not for Navigation

Joemma Beach State Park dock

Harbor Marina. The bay has limited anchorage. The channel north of the marina, under a bridge with a mean high water clearance of 16 feet, dries on a minus tide.

⑨ **Fair Harbor Marina.** 5050 E. Grapeview Loop Rd., P.O. Box 160, Grapeview, WA 98546; (360) 426-4028; info@fairharbormarina.com; www.fairharbormarina.com. Open during the summer months with limited side-tie guest moorage on an 88-foot dock. Concrete launch ramp, water, 20 & 30 amp power, garbage, Wi-Fi, restrooms and showers. Picnic areas. Owners Susan and Vern Nelson have retired and the marina is currently for sale. Best to call ahead for moorage. The fuel dock and gift store are closed. Permanent moorage during the winters.

⑩ **Allyn Waterfront Park (Port of Allyn).** P.O. Box 1, Allyn, WA 98524; (360) 275-2430; portofallyn@aol.com; www.portofallyn.com. Open all year, launch ramp, 250 feet of moorage for boats to 45 feet on a "T" shaped float at the end of a public pier. Restrooms on site. The dock is exposed to winds. No fuel. Allyn is surrounded by shoal water, but can be approached by favoring the east side of the channel until opposite the wharf, then turning in. Depth at the mooring float is 5.25 feet at zero tide. Office hours are Monday through Friday, 11:00 a.m. to 4:30 p.m.

A waterfront park, 100-year-old church, grocery and liquor store, post office, restaurants, wine tasting room, kayak rentals, and the George Kenny School of Chainsaw Carving are a short walk ashore.

If you're experiencing a craving for a manly, heart-stopping burger and shake, visit Big Bubba's Burgers, an Allyn landmark, across the road from Waterfront Park. Golfing available at nearby Lakeland Village Golf Course.

Rocky Bay. The best anchorage is behind a small sandspit extending from Windy Bluff. Enter with caution and round the little rocky islet off the end of the spit before circling in to anchor.

Vaughn Bay. Vaughn Bay can be entered at half tide or higher. Take a mid-channel course past the end of the spit, then turn to parallel the spit until safe anchoring depths are found near the head of the bay. Jet skis and water skiers sometimes roar around during the day, but they quit at sundown and leave the bay peaceful at night. A launch ramp is on the north shore of the bay.

Herron Island. Privately owned.

⑪ **McMicken Island Marine State Park.** (360) 426-9226. On Case Inlet, off the east side of Harstine Island. Open all year, day use only, no overnight camping. Toilets and 5 overnight mooring buoys, for boats 45 feet and under. Mooring buoys are on the north and south sides of 11½-acre McMicken Island. The buoys on the north side are a little close to shore on minus tides. Self register and pay mooring buoy fee on shore. Anchorage is on either side of the island, good holding bottom.

A trail on McMicken Island leads to a nice view of the beach and surrounding waters. A sign says to watch for poison oak. An artificial reef is north of the island. Fishing, good clamming and oyster gathering, swimming. McMicken Island is accessible only by boat except on low tides, when it and Harstine Island are connected by a drying spit. The spit comes up quickly, and you could find yourself aground if you try to pass between the two islands. The park has no garbage drop and a "Pack it in–Pack it out" policy.

Harstine Island State Park. This park is across the bay from McMicken Island. Open all year, day use only. No power, water, or toilets. At low tide you can cross to McMicken Island State Park. Anchoring only. Clamming, beachcombing.

⑫ **Joemma Beach State Park.** (360) 902-8844. Formerly Robert F. Kennedy Recreational Area, southeast Case Inlet, just north of Whiteman Cove. Cascadia Marine Trail campsite, 500 feet of dock space in place from mid-May through mid-October, 4 mooring buoys (boats 45 feet and under), boat launch, vault toilets. No power, no showers. The docks are good. Camping and picnic sites (including a covered shelter) on shore. Red Rock crabbing has occasionally been reported as excellent, right at the dock. The docks are exposed to southeast storms.

DRAYTON PASSAGE, PITT PASSAGE, BALCH PASSAGE

Taylor Bay. Taylor Bay, on Anderson Island, offers limited anchorage near the entrance, but is exposed to southerlies.

Oro Bay has a shallow, well-marked entrance with good anchorage inside. Oro Bay has a tranquil, rural feeling about it. Entering, the first dock you come to is a Tacoma Yacht Club outstation. Burwell's Landing is a Bremerton Yacht Club outstation. The Oro Bay Marina is home to Oro Bay Yacht Club, with some reciprocal moorage.

Amsterdam Bay indents Anderson Island and is very shallow. Safe anchoring depths are right in the middle, when that spot is not already occupied by local residents' boats. The shores are rural and picturesque. If low tide isn't too low, it's a good place to spend the night. Observe a 5 mph or lower no-wake speed to prevent damage along the shoreline.

⑬ **Eagle Island Marine State Park.** (360) 426-9226. Ten-acre island on Balch Passage, off north side of Anderson Island. Open all year, day use only, 1 overnight mooring buoy on the east side, 2 overnight mooring buoys on the west side. Mooring buoys for boats 45 feet and under, self-register and pay mooring buoy fee on shore. No toilets, power, or water. Boat access only. Avoid the reef, marked by a buoy, off the west side of the island. Fishing and clamming. Watch for poison oak. No fires, no garbage drop and a "Pack it in–Pack it out" policy, no camping.

Eagle Island is a lovely spot. Except for the current, which can roar through, this is an excellent South Sound layover location. Lots of seals, a fine view of Mt. Rainier, and good anchoring on the east side. The island is covered with dense forest, but well-maintained trails lead through the trees. Correspondents James and Jennifer Hamilton call Eagle Island "a gem." Don't be oversold, but do expect a good place to spend some time.

Filucy Bay. Filucy Bay is a popular destination and a fine anchorage. Anchor inside the spit to the south of the entrance, or in the north section, farther in. The north section is wooded, quiet, and protected with good holding over a mud bottom. The view of Mt. Rainier from the entrance of Filucy Bay is stunning. Longbranch Improvement Club Marina welcomes visiting boaters.

⑭ **Longbranch Improvement Club Marina.** 5213 Key Penninsula Hwy. S., Longbranch, WA 98351; (253)884-5137; (253) 307-1873 cell; licdockmaster@gmail.com; www.longbranchimprovementclub.org. Longbranch is a good South Sound stopover, and especially popular as a destination for boating club cruises. Open all year, but hours vary in winter. The marina has 540 feet of side-tie dock space for guest moorage, 30 amp power, ice, Wi-Fi, garbage drop, water, portable toilets. No showers. No charge for 4-hour day moorage. Advance notification for groups is requested. Group cruises stack the boats in tightly, and raft several deep. Check their website for the schedule of group cruises. The guest moorage bull rails are painted yellow. The docks have a large covered area with roll-down canvas sides, lights, tables, chairs, heaters, barbecues, book exchange. This marina has a warm, friendly atmosphere.

If you've anchored out, the dinghy dock is on the west side of the main dock, next to the ramp. Mechanic and divers are on call. Dances are held Memorial Day, July 4th, and Labor Day at the historic Longbranch Improvement Club Hall, located about a half-mile away. The dances are popular and usually sell out.

Pitt Passage is a winding, shallow passage between McNeil Island and the mainland. Because the passage is shoal, many skippers avoid it. Safe transit, however, can be made by following the navigation aids between tiny Pitt Island and McNeil Island. The waters west of Pitt Island are shoal.

Red, Right, Returning assumes you are returning from the north. This means that from the north, run an S-shaped course to leave the green can Wyckoff Shoal Buoys 1 and 3 to port, then turn east across the north side of Pitt Island to leave the red Daybeacon 4 to starboard. Continue between Pitt Island and McNeil Island, to leave the red nun Buoy 6 to starboard. Study the chart carefully before making your first run through Pitt Passage. Note how Wyckoff Shoal extends westward from McNeill Island almost across the mouth of the passage.

McNeil Island was a major state prison. It closed in 2011.

CARR INLET

Mayo Cove. Mayo Cove is pretty. The bay is shallow, however, and drying shoals are on either side. For exploring, take the dinghy part way up the inlet leading to Bay Lake.

Lakebay Marina & Resort. 15 Lorenz Road, Lakebay, WA 98349; (253) 884-3350; www.lakebaymarina.com. Located across Mayo Cove from Penrose Point Marine State Park. Lakebay

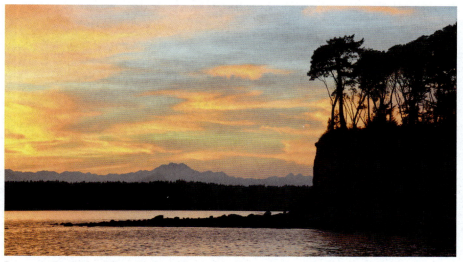
Sunset at Cutts Island State Park

Marina was built on a historic Mosquito Fleet landing. Open all year with 30 guest slips, 30 amp power, water, restrooms, boat launch, a small store, and a large meeting/dining room. Free Wi-Fi. Pumpout planned for 2018. Ethanol-free gasoline at the fuel dock, no diesel. Campsites and cabins for rent. A tandem bicycle is available for overnight guests. Kayaks and stand-up paddleboards can be rented.

The Lakebay Cafe is on site and has good meals, bar, fishing tackle and clothing items. It is open 7 days a week in summer; closed Mondays and Tuesdays in winter. Breakfast Saturday and Sunday. A large dining room using theater seats and surrounded by old pictures of the marina is good for groups.

Clam digging for overnight guests. The marina has a cocktail bar and regularly hosts beer tastings and live music in the summer. See their website for a schedule.

⑮ **Penrose Point Marine State Park.** (253) 884-2514. In Mayo Cove, west shore of Carr Inlet. Open for mooring and camping year-round. The 158-foot dock has 270 feet of side-tie space. The inner side of the dock grounds on lower tides. 8 mooring buoys for boats 45 feet and under. Self register and pay mooring fee on shore. Facilities include Cascadia Marine Trail campsite, picnic sites, restrooms, seasonal showers, pumpout, portapotty dump. No power. Standard campsites, 2.5 miles of hiking and biking trails, clamming, oyster picking, swimming, fishing. At low tide enter the cove with care.

Von Geldern Cove. Von Geldern Cove is a shallow bay, but anchorage, exposed to northerly winds, is possible near the entrance. Most of the shoreline is residential. The town of Home, with a launch ramp, has some supplies. Take the dinghy under the bridge at the head of the bay and explore the creek until it's too shallow.

Glen Cove is protected by a spit, but is very shallow and not recommended for overnight anchorage.

Rosedale. Rosedale is a small community tucked in behind **Raft Island**. Good anchorage.

Enter the bay to the north of Raft Island, since a causeway connects the island to the mainland across the very shoal south side. The small and quaint Island View Market, with groceries and liquor, has a dinghy dock.

Cutts Island Marine State Park. (253) 265-3606. Open all year, day use only, 8 overnight mooring buoys for boats 45 feet and under. Self-register and pay mooring fee on shore. Accessible by boat only. No power, no water, no toilets, no camping or fires allowed. Easy row to Kopachuck Marine State Park. Cutts Island is connected to Raft Island by a drying shoal. Watch your depths if you try to cross between Cutts Island and Raft Island. We are told that in bygone days, Cutts Island was an Native American burial ground, and its local name is Dead Man's Island.

⑯ **Kopachuck Marine State Park.** (253) 265-3606. Three miles north of Fox Island, just north of Horsehead Bay. Open all year for day use and mooring. 2 overnight mooring buoys for boats 45 feet and under. Self-register and pay mooring fee on shore. Good bottom for anchoring, but unprotected. Underwater park with artificial reef for scuba diving. Kitchen shelters, picnic sites. Playground, trail, clamming, fishing. Swimming in shallow water off the beach area.

Longbranch Marina

Penrose Point State Park & Lakebay Marina

2018 WAGGONER CRUISING GUIDE

SOUTH AND CENTRAL PUGET SOUND   See Area Map Page 75 - Maps Not for Navigation

The shore of Wollochet Bay is lined with homes, many with docks and mooring buoys, but good anchorage is available.

The campgrounds are permanently closed due to hazardous trees.

Horsehead Bay. Horsehead Bay is an excellent anchorage, surrounded by fine homes. A launch ramp is near the harbor entrance. Good holding ground is a short distance inside the bay.

Hale Passage separates Fox Island from the Olympic Peninsula, and is crossed by a bridge with a mean high water clearance of 31 feet. A short distance east of the bridge, a green can buoy marks a drying, boulder-studded shoal. Pass to the north of the buoy. Currents run strongly through Hale Passage, with 1 to 2.5 knots common, flooding west and ebbing east. The ebb current is stronger than the flood.

Fox Island is connected to the mainland by a bridge with a mean high water clearance of 31 feet. Good anchorage can be found behind **Tanglewood Island**, which has a pavilion used by yacht clubs and other groups for special occasions. Residents of Fox Island are protective of their privacy, so it is a good idea to stay aboard unless invited ashore.

Wollochet Bay. Wollochet Bay winds a couple of miles into the mainland off Hale Passage. The shores of the bay are lined with homes, many with mooring buoys, but good anchorage can be found. The mouth of the bay is open to southerly winds. Inside, the waters are protected. Tacoma Yacht Club has an outstation near the head of the bay.

We've had good luck catching crab at the mouth of the bay.

A favorite pastime while visiting Wollochet Bay is launching the dinghy and exploring the saltwater marsh and estuary area at Wollochet Bay Estuary Park. The park, at the very head of the bay, has 854 linear feet of shoreline including the confluence of Artondale Creek.

Ketron Island. Privately owned.

HENDERSON INLET, NISQUALLY, STEILACOOM, TACOMA NARROWS

Henderson Inlet extends about 5 miles south from Itsami Ledge. The inlet has been the site of major logging operations over the years, and log rafts are still stored along the west side. Anchorage is good along about half of the inlet before it becomes too shallow near the entrance to Woodward Creek.

⑰ **Zittel's Marina Inc.** 9144 Gallea St. NE, Olympia, WA 98516; (360) 459-1950; www.zittelsmarina.com. Open all year, hours may vary in the winter. Ethanol-free gasoline and diesel at the fuel dock. Guest moorage in unoccupied slips and side-tie up to 65 feet when available (don't count on availability), 30 amp power, launch ramp, restrooms, pumpout, portapotty dump, showers. Haulout and repairs, limited marine supplies, boat rentals, groceries, bait and tackle. Owned and operated by Mike and Kathi Zittel.

Johnson Point is a popular salmon fishing area. Two launch ramps are at Johnson Point, but no facilities for visiting boaters.

Tolmie Marine State Park. (360) 753-1519. Eight miles northeast of Olympia. This 105-acre park is open all year for day use and overnight moorage, except closed for day use Mondays and Tuesdays in winter. Restrooms and showers. 5 mooring buoys for boats 45 feet and under are well offshore; beach and shallows extend out some distance. Self-register and pay mooring fee on shore. The underwater park for scuba diving includes sunken wooden barges. Hiking trails, picnic sites with barbecues, meeting room. Nice sandy beach. The park includes a small saltwater lagoon marsh area good for watching wildlife. No camping.

Nisqually Reach is the body of water south of Anderson Island, between the island and the mainland. The channel is marked by buoys along the extensive mudflats of the Nisqually River delta. The delta is a wildlife refuge, and is accessible by boat at half tide or better, by way

Days Island

82   www.WaggonerGuide.com

See Area Map Page 75 - Maps Not for Navigation   SOUTH AND CENTRAL PUGET SOUND

of the Luhrs Beach launch ramp near Nisqually Head. Contributing Editor Tom Kincaid has entered the river itself by dinghy, but from the water side the entrance is hard to spot.

Steilacoom. Picnic area on a small pebble beach, launch ramp, and fishing pier adjacent to the ferry landing. A year-round 60-foot day-use dock available for hourly moorage, limited to boats 23 feet and under, adjacent to the ferry landing. Steilacoom, incorporated in 1854, is the oldest incorporated town in Washington. A museum, restaurants, and other services are nearby. Steilacoom Marina, at Gordon Point, is abandoned and dilapidated.

Tacoma Narrows. All of the water in southern Puget Sound flows through Tacoma Narrows, with 4- to 6-knot currents common. Day Island Yacht Club, Narrows Marina, and Day Island Marina are on the east side of the south end of the Narrows. The Tacoma Narrows bridges, more than a mile long and 180 feet above the water, are two of the world's longest suspension bridges.

Back eddies form along the sides of the narrows, useful when transiting with an opposing current.

⑱ **Narrows Marina.** 9007 S. 19th St. Suite 100, Tacoma, WA 98466; (253) 564-3032; nmbt@narrowsmarina.com; www.narrowsmarina.com. Open all year except Christmas

Gig Harbor

2018 WAGGONER CRUISING GUIDE

SOUTH AND CENTRAL PUGET SOUND   See Area Map Page 86 - Maps Not for Navigation

Tasty food can be found at The Trolley.

week, three days during Thanksgiving, and Easter Sunday. Ethanol-free gasoline and diesel at the fuel dock, restrooms, pumpout, transient moorage, long term parking, convenience store, tackle and live bait. Full service repairs on-site with a 9-ton lift.

Colored tape along the docks indicates where you can tie up. Green indicates free moorage for visits less than three hours. Blue indicates reserved transient moorage; call ahead for a slip assignment. The fuel dock is inside the breakwater in the northeast corner of the marina. Currents can run strongly at the docks.

The Boathouse 19 restaurant and Narrows Brewing Company are on site. The top of the bar at Boathouse 19 is made from the old Day Island Bridge and the table tops are from Nalley Valley pickle barrels. Narrows Brewing Company has a tasting room where you can bring your own food and sample a variety of beers.

Narrows Marina is a 10 minute taxi ride from Chambers Bay Golf Course, the site of the 2015 U.S. Open.

Days Island. If your destination is the Day Island Yacht Club at the back of the lagoon, run down the west side, close to Days Island and its boathouses. At lower tides this will be obvious, because a big drying shoal blocks the middle. Time your passage for mid-tide or higher. Least depth at zero tide is said to be 4 feet.

Titlow Park. Tacoma Narrows Waterway. Located on the Tacoma side, about 1 mile south of the Tacoma Narrows Bridge. Open all year, park with tennis courts and 'Spray Ground' (splash park). Restaurants a short walk away. Titlow Park is a marine preserve with excellent diving.

CENTRAL PUGET SOUND

LOCAL KNOWLEDGE

SPEED LIMIT: A no-wake speed of 5 mph or less is enforced within Gig Harbor and 200 feet outside the entrance.

⑲ **Gig Harbor.** www.gigharborguide.com. Gig Harbor is one of the most perfectly protected harbors in Puget Sound, and one of the most charming towns. The south shore is lined with moorages for the substantial commercial fish boat and pleasure boat fleets. The entrance to Gig Harbor is narrow, especially at low tide. Maintain a mid-channel course around the end of the spit.

Gig Harbor has overnight moorage, marine supplies, major repairs, and haulout. Anchorage is in 20 to 42 feet with good holding, although

Gig Harbor Marketplace

RESTAURANTS, SHOPS & SERVICES

ANTHONY'S
Anthony's at Gig Harbor serves premium NW seafood and offers a spectacular view of the harbor and Mt. Rainier. Enjoy the view from our expansive deck. Downstairs in our Shoreline Room lounge is a lighter menu and a more casual dining experience.
253-853-6353 • 8827 Harborview Dr. N., Gig Harbor, WA 98335
www.anthonys.com

DEVOTED KISS CAFE
Devoted Kiss Cafe is located in Downtown Gig Harbor at the end of the Bay in the Finholm District. Join us for a mouth-watering breakfast or lunch while enjoying our sweeping views of Gig Harbor and Mt. Rainier. Our staff is ready to welcome and guide you through the greatest dining experience this side of the bridge.
253.851.0055 • 8809 North Harborview Drive, Gig Harbor, WA 98332
www.devotedkisscafe.com

GIG HARBOR MARINA
Gig Harbor Marina & Boatyard is the only full-service boatyard with 50-metric ton travelift in Gig Harbor. We offer transient moorage, luxury guest lodging, brand new restrooms with showers, on-site food trolley and private event space. GHMB is also home to The NW Maritime Academy, a certified USCG training facility. We are close to incredible shops, parks, restaurants, bars or breweries in downtown Gig Harbor.
253-858-3535 • 3117 Harborview Dr., Gig Harbor, WA 98335
GigHarborMarina.com • VHF 69

HARBOR HISTORY MUSEUM
Harbor History Museum creates opportunities to experience the heritage of the greater Gig Harbor communities by collecting, preserving, and sharing the rich history of the area. Artifacts, video kiosks, hands-on exhibits, computer interactives, and a small theater bring Peninsula history to life in our permanent galleries. In addition, the Museum provides 3-5 special exhibits throughout the year so there is always something new to see and experience for our members and visitors.
253.858.6722 ext. 5 • 4121 Harborview Drive, Gig Harbor, WA 98332 • www.harborhistorymuseum.org

HERITAGE DISTILLING CO.
Heritage Distilling Company (HDC) is a craft distillery with 2 tasting room locations in Gig Harbor. HDC makes award winning vodkas, gins, and whiskeys. Learn more at www.heritagedistilling.com.
253.509.0008 • 3207 57th St Ct NW & 3118 Harborview Dr., Gig Harbor, WA 98335 • www.heritagedistilling.com

SHIP TO SHORE MARINE & KAYAK
Located at Arabella's Landing in Gig Harbor, Ship to Shore Marine, a family owned business, is South Puget Sound's premier marine supply and kayak store. The store has just expanded into two new custom buildings stocked with everything boaters need. Store crew members also offer excellent customer service because they are all experienced sailors, boat owners and kayakers.
253-858-6090 • 3403 Harborview Dr., Gig Harbor, WA 98332
www.shiptoshoremarine.com

GIG HARBOR COMMUNITY EVENTS
Monthly First Saturday FREE Art Walk at various downtown galleries www.gigharborwaterfront.org
April 28 & 29 - 7th Annual Gig Harbor Paddlers Cup www.gigharborpaddlerscup.com
May 26 - Street Scramble - An urban scavenger hunt! www.gigharborguide.com
May 12 - Gig Harbor Beer Festival www.gigharborbeerfestival.com
June 2 & 3 - Maritime Gig Festival www.maritimegig.com
June 26 – Aug 14 Summer Sounds at Skansie Every Tuesday - Enjoy an outdoor concert! www.gigharborguide.com
July 1 - Gig Harbor Wings and Wheels Air Show and Car Show www.freedomfair.com
July 21 - Chalk the Harbor www.gigharborwaterfront.org
July 21 & 22 - Peninsula Art Leauge's ArtFest www.peninsulaartleague.com
July 28 - Gig Harbor Wine & Food Festival www.gigharborwaterfront.org
September 23 - Race for a Soldier Half Marathon and 5K www.raceforasoldier.org
October 27 & 28 11th Annual Gig Harbor Film Festival www.gigharborfilmfestival.org
November 8 - 9th Annual Girls Night Out www.gigharborwaterfront.org
November 17 - Donkey Creek Chum Festival www.harborwildwatch.org
November 22 - Turkey Trot www.gigharborturkeytrot.com
December 8 - Lighted Boat Parade gigharboryachtclub.wildapricot.org/

SOUTH AND CENTRAL PUGET SOUND   Reference Only – Not for Navigation

Central Puget Sound

86   www.WaggonerGuide.com

See Area Map Page 86 - Maps Not for Navigation

SOUTH AND CENTRAL PUGET SOUND

the bay shoals close to both shores and toward the head. In some areas, weed on the bottom can foul anchors.

The City of Gig Harbor maintains Jerisich Park with its dinghy dock, long moorage float, 30 amp power, water and holding tank pumpout. The Gig Harbor Maritime Pier, 40-feet, next to Tides Tavern, has temporary moorage, restrooms and pumpout.

We enjoy walking Gig Harbor's village-like commercial streets. The harbor is lined with shops, galleries, specialty shops and antiquing are excellent, and the architecture turn-of-the-20th-century. At least two shops serve enormous ice cream cones and have chairs out front where you can enjoy your treat in the shade. Several good restaurants, from casual to elegant. On the casual side, Tides Tavern, a short distance inside the mouth of the bay, is a longtime favorite. If you are lucky, you'll find room to tie the boat at their private dock. Tides Tavern personnel can come to your boat to take your order and deliver your meal dockside, a nice option for families. Anthony's, near the head of the bay, also has a dock. More likely, you'll take the dinghy or approach by land. The JW Trolley @ The Boatyard is a new addition at the Gig Harbor Marina & Boatyard and has become a local Gig Harbor favorite for informal dining. Open 8:30 a.m. to dusk.

Finholm's Market and Deli, The Harbor General Store, and The Waterfront Natural Market offer some groceries within easy walking distance of the waterfront. Several supermarkets are uptown, best reached by bus or taxi. In the summer months a trolley-themed bus service runs, seven days a week, frequently between the waterfront and uptown areas.

For a great view of Gig Harbor and Mt. Rainier, the local Lions Club built an observation area called the Finholm View Climb. The stairway is at the head of the bay, across the street from Anthony's Restaurant. Lee's SUP & Kayak rentals are located in front of Anthony's Restaurant.

For a romantic time with someone special, grab your favorite refreshment and take a gondola tour of the harbor (gigharborgondola.com). A small snack box of cheese, fruit and chocolates is provided.

The recently renovated Gig Harbor History

Arabella's Landing

Museum (www.harborhistorymuseum.org) is superb. Located at the west end of Harborview Drive, the main road along the waterfront.

⑲ **Gig Harbor Marina and Boatyard.** 3117 Harborview Drive, Gig Harbor, WA 98335; (253) 858-3535; www.gigharbormarina.com. Monitors VHF 69. Open all year with guest moorage in unoccupied slips, 30 amp power, water, garbage drop, and free Wi-Fi. New restrooms with showers. Reservations accepted. Full service boatyard with haulout to 50 tons. "The Club" building and classroom space are available for rendezvous and other events.

⑲ **Arabella's Landing.** 3323 Harborview Drive, Gig Harbor, WA 98335; (253) 851-1793; info@arabellaslanding.com; www.arabellaslanding.com. Open all year, 225 feet of guest side-tie moorage for boats up to 175 feet, six 50-foot slips, and one 60-foot slip; 30 & 50 amp power, water, Wi-Fi, restrooms, showers, laundry, secured gate, pumpout. ADA accessible. Reservations recommended.

Stan and Judy Stearns developed this classy marina, located a short distance past the city dock, close to shopping, restaurants, services, and groceries. Excellent concrete docks, beautiful grounds, and brick walkways. They have a well-trained crew to help with landings, make dinner reservations, or assist in finding someone to repair your boat if necessary. The moorage fee includes power, water, and showers. Group gatherings may make use of the clubhouse with lounge, fireplace, and coffee service.

Enjoy Netshed No. 9 restaurant at the top of the docks for breakfast and lunch, and make reservations for a 5-star dinner at Brix 25. Ship to Shore Marine Supply, on site, has an excellent stock of marine supplies and kayaks which you may try-out in their infinity pool. In 2017 Arabella's added two Airbnb suites for their guests that want to stay ashore. See GigHarborAirbnb for reservations for the "The Sail Loft" and "The Cove Suite".

Bayview Marina, just east of Arabella's Landing, is under the same ownership, with 250 feet of dock, 30 & 50 amp power and water on the dock.

⑲ **Jerisich Dock.** 3211 Harborview Drive, Gig Harbor, WA; (253) 851-6170; www.cityofgigharbor.net. Open all year, 420 feet of first-come, first-served dock space, 30 amp power, seasonal water, free seasonal pumpout. Two mooring buoys for vessels 32 feet and under (no charge), but required to register. This is an attractive and well-used public dock and park, located just west of Tides Tavern on the downtown side of Gig Harbor. Maximum 3-night stay within a 10-day period. Pay overnight moorage fees at self-payment kiosk adjacent to the dock, credit and debit cards accepted. Dinghy dock is near shore on the west side. Restaurants, groceries, and a seasonal trolley café are all within walking distance. Check your tide table; close to shore you could touch at low tide.

The Welcome Plaza, upland from the Jerisich Dock in Skansie Brothers Park, was refurbished in 2017. Large restrooms were constructed to include showers for visiting boaters along with laundry facilities. The Splash Fountain is popular with children. A viewing deck, with tables and chairs, is located above the restrooms.

⑲ **Peninsula Yacht Basin.** 8913 N. Harborview Drive, Gig Harbor, WA 98332; (253) 858-2250; dockmaster@peninsulayachtbasin.com; www.peninsulayachtbasin.com. Open all year, no transient moorage, reciprocal privileges with Gig Harbor Yacht Club only. Maximum boat length 85 feet, 6-foot depth at zero tide, 20 & 30 amp power, restrooms, showers. Located on the north shore of Gig Harbor, next to Anthony's Shoreline Restaurant.

ANTHONY'S AT GIG HARBOR
8827 Harborview Dr. N.
(253) 853-6353

TACOMA AREA

Commencement Bay. The southern shoreline of Commencement Bay is mostly parks, interspersed with buildings, housing, restaurants, and other facilities. At least two restaurants provide moorage for their patrons. Following this shoreline southeastward leads to the Thea Foss Waterway.

Tacoma's Commencement Bay is busy with commercial traffic. Most visiting boats choose to moor at one of several marinas in the Thea Foss Waterway. Museums, restaurants, and other attractions are a short walk from the docks.

Point Defiance. Point Defiance marks the northern end of Tacoma Narrows and is noted for swirling currents and excellent salmon fishing. The entire point is a major Tacoma park, complete with trails, a zoo, aquarium, gardens, sports facilities, and picnic areas.

⑳ **Breakwater Marina.** 5603 N. Waterfront Drive, Tacoma, WA 98407; (253) 752-6663 (office); (253) 752-6685 (service); www.breakwatermarina.com. Certified Clean Marina. Open all year, 15 & 30 amp power, restrooms, showers, laundry, portapotty dump, pumpout, propane, store. Guest moorage is in unoccupied slips for boats up to 45 feet, call ahead. Repairs available.

ANTHONY'S AT POINT DEFIANCE
5910 N. Waterfront Drive
(253) 752-9700

⑳ **Point Defiance Boathouse Marina.** 5912 N. Waterfront Drive, Tacoma, WA 98407; (253) 591-5325; pointdefiancemarina.com. Certified Clean Marina and 5-Star EnviroStar rating. Open 7 days a week all year except Thanksgiving and Christmas. Guest moorage is on the dock between the ferry landing and the 8-lane boat launch, 72 hour maximum stay. Pay at the boat launch kiosk. Ethanol-free gasoline, restrooms, free pumpout, some 30 amp power, dry storage for small boats, boat rentals. Bait, tackle, snacks, souvenirs and gift items at Point Defiance Boathouse Tackle Shop. Public fishing pier. Anthony's Restaurant is at the east end of the marina. The marina is within walking distance of the Point Defiance Zoo & Aquarium and Point Defiance Park. Bus service to greater Tacoma.

Commencement Bay

CHARTS

18441	Puget Sound – Northern Part (1:80,000)
18446	Puget Sound – Apple Cove Pt. to Keyport (1:25,000) & Agate Passage (1:10,000)
18447	Lake Washington Ship Canal (1:10,000) & Lake Washington (1:25,000)
18448	Puget Sound – Southern Portion (1:80,000)
18449	Puget Sound – Seattle to Bremerton (1:25,000)
18453	Tacoma Harbor (1:15,000)
18474	Puget Sound – Shilshole Bay to Commencement Bay (1:40,000)

Ruston. Point Defiance below the community of Ruston is the Tacoma terminus of the ferry to Vashon Island. The Point Defiance Boathouse Marina and Anthony's Harbor Lights restaurant are west of the ferry dock. A large launch ramp, operated by the Parks Department, is east of the ferry dock. Long-term tow vehicle and trailer storage is available a couple of blocks up the hill from the launch ramp.

The small town of Ruston was the site of a smelter. The site has recently been redeveloped, and a substantial footbridge now leads to the ferry terminal. A half-mile east of Point Defiance is the impressive new Point Ruston development, consisting of classy condos and apartments, shops, cafes, and a theater. A 'splash pad' overlooks the waterfront and pathway that connects Point Ruston to Point Defiance. Point Ruston is definitely worth a visit for the grand views, eateries, and park-like atmosphere.

Looking south in the Thea Foss Waterway, as seen from the 11th St. bridge

Old Town Dock. Next to Jack Hyde Park (formerly Commencement Park). The docks are usable, but don't appear to get much traffic. Smaller boats only.

LOCAL KNOWLEDGE

STRONG CURRENTS: Currents, especially on large tides, can run stronger than expected in Foss Waterway. Plan landings and departures accordingly.

Thea Foss Waterway. The Thea Foss Waterway (formerly City Waterway) has gone through a major renewal and revitalization.

Just inside the mouth of the waterway, the Foss Waterway Seaport is a fascinating stop. It is housed in the century-old Balfour warehouse, once part of a mile-long row of wheat warehouses. The 300-foot-long by 150-foot-wide building itself is a museum exhibit. Displays inside include a lab, a working boat building shop, Willits canoe exhibit, marine biology exhibit, and an extensive display detailing Puget Sound's maritime history. Some 1200 feet of public floats make boat access easy.

Up on Pacific Avenue, the Union Railroad Station has been restored and rebuilt as the Federal Courthouse, and decorated with Dale Chihuly glass sculpture. The must-see Washington State History Museum, which shares the courthouse's beautiful architecture, is next to the courthouse.

The Washington State History Museum is excellent. Allow at least two hours to see it; three or four hours is better. Adult or child, it's a knockout.

At the head of the waterway, the Museum of Glass fronts on the waterway, immediately east of the courthouse and the Washington State History Museum.

The Chihuly Bridge of Glass connects the courthouse and history museum complex with the Museum of Glass. You can spend several hours there. The hot shop furnaces roar, and the crew may create a bowl, a vase, or candlestick holders before your eyes. Exhibits in the galleries rotate. The works on display are impressive.

The Tacoma Art Museum features regularly rotating exhibits, and the building itself is a work of architectural art.

LeMay-America's Car Museum, across the road from the Tacoma Dome, draws large crowds. More than 350 cars, trucks and motorcycles are on display, dating from the beginning

Thea Foss Waterway

Breakwater Marina

Your Bridge to Culture

LeMay – America's Car Museum

Washington State History Museum

Museum of Glass

Foss Waterway Seaport

Tacoma Art Museum

Children's Museum of Tacoma

Six great museums. One low price.
www.TacomaMuseumDistrict.org

TACOMA REBORN

For years Tacoma was an industrial port not friendly to recreational boaters. The city waterfront had been neglected, facilities were limited and there wasn't much to do. The city was famous more for its pulp mills than its historic buildings, museums, and restaurants.

In the late 1980s Tacoma's political leaders got serious about rejuvenating their city. The Simpson Paper Mill spent tens of millions of dollars on renovations, reducing emissions and sweetening the air. In 1990 the University of Washington established its Tacoma campus, which now has more than 4000 students just up the hill from the Thea Foss Waterway. Tacoma Link light rail was built to help the growing population get around the city.

Foss Waterway Seaport

Museum of Glass and waterfront walk

Much of Tacoma's redevelopment has been centered around the Thea Foss Waterway. In 1992 the former president of University of Puget Sound conceived of the idea for a glass museum. Working with Dale Chihuly, a Tacoma native, he proposed the glass museum be built in Tacoma. In 2002 the high-profile, 75,000 square foot Museum of Glass opened a few steps up from the Thea Foss Waterway. Exhibits show a variety of glass, from both Chihuly and other artists. The working hot-shop, visible to visitors, is a highlight.

Part of Tacoma's revitalization is the emergence of its museum district, conveniently located just upland from the Thea Foss Waterway. Above the Glass Museum is the outstanding Washington State History Museum, housed in a distinctive brick building. The Tacoma Art Museum is just north of the History Museum.

Tacoma Waterfront

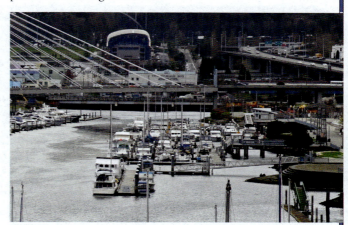
Looking south from the 11th Street bridge to the LeMay Museum

Slightly further away is LeMay—America's Car Museum. Harold LeMay, now deceased, was a garbage pioneer. He started LeMay Inc. in 1942 and grew it into the 10th largest garbage hauler in the country. The wealth generated from his business endeavors allowed him to indulge his automotive hobby. Over time he and his wife collected more than 3,300 cars, trucks, and motorcycles—the largest private collection in the world. Today, more than 700 of his cars are on display in his namesake museum.

At the entrance to Thea Foss Waterway is Foss Waterway Seaport. The century-old Balfour Dock building was originally built for cargo arriving by rail and departing by sail. After a recent renovation, it now houses the Working Waterfront Maritime Museum. Inside you'll find notable classic boats and sailing vessels along with displays of boat building and restoration. The extensive guest dock along the waterfront offers four hours of free moorage, perfect when visiting the museum.

What would any progressive city be without a Children's Museum? The Children's Museum of Tacoma believes in the "Power of Play" and "Play to Learn", and play is the right of every child. The museum is new and bright, a fun place for kids. It moved to its current location on Pacific Avenue in 2012.

A single, discounted admission ticket to the Tacoma Art Museum, Museum of Glass, the LeMay America's Car Museum and the Washington State History Museum is available for $52.50, or $42 for students, active duty military, and seniors aged 65 and over. The pass is good for a seven day period while visiting Tacoma and includes a discount for the Foss Waterway Seaport. The Children's Museum of Tacoma is a "pay-as-you-will" museum.

Union Station

Tacoma has grown into one of the region's best urban destinations with an esplanade, restaurants and museums to explore, all within a short walk from marinas of the Thea Foss Waterway.

of motorized transport. Open 7 days a week, 10:00 a.m. to 5:00 p.m. Check website for weekly events. Highly recommended.

Downtown Tacoma is very different from other Puget Sound cities. Many of the old buildings are beautiful, and some are historic. One building has a plaque commemorating Russell G. O'Brien, who on October 18, 1893, originated the custom of standing during the playing of the *Star Spangled Banner*. We learn the most interesting things when we walk around.

Guest moorage: Modern, Dock Street Marina, with guest moorage, is in front of the Museum of Glass. Guest moorage is also available at Foss Harbor Marina. Side-tie guest moorage is available at Foss Waterway Seaport.

No Anchoring Zone: All of the Thea Foss Waterway is a no anchoring zone.

Breweries: Area breweries include McMenamins Elks Lodge on 565 Broadway; Odd Otter Brewing at 716 Pacific; Pacific Brewing & Malting at 610 Pacific Ave.; and 7 Seas Brewing at 2101 Jefferson Ave.

The dramatic highway 509 bridge is just south of Dock Street Marina.

Farmers market: On Broadway between 9th and 11th Streets, a farmers market with 70 to 90 vendors. Thursdays, May through October from 10:00 a.m. to 3:00 p.m.

Light rail: Light rail runs from the theater district at the north end of downtown Tacoma to a last stop, 2½ blocks from the Tacoma Dome and LeMay-America's Car Museum. At the museum district, the tracks are in the middle of Pacific Avenue, fronting the Washington State History Museum. The free trains are clean and safe. They run every 12 minutes from morning to evening.

With the accomplishments and ongoing efforts of the Port of Tacoma, city leaders and others, The Foss Waterway and downtown Tacoma is a first class urban boating destination.

Things to Do

1. **LeMay-America's Car Museum.** This museum is housed in a dramatic building, just up from the waterfront. See over 350 cars, trucks and motorcycles on display in the world's largest auto museum.

2. **Museum of Glass.** With its iconic architecture near the waterfront and beautiful glasswork, this has become a key part of the Tacoma art scene.

3. **Tacoma Art Museum.** Art in Tacoma continues with photography, paintings, and Chihuly glass.

4. **Washington State History Museum.** Learn about Washington's past.

5. **Tacoma Glassblowing Studio.** See how glass art is made.

6. **Point Defiance Zoo & Aquarium.** See an Asian Forest Sanctuary, elephants and tigers. The large aquarium has octopi, sharks, and a beluga whale.

7. **Children's Museum of Tacoma.** The museum serves young children and their parents through self-directed play.

㉑ **Foss Waterway Seaport.** 705 Dock St, Tacoma, WA 98402; (253) 272-2750; info@fosswaterwayseaport.org; www.fosswaterwayseaport.org. Located at the mouth of Foss Waterway. Visitor moorage along 1200 feet of floating dock. From the middle gangway to the south end, 30 & 50 amp power and water are available. No power or water north of the

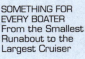

J&G MARINE SUPPLY

SOMETHING FOR EVERY BOATER From the Smallest Runabout to the Largest Cruiser

YOUR ONE STOP SHOP for

ELECTRONICS SALES • SERVICE • INSTALLATION

Autopilots • Antennas • Chart Plotters • GPS • Inverters • Radars
Sat. Receivers • Sounders • VHF & SSB Radios

ComNav · ICOM · Digital Antenna · Shakespeare · SIMRAD
Furuno · SEA · JRC · Nobeltec · SI-TEX
Garmin · Big Bay Technologies · C-MAP · Northstar · KVH
Lowrance · OceanLED · Maretron · Magnum Energy · Raymarine · Standard Horizon · Rose Point

FIBERGLASS SUPPLIES

| Polyester & Epoxy Resin | Cloth Cleaners | Mat Waxes | Tape Tools |
| Fillers | Paint | Varnish | Sealants |

and MARINE ACCESSORIES!

Anchors · Charts— · Fenders · Life Vests · Shorepower Cords
Battery Switches · U.S. & Canadian · Flares · Mooring Buoys · & Connectors
Bilge Pumps · Crab & Shrimp Pots · Fuel Tanks · Paint & Varnish · Trailer Accessories
Boat Hooks · Docklines · Heaters · Plumbing · Zincs
Books · · Horns · Rod Holders

M-F 8:30-5:00
SAT 9-1:00

1690 Marine View Dr. Tacoma WA 98422

253-572-4217   800-381-4217

TACOMA MARKETPLACE

RESTAURANTS, SHOPS & SERVICES

ALFRED'S
We serve Breakfast, Lunch and Dinner all day, and we have a full service bar. Want a great breakfast, come see us. With its great food, generous cocktails, fun, old fashioned atmosphere and friendlier than average staff, Alfred's is a favorite with locals and visitors alike. Take the free link train to the Dome District.
253-627-5491 • 402 Puyallup Ave • One block west of the Dome at the corner of East D St and Puyallup

CHILDREN'S MUSEUM OF TACOMA
We encourage all ages to celebrate play with our playscapes and innovative design that celebrates imagination and encourages creativity. The museum has five main play areas – Woods, Water, Voyager, Invention and Becka's Studio. We are open Wednesday to Sunday from 10am to 5pm. Admission is by donation. Come play with us!
253-627-6031 • 1501 Pacific Ave. • www.playtacoma.org

DOCK STREET MARINA
Dock Street Marina is Tacoma's only dedicated guest moorage facility. Located in front of the Museum of Glass and just steps away from the Chihuly Bridge of Glass that leads to more museums, shops and restaurants. Reservations recommended. Please call.
253-250-1906 • www.dockstreetmarina.com.

FOSS WATERWAY SEAPORT
The Foss Waterway Seaport celebrates Tacoma's rich maritime heritage—past, present and future. Located on the waterfront in a century-old wheat warehouse built cargo arriving by " rail and departing by sail!" Features maritime heritage exhibits, land and boat based marine science, heritage boat shop and hands on activities for ages. Short term moorage, power & water. Home of Festival of Sail (tall ships) June 15 -18, 2017.
253-272-2750 ext 100 • 705 Dock Street • www.fosswaterwayseaport.org

LEMAY – AMERICA'S CAR MUSEUM
Celebrating America's love affair with the automobile. The four-level, 165,000 sq. ft. museum features rotating exhibits and 300 cars, trucks and motorcycles on display. Free Tacoma Link Light Rail from Union Station to the Dome District.
253-779-8490 • 2702 E. D Street • www.americascarmuseum.org

MUSEUM OF GLASS
The world famous Museum of Glass is located at the south end of the Foss Waterway with adjacent guest moorage. Featuring multiple exhibitions and art installations, hands-on art studio, diverse educational programs, and a fully functioning glass blowing Hot Shop, the museum offers a unique and entertaining experience for all. Hours are 10am to 5pm, Tuesday through Sunday.
253-284-4750 • 1801 Dock St. • www.MuseumofGlass.org

NORTHWEST YACHTNET BROKERAGE
Our brokers have the knowledge, contacts and yachting expertise to give you optimal service in any area that you require. NW Yachtnet Brokerage brokers complete the continuing education required to be "Certified Professional Yacht Brokers." Our highly skilled team will treat you with honesty and respect. We are here to make boating the enjoyable experience it is meant to be. We have offices in Tacoma, Seattle, and Olympia.
1-888-641-5901 • www.nwyachtnet.com
1717 Dock Street (next to the Museum of Glass)

ROCK THE DOCK
Always great food, friends and fun on the Thea Foss Waterway! Live music every weekend - never a cover charge. Dock side outdoor seating. Full menu on line, find us on Facebook or visit our website for a full calendar of events.
253-272-5004 • 535 Dock St. • www.RocktheDockPub.com

TACOMA ART MUSEUM
Tacoma Art Museum serves the diverse communities of the Northwest through its collection, exhibitions, and learning programs, emphasizing art and artists from the Northwest and broader western region. We are open Tuesday to Sunday from 10am to 5pm.
253-272-4258 • 1701 Pacific Avenue • www.tacomaartmuseum.org

WASHINGTON STATE HISTORICAL SOCIETY
Our museum is dedicated to collecting, preserving and vividly presenting Washington's rich and storied history. We invite you to explore our interactive exhibits and high-tech displays, listen to theatrical storytelling, discover dramatic artifacts and learn about Washington State's unique people and places.
253-272-9747 • 1911 Pacific Ave. • www.washingtonhistory.org

TACOMA COMMUNITY EVENTS

April	Daffodil Festival • Sailing Schooner Zodiac Easter Brunch Cruises www.fosswaterwayseaport • Tacoma City Marathon
May	Apple Blossom Festival
June	NW Pinball Show • Festival of Sail (tall ships) * Scottish Highland Games • www.tacomagames.org
July	Freedom Fair • Tacoma Pride Festival - 2nd week in July Tacoma Food Truck Fest • www.metroparkstacoma.org/foodtruckfest Vintage Motorcycle Festival • www.americascarmuseum.org
August	Brew Five Three, Tacoma's Beer and Blues Festival www.broadwaycenter.org
Oct.	Tacoma Film Festival • www.TacomaFilmFestival.com
Nov.	Annual Holiday Tree lighting at the Broadway Center Day after Thanksgiving
Nov-Jan	Ice Skating Rink in Tacoma Polar Plaza

SOUTH AND CENTRAL PUGET SOUND See Area Map Page 86 - Maps Not for Navigation

Chinook Landing Marina

Dockton Park has extensive moorage.

middle gangway. No restrooms or garbage drop. Pumpout available April through September. Reservations only for groups. Payment is made at the Seaport office, or drop box after hours, 4 hour free stay. A dock for floatplanes is attached to the northwest end of the Seaport Facility; watch for floatplane activity.

㉑ **Foss Harbor Marina.** 821 Dock Street, Tacoma, WA 98402; (253) 272-4404; info@ fossharbor.com; www.fossharbormarina.com. Certified Clean Marina. Monitors VHF 71. Open all year, ethanol-free gasoline and diesel at end of D dock. Visitor moorage to 95 feet in unoccupied slips. Restrooms, showers, laundry, water, fixed and slip-side pumpout, portapotty dump, 30 & 50 amp power, free Wi-Fi in lounge area, Wi-Fi on the docks for a fee, kayak and SUP rentals. The restrooms have been redone and two showers have been added. The docks have been redecked and improved, and are excellent. Store has expanded beer and wine selection, deli sandwiches, convenience groceries, bait, tackle, marine supplies. An indoor lounge and outdoor patio are available for customers. Convenient walk to downtown.

㉑ **Dock Street Marina.** 1817 Dock St., Tacoma, WA 98402; (253) 250-1906; info@ dockstreetmarina.com; www.dockstreetmarina.com. Call ahead by phone for slip assignment. Certified Clean Marina. Concrete docks, security gates, 30, 50 & 100 amp power, water, slip-side pumpout, garbage, recycling drop, laundry, restrooms, free showers, free cable TV, some wheelchair access, kayak rentals. Complimentary bicycles for marina guests. This is the marina in front of the Museum of Glass. It is made up of two sets of docks—G and H docks are the southern, guest moorage docks. The permanent moorage 17th St. docks are immediately north.

The office, showers, and laundry are above the guest moorage docks, 30 slips 36-60 feet, with 127-foot pier ends. Concierge service. Pet-friendly. Moorage in the north docks is by assignment in unoccupied slips only. A 320-foot dock is in the north moorage.

Special events such as the Daffodil Marine Parade completely fill the marina. See their website for the complete list of special events. Rendezvous sometimes fill the marina, too. Reservations recommended, even in the off season.

Dock Street Marina is first-class, with an easy walk to many Tacoma restaurants and museums. Don't be surprised to find a courtesy newspaper in the cockpit on Sundays, or a red rose on Valentine's Day.

㉑ **Dock Street North Pier.** (253) 272-4352; This is the long concrete float north of Dock Street Marina. No power, water, or garbage, reservations 24-hours in advance. Watch your depths at zero tide or lower.

㉑ **Delin Docks.** 1616 East D St., Tacoma, WA 98421; (253) 572-2524; info@delindocksmarina.com; www.delindocksmarina.com. Certified Clean Marina. Open all year, 30 & 50 amp power, water, restrooms, free showers, laundry, pumpout, portapotty dump. These are new docks with 30- to 60-foot slips, located immediately north of Johnny's Dock on the east side of Foss Waterway. They're primarily permanent moorage, although occasionally unoccupied slips might be used for guest moorage.

Note: Dock Street Marina and the Delin Docks are under the same management.

㉑ **Johnny's Dock.** 1900 East D St., Tacoma, WA 98421; (253) 627-3186; www.johnnysdock.com. Open all year with limited moorage to 55 feet, power, and water. Transient moorage primarily serves Johnny's Dock restaurant.

㉑ **Tacoma Fuel Dock.** 820 East D St., Tacoma, WA 98421; (253) 383-0851; (800) 868-3681, www.cbmsi.com. Fuel dock open all year except Thanksgiving, Christmas, and New Year's Day. Summer hours 8:00 a.m. to dusk, winter hours 8:00 a.m. to 4:30 p.m. Monitors VHF 69, summer only. Gasoline, diesel, ice, frozen herring, soft drinks, snacks. Located on the east side of Thea Foss Waterway; look for the large Tacoma Fuel Dock sign. The uplands house Commencement Bay Marine Services and the Tacoma Youth Marine Center training young people in the skills needed for work on boats and along the waterfront. A portion of fuel sales supports the Sea Scouts and Tacoma Youth Marine Center.

Hylebos Waterway. The Hylebos Waterway follows the north shore of Commencement Bay and includes a number of moorages, boat builders, and boat service businesses. The shores are lined with heavy industry of many kinds, not all of it scenic. Still, an interesting exploration.

Guest moorage is at Chinook Landing Marina, a short distance up the waterway.

㉒ **Chinook Landing Marina.** 3702 Marine View Drive Suite 100, Tacoma, WA 98422; (253) 627-7676. Monitors VHF 79. Certified Clean Marina. Open all year, guest moorage available. Snacks and ice cream at the office. This is an excellent facility, 30 & 50 amp power, restrooms, showers, laundry, free Wi-Fi, pumpout, portapotty dump, 24-hour security. Larger boats should call ahead for availability. No shops or restaurants nearby. The well-stocked J&G Marine Supply chandlery is located about a mile away.

Tyee Marina. 5618 Marine View Dr. Tacoma WA 98422; (253) 383-5321. Permanent moorage only.

Browns Point Park. Open all year, day use only. Picnic tables and a swimming beach. The lighthouse is the focal point, with free tours of the light keepers cottage on Saturdays 1:00 p.m. to 4:00 p.m., May to October. For more information call the Points Northwest Historical Society (253) 927-2536.

VASHON ISLAND, COLVOS PASSAGE, EAST PASSAGE, DES MOINES, BLAKE ISLAND

Colvos Passage. The current always flows north in Colvos Passage, so heading north on a flood tide is a good choice. Colvos Passage offers little to entice a boater to stop, although Contributing Editor Tom Kincaid has anchored off Olalla and dinghied to the little store for a snack.

Dockton Park

Des Moines Marina is protected by a rock breakwater.

Inside the breakwater at Des Moines Marina. Fuel dock on the right, guest moorage on the left.

Harper State Park. Located 1.5 miles west of the ferry landing at Southworth. Open all year, day use only. Anchoring only. The gravel launch ramp is usable at high tide only, but is the closest launch to Blake Island, 1 mile away.

Quartermaster Harbor. Quartermaster Harbor indents the south end of Vashon Island about 4 miles. It is protected on the east side by Maury Island, which connects to Vashon Island by a narrow spit of land. Dockton Park is a popular destination.

Anchorage is good throughout most of Quartermaster Harbor, including the village of Burton, beyond Burton Peninsula. Anchorage at Burton is well-protected, with excellent holding on a sticky mud bottom. Be prepared to spend extra time cleaning the anchor and chain. The Quartermaster Yacht Club (members of reciprocal clubs welcomed) is at Burton, as is the Quartermaster Marina. The village of Burton has a well-stocked convenience store and several small shops. Taxi service is available on Vashon Island (Vashon Taxi (206) 434-1121), and buses run to Tacoma and Seattle.

Jensen Park, on Burton Peninsula, has a launch ramp, beach, picnic tables and barbecues. Vashon Watersports rents kayaks, canoes, and stand-up paddleboards at the park.

㉓ **Dockton Park.** 9500 SW Dock Road, Dockton, WA 98070; (206) 477-6150. Operated by King County Parks. Open all year, concrete launch ramp, 58 guest slips, rafting okay, restrooms, free showers, no power, no garbage pickup, no services within walking distance. Four days maximum stay. Dockton is a popular 23-acre park on the west side of Maury Island in Quartermaster Harbor. The park has play equipment, trails, fire pits, picnic shelters, picnic tables, barbecue areas. Call for group reservations.

About two blocks down 260th street, which runs eastward just above the dock, trailheads lead southward into 152-acre Dockton Forest, with one of the largest madrona forests in the area.

Anchoring note: Holding can be fair to poor in the area north of the Dockton Park docks. If anchoring, be sure of your set.

Quartermaster Marina. 23824 Vashon Highway SW, Vashon, WA 98070; (206) 919-2318 (manager); (206) 463-3624 (office). Open all year, transient moorage in unoccupied slips. Call ahead for availability. Water, 30 & 50 amp power, restrooms, garbage drop, pumpout, Wi-Fi.

East Passage is between Vashon Island and the mainland. Large ships bound to or from Tacoma or Olympia use this route. Tidal currents flood south and ebb north, and normally are a little stronger in East Passage than in Colvos Passage on the west side of Vashon Island.

Dash Point State Park. 5700 SW Dash Point Rd., Federal Way, WA 98023; (253) 661-4955. Open all year, 398 acres, restrooms, showers, no power. Sandy beach, swimming, and primitive, partial utility, and full utility campsites.

Redondo. A launch ramp, with 2 floats and a floating breakwater, is operated by the city of Des Moines. Fishing pier with coffee hut. Highline Community College operates the Marine Science and Technology Center (MaST), open to the public Saturdays 10:00 a.m. to 2:00 p.m. Anchor out and take the dinghy in.

Saltwater Marine State Park. 25205 8th Place South #1, Des Moines, WA 98198; (253) 661-4956. Two miles south of Des Moines. Open all year, overnight camping. Two day-use-only mooring buoys. Restrooms, showers, no power. Artificial reef for scuba diving, and outside shower for scuba rinse-off.

Traditional salmon bake dinner is a popular event at Tillicum Village.

City of Des Moines Marina

SOUTH AND CENTRAL PUGET SOUND   See Area Map Page 86 - Maps Not for Navigation

Blake Island Marine State Park

421 South 227th St.
(206) 824-1947

Sandy swimming beach. Vault toilets, primitive campsites, picnic tables and shelters, kitchen shelter, children's play equipment. Seasonal concession stand.

Maury Island Marine Park. 5405 SE 244th Street, Dockton, WA. This is a 300-acre park at the site of what once was a sand and gravel operation, 1.5 miles south of Point Robinson. Trails lead through the park. The anchorage, with fair holding, is well protected in a northerly breeze. Popular with locals. On sunny days the winds are warmed as they cross Maury Island, making for good sunbathing. Operated by King County Parks.

Point Robinson. Point Robinson is surrounded by a 10-acre county park that can be approached by dinghy. The lighthouse is beautiful and the park has a nice beach, but no facilities for boaters.

Tramp Harbor, where Vashon Island joins Maury Island, has convenient anchoring depths, but only minimal protection from winds, particularly from the north. It is seldom used for overnight anchorage.

㉔ **Des Moines.** The City of Des Moines, between Tacoma and Seattle, is a good destination for clubs and groups. The Des Moines Marina has full services available.

Des Moines Beach Park is next to the marina and provides boater beach access.

㉔ **City of Des Moines Marina.** 22307 Dock Ave. S., Des Moines, WA 98188; (206) 824-5700; marinainfo@desmoineswa.gov; www.desmoinesmarina.com. The marina does not monitor VHF. Certified Clean Marina. Open all year. Gasoline, diesel, propane, 30 amp power, free Wi-Fi. This 840-slip marina and public pier has 1500 feet of guest moorage, much of it side-tie, for boats to 100 feet. Maximum boat length in permanent slips is 62 feet. The parking lot is now paid parking. Channel depth is 13 feet at zero tide. Stop at the fuel dock for directions to an empty berth. Free moorage for 4 hours. Restrooms, free showers, 2 free pumpouts. Reservations accepted for boats 32 feet and larger, or groups of 5 or more boats, 1 day in advance.

The marina can assist yacht clubs or rendezvous with planning and special needs, including free shuttle service upon request.

Des Moines Marina is the closest marina to Sea-Tac Airport. The marina can provide shuttle service to and from the airport.

The guest moorage area now has a 25×100-foot concrete activity float with shelter, and all-new concrete floats. An 80-foot-long ADA-compliant ramp has been installed. The boatlift was removed. The grounds have been landscaped. Des Moines, already a popular destination for clubs and groups, is now even more attractive.

All services, including laundry, groceries, and several restaurants, are within walking distance. Shuttle service by request. The 670-foot public fishing pier runs east-west. To enter the marina, leave the fishing pier to port and turn to starboard at the north end of the breakwater. At low tide the entrance is tight, especially with opposing traffic. At the south end of the marina Des Moines Yacht Club has guest moorage for visiting members of reciprocal clubs.

Farmers market on Saturdays, June through September. July 4th "Fireworks over Des Moines."

CSR Marine, a highly regarded boatyard on Seattle's Lake Washington Ship Canal, operates the repair yard at the Des Moines Marina. Travelift haulout to 25 tons.

Yukon Harbor offers good anchorage, well protected from the south but open to the northeast.

㉕ **Blake Island Marine State Park.** (360) 371-8330. Open all year, 475 acres with 1500 feet of dock space in the breakwater-protected marina. 24 mooring buoys for boats 36 feet and under ring the island. Pumpout, water, 30 amp power. No garbage drop and a "pack it in–pack it out" policy. Moorage is limited to 7 consecutive days. Buoys on the east side are exposed to wakes from passing ships. Self-register and pay mooring buoy fee on shore.

The marina is on the northeast shore of the island. To enter, follow the dredged channel marked by red and green beacons. Stay in the marked channel; the water is shoal on both sides of the beacons. Immediately inside the breakwater, one float is for the boat that brings guests to Tillicum on Blake Island, and another is for the State Parks boat. The rest of the floats are available on a first-come, first-serve basis. Expect to find them full during high season and on weekends year round.

Blake Island has primitive campsites, including a Cascadia Marine Trail campsite. An underwater reef is good for scuba diving. The park has picnic shelters, volleyball courts, nature trail, approximately 16 miles of hiking trails through dense forest, and 5 miles of shoreline to explore. The Tillicum restaurant is a replica of an Indian longhouse. It is open only when tours are scheduled, and features dinner with fish cooked on stakes facing an open fire. Tours include dinner and a show with dancing and masks, and compares favorably with the show at Alert Bay. Call Argosy Tours (888) 623-1445; (206) 623-1445. Internet search, Argosy Cruises Tillicum Excursion. Individuals arriving by private boat should call ahead for dinner reservations.

Sailboat races are held in Elliott Bay.

Ride the Great Wheel on the Seattle waterfront.

www.WaggonerGuide.com

SOUTH AND CENTRAL PUGET SOUND

Bell Harbor Marina offers easy access to downtown Seattle.

Wildlife is abundant, including a high raccoon population not fearful of people. They roam the grounds and docks day or night looking for food. As in all state parks, there is a policy not to feed the animals. Park rangers recommend securing all garbage, pet food and ice chests, yes they can open an ice chest. Do not leave hatches open or you might find an unwelcomed surprise in your salon.

Blake Island is just a short hop from Elliott Bay Marina or Shilshole Bay Marina. The park is accessible only by boat and is one of the most popular stops on Puget Sound. A gem of a park.

SEATTLE

Elliott Bay, the center of Seattle's shipping industry, is a busy ocean port. Keep a sharp watch for ferries coming and going from Colman Dock, for tugs with tows, and for commercial vessels of all kinds. Large vessels are slow to maneuver, and should always be given a wide berth. When there's any doubt at all, *any* doubt, cross *behind* commercial vessels, not in front of them.

Piers 89, 90, and 91 in Smith Cove are heavily used by commercial ships. The Port of Seattle's grain terminal occupies part of the shoreline north of the regular commercial piers. Myrtle Edwards Park, including a fishing pier, stretches along about a mile of the Elliott Bay waterfront. The piers on the central waterfront, too small for modern maritime commerce, have been converted to other uses, including a hotel, shops, museums, an aquarium, and places to sit and watch the harbor activity.

At Pier 36, south of the Colman ferry dock, the U.S. Coast Guard has its Seattle headquarters, including the Coast Guard Museum and Vessel Traffic Service.

Downtown Seattle is served by two excellent marinas: Elliott Bay Marina on the north shore below Magnolia Bluff, and Port of Seattle's Bell Harbor Marina at Pier 66. These two marinas make downtown Seattle easy and safe to visit.

Seattle is often referred to as the "Boating Capital of America" and with little wonder. With abundant first-class visitor moorage, there is good reason to cruise to the Emerald City to find out what makes it so special.

THINGS TO DO

1. **Pike Place Market**. Unique shops with many specialty food items, even the first Starbucks. You can see cheese being made at Beechers. Watch out for flying salmon in the market. Don't miss the nearby Olympic Sculpture Park.

2. **Seattle Aquarium**. See a coral reef, giant Pacific octopus, pinecone fish, and potbellied seahorses. Located at Pier 59, a few blocks south of Bell Harbor Marina.

3. **Seattle Art Museum (SAM)**. Locally curated exhibits and rotating exhibitions from the best art collections of the world.

4. **Fremont Farmers Market**. Year-round on Sundays in this funky neighborhood. You never know what you might find.

5. **Burke-Gilman Trail**. Rent a bike and see Seattle from Shilshole to Kenmore, mostly along the city's lakefront. Some detours on streets through Ballard.

6. **Seattle Center**. Tour the Space Needle, or MoPop, the museum of pop culture formerly known as EMP—the Experience Music Project, and the new Chihuly Garden and Glass Museum.

7. **Pacific Science Center** at **Seattle Center**. Enjoy the IMAX Theater, the Planetarium or unique exhibits. Great for kids and adults.

8. **Tillicum, Blake Island**. Take your boat to Blake Island State Park and make a reservation for a tribal salmon buffet dinner and show. Experience the Coast Salish people through storytelling and dance.

9. **Center for Wooden Boats**. Walk around the antique restored boats on South Lake Union. With

Elliott Bay Marina

2018 WAGGONER CRUISING GUIDE

SOUTH AND CENTRAL PUGET SOUND   See Area Map Page 86 - Maps Not for Navigation

Mount Rainier is a prominent landmark throughout south and central Puget Sound. This is the Seattle waterfront from Bell Harbor Marina.

membership and checkout you can even rent a classic sailboat or powerboat for a cruise on the lake.

10. Museum of History and Industry (MOHAI). Newly relocated to South Lake Union. Many exhibits on Seattle's heritage.

11. Kenmore Air Tour. What better way to learn the islands and waterways of this spectacular cruising area than from the air? Stay local or take an extended flight from Lake Union to the San Juan Islands and back.

12. Museum of Flight. A short taxi ride away is one of the nation's best flight museums. The Concorde, WWII aircraft, a Space Shuttle Simulator, a Boeing 707 and 787, and more.

13. Seattle Zoo. An outstanding zoo for the day or an afternoon, just a cab ride away.

14. Seattle Children's Museum. Over 22,000 sq. ft. of hands-on exhibits for kids, ages 10 months to 10 years, to explore, and daily educational programs.

15. Seattle Great Wheel. Take a ride on one of Seattle's newest attractions. Great views day or night. Located at Pier 57.

㉖ **Elliott Bay Marina.** 2601 W. Marina Place, Seattle, WA 98199; (206) 285-4817; info@elliottbaymarina.net; www.elliottbaymarina.net. Monitors VHF 78A. Certified Clean Marina. This is a beautiful marina, immaculately maintained, open all year. The fuel dock has gasoline, diesel, free pumpout, and a store with convenience groceries. Transient moorage available in unoccupied slips, first-come, first-served. Reservations can be made for vessels 50 feet and longer. The marina has free cable TV, 30 & 50 amp power, up to 100 amp on outside moorage, restrooms, laundry, pumpout, free showers, free use of kayaks, SUPs and bikes, and excellent 24-hour security.

Enter through either end of the breakwater. The marina office is on the ground level of the main building, near Maggie Bluffs marina grill. Elegant dining at Palisade and casual dining at

ELLIOTT BAY MARKETPLACE

RESTAURANTS, SHOPS & SERVICES

BOAT INSURANCE AGENCY
Boat Insurance is what we do at the Boat Insurance Agency, and we have been doing just that for over 30 years! Owned by Neal Booth and staffed by knowledgeable boaters and insurance folks, we are the first choice for thousands of boaters in the West. Representing all of the best markets, we do the shopping for you so you don't have to! Ask about our yacht club discounts, education and experience credits!
206-285-1350 • 2601 W Marina Pl. #B • www.boatinsurance.net

ELLIOTT BAY MARINA
With 360 degree views of downtown Seattle and the Olympic Mountains, Elliott Bay Marina offers a relaxing place to moor. Enjoy two restaurants, repair facilities, 24-hour security, fuel dock, convenience store, year round events, and friendly customer service from our marina staff.
206-285-4817 • 2601 West Marina Place • www.elliottbaymarina.net

EMERALD HARBOR MARINE
Emerald Harbor Marine is a yacht systems and services company based in Seattle and operating throughout the Pacific Northwest. We work with the best marine manufacturers to ensure you get the right product, expert installation and the best value. From communications equipment to watermakers and everything in between, we'll ensure it's right for you and right for your boat.
206-285-3632 • 2601 W. Marina Place #T • www.emharbor.com

MONKEY FIST MARINE
Keeping you on the water. Providing quality services from stem to stern; heating, bow and stern thrusters, electronics, plumbing, electrical, head systems, propulsion/engine, and generator.
206-285-2600 • 2601 West Marina Place Ste. K • www.monkeyfistmarine.com

NORDHAVN YACHTS NORTHWEST
Nordhavn Yachts Northwest are the official representatives for new and used Nordhavns in the Pacific Northwest. Since opening our doors in 2005, we have helped countless buyers step into the boat of their dreams. We're proud to say that we have sold more Nordhavns than any other boat dealer in the area and our expertise in the trawler marketplace is unsurpassed.
206-223-3624 • 2601 W. Marina Pl., Suite S • www.nordhavn.com

PALISADE RESTAURANT
Palisade, where Seattle celebrates! Come up from the marina and join us for lunch, happy hour, dinner or weekend brunches with endless mimosas. Dining overlooks the marina with indoor and outdoor seating. Palisade is Seattle's landmark destination for elegant catering, inspiring views and memorable dining experiences. Let us be your onshore galley.
206-285-1000 • 2601 West Marina Place • www.palisaderestaurant.com

See Area Map Page 86 - Maps Not for Navigation

SOUTH AND CENTRAL PUGET SOUND

Maggie Bluffs. The fuel dock has a mini-mart. It's 5 minutes by cab or Uber to downtown Seattle. There is easy access to the Seattle public transportation system within walking distance.

The marina is headquarters for the Downtown Sailing Series, 10 informal races Thursday evenings during the summer, with barbecue and awards afterward.

Whole Foods Market and West Marine are about 1 mile away. A bike and walking path runs from the marina along scenic Myrtle Edwards waterfront park to the downtown waterfront. We took about an hour each way to walk between the marina and Pier 70. Seattle Yacht Club has an outstation (no reciprocal moorage) at the marina. Views of downtown, Mt. Rainier, Olympic Mountains.

㉗ **Bell Harbor Marina.** Pier 66, 2203 Alaskan Way, Seattle, WA 98121; (206) 787-3952; bhm@portseattle.org; www.portseattle.org. Monitors VHF 66A. Certified Clean Marina. Open all year, 30, 50 & 100 amp power, water, restrooms, free showers, garbage/recycling drop, pumpout, 24-hour security. Entrance at 47°36.55'N/122°20.85'W—look for the distinctive spire as a landmark. Moorage reservations can be made by telephone or email.

The Port of Seattle's Bell Harbor Marina, with 37 slips, is part of Seattle's Central Waterfront Development, and is an easy cruising destination. Depending on the mix, the docks will hold as many as 70 visitor boats, 30 feet to 70 feet. The waterfront, with the Seattle Aquarium, a variety of shops, and the Seattle Great Wheel, is just outside the marina. It's a safe, 2-block walk to the always interesting Pike Place Market.

Visitors can leave their boat at Bell Harbor and take in a game at Safeco Field for the Mariners or CenturyLink Field for the Seahawks or the Sounders. Three restaurants are just above the marina with many more restaurants and shops within walking distance.

Bell Harbor's facilities are top-notch, with excellent wheelchair access. The staff is professional and alert.

Because of rough water in Elliott Bay, the breakwater entry is narrow. Boats larger than 70 feet will find the entry and turning basin a little tight. The Port of Seattle provides approximately 1900 feet of outside pier apron devoted to large vessels including superyachts and cruise ships.

2201 Alaskan Way
(206) 448-6688

East Waterway. Both sides of East Waterway are lined with docks for commercial vessels, most of them loading or unloading containers. The waterway is navigable to Spokane Street, where a fixed bridge and foul ground block further navigation.

West Waterway. West Waterway and the connecting Duwamish River make a splendid sightseeing voyage. Use large-scale Chart 18450.

Enter past busy Vigor Industrial shipyard (formerly Todd Shipyard) and the now-closed Lockheed Shipyard at the mouth, and motor along a fascinating variety of docks, ships, barges, small pleasure boats, mega-yachts, and abandoned hulks. Commercial buildings and the modest homes of South Park are on both sides.

You will go under the 1st Ave. S. Bridge, vertical clearance 39 feet, and past the former site of the Boeing Company's Plant 2, to the 16th Ave. S. Bridge (renamed the South Park Bridge). The 1st Ave. S. Bridge will open on signal, except during rush hour traffic. The famed Delta Marine facility, builder of commercial fish boats and megayachts, is a short distance beyond the 16th Ave. S. (South Park) Bridge.

Not far past Delta Marine, a low bridge blocks progress to all but small, open boats.

Don Armeni Park and Seacrest Park are located between Harbor Island and Duwamish Head. Don Armeni Park has a 4-lane launch ramp with floats. Seacrest Park has a fishing pier.

Bell Harbor Marina

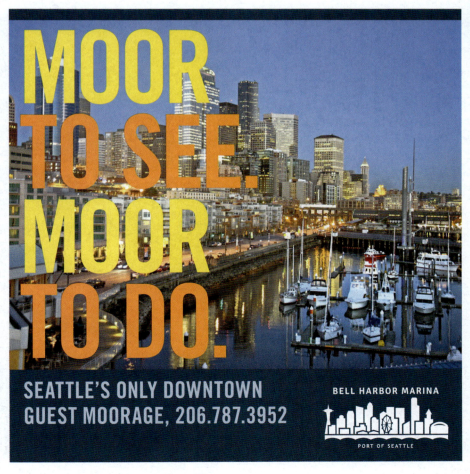

2018 WAGGONER CRUISING GUIDE

SOUTH AND CENTRAL PUGET SOUND

See Area Map Page 86 - Maps Not for Navigation

Harbor Island Marina. 1001 Klickitat Way S.W., Seattle, WA 98134; (206) 787-3006; him@portofseattle.org; www.portofseattle.org. This Port of Seattle marina is located on the south end of Harbor Island and caters to long term tenants. No transient moorage.

SHILSHOLE BAY

LOCAL KNOWLEDGE

Shallow Area: Do not stray south of the buoyed channel in Shilshole Bay. The water between the channel and Magnolia Bluff shoals rapidly.

Shilshole Bay indents the shoreline of Puget Sound north of West Point, and leads via a dredged channel to the Hiram M. Chittenden Locks (Ballard Locks) and the Lake Washington Ship Canal. Shilshole Bay Marina is north of the dredged channel, with entrances around the north and south ends of a long rock breakwater.

Lacking local knowledge, boats bound for the locks should follow the channel, marked by buoys, to the locks.

㉘ **Shilshole Bay Marina.** 7001 Seaview Ave. NW, Suite 100, Seattle, WA 98117; (206) 787-3006; (800) 426-7817; sbm@portseattle.org; www.portseattle.org. Certified Clean Marina. Monitors VHF 17. Open all year, office hours 8:00 a.m. to 4:30 p.m., Monday through Saturday. This is a large, busy, well-equipped marina, operated by the Port of Seattle. The marina has guest moorage for more than 100 boats to 250 feet, 30, 50, & 100 amp power, restrooms, showers, laundry, free cable TV on the guest docks, pumpout, portapotty dump. Complimentary bikes and shuttle. The marina shuttle provides transportation for guests to Ballard shopping and dining. Waste oil disposal stations, recycling and garbage drop.

A complete boatyard (Seaview West) with 55-ton Travelift haulout is at the south end of the marina. The boatyard has repair-yard supplies and propane. A wide launch ramp is at the north end of the marina.

A coffee shop is onsite. Walking distance to restaurants, a fast-food stand, and a West Marine store. Golden Gardens Park, with beach and picnic areas, is a short walk north of the marina.

The large Central Plaza, in front of the office building and adjacent to the guest docks, is nice for gatherings. Contact the office for event planning.

㉘ **Shilshole Bay Fuel Dock.** 7029 Seaview Ave. NW, Seattle, WA 98117; (206) 783-7555. Open 7 days a week except Thanksgiving and Christmas. Ethanol-free gasoline, diesel, kerosene. At the end of H dock, the Port of Seattle operates a pumpout, bilge pumpout, and portapotty dump at the outer end of the dock. Convenience store carries ice, beverages, snacks, local guidebooks. Friendly people, clean and efficient operation.

LAKE WASHINGTON SHIP CANAL

The Lake Washington Ship Canal connects the Hiram Chittenden Locks with Lake Washington, a distance of approximately 5.5 miles. Except for a marked course in the middle of Lake Union, a 7-knot speed limit is enforced all the way to Webster Point, at the entrance to Lake Washington. Most boats travel about 6 knots. If no bridge openings are needed, allow about 30 minutes between Lake Union and the locks, and about an hour between Lake Washington and the locks. The Lake Washington Ship Canal has fuel docks, ship repair yards, boatyards, and moorages. Keep an alert lookout for vessels pulling out or turning. This can be an active area.

LOCAL KNOWLEDGE

SOUND SIGNALS: For all of the bridges, the sound signal to request an opening is 1 long blast and 1 short. The bridge tender will answer with 1 long and 1 short blast if the bridge can be opened or 5 short blasts if it cannot.

Ship Canal Bridge Information. From west to east, the Lake Washington Ship Canal is crossed by the Ballard Bridge, vertical clearance 44 feet at the center; Fremont Bridge, vertical clearance 30 feet at the center; University

We're not just a marina.
We're a super fun destination.

SHILSHOLE BAY MARINA
PORT OF SEATTLE
Call us: 206 787 3006

www.WaggonerGuide.com

See Area Map Page 86 - Maps Not for Navigation

SOUTH AND CENTRAL PUGET SOUND

Hiram M. Chittenden Locks

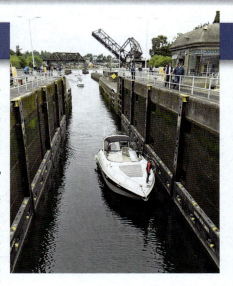

The dredged, well-marked channel leading to the Hiram Chittenden Locks passes under the Burlington Northern bascule bridge. *Caution: Although Chart 18447 shows vertical clearance of this bridge to be 43 feet from mean high water, Local Notice to Mariners reports that the actual clearance may be closer to 41 feet. Clearance gauges have been installed at the draw.* The bridge is kept open unless a train is due. The opening signal is one long and one short blast, the same signal as for the Ballard, Fremont, University, and Montlake Bridges. Remember, though, if a train is due you will be ignored.

Your wait at the locks, in either direction, can be as short as zero or as long as several hours depending on the flow of commercial traffic.

Approaching from Puget Sound: If you are approaching from Puget Sound, you'll starboard-side tie to the wall on the south side of the channel under the railroad bridge. If traffic is heavy, as it often is at the end of fair weather summer weekends, you may end up port-side tying to the wall west of the railroad bridge. Normally, only large commercial craft tie to that wall, but if the waiting area is crowded, you may be there, too. The current always flows from the lake into the Sound. Approach carefully and be ready with extra fenders. Wait your turn and do not crowd ahead. Government vessels and commercial vessels have priority over pleasure craft, and will be directed into the locks ahead of pleasure craft.

Red and green lights on the large and small locks signal when you can enter. Red light means no; green light means yes. A loud hailer system also announces directions to the traffic waiting to transit.

Lock attendants do not respond to most radio calls from pleasure craft, but if you must communicate with them, call on VHF 13, using the 1-watt low-power mode. If you need help, they will answer. If you're calling to complain, forget it.

There are two locks: a large lock 825 feet long and 80 feet wide, and a small lock 150 feet long and 30 feet wide. On a busy summer weekend, the large lock can take a half-hour or more to fill with vessels. Lock attendants will direct entering vessels to one lock or the other by light signals and the loud hailer. Each vessel should have bow and stern mooring lines at least 50 feet long with a 12-inch eye in one end. Fenders should be set out on both sides of the boat. You may be placed against the lock wall or rafted to another boat.

The lock attendants are conscientious, experienced, and helpful. They make eye contact with the helmsman of each vessel as it enters, and signal their intentions clearly. They are polite, but they give direct orders. Do exactly what they tell you to do. They have seen everything and know how to deal with problems.

If directed into the large lock, larger vessels will be brought in first and tied along the walls. Smaller vessels will raft off. Large vessel or small, be sure you have 50-foot mooring lines bow and stern in case you are put along the wall. The lock attendants will throw messenger lines to you. Tie your mooring lines to the messenger lines and they will take them to bollards on top of the lock wall.

There is usually some current in the locks, flowing from the lakes toward the Sound. Enter slowly but with enough speed for steerage. Once your lines are made fast, prepare to assist boats that lie alongside you. When the lock is closed and the water begins to rise, the vessels along the wall must keep a half-turn on their cleats and continuously take in slack. When the water has stopped rising, make all lines fast until you are told to leave.

If directed into the small lock, you will lie alongside a floating wall equipped with yellow-painted "buttons." Loop your bow and stern lines around the buttons, bring the lines back, and make them fast to cleats. The floating walls rise or fall with the water level, so you don't need to tend your lines during the transit. *Caution:* It is always possible that a floating wall could jam in its tracks. Stand by to slack your lines quickly if that happens.

When directed to do so, loosen your lines and move out of the locks slowly but with good steerage.

Approaching from the lake: If you are westbound from the lake to the Sound, you still need 50-foot mooring lines bow and stern in case you lie along the wall of the large lock. However, you will be able to hand your lines to the attendant instead of tying them to messenger lines. Boats along the large lock wall will slack their lines as the water drops.

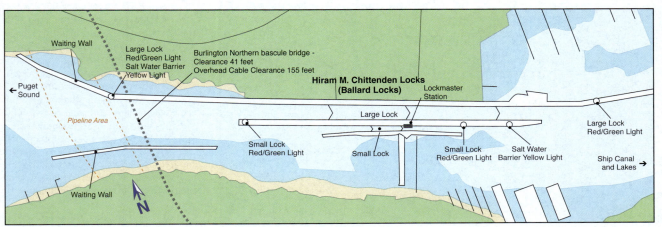

Hiram M. Chittenden Locks

2018 WAGGONER CRUISING GUIDE

SOUTH AND CENTRAL PUGET SOUND   See Area Map Page 86 - Maps Not for Navigation

Shilshole Bay Marina

Bridge, vertical clearance 42 feet at the center; and the Montlake Bridge, vertical clearance 46 feet at the center.

Rush hour restricted openings: The Ballard, Fremont and University Bridges do not open for recreational vessel traffic weekdays from 7:00 a.m. to 9:00 a.m. and 4:00 p.m. to 6:00 p.m., except holidays.

Nighttime bridge openings: The Ballard, Fremont and University Bridges are untended at night between 11:00 p.m. and 7:00 a.m. One crew, based at the Fremont Bridge, stands by to open bridges for vessel traffic. For openings call one hour ahead on VHF 13, or by telephone (206) 386-4251.

The Montlake Bridge is tended 24 hours a day, but between 11:00 p.m. and 7:00 a.m. vessels needing an opening must call ahead on VHF 13 or by telephone, (206) 720-3048.

㉚ **24th Avenue Landing.** At the foot of 24th Ave. NW on the north side of the Ship Canal, east of locks. Open all year, day-use only up to 2 hours free of charge; no overnight stays. Dock has 300 feet of space, 40-foot maximum boat length. No power, water or showers. The Ballard business district is within walking distance.

㉚ **Ballard Oil Co.** 5300 26th Ave. NW, Seattle, WA 98107; (206) 783-0241; info@ballardoil.com; www.ballardoil.com. Open Monday through Saturday. Just east of the locks, on the north side of the Ship Canal. Diesel only. Set up to handle larger and commercial vessels.

㉛ **Salmon Bay.** The Port of Seattle's Fishermen's Terminal is located on the south side of the Lake Washington Ship Canal at Salmon Bay, a half-mile east of the locks. Although Fishermen's Terminal caters primarily to the large Seattle-based fishing fleet, guest and permanent moorage is available for pleasure craft. A short term guest float is located along the inner bulkhead at the head of the west wall, often used by boaters while dining at Chinook's restaurant. Major repair facilities are nearby, as are stores offering a variety of marine services and supplies.

㉛ **Salmon Bay Marine Center.** 2284 W. Commodore Way #100, Seattle, WA 98199; (206) 450-9100; www.sbmc.com. On the south side of the Ship Canal, this facility has 18 slips to accommodate vessels from 60 to 240 feet. Most slips are sold or on long term lease. Short term moorage for large vessels may be available by reservation. Slips are 30 feet to 45 feet wide with a minimum depth of 12 feet. Power is single and 3-phase 240/480 and 208 volt–200 amp. A 50-cycle transformer is available. Black water connection at each slip with gray water pumpout. Free Wi-Fi, parking, and 4 electric utility cars for dock use. Marine repair companies and several large yacht brokerages are in the shoreside building.

㉛ **Salmon Bay Marina.** 2100 W. Commodore Way, Seattle, WA 98199; (206) 282-5555; sales@salmonbaymarina.com; www.salmonbaymarina.com. Open 8:00 a.m. to 5:00

See Area Map Page 86 - Maps Not for Navigation SOUTH AND CENTRAL PUGET SOUND

Water, Pure & Simple.

Spectra has engineered simplicity and reliability into watermaking. The best pump means the quietest and most efficient operation. There isn't even oil to change! Run it off the batteries, alternator or genset through a charger.

Whether your needs are 10 gallons a day or 10,000, we have a model for you.

And, of course, Spectra stands behind all its watermakers with the industry's best warranty.

When it comes to planning and installing a Spectra, the most experienced team anywhere is Emerald Harbor Marine.

Simply put, Spectra makes the most versatile, quiet, compact and efficent watermakers.

At Elliott Bay Marina in Seattle
206-285-3632
www.emharbor.com

SELF SERVICE & FULL SERVICE FACILITIES IN SEATTLE & BELLINGHAM

Seaview West work building

Seaview Fairhaven work building

Seaview North 165 travelift

Refit & Restoration
Yacht Commissioning
Topside Refinishing
Custom Metal Fabrication
Mechanical & Electrical Systems

Seaview Fairhaven indoor storage

Shipwright Services
Fiberglass Repair
General Maintenance & Detailing
Dry Moorage & Long Term Storage
Navigation, Entertainment & Communication Systems

AUTHORIZED WARRANTY CENTERS FOR
PRESTIGE   GRAND BANKS   HINCKLEY

SEAVIEW WEST
At Shilshole Bay Marina / 80 Ton
206-783-6550
west@seaviewboatyard.com

SEAVIEW NORTH
At Squalicum Harbor Marina / 165 Ton
360-676-8282
north@seaviewboatyard.com

SEAVIEW YACHT SERVICE FAIRHAVEN
In the Fairhaven District / 35 Ton
360-676-8282
north@seaviewboatyard.com

www.seaviewboatyard.com

SERVING NORTHWEST BOATERS FOR 44 YEARS

2018 WAGGONER CRUISING GUIDE

SOUTH AND CENTRAL PUGET SOUND   See Area Map Page 86 - Maps Not for Navigation

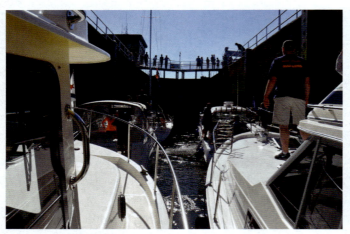
Heading up in the small lock

The Lake Washington Ship Canal is lined with moorages and marine service providers.

p.m. Monday through Saturday. Restrooms, showers, and laundry facilities, 30 & 50 amp power. This marina is primarily full time leased moorage, but they do rent slips for temporary moorage with prior reservations. Seattle Marine & Fishing Supply, a large chandlery, is across the street. Walking distance to restaurants and Fishermen's Terminal.

㉚ **Covich-Williams Chevron.** Dock Office, 5219 Shilshole Ave. NW, Seattle, WA 98107; (206) 784-0171; www.covichwilliams.com. On the north side of the Ship Canal, next to Salmon Bay Sand & Gravel. Open weekdays 8:00 a.m. to 5:00 p.m., Saturdays until noon; closed Sundays. Gasoline, diesel, kerosene. Carries filters, absorbent products, antifreeze, environmental products, fuel additives.

㉚ **Ballard Mill Marina.** 4733 Shilshole Ave. NW, Seattle, WA 98107; (206) 789-4777; ballardmillmarina@gmail.com; www.ballardmillmarina.com. Open all year, no guest moorage, 28 to 60 feet. Restrooms, pumpout, 20 & 30 amp power, showers. East of Covich-Williams Chevron fuel dock on the north side of the Ship Canal. Free pumpout on the east dock. Stores, restaurants, marine supplies, haulout and repairs nearby.

㉛ **Fishermen's Terminal.** 3919 18th Ave. W., Seattle, WA 98119; (206) 787-3395; (800) 426-7817; ft@portseattle.org; www.portseattle.org. Monitors VHF 17, 24 hours a day, 30, 50 & 100 amp power, water, restrooms & showers, security cameras, free pumpout (sewage and bilge), recycling, waste oil dump. Major repair and supply facilities nearby. Restaurants, fish sales, shops, small grocery store, chandlery, postal service on site. The marina is on the south side of the Ship Canal, immediately west of the Ballard Bridge. Guest moorage welcomed, first-come, first-served, call for slip assignment. Make payment at building No. C15 located at 3919 - 18th Ave. West.

Dining: Chinook's at Salmon Bay is good for sit-down dining. A takeout seafood window is on the east side of the building. Tables and chairs are on the deck or in a covered area. An excellent fish market is in the front of the building. The Highliner Pub and the Bay Café also offer dining. The side-tie guest mooring float is in front of the restaurant building, 4 hours moorage complimentary.

Lake Union is lined with ship and boat moorages, houseboat moorages, and boating related businesses. It's the center of Seattle's boat sales industry. In the middle of the lake, a speed range marked by 4 buoys, is for sea trials. Other than the speed range, a 7-knot speed limit is enforced. A launch ramp is on the north shore, east of Gas Works Park. Gas Works Park is easily identifiable by the painted remnants of an industrial coal gas plant. Tyee Yacht Club and Puget Sound Yacht Club have moorages on Lake Union. The large Fisheries Supply marine store is located near Gas Works Park. Transient moorage is limited on Lake Union.

The south end of Lake Union is the home of Northwest Seaport. Next door is the Center for Wooden Boats and the new Lake Union Park with the Museum of History and Industry (MOHAI). Kenmore Air's seaplane base is on the southwest shore, just across from the park. Flight operations are in the center of the lake and may change with wind direction or due to traffic on the lake. Be aware of floatplanes. A major ship repair yard, Lake Union Drydock, is on the eastern shore near the south end of the lake. Ivar's Salmon House, a popular waterfront restaurant, is at the north end of the lake under the I-5 freeway bridge, with temporary moorage for tenders and small boats while dining.

㉜ **Morrison's North Star Marine.** 2732 Westlake Ave. N., Seattle, WA 98109; (206) 284-6600; www.morrisonsfueldock.com. Open all year, 7 days a week. Fuel dock with ethanol-free gasoline and diesel, no guest moorage. Restrooms, free pumpout, water. Handles oil changes; call for appointment. Limited marine

Fishermen's Terminal

104   www.WaggonerGuide.com

SOUTH AND CENTRAL PUGET SOUND

Lake Union can be busy with all types of watercraft.

hardware, local charts, groceries, beer, wine, ice. Friendly and well-run.

㉜ **Nautical Landing Marina.** 2500 Westlake Ave. N., Seattle, WA 98109; (206) 464-4614; info@nautical-landing.com; www.nautical-landing.com. Open all year for permanent and transient use with 1900 feet of moorage, 30, 50 & 100 amp power, security, Wi-Fi, garbage and recycling drop. This facility is popular with superyachts and has services to match. Plans are underway to add tanker truck fueling at the docks.

㉝ **MOHI Docks** - Center for Wooden Boats. Docks located in front of the Museum of History and Industry, on the south end of Lake Union, are managed by the Center for Wooden Boats (206-382-2628). The North Wall has 160 feet of side-tie moorage and one 61-foot slip. Overnight stays at $1.20 per foot. Call ahead for space. An invoice will be sent by email. 30 amp power no water. Two-week maximum stay. Reservations available by phone or email knanen@cwb.org. The small concrete Art Float in front of the gazebo structure is for human-powered craft only. The West Wall has 140 feet of side-tie moorage on a first-come, first-serve basis, no charge. Day-use only from sunrise to sundown, no overnight moorage. The West Wall is occasionally reserved for historic vessels, festivals, and special events.

㉝ **Chandler's Cove.** 901 Fairview Ave. N., Seattle, WA 98109. An 85-foot guest float at the north end of the pier, two-hour day moorage limit, no overnight stays. Several restaurants, snacks, ice. Easy walk to the Center for Wooden Boats, Northwest Seaport, and the Museum of History and Industry (MOHAI).

㉝ **H.C. Henry Marina.** 809 Fairview Place N., Seattle, WA 98109. Located at the south end of Lake Union. Guest moorage space on the south side of H dock, 2-hour limit while dining at Daniel's Broiler, no overnight stays.

㉝ **Marina Mart.** 1500 Westlake Ave. N., Seattle, WA 98109; (206) 268-3322; www.marinamart.com. Permanent moorage only, no guest moorage.

Portage Bay. East of the University Bridge, vertical clearance 42 feet at the center, Portage Bay is the home of Seattle Yacht Club and Queen City Yacht Club. The University of Washington has several facilities along the north shore. The University Bridge opens to 1 long blast and 1 short.

Montlake Cut. East of Portage Bay, the Montlake Cut connects to Union Bay and Lake Washington. The cut is narrow. When boat traffic is heavy, boat wakes can be turbulent as they bounce off the concrete side walls. Slow, steady speeds are called for. The Montlake Bridge, which crosses the cut, has a vertical clearance of 46 feet at the center. The bridge opens to 1 long blast and 1 short.

Union Bay. Union Bay is just east of the Montlake Cut and connects with Lake Washington. The dredged channel is well buoyed. The University of Washington's waterfront activities center is on the north shore, and the arboretum is on the south shore. Except for the dredged channel, the bay is shoal.

LAKE WASHINGTON

Lake Washington, 16 miles long, defines the eastern border of Seattle, and washes the edges of Kenmore, Bothell, Kirkland, Medina, Bellevue, Mercer Island and Renton. The SR 520 floating bridge replacement is in the final stages. The floating span from the west high-rise to the eastern shore is complete and does not have an opening for boat traffic. Vertical clearance is 65 to 70 feet at the east high-rise and 44 feet at the west high-rise. Construction activity is between the west high-rise and Montlake. Vertical clearance is subject to change throughout construction.

The I-90 floating bridge has maximum vertical clearance of 34 feet at the west end and 37 feet at the east end. Least clearance at each end is 28 feet.

Summer weekends can be busy. Seafair weekend borders on madness.

Sand Point. North from Webster Point, the first notable landmark is the former Naval Aviation base of Sand Point. Sand Point now includes Magnuson Park, which has a 2-lane launch ramp with floats. It is also the Northwest District headquarters for the National Oceanic and Atmospheric Administration (NOAA), which has a long piling pier along its north shore. The small marina west of the NOAA pier belongs to the Navy.

Kenmore. North Lake Marina in Kenmore provides access to a restaurant, and anchorage is possible in the area. Kenmore is home to Kenmore Air, a major seaplane operation. Stay well clear of seaplane operating areas. Kenmore is also the mouth of the Sammamish River. Shoal water abounds. Find the buoys and stay in the dredged channel. The river is navigable by small, low, shallow-draft boats all the way to Lake Sammamish.

㉞ **North Lake Marina.** 6201 NE 175th St., Kenmore, WA 98028; (425) 482-9465; susan@northlakemarina.com; www.northlakemarina.com. Open all year, closed weekends November

SHIP CANAL BRIDGE OPENINGS			
BRIDGE	**HEIGHT**	**CLOSED HOURS**	
Burlington-Northern Railroad Bridge	41 feet		
Ballard Bridge	44 feet	Weekdays 0700-0900, 1600-1800 and Special Events	1-hour notice 2300-0700
Fremont Bridge	30 feet	Weekdays 0700-0900, 1600-1800 and Special Events	1-hour notice 2300-0700
University Bridge	42.5 feet	Weekdays 0700-0900, 1600-1800 and Special Events	1-hour notice 2300-0700
Montlake Bridge	46 feet	May 1- Aug. 31: Weekdays 0700-0900, 1530-1800; Sept. 1-April 30: Weekdays 0700-1000, 1530-1900	May 1-Aug 31: 1230-1530 and 1800-1830 opens only on the hour and half hour
SR 520 *West End*	44 feet	SR 520 replacement bridge no longer has an opening span.	
SR 520 *East End*	65 feet 70 feet	on the shore side of the channel on the deep water side of the channel	

2018 WAGGONER CRUISING GUIDE

SOUTH AND CENTRAL PUGET SOUND   See Area Map Page 86 - Maps Not for Navigation

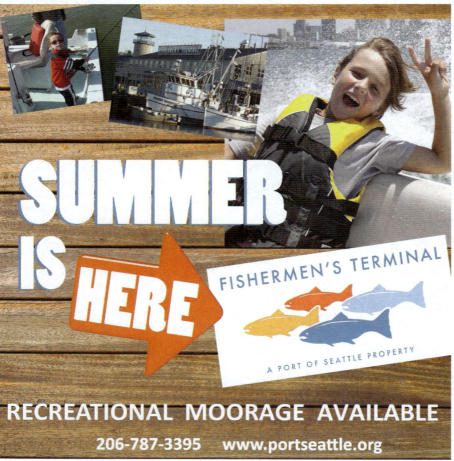

through March. Ethanol-free gasoline at the fuel dock, no diesel. Permanent moorage only, no transient space. Restrooms, pumpout next door at Harbor Village Marina. Parts, accessories, ice. Complete repairs available. Haulout to 20 tons.

Logboom Park. North shore of Lake Washington, Kenmore. Open all year, day use only, moorage available. Restrooms, no power, no showers. Trails, fishing pier, children's play equipment, picnic areas, and outdoor cooking facilities. The park is on the Burke-Gilman Trail, a walking and cycling trail that runs from Lake Union to the Sammamish River Trail.

Saint Edward State Park. 14445 Juanita Drive NW, Kenmore, WA 98028; (425) 823-2992. Northeast shore of Lake Washington. Open all year, day use only. Restrooms, showers, no power. Anchoring or beaching only. Picnicking, trails, fishing, indoor swimming pool. Tennis courts, gymnasium. An approximately 300-acre park is at the top of a bluff; trails lead down to a sandy beach.

Juanita. Anchorage is possible in Juanita Bay, which shoals gradually toward all shores.

Kirkland. Kirkland is an outstanding cruising destination. The City of Kirkland's Marina Park visitor docks are well maintained, and connect directly with downtown. A good launch ramp is immediately north of the docks. If you enjoy tree-lined streets, superb dining, interesting boutiques and upscale galleries, you will not be disappointed. Kirkland is prosperous and it shows.

Next to Marina Park is the **Kirkland Homeport Marina**, which is primarily full-time, leased moorage; www.kirklandhomeport-marina.com.

A mile south of Marina Park is privately-owned Carillon Point Marina, with some guest moorage and access to restaurants and other businesses. Several restaurants in the area have their own docks for patrons.

㉟ **Marina Park.** 25 Lakeshore Plaza Drive, Kirkland, WA 98033; (425) 587-3300; www.kirklandwa.gov. Launch ramp adjacent. Open all year, 90 guest slips, restrooms, 30 amp power in some slips, Wi-Fi. No showers. This is a large and popular Lake Washington destination. Moorage is first-come, first-served and paid through electronic public pay stations located on the dock. Between 8:00 a.m. and 10:00 p.m. the first 3 hours free, ticket provided at pay station. Excellent access to downtown Kirkland. Nearby groceries, ice, and post office.

Use of the launch ramp can be purchased for a fee (each way) at the on-site pay station; a bollard in front of the ramp will lower upon payment. A key card for the season can be purchased from the city office at 123-Fifth Avenue. Use of the ramp is free from November 1st through March 31st. For additional information call (425) 587-3300.

Guest moorage can also be found along 150 feet of side-tie on Anthony's Restaurant dock, managed by the city. The dock is located on the

106   www.WaggonerGuide.com

SOUTH AND CENTRAL PUGET SOUND   See Area Map Page 86 - Maps Not for Navigation

south side of a private marina. Make payment at the public pay station at the Marina Park.

135 Lake Street South
(425) 822-0225

㊱ **Carillon Point Marina.** 4100 Carillon Point, Kirkland, WA 98033; (425) 822-1700; www.carillon-point.com. Certified Clean Marina. Open all year, guest moorage, 30 & 50 amp power, Beacon/BBX Wi-Fi, restrooms, showers, pumpout, portapotty dump. The public pier on the north end of the marina has 150 to 200 feet of side-tie 2-hour tie-ups at no charge. The inside of the pier is for boats 32 feet and under and the outside of the pier is for larger vessels. Overnight moorage in unoccupied slips as available. This is a nice marina adjacent to a high-quality hotel with restaurants, spa, and shopping. Downtown Kirkland is 1.5 miles away by road.

㊱ **Yarrow Bay Marina.** 5207 Lake Washington Blvd. NE, Kirkland, WA 98033; (425) 822-6066; service@yarrowbaymarina.com; www.yarrowbaymarina.com. Open all year with ethanol-free gasoline and diesel, no guest moorage. Marine parts, restrooms, pumpout, haulout and repairs.

Montlake Bridge has a clearance of 46 feet. On sunny summer days boat traffic ranges from heavy to very heavy.

Cozy Cove and Fairweather Bay. Cozy Cove and Fairweather Bay are entirely residential, but anchorage is possible.

Meydenbauer Bay. Maydenbauer Bay is the home of Bellevue Marina and the Maydenbauer Bay Yacht Club, which has some moorage for reciprocal clubs. Maydenbeauer Beach Park underwent extensive renovation in 2017. Downtown Bellevue, with outstanding shopping, is nearby.

Anchorage is possible in Meydenbauer Bay, although the water is deeper than most pleasure craft prefer. The marina off **Beaux Arts Village**, a short distance south of Meydenbauer Bay, is reserved for Beaux Arts residents.

Bellevue Marina. 99th Avenue NE, Bellevue, WA 98004; (425) 443-1090 Dock Master. Small boat visitor moorage between Pier 2 and Pier 3, day-use only up to 4 hours between 8:00 a.m. and 9:00 p.m. daily. Seasonal portable toilets. City park Rangers monitor the facilities.

Luther Burbank Park. 2040 84th Avenue SE, Mercer Island, WA 98040; www.mercergov.org. Open all year, day use only, dock space for 30 or more boats. Restrooms, no power, no showers. No anchoring. Park has picnic areas, swimming areas, trails, tennis courts, amphitheater.

East Channel Bridge. Vertical clearance is 65 feet.

㊲ **Newport Shores.** Newport Shores has a large private marina with an adjacent public launch ramp and fuel dock.

㊲ **Seattle Boat - Newport.** 3911 Lake Washington Blvd. SE, Bellevue, WA 98006; (425) 641-2090; www.seattleboat.com. Open all year, call or visit website for hours. Fuel dock with gasoline and diesel, located just south of the I-90 East Channel bridge at Newport Yacht Basin; snacks, beverages, and ice. Complete repairs available. Marine supplies and parts, new and used boats, self-serve storage. Haulout to 35 tons.

㊳ **Gene Coulon Memorial Beach Park.** 1201 Lake Washington Blvd., Renton, WA 98055; (425) 430-6700; www.rentonwa.gov. Open all year, day use only. Restrooms, showers, no power. Pay at the automated pay box. Showers in summer only, at the swim center. Ivar's and Kidd Valley restaurants in the park. Eight lanes for boat launching,

Ivar's Salmon House Features:
- Fresh, alder grilled salmon and seafood
- Outdoor dining (weather permitting)
- Free moorage while dining with us
- Happy Hour 7 days a week (call for details)
- Banquet facilities available

401 NE Northlake Way
On north Lake Union next to the Ship Canal Bridge
(206) 632-0767
Ivars.com

108   www.WaggonerGuide.com

Carillon Point Marina, Kirkland

The annual Seafair festivities draw thousands of people to Lake Washington for air shows, hydroplane races, and parties.

very well organized, credit and debit cards only. No overnight parking in winter. This is a big, attractive, and much-used park with picnic shelters, playground equipment, tennis courts, horseshoe pits, volleyball courts, grassy areas and beaches. It has a fishing pier and a paved walkway along the water. Popular with everyone, especially families. Located on the southeast shore of Lake Washington, next to Boeing's Renton 737 complex.

Rainier Beach. Has a launch ramp and a private marina. It is the home of the Rainier Yacht Club. Limited guest moorage for visiting members of reciprocal clubs.

Andrews Bay. 5895 Lake Washington Blvd. S., Seattle, WA 98118; (206) 684-4396; www.seattle.gov. Andrews Bay is a popular anchoring spot, with room for many boats. Nestled in between **Seward Park** on Bailey Peninsula and the mainland, it is the only authorized pleasure boat anchorage in Seattle. Signs on the Seward Park shoreline mark the anchorage area. Put the hook down in 25 to 50 feet, excellent mud bottom, 72-hour maximum stay in 7-day period. A Seattle Parks swim area with bathhouse and lifeguards is at the head of the bay. A large grassy playfield is adjacent. Miles of trails lead through dense forest. Excellent stop, especially for families.

㊴ **Lakewood Moorage.** 4400 Lake Washington Blvd. S., Seattle, WA 98118; (206) 475-6559; www.seattle.gov. Open all year. No guest moorage. Permanent moorage only.

Stan Sayers Memorial Park. www.seattle.gov. Open all year. Temporary, day use moorage only, not enough depth for larger boats. Restrooms, no power, no showers. Launch ramp with boarding floats. Tie up to the floats. This is the pit area for hydroplanes during the annual Seafair races.

RICH PASSAGE, PORT ORCHARD, BREMERTON, SILVERDALE

LOCAL KNOWLEDGE

HEAVY TRAFFIC: Rich Passage is the ferry route between Seattle and Bremerton. Keep a sharp lookout ahead and astern and stay well clear of the ferries. Naval vessels also use Rich Passage to and from the Bremerton Naval Shipyard.

Rich Passage is winding but well-buoyed. From the west entrance, the city of Bremerton and the Naval Shipyard are clearly visible. For security reasons, stay well off the Naval facilities.

Currents run to 2 knots at the east entrance and 5.5 knots at the west entrance, flooding west and ebbing east.

Manchester State Park. 7767 E. Hilldale, Port Orchard, WA 98366; (360) 902-8844; www.parks.wa.gov. Open 7 days a week in the summer, 111 acres, day use and overnight camping. Open weekends and holidays in winter. Restrooms, showers, no power. Anchoring only; a bit rough because of boat traffic in Rich Passage. Park is in a shallow cove, good for wading in summer and scuba diving offshore. Picnic tables and shelters with fireplaces, campsites, nature and hiking trails. Old gun battery and emplacements are fun to explore.

㊵ **Port of Manchester.** P.O. Box 304, Manchester, WA 98353; (360) 871-0500; www.portofmanchester.com. Open all year, 400 feet of guest dock space, restroom, no overnight moorage. Dock can be dry on zero or minus tide. A launch ramp is adjacent to the dock. Overnight parking allowed. No power or other facilities at the dock. A restaurant and pub are a short walk away.

Fort Ward Park. 2241 Pleasant Beach, Bainbridge Island, WA 98110; (206) 842-2306; www.biparks.org. Open all year. Anchorage is exposed to wind and wakes from passing boat traffic. Toilets, launch ramp and hiking trails. Because of strong currents in Rich Passage, the underwater park is for expert scuba divers only. Bird watching from 2 bird blinds. Remains of historic fort emplacements to explore. No camping.

Port Orchard. The city of Port Orchard has long been a popular destination for Puget Sound boaters. It has a number of marinas that welcome visiting boats, including one, Port Orchard Marina, that is operated by the Port of Bremerton. Port Orchard Yacht Club, which welcomes visiting reciprocal yachts, is west of the Port Orchard Marina. Several other marinas have permanent moorage. Anchorage is in 50 to 60 feet, mud bottom. A passenger ferry runs between Port Orchard and Bremerton. Water Street boat launch has long term parking for tow vehicles and trailers.

Downtown Port Orchard has several antique and collectibles shops, and restaurants. Seasonal farmers market, 9:00 a.m. to 3:00 p.m. on Saturdays, mid-April through mid-October. The Port Orchard Public Market is open daily with a variety of local food and beverage vendors. Concerts by the Bay are held at Marina Waterfront Park June through September.

Golf: McCormick Woods (800) 323-0130; Trophy Lakes (360) 874-8337; and Gold Mountain (360) 415-5432 are nearby. The courses have transportation available.

Besides a walkable waterfront featuring family friendly activities, playgrounds, parks and an array of excellent dining and shopping options, there are many events and festivals year round, www.exploreportorchard.com.

㊶ **Port Orchard Marina.** 707 Sidney Pkwy., Port Orchard, WA 98366; (360) 876-5535;

SOUTH AND CENTRAL PUGET SOUND   See Area Map Page 86 - Maps Not for Navigation

Port Orchard Marina

kathyg@portofbremerton.org; www.portofbremerton.org. Certified Clean Marina. Monitors VHF 66A. Enter the marina around the west end of the breakwater. The entrance is marked with navigation lights. Open 7 days a week all year, except for fall/winter holidays. Gasoline and diesel at the fuel dock, guest moorage in 50 slips (40-foot), and side-tie moorage along 1500 feet of inside breakwater with another 1500 feet available on the outside as well. The marina is well-managed and well-maintained, with clean restrooms and beautiful landscaping.

The marina has 30 amp power, water, restrooms, laundry, free showers, free pumpout, portapotty dump, and free Wi-Fi. An excellent children's play area is at the north end of the marina grounds. This is one of Puget Sound's popular destinations. Reservations accepted, 4 hours of day use free. It's one block to downtown Port Orchard. Repairs are nearby. Shuttle service by appointment.

Bremerton. The Bremerton waterfront was redeveloped several years ago and offers excellent facilities. The Bremerton Harborside Kitsap Conference Center, with a Starbucks, Anthony's Restaurant, and Cold Stone Creamery, overlooks the marina. The Hampton Suites Hotel is next door. Bremerton is doing its best to shed a dowdy image and make a name for itself.

Points of interest include the Naval Museum, the historic destroyer USS *Turner Joy*, and the attractive city boardwalk. Many boaters take the passenger ferry for the 10- to 12-minute ride to Port Orchard, where the dining, seasonal farmers market, antiques shopping, and boutiques are popular. Bremerton Marina is secured by a locked gate. Kitsap County buses in the adjacent transportation center can take you anywhere you wish to go, or take the ferry to downtown Seattle.

There is always something happening in Bremerton with its line-up of festivals and concerts. The Blackberry Festival is held Labor Day weekend, with booths ashore selling wonderful blackberry treats and more. We just happened to be there, and the festival was a hoot.

LOCAL KNOWLEDGE

STRONG CURRENTS: Tidal currents can make boat handling tricky in Bremerton Marina. It is best to time arrival and departure to coincide with slack water.

 Bremerton Marina. 120 Washington Beach, Bremerton, WA 98367; (360) 373-1035; kathyg@portofbremerton.org. www.portofbremerton.org. Monitors VHF 66A. Certified Clean Marina. Located next to the ferry dock. Open all year, except for fall/winter holidays. Guest moorage in 80 to 100 slips and 990 feet inside of side-tie dock space, 30 & 50 amp power, water, garbage, restrooms, free showers, laundry, free Wi-Fi, 2 portapotty dumps. Shuttle service by appointment.

No fuel is available. The nearest fuel dock is at Port Orchard.

This quality marina has excellent docks and a breakwater to protect against ferry wakes. Fountain Park, a short walk to the other side of the ferry dock, is lovely. The dramatic fin-like sculptures are fountains meant to resemble the superstructure (called the sail) of a modern submarine.

110

ANTHONY'S AT SINCLAIR INLET
20 Washington Ave.
(360) 377-5004

Washington Narrows connects **Sinclair Inlet** with **Dyes Inlet**. The narrows are crossed by two bridges with a minimum vertical clearance of 80 feet. Tidal currents, averaging over 2 knots, flood west and ebb east. Signs ask boaters to maintain minimum speed to reduce wake damage to the shore and to boats moored at the marina. A launch ramp with float and fishing pier is on the north side of the narrows about halfway along, part of the Lebo Street Recreation Area.

Bridgeview Marina. (360) 876-2522; Permanent moorage only, no transient space; pumpout is for moorage customers only.

Phinney Bay. Phinney Bay is the home of the Bremerton Yacht Club, with guest moorage for visiting reciprocal boats. Anchorage is good throughout the bay, which shoals toward each shore.

Ostrich Bay. Ostrich Bay offers good anchorage, mud bottom. The most popular anchorage is along the west side of the bay, facing dense forest. We have spent several pleasant nights at this spot. For some reason this entire area is overlooked. Even when the docks at Port Orchard and Bremerton are full on summer holiday weekends, Ostrich Bay has been almost empty.
Caution: Unexploded ordnance from years ago, when the Navy pier was used for loading munitions, has been found in the bay, especially in the vicinity of the pier.

Oyster Bay. A narrow but easily-run channel leads off Ostrich Bay into Oyster Bay, where perfectly protected anchorage is available toward the center of the bay. To enter, keep between the lines of mooring buoys and mooring floats on both sides of the channel. The channel shoals to about 6 feet at zero tide. Oyster Bay is surrounded by homes.

Dyes Inlet indents the Kitsap Peninsula northwest of Bremerton. Silverdale is on the north shore of Dyes Inlet and has a marina, waterfront park, boat ramp, and boardwalk. Dyes Inlet is connected to Sinclair Inlet via Port Washington Narrows.

㊸ **Silverdale Marina (Port of Silverdale).** P.O. Box 310, Silverdale, WA 98383; (360) 698-4918; portofsilverdale@wavecable.com; www.portofsilverdale.com. Open all year. Guest moorage along 1300 feet of wide, side-tie dock with a least depth of 10 feet at zero tide. No rafting. Moorage is on the honor system, but confirmed by security patrols that record the moored boats. Three-night maximum stay. Group reservations accepted online for a $75 fee. Restrooms, 30

See Area Map Page 86 - Maps Not for Navigation

SOUTH AND CENTRAL PUGET SOUND

Bremerton Marina

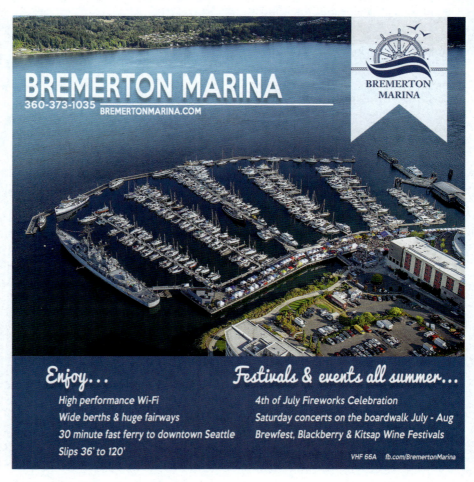

SOUTH AND CENTRAL PUGET SOUND

See Area Map Page 86 - Maps Not for Navigation

amp power, seasonal potable water, pumpout, showers, 2-lane concrete launch ramp. No long-term parking. The pumpout operates 8:00 a.m. to 10:00 p.m., weekends, May to October.

The marina is adjacent to county-run Silverdale Waterfront Park. The park has picnic tables, restrooms, fire pits, children's play area, pavilion and a Veterans Memorial. Interesting shops and dining are in adjacent Old Town Silverdale. Complete shopping is at the Kitsap Mall about a mile away. The Trails shopping center is about 1.5-miles away. The nearby Clear Creek Trail & Interpretive Center is a good walk.

Whaling Days, a 3-day celebration the last weekend of July, draws big crowds, both from land and the water. Plan to anchor out. If you're on the dock, expect to be included in the carnival atmosphere. It's a big fair with live bands all weekend, activities for kids, outrigger canoe races, a fun run and more. See their website at www.whalingdays.com. Silverdale hosts the Kitsap Peninsula Water Trails Festival during the fourth weekend in June. Events include a 50K triathlon, kayak races, and waterfront activities.

BROWNSVILLE, POULSBO, NORTHERN PORT ORCHARD

Northern Port Orchard separates Bainbridge Island from the Kitsap Peninsula. Rich Passage and Sinclair Inlet are at the south end; Agate Passage is at the north. Brownsville and Poulsbo are the major marina destinations. The Agate Passage bridge has a vertical clearance of 75 feet. Currents in Agate Passage run to 6 knots on spring tides, flooding south and ebbing north.

LOCAL KNOWLEDGE

ROCK: A nasty rock, almost awash at zero tide, is inshore from the mooring buoys at Illahee Park, approximately between the buoy nearest the dock and shore. Thanks to Correspondents Al & Becca Szymanski, S/V *Halona*, for the report.

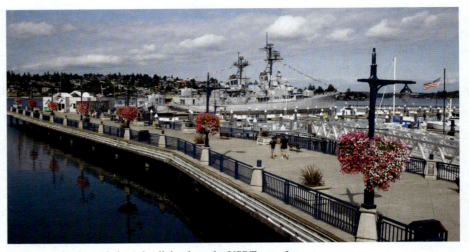

Bremerton harborside boardwalk leads to the USS Turner Joy.

 Illahee Marine State Park. 3540 NE Bahia Vista Drive, Bremerton, WA 98310; (360) 478-6460. Located 3 miles northeast of Bremerton. Open all year, mooring and overnight camping. Guest moorage with 356 feet of side-tie dock space, 5 mooring buoys for boats 45 feet and under. Restrooms and showers, no power. The dock is protected by a floating concrete breakwater. Park has 3 kitchen shelters, picnic tables, campsites, horseshoe pits, ball field, hiking trails, and portable toilet. Popular for fishing and sunbathing. Most services are in the upland area, reached by a steep trail.

 Port of Brownsville. 9790 Ogle Rd. NE, Bremerton, WA 98311; (360) 692-5498; jerry@portofbrownsville.org; www.portofbrownsville.org. Certified Clean Marina. Monitors VHF 16, switch to 66A. Open all year, 7 days a week. Fuel dock has ethanol-free gasoline, diesel, and propane. Guest moorage in 25 24-foot slips, 20 40-foot slips, and 550 feet of side-tie moorage along the breakwater, 30 & limited 50 amp

Port of Brownsville

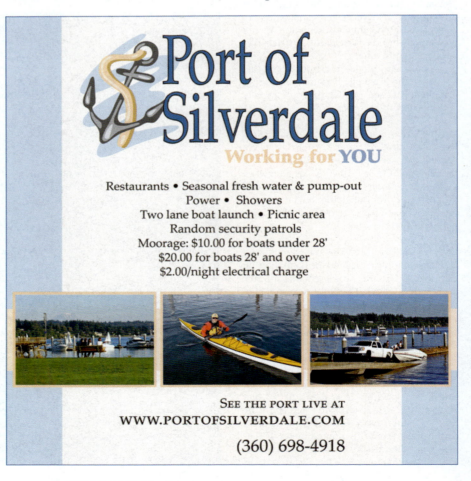

See Area Map Page 86 - Maps Not for Navigation   SOUTH AND CENTRAL PUGET SOUND

Harborside Park is a favorite in Bremerton.

power, free Wi-Fi, restrooms, showers, laundry, book exchange, free pumpout, portapotty dump, in-slip pumpout service (MV Ms le Pew). Paved 2-lane launch ramp with ample parking.

Up on the wharf, a covered picnic/gathering pavilion, with tables, is inviting. Additional picnic tables are on the docks and in Burke Bay Overlook Park above the wharf, with barbecue. This is a popular destination for club cruises. Group reservations invited.

A breakwater marks the entrance to the marina. The channel and area around the fuel dock has been dredged to 9 feet at minus tide and well marked with green buoys to port on entrance, so you don't have to hug the south side of the dock. The Deli has snacks, beer, and wine selection. They make take-out food and can cater a gathering. This is a pleasant, friendly marina.

Groceries are available a short walk (city block) up the road at the Daily Stop.

Brownsville Appreciation Day: Fourth Saturday of September. Folksy and fun, small community at its best. Classic boats and cars, treasure hunt, unicycles, hot dogs and hamburgers. All proceeds (not just profits) divided among the local elementary schools.

Savory treat: A short walk up the road from the marina, Sweeney's Country Meats has mouth-watering specialty meats. We tried a marinade, jerky, and some of the bacon. All were delicious and well worth a visit.

㊻ **Port of Keyport Marina.** P.O. Box 195, Keyport, WA 98345; (541) 760-0176; www.portofkeyport.com. Concrete docks with five 50-foot slips for guest moorage, first-come, first-served. Water, 30 amp power. No restrooms. Six hours free, 3-day maximum stay. Be mindful of the current when approaching the dock. Boat launch ramp. Make payment at the Keyport Mercantile, located upland. There are several restaurants in the area, and the must-see Naval Undersea Museum (360-396-4148).

A pedestrian gate, open 10:00 a.m. to 4:00 p.m., is about a quarter of a mile straight up Washington Street from the dock. The gate leads onto the Naval Base and the Naval Undersea Museum. You can view a simulation of a nuclear fast attack submarine, torpedoes and torpedo tubes, a Confederate mine from the Civil War, and learn the history of naval diving. The museum is open daily. Admission is free.

Fletcher Bay. Fletcher Bay is shallow and not a good anchorage.

㊼ **Manzanita Bay.** Manzanita Bay is a good overnight sheltered anchorage for Seattle-area boats. The bay is all residential and has no public facilities, but the holding ground is excellent. Observe the 5-knot no-wake speed limit beginning halfway down the bay. Although the bay is lined with lovely homes, the surrounding hills give a feeling of seclusion.

At the north end of the bay, Manzanita Landing, a former Mosquito Fleet landing, provides access to the trail system of Manzanita Park. From the landing take Manzanita Road NE to NE Day Road West. Walk east to the park, which is on the left (north) side of the street.

Liberty Bay. The entrance to Liberty Bay is past the Keyport Naval torpedo research and testing facility and around Lemolo Point. The Navy requests boats travel at no-wake speed past its facility. A power cable with 90-foot clearance crosses overhead. A sign on the beacon off Lemolo Point asks boaters to slow down in all of Liberty Bay; buoys post the speed limit. Much of Liberty Bay is covered by Wi-Fi. Three major marinas are along the north shore of Liberty Bay: a private marina; the Poulsbo Yacht Club; and the Port of Poulsbo Marina.

The private marina has no guest moorage. At the Poulsbo Yacht Club, reciprocal moorage is along the northwest perimeter of the floating breakwater. Some reciprocal moorage is still available on the inside of the older breakwater.

㊽ **Poulsbo.** Poulsbo, on Liberty Bay, is one of the most popular destinations on Puget Sound, partly because it is close to the major population centers, and partly because it is such a delightful place to visit. Settled originally by Scandinavians, the downtown business district still loudly (to say the least) maintains its Norwegian heritage. Everything most visitors need is available either near the water or at the malls located on the highway about a mile away.

The waterfront portions of Poulsbo make for a lovely walk. Victorian homes and gardens have been restored and preserved to perfection.

Restaurants, bakeries and many shops that specialize in gifts, collectibles and home accesso-

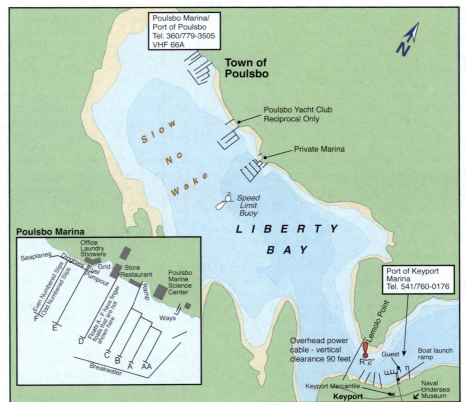

Poulsbo

2018 WAGGONER CRUISING GUIDE

Port of Keyport Marina. Transient moorage is to the left of the boathouse.   *Who can resist stopping in for fresh bakery treats from the Poulsbo Bakery?*

ries are a few steps away in downtown Poulsbo. Dining and shopping are popular. Sluys' Bakery is a favorite. Longship Marine is one of the few remaining second hand marine stores offering marine supplies. The nearby Poulsbo Marine Science Center is excellent, especially for families. Shopping centers, with supermarkets and the usual stores, are a few blocks away. Special events include Saturday Farmers Market, May - October; Viking Fest, 3rd weekend in May; Scandinavian Midsommer Fest, June; 3rd of July Celebration; Traditional Street Dance, August; and Yule Fest, December.

Looking for a great day trip or a weekend getaway? Look no further, Poulsbo has it all.

㊽ **Poulsbo Marina / Port of Poulsbo.** 18809 Front St., P.O. Box 732, Poulsbo, WA 98370; (360) 779-9905; (360) 779-3505 ext. 1 (for reservations) office@portofpoulsbo.com; reservations@portofpoulsbo.com (for reservations); www.portofpoulsbo.com. Monitors VHF 66A. Open 7 days a week, all year, except Christmas Day and New Year's Day. Register by 4:00 p.m. to get the combination for the showers and restrooms. The fuel dock has ethanol-free gasoline and diesel. The marina has 130 guest slips, 10-foot depths at low tide, and 30 amp ELCI-protected power on all docks. Good restrooms and showers, laundry, pumpout, portapotty dump, launch ramp, free Wi-Fi. A meeting room and activity float are available. Groceries, fine restaurants and shops within walking distance.

If anchored out, dinghy tie-up is on the shore side of the dock closest to shore.

Agate Passage connects Port Orchard with Port Madison, and is crossed by a highway bridge with a vertical clearance of 75 feet. Currents in the pass run as high as 6 knots at spring tides, flooding south and ebbing north. The channel through the pass is well marked, but in general, a mid-channel course will serve.

For some reason, many craft go through Agate Passage too fast, creating havoc for slower craft. Agate Passage isn't very long. Keep the speed down, look astern to judge your wake, and give fellow boats a break.

PORT MADISON AND BAINBRIDGE ISLAND

Miller Bay. Miller Bay indents the Northwest corner of Port Madison. It is very shallow and should be entered only at half tide or better, or with local knowledge. Like many bays on Puget Sound, Miller Bay has a drying shoal in the middle, so navigable water can be found only around the perimeter.

Mattson's Bay Marine. 20622 Miller Bay Rd. NE, Poulsbo, WA 98392; (360) 598-4900; mattsonsbaymarine@gmail.com. Open Tuesday through Saturday all year. Haulout to 30 feet, parts and complete repairs. Launch ramp, dry storage.

Suquamish. Suquamish is best known as the winter home of Chief Seattle and the former site of his longhouse, the Old Man House village. With its restaurants and other cultural attractions, it makes a good day trip from Seattle.

The Suquamish community dock and float, just north of Agate Pass, provides short-term moorage for visiting boats. The east side of the float is exposed to chop from boat traffic and weather in outer Port Madison. If the protected space on the west side is not available, boaters can anchor and take the dinghy to the float. Good anchorage is northeast of the float. A boat ramp is south of the float; it's not usable at low tide.

Today, the town of Suquamish is the center of the Suquamish Indian Reservation. A new community center across the street from the dock is patterned after the Old Man House. The Suquamish Museum is up the hill.

Visible above the community center is an impressive veterans memorial, with carved figures honoring Chief Kitsap, Chief Seattle, and Suquamish veterans.

From the veterans memorial, follow signs to Chief Seattle's grave in the Suquamish Tribal Cemetery behind the white church of St. Peter's Catholic Mission. The original gravestone placed by Seattle pioneers is still there, along with more recent Native carvings and inscriptions of Chief Seattle's words.

From Chief Seattle's grave, continue walking uphill to the new Suquamish Museum. The museum is open 10:00 a.m. to 5:00 p.m., daily.

Since 1911, the Suquamish Tribe has been celebrating Chief Seattle Days on the third weekend of August. Activities include a traditional salmon bake, canoe races, baseball, drumming and dancing, and a memorial service honoring Chief Seattle.

Agate Pass Cafe, Sully's Bistro and Bar, and Scratch Kitchen are within easy walking distance of the dock, and excellent.

Indianola. Indianola is distinguished by the long pier that served passengers and freight during Mosquito Fleet days. A float is installed during the summer to give access to the town, max boat size 30 feet, max stay 30 minutes.

PETER PUGET (1765-1822)

Peter Puget joined the British Navy as a midshipman at the age of 12 in the year 1778 and served on numerous ships of the day gaining valuable experience. In 1790 Peter Puget became lieutenant-in-command of the *Chatham* and sailed alongside the *Discovery* in the South Pacific before starting a detailed survey of the Pacific North American coast. During the Americas coastal voyage, many sites and features were named after friends or persons of influence. Captain George Vancouver anchored the ships near present day Seattle and sent Peter Puget south with two rowing craft which included Joseph Whidbey. Peter Puget had also explored the Columbia River by small craft; Puget Island, opposite the Native village of Cathlamet, Washington, was named in his honor. Peter Puget later assisted George Vancouver in negotiations with the Spanish in 1792 at Nootka Sound. After returning to England in 1795, Puget was given the rank of Commander and continued to serve in the British navy.

Source: Wikipedia, Wikimedia Foundation

Poulsbo fuel dock

The cold water didn't deter these swimmers at Indianola.

The float grounds on low and minus tides. The Indianola Country Store, just a few blocks from the pier, has been in business since the 1920s. It has a good selection of grocery items, beer and wine, and a popular deli.

Inner Port Madison. The inner, residential bay extends for about 1.5 miles into the north end of Bainbridge Island. This is where Port Madison Yacht Club and a large Seattle Yacht Club outstation (no reciprocals) are located. Anchorage is good throughout, with a wide bight about 0.75 mile inside the entrance. Shore access is possible from a dinghy dock at Hidden Cove Park just west of the SYC outstation. Farther in, **Hidden Cove** is a lovely spot. For Seattle area boats, this is an often-overlooked area to have a picnic lunch or a quiet night at anchor. The shores are private but the setting is idyllic.

Fay Bainbridge Park. www.biparks.org. South of Point Monroe on Bainbridge Island. Open all year; exposed, anchoring only. Restrooms, showers. The park has 3 kitchen shelters, fireplaces, fire rings, a beach area, launch ramp, utility and primitive campsites, children's play equipment, horseshoe pits, fishing, clamming, and a concession stand in summer.

Murden Cove. Murden Cove has convenient anchoring depths, but little protection from winds. It's a long row to shore, partly over drying flats. The residential community of Rolling Bay is at the head of the bay.

LOCAL KNOWLEDGE

NO ANCHOR ZONE: The bottom around the south entrance to Eagle Harbor has been capped to prevent the spread of pollutants from a former creosote facility. Do not anchor in this area.

Eagle Harbor. Eagle Harbor is the location of the City of Bainbridge Island. The city changed its name from Winslow a number of years ago and is sometimes referred to by its old name. To further complicate matters, the City of Bainbridge Island is on the island which also takes the name of Bainbridge. The City of Bainbridge Island is the western terminus of a ferry from downtown Seattle.

The City of Bainbridge has a guest dock and boat launch at the Eagle Harbor Waterfront Park. Linear moorage and mooring buoys are located in the harbor. Anchorage in Eagle Harbor is available west of the Ferry Maintenance Yard, and at least 200 feet south of the marinas on the north shore. Anchorage for the first 2 days is without charge, a fee is charged for additional days, maximum 30-day stay. The nominal anchorage fee provides access to showers and garbage drop at the Park. Moorings in the harbor are part of the Eagle Harbor Waterfront Park facilities. A self-registration payment box for dock moorage, buoys, linear moorage and extended anchorage is located at Eagle Harbor Waterfront Park.

Several marinas in the area provide guest moorage if a permanent tenant is away. All but one marina, Eagle Harbor Marina on the south shore, are on the town side of the harbor. Queen City Yacht Club, Meydenbauer Bay Yacht Club, and Seattle Yacht Club have outstations in Eagle Harbor. A pumpout station is located at Eagle Harbor Waterfront Park, and in-slip pumpouts are provided at Eagle Harbor Marina.

We enjoy walking the streets of town, which offer boutiques, art shops, and a variety of good restaurants. The grocery store, within walking distance, has everything. The Bainbridge Island Museum of Art (with a cafe) opened in 2014. The Alehouse on Winslow, located next to the museum, has a nice selection of beer and cider on tap; patrons may bring in outside food. The grounds and gardens at Bloedel Reserve, on the north end of the island, are worth a visit. Kitsap Transit, at the ferry terminal, provides service during weekdays and Saturdays.

Eagle Harbor is entered through a marked channel past foul ground that extends south from Wing Point. Nun Buoy 2 is at the end of this foul ground, and the Tyee Shoal Beacon is a short distance south of Buoy 2. The ferries round Tyee Shoal Beacon, but other craft can use Buoy 2 safely, following the rule of Red, Right, Returning. Follow the markers all the way in. Shoal water extends out to the channel on both sides. Observe the 5-knot speed limit from Buoy 5. The far west end of the inner harbor is an Aquatic Conservancy area where power boats are not allowed.

No Discharge Zone.

㊾ **Eagle Harbor Waterfront Park.** 280 Madison Ave. N., Bainbridge Island, WA 98110; (206) 786-7627; www.ci.bainbridge-isl.wa.us. Open all year. 500 feet of transient side-tie moorage at the dock. Water, 30 & 50 amp ELCI-protected power, and pumpout. 400 feet of linear moorage and 4 mooring buoys in the harbor. All moorage facilities are first-come, first-served. Washrooms, free showers, and garbage drop are located upland from the dock in the Waterfront Park. Rafting is encouraged. Boat launch ramp is next to the dock. Public washrooms are open all hours. Showers are accessible with an entry code available by calling the harbormaster. Payment for these City moorage facilities is made at the self-registration payment box located at the Park. Maximum 2-day stay in a seven-day period at the dock.

A short quarter-mile walk north from the Waterfront Park brings you to the center of town and the grocery store on Winslow Way. Half-mile long Winslow Way is lined on both sides with small shops, restaurants, pubs, and a bakery. One block north of Winslow Way on Ericksen Avenue is the Bainbridge Island Historical Museum.

In late 2017 and early 2018 the dock moorage facilities were upgraded and enlarged. The main dock was lengthened by 100 feet and a 200-foot end cap added. Water and GFI-protected shore power were added.

㊾ **Winslow Wharf Marina.** P.O. Box 10297, 141 Parfitt Way SW, Bainbridge Island, WA 98110; (206) 842-4202; dave@winslow-wharfmarina.com; www.winslowwharfmarina.com. Monitors VHF 09. Open Tuesday through Saturday, 9:00 a.m. to 5:00 p.m. Guest moorage in unoccupied slips. Maximum boat length 50 feet, 30 & 50 amp power, clean remodeled restrooms, free showers. Wi-Fi, laundry, book exchange, pumpout, portapotty dump. Reservations required. Chandlery Marine, a well-

SOUTH AND CENTRAL PUGET SOUND

See Area Map Page 86 - Maps Not for Navigation

Linear moorage in Eagle Harbor

stocked marine supply store, has a little bit of everything, (206) 842-7245. Seattle Yacht Club and Meydenbauer Bay Yacht Club have dock space reserved for their members. The spaces are clearly marked, and non-member boats may not use them.

㊾ **Harbour Marina.** 233 Parfitt Way SW, Bainbridge Island, WA 98110; (206) 550-5340; info@harbour-marina.com; www.harbour-marina.com. Open all year. Unoccupied slips used for guest boats, call ahead for availability. Facilities include 30 amp power, restrooms, free showers, laundry, pumpout. Located directly below Harbour Public House, an English-style pub with beer, wine, and food. No kids allowed in the pub. Moorage for visiting the pub and Pegasus Coffee House is clearly marked. Close to the Waterfront Trail and a short walk to downtown.

㊿ **Eagle Harbor Marina.** P.O. Box 11217, 5834 Ward Ave. NE, Bainbridge Island, WA 98110; (206) 842-4003; harbormaster@eagleharbormarina.com; www.eagleharbormarina.com. Open all year. Primarily permanent moorage with limited transient moorage, call ahead. Marina has 30, 50 & 100 amp ELCI-protected power. Restrooms, showers, laundry, pumpout, free Wi-Fi. Docks were replaced and upgraded in 2017 including new monitored shore power, in-slip portable pumpout, year-round water, and security. This marina is on the south side of Eagle Harbor away from town; there are no restaurants or stores in the immediate area.

㊽ **Blakely Harbor.** In the early days Blakely Harbor was the site of major lumber and shipbuilding activities. Now it is a quiet residential neighborhood. Some stub pilings remain from the old docks. The head of the bay, including the old mill pond and ruins of the concrete powerhouse, is now a park. Good anchorage in 35 to 50 feet can be found far enough into the bay to be well protected, yet still have a view of the Seattle skyline. Sunset on a clear evening is beautiful. Blakely Rock is 0.5 mile off; give it a good offing. Enter Blakely Harbour in the middle of the mouth of the bay. A drying reef extends from the north shore, and shoals are along the south side.

Eagle Harbor

116 www.WaggonerGuide.com

Hood Canal

CHAPTER 3

HOOD CANAL
Dabob Bay • Pleasant Harbor • Alderbrook

HOOD CANAL

Hood Canal is a 65-mile-long glacier-carved fjord. Because the shorelines are fairly straight with few protected anchorages, Hood Canal is less used by pleasure craft than many other waterways. Most boaters don't realize that shrimping, oyster gathering, clamming and fishing can be outstanding. The shrimping season is short: usually 3 weeks in May, just 2 days each week. But on those days, the boats are thick. In clear weather the views of the Olympic Mountains from Hood Canal are outstanding. Other than shrimpers and knowing fishermen, however, Hood Canal is largely undiscovered.

Several rivers flow from the Olympic Mountains into Hood Canal, and each has formed a mudflat off its mouth. Although the shoal off the Dosewallips River, a couple of miles south of Pulali Point, is marked, the shoals off the Duckabush, Fulton Creek, Hama Hama, and Lilliwaup rivers are not marked, nor is the extensive shoal off the Skokomish River at the Great Bend. Care must be taken to avoid running aground.

Pleasant Harbor and the Alderbrook Inn Resort can take larger boats, but many of the other marinas and parks on Hood Canal are aimed at trailerable boats. This has disappointed some people in larger boats, who had hoped for more facilities for boats their size.

Hood Head. Anchorage can be found behind Hood Head on the western shore of Hood Canal, but the water shoals rapidly to drying flats near the head of the bay.

Shine Tidelands State Park. Stretches 1 mile north of the Hood Canal Bridge into Bywater Bay on the west shore of Hood Canal. Day use only, toilets, no power, water or showers. Anchoring only, well offshore. Launch ramp, crabbing and clamming, hiking trails.

Bywater Bay. Anchor in 6 to 12 feet, good holding on a soft bottom with room to swing. The spit provides wave protection from north winds. A shallow draft boat can easily enter the lagoon in the undeveloped Wolfe Property State Park at the northwest corner of the bay. [*Hamilton*]

CHARTS	
18441	Puget Sound – Northern Part (1:80,000)
18448	Puget Sound – Southern Part (1:80,000)
18458	Hood Canal – South Point to Quatsop Point including Dabob Bay (1:25,000)
18473	Puget Sound – Oak Bay to Shilshole Bay (1:40,000)
18476	Hood Canal to Dabob Bay (1:40,000)
18477	Puget Sound – Entrance to Hood Canal (1:25,000)

Main street in historic Port Gamble

Port Gamble. Port Gamble is a fine anchorage, protected from wave action by a sandspit at the entrance. Anchorage in 18 to 30 feet is possible everywhere. Many people prefer the area just inside the spit. Port Gamble is charming and historic. The remnants of the sawmill are being removed, and the town has been restored. A museum, restaurants and small shops are on the tree-lined main street. Having established a sawmill, Port Gamble began as a company-owned town, founded in 1853. The mill was in operation until 1995. The Port Gamble Historic Museum (360) 297-8078 covers the history of the mill and town site. The museum is open daily, May through September, and on weekends only during the winter months.

LOCAL KNOWLEDGE

DANGEROUS ROCKS: Sisters, two substantial rocks about 200 yards apart, lie 0.4 mile south of the Hood Canal bridge on the west side. The rocks dry at half tide. The southern rock is marked by a large lighted beacon, yet from time to time an unwary boat manages to go up on these rocks. For safety, if you have passed under the western end of the bridge, turn eastward at once and run parallel to the bridge to the middle before turning south into Hood Canal.

Hood Canal Floating Bridge. The east end of the Hood Canal Floating Bridge has 50 feet of vertical clearance. Clearance on the west end is 33 feet. The bridge can be opened for larger vessels, but it is not manned. To arrange an opening call (360) 779-3233, which connects to a State Department of Transportation office in Tacoma. They will take your name, telephone number, name of your vessel, date and time of desired opening, and whether you are inbound or outbound. They also will ask what width opening you need (300 feet or 600 feet). One hour's notice is needed to get a crew to the bridge and prepare it for opening. No bridge openings between 3:00 p.m. and 6:15 p.m. daily, from Memorial Day to Labor Day.

Salsbury Point County Park. Just off the northeast end of the Hood Canal Bridge. Day use only, restrooms, no power. Anchoring only, 2 launch ramps. Picnic tables, fireplaces, children's play area. Nature trail. Sandy beach for experienced divers only because of strong currents.

Kitsap Memorial Marine State Park. (360) 779-3205; Four miles south of Hood Canal Bridge. Open all year, day use and overnight camping, 2 mooring buoys for boats 45 feet and under. Self-register and pay mooring buoy fee on shore. Restrooms, showers, no power. Picnic sites, kitchen shelters, fireplaces. Standard campsites, swimming beach, playground, horseshoe pits, volleyball courts, baseball field. Buoys are exposed to tidal currents and wind.

Squamish Harbor. Squamish Harbor has convenient anchoring depths, but the harbor is quite open and has numerous rocks and reefs that must be avoided. It is seldom used for overnight anchorage.

Thorndyke Bay. Thorndyke Bay is too open to provide a snug anchorage.

LOCAL KNOWLEDGE

RESTRICTED AREAS: Boaters should take great care not to enter the Restricted Area in front of the Bangor Naval Station on the east side of Hood Canal, about 4 miles south from Vinland, which is patrolled constantly to keep passing vessels well away. The patrol craft are fitted with guns and are authorized to shoot. Best practice is to stay west of mid channel when transiting this area. A second Naval Restricted Area is located off Point Whitney in Dabob Bay.

NAVAL OPERATING AREAS: Two adjoining Naval Operating areas cover a majority of Hood Canal, from South Point to Hazel Point. When transiting this area, boaters should monitor Channel 16. Look for Naval vessels flying a

HOOD CANAL

See Area Map Page 119 - Maps Not for Navigation

Stay well clear of Bangor Naval Station.

"Bravo" (red) flag during periods of Naval operations. A passage corridor outside the Operating Areas follows the west side of Hood Canal, hugging the eastern shoreline of Toandos Peninsula. Another Naval Operating & Exercise Area is in Dabob Bay, where flashing lights along the shoreline indicate the status of operations.

Naval Base Kitsap (Bangor). This is the location of Bangor Naval Station, homeport for a fleet of nuclear submarines. Several of these awesome machines often are visible to passing craft. Stay outside of the marked restricted area.

Seabeck Bay. Anchorage is possible behind Misery Point, with good protection from the south and west. The Seabeck General Store can be accessed by dinghy. A new marina, Olympic View Marina, is for permanent moorage only.

Scenic Beach State Park. South of Seabeck. Open for day use all year and overnight camping in summer only. Anchoring only. Standard and primitive campsites. Kitchen shelter, fireplaces, fire rings, horseshoe pits, volleyball areas. Scuba diving, swimming, hiking, shellfishing.

Fisherman Harbor. Fisherman Harbor can be entered only at high water, but once inside offers protected anchorage in 5 to 15 feet. Follow the natural channel into the bay, then turn south and follow the spit until anchoring depths are found. All the land around the bay is privately owned. Years ago, we tiptoed into Fisherman Harbor in a sailboat at something less than high tide. It was careful going, with a close watch from the bow and a bit of luck, but the boat got in without touching. Less foolish souls should wait for higher water. [*Hale*]

Dabob Bay. Most of Dabob Bay is a Naval Operating & Exercise Area with 5 warning lights. Flashing amber lights indicate Naval operations are in progress; boaters may enter the area on an amber light but should keep well clear of Navy vessels. Flashing red lights indicate the area has been closed to navigation. If the lights turn red while you are inside the Operations Area, shut down engines and depth sounder until operations have ended. The 5 warning lights are located at Whitney Point, Pulali Point, and Sylopash Point on the west side of the bay; Zelatched Point on the east side of the bay; and at the north end of the bay on the southeast side of Bolton Peninsula. South of Pulali Point (western shore of Dabob Bay) is outside the Operating Area and includes Jackson Cove, where good anchorage can be found. Correspondent Jim Norris reports "We anchored two nights just north of Broad Spit in Dabob Bay. The wind was SE 20-25 all day. Given the full fetch of Hood Canal for waves to develop, I feared a nasty swell would bend around the spit and make life uncomfortable. Not so. The spit offered good protection from the waves, but not the wind. We swung around on the anchor, but no other motion in the boat." Boaters should be aware of the Restricted Area just off Point Whitney, a charted no anchoring zone.

A State Department of Fish and Wildlife oyster research laboratory is at Whitney Point with a good launch ramp alongside. A breakwater-protected marina is at the village of Quilcene. Caution should be exercised when transiting Dabob Bay and Quilcene Bay to avoid the large number of shrimp pots during the season.

Broad Spit Park. On the east shore of Bolton Peninsula in Dabob Bay. Anchor on either side of the spit, depending on wind direction. Easy beach access, trails ashore. Lagoon that fills at high tide. [*Thanks to readers David and Sharon von Wolffersdorff.*]

Pleasant Harbor Marina

Experience Your Cruising Dreams

Waggoner Guide Books, Flotillas and Seminars

BOOKS AND MAPS:
Waggoner Cruising Guide
Ports and Passes
Over 300 Cruising Guides and Maps
Seafood Cookbooks
Children's Nautical Books too
Shop at waggonerguide.com or stop by our store in Anacortes

CRUISE THE INSIDE PASSAGE TO SOUTHEAST ALASKA FLOTILLA
May 12 - May 31, 2018 - $2900
May 18 - June 7, 2019 - $2900
Includes Cruising Guides and 50% off the 3 day seminar

Cruising Desolation Sound Flotilla
June 16-July 1, 2018 - $2000
Includes Guide Books

Waggoner Seminars
Cruising the Inside Passage to SE Alaska
April 16-18, 2018 - Anacortes
$395 per couple/$225 per person. Held in Anacortes

See WaggonerGuide.com for more information on Flotillas and Seminars

Also see our other informative seminar programs at: CruisersCollege.org

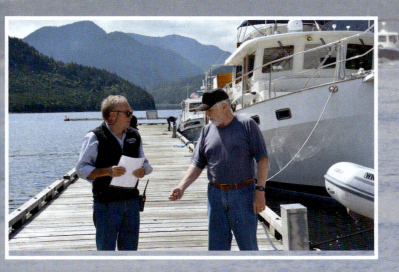

**See WaggonerGuide.com for more information, our store, flotilla and seminar information and many informative articles and cruising tips.
425.780.5015**

HOOD CANAL

See Area Map Page 119 - Maps Not for Navigation

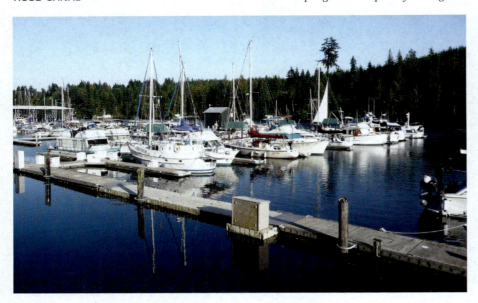

Pleasant Harbor Marina, a clean, attractive facility with guest moorage

Quilcene Bay. Anchor in 12 feet, good holding in mud along the east shore opposite the marina, with protection from moderate southerly winds. On a 10-foot tide, a shallow draft vessel can travel at least a quarter mile up Donovan Creek through winding grasslands at the head of the bay. *[Hamilton]*

① **Herb Beck Marina.** 1731 Linger Longer Rd., Quilcene, WA 98376; (360) 765-3131; www.portofpt.com/marinas/. Managed by the Port of Port Townsend. Monitors VHF 66A. Open Wednesday through Sunday 8:00 a.m. - 4:30 p.m. in the summers; Tuesday, Friday, and Saturday 8:00 a.m. - 4:30 p.m. winters. Ethanol-free gasoline and diesel at the fuel dock. Limited guest moorage to 40 feet, 20 & 30 amp power, water, showers, restrooms, pumpout, garbage drop. Reservations accepted. This is a small, rustic marina.

Dosewallips State Park. (360) 796-4415; South of Brinnon. Park open all year for day use and overnight camping. Accessible by kayak or canoe. Restrooms, showers. Hiking trails, picnic areas, standard, utility, and primitive campsites.

Pleasant Harbor. Pleasant Harbor is a major stopping point on Hood Canal with a good destination resort marina and a state park dock. Enter through a narrow channel with least depth of 8.5 feet at zero tide. Inside, there's room to anchor, 18 to 42 feet, mud bottom. Pleasant Harbor Marina has excellent facilities for visiting boaters. Home Port Marina of Pleasant Harbor (formerly, Pleasant Harbor "Old" Marina) has no guest moorage.

Pleasant Harbor is full of boats in May, when the annual shrimping season is under way. For dates, go to www.wdfw.wa.gov.

② **Pleasant Harbor Marina.** 308913 Hwy 101, Brinnon, WA 98320; (360) 796-4611; (800) 547-3479; reservations@phmresort.com; www.pleasantharbormarina.com. Monitors VHF 09 & 16. Open all year. Closed Thanksgiving and Christmas. Ethanol-free gasoline, diesel and propane at the fuel dock. The marina has approximately 60 guest slips and unoccupied slips as available, 30 & 50 amp power. Side-tie moorage to 150 feet. Facilities include sparkling clean restrooms and free showers, laundry, free Wi-Fi, on-site security, and free pumpout at fuel dock. A floating washroom called "The Caboose" is moored at the north docks with a clean shower and two toilets.

The main building houses the marina office, restaurant, lounge, and store. The store has a selection of gifts, clothing, some groceries, beer and wine. At the fuel dock you'll find ice cream, ice, crab and shrimp bait, tackle, and marine hardware.

A shuttle van can take you to several local hikes that range in length from a 0.2 mile trail to 130-foot-high waterfall, to a 3.5- mile loop of Dosewallips State Park.

This is a popular destination. Reservations strongly recommended, especially on weekends and holidays. Many of the permanent tenants spend considerable time at the marina, and life on the docks is quite friendly. Amenities include a barbecue and picnic area, swimming pool, hot tub, laser skeet range, and children's play area. Kayak, and SUP rentals. Live music May through September. Diane and Christy are the very capable managers.

③ **Pleasant Harbor Marine State Park.** (360) 796-4415. Open all year for day use and overnight mooring. No camping. Dock has 120 feet of space, 3-night maximum stay, first-come, first-serve. This is the first dock on the right as you enter Pleasant Harbor.

Triton Head. A state park launch ramp is at Triton Head, and anchorage is possible off this little bight.

④ **Triton Cove State Park.** (360) 796-4415; West side of Hood Canal, south of the Dosewallips River. Open all year, day use only. Vault toilet, no power, no showers. Concrete launch ramp, picnic area.

⑤ **Hoodsport.** Hoodsport is popular with scuba divers as a place to view the giant Pacific octopus. Local marine preserves such as Octopus Hole and Sund Rock offer divers the chance to see octopus, wolf eels, rockfish, anemones and other marine life.

The town has a grocery store, hardware store, restaurants, an espresso shop, a dentist, a beauty salon, and gift shops. The Washington Department of Fish and Wildlife operates a fish hatchery in town.

⑤ **Port of Hoodsport.** P.O. Box 429, Hoodsport, WA 98548; (360) 877-9350; portmail@hctc.com; www.portofhoodsport.us. Docks with guest moorage, no power, no water. Garbage drop. Self-register at head of dock. Grocery store is located across the highway from the dock; other Hoodsport businesses are within walking distance. There is also a public dock with 6 slips to 16 feet.

Sunrise Motel & Resort. 24520 Hwy 101, Hoodsport, WA 98548; (360) 877-5301; sunrise@hctc.com; myweb.hcc.net/sunrise. Open all year, no power, laundry. Restrooms and showers in motel rooms. Stay on your boat or rent rooms. Maximum length 20 feet. Underwater park, scuba air station, barbecue, hot tub.

Potlatch Marine State Park. (360) 877-5361. South of Hoodsport. Open all year, day use and overnight camping and mooring. Restrooms, showers, no power. Five mooring buoys (boats 45 feet and under) are offshore in deep water, except the second buoy as you approach from the north. We are told this buoy swings into 5-foot depths at zero tide. Self-register and pay mooring buoy fee on shore. The park has a picnic area, an underwater park for scuba diving, short hiking trails, campsites. Good wildlife-watching.

⑥ **Hood Canal Marina.** P.O. Box 305, 5101 E. Hwy 106, Union, WA 98592; (360) 898-2252; hoodcanalmarina@hctc.com; www.hood-canal-marina.com. Certified Clean Marina. Open all year. Fuel dock with ethanol-free gasoline and diesel, open daily 8:00 a.m. to 5:00 p.m.; 30 amp power, free Wi-Fi, washrooms, and pumpout. Limited transient moorage, maximum 40-foot vessels. Call ahead for moorage. Moorages fill quickly in May during shrimp season. The Union launch ramp is adjacent and has off-site secured parking. The Union City Market is the newest addition at Hood Canal Marina offering food items, crafts, books and clothing.

⑦ **Alderbrook Resort & Spa.** 10 E. Alderbrook Drive, Union, WA 98592; (360) 898-2200; (360) 898-2252; cindy.sund@alderbrook.com; www.alderbrookresort.com. Monitors VHF 16, then switch to a working channel. Open all

PLEASANT HARBOR
— MARINA & RECREATION COMMUNITY —

CALL NOW
360-796-4611

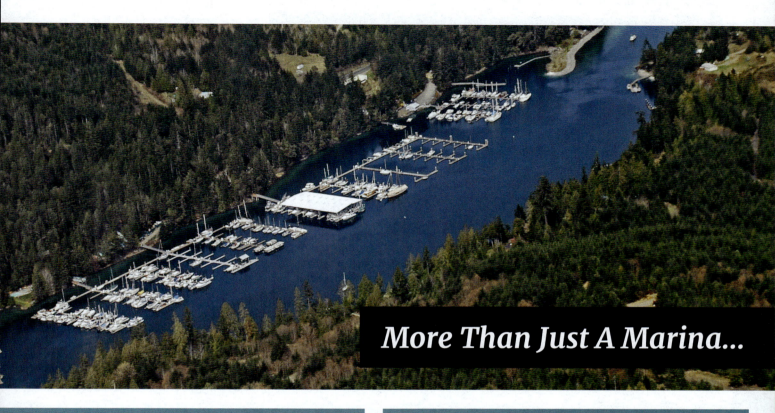

More Than Just A Marina...

YEAR ROUND MOORAGE

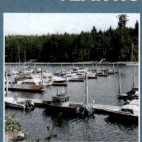

- 312 Slip Protected Marina
- 30 & 50 Amp Power
- Non-Ethanol Gas & Diesel
- Vacuum Pump Out
- Heated Pool & Hot Tub
- Permanent / Guest Moorage
- Boats Up To 150'

LUXURY ACCOMMODATION

- 4 Suites
- Queen Size Beds
- En-Suite Bathrooms
- Outside Deck with BBQ
- Heated Pool & Hot Tub
- TV + WiFi
- Full Kitchen

GALLEY & PUB

- Delicious Food
- Local Beers On Tap
- Local Wine Selection
- Groceries / Gift Shop
- Roof Top Patio
- Live Music
- 3 Big Screen **TVs**

ACTIVITIES & ADVENTURES

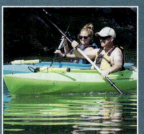

- Children's Play Area
- Kayak Racing
- Kayak & SUPs
- Laser Skeet Shooting
- Horseshoes
- Hiking
- Boating
- Lawn Games
- Shrimping/Crabbing

Play, Relax, Enjoy
www.pleasantharbormarina.com

HOOD CANAL See Area Map Page 119 - Maps Not for Navigation

Docks at Alderbrook Resort & Spa

year, 1500 feet of guest moorage. Restrooms, showers, 30 & 50 amp power, water, swimming pool and whirlpool spa, free Wi-Fi. Pumpout available, check for availability in advance. Seaplane dock. Kayak, paddleboard, hydrobike and seacycle rentals. The classic schooner *Pleiades* is available for scheduled trips and charters.

If you're looking for a quality resort experience, you'll find it here. The rooms are beautifully appointed, the grounds are immaculate, and the dining room is superb. Moorage is free while dining. They have an indoor pool, with a spa adjacent. Hiking trails surround the property. Everything you're looking for in a weekend getaway is here, including golf. Best to call ahead for reservations and prices.

Golf: Alderbrook Golf & Yacht Club, 18 holes, par 72, (360) 898-2560.

⑧ **Twanoh Marine State Park.** (360) 275-2222. Eight miles west of Belfair. Open all year, day use and overnight camping and mooring, except no camping in winter. Has 200 feet of overnight and day-use moorage dock, 6 mooring buoys for vessels 45 feet and under. Self-register and pay mooring fees on shore. Restrooms, showers, pumpout, portapotty dump, power, no water. Be aware that water depth at the dock is only 3 feet at zero tide. This is a large and popular park, with launch ramp, playground, picnic areas, kitchen shelters, fireplaces. Launch ramp docks removed from November through April. Standard, utility and primitive campsites, tennis courts, hiking trails.

⑨ **Summertide Resort & Marina.** P.O. Box 450, 15781 NE Northshore Rd. Tahuya, WA 98588; (360) 275-9313; www.summertideresort.com. Guest moorage, 50-foot maximum boat length. Restrooms, showers, Wi-Fi, no power. Launch ramp, RV spaces with hookups. Rental cottages available. Store carries groceries, beer and wine, snacks, ice, bait, tackle. Reservations necessary.

Belfair State Park. (800) 452-5687. Three miles southwest of Belfair on the north shore of Hood Canal. Open all year for day use and overnight camping. Restrooms and showers. Anchor far offshore if at all. Drying mudflats restrict approach to small, shallow-draft boats only. Popular park, camping reservations required in summer.

⑩ **Port of Allyn Hood Canal.** P.O. Box 1, Allyn, WA 98524; (360) 275-2430; www.portofallyn.com. Open all year with 240 feet of side-tie dock space. Water, 30 amp power, portable toilets, seasonal pumpout and portapotty dump, no showers. Overnight moorage for boats up to 45 feet with a 14-day limit. Self-registration payment box on-site. Launch ramp with credit, debit card payment.

Hood Canal with splendid views of the Olympic Mountains

124 www.WaggonerGuide.com

North Puget Sound

CHAPTER 4

NORTHWEST PUGET SOUND
*Kingston • Admiralty Inlet
Port Ludlow • Port Townsend*

NORTHEAST PUGET SOUND
*Edmonds • Everett • Langley
Saratoga Passage • Coupeville
Oak Harbor • La Conner • Deception Pass
Anacortes • Bellingham • Semiahmoo Bay
Blaine • Point Roberts*

NORTH PUGET SOUND

See Area Map Page 127 - Maps Not for Navigation

Kingston. Kingston, in Appletree Cove on the west side of Puget Sound, is the western terminus of the ferry run to Edmonds, and possibly the only city in Washington State where you can get an authentic French crepe at five o'clock in the morning while waiting for the ferry. A Port-owned marina, with a park, is located behind the breakwater. The park's meticulously maintained lawn and gardens are inviting. Kingston's tree shaded main street is lined with cafés with great food and colorful names, many with outdoor seating. Farther uptown is a grocery store and hardware store. On the north side of the ferry holding area a deck overlooks Puget Sound. A path leads to a Port-owned broad sandy beach filled with driftwood. It's a pleasant walk and great for families. On the the park grounds next to the marina a farmers market, quite popular, is open 9:00 a.m. to 2:00 p.m. Saturdays, May to mid-October. Concerts on the Cove, with a beer garden, are held Saturday evenings during July and August.

A pavilion on the park grounds, just up from the marina, is used for music concerts, gatherings, and weddings.

Anchoring is good south of the marina breakwater. Watch your depths. It gets shallow close to shore.

① **Port of Kingston.** P.O. Box 559, Kingston, WA 98346; (360) 297-3545; info@portofkingston.org; www.portofkingston.org. Monitors VHF 65A but prefers telephone calls. Open year-round, 49 guest slips to 50 feet, water and 30 amp power. At the outer end of the guest dock an 86-foot-long float, with water and 30 & 50 amp power, accommodates larger boats. The marina has restrooms, laundry, portapotty dump, free showers, free pumpout, in-berth pumpout on the guest dock, and free Wi-Fi. The fuel dock has ethanol-free gasoline, diesel and Delo lubricants. A dual-lane concrete launch ramp, with a float between the two lanes, is available. A kayak center is located on A Dock; key cards issued by the Port office are required for access. Parking (fee charged) for tow vehicles and trailers. Two electric courtesy cars are available through the Port office for local trips to shopping several blocks away. They are fun to drive and popular; 30-minute usage recommended.

Four mooring buoys for boats to 35 feet are outside the breakwater north of the ferry dock. They are exposed to winds and the wakes of passing boat traffic.

Moorage reservations are accepted with one day advance notice; call the Port office during business hours. Kingston is quite popular during the summer months, reservations are important. Reserved slips are marked and are not available, even for temporary use.

Enter the marina around the end of the rock breakwater. Leave two pilings that mark the

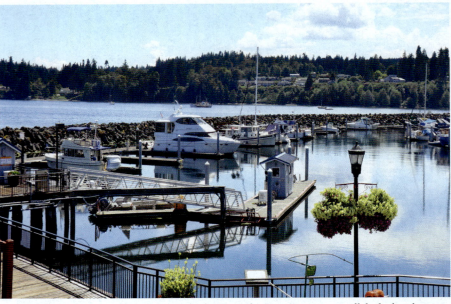

Port of Kingston marina. Fuel dock is in the foreground; visitor moorage parallels the breakwater.

Kingston

Northwest Puget Sound

NORTH PUGET SOUND

edge of the dredged channel to port. Leave the red buoy marking the end of the breakwater to starboard. Guest moorage is in slips extending from the dock that runs parallel to the breakwater, plus the side-tie float for larger boats at the outer end. The fuel float is at the shore end of the guest dock. Working from the shore end of the guest dock: the first five are 20-foot slips; then two 50-foot Kingston Cove Yacht Club reciprocal slips; then the 50-foot slips; then the 40-foot slips; and then the 30-foot slips. Moor in any unreserved guest dock slip and register at the Port office.

See the website for a schedule of music events. On the guest dock, two 22'x8' gazebos with picnic tables and power are popular with visiting boaters. First-come, first-served.

Golf: The White Horse Golf Club has a free shuttle to the marina. Call (360) 297-4468. The Point No Point Casino (360) 297-0070 and the Clearwater Casino (360)598-8700, also offer shuttle service.

ADMIRALTY INLET

Admiralty Inlet begins at Point No Point in the south and ends at Point Wilson in the north. Admiralty Inlet is wide, deep, and straight, with no hazardous reefs or shoals. It makes up for this good design by often being the only patch of rough water for miles. Flood current or ebb, Admiralty Inlet waters swirl and lump up. If the wind is light, you'll see the swirls. If the wind is blowing, you'll be in the lump. Use the Bush Point current tables to predict the times of slack water, and the time and strength of maximum current.

If Admiralty Inlet is rough and you have to be there anyway, try to favor the eastern or western shores. The western shore is preferred. A suggested route is along Marrowstone Island, far enough off to avoid the rocks shown on the chart. Approach around Marrowstone Point inside the rough water just outside, and into Port Townsend Bay.

If you are northbound past Point No Point and you can see that Admiralty Inlet is rough (you can see it), head west across the south tip of Marrowstone Island, and go through Port Townsend Canal into Port Townsend Bay. Port Townsend Canal currents are based on the Deception Pass current tables.

Point No Point. Point No Point, on the west side of Puget Sound, is a popular salmon-fishing spot and a place where boats heading up-sound and down-sound tend to converge. Boat traffic can get heavy, especially when the salmon are running and the waters are literally covered with small sport fishing boats working along the tide-rip.

Watch out for this tide-rip. When a strong wind opposes a big tide, the waters off Point No Point can turn dangerous.

LOCAL KNOWLEDGE

NAVIGATION NOTE: Check your chart before entering the landlocked Port Ludlow inner harbor and be sure to pass between the two islets. Passing outside of either islet could put you aground.

SPEED LIMIT: A 5-mph "no wake" speed limit is in effect throughout Port Ludlow and applies to all vessels, including dinghies.

② **Port Ludlow.** Well-protected Port Ludlow indents the western shore of Puget Sound. It was once the site of a major Pope & Talbot sawmill, and now is a nice residential area, a destination resort and a marina. Anchorage is in the landlocked inner harbor, reached by passing between two little islands near the head of the bay. Deeper draft boats should watch the depth sounder closely when entering the inner harbor at low tide. The passage is shallower than the bays it connects. Good anchorage, mud bottom, is in about 15 feet. An 8-foot shoal area a short distance northeast of the entrance is noted on large scale Chart 18477. Anchorage can also be found south of the marina; note the charted cable area immediately west of the marina.

The inner harbor is a favorite destination in Puget Sound, protected from all winds. Upscale homes are set well back and often screened by trees, providing privacy and a lovely harbor charm. Meydenbauer Bay Yacht Club has an outstation on the peninsula that forms the inner harbor. A level, scenic one-mile pathway parallels Oak Bay Road, leading west from the marina to the Village Center which has a grocery, gift shop, pizza shop, and a café.

② **Port Ludlow Resort and Marina.** 1 Gull Drive, Port Ludlow, WA 98365; (360) 437-0513; (877) 344-6725; marina@portludlowresort.com; www.portludlowresort.com. Monitors VHF 68. Certified Clean Marina. Open 7 days a week, all year. Ethanol-free gasoline and diesel at the fuel dock. Excellent concrete docks. Guest moorage in 50 slips and along 460 feet of dock, plus unoccupied slips as available, 30 & 50 amp power, water, restrooms, laundry, Wi-Fi, gazebo with barbecue, pumpout, portapotty dump, free showers. Pavilion tent for groups. Kayak, SUPs, and skiff rentals. Reservations recommended.

A resort restaurant and lounge are within walking distance. Locals speak highly of the restaurant. Free shuttle for marina guests to the

Port Ludlow

Port Ludlow Resort and Marina

JAMES COOK (1728-1779)

James Cook is known the world over for his significant explorations as well as for his incredible leadership. He joined the British merchant navy as a teenage and then the Royal Navy in 1755. Gaining experience and skills in navigation and cartography, he was assigned commander of HM Endeavour for his three Pacific voyages.

Cook's First Voyage (1768-71) was a scientific voyage, circumnavigating the world from England to Cape Horn and continuing westward across the Pacific, reaching Tahiti, New Zealand, and Australia. Cook chose individuals of noted expertise to be part of his team, including two botanists who collected over 3,000 plant species and who helped promote the British settlement of Australia. An artist selected for his First Voyage of exploration documented 264 drawings of the botanists' findings. Thanks to Cook's leadership, not a single man lost his life to scurvy, having understood the importance of replenishing fresh foods when needed. Cook's journals were published after his return, which brought him recognition among the scientific community.

On Cook's Second Voyage (1772-75), he engaged artist William Hodges, who produced notable landscape paintings. This Second Voyage covered the extreme southern latitudes of South America, crossing of the Antarctic Circle, then on to Australia and New Zealand before rounding Cape Horn, sailing back to England. During this voyage, Cook discovered and named Clerke Rocks and the South Sandwich Islands; and he had claimed South Georgia as a possession for Britain.

Today's boaters in the Pacific Northwest hold equal admiration for Cook's Third Voyage (1776-79). From the Hawaiian Islands, Cook sailed north, northeast to explore the west coast of North America. Exploring the coastline of today's California, he landed on the Oregon coast, naming the spot Cape Foulweather. Due to poor visibility and bad weather, he unknowingly sailed past the Strait of Juan de Fuca, eventually reaching Nootka Sound on the west coast of Vancouver Island. Cook's two ships, the *HMS Resolution*, and the *HMS Discovery* captained by Charles Clerke, stayed at Nootka Sound for a month trading with the Yuquot Natives, who desired metal objects in exchange for sea otter pelts. Departing Nootka Sound, Cook sailed northwest to the Bering Strait continuing his mapping of the Northwest coastline. Among his accomplishments, Cook charted the majority of the North American coastline on world maps for the first time.

Unfortunately, Cook met his demise when returning to Hawaii in 1779. His arrival coincided with a Native Hawaiian festival and worship of the Polynesian god Lono. The Natives, finding similar worship symbols in the shape of the sails and rigging along with Cook's procession around the island, led the Natives to treat Cook as an incarnation of Lono. (The evidence to support this theory was challenged in 1992). Cook's plan was to resume his exploration of the Northern Pacific, but as he departed the island of Hawaii, the Resolution's foremast broke and he returned to Kealakekua Bay to make repairs. Tensions and quarrels between the Europeans and Hawaiians ensued. Cook and some of his officers came ashore to retrieve the Hawaiian King, a large crowd of Natives assembled on the beach; Cook was struck on the head from behind and stabbed. Accounts of the voyage were completed by James King who took command of the ship Discovery.

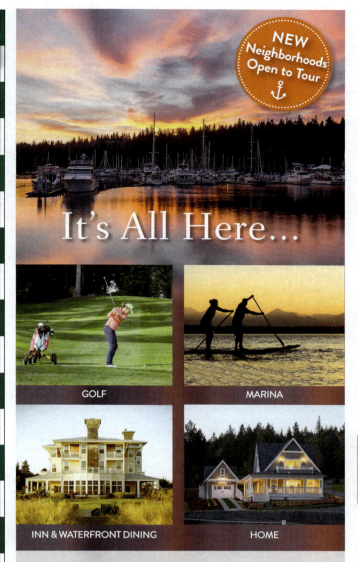

NEW Neighborhoods Open to Tour

It's All Here...

GOLF · MARINA · INN & WATERFRONT DINING · HOME

Port Ludlow Marina is open year round & offers:

- Boat In and Golf Packages
- Shuttle Service to the Golf Course
- Covered Pavilion and BBQ Fire Pit
- 30 miles of hiking trails
- 24 miles of biking trails
- Waterfront Dining
- Fuel Dock and Pump Out
- Free WiFi
- Marina Store

Port Ludlow
golf. marina. inn. home.

360.437.0513
www.PortLudlowResort.com

NORTH PUGET SOUND

resort's 18-hole golf course. The marina store carries limited groceries, hot dogs, ice cream, beer, wine, ice, books, propane and limited marine hardware and supplies. Shops, medical services, and a post office are nearby. Marine mechanics from Port Townsend may be available. With its large grounds, pavilion tent, dining and golf, this a popular destination for groups and rendezvous.

The marina often runs cruise-in specials that include moorage, golf, and restaurant credit. Check the marina website.

③ **Mats Mats Bay.** A course between Port Ludlow and Mats Mats Bay should avoid Snake Rock, close to shore, and Colvos Rocks and Klas Rocks, farther offshore. Colvos Rocks are marked by flashing lights at the north and south ends, and Klas Rocks by a diamond shape dayboard with a flashing white light. Snake Rock is not marked.

Mats Mats Bay has a dogleg entrance with a least depth of 5 feet at zero tide. A lighted range shows the center of the narrow channel. A rock once almost blocked the entrance to the bay. It was blasted out years ago, and buoys now mark the channel. Pay attention to all buoys, and do not stray from the marked channel, especially at low water. Anchor in 18 feet in the middle or south part of the bay. The large number of boats on permanent moorings restrict anchoring options. Mats Mats Bay is well protected from almost any wind. A launch ramp is at the south end of the bay.

Point Hudson Marina entry at the east end of Port Townsend

Oak Bay. Oak Bay, with convenient anchoring depths, is at the southern approach to Port Townsend Canal. Oak Bay County Park is on the west side of the channel, approximately one mile south of the entrance to the canal.

Oak Bay County Park. Northwest shore of Oak Bay. Open all year, restrooms, launch ramp, campsites, picnic tables, no power, no water. Anchoring or beaching only. Marked by a rock jetty. Swimming, scuba diving, clamming, crabbing.

Port Townsend Canal. Port Townsend Canal (also known as Hadlock Canal) runs from

CHARTS	
18441	Puget Sound – Northern Part (1:80,000)
18446	Puget Sound – Apple Cove Pt. to Keyport (1:25,000)
18464	Port Townsend (1:20,000)
18471	Dungeness to Oak Bay (1:40,000)
18473	Puget Sound – Oak Bay to Shilshole Bay (1:40,000)
18477	Puget Sound – Entrance to Hood Canal (1:25,000)

See Area Map Page 127 - Maps Not for Navigation   NORTH PUGET SOUND

There are many fine eateries and shops in the Port Townsend Victorian buildings.

An incredibly wide variety of boats are seen in the harbor.

Oak Bay to Port Townsend Bay through a relatively narrow dredged channel. The canal is well marked, easy to transit, and spanned by a bridge with 58-foot vertical clearance. Currents run to 3 knots. Port Townsend Canal is a secondary station under the Deception Pass reference station in the current tables.

Port Hadlock Marina

Port Hadlock and Irondale. The towns of Irondale and Port Hadlock are west of the northern entrance to Port Townsend Canal. The hotel and restaurant at Port Hadlock are closed, but the marina is fully operational. Anchorage is good, sand bottom. Stay north of Skunk Island, due west from the marina.

The **Ajax Café**, (360) 385-3450 www.ajax-cafe.com; the popular Ajax Cafe is located one quarter mile northwest of Port Hadlock Marina, across the street from a 75-foot public dock. Ajax Café is currently closed indefinitely for a re-design of their septic system. Fundraising efforts for upgrades to the historic 1878 Galster House, which houses the Café, have been beneficial. More recently, the Ajax Café partnered with the adjacent **Northwest School of Wooden Boat Building** to develop a plan that resolves the septic issues and allows the café to move forward toward re-opening.

Guided tours of the Northwest School of Wooden Boat Building (360-385-4948) are offered to the public on the first Friday of every month, starting at 3:00 p.m. The tour is approximately an hour and a half, covering boat building techniques and the school itself, which attracts students from around the world. The accredited school provides instruction for both traditional and contemporary wooden boatbuilding.

④ **Port Hadlock Marina.** 173 Hadlock Bay Rd., Port Hadlock, WA 98339; (360) 385-6368; harbormaster@porthadlockmarina.com; www.porthadlockmarina.com. Contact on VHF 16, switch to 66A; phone calls preferred. Open all year, 30 & 50 amp power, call for availability of transient moorage. New restrooms with showers. Laundry, garbage, in-slip pumpout, free Wi-Fi. Mostly permanent moorage. The marina has 600 feet of nice beach and 3 picnic areas with tables, power, barbecues, and a 6-foot fire pit. No groceries, repairs, or marine supplies at marina, but a QFC grocery store is a one-half mile away.

Kilisut Harbor. Kilisut Harbor is entered through a channel between Walan Point and the spit protecting the harbor. When approaching the entrance, stay clear of the Navy restricted area off Walan Point. The channel is well marked though shallow, averaging about 11 feet. Currents can run strongly. The channel swings past Fort Flagler State Park on the north shore, with launch ramp and dock. Picnicking and camping facilities are ashore. The channel continues through Kilisut Harbor to Mystery Bay. Mystery Bay State Park, on the north shore, has a long dock and mooring buoys. At the head of Mystery Bay is the village of Nordland, and a great old general store with its small

2018 WAGGONER CRUISING GUIDE

PORT TOWNSEND MARKETPLACE

RESTAURANTS & SHOPS

ELEVATED ICE CREAM & CANDY SHOP
We use the freshest local Ingredients in our flavorful ice creams, ices and sherbets, and handcraft our own chocolates and truffles. See our assortment of dark chocolate bars, candies and gifts. We're open late during boating season! Just two blocks west of Point Hudson. Find us on Facebook.
360-385-1156 • 627 Water St. • www.elevatedicecream.com

THE FOUNTAIN CAFE
Downtown Port Townsend is a casual and intimate cafe known for its excellent lunches and dinners enjoyed in a cozy setting one block from the hustle and bustle of Water Street. This popular eatery is located in the entertainment zone around Haller Fountain, a historic landmark famous for its statuesque, nude maiden and her attending sprites.
360-385-1364• 920 Washington St.
www.fountaincafept.com

MARINE THRIFT
Marine Thrift is a place where builders, sailors, DIYers, and the curious can find amazing deals on hardware, tools, and all kinds of other interesting boat gear. We keep good materials out of the landfill and in circulation while ensuring costs of boating stay accessible to many.
360-379-5807 • 315B Haines Place, Port Townsend
info@marinethrift.com • www.nwmaritime.org/marine-thrift

THE SWAN HOTEL AND COTTAGES
Located on the water front near the Point Hudson Marina, the NW Maritime Center and Historic Downtown. The Swan features suite, studio, and hotel-style rooms, as well as deluxe cottages. Within walking distance of most of Port Townsend's restaurants, shops & attractions.
360-385-1718 • 222 Monroe at Water Street
frontdesk@theswanhotel.com • www.theswanhotel.com

THE WINE SELLER
The Small Town Wine Shop With a Big City Selection, since 1982. Amazing selection of fine wines, champagne, beer & ale, ciders, gourmet foods, cheese, coffee chocolate & cigars. Surprisingly competitive prices! Generous mixed-whole and 1/2 case discounts. Knowledgeable friendly wine specialists!! OPEN 7 DAYS a WEEK. Marina delivery available!
360-385-7673 • 1010 Water St. • www.PTwineSeller.com

THE WOODEN BOAT CHANDLERY
Everything for wooden boats and the people who love them. For boat owners, we have bronze hardware, copper nails, rope, oakum, varnishes and more. For boat lovers, we have NOAA charts, cruising guides, galley ware, maritime books, nautical gifts and toys, and affordable apparel and more.
360-379-2629 • 431 Water Street • Yellow Building at NW Maritime Center • woodenboatchandlery.com

PORT TOWNSEND COMMUNITY EVENTS

Strange Brew festival	January
Shipwrights' Regatta	February
WBF Maritime Swap Meet	April
Port Townsend Rhododendron Festival	May
Classic Mariner Regatta	June
Steampunk Festival	June
Raker's Car Show	June
Centrum's Jazz Festival	July
Centrum's Acoustic Blues Festival	July
Wooden Boat Festival	September
Crafts By the Dock Fair	September
PT Film Festival	September
Kinetic Skulpture Weekend	October
Holiday Craft Fair	November
Festival of Lights	December

dock. Mystery Bay is a voluntary no anchoring zone to protect local shellfish.

⑤ **Fort Flagler Marine State Park.** (360) 385-1259. On Marrowstone Island. Open all year, 784 acres, day use, overnight mooring and camping. Has 256 feet of dock space with 6-foot depths at zero tide (docks removed in winter), 6 mooring buoys for boats 45 feet or less, launch ramp. The current can run strongly through this area; allow for it when mooring. Restrooms, showers, portapotty dump, no power. Self-register and pay mooring fee on shore. Easy trails lead to old fortifications along the north shore of Marrowstone Island. Underwater park for divers. Snack and grocery concession. Boat rentals, fishing supplies. Standard, utility, and primitive campsites. Campsite reservations are a good idea in summer, call (800) 452-5687.

⑥ **Mystery Bay Marine State Park.** (360) 385-1259. In Kilisut Harbor on Marrowstone Island. Open all year, 10 acres, 683 feet dock space with 4.5-foot depth at zero tide, 7 mooring buoys for boats 45 feet or less. Pumpout, portapotty dump, toilets, launch ramp, no power, no showers. This park is open for day use only, but overnight mooring is permitted at the dock. The dock runs parallel to shore. Call Fort Flagler office for more information (360) 388-1259. Self-register and pay mooring fee on shore. The charming Nordland General Store is at the shallow end of the bay with a dock in front. Dinghy landing only.

Port Townsend. Port Townsend has two Port-owned marinas, Point Hudson Marina and the Port of Port Townsend's Boat Haven. Boat Haven is closer to a supermarket, but Point Hudson is closer to downtown.

Port Townsend is a major boatbuilding and repair center with craftsmen skilled in every nautical discipline. It is the home of the annual Wooden Boat Festival at Point Hudson Marina, held the weekend after Labor Day. Next to the Point Hudson Marina is the Northwest Maritime Center and the Wooden Boat Chandlery. Northwest Maritime Center often has boat building projects underway, visitors welcome. Wooden Boat Chandlery carries an array of

Point Hudson Marina

Port Townsend Boat Haven

Port Townsend Boat Haven Marina & Boat Yard

The West Coast's premier location for marine services.
A full-service yard with 300 & 75 ton lifts, that also welcomes DIY work.
Over 100 vendors for services and supplies.
Fuel dock, laundry, showers, provisions, chandleries.

360-385-2355
PortofPT.com
info@portofpt.com

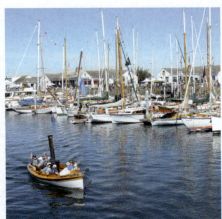
The Wooden Boat Festival in Port Townsend

NORTH PUGET SOUND

nautical items. A Maritime Thrift Store for used gear is located in Boat Haven, 315 B Haines Place.

Port Townsend is a favorite destination. The commercial district is lined with imposing stone and brick buildings from before 1900. At that time, residents hoped Port Townsend would become the western terminus of the transcontinental railroad and the principal city on Puget Sound. Victorian homes, many of them beautifully restored and cared for, are on the hill above the business district. Port Townsend's upper business district is at the top of a long flight of stairs from the lower district on Water Street. The town of Port Townsend is a haven for writers, craftspeople and artists of all kinds. Tourists overwhelm the town during the summer, but that shouldn't keep anybody away.

Golf: The Port Townsend Golf Club is within walking distance of Boat Haven Marina. Call (360) 385-4547.

Whether you're a woodenboat fan, history buff or antique collector, Port Townsend has a little bit of everything. Even with limited time to spare, the town's distinctive charm and spectacular views of Admiralty Inlet are enough to make the trip worth it.

⑦ **Port of Port Townsend Boat Haven.** P.O. Box 1180, 2601 Washington Street, Port Townsend, WA 98368; (360) 385-2355; (800) 228-2803; info@portofpt.com; www.portofpt.com. Monitors VHF 66A. Open all year. Guest moorage along 900 feet of side-tie linear dock and unoccupied slips as available, 30 & 50 amp power, restrooms, showers, laundry, pumpout, portapotty dump, for-fee Wi-Fi, launch ramp. Ethanol-free gasoline and diesel fuel at the fuel dock (The Fish'n' Hole).

The marina is west of the ferry dock, and entered between a rock breakwater and a piling wavebreak. The first basin on the right has the Coast Guard float and slips for commercial vessels. The next basin is the recreational basin with combination fuel dock and registration dock, moorage slips, linear dock, launch ramps, and haulout facilities. Fuel/registration dock is on the right, after passing the Coast Guard float.

Call ahead or check-in at the marina office for guest moorage availability and slip or side-tie assignment, which may be in the recreational basin or commercial basin. Vessels over 50 feet should call a day in advance. Spaces may be available through the marina for reciprocal yacht club members with Port Townsend Yacht Club. After hours, empty slips are marked on a map board at the top of the launch ramp and fuel dock. Temporary tie-up is just past the fuel dock, towards the launch ramps, for use only while checking for an empty slip, 15-minute limit.

Customs clearance by appointment only during standard business hours 8:00 a.m. to 4:00 p.m.; call (360) 385-3777. There is only one CBP agent stationed in Port Townsend in an office at Point Hudson. Please plan accordingly.

A hardware store and a large Safeway supermarket are across the highway. The local co-op market is a few blocks closer to town. The Chamber of Commerce Visitor Information Center is just beyond Safeway. Key City Fish, an excellent fish market, is in the repair yard area. Several good restaurants are nearby. More restaurants and a brew pub are in the Boat Haven. The main part of the town, with more restaurants and shops, is a 5-7 block walk.

A 300-ton Travelift and a smaller Travelift are available for haulout. Major boatbuilding and repair facilities and a chandlery (Admiral Ship Supply) are at the Boat Haven, and a West Marine store is nearby.

Point Hudson Marina

⑦ **The Fish'n' Hole.** (360) 385-7031. Ethanol-free gasoline and diesel fuel, open all year. Located inside the Boat Haven breakwater. Floating store carries soda, snacks, ice, bait, tackle.

⑧ **Point Hudson Marina & RV Park.** P.O. Box 1180, Port Townsend, WA 98368; (360) 385-2828; (800) 228-2803; pthudson@portofpt.com; www.portofpt.com. Monitors VHF 09. Open all year, moorage slips to 70 feet. Side-tie dock space accommodates larger boats. Water, 30 & 50 amp power, restrooms, showers, pumpout, laundry, for-fee Wi-Fi. Reservations recommended. Temporary tie-up is available for up to 4 hours, call ahead for space assignment. Ice, event facility, RV park and restaurants are on the property or nearby. The marina is within easy walking distance to town.

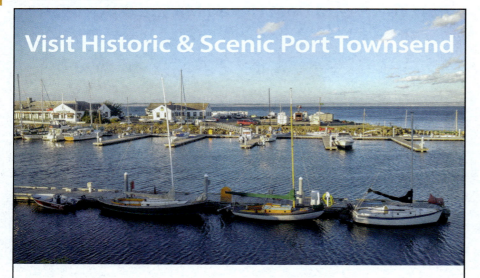

Stay at Point Hudson Marina & RV Park. Just steps away from the heart of downtown. Walk to shops, restaurants & more!

Reservations: 360-385-2828
PortofPT.com
pthudson@portofpt.com | VHF 09

Point Hudson Marina & RV Park

See Area Map Page 127 - Maps Not for Navigation   NORTH PUGET SOUND

The Port of Edmonds building with restaurant and showers

Enter the marina between two piling breakwaters that force the channel into a distinct bend, directly into the prevailing northwesterly summer winds. The limitation on the size of boats is mainly due to the turns required to enter the breakwater. Breakwater repairs are planned for summer of 2018, a barge may temporarily block the marina entrance; call the marina for current status. The marina office is in a white building on the north side.

The Sea Marine haulout and boatyard facility is at the north end of the basin. There's no grocery store nearby, so Sea Marine has ice, propane, and beer. Three restaurants are in the historic white buildings on the north side of the harbor. Other marine businesses around the harbor include Hasse & Co. sailmakers, Brian Toss Rigging, several wooden boat shops, and the Wooden Boat Chandlery located in the NW Maritime Center on the south side of the harbor entrance. The coffee shop at the Wooden Boat Chandlery has free Wi-Fi.

Customs clearance by appointment only during standard business hours 8:00 a.m. to 4:00 p.m.; call (360) 385-3777. There is only one CBP agent stationed in Port Townsend in an office at Point Hudson. Please plan accordingly.

Fort Townsend Marine State Park. (360) 385-3595. Open summers only, 367 acres, 3 mooring buoys for boats 45 feet or less, restrooms, showers, no power. The park has campsites, swimming, playgrounds, hiking trails, picnic tables, fire rings, and kitchen shelters. Self-guided nature trail, clamming, fishing and scuba diving. Self-register and pay mooring buoy fee on shore.

Fort Worden Marine State Park. (360) 344-4400. North of Port Townsend. Open all year, 120 feet of dock space, 5 mooring buoys. Restrooms, showers and no power. The dock is protected by a wharf. Use the dock or a buoy—this is not a good anchorage, although a friend found good sand bottom in about 18 feet. He also reported that the wakes from passing ship traffic rolled him out of his bunk all night, and he won't overnight there again. Others say they've had no trouble at all. Underwater park for scuba diving. Boat launch with two ramps. Tennis courts, picnic areas, snack bar concession near moorage area. Hiking trails, swimming, fishing. Utility and primitive campsites. Campsite reservations taken year-round. Call (800) 452-5687. Self-register and pay mooring fees on shore.

Upland, the old officers' quarters can be rented overnight. Fort buildings house the Marine Science Center and the Centrum Foundation, which conduct workshops and seminars on the arts each summer.

LOCAL KNOWLEDGE

TIDE-RIP: The tide rip at Point Wilson can be dangerous to cruising boats. The bigger the ebb, the greater the chance for a tide-rip. A small ebb can produce no rip at all, particularly if the wind is light. Use the Bush Point current tables to predict the time of slack water and strength of maximum current. Those who think that a fast boat makes current tables unnecessary are wrong, and Point Wilson will prove them so.

Point Wilson. Point Wilson is the corner where Admiralty Inlet turns into the Strait of Juan de Fuca. On an ebb, a nasty tide-rip can build immediately north of Point Wilson, and stretch well across the mouth of Admiralty Inlet. If it's a big ebb and opposed by strong westerly winds, the seas in this area are not merely nasty, they are dangerous. They are high, steep and close together. They break. They are not long rollers; they are pyramid-shaped, and have no consistent pattern except for being ugly.

Since boats bound for the San Juan Islands or out the Strait of Juan de Fuca often

CHARTS	
18423 sc folio smallcraft	Bellingham to Everett including San Juan Islands (1:80,000) Blaine (1:30,000)
18441	Puget Sound – Northern Part (1:80,000)
18443	Approaches to Everett (1:40,000)
18444	Everett Harbor (1:10,000)
18445 sc folio smallcraft	Puget Sound – Possession Sound to Olympia including Hood Canal

2018 waggoner CRUISING GUIDE   135

NORTH PUGET SOUND — Reference Only – Not for Navigation

Northeast Puget Sound

See Area Map Page 136 - Maps Not for Navigation

NORTH PUGET SOUND

schedule their passages to take advantage of the ebb, skippers must be aware of what can happen at Point Wilson, especially if a westerly is blowing. In such conditions, the wise approach is to favor the Whidbey Island side. The even wiser choice is to wait until slack water or the beginning of the flood. Better yet, wait for the wind to drop and then go at slack water.

For information on crossing the Strait of Juan de Fuca, see Chapter 5, Strait of Juan de Fuca.

WEST WHIDBEY ISLAND

South Whidbey State Park. On Admiralty Inlet on the Whidbey Island side, just south of Lagoon Point. Open all year, day use only. Campground closed October 15 to March 15. Restrooms, showers, no power. Anchoring in calm conditions or beaching only. Picnic sites, hiking trail, underwater park for scuba diving.

The Port of Everett Marina is excellent, with attractions nearby.

Fort Casey State Park. (360) 678-4519. Admiralty Head, adjacent to Keystone Harbor on Admiralty Inlet. Open all year, day-use and overnight camping, restrooms, no power, no showers. Has a 2-lane launch ramp with boarding floats. Not a good anchorage; beachable boats are best. Underwater park with artificial reef for scuba divers. Picnic areas, standard and primitive campsites. Lighthouse and interpretive center. Historic displays and remains of the old fort to explore. Guided tours during summer.

Fort Ebey State Park. (360) 678-4636. Open all year for day use and overnight camping. The park has restrooms and showers, no power. Anchoring only, or small boats can be beached. Standard campsites, picnic sites. Interesting bunkers and gun batteries are in the old fort.

Joseph Whidbey State Park. (360) 678-4636. Northwest shore of Whidbey Island on Admiralty Inlet. Open April through September, day use only. Toilets, no power, water or showers. Anchor or beach only. One mile of sandy beach on Puget Sound. Picnic sites.

NORTHEAST PUGET SOUND

⑨ **Edmonds.** Edmonds, a prosperous community with a small-town feel to it, is about 8 miles north of Shilshole Bay on the east side of Puget Sound. Edmonds has a major rock breakwater-protected marina (the Port of Edmonds Marina) with excellent facilities for visiting boats. At the marina and in the town a short distance away you'll find a number of very good restaurants, antiques stores, a lively art scene, a historic 252-seat movie theater, art museum, performance theaters, and interesting shops and galleries. Edmonds "walks" well. This is an ideal destination for a weekend getaway, year-round.

THINGS TO DO

1. **Edmonds Waterfront Festival** (June)

2. **Marina Concert Series:** Wednesday evenings and Sunday afternoons (June - mid-September).

3. **Taste of Edmonds** (Around the second week of August.)

4. **Edmonds Public Art Walking Tour:** Twelve of 15 art pieces are in the city's central core.

5. **Edmonds Historic Site Walking Tour:** This self guided tour takes you past 29 sites in a one-square-mile section of the city's historic center.

6. **Scratch Distillery:** Learn about the distilling process for handcrafted vodkas and gin in a relaxed contemporary atmosphere. Tour & Tasting on Saturdays and Sundays.

7. **Cascadia Art Museum** opened in the fall of 2015. It showcases American regional art from the mid-19th to the mid-20th century.

8. **Edmonds Center for the Arts** has theatre productions, comedy, film series, and live music.

9. **Edmonds Segway Tours:** Learn about Edmond's history or take a sunset tour. Book online or call (206) 947-5439.

⑨ **Port of Edmonds.** 336 Admiral Way, Edmonds, WA 98020; (425) 775-4588; info@portofedmonds.org; www.portofedmonds.org. Monitors VHF 69. Certified Clean Marina and Certified Clean Boatyard. Open 7 days a week all year. The fuel dock has ethanol-free

Port of Edmonds

NORTH PUGET SOUND See Area Map Page 136 - Maps Not for Navigation

gasoline & diesel. The marina has 500 feet of guest side-tie dock space, plus unoccupied slips when available. They can accommodate boats to 100 feet. The docks are served by 30 & 50 amp power, free Wi-Fi, restrooms, showers, two pumpouts, a covered outdoor weather center, and public plaza.

Enter through the middle of the breakwater. Guest moorage and the fuel dock are immediately to the south. The marina has a large do-it-yourself work yard, a 10,000-pound public sling launch and a 50-ton Travelift. Close to two popular public beaches and a public fishing pier. An artificial reef for scuba diving (the first such site in the state) is next to the ferry dock just north of the marina. Fishing charters are available. It's a short walk to several restaurants. Groceries and shops are in town, about 9 blocks away. When you register at the marina you will be given a welcome bag with discount coupons for Edmonds businesses. On Saturdays a market is set up near the downtown business district. The marina provides courtesy van service to downtown Edmonds. The marina personnel are friendly and helpful.

**456 Admiral Way
(425) 771-4400**

**456 Admiral Way
(425) 771-4400**

Possession Sound is on the southeast side of Whidbey Island between Possession Point and Mukilteo.

Mukilteo. (425) 263-8180. Mukilteo Lighthouse Park has a 4-lane launch ramp with floats in summer. It is exposed to ferry wakes and waves generated by winds on Possession Sound and Port Gardner. A launch fee is charged. Call for more information. Tucked behind the ferry wall and pilings next to Ivar's Restaurant are 3 seasonal, 24-foot Port of Everett floats for access to restaurants and other businesses ashore; caution is advised, floats shift forward and back between pilings. The Mukilteo Lighthouse is open for visitors April through September.

Gedney Island. (425) 327-2607. Gedney Island, known locally as Hat Island, is privately owned. The marina on the north shore is for Gedney Island property owners and their guests, and members from reciprocal yacht clubs.

Tulalip Bay. Anchorage is possible, but Tulalip Bay is very shallow, with a reef guarding the entrance and drying shoals inside. Several private floats and mooring buoys owned by members of the Tulalip Indian Tribe often occupy the bay.

LOCAL KNOWLEDGE

STRONG CURRENTS: Currents in the Snohomish River can be quite strong, particularly on an ebb tide. Allow for the current as you maneuver.

Night Lights: At night, lights ashore in Everett's Navy facilities make the entrance channel buoys very difficult to see and identify. A vessel approaching at night should be extremely cautious.

⑩ **Everett.** The Port of Everett Marina is home to a substantial fishing fleet as well as private pleasure craft. Entry is about a mile upstream from the marked mouth of the Snohomish River. Information about moorage can be obtained from the fuel dock just inside the piling breakwater.

When you are in the river and approaching the marina entrance, watch for debris in the water and pay close attention to your navigation. Several aids to navigation, including one buoy marking a sunken ship, can be confusing. Although the channel can be entered between Lighted Buoy 3

EVERETT MARKETPLACE
RESTAURANTS, SHOPS & SERVICES

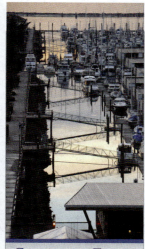

Calendar of Events

ALL SUMMER LONG:
Waterfront Farmer's Market
Music at the Marina
Jetty Island Days
Harbor Tours

APRIL 8:
Everett Half Marathon

APRIL 21:
Milltown Sailing Swap Meet

MAY 5:
Opening Day of Boating

JUNE 9:
Marina Cleanup Day

JULY 4:
Fourth of July Celebration

AUGUST 18-19:
Fresh Paint Festival of Artist at Work

SEPTEMBER:
Mukilteo Lighthouse Festival • Wheels on the Waterfront Car Show

DECEMBER 1:
Holiday on the Bay

Port of Everett
www.portofeverett.com/events
or 800-729-7678

Photos courtesy of Port of Everett

ANTHONY'S HOMEPORT EVERETT
Located on Port Gardner Bay, the restaurant offers fresh northwest seafood with majestic views of Puget Sound islands and the Olympic Mountains. Lunch served Monday-Saturday, Sunday brunch and dinner served daily. Located at Everett Marina Village. Visitor moorage along the dock in front of the restaurant.
425-252-3333 • 1726 West Marine View Drive, Everett Marina Village
www.anthonys.com

ANTHONY'S WOODFIRE GRILL
Featuring specialties from its custom-built rotisserie, applewood-burning oven and applewood grill. Serving signature fresh northwest seafood selections, as well as northwest beef selections at lunch and dinner daily. Located at Everett Marina Village. Visitor moorage along the dock in front of Anthony's HomePort.
425-258-4000 • 1722 West Marine View Drive, Everett Marina Village
www.anthonys.com

BAYSIDE MARINE AND DRYSTACK
Offering consignment brokerage, used boat sales, parts and service for most major brands of pleasure boats and inside boat drystack. Keep your boat inside with secure rack storage with private dock and launching.
425-252-3088 • 1111 Craftsman Way •
www.baysidemarine.com

EVERETT YACHT SERVICE
Our mission is to provide top quality maintenance and repair at our indoor facility in a timely manner for a fair price. Our experienced technicians provide service in the following: mechanical, electrical, gel coat and fiberglass repairs, bottom painting and electronic installations.
425-212-9923 • 1205 Craftsman Way Suite 116 •
phil@everettyachtservice.com

SCUTTLEBUTT BREWING COMPANY
Brewing handcrafted beer from the Northwest's finest ingredients since 1995. Come visit our family friendly brewery and pub. Offering a variety of handcrafted ales and root beer and a full menu, we have something for everyone. Just steps from the dock, on the water at the north end of the Everett Marina.
425-257-9316 • 1205 Craftsman Way •
www.scuttlebuttbrewing.com

NORTH PUGET SOUND   See Area Map Page 136 - Maps Not for Navigation

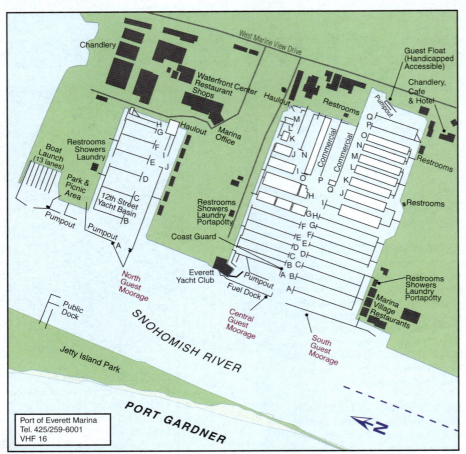

Port of Everett Marina

7. **Everett Farmers Market**. Every Sunday at Boxcar Park, just up from the marina.

8. **Port Gardner Landing**. Summer Concerts.

9. **Legion Memorial Golf Course**. Close to the marina.

⑩ **Port of Everett Marina.** 1205 Craftsman Way, Suite 105, Everett, WA 98201; (425) 259-6001; marina@portofeverett.com; www.portofeverett.com. Monitors VHF 16. Certified Clean Marina. Open all year, gasoline and diesel at fuel dock. Over 5000 feet of guest moorage with depths 10 to 16 feet, unoccupied slips used when available. Moorage is first-come, first-served, and self-pay stations are on the docks. If staying less than six hours before 10 p.m., guest moorage is free. Water, 20, 30 & 50 amp power, restrooms, showers, laundry, multiple free pumpout stations, free portapotty dump, Wi-Fi.

Handicapped-accessible guest moorage available. Watch for strong currents when landing at the guest dock. The Port's Craftsman District has a Travelift haulout to 75 tons with yard storage, a boatyard for repairs and maintenance. The Travelift is at the east end of the moorage. The Everett Marine Park, a 13-lane launch ramp (largest in the state) is just north of marina.

The Port of Everett's North Marina opened in 2007 with its first-class 42-slip guest moorage dock. The concrete docks are wide, stable and heavily built. Power is 30 & 50 amp, with 100 amp at the end moorages. A pumpout line is built into the main docks with attachments at each slip. The basin has its own restrooms, showers, and laundry. The Port of Everett is a large, complete marina, with shops, full repairs, services nearby, and and two chandleries. An attractive marina village with a hotel, shops, a West Marine store and good restaurants is adjacent to the south mooring basin. The wheelchair-accessible float is next to the street in the east end of the south basin. The new Waterfront Center Building on the north side of the marina has an inside coffee area, a brew-pub restaurant and a distillery. Harbor Marine, a complete marine supply store and chandlery, is on 10th Street between the north docks and the Everett Marine Park launch ramps. They have added a snack bar and cafe with daily specials. The northeast corner of the Port is being re-developed over the next few years to include a hotel, apartments, and splash park.

and Light 5 off the south end of Jetty Island, the water between them is somewhat shoal. For complete safety we recommend entering by leaving Lighted Buoy 3 to port. The channel leads past the U.S. Navy homeport facilities.

The marina is a long hike from the central business district, but bus and taxi service are available.

Everett offers numerous activities of interest. The Everett Marina hosts a farmers market in Boxcar Park at the disabled-access dock, Sundays, 11:00 a.m. to 4:00 p.m. May through October. The Port of Everett hosts a summertime waterfront concert series at Port Gardner Landing June through August, from 6:30 p.m. to 8:30 p.m. on Thursday and Saturday. The Xfinity Arena at Everett (www.xfinityarenaeverett.com) brings big-name entertainment. For professional sports with an intimate feeling, take in a minor league baseball game and cheer on the Aquasox. The July 4 fireworks show is Puget Sound's largest outside Seattle, and right in the laps of the Everett moorage. A courtesy shuttle bus, 4-guest minimum, connects to the Tulalip Casino with return service to the marina as late as 2:00 a.m. Call (888) 272-1111 to arrange.

Across the river from the marina is a Port-owned float at Jetty Island, which has what is probably the largest pure sand beach on Puget Sound. The Langus Waterfront Park, with good launching facility, is on the north shore of the main river channel, a short distance up the river from the Port of Everett Marina.

Farther up the Snohomish River, Dagmar's Landing is a large dry-land storage facility with a huge fork lift truck and a long float. A detailed chart or local knowledge are required before continuing beyond Dagmar's.

THINGS TO DO

1. **Boeing Aircraft Factory**. Take a 90-minute tour of the world's largest aircraft plant. Children must be at least 4 feet tall. A cab ride away.

2. **Flying Heritage Collection**. A remarkable collection of one-of-a-kind military aircraft from the past 75 years. Located at Paine Field, adjacent to the Boeing factory.

3. **Tulalip Casino Resort**. Adult gaming and good restaurants. The Tulalip Amphitheatre often has live music. Call 360-716-6640 to arrange a free shuttle for groups of 4 or more.

4. **Seattle Premium Outlet Stores**. Features over 130 designer names; outlet stores next to the Tulalip Casino.

5. **Imagine Children's Museum**. Hands-on activities for kids and many special events. About 1.5 miles from the marina.

6. **Port Gardner Bay Winery**. A boutique winery with relaxed tastings. They also offer classes in winemaking. About 1.5 miles from the marina.

Langley Boat Harbor with floating breakwater moorage and inner harbor docks

Langley Boat Harbor

Everett Marine Park. On the Snohomish River, north of the Port of Everett Marina. Open all year, 700 feet of overnight guest moorage, restrooms, pumpout, portapotty dump. Pay station on shore. No power, no showers. The park has a 13-lane launch ramp with boarding floats. An attendant is on duty summer and fall.

Jetty Island. (425) 257-8304; www.everettwa.org. Jetty Island is a lovely low sand island across the river from the Everett Marina and Everett Marine Park. Jetty Island is open all year. Two large docks provide space for a number of boats. Boats can overnight at the dock. Jetty Island has toilets but no showers, no power, and no water for boats. The toilets are closed in winter. Pay station on shore.

River currents can make landing at the docks challenging. Before approaching the dock, be sure your boat is well fendered, dock lines ready, and contingency plans agreed upon.

Jetty Island is a wildlife preserve with great birdwatching. The Parks Department offers nature programs during the summer, and runs boats from the launch ramp to the island, no charge, July 4 through Labor Day.

Snohomish River Delta. The Snohomish River Delta has three main mouths—Steamboat Slough, Ebey Slough, and the main river—each of which is navigable for all or part of its length. Cautious boaters can cruise the delta.

Contributing Editor Tom Kincaid has cruised all of this area, some of it several times, in a 30-foot sailboat, a 36-foot powerboat, and an outboard-powered dinghy. The waters are subject to tidal action. Drying flats are off the river mouths. Enter only during the hours of highest tides. The Snohomish River Delta is a fascinating place with wildlife, calm anchorages, and quiet.

Langus Waterfront Park. North shore of the Snohomish River. The park is open all year and has restrooms, but no guest moorage, power or showers. This is a City of Everett park with a 2-lane concrete launch ramp and boarding floats. A wide concrete float is for fishing and launching rowing shells.

Port Susan. Port Susan is surrounded by Camano Island to the west and the mainland to the east. A swampy waterway connects the northern end of Port Susan with Skagit Bay.

Kayak Point in Port Susan is a Snohomish County Park. North of Kayak Point, Port Susan shoals to drying flats, through which meander the two mouths of the Stillaguamish River. At high tide it is possible to cross over these flats and enter South Pass to Stanwood, although the bridge just beyond Stanwood is very low.

Kayak Point County Park. 15610 Marine Drive, Stanwood, WA 98292; (360) 652-7992. Open all year, restrooms but no showers. Anchorage only close to shore. The anchorage is exposed to southerly winds. Launch ramp with boarding floats. Fishing pier, no overnight moorage at the pier.

Saratoga Passage. Saratoga Passage separates Camano Island from Whidbey Island. The waters are better protected and often smoother than Admiralty Inlet, and the current is less. Boats running between Seattle and the San Juan Islands often choose this inside route via Deception Pass or La Conner when the wind and seas are getting up in Admiralty Inlet.

This is not to say the waters are always smooth. One year, Bob and Marilynn Hale ran into uncomfortable seas while southbound in Saratoga Passage during a 25-knot southerly storm, and were forced to run back to Oak Harbor for shelter.

Saratoga Passage is relatively free of dangers, but it does have two tricks: Rocky Point(s) and Holmes Harbor. A study of the chart shows two Rocky Points in Saratoga Passage. One is on Whidbey Island at the entrance to Holmes Harbor; the other is at the north end of Camano Island.

Southbound boats may be tempted to go straight into Holmes Harbor instead of turning southeast past the Whidbey Island Rocky Point. If

Glass art at the Langley fire station

Unique shops and boutiques are found at the seaside village of Coupeville.

NORTH PUGET SOUND   See Area Map Page 136 - Maps Not for Navigation

Coupeville Wharf is steps away from town.

Sailboats lined up during Whidbey Island Race Week

you're not watching your chart, the appeal is quite strong. Follow the Camano Island shoreline.

Cama Beach State Park. (360) 387-1550. Twelve miles southwest of Stanwood. Open all year, anchoring only. Restrooms, showers, small store, 15 miles of hiking and biking trails, 24 cabins, 7 deluxe cabins and 2 bungalows. The Center for Wooden Boats runs the boathouse and boat rental operation, first-come, first-served. Many classic rowboats and sailboats are available for hourly or daily rentals. The workshops on shore may have a boat building project or two underway. See the CWB website (www.cwb.org) for information on classes offered at Cama Beach and available boat rentals. Advance contact is recommended for hours and days of operation (360) 387-9361 or cama@cwb.org.

Elger Bay. Elger Bay is a good anchorage, mud bottom, with surprisingly good protection from northerly winds. Watch your depths close to the head of the bay.

Camano Island State Park. (360) 387-3031. Fourteen miles southwest of Stanwood. Open all year for day use and overnight camping, first-come, first-served.. Restrooms, showers, no power. Anchoring only. Launch ramp. Underwater park for scuba diving. Cabins, standard and primitive campsites.

⑪ **Langley.** The Langley Boat Harbor serves the delightful village of Langley. If the boat harbor is crowded, as it usually is during the summer, anchorage is good south and east of the harbor, unless strong northerly winds make the area uncomfortable. Before giving up, however, remember that the Langley Boat Harbor has a long history of being creative about getting another boat tied up. Their motto is, "We'll try to fit you in." *Be sure you have fenders set on both sides.*

The town of Langley itself has streets lined with old buildings housing interesting shops, excellent galleries, fine restaurants, a whale museum, a craft brewery, and a vintage 250-seat movie theater. Langley is a good walking town. You'll find beautiful views of Saratoga Passage from the bluff above the marina. A couple blocks from the cozy commercial district the farms begin.

⑪ **Port of South Whidbey/Langley Boat Harbor.** P.O. Box 872, Freeland, WA 98249; (360) 221-1120; harbormaster@portofsouthwhidbey.com; www.portofsouthwhidbey.com. Monitors VHF 66A. Guest moorage year-round. A 300-foot floating breakwater was installed in 2014 and D and E docks were added, significantly increasing available moorage. Approximately 1,100 feet of moorage. Depths shallow to approximately 8 feet at zero tide south of the breakwater. Check your depth.

Reservations accepted online and are highly recommended during the peak season. Restrooms, showers, 20, 30, 50 & 100 amp power, launch ramp (higher tides only), pumpout barge, free Wi-Fi. Friendly service staff tries to help every boat dock. Nearby groceries, unique shops, boutiques, bakery, laundromat, post office, doctor, vet are up the hill in town. Free shuttle to town in season. Crabbing for every-

Oak Harbor Marina

CHARTS	
18421	Strait of Juan de Fuca to Strait of Georgia (1:80,000)
18427	Anacortes to Skagit Bay (1:25,000)
18428	Oak and Crescent Harbors (1:10,000)
18441	Puget Sound – Northern Part (1:80,000)
18443	Approaches to Everett (1:40,000)

one at the upper wharf, and by reservation only off D and E docks at the marina.

Holmes Harbor. Holmes Harbor indents the eastern shore of Whidbey Island for about 5 miles in a southerly direction. It is deep and relatively unprotected from strong northerlies. The harbor has a good launch ramp at the head and anchorage along either shore. Honeymoon Bay is a good anchorage. Holmes Harbor is subject to williwaws, the unusually strong gusts of wind that spill across the lower portion of Whidbey Island.

⑫ **Honeymoon Bay.** Honeymoon Bay is a favored anchorage on the west shore of Holmes Harbor. Private mooring buoys take up most of the good spots; but with a little diligence, satisfactory anchoring depths with adequate swinging room can be found. Honeymoon Bay is exposed to northerly winds.

Penn Cove. Penn Cove is about 10 miles north of Holmes Harbor. The cove extends nearly 4 miles west from Long Point, with the town of Coupeville on the southern shore. Anchorage is good along both shores and toward the head of the bay, but be aware that strong winds from the Strait of Juan de Fuca can blow across the low neck of Whidbey Island at the head of the cove. This is where the famous Penn Cove mussels come from. Watch for mussel-growing pens.

⑬ **Coupeville.** The town of Coupeville is served by the Coupeville Wharf, a 415-foot-long causeway on pilings extending over the beach to deep water. Coupeville is quaint, old, and friendly, with a variety of shops, galleries, and restaurants. A display of tribal canoes is 200 feet from the head of the wharf.

Oak Harbor Marina, with picnic tables along the water, is a good place for gatherings.

⑬ **Coupeville Wharf.** P.O. Box 128, Green Bank, WA 98253; (360) 678-6379. Open all year, 450-plus feet of dock space, first-come, first-served, free moorage before 5:00 p.m. Watch depths at low and minus tides. Gasoline and diesel at the fuel dock. There is also room to anchor in front of town. Pumpout, restrooms and showers are on the wharf, no power or water on the float. Free Wi-Fi is available on the float and throughout town. A gift shop, a coffee shop, and a restaurant are at the outer end of the wharf. The town's shops and restaurants are within easy walking distance. Island Transit, with stops nearby, offers free bus service to key points on Whidbey Island.

Captain Coupe Park. 602 NE Ninth St., Coupeville, WA 98239-0577; (360) 678-4461. Open all year with restrooms and nearby portapotty dump, no power, no showers. Anchoring only. A launch ramp with a float is installed in the summer. The park is one-quarter mile by water from Coupeville wharf. It's better to anchor closer to the wharf. Mud flats surround the launch area at low tide.

NORTHEAST PUGET SOUND

⑭ **Oak Harbor.** Oak Harbor is a shallow and well protected port with a major, city-owned marina. The entrance channel is marked by red and green buoys and beacons, beginning with Buoy 2, offshore about 1 mile south of Maylor Point. From Buoy 2 the entry channel runs northward into Oak Harbor, and makes a 90-degree turn to the east for the final mile that leads to the marina.

Do not pass between Buoy 2 and Maylor Point. The water there is shoal and littered with large boulders that have been known to tear stern drive units out of boats.

The only moorage is at the spacious Oak Harbor Marina. The marina has complete facilities and park grounds ashore for dog-walking, games, or strolling. It's a bit of a walk to town, and the nearest grocery store is 1½ miles away.

Free bus service runs Monday through Saturday, or you can call a cab.

Anchorage can be found just outside the marina close to the entry channel. The bottom is soft; be sure your anchor is well set. A small float for dinghies is in front of the business district, about a 1-mile walk from the marina. The float dries at low tide.

Events: Holland Happening is the last weekend of April; the town's celebration of their Dutch heritage. Whidbey Island Race week is mid-July.

Festivals: Oak Harbor Music Festival is Labor Day weekend; free admission.

Golf: The 18-hole Gallery Golf Course at the Whidbey Island Naval Air Station is open to the public year-round. The course overlooks the east end of the Strait of Juan de Fuca. Smith Island is clearly visible; (360) 257-2178. Also the Whidbey Golf & Country Club, open play after 1:00 p.m.; (360) 675-5490.

Taxi: (360) 682-6920 or (360) 279-9330.

LOCAL KNOWLEDGE

ENTRANCE CHANNEL: Shoals line each side of the channel all the way into Oak Harbor. At low tide especially, you will go aground if you stray.

⑭ **Oak Harbor Marina.** 865 SE Barrington Dr., Oak Harbor, WA 98277; (360) 279-4575; csublet@ohmarina.org; www.ohmarina.org. Monitors VHF 16, switch to 68. Open all year (closed Sundays & holidays, October through March) with at least 26 slips for guest moorage. The fuel dock has mid-grade ethanol-free gasoline, diesel and propane. The marina has 20 & 30 amp power, restrooms, showers, laundry, pumpout, porta-potty dump, and free Wi-Fi. The guest moorage dock has picnic tables along the breakwater. In the adjacent park, there are Bocce ball and Petanque courts. One set of restrooms and showers is on the lower level of the administration building at the head of the

---

JOSEPH WHIDBEY (1757-1833)

Joseph Whidbey was a member of the British Royal Navy and served on Captain George Vancouver's Expedition of 1791-95. In 1792 Whidbey, along with Peter Puget, explored a large Sound to the south of present-day Port Townsend with two small boats launched from the mother ship, *Discovery*. Captain Vancouver attributed the names Whidbey Island and Puget Sound in honor of his officers who explored and identified landmarks in the area. Joseph Whidbey later received wide recognition as a Naval Engineer. He helped John Rennie plan the massive stone breakwater at Plymouth Sound near Plymouth, Devon England to shelter ships during the Napoleonic Wars (1803-1815).

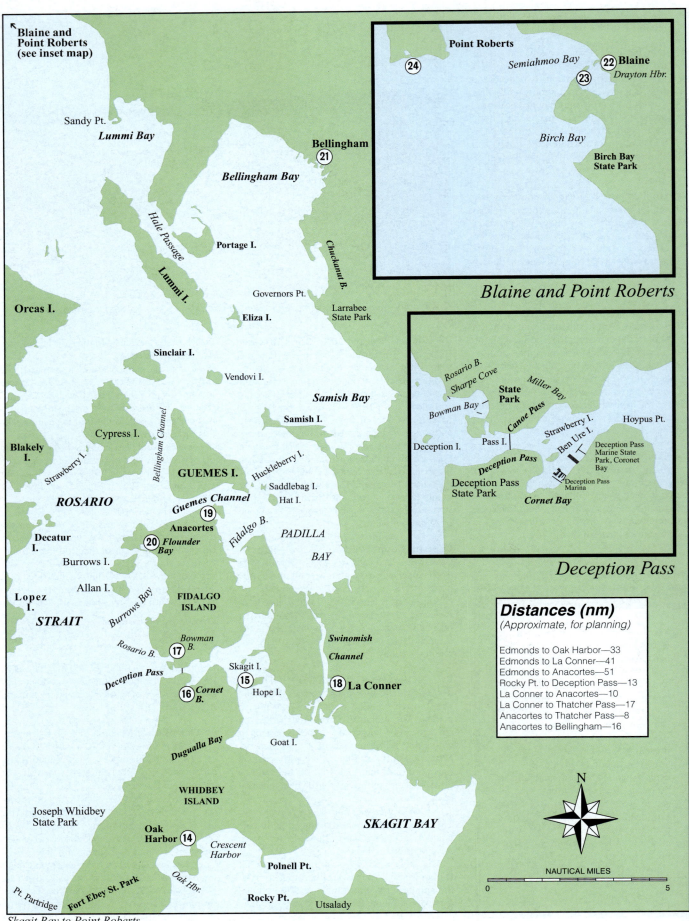

docks. Additional restrooms, showers, and laundry are in buildings a short distance away. A floating restroom facility is on the guest moorage F-dock. Military and retired military (with DoD I.D.) can walk onto the Navy base area and use the Navy Exchange for shopping and provisioning. The Exchange is in one of the large buildings that formerly was a hangar. A seasonal convenience store is open in the summer. A 100-foot-wide concrete launch ramp, built in 1942 to launch PBY Catalina patrol seaplanes, is at the south end of the marina. Extended parking for trailers and tow vehicles. Mariners Haven has repairs and a chandlery. Free bus service to town. Whidbey Island Race Week is held mid-July. Reservations recommended for the Oak Harbor Music Festival on Labor Day weekend. Hydroplane races are held mid-August.

Oak Harbor Marina is protected by a floating concrete breakwater. Guest moorage is in slips on the inside of this breakwater and along the long float leading to shore. A dredged channel, 100 feet wide with a least depth of 12 feet at zero tide, leads along the west face of the breakwater and around the end, to side-tie moorage on the float that leads to shore. Water outside the channel is shoal. Entering Oak Harbor, keep red buoys and beacons close to starboard (see Local Knowledge Entrance Channel). If you plan to moor along the north side of the marina, the safest approach is to head directly for the entrance light at the south end of the breakwater. When you reach the breakwater, turn to port and proceed along the outside (west side) of the breakwater to the north moorage. The Oak Harbor Marina is well maintained, easygoing, and friendly.

Crescent Harbor. Just east of Oak Harbor. The Navy facility along the western shore near the head of the bay has large old hangars that once housed PBY Catalina flying boat patrol aircraft. Crescent Harbor is exposed to southerly winds, but in northerlies or westerlies it's a good anchorage.

Rocky Point. Tidal currents meet off Rocky Point. North of the point they flood south out of Deception Pass and Swinomish Channel. South of the point they flood north out of Saratoga Passage.

Skagit Bay. Skagit Bay extends from Polnell Point and Rocky Point to Deception Pass. The bay becomes increasingly shoal toward the east due to Skagit River outflow. The navigable channel parallels the Whidbey Island shore, and is well marked by buoys. Use caution in this channel; buoys can be dragged out of position by tugs with tows. The village of Utsalady, with a launch ramp, is on the Camano Island side of the channel. Anchorage there is not protected from northerly winds and waves, but Correspondents James & Jennifer Hamilton report anchoring through a southeast gale without difficulty.

⑮ **Skagit Island, Hope Island, Similk Bay. Hope Island** is a state marine park with 4 mooring buoys on the north side and good anchorage, particularly along the south shore. Check the depths before using the buoys. No power, water, restrooms or showers. Trails lead around and through the island. **Skagit Island**, just to the north, has 1 mooring buoy along its north side. **Similk Bay** is shoal but navigable in shallow draft boats. Anchorage is possible anywhere. Self-register and pay mooring buoy fee on shore.

Kiket Island/Kukutali Preserve. Located just east of Skagit Island. Kiket Island was acquired by Washington State Parks and the Swinomish Tribe in 2010 and renamed Kukutali Preserve. Until a management plan can be finalized, it is closed to visitor boat traffic. Even if it is opened to boat visitors, landing will be in human-powered craft only, at a designated location.

⑯ **Cornet Bay.** Cornet Bay, tucked in behind Ben Ure Island, indents the north shore of Whidbey Island just east of Deception Pass. A dredged channel marked by pilings leads to Deception Pass Marina and a state park, both of

Note the currents in this view of Deception Pass looking west.

Deception Pass Marina

La Conner Marina

NORTH PUGET SOUND

See Area Map Page 144 - Maps Not for Navigation

SWINOMISH CHANNEL

Swinomish Channel

In October, 2013, the U.S. Coast Guard changed the buoyage in Swinomish Channel. The "change point," noting "return from the sea (Red Right Returning)" was moved to the center of La Conner. It previously was about 2 miles north of La Conner. Old charts do not reflect this change. Buoy R22 has been changed to G35; G23 to R34; R26 to G31; and G25 to R32.

The general rule of thumb when transiting the Swinomish Channel is to use Seattle tides and add 30 minutes in addition to any adjustments for daylight saving. Time of slack water and the duration of current flow are dependent on the range between high and low water (tide). Helpful information for transiting the Swinomish Channel is found in Ports and Passes in the La Conner section.

The southern entrance to Swinomish Channel is just north of Goat Island. Do not turn into the channel until the range markers in Dugualla Bay, to the west, are in line. The channel is well marked but narrow, particularly if you meet a tug with a tow of logs. Once when transiting the channel, we had 8.0 feet of water in the southern entrance at a zero tide. Check the range as you go. Rock piles lie immediately outside of the dredged channel. Tidal currents flow across the channel and can sweep a boat off course. Occasionally a deadhead log will imbed itself in the shallow bottom. At Hole in the Wall the channel bends sharply around a high rock outcropping. Swirling currents in this area can call for close attention.

From Hole in the Wall to the railroad swing bridge north of La Conner the channel is a no wake zone. Be particularly mindful of your wake when passing through the town of La Conner.

Red, Right, Returning: The buoyage system for Swinomish Channel south of the town of La Conner assumes "return" is from the south. North of La Conner and in Padilla Bay, the dredged channel assumes "return" is from the north. Red navigation aids in Padilla Bay are on the west side.

Rainbow Bridge (now painted orange), located just south of La Conner, has an overhead clearance of 75 feet.

Swinomish Channel is dredged every few years, but it silts up between dredgings. A much-needed dredging was completed in January 2013, with additional re-dredging during the winter of 2014. Keep in mind that the silting occurs at the same locations each time, so at low tide the wary boater can avoid them. Here are the troublesome locations

1. West of Goat Island, the very entrance to Swinomish Channel is shoal. Especially on a low tide, swing wide and don't cut any of the entry buoys close. The channel leading past Goat Island is quite shoal. On very low tides deep draft vessels such as sailboats should wait for more water.

2. South of town at Shelter Bay, a shoal extends from the west side of the channel, approximately in line with the southernmost house of the Shelter Bay development. Favor the center of the channel.

3. About midway along the main La Conner waterfront, a shoal extends from the west side of the channel, approximately between the middle of the restaurants on the La Conner side and a tall pole with antennas on the west side. Favor the east side of the channel.

4. Just south of the highway bridges and the railroad swing bridge, at the location marked "Pipeline Area," sand accumulates on top of the pipeline to create another shoal.

5. The most troublesome shoal is opposite Buoy 29, north of the railroad swing bridge and the highway bridges. This shoal stretches across the entire channel.

Shelter Bay, with its private moorage, indents the western shore of Swinomish Channel just north of Hole in the Wall.

Then comes lovely Rainbow Bridge (now orange), vertical clearance 75 feet in the center. North of Rainbow Bridge the town of La Conner stretches along the eastern shore of the channel. Across from La Conner the Swinomish Indian Reservation occupies most of the west side of the channel. On the La Conner side, several privately-owned floats serve restaurants and other businesses along the La Conner waterfront.

Just north of La Conner is another point where the flood and ebb currents meet, ebbing south past La Conner and north toward Anacortes. The channel is marked by buoys and ranges, but follows a generally northerly direction until it passes under a swinging railroad bridge and fixed highway bridges to enter Padilla Bay. The highway bridges are high enough that they don't impede boat traffic. The railroad bridge is very low. Hundred-car-long crude oil trains headed to the local refinery can close the bridge for 20 minutes or more, holding up boat traffic. If you are there at the wrong time consider dropping the anchor until the train has passed. Currents can be strong.

LA CONNER MARKETPLACE
RESTAURANTS, SHOPS & SERVICES

CALENDAR OF EVENTS

JANUARY
Skagit Valley Winter Birds Festival

FEBRUARY
52rd Annual Smelt Derby

MARCH
4th Annual La Conner Daffodil Festival

APRIL Skagit Valley Tulip Festival

MAY Opening Day Boating Season Parade

JUNE MoNA Auction

JULY Hometown 4th of July Celebration

AUGUST 18th Annual Classic Boat & Car Show

OCTOBER
Festival of Family Farms
4th Annual Brew on the Slough – La Conner's Beer Fest

NOVEMBER Arts Alive!

DECEMBER
Community Tree Lighting
Lighted Boat Parade

Dates may change, check website
www.lovelaconner.com

LA CONNER CHAMBER
A beautiful village on the banks of the Swinomish Channel. Shop, Dine, Art and Wine! Come experience the LaConner love. Located just 60 miles north of Seattle in the heart of Skagit Valley
360-466-4778 • 413 Morris Street, La Conner, WA • www.lovelaconner.com

LA CONNER CHANNEL LODGE & COUNTRY INN
Enjoy Deluxe Accommodations! The Channel Lodge features water views and private balconies. The Country Inn on Second Street is charming with spacious rooms. Enjoy continental breakfast, free parking, and Wi-Fi at both locations!
1-888-466-4113 • 360-466-1500 • 205 N. First St. & 107 S. Second St., La Conner, WA www.LaConnerLodging.com

LA CONNER LANDING FUEL DOCK
The friendliest and most convenient fuel dock around! Fuel up and pump out at the same time. Quality marine diesel and ethanol free gas. Located on the Swinomish channel just north of town. Ice, bait, food and marine supplies. Hours vary by season.
360-466-4478 • 541 North 3rd Street, La Conner, WA

LACONNER MARITIME
Servicing, building and equipping boats for nearly 40 years, we take pride in our reputation as a friendly, professional boat yard that can handle every customer need from pressure washing the hull to rebuilding the engine.
360-466-3629 • 920 West Pearle Jensen Way www.LaConnerMaritime.com

MUSEUM OF NORTHWEST ART
MoNA collects collects, interprets and presents contemporary art from Alaska, British Columbia, California, Idaho, Montana, Oregon and Washington. MoNA is free and open seven days a week. The museum store features gifts handmade by local artists.
360-466-4446 • 121 S. First St., La Conner, WA www.monamuseum.org

LA CONNER BREWING COMPANY
Unique Northwest-style family-friendly brewpub featuring wood-fired pizzas, burgers and other fresh local pub fare served with our small-batch, hand-crafted beers. Enjoy by the fireplace or on the garden terrace.
360-466-1415 • 117 S. First Street, La Conner, WA
www.laconnerbrewery.com

Boardwalk photo courtesy of La Conner Chamber of Commerce
Town photo courtesy of Aimee Beckwith

which offer visitor moorage. The passage west of Ben Ure Island should not be attempted except at high tide, and then only by shallow draft boats. Vessel Assist towing and emergency rescue office nearby.

⑯ **Deception Pass Marina.** 200 West Cornet Bay Road, Oak Harbor, WA 98277; (360) 675-5411. Open all year. The marina has some slips reserved for visiting boats and uses unoccupied slips as available. The docks have 30 amp power, but only limited room for larger boats up to 65 feet. Ethanol-free gasoline, diesel, and propane at the fuel dock. The store carries convenience groceries, bait, tackle, charts, books, beer and wine. Restrooms, no showers (showers are available at the state park next door). Call ahead for availability of guest moorage. Nearby laundry and haulout.

⑯ **Deception Pass Marine State Park, Cornet Bay area.** Open all year for day use and overnight moorage. The park has 600 feet of side-tie dock space, restrooms, showers and pumpout, but no power. Two additional 100-foot floats are anchored offshore and not connected to land. A 5-lane launch ramp has boarding floats. Hiking trails and picnic areas nearby. Groceries, laundromat and services are at Deception Pass Marina. Park has campsites, but not near this area. On Ben Ure Island, a single cabin is available for rent. Reservations online or call (888) 226-7688.

CHARTS	
18421	Strait of Juan de Fuca to Strait of Georgia (1:80,000)
18423 sc folio small-craft	Bellingham to Everett including San Juan Islands and Blaine – Cancelled
18424	Bellingham Bay (1:40,000) Bellingham Harbor (1:20,000)
18430	Rosario Strait—Northern Part (1:25,000)
18429	Rosario Strait—Southern Part (1:25:000)

La Conner, on Swinomish Channel, is a small, charming town with shops and restaurants.

LOCAL KNOWLEDGE

STRONG CURRENTS: Currents run to 8 knots in Deception Pass with strong eddies and overfalls. Dangerous waves can form when a big ebb current meets strong westerly winds. It is best to time an approach to enter the pass at or near slack water. Try to travel single-file.

Deception Pass. Deception Pass narrows to 200 yards at Pass, Island, one of the anchors for the spectacular 144-foot-high bridge that connects Whidbey Island and Fidalgo Island.

Tidal current predictions are shown under Deception Pass in the tide and current books. An even narrower pass, Canoe Pass, lies north of Pass Island. Kayaks use Canoe Pass, but lacking local knowledge we wouldn't run our boat through it.

From the west, the preferred route to Deception Pass is just to the south of Lighthouse Point and north of Deception Island.

North of Lighthouse Point, **Bowman Bay**, also known as Reservation Bay, is part of Deception Pass State Park.

⑰ **Deception Pass Marine State Park, Bowman Bay (Reservation Bay).** Open all year for day use and overnight camping and mooring. Restrooms with showers, no power. Bowman Bay has a gravel 1-lane launch ramp. Standard campsites are on the north shore. The park has picnic sites and outdoor kitchens. An underwater park for diving is near the mouth of Bowman Bay, near Rosario Head. When entering take care to avoid Coffin Rocks and Gull Rocks, which cover at high tide. Safe entry can be made by staying fairly close to the Reservation Head side of the entrance.

A mooring float, approximately 100 feet long and not connected to shore, is located behind Reservation Head. On the east side of the bay the 40-foot-long float on the park dock is for dinghies.

Anchorage is also possible in the bay north of Rosario Head, but it is exposed to wave action from Rosario Strait.

Deception Pass Marine State Park, Sharpe Cove. Open all year for day use and overnight camping and mooring. The park has 160 feet of dock space, no power. Restrooms, showers, portapotty dump, picnic sites, kitchen. Campsites are east of Sharpe Cove. The onshore facility is the Walla Walla University Rosario Beach Marine Laboratory.

Shelter Bay Marina. 1000 Shoshone Drive, La Conner, WA 98257; (360) 466-3805; www.shelterbay.net; kemerson@shelterbay.net. Shelter Bay Marina is on the west side of Swinomish Channel just south of La Conner. Primarily permanent moorage, but some transient space is available. Water, 30 & 50 amp power, pumpout, restrooms, showers, no laundry.

⑱ **La Conner.** The Port of Skagit's La Conner Marina, with two large moorage basins, is a short distance north of downtown La Conner. Both moorage basins have guest moorage and

NORTH PUGET SOUND

See Area Map Page 144 - Maps Not for Navigation

Cap Sante Marina

full facilities for visitors. Fuel is available adjacent to the marina at La Conner Landing, and propane is available at Boater's Discount marine supply store between the two basins. Current in Swinomish Channel can be strong and difficult to predict. Allow for current before landing anywhere along the channel.

The town of La Conner is thoroughly charming. It has excellent restaurants, galleries, museums, wine tasting rooms, and shops. Public floats line the business district. During the summer, hordes of visitors arrive by car and tour bus. Even when crowded, the town is enjoyable. Free outdoor concert, parade, food vendors and fireworks on the 4th of July. On summer Sundays in Gilkey Square, live music from mid-June to August.

⑱ **La Conner Marina.** P.O. Box 1120, 613 N. 2nd St., La Conner, WA 98257; (360) 466-3118; www.portofskagit.com/la-conner-marina. Monitors VHF 66A. Open all year with 30 & 50 amp power, free Wi-Fi, restrooms, showers, laundry, pumpout. Haulout to 82 tons. Complete repairs available through La Conner Maritime.

All shopping and services are within walking distance. A monorail launch can handle boats to 14,000 lbs. Trailers must be roller style, no bunks. A paved and lighted storage yard is available for trailers and tow vehicles.

This marina, owned by the Port of Skagit, is where most visiting boats tie up. F dock at the south basin has 1200 lineal feet of side-tie guest moorage. G dock at the north basin has another 1200 feet of side-tie moorage. E dock, near shore in the south basin, has 450 feet of guest moorage for the Swinomish Yacht Club. Reservations accepted. Unoccupied slips are used when available. If the moorage appears full, call anyway. They try to fit everybody in.

La Conner Landing Marine Services. P.O. Box 1020, La Conner, WA 98257; (360) 466-4478. Open all year. Summer hours from 8:00 a.m. to 6:00 p.m. daily. Hours and days vary during the fall and winter, call ahead. Fuel dock with ethanol-free gasoline and diesel, pumpout. The store has tackle, bait, ice, marine items, and snacks.

Caution: Strong current flows past the dock. Look for the directional sign on the fuel shed labeled 'CURRENT' with an arrow indicating which way the current is running.

Padilla Bay. The well-marked channel through Padilla Bay is about 3 miles long between drying flats. Don't take any shortcuts until north of Beacon 2, which marks the edge of Guemes Channel. Deeper draft boats, such as sailboats, should hold to a mid-channel course, especially at low tide. To the west of the channel are long docks serving ocean-going tankers calling at the two major oil refineries in Anacortes. Often tankers, barges, or tug boats lie at anchor in the bay awaiting room at the docks.

Red, Right, Returning: In Padilla Bay, Red, Right, Returning assumes "return" is from the north. Red navigation aids are on the west side of the channel from Padilla Bay to La Conner. South of La Conner, red navigation aids are on the east side of Swinomish Channel. Approaching La Conner from north or south, remember Red, Right, Returning.

Saddlebag Island Marine State Park. Open all year for day use and overnight anchoring and camping. Boat access only. Anchorage is good off the north or south shore. Water depths are inconveniently deep on the west side, and inconveniently shallow on the east. Vault toilets, primitive campsites. Cascadia Marine Trail campsite. One-mile hiking trail. "Hot spot" for crabbing.

Huckleberry Island. North end of Padilla Bay, owned by the Samish Indian Nation. Open all year, day use only. No services. Undeveloped 10-acre island with anchoring or beaching only. No fires or camping. Pack out all garbage. Attractive to kayakers and scuba divers. Gravel beach on the southwest side of the island.

⑲ **Anacortes.** www.anacortes.org. Anacortes is a major boating center, with fishing and pleasure craft facilities in Fidalgo Bay and along Guemes Channel. The city's marine businesses can provide for a boater's every need, including food, fuel, and repairs. With seven haulout yards, Anacortes has the marine trades for any repair.

U.S. Customs: Anacortes is a U.S. Customs port of entry with an office in the Cap Sante Marina harbormaster's building. There is no U.S. Customs dock. Call the marina office for a slip assignment and proceed to the slip. Then call the Anacortes customs office at (360) 293-2331 for instructions. Between 1:00 p.m. and 3:00 p.m. during the summer agents are apt to be 4 miles away at the Washington State Ferry

---

SALVADOR FIDALGO (1756-1803)

The lands claimed for Spain along the Pacific Coast of the Americas by Vasco Nunez de Balboa in the 1500's went unchallenged for 250 years; but by the late 1700's, Russian and British ships had begun to arrive. Juan Vicente de Guemes, the second Count to the Viceroy of New Spain in San Blas, sent Salvador Fidalgo north to learn the extent of the Russian and British encroachments. Fidalgo arrived at Nootka Sound on the west coast of Vancouver Island in 1790, and departed in May to continue north, reaching Prince William Sound where he anchored off Cordova (Puerto Cordova), Alaska. Fidalgo erected a wooden cross and re-asserted Spain's claim; other similar ceremonies were performed in the region. Contact with the Russians was made in July 1790 on the southwestern coast of the Kenai Peninsula which he named Puerto Revillagigedo. He also arrived at the Russian outpost on Kodiak Island in Three Saints Bay, and at Alexandrovsk (today's English Bay). After sailing back to San Blas, Fidalgo was sent to Neah Bay in 1792 to establish a Spanish outpost consisting of a stockade with a small garrison. A garden was created and livestock contained. It was thought that this new post may be needed if negotiations over the 'Nootka Crisis' at Nootka Sound did not end favorably for Spain. The post at Neah Bay was eventually abandoned due to a conflict with the Native Makah. Fidalgo Island, Salvador Fidalgo's namesake, serves as a remembrance of this Spanish explorer.

terminal, clearing arrivals on the international ferry from Sidney, B.C. You'll have to wait aboard for the agents to return. Otherwise, they will ask the captain to walk up to the Customs office, Suite F, to the right of the harbormaster's office for clearance.

Fidalgo Bay is shallow. If you stray from the dredged and marked channels during low water, you could find yourself aground.

Four marinas are located on the Fidalgo Bay side of town. Three additional marinas are located on the west end of Fidalgo Island. From north to south on Fidalgo Bay, the first is Cap Sante Marina, owned by the Port of Anacortes, with guest moorage, fuel, water, electricity, pumpout and haulout facilities. Enter between the arms of a piling breakwater due west of Cap Sante.

The second, behind a prominent breakwater, is Anacortes Marina, where Marine Servicenter has fuel, pumpout, 55 ton Travelift haulout, and repairs. Open seven days a week from 8:00 a.m. to 4:30 p.m. and 8:00 a.m. to 8:00 p.m. from Memorial Day weekend to Labor Day weekend. Permanent moorage only. Anacortes Yacht Charters and many bareboat charter boats are based in this marina. Follow the dredged channel to the marina entrance on the south side. The north entrance in the breakwater is for exiting boats only.

Next is the 360-foot-long dock and haulout ramp for Pacific Marine Center (360) 299-8820. In 2016 they completed facilities for a new 200 ton Travelift. Now large vessels can be hauled out and blocked in their extensive yard complex

The Anacortes Farmers Market is open Saturdays from 9:00 a.m. to 2:00 p.m. May to October.

for maintenance and repairs. In addition they have multiple KMI Sea-lift machines for haulout on their ramp for vessels up to 65 feet. Limited moorage is available on their docks, typically reserved for repair or dry storage customers.

The fourth is Fidalgo Marina, where Cap Sante Marine has a 50 ton Travelift and the haulout ramp for North Harbor Diesel. The marina is protected by a piling breakwater, and is entered through the dredged channel marked by pilings extending from deeper water near Cap Sante.

Moving east to west, Dakota Creek Industries is a large shipyard on Guemes Channel with Syncrolift ship lift and drydock for vessels to 400 feet.

Just past the Guemes Ferry is Anchor Cove, a private marina with no transient moorage.

Lovric's Sea-Craft is on Guemes Channel, with two marine ways for haulout, and a small dry dock.

Skyline Marina is in Flounder Bay on the west side of Fidalgo Island, 3 miles from downtown Anacortes. It has some transient moorage and a DIY yard with 55 ton Travelift haulout and a stationary lift accommodating 16,000 pounds.

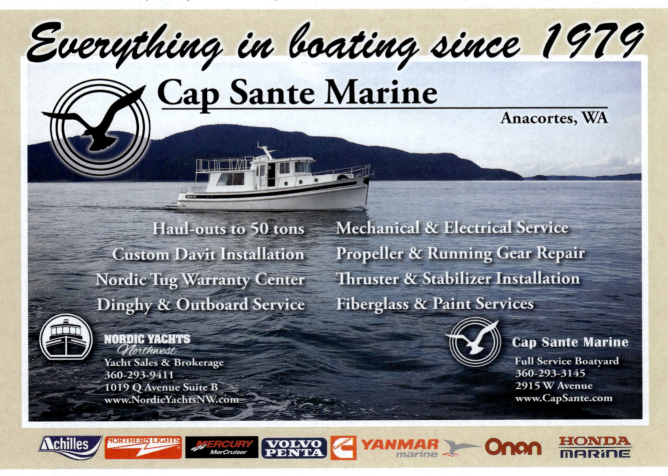

ANACORTES MARKETPLACE

RESTAURANTS, SHOPS & SERVICES

CALENDAR OF EVENTS

JANUARY First Friday Gallery Art Walk

FEBRUARY First Friday Gallery Art Walk
Daddy-Daughter Dance

MARCH First Friday Gallery Art Walk
Anacortes Salmon Derby

APRIL First Friday Gallery Art Walk
Spring Wine Festival
Anacortes Spring Boat Show
Art in Bloom, The Depot
Island Chicks Antique & Vintage Show, Port Warehouse
Art of Gardening Event at the Depot
Skagit Valley Tulip Festival
Anacortes Annual Quilt Walk

MAY First Friday Gallery Art Walk
An-O-Chords Barbershop Concert
TrawlerFest, Cap Sante Marina

JUNE
Waterfron Festival Kick-Off Dinner
Chamber Gallery Art Walk
Kids Fishing Derby
Chamber Gallery Art Walk
Anacortes Waterfront Festival, Cap Sante Marina
St. Mary's "Merry Festival"
Bark-in-the-Park Dog Festival, Storvik Park
Doyle Geer Golf Tourn.
Relay for Life

Dates may change, check website
www.anacortes.org
360-293-3832

Statue Photo Courtesy of Anacortes Chamber of Commerce, Steve Berentson, photographer

ACE HARDWARE
Ace Hardware of Anacortes AND Friday Harbor is your locally owned and operated hardware store, specializing in marine hardware, stainless fasteners, electrical, Craftsman Tools, fishing licenses, tackle, bait, rain gear and all your hardware needs.
360-293-3535 • 1720 Q Avenue, Anacortes, WA 98221 • 360-378-4622 • 340 Argyle Ave, Friday Harbor, WA 98250
www.AceAnacortes.com

Mary LaFleur

ALT INSURANCE GROUP
An all lines broker with a specialty niche in yacht insurance, Mary LaFleur has over 30 years in the insurance industry, represents over 30 insurance carriers, and is a life-long boater. "Most times we can save our boaters enough on their auto, home, commercial and RV insurance to put fuel in their tanks." Customer Service is second to none.
253-222-7519 • 360-899-4653
819 Commercial Avenue, Ste D,
mary@altinsurancegroup.com
www.altinsurancegroup.com

ANACORTES MARINE ELECTRONICS
We offer custom navigation and communication solutions. Service and installations are our specialty using NMEA certified technicians. Serving Everett to Bellingham. Call us today for a free consultation.
A division of Marine Services Group.
360-293-2565 • 1910 Skyline Way
www.anacortesmarine.com

ANACORTES MARINE INSURANCE
One of only a few Insurance agencies in Washington State, and the only one in Skagit County/Anacortes, offering direct access to the top Yacht Insurance markets in the world. Featuring CHUBB(formerly ACE), REDSHIELD, FALVEY, and PANTAENIUS, as well as PREMIER, SAFECO, and TRAVELERS, our experienced staff can find the best coverage/best pricing to fit your needs. Additional access to brokers allows us to handle all types of Marine-related Business Pursuits.
360-588-8112 • 2517 Commercial Avenue
www.AnacortesMarine-Ins.com

ANACORTES RIGGING & YACHT SERVICES
Pleasure marine, industrial, and architectural wire and rope rigging services. Standing rigging, running rigging, mooring, tow lines, lifting bridles, davit service. Large selection of rope in stock and fast turn around. Consultation, inspection, refits.
360-293-2030 • www.AnacortesRigging.com

ANTHONY'S
Anthony's at Cap Sante Marina - Lunch and dinner daily in a scenic waterfront setting, overlooking the marina with two view decks. Serving fresh northwest seafood from our own seafood company. Adjacent is The Cabana by Anthony's, a casual seafood restaurant with a classic "to-go fish & chips" bar. Both restaurants are steps from the marina.
360-588-0333 • 1207 Q Avenue •
www.anthonys.com

ANTHONY'S THE CABANA
The Cabana is located adjacent to Anthony's at Cap Sante Marina. The Cabana offers casual family-friendly dining as well as a classic fish & chip "to-go" bar for quick service dining. The Cabana has two full-size Bocce Ball courts available for guests while dining.
360-588-0333 • 1207 Q Avenue • www.anthonys.com/restaurants/detail/anthonys-cabana

THE BROWN LANTERN ALE HOUSE
Serving the locals & visitors to Historic Anacortes since 1933, just steps from the waterfront in the heart of oldtown. Featuring outstanding burgers, creative pub fare, 15 beers on draft, and over 50 different whiskies alone! See why we are voted the "Best Tavern in Anacortes" year after year. Now family friendly.
360-293-2544 • 412 Commercial Ave.
www.brownlantern.com

CAP SANTE INN
"The Best Value" and "Most Fun" in Anacortes. Located in Historic Old Town across the street from the Cap Sante Marina, restaurants, shops, & galleries. Walk to everything!
360-293-0602 • 906 9th St. •
www.capsanteinn.com

CAP SANTE MARINE
Over 30 years of experience with professional service and factory-trained and authorized service technicians. We offer full mechanical services, electrical installation and repair, Fiberglas, gelcoat, and paint in our heated shop. Fully-stocked parts department and haulout up to 50 tons on our Travelift.
360-293-3145 • 2915 W Avenue •
www.capsante.com

ROCKFISH GRILL / ANACORTES BREWERY / H2O
The Rockfish Grill serves NW food including wood fired pizza made with fresh local ingredients. Live music weekly. Family friendly. H2O features craft cocktails using house made liquors, 24 draft handles and a full menu with live music and a dance floor. Both establishments serve Anacortes Brewery beers made right next door.
360-588-1720 • 320 Commercial Avenue •
www.anacortesrockfish.com
360-755-3956 • 314 Commercial Ave •
www.anacortesH2O.com

NORTH HARBOR DIESEL
& Yacht Service Inc.

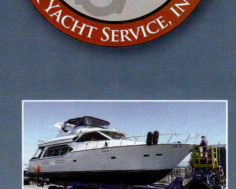

Service • Sales • Storage

AWARD WINNING YACHT SERVICE
- Complete diesel & gas Engine Services & Repowers
- Complete Interior Remodel & Design
- Custom Hull Modifications
- Fully Stocked Marine Store
- 22,000 Sq. Ft. Shop

SHORESIDE MARINA
- 5 Acres of dry outdoor storage
- Low monthly storage fees
- 4 Sea-Lifts - up to 65 Ft. & 45 Tons

360-299-1907
For Shoreside Marina Information,
Call Robyn at 360-899-9274

INSIDE PASSAGE YACHT SALES
Now located at North Harbor Diesel
We match perfect boats to individual buyers. It is our passion! New boats from Lindell Yachts, Parker, and Sargo. Large inventory of used boats from center consoles to cruisers and pilot houses. It's not about the boat...it's about the lifestyle.

360.468.4997 • InsidePassageYachtSales.com

360-293-5551
Anacortes, WA
NorthHarborDiesel.com
service@northharbordiesel.com

ANACORTES MARKETPLACE
RESTAURANTS, SHOPS & SERVICES

CALENDAR OF EVENTS

JULY
First Friday Gallery Art Walk Town Photo | 4th of July Parade | Kids 'R Best Fest Shipwreck Day Anacortes Art Dash Half Marathon

AUGUST
First Friday Gallery Art Walk Anacortes Arts Festival
Annual Eagles Bar-B-Q
Work Boat Races
Fidalgo Bay Day

SEPTEMBER
First Friday Gallery Art Walk Antique Machinery Show
Oyster Run Motorcycle Rally

OCTOBER
First Friday Gallery Art Walk
Bier on the Pier
Anacortes Fall Boat Show
Trick or Treat Downtown

NOVEMBER
First Friday Gallery Art Walk Friends of the Forest Annual Fall Event | Island Chicks Fall Vintage Market

DECEMBER
Tree Lighting, Parade & More
Holiday Art Walk
Lighted Boat Parade

Dates may change, check website
www.anacortes.org
360-293-3832

NORTH HARBOR DIESEL & YACHT SERVICE
North Harbor Diesel and Yacht Service has been in Anacortes since 1985. Come see us for boat storage, engine services, hull and bottom repairs, maintenance and modernizing. Open year round Monday–Friday, we are the region's premier boat yard.
360-293-5551 • 720 30th Street • www.northharbordiesel.com

NORTH HARBOR YACHT BROKERS
Our staff is friendly, responsive, and, above all, service oriented. Whether buying or selling, you'll receive expert, timely, market advice and research, and successful sales strategies to make your purchase or sale stress-free and fun!
360-299-1919 • 409 30th St. - Off R Ave. www.northharboryachtbrokers.com

NORTH ISLAND BOAT
We are a full service boat yard offering haul out and repair. Skilled in diesel, gas, hydraulic and electrical systems. Closest boat yard to the San Juan Islands!
A division of Marine Services Group
360-293-2565 • 1910 Skyline Way • www.northislandboat.com

SALISH MARINE LLC
Marine maintaince and repair. Working Anacortes and Laconner.
360-707-1257 • 16840A Bennett Rd, Burlington, WA 98273 • www.facebook.com/Salishmarine

SEATTLE YACHTS
Serving the Pacific Northwest for over 33 years, Seattle Yachts is the premiere dealership for trawlers, cruising sailboats and motoryachts, both new and brokerage. Now with 2 offices to serve you; one at Shilshole Marina in Seattle and the other at the Anacortes Marina.
844-692-2487 Ext 2 • Anacortes Marina 2415 T Ave, Suite 112 • www.SeattleYachts.com

TIDES OF ANACORTES
Your destination for Island apparel. Whether you're needing an outfit for a morning hike, an afternoon on the water, or an evening out, Tides has it! Come by and visit.
360-873-8785 • 804 Commercial Avenue • www.tidesofanacortes.com

UNION TAVERN
A classic American Tavern in the heart of downtown Anacortes. The menu boasts a delicious collection of both traditional pub fare and comfort food. We have a friendly staff serving 18 constantly rotating taps and a great selection of wine and classic cocktails.
360-873-8245 • 902 Commercial Avenue

CRUISERS COLLEGE
INCREASE YOUR NAUTICAL KNOWLEDGE AND DIY CLASSES

To see a schedule of our up coming classes go to www.WaggonerGuide.com/CruisersCollege Or call the Waggoner Guide office to register at 425.780.5015

Cruisers College is brought to you by

Great experiences come in small islands

Relax and enjoy a weekend (or more!) on Fidalgo Island. With mild temperatures, lush forest lands to explore, and water that surrounds, staying here is a great way to spend your time away from home. Visit by car, ferry, plane or boat. Experience amazing restaurants, boutique shopping in historic downtown, nature viewing, and luxurious spas.

From Anchors to Zincs you can cover all of your boating needs in Anacortes! We have first class marinas and over 50 marine trades companies and professionals that are dedicated to providing quality parts and services. Let us help you buy, insure, store, moor, maintain, repair, and enjoy your boat, right here on beautiful Fidalgo island.

       360-293-3832

NORTH PUGET SOUND   See Area Map Page 144 - Maps Not for Navigation

Mount Baker above Padillia Bay

Build your own boat at the Anacortes Waterfront Festival

Farmers market: Saturdays 9:00 a.m. to 2:00 p.m. next to the Depot Arts & Community Center.

Events: Wine Festival, April 7; Anacortes Waterfront Festival, early June at Cap Sante Marina; Shipwreck Day, July 21; Anacortes Arts Festival, early August; Oyster Run, September 23; Bier on the Pier, early October. www.anacortes.org; info@anacortes.org; (360) 293-7911.

Things to Do

1. **Charming downtown**. Visit the shops, galleries, antique stores, and restaurants along Commercial Avenue.

2. *W. T. Preston*, an old snag boat, is now part of the Anacortes History Museum. Located across from the north end of Cap Sante Marina.

3. **Live music**. On Fridays and some Saturdays in July and August, the Port of Anacortes hosts free concerts at Seafarers' Memorial Park.

4. **Skagit Cycle**. Rent a bike and ride the Tommy Thompson Trail, or just around town. Catch the Tommy Thompson Trail from R Avenue at Cap Sante Marina.

5. **Cap Sante Park**. Walk to the top and view Mt. Baker and the marina from this scenic vantage point. Sunsets from here are particularly beautiful. A steep switchback trail leads from the gazebo on the point at Cap Sante.

6. **Seabear Smokehouse**. Learn the difference in taste between smoked pink, king and sockeye salmon at their processing plant and factory store at 30th Street and T Ave.

7. **Crabbing**. Fidalgo Bay often has great crabbing.

⑲ **Cap Sante Marina/Port of Anacortes.** 100 Commercial Ave., 1019 Q Ave., Anacortes, WA 98221; (360) 293-0694; (360) 661-5000; marina@portofanacortes.com; www.portofanacortes.com. Monitors VHF 66A. Formerly Cap Sante Boat Haven. Open all year with moorage to 120 feet. Call or radio ahead for slip assignment. There is a $5 fee for reservations. No fee for same-day reservations. The 18×120-foot fuel dock, with ethanol-free gasoline, and diesel is to port inside the breakwater. A high-volume fuel delivery hose is available. Propane at boat launch. The marina has 20 & 30 amp power with some 50 & 100 amp power available, 5 pumpout carts (free), 2 portapotty dumps, excellent restrooms, showers, and laundry. A pumpout float is located just inside the harbor entrance. Free Wi-Fi throughout the marina. Complimentary bicycles with baskets are available for marina guests. A monorail launch can handle boats to 25,000 pounds. A small hoist and dry storage yard for hand launching small boats is in the North Basin on P-Q dock. Call (360) 293-0694. Most of the transient area marina floats have been replaced by wide, stable concrete floats, with wide slips and wheelchair accessible ramps to shore. The floats are first-class in every way.

Follow the dredged and marked channel, and enter between the arms of a piling breakwater due west of Cap Sante. The area to port just inside the breakwater, towards Seafarers' Memorial Park, is shoal and should not be attempted. The harbormaster's office and U.S. Customs office are just north of C & D floats.

This is a clean and popular stop, located in the heart of downtown Anacortes. Complete facilities, including many good restaurants, large Safeway and Marketplace grocery stores, well-stocked Ace Hardware and Sebo's hardware stores, and two marine stores (West Marine, Marine Supply & Hardware) are within walking distance. An esplanade leads from the marina to the new Seafarers' Memorial Park and building, and around the marina to Rotary Park. A new dock for dinghies is behind a small breakwater at Seafarers' Memorial Park. The lawn and beach area is used as a kayak launch.

Cap Sante Marina is one of the top three most popular marina (rated by marina moorage nights) in the state. It is considered the homeport of the San Juan Islands and is often used as a supply and provisioning jumping-off point for cruises into the islands and further north.

ANTHONY'S CAP SANTE MARINA
1207 Q Avenue
(360) 588-0333

THE CABANA
1207 Q Avenue
(360) 588-0333

⑲ **Anacortes Marina.** 2415 T Avenue, Anacortes, WA 98221; (360) 293-4543. Primarily private moorage. Marine Servicenter, with fuel dock, haulout, and repairs, is lo-

NAVIGATION & COMMUNICATIONS
Component-Level Repairs
On-Board Debugging
System Designs
New Product Installation

Our team of experts can help you design a system for your boat.

360.293.2565
1910 Skyline Way • Anacortes
www.AnacortesMarine.com

Anacortes Marine Electronics
A division of the Marine Services Group

156   www.WaggonerGuide.com

CAP SANTE MARINA

Visit Cap Sante year-round. Our all-weather Marina, in Anacortes, is centrally located between Victoria BC and Seattle, Cap Sante Marina offers the ultimate location for guests planning to explore the region or stay local year round. Within walking distance from downtown, you can enjoy our many local restaurants, shops, festivities and amenities any time of year.

In my book, Cap Sante is the #1 Marina in the Pacific Northwest.

Rod Macaya
Camas, WA

This was my first time using Cap Sante. I was blown away by the customer service!!! Don't change anything. The place is perfect! Thank You!

Sean Maloney
Portland, OR

1019 Q Avenue, Anacortes, WA 98221 • 360-293-0694
www.portofanacortes.com • marina@portofanacortes.com

NORTH PUGET SOUND   See Area Map Page 144 - Maps Not for Navigation

Skyline Marina

cated there. Enter through the dredged channel to the south opening in the pilings. Exit the marina through the north opening in the breakwater. Marine Servicenter's fuel dock, pumpout and and 55ton Travelift are straight ahead when you enter the marina.

⑲ **Marine Servicenter.** 2417 T Avenue, Anacortes, WA 98221; (360) 293-8200; service@marinesc.com; www.marinesc.com. Open all year. Fuel dock with ethanol-free gasoline, diesel, propane, pumpout, portapotty dump, lubricants, engine oil. Complete repair facilities with yard and haulout to 55 tons.

⑲ **Fidalgo Marina.** 3101 V Place, Anacortes, WA 98221; (360) 299-0873. No transient overnight moorage, but a number of marine businesses are located there. Enter through the opening at the end of the dredged channel on the north side. First, to starboard, is the dock with a 50-ton Travelift for Cap Sante Marine, a full-service boatyard for repairs and refits (360) 293-3145.

Next are the staging docks with temporary moorage for the marine repair businesses. The city dock has marked temporary hourly moorage but no overnight. The ramp at the end of the small basin is for the 45-ton capacity KMI Sea-Lifts for North Harbor Diesel's repair yard and dry storage yards, and Banana Belt Boats brokerage storage yard.

Guemes Channel. On an ebb tide, waters in Guemes Channel can be very rough, especially west of the mouth of Bellingham Channel.

Watch for the Guemes ferry, a small car and passenger ferry that makes frequent crossings between Anacortes and Guemes Island.

Next to the ferry dock is Anchor Cove Marina, a private condo marina with covered and open slips.

Farther west is Lovric's Sea-Craft (360) 840-3271, a commercial shipyard and moorage with large marine ways for haulout. Ship Harbor was once the primary harbor for Anacortes and offers some protection and reasonable anchorage. Watch for ferry traffic from the busy Washington State Ferries terminal in Ship Harbor. *Cross behind the ferries, not in front.*

Guemes Island. Guemes Island has no facilities specifically for boaters, although anchorage can be found along the north shore. Anchorage also can be found on the eastern shore in a tiny notch called Boat Harbor. A ferry connects Guemes Island to Anacortes.

Washington Park. www.cityofanacortes.org. West shore of Fidalgo Island on Guemes Channel. Open all year for day use and overnight camping. Restrooms, portapotty dump, showers. Anchoring or beaching only. Two-lane launch ramp, parking area, picnic tables, picnic shelters, fireplaces, campsites. Playground equipment. The loop road is 2.2 miles in length and is good for walking or jogging. The park has forested areas and viewpoints along the beaches overlooking Rosario Strait to Burrows Bay.

Flounder Bay. Flounder Bay has been dredged to provide moorage for the Skyline real estate development. Skyline Marina and several charter companies are inside the spit. Also a small chandlery, Travelift, and other facilities, including a large dry storage building. Entry is from Burrows Bay along a dredged channel marked by lighted pilings.

⑳ **Skyline Marina.** 2011 Skyline Way, Anacortes, WA 98221; (360) 293-5134; info@skylinemarinecenter.com; www.skylinemarinecenter.com. Open all year, guest moorage, 30 amp power (ELCI-protected power on some docks), laundry, showers. Fuel dock with ethanol-free gasoline, diesel and pumpout. A seaplane float is at the fuel dock. Propane and a coffee bar at the new marina office.

Complete boat repairs and services are available. The yard has space for DIY repairs. A convenience store with grocery items is a block away. Other marine services nearby. Secure inside and outside storage for boats, vehicles, and trailers. Water taxi to the San Juan Islands. The marina is 4 miles from downtown Anacortes.

In 2017, the inner area around TA-TC docks was dredged and new docks installed. A 16,000 pound stationary lift was added and the nearby 55 ton Travelift area was rebuilt. A new building housing a kayak tour operator, a marine brokerage, bareboat charter and other marine related businesses was completed in 2017. The upland marina office building and shop were renovated in 2015.

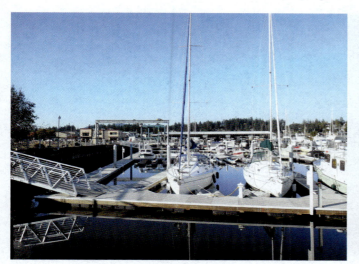
Skyline Marina in Fidalgo Bay is one of the closest marinas to the San Juan Islands.

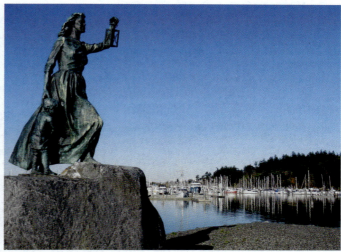
Cap Sante Marina seen from waterfront pathway and Lady of the Sea statue

Burrows Island State Park. Open all year, no facilities. Undeveloped 330-acre state park. Anchor in Alice Bight on the northeast shore, or beach. No camping or fires. Pack out all garbage. Do not disturb wildlife or surroundings. Most of the shoreline is steep cliffs. The Burrows Island Lighthouse is on the west tip of the island.

Allan Island. Allan Island is privately owned, but anchorage can be had in the little bight on the east shore.

Cypress Island. A park ranger told us he considers Cypress Island to be the "crown jewel" of the San Juans, we agree. This island, now largely in public ownership, is beautiful, and is an excellent place to stretch the legs. Access is hindered by a shortage of good anchorages, so you won't be bothered by large crowds. Several trails lead off from Pelican Beach at the northeast corner of the island. They can provide leisurely walks or vigorous hikes, with beautiful views.

About a half-mile south of Pelican Beach, just past a small headland, two little coves are quite pretty and have room for one or two boats each.

Pelican Beach Recreation Site. Dept. of Natural Resources (DNR) park on the northeast side of Cypress Island. Open all year for day use and overnight camping and mooring. The park has 6 mooring buoys, a gravel beach, 5 campsites, compost toilets, picnic shelter, fire pit, information board. Many kinds of wildlife and birds can be observed. Public DNR beaches extend from the park around the north end of Cypress Island for 1.5 miles until just south of Foss Cove, and south of the park for 0.5 mile to Bridge Rock. The moorage is unprotected to the north. If anchored or moored to a buoy and the northerly wind comes in, you'll not want to stay. Current runs through the moorage, and is subject to wakes from passing traffic.

Eagle Harbor. East side of Cypress Island. Eagle Harbor is shallow, especially at low tide, but has 15 mooring buoys. Use care in approaching all but the outermost of these buoys. The bay's shallow spots are truly shallow. The innermost 4 buoys display red tags cautioning the user to verify depths at lower tide levels. Convenient beach access to the island's trails. No fires, no camping. If you have sufficient depth, Eagle Harbor is quite protected. Views of Mount Baker are breathtaking.

Cypress Head. East side of Cypress Island. Open all year for day use and overnight camping and mooring. The park has 4 mooring buoys and 5 campsites, picnic sites, compost toilets, no other facilities. Three miles of public tidelands extend from the moorage/recreation area. Many types of birds and wildlife, good fishing. Tide-rips at the south end of the island cause high wave action.

Deepwater Bay. East side of Cypress Island. Deepwater Bay has several fish farms.

Strawberry Island State Park. West of Cypress Island in Rosario Strait. Open all year. Anchoring or beaching only, anchorage in settled weather only. Strong currents and submerged rocks make landing difficult; skiffs or kayaks are best for landing. Park has three Cascadia Marine Trail campsites, vault toilet.

Vendovi Island. San Juan Preservation Trust, www.sjpt.org. Day use only, open April 15 through October 15, 10:00 a.m. to 6:00 p.m Thursday through Monday. No anchoring. A 70-foot dock behind a rock breakwater is on the north shore. All visitors must sign in and review visitor guidelines at the head of the dock upon arrival. A public restroom is in the building at the top of the hill.

Sinclair and Eliza Islands. A piling breakwater protects a loading and unloading dock on the south shore of Sinclair Island, but there are no facilities specifically for pleasure boaters. Eliza Island is privately owned, with a private dock and float on the north side. Anchorage is possible several places around the island.

Larrabee State Park. (360) 676-2093. Seven miles south of Bellingham on Samish Bay. Open all year for day use and overnight camping. The park has restrooms and show-

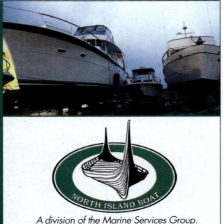

NORTH PUGET SOUND

See Area Map Page 144 - Maps Not for Navigation

Fairhaven Moorage

Village Books, in Fairhaven, is an excellent bookstore.

ers. This was Washington's first official state park, dedicated in 1923. It covers 2000 acres and is heavily used. Facilities include a launch ramp, kitchen shelters, picnic tables, standard, utility, and primitive campsites. Fishing, clamming, crabbing, scuba diving. Trails provide access to two freshwater lakes within the park. A 5.5-mile walking/bicycling trail connects with Bellingham.

Chuckanut Bay. Chuckanut Bay is a good anchorage with protection from prevailing winds in the north or south arms. Enter close to Governors Point to avoid extensive rocky shoals that partially block the entrance. The land around the bay is privately owned. Correspondents James and Jennifer Hamilton anchored in Pleasant Bay, just inside Governors Point, during a southeast gale. "The winds howled up to 49 knots, but the water was reasonably calm. Good holding over mud." [*Hamilton*]

㉑ **Fairhaven Moorage.** (360) 714-8891; www.boatingcenter.org. Nine mooring buoys, a side-tie linear mooring system, and two boat launch ramps at Fairhaven are managed by the Community Boating Center. Moorage and boat launch May through October, 38-foot maximum. Launch ramps are tide-dependent and best suited to smaller boats. Pay moorage at the CBC office or pay box. Walk up to shops and restaurants in Fairhaven's lovely Victorian buildings. Just south of the business district you'll find a beautiful old park with mature plantings and great expanses of lawn. The Seaview Boatyard Dock (360) 676-8282 is located east of the Bellingham Cruise Terminal and transient linear moorage. The boatyard dock is used for staging in preparation for Travelift haulout.

㉑ **Bellingham.** Bellingham is the largest city between Everett and the Canadian border, and has complete facilities for commercial and pleasure craft. Moorage, fuel, marine supplies, and repairs are available at the Port of Bellingham's Squalicum Harbor. Bellingham Yacht Club and Squalicum Yacht Club are nearby. BYC has moorage for members of reciprocal yacht clubs.

Charming Hotel Bellwether is near the mouth of the Squalicum Harbor south basin, adjacent to the Marina Restaurant and shops. The port runs a courtesy shuttle to downtown grocery stores, and the historic Fairhaven area shops and restaurants.

Mooring buoys and a linear moorage system are at Fairhaven, in the south part of Bellingham Bay. Fairhaven is a delightful stop with turn-of-the-20th-century Victorian buildings, boutiques, a large bookstore and other interesting shops. Fairhaven is also the southern terminus of the Alaska Marine Highway Ferry System. As with Squalicum Harbor, you can take a bus or taxi to downtown Bellingham. Many shops, restaurants and a supermarket are within walking distance in this historic area. The Bellingham International Airport is convenient for arriving or departing guests.

Bellingham's scenic surroundings and its proximity to the San Juan Islands alone would be enough to draw many boaters. Bellingham is a college town with incredible shopping opportunities including provisioning for the galley. Squalicum Harbor has comfortable moorage and is a convenient base for cruising.

Things to Do

1. **Spark Museum of Electrical Invention.** Over 1,000 radios and many other electrical devices on display.

2. **Bellingham Railway Museum.** Model and actual trains, including a simulator.

3. **Whatcom Museum.** Art, photography, and a family interactive gallery. Downtown.

4. **Historic Fairhaven.** Good shopping and restaurants surrounded by period buildings. Peruse Village Books.

NORTH PUGET SOUND

25 Bellwether Way
(360) 647-5588

7 Bellwether Way
(360) 527-3473

5. Bellingham Farmers Market. Held in Depot Square, a glass and steel building modeled after a railroad station, with beams and arches salvaged from a local highway bridge. Wonderful local vendors every Saturday from 10:00 a.m. to 3:00 p.m. One of the largest markets in the state.

6. Boundary Bay Brewery & Bistro. Across from the farmers market. Great beer garden and good food.

7. Mount Baker Theatre. Enjoy a performance in this magnificently restored art deco theater built in 1927.

8. Mindport. Not quite a science museum. Exhibit themes are exploration, observation, creativity, play, and of course, fun.

9. The Big Rock Garden. More than 37 sculptures in this 2.5-acre park. Local and internationally acclaimed artists represented. Near Lake Whatcom, a cab ride away.

LOCAL KNOWLEDGE

SHALLOW AREA: A shoal habitat enhancement bench (4-foot depth at zero tide) is along the breakwater protecting the western basin of Squalicum Harbor. The bench extends approximately 200 feet out from the breakwater and runs approximately 400 feet along the breakwater. White cylindrical can buoys mark the outer corners. From its outer edge, the bench slopes another 100 feet into Bellingham Bay until it meets the sea floor. Give the buoys a good offing when running along the face of the breakwater.

㉑ **Squalicum Harbor/Port of Bellingham.** 722 Coho Way, Bellingham, WA 98225; (360) 676-2542; squalicum@portofbellingham.com; www.portofbellingham.com. Certified Clean Marina. Monitors VHF 16, switch to 68. Open all year, guest moorage along 1000 feet of dock in two basins. Unoccupied slips are used when available, please call ahead. The marina has 20, 30 & 50 amp power (mostly 30 amp), restrooms, showers, laundry, pumpout, portapotty dump, and fee-based Ecco Wi-Fi. Three-day maximum stay in any 7-day period for visiting boats with longer stays subject to approval. The docks in both basins are gated for security. Restaurants and a snack bar nearby. Also chandleries and repair shops.

Seaview Boatyard runs the shipyard adjacent to the westernmost moorage basin. The yard has a 150-ton Travelift and a 35-ton Travelift.

Squalicum Harbor is divided into two moorage basins, each with its own entrance and guest moorage. The westernmost has restrooms located about halfway out the main pier, and onshore at the top of the dock ramp. Portable pumpout carts are kept at the restroom station.

In the eastern basin, guest moorage is just inside the breakwater entrance. Hotel Bellwether, with its dock, is located on the east side near the entrance. The hotel is part of a larger Port of Bellingham Bellwether development with park grounds, restaurants, boutiques, and a coffee shop. Seasonally, you can buy fresh fish right off the boat. A marine life tank (great for kids) also is near the streetside parking lot. A 3-lane launch ramp, with extended-term parking for tow vehicles and trailers, is just east of the east basin.

Harbor Marine Fuel. (360) 734-1710. Open all year. Fuel dock with diesel and gasoline (containing ethanol). Store carries motor oils. Located in northern Squalicum Harbor, behind the breakwater.

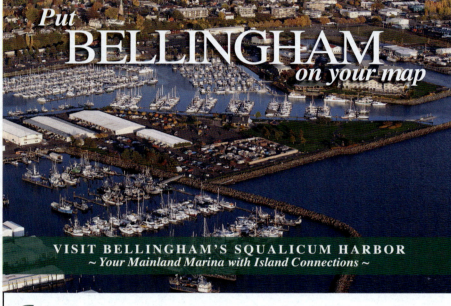

VISIT BELLINGHAM'S SQUALICUM HARBOR
~ *Your Mainland Marina with Island Connections* ~

A variety of restaurants, Hotel Bellwether, chandlery, trails and parks alongside our harbor and more than 1,000 feet of visitor dock space make Squalicum Harbor an ideal visitor destination.

- Friendly dockside service
- Several charter boat operations
- 4-lane boat launch open year-round
- Courtesy shuttle service and other ground transportation options
- Over-the-dock fuel service for bulk pricing
- Available Fuel Dock
- Diverse marine repair and supply services in the harbor
- Full Service Boatyard
- Restrooms, laundry and showers
- Holding tank pump-outs

- Closest U.S. port to Alaska
- Minutes away from the San Juan and Gulf Islands and midway between Seattle and Vancouver, B.C.
- An expanded Bellingham International Airport, providing more commercial flights to a growing number of destinations
- Outstanding visitor amenities:
  Vibrant downtown with entertainment, microbreweries, shopping, museum, seasonal farmers market
  Unsurpassed recreation opportunities – Mt Baker, golfing, bike trails

SQUALICUM HARBOR OFFICE: 722 Coho Way, Bellingham, WA 98225 • (360) 676-2542
squalicum@portofbellingham.com • www.portofbellingham.com

NORTH PUGET SOUND   See Area Map Page 144 - Maps Not for Navigation

Port of Bellingham, Squalicum Harbor

BELLINGHAM MARKETPLACE

RESTAURANTS, SHOPS & SERVICES

ANTHONY'S AT SQUALICUM HARBOR
Located in Bellwether on the Bay, offering spectacular views of the San Juan Islands. Serving fresh Northwest seafood from our own seafood company along with seasonal local produce - lunch, Monday through Saturday; Sunday brunch; and dinner served daily. Visitor moorage nearby on side-tie docks.
360-527-3473 • 360-647-5588 • 25 Bellwether Way, Bellingham
www.anthonys.com

ANTHONY'S HEARTHFIRE GRILL
On Squalicum Harbor in Bellwether on the Bay, offering guests spectacular views of the San Juan Islands. Serving premier northwest beef and fresh northwest seafood, this high-energy restaurant specializes in hearthfire cooking. Lunch and dinner served daily. Visitor moorage nearby on side-tie docks.
360-527-3473 • 7 Bellwether Way, Bellingham
www.anthonys.com

BELLHAVEN YACHT SALES AND CHARTERS
The premier choice for sail or power boat charters, certified sailing and power instruction, and yacht sales. Boats of varied specifications are available to suit your cruising style and preferences. Your exclusive dealer for Bali catamarans.
877.310.9471 • 700 Coho Way, Bellingham, WA 98225
www.bellhaven.net • bellhaven@bellhaven.net

LFS MARINE & OUTDOOR
Located within easy walking distance of Squalicum Harbor docks. Boaters will appreciate the wide selection of fishing gear and crab pots, boat equipment and supplies, safety supplies, outdoor clothing, boots, and rain gear, plus Pacific Northwest gifts, nautical books, and cards.
Open Weekdays 8 to 5, Saturdays 9 to 5.
800-426-8860 • 360-734-3336 • 851 Coho Way
Bellingham, WA 98225 • www.LFSmarineoutdoor.com

NW EXPLORATIONS
NW Explorations is a premier brokerage, charter and marine services company offering first class customer service in all areas. Whether you want to charter, buy/sell a vessel, or care for your existing boat, NW Explorations can help meet your needs.
360-676-1248 • 2623 South Harbor Loop Dr., Bellingham, WA 98225 • www.nwexplorations.com

SAN JUAN SAILING
A family run business for over 30 years, we strive to provide our guests with sail and power instruction, charters (sailboats, trawlers, motoryachts, sail and power catamarans), and brokerage services in a manner that consistently exceeds their expectations.
360-671-4300 • Gate 3, Squalicum Harbor, Bellingham
www.sanjuansailing.com

SEAVIEW NORTH BOATYARD
A full service and do-it-yourself boat repair facility for vessels up to 160 tons and 120'. We offer all disciplines of work including wood, fiberglass, topside paint, fabrication, mechanical and general maintenance. Seasonal dry storage is also available.
360-676-8282 • 2652 Harbor Loop Dr., Bellingham, WA 98225
north@seaviewboatyard.com

TRI-COUNTY DIESEL MARINE
We're factory trained and authorized for servicing the top brands covering maintenance, repair, and repower of marine propulsion and power generation. With over 100 years of combined experience, no job is too big or too small for our friendly team of professionals.
360.733.8880 • • 2696 Roeder Ave. , Bellingham, WA 98225
care@tricountydieselmarine.com
www.tricountydieselmarine.com

Harbor Events
Ski-to-Sea - May 27th

Haggen Family 4th of July - Fireworks & fair

Farmers Market - Saturdays April-Christmas

Sea Feast - Sept. 22

Contact the Port of Bellingham
www.portofbellingham.com • 360-676-2500

Maintenance tips
Basic engine service: Oil change, fuel filter change, refrigeration re-charge and diagnosis, battery maintenance, stuffing box adjustment, prop cleaning, and new zincs installed.

Inspect and service the tender: check for leaks in the inflatable, have the outboard serviced, ensure that all davit and hoist systems onboard are functioning.

Electronics: Ensure that all local charts are loaded onto nav gear, and or charts are procured. Keep an updated version of the Waggoner Guide in the chart table.

Inspect and service all charging gear: High output alternator, regulator, inverter, and genset service.

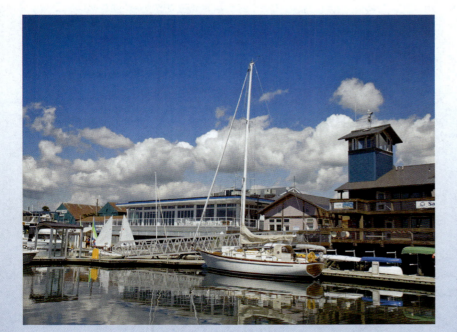

NORTH PUGET SOUND

㉑ **Hotel Bellwether.** 1 Bellwether Way, Bellingham, WA 98225; (360) 392-3178; reservations@hotelbellwether.com; www.hotelbellwether.com. Open all year, side-tie moorage along 220-foot concrete float, 30, 50 & 100 amp power. Larger boats tie outside, smaller boats tie inside. This is a classy small hotel, done to 5-star standards. Outstanding dining. Located just inside the mouth of the Squalicum Harbor east basin. Reservations required. Dog friendly.

Hilton Harbor Marina. 1000 Hilton Ave., Bellingham, WA 98225; (360) 733-1110; info@hiltonharbor.com. Fuel dock with gasoline only. Located at the south entrance to Squalicum Harbor at the foot of Hilton Avenue. Two 3 ton hoists., repairs. Oil disposal available.

Lummi Island. Lummi Island is high (1480 feet) and has no facilities specifically for visiting boaters. Anchorage is good in several places, including Inati Bay and along both shores of Hale Passage. A ferry connects Lummi Island to the mainland. Restaurants and other businesses are near this dock. The Lummi Nation's people haul their boats, including reef net boats, on the beach south of the ferry dock.

Inati Bay. Inati Bay is on the east side of Lummi Island, approximately 2 miles north of Carter Point. It is the best anchorage on Lummi Island, protected from all but northeasterly winds (rare in the summer) with good holding. Members-only allowed at the Bellingham Yacht Club outstation property (change from earlier years, when all were welcome ashore).

When entering Inati Bay, leave the white cautionary buoy well to starboard to avoid the rock that extends northward from the buoy. Stay close to the point of land on the south side of the entrance. In 2016, we noted a log booming operation just inside the entrance late in the summer season.

Lummi Island Recreation Site. Southeast shore of Lummi Island. Open all year, toilets, campsites.

Sandy Point. Sandy Point is a private real-estate development consisting of several canals with homes on them. No public facilities. Long docks serving a refinery and an aluminum plant extend from shore north of Sandy Point.

Birch Bay. Birch Bay at the southeastern end of Strait of Georgia is a large bay with excellent anchoring depths over a flat mud bottom. However, the bay is so large that it affords little protection from wind and waves. Open to the northwest, west, and southwest, Birch Bay is best used in calm conditions. Popular in the summer, you will find almost as many small craft as crab pot buoys. Large sections of the head of the bay are drying tidal areas. The cluster of buildings on the east shore marks the town of Birch Bay and the group of masts on the north shore marks the private Birch Bay Marina with no services for transient boaters.

See Area Map Page 144 - Maps Not for Navigation

LOCAL KNOWLEDGE

SHOAL ENTRY: The approach to Blaine through Semiahmoo Bay is shoal at all stages but high tide. Pay close attention to the buoys along the drying bank on the south side of the bay, and turn into the entrance channel before getting too close to the eastern shore.

㉒ **Blaine.** Blaine has two moorages in Drayton Harbor. One is owned by the Port of Bellingham; the other, Semiahmoo, is privately owned and has both permanent and transient moorage at this nice resort.

The Port of Bellingham's Blaine Marina is on the east (port) side as you enter. Entry to that marina is through an opening in the piling breakwater. Once through the breakwater follow the signs to the guest moorage in the middle of the harbor.

The Semiahmoo Marina is on the west side of the entrance channel and has fuel. Both marinas have water, power, and other facilities ashore. The Port's marina gives access to the town of Blaine and a number of boating-related businesses and a good selection of restaurants. Semiahmoo Marina has access to two world-class golf courses. In the summer, Friday through Sunday, the classic foot ferry *Plover* operates between the two marinas or you can dinghy between the two.

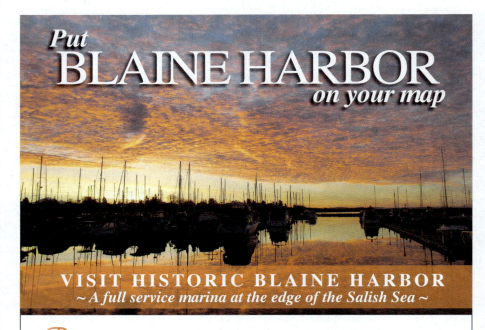

Put **BLAINE HARBOR** on your map

VISIT HISTORIC BLAINE HARBOR
~ *A full service marina at the edge of the Salish Sea* ~

Relax and re-provision on your Inside Passage Adventure Strategically located on the US - Canadian Border, 1 minute to Interstate 5!

Blaine Harbor promenade.

- Over 800 feet of visitor moorage
- No reservations required
- Post office & marine supplies
- Provisions & liquor store,
- 30 minute drive to Bellingham & Vancouver BC
- Friendly dockside service
- 70 person Meeting Room for your group events
- Restrooms, laundry & showers
- New Children's Playground
- 2 lane boat launch with ample parking
- Boatyards & Marine Trades Services

BLAINE HARBOR *Port of Bellingham*

BLAINE HARBOR OFFICE • 235 Marine Drive Blaine, WA 98230
360-647-6176 • www.portofbellingham.com • blaineharbor@portofbellingham.com

www.WaggonerGuide.com

See Area Map Page 144 - Maps Not for Navigation   NORTH PUGET SOUND

Drayton Harbor

With all that Blaine has to offer, no lack of things to do and fantastic sunsets, it makes a nice cruising destination.

Drayton Harbor is a sensitive shellfish harvesting area.

No Discharge Zone. Gray water okay.

㉒ **Blaine Harbor/Port of Bellingham.** P.O. Box 1245, 235 Marine Drive, Blaine, WA 98230; (360) 647-6176; blaineharbor@portofbellingham.com; www.portofbellingham.com. Monitors VHF 16, switch to 68. Certified Clean Marina. Side-tie guest moorage along 800 feet of wide dock, unoccupied slips up to 120' used when available. Services include 30 & 50 amp power, water, restrooms, showers, laundry, pumpout carts, portapotty dump, and fee-based Ecco Wi-Fi. Repairs, haulout, supplies available. Waste oil disposal. Two blocks to town. Concrete launch ramp with parking. Restaurants nearby. Courtesy shuttle to grocery store in town.

The side-tie guest (visitor) dock is served by a wide fairway for easy maneuvering. The shoreside facilities are built to a turn of the 20th century theme. The marina office is in the Boating Center building. A 65-person public meeting room, with kitchen, is also in this building at Gate 2. An attractive park with a children's playground and beach access is across the road on the north side of the spit. Walking distance to the Peace Arch at the border.

㉒ **Blaine Marina Inc.** The fuel dock is closed.

㉓ **Semiahmoo Marina.** 9540 Semiahmoo Parkway, Blaine, WA 98230; (360) 371-0440; moorageoffice@semiahmoomarina.com; www.semiahmoomarina.com. Monitors VHF 68. Open all year. Ethanol-free gasoline and diesel at the Semiahmoo Marina fuel dock, which offers a fuel discount for guests; propane, free pumpout. Guest moorage in unoccupied slips when available. One 50-foot slip is reserved for reciprocal yacht clubs. Call for availability for all guest moorage, reservations accepted. Services include 30 & 50 amp power, restrooms, free showers, laundry, pumpout, portapotty dump, Wi-Fi. Marina store with gifts, clothing, beer, wine, and marine items. Marina Cafe serves breakfast and lunch.

The Semiahmoo Resort has a hotel, spa with pool, restaurants and kayak, SUP, and bicycle rentals. It is a full resort with all the amenities. If you have bicycles on board or have rented a bike, you can ride the 1.2-mile scenic pathway to the Alaska Packers Association Cannery & Fishing Museum, located at 9261 Semiahmoo Parkway. Museum displays, housed in an original cannery building, include machinery and historic photos. Open weekends 1:00 p.m. to 5:00 p.m., Memorial Day through September.

Golf: The par 72 Semiahmoo course is outstanding. Day passes available for marina guests. Telephone (360) 371-7015.

㉔ **Point Roberts.** Point Roberts is a low spit of land extending south from Canada into U.S. waters. Although physically separated from the U.S., Point Roberts is U.S. territory and part of the state of Washington. The Point Roberts Marina is on the south shore. Enter via a dredged channel through drying flats. Four ocean-front parks, one located at each corner of 4.9 square mile Point Roberts, can be reached by bicycle. Bicycle rentals are available through Peddle Pushers Bike Rentals (360-990-0193).

㉔ **Point Roberts Marina Resort.** 713 Simundson Drive, Point Roberts, WA 98281; (360) 945-2255; prmarina@pointrobertsmarina.com; www.pointrobertsmarina.com. Monitors VHF 66A. Open all year. Fuel dock with mid-grade gasoline, diesel, propane, ice, beer & wine, fishing licenses, tackle, convenience items. The fuel dock is open daily during the summer

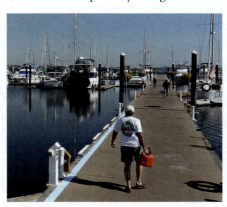

Blaine Harbor's docks are wide and sturdy.

2018 waggoner CRUISING GUIDE   165

NORTH PUGET SOUND — See Area Map Page 144 - Maps Not for Navigation

The Point Roberts US Customs dock

The broad fairway at Point Roberts Marina leads to transient moorage in assigned unoccupied slips.

season until 5:00 p.m., Sunday through Thursday; and until 8:00 p.m. on Friday and Saturday. Transient moorage in unoccupied slips. Phone ahead for slip assignment, reservations required. Services include 30 & 50 amp power, (ELCI-protected power on some docks) free Wi-Fi, restrooms, showers, laundry, garbage drop, free pumpout. The remodeled Compass Rose Bar & Grill at the marina is delightful, reservations recommended for large groups; (360) 945-7673. Other restaurants, golf and groceries are nearby. Haulout to 35 tons. Westwind Marine Services, with repairs and a chandlery, is in the main building and has seasonal hours.

Point Roberts is a U.S. Customs port of entry. The first dock to starboard has a direct-dial telephone to customs. Agents typically drive over from the Point Roberts border office. Summer hours 8:00 a.m. to 8:00 p.m., winter hours 8:00 a.m. to 5:00 p.m. Consider calling ahead at (360) 945-5211.

Lighthouse Marine County Park. (360) 945-4911; lthouse@pointroberts.net; www.whatcomcounty.us. Open for day use and overnight camping in summer, day use only in winter. On the southwest corner of Point Roberts. Anchor north of the park and row in, or moor at Point Roberts Marina and walk or ride a bike over. Facilities include boat launch ramp with seasonal staging float, campsites, picnic shelters, fire pits, barbecues, restrooms, showers, sand and gravel beach. Also a whale exhibit, playground, boardwalk, and picnic shelters. Whales can sometimes be seen from the park. A small public airstrip is along the eastern perimeter of the park.

GET YOUR WAGGONER GUIDE UPDATES & CHANGES
Visit www.WaggonerGuide.com

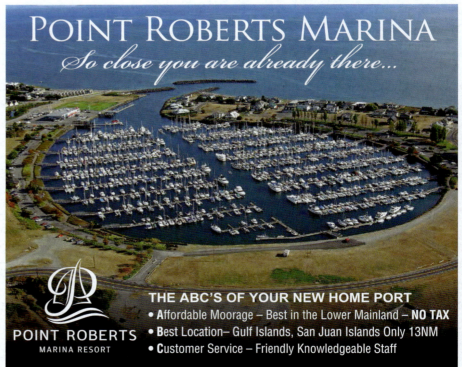

Point Roberts Marina

POINT ROBERTS MARINA
So close you are already there...

POINT ROBERTS MARINA RESORT

THE ABC'S OF YOUR NEW HOME PORT
- **A**ffordable Moorage – Best in the Lower Mainland – **NO TAX**
- **B**est Location– Gulf Islands, San Juan Islands Only 13NM
- **C**ustomer Service – Friendly Knowledgeable Staff

WWW.POINTROBERTSMARINA.COM
PH: 360-945-2255 | FAX: 360-945-0927 | PRMARINA@POINTROBERTSMARINA.COM

166 — www.WaggonerGuide.com

Strait of Juan De Fuca

CHAPTER 5

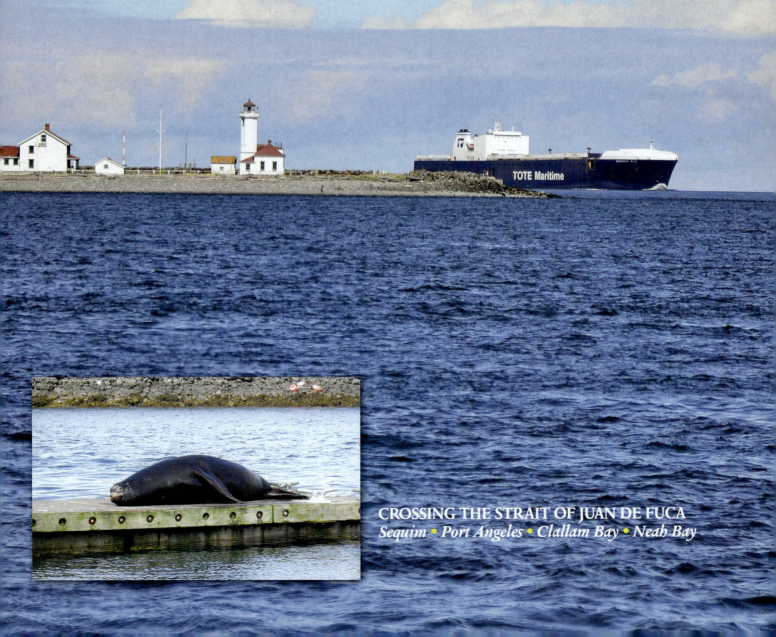

CROSSING THE STRAIT OF JUAN DE FUCA
Sequim • Port Angeles • Clallam Bay • Neah Bay

STRAIT OF JUAN DE FUCA

See Area Map Page 170 - Maps Not for Navigation

The Strait of Juan de Fuca is about 100 miles long and 12 miles wide. Depending on the weather it can be flat calm or extremely rough. The typical summertime pattern calls for calm mornings with a westerly sea breeze rising by mid-day, increasing to 30 knots or more late in the afternoon. If this sea breeze opposes an outflowing ebb current, the seas will be unusually high, steep, and close together. Often, however, the "typical" weather pattern does not prevail, and the wind blows around the clock. Or, it can be calm, even on a warm summer afternoon. Weather reports must be monitored. If wind is present or predicted, we stay off the strait.

Discovery Bay. Discovery Bay is west of Point Wilson. It is somewhat protected from the Strait of Juan de Fuca by Protection Island, a wildlife refuge. Discovery Bay is open and unobstructed, but it is seldom used by pleasure craft as an overnight anchorage. Gardiner, halfway down the bay, has a launch ramp.

Sequim Bay. Sequim Bay is a beautiful, quiet anchorage with a public marina and a state park with floats. The bay is protected by Travis Spit, extending from the eastern shore. To enter, steer for the middle of this spit, then turn sharply west and run parallel to the spit.

Actor John Wayne, who visited Sequim Bay often aboard his yacht *Wild Goose*, donated 22 waterfront acres to the Port of Port Angeles on condition that the Port build a marina on the site.

LOCAL KNOWLEDGE

SHOAL AREA: Sequim Bay has a large shoal in the middle with passage around the eastern and western sides. The marked channel, which leads to John Wayne Marina, is on the west side. This route is best when approaching Sequim Bay State Park.

① **John Wayne Marina.** 2577 W. Sequim Bay Road, Sequim, WA 98382; (360) 417-3440; rona@portofpa.com; www.portofpa.com. Open all year, gasoline and diesel at the fuel dock, guest moorage in 22 slips and 200

John Wayne Marina harbor office building also includes a restaurant with a deck overlooking the marina.

feet of dock. Services include 30 amp power, restrooms, showers, Beacon free Wi-Fi, laundry, pumpout, portapotty dump, and launch ramps. The Dockside Grill restaurant is ashore. Picnic area and beach access are nearby. Check in at the first float inside the breakwater. John Wayne Marina is operated by the Port of Port Angeles. For those desiring onshore accommodations, the John Wayne Waterfront Resort (360-681-3853) has cabins and camp sites a short walk away.

① **Sequim Bay Marine State Park.** (360) 683-4235; Sequim Bay Marine State Park occupies 92 acres along the western shore of Sequim Bay. Open all year, day use and overnight mooring and camping, 424 feet of dock space and 5 buoys (for boats 45 feet and under). Facilities include restrooms, showers, portapotty dump, picnic sites, campsites, kitchen shelters, and launch ramp. No power. The mooring buoys are in deep water. Pay nightly mooring buoy fee on shore. The water around the dock and mooring float is shallower. Watch your depths at low tide. Boarding floats at the launch ramp are removed in the winter.

Dungeness Spit. Beautiful Dungeness Spit, 5.5 miles long, is the world's longest natural sand spit. The spit provides protection from westerly weather, and convenient anchoring depths along its inner edge before an attached cross-spit forces the channel south. Shallow draft boats can continue into the inner harbor, where there is a launch ramp and protected anchorage. Dungeness Spit is a wildlife refuge and open to hikers but has no public facilities.

② **Port Angeles.** Port Angeles is a substantial small city on a bay protected by Ediz Hook. The Port Angeles City Pier, with visitor moor-

CHARTS	
18460	Strait of Juan de Fuca Entrance (1:100,000)
18465	Strait of Juan de Fuca – Eastern Part (1:80,000)
18468	Port Angeles (1:10,000)
18471	Approaches to Admiralty Inlet – Dungeness to Oak Bay (1:40,000)
18484	Neah Bay (1:10,000)
18485	Cape Flattery (1:40,000)

John Wayne Marina

168

STRAIT OF JUAN DE FUCA

See Area Map Page 170 - Maps Not for Navigation

The entrance to John Wayne Marina is unusual and requires close attention.

Port Angeles Boat Haven, with guest moorage, has a log yard outside the marina.

age, is near the south end of the business district. Guest moorage with full services is available at the breakwater-protected Port of Port Angeles Boat Haven marina at the southwest corner of the bay.

Port Angeles is a U.S. Customs port of entry. The *Coho* car and passenger ferry runs from Port Angeles to Victoria (www.cohoferry.com). It is possible to moor the boat in Port Angeles, take the *Coho* ferry as a walk-on passenger in the morning, tour Victoria, B.C. for the day, and return to Port Angeles in the late afternoon.

The outer end of Ediz Hook is a Coast Guard station. Just west of the Coast Guard station is the Port Angeles Pilot Station, where Puget Sound Pilot tenders shuttle pilots to ships bound to or from Puget Sound ports.

Port Angeles has a number of attractions. The walkable town has many shops and restaurants to explore. The Feiro Marine Life Center, on the city pier, focuses on the marine life in the Strait of Juan de Fuca. Open daily, 10:00 a.m. to 5:00 p.m. in summers and 12:00 p.m. to 5:00 p.m. in winters. In late June, free summer concerts begin on the pier, Wednesdays 6:00 p.m. to 8:00 p.m. The Juan de Fuca Festival with music, workshops and crafts is on Memorial Day weekend. For general tourist information see the North Olympic Peninsula Visitor & Convention Bureau website: www.olympicpeninsula.org.

Farmers market: Saturdays year-round, from 10:00 a.m. to 2:00 p.m at the corner of Front Street and Lincoln Street.

Olympic Discovery Trail: The Olympic Discovery Trail for walking and bicycling, runs

PORT ANGELES: Northwest cruising starts here.

The Port Angeles Boat Haven
on the Strait of Juan de Fuca

Closer to the Pacific Ocean than any other port on Puget Sound, the Port Angeles Boat Haven is the **best option** for no-hassle access to all points northwest.

- Easy in and out, US Customs on site
- International airport minutes away
- Convenient services and supplies: provisioning, fueling, boat maintenance
- Great recreation in adjacent Olympic National Park

For more information, visit
www.portofpa.com/boathaven
or call the Port Angeles Boat Haven:
(360) 457-4505

2018 WAGGONER CRUISING GUIDE 169

STRAIT OF JUAN DE FUCA

Reference Only – Not for Navigation

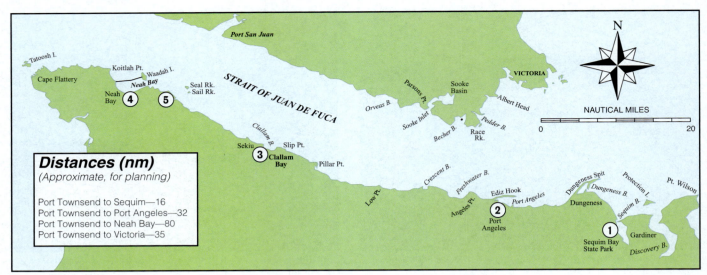

Strait of Juan de Fuca

from Port Angeles to the town of Blyn. Eventually this trail will extend all the way from Port Townsend to La Push. Bike rentals are available in Port Angeles.

② **Port Angeles Boat Haven.** 832 Boat Haven Drive, Port Angeles, WA 98362; (360) 457-4505; pamarina@olypen.com; www.portofpa.com. Open all year, ethanol-free gasoline and diesel at the fuel dock, and high-volume fuel delivery for larger vessels. The marina has concrete docks, side-tie guest moorage, and a guest arrival float. Maximum boat length 164 feet. Services include 30, 50, and 100 amp power, restrooms, Wi-Fi, showers, waste oil disposal, pumpout. Security system with locking gates. Call ahead for after-hours arrival. Online reservations available through Dockwa.com. Excellent 2-lane launch ramp with ample room for tow vehicles and trailers. Customs clearance is available from a dedicated phone on the water side of the harbor office, (360) 457-4311. Haulout on a 70-ton Travelift. Groceries, doctor, post office, and laundry are nearby. The Castaway Restaurant, located on the northwest end of the moorage basin, is a full service restaurant and night club frequently featuring live music.

② **Port Angeles City Pier.** Foot of North Lincoln St., Port Angeles, WA 98362; (360) 417-4550; www.cityofpa.us. Six new floats, one of which is ADA accessible, have been constructed for Port Angeles City Pier with a planned installation in time for the 2018 boating season. Transient overnight side-tie moorage for boats up to 80 feet. No power, no water; first-come, first-served. A self-registration pay station is located near the docks. Maximum 10-day stay.

Crescent Bay. Crescent Bay is a possible anchorage if conditions on the Strait of Juan de Fuca become untenable. Close to the western shore it offers a little protection from westerlies, but swells can still work into the bay and make for an uneasy stay.

Pillar Point. Pillar Point has a fishing resort with launch ramp and float but is not available for transient moorage. In a westerly, the area close to and a little east of the point is a notorious windless spot—a "hole" in sailboaters' language. A Waggoner reader wrote to tell us anchorage is good along the eastern shore.

CLALLAM BAY AND SEKIU

Clallam Bay. Clallam Bay, with Sekiu on its western shore, is somewhat protected from westerlies and has convenient anchoring depths along the shore. A serious reef, marked by a buoy at its outer end well offshore, extends from the eastern point. Leave the buoy to port when entering the bay. Three marinas offer transient moorage.

③ **Van Riper's Resort.** P.O. Box 246, 280 Front Street, Sekiu, WA 98381; (360) 963-2334; www.vanripersresort.com. Open summers, closed winters. Guest moorage on five docks with 450 feet each. Facilities include restrooms, showers, free Wi-Fi, campground, concrete launch ramp. No power. Boat and motor rentals, charter service, ice, groceries, charts, and books. Nearby post office, restaurant and bar, and marine supplies.

③ **Olson's Resort.** P.O. Box 216, 444 Front St., Sekiu, WA 98381; (360) 963-2311. Open March through September. Gasoline and diesel at the fuel dock. Guest moorage in 300 slips behind a breakwater, 35-foot maximum boat length. No power. Services include restrooms, showers, laundry, 3-lane concrete launch ramp, and Wi-Fi near the office. Motel units available. Busy during salmon season. After 80 years of family ownership, the Olson family sold the resort in late 2014. The Mason family now owns and operates the resort.

③ **Curley's Resort.** P.O. Box 265, Sekiu, WA 98381; (360) 963-2281; (800) 542-9680; www.curleysresort.com. Open May through September, guest moorage while staying in one of the cabins. 750 feet of dock space, 30-foot maximum boat length. This is a private resort with moorage, motel rooms, and cabins for rent. Pets must remain on the boat.

NEAH BAY

The Makah Tribe town of Neah Bay is popular with sport fishermen, who trailer their boats

Port Angeles Boat Haven

See Area Map Page 170 - Maps Not for Navigation   STRAIT OF JUAN DE FUCA

A tribal mask in the Makah Museum at Neah Bay

Totems at Makah Cultural Center

in during the summer. It's also a good place to wait for a favorable weather window to round Cape Flattery and head down the Pacific Coast. Most boats bound to or from Barkley Sound, however, choose to stay along the Vancouver Island side of the Strait of Juan de Fuca. For cruising boats that do stop, moorage is at the Makah Marina docks, managed by Big Salmon Resort.

A long breakwater connects the mainland and Waadah Island, blocking ocean waves from getting in. Anchorage is good, sand bottom, throughout the bay. A second breakwater protects the Makah Marina. The Coast Guard station at the entrance to the bay serves the west end of the Strait of Juan de Fuca and the northern Pacific Ocean coast.

Neah Bay is not a U.S. Customs port of entry, although entrants with Nexus cards can phone in from there. Those without Nexus must clear at a designated port of entry. Port Angeles is the nearest location.

The Makah Cultural & Research Center Museum features artifacts from the Ozette archaeological dig site. The museum is world-class—a must see. The Ozette dig was a village buried by a mudslide 500 years ago, before European contact. It is a time capsule of coastal Native life. The tools, clothing, furniture, weapons, and fishing implements are exquisitely preserved and displayed.

Neah Bay's general store is well-stocked, except for spirits. Neah Bay is dry.

④ **Makah Marina.** P.O. Box 137, Neah Bay, WA 98357; (360) 645-3015. www.makah.com/activities/marina Open all year, guest moorage, 30 & 50 amp power, free Wi-Fi, potable water, restrooms, showers, laundry nearby, pumpout station, portapotty dump, 2-lane launch ramp with extended parking available for tow vehicles and trailers. Summertime visitor moorage is managed by Big Salmon Resort, see listing below. Shopping (on the rough and ready side) and lodging are nearby. The extraordinary Makah Museum is an easy walk.

The marina is spacious and well-built. The concrete docks are stable, and each mooring slip is served by sturdy mooring cleats. The slips and the fairways between docks are wide. On shore, the administration building has restrooms and showers. Summertime moorage can be crowded with commercial boats and their gear, however, so don't expect a resort environment.

④ **Big Salmon Resort.** P.O. Box 140, 1251 Bay View Ave., Neah Bay, WA 98357; (360) 645-2374; (866) 787-1900; www.bigsalmonresort.net. Open April 1 to September 15. Gasoline and diesel at fuel dock. Pumpout. Haulout to 30 tons and 2-lane concrete launch ramp with long-term parking. Guest moorage at Makah Marina. A small store carries tackle, some groceries, local charts. Motels, doctor, post office nearby.

JUAN DE FUCA (IOANNIS PHOKAS) 1536-1602

Juan de Fuca was a Greek explorer and pilot in the service of the King of Spain, Philip II. The name Juan de Fuca is a Spanish translation of his Greek name, Ionnis Phokas. DeFuca's early voyages were to the Far East before arriving in New Spain near Cabo San Lucas around 1587. Under order of the Viceroy of New Spain, DeFuca undertook two voyages to the Pacific Northwest, the first reported to end in a mutiny and a return to California. His second voyage in 1592 was considered a success by the Viceroy who wanted DeFuca to find the Strait of Anian, the fabled Northwest Passage. DeFuca had returned to Acapulco with the news that he had found the Strait at 47 degrees latitude, now known as the Strait of Juan de Fuca (48 degrees latitude). DeFuca also made note of the tall pinnacle rocks at the entrance to the strait. Although not given any significant reward from the Viceroy for his discovery, we remember Juan de Fuca's contribution through well-known place names such as the Juan de Fuca Plate, Juan de Fuca Provincial Park on West Vancouver Island, and the Strait itself which carries his name.

Port Angeles City Pier

2018 WAGGONER CRUISING GUIDE   171

STRAIT OF JUAN DE FUCA

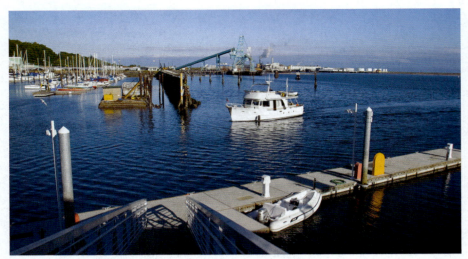

Check-in dock for Port Angeles Boat Haven

If the fuel dock is closed for the season, fuel is available at the Makah Mini Mart's commercial dock just beyond the commercial fish offloading pier.

⑤ **Snow Creek Resort.** P.O. Box 248, Mile Marker 691, Hwy 112, Neah Bay, WA 98357; (360) 645-2284; snowcreek@gmail.com. Open from April 15 to October 1. Guest moorage for up to 40 boats plus 25 buoys. Maximum boat size 26 feet. Restrooms, showers, campsites and RV parking, cabins, limited groceries, diving air, haulout, beach launch, and hoist launch.

CROSSING THE STRAIT OF JUAN DE FUCA

Important: *Routes suggested below are approximate and for reference only. They assume good conditions and the absence of current. Since current is always present, appropriate course adjustments will be needed.*

The Strait of Juan de Fuca has a well-earned reputation for being rough at times. It's true that a boat crossing the strait can take a beating that its crew will not want to repeat, but often the crossing can be almost flat. If conditions truly are foul, alternate routes exist. The secret to an easy crossing lies in picking your times and not being foolhardy.

Summer weather pattern. During the high summer cruising season, the "typical" weather pattern calls for near-calm conditions in the early morning, when the air over the entire region is cool. As the summer sun heats the land, air over the land rises, and colder ocean air funnels down the Strait of Juan de Fuca to replace the rising land air. This is called a sea breeze, and it usually develops in the late morning or early afternoon. By late afternoon the sea breeze can be quite strong, creating short, high seas, especially on an ebb. After sundown, as air in the interior cools, the sea breeze dies away.

Given this pattern, early morning crossings are preferred. Carefully monitor the official weather reports and forecast. If the morning report says the wind already is blowing 15 to 20 knots, and more wind is expected, don't cross. Wait until the wind subsides or take an alternate route.

Fog can develop unexpectedly. Sometimes it is only a thin mist, other times it can be pea-soup thick. Normally when the wind moves in, the fog blows out.

LOCAL KNOWLEDGE

BEWARE OF THE EBB TIDE. Ebbing tidal currents can set up dangerous tide-rips at Point Wilson, and at the south end of Rosario Strait, at Cattle Pass, and off Discovery Island. Do not underestimate the viciousness of these tide-rips. Whenever possible, plan your passage to transit these danger spots near the turn of the tide or on a flood.

Point Wilson to San Juan Channel. The most direct route from Point Wilson to Friday Harbor is via San Juan Channel. A direct course between the two intersects Smith Island. Shoals, covered with dense kelp, extend westward from Smith Island for nearly 2 miles. Partridge Bank, between Point Wilson and Smith Island, should be avoided. Heavy kelp is an obstacle, and if the wind is up, seas are worse in the shallow water over the bank.

At Point Wilson you'll set a course of approximately 301° magnetic until you're abeam the Smith Island light, where you'll turn to a course of 330° magnetic to fetch Cattle Pass. (From Cattle Pass to Point Wilson reverse the process: run 150° magnetic until the Smith Island light bears abeam to port, then turn to 121° magnetic to fetch Point Wilson.)

When using this route, it's best to time your arrival at Cattle Pass for shortly after the current turns to flood. The current can run hard through Cattle Pass, so it's best not to fight it. Use the San Juan Channel current predictions.

If you do it right, you'll carry the last of a dying ebb out Admiralty Inlet, past Point Wilson, and well across the strait.

Just before reaching Cattle Pass, the current will turn to flood, flushing you nicely through the pass and into San Juan Channel. Since you can have 2 to 4 knots of current in Admiralty Inlet, and a couple knots of current in the strait, riding the ebb can save considerable time, even in a fast boat. The less time you're exposed, the less time you have to meet trouble.

To Rosario Strait or Deception Pass. From the mouth of Admiralty Inlet, plot a course that leaves Point Partridge bell buoy off Whidbey Island to starboard. If you're bound for Rosario Strait, stay out of the traffic lanes as much as possible. As noted above, the mouth of Rosario Strait can be filled with dangerous tide-rips on an ebb tide. Be prepared to favor the eastern shore.

FRANCISCO DE ELIZA (1759-1825)

Francisco de Eliza was commandant of the Spanish post in Nootka Sound, located on West Vancouver Island. The post had been established by Estaban Jose Martinez in 1789 but abandoned in October that same year due to the 'Nootka Incident.' Both Spain and Great Britain had claimed ownership of the territory, setting off a political dispute. Francisco de Eliza arrived in Nootka Sound (Santa Cruz de Nuca) in 1790 to reoccupy the site and establish a permanent settlement. He arrived with three ships: the *Concepcion*, the *San Carlos*, and *The Princesa Real*. Eliza dispatched several explorations in the region, which included the Strait of Juan de Fuca and the Strait of Georgia. In 1790, he sent Salvador Fidalgo to the Russian outposts in Alaska, and Manuel Quimper to the Strait of Juan de Fuca with pilot Gonzala Lopez de Haro. Quimper's expedition found and charted Neah Bay, Esquimalt Harbour, Admiralty Inlet, Haro Strait, Rosario Strait, and Deception Pass. In 1791, Jose Maria Narvaez further explored the Strait of Juan de Fuca, Haro Strait, and followed the Strait of Georgia northward reaching as far as Texada Island. The inlets of the Strait of Georgia rekindled the hope of a Northwest Passage to the Atlantic, which led to the 1792 expedition of Dionisio Alcala Galiano and Cayetano Valdes. While sailing back to Nootka Sound, Eliza's expedition led by Narvaez, entered the deep harbor of 'Puerto de Nuestra Senora de Los Angeles,' present-day Port Angeles.

STRAIT OF JUAN DE FUCA

To Haro Strait (Roche Harbor). Leaving Point Wilson, run a course of approximately 301° magnetic until the Smith Island light is abeam to starboard. Then turn to approximately 305° magnetic to run toward Lime Kiln Point on the west side of San Juan Island. Once near Lime Kiln Point, follow the San Juan Island shoreline north.

If you're returning south from Roche Harbor, follow the San Juan Island coastline until you're a little south of Lime Kiln Point, then turn to approximately 125° magnetic until the Smith Island light is abeam to port. At Smith Island turn to 121° magnetic to fetch Point Wilson.

Both the flood and ebb currents run strongly along the west side of San Juan Island. Even in a fast boat it is best to make this passage with favorable current. The Canadian Hydrographic Service book *Current Atlas: Juan de Fuca Strait to Georgia Strait* illustrates these current flows in convincing diagram form. *Waggoner Tables*, published annually, provide the time schedule for the Current Atlas.

To Victoria. From Point Wilson, a course of approximately 275° magnetic takes you 30 miles to Victoria. Returning from Victoria, a course of about 095° magnetic should raise Point Wilson in time to make late-run corrections for the effects of current. In slow boats, the trip between Victoria and Point Wilson usually can be made on a single favorable tide. In all boats, utilizing favorable current can save significant time.

Even the best plan can go awry. While over the years we have made many easy crossings of the strait (only a few have been "memorable"), it's important to understand that conditions can change with little warning. When you're several miles offshore and the wind decides to kick up, you can't pull over until things improve.

The Strait of Juan de Fuca is not to be feared, but it should be respected. Be sure your boat is seaworthy, well-equipped, and in excellent condition. Carry plenty of fuel. Check the typically easterly flowing offshore weather systems. Let the weather and tide and current tables set your plans. Don't be afraid to wait, but be confident enough to seize opportunities as they arise.

Waiting for a freighter to pass

THE POINT WILSON RIP

One of the more frustrating pieces of water we face in the Northwest is the infamous Point Wilson tide-rip just off Port Townsend. The rip usually (but not always) forms on an ebb tide, and may or may not be accompanied by westerly wind. The patch of rough water can extend for several miles north and west of Point Wilson. We have learned three ways to avoid being bounced around by the Point Wilson rip.

The first is to round Point Wilson at or near slack water. Usually, the rip doesn't form until well into an ebb cycle, so timing your arrival to coincide with slack water should get the job done.

If, however, you must go that way while the rip is tearing the Strait of Juan de Fuca to shreds, you can pick one of two routes around it.

The first is to hug the Point Wilson shore as closely as you dare, keeping close to shore until you pass McCurdy Point, before heading across to the San Juan Islands or heading west to Victoria. The fact that the current runs more slowly close to shore prevents the tide-rip from having the same wild effect as farther out.

The other route is to stay close to the Whidbey Island shore (avoiding the shoal water off Partridge Point and staying east of Partridge Bank) until past Smith Island before turning toward your destination.

It doesn't take much ebb current to create the Point Wilson Rip. On July 26, 2001 we were returning to Seattle from the San Juan Islands, reaching Point Wilson at noon. Bush Point maximum ebb of 2.3 knots would not be until 1347, yet already the rip was visible and working its way eastward across the mouth of Admiralty Inlet. Although there was no wind and the water around us was calm, inside the rip ugly black seas reared up and broke.

A white powerboat entered the far side of the rip. The boat was about 40 feet long, perhaps coming down from Victoria. Once in, it was trapped. It rolled and plunged, taking water up to the fly bridge.

The longer it was in the rip, the bigger the rip became. Rolling and crashing, the boat had no choice but to carry on. The bow lifted out on the crests and disappeared in the troughs, burying in the waves ahead. Eventually the boat got through. We don't know if it suffered damage, but we're sure the people suffered. This rip should not be trifled with.

— Tom Kincaid and Robert Hale

San Juan Islands

CHAPTER 6

SAN JUAN ISLAND
Friday Harbor • Roche Harbor • Garrison Bay

LOPEZ ISLAND
Fisherman Bay • Spencer Spit • Watmough Bay

ORCAS ISLAND
Eastsound • Deer Harbor • Rosario Resort

Blakely Island • Sucia Island • Jones Island
Shaw Island • Stuart Island • James Island

SAN JUAN ISLANDS

See Area Map Page 176 - Maps Not for Navigation

The world-famous San Juan Islands are the dream destination for thousands of boaters each year. The scenery is stunning, the fishing is good, the anchorages are plentiful, and the amenities—marine resorts, settlements, villages and towns—are many and varied. The islands contain large flocks of bald eagles. Sailing in the company of porpoises and whales is almost commonplace.

The San Juans have a feel about them that is different from most other coastal cruising areas. In the San Juans we don't just head down the coast to another bay, or out to a little clutch of islets for the night. Instead, we are cruising among the peaks of a majestic sunken mountain range, and each island peak is different from the others. We've truly left the bustle of civilization behind and found a corner of paradise.

The San Juans have so much to see and do that a first-time visitor can be overwhelmed. We have a short list of stops that we recommend. They are not the only places to experience, but nothing like them exists anywhere else. Our short list is as follows: Rosario Resort, Roche Harbor, English Camp (Garrison Bay), Stuart Island (Prevost Harbor and Reid Harbor), Sucia Island, Friday Harbor. You will make many other stops as well. But these six are highly recommended, especially for the first-time visitor, or when you have guests.

Rosario Resort is a mansion and estate built in the early 1900s by Robert Moran, a turn-of-the-20th-century pioneer ship builder. The facilities include a luxury resort hotel and marina. Roche Harbor is another century-old monument, this one built around limestone quarrying. It's now a deluxe resort and a don't-miss experience. English Camp is at Garrison Bay, a short distance from Roche Harbor. This is where the British garrison was stationed during the historic 1859–1872 Pig War. The blockhouse, formal gardens, and several buildings remain. They are now a National Historical Park, with an interpretive center. You can anchor in the bay and visit by dinghy.

Stuart Island is a gem. In both Prevost Harbor and Reid Harbor you can anchor, tie to a mooring buoy, or moor on the coveted, but space-limited, State Park docks. Whichever you do, you will be surrounded by beauty. A hike along a well-marked, up-and-down trail leads to the dirt road that runs out to Turn Point Lighthouse. Along the way are the Stuart Island one-room school, library, and museum.

Sucia Island, with its weather- and water-sculpted sandstone, its fossils and fascinating shoreline, is the definitive anchorage of the San Juans. The problem will be choosing which of Sucia Island's five bays to stay in.

Friday Harbor is a lovely little town where you can browse the shops, or enjoy one of the many restaurants or pubs. Friday Harbor is the commercial hub of the San Juans, with more services than any other destination.

No, we've not mentioned the charming village of Eastsound on Orcas Island, or Lopez Village on Lopez Island, or the Shaw General Store at the Shaw Island ferry landing, or Spencer Spit, or a dozen other delightful places to see, although we certainly describe them in detail later in the chapter. This is the problem with the San Juans. There are so many choices.

Although summertime tourism is a major industry in the San Juan Islands, the settlements have retained a small village atmosphere. Minutes out of town, you will be on winding roads in pastoral farm country. Island people are easygoing and friendly, and many of them are highly accomplished. Movie stars and industrialist families have estates there. The late author Ernest Gann lived on San Juan Island. One famous author's book bio says simply that he lives on an island. What it doesn't say is that the island is in the San Juans.

Drinking water is in short supply in the San Juan Islands. In almost every case you'll find no water for boat washing. Go to the San Juans with full water tanks, and conserve while you are there.

Personal watercraft restriction: Because some people were hot-dogging on their PWCs and harassing whales and other wildlife, San Juan County has banned PWC use in the San Juan Islands.

San Juan Islands National Wildlife Refuge. The San Juan Islands National Wildlife Refuge consists of 83 islands, islets, rocks and reefs. Boaters must remain 200 yards offshore from any refuge property.

Getting to the San Juan Islands. If you are approaching from the east, you'll enter the San Juans through one of four passes: Lopez Pass, Thatcher Pass, Peavine Pass, or Obstruction Pass.

At times the waters outside these passes can be turbulent, dangerously so, the result of tidal current and wind opposing each other. Be sure you have a complete tide and current book, and are able to read it. You can't go wrong with the official government publications, but our preferred tide book is *Ports and Passes*, available at marine supply stores or www.WaggonerGuide.com. *Ports and Passes* uses a tabular format, covering the area from Olympia to the Alaska border and is corrected for Daylight Saving Time.

The San Juan Islands are understandably popular. The scenery is impressive.

CHARTS	
18421	Strait of Juan de Fuca to Strait of Georgia (1:80,000)
18429	Rosario Strait, Southern Part (1:25,000)
18430	Rosario Strait, Northern Part (1:25,000)
18431	Rosario Strait to Cherry Point (1:25,000)
18432	Boundary Pass (1:25,000)
18433	Haro Strait – Middle Bank to Stuart Island (1:25,000)
18434	San Juan Channel (1:25,000)
3462	Juan de Fuca Strait to Strait of Georgia (1:80,000) (Canadian)

WATCH FOR FERRY TRAFFIC

Ferry traffic is heavy and the routes are confusing in the Lopez Island/Shaw Island/Orcas Island section of Harney Channel. Ferries may pull away from a landing in one direction, then turn and head a different direction.

Ferry captains ask that pleasure craft watch for ferries at all times, and not assume that a ferry will maintain the course it is on at the moment.

San Juan Islands

Sylvan Cove is a lovely anchorage, but the land ashore is all private.

Visitors stand at the end of Spencer Spit.

① **James Island Marine State Park.** (360) 376-2073; Open all year for day use, overnight mooring, and camping. James Island is a favorite spot, with trails to hike and wildlife to view. Visiting boats can use both sides of a 44-foot-long float on the west side of the island. Toilets, no power or water. Strong currents and a rocky bottom make anchoring difficult in the west cove. Use the float (removed in winter).

The east cove is exposed to wakes from passing traffic in Rosario Strait, but has 4 mooring buoys for boats 45 feet or less. Self-register and pay nightly mooring buoy fee on shore. The park has a picnic shelter and 13 primitive campsites. A Cascadia Marine Trail campsite is at Pocket Cove (high bank gravel beach). Excellent hiking, picnicking, scuba diving. Pack out all garbage. If at the dock, raccoons will go aboard unattended boats if food or garbage is left in the open. Best to stow food well and close the boat tight.

LOCAL KNOWLEDGE

TIDE-RIP: When the current is ebbing and the wind is blowing from the south, be particularly mindful of the tide-rips that form at the eastern entrance to Thatcher Pass.

CAUTION IN ROSARIO STRAIT

Lopez Pass, Thatcher Pass, Peavine Pass and Obstruction Pass all connect with Rosario Strait. Especially on an ebb, when current in Thatcher Pass and Lopez Pass flows east into Rosario Strait, expect rougher water off their mouths. If a big southflowing ebb in Rosario Strait is opposed by a fresh southerly wind, expect severe turbulence. The tide-rips and heavy seas can persist completely across the strait.

We have seen some vicious rips at the south end of Rosario Strait. Walt Woodward (*How to Cruise to Alaska without Rocking the Boat Too Much*) recalls that a rip outside Lopez Pass was the worst he had ever encountered.

The waters between Guemes Channel and Thatcher Pass can be rough or even dangerous in these conditions (southflowing ebb in Rosario Strait opposed by fresh southerly wind). Guemes Channel enters Rosario Strait from the east, and Thatcher Pass enters from the west. Bellingham Channel angles in from the northeast. The conflict of the four currents, combined with the opposing wind, creates confused, high and steep beam seas as you cross. It seems that all experienced local yachting families (ourselves included) have their own horror stories of crossings in such conditions.

We have learned to treat Rosario Strait with great respect. Thus, one year when a 20-knot southerly was blowing, we left the San Juans for Seattle via Peavine Pass, at the north end of Blakely Island. As we suspected, Rosario Strait was rough, especially to the south. We angled northward and eastward across the top of Cypress Island, and looked down Bellingham Channel. It too was a mass of whitecaps.

So we continued eastward, and found calm water on the east side of Guemes Island. Our route plan back to Seattle then went past La Conner and south through Saratoga Passage. It was longer and slower than a fast run across the Strait of Juan de Fuca and down Admiralty Inlet, but it was unruffled.

– *Robert Hale*

Thatcher Pass. Thatcher Pass runs between Blakely Island and Decatur Island, and is one of the main entrances into the San Juan Islands. Currents can run strongly. Washington State Ferries use Thatcher Pass, so keep a sharp lookout.

Decatur Island. Decatur Island is east of Lopez Island and south of Blakely Island. Decatur Island has three vacation communities and about 50 full-time residents. No public services.

Sylvan Cove. Sylvan Cove, at the northwest corner of Decatur Island, has good holding bottom in convenient depths. The bay is truly beautiful, with New England-style buildings ashore. All the land is private, as are the mooring buoys, the dock, and float that serve homeowners on the island.

Brigantine Bay. The area between Trump Island and Decatur Island is pretty, and has anchorage in 24 to 42 feet. The dock and all the land ashore are private. **Center Island.** Good anchorage can be found by simply cruising around Center Island into **Reads Bay** until you find an area out of the prevailing wind.

Unnamed Island #3 (Reads Bay Island). This island, an undeveloped Bureau of Land Management property, is in the little bay at the south tip of Decatur Island, and joins Decatur Island at low tide. Open all year, day use only. Anchor out. No fires or overnight camping. Pack out all garbage. Do not disturb wildlife or alter the surroundings. This is one of Contributing Editor Tom Kincaid's favorite anchorages. When the Kincaid children were small, they used the concrete structure on the island as a fort.

Lopez Pass. Lopez Pass connects Rosario Strait to Lopez Sound. Currents can flow strongly through Lopez Pass and the area calls for careful navigation.

Lopez Island. Lopez Island offers a variety of anchorages and moorages. On the northern end, sandy Spencer Spit is a favorite. Fisherman Bay, on the west side, has the village of Lopez, with marinas, a museum, a grocery store, and restaurants.

SAN JUAN ISLANDS

The southern end of Lopez Island is indented by several bays, and guarded by rocks and reefs. The geography is rugged and windblown, the result of the prevailing westerly winds from the Strait of Juan de Fuca. It's an interesting shore to explore when the wind is down.

Lopez Sound. Lopez Sound is the large body of water between Decatur Island and Lopez Island. This broad area has easy anchoring depths with few hazards. A selection of anchoring locations in Lopez Sound affords wind protection from a variety of directions. Among them are Hunter Bay and Mud Bay. Although Lopez Sound is surrounded by private homes and docks, it's very picturesque and feels special. A variety of scenery captures the mind's eye, everything from wind swept slopes and rocky beaches, to tree-covered hillsides and open pastures. Crabbing and clamming are popular local past-times.

Mud Bay. South end of Lopez Sound. This large bay has ample room for anchoring with good holding in 12 - 14 feet over a mud bottom. Watch your depths, charted shallow areas in the bay. Good protection except in strong northeast and southeast winds. Buoys in the bay are private. Tiny Mud Bay County Park (360) 378-8420, located along the southeast side of the bay, is open all year for daytime use. No shore side signage at the park. The park beach is a popular departure point for kayakers. Clamming on the mud flats is reported to be good.

Hunter Bay. Southwest corner of Lopez Sound. Hunter Bay is a good place to anchor, consistent depths of 15 feet over a mud bottom. The bay is surrounded by forest and protected from all but northeast winds. Located on the southeast side of the bay, just south of Crab Island, is a public launch ramp and public pier with a 45-foot float for day use, no overnight moorage.

② **Spencer Spit Marine State Park.** 521 A. Bakerview Road, Lopez Island, WA 98261; (360) 468-2251; www.parks.wa.gov. On the northeastern shore of Lopez Island. Open all year, day use and overnight moor-

Fisherman Bay, Lopez Island

ing and camping. The park has 12 mooring buoys; self-register and pay nightly mooring buoy fee on shore. The buoys, for boats 45 feet and under, typically fill up quickly during the summer, but anchoring is good. Restrooms are located upland, no showers. Restrooms are closed from the end of October to March. Water is available at the bottom of the trail to the uplands.

Spencer Spit is a popular park. A saltwater lagoon, fed from the north side, is in the middle of the spit. If you are on the north side, you must walk around the tip of the spit and back down the south side to get to the upland areas of the park. The park has standard and primitive campsites. To reserve a campsite call (888) 226-7688. Rabbits abound, and interpretive signs aid exploration. Spencer Spit is a Cascadia Marine Trail campsite. Although the pass between Spencer Spit and Frost Island is narrow, it is deep and safe.

Swifts Bay. Swifts Bay, behind Flower Island and Leo Reef, is shallow, but a usable anchorage in settled weather. Anchor on a sand bottom in 10 to 20 feet.

Spencer Spit State Park

Large Mud Bay, on the south end of Lopez Sound, has ample room for many boats at anchor; mooring buoys in the bay are private.

See Area Map Page 176 - Maps Not for Navigation   SAN JUAN ISLANDS

Shoal Bay. Shoal Bay indents the northern tip of Lopez Island between Humphrey Head and Upright Head offering good, fairly protected anchorage. We think the best spot is behind the breakwater and off the private marina along the east shore. Numerous crab pot floats must be avoided in picking an anchorage.

LOCAL KNOWLEDGE

SHOAL ENTRY: The entrance to Fisherman Bay should not be attempted by deep draft boats at less than half tide.

③ **Fisherman Bay.** Fisherman Bay extends southward about 1.5 miles into the western shore of Lopez Island. The entrance is winding and shallow. About 200 yards off the entrance, a non-lateral sector light marks the center of the entrance channel; you can pass on either side, but stay close to remain in the deepest water. Caution: watch for the charted rock awash approaching red Daybeacon 4. Leave this beacon to starboard, then follow the well-marked channel into the bay. Cutting any of the corners risks grounding.

The northernmost marina in Fisherman Bay belongs to Islands Marine Center. The docks next door belong to the Lopez Islander Resort. About one-half mile south of the Lopez Islander, the Galley Restaurant, (360) 468-2874, has two mooring buoys and a dock where moorage often can be arranged.

Anchorage in Fisherman Bay is shallow,

Islands Marine Center in Fisherman Bay offers moorage and full-service repairs.

with a mud bottom. When entering or departing, resist the urge to cut inside any navigation marks. Departing, it's tempting to cut inside red nun Buoy 8, and there you are, aground. Remember: Red, Right, Returning, also means Red, *Left, Departing.*

Lopez Village is a little less than a mile away. You'll find excellent dining, a new, splendidly stocked grocery store, galleries, all the usual services, and the famous Holly B's Bakery.

The Lopez Historical Museum is open noon to 4:00 p.m., Wednesday to Sunday, May through September, with exhibits inside and on the field outside. A farmers market takes up an entire field at the village, 10:00 a.m. to 2:00 p.m. on Saturdays, May through September.

Keep one hand free to wave to passing vehicles as you walk or cycle the roads. It's the custom on Lopez Island. Everybody waves.

Note. Floatplanes typically use the northwest side of the bay for landing. This is also where local boat repair centers conduct on-water testing. Consider anchoring in other areas of the bay.

Golf: The Lopez Island Golf Course, 9 flat holes next to the airport, is kept up entirely by volunteers. You'll need a ride to get there. (360) 468-2679.

③ **Islands Marine Center.** 2793 Fisherman Bay Rd., Lopez, WA 98261; (360) 468-3377; imc@rockisland.com; www.islandsmarinecenter.com. Monitors VHF 69. Open all year, Monday through Saturday. Guest moorage along 1000 feet of dock space, 30 amp power, Wi-Fi, restrooms, showers, garbage, recycling, pumpout. Call ahead.

This is a well-run, full-service marina, with

ISLANDS MARINE CENTER
YOUR HOME PORT IN THE SAN JUANS

100 SLIP MODERN MARINA WITH WATER, POWER, ICE, PUMPOUT, HIGH SPEED INTERNET

MARINE PARTS • NAPA AUTO SUPPLY

FISHING TACKLE & BAIT

FULLY STOCKED CHANDLERY

PURSUIT & OCEAN SPORT DEALER

VOLVO, MERCRUISER, YAMAHA, & YANMAR

FULL SALES & SERVICE

FACTORY TRAINED SERVICE DEPARTMENT

HAULOUTS TO 25 TONS

RESTAURANTS & SHOPPING NEARBY

P.O. Box 88 • Fisherman Bay • Lopez Island, WA 98261
Phone (360)468-3377 • Fax (360)468-2283 • VHF 69
E-mail imc@rockisland.com • www.islandsmarinecenter.com
Call or Radio for Reservations

2018 WAGGONER CRUISING GUIDE

SAN JUAN ISLANDS   See Area Map Page 176 - Maps Not for Navigation

Rental kayaks are available on the beach at the Lopez Islander Resort.

haulout to 25 tons, launch ramp, repairs, fishing supplies, and a fully stocked chandlery. One view guest room available for overnight lodging. Good depth at all docks. The marina offers a 2-hour tie-up fee for boaters going to the nearby Lopez Village for shopping.

③ **Lopez Islander Resort & Marina.** P.O. Box 459, 2864 Fisherman Bay Rd., Lopez, WA 98261; (360) 468-2233; (800) 736-3434; desk@lopezfun.com; www.lopezfun.com. Monitors VHF 78A. Open all year, gasoline & diesel at the fuel dock. Guest moorage in 64 slips plus 600-foot dock. Reservations recommended on busy weekends. Services include 30 & 50 amp power, restrooms and showers, laundry, swimming pool (heated June through September), year-round Jacuzzi, free Wi-Fi in the lodge. The seasonal dock store has ice, beer, wine, and bait, along with basics like milk, eggs, cheese, and snacks. Nearby bicycle and kayak rentals.

The resort has a good restaurant with an outdoor deck and sports lounge, a workout facility, a spa, massage, camping, and water-view lodging by reservation. Live music in the Tiki Bar most weekends June through September. The docks are solid, and the management is attentive. Shuttle service available for a fee.

Odlin Park. 350 Court St. #8, Friday Harbor, WA 98250; (360) 378-8420; parks@sanjuanco.com. sanjuanco.com/495/Lopez-Island. West side of Lopez Island. Located between Flat Point and Upright Head. Open all year. Good bottom for anchoring, but exposed to northwest winds. Five mooring buoys are available, a nightly use fee is payable at the park office, located up the road past the baseball field. Small float for boats 30 feet and under with a 2-hour limit, or take your small craft ashore. Campsites, restrooms. Beach area and sea wall, baseball diamond, picnic sites, cooking shelter, fire pits.

Upright Channel Park. Northwest side of Lopez Island. Day use only. Restrooms, 4 picnic sites, no other facilities.

④ **Mackaye Harbor.** Mackaye Harbor and Barlow Bay at the south end of Lopez Island are a good overnight anchorage for boats planning an early morning crossing of the Strait of Juan de Fuca. Swells from a westerly wind can make their way into the harbor.

A county dock/boat launch is located at the northeast end of Mackaye Harbor. The Southend General Store & Restaurant (360) 468-2315 is located a half mile away. The restaurant is open for lunch and dinner noon to 8:00 p.m., Wednesday through Saturday. The well-stocked grocery includes a collection of local foods, art and jewelry. Docks and mooring buoys in Barlow Bay are private. Dinghy or kayak ashore at Mackaye Harbor.

Dangerous wreck: A sunken boat is on the east side of the entry to Barlow Bay, approximately at the 2 fathoms, 5 feet sounding on Chart 18429. The wreck is visible at low tide. Mackaye Harbor is the site of a fish boat marina, and during the summer months a large fish boat fleet can be found in the harbor.

Iceberg Island. An undeveloped state park in outer Mackaye Harbor. Open all year, day use only. Anchor out. No facilities, no fires, no overnight camping. Pack out all garbage. Do not disturb wildlife or alter the surroundings.

Aleck Bay. Aleck Bay is not particularly scenic, but it is big and easy to get into. Anchor close to the head of the bay in 30 to 36 feet.

Hughes Bay. Hughes Bay is exposed, but Contributing Editor Tom Kincaid has anchored overnight as far into the bay as he could get and still have swinging room.

McArdle Bay. McArdle Bay provides good anchorage in 24 to 30 feet, but is completely exposed to southerly winds coming off the Strait of Juan de Fuca. Lovely homes are on the hills above the bay. Just outside, the chart shows a rock in the passage between Blind Island and Lopez Island. The rock is actually a reef.

Castle Island. Castle Island is part of the San Juan Islands National Wildlife Refuge. Boats must stay 200 yards from shore to protect wildlife; no shore access.

Watmough Bay. A beautiful high sheer rock wall is on the north side of Watmough Bay.

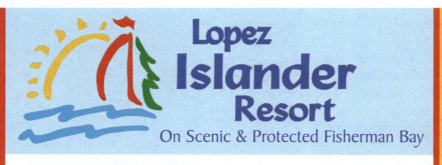

Lopez Islander Resort
On Scenic & Protected Fisherman Bay

Excellent Guest Moorage
Island Restaurant & Lounge
New Pool, Jacuzzi & Boater's Showers

- Weekly live music
- Gas, diesel, power & water
- Adjacent pumpout facilities
- Dock store
- Laundry facilities
- On island golf
- Bicycle & Kayak rentals
- Workout facilities & spa
- Village grocery & liquor store
- Water view hotel lodging

Lopez Islander Resort
Ch. 78A
(360) 468-2233
www.LopezFun.com

See Area Map Page 176 - Maps Not for Navigation   SAN JUAN ISLANDS

The chart shows the bottom as rocky, but we have found excellent holding in blue mud in 12 to 18 feet about halfway in. Three public mooring buoys are for boats 45 feet and under. They are free to use for up to 72 hours. The bay looks sheltered from southerly weather, but we've found waves work their way into the bay.

A pretty trail leads back through the woods from the head of the bay. A short but steep trail leads to the top of Chadwick Hill. The head of the bay and the trails are part of a San Juan County Land Bank preserve, made possible by donations from private citizens.

LOCAL KNOWLEDGE

TIDE-RIP: Nasty tide-rips can form off the eastern entrance to Peavine and Obstruction Passes when the wind is blowing from the south and the tide is ebbing.

Stop at Blakely Island for a fresh donut and fuel. Fuel self-pay station is at the top of the ramp.

Obstruction Pass and Peavine Pass. Obstruction Pass runs between Obstruction Island and Orcas Island. Peavine Pass runs between Obstruction Island and Blakely Island. Both passes connect the inner San Juan Islands to Rosario Strait. Currents run to 6.5 knots, and can make these passes challenging. Peavine Pass is preferred, but be alert for occasional ferry traffic. The ferries usually use Thatcher Pass. Peavine Pass is their storm route, although sometimes it is used in fair weather as well.

Blakely Island. Blakely Island is east of Lopez Island and Shaw Island. Both Blakely Island and tiny Armitage Island off the southeast corner of Blakely Island are privately owned, with no shore access. Anchorage is possible in Thatcher Bay, and, with care, behind Armitage Island. The Blakely Island Store & Marina, at the north end of Blakely Island, has guest moorage. Blakely Island is private, including the roads. Please confine your stays to the marina property.

⑤ **Blakely Island Store & Marina.** #1 Marina Dr., Blakely Island, WA 98222; (360) 375-6121; blakelyislandmarina@gmail.com. Monitors VHF 66A. Moorage in 12 guest slips and in permanent slips as available. Phone or email reservations a must. Fuel dock has gasoline and diesel, with a kiosk for self-serve credit card purchases from 6 a.m. to 8 p.m. Facilities include excellent concrete docks, 30 amp power, Wi-Fi, water, restrooms, showers, laundry and covered picnic area.

The store is open from June until mid-September. It serves dinner on Friday, and breakfast and deli lunch daily. Fresh donuts, made on site, are available in the morning. Beer on tap. They also carry a good selection of books and some gift items.

The channel leading to the boat basin is shallow, and may restrict deep draft vessels at the bottom of a very low tide. Other than those conditions, you should have plenty of water. If in doubt, call the marina office for guidance.

Shaw Island. The marina is adjacent to the Shaw Island ferry terminal. Resident boats occupy most of the dock space. Maximum length for short term guest moorage is 25 feet, call ahead at the Shaw General Store. It's better to anchor in Blind Bay and take the dinghy over. Tie up in a place that doesn't block a permanent boat. Wakes make their way into the moorage, either from the ferries or from boat traffic in the channel. Consider this when tying up to the dock.

Safety note: *Do not under any circumstances run the dinghy under the bow of a ferry tied up at the landing.*

LOCAL KNOWLEDGE

DANGEROUS ROCKS: Charted rocks obstruct the waters west of Blind Island. While

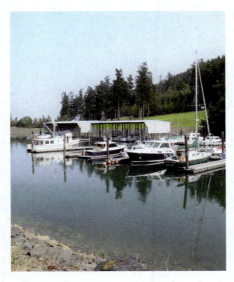
Protected guest moorage at Blakely Island Marina is tucked behind the store, accessed through a narrow passage near the fuel dock.

Blakely Island Marina

2018 Waggoner Cruising Guide   181

SAN JUAN ISLANDS

it's possible to get through safely, our advice is do not pass west of Blind Island.

Blind Bay/Blind Island Marine State Park. Blind Bay, on the north side of Shaw Island, has good anchorage throughout the center portion. Blind Island is a minimally developed state park and Cascadia Marine Trail campsite, with 4 mooring buoys on its south side for boats 45 feet and under. Self-register and pay nightly mooring buoy fee on shore at Blind Island. Toilets are on the island. Pack out all garbage.

East of Blind Island a white daymark, installed and maintained by Bellingham Yacht Club since the 1950s, marks a rock that lies between Blind Island and the Shaw Island shore. Enter Blind Bay midway between that mark and Blind Island. The water shoals abruptly as you enter, but there's no danger unless you are close to the island. Several rocks are just under the surface on the west side of Blind Island. Transit should not be attempted on the west side without local knowledge.

⑥ **Shaw General Store.** P.O. Box 455, Shaw Island, WA 98286; (360) 468-2288; www.shawgeneralstore.com. Open 7 days a week in summer, closed in winter. Very limited short-term, day-use guest moorage, maximum 25 feet, call ahead. Groceries, beer and wine, ice, gift items, soup, sandwiches, ice cream cones in summer, local organic produce, and coffee roasted in-house. The back area of the store is a coffee shop. Restrooms adjacent to the ferry dock.

You'll enjoy anchoring in Blind Bay and taking the dinghy over to meet Steve and Terri Mason, who have owned the store for 15 years. The store was built in 1924. It's as charming as can be, with its straight-grain wood floors, old shelving and displays, and posters and signs from days gone by. The store is a local hangout for Shaw Island residents.

Parks Bay. Parks Bay is a fine anchorage, but you can't go ashore. Except for three privately-owned parcels at the north end and a single parcel at the south end, the land surrounding Parks Bay is owned by the University of Washington as a biological preserve, and is off limits to visitors. Stub pilings are at the closed end, but there is plenty of anchoring room, mud bottom, throughout the bay. Parks Bay Island, at the mouth of the bay, is no longer a state park.

Hicks Bay. Hicks Bay has good anchorage, although it is exposed to southerlies. When entering, take care to avoid a reef extending from the southern shore.

Indian Cove. Indian Cove, a popular anchorage area has a big open feeling. Somewhat protected from southerlies by nearby Lopez Island and Canoe Island. Watch for drying rocks between Canoe Island and Shaw Island, and a shoal 200 yards west of the southern point of Canoe Island. The Shaw Island County Park, with launch ramp, has an excellent beach.

Shaw General Store next to the Shaw Island ferry landing serves ice cream, sandwiches and more.

Blind Island and Shaw Island

BE WHALE WISE

One of the best parts of cruising in the Northwest is the opportunity to see whales, including humpback, minke, and occasionally gray. "Whales" in regards to orcas is actually a misnomer: so called "killer whales" are, in fact, the largest members of the dolphin family.

This story is all about respectful whale and orca viewing.

As a cruiser, I've watched whales from our own boat. As a professional captain, I've run whale watch boats for San Juan Safaris in Friday Harbor and San Juan Outfitters in Roche Harbor. As you might imagine, boaters have a lot of questions about viewing these magnificent animals.

Where are the whales? If I could answer that question with absolute certainty, I'd be buying lottery tickets. The Southern Resident Killer Whales, common to this area, are always on the move. No, they aren't always on the west side of San Juan Island. They can (and do) travel 70 to 100 miles per day searching for food. Their primary diet is salmon. Transient orcas are mammal-eaters.

When looking for whales, I follow the food. The "residents" (J, K & L Pods) are not always "in residence" in the San Juan Islands. If their food source is elsewhere, so are they.

No, whales are not "tracked." No radio transmitters, no spotting planes. As a professional whale watch operation, our company belongs to the Pacific Whale Watch Association. Members work together to find the whales. We report sightings and locations among our members. The captains are cooperative and work together to ensure guests on all member whale watch boats have the opportunity to view whales.

It's tacky to ask a professional whale watch captain, "Where are the whales?" If you want to utilize their knowledge, buy a ticket on a whale watch boat. The naturalists on our boats can explain the behavior you are viewing and answer questions, making the trip educational as well as entertaining. The captains position the boats for best viewing.

How close can we get to the whales? This is the most asked question when guests first board our boats. And, from what I see on a daily basis, many boaters are unfamiliar with laws governing operating near whales. Orcas are endangered and protected. Distance regulations are not suggestions. Violate them and you may be boarded by law enforcement, usually NOAA, Washington Department of Fish and Wildlife (WDFW), or the San Juan County Sheriff's Department.

The three resident pods collectively have fewer than 85 whales. Enforcement is a serious matter. The boating and whale watch businesses in the Pacific Northwest, and many local economies, depend on whale watching. We all want these animals around for future generations to see.

With that in mind, this graphic illustrates how close boats can get to whales. Laterally, vessels can approach no closer than 200 yards. Often, the whales are moving, and professional whale watch boats move along with them, always mindful of that 200-yard distance. That's two football fields. Binoculars are your friend.

Most professional captains use rangefinders to ensure they maintain 200 yards of separation. If you aren't a good judge of distance, follow the lead of the professional operators, and stay at least as far away as they do.

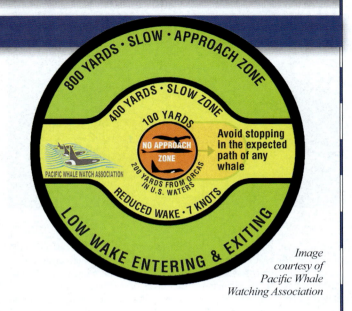

Image courtesy of Pacific Whale Watching Association

No, you aren't allowed to "get ahead of the whales and shut down," with the idea that they will come to you. The law requires vessels give 400 yards of clearance in front of the whales, and vessels may not impede their progress.

Some of my fishing friends have questioned whether they have to move when they have lines in the water and they see whales moving towards them. I quote the, "200 yards laterally, 400 yards in front of" law. In the eyes of the law, a recreational boat with lines in the water is not a fishing vessel. Interpret that any way you want, but understand that if you are closer than the law allows, you may be cited and fined. I don't take the chance; my captain's license could be jeopardized, fines can be steep, and it's important to respect wildlife.

Despite the regulations, we see boaters run too close to whales almost every day during summer. Bad behavior is reported. If violators are lucky, they may just get an educational visit from the Sound Watch boat (or the Canadian equivalent, Strait Watch). If they're not lucky, they may get an expensive visit from NOAA or WDFW. Learn the rules, follow the rules. The laws apply to all, whether you are a professional captain, a private boater (sail or power), or a kayaker.

Speed limits are also enforced. When within half a mile of whales, keep your speed to 7 knots or less. Have you seen someone speed right up to the whales? Yep, that's illegal. Don't be that guy.

In Canadian waters vessels must maintain 100 yards of separation.

What if the whales come up too close to me? Whales don't get the same memo we do. Sometimes they'll be running a straight course, then dive and change course.

The following is a recommendation, not the law. If whales surface unexpectedly within 100 to 200 yards, try to slowly move away perpendicularly to the whales' direction of travel. If they're within 100 yards, shut down until the whales are a safe distance away, then slowly move away. Even if the incident was not intentional, you can be cited.

Seeing these mammals is breathtaking. You may see them milling or feeding, resting or on a hunt. You might see a calf learning new skills. If the timing is right, you may see a breach. Or two—they often breach a second time, so keep the camera ready.

Enjoy the whale viewing, but be whale wise.

– Captain Jim Bathurst

Be Whale Wise. Related info may be found at:
http://wdfw.wa.gov/conservation/orca/
http://www.bewhalewise.org/new-regulations/

SAN JUAN ISLANDS

See Area Map Page 176 - Maps Not for Navigation

Anchoring at Turn Island can be tricky due to strong currents. Several mooring buoys provide an alternative.

Picnic Cove. Picnic Cove is immediately east of Indian Cove. It's a pretty little nook with room for a couple boats. A mid-channel entrance is best, to avoid reefs on each side of the cove. The head of the cove shoals to drying flats. Anchor in 20 to 25 feet. The mooring buoys in the cove are private.

SAN JUAN ISLAND

San Juan Island is the second largest of the San Juan Islands, and has the largest population. Friday Harbor, the only incorporated town, is the seat of county government.

Cattle Pass. Cattle Pass is the local name for the narrow channel between the south end of San Juan Island and Lopez Island. It is the only southern entrance to the San Juan Islands, and connects with San Juan Channel. Whale Rocks lie just south of Cattle Pass. It's easy to get close to them if you're not careful. When we enter Cattle Pass from the south, we try to favor gong Buoy 3, marking Salmon Bank, to port, and make a course for the middle of the entrance. This avoids Whale Rocks.

After we clear Cattle Pass northbound, we've felt a definite tendency to favor the Lopez Island shore. Maybe it's just us. In any case, this course leads dangerously close to *Shark Reef*, about one-half mile north of Cattle Pass. We recommend sagging west a little toward Griffin Bay until past Shark Reef.

Tidal currents can run strongly through Cattle Pass, and the waters can be turbulent with rips and eddies. Watch out for a big ebb current flowing out of San Juan Channel against a fresh westerly wind in the Strait of Juan de Fuca. We've seen this ebb current as much as a mile outside Cattle Pass. Against a fresh westerly it will create high, steep seas, the kind you definitely want to avoid. Current predictions are shown under San Juan Channel in the tide & current books.

In Cattle Pass, it's possible to run behind Goose Island and avoid foul current, but local knowledge is called for.

Fish Creek. Fish Creek is a tiny indentation near the southern tip of San Juan Island, lined with the docks and mooring buoys of the homes along its shores. Fish Creek has no public facilities, and swinging room is very restricted between the homeowners' floats.

Griffin Bay. You can anchor in several places in Griffin Bay. A stretch of beach inshore from Halftide Rocks is Griffin Bay Park, a public campground. American Camp, maintained by the U.S. Park Service as an historical monument to the 1859-72 Pig War, is a short walk from the campground. The Pig War resulted in setting the boundary between the U.S. and Canada in Haro Strait, keeping the San Juan Islands in the U.S.

Griffin Bay Park. Next to American Camp. Open all year. Toilets, no other facilities. Four campsites and a picnic area. Two inland campsites are exclusively for boaters arriving by human- or wind-powered watercraft. Vessels with motors are not allowed to moor at the park overnight. Watch for shallow water and pilings.

Unnamed Island #119. Griffin Bay, south of Dinner Island. This island is part of the San Juan Islands National Wildlife Refuge. Boats must stay 200 yards from shore; no shore access.

⑦ **Turn Island State Park.** (360) 376-2073; In San Juan Channel, at the southeast entrance to Friday Harbor. Turn Island is open all year for day use and overnight mooring. Boat access only; *land only on the west or southwest beach*. Pets are not permitted on shore. Outhouse and campsites. No fires. Pack out all garbage. Hiking, fishing, crabbing.

Turn Island is a beautiful park, completely wooded, with many trails. It's a popular stop for kayaks and beachable boats. Along the south side of the island the trees (madrona, cedar, hemlock, cypress) are bent and twisted, with much evidence of blowdown. The wind must howl though here in the winter.

Three mooring buoys, for boats 45 feet and under, are placed along the west side, at the mouth of the pass separating Turn Island from San Juan Island. Currents can be quite strong in this pass, but these buoys are located safely out of the current. If you anchor to seaward of them you will be in the current. We recommend the buoys. Self-register and pay nightly mooring buoy fee on shore.

Friday Harbor

184

www.WaggonerGuide.com

Friday Harbor Seafood, on a float at the Port of Friday Harbor

Correspondents James and Jennifer Hamilton have anchored off the southwest tip of Turn Island in about 10 feet of depth at zero tide. Although the current ran noticeably, the anchor held perfectly. Other boats, anchored farther out and closer to the eastern mouth of the pass, appeared to have less current.

Turn Island is part of the San Juan Islands National Wildlife Refuge. Do not disturb animals in their natural habitat.

⑧ **Friday Harbor.** www.fridayharbor.org. Friday Harbor is the government and commercial center of the San Juan Islands. It is a U.S. Customs port of entry, and the terminal for ferries from Anacortes that also serve Sidney, B.C. The town swells with tourists during the summer months and has many boutiques, shops, galleries, restaurants and pubs to serve them. The post office is close to the marina. King's Market, a well stocked grocery store, is on the main street (Spring Street) two blocks up from the waterfront. They will drive you back to the marina with a sizable purchase.

Kenmore Air flies in from Lake Union and Boeing Field in Seattle, with a shuttle to Sea-Tac Airport. NW Seaplanes flies in from their location on south Lake Washington in Renton. Check their websites for seasonal schedules.

Moor at the Port of Friday Harbor marina or anchor out. Anchorage is good in the cove north of the marina, and behind Brown (Friday) Island. Do not anchor in the cable-pipeline area between San Juan Island and Brown Island. Our friend John Mifflin cautions that the water close to Brown Island contains several sunken wrecks, "requiring diver assistance when raising anchor."

Enter Friday Harbor around either end of Brown Island. An unlighted daybeacon marks the end of a drying reef off the southwest corner of Brown Island. Brown Island is privately owned, and has its own dock and floats.

Take care to avoid interfering with the ferries and the large number of float planes taking off and landing in the harbor. The fuel dock is located between the Port marina and the ferry dock. The floats just south of the ferry dock are owned by the condominium apartments ashore. Jensen's Marina, at the south end of the harbor, can handle repairs. The Port marina office has a list of repair people, too. For marine supplies, stop by Friday Harbor Marine, located at 655B Mullis Street, near the airport. They also have a new craft brewery right alongside the marine supplies and boat repairs. It goes together, right? Kings Marine carries marine supplies, fishing gear and apparel. There is also a West Marine Express store about four blocks up Spring Street.

The Downriggers Restaurant is in a new building on the same site after a devastating fire destroyed the earlier historic building. Other businesses in the new building include San Juan Excursions, San Juan Safaris, and the Rip Tide Cafe.

Bus transportation: San Juan Transit, next to the ferry landing, has scheduled service and tours all around San Juan Island; www.sanjuantransit.com; (360) 378-8887.

Taxi: Classic Cab, (360) 378-7519; Bob's Taxi, (360) 378-6777; Friday Harbor Taxi, (360) 298-4434; Rhodes Trips Taxi & Tours, (360) 298-6975; San Juan Taxi, (360) 378-8294.

Mopeds: Susie's Mopeds (800) 532-0087 (cars, mopeds, ScootCoupes).

Bicycles: Island Bicycles Transportation (360) 378-4941.

Trolley: Friday Harbor Jolly Trolley Transportation (360) 298-8873. Offers guided rides to island attractions with hop on/hop off all-day passes.

Golf: San Juan Golf & CC, 9 interesting holes with separate tee boxes for 18, par 71, is a short taxi ride away; (360) 378-2254.

Summer concerts: Live music Sundays at 2:00 p.m. and Fridays 5:00 p.m. to 7:00 p.m. July and August in the small park next to the marina.

Farmers market: San Juan Farmers Market Saturdays 10:00 a.m. to 1:00 p.m. mid-April through mid-October in the Brickhouse Plaza, 150 Nichols St., about 5 minutes from the marina.

Things to Do

1. **The Whale Museum.** In Friday Harbor. Learn about orca whales that frequent the San Juan Islands.

2. **Lime Kiln Point State Park.** Watch for whales that often cruise by this park.

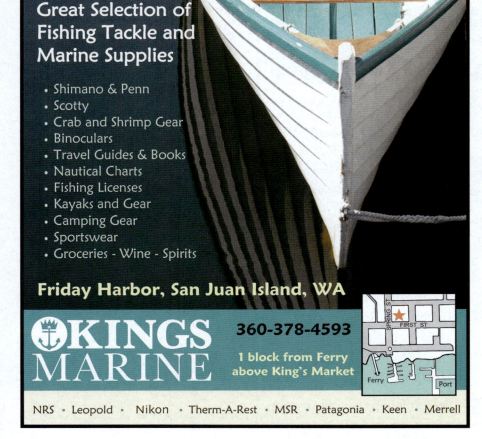

SAN JUAN ISLANDS

See Area Map Page 176 - Maps Not for Navigation

Spring Street in Friday Harbor is lined with shops and restaurants. Photo by Michael Bertrand.

One of many good eats in Friday Harbor, ranging from breweries to fine dining to ice cream worth standing in line for

3. **Tastings.** San Juan Vineyards has a tasting room near Friday Harbor. San Juan Island Distillery, with a variety of apple-based spirits, has a tasting room within walking distance of Roche Harbor.

4. **Westcott Bay Sculpture Park.** More than 100 superb sculptures in iron, bronze, stone and wood displayed in a 20-acre park near Roche Harbor.

5. **Pelindaba Lavender Farms.** Walk through fields of purple lavender and shop for all things lavender.

6. **San Juan Golf Course.** Attractive 9 hole par 71 course, with tee boxes for 18 holes.

7. **Saturday Farmers Market.** Fresh vegetables, flowers, plants, honey and more at the Brickworks in Friday Harbor.

8. **English Camp.** See the gardens, hike the trails, learn the history. In Garrison Bay near Roche Harbor.

9. **Roche Harbor Mausoleum.** Walk from Roche Harbor resort to this beautiful setting steeped in mythology.

10. **Blackberries.** In late summer they are everywhere, big, tasty, and free.

11. **Krystal Acres Alpaca Farm.** See alpacas and learn what they can be used for.

12. **Susie's Mopeds.** Rent mopeds or electric bicycles. Rental office in Friday Harbor 360-378-5244.

13. The "**Retirement of the Colors**" ceremony at Roche Harbor at sunset is unforgettable.

14. **Friday Harbor Seafood.** Fresh shrimp, oysters, crab, or fish for sale on the main dock.

15. **Shuttle Bus Tour.** Regular schedule in the summer. Ride the bus, getting on and off at locations such as the lavender farm, Lime Kiln Point, and English Camp.

⑧ **Port of Friday Harbor.** P.O. Box 889, 204 Front Street, Friday Harbor, WA 98250; (360) 378-2688; tamih@portfridayharbor.org; www.portfridayharbor.org. Monitors VHF66A. Certified Clean Marina. Open all year, gasoline and diesel at the fuel dock. Side-tie guest moorage along 1500 feet of dock, plus moorage on the guest dock and in unoccupied slips. Reservations accepted. Only 30% of the transient space is available for reservations; 70% is first-come, first-served. If reservations are full, space may be available on the day you arrive.

The slips handle boats to 44 feet. Longer boats (to 200 feet) side-tie along the breakwaters (see marina diagram). Breakwater A has no power or water. Marina services include 120-volt 30 & 50 amp power, 240-volt 50 amp power, and some 240-volt 100 amp power, free Wi-Fi, newly renovated restrooms and showers, excellent laundry, garbage and recycling drop. Seasonally, the Pumpty Dumpty pumpout service is available to come to your boat for a small charge, or you can use the self-serve pumpout carts. An ADA-compliant ramp connects the wharf above with the floats and slips below. A floating restroom is on the long float leading to guest moorage, dock G. A covered activity barge is available for groups or rendezvous. Ten or more vessels earn a group moorage discount. Individual boats staying four nights get a fifth night free from September 15 to June 15. Check the Port's website for seasonal specials and events.

If you do not have reservations, call on VHF 66A for a moorage assignment, but wait until you are within sight of the marina before calling. In the summer, a slip assignment station is staffed at the end of Breakwater A. A dinghy

REPAIR SERVICES
After Hours & Weekends
Mercury Authorized
ABYC & NMEA Cert
Diesel & Gasoline
Cooling & Fuel
Starting and Charging
Diesel Fuel Polishing

PARTS- SUPPLIES
4 Hour Parts Service
Start/House Batteries
Impellers & Pumps
Inverters & Chargers
Oil and Fuel Filters
NMEA Networks
Hobie Mirage Kayaks

665 B Mullis St   360-378-6202   fridayharbormarine.com

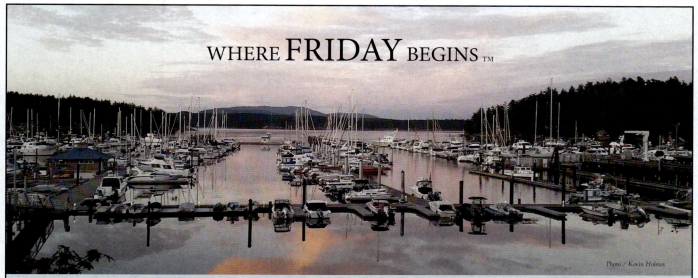

WHERE FRIDAY BEGINS ™

Photo / Kevin Holmes

Escape the hustle and bustle of the mainland and consider the jewel-like cluster of the San Juan Islands! Explore the natural beauty of pristine beaches and hiking trails. Enjoy wildlife and eco-tours, with knowledgeable nature guides. Go fishing from kayaks, charter boats or... simply relax and enjoy the scenery! Keep in mind we're the convenient transportation hub to British Columbia, Bellingham, Anacortes, Port Townsend and Seattle!

PORT OF FRIDAY HARBOR

Post Office Box 889 • Friday Harbor, WA 98250
VHF66A • 360-378-2688 • Fax: 360-378-6114
www.portfridayharbor.org

HOW YOU CAN HELP THE ORCAS

The diversity and complexity of marine life in the coastal waters off of British Columbia and Washington are truly extraordinary. Seeing killer whales and other marine wildlife in their natural environment is a magnificent experience. Killer whales, also known as orcas, are an icon of the Pacific Northwest.

Southern Resident killer whales (SRKW) are classified as an endangered species by the U.S. and Canadian federal governments and by Washington State. Vessel disturbance and sound are contributing factors in the population's decline. Other threats identified are reduced quantity and quality of prey, persistent pollutants that cause immune or reproductive system dysfunction, and oil spills.

There are three ecotypes of killer whales on the West Coast of North America: resident killer whales (Alaskan, Northern and Southern Resident killer whales; fish-eaters, predominantly salmon); transient killer whales, also known as Biggs killer whales (feed on marine mammals like seals, sea lions, whales, dolphins, and porpoise); and offshore killer whales (feed on fish, squid, and maybe sharks).

Give whales space. Admiring whales from a distance is the safest and most responsible way to view them in their natural habitat. They are wild, unpredictable animals that can move surprisingly fast. Many boaters believe if they shut down their engine, they then reduce the disturbance to the whales if they are within 200 yards. If you are not able to remain in compliance with the 200-yard rule, it is advised to place your engine in neutral. If needed, put your engine in gear to slowly and carefully maneuver out of the path of whales. It is suggested to reduce speed to less than 7 knots when within 400 yards of the nearest marine mammal to reduce your engine's noise and vessel's wake. Another key guideline is to remain on the offshore side of whales when they are traveling close to shore. Too many times, vessels have been observed altering the course of whales because the vessel is blocking the path to a nearby seal haul-out or interrupting a salmon chase where the shoreline is used to assist in foraging. How many obstacles (vessels) might a whale have to avoid and potentially risk losing their prey, or interfere with important foraging strategies lessons for younger whales.

Research vessels are exempt from designated regulations. If you observe a vessel in close proximity to the whales, look for a yellow pennant (triangle flag) which identifies the vessel as a National Marine Fisheries Service (NMFS) permitted research organization. Please do not interfere with the research being conducted. Keep a lookout out for Soundwatch or Straightwatch (Boater Education vessels). During the summer season, both groups standby on VHF 16. You can contact them for detailed information on the behavior and travel patterns of the whales.

There are many ways you can contribute to minimize your impact and to improve our understanding of marine mammals. Some suggestions are:

1) Be current on regulations and guidelines,

2) Report wildlife sightings,

3) Report stranded or entangled animals, and

4) Report violators.

Sadie Youngstrom

Note: For contact phone numbers, see Chapter 1

SAN JUAN ISLAND MARKETPLACE

RESTAURANTS, SHOPS & SERVICES

ACE HARDWARE
Ace Hardware of Anacortes AND Friday Harbor is your locally owned and operated hardware store, specializing in marine hardware, stainless fasteners, electrical, Craftsman Tools, fishing licenses, tackle, bait, rain gear and all your hardware needs.
360-293-3535 • 1720 Q Avenue, Anacortes, WA 98221
360-378-4622 • 340 Argyle Ave, Friday Harbor, WA 98250
www.AceAnacortes.com

BACKDOOR KITCHEN
We serve high-quality international food and drink in a unique and tranquil atmosphere. We utilize only the freshest ingredients, use local farms when possible, and prepare all our dishes from scratch. Join us for dinner or drinks in our cozy bar, dining room or heated patio. While only two blocks from the ferry landing, we're a little hard to find – but well worth the trouble. Just ask a local!
360-378-9540 • 400b "A" Street, Friday Harbor, WA
www.backdoorkitchen.com

THE GOURMET'S GALLEY
Since 1969 a favorite source of rare ingredients for the adventurous cook. Proper teas, teapots, and kettles. Quality tools for the serious chef. Whimsical gifts with food and marine themes.
Monday-Saturday 10 - 5:30.
360-378-2251 • 21 Spring Street, PO Box 578

KING'S MARINE CENTER
Best selection for your outdoor adventure gear. Everything from fishing gear, kayak accessories, marine supplies and camping gear to sportswear, shoes & boots, sunglasses, books and more.
360-378-4593 • 110 Spring St. W • Above King's Market

LAVENDERA MASSAGE
Rest, renew, revitalize with a smoothing massage: Therapeutic, relaxation, combo, hot stone, couples, prenatal massage. Prices: 60 min $95, 75 min $120, 90 min $135. *Clothed massage and chair massage $1 per minute.* Body wrap, body exfoliation, foot therapy, and energy work also available. Call or email to book, go to our website for more info.
360-378-3637 • 285 Spring Street, Friday Harbor, WA 98250 info@lavenderamassage.com
www.lavenderamassage.com

SAN JUAN ISLANDS MUSEUM OF ART
The museum is committed to promoting the arts of the Pacific Northwest and Southwest British Columbia. We offer rotating exhibitions through our three galleries, with approximately 8-10 exhibitions per year, as well as a lecture series titled Art as a Voice.
360.370.5050 • 540 Spring St. www.sjima.org

SUSIE'S MOPEDS
Explore San Juan Island at your leisure with an electric bike, moped, Scoot Coupe, or car. Let our professional and friendly staff help plan your island adventure which includes plenty of spectacular scenic stops. Hourly and daily rates. An island tradition since 1986. Reservations suggested.
360-378-5244 • At the Ferry Landing
www.susiesmopeds.com

WHALE MUSEUM
Be Whale Wise! Founded in 1979, The Whale Museum in Friday Harbor is a natural history museum. Our mission is to promote stewardship of whales and the Salish Sea ecosystem through education and research programs. Come learn about the endangered Southern Resident Orcas and other marine mammals. Find the perfect gift or adopt an orca.
360-378-4710 ext. 30 • 62 First St. N.
www.whalemuseum.org

SAN JUAN ISLAND COMMUNITY EVENTS

April
Island-wide Earth Day clean ups

May
National Historic Preservation Month
Opening Day Boat Parade, Friday Harbor
Memorial Day Parade & Ceremony, Friday Harbor

June
San Juan Island Artists' Studio Tour
Three Lakes Triathlon & San Juan Island Marathon, Half Marathon & 10K Day
Orca Sing Annual Concert

July
July 4th Parade, Pig War Picnic, Friday Harbor
Rock the Dock dance, Fireworks, Port of Friday Harbor
Roche Harbor Old Fashioned Fourth - Games and Fireworks
San Juan Island Lavender Festival & Summer Arts Fair
San Juan Island National Historical Park Encampment
Summer Concert Series "Music in the Park" Port of Friday Harbor (July-Labor Day)
Music on the Lawn, July - August at the San Juan Historical Museum grounds

July – August
Shakespeare under the Stars

August
Shaw Island Classic Sail Boat Race, Jazz at the Labs
San Juan County Fair
Concours d'Elegance of the San Juan Islands

September
Friday Harbor Fly-In & Open House
San Juan Vineyards Harvest Festival
Savor the San Juans

October
Savor the San Juans
Friday Harbor Fall Farm Parade

November
Friday Harbor Film Festival
Artisans' Holiday Marketplace

December
Island Lights Festival – Friday Harbor
Lighted Boat Parade & Santa's Arrival – Friday Harbor
San Juan Historical Museum – Old Fashioned Christmas Celebration (not 100% sure)
Nutcracker Ballet

float and day moorage are available. Nearby haulout and repairs.

This is one of the busiest marinas in the Northwest, and the pressure on staff and facilities is enormous. To their credit, they maintain the docks, showers and restrooms quite well. Because they are so busy, when you depart it is courteous to call the marina on VHF 66A to let them know your slip is available.

Customs: U.S. Customs clearance is on Breakwater B. Tie up in the designated customs area and check in at the direct-phone kiosk on the dock. During the summer months the kiosk may be manned by a CBP agent. Occasionally customs officials will have you walk to the U.S. Customs office. The office has moved to the corner of Spring Street and First Street, about 3 blocks from the marina.

⑧ **Port of Friday Harbor Fuel Pier.** 10 Front Street, Port of Friday Harbor, Friday Harbor, WA 98250; (360) 378-3114; www.portfridayharbor.org. Between the Port of Friday Harbor marina and the ferry dock. Open 7 days a week, all year. Ethanol-free gasoline, diesel, oil, lubricants, propane, and ice.

Rocky Bay. Rocky Bay, close inshore from O'Neal Island, is a good anchorage and fairly well protected. Take care to avoid a drying shoal and a covered rock.

Roche Harbor Marina

SAN JUAN ISLANDS

See Area Map Page 176 - Maps Not for Navigation

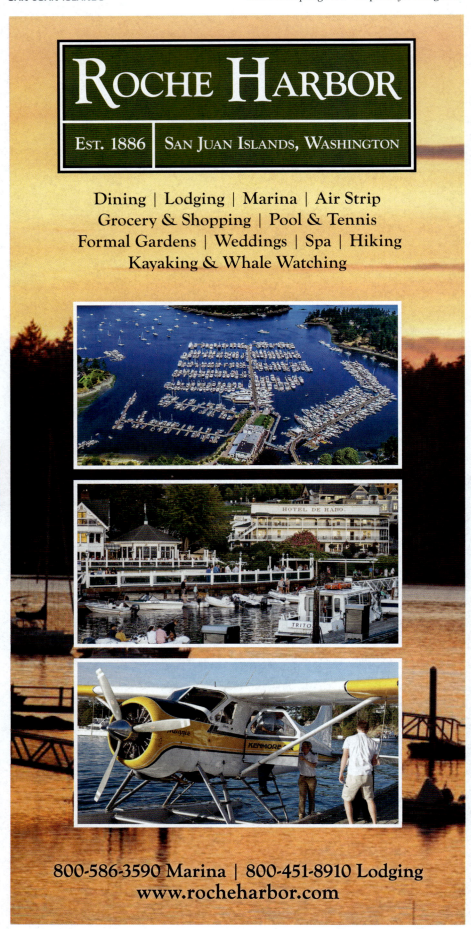

⑨ **Roche Harbor.** Roche Harbor, (pronounced Rohsh Harbor) on the northwest corner of San Juan Island, is popular, attractive, and has a number of interesting anchorages and moorages. From the north (Spieden Channel), enter Roche Harbor on the *west* side of Pearl Island. The passage east of Pearl Island is shallow, and is in line with dangerous rocks outside. From the south (Haro Strait), entry is through Mosquito Pass.

Roche Harbor is one of the busiest U.S. Customs ports of entry for boats. During the prime summer season, the floating customs office and the harbormaster's office are located on G-dock. The customs landing area on G-dock is noted with signs on the pilings. Outside of the summer months, the floating customs office and harbormaster's office are located just north of the fuel dock on the main pier below the flag pavilion. Moor between the signs only when clearing customs. On busy days, boats tend to create an informal line on the water waiting for the customs dock. Be patient. It can be a challenge to maintain a place in line among boats at anchor, especially when a good breeze kicks up. Note that the seaplane dock is near the customs dock, and arriving seaplanes will need to cut through the line of boats. One summer we watched as one of the area's large wooden sailing schooners pulled up to the dock to clear customs. The space was much too small to lie alongside. The captain commanded her crew of high school students to drop the anchor at the right time, as she turned stern-to the dock. With an audience watching, she backed down and tied off, stern-to. She placed a 133-foot vessel into less than 20 feet of dock space.

Note: During the winter, early spring, and late fall months the customs and harbor offices are floated inshore to the dock area below the ramp to the main dock. The customs landing area is designated across from the customs office. In winter, approach as though you are going to the fuel dock. The customs dock is to starboard, marked with signs, just below the ramp. *Note:* Once tied to the dock, all crew must stay on the boat until cleared. The U.S. Customs agents are particular about procedure here.

Many boats anchor in Roche Harbor, but we've heard of anchors dragging in strong winds. Check your set and use ample scope. Anchorage is also possible in Open Bay on Henry Island, although it is exposed to southerly winds.

Bus transportation: San Juan Transit has scheduled service to Friday Harbor and all around San Juan Island. The pick-up area is on the road across from the Roche Harbor store. Call (360) 378-8887; www.sanjuantransit.com.

⑨ **Roche Harbor Marina.** P.O. Box 4001, Roche Harbor, WA 98250; (800) 586-3590; (360) 378-2155; marina@rocheharbor.com; www.rocheharbor.com. Monitors VHF 78A. Open all year, up to 250 guest slips, including moorage for boats to 150 feet. Call ahead for reservations. They work to fit everyone in, even on busy holidays. Last-minute holiday moorage may mean Med-tying stern-to on the cross docks. The dock crew provides plenty of help.

SAN JUAN ISLANDS

A view of the gardens, blockhouse, and dinghy dock at English Camp National Historical Park.

Ethanol-free gasoline and diesel at the fuel dock, open 9:00 a.m. to 6:00 p.m. Services include 30, 50, and some 100 amp power (ELCI-protected power on some docks), restrooms, showers, laundry, portapotty dump, propane, and free Wi-Fi (best reception is in the hotel lobby). Pumpout is at the north end of the fuel dock, or call for the "Phecal Freak," for a courtesy pumpout at your slip. Their motto: "We take crap from anyone." Tips are appreciated. The moorage fee includes water, power, pumpout, trash disposal, and use of the pool and resort facilities. Excellent management. When we visited at the end of a busy day at the end of summer, we found all the facilities, including the showers, to be clean and in good condition.

This is one of the most popular spots in the islands, and in our opinion is a must-see destination. The historic Hotel de Haro, the heated swimming pool, formal gardens, tennis courts, Afterglow Spa, well-stocked grocery store, gift shops, and excellent restaurant and lounge are something apart from the usual tourist fare. An informal café also is available. Try the Roche Harbor donuts at the café, made fresh each morning.

Be sure to take a walk up to the Afterglow Vista Mausoleum. You've never seen anything like it. Another good walk is up the small mountain behind the resort, past the limestone quarries, to a lookout. The trail is easy and well-maintained, and the view is excellent. The entire loop took us approximately a half-hour. If we had stopped to smell the flowers it would have taken an hour. The hotel lobby has complimentary walking tour maps. For $1.00 they also have a pamphlet detailing the remarkable history of Roche Harbor. See the guest registry on display, and the pictures on the wall showing the history of Roche Harbor.

The Westcott Bay Sculpture Park is on the edge of the Roche Harbor property, across the road from the airstrip. The park is a display of outdoor sculpture—approximately 100 pieces—set in a large grassy field and along several trails through the woods. This description completely understates how impressive the display is. We spent an hour in the park and should have spent three more hours. It's magnificent. The pieces are first-rate and the setting works.

Major development continues on the hillside up from the hotel. Great effort has been made to design the new construction in keeping with the classic century-old style of the existing buildings. Many of the units are available for overnight or longer stays. Contact Roche Harbor Lodging at www.rocheharbor.com. The Afterglow Spa offers massage and other treatments for the crew. Advance reservations recommended.

A lovely bell concert rings out from the church at 9:00 a.m., noon, and late afternoon. At sundown each evening during the summer season the marina conducts a formal retirement of the colors. The Roche Harbor flag is lowered, followed by the British flag to "God Save the Queen," and the Canadian flag to "O Canada." Then the cannon fires—BOOM!—and the U.S. flag is lowered to "Taps." Against a fiery sunset backdrop the ceremony is inspiring. It puts a lump in our throat.

Dinghy docks: Dinghy docks are at the bottom of the ramp to the main wharf, or to port just past the fuel dock.

Bus transportation: San Juan Transit has scheduled service all around San Juan Island, with regular stops at Roche Harbor. Guests can take the shuttle from the ferry landing in Friday Harbor to Roche Harbor; www.sanjuantransit.com; (360) 378-8887.

Mopeds: Susie's Mopeds is near the airstrip; www.susiesmopeds.com; (360) 378-6262.

Posey Island Marine State Park. www.parks.wa.gov. North of Roche Harbor. Day use and overnight mooring and camping. Pit toilet, no other facilities. Cascadia Marine Trail campsite (primitive). The island is less than 1 acre in size. Water surrounding the island is shallow. Motorized vessels are not permitted; anchor out and row in. Great sunset views on the west side.

Mosquito Pass. Mosquito Pass connects Roche Harbor to Haro Strait, and provides access to Westcott Bay and Garrison Bay. The flood current sets north in Mosquito Pass and the ebb sets south, out of Roche Harbor. Currents can be strong at times. The channel is narrow but well-marked. Navigate carefully. See Mosquito Pass Route map.

Westcott Bay. Westcott Bay has good anchorage, but is partly taken up with a shellfish culture business. Although the bay is shallow, adequate anchoring depths can be found throughout. The beach has excellent clamming.

Westcott Bay Shellfish Co. (360) 378-2489). Located on the southeast shore of Westcott Bay, open daily in the summer months 11:00 a.m. to 5:00 p.m. from Memorial Day weekend through Labor Day. Retail shellfish sales. As time permits, staff will show you how to shuck your oysters. Local bakery bread, cheeses, and charcuterie are available for purchase from their deli to enjoy with your hand-shucked shellfish along with beer, wine, sodas or water. Picnic tables overlooking the bay complete this unique experience. Anchor in the bay; boaters are welcome to tie dinghies (bow-tie only) to the Shellfish Company's working docks to go ashore and make purchases. Barbequed oysters are available on select days. During the 1970's, Westcott Bay oysters were known in oyster bars around the world. This family-run aquaculture farm continues the legacy of providing quality oysters as well as clams and mussels.

Garrison Bay. Garrison Bay, the site of English Camp, is a popular and excellent anchorage, with room for a large number of boats.

Mosquito Pass Route

2018 WAGGONER CRUISING GUIDE — 191

SAN JUAN ISLANDS

English Camp National Historical Park. P.O. Box 429, 4668 Cattle Point Road, Friday Harbor, WA 98250; (360) 387-2240 ext. 2244; www.nps.gov. Open all year; Visitor Center open seasonally. Anchor in the bay and dinghy to the park dock. British troops were garrisoned here during the 1859-72 Pig War, and the U.S. Park Service has restored the buildings and grounds as a historical site. You can tour the grounds, some of the buildings, and the cemetery, where several people from that era are buried. Rangers are on duty to provide information, and a film tells the history. It's a good stop for families with children. Restrooms, no other facilities. A steep trail leads to the top of 650-foot-high Young Hill, for a marvelous view.

Mitchell Bay. A shoal extends from the south shore almost to the middle of the entry. A rock is at the outer end of the shoal. Leave this rock to starboard when entering. Large scale Chart 18433 shows the entrance clearly.

⑩ **Snug Harbor Resort.** 1997 Mitchell Bay Road, Friday Harbor, WA 98250; (360) 378-4762; sneakaway@snugresort.com; www.snugresort.com. Monitors VHF 66A. Snug Harbor is open all year and welcomes visitors. Maximum boat length 60 feet. Depth at zero tide is 9 feet. Services include 30 amp power, Wi-Fi, restrooms, showers, garbage drop, recycling, barbecues, fire pits. Reservations recommended. The on-site convenience store has ice and limited groceries, gifts, propane, fishing and boating supplies. Mitchell Bay Coffee has free Wi-Fi, espresso, fresh pastries, waffles and soup. Canoes and kayaks available for guest use free of charge.

The resort has undergone extensive renovations. They've built beautiful new cabins, with barbecues and fire pits.

Lime Kiln Point. Lime Kiln Point is a favorite place to watch for orcas, the so-called "killer whales," that often cruise within a few yards of shore. Anchorage offshore from this park would be very difficult and is not recommended. A small interpretive center with information about orca whales is in the park. Best visited by taking the San Juan Transit shuttle bus from Roche Harbor or Friday Harbor.

San Juan County Park. 4289 West Side Road N., Friday Harbor, WA 98250; (360) 378-2992; www.sanjuanco.com. Open all year. Facilities include launch ramp and restrooms. No power, no showers. A popular park for kayak campers who can pull up on the beach.

Henry Island. A Seattle Yacht Club outstation (no reciprocals) is in Nelson Bay. Nelson Bay is shallow, so use your depth sounder and tide table

Lime Kiln Point lighthouse. Orca whales are often spotted offshore.

before anchoring. The rest of the island is private.

Unnamed Island #40. On the southwest side of San Juan Island, approximately 1 mile northwest of Pile Point. Open all year, day use only, no facilities. Anchor out at this undeveloped DNR (Dept. of Natural Resources) property. No fires or overnight camping. Pack out all garbage. Do not disturb wildlife or alter the surroundings.

Unnamed Island #38. On the southwest side of San Juan Island, near the center of Kanaka Bay. Open all year, day use only, no facilities. Anchor out at this undeveloped DNR property. No fires or overnight camping. Pack out garbage. Do not disturb wildlife or alter the surroundings.

LOCAL KNOWLEDGE

DANGEROUS REEFS: TowBoatU.S. reports the Wasp Islands are the number-one area for groundings in the San Juan Islands.

Wasp Islands. The Wasp Islands on the east side of San Juan Channel are a rock and reef-strewn area requiring careful navigation. The underwater hazards are charted but not all of them are marked, and the unwary can come to grief. Wasp Passage, however, is free of hazards, and the skipper who stays in the channel will have no problems.

All the major Wasp Islands are privately owned except Yellow Island, which is owned by The Nature Conservancy.

Yellow Island. (206) 343-4344; www.nature.org. Open all year, 10:00 a.m. to 4:00 p.m. Yellow Island is owned by The Nature Conservancy and administered as a wildlife preserve. No pets. Land dinghies on the southeast beach, below the wooden Dodd cabin.

Northwest McConnell Rock. Northwest of McConnell Island. Part of the San Juan Islands National Wildlife Refuge. Boats must stay 200 yards from shore; no shore access.

⑪ **Jones Island Marine State Park.** (360) 376-2073; Open all year, day use and overnight mooring and camping. The bay at the north end of Jones Island is an excellent an-

Garrison Bay and English Camp

chorage. Boats anchoring near the beach run stern-ties ashore, leaving swinging room for boats anchored in the middle. Currents can swirl through the bay, so leave ample room when you anchor.

Normally, 7 mooring buoys, for boats 45 feet and under, are in the bay. A seasonal 160-foot-long mooring float connects to a wharf that leads to shore. Self-register and pay mooring buoy fee at the head of the wharf. Composting toilet facilities are ashore. A well provides drinking water, but may run dry in late summer. Use the water sparingly.

A few mooring buoys are in the small bay on the south side of the island. Self-register and pay mooring buoy fee on shore. In the middle of this bay, watch for a rock that lies awash at zero tide. The rock is shown on the charts, but the symbol is easy to overlook. Choose your anchorage based on which side of the island provides the best protection from the wind. We've had a pleasant night in the south anchorage when the wind was blowing from the north, while cruisers anchored in the north bay reported a difficult night.

The south bay is a Cascadia Marine Trail site, with 24 primitive but excellent campsites, and toilet facilities. It's a popular kayak destination. Excellent views.

Jones Island suffered a blowdown of mature trees during a severe storm in 1990. For environmental reasons, most of the downed trees were left to rot on the ground, although campsites and trails were cleared and the logs bucked up for firewood. Ample evidence of the blowdown can be seen on the northeast side of the island.

This is a wonderful park, popular for families with children. An easy trail connects the north and south moorages, with a 1.2-mile south loop trail branching off through forest and along rock headlands over the water. If you look carefully along this trail, you'll see low patches of prickly pear cactus growing along the way. At the north moorage especially, you probably will meet tame deer. If you dine at a picnic table they may try to join you. During the summer, mooring buoys and float space can be hard to get.

Caution: Raccoons will go aboard unattended boats at the dock if food is left in the open. Stow food well, and close the boat tightly.

Orcas Island. Orcas Island is the largest island in the San Juans, deeply indented by Deer Harbor, West Sound and East Sound. Various locations around the island offer services ranging from float plane flights, to groceries, to luxurious spa experiences, to boat repairs. The island hosts several festivals and has a seasonal Saturday farmers market. See www.orcasislandchamber.com/orcas-island-events for more information.

Getting around: Car rental delivery service is available through "Orcas Island Shuttle" (360-376-RIDE), offering a variety of interesting vehicles. We spotted a 2-seater Miata with the company logo; cars can be delivered anywhere on the Island. For taxi service, call (360) 376-TAXI. San Juan Transit has shuttle bus service around the island on weekends.

Golf: The 9-hole Orcas Island Golf Club is hilly but easily walked. During dry summer months even well-played shots can roll into oblivion. Fun course. (360) 376-4400.

⑫ **Deer Harbor.** Deer Harbor is a quiet, protected bay on the west end of Orcas Island that is home to two marinas. Deer Harbor Marina is the first marina entering the bay from the south with transient moorage, guest services, and outstations for several yacht clubs. At the north end of the bay is Cayou Quay Marina with permanent moorage only and no transient services. The entire bay north of Fawn Island has good anchorage. A charted Cable Area surrounds Fawn Island and extends westward to the shore of Orcas Island.

⑫ **Deer Harbor Marina.** P.O. Box 344, 5164 Deer Harbor Road, Deer Harbor, WA 98243; (360) 376-3037; mbroman@deerharbormarina.com; www.deerharbormarina.com. Monitors VHF 78A. Certified Clean Marina. Open all year. Facilities include ethanol-free gasoline and diesel at the fuel dock, guest moorage for vessels up to 120 feet, 30 & some 50 amp power, free Wi-Fi, restrooms and showers, pumpout, laundry, barbecue floating dock for parties and rendezvous. Air service by Kenmore Air.

The docks are excellent, and the restrooms and showers are clean and spacious. A small store at the outer end of the wharf carries groceries, beer, wine, espresso, Lopez Island Ice Cream cones, and has an ATM. A small cafe in the store serves breakfast, lunch, and snacks.

Deer Harbor Marina

Whether you're here for a vacation or are looking for permanent moorage in a Pacific Northwest paradise, Deer Harbor Marina should be a key waypoint on your journey. Come enjoy the beauty of Deer Harbor throughout the season.

- Winter Rates at $6 per foot
- Slips to 50'
- Guest side ties up to 150'
- 30 amp power/limited 50 amp
- New pool, showers & laundry
- Fuel dock (gas & diesel)
- Deli, groceries, beer, wine, ice cream, coffee, prep food, DVD rentals & ATM
- Whale watching, kayaks, bike & boat rentals, tours and charters
- Fresh water
- Pump-out
- Nearby restaurants
- Apparel, gifts, books, maps & charts

Deer Harbor Marina
Orcas Island, WA
Lat 48° 37' 135" • Lon 123° 00' 166"

CONTACT: 360.376.3037 • VHF 78A
EMAIL: mbroman@deerharbormarina.com
ONLINE: www.DeerHarborMarina.com

SAN JUAN ISLANDS   See Area Map Page 176 - Maps Not for Navigation

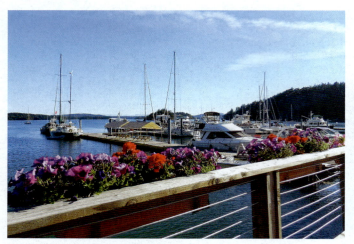
Deer Harbor Marina is a popular destination for families.

Looking east toward Orcas Landing from Wasp Passage. Watch for ferry traffic, current, and charted rocks.

Fresh donuts made before your eyes on Saturdays and Sundays. A gift store on the dock has books and items for kids. Kayaks and SUPs for rent. Whale watching, boat charters, and fishing charters available. 12-passenger loaner van is available (weekdays only during summer), inquire at the office. We took the van to Turtleback Mountain for a hike with an impressive view of the area. We have also used it to pick up crew arriving by ferry at Orcas Landing.

A beautiful sand beach next to the wharf will entertain the little ones. At the north end of the beach, a small but lovely park has been built. The Resort at Deer Harbor is across the road. Marina guests have access to the resort's swimming pool. The Deer Harbor Inn Restaurant, a ten-minute walk north, is excellent. If you don't want to walk, you can ride the restaurant's courtesy "limousine." The entire area has an easy and relaxed "vacation" feeling. Even the quaint post office fits right in. During the busy months it's best to call ahead for mooring reservations. The marina purchased the restaurant building across the street from the marina. The Island Pie, with indoor and outdoor dining on the deck, serves pizza, beer, cider and wine.

Cell phones: Cell phone service is spotty at the marina. A free courtesy phone is available in the laundry room.

LOCAL KNOWLEDGE

SPEED LIMIT: A 7-knot zone marked by white cylindrical buoys extends from just west of Pole Pass eastward almost to Bell Island.

Pole Pass. Boats transiting between Harney Channel and Deer Harbor usually go through Pole Pass, a narrow notch separating Crane Island from Orcas Island. Rocks obstruct the edges and approaches, and currents can run swiftly through the pass. A mid-channel course is safe. For most skippers, good sense dictates slow speeds. Unfortunately, not all skippers have seen it that way, and wakes have damaged docks along the shoreline. So now speeds are limited by county law to 7 knots maximum. Sometimes the sheriff is there, ticketing speeders.

⑬ **West Sound.** West Sound is the middle inlet of Orcas Island, where the Wareham family's West Sound Marina offers limited overnight moorage and complete service facilities. Next to the marina is the Orcas Island Yacht Club, with reciprocal moorage for visiting members. A day-use-only public dock is west of the Orcas Island Yacht Club dock. At press time, the Westsound Inn and Cafe located upland from the public dock was for sale. It is not known if the Inn and Cafe will be open for the 2018 season.

Good anchorage is available at the head of the bay (stay well clear of Harbor Rock, marked by a daybeacon). Anchorage is also good off the village of West Sound, and behind Double Island.

⑬ **West Sound Marina.** P.O. Box 119, 525 Deer Harbor Road, Orcas Island, WA 98280; (360) 376-2314; info@westsoundmarina.com; www.westsoundmarina.net. Monitors VHF 16, switch to 09. Open all year, except closed Sundays in the winter. Facilities include ethanol-free gasoline and diesel at the

Deer Harbor Marina

The pool at Deer Harbor is available for marina guests.

See Area Map Page 176 - Maps Not for Navigation SAN JUAN ISLANDS

West Sound Marina

County Dock at Orcas Landing, a convenient stop for grocery and gift shopping. East end of the dock is reserved for a whale watch boat.

fuel dock, propane, 400 feet of guest moorage, reservations 24 hours in advance, 30 amp power, restrooms, shower, pumpout. Haulout to 30 tons with full service and repairs, including an enclosed area for major work. The chandlery has most boating supplies. When approaching, stay well off Picnic Island. A rock ledge extends into West Sound from the island. Once at the marina, stay close to the docks. The water shoals toward Picnic Island.

Victim Island. West side of West Sound. Open all year, day use only, no facilities. Anchor out at this undeveloped BLM property. No fires or overnight camping. Pack out all garbage. Do not disturb wildlife or alter the surroundings.

Unnamed Island #80 (Massacre Bay Rocks). West of Indian Point in West Sound. Open all year, day use only, no facilities. Anchor out at this undeveloped Bureau of Land Management (BLM) property. No fires or overnight camping. Pack out all garbage. Do not disturb wildlife or alter the surroundings.

Skull Island. North end of Massacre Bay. Open all year, day use only, no facilities. Anchor out at this undeveloped BLM property. No fires or overnight camping. Pack out all garbage. Do not disturb wildlife or alter the surroundings.

Unnamed Island #81 (Trinka Rock). South of West Sound Marina, north of Picnic Island. Open all year, day use only, no facilities. Anchor out at this undeveloped BLM property. No fires or overnight camping. Pack out all garbage. Do not disturb wildlife or alter the surroundings.

⑭ **Orcas Landing.** Orcas Landing has a float next to the ferry dock, but stays are limited to 30 minutes. The grocery store at the head of the ferry dock is well stocked, and has a good selection of wine and cheese. Other shops in the village, aimed at serving the summer ferry lineup, are good. Great sandwiches and ice cream cones, too. Be well-fendered and securely tied to the dock at Orcas Landing. Passing boat and ferry traffic in Harney Channel throw a lot of wake towards the dock.

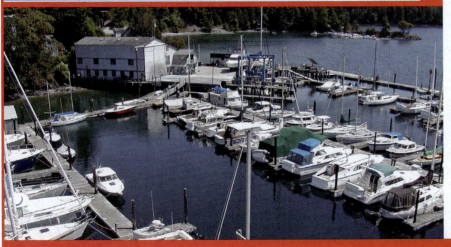

WEST SOUND MARINA
The Service Center of the San Juans
"We Fix Boats"

- Haulouts to 30 tons, 64' LOA, 18' beam at any tide
- Engine Service and Sales
- Factory Certified Mechanics
  Volvo • Mercruiser • Evinrude • Yanmar
- Complete Chandlery
  Most everything you need for boat and crew
- Moorage
  180 year-round slips
  Overnight moorage by reservation
- Gas • Diesel • Propane • Ice

P.O. BOX 119 • ORCAS, WASHINGTON • 360/376-2314 • FAX 360/376-4634
INFO@WESTSOUNDMARINA.COM • WWW.WESTSOUNDMARINA.NET

2018 WAGGONER CRUISING GUIDE

SAN JUAN ISLANDS　　　　See Area Map Page 176 - Maps Not for Navigation

A collection of historic log cabins make up the Orcas Island museum in Eastsound.

Rosario Resort's new dock configuration accommodates more boats and improves access.

Grindstone Harbor. Grindstone Harbor is a small, shallow anchorage, with two major rocks in its entrance. One of these rocks became famous a number of years ago when the Washington State ferry *Elwha* ran aground on it while doing a bit of unauthorized sightseeing. Favor the east shore all the way in. Private mooring buoys take up much of the inner part of the bay, but there's room to anchor if you need to.

Guthrie Bay. Guthrie Bay indents Orcas Island between Grindstone Harbor and East Sound. It's a pleasant little spot with private mooring buoys around the perimeter and homes on the hillsides. Anchor in 24 to 42 feet.

East Sound. East Sound, the largest of Orcas Island's indentations, extends about 6 miles north from Foster Point. The shores on both sides are steep, and offer few anchorage possibilities. Rosario Resort is on the east side, a short distance up the sound past the village of Olga. The village of Eastsound is at the head. Fresh winds sometimes blow in East Sound, while outside the air is calm. Anchorage is also possible in Fishing Bay on the west Shore.

Eastsound. The village of Eastsound, at the head of East Sound, is the largest settlement on Orcas Island. A 40-foot seasonal county dock is on the eastern shore, small boats or dinghies only. A 10-minute walk leads to town. Eastsound has several very good restaurants, a large grocery store, an excellent museum, many interesting shops, and on Saturdays during the summer, a busy farmers market.

Anchoring note. A sign on the county dock announces that the bottom inshore, from a line between the dock and the small islet off the town, is sensitive eelgrass habitat. It requests that you anchor to seaward of that line. Anchorage is possible in Fishing Bay on the west shore.

⑮ **Rosario Resort & Spa.** 1400 Rosario Rd., Eastsound, WA 98245; (360) 376-2222; (800) 562-8820; harbormaster@rosarioresort.com; www.rosarioresort.com. Monitors VHF 78A. Certified Clean Marina. Open all year, diesel and ethanol-free unleaded gasoline at the fuel dock (fuel dock by appointment October through April), over 30 slips with unlimited water for filling tanks and boat washing, 30 & 50 amp ELCI-protected power, 8 mooring buoys, garbage drop, restrooms, showers, café, convenience store, swimming pools, Wi-Fi, seaplane service to Seattle via Kenmore Air and NW Seaplanes. Reservations for moorage are strongly recommended. Buoys are first-come, first-served, with room to anchor, though the sound is exposed to southerlies. The outdoor swimming pool, nearest the docks, welcomes families as does the spa-pool inside the resort's Mansion; the Mansion's outdoor pool is for adults only. Two hours of day use moorage is free if space is available. For those wanting to explore Eastsound or the island, car rental delivery service is available through "Orcas Island Shuttle" (360-376-RIDE).

A 200-foot breakwater dock accommodates larger vessels up to 180 feet. The outer end of the breakwater is for seaplanes only. New docks in a U-shape configuration allow easy access into the marina through a center fairway. Moorage includes power, water, restrooms and showers. Boats on buoys pay a buoy fee and boats anchored out pay a landing fee for use of the marina pool, shower and restrooms; spa facilities are extra. The Cascade Bay Grill and Store at the head of the dock is open from Memorial Day through mid-September and has snacks, sodas, beer and wine, limited groceries. The Grill serves great burgers, fish & chips, and

See Area Map Page 176 - Maps Not for Navigation   SAN JUAN ISLANDS

The Moran Mansion is a distinctive landmark when approaching Rosario Resort.

The public dock and pier at the charming village of Olga on Orcas Island

casual fare, inside or out. Live entertainment two nights a week, check their website.

The centerpiece of the resort is the magnificent Moran Mansion, listed on the National Register of Historic Places. The mansion houses a restaurant, lounge and the spa. The mansion itself is also a fascinating museum (open 8:00 a.m. to 9:00 p.m. daily), a chronicle of Robert Moran's history as a shipbuilder, the mayor of Seattle, then as the builder of Rosario. Christopher Peacock, longtime resident artist and musician and now resort manager, presents a slide presentation on the history of the resort, with musical accompaniment performed on the giant room-sized Wurlitzer pipe organ. The concert begins at 4:00 p.m. Tuesdays to Saturdays mid-June through mid-September, and Saturdays only through the winter. It's wonderful. Don't miss it. Moran State Park is about a 30-minute walk.

Figurehead: The beautiful figurehead above the marina is a replica from the wreck of the *America*, a wooden clipper ship converted to barge use. The ship went aground near False Bay on San Juan Island in 1914 while under tow from Seattle to Vancouver. During periods of small tides and slack water, the wreck's bones are still a dive site at False Bay (from *Northwest Dive News*).

⑯ **Olga.** Olga, a tiny pastoral village, is near the entrance to East Sound, on the east shore. Olga has a dock and 105-foot-long mooring float, but no power, restrooms, or showers. The float is removed in winter. A box for overnight moorage payment is at the bottom of the ramp. Three-day overnight limit. Day-use stay up to two hours. Limited anchorage offshore exposed to southeasterly winds. Numerous private mooring buoys and charted cable area limit the possible anchoring opportunities.

A sign above the dock lists local stores and locations. Olga Village has a post office. Up the road you will find the Artworks co-operative, the James Hardman Gallery, and the new Catkin Café housed in the recently reconstructed Strawberry Barreling Plant building.

Twin Rocks. West of Olga. Open all year, day use only, no facilities. Anchor out at this undeveloped state park property. No fires or overnight camping. Pack out all garbage. Do not disturb wildlife or alter the surroundings.

Lieber Haven Resort. P.O. Box 127, Olga, WA 98279; (360) 376-2472; www.lieberhavenresort.com. In the middle of Obstruction Pass. Overnight moorage on the resort docks for cottage guests only. Two rental cottages along a nice sandy, light gravel shoreline. Store carries some groceries, beer and wine, and some marine supplies.

Obstruction Pass State Park. www.parks.wa.gov. Southeast tip of Orcas Island. Open all year, moorage at 3 buoys for boats 45 feet and under. Self-register and pay moorage buoy fee on shore. Toilets, no power or showers. Good anchoring on a gravel bottom. Campsites with fireplaces, picnic tables, hiking trails.

⑰ **Doe Island Marine State Park.** (360) 376-2073; On the southeast side of Orcas Island. Normally, open all year for day use and

Rosario Resort

Doe Bay

2018 waggoner CRUISING GUIDE

SAN JUAN ISLANDS

See Area Map Page 176 - Maps Not for Navigation

Though small, Matia Island has a cove for anchorage and a public dock.

Exploring the caves on Sucia Island.

camping. This is a beautiful tiny island with a rocky shoreline dotted with tidepools. A trail leads around the island, through dense forest and lush undergrowth. Toilets, but no power, water, or showers. Pack out all garbage. Adjacent buoys are privately owned. Currents run strongly between Doe Island and Orcas Island. The 30-foot mooring float was damaged in a storm in 2010. As of 2017, the dock has not been replaced. The park is still open to small boats and kayaks.

⑰ **Doe Bay Resort and Retreat.** 107 Doe Bay Road, Olga, WA 98279; (360) 376-2291; office@doebay.com; www.doebay.com. Doe Bay is an interesting off-the-beaten-path destination, with 2 guest buoys and anchorage space for 3 to 6 boats. Dinghy ashore to the rocky beach to visit the café or use the creekside soaking tubs and cedar sauna. The café has an intriguing menu and is open for breakfast, lunch and dinner, with indoor and outdoor seating. A store has convenience groceries and items from local artisans. The resort has cabins, geodesic domes, yurts, a beautifully crafted treehouse, and campsites for rent. Doe Bay Fest, a popular music festival, is held in August.

Smuggler's Villa Resort. P.O. Box 79, Eastsound, WA 98245; (360) 376-2297; smuggler@rockisland.com; www.smuggler.com. No transient moorage. Smuggler's Village has condos for rent, a swimming pool and hot tubs. Reservations required. Good base for trailer boaters who can rent a condo for overnights and explore the northern San Juans during the day.

⑱ **Barnes and Clark Islands.** These two beautiful islands lie parallel to each other in Rosario Strait, between Orcas Island and Lummi Island. Barnes Island is privately owned, but Clark Island is a state park, with mooring buoys installed during the summer. Camping and picnicking sites are ashore, and trails meander along the island.

⑱ **Clark Island Marine State Park.** (360) 376-2073; Open all year, day use and overnight mooring and camping. Clark Island is exposed to Rosario Strait and the Strait of Georgia, and is best in settled weather. Mooring buoys are deployed between Clark Island and Barnes Island, and in the bay on the east side. The park has 9 mooring buoys for vessels 45 feet and under: 6 on the east side and 3 on the west side. Self-register and pay mooring buoy fee on shore. Toilets, picnic sites, fire rings, and primitive campsites. No power, no water. Pack out all garbage.

Note. A nasty rock is in the entrance to the bay.

Visitor report: Correspondents Bruce and Margaret Evertz spent a night on a buoy on the east side of Clark Island and ". . .woke up three times in the middle of the night hanging onto the mattress as we rolled in the wake of something big. Next time we'll try one of the buoys on the west side."

Sucia, Patos, and Matia Islands

See Area Map Page 176 - Maps Not for Navigation   SAN JUAN ISLANDS

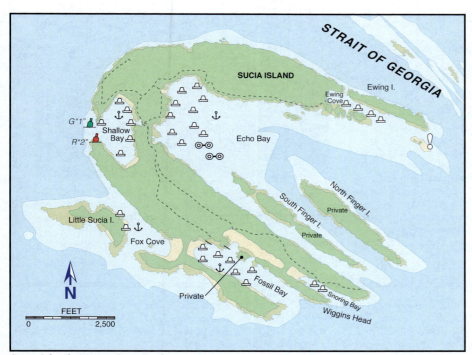

Sucia Islands Marine State Park

⑲ Matia Island. (360) 376-2073; Open all year, day use and overnight mooring. Matia Island is part of the San Juan Islands National Wildlife Refuge. All access is restricted except the loop trail and the designated 5-acre moorage and picnicking area at Rolfe Cove. The rest of the island is off-limits to protect wildlife. Pets are not allowed on shore.

The favored Matia Island anchorage is in **Rolfe Cove**, which opens from the west. Strong currents can run through Rolfe Cove and the bottom is rocky. Be sure the anchor is well set and swinging room is adequate. Facilities include a 64-foot-long moorage float, 2 buoys (limit 45 feet), 6 campsites, toilet. No power, water or showers. The mooring float is removed in winter. Self-register and pay mooring buoy fee at the head of the dock.

Those confident in their anchoring ability might try the little 1-boat notch between Rolfe Cove and Eagle Point, although you can't go inland from there. A stern-anchor will be required to keep the boat positioned. High cliffs surround this cove. It's very secluded and serene.

Anchorage is good in the bay indenting the southeast corner of the island. The remains of an old homestead are located at the head of that bay.

There is some disagreement about the pronunciation of Matia. Bruce Calhoun's book, *Cruising the San Juan Islands*, says it's pronounced "Mah-TEE-ah." We've been told, however, that a number of genuine old hands have always pronounced it "Mah-CIA," as in "inertia" or "militia." However the name is pronounced, Matia Island is a popular destination, beautiful and interesting.

LOCAL KNOWLEDGE

DANGEROUS REEFS: A reef extends westward from Little Sucia Island nearly to the shoal water near West Bank. Sucia Island is surrounded by such hazards. We strongly recommend that vessels in these waters carry and use Chart 18431.

⑳ Sucia Island. Open all year, day use and overnight mooring and camping. For information call (360) 902-8844; for campsite reservations call toll-free (888) 226-7688. Facilities include dock space, linear tie mooring systems, numerous mooring buoys, and toilets. Water, but no power, no showers. This probably is the most heavily used marine park in the system. As many as 500 boats can visit on one weekend in the high summer season.

Like Matia and Patos Islands, Sucia Island is made of sandstone carved by water and wind into dramatic shapes. Many fossils can be found in Sucia Island's sandstone. It is illegal to disturb or remove fossils.

The park has 55 primitive campsites and 2 group campsites, which can be reserved. Camping is permitted in designated areas only. A day use/picnic area, with picnic shelters, is on the neck of land separating Echo Bay and Shallow Bay, and can be reserved. The park has several miles of hiking trails and service roads. Fresh water is available at Fossil Bay and near Shallow Bay April through September. The most developed facilities are at Fossil Bay.

Sucia Island has several fingers that separate small bays. Facilities are as follows: Fox Cove: 4 mooring buoys; Fossil Bay: 2 docks, 16 mooring buoys; Snoring Bay: 2 mooring buoys; Echo Bay: 14 mooring buoys, 2 linear moorings; Ewing Cove: 4 mooring buoys; Shallow Bay: 8 mooring buoys. All mooring buoys are limited to boats 45 feet or less. All docks and moorings are Washington State Parks facilities, self-register and pay a fee at the designated on-shore stations. The mooring buoy count can change based on winter weather and repairs.

Shallow Bay. Shallow Bay is an excellent, popular anchorage. Lots of room except on minus tides. Mooring buoys take most of the obvious good spots, so if they are taken you'll be looking at the south side of Shallow Bay. Check the tides before anchoring, and be sure you'll have enough water under the keel at low

Eroded sandstone on Sucia Island

Active Cove on Patos Island is one of the most scenic anchorages in the San Juan Islands.

2018 WAGGONER CRUISING GUIDE

SAN JUAN ISLANDS See Area Map Page 176 - Maps Not for Navigation

Turn Point Special Operating Area

The Turn Point Special Operating Area was created in 2001 to manage the high volume of commercial ship and recreational boat traffic around Turn Point. Ships longer than 100 meters (328 feet) must call in to Victoria Traffic on VHF channel 11 prior to entering the area and report their intended navigation movements and any other information necessary to comply with standards of care.

Recreational vessels should monitor VHF channel 11 in this vicinity so they can be aware of any ships. If ships are in the Special Operating Area, stay well clear until they are past. In a crossing situation, *cross behind the large ship*, not in front of it.

Turn Point is a blind corner. A recreational vessel could be completely unaware of a fast approaching ship on the other side. Monitor VHF channel 11. We had a near-miss in fog a few years ago. It was scary.

Also see "What Recreational Boaters Need to Know about VTS" in Cruising Information section in the front of the Waggoner.

— *Robert Hale*

tide. Easy entry as long as you pass between the two buoys marking the entrance. The best place to beach the dinghy is on the narrow neck of land separating Shallow Bay from Echo Bay. Sunsets in Shallow Bay are beautiful.

Fox Cove. Enter Fox Cove from either side. Waters off the southern entry can be turbulent. At the west entry foul ground extends west farther than you expect. Tie to mooring buoys or anchor behind Little Sucia Island. A pretty spot with sandstone cliffs.

Fossil Bay. Fossil Bay is easy to enter, nicely protected, and beautiful. Anchor out, tie to one of the mooring buoys, or moor at the docks. In winter one of the docks is moved to a more protected area of the park. At the head of the outermost dock a plaque commemorates the yacht clubs that were members of the Interclub Boating Association of Washington, when Interclub worked to collect funds from ordinary citizens, then bought the island and gave it to the state as a state park. One of the points of land overlooking Fossil Bay is named for Ev Henry, the first president of Interclub, who conceived the idea and carried out the project.

Depths in Fossil Bay at zero tide are 6 feet at the outer end of the innermost dock, and they shoal rapidly toward the head of the bay. The park ranger told us depths are only 5 feet at zero tide near the outer dock. Be careful on low tides. A substantial day use shelter, excellent for group functions, has been built at the head of the dock. Call (360) 376-2073 for reservations.

Snoring Bay. Snoring Bay is easy to enter and has 2 mooring buoys. A good spot. As we understand the story, a park ranger was caught sleeping on duty in this bay, hence the name.

Echo Bay. Echo Bay is the largest of Sucia's bays. Although it is the most exposed, it is the most popular. Mooring buoys line the western shore, and 2 linear mooring systems are just outside the buoys. Picnic facilities are on the narrow neck of land separating Echo Bay from Shallow Bay.

The fine gravel beach at the head of Echo Bay is fairly steep, making dinghy landing much more convenient. We were able to step ashore without getting our feet wet.

The two long islands in Echo Bay (North Finger and South Finger Island) are privately owned. The south half of Justice Island (the small island off South Finger Island) is park-owned but closed to the public as a nature preserve.

Caution: A reader reported that he grounded his Cal 39 sailboat, which draws 6 feet 8 inches, on an uncharted rock in Echo Bay. The grounding occurred in the area marked 1 fathom, 5 feet extending from the small islet northwest of South Finger Islet, as shown on large scale Chart 18431. He sounded the area carefully after the grounding, and found the depths to be somewhat less than charted. The keel of his boat confirmed the soundings. On low tides especially, give the tip of this islet a good offing.

Despite occasional stories of anchor dragging in Echo Bay, we have found the bottom to be heavy, sticky clay, with excellent holding.

No-anchor zone: A no-anchor zone is marked by buoys near the head of Echo Bay. They want to protect eelgrass from boat anchors and dragging chain rode. Mooring buoys in the bay use eco-friendly anchors that do not disturb eelgrass.

Ewing Cove. In our opinion, cozy little Ewing Cove, tucked in behind Ewing Island on the north side of Echo Bay, is the most charming of Sucia Island's bays. The cove has 4 mooring buoys and a lovely beach at the western end. We have reports of a rock in Ewing Cove's southern entrance, from Echo Bay. The rock is east of a white can that marks a fish haven, shown on large scale Chart 18431. We're told the rock is black and hard to see, and feeds on propellers at low tide. Be extra cautious. Reader Bruce Farwell sent lat/lon coordinates of 48°45.794'N/122°52.924'W. We've found the narrow pass at the northwest end of Ewing

Fossil Bay offers picnic areas and beaches within close proximity to mooring buoys, anchoring, and two docks.

See Area Map Page 176 - Maps Not for Navigation

SAN JUAN ISLANDS

Cove to be deep and easily run as long as you pay attention. Danger Reef lies just outside.

㉑ **Patos Island.** (360) 376-2073; Open all year, day use and overnight mooring and camping. Facilities include 2 mooring buoys (limit 45 feet) in Active Cove, toilets, primitive campsites. Self-register and pay mooring buoy fee on shore. The remains of the dock that served the lighthouse on Alden Point are still there, but barely recognizable. A one-mile trail leads from the beach at the head of Active Cove to the lighthouse. Pack out all garbage. The island is a breeding area for birds.

㉑ **Active Cove.** The only possible Patos Island anchorage is in Active Cove, on the west tip of the island. The cove, with its sculpted sandstone walls, is one of the most scenic spots in the San Juans. Considerable current activity is outside the entrances. Inside the cove the currents are reduced, but it's tight. Use the mooring buoys when possible. If the mooring buoys are taken, anchoring gets interesting. A stern-tie to shore probably will be called for.

Freeman Island. On President Channel. Open all year, day use only, no facilities. Anchor out at this undeveloped state park property. No fires or overnight camping. Pack out all garbage.

㉒ **West Beach Resort.** 190 Waterfront Way, Eastsound, WA 98245; (360) 376-2240; (877) 937-8224; vacation@westbeachresort.com; www.westbeachresort.com. Open all year, ethanol-free premium gasoline at the fuel dock, 10 mooring buoys in the summer and 3 in the winter, restrooms, showers, pumpout. Floats in deeper water accommodate larger boats. Larger powerboats and keel sailboats tie to mooring buoys. Most of the docks are removed from mid-September to late May, limited moorage in the winter. The fuel dock is open year round. The store has a little bit of everything, including groceries, ice, beer, wine, espresso, ice cream, and free Wi-Fi. Limited dock space in the off-season.

West Beach is a popular fishing resort with cabins, tent cabins, RV, camping, children's activities, food service, private launch ramp (free for guests, a fee is charged for non-guests) and parking. Be careful if you anchor out. The eelgrass bottom does not offer good holding in many places and you can drag.

Waldron Island. Waldron Island has no public facilities. In settled weather anchorage is good in Cowlitz Bay and North Bay. Mail Bay, on the east shore, is rocky but usable. The mail boat from Bellingham used to arrive here, leaving the mail in a barrel hung over the water.

㉓ **Stuart Island.** The center portion of Stuart Island, including Reid Harbor and Prevost Harbor, is a state park with campsites, potable water, and clean, spacious composting toilets. A trail and dirt road from Reid Harbor and Prevost Harbor lead out to the automated Turn Point lighthouse. The distance is about 3 miles, each way. It's an excellent walk, although the trail to the road goes over a mountain, and will have you puffing. The view down into Reid Harbor is excellent, however.

Once you get to the road, it's 0.7 mi. to the school house (1 room, K-8), library and museum, which in our opinion are on the must-see list. The school house is modern, but the library and museum buildings go back to earlier days. The museum is filled with information about island life, which, despite being close to big cities, is pretty primitive. There is no public electric power, for example. Every resident is

One of the small, intimate marinas among the San Juan Islands; West Beach Resort has mooring buoys and seasonal dock moorage.

Stuart Island Marine State Park

2018 WAGGONER CRUISING GUIDE   201

SAN JUAN ISLANDS

responsible for his or her own electricity, and a few choose to do without. Ditto water and telephone, although cell phones have filled that void. Handmade postcards are for sale in the library on the honor system.

One island family, Ezra and Loie Benson and their children, have created a small business called Boundary Pass Traders. They operate the Treasure Chest, near the schoolhouse. T-shirts, stationery, and the like have been enhanced with local scenes. Strictly the honor system. Select the items you like and mail a check for your purchases. We did it, and got a nice thank-you note in reply.

Stuart Island's one-room Schoolhouse is among the many hiking destinations on the Island.

Prevost Harbor. Open all year, day use and overnight mooring and camping. Facilities include 256 feet of dock space, 7 mooring buoys (limit 45 feet), a linear mooring system, 18 primitive campsites, toilets. Self-register and pay dock moorage, mooring buoy, and linear mooring fee at the head of the state park dock. The favored entrance to Prevost Harbor is around the west end of Satellite Island. A county dock on the northwest end of Prevost Harbor, suitable for dinghies, shortens the walk to the Island school and Turn Point lighthouse. No overnight stays at the county dock.

Caution: Two reefs in the Prevost Harbor entrance cover at high tide. One is off the Stuart Island shore and dries at 6 feet. The other is off Satellite Island and dries at 4 feet. The reefs are clearly charted, but when they cover, the route to the dock looks to be wide open. If you're entering at higher tide when the reefs are covered, don't wrap tightly to port around the tip of Satellite Island. That's where one of the reefs is lying in wait. Proceed a short distance straight into the harbor (but not too far; that's where the other reef is located), then turn to port.

Except for the reefs noted above, anchoring is good throughout Prevost Harbor. After dinner we took a slow dinghy ride around the shoreline. A grass airstrip is at the east end of the harbor, beyond the docks. As we putt-putted along we found the houses, rock forms, and beaches fascinating.

The passage to the east of Satellite Island is foul. Contributing Editor Tom Kincaid, however, reports that with care these waters are passable at half tide or better, or by shallow draft boats. Use caution. Shoreside facilities are shared with Reid Harbor, on the narrow but steep neck of land that separates them.

Satellite Island East Cove. "The little cove on the eastern shore of Satellite Island has good holding in mud in about 40 feet. Wonderful view across Boundary Pass. Inside, Prevost Harbor was packed with boats; we were alone." [*Hamilton*]

Reid Harbor. Open all year, day use and overnight mooring and camping. The entrance is straightforward. A 192-foot mooring float is on the north shore, 13 mooring buoys (for boats 45 feet and under) dot the bay, and mooring floats and a linear mooring system are placed within easy dinghy distance of the landing pier. Self-register and pay mooring fees at the head of the dock. Facilities include toilets, pumpout, portapotty dump. Reid Harbor is long and narrow, and protected by high hills. The bottom is excellent for anchoring, and the harbor holds a great number of boats. It's a popular destination. The setting is beautiful. Shoreside facilities are shared with Prevost Harbor, on the narrow but steep neck of land separating them. The county dirt road leading to the Turn Point Lighthouse, with its museum (and the school house, museum and library along the way), begins at the head of Reid Harbor. No dock at the head of the bay, but if tides are favorable you could beach your dinghy there without having to carry it back through the mud.

Gossip Island. "Reid Harbor had too many boats for our taste. Preferring a view anyway, we dropped anchor just outside, in the cove formed by Gossip Island and the unnamed island immediately northwest of Gossip Island. It was very private, with two white sand beaches nearby. Good holding ground for the anchor. Southerly swells rocked us a couple times, but no worse than in the east cove of James Island. We had an excellent view through the islets to the Olympic Mountains, and of large ship traffic away off in Haro Strait." [*Hamilton*]

Johns Pass. Johns Pass separates Stuart Island and Johns Island, and is used regularly. At the south end of the pass foul ground, marked by kelp, extends about half of a mile southeast from Stuart Island. Boats heading southeast through Johns Pass should head for Gull Reef, then turn when well clear of the kelp. Anchorage is possible in Johns Pass and along the south side of Johns Island.

The buoys and anchorage in Reid Harbor on Stuart Island are popular, but there's ample space for lots of boats.

Waggoner eNews
Boating, Maintenance Tips & Destinations
www.waggonerguide.com

Gulf Islands

CHAPTER 7

GULF ISLANDS
*Victoria • Sidney • Butchart Gardens • Chemainus
Wallace Island • Pirates Cove • Nanaimo*

SALTSPRING ISLAND
Ganges • Vesuvius • Fulford Harbour

NORTH & SOUTH PENDER ISLAND
Bedwell Harbour • Port Browning • Otter Bay

GALIANO ISLAND
Sturdies Bay • Montague Harbour

GULF ISLANDS

For convenience, the Gulf Islands section of this book includes the southern tip and the east side of Vancouver Island as far up-island as Nanaimo.

The Gulf Islands are British Columbia's version of the Washington's San Juan Islands. The San Juan Islands are the peaks of a sunken mountain range. The Gulf Islands, for the most part, are a different geology, made of sandstone that has been folded and uplifted until it sticks out of the sea. Together, the San Juan Islands and Gulf Islands create a superb cruising area.

Like the San Juan Islands, the Gulf Islands are in the lee of mountains. They receive much summertime sun and little summertime rainfall. Water is in short supply. Boat washing is something that just isn't done, at least in the islands themselves.

The Gulf Islands are blessed with dozens of anchorages, from one-boat notches to open bays that hold many boats. Marine parks provide anchorage, mooring and docking possibilities, and facilities ashore. Private marinas run the spectrum from rustic to deluxe, many with excellent dining on-site or nearby.

The largest town in the Gulf Islands proper is Ganges on Saltspring Island. If your definition of the islands expands (as ours does) to include southern and eastern Vancouver Island, then Victoria, Sidney, Ladysmith and Nanaimo are larger than Ganges.

The best provisioning stops are Victoria, Sidney, Ganges, Ladysmith, Chemainus, and Nanaimo. Fuel is available throughout the islands.

Victoria Harbour Authority's Causeway Floats are right in front of the Empress Hotel.

Navigation is straightforward, but pay attention. It's easy to get confused, and the waters are dotted with rocks and reefs. You want to know where you are at all times. Unfortunately for those who rely solely on paper charts, no single chart sheet covers all the waters, so you will be working among the 1:40,000 scale Charts 3440, 3441, 3442 and 3443, plus several large-scale charts and plans charts. Plans charts are a collection of large-scale charts all on one sheet.

The Canadian Hydrographic Chartbook 3313 is an excellent chartbook for the Gulf Islands. At $90 Cdn. this chartbook is not inexpensive, but it has everything.

Customs – Entering Canada. Vessels entering Canada are required to clear Canadian Customs at their first stop in Canada. Most boats will clear customs at Bedwell Harbour on South Pender Island, Victoria (includes Victoria Inner Harbour, Oak Bay and Cadboro Bay), Sidney, or Nanaimo. Bedwell Harbour is just 4 miles north of Stuart Island in the San Juan Islands, but its station is open only from May 1 through September 30. See page 18 for a more detailed explanation on the process of clearing Canadian Customs.

Gulf Islands National Park Reserve. The Gulf Islands National Park Reserve came into

Greater Victoria Harbour

See Area Map Page 205 - Maps Not for Navigation

GULF ISLANDS

Enjoy the views along the Westsong/Songhees mile-long pathway, where you can get on and off at various foot ferry landings.

being in 2004. Many former provincial parks, and most of the uninhabited islands and islets south of Active Pass, were transferred to the new national park, plus a number of other properties that were purchased. Land continues to be purchased and added to the Reserve. Park lands have green and white location signs, or small yellow boundary signs bearing the stylized beaver symbol of Parks Canada. Dogs must be on leash. Camping is in designated areas only. Nominal usage fees are charged, often collected through honor boxes on shore.

For more information see www.pc.gc.ca/gulf; gulf.islands@pc.gc.ca; (250) 654-4000; (866) 944-1744. For emergencies or to report problems on park lands, call toll-free (877) 852-3100.

iOS and Android App: The Parks Canada Explora app, available free for iOS and Android, provides geo-tagged maps, photos, information, and quizzes about sites throughout the Gulf Islands National Park Reserve.

VICTORIA AREA

Esquimalt Harbour. Esquimalt Harbour is a wonderful but often overlooked anchorage, with excellent holding in thick mud southeast of Cole Island, with room to swing. Protection is reasonable, even with big winds blowing in the Strait of Juan de Fuca. With this bottom you're not going anywhere, anyway. At night the lights from the shipyard reflect on the still water—magic. The Canadian Navy guards the entrance with a high speed inflatable and will advise you to keep 100 meters away from their ships and property. Anchor north of a line between the south end of Richards Island and the north end of Smart Island.

The British Navy once used Cole Island for munitions storage. The large brick buildings from the late 1800s on the island are still intact and make interesting exploration. Cole Island is a National Historic Site where visitors are welcome. A dinghy dock is located on the southwest side of Cole Island and boardwalk pathways connect all the buildings. For a map of the buildings on the island, go to www.coleisland.ca. Our sister publication, *Cruising the Secret Coast*, by Jennifer and James Hamilton, devotes an entire chapter to Esquimalt Harbour and vicinity.

Security zone: All vessels entering or departing Esquimalt Harbour are requested to contact QHM Operations on VHF channel 10 or by telephone (250) 363-2160. Give your vessel name, make, and direction of travel at Fisgard Lighthouse and Duntze Head. Fisgard Lighthouse was the first lighthouse on Canada's west coast (1860) and is still in operation.

Fleming Beach at Macaulay Park. West of Victoria Harbour, in Esquimalt. Open all year. Facilities include launch ramp (fee charged) and washrooms. This is a charming little cove, protected by a rock breakwater, overlooked by most boating people. It is the home of Esquimalt Anglers' Association, a private sportfishing and fish enhancement group. The boarding floats at the launch ramp have room for temporary moorage while shopping nearby, or you can anchor out. Walkways and picnic areas have been built. Fleming Beach is adjacent to old coastal gun emplacements, which make for good exploring.

LOCAL KNOWLEDGE

Victoria Mandatory Traffic Lanes: All vessels 65 feet LOA and less must enter and depart Victoria's Inner Harbour between Shoal Point and Laurel Point along the south shore, as shown in the accompanying harbor map. Inbound vessels favor the docks; outbound vessels a little farther out. The traffic lanes are marked by buoys (keep the buoys to port when entering and exiting). The more open water in the middle of the harbor is used by the large number of float planes that land and take off constantly. Because of the volume of boat and float plane traffic, no sailing is allowed inside the breakwater. Sailboats under power must have sails lowered.

① **Victoria.** Victoria is the provincial capital of British Columbia, and the largest city on Vancouver Island. Vancouver Island is served by ferries from Port Angeles, Wash. to Victoria; from Tsawwassen to Sidney and Victoria through Swartz Bay; and from Vancouver (Horseshoe Bay) to Nanaimo. The fast-running Victoria Clipper passenger ferry connects Victoria and Seattle. Scheduled float planes also connect with Vancouver and Seattle, and other destinations.

Victoria is beautiful. The Empress Hotel, for which the word "majestic" could have been created, dominates the Inner Harbour. The Empress

What do you say to the best room in town in one of the world's most perfect harbours?

HELLO VICTORIA.

 4 MOORAGE LOCATIONS FOR VESSELS UP TO 375 FT

 SHORT & LONG TERM MOORAGE

 PRIVATE LAUNDROMAT, WASHROOM & SHOWERS

30, 50 AND 100 AMP AVAILABLE

WI-FI ACCESS

FULL DOCK SECURITY WITH GATE ACCESS

GREATER VICTORIA HARBOUR AUTHORITY

FOR INFO ON YEAR ROUND EVENTS VISIT GVHA.CA
250 383 8326 EXT. 235 | 1 877 783 8300 EXT. 235 | ONLINE RESERVATIONS AT GVHA.CA

2018 WAGGONER CRUISING GUIDE

GULF ISLANDS

See Area Map Page 205 - Maps Not for Navigation

Oak Bay Marina

is flanked on the south by the B.C. provincial parliament buildings, themselves the embodiment of dignity, thoughtful deliberation, and orderly progress—the buildings, that is. Between the Empress and the parliament buildings stands the Royal British Columbia Museum, a must-see, especially for families. A giant ice-age mammoth dominates the entry, and the rest of the museum delights with a re-creation of Capt. Vancouver's ship, a Victorian town exhibit, a west coast seashore, a First Nations Big House and much, much more. *Highly recommended.*

The Maritime Museum of British Columbia (250) 385-4222 is located downtown in Nootka Court at 634 Humboldt Street, across from the Empress Hotel. This excellent museum is open 10:00 a.m. to 4:00 p.m. Tuesday through Saturday.

The Visitor Information Centre is on top of the causeway at the head of the Inner Harbour, across from the Empress Hotel. It's easy to find. The entire Victoria Inner Harbour is covered by Wi-Fi.

Inside Ogden Point, marinas and public wharves begin with Erie Street Wharf (Fisherman's Wharf) and progress inward to the well-marked customs dock at Raymur Point. East of the customs dock is the Coast Victoria Harbourside Hotel & Marina. Next, in James Bay, comes the Causeway Floats, in front of the Empress Hotel. These docks are popular and fill first. Northward from the Causeway Floats comes Ship Point Wharf floats. Continuing north is the Broughton Street Wharf, Wharf Street Floats, and Johnson Street Float. On the north shore of the Middle Harbour is the Victoria International Marina. With the exception of Harbourside Hotel & Marina and Victoria International Marina, all moorage facilities are managed by the Greater Victoria Harbour Authority. Details regarding these facilities are described below.

For an interesting side trip, take the dinghy through Gorge Waters to Portage Inlet. You'll travel through the industrial part of the city, then through park and residential areas. It's about a 3-mile trip; currents are a factor if you intend to row.

Customs: The customs dock is located at Raymur Point, just east of Fisherman's Wharf in front of the Harbourside Hotel & Marina. When arriving, check in using the dedicated phone at the customs dock.

Greater Victoria Harbour Authority: The Greater Victoria Harbour Authority operates 6 facilities, 3 of which have transient moorage: Causeway Floats, Ship Point Wharf (large vessels), and Wharf Street Floats. Laundry, showers, and washrooms for all three transient facilities are located on the Broughton Street Wharf—look for the gray building with a red roof. The Harbour Authority has a "meet and greet" program for visiting boats. When you enter the Inner Harbour, call on VHF 66A and they will direct you to available guest moorage.

Reservations: The Coast Victoria Harbourside Hotel & Marina, adjacent to the Erie Street Wharf, accepts reservations. The Greater Victoria Harbour Authority accepts reservations for any size vessel. The Harbour Authority recommends that vessels greater than 60 feet LOA call ahead so space can be found: (250) 383-8326; (877) 783-8300; reservations@gvha.ca.

Symphony Splash: On the first weekend in August enjoy symphony music from a barge in the Inner Harbour, punctuated with cannons and fireworks. Over 40,000 people line the Inner Harbour for the evening event.

No Discharge Zone. Discharging raw sewage is prohibited in Victoria Inner Harbour, defined as beginning at the Ogden Point breakwater. This applies to "black water" only. "Gray water," such as from dishwashing or showers, is okay (if biodegradable).

Pumpout: A for fee pumpout station is located on the B Dock of Fisherman's Wharf. Tokens to operate the pump are available at Victoria Marine Fuels and the Harbour Authority seasonal kiosk at the Causeway Floats.

Things to Do

1. **Royal British Columbia Museum**. An extraordinary museum covering the human and natural history of British Columbia is just above James Bay in Victoria.

2. **B.C. Maritime Museum**. Displays on B.C. marine history, the voyages of Captain George Vancouver, and other rotating exhibits..

3. **Afternoon tea at the Empress Hotel**. A special treat, high tea offers pastries and piano music in an elegant setting.

4. **Victoria Inner Harbour**. Watch street musicians, mimes, and artists. The waterfront comes alive in the summer. Great boat watching, too.

Greater Victoria Harbour Authority - GVHA. The Victoria Harbour Authority operates six marina facilities in the Victoria harbour area, three of which have short and long-term transient moorage.

① **Erie Street Wharf (Fisherman's) - GVHA.** Erie Street Wharf is reserved primarily for commercial and monthly moorage. No transient space.

① **Causeway Floats - GVHA.** (250) 383-8326 ext. 235 or 265; (877) 783-8300 ext. 235 or 265; reservations@gvha.ca; www.gvha.ca. Monitors VHF 66A. Open all year with 2000+ feet of side-tie dock space for vessels to 60 feet, 30 amp power, potable water, free Wi-Fi, garbage and recycling drop. Limited transient moorage October 1 through May 15. Docks are gated at night, June-September, gated all hours October-May. The check-in kiosk, located beside the ramp to shore, is open June 15 through September 15.

These are the picturesque and popular docks directly in front of the Empress Hotel. Downtown Victoria beckons with fabulous restaurants, shopping, hotels, museums, and sightseeing. Public washrooms (no showers) are located under the Visitors Centre building. Private, clean Harbour Authority operated showers, laundry, and washrooms are at the Broughton Street Wharf.

① **Ship Point Floats - GVHA.** (250) 383-8326 ext. 235 or 265; (877) 783-8300 ext. 235 or 265; reservations@gvha.ca; www.gvha.ca. Monitors VHF 66A. Open all year for larger vessels to 280 feet, slips and side-tie, gated all-hours. Reservations highly recommended. Potable water, 30, 50, 100 amp single phase/208 & 3-phase/480 power, free Wi-Fi, garbage, recycling drop. Public washrooms (no showers) are located under the Visitors Centre building. Private and clean Harbour Authority-operated showers, laundry and washrooms are at the Broughton Street Wharf.

① **Broughton Street Wharf - GVHA.** Showers, washrooms, and laundry facilities, serving Harbour Authority transient moorage guests, are located on the Broughton Street Wharf (site of the old customs dock). No transient moorage at the Broughton Street Wharf.

See Area Map Page 205 - Maps Not for Navigation

GULF ISLANDS

① **Wharf Street Floats - GVHA.** (250) 383-8326 ext. 235 or 265; (877) 783-8300 ext. 235 or 265; reservations@gvha.ca; www.gvha.ca. Monitors VHF 66A. Open all year for vessels to 375 feet, more than 1000 feet of side-tie visitor dock space. Limited guest moorage October 1 to end of May. Potable water, 30, 50 & 100 amp power (single phase/208), free Wi-Fi. Power availability varies depending on location. Washrooms, showers, laundry, garbage & recycling drop are located on the adjacent Broughton Street Wharf. Conveniently located downtown, just not quite as picturesque as the Causeway Floats in front of the Empress Hotel.

① **Johnson Street Float- GVHA.** This marina facility is for monthly moorage only, primarily used by fish boats and commercial vessels.

① **Victoria Marine Fuels Ltd.** (250) 381-5221; www.marinefuels.com. Fuel dock with gasoline and diesel, located at Erie Street Fisherman's Wharf at 1 Dallas Rd. Open all year, but with shorter winter hours, closed Christmas Day and New Year's Day. Store stocks snacks, food items, charts. This is the only fuel dock in the Inner Harbour.

① **Coast Victoria Harbourside Hotel & Marina.** 146 Kingston Street, Victoria, V8V 1V4; (250) 360-1211; coastvictoria@coasthotels.com; www.coasthotels.com. Guest moorage May through September, limited availability October through April; 30 & 50 amp power, potable water on the docks, washrooms and showers. Marina guests have full access to the dining room and lounge, indoor/outdoor pool, Jacuzzi, sauna, and fitness facilities. Reservations accepted. Within walking distance of downtown.

① **Victoria International Marina.** 1 Cooperage Place, Victoria, BC V9A 7J9; (778) 432-0477; info@vimarina.ca; www.vimarina.ca. On the north shore of Victoria Harbour, northeast of Pelly Island, two symmetrical one-story buildings sit on either side of this 28-slip marina designed to accommodate boats 65 to 175 feet in length. Seven slips are leased for 40 years; seven slips are available for one-year renewable leases; seven slips for monthly leases with a 3-month minimum stay; and seven slips are reserved for transient moorage with a 3-day minimum stay. This is a world-class marina with first-class marina services and crew quarters. The marina is designed and built with luxury yachts in mind. Due to Victoria Harbour traffic restrictions imposed by Transport Canada, this marina is currently for yachts 65 feet and over. Future plans for the marina include a restaurant that will be open to the public. The beautiful Westsong/Songhees Walkway meanders along the shore offering outstanding views. Three water-taxi landings are located along the Walkway with departures to Victoria's downtown waterfront.

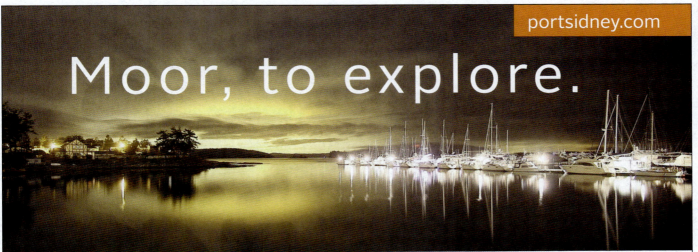

Come and visit the new Port Sidney marina, located at the best entrance to Beacon Ave. The marina now offers special group bookings, custom docks with a large covered tent, showers and laundry and wifi. So whether you stay for a night or a month it's the perfect location to Moor, and explore Sidney and the surrounding Gulf Islands.

MILL BAY **MARINE** GROUP

Bridgemans Bistro	**Mill Bay Marina**	**Pacific Gateway Marina**	**Port Browning Marina**	**MK Bay Marina**
Mill Bay BC	Mill Bay BC	Port Renfrew BC	Pender Island BC	Kitimat BC

2018 waggoner CRUISING GUIDE

GULF ISLANDS   See Area Map Page 205 - Maps Not for Navigation

The dog and people friendly Beacon Park along Sidney's waterfront

① **Westbay Marina.** (250) 385-1831; www.westbay.bc.ca; located in Victoria Harbour, west side; permanent moorage with transient slips occassionally available.

② **Oak Bay.** Oak Bay is on the east side of the south tip of Vancouver Island, west of the Chatham Islands. The channels between the various rocks and reefs are well marked. This is the route taken by many tugs with tows, and commercial fish boats of all sizes. The Oak Bay Marina and a separate small repair yard are located behind the breakwater.

② **Oak Bay Marina.** 1327 Beach Drive, Victoria, BC V8S 2N4; (250) 598-3369; (800) 663-7090 ext. 247; obm@obmg.com; www.oakbaymarina.com. Open all year with gasoline and diesel at the fuel dock. Customs clearance telephone at the fuel dock. Guest moorage for boats to 80 feet, 15 & 30 amp power, washrooms, showers, laundry. Call ahead for availability.

The marina has excellent docks and a good licensed waterfront restaurant. Outdoor seating on the deck overlooking the marina. The restaurant offers a coffee house for quick casual dining, and a gift shop with local products and sundry items. A small chandlery carries essential boating supplies. Repairs are at the Gartside Marine boatyard in a neighboring building, no haulout. The Oak Bay Beach Hotel is nearby for elegant dining. Complete shopping at quaint Oak Bay Village a short distance away. Regular bus service to downtown Victoria.

Discovery Island Marine Park. Open all year. An undeveloped park suitable for beachable boats only. The island was once the home of Capt. E.G. Beaumont, who donated the land as a park. The northern part of Discovery Island, adjacent Chatham Island, and some of the smaller islands nearby are Indian Reserve lands: no landing.

Cadboro Bay. Cadboro Bay is entirely residential except for the Royal Victoria Yacht Club, which has a breakwater-protected marina on the western shore. Moorage at Royal Victoria Yacht Club is for members of reciprocal clubs only. Customs clearance is available.

Anchorage in Cadboro Bay is excellent, mud and sand bottom. A 100-foot long concrete replica of Cadborosaurus, the elusive sea monster of Cadboro Bay, is prominent in the playground above the broad sandy beach at Cadboro-Gyro Park.

③ **D'Arcy Island (Gulf Islands National Park Reserve).** Open all year. This is an undeveloped island with no facilities other than some primitive campsites and a toilet. Dogs must be on leash. The island is surrounded by intimidating rocks, reefs, and shoals. Even if you study the chart carefully, kelp-covered rocks will pop up and surprise you. Approach with great caution.

As far as we are concerned, there are no "good" anchorages at D'Arcy Island, only acceptable spots in the right weather. If conditions allow, the cove on the west side of the island, south of the light, will work. Two coves on the northwest end look okay, but we didn't put the anchor down to confirm. The single Parks staff mooring buoy is in the cove on the east side of the island. This cove is closest to the island's campsites. We have not explored it ourselves.

D'Arcy Island was B.C.'s first leper colony; from 1891 until 1925 it housed Chinese lepers. The colony was closed in 1925 and the island reverted to provincial jurisdiction. Plans for the island as a federal penitentiary were never realized. D'Arcy Island remained undeveloped, and was established as a marine park in 1961. *A Measure of Value,* by Chris Yorath, provides a good history of D'Arcy Island.

To the east, Little D'Arcy Island is private property.

④ **Sidney Spit (Gulf Islands National Park Reserve).** The park, open all year occupies about one-third of Sidney Island, and all of the mile-long Sidney Spit with its white sand and shell beach extending northwest from the island. Anchor or tie to one of 12 mooring buoys, or moor on the seasonal dock. Anchoring depths are shallow and the area has considerable eel grass. Self-registration and payment box located at the dock. Buoys are limited to vessels of 50 feet or less in winds up to 30 knots; 40 feet for winds up to 37 knots; no mooring in large waves. In the summers, a passenger ferry runs between Sidney Spit dock and Sidney Beacon Ave dock.

Picnic and camping areas are ashore. Dogs must be on leash. An easily walked 2-km loop trail winds around the park through a dense forest of cedar, hemlock, fir, big-leaf maple and vine maple. A herd of fallow deer is reported to be on the island. A large saltwater lagoon is habitat for many animal and plant species and is off limits; markers show its borders. The remains of a brick-making factory are near the lagoon, where a beach is covered with broken red bricks.

⑤ **Isle-de-Lis at Rum Island (Gulf Islands National Park Reserve).** Open all year, anchoring only, campsites and a pit toilet. This is a small, undeveloped, and very pretty park with a walking trail and beaches. Dogs must be on leash. Rum Island is located at the east end of Gooch Island (private), where Prevost Passage meets Haro Strait. Anchorage is on either side of the gravel spit connecting Rum Island and Gooch Island. The northern anchorage is preferred. Rum Island is said to have come by its name honestly during Prohibition. In 1995 the warship HMCS *Mackenzie* was sunk in approximately 100 feet just north of Gooch Island to create an artificial reef for divers. It is marked with 2 cautionary/information buoys.

Roberts Bay. Good anchorage, centrally located about a mile from both Sidney and Tsehum Harbour. Anchor in the center of the bay where the large shallow bay gives separation from the homes lining the shore. Good holding on a flat mud bottom, but exposed to north and northeast winds. Large wakes from boats entering and exiting Tsehum Harbour occasionally find their way into the anchorage but the bay becomes settled in the evening.

THINGS TO DO

1. **Butchart Gardens in Brentwood Bay.** A 55-acre display of flowers and gardens. Fireworks on Saturdays in the summer. Take the bus from Victoria or visit the area by boat.

2. **Shaw Ocean Discovery Centre in Sidney.** Learn more about the ecosystem of the B.C. coastal waters.

3. **Bookstores.** Downtown Sidney has numerous bookstores, everything from books for kids to collectors. Even a haunted bookstore. See why Sidney is called Booktown.

4. **Lochside Regional Trail along the waterfront.** Rent bikes for this flat and easy-to-ride trail from Victoria to Sidney.

⑥ **Sidney.** For boats crossing from Roche Harbor or the northern San Juan Islands, Sidney is a natural first stop to clear customs, stroll around, and restock with fresh produce, meat, spirits, and more. Downtown Sidney and nearby Tsehum Harbour have much to attract boaters, including excellent bakeries just up Beacon Avenue (Sidney's main street). The town also has art galleries, interesting shops, liquor stores, several bookstores, several museums, and three supermarkets. Summer concerts are held on the lawn at the base of Beacon Street. A paved walkway stretches 2.5 km along the Sidney waterfront between Port Sidney Marina and south beyond the Washington State Ferries terminal. It is part of the 29 km multi-use Lochside Regional Trail stretching from Swartz Bay to Victoria.

The Sidney Historical Museum occupies the lower floor of the old Post Office Building, up at the corner of 4th and Beacon. The museum has an excellent exhibit of early history in Sidney, admission by donation. Highly recommended, especially for families. Located at the nearby Sidney airport is the BC Aviation Museum a short cab ride away.

The Shaw Ocean Discovery Centre in the Sidney Pier building has outstanding exhibits of marine life from local waters.

Port Sidney Marina

For an entirely different feeling from downtown Sidney try Tsehum Harbour, a short distance north of downtown. The pace in Tsehum Harbour is much slower, and many of the moored boats are funkier. This is where the fishing fleet moors, and where the boat yards are. Van Isle Marina is the major marina.

Something about Tsehum Harbour attracts good restaurants, too. Tsehum Harbour's only disadvantage is the long walk to major shopping. Regular bus service runs into Sidney, or you could take a taxi or rent a car. Thrifty Foods charges $5 per order for delivery.

Market: The Sidney Street Market takes over the lower part of Beacon Avenue Thursday evenings May through September, 5:30 p.m. to 8:30 p.m.

Customs: Sidney is the western terminus of the Washington State Ferries that run from Anacortes and Friday Harbor, and is a Canada Customs port of entry. Customs can be cleared by telephone at Port Sidney Marina, Van Isle Marina or Canoe Cove Marina.

GULF ISLANDS   See Area Map Page 205 - Maps Not for Navigation

Delta
MARINE SERVICE

2075 Tryon Rd Sidney BC Canada V8L 3X9
Tel: 250.656.2639   Fax: 250.656.2619
Westport Marina in Tsehum Harbour

tracy@delta-marine.com   www.delta-marine.com   brian@delta-marine.com

- Absentee owner care
- Custody & provisioning
- Bright work & detailing
- Professional paint & varnish facility
- Structural & cosmetic fiberglass repair
- Custom cabinet shop
- Interior yacht design
- Full mechanical & electrical service
- Stainless steel & aluminum fabrication
- 55 ton local travel lift & 100 ton option mid island

FLEMING

GB AUTHORIZED SERVICE CENTER

PHILBROOK'S BOAT YARD LTD.
Experience a Higher Standard

WE ...
- Do It Once
- Do It Right
- Do It On Time
- Do It On Budget
- Do It All

Haulouts
Canvas
Mechanical
Electrical
Paint
Composites
Wood
Metal Fabrication

Toll Free 1-877-656-1157
Phone 250-656-1157 FAX 250-656-1155
Sidney, B.C. Canada
www.philbrooks.com • yachts@philbrooks.com

We Guarantee It

CANADIAN SERVICE AND WARRANTY PROVIDERS FOR NORDHAVN AND SELENE

GULF ISLANDS

Wi-Fi: Free Wi-Fi throughout town. Select Sidney WiFi network and accept terms to connect.

Golf: Glen Meadows, 18 holes, (250) 656-3921; Ardmore, 9 holes (250) 656-4621. Both are said to be good courses.

⑥ **Port Sidney Marina.** 9835 Seaport Place, P.O. Box 2338, Sidney, BC V8L 4X3; (250) 655-3711; admin@portsidney.com; www.portsidney.com. Monitors VHF 66A. Open all year. Facilities include 30, 50 & 100 amp power, water, excellent washrooms, showers, laundry, Shaw Go Wi-Fi on the docks and free Wi-Fi in the comfortable marina lounge. This is a popular marina, modern and well-maintained, adjacent to downtown Sidney. Reservations recommended. A for-fee pumpout, located between D and E docks, accommodates boats up to 40 feet. The marina is part of the Mill Bay Marine Group, a company that owns several marinas throughout B.C.

Call on VHF 66A low power before entering and exiting the breakwater. When approaching from the north, pass between the two buoys just outside the breakwater entrance. The easternmost of these buoys marks a reef. Do not try to enter between the north end of the breakwater and shore. If you are directed to the shore side of the long, main pier, do not stray outside the marked channel. The bottom has been dredged alongside the shoreside dock, but shoal water lies just a few feet inshore.

Customs: The customs check-in dock is on the end of G dock. Customs can be cleared by using the direct-line telephone on the dock. During summer months customs officers may be stationed there for inspections after calling in. Space at the dock is limited to one or two boats and once inside the breakwater maneuvering room is limited. The marina office has a video camera pointed at the dock and they can advise over the VHF if boats are waiting to clear customs.

⑥ **Sidney Beacon Ave. Public Wharf.** Sidney Beacon Avenue Public Wharf is used only for the summertime ferry to Sidney Spit Marine Park and does not have public dock space. A snack bar, café and a fresh fish market are at the end of the pier.

⑦ **Tsehum Harbour.** Tsehum Harbour (Tsehum is pronounced "See-um"), a shallow but navigable inlet about 1.5 miles north of downtown Sidney, contains a number of public, private, and yacht club moorages as well as chandleries. Enter favoring the Armstrong Point (south) side to avoid a marked rock. This is the working waterfront of Sidney, with several excellent boatyards. Van Isle Marina, the first marina on the south side, has a customs check-in telephone, fuel, and guest moorage. Westport has guest moorage, and many services including haulout and free showers. Other moorages in Tsehum Harbour are North Saanich Marina, Capitol City and Sidney North Saanich yacht clubs, a Royal Victoria Yacht Club outstation, and private marinas. The main fuel dock is in Van Isle Marina. Fuel is also available at North Saanich Marina.

Speed limit: A speed limit of 4 knots is in force in Tsehum Harbour. Watch your wake.

Repairs: Haulout and complete repairs are available.

LOCAL KNOWLEDGE

ROCKS: Stay close to the end of the dock when rounding the west end of the fuel and customs dock at Van Isle Marina. A substantial drying rock lies a short distance off, and each year a few boats manage to find it. The rock is marked by a beacon, but the rock extends toward the dock from the beacon.

⑦ **Van Isle Marina.** 2320 Harbour Road, Sidney, V8L 2P6; (250) 656-1138; info@vanislemarina.com; www.vanislemarina.com. Monitors VHF 66A. Open 7 days a week, all year. Gasoline and diesel at fuel dock, customs clearance with dedicated phone in the small shed at the end of the fuel dock, Shaw Go Wi-Fi, 15, 30, 50 & 100 amp power, excellent washrooms, showers and laundry, pumpout, launch ramp for marina guests, oil pumpout. Internet is provided free through an installation by Shaw Go. Passwords available from the office. A business center with computer connections, copy machine, fax machine, and conference room is available for marina guests.

A side-tie dock, 451 feet long and 15 feet wide, runs parallel to the breakwater on the east side of the marina. It is set up for yachts up to 200' and more, with 100 amp power,

Tsehum Harbour

2018 waggoner CRUISING GUIDE   213

GULF ISLANDS

telephone, cable, and internet connections. Large boat or small, it's best to call ahead for guest moorage availability.

Van Isle is a large and busy marina, about a mile from downtown. Full repair services, haulout to 45 tons, and dry storage are available. The Thrifty Foods in Sidney will deliver groceries to the marina. The Sea Glass Waterfront Grill is at the head of the dock, call (778) 351-3663 for reservations. The famous Latch Country Inn Restaurant is a short walk away. The marina offers bicycles at no charge to ride into Sidney or on the popular Lochside Trail, nearby.

Since 1955 Van Isle Marina has been owned and managed by three generations of the Dickinson family. The family's long-term commitment to doing things right is evident. The staff is excellent, and the facilities are top-notch.

⑦ **Tsehum Harbour Public Wharf.** (250) 655-4496. Open all year, 1043 feet of dock space, power, washrooms, no showers. This is a commercial fish boat harbor that accepts very limited transient moorage. Call in advance.

⑦ **Westport Marina.** 2075 Tryon Road, Sidney, BC V8L 3X9; (250) 656-2832; westport@thunderbirdmarine.com; www.thunderbirdmarine.com. Open all year, 15, 20 & 30 amp power, washrooms, free showers, Wi-Fi. Guest moorage in unoccupied slips, call ahead for availability. Haulout to 55 tons. Well stocked chandlery, charts, limited groceries.

⑦ **North Saanich Marina.** P.O. Box 2001, 1949 Marina Way, North Saanich, BC V8L 3S3; (250) 656-5558; nsm@obmg.com; www.northsaanichmarina.com. Open all year, gasoline and diesel at fuel dock, not always attended. Washrooms at main office. Permanent and visitor moorage usually available for vessels to 70 feet, 15, 30 & 50 amp power. Recent dock refurbishments, large dog walking area, and a short taxi ride to the nearby town of Sidney. Store carries sundries, fishing tackle, boat cleaning supplies, ice. Call ahead for moorage availability. The marina is part of Oak Bay Marine Group, a company that owns several marinas and fishing resorts throughout B.C.

⑧ **Canoe Bay.** Canoe Bay, commonly called Canoe Cove, is tucked in behind a group of islands, only some of which have navigable passages between them. The clearest passage is **John Passage**, along the west side of Coal Island. From John Passage turn west into **Iroquois Passage**, and follow Iroquois Passage between Fernie Island and Goudge Island into Canoe Bay. From the south, **Page Passage**, west of Fernie Island,

Van Isle Marina

Westport Marina

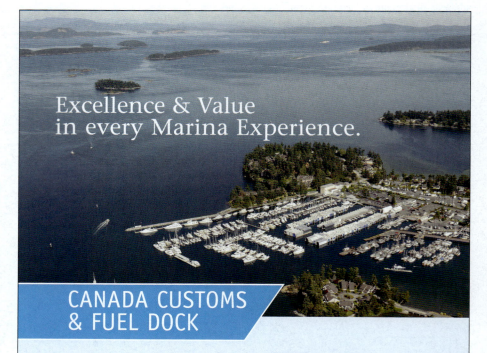

Excellence & Value in every Marina Experience.

CANADA CUSTOMS & FUEL DOCK

- 500 berths for annual, monthly or nightly moorage
- Service for boats 20' to 200'
- Fuel dock and marine store
- Canada Customs Port of Entry
- Haul outs and full repair facilities
- Yacht Park - 90 spaces for dry land storage and maintenance
- 15/30/50/100 amp shore power
- Casual dining at Sea Glass Grill
- Business centre and meeting room
- Laundry, showers and washrooms
- Yacht brokerage and sales
- Free WiFi

Situated in beautiful Tsehum Harbour by Sidney, British Columbia, Van Isle Marina is just 5 minutes from ferries, Victoria International Airport and shopping.

VAN ISLE MARINA
family owned & operated since 1955

Tsehum Harbour, Sidney, BC | 250.656.1138 | info@vanislemarina.com

vanislemarina.com

SWIMMING POOLS OF THE INSIDE PASSAGE

Swimming pools are a welcome treat at a marina. Over the years we've had many readers request a list of boat-accessible swimming pools in the Northwest. As it turns out, there are many choices, from Hood Canal to Gorge Harbour, and most of the pools are heated. You just need to know how to find them.

ALDERBROOK RESORT & SPA
The indoor heated pool is in a greenhouse adjacent to Hood Canal, with a beautiful view of the area.

Pleasant Harbor Marina

PLEASANT HARBOR MARINA
The heated outdoor pool and hot tub are tucked among the trees above the marina. Open seasonally.

ROSARIO RESORT & SPA
Three pools are located around the property. The family pool is adjacent to the marina. The adults-only pool is in front of the resort on a sun deck. A lap pool is tucked into the spa in the basement of the historic mansion.

LOPEZ ISLANDER RESORT & MARINA
Pool and hot tub are located across the street from the marina and main lodge building.

Deer Harbor Marina

DEER HARBOR MARINA
The seasonal outdoor pool is up the hill and overlooks the marina.

Roche Harbor Marina

ROCHE HARBOR MARINA
The large heated pool is on the hill overlooking the marina. A dinghy dock provides access, or walk around from the main docks.

SEMIAHMOO MARINA
The spa and pool are part of the Semiahmoo Health Club at the resort, and are available for a fee.

Poets Cove Marina

POETS COVE MARINA
The pool and hot tub overlooks the marina. Laundry is just a few steps away, so you can catch up with the wash while lounging at the pool.

PORT BROWNING MARINA
The pool is on the sloping hillside next to the pub. Kids love this pool.

Otter Bay Marina

OTTER BAY MARINA
The adults-only pool is just up the way, next to the main building and snack bar. The family pool is up the hill.

BRENTWOOD BAY RESORT & MARINA
The pool and hot tub are just outside the main building, overlooking the marina. The focus is on serenity and relaxation for adults.

GANGES
The new community center has a pool and shower facility for visitors. Ask the marina for directions.

OCEANFRONT SUITES AT COWICHAN BAY
Oceanfront Suites has moorage and an indoor pool. Guests of other marinas can use the pool for a fee.

BEACH GARDENS RESORT & MARINA
You can enjoy the indoor pool year round.

GORGE HARBOUR MARINA RESORT
The pool and hot tub look over the marina and the harbor.

Gorge Harbour Marina Resort

GULF ISLANDS

See Area Map Page 205 - Maps Not for Navigation

leads to Canoe Bay, and many boats use Page Passage. Canoe Bay has moorage with all amenities.

Caution: Page Passage should be run only with local knowledge or close study of large-scale Chart 3479. Tidal currents can run strongly, especially on spring tides.

⑧ **Canoe Cove Marina & Boatyard.** 2300 Canoe Cove Road, North Saanich, BC V8L 3X9; (250) 656-5566; (250) 656-5515; www.canoecovemarina.com. Monitors VHF 66A. Open all year, gasoline, diesel, propane at fuel dock, 30 & 50 amp power, washrooms, showers, laundry, 24-hour customs clearance at fuel dock, free Wi-Fi. This is a 450-berth marina with permanent and visitor moorage. Best to call ahead.

Navigate carefully on approach. A number of islands and rocks surround the entrance to Canoe Cove. They are well marked on the charts and easily avoided as long as you pay attention.

Canoe Cove Joe's Cafe is in the center of the marina, and the excellent Stonehouse Restaurant is nearby. A short trail leads to the Swartz Bay ferry terminal for arriving or departing guests from Tsawwassen, on the B.C. mainland. A harbor taxi shuttle connects the marina with Sidney. Pacifica Paddle Sports (250) 665-7411 at Canoe Cove offers kayak, canoe, and paddleboard rentals along with lessons and tours.

Canoe Cove's major thrust is its environmentally friendly full repair facility. They recently added a new 83-ton Travelift, and they have extensive covered work areas and a well-stocked chandlery now run by Vector Marine. The staff and management are friendly and competent. Together with Vector Marine, Blackline Marine, Raven Marine, Sea Power Marine Centre, Jespersen Boat Builders, Reyse Marine, and Lightship Marine Mobile, they can do anything.

Customs: The customs clearance dock is located on the fuel dock pier.

Swartz Bay Public Wharf. Open all year, adjacent to the ferry terminal, with 85 feet of dock space. No facilities. Watch for heavy ferry traffic near Swartz Bay.

Piers Island Public Wharf. Open all year with 200 feet of dock space, no facilities.

⑨ **Portland Island (Gulf Islands National Park Reserve).** Formerly Princess Margaret Provincial Marine Park. Open all year, picnic and campsites, toilets, no other facilities. Dogs must be on leash and cleaned up after. In honor of her last visit to Victoria, Portland Island was donated to Her Royal Highness Princess Margaret, who later deeded the island to British Columbia. The park is now part of the Gulf Islands National Park Reserve.

Portland Island is wooded and hilly. Hiking trails follow the coastline. Easy-walking service roads and trails crisscross the center of the island. It would be easy to spend an entire day exploring. Reader Tyson Nevil says the coastline trail is easier to follow when walking in a counter-clockwise direction.

Anchor in Royal Cove (behind Chads Island) on the north side of the island, or in Princess Bay,

Poets Cove Resort in Bedwell Harbour is one of the most popular clearance points when entering Canada.

behind Tortoise Island on the south side. The Royal Cove anchorage is exposed to the wakes of passing BC ferries, and Princess Bay also gets wakes. At Royal Cove you can have a quiet night if you can get well inside. Poorly marked stern-tie rings are along the high tide line in Royal Cove.

There's room for a couple of boats behind Brackman Island, off the southwest corner of Portland Island. Watch your depths at low tide. Brackman Island is a protected wildlife and bird sanctuary. No access is allowed above the high tide line and no pets are allowed.

Princess Bay is roomier and far more popular, but somewhat exposed to southerly winds. In summer it's usually fine. With its shallow depths, not much anchor rode need be paid out, and the boats squeeze in pretty tightly. Watch your depths as you approach the head of Princess Bay. The bottom shoals rapidly, farther from shore than you might expect. Dinghy docks in Royal Cove and Princess Bay provide shore access.

The host float in Princess Bay is staffed by yacht club volunteers during the summer. They answer questions and give out information.

The *G.B. Church*, a sunken freighter off the southwest shore of the island, is an artificial reef for divers. The freighter lies in 100 feet and is marked with bow and stern buoys.

PLUMPER SOUND AREA

Bedwell Harbour. Bedwell Harbour has a luxury marina resort, Poets Cove, with docks that give complete access to the facilities ashore. North of the resort, anchorage is good (except in a southeasterly) off the Beaumont/Mount Norman portion of Gulf Islands National Park Reserve. Anchorage also is good, if tight, in Peter Cove, on the west side of the harbor.

Slow Coast Coffee and Medicine Beach Liquor store are located a short walk from Medicine Beach, at the north end of Bedwell Harbour. No dock, but easy anchoring just offshore, and a sandy beach for the dinghy.

Customs clearance: The Canada Border Services Agency (Canada Customs) dock is adjacent to Poets Cove Marina and well marked. Open from May 1 to September 30. Except for landing, only the skipper can leave the boat until customs is cleared. The procedure is for the captain to go up the ramp to the direct-line telephones along the wall of the customs office. Have all of the vessel's paperwork and crew's

Canoe Cove Marina

CANOE COVE MARKETPLACE

RESTAURANTS & SHOPS

ALL THINGS MARINE THRIFT STORE
The Maritime Museum of BC has opened the marine focused thrift store which will take in donated surplus marine equipment to be sold by volunteers of the Museum. This is a great way to reuse and recycle the many extra pieces of marine equipment that most boaters gather and see them go to a good use. The MMBC will be accepting donations of saleable marine equipment and tools at their location at Canoe Cove Marina on Fridays and Saturdays.
Open Fridays and Saturdays • 250-385-4222 ext. 102
www.mmbc.bc.ca

BLACKLINE MARINE INC.
Blackline delivers industry leading service in yacht rigging, composite repair, AwlGrip paint refinishing, custom metal fabrication, and seasonal maintenance. Canoe Cove Marina has been our home for 37 years and we are proud to be an active member of this service community.
Service & Haul Outs: 250-656-6616
info@blacklinemarine.com

CANOE COVE MARINA & BOATYARD
Canoe Cove Marina has been a preferred "one-stop" full service marina for over 75 years. Commitment to customer service, ongoing upgrading of technical skills, and regular expansion of facilities, has been the hallmark of the Marina's success.
250-656-5566 • 2300 Canoe Cove Rd., North Saanich, BC V8L 3X9. • info@canoecovemarina.com

JESPERSON BOAT BUILDERS
Jespersen Boat Builders has been building, refitting, and repairing boats for over 45 years. Conveniently located at Canoe Cove Marina, Jespersen provides the highest quality craftsmanship in all areas of marine woodworking; including cold molded construction, traditional planking, interior and exterior joinery, teak decking, and wooden spars.
250-656-2581 • jespersenboats@telus.net

RAVEN MARINE
Providing professional yacht services to the Pacific Northwest for over 20 years. Our accredited technical teams are experienced with installations, maintenance, and repairs. Our professional brokers will provide the advice and expertise you need to make an informed decision.
250-655-3934 • info@ravenmarine.ca

M. MORGAN WARREN STUDIO
M. Morgan Warren lives and maintains a working studio at Canoe Cove. She is well known for her highly detailed realistic watercolours of the birds of North America and her native Britain. Over the past thirty years she has made an in-depth study of the flora and fauna of this region, and has recorded those observations in her art and her writing, striving to give people a special glimpse into the hidden lives of her subjects.
778-678-3581 • www.morganwarren.com

TOTAL BOAT MARINE SURVEYORS
Total Boat Marine Surveyors Limited has a long standing reputation for quality marine surveying and marine claim damage reporting on Vancouver Island. The company is a member of the NAMS Global and ABYC and conducts regular continuing education to keep up to date on the latest standards and developments in the boat repair and maintenance field. We think you will enjoy our personal approach to your marine survey.
250-508-4418 • Kelly Thody - Marine Surveyor and Owner
kelly@totalboatmarine.com

VECTOR YACHT SERVICES
Vector Yacht Services is the premier marine repair, service, and repower center for Vancouver Island. With over 30 years of service, our factory trained service technicians are experienced in all aspects of boat systems. We pride ourselves on providing quality workmanship and exceeding customer expectations.
Chandlery & Service 250-656-5515 • cc@vectoryacht.com

GULF ISLANDS

passport information ready. Call in for clearance. In most cases the agent on the telephone will give you a clearance number, but you may be asked to stand by for agents to inspect your vessel. Canpass or Nexus permits only from October 1 through April 30. See the U.S. and Canadian Customs Information section for more information on clearing Canadian Customs.

Peter Cove. Peter Cove is at the southern tip of North Pender Island. It is a well protected little anchorage, but permanently moored boats make anchoring a bit tight. A significant reef guards the mouth of the cove. Enter and depart north of the reef.

⑩ **Poets Cove Marina.** 9801 Spalding Road, RR #3, South Pender Island, BC V0N 2M3; (250) 629-2100; (250) 629-2111 marina; marina@poetscove.com; www.poetscove.com. Open all year, gasoline, diesel, and ice at the fuel dock. Guest moorage to 100 feet in 95 slips and side-tie, 30 amp power. If slips are filled, a floating dock is available at a reduced rate. Liquor store, cafe, pub with dining, heated pool, hot tub, spa, Eucalyptus Steam Cave, fitness center, and free Wi-Fi. Coin-operated laundry machines are located adjacent to the pool.

This popular resort is first class in every way, including the well trained staff. The casual Moorings Cafe is located in the building adjacent to the pool, and serves sandwiches and coffee, has convenience items, and sells liquor. Syrens Bistro and Lounge, open April through October, serves lunch and dinner noon to 9:00 p.m. and has seating indoors or out on the patio. Aurora, a fine dining venue, serves breakfast and dinner, open May through September.

Poets Cove has plenty of activities. Book an aerial whale watching excursion, rent a bike or kayak and explore the island, play a round of golf, or try out the disc golf course. Kids Camp programs are available through Dog Mermaid Eco Excursions (250) 222-0015. Shuttle service is available.

Beaumont/Mount Norman Park (Gulf Islands National Park Reserve). In Bedwell Harbour, west side of South Pender Island, in Bedwell Harbour. Open all year. Facilities include 15 mooring buoys (pay buoy fees at honor box top of staircase above the beach northwest of the buoys, no charge before 3:00 p.m.). Mooring buoys accommodate boats up to 50 feet, or 40 feet depending upon wind conditions. Signage for size limits are posted on the buoys. Toilets, no showers or fresh water. Walk-in campsites, picnicking, excellent walking and hiking trails. Hike to the top of Mount Norman, elevation 800 feet, for a memorable view. Dogs must be on leash.

Enter from Swanson Channel from the south, or from Plumper Sound and Port Browning through Pender Canal (27-foot clearance).

Pender Canal. Pender Canal is a man-made dogleg channel between North Pender Island and South Pender Island, connecting Bedwell Harbour and Port Browning. The canal is crossed by a bridge with 27 feet of vertical clearance. Pender Canal is narrow, shallow, and often has a swift current running through it. Because of its dogleg shape, vessels approaching from opposite directions cannot see each other until they are in the narrowest section.

Before entering, signal your intentions on VHF 16, low power: *Securite, Securite, this is the 34-foot motor vessel Happy Days, northbound from Bedwell Harbour to Port Browning. Any concerned traffic please advise, channel one-six.*

⑪ **Port Browning.** Port Browning has a resort (Port Browning Marina) with moorage and other facilities. Anchorage is good

Bedwell Harbour

Overlooking the marina at Port Browning

Bridgeman's Bistro at Port Browning features beer on tap and specialty wines.

throughout the harbor. The Driftwood Centre shopping area is about a half-mile walk from the marina or you can call the Pender Island Cab at (250) 629-2222. The center has a beautiful Tru-Value Foods, a bank, gift shop, book store, bakery, liquor store, pharmacy, and post office. The gas station now has marine supplies.

⑪ **Port Browning Marina.** PP.O. Box 126, North Pender Island, BC V0N 2M0; (250) 629-3493; contact@portbrowning.ca; www.portbrowning.ca. Monitors VHF 66A. Canpass/Nexus-only reporting station. Open all year, 3000 feet of guest moorage, 15 & 30 amp power, free Wi-Fi, ATM, excellent washrooms, laundry, launch ramp, seasonal swimming pool, beer & wine sales. Kayak and SUP rentals.

Port Browning Marina offers two dining venues: the licensed family Port Browning Pub, with large picture windows facing east, overlooks the bay; and the adults-only bar named Bridgeman's Bistro, with a separate entrance, occupies the back portion of the restaurant building. Completed in 2017, Bridgeman's Bistro is classy with modern finishes, offering beer-on-tap and specialty wines. A glass-enclosed side-patio provides partial views of the marina and kayaking activities. Similar menu selections are available at both dining venues. Port Browning Marina is a local's favorite.

The Mill Bay Marine Group recently purchased the property with future plans to install new docks in a new configuration. Improvements in the upcoming years include a fuel dock, pumpout, water at the docks and 50 amp power.

Browning Harbour Public Wharf. Open all year, 89 feet of dock space, no facilities. Commercial fishing vessels have priority.

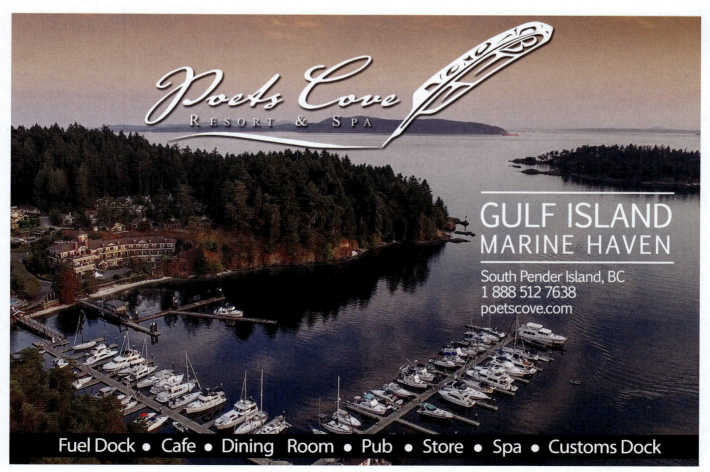

GULF ISLANDS

Shingle Bay (Gulf Islands National Park Reserve). This is a recent addition to the Gulf Islands National Park Reserve. Open all year, picnic tables, campsites, composting toilets. Dogs must be on leash and cleaned up after. See the remnants of the Shingle Bay fish reduction plant that operated intermittently between 1927 and 1959. It served as an important part of the local economy, employing 15 to 20 men at a time, mainly Pender Island residents.

Because the bay shoals rapidly, you must anchor well out, in line with the old reduction plant. Favor the north side, as a reef extends on the south. Anchorage is exposed to the southwest. The community park at the head of the bay is a welcome place to walk dogs, picnic, and access the island. A jungle gym is popular with children.

⑫ **Otter Bay Marina.** 2311 McKinnon Rd., North Pender Island, BC V0N 2M1; (250) 629-3579; info@otterbaymarina.ca; www.otterbaymarina.ca. Monitors VHF 66A. Moorage open all year, full services May 15 to September 30. Washrooms, showers, laundry, 15 & 30 amp power, 50 amp power on "A" dock, launch ramp, gazebo, children's play area, two heated pools, free Wi-Fi. Scooters for rent. The mooring buoys off the dock are private.

The upper pool is for families and is open mid-May through Labour Day. When both pools are operating, the lower pool is for adults. The small convenience store carries baked goods, some groceries, frozen meat, poultry and fish, gifts, clothing, and some boating supplies. Motor scooters, kayaks, and SUP rentals. A daily or weekly day camp is offered for children through Dog Mermaid Eco Excursions (250) 222-0015.

This popular marina is on the west side of North Pender Island, facing Swanson Channel. Look for the tall flagpoles on the observation deck, just past the ferry landing. The marina was taken over by new owners in the fall of 2017. Upgrades to the lower pool and washrooms have been completed. Cozy fire pits with seating were added along the walkways among the colorful flower beds. Scheduled weekend BBQ's begin in June. It just keeps getting better.

Otter Bay Marina is a great place to relax and enjoy the views.

An enclosed activity center with a stone fireplace and barbecue is a nice venue for group events and rendezvous, even in the off-season.

The coffee shop is open for breakfast and lunch daily during the season. For a short excursion, take the dinghy across the bay to Roe Island Park, a lovely spot to stretch the legs.

Caution: A green spar buoy is off the corner of the marina docks. Red, Right, Returning means you leave this buoy to port as you enter. Do not pass between the buoy and the dock. A rock 2 feet below the surface at zero tide lurks between the buoy and the dock.

Golf: The 9-hole Pender Island Golf Course is about a 15-minute walk from the marina. No tee times needed. The marina can give you a ride up the hill to the course for a small fee. The golf course has a new restaurant, Zuppa's (250) 629-3124.

Roesland/Roe Lake (Gulf Islands National Park Reserve). Located on North Pender Island, deep in Otter Bay. Correspondent Deane Hislop reports: "We set the anchor, good hold-

Otter Bay Marina

220

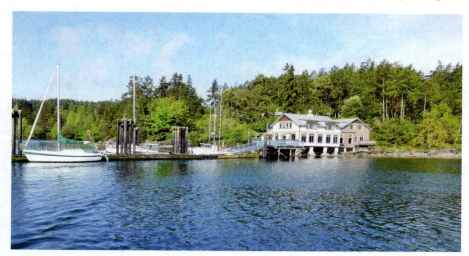
Philly's Diner at Hope Bay Public Wharf

ing, and took the dinghy to the park's dinghy dock. We discovered a former 1908 farmhouse that now serves as the Pender Island Museum, offering a glimpse into the island's past. This is also the location of Parks Canada's field office. We took the short walk to the end of Roe Islet to take in an amazing view of Swanson Channel, Saltspring Island, and Vancouver Island. Then it was back along the islet and up Shingle Bay road to the Roe Lake trail head and through the forest to beautiful Roe Lake, making for a full day of hiking and exploring."

Port Washington Public Wharf. On North Pender Island. Open all year, 147 feet of dock space, unoccupied slips used when available. No facilities. Watch for a rock off the southeast dock. One float is designated for aircraft.

⑬ **Hope Bay Public Wharf.** (250) 813-3321 Wharfinger. East side of North Pender Island, facing Navy Channel. Open all year, 300 feet of dock space, 2 day-use mooring buoys marked "Hope Bay Store". If the dock is full (it often is), tie to the mooring buoys and dinghy in. Wakes from passing ferries make rafting undesirable, and depths on the inside of the dock are shallow at low tide.

This historic landing has attractive buildings on the pier which house a number of small businesses, including the Red Tree Gallery, the Pender Island Veterinary Clinic (250) 629-9909, and the Dockside Realty. The popular cafe that closed in 2016 has re-opened as Philly's Diner (250) 629-2090 and carries on the tradition of tasty well-prepared meals.

Breezy Bay – Saturna Island Family Estate Winery. 8 Quarry Road, Saturna Island, BC V0N 2Y0; (250) 539-3521; (877) 918-3388; www.saturnavineyards.com. The winery and bistro are no longer open, however, visitors can hike the winery grounds and enjoy the spectacular views. Access from a small dock in Breezy Bay, just north of Croker Point. When looking toward shore, two docks are visible. The winery dock is the one on the right; look for the sign on the ramp. A 15-minute walk through 60 acres of vineyards takes you to the winery buildings overlooking the vineyards with views of Plumper Sound.

Irish Bay. Irish Bay, on the west side of Samuel Island, is a good anchorage with scenic rock walls, but the island is privately owned. If you venture above the foreshore, the caretaker will shoo you off.

Winter Cove. Winter Cove, between Samuel Island and Saturna Island, has an attractive park (part of the Gulf Islands National Park Reserve) on the Saturna Island side, and shallow anchorage. We think the best anchorages are behind Winter Point, north of the cable line, or just off the National Park Reserve lands. The charts show shallow water in the middle of the cove, but you can patrol around—carefully—with the depth sounder and find anchoring sites away from the preferred spots. The mooring buoys in the southwest corner of the cove are private. A public dinghy dock is on the eastern shore. It has been reported that a sunken boat lies in the middle of Winter Cove.

Minx Reef partially blocks the Plumper Sound approach to Winter Cove. Entering, we have found the best way to avoid the reef is to point the bow at the northern shore of Irish Bay, and run well past Winter Point before turning south into the cove.

The annual Canada Day (July 1) Saturna Island Lamb Barbecue at Winter Cove is a big event. The cove is packed with boats; islanders shuttle visitors ashore and back. For more information go to www.saturnalambbarbeque.com.

The annual Saturna Lions Club Dog & Dogs Show is in early September. Prizes for best dog and owner look-alike, best puppy, best tail-wagger, and more. Bribes encouraged. Correspondents Bruce and Margaret Evertz happened upon the show and say it's wonderful. Bring your dog. For information see www.saturnalionsclub.net.

Boat Pass. Boat Pass connects Winter Cove with the Strait of Georgia. Currents in Boat Pass can run to 7 knots past several nasty rocks and reefs. Take this pass only at or near high water slack, preferably after seeing it at low water so you know where the rocks are.

⑭ **Lyall Harbour.** www.saturnatourism.com Lyall Harbour, on Saturna Island, is a large, well protected anchorage, with a ferry landing and store near the entrance. Nearby **Boot Cove** is a beautiful spot with anchorage in 12 to 18 feet, but it is crowded with resident boats on mooring buoys, and can be subject to williwaws blowing over a low swale on Saturna Island.

Contributing Editor Tom Kincaid anchored there one afternoon, and before night his anchor line was stretched tight by 40-knot winds that were still blowing the next morning. "I dinghied to the nearest beach that afternoon and walked to the store for a loaf of bread," he reports. "I asked the proprietor if he'd heard when the wind was supposed to die down. 'Oh, you must be in Boot Cove,' he said. 'It always blows in Boot Cove.' So we weighed anchor, set sail, flew out the entrance and coasted to a stop, windless, just outside."

Lyall Harbour is off the beaten path for the Gulf Islands. It is quiet and gradually being discovered. Your choice, anchor in the bay or tie at the dock. Nothing fancy. This is not Ganges. The Saturna Point Store is the center of activity in Lyall Harbour and just up the road from the Public Wharf. The Lighthouse Pub is downstairs in the same building and has very good food with fish and chips being their signature item, though some say their lamb burger is to die for. Lamb carries a special reverence on Saturna Island. Dine inside or out on the deck. The beer is cold and the drink menu is imaginative and available by the drink or by the pitcher. You get the idea. The people are very nice. They say hello. They like your business. The Pub is family friendly.

Need a "wake-me-up" in the morning? Hike a mile up the hill from the marina. Then treat yourself to darn good organic coffee and, sweet and savory baked goods, or breakfast items at Wild Thyme. You can't miss it on the left. It is the pleasant green double-decker bus. If it is raining, sit on the upper deck of the bus and join the locals. You might need to get up to date on your Canadian politics - Saturna's point of view. Or enjoy the sun outside in a patio area. Visitors and locals rave about their food. Open for breakfast and lunch. Free Wi-Fi. After a hearty breakfast, it is downhill back to the boat. For the day, rent a bike (inquire at Saturna Point Store & Fuel), or rent a kayak, or SUP, or take a kayak guided tour of the area (Saturna Paddle Shack 250-539-5553 and on the dock) saturnacan.net/activities/kayaking), or visit the three artist galleries up the hill past Wild Thyme. An Outdoor Market is open seasonally on Saturdays in the store parking lot from 10:00 a.m. to 1:00 p.m. Relax and enjoy the laid-back Gulf Islands.

⑭ **Lyall Harbour Public Wharf.** Next to the ferry dock. Open all year, 200 feet of dock space. No power, water, washrooms or showers. Commercial fishing vessels have priority. Gasoline and diesel at nearby fuel dock. Pay for fuel at the Saturna Point Store, just above the dock. Moorage is collected at the honor box at the top of the dock. Note, there are day rates and overnight rates. Floatplanes arrive three times per day from the

GULF ISLANDS

Vancouver airport for your guests. Laundry and showers are located at the campground ¼ mile up the road from the wharf. Wild Thyme Coffee House is up the road a bit in a cute converted double-decker bus named Lucy. Stay overnight and treat yourself and your crew to an evening at the Lighthouse Pub.

⑭ **Saturna Point Store & Fuel.** 100 E. Point Rd., P.O. Box 80, Saturna Island, BC V0N 2Y0; (250) 539-5726. saturnapointstore.com Open daily in summers. Gasoline and diesel at fuel dock, washrooms, grocery store with essentials and snack items, ice, ice cream, fishing gear, ATM and a small bookstore and gallery. The Saturna Lighthouse Pub downstairs (250-539-5725) offers sit-down dining inside or out, take-out and off-premises sales. The pub is now fully licensed for family dining.

Georgeson Passage. Georgeson Passage, between Mayne Island and Samuel Island, is short and pretty. Currents, based on Active Pass, are about half as strong as those in Active Pass, both flooding and ebbing. Still, they run vigorously. See the Georgeson Passage secondary station under Active Pass in the Tide & Current Tables Vol. 5, and Ports and Passes. If entering from the Strait of Georgia through the narrow pass between Campbell Point and Georgeson Island, be aware that a drying reef extends from Campbell Point into the pass. Favor the Georgeson Island side. Watch for rapids.

⑮ **Horton Bay.** The public wharf is a Canpass/Nexus-only customs reporting station, and has room for a dozen 30-foot boats, plus rafting. Entering the area between Mayne and Samuel Islands requires some care but is completely navigable.

From the Gulf Islands side, the best route is through Georgeson Passage, east of Lizard Island. Be careful of a kelp-covered rock in less than 6 feet, fairly close to Mayne Island. If entering west of Lizard Island, the rock is in the middle of your path into Horton Bay. A reef extends from Curlew Island into Robson Passage, which separates Curlew Island from Mayne Island. Use Plans Chart 3477 (larger scale, much recommended) or 3442. A study of Chart 3477 shows a mid-channel course is called for. The bay is filled with crab pots and private mooring buoys in the best part of the bay. We have received reports of current running through the bay.

⑯ **Cabbage Island (Gulf Islands National Park Reserve).** Open all year, 10 mooring buoys, toilets, no water, no showers. Dogs must be on leash. In 2016 it was reported that several of the buoys were out of place, making some of them potentially unusable. No rafting on the buoys. Maximum vessel size: 50 ft for winds 30 knots or less; and 40 ft for winds of 37 knots or less. This is a pretty anchorage between Cabbage Island and Tumbo Island, out on the edge of the Strait of Georgia.

The chart shows the entrance from the north, between two long reefs. Local knowledge advises to cross the reef on the Tumbo Channel side, between two patches of kelp, a short distance from the north tip of Tumbo Island. This should show 30 feet under the keel all the way across. Chartbook 3313 shows good depths at that location. The island has picnic sites, campsites, and a wonderful sandy beach. Crabbing is reportedly good.

Cabbage Island is interesting to explore. It isn't very big, so you can walk around the entire island in a reasonable time. Though tiny, the island is hardly dull. The beaches are different on every side, ranging from white sand, to sandstone reefs, to an aggregate of small rocks embedded in sandstone, to fine gravel.

Inland, you'll find forests of arbutus (madrona), Garry oak and western red cedar.

⑯ **Tumbo Island (Gulf Islands National Park Reserve).** Tumbo Island, privately owned until recently, is now part of the Gulf Islands National Park Reserve. Dogs must be on leash. Trails lead through the island, although getting to them can be a challenge. The entire island goes straight up from the water, so you'll have to climb some rocks. Once there, you can find remnants of the island's commercial past in the forests and fields.

Coal mining was attempted in the early 1900s, but the shafts flooded and the effort was abandoned. In the 1920s and 1930s foxes were raised. The original fox farm homestead can still be seen on the island. Horses were kept on Cabbage Island for feed for the foxes. At low tide the horses were brought across the sandbar between the two islands, then slaughtered and butchered. One horse, flesh and bone ground to mash, was consumed every three days.

The landowner who sold Tumbo Island to the reserve has a life tenancy for the house and a small area surrounding the house. If someone is in residence there, please respect their privacy.

⑰ **Narvaez Bay (Gulf Islands National Park Reserve).** Picnic tables and toilet, camping in 7 sites, ideal for kayakers. Dogs must be on leash. Beautiful Narvaez Bay indents the rock cliffs on the south shore of Saturna Island, and is open to southeasterly winds and the wakes of passing ship traffic in Boundary Pass. Parts of the bay's shoreline were added to the Gulf Islands National Park Reserve, including the small peninsula parallel to the western shore, a short distance in.

You can anchor in the little bight behind this peninsula and have shelter from wind and waves, although a reader wrote that in a northerly, they experienced williwaw winds of 20+ knots from the head of the bay. The wind in the Strait of Georgia was only 12 knots. The holding ground is not very good. It appears to be loose mud, the kind that washes off easily. It felt like a thin layer on top of rock—fine for a picnic in settled weather, but chancy for overnight.

The neck of land separating the peninsula from the rest of Saturna Island holds the ruins of an ambitious homestead. We didn't find any buildings, although fruit trees and the remnants of fences are there. A dirt service road runs the length of the peninsula and leads up the hill to a main Saturna Island road.

ACTIVE PASS AREA

Active Pass. Active Pass separates Mayne Island and Galiano Island, and has long been one of the most popular fishing areas in the Gulf Islands. It also is the route taken by commercial traffic, including BC Ferries that run between Tsawwassen and Swartz Bay. Currents in Active Pass run to 7 knots on a spring tide. They flood eastward toward the Strait of Georgia. See the Tide and Current Tables Vol. 5, or Ports and Passes. Unless your boat is quite fast, slack water passage is recommended. If you are in the current, you can minimize turbulence by favoring Miners Bay.

Dinner Bay. Dinner Bay, between Crane Point and Dinner Point, looks to be a good anchorage, but is exposed to ferry wakes and northwest winds.

Village Bay. Village Bay is wide and deep, with convenient anchoring depths near the head. The bay is open to northwest winds and waves, but well protected from everything else. Village Bay has a ferry terminal.

Land your dinghy on the gravel beach at Cabbage Island, hike the short trail and enjoy the views of the Strait of Georgia.

See Area Map Page 205 - Maps Not for Navigation

GULF ISLANDS

Moorage at Fulford Public Wharf

⑱ **Miners Bay.** A public wharf is in the bay on the south side of Active Pass, and is subject to swirling tidal currents and the wakes from passing ferries. A float is on each side of the main dock. Convenient anchoring depths are close to shore—most of the bay is quite deep. The wharf is a Canpass/Nexus-only customs reporting station.

A bakery, inn, pub, and two grocery stores, one with a liquor agency, are up the hill from the dock. A small museum on Fernhill Road covers the history of this area with indoor and outdoor exhibits. Across from the museum, on Saturday mornings, from 10:00 a.m.-1:00 p.m., the Mayne Island Farmers Market, has local produce, handicrafts, baked goods, and art work. Beginning in the 1800s, this was a popular stop for miners on their way to the gold mines. The Springwater Lodge, built in 1892, overlooks the bay. It remains the oldest continuously operated hotel in British Columbia.

⑱ **Active Pass Auto & Marine.** (250) 539-5411; www.activepassautoandmarine.com. Open all year. Propane, stove alcohol, tackle, bait, ice, snacks, ice cream, marine supplies, haulout, 24-hour towing and moped and bicycle rentals. Located at the service station 200 yards from the dock.

⑲ **Sturdies Bay.** Sturdies Bay, on Galiano Island toward the eastern end of Active Pass, is a landing for ferries coming to and from Tsawwassen and continuing on to the other Gulf Islands. A public float is alongside the ferry dock. The community of Sturdies Bay, just up the road, has a grocery store, shops and a post office. Galiano Oceanfront Inn & Spa is south of the ferry landing and has its own dock.

Sturdies Bay is a convenient stop to exchange crew arriving from or departing to the mainland on the BC Ferries. They can disembark the ferry, walk across to the provincial dock, and board the boat.

⑲ **Galiano Oceanfront Inn & Spa.** 134 Madrona Drive, Galiano Island, BC V0N 1P0; (250) 539-3388; info@galianoinn.com; www.galianoinn.com. Located in Sturdies Bay, north of the ferry landing. Open all year but dock in place May to October only, call for exact dates. Wi-Fi, but no power or water on the dock. The dock is subject to wakes from passing ferries in Active Pass. Set fenders accordingly. Reasonable dock rates; free if using spa, restaurant, or inn.

This is a high-quality inn and spa, with casual fine dining, natural spa, and gardens. Pizza from a wood-fired oven is served for lunch and early dinner from a pizza terrace overlooking the bay (seasonal). Village shops are a block away with more choices for dining, shopping and liquor store. Smart cars are available for rental (inquire in advance). If you're in Montague Harbour and want to dine at Atrevida Restaurant at the Inn, or have spa treatments, call for pick-up and reservations, (250) 539-3388.

The Kunamokst Mural from the 2010 Olympic games is displayed in the lobby of the Inn. The mural is made from individual tiles, each independently illustrated by a different artist. Collectively they form an image of an orca whale and calf. It's quite striking.

Whaler Bay. Whaler Bay is on the east side of Galiano Island, just north of Active Pass. It is full of rocks and shoal water. Enter carefully through a rock-strewn passage from the south, or through a more open passage around the north end of Gossip Island. Whaler Bay has a public wharf. Good protection is near the wharf, but there's very little swinging room.

Whaler Bay Public Wharf. (250) 539-2264. Open all year, 350 feet of dock space, no facilities. Commercial fishing vessels have priority.

MAYNE ISLAND, CAMPBELL BAY TO HORTON BAY

Campbell Bay. Campbell Bay, on the northeast side of Mayne Island, is entered between Edith Point and Campbell Point. It is open to southeasterly winds, but has anchoring depths near the head, mud bottom.

Bennett Bay (Gulf Islands National Park Reserve). Bennett Bay, south of Campbell Point, has good anchorage but is exposed to southeast winds. Curlew Island and Samuel Island are privately owned.

Note: Campbell Point, a portion of the waters of Bennett Bay, Georgeson Island, and the Belle Chain Islets including Anniversary Island, are part of Gulf Islands National Park Reserve. To protect sensitive ecosystems, access to Georgeson Island and the islets is prohibited.

SALTSPRING ISLAND, FULFORD HARBOUR TO LONG HARBOUR

Russell Island (Gulf Islands National Park Reserve). Russell Island is just outside Fulford Harbour. Anchor on the northwest side of the island, fair holding, with views of mountains above Fulford Harbour. A trail leads through open meadows and a forest of Douglas fir, arbutus (madrona) and Garry oak. The original house dates back more than a century. A caretaker lives on the island. A boater we trust reports, "Russell Island is wonderful!"

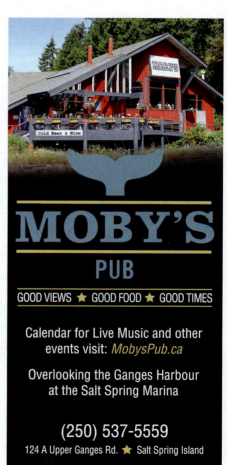

Miners Bay Public Wharf

2018 WAGGONER CRUISING GUIDE

GULF ISLANDS

See Area Map Page 205 - Maps Not for Navigation

A moonlit night over Ganges Harbour

Fulford Harbour. Fulford Harbour is wide and open. A public dock for locals only is located on the north side of the ferry terminal. On the south side of the ferry terminal is a public float with transient moorage that is exposed to wind and ferry wash. No services at the float. The charming village of Fulford has a restaurant, a good grocery store at the Salt Spring Mercantile, and an assortment of art galleries and stores specializing in crafts and country clothing. Everything feels very "island."

By all means take a 15-minute walk down the road to St. Paul's Catholic church (called the Stone Church), built in 1880. The graveyard, with island history chiseled into its headstones, is adjacent. On one visit we found the church's door unlocked, and stepped inside. It was lovely. "This is where God lives," we thought.

Bus transportation: Regular bus service on Saltspring Island connects Fulford Village, Ganges, Long Harbour, Vesuvius and Fernwood. For schedule see www.busonline.ca; (250) 537-6758.

Fulford Harbour Marina. Docks have been removed and this marina is no longer available due to storm damage years ago, no guest moorage until further notice.

Fulford Outer Harbour - Harbour Authority of Salt Spring Island. (250) 537-5711 Open all year. www.saltspringharbours.com A public wharf and float is located immediately south of the BC Ferries terminal, managed by the Harbour Authority of Salt Spring Island. The 54-foot public float provides moorage on both sides. Overnight moorage permitted. No water, no power. Payment envelopes, moorage rates, and a self-pay box are located on the wharf. Locals tend to use this float primarily for loading and unloading purposes.

Fulford Inner Harbour - Harbour Authority of Salt Spring Island. Located just north of the BC Ferries terminal is a public dock filled with local boats; no space for transient boats.

Isabella Island (Gulf Islands National Park Reserve). A smallish anchorage is available behind Isabella Island, a short distance west of the mouth of Fulford Harbour. Although exposed to the west, it's a cozy little spot for one or two boats. Anchor in 24 feet.

Ruckle Park. Beaver Point on Saltspring Island. Open all year, day use and overnight camping. No mooring facilities, exposed anchorage on each side of Ruckle Point. Probably the best of these anchorages is in the first cove south of Ruckle Point. Swinging room is limited, and the cove is exposed to ferry wakes and southeast winds. The anchorage is pretty, though, and in settled weather could be a good day stop. This is an extensive park, with miles of shoreline and rocky headlands. Walk-in campsites. Great views of the southern Gulf Islands.

LOCAL KNOWLEDGE

ENTRANCE CHANNEL: There's only one safe way to get into Ganges by water, and that is to leave all the Chain Islands to starboard. This will put you in a safe fairway, amply wide and easily run. Do not cut through any of the islands, either. No short-cuts. Money Makers Reef, which extends northwest from Third Sister Island, is well-named, but Money Makers Reef is not the only problem. "It's a minefield out there," as one local put it.

The entry channel itself can be a minefield, too. It's filled with crab pot floats, many in dark colors, and you have to pay attention every inch of the way to avoid them.

⑳ **Ganges.** Ganges, at the head of Ganges Harbour, is a favorite destination. This bustling seaside village has marinas, good anchorage, shops, galleries, restaurants, and two large supermarkets with marina delivery. There is a dedicated centrally located dinghy dock. Thrifty Foods is the closest to the marinas. Above the store, entered from the street side, is "The Local," a liquor store associated with Thrifty Foods that also delivers to the marinas. Country Grocer (Liquor Agency in the store), at 374 Lower Ganges Road, has a van with pick-up, drop-off services at any Ganges marina.

Mouat's, a huge old hardware and household goods general store with a separate gift shop and apparel section, is a longstanding favorite.

The sprawling Salt Spring Island Saturday Market, also called the Farmers Market, is held in Centennial Park at Grace Point on Saturdays 9:00 a.m. to 4:00 p.m., April through October. A Tuesday farmers market, no crafts, is held in the same location, 2:00 p.m. to 6:00 p.m. from June to the end of October. Although boats and tourists are important to summer trade, Ganges is not just a summer resort village. It's a bustling center of year-round local commerce.

Boats can anchor out in the bay. All buoys in the harbour are private. Moorage is available at Saltspring Marina, Ganges Marina, or the town's Kanaka Wharf. Larger vessels might side-tie along the 240-foot-long floating breakwater that extends into the bay from the Coast Guard dock. An airplane float, pumpout station, and some power and water are on the breakwater. A ramp leads to shore. Because of the breakwater's high freeboard, it is best suited to larger boats. If the wind blows (especially a southeasterly), expect some movement.

The Saltspring Island Sailing Club's docks, to port as you approach Grace Point, have some space for reciprocal clubs. It's about a 1-mile walk to town. The Centennial Wharf public dock behind Grace Islet is permanent moorage only with some transient "hot berths" available if you call the Harbour Authority office. Off Mouat's, the Kanaka Visitors' Dock has close proximity to shopping; Kanaka Dock moorage frequently opens up during the day as boats come and go.

More than 40 artists' studios are in Ganges and scattered around Saltspring Island. In addition to painters and sculptuors, they include artisan cheese makers, bakers, wineries, and now a microbrewery. Rental cars and vans are available at Saltspring Marina. A local map identifies stops and hours.

Artspring: Locally supported arts and theater, an easy walk from the village. See www.artspring.ca.

Bird sanctuary: While you can anchor a short distance south of the Sailing Club's docks, Walter Bay and the spit that creates it are a sanctuary for black oystercatchers. Please leave the sanctuary area alone.

Golf: Salt Spring Island Golf & Country Club (250) 537-2121. Blackburn Meadows (250) 537-1707. Both courses are 9 holes.

Swimming pool: The recently opened Rainbow Road Indoor Public Pool is an easy walk away. Call (250) 537-1402 for hours. The pool has showers.

Bus transportation: Regular bus service on Saltspring Island connects Fulford Harbour, Ganges, Long Harbour, Vesuvius and Fernwood. For schedule see www.busonline.ca; (250) 538-4282.

Taxi: Silver Shadow Taxi (250) 537-3030; Amber Cab Co. (250) 537-3277

Car rental: Salt Spring Car Rentals (250) 537-3122

SALT SPRING ISLAND & GANGES HARBOUR MARKETPLACE

RESTAURANTS & SHOPS

BLACK SHEEP BOOKS
Get lost in a good bookstore. Explore two floors packed with volumes of enduring value, including familiar favorites, contemporary fiction, guides, and non-fiction titles covering everything from outer space to inner peace. Authorized dealer for CHS marine charts.
250-538-0025 • 3101-115 Fulford Ganges Rd., In Grace Point Square • www.blacksheepbooks.ca

LI READ SEA TO SKY PREMIER PROPERTIES
You love boating among the Gulf Islands. See Li Read to find your new dream home port. Visit Li for what is for sale, an island map and market conditions. Office located across the street from Ganges Marina, Salt Spring Island. Welcome!
250-537-7647 • #4 - 105 Rainbow Road • LiRead33@Gmail.com • www.LiRead.com

MOBY'S PUB
Moby's Pub offers a comfortable atmosphere. The friendly staff, great food, legendary live entertainment, waterfront patio, and excellent location make Moby's the best place on Salt Spring Island to meet people.
250-537-5559 • 124 A Upper Ganges Rd. • www.mobyspub.ca • mobyspub@gmail.com

EAGLE EYE MARINE
Eagle Eye Marine Services is the largest commercial assistance company in the southern gulf islands. We are the southern gulf islands' marine towing and salvage team. We pride ourselves on our professionalism and on being the right fit for any job.
250-883-SUNK (7865) • www.eagleeyemarine.ca

Salt Spring Island Community Calendar

Famous Saturday Market: April to October
Tuesday's Farmers Market: June to October
All Summer Long: Music under the Stars, ArtCraft, Salt Spring Studio Tours, ArtSpring Summer Performances, Live Music at Oystercatcher, Moby's Pub and Salt Spring Vineyards – and more!
January: Salt Spring Polar Bear Swim
February: February Festival • Family Day Concert • Seedy Saturday • Indoor Market
March: Documentary Film Festival • Salt Spring Home & Garden Show
April: Salt Spring Blooms in April • Easter Art Festival • Blossom Festival
May: Round Salt Spring Sailing Race • Ruckle Farm Day
June: Tour des Iles Festival Taste of Salt Spring • Solstice on Salt Spring
July: Canada Day Festivities • Classic Car Show • Lavender Festival
August: Firefly Lantern Festival • Movies in the Park
September: Pride Festival • Fall Fair Weekend • Working Boat Festival
October: Harvest Food and Drink Festival • Apple Festival • Sip & Savour Salt Spring • Harvest Grape Stomp • Halloween in Ganges Village
November: Remembrance Day Parade & Ceremonies • Christmas Light Up Events
December: Christmas on Salt Spring • WinterCraft at Mahon Hall
Christmas Craft Fairs:
   WinterCraft at Mahon Hall • Beaver Point Hall • Fulford Hall
ArtSpring Christmas Concerts • Annual Glowtini Contest • Community Christmas Dinner • New Year's Eve Celebrations
Plus… Special Events during most Canadian Holiday Long-weekends!

www.SaltSpringTourism.com • 250-537-4223

GULF ISLANDS See Area Map Page 205 - Maps Not for Navigation

Saltspring Marina at the head of Ganges Harbour

The popular Salt Spring Island Fair, held in mid-September, is within easy walking distance from town.

Things to Do

1. **Studio Tour.** Map available at the Visitor Centre. Rent a car, van, or moped at the Saltspring Marina and visit some of the 40 artist studios. Most are open every weekend.

2. **Salt Spring Island Cheese Company.** See the many steps needed to make artisan cheese. Then taste 20 different cheeses.

3. **Wine Tasting.** Three wineries are on Saltspring Island and they regularly have tastings. Wine and farm tours available at TourSaltSpring.com.

4. **Salt Spring Island Saturday Market.** The largest farmers market in the islands.

5. **Hastings House.** Reserve for an elegant dinner or lunch. Walk the grounds of this manor style resort. A special experience.

6. **Barb's Buns.** Delicious coffee and fresh baked goods. Bring some back to the boat. Their breakfasts and lunches are also very good.

7. **Embe Bakery.** A "old style" full service bakery serving up freshly baked breads, pastries, dessert pies, meat pies, and other baked goods.

㉔ **Harbour Authority of Salt Spring Island.** 127 Fulford Ganges Road, Salt Spring Island, BC V8K 2T9; (250) 537-5711. Monitors VHF 09. www.saltspringharbours.com

The Harbour Authority of Salt Spring Island manages eight marina facilities on Salt Spring Island: Ganges Centennial Wharf; Ganges Breakwater Float (which also includes the Wharfhead where the Coast Guard building is located); Ganges Kanaka Wharf; Vesuvius Bay; Fulford Inner Harbour; Fulford Outer Harbour; Burgoyne Bay; and Musgrave Landing. The Harbour Authority office and wharfinger are located at Ganges Centennial Wharf.

㉔ **Ganges Centennial Wharf - Harbour Authority of Salt Spring Island.** (250) 537-5711. Monitors VHF 09. www.saltspringharbours.com This is the Grace Point facility. Mostly commercial and permanent moorage, but sometimes transient space is available, call the Harbour Authority Office.

㉔ **Ganges Breakwater Float - Harbour Authority of Salt Spring Island.** (250) 537-5711. Monitors VHF 09. www.saltspring-harbours.com. This is the dock below the Coast Guard station. Moorage on the outside of the floating breakwater or in several slips on the inside. Be sure to avoid the marked seaplane and Coast Guard areas. Limited 30 amp power and water. Washroom, shower and garbage drop at the Harbour Authority office at Centennial Wharf. Two hours free moorage before 4:00 p.m.

Wharfingers collect moorage daily, or pay in the drop box at the head of the docks or at the Harbour Authority office.

㉔ **Ganges Kanaka Wharf - Harbour Authority of Salt Spring Island.** (250) 537-5711. Monitors VHF 09. www.saltspringharbours.com. These docks are immediately north of the floating breakwater, with 1400 feet of visitor moorage, water, 30 amp power, and pumpout. Good free Wi-Fi on the docks or from nearby cafés. Washroom, shower and garbage drop at the Harbour Authority office at Centennial Wharf, about a block away. Free moorage for 2 hours. Boats come and go all day and moorage opens up after crews complete their shopping.

Ganges Harbour

226 www.WaggonerGuide.com

Ganges & Salt Spring Island – Foodie Heaven!

Salt Spring Island has been a foodie heaven since the late 1800s. Back then, fresh produce grown on the island was delivered to Hope Bay, where it was loaded on the ferry and shuttled to Vancouver.

Today, Salt Spring Island is home to brewers and vintners, farmers, cheesemakers, artisan bakers, and restaurateurs. If you love delicious food, Salt Spring Island is a fantastic destination.

Farmers Market

Ganges hosts the best farmers market in the Gulf Islands. Each Saturday from March through October, the "Market in the Park" at Centennial Park is open for business. More than 100 vendors sell their wares, ranging from fresh produce to seafood to pastries and crafts. The variety is outstanding and everything is made locally.

Another, smaller, market is held Tuesday afternoons at the same location.

Both markets are perfect places for provisioning. We've found fresh seafood, unusual mushrooms, heirloom tomatoes, ripe melons, berries, a variety of sprouts, and more. Four artisan bakeries—ranging from Rendezvous French Patisserie (superb desserts) to the Salt Spring Island Bread Company and the Bread Lady—attend the market. Fair warning: it's best to go early, since many items sell out by closing time.

Wine and Beer

Salt Spring has three wineries: Garry Oaks Estate Winery, Salt Spring Vineyards, and Mistaken Identity Vineyards. Each has a tasting room.

Both Garry Oaks and Salt Spring Vineyards require car transportation. Mistaken Identity Vineyards can be reached by walking 1.5 miles up Lower Ganges Road from Saltspring Marina.

Each winery hosts a variety of tasting events throughout the summer, some including food pairings or live music. Check their websites for a schedule of events.

The Sip and Savour festival in September celebrates Salt Spring Island's wineries.

If beer is your preference, stop by one of B.C.'s smallest breweries: Salt Spring Island Ales, outside of Ganges. You can enjoy beer on tap, or pick up a bottle or growler for later. The beer is organic and made with locally grown ingredients—even the hops are from Salt Spring Island.

Restaurants

Hastings House is one of the finest restaurants we've ever dined at. They've hosted movie stars and sports stars, royalty and heads of state. Almost everything, including bread and crackers, is prepared fresh in their kitchen. They grow many of their ingredients on site, and the garden is open to patrons. We recommend wandering through, either before or after your meal. It's not uncommon to see the chef gathering herbs, fruits, or vegetables.

An optional cocktail hour in the Manor House precedes dinner. Recommended.

Still hungry?

If you're willing to travel beyond walking distance from Ganges, another world opens up. Salt Spring Auto Rentals (250 537-3122) provides maps highlighting more than 40 destinations on Salt Spring Island. Many of these places are artisan food businesses, ranging from cheese makers to beekeepers.

One of our favorites is Salt Spring Island Cheese Company, near Fulford Harbour. A tour includes petting the goats and sampling some of their 20+ cheeses in a tasting room overlooking the production area. Afterword, customers can relax at outdoor tables and enjoy goat milk gelato.

Salt Spring Island's wide variety of food producers and restaurants, and their consistently high quality, make it the ideal destination for foodie boaters.

– Mark Bunzel

GULF ISLANDS See Area Map Page 205 - Maps Not for Navigation

The Hastings House gardens are outstanding.

Classic boats in Glenthorne Passage

Wharfingers collect check or cash for moorage daily, or pay in the drop box at the head of the docks, or at the Harbour Authority office.

LOCAL KNOWLEDGE

TWO DANGEROUS ROCKS: Zachary Rock, 5 to 6 feet deep at zero tide, is approximately 50 feet off the end of C dock at Ganges Marina.

Money Makers Rock, a short distance off the Saltspring Marina entrance, is marked by two buoys. The rock is about 50 feet long, more like a short reef than a rock. Approach the Saltspring Marina on either side of the two buoys, not between them. In 2018, the new breakwater for the Saltspring Marina may be covering Money Makers Rock.

⑳ **Ganges Marina.** 161 Lower Ganges Road, Salt Spring Island, BC V8K 2L6; (250) 537-5242; gangesmarina@gmail.com; www.gangesmarina.com. Monitors VHF 66A. Moorage for vessels up to 120 feet. Open all year, gasoline, diesel and limited lubricants at fuel dock, ample guest moorage. Reservations recommended in summer. Facilities include 30 & 50 amp power, washrooms, showers, laundry, free Wi-Fi, garbage drop. On-site marine mechanic. Groceries, restaurants, propane, and other services nearby.

A floating breakwater, 500 feet long and 24 feet wide, can handle vessels to 400 feet.

Complimentary muffins and coffee served every morning during the high season at the marina office; bring your own cup.

⑳ **Saltspring Marina.** 124 Upper Ganges Rd., Salt Spring Island, BC V8K 2S2; (250) 537-5810; (800) 334-6629; info@saltspringmarina.com; www.saltspringmarina.com. Monitors VHF 66A. Guest moorage for all sizes of boats, 15 & 30 amp power, washrooms, showers, laundry, water, ice, recycling and garbage drop, portable pumpout, Shaw Go Wi-Fi, concrete launch ramp. No long term parking.

Adjacent Moby's Pub (take-out & offsales) has a terrific menu, music, and dancing. Check their website. Rendezvous French Bakery has

See Area Map Page 205 - Maps Not for Navigation   GULF ISLANDS

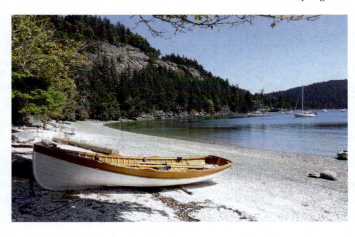

White shell beach at Montague Harbour Marine Park

fresh baked goods. Harbours End is a full-service repairs and haulout to 40 feet (250-537-4202). Car, van, scooter, bicycle, and kayak rentals.

Upgrades are planned for Saltspring Marina from 2018 to 2020. At press time, work has begun on the first phase, which includes addition of a new floating breakwater to be located southeast of the marina at or over Money Makers Rock. Breakwater construction, which will also include additional moorage space, should be completed in time for the 2018 boating season. Moorage may be limited during fall and winter. Contact the Marina regarding access to the docks around the new breakwater. The second phase of planned upgrades, scheduled for 2020, includes replacing the existing docks with new and upgrading power. The prospect of getting rid of Money Makers Rock hazard will be much appreciated. These welcome upgrades to the marina are long overdue for this proud member of Clean Marina™.

Long Harbour. Long Harbour lies parallel to Ganges Harbour, but is much narrower. The ferry from Tsawwassen lands there. Good anchorage is beyond the ferry dock, taking care not to anchor over a charted cable crossing. Royal Vancouver Yacht Club has an outstation in Long Harbour.

PREVOST ISLAND

㉑ **Prevost Island.** Prevost Island is a favorite of many. Annette Inlet and Glenthorne Passage, on the northwest end, are particularly attractive. The bays indenting from the southeast also look inviting, but with a southeaster always possible and with ferry traffic flying by in Swanson Channel, they might get a little lumpy.

Acland Islands. The passage between the Acland Islands and Prevost Island is a pleasant anchorage, with dramatic sheer rock walls on the Prevost Island side. Anchor in 25 to 35 feet with enough room to swing, or stern-tie to Acland Island.

Glenthorne Passage. Glenthorne Passage is the westernmost of the northern bays on Prevost Island. Well protected anchorage in 15 to 30 feet, good holding. Even though cabins line Secret Island, the surroundings are agreeable and the anchorage is popular. In summer months the sun sets in the narrow passage between Glenthorne Point and Secret Island.

Annette Inlet. Annette Inlet is a little wider than Glenthorne Passage, with few houses and a good sandy beach at the head. As you approach, note the charted rock that dries at 0.9 meter, off the mouth of the inlet. A rock at the point is marked by a small, private beacon. Approach from the Glenthorne Passage side and wrap around the point, leaving the beacon to starboard. The head of the bay shoals to drying flats. Anchor in 8 feet (zero tide) anywhere, gray mud bottom. Southeast winds can blow across the low swale separating Annette Inlet from Ellen Bay on the other side of Prevost Island, but there isn't enough fetch to build waves.

Selby Cove & James Bay. A house and dock are on the right side as you enter **Selby Cove**. Anchor in 18 feet and be sure of your set. We found poor holding in one spot. **James Bay** is the most northeast bay, open to northwesterlies. It is a little deep for anchoring until close to the head. The lands surrounding James Bay and a portion of the north shore of Selby Cove are part of Gulf Islands National Park Reserve, as are the lands surrounding Richardson Bay and the Portlock Point light station at the southeast corner of Prevost Island. Ferries do not serve Prevost Island, thus it is less populated than the larger islands.

MONTAGUE HARBOUR

㉒ **Montague Harbour.** Montague Harbour is a popular stopping spot in the central Gulf Islands. It is well protected and has an outstanding marine park. Depending on wind direction, you can find good anchorages around the bay.

Entry is unobstructed, either from the southeast, past Phillimore Point, or from the northwest, between Parker Island and Gray Peninsula.

Caution: A shoal extends southeast from the tip of Gray Peninsula into Montague Harbour. We've seen a boat thoroughly grounded on that shoal, awaiting a rising tide. Continue well into the harbor before turning east to anchor or pick up a mooring.

Montague Harbour will hold a huge number of boats. We have anchored there during high

Montague Harbour

2018 WAGGONER CRUISING GUIDE

GULF ISLANDS   See Area Map Page 205 - Maps Not for Navigation

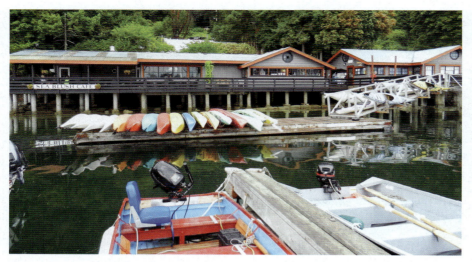

Montague Harbor Marina

season surrounded by more than 100 boats, yet no one was crowded. Anchor in about 40 feet over a mud bottom. The marina has a fuel dock, store, gift shop, scooter and kayak rentals, and restaurant. Wi-Fi is available throughout the harbor.

No Discharge Zone, Gray Water okay.

Customs: Montague Harbour is a Canpass/Nexus-only call-in customs clearance location.

Dining: Everybody enjoys the Hummingbird Inn Pub. A visit to Hummingbird Pub begins with a memorable ride on the Hummingbird Pub bus. Catch the bus on the road above the marina, about 300 yards to the right of the intersection. The bus also stops at the front gate of the marine park. Check the Hummingbird Pub website or signs at the marina and park entrance for the scheduled times for bus pick-up. The Hummingbird Pub serves food and is family friendly.

The Pilgrimme Restaurant now operates in the former location of the French restaurant La Berengerie. It gets great reviews from visiting boaters. Reservations recommended. Walking distance from Montague Harbour Marina.

㉒ **Montague Harbour Marine Park.** Montague Harbour Marine Park, at the north end of Montague Harbour, is beautiful and very popular. The park is open all year. It has excellent white sand beaches on the south side and astonishing rock beaches on the north and west sides. If you walk along the beach on the north side, opposite the head of the lagoon, you'll find a midden beach with numerous shells. There's no hint of the midden on the trail above, but it's obvious from the beach. A tiny, secluded beach is on Gray Peninsula, facing Parker Island. The park has walk-in campsites and toilets. A dock with a 300-foot-long float is for dinghies and boats up to 11 meters (36 feet). Designated dinghy area is on the shore end of the float. There are approximately 40 mooring buoys off the dock. No boat size limitation is marked on the buoys but it is a practical matter, be careful not to endanger other boats or damage buoy equipment. An honor box for paying moorage at the top of the stairs. The park has anchorage for many boats on both sides of Gray Peninsula depending on wind direction. Garbage disposal for a fee is available, located up the stairs from the dock.

㉒ **Montague Harbour Marina.** 3451 Montague Rd, Galiano Island, BC V0N 1P0; (250) 539-5733; montagueharbourmarina@gmail.com www.montagueharbour.com. Monitors VHF 66A. Open May 1 to September 30. Guest side-tie moorage, 15 & 30 amp power, free Wi-Fi, and washrooms. Reservations strongly recommended during the high season. Garbage and recycle drop-off with overnight moorage. Dog friendly. Licensed restaurant, groceries, marine supplies, and gift shop. Diesel and ethanol-free gasoline at the fuel dock. Fuel is available during the off-season on Saturdays from 10:00 a.m. to 2:00 p.m. or by arrangement. Moped, kayak, and motor boat rentals.

New owners purchased the marina in 2014 and promptly set about refurbishing most of the facility. The store has been renovated and now carries an expanded variety of goods, including smoked fish, meats, and local produce, charts, fishing tackle, books, souvenirs, and hand-dipped ice cream cones. The licensed Crane & Robin is open for breakfast, lunch and dinner. Check their happy hour specials. Dinghy dock available for any boaters on anchor or mooring buoys who want to enjoy the marina's shopping and dining. Check in with store if you plan to leave the property. Limited Wi-Fi for anchored boats is available for a fee.

㉒ **Montague Harbour Public Wharf.** Open all year, 160 feet of dock space, no facilities. 2-hour complimentary tie-up for dingies and boats. Fee for additional stays, pay at self-registration payment box at head of the ramp. Video monitoring and the wharfinger enforce the 2-hour free limit. Surveillance ensures that everyone has an opportunity to use the dock. Wharfinger always greets you with a smile.

Walker Hook. Walker Hook, on the west side of Trincomali Channel, has a beautiful beach on its

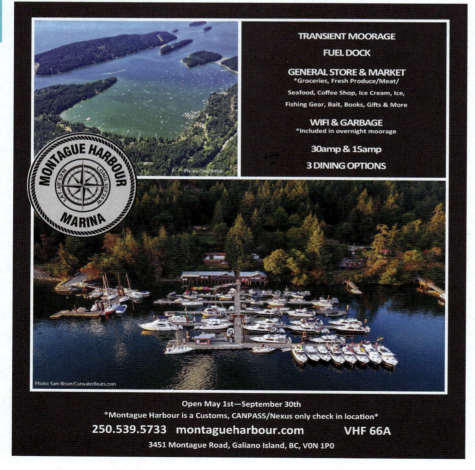

eastern shore, where it connects with Saltspring Island. Anchor in 24 feet. An approach between Atkins Reef and Saltspring Island takes the worry out of identifying just where the various rocks are.

Fernwood Public Wharf. Located on the Trincomali Channel side of Saltspring Island north of Walker Hook, opposite Victoria Shoal and just south of Wallace Island. Open all year, 44 feet of dock space, no facilities. Correspondents Fred and Judy Triggs visited and say they'd stop again. They enjoyed the locals who came down to visit, and concluded, "A pleasant and unexpected surprise was the Fernwood Road Café, located at the head of the pier, 50 meters up the road. Well stocked, good bakery items, sandwiches and pizza – excellent food." We visited, and agree.

SAANICH INLET

Saanich Inlet extends south into Vancouver Island for about 12 miles. The northern part of the inlet is fairly civilized, especially along the Saanich Peninsula shore to Brentwood Bay, where Butchart Gardens is located. For a beautiful and often-overlooked trip, continue south through Squally Reach and Finlayson Arm. Boat traffic usually is minimal.

Holding tank pumpout service: J.R. Pump Out, a mobile pumpout boat, serves the Brentwood Bay/Butchart Gardens area of Saanich Inlet. Because of a sill at the mouth of the inlet, Saanich Inlet does not exchange its water well and is growing increasingly lifeless along the bottom. Saanich Inlet is not a good place to pump overboard. J.R. Pump Out at (844) 507-3451 or VHF 88 (seasonally). During the summer season the pumpout boat goes out every evening. In winter, every two weeks.

Restricted area: In Saanich Inlet, Area Whiskey Delta (WD) is restricted when the government is conducting certain operations. Before entering, listen to the continuous marine broadcast or call the Coast Guard on VHF 83 to ensure the area is not restricted before entering.

Deep Cove. Wain Rock, with good water on both sides, lies about 0.2 mile off Moses Point. The remains of a public wharf are in the south

Dinghies on one side of Butchart Gardens dock, the other side is reserved for floatplanes.

part of the cove. Deep Cove Marina is adjacent to this pier and is for permanent moorage; transient moorage available only when there is space available which is rare, call (250) 733-2991 Ext 300.

Boaters can anchor in front of The Chalet restaurant on the north end of Deep Cove and land the dinghy on their private beach, while enjoying lunch or dinner. Call ahead for reservations (250) 656-3541, open Wednesday-Sunday. This is a unique venue overlooking Deep Cove and Saanich Inlet. The home was built as a teahouse for the B.C. Electric Rail Line in 1913 and has been a restaurant ever since. After coming ashore, leave your boots behind and slip on your nice shoes; this is a fine dining venue with prices to match. Remains of several pilings in front of The Chalet help locate the restaurant; see www.deepcovechalet.com for more details.

DIONISIO ALCALA GALIANO (1760-1805)

Alcala Galiano was a Spanish explorer and cartographer. He learned hydrography by participating in several surveys and later studied astronomy. From 1789-1794, he served as the hydrographer for Malaspina's Scientific Expedition which rivaled that of Cook's earlier expedition. Aboard the ship Atrevida, Galiano helped map the coastline of Patagonia and mapped extensive areas of the Pacific Coast. Malaspina and Galiano arrived in Mexico in 1791 and the following year departed for Nootka Sound with Galiano in command of the ship Sutil, and Valdes in command of the Mexicana. They arrived at the Spanish outpost of Nootka Sound on West Vancouver Island in May, 1792. The outpost was under the direction of Francisco e Eliza and his senior officer Juan Francisco de la Bodega y Quadra. After resupplying their ships and making repairs, Galiano and Valdes left Nootka Sound and entered the Strait of Juan de Fuca, stopping at today's Neah Bay, where Salvador Fidalgo was establishing another Spanish outpost. Galiano wanted to reach waters yet unexplored and moved quickly along the Strait and along the coast of Vancouver Island. Sailing through the night, they reached Race Rocks and anchored in Esquimalt Harbour. The following day, they made the push to Lopez Island, anchoring near Point Colville, then through Guemes Channel to Bellingham Bay. It was near Point Roberts on June 13th when they encountered the HMS Chatham, under William Robert Broughton, second in command for the British expedition led by George Vancouver. A week later they met Captain George Vancouver near present-day Vancouver British Columbia. Galiano and Vancouver struck up a friendly relationship and agreed to share charts and divide up their surveying efforts until parting ways. The flotilla, including the Discovery, Chatham, Sutil, and Mexicana, sailed along the Sunshine Coast through Welcome Pass and Malaspina Strait to an anchorage in Desolation Sound. After separating, Galiano and Valdes became the first Europeans to circumnavigate Vancouver Island. Boaters today can visit the memorial in Galiano's honor located in Montague Park on Galiano Island. To find the memorial from the park dock, stay right at the top of the stairs and follow the shoreline towards the flagpole and park entrance road. The monument is below the park entrance signage board, somewhat hidden in the grass.

CHARTS

3313 Small craft charts (chartbook)	Gulf Islands and adjacent Waterways
3442	North Pender Island to Thetis Island (1:40,000)
3443	Thetis Island to Nanaimo (1:40,000)
3447	Nanaimo Harbour & Departure Bay (1:8,000)
3458	Approaches to Nanaimo Harbour (1:20,000)
3473	Active Pass, Porlier Pass & Montague Harbour (various)
3475 Plans	Stuart Channel Chemainus Bay, Ladysmith Harbour, Dodd Narrows to Flat Top Islands, Dodd Narrows, Osborn Bay
3477 Plans	Gulf Islands Telegraph Harbour & Preedy Harbour, Pender Canal, Bedwell Harbour to Georgeson Passage

GULF ISLANDS See Area Map Page 205 - Maps Not for Navigation

Stay in luxury at Brentwood Bay Resort, near Butchart Gardens.

Patricia Bay. Patricia Bay, locally called Pat Bay, is open, but all the facilities are reserved for the Canadian Government's Institute of Ocean Sciences. It is here that the Canadian Hydrographic Service develops and maintains charts and related publications for western Canada and the Arctic.

Coles Bay. Coles Bay is east of Yarrow Point. It is good for temporary anchorage but open to southerly winds. If approaching from the north, the Canadian Small Craft Guide recommends that you give Dyer Rocks, off Yarrow Point, a 0.5-mile berth to avoid shoals extending south from the rocks.

LOCAL KNOWLEDGE

DANGEROUS ROCKS: A reef, marked by red nun buoy *U22*, is a short distance off the Brentwood Bay ferry dock. Approach Brentwood Bay Resort & Marina from the north, leaving buoy *U22* to starboard. Dangerous rocks lie on the other side of the buoy, and west and south of the lodge's docks. Locals report that these rocks are hit frequently.

㉓ **Brentwood Bay.** Although Brentwood Bay can be entered on either side of Senanus Island, prawn trap floats often clog the water between the north end of the island and Henderson Point. Best to leave Senanus Island to port. The Mill Bay ferry departs a short distance south of Sluggett Point. The Seahorses Cafe, with a dinghy dock, is north of the ferry dock. Nearby Blue's Bayou Café to the south has Cajun/Creole style food. Open for lunch and dinner, reservations recommended (250) 544-1194. The Brentwood Bay Public Dock, next to the Cafe, is suitable for dinghies and small watercraft.

Pumpout is available throughout Brentwood Bay for free (donations appreciated) through J. R. Pumpout, (844) 507-3451 or VHF 88. This program is funded by Butchart Gardens.

The village up at the highway has some shopping. Moorage is at Brentwood Bay Resort & Marina.

㉓ **Portside Marina.** 789 Saunders Ln., Brentwood Bay, BC V8M 1C5; (250) 652-2211; info@portsidemarina.net; portsidemarina.net. Open all year with limited guest moorage for boats up to 50 feet, reservations accepted. 30 amp power, water, washrooms, showers, and laundry. The marina is located in Brentwood Bay north of the BC Ferries terminal and next to the Seahorses Café. New owners took over the marina in 2017 and have been steadily making improvements. Transient moorage space for 2018 will be expanded from two to six slips. A small marine ways and boatyard that specializes in wooden boat building and repair is adjacent to the marina. Pacifica Paddle Sports (250-665-7411) is located at the marina and has rental kayaks, canoes, and SUPs.

㉓ **Brentwood Bay Resort & Marina.** 849 Verdier Ave., Brentwood Bay, BC V8W 1C5; (250) 652-3151; (888) 544-2079; marina@brentwoodbayresort.com; www.brentwoodbayresort.com. Monitors VHF 66A. The reservation-only marina has 22 slips of guest moorage and side-tie moorage for vessels to 125 feet, 15, 30 & 50 amp power, water, washrooms, laundry, garbage, recycling, showers, adult pool with drinks and pub food service, sushi and sake, cold beer & wine off-sales in the pub, free Wi-Fi. 'Patio Party' is held at the pub on weekends as scheduled in the months of July and August, live music and beer samplers.

This is a highly rated resort and spa, with excellent views of Saanich Inlet, beautiful landscaping, a pub and dining room. A shuttle boat runs to Butchart Gardens for a fee (make reservations at the marina office), or it's a short dinghy ride away. Kayak and SUP rentals, bicycle rentals, guided diving trips, and Paddle Sports eco-adventure tours available.

㉓ **Angler's Anchorage Marina.** (250) 652-3531; www.anglersanchoragemarina.com. Some transient moorage available in slips to 50 feet, call ahead, 30 & 50 amp power, washrooms, showers, laundry, garbage drop, pumpout. Reservations are accepted and recommended. A new patio and ramp were added in 2017 to create a welcoming entrance to the refurbished marina office.

㉓ **Butchart Gardens.** 800 Benvenuto Avenue, Brentwood Bay, BC V8M 1J8; (250) 652-5256; (866) 652-4422; www.butchartgardens.com. Locally named **Butchart Cove** just outside the mouth of Tod Inlet is the back door to the celebrated and astonishing Butchart Gardens. The Gardens are a must-see attraction. They are lighted at night, creating an entirely different effect from the day. On Saturday evenings during the summer a fireworks display is held on a large field in the gardens. Many people arrive early and have a picnic dinner while waiting for darkness. A little known secret is — The Dining Room restaurant will prepare a special picnic basket to enjoy on the grounds — see their website for the menu. Bring blankets and cushions. Even for jaded viewers, it's worth the trip. The most interesting fireworks are done at ground level, accompanied by music — you have to be at the field for the full experience.

The Gardens' dinghy dock is in tiny Butchart

Brentwood Bay Marina

www.WaggonerGuide.com

Cove with 4 free mooring buoys for boats 40 feet and under (a fifth mooring ball for vessels 18 feet and under) that are first-come, first-served, maximum 24 hour stay. Eyes for stern-ties are set into the rock wall. Most visitors put the anchor down in adjacent Tod Inlet and go by dinghy to the dinghy dock. Dinghy dock is closed from December 1 to January 6.

Tod Inlet. *No Discharge Zone, Gray water okay.* Tod Inlet reaches back behind Butchart Gardens into Gowlland Tod Provincial Park, and has ample anchoring room. Anchor in water deeper than 20 feet to protect eelgrass. Green can Buoy *U21* marks a rock. Leave the bouy to port when entering. The inlet is narrow when seen from Brentwood Bay, but opens somewhat after a bend. In the narrow sections you should plan to run a stern-tie to shore. Boats in the more open sections around the bend often can swing without a stern-tie. On Saturday nights the inlet is crowded with boats that come to see the fireworks display at the Gardens.

The dinghy dock on the southeastern shore of the inlet is provided by the Marine Conservation Society and BC Parks, look for the green Marine Ecology float building. A trail to the south leads to the main entrance of Butchart Gardens, about a 10 minute walk. Stay left at the 'Y' in the trail. It's also a short dinghy ride to Butchart Cove where you can tie to the shore side of the dinghy dock and pay admission to the gardens at the backdoor entrance. The dinghy dock in Tod Inlet serves as an access point for the Gowlland Tod Provincial Park with hiking trails connecting through the Gowlland Range. During the summer months, volunteers set up a float in Tod Inlet to provide information and answer questions. The float is staffed by members of the Capital City Yacht Club on behalf of BC Parks.

Finlayson Arm. Goldstream Boathouse is located at the head of Finlayson Arm, at the edge of drying flats off the mouth of the Goldstream River. The shoal water seems to be extending farther north, so come in close to the docks. If the approach is made from mid-channel, an unsuspecting skipper could find his ship aground. Unique homes dot the hillsides and shoreline along Finlayson Arm. Look for the cute 'crooked little house' on a small point just before the power lines on the western shore at 48°31.14'N/123°32.5'W.

㉔ **Goldstream Boathouse.** 3540 Trans-Canada Hwy, Victoria, BC V9B 6H6; (250) 478-4407; admin@goldstreamboathousemarina.com; www.goldstreamboathousemarina.com. Open all year, gasoline and diesel at fuel dock. Minimal guest moorage available, but even during the summer season they usually have room, call ahead. Complete repair facility and haulout by trailer up to 50 feet, small convenience store, 2-lane concrete launch ramp, 15, 30 & 50 amp power, washrooms, no showers.

㉕ **Mill Bay.** Mill Bay is a good anchorage. The west shore provides a lee from the usual summer west or northwest winds. The bay is, however, open to southeast winds. Just north of the Mill Bay Marina is a spar buoy zone marking a no-anchoring area. A charted pipeline extends from the northwest corner of the bay.

㉕ **Mill Bay Marina.** 740 Handy Road, Mill Bay, BC V0R 2P1; (250) 743-4303; contact@millbaymarina.ca; www.millbaymarina.ca. Monitors VHF 66A. 700 feet of transient moorage to accommodate boats to 200 feet, 30 & 50 amp power, water, gasoline, diesel, pumpout, laundry, showers, free Wi-Fi. Reservations recommended in season. Wide roomy slips and side-tie moorage on concrete docks. State-of-the-art marina with great views of Mt. Baker.

Picnic tables and propane barbeques for guest use are on the docks. The Bridgemans Bistro restaurant, open for lunch and dinner, and brunch on weekends is a hit. Soft drinks, ice cream. Live music on Sundays. Blue Dog Kayaking (250) 710-7693 located at Mill Bay Marina offers kayak and SUP rentals, instruction, and expeditions.

The Mill Bay Shopping Centre is a short walk up the hill. The center has a supermarket, drug store, liquor store, hardware store, bank and gift stores. Several restaurants and the Visitor Centre are also located there.

A public launch ramp is on the north side of the marina. Spar buoys north of the marina and boat launch, located in front of the Brentwood College School (a college prep boarding school), mark a no-anchoring area. The no-anchoring area

Goldstream Boathouse

protects an ocean loop geo-exchange system used for heating and cooling the school's buildings.

㉕ **Mill Bay Community Wharf.** Open all year, 50 feet of dock space, no facilities. Three hour maximum stay, no overnight moorage.

㉖ **Cowichan Bay.** www.cowichanbay.com. The picturesque waterfront village of Cowichan Bay is located near the southwest corner of Cowichan Bay. Docks at Fishermen's Wharf are behind a floating breakwater. The floating breakwater dock is not connected to land. A dinghy is needed for shore access. The privately owned marinas are west of the public wharf. At the other end of town, Hecate Park has a launch ramp with ample trailer storage. In settled weather anchorage is possible but not advised. We are told crabbing and prawning are good.

The annual Cowichan Bay Regatta is held the first weekend in August, a popular event drawing many participants. The village is full of life. It has numerous shops and businesses, including liquor stores and good restaurants, not one of them part of a major chain. Interesting little shops are tucked away everywhere. The Grain Mill Bakery is superb as is Hilary's Cheese Shop. Udder Guys Ice Cream has some of the best ice cream on the coast. The Cowichan Bay Maritime Centre, built on a wharf extending from shore, has many interesting displays.

The Ocean Front Suites has a pub and restaurant. Visitors can use the hotel pool for a daily membership charge. A grass tennis court, just like Wimbledon, is 3 miles west of town at 2290

GULF ISLANDS

Cowichan Bay Rd (250) 746-7282. For brewery tours of the area, see CheersCowichanTours.com (250) 710-7391.

Water Shuttle: The Genoa Bay Shuttle (250-812-7543) provides water taxi service between Genoa Bay Marina and Cowichan Bay Bluenose Marina.

㉖ **Cowichan Bay Fishermen's Wharf Association.** P.O. Box 52, Cowichan Bay, BC V0R 1N0; (250) 746-5911; cbfwa@shaw.ca. Monitors VHF 66A. Open all year, 900 feet of dock space for vessels to 100 feet, 30 amp power, free Wi-Fi, clean washrooms, laundry, showers, free pumpout, garbage and recycling drop, waste oil disposal. Short-term shopping stops are encouraged until 2:00 p.m.; check-in at the harbor office.

㉖ **Oceanfront Suites at Cowichan Bay.** 1681 Cowichan Bay Rd., Cowichan Bay, BC V0R 1N0; (250) 715-1000; info@oceanfrontcowichanbay.com; www.oceanfrontcowichanbay.com. Full service resort hotel. Overnight stays at the dock for hotel guests; hourly stays for restaurant and pub patrons; dock suitable for shallow draft boats only. No power on the docks. The Oceanview restaurant overlooking the bay is open seasonally. Located immediately south of the Fishermen's Wharf dock. Watch your depths on very low tides.

㉖ **Pier 66 and Pier 67 Marina.** 1745 Cowichan Bay Rd., Cowichan Bay, BC V0R 1N0; (250) 748-3800. Gasoline and diesel. The fuel dock is managed by Ocean Ecoventures; hours vary, call ahead. Fuel dock suited for small vessels only. Permanent moorage only, no transient moorage.

㉖ **Dungeness Marina.** 1759 Cowichan Bay Rd., Box 51, Cowichan Bay, BC V0R 1N0; (250) 748-6789; info@dungenessmarina.com; www.dungenessmarina.com. Permanent moorage, no transient moorage. The marina changed ownership in 2017 and no longer has transient moorage.

㉖ **Bluenose Marina.** 1765 Cowichan Bay Rd., P.O. Box 40, Cowichan Bay, BC V0R 1N0; (250) 748-2222; deven@thebluenosemarina.com; www.thebluenosemarina.com. Open all year. Guest moorage available on a 100 foot dock, reservations accepted. 15 & 30 amp power, washrooms, showers, laundry. Nearby launch ramp, public playground, and kayak shop. The Cow Cafe & Cookhouse serves seafood and steaks. The Vine Restaurant and Creperie, and Udder Guys Ice Cream shop are nearby.

㉗ **Genoa Bay.** Genoa Bay indents the north shore of Cowichan Bay. Anchorage can be found off the marina docks. The Genoa Bay Marina has transient moorage.

Water Shuttle: The Genoa Bay Shuttle (250-812-7543) provides water taxi service between Genoa Bay Marina and Cowichan Bay Bluenose Marina, departing six times a day; call to book a seat.

㉗ **Genoa Bay Marina.** 5000 Genoa Bay Rd., Duncan, BC V9L 5Y8; (250) 746-7621; (800) 572-6481; info@genoabaymarina.com; www.genoabaymarina.com. Monitors VHF 66A mid-May through end of October. Open all year, guest moorage in 30 slips and along 1200 feet of dock space, call ahead. Excellent washrooms, showers and laundry, 15, 30 & 50 amp power, limited water. Launch ramp, covered picnic shelter, Wi-Fi. This is a popular summer stop. The Genoa Bay Gallery has lovely paintings, prints, and sculpture. The Genoa Bay Café is busy, reservations recommended. During July and August the "breakfast cabana" on the dock offers coffee, fresh baked goods, and other breakfast items.

The unusually good store carries convenience items, souvenirs, books, cruising guides, and snacks. Good crabbing in the bay. Scheduled shuttle runs to the Cowichan waterfront.

Musgrave Landing - Harbour Authority of Salt Spring Island. (250) 537-5711 saltspringharbours.com/musgrave-landing/ Musgrave Landing is on the southwest corner of Salt Spring Island, at the mouth of Sansum Narrows. It is managed by the Harbour Authority of Salt Spring Island. Musgrave Landing is a popular stopover, although it has only a small public float for visitor moorage, no facilities, and very restricted anchorage nearby. Upland you'll find good hiking along miles of logging roads. On a pleasant roadside walk we picked a bouquet of thistle, foxglove, dandelion, fern, salal, nicotiana and pearly everlasting for the galley table. A housing development, with private dock, is on Musgrave Point.

SANSUM NARROWS TO DUCK BAY

Sansum Narrows. Sansum Narrows connects Satellite Channel to the south with Stuart Channel to the north, and leads between high hills on Saltspring Island and Vancouver Island. The wind funnels down the axis of the narrows, turning at the bends. It also funnels down the valleys leading to the channel, so wind directions can be erratic. Currents seldom exceed 3 knots; usually they are less.

Burgoyne Bay - Harbour Authority of Salt Spring Island. saltspringharbours.com/burgoyne-bay/; Burgoyne Bay has ample anchorage in 18 to 30 feet at its inner end, but is subject to williwaws that blow across a low swale on Saltspring Island. Most of the bay is too deep for convenient anchoring. A 65-foot public float for visitor moorage is at the head of the bay, next to the anchorage, no facilities. One side of the float is available for transient moorage stays up to 48 hours. The other side is reserved for local use.

㉘ **Maple Bay.** Maple Bay is a major pleasure boat center, with public moorages and all necessary facilities and services. Birds Eye Cove, off the southwest corner of Maple Bay, is home to the Maple Bay Yacht Club, with reciprocal moorage, and the Maple Bay Marina and Birds Eye Cove Marina, both with fuel docks. Anchoring is good in Birds Eye Cove, but avoid anchoring in the area just off the dock on the east side of the cove, opposite the marina docks. Markers designate the navigation channel. Do not anchor in the channel.

Birds Eye Cove Farm, located a half-mile south of Maple Bay, is a favorite local attraction. The Farm raises beef, pork and chickens as well as farm-fresh produce. Visitors can purchase vegetables, eggs, pies and meat dishes from the "Gypsy Wagon" open daily from 9:00 a.m. to 5:00 p.m. Food items are created on their spit grill and wood-fired pizza oven. "Pizza Nights" are held from 4:00 p.m. to 8:00 p.m. on Mondays in May, and from June until Labor Day on Mondays and Wednesdays. It's a treat to join the social events among 300 acres of beautiful rolling

Genoa Bay Marina

GULF ISLANDS

See Area Map Page 205 - Maps Not for Navigation

The friendly staff at Maple Bay are ready to assist.

fields. Gatherings are held in the large hand-cut timber frame barn and there are two timber frame cabins to rent. For more information go to www.birdseyecovefarm.com or call (250) 748-6379. One of the best farmer's markets on Vancouver Island is held in downtown Duncan on Saturdays at the Market Square, look for the Clock Tower. The market is open year-round, spring/summer hours 9:00 a.m. to 2:00 p.m. Taxi service is available through Duncan Taxi (250) 746-4444 or make reservations for the shuttle service from Maple Bay Marina.

㉘ **Maple Bay Marina.** 6145 Genoa Bay Rd., Duncan, BC V9L 5T7; (250) 746-8482; (866) 746-8482; info@maplebaymarina.com; www.maplebaymarina.com. Monitors VHF 66A. Open all year. Gasoline, diesel, lubricants and propane at the fuel dock. New fuel tanks and fuel lines were added in the spring of 2017 along with high-flow pumps. Mostly 15 & 30 amp power, some 50 amp, garbage, washrooms, showers, laundry, water, waste oil disposal, Shaw Go Wi-Fi, and free Wi-Fi. Mariners Market & Espresso Bar has coffee, hot breakfast items, muffins, sandwiches, convenience groceries and local art and crafts. The marina office is in the Mariners Market store. A chandlery has marine supplies and charts. Call ahead for slip assignment. Reservations recommended.

A 55-ton Travelift provides haulout for repairs. It is run by Lindstrom Marine, who has the small marine supply store at the marina.

The washrooms are spacious and clean, with good showers. The Shipyard Restaurant & Pub has good food, with daily specials and live music on Friday evenings. The pub offers off-sale beer and wine. Shuttle service is available to downtown Duncan twice a day on weekdays and on Saturdays for a fee. There is charter shuttle service to two different local golf courses. Ask for a schedule at the marina office. Hiking trails and map are available for Mount Tzouhalem.

The marina offers float home and kayak rentals. Check the website for special events.

Harbour Air has scheduled float plane service to Vancouver Harbour. Saltspring Air has scheduled service to Vancouver Airport and Vancouver Harbour.

㉘ **Birds Eye Cove Marina.** 6271 Genoa Bay Rd., Duncan, BC V9L 5Y8; (250) 746-5686; info@birdseyecoveduncan.ca. Gasoline and diesel at fuel dock. Limited guest moorage with 15 & 30 amp power, washrooms. No showers. In 2017, the fuel dock was closed for renovations.

㉘ **Maple Bay Public Wharf.** Open all year. Located in Maple Bay, not in Birds Eye Cove, which extends from the south side of Maple Bay. Moorage along 300 feet of dock space, water to the bottom of the ramp but not out the dock, no power. Self-register at kiosk. A nice beach is nearby. An underwater park is about 200 feet off the end of the dock. The wharf is managed by the Chemainus Harbour Authority and checked daily.

Crofton Public Wharf. Open all year, 1000 feet of dock space, 20 & 30 amp power, washrooms, showers, laundry, garbage drop. Breakwater protected. The docks are usually full with local boats. Crofton is the pulp and paper mill town on the west side of Stuart Channel. The public dock is next to the terminal for the ferry to Vesuvius on Saltspring Island. Walking distance to all services including groceries, restaurants, fishing supplies and licenses. Playground two blocks away. Nearby outdoor swimming pool, tennis courts, hiking trails.

㉙ **Vesuvius.** Located on the northwest side of Saltspring Island, the village of Vesuvius is the terminus for the ferry to Crofton on Vancouver Island. Vesuvius has a public wharf, coffee shop with tasty lunch items, and a restaurant all within easy walking distance. The Seaside restaurant has its own private dock suitable for dinghies and small craft. Vesuvius Bay has anchorage that is open to the northwest with limited protection to the south and southeast. The bay is regularly rocked with wakes from the arriving ferry. More

Cowichan Bay

Genoa Bay Marina

Birds Eye Cove and Maple Bay Marina

2018 Waggoner Cruising Guide — 235

GULF ISLANDS   Reference Only – Not for Navigation

Northern Gulf Islands

protected anchorage can be found nearby in Duck Bay.

㉙ Vesuvius - Harbour Authority of Salt Spring Island. (250) 537-5711 saltspringharbours.com/vesuvius-bay. The public wharf at Vesuvius, located behind the ferry landing, has side-tie visitor moorage on a 40 foot float; no power, no water. Self-registration, moorage rates and payment box are located at the wharfhead; first 2 hours stay at no charge 8:00 a.m. to 4:00 p.m. This is a popular location and well used by smaller transient boats.

Duck Bay. Just north of Vesuvius Bay, Duck Bay has good anchorage with steep, wooded cliffs rising on its east side. The bay is well-protected, except from northwest winds. A number of private docks, mooring buoys and homes surround the bay.

NORTHERN GULF ISLANDS
Stuart Channel. Stuart Channel runs from Sansum Narrows to Dodd Narrows. It is bordered on the west side by Vancouver Island, and on the east side by Saltspring, Kuper, Thetis and De Courcy Islands. Stuart Channel tends to be littered with drift because of extensive log towing to Crofton, Chemainus and Ladysmith. Keep a sharp watch ahead.

㉚ Chemainus. Chemainus is on the Vancouver Island side of Stuart Channel. It has a good public wharf and floats. Chemainus Bay, south of the Municipal Dock, is filled with commercial log boom operations and commercial maritime activities. The bay is not suitable for anchoring.

Chemainus is filled with boutiques, galleries, antique shops, and interesting-looking restaurants. More than 30 of the town's buildings have large, well-done murals, most of them depicting Chemainus' distant past as a Native

seasonal campground and its more recent history as a mining, logging, and mill town. The mural project is now focused on celebrating Canadian artist Emily Carr's work. The first mural is a remarkable three-dimensional piece on the west side of the Chemainus Theatre Festival building. This is the initial step in a planned million-dollar outdoor gallery of Carr's art, both paintings and sculpture.

Chemainus has grown so popular that a large parking area has been built for tour buses, and in they roll, filled with visitors from around the world. Horse-drawn tours are available. Two 49th Parallel grocery stores are located on Oak Street. The original historic general store is immediately above the municipal dock, and the new well-stocked store is about half a mile up Oak Street from the dock. Also on Oak Street is the Chemainus Bakery with a good selection of fresh backed goods.

A ferry crosses between Chemainus and Thetis Island, about a 10-minute walk from

See Area Map Page 236 - Maps Not for Navigation

GULF ISLANDS

Enjoy the good pub food and view of Stuart Channel from the Seaside Restaurant on Vesuvius Bay, west side of Saltspring Island

either Thetis Island Marina or Telegraph Harbour Marina. This is a good way to visit Chemainus. If you take in an evening show in Chemainus, be sure you can get to the ferry before the last departure. Chemainus Water Taxi is another option (250) 246-7866 or (250) 246-9559.

Live theater: The Chemainus Theatre Festival mounts live matinee and evening performances year-round (closed Mondays). Highly recommended. Call for tickets in advance: (250) 246-9820 or (800) 565-7738.

㉚ **Chemainus Municipal Dock.** P.O. Box 193, Chemainus, BC V0R 1K0; (250) 715-8186; (250) 246-4655; harmen.chemainus.munimarina@gmail.com. Monitors VHF 66A. Day and overnight moorage, 30 & 50 amp power, water, washrooms, showers, garbage drop, pumpout and Wi-Fi. Make moorage reservations directly with the marina by phone or email; they have no relationship with third-party booking services.. A nice laundromat is 1½ blocks away at 9870 Cross Street. This marina, with slips and side-tie, is next to the ferry terminal. Reservations recommended. Every two hours from morning to night, the ferry arrives and rolls things around a little. It's not bad, but first-time visitors should be aware of the wake.

Visitor boats will tie along 175 feet on the outside of the main dock or moor in slips on the inside of the main dock. Because Chemainus is a popular day stop, landing fees have been instituted—$6 under 40 feet; $12 over 40 feet. They found that the docks were full during the day then empty at night, and they need moorage income to maintain the facility. The irrepressible Harmen Bootsma is the manager.

Mooring buoys: Eight mooring buoys are available off the park at the entrance to the bay. One boat per buoy, 45-foot maximum length. Cost is $10 per night if you pay at the Chemainus Municipal Dock office; $20 if they have to come out to collect. Private mooring buoys are also in the bay; look for the buoys labeled 'public.'

㉚ **Jones Marine Services Ltd.** Box 29, Chemainus, BC V0R 1K0; (250) 246-1100. Diesel and mid-grade gasoline. Open 8:00 a.m. to 3:30 p.m. Monday through Saturday. Accepts cash and

Chemainus

2018 WAGGONER CRUISING GUIDE

GULF ISLANDS

Visa/MasterCard. This dock services the 9-vessel Jones tugboat fleet, and offers fuel to pleasure craft as well. The docks may be taken up with Jones's own boats.

Evening Cove. Evening Cove, at the mouth of Ladysmith Harbour, is a possible anchorage. Correspondent Bruce Evertz reports: "We found good protection from northwest winds, but did have a few wakes from passing boats. There are several houses around the bay so it's not a good spot to take Fido ashore."

㉛ **Ladysmith Harbour.** Ladysmith is on Vancouver Island, approximately 6 miles north of Chemainus. Ladysmith is an active sawmill town. Logs are stored on the north side of the harbor and in front of the mill on the south side.

Ladysmith itself is about one-half mile from Ladysmith Community Marina and Fisherman's Wharf, up the hill and across the highway. It's a bit of a hike, but worthwhile. Before reaching the highway, the big blue building is the Ladysmith Waterfront Arts Centre, with interesting galleries and the Ladysmith Maritime Society's office and historical collection of outboard motors. The building used to be a railroad equipment repair facility. The tracks are still there. A train occasionally rumbles by.

The main street of Ladysmith looks as if time passed it by. Movie scenes have been filmed here. A large and friendly 49th Parallel Grocery is several blocks west from the main downtown

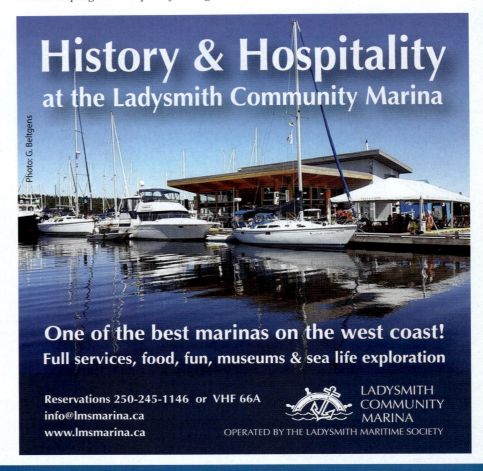

History & Hospitality
at the Ladysmith Community Marina

Photo: G. Beltgens

One of the best marinas on the west coast!
Full services, food, fun, museums & sea life exploration

Reservations 250-245-1146 or VHF 66A
info@lmsmarina.ca
www.lmsmarina.ca

LADYSMITH COMMUNITY MARINA
OPERATED BY THE LADYSMITH MARITIME SOCIETY

LADYSMITH MARKETPLACE

49th PARALLEL GROCERY AND CAFÉ
The 49th is a full-service grocery store, including fresh produce, meat, deli, bakery, café, and flower shop. We offer a delivery service back to your vessel– check with the wharf for details. Located next to the Liquor Depot and a short hike from Ladysmith Marinas. Open 7 days a week!
250-245-3221 • 1020 First Ave. • www.the49th.com

FOX & HOUNDS
Our Tudor style British Pub offers 16 English, European and local craft beers on tap, and a full British menu with all your favourites. We are family-owned and family-friendly. Open seven days a week from 11.30am to 10pm. Look for the British red phone box on High Street.
250 924 1747 • 11 High Street
www.foxandhoundsladysmith.com

CHAMBER OF COMMERCE AND VISITOR CENTRE
The information hub of our community. Discover all the wonderful things there are to see and do in Ladysmith including some of the hidden hotspots. Find out where to dine, shop or what's going on around town. Visit us for all these questions and more.
250-245-2112 • 33 Roberts Street •
www.ladysmithcofc.com or www.tourismladysmith.ca

LADYSMITH COMMUNITY MARINA
"The friendliest marina on the west coast"
Ladysmith Community Marina is all about community and making your stay enjoyable. Our 3000 sf floating Welcome Centre has beautiful amenities that will make you feel at home as you explore local islands, vineyards, forests and towns. Located 55 nautical miles north of Victoria, Ladysmith Community Marina is the first marina port side as you enter Ladysmith Harbour.
250-245-1146 • 610 Oyster Bay • www.lmsmarina.ca

LADYSMITH MARINA
Located on the protected east coast of Vancouver Island just outside of Nanaimo, BC, Ladysmith Marina is the perfect gateway to some of the most breathtaking boating grounds in British Columbia, including the Gulf Islands. With a waterfront picnic area and ample parking, this ocean paradise is easily accessed from nearby Nanaimo Airport and two BC Ferries terminals.
250-245-4521 • 901 Gladden Rd. • www.ladysmithmarina.com

PHARMASAVE LADYSMITH
Located at the top end of First Avenue, Pharmasave has been serving Ladysmith for over 35 years. More than a drug store, Pharmasave has a great selection of products & services ranging from full service pharmacy and cosmetic departments to beautiful giftware, greeting cards and a Post Office. Visit us today and "Live Well" with Pharmasave.
250-245-3113 • 441 1st Ave. • www.ladysmithpharmasave.com

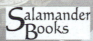

SALAMANDER BOOKS
Visit our independent bookstore in historic downtown Ladysmith. Come in to our store, relax and browse. We have an interesting selection of both new and used books, including cookbooks, travel guides, local authors, and children's books. Open Monday to Friday from 9:30am to 5:30pm, and Saturdays from 10am to 5pm.
250-245-4726 • 535 1st Ave. • Find us on Facebook!

GULF ISLANDS

area, and will deliver to the docks. A private liquor store is next door to the grocery.

The Old Town Bakery at 510 First Avenue (main street through town) is "to die for," with the widest variety of fresh-baked cinnamon buns we've ever seen. Note that in 2106, the bakery moved to remodeled space literally next door. We had an excellent and reasonably priced deli lunch there, too. Buoma Meats, at 412 First Avenue, is an old-fashioned butcher shop, all weights in pounds and ounces. The Beantime Cafe serves fresh roasted coffee. A broad selection of restaurants are in town. Several restaurants will deliver to the marinas.

Ladysmith Community Marina, run by the Ladysmith Maritime Society, behind Slag Point on the south side of the harbor, is the first major set of docks. Ladysmith Fisherman's Wharf is adjacent, followed by Ladysmith Marina, farther into the harbor. Page Point Marina, on the north shore, sometimes has transient moorage available. Ladysmith Yacht Club, located at Ladysmith Marina has reciprocal moorage. Near the mouth of Ladysmith Harbour the long float in Sibell Bay, on the north side of the Dunsmuir Islands, is a Seattle Yacht Club outstation, member boats only, no reciprocal moorage.

The best anchoring is either in Sibell Bay or just west of Sibell Bay, inside the westernmost of the Dunsmuir Islands. Because of shoal water between Sibell Bay and the latter anchorage, it's a good idea to loop around the west end of the Dunsmuir Islands. Anchorage can also be found at the head of Ladysmith Harbour, off of Page Point Marina.

Repairs: Ladysmith Marine Services offers marine repairs and haulout to 40 feet, (250) 714-6206.

Sealegs Kayaking Adventures, located upland from Ladysmith Community Marina, offers equipment sales, tours and lessons. The office, located at 200 Transfer Beach Blvd., is a short hike up the hill, phone (250) 245-4096.

No-Discharge Zone. Gray water okay.

㉛ **Ladysmith Community Marina.** P.O. Box 1030, Ladysmith, BC V9G 1A7; (250) 245-1146; info@lmsmarina.ca; www.lmsmarina.ca. Monitors VHF 66A. Best to phone or email for availability. Open all year, 800 feet of guest moorage with 30 amp power, water, block and cube ice, pumpout, free Wi-Fi. Garbage, recycling, and compost accepted (donations appreciated). Reservations recommended. The impressive Ladysmith Maritime Society Welcome Centre, on a float at the docks, has a fireside lounge, washrooms, showers, laundry, and the seasonal Oyster Bay Cafe, which is open from mid-May to Sept. from 8:00 a.m. to 3:00 p.m daily. Adjacent to the Oyster Bay Cafe is the new Sea Life Center with interpretive displays and an underwater portal to view the marine life. It is a hit with the kids. The dinghy dock is on the cross dock by the Welcome Centre.

These are the first set of docks on the southwest side as you enter Ladysmith Harbour. The docks are very good and the historical displays, including restored museum boats and equipment, are fascinating. The new Harbour Heritage Centre and an art gallery are up the hill in the large blue building. They have drop-in art classes, too. The town of Ladysmith is a short walk away, up the hill. Bus service runs to nearby shopping and a mall outside of the town center.

The community is justifiably proud of this new facility and its large meeting spaces. A large covered 40 X 20 foot picnic area with tables and grills, located on the docks, can accommodate up to 100 people. At the end of the day it is not unusual for a group to gather round, some grilling their dinners and some visiting others. Dine on the Dock programs are every other Friday during the summer. Music on the Dock events are held every Thursday. Check the website for more information. The Ladysmith Maritime Society Community Marina really is a community marina, run by a small staff and over 250 volunteers. As guests, we could feel their enthusiasm.

㉛ **Ladysmith Fisherman's Wharf.** P.O. Box 130, Ladysmith, BC V9G 1A1; (250) 245-7511 or (250) 618-4720 after hours; office hours 10:00 a.m. to 1:00 p.m. Monday through Saturday. lfwa@telus.net; www.ladysmith-fishermanswharf.com. Open all year, 1200 feet of dock space, 30 amp power, garbage drop, washrooms, showers, laundry services, waste oil disposal, trailer parking. Marine repairs, tidal grid and launch ramp. Limited transient moorage. Commercial fishing vessels have priority during the winter months. Stairs lead up the hill toward the town of Ladysmith, about one-half mile away.

㉛ **Ladysmith Marina.** 901 Gladden Rd., Ladysmith, BC V9G 1K4; (250) 245-4521; ladysmithmarina@obmg.com; www.ladysmith-marina.com. Monitors VHF 66A. Open all year, washrooms, showers, and a public laundry. 30 & 50 amp power. Picnic area. This marina has permanent moorage, but guest moorage is often available in unoccupied slips, call ahead for availability; reservations accepted. Dock A on the east side of the marina is occupied by the Ladysmith Yacht Club. The marina is part of Oak Bay Marine Group, a company that owns several marinas and fishing resorts throughout B.C.

㉜ **Page Point Marina Inc.** 4760 Brenton-Page Rd., Ladysmith, BC V9G 1L7; (250) 245-2312; (877) 860-6866; moorage@pagepointmarina.com; www.pagepointmarina.com. Monitors VHF 66A. Open all year. Permanent and guest moorage to 66 feet, 30 amp power, water, free Wi-Fi, garbage drop, compost & recycling. Can prearrange kayaks and bicycle rentals. Free shuttle service to the airport. Pet-friendly. Reservations recommended. The dinghy dock is next to the ramp at

Ladysmith Harbour

Ladysmith Maritime Society and Community Marina

Thetis Island Marina

2018 WAGGONER CRUISING GUIDE

GULF ISLANDS

the head of G dock.

A cozy inn is available for short or long-term accommodations and private functions.

Tent Island. Tent Island is off the south tip of Penelakut Island (formerly Kuper Island), at the junction of Houstoun Passage and Stuart Channel. The small bay on the west side of Tent Island is a popular anchorage in settled weather.

Preedy Harbour. Preedy Harbour indents the southwest corner of Thetis Island, due west of Telegraph Harbour. The ferry from Chemainus calls there. From the south, enter between Hudson Island and three long, thin reefs, marked with red (starboard hand) lights and day beacons. From Stuart Channel enter between Hudson Island and Dayman Island. Reefs, marked by green buoys on the Dayman Island side and a light on the Hudson Island side, extend from both these islands. Because the Hudson Island light is positioned upland from the toe of its reef, favor the Dayman Island buoys.

Entry from the north is clear as long as you stay mid-channel. For all three entries, check the chart carefully so you know where the reefs are, and how to avoid them.

A day-use-only community dock is in the northwest corner of Preedy Harbour, near the ferry landing. Anchorage is good in this area, keeping in mind the ferry comings and goings.

㉝ **Telegraph Harbour.** Telegraph Harbour is one of the Gulf Islands' most popular stops. It is located across Stuart Channel from Chemainus, between Thetis Island and Penelakut Island (formerly Kuper Island). Two marinas are in Telegraph Harbour: Thetis Island Marina and Telegraph Harbour Marina. Both marinas are walking distance to an inter-island ferry to Chemainus. While you're at Telegraph Harbour, you may enjoy walking the roads of Thetis Island. You'll find a number of interesting stops, including the Pot of Gold Coffee Roasting Co.

White Restricted Operations buoys mark the edges of the anchoring area. Note the shoal areas on the starboard side of the channel and across from the Thetis Island Resort.

Penelakut Island (formerly Kuper Island) is an Indian Reserve.

Farmers market: A farmers market is held 10:00 a.m. to 12:00 p.m. on Sundays, May through September at Telegraph Harbour Marina.

LOCAL KNOWLEDGE

ENTRANCE CHANNEL: New channel markers indicate the channel between Thetis Island Marina and Telegraph Harbour Marina. Keep the marks to starboard when entering. On very low tides hug the breakwater outside the Thetis Island Marina fuel dock as you enter Telegraph Harbour. The channel has about 9 feet of depth at zero tide.

㉝ **Thetis Island Resort.** 46 Harbour Rd., Thetis Island, BC ; (250) 246-1443; marina@thetisisland.com; www.thetisisland.com. Monitors VHF 66A; (250) 246-3464 (pub, year round). To port, this is the first marina as you enter Telegraph Harbour. Open all year, gasoline and diesel at the fuel dock, propane on shore, over 3000 feet of side-tie dock space, 15 & 30 amp power, washrooms, showers, laundry, ATM. New docks were added in 2017 with plans to add additional docks in the near future. The marina has three rental suites, and they're quite nice. This is a full-service marina with a liquor store, convenience groceries, snacks, ice, and post office. Wi-Fi on the docks; get the password at the pub or the fuel dock. A cell phone booster covers the pub and deck areas. It's a 10- to 15-minute walk to the BC Ferries to Chemainus.

The fully-licensed pub has inside and outside dining and separate areas for families. The pub has good food and an excellent selection of beers, porters, stouts, and single-malt scotches.

The Resort has its own water desalination system. A covered picnic and barbecue area with seating is available for groups. There is a Saturday Market from 10 a.m. to 2 p.m.

㉝ **Telegraph Harbour Marina.** Box 7-10, Thetis Island, BC V0R 2Y0; (250) 246-9511; (800) 246-6011; sunny@telegraphharbour.com; www.telegraphharbour.com. Monitors VHF 66A. This is the marina at the back of the bay. Although close to drying flats, the docks have at least 6 to 8 feet on all tides. Open 7 days a week, mid-June through mid-September, and weekends only from Easter through mid-June. In winter no facilities are

240

240   www.WaggonerGuide.com

See Area Map Page 236 - Maps Not for Navigation   GULF ISLANDS

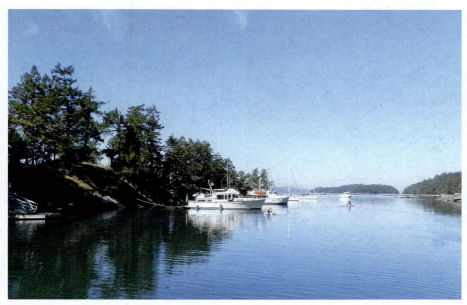
Stern-tied in lovely Princess Cove on Wallace Island

available except moorage and electricity. Gasoline & diesel, oil, stove alcohol, and kerosene at the fuel dock. Moorage along 3000 feet of dock, 15 & 30 amp power, washrooms, showers, laundry, Wi-Fi, garbage drop, limited water.

The store carries convenience groceries including a variety of specialty meats, deli items to go, marine guides, books and gifts, and fresh-baked pies. The marina has pre-ordered homemade pizzas and fresh baguettes to go, and is the exclusive outlet for Thetis Island's Pot of Gold coffee. They have an old fashioned soda fountain where you can still get guilt-filled hard ice cream milk shakes, sundaes, and ice cream specialties.

Telegraph Harbour

The marina is clean and well-maintained. Staff helps arriving boats land. They have a playground for kids, a dog run, a large covered area for group functions, and a picnic area with tables and barbecues. It's a 10 to 15 minute walk to the BC Ferries to Chemainus. Boaters are permitted to use the community trail system, accessible from the marina. The Domaine Jasmin Winery (250) 246-9494 is a recent addition on the island located several miles north. Arrangements for group transportation to the winery are possible through the Telegraph Harbour Marina with a return trip provided by winery personnel.

Rendezvous: Many rendezvous are held here in spring or early fall, best to call ahead for reservations on weekends and during the peak season. A few rendezvous fill the marina, but most do not. Moorage space is usually available.

The Cut. The Cut is a straight and uncomplicated drying pass connecting Telegraph Harbour with Clam Bay. Red, Right, Returning assumes you are returning from Clam Bay. Cruising boats should only try The Cut at or near high water, with local knowledge. Signs at each end purport to show the depth, but they read approximately 3 feet too deep. We took the dinghy through at the bottom of a 4.3-foot tide, sounding the shallow spots with a leadline. Although the two signs said 6 feet of water was in the channel, we found only 2 to 2.5 feet in the shallow spots near the Telegraph Harbour entrance and at a couple of narrow places on the Clam Bay side.

North Cove. North Cove indents the north end of Thetis Island and is a good anchorage, although it is open to northwesterly winds. A substantial rock breakwater protects a private float and boathouse at Fraser Point, the entrance to North Cove. Camp docks are in the southwest corner of the cove. Anchor in 24 to 36 feet (zero tide) along the south shore. High tide covers fingers of rock that extend from the south shore, but the rock reappears when the tide drops. Don't get too close. Stay clear of the rocks in the middle of the entry. The charts show them as ++, for dangerous rocks 6 feet or less beneath the surface.

Cufra Inlet. Cufra Inlet, about a mile long, extends into Thetis Island from the southeast corner of North Cove. Most of the inlet dries, but is good for dinghy exploring at higher water.

Clam Bay. Clam Bay is a large, relatively open bay with good anchoring in convenient depths. Reader Jerry Williams, who lived there, says his favorite spot is the little bight on the north shore, between Leech Island and Thetis Island. The mouth of the Clam Bay is partly blocked by Centre Reef. Rocket Shoal is in the middle of the bay. Lacking familiarity, the safest entry is south of Centre Reef, between Buoy *U42* and Penelakut Spit, which extends from Penelakut Island (formerly Kuper Island). The charts show everything. Large scale Plans Chart 3477 is especially useful. Clam Bay is at one end of The Cut, the drying channel that separates Thetis Island from Penelakut Island.

Southey Bay. At the north tip of Saltspring Island, tucked in beside Southey Point, is a little notch that Contributing Editor Tom Kincaid used as an anchorage in past years. An increasing number of private mooring buoys have restricted swinging room, but it's still a possible anchorage.

Secretary Islands. The Secretary Islands have several nice little anchorages, with the emphasis on *little*. One of the easiest is in the notch on the Trincomali Channel side between the two Secretary Islands.

Mowgli Island. Mowgli Island, off the northwest tip of the Secretary Islands, has good anchorage in a cozy bay between it and the first Secretary island. Swinging room is limited. We suggest a stern-tie across the gravel beach to driftwood ashore. The island is surrounded by reefs. They are easily seen at low tide, but be cautious at high tide.

㉞ **Wallace Island Marine Park.** www.env.gov.bc.ca/bcparks/explore/parkpgs/wallace/ Open all year. Wallace Island, a marine park purchased with the help of the local boating community, is a low and beautiful tree-covered island in Trincomali Channel. Enter from Houstoun Passage. You'll find sheltered anchorage and a dock at Conover Cove, anchorage for many boats in locally-named Princess Cove, and room for a couple of boats just inside Panther Point. The park has toilets, campsites and picnic areas, and trails crisscrossing the entire island. It's a fine place to walk through the forest and stretch the legs. Raccoons roam the area–especially at night, lock up all food items aboard and pack out refuse. Old cabins set in an orchard near Conover Cove are locked shut, awaiting funds for restoration. One cabin is festooned with carved name boards from visiting yachts. Please respect the two private properties on the island.

㉞ **Conover Cove.** A reef directly offshore from the entrance to Conover Cove on Wallace

2018 WAGGONER CRUISING GUIDE

Stern-ties are the rule at popular Pirates Cove Marine Park.

Island can be avoided by going around either end. Especially from the southeast, give the reef ample room. When you leave, remember the reef is there. We are told that each year boats depart at high tide and drive up on the rocks. A dock for boats 36 feet and under provides access to the island, nominal fee is charged. An honor-system pay-box is located at the head of the ramp. Conover Cove is fairly shoal at the dock and shoals even more toward both ends of the bay. You can anchor and stern-tie to rings set in the rocks on shore; the rings are marked with red painted arrows. Be sure to check your depths. The entrance to Conover Cove is shallow at low tide.

㉞ **Princess Cove.** Princess Cove is just northwest of Conover Cove, and has room for quite a few boats to anchor. Mooring eyes for stern-ties, usually marked with red or yellow-painted arrows, are set in the rock along the shoreline. Chain hangs from some of the mooring eyes. Absent the chains, at low water you have to be part mountain goat to get to several of those eyes. Set the anchor carefully in 18 to 24 feet (deeper toward the mouth of the cove), and maintain an anchor watch if the wind comes up. A dinghy dock is on the west side of the cove for convenient access to hiking.

㉞ **Panther Point.** Panther Point is the southeast tip of Wallace Island. There's room for one or perhaps two boats in 30 to 36 feet just inside the mouth of the cove. If you anchor any farther inside, a rock on the north side will restrict your swing. The anchorage is exposed to southeast winds but protected from other winds.

Retreat Cove. Retreat Cove, a small notch protected by off-lying Retreat Island, indents Galiano Island across Trincomali Channel from the south tip of Wallace Island. The approach around the north side of Retreat Island is shallow and foul with rocks and reefs. Enter only from the south. The head of Retreat Cove shelves sharply. Anchor in 18 to 24 feet, but plan your swing to avoid the shelf. An 80-foot-long public dock, no facilities, is on the southern shore of the cove. Local boats take much of the space on the dock.

North Galiano. North Galiano is on the west side of Galiano Island. It lies to the northeast of Hall Island and has anchorage and a small public dock, no facilities.

Dionisio Point Park. Open all year, day use and overnight camping, toilets, no power, no showers. Anchor only. The park overlooks Porlier Pass. It has sandy beaches, rocky headlands and forested uplands.

Porlier Pass. Porlier Pass separates Galiano Island and Valdes Island. Several times a year, currents on large tides reach 9 knots. Current predictions are shown in the Tide and Current Tables Vol. 5, and Ports and Passes. The current floods north into the Strait of Georgia, and ebbs south into the Gulf Islands. The best time to transit is at slack water. A study of the chart shows it is safest to transit Porlier Pass on the south sides of Black Rock and Virago Rock, staying toward the Galiano Island side of the pass.

From the Strait of Georgia, begin your approach near Lighted Bell Buoy *U41*. South of the buoy, pick up the range on Race Point and Virago Point. Follow that range into Porlier Pass to clear the rocks extending from the northeast tip of Galiano Island. Once clear of the rocks, you can turn to follow a mid-channel course between Virago Rock and Galiano Island. Charts 3442 and 3443 show the range and the rocks to be avoided on both sides, but the larger scale Chart 3473 really helps understanding. Chartbook 3313 also shows the pass in excellent detail.

De Courcy Group. The De Courcy Group has several interesting small anchorages. **Whaleboat Island**, just off the southeast shore of **Ruxton Island**, is a relatively undeveloped provincial park. The preferred anchorage is south of the island, taking care to avoid a drying rock. The north end of Ruxton Island has **Herring Bay**, one of the more attractive small anchorages in the northern Gulf Islands, and frequently used when the anchorage at **Pirates Cove** on De Courcy Island is full (which it often is in the summer). Herring Bay has a white sand beach to enjoy. The De Courcy Group is named after Michael de Courcy, captain of the H.M.S. Pylades, who charted these waters from 1859 to 1861.

Whaleboat Island Marine Park. Just south of Ruxton Island. No facilities. Whaleboat Island is undeveloped, but provides an extremely limited alternate anchorage to Pirates Cove Marine Park. The preferred anchorage is south of the island, taking care to avoid a drying rock.

Pylades Island. Reader Jerry Williams, who grew up on Pylades Island, tells us the little hole just north of the dot islet off the northeast corner of Pylades Island is "magical." Most of the land is private, please do not take dogs ashore. A drying shoal is between Pylades Island and the dot islet, so approach from the north. In Whaleboat Passage, between Pylades Island and Ruxton Island, note the drying rock a short distance off Pylades Island.

Herring Bay. Herring Bay indents the northwest end of Ruxton Island, off Ruxton Passage. The bay is bordered by weather-carved sandstone walls and has a beautiful sand beach on the southeast side. Good anchoring in 24 feet, much to explore.

A charted rock ledge that dries at 1 foot is in the west entrance to Herring Bay at 49°05.08′N/123°43.01′W. We use the north entrance exclusively.

LOCAL KNOWLEDGE

DANGEROUS REEFS: The entrance to Pirates Cove is guarded by a reef that extends parallel to the shoreline to a point a little beyond a concrete beacon. When entering, you must leave this beacon to port. A range, consisting of a white-painted arrow on the ground and a white × on a tree above, shows where to make your approach. Align the × on the tree above the arrow on the ground and proceed slowly until just past the concrete beacon to port. Turn sharply to port and leave the red Spar Buoy *U38* to starboard. The entry is shallow. At lower tides deep-draft boats should be especially cautious.

㉟ **Pirates Cove Marine Park.** Pirates Cove is open all year, campsites, pit toilets, hand pump water (boil before use) on the south beach, no other facilities. It's a lovely little harbor, protected from seas but not all winds, with room for many boats (on a short scope). 24 mooring rings for stern-ties are set into the sandstone cliffs that encircle the bay. Do not use trees for stern tie. Two dinghy docks are for shore access, one on the northeast and the other on the southwest side of the cove. Dinghies may go ashore at the south end beach. The small marina on the right as you enter is private.

Most of the land is a marvelous provincial park. The cove is surrounded by a forest of Douglas fir, Garry oak and arbutus (madrona). Well-maintained trails lead through the forest and along the rock shoreline with its sculpted sandstone formations and tide pools. Be sure to stay on designated trails to avoid brushing against poison oak, a rash-causing plant species protected by the Provincial Marine Park. Pirates Cove has only a fair holding bottom of sticky mud. If the wind comes up during the night, you can expect a fire drill as boats drag anchor. It's best to stern-tie. When departure time arrives, be prepared to spend extra time cleaning the anchor as it comes aboard.

No Discharge Zone, No Gray Water Discharge.

On Ruxton Passage, the little notch at the south end of De Courcy Island is also part of the park, and you can anchor there. The beach is good for dinghy or kayak landing, and campsites are ashore. Additional anchorage is available at Whaleboat Island Marine Park, nearby. Another "Pirates Cove overflow" notch is just north of Pirates Cove off Link Island.

Boat Harbour and Kenary Cove. Boat Harbour, across Stuart Channel from the De Courcy Group, is almost filled with spar buoys posted with 'No Anchoring' and 'Private Seabed'. Kenary Cove within the harbour is home to a private marina and private moorings. The head of Kenary Cove dries on low tide.

GABRIOLA PASSAGE TO NANAIMO

Gabriola Passage. Gabriola Passage (Gabriola is pronounced "GAY-briola") is the northernmost entrance to the Gulf Islands from the Strait of Georgia. From Bowen Island on the east side of the strait, it is 14 miles to Gabriola Passage, the shortest crossing between the lower mainland and the islands.

Tidal currents on spring tides can run to 8 knots in Gabriola Passage, both flood and ebb. Typical maximum currents are around 4 knots.

Silva Bay

Quick Silva fuel dock

Transiting is best at slack. The current sets east on the flood and west on the ebb. Times of slack and maximum currents are given in the Tide & Current Tables, Vol. 5 and Ports and Passes.

Degnen Bay. Degnen Bay, on Gabriola Passage at the south end of Gabriola Island, is a good anchorage but a little crowded with boats on moorings. Entering Degnen Bay, favor the east side, close to Josef Point, to avoid rocks in the middle. A petroglyph of a killer whale is on a slab of rock near the head of the bay. Correspondents John and Lorraine Littlewood report additional petroglyphs on the United Church grounds. A public dock provides access to Gabriola Island. All other docks are private.

Degnen Bay Public Wharf. Has 190 feet of dock space, power, garbage drop, but no other facilities. Commercial fishing vessels have priority.

Wakes Cove. Wakes Cove, on Gabriola Passage at the north end of Valdes Island, has a beautiful new provincial marine park occupying almost the entire north end of Valdes Island. The park has trails and historical interpretation information. It is served by a small dock. Anchorage is a little iffy.

Dogfish Bay. Kendrick Island, on the northeast side of Valdes Island, creates a narrow and shallow bay known locally as Dogfish Bay. Dogfish Bay is well protected and the holding ground is good. West Vancouver Yacht Club has an outstation on Kendrick Island, members only, no reciprocal moorage.

Drumbeg Provincial Park. South end of Gabriola Island, overlooking Gabriola Passage. Open all year, day use only. Toilets, no other facilities. Has shelving sandstone rocks and a small sandy beach.

Flat Top Islands. The Flat Top Islands are appropriately named, and from the north or east they're a little hard to tell apart. If approaching from the Strait of Georgia, pass north of **Thrasher Rock Light**. The light marks the northern end of Gabriola Reefs. All the Flat Top Islands are privately owned.

LOCAL KNOWLEDGE

DANGEROUS ROCK: When entering Silva Bay between Vance Island and Tugboat Island, leave the beacon marking Shipyard Rock to port. Do not turn at once for the Silva Bay floats or

CHARTS			
3313 Small craft charts (chartbook)	Gulf Islands and adjacent Waterways	3477 Plans	Gulf Islands Bedwell Harbour to Georgeson Passage (1:15,000) Telegraph Harbour & Preedy Harbour (1:15,000) Pender Canal (1:4,000)
3412	Victoria Harbour (1:5,000)		
3419	Esquimalt Harbour (1:5,000)		
3424	Approaches to Oak Bay (1:10,000)	3478 Plans	Saltspring Island Cowichan Bay to Maple Bay (1:20,000) Birds Eye Cove (1:10,000) Genoa Bay (1:10,000) Ganges Harbour & Long Harbour (1:20,000) Fulford Harbour (1:15,000)
3440	Race Rocks to D'Arcy Island (1:40,000)		
3441	Haro Strait, Boundary Pass & Satellite Channel (1:40,000)		
3442	North Pender Island to Thetis Island (1:40,000)	3479	Approaches to Sidney (1:20,000)
3473	Active Pass, Porlier Pass & Montague Harbour		

GULF ISLANDS   See Area Map Page 236 - Maps Not for Navigation

A boat northbound through Dodd Narrows

other facilities. Shipyard Rock is larger than it appears on the charts. Continue instead until about halfway to Law Point before making your turn. A buoy marks the inner end of Shipyard Rock, but give the rock plenty of room anyway.

㉟ **Silva Bay.** Silva Bay is a popular destination in the Flat Top Islands area, well protected, with good holding bottom. From the north, enter behind Vance Island; from the south, through Sear Island Passage between Gabriola Island and Sear Island. Most boats, however, go through Commodore Passage, between Acorn Island and Tugboat Island, and enter Silva Bay between Tugboat Island and Vance Island. Notorious Shipyard Rock lies along the south side of this passage.

Silva Bay Shipyard, with marine railway and 12-ton Travelift, is next to Silva Bay Marina.

Anchoring: Anchoring is tight. A float plane take-off and landing channel has been designated along the front of the docks, where anchoring is not allowed.

㊱ **Silva Bay Resort & Marina.** 3383 South Road, Gabriola Island, BC V0R 1X7; (250) 247-8662 ext. 8; info@silvabay.com; www.silvabay.com. Monitors VHF 66A. Open all year with guest moorage, 30 amp & limited 100 amp power, water, garbage drop, washrooms, showers, laundry, liquor store with snack items. Reservations recommended. Diesel and mid-grade gasoline at the fuel dock.

Daily floatplane flights to Vancouver.

The Silva Bay Bar & Grill is a pub with a separate, quieter dining room (families welcome). It is open for lunch and dinner year-round.

㊱ **Page's Resort & Marina.** 3350 Coast Road, Gabriola Island, BC V0R 1X7; (250) 247-8931; info@pagesresort.com; www.pagesresortgroup.com. Monitors VHF 66A. Open all year, visitor moorage was expanded in 2015 and accomodates vessels up to 65 feet. Mid-grade marine gasoline and diesel at the fuel dock. 30 amp power, washrooms, showers, laundry, garbage, recycling, bicycle and scooter rentals, ice, free Wi-Fi. Cottages and tent sites for rent. The grounds are well maintained.

Cab service and a community shuttle bus service can take you to Gabriola Island's shopping center, or you can rent bicycles or motor scooters at Page's. You can walk or dinghy over to the Silva Bay Resort and Marina's pub or liquor store.

For those interested in books, Page's is an attractive stop. The office feels more like a peaceful library or bookstore (which it is) with an extensive range of titles, especially books about local subjects and by local authors. The shop also carries essential groceries, sundry items, bait, marine charts, and cruising guides.

This marina resort is friendly and well managed. Gloria and Ken Hatfield are the owners.

244

SILVA BAY . GABRIOLA ISLAND . BC

Page's Resort & Marina Ltd is delighted to announce the purchase of Silva Bay Inn. Both are located on Gabriola Island overlooking Silva Bay and the Flat Top Islands. Start Exploring Today!

PAGE'S RESORT AND MARINA
Silva Bay • VHF 66A • 250-247-8931

PAGE'S INN ON SILVA BAY
Silva Bay • 250-247-9351

Open year round • Moorage • 30Amp • Fuel Dock • WiFi • Shower & Laundry • Marine Chart Dealer
Cottages • Suites • Campground • Scooter, Mountain Bike & Kayak Rentals

PAGESRESORTGROUP.COM

See Area Map Page 236 - Maps Not for Navigation

GULF ISLANDS

Every day at noon the cannon is fired from the historic Bastion above the moorage area.

Nanaimo Harbour & Newcastle Island Passage

㊱ **Page's Inn on Silva Bay.** 3415 South Rd., Gabriola Island, BC V0R 1X7, (250) 247-9351; info@silvabayinn.ca; www.pagesresortgroup.com. This lovely Inn, formerly the Boatel, was recently purchased by Page's Resort & Marina. Located adjacent to Page's Marina, the docks at Page's Inn offer transient moorage for boaters staying ashore in one of the suites.

Silva Bay Shipyard. 3445 South Road, Gabriola Island, BC V0R 1X7; (250) 247-9800; info@silvabayshipyard.com; www.silvabayshipyard.com. A do-it-yourself boatyard with a 12-ton travelift and 80-ton railway. Ships chandlery, mechanical & electrical repairs, stern drive mechanics, and wooden boat repair.

False Narrows. False Narrows is east of Dodd Narrows, and is an alternate connection between the Gulf Islands and Northumberland Channel. If you choose to make this passage, you will be traveling between reefs in a shallow channel that is best used at half tide or better. Local knowledge says if you strictly follow the two ranges shown on the chart you'll be okay. Go slowly to keep your wake down. Maximum currents in False Narrows are about half of those in Dodd Narrows.

We navigated False Narrows for the first time in 2014. With a careful eye on the ranges and the chartplotter, the transit was uneventful. Kelp marked the reefs.

㊲ **Dodd Narrows.** Currents in Dodd Narrows run to 9 knots as water swirls through the narrow deep passage between cliffs. The narrows are best taken at slack water. For the hour or so before the predicted turn, boats collect at each end waiting for the right time. These boats include commercial craft, even tugboats with log tows or large barges, so the period around slack water can get pretty interesting. Generally, the boats on the upstream side go first, catching the last of the dying fair current. When they are through, boats on the other end go through, picking up the beginnings of the new (for them) fair current. It all works well as long as no one gets pushy.

Because Dodd Narrows is a dogleg, it's a good idea to broadcast a *Securité* before transiting (*Securité, Securité, this is the 34-foot motor vessel Happy Days entering Dodd Narrows southbound. Any concerned traffic please advise, channel one-six*). If you're dropping in behind a string of boats going through, you shouldn't need to broadcast a *Securité*. On busy days with a lot of traffic, redundant broadcasts clog up Channel 16. *Be sure to use 1-watt low power.*

Don't be in a hurry, and don't try to pass a slower boat. Dodd Narrows is short. Travel single-file and leave room between your boat and the boat ahead.

Northumberland Channel. Northumberland Channel is the passage from the Gulf Islands to Nanaimo. It begins at False Narrows and runs northwest between Gabriola Island and Vancouver Island. Northumberland Channel exits in the Gulf of Georgia, or, at Jack Point, makes the turn to Nanaimo. Because of considerable

2018 WAGGONER CRUISING GUIDE

log boom towing in the area, watch for floating debris. If you are not yet ready for civilization, you might lay over at Pilot Bay, on the north end of Gabriola Island.

Pilot Bay. Pilot Bay is on the north end of Gabriola Island. It's a good anchorage in a southeasterly, but is open to northwesterlies. *No discharge zone*, gray water okay.

Gabriola Sands Park. North end of Gabriola Island. Open all year, day use only. Toilets, but no other facilities. This park fronts on Taylor Bay and Pilot Bay. It has a sandy swimming area and a playfield. Good for kids.

Sandwell Park. Northeast side of Gabriola Island. Open all year, day use only, toilets but no other facilities. This is a small seafront park with a sandy beach and forested uplands.

㊳ **Nanaimo.** As you pass Jack Point the city of Nanaimo opens up. Head for the prominent high rise condominium building, easily seen from Jack Point. The harbor is wide and sheltered from the Strait of Georgia by Protection Island and Newcastle Island.

The Nanaimo Port Authority public marina is at the south end of the business district near Nanaimo's famous Bastion (blockhouse), with access to downtown Nanaimo. The Bastion was built in 1853 by the Hudson's Bay Company, and is Nanaimo's oldest man-made landmark still standing. A Thrifty Foods supermarket, London Drug, Pacific Place, ATM, B.C. liquor store, Starbucks and several fast-food and sandwich shops are in the shopping mall near the Port Authority marina. The Nanaimo Museum is in the Conference Centre, one block from the public marina.

The Canada Customs dock is marked at the head of E dock on the north side of the public docks, just behind the fuel dock area. Other moorages, including the Nanaimo Yacht Club, are in Newcastle Island Passage, the channel leading behind Newcastle Island to Departure Bay. The Nanaimo Yacht Club has guest moorage for visiting members of reciprocal clubs. Waterfront Suites & Marina has transient moorage and Stones Marina occasionally has room for transient boaters.

Satellite Reef caution: Buoy *PS* is west of Satellite Reef, approximately where boats entering from Northumberland Channel would plan to turn to anchor at Newcastle Island or continue through Newcastle Island Passage. Satellite Reef dries at zero tide and should be considered hazardous at all times. Stay west of Buoy *PS*.

Repair and haul-out facilities capable of handling any needed job are located along Newcastle Island Passage, known locally as Newcastle Channel.

Nanaimo is a natural point of departure for boats headed across the Strait of Georgia or north to Campbell River or Desolation Sound and beyond. It is the second largest city (behind Victoria) on Vancouver Island. Shops of all kinds line the narrow, winding streets of old town Nanaimo. We've prowled through several impressive bookstores—new and used—in downtown.

Nanaimo offers excellent dining, from casual to elegant. Several restaurants are on the water in the marina. A winding promenade takes walkers along the waterfront for 4 km (2.5 miles), from the marina to the B.C. Ferry Terminal in Departure Bay.

An 1853 cannon, intended in its day to protect the Bastion but used instead to welcome ships into the harbour, is fired at noon each day at the Bastion beginning in May. It's a ceremony complete with a piper in full regalia and a booming explosion with a cloud of white smoke. Beginning in June the Brigadoon Dance Academy's highland dancers perform from 11:15 a.m. to 11:45 a.m. Get there early and bring your camera.

Nanaimo is home to the Annual 'World Championship Bathtub Race' held during the third weekend in July. The event is preceded by a parade of bathtub race participants, games, food, and concerts. See www.bathtubbing.com.

Chandlery: Harbour Chandler, south of the boat basin, is an excellent chandlery. At the north end is Stones Boatyard Marine Store.

Farmers market: Just north of the Bastion, a farmers market, often with entertainment, is open 10:00 a.m. to 2:00 p.m. Fridays, May to mid-October.

Golf: Pryde Vista (250) 753-6188 is a pretty and easily-walked 9-hole par 33 course, a short cab ride away. Nanaimo Golf & Country Club (250) 758-2451 is a first-class 18-hole course, a slightly longer cab ride away. Both are recommended.

Taxi: AC Taxi, (250) 753-1231

Nanaimo Port Authority

Things to Do

1. **Nanaimo Bastion**. Located above the marina, the Bastion is the oldest standing building in Nanaimo. You can explore it, or watch the cannon ceremony at noon.

2. **Newcastle Island**. Hike to the sandstone quarry or rent a kayak, SUP, or bike. A foot ferry provides regular access to Newcastle Island from the Nanaimo waterfront or take your dinghy. A children's playground was recently added. Walking tours and a traditional tribal salmon bake are available on the island by reservation. See www.newcastleisland.ca for reservations information.

3. **Fresh seafood on the dock**. Fishermen return to the Port Authority marina and sell their catch. You can prepare a fresh seafood dinner on your boat. Or, stop by Trollers for fish and chips.

4. **Nanaimo Museum**. Just up from the marina at 100 Museum Way. Learn the history of Nanaimo from its First Nations roots to the discovery of coal in the area.

5. **Petroglyph Provincial Park**. A taxi ride from the docks. See carvings of animals and sea creatures immortalized in the sandstone hundreds and thousands of years ago.

6. **Dinghy Dock Pub**. On Protection Island. Take your dinghy or the ferry ($9). Great sun deck, good food, and of course cold beer.

7. **Walk or bike** the multi-use Harbourfront Walkway trail along the downtown waterfront, and on north along the Newcastle Channel.

㊳ **Nanaimo Port Authority.** 100 Port Drive, P.O. Box 131, Nanaimo, -BC V9R 5K4; (250) 755-1216; (250) 754-5053; marina@npa.ca; www.npa.ca. During July and August call (250) 755-1216. Monitors VHF 67 (*not 66A*). Open year-round. Three hours of moorage complimentary, but call on VHF 67 for slip assignment. Fewer spaces have been reserved for transient moorage than in the past. Reservations recommended. Reservations must be made 48 hours in advance. Rafting is permitted. Dock assistants are available during the summer months to help you tie up. Numerous commercial fishing vessels are in the basin during the winter months, but pleasure craft moorage is available. Water at selected docks in the winter. Customs clearance available at the customs dock, just behind the fuel dock.

A floating breakwater dock is in the center of the harbour entrance, and the Eco Barge pumpout and portapotty dump is tied to the shore side of this dock. No charge for the Eco Barge. Arriving and departing vessels must pass south of the floating breakwater dock. The northern entrance is reserved for aircraft. *No Discharge Zone, Gray water okay.*

The Port Authority harbour is actually two marina facilities: **Inner Boat Basin** and **W.E. Mills Landing & Marina** (formerly and locally known as Cameron Island Marina). We have used both and are happy either place.

Inner Boat Basin is mostly permanent moorage with some transient space. Facilities include extensive dock space, 20 & 30 amp power on all floats, some 50 & 100 amp power, water, free Wi-Fi, and waste oil disposal. Washrooms, showers with heated tile floors, and laundry are next to the wharfinger office.

㊳ **W.E. Mills Landing & Marina,** the newer docks just inside the breakwater pier. Larger vessels and ships will tie on the outside of the breakwater pier, smaller boats on the inside. Facilities include 20, 30, & 50 amp power and water. Free Wi-Fi. Washrooms, showers, and laundry are located in the Inner Boat Basin near the wharfinger office, a short dinghy ride but a long walk. Wakes from boats headed for the fuel dock or the Inner Boat Basin rock boats at W.E. Mills Landing & Marina. The docks have a security gate that is open 7:00 a.m. to 11:00 p.m. Between 11:00 p.m. and 7:00 a.m., you'll have to use the combination supplied by the dock help or call security to let you in. Watch the current when landing at W.E. Mills Landing & Marina. Usually there's no problem, but be aware.

WATERFRONT SUITES & MARINA
NANAIMO'S NEW, PREMIERE MARINA

- Located in the heart of Nanaimo along Newcastle Channel (in front of buoy P-13)
- Brand new docks constructed of marine-grade aluminium
- 30 and 50 Amp Metered Power and Water service
- Comfortable, economical accommodations
- Annual and Transient Moorage available
- Marina Lounge for Moorage clients
- Waterfront Club Concierge Service
- Home of the Nanaimo Boat Show
- Washroom and Shower Facilities
- Laundry Facilities

1000 Stewart Avenue, Nanaimo, BC V9S 4C9 | 250-753-7111 | www.waterfrontnanaimo.com | moorage@waterfrontnanaimo.com

GULF ISLANDS

Museum inside the Nanaimo Bastion

Seasonally, fresh fish is sometimes sold at the Nanaimo Fisherman's Market dock at the entrance to the Inner Boat Basin. The dock is 250 feet long, 15 feet wide, and wheelchair accessible. With its flags and specially designed gazebos, you can't miss it. Fish & chips, Mexican food, and other delights are available at floating restaurants. Theaters, a waterfront promenade, and tennis courts are nearby. The seaplane terminal is north of the Inner Boat Basin.. All of the Nanaimo commercial district is within a five-minute walk.

No designated dinghy dock. If coming by dinghy, call the marina office on VHF 67 for tie-up instructions.

㊳ **Petro-Canada Coastal Mountain Fuels.** 10 Wharf St., Nanaimo, BC V9R IP2; (250) 754-7828. Open all year, gasoline and diesel at the fuel dock. Lubricants, accessories, ice, snacks. At the end of "E" dock. May to mid-September, 7:00 a.m. to 7:00 p.m.; October to May, 8:00 a.m. to 5:00 p.m.

㊳ **Waterfront Suites & Marina.** 1000 Stewart Ave., Nanaimo, BC V9S 4C9; (250) 753-7111; moorage@waterfrontnanaimo.com; www.waterfrontnanaimo.com. Monitors VHF 67. Open all year, moorage to 100 feet, 30 & 50 amp power, washrooms, showers, laundry, Wi-Fi, 24-hour service and security. Reservations encouraged. This new marina opened in 2015. The docks are modular and staff can configure a dock for odd sized boats. Often has space for transient boats when the other marinas are full.

㊳ **Stones Marina.** 1690 Stewart Ave., Nanaimo BC V9S 4E1; Marina (250) 753- 4232; www.stonesmarina.com. Open all year, 30 & 50 amp power, washrooms, showers, laundry, cable & internet, fuel dock. Limited transient overnight moorage by reservation only. The marina office is located in the white building up the driveway and along the main road. The marina complex has a pub and restaurant, liquor store, marine supplies store, boatyard, yacht charters, and day-use guest moorage dock. The 140 foot float in front of the pub restaurant has side-tie space for vessels visiting the Stones Marina complex. Stones Boatyard & Marine Store www.nanaimoboatyard.ca (250-716-9065) are located in the Stones Marina complex. The do-it-yourself or yacht services boatyard with 83-ton Travelift is available for scheduled and emergency repairs. Stones Boatyard & Marine Store is under separate ownership.

Caution: Waters are shallow around the day-use guest dock and Travelift; check your depth.

㊳ **Departure Bay Gas N Go.** 1840 Stewart Ave., Nanaimo, BC V9F 4E6; (250) 591-0810. Open all year. Fuel dock with gas and diesel at north end of Newcastle Channel. Small store carries snacks, tackle, some lubricants.

㊴ **Newcastle Island Marine Park.** www.env.gov.bc.ca/bcparks/explore/parkpgs/newcastle/ Open all year, moorage with 1500 feet of dock space, excellent washrooms and showers, no power. Anchoring is prohibited in Mark Bay; 43 mooring balls are available for vessels 40 feet and under (some are limited to 30 feet). A nightly mooring fee is paid onshore at the head of the dock. Extensive anchorage is still available just beyond Mark Bay and the docks. Several small bays, beaches, and playing fields. Many hiking trails. Walk-in campsites and picnic areas. Seasonal kayak, canoe, SUP and bicycle rentals. In summer a passenger ferry connects the island with Nanaimo.

The 1931 pavilion houses a dance floor, snack bar, visitor center, and excellent interpretive displays on the natural and human history of the area.

This is an extraordinary park. The pulpstone quarry astonishes. The bays and beaches intrigue. Before European settlement, Newcastle Island was a summer campsite for First Nations people. Since European settlement, it has supported a shipyard and been mined for coal. In the early 1870s it was quarried for sandstone that built the San Francisco Mint. Between 1923 and 1932 its sandstone was quarried for pulpstones, giant cylinders that ground wood into pulp for making paper. Before WWII, Japanese fishermen ran herring salteries here. Through it all, Newcastle Island has been a popular holiday spot.

You might see rare albino raccoons, and dozens of bunny rabbits. If moored at the dock, raccoons will try to board vessels searching for food. Secure your boat well, and don't leave any food or garbage out. Arrive early enough to get literature from the visitor center. Try to spend the night. The lights of Nanaimo are beautiful. The Dinghy Dock pub is a short dinghy ride away.

Newcastle Island Marine Park

Pulp stones from the sandstone quarry on Newcastle Island

Strait of Georgia

CHAPTER 8

CROSSING THE STRAIT OF GEORGIA

STRAIT OF GEORGIA
*Schooner Cove • French Creek • Denman Island
Hornby Island • Comox • Oyster River
False Bay • Squitty Bay*

STRAIT OF GEORGIA

Crossing the Strait of Georgia. The Strait of Georgia is not to be trifled with. It's a big body of water, 110 miles long and 15 to 20 miles wide. Pleasure craft cross the strait all the time, but locals know better than to go out when the wind is blowing. They are especially careful when wind blows against strong currents.

When conditions are right, the strait need not be intimidating. The "typical" summertime fair weather wind pattern calls for calm mornings followed by a rising northwesterly sea breeze by early afternoon. By mid-afternoon the sea breeze can be 20 to 25 knots. In the evening the wind dies down. We have crossed early in the morning and in the evening and had no problems.

Frequently though, the typical pattern doesn't hold. If a weak frontal system passes over the area, the higher pressure behind the front will produce northwesterlies of 20 to 25 knots, sometimes reaching gale force. These winds can blow around the clock for three days or even longer, effectively closing the strait to small craft.

Summer afternoon southwesterly winds known as Qualicums can blow across the strait between Qualicum Beach and False Bay at the northern tip of Lasqueti Island. Qualicum winds resulting from the passage of a cold front can reach 40 knots but are short-lived.

When wind opposes current in Sabine Channel, between Lasqueti Island and Texada Island, 8-foot seas can result. Malaspina Strait can be rough, especially when wind is against current. Currents from Howe Sound and Burrard Inlet meet off Point Atkinson, and create rough seas. Wind makes them worse.

When the wind is up it produces a difficult 4- to 5-foot chop—sometimes higher—in the middle of the strait away from land influences. These aren't long, lazy ocean swells. Strait of Georgia

The Strait of Georgia on a calm day

seas are steep and close together. In southeasterly winds, the largest seas are found near Chrome Island and Cape Mudge, both locations with significant fetch. When the wind blows from the northwest, the largest waves are found in Sabine Channel and near Sand Heads. A well-handled boat might run with these seas, but taken on the bow or beam they are no fun at all.

Sometimes, the afternoon winds never materialize and the strait can be crossed all day. It's best to avoid being forced into crossing at a specific time or on a specific day. Wait for calm conditions and know that they don't always appear in the morning and evening. When the conditions are right, go. Be cautious yet decisive.

Even in calm conditions, you may find tide-rips off many of the points, and wherever passes or channels join the strait. When the current flows out of a pass or inlet into the strait, confusion results. Add wind, and big confusion results. While the ebb current flows from inlets into the strait, note that the *flood current* flows out of the Gulf Islands into the strait. At the eastern mouths of Active Pass, Porlier Pass, and Gabriola Pass, look for rough seas on the flood, especially when the wind is blowing.

We list these cautions not to frighten the reader but to inform. Weather patterns do exist and the bad spots are known. The skipper who monitors the VHF continuous marine broadcast will gather a sense of what is happening, where it is happening, and why it is happening. Go and no-go decisions get easier.

Here are a few tips for a safe and comfortable crossing:

• Monitor the buoy reports for Halibut Bank (Buoy 46146, off Gibsons) and Sentry Shoal (Buoy 46131, between Comox and Campbell River and below Mitlenatch Island). These reports provide frequent updates on sea state and wind conditions. They can be found online on Environment Canada's website, on the continuous marine broadcast, or by calling Dial-A-Buoy at (888) 701-8992.

• Monitor lightstation reports. Lightstations are at Chrome Island, Merry Island and Entrance Island. The lightkeepers provide information on visibility, wind speed and direction, and sea state, updated every three hours and broadcast on the VHF WX channels. You can also call directly on VHF 82.

• Based on the wind direction and sea state, choose the best angle and direction for your crossing. The most direct course may not be the most comfortable. Don't be afraid to change your destination if the weather isn't cooperating.

• The north-flowing flood current from Strait of Juan de Fuca meets the south-flowing flood from Discovery Passage near Mitlenatch Island. When traveling the length of the strait, time your departure to take advantage of currents flowing in the same direction as the wind. When crossing, especially in the south, try to time your departure to hit slack in the middle of the strait. Both strategies will minimize the effect of wind against current.

• The area between Qualicum Beach and Lasqueti Island can be subject to southwesterly winds coming through the Alberni "notch" in the Vancouver Island mountains. Check Chrome Island for local southwesterly winds. Old salts also recommend checking winds at Cape Beale, on the west coast of Vancouver Island. If a strong southwesterly wind is blowing there, often it will flow right over Vancouver Island through the Alberni "notch," affecting the waters off Qualicum Beach.

• Take advantage of lees along the way. For example, you may choose to go up one side or the other of 27-mile Texada Island to stay in the lee of a southwesterly or northeasterly wind. Always be prepared to turn around and go back if things do not look right.

Whiskey Golf. Boats headed north from Nanaimo often must navigate through or around the restricted area "WG" (Whiskey Golf) when it is "live." Whiskey Golf is a deepwater range operated by the Canadian and U.S. Navies, and is used to test torpedoes (always unarmed) and various ships' systems. The area consists of a network of underwater sensing devices joined by cables to a control site on Winchelsea Island. Torpedoes are fired from range vessels or aircraft along a predetermined course, and are tracked

CHARTS	
3312 Small-craft chart (chart-book)	Jervis Inlet & Desolation Sound
3443	Thetis Island to Nanaimo (1:40:000)
3447	Nanaimo Harbour & Departure Bay (1:8,000)
3456	Halibut Bank to Ballenas Channel (1:30,000)
3458	Approaches to Nanaimo Harbour (1:20,000)
3459	Approaches to Nanoose Harbour (1:15,000)
3512	Strait of Georgia, Central Portion (1:80,000)
3513	Strait of Georgia, Northern Portion (1:80,000)
3527	Baynes Sound (1:40,000); Comox Harbour (1:15,000)
3536 Plans	Strait of Georgia (various scales)

Strait of Georgia

from the Winchelsea control center. After the run, the torpedoes are recovered either by helicopter or range vessels. Unauthorized craft are not permitted in the area while the range is in operation.

Typically, the range is active Mondays through Fridays, sometimes Saturdays, 7:00 a.m. to 5:30 p.m. Winchelsea Range Control monitors VHF channel 10 during operations. Notice of operation is included as part of the Canadian continuous marine broadcast on the weather channels. The Coast Guard (VHF channel 83A) also knows if the range is active. If unsure, contact Winchelsea Range Control or the Canadian Coast Guard.

The Whiskey Golf restricted area is on the direct course across the Strait of Georgia from Nanaimo to Secret Cove, Smugglers Cove, Pender Harbour, and other destinations along the Sunshine Coast. We once saw an oblivious skipper cross right through the active range. Winchelsea Control made multiple calls to the offending vessel with no response. A patrol helicopter quickly flew over, hovered just in front of the offending vessel, and redirected it to safe water. Such encounters are best avoided.

The Canadian Navy established a safe transit route along the edges of the restricted area when the range is in use. After clearing Nanaimo Harbour or Departure Bay (being careful to avoid Hudson Rocks and Five Finger Island), head directly for the Winchelsea Islands. Pass east of Winchelsea Islands within 1000 yards. Turn to pass east of the Ballenas Islands within 1000 yards. Once well past the Ballenas Islands, steer a course for your destination on the mainland side of the strait, or northwest along the Vancouver Island side.

Nanoose Harbour. Anchorage is good just inside the sandy spit on the south side of the entrance. The docks and mooring buoys along the north shore are the base for Royal Canadian Navy and U.S. Navy vessels engaged in activity on the Winchelsea (Whiskey Golf) torpedo range.

Schooner Cove. Schooner Cove is north of Nanoose Harbour. The cove is well-protected with a breakwater on the northwest entrance. The Fairwinds Marina fills most of the cove.

① **Fairwinds Marina at Schooner Cove** 33521 Dolphin Dr., Nanoose Bay, BC V9P 9J7; (250) 468-5364; marina@fairwinds.ca; www.fairwinds.ca. Monitors VHF 66A. Fairwinds Marina at Schooner Cove is open all year with gasoline and diesel at the fuel dock. Guest moorage for vessels up to 80 feet, 15, 30 & 50 amp power, washrooms, showers, and pumpout. Fairwinds Marina is a large, mostly permanent moorage facility with space for transient boats. Easily accessed off of Ballenas Channel and Strait of Georgia, the marina has picturesque views of the Strait of Georgia and coastal mountains. Reservations recommended. Watch for a rock marked by a red buoy just inside the breakwater. Keep the buoy well to starboard when entering. The outstand-

STRAIT OF GEORGIA See Area Map Page 251 - Maps Not for Navigation

Tribune Bay, with its sandy beach, is a busy spot in summer.

ing Fairwinds Golf club is part of the resort. A courtesy shuttle takes you there. No charge for rental clubs for overnight moorage guests (they encourage drop-in golfers).

Correspondents Bob and Shino Posey report that in 2017 renovation started on the main hotel building upland from the marina that houses the marina office. During renovation, the marina office, washrooms, and showers are located in mobile buildings adjacent to the main building. 2017 was also the start of a multi-year sectional renovation project to repair and replace aging floats at the marina. The marina remains open during renovation.

Schooner Reef. Schooner Reef is a short distance northward off the mouth of Schooner Cove and has caught a number of boats unaware. The light marking the reef is on the southernmost of its rocks. More rocks lie up-island from the light.

Nuttal Bay. Nuttal Bay is protected from southeasterly winds but exposed to northwesterlies. To enter Nuttal Bay, leave Dorcas Rock Buoy *P27* to port. Do not pass between Dorcas Rock Buoy *P27* and the land south of it. Buoy *P27* lies a good deal farther out than one might expect. If you are traveling up- or down-island, locate that buoy and pass to seaward of it.

Mistaken Island. Privately owned and posted with "No Trespassing" signs.

Parksville. Parksville has a nice beach, but shoal water extends out some distance. Except for the marina at French Creek at the north end of Parksville, no facilities are available for boaters.

② **French Creek Harbour Authority.** 1055 Lee Rd., Parksville, BC V9P 2E1; (250) 248-5051; hafc@frenchcreekharbour.ca. Monitors VHF 66A. Open all year with gasoline & diesel. Commercial vessels have priority for moorage, but room may be available for pleasure craft. No reservations; rafting is required. Washrooms and shower, 20 & 30 amp power, waste oil disposal. Office hours are 8:00 a.m. to 5:30 p.m. Restaurant, pub, marine supplies, nearby launch ramp and haulout. A fish market in the large white processing building sells fresh seafood. Groceries are at the mall, a 15-minute walk away.

French Creek is the only breakwater-protected harbor in the 25-mile stretch between Northwest Bay and Deep Bay. The breakwater has been moved out and the entrance changed recently, and additional docks are planned for the future. French Creek is the western terminus of the passenger ferry to Lasqueti Island.

Hornby Island. Hornby Island has anchorages in Tribune Bay, Ford Cove, and south of Shingle Spit (where a small ferry runs to Denman Island). Tribune Bay and Shingle Spit are exposed to southeast winds.

A seasonal dock for dinghies and shallow draft water craft is located next to the ferry terminal. The dock is for guests dining at the Thatch Pub and Restaurant located above the dock. The fully licensed Pub and Restaurant has live entertainment, (250) 335-0136; thatchpub.com.

The annual Hornby Festival held in early August is a well-organized event drawing professional, award-winning musicians from around the country, see hornbyfestival.com.

Tribune Bay. Tribune Bay is a wonderful place to visit and justifiably popular. Anchor offshore in 18 to 30 feet and dinghy to a splendid sand beach. Visit Tribune Bay Provincial Park. Take the 3-mile hike to Helliwell Provincial Park, on St. John Point.

Caution: Tribune Bay has excellent protection from northwesterlies, but in a southeasterly the bay can get very rough. For a more private nook, try the little cove near St. John Point. Anchor in 20 to 30 feet.

Fairwinds Schooner Cove Marina

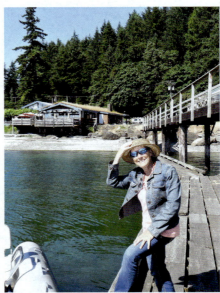

The dinghy dock at lively Thatch Pub is seasonal and dries on low tides.

③ **Ford Cove.** Upgraded harbor with greater capacity at the Harbour Authority public dock. A green spar buoy marks the southern end of Maude Reef. You'll see a rock breakwater and a floating breakwater. To enter, leave the rock breakwater to starboard. No fresh water on the dock. Good anchorage on rocky bottom.

A well-stocked grocery (250) 335-2169 is upland from the docks and sells fresh take-out pizza year-round. A seasonal fish & chips hut is adjacent. The store and eatery along with cottages, campsites, and RV parking make up a small resort called Ford's Cove Marina & Store.

There are numerous trails in the area. A well-traveled 1.5 mile trail leads northwest along the shore to Shingle Spit and the popular Thatch Pub.

③ **Ford Cove Harbour Authority.** 10800A Central Rd., Ford Cove, Hornby Island, BC V0R 1Z0; (250) 335-0003; VHF 66A; fordcoveharbour@gmail.com; www.fordcoveharbour.com. Open all year, guest moorage along 3000 feet of dock space and inside of the floating breakwater, 20 & 30 amp power, toilets, garbage drop, no water, no showers. Reservations accepted or call ahead for availability. Rafting allowed up to 20 feet deep. No rafting on the breakwater. Wi-Fi planned for 2018. Kayak and boat rentals.

Baynes Sound. Chart 3527 shows navigation aids not shown on Chart 3513. These aids are buoys marking extensive shoals off Gartley Point, Union Point, Denman Point and Base Flat (Buckley Bay); 2 buoys near Repulse Point; and 2 buoys marking the shoal off Mapleguard Point. Baynes Sound, a 12-mile-long refuge, is protected from the Strait of Georgia by Denman Island. A ferry to Denman Island crosses from Buckley Bay. Comox is at the north end of Baynes Sound and Deep Bay is at the south end. The northern entry to Baynes Sound is across the Comox Bar, marked by buoys and a lighted range on the Vancouver Island shore. The southern entry is past Chrome Island.

French Creek Boat Harbour

LOCAL KNOWLEDGE

NAVIGATION NOTE: A considerable shoal extends into the mouth of Baynes Sound outside Deep Bay. The shoal, and shoaling along the shoreline of Denman Island, opposite, are marked by buoys shown on Chart 3527 but not on Chart 3513.

④ **Deep Bay.** Anchorage is good in Deep Bay, though in deeper water than most boaters like. Permanently anchored boats occupy most of the anchoring area. Ship & Shore Cafe and Store with convenience supplies, fishing tackle, hardware, laundry and a lunch counter is near the head of the public wharf. The store has gasoline available upland and delivered dockside.

④ **Deep Bay Harbour Authority.** 164 Burne

Boaters should check the red/green light at each of the Denman-Buckley cable ferry terminals before crossing the ferry route in Baynes Sound.

Ford Cove

The Denman-Buckley ferry runs on three underwater cables across Baynes Sound.

2018 **waggoner** CRUISING GUIDE

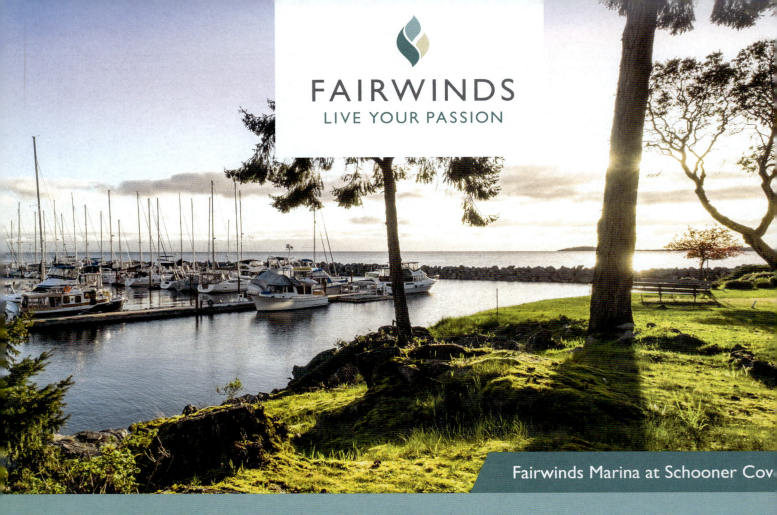

Fairwinds Marina at Schooner Cove

MOORAGE AVAILABLE! Start planning your adventure now.

Amenities of the fully serviced Fairwinds Marina include:

- Gas and Diesel Fuel
- Annual, Monthly and Transient Moorage
- Wi-Fi and Laundry facilities
- Washroom facilities with showers
- Pump out station
- Secured dock facilities
- Boat launch ramp
- 25' to 50'+ slips

COMING SOON TO FAIRWINDS!

- A variety of shops and services at Fairwinds Landing including a new waterfront pub/restaurant
- 39 concrete suites with panoramic views of the ocean and our 350 slip marina

To learn more and to register, please visit **www.fairwinds.ca**

3521 Dolphin Drive, Nanoose Bay, B.C. | *call* **250-468-5364** or *visit* **fairwinds.ca**

Comox Valley Harbour Authority

Rd., Bowser, BC V0R 1G0; (250) 757-9331; deepbay-mgr@shawcable.com; www.dbha.ca. The government wharf and floats are open all year with moorage along 1130 feet of dock. Garbage drop, 20 & 30 amp power, free Wi-Fi, free pumpout, waste oil disposal, tidal grid, rafting dock, washrooms, showers. The pumpout is located at the loading zone on the main pier. Space is very limited and rafting is required, call ahead to see what is available.

Fanny Bay. Fanny Bay is primarily a camping area, but does have a small public mooring float.

LOCAL KNOWLEDGE

CABLE FERRY: The new *Baynes Sound Connector* cable ferry runs between Buckley Bay and Denman Island. Red and green lights are at each terminal. When the green lights are illuminated, vessels may cross the ferry lane. When red lights are illuminated, the ferry is in transit and vessels may not cross the ferry lane.

Denman Island. www.denmanisland.com. A new public dock and 60-foot float are alongside the landing for the cable ferry that runs to Buckley Bay on Vancouver Island. Six hours of moorage is free, 2-day maximum stay. No power or water; 5 mooring buoys. Self-registration and payment box at the top of the ramp. Denman Village is a one-third mile walk up a steep hill. The Denman General Store with groceries, a post office, and liquor store is in Denman Village. A small museum, community center, bistro, and a craft shop are also in the Village.

The north end of Denman Island stretches out into a long spit, dotted with small islands and rocks. One of these islands, Sandy Island, is a provincial park. Off the south end of Denman Island is Chrome Island lighthouse, a dramatic landmark.

Sandy Island Marine Provincial Park. This park includes the Seal Islets, and is accessible only by boat. Anchor in Henry Bay, south of Longbeak Point. Picnic areas, swimming, fishing, hiking trails, and wilderness campsites. Sandy Island is a popular overnight stop for kayakers. At low tide it is possible to walk along the sandy spit all the way to its end—halfway to Comox.

LOCAL KNOWLEDGE

NAVIGATION TIP: If you follow the buoyed channel over the Comox Bar in a fresh southeasterly you will have 4- to 5-foot seas on your beam. In these conditions it's better to ignore buoys *P54* and *P52* and instead work your way south until you can turn to fetch the inner Buoy *P50* while running with the seas. The chart indicates ample depths. Large scale Chart 3527 shows Buoy *P50*, but small scale Chart 3513 does not.

Comox Bar. The Comox Bar nearly joins Denman Island and Cape Lazo, with a shallow channel (least depth 15 feet) across the bar. A lighted range—white, with red vertical stripes—is on the Vancouver Island shore. The range's lights are visible in cloudy weather and at night, but in sunlight they are hard to see. Lighted red Bell Buoy *P54* marks the Strait of Georgia end of this channel. Red Buoys *P52* and *P50* show the course across the bar.

⑤ **Comox.** If you plan to go to Comox, we urge that you have Chart 3527 (1:40,000), with its 1:15,000 inset of Comox Harbour and the Courtenay River up to the Lewis Bridge. Chart 3527 shows the various ranges and other navigation aids in excellent detail, and could save you from much uncertainty.

Marine services at Comox include Desolation Sound Yacht Charters (250) 339-4919 offering cleaning, maintenance, hull inspection,

STRAIT OF GEORGIA   See Area Map Page 251 - Maps Not for Navigation

Comox Harbour Authority docks   *The new Pavilion at Comox Harbour, a place for group gatherings near the docks.*

and bright work (after-hours calls accepted); and Wills Marine Supply (250) 941-7373 offering electrical, mechanical, diving and repair services.

Comox is a busy little city, population 13,600, with breakwater-protected marina docks. HMCS *Quadra*, a Canada Sea Cadet camp, is on Goose Spit, across the bay from Comox.

The Comox Valley is a popular retirement area. Albertans from the oil patch can take daily flights to the Comox airport and enjoy golf and skiing within an hour of one another on Vancouver Island.

From Baynes Sound the entrance to Comox is well marked, but be careful of drying flats off Gartley Point and in the inner half of the bay. The breakwater in front of the town will be clearly visible. As the harbor map shows, the breakwater shelters four sets of docks: the Comox Bay Marina; the Gas N Go fuel dock and marina; the municipal marina; and one set of Comox Harbour Authority public docks used entirely by commercial fishing boats. A launch ramp and two tidal grids are behind the breakwater. The other set of Harbour Authority public docks, where pleasure craft are welcomed, is around the east end of the breakwater.

Showers and laundry are in the Harbour Authority's building at the head of its docks. A beautiful pavilion with meeting space overlooks the Comox Harbour Commercial Wharves. This new pavilion acts as a nice venue for yacht club rendezvous. A Splash Park located behind the pavilion is a hit with the kids. The seasonal food truck has been relocated near the pavilion.

Comox has good shopping and a number of restaurants within walking distance of the marina. The downtown area includes a supermarket and chandlery. A hospital overlooks the bay. Regular bus service runs from Comox Mall downtown to the town of Courtenay with more shops, restaurants and a museum. You can also go by dinghy up the slough to Courtenay. See the Courtenay section for more information.

When you're in Comox, take the short walk to the Filberg Heritage Lodge & Park. It's a 9-acre estate built in the 1930s by logging baron R. J. Filberg, furnished and maintained in its original splendor. The heavy wood construction, fabulous gardens, and interesting outbuildings (root cellar, chicken coop, dairy barn, potting shed, and so forth) are must-see attractions. Weddings and art shows are held there.

Float planes: A float plane landing and take-off zone is southwest of the marina breakwaters, with regularly scheduled flights. It does not affect anchoring behind Goose Spit or the approach to the marinas.

Golf: The Comox Golf Club, a well-maintained, flat and fun 9-hole course, is within walking distance of the docks. Call (250) 339-4444. A number of other courses (from good to outstanding) are a taxi ride away, or rent a car and have complete mobility.

Festival: The Filberg Festival, an arts, crafts, food, and entertainment celebration, draws 20,000 to 25,000 visitors each year. It's held at Filberg Park, east of the public floats in Comox Harbour. Dates coincide with Comox Nautical Days and B.C. Day long weekend in early August. The park will be closed the week prior to the festival and the week following. Special events also can result in closures. Call first to confirm they are open (250) 941-0727. www.filbergfestival.com.

⑤ **Comox Valley Marina.** 1805 Beaufort, Box 20019, Comox, BC V9M 1R9; (250) 339-2930; manager@comoxvalleymarina.com; www.comoxvalleymarina.com. Side-tie moorage at a guest dock and in unoccupied slips. Water, 15, 30 & 50 amp power, shower, washroom, free Wi-Fi, 24-hour access to laundry, garbage, and nearby floatplane service. The amenities building and marina office are on the float at the base of the ramp.

⑤ **Gas N Go Marine Ltd.** 11 Port Augusta St., Comox, BC V9M 7Z8; (250) 339-4664; (888)

Comox Valley Harbour Authority

Fisherman's Wharf

20, 30 & 50 Amp Power Available
Free Wi-Fi, Sewage Pumpout
Garbage, Recycling and Oil Disposal
www.comoxharbour.com   info@comoxharbour.com
VHF 66A or 250-339-6041

Enjoy our working harbour, just one block from downtown Comox's shopping, galleries, dining, pubs, parks and golf course. Buy fresh seafood direct from the fishermen. Visit our webpage to see what's available.

256   www.WaggonerGuide.com

575-4664; gasngomarine@gmail.com; www.gasngomarine.com. Monitors VHF 66A. Open all year. Fuel dock with gasoline & diesel. Transient moorage when slips are available (call ahead), 15 & 30 amp power, washrooms, small store, Wi-Fi. As you approach, look for the Gas N Go sign.

⑤ **Comox Municipal Marina.** 1809 Beaufort Ave., Comox, BC V9M 1R9; (250) 339-3141. Permanent moorage only.

⑤ **Comox Valley Harbour Authority.** 121 Port Augusta St., Comox, BC V9M 3N8; (250) 339-6041; info@comoxharbour.com; www.comoxharbour.com. Monitors VHF 66A. Located at east end of the Comox breakwater. Guest moorage available on 2100 feet of docks, 20, 30 & 50 amp power. Holding tank pumpout, garbage drop, cardboard recycling, waste oil disposal, free Wi-Fi (get the password at the office). Clean washrooms, showers, laundry, and an air-conditioned lounge with a bucket of biscuits for visiting boat dogs.

This is a working waterfront facility, only two blocks from downtown Comox. In the summer, harbor staff move the fishing boats to one float and set aside the other docks for overnight pleasure craft. Fresh seafood is available "off the boat," usually in the evening. The Harbour Authority staff works hard to make visiting pleasure boaters feel welcome and comfortable.

⑤ **Comox Harbour.** Anchorage can be found in Comox Harbour; with northerly winds, anchor south of the marina breakwater, taking care to avoid channel entrances on either end of the breakwater; in southerly winds, the favored anchorage is tucked into the cove north of Goose Spit. Mud bottom. The harbour is not as well protected as charts might suggest and can get uncomfortable in southerly winds.

⑥ **Courtenay.** For a pleasant diversion, take the dinghy a short distance up the Courtenay River to the town of Courtenay. A dredged channel, marked by ranges, leads through the delta to the river mouth. The river is an interesting break from the saltwater experience out on the strait.

Just before you reach Lewis Bridge (vertical clearance 10 feet) Courtenay Slough leads off to the right. Inside, an extensive Comox Valley Harbour Authority float parallels the shore, and a city float is at the head. Enter the slough at high tide only. The mouth is blocked by a weir that dries at 8 feet; without the weir the slough would empty completely at low tide.

The slough's Harbour Authority dock is gated and locked. Pick up a re-entry key at the Harbour Authority office in Comox. An imposing restaurant dominates the view at the head of the slough. Excellent shopping and several restaurants are within easy walking distance.

Museum: We highly recommend a visit to the Courtenay & District Museum, a 4-block walk from the slough. There, hung from the ceiling, is the 40-foot-long skeletal reconstruction of an 80-million-year-old elasmosaur, excavated from the banks of the nearby Puntledge River. This is the most dramatic exhibit in an outstanding paleontological display. Other things you will see are dinosaur footprints, an extinct marine reptile that resembles a 15-foot-long alligator, and an ancient fish they call a "sabre-toothed salmon." We toured the museum and were impressed. Families with inquisitive children will be rewarded. There's much more than we can cover here. The museum is in the old brick post office building at 4th St. and Cliffe Avenue. From Comox you can get to the museum by bus or cab, or take the dinghy to Courtenay. Call for information: (250) 334-0686.

Cape Lazo. Cape Lazo is marked by a high cliff. *Be sure to stay to seaward of Buoys PJ and PB.* The buoys are well offshore, but shoals studded with boulders reach almost all the way out to them.

Somewhere just north of Cape Lazo is the point at which the tidal currents change direction and begin flooding south from the north end of Vancouver Island, rather than north from Victoria.

Little River. Little River, 3 miles up-island from Cape Lazo, is the western terminus for the ferry to Westview/Powell River. Marginal moorage for a few small craft can be found behind the ferry dock.

Oyster River. A channel, dredged annually and marked by pilings, leads to the protected Pacific Playgrounds Marina next to the mouth of the Oyster River.

⑦ **Pacific Playgrounds Resort & Marina.** (250) 337-5600; info@PacificPlaygrounds.com; www.PacificPlaygrounds.com; open year-round, secure marina with transient and permanent moorage up to 40 feet, a few 46-foot spaces; 15 amp power, water at the docks, restrooms, showers; reservations accepted. Payment made at the upland office open 9:00 a.m.-8:00 p.m. summer months. Payment can also be made at the dockside "fishing shack" summer hours 6:00 a.m.-8:00 p.m.; hours vary off-season. Located 16 miles south of Campbell River (49° 52' N / 125° 7' W), Pacific Playgrounds is accessed through a channel alongside, and south of Oyster River. This is a challenging entrance, check the tide tables; marina personnel advise that a minimum tide of 7 feet is needed for a boat with a 4.5 foot draft; the depth is shallowest at the outermost channel marker; access is not advised during high winds and swells. Oyster River Plaza is a short walk from the marina, with shops, cafes, a supermarket, and other services. A beautiful trail from the marina leads to a one-lane timber truss bridge over Oyster River, where you will find the Fishermen's Lodge Pub.

⑦ **Salmon Point Resort.** (250) 923-6605; sales@salmonpoint.com; www.salmonpoint.com. Gas, propane, launch ramp, store, laundry, pool, jacuzzi and kids' activity areas. Located 15 miles south of Campbell River on the western shore of Discovery Passage, this marina, built behind a riprap breakwater, has room for powerboats up to 32 feet. The entrance is very shallow and dries at low tide. "Stay-aboards" (overnighting on boat) not permitted. The resort is an RV park primarily serving recreational fishermen, with 1 to 2 bedroom cottages, rental RVs, and a licensed restaurant and pub on site.

LASQUETI ISLAND

Lasqueti Island is often overlooked by pleasure craft as they hurry across the strait between Nanaimo and the Sunshine Coast, or run along the Vancouver Island shore between Nanaimo and Campbell River. The island has a number of good anchorages. A convenience store is at the village of False Bay, located upland from the ferry landing on the left. The shores of Lasqueti Island are indented by a number of bays that invite anchorage. Along the south shore are Boat Cove, Old House Bay, Richardson Cove and Jenkins Cove, all of which are somewhat open to southerlies, but offer good protection from northerlies or in settled weather. This part of the Lasqueti shoreline is rugged and beautiful. Squitty Bay is at the southeast end of Lasqueti Island—tiny, but with a public float. Several little dogholes for anchoring can be found in Bull Passage. Little Bull Passage, between Jedediah Island and Bull Island, has a number of good anchorages in both ends, and is passable for most boats. Other anchorages are Boho Bay, Tucker Bay and Scottie Bay. Spring Bay is only partially protected from the north by a group of small islands offshore.

Passenger ferry arriving in Lasqueti after crossing Strait of Georgia from French Creek

STRAIT OF GEORGIA

⑧ False Bay. False Bay is the primary settlement on Lasqueti Island with a public float offering limited dock space and a float plane tie-up. A passenger-only ferry runs between False Bay and French Creek on Vancouver Island. Island residents transport not only themselves by ferry but also bring a large quantity of supplies, everything from food and clothing to appliances. It's quite a scene when the ferry arrives at False Bay. An open-air market is held at the arts center, a quarter mile up the road from the ferry landing, from mid-June to September.

Buoys adjacent to the ferry landing are private and fill most of the anchoring area near the public float. The preferred anchorage is the north shore of the bay, an easy dinghy ride to the public float. On warm summer afternoons strong winds, called Qualicums, can blow through False Bay; waves break at the dock, making tie-up difficult. If you must tie in these conditions, make sure you have robust dock lines and fenders. Kevin Monahan, a long-time resident of Lasqueti Island, reports that southwest gale force winds at Cape Beale often serve as a presage of Qualicum winds arriving at False Bay.

⑨ Squitty Bay. Squitty Bay is a tiny, narrow and shallow notch at the southeast corner of Lasqueti Island. It would be harrowing to enter Squitty Bay in a roaring southeasterly, but at other times entry should be easy. Rocks border the north side of the entrance; favor the south side. The unnamed point on the south side of Squitty Bay is an ecological reserve, noted for prickly pear cacti and Rocky Mountain juniper. The public dock, 150 feet long, may be largely occupied by local boats. Rafting is permitted. Ashore, the trees in this area are bent and broken, obviously by strong winds. Tall trees are rare. A walk along the road is fascinating.

Bull Passage. Bull Passage and the islands that lie off the south end of Jedediah Island are rugged and scenic.

Little Bull Passage. Between high rock cliffs, Little Bull Passage is narrow and beautiful. Watch for the charted rock on the Jedediah Island side. It hides at high tide. Our notes say, "The east end of Little Bull Passage is absolutely fabulous. So much variety and strength in the rock walls and islands. Worth a side trip just to see the sights."

Jedediah Island. Jedediah Island is a marine park. Although good anchorages are scarce and tight, Jedediah Island is increasingly popular. One of the best anchorages is in the little notch, called Deep Bay, opposite the south end of Paul Island, where chains have been installed around this small bay to facilitate stern-ties. It is impractical that all these stern-ties could be used at the same time in this tiny, v-shaped bay, except for the smallest of boats. The large number of stern-ties are provided to allow different options for boaters. Long Bay just south of Deep Bay is usable, too. Long Bay goes dry a short distance inside the mouth. Codfish Bay on the southeast side of Jedediah Island has room for two or three boats to stern-tie. If nothing looks good at Jedediah Island itself, Boho Bay at Lasqueti Island, about 1 mile away, is an alternative.

One interesting spot is the narrow and protected steep-sided notch at the southeast end of Jedediah Island. Although its sheer walls might discourage much on-shore exploration, it is possible to scramble from the head of the notch up the bluffs on the north side. You will be rewarded not only with access to the rest of the island but also an excellent view toward Texada Island. [Hamilton]

For easy access to the island, take the dinghy ashore at Deep Bay and hike the short, well-marked trail across the island. A map of the island is posted at the head of the trail from both Deep Bay and Long Bay. A trail also leads from Codfish Bay. A visit to the old homestead on the east side of Jedediah Island is an exciting adventure and should not be missed. The homestead is frozen in time and left undisturbed. Please respect the property and leave things as found for others to enjoy. The island was owned by three different families over the years; first, the Foote Family who purchased the island in 1890 and lived here for over 30 years. Next came Henry Hughes from Ireland and his wife, who lived here for 29 years. The last owners, Alan and Mary Palmer, bought the property in 1949. Not wanting this island paradise to be developed, the Palmers sold Jedediah Island to the Provincial Government in 1994 to be used as a Marine Park. A plaque on the island commemorates their generous forethought. You can learn more about the history of Jedediah Island in the book - *Jedediah Days, One Woman's Island Paradise*, by Mary Palmer.

TEXADA ISLAND

Texada (pronounced "Tex-AY-da") Island has three main anchorages: Anderson Bay on Malaspina Strait at the south end; Blubber Bay at the northern tip; and Sturt Bay, a couple miles south along the Malaspina Strait (eastern) side. Although it has a ferry landing and public float, **Blubber Bay** is dominated by an enormous quarry and is not inviting, although anchorage is possible if needed.

Anderson Bay. Anderson Bay is at the south end of Texada Island on Malaspina Strait. It is a beautiful spot, lined with sheer rock walls. Anchor in 24 feet near the head.

The safest approach is from the southeast. In our opinion, the pass between Texada Island and the unnamed 20-meter island is not as open as the charts suggest. We explored this pass at the bottom of a 1.6-foot low tide and found rock shelves extending from the Texada Island side well into the pass. Be especially careful of the reef that extends from the southwest point of Texada Island. The reef dries at low tide, but at higher stages of tide it could be a nasty surprise.

⑩ Sturt Bay. Locally called Marble Bay, on Malaspina Strait near the north end of Texada Island. Sturt Bay has the best anchorage and moorage on Texada Island. The Texada Boat Club has extensive floats, visitors welcomed. The floats have water and 15 amp power. Bob and Maggie Timms are the wharfingers, (604) 414-5897. Anchorage is elsewhere in the bay.

Hiking trails are close to the docks. The Centennial Service Garage (gas station) has Wi-Fi. A new RV campground just up the hill from the garage has laundry facilities, coin-operated showers, and Wi-Fi. The full service grocery store has liquor and good meats. A farmers market is held Sundays from noon to 1:30 p.m. at Gillies Bay Ballpark. Correspondents Al and Becca Symanski tell us the Texada Island Museum, housed in a wing of the local school, is a "must see."

Caution: Sturt Bay is a welcome haven if a northwesterly is kicking up Malaspina Strait, but not suitable in a fresh southeasterly. Swells from a southeasterly bounce back from the north shore of the bay, making it and the guest moorage dock lumpy. Blubber Bay is a better anchorage in a southeasterly.

Vananda/Sturt Bay Public Wharf. Dock has 98 feet of mooring space. Exposed and not very interesting. Nearby Sturt Bay is preferred.

Harwood Point Regional Park. Gillies Bay, Texada Island. Anchor out only and dinghy in to a 40-acre park. Grass fields, picnic tables, campsites, pit toilets.

Jedediah Island is a small island that can easily be explored by dinghy or by foot.

Vancouver, Mainland B.C. & The Sunshine Coast

CHAPTER 9

WHITE ROCK TO VANCOUVER
Boundary Bay • Fraser River • Steveston

VANCOUVER AND HOWE SOUND
*False Creek • Vancouver Harbour • Indian Arm
Horseshoe Bay • Gibsons*

GOWER POINT TO SECHELT INLET
*Buccaneer Bay • Smuggler Cove • Secret Cove
Pender Harbour • Egmont • Sechelt Rapids • Sechelt*

JERVIS INLET
*Blind Bay • Ballet Bay • Hotham Sound • Jervis Inlet
Princess Louisa Inlet*

MALASPINA STRAIT TO SARAH POINT
Grief Point • Westview • Lund • Copeland Islands

Vancouver, Mainland B.C. & The Sunshine Coast

WHITE ROCK TO VANCOUVER

The coastline between Boundary Bay and Vancouver is an uninteresting river delta and the waters are often rough. Fraser River sediment, locally known as Sand Heads, has created shoal depths for some distance offshore. The prevailing winds tend to blow against the river current in the shallow water, and steep seas build quickly. Stay well off in deeper water, but even there, a 20-knot wind can make for a rough ride.

We listened to the VHF one day when a storm front blew through, and we sympathized with a terrified woman aboard a chartered 45-foot powerboat caught in steep seas near Roberts Bank. She kept repeating their lat/lon coordinates from the GPS and begging for help. The boat wasn't taking on water and no one was injured, but conditions were awful and they were scared. There was nothing another boat could do.

A few weeks earlier we spoke with a couple who had gone up that shore to Vancouver and had a very rough ride, the kind of ride they never wanted to repeat—period. We have run that coast in calm conditions and had no problems. If you decide to go that way, be sure conditions are favorable. [*Hale*]

Most pleasure craft choose to go north through the Gulf Islands, then pick a patch of good weather to cross the Strait of Georgia to Vancouver or Howe Sound. The shortest distance across the strait, from Gabriola Pass to Howe Sound, is 14 miles. Even slow boats can make the crossing in two or three hours; faster boats can cross in an hour or less. Listen for the weather report for the Halibut Bank buoy, or call Dial-a-Buoy at 888/701-8992 and enter 46146 for the wind and wave conditions in the Strait of Georgia, off Sechelt.

Boundary Bay. The U.S./Canada border runs through Boundary Bay. Delta, B.C. is located on the northwest shore. Point Roberts, Washington, is to the southwest. White Rock and the Semiahmoo First Nation's reserve are on the southeast shore. The southeastern section of Boundary Bay, straddling the U.S./Canada border is known as Semiahmoo Bay. The northern tip of Boundary Bay is known as Mud Bay.

① **White Rock.** White Rock, in Canada, is almost due north of Blaine, in Boundary Bay. A long pier, with floats at the outer end, crosses

White Rock to Vancouver

CHARTS	
3463	Strait of Georgia, Southern Portion (1:80,000)
3488	Fraser River, Pattullo Bridge to Crescent Island (1:20,000)
3489	Fraser River, Crescent Island to Harrison Mills (1:20,000)
3490	Fraser River, Sand Heads to Douglas Island (1:20,000)
3491	Fraser River, North Arm (1:20,000)
3492	Roberts Bank (1:20,000)

tide flats. The waterfront village has interesting restaurants, shops, and galleries.

① **City of White Rock Pier.** (604) 626-5330. White Rock is a Canada Customs port of entry; call (888) 226-7277. The south side of the eastern float has about 50 feet of space reserved for transient moorage, 2 hours maximum stay, no power or water.

② **Crescent Beach.** North of White Rock, the Nicomekl River empties into Boundary Bay, creating a channel that leads to the village of Crescent Beach and the Crescent Beach Marina. The channel is marked by port and starboard daymarks. The marina is located just beyond the Burlington Northern Railway swing bridge that crosses the river to Blackie Spit. Depending on tide, bridge clearance ranges from 9 to 20 feet. The bridge is manned 7 days a week, from 6:30 a.m. until 10:30 p.m., and will open to 3 horn blasts. Call the bridge at (604) 538-3233 or call the Crescent Beach Marina at (604) 538-9666, and they will contact the bridge tender.

② **Crescent Beach Marina Ltd.** 12555 Crescent Road, Surrey, BC V4A 2V4; (604) 538-9666; info@crescentbeachmarina.com; www.crescentbeachmarina.com. Open all year, gasoline & diesel at the fuel dock. Guest moorage for boats to 60 feet; call first. Haulout on hydraulic trailers to 30 tons, 15, 20 & 30 amp power, washrooms, ice, repairs, chandlery, launch ramp, showers, laundry, pumpout, dry storage.

Canoe Passage. Canoe Passage is the southernmost mouth of the Fraser River. The seaward entrance is marked by a government buoy, but private dolphins mark its winding path through Roberts Bank. Although mainly used by commercial boats with local knowledge, Canoe Passage can be used by small craft, especially at half tide or better on a rising tide. The swing bridge connecting Westham Island with the mainland is manned 24 hours a day, and opens to 3 whistle blasts. Contact the bridge tender on VHF 74 or by telephone at (604) 946-2121. In 1997 the Canadian Hydrographic Service published large scale Chart 3492 (1:20,000) showing Canoe Passage, but we are skeptical. Locals who use the passage remark the channel yearly, after major runoff has moved the sand bars.

South Arm Fraser River. Sand Heads marks the mouth of the South Arm (also called the **Main Arm**) of the Fraser River. The South Arm is the Fraser's major entry, and is protected on its north side by the Steveston Jetty. Currents in the Fraser River can run to 5 knots, depending on the volume of water in the river, which in turn depends on rain and snow melt upstream. Large flood tides will at times slow or reverse the current.

Caution: An on-shore wind meeting an ebb current, combined with heavy outflow from the river, will create dangerously steep and high seas in the river mouth. Friends who keep their boats on the river tell of their entire boat being

VANCOUVER, MAINLAND B.C. & THE SUNSHINE COAST

Transient moorage is on the opposite side of the dock from the whale watch tour boats.

airborne in these conditions.

The lower part of the Fraser River is delta country, low and flat. The marshlands are havens for wildlife, and you'll see many eagles. The river itself contains much drift. The river is used heavily by fish boats, tugs towing barges or log booms, Coast Guard boats, work boats of all description, and freighters. Water-oriented industrial companies are located along the shores.

Relatively few cruising boats go up the Fraser River, in part because the entire coast between Point Grey and Point Roberts is uninteresting to view, and hostile in any kind of wind. Most of the marinas on the Fraser River exist primarily for permanent moorage tenants, with few facilities for visitors.

③ **Steveston.** The first stop on the Fraser River is Steveston, a long, slender harbor on the north side of Cannery Channel, protected by a sand island (Steveston Island). Although Steveston is primarily a fishing town with moorage and other services for commercial fishermen, it has become a lively tourist destination as well. Transient moorage is available at the Steveston Wharf and at Imperial Landing located a third of a mile east of the wharf. Steveston has a fuel dock. A chandlery, antique shops, bookstores, plenty of dining and all the other facilities of a small city are ashore. The streets of Steveston are quaint; the local movie industry sometimes films scenes there. Steveston has much to offer above and beyond its attractive shops and cafes. The excellent Gulf of Georgia Cannery Museum on the west end of the Public Wharf is a must see, as is the Britannia Shipyards National Historic Site on the east end of the village (reached by a beautiful new promenade along the shoreline). Hikers and bicyclists make use of the extensive trail system that leads to the North Arm of the Fraser River and to the City of Richmond. For a short hike, walk the trail west of town to Garry Point Park with beach access and great views over the South Arm and the Gulf Islands.

③ **Steveston Harbour Authority Wharf.** 12740 Trites Rd., Richmond, BC V7E 3R8; (604) 272-5539; www.stevestonharbour.com. Open all year, 30 amp power, water, washrooms, and showers. No WiFi. Side-tie transient moorage is available by reservation only on the east side of the unlabeled float, east of the fish sales float (the eastern most Wharf float.) Additional side-tie transient moorage is available on the shore side of A-dock on a first-come, first-serve basis. All transient guests must register and make payment by phone; the Harbour Authority office is located more than a mile away, at their Paramount Basin site. A key to the showers is provided upon request. Showers and public washrooms are located next to the Gulf of Georgia Cannery Museum.

③ **Steveston Chevron.** (604) 277-4712. Fuel dock with ethanol-free gasoline, diesel, washrooms. Limited marine supplies, lubricants, snacks.

③ **City of Richmond Imperial Landing.** Located a third of a mile east of the Steveston Harbour Authority docks; britannia@richmond.ca; www.richmond.ca/parks. A Richmond City Parks Department facility (604) 244-1208. Transient side-tie moorage on this substantial 600-foot concrete dock; 30 amp power, no water, no washrooms, or showers. First three hours are free. Rates for stays over three hours are posted at the automated pay-station at the head of the ramp. Maximum stay is three consecutive days. This dock offers a more secluded moorage option when visiting the community of Steveston. Charted depths are deeper off the west end of this dock than around the Steveston Harbour docks.

Caution: Hazardous submerged piles are reported near the inside (shore side) of the east half of the dock.

④ **Ladner.** Ladner is a pretty town. Leave the main branch of the Fraser River and take

Steveston Harbour

VANCOUVER, MAINLAND B.C. & THE SUNSHINE COAST

See Area Map Page 260 - Maps Not for Navigation

Sea Reach to Ladner Harbour, fronted by float homes. Moorage for fish boats is on the port side, and pleasure craft are welcome when the fleet is out. Strongly favor the south shore as you enter Ladner Harbour, skirting the docks of marinas and businesses located along River Road. A drying mud bank, studded with deadheads, extends a considerable distance from the north side of the harbor.

④ **Ladner Yacht Club.** (604) 946-4056; www.ladneryachtclub.ca. Reciprocal boats only if space is available. Water, restrooms, 30 amp power, secured marina.

Deas Slough. A little farther up the river from Ladner, Deas Slough is home to Captain's Cove, located behind Deas Island. A low bridge (Hwy. 99) blocks passage any farther up Deas Slough, except for small boats with no masts.

⑤ **Captain's Cove Marina.** 6100 Ferry Rd., Ladner, BC V4K 3M9; (604) 946-1244; info@captainscovemarina.ca; www.captainscovemarina.ca. Open all year, guest moorage available for boats from 24 to 60 feet, best to call ahead. The fuel dock has gasoline and diesel. Washrooms, showers, laundry, water, 30 & 50 amp power, waste oil disposal, pumpout, Wi-Fi. The facility is large and well cared for. Haulout to 60 tons, and a yard for repairs.

Golf: Cove Links, a pretty (and pretty challenging, we're told) 9-hole par 29 golf course next to Captain's Cove Marina, is part of a development that includes homes and condos.

⑥ **Shelter Island Marina Inc.** 6911 Graybar Rd., Richmond, BC V6W 1H3; (604) 270-6272; www.shelterislandmarina.com. Open all year, some guest moorage, call ahead. Washrooms, showers, laundry, water, 15, 30, & 50 amp power, several Travelifts for boats up to 220 tons, chandlery with hardware section in the marina office and a full-service chandlery across the parking lot. Restaurant and pub with free Wi-Fi, beer and wine store, and a full liquor store two blocks away.

Shelter Island Marina is behind Don Island at the south entrance to Annacis Channel. It is a busy facility with a number of boat repair companies.

New Westminster. New Westminster is located at the confluence of the North and South Arms of the Fraser River, and is heavily industrialized along the waterfront.

Contributing Editor Tom Kincaid has run the river past New Westminster to the Pitt River, where he spent the night at the Pitt Meadows Marina. A few friends have continued to the Harrison River, running up the Harrison River to Harrison Lake and Harrison Hot Springs. All recommend having a fast boat and a knowledgeable pilot aboard before attempting to run either of these rivers. The Fraser River beyond Richmond is poorly marked, and sand bars are constantly changing. The river is navigable as far as Hope during high water stages, but mariners should rely on local knowledge before attempting this run.

North Arm Fraser River. The North Arm of the Fraser River is lined with boatbuilding and repair yards and other businesses that serve the marine community. A jetty runs through Sturgeon Bank along the south side of the North Arm, parallel to the Point Grey shoreline. A dredged basin, known locally as "Coward's Cove" or the "Chicken Hole," is on the north side of the channel, just before the North Arm enters the Strait of Georgia. The basin gives good protection to skippers while they assess conditions out on the strait.

⑦ **Richmond Chevron.** 7891 Grauer Rd., Richmond, BC V7B 1N4; (604) 278-2181. Beneath Arthur Laing Bridge. Open all year, gasoline, diesel, lubricants and waste oil disposal.

Middle Arm Fraser River. The Middle Arm of the Fraser River runs along the south side of Sea Island, which is almost entirely taken up by Vancouver International Airport. The west entrance is blocked by Sturgeon Bank with no marked channels. We have seen a small, fast cruiser enter the Middle Arm, but the tide was high and perhaps the skipper had local knowledge (or maybe he was just lucky). Prudence dictates entry from the North Arm only. The Delta River Inn Marina and Vancouver Marina are on the Middle Arm near a low swing bridge connecting the city of Richmond with the airport.

⑦ **Pier 73 Marina & Yacht Club.** 3500 Cessna Drive, Richmond, BC V7B 1C7; (604) 970-4882; info@pier73marina.com; pier-73marina.com. Located 8 miles up the North Arm of the Fraser River in Moray Channel at the Pacific Gateway Hotel Vancouver Airport. Open all year, limited guest moorage, call ahead. This fully refurbished marina has slips from 30 to 80 feet, 30 & 50 amp power, water. The hotel has several restaurants, a bar, and a pool. They run a bus to the airport.

⑦ **Vancouver Marina.** #200-8211 River Road, Richmond, BC V6X 1X8; (604) 278-9787; mooring@vancouvermarina.com; www.vancouvermarina.com. Monitors VHF 66A. Open all year, call ahead for guest moorage. Gasoline & diesel at the fuel dock, 15, 20 & 30 amp power, garbage, pumpout, recycling and waste oil disposal, washrooms, no showers. They carry marine supplies, snacks, bait, and ice. Restaurant, mechanic and parts department, haulout to 30 feet, 24-hour security. Located in the heart of Richmond on the Middle Arm of the Fraser River.

⑦ **Skyline Marina.** 8031 River Road, Richmond, BC V6X 1X8; (604) 273-3977; www.skylinemarina.ca. Open all year, no transient moorage. The marina has a boatyard and 30 ton Travelift.

VANCOUVER

Vancouver is the largest city in British Columbia, and the major deepwater port on the west coast of Canada, handling cargo from across Canada and around the world. The city is clean,

False Creek Harbour Authority

- Clean Marine Certified
- Walk to Granville Island
- Electrical & Water Hookups
- Washrooms & Showers
- Laundry Facilities
- Free Wifi
- 24-hour Security
- Snacks, Pop & Ice

VHF: 66A
tel: 604.733.3625
fax: 604.733.3628
www.falsecreek.com

Visitor Moorage Welcome!

False Creek Harbour Authority • 1505 West 1st Avenue • Vancouver BC V6J 1E8

VANCOUVER, MAINLAND B.C. & THE SUNSHINE COAST

See Area Map Page 264 - Maps Not for Navigation

safe, and thoroughly cosmopolitan. Its architecture is exciting. Vancouver's parks, museums, hotels, and dining are wonderful.

If you are approaching Vancouver from the south, you could go up the North Arm of the Fraser River to a number of marinas in the Richmond area, and take a bus into the city. If you are approaching from the north, you could tie up at Horseshoe Bay on the north shore of West Vancouver, or at Snug Cove on the south side of Bowen Island. A private foot ferry runs between Snug Cove and Granville Island during the summer months. Or take the BC Ferries from Snug Cove to Horseshoe Bay, then board a bus for the trip into Vancouver—or as far south as White Rock if that's where you wanted to go. The Vancouver bus system is excellent and affordable.

For moorage in Vancouver proper, choose either the Vancouver Harbour area or the False Creek area. Each has advantages, and each is good. Once you're settled, Vancouver's bus system allows you to get around the entire area with minimum delay. A Costco store is located near the northeast end of False Creek at 605 Expo Blvd. (604) 622-5050.

Anchoring restriction: A permit, at no cost, is required for all vessels anchoring in False Creek (see False Creek area description for details).

Point Grey. Point Grey marks the southern entrance to Burrard Inlet. When approaching from the south, cutting too close to Point Grey risks grounding on Spanish Bank. Leave the buoys to starboard when entering.

Spanish Bank. Spanish Bank is an extensive drying bank off the north shore of Point Grey. The outer edge of the bank is marked with buoys. Royal Vancouver Yacht Club has its main clubhouse and sailboat moorage about 3 miles from Point Grey along the south shore of English Bay. A launch ramp is close to the former Kitsilano Coast Guard station near the entrance to False Creek.

First Narrows under Lions Gate Bridge

FALSE CREEK

False Creek is an ideal centrally located bay with a number of marina moorage options, well-protected anchorage and a full service boatyard with Travelift. A well-monitored anchoring permit system helps to keep anchoring space available and prevents permanent anchorage abuses. Anchoring permits (free) are required for day anchoring longer than 8 hours and overnight anchoring. Permits can be picked up at Heather Civic Marina or online at http://vancouver.ca/streets-transportation/anchoring.aspx. Boats without permits are subject to ticketing and fines up to $500.

False Creek Yacht Club, on the north shore of False Creek, usually has guest slips available. Quayside Marina, also on the north shore, has excellent facilities with guest slip and side-tie moorage. Foot ferries stop at Quayside. On the south shore, the Fishermen's Wharf marina, managed by the False Creek Harbour Authority, has transient moorage and good facilities. It is a short walk from the marina to the Granville Island Market, shops, and restaurants. False Creek is covered by Wi-Fi.

Blue Pacific Charters (604-682-2161), on the west side of Granville Island near the Granville Market, sometimes has moorage available in unoccupied slips, reservations required. To reach these docks turn just before the Bridge Restaurant, on the south side when you enter False Creek, and work your way towards the docks. On the east side of Granville Island the Pelican Bay Marina, next to the Granville Island Hotel, has some guest moorage.

Granville Island is an active and vibrant place, full of people. You'll find a busy food market (similar in many ways to Seattle's Pike Place Market), many restaurants, galleries, shops, and a variety of marine supplies, both on the island and a short walk away. Docks face the waterway, and are posted for 3-hour maximum stay.

Two harbor foot ferry franchises serve False Creek. If anchored, you can hail a passing ferry for transportation around the creek. Great for a tour of the harbor too.

Fuel: Fuel is available at the False Creek Fuels.

Pumpouts: Pumpouts are located at Burrard Bridge Civic Marina, False Creek Harbour Authority Fishermen's Wharf, Heather Civic Marina (under the large "Monk's" sign), and Quayside Marina. The City of Vancouver and the Vancouver Park Board started a free mobile pump-out service pilot project in 2017. To schedule the service, contact Skookum Yacht Services at (778) 683-7867 or email at pumpout@skookumyachtservices.com.

No Discharge Zone. Gray Water Okay.

THINGS TO DO

1. **Granville Market**. On Granville Island, a delight to the senses with flowers, spices, teas, fruit and other food markets, restaurants and crafts.

2. **Foot Ferries**. Crisscross the water from False Creek. Travel to different attractions or stay aboard to tour the entire harbor area. Some ferries allow bicycles.

3. **Vancouver Maritime Museum**. Learn more about B.C. maritime history from Vancouver to the Arctic. See tugboats, fireboats and even pirates. Easily reached by foot ferry.

4. **Stanley Park**. Several bike rental shops are on Denman Street, near Coal Harbour. Rent a bike and ride the trail along the seawall. Or, take a walk around the park. While in Stanley Park, learn more about B.C.'s First Nations people in Klahowya Village.

5. **Vancouver Aquarium**. Located in Stanley Park. Excellent. Don't miss the white Beluga whales.

CHARTS	
3311sc Small craft charts (strip charts)	Sunshine Coast to Desolation Sound
3463	Strait of Georgia – Southern Portion (1:80,000)
3481	Approaches to Vancouver Harbour (1:25,000)
3493	Vancouver Harbour, Western Portion (1:10,000)
3494	Vancouver Harbour, Central Portion (1:10,000) Second Narrows (1:6,000)
3495	Vancouver Harbour, Eastern Portion (1:10,000) Indian Arm (1:6,000)
3512	Strait of Georgia, Central Portion (1:80,000)
3526	Howe Sound (1:40,000)
3534 Plans	Howe Sound: Mannion Bay, Snug Cove, Fishermans Cove, Horseshoe Bay, Shoal Channel, Squamish Harbour

2018 WAGGONER CRUISING GUIDE

VANCOUVER, MAINLAND B.C. & THE SUNSHINE COAST

Reference Only – Not for Navigation

Vancouver and Howe Sound

6. Spirit Catcher Miniature Train. Take a ride and see the story of Sasquatch.

7. Science World. The distinctive domed glass building on False Creek with imaginative exhibits and hands-on experiments for young and old.

8. Bloedel Floral Conservatory. In Queen Elizabeth Park. Tropical plants; colorful birds flying about.

9. Museum of Anthropology. On the University of British Columbia campus. Study of First Nations people and other B.C. cultures.

10. Deeley Motorcycle Exhibition. Over 250 motorcycles on exhibit, spanning 115 years and 59 different manufacturers.

11. Yaletown or **Gastown.** Key shopping areas with many shops and boutiques.

Vancouver Maritime Museum. 1905 Ogden Avenue in Vanier Park, Vancouver, BC V6J 1A3; (604) 257-8300; www.vancouvermaritimemuseum.com. Vancouver Maritime Museum is on the south shore of English Bay at the entrance to False Creek. The museum's docks are for display boats only. The vessel *St. Roch*, which explored the Northwest Passage, is on display in its own building. The False Creek Ferry stops at the museum docks.

⑧ **Vancouver Boating Welcome Centre.** 1661 Granville St., Vancouver, BC V6Z 1N3; (604) 648-2628; welcome@fcyc.com. Hours 9:00 a.m to 5:00 p.m. Located in a boat at False Creek Yacht Club. The Welcome Center is a good resource to help with boating related matters. Anchor permits for False Creek are no longer available through the Welcome Centre. The Yacht Club may be phasing out of their participation in the Welcome Centre over the next couple of years.

⑨ **Burrard Civic Marina.** 1655 Whyte Ave., Vancouver, BC V6J 1A9; (604) 733-5833 (604) 505-5833 cell; burrard.marina@vancouver.ca. The first marina in False Creek, with over 420 berths. Open 7 days a week all year. Operated by the City of Vancouver. Permanent moorage with some space for transient boats in vacant slips to 36 feet (occasionally up to 45 feet). Call for availability. Water, 15 amp power, washrooms, showers, laundry, pumpout, waste oil disposal, tidal grid, security gate with keycard, free Wi-Fi. The marina is convenient to the Vancouver Maritime Museum, walking and bike paths, and the False Creek foot ferries.

⑨ **False Creek Fuels.** 1655 Whyte Avenue, Vancouver, BC V6J 1A9; (604) 638-0209; fillup@falsecreekfuels.com; www.falsecreekfuels.com. Monitors 66A. Just west of the Burrard Street Bridge, the fuel float carries gas, diesel, oil, lubricants. Open 7 days a week. Accommodates vessels to 165 feet. The store has drinks, snacks, ice cream, sandwiches (seasonal), and a

264   www.WaggonerGuide.com

See Area Map Page 264 - Maps Not for Navigation

VANCOUVER, MAINLAND B.C. & THE SUNSHINE COAST

coffee bar. It also has ice, bait, tackle, marine supplies, guidebooks.

⑨ **False Creek Harbour Authority Fishermen's Wharf.** 1505 W. 1st Ave., Vancouver, BC V6J 1E8; (604) 733-3625; info@falsecreek.com; www.falsecreek.com. Monitors VHF 66A. This is a 5-Anchor Clean Marina, open all year, around the clock. It is on the south shore of False Creek, west of Granville Island. Contact the wharf office for tie-up instructions before landing. Water, 20, 30, 50 & 100 amp power, washrooms, showers, laundry, ice, pumpout, recycling, waste oil disposal, 24-hour security, free Wi-Fi. The ramps to shore are 75 feet long and 5 feet wide, and fitted with transition plates at each end to make them fully handicap compliant. Go Fish is a popular takeout in the parking lot area. Expect long lines at noontime. Dine outside on picnic tables.

Fish boats have moorage priority, but transient moorage is available in the summer. A fish sales dock is just east of the main dock. Fresh fish and prawns right off the boat are sometimes available. Do not tie to the fish sales dock, even if it is empty.

Customs Clearance. A courtesy customs clearance area is located in the yellow painted bull-rail area on the 'T' end of F-dock. There is no dedicated phone, you will need to use your cell phone.

⑨ **Blue Pacific Yacht Charters.** 1519 Foreshore Walk, Vancouver, BC V6H 3X3; (604) 682-2161; info@bluepacificcharters.ca; www.bluepacificcharters.ca. Open all year, moorage in unoccupied slips as available, 30 & 50 amp power, washrooms, and showers. Located on the west side of Granville Island.

⑨ **Granville Island Boat Yard.** (604) 685-6924; www.granvilleislandboatyard.com. A full service boatyard with 55 ton Travelift is located on the west side of Granville Island. The boatyard has repair service trades people available and welcomes do-it-yourself.

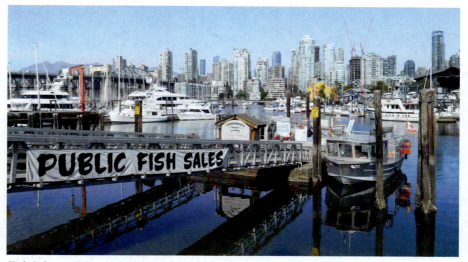
Fish Sales and Customs Dock at Fishermen's Wharf in False Creek

⑨ **Pelican Bay Marina.** 1708 W. 6th Ave., Vancouver, BC V6J 5E8; (604) 729-1442; pelicanbaymarina@mail.com. Open all year, adjacent to the Granville Island Hotel on the east end of Granville Island. Moorage in unoccupied slips when available, call ahead. Water, 15, 30 & 50 amp power, washroom, ice.

⑨ **Heather Civic Marina.** 600 Stamps Landing, Vancouver, BC V5Z 3Z1; (604) 874-2814; heather.marina@vancouver.ca; www.vancouver.ca/streets-transportation/heather-civic-marina.aspx. Open all year with guest moorage to 42 feet in unoccupied slips, call for availability. Washrooms, showers, pumpout, 15, 30 & 50 amp power. Restaurants and pub nearby. A passenger foot ferry runs to both sides of False Creek. The Heather Civic Marina office issues anchoring permits for False Creek.

⑧ **False Creek Yacht Club.** 1661 Granville St., Vancouver, BC V6Z 1N3; (604) 648-2628 dockmaster; (604) 682-3292 administration & event scheduling; www.fcyc.com; welcome@fcyc.com. Washrooms, showers, laundry, pumpout, free WiFi, 30 amp power, and lounge. Open all year on the north side of False Creek, directly under the Granville Street Bridge. Guest moorage in unoccupied slips. Reciprocal and public guest moorage. Guest moorage in unoccupied slips. Call the dockmaster upon arrival. A passenger foot ferry runs regularly to Granville Island.

⑧ **Quayside Marina.** 1088 Marinaside Crescent, Vancouver, BC V6Z 3C4; (604) 681-9115; (604) 209-6456; qsmarina@ranchogroup.com; www.ranchovan.com/marina. Monitors VHF 66A. Open all year for vessels to 125 feet, 30, 50 & 100 amp power, water on the docks, washrooms, showers, laundry, pay telephone, pumpout, garbage and recycling, ice, security. Wheelchair accessible. Online Reservations are available on their website. Slip sales and long-term lease information also found on their web site.

False Creek, Vancouver

2018 WAGGONER CRUISING GUIDE   265

VANCOUVER, MAINLAND B.C. & THE SUNSHINE COAST

See Area Map Page 264 - Maps Not for Navigation

Coal Harbour Marina is in the middle of downtown Vancouver and the most centrally located.

The Quayside (pronounced "Keyside") Marina is on the north shore of False Creek, in the middle of Vancouver's cosmopolitan Yaletown district. Most of the slips are for permanent moorage, but guest moorage is available on a 500-foot-long float extending from shore, or in vacant slips. Colorful Aquabus foot ferry boats come and go from their spot near the head of that float as do the small passenger False Creek Ferries. Moorage reservations are essential during high season and requested year-round. Although it's a bit of a walk from the guest dock to the office, check in promptly after you arrive.

Pacific Boulevard Marina. Box 26, 750 Pacific Blvd., Vancouver, BC V6B 5E7; (604) 683-7035; info@pacblvdmarina.com; www.pacblvdmarina.com. Permanent moorage marina with transient space when available for vessels up to 40 feet; 30 amp power, water, security gates. Located at the northeast end of False Creek. Reservations requested no more than one week in advance. Transient space is most likely available during March and April.

LOCAL KNOWLEDGE

STRONG CURRENTS: Currents run strongly in both First and Second Narrows. Use caution, especially because of the heavy traffic that frequents the area.

Vancouver Harbour (South). Vancouver Harbour is entered under the Lions Gate Bridge through First Narrows, in the northeast corner of Burrard Inlet. Because of heavy commercial traffic, strong currents and narrow channels, sailing craft must be under power from westward of First Narrows until well into Vancouver Harbour. No sailing is permitted through Second Narrows, either. In First Narrows, a strong ebb current meeting a fresh onshore breeze can create high, steep seas. Current predictions are shown in the Tide and Current Tables Vol. 5, and Ports and Passes. Monitor VHF 12 for Vessel Traffic Services (VTS) information.

Watch for drifting logs, float plane traffic, and Vancouver Rowing Club rowers in Vancouver Harbour. Approaching Coal Harbour, leave Burnaby Shoal and the Chevron fuel barge to starboard. Observe a 5-knot speed limit.

Once into Vancouver Harbour, your best bet for moorage is along the southern shoreline in the Coal Harbour area. Vancouver Rowing Club, located adjacent to Stanley Park, has moorage for members of reciprocal yacht clubs. The Coal Harbour area, from the Vancouver Rowing Club to Coal Harbour Marina, is covered by Wi-Fi. Stanley Park is nearby.

Bayshore West Marina, next to the Harbour Ferries docks, has all new facilities.

Coal Harbour Marina, just east of the Bayshore Hotel, makes a visit to Vancouver a real pleasure. It is first class in every way, and is an excellent base for a few days in town.

These marinas are close to downtown Vancouver, a pleasant walk or short cab ride away. Wright Mariner Supply, occupying a floating structure in the Coal Harbour Marina, sells a complete range of marine supplies, clothing, charts, and books.

Robson Street's shops, galleries and wide range of restaurants are just a few blocks away.

Anchoring restriction: Pleasure craft may not anchor in Vancouver Harbour between First Narrows and Second Narrows.

Customs dock: (888) 226-7277 The customs dock is a Parks Board dock called "Harbour Green," east of Coal Harbour Marina. Day moorage up to 3 hours, no overnight.

⑩ **Coal Harbour Chevron.** (604) 681-7725. Fuel barge in Coal Harbour open 7 days a week 7:00 a.m. to 11:00 p.m., gasoline & diesel, washrooms, showers. They do oil changes and have waste oil disposal.

⑩ **Coal Harbour Marina.** 1525 Coal Harbour Quay, Vancouver, BC V6G 3E7; (604) 681-2628; guestservices@coalharbourmarina.com; www.coalharbourmarina.com. Monitors VHF 66A. Open all year, guest moorage for boats to 330 feet, reservations recommended. Facilities include 30, 50 & 100 amp single/3-phase power, Wi-Fi, pumpout, washrooms, showers, laundry. This is a first-class marina with wide concrete docks, 24-hour staff, security gates, a restaurant, marine supply store, and easy access to downtown Vancouver. Reservations in season highly recommended.

⑩ **Bayshore West Marina.** 450 Denman St., Vancouver, BC V6G 3J1; (604) 689-5331; info@bayshorewestmarina.com; www.bayshorewestmarina.com. Open all year, limited guest moorage to 80 feet; 30, 50 & 100 amp

Coal Harbour

See Area Map Page 264 - Maps Not for Navigation

VANCOUVER, MAINLAND B.C. & THE SUNSHINE COAST

Coal Harbour Marina

Bayshore West Marina

Mosquito Creek Marina

power, garbage, recycling Wi-Fi, washrooms, and pumpout. Located in Coal Harbour between Stanley Park and the Westin Bayshore Resort. Restaurants and shopping within easy walking distance. Guided fishing excursions available. The slips and fairways are wide for easy maneuvering.

Vancouver Harbour (North). With the exception of the re-developed Lonsdale area, the north shore of Vancouver Harbour is mostly heavy commercial. Transient moorage is available at Mosquito Creek Marina and at the City of North Vancouver's St. Roch dock. Both are near the Lonsdale area which has a selection of restaurants and pubs, grocery, and shopping. SeaBus foot ferry service at Lonsdale Quay in North Vancouver runs to downtown Vancouver. The crossing takes 12 minutes and connects with other transportation options in downtown Vancouver. For more information see the Vancouver transit planning website: www.translink.ca.

A number of good marine repair shops are in Mosquito Creek Marina and at Lynnwood Marina, just west of Second Narrows.

Saturday Summer Concerts: July through August at Shipbuilders' Square at the foot of Lonsdale. Shipyards Night Market: May through September from 5 to 10 p.m. on Fridays. Live music, fresh food and locally made products.

Caution: The SeaBus north terminus is just west of Lonsdale Quay with frequent arrivals and departures of two foot-passenger catamaran SeaBus ferries.

St. Roch Dock. (604) 982-3910; www.cnv.org. 80 feet of floating dock for short-term and overnight moorage. Located east of Lonsdale Quay with its "Q" on top of the tower, just below the historic yellow crane and next to the re-developed 700x50 feet Burrard Dry Dock. This pleasure craft float is conveniently

267

- GUEST MOORAGE AVAILABLE 30' TO 330'
- 30, 50 & 100 AMP POWER
- DOCKSIDE ASSISTANCE 24 HRS
- GUEST SERVICES 8:30 AM – 5:00 PM
- SECURITY GATES & VIDEO CAMERAS

Coal Harbour Marina
LOCATION • QUALITY • SERVICE

- LAUNDRY, WASHROOMS & SHOWERS
- CHANDLERY & SHIPWRIGHT SERVICE
- MARINE PUB & RESTAURANT
- ADJACENT FUELING STATION

Coal Harbour Marina is Vancouver's premier provider of salt-water moorage offering a range of amenities in one of the most spectacular harbours in the world. Shopping, restaurants, sporting events, live theatre, museums and Stanley Park are just a short jaunt away. Follow the Seawall Trail on foot, bike or blades! Find us on Facebook and Twitter.

Telephone **604.681.2628** • Fax 604.681.4666 • VHF **66A (24 hrs)** • WWW.COALHARBOURMARINA.COM
1525 Coal Harbour Quay Vancouver, BC V6G 3E7 • 49°17.500'N 123°07.600'W • guestservices@coalharbourmarina.com

2018 WAGGONER CRUISING GUIDE — 267

VANCOUVER, MAINLAND B.C. & THE SUNSHINE COAST

located but exposed to Vancouver Harbour on the south. No charge for the first 3 hours of stay. Thereafter, call the City of North Vancouver (604) 982-3910 to make payment.

The City of North Vancouver has two other docks nearby. The Goldsworthy Pier float has 36 feet of day-use only space with stays limited to 3 hours at no charge. The Burrard Dry Dock is for large vessels and requires prior arrangement scheduling and a signed agreement.

⑪ **Mosquito Creek Marina.** 415 West Esplanade, North Vancouver, BC V7M 1A6; (604) 987-4113; mcmb_dockmaster@squamish.net; www.mosquitocreekmarina.com. Open all year with guest moorage in unoccupied slips, reservations recommended. 15, 30 & 50 amp power (100 amp on Dock A), washrooms and laundry, Wi-Fi, 50-ton Travelift, water, pumpout, marine repairs, security gates, 24-hour security. Fuel dock with mid-grade gasoline, high-speed diesel, ice, bait and fishing supplies. On-site cafe located in a double-wide trailer near the office.

The marina is operated by the Squamish Nation. A mixture of open moorage and covered moorage with a variety of slip sizes. Know your assigned slip and study the Mosquito Creek Marina dock diagram before entering the marina as dock and slip signage is lacking. Replacement of finger piers and decking is on-going. Future plans include removal of F-dock allowing a wider entrance to the marina.

A foot path connects the marina with Lonsdale Quay shopping, with restaurants and a farmers market. Several boat repair companies with complete services are on-site. It's a 10-minute walk to the SeaBus foot ferries to downtown Vancouver.

⑪ **Lynnwood Marina.** 1681 Columbia St., North Vancouver, BC V7J 1A5; (604) 985-1533; info@lynnwoodmarina.com; www.lynnwoodmarina.com. Moorage for repair customers only. The marina has 15 & 30 amp power, complete repairs, and haulout to 60 tons. Shopping is about a 10-minute walk away.

See Area Map Page 264 - Maps Not for Navigation

BURNABY, PORT MOODY, INDIAN ARM

Second Narrows. To proceed eastward from Vancouver Harbour to Burnaby and Port Moody, you first must go through Second Narrows. On spring tides, flood currents can reach 6.5 knots and ebb currents 5.5 knots. The narrows are not to be treated lightly. Wind and current opposing each other can create standing waves and difficult seas. The best advice is to go through near times of slack, although on small tides the current should present few problems for boats with adequate power. Current predictions are shown as a secondary station in the Tide and Current Tables Vol. 5, and Ports and Passes. Due to extensive heavy displacement commercial traffic, monitor Vessel Traffic Service on VHF channel 12. Sailing is not permitted in Second Narrows.

Cates Park. Cates Park is at Roche Point, near the entrance to Indian Arm. The park has a paved launch ramp, beach, trails, playground, changing room, and picnic shelter. Temporary anchorage only.

Burnaby. The park at Burnaby is the site of an old sawmill. The park has no public float, but anchorage is good just east of the fishing pier.

Port Moody. Port Moody ends in drying flats, but a dredged channel on the south shore leads through the flats to Rocky Point Park. The park has a launch ramp, swimming pool and picnic areas, and is the location of the Port Moody Museum. A large designated anchorage area is located at the head of the bay with protection from all except northwesterly winds. This is an industrial area with commercial traffic.

⑫ **Reed Point Marina.** 850 Barnet Highway, Bldg. #1, Port Moody, BC V6H 1V6; (604) 937-1600; office@reedpoint.com; www.reedpoint.com. Open all year, mid-grade gasoline and diesel. Washrooms, showers, pumpout, haulout to 55 tons, chandlery, sundries, restaurant, marine supplies and service. Permanent moorage only.

INDIAN ARM

Indian Arm extends 11 miles into Coast Range mountains soaring to 5000 feet. Indian Arm is largely unpopulated beyond Deep Cove, because Deep Cove is the end of the road from North Vancouver. The waters in Indian Arm generally are calm, but can be ruffled by local downdraft winds off the mountains. Indian Arm is a little secret that Vancouver boaters cherish. It feels remote, yet it is close to the city.

Indian Arm Marine Park. In 1996 the Indian Arm Marine Park was expanded from the Twin Islands and Racoon Island to include most of the fjord. Croker Island and Granite Falls are part of the park.

Belcarra. Belcarra Regional Park is located on the east shore of Indian Arm, near the entrance. The public float is for loading and unloading only. Anchorage is good. The park has 2 lakes, 4 miles of shoreline, and complete facilities. It's a popular stop.

Strathcona. The small Strathcona municipal float is at the mouth of Indian Arm across from Belcarra, behind White Rock and the Grey Rocks Islands. The float dries at low tide.

⑬ **Deep Cove.** Deep Cove is a city of about 5,000 people. The public float provides access to shopping in the town of Deep Cove for vessels up to 36 feet, no overnight moorage. The commercial village, adjacent to the public float, is upscale. Deep Cove is the location of the Deep Cove Yacht Club. Deep Cove Northshore Marina has moorage, fuel, and other amenities. Speed limit in Deep Cove is 5 knots.

⑬ **Deep Cove Public Wharf.** The dock is 145 feet long, and is within walking distance of grocery stores, restaurants, live theater, and other facilities. Day use only, for boats up to 36 feet, no overnight moorage.

⑬ **Deep Cove North Shore Marina.** 2890 Panorama Drive, North Vancouver, BC V7G 1V6; (604) 929-1251; info@deepcovemarina.com; www.deepcovemarina.com. Open all year, gasoline and diesel at the fuel dock, limited guest moorage in unoccupied slips and side-tie. Call ahead. Facilities include washrooms, showers, laundry, and convenience store. Deep Cove Village with restaurants and shopping is located a mile to the west.

Bedwell Bay. Bedwell Bay has the best anchorage in Indian Arm. The bay is sheltered from southerly winds. The anchorage can be crowded during peak season. Speed limit 5 knots.

Twin Islands and Racoon Island. The larger of the Twin Islands has a dinghy float on its east side, and picnic and sanitary facili-

Remote and scenic Deep Cove is a surprisingly short distance from metro-Vancouver.

ties ashore. Anchorage offshore is quite deep (between 80 and 150 feet). Twin Islands and Racoon Island are used by kayakers and canoeists who pull their craft ashore.

Granite Falls. Granite Falls, the largest of the falls entering Indian Arm, tumbles off a cliff along the east bank. A small day dock makes access easy and serves campsites ashore. Anchorage is fair just offshore. The climb up the cliff is good exercise for cramped muscles. Because of the questionable anchoring bottom, overnight anchoring is not recommended if outflow winds are expected.

Wigwam Inn. The Wigwam Inn, at the head of Indian Arm, was a luxury resort whose rich history goes back to 1906. Today it is a Royal Vancouver Yacht Club outstation. RVYC members only. Burrard Yacht Club and Deep Cove Yacht Club have outstations nearby—members only, no reciprocals.

POINT ATKINSON TO HORSESHOE BAY

Caulfeild Cove. Caulfeild Cove is a tiny bight, protected from nearly all winds and seas, tucked into the shoreline just east of Point Atkinson. A 52-foot public float lies along the east side of the cove with 6 feet of depth alongside.

Point Atkinson. Point Atkinson is the north entrance to Burrard Inlet.

LOCAL KNOWLEDGE

TIDE-RIPS: The waters just off Point Atkinson can be very rough, especially on a large ebb flowing against a fresh onshore wind. Often, a course well to seaward is called for, and even that can be heavy going. Point Atkinson is well known to Vancouver boaters, who give this area great respect.

Eagle Harbour. Eagle Harbour is the home of the Eagle Harbour Yacht Club. No guest moorage.

Fishermans Cove. Fishermans Cove, the home of West Vancouver Yacht Club, is filled with Thunderbird Marina. West Vancouver Yacht Club has some guest moorage for members of reciprocal clubs.

Important: Enter on the northwest side of the 39-meter island and Eagle Island, leaving the flashing red light to starboard. A "false entrance" between the 39-meter island and Eagle Island could put you in real trouble.

The passage from Eagle Harbour east of Eagle Island is shown clearly on Plans Chart 3534 but not on smaller scale Chart 3481.

The daymark in the northern mouth of the passage east of Eagle Island has been changed from port hand to starboard hand. This daymark relates to craft approaching from the north side of Eagle Island. Those craft should leave that daymark to starboard, to stay between the daymark and the docks on the north side of Fishermans Cove. Vessels northbound from Eagle Harbour should leave the daymark to port.

⑭ **Thunderbird Marina.** 5776 Marine Drive, West Vancouver, BC V7W 2S2; (604) 921-7484; thunderbird@thunderbirdmarine.com; www.thunderbirdmarine.com. Permanent moorage only. Haulout to 25 tons for boats to 50 feet. Do-it-yourself or use trades people boatyard. Thunderbird Marine Supplies carries marine supplies and hardware.

HOWE SOUND

Howe Sound, about 12 miles from Vancouver, is the "backyard" for Vancouver area boaters. Stunning Coast Range mountains surround Howe Sound. Since the sound is largely unpopulated, it provides a wilderness setting close to the city.

Watch for the considerable drift floating in Howe Sound.

⑮ **Horseshoe Bay.** Horseshoe Bay is the eastern terminus of ferries serving the Gulf Islands, Sunshine Coast, and Vancouver Island. Sewell's Marina, a large breakwater-protected public marina, is located to the west of the ferry docks. Boaters transiting this area are urged to use caution because of the steady procession of large ferry boats.

⑮ **Sewell's Marina Ltd.** 6409 Bay St., West Vancouver, BC V7W 3H5; (604) 921-3474; info@sewellsmarina.com; www.sewellsmarina.com. Open all year, gasoline and diesel fuel, ice, limited 15 & 30 amp power, concrete launch ramp, frozen bait. Limited guest moorage, mostly for boats 45 feet and under, call ahead. Fishing charters. Restaurants, groceries, and a post office nearby.

⑮ **Horseshoe Bay Public Wharf.** (604) 925-7129. Guest float, approximately 100 feet, on the south side of the wharf for short-term tie-up, maximum 4 hour stay. A float on the east end of the wharf is a 10-minute pick-up, drop-off area.

⑯ **Sunset Marina Ltd.** 34 Sunset Beach, West Vancouver, BC V7W 2T7; (604) 921-7476; sunsetmarina@shawlink.ca; www.sunsetmarinaltd.com. Open from March 1 to October 15. Gasoline, guest moorage to 24 feet, haulouts to 25 feet (power boats only), repairs, launch ramp with long term parking, washrooms. They carry marine supplies, tackle, and bait.

Bowen Island. Bowen Island is served by ferry from Horseshoe Bay. Snug Cove has a public wharf and two marinas. It's a wonderful destination with shops, a number of good restaurants, and a 600-acre park. A co-op store up the hill from the harbor has provisions. On the northeast corner of Bowen Island, Columbine

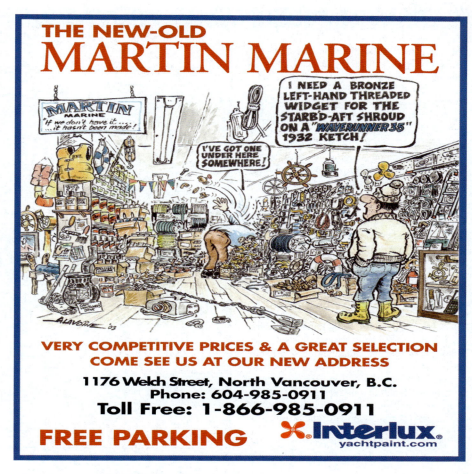

VANCOUVER, MAINLAND B.C. & THE SUNSHINE COAST

Bay and Smugglers Cove offer good anchorage. Galbraith Bay has a public float. Anchorage is in Bowen Bay and Tunstall Bay.

⑰ **Snug Cove.** Snug Cove on Bowen Island is a favorite stop. It has a public dock and two marinas, and is served by ferry from Horseshoe Bay. From there you can take a bus to downtown Vancouver. Or take the seasonal foot ferry that runs directly to Granville Island.

The commercial village at Bowen Island has several boutiques, restaurants, grocery store, bakery/coffee house, pharmacy, wine store and liquor agency, and a couple of pubs. Bowen Island residents are artistic, interesting, and eclectic, and the local shopping reflects the character of the population. A public market with bakery, locally grown items, crafts and artwork is in the green building above the marina, open Saturdays and Sundays in July and August.

Pubs: New for 2018, visit Bowen Island Pub located in an impressive building up the hill; also new at Snug Cove is the Copper Spirit Distillery with a selection of locally crafted vodka, gin and whisky.

Dock Dance: The annual Dock Dance, a benefit dance for the local volunteer firefighters, is held in early August. Participants take over the dock at Snug Cove for a party that literally rocks the dock with music and dancing.

Golf: The 9-hole par 35 Bowen Island Golf Club is challenging and beautiful, with greens that are devilishly hard to read. Call (604) 947-4653. Union Steamship Co. provides transportation for its guests.

Ferry Noise: Ferry propellers make underwater noise that can sometimes be heard throughout Snug Cove. If you hear what you think is an onboard pump cycling ON whenever a ferry is at the dock, realize that it may actually be noise transmitted from the ferry's props to your hull.

⑰ **Bowen Island Marina.** 375 Cardena Dr., RR 1 A-1, Bowen Island, BC V0N 1G0; (604) 947-9710; norma@bowen-island.com; www.bowen-island.com. Open all year, limited guest moorage, reservations required, 15 amp power. Located on the starboard side when entering Snug Cove. Shops with ice cream, pies, pastries, gifts and kayak rentals.

⑰ **Snug Cove Public Wharf.** (604) 328-5499. This wide concrete dock, with 350 feet of space, is next to the ferry landing in Snug Cove and exposed to ferry wash. No water or electricity.

⑰ **Union Steamship Co. Marina.** P.O. Box 250, Bowen Island, BC V0N 1G0; (604) 947-0707; marina@ussc.ca; www.unionsteamshipmarina.com. Monitors VHF 66A. Open all year, ample guest moorage, pumpout, 30 & 50 amp power, a boaters lounge with washrooms and showers, laundry, free Wi-Fi. The washroom and shower building, one of the finest on the coast, also includes a comfortable lounge with big screen TV and a computer station, all near the showers and laundry.

This is an excellent place to stop. Rondy Dike, an architect by training, and his wife Dorothy have restored the Union Steamship Co. landing into a wonderful destination resort. Their daughter, Oydis Dike Nickle, and her husband Dean, now manage the resort and marina. The staff is attentive and standing by to help. A lovely boardwalk leads from the marina, connecting several shops, cafes, and Doc Morgan's Pub & Restaurant. Easy walking trails are found through the adjacent 600-acre park. It seems that everyone who stays at Union Steamship has a good report. Reservations recommended.

The marina has 8 cottages available, reasonable rates.

Mount Gardner Park Public Dock. Galbraith Bay, northwest side of Bowen Island. Has 110 feet of space.

Gambier Island. Gambier Island has three significant inlets, all opening from the south: West Bay, Centre Bay, and Port Graves. A smaller inlet, Halkett Bay, is at the southeast corner of the island. Thornbrough Bay, on the west side of the island, has a public dock. We are told that boats often tie to log booms on the western (Port Mellon) side of the island. In the summertime the water around Gambier Island warms to swimming temperatures. We know, we tried it.

Gambier Harbour Public Wharf has 100 feet of dock space.

Burrard Yacht Club and Thunderbird Yacht Club have outstations at Eakins Point at the north end of Gambier Island. Members only, no reciprocals.

West Bay. Favor the west shore when entering West Bay to avoid the reef extending from the eastern shore. West Bay once was a major log booming site and the bottom is apt to be foul with old cable and equipment.

Anchorage in West Bay is in at least two places. The first is on the north side of the reef, close to the reef. The second is in the bight at the northeast corner of the bay. Easy anchoring depths are close to shore in this bight, but because of real estate development, you probably shouldn't run a stern-tie to shore.

Centre Bay. Most of Centre Bay is deep, but the little bight on the west side, just inside the entrance, has 18- to 24-foot anchoring depths, and is delightful. Royal Vancouver and West Vancouver yacht clubs have outstations in Centre Bay. The docks belonging to the Centre Bay Yacht Station are at the head of the bay.

Port Graves. Port Graves is definitely the most scenic of Gambier Island's inlets and has good anchoring depths at the head. Because of real estate development in West Bay and Centre Bay, Port Graves is the best anchoring spot on the island. A public wharf with a small float is located at the head of the bay, and a private dock is a short distance to the west. Anchor in the area off the docks and between them to avoid snagging logging cables on the bottom.

Halkett Bay. Halkett Bay at the southeast corner of Gambier Island has room for 4 to 5 boats, but chop can be somewhat active in southerly winds. Rocks are on the west side of the bay. Approach along the east shoreline. A small float provides access to Halkett Bay Marine Park with pit toilets, primitive campsites, and trails.

Snug Cove

See Area Map Page 264 - Maps Not for Navigation

VANCOUVER, MAINLAND B.C. & THE SUNSHINE COAST

Brigade Bay. Brigade Bay is on the eastern shore of Gambier Island. Anne Vipond, reporting in Pacific Yachting, suggests that because of deep water fairly close to shore, a stern anchor be set toward the beach and the main anchor set offshore.

Thornbrough Bay. The New Brighton Public Wharf in Thornbrough Bay has 390 feet of dock space.

⑱ **Plumper Cove Marine Park.** Plumper Cove Marine Park is in a cove formed by Keats Island and two small nearby islands. The park has 400 feet of dock space and several mooring buoys. Correspondent Jim Norris reports wave action at the dock. The bay has anchorage for quite a few boats. A rock, marked by a yellow buoy, lies a dozen yards off the dock.

Porteau Cove. Porteau Cove is on the east shore of Howe Sound in Montagu Channel at latitude 49°33'N. The park is open all year; toilets, launch ramp, walk-in campsites, hiking trails and a picnic area. Tiny Porteau Cove itself has 1 mooring buoy. Sunken ships and man-made reefs provide excellent scuba diving. White caution buoys mark the yellow-buoyed diving area. Watch your depths; some of the cove dries at low tide.

⑲ **Lions Bay Marine Ltd.** 60 Lions Bay Ave., P.O. Box 262, Lions Bay, BC V0N 2E0; (604) 921-7510; www.lionsbaymarina.com. Open all year, except closed December 15 to January 15. In winter, closed on Tuesday and Wednesday. Gasoline, diesel and propane available. In summer they have transient moorage on 400 feet of dock space. Haulout to 30 feet (powerboats only) with repairs on site. Groceries and a post office are nearby.

⑳ **Squamish.** www.squamish.ca. The town of Squamish, pop. 15,000, is nestled against the Coast Range mountains at the north end of Howe Sound, on the road between Vancouver and Whistler. Since the 2010 Winter Olympics at nearby Whistler, Squamish has become a pretty vibrant place. A bus runs to Whistler, or you can rent a car. Shopping and two golf courses are an easy drive away. The superb Furry Creek course is a little farther. The new Sea to Sky Gondola is about 2.5 miles from the docks and the views from the top are outstanding. The shopping district is about one-quarter mile from the docks, and the pub is closer. Summertime inflow winds usually begin between 11:00 a.m. and noon. By 2:00 p.m., the wind can make landing tricky. Best to go to Squamish in the early morning.

⑳ **Harbour Authority of Squamish Boat Harbour.** P.O. Box 97, Squamish, BC V8B 0A1; (604) 892-3725. Open all year. Located near downtown Squamish with 2000 lineal feet of dock space and 200 feet of summer transient moorage. Next to the Squamish Yacht Club. Pumpout, 15 amp power, washrooms, showers, boat launch. The docks are full in the winter, but open up a little in the summer; definitely call

Plumper Cove Marine Park has an excellent dock, but no power or water. The yellow buoy pictured here marks a rock.

ahead. Expect a relaxed, informal experience. They don't get many visitor boats. The Port Captain for SYC can be reached at (604) 815-9533; reciprocals are available for just about any yacht club. Within walking distance of downtown.

Shoal Channel (The Gap). The Gap is a sandy shoal with a least depth of approximately 5 feet at zero tide, between Keats Island and Steep Bluff, at the mouth of Howe Sound. Although waves off the Strait of Georgia tend to break on this shoal, if you know your draft and the state of the tide you can approach Gibsons from the strait via The Gap and have no problems—unless it's rough, and then you should go around Keats Island. Stay mid-channel. Boulders line the edges of the passage. The distance to Thrasher Rock, outside Gabriola Pass in the Gulf Islands, is approximately 16 miles. Use Chart 3463 for the crossing, changing to Chart 3526 as you approach Popham Island. This approach, with Howe Sound islands backed up by the Coast Range mountains, is magnificent.

Correspondent Pat Shera says you can cross Shoal Channel at anything but low tides

UNION STEAMSHIP MARINE RESORT BOWEN ISLAND

JUST OFF THE COAST OF ORDINARY

- The "Best" showers on the West Coast
- Guest moorage for vessels up to 210'
- 8 nautical miles from downtown
- Doc Morgan's Pub & Restaurant
- Chandlery & Gift Store
- 30 & 50 amp service
- Free Wi-Fi

Union Steamship Marine Resort
Bowen Island, BC
email: marina@ussc.ca
Marina: 604.947.0707 • VHF: 66A

www.unionsteamshipmarina.com

2018 WAGGONER CRUISING GUIDE   271

VANCOUVER, MAINLAND B.C. & THE SUNSHINE COAST

See Area Map Page 264 - Maps Not for Navigation

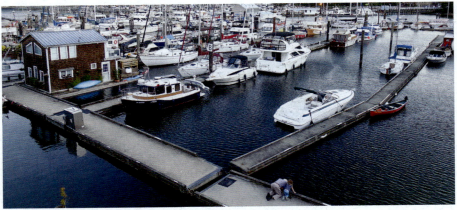

Docks at Gibsons Landing Harbour Authority

using a natural range. Keep the FlG (flashing green) light located east of the Gibsons Harbour entrance just barely visible in line with the base of Steep Bluff in the foreground. This transit takes you across the shoals with a minimum depth of 7 feet at zero tide. Travel along the 20- to 30-foot depth contour from either side until this natural range lines up, then stay on the range until you reach 20- to 30-foot depths on the other side. Not recommended when a strong southerly is blowing.

㉑ **Gibsons.** Gibsons is a charming seaside village, a good place to take the day off and stretch your legs. The lower Gibsons downtown area is filled with shops, restaurants, and pubs ranging from elegant to funky. The Sunshine Coast Museum & Archives is excellent. Hours are 10:30 a.m. to 4:30 p.m., Tuesday through Saturday.

The nearest supermarket is SuperValu in upper Gibsons. You'll need a ride. Be sure to see Fong's Market & Gifts in lower Gibsons, one of the more unexpected places on the coast. They have many of the essential grocery items, a good selection of Asian foods and a broad array of bowls, tea pots and other imported items. The Gibsons Market is just up from the Gibsons Marina. Some may remember the Market from earlier visits. In 2016 they expanded (rebuilt) the Gibsons market to be a 2-story building with more local produce, crafts and an aquarium. They re-used the cupola from the old building by lifting it up to the top of the new building by crane.

As you enter the marina complex at Gibsons you will see The Gibsons Landing Harbour Authority public dock to the north. Gibsons Marina and Fuel Dock are ahead and to the south; the fuel dock is straight ahead and the marina is to the left. There are several private docks and a private marina behind the breakwater at Gibsons. A shoal extends from the shore between the public dock and the fuel dock. Approach each moorage directly from seaward.

Some boats anchor outside the breakwater and to the east of the pier, in front of the townsite. This is unprotected and suitable only in settled weather.

Sea Cavalcade: The Sea Cavalcade festival, featuring food, dancing, fireworks and other events, is held each July. See www.seacavalcade.ca.

㉑ **Gibsons Landing Harbour Authority.** P.O. Box 527, Gibsons, BC V0N 1V0; (604) 886-8017; glha@telus.net; www.gibsonsha.org. Monitors VHF 66A. Open all year, guest moorage, 15, 30, 50 and 100 amp power but mostly 15 amp with 20 amp receptacles, 3-ton crane, washrooms and showers, laundry, pumpout, garbage dumpster. The public wharf has been upgraded with beautiful offices, improved shoreside amenities, and surveillance television security. Much of the moorage space is taken by permanent tenants, but they work to fit visitors in. Reservations for vessels 45 feet and up are accepted. A year-round 80-foot long float for short-term stays up to 4 hours is on the shore side of the wharf, outside of the breakwater protected harbour. Register and pay at the Harbour Authority Office.

㉑ **Gibsons Marina and Fuel Dock.** P.O. Box 1520, Gibsons, BC V0N 1V0; (604) 886-8686 (marina), (604) 886-9011 (fuel dock). Monitors VHF 66A. Both Gibsons Marina and Hyak Marine were purchased by a local developer in 2015 and have been combined into Gibsons Marina and Fuel Dock. In 2016, the fuel dock still carried the name Hyak Fuel Dock. Open all year except Christmas Day. Guest moorage, call ahead for availability, 15 and some 30 amp power, free Wi-Fi, washrooms, showers, well-stocked chandlery, laundry, pumpout, garbage, recycling, concrete launch ramp. The fuel dock has gasoline and diesel. The store on the fuel dock has lubricants, snacks, and ice cream.

GOWER POINT TO SECHELT INLET

From Howe Sound to Pender Harbour the coast is largely a barren run. The exceptions are Buccaneer Bay, Secret Cove, Smuggler Cove, and to a lesser extent, Halfmoon Bay. When the weather gets up the going can be wet and slow; but with a weather eye, the passages can be easy.

Trail Bay. A rock breakwater protects a small moorage at **Selma Park** on the south shore of Trail Bay. We once waited out a nasty southeasterly, riding on the hook in this hideout.

LOCAL KNOWLEDGE

STRONG CURRENTS: Currents run to 3 knots at the north end of Welcome Passage and

Gibsons Landing

Sunshine Coast and Jervis Inlet

VANCOUVER, MAINLAND B.C. & THE SUNSHINE COAST

See Area Map Page 273 - Maps Not for Navigation

2 knots off Merry Island at the south end. When wind and current oppose each other the waters can be rough and uncomfortable. Watch for drift.

Welcome Passage. Welcome Passage separates South Thormanby Island from Sechelt Peninsula and is used by boats of all types bound up or down the Sunshine Coast. The passage west of Merry Island is deep and easily navigated.

Halfmoon Bay. A public dock with 170 feet of mooring space is at the head of Halfmoon Bay. It is very shallow on the land side of the mooring float. Onshore, walk about a half block through a residential neighborhood to an area with a store (a longtime landmark) and a cafe with fresh bakery. Henry Hightower, a resident of Halfmoon Bay and a Grenfell 32 owner, provided us with the following insider's view of the facilities and anchorage possibilities. He writes:

"The store at the Halfmoon Bay government wharf is well stocked, and has the best bacon and free-range eggs, as well as fresh and packaged meat, fruit, vegetables and staples, fishing gear, beer, wine and liquor, convenience store stuff, and a gift shop." After visiting, we agree.

If a strong wind is blowing or forecast, there will almost certainly be at least one tug and log boom fixed across the open south side of Priestland Cove, between the shore and the charted rocks. There is quite a bit of room to anchor behind its shelter.

Dockside dining at Smitty's Oyster House

Priestland Cove is southeast of the government dock.

㉒ **Smuggler Cove.** Smuggler Cove has a narrow entrance through the rocks, but opens to a beautiful anchorage that is protected from most weather. We have received reports that the cove is not protected from northwesterlies. Before entering, first-timers should have in hand Sheet 3 from Sunshine Coast Strip Chart 3311 or Plans Chart 3535. Both charts show Smuggler Cove clearly, but Chart 3311's scale of 1:6000 is even clearer than Chart 3535's 1:10,000 scale. As both charts show, the channel is very close to the Isle Capri side of the entrance in order to avoid rocky shoals extending from the south shore. Inside is Smuggler Cove Marine Park, which has no facilities for boaters or campers, but does have trails through the park's 400 acres of woodlands. A favorite activity is paddling a kayak or dinghy among the little islets and coves. Reduce swinging room by taking a stern-tie to yellow painted rings set in the rock ashore.

No Discharge Zone. Gray water okay.

Buccaneer Bay. Buccaneer Bay is between North Thormanby and South Thormanby Is-

274

secretcove MARINA

The sunshine coast's best kept secret for moorage, fuel, dining & supplies . . .

marina
visitor moorage
up to 150', with
water, power

fuel dock

services
showers, recycling
BroadbandXpress Wireless

store
B.C. liquor agency
groceries, meats & produce
marine supplies & hardware
tackle, fishing licences
baked goods, organic coffee
books, magazines
charts & clothing
giftware, cuban cigars

close to Smugglers Cove & the beaches of Thornamby Island

+ the upper deck restaurant

monitoring VHF channel **66A**
www.secretcovemarina.com
1-866-885-3533
5411 Secret Cove Road, Box 1118 Sechelt B.C. V0N 3A0
reservations recommended in summer months

the upper deck restaurant
fully licenced
gourmet dinners
weekend brunch
casual breakfasts & lunches

www.WaggonerGuide.com

See Area Map Page 273 - Maps Not for Navigation

VANCOUVER, MAINLAND B.C. & THE SUNSHINE COAST

lands, and has a beautiful white sand beach at the south end and west side.

Be careful to enter Buccaneer Bay by leaving the Tattenham Ledge Light Buoy Q51 to port. The buoy is well north of South Thormanby Island, but it marks the end of Tattenham Ledge and should be respected.

Once in Buccaneer Bay, anchor in 30 to 40 feet behind the Surrey Islands or in 20 to 30 feet in Water Bay. The Surrey Islands anchorage is particularly cozy and attractive.

A private moorage is in Water Bay. During the day small boat traffic to and from the dock will rock you some, but it dies down at night. The dock is posted for loading/unloading only, 2-hour maximum.

Watching your depths, you can also snug up to the shoaling waters off Gill Beach at the south end of the bay. In a southeasterly, you'll get some wind but no seas. There's no protection from a northwesterly, however. One year we anchored in calm conditions, only to have a northwesterly come in around midnight and ruin our night's sleep. It was pretty bouncy.

Secret Cove. Secret Cove has three branches, each with excellent weather protection and easy anchoring depths. Unfortunately, the Secret Cove bottom is notorious for anchor dragging in strong winds, so be sure you are well set if you do anchor.

Enter Secret Cove north of a light on a small rock in the middle of the entrance. Inside are the three arms. The southern arm has a very narrow entrance but adequate depths inside. This arm is lined with private docks that restrict swinging room in the middle. You can find room, however, off the Royal Vancouver Yacht Club outstation docks about halfway in. Correspondents James and Jennifer Hamilton have anchored there and report the holding ground is excellent. The center arm has Buccaneer Marina. The north arm is occupied almost entirely by Secret Cove Marina, but there is still

Public pier and beautiful Vaucroft Beach on North Thormanby Island

plenty of room for anchoring, using stern-ties to shore if needed. A public float is adjacent to Secret Cove Marina. It is primarily used by local commercial fish boats.

㉓ **Secret Cove Public Wharf.** Dock has 144 feet of moorage with 20 amp power, no water. Primarily used by local commercial fish boats.

㉓ **Secret Cove Marina.** 511 Secret Cove Road, Sechelt, BC V0N 3A0; (866) 885-3533; info@secretcovemarina.com; www.secretcovemarina.com. Monitors VHF 66A. Open April 1 through Canadian Thanksgiving. This is a full service marina in the north arm of Secret Cove, with gasoline and diesel fuel, guest moorage, 15 & 30 amp power, washrooms, clean showers, liquor agency, restaurant, store with groceries, gift items, clothing, block and cube ice, boating and fishing supplies, Wi-Fi. Fishing charters, golf shuttles, moped, canoe, and paddleboat rentals. Reservations requested. This marina resort is well managed and continues to receive excellent reviews.

The store has a wide range of foods and other essentials, including gifts and a good liquor and wine selection.

㉔ **Buccaneer Marina & Resort Ltd.** 5535 Sans Souci Rd., Halfmoon Bay, BC V0N 1Y2; (604) 885-7888; buccaneermarina@telus.net; www.buccaneermarina.com. Open all year,

CHARTS	
3311 Small craft charts (strip charts)	Sunshine Coast to Desolation Sound
3312 Small craft chart (chartbook)	Jervis Inlet & Desolation Sound
3512	Strait of Georgia, Central Portion (1:80,000)
3514	Jervis Inlet (1:50,000); Malibu and Sechelt Rapids
3535 Plans	Malaspina Strait: Pender Harbour, Secret Cove/ Smuggler Cove, Welcome Passage

gasoline and diesel fuel, limited guest moorage with 15 amp power, chandlery, engine and outboard repairs (weekdays), propane, haulout to 40 feet, paved launch ramp with long term parking. Fishing tackle and one of the few places with live herring bait. Water taxi to Thormanby Islands. Located in the center arm of Secret Cove. Owned and operated by the Mercer family since 1968.

Bargain Bay. Although its entry is actually off the Strait of Georgia, Bargain Bay is properly a part of the complex of bays that make up Pender Harbour. Enter between Edgecomb Island to the east and Francis Peninsula to the west. The entry is easy and open until you are part way inside, where a drying reef and an underwater rock extend from the west shore to the middle of the channel. Another underwater rock lies off the east shore. Pass between the two rocks and proceed into the bay.

Bargain Narrows, called Canoe Pass, is a drying channel spanned by a bridge with 4 meters (13.12 feet) vertical clearance. The pass runs between Bargain Bay and Gerrans Bay inside Pender Harbour.

PENDER HARBOUR

Pender Harbour is a natural stopover for boats heading north or south in the Strait of Georgia. For northbound boats, it's just the right distance for a day's run from Nanaimo, Silva Bay, or Howe Sound. For boats southbound from Desolation Sound, it's a good place to prepare for the long, exposed legs across the Strait of Georgia or down the Sunshine Coast. Boats bound to or from Princess Louisa Inlet often use Pender Harbour both going and coming.

Pender Harbour has good marinas, good anchorages, good eating, and good shopping. It has fuel and a haulout and repair facility. Diving services available through Wet Dock Divers (604-740-5969). The harbor is nestled against steep mountains; the scenery is beautiful. It's a good place for walking and hiking. If you carry trail bikes, the Madeira Park Public Wharf has a map of the nearby Suncoaster Trail, built and maintained by volunteers.

Pender Harbour is not a single large bay. It is a complex of coves, each with its own personality. Most cruisers will go down the north side. At the back, Hospital Bay and Garden Bay

Secret Cove

2018 WAGGONER CRUISING GUIDE

VANCOUVER, MAINLAND B.C. & THE SUNSHINE COAST

Reference Only – Not for Navigation

Pender Harbour

have marinas, fuel, shopping, and dining. The best anchorage is in Garden Bay. John Henry's Resort & Marina is the only place for fuel in Pender Harbour. Madeira Park, in the southeast corner of Pender Harbour, has moorage, haulout and repairs. A shopping center is a short walk from the Madeira Park dock.

Pender Harbour has several drying and underwater rocks throughout, but most of them are marked. With Chart 3535 (or good electronic charts) and a little care, you should have no problems.

Pender Harbour Blues Festival: Early June, www.penderharbourbluesfestival.com.

Pender Harbour Jazz Festival: September. Musicians and audiences from around the world. Performances in venues all around Pender Harbour. About one-quarter of the events are ticketed, the rest are free. *Pender Harbour Chamber Music Festival*, mid- August. For both festivals and more see www.penderharbourmusic.ca.

Transportation: There's no bus or taxi service. Use your dinghy, or try the **Slo-Cat Harbour Ferry**, based in Madeira Park, for excursions or shopping trips. Call Slo-Cat on VHF 66A.

Golf: The Pender Harbour Golf Club 9-hole course is terrific, but you'll have to find a ride to get there.

Irvines Landing Marina & Pub. Closed.

㉕ **Pender Harbour Resort and Marina.** 4686 Sinclair Bay Road, Garden Bay, BC V0N 1S1; (877) 883-2424; (604) 551-2742 (phone or text); info@phrm.ca; www.phrm.ca. Open all year with moorage to 50 feet. Water, 15 & 30 amp power, Wi-Fi, showers, laundry, launch ramp, garbage and recycling drop. Marina guests have access to all resort amenities, including heated seasonal swimming pool, fire pit, gazebo, and sports field. Cottages, motel rooms, yurts, campsite, boats, stand-up paddleboards, and kayaks are available to rent. There is a small store in the office with snacks, essentials, bait and gifts.

Hospital Bay. Hospital Bay is on the west side of Garden Peninsula, facing the mouth of

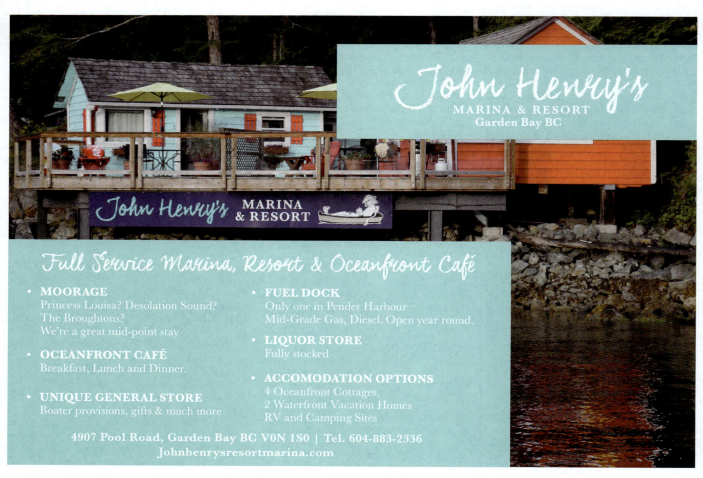

Pender Harbour. The harbor is home to the former Fisherman's Resort and Marina (now part of John Henry's), John Henry's store and fuel dock, and a public dock. John Henry's store is not quite a supermarket, but it is very well stocked with food items, gifts, books and a liquor agency. Hospital Bay is also the site of the St. Mary's Columbia Coast Mission Hospital building, built in 1929 and now the newly renovated Sundowner Inn.

A narrow isthmus divides Hospital Bay from Garden Bay with a walkway between the two. LaVerne's, a local favorite diner, is located here. The milkshakes are legendary. Locals rave about breakfasts, too.

㉖ **Fisherman's Resort & Marina.** Fisherman's Resort and Marina was purchased in 2015 and is now part of John Henry's. See the listing below.

㉖ **John Henry's Resort & Marina.** P.O. Box 40, 4907 Pool Lane, Garden Bay, BC V0N 1S0; Moorage: (604) 883-2336 Store: (604) 883-2253; info@johnhenrysresortmarina.com; www.johnhenrysresortmarina.com. Monitors VHF 66A. John Henry's and Fisherman's Resort are now operated as a single entity. Open all year with 2300 feet of moorage, water, 20, 30 & 50 amp power, washrooms, showers, laundry, Wi-Fi, garbage, recycling, ice, launch ramp. Gasoline, diesel, 50:1 pre-mix, and propane at the fuel dock. Moorage guests receive a fuel discount. Kayak, SUPs, powerboat, cottage, and RV site rentals available. Kenmore Air and Harbour Air provide float plane service from Seattle and Vancouver.

This is a quiet, well-cared-for marina and resort with beautiful lawns and flower gardens. The well-stocked store above the fuel dock has fresh produce, meats, sandwiches, charts, cruising guides, books, liquor agency, post office, and an ATM. The store also carries tackle, bait, ice, gift items and hand-scooped ice cream. The store at the fuel dock carries snack items, fishing tackle, and boat supplies.

New owners took over the property in 2015. They built a new deck and restaurant at the store and improved the selection throughout the store in 2016. The restaurant with indoor and outdoor seating on the new deck is very good and the portions are substantial. For those familiar with the old John Henry's, it is quite an improvement.

Hospital Bay Public Wharf. Across from the fuel dock in Hospital Bay, 150 feet of overnight moorage, 20 & 30 amp power on all floats, water, garbage disposal at the top of the dock. Portapotties are in the pocket park 200 feet up the road. Close to John Henry's, LaVerne's and the pub in Garden Bay.

Garden Bay. Garden Bay is at the northeast corner of Pender Harbour. The Garden Bay Hotel hasn't been a hotel for a long time, so don't look for rooms to rent. The restaurant and pub have indoor and outdoor seating.

Seattle Yacht Club, Burrard Yacht Club and Royal Vancouver Yacht Club have outstations in Garden Bay—members only, no reciprocals. Many boats anchor out in Garden Bay and dinghy either to the marinas, John Henry's, or to Madeira Park. The Garden Bay holding ground is good and the protection is excellent in most weather.

Garden Bay Provincial Park has about 50 feet of frontage on the north shore. The park has a dinghy dock, toilets, and a network of excellent walking trails, but no other facilities for boaters. Garden Bay Lake, a popular swimming destination, is within walking distance of the Provincial Park.

㉗ **Garden Bay Hotel Marina & Pub.** P.O. Box 90, Garden Bay, BC V0N 1S0; (604) 883-2674; gbhm@dccnet.com; www.gardenbay-pub.com. Monitors VHF 66A. Open all year, 900 feet of moorage, 15 & 30 amp power, washrooms, showers on shore across from the pub entrance, Wi-Fi. This is a large, full-service marina with a popular pub and separate dining area. The pub is open 7 days a week all year, live bands on most summer weekends.

On a beautiful day, the deck overlooking Garden Bay is quite pleasant. A road leads from the pub to Hospital Bay and John Henry's store. A separate walking trail leads along the shore to the Royal Van outstation, and connects with the road to John Henry's.

Hospital Bay

Garden Bay

VANCOUVER, MAINLAND B.C. & THE SUNSHINE COAST

See Area Map Page 276 - Maps Not for Navigation

Guest moorage at Pender Harbour Painted Boat Resort

㉗ **The Pilothouse Marina.** P.O. Box 6, Garden Bay, BC V0N 1S0; (604) 883-2479; (877) 856-2479; office@thepilothousemarina.com; www.thepilothousemarina.com. The marina is closed; see WaggonerGuide.com for updates.

Gunboat Bay. Gunboat Bay, surrounded by high, steep mountains, is entered through a narrow channel with a least depth of 4 feet. An underwater rock lies just to the north of the centerline of the entry channel. Currents in the entry channel are quite strong except at slack water. Although the bay is open and good for anchorage before it peters out into drying flats, few boats anchor there because Garden Bay is so much easier.

㉘ **Sunshine Coast Resort & Marina.** P.O. Box 213, Madeira Park, BC V0N 2H0; (604) 883-9177; (888) 883-9177; vacation@sunshinecoast-resort.com; www.sunshinecoast-resort.com. Monitors VHF 66A. Open all year with moorage for boats to 100 feet, call for reservations, 15 & 30 amp power, water, washrooms, showers, free Wi-Fi, hot tub on the deck, laundry, bait, small boat and kayak rentals, and a hillside lodge with 16 truly outstanding rooms.

The entire property is tidy and well-maintained. Manager Ralph Linnmann is committed to providing attentive customer service.

A steep mountainside rises above the docks. The laundry, showers, and road to town are a considerable climb up the hill, although the office and additional showers are in the new lodge about halfway up. The marina is in the small bay to the right as you approach Gunboat Bay, about a half-mile north of Madeira Park shopping. You can walk to Madeira Park down the hill (and back up to return) or take the dinghy (we'd take the dinghy). Free transportation to the challenging Pender Harbour Golf Club.

㉙ **Madeira Park.** If you want to provision, Madeira Park is where you'll do it. The Harbour Authority Public Wharf is close to two grocery stores (the well-stocked IGA, and the Oak Tree Market with excellent meats and cheeses). The IGA is open 7 days a week 8:30 a.m. to 7:00 p.m., and 8:30 a.m. to 8:00 p.m. in July and August; delivery to the wharf by request. A drugstore, liquor store, bank with ATM, book store, and veterinarian are close by. No laundromat. Madeira Park has a full-service medical clinic. The Grasshopper Pub has been rebuilt and has temporary moorage at their dock while dining or shopping at their liquor store.

㉙ **Harbour Authority of Pender Harbor Madeira Park Public Wharf.** P.O. Box 118, Madeira Park, BC V0N 2H0; (604) 883-2234; penderauthority@telus.net. Monitors VHF 66A. Open all year, 600 feet of dedicated visitor moorage space, 15, 20, 30 and 50 amp power, washrooms, showers, garbage drop for fee, recycling, pumpout, aircraft float, free Wi-Fi. The dinghy dock faces shore, adjacent to the launch ramp. No dinghy check-in is needed and no charge for daytime dinghy tie-up. Marine repair, chandlery, and mechanics nearby.

In recent years considerable upgrading has been done to make Public Wharf not just a dock for the dinghy but a destination in its own right. With donations from local businesses and mostly volunteer labor, walls were built, walkways laid, landscaping installed, new offices constructed with washrooms and showers, a gazebo added, and the docks improved.

㉙ **Madeira Marina.** P.O. Box 189, Madeira Park, BC V0N 2H0; (604) 883-2266; madeiramarine@telus.net. Open all year. Marine railway with haulout to 40 tons, complete marine repairs, parts, indoor painting facility for boats up to 30 feet, and chandlery. Prompt, competent repair service.

Pender Harbour Hotel & Grasshopper Pub. 12671 Sunshine Coast Hwy, Madeira Park, BC V0N 2H0; (604) 883-9013; penderharbourhotel.com. Located in Madeira Park high above Welbourn Cove. The Hotel's private dock has space for temporary moorage while visiting the Grasshopper Pub or shopping at their liquor store. Call for moorage and courtesy pickup at the dock; it's a short but steep walk up the driveway to the Hotel and Pub. Good food and drink with outstanding views.

Gerrans Bay. Gerrans Bay is dotted with rocks, but all of them are marked. It is mostly residential, with some of the homes obviously in the commercial fishing business. Two resorts, the

Madeira Park

278   www.WaggonerGuide.com

Coho Marina (no guest moorage) and the new and lavish Painted Boat Resort & Marina, are in Gerrans Bay.

㉚ **Painted Boat Resort Spa & Marina.** P.O. Box 153, 12849 Lagoon Rd., Madeira Park, BC V0N 2H0; (604) 883-2456; (866) 902-3955; reservations@paintedboat.com; www.paintedboat.com. Open all year with guest moorage to 70 feet, reservations needed. The approach winds through rocks and reefs. We suggest entering carefully with a bow watch. The docks have 15, 30 & 50 amp power. This is a high quality resort with moorage. The upscale but relaxed Restaurant at Painted Boat is open seasonally for dinner, with 280 feet of short term moorage for restaurant patrons. Reservations required. It is elegant with a great view. The full-service spa is beautiful and has eight treatment rooms, two pools and hydrotherapy, available for an additional charge.

㉛ **Whiskey Slough Public Wharf.** Guest moorage along 60 feet of dock, 20 & 30 amp power, no facilities or services. Mostly commercial fish boats here.

Agamemnon Channel. Agamemnon Channel runs northeast between Nelson Island and the mainland, and is the shortest route for those heading for Princess Louisa Inlet, Egmont, or Sechelt Inlet. The only reasonable anchorage is at Green Bay. A private marina is in Agamemnon Bay.

Green Bay. Green Bay is a well-protected small bay on the northwest side of Agamemnon Channel. Prime anchorage is at 30 feet in the cove on the west side of Green Bay in front of the lake shown on the chart. A stream with a waterfall runs from the lake to the cove. A drying reef nearly closes the pass to the back cove to the north of the prime anchoring area.

Backeddy Marina is on the way to Princess Louisa or Sechelt and Sechelt Rapids.

Holding is fair on a hard mud bottom. Use caution approaching and within Green Bay as it is not well charted. Sailing Directions warns of rocks on the east side of the entry to Green Bay which are not shown on the chart. A large uncharted rock/pinnacle with 6 feet of water at zero tide is located mid-channel off a cabin with a small float, on the northeast side of Green Bay, east of the prime anchoring area. We entered favoring the west side of Green Bay. Several cabins, some with private docks, cling to the shore. The gentle sound of the waterfall makes for a restful anchorage.

SECHELT INLET

Egmont. Egmont, on the Sechelt Peninsula, is near the entrance to Skookumchuck Narrows and Sechelt Rapids. Sechelt Inlet lies beyond the rapids. Backeddy Resort & Marina and Bathgate General Store & Marina both have fuel. Backeddy Resort & Marina fronts on Skookumchuck Narrows; Bathgate is closer to the rapids, behind a well-marked reef in Secret Bay. The public dock is adjacent. Beautiful West Coast Wilderness Lodge, with fine dining and more, is immediately south and up the hill from Backeddy Resort & Marina. It's an easy walk between the two, and the view from the dining room and deck at West Coast Wilderness Lodge is a knockout. One of our correspondents reports that their dinner was as good as the view—world class, they said. We agree.

The Egmont Heritage Centre is a short walk up the main road from the marinas.

LOCAL KNOWLEDGE

STRONG CURRENTS: Strong currents can whip through Backeddy Marina. Watch the current as you approach the dock, although dockhands are usually available to assist. Sechelt Rapids currents in the Tide and Current guides will give you an idea of the current direction and force.

DANGEROUS ROCKS: The red triangle day beacon off Backeddy Marina's south docks means Red, Right, Returning for the channel outside. Approaching the docks, leave the beacon to port or you will run up on a rock shelf that extends from shore.

㉜ **Backeddy Resort & Marina.** 16660 Backeddy Rd., Egmont, BC V0N 1N0; (604) 883-2298; (800) 626-0599; info@backeddy.ca; www.backeddy.ca. Monitors VHF 66A. Open all year with guest moorage and services, reservations recommended. Gasoline and diesel fuel, 400 feet of moorage for vessels up to 120 feet. 15 & 30 amp power, washrooms, showers, laundry, garbage drop with fee, Wi-Fi, water at the fuel dock. Cabins, 5 geodesic domes for luxury camping, concrete launch ramp. Float plane access for Kenmore Air and West Coast Air. Small convenience store on site with ice. Backeddy Pub open for

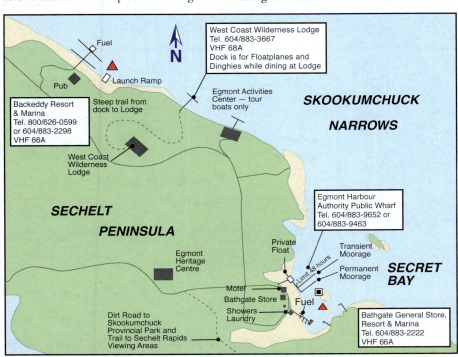
Egmont (Backeddy, Bathgate, Egmont Marinas & Wilderness Lodge)

lunch and dinner, hours vary between October and April, call ahead.

The marina is opposite the Sutton Islets. This is a well-run marina, its rustic exterior hides the well-appointed pub and accommodations. Kayak and bicycle rentals available at the marina. Tours for Princess Louisa Inlet leave from the Backeddy dock. Water taxi service available. The Backeddy fuel dock is the first and last on the way to and from Princess Louisa Inlet.

㉜ **West Coast Wilderness Lodge.** 6649 Maple Road, Egmont, BC V0N 1N0; (604) 883-3667; lodge@wcwl.com; www.wcwl.com. This beautiful luxury lodge is located within easy walking distance from Backeddy Marina and offers a fine dining venue for boaters and lodge guests. Open for breakfast and dinner during the shoulder seasons; breakfast, lunch, and dinner during the summer. Reservations highly recommended during peak season, July and August. The float below the lodge is for seaplanes; however, dingies may tie-up while dining at the lodge, contact on VHF 68A. A steep trail leads from the dock to the lodge. Adventure tours can be booked through the Egmont Adventure Centre located below the Lodge (778-280-8619). Moorage can be found near the Lodge at Backeddy Marina or at Egmont Public Wharf.

㉝ **Bathgate General Store, Resort & Marina.** 6781 Bathgate Rd., Egmont, BC V0N 1N0; (604) 883-2222; info@bathgate.com; www.bathgate.com. Monitors VHF 66A. Open all year, gasoline and diesel at the fuel dock, limited guest moorage, 15, 20 & 30 amp power, showers, washrooms, laundry. Reservations recommended. The docks are beginning to show their age at this popular stop. The store has fresh produce and a good selection of groceries, propane, marine supplies, liquor agency, bait and tackle, block and cube ice. It's the only well-stocked store for miles. Deluxe wheelchair-accessible waterfront motel unit available. Short and long term parking. New owners purchased the property in spring 2015, and have made upgrades to the fuel dock, store, and hotel.

The reef in Secret Bay can confuse a first-time visitor, especially one who isn't that familiar with navigation aids. Remember: Red, Right, Returning. When entering, leave the red daymark well to starboard and you'll have no problems. If you still aren't sure, just remember to go around the ends, not between the two beacons.

㉝ **Egmont Public Wharf.** Managed by the Egmont Harbour Authority, 604-883-9652 or 604-883-9463, two public floats and one private float are accessed from the public wharf. The small float northwest of the wharf is private with no public access. The two large floats south of the wharf are public with permanent moorage on the southerly of these two floats and 150 feet of transient moorage for up to 48 hours on the northerly side of the north float. Self-registration and payment is at the head of the ramp. 20 & 30 amp shore power.

Sechelt Inlet. Beautiful Sechelt Inlet, with few anchorages and limited facilities for pleasure craft, is often passed by—especially with Princess Louisa Inlet at the end of nearby Jervis Inlet. Sechelt Rapids also serve as a gate to keep out all but the determined.

To explore Sechelt Inlet and its arms, use Chart 3512 (1:80:000) or Chartbook 3312. The inlet is shown at 1:40,000 in Chartbook 3312. Sechelt Inlet extends about 15 miles south of Sechelt Rapids. It ends at Porpoise Bay, the back door to the village of Sechelt, where there is a public float and easy anchorage. Two arms, Salmon Inlet and Narrows Inlet, run from the eastern side of Sechelt Inlet into the heart of the Earle mountain range. A number of provincial park sites are in Sechelt Inlet, most of them best suited to small boats that can be pulled up on the beach.

Inflow winds can blow from south to north in Sechelt Inlet and up Salmon Inlet and Narrows Inlet. Even when the northern part of Sechelt Inlet is near calm, the southern part can be increasingly windy. In Salmon Inlet and Narrows Inlet, the inflow winds will grow stronger as the inlets deepen and narrow. Outflow winds can develop at night, but in the summer they often don't unless a strong southeasterly is blowing out on the strait.

The tidal range does not exceed 10 feet in Sechelt Inlet, and the times of high and low

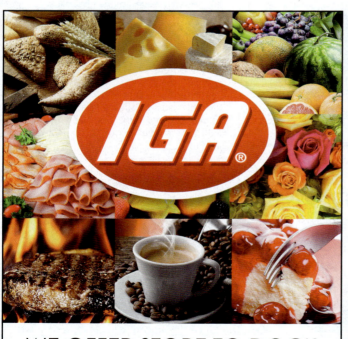

WE OFFER STORE TO DOCK CART SERVICE!

BAKERY · DELI · PRODUCE · MEAT · FLORAL

12887 Madeira Park Road, Pender Harbour, BC
604.883.9100 | iga078@igabc.com

SALES · PARTS · SERVICE

PENDER HARBOUR'S COMPLETE MARINE SUPPLIES & SERVICES

MADEIRA MARINA
(1980) LTD.

WELL STOCKED MARINE STORE

Sales & Service for:
Mercury & Honda Outboards
Mercruiser · Volvo Penta
and Other Major Brands
International Paints
Navigational Charts

MARINE HAULOUT & SERVICES

40-Ton Marine Ways
Trailer Haulout To 30 Feet
Welding & Fabrication/
Steel & Aluminum
Light Machining
Dry Storage

604-883-2266
fax: 604-883-9250 · madeiramarine@telus.net
12930 Madeira Park Rd. PO Box 189
Madeira Park, BC V0N 2H0

Rick & Karen King, owners

tide are 2 to 3 hours after Point Atkinson. Two secondary ports, Porpoise Bay and Storm Bay, are shown in Tide & Current Tables, Vol. 5. Current predictions for Tzoonie Narrows, in Narrows Inlet, are shown under Secondary Stations in Tide & Current Tables, Vol. 5 and Ports and Passes. Depths at the head of the Inlet are shallow enough for easy anchoring over a mud bottom. Usually there are other boats at anchor and a number of private buoys, but it's a large area with ample space.

For a complete description of Sechelt Inlet cruising, including excellent hiking trails, see our sister publication, *Cruising the Secret Coast,* by Jennifer and James Hamilton.

LOCAL KNOWLEDGE

DANGEROUS CURRENTS AND INCORRECT TIDE DATA: We've had reports that some current tables contained in electronic navigation programs don't agree with the printed tables for Sechelt Rapids. Use the Canadian Hydrographic Service or Ports and Passes tables.

Sechelt Rapids. On large tidal exchanges, Sechelt Rapids can run 16.5 knots, the world record holder. Sechelt Rapids, also known as the Skookumchuck Rapids (Sechelt is pronounced "SEE-shelt"; skookum means "big" or "strong," and chuck means "body of water"), provide the only water access to Sechelt Inlet.

Times of turn and maximum current are shown in the Tide and Current Tables, Vol. 5 and in Ports and Passes. Sechelt Rapids can be extremely dangerous except at or near slack water. At full flow the rapids are boiling cauldrons with 8-foot overfalls and 12- to 16-knot currents. Even an hour before slack, when many other rapids may have calmed down, the Sechelt Rapids can be menacing. Traverse the rapids only at slack water. Be aware of where you are time-wise in the lunar cycle. When close or on a full moon or a new moon, the period of slack water is short. When the rapids are running at full strength this area is deadly.

Lacking prior experience, do not go through without accurate charts for Sechelt Rapids and Secret Bay. Sailing Directions says the best route through the rapids is west of Boom Islet (choked with kelp, but safe) and west of the Sechelt Islets light.

We, however, have run a dogleg course without discomfort through the middle of the channel, between the Sechelt Islets and the unnamed islet directly north of the Sechelt Islets. This area is where dangerous whirlpools can develop on ebbs, so be careful. Give Roland Point a wide berth, especially on a flood.

Either direction, Sechelt Rapids are just fine at slack, and if you time it well (easily done) you'll slide through with no problems at all. But when the rapids are running, their roar can be heard for miles. Lives have been lost there.

Before making your own entrance it can be instructive to walk to the rapids from the public dock in Egmont to watch the channel in full boil.

㉞ **Poise Cove Marina.** 5991 Sechelt Inlet Rd., Sechelt, BC V0N 3A3; (604) 885-2895. Open all year with limited guest moorage for boats to 25 feet, limited 15 amp power, concrete launch ramp for boats 25 feet or less. No long term parking. Located on the east side of Sechelt Inlet near Porpoise Bay Marine Park.

㉞ **Choquer & Sons Ltd.** 5977 Sechelt Inlet Rd., Sechelt, BC V0N 3A0; (604) 885-9244; choquerandsons@telus.net. Good docks with guest moorage for boats to 75 feet, deep enough for sailboats, 15 & 30 amp power, bathroom, showers. Launch ramp and trailer lift. Full marine repair. Their primary business is a machine and metal fabrication shop upland.

㉟ **Lighthouse Pub & Marina.** 5764 Wharf Rd., Sechelt, BC V0N 3A0; (604) 885-9494; info@lighthousepub.ca; www.lighthousepub.ca. Located at the south end of Sechelt Inlet with easy access to Sechelt village. Docks with slips from 16 to 40 feet plus side-tie moorage, 30 amp power, showers, laundry, washrooms. Call ahead for moorage, make payment at the pub. The long and often empty dock extending from the pub is reserved for Harbour Air floatplanes. The dock to the east, marked 'Day Use' is used for transient side-tie. Dinghies may tie-up on the fuel dock, near shore, when dining at the pub or visiting in town. For taxi service call (604-885-3666). Gasoline and diesel at the fuel dock. Lighthouse Marine Store (778-458-3625) carries marine hardware, charts, fishing supplies, snacks, ice. Look for the lighthouse on top of the pub. We've heard the food at the pub is excellent. Three 2-bedroom "Bed & Boat" cottages are available for rent, reservations at bedandboatcottages.com.

㉟ **Royal Reach Marina & Hotel.** 5758 Wharf Rd., Sechelt, BC V0N 3A0; (604) 885-7844. Open all year, moorage to 30 feet is for hotel guests only, limited 15 amp power, must call ahead. Located at the head of Sechelt Inlet. Watch your depths at low water.

㉟ **Porpoise Bay Government Wharf.** 5770 Wharf Street, Sechelt, BC V0N 3A0; (604) 740-7528. Next to the Lighthouse Pub & Marina. This dock usually is completely taken by local boats, but space does become available from time to time. Call Les, the Wharfinger, regarding available space. Docks accommodate boats up to 30 feet; 20 & 30 amp power, water, pumpout, and grid. Self-registration and payment box at the head of A-dock. Dinghies may tie-up in available space at the dock.

Narrows Inlet. Narrows Inlet is mostly 150 to 180 feet deep except at the head, where the Tzoonie River makes a delta. Tzoonie Narrows, about a third of the way along, is a spectacular cleft in the high mountains that surround the inlet. Tidal currents run to a maximum of 4 knots through Tzoonie Narrows, but the passage is free of hazards. All but the slowest or lowest-powered boats could run them at any time. Arguably the best anchorage in this area is in Storm Bay at the mouth of Narrows Inlet. Storm Bay is very pretty with a dramatic rock wall on its eastern shore. Anchor behind the little islets at the entrance or near the head of the bay.

Tzoonie Narrows Park. This park takes in both sides of the narrows and is good for swimming, fishing, diving, and picnicking. Walk-in campsites. The 1-meter islet shown on the chart is a long, narrow reef with large extensions under the surface. You can anchor inside the reef, or in the deep bight on the other side of Narrows Inlet.

Salmon Inlet. Salmon Inlet is very deep, although anchorage is good in Misery Bay, where the water is warm enough for swimming. A drying shoal almost blocks the passage across the inlet at Sechelt Creek. The shoal can be passed safely by staying close to the north shore.

MALASPINA STRAIT TO JERVIS INLET

Quarry Bay. Quarry Bay faces the Strait of Georgia and is too deep and exposed to be a destination of first choice. If you must anchor

Sechelt (Skookumchuck) Rapids running at a 12 knot flood, less than full boil at almost 16 knots

VANCOUVER, MAINLAND B.C. & THE SUNSHINE COAST

See Area Map Page 273 - Maps Not for Navigation

there, you could work your way in among the rocks in the southeast corner of the bay. It would be a good idea to run a stern-tie to keep from swinging onto a rock. At the north end of Quarry Bay a little cove, surrounded by homes, is well protected and has good anchoring depths. It would be a good hideout. Chart 3512 (1:80,000) and Chartbook 3312 (1:40,000) show a stream connecting this cove with Quarry Lake. Three rocks in this cove are shown in Chartbook 3312.

Cape Cockburn. An unmarked drying rock is a short distance off Cape Cockburn. Give the cape a good offing.

Cockburn Bay. Cockburn Bay is completely plugged by drying rocks and is accessible only by small craft at or near high water.

Hidden Basin. Hidden Basin is blocked by drying shoals and rocks, and currents run strongly through the restricted entrance. Chartbook 3312 (1:40,000) shows Hidden Basin better than Chart 3512 (1:80,000). Entrance to Hidden Basin should be made—carefully—at high water slack. Secure anchorage is available once inside.

㊱ **Blind Bay.** Blind Bay once had a number of good anchorages, especially along the Hardy Island side. Most of them now are taken with private homes and their docks, so the choices are fewer. One good spot on the south side is popular Ballet Bay. On the north side, Hardy Island Marine Park (formerly Musket Island Marine Park) has anchoring. Nearly all anchorages require a stern-tie. Use your chart and depth sounder, watch for rocks, and go slowly.

㊱ **Ballet Bay.** Ballet Bay, on Nelson Island, is a popular, well-protected anchorage in Blind Bay.

Ballet Bay can be entered from the north, but many rocks obstruct the path and close attention is called for. The easier entry is from the west, between Nelson Island and Clio Island. If you do enter from the west, the rock shown at the point before you turn into Ballet Bay truly is there, and farther offshore than you might expect. Give it a wide berth. Many rocks in the area around Ballet Bay are marked with sticks or small floats, but don't count on all of the rocks being marked. Not all the rocks are charted. Go slowly and pay attention.

The center of Ballet Bay is good-holding mud, but the bottom grows rockier toward shore ("a boat-eating rockpile" —*Evertz*). A trail

The view from the West Coast Wilderness Lodge. Backeddy Marina can be seen below.

JOSE MARIA NARVAEZ (1768-1840)

Jose Maria Narvaez was a Spanish naval officer and explorer. He explored the San Juan/Gulf Islands and the lower mainland B.C. coast. He was assigned to San Blas in New Spain, present-day Mexico, in 1788 and soon sailed north as pilot for Gonzalo Lopez de Haro, commander of the ship *San Carlos*. The Spanish were concerned about Russian fur trading in Alaska and ships were sent to investigate. Arriving in Prince William Sound, Narvaez was able to confirm a Russian presence and continued to Kodiak Island where he discovered a Russian outpost. In an exchange of gifts, he was given a map of the Alaskan coast which depicted several Russian outposts. Narvaez also learned that the Russians planned to occupy Nootka Sound on the northwest coast of Vancouver Island. He returned to San Blas with the news and was sent on a second expedition in 1789 to explore Nootka Sound and subsequently explored Clayoquot Sound, Barkley Sound, and the Strait of Juan de Fuca. In hopes of discovering the Northwest Passage, Narvaez was sent on a third mission to Nootka Sound as pilot of the ship *Princesa*. From Nootka Sound, Narvaez continued exploring the area, including further exploration of the Strait of Juan de Fuca in 1791 as commander of the ship *Santa Saturnina*. By mid-June his base of operations was moved to Esquimalt Harbour near present-day Victoria. Sailing between Pender and Saturna Islands, he entered "a grand canal," (the Strait of Georgia), and became the first European to see the Strait; he speculated that this might be the prized Northwest Passage. His base of operations was later moved to present-day Port Discovery on the south side of the Strait of Juan de Fuca. From here Narvaez set out to explore Rosario Strait and the Strait of Georgia more fully. Before heading north into the Strait of Georgia, Narvaez surveyed Guemes Island, Cypress Island, and Lummi Island; and explored Padilla Bay and Bellingham Bay. Anchorages along the way included Chuckanut Bay (Puerto Socorro), Birch Bay, and Drayton Harbour. Sailing west across Boundary Bay, he rounded Point Roberts, anchoring off Point Grey before entering Burrard Inlet, today's Vancouver harbour. Narvaez continued northward along the Sunshine Coast and anchored off Mission Point in Sechelt, where he came ashore with a skiff. Today, boaters can visit the marker at Sechelt in honor of his 1791 explorations; the marker is located at the south end of the Davis Bay seawall near the spot where Narvaez became the first European explorer to set foot on the mainland coast of present-day British Columbia. Narvaez returned to Port Discovery, his base of operations, in mid-July 1791. At the start of his voyage, Narvaez had passed Admiralty Inlet, the entrance to Puget Sound and had planned to explore it later; however, Commandant Eliza was eager to return to his post at Nootka Sound, resulting in a missed opportunity for the Spanish to explore this area. Captain George Vancouver entered Puget Sound the following year.

reportedly connects Ballet Bay and Hidden Basin, although all Evertz found were "No Trespassing" signs.

Hardy Island Marine Park. Formerly Musket Island Marine Park. Located behind Fox Island, near the western entrance to Blind Bay. The upland area of the park is on Hardy Island. A beautiful spot. Anchor behind the tiny islet, or in the bay that opens up to the north of the islet. In most cases you'll stern-tie to shore. The bottom can be rocky, so be sure you have a satisfactory set. You also can anchor in the narrow, vertically sided, almost landlocked cove indenting Hardy Island immediately northwest of the park itself. A reader who dove this cove to recover a lost item reports a mud bottom. Rock has been quarried on the peninsula high above the cove. It's quite dramatic. The area is poorly charted and some of the depths are deeper than charts show.

Telescope Passage. Telescope Passage connects Blind Bay with Jervis Inlet, but is partly blocked by underwater rocks that extend from the 70-meter island at the north entrance. Strongly favor the Nelson Island side until past the 70-meter island. Then, trend toward the middle of the passage to avoid charted and uncharted rocks along the Nelson Island side. When approaching Telescope Passage from Jervis Inlet, you might be confused (we were) by the presence of a tiny islet almost 100 feet high just outside the entrance. Check the chart closely; the islet is shown as the smallest oval imaginable with (26), for 26 meters high, directly beside it.

JERVIS INLET

Jervis Inlet extends 46 miles into Coast Range mountains and is the route to fabled Princess Louisa Inlet. Jervis Inlet is 1 to 1.5 miles wide and often more than 600 feet deep. Steep-to shores, with mountains rising directly above, make for few good anchorages. Currents in Jervis Inlet are light, and are often affected by winds. Watch for drift. Heading up-inlet, Backeddy Resort & Marina and Bathgate Marina in Egmont are the last fuel stops.

Once beyond Foley Head and Egmont Point, you'll find only indifferent anchorages at Vancouver Bay, Deserted Bay, and Killam Bay. The 30 miles of Princess Royal Reach, Prince of Wales Reach, and Queen's Reach do not have useable anchorages. Unlike the other deep fjords that penetrate from the sea, however, Jervis Inlet has a spectacular prize at the end: Princess Louisa Inlet.

Pictograph: Correspondent Pat Shera reports a good pictograph of what appear to be a group of salmon and other figures on the north side of Princess Royal Reach, midway between Osgood Creek and Patrick Point, 50°03.42'N/123°50.65'W.

Thunder Bay. Thunder Bay, immediately inside the north entrance to Jervis Inlet, has anchorage in the protected cove on the south shore, and in the open cove at the northwest corner. Correspondent Capt. Fred Triggs reports that in the southern cove, the rock drying at 2.1 meters appears to be farther offshore than charted. The cove looks a little small on the chart, but Capt. Triggs says it has room for several boats and good holding. The shores are lined with vacation cabins. Mooring floats restrict anchoring room. Rocks extend from the point as you approach. Give the point a good offing. At low tide the charted rock looks like a small haystack. If you stay off the west shore you'll be fine.

Saltery Bay. Saltery Bay has a public float, a boat launch, and picnic sites. It is the ferry landing for road travel along the Sunshine Coast.

Saltery Bay Public Wharf. Adjacent to the ferry landing. Visitor moorage available along 435 feet of dock space. Garbage pickup. Commercial vessels have priority.

Saltery Bay Provincial Park. Open all year, anchor only or moor at the public wharf, a 1-km walk from the park entrance. Picnic facilities and a dive rinse station are located above the small sandy beach. Most of the shoreline is rock, however, and very impressive. In Mermaid Cove, scuba divers can look for the underwater statue of the mermaid. The dive reef is marked by white buoys. A launch ramp is a short distance west of Mermaid Cove.

St. Vincent Bay. Much oyster culture activity. Sykes Island and Junction Island may have anchorage.

Hotham Sound. Hotham Sound is a beautiful, 6-mile-long body of water, surrounded by high, rugged mountains. The sound is sheltered from most strong winds, and in the summertime the water is warm enough for swimming. Friel Lake Falls tumble 1400 feet down sheer mountainside near the Harmony Islands. Unfortunately, good anchorages in Hotham Sound are few.

Wolferstan (*Cruising Guide to British Columbia Vol. 3, Sunshine Coast,* now out of print) devotes an entire chapter, with superb aerial photos, to Hotham Sound; but for the most part, even his advice comes down to finding little niches along the shoreline. Suitable anchorage is found in Baker Bay at the head of Hotham Sound.

Harmony Islands Marine Park. The Harmony Islands in Hotham Sound are a lovely spot. The best anchorage is in locally-named Kipling Cove, a nook surrounded by the three northern islands that make up the Harmony Islands. The bottom is rocky, so be sure you have the right ground tackle and it's well set. You'll run a stern-tie to shore.

Two of the three islands that make up Kipling Cove are privately owned and posted with "Private Island, No Stern Ties, No Fires, No Kayakers" signs. The signs mean what they say, and private property must be respected. The northeasternmost island that makes up Kipling Cove is owned by B.C. Parks, however, with no restrictions on going ashore or stern-tying. The southernmost of the Harmony Islands (separate from Kipling Cove) is also part of the marine park.

Because anchoring inside Kipling Cove can be tight, some boats choose to put the hook down in the channel on the east side of the islands. Close to the islands the depths are fine, but the channel itself is around 100 feet deep.

At anchor in Hardy Island Marine Park.

Blind Bay

VANCOUVER, MAINLAND B.C. & THE SUNSHINE COAST

As long as you are set up for deeper anchorages, you should be okay. Rings for stern ties are along the high tide line.

We have been told that williwaws can blow down from the mountains and make anchoring interesting. And we have heard that flies can be aggressive. Our visits have been in late June. On our one overnight we were troubled by only a few flies in the evening—but they were definitely determined.

Dark Cove. Dark Cove is a little notch between Foley Head and Goliath Bay, and was recommended to us by an experienced sailboater we met at Princess Louisa Inlet. We motored through Dark Cove the next day but didn't stop. At 90 feet deep, Dark Cove isn't ideal for anchoring, although protection behind Sydney Island is excellent.

Malibu Rapids. Malibu Rapids mark the entrance to Princess Louisa Inlet. The rapids are narrow and dogleg-shaped, and boats at one end cannot see boats at the other end. It is courteous—and wise—to warn other vessels via VHF radio that you are about to enter the rapids, and the direction you are traveling. Most boats use channel 16 because it is the one VHF channel everyone is supposed to monitor. The transmission can be brief: "*Securité, Securité. This is the 34-foot motor vessel Happy Days, inbound to Princess Louisa Inlet. Any concerned traffic please respond on channel one-six.*"

A VHF securite call is a notice of safety to boaters. When making a securite call at Malibu Rapids, it is for safety reasons and not for any right-of-way statement. Rules of the road for vessels operating in current flow are determined by current flow direction. Vessels traveling with the current are the 'stand-on' and vessels traveling against the current flow are the 'give-way.' The path through Malibu Rapids is 'S' shaped. While it might be tempting to 'cross over' the opposing traffic path to get a look at the rapids, this may create a conflict with boats coming in the opposite direction.

Currents in Malibu Rapids run to 9 knots and create large overfalls. Run this passage at slack water. High water slack occurs about 24 minutes after high water at Point Atkinson, and low water slack about 36 minutes after low water at Point Atkinson. High water slack is preferred because it widens the available channel somewhat. High slack or low, before entering or leaving Malibu Rapids, local knowledge says to wait until the surf created by the overfall subsides entirely.

Important: Use the Volume 5 Canadian Hydrographic Service or Ports and Passes tide tables for Point Atkinson tides.

Princess Louisa Inlet. Princess Louisa Inlet, 4 miles long, is the "holy grail" for cruising people from all over the world. Entered through Malibu Rapids, the inlet is surrounded by 3000-foot-high mountains that plunge almost vertically into 600-foot depths below. Entering Princess Louisa Inlet is like entering a great cathedral. The author Earle Stanley Gardner wrote that no one could see Princess Louisa

Running against a couple knots of current at Malibu Rapids

Inlet and remain an atheist. It is one of the most awesome destinations on the coast. What words can describe this place? All the superlatives have been used up on lesser subjects.

Please observe a no-wake speed limit. Larger wakes bounce off the sides of the inlet.

Malibu Club, a Young Life Christian summer camp for teenagers, is at the entrance to the inlet, just inside Malibu Rapids. The kids and staff are welcoming and polite. Tours are possible. It's probably best to visit by dinghy after your boat is settled at MacDonald Island or the park dock at Chatterbox Falls.

As you clear Malibu Rapids and motor up Princess Louisa Inlet, you will be treated to waterfalls streaming down the mountainsides. About halfway along, 5 mooring buoys are behind MacDonald Island.

Princess Louisa Park is at the head of the inlet, surrounded by a bowl of high sheer cliffs that astonish even repeat visitors. The 650-foot-long park dock will hold a large number of boats. The dock is available at no charge; maximum boat length is 55 feet and stays are limited to 72 hours. Snug up close to the boat in front to leave room for others. The float at the end of dock is for floatplanes.

If the dock is full you will need to make use one of the five mooring buoys at MacDonald Island. Anchorage is possible at MacDonald Island but may not be practical due to depths and lack of swinging space. Two dinghy docks are provided on the mainland shore opposite MacDonald Island for visitors to access a 1.5 km loop trail.

Since most people don't stay longer than a day or two, there's good turnover. A boat at anchor or on a mooring buoy need only wait for the twice-daily departure of boats from the dock running for slack at the Malibu Rapids. Space then can be found before the next fleet arrives from the rapids. Water (not potable) is available all the way out the dock (May 1 - Oct 30) but no power. Up-inlet thermal winds can develop on warm afternoons. Be aware if you're out in the dinghy.

The park is beautifully developed and maintained. Use the shoreside toilets. Limit generator use to 9:00 a.m. to 11:00 a.m. in the morning and 6:00 p.m. to 8:00 p.m. in the evening. Quiet hours are 11:00 p.m. to 7:00 a.m. The water is warm enough for swimming, even by adults who usually don't go in anymore.

No discharge zone. Gray water okay.

There's a covered fire pit for group get-togethers. For those who wish, a short walk to the pools near the base of Chatterbox Falls will yield a bracing bath/shower followed by a power rinse.

A delightful waterfall-fed pool is hidden in the forest on the north side of the inlet. From the dock you can see a large boulder that marks the spot. Land the dinghy on the small beach just beyond the boulder and walk a few steps to the pool. A bather we met yelped when he jumped in, but a moment later said the water was fine.

No hook-and-line fishing. Princess Louisa Inlet is a rockfish conservation area.

Trapper's Cabin is about a 2-hour very demanding hike from the dock area. The cabin is now completely collapsed. The trail is steep, and often muddy and slippery. We're not kidding about the hike being demanding, serious injuries have occurred.

With a fast boat, Princess Louisa Inlet could be seen in one day. Zoom up for the morning slack at Malibu Rapids, see the sights for a few hours, and zoom out on the afternoon slack. That, however, would be seeing Princess Louisa Inlet but not experiencing it. Something good happens to people when they're at Princess Louisa Inlet. We suggest at least three days for the trip: one day up 46-mile-long Jervis Inlet; the next day at the park; and the third day back down Jervis Inlet on the morning slack.

Princess Louisa Society. The Princess Louisa Society was formed to buy and preserve the area around Chatterbox Falls for perpetuity. The Society gave the property to B.C. Parks, but maintains an active role in the care of the facilities. Fundraising continues to maintain and develop the facilities at docks and in the area. Annual memberships are $40 U.S or Cdn.; life memberships are $200 U.S. or Cdn. The Society website is www.princesslouisa.bc.ca.

See Area Map Page 287 - Maps Not for Navigation

VANCOUVER, MAINLAND B.C. & THE SUNSHINE COAST

Princess Louisa Inlet on a high-speed tour boat

Chatterbox Falls visible from the dock at Princess Louisa Inlet

MALASPINA STRAIT TO SARAH POINT

Malaspina Strait, 36 miles long, separates Texada Island from the mainland. Although the strait looks protected from the open water of the Strait of Georgia, storms can create high seas. Especially on an ebb tide, confused seas often build up off the mouth of Jervis Inlet and extend almost to Texada Island. Grief Point, at the north end of Malaspina Strait, is another bad spot in a southeasterly. Other than the mouth of Jervis Inlet, however, Malaspina Strait poses no threat in settled weather.

McRae Cove faces Malaspina Strait, just west of Scotch Fir Point at the mouth of Jervis Inlet. The cove is well protected but shallow. The charts show a straightforward entry between the 27- and 29-meter islands, then along a 36-meter island. Anchoring is in the vicinity of the 36-meter island in 6 feet at zero tide. Don't go much farther in—the bottom shoals quickly.

㊲ **Beach Gardens Resort & Marina.** 7074 Westminster St., Powell River, BC V8A 1C5; (604) 485-6267; (800) 663-7070; beachgardens@shaw.ca; www.beachgardens.com. Monitors VHF 66A July & August. Open all year, moorage, 15 & 30 amp power, water, free Wi-Fi, washrooms, showers, coin laundry, fitness center, indoor pool, ice, well-stocked beer and wine sales store. Gasoline, diesel and lube oil at the fuel dock, seasonal only. New fuel pump. This is a breakwater-protected marina with good docks, just south of Grief Point. Deluxe waterfront rooms are available. Kayak and paddle board rentals available.

Beach Gardens Resort features a new building overlooking the marina and fronting the older buildings of the resort. The laundry, beer and wine store, and The Seasider Bistro, (604) 485-0996, are on the bottom level of the new building with a beautiful view of Malaspina Strait. Check www.theseasider.ca. for seasonal hours. Free shuttle service to Town Centre Mall in July and August. The city bus and bus service to Vancouver stop is a short walk away. A new market with specialty coffee is within walking distance.

The Myrtle Point Golf Course is nearby and will pick up marina guests.

Grief Point. Grief Point marks the northern end of Malaspina Strait on the mainland side. The seas around Grief Point get particularly rough when the wind blows.

㊳ **Westview/Powell River.** There are two main moorage areas at Powell River's Westview area: the North Harbour for permanent moorage located north of the ferry landing with its own entrance; and the working harbour and transient guest moorage facility with an entrance located south of the ferry landing. The guest moorage facility consists of two basins referred to as Westview and South Harbour; these two basins are accessed through the shared south entrance and the floats are used by working vessels and transient pleasure craft. Fuel, water and power are available at the Westview and South Harbour basins; nearby stores have marine supplies. Grocery stores and a major shopping center are a taxi or a free seasonal shuttle from the marina.

The section adjacent to the ferry loading area between the two main moorage areas, north and south, has been redeveloped and now houses the harbor office, new washrooms, showers, and laundry. Access to excellent restaurants, the Willingdon Beach Trail, and the historic "Townsite" district makes Powell River a destination worth visiting.

An excellent stock of marine and fishing supplies is available at nearby Marine Traders chan-

Beach Gardens Resort & Marina

2018 waggoner CRUISING GUIDE

VANCOUVER, MAINLAND B.C. & THE SUNSHINE COAST

See Area Map Page 287 - Maps Not for Navigation

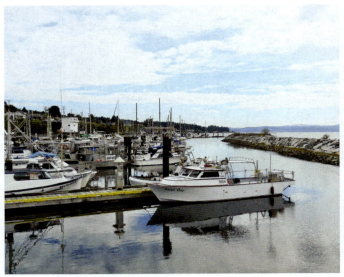
Westview basin at Powell River

Willingdon Beach in Powell River

dlery. Shops and a range of restaurants are on the main commercial streets, a short walk away. The Chopping Block, an old-fashioned butcher shop, is at the north end of Marine Avenue. Their meats, seafood, homemade smoked sausage, and cheese are delicious. The Town Centre Mall, with Save-On Foods, Safeway, Shoppers Drug Mart, Walmart, liquor store and other shops, is located some distance away, up a steep hill on Courtenay Street (they call it Cardiac Hill). It's a hike. Another shopping center has a QF grocery store that will deliver to the marina.

The original Powell River townsite is a couple of miles up the road from Westview. Visitors can walk or bicycle along the shoreline through a beautiful forested trail starting at Willingdon Beach on the north end of downtown Powell River. Numerous pieces of historic logging equipment are on display along the Willingdon Beach Trail, serving as a fascinating outdoor museum complete with interpretive signage. For energetic hikers, you can access the old "Townsite" district above the Mill off the end of the trail. Take a taxi for the return trip to Powell River. Townsite is the original settlement of Powell River and is a designated National Historic District. Four hundred of the original buildings from the early 1900s remain. Many have been refurbished and are still in use. A row of large oak trees and grand homes from the era stand proudly overlooking the mill and Malaspina Strait. Several cafes are found in Townsite and a brewery offering craft beer samplers.

In Powell River, history buffs may want to visit the small history museum adjacent to Willingdon Beach. The Blackberry Festival is in early August. Check the town's website (www.discoverpowellriver.com) for a schedule of activities.

Golf: The 18-hole Myrtle Point Golf Club is a short distance south of Westview. Call (604) 487-4653.

㊳ **Westview Harbour.** 6790 Wharf Street, Powell River, BC V8A 1T9; (604) 485-5244; jkinahan@powellriver.ca. Monitors VHF 66A. Open all year, potable water, 30 & 50 amp power, washrooms, new large showers, laundry, garbage drop, recycling, waste oil disposal, free Wi-Fi. Pumpout by appointment. Leave the daymark inside the harbor entry to port when entering. Guest moorage is available at both Westview Harbour and South Harbour basins, which share the same south entrance. Westview Fuels is the demarcation between the two moorage areas.

Westview Harbour (floats 1-6) is the primary guest moorage basin; effort is made to accommodate most transient boats in Westview, rafting may be required or stern-tie to the main dock. South Harbour (floats 7-11) can accommodate vessels up to 200 feet (20-foot draft at zero tide). A short trail connects the South Harbour basin and the Westview Harbour basin.

Washrooms, showers, and garbage drop are available at both Westview and South Harbour; the newest facilities are located at Westview with the older more basic facilities at South Harbour.

One-hour complimentary moorage, call

Westview Harbour

CHARTS	
3311 Small craft charts (strip charts)	Sunshine Coast to Desolation Sound
3312 Small craft chart (chartbook)	Jervis Inlet & Desolation Sound
3512	Strait of Georgia, Central Portion (1:80,000)
3514	Jervis Inlet (1:50,000) Malibu Rapids (1:12,000) Sechelt Rapids (1:20,000)

Westview Fuels

South Harbour • Powell River
Ph: 604-485-2867 Eve: 604-485-4641

Debbie & Joe Hooper
Owners/Operators

A Complete Line of Marine Fuels, Lubricants & Much More

P.O. Box 171, Powell River, B.C. V8A 4Z6

Reference Only – Not for Navigation

VANCOUVER, MAINLAND B.C. & THE SUNSHINE COAST

CHARTS	
3311sc Small craft charts (strip charts)	Sunshine Coast to Desolation Sound
3512	Strait of Georgia, Central Portion (1:80,000)
3513	Strait of Georgia, Northern Portion (1:80,000)
3536 Plans	Strait of Georgia (various scales)
3538	Desolation Sound and Sutil Channel (1:40,000)

Powell River & Lund

ahead. Free scheduled shuttle to the mall picks up outside the harbor office four times per day during the ten-week season. Schedule is posted at the marina office.

㊳ **Westview Fuels.** P.O. Box 171, Powell River, BC V8A 4Z6; (604) 485-2867. Monitors VHF 66A. Gasoline, diesel, lubricants, washrooms, and ice. Located between Westview Harbour and South Harbour. Joe and Debbie Hooper are the owners and they're great.

Dinner Rock. Dinner Rock, exposed at all tides, is approximately 0.2 mile off the mainland shore, slightly southeast of Savary Island. In 1998 a 1000-lb. cross was erected on the rock. It is a memorial to the five people who died there in October 1947, when the vessel *Gulf Stream*, proceeding in darkness with rain falling, struck the rock and sank.

Savary Island. Savary Island is a 4-mile-long sandy island that lies approximately east and west, and is served by water taxi from Lund. The island is a favorite destination for Vancouverites. The small public dock on the north shore is for loading and unloading only. Anchorage is good, sand bottom, within easy dinghy distance of shore. Savary Island has no real protected harbor, but the beaches are some of the best in B.C.

In summer months, Riggers a licensed pub-style restaurant, and a small general store are open. From the public dock turn right and follow the road for about one-half mile. Bicycles can be rented nearby. A number of years ago Bob Hale anchored off the north shore for the night and "got away with it." By contrast, Contributing Editor Tom Kincaid once anchored overnight in the same area, but by morning the wind had come in from the north and he was on a lee shore. We visited Savary Island recently and anchored in 50-70 feet just off the dock and mooring field. We took the dinghy to shore and explored the island. The gently sloping beach makes landing and mooring the dinghy a challenge. Visiting by water taxi from Lund might be a better idea if you plan to spend the day there.

Nearby **Hernando Island** is surrounded by rocky shallows, and is seldom visited by cruising boats. Renowned authors Lin and Larry Pardey, however, report excellent anchorage with protection from southeast winds in Stag Bay, northwest of the pier. Anchor in 18 to 24 feet on a firm sand bottom.

Mitlenatch Island. Roughly west of Hernando Island, Mitlenatch Island appears to be an uninviting rock out in the middle of the Strait of Georgia. It is in fact a thriving and ruggedly beautiful wildlife refuge, with a small, protected anchorage on its east side. Park volunteers spend a week in turn each year on the island doing trail maintenance and guiding tours. Visitors are asked to stay on the trails to avoid disturbing birds. Those who visit will be rewarded, as this note from Correspondents John and Lorraine Littlewood suggests:

"If you can get there on a calm clear day in September, you'll see an incredible variety of wildlife, from Goshawks to huge sea lions. An additional benefit is water so clear that we could actually watch our Bruce anchor deploy. It hit the bottom in about 20 feet, flipped over, bit, and buried itself. This was on only 2:1 scope, although we later paid out to our normal 3:1."

We thank reader Sharl Heller for increasing our awareness of Mitlenatch Island.

㊴ **Lund.** Lund is the north end of the Pacific Coastal Highway, the road that leads all the way to the tip of South America. Lund is a busy place in the summer, a jumping-off point for Desolation Sound with fuel, provisions, and pumpout.

The historic Lund Hotel, with restaurant and pub, is at the head of the fuel dock. The small but well-stocked store, in the same building as the hotel, has a good deli, fresh (often local) vegetables, ice cream, frozen meats, liquor agency with good wine and beer selection, pet supplies, prawn bait, frozen herring, camping and picnic supplies, and more.

Lund is the mainland's closest launch site to Desolation Sound. Long-term auto, trailer and tow vehicle storage are available at Dave's Parking (604) 483-3667 and Lund Auto & Outboard a few blocks away. Nancy's Bakery is in the modern, larger building overlooking the public docks. Nancy's pastries, pizzas, and other specialties are famous. Nancy's also has good Wi-Fi. Upstairs from Nancy's is Pollen Sweaters, specializing in locally made sweaters, and Terracentric Adventures, a kayak tour operator. Guests can drive up from Vancouver or Seattle and leave their car with Dave's Parking while out cruising.

The town assumed operation of the public docks following divestiture by the federal government several years ago. With commercial fishing in decline, the docks and shoreside facilities were upgraded to make them more inviting to visiting pleasure craft. Rafting may be required. When the docks are full, you can moor along the inside of the breakwater and dinghy to the dinghy dock. There's a good launch ramp, and modern public washrooms with excellent showers.

Over on the north side of the bay a public float, with no access to shore, is in the middle of Finn Cove.

Fuel: The busy Lund Hotel fuel dock has gasoline and diesel.

Garbage: During the season a truck at the top of the boat launch that will take your garbage for a fee. Recycling is available behind the hotel.

Haulout: Jack's Boatyard in Finn Cove has a repair yard, haulout to 50 tons and boat storage.

Lund Small Craft Harbour

2018 WAGGONER CRUISING GUIDE 287

VANCOUVER, MAINLAND B.C. & THE SUNSHINE COAST

See Area Map Page 287 - Maps Not for Navigation

Nancy's Bakery above the harbour at Lund

About Finn Cove. Sailing Directions and the charts call it Finn Cove, but the locals call it Finn Bay. The road that leads from the village to the cove is named Finn Bay Road. The Waggoner will call it Finn Cove, however, to be consistent with the charts. No anchoring in Finn Cove.

㊴ **Lund Small Craft Harbour.** P.O. Box 78, Lund, BC V0N 2G0; (604) 483-4711; lundharbour-wharfinger@twincomm.ca; www.lundharbourbc.wordpress.com. Monitors VHF 73. Open all year, more than 1700 feet of breakwater-protected dock space, 20, 30 & some 50 amp power. The harbor has one of the only pumpout stations in the area. Garbage drop, $3 to $6 per bag, is above the fuel dock during the season; off-season, use the garbage drop at the general store. No oil disposal. Excellent washrooms and showers. Wide concrete launch ramp with 4 lanes, good for most launchings down to about 5 feet above zero tide. (Some say 3 feet, but that's cutting it close.) The new configuration provides 600 more feet for this popular harbor.

Enter north of the floating breakwaters. The northern dock located inside the breakwater is reserved for pleasure craft, rafting required. Don't give up if the docks appear full. Office hours are 8:00 a.m. to 11:00 a.m. and 3:00 p.m. to 5:00 p.m. October to May, 8:00 a.m. to 5:00 p.m. June and September, 8:00 a.m. to 8:00 p.m. July 1 to Labour Day. Moorage is free for the first hour, 1 to 3 hours are charged at the half-day rate. Radio ahead for a slip assignment when near the entrance, even for short stays.

The floating concrete breakwater noted above (no power or water) protects the inner docks. You can tie inside of these floats and dinghy to the marked dinghy dock area below the ramp. Overnight moorage is charged on the breakwater.

The area near the launch ramps had a green buoy to mark a shallow spot for years. It has been removed. Local knowledge says to be aware of a high spot there, about 4 feet at its shallowest.

㊴ **Lund Hotel.** 1436 Highway 101, Lund, BC V0N 2G0; (604) 414-0474; (877) 569-3999; info@lundhotel.com; www.lundhotel.com. Open year-round; An 80-foot dock provides limited overnight moorage on a first-come, first-serve basis. Free moorage for hotel guests. Free Wi-Fi. The laundry facility is clean, with good machines. The store and deli are well stocked. The fuel dock has gasoline, diesel, and lubricants.

The historic hotel, which dates back to 1905, has been restored and remodeled with a pub and separate dining area. The hotel has 31 rooms, all renovated in 2017, ranging from budget-sensitive to four "boutique superior oceanfront" rooms overlooking the water. Rooms feature unique hand-painted murals. The hotel, pub, general store, and fuel dock are under the new ownership of the Tla'amin Band. Tug Guhm Gallery & Studio, well known for lifelike seal heads carved from a single block of stone, is in the lower part of the hotel.

㊴ **Lund Water Taxi.** (604) 483-9749. Scheduled service to Savary Island. Can deliver parts or people to Desolation Sound and surrounding areas.

㊴ **Dave's Parking.** P.O. Box 94, 1440 Lund Rd., Lund, BC V0N 2G0; (604) 483-3667. Daily and long-term vehicle and trailer parking in secure lots off-site.

㊴ **Lund Automotive & Outboard Ltd.** 1520 Lund Hwy, Lund, BC V0N 2G0; (604) 483-4612. Long-term tow vehicle and trailer parking in secure lots. Call ahead for reservations. Mechanics are on staff for mechanical and electrical repairs and they are an authorized service facility for several engine brands. Haulout to 30 feet.

㊴ **Jack's Boatyard (Finn Cove).** 9907 Finn Bay Road, P.O. Box 198, Lund, BC V0N 2G0; (604) 483-3566; info@jacksboatyard.ca; www.jacksboatyard.ca. Haulout to 50 tons, storage available. Can haul sailboats. Washrooms, showers, laundry, supply store, garbage and recycling drop, Wi-Fi in the boatyard well above the water. Owner Jack Elsworth blasted the boat storage yard out of solid rock and welded up the darndest haulout machine imaginable. Think Travelift, then make it completely different. You have to see it to understand.

In 2013, they added the structure to support a 50-ton Travelift, and a lower yard was cleared to allow for blocking four or more medium to large boats. The old lift will still be used to haul boats to 30 tons up the hill to the expansive upper yard. Since Quarterdeck Boatyard in Port Hardy closed in 2014, this lift and the lift in Campbell River are the only lifts until Shearwater, some 200 miles north.

ALESSANDRO MALASPINA (1754-1810)

Alessandro Malaspina was an Italian explorer who served as a Spanish naval officer and is best known for his circumnavigation of the world in 1786-1788 along with his scientific voyage of discovery in 1789-1794. The scientific data collected during Malaspina's expedition is regarded as equal to that of Cook's earlier voyage. Noted naturalists, astronomers, geographers, and artists of the day accompanied Malaspina on his scientific voyage. The medical officer, Pedro Gonzales, was convinced that fresh oranges and lemons prevented scurvy; as a result, Malaspina's expedition had no significant cases of scurvy. Scholars under Malaspina recorded Native languages and social practices in addition to rendering exceptional sketches of people and places. In search of the Northwest Passage, Malaspina sailed to Yakutat. On his return from Yakutat, he entered the Spanish outpost of Nootka Sound on West Vancouver Island and spent time improving relationships with the Nootka prior to the arrival of Bodega y Quadra the following year. Like Cook, Malaspina achieved a precision in mapping America's western coastline. Unfortunately, Malaspina's maps and reports went unpublished for 80 years after his extensive voyages and a number of documents were lost. Malaspina had suggested that Spain should free its colonies and form a confederation of states bound by international trade along with other suggestions which were seen as criticisms against Spain; his suggestions landed him in prison from 1796-1802. Today, Alessandro Malaspina is honored through the many place names that pay tribute to his accomplishments, including Malaspina Strait, Malaspina Peninsula, Malaspina Peak, and Malaspina Glacier.

The new Salish Orca, BC Ferries orca class boat, departing Malaspina Strait for Comox

Copeland Islands. The Copeland Islands (locally known as the Ragged Islands) are a provincial park with no facilities specifically for boaters. Anchorage is possible in several nooks and coves among the islands, although some of the coves are exposed to wakes of boats transiting Thulin Passage. Because of remnants of booming cable on the bottom, a buoyed trip line to the anchor crown is a good idea. Check your swing when you anchor. On low tide a few years ago we saw a Grand Banks 42 high and dry, propped up with driftwood. Please watch your wake in Thulin Passage. There are environmentally sensitive areas in the Copeland Islands.

Sharpe's Landing. A private marina with no facilities for transient boaters is located in a small bay on the north end of Thulin Passage on the Malaspina Peninsula side. Please watch your wake as you go by.

㊵ **Bliss Landing Estates.** (604) 414-9417; (604) 483-8098; bliss@twincomm.ca. Located in Turner Bay, north of Lund. Open all year. Guest moorage first-come, first-served. The docks belong to the development and space cannot be guaranteed. Washrooms, showers, laundry, 30 & 50 amp power, water, free Wi-Fi. The docks are exposed to westerly winds; moor bow-out. It's about a 15-minute dinghy ride to Lund. Limited to boats under 60 feet LOA.

GEORGE VANCOUVER (1757-1798)

George Vancouver is widely known among boaters of the Pacific Northwest. A British maritime explorer and surveyor, Captain George Vancouver circumnavigated the World in 1791-1795 including extensive charting of the Pacific coastlines from Baja to the Gulf of Alaska. His charts depicted principal rivers and bays and ended the speculation of a passage through North America. These charts or maps were included in his published account, "A Voyage of Discovery" (1798). He had begun his career as a midshipman during James Cook's second and third voyages to the Pacific. During Vancouver's own four-year voyage, he commanded the ship Discovery, and William Broughton captained the Chatham. In 1793 Vancouver's surveys of the Pacific Northwest included the Strait of Juan de Fuca, Puget Sound, and the Strait of Georgia as well as a circumnavigation of present-day Vancouver Island. In 1792, 100 miles of the Columbia River were surveyed; Howe Sound and Jervis Inlet were also explored. Vancouver was dispatched to Nootka Sound to handle negotiations with the Spanish over disputed territorial claims of the area. In 1793, Vancouver explored southeast Alaska and in 1794 conducted a survey of Prince William Sound. He sailed to Mexico and then home to England in 1795. Unfortunately once home in England, Vancouver, one of Britain's greatest explorers, faced difficulties from those whom he had disciplined and died in obscurity at the age of 40, in May of 1798. Today, George Vancouver is honored through various place names including the City of Vancouver, Vancouver Bay, and Vancouver Island in British Columbia; in Washington State, the town of Vancouver takes his name as does historic Fort Vancouver, a Hudson's Bay Co. trading post that was established in present day Vancouver, Washington around 1825.

Happy Hour Pot Luck Favorites

I love Potlucks! I also love eating and preparing food and potlucks are full of surprises. Where else can you try many varieties of unusual dishes that are other people's favorites. Also, if you like to cook, potlucks are the place to show off. Yes, potlucks are the un-said competition with the prize being the comments, "I can't believe you made this on your boat…," or "Can I have that recipe…" Success at potluck cooking is making something fast and easy. After all, we are on our boats to relax.

I will admit I like the fun of preparing the visual presentation and something that tastes really good, a treat you do not always find in a restaurant. I also vary my recipes with different toppings or fillings. And my last secret, I double up the recipe or split it and keep one-half in the fridge for the potluck two days later.

Lastly, Savory or Sweet - or Both. If the afternoon event is an Appetizer Potluck, I often go for the savory finger food. Though I will say, when I bring something sweet for an appetizer potluck, I have never seen it turned down, and my platter always goes home empty.

Here are two quick and easy recipes to inspire you. They have good visual appeal and your friends will be asking for more. With a supply of Puff Pastry and cream cheese in the freezer, you have many options for recipes or adaptations you can make. Experiment and enjoy!

Smoked Salmon Puffs

I stock 3-4 bricks of cream cheese in my boat's freezer before I leave for summer cruising. It is not very expensive in the warehouse stores. I swear, the only reason I have the extra freezer is for cream cheese and the occasional salmon I catch during the summer. I also stock several packages of smoked salmon. It doesn't need to be refrigerated, is healthy, and tastes great.

Here is a recipe that will have the others at a Happy Hour Potluck salivating for a taste, and others envious of your prowess in the galley. It has color, is savory, and the easy to use puff pastry makes it visually very appealing.

Ingredients:
1/3 cup cream cheese softened to easily mix and spread
1/4 teaspoon of Old Bay or your favorite salmon rub
1 1/2 teaspoon grated lemon zest (I pre-zest and freeze 1 teaspoon portions)
1/4 teaspoon freshly ground black pepper
1/2 of a 17.3-ounce package Puff Pastry Sheets (1 sheet), thawed
1 each of a 4-ounce package thinly sliced smoked salmon, cut into 12 pieces
12 sprigs fresh dill weed or dried dill
3 teaspoons jarred tobiko or salmon roe (optional for color and crunch)

Directions:
Heat the oven to 400°F. Stir the cream cheese, lemon zest, black pepper and optional Old Bay or salmon rub seasoning in a small bowl.

Unfold the pastry sheet on a lightly floured surface. Cut the pastry sheet into 12 (2-inch) squares or use a circle cutter. Place the pastry squares onto a baking sheet. Prick the pastry thoroughly with a fork.

Bake for 12 minutes or until the pastries are golden brown. Let the pastries cool on the baking sheet for 10 minutes.

Spoon 2 teaspoons cream cheese mixture on each pastry. Top each with 1 piece of salmon and dill. Top with tobiko or salmon roe if desired.

Adapted from Pepperidge Farm Puff Pastry Recipes

Quick and Easy Pot Luck Cheese Cake

Cheese cake is a special indulgence and many think it is hard to make. This is a quick and easy recipe that does not require a spring form pan. You can make it with a hand mixer or stir by hand. I make it in either a foil lined 13"x9" pan for large groups or I surreptitiously put it into two foil-lined pans and leave one in the fridge for another day's potluck at a new destination. If you want to make this gluten free, make the crust from ground almonds instead of graham crackers. Grind your own almonds in a blender or food processor and mix in melted butter and sugar. I like it better than graham crackers. If you do not have sour cream on board, make it without. You lose a little tang - but it works.

Ingredients:
6 graham crackers, finely crushed (about 1 cup) or crushed almonds
3 Tbsp sugar
3 Tbsp butter (or margarine), melted
5 (8-oz) packages cream cheese, softened
1 cup sugar
3 Tbsp flour
1 Tbsp vanilla
1 cup sour cream (ok if you don't have any)
4 eggs
1 (21-oz) can cherry or blueberry pie filling, your favorite preserves from a jar, or fresh berries picked on the trail.

Directions:
Heat oven to 325°F. Line a 13x9-inch pan with foil, with ends of foil extending over sides. Mix graham crumbs, 3 Tbsp. sugar and butter; press onto bottom of pan. Bake 10 min.

Meanwhile, beat cream cheese, 1 cup sugar, flour and vanilla with mixer until well blended. Add sour cream; mix well. Add eggs, 1 at a time, mixing on low after each just until blended. Pour over crust.

Bake for 40 min. or until center is almost set. Cool completely. Refrigerate 4 hours. Use foil handles to lift cheesecake from pan before cutting to serve. Top with pie filling, preserves, or fresh berries.

Adapted from Philadelphia Brand Cream Cheese

Desolation Sound & Discovery Passage

CHAPTER 10

DESOLATION SOUND
*Prideaux Haven • Homfray Lodge • Pendrell Sound
Refuge Cove • Teakerne Arm • Toba Inlet*

CORTES ISLAND
*Squirrel Cove • Cortes Bay • Von Donop Inlet
Gorge Harbour*

QUADRA ISLAND
*Rebecca Spit • Heriot Bay • Octopus Islands
Okisollo Channel*

DISCOVERY PASSAGE
Campbell River • April Point • Brown Bay • Small Inlet

DESOLATION SOUND & DISCOVERY PASSAGE

See Area Map Page 293 - Maps Not for Navigation

Captain George Vancouver had it all wrong when he explored and wrote about this area during his cruise in 1792. He named it Desolation Sound, saying, "there was not a single prospect that was pleasing to the eye." Granted, his crew did have a challenging time with weather, fleas, and even shellfish poisoning. In reality, Desolation Sound, located today literally just beyond the end of the road, is a place of extraordinary beauty. It's one of the Northwest's most dreamed-about and sought-after cruising destinations.

Officially, Desolation Sound is the body of water north of Sarah Point and Mary Point, and south of West Redonda Island. When most people think of cruising these waters they consider Desolation Sound to include the entire area north of Cape Mudge and Sarah Point, and south of Yuculta Rapids and Chatham Point, including Discovery Passage (Campbell River).

For those departing from the Seattle or Vancouver areas, the trip to or from Desolation Sound might take as long as a week, depending on boat speed, weather, and stops along the way.

Desolation Sound is not a huge area. Even slow boats can go from one end to another in a day. But Desolation Sound offers a wilderness setting, generally easy waters, many bays and coves to explore and anchor in, and marinas where fuel and supplies are available. On the west side of these cruising grounds, Campbell River on Vancouver Island is a vibrant small city. Campbell River has complete supplies and even a boatyard for haulout and repairs. Lund, on the B.C. mainland, is at the eastern entry to Desolation Sound. Lund is a quaint, small village that has several services vacationing boaters are apt to need, including a nearby boatyard and lift. Lund also is the northern terminus of Highway 99, a road that extends to Tierra del Fuego on the tip of South America. Small marinas scattered throughout Desolation Sound offer fuel, water, and limited supplies.

Okeover Harbour Authority docks

Since it is close to the point where the tidal currents meet on the inside of Vancouver Island, the water in Desolation Sound is not regularly exchanged with cold ocean water. During the summer, water temperatures of 70° to 80°F are not unusual in some of the bays, making for comfortable swimming.

Navigation is straightforward, with few hazards in the major channels. Closer to shore it's a different story, but the rocks and reefs are charted.

The most popular time to cruise Desolation Sound is from mid-July through the end of August, when the prospects for sunny, warm weather are best. It's also when the anchorages and facilities are most crowded. June weather can be cool and rainy, but crowds are not a problem. It's then that the waterfalls are most awesome and the resorts and businesses, while open and stocked, are the least harried.

If your calendar permits, the very best time to cruise Desolation Sound might be early- to mid-September. By then the high-season crowds have departed, yet summer usually hangs on for a last and glorious finale. Stock in the stores may be thin and the young summertime help has headed back to school, but the low slanting sunlight paints the hills and mountains with new drama, and the first colors of autumn make each day a fresh experience. Watch the weather closely. Leave before the fall storm pattern begins, although usually that's not before October.

Navigation note. Tide information for locations in Desolation Sound is shown in Ports and Passes and Canadian Tide and Current Tables, Vol. 5 (they are shown as secondary ports based on Point Atkinson Tides). Currents for Beazley Passage, Hole in the Wall, and Discovery Passage are shown in Vol. 6 and Ports and Passes as are corrections for Upper Rapids and Lower Rapids in Okisollo Channel. Owen Bay tides and Okisollo Channel secondary port tide corrections also are in Vol. 6 and Ports and Passes.

Sarah Point. For boats running north through Thulin Passage, Sarah Point, at the tip of the Malaspina Peninsula, is the dramatic entrance to Desolation Sound. The high hills of the Malaspina Peninsula hide the Coast Range mountains. But on a clear day, once Sarah Point is cleared, the mountains come into magnificent view.

MALASPINA INLET

Malaspina Inlet, Okeover Inlet, Lancelot Inlet and Theodosia Inlet all are entered between Zephine Point and Myrmidon Point. On a spring flood tide you will most likely find current at the mouth of Malaspina Inlet, all the way to Grace Harbour. Much of Gifford Peninsula, to the east of Malaspina Inlet, is Desolation Sound Marine Park. Several good anchorages are in this area. You'll also find rocks and reefs, most of them covered in kelp in summer and easily identified. They'll keep you alert, though.

Aquaculture occupies several otherwise inviting anchorages, but there are still plenty of choices in this area. Many of the aquaculture sites indicated on charts are no longer active, but debris left behind can foul ground tackle.

Malaspina Inlet is popular with kayakers. Be mindful of your wake.

① **Grace Harbour.** Grace Harbour is a popular anchorage. The inner bay is surrounded by forest and almost completely landlocked, with anchorage for quite a few boats. Many of the anchorages are along the shore, so be prepared to run a stern-tie. A fire pit is in a little, park-like area at the north end. A rock, shown on the charts, is in the middle of this innermost bay. The anchor just skids across the rock before finding holding ground on the other side. On a crowded summer weekend, the empty spot in the middle is there for a reason.

Treven Bay. The head of Trevenen Bay looks like a good anchorage on the chart, but the bay is largely taken by aquaculture.

Penrose Bay. Anchorage at the head of the bay. The Okeover Harbour Authority docks are on the west shore to the south.

② **Okeover Harbour Authority.** Okeover Inlet borders the Desolation Sound Marine Park area. The Okeover Harbour Authority docks are located on the western shore of Okeover Inlet a short distance south of Penrose Bay with road access to Lund. Oysters and other seafoods are grown in several places along beautiful Okeover Inlet.

The docks at Okeover are managed by the Okeover Harbour Authority (604) 483-3258,

CHARTS

3312 Small craft chart (chartbook)	Jervis Inlet & Desolation Sound
3513	Strait of Georgia – Northern Portion (1:80,000)
3537 Plans	Okisollo Channel (1:20,000); Whiterock Passage (1:10,000)
3538	Desolation Sound and Sutil Channel (1:40,000)
3539	Discovery Passage (1:40,000) Seymour Narrows (1:20,000)
3540	Approaches to Campbell River (1:10,000)
3541	Approaches to Toba Inlet (1:40,000)
3542	Bute Inlet (1:40,000)
3555 Plans	Vicinity of Redonda Islands & Loughborough Inlet
3559	Malaspina Inlet, Okeover Inlet & Lancelot Inlet (1:12,000)

www.WaggonerGuide.com

Reference Only – Not for Navigation   **DESOLATION SOUND & DISCOVERY PASSAGE**

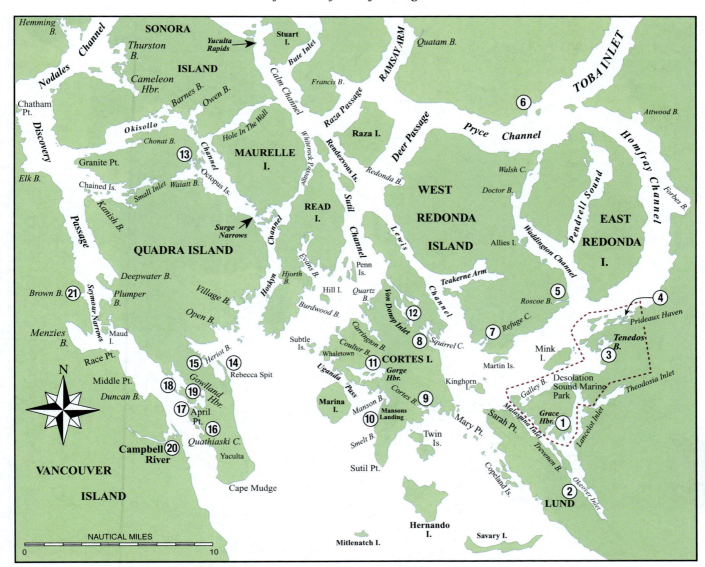

Desolation Sound and Discovery Passage

contact via VHF 66A. Docks located behind the L-shaped breakwater are for local working boats. The large outer breakwater (440 feet each side) provides plenty of space for transient moorage, no power, no water; the seaward side of the breakwater is exposed to northerly winds. Moorage is on a first-come, first-serve basis; payment made to wharfinger or fill out the self-registration envelope and deposit at the office door-drop. Office located on the wharf is open 12:30 p.m.-6:30 p.m. daily during the summer months, hours vary during the off-season. Launch ramp on-site.

The Laughing Oyster Restaurant (604) 483-9775 is located above the docks. It is an excellent restaurant with outstanding cuisine, lovely surroundings and a stunning view. Reservations recommended. It's one of those gems not to be missed.

Lancelot Inlet. Isabel Bay in Lancelot Inlet is popular. The best anchorage is behind Madge Islands, with a beautiful view and room for one or two boats among the large rock formations. Good anchorage is also in Thors Cove. The bay is deep, except in nooks or close to shore.

Correspondent Pat Shera, from Victoria, wrote to tell us that in Isabel Bay he fouled his anchor on a section of bulldozer track at the head of the anchorage, just west of the north tip of Madge Island. If you have Chartbook 3312, it's where the 4.2-meter sounding is shown. He says another section of track was high and dry on a nearby rock.

Theodosia Inlet. Theodosia Inlet has a narrow, shallow, and kelp-choked entrance, but is navigable by most boats at all stages of the tide. Once inside, the bay opens up. Logging activity takes away from the remote feeling of the bay. Boomed logs can occupy much of the shoreline. Anchorage is in a number of gunkholes along the shoreline.

MINK ISLAND AREA

Galley Bay. Galley Bay is just east of Zephine Head. It is a good anchorage, particularly in the eastern end.

Mink Island. Mink Island is private property, but you'll find excellent anchorage in the bay that indents the southeast shore, particularly if you work in behind the little island in the center of the bay. You'll probably run a stern-tie to shore.

Curme Islands. Wolferstan describes navigation in the Curme Islands, east of Mink Island, as "challenging." Bailey and Cummings, in their *Gunkholing* book (now out of print), described the Curme Islands as extremely tight with shallow waterways, but with anchoring possibilities if the boat uses 4-way ties to hold position. For most people, dinghies and kayaks are probably the way to go.

③ **Tenedos Bay.** Tenedos Bay (also called Deep Bay) is a favorite, for a couple of reasons. First, it's a good, protected anchorage, with a landlocked basin behind the island off the northwest shore. This island is joined with the mainland by a drying shoal, shown on the charts. Second, it's just a short dinghy ride to the mouth of the stream that runs from Unwin Lake, a popular freshwater swimming hole. A path beside the stream leads to the lake. Several of the stream's pools, screened by vegetation, make good bathing places.

2018 WAGGONER CRUISING GUIDE

DESOLATION SOUND & DISCOVERY PASSAGE

See Area Map Page 293 - Maps Not for Navigation

See Area Map Page 293 - Maps Not for Navigation   **DESOLATION SOUND & DISCOVERY PASSAGE**

Melanie Cove, a quintessential Desolation Sound anchorage with jaw-dropping views. Stern ties are the rule, made easier with anchors along the north shore.

Exploring the rocky shores of Prideaux Haven

In addition to the landlocked basin noted above, you'll find anchorages in coves along the shore of Tenedos Bay. We like the little notch at the northernmost corner. Stern-ties to shore are the norm. The center of Tenedos Bay is too deep (300 to 600 feet) for anchoring.

Caution: As you enter Tenedos Bay, a nasty rock lies submerged off the south side of Bold Head. Especially if you are headed to or from Refuge Cove, Mink Island, or around Bold Head to Prideaux Haven, this rock is right on your probable course. The rock lies farther offshore than you might expect. Give it an extra wide berth, just to be sure. Remember to study your charts before proceeding in these waters. A number of rocks are shown. All are easy to avoid if you are aware of them.

Otter Island. A very narrow but navigable channel runs between Otter Island and the mainland. Ample space for a few boats to anchor on the north side, using stern-ties to shore.

PRIDEAUX HAVEN AREA

The coves that make up the area generally known as Prideaux Haven are the most popular spots in Desolation Sound, with several requiring stern-ties to increase the number of boats accommodated. The area is described in great detail by M. Wylie Blanchet in her classic book *The Curve of Time.*

At the head of Melanie Cove you can find the remains of Mike's place, and in Laura Cove traces of old Phil Lavine's cabin site are visible (both from *The Curve of Time*). The evidence, however, is getting pretty faint.

The entire clutch of islands and shallow waterways invites exploration by dinghy or kayak. The narrow pass between Scobell Island and the William Islands, for instance, is beautiful. During high season, the only thing missing is solitude. You'll have lots of company.

No Discharge Zone. Gray water okay.

Eveleigh Island. Anchorage is in Eveleigh Anchorage, the western cove behind Eveleigh Island. A drying reef connects Eveleigh Island with the mainland. Entry to the other Prideaux Haven anchorages is around the east end of Eveleigh Island. A reef almost, but not quite, closes this entrance. Use Chart 3555 (recommended) or Chartbook 3312. Smaller scale Chart 3538 (1:40,000) shows the entry but with too little detail to inspire confidence. After rounding Lucy Point, strongly favor the Eveleigh Island side of the passage to clear the reef.

④ **Prideaux Haven.** Inside Eveleigh Island is the main Prideaux Haven anchorage and also Melanie Cove. Except in the very middle of Prideaux Haven and Melanie Cove, stern ties are the rule during the summer. There are 13 stern-tie mooring eyes with chain along the southwest shore of Eveleigh Island and 3 stern-tie mooring eyes with chain on the southeast side

Prideaux Haven Stern-tie Anchors

2018 WAGGONER CRUISING GUIDE   295

of Scobell Island. In 2016 seven new stern-tie mooring eyes were installed in Melanie Cove.

No Discharge Zone. Gray water okay.

④ **Melanie Cove.** Melanie Cove is perfectly protected, with ample room along both shores for boats to anchor and stern-tie. Stern-ties along the north shore are made easier with recently installed stern-tie mooring eyes, while the south shore requires a scramble up-shore to find a tree or rock anchor. A few boats can anchor in the middle without a stern-tie. An overgrown apple orchard and the site of Mike's cabin, warmly described in *The Curve of Time*, are at the head of the cove. A small creek on the south shore, near the head, has a flowing hose. The water is untreated, and not recommended for human consumption.

Correspondent Gil Flanagan tells us a trail runs between Melanie Cove and Unwin Lake, with a new section that bypasses an earlier hand-over-hand section. He says the first half-mile is easy, and has a nice view at the end.

④ **Laura Cove.** Laura Cove has a fairly narrow entrance, with a least depth of approximately 10 feet at zero tide. Rocks extend from both sides. Enter cautiously. Once you're inside, the bay is beautiful. A few cherry trees and English Ivy mark Old Phil, the Frenchman's cabin site mentioned in *The Curve of Time*, at the head of this bay. Anchorage is to the east of Copplestone Point; there are a number of stern-tie opportunities along the north and south shores of the cove, the west end of the cove is a maze of rocks and reefs.

Roffey Island. If you can't find a place at Prideaux Haven, Melanie Cove, or Laura Cove, try the little bay behind Roffey Island. Room for one or more boats away from the crowd.

Homfray Channel. Homfray Channel curves from the south end of West Redonda Island and around East Redonda Island, until it merges with Toba Inlet. The only bays of consequence are Forbes Bay and Atwood Bay. The center of Atwood Bay is too deep for convenient anchoring, though we've successfully anchored in the nook indenting the north shore. Bob Stephenson, the former owner of Desolation Sound Yacht Charters, says Forbes Bay can be good for anchoring.

In Bill Wolferstan's book, *Desolation Sound and the Discovery Islands*, he tells of two Native pictographs on the west shore of Homfray Channel—one of a single fish, the other unidentified. Actually, there are several pictographs located about 10 feet above the high water line. Correspondent Pat Shera gives coordinates of 50°11.698'N/124°39.514'W.

Homfray Lodge. (604) 740-6032; info@homfraylodge.com; www.homfraylodge.com. Just north of Forbes Bay. Beautiful and remote location with 250 feet of moorage and two mooring buoys. Moorage is for guests who have booked overnight stays at the lodge. Potable water, showers, Wi-Fi at the lodge. No power or food service. Guests can sit on the covered porch and enjoy a beautiful view up the channel. Cabins are available for rent. Fishing and sightseeing charters can be arranged. Reservations recommended during the high season.

WADDINGTON CHANNEL

⑤ **Roscoe Bay/Roscoe Bay Marine Park.** Roscoe Bay, on West Redonda Island where Waddington Channel meets Homfray Channel, is an excellent, protected, and popular anchorage. The bay is divided into an inner cove and an outer cove, separated by a drying shoal easily crossed by shallow draft boats at half tide or better. If in doubt, go in on a rising tide. At high tide most sailboats can get in.

The inner cove is pretty, and except for the other boats enjoying the bay with you, it's a good example of what cruising in these waters is all about. Dinghy ashore and take the short hike up to the knob dividing the two bays.

At the head of the inner cove an old logging road with a short stream beside it connects with Black Lake. During summer months the water in Black Lake is warm and excellent for swimming or bathing. Trout fishing is reportedly good. If you carry your dinghy up the road you can launch it along the lake's shoreline.

On the west side of Roscoe Bay a large red float (a "scotsman") hangs in a tree marking the beginning of a trail to the top of a 2200-foot-high mountain. A rock cairn has been built at the summit, and on the cairn is a bottle with pencil and paper inside. Write your name on the paper and add it to the collection. The hike is demanding and a round trip takes several hours, so use your judgment.

No Discharge Zone. Gray water okay.

LOCAL KNOWLEDGE

SPEED LIMIT: Seed oyster growers in Pendrell Sound ask for a 4-knot speed limit in the vicinity of their operations to prevent damage.

Pendrell Sound. With summer water temperatures dependably in excess of 68°F, Pendrell Sound has been called the "warmest saltwater north of Mexico." Major oyster culture operations are in the sound, providing seed oysters to growers all along the coast.

Strings of cultch material (often empty oyster shells) are suspended from floats in the bay until the oyster spat adheres to them, at which point they are shipped.

The favored anchorage is at the head of Pendrell Sound, probably stern-tied to trees ashore. Wear good shoes and sturdy gloves when you're clambering around on the rocks.

Another anchorage is on the western shore, about three-quarters of the way up the sound, tucked in behind a small islet at the outfall from a saltwater lagoon. "We tried this anchorage in deteriorating weather a few years ago, but found the best spots, close to the islet, taken. With nightfall approaching and conditions worsening, we got creative. The charts show the shore on the north edge of this cove as reefs, but we found a nice opening, perhaps 50 feet wide, between two fingers of reef. We were able to set the anchor in front of the opening and back in. A long stern-tie was run to rocks on shore. It took several changes in the stern-tie termination point to align the boat just right, but once done, the anchorage was snug and safe for the night—a windy night filled with rain, thunder and lightning. We were rather proud of ourselves." [*Hale*]

Elworthy Island. A delightful cozy anchorage lies behind Elworthy Island, a mile north of Church Point, roughly across Waddington Channel from the entrance to Pendrell Sound. The aquaculture noted on charts no longer is present. The island is called Alfred

Sailboats stern-tied in cozy Laura Cove. Note: Tying to live trees is discouraged.

Roscoe Bay is a scenic and popular anchorage. A lake is a short walk from the head of the bay, seen in this photo.

See Area Map Page 293 - Maps Not for Navigation   **DESOLATION SOUND & DISCOVERY PASSAGE**

Toba Wilderness Marina updated their docks and added a new Welcome House.

Island by Wolferstan, but in 1992 it was renamed Elworthy Island for seaman Richard Elworthy, who died serving freedom in 1942. A handsome plaque is set into rock on the northeast corner of the island. Enter the anchorage from either end, but watch for a drying rock near the north entrance. The south entrance shallows to about 12 feet. The island's shoreline is covered with oysters.

Allies Island. Allies Island is connected to West Redonda Island by a drying reef. The north cove is pretty well choked with aquaculture; anchorage is possible in the south cove. The south cove offers a secluded anchorage for 1 to 3 boats and is exposed to the southeast. The rocks around the cove are full of oysters.

Doctor Bay. Doctor Bay is mostly filled with aquaculture. Correspondent Fred Triggs reports good anchorage in 35-40 feet north of the aquaculture operation. We've also heard reports that the aquaculture operation allows pleasure boats to tie up to some floats; check with an employee for instructions.

Walsh Cove Marine Park. Walsh Cove Marine Park is a beautiful little spot with room for a few boats to anchor on a rocky bottom. Enter Walsh Cove from the south. At the north end of the cove, a rock-strewn reef connects Gorges Island to West Redonda Island. The middle of the cove is deep. Most boats anchor near shore with stern-ties to rocks or trees.

The cove is well protected from down-channel winds but open to up-channel winds from the south. Two sets of Native pictographs are at Butler Point.

⑥ **Toba Wilderness Marina.** (250) 830-2269; inquiries@tobawilderness.com; www.tobawilderness.com. Contact VHF 66A ahead of time for tie-up instructions upon approach. Reservations highly recommended during July and August. This is a quiet marina, located behind Double Island at the mouth of Toba Inlet. The views up Toba Inlet are breathtaking. The marina expanded their dock space in 2016 and now has 1400 feet of moorage, on concrete floats, for vessels up to 200 feet, with no requirement for rafting. At the top of the dock ramp, enjoy the new Welcome House for afternoon and evening get-togethers. 5 km of hiking trails, Wi-Fi, washroom, showers, and garbage drop-off (1 bag only per day with overnight moorage). Abundant clean clear water is available on the dock, with 30 and 50 amp power. Scheduled float plane service is available by Kenmore Air. NW Seaplanes and Corilair also stop there. Secure long-term moorage and boat watch available. Please do not go into the water while hiking to the base of the falls, as this is the source of the marina's drinking water. This marina is not setup for day visits or tours. Overnight guests only please. Anchoring in the bay adjacent to the dock is not recommended.

Toba Inlet. Toba Inlet extends 20 miles into the 8,000-foot-high Coast Range mountains until it ends in drying flats at the mouth of the

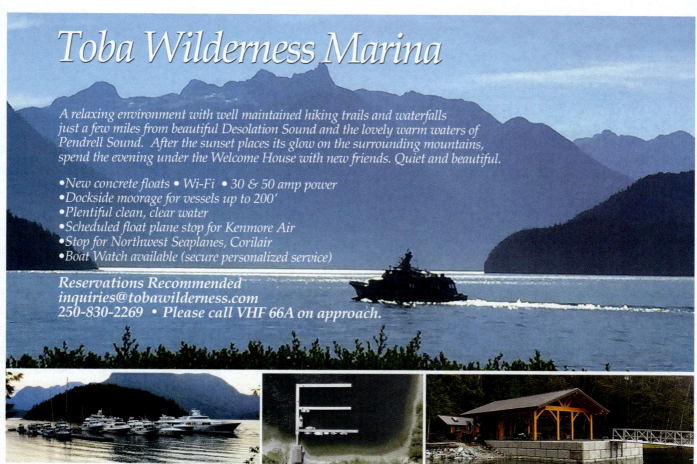

2018 waggoner CRUISING GUIDE   297

DESOLATION SOUND & DISCOVERY PASSAGE See Area Map Page 293 - Maps Not for Navigation

Refuge Cove Store has food, supplies and a selection of marine hardware.

A trail overlooking the falls leads from the dinghy dock at Teakerne Arm.

Toba River. The water is very deep right up to the rock wall shores. Look for two Native pictographs in Toba Inlet: one along the west shore at 50°25'N/124°40.7'W and another on the north shore at 50°25.2'N/124°34.4'W of the inlet. Magnificent waterfalls crash into the sea, especially early in the season when the snowpack is rapidly melting. Toba Inlet reminds us of the inlets north of Cape Caution. Limited anchorage is possible at the head of the inlet, and in Brem Bay off the mouth of the Brem River. We observed a boat stern-tied in a small bight off the north shore near a river inlet at approximately 50°26'N/124°32'W.

After being unused for some time, we found the log dump in Brem Bay partially active again in 2014. Correspondent Gil Flanagan reports that he has anchored, stern-tied, on the northeast side of Brem Bay, at the mouth of a cove created by a rock breakwater not shown on the chart. The views were beautiful.

Toba Inlet's most dramatic waterfalls are on the north side, about 3 miles past Snout Point, opposite Brem Bay, on the south side of the inlet.

LEWIS CHANNEL

Lewis Channel runs between West Redonda Island and Cortes Island.

⑦ **Refuge Cove.** Refuge Cove, with a public marina, fuel dock, shops and well-stocked store, is a good resupply stop in the heart of Desolation Sound. The busiest times are between 11:00 a.m. and 3:00 p.m. For easiest moorage and fuel dock use, early morning and late afternoon are recommended. Several homes, joined by boardwalks, surround the cove. Ample moorage is available. A floating dock, just off the fuel dock, is for overflow moorage, with no power or water. Dogs should be on a leash. A pet path is beside the used-book stand. Anchorage is possible toward the head of the bay.

Traffic can be heavy during high season. Approach slowly, and wait your turn for dock space or fuel. Turnover is rapid; you shouldn't have to wait long. Refuge Cove is a scheduled stop for float plane service.

Garbage barge: Around mid-June, an enterprising chap named Dave Cartwright moors a barge near the mouth of Refuge Cove. For a reasonable fee charged by the pound he accepts bagged garbage and responsibly takes it away. If you have accumulated garbage from several days in Desolation Sound, this is one of the few places to dispose of it.

⑦ **Refuge Cove General Store.** General Delivery, Refuge Cove, BC V0P 1P0; (250) 935-6659; refcov@twincomm.ca; www.refugecove.com. Guest moorage along 2000 feet of side-tie dock space. No reservations; first-come, first-served. The fuel dock has gasoline, diesel, and propane. Washrooms, showers and laundry are up by the store. Free purified water, 15 amp power, fee-based Wi-Fi.

The store carries groceries, fresh produce, deli items including cheeses and meats, hand-dipped ice cream, a complete liquor agency with interesting wine selections, some marine supplies and gear, charts, cube and block ice, a good selection of books and magazines. It is also a post office. If Judith Williams' delightful book *Dynamite Stories* is in stock, pick up a copy. The stories are a blast, literally. The store has limited operating hours in the fall.

Most businesses, including the art gallery and gift shop, are open June through August. The cafe has bakery items and fresh bread; open for breakfast, lunch and dinner. Licensed for wine and beer with Happy Hour specials.

Teakerne Arm. Teakerne Arm is a deep inlet extending from Lewis Channel into West Redonda Island. Anchorage is just inside the en-

Refuge Cove

Replenish Refuel Refresh
in the Heart of Desolation Sound

- Complete Groceries including Fresh Produce, Meats, Dairy Products, Deli
- Gas, Diesel, Oil, Propane
- Large Liquor & Wine Selection
- Block & Party Ice
- Showers, Laundry, Post Office
- Gifts, Books & Charts
- Fishing Tackle & Bait
- Espresso, Desserts, Burgers
- Wireless Internet
- Float Plane Service
- Moorage – no reservations necessary – 4hr courtesy stopover

Seasonal Hours
June: 9am-5pm
July & Aug: 9am-6pm
Sept. 1-15: 9am-5pm

Famous Friendly Service
250-935-6659
refcov@twincomm.ca

trance in Talbot Cove, or in front of the waterfall from Cassel Lake at the head of the north arm, or in the south arm. Both arms are deep, except very close to shore.

The area near the waterfall is a provincial park, with a dinghy float connected to shore by an aluminum ramp. Anchorage is in 90 to 150 feet. A cable in fair but serviceable condition hangs down the rock wall west of the waterfall for stern-ties. Several rings are set in the rock just above the high tide line and on either side of the dinghy dock. The waterfall is stunning, about 2½ stories high. Taking the short, vigorous hike from the dinghy float to Cassel Lake for a swim is a popular pastime. The water warms in the summer.

Talbot Cove. Talbot Cove is near the entrance to Teakerne Arm, on the south shore. The cove is marked with large yellow propane floats for a commercial operation. Anchor with a stern-tie in the southeast corner.

CORTES ISLAND

Recommended book: Destination Cortez Island, by June Cameron, describes the early days on Cortes Island. In our opinion this book joins *The Curve of Time* as entertaining background reading about the B.C. coast. After reading *Destination Cortez Island* you will have an entirely different outlook about your explorations of Cortes Bay, Squirrel Cove, Von Donop Inlet, Whaletown, Gorge Harbour, Mansons Landing, and the entire Desolation Sound area.

Published in Canada by Heritage House and in the U.S. by Fine Edge Nautical Publishing.

⑧ **Squirrel Cove.** Squirrel Cove is made up of an outer bay and an inner bay. The outer bay provides access to the public wharf and the Squirrel Cove Trading Co. general store dock. The Flying Squirrel take-out stand and The Cove restaurant are located upland. A farmers market is held Sundays from 11:00 a.m. to 3:00 p.m. The inner bay, consisting of two anchorage areas, has better protection and during the summer is often full of anchored boats. A saltwater lagoon is at the head of the inner bay. A connecting rapids runs into the lagoon at high tide and out of the lagoon at low tide. Be sure to plan an exit strategy if you enter the lagoon by dinghy.

Gorge Harbour

At one time the inner bay was used for log booming. June Cameron wrote an article in Pacific Yachting telling of a tangle of sunken logs on the bottom. Our side-scan sounder showed the bay filled with logs scattered like matchsticks. A trail leads from the northwest corner of Squirrel Cove to Von Donop Inlet.

The large building on the west shore is a Native Cultural Centre and offices.

No Discharge Zone. Gray water okay.

⑧ **Squirrel Cove Public Wharf.** Guest moorage with 15, 20 & 30 amp power along 200 feet of dock. The dock is close to the Squirrel Cove Trading Co. store, The Cove Restaurant and the Flying Squirrel Take-Out window. Garbage drop (charge assessed at an honor box) and pay telephone available.

At very low tides the ramps from the wharf to the floats are quite steep. Local boats often take much of the dock space, although by being patient we've found room. Rafting permitted. There's always room for a dinghy. A full-time diver is nearby for maintenance and recovery. The phone number posted at the dock.

⑧ **Squirrel Cove Trading Co. Ltd.** P.O. Box 1, Squirrel Cove, BC V0P 1T0; (250) 935-6327; squirrelcovetrading@yahoo.ca; www.squirrelcove.com. Open all year. Washrooms, showers and laundry are in a separate building just west of the store. Gasoline, diesel, propane and kerosene available upland. Gas and diesel available at the store's dock which is small and only accessible at higher tides. Picnic tables available. This is a good provisioning stop, with fresh produce, meat and fish, groceries, ice, books, marine hardware, post office, pay phone, Wi-Fi, liquor, and ATM. The expanded hardware section downstairs has just about anything a person might need.

A crafts shop and gallery is next to the store, stocked with island-made (or designed) goods and clothing. Artists take turns staffing the shop. A Sunday market, with crafts, local produce, baked goods and musicians, runs from 11:00 a.m. to 3:00 p.m., summers only.

The Cove Restaurant was closed in 2017. At press time the restaurant is planned to be open in 2018. The Flying Squirrel is a take-out stand serving fresh fish, bannock "native fry bread," and several gluten-free options. You can dine on the picnic tables. In the off season sandwiches are available at the store. New owners purchased Squirrel Cove in 2016. The store was refreshed with improvements in the mix of merchandise and the layout.

⑨ **Cortes Bay.** Cortes Bay is well protected, but in some places the soft mud bottom doesn't

Squirrel Cove Store is under new management. The gift shop, on the right, carries locally-made items.

DESOLATION SOUND & DISCOVERY PASSAGE   *See Area Map Page 293 - Maps Not for Navigation*

hold well. Use Chart 3538 when approaching. Several charted rocks and reefs near the entrance have claimed the inattentive. These include Central Rock, north of Twin Islands, several rocks around Three Islets, and a rock off the headland midway between Mary Point and the entrance to Cortes Bay. To be safe, we always pass south of Three Islets.

Pay close attention to the beacon in the middle of the narrow entry to Cortes Bay. This beacon, with its red triangle dayboard, marks the south end of a nasty reef. Leave the beacon to starboard (Red, Right, Returning) as you enter. If you doubt the existence of this reef, one look at low tide will convince you. A small public wharf is at the head of Cortes Bay. It is usually full during the summer. Rafting is required.

Seattle Yacht Club has an outstation on the south shore of Cortes Bay, at the location of a former marina. Royal Vancouver Yacht Club has an outstation on the north shore. No reciprocals at either outstation.

Local knowledge says good holding ground is east of the Royal Van outstation, off the mouth of a small drying cove. During a 30- to 40-knot southeasterly blow we saw several boats anchored successfully off the SYC outstation as well.

No Discharge Zone. Gray water okay.

Twin Islands. Twin Islands, located off the southeast side of Cortes Island, are really a single island divided by a drying spit. Anchorage is possible close to the drying spit on either side.

Sutil Point. Sutil Point is the south end of Cortes Island. A long, drying spit dotted with boulders extends south from the point, almost to buoy Q20. Give this buoy plenty of sea room.

A fresh southeast wind, especially if it is blowing against an ebb current (see Point Atkinson tides), will set up high steep seas south of Sutil Point and east past Mitlenatch Island. Sutil Point can be dangerous in a southeasterly.

Smelt Bay Provincial Park. One mile north of Sutil Point on the west side of the peninsula. Good temporary anchorage is close to shore. The park has 23 campsites, picnic tables, and a white sand beach.

⑩ **Mansons Landing.** The historic store at Mansons Landing has been closed and the building moved about three-quarters of a mile up the hill. It is now a co-op with a broad selection of organic foods and a coffee shop with Wi-Fi. An excellent small bookstore is next to the co-op. The post office, community center and library, a snack stand and a small market are across the street. A farmers market is held Fridays from 12:00 p.m. to 3:00 p.m at Manson's Hall.

The 177-foot public dock is still there, and garbage can be left for a fee. Anchorage is good north of the public dock. The entire area is exposed to the south.

No Discharge Zone. Gray water okay.

⑩ **Mansons Landing Marine Park.** Open all year, 117 acres. The park has no dock of its own, but can be reached from the Mansons Landing public dock, or you can anchor out. Hague Lake, with warm water and swimming beaches safe for small children, is a 10-minute walk from the public dock.

⑪ **Gorge Harbour** is a large bay with many good spots to put the hook down. The entry is through a narrow cleft in the rock cliff. Orange-colored Native pictographs, including a stick figure man, a man on what appears to be a turtle or fish, and several vertical lines, are on the rock wall to port as you enter. You have to look closely to identify them. Current runs through the entrance, but boats go through at any time. Inside you'll find good, protected anchorage. An aquaculture operation is to starboard just inside the entrance. The Gorge Harbour Marina Resort, on the northwest shore, has many amenities, including a restaurant. If the marina is full, anchor in the protected bay in 55 to 60 feet.

No Discharge Zone. Gray water okay.

⑪ **Gorge Harbour Marina Resort.** P.O. Box 89, Whaletown, BC V0P 1Z0; (250) 935-6433 ext. 4; moorage@gorgeharbour.com; www.gorgeharbour.com. Monitors VHF 66A. Open all year, gasoline and diesel at the fuel dock, guest moorage along 1800 feet of dock. Reservations are recommended May 15 to September 15; held-back moorage space is released daily at 4:00 p.m., first-come, first-served. Facilities include 30 & 50 amp power, water, swimming pool, hot tub, barbecue areas, washrooms, showers, laundry, Wi-Fi, pay phones. A well-stocked convenience store has fresh vegetables, meats, dairy products, liquor, ice, propane, DVD movie rentals. Four lodge rooms and a poolside cottage for rent. Garbage disposal is available for marina guests for a fee, no charge for recycling. Complete recycling instructions available. The resort has an RV park, 2 trailer rentals, campground, lodge accommodations, and float plane service. Boats, kayaks, stand-up paddleboards, and cars for rent.

The resort features a pool and hot tub surrounded by attractive landscaping. A patio with a fireplace and barbecue area are available for guest use. Both overlook the harbor. Live music is often performed in the evening on the patio. There is an elaborate children's play area. Many boaters consider Gorge Harbour Marina & Resort to be on the list of special destinations. The Gorge Harbour Marina farmer's market is open from 10 a.m. to 1:00 p.m. Saturdays during summer.

The Floathouse Restaurant always gets excellent reviews. The atmosphere is cozy and conducive to multi-table conversations. Open from May through September, with reduced hours in winter. During peak season the restaurant offers breakfast, lunch, tapas (3:00p.m. to 5:00p.m.), dinner and a Sunday brunch. Espresso and pastries at the bar all day long. Year after year, they have a great chef. The restaurant has two areas, one part is covered with a bar and cocktail area; the other part is open with seating overlooking the harbor. Restaurant reservations recommended in the high season, outdoor seating can be requested.

⑪ **Gorge Harbour Public Dock.** Located a short distance east of the Gorge Harbour Marina. Commercial vessels have priority. A new boat launch ramp is located adjacent to the public dock.

Uganda Passage. Uganda Passage separates Cortes Island from Marina Island. The pass is narrow and winding, but well marked and easy to navigate as long as you pay attention. Red, Right, Returning assumes you are returning from the south. See the Uganda Passage map showing the route through the passage. Shark Spit is long and low, with a superb sand beach. Swimming is good. Anchorage is south of the pass, on either the Cortes Island side or the Marina Island side.

Whaletown. Whaletown is the terminus of the ferry between Cortes Island and Quadra Island. The ferry dock is on the north side of the bay, and a small public float is on the south side. Watch for several marked and unmarked rocks, normally covered by kelp. The small post office is open limited hours, but outgoing mail can be deposited anytime.

Subtle Islands. The two Subtle Islands are separated by a drying shoal. Good anchorage is off this shoal on the east side, particularly in settled weather. The little bay on the north side is very deep except at the head. It has a lovely (and exposed) view to the north. The islands are privately owned and marked with "stay off" and "keep away" signs.

Coulter Bay. Coulter Bay is pretty, but as the chart indicates, much of the bay is too shallow for anchoring. Most of the good spots are taken by local boats. You could anchor in the tiny nook behind Coulter Island, beside a little unnamed islet to the west. Some cabins are nearby, but they are screened from view and you won't feel as if you're in their kitchens.

Carrington Bay. Carrington Bay is pretty, and well protected except from the north. The bottom is rocky so be sure your anchor is properly set before turning in for the night.

Uganda Passage

See Area Map Page 293 - Maps Not for Navigation

DESOLATION SOUND & DISCOVERY PASSAGE

Whiterock Passage is narrow, with leading and following range markers to guide you through safely.

Carrington Lagoon, at the head of the bay, is interesting to explore. Drag the dinghy across the logs that choke the entrance to the lagoon. June Cameron, in *Destination Cortez*, says the lagoon entrance was blasted out of rock, with amazingly smooth sides—a tribute to the skills of the man who did the blasting. A good anchorage is to the right, near the entrance to the lagoon, with a stern-tie ashore. We've seen other boats anchored in the little bight a short distance to the left of the lagoon entrance and behind the tiny island just off the eastern shore of the bay.

No Discharge Zone. Gray water okay.

Quartz Bay. Quartz Bay is unusually pretty, with good holding bottom. The eastern cove of the bay has several homes and two private docks along the shoreline. You can anchor with swinging room in 30 to 42 feet near the head, but you're in their front yards. The western cove has some aquaculture, one cabin on the shore, and anchoring depths near the south and west shores. You may have to run a stern-tie to shore. It is exposed to north winds, but it's a nice spot.

LOCAL KNOWLEDGE

DANGEROUS ROCK: About halfway into Von Donop Inlet, a rock lies in the narrowest part of the channel. Look for two prominent rock outcroppings covered with lichen, moss and grass on the left side of the channel. The rock is opposite the second, or inner, of these outcroppings. Hug the right side and keep that rock to port, even if tree branches try to brush the starboard side of the boat or rigging.

⑫ **Von Donop Inlet.** Von Donop Inlet, on the northwest corner of Cortes Island, is entered through a narrow, 2-mile-long channel with reversing tidal overflows. Entry and exit should be at high-water slack. Once inside, several coves provide protected anchorage. The largest of these coves takes up the entire head of the inlet and has room for many boats. The bottom in this area is sticky mud. It is ideal for holding, but requires extra cleaning time when the anchor is brought aboard. Several maintained trails lead from the head of Von Donop Inlet to lakes, other destinations, and Squirrel Cove.

⑫ **Háthayim Provincial Marine Park (Von Donop).** This 3155-acre park includes Von Donop Inlet, Robertson Lake and Wiley Lake.

Read Island. The east side of Read Island is indented from the south by Evans Bay, where several little notches are worth exploring as anchorages. Most have drying flats at their heads. Bird Cove is probably the best protected, although Contributing Editor Tom Kincaid has spent a quiet night behind the little islets in the bay just to the north of Bird Cove. A small public float is near the entrance to Evans Bay.

Hill Island. Hill Island is privately owned. According to Sailing Directions, a private lodge with a floating breakwater is in Totem Bay. The island is not open to the public.

Burdwood Bay. Burdwood Bay has several possible anchorages, particularly on the lee side of the little islands that extend from the south side of the bay, and in a notch in the north end. Burdwood Bay is not particularly pretty, but could be a hideout in a storm.

Hoskyn Channel. Hoskyn Channel runs between Read Island and Quadra Island and connects at the north with Whiterock Passage and Surge Narrows.

Bold Island Anchorage. Bold Island is just north of Village Bay on the west side of Hoskyn Channel, located at approximately 50°10'N/125°10'W. Correspondent Carol-Ann Giroday reports that they enter through Crescent Channel, and have good anchorage in the basin at the northwest corner of Bold Island, approximately between the two drying reefs. She says two oyster farms are in the area, but there is room for several boats to anchor, and that a wonderful oyster and clam beach is in the green-colored drying nook on Quadra Island. She adds, "We have gone ashore at this location and walked along Surge Narrows Road to nearby Village Bay Lake, where we enjoyed a fresh water swim. From the anchorage, the view southward across to Read Island and Dunsterville Islet is spectacular." This anchorage might be exposed to southerlies.

Hjorth Bay. Hjorth Bay, on Hoskyn Channel along the west side of Read Island, is a good anchorage except in a strong southerly. Anchor in 50 to 60 feet, probably with a stern-tie to shore. A small cabin is on shore behind the island.

Whiterock Passage. Whiterock Passage is narrow, and the dredged channel is bounded on both sides by drying shoals studded with angry boulders. Least depth at zero tide is 5 feet. Maximum currents are 2 knots. Running Whiterock Passage at half tide is a good idea—it exposes the shoals on both sides but provides a little extra depth. The uninitiated tend to avoid Whiterock Passage, but it's easy to run if you pay attention and know how. Here's how:

Carefully study Plans Chart 3537 or Chartbook 3312, both of which detail Whiterock Passage at a scale of 1:10,000. As the charts show, two ranges are on the Read Island side of the passage. Going either direction, one will be a leading range as you enter, and the other a back range as you depart. Approaching, find the leading range and stay exactly on it. Proceed slowly and watch astern as the back range comes into view. When the back range lines up, turn the appropriate direction and let the back range keep you on course as you complete your transit.

Remember that the course lines on the charts are true, not magnetic. You must subtract the magnetic variation from the true heading to get the magnetic course. Before entering, make sure you have a clear view astern from the helm to view the back range markers.

Rendezvous Islands. The Rendezvous Islands have a number of homes along their shores. Anchorage may be possible in a bight between the southern and middle islands, but a private float and dolphins restrict the room available.

CALM CHANNEL

Calm Channel connects Lewis Channel and Sutil Channel to the south, and with Bute Inlet and the Yuculta Rapids to the north. It is appropriately named, often being wind-free when areas nearby are breezy.

Frances Bay. A logging road and logging dump area are located on the westerly side at the head of the bay, indicating past logging operations. In 2017 no logging operations were observed and boats were seen anchored at the head of the bay in the eastern portion. It has been reported that the bottom is rocky throughout the rest of the bay and an anchor fouling cable is near the log dump.

Church House. Church House is an abandoned Indian Reserve opposite the entrance to Hole in the Wall on Calm Channel, and near the mouth of Bute Inlet. The white-painted church, an often-photographed landmark, has collapsed in a heap.

Redonda Bay. Redonda Bay has the ruins of an old wharf left over from logging days, but

2018 WAGGONER CRUISING GUIDE

DESOLATION SOUND & DISCOVERY PASSAGE   See Area Map Page 293 - Maps Not for Navigation

Okisollo Channel

otherwise is not a good anchorage. The wharf is no longer usable and the ramp leading from the float to the wharf is gone. Several rocks in the bay are charted.

Bute Inlet. Bute Inlet, approximately 35 miles long, is very deep. Except in small areas near the mouths of rivers and at the head of the inlet, it is not good for anchorage. Usually, the bottom drops away steeply, making a stern-tie to shore necessary. Anchorages should be chosen with an eye to strong inflow winds during the afternoon, followed by calm, then by icy outflow winds in the morning. Correspondents Gil and Karen Flanagan explain:

"The glaciers around Bute Inlet were melting and there are a lot of them. The water was milky by Stuart Island, and got darker and darker the farther up we went, turning from light green to gray to brownish. We saw considerable drift, including complete trees with roots sticking 8 feet or so into the air. At times we had to slow to idle, shift to neutral and coast through bands of drift. Jack Mold, the caretaker at Southgate Camp, said what we experienced was normal.

Waddington Harbour, at the head of Bute Inlet, has a lot of good anchoring spots in 10 to 50 foot depths. We anchored as close to the northeast shore as we could get, and still were at least 100 yards from the beach (don't bother trying to stern-tie). There is no protection from wind, but we had no wind. We didn't see much driftwood on the beach, either. We doubt if inflow winds blow hard or long, probably because even on hot days the massive ice fields in the mountains above preclude high land temperatures.

Because of the ice fields, we had an overnight low in the upper 40s on September 1. It was 10 to 20 degrees lower than temperatures we had been experiencing in Desolation Sound. The morning air was cold enough that we needed heavy coats, even in the sun.

Mountains 6,000 to 7,000 feet high rise directly from the head of the inlet. They have snowfields, and are spectacular.

The milky water, drifting logs, huge harbor and high mountains create an environment that felt wild and different from anywhere we have been on the coast. We spent only 19 hours in Waddington Harbour, which wasn't long enough to take the dinghy up either river. We did see a grizzly bear on the beach near our anchorage. We definitely will go back." [*Flanagan*]

Reader Richard McBride sent a note about a tiny anchorage he calls "The Nook," just outside Orford Bay:

"It is a small crack in the mountain wall about 100 feet wide at the opening and about 150 feet deep, with a little waterfall at the head. This is a terrific spot for a couple of small boats to tuck in. Lat/lon 50°34.368'N/124°52.439'W."

OKISOLLO CHANNEL/ SURGE NARROWS

Owen Bay tides and Okisollo Channel Secondary Port tide corrections are contained in Canadian Tide and Current Tables Vol. 6, and Ports and Passes. Okisollo Channel runs along

Quiet anchorage in Octopus Islands Marine Park, northwest of the northerly narrow entrance channel

See Area Map Page 293 - Maps Not for Navigation

DESOLATION SOUND & DISCOVERY PASSAGE

Juan Francisco de la Bodega y Quadra (1743-1794)

Born in Lima, Peru and not included as part of the Spanish elite, Bodega y Quadra worked his way up to eventually becoming a naval officer. Like other Spanish explorers of the time, he was dispatched from San Blas to find Russian settlements in the north. Bodega y Quadra sailed in the vicinity of Point Grenville and Destruction Island near Grays Harbor on the coast of Washington State with the ship Sonora, and continued north near present-day Sitka in search of the Russians. He arrived in August 1775 and concluded that there was no significant Russian settlement at that time in the Pacific Northwest; the journey enabled Bodega y Quadra to draw a reasonably accurate map of the West Coast of North America. Moving up to second in command, Bodega y Quadra again left San Blas in 1779 with the mission to chart every bay and inlet of the northwest coast in search of the Northwest Passage. He went as far as Port Etches (Puerto de Santiago) near Prince William Sound, which helped to support Spain's claim in the North Pacific. He was later promoted to Ship Captain and commandant of the Naval Department in San Blas, New Spain. Faced with the aftermath of the 'Nootka Crisis,' he was appointed to serve as Spanish Commissioner to negotiate the terms of the Nootka Convention with Captain George Vancouver at Friendly Cove. Quadra was instrumental in keeping the situation under control by entertaining every ship that came into port, along with their crew, no matter what country they were from. Today, various place names in his honor, including Quadra Island and Bodega Bay in northern California, are reminders of Quadra's contributions.

the east and north sides of Quadra Island, from Surge Narrows to Discovery Passage.

Surge Narrows & Beazley Passage. Surge Narrows and Beazley Passage should be run at or near slack water. Spring floods set eastward to 12 knots and ebbs set westward to 10 knots. Current predictions are shown under Beazley Passage in the Canadian Tide and Current Tables Vol. 6, and Ports and Passes.

Although Beazley Passage, between Peck Island and Sturt Island, has the strongest currents in the Surge Narrows area, it is the preferred route between Hoskyn Channel and Okisollo Channel. Especially on an ebb current in Beazley Passage, watch for Tusko Rock, which dries at 5 feet, on the east side of the pass at the north end. Stay well clear of Tusko Rock.

According to Sailing Directions, the duration of slack at Surge Narrows varies between 5 and 11 minutes. The passage north of the Settler's Group is useable following the deeper channel, avoiding the charted rocks and shoals.

⑬ **Octopus Islands Marine Park.** This is a beautiful, popular anchorage and exploration area, wonderfully protected. You can enter from Waiatt Bay, but the usual entry is by a narrow channel from the north. Anchor in any of several coves and run a stern-tie to shore.

At the end of the channel as you enter from the north, a rock, clearly shown on Plans Chart 3537, obstructs part of the entry to the first cove on the right. This rock is easily seen as a white smear under the water. You'll be going slowly anyway; watch for it and you'll have no trouble.

Waiatt Bay. Waiatt Bay is broad and protected, with convenient anchoring depths behind the Octopus Islands. The bay's entrance is choked with islets and rocks, and Sailing Directions (written for large vessels) warns against entering. With the aid of large scale Plans Chart 3537 (1:20,000), however, a small boat can pick its way in along the south shore, or in the middle of the islets, or along the north shore. The chart shows the possibilities. You might anchor in a notch along the shore, or at the head of the bay.

A trail connects the head of Waiatt Bay with Small Inlet. The trail splits about halfway along. Both branches go through, but Correspondent Pat Shera says the branch to the northwest is the drier of the two. Correspondent Carol-Ann Giroday adds that the trail continues along the south shore of Small Inlet to beautiful Newton Lake and to Granite Bay. She cautions hikers not to confuse a pond along the way with substantial Newton Lake.

Hole in the Wall. Hole in the Wall connects Okisollo Channel with Calm Channel to the east. Boats accumulate on each side of the rapids at the western entrance to Hole in the Wall, waiting for slack water. In general, boats on the upstream side will catch the last of the fair current when the rapids calm down, leaving room for the boats on the other side to pick up the new fair current in the opposite direction. Slacks occur 50 to 55 minutes before Seymour Narrows, and last about 4 minutes (Seymour Narrows currents are shown in Canadian Tide and Current Tables Vol. 6, and Ports and Passes). The flood current sets northeast. Maximum currents run to 12 knots on the flood and 10 knots on the ebb.

LOCAL KNOWLEDGE

DANGEROUS CURRENTS: Upper Rapids and Lower Rapids in Okisollo Channel can be dangerous and should be run at or near slack. Slacks occur 50 to 55 minutes before slack at Seymour Narrows.

Upper Rapids. These are the first rapids in Okisollo Channel north of Hole in the Wall, and they are dangerous unless run at or near slack water. Slack occurs 55 minutes before Seymour Narrows (Seymour Narrows currents are shown in Canadian Tide and Current Tables Vol. 6, and Ports and Passes). At full rush on a spring tide, the rapids running at 9 knots are frightening to watch. A wall of white water stretches nearly across the channel almost until slack. When it's time to go through, steer a little east of mid-channel to avoid Bentley Rock. Chart 3537 makes the course clear.

Barnes Bay and several small indents in this part of Okisollo Channel could be good anchorages, except for the large amount of log booming and aquaculture. Owen Bay is the preferred anchorage.

LOCAL KNOWLEDGE

STRONG CURRENTS: Currents run strong through the islands that separate Owen Bay

Middle entrance to Waiatt Bay in Octopus Islands Marine Park

2018 WAGGONER CRUISING GUIDE

DESOLATION SOUND & DISCOVERY PASSAGE

See Area Map Page 293 - Maps Not for Navigation

Anchorage can be found on the Drew Harbour side of Rebecca Spit Provincial Marine Park, with dinghy access to the long beaches.

Heriot Bay Inn & Marina

from Upper Rapids. If you explore these islands, exercise caution to avoid getting sucked into the rapids.

Owen Bay. Owen Bay is large and pretty. Our recommended anchorage is in the second little notch on the west side of the bay. This notch is quite protected, and has room for about 5 boats if the spots are well chosen and stern-ties are used. Enter Owen Bay through a narrow channel between Walters Point and Grant Island. A reef, marked by kelp, extends from Walters Point nearly halfway across this channel. It will inspire you to hug the Grant Island side. Correspondent Pat Shera adds that there is good holding and shelter near the small public float on the east side of the bay. Shera also says that the northeastern head of Owen Bay has "acres of good holding on a flat bottom." That area, however, is subject to being hit by strong (and cold) outflow winds from Bute Inlet. He was "kissed by the Bute" one sleepless night and knows what he's talking about.

A trail leads from the public float to Hole in the Wall. Correspondent Bruce Evertz informs us that for most of the distance the trail is a road that passes several homes and homebuilding sites, and then gets overgrown. Shortly before reaching the water in Diamond Bay, it becomes a plank road that turns 90 degrees to the right. Don't turn. Continue ahead, onto a footpath, which leads to a good view of Hole in the Wall rapids, part of Upper Rapids, and the Octopus Islands.

Lower Rapids. Lower Rapids turns at virtually the same time as Upper Rapids—55 minutes before Seymour Narrows (Seymour Narrows currents are shown in Canadian Tide and Current Tables Vol. 6, and Ports and Passes). Currents run to 9 knots on spring tides, and you must steer a course to avoid Gypsy Shoal, which lies nearly in the middle. Transit at slack water only.

We recommend avoiding Lower Rapids altogether by going through Barnes Bay, north of the Okis Islands. At times other than slack you will still see considerable current, but you will avoid the hazards of Lower Rapids.

Barnes Bay. Barnes Bay and several small indents in this part of Okisollo Channel could be good anchorages, except for the large amount of log booming and aquaculture. Anchorage may be possible to the west in **Chonat Bay** and in the notch behind **Metcalf Island**.

QUADRA ISLAND, SOUTH

⑭ **Drew Harbour/Rebecca Spit Marine Park.** Drew Harbour is large, and in the right winds the open harbor can be lumpy. The preferred anchorage is in the bight immediately inside the north tip of Rebecca Spit. A drying shoal defines the south side of this bight. The shoal extends a considerable distance from shore, and it could fool you at high tide.

If the preferred bight is full, anchor south of the drying shoal in 24 to 36 feet, although it isn't as protected. Rebecca Spit Marine Park is popular. The Drew Harbour side of the spit has a lovely sand beach. Trails with picnic tables run the length of the spit. The exposed Sutil Channel side has a beach of remarkable small round boulders.

Bill Wolferstan's cruising guide to Desolation Sound contains an excellent section describing silvered tree snags on the spit, the result of subsidence during a 1946 earthquake. Wolferstan also describes the mounded fortifications, thought to be defenses built 200 to 400 years ago by the local Salish tribe against attacks from the Native Kwakiutl.

⑮ **Heriot Bay.** Heriot Bay has a public wharf, a supermarket, the Heriot Bay Inn & Marina, and the Taku Resort. During the summer high season the public dock usually is full with boats rafted several deep. Anchorage area north of the public wharf is filled with private mooring balls. Transient anchorage is found further east in 50 to 60 feet of water. The Heriot Bay Inn & Marina is between the ferry dock and the public dock. Just south of Heriot Bay, in Drew Harbour proper, Taku Resort has excellent docks and facilities. Heriot Bay Tru-Value Foods, a short walk from the Heriot Bay or Taku resorts, is the best-stocked grocery store in Desolation Sound, with complete groceries, including fresh vegetables and meats, a post office, gift shop, and liquor store;

Heriot Bay

See Area Map Page 293 - Maps Not for Navigation

DESOLATION SOUND & DISCOVERY PASSAGE

The Heriot Bay Inn & Marina has a pub, restaurant, and gift shop.

Java Bay Cafe is located in the same building. Free grocery delivery to the docks from Tru-Value Grocery (250) 285-2436. Bicycles can be rented from a shop on the road above Taku Resort. The Quadra Island Golf Course is a short ride away.

⑮ **Heriot Bay Public Wharf.** (250) 285-3622; www.qiha.ca. Open all year, 670 feet of dock space, power, water, portable toilets, Wi-Fi, garbage drop, launch ramp. The docks have recently been rebuilt. Watch for ferry wash on the outer face. Heriot Bay Inn and shopping nearby. The dock is managed by the Quadra Island Harbour Authority.

⑮ **Heriot Bay Inn & Marina.** P.O. Box 100, Heriot Bay, BC V0P 1H0; (250) 285- 3322; (888) 605-4545; info@heriotbayinn. com ; www.heriotbayinn.com. Monitors VHF 66A. Open all year, gasoline, diesel, propane, ice and fishing tackle. Guest moorage available on 1800 feet of side-tie dock, mostly 15 amp power with some 30 amp, washrooms, showers, laundry, limited Wi-Fi. Reservations recommended June through September. Fairways between the finger floats are narrow, larger vessels should 'starboard-tie' on the outside of float "1". The outer docks and fuel dock are subject to wakes from passing ferries.

Two of the docks were replaced in 2016 and in 2017 a new walkway and longer ramp improved access to the docks. Plans to upgrade the fuel dock and shed were in the works during the fall of 2017.

The hotel is delightful. This 1913 historic hotel has ten rooms, three cabins, and a suite. The restaurant has outdoor seating overlooking the bay, and the pub has live music on many nights. The gift store off the lobby has local guidebooks, local artisan jewelry, crafts, and souvenirs. The office can provide contact information for local tours and fishing guides. Heriot Bay Tru-Value Foods is a short walk up the hill. Bicycle and kayak rentals nearby.

In 2008 a group of 20 Quadra Island residents ("old hippies," one of them said) bought the property and set about making improvements. Among them they had all the needed skills: carpentry, electrical, painting, administrative, whatever else was required. In recent years the Heriot Bay Inn's public areas have been upgraded with lovely flower beds and walkways. The goal of this working community is to maintain the property with the spirit of welcoming the traveling public.

⑮ **Taku Resort & Marina.** P.O. Box 1, Heriot Bay, BC V0P 1H0; (250) 285-3031; info@takuresort.com; www.takuresort.com. Monitors VHF 66A. Open all year. The docks have 30 & 50 amp power, potable water and Wi-Fi. Washrooms, coin showers, laundry and a 14-room resort are ashore, as are RV sites, tennis, volleyball, badminton and horseshoes. The docks are exposed to southeast winds across the bay, but the inside moorage is protected. The views and proximity to Rebecca Spit Marine Park make this a popular marina. A shopping center and Tru-Value Foods grocery store is a short walk away. A kayak tour operator is on site and a bicycle rental store is just up the road. The resort offers kayak, paddleboard rentals, and cooking classes. The facilities and service are high quality. Lynden McMartin is the manager.

DISCOVERY PASSAGE

Discovery Passage is approximately 20 miles long, and separates Quadra Island and Sonora Island from Vancouver Island. It is the main route for commercial traffic north and south along the east side of Vancouver Island. Cape Mudge is the south entrance to Discovery Passage. At the north end, Discovery Passage connects with Johnstone Strait at Chatham Point. An enormous amount of water flows through Discovery Passage, flooding south and ebbing north. Tide-rips are frequent.

Cape Mudge. The area around Cape Mudge and Wilby Shoals is a famous hot spot for salmon fishing and often full of small fishing craft during the summer months. Several resorts in the area cater to sport fishermen. Guides are available for hire in Campbell River.

On a flood tide, a backeddy often sets up at Cape Mudge running north along the western edge of Wilby Shoals all the way to the Cape Mudge Lighthouse.

LOCAL KNOWLEDGE

TIDE-RIPS: A strong southeasterly wind blowing against a large, south-flowing flood tide can set up high and dangerous seas. Lives have been lost off Cape Mudge in such conditions. Cape Mudge, at the south end of Quadra Island, has been a graveyard for vessels of all sizes, particularly in the winter months. If a southeaster is blowing, Sailing Directions recommends entering at or after high water slack. Good advice.

Yaculta. The First Nations settlement of Yaculta, located on Quadra Island, is the site of the Nuyumbalees Cultural Centre, with its splendid collection of potlatch regalia and historical artifacts and photos. Open 7 days a week, May to September. The Centre is a 3-block walk south from the public dock. We urge a visit. **Cape Mudge Boatworks** (250) 285-2155 is located here. They have a large marine ways and often work on recreational boats.

Yaculta Public Dock. Located at 50°01.4'N on the east side of Discovery Passage, next to the Cape Mudge Boatworks marine ways; public dock with 220 feet of float; 30 amp power and water. No charge. Not recommended for overnight stays, exposed to winds and boat wakes, use at your own risk. Near the Yaculta village and the Nuyumbalees Cultural Centre.

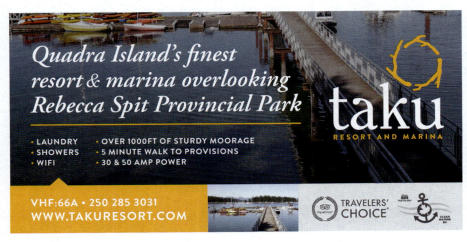

DESOLATION SOUND & DISCOVERY PASSAGE

See Area Map Page 293 - Maps Not for Navigation

Moorage space on the more protected inside of the floats is normally occupied by local boats.

⑯ **Quathiaski Cove.** Quathiaski Cove (known locally as Q-Cove) is the Quadra Island landing for the ferry to Campbell River. A public dock is next to the ferry landing and may be rolly from ferry wakes and passing vessels. A seasonal snack stand is in the ferry parking lot; a pub and restaurant are a short walk away. A shopping center with a good grocery store, a tasty informal café, pizza restaurant, bank with an ATM, and a variety of stores to peruse are a few blocks up the hill from the ferry landing. The grocery store will deliver to the dock. The Visitor Centre is next to the bank. A farmers market adjacent to the Visitor Centre is open Saturday mornings during the summer months.

Because of ferry traffic the best anchorage is farther north, in the cove behind Grouse Island. Fingers of current from Discovery Passage work into Quathiaski Cove at some stages of the tide, so be sure the anchor is well set.

⑯ **Quathiaski Cove Public Wharf.** (250) 285-3622; www.qiha.ca. Adjacent to the ferry landing. The dock has 20, 30 & 50 amp power, water, Wi-Fi, pay telephone, and launch ramp. Above the dock there are new washrooms and shower facilities, with a number to call for the keycode after hours. The dock has considerable mooring space, but we often find it crowded with local and commercial fishing boats. Commercial fishing boats have priority. South side of the south float is for seine fishing vessels. Managed by the Quadra Island Harbour Authority.

⑰ **April Point Resort, Spa & Marina.** P.O. Box 381 Quathiaski Cove, BC V0P 1N0; (250) 285-2222 x264; marina@northcoasthotelresort.com; www.aprilpoint.com. Monitors VHF 66A. Resort and spa open mid-May to October, moorage open all year. The resort lodge and spa are located at April Point and the marina is located in the cove a half mile southeast. The marina has moorage for vessels up to 200 feet, Wi-Fi, water, garbage, and 30, 50, & 100 amp power. Laundry, showers, and a picnic area are available at the resort lodge along with kayak and bike rentals; the resort lodge is a 10-minute walk from the marina or an easy commute by dinghy. In 2017 the G/H dock at the marina was replaced for an additional 600 feet of moorage.

Approaching, you will see a red spar buoy at the entrance to the bay. The buoy marks a shoal, keep the buoy to starboard as you enter (Red, Right, Returning). The proper channel will appear narrow, especially at low tide. You will be strongly tempted to leave the buoy to port, which might put you aground. The docks in front of the lodge are for resort boats and dinghies only; however, boats under 25 feet may be allowed to tie-up while dining at the lodge.

April Point Resort & Spa is a deluxe destination vacation resort. It has everything for the most demanding guest, including excellent rooms, a beautiful spa, fishing guides, renowned dining, and scheduled air service by Kenmore Air. The marina and resort are owned by North Coast Hotel Resort Ltd, which operates a num-

Campbell River

ber of high-quality resorts. Painter's Lodge, north of Campbell River on the west side of Discovery Passage, is a North Coast Hotel resort and is accessible by water taxi from April Point. April Point moorage guests have full access to the amenities at Painter's Lodge, including dining, swimming pool, hot tub and tennis courts.

Limited anchorage can be found in the cove near the marina. A rock-strewn passage, suitable for kayaks and dinghies only, leads between the cove and adjacent Gowlland Harbour.

⑱ **Steep Island Lodge.** P.O. Box 699, Campbell River, BC V9W 6J3; (250) 830-8179; info@steepisland.com; www.steepisland.com. Open May 15 to September 30. Limited guest moorage by reservation only, 15, 30 & 50 amp power, no water. This is a beautiful resort with private cabins. It is on the east side of Steep Island, off the northwest corner of Gowlland Island. Fishing and kayak charters available. Float plane service. Jacuzzi. Dinner is all-inclusive and by reservation only.

Gowlland Harbour. Gowlland Harbour is a large, protected bay behind Gowlland Island, with considerable log booming activity along the shoreline. Before entering, study the chart so you can avoid Entrance Rock, north of Gowlland Island.

You'll find good anchoring depths at the north end of the bay, but it's much prettier at the south end, especially behind Stag Island. Although homes and docks are on the shores,

See Area Map Page 293 - Maps Not for Navigation

DESOLATION SOUND & DISCOVERY PASSAGE

April Point marina with ample side-tie moorage is a short walk to the Resort Lodge and Spa (inset).

we didn't feel closed-in-upon. Good anchoring is also behind Wren Islet, Crow Islet, and the Mouse Islets, all of them a little to the north of Stag Island. These islets, which are protected as provincial park preserves, make good picnic spots.

⑲ **Seascape Waterfront Resort.** P.O. Box 566, Quadra Island, BC V0P 1N0; seascapequadra@gmail.com; www.seascapewaterfrontresort.com. Located north of Stag Island. in Gowland Harbour; 50°04.9'N 125°13.4'W Open all year, 1000 feet of guest moorage, 15 & 30 amp power, washrooms, showers, laundry, kayak rentals. In 2017, Seascape Waterfront Resort began renovations on their cabins and docks. At press time it was not known if the resort would be open for the 2018 boating season.

CAMPBELL RIVER

Campbell River calls itself the "Salmon Capital of the World," and is working to become an important tourist destination. While dozens of guideboats take sportfishermen to prime fishing areas in Discovery Passage and off Cape Mudge, lunker-size salmon are still caught from marina breakwaters and the public fishing pier.

Campbell River has complete shopping, dining, and marine facilities, all close to the waterfront. Fisherman's Wharf and the Coast Marina are close to Tyee Plaza with drugstore, liquor store, excellent laundromat, and more. Discovery Harbour Marina is part of the extensive Discovery Harbour Centre with grocery and big-box general merchandise stores, liquor store, fast food, restaurants, and pubs.

An attractive promenade runs the length of the shoreline from Fisherman's Wharf marina to the ferry dock. The promenade is scheduled to be extended to the Discovery Harbour Marina; for now follow the sidewalk along the highway. At the north end of Discovery Harbour Marina, a Native-owned cruise ship terminal has been built.

As you approach Campbell River from the south you will find four marinas, with transient moorage, each protected by a breakwater. The southernmost marina is Fisherman's Wharf (formerly the Government Dock, now Campbell River Harbour Authority).

Coast Marina is the second breakwater protected marina, offering guest moorage as you progress northward. The ferry run between Quathiaski Cove on Quadra Island and Campbell River lands adjacent to Coast Marina. Coast Marina is closest to downtown Campbell River.

The third marina is Discovery Harbour Marina with considerable moorage, including slips and side-tie. The 52-acre Discovery Harbour Centre adjoins the marina for convenient shopping, including Ocean Pacific Marine Supply, a well-stocked chandlery. Pacific Marine Supply, a well-stocked chandlery. Adjacent to the shopping center is a repair yard with 110-ton Travelift haulout.

The fourth marina named Discovery Harbour Authority Small Craft Harbours is located behind the same breakwater that protects Discover Harbour Marina. This fourth marina is located on the north side of Discovery Harbour Fuels sales dock and provides transient moorage and a boat ramp. All four marinas monitor VHF 66A. Located one half-mile up the Campbell River is Freshwater Marina and Boatyard, offering permanent moorage, repair services and a 50 ton Travelift.

Marine Parts & Supplies: Well-stocked Ocean Pacific has overnight delivery from major suppliers in Vancouver for just about anything.

Museums: The Campbell River Museum & Archives, at 470 Island Hwy, is in the "don't miss" category. The care and imagination of the exhibits remind us of the Royal British Columbia Museum in Victoria, only smaller, and without the giant ice age mammoth.

The Maritime Heritage Centre, a short walk south from Fisherman's Wharf, features a number of fishing and maritime exhibits.

The new Discovery Passage Aquarium is just above the docks at Fisherman's Wharf. It is small, but the exhibits are well done. Younger crew will enjoy it.

Farmers market: Sundays, May through September, 10:00 a.m. to 2:30 p.m. in the fishing pier parking lot at the Fisherman's Wharf docks. Fresh farm produce, baked goods, fresh fish, all the things you'd expect.

Golf: The 18-hole Story Creek golf course, south of town, is outstanding, a must-play for serious golfers. Call (250) 923-3673. Sequoia Springs, a short cab ride from the marinas, is a flat but serious 18-hole course with lots of water and deep rough, well maintained and fun to play. Call (250) 287-4970.

⑳ **Fisherman's Wharf (Campbell River Harbour Authority).** 705 Island Highway,

MARINA
- Campbell River's only Fresh Water Marina
- Holds up to 162 boats overall
- All covered boathouses with hydro & water
- Boats up to 55ft long
- Dryland Storage
- Boat launch available

TRAVEL LIFT
- 50 Ton Travel Lift
- Do it yourself boatyard
- Contractors Welcome
- River Pilot available
- Hydro & water available upon request
- (2) 60ft covered sheds available

2018 WAGGONER CRUISING GUIDE

DESOLATION SOUND & DISCOVERY PASSAGE

See Area Map Page 293 - Maps Not for Navigation

Campbell River, BC V9W 2C2; (250) 287-7931; fishermans@telus.net; www.fishermanswharfcampbellriver.com. Monitors VHF 66A. Open all year, water on docks, 20, 30, limited 50 & one 100 amp power, pumpout, ample dock space, washrooms, showers, tidal grid, Wi-Fi, garbage, recycling. Reservations accepted. All but one of the docks are side-tie only, rafting permitted. Docks A,B, and C are in the North Basin and docks 1-6 are in the South Basin. Docks A,B,1,2 and the west side of 3 are reserved. Transient space is located on docks 4,5,C, and east side of 3. The pumpout is on dock C in the north basin in the area marked "Loading Zone."

This was almost entirely a commercial fishing boat moorage basin until the harbor authority took over operation. Several improvements have been made to attract pleasure craft. All the docks have been recently re-decked, and a new building completed with washrooms, showers, and the harbor office. The well known Dick's Fish and Chips moved from the Coast Marina to a new storefront across from the Wharf. Crabby Bob's on finger 6 on the south wharf has fresh and frozen seafood on the dock. Other boats sell fresh fish on the floats between fingers 2 & 3. Call the office for a heads-up on what's available. Office hours are 8:00 a.m. to 5:00 p.m., 7 days a week. If the office is closed, take an empty space and register in the morning.

㉑ **Coast Marina.** 1003 Island Highway, Campbell River, BC V9W 2C4; (250) 287-7455; coastmarina@gmail.com; www.coast-marina.ca. Monitors VHF 66A. The Coast Marina is located behind the middle of Campbell River's three breakwaters, and has facilities for boats to 180 feet in length. Open all year, guest moorage, 30, 50 & 100 amp power, washrooms, showers, excellent laundry across the street in the plaza, garbage, recycling, water, and free Wi-Fi. Water taxi, whale watching, charter fishing, and adventure tours.

The marina has wide concrete docks with power and water to each slip. Work began in 2017 to expand moorage space on C and D docks, planned to be available for 2018 season.

Campbell River's Discovery Harbour Marina with ample moorage near shopping, restaurants, and pubs is located behind protective breakwaters.

A 'Hydro Clean Hull Wash' system was added, located on P-dock. For information on how it operates, see Hydrochw.com. The marina is just steps away from Foreshore Park and downtown Tyee Plaza shopping. Dockside Fish & Chips is a fully licensed restaurant with indoor and outdoor seating. In 2016/2017 the restaurant was refurbished, and a new menu established,

---

Fisherman's Wharf
Campbell River Harbour Authority

FISHING, COMMERCIAL & PLEASURE BOATS ARE WELCOME!

- Open all year
- Permanent & transient berthage available
- Reservations available
- 20, 30, 50 & 100 amp power
- Hydraulic winches
- Seafood sales
- Laundry
- Potable Water
- Washrooms & Showers
- Garbage & Pumpout
- Beside the Discovery Fishing Pier
- Walking distance to downtown
- Marine hardware & supplies
- Restaurants & Shopping
- Office phone & Internet

Phone: 250-287-7931 • Fax: 250-287-8495 • 705 Island Hwy, Campbell River, BC
www.fishermanswharfcampbellriver.com • Email: fishermans@telus.net • VHF CH. 66A

Discovery Harbour

Coast Marina

Fisherman's Wharf, Campbell River

308   www.WaggonerGuide.com

A great marina destination in a great little city with great shopping next door

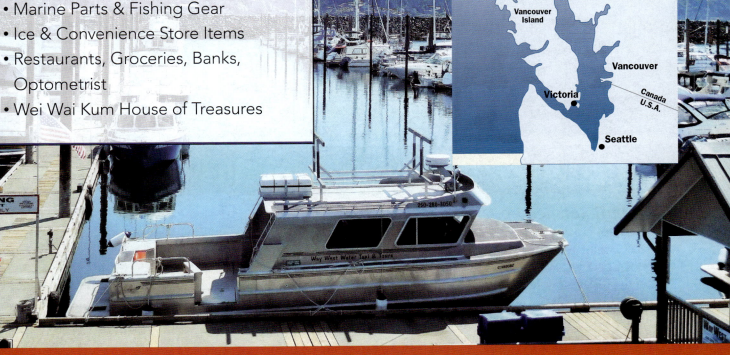

- Full Line of Oil and Filters
- Marine Parts & Fishing Gear
- Ice & Convenience Store Items
- Restaurants, Groceries, Banks, Optometrist
- Wei Wai Kum House of Treasures

phone 250.287.2614 | fax 250.287.8939 | VHF 66A
www.discoveryharbourmarina.com | email info@discoveryharbourmarina.com

DESOLATION SOUND & DISCOVERY PASSAGE

including Benino Gelato treats. An art gallery is located next door.

⑳ **Discovery Harbour Marina.** Suite 392-1434 Ironwood St., Campbell River, BC V9W 5T5; (250) 287-2614; info@discoveryharbourmarina.com; www.discoveryharbourmarina.com. Monitors VHF 66A. Open all year. Fuel dock with gasoline and diesel. Washrooms, showers, laundry, garbage drop, ample guest moorage, 20, 30, 50 & 100 amp single/3- phase power, Wi-Fi. In-slip pumpout service to be provided in 2018. The G, H, I and J floats have side-tie moorage that can handle mega-yachts. Customs clearance available. This is the largest of Campbell River's four breakwater-protected marinas. The marina has excellent docks, landing assistance and friendly people.

The marina office, with showers, washrooms, and laundry, is in a 2-story floating facility at the foot of the north ramp on K dock. New floating washrooms are near E dock to save the long walk to the main washrooms. The docks can be busy with whale and bear tour operators. Water taxi located on the main dock.

The extensive Discovery Harbour Centre shopping plaza is adjacent to the marina, with everything you would expect to find in a major center.

⑳ **Discovery Harbour Fuels.** Box 512, Campbell River, BC V9W 5C1; (250) 287-3456; dhfs@telus.net; www.discoveryharbourfuel.com. Monitors VHF 66A. Fuel dock open all year, gasoline, diesel, propane exchange, self-service oil change system, and fresh water fill. Located straight ahead as you enter the Discovery Harbour Marina breakwater. A full line of cruising guides, maps, extensive charts, fishing gear, marine parts, ice, kerosene and convenience supplies.

⑳ **Discovery Harbour Authority Small Craft Harbours.** (250) 287-7091. Monitors VHF 66A. This marina was formerly for commercial boats only but is now open to recreational vessels; the marina is managed by the Discovery Harbour Authority. Open all year with 4000 feet of dock space located north of the fuel sales just inside the Discovery Harbour breakwater. Transient moorage with mandatory rafting; permanent slips for commercial vessels; launch ramp on site. 30 & 50 amp power and two 100-amp stations; no reservations, may call ahead for availability. Washrooms, showers, laundry, garbage drop with recycling and waste oil disposal; no Wi-Fi. Payment made at wharfinger office on site open 8 a.m.-4 p.m. daily; after hours use envelope payment drop at office door. Marina has a night watchman and camera surveillance.

Freshwater Marina and Boatyard. 2705 N Island Hwy, Campbell River, BC V9W 2H4; (250) 286-0701 Marina; (250) 203-2635 Boatyard; jwtimber@uniserve.com Marina; darcybain@gmail.com Boatyard; www.freshwatermarina.ca. Open all year Monday – Friday. Freshwater Marina is located about half a mile up the Campbell River from Discovery Passage; the Marina and Boatyard are accessible on a 6 foot tide or better for small craft and higher tides for larger vessels. River pilots are available, contact Freshwater Marina. Permanent moorage is available for vessels up to 65 feet, dryland storage for smaller craft. Tide dependent launch ramp. No transient moorage. Freshwater Boatyard has a 50 ton Travelift and do-it-yourself boatyard that also welcomes trades contractors.

Seymour Narrows. Currents in Seymour Narrows run to 16 knots on the flood and 14 knots on the ebb, flooding south and ebbing north.

Northbound, you can wait for slack either in Menzies Bay on the Vancouver Island side, or in the good-size unnamed bay behind Maud Island on the Quadra Island side. South of Maud Island the flood forms a backeddy along Quadra Island, easily sweeping northbound boats toward Maud Island. Southbound, Plumper Bay is a good waiting spot on the east side, as is Brown Bay on the west side. Brown Bay has a floating breakwater, and a marina with a fuel dock and restaurant.

Both **Deepwater Bay** and **Plumper Bay** are too exposed and deep to be attractive as anchorages. **Menzies Bay** may have good anchorage, being careful to go around either end of a drying shoal which almost blocks the entrance. This area is used as a booming ground for the pulp mill in Campbell River.

Seymour Narrows is the principal route for northbound and southbound commercial traf-

---

OCEAN PACIFIC
MARINE STORE & BOATYARD

The North Island's Largest Marine Supply Store & Boatyard
LOCATED IN DISCOVERY HARBOUR MARINA & SHOPPING CENTRE

www.oceanpacificmarine.com

Our Full-Service Boatyard Offers:
- 110 Ton Travelift
- ABYC Certified Marine Technicians & Electricians
- CWB Certified Welders
- Certified Diesel Mechanic,
- Fibreglassers, Painting and Detailing
- Shipwrights & Fine Wood Workers
- Emergency Services Available

ABYC CERTIFIED TECHNICIAN

CWB CERTIFIED

ISO 9001:2008 QUASAR REGISTERED

Toll-Free: 800-663-2294
Local Phone: 250-286-1011
Fax: 250-286-6254
102-1370 Island Highway
Campbell River, B.C. V9W 8C9

fic, including cruise ships. Give large vessels ample room to maneuver. Before going through, we urge you to read the Sailing Directions section on Seymour Narrows. Especially on a flood, Sailing Directions counsels against the west side because of rough water. Monitor the passage times of commercial traffic on VHF 71, the area Vessel Traffic Services (VTS) frequency.

The warship HMCS *Columbia* was sunk off Maud Island to create an artificial reef.

㉑ **Brown's Bay Marina & RV Park.** 15021 Brown's Bay Road, Campbell River, BC V9H 1N9; (250) 286-3135; marina@brownsbayresort.com; www.brownsbayresort.com. Monitors VHF 12 & 66A. Open all year, gasoline and diesel, side-tie moorage to 100 feet along 2000 feet of dock, 50 slips for boats to 24 feet, 15, 30 & 50 amp power, free Wi-Fi, washrooms, showers, laundry, ice, cable television, phone, garbage drop, marine & RV store, boat launch. Four rental cabins and tent cabins for camping available.

This marina is on Vancouver Island, at the north end of Seymour Narrows. Enter around the north end of the breakwater. Strong currents can sweep through the marina; be sure to take the current into account when maneuvering, and tie your boat to the dock securely.

The store has a variety of snack items, clothing, and fishing gear. The seasonal floating restaurant is newly remodeled and quite pleasant. All-you-can-eat crab feed specials on Thursdays and Fridays are signature events in season along with their annual Luau. Call or check their website for the schedule.

Kanish Bay. Kanish Bay has several good anchorages. You could sneak behind the **Chained Islands**, and with some thought and planning find a number of delightful spots, especially in settled weather. **Granite Bay** is well protected with a good bottom, houses dot the shoreline. The small bay between Granite Bay and Small Inlet offers protection from westerlies. An aquaculture operation is in the mouth of this bay.

Correspondents James & Jennifer Hamilton anchored in the cove behind Bodega Point, just south of the 2-meter rock. "Really beautiful. Birds calling. Good holding in sticky mud."

Small Inlet. A narrow but easily-run channel with a least depth of 8 feet leads from the northeast corner of Kanish Bay to Small Inlet. This inlet, surrounded by steep, wooded mountains, is beautiful, although we can confirm that a strong westerly from Johnstone Strait can get in and test your anchoring. Once through the kelp-filled entrance channel, a number of good anchorages can be found along the north shore. A couple of boats can fit behind a little knob of land near the southeast corner. The chart shows 3 rocks in this anchorage—actually, it's a reef with 3 high points. You also can anchor in the cove at the head of Small Inlet, behind 2 small islands.

A trail runs from the head of Small Inlet to Waiatt Bay, with a branch that continues to Granite Bay.

Granite Point. If you are traveling between Discovery Passage and Okisollo Channel, you can safely steer inside Min Rock, north of Granite Point, and run close to Granite Point itself. You will be treated to the sight of some extraordinary rock formations on Granite Point.

Rock Bay Marine Park (Otter Cove). Otter Cove is just inside Chatham Point. It's a useful little anchorage, with convenient depths and protection from seas rolling down Johnstone Strait. If you need a place to hide until the wind or seas subside, it's a good spot.

SEYMOUR NARROWS

Seymour Narrows is a wide pass, clear of hazards, and offers a direct route north past the important provisioning town of Campbell River. It is the easiest connection from the Strait of Georgia to Johnstone Strait or Cordero Channel.

Most commercial vessels stay clear of Seymour Narrows except at slack. A ship or barge-towing tug cannot afford to go sideways for even a few seconds. Small fishboats and recreational vessels, however, often transit Seymour Narrows within an hour of the turn, especially if going with the current. We always take Seymour Narrows going with the current and we've rarely had an anxious moment.

Smaller tides, where maximum current is predicted at six knots or less, can be taken at any time for most boats (again, going with the current). Larger tides should be taken within a half-hour of the turn. If it's a strong current cycle, in the 14- to 16-knot range, arrive at the pass within 15 minutes of slack water and the current will be manageable. The strongest current doesn't extend very far in either direction, so the transit past whirlpools lasts only a few minutes.

Hydrographers say the strongest currents at the Narrows are in the vicinity of Ripple Rock (slightly west of mid-channel, directly beneath the hydro lines strung between Vancouver Island and Maud Island). On a flood, the strongest turbulence will be along the west wall and in the area south of Ripple Rock. On an ebb, the turbulence and the set starts between Maud Island and Ripple Rock. The ebb current sets northwest to the west wall.

Northbound vessels: On small tides, northbound vessels should arrive off the Maud Island light an hour before the end of the ebb, or an hour prior to high water slack, before the ebb begins. Once into the narrows, steer toward the tongue of the current stream (east of mid-channel) to avoid the whirlpools and eddies north of Maud Island up to North Bluff. On big tides, low-powered vessels will find it prudent to be at the Maud Island light at high water slack, or just a few minutes into the north flowing ebb.

Note how the current is pushing the barge to one side in Seymour Narrows.

If the slack is at low water, arrive at the pass before the end of the ebb. Slack on large tides is not very long, five to ten minutes at most. You'll want to be past Brown Bay before the southflowing flood gets underway. It can be brutal in a slow-moving boat. You may find a back eddy along the eastern shore. On a large flood, Seymour Narrows can reach 16 knots, no place to be in any kind of boat.

Southbound vessels: Southbound boats should be opposite Brown Bay within an hour of the beginning or end of a neap (small) flood. On a large spring flood, it would be wise to be opposite Brown Bay within a half-hour of its end or beginning. Keep well off the sheer rock wall on the west shore of the narrows. Current turbulence can set a vessel onto that wall. The worst turbulence is usually south of Ripple Rock, especially if wind is against current. Stay on your side of the channel (i.e. to starboard) to be clear of any tugs or large ships headed the other way. The good news about Seymour Narrows is that there are no obstructions and just one strong, main stream.

– Bill Kelly

Anne Vipond and Bill Kelly are the authors of *Best Anchorages of the Inside Passage*.

Johnstone Strait

CHAPTER 11

JOHNSTONE STRAIT
*Yuculta Rapids • Stuart Island
Cordero Channel • Nodales Channel
Blind Channel • Greene Point Rapids
Whirlpool Rapids • Sunderland Channel
Johnstone Strait • Port Neville*

JOHNSTONE STRAIT

See Area Map Page 314 - Maps Not for Navigation

The southern tip of Stuart Island marks the northern boundary of Desolation Sound. North of Desolation Sound, you'll find colder water, harsher weather, fewer services, and a greater number of rocks, reefs and tidal rapids. You should have good ground tackle and know how to use it.

Fewer boats venture north of Desolation Sound. A greater percentage of those boats are 32 feet in length and larger. Many stay out for four to eight weeks or more, and the larger boats provide more comfortable accommodations. On average the occupants are older, too. The farther north you go, the more remote conditions become, all the way to Alaska.

It is possible to do a quick two- to three-week trip from Seattle to this area, although it might require long days on the water to get there. The reward is experiencing beautiful cruising grounds few others will see.

Garbage Drops. While occasionally you will find a lack of garbage drops in Desolation Sound and south, garbage becomes a much greater problem farther north. Garbage must be hauled from marinas and settlements to authorized dumps, usually on Vancouver Island. Since marinas must pay for hauling and disposal, most charge a fee for garbage, if they accept it at all. Those that do will sometimes take recyclables at no charge. Use as little glass as possible, wash and flatten cans, and pack paper out.

Fresh Water. Fresh water can be a problem even in Desolation Sound, and northward the supplies are fewer. This was especially true during the 2015 drought. Many marinas prohibited boat washing. Some marinas limited the amount of water for filling tanks. Check with marina staff before washing the boat or filling the tanks.

Chatham Point marks the Southern end of Johnstone Strait.

Some stops, such as Lagoon Cove or Blind Channel, have sweet spring water from deep wells. In some places, the potable water has a brown cast from cedar bark tannin. We don't know of anybody who has had a bad experience from it. We use an RV filter on the hose when filling the tank and a filtration system to a special tap in the galley for clean good tasting water. Others purchase large jugs of water for cooking and drinking.

Prices. The season is short and the costs are high. Everything must be brought in by water taxi, barge, or air. Don't be upset when prices are higher than at home. Remember too that during the season the marina personnel's workday starts early and ends late, and calls for a smile at all times.

Provisions. Going north there are major shopping centers and large grocery stores in Campbell River, Port McNeill and Port Hardy. There are small stores with many items and the essentials in Telegraph Harbour, Port Harvey (depending on new construction for 2017), Pierre's Echo Bay, Sullivan Bay, Sointula, and Alert Bay. You will not starve, though you may not always find those special ingredients for a unique recipe, like Old Bay for a prawn boil. Everything must be brought in by boat and occasionally floatplane. Prices are higher and some resorts are now reserving perishables and other products for their marina guests only.

Recommended books. Peter Vassilopoulos's cruising guide, *Broughton Islands Cruising Guide*, is excellent. The book covers the waters from Yuculta Rapids to Port Hardy, and is packed with maps, history, and hundreds of aerial color photos.

A second book, *Local Knowledge: The Skipper's Reference, Tacoma to Ketchikan* by Kevin Monahan, is a compilation of useful navigation and trip-planning information, including mileage and conversion tables. It has a comprehensive section on tidal rapids, recommended strategies, and how to calculate timing for transit. We use the mileage charts regularly. Monahan's excellent Johnstone Strait diagrams have been reproduced on page 316.

Exploring the South Coast of British Columbia, by Don Douglass and Réanne Hemingway-Douglass, is another excellent book covering this area.

THE INSIDE ROUTE TO THE BROUGHTONS

Most cruisers heading north choose the sheltered inside route through Cordero Channel, Chancellor Channel, Wellbore Channel and Sunderland Channel rather than face a long, possibly rough passage in Johnstone Strait against the prevailing northwest winds. Often the Johnstone Strait route is taken on the way home with the winds from astern and ideally on a flood tide. The inside route runs from the north end of Calm Channel (the south tip of Stuart Island), through five sets of rapids: Yuculta Rapids, Gillard Passage, Dent Rapids, Greene Point Rapids and Whirlpool Rapids. The route includes an open stretch of approximately 13 miles in Johnstone Strait (which cannot be avoided) between Sunderland Channel and Havannah Channel, after which the currents of Chatham Channel must be negotiated. Careful planning is paramount. You need to know the times of slack water at each rapids, and you need to know how long it will take to get to each rapids.

Up-to-date charts and a copy of the Canadian Tide and Current Tables Vol. 6 or Ports and Passes are critical for safe navigation. Using the corrections shown in the Reference and Secondary Current Stations in the front part of the Tide and Current Tables (back of Ports and Passes), you must be comfortable calculating the times of slack water at the various rapids. For anchoring or transiting shallow channels, use the corrections in the Reference and Secondary Ports pages to calculate times and heights of tides.

The calculations can be daunting at first, but an evening spent reading the excellent instructions will clear matters considerably. For clari-

CHARTS

3312 Small-craft chart (chartbook)	Jervis Inlet & Desolation Sound
3539	Discovery Passage (1:40,000)
3543	Cordero Channel (1:40,000) Greene Point, Dent, & Yuculta Rapids (1:20,000)
3544	Johnstone Strait, Race Passage & Current Passage (1:25,000)
3545	Johnstone Strait, Port Neville to Robson Bight (1:40,000)
3546	Broughton Strait (1:40,000)
3555 Plans	Vicinity of Redonda Islands & Loughborough Inlet
3564 Plans	Johnstone Strait; Port Neville, Havannah Channel & Chatham Channel

2018 WAGGONER CRUISING GUIDE — 313

JOHNSTONE STRAIT — Reference Only – Not for Navigation

Distances (nm)
(Approximate, for planning. Distances from end of one rapids to beginning of next rapids will be less.)

Harbott Pt. (south tip of Stuart Is.) to Gillard Passage—2.0
Gillard Passage to Dent Rapids (Devils Hole)—2.0
Dent Rapids (Devils Hole) to Shoal Bay—7.4
Shoal Bay to Greene Pt. Rapids (Griffiths Islet Lt.)—6.0
Greene Pt. Rapids (Griffiths Islet Lt.) to Whirlpool Rapids—11.0
Whirlpool Rapids to Port Neville—13.0
Port Neville to Havannah Channel—9.0
Havannah Channel entrance to Chatham Channel E entrance—6.6
Chatham Channel E entrance to Minstrel Is (Blow Hole)—4.5

Johnstone Strait

fications, don't be shy about asking a few old salts on the docks. They (we) love to help.

Since the waters north of Desolation Sound flood southward from the top of Vancouver Island and ebb northward, the northbound boat (if it wishes to clear a number of rapids in one run) has a timing problem. Assuming a start with Yuculta Rapids, all the rapids to the north will already have turned before slack water occurs at the Yucultas. It is best to approach Yuculta Rapids before the southbound flood turns to the northbound ebb, and utilize two backeddies (described below) to help your way against the flood for the two or so miles to Gillard Passage and Dent Rapids. Done correctly, you'll go through Dent Rapids against the last of the flood current, and let the new ebb current flush you out Cordero Channel.

The ebb will already have been running 13 miles away at Greene Point Rapids, which turned earlier. Depending on your boat's speed, the ebb could be at full force when you arrive. Rather than go through in these conditions, many choose to overnight at Blind Channel Resort. Shoal Bay and the Cordero Islands are other good places to wait for Greene Point Rapids to turn to slack.

The next day you can depart before high water slack and push through Greene Point Rapids in the dying flood current. Then you'll hurry to Wellbore Channel, to take Whirlpool Rapids early in the favorable ebb current. If this is done early in the morning, it is possible the wind will not have started building for the stretch in Johnstone Strait. With luck it can be a pleasant run down Sunderland Channel and into Johnstone Strait for the 13-mile run to Havannah Channel. How well this works depends on the speed of your boat, the time of day, the conditions, and the flexibility of your schedule.

Southbound the options are greater. Take your first rapids against the last of the dying ebb, and let the new flood current flush you south. Each rapids in succession turns at a later time. Given the right conditions even a slow boat can take all the rapids on one tide, with only a few hours' wait if the boat arrives at any given rapids when they are running too hard to risk transit.

Note: Canadian Tide and Current Tables do not adjust for Daylight Saving Time. Ports and Passes tide and current times are adjusted for Daylight Saving Time.

Caution: A tight schedule is not justification for taking a chance with bad conditions. The dangers are real.

① **Yuculta Rapids.** The Yuculta (pronounced "YEW-cla-ta") Rapids separate Stuart Island and Sonora Island. Taken at slack they are benign, but at full force on a spring tide, especially against an opposing wind, they can be extremely dangerous. Northbound, Sailing Directions recommends that slow and low-powered boats arrive at the rapids an hour before high water slack, and use a backeddy along the Stuart Island shore until off Kellsey Point. Then cross to the Sonora Island shore to use a prevailing northerly current. This should position the boat to go through Gillard Passage and Dent Rapids satisfactorily. If you are late and unsure about transiting Dent Rapids, wait in Big Bay for the next slack.

② **Big Bay (Stuart Island).** For decades, Big Bay on Stuart Island has been a major fishing resort center. The public floats are behind a plank and piling breakwater at the head of Big Bay. The former Big Bay Marina is now a private fishing resort with no services for cruising boats. The Stuart Island Community dock has moorage and a store. Big Bay has seen an increase in development of exclusive, high-end fishing resorts and lodges over the past few years. Many boats criss-cross the bay during the summer and peak fishing seasons.

② **Stuart Island Community Dock.** P.O. Box 5-6, Stuart Island, BC V0P 1V0; (250) 202-3625; postmaster@stuartisland.info; www.stuartislandca.info. Monitors VHF 66A. Moorage, water, liquor, laundry, post office, store, ice, community kitchen, fishing guides, good cell phone coverage, free Wi-Fi. No power, no fuel. Staff is on call 24 hours a day in season.

The docks were rebuilt and expanded to accommodate boats to 100+ feet. The store carries convenience items, liquor, locally made goods. Store hours are 8:00 a.m. to 5:00 p.m. seven days a week in season. A large deck with covered picnic area connects to the store.

A well-marked road and trail lead to Eagle

www.WaggonerGuide.com

RUNNING THE RAPIDS

The cautious advice—the first rule of thumb—for transiting tidal current rapids is to wait for slack water and go through then. This rule of thumb is fine but imperfect. There you sit, watching other boats go through before slack and after slack.

A second rule of thumb is a corollary of the first. It says that boats should arrive at a rapids an hour before predicted slack, so they're ready to go through as soon as the rapids grow quiet. Like most rules of thumb, this one doesn't always work either. Sometimes it appears as if the rapids would be safe much longer than an hour before or after. Sometimes one look tells you it's smarter to wait. With a little study, however, it's possible to predict when the window of opportunity will be wider or narrower.

Before going further, two definitions:

Slack water. Slack water is the time when rapids cease flowing one direction but haven't begun flowing the opposite direction. Another word for slack is turn, meaning the time when the water's flow turns from one direction to the other.

Window, or window of opportunity. For purposes of this article, window means a time when most boats can transit a rapids safely, without too much excitement.

This article gelled with me in Malibu Rapids at the mouth of Princess Louisa Inlet. It has its origins in the successful running of the Pacific Northwest's tidal current rapids over a span of nearly four decades.

Understand that my wife and I are the original cautious and conservative boaters when it comes to rapids. Several years ago we hiked from Big Bay, on B.C.'s Stuart Island, to Arran Rapids, one of the most deadly rapids on the coast. We arrived in what must have been the middle of a large tide exchange, with its frightening whitewater overfalls, upwellings and whirlpools that no sensible boat could be expected to survive. White water is full of air, and less buoyant than green water. Boats float lower, with less freeboard. Rudders lose effectiveness and propellers lose their bite. We got the message: Rapids are not to be trifled with.

With experience, we have developed a loose sense of when a rapids could be run at times other than slack. Until our transits of Malibu Rapids, however, this sense was not refined to any kind of structure.

For what it's worth, here's our thinking. But first,

Caution: Every rapids has its own personality and characteristics. What follows is general in nature, and may not apply to any given rapids. It is a way of looking at things, an approach to the problem. It is not a guarantee.

The determining factors are 1) high water slack vs. low water slack; 2) neap tides vs. spring tides; 3) the size of the exchange on each side of slack.

High water slack vs. low water slack. We entered Princess Louisa Inlet through Malibu Rapids without drama nearly two hours before high water slack. When we departed two days later we found definite swirls, overfalls and whirlpools only 20 minutes before low water slack. The two transits were entirely different.

Our entry to Princess Louisa Inlet was at high water, when the narrow, shallow channel was full. Our departure was at low water, when the channel was much less full and much narrower. The less water in the channel, the faster the current must run.

General Rule: The window of opportunity is wider at high water slack. The narrower and shallower the channel, the more this is true.

Neap tides vs. spring tides. Neap tides are small tides that occur around the times of half moon. Neaps often show only a small dip from one high water to the next. The widest windows of opportunity occur on that small dip.

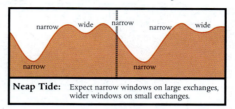

Neap Tide: Expect narrow windows on large exchanges, wider windows on small exchanges.

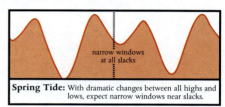

Spring Tide: With dramatic changes between all highs and lows, expect narrow windows near slacks.

Spring tides occur around the times of full moon or no moon. Low tides can be very low and high tides very high. On springs even the dip between two high tides can be significant. The windows of opportunity are narrower on spring tides than on neap tides.

Since it takes only a week to go from neap tide to spring tide (and another week to go from spring tide to neap tide), the experience from just a few days earlier has no bearing on the day you're going through. Each day, each transit, must be evaluated on its own.

Size of the exchange. Imagine this exercise. Using a garden hose, fill a five-gallon container in a minute. Then fill a one-gallon container in a minute. You had to turn the flow of water way down for the one-gallon can. Our neap tide entry through Malibu Rapids was near the top of a fairly small rise from lower low water to high water. The smaller the rise or fall, the less the current.

Conclusions

1. The window is narrowest at lower low water slack. The tide has dropped a long way and will be rising a long way. The farther the tide has dropped and the farther it is to rise, the narrower the window. Also, the shallower and narrower the rapids, the narrower the window at lower low water. At lower low water, plan to go through fairly close to slack.

2. The window at high water slack is wider on neap tides than on spring tides. The window is widest in the "dip" between the two high waters on neap tides.

3. At high water slack, the window is narrower on the rise from lower low water. The window is wider between the next two high waters.

Disclaimer. Skippers are responsible for the welfare and safety of their vessels and passengers. The purpose of this article is to provide tools for evaluating situations. It is not the purpose of this article to tell a skipper when he should transit a rapids before or after slack water, or how much before or after. When in doubt, the safest course is to transit at slack water, regardless of what other boats are doing.

– Robert Hale

JOHNSTONE STRAIT

See Area Map Page 314 - Maps Not for Navigation

MONAHAN'S LOCAL KNOWLEDGE

LEGEND
Boils (upwelling) Whirlpool Turbulence (Tide Rip)
← Direction of ebb current   ⇢ Direction of flood current

LOCAL EFFECTS – EBB

West of Port Neville, the ebb begins along the mainland shore and takes almost two hours to completely cover the strait from one side to the other.

Turn to flood occurs in Sunderland Channel 1h 40m before Johnstone Strait Central and 1h 20m before Camp Point.

To avoid heavy weather in Johnstone Strait (especially when wind opposes currents) Sunderland, Wellbore and Cordero Channels offer calmer conditions.

Current Passage turns to ebb 50m after Johnstone Strait Central, but 1h 15m before Camp Point.

Turn to ebb at Vansittart Point occurs up to 30m before Current Passage, almost two hours before Camp Point.

Freshet conditions in mainland rivers may encourage a premature turn to ebb in the vicinity of Mayne Passage.

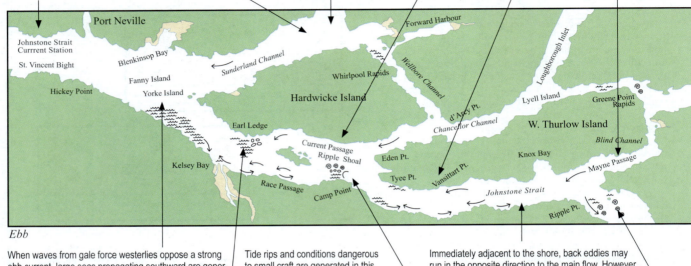

Ebb

When waves from gale force westerlies oppose a strong ebb current, large seas propagating southward are generated in this area. In this case, smaller boats should seek shelter at Port Neville or enter the harbour at Kelsey Bay and wait for the contrary current to moderate.

Tide rips and conditions dangerous to small craft are generated in this area during large tides, especially when strong westerlies oppose the ebb current.

A steep underwater ridge extends southward from Earl Ledge across the channel to the Vancouver Island shore. Deep tidal currents meet this steep topography and are deflected to the surface, causing extreme turbulence west of Helmcken Island during large tides.

Stay clear of Ripple Shoal. Dangerous whirlpools form to the west of the shoal during the ebb.

Immediately adjacent to the shore, back eddies may run in the opposite direction to the main flow. However, at headlands between back eddies, the ebb current is strong right up to the shore.

Tide rips and turbulent conditions are generated in this area during large tides, especially when strong westerly winds oppose the ebb current.

LOCAL EFFECTS – FLOOD

Near Port Neville, the mainland and Vancouver Island shores turn to flood up to one hour before the center of the channel.

In Current Passage, turbulence is weaker near the north shore.

To avoid heavy weather in Johnstone Strait (especially when wind opposes currents) Sunderland, Wellbore and Cordero Channels offer calmer conditions.

Stay clear of Ripple Shoal. Dangerous whirlpools form to the east of the shoal during the flood.

First ebb current in eastern Johnstone Strait begins between Mayne Passage and Vansittart Point, up to two hours before turn to ebb at Camp Point.

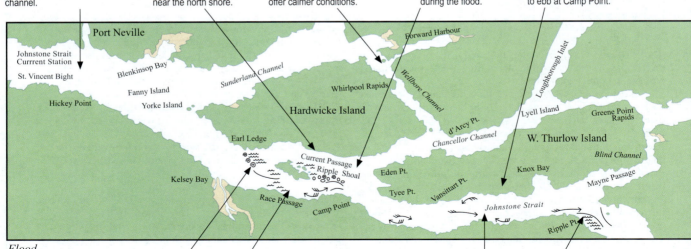

Flood

Tide rips and conditions dangerous to small craft are generated in this area during large tides, especially when strong southeasterlies oppose the flood current.

The ebb current in Current and Race Passages persists approximately 1h 20m longer than in Sunderland Channel.

Immediately adjacent to the shore, back eddies may run in the opposite direction to the main flow. However, at headlands between back eddies, the flood current is strong right up to the shore.

Tide rips and turbulent conditions are generated in this area during large tides, especially when strong southeasterlies oppose the flood current.

Copyright © Kevin Monahan, *Local Knowledge: A Skipper's Reference, Tacoma to Ketchikan*

Lake, where a skiff is kept. It's a good walk, through beautiful forest.

Shoal: An important shoal lies a short distance off the dock. Approach from the south.

Gillard Passage. Currents run to 13 knots on the flood and 10 knots on the ebb. Transit near slack water. Times of slack are shown in Canadian Tide and Current Tables Vol. 6 and Ports and Passes. Pass south of Jimmy Judd Island. Big Bay is a good place to wait if the current is too strong.

If you're lucky, you might find the trees on and near Jimmy Judd Island filled with eagles that swoop down to the swirling waters to feed on hake, whose air bladders have brought them to the surface. It's a real sight.

③ **Morgan's Landing Retreat.** P.O. Box 5-3, Stuart Island, BC V0P 1V0; (250) 287-0237; morganslanding@hotmail.com. Monitors VHF 66A. Construction and installation of all new concrete docks began in the fall of 2017. 600 feet of guest moorage is anticipated to be available for the 2018 boating season with 30, 50, and 100 amp power. Water, washrooms, showers, laundry and ice. Reservations suggested. Happy Hours are becoming a new event at Morgan's. Facilities include accommodations, eco tours and guided fishing charters, and meals by reservation. This is an upscale fishing lodge located at the mouth of the little bay that separates Dent Island from the mainland. Bob Morgan is a third-generation resident of Stuart Island, with 45 years of experience as a fishing guide. Jode (pronounced Jody) Morgan is a baker by trade and has been a fishing guide for 35 years. Fishing charters are their specialty. Floatplane and water taxi service available.

③ **Dent Island Lodge.** P.O. Box 8, Stuart Island, BC V0P 1V0; (250) 203-2553; info@dentisland.com; www.dentisland.com. Monitors VHF 66A. Open late May to mid-September, guest moorage for boats to 200 feet on wide, stable concrete docks, 30 & 50 amp power at every dock pedestal, plus single-phase 100 amp power upon request. Potable water on the docks, Wi-Fi, good cell phone service, fishing guides, restaurants, gift shop, sauna, showers, exercise room, hot tub.

The service at Dent Island Lodge is first class, with moorage and dinner prices to match. The main lodge was removed in 2017 for the construction of a new bigger and better lodge to be open sometime in 2018. The professional staff treats you like a special guest in a small, quiet, private retreat. At the end of the day after the guide boats have returned from fishing, an elegant appetizer table is set out. The dinner menu in the main dining room is limited but very well done. Less formal, the Rapids Outdoor Grill is

The Reversing rapids in Canoe Pass beside Dent Island Lodge are fascinating to watch.

DENT ISLAND

"The Place To Be"

When cruising north of Desolation Sound this season, make your reservations at our premier resort. Dent Island, well known for outstanding accommodations, friendly staff, and amazing culinary experiences. **Come and see what all the talk is about!**

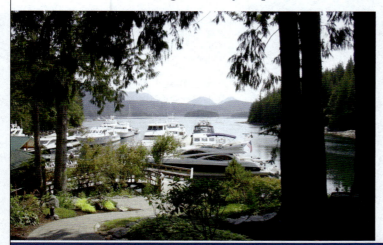

Amenities available to our moorage guests include:
- Fine dining restaurant & full-service bar
- 24 hour hot tub, sauna, laundry, showers and exercise facility
- 30, 50 & 100 amp power and unlimited supply of fresh water
- Professional experienced fishing guides
- Fish packing facility and ice
- Wireless internet throughout the marina
- Scheduled sea plane and water taxi services
- Accommodation packages also available
- Scenic jet boat tours
- Marina monitors VHF Channel 66A
- Reservations highly recommended

www.dentisland.com   250-203-2553   info@dentisland.com

JOHNSTONE STRAIT

See Area Map Page 314 - Maps Not for Navigation

Small plate dinners at the Rapids Outdoor Grill at Dent Island Lodge are a special treat for the crew

a small-plate-style dining area with a view of Canoe Pass rapids. Tables surround the kitchen and the chef personally prepares each dish directly in front of you. Both dining options are popular; reservations recommended.

A hiking trail, rough in places, is a good place to work off some of the calories.

The lodge is at the back of a little bay separating Dent Island from the mainland, next to Canoe Pass rapids, where 10- to 12-knot whitewater tidal currents churn. A spacious deck overlooks the pass. Another deck, screened by forest, holds a hot tub.

The lodge has a fast jet boat for eco-explorations and thrilling rides in the rapids. They offer tours to the head of Bute Inlet, including runs up the rivers in the inlet. Resort manager Justin Farr is an experienced fishing guide in these waters, and he knows every swirl, overfall and calm spot. The boat turns in its own length and dances through rough waters. The tour will make you respect the waters around Dent and Arran Rapids.

Schedule arrivals and departures to coincide with slack water in Gillard Passage, and approach from the southeast. The 1:20,000 inset on Chart 3543 shows the lodge location including the dock. As the inset shows, a shoal area 0.9 meter deep at zero tide is on the east side of the entry. Stay mid-channel. It is best to make reservations, even in the less-busy weeks of the season. Reservations are just about essential during high season.

④ **Dent Rapids.** Currents run to 9 knots on floods and 8 knots on ebbs. Time corrections are shown under Reference and Secondary Current Stations in Tide and Current Tables Vol. 6 and Ports and Passes. Per Sailing Directions, "In Devils Hole, violent eddies and whirlpools form between 2 hours after turn to flood and 1 hour before turn to ebb." People who have looked into Devils Hole vow never to run that risk again. Favor the Sonora Island shore of Dent Rapids.

Tugboat Passage, between Dent Island and Little Dent Island, avoids the potential problems of Devils Hole, and the current is less. Use the large-scale inset on Chart 3543, and favor the Little Dent Island side.

Arran Rapids. Arran Rapids separate the north side of Stuart Island and the mainland, and connect Bute Inlet with Cordero Channel. Current predictions for Arran Rapids are shown in Canadian Tide and Current Tables Vol. 6, and Ports and Passes. Arran Rapids are unobstructed, but tidal streams run to 13+ knots. These rapids have a long history of killing the unknowing or foolhardy. *Run Arran Rapids at slack water only*, if at all. We have hiked from Big Bay to Arran Rapids and watched the water during a spring tide. The enormous upwellings, whirlpools, and overfalls were frightening.

⑤ **Denham Bay.** (250) 703-6978 (Peter); (250) 218-8538 (Sarah); denhamdocks@gmail.com; www.denhambay.com. Monitors VHF 66A. Denham Bay is located in a lovely setting with park-like grounds offering several well-appointed vacation cabins. Be sure to stay clear of Secord Rock located approximately 400 yards offshore lying northwest of Horn Point; there is currently no buoy marking this rock. Open May 15 to October 15, water, Wi-Fi, no power.

Owners Peter Geneau and Sarah Askwith are friendly and welcoming. Peter has worked in the salmon enhancement and as a fishing guide in the area. Sarah worked as a high-end pastry chef for some of the local resorts.

A new dock was added in June of 2017, increasing moorage space to approximately 500 feet. Reservations are taken for group events, priority is given to boats making use of the cabins. Denham Bay primarily caters to smaller boats but can accommodate boats up to 60 feet as space allows, call ahead for availability. A beautiful outdoor kitchen area with granite countertops is available for cabin guests, and boaters moored at the marina can make use of a separate shore-side kitchen area and the wood-fired pizza oven. The grounds are a delight, with lovely walkways and a shore-side boardwalk. Hiking trails in the area. Salmon charters can be arranged with prior notification.

Frederick Arm. Frederick Arm is deep, with almost no good places to anchor. You can anchor in several nooks along the eastern shoreline, or near the head, where the bottom shoals rapidly.

Oleo's. Oleo's is now closed, buildings have been removed except for two small structures which have collapsed; commercial business is no longer present at the site.

Estero Basin. If the crowds are getting to you, uncharted Estero Basin, at the head of Frederick Arm, is where you can avoid them. The narrow passage into the basin, called "The Gut," is passable only at high water slack (very high water slack, we now are told), and slack doesn't last long. A dinghy with outboard motor is a good way to go, and you may have to drag it part of the way. We have not been in Estero Basin, but Wolferstan has. He writes convincingly about the strong currents in The Gut and the eerie stillness of the 5-mile-long basin with its uncharted rocks. Friends tell us that Estero Basin is absolutely beautiful, usually deserted, with small islands, sheer cliffs, and water that grows fresher the farther you

Denham Bay docks just above Dent Rapids overlooking Cordero Channel

go. "Bring your lunch and shampoo," we're advised.

Waggoner reader Patrick Freeny reported that he had just enough water for his inflatable dinghy on a 13-foot tide. On a 10-foot tide the dinghy had to be dragged in. Dinghies or skiffs only, no larger boats.

NODALES CHANNEL

Thurston Bay Marine Park. Thurston Bay Marine Park is large enough to hold many boats without feeling too crowded. We've had good overnight anchorages in Handfield Bay, and in 36 feet behind Block Island.

The landlocked inlet behind Wilson Point, on the south side of Thurston Bay, is best entered at half tide or higher. Wolferstan calls this inlet Anchorage Lagoon. At the entrance, least depth at zero tide is 2 feet or less. We tiptoed in near the bottom of a 2.9-foot low tide with the depth sounder showing 6 feet (our boat drew 3 feet). Inside we found four boats at anchor in a pretty setting, with 9 to 10 feet of depth. This is a good place to know your vessel's draft and the tidal range during your stay.

Be bear aware when ashore.

LOCAL KNOWLEDGE

Dangerous Rocks: Note that in the entrance to Cameleon Harbour, **Douglas Rock**, which dries at 1.5 meters, is detached from Bruce Point. Give Bruce Point ample room.

Handfield Bay. Handfield Bay is entered from Binnington Bay, located to port as you enter Cameleon Harbour. Chart 3543 (1:40,000) makes it clear that you should enter Handfield Bay leaving Tully Island to port. Once inside you'll find excellent protection, good anchoring depths, and shore access. From the upper helm the rock north of Tully Island was easy to spot at half tide. Handfield Bay is a favorite stop for many cruisers.

Cameleon Harbour. Cameleon Harbour is a big, open bay with ample protected anchorage, depending on where you need the shelter.

Hemming Bay. Hemming Bay is pretty, especially at the north end, near the head. Enter leaving the Lee Islands well to starboard to avoid Menace Rock in the middle of the bay. Most of Hemming Bay is deep, but you can find anchoring depths near the head. Correspondent Carol-Ann Giroday reports that the land at the head of Hemming Bay is private, and posted with no-trespassing signs.

⑥ **Shoal Bay.** Shoal Bay has a public float with good anchorage off the outboard end. The water shallows dramatically at the head of the bay. Shoal Bay is protected from most winds blowing down Cordero Channel, but is open to wakes from passing boats. It has a beautiful view up Phillips Arm. It's a good place to wait for slack water at the rapids north or south. Rafting is mandatory; set out fenders on both sides. The docks fill quickly during the summer, so arrive early or be prepared to anchor out. No power or water at the docks. Mark MacDonald is the wharfinger, and moorage fees are collected at the Shoal Bay Pub, just up from the head of the wharf.

⑥ **Shoal Bay Pub.** General Delivery, Blind Channel, BC V0P 1B0; (250) 287-6818; shoalbay@mac.com; www.shoalbay.ca. Open May 1 to October 1. Free Wi-Fi at the pub, washrooms, showers, laundry, guest cabins. The pub has cold beer and other beverages, indoor seating, and a deck with breathtaking views up Phillips Arm.

A large vegetable patch, adorned with sculpture, is available for garden-deprived cruisers who like to get their hands dirty. All tools are provided. Pay by donation for what you pick. Mark's wife Cynthia is a talented potter, and her locally thrown and fired pottery is available for sale. Her work adorns the property.

For exercise, take the sometimes challenging hike up the mountain to the abandoned gold mine.

The Shoal Bay International Blues Festival is held in early August, check their web site for dates. What started out as a bunch of friendly folks jamming now has a stage with a schedule of acts. The dock and anchorage fill quickly, so arrive early. The music goes on into the wee hours and echoes across the bay.

Phillips Arm. Phillips Arm is deep, with little protection along the shores. **Fanny Bay** looks good on the chart, but has log booming activity. A northwest wind can blow through a saddle in the mountains at the head of Fanny Bay. On an earlier visit we found a stiff breeze in the bay; in Phillips Arm the air was calm. Large logging operations are located near the head of the inlet. A friend, much experienced, tells us not to anchor in the area of Dyer Point. The bottom there is foul with a tangle of sunken logs. [*Hale*]

Bickley Bay. Bickley Bay on Cordero Channel has anchoring depths toward the head of the bay. Favor the east shore to avoid a shoal area. Friends who have cruised in the area extensively warn of poor holding ground and won't go in anymore. Phil Richter at Blind Channel Resort also warns of poor holding. Caution advised.

The view of Phillips Arm and Shoal Bay public floats from the Shoal Bay Pub

JOHNSTONE STRAIT

See Area Map Page 314 - Maps Not for Navigation

Blind Channel Resort's tidal turbine power generator is anchored just north of the resort.

⑦ **Cordero Lodge.** Cordero Lodge, General Delivery, Blind Channel, BC V0P 1B0; (250) 287-0917; corderolodge@gmail.com; www.corderolodge.com. The Lodge and restaurant closed in 2017 due to health issues. At press time it was not clear what services will be available at the resort for the 2018 season and beyond. See www.WaggonerGuide.com for update information.

Please, please slow down. Passing boat traffic in Cordero Channel can put out damaging wakes that roll into boats moored at Cordero Lodge. As you approach the lodge location, throttle back to no-wake speed and hold that speed until you're past. It's only a short distance.

Crawford Anchorage. Crawford Anchorage, between Erasmus Island and East Thurlow Island, is chancy at best, with a rocky and poor holding bottom. Friends report they have anchored in Crawford Anchorage successfully, using a Bruce anchor and a stern-tie to Erasmus Island. We tried anchoring with indifferent results. Enter Crawford Anchorage from the west—rocks lie in the eastern entrance. Rocks also lie southeast of Mink Island.

Mayne Passage (Blind Channel). Mayne Passage connects Cordero Channel with Johnstone Strait. From Johnstone Strait, the entrance can be hard to spot, hence the local name "Blind Channel." The current in Mayne Passage reaches 5 knots at springs, flooding north and ebbing south. Chart 3543 (1:40,000) shows rips in the northern part of Mayne Passage, and Sailing Directions warns of whirlpools and overfalls. Passages near slack are recommended. Blind Channel Resort, on the west shore of Mayne Passage, is popular. On the east side of Mayne Passage, Charles Bay is a good anchorage.

Charles Bay. On the east side of Mayne Passage, Charles Bay has convenient anchoring depths around Eclipse Islet in the center of the bay. Just east of Eclipse Islet, however, the bay shoals to drying flats.

LOCAL KNOWLEDGE

Strong Currents: Current runs across the face of the floats at Blind Channel Resort and landing can be a little tricky. At the fingers themselves, the current runs from north to south about 90 percent of the time, regardless of the current in the middle of the channel. A short distance off the fingers, however, the current usually runs from south to north. You can verify the current direction at the docks by observing which way the fingers press against the pilings at the outer ends. Call on the VHF for docking instructions. One of the staff always comes down to help with landings. They know what to do.

⑧ **Blind Channel Resort.** Blind Channel, BC V0P 1B0; (888) 329-0475; info@blindchannel.com; www.blindchannel.com. Monitors VHF 66A. Open all year, gasoline, diesel, propane. Ample moorage on 2000 feet of dock, 15, 30 & some 50 amp power, washrooms, showers, laundry, UV-treated spring water, free Wi-Fi. Garbage drop for fee, no charge for glass and cans. Float planes stop here. This is a complete, well-run, and popular marina and resort, with water taxi, adventure tours, accommodations, excellent fully-licensed restaurant open June through Labour Day, well-stocked store, fresh-baked goods during the high season, post office, liquor agency, gift items. The new gazebo overlooking the marina is a welcome addition in rainy weather. Several events are held throughout the summer months, check their website for the season's schedule.

The resort is surrounded by hiking trails, developed and maintained by Interfor. One trail leads to an 900-year-old cedar, 16 feet in diameter. It's a good hike and a splendid old tree. Recommended.

The Cedar Post Restaurant is excellent, akin to something that might be found in Whistler or Vancouver. The servers are well-dressed and the menu is varied. The Grill Shack on the seaside patio is open for lunch in July and August.

This is a real family enterprise, now spanning four generations. Edgar and the late Annemarie Richter bought Blind Channel in the early 1970s. Edgar designed and built all the buildings, and Annemarie's distinctive and lovely artwork decorates the dock and the restaurant. What they built, with long hours and hard labor, is a long way from what they bought 40 years ago.

Their son Phil Richter is general manager. Phil and Jennifer's sons Eliot and William grew up working on the docks and in the dining room. Eliot is now a partner in the business and lives on-site. You will most likely see Eliot's children running around the property, learning and having fun.

LOCAL KNOWLEDGE

Tidal Current Turbine Generator: July 2017, Blind Channel Resort added a tidal current turbine generator anchored in Mayne Passage less than 1/4 mile north of the resort and 400 feet from the West Thurlow Island shore. Most of the turbine generator is below the water's surface with part of the frame floating above. The turbine supplies electrical power to the resort.

⑨ **Greene Point Rapids.** Currents in Greene Point Rapids can run to 7 knots on spring tides. On small tides currents are much less. Sailing Directions warns of "considerable overfalls, whirlpools and eddies," and recommends transiting near slack. Slack water occurs about 1 hour and 30 minutes before slack water at Seymour Narrows. Current corrections are shown under Seymour Narrows in the Secondary Stations section in Tide and Current Tables Vol. 6, and in Ports and Passes. When eastbound on flood tides, low-powered boats and boats with tows are cautioned against being set against Erasmus Island.

Loughborough Inlet. Loughborough (pronounced "Loch-brough") Inlet, off Chancellor Channel, is deep, with steep-to sides and few good anchorages. The best anchorage used to be in **Beaver Inlet**, a short distance from the mouth on the western shore. Beaver Inlet is now a log booming ground with significant commercial activity, making it ill-suited to pleasure boats. Edith Cove in Beaver Inlet is occupied by a float home and log raft, so it's not an anchorage.

Sidney Bay. Sidney Bay indents the western shore of Loughborough Inlet, where resident homesteaders Dane Campbell and Helen Piddington operate a rustic 120-foot float for visiting boats, located on the south side of the bay 50°30.88'N/125°36.06'W. Payment can be made at the float shed, or across the bay at their home on the north shore. Dane most likely will be ready to receive your painter line and provide good conversation. Correspondent Deane Hislop writes, "It's well protected from the wind and a beautiful location. We've stayed many times." Dane is a soft spoken commercial fisherman that we have found quite interesting to talk to. In 1975 he and his wife moved to Sidney Bay, where they raised their two children. Helen's book, *The Inlet*, describes life and their experiences in Loughborough Inlet." Her other book, The Rumble Seat, describes growing up in the 1930's near Victoria BC. The Landons report that Helen's health is failing; boaters may wish to visit this pioneer outstation, one of the last remaining from a bygone era, before it too passes with time.

WELLBORE CHANNEL

⑩ **Whirlpool Rapids.** Whirlpool Rapids on **Wellbore Channel** has currents to 7 knots. The time of turn is based on Seymour Narrows, and corrections are shown under Secondary Current Stations in the Tide and Current Tables Vol. 6, and Ports and Passes. The flood sets southeast and the ebb sets northwest. When the current is running, expect strong whirlpools, upwellings and back eddies on the downstream side. The turbulence occurs south of Carterer Point on the flood, and north of Carterer Point on the ebb. It is best to transit within a half-hour of slack, although on small tides boats seem to go through anytime. At low tide you might see bears on the beach near the south entrance to Wellbore Channel.

Forward Harbour. The entrance to Forward Harbour is narrow but unobstructed. Most of the harbor is 60 to 90 feet deep. Douglas Bay is a pretty anchorage, sheltered from Johnstone Strait westerlies that turn and blow through Sunderland Channel. The bottom of Douglas Bay drops off quickly, and you may find yourself anchored in 60 feet of water instead of 30 feet—a good reason to carry at least 300 feet of anchor rode. We've had a report that a southeast wind can make for a rough time for boats anchored along the northern shore.

A trail leads from Douglas Bay to a white sand beach at Bessborough Bay. In the past the trail was well marked and easy to walk, but we received a report that winter blowdown has made the trail much more challenging.

If Forward Harbour is too full, good anchorage can be found in the little bay on Hardwicke Island, directly across from the mouth of Forward Harbour.

Bessborough Bay. Although you can find anchoring depths in the southeast corner, the entire bay is open to strong westerlies blowing up Sunderland Channel.

Topaze Harbour. Big and pretty enough, but little shelter for small boats.

Sunderland Channel. Sunderland Channel connects Wellbore Channel with Johnstone Strait. If the westerly is blowing and whitecaps are in Sunderland Channel, it will likely be worse in Johnstone Strait. Many boats wait out these conditions in Forward Harbour.

All of the channels north of Yuculta Rapids—Nodales Channel, Mayne Passage, Chancellor Channel, and Sunderland Channel—lead to Johnstone Strait. Each provides some protection and a chance to observe conditions on Johnstone Strait before venturing out. A strong westerly wind opposed by an ebb current can make Johnstone Strait difficult.

JOHNSTONE STRAIT

Johnstone Strait is a seductive and difficult body of water. The strait begins at Chatham Point in the east, and stretches 54 miles along the northeast side of Vancouver Island to Blinkhorn Peninsula. It is the shortest route up- or down-island. Especially on the Vancouver Island side, Johnstone Strait is bounded by steep, high and beautiful mountains. On a clear day the scenery is awesome.

That is the seductive part. The difficult part is what the wind and current in Johnstone Strait do to each other. The flood current flows eastward, down-island, toward Discovery Passage and Campbell River. The ebb current flows westward, up-island, toward Queen Charlotte Strait and the North Pacific Ocean. A residual ebb surface current exists in Johnstone Strait, increasing the west-flowing ebb current's strength and duration. In the summer, the prevailing wind in Johnstone Strait is a westerly, often a gale-force westerly, funneled by the mountains. The result is a classic wind-against-current heaping up of the seas.

Conditions are worst where the meeting of currents creates tide-rips, even in calm conditions. This stretch begins at Ripple Shoal, east of Kelsey Bay. It extends westward past Kelsey Bay, through Race Passage and Current Passage, and across the mouth of Sunderland Channel. Especially on an ebb, when the westerly is blowing you don't want to be there—period. Leave the heroics to others. Johnstone Strait can take all the pleasure out of a pleasure boat. Kevin Monahan's excellent diagrams on page 316 illustrate Johnstone Strait's trouble spots.

Despite the potential problems, we have run the length of Johnstone Strait, both directions, many times, and often had an excellent ride. But we listened to the weather and went when conditions were calm or near-calm. If the wind had come up, we were prepared to run for cover in a bay or seek out a friendly point to hide behind until conditions improved. We always keep a bail-out point in mind. Conditions can change quickly.

Watch for drift in Johnstone Strait. There's considerable current activity, and many shear lines where scrap wood, tree limbs, logs, and even entire floating trees accumulate.

Turn Island. Turn Island is off the southern tip of East Thurlow Island, at the intersection of Johnstone Strait and Discovery Passage. Anchor behind Turn Island, about where the 5.8-meter sounding is shown on the chart, with good holding and room to swing. The anchorage has nice views to Johnstone Strait and the mountains on Vancouver Island. [*Hamilton*]

Knox Bay. Knox Bay is located on the north side of Johnstone Strait, near the mouth of Mayne Passage. Knox Bay would be a poor choice for an anchorage, but a good hideout to escape a strong westerly in the strait. The northwest corner of the bay is best protected. Unfortunately, it is deep and occasionally has log booming.

Fanny Island. When the Environment Canada weather station was moved from Helmcken Island to Fanny Island a few years ago, Johnstone Strait weather reports improved dramatically (Helmcken Island could report 8 knots of wind when it was blowing 30). We're told, however, that while Fanny Island reports of northwest winds are fairly accurate, south and

Blind Channel RESORT

TIE UP A favourite destination for boaters for generations. Stay on your boat, or in a deluxe rental cabin overlooking the harbour. Full service marina with 15, 30, and 50 amp power, marine gas, diesel, and propane, filtered spring water, and Wi-Fi. General store offering groceries, gifts, liquor, fishing tackle, ice, a post office and much more. Laundry and shower facilities.

DINE OUT A memorable dining experience, showcasing the owners' German heritage and creative use of fresh, local ingredients. Stunning views from all seats.

EXPLORE Tranquil hiking trails. Guided fishing and marine adventure tours. Water taxi service.

info@blindchannel.com   VHF Channel 66A   1-888-329-0475
www.blindchannel.com

JOHNSTONE STRAIT

east winds can be reported less than what's actually going on.

Helmcken Island. Helmcken Island has protected anchorage on its north side in Billygoat Bay. Currents in this part of the strait run at 5 knots. When opposed by wind from the opposite direction large, dangerous seas can build rapidly. Billygoat Bay is a good place to hide out. Anchor in approximately 30 feet, although Correspondents James and Jennifer Hamilton found only poor holding over rock. Instead, they recommend the cove northwest of Billygoat Bay. They go up to the head of the cove, where they have found calm water, with an "awesome" view eastward. The cove is unnamed in Sailing Directions or on the chart. The Hamiltons call it Helmcken Cove.

⑪ **Kelsey Bay.** (250) 282-3623. Kelsey Bay, on the north side of Vancouver Island, has a breakwater southeast of the harbor, made of old ship hulks—the Union Steamship *Cardena* and three WWII frigates: HMCS *Runnymede*, HMCS *Lasalle*, and HMCS *Longueil*. Enter leaving the light green breakwater to starboard and the old ships to port. Watch for current entering the breakwater. Transient moorage is on A, B, and C docks, maximum length 60 feet. Water, 20 and 30 amp power, garbage drop, recycling, oil disposal. Most of the moorage is occupied by commercial fish boats. Rafting may be required. Moorage is paid at the honor box at the top of the ramp, an attendant is on site during the summer months. We found the docks to be clean and well maintained The Straits View Cafe, located behind the breakwater, welcomes boaters at their 100-ft dock while enjoying breakfast, lunch, or dinner; the cafe is closed on Tuesdays. Overnight stays are permitted on the Cafe dock, moorage charged, 20-amp power, reservations accepted, call (250) 282-0118.

A small gift shop that doubles as a tourist office is located on the wharf at the north end of the marina. The small village of Sayward is approximately one mile south, some services but the grocery store is no longer open.

Yorke Island. Located in the middle of Johnstone Strait, west of Hardwicke Island, Yorke Island is the site of several gun emplacements which were installed in 1937. These ruins from WWII were originally intended to block enemy backdoor approach to the Strait of Georgia and the cities of Vancouver and Victoria. Well maintained trails by BC Parks lead from the south cove on the island to various gun and battery sites. The main gun emplacement is at the highest point on the island with great views of the Strait and is visible from passing boats. Yorke Island is a haunting place to visit and worth the stop in the right conditions. Maps of the island and more historical information can be found at www.wikipedia.org/wiki/Yorke_Island_(Canada). Temporary anchorage can be found in 30 to 45 feet of water, east of the unnamed cove on the south side of the island. The cove is often covered with kelp and the bottom is rocky with poor holding. Wind and current are a consideration. Leaving the boat unattended is not recommended, best to leave someone aboard as anchor watch. Charted rocks lie south of the cove.

Blenkinsop Bay. Blenkinsop Bay has reasonably protected anchorage along the north shore of Johnstone Strait, but swells from westerly winds work into the bay. The chart shows tiderips off Blenkinsop Bay. The chart isn't kidding. McLeod Bay and an unnamed bay inside Tuna Point are possible temporary anchorages.

⑫ **Port Neville.** Port Neville is an 8-mile-long inlet, a popular hideout for the fishing fleet, and an excellent spot to duck into if the weather in Johnstone Strait deteriorates. The inlet is a good anchorage. A government dock and float are a short distance inside, along the eastern shore. Boomed logs are stored in several places toward the inner end of the inlet. No public facilities or services are in the vicinity. The current can run swiftly past the government float, so plan your approach carefully. Remember, there's no shame in making several attempts before you get your landing right.

For years Olaf "Oly" Hansen, at the government dock post office, could be reached by radio for a report on conditions on Johnstone Strait. Oly died in January, 1997 at age 87, another legend gone from the coast. Oly's widow Lilly lived on in the family house for a few years, but finally had to move down-island. In 2003, shortly after her 90th birthday, she too left us. Their daughter Lorna (Hansen) Chesluk raised her daughter Erica in the house at the head of the wharf. Lorna was the postmaster, and she happily looked out on the strait and gave a report if you called on the radio.

The post office was closed in 2010, and Lorna moved to Campbell River to be closer to family. The Hansen family had lived at Port Neville since 1891. Until it closed, the Port Neville post office was the longest continuously-operating post office in the province. Yet another page of coastal history is turned. A caretaker now looks after the property. The wonderful old store building is at the head of the wharf. Occasionally tour and whale watching groups stop by to see the old post office, still frozen in time.

If you go ashore, keep pets on a leash. Wild animals (grizzly bears and black bears) and protective mother deer are in the area.

On the west side of Robbers Nob, near the tip, several petroglyphs can be seen below the high tide line. The property above the high tide line is private.

Anchoring: Correspondents James and Jennifer Hamilton recommend Baresides Bay. "Anchor directly south of the *MSh* symbol on Charts 3545 and 3564. You will be in 15 feet of water at zero tide, about 200 feet from shore. Excellent holding. Not super-protected, but out of the teeth of the westerly." [*Hamilton*]

LOCAL KNOWLEDGE

RESTRICTED AREA: Robson Bight, on the Vancouver Island side near the north end of Johnstone Strait, is an Ecological Reserve, a gathering place for Orcas. Unauthorized vessels (meaning yours and ours) are not allowed. Stay outside of the Reserve's boundary lines noted on the charts.

Robson Bight. The Robson Bight Ecological Reserve is a restricted area that runs 0.5 mile offshore and for 5 miles off Robson Bight. It is part of a reserve for Orca whales. The Reserve is not centered on the Bight and extends more to the east. The Reserve is shown on most charts but may be hard to see. If you stray into the restricted area, wardens will intercept your boat and instruct you to leave immediately.

Views of Johnstone Strait from Yorke Island's WWII gun emplacements

The view from the Straits Bay Cafe at Kelsey Bay

The Broughtons

CHAPTER 12

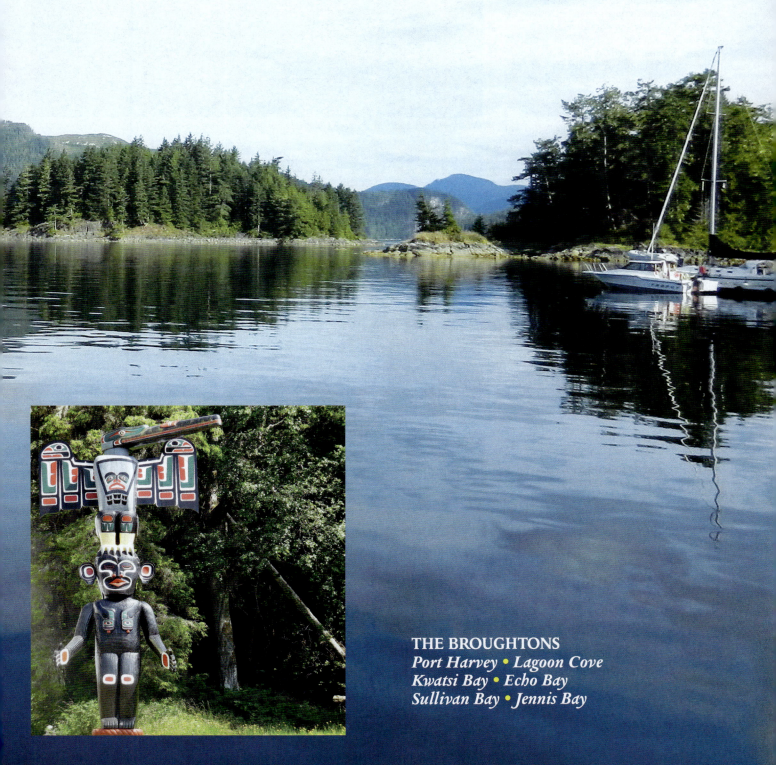

THE BROUGHTONS
*Port Harvey • Lagoon Cove
Kwatsi Bay • Echo Bay
Sullivan Bay • Jennis Bay*

THE BROUGHTONS

See Area Map Page 325 - Maps Not for Navigation

"The Broughtons" is an all-encompassing term for the inlets, islands and waterways on the mainland side of Queen Charlotte Strait, north of Johnstone Strait. This area includes the islands adjoining Blackfish Sound and Fife Sound. It also includes Knight Inlet, Kingcome Inlet, Tribune Channel, Drury Inlet, and Mackenzie Sound. For convenience we include Havannah Channel and Chatham Channel. Locals call this area the Mainland, to distinguish it from the Vancouver Island side from Sayward (Kelsey Bay) to the top of Vancouver Island, which they call North Island.

The Broughtons, or the Mainland, is one large, complex cruising ground. It offers anchorages from raw and wind-swept Fife Sound and Blackfish Sound, to the gentler waters of Simoom Sound, Greenway Sound and Drury Inlet. Small, family-owned resorts—no two of them alike—are spread throughout the Broughtons. Most cruisers anchor out some of the time and enjoy the social side of marina life the rest of the time. During the course of a cruising holiday, most cruisers either stop at or overnight at all the marinas: Port Harvey, Lagoon Cove, Kwatsi Bay, Pierre's at Echo Bay, Sullivan Bay, and Jennis Bay.

Resupply and repairs are on the North Island side, at Port McNeill, Alert Bay, Sointula, and Port Hardy. North Island is described in a separate chapter.

The rich history of the Broughtons begins with Native habitation dating back thousands of years. On Mound Island, 14 depressions in the earth are evidence of Native Big Houses and Long Houses, each of which held extended families. We're told that trading beads, the colorful glass beads exchanged for valuable pelts by early traders, still can be found on beaches throughout the Broughtons, although we've never found any.

The Broughtons were homesteaded in the late 1800s and early 1900s. Families were raised on rude farms. The men rowed across Queen Charlotte Strait to Alert Bay, or rowed—*rowed*—200 miles south to Vancouver or Victoria to conduct business and bring back supplies.

In most cases, the forest has erased all traces of the homesteaders' now-abandoned efforts.

Beautiful Lacy Falls in Tribune Channel near Watson Cove and Kwatsi Bay

One notable exception is remarkable "Monks' Wall," at the north end of Beware Passage. There, hidden in the trees, are the remains of rock walls from William and Mary Anne Galley's wilderness trading post that was active from the late 1800s until after the First World War.

The Broughtons are a destination. Take your time and don't hurry through. See Billy Proctor's museum in Shoal Harbour. Marvel at Lacy Falls on Tribune Channel. Anchor out in the coves and lagoons. Visit the marinas and meet the families who run them.

Ask questions, read the history, and take time to explore. If you spend your entire cruise in the Broughtons, you might—you just might—scratch the surface.

Marinas: Marinas in the Broughtons are different from marinas elsewhere on the coast. They're small and often family run. Some cruisers develop friendships with the owners, and come back year after year to catch up. The marinas may be a little rough around the edges, but that's part of their charm. These are wilderness marinas, and the owners make do with what they have.

Wi-Fi: Internet in the Broughtons is provided by satellite, and bandwidth is limited. Marina owners request that visitors refrain from downloading videos, sending large email attachments, using Skype, or engaging in other high bandwidth activities.

Potluck hour: Many of the marinas in the Broughtons have a potluck hors d'oeuvre—or even a potluck dinner—gathering around 5:00 p.m. Bring your own beverages, leaded or unleaded and your own plate with utensils.. It's an ideal time to meet other boaters and exchange information. Kids usually are more than welcome, although if they're the only ones they might get bored with grownups' chit-chat. You'll want to carry a stock of suitable fixings for your hors d'oeuvre or potluck contribution. The fixings don't have to be fancy. If you're down to Doritos and salsa, they'll be hoovered into mouths in short order. If you enjoy preparing something special, this is a good time to show your stuff.

Good Books: Tide Rips and Back Eddies; and *Full Moon, Flood Tide*. Both by Bill Proctor, edited and illustrated by Yvonne Maximchuk. Pub-

CHARTS

3515	Knight Inlet (1:80,000); Simoom Sound (1:20,000)
3544	Johnstone Strait, Race Passage & Current Passage (1:25,000)
3545	Johnstone Strait, Port Neville to Robson Bight (1:40,000)
3546	Broughton Strait (1:40,000)
3547	Queen Charlotte Strait, Eastern Portion (1:40,000)
3564 Plans	Johnstone Strait: Port Neville, Havannah Channel, Chatham Channel

Small intimate marinas are found among the Broughtons Islands.

The Broughtons - East

The docks at Port Harvey

lished by Harbour Publishing. These books are highly recommended reading before or during a cruise to the Broughtons. If you are hungry for a little more, consider Yvonne's recently released book, *Drawn to Sea,* for more insights on life and the people of this area.

HAVANNAH CHANNEL

Havannah Channel leads northward toward Knight Inlet and other channels to the north and west.

① **Port Harvey.** Port Harvey is large, and although it is open to westerlies from Johnstone Strait, it is an excellent anchorage. If you're planning an early morning run on Johnstone Strait it's a good place to overnight. You'll find anchorage in several notches along the east side before you reach the head of the bay, and ample anchorage at the head.

A big logging operation is on the west side of Port Harvey. A permanent house with private mooring floats is on the shore. The wind blows through Cracroft Inlet, and a gentle, low surge can come in if the wind is blowing on Johnstone Strait.

Caution: Do not attempt the narrow canal that leads between Port Harvey and Cracroft Inlet. The channel dries and is studded with boulders.

Port Harvey Marine Resort is located at the head of Port Harvey. They charge a fee for landing the dinghy.

① **Port Harvey Marine Resort.** St. 108, 1434 Ironwood St., Campbell River, BC V9W 5T5; (250) 902-9003; portharveymarine@gmail.com; www.portharvey.blogspot.com. Monitors VHF 66A. Guests welcomed with ample 1000 feet of side-tie moorage on good docks, with 15 & 30 amp power, water, and Wi-Fi. Easy access to shore for walking the dog or walking the trail through the forest. Day pass available for guest moorage. Owners are George and Gail Cambridge. The beach in front of the Cambridge's house has clams and geoducks for those willing to do a little digging.

George and Gail Cambridge opened this well-positioned marina in 2009 and it was instantly popular. Sadly, in late 2015, the barge holding the store and Red Shoe Pub & Restaurant sunk. The docks were undamaged. In the summer of 2016, George and Gail were open for business with happy hours in a large tent on the dock. Construction on a new general store was in progress in 2017 with plans to be open for the 2018 season. Pizza from their pizza oven will be offered for impromptu gatherings at the dock. New washrooms, showers, and laundry facilities are in the planning stages. See WaggonerGuide.com for updates.

The marina isn't visible until you get all the way to the head of Port Harvey, beyond Range Island, so don't give up. You will see the industrial operation on the shore first. Port Harvey Marina is just across the bay.

Bockett Islets. Contributing Editor Tom Kincaid has anchored for a few hours among the Bockett Islets awaiting favorable current in Chatham Channel.

Boughey Bay. Anchorage is toward the south end of Boughey (pronounced "boogie") Bay. John Chappell (*Cruising Beyond Desolation Sound*) says easterly winds can spring up suddenly in the bay.

Matilpi. Matilpi (pronounced MAT-il-pi) is an abandoned Indian village site. It is beautiful, with a white shell beach backed by dense forest. Anchor behind the northern of the two islands, or between the islands. Protection is excellent.

Burial Cove. Burial Cove is pretty, though open to most winds. It is well-protected from seas and has good holding in 25 feet. A few houses are on shore. We've anchored there twice.

Call Inlet. Call Inlet is approximately 10 miles long, and runs through beautiful, steep-sided mountains. You can find anchoring depths in the Warren Islands, near the mouth of the inlet. They are a pretty spot to wait for the current to change in Chatham Channel. A stern-tie to shore is a good idea for overnight anchorage.

Chatham Channel. Chatham Channel is easier to run than it appears from the chart.

Moorage & General Store
Bakery • Pub & Restaurant
Ice Cream • Laundry & Showers
(under construction call ahead)
Power & Water • Wireless Internet
Walking Trails • Pet Friendly

East Cracoft Island
N50°34.057' W126°16.086'

At the Head of Port Harvey tucked in behind Range Island

George & Gail Cambridge
250-902-9003 or 780-524-6520
Channel 66A
portharveymarine@gmail.com
www.portharvey.blogspot.com

THE BROUGHTONS

See Area Map Page 326 - Maps Not for Navigation

Lagoon Cove docks and office with Clio Channel in the distance

Popular Happy Hour at Lagoon Cove is held at the historic workshop

The southern section is the narrowest, with the least room in the channel, and requires the greatest attention. The current floods east and ebbs west. Near slack water is the most pleasant time to transit this southern section.

Slacks are based on Seymour Narrows predictions. Correction factors for the times of slack water are found under Secondary Stations in the Tide and Current Tables, Vol. 6, and Ports and Passes. Chart 3545 (1:40,000) shows the area, including the range locations. Chart 3564 (1:20,000), with its 1:10,000 insert of the southern section, really helps understanding. We highly recommend Chart 3564.

If you are running compass courses through the southern section, remember that the headings shown on the chart are true, and must be corrected to magnetic. We have found that in some lighting conditions, or if the trees are not trimmed, the ranges are hard to locate from the far ends of the lower channel. Going either direction, a sharp-eyed crew should sight astern at the back range until it grows difficult to see. By then the leading range should be visible. Maximum currents in the southern section run to 5 knots on a spring tide, with no significant swirls or overfalls. In our experience, the current usually is much less than shown (but not always; twice, we have found considerable current). Chatham Channel can be taken at times other than slack water, but you should know what you are doing, and in the southern section *keep your boat lined up on the range.* Keep your eyes open. We encountered a bear swimming across Chatham Channel one morning.

Cutter Cove. Cutter Cove, located across from Minstrel Island Resort (now closed) at the north end of Chatham Channel, is very pretty and a good anchorage. A fresh west or northwest wind can enter the cove. No swells, but aggressive little whitecaps. The bottom looks flat, as if it's pure mud. "At least one noisy old rock is down there, though, because the anchor chain dragged across it all night long." [*Hale*] Anchor in 24 feet (zero tide).

In 2014, Correspondent Richard Spore anchored in Cutter Cove and was entertained by a mama bear and her four cubs foraging on the beach.

Minstrel Island Resort. The sad story of this once great stop continues. The buildings appear abandoned and vegetation is growing on the docks as they slowly decay, due to lack of maintenance. You may see several boats moored there.

LOCAL KNOWLEDGE

CAUTION: When entering Lagoon Cove from Blow Hole, give the Islet and shoal across the channel from Perley Island a wide berth as the shoal extends further west than chart 3564 indicates. Look for a private orange and/or green round plastic float which should pass to your port side entering Lagoon Cove.

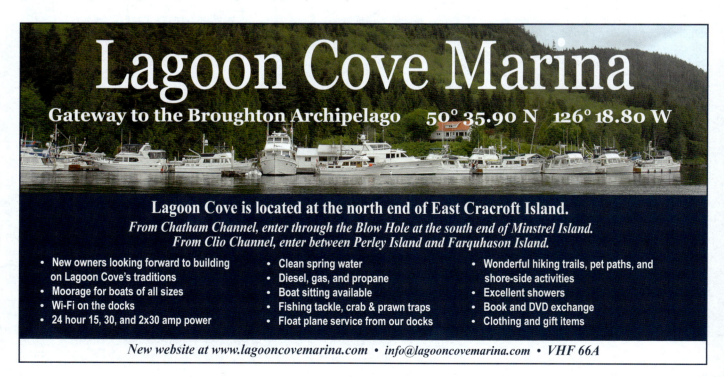

Lagoon Cove Marina

Gateway to the Broughton Archipelago   50° 35.90 N   126° 18.80 W

Lagoon Cove is located at the north end of East Cracroft Island.
From Chatham Channel, enter through the Blow Hole at the south end of Minstrel Island.
From Clio Channel, enter between Perley Island and Farquhason Island.

- New owners looking forward to building on Lagoon Cove's traditions
- Moorage for boats of all sizes
- Wi-Fi on the docks
- 24 hour 15, 30, and 2x30 amp power

- Clean spring water
- Diesel, gas, and propane
- Boat sitting available
- Fishing tackle, crab & prawn traps
- Float plane service from our docks

- Wonderful hiking trails, pet paths, and shore-side activities
- Excellent showers
- Book and DVD exchange
- Clothing and gift items

New website at www.lagooncovemarina.com • info@lagooncovemarina.com • VHF 66A

THE SURPRISE ON KNIGHT INLET

More times than not, we have been cruising the calm protected waters of Chatham Channel when headed north, or down Tribune Inlet when headed south, and broken out into Knight Inlet to find 4-6 foot seas and 20+ knots of wind. What happened? When you look at the charts you can see what is happening. Winds typically come from the west or northwest during the popular summer cruising months. From Queen Charlotte Sound and Blackfish Sound there is 16 miles of fetch for wind-driven waves to build. This is enough to set up challenging wave conditions. If your timing adds an ebb current, you can see how you can go from fairly calm conditions to a 2 mile crossing of Knight Inlet that is very uncomfortable, especially when headed south. Consider timing your crossing of Knight Inlet early in the morning before winds pick up and on a flood tide.

The Blow Hole. The Blow Hole is a short, shallow, easily-navigated channel between Minstrel Island and East Cracroft Island. The channel gets its name from strong westerly winds that sometimes blow through. Near the west end a reef, shown clearly on Chart 3564, extends from East Cracroft Island on the south side of the channel. Brave the kelp and favor the north side of the channel and you'll have no problems.

② **Lagoon Cove.** Lagoon Cove has good anchorage along the shorelines, although the middle of the bay is a little deep for most boats. Lagoon Cove Marina is on the east side of the bay. Locals recommend against anchoring on the west side of the bay, which they say is foul with logging cable. We got a note from a reader who said at least one cable can be found on the east side as well.

② **Lagoon Cove Marina.** c/o Minstrel Island P.O., Minstrel Island, BC V0P 1L0; info@lagooncovemarina.com; www.lagooncovemarina.com. Monitors VHF 66A. Open all year. Lagoon Cove has gasoline, diesel, propane, stove oil, 15, 30, & 2×30 amp power, water, washroom & showers, gift shop. Wi-Fi has been extended to the docks with a separate repeater located on 'honeymoon dock.' Wired internet connection is available in the workshop area. Kenmore Air and NW Seaplanes service to Seattle.

A do-it-yourself burn barrel is available for burnable garbage (no fair just dropping a bag of garbage in, for someone else to deal with). The fuel dock office carries fishing tackle, prawn and crab traps, ice, charts, a few essentials. A separate store with the grand name "Edgewater Emporium" carries Lagoon Cove branded clothing.

The entire property has a whimsical quality about it. The workshop is a "historic" workshop full of old tools. A totem pole is made from pieces of outboard motors and all sorts of other junk. Two "exercise stations," one of them a pile of wood with an axe, the other a brightly painted lawnmower, invite the eager. Several hiking trails are maintained. A pet path is available for the four-legged crew.

Lagoon Cove Marina is one of the most popular stops on the coast and fills during the summer months. Reservations accepted. Happy hour appetizer potlucks for marina guests are held almost every day in the "historic" workshop. Guests bring treats from their boats. Marina guests often volunteer to set and retrieve the marina's prawn traps. Happy hour often morphs into a casual potluck dinner. Weather permitting, a marshmallow roast might be organized at sunset. Over the years singing around the campfire has been a big part of Lagoon Cove. Bring your instrument and join in.

Everybody, by the way, goes to the happy hour and marshmallow roasts. "This is summer camp for adults," an enthusiastic lady told us.

Current owners, Jim and Lou Ryan, purchased the property in 2016 and began their first season in 2017 with lots of energy, making improvements to the marina while maintaining the beloved character and charm of Lagoon Cove. Their daughter Kelley and son-in-law Dan round out the family team. The Ryans are committed to "enhancing but not changing" this popular destination.

Knight Inlet. Knight Inlet (locally called Knight's Inlet) extends from its mouth at Midsummer Island to its head, at the mouth of the Klinaklini River. The inlet is about 70 miles long and 2 miles wide, the longest of the fjords indenting the B.C. coast. Along most of its length the shores rise steeply to 6,000-foot-high mountains. Anchorage is iffy at best, so for many, the inlet's upper reaches are explored mainly by fast boats able to make the round trip in a single day. Boats with limited fuel capacity should top off at Lagoon Cove before making the trip. Extensive logging activity has put considerable debris in the water. Watch carefully.

The section above Glendale Cove is reported to be more dramatic than Jervis or Bute inlets. Reader John Tyler reports, "Even with the distances involved, it's well worth the time to cruise up there."

In Knight Inlet, **Tsakonu Cove** is a pretty anchorage, protected from westerlies but exposed to the east. Several years ago we anchored near the head of Tsakonu Cove for a quiet lunch, while outside a 20-knot inflow wind blew Knight Inlet into an uncomfortable chop. Driftwood logs on the shore suggest that outflow winds in Knight Inlet probably roar into Tsakonu Cove, accompanied by substantial seas.

Hoeya Sound. Hoeya Sound is pretty, but deep and completely exposed to the westerly winds that are prevalent in the summer.

Glendale Cove. Glendale Cove offers minimal protection from strong northeast winds that often blow down the inlet. "We anchored on a sloping bottom off the east side, just north of some old pilings. The second night four other pleasure boats were there. Every place else seemed to be less than 6 feet or more than 150 feet." [*Evertz*]

Glendale Cove has one of the highest concentrations of Grizzly Bears, also referred to as Brown Bears, on the west coast of British Columbia. In spring, bears are feeding on tidal area sedge; and by mid-August, they are feeding continuously on salmon. Pleasure boaters anchored in the cove are often approached by the First Nations, who hand out bear viewing guidelines established by the Commercial Bear Viewing Association. These helpful guidelines are intended to protect the bears from feeling crowded and becoming displaced, as well as common sense safety tips for those viewing the bears. Dogs should never be brought ashore. Boaters should be respectful of boat speed, noise, distance, and viewing time. Being good stewards and respectful boaters is always important for future preservation of these special places. Knight Inlet Lodge, located on the east side of Glendale Cove, is a private resort providing Grizzly Bear tours to their fly-in guests. Reservations are booked well in advance for this distinctive lodge. The Lodge does not provide transient moorage and doesn't have any services for boaters visiting the area.

Wahshihlas Bay. Located at the mouth of the Sim River, Wahshihlas Bay is a possible anchorage. Although we've never tried it, Correspondents Bruce and Margaret Evertz have. "It was settled weather and we anchored in the northwest corner, just off the shoal. There were some snags to avoid. If we expected any winds we could have

THE BROUGHTONS   See Area Map Page 326 - Maps Not for Navigation

The happy hour potlucks are legendary at Kwatsi Bay Marina.

At Kwatsi Bay take the dinghy over to the beach and hike to the waterfalls.

moved away from the shoal a little and anchored with a stern tie to shore or to some old pilings. The bay is far from 'bomb proof,' but we felt secure with the weather we had." [*Evertz*]

Port Elizabeth. Port Elizabeth is a great big bay bounded on the west by low hills that let westerlies in. A substantial log booming operation is in the cove in the northwest corner. You can find good anchorage near the booming site and along the western shore, west of the largest of the three islands. The two smaller islands are joined on the west by drying flats.

Correspondents John and Lorraine Littlewood provided us with the following extra information:

"The unexpected difficulty with the anchorage in Duck Cove at the west end of Port Elizabeth is that in any winds from 0 to 180 degrees you will feel the full force. We were getting gusts to 30 knots in a southeaster, supposedly sheltered. The only real shelter is in the extreme southeastern end of Port Elizabeth, except in a northwest blow." [*Littlewood*]

Sargeaunt Passage. Sargeaunt Passage connects Knight Inlet and Tribune Channel, and has anchorage at either end of the narrows, although one cruiser warned us about old logging cables fouling their anchor on the southeast side. The passage runs between steep-sided mountains, and is beautiful. The shoal in the middle extends from the east shore across much of the passage. Favor the west shore. We found the depth at the narrow part was less than shown on the chart.

Tribune Channel. Tribune Channel borders the east and north sides of Gilford Island. The only marina on Tribune Channel is at Kwatsi Bay. Lacy Falls can be stunning.

Kumlah Island Anchorage. Kumlah Island is in Tribune Channel, roughly across from the mouth of Thompson Sound. Waggoner reader Joel Erickson found suitable anchorage in 16 to 24 feet behind Kumlah Island, between it and Gilford Island. We haven't spent the night, but would consider anchoring there in settled weather. The view is beautiful.

Thompson Sound. Thompson Sound is surrounded by forested mountains so steep that the hillsides are scarred by many landslides. Earlier editions of the Waggoner said Thompson Sound has no good anchorages, but Correspondents John and Lorraine Littlewood set us straight with this email: "There is excellent anchorage at the head of Thompson Sound, on the shelf between the mudflats at the mouth of the Kakweiken River. You can explore the river for a couple miles at high tide; there is lots of bear sign, and we don't mean black bears, either!"

A reader reported that when they tried to anchor they found the shelf dotted with crab trap buoys, leaving no room. They anchored briefly in the lee of Sackville Island, with a stern-tie to shore.

Bond Sound. In the past, we reported that Bond Sound had no good anchorages. But inspired by Bill Proctor's wonderful book, *Full Moon, Flood Tide*, readers Jim and Marsha Peters anchored their Grand Banks 42 *Dev's Courage* at the head of the sound in settled weather and took the dinghy some distance up the Ahta River. They said it was beautiful. Correspondents Steve and Elsie Hulsizer say to go up about two hours before high water. Another reader (Bill Cooke, Eastbay *Pop Pie*) told us that cutthroat trout fishing is good at the head of the sound. Correspondents John and Lorraine Littlewood add this note from an early September cruise:

"Bill Proctor's book, *Full Moon, Flood Tide*, led us to the Ahta River at the head of Bond Sound, an absolutely pristine salmon spawning river teeming with every sort of wildlife, from very large, dead salmon that have just completed their life cycle, to very much larger hairy brown mammals that feed on them (and just about anything else they want to). The place is like something from a fairy tale. It is not all that easy to find and explore, but very much worth it. Anchorage is tricky just off the drying bar at the mouth of the rivers (there are two: Ahta Creek on the left as you face the estuary and the Ahta River on the right). The Ahta River, with a smaller opening, is deep, fast and clear. Don't tell a soul."

Note: Strong winds can funnel through Bond Sound, making it mostly unsuitable for overnight anchorage.

③ **Kwatsi Bay.** The inner cove of Tribune Channel's Kwatsi Bay is a stunning anchorage, one of the most impressive on the coast, surrounded by a high, sheer bowl of rock. Sunrises and sunsets are magnificent. Our log says,

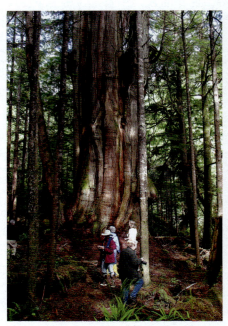
It's worth the trek through the forest to see the 1000-year-old cedar tree at Watson Cove.

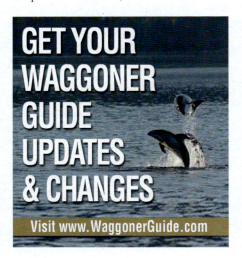

330   www.WaggonerGuide.com

See Area Map Page 326 - Maps Not for Navigation

THE BROUGHTONS

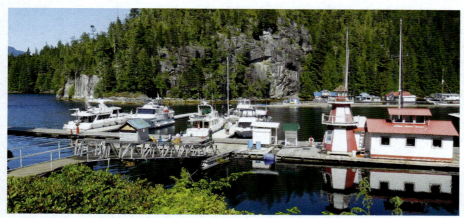

Reserve your space at Echo Bay's popular marina docks or try their Cliffside option on the other side of the bay.

"Wow!" The bay is deep, though, over 100 feet deep in much of the inner cove. We had a peaceful night in 60 feet with good holding off the two streams that empty into the western bight of the inner cove. The next morning, we found several other possible places to anchor in 48 to 72 feet. We have been told that the spot we anchored in is rocky and we should have anchored on the south side of the back bay, east of the entrance. [*Hale*]

③ **Kwatsi Bay Marina.** Simoom Sound P.O., Simoom Sound, V0P 1S0; (250) 949-1384; kwatsibay@kwatsibay.com; www.kwatsibay.com. Monitors VHF 66A. Moorage, water, small gift store, Wi-Fi during set hours. No shore power. Visa and Mastercard accepted. Plans for 2018 include replacing the bull rails with cleats.

Max Knierim and his wife Anca Fraser opened Kwatsi Bay Marina in 1998. Together with their daughter Marieke and son Russell, they carved out a place to live in the bush. Marieke and Russell have grown up and are now off in their own lives. Max and Anca are empty nesters, except for the many friends and guests who visit Kwatsi Bay during the summer.

The store is small but classy, with a selection of local arts and crafts ranging from pottery to woodwork. It also carries souvenir T-shirts, caps and sweatshirts. Reservations are recommended for July and August, email is best. Short hiking trails are nearby, reached by dinghy. One leads to a beautiful waterfall. Max or Anca can provide directions. Kwatsi Bay often hosts a potluck happy hour on the dock in the evening.

This is not a luxury resort; this is the wilderness, at its gentle but hardworking best. Recommended.

Watson Cove. Watch for a rock in the entrance, and favor the north shore when entering. Watson Cove is surrounded by beautiful rock, stunning waterfalls, and dense forest. A fish farm and floathouse have been moved from inside the cove to just outside. This makes the cove accessible for anchoring (60 feet, about halfway in), although we've heard the bottom is foul with logging debris. Don't tie to the aquaculture float; a barge is moored there overnight.

At the head of Watson Cove a dinghy can be tied to a length of large logging chain and you can scramble up the rock to a trail leading to the 1000-year-old cedar tree mentioned on p. 164 of Billy Proctor's *Full Moon, Flood Tide*. On an otherwise quiet afternoon at Kwatsi Bay, Anca took a bunch of us over in the speedboat to see the tree. The forest was beautiful and the tree was a memorable sight.

Lacy Falls. Just west of Watson Cove, Lacy Falls washes down an expanse of smooth black rock and tumbles into the sea. The boat can be brought up close, but not too close. The bottom at the base of the falls is rocky. *Note*: During dry periods water does not fan across the rocks.

Wahkana Bay. The inner cove of Wahkana Bay is attractive, but 120 feet deep except near shore. The south shore has spots where you can anchor in 48 to 72 feet with swinging room, however. Parts of the east shore are reported to be foul with logging debris and old pilings beneath the surface. The head of the inner cove shoals rapidly so watch out. Wind can blow through the saddle that reaches to Viner Sound.

Viner Sound. Viner Sound is pretty, but narrow and shallow. An indent on the north side, a short distance down the narrow channel, will hold one boat near the opening. Just inside that indent the water shoals immediately. Two public mooring buoys are in the little cove on the north side. The long shoaling area shown on the chart at the head of Viner Sound is real. Watch your depths as you explore.

Scott Cove. Scott Cove once was a busy logging camp, but the camp is now closed. This was the location of Pierre's Bay Marina, which moved to Echo Bay in 2008. We're told a surprising number of people still show up every summer looking for Pierre's Bay Marina.

LOCAL KNOWLEDGE

POWELL ROCK WARNING: A nasty drying rock lies off Powell Point, the southwest corner of Scott Cove. A boat running between Tribune Channel and Echo Bay or Cramer Passage could easily run up on this rock. Give Powell Point (and the rock) a big, wide offing.

④ **Echo Bay.** Echo Bay has been a gathering place for thousands of years, and for more than 100 years it has been a center for loggers, fishermen, and now summertime boaters. In 2008 Pierre and Tove (pronounced "Tova") Landry bought the Echo Bay Resort and moved Pierre's Bay Marina from nearby Scott Cove to Echo Bay. The Echo Bay Resort docks were scrapped and new docks, with upgraded power, were built and installed. The store was refurbished and restocked. A new fuel dock was built. In a span of about three months the resort was transformed—a remarkable achievement in a remote location where help is scarce and everything must be barged in.

Since then Pierre has continued expanding and improving the facilities. The blue roofed

Guests relax around a cozy fire at Pierre's.

Pierre's Echo Bay
Lodge & Marina

Family & Pet Friendly!

All Size Yachts Welcome!

- Fuel
- Moorage
- Grocery Store
- Post Office
- Walking Trails

- Rental Suites
- Laundromat & Shower
- 15, 30, & 50 Amp Power
- Cell Phone Coverage
- Internet

- Dinners June to Sept., Mon., Wed., Thurs., Sat.
- Prime Rib Mon. & Thur.
- Fish & Chips Wednesday
- Pig Roast Saturdays

We're located in the Broughton Archipelago
50°45.115'N/126°29.730'W

Visit us online at:
www.pierresbay.com

250.713.6415
info@pierresbay.com

See Area Map Page 326 - Maps Not for Navigation

THE BROUGHTONS

Billy Proctor's museum is filled with artifacts from a lifetime in the Islands. The Gift Shop has an impressive selection of local and nautical books.

event building, on the concrete breakwater, is the first sight upon entering. What used to be called Windsong Sea Village, under the cliff opposite Pierre's, is now part of Pierre's, known as The Cliffside. In 2017 the event building was expanded out towards the water and is now connected to the building where the store is housed.

Echo Bay has much to offer. Visit Billy Proctor's museum of local artifacts. A short but steep trail leads from Pierre's to the museum. An easier trail begins at the Cliffside docks. Book an Eco-Tour with Nikki Van Schyndel (see Echo Bay Eco Ventures www.echobayecoventures.com). Or take the dinghy over to Shoal Harbour and see local author and artist Yvonne Maximchuk's SeaRose Studio www.yvonnemaximchuk.com.

A deep midden at the head of Echo Bay is easily investigated from the beach. A schoolhouse once stood on shore, but the school-age population of the area has fallen below the threshold needed to keep the school open. The school closed in 2008, and was removed in fall 2014. A good hike begins behind where the former schoolhouse stood, and leads back into the hills past two dams, across a couple of bridges, and onto a logging road. The logging road is heavily overgrown with alder, however, and you probably won't go much farther.

Slow down: The wakes from passing vessels and the following wake from approaching vessels can get inside the bay and set things a-rocking. Please slow down well outside the marina when approaching.

Caution: See Pym Rocks warning.

GET YOUR WAGGONER GUIDE UPDATES AT www.WaggonerGuide.com

④ **Pierre's Echo Bay Lodge & Marina.** c/o General Delivery, Simoom Sound PO, BC V0P 1S0; (250) 713-6415; info@pierresbay.com; www.pierresbay.com. Monitors VHF 66A. Phone coverage is spotty in the area. Best to contact the marina by email. Open all year, gasoline, diesel, propane, 15, 30 & 50 amp power, rental cabins, store, ice, water, washrooms, showers, laundry, Wi-Fi. Ample guest moorage, reservations recommended mid-July through mid-August. Floatplane service by Kenmore Air and NW Seaplanes.

This is a busy destination in the Broughtons, with wide, sturdy docks, ample electric power, fuel dock and a well-stocked store for marina guests. The protected bay, with dramatic sheer rock faces, is beautiful. Pierre and Tove Landry have made Echo Bay a popular destination.

Pierre's is a social place. Happy hour gatherings are common and sometimes lead to potluck dinners. Visitors enjoy sitting around a cozy fire pit located onshore above the docks. During summer, Pierre and Tove host several weekly food events, such as fish n' chips night and prime rib night. Saturday night pig roasts, their signature event, run from the last weekend in June to the first weekend in September. Many visitors arrive on Fridays to get a good spot on the dock. Reservations are just about essential. Check their website for schedules and themes, some of which merit a costume or funny hat.

This might sound too structured and busy for some people, but Pierre and Tove, and the rest of the crew, make it pure fun.

④ **Pierre's Echo Bay - The Cliffside.** Formerly Windsong Sea Village, acquired by Pierre's at Echo Bay in 2013. The Cliffside offers overflow moorage for Pierre's at Echo Bay. Water, no power. For cruisers who prefer less hustle-and-bustle, The Cliffside is a good alternative to the main docks at Pierre's. A ramp to shore leads to a trail through the woods to Billy Proctor's Museum.

④ **Echo Bay Marine Park.** The dock has been condemned and is now closed. The holding bottom can be poor; anchor with care. The park has walk-in campsites and picnicking. A nice beach is often used as a landing for kayakers.

Shoal Harbour. Shoal Harbour has good, protected anchorage, mud bottom. We would anchor just to the right, inside the entrance. Wherever you anchor, check the depths before retiring—parts of the bay are quite shoal.

Billy Proctor's Museum. Open 10:00 a.m. to 5:00 p.m. A trail, rough in places, leads from Pierre's at Echo Bay. An easier trail begins at The Cliffside. By boat, if you leave Echo Bay and turn left toward Shoal Harbour, you can follow the shoreline around the peninsula and into a cozy bay with a home, small dock and marine railway haulout. This is where legendary Billy Proctor, who has logged, trapped and fished on the coast all of his many years, lives and has his museum.

Over a lifetime, Billy Proctor has collected a treasure of Chinese opium bottles, Chinese and Japanese beer bottles, engine plates, tools, arrowheads, bone fish hooks, a 1910 mimeograph machine from Minstrel Island, a crank telephone, a scale from the old Simoom Sound post office, and thousands of other artifacts of the coast's past.

Finally, in a structure he built from lumber he milled himself, the remarkable collection is displayed. Out the back door is a fish pond. Out the front door is another building he put up himself, housing a small book and gift shop, and more treasures. Everything has a story, even the windows and doors.

A few years ago, Billy built a replica of a hand logger's cabin, circa 1900. All the wood came from a single cedar log he found floating. Recently, he built a small schoolhouse and filled it with items from the old Echo Bay schoolhouse. Visitors can write on the old blackboards and look through old pictures. The kids love it.

No admission charge for the museum or schoolhouse, but a box marked "donations," which go to salmon enhancement, is next to the door. Billy also has an excellent selection of books on the area, including his own.

If you want to call ahead, try *Ocean Dawn* on VHF 16. Hike the occasionally challenging trail from Pierre's. Meet Billy and go have a look. We think you'll be glad you did.

Pym Rocks. *Caution*: When crossing from the vicinity of Echo Bay bound for Simoom Sound, Shawl Bay, Greenway Sound and so forth, Pym Rocks, off the northeast tip of Baker Island, lie very close to your probable course. We know of one experienced skipper whose attention wandered briefly and he went right up on the rocks. We had a close call with the rocks ourselves, but steered clear in time. The rocks are farther out than they ought to be, and unless you're on autopilot they keep drawing the boat toward them. [*Hale*]

Burdwood Group. The Burdwood Group is a beautiful little clutch of islands, a gunkholer's dream. The group is dotted with rocks and reefs, and Chart 3515 (1:80,000) doesn't show a lot of detail. With a sharp lookout, however, small boats can slowly maneuver among the islands. Anchorages are scarce, deep and rocky, and recommended in settled weather only. Given the opportunity, the

2018 WAGGONER CRUISING GUIDE — 333

THE BROUGHTONS   See Area Map Page 326 - Maps Not for Navigation

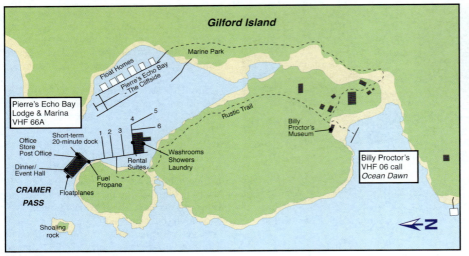

Echo Bay

FLAG ETIQUETTE

The National Flag
Vessels should fly the National Flag in which they are registered. As a general rule, the ship's National Flag should be 1 inch for each foot of the vessel's overall length; be sure this flag is not too small in proportion to your vessel. The National Flag is properly flown from a staff pole at the stern of a power boat, and from the leech of the most aftersail of a sailboat. Older tradition called for the flag to be removed from the gaff or leech when not under sail, and the flag placed on a staff pole at the stern. Most sailboats today fly the National Flag from the stern when under sail and under power. The Flag should be flown from 0800 to sunset, and at half-staff on Memorial Day until 12:00.

Courtesy Flag
As a courtesy, vessels should fly the National Flag of a foreign nation when cruising in their waters. Proper placement is on the mast of a power boat, or on the end of the starboard spreader for sailboats. For sailboats with more than one mast, the Courtesy Flag is flown from the starboard spreader of the forward mast. A power vessel without a mast, may fly the Courtesy Flag from the bow in lieu of a burgee; or preferably, on the starboard antenna strong enough to support it. Be sure your Courtesy Flag is not torn or in disrepair, and not too small. For sizing purposes, use one-half inch for each foot of the vessel's overall length. Most importantly, never fly a Courtesy Flag from the bow of your vessel unless you are a power boat without a mast. The Courtesy Flag is raised only after clearing customs, and usually takes the place of the yellow quarantine flag. Don't forget to remove the Courtesy Flag once you leave the waters of your host country.

Burgee
A burgee is a small flag with a symbol indicating membership in a yacht club or boat club. The burgee is flown from the bow on power boats and usually at the end of the lowest starboard spreader on sailboats. Only one burgee should be flown at a time, indicating the group or activity in which you are participating. Burgees can be sized to one-half inch for each foot of the vessel's overall length.

Quarantine Flag
In early times, a yellow flag indicated that there was a disease or illness aboard the ship, which was then isolated for 40 days. In modern times, it's the opposite, the yellow flag signals that the ship is free of disease and requests boarding and inspection. Boaters should fly the yellow Quarantine Flag from the mast just prior to reaching a customs dock or assigned slip, and the flag should be removed once you have cleared customs. There's a side benefit to the bright yellow flag, it's often easier for a customs agent to locate your vessel in a large marina, resulting in a quicker response to your request for clearance.

WILLIAM ROBERT BROUGHTON (1762-1821)

As a British Naval officer, W. Robert Broughton served as Commander of *HMS Chatham* during Captain George Vancouver's 1791-1795 Expedition of North America's Pacific Coast. In 1792, Broughton was given the assignment of exploring and charting a group of islands in the Queen Charlotte Sound, known today as The Broughtons, named in his honor by George Vancouver. Robert Broughton also explored the lower reaches of the Columbia

River, navigating upstream as far as the Columbia River Gorge, east of present day Portland, Oregon. Broughton's map of the Columbia River was later used as a planning tool by the Lewis and Clark expedition. Today, a plaque along Interstate 84 commemorates the spot where Broughton landed in 1792. In 1793 Broughton served as Commander of *HMS Providence* which began a four-year survey of the Asian coast, including Japan. After reaching England in 1799 and writing his book, "*A Voyage of Discovery to the North Pacific Ocean*," he resumed his naval career and served as Commander of several gun boats. Today, boaters in the Pacific Northwest include The Broughton Island Group among their favorite cruising destinations.

See Area Map Page 326 - Maps Not for Navigation

THE BROUGHTONS

Laura Bay

cruising boat should at least patrol through these islands.

Simoom Sound. Simoom Sound is a dogleg inlet, very scenic, but most of it is too deep for convenient anchoring. The best anchorages are in **O'Brien Bay** at the head of Simoom Sound, and in **McIntosh Bay** and the bays adjacent, along the north shore. You'll be in 48 to 60+ feet in O'Brien Bay, and 18 to 36 feet in the McIntosh Bay area. We spent a quiet night in McIntosh Bay behind the small island. The views took our breath away. In an emergency you could find anchorage off the northeast corner of Louisa Islet, and near the mouth of a creek on the Wishart Peninsula side.

Hayle Bay. After a visit to Hayle Bay our log reads, "Too deep, too exposed." [*Hale*]

⑤ **Laura Bay.** Laura Bay is a pretty and popular anchorage. Anchorage is in two sections: one, with a challenging entry, is in the long neck that extends westward behind the outer anchorage; the other is the outer anchorage in the cove between Trivett Island and Broughton Island. The cove behind Trivett Island is lovely. A little islet is in the cove, but the chart incorrectly shows good water all around. A rock is in the narrow passage to the east of the islet. Entering the cove, leave the islet to starboard. Our charlet shows the rock and best anchorages.

Caution: A major drying reef lies a short distance inside the entry to the neck that extends westward from the outer anchorage. This reef is shown on small scale Chart 3515, but without enough detail to indicate how to get around it. Our observations indicate that the reef extends from the south shore until somewhat past the middle of the channel. Approaching the reef, favor the north side at dead slow with an alert bow watch.

The diagram here is courtesy of longtime Northwest cruising couple Fred and Mike Hayes, who felt their way in and anchored. Fred suggests a familiarization run by dinghy before taking the bigger boat in. Low tide would be best, when the rocks are visible.

Sir Edmund Bay. Sir Edmund Bay should be entered east of Nicholls Island, to avoid a rock west of the island. This rock is farther offshore than you might expect. Fish farms take up considerable space, but anchorage is possible in a cove at the northwest corner of the bay, and in another cove at the south corner.

The northwest cove is 48 to 60 feet deep until well in. Then it shoals to 30 feet before the shelf is reached. An all-chain anchor rode would yield a small enough swinging circle; boats with combination chain and rope may need to stern-tie to a tree. The cove is not very pretty and wouldn't be our first choice.

The southern cove has anchorage behind a charted drying rock. Some years ago, we visited near the bottom of a 7-foot low tide and failed to locate the rock. Others who have anchored there say the cove is a good spot, however. Until we know more we neither recommend nor discourage anchoring.

⑥ **Shawl Bay & Moore Bay.** Shawl Bay and Moore Bay are a short distance inside the entrance to Kingcome Inlet on the east side. The bays are connected by a narrow channel that reportedly is navigable at half tide or better. Moore Bay has no marinas. Anchorage is behind Thief Island in the south part of Moore Bay, or in 36 feet close behind the 55-meter island near the north shore. Two other nooks along the east shore might also be workable anchorages, depending on the weather. Along the north shore, near where a stream from Mt. Plumridge enters the bay, the Ministry of Forests installed a dinghy dock and four campsites with picnic tables and an outhouse.

Shawl Bay Marina. c/o General Delivery, Simoom Sound, BC V0P 1S0; (250) 483-4022; shawlbaymarina@gmail.com; www.shawlbaymarina.com. New owners purchased Shawl Bay Marina in 2016 and closed the marina for renovations, which began in 2017. At press time it is not known if the new facilities will be open for the 2018 boating season. See WaggonerGuide.com for updates.

Reid Bay. Reid Bay, on the western shore just inside the entrance to Kingcome Inlet, is open, deep, and uninteresting. It is no place to anchor. Just south of Reid Bay, however, an unnamed cove has possibilities. It is rather pretty and has good protection from westerlies. The chart indicates depths of approximately 6 fathoms throughout the bay, but our depth sounder showed 60 to 80 feet, except about 36 feet close to the head. If you go into this cove, give a wide berth to the point at the south entrance. We saw one uncharted rock just off the point; Chappell's guidebook says there are two.

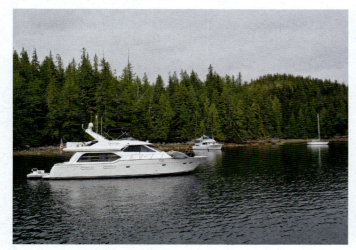

Laura Bay has room for several boats to anchor.

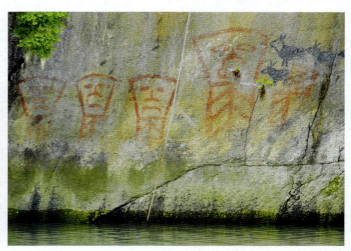

At the head of Kingcome Inlet you can see this native pictograph.

2018 WAGGONER CRUISING GUIDE

KINGCOME INLET

Kingcome Inlet extends 17 miles inland between high and beautiful mountains, terminating at the delta of the Kingcome River. The water is milky from glacier runoff and the surface band of water can be surprisingly fresh. Just beyond Petley Point at the head of the inlet, a magnificent new pictograph, a real work of art, is painted high on a rock cliff on the north shore. It is the work of Native artist Marianne Nicolson. The pictograph is brilliant red in color, and measures 28 feet wide and 38 feet high. A half mile south of the new pictograph, there is a much older Native pictograph at 50°55.540'N/126°13.478'W. The book, *Two Wolves at the Dawn of Time*, by Judith Williams, describes the project. The book's prose is a bit rich, but the story is interesting.

Kingcome Inlet's great depths and sheer rock walls allow virtually no suitable anchorages in the upper portions, except in settled weather.

Wakeman Sound. Wakeman Sound branches off Kingcome Inlet and extends about 7 miles north into the mountains. Although it has no good anchorages, on a clear day the scenery is beautiful. Wakeman Sound is a center for logging activity. Watch for drift in the water.

Belleisle Sound. Belleisle Sound branches off Kingcome Inlet to the south. Entry is between two high green mountains—the kind that make you feel small. Belleisle Sound is beautiful and remote-feeling, but generally too deep for easy anchoring. Only a small area just inside the entrance is usable. Chappell and Sailing Directions warn that strong westerlies can blow through. On the day of our visit the surface was mirror-calm. The water was warm and people on another boat took a swim, right out in the middle. Way back in 1981 we spent the night in Belleisle Sound without difficulty, anchored and stern-tied to the little islet across from the entrance. [*Hale*]

SUTLEJ CHANNEL

Cypress Harbour. Cypress Harbour is a pretty spot, but a large fish farm occupies part of Miller Bay, and an old logging operation is in Berry Cove farther in. Good anchorage, removed from the fish farm and logging, is in lovely Stopford Bay, in the southeast corner of Cypress Harbour. Be sure to avoid the charted rock. We've had a report of a stretch of logging cable lying on the bottom a short distance before the rock is reached. Correspondent Gil Flanagan reports that a pleasant ¼-mile walk leads from the campground to a rock grotto and pond. The old road continues to a meadow about a mile farther along, and keeps going. Watch the depths in Stopford Bay; the bottom grows increasingly shoal until it becomes drying flats. Recommended if you want a quiet, tucked-away anchorage.

Broughton Lagoon. "The entrance to Broughton Lagoon is a reversing tidal rapids. At Alert Bay high slack, water pours in through the narrow passage, trying to fill the lagoon. At Alert Bay low slack, water pours out at a ferocious rate. The calmest time to enter Broughton Lagoon is about 1 hour 15 minutes after Alert Bay high slack. For about 30 minutes around that time the rapids are at their least flow. Use the north entry channel only. The other channel often dries. This is a beautiful lagoon. It has plenty of width and depth for powerful dinghies. Not recommended for larger craft without local knowledge." [*Tom Taylor*]

Greenway Sound. Greenway Sound has several good anchorages. In 2016, the remaining buildings and docks for the now-closed Greenway Sound Marine Resort were removed. The bay behind Broughton Point, at the east end of Carter Passage, is pretty.

Depending on conditions, anchorage is in a number of little nooks on both sides of Greenway Sound and behind Simpson Island, near the head of the sound. Leave Simpson Island to starboard when approaching the head of Greenway Sound. For exercise, Broughton Lakes Park, with access

Planning for Happy Hour

The primary social gathering when cruising in the Broughtons is Happy Hour. This ritual typically begins around 4:00 to 5:00 p.m. and can extend well past dinnertime. I am told a movement is underway at some marinas to move the start of happy hour to 3:00 p.m., or maybe sometime after lunch.

If a Happy Hour is not scheduled it could happen spontaneously when a group is hanging around the dock with nothing to do. All of a sudden someone gasps, "Hey, we ought to have a Happy Hour!" The drinks start flowing and food emerges.

During our early years of cruising the Inside Passage, we never seemed to have the right provisions for a proper Happy Hour contribution. We once showed up at an impromptu Happy Hour with a plate of store bought Oreo cookies (oh, the horror!), though the Oreos always disappeared. No one had briefed us on Happy Hour etiquette, and our cruising guides lacked this critical information.

With a few seasons under my belt I now begin preparing for Happy Hour at the beginning of the cruising season. In addition to making sure we have an adequate supply of oil, filters, and belts, I make sure we have plenty of items for whipping up a jaw-droppingly impressive Happy Hour hors d'oeuvre, preferably something that will stack or mound to 8-12 inches high or more.

What is my secret? A good supply of cream cheese and crackers!

At the beginning of the season I make a special trip to my local warehouse store for bricks of cream cheese. In order to carry sufficient quantities, I purchased and installed a dedicated refrigerator. I also buy a variety of crackers, boxes of them. I stock onion soup mix, different spice combinations, canned smoked salmon, canned crab, and even canned shrimp. Just in case I end up cruising to multiple locations with the same people, I also have a number of sweet mixes for cream cheese to change things up. Dried cherries, cran-raisins, dried apricots, and a

few syrups to add color and flavor.

Now, cream cheese adaptations go over well, but I have noticed some captain and first mate teams look for extra points in the unspoken Happy Hour competition. They bring a dip with fresh caught crab (sometimes even artfully arranged in the shell) with chunks of crabmeat. Or, they show up with a bowl of fresh prawns caught that morning, still warm from a spiced boil. I really hate the guy who shows up with his salmon caught that morning and smoked on the dock next to his boat. How does he do this? He is one competitive Happy Hour cruiser!

Other Happy Hour recipes show up too. I long for the pea salad like my mother used to make, or the spicy coleslaw someone brings in an antique bowl. Sometimes someone will bring a simple green salad with fresh tomatoes and basil brought over from Vancouver Island that morning, garnished with pine nuts. Fresh brownies are a wonderful contribution, and yes, I might even sneak an Oreo cookie or two when one of the newbies joins the party on the dock.

Our best galley advice for cruising in the Broughtons? Be ready and go bold for Happy Hour. Mix it up, mound it high, and watch it fly. Fellow cruisers will love the end result!

– Anonymous

See Area Map Page 325 - Maps Not for Navigation   THE BROUGHTONS

Sullivan Bay Marina Resort

from a dinghy dock on the west shore of the bay due east of Greenway Point, received much work in recent years and has excellent hiking. The bay itself is a little deep for anchoring, so anchor elsewhere and take the dinghy over. Good trout fishing at the lakes (fresh water license required), beautiful views.

Greenway Sound Marine Resort. The resort closed several years ago and the marina docks and buildings were removed in 2016.

Cartwright Bay. This bay is open to the wakes from passing traffic in Sutlej Channel, but offers easy anchorage at its inner end.

⑦ **Sullivan Bay Marina Resort.** Box 6000, Port McNeill, BC V0N 2R0; (604) 484-9193; sullivanbaymarina@gmail.com; www.sullivan-bay.com. Monitors VHF 66A. Fuel open year-round, store and moorage seasonal. Services include gasoline, diesel, propane, 15, 30 & 50 amp power, water, washroom, showers, laundry, exercise room, and free Wi-Fi at the happy hour tent for moored guests.

Everything except the fuel storage tanks is on floats, in cozy float houses that date from the mid-20th century. Guests often gather around 5:00 p.m. for drinks and appys at the "Sullivan Square" area. Golfers can try their hands on the 1-hole golf course. Depending on tide and wind, the floating target is 100 to 140 yards out.

Sullivan Bay is legendary among cruising boaters. It has ample moorage (3000 feet), a well-stocked store with liquor agency, bait and tackle, and is pet friendly. They also offer fresh-baked pastries, pies, and cinnamon buns. The restaurant is open Monday, Wednesday and Friday with a fixed price, buffet style dinner; we are told it is quite good.

This is a popular turnaround point for Broughtons cruisers. Daily floatplane service to Seattle and elsewhere. Boat sitting available. The resort offers fishing charters.

The annual July 4th celebration and parade on the docks is hugely popular. Reservations recommended.

A community of handsome vacation float homes occupies a portion of the Sullivan Bay moorage. Improvements continue every year. Debbie Holt and Chris Scheveers are the attentive managers. Tucker, their Assistant Manager, is an enthusiastic member of the community. He is happy to show other dogs the 'poop deck' located behind the fuel dock.

337

SULLIVAN BAY • MARINA RESORT

WELCOME TO OUR UNIQUE FLOATING VILLAGE!

Sullivan Bay Marina Resort is located off Wells Passage on North Broughton Island, in the midst of mountains and channels. Sitting at the edge of the Broughton Archipelago, Sullivan Bay Marina Resort enjoys the many wonders of this magical area. With the beauty of nature at every turn, visitors are bound to see whales, dolphins, eagles and many more wonders.

The Marina Offers:

- Gasoline, Diesel, Propane
- Showers & Laundry
- 30, 50 Amp Power
- Free Internet with Moorage
- Fishing Tackle
- Boat Babysitting Our Specialty

- Liquor Agency
- Well-stocked Store with Fresh Baked Goods Daily
- Regular International & Local Float Plane Service
- Buffet Style Restaurant
- Exercise Room

Cruise on over and enjoy the marina and hospitality.

SullivanBayMarina@gmail.com
WWW.SULLIVANBAY.COM

604.484.9193
VHF CH. 66A

SULLIVAN BAY MARINA
BOX 6000
PORT MCNEILL, B.C. V0N 2R0

2018 WAGGONER CRUISING GUIDE

THE BROUGHTONS

Atkinson Island. Find anchorage in either end of the passage south of Atkinson Island.

GRAPPLER SOUND

Grappler Sound, north of Sutlej Channel and Wells Passage, has several good anchorages.

Kinnaird Island. The bay in the northeast corner of the island is reported to be good in settled weather.

Hoy Bay. Some anchorage is possible in Hoy Bay, behind Hopetown Point, west of Hopetown Passage.

LOCAL KNOWLEDGE

DANGEROUS CURRENTS: If Hopetown Passage is attempted at all, it should be done cautiously, at high water slack in a shallow draft boat.

Hopetown Passage. The eastern entrance to Hopetown Passage is blocked by a drying reef. Strong currents, tidal overfalls and shallow depths make this a challenge. Explore by dinghy first.

⑧ **Carriden Bay.** Carriden Bay is located just inside Pandora Head, at the entrance to Grappler Sound. The holding is reportedly good, if a little deep when away from the shoreline. One reader calls Carriden Bay "a special spot." As you look in, the spectacular knob of Pandora Head rises on the left, and when you're in, you see a beautiful vista of mountains out the mouth of the bay. This vista makes Carriden Bay exposed to east winds, however. It could be an uncomfortable anchorage in such winds.

⑨ **Claydon Bay.** This is a popular anchorage. Entering or leaving, favor the Morton Point side. Foul ground, shown on the chart, extends from the opposite side of the entry. In Claydon Bay you can pick the north arm or south arm, depending on which way the wind is blowing. An islet is in the entry to the north arm. Leave this islet to starboard when entering. Note also that the drying reef surrounding the islet extends a considerable distance southeast of the islet. We are told aggressive flies can be a problem in Claydon Bay, especially in the north arm. Crabbing is reportedly good.

Woods Bay. Woods Bay is deep until close to shore, and exposed to westerly winds. This bay has been reported to be a good spot in settled weather, but we think other anchorages in the area are more appealing.

Embley Lagoon. Too shallow for anything but dinghies, but an interesting exploration.

Overflow Basin. Dinghies only.

See Area Map Page 325 - Maps Not for Navigation

⑩ **Turnbull Cove.** Turnbull Cove is a large, popular, and beautiful bay, with lots of room and good anchoring in 30 to 50 feet. Avoid the areas in front of recent slides. The bottom there probably is foul with debris. Chappell warns that an easterly gale can turn the entire bay into a lee shore, so be aware if such winds are forecast.

The Ministry of Forests built a trail from Turnbull Cove over the mountain to Huaskin Lake. A large float for swimming, a picnic table, a tent platform, and a fire pit are at the lake. It's really nice. The trail goes straight up and straight back down, and it's muddy in places. Steps and even a handrail are on the lake side. They make a big difference. The lake is scenic and looks as if it goes forever.

Approach: Currents of 2+ knots flow through the channel leading to the entry. The currents are not hazardous, but they can come as a surprise. The west side of the entry to Turnbull Cove is charted as clear, but lots of kelp is growing there. A mid-channel course is recommended.

Nepah Lagoon. The adventuresome might want to try Roaringhole Rapids into Nepah Lagoon. Transit, by dinghy with an outboard motor, should be attempted only at high water slack, which lasts 5 minutes and occurs 2 hours after the corresponding high water at Alert Bay. The channel is only 3 feet deep at low water. Nepah Lagoon doesn't appear to have any useable anchorages, except possibly a little notch about a mile from the rapids.

MACKENZIE SOUND

Kenneth Passage. Kenneth Passage has sufficient depths at all stages of tide, being careful of a covered rock off Jessie Point. Currents can be quite strong and whirlpools sometimes appear. Slack water entry is advised, especially on spring tides. The best advice is to take a look and decide if conditions suit you and your boat.

Steamboat Bay. Steamboat Bay is a good anchorage, with room for a few boats. The bay shoals to drying flats all around. Watch for the drying rocks along the east shore at the entrance.

Burly Bay. Burly Bay is a good anchorage, mud bottom, but the muddy shoreline makes going ashore difficult. The little notch just to the west of **Blair Island** is better. Chappell (*Cruising Beyond Desolation Sound*) was not excited about Burly Bay. Bob and Marilynn Hale noted in their log, "Spectacular scenery, Ansel Adams photograph stuff, with rock wall on eastern shore falling straight into the sea." We've heard reports of grizzly bears on shore at Burly Bay. Guidebooks often are influenced by who visited, and what kind of day was had.

Little Nimmo Bay. Little Nimmo Bay is a pretty anchorage, and the rock-strewn entrance is not as difficult as it appears on the chart—except on a low tide. The Nimmo Bay Wilderness Resort is located there. Anchor in 24 feet, mud bottom. Several small

Explore the Inside Passage
Cruising and Planning Information
See WaggonerGuide.com

Exploring Southeast Alaska

Exploring the North Coast of British Columbia

Exploring the South Coast of British Columbia

Exploring the Pacific Coast

Exploring the San Juan and Gulf Islands

FINE EDGE
Nautical & Recreational Publishing

The complete Exploring series by Don Douglass and Reanne Hemingway-Douglass is available at your local nautical bookstore, and WaggonerGuide.com or at 360-299-8500. In Canada available through Chynasea at 250-594-1184 and portsandpasses.com. Also on Amazon.

Exploring Vancouver Island's West Coast

waterfalls tumble through the forest. Grizzly bears are reported to be in the area. Make lots of noise if you go ashore. With care it is possible to go through to Nimmo Bay, also a good anchorage.

⑪ **Nimmo Bay Wilderness Resort.** Box 696, Port McNeill, BC V0N 2R0; (800) 837-4354; heli@nimmobay.com; www.nimmobay.com. Nimmo Bay Wilderness Resort is a high-end destination resort that specializes in Heli-fishing and Helicopter Day Trips with gourmet lunches. While the resort has been open to visiting boaters in the past, it is now limited to boating guests staying in the on-shore resort accommodations, or booking spa massage services with advance reservations. Larger vessels can anchor in Mackenzie Sound or Nimmo Bay and take the tender to the resort's dock. Floatplane service available from Kenmore Air, and NW Seaplanes.

DRURY INLET

Drury Inlet is much less visited than other waters in the area. The entrance, off Wells Passage, is clearly marked on the charts, as is Stuart Narrows, 1.5 miles inside the entrance. Good anchorage is in two arms of Richmond Bay (choose the one that protects from the prevailing wind); near Stuart Narrows; in Jennis Bay; and in Sutherland Bay, at the head of Drury Inlet. Approach Sutherland Bay around the north side of the Muirhead Islands, after which the bay is open and protected.

We anchored for the night in the southwestern cove of Richmond Bay, near Stuart Narrows, and found it superb. The cove was protected, tranquil and private.

Our sister publication, *Cruising the Secret Coast*, available at WaggonerGuide.com, by Jennifer and James Hamilton, devotes an entire chapter to exploring Drury Inlet and Actaeon Sound, with details about interesting hikes.

Helen Bay. Helen Bay is just east of Stuart Narrows. It is reportedly a good anchorage. Halibut are said to be caught in the area.

Stuart Narrows. Currents in Stuart Narrows run to a maximum of 7 knots, although on small tides they are much less. Times of slack are listed under Alert Bay, Secondary Current Stations, in the Tide & Current Tables Vol. 6, and Ports and Passes. The skipper of a tug towing a log boom through Stuart Narrows advised us that he times slack for 10 minutes after both high and low tides at Alert Bay, which is in line with the tide and current tables information. The only hazard is Welde Rock. You will most likely see the kelp. Get way over to the south side of the channel. The current flows faster south of Welde rock, although passage can be made north of the rock as well. Leche Islet should be passed to the north. A study of the chart shows a rock patch to the south.

Note that Stuart Narrows is well inside the mouth of Drury Inlet.

⑫ **Jennis Bay.** Jennis Bay is the site of a logging camp and booming ground, with good anchorage in the cove northwest of Jennis Bay Marina.

⑫ **Jennis Bay Marina.** P.O. Box 456, Port McNeill, BC V0N 2R0; (778) 762-3037, jennismarina@gmail.com; www.jennisbay.com. VHF 66A. Moorage available year-round, 300 feet of transient moorage space for up to 11 boats depending upon size and rafting options. Limited free Wi-Fi. No power. TV room, washroom and shower. Four cabin rentals. Kayaking, mountain biking, hiking, and miles of logging roads and trails for exploring. Happy Hour potlucks are ad-hoc, organized by visiting pleasure boaters at the covered barbecue area.

Eugene Larson is the new year-round, on-site general manager. He has started sprucing up the grounds and buildings while maintaining the character of this historic logging camp. Eugene comes to Jennis Bay with a background in commercial fishing. Eugene offers a truck for rent to drive the 4-mile road to Huaskin Lake for fishing, swimming or picnicking.

From Drury Inlet, enter Jennis Bay around either end of Hooper Island. If entering during limited visibility, the west end may be safest. Keep to a mid-channel course to avoid rocks along the shores. Leave the floating log breakwater and yellow buoys to starboard entering the marina.

Caution: Obstructions in the water lie about 500 feet southeast of the marina's log boom breakwater, consisting of a float plus a separate 'standing boom,' neither of which are lit.

Davis Bay. Davis Bay looks inviting on the chart, but is not very pretty and is open to westerlies. Enter on the south side of Davis Islet, strongly favoring the Davis Islet shore.

Muirhead Islands. The Muirhead Islands, near the head of Drury Inlet, are rock-strewn but beautiful. They invite exploring in a small boat or kayak. The cove on the northeast side, behind the dot island, is a suitable anchorage, as is the cove on the south side, immediately west of the 59-meter island.

Actress Passage and Actaeon Sound. Actress Passage, connecting Drury Inlet with Actaeon Sound, is rock- and reef-strewn, narrow and twisting. Careful navigation is required. There are two theories: some feel high water slack is best to have more water; others feel low water slack is best to allow a better chance of seeing the rocks and hazards in the water. One approach is to enter Actress Passage between Dove Island and the mainland to the north, avoiding the charted rock. Tugs and tows and other commercial traffic, however, use the shorter channel east of Dove Island, splitting rocks marked with sticks at the entrance to Drury Inlet.

Once into Actress Passage, the overriding navigation problem is the area between Skene Point and Bond Peninsula, where a careful S-shaped course around the rocks is required, hence the local name Snake Passage. Another choice is to follow Chappell's suggestion of crossing from Skene Point to Bond Peninsula, and working past the charted hazards around the corner.

In our sister publication, *Cruising the Secret Coast*, the Hamiltons have extensively explored this area and present specific directions for this passage and the area.

Covered patio and BBQ for impromptu happy hour gatherings at Jennis Bay

WELLS PASSAGE

Tracey Harbour. Tracey Harbour indents North Broughton Island from Wells Passage. It is pretty and protected. No anchorage is viable, however, until near the head of the bay. There, you can find anchorage on mud bottom in Napier Bay, or on rocky bottom in the bay behind Carter Point. You're apt to find log booms in Napier Bay, and leftover buildings from an old logging operation. Anchor near the head of the cove behind Carter Point. The cove is beautiful and cozy-feeling, but the bottom feels like a thin layer of mud on top of rock and it wouldn't take much to drag the anchor.

Carter Passage. Since Carter Passage is blocked in the middle by a boulder-strewn drying shoal, it is actually two harbors, one off Wells Passage and one off Greenway Sound, with good anchorages in each end. The west entrance has tidal currents to 7 knots, and should be taken at or near high water slack. A reef extends from the south shore, so keep north of mid-channel. Two pleasant anchorages are in this west end.

The east entrance, off Greenway Sound, is somewhat easier, in terms of both tidal currents and obstructions. John Chappell's *Cruising Beyond Desolation Sound* describes how to safely transit the drying shoal between the two ends of Carter Passage.

Dickson Island. Dickson Island is near the mouth of Wells Passage. The small anchorage on the east end of the island provides good protection from seas, but the low land allows westerly winds to blow across the bay. Two other bays along the west side of Broughton Island are too exposed to westerly weather to be good anchorages.

Polkinghorne Islands. The Polkinghorne Islands are outside the mouth of Wells Passage. A channel among the islands is fun, particularly on the nice day. The anchoring bottom we've found is not too secure, so an overnight stay is not recommended. [*Kincaid*]

FIFE SOUND

Cullen Harbour. Cullen Harbour is on the south side of Broughton Island, at the entrance to Booker Lagoon. It is an excellent anchorage, with plenty of room for everyone. You might rock a little if the wind is blowing from northwest. The bottom is mud, and depths range from 24 to 50 feet.

LOCAL KNOWLEDGE

UNCHARTED ROCK: Correspondents John and Lorraine Littlewood did some independent chart work surveying Booker Lagoon, and found a ledge of rock not shown on the charts (see Booker Lagoon map). Its presence was confirmed by two bent props, one bent skeg and one bent rudder— "a real boat-eater," according to John.

Booker Lagoon. The entrance to Booker Lagoon is from Cullen Harbour through **Booker Passage**, a narrow channel bounded by reefs on both sides. The channel is about 50 feet wide and has ample depths. Best to transit at slack water. Use the Sunday Harbour secondary station in Canadian Tide and Current Tables Vol. 6, or Ports and Passes. On big tides the duration of slack water is about 10 minutes, and the stream can build to 7 knots or more. The aquaculture pens that once occupied the four arms of Booker Lagoon have been removed, so it's a good anchorage again on a sticky mud bottom. Don't enter Booker Lagoon through the passage on the west side of Long Island. The passage is shoal and choked with kelp.

Once in Booker Lagoon you'll be in a secluded coastal paradise. The lagoon is quite large, and deep in the middle. Explore around, then anchor in one of the arms—away, we suggest, from other anchored boats. It's that kind of place.

Deep Harbour. In the past the inner part of Deep Harbour was blocked by boomed logs and the center of the bay taken over by aquaculture pens. It is now clear and there are little nooks around the edges with room for one boat.

BROUGHTON ARCHIPELAGO

Much of the Broughton Archipelago is now a marine park. Some of the islands are private, however, so use discretion when going ashore.

Our journal, written while at anchor after a day of exploring, reads, "A marvelous group of islands and passages, but few good anchorages. We navigated around Insect Island and through Indian Passage. Very pretty—many white shell beaches. Rocks marked by kelp. A different appearance from Kingcome Inlet or Simoom Sound. The trees are shorter and more windblown. The west wind is noticeably colder than farther east. Fog lay at the mouth of Fife Sound; a few wisps blew up toward us. Great kayaking, gunkholing country." [*Hale*]

This large group of islands west of Gilford Island does have anchorages, including Sunday Harbour, Monday Anchorage, and Joe Cove. The area is dotted with rocks, reefs, and little islands, which in total provide good protection, but also call for careful navigation.

M. Wylie Blanchet (*The Curve of Time*) was blown out of Sunday Harbour, and we've heard mixed reports about Monday Anchorage. Chappell wasn't impressed with either one. Joe Cove is considered to be a good anchorage. Chart 3546 (1:40:000) should be studied carefully before going into these waters, and kept close at hand while there. Currents run strongly at times through the various passages.

⑬ **Sunday Harbour.** Sunday Harbour is formed by Crib Island and Angular Island, north of the mouth of Arrow Passage. The bay is very pretty, although exposed to westerly winds. We would anchor in the middle for a relaxing lunch on a quiet day. The little cove in the northeast corner looks attractive but is full of rocks.

⑭ **Monday Anchorage.** Monday Anchorage is formed by Tracey Island and Mars Island, north of Arrow Passage. It is large and fairly open. Chappell says you can anchor behind the two small islands off the north shore of the bay. When the Hales visited they anchored for lunch fairly deep in the first large cove on the south shore. The anchor bit easily in 40 feet, and they had good protection from the westerly that was blowing.

⑮ **Joe Cove.** Joe Cove, perfectly protected and private feeling, indents the south side of Eden Island. The best anchorage is near the head. A little thumb of water extends southeast near the head of the cove, but access is partially blocked by several rocks. It is possible, however, to feel your way in by hugging the shore to starboard as you enter. The passage is narrow but clear. Tie to the float in the cove.

East of Eden (Lady Boot Cove). Lady Boot Cove is what Don and Reanne Douglass call this nice little anchorage in *Exploring the South Coast*

Wells Passage connects western Broughtons with Queen Charlotte Strait.

of *British Columbia*. Locals tell us the correct name is East of Eden. The cove indents the northeast corner of Eden Island, with Fly Island directly off the mouth. As the chart shows, the southern indent is shoal and foul with a drying reef. The northern indent is beautifully protected with room for a couple of boats.

RETREAT PASSAGE

Seabreeze Cove. This otherwise unnamed lovely little anchorage in Gilford Island was suggested by Correspondents James and Jennifer Hamilton. It lies behind the 70-meter island due east of Seabreeze Island, at the western entrance to Retreat Passage. Their report: "We anchored in 18 feet south of the 70-meter island and held very well in sticky mud. Some southwest winds did blow through, but nothing major. The water was barely rippled. Caught three big Dungeness crabs overnight."

Be aware that the bottom shoals rapidly once past the 70-meter island.

Bootleg Bay. South of False Cove, a thumb-like island protrudes northwest from Gilford Island. The cove south of that island has about 30 feet at the entrance, shoaling gently toward the head. No name appears on the charts. According to Chappell it is known locally as Bootleg Bay. A wrecked fish boat has been reported at the head of the bay.

⑯ **Waddington Bay.** Waddington Bay indents the northeast corner of Bonwick Island. The bay is popular, with room for several boats. It has good holding in 18 to 30 feet. The approach is off the little pass that connects Retreat Passage and Arrow Passage. Turn to leave the 46-meter island to starboard, and go on in. Be sure you have the right island; they all look alike. The approach is wide enough, but rocks are all around and careful piloting is called for. Know your position at all times. Waddington Bay shoals at the head. The wind direction and your depth sounder will tell you where to put the hook down. Wind will get in when the westerly is blowing, but there's no fetch for seas to build. This is a tranquil anchorage—a good place to hide out for a few days.

Grebe Cove. Grebe Cove indents the east side of Bonwick Island off Retreat Passage. The cove shallows to 40 to 50 feet about 200 yards from the head, and 30 to 40 feet near the head, mud bottom, with good depths side to side. A saddle in the hills at the head might let westerlies in, but the seas would have no fetch. On one visit, a couple in a 20-foot pocket cruiser called out, "Great anchorage! The otters will entertain you!"

Carrie Bay. Carrie Bay indents Bonwick Island across Retreat Passage from Health Bay. The head of the bay is pretty and protected from westerly winds. The bottom shoals rapidly from 40 to 50 feet in much of the bay to around 20 feet at the head.

Health Bay. The Health Bay Indian Reserve, with a small dock, fronts on Retreat Passage. Health Bay itself is strewn with rocks. Anchorage is best fairly close to the head of the bay, short of the first of the rocks.

BLACKFISH ARCHIPELAGO

The name Blackfish Archipelago does not appear on the charts or in Sailing Directions, but generally refers to the myriad islands and their waterways adjacent to Blackfish Sound.

Goat Island Anchorage. You'll find a good anchorage in the cove that lies off the southeast corner of Crease Island.

Clarification: Two islands make up this cove—a larger island to the north and a much smaller one to the south. Chart 3546 seems to label the smaller, southern island as Goat Island, but until now we—and Chappell and Douglass—have meant the larger island to be Goat Island. In their book, Vipond and Kelly label the smaller, southern island as Goat Island. A careful study of the chart shows Vipond and Kelly to be correct. Whatever the islands are named, the entry suggestions are unchanged.

Enter Goat Island Anchorage between Crease Island and the larger, northern island, leaving the northern island to port. The chart makes the preferred entry clear. Anchor in 12 to 18 feet on a sometimes rocky bottom, wherever it looks good. The cove is excellent for crabbing. Weed on the bottom might foul some anchors. A reader reported that their anchor found a large diameter line on the bottom, probably left over from earlier logging. Where there's one cable there might be more. It would be a good idea to rig a trip line to the crown of the anchor. The view to the southeast is very pretty.

Leone Island. A bay lies between Leone Island and Madrona Island. Contributing Editor Tom Kincaid has anchored there and recommends it.

Booker Lagoon

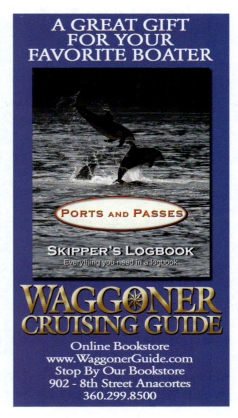

THE BROUGHTONS

See Area Map Page 325 - Maps Not for Navigation

"'Friends, with extensive experience, also recommend it. We, however, tried to set our anchor four times over a 2-day period, and failed each time. Twice the anchor did not penetrate large, leafy kelp. Once it refused to set in thin sand and reedy weed. On the last try the anchor seemed to set, but it dragged with only moderate power in reverse." [*Hale*]

Mound Island. The cove behind Mound Island is a good anchorage, paying mind to the rocks (shown on the chart) that line the shores. Tom Sewid at Village Island told us that 14 depressions in the earth were once the sites of big houses. Correspondent Pat Shera reports that the depressions are obvious, just inland from the beach at the western end of the island.

⑰ **New Vancouver.** (250) 974-2703. Monitors VHF 78. Moorage, with 30 amp power. Washrooms, showers and laundry are located in a trailer unit. Trails to camp sites are in the area. The store has gifts and convenience groceries. Open June 1 through September 15. New Vancouver, traditionally known as Tsatsisnukwomi Village, is on the north side of Harbledown Island, a short distance west of Dead Point, the entrance to Beware Passage. The location is marked IR on the chart, for Indian Reserve. It is the ancestral home of the Da'naxda'xw Native Band, who moved from Knight Inlet in the 1960s. The band is welcoming and offers cultural tours of the village and bighouse for a fee.

Farewell Harbour. You'll find good anchorage in Farewell Harbour close to the Berry Island side. The Farewell Harbour Marine Resort, shown on the chart, is actually a luxury fishing resort and doesn't cater to visiting yachties.

Chiefs Bathtub. The Chiefs Bathtub is located on Village Channel on the north side of Berry Island, at approximately 50°36.45'N /126°39.56'W (NAD 83). It's a sculpted-out depression in a rock cliff, a little below the high water line. According to Tom Sewid, up-and-coming chiefs had to sit in this bathtub four times a day for four days as the cold waters of the tide washed in. If you take the dinghy to see the tub more closely, don't touch the pictographs on the rock. Skin oils attack the paint.

⑱ **Village Island.** (250) 287-2955; viband@telus.net; A site on the western shore of Village Island is often known incorrectly as Mamalilaculla. This site is an abandoned, collapsing Indian village. Anchor in the bay north of the village (be sure of your set).

First Nations Watchmen are ready to assist during the peak season; contact them on VHF 79A. The Native band charges $20 per person to see the village, with its empty hospital building, collapsing houses, fallen totem pole and Big House remains. All fees go towards the cleanup of village site and support for the Native Watchmen.

If watchmen are not present or you arrive

Docks at the Native Village of New Vancouver

outside the peak period of July and August, the Mamalilikulla First Nation asks that you call their office at (250) 287-2955 for permission to go ashore. Mail your check for fees to 1441 B 16th Ave., Campbell River, BC V9W 2E4; fees collected go towards developing the Guardian Watchmen program.

Native Anchorage. Native Anchorage is located at the southwest corner of Village Island. It's no place to be in a southerly storm, but in all other winds it's a fine anchorage. Put the hook down in 18 to 24 feet. Excellent mud bottom.

Canoe Passage. Canoe Passage runs east-west between Turnour Island and Village Island. The waterway dries at low tide, but can be transited at higher tides, depending on a vessel's draft.

CLIO CHANNEL

Cracroft Inlet. Cracroft Inlet is on the south side of Dorman and Farquharson Islands. While we have not anchored there (yet), it is reportedly well protected, with good holding bottom on either side of the large charted rock. Lagoon Cove, on the other side of Farquharson Island, can be reached by taking the dinghy around the east end of the island. The passage is shallow, so check the tides and be sure of your depths.

Bones Bay. The entire bay is fairly open, although you may find temporary anchorage behind the islets along the south shore. Watch for rocks around the islets. A floating fishing lodge is moored behind these islets.

Bend Island. Bend Island is connected to West Cracroft Island by a drying ledge, but good anchorage is in either end. Friends have anchored in the tiny nook just east of Bend Island, with a stern-tie to shore.

⑲ **Potts Lagoon.** The outer bay behind Klaoitsis Island and the 119-meter headland is filled with a logging and log booming operation. But two inner bays are open and provide good anchorage from all winds. The inner bay to the southeast of the 41-meter island is the more popular and spacious with anchoring depths of 18 to 24 feet. Ruins from an old pier along with a few float homes add to the character of this hidden scenic anchorage. A smaller but more private cove is found to the northeast of the outer cove.

Klaoitsis Island. Anchorage might be found in the bay northwest of Klaoitsis Island, and in a notch on the south shore of Jamieson Island. Currents can run through these anchorages. For most boats, Potts Lagoon is a better choice.

Beware Passage. If you read the place names from Chart 3545, Beware Passage might scare you away; Beware Passage, Care Rock, Caution Rock, Caution Cove, Beware Rock, Beware Cove, and Dead Point. Beware Passage is aptly named, but you can get through safely. Sailing Directions recommends transiting at low water when rocks are visible. There are two routes through Beware Passage; Care Island route and Harbledown Island route. Both routes are shown on the Beware Passage map. Locals prefer the Harbledown Island route and suggest only using the Care Island route at low water slack, when rocks can be seen and current isn't making course changes difficult. We recommend proceeding dead slow with a careful watch on depth sounder and a bow watch for both routes. Assuming a passage from east to west, both routes start by entering just off Nicholas Point on Turnour (pronounced "Turner") Island. There are several Native pictographs on a rock face 300 yards west of Nicholas Point at 50° 34.55N 126° 29.64NW. After Nicholas Point and the pictographs, both routes follow mid-channel between Kamano Island and the unnamed islet north of Kamano Island. At the west end of Kamano Island, the two routes separate. For Harbledown Island route, turn to heading 275° magnetic when the west end of Kamano Island is abeam your port side. Proceed to the Harbledown Island side of Beware Passage and a narrow channel between Harbledown Island and pair of small islands that lie just offshore from Harbledown Island. This narrow channel

See Area Map Page 325 - Maps Not for Navigation   THE BROUGHTONS

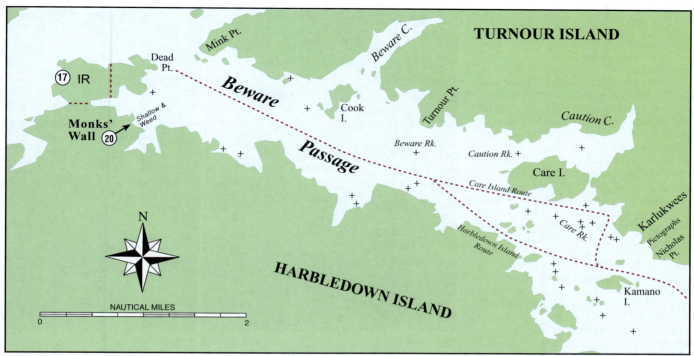

Beware Passage

has kelp, and a charted shoal on the Harbledown Island side. Exit this narrow channel on a heading of 305° magnetic. Turn to port and continue northwest on Beware Passage when Dead Point is on a course of 273° magnetic. For Care Island route, when the west end of Kamano Island is abeam your port side, turn to a heading of approximately 346° magnetic. Turn to a heading of approximately 266° magnetic when you see a forested rock outcropping on Turnour Island shore to your starboard. Check your GPS chartplotter to confirm this critical turn to the west making sure you avoid the rock awash to port and the charted rock that dries at 1.2 meters. Proceed, favoring the Care Island side until past Care Island. Then turn to heading 271° magnetic. For both routes, pass between Beware Rock and the charted rock that dries at 0.9 meters and proceed to Dead Point.

Caution Cove. Caution Cove is open to prevailing winds, but the bottom is good. Caution Rock, drying at 4 feet, is in the center of the entrance. The rock is clearly shown on Chart 3545, as are the rocks just off the drying flats at the head of the cove. An extensive logging operation may be operating in the cove. Beware Cove might be a better option.

Beware Cove. Beware Cove is a good anchorage, very pretty, with protection from westerlies but not southeasterlies. Easiest entry is to the west of Cook Island, leaving Cook Island to starboard.

⑳ **Monks' Wall.** The ruins of a massive and mysterious rock wall lies hidden just inside the treeline on Harbledown Island, at the north end of Beware Passage. Chinese Buddhist monks are reported to have been on the island more than a century ago, and some have speculated that they are the ones who built the wall. It makes an intriguing story: far from their homeland, devout Buddhists in their robes carrying and positioning huge stones for what?—a temple, perhaps.

The real story is not as intriguing, but it is at least as inspiring. The wall was not built by monks. It was built by white settlers, William Herbert Galley and his wife Mary Anne Galley. In the late 1800s Galley acquired 160 acres on Harbledown Island and built a trading post there. According to Galley's great-granddaughter, great-grandfather Galley married Mary Anne Wharton in 1889. Together they cleared the land, planted 125 fruit trees, and kept cows, pigs, chickens, ducks and sheep. The homestead was defined by carefully-built rock walls, straight

Native village ruins and midden beach at Village Island

Native Pictograph near Karlukwees on the east end of Beware Passage

2018 WAGGONER CRUISING GUIDE   343

THE BROUGHTONS   *See Area Map Page 325 - Maps Not for Navigation*

and solid. An archway marked the entrance to the trading post. It is said that Mary Anne Galley carried rocks in her apron. Those rocks are big. Some apron. Some great-grandmother.

The Monks' Wall is located on the west side of Beware Passage, a short distance south of Dead Point. It is on the point of land separating two large, shallow bays, at lat. 50°35.40'N. (This latitude was measured on the chart, and is approximate.) Anchor in the bay north of that point of land and row the dinghy in. The bottom shoals when approaching the cove, and is dense with weed that could foul a propeller. Working from north to south, identify the third little nook on the point of land. It's a definite indent. At the treeline, a tangled rootball from a blown-down tree marks the entry. The ruins of the magnificent walls are just inside.

If you hike through the woods around the area you'll find more walls; taken together they're impressive. All built by hand. Straight and true. Enveloped now by the relentless forest. The archway has since collapsed.

Although Monks' Wall is a misnomer, it looks like the name will stick. Our thanks to Galley great-granddaughter Kathy Young for her historical background, and to Billy Proctor for his quickly-drawn map that showed us where to find the site.

Request: The wall and the lesser walls in the surrounding forest are a treasure. Please, no souvenirs, no destruction, no litter.

Dead Point. The unnamed cove just inside Dead Point offers protection from westerlies.

Walls from an old trading post established by the Galley family more than 100 years ago

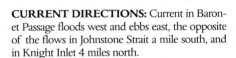

CURRENT DIRECTIONS: Current in Baronet Passage floods west and ebbs east, the opposite of the flows in Johnstone Strait a mile south, and in Knight Inlet 4 miles north.

Baronet Passage. Baronet Passage is very pretty. It's partially obstructed by Walden Island, with the preferred passage in the deeper channel to the north of Walden Island. This is a well-used passage for boats heading to and from Blackfish Sound.

㉑ **Growler Cove.** Growler Cove, on the west end of West Cracroft Island, is an excellent anchorage, with ample room and good protection from westerlies and easterlies. It is popular with commercial fishermen who work Johnstone Strait and Queen Charlotte Strait. During prime commercial fishing months of July and August, Growler Cove is apt to be full of commercial boats, with little room for pleasure craft.

If you're approaching from the east, enter along West Cracroft Island, favoring the island as you work your way in. We saw an extensive kelp bed, not shown on the chart, off the point that leads to the entrance. We would keep clear of that kelp. If you're approaching from the west, enter between Sophia Islands and Baron Reef, both shown on the chart. Inside, keep a mid-channel course, favoring the north side to avoid a charted rock about halfway in. Good anchoring near the head in 18 to 24 feet.

Hanson Island. The rugged and beautiful north shore of Hanson Island is indented by a number of bays and coves that are a gunkholer's paradise. The most popular anchorage is in Double Bay, also the location of the Pacific Outback Resort, a private fishing lodge. Enter only along the west side of the bay. The bay behind Spout Islet, to the east of Double Bay, is also a good anchorage. Correspondent Deane Hislop writes: "We spent a night in the beautiful bay to the east of Spout Islet. The holding was good and provided protection from the summer afternoon westerlies. The view of the whales in Blackfish Sound, the Miriam Range, and 1238-meter Mt. Mathison were spectacular."

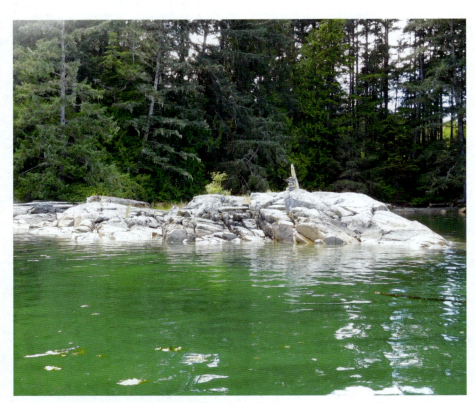
Land your dinghy here to visit Monks' Wall on the south shore at the north end of Beware Passage.

344   www.WaggonerGuide.com

North Vancouver Island

CHAPTER 13

WEYNTON PASSAGE
Bauza Cove • Telegraph Cove
Beaver Cove • Pearse Islands

BROUGHTON STRAIT
Port McNeill • Alert Bay • Sointula

QUEEN CHARLOTTE STRAIT
Beaver Harbour • Port Hardy • Bear Cove

NORTH VANCOUVER ISLAND

See Area Map Page 347 - Maps Not for Navigation

North Island refers to the eastern side of Vancouver Island from Sayward (Kelsey Bay) to the top of the island. North Island is served by Highway 19 and is the center of commerce for both sides of the Inside Passage in this area. Port McNeill and Port Hardy are the principal towns. Alert Bay on Cormorant Island and Sointula on Malcolm Island also have facilities.

Boats cruising the Broughtons or continuing farther up the coast usually stop at one or more of the North Island towns for supplies, repairs, fuel, and water. For this reason, the North Island chapter opens with comments about crossing Queen Charlotte Strait.

Kelsey Bay and Robson Bight are covered in the Johnstone Strait section.

Hospitals: Port McNeill and Port Hardy have fully-staffed hospitals. The Cormorant Island Community Health Centre in Alert Bay is in a new building, behind the U'mista Cultural Centre. It has a doctor on duty every day.

Queen Charlotte Strait. Queen Charlotte Strait is about 15 miles wide. The prevailing winds are from the northwest in the summer and the southeast in the winter. In the summer, winds are often lighter in the morning.

Typically, by late morning or early afternoon a sea breeze will begin, and by mid-afternoon it can increase to 30 knots with very rough seas. The sea breeze usually quiets at sundown.

Tom Taylor, owner of the now-closed Greenway Sound Marina Resort, has crossed the strait between Wells Passage and Port McNeill hundreds of times, and tells us that in good weather he could go (in a fast boat) as late as 2:00 p.m. Any given day can go against the norm, however. Skippers should treat Queen Charlotte Strait with great respect.

Weather information: The wind report from Herbert Island, in the Buckle Group, can be a good reference for approaching northwesterly winds. If it's not blowing at Herbert Island, there's a good chance Queen Charlotte Strait will be okay. If Herbert Island is windy, however, Queen Charlotte Strait probably will be next.

Bauza Cove. Bauza Cove is an attractive but deep bay with good protection from westerly swells. It is open to the wakes of passing traffic in Johnstone Strait.

CHARTS	
3546	Broughton Strait (1:40,000); Port McNeill & Alert Bay (1:20,000)
3547	Queen Charlotte Strait, Eastern Portion (1:40,000)
3548	Queen Charlotte Strait, Central Portion (1:40,000); Blunden Harbour & Port Hardy (1:15,000)

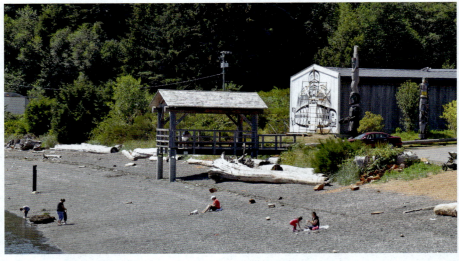

Locals relax on the beach in front of U'mista Cultural Centre.

① **Telegraph Cove.** Telegraph Cove is postcard picturesque. The boardwalk is lined with old, brightly painted buildings on pilings, including a good restaurant and pub. The old homes are now cottages for resort guests. The place is the embodiment of the word "charming." A whale museum is located at the end of the docks and a whale watch excursion boat leaves several times each day. Tide Rip Grizzly Tours takes groups up Knight Inlet by fast boat to see grizzly bears. Charter fishing boats head out to fish for salmon, and a kayak operator takes groups out to the islands and Johnstone Strait.

The Telegraph Cove Resort moorage is to starboard as you enter. Moorage is primarily for small boats, but some room is available for larger boats at the dock near the entrance. To port as you enter, Telegraph Cove Marina has some side-tie guest moorage for larger boats, and a considerable number of guest slips for boats to 30 feet.

Telegraph Cove

North Vancouver Island

Be advised, though, that Telegraph Cove isn't very big. There's room to maneuver, but "spacious" is not the word that comes to mind, especially when the wind picks up.

① **Telegraph Cove Marina.** Box 1-8, 1642B, Telegraph Cove, BC V0N 3J0; (250) 928-3163; (877) 835-2683; reservations@telegraphcove.ca; www.telegraphcove.ca. Monitors VHF 66A. Open all year, 130 slips to 30 feet, limited side-tie moorage to 65 feet. Mostly permanent moorage, limited transient space. Potable water, some slips have 15, 30 & 50 amp power. Concrete launch ramp. Showers, laundry, and washrooms. Wi-Fi available for a fee. Reservations requested.

It's an easy walk around the cove to amenities and tour operators such as whale watching, grizzly bear viewing, and kayak tours. The Seahorse Cafe has good food and a great view over the marina.

① **Telegraph Cove Resort.** Box 1, Telegraph Cove, BC V0N 3J0; (250) 928-3131; (800) 200-4665; info@TelegraphCoveResort.com; www.telegraphcoveresort.com. Open seasonally with gasoline (no diesel), launch ramp, restaurant, pub, two coffee shops, general store with gifts and fishing tackle. Slips for boats to 25 feet. Larger boats may be able to overnight on the fuel dock, check with management. No power or water. Cabins and campsites available for rent. The resort maintains the historic boardwalk, with cottages and buildings from when this was a telegraph station during the early 1900s. Attractions include fishing charters, whale and bear watching tours, and the Whale Interpretive Centre. The restaurant and pub are good.

Beaver Cove. Fairly deep anchorage can be found along the shores of Beaver Cove, the site of an old sawmill. Logs may be boomed in the bay, and the bottom is almost certainly foul with sunken logs and debris.

Pearse Islands (Cormorant Channel Marine Park). Careful piloting is called for when exploring this area because of rocks, reefs, and strong currents in the narrow channels between the islands. Correspondents James and Jennifer Hamilton report:

"We anchored in 30 feet (zero tide) just north of the 72-meter islet, about where the 9.8-meter sounding is on Chart 3546. A little wind blew through from the northwest, but we saw very little boat traffic. It was a lovely spot with an excellent view down Broughton Strait. Good holding—the anchor set instantly with 150 feet of rode out. It looks like excellent dinghy-exploring country, but it had been a long day and we didn't have the strength.

The next morning the current was really whipping through the passage, but we held just

Alert Bay
Discover our World

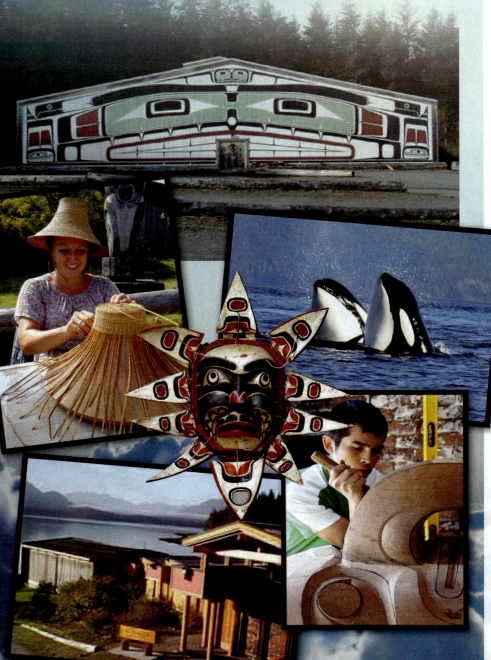

Arts | Culture | Heritage
U'mista Cultural Centre
Alert Bay Visitor Centre
and Art Gallery
Alert Bayi Museum
Big House & World's
Tallest Totem Pole
'Namgis Burial Ground with
stand of totems
Traditional dance performances
in Big House

Activities
Whale watching
Fishing
Nature Trails
Traditional Canoes
Skate Park
Cultural Playground

Health
Hospital and Health Centre
Personal Care Services

Business
Full service Marina
Accommodations -
Hotels, B&B's Cabins
Campground
Grocery Store | Pharmacy
Restaurants | Pubs
Liquor Store | Post Office
Churches | Banking | Hair Salon

For general inquiries and cultural planning:
Alert Bay Visitor Centre

Phone: (250) 974-5024
Fax: (250) 974-5026
E-mail: info@alertbay.ca
www.alertbay.ca

U'mista Cultural Centre
For events and cultural activities check here
www.facebook.com/Umista.Cultural.Society
(250) 974-5403 or 1-800-690-8222 | www.umista.ca

Alert Bay — The Spirit of U'mista

The heritage of the Inside Passage is a rich tapestry of man's life on the land and his utilization of its waters for both transportation and sustenance. Today we enjoy the beauty of the islands and animals, the fjords and waterfalls. And, occasionally, nature's bounty, hauled to the surface in a crab pot or caught on the end of a fishing line. But for thousands of years, since long before Europeans arrived, the area was carefully occupied by First Nations people.

Their culture is different than ours. They depended on the environment around them in ways often lost in modern life. Their beliefs and customs are inextricably linked to the Inside Passage. A glimpse into their culture reveals a belief in family and clan and an interest in preserving life and land. They believe in sustaining their people by maintaining nature's balance.

They are also a giving people, always ready to share. Perhaps there is no better example of their culture of sharing than their potlatch ceremonies.

Potlatches bring together neighboring families and nearby tribes. Cultural traditions, like songs and dances, are performed and ceremonial regalia, like coppers, masks and robes, are shown off. Feasts are prepared. Gifts, ranging from blankets to berries, are given. Successful potlatches can be reminisced about for years. Potlatches may celebrate marriage, birth, death or other rites of passage. Regardless of the reason for celebration, potlatches are a vehicle for giving. The more a family shares, the better the event is remembered.

In 1885, the government of Canada banned potlatches. Unwilling to give up centuries old traditions, the celebrations secretly continued. But in the early 1920s a new Director of Indian Affairs gave orders to enforce the potlatch laws. First Nations members were arrested and some were jailed for up to two months. Regalia was confiscated, packed and shipped to Ottawa for storage. Some masks were kept for the personal collection of the Superintendent General of Indian Affairs.

Beginning in the 1960s the Canadian government slowly repatriated the items they had taken. They reached an agreement where the regalia would be returned and placed on display in two museums, the Nuyumbalees Cultural Centre near Cape Mudge, and the U'mista Cultural Centre in Alert Bay. When a person returns from enslavement, they are said to have "u'mista," and the same can be said for the potlatch regalia that has now been returned to the First Nations people.

Today, the spirit of u'mista is alive in the coppers, robes and masks on display in the U'mista Cultural Centre.

NORTH VANCOUVER ISLAND

See Area Map Page 347 - Maps Not for Navigation

Welcoming office and docks at Sointula on Malcolm Island

Baked goods and coffee are featured at the cafe on First Street.

fine. When we left we found the current very strong off the tip of the 88-meter island, with whirlpools and upwellings." [*Hamilton*]

Correspondent Pat Shera reports that when the current is flooding east in Broughton Strait, a strong westward countercurrent is present when approaching the Pearse Islands from the south.

② **Alert Bay.** One can learn more about native culture here, in less time, than anywhere on this part of the coast.

Chart 3546 shows Alert Bay in good detail and shows where current runs up to 4 knots. Protected moorage is available in the Boat Harbour basin at the head of the bay.

A small public float is in front of the main part of town. The float is exposed to all winds and currents can run swiftly, but it is convenient when provisioning at the nearby grocery. Deeper in the bay, the breakwater-protected Boat Harbour basin, northwest of the ferry landing, has moorage. Anchorage is available in the bay; be sure to anchor clear of the ferry dock and its approach.

The Alert Bay village is about a half-mile walk from the Boat Harbour. At the top of the dock, take a right and walk along the waterfront. The village has a grocery store, pharmacy, pub, liquor store, restaurants, salon and spa, ATM, post office, and walk-in emergency clinic. An excellent Visitor Centre is on the water side of the road, about midway into the commercial area. It's open 7 days a week during the season. You will get good information about the attractions in Alert Bay: the world's tallest totem pole (whose top blew off in a 2007 winter storm); the U'mista Cultural Centre and gift shop; the Ecological Park, where you can see culturally modified cedar trees (trees partly stripped of bark to make baskets, regalia, and clothing); the burial grounds; the Anglican church that dates back to 1879. Brochures give information and map routes for self-guided tours. Interpretive displays have been installed. U'mista Cultural Centre is about a one-mile walk to the left from the Boat Harbour docks. Five awakwas (places to meet) along the way represent the five clans of the 'Namgis First Nation.

Cruisers moored at Port McNeill can walk-on the BC ferry to Alert Bay. Catch the 8:40 a.m. ferry from Port McNeill and return on the 5:55 p.m. or 8:25 p.m. ferry from Alert Bay. Bring your camera. The entire town of Alert Bay is walkable and photogenic.

Hiking trails: Cormorant Island has an extensive system of predator-free hiking trails. Ask for a map in the Visitor Centre or harbor office.

Seafest: Fourth weekend in July along the boardwalk. Table vendors, music, fun contests, and Artfest.

Alert Bay 360: B.C. Day is the first Monday of August. Observe or take part in the paddling race around Cormorant Island.

② **Alert Bay Boat Harbour.** 20 Fir Street, Bag 2800, Alert Bay, BC V0N 1A0; (250) 974-5727; boatharbour@alertbay.ca; www.alertbay.ca. Monitors VHF 66A. Good docks, 30 amp power, water, pumpout. This is the breakwater-protected public wharf and floats in Alert Bay, located next to the ferry landing. The harbor manager's office features showers and flat-rate laundry.

② **U'mista Cultural Centre.** P.O. Box 253, Alert Bay, BC V0N 1A0; (250) 974-5403; (800) 690-8222; info@umista.ca; www.umista.ca; www.facebook.com/umista.cul tural.society. We doubt that anyone could see this collection of historical coppers, masks and other ceremonial regalia without being affected. Open daily 9:00 a.m. to 5:00 p.m. from Canada Day to Labor Day, and Tuesday through Saturday, 9:00 a.m. to 5:00 p.m. in winter.

The displays portray the history of the area and the significance of the potlatch. In 1884 the government attempted to outlaw potlatch ceremonies, but the law was generally ignored and unenforced. In 1921, however, 45 people in the village were charged with violating a revised version of the law. Twenty-two people received suspended sentences, in an agreement where potlatch paraphernalia and ceremonial regalia, including masks and coppers, were turned over to the Indian Agent at Alert Bay. The items were sent to museums; some ended up in the personal collection of a government official. The people of Alert Bay successfully negotiated the return of their property in the 1960s, with the stipulation that museums be constructed for their display in Alert Bay and in Yaculta, near Cape Mudge. The result in Alert Bay is the U'mista Cultural Centre.

If you can, schedule your visit to see the T'sasała Cultural Group dance performance, Thursdays through Saturdays at 1:15 p.m. in the 'Namgis Bighouse: $20 adults, $10 for 3-12 year olds; no charge for children under 3. They explain and perform traditional dances, complete with regalia and masks. The audience joins in a dance at the end. Afterward, a visit to the U'mista Cultural Centre takes on greater importance. The artifacts on display are extraordinary. You can participate in a variety of free drop-in programs such as cedar bark weaving, traditional medicine, and story telling, to name a few. New for 2018 is a children's playground. Check their Facebook page for free events and classes during the summer.

Alert Bay Boat Harbour

See Area Map Page 347 - Maps Not for Navigation NORTH VANCOUVER ISLAND

Malcolm Island (Sointula)

③ **Sointula**. Sointula is a pleasant stop with amenities including an Info Centre, Co-op grocery store and bakeries. The Malcolm Island Lions Harbour Authority marina has space in the summer for visiting boats in both the north and south sections. The Sointula Co-op, across the road from the south docks, carries charts and a good selection of marine hardware. A Co-op grocery store in the village, closed on Sundays and Mondays, has a small liquor agency. The Co-op does not use plastic bags. Bring your own bags for purchases. A farmer's stand, actually a box on the side of the Info Centre, carries local items including eggs and breads and uses an honor box for payment. An ATM is in the co-op store in the village and at the hotel, which also has a restaurant and gift shop featuring local artisans.

Sointula means "place of harmony" in Finnish, and was settled by Finnish immigrants as a utopian cooperative shortly after the turn of the 20th century. Utopia didn't last, but the Co-op store is a reminder of earlier days. There's no doubting the Finnish influence as you walk around—the town is clean, well-maintained and orderly. You'll find well-tended lawns and gardens, with unique wood fencing.

Schedule time to see the museum. It's lovingly done, and volunteers on duty are full of information.

Sointula is a place where drivers wave as they go by, and are apt to stop and ask if you'd like a ride. It's a place where people put down what they are doing to chat briefly and exchange a small joke or two.

You can also visit Sointula by walking on the BC ferries from Port McNeill.

Note: the concrete float that used to be next to the BC Ferries dock in front of the town center has been removed.

③ **Malcolm Island Lions Harbour Authority.** P.O. Box 202, Sointula, BC V0N 3E0; (250) 973-6544; milha@cablerocket.com; www.sointulaharbour.com. Monitors VHF 66A. Excellent docks with 20 & 30 amp power, water, laundry, showers, garbage drop, Wi-Fi. Office hours are 8:30 a.m. to 4:30 p.m. in summer, 8:30 a.m. to 12:30 p.m. in winter. Downtown Sointula is an easy bike ride away, loaner bicycles are available at the Harbour Office.

Sointula's extensive public docks are behind a rock breakwater at the head of Rough Bay, 1 mile north of the ferry landing. The docks are divided into north and south sections. Both sections are available to visiting boats and it's an easy walk on the road between the two. Each set of docks has a garbage drop and pay phone. The north docks

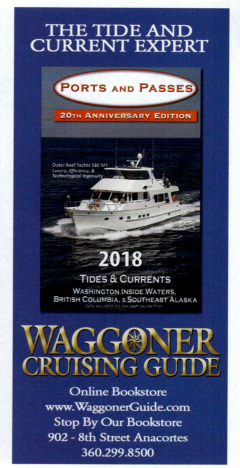

2018 WAGGONER CRUISING GUIDE   351

NORTH VANCOUVER ISLAND

also have washrooms, showers, and laundry, built and maintained by the Malcolm Island Lions Club. Solar panels on the roof provide the hot water. Both sections have potable water on the docks. All moorage is first-come, first-served, side-tie only, no reservations, rafting allowed. Moor where it makes sense. Pay at the newly built office in the north section. Lorraine Williams is the manager. The office staff is happy to provide you with more information on the town.

The Burger Barn, a local favorite, with good hamburgers, wraps, and fish & chips, is in the bright red building in the parking lot.

Tarkanen Marine Ways (250) 973-6710, capable of major and emergency work, is located near the boat basin. Tarkanen has three marine ways with varying size cradles that can accommodate vessels up to 60 feet. With the closing of the Quarterdeck Boatyard in Port Hardy, this is the only marine ways between Campbell River or Lund and Shearwater. It is often busy serving commercial fishing boats. Tarkanen Marine Ways was completely rebuilt after a fire in 2016 and re-opened for business in 2017.

Mitchell Bay. Mitchell Bay, near the east end of Malcolm Island, is a good summertime anchorage, protected from easterlies and northwest winds. Not suitable in south or southwest winds. A public dock managed by the Malcolm Island Lions Harbour Authority is located on the east side of the bay; first-come, first-served. The L-shaped public dock has approximately 150 feet of moorage on the outside. Inside portion of the docks are usually occupied by smaller, local boats. Self-registration and payment box located at the head of the ramp. Don't miss visiting the bright 'Red Net Shed' at the head of the pier, where you can purchase antiques and other collectibles. A log boom area is north of the public dock.

④ **Port McNeill.** Port McNeill is a modern small city on Highway 19, which runs the length of Vancouver Island. It has banks, stores, hotels, restaurants, and transportation to the rest of Vancouver Island. With nearly all services located within easy walking distance of the boat harbor, Port McNeill is an excellent resupply point for boats headed north, south, or into the Broughton Islands.

Port McNeill has two marinas: the North Island Marina, formerly Port McNeill Fuel Dock and Marina, and the Town of Port McNeill Harbour. Both are protected by an extensive breakwater. The Town docks are the first, to port as you round the end of the breakwater. North Island Marina and fuel dock is to starboard. Both facilities are close to shopping, restaurants and a modern laundromat. The laundromat also has free Wi-Fi.

A large, drive-on loading float was installed between the town docks and the North Island Marina fuel dock, reducing maneuvering room, particularly at low tide. While there is no boat yard, there are a number of resources for marine services and repairs. Both marinas can provide a list of boat service providers.

The well-stocked IGA is in a shopping center a few blocks from the docks. The IGA has a van and will deliver to the dock. Fishing tackle, post office, large liquor store, drug store, marine supplies and more are within a few minutes' walk. A hospital is nearby. The Shop-Rite marine and logging store near the marina carries just about everything and handles outboard repairs.

Regular floatplane service connects down-island. Kenmore Air and NW Seaplanes fly to Seattle from North Island Marina. The Port Hardy International Airport, with air service north and south, is a 30-minute taxi ride from town.

If the town marina and the North Island Marina are full, anchorage is possible across the bay from the marinas. Good holding in thick, sticky mud.

Be sure to see the Port McNeill and District Museum, which showcases the history of logging in the area. It is a short walk from the docks. Nearby, the world's largest burl is on display.

BC Ferries operates a ferry from Port McNeill with service to Sointula and Alert Bay. Many dock their boat in Port McNeill and walk-on the ferry to Sointula and Alert Bay.

Golf: Seven Hills Golf & Country Club, par 35, 9 interesting and hilly holes halfway between Port McNeill and Port Hardy, on the road to Port Alice. Call (250) 949-9818; they may be able to arrange a ride. Also the Cedar Park 9-hole par 3 course just outside Port McNeill. Call (250) 956-2270.

④ **Port McNeill Harbour.** 1594 Beach Drive, P.O. Box 1389, Port McNeill, BC V0N 2R0; (250) 956-3881; info@portmcneillharbour.ca; www.portmcneillharbour.

MARINA OFFICE: 250-956-4044 - WINTER OFFICE: 250-956-3336 - VHF/66A
TRANSIENT MOORAGE FOR YACHTS UP TO 285' - FRIENDLY SERVICE
IN BERTH FUELING FOR MARINE DIESEL - MARINE GAS - AVGAS - JET FUEL
PROPANE - CHANDLERY AND PARTS STORE - BBQ & PATIO AREA
WWW.PORTMCNEILL.COM   RESERVATIONS: 1-855-PORT-MAC(767-8622)

See Area Map Page 347 - Maps Not for Navigation

NORTH VANCOUVER ISLAND

Port NcNeill

ca. Monitors VHF 66A. When approaching, call on the VHF for a slip assignment. Open all year, guest moorage, 20, 30, 50 & 100 amp power, water, washrooms, showers, pumpout, waste oil disposal, garbage drop. This is a comfortable marina, with friendly management and room for all sizes of boats. No reservations; first-come, first-served. The marina office is in the Visitor Centre building, above the marina. The BC Ferries landing, with service to Alert Bay and Sointula, is east of the marina.

The Harbour showers are located above the BC Ferries landing and are $5 per day, payable at the Harbour Office. A passcode for the combination lock to the showers is provided with payment.

④ **North Island Marina.** P.O. Box 488, Port McNeill, BC V0N 2R0; (250) 956-4044; info@portmcneill.com; www.portmcneill.com. Monitors VHF 66A. Formerly Port McNeill Fuel Dock and Marina. Open all year with 2100 feet of guest moorage for vessels to 285 feet, 30, 50 (120/208 volt) and 100 amp (single and three phase) power, water, Wi-Fi. Garbage and recycling at the head of the dock. The main dock has a security gate; get the passcode from the marina office. Reservations highly recommended.

The fuel dock has gasoline, diesel, 100 LL and Jet A aviation fuel, propane. A long fuel hose and reel allows for in-berth fueling. The dock store has ice, lubricants, some marine parts. An auto parts store is just beyond the head of the dock with marine parts, batteries and lubricants. If parts are not available locally, they can be ordered and often flown in the next day. Diver available. A first-rate laundromat with Wi-Fi is across the street from the auto parts store. This is a friendly and well-staffed marina located adjacent to the Municipal Floats.

You can't miss the large "Happy Hour" float with wind-break and awning cover, which has become the gathering place for special events. The 10-foot long custom made charcoal grill is started each evening during the summer season for your steak, burgers, or just-caught salmon. The custom-made tables have built-in stainless tubs for ice to keep beverages chilled.

North Island Marina offers many services, including a courtesy car, and pick-up and drop-off at the Port Hardy airport, about 24 miles away. The marina staff can arrange for heli-tours, golf or other services, including boat watch. For those who need to return home, North Island Marina is a good spot to leave your boat. Their customer service is outstanding with concierge type services. Kenmore Air and Northwest Seaplanes leave directly from the North Island Marina floatplane dock with flights to Seattle. Steve Jackman and his wife Jessica are the personable and capable marina managers along with other family members on site, Bruce, Nancy, Alan and Katie and the staff members. Check with them if you have maintenance issues or special requests.

Beaver Harbour. The islands in Beaver Harbour are picturesque. The west side of the Cattle Islands is protected; anchor on a mud bottom in 30 to 45 feet. Patrician Cove has been recommended to us. Several white shell midden beaches are located throughout the islands. Reader Jack Tallman reports fresh northwesterly winds get in and can make for a "troublesome night."

Our sister publication, *Cruising the Secret Coast*, by Jennifer and James Hamilton, devotes a chapter to Beaver Harbour and the Native village of Fort Rupert.

Fort Rupert. Located in Beaver Harbour past Thomas Point. Exposed to north and east winds, but with several areas that serve well for day anchorage or overnight in settled weather. The town of Fort Rupert consists of two distinct areas, the newer town on the southwest shore of Beaver Harbour and the Native Reserve on the southern-most shore. Both areas are accessible by dinghy or kayak. Storey's Beach Park on the southwest offers a sandy beach and picnic tables. The south shore is the site of the Kwakiutl Band Longhouse and cemetery with exceptional carvings and paintings by Calvin Hunt, a well-known Master Carver and local resident. Visitors are welcome at the community carving shed located near the Longhouse and at Calvin Hunt's art gallery located on Copper Way.

Anchor off the south beach in 16 to 30 feet of water and dinghy to shore, look for the public gazebo for a landing spot. Position the dinghy appropriately for the charted extensive drying beach. A short trail leads to the cemetery and longhouse; the small Fort Rupert General Store is nearby.

This area was once the site of a Hudson's Bay Company fort, built in 1849, first commanded by William Henry McNeill. The fort burned down in 1889. One of the remaining eight-pound cannons is displayed in front of the Longhouse.

NORTH VANCOUVER ISLAND   See Area Map Page 347 - Maps Not for Navigation

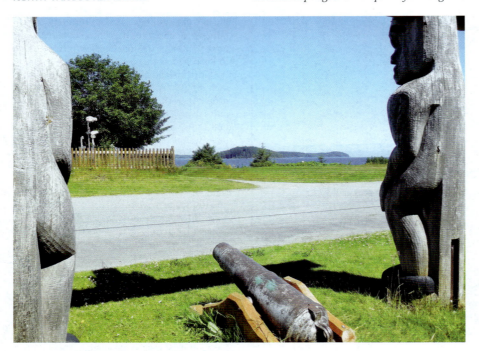

Historic Fort Rupert overlooking Beaver Harbour and Deer Island

⑤ **Port Hardy.** Port Hardy is the northernmost community on Vancouver Island. Moorage is at the seasonal Seagate T-Floats, formerly called the City Dock (summer only), Quarterdeck Marina, and Port Hardy Harbour Authority.

The seasonal Seagate T-Floats are adjacent to the Coast Guard wharf, and have the closest access to town and shopping. If the floats are full, you can anchor out and take the dinghy in.

The Quarterdeck Marina and the Harbour Authority floats are a mile or so farther into Hardy Bay, past a narrow entry channel. It's a one-mile walk from this inner bay to downtown. Stryker Electronics Ltd. (250) 949-8022, with marine electronics, repairs and a chandlery is across the street.

A large Save-on Foods supermarket is at Thunderbird Mall. For items with "Regular price/Member price" shelf tags, we found that non-members can get the Member price by asking the checker for a tourist card. The store will pay the cab fare to deliver large orders to the Seagate Summer Floats, Harbour Authority floats, and Quarterdeck Marina. They didn't give us an exact amount, but something around $100 probably would qualify.

Port Hardy is clean and friendly. A park is along the shore with a seaside promenade past tidy waterfront homes. The Visitor Centre is next to the park. Be sure to read the sign commemorating completion of the Carrot Highway. A nearby library houses a small but excellent museum.

Port Hardy has city amenities, including a hospital and airport with scheduled flights to and from Vancouver. Nearby Bear Cove is the terminus for the BC Ferry that runs to Prince Rupert during the summer. Coastal Mountain Fuels is in Bear Cove. There is a recreational boat marina in Bear Cove with portapotties and two lane boat ramp.

Dining: Port Hardy has several restaurants. We've had a good lunch and dinner at the Quarterdeck Pub at the Quarterdeck Marina. In town, breakfast at Captain Hardy's is a local favorite, complete with oversized portions. Cafe Guido has excellent coffee, sandwiches and baked goods. The Book Nook, the West Coast Community Craft Shop and The Drift are co-located with Cafe Guido. A local favorite, The Sporty Bar & Grille is down the street. A recent addition to Port Hardy is the beautiful Kwa'LiLas Hotel, formerly the Port Hardy Inn. Three Native tribes; Nakwaxda'xw People, Gwa'sala People, and Kwakiutle People came together to completely rebuild the structure, making extensive use of local cedar as an expression of native culture. The Kwa'LiLas Hotel houses the fine dining Ha'me' Restaurant with an excellent menu. Ha'me' is open for lunch and dinner; (250) 949-8884 for reservations. Taxi transportation is available in the area; Town Taxi (250) 949-7877; Waivin Flags Taxi (250) 230-7655.

Museum: The museum on the main street in town is small but superb. It also houses the finest collection of local history and local interest books we've seen. We recommend it.

Golf: Seven Hills Golf & Country Club, par 35, 9 hilly holes halfway between Port Hardy and Port McNeill on the road to Port Alice. A nice course. Call (250) 949-9818; they may be able to arrange transportation.

Fuel: Fuel is available on the east side of Hardy Bay at Coastal Mountain Fuels in Bear Cove, and at Quarterdeck Marina farther in the bay.

Walkway & Nature Trail: A walking trail with picnic tables and viewpoints starts near the Quarterdeck Marina, leads past the Glen Lyon Inn, and continues along the edge of Hardy Bay. At the head, you can turn north and walk to the Quatse River estuary, or take the Quatse River loop through the woods to the Quatse River Salmon Hatchery (www.quatsehatchery.ca or call (250) 949-9022 to arrange a tour). The trail is very easy, and much of it is wheelchair-accessible. It's a great side-trip that offers a different perspective of Port Hardy. [Hamilton]

LOCAL KNOWLEDGE

FLOATPLANE OPERATIONS FLASHING LIGHTS: Two floatplane pilot-activated white flashing lights in Port Hardy's inner harbour, when flashing, indicate floatplane

Port Hardy

See Area Map Page 347 - Maps Not for Navigation   NORTH VANCOUVER ISLAND

Port Hardy's Quarterdeck Marina has transient moorage.

aircraft take-off and landing activity. Both lights are charted, one is located on the east shore 300 yards south of red and green inner harbour entrance markers, and the other is located on the tip of the south shore breakwater.

DANGEROUS REEF: South of the Port Hardy Seagate T-Floats in the outer bay, yellow buoys mark a large drying reef. If proceeding to the inner bay, pass well east of the reef.

⑤ **Fisherman's Wharf - Port Hardy Harbour Authority.** 6600 Hardy Bay Rd., Port Hardy, BC V0N 2P0; (250) 949-6332; (250) 949-0336 cell; porthardyharbour@gmail.com; www.porthardy.ca. Monitors VHF 66A. The finger floats have mostly 20 amp power, some 30 amp. The main float has increased the number of 30 and 50 amp outlets. Although this basin is primarily for commercial fishing vessels, there is limited room for pleasure craft in the summer when the fleet is out. The facility has washrooms, no showers, no laundry, pumpout, and launch ramp.

⑤ **Quarterdeck Inn & Marina Resort.** 6555 Hardy Bay Rd., P.O. Box 910, Port Hardy, BC V0N 2P0; (250) 949-6551; (250) 902-0455; marina@quarterdeckresort.net; www.quarterdeckresort.net. Monitors VHF 66A. Open all year, gasoline, diesel, propane, guest moorage, 15, 30 & 50 amp power, washrooms, showers, laundry, Wi-Fi access, liquor store. During winter the fuel dock and marina office are closed on Sundays.

This is a busy marina, with a fuel dock and liquor agency. The Quarterdeck Pub & Restaurant is on the same property.

Quarterdeck's 40-room hotel is attractive and well-appointed. It has full wheelchair access, ocean views, and a covered walkway to the pub, with a nice area for families.

The boatyard and Travelift are no longer operating.

⑤ **Seagate T-Floats -Port Hardy Harbour Authority.** (250) 949-6332; (250) 949-0336 cell; porthardyharbour@gmail.com; www.porthardy.ca. Monitors 66A. Seasonal floats with 30 amp power, water, and garbage drop. Close to town and shopping. Side-tie for boats up to 60 feet. Docks are best used in settled weather as the area is exposed to the north. Docks are managed by Port Hardy Harbour Authority; moorage payment can be made with credit card by telephone or to Harbour Authority staff who come to the floats twice daily. This is a convenient place to stop and fill water tanks before heading around Cape Caution or into the Broughtons.

⑥ **Coastal Mountain Fuels (Bear Cove).** 6720 Bear Cove, Port Hardy, BC V0N 2P0; (250) 949-9988. Monitors VHF 16. Open all year, gasoline, diesel, kerosene, propane. Despite commercial appearance, they welcome pleasure boats. Washrooms, bait, ice, waste oil pump and disposal. Located near the BC Ferries terminal. Launch ramp and convenience store.

West Coast of Vancouver Island

CHAPTER 14

HARDY BAY TO QUATSINO SOUND
*God's Pocket • Goletas Channel • Nahwitti Bar
Cape Scott • Sea Otter Cove*

QUATSINO SOUND TO KYOQUOT
*Winter Harbour • Quatsino Narrows • Coal Harbour
Brooks Peninsula • Bunsby Islands*

KYOQUOT SOUND TO ESPERANZA INLET
Clear Passage • Zeballos • Esperanza • Tahsis Narrows

NOOTKA SOUND TO HOT SPRINGS COVE
Tahsis • Critter Cove • Friendly Cove • Estevan Point

CLAYOQUOT SOUND
Bacchante Bay • Ahousat • Lemmens Inlet • Tofino

BARKLEY SOUND
Ucluelet • Broken Group • Port Alberni • Bamfield

Cuising the **west coast of Vancouver Island**. For many, the area from Port Hardy, at the top of the east coast of Vancouver Island, down the west coast of Vancouver Island to the mouth of the Strait of Juan de Fuca, is the finest cruising ground in the Northwest—except, perhaps, Alaska. Little can compare with the variety, beauty, ruggedness, remoteness, and sheer satisfaction of this voyage. Please allow enough time when you make the trip. Plan for three weeks, two weeks at a minimum. This is a large cruising area to cover and you may have to allow for being weathered in.

The West Coast is broken into five inlets and sounds that snake their way into the heart of Vancouver Island. Mountains rise all around. Rocks lurk in the waters. Fish and wildlife abound. Only the hardy (and occasionally the foolhardy) are out there with you. This is Northwest cruising writ large.

Except for the rounding of Cape Scott and the long run down the Strait of Juan de Fuca, the distance between inlets and sounds is in the 20- to 30-mile range. Wait for good weather and dash around. Once inside, let the wind outside blow. You're safe.

Clockwise or counter-clockwise? Most boats travel the west coast of Vancouver Island traveling counter-clockwise. For sailboats, the prevailing summertime westerly winds combine with the westerly swells of the Pacific Ocean, and create some splendid downwind offshore sailing. Most powerboats have an easier time running with the seas than into them, so they prefer the prevailing conditions. "Prevailing," though, does not mean guaranteed, and the wind can blow from the south.

The difficulty with a counter-clockwise trip is the time it takes. To go down-island on the outside, you first must go up-island on the inside, and the weeks go by. Those who do not have the luxury of time to circumnavigate Vancouver Island can cruise the West Coast by running out the Strait of Juan de Fuca to Barkley Sound. They begin their explorations from Barkley Sound, traveling clockwise up the coast, perhaps only as far as Nootka Sound and then back down the coast. They must pick their weather for outside passages up-island into the prevailing swells, but that can be done. And if weather delays a passage for a day or even a few days, at least the time is spent on the West Coast, not in traveling up the Inside Passage.

Strait of Juan de Fuca. For boats coming from Puget Sound or Vancouver/Victoria, the Strait of Juan de Fuca can be a difficult body of water. The typical summer weather pattern calls for calm conditions in the early morning, with a sea breeze building by afternoon, often to 30+ knots. When wind and tidal current oppose, large, steep seas result.

On the American side, boats can leave Port Townsend at first light and get to Sequim Bay, Port Angeles, Pillar Point or even Neah Bay before the wind builds. From there they can cross to the Canadian side for the run to Ucluelet Customs the next day. Weather permitting, a fast boat can make it in one day.

On the Canadian side, boats can depart Victoria or Sooke at first light, and reach Port San Juan or even Barkley Sound, conditions and boat speed permitting. The distance from Victoria to Bamfield is approximately 92 nautical miles.

These thoughts are for typical conditions. Variations often change typical conditions. We have seen the strait windy all day and calm all day. Listen to the weather broadcasts, watch the barometer and sky, and be cautious.

The boat. Large or small, a boat for the West Coast should be seaworthy, strong, and well-equipped. The seas encountered on the offshore passages will be a test, especially at Cape Scott, Brooks Peninsula, Tatchu Point, Estevan Point, the entrance to Ucluelet, Cape Beale, and in the Strait of Juan de Fuca.

The wind accelerates as it is diverted at the capes and points, and the ocean's currents grow confused. Between wind and current, the seas grow noticeably higher and steeper. Even on moderate days, a boat can be suddenly surrounded by whitecaps. At Cape Scott and off Brooks Peninsula, pyramid-shaped waves can appear, break (or crumble into foam), and sweep past.

These 'rogue' waves can come from directions different from the prevailing seas. Assuming a summertime westerly wind and a course in following seas, they can grab the broad sterns of many powerboats and make broaching a hazard. A double-ender, especially a double-ended sailboat with a large rudder, will not be affected as much. In fact, sailing in these seas with a 25-knot breeze from astern could be high points of the trip. But a planing-hull powerboat skipper will pay close attention to the waves and their effect

It is at times such as these that the skipper and crew know they are in serious water, and that their boat and equipment must be dependable. It is no place for old rigging, uncertain engines, sticky steering, intermittent electrical power, broken antennas, small anchors, unswung compasses, or clogged pumps. For a lifelong city-dweller, the West Coast is a wild coast with open seas and rocks a mile offshore. It pays to be prepared.

There are essentially no repair services between Port McNeill/Port Hardy and Ucluelet. Where service is available, it is oriented towards sport fishing vessels, with limited capabilities and parts to service inboard engines, onboard auxiliary systems and electronics. Even if you have the parts, the shop will very likely not have the time to help you since their bread and butter is the sport and commercial fishery.

You, the owner and operator of the boat, must decide which systems are critical to continuing the voyage and carry your own spares and learn how to install them. Parts not common to sport fishing vessels may be available from Campbell River, the nearest large town with an industrial base. Make sure that you have the maintenance and parts books available and the tools needed. With the right parts and tools, another cruiser may be able to help.

Most consider radar all but essential. The local boats, even the little ones, have radar. A GPS chartplotter will add to your navigational peace of mind. Even on clear days in mild conditions, GPS can identify turning points and confirm visual navigation. A chartplotter can take the anxiety out of navigating among ugly black rocks. In thick weather or fog, radar and electronic navigation will raise the comfort level aboard dramatically.

Weather. Winter on the West Coast is stormy, and not a place for pleasure craft. In early spring, conditions begin to improve, and by June or July the pattern of calm early mornings followed by rising westerly winds establishes itself. In the evening the winds subside. That said, even in summer, serious storms can hit the West Coast.

Northwest winds coming down the coast tend to turn inland at the entrances to sounds and inlets. Sailors making a downwind run along the coast will often be able to carry that wind into the sounds, ending their day with a glorious sail on smooth water.

Fog can be a problem, particularly in August and September. We've heard the month of August referred to as "Foggust." The typical fog forms in early morning and burns off in late morning or early afternoon—just as the westerly fills in. If an outside passage is planned but the morning is blanketed in fog, the skipper will appreciate having radar and a chartplotter. He also will be glad he did his chart navigation the day before, with waypoint coordinates plot-

Uchuck III delivers supplies and passengers to Walters Cove.

2018 WAGGONER CRUISING GUIDE

ted and loaded, distances measured, and compass courses laid.

Plan for rain and cool temperatures as well as sunshine during a visit of two to four weeks or more.

The Coast Guard broadcasts continuous weather information from several locations along the way. The reports are limited in scope to weather that affects the West Coast, and include wind and sea state reports from lighthouses and weather-monitoring stations. In surprisingly short time, a visitor who's paying attention learns how to interpret the weather broadcasts and decide whether the time is right for an outside passage.

Lighthouse weather reports are particularly valuable. These reports include visibility, wind speed and direction, human-observed sea state, and swell height and direction. Reports are issued every three hours, but light keepers can often be reached on VHF 82 for up-to-the-minute weather information.

Fuel. Although the West Coast is a wilderness, it is a wilderness with fuel. Gasoline and diesel are available all along the way, within workable ranges for virtually any boat capable of safely being out there. The fuel stations exist to serve the fishing fleet, logging camps, and the pockets of permanent residents, especially Native communities. Fuel can be found at Winter Harbour, Coal Harbour, Fair Harbour, Zeballos, Esperanza, Tahsis, Critter Cove (gasoline only), Newston Cove, Moutcha Bay, Ahousat, Tofino (gasoline and biodiesel only), Ucluelet, Bamfield, Poett Nook (gasoline only), Port Alberni, Port San Juan (gasoline only), Sooke, and Victoria.

Note: The above list of fuel stops is subject to change. Check for the latest updates at www.WaggonerGuide.com.

Ice. Although finding block ice can be a challenge, it is becoming more common on the west coast. Where commercial fishing is allowed, the fish processing plants may have flaked ice for the fish boats, which take it on by the ton. A polite inquiry usually will yield enough ice for the icebox or cooler—sometimes for a charge, often not. Fish ice is "salt ice," and not recommended for the cocktail hour.

Water. Ask locals before filling the tank.

Fresh vegetables. Uneven quality. Best to plan ahead and stock accordingly. Port Alice, Tofino and Ucluelet are the only towns with real supermarkets.

Public docks. Every community has a public dock with moorage fees collected by a local resident. At some of the docks the local resident isn't around, or doesn't bother to come collecting. Accept the no-charge tie-ups where you find them, pay gladly where the charge is collected.

Reference books and guidebooks. The Canadian Tide and Current Tables, Vol. 6 (blue cover) gives tides and currents south to Port San Juan. Vol. 5 (green cover) covers the Strait of Juan de Fuca and inland waters of Strait of Georgia and Puget Sound. *Ports and Passes Tides and Currents* covers the entire west coast. *Sailing Directions,* B.C. Coast, South Portion, is the official government publication, and should be considered essential. Note that *Sailing Directions* is intended for large vessels. A cove listed as good for anchoring may be too deep or exposed for small craft, but a passage listed as tortuous may be easily run by small craft.

Useful book: *Voyages to Windward* by Elsie Hulsizer, paperback edition, 2015. Well-told stories of West Coast adventures packed with information about the coast's history, people, and natural history. Excellent photos. Provides a good sense of what it's like to cruise this challenging and interesting coast.

Three good guidebooks exist, and we carry all three. For those with limited space, we recommend carrying the the most current edition of the Waggoner Cruising Guide for updated information on facilities (only the Waggoner is truly up-to-date) and a second guide of your choice. The three are very different. Look for the one that most matches your cruising style.

The first is Don Watmough's *Cruising Guide to the West Coast of Vancouver Island*. It was published in 1984 as part of the Pacific Yachting series on British Columbia cruising, and republished (unrevised) in 1993 by Evergreen Pacific Publishing Co. The rocks have not moved since 1984, and the excellent aerial photos by George McNutt will help with navigation. The book was written before boats had GPS and radar. The author's dependence on traditional coastal navigation skills is instructive. Watmough gives a good picture of what the coast was like in the 1980s. Keep in mind that the coastal towns have gone through dramatic economic changes with declines in both fishing and logging and the closing of pulp and sawmills. The second is Don and Reanne Douglass', *Exploring Vancouver Island's West Coast*, 2nd ed., published in 1999. The book is clear, easy to understand, and describes a large percentage of bays and coves along the West Coast. Not every bay described is a desirable anchorage, but the Douglasses tell the reader what to expect if he is forced to enter.

The third and newest is Anne and Laurence Yeadon-Jones' *Dreamspeaker Cruising Guide, Vol. 6: The West Coast of Vancouver Island*, published in 2009 by Fine Edge in the U.S. and Harbour Publishing in Canada. It has the most up-to-date information of the cruising guides and includes the most information on shoreside attractions such as hiking trails They favor stern-tieing and tight anchorages which some boaters may not care for, particularly since stern-tieing is rarely necessary on the west coast.

Charts. The Canadian Hydrographic Service has more than 30 charts that cover the coast between Port Hardy and Trial Island. Buy them all. Let the few that you don't use be insurance that you will have the chart you need, regardless of where you are. The charts are of excellent quality and easy to read. The West Coast is no place for approximate navigation. If a $20 chart can take even a moment's anxiety out of a passage, the $20 is well spent.

Helpful maps. Correspondents James and Jennifer Hamilton recommend the Coast Recreation Maps (www.coastalwatersrec.com). The maps cover all the major inlets.

Coast Guard. The Canadian Coast Guard stationed along the West Coast is simply incredible. They watch like mother hens over the fleets of fish boats, pleasure boats and work boats, ready to deploy helicopters and rescue craft instantly. They know what the weather is doing and where the traffic is. They know where to find help. A call to the Coast Guard brings action.

Local communities can often respond even faster than the Coast Guard. In the area off Kyuquot Sound, for example, we were told that a call to Walters Cove on VHF 06 or 14 would bring help a-running. Be sure to call the Coast Guard on channel 16, too.

Insurance. Insurance policies for most inshore boats do not cover the west coast of Vancouver Island. Read your policy and check with your agent about extending the coverage for the period of your trip.

Communications. Unless you have a satellite phone, be prepared to be out of communication with civilization for much of your stay on the coast. Cell phone service is found only

Nootka Light Station at Friendly Cove.

Reference Only – Not for Navigation WEST COAST OF VANCOUVER ISLAND

Hardy Bay to Cape Scott

in Ucluelet, Tofino, Hot Springs Cove and in many locations in Quatsino Sound. Wi-Fi, found at marinas, coffee shops, restaurants and as commercial services is usually satellite based, which is slower than you may be used to.

Oregon's Secret. Many of the boats cruising the West Coast come from Oregon. For years it's been their playground, their little secret. The reason is obvious. After the trip along the Washington coast, their first stop is the west coast of Vancouver Island. In good weather it's a long but easy run. Boats from the population centers of Puget Sound or Vancouver/Victoria must fight the Strait of Juan de Fuca or go around the top of Vancouver Island. Often, it is easier for them to enjoy cruising in the protected waters inside Vancouver Island.

Trailer Boats. Launch ramps are available on each of Vancouver Island's sounds and inlets. Many kayakers choose whatever part of the West Coast they wish without making a summer of it. The West Coast truly is kayak country, with kayak delivery services from small speedboats with kayak racks, to the coastal freighters the *Frances Barkley* and *Uchuck III*.

HARDY BAY TO CAPE SCOTT

We will start from the north as though leaving from Port McNeill or Port Hardy, both excellent ports with provisioning and other services. Most importantly, you can watch the internet for the right weather window. Many cruisers like to watch for a 1-3 day settled weather window for the trip leg from the top of Vancouver Island south past Brooks Peninsula.

Goletas Channel stretches west-northwest 23 miles between Duval Point (entrance to Hardy Bay) and the western tip of Hope Island. At the west entrance of Goletas Channel the notorious Nahwitti Bar blocks westerly swells from entering. Goletas Channel's shorelines are steep-to. Winds can funnel between them and grow stronger, but in usual summer conditions the channel, while it can get pretty choppy, is not known for dangerous seas. Be alert, however, for turbulence and debris in the water where Christie Passage, Browning Passage and Bate Passage join Goletas Channel. The mouth of Hardy Bay can be slow going as you pick your way through drift. Bull Harbour indents Hope Island at the west entrance to Goletas Channel. It is the usual waiting point for slack water on Nahwitti Bar.

God's Pocket is a favorite layover in Christie Passage on the west side of Hurst Island, just off Goletas Channel. Boats bound around Vancouver Island probably will not see God's Pocket unless to escape a chop in Goletas Channel. But boats planning a direct crossing of Queen Charlotte Sound to Haida Gwaii (Queen Charlotte Islands), or boats bound past Cape Caution, find God's Pocket to be a good departure spot. God's Pocket is a local name, not shown on the chart.

God's Pocket Resort. P.O. Box 130, Port Hardy, BC V0N 2P0; (250) 949-1755; info@godspocket.com; www.godspocket.com. This is primarily a diving resort with friendly people. Room for three to four boats at the dock, or anchor out. No power or water on the docks. Washrooms and showers. Breakfast, lunch and dinner are available for the resort's diving guests; others can be accommodated on an as-available basis, with reservations.

Port Alexander. Port Alexander, indenting Nigei Island west of Browning Passage, is a good anchorage for boats bound for Cape Scott or around Cape Caution. Anchor near the head in 50 to 60 feet. The beach is good for dog

CHARTS	
3549	Queen Charlotte Strait, Western Portion (1:40,000)
3598	Cape Scott to Cape Calvert (1:74,500)
3605	Quatsino Sound to Queen Charlotte Strait, 1:150,000
3624	Cape Cook to Cape Scott (1:90,000)
3625	Scott Islands, 1:80,000
3679	Quatsino Sound (1:50,000)
3681 Plans	Quatsino Sound
3686	Approaches to Winter Harbour (1:15,000)

God's Pocket Resort has space for a few boats and is a good jumping-off point when rounding Cape Scott.

2018 WAGGONER CRUISING GUIDE

WEST COAST OF VANCOUVER ISLAND

See Area Map Page 359 - Maps Not for Navigation

Protected anchorage in Bull Harbour.

When the wind and current are calm, Nahwitti Bar can be easily negotiated.

walking. The westerly wind blows in across the island, but has no fetch for seas to build. The west side of the bay seems more protected than the east. The accumulation of large logs on the beach indicates that this is no place to be in a southerly storm.

Clam Cove. Clam Cove is a local name, not shown on the chart, for an anchorage on the Gordon Channel side of Nigei Island, where Browning Passage meets Gordon Channel. The entrance is approximately 0.7 miles southeast of Hougestal Point. The entrance is guarded by rocks, but Correspondent Bruce Evertz reports that with attention, entry isn't a problem. Correspondents Carol-Ann Giroday and Rick LeBlanc tell us the entry is wider than it appears on the chart and kelp marks the shallow spots. The basin has room for several boats, with protection from all winds. An easily-walked trail leads from the south end of Clam Cove to Port Alexander. A cluster of float homes is located at the north end of the inner-most part of the cove.

Shushartie Bay. "We stopped for breakfast in Shushartie Bay after rounding the top end of Vancouver Island (clockwise circumnavigation). A 30-knot southeasterly wind was blowing against a strong flood current, making Goletas Channel very rough. We went deep into the bay and dropped the hook in 50 feet just inside the 30-meter line, west of some dolphins marked 'Dns' on the chart. Holding was good in thick mud. This is no Prideaux Haven, but considering the conditions outside, the swell that came in wasn't too bad. The Douglasses description of Shushartie Bay is fairly negative, and we don't know how it would be in a westerly. But it worked for us that day." [*Hamilton*]

Bull Harbour. Bull Harbour is a lovely bay almost landlocked in Hope Island. It is the place to wait for weather and for slack water on Nahwitti Bar.

Enter Bull Harbour around the east side of Norman Island, which blocks the southern entrance. Parts of Bull Harbour grow quite shoal on a low tide. Check the depths and tide tables before anchoring for the night. The bottom is mud and holding is excellent. Sailing Directions says the southern portion of the harbor is reported to be foul with old chain and cable. During the fishing season, commercial fish boats often crowd the harbor.

All of Hope Island, including Bull Harbour, at the west end of Goletas Channel, is the property of the Tlatalsikwala Native band. Depending on the time of year, between two and 30 band members are apt to be on Hope Island. Visitors are no longer allowed to use the dock or go on shore.

Westerly winds can enter Bull Harbour, as can southeast gales. If you are anchored, be sure the anchor is well set, with adequate scope. In crowded conditions, achieving adequate scope can be a problem.

Nahwitti Bar. Nahwitti Bar should be attempted only at or near slack. Slack water and current predictions are shown in Tide and Current Tables, Vol. 6. Maximum tidal currents over the bar reach 5.5 knots. From seaward, the bar shoals gradually to a least depth of approximately 35 feet. When ocean swells from deep water hit the bar, friction from the shallowing bottom slows the water there, while the top of the swell continues its pace. As a result the waves grow high and steep. If a strong ebb current opposes westerly winds, dangerous and heavy breaking seas will develop.

It is often said that the ideal time to cross Nahwitti bar is at high slack water, when the typical westerly wind blows with the flood current. This tends to keep seas down and permits crossing a few minutes before the slack. The subsequent ebb current flows to 3 knots along the coast all the way to Cape Scott.

A crossing at high slack is not without its disadvantages, though. First, the ebb that follows will oppose the prevailing westerly wind, and could build a steep chop along the run to Cape Scott. Second, if you cross Nahwitti Bar at slack, you are almost guaranteed to arrive at Cape Scott around mid-tide, when currents there could be kicking up the seas. One alternative is to take the inner route around Nahwitti Bar prior to high or low slack at the bar, timing your arrival at Cape Scott for high or low water.

Thus the wise skipper considers all factors before crossing Nahwitti Bar: current direction and speed, weather, time of day, and the speed and seakeeping qualities of his vessel. At least 30 minutes should be allowed to get through the swells on the bar. Even fast boats usually must proceed slowly. At slack water in windless conditions, we found impressive swells extending 2.5 miles out to Whistle Buoy *MA* before they died down.

Nahwitti Bar Inner Route. A September 1992 *Pacific Yachting* article by June Cameron describes a quieter inner route that avoids Nahwitti Bar altogether. While in Bull Harbour, an old and grizzled commercial fisherman told us he hadn't gone across the bar in years, and we were nuts if we didn't take the inner route. Cross to the bay on the south shore of Goletas Channel and work in behind Tatnall Reefs. Follow the Vancouver Island shoreline around the bay, passing on either side of Weser Island. If the westerly is blowing, you can hide in the little nook behind Cape Sutil. We did it and it works. We don't plan to cross Nahwitti Bar again. [*Hale*]

Cape Sutil to Cape Scott. Sailing Directions says the distance from Cape Sutil to Cape Scott is 15 miles, but this understates the actual running distance after crossing Nahwitti Bar. A more realistic distance would be measured from Whistle Buoy *MA*, and would be approximately 16.5 miles. Although the run across the bottom of Queen Charlotte Sound is exposed to westerlies, except for the relentless Pacific swell the early morning conditions are often quiet. Rocks extend as much as a mile offshore all along the way. Stay well off.

According to Sailing Directions, temporary anchorage can be found in Shuttleworth Bight, Nissen Bight, Fisherman Bay (southwest corner of Nissen Bight), Nels Bight, and Experiment Bight. Study the chart before entering, and watch the weather.

Cape Scott is the westernmost point of Vancouver Island. Dangerous rocks extend 0.5 mile offshore, northward and westward. The cape itself is a low piece of land connected by a narrow neck with the main body of Vancouver Island. The Cape Scott Light, on a square tower 13 feet high, is on higher ground about a quarter-mile inland from Cape Scott.

Currents flowing on both sides of the cape meet at Cape Scott. Especially when opposed by wind, the currents can produce heavy seas and overfalls, dangerous to small craft. Even in calm conditions, seas can emerge seemingly from nowhere, the result of colliding currents. With its seas, rocks, and shortage of convenient hidey-holes, Cape Scott is not a place to treat lightly. A vessel in trouble at Cape Scott could be in serious trouble, and quickly.

It is with good reason that guidebooks (including this one) and magazine articles emphasize the dangers and cautions at Cape Scott. The waters can be treacherous. Yet in settled summer conditions, a well-managed seaworthy vessel, with a good weather eye, can make a safe and satisfying rounding. The standard advice is to round Cape Scott at slack. Other factors may persuade a skipper to round at times other than slack. Each situation, each boat, is different. What worked yesterday may not work today. A careful skipper, fully aware that the safety of his vessel and crew truly are at risk at Cape Scott, must judge conditions and make the right choices.

Weather information: The Cape Scott lighthouse weather report is regularly updated with wind speed and direction, sea conditions, and visibility information. The automated weather station on Sartine Island provides wind speed and direction. Listen to the continuous marine broadcast for the latest weather information.

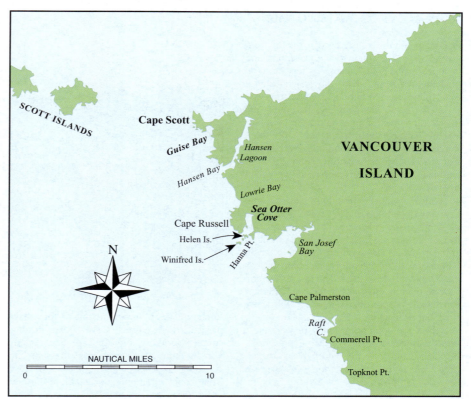

Cape Scott to Quatsino Sound

CAPE SCOTT

For 25 years Cape Scott, the remote far north tip of Vancouver Island, had been a dream of mine. Cape Scott is exposed to weather and current, and to seas that could have begun thousands of miles away. It is the most significant landmark in a circumnavigation of Vancouver Island—one of the events that marks a *compleat* Northwest boatman.

Cape Scott can be rough. At their worst, Cape Scott's seas have capsized and sunk substantial vessels. Even quiet days can be uncomfortable, the result of swells that sweep in from the Pacific to meet colliding currents. Rocks lie offshore. If you find yourself in trouble off Cape Scott, you are in trouble.

Mrs. Hale, ever stalwart before, refused to face Cape Scott. So longtime friend Tom Hukle came aboard for my first voyage around the north face of Vancouver Island and down the West Coast. Tom is a former sailboat skipper of the year at Seattle Yacht Club, an excellent seaman, knowledgeable navigator, and superb shipmate (but lousy cook).

On a breakfast of buns from the bakery and hot coffee, Tom and I departed Port Hardy at first light and ran out Goletas Channel. *Surprise*, a well-equipped Tollycraft 26 repowered with a "big-block" 454 V-8 Crusader engine, cruised at an easy 15 knots. We made all 15 knots in the flat water of a windless Goletas Channel, and reached Bull Harbour an hour and 15 minutes before the predicted turn at Nahwitti Bar. With time to kill, we inspected and took pictures at Bull Harbour. A few minutes before the turn, we followed two fish boats into the up-and-down rollers of the bar.

We rolled across at slow speed, steering a course for Whistle Buoy *MA*, 2½ miles away. A short distance beyond the buoy the bottom grew deeper and the seas flattened. We powered back up to 15 knots for the run to Cape Scott, confirming major landmarks as we progressed: Cape Sutil, Northwest Nipple, Christensen Point, Nahwitti Cone, Frederickson Point. At last Cape Scott lay ahead, with the uninviting Scott Islands offshore. Cape Scott itself was uninviting. Rocks extended from the land. Seas broke heavily on the shore. A low salt mist hung over all.

Out where we were, in only 10 to 15 knots of wind, the seas began to lump up. They were not towering, but for a small boat their closeness and steepness made even modest height significant. It had to be the currents. At first *Surprise* shouldered into the seas well, but after a brief time Tom Hukle, who was on the helm, said, "I'd like to slow down."

Tom and I agreed that if this is what Cape Scott was like in good conditions, it could be unrelenting hell in foul. Speed reduced, we bucked along. Charts slid onto the cabin sole, and a few books rearranged themselves. The wipers cleared spray from the windshield.

At last, at 10:15 that morning, in erratic writing clearly affected by the motion of the boat, I made the log entry I had waited 25 years to make: "Cape Scott abeam to port 1.5 miles. Light wind. Confused 4 to 6 foot seas. We're going home. A major moment."

A major moment indeed. Tom turned chatty, but I stared out the side window at Cape Scott, watching it move past as we began our voyage down the west coast of Vancouver Island. "Give me a few minutes," I said to Tom. "I know it's corny, but I've waited a long time for this. I want to savor it."

– *Robert Hale*

WEST COAST OF VANCOUVER ISLAND

CAPE SCOTT TO QUATSINO SOUND

Depending on the courses chosen, the run from Cape Scott to the entrance of Quatsino Sound is approximately 28.5 miles. To stay clear of off-lying rocks and reefs, the general advice is to follow the 20-fathom curve all the way down the coast. Douglass says he prefers the 30-fathom curve for an extra margin of safety. We are inclined toward Douglass' 30-fathom standard. In moderate conditions with excellent visibility, we felt comfortable in 25 to 30 fathoms. Had conditions worsened, we would have moved out.

With the summer westerly in place, the run between Cape Scott and Quatsino Sound is a downhill sleigh ride. Powerboaters, especially those with planing hulls, will have to saw away at the helm and play with the throttle to stay in harmony with the relentless procession of rollers. They will arrive tired. The sailboaters will have all the fun, especially if the boat and crew can handle a spinnaker. They too will arrive tired, but exhilarated.

Given the conditions, many boats make a direct passage between Cape Scott and Quatsino Sound, and leave the bays between for another day. Sailboats, after a long passage at 6 knots, will be apt to put into one of those bays, particularly Sea Otter Cove. Boats heading counter-clockwise, toward Cape Scott, might also be more apt to investigate the shoreline, choosing to spend the night in Sea Otter Cove. They could make an early departure the next morning and round Cape Scott before the westerly fills in.

Weather information: At the north end, the Cape Scott lighthouse weather report informs mariners of wind and sea conditions. At the south end, the Quatsino lighthouse report does the same. Listen to the continuous marine broadcast for the latest weather information.

Guise Bay. Guise Bay is just south of Cape Scott. Sailing Directions says the entrance to Guise Bay is encumbered with rocks, and local knowledge is called for. The chart suggests that entrance is possible, but Douglass says that the rocks are often covered with foam and a strong heart is needed. Correspondents Gil and Karen Flanagan, however, put in to Guise Bay, and here is their report:

"Guise Bay is a great anchorage. The shore is so interesting we would consider overnighting there. The walk to the lighthouse is well used, and pretty easy. The anchorage area is about 600 yards long by 600 yards wide. The swell that day was only a few inches. Behind the island, the main south entrance channel is 1000 feet wide and 42 feet deep. If it is a reasonably nice day, don't pass it by." [*Flanagan*]

Hansen Bay. Hansen Bay was the location of a Danish settlement around 1900. Supply vessels could anchor in good weather only. The settlement failed. Sailing Directions says Hansen Bay "affords no shelter," although commercial fish boats do hole up there.

Sea Otter Cove. Sea Otter Cove, south of Cape Scott, is described in Sailing Directions as "indifferent shelter." Nevertheless, Sea Otter Cove is a favorite of fish boats, and well-known to yachtsmen. The rocks and islets outside the entrance are awesome in their ruggedness. Inside, you feel safe but surrounded by hostile ground. Sea Otter Cove is an exciting place to be. We recommend it.

Enter from the south, between Hanna Point and the Helen Islands. Watmough's book shows swells breaking almost across the entrance, but careful attention to the chart will bring you through. The channel is narrow, and grows shallower as you go in. Contributing Editor Tom Kincaid says he stopped watching the depth sounder because it scared him. Deep draft sailboats, especially, should be careful if they anchor there. Four storm mooring buoys were in place in 2015; least depth was about 8 feet at zero tide.

San Josef Bay. San Josef Bay is protected from northerly winds, but open to westerly and southerly winds. Anchor in settled weather.

QUATSINO SOUND

Quatsino Sound is the northernmost of the five sounds that indent the west coast of Vancouver Island. Despite fish farms, logging operations, a pulp mill (closed January, 2015) and former mining sites, Quatsino Sound still provides scenic coves and interesting anchorages. With the exception of North Harbour and Winter Harbour on the north side near the entrance, Quatsino Sound is probably the sound least explored by cruising yachts.

Quatsino Sound is, however, the first quiet anchorage after the 50-mile run from Bull Harbour, and a welcome sight it is after anxiety

A community boardwalk skirts the shoreline at Winter Harbour.

PAST & PRESENT: SEA OTTER COVE

For boats rounding Cape Scott heading down the West Coast, the first fully protected harbor is Sea Otter Cove. Kayakers and rowers sometimes stop in Hansen Lagoon, where they can more easily pull their boats up on the beach. But for boats that need to anchor, Sea Otter Cove is a welcome retreat, safe from whatever might be going on out on the ocean.

Boats can enter and leave Sea Otter Cove from either the north or south. The south entrance to Sea Otter Cove is protected by a group of small islands, each one of which is surrounded by a reef. Using care, entry can be made on either side of these islands. If you choose the southernmost route, a single red light kept to starboard (Red, Right, Returning) provides a reference point for the very narrow channel between the reefs. The northern-most route is broader and deeper, but more exposed to the ocean swells until you're well into the bay.

Once inside, you'll note that the entire bay is quite shallow, in many places less than 5 feet at zero tide. Be very careful during extreme low tides.

CHARTS	
3624	Cape Cook to Cape Scott (1:90,000)
3679	Quatsino Sound (1:50,000)
3681 Plans	Quatsino Sound
3686	Approaches to Winter Harbour (1:15,000)

at Cape Scott and hours of rolling seas. The entrance is straightforward. Using large-scale Chart 3686, identify South Danger Rock and Robson Rock (both of them well away from land), stay close to Kains Island, and proceed into Forward Inlet. North Harbour and Browning Inlet are good anchorages, or you can continue to Winter Harbour.

For those coming from Haida Gwaii or the Central Coast, Quatsino Sound offers the opportunity to do major provisioning, either at Port Alice or by taking a bus to Port Hardy from Coal Harbour.

VHF: We are told the fishermen work on channels 73, 84, and 86.

Cell phones: In 2013, we found good Telus service throughout most of Quatsino Sound. A surprising exception is Winter Harbour.

① **Winter Harbour.** Winter Harbour once was a commercial fishing outpost, and B.C. Packers owned the first major set of docks as you enter, including the fuel dock. With the closing of fishing, their docks and fuel facility have been taken over by the company that owns and runs the Outpost store. Today Winter Harbour has 12 full time residents and about 70 summer residents.

Beyond the Outpost and its facilities is the campground of the Winter Harbour Lodge, followed by the Qualicum Rivers Fishing Resort (the large white building), and finally, the Winter Harbour Authority public dock.

The library, located above the public dock, has irregular hours. Pay phones are on the far side of this building. A post office and book exchange is located in a small building to the right of the public wharf. Pay-for-use Wi-Fi is available in Winter Harbour, although in 2016 it was not available at the public dock.

Van Isle 360: The Van Isle 360 sailboat race, held in odd-numbered years, visits Winter Harbour. They fill the docks when they arrive.

① **Outpost at Winter Harbour, Grant Sales Ltd.** 108 Winter Harbour Rd., Winter Harbour, BC V0N 3L0; (250) 969-4333; winterharbour@telus.net; www.winterharbour.ca. Monitors VHF 19. Open all year, moorage for boats to 75 feet, gasoline, diesel, oil, laundry, washrooms & showers, general store, water at fuel dock, campsites. The showers are in a small building on a dock near the Outpost. The general store has frozen foods including some frozen meat, canned goods, packaged foods and ice. Produce is limited. Grocery availability may depend on delivery schedules. The Outpost also carries liquor, clothing, charts, fishing equipment, and miscellaneous tools. The liquor agency has a decent wine selection. Wi-Fi can be purchased and used at an attractive patio area overlooking the harbor. Greg Vance is the owner.

① **Winter Harbour Authority.** (800) 960-2646 rob@qualicumrivers.com; Moorage on 450 feet of dock, water, waste oil disposal, garbage drop, recycling, 15, 20, & 30 amp power. Power is run to the dock by extension cord; quality varies. A pay phone is at the top of the dock. Cruisers may need to go to the Outpost to use the for-fee WiFi. A tidal grid is available. Qualicum Rivers, the fishing lodge next door, operates June through September and sells flaked ice to cruisers and has a restaurant. Reservations required at the seasonal restaurant.

A sign on the dock asks shallow draft boats to allow deeper draft boats priority on the outer side. Larger boats also anchor to the north of the public dock and at the head of Winter Harbour.

North Harbour. North Harbour, north of Matthews Island in Forward Inlet, is an excellent anchorage, popular with boats planning a morning departure from Quatsino Sound. A small float house is moored close to shore and does not significantly interfere with anchorage. North Harbour is sheltered and quiet, yet close to the mouth of Quatsino Sound.

Browning Inlet. Browning Inlet is narrow and sheltered from seas and swells, with good holding in 18 to 30 feet. Crabbing is reportedly good. In strong northwesterlies, winds blow from the valley to the north. In those conditions North Harbour or Winter Harbour are preferable.

Koskimo Bay. Koskimo Bay has a couple of anchorages, one behind Mabbott Island and one at Mahatta Creek. The Koskimo Islands are at the east end of Koskimo Bay.

Mabbott Island. The little area behind Mabbott Island would be a cozy spot to drop the hook if the large fish farm and float house didn't take much of the anchorage.

Mahatta Creek. In Koskimo Bay. Work your way east of the mouth of the creek, anchor in 30 to 45 feet. At high tide you can explore the creek. Waves can build across the sound in strong northwesterlies. On those days it's best to move north to East Cove.

Koskimo Islands. Explore by dinghy. The narrow passage between the largest of the islands and Vancouver Island can be run (carefully), but with safe water just outside the islands we see no need to.

Koprino Harbour. Most of Koprino Harbour is too deep for pleasure craft to anchor, but the area of East Cove, near the northeast corner of Koprino Harbour, is excellent.

East Cove. East Cove is tranquil, snug and tree-lined, with good dinghy access to shore—cruising as it should be. If East Cove were in Desolation Sound instead of Koprino Harbour, it would be filled with 25 boats every night, all stern-tied to shore. But because East Cove is on the west coast of Vancouver Island, you will probably be the only boat at anchor and won't need a stern-tie. Another cove, almost as delightful, is just to the north, behind a group of little islets. The largest of these islets is identified on the chart as Linthlop Islet.

Pamphlet Cove. Pamphlet Cove, part of a provincial recreation reserve, is located on the north side of Drake Island, about 3.5 miles west of Quatsino Narrows. Pamphlet Cove is scenic and protected, an ideal anchorage. You can go ashore and enjoy the reserve. At high tide several small lagoons make for good exploring by dinghy or kayak. Watmough reports a trail leading from Pamphlet Cove to the south side of Drake Island, but we couldn't find it in 2013.

Julian Cove. Southeast of Drake Island and east of Kultus Cove. Protection is excellent and

Moorage at the Winter Harbour Harbour Authority.

Julian Cove is an outstanding anchorage.

WEST COAST OF VANCOUVER ISLAND   Reference Only – Not for Navigation

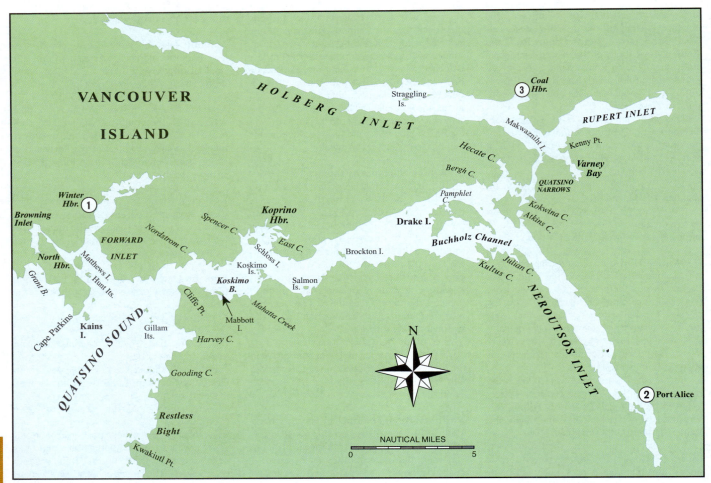

Quatsino Sound

holding is good. Probably the most pristine cove in Quatsino Sound, Julian Cove has room for four or five boats. Beautiful forested hills surround it without a clearcut in sight. At the head of the bay a stream crosses a marsh and salmonberries grow along the shore. Watch for bears. Entry is direct and easy.

Smith Cove. In 2013, a large float and separate float house with cables running to shore occupied much of Smith Cove. Nearby Julian Cove is a better choice.

Atkins Cove. Atkins Cove is well protected except south. Good holding over a mud bottom.

"Early Bird Cove," Douglass' name for the almost-landlocked cove accessed through the narrows on the north side of Atkins Cove, is also a good anchorage. We went through the narrow, shallow entrance strongly favoring the west shore. On an 8.5-foot high tide we saw depths of 6.5 feet. In 2013, a float was anchored inside, near the entrance, but there is still plenty of room for anchoring.

Neroutsos Inlet. "The wind blows hard every afternoon in Neroutsos Inlet," one knowledgeable local told us. Neroutsos Inlet is long and straight-sided, with little diversion along the way. An former pulp mill is at Port Alice near the south end.

② **Port Alice.** Port Alice, properly Rumble Beach, but locally called Port Alice, is a friendly, former cellulose-mill town struggling to adjust to the recent sale and subsequent closure of the mill. Amenities include a liquor store, and a grocery market that almost qualifies as a supermarket (and the best grocery shopping between Port Hardy and Tofino). Currently, restaurants are scarce. Fuel is available from a service station near the public dock at the north end of town for a $20 fee. A tricky 9-hole golf course is located at the site of the former mill, the *real* Port Alice, about a mile south of the town. Showers and laundry are available at the campground half a mile south of the yacht club and Rumble Beach Marina.

Visitors are warmly welcomed in Port Alice. It is a delightful stop and a good alternative to a bus ride into Port Hardy from Coal Harbour for provisioning.

② **Rumble Beach Marina.** (250) 209-2665; (250) 284-3391. Open all year with moorage to 100 feet. This new marina, just south of the Port Alice Yacht Club, is the best moorage prospect in Port Alice. Potable water and garbage drop. No power.

The marina is operated by the city and is walking distance of all Port Alice amenities.

② **Port Alice Yacht Club.** You must belong to a yacht club with reciprocal privileges to tie up here. A log breakwater protects the yacht club and the new public dock/launch ramp to the south. Moorage is available in members' vacant slips. Slips are generally not available in July and August. Boats that have been trailered to Port Alice cannot stay at the yacht club.

Although the yacht club is designed primarily for smaller boats, it may have room for larger boats if two adjacent moorage spaces are open. A volunteer worker may point you to your slip, help you tie up, then show you around town. Good water and 20 amp power on the docks. If you come in after hours, the gate is locked but the phone numbers of volunteers are posted. A public park with picnic tables and playground equipment is immediately to the north. We were told that boats can anchor south of the Frigon Islets.

Quatsino Narrows. Quatsino Narrows connects with Rupert Inlet and Holberg Inlet, and the village of Coal Harbour. With tidal streams near Makwazniht Island running to 9 knots on the flood and 8 knots on the ebb, it is best to take the narrows near slack. Predictions for Quatsino Narrows are shown as a secondary station based on Tofino in Canadian Tide & Current Tables Vol. 6, and Ports and Passes. You'll find considerable turbulence near Makwazniht Island. The range on the eastern shore of the narrows is for large ships with

364   www.WaggonerGuide.com

Docks at Rumble Beach Marina within walking distance to Port Alice. *The entrance to Klaskish Basin is narrow.*

30-foot drafts; small boats need not stay on the range. Turbulence, though less than that found near Makwazniht Island, is present near the south entrance to Quatsino Narrows. At slack water watch for tugs with log boom tows.

Varney Bay. Varney Bay, at the mouth of the Marble River and east of the north entrance to Quatsino Narrows, is scenic, tranquil and protected. A dinghy ride up the Marble River is worth a trip through Quatsino Narrows. Anchor inside Kenny Point behind the 3-meter island, and watch for rocks and deadheads as you enter. Varney Bay is a fish preserve. No fishing. Correspondents Gil and Karen Flanagan add this report: "After you cross the rather large delta, the Marble River flows through a canyon. The river has undercut some of the canyon walls, forming fantastic caverns. We went up the river about 2.7 miles to a rapids, where we found a huge cavern, measuring at least 30 feet by 30 feet. A must-see." To ensure enough water to safely cross the delta and reach the cavern, plan to be at the rapids as close to high tide as possible.

Rupert Inlet. Rupert Inlet is the site of the giant Utah Mines open pit copper mine, now closed and flooded.

③ **Coal Harbour.** Coal Harbour has a small village with launch ramp, marina, small general store, and museum. It is 8 miles by road from Port Hardy.

Thrice-daily bus service to Port Hardy, with connections to Port McNeill, leaves from the Whales Reach development.

During World War II, Coal Harbour was a Royal Canadian Air Force seaplane base. The large building on the waterfront was the hangar. The Coal Harbour Whaling Station, the last whale-processing site on the West Coast, later operated out of these same facilities. Whaling operations ceased in 1967. The hangar and adjacent land now serve as seaplane storage, launching facilities, and water taxi service.

One room in the hangar is a museum, with artifacts, newspaper clippings and photographs from Coal Harbour's years as an RCAF base and a whaling station. Ask at the desk to see it. If you're lucky you'll get a guided tour. No charge. The large whale jawbone shown in photos of Coal Harbour has been repaired and is on display. Recommended.

The old assembly building for the air base has been renovated as the Whales Reach Development to include a coffee shop, general store, and lodging.

③ **Quatsino First Nations Dock.** 322 Quattishe Road, Coal Harbour, BC V0N 1K0; (250) 949-6870; Moorage, gas, diesel, water, some 20 amp power. Showers and laundry facilities available beyond the wharfinger office. The floats can be busy with commercial boats. Floats can accommodate vessels up to 60 feet.

Holberg Inlet is 18 miles long, narrow and deep, a classic fjord. It has few places to anchor, and not much for the cruising yachtsman. With its 36-mile round trip and no facilities or attractions, it is seldom traveled by cruising yachts.

Quatsino Village. The public dock at Quatsino Village is mostly for smaller boats and loading/unloading. We tucked into the only larger space available only to be shouted at by a taxi boat operator who appeared to have plenty of space to maneuver. We walked into the village and to the 1898 Anglican church, open for visitors. A small museum and snack shop are open one hour per day, several days a week. Chart 3681 shows the details for entry. Room to anchor off the dock if necessary.

BROOKS BAY

Brooks Bay is between Quatsino Sound and Brooks Peninsula. It's about 19 miles from a departure point south of Kains Island (at the entrance to Quatsino Sound) to a point about 2 miles west of Solander Island. Depending on the course chosen, it's another 22 to 25 miles from Solander Island to Walters Cove—a total of at least 40 miles in the open sea. If wind and seas are favorable, those heading south will want to seize the opportunity to round Brooks Peninsula. They can be excused for not exploring Brooks Bay. If the weather is unfavorable, Brooks Bay is a good place to explore while waiting for a weather window. If you have the time, it is recommended.

Two inlets, Klaskino Inlet and Klaskish Inlet, are beautiful and have good anchorage, although portions of Klaskino Inlet have been logged. Brooks Bay is dotted with unmarked (but charted) rocks and reefs that make navigation exciting. Plot courses carefully.

④ **Klaskino Inlet.** Assuming an approach from the north, leave Lawn Point approximately 2 miles to port. (Lawn Point's grassy-looking slopes are in fact covered with low bushes). Continue, leaving Scarf Reef to port. Then turn to leave Rugged Islets to starboard. Turn to pass midway between Buoys *M17* and *M18*, then turn to enter Klaskino Inlet.

For a quick anchorage, skirt around Anchorage Island into Klaskino Anchorage or into the small bight north of Klaskino Anchorage.

If you'd like to explore further, go through Scouler Pass. Use the more open northern channel, leaving Buoy *M23* to port. The kelp will be close enough to hold your attention. Anchor in the bight between the 67- and 53-meter islands, in the area shown as 7 meters at zero tide. The drying flats of the river mouth come up sharply. Be sure you don't swing onto them.

Correspondent Gil Flanagan went all the way to the head of Klaskino Inlet (about 4 miles from Scouler Pass), and recommends the

CHARTS	
3623	Kyuquot Sound to Cape Cook (1:80,000)
3624	Cape Cook to Cape Scott (1:90,000)
3651	Scouler Entrance and Kyuquot
3677	Kyuquot Sound, 1:40,000
3679	Quatsino Sound (1:50,000)
3680	Brooks Bay (1:38,300)
3683	Checleset Bay (1:36,500)

WEST COAST OF VANCOUVER ISLAND

Reference Only – Not for Navigation

Quatsino Sound to Kyoquot Sound

anchorage behind the little island near the head. He says shore access is excellent, with logging roads for walking. Make noise; bears frequent the woods.

Leaving Klaskino Inlet, the safest route is back between Buoys *M17* and *M18*. Although it's possible to take a route westward through Steele Reefs, we're not sure we'd do it again. Our course took us directly over the word "Steele" on the chart. We had good depths, but even on a quiet day the surf crashing on the rocks seemed closer than we expected. [*Hale*]

⑤ **Klaskish Inlet.** If you run from Quatsino Sound directly to Klaskish Inlet, your probable course will take you very near to Hughes Rock, which dries 5 feet. Hughes Rock is clearly shown on the chart. Don't run over it.

Consider anchoring in magnificent Klaskish Basin, reached through a knockout, must-see narrow gorge with vertical rock sides overhung with dense forest. Once through, you are separated from the rest of the world. All the mooring buoys shown on the chart have been removed.

Brooks Peninsula. Brooks Peninsula and the waters off Cape Cook are, together with Cape Scott, the most hostile on the west coast of Vancouver Island. Like rounding Cape Scott, rounding the Brooks is a milestone in a circumnavigation. The peninsula itself is a mountainous, rectangular promontory that extends 6 miles out from Vancouver Island, like a growth on the side of an otherwise handsome face. Rocks and reefs guard much of the shoreline. Tangles of driftwood make beaches impassable. Cliffs rise from the beaches. At the tops of the cliffs, wilderness. Much of the peninsula is a provincial park, preserved for its wildness. Twenty thousand years ago, when glaciers covered most of Vancouver Island, the Brooks Peninsula remained ice-free. Plant species wiped out in glaciated areas are still found here. Park status helps preserve those species.

Cap on the Cape: When a cloud forms on top of Brooks Peninsula over Cape Cook, it often means that strong northwesterly winds will follow.

Cape Cook & Solander Island. Cape Cook is the northwestern tip of Brooks Peninsula. Rocks and shoals extend offshore from Cape Cook nearly to Solander Island.

The Cape Cook/Solander Island area can be a dangerous patch of water. When conflicting currents meet accelerating winds, conditions can sink a boat. Cape Cook has driven back large steamships. The marine weather broadcasts often talk of "local winds off the headlands" of 35 knots. The headland they have in mind is Cape Cook. While no headland on the West Coast should be taken lightly, Cape Cook (and Cape Scott) should be given the greatest respect. Listen to the weather broadcasts. If conditions sound questionable, wait. When your opportunity comes, seize it.

On all but the quietest days, the safe route past Cape Cook is well offshore from Solander Island. If you are one of the rare lucky ones to round the Brooks on a quiet day and can approach Solander Island more closely, you'll see Steller sea lions hauled out on the base of the island and puffins swimming near your boat.

www.WaggonerGuide.com

Weather information: An automated weather station on Solander Island provides wind speed and direction, updated hourly. Listen to the continuous marine broadcast for the latest weather information.

Clerke Point. Clerke Point marks the southeast corner of Brooks Peninsula. Shoals extend at least 0.5 mile offshore. Following the 20-fathom curve will leave ample room for safety. The pyramid-shaped seas we had battled at Solander Island disappeared completely by Clerke Point.

Once past Brooks Peninsula, the winds slacken, the weather warms and conditions improve.

CHECLESET BAY

Checleset Bay has a number of anchorages, including the Shelter Sheds, Columbia Cove, and the Bunsby Islands. If you have just rounded Brooks Peninsula, Shelter Sheds or Columbia Cove are good stops. Columbia Cove is exceptional.

Shelter Sheds. The Shelter Sheds are lines of reef extending from Brooks Peninsula into Checleset Bay. Fishermen have found shelter in their lee, hence the name. Correspondent Gil Flanagan reports that Shed 4 has by far the finest beach his family has found—better even than West Beach at Hakai. The water was near 70° F. A trail leads to Columbia Cove, but Correspondents Steve and Elsie Hulsizer report that windfall has made the trail difficult, especially the first 200 yards.

⑥ **Columbia Cove.** Beautiful Columbia Cove is known locally as Peddlers Cove. Neither name is on the chart. The cove is immediately north of Jackobson Point, snugged up against the base of Brooks Peninsula.

Be sure to enter between Jackobson Point and the 215-foot island. Columbia Cove has experienced some silting over the years and anchoring room has become limited. The mouth of the cove, between Jackobson Point and the 215-foot island, is safe in a northwesterly. In southerlies, winds and waves make this area uncomfortable, leaving room for only about three boats in the cove itself. Columbia Cove is a voluntary no-discharge zone. Please volunteer.

Brooks Peninsula is famous for high winds and rough water. It demands respect.

The name Columbia Cove comes from Captain Robert Gray's ship *Columbia*, which overnighted here twice. If you think Columbia Cove is crowded with three boats, now imagine it with the *Columbia*, the schooner *Adventure*, and the ship *Margaret*, of Boston, all at the same time. A sometimes muddy trail across the small peninsula formed by Jackobson Point leads to a beautiful sandy ocean beach. Great beachcombing. Take the dinghy up the stream to the trailhead, but watch the tide. You can be stranded, with a long walk across tideflats.

Weather note: When strong winds from the northwest are forecast south of Brooks Peninsula, the Brooks provides a lee for Columbia Cove and adjacent waters. Winds may be strong but seas will be quiet. It's a good place to wait out a northwest gale. It's not a good place to wait out a southeast gale.

⑦ **Battle Bay.** Battle Bay, north of the Bunsby Islands, has acceptable anchorages roughly off the Indian reserve, and in the nook that makes up the northeast shore. Approach the Longback Islands before making your turn into Battle Bay. One interesting anchorage is immediately west of Battle Bay, against the east shore of Acous Peninsula. To reach that anchorage, leave the Skirmish Islands to starboard as you approach. From there you'll look across a sea of islands and rocks to the Bunsbys.

The Indian Reserve on the Acous Peninsula is the former home of the Checleset Band, now located in Walters Cove. You can find fallen totem poles serving as nurse logs, and the depressions of old longhouses.

⑧ **Bunsby Islands.** "Did you get to the Bunsbys?" That's what people ask when they learn you've been down the west coast of Vancouver Island. Don't disappoint them by saying no. The Bunsby Islands are rocky, rugged, and beautiful. They were named for a character in the Charles Dickens novel *Dombey and Son*. A number of other features in the area also carry names from that novel.

Study the chart and know your location at all times. Enter the Bunsby Islands only through Gay Passage. Two anchorages are off this passage: either the cove in the southern island or the slightly larger bay in the northern island. Enter the northern island's bay favoring the north shore to avoid a shoal extending from the south side. In this larger bay, note the rock

Solander Island off Cape Cook, the Cape of Storms, on a rare calm summer afternoon.

This beach is a lovely hike from Columbia Cove.

WEST COAST OF VANCOUVER ISLAND

See Area Map Page 369 - Maps Not for Navigation

The Bunsby Islands are not to be missed. The rugged scenery and sandy beaches are a highlight of the west coast of Vancouver Island.

directly beneath the 6-fathom sounding. The lagoon adjacent to this bay may be fine for an adventuresome trailerable boat.

The cove on the west side of Gay Passage is guarded by two rocks that dry 4 feet. The rocks are easy to identify and avoid if you're paying attention. The cove has room for several boats.

Checleset Bay has a large population of sea otters, the successful result of a 1969 effort to re-establish these delightful creatures. From the Bunsbys, where they were first reintroduced, the sea otters have spread up and down the coast, as far south as Barkley Sound and as far north as the Cape Caution area on the mainland. You'll sometimes see them in "rafts," groups of otters hanging together, in kelp beds.

If weather allows, take the dinghy or kayak around the islands. The rugged, windswept rocks and islets are too stunning to try to describe. It's easy to get disoriented. Carry a chart, compass, handheld GPS and handheld VHF radio.

KYUQUOT SOUND

With the exception of the outer islands and Rugged Point, Kyuquot (pronounced "Ki-YU-kit") Sound is protected and pretty, surrounded by high mountains, with easy waters. On the inside, Dixie Cove and Don Douglass' "Petroglyph Cove" (known locally as Blue Lips Cove) are excellent anchorages, and several others are attractive. The settlement of Walters Cove is a favorite.

From the south, enter Kyuquot Sound past Whistle Buoy *M38*. Leave the buoy to starboard, and proceed through Kyuquot Channel. Most visiting pleasure craft, however, will approach from the north and stop at Walters Cove before entering Kyuquot Sound proper.

⑨ **Walters Cove.** For communication, call on VHF channels 06 or 14. The little settlement of Walters Cove has almost everything you might need after a week or two of working your way along the coast: outpost hospital, ice, charts, a small general store, pay phone, a restaurant and coffee shop, relaxed and friendly people, happy kids and lazy dogs.

One thing Walters Cove does not have is liquor. Walters Cove is dry, by vote of the Kyuquot Native community, and there's not a drop to be bought. Nor is liquor in evidence, even on the dock.

Another thing you won't find is fuel. Be sure you have enough fuel in your tanks. The nearest fuel is in Fair Harbour.

From seaward, the safest approach to Walters Cove in all weather is from Whistle Buoy *MC*, at the entrance to Brown Channel. Use Chart 3683. Go through Brown Channel and turn to starboard on a course to leave Gayward Rock to starboard. At Gayward Rock go to large scale Chart 3651 to work your way past the east side of Walters Island and into Walters Cove.

Boats coming down from the Bunsby Islands probably will follow Chart 3683's rather obvious passage along the Vancouver Island shoreline, leaving Cole Rock to starboard, and McLean Island and Chief Rock Buoy *M29* to port. At Gayward Rock they would move to large-scale Chart 3651.

New rock: On Charts 3623 and 3683 the 41-foot sounding at 50°03'03.0"N/127°27'01.0"W should be replaced with a sounding of 10 feet. This rock is along your probable shoreline passage course. At a depth of 10 feet at zero tide the rock is not a concern for most boats, but you should know it's there.

Without Chart 3651, entry to Walters Cove would be a tricky matter. Although it is marked by buoys and a daybeacon, the channel past the east side of Walters Island is easy to misread, and the unwary skipper could find himself on a rock. With Chart 3651 the channel is apparent, and following the rule of Red, Right, Returning, entry is safe. The one daybeacon along the way marks the narrow passage that leads directly into Walters Cove. Don't cut it close. Remember that beacons are attached to the earth; rock extends well into the passage from the beacon. Use a mid-channel course favoring the north side between the beacon and the 51-meter island opposite. The chart makes the route clear.

Several locals insist, "Don't anchor in Walters Cove!" The bottom, they say, is foul with debris. Furthermore, the floor of the bay is crisscrossed by high voltage submarine electrical cables, a Telus phone line, and the water lines serving the community.

Instead of anchoring, tie up at the public wharf to port as you enter. Long mooring floats are on each side of the public wharf. The general store and post office is at the head of the wharf. Open Monday, Wednesday, and Friday 1:00 p.m. to 5:00 p.m. Stock arrives once per week. Walters Cove Resort also offers moorage, reservations recommended.

Java the Hutt Coffee Shop, which began its life as a "boat-through" rather than "drive-through" coffee shop on the Kyuquot Inn dock, is now located in the renovated school house at the inn with an expanded menu. In 2016 it was open Tuesday through Saturday 11:00 a.m. to 7:30 p.m. except closing on Thursday to serve the *M/V Uchuck III* passengers who arrive in the late afternoon. They serve coffee, pastries and a variety of burgers and salads. Free Wi-Fi is provided. Showers are available at the inn. Owner Eric Gorbman is among one of the friendliest people on the coast and the Java the Hutt is popular with residents, boaters, and guests at the Inn.

The best time to arrive at Walters Cove is Thursday afternoon. The *Uchuck III* arrives that day, sometime around 5:00 p.m., depending on the other stops they have scheduled. Walters Cove becomes a bustle of activity when the ship lands, with skiffs arriving from all over the cove and outlying areas. Watching the *Uchuck*

CHARTS	
3651	Scouler Entrance
3677	Kyuquot Sound (1:40,000)
3683	Checleset Bay (1:36,500)

The public dock at Walters Cove. The building at the head of the dock is a post office and well stocked store.

Kyoquot Sound

III unload its cargo is a slice of West Coast life you won't want to miss. Everyone pitches in. Fuel barrels, boxes, even washers and dryers are loaded off the boat's starboard side into waiting skiffs. Pallets of groceries are loaded off the port side onto carts on the dock.

Because the ship overnights at Walters Cove, passengers spend the night at lodges and B&Bs. For dinner, passengers eat at the Java the Hutt Coffee Shop. When there is space, the Java the Hutt also feeds boaters, guests at the lodges, and anyone else who asks by mid-afternoon. Dinner is delicious. Guests eat family-style at a long table.

For medical matters, contact the VIHA (Vancouver Island Health Authority) outpost hospital at Walters Cove, (250) 332-5289.

Good water is available at the store for a small fee.

The Kyuquot Band Native community of approximately 200 is across the bay, served by its own public dock. We met a resident of the Native community who told us that she operates a small store near the head of the dock selling snacks, soft drinks, some groceries and native crafts.

All transport is by boat in Walters Cove, and from an early age the Kyuquot children (and Native children all along the coast) are accomplished boat handlers. Their outboard-powered craft seem to have but two directions: forward and reverse; and two throttle settings: full-power and off.

Walters Cove has been a popular gathering place for decades. Years ago it was home to five fish camps in the summer. When people were stuck in port waiting for the weather to break, the talk flowed. Long ago Walters Cove got its local name of Bull---t Bay, BS Bay in polite company. A cafe in Walters Cove was called the BS Cafe. (The BS Cafe, with its memorabilia-laden walls, burned in 1998.)

⑨ **Walters Cove Resort.** (250) 332-5274; (250) 287-2223; gofishing@walterscoveresort.com; www.walterscoveresort.com. Monitors VHF 78A. Open in summer with moorage, water, ice, Wi-Fi. No power. Reservations required. This is a first class fishing lodge that provides transient moorage when space is available. Showers available with room rental. A take-out menu from Walters Cove Bistro is available with dine-in options as space allows. Moorage guests have full access to resort amenities, including hot tub, lounge, kayaks, and SUPs. Fishing charters and fish packing available.

Barter Cove. Barter Cove, in the Mission Group islands outside Walters Cove, is open, unprotected and not as interesting as anchorages inside Kyuquot Sound. Leave Ahmacinnit Island and the tiny islet east of Ahmacinnit Island to starboard, and feel your way in.

Kamils Anchorage. Kamils Anchorage in the Mission Group islands is more exposed than Barter Cove. Enter, very carefully, through Favourite Entrance.

Amos Island. From Walters Cove, the easiest entrance to Kyuquot Sound is around the east side of Amos Island into Crowther Channel. Use Chart 3651 to identify the channel between Walters Cove and Nicolaye Channel, then Chart 3682 to find the route past Amos Island. The passage east of Amos Island is deep but narrow, and bounded by rocks. The first time through can be unsettling, but after you've done it once it's easy.

Surprise Island. Surprise Island, steep, round, and logged off to stumps, is located in Crowther Channel. On the south side of Surprise Island, Crowther Channel is deep and open, but on the north side a narrow passage is interesting. At zero tide least depths in this passage are approximately 18 feet. A ledge of rock, shown on the chart, extends from the north shore. Favor the Surprise Island side all the way through.

Hankin Cove. Hankin Cove is located near the mouth of Kashutl Inlet, on the east side. It is a beautiful little cove with good holding and completely protected. Stands of small trees covering the hillsides show evidence of past logging. Correspondents Gil and Karen Flanagan anchored in the southeast cove, and add, "Chart 3682 is way off on the shoal in this cove. The shoal extends only halfway across from the east shore. Depths are 12 to 18 feet along the west shore, almost to the south end of the cove."

Walters Cove Resort caters to fishing guests but accommodates cruising boats by reservation. Meals are excellent.

⑩ **Fair Harbour.** Enter Fair Harbour south of Karouk Island, leaving the two lighted beacons to port. The passage north of the island has two newly-reported rocks, not shown on the chart.

Fair Harbour has a wide dirt launch ramp at the head, with a small campground and ample parking. A dirt road leads from Zeballos to Fair Harbour, the only road access to Kyuquot Sound. This is a popular trailer boat launch point. A good-sized public wharf, with a long float, is at the head. If the float is full, anchor in approximately 60 feet.

⑩ **Fair Harbour Marina & Campground.** (250) 483-3382; fairharbourmarina@gmail.com; www.gatewaytokyuquot.com. Open all year. Limited moorage, gas, diesel, propane, water, garbage drop, boat launch. No power on the docks. This is the only fuel in Kyuquot Sound. A small store carries fishing tackle, ice, convenience food.

⑪ **Dixie Cove.** Dixie Cove indents the east side of Hohoae Island, and is a wonderful anchorage. Enter south of Copp Island, through a narrow but deep passage to the first of two anchorages. The outer anchorage is approximately 30 feet deep, with good holding. Another narrow passage leads to the inner cove, completely secluded, with rock cliffs on one side. Depths here are approximately 18 feet, mud bottom with excellent holding. Landing on shore is a problem, so you're restricted to the boat. As a place to put the hook down, though, Dixie Cove is highly recommended.

⑫ **Petroglyph Cove (Blue Lips Cove).** In his excellent book, *Exploring Vancouver Island's West Coast,* Don Douglass describes this previously-unnamed anchorage and calls it "Petroglyph Cove." In the second edition of his book, Douglass acknowledged that others had not been able to find the petroglyphs. Hulsizer reported finding what looked like a faded pictograph (red ochre painting) and noted that the local name for the cove is Blue Lips Cove—because when residents went swimming the water was so cold their lips turned blue. Petroglyph, Pictograph or Blue Lips, the cove is located near the mouth of Amai Inlet, roughly due west of Amai Point. The narrow entry is hidden until you're right on it. The channel shallows to a least depth of 12 to 18 feet, but has no hazards. Once inside you are protected. While in our opinion Petroglyph Cove is not as pretty as Dixie Cove, it is an excellent spot.

Volcanic Cove. Exposed to the north, small, no room to swing. Temporary only for small boats, in our view.

⑬ **Rugged Point Marine Park.** Rugged Point marks the southern entrance to Kyuquot Sound. Our notes read, "Wow!" The beaches on the ocean side are spectacular, and deserve a visit. Anchor along the inside beaches in 18 feet on a kelp-covered hard sand bottom, and dinghy ashore. The Pacific swell, though diminished, can get into the anchorage. The anchorage is protected from southeasterlies and westerlies but is subject to occasional nighttime outflow winds. Be sure you anchor far enough offshore to avoid swinging onto shallows if outflow winds develop.

A trail, now upgraded with a boardwalk, leads through the park to the ocean beaches. Bear and cougar prints have been sighted, so be noisy. Once on the ocean beach, you will find a series of paths leading around headlands all the way to the Kapoose Creek. Some of the paths are steep and involve climbing ladders or using ropes for assistance.

Cachalot. Cachalot, the site of a former industrial whaling center, makes an interesting lunch stop or afternoon exploration. Locate it by finding the abandoned pilings between Cachalot Inlet to the east and Cachalot Creek to the west. Although pronounced locally as "catch a lot," the name means sperm whale in French (and in French would be pronounced "caa-shaa-low"). The whaling center operated between 1907 and 1926, then served as a pilchard reduction plant until the 1940s.

Anchor off the old pilings in 30 to 60 feet of water and take the dinghy ashore. You'll find old whale bones, crockery, and miscellaneous hardware on the beach, and rusty equipment in the forest. Next to the creek, a ferrocement statue of a sperm whale serves as a memorial to the whales that were processed at this site. The statue was placed there by Vancouver Island artist Wayne Adams in the 1970s. Hulsizer gives the history of the site in in her book *Voyages to Windward*.

When anchoring, avoid the drying shoal on the north end of the site near the river and be sure to anchor in at least 30 feet of water to avoid your anchor being entangled in kelp.

Kyuquot Sound to Esperanza Inlet. Depending on the course chosen, it is approximately 13.5 miles between Rugged Point and the entrance to Gillam Channel, which leads into Esperanza Inlet. In good visibility the route through Clear Passage is smooth and interesting. In poor visibility, we would head seaward from Rugged Point to entrance Buoy *M38*, then turn southeastward toward Gillam Channel.

Clear Passage to Tatchu Point. Clear Passage takes you about 4 miles along the coast in waters protected by the Barrier Islands, past a steady display of rugged rocks and rock islets. The channel is free of hazards. To enter Clear Passage, leave Grogan Rock to starboard, watching carefully for the rock to port, marked by kelp, that dries at 4 feet. Heading down-island, we got a little close to Grogan Rock, and the depths came up sharply. We moved off to port and they went back down. You will have no trouble identifying Grogan Rock. It is an awful 23-foot-high black pinnacle and it commands attention. Lay a course to take you north of McQuarrie Islets, and exit Clear Passage leaving McQuarrie Islets to starboard. The rocks and islets along Clear Passage all look alike. It helps to plot a waypoint at the spot where you intend to turn to exit past McQuarrie Islets. Clear Passage is also a good route when heading north. Leave McQuarrie Islets and Grogan Rock to port.

At anchor in lovely Hankin Cove.

The island just south of Grassy Isle is a good place to hunt fossils. "We anchored south of Clark Island and took the dinghy ashore to a shell beach on the southeast corner of the island. The fossils were just lying on the beach. We recommend doing this on a calm day only. With the new, more detailed, metric chart, it might be possible to find anchorage between Grassy Isle and Clark." [*Hulsizer*]

Local fishermen say the waters from Jurassic Point past Tatchu Point can be an "ugly patch of water." Use caution and careful judgment.

⑭ **Rolling Roadstead (Catala Island Provincial Park).** Rolling Roadstead offers acceptable anchorage in fair weather. From the west the approach can be tricky. Douglass and Watmough describe the approach in their books. Careful navigation is called for, including the finding and identifying of the various rocks and reefs in the entrance. The hazards are easily identified, either by the breaking surf or kelp growing in the shallows. With the hazards accounted for, the entry is reported to be safe. All agree that it should be run in fair weather only, with good visibility.

If you're coming down from Tatchu Point, especially in a fresh westerly, it's easier to enter via Gillam Channel, leaving Black Rock and Entrance Reef to port and approach Rolling Roadstead from the southwest. Anchor in the lee of the point of land that juts abruptly from Catala Island.

Catala Island, which protects Rolling Roadstead, is a provincial marine park. The beach on Catala Island is beautiful. Several sea caves are accessible.

Gillam Channel. Gillam Channel, more than one-half mile wide and well-buoyed, is the safe entrance to Esperanza Inlet. Approaching, leave the entrance buoy *M40* and buoy *M42*, which marks the west end of Blind Reef, to starboard. Leave buoy *M41* to port, and continue into Esperanza Inlet.

ESPERANZA INLET

Esperanza Inlet is on the west side of Nootka Island, and ultimately connects with Nootka Sound. The inlet is part of the "inside route" through this portion of the coast. This route is served by three communities—Zeballos, Tahsis, and Gold River—and by the Esperanza Mission, with its fuel dock and excellent water. The waterways are beautiful, and contain several good stopping places. Tahsis Narrows connects Esperanza Inlet with Tahsis Inlet on the Nootka Sound side, and is not difficult to run.

Nuchatlitz Inlet. Reader Don Thain reports that Mary Basin is a delightful and protected anchorage with good holding in mud. A pretty waterfall on Laurie Creek is reachable by dinghy on a 7-foot tide. The inner basin is a tidal lagoon.

⑮ **Nuchatlitz Provincial Park.** Nuchatlitz Provincial Park is a beautiful and interesting stop with a well-protected anchorage. It's a favorite among kayakers and campers. The area contains a number of archeological treasures, including burial canoes on land and burial caves on the outer islands.

The entry to Nuchatlitz is very complex with numerous rocks and reefs; a careful study of the charts is warranted. Inside, a large bay has a uniform bottom with approximately 30- to 40-foot anchoring depths. In good weather, if you choose an anchoring spot where you can see over the islands towards the northwest, you may be rewarded with a magnificent sunset. The anchorage can be absolutely calm when the wind dies in the evening, but you can hear the surf breaking on the outer islands.

The abandoned Indian village of Nuchatlitz is on the shore of a 44-meter island marked Indian Reserve, above a marvelous beach. At low tide you can walk the drying sand bar from the reserve island to a second 44-meter island to

CHARTS	
3677	Kyuquot Sound, 1:40,000
3675	Nootka Sound (1:40,000)
	Gold River (1:10,000)
	Princesa Channel (1:10,000)
3676	Esperanza Inlet (1:40,000)
	Tahsis (1:12,000)

See Area Map Page 372 - Maps Not for Navigation   WEST COAST OF VANCOUVER ISLAND

Zeballos is bounded by impressive mountains.

the west. Although the village was moved from this site to Espinosa in the 1980s, the site is still visited by the band. Local kayak tours use it as a landing site.

A number of private homes dot the shores of a privately-owned unmarked island on the south side of the anchorage. Private buoys mark the route past submerged rocks to homes on the island's back side and to a shallow lagoon. Use Chart 3676, which reflects hydrographic survey work performed between 1992 and 1996 at the cost of many survey launch propellers.

The easy but long entry to Nuchatlitz is from the northeast, passing east of Rosa Island. From there the chart makes the course clear: Follow the winding channel east of the 37-meter and 34-meter islands, and east of the two red spar buoys *M46* and *M48* (Red, Right, Returning). At Buoy *M48* the bay opens up. Both Douglass and Yeadon-Jones describe a second, more direct entrance, leaving the light on the 37-meter island (known locally as Entrance Island) to starboard as you enter.

⑯ **Queen Cove.** Queen Cove is a short distance inside the entrance to Port Eliza, the first inlet to port as you enter Esperanza Inlet. It is a safe and satisfying spot to put the hook down and go exploring, although not as beautiful as Nuchatlitz on the east side of Gillam Channel. Queen Cove is a popular anchorage among island circumnavigators. Anchor here and you'll soon have company. The cove is well protected, and has excellent holding in 20 to 40 feet. It is large enough for several boats to swing. A cabin with dock is at the north end of Queen Cove. The Park River enters at the north end, and makes a good dinghy exploration. In 2016 we heard reports that the Queen Cove Band was charging $5.00 per boat to anchor.

The most protected anchorage is the nook at the south end of Queen Cove, between the little island and the rock that dries at 3.4 meters (11 feet). Swinging room is a little restricted, but the anchorage is workable. We overnighted in Queen Cove, anchored in the wider and much more exposed northern area. At 5:00 p.m. the wind came in, and built to about 25 knots before dying at sundown. We sailed back and forth on our anchor, but we didn't budge. [*Hale*].

Espinosa Inlet. Espinosa Inlet is deep and high-walled. No place to anchor. The Native village of Ocluje is located at its head.

Newton Cove Resort. (877) 337-5464; info@nootkamarineadventures.com; www.nootkamarineadventures.com. Monitors VHF 06. Call ahead for availability. Moorage, 30 & 50 amp power, restaurant, lodging, fishing charters, fish packing. Fuel dock has gas and diesel, ice, and bait. Located near the mouth of Espinosa Inlet.

⑰ **Zeballos.** www.zeballos.com. Zeballos (pronounced "Ze-BAH-los") is the most unexpected town on the west coast of Vancouver Island. While other settlements range from fishing camp (Winter Harbour) to bustling town (Tofino), Zeballos stands alone.

The trip up Zeballos Inlet is an especially scenic one, with bulbous-topped odd-shaped mountains, and sheer rock faces rising above the shores. Zeballos is a mining town that looks like Cicily, Alaska, the fictional town made famous by the television show *Northern Exposure*, with wandering streets, false-fronted buildings, and a museum. The town is built at the mouth of the Zeballos River, next to mountains that go *straight up*.

The museum, located on the main road heading out of town, is one of the town's main attractions. It's small but fascinating, with mining paraphernalia, photographs, and a full-scale model of a mine entrance. In 2016 it was staffed by a full-time curator, but in previous years has not always been open regularly. If you arrive at the museum during the workweek and no one is there, inquire at the municipal hall and someone will give you a tour.

The town recently constructed a boardwalk trail through the Zeballos River estuary. It's a beautiful walk along the river.

Much gold has been taken out of the highly mineralized mountains around Zeballos. Over dinner at the hotel on our first visit, we talked with a wildcat prospector whose eyes burned bright as he told of pockets of gold still waiting to be taken. He insisted that he didn't have gold fever, *but he knew where the gold was*. [*Hale*]

The floats at Zeballos are well maintained, with power and water.

Zeballos

2018 WAGGONER CRUISING GUIDE

WEST COAST OF VANCOUVER ISLAND — Reference Only – Not for Navigation

Nootka Sound

374

Tie up at the public dock, to the right of the fuel dock as you approach. Pay telephones are at the head of the dock and on the seaplane dock. The village has built a new wharf to the left of the fuel dock, but it is for large vessels, loading and unloading only. The small float next to the wharf is for short-term (a few hours) tie-up. A bird-viewing platform overlooks the estuary.

A fish-processing plant is shoreward of the fuel dock and is one of the town's economic mainstays. It's a good place to purchase chipped ice.

Provisioning: Cruising boaters often ask whether they should stop at Zeballos or Tahsis for provisioning. The answer is you may need to stop at both for everything you need. At present, no good store exists in Zeballos. The store near the fuel dock carries ice cream and convenience foods, as well as frozen meat and bread, and liquor. The Rosa Island General Store also offers limited items including staples, snacks, and cigarettes. Fruits and vegetables were in short supply at both stores. Zeballos is a good place to spend the night. The inlet leading to the town is long and beautiful. There's no point going both ways in one day.

⑰ **Zeballos Fuel Dock Inc.** P.O. Box 100, Zeballos, BC V0P 2A0; (250) 761-4201. Monitors VHF 68. Open all year. Gasoline, diesel, propane, kerosene, petroleum products, some marine supplies. Tim and Candace Saulkner are the owners.

⑰ **Village of Zeballos Municipal Wharf.** (250) 761-4229. Open all year. For large vessels, loading and unloading only. The small float next to the wharf is for short-term (a few hours) tie-up. Some overnight moorage with permission. Access to power and water if absolutely necessary.

⑰ **Zeballos Small Craft Harbour.** P.O. Box 99, Zeballos, BC V0P 2A0; (250) 761-4333. Monitors VHF 06. Open all year with 400 feet of moorage, 30 amp power, year-round washrooms & showers, water, waste oil collection, all tide launch ramp, long term parking (launch ramp is run by the village). A sign on the east side of the easternmost dock warns of shallow water, but the Hulsizers report finding 2.7 meters when sounding the depth with a lead line at low tide.

⑱ **Esperanza (Nootka Mission).** P.O. Box 368, Tahsis, BC V0P 1X0; (250) 483-4162; www.esperanza.ca. info@esperanza.ca Monitors VHF 06. Fuel dock with gasoline, diesel, lube oil. Excellent water, phone service and free Wi-Fi. A small store, with fishing gear and limited food, is on the fuel dock. Moorage is available at the dock for boats up to 120 feet in front of the old boathouse, except during the month of July; call ahead. The mission runs camps for local children. When a camp is in session, facilities may not be available.

Esperanza is the home of the Nootka Mission. Its story goes back to 1937, when the Shantyman Mission began a hospital at Esperanza. This was in the tradition of the Mission, founded in northern Ontario in 1907 to serve shanty dwellers in outlying areas. The Esperanza hospital no longer operates and the property is now owned by the Esperanza Ministries Association, serving people of the west coast of Vancouver Island. The property is immaculately kept. The fuel dock is an important source of revenue.

Inquire about availability for visiting boaters. Showers, washrooms, some 15 amp power, water, ice, and laundry are available. Sometimes, fresh Esperanza-grown produce and canned cheesecake are available for purchase.

Tahsis Narrows. Tahsis Narrows connects the Esperanza Inlet side of Nootka Island with the Nootka Sound side. From the chart, one would think reversing tidal currents rage through the narrows four times a day, but they do not. The narrows are deep and free of hazards, with little tidal current activity. Passage can be made at any time.

TAHSIS INLET

Tahsis Inlet (Tahsis is pronounced with a short-*a*, as in *cat*) is long and narrow, and bounded by mountains. The wind funnels and blows up-inlet or down, depending on conditions. The normal situation in prevailing westerly winds is for light or outflow winds in the morning and strong inflow winds in the afternoon, building stronger as you approach the town. But during extended periods of warm weather, strong outflow winds can also develop, especially at night and early morning. Gale-force easterlies rarely reach upper Tahsis Inlet, making it a good place to wait out a storm.

⑲ **Tahsis.** At the head of the inlet the sawmill town of Tahsis once had full facilities, but the mills closed and have been dismantled. The loss of the mills just about killed the town. Now, Tahsis is struggling but surviving. Outsiders bought the houses at bargain prices, which, at least initially, gave the economy a small boost. Through it all, the Westview Marina has remained an outstanding operation.

In town, the Tahsis Supermarket has consolidated many of the operations previously run by others. The Supermarket sells groceries, liquor and fuel. It also has a small cafe. This is a small town and grocery selection is limited. Tahsis Building Centre, a hardware store, is just north of the Supermarket. A post office is located at the other end of town, near the seaplane dock.

The Tahsis library, in the municipal building, has free Wi-Fi and an excellent view. It's a wonderful place to while away a stormy afternoon.

⑲ **Westview Marina & Lodge.** P.O. Box 248, Tahsis, BC V0P 1X0; (250) 934-7672; (800) 992-3252; info@westviewmarina.com; www.westviewmarina.com. Monitors VHF 06. The fuel dock has gasoline, diesel, lubricants, and marine parts. Mechanic available 24/7. Washrooms, showers, laundry, free Wi-Fi, small store with ice and good gift selection, licensed restaurant with patio, and the Island Attitude Coffee Café. The Café opens at 5:00 a.m. during the summer. Moorage with 15, 30 & 50 amp power and potable water. Kayak rentals and eco tours. Courtesy car available. Email your provisioning list a week ahead and they'll have it ready for you.

This marina, at the head of Tahsis Inlet, is set up to serve the summer flotilla of small sport-fishing boats. Cruisers are welcome, too, and the marina has just about anything a cruising boater might need. Reservations recommended May to September, but the marina will always try to fit you in. The restaurant has live music and steak dinners on Friday nights, June through September. Each year, we receive positive reviews from readers, praising the facilities and the treatment they receive. The marina is neat and attractive, the people helpful, and the fuel dock easy to approach.

Tsowwin Narrows. The major navigation danger in Tahsis Inlet is Tsowwin Narrows, created by the outfall from the Tsowwin River. A

CHARTS	
3675	Nootka Sound (1:40,000) Gold River (1:10,000) Princesa Channel (1:10,000)
3676	Esperanza Inlet (1:40,000) Tahsis (1:12,000)

Tahsis Inlet

WEST COAST OF VANCOUVER ISLAND

beacon marks the edge of the shoal. Pass between that beacon and another beacon on the west shore of the inlet. Remember that beacons are attached to the earth, and shoal water can extend into a channel from a beacon. Give each beacon a good offing. While we did not see much debris, Tahsis Inlet is reported to have considerable drift and deadheads, depending on logging activity. Keep a close watch on the water ahead.

Princesa Channel. Princesa Channel runs between Bodega Island and Strange Island, and connects Tahsis and Kendrick inlets. A route through Princesa Channel gets a boat out of the Tahsis Inlet chop and cuts some distance off a passage for southbound boats heading to Friendly Cove, but the Tahsis Inlet entrance to Princesa Channel is narrow and partly guarded by underwater rocks.

From Tahsis Inlet to Kendrick Inlet (east to west) the problem is the flood tide. The flood current flows northward into Tahsis Inlet, and a boat entering Princesa Channel will find a definite northward set to its course. This northward set will tend to put the boat onto a submerged rock charted about 200 feet north of the Princesa Channel light, at the east entrance to Princesa Channel. Don Douglass, in his book *Exploring Vancouver Island's West Coast*, believes the rock is closer to 100 feet from the light. Whether 100 feet or 200 feet, the rock is not far away. The goal is to wrap around the Princesa Channel light but avoid yet another charted rock south of the light, while not being set onto the rock 100 to 200 feet north of the light. Chart 3675 shows the rocks clearly. Study the chart and you will understand not only the challenge but the decisions required to meet the challenge.

We ran Princesa Channel in a stout flood current and had no problems. In our case, we ran south in Tahsis Inlet until the Princesa Channel light bore 235° magnetic, then turned toward the light. We kept the light on our nose (we had to crab to make good our course) until the light was close aboard, then laid off to starboard to give the light 50 feet of clearance, and entered the channel. The key was to be aware of the rock 100 to 200 feet north of the light and keep our course south of that rock. Once past the light we held a mid-channel course and waltzed on through. [*Hale*]

Bodega Cove. Douglass calls this previously unnamed anchorage "Bodega Cove" and we see no reason to argue. Bodega Cove lies at the head of Kendrick Inlet, between Nootka Island and Bodega Island. The area has been logged, so the scenery is not that of primeval forest. Protection is excellent, however, and the shores are accessible. A reef extends from the Nootka Island side of the entrance. Favor the eastern, Bodega Island, side. The recommended approach is to divide the entry channel in half, then split the eastern, Bodega Island, portion in half again (in other words, three-quarters of the way toward the eastern shore), and run down that line.

A large log dump and booming ground is on Nootka Island near the head of Kendrick Inlet. When it's in operation, you can watch huge machines dumping piles of logs into the water.

The Island Attitude Coffee Café at Westview Marina.

It is a short walk from Friendly Cove to this beautiful beach overlooking Nootka Sound.

WEST COAST OF VANCOUVER ISLAND

NOOTKA SOUND

Nootka Sound is where European influence in the Northwest began. Although Captain Cook first landed at Resolution Cove in 1778, it was at Friendly Cove that Captain Meares built the *Northwest America*, 48 feet on deck, the first ship ever built on the west coast, and launched it in 1788.

The long arms (Muchalat Inlet and Tlupana Inlet) that reach out from Nootka Sound have few anchorages, and they tend to be deep. The Port of Gold River is at the head of Muchalat Inlet. The town of Gold River is 9 miles from the dock. Trailerable boats, most of them here for salmon fishing in Nootka Sound, are launched at Gold River.

⑳ **Critter Cove.** Critter Cove is the name given by Cameron Forbes to this previously unnamed spot about 1 mile south of Argonaut Point on Tlupana Inlet. Cameron has established a sportfishing resort in the cove and named it after his nickname of "Critter," when he played hockey. The inner cove is no longer suitable for anchoring.

⑳ **Critter Cove Marina.** P.O. Box 1118, Gold River, BC V0P 1G0; (250) 412-6029; info@crittercove.com; www.crittercove.com. Fuel dock carries mid-grade gasoline, oil, ice, bait, coffee, convenience food, fishing tackle, and ocean-themed pottery. Fuel dock hours are 10:00 a.m. to 6:00 p.m. in June, and 8:00 a.m. to 9:00 p.m. in July and August. Moorage, cabins, lodge rooms, suites, restaurant, showers, washrooms. No power or water on the docks. Showers are for overnight guests only.

Cameron Forbes, one of the nicest guys you'll meet, has quite a sportfishing camp here. Most of Critter Cove is on floats, including the licensed restaurant and some of the accommodations. The Critter Cove Cafe is open for breakfast, lunch and dinner. Boaters who are not overnight guests are welcome at the cafe. There are also self-contained beach cottages on the land adjacent to and behind the floating portion of the resort. Most of the boats at Critter Cove are trailered into Gold River, where they are launched. They do have room for a few visiting cruisers.

Nootka Sound Resort. (877) 337-5464; VHF 06 info@nootkamarineadventures.com; www.nootkamarineadventures.com. Call ahead to check moorage availability. Moorage, power, water, restaurant, lodging, fishing charters. Located in Galiano Bay.

Hisnit Inlet. Hisnit Inlet extends north from Tlupana Inlet. Hisnit is one of the few anchorages in Nootka Sound that is well-protected, shallow enough for convenient anchoring, and large enough for a number of boats. Two submerged rocks lie almost mid-channel a short distance into Hisnit Inlet. Do not be deceived by the open and safe appearance of the inlet as you arrive or depart. Favor the south shore.

Extensive clear cutting mars the hills. In 2013, logging was underway high on the hills and noise filtered into the anchorage. Still, the view of mountains up the stream at the head of the inlet is stunning. A marble quarry once operated on the east shore. Piles of white marble are visible on the beach and in the nearby forest. The quarry itself is buried under fallen trees and is difficult (and dangerous) to locate. Near the head of the inlet on the same east shore is a large rock shaped like a human head.

Anchorage at the head of the inlet is in 40 to 60 feet. It is open but protected. The shoreline is accessible.

㉑ **Moutcha Bay Resort.** (877) 337-5464; info@nootkamarineadventures.com; www.moutchabay.com. Newly constructed Moutcha Bay Resort is a full service marina, with moorage to 150 feet, fuel dock with gasoline, diesel and propane, water, 15 & 30 amp power, pumpout, Wi-Fi, and a concrete launch ramp. Washrooms and showers are at the top of the docks. The docks are brand new, beautifully built, wide and stable. A small store carries limited groceries, gift items, and ice.

The restaurant is good and features local seafood, meat, and produce. Fishing charters, guided and unguided, are available on a fleet of rental boats. Fish processing and packing is offered. Yurts, chalets, and campsites can be rented. The staff is helpful and courteous. This is a luxury resort with facilities to match.

Ewin Inlet. Ewin Inlet indents the south side of Bligh Island some 3 miles, with no anchorages until the head is reached. The cove to the west at the head of the inlet is quite protected and has depths of 30 to 40 feet. "We rounded the little islet in the cove at low tide, about 100 feet off, and the depth sounder abruptly but briefly showed a depth of 15 feet. We suspect it found an uncharted rock." [*Hale*]

Resolution Cove. Historic Resolution Cove is on Bligh Island, near the south end of Clerke Peninsula. In March, 1778, Captain Cook anchored his two ships there and found and fitted a new foremast for the *Resolution*. A flagpole and plaques commemorating Cook's visit have been placed on a knoll above the cove. Anchor in 40 to 50 feet, either with a stern-tie to shore or enough room to swing. You'll probably make your visit a short one. Swells from the ocean wrap around the Clerke Peninsula into the cove.

Santa Gertrudis Cove. The western cove in Santa Gertrudis Cove is an excellent anchorage: cozy, good holding, protected. As you enter you will see an island in the northern cove. A submerged rock extends from that island a considerable distance toward the south shore, farther than we expected. Be sure to identify this rock and give it room as you favor the south shore. There is sufficient room to pass between this rock and the drying rock shown off the south shore on the chart. The north cove of Santa Gertrudis Cove, around the island, is foul and tight.

㉒ **Friendly Cove.** Friendly Cove is where Captains Vancouver and Quadra met in 1792 and attempted to negotiate the final details of the Nootka Convention of 1790, in which Spain relinquished to England all its claims to Northwest lands. Hulsizer, in her book *Voyages to Windward*, gives an interesting and succinct explanation of the complicated events in Friendly Cove that brought Spain and Great Britain to the brink of war before they worked out their differences in the Nootka Convention.

Friendly Cove is shallow and fairly protected from typical summertime winds, with good anchoring for four or five boats on a sand bottom. Outflow winds can make Friendly Cove bumpy. Nearly all the land ashore belongs to the Mowachaht Band, and a fee ($12 per person, no credit cards) must be paid for landing. The band has summertime staff on hand who monitor VHF 66A and collect the fee. The landing fee is the same, whether you dinghy in from an anchored boat or tie up at the wharf and floats on the west side of the bay.

When you anchor, be aware that the *Uchuck III* delivers tourists and freight to the dock regularly. To watch the *Uchuck* wind its way through anchored boats is awe-inspiring—and terrifying if you're on one of the boats.

A trail runs through campgrounds and above the ocean beach. It passes the Native graveyard and leads to a lake that's good for swimming. Six rental cabins, small and rustic, are just beyond the lake. The spired Catholic

Moutcha Bay Resort's lodge is first class.

2018 WAGGONER CRUISING GUIDE

WEST COAST OF VANCOUVER ISLAND   *See Area Map Page 374 - Maps Not for Navigation*

BOARDWALK PLANKS BEING REPLACED AT HOT SPRINGS COVE BC

Boardwalk at Hot Springs Cove is being rebuilt.
In the fall of 2018, BC Provincial Parks will begin a project to replace and widen the failing boardwalk at Hot Springs Cove. Located on the West side of Vancouver Island, this remote park site was originally accessible only by boat. Today, a number of Tofino based tour operators bring large numbers of visitors to this park by seaplane and high-speed tour boat. The 2 km (1 ¼ mile) boardwalk, from Maquinna Marine Park dock to the hot springs, has hundreds of individually carved planks commemorating boaters' visits to the park and hot springs. The long history of carved boardwalk planks holds an often surprisingly artistic dated chronology of boat names, dates, and trivia.

History of Carved Planks at Hot Springs Cove
A long time ago, when boats were wood or steel, boaters came to enjoy the hot springs at Hot Springs Cove. The 2 km trail from the anchorage area to the hot springs was a rustic muddy trek. Locals and visiting boaters over time constructed the first boardwalk path by voluntarily bringing individual planks to add to the growing boardwalk. Reportedly, the very first planks were hand-split from sections of logs on-site. Boat names, dates, and messages were inscribed on the planks; and thusly, the record of this unique boardwalk was created.

After a number of years — probably about the time the first fiberglass boats appeared — the original boardwalk and planks needed to be replaced. The boardwalk was rebuilt with all new 2x6 planks and the history of the first planks went with it. However, the tradition of carved planks with boat names didn't die; and very soon after the construction of the new boardwalk, carved boat names and dates began to appear once again.

It's okay to Carve the Planks – But Don't Pick the Flowers
In the more recent past, BC Parks facilitated carved boardwalk planks. BC parks had been providing plank dimensions for those who wanted to pre-carve a plank and leave with park rangers for later installation. To make it even easier, BC Parks sold bare planks which you could carve and leave with them for installation. This is one of those rare instances where it was okay to leave your mark at a park.

As access by seaplanes and tour boats brought increasing numbers of vistors, carved planks appeared from other than boaters. In 2012, a romantic suitor had a carved plank placed on the boardwalk that read "Clara, Will you marry me?" For those who immediately ask the question; it is reported that Clara said "yes."

Where are the artfully carved planks going?
We at Waggoner Guide learned of the boardwalk replacement project during the summer of 2017 and at that time, the future plans for individually carved planks was undetermined. Following the suggestion of the Waggoner Guide team, BC Parks intends to consolidate the best planks and re-purpose them in a special feature within the park. Plans include interpretive signage capturing the history of the carved planks.

Will the Carved Plank Tradition Live-On?
The answer is, NO. Today's safety and construction standards preclude future carvings along the boardwalk. BC Parks expresses their appreciation and thanks the public for participating in the past boardwalk program. The Waggoner Guide team is appreciative that BC Parks is preserving this piece of northwest boating history.

Visitors will continue to have access to the park and hot springs during construction.

- Leonard and Lorena Landon, Managing Editors

---

church is filled with Native carvings, and has two marvelous stained glass windows. They depict the transfer of authority over the area from Spain to England in 1792, and were a gift from the government of Spain.

A carved welcome figure stands on the far shore of the cove, facing the open sea.

㉒ **Nootka Light Station.** You can walk from the Friendly Cove beach to the Nootka Light Station on San Rafael Island. A well-maintained series of stairs leads up from the beach to the light station. Once at the station, be sure to sign the guest book.

Nootka is a repeater station for Prince Rupert Coast Guard radio, and has considerable radio equipment. Every three hours from early morning until nightfall, the Nootka station reports weather conditions for the marine weather broadcast, including estimated wind strength and sea conditions offshore.

Thanks to the miracle of the Fresnel lens, the light uses only a 35-watt LED bulb to cast a beam that can be seen for 15 miles.

The Nootka Light Station and its light keepers are powerful arguments for retaining manned light stations along the coast. They are invaluable for timely and accurate weather information, and for communication in areas that

may not have good cell phone coverage. The lightkeepers monitor VHF channel 82. We are told that many of the lightkeepers maintain an open Wi-Fi signal for visiting boaters.

Estevan Point. Estevan Point is the southwest corner of Hesquiat Peninsula, another of the headlands where winds and seas build and become confused. Estevan Point can be ugly in a storm, but in more settled conditions does not present the challenge found at Cape Cook or Cape Scott. In fog, the problem with Estevan Point is its low, flat terrain, which makes its shoreline a poor target for radar. The rocks more than a mile offshore make Estevan Point unforgiving for the navigator who is off-course.

From Nootka Sound, a rounding of Estevan Point first must clear Escalante Rocks and Perez Rocks, both of them on the west side of Hesquiat Peninsula. Unfortunately for the navigator, no single chart shows all of Estevan Point from Nootka Sound to Hesquiat Bay in large scale. You will be forced to plot your course on small scale Chart 3603, which doesn't give much close-in detail. Once at Estevan Point, you can use Chart 3674 to continue to Hot Springs Cove.

Especially with the lack of a single good large scale chart for the west side of Hesquiat Peninsula, the general advice is to give Estevan

Point "lots of room." Give Escalante Rocks and Perez Rocks lots of room, too. This applies when heading north as well.

Weather information: The Estevan Point lighthouse provides updated wind, sea, and atmospheric conditions every three hours. Listen to the continuous marine broadcast for the latest weather information.

Hesquiat Harbour. Hesquiat Harbour is protected from westerly winds, and Hesquiat Bar, 24 feet deep, knocks down the Pacific swell. Beware the bar in a southeasterly; storm seas can break over it. Rae Basin is a well-protected anchorage in the northeast corner of Hesquiat

CHARTS	
3603	Ucluelet Inlet to Nootka Sound (1:150,000)
3674	Clayoquot Sound, Millar Channel to Estevan Point (1:40,000) Hayden Passage (1:20,000) Hot Springs Cove (1:20,000) Marktosis (1:10,000)
3675	Nootka Sound (1:40,000) Gold River (1:10,000) Princesa Channel (1:10,000)

Reference Only – Not for Navigation   WEST COAST OF VANCOUVER ISLAND

Hot Springs Cove

Harbour. From there you can take the dinghy to Cougar Annie's Garden for an interesting tour. Tours are arranged through the Boat Basin Foundation; email abby@ecotrust.ca a couple of days before your arrival. Admission is charged, to pay for the restoration and ongoing research there. We're told the visit is well worth the cost.

Hot Springs Cove Area. Hot Springs Cove is adjacent to Sydney Inlet, the northern entrance to Clayoquot Sound. Depending on the points of departure and arrival and the exact course chosen, the distance from Nootka Sound around Estevan Point, past Hesquiat Peninsula, and east to Hot Springs Cove, is approximately 30 to 31 miles. When traveling south, once you are past Chief Matlahaw Point, you can duck into the lee of Hesquiat Peninsula to avoid the worst of the ocean swells.

㉓ **Hot Springs Cove.** www.env.gov.bc.ca/bcparks/explore/parkpgs/maquinna/. Hot Springs Cove is one of the reasons cruising boats do the West Coast. The challenge of getting to Hot Springs is sufficient to make the reward—a soothing bath in comforting water (no soap, please)—worth the entire trip. In earlier times most visitors came the hard way, up from Barkley Sound or down from Cape Scott. Now tour boats, float planes, and even helicopters carrying visitors who have arrived without effort at Tofino, visit Hot Springs Cove many times a day. An hour by high-speed boat and they are there.

The cove is easy to enter. Chart 3674 shows that the mouth is open and the channel free of dangers. The marine park public dock is approximately 1.7 miles farther into the cove from the hot springs themselves. You can anchor in 24 feet, or boats less than 12 meters (40 feet) can tie to the BC Parks dock. Moorage on the dock is $2.00/meter; self-registration and fee payment on shore at the park Information Shelter.

The B&B boat Innchanter, with attached dinghy floats, is normally anchored nearby and may have space for visiting boaters for dinner or breakfast. Call Shaun on the Innchanter at (250) 670-1149.

A 1.2-mile walk along a well-maintained boardwalk and path leads to the hot springs. A $3 per person park fee is payable at a dropbox

2018 WAGGONER CRUISING GUIDE

ESTEBAN JOSE MARTINEZ (1742-1798) AND THE NOOTKA CRISIS

The Spanish had claimed the Pacific Northwest region under the 1774 explorations of Juan Perez and the subsequent explorations of Jose Maria Narvaez and Bodega y Quadra. The Russian colonization in Alaska was seen as a threat by Spain who wanted to maintain their claims in the region. In 1789 the Viceroy of New Spain, headquartered in San Blas, instructed Esteban Jose Martinez to build a settlement and fort at Nootka Sound on the west coast of Vancouver Island. The settlement included houses, a hospital, and Fort San Miguel. A number of fur trading vessels, both British and American, arrived in Nootka Sound that same summer of 1789. The Spanish laid claim to the area and issued warnings to ships from other countries; the American ships departed, but by the end of the summer, Martinez had seized several British ships and arrested their crews. These events led to the 'Nootka Crisis,' or conflict between Spain and Great Britain. Due to these actions, Martinez lost his position under the new Viceroy, Juan Vicente de Guemes. In 1790, Francisco de Eliza was sent to reoccupy Nootka Sound and war was averted by a series of meetings or conventions. In 1791 it was agreed that the Northwest Coast would be open to traders of both Britain and Spain but the details were yet to be worked out; in the meantime, Spain retained control of Nootka Sound and maintained the fort at Friendly Cove. In 1792, Bodega y Quadra and George Vancouver met at Friendly Cove in Nootka Sound to work out the details of an agreement. Although friendly with each other, they could not reach terms they both agreed upon as representatives of their country. By 1793, Britain and Spain had become allies in a war against France and the 'Nootka Crisis' had become less important. The details of the Nootka Convention were worked out in which Spain relinquished to England all its claims to Northwest lands. Today, visitors to Nootka Sound can imagine the scene that took place here in 1792 as depicted on one of the stained-glass windows in the church at Friendly Cove.

---

near the head of the dock. A park attendant lives in the cabin next to the public dock.

In the past, visiting craft had a tradition of bringing a plank to add to the boardwalk. On the plank would be carved the name of the boat and the year of the visit. Many of the planks showed remarkable artistic talent. This practice has been discontinued by the parks department.

A multi-year project to replace and widen the boardwalk (from the dock to the hot springs) is slated to begin in 2018. Access to the hot springs will be open during construction.

The hike through the rainforest to the hot springs is easy and beautiful. Toilets are available at the end. The modest will find a pleasant changing room in which clothes may be doffed and a bathing suit put on. Traditionalists will lament that the hot springs no longer can be enjoyed in the old way, sans bathing suit. The place is popular.

Although a constant stream of bathers hike the trail and soak in the springs during the day, savvy boaters know that if they come before 9:00 a.m. or after 6:00 p.m., they'll share the springs only with other boaters.

The kids from the village across the cove play at Hot Springs, in part (as Contributing Editor Kincaid suggests) to further their study of anatomy, and in part to show off for the *touristas*. The braver lads dive off the rocks into the surf. It's not Acapulco, but it's not bad.

Watch your belongings. We lost a towel.

Hot Springs has campsites, often used by kayakers. During an earlier visit, a kayak-borne fisherman brought several catches to the dock and gave them away. They included rockfish, sea bass and coho salmon. He went out to the rocks just outside the cove, made a pass, and came back with his catch. Each time his line went in the water it came up with a fish.

A cell phone tower in the Native village across from the park now provides four to five bars of cell phone service (Telus).

CLAYOQUOT SOUND

Clayoquot Sound is a series of inlets and passages with entrances at both its north and south ends. By traveling inside Clayoquot Sound you can explore many coves and anchorages, and avoid 20 miles of ocean swells. Tofino is the only major town, although fuel and some groceries are available at Ahousat.

Much of Clayoquot Sound is within the traditional territory of the Ahousaht First Nation, who have established a Stewardship Guardian Program. First Nation representatives of the Ahousaht Stewardship Program collect donation fees at various anchorages within the Clayoquot Sound in support of their programs which include care for beaches and trails, search and rescue support, management and cultural interpretation for visitor access, and training in first aid. Guardians monitor VHF channel 65A and may be contacted if you are in need of support. For more information call Ahousaht Stewardship Operations at (250) 731-6957.

Sydney Inlet. Sydney Inlet is the northern entrance to Clayoquot Sound. It is adjacent to Hot Springs Cove and leads approximately 11 miles into the mountains of Vancouver Island, with several good anchorages. Rounding Sharp Point after leaving Hot Springs Cove, be aware of two charted but unmarked off-lying rocks. The first is fairly close to Sharp Point and easy to avoid. The second is about 0.2 mile off. Most boats will choose to pass between the two rocks. Be sure you know where you are. Once in Sydney Inlet, the fairway is open and unencumbered. Reader Don Thain reports that sea otters are now well established in Sydney Inlet and that crabbing is poorer where the sea otters have colonized.

Sydney Inlet Unnamed Cove. This is the cove that lies behind the 65-meter island about 0.5 mile south of Hootla-Kootla Bay, at latitude 49°21.85'N on the east shore of Sydney Inlet. (Douglass, in both editions of *Exploring Vancouver Island's West Coast*, mistakenly calls this cove Hootla-Kootla, but the chart leaves it unnamed and calls the next cove to the north Hootla-Kootla.) Enter from the south. You'll see a beautiful white beach. Although the water is a little shallow near the beach, it's the prettiest spot in the cove. You could also anchor at the north end of the cove, behind the 65-meter-high island. Do not attempt to enter the cove at the north end. It is foul.

Young Bay. Young Bay, on the east side of Sydney Inlet, is a lovely place to anchor, although a little deep until you get close to shore. The middle is 50 to 60 feet deep, but along the shore it's easy to find 35- to 40-foot depths. On the south shore a stream connects with Cecilia Lake, one-half mile away. A rough trail leads up the stream to the lake. Trout fishing at the lake is reported to be good. A copper mine and a pilchard reduction plant both operated here in the past. Only a few concrete platforms and pieces of machinery remain.

Enter Young Bay right down the middle, to avoid shoals that extend from either side. Once inside you will see a small islet with trees on it. Pass to the south of that islet.

CHARTS	
3673	Clayoquot Sound, Tofino Inlet to Millar Channel (1:40,000)
3674	Clayoquot Sound, Millar Channel to Estevan Point (1:40,000) Hayden Passage (1:20,000) Hot Springs Cove (1:20,000) Marktosis (1:10,000)
3685	Tofino (1:20,000)

Clayoquot Sound

Bottleneck Bay (Coyote Cove). This is an otherwise unnamed bay that cruising guide author Don Watmough fell in love with. Bottleneck Bay is located just north of Young Bay, east of Adventure Point. The entrance is narrow but deep. Inside, the high, treed hills make the feeling of seclusion complete. Easy anchoring in 30 feet.

Holmes Inlet Nook. Occupied now by aquaculture and a floathouse and dock with a very possessive dog. No longer an anchorage.

Hootla-Kootla Bay. Hootla-Kootla Bay is located about 0.25 mile north of the 65-meter-high island on the east shore of Sydney Inlet, approximately 1.6 miles from the mouth of the inlet. This cove is known locally as Baseball Bay, but the chart shows it as Hootla-Kootla Bay. The entrance is shallow, and is partly blocked by a charted rock just south of mid-channel. Divide the channel north of the rock in half, and enter the northern half "mid-channel." "Least depth on the depth sounder was 12.5 feet near the bottom of a 3.6-foot low tide at Tofino. Anchorage is good once inside." [*Hale*]

Riley Cove. Riley Cove is just east of Starling Point, on the northwest tip of Flores Island. It may not be the best choice for an anchorage. The cove is open and uninteresting, and a little deep for anchoring until close to the head. At the head, Riley Cove is divided into two smaller coves; the cove to the west has a sandy beach. A rock, not shown on the chart, is just off the point that separates the two coves. A shoal extends from the east shore near the entrance of Riley Cove. Favor the west shore.

Steamer Cove. Steamer Cove is on the north side of Flores Island, behind George Island. The small cove at the southwest corner of Steamer Cove is well protected and has easy anchoring depths. Unfortunately, the hillsides around the anchorage have been logged clean, right down to the water, so the outlook is uninteresting. If you're looking for shelter in a storm, the outlook would be irrelevant. In that case Steamer Cove would be excellent.

Lennard Island Lighthouse along the west coast of Vancouver Island. Photo by John Forde, The Whale Centre.

WEST COAST OF VANCOUVER ISLAND

Sulphur Passage requires careful navigation for a safe transit.

㉔ **Bacchante Bay.** Bacchante Bay, at the east end of Shelter Inlet, is a dramatic anchorage, with steep cliffs on both sides, an inviting grassy meadow at the head and a snow-capped mountain beyond. The narrow, shallow entrance is hidden until you are close. Bacchante Bay is part of Strathcona Provincial Park.

Bacchante Bay has ample room to anchor in 40 to 50 feet. Holding is excellent. If you run to the head of the bay, watch for abrupt shoaling off the meadow. At high tide explore Watta Creek by dinghy.

Readers Mike and Sandy Cecka report fouling their anchor in Bacchante Bay. They anchored on the west side of the bay, below steep cliffs. We've had no problem anchoring in the middle of the bay.

Hayden Passage. Hayden Passage is on the west side of Obstruction Island, and connects Shelter Inlet with Millar Channel. Tidal current predictions are shown with Hayden Passage as a secondary station based on Tofino in the Tide and Current Tables, Vol. 6 and Ports and Passes. The flood sets southeast; the ebb, northwest. Be sure to pass west of the red daymarker beacons (Red, Right, Returning).

Because the flood currents meet at Hayden Passage, you may find that the currents don't behave as predicted. The cautious passage would be at slack water. If transiting sometime other than slack water, maintain a constant watch for current set, and crab as needed to stay in the channel.

Sulphur Passage. Sulphur Passage connects Shelter Inlet and Millar Channel on the east side of Obstruction Island and is far more tortuous than Hayden Passage. The northern portion of Sulphur Passage is the tricky part. There, the channels twist and turn and are bounded by submerged rocks. Don Douglass ran Sulphur Passage along the east side of the 38-meter island in the northern portion, and reported it to be a period of "high anxiety."

With Douglass' experience in mind, we ran a dogleg course from north to south on the west side of the 38-meter island. We found it to be straightforward—albeit with careful planning and cooperation between navigator and helmsman. For reference, the course is described here. (Following this course on Chart 3674 will be helpful. The directions North, South, East and West in this description are true, not magnetic.)

Our course leaves Belcher Point close to port and continues to the south corner of the charted fish farm. Cross to a point of land northeast of a 290-foot hill on the west shore. Turn south again and favor the west shore until past the 38-meter island and the tiny islet south of it. Then turn east, point the bow at the mouth of a creek that enters on the eastern shore. Once in the middle, and approximately due south of the 38-meter island's western tip, turn south once more and motor through. While other courses probably would be safe, this course has the advantage of using easily-identified landmarks (the fish farm, the point under the high hill, the stream outlet, the tip of an islet) either as turning points or as points to aim for. [*Hale*]

Friendly Dolphin Cove. Friendly Dolphin is Douglass' name for the cove that indents Obstruction Island, just inside the south entrance to Sulphur Passage. The cove is pretty, private and appealing. Anchor near the head in 40 to 50 feet, probably with a stern-tie ashore to control swinging. Dave Letson, a former wharfinger at Hot Springs Cove, said he thought this cove was "too deep and too buggy."

Shark Creek. 49°23.95'N/126°04.00'W. "This is a kayakers' secret: a beautiful 70-foot-high waterfall in a chimney, accessible at high tide by dinghy only. It is located in Millar Channel, just north of Atleo River. Anchor north of the small island and dinghy in. Best in late afternoon when sunlight makes a rainbow on the rocks behind the falls." [*Hulsizer*]

Matilda Inlet indents the southeast corner of Flores Island and is bordered on the east by McNeil Peninsula. Anchorage is possible near the head of Matilda Inlet. From the anchorage, a warm springs in Gibson Marine Park can be visited (best at high tide; at low tide it's a muddy hike) or a trek made to the beach. Don Watmough describes the area in fond detail. The Native community of Marktosis is on McNeil Peninsula. Across the inlet and a short distance north are the store and fuel dock of Ahousat.

㉕ **Ahousat.** General Delivery, Ahousat, BC V0R 1A0; (250) 670-9575. Ahousat, with its general store, fuel dock, cafe, and marine ways, is on the west shore of Matilda Inlet, at the southeast corner of Flores Island. Gasoline, diesel and stove oil at the fuel dock, washrooms, 15 amp power, showers and laundry, haulout to 40 feet. Potable water, pay phone, post office, and motel rooms are available. The store is a rough-and-ready place, with a cougar head on the wall, but with luck, it may have what you need: groceries, miscellaneous hardware and marine supplies. No charts or liquor.

Example of a route through Sulphur Passage

You can visit the large red boathouse near the main public dock and see Native canoes in various stages of restoration.

Marktosis. Marktosis is the Native village across Matilda Inlet from Ahousat. Correspondents Steve and Elsie Hulsizer report that the village has a cafe and a small Native arts shop. Permits for the Wild Side Trail can be purchased there; the trail is mostly boardwalk to White Sand Cove. They suggest that you anchor south of Ahousat in the bay near the "slightly warm" springs, and take the dinghy back to the village. Leave the dinghy at the first pier on the right as you enter, and touch base with the band office before exploring further. The Hulsizers found several Native canoes, ranging from new to under restoration, in the old boat shed on the far side of the village.

Gibson Marine Park. Gibson Marine Park is at the head of Matilda Inlet, past Ahousat. At one time, Hugh Clarke, at the Ahousat General Store, hacked out a trail from the head of the inlet to the hot springs. Boots are necessary on the trail, which transits some boggy areas. Clarke recommends going in at half tide on a rising tide, to avoid tramping across the mud flats. Correspondent Gil Flanagan tells us that you can hike for many miles on the ocean beach to the west. The only problem, Flanagan says, are bands of gravel that make barefoot walking uncomfortable. He adds that the beach is popular with kayakers and tourists from Tofino. The park requests that dogs are kept out of the park as there have been incidents of wolves killing the dogs.

Herbert Inlet. The run up Herbert Inlet is even more spectacular than many other inlets along the coast. High mountains and rock walls line the shores. Deep alpine river valleys lead away into the mountains. Snowcapped peaks can be seen in the distance.

West Whitepine Cove. Although unnamed, both Watmough and Douglass call this delightful anchorage West Whitepine Cove, and we shall do the same. West Whitepine Cove lies to the west of Whitepine Cove, near the mouth of Herbert Inlet. Entry to the inner bay is along the south side of the 67-meter island. We entered slowly, strongly favoring this island. Rocks were visible underwater and easily skirted. Once inside, the cove is lovely and protected. Bears are reported to frequent the south shore.

A charted rock is in the cove, off the tip of the little peninsula that extends southeast from the 94-meter island. When anchoring, stay away from it.

Gibson Cove. Gibson Cove indents the west side of Herbert Inlet, about 5 miles north of Whitepine Cove. Since Gibson Cove is not on the way to anyplace else, we suspect it sees few visitors. Those who do visit are in for a treat. Gibson Cove is beautiful, but a little deep for anchoring. Although it appears protected, strong afternoon westerlies can bring wind and waves.

Ahousat has a general store, café, fuel and haulout.

Quait Bay. Quait Bay is located on the east shore of Cypress Bay. With its 35-foot depths, anchoring is good just about anywhere. The most popular spot, though, is in the little cove in the east corner, in about 10 feet.

A submerged concrete structure lies in the mouth of the two nooks at the back of this cove at 49°16.603'N/125°50.843'W. A reader reports the structure dries at 2 feet. Enter Quait Bay on the northwest side of the 45-meter island, favoring the northwest shore. The chart makes the course clear. In 2016 the large floating lodge building just inside the entrance was closed but occupied by a caretaker. For a peek at what life is like for Clayoquot Sound's year-round residents, take your dinghy out the east entrance of Quait Bay to the next unnamed cove to the east and visit Wayne Adams and Catherine King in their floating garden on their magenta and turquoise floating home. Wayne and Catherine must hold the record for interviews and feature articles about Clayoquot Sound residents.

Matlset Narrows. Matlset Narrows runs to a maximum of 4 knots on spring tides. The flood sets east. Sailing Directions warns of strong tide-rips in the vicinity of the Maltby Islets at the east end of the narrows. We ran the narrows against a west-flowing ebb. We saw definite current activity, but had no problem. We suspect any tide-rips would be on a flood.

Calmus Passage to Heynen Channel. The route from Millar Channel to Heynen Channel via Calmus Passage and Maurus Channel is the beginning of shallower water. The channels are well marked by buoys and beacons but the navigator must stay alert, keep an eye on the depth sounder, and know the vessel's position at all times. Large-scale Chart 3685 is extremely helpful.

Cell phones: In 2013, on our counter-clockwise circumnavigation of Vancouver Island, Calmus Passage was the first place with cell phone reception since leaving Quatsino Sound.

Lemmens Inlet. Lemmens Inlet indents Meares Island, just a few miles from the town of Tofino. Be sure to use large scale Chart 3685 while navigating around Tofino and into Lemmens Inlet. The entry channel to the inlet is amply deep, but bordered by drying flats. Once inside, you have your choice of three possible anchorages—although float homes now are moored in all of Lemmens Inlet's coves, so anchoring may be a challenge.

Adventure Cove. Adventure Cove, where Capt. Robert Gray built the small schooner *Adventure* in 1792, is filled with history. The beach is easy to land on. While walking in the woods we could almost feel the presence of Gray's Fort Defiance and the shipbuilding activity. Though the area is now overgrown with large trees, some say you can feel as though *something went on here*. Watmough and Douglass describe the history well. Hulsizer discusses it more thoroughly in *Voyages to Windward*. Unfortunately, a floathouse and a fish farm take up most of the cove, leaving little room for anchoring. Discarded fish farming equipment on the beach makes beach access challenging. A reader tells us an uncharted rock lies SSW of the island in the mouth of Adventure Cove.

Lemmens Northwest Cove. Lemmens Northwest Cove is Douglass' name for this anchorage in the northwest corner of Lemmens Inlet. It is identified on the chart by the 38-meter island and the fish pens in the mouth. Drying rocks obstruct the entrance. Locate them and then run midway between the rocks and the 38-meter island. Once inside, you'll find good anchoring depths and adequate protection. We were not charmed by the cove, however.

Gods Pocket. Gods Pocket is the cove northwest of Lagoon Island, on the west side of Lemmens Inlet. Protection is good, with anchorage in 25 to 30 feet. Two very nice float homes occupy the cove, however. You'll be anchoring in their front yards.

Fortune Channel. Fortune Channel connects Tofino Channel with Matlset Narrows, which in turn connects with the waters of upper and western Clayoquot Sound. In Fortune Channel you can choose from three good anchorages: Windy Bay, Heelboom Bay and Mosquito Harbour. Chances are, you won't see much boat traffic in this area.

WEST COAST OF VANCOUVER ISLAND

See Area Map Page 381 - Maps Not for Navigation

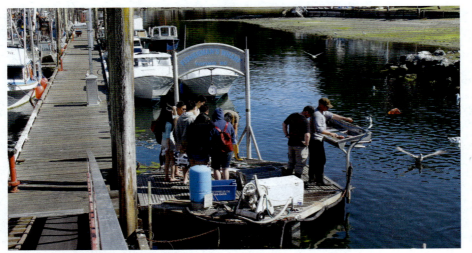

Fishing is a popular pastime in Tofino.

Mosquito Harbour. Although not as scenic and cozy as Heelboom Bay, Mosquito Harbour is big and open and easily entered. Anchor in 20 feet behind the Blackberry Islets. Approach on either side of the Wood Islets, but from Fortune Channel you'll probably approach by way of Plover Point or Dark Island. Kelp marks the rocks off the north end of Dark Island. Note the location of Hankin Rock. We would trend toward Plover Point before turning to enter Mosquito Harbour.

Heelboom Bay. Heelboom Bay, located near the south end of Fortune Channel, is a good anchorage, surrounded by lush evergreen forests. We found outstanding holding in 35 feet. This Bay was the site of a major protest against logging in Clayoquot Sound and is considered almost sacred by some residents. Approaching, favor the east shore and stay well clear of rocks off the western shore. One of these rocks is considerably detached from the shoreline. Chart 3685 helps understanding.

Windy Bay. Windy Bay is beautiful. The south shore is heavily forested, and the north shore is sheer rock wall. Westerly winds accelerate over the saddle at the head of the bay, but they have no fetch to build up seas. With 15 knots of wind outside Windy Bay, we had gusts to 30 knots inside. Anchor in 30 to 35 feet with excellent holding.

Browning Passage and Tsapee Narrows. Rocks abound and shoals threaten. The larger scale Chart 3685 will show you the way. If you are coming from Heynen Channel or Lemmens Inlet, the course will be clear: Pass west of Morpheus Island and east of Buoy *Y35*, and continue down Browning Passage and through Tsapee Narrows. Note that currents on springs can run to 5 knots near Morpheus Island and 4 knots at the narrows. Go slowly. Look ahead and identify all buoys, islands and visible rocks well in advance. Keep a close reference between your charts and your navigation electronics. Done this way, the passage should not be difficult.

If you are departing Tofino, leave Buoy *Y29*, opposite the 4th Street dock, to starboard, and run toward Arnet Island until you can safely turn to run south, along the west side of Riley Island. Favor Riley Island to pass clear of the rocks shown on the chart. Once south of Riley Island you are in Browning Passage.

TOFINO INLET

Not a lot of boat traffic here and only a few attractive anchorages.

Island Cove. Island Cove is easy to enter around either side of Ocayu Island. Study the chart to avoid the rocks that lie off the southwest shore of the approach. Unfortunately, the hillsides surrounding Island Cove have been logged down to the water's edge and the cove isn't very pretty. Anchor in 40 to 50 feet, close to the west shore.

Gunner Inlet. It's tricky to get into the inlet and not very scenic when you make it. Approach favoring the east shore and use a small low islet with a distinctive white top as your leading mark. Make an S-turn around the islet and follow the chart in.

Tranquilito Cove. Tranquilito Cove is the name Douglass gave this unnamed cove on the east side of Tranquil Inlet, near the head. This cove is secluded and beautiful. The rock wall on the north side has been strikingly sculpted by glaciers. Favor the northern side of the entry to avoid a shoal that extends from the point of land on the south side. Anchor in 20 feet.

Cannery Bay. Cannery Bay, at the mouth of the Kennedy River, is easy to get into and despite its flat terrain is rather pretty. Consider the nook just to port as you enter. Anchor in 15 to 20 feet.

Kennedy Cove. Kennedy Cove is easy to enter by favoring the 68-meter island. Anchor wherever you like in 15 to 30 feet. It's a pretty spot.

㉖ **Tofino.** If you come from up-island, Tofino will be your first major town since Port McNeill or Port Hardy, and it's more vibrant than either of them. During the summer season, Tofino's bustle and busyness may surprise you. After growing accustomed to the slower life up-island, Tofino, with its commerce, tourists, fast traffic and loud engines, can cause culture shock. Welcome to the city.

As long as you're in the city you might as well spend some money. You can choose from several good restaurants, the kind that serve meals without french fries. Gift shops and galleries—at last!—are available for mementos and

Tofino

384   www.WaggonerGuide.com

See Area Map Page 381 - Maps Not for Navigation   WEST COAST OF VANCOUVER ISLAND

Method Marine Supply is Tofino's fuel dock and marine supply source.

presents. The Co-op store, close to the waterfront, is a complete supermarket and will deliver if asked. The Co-op also carries clothes. Showers are available at the 4th Street Dock and at the laundromat at 4th & Campbell. The laundromat has enough machines to do all the crew's laundry in one cycle. Common Loaf is all-organic and features a local favorite: peasant bread. SoBo, open for lunch and dinner, uses locally grown ingredients in their dishes; reservations recommended (250) 725-2341. Correspondents Dick and Judy Juntunen strongly recommend a visit to the Tofino Botanical Gardens, approximately 1.5 miles out of town. They say the Gardens' excellent guidebook will explain everything you see. Seasonal breakfast, lunch or snacks are available at Darwin's Cafe. "A nice change from the tourist activity on the waterfront."

The free Tofino Transit Shuttle runs throughout town. The Tofino Beach Bus stops at all the local beaches and parks between Tofino and Ucluelet; $17 one way, $25 for same day round trip. The same company runs busses to many other destinations on Vancouver Island. Bike rentals are available.

From seaward, enter Tofino via Templar Channel. While Chart 3673 gives a good overall view, for the close navigation needed we strongly recommend large scale Chart 3685. Note how the buoyed fairway twists and turns to avoid shallows. Identify each buoy as you proceed, and leave the buoys off the proper hand.

From the north, enter Tofino via Deadman Pass, narrow and bordered on both sides by drying flats. Be sure to use large scale Chart 3685. Note that while you may be returning to Tofino, the buoyage system in Deadman Pass is not. As you head south in Deadman Pass you will leave the red buoys to port.

The approach to Tofino, whether through Templar Channel or Deadman Pass, is one of the few places on this coast where you need to carefully watch the currents. Time your arrival for slack water to avoid the strong currents that swirl around the docks.

Stay close to the docks once at Tofino. A serious drying reef lies a short distance off.

Anchoring can be a challenge because of strong currents that sweep through the harbor. Although Tofino has several public docks, moorage for visiting boats is limited. The District of Tofino Dock (called the Whiskey Dock) near Grice Point is closest to the Co-op and the liquor store, but is busy day and night with water taxis and locals. Moorage may be available at the Method Marine Supply fuel dock. It tends to be full during the busy season, but you can check.

The most popular moorage is the Tofino Harbour Authority 4th Street Public Dock. Farther east, Marina West Motel may have space, but without advance reservations the docks often are taken by their sport fishing guests. The easternmost public dock is called the Crab Dock. The Crab Dock is a longer walk from the commercial district, however. Currents can make landing on a flood tide tricky. Do not proceed eastward past the Crab Dock. A major rock blocks the channel.

㉖ **Tofino Harbour Authority 4th Street Public Dock.** P.O. Box 826, Tofino, BC V0R 2Z0; (250) 725-4441; tofharbour@gmail.com; Monitors VHF 66A. Maddy Prince is the harbormaster. Open all year, 20 & 30 amp power, water, pumpout, washrooms, showers, laundry, Wi-Fi. This is the best moorage prospect in Tofino, well-signed and convenient to the commercial district. Watch the current.

A shoal extends into the channel from a piling east of the easternmost dock, and leads across the ends of B, C and D docks. Dredging was completed in 2017. Minimum depth is 8 feet at 0 tide.

This is a commercial fishing harbour with some recreational moorage available on E-dock, first-come, first-served.

The dock water system operates by a 'loonie' timer, similar to pay showers. Make sure all the other faucets are closed, then feed a loonie to the timer, which pressurizes the dock system for about 15 minutes. Water pressure is good and one dollar should get you about 100 U.S. gallons of water. Be all set up before you start the system.

㉖ **Method Marine Supply.** Box 219, 380 Main Street, Tofino, BC V0R 2Z0; (250) 725-

Full Service Marine Supply including...
- Fuels & Lube Oil
- Hardware
- Hydraulic Repair
- Fishing Gear, Bait & Ice
- Dive Gear & Air Fills
- Electronics & Charts
- Raingear & Boots
- Mustang Survival Gear
- Convenience Store

Special orders – 1 day: Access to all major marine lines & suppliers

Method Marine Supply • Tofino • 380 main st.
250.725.3251 • fax: 250.725.2111
www.methodmarine.com

GEAR FOR OUT HERE Outdoor Gear and Clothing
Hiking/Camping/On-Water
Next to Method Marine
Phone: 250.725.3342

2018 WAGGONER CRUISING GUIDE   385

FROM THE LIGHTHOUSE

Scattered along British Columbia's 27,000 kilometres (16,875 miles) of coastline are twenty-seven staffed lightstations. Boaters usually spot the iconic lighthouse tower and perhaps a red and white building or two when cruising by–mindful of the fact that most lighthouses were built to warn mariners away from nearby hazards. Coastal aviators have a stellar view of an entire station and its infrastructure: depending on the station, there are anywhere between six to twelve buildings plus engines and derricks for the keepers to maintain. And who are these Canadian Coast Guard lightkeepers and what do they actually do? Especially those of you confused by erroneous information in the 2016 Tide Tables stating that the Entrance Island station had been destaffed in 2009, when lightkeepers have been stationed on Entrance non-stop since 1874. In 2014, in fact, lightkeepers Glenn Borgens and Jake Etzkorn pulled nine people from the water after their pleasure boat sank nearby.

Lightkeepers come in all shapes, sizes, and ages, just like our lighthouses. There is a definite affinity among prairie-born flatlanders, as well as grizzled west coasters, for lightstation work. It could be the wide skies and far horizons or a genetic tendency for necks cranked upwards, the better to study clouds as harbingers of incoming weather, fair or foul. We work seven days a week and only get "off the rock" for annual leave, training, and medical/dental appointments. Relief keepers like myself fill in for the absentee lightkeepers.

Lightkeepers seem to have creative outlets and also contribute as "citizen scientists," i.e., daily, monthly and seasonal observations for environmental and marine life scientific agencies. Many of us are experienced boaters—Cape Beale principal lightkeeper Karen Zacharuk and husband Kyle sailed to Alaska and back in 2015.

Mariners can hail us on VHF 82A and, provided we are not preoccupied (check for Coast Guard ships or helicopters in the vicinity), or rendered temporarily deaf by ear protectors worn while mowing lawns, operating pressure washers or working in our engine rooms, we can provide you with the latest weather report. An on-shore visit may be possible, but radioing us for permission and instructions to land is much appreciated.

Scarlett Lighthouse

Our weather reports, prepared every three hours from 4:30 a.m. to 10:30 p.m. PDT, are transferred to the continuous marine broadcast channel VHF radio as well as to the Environment Canada website*. Each report includes visibility, precipitation, wind speed and direction, wave height, swell height and direction. We also call in "special weathers" to warn mariners and aviators of worsening visibility, wind speed, or sea conditions.

At Ivory Island Lightstation on the Inside Passage, bilingual lightkeepers Lise and Rob Desmanche have set up a Facebook page where they post photos of boats cruising by so call ahead if you'd like your vessel photographed, a weather update or just to chat, says Lise. (https://www.facebook.com/IvoryIsland)

Lightkeepers Mark and JoAnne Tiglmann at Nootka Lightstation have often helped locate recreational boaters with urgent communications pertaining to family emergencies and directly assisted with medical emergencies. Even the formidable Triple Island Lightstation has cell phone service as well as the ALN (Automated Lighthouse Network) and VHF connection to boaters. We've all heard the old joke about the rich guy in the yacht with a road map calling a lightkeeper for directions to Alaska but there has always been contact between lightkeepers and mariners, due to mechanical breakdowns or personal or medical situations. We may not all be able to offer a calm harbour in a storm, like Friendly Cove below Nootka Lightstation, but we often have our eyes on you, and our ears on the VHF radio 24/7 too. We can and do summon help, by land, sea and sky. And as one lightkeeper says, it's just so nice to wave at a boat and to have the people on the boat wave back, like a silent hello out there.

Caroline Woodward, Photos by Jeff George, Lennard Island Lightkeepers. Caroline is the author of *Light Years: Memoir of a Modern Lighthouse Keeper*, an interesting book about her experiences, together with her husband, Jeff George, managing lighthouses up and down the BC coast.

Nootka Lighthouse

3251; sbernard@methodmarine.ca; www.methodmarine.ca. Open all year. Gasoline, bio-diesel, lube oils, propane, water, ice, divers' air, vacuum waste oil disposal. Moorage has electrical hook-up, but moorage often is fully reserved in the busy season. This is a modern, well-run facility, with a good chandlery that carries a wide range of equipment and supplies, including sport fishing gear, fishing licenses, bait, snacks, foul weather wear, and charts. Storm Light Outfitters, a well-stocked outdoor gear store, is right behind, up on the street.

㉖ **Tofino Resort & Marina.** P.O. Box 69, 634 Campbell, Tofino, BC V0R 2Z0; (844) 680-4184 ext 002; (250) 726-6130; marina@tofinoresortandmarina.com; www.tofinoresortandmarina.com. Newly constructed docks have water, 15 & 30 amp power. Showers, laundry, and Wi-Fi. Primarily a sport fishing resort with lodging, restaurant, fish packing facilities and adventure tours (hot springs, whale watching and bear watching). Transient and annual moorage; reservations requested.

㉖ **Tofino Harbour Authority Crab Dock.** P.O. Box 826, Tofino, BC V0R 2Z0; (250) 725-4441; tofharbour@gmail.com Monitors VHF 66A. Maddy Prince is the harbormaster. This is the easternmost dock on the Tofino waterfront. Some transient recreational moorage, 20 & 30 amp power, water. First-come, first-served.

CLAYOQUOT SOUND TO UCLUELET

It is approximately 19 miles from Lennard Island, at the southern entrance to Clayoquot Sound, to Whistle Buoy *Y42* offshore from Ucluelet Inlet. These 19 miles cross the ocean face of the Pacific Rim National Park; but since you'll probably be about 3 miles out, you won't see much of the park. Sailing Directions says to stay 2 miles off the coast; Watmough likes 3 miles. So do we. Plot a waypoint for Whistle Buoy *Y42*, go 3 miles offshore from Lennard Island, turn left, and make for the buoy. In fog, radar is a big help in avoiding the many fish boats that work these waters. Sport fishing boats that travel full speed even in thick fog are especially worrisome. Absent a GPS and radar, in fog we would go out to at least 30 fathoms deep and follow the 30 to 40 fathom curve to Buoy *Y42*.

Weather information: The Lennard Island lighthouse, just outside of Clayoquot Sound, and the

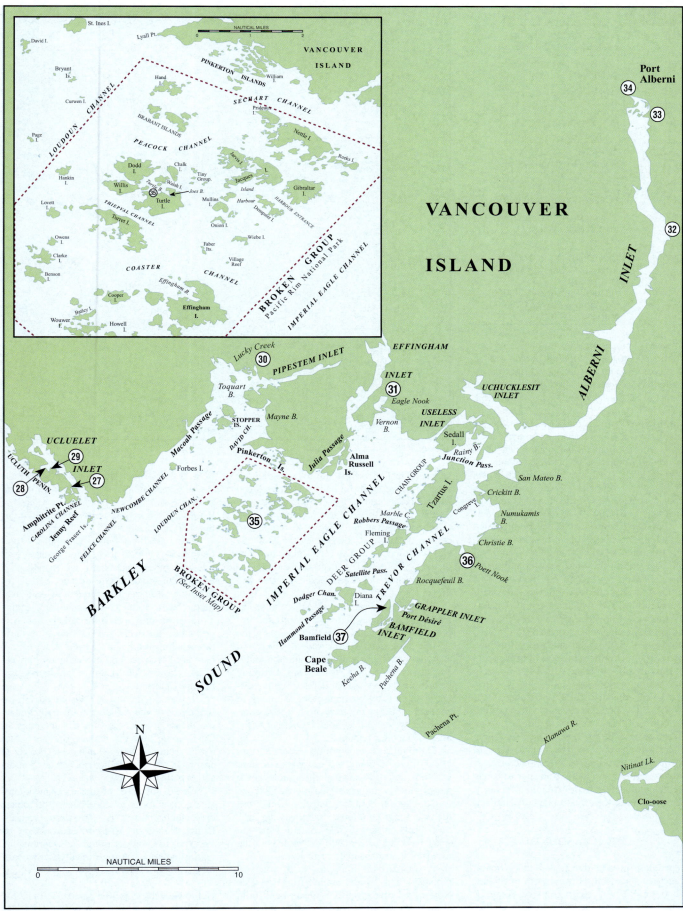

Barkley Sound

WEST COAST OF VANCOUVER ISLAND

See Area Map Page 387 - Maps Not for Navigation

CHARTS

3602	Approaches to Juan de Fuca Strait (1:150,000)
3603	Ucluelet Inlet to Nootka Sound (1:150,000)
3646 Plans	Barkley Sound
3647	Port San Juan and Nitinat Narrows
3668	Alberni Inlet (1:40,000) Robbers Passage (1:10,000)
3670	Broken Group (1:20,000)
3671	Barkley Sound (1:40,000)
3673	Clayoquot Sound, Tofino Inlet to Millar Channel (1:40,000)
3674	Clayoquot Sound, Millar Channel to Estevan Point (1:40,000) Hayden Passage (1:20,000) Hot Springs Cove (1:20,000) Marktosis (1:10,000)

Ucluelet Harbour

Amphitrite Point lighthouse, just outside of Barkley Sound, provide a picture of outside weather conditions. Listen to the continuous marine broadcast for the latest weather information or you can attempt to call the lighthouse keepers on VHF 82.

Amphitrite Point. Amphitrite Point, at the end of the Ucluth Peninsula, can present a challenge. The essential navigation problem is to get around Amphitrite Point while staying well clear of Jenny Reef, shown on the chart, yet staying off the Amphitrite Point shoreline. The problem is made more difficult in fog, when the radar may lose Buoy Y43 against the shoreline.

Carolina Channel is the entry suggested by Sailing Directions, except in thick weather, when Carolina Channel can be too rough for safe navigation. The outer entrance to Carolina Channel is marked by Whistle Buoy Y42, about 0.5 mile offshore. The channel leads past Bell Buoy Y43, which lies but 300 meters off the rocky shore. In reduced visibility, life can get interesting when you're trying to raise Buoy Y43. If you have trouble seeing the buoy against the rocky shoreline, the light structure on the east side of Francis Island could serve as a leading mark.

As you approach Carolina Channel, leave Whistle Buoy Y42 close to starboard, and turn to a course of 037° magnetic to raise Buoy Y43. After passing close south of Buoy Y43, Sailing Directions suggests using the summit of South Beg Island as a leading mark. It should bear approximately 075° magnetic. Run approximately 0.2 mile until the eastern extremity of Francis Island is abeam, then round Francis Island and enter Ucluelet Inlet.

BARKLEY SOUND

Depending on your direction, Barkley Sound is the first sound on the way north or the last sound on the way south. Barkley Sound is named after English Capt. Charles William Barkley, who in 1787 sailed into the sound on his ship *Loudoun*, which he had illegally renamed *Imperial Eagle* (Austrian registry) to avoid paying a license fee to the East India Company. With Capt. Barkley was his 17-year-old bride Frances Trevor Barkley. Capt. Barkley came to trade with the Indians for furs. You'll find reminders of the Barkleys in many names around Barkley Sound, including Imperial Eagle, Loudon and Trevor Channels.

Barkley Sound is roughly square in shape, measuring 15 miles across its mouth and approximately 12 miles deep, not counting the 20-mile-long canal to Port Alberni. The sound is dotted with rocks and islands, and the waters are famous for their excellent fishing. A cruising boat could spend weeks in Barkley Sound, fishing, exploring, and moving from one nook to another. In fact, many boats do just that, coming directly from Puget Sound, Oregon, or the Strait of Georgia region.

During the summer months fog often forms just offshore. In minutes, it can sweep in, even with no wind. It is essential, therefore, that the navigator know the vessel's position at all times. A GPS and electronic navigation will prove useful in foggy conditions. Radar is a big help. Most boats cruising Barkley Sound, large and small, have radar. Even with electronic help, the navigator must remain alert and aware.

If approaching from up-island, you will probably enter Barkley Sound from Ucluelet. Note that a course across Sargison Bank from Ucluelet to the Broken Group takes you very close to a rock that lies approximately 0.7 miles east of Chrow Island. The rock is shown on the chart not with a rock symbol, but by a depth of 0.5 meters. It is easy to overlook while scanning the chart for hazards.

If approaching from the Strait of Juan de Fuca or Oregon, leave Cape Beale at least one-half mile to starboard, which will leave the offshore rocks a safe distance off. If the boat is coming from the United States, it must go directly to Ucluelet for Canadian Customs, although it may duck into Barkely Sound to get out of the ocean swells. A good option is to enter Imperial Eagle Channel, leave Effingham Island to port, and proceed west between Clarke and Benson Islands to Loudoun Channel and Ucluelet.

In Barkley Sound you will find superb exploring everywhere: Pipestem Inlet, the Pinkerton Islands, Julia Passage, the Chain Group, the Deer Group and the famous Broken Group. Settled summer weather makes it possible to anchor in any of hundreds of coves or nooks and explore by dinghy.

We do not cover all the areas mentioned above, an unfortunate consequence of limited exploration time. Other references—especially Douglass' *Exploring Vancouver Island's West Coast* are excellent resources. In the end, your own inquisitiveness and derring-do will determine the range of your exploring.

Ucluelet. Ucluelet is pronounced "You-CLOO-let." With moorage, fuel, provisions, repairs and

See Area Map Page 387 - Maps Not for Navigation   WEST COAST OF VANCOUVER ISLAND

The Ucluelet Small Craft Harbour grounds are inviting.

good dining, the village of Ucluelet (pop. approx. 1800) is the commercial center of Barkley Sound. The channel leading into Ucluelet is well buoyed. Following the rule of Red, Right, Returning, you will have no problems. Spring Cove, to port a short distance inside the channel, is where fish boats used to discharge their catches. The plant deep in the cove is closed and the docks are posted with No Trespassing signs. Spring Cove is a good anchorage.

Ucluelet has one fuel dock, located on the town side. Several fish processing plants and public docks used by large commercial boats are also on the town side of the inlet. Small public docks used by the Ucluelet Native Band are on the east side of the inlet, across from town.

West of the north tip of Lyche Island, the Ucluelet Small Craft Harbour is the principal marina, and the one we recommend. The Canadian Princess, a former Canadian Hydrographic Service survey ship, has been removed and is no longer an option as a local floating hotel. Another marina to consider is Island West Resort, on the west side of the inlet just before the turn to the small craft harbor. The docks are built almost entirely for trailerable boats. They have no designated guest dock, so call ahead by phone.

In town, halfway up Ucluelet Inlet, Pioneer Boat Works has a marine railway for haulout and repairs. Their chandlery, next to the ways, has a good stock of marine supplies, commercial and sportfishing tackle, and charts. Pioneer Boat Works serves the commercial fishing fleet. Cruisers will find what they need there. Around the winding streets of Ucluelet you will find gift shops, art galleries, including an excellent Native Gallery, the Ucluelet Aquarium, dining from casual to quite nice, a large co-op grocery and general merchandise store, and other essential services. It's a pleasant hike out the road to the Coast Guard station at Amphitrite Point. We've walked it and recommend it. The Wild Pacific Trail begins just beyond He-Tin-Kis Park, near the Coast Guard station.

In Ucluelet Inlet, Lyche Island can be passed on either side. If passing on the west side (the town side), check Chart 3646 and leave the buoys and beacons off the proper hands.

Customs: Ucluelet is the only customs reporting station on the west coast of Vancouver Island. Open all year. The 52 Step Dock in Ucluelet Inlet, a short distance beyond buoy Y44, is the official Customs dock. Call (888) 226-7277 by cell or at the on-dock payphone.

㉗ **Eagle Marine, Ltd./Columbia Fuels.** 1231 Eber Road, Ucluelet, BC V0R 3A0; (250) 726-4262; www.columbiafuels.com. Open 7 days a week all year, summer 7:30 a.m. to 7:30 p.m., winter 8:00 a.m. to 5:00 p.m. Gasoline, diesel, lubricants, water, ice, bait, tackle, convenience items, garbage drop.

52 Steps Dock. This is the customs dock. Moorage on west side, water, no power.

Whiskey Landing. 1645 Cedar Rd, Ucluelet, BC V0R 3A0, Canada; (250) 726-2270; www.whiskeylanding.com; info@whiskeylanding.com. Guest moorage for hotel guests.

㉘ **Ucluelet Small Craft Harbour.** 200 Hemlock St., Ucluelet, BC V0R 3A0; (250) 726-4241; (250) 725-8190; kcortes@ucluelet.ca. The marina has 30 amp and some 50 amp power, water, washrooms, excellent showers and laundry, pumpout, waste oil disposal, Wi-Fi. The outside basin, before entering the large main basin, has two floats marked for recreational and commercial boats. Although the floats are inviting, we'd continue inside. Docks B & C are marked for commercial boats only; docks D, E & F are for recreational and commercial boats. The facility is completely protected, well maintained, and quiet. It's where most cruising boats tie up. The staff is attentive and helpful.

㉙ **Island West Resort.** Box 879, 1990 Bay St., Ucluelet, BC V0R 3A0; (250) 726-7515; fish@islandwestresort.com; www.islandwestresort.com. Call ahead. A busy sportfishing resort, often fully reserved a year ahead for July and August. Limited 15 amp power, washrooms, showers, free Wi-Fi, laundry, portapotty dump, launch ramp, marine supplies, ice, convenience groceries, excellent pub. Fishing charters.

2018 WAGGONER CRUISING GUIDE

The Wild Pacific Trail leads to Amphitrite Point Lighthouse.   Lucky Creek is a magical spot.

WESTERN BARKLEY SOUND

The western part of Barkley Sound, from Ucluelet to Pipestem Inlet and over to the Pinkerton Islands, is relatively open and easily run. As long as you stay in the middle, Newcombe Channel and Macoah Passage present no problems. They lead to the Stopper Islands and, beyond them, to Pipestem Inlet. Pipestem Inlet is where the magical falls at Lucky Creek await.

Stopper Islands. The Stopper Islands are quite pretty and beg exploration by dinghy or kayak. Anchor between Larkins Island and the large island.

Toquaht Bay Marina. www.secretbeachcampground.com. On the west side of Toquaht Bay behind a breakwater constructed of orange railroad tankers. Boat launch and moorage for trailerable boats.

Pipestem Inlet. Pipestem Inlet is beautiful and deep, bordered by high mountains and lined with forest. With one possible exception, though, the only anchoring possibilities are near the mouth. That exception is the little cove near the head of the inlet, behind the 32-meter island. We saw a 20-foot trailerable boat anchored in there and stern-tied to shore, but we didn't have the courage to take the 37-footer in. Maybe this cove is okay—we don't know. [*Hale*]

Near the mouth of Pipestem Inlet, the good anchorages are behind **Bazett Island**, either southwest or southeast, or behind **Refuge Island**. If you choose Bazett Island, the southwest anchorage is well into the southwest cove, off the mouth of the drying inlet colored green on the chart. The southeast anchorage is in the little thumb-shaped inlet, or along the adjacent shore, stern-tied. Reader Dick Drinkow reports that a number of large yellow buoys are in Bazett Island's southwest cove.

The Refuge Island anchorage is directly north of Refuge Island, a bit east of the 16-meter island. This anchorage and the Bazett Island anchorages are within easy dinghy commute to Lucky Creek. Aquaculture buoys occupy part of this cove but still leave room for boats to anchor.

㉚ **Lucky Creek.** The late John Schlagel, fearless longtime explorer, did not suggest that we see Lucky Creek, he *instructed* us to see Lucky Creek, and he was right. This is a window-of-opportunity trip and the window corresponds with high tide.

We suggest taking the outboard-powered dinghy up to the falls an hour before high water and coming out an hour after. Former Managing Editor Sam Landsman took a shallow-draft, outboard powered 22' C-Dory in, and wouldn't want to go in anything much bigger.

The entrance is directly across Pipestem Inlet from Bazett Island. After crossing the shallow entry (bordered by meadow grass and wildflowers), the channel winds through marvelous mature forest, with overhanging cedars. The deeper part of the channel tends to follow the outside of the bends, river-style. The water is clear. We kept our eye on the bottom. Close to the falls the bottom shoals and we sought out the narrow, U-shaped channel to follow.

Suddenly, before our eyes was a storybook waterfall directly out of Walt Disney's imagination. Seeing that waterfall, we knew Tinker Bell was around; she was just too quick for us to see. When you go, tie the dinghy off to the side and climb up to a series of bathing pools. Be careful, the rocks can be slippery. And remember, just as Cinderella had to run when the clock tolled twelve, you cannot stay. If you tarry too long the falling tide will close you in.

You probably won't be alone at Lucky Creek. The lodges and resorts in the area are fully familiar with Lucky Creek and the boat drivers know the channel well. We got to Lucky Creek a half-hour after high tide, and the guests were all leaving—at top speed in the narrow waterway that was unfamiliar to us. They came right at us and swooped past, all smiles and happiness as we splashed through their wakes. No matter, the trip was worth it. [*Hale*]

Entrance Inlet. Entrance Inlet indents Vancouver Island at the northeast corner of Mayne Bay. Anchor in the outer basin in 40 feet. During the day you will have boat traffic from the fishing resort in Cigarette Cove.

Cigarette Cove. You can anchor in Cigarette Cove, but the resort takes up much of the space. The entry is narrow and bounded by rocks. If you pay attention, you will have no problems.

Southeast Cove. This cove is open to the west, but is good in settled weather. Anchor in 35 to 40 feet.

Pinkerton Islands. Far from the wildness of the outer islands, the Pinkerton Islands are north of the Broken Group, next to Vancouver Island. The Pinkertons are small and protected, with narrow channels, and are ideal for gunkholing. Watch for rocks. The easiest anchorage is in the cove northwest of Williams Island. Unless several boats want to share the cove, no stern-tie is required. A study of the chart will suggest a number of other possibilities, most of which will require a stern-tie to shore.

UPPER BARKLEY SOUND

Effingham Inlet. Sailing Directions says Effingham Inlet is high, steep and deep, with few if any anchoring possibilities. Correspondents Bruce and Margaret Evertz explored Effingham Inlet and here is their report:

"We found anchorage in the bay on the west side of Effingham Inlet about one-quarter of the way in. The center of the bay is fairly flat and approximately 75 feet deep. Our anchor set well at 49°00.959'N/125°10.659'W. Another secure spot would be at the south corner of the bay in 30 to 40 feet with a stern-tie. We were told that boats often anchor on the north side of the small peninsula near John Islet, at the entrance.

"While several oyster farms are in the lower part of Effingham Inlet, we saw few signs of man farther in. It isn't Princess Louisa, but like Pipestem Inlet it's still pretty. The sides are high, steep and forested, with many interesting cliffs. We saw only two waterfalls. We didn't see many anchoring opportunities unless you want to stern-tie, and there were many small bights for that. We were told that afternoons can be windy, but the trees grow right to the high water line so we don't think the winds amount to much." [*Evertz*]

㉛ **Jane Bay/Franks Bay.** This bay, known locally both as Jane Bay and Franks Bay, is not named on the chart. It is located at the back of Barkley Sound, connected by a narrow but safe passage with Vernon Bay at 48°59.80'N/125°08.80'W. Anchor, care-

See Area Map Page 387 - Maps Not for Navigation   WEST COAST OF VANCOUVER ISLAND

Harbour Quay Marina in Port Alberni is close to downtown. Showers and laundry are in the new building, top of ramp.

fully, near the head before the flats shoal too much. A water line is clearly marked with yellow buoys. Or tie up at Eagle Nook Lodge.

㉛ **Eagle Nook Resort and Spa (Vernon Bay).** P.O. Box 289, Ucluelet, BC V0R 3A0; (800) 760-2777; (604) 357-3361; info@eaglenook.com; www.eaglenook.com. Monitors VHF 73. Marina is immediately to starboard as you enter the bay. Moorage to 100 feet, 30 & 50 amp power, water, Wi-Fi, washrooms and showers. Reservations recommended, especially for larger boats. The lodge's exterior is Pacific Northwest style, interior is traditional lodge. Open May to mid-September. An elite high-end restaurant, spa, and guided fishing are available to visiting boaters. Well-maintained walking trails lead through the forest.

Useless Inlet. Useless Inlet contains a number of aquaculture leases and recreational float homes. Entry to the inlet is made interesting by a series of large rocks that are covered except at lower stages of the tide. The rocks were covered when we were there and the wind rippled the water, making them hard to see. The obvious safe entry is along the north shore, to avoid the rocks in the middle. We attempted that route twice but didn't feel comfortable. We did see several trailerable sport fishing boats roar in and out of Useless Inlet, running between the rocks in the middle. They knew where the channel was; we didn't.

Correspondents Bruce and Margaret Evertz went into Useless Inlet. They report that "Useless Nook," described in the Douglass book, has an oyster farm in it, and a sign on shore that says, "No anchorage or trespassing in bay—oyster farm."

ALBERNI INLET

Alberni Inlet begins between Chup Point and Mutine Point, where it meets with Trevor Channel and Junction Passage. The inlet continues some 21 miles into the heart of Vancouver Island to the town of Port Alberni. Alberni Inlet is narrow and high-sided, with little to interest the cruiser along the way. A well-protected detached public float is in San Mateo Bay, near the mouth of the inlet. In Alberni Inlet itself, the only good stopovers are at the public float at Hook Bay or at China Creek, about 6 miles down-inlet from Port Alberni. Tidal current flows are less than 1 knot both directions, but the surface current can flow as fast as 3 knots when wind and current direction are the same. Except for trailer boats (see Port Alberni entry below) boats without a reason to go to Port Alberni seldom make the trip, preferring instead the many pleasures of Barkley Sound.

In the summer, an up-inlet thermal wind develops at 1:00 p.m. ("You can set your clock by it," says a friend in Port Alberni), and will increase to 25 to 30 knots by mid-afternoon. The wind produces a short, uncomfortable chop. We would run Alberni Inlet in the morning.

Port Alberni. *Port Alberni is the best single saltwater trailer boat destination in the Northwest.* We say this because Port Alberni gives the trailer boater safe and easy access to Barkley Sound, the most diverse and interesting cruising ground in the Northwest. (Note that by trailer boat, we still mean cruising boats with sleeping, cooking and toilet facilities, or at the very least, boats suitable for camping out. It's a 21-mile run down the Alberni Inlet to Barkley Sound; once in Barkley Sound you won't be coming back for a few days).

To get to Port Alberni from the mainland, trailer the boat to the BC Ferries terminal at Tsawwassen, near the U.S. border, or to the Horseshoe Bay terminal, north of Vancouver. Large, comfortable ferries will take you to Nanaimo's Duke Point or Departure Bay terminals. (Or, if you are coming from the south, take the private ferry Coho from Port Angeles, Wash. to Victoria.) Our trailer boat friends tell us the fares for trailered boats are not inexpensive, so be prepared. From the Duke Point ferry terminal at Nanaimo, an easy and often beautiful 1½- to 2-hour drive on paved highway will take you to Port Alberni.

Along the way, be sure to stop at Cathedral Grove for a walk through a towering forest of 1000-year-old cedar, hemlock and Douglas fir. The trail is easy and well-maintained. If you hurry along, you can walk it in 20 minutes. If you linger to absorb more of the majesty, it could take about an hour. Interpretive signs explain everything.

To reach Port Alberni you do have to go over a 1230-foot-high mountain pass, with an 8 percent grade on the east side and a 6 percent grade on the west. Be sure your rig has enough power and brakes.

Once at Port Alberni, you'll find good launch ramps at Clutesi Haven Marina at the mouth of the Somass River, and at China Creek, located 6 miles down the Alberni Inlet. Long-term parking is available at both locations. All the marinas are operated by the Port Alberni Port Authority; www.portalberniportauthority.ca.

In Port Alberni you'll find complete services including hospital, shopping, marine supplies and repairs, and dinner out.

A steam locomotive pulls a train that runs from downtown Port Alberni to the McLean Mill National Historic Site, the only working steam-operated sawmill in Canada. It takes about 35 minutes each way. The McLean Mill is a fascinating tour, with interpretive signs to explain what you are looking at. The cookhouse, blacksmith shop, workers' housing and other buildings have been restored. Mill demonstrations and a guided theatrical experience are offered daily. Logs are in the mill pond. A trip to the McLean Mill is a step back in time. The entire family will enjoy it. Call (250) 723-1376. Better yet, for latest information and schedules see www.alberniheritage.com.

For information on other attractions and events, contact the Alberni Valley Chamber of Commerce, (250) 724-6535.

Salmon festival: Port Alberni's Salmon Festival & Derby (www.salmonfestival.ca) is held Labour Day weekend each year at Clutesi Haven Marina. We are told that the Somass River is the third largest salmon stream in B.C. Only the Fraser River and the Skeena River have larger returns.

Haulout: Alberni Engineering and Shipyard has haulout and complete repairs for boats to 100 feet. Call (250) 723-0111.

Golf: The Alberni Golf Club is an 18-hole par 70 course, with deep rough and excellent greens. Call (250) 723-5422. Hollies Executive Golf Course is a 9-hole, par 30 track. Call (250) 724-5333.

Fuel: No marine diesel fuel is available in Port Alberni itself, although diesel and gasoline are available at China Creek. Gasoline is available at Clutesi Haven.

㉜ **China Creek Marina & Campground.** (250) 723-9812; www.campchinacreek.com; chinacreek@alberniport.ca. Open April through September, 88 slips and 2300 feet of side-tie moorage, 4-lane launch ramp. Gasoline, diesel, propane, 15, 20 & 30 amp power, washrooms, showers, laundry, ice, garbage drop, fish cleaning stations, playground. Campsites and RV sites are adjacent.

㉝ **Harbour Quay.** 2900 Harbour Rd., Port Alberni, BC V9Y 7X2; (250) 723-1413; www.portalberniportauthority.ca; harbourquay@alberniport.ca. Harbour Quay has 15 slips and 2000 lineal feet of side-tie moorage, 20 & 30 amp power, washrooms, showers, laundry, potable water on the floats, garbage drop. This is a breakwater-protected marina close to down-

2018 WAGGONER CRUISING GUIDE

WEST COAST OF VANCOUVER ISLAND

See Area Map Page 387 - Maps Not for Navigation

CHARLES WILLIAM BARKLEY (1759-1832)

Charles Barkley was an English ship captain and fur trader. He learned his trade at the age of 11 from his father who was a commander of the East India Co. ship, *Pacific*. After making several voyages as a young man for the East India Co., Charles left the business to command his own ship, the *Loudoun,* later re-named *Imperial Eagle*, to engage in fur trading on the northwest coast of North America. In 1787 Charles Barkley entered Friendly Cove in Nootka Sound and stayed for about a month. He acquired several hundred prime skins and then sailed south exploring and naming parts of the coast between Nootka Sound and the Strait of Juan de Fuca, giving the names Barkley Sound, Loudoun Channel, and Cape Beale. His ship, *Imperial Eagle,* was the first European vessel to enter Neah Bay in July, 1787. That same year, Barkley headed for China to sell his sea otter pelts and arrived in Macau in December. In the following years, Barkley commanded the *Princess Frederica* and sailed the Indian Ocean (1791), then returned to the Pacific Northwest coast in command of the *Halcyon* to trade in sea otter pelts at Sitka Sound, departing once again for the Hawaiian Islands and China.

---

town. The docks have been reconfigured to create more side-tie moorage, making it attractive for larger boats. Check ahead for availability. Adjacent to the Maritime Heritage Discovery Centre, located in a genuine west coast lighthouse.

㉝ **Fisherman's Harbour.** 3140 Harbour Rd., Port Alberni, BC V9Y 7X2; (250) 723-2533; www.portalberniportauthority.ca; fishermansharbour@alberniport.ca. Open all year, 7600 feet of moorage, 20, 30 and some 50 amp power, water, new washrooms & showers, garbage drop, pumpout, 2 winches on the wharf. Fisherman's Harbour is adjacent to downtown Port Alberni, with all the services of downtown close by. They never turn anyone away, but be prepared to raft. June is the busiest month.

㉞ **Clutesi Haven.** (250) 724-6837; www.portalberniportauthority.ca; clutesihaven@alberniport.ca. Open all year. Moorage sometimes available, call ahead. Water, 15, 20 & 30 amp power, washrooms, garbage drop, 4-lane launch ramp. Clutesi Haven is located behind a breakwater near the mouth of the Somass River. Best suited to boats 40 feet or less. This is a popular launching spot for trailerable boats. Hotels, pubs, and liquor store are nearby. Groceries are 5 blocks away.

BROKEN GROUP

The Broken Group extends from the wind-and-wave-lashed outer islands to peaceful islands deep inside Barkley Sound. The Broken Group is part of the Pacific Rim National Park, to be preserved in its natural state in perpetuity. For many Northwest boaters, a holiday spent in the Broken Group is the fulfillment of a lifelong dream.

Boats visiting the Broken Group will find dozens of little nooks and bights to put the hook down, depending on weather and the mood on board. Don Watmough, Don Douglass, and the Yeadon-Joneses all describe a number of them in their guides. The major anchorages are Effingham Bay, Turtle Bay and Nettle Island.

Chart note: On Chart 3670, the water faucet symbols on Effingham Island, Benson Island, Clarke Island, Turret Island, Willis Island and Gibraltar Island should be deleted.

Pets: The Broken Group is part of Pacific Rim National Park. In order to protect native flora and fauna, pets are not permitted on shore anywhere in the Broken Group.

Effingham Bay. Effingham Bay is large, pretty, and protected. On the nights of our visits we have shared the bay with 10 to 20 other boats, yet everyone had room to swing and we didn't feel crowded. The chart shows the entrance. Anchor in 30 to 50 feet, good holding. Sunsets, seen out the mouth of the bay, can be dramatic. Because Effingham Bay is open to the west, westerly winds can make the anchorage a bit bumpy.

Take the time to dinghy ashore and hike to the ancient Native village site on the east side of Effingham (Village) Island. The trail begins on the right side (as you face the land from the water) of the little thumb of water at the head of Effingham Bay and leads through lush and mature forest. Take care to turn right, the left side leads in the wrong direction. Don't be fooled; the wrong trail leads to mud, fallen trees and other obstacles. The sign warns of wolves on the island. Do pay attention to what it says:

"When in a group, act in unison to send a clear message to the wolves they are not welcome.

"Back away slowly, do not turn your back on the wolf.

"Make noise, throw sticks, rocks and sand at the wolf."

The trail across the island is generally easy, but a little primitive and challenging in places. The village site, on the eastern shore, is mystical. Widely-spaced trees suggest the location of the main village. The large midden, with shells poking out of it, indicates a long and populous habitation. Near the beach you can find an old longhouse beam that now serves as a nurse log. A sea cave is located there, but is inaccessible at high tide. Late in the day the view eastward from the beach—the sea, with the mountains of Vancouver Island painted in low reddish light—is inspiring.

Benson Island. In settled weather you can take anchorage off the east shore of Benson Island, in the cove opposite the water faucet icon on the chart. A trail leads across the island to a scenic rocky beach with a blowhole that sounds just like a whale blowing.

Clarke Island. Temporary or settled weather anchorage can be found on the east side of Clarke Island.

Turret Island. The cove formed by the 36-meter island on the southwest side of Turret Island is okay for anchoring, though the bottom is thick with kelp. The surrounding area has interesting rock formations and is good for exploring by dinghy or kayak.

㉟ **Turtle Bay.** Turtle Bay is a local name for the bay formed by Turtle Island, Willis Island, and Dodd Island. Joes Bay, an appendage of Turtle Bay, indents Turtle Island. It is the little nook where Salal Joe, the Hermit of Barkley Sound, made his home.

The best entrance to Turtle Bay is from the north, off Peacock Channel, between Dodd Island and Chalk Island. A study of the chart shows the entrance channel bounded by rocks and drying rock outcroppings along the way. A careful entry, proceeding slowly and identifying the hazards, will bring you in safely. Those who have been in a few times know where the rocks are and roar right in.

Anchor in 25 to 30 feet on a mud bottom, good holding.

Nettle Island. Nettle Island has three good anchorages—one in the large bay that indents the southern shore, and the other two in the channel between Nettle Island and Reeks Island to the east. In Nettle Island's large bay we prefer the eastern portion, off the park ranger's float cabin. The center of the bay is a little deep (50 to 60 feet, depending on state of tide), but you can find depths of 20 to 30 feet near the shore north of the ranger's cabin. Reader Dick Drinkow reports that the park ranger warns that boats have grounded on the shelf, and recommends anchoring in the center of the bay.

Watmough describes two other anchorages along the east side of Nettle Island, opposite Reeks Island. These nooks will hold a couple of boats each, and Watmough says they are delightful. The charted rocks are easy to identify and avoid.

Outer Islands. The outer islands of the Broken Group are marked by twisted trees, the result of relentless onshore winds, especially in the winter. If your needs include the de-

---

www.WaggonerGuide.com

sire to navigate "at the edge," the outer islands can satisfy that need. Here, you'll have your opportunity to run in wind and fog, with the Pacific Ocean swells beating against the rocks. Navigate carefully. The low islands are easy to get mixed up. Rocks and reefs are charted, but they're everywhere. This is beautiful, raw country. The kayakers have it best. The favored anchorage is at Wouwer Island.

Wouwer Island. Wouwer Island is breathtaking, both in its scenery and gunkholing. At half tide or higher, most boats can make it through the slit between Batley Island and Wouwer Island. A bow watch will only scare you.

We anchored temporarily in a nook south of two islets, west of the slit between Batley and Wouwer Islands. A trail leads across the island to a lovely beach with great beachcombing.

EASTERN BARKLEY SOUND

Limestone Bay, located at the mouth of Uchucklesit Inlet, has satisfactory anchorage in 12 feet with some protection. Use the southwest entrance only.

㊱ **Poett Nook.** Poett Nook is on the eastern shore, at lat 48°53'N. It doesn't look like a nook when you see it. It is a spacious, rather pretty bay, with good anchoring in 25 feet. The entry is narrow but deep. The Poett Nook Marina, a large sport fishing resort, is on the eastern side of the bay.

㊱ **Poett Nook Marina & Campground.** Mailing: P.O. Box 1083, Port Alberni, BC V9Y 7L9; (250) 758-4440; (250) 720-9572; poettnookmarina@gmail.com; www.poettnook.com. Gasoline at the fuel dock, washrooms, showers. No power, non-potable water. A small store carries convenience food, ice, and tackle. Fee-based garbage drop. This is a busy small-boat sportfishing resort, with 123 RV/camping sites and berths for 174 boats. Maximum length 36 feet. Most boats launch at Port Alberni or China Creek.

Robbers Passage. Robbers Passage leads between Fleming Island and Tzartus Island in the Deer Group, and is a likely route for boats bound between points near the head of Barkely Sound and Bamfield. A rock that dries 1 meter is in the western approach to Robbers Passage. Although the rock is clearly charted, people at the Port Alberni Yacht Club swear this is one rock that moves. Give the rock a wide berth. The S-shaped channel leading into Robbers Passage requires close attention, but with attention it is safe. A study of large-scale chart 3668 will make the route clear. Inside the passage, the Port Alberni Yacht Club has its floating clubhouse and docks.

Port Alberni Yacht Club. Consider spending at least one night at the Port Alberni Yacht Club. The facility is clean and well-maintained, and the folks are friendly and helpful. They have a wealth of local knowledge to share. Be sure to walk the beautiful trail around the

Turtle Bay is a large, scenic anchorage.

peninsula behind the yacht club. The moorage charge is modest and goes back into the facility. All are welcome; no yacht club membership needed. Washrooms, showers, and non-potable water available.

Aquaculture ventures have left considerable debris on the seafloor. Anchoring not recommended, although Elsie and Steve Hulsizer report that on several occasions when the moorage was full they anchored off the docks without any problems. Several large buoys might be mistaken for mooring buoys. These buoys are not designed for mooring and have dragged when boats tied to them.

Fleming Island. The day was sunny with only a gentle breeze, so we left the boat at the yacht club and motored the dinghy around Fleming Island. The impossibly rugged shoreline is dotted with sea caves. We were told that some of the caves extend far into the rock. For thousands of years the First Nations people in Barkley Sound put some of their dead in bentwood boxes and hid them in sea caves. We were fascinated by the stories.

We did, however, ease the dinghy through a narrow cleft in the rock and up to the mouth of one cave. The opening loomed above us, and we could see the floor of small boulders rise and disappear in darkness. The rock walls of the cleft were covered with orange and purple sea stars. Other neon-hued sea life waved in the surge. The word *impressed* does not begin to describe the effect on us. [*Hale*]

Tzartus Cove. Tzartus Cove (our preferred anchorage on Tzartus Island) is the name Douglass gives to this excellent anchorage about 0.5 mile north of Marble Cove. Rocks extend from both shores, so go right down the middle when you enter. Anchor near the head in 25 to 30 feet. Sea caves are nearby. Reader Dick Drinkow reports that a bit of northwest swell can get into the cove and that kelp fouled their anchor.

Marble Cove. Marble Cove is on the west side of Tzartus Island, and often is mentioned as a good anchorage (we would choose instead the cove one-half mile north). A rock stack between two islands and reddish rocks on the shore add to the scenic nature of the cove. A float house is on the north side of Marble Cove. Anchor in 25 to 30 feet off the gravel beach on the island opposite the float house. This is a good place to explore tidepools at low tide.

Grappler Inlet. Grappler Inlet joins near the mouth of Bamfield Inlet and leads to **Port Désiré**, a protected anchorage with a launch ramp and a public dock. Although Grappler Inlet is beautiful, it is surrounded by homes.

㊲ **Bamfield Inlet.** Bamfield Inlet is open and easy to enter. The village of Bamfield is along the shores of the inlet. Several public docks are located on each side. Commercial fish boats have priority, but space usually can be found for pleasure craft. At the head of the inlet, past Rance Island, is a quiet basin where boats can anchor, although an overhead power cable lim-

Wolf spotted on Turtle Island

WEST COAST OF VANCOUVER ISLAND

See Area Map Page 387 - Maps Not for Navigation

The Port Alberni Yacht Club docks are in Robbers Passage.

The Bamfield Market is well stocked.

its mast height to 17 meters (55 feet). Larger boats anchor off the East Bamfield public dock. The mooring buoys shown on the chart have been removed. The West Bamfield public dock is largely reserved; even a dinghy may have trouble finding a spot.

㊲ **Bamfield.** They call the inlet "Main Street." The village of Bamfield covers both sides of the inlet, and the west side is not connected by road with the east side. You cross by boat or you don't cross. The Bamfield General Store, with liquor agency, is on the west side of the inlet. A boardwalk runs along the homes and businesses on the west side, and folks get around by walking. The Boardwalk Bistro located near the West Bamfield public dock serves espresso drinks and delicious salmon burgers.

The east side has roads that tie its businesses and homes together. They connect with the 60-mile-long dirt logging road that leads to Port Alberni. The east side has a hardware store and a marine store, pub, a small grocery store with deli counter and small cafe. In 2016 the pub was purchased by new owners who have refurbished the interior, it's attractive and inviting. The trail to Cape Beale begins on the east side of the inlet. A launch ramp is at Port Désiré.

A small Outpost Hospital is located on the east side. It is set up to treat illness or injury, deliver babies, and dispense medication. The hospital is operated by registered nurses, and a visiting physician calls on a regular schedule. They work closely with the Coast Guard for emergency helicopter transport when needed. A fee schedule accommodates non-Canadians who need medical attention.

Wi-Fi is available through Community Wireless Networks, (250) 728-3647.

The large building on the east side of the inlet near the entrance houses the Bamfield Marine Research Station. The station is owned by five universities in British Columbia and Alberta, and began operation in 1971. Visitors are welcome and tours are offered during the summer, 1:00 p.m. to 2:30 p.m. Wednesdays, Fridays and Sundays, no charge, donations appreciated. This facility once was the eastern terminus of the trans-pacific cable that connected North America with Australia. Its first message was sent on November 1, 1902; its last message was sent in 1959. See their website at www.bms.bc.ca.

Bamfield offers several events during the year, including the Music by the Sea Festival, with classical and jazz musicians from all over. Lodging is at a premium, but boaters can stay on board. See www.bamfieldchamber.com/events.html for events and dates. The festival welcomes boaters. The first time you attend, they will award you a festival burgee to fly from your boat. Come a subsequent year, and they'll give you a second burgee with two stars on it. Repeat as many times as you want and get as many burgees as your number of visits, each with more stars. The experience of sitting in the Bamfield Marine Research Station's modern auditorium and watching the sun set over Barkley Sound through floor to ceiling glass windows while listening to wonderful music is well worth repeating.

While in Bamfield, be sure to visit the small historical museum at the Bamfield Centennial Park on the road from East Bamfield to Grappler Inlet.

㊲ **East Bamfield Public Dock.** Moorage, water, garbage drop, limited power. No washrooms. The docks have recently been resurfaced. Nearby market and cafe.

㊲ **Bamfield Fuel Barge.** Located on the east side of the inlet, just past the government wharf. Gasoline, diesel, ice, convenience food. Open 8:00 a.m. to 8:00 p.m. in the summer.

㊲ **West Bamfield Public Dock.** (250) 720-7548; bhadockmanager@gmail.com. Moorage, 20 & 30 amp power, water. No washrooms. Reservations recommended during July and August.

㊲ **Harbourside Lodge.** (250) 728-3330; requests@harboursidelodge.com; www.harboursidelodge.com. Moorage, 30 & 50 amp power, water, washroom, showers, laundry. Gasoline and diesel. Store has ice, bait, tackle. Located on the west side of the inlet, just past the government dock.

㊲ **McKay Bay Lodge.** (250) 728-3323; mckaybay@island.net; www.mckaybaylodge.com. Located on the west side of the inlet. Gasoline, diesel, tackle, ice. Limited moorage, washroom, guest rooms.

BARKLEY SOUND TO BECHER BAY

The final leg of a counter-clockwise circumnavigation of Vancouver Island is from Barkley Sound into the Strait of Juan de Fuca. On the Canadian side, Port Renfrew is the only protection between Barkley Sound and Sooke.

The typical summer weather pattern calls for calm conditions in the early morning, with a westerly sea breeze building by afternoon, often to 30+ knots.

Currents in the Strait of Juan de Fuca can be strong. This can speed up the passage, especially for sailboats. Or, they can substantially slow the trip. When the wind blows against the current, steep, sometimes-dangerous seas result. Pay attention to the current when planning to transit the Strait of Juan de Fuca.

Several weather resources make the trip less nerve-racking. Lighthouses at Cape Beale, Pachena Point and Carmanah Point provide regular weather updates. Automated stations at Shearingham Point and Race Rocks report hourly wind speed and direction. The Neah Bay weather buoy (46087) provides regular wind speed updates, and the New Dungeness buoy (46088) provides wind speed, direction, and sea state. Put together, you can get picture of conditions on the Strait before venturing out.

Cape Beale. Cape Beale, surrounded by off-lying rocks, marks the eastern entrance to Barkley Sound. Trevor Channel exits at Cape Beale, and is the safest entry to, or exit from, Barkley Sound in thick weather or poor visibility. Seas can be difficult off Cape Beale when an outflowing current from Barkley Sound meets the longshore current outside. The collision of currents, combined with wind and shallow depths around the cape, can make for heavy going.

The usual advice is to round Cape Beale in early morning, before the summertime westerly wind gets up.

The local lightkeepers have provided this bit of local knowledge: A nasty reef is one-quarter of a mile in front of the lightstation. Beware of coming in close to take photos. Lightkeepers have had to summon the Bamfield Lifeboat crew a good many times to rescue overturned sports-fishing and pleasure craft occupants.

Nitinat Narrows. Nitinat Narrows connects Nitinat Lake with the Pacific Ocean. Entrance to the narrows is obstructed by rocks and a shallow bar. An onshore wind can cause breaking seas. A crossing of this bar and negotiation of the narrows to Nitinat Lake is considered a supreme Northwest navigation challenge by a small number of adventurers. Each year a few boats do make it through.

Many years ago Don Douglass took his Nordic 32 tug across the bar, through the narrows, and into Nitinat Lake. His guidebook, *Exploring Vancouver Island's West Coast, 2nd Ed.* describes the experience, including the comment that his crew refused to ever try it again.

㊳ **Port San Juan.** For shelter off the Strait on the Canadian side consider Port San Juan, about halfway between Victoria and Barkley Sound. Port San Juan is a rectangular notch in Vancouver Island, with Port Renfrew on the eastern shore near the head of the bay. A public dock at Port Renfrew has limited moorage.

You can also anchor, with some protection, close to shore along the west side of Port San Juan, or tie to one of the log rafts boomed in the mouth of the Gordon River, at the northwest corner of the bay.

Readers Mike and Sandy Cecka report good anchorage close to shore behind Woods Nose. Woods Nose breaks up the swell, and trees ashore block much of the wind. A well-maintained trail leads from this anchorage to a paved road. Take a right at the road, walk another 15 minutes, and arrive at Botanical Beach Provincial Park.

The old hotel and pub at the head of the public dock has rooms, and just beyond is the Lighthouse Pub, modern and up-scale. Port Renfrew is the end of the road and the large Lighthouse Pub seems out of place until it's ex-

Rafting is encouraged at Sooke Harbour Authority docks.

plained that in the summer some 2,000 people per day—hikers, kayakers and sight-seers—pour through the town.

㊳ **Port Renfrew Community Dock.** 17280 Parkinson Rd., Port Renfrew, BC V0S 1K0; (250) 647-5431. VHF 06 & 68 "Medd-O Base." Floats with room for 20 boats are installed from mid-May through mid-September. All are taken by charter boats. No electrical power; water is on the wharf but not on the floats. Best to call ahead for availability and reservations. Stan Medd is the harbormaster.

㊳ **Pacific Gateway Marina.** (250) 412-5509; contact@pacificgatewaymarina.ca; www.pacificgatewaymarina.ca. Now open year round. Gasoline and diesel. No washrooms, power or water. Moorage to 70 feet, but most slips are designed for small sport fishing boats. Large vessels should call ahead for availability. This marina is now owned and managed by the Mill Bay Group and improvements are underway.

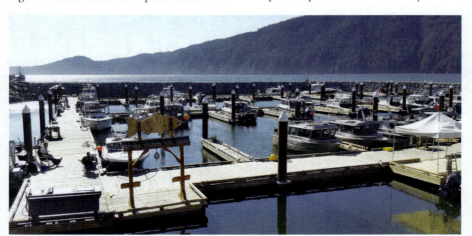

Pacific Gateway Marina at Port Renfrew

SOOKE AND BECHER BAY

㊴ **Sooke Harbour.** Enter between Company Point and Parsons Point. The harbor is protected by Whiffen Spit, which nearly blocks the passage. Enter by keeping Whiffen Spit (with its small lighthouse) close to port, and follow the marked channel to town. An area just inside Whiffen Spit has good anchorage, although wakes from passing boats make it rolly. The Sooke Harbour Marina, with guest moorage and other facilities, is south of the Sooke Harbour Authority wharf. The city floats usually are taken by commercial fishboats, but pleasure craft will find room when the fleet is out.

Sooke has a wide variety of services close to the city floats, including a marine railway and machine shop, groceries, fuel, and restaurants. Currents run quite strongly along the city waterfront. Be careful when landing.

Sooke Basin, the innermost harbor, is seldom visited by pleasure craft. The shallow channel follows the curve of the shoreline east of Middle Ground, between Eliza Point and Trollope Point. Notices to Mariners advises that entry to Sooke Basin be made after low water during daylight hours, when the drying banks are visible. Contributing Editor Tom Kincaid has anchored in a little, almost landlocked, bay behind Pim Head.

Sooke is the only completely protected harbor between Victoria and Barkley Sound. It is 15 miles closer to Barkley Sound than downtown Victoria, and often used as a departure point for boats heading up the west coast of Vancouver Island.

No customs clearance is available in Sooke. The nearest Canadian Port of Entry is Victoria.

㊴ **Sooke Harbour Resort & Marina.** 6971 West Coast Road, Sooke, BC V9Z 0V1; (250) 642-3236; reservations@sooke-

WEST COAST OF VANCOUVER ISLAND   Reference Only – Not for Navigation

Sooke

Pedder Bay Marina

harbourmarina.ca; www.sookeharbourmarina.ca. Open all year with guest moorage to 50 feet. Services include washrooms, showers, 30 & 50 amp power, Wi-Fi on shore, and 2-lane concrete launch ramp. No long term parking. This is the first marina as you come into the harbor.

㊴ **Sooke Harbour Authority.** Open all year, guest moorage along 797 feet of dock, 30 amp power, no washrooms or showers.

㊵ **Sunny Shores Resort & Marina.** 5621 Sooke Rd., RR 1, Sooke, BC V9Z 0C6; (250) 642-5731; www.sunnyshoresresort.com. Open all year. Gasoline and diesel at fuel dock. Guest moorage for 6 to 10 average size boats, call ahead for availability. Washrooms, showers, laundry, 15 amp power, haulout. Motel accommodations and campground. Mini-golf, playground. Store carries ice, fishing tackle, limited groceries. Taxi to town 3 miles away; bus to Victoria, 28 miles away.

Becher Bay. Becher Bay is a good alternative to Sooke for boaters wishing to avoid a difficult entry in fog. Although Becher Bay is farther east than Sooke, the time not spent winding your way past Whiffen Spit makes up for it. Campbell Cove on the west side of Becher Bay is a pleasant anchorage, but be careful of a drying rock near the south end. It's a good departure point for the run to Barkley Sound. Kelp is on the bottom; be sure of your set. Murder Bay, at the north end, is another recommended anchorage, also with kelp, though.

Another pleasant anchorage lies to the east of Wolf Island. For a bit of gunkholing, enter between Wolf and Lamb Islands. Be sure to avoid the submerged power cable when anchoring.

㊶ **Becher Bay Marina & Campground.** 241 Becher Bay Rd., Sooke, BC V9Z 1B7; (250) 642-3816. Open May 1 to September 30. Limited guest moorage by reservation only, maximum boat length 30 feet. Services include washrooms, no showers, 2-lane concrete launch ramp, no power. Smokin' Tuna Cafe on site. RV parking.

Pedder Bay. Pedder Bay is a mile-long inlet, shallow and narrow, just south of William Head. No anchoring in bay due to submerged utility pipes. A launch ramp with floats is at the head.

㊷ **Pedder Bay Marina.** 925 Pedder Bay Drive, Victoria, BC V9C 4H1; (250) 478-1771; pbm@obmg.com; www.pedderbay.com. Monitors VHF 66A. Open all year, gasoline only at fuel dock. Permanent and visitor moorage available for vessels up to 50', call ahead for larger boats. Washrooms, showers, laundry, 30 amp power, free Wi-Fi, 3-lane concrete launch ramp, year-round RV resort, camping, coffee shop, chandlery with bait, tackle, and ice. Approaching, use Chart 3410; watch the wind. Located between Pearson College and Dept. of National Defence (don't stop there; it's a prison). The marina is part of Oak Bay Marina Group.

FIRST-AID SUPPLIES & PREPAREDNESS

A good first-aid kit is critical when cruising in some of the more remote places. Medical help could be a day or more away. Consider adding a few additions not always included in First Aid kits that fit your lifestyle. We try to cover a reasonable range of potential medical emergencies or discomfort.

Dressings:
Hydroxide Wipes & Hydrogen Peroxide
Adhesive Bandages
Band-Aids (various sizes)
Gauze Pads, Rolls & Tape
Blister Pads such as Moleskin

Equipment:
Surgical Gloves
Tweezers and Scissors
Splinting Material
Thermometer
Gel Packs (heat/cold)

Ointments:
Antibacterial ointment such as Polysporin
Aquaphor for cracks and dry skin
Insect sting relief (medicated pads)

Medications:
Pain Relivers
Anti-acids such as Tums or Pepto Bismol
Allergy medication such as Benadryl
Sea Sickness medication - Dramamine
Cold & Flu medications, Cough Drops

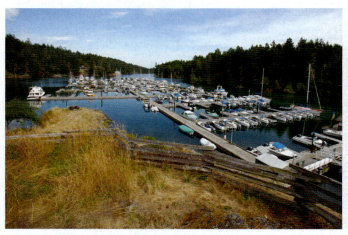
The Pedder Bay Marina has few spots for boats larger than 26 feet.

Rounding Cape Caution

CHAPTER 15

PINE ISLAND ROUTE
Pine Island • Egg Island

WALKER GROUP ANCHORAGE
Kent Island • Staples Island

PULTENEY POINT–JEANETTE ISLAND ROUTE
*Malcolm Island • Jeanette Islands • Harris Island
Hot Spring Island • Richards Channel • Allison Harbour*

MAINLAND ROUTE
*Blunden Harbour • Allison Harbour • Miles Inlet
Nakwakto Rapids • Southgate Group*

CAPE CAUTION

For many, Cape Caution is a fearsome barrier to exploring the remote and beautiful northern areas of British Columbia and on to Southeast Alaska. Like many of the challenging cruising areas of the Inside Passage, careful planning, attention to the weather reports, patience and time can lead to a smooth and uneventful crossing. We have met cruisers who may wait for days for the right settled conditions. Good weather for a crossing happens more often than you might think.

To get to the central and northern B.C. Coast you first must round Cape Caution. Although the distance in open water is only about 40 miles, the seas can be high and steep. The bottom shoals from 100+ fathoms off the continental shelf to 20-70 fathoms in Queen Charlotte Sound itself, causing seas to heap up. The problem is made worse when these seas are met by the outflowing ebb currents from Queen Charlotte Strait, Smith Sound, Rivers Inlet and Fitz Hugh Sound.

After more than 30 crossings, we've refined our "go, no-go" decisions to six factors: weather forecast; time of day; lighthouse wind and sea reports; flood or ebb tide; size of tidal exchange (spring tide or neap tide); and the automated combined wave (wave and swell) height reports from the West Sea Otter Buoy.

Weather forecast. Regardless of other factors, we want a favorable forecast or we're not going. Fog, while limiting visibility, often indicates little to no wind, favorable for a crossing if you are skilled operating your radar. Radar is very helpful as it is not unusual to have opposing traffic in this area during periods of settled conditions when others want to round Cape Caution.

Time of day. The typical summertime weather pattern calls for calm early mornings, followed in late morning or early afternoon by a rising westerly sea breeze, sometimes to gale force. "Typical," however, does not mean every day. We've seen windy mornings and flat-calm late afternoons.

Lighthouse wind and sea reports. From south to north, lighthouses, and automated stations, at Scarlett Point, Herbert Island, Pine Island, Egg Island, and Addenbroke Island report conditions approximately every four hours, posted on the Continuous Marine Broadcast. Pine Island and Egg Island are the most relevant. Addenbroke Island, inside the mouth of Fitz Hugh Sound, often reports quiet conditions when Pine Island and Egg Island are much rougher. Scarlett Point, just off the north part of Vancouver Island, usually is quieter than Pine Island and Egg Island. In our case, we can tolerate "3-foot moderate" seas, but we don't like them. "Two-foot chop, low westerly swell" is our preferred upper limit for crossing.

Flood or ebb tide. Flood tide is preferred. On a flood, the incoming swells and prevailing westerly wind are aligned and the seas are flattened. The ebb is the reverse: outflowing ebb currents meet the westerly swells, making them higher and steeper. One year we made the mistake of crossing the mouth of Rivers Inlet in a mounting sea breeze that was blowing against a strong outflowing ebb, and we took a beating. We *will not* do that again.

Size of tidal exchange. If possible, cross during a time of neap tides (half moon). If that can't be done, try to cross on a flood. If that can't be done, try to cross at the end of one tide, when currents are growing less, and the beginning of the next tide, while currents are still low. Avoid crossing the mouth of Rivers Inlet on an ebb.

West Sea Otter Buoy. When West Sea Otter Buoy reports seas 1.3 meters or less, with a dominant wave period greater than 8 seconds, crossing is likely to be pleasant. Combine this information with the weather forecast, lighthouse reports, and flood and ebb tides. We learned about West Sea Otter from a towboat skipper who had been waiting for days for the buoy to report 1 meter or less so he could tow a raft of precious cedar logs south.

VTS Radio note. South of Cape Caution, Victoria VTS, channel 71, controls large vessel traffic. North of Cape Caution, traffic is controlled by Prince Rupert VTS, channel 11. Especially in reduced visibility, one radio should be monitoring VHF 16 and a second radio should be scanning channels 11 and 71. If large vessels or tugs with tows are around, you want to know about them.

Pine Island Route. This is the most popular route from Vancouver Island. It begins at Scarlett Point at the mouth of Christie Passage on Gordon Channel, and ends at Fury Cove, at the north end of Rivers Inlet. The distance is approximately 40 miles. Boats often provision and refuel in Port McNeill or Port Hardy, and move to a departure point near Christie Passage for a crossing the next morning. God's Pocket in Christie Passage, Port Alexander in Browning Passage, or Clam Cove in Gordon Channel just west of Browning Passage, are often used. Another good spot is the cove between Staples Island and Kent Island in the Walker Group.

The Pine Island route leads westward in Gordon Channel to Pine Island, then northward past the tip of the Storm Islands, past Egg Island, and on to Smith Sound, Rivers Inlet or Cape Calvert. This route will give Cape Caution an offing of 1.5 to 2.5 miles.

Gordon Channel is a principal passage for commercial vessels. Display a radar reflector. In thick weather or fog, radar and GPS are extremely useful. Especially in low visibility or fog, most commercial traffic can be avoided by crossing Gordon Channel to the Redfern Island/Buckle Group side, and favoring that side to Pine Island.

Pulteney Point to Jeanette Islands Route. If Queen Charlotte Strait is behaving, this can be a good route from Port McNeill, on Vancouver Island, to the mainland side. From Pulteney

Cape Caution has a reputation for challenging weather, but it's not always rough. We often cross Queen Charlotte Sound in conditions like this.

The Pine Island Lighthouse provides useful weather updates.

398　　　　　www.WaggonerGuide.com

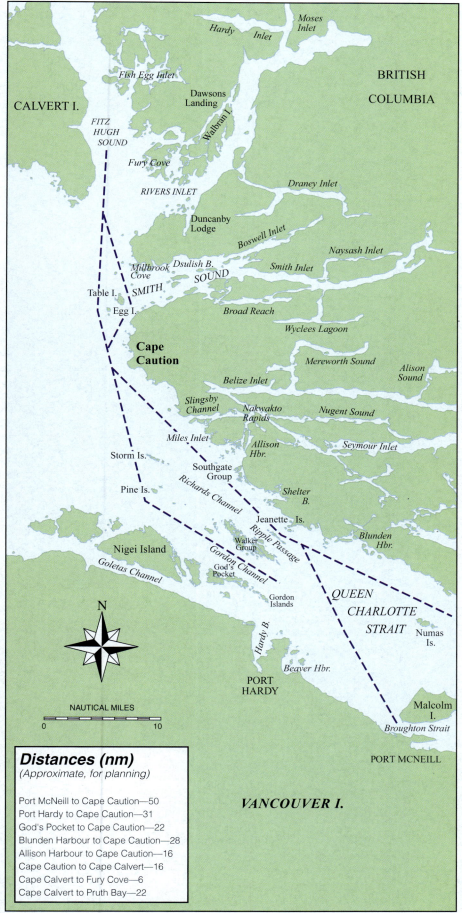

Distances (nm)
(Approximate, for planning)

Port McNeill to Cape Caution—50
Port Hardy to Cape Caution—31
God's Pocket to Cape Caution—22
Blunden Harbour to Cape Caution—28
Allison Harbour to Cape Caution—16
Cape Caution to Cape Calvert—16
Cape Calvert to Fury Cove—6
Cape Calvert to Pruth Bay—22

Point at the west tip of Malcolm Island, turn to a course of 309° magnetic. This will leave the charted kelp patch to port. Twenty miles later you will arrive at the Jeanette Islands on the mainland side of Queen Charlotte Strait. Turn to approximately 290° magnetic and proceed through Richards Channel until flashing green Whistle Buoy N31 is abeam to port. Alter course slightly to leave Harris Island to starboard and Allen Rocks Lighted Whistle Buoy N33 to port. From there a course of approximately 293° magnetic will take you to a common intersection point west of Cape Caution.

Caution in Richards Channel. On an ebb, especially a big ebb, Richards Channel can be difficult. One year, although the wind was calm, a big ebb set up a 2.5-knot outflowing current that opposed the incoming swells, creating larger and more threatening seas. We aborted our crossing and anchored instead in Allison Harbour. High winds kept us in Allison Harbour the following day and night.

Mainland Route. The mainland route offers more shelter in case of a blow and lets you visit Blunden Harbour, Allison Harbour, Miles Inlet, and Milbrook Cove in Smith Sound. You could even take a major side trip through famed Nakwakto Rapids (at slack) and spend time in Seymour Inlet and Belize Inlet. Many boats prefer the mainland route for its greater interest and possibility of shelter. The major cautions are Richards Channel on an ebb (above) and the waters off Slingsby Channel on an ebb.

Slingsby Channel Caution. Slingsby Channel is the primary drain for the hundreds of miles of inlets behind Nakwakto Rapids. What Slingsby Channel does to Queen Charlotte Strait on a big ebb can be terrifying. Outer Narrows at the mouth of Slingsby Channel runs to 9 knots on an ebb. The water fire-hoses into Queen Charlotte Strait, where it collides with the Pacific Ocean's incoming swells. If a westerly is blowing against this vast outpouring, conditions can be as bad as the worst at Cape Mudge.

Outer Narrows currents turn 10 minutes before Nakwakto Rapids, both flood and ebb. We departed our anchorage in Allison Harbour at 8:00 a.m., not realizing that two hours earlier the maximum ebb at Nakwakto Rapids was 11.4 knots. Shortly after 8:00 a.m. Slingsby Channel was still roaring. Although not a breath of wind was stirring, we found ourselves in large, steep seas that lifted the bow high, then crashed us down into the troughs. We pressed on, hoping not to meet a log in the bottom of a trough, and got through without injury or damage. The turbulence diminished but persisted all the way to Cape Caution, which we rounded at 10:10 a.m., a half-hour after the turn to flood in Slingsby Channel.

Summing up. We have rounded Cape Caution 30 times, and only twice have the crossings been unpleasant. The first was the beating we took when we were off Rivers Inlet. We knew we were pressing our luck and we paid dearly. The second was the frightening conditions off Slingsby Channel, even with the wind calm. In both cases it was the ebb that led to the trouble. [*Hale*]

Northern B.C. Coast

CHAPTER 16

BLUNDEN HARBOUR TO SLINGSBY CHANNEL
Allison Harbour • Miles Inlet • Nakwakto Rapids

SMITH SOUND
Table Island • Millbrook Cove • Ahclakerho Channel

RIVERS INLET AND FISH EGG INLET
Duncanby Lodge • Dawsons Landing • Fury Cove

FITZ HUGH SOUND & FISHER CHANNEL
Pruth Bay • Ocean Falls • Shearwater

BURKE & DEAN CHANNELS, BELLA COOLA
Eucott Hot Springs • Elcho Harbour

SEAFORTH CHANNEL & MILBANKE SOUND
Roscoe Inlet • Reid & Jackson Passages • Fiordland

FINLAYSON CHANNEL TO PRINCE RUPERT
Klemtu • Butedale • Bishop Bay • Hartley Bay

NORTHERN B.C. COAST

Planning a Trip to the Northern B.C. Coast. Most cruisers limit their voyages to the waters south of a line that runs between Wells Passage on the mainland to Port Hardy on Vancouver Island. North of this line the northern part of Queen Charlotte Sound is a natural barrier. It takes time, a strong boat, and good navigation skills to proceed farther up the coast. To be fair, a lifetime of cruising could be spent south of that line with complete satisfaction.

But—to those with the time and inclination—the coast north of Wells Passage is a special experience. The scenery is magnificent, the population is small and self-sufficient, the fishing can be exceptional and you can even take a warm soak at one of several hot springs. You can anchor in bays with no other boats and take in the scenery all by yourself.

This is the part of the coast where you'll find the famous names: Nakwakto Rapids, Rivers Inlet, Fish Egg Inlet, Hakai, Bella Bella, Ocean Falls, Ivory Island, Fiordland, Butedale, Grenville Channel, Prince Rupert. It's a coast filled with history and possibilities. If it's wilderness you seek, you can find it here.

Be self-reliant. Between Port Hardy and Prince Rupert, there are few marinas with services for pleasure boats. Be glad the facilities are there, and don't complain if they're a little rough and maybe a bit more expensive. Don't expect marina help to come down to take your lines as you land.

Most facilities and businesses are set up to take credit cards. ATMs are limited except for a machine at Shearwater and sometimes in Klemtu, and you have full banking in Prince Rupert. You'll still have telephones, but not as often. Cell phone coverage is spotty. To determine whether you have cell phone coverage or roaming in this area, check with your provider. There are several areas with cell phone coverage between Port Hardy and Prince Rupert. Generally speaking you will find coverage at Shearwater/New Bella Bella, Klemtu, Hartley Bay, Kitimat, and Bella Coola. Some boats rent or purchase satellite phones when cruising this area. Satellite based messaging devices, such as the Garmin InReach system, with weather forecast delivery options, are useful in isolated areas with no VHF radio reception. Land line pay phones are in Bella Coola, Shearwater, New Bella Bella, Ocean Falls, and Klemtu.

Insurance. Some vessel insurance policies don't cover these waters without a special rider. Check with your marine insurance broker before you leave.

The boat. Not many small boats cruise the northern coast. You'll sometimes see jerry cans filled with extra fuel or water lashed to the rails or in the cockpits. Radar and GPS should be considered standard equipment. This is remote country. The boat should be in top mechanical condition. Complete spares should be carried.

Many anchorages along this coast are 60 to 90 feet deep, with shallower water too close to shore to swing in comfort. You'll need ample anchor rode—300 feet should be considered the minimum.

Dall's Porpoise love to accompany boats.

Bottoms often are rocky. Because of its resistance to bending and its ability to set and hold in nearly any bottom, including rock, Bruce is a popular anchor. Manson Supreme, Rocna, CQR, Ultra and Delta anchors also are popular. You don't see as many Danforth style anchors. Danforth style anchors are good in sand and mud, but they have trouble setting in rock, and once wedged they are easily bent.

Be sure to carry at least two anchors. Whatever the style of anchors chosen, they should be big, strong, and ready to deploy.

Fuel and water. Fuel is plentiful, both gasoline and diesel, all the way up the coast. Rivers Inlet has gasoline and diesel at Duncanby Lodge & Marina and at Dawsons Landing. You can get gasoline and diesel at Bella Coola, Shearwater, New Bella Bella, Klemtu, Kitimat, Hartley Bay, and Prince Rupert. The longest distance between fuel stops is roughly 70 miles.

Water is available all along the way. Some of it may be tinged brown from cedar bark tannin, but people have been drinking cedar water for decades with no ill effects. Ocean Falls has sparkling clear, purified water. New Bella Bella, Klemtu and Hartley Bay have multi-million-dollar water treatment plants that deliver clear, pure water.

Weather. Bring clothes for all conditions, from cold and rainy to hot and sunny. Expect wet weather at least part of the time. The residents of Ocean Falls call themselves "The Rainpeople" for good reason. Some years have been so wet that a few boats quit their cruise.

Plan for clouds down on the deck, for fog, for rain (both vertical and horizontal), and for storms. Leave enough flexibility in the schedule to anchor through serious foul weather. Be sure the boat is well-provisioned and equipped with generator or battery power to spend several days at anchor in one location.

Plan on sunshine, too, maybe a lot of sunshine. It can get *hot*. Bring bug spray, and equip the boat with screens on doors, hatches, opening ports, and windows.

Cabin heat is essential. Many boats use a Red Dot-style truck heater while under power, and a second heat source at anchor. Depending on the boat, secondary heat can be electric (generator required), diesel furnace, diesel heater, oil galley stove, wood stove, or propane catalytic heater.

Sailboaters will want some sort of cockpit protection, from a companionway dodger to full cockpit enclosure. Keep the cabin warm and dry, or you'll be miserable.

Marinas. There aren't many marinas on this coast. In Rivers Inlet, Duncanby Lodge & Marina has guest moorage, fuel and dining. Dawsons Landing has moorage, fuel and supplies. The Native band stores at New Bella Bella and Klemtu have a good grocery selection. Shearwater, near New Bella Bella, has moorage, a restaurant and pub, groceries, chandlery, fuel, water, haulout and repairs. Ocean Falls has moorage, power, water, Wi-Fi and a pub in nearby Martin Valley. Farther north, Hartley Bay has fuel, water, and limited moorage. Prince Rupert has just about everything.

If you're in a jam, you could seek help at one of the sportfishing lodges along the coast, but remember that their business is serving their fly-in fishing guests, not recreational boats.

Dogs and hiking. Shorelines often are steep and rocky along this part of the coast, with few good places to walk the dog or take a walk yourself. Although we have seen many pets on board, we've met a number of cruisers who feel it's just too difficult to get a dog ashore. People who enjoy regular walks and hikes will find their options limited. All agree that the coast is beautiful, but some would welcome more opportunity for exercise.

Repairs. While it's best to carry complete spares and know how to fix whatever goes wrong, nobody can be ready for everything. Parts and mechanics can be flown in anyplace along the coast between Port Hardy and Prince Rupert. The only full-service shipyard is at

NORTHERN B.C. COAST

Shearwater. Kitimat has facilities and a yard for repairs. Prince Rupert has full services, though they primarily serve the fishing fleet.

Charts and reference books. The Canadian Hydrographic Service has more than 65 charts that cover the coast from Wells Passage to Prince Rupert. Many boats that like to use paper charts will make the passage with fewer than 65 charts, but the number of charts on board likely will be closer to 65 than 35. Despite their cost ($20 Cdn.), consider buying every chart, both small scale and large scale, in the area you plan to cruise. Include a few extra charts for unplanned side trips, unless your schedule calls for a straight passage up the main route (Interstate 5, as it is sometimes called). It takes a capital investment to cruise this coast safely and enjoyably.

Many boats carry a copy of Marine Atlas, Vol. 2, especially for those who rely on their chartplotter or laptop navigation system. The charts in the atlas are long out of date and many of the place names have changed, but the course lines are helpful. The book is a good quick reference and backup.

Tides and currents are shown in Ports and Passes and Canadian Tide and Current Tables, Vol. 7, (the purple book). North of Cape Caution you may want to consider getting the new 3-volume set of Sailing Directions for the North Coast, PAC 200, 205, and 206.

The most complete guidebook is *Exploring the North Coast of British Columbia*, 3rd Ed., by Don Douglass and Réanne Hemingway-Douglass, published and updated in 2017. Check www.WaggonerGuide.com for information on the updated edition. *Cruising the Secret Coast*, by Jennifer and James Hamilton, opens up anchorages in some of the most scenic, out-of-the-way locations for this area and others.

For the latest updates, sign up for WaggonerGuide.com email alerts. We also recommend a subscription to *Pacific Yachting* magazine, published in Canada. This is a well-done monthly magazine with cruising articles and updates on boating along the B.C. coast.

CHARTS

3547	Queen Charlotte Strait, Eastern Portion (1:40,000)
3548	Queen Charlotte Strait, Central Portion (1:40,000)
3549	Queen Charlotte Strait, Western Portion (1:40,000)
3550	Approaches to Seymour Inlet & Belize Inlet (1:40,000)
3552	Seymour Inlet & Belize Inlet (1:50,000)
3598	Cape Scott to Cape Calvert (1:74,500)
3921	Fish Egg Inlet & Allison Harbour (1:20,000)
3934	Approaches to Smith Sound & Rivers Inlet (1:40,000)

Blunden Harbour is a beautiful anchorage, with room for many boats. It's a good starting point for an early morning rounding of Cape Caution.

BLUNDEN HARBOUR TO SLINGSBY CHANNEL

Wells Passage to Blunden Harbour. The entrance to Blunden Harbour is approximately 11 miles northwest from the mouth of Wells Passage.

Blunden Harbour. Blunden Harbour is a lovely, well-protected bay, with excellent holding ground. As you approach the entrance it is important to identify Siwiti Rock and leave it to starboard. Study the 1:15,000 Blunden Harbour inset on Chart 3548 or your chartplotter. Note the several rocks along both sides of the passage into Blunden Harbour. These rocks make a somewhat serpentine route necessary as you go in.

Anchor anywhere in the large basin, or between Moore Rock and Byrnes Island. We feel that Moore Rock is closer to Byrnes Island than the chart suggests. An abandoned Indian village is on the north shore, and the beach is littered with relics. A large "no trespassing" sign warns against exploring the uplands, however.

You can explore Bradley Lagoon in the northeast corner of Blunden Harbour. Those who have say it's interesting. Take the dinghy through the rapids at high water slack.

Southgate Group. The Southgate Group is a cluster of islands at the corner of the route between Blunden Harbour and Allison Harbour. A passage between Southgate Island and Knight Island makes for a scenic, sheltered shortcut. Basins on either side of the narrows appear just right for anchoring. Chart 3921 shows the passage in large detail.

Allison Harbour. Allison Harbour is large, long and nicely protected, with room for many boats. Log booms may be tied to shore. Crabbing is said to be good. The best holding ground is toward the head, in 20 to 25 feet. *Favor the western shore as you enter and leave, to avoid a rock that lies almost mid-channel, about halfway in.*

Murray Labyrinth. This one is for the brave, who will be rewarded. *Exploring the North Coast of British Columbia* has a good description of Murray Labyrinth, and *Best Anchorages...* authors Kelly and Vipond describe Murray Labyrinth in glowing terms. Waggoner Correspondents Lorraine and John Littlewood report:

"The inner cove is a special place to us and nearly a perfect anchorage. It's guarded by what looks to be an impossibly tortuous, kelp-choked entrance, so most boats pass on by (in 10 years, we've not seen another boat there). It's not that hard, though, and the reward is that extreme rarity on the coast: a landlocked, completely protected anchorage with access at any tide and endless exploration potential by kayak or dinghy.

"We took our 43-foot Ocean Alexander in twice, and other boats before. It was a piece of cake each time—just keep a bow watch and go dead slow, in and out of gear as necessary to give yourself plenty of time to react. All obstacles are plainly visible or charted. Use the south entry only. Do not attempt to enter or leave through the northern passage in anything other than a kayak or dinghy. It's foul, and what appear to be two rocks are really one rock with the middle part awash at low tide." [*Littlewood*]

Skull Cove. Skull Cove is on Bramham Island, roughly opposite Murray Labyrinth. It is one of the prettier anchorages you will find. If approaching from the south, we would pass behind Southgate Island and follow the eastern mainland shore almost to City Point. Then we would turn northwest, leaving Town Rock to port, and go through the passage between the Deloraine Islands and Murray Labyrinth, thus avoiding all the rocks and reefs that lie offshore. If approaching from the north, follow the Bramham Island shore.

Enter Skull Cove on the east side of the unnamed island and take anchorage in the cove immediately to port, in 20 to 25 feet. The view on the west side of the island is superb.

Miles Inlet. Miles Inlet indents the west shore of Bramham Island and is beautiful. The narrow passage is lined with silver snags. The trees are not tall, suggesting wind from winter storms blows strongly in the inlet. The entrance is narrow, but using McEwan Rock as a reference, the entrance is easy to locate. Offlying rocks are on each side of the entrance. Go directly down the middle. Once inside, anchor in a little nook on the north side of the entrance channel or at the T intersection. The two arms of the T shoal rapidly, but the north arm has more room.

NORTHERN B.C. COAST

Boat name signs attached to trees on Turret Rock in Nakwakto Rapids

Schooner Channel. Schooner Channel, along the east side of Bramham Island, is narrow and requires constant attention to avoid rocks and reefs. With attention, however, the channel is not difficult to run. Watch tidal currents closely. The flood runs to 5 knots and the ebb to 6 knots. Schooner Channel currents are shown in Ports and Passes and Canadian Tide and Current Tables, Vol. 6, as a secondary station based on Nakwakto Rapids.

An unnamed bay opposite Goose Point at the north end of Schooner Channel is mentioned in Sailing Directions as a good anchorage for small craft.

LOCAL KNOWLEDGE

Tide-Rip: Mike Guns, a commercial fisherman with much experience in these waters, reports that when an ebb current opposes a westerly wind, the entrance to Outer Narrows and Slingsby Channel is on par with the worst conditions that Nahwitti Bar or Cape Mudge can produce. He has seen "noticeable turbulence" as long as 3 hours after maximum ebb at Nakwakto Rapids. Take this patch of water seriously.

Slingsby Channel. Slingsby Channel runs between the mainland and the north side of Bramham Island. Currents in Outer Narrows, between the Fox Islands and Vigilance Point, run to 7 knots on the flood and 9 knots on the ebb. Outer Narrows is shown as a secondary station based on Nakwakto Rapids in Canadian Tide and Current Tables, Vol. 6 or Ports and Passes.

You can enter Slingsby Channel via a narrow, scenic channel that runs between the Fox Islands and Bramham Island, thus avoiding Outer Narrows entirely. Sailing Directions mentions the channel but does not encourage it. We found the channel easy to run, and deeper than the chart shows. [*Hale*]

Treadwell Bay. Treadwell Bay is a good, protected anchorage at the east end of Slingsby Channel. It is often used by boats awaiting slack water at Nakwakto Rapids. Favor the east shore as you enter to avoid rocks off the Anchor Islands. The rocks are shown clearly on the charts. Inside, beware of rocks shown on the chart off the south shore of the bay.

Nakwakto Rapids. Nakwakto Rapids is among the world's fastest. Especially on spring tides, they must be transited at slack water only. At neap tides the window of safety opens a little wider. We have been told that high water slack is much preferred over low water slack. On big tides in particular, take this advice very, very seriously.

During the full rush of a maximum tidal current, the sound and action of the rushing water give the impression that Turret Rock actually trembles. Brave mariners have nailed boards with their boat names to trees on Turret Rock. Favored passage is on the west side.

Behind Nakwakto Rapids lie the extensive

Blunden Harbour to Slingsby Channel

2018 WAGGONER CRUISING GUIDE

NAKWAKTO RAPIDS AND BELIZE INLET

If you are looking for a much less-traveled area with remote anchorage and intriguing, majestic scenery, the labyrinth of waterways lying southeast of Cape Caution is the place to be. How often do boaters on their way to or from Southeast Alaska focus on getting around the Cape Caution gate instead of seeing the cruising opportunities awaiting in the variety of inlets behind Cape Caution?

Allison Harbour, located south of Bramham Island, serves as a starting point for timing a passage through Nakwakto Rapids, the gate to this labyrinth of remote inlets.

On a recent trip, we anchored for the night in Allison Harbour and departed the following day, allowing 40 minutes to reach Nakwakto Rapids before slack. One of the world's fastest rapids, Nakwakto can attain speeds of 14.5 knots on large ebb tides and holds a record second only to Sechelt Rapids. Like other boaters, we had heard about these rapids and had seen photographs which tend to deter boaters from taking this passage. As we discovered, however, transiting the rapids at slack is a non-event; admittedly, timing the rapids is crucial. Not only is it the speed that makes Nakwakto treacherous, but also the whirlpools and eddies. Nakwakto Rapids is not one to challenge in anything but slack; within 15 minutes of slack, you can see turbulence and eddies. While transiting the rapids at slack is easily done, it's not uncommon to meet a tug pulling a raft of logs. As we neared the entrance to Nakwakto Rapids, we saw a tug approaching from the opposite direction and circled around a small islet to wait for the tug to be well clear before continuing into the passageway. Normally, seeing tugs at rapids is often a concern; but in this case, they serve as a confirmation that it's time to go through. Turret Rock, known locally as 'Tremble Island' lies in the middle of the narrow Nakwakto Rapids. Boaters can pass around either side of Turret Rock; the west side is considered the preferred side. On our return trip, however, we passed on the east side with equal ease. Transiting each side allowed us to see all of the boat names attached to trees on this tiny rock island, a long-standing tradition.

Once through Nakwakto Rapids, boaters have three main headings to explore: east into Nugent Sound; southeast into Seymour Inlet which includes Frederick Sound; or northeast into Belize Inlet which includes Mereworth Sound and Alison Sound. Seldom visited by pleasure boaters, we found ourselves completely alone among these isolated scenic inlets, hidden from the outside world. With limited time, we chose the beautiful Belize Inlet route, a fjord-like channel with steep mountains and numerous waterfalls. Putting the nose of Got d' Fever up close to one of the falls, we took in the quiet, undisturbed majesty of this remote backcountry.

While traversing through the bends and turns admiring the variety of geological formations and vegetation, we couldn't help but marvel that this area was once home to the Nakwaktok people. Pictographs in the area give evidence of their previous life here. A pictograph on the northern shore of Belize Inlet (near the entrance to Alison Sound) depicts a sailing ship and some canoes, men in the canoes appear to be holding what looks like rifles. As we turned up Alison Sound following the narrow, twisting channel lined with more mountain peaks and cascading waterfalls, we found a second pictograph on the north shore showing a row of canoes with one lone canoe approaching. It is reported that a Native Nakwaktok camp in Village Cove of Mereworth Sound was fired upon in 1868 in retaliation for an assault on a trading vessel named Thorton; perhaps these pictographs record this incident. History indicates that a main village as well as summer camps were established throughout these inlets.

For us, our journey took us to the head of Belize Inlet ending at a delta. Backtracking a short distance, we found anchorage at Summers Bay over an irregular bottom in about 60 feet of water. The still quiet evening was interrupted only by the sound of a nearby waterfall and the chirping of birds as the sun went behind the peaks above Chief Nollis Bay at the western end of Alison Sound.

– *Lorena Landon*

One of many scenic stops on Belize Inlet on the way to Alison Sound

Dramatic scenery on Belize Inlet where very few boaters venture

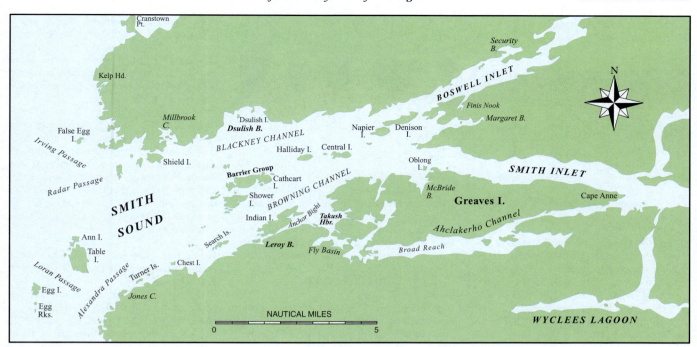
Smith Sound

waterways of Seymour Inlet, Belize Inlet, Nugent Sound, and Alison Sound.

Note: Our sister publication *Cruising the Secret Coast*, by Jennifer and James Hamilton, devotes three chapters to the approaches to Nakwakto Rapids and the extensive waters of Seymour Inlet and Belize Inlet. Highly recommended.

SMITH SOUND

Smith Sound doesn't see many pleasure boats, but it's reputed to be full of fish. We visited during an opening for gillnet commercial salmon fishing, and the boats turned out in force. Picking our way among the nets required close attention, but all went well.

You're on your own in Smith Sound itself. There are no resorts or settlements. Several bays are good for anchoring, although only one, Millbrook Cove, really appeals to us.

From the south, enter Smith Sound through Alexandra Passage, between North Iron Rock and Egg Rocks. From the west, enter through Radar Passage. From the north, enter through Irving Passage. We suggest that you plot waypoints to keep clear of rocks. This is especially true in reduced visibility.

Table Island. Table Island is in the mouth of Smith Sound, and the casual visitor would not think of it as an anchorage. But fish boats anchor there and have no problems. A boat waiting to make a southerly dash around Cape Caution could find this anchorage useful, as could

CHARTS	
3931	Smith Inlet, Boswell Inlet & Draney Inlet (1:40,000)
3932	Rivers Inlet (1:40,000)
3934	Approaches to Smith Sound & Rivers Inlet (1:40,000)

a boat seeking shelter from a westerly in Queen Charlotte Sound.

Jones Cove. Jones Cove is on the south shore of Smith Sound, near the mouth. The cove is cozy and well protected and often used by commercial fish boats. Anchor in 20 feet with limited swinging room. Depending on the rise and fall of the tide and the presence of other boats, you may choose to run a stern-tie to shore.

Fly Basin. Fly Basin is on the south side of Smith Sound at 51°16.35'N/127°36.20'W. "It is very private and protected, but entry requires care. Study of the chart will show that you should favor the western shore until opposite the point of land extending from the eastern shore. Then swing to the east side of the channel. The charted rocks can be difficult to see except at low water. Once in, anchor in 15 to 25 feet (zero tide) in the eastern section of the bay, excellent holding in mud." [*Hamilton*]

Correspondents John and Lorraine Littlewood report the western basin is also good. Work your way in past the rocks, and anchor in pristine surroundings on a good mud bottom. They begged us to not tell a soul about this anchorage, but since we are friends we feel safe letting you in on it.

McBride Bay. This bay is on the north side of Greaves Island, at the east end of Browning Channel. It is deep until near the head, which has 30 to 40 foot anchoring depths. Protection is excellent, but swinging room is a little limited.

Ahclakerho Channel. Ahclakerho Channel leads along the south side of Greaves Island. The current runs hard in the channel. Transit at slack water, especially on big tides. Slack appears to be around the time of high and low water at Bella Bella. Correspondent Gil Flanagan reports: "This is an overlooked gem. The narrow part of the channel is probably 200 feet wide. The anchorage on the east side of the 78-meter east Ahclakerho Island gives good protection from west winds in Smith Sound. We stern-tied among numerous rocks and small islands. It was beautiful."

Margaret Bay. Margaret Bay is at the head of Smith Sound, on the point of land that separates Boswell Inlet and Smith Inlet. Chambers Island, rather small, is in the middle of the bay, about halfway in. West of Chambers Island depths are too great for anchoring. East of the island they shallow to 50 to 55 feet. The head shoals sharply, and old pilings take up much of the room at the head. Protection is excellent.

Ethel Cove. Ethel Cove is just outside the mouth of Margaret Bay. It looks right out to sea, however, and we found a very low surge coming in. Get close to shore or anchor in 50 to 60 feet farther out.

Finis Nook. Finis Nook is located near the mouth of Boswell Inlet, on the south shore, sort of "around the corner" from Margaret Bay. It is nearly landlocked and completely protected; it seems a perfect anchorage. A log boom blocks the back bay, however, and a float house is on the east side, with the wreck of a fish boat. Anchoring depths in the area not already taken are approximately 35 feet. We were disappointed, and went back to Millbrook Cove to overnight. (In *Cruising the Secret Coast*, the Hamiltons like Finis Nook).

Dsulish Bay. Dsulish Bay, with beautiful white sand beaches, is on the north shore of Smith Sound. A trail reportedly leads to Goose Bay to the north. The best anchorage is behind the 46-meter island, deep inside the bay. It is a little open but workable. We have seen fish boats anchored along the west side of Dsulish Bay. In

NORTHERN B.C. COAST

See Area Map Page 407 - Maps Not for Navigation

Millbrook Cove a quiet, protected anchorage at the entrance of Smith Sound.

the right conditions it would be a good lunch stop, though we're not so sure about overnight.

Millbrook Cove. This is the outermost anchorage on the north side of Smith Sound. To us it is the favored anchorage. The cove is completely landlocked, with 25 to 35 foot depths, good holding ground, and ample room.

Getting in will hold your attention, at least the first time. Find the red spar buoy E6 marking Millbrook Rocks. The buoy has a small radar reflector on top. Leave this buoy to starboard (Red, Right, Returning), and aim the boat toward the 30-meter island. Keep a sharp lookout for rocks on both sides, especially the west side, as shown on the chart. The 30-meter island can be passed on either side, although the east side is a little deeper.

Once in, watch for a drying rock a short distance off the northeast corner of the 30-meter island. Minding your depths, anchor anywhere.

RIVERS INLET

Note: Cruising the Secret Coast, by Jennifer and James Hamilton, contains an entire chapter devoted to cruising the parts of Rivers Inlet not covered here, with a little overlap.

Rivers Inlet is a famed salmon fishing area and, at one time, had 18 salmon canneries. All the canneries are closed now and most are sinking into ruin. Absent its commerce of former years, Rivers Inlet is prime cruising ground. The scenery is beautiful and the anchorages excellent. The area is served by two marinas: Duncanby Lodge & Marina and Dawsons Landing. In Goose Bay, a substantial concrete dock provides access to the Goose Bay Cannery, but no amenities.

Open Bight. Open Bight, well named, is just inside Cranstown Point at the entrance to Rivers Inlet. Anchorage, with protection from westerlies but not easterlies or northerlies, is along the south and west shores. The west shore is preferred. We would put the hook down outside the kelp line in 25 to 30 feet, within view of a stunning white shell midden beach. Gentle swells will rock the boat.

Home Bay. Home Bay, on the south shore a short distance inside the mouth of Rivers Inlet, is a pretty spot.

Just west of Home Bay is another nook, which Douglass calls West Home Bay in *Exploring the North Coast of British Columbia*. The bay has anchorage behind the first of two islets inside. Contrary to Douglass's illustration, however, low tide reveals rocks that foul the western side of that first islet. We would pass the islet only to the east.

Other anchoring possibilities lie in the unnamed group of islands just west of Duncanby Lodge & Marina. Larger boats will find good anchoring in deep water in the unnamed cove marked with 29-meter and 35-meter soundings. The large island with the 105-meter hill is at the north end of this cove. Smaller boats can creep into the unnamed cove east of the deep water cove. This cove is marked with a 9-meter sounding in the mouth and a 16-meter sounding inside. A fishing resort outpost is moored on the eastern shore. The little nook at the northeast end of the cove offers quiet anchorage in 60 to 120 feet, but be careful when you enter this nook. A reef extends northward nearly halfway across the entrance, much farther than the chart suggests. Favor the north side.

① **Duncanby Lodge & Marina.** (604) 628-9822; (877) 846-6548; www.duncanbylodge-marina.com. Monitors VHF 06. Open 7 days a week, June 1 through early-September. Gaso-

---

CLOSE ENCOUNTER IN FITZ HUGH SOUND

We were southbound in thick fog and calm seas in Fitz Hugh Sound, having left our anchorage in Kisameet Bay early and hoping the fog would lift and the seas would remain calm for an uneventful rounding of Cape Caution later in the day.

The fog did begin to lift as we motored along the eastern shore. A mile in front of us, in front of Fairmile Passage, the northern entrance to Fish Egg Inlet, we could see two humpback whales close together, spouting and apparently feeding.

We altered course, but it seemed the whales were moving in that direction as well, so we altered course again in the opposite direction. The whales moved in that direction, too, as if to intercept us.

Finally, the whales were very close. Each of them was easily the size of our boat, a 1982 43-foot Ocean Alexander. We had slowed to idle and then into neutral as one of the whales broke off and slid past us, about 25 feet off to port. We were looking frantically for the other one when, without warning, there was a spout directly under our bow with an accompanying loud whoosh. The mist drifted over the foredeck and onto the cabin windows, and we felt a gentle but very discernible bump as our new friend decided to have a close encounter of the third kind (apologies to Spielberg). The boat lifted slightly and slid off to starboard, while we, in no particular order, shouted to each other to: (a) Watch Out! (b) Get the Camera! (c) Hold On! We managed only (c). Suddenly our heavy old Ocean Alexander didn't feel so substantial.

We've been told that humpbacks sometimes like to do this and it doesn't appear to be accidental, but this was the first time for us. You simply cannot believe how big these animals are until you see/hear/smell/feel them at this range. "Immense" is the first word that comes to mind. Clearly, they knew we were there. With two engines running and two depth sounders pinging at two different frequencies, we weren't exactly stealthy. The whales just delivered a gentle reminder about who belongs where. We got the message.

— Lorraine & John Littlewood

CHARTS

3727	Cape Caution to Goose Island (1:73,584)
3935	Hakai Passage & vicinity (1:40,000)
3939	Fisher Channel to Seaforth Channel & Dean Channel (1:40,000)
3936	Fitz Hugh Sound to Lama Passage (1:40,000)
3921	Fish Egg Inlet & Allison Harbour (1:20,000)
3932	Rivers Inlet (1:40,000)
3934	Approaches to Smith Sound & Rivers Inlet (1:40,000)

Rivers Inlet & Fish Egg Inlet

NORTHERN B.C. COAST

line and diesel (available year round), water on the docks (filtered but still tinted brown). Guest moorage is located on the outside of the south floats, and are exposed to wind and waves. No power, no water. Make reservations online or by phone. Showers and drop-off laundry services are available. The restaurant serves breakfast, lunch, dinner, and is very good. Restaurant is closed to the public Monday and Friday evenings, and from 10:00 a.m. to 5:00 p.m. on Tuesdays and Saturdays. A computer located in the foyer is available for internet access for a daily fee.

Duncanby is a high-quality destination fly-in fishing resort. Meals at the restaurant are delicious and priced attractively. The resort offers a quality experience, priced at the upper end of typical, but still affordable.

Goose Bay. Anchorage is good in 20 to 50 feet on a sticky bottom across the bay from the cannery buildings. Crabbing is reported to be good, too.

Goose Bay Cannery Dock. (778) 373-6346; Monitors VHF 06. Open during peak summer season. This is a private facility which is at the discretion of the owners to permit visitors to come ashore. The historic cannery in Goose Bay built in 1926 processed and canned salmon from 1927-1957 and 350 people once worked and lived at the cannery. A clean, sturdy 175-foot concrete dock is available for short-term and overnight stays on a first-come, first-serve basis; no power; no water. Leave space on the dock for floatplanes. A self-registration payment box is located at the end of the dock ramp, expect a donation fee of $1 per foot. Fees collected go towards making improvements on the cannery buildings. Projects are ongoing and shared among the multiple owners of the property. Depending on which owner you meet and the work scheduled for that day, you might be able to finesse an invitation for a brief tour of the grounds and cannery. With permission, hiking the 1 mile trail to a dam located above the cannery may be of interest, but be "bear aware" and take appropriate precautions. A waterfall, and a suspension bridge built in the 1940's can be seen near the dam. Correspondents Knut and Christine Hildebrand report that the trail is challenging. Use at your own risk.

Hemasila Inlet. "Entry to the inner basin looks impossible on the chart, but isn't. The charted rock is central in a 200-foot-wide channel and is visible except at very high tides. Favor the east side—it has slightly more room and the shore is steep. We anchored in 35 feet just north of the 9.1-meter sounding with plenty of room to swing. Holding was excellent in thick mud. It was sheltered and pretty, with a small creek at one side and a small waterfall at the other side. Watch for a rock 2.5 meters deep at zero tide in the mouth of the inlet where the *R* symbol and 24 meter sounding are located." [*Hamilton*]

Taylor Bay. Taylor Bay indents the east shore of Walbran Island and has tranquil, lovely anchorage in 35 to 50 feet, although swinging room is limited. Anchor all the way in or try the nook behind the north end of the inner island, between the inner island and Walbran Island. Protected from most winds except east and southeast.

Draney Narrows & Draney Inlet. The current runs hard in Draney Narrows. We looked in 1½ hours before the predicted turn and decided against it. Fifteen minutes before the turn the narrows were flat. Predictions are shown in Canadian Tide & Current Tables, Vol. 7 and Ports and Passes as a secondary station based on Prince Rupert Tides.

Draney Inlet, approximately 24 miles long, is surrounded by high, steep mountains. It's beautiful. Because it is not on the way to anyplace else, it sees little pleasure craft traffic. Good anchorage in 30 to 35 feet is available in Fish Hook Bay, a short distance inside the narrows. When we visited, a float home with two floating outbuildings was on the south shore of Fish Hook Bay, near the entrance. A large sign read, "Warning, Private Property, No Trespassing." A convincing watchdog greeted our boat with don't-mess-with-me barks and growls. We didn't argue.

Note: Our sister publication, *Cruising the Secret Coast*, by Jennifer and James Hamilton, devotes a chapter to Draney Inlet, with much information about anchorages and what to see.

Johnston Bay. Johnston Bay, on the east shore of Rivers Inlet just south of Wadhams, is a former cannery site. The bay is quiet and beautiful, but deep until very near the head. As the chart

Duncanby Lodge & Marina, a fishing resort with moorage and nice restaurant.

Informal owner conducted tours of the Goose Bay Cannery might be available as owner's time permits.

Visitor moorage at Goose Bay Cannery. Sign in at the head of the dock.

Relax and enjoy the view of Rivers Inlet at Dawsons Landing. *Dawsons Landing has plenty of dock space.*

shows, a reef lies in the center of the outer part of Johnston Bay, and a rock is close to the eastern shore at the entrance. Favor the western shore all the way in and you'll have ample depths with no hazards.

Sandell Bay. "North shore of Rivers Inlet, where the inlet takes that east bend. Anchor well into the bay in 25 feet, zero tide. Excellent holding in mud/sand/rock/shell. Kind of like a cement mix, and held like it, too. Sandell Bay looks exposed on the chart, but is actually protected. It was blowing 30 knots in Rivers Inlet when we came in, and from the anchorage we could see a line of whitecaps out there. But hardly any wind or fetch reached us." [*Hamilton*]

Good Hope Cannery. Good Hope Cannery is the large, white building visible when cruising past Draney Inlet. The facility is a high-end fly-in sport fishing resort. No services for cruising boats.

② **Dawsons Landing (Dawsons Landing General Store).** (604) 629-9897; dawsonslanding@gmail.com; www.dawsonslanding.ca. Monitors VHF 06. Phone service is spotty; it's often best to communicate by email. Open all year, gasoline and diesel fuel. Guest moorage, hardware, groceries, charts, ice, fishing licenses, fishing and hunting gear, liquor, washroom, showers, laundry, post office, two rental cabins with kitchenettes. Satellite based Wi-Fi available for a fee, pay at the general store. Locally produced water available on the dock. A heli-pad takes up part of the south end dock. They have scheduled air service from Wilderness Seaplanes and NW Seaplanes.

Dawsons Landing is owned by Rob and Nola Bachen, and has been in the family since 1954. This is a real general store, with an excellent stock of standard grocery items and an astonishing accumulation of tools and hardware. One year, for example, we needed an in-line fuse holder to replace a spare we had used. Dawsons had it.

Note that instead of cleats, you'll tie to loops of rope set into the planks. Absent bull rails, it's easier and safer to clear the docks of snow in the winter. The one dock with bull rails is used by float planes.

Rob and Nola are friendly and helpful, two of the most genuine people we know. The more we are around them the better we like them. Both have an impish good humor. They're a treat.

Smoked salmon: It's almost worth a trip to Dawsons Landing simply to stock up on the Bella Coola Valley Seafoods smoked wild Pacific salmon that Nola carries in the store. Several smoke flavors to choose from; time of year varies depending on commercial fishing season.

Darby Channel (Schooner Pass). Darby Channel, locally called Schooner Pass, borders the west side of Walbran Island, and is easily run. Southbound boats should favor the west shore of the channel to avoid being lured into foul ground behind Pendleton Island. The rock off the southwest corner of Pendleton Island is clearly marked by a beacon and easily avoided.

Supplying Rivers Inlet for Over 65 Years

DAWSONS LANDING
GENERAL STORE LTD.

A GENUINE OLD-TIME GENERAL STORE

Fuel • Complete Grocery
Well-Stocked Liquor Agency
Block & Cube Ice
Bottled Water • Water on Dock
Internet Hookup
Bait • Souvenirs
Moorage • Post Office
Showers & Laundry
Rental Cabins
Scheduled Air Service
We Freeze Fish

IN THE MIDDLE of the WORLD-FAMOUS RIVERS INLET FISHING GROUNDS

WWW.DAWSONSLANDING.CA
dawsonslanding@gmail.com • Phone 604/629-9897
Proprietors Rob & Nola Bachen • Dawsons Landing, BC V0N 1M0 • VHF 06

NORTHERN B.C. COAST

See Area Map Page 407 - Maps Not for Navigation

Pierce Bay. Exercise caution, because Pierce Bay contains dangerous rocks not necessarily shown on the chart. One of the rocks is east of the south tip of the largest island, at 51°31.665'N/127°45.667'W. This rock is in relatively open water, and could surprise a person. Another is off the northwest point of the large island, where the anchorage opens up.

Frypan Bay. Frypan Bay, spacious, scenic and well protected, is at the northeast corner of Penrose Island. Anchoring depths, along the south shore, are 25 to 40 feet and, in the middle, 50 to 85 feet with good holding. This anchorage is a favorite of many cruisers. The narrow entrance has an uncharted shoal on the port side shore as you enter.

Big Frypan Bay. Located on the east side of Penrose Island, this large bay has ample room for numerous boats; anchoring depths of 68 feet on a sand-mud bottom. Shallower depths can be found in a couple of coves within the bay. The short, narrow entrance to Big Frypan is straight-forward and easy to transit.

Finn Bay. Finn Bay, on the north side of Penrose Island, is well protected. An abandoned sport fishing camp is in the bay.

Sunshine Bay. Tucked in the middle of Ripon Island, the bay is entered through a narrow channel off of Klaquaek Channel. The charted shoal on the south shore at the neck of the entrance is not as extensive as depicted on the charts. Anchoring depths are 25 to 30 feet over a flat mud bottom. This intriguing bay is home to a hidden community of float-homes. During the off-season, this bay is the parking location for several floating fishing lodge buildings.

Fury Cove. The cove behind Fury Island is a beautiful and a popular anchorage, with a perfect white shell beach. Fury Cove, as it is commonly called, is entered by leaving Cleve Island to port, then turning to port towards the narrow entrance.

Fury Cove is a good place to spend the night before a southbound rounding of Cape Caution, or when headed north after crossing Cape Caution. It is popular and occasionally fills up; consider Big Frypan Bay as an alternative. While at anchor, you can look across the beach and see the conditions on Fitz Hugh Sound. Inside, avoid the charted rock that dries at 10 feet close to Fury Island. Consider taking the dinghy to shore to explore the beach and tide pools. A cabin used by kayakers is nestled in the woods on the north shore of Fury Island.

Overboard discharge: No black water overboard discharge, please. Fury Cove does not flush well.

Cleve Island is mentioned in Sailing Directions, but shown on the chart only as a 61-meter island—no name.

Breaker Pass: Breaker Pass separates Fury Island from Cleve Island. We have run through the pass in calm weather, but we could tell it wouldn't take much of a southwesterly for Breaker Pass to live up to its name.

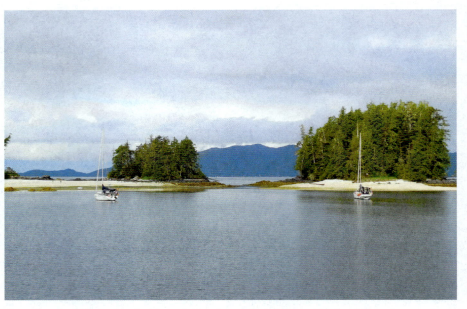

Fury Cove is well-protected with sandy beaches and windows to Fitz Hugh Sound.

Philip Inlet. Philip Inlet indents the mainland side of Fitz Hugh Sound approximately 3 miles south of Addenbroke Island. On a sunny afternoon we found the entrance hard to identify. Use caution when entering: the chart does not show the ledges of rock that extend from each side of the inlet near the mouth.

About halfway in, a small island creates a rock-strewn, tight and tricky narrows. We would not want to go through the narrows without a bow watch or good visibility from a fly bridge helm.

Once past the narrows the inlet becomes rather open-feeling and uninteresting. Depths near the head are approximately 30 feet. We went in planning to anchor for the night, but decided instead to anchor in Green Island Anchorage at the mouth of Fish Egg Inlet. [*Hale*]

Fifer Bay. Fifer Bay indents the western side of Blair Island, with lovely 6- to 12-foot anchorage for small craft at the head of the southernmost cove. There's room for one boat if it swings, more if all stern-tie to shore. When entering, favor Sweeper Island to avoid the rocks lying off the southern side of the entrance. When clear of the rocks, turn south and work your way into the anchorage.

FISH EGG INLET

Fish Egg Inlet indents the east side of Fitz Hugh Sound, behind Addenbroke Island. This is beautiful cruising country, and is becoming one of the popular spots on the coast. Those who say you'll be all alone are wrong. The gunkholing possibilities are many, but here are notes on some of the better-known anchorages.

Mantrap Inlet. Once you're inside, Mantrap Inlet offers good anchorage. The entrance, however, is narrow, made narrower by an uncharted ledge of rock that extends from the west shore. Consider going through at half tide or higher, dead slow, with a lookout.

Oyster Bay. Oyster Bay, next to Fish Trap Bay at the head of Fish Egg Inlet, is a nice anchor-

Entrance to very well-protected Sunshine Bay on Ripon Island

410   www.WaggonerGuide.com

SIR FRANCIS DRAKE (1540-1596)

Francis Drake was an English sea captain who lead a circumnavigation of the world from 1577 to 1580 as a single expedition. Believed to have landed at today's Drake Bay, Drake claimed California for the English. Encroaching upon the activities of the Spanish and plundering their ships, Drake was branded a pirate (El Draque) by the King of Spain, who put an exorbitant price on his head. In the eyes of the English, he was a hero.

In 1563, Drake made his first voyage to the Americas followed by a third expedition in 1568. Influenced by his own bold nature, he began making raids in 1572 of the Isthmus of Panama, known as the Spanish Main, where he captured incredible treasures of silver and gold. After his successful raids, Drake set out in 1577 for the Pacific Coast seeking further Spanish treasures and new lands. The northern limit of Drake's exploration has been in dispute, but recent research strongly suggests that he had gone as far as Southeast Alaska, sailing through today's 'Inside Passage.' Descriptions found in crew journals match objects which have been discovered, giving testament to his explorations. An array of stone cairns, inscribed in Latin, were found on a hillside above Nehalem Bay in Oregon. Stone cairns arranged in the shape of a large triangle, marked with compass bearings, was the system used in Drake's time to determine Longitude. In 1954 a cave, containing Tlingit burial boxes and a rectangular piece of metal with rusted holes in each corner, was discovered on Kuiu Island in Southeast Alaska. The holes seemed to indicate that the plate had been nailed to something. A rubbing was made of the Latin inscription and sent to the Smithsonian. The inscription stated that Drake had named some place 'Port Discovery' and had taken possession of the surrounding country in the name of Queen Elizabeth.

Drake's writings include accurate descriptions and drawings of the Columbia River, Grays Harbor, Fraser River, Comox Bar, Dixon Entrance, and the Stikine River. It is fascinating to contemplate the likelihood of Francis Drake exploring the Pacific Northwest 200 years before other notable early English and Spanish explorers. Frances Drake returned to Plymouth, England in 1580 and was awarded knighthood aboard his ship, the Golden Hinde, in 1581. Fortunately, or unfortunately, Queen Elizabeth forbade any detailed publication of Drake's explorations. Upon penalty of death, his destinations and maps were to be kept secret, out of reach from rival Spain. Details of his explorations were falsified at the time to misdirect the competition. Sir Francis Drake died of dysentery at sea off the coast of Panama in 1596; his body was sealed in a lead coffin and sent to the deep a few miles off the coastline. His coffin has never been found.

---

age with a remote feel to it. We had a late and relaxed lunch there, anchored in 20 feet near the head of the bay. Recommended. [*Hale*]

Fish Trap Bay. Awfully tight, but room for one boat, stern-tied. At lower water levels the Native fish trap is clearly visible.

Waterfall Inlet. Pretty spot, but we couldn't find any comfortable anchorages. We felt that the west entry, leaving the 99-meter island to starboard, was safest. Go slowly and watch for rock ledges that extend from each side of the narrow pass.

Joe's Bay. Joe's Bay has become quite popular. When we visited in early July one year, five other boats were already anchored. Joe's Bay is worth the crowds, though. It's tranquil, tree-lined and snug. Anchoring is straightforward in the southern basin; rocks and reefs make the northern portion somewhat trickier. A stern-tie to shore might be called for to keep the boat from swinging onto a rock. Once anchored, the tidal rapids leading to Elizabeth Lagoon and Sulphur Arm are worth exploring with the dinghy.

Souvenir Passage. Sailing Directions says that Souvenir Passage is very narrow at its eastern end and the chart shows a rock on the north shore. We have found good water all the way by favoring the south side of the passage.

Illahie Inlet. The head of Illahie Inlet would be a delightful anchorage in 30 to 40 feet, mud bottom, with good protection. Favor one shore or the other as you enter Illahie Inlet. Rocks lie in the middle of the channel, partway in.

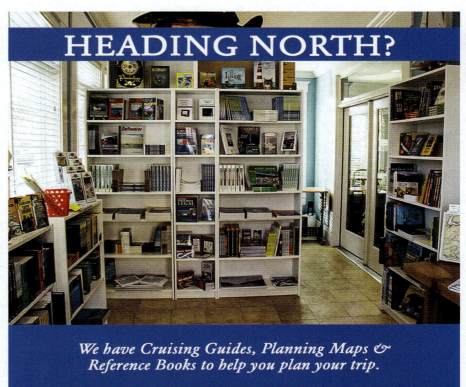

NORTHERN B.C. COAST — Reference Only – Not for Navigation

Fitz Hugh Sound to Burke Channel

Green Island Anchorage. Green Island Anchorage, just off Fitz Hugh Sound at the mouth of Illahie Inlet, is about as cozy as an anchorage needs to be. Excellent holding in 35 to 40 feet. From seaward, wrap around the 70-meter island and follow the shoreline in. This is a good spot to rest after crossing Queen Charlotte Sound.

FITZ HUGH SOUND

Fitz Hugh Sound begins at Cape Calvert and continues north to Fisher Channel. Boats crossing Queen Charlotte Sound from the south will find the ocean swells quickly vanish once Cape Calvert is behind them. A southwesterly can still make things nasty, especially in a south flowing ebb current. Even in settled conditions, expect to find rougher water where Hakai Passage joins Fitz Hugh Sound.

Northbound boats that don't stop at Rivers Inlet probably will stop in Fifer Bay, Safety Cove, or Pruth Bay. Green Island Anchorage is another good choice for passing traffic.

Safety Cove. Safety Cove is a steep-walled, uninteresting bay that indents Calvert Island approximately 7 miles north of Cape Calvert. The bottom shoals sharply a fair distance from the head of the bay. Sailing Directions recommends anchoring immediately when the depth reaches 100 feet. If you press in to find shallower water, watch your swing or you could find yourself aground on the shelf at low tide. Despite its name and regular use, Safety Cove is not our first choice of anchorages in the area.

③ **Pruth Bay.** Pruth Bay is at the head of **Kwakshua Channel**, some 7 miles north of Safety Cove. Pruth Bay has long been a favorite stopover point. It offers ample room, 40- to 50-foot anchoring depths, and a flat bottom with good holding. Storms coming off the ocean can make the bay quite windy.

This entire area is part of the **Hakai Luxvbalis Conservancy Area**, a huge provincial

CHARTS	
3727	Cape Caution to Goat Island (1:73,584)
3921	Fish Egg Inlet and Allison Harbour (1:20,000)
3934	Approaches to Smith Sound and Rivers Inlet (1:40,000)
3935	Hakai Passage and Vicinity (1:40,000)
3936	Fitz Hugh Sound to Lama Passage (1:40,000) Namu Harbour (1:20,000)
3937	Queens Sound (1:40,000)
3938	Queens Sound to Seaforth Channel (1:40,000)
3939	Fisher Channel to Seaforth Channel and Dean Channel (1:40,000)
3974	Dean Channel, Burke Channel and Bentinck Arms, 1:80,000

West Beach near Pruth Bay is arguably the best beach anywhere on the west coast.

park that includes the northern half of Calvert Island, the southern two-thirds of Hunter Island, and Goose Island.

Correspondents James and Jennifer Hamilton have anchored in about 50 feet with good holding in the unnamed cove west of Keith Anchorage, on the south shore of Kwakshua Channel, a short distance east of Pruth Bay. Anchor in this cove or one of the others that indent that shore, in Pruth Bay itself, or in the bay north of the thumb of land marked by Whittaker Point.

Southbound, we often overnight at Pruth Bay before rounding Cape Caution. Hakai Beach Institute provides free Wi-Fi in the bay, handy for downloading weather information.

Note: Our sister publication, *Cruising the Secret Coast*, by Jennifer and James Hamilton, devotes a chapter to this area. It describes anchorages not included in the Waggoner, and includes coverage of anchorages at the mouth of Hakai Passage.

③ **Hakai Beach Institute.** In 2010 the luxury fly-in fishing resort at the head of Pruth Bay was purchased by the Tula Foundation and became the Hakai Beach Institute. The facility is now used for research and as a conference center. Visitors are welcome.

No fuel or commercial services are available at Hakai Beach Institute. When arriving by dinghy, moor only at the clearly marked "dinghy dock" section of the float. The Institute requests that visitors sign the guest log at the Welcome Centre, at the head of the dock. A public washroom is adjacent.

The grounds are immaculate. Follow the signs for the trail to West Beach, one of the finest beaches on the coast. The trail is substantially covered with a boardwalk, but unfinished and muddy in some places. Carry bug spray. After a pleasant and flat hike of almost a half-mile, you hear the ocean and break out of the forest to a beautiful beach, with white sand extending in both directions. On a sunny day it seems almost tropical. On an overcast day, with crashing waves, it carries the beauty and furor of the wild Pacific Ocean. A less-developed trail leads north to North Beach, a sandy beach facing Hakai Pass; and a longer more challenging trail leads south to nine scenic west facing beaches.

Visiting boats are welcome to anchor in Pruth Bay, as long as they stay 100 meters from the dock so seaplanes have room to maneuver. Free

Easy trail from Pruth Bay brings you to West Beach.

HAKAI BEACH INSTITUTE – PRUTH BAY

Pruth Bay has always been a good overnight stop along the Inside Passage. The bay, at the head of Kwakshua Channel, is well protected and scenic. But the real attractions are West Beach and North Beach, two of the most beautiful sand beaches in the Northwest.

Access to the beach areas, however, has not always been easy. As the owners of the property have changed, the state of the trail leading across Calvert Island has ranged from poor to acceptable.

A few years back the property, formerly a fishing lodge, was acquired by the Tula Foundation and rechristened as the Hakai Beach Institute. Eric Peterson and Christina Munck, the principals of the Tula Foundation, have since transformed the property into a world-class conference and research center.

The improvements are apparent as soon as you arrive. Beautiful new docks have been installed, welcoming signage posted, and top-notch facilities constructed. Signs direct visitors to the

West Beach trail, now a well-maintained gravel and boardwalk.

Researchers and educators use the facilities to investigate and collaborate. Areas of research include local archaeology, ecology, and First Nations culture. The institute has a fleet of boats available to transport personnel and equipment throughout the area and scientific labs to support research activities.

Due to its location, the Hakai Beach Institute is totally off the grid. Electricity is generated by a 50 kW solar farm feeding into a nearly 10,000 amp hour battery bank. Water is collected on site. Sewage is heavily treated before being released. And perhaps most welcome for visiting boaters, internet is piped in through nine satellite links and distributed wirelessly throughout the property and anchorage (please, no streaming video or other bandwidth intensive tasks).

We are fortunate to have people like Eric and Christina, focused on understanding our environment and sharing the beauty of this area with visiting boaters.

You can learn more about the Hakai Beach Institute and the work of the Tula Foundation on their blog and website, www.hakai.org.

– *Mark Bunzel*

Wi-Fi covers the entire bay. Wi-Fi internet use is limited to 300mb of data per device per day. The best reception is close to the head of the bay.

Meay Inlet. Meay Inlet leads north from Kwakshua Channel to Hakai Pass. Immediately after the turn past Whittaker Point is a small scenic cove with room for 4 or 5 boats. The Hamiltons, in *Cruising the Secret Coast*, named this cove Whitaker Point Cove and report anchorage in 40 to 60 feet, with good holding in mud mixed with shell.

The Hakai Lodge fly-in fishing resort, owned by the principals of NW Seaplanes, is in a nearby cove from late June until September. The resort has almost daily floatplane service to the Renton/Seattle area, making this a good place to drop off or pick up crew or parts. In 2014 the lodge began serving meals to visiting boaters, reservations required. Email ccarlson@hakailodge.com for meal reservations. This is a seasonal resort, floats are removed in the off-season.

Hakai Passage. Hakai Passage is one of the great fishing spots, yielding 50- to 60-pound salmon and large bottom fish. Since Hakai Passage opens to the Pacific Ocean, it can get rough. Treat it with respect. On an otherwise pleasant afternoon we overheard two well-managed boats discussing on the radio whether the swells they were facing in Hakai Passage began in Japan or just Hawaii.

Goldstream Harbour. Goldstream Harbour is a lovely little anchorage at the north end of Hecate Island. Enter from the east favoring Hat Island, which extends from the south shore about 0.2 mile inside. Don't favor Hat Island too closely, though; rocks extend out from it. Hat Island is not named on the chart, but its height (39 meters) is shown. Once past Hat Island, pass Evening Rock, which dries at 1.2 meters, leaving it to starboard. Evening Rock lies about 300 feet off the northwest corner of Hat Island (it helps to refer to the chart as you read these instructions). Inside, the middle of Goldstream Harbour is about 30 feet deep. Rocks extend out from the shore, so pick your anchoring spot carefully to swing safely. This is a nice protected spot with an opening in rocks to look out at the conditions in Hakai Pass.

Ward Channel. Ward Channel connects Hakai Passage with Nalau Passage. Running it is straightforward as long as you follow the chart to keep track of the rocks.

Edward Channel. Edward Channel, west of Ward Channel, also connects Hakai Passage with Nalau Passage, but the southern entry is much tighter than Ward Channel. Pass between the 27-meter and 31-meter islets, staying well clear of the detached rock that dries at 1.6 meters off the south tip of the 27-meter islet. Chart 3935 (1:40,000) is quite clear. Don't try the south entry with the older Chart 3727 (1:73,584). It doesn't show enough detail where you need it. The primary reason to be in Edward Channel is the lovely anchorage of Lewall Inlet.

Lewall Inlet. Lewall Inlet indents the east shore of Stirling Island and is a delightful anchorage. Run all the way to the bend and anchor in 10 to 20 feet, north of the north shore of the entry channel. Stay well off the little treed islet near the south shore. A ledge of drying rock reaches out from that islet.

Uncharted rock: An uncharted rock lies mid-channel just north of the anchorage bend at approximately 51°46.150'N/128°06.266'W. The rock dries on a +2 foot tide. Use extreme caution if going north of the bend at the anchorage.

Nalau Passage. Nalau Passage, scenic and open, separates Hunter Island and Stirling Island, and connects Fitz Hugh Sound with Kildidt Sound. A conservative, mid-channel course has no hazards. The western entrance, however, is made interesting by drying rocks offshore from the north side of the passage. Eastbound boats crossing Kildidt Sound may have anxious moments finding the exact entrance. We used the following waypoint for the western entrance successfully: 51°47.10'N/128°07.20'W.

SPIDER ISLAND AREA

Note: Our sister publication, *Cruising the Secret Coast*, by Jennifer and James Hamilton, contains extensive coverage of these cruising grounds, including Kildidt Sound, Kildidt Inlet, the Goose Group, the McNaughton Group, and other wild areas between Hakai Passage and Seaforth Channel.

Kildidt Sound. Kildidt Sound is remote and beautiful with many anchorage possibilities. Consult *Cruising the Secret Coast* for more information on the numerous islets and anchorages in this area.

Serpent Group. Correspondents James and Jennifer Hamilton have anchored successfully in the cove on the easternmost side of the 57-meter island, southwest of the 31-meter island. Their anchorage was tranquil, but when they dinghied ashore and climbed to the seaward side they found windblown trees barely holding to the shore.

Kildidt Narrows. Kildidt Narrows is the reversing tidal rapids at the entrance to Kildidt Inlet, which the Waggoner does not yet cover. We include it here only because observations by Waggoner Correspondents James and Jennifer Hamilton, and confirmed by Canadian Hydrographic Service, indicate that the Sailing Directions times are incorrect. High water slack occurs approximately 1.5 hours after high water at *Bella Bella*. The time difference for low water slack varies with the height of the tide. For a low water of 0.4 meter, slack occurs approximately 2 hours after low water at *Bella Bella*; for a low water of 2.5 meters, slack occurs approximately 1 hour after low water at *Bella Bella*. Bella Bella is italicized because Sailing Directions calls for Prince Rupert tides.

For complete coverage of Kildidt Narrows and Kildidt Inlet, see *Cruising the Secret Coast*.

Brydon Channel. Brydon Channel connects Kildidt Sound and Spider Anchorage. Westbound across Kildidt Sound, lay a course well south of Lancaster Reef, then turn north toward the Brydon Channel entrance. When studying the chart, you will see the easternmost dogleg in Brydon Channel is foul with rocks. Mike Guns, a commercial fisherman with much experience in these waters, told us the safe route through is to hug the northwest end of the 72-meter island at the eastern end of the channel. This keeps you clear of the rocks farther out. See the reference map.

Brydon Anchorage. Brydon Anchorage extends northward into Hurricane Island at the west end of Brydon Channel at 51°50.25'N/128°12.25'W (NAD 83). Cor-

James & Jennifer Hamilton found this perfect anchorage in Kildidt Sound's Serpent Group. Photo by James Hamilton.

Kildidt Sound and Brydon Channel

NORTHERN B.C. COAST

See Area Map Page 412 - Maps Not for Navigation

respondents James and Jennifer Hamilton anchored in 30 feet near the very head. They report, "An amazing view to the south, not a soul around. It was an astonishingly quiet and beautiful anchorage—like no other. Most places remind us of somewhere else. This one stands alone." [Hamilton]

Spider Island area. This area is beautiful, raw, remote feeling, and little visited. The waters are also full of rocks. This is perfect gunkholing country, a paradise for kayakers.

You have a choice of two ways to get there, outside or inside. The outside route goes out the mouth of Hakai Passage into Queens Sound, then bends northwest toward the west side of Spider Island. Breadner Point, on the west side of Spider Island, is a famous hot spot for spring salmon. South of Spider Island, enter through Fulton Passage, or north of Spider Island through Spider Channel.

The inside route goes through Nalau Passage, across Kildidt Sound, and through rock-choked Brydon Channel into Spider Anchorage. An alternate to the Brydon Channel portion is Spitfire Channel, along the north side of Hurricane Island. Spitfire Channel has one spot so tight, however, we recommend you explore by dinghy before committing the mother ship. Near high tide, and with a lookout on the bow, we squeezed through in a 52-foot Grand Banks.

The following information is an overview of the main places. It would take several days to poke around all the delights of this area.

Passage between Spider Anchorage and Spitfire Channel. This passage separates Spitfire Island and Hurricane Island. The route shown was recommended to us by Mike Guns. The passage is clear until the north end, where rocks extend from Spitfire Island. This area is fairly well covered with bull kelp floating on

Spitfire Passage is narrow, challenging and beautiful. Here three Grand Banks yachts from NW Explorations pass through carefully with a bow watch ready to call out the clearance to the rocks.

the surface and thick leaf kelp below. We went in near the top of a high tide without difficulty. Next morning we departed 1½ hours after a 3.3-foot low tide and gathered a heavy glop of leaf kelp on our props and rudders. A low-powered fin keel sailboat could have been stopped dead. This passage is best run near high water.

Hurricane Anchorage. "Hurricane Anchorage" is Douglass' name for the otherwise unnamed cove in the hook formed by the south end of Hurricane Island. As shown on the reference map, enter north of the group of islets that make up the hook. Well protected and scenic.

Spitfire West Anchorage. This is Douglass' name for the otherwise unnamed cove that indents Hurricane Island, immediately west of the Spitfire Channel narrows. Several people have recommended it to us. Douglass says the bottom offers only fair to poor holding, however.

Spitfire North Anchorage. This is our name for the otherwise unnamed cove that indents Hunter Island, west of the Spitfire Channel narrows. Mike Guns recommended it to us. We would anchor in the outer part only. At low water the mouth leading to the inner lagoon appeared to be impassable or nearly so. The east side of the outer cove had a bottom that felt like a thin layer of mud on top of rock, and we dragged easily. The west side of the cove yielded good holding in 50 to 55 feet.

Spitfire Channel. Spitfire Channel separates Hurricane Island and Hunter Island, and except for the narrows at the west end, is easily run. The narrows are another matter. A medium-size cruiser can go through these narrows without difficulty, but with great caution and a sharp lookout. Underwater rocks extend into the channel, especially from the north side. Plan your transit at high water slack—high water, to get the greatest width possible; slack because we wouldn't want current pushing us where we didn't want to go. Least depth is 1.9 meters (approximately 6 feet) at zero tide.

FITZ HUGH SOUND, CONTINUED

Kwakume Inlet. Kwakume Inlet is a beautiful and roomy anchorage, but study your chart closely before entering. A rock awash at zero tide is shown outside the entrance, and you'll want to steer a course to avoid it. Mike Guns, a commercial fisherman with 35 years' expe-

Bonsai tree on wind-swept island near Spider Anchorage and Spitfire Channel

416 www.WaggonerGuide.com

rience in these waters, says the preferred approach is from the north. He recommends favoring the mainland shore, to pass between the rock and the shore.

Once past the rock, pass between the larger islet in the entrance and the little dot islet south of the larger islet. Inside, two rocks are shown a short distance along the north shore, one of them dries at 1.5 meters. Near the head of the main basin and south of its islet, another rock is shown, this one dries at 1.8 meters.

The south cove immediately inside the entrance has been recommended as an anchorage, but might be filled with aquaculture. Other aquaculture is located along the north side of Kwakume Inlet. Fortunately, it doesn't occupy any favored anchorages.

With the south cove taken, the best anchorage is in 25 to 30 feet (zero tide) at the head of the inlet, between the shore and a rock shown as drying at 1.8 meters. Anchor either there or in the inner basin.

If you can get into it, the inner basin is unusually secluded and snug feeling. Be aware, however, that the short fairway leading to the inner basin is narrow, and that a substantial drying rock lies in the middle, with more rocks on each side. *High water only, this little pass, dead slow bell, with alert lookouts.* We favored the north side.

Having a high tide when we arrived in early evening, we felt our way into the inner basin for the night. We were treated to glass-smooth water and the most plaintive loon's call we've ever heard. As we slipped out at high water early the next morning we were stopped cold by a wolf's cry—a long lonesome troubled howl, repeated just once. [*Hale*]

Koeye River. A charted rock lies north of Koeye Point. Enter north of that rock and wrap around into the cove behind the point. A lodge is near the point.

A few years ago we talked with the lodge caretaker, who told us that an onshore wind blowing out of Hakai Passage creates large seas that roll into the bay. He also said this is grizzly bear country. Later, we talked with a boat that experienced the seas mentioned above. The skipper said the seas were awful. They had come back from the mine and had much trouble getting from the dinghy to the boat. Stay away in a westerly.

Although in our opinion Koeye (pronounced "Kway") River is not a good spot for overnight anchoring, several people have told us a dinghy trip up the river to the mine ruins is beautiful. At the mine you'll find two open pits connected by a tunnel. The remains of a shop are there, and a huge old 1-cylinder steam engine. The buildings on the point at the mouth of the river are a Bella Bella Native band summer camp. [*Hale*]

Sea Otter Inlet & Crab Cove. Sea Otter Inlet, on Hunter Island, has two arms that form a "T" at the entrance. Crab Cove, the northern arm, was recommended by a park ranger at Pruth Bay. Anchor near the head in 30 to 35 feet. The south arm is prettier than Crab Cove and more private feeling. Anchor near the head of the south cove in 35 to 40 feet.

Kiltik Cove. Mouth of cove at 51°53.80'N /128°00.05'W. Kiltik Cove indents the east side of Hunter Island, approximately across from Namu. It is extremely well protected. The bottom shoals abruptly just past the tiny rock islet on the east shore of the arm. We would anchor in 35 to 40 feet a short distance north of that rock.

Warrior Cove. Warrior Cove is on the mainland (east) side of Fitz Hugh Sound, approximately 1.5 miles south of Namu. With a typical westerly wind, a following sea will chase you into the cove, but the seas subside when you pass the 82-meter island (in a southeast gale a lump may get in). The inner cove is pretty and protected. Scout around for just the right spot, and put the hook down in 20 to 25 feet, good holding.

Namu. The falling-down cannery at Namu has gone through another transition. For many years caretakers Pete and Rene (pronounced "Reenie") Darwin, and Rene's longtime friend Theresa, managed the facility. They created a unique destination on a collection of floats, complete with a covered common area, gift store, workshop, greenhouse, and docks. They transformed the uplands of the old cannery with art and and creative landscaping. Pete and Rene have moved on, physically moving their floats to Lizzie Cove on Lama Passage. See Lizzie Cove entry for more information.

Anchorage is still available at Namu or in nearby Rock Inlet. When we visited in 2014, windows were broken, doors were open, and some of the buildings had been ransacked. Visit the cannery at your own risk.

Navigation note: The beacon is gone from Loo Rock, between the Namu floats and the entrance to Rock Inlet, but Loo Rock still exists. In 2013 it was marked by a round float. The Namu Harbour inset on Chart 3936 shows the rock's location. Another rock, located in front of the abandoned cafe building, was marked with a ball in 2013.

Rock Inlet. Rock Inlet extends northeast from Whirlwind Bay (Namu), and it's a good, protected spot. Entering or departing, be sure to identify Verdant Island, near the mouth, and pass east of it. Keep a mid-channel course and watch for rocks. The chart shows the way. Inside, anchor in 25 to 40 feet. The bottom is rocky, and our anchor skipped across for some distance before setting.

FISHER CHANNEL

The north end of Fitz Hugh Sound divides into Burke Channel and Fisher Channel. Burke Channel leads eastward to Bella Coola, which is connected by road to Williams Lake and the highways inland. Bella Coola has facilities and is mentioned often by the few residents on this part of the coast, but is little visited by pleasure craft.

Fisher Channel is a continuation of the Inside Passage route, although the Inside Passage soon leads west and north, via Lama Passage or Gunboat Passage, to Bella Bella and Shearwater. If you remain in Fisher Channel you will reach Cousins Inlet. Ocean Falls, at the head of Cousins Inlet, is the most complete and interesting ghost town on the coast.

Humchitt Island. Humchitt Island is immediately off the south tip of King Island, at the intersection of Fitz Hugh Sound, Burke Channel and Fisher Channel. "With 15-knot southeasterlies blowing up Fitz Hugh Sound, we overnighted in the cove on the northeast shore of Humchitt Island. The seas were 2 to 3 feet outside, but our anchorage was tranquil and calm, with an amazing view up Fisher Channel. Anchor in 10 to 20 feet, moderate to good holding over rock, with a 150-foot swing radius." [*Hamilton*]

Kisameet Bay. Kisameet Bay is on King Island, about 3.5 miles north of the mouth of Burke Channel, roughly east of Fog Rocks. Correspondents John and Lorraine Littlewood report: "A splendid anchorage. The northernmost part of the bay, behind the island, is the place to be. It's quiet and fully protected from wind and sea, with a 'window' out into Fisher Channel to observe conditions." This is a very pleasant place to hide out. Anchor in 30 to 40 feet. We overnighted in this anchorage three seasons ago before heading south to cross Cape

The Kisameet Bay anchorage is somewhat smaller than this photo suggests. Work your way in around rocks, all of them charted.

NORTHERN B.C. COAST   See Area Map Page 412 - Maps Not for Navigation

This sandy beach at Sagar Lake is reached by trail from Codville Lagoon.

Caution. We found it to be just as the Littlewoods described and recommend it.

Codville Lagoon. Codville Lagoon is a provincial park on the east side of Fisher Channel. It is a popular anchorage, protected and pretty. Readers John and Deb Marshall reported that strong winds will work their way to the back cove. The narrow entrance is hard to locate, but Codville Hill, its moonscape of three peaks and barren rock slopes, is a good landmark. Favor the south side of the entrance to avoid a rock off the north shore. Anchor in 40 to 50 feet at the eastern head of the inlet. A trail runs from the northeastern shore of the anchorage to sandy beaches at beautiful Sagar Lake. Correspondent Jim Norris warns of vicious sand fleas. This is bear country. Make noise as you walk.

The Trap. The Trap is located behind Clayton Island on the west side of Fisher Channel, about 2 miles south of Lama Passage. North entrance at 52°02.35'N/127°56.80'W. South entrance at 52°01.05'N/127°56.80'W. We read about this spot in Iain Lawrence's *Far Away Places* (now out of print). Southbound on a windy, rainy afternoon we decided to tuck in for a look. The passage behind Clayton Island is as Lawrence describes it: deep, but protected from the wind. Lawrence says the bottom is rocky and requires a stern-tie to shore to prevent swinging. The Trap itself is the bay at the very south end of the passage. Lawrence says this bay empties at low tide, revealing a labyrinth of ancient fish traps.

Long Point Cove. Long Point Cove is located on the west side of Fisher Channel, approximately 1 mile south of Lama Passage. Although Sailing Directions mentions Long Point Cove as a good anchorage for small craft, it isn't as scenic or interesting as other anchorages in the area. On entering, favor the west shore to avoid a rock that dries some 250 to 300 yards north of Long Point. The rock is shown on the chart.

④ **Ocean Falls (Cousins Inlet).** Ocean Falls is a favorite destination. Although a ghost town, Ocean Falls is a busy ghost town. The winter population of 25 swells to 100 in the summer, but services are limited. Darke Waters Inn & Adventure Lodge offers showers, laundry, and ice. Meals are offered at Darke Waters with advance notice. Saggo's Saloon in nearby Martin Valley is usually open Mondays, Wednesdays, and Fridays from 4:00 p.m. to 7:00 p.m.; check the bulletin board at the top of the dock.

A right turn at the top of the ramp from the Small Craft Harbour leads to Ocean Falls proper. Other than the small gift store in the corner of the marine ways building, Darke Waters is the only operating business.

The dam dominates the head of the inlet and supplies electrical power for Ocean Falls, Shearwater, and New Bella Bella. The dam also provides water and power for the town's multi-million dollar hatchery and rearing pen facility for Atlantic salmon smolt for fish farms. Some 30 large green fiberglass rearing pens have been installed beside the former Crown Zellerbach mill site. Mixing ponds, where freshwater and saltwater are blended in exact proportions for the developing smolt, have been blasted out of the rocky mountainside leading to the dam.

A trip to Ocean Falls is not complete without a hike to the dam with vistas of Link Lake and views of the once busy mill town below, a walk through this "ghost town" can't help but stir the imagination. Make noise—you might meet a bear. Trout fishing in Link Lake is said to be excellent.

A left turn at the top of the dock leads visitors on a 1.5-mile road to Martin Valley. It's an easy, scenic stroll. The first house you come to is Saggo's Saloon. A little farther along, a concrete launch ramp serves amphibious planes.

The houses in Martin Valley were taken over by the province when Ocean Falls was abandoned. They have since been sold to people who enjoy the beauty and solitude of the area. Visitors as well as locals arrive at Ocean Falls by ferry service from Bella Bella, Shearwater, and Bella Coola.

Crabbing is excellent off the mill site. Halibut and salmon can be caught in Cousins Inlet. Consider dropping a prawn trap in Wallace Bay on your way up the inlet. We think Ocean Falls is a "don't miss" stop for its unique charm and beauty.

Air service to and from Ocean Falls is available through Wilderness Seaplanes.

④ **Ocean Falls Small Craft Harbour.** General Delivery, Ocean Falls, BC V0T 1P0; (250) 289-3859; www.oceanfalls.ca/blog/ofha. Open all year, public dock with ice, potable water, free Wi-Fi, 20 & 30 amp power, no fuel.

Ample dock space with reasonable rates and all the Link Lake water you need. The water is sweet and pure and has gone through a further purification process.

"The Shack," a yellow float house next to the ramp, has a book exchange, computer with internet, and tables and chairs. Pay moorage

The view of Ocean Falls from the Small Craft Harbour.

418   www.WaggonerGuide.com

Ocean Falls

Ocean Falls, at the head of Cousins Inlet, is a ghost town, lost on the B.C. coast. When you round Coolidge Point in the inlet you see the "falls," the spillway from the dam. Below the dam are extensive docks, and on top of the docks is a huge mill. To the left of the mill are tall, modern buildings. It is only after you land and walk uptown that you realize most of the buildings are empty, and the north coast wind is whistling through their open windows.

Until it closed more than 35 years ago, the Crown Zellerbach mill was the second largest on the coast, and Ocean Falls was a busy community of more than 5,000. Championship swimmers came from its Olympic-size swimming pool. The pool is filled in now. When Crown Zellerbach gave up the mill in 1973, the province, unwilling to lose the jobs, tried to run it. On May 31, 1980 it gave up too. The mill's machinery was removed, and in 1986 bulldozers came to level the town. The town's residents stood in front of the bulldozers and backed them down, though not until many of the houses and buildings had been destroyed.

Downtown, fortunately, was largely spared. The Martin Inn

The mermaid welcomes you to Ocean Falls. Herb Carpenter, a local resident, created the sculpture.

Kids can find coins burried around Fairy Rock.

hotel, tall and imposing, is empty. Its doors are chained shut and signs warn off trespassers. Inside are papers from 1976. The Lions Club room has literature illustrated with drawings of briefcase-carrying businessmen dressed in suits and snap-brim hats. In the lounge, veneer lifts off the mantel above the fireplace dedicated to Archie Martin, the legendary mill manager. The car-

pets are soaked and rotting. Paint peels off the walls.

A dormitory where mill workers lived looks almost ready to accept a new crop of college students. Its doors too are chained shut. A two-story garden-court apartment complex, 1970s style, is overgrown with weeds. The windows are broken, the plumbing fixtures are torn out, and the roof is falling in. We watched as a lonesome wind fluttered the few ragged and water-stained curtains that remained. We thought, a story longs to be written. A film waits to be made.

On our first visit to Ocean Falls we met bearded Norman Brown ("Nearly Normal Norman Brown, they call me"), who befriended us and showed us around. For several years the historical artifacts Norman collected were moved to the old Hudson's Bay (then Co-op) building. A sagging corner of the building was jacked up, and Norman, who is a glazier by trade, reinstalled windows. Heavy snowfall in the 2007–08 winter collapsed the roof of the building, and now Norman's displays have been moved to an upper floor in the marine ways.

With its infrastructure and deepwater harbor, Ocean Falls has sought new industry. A number of years ago a company tried to sell bottled water from the pure offerings of Link Lake, behind the dam. Stock was sold and publicity went out. The venture failed. Now the hatchery is in place, which, unfortunately, has failed to provide new local jobs.

For the present, Ocean Falls remains essentially a ghost town with a dam and a big fish hatchery. A short distance from the company guest house, a failing boardwalk fronts on what once were pleasant homes with a view of the inlet. The boardwalk is rotting and sagging and most of the houses are empty. Nearly Normal Norman Brown greets visitors and sells or barters antiques he has collected. Around the edges, Nature reclaims the land.

– Robert Hale

Nearly Normal Norman Brown welcomes visitors in his museum on the second floor of the marine ways.

"The Shack" is a homey place to hang out on the docks.

NORTHERN B.C. COAST   See Area Map Page 412 - Maps Not for Navigation

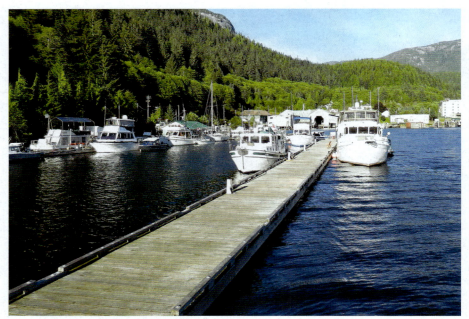
Ample side-tie at Ocean Falls Small Craft Harbour

in The Shack, or wait for the wharfinger to come down the docks in the morning or late afternoon. Visa and MasterCard accepted. After a one-year leave of absence, Ken returned in 2017 to his post as wharfinger.

Harbor owner Herb Carpenter runs the marine ways. Herb built Melissa, the gold-colored mermaid who welcomes boats to the docks. In the downstairs corner of the marine ways building, Herb's wife Lena has set up a little gift shop called C' shores Gift Shop.

Upstairs is Nearly Normal Norman's Ocean Falls Museum, filled with items left behind by former residents of Ocean Falls. Those of us over 50 will recognize many of the objects. If the door is not open, ask around. Norman will open up for visitors. Donations accepted. Children will love visiting the "Fairy Rock" located a short distance from the docks on the road to Martin. Children take great delight in finding coins hidden in the Rock. Be sure to let the wharfinger know if you plan to visit Fairy Rock so the fairies can be alerted; you can contribute coins at The Shack in support of this long-standing tradition at Ocean Falls. Another fun tradition is the Annual Salmon Derby Barbecue weekend held in late August, a popular event drawing participants from other nearby communities. Tickets for the barbeque can be purchased at The Shack.

No garbage drop: Recycling bins are located at The Shack. Anything fish or crabs can eat can be put in the chuck for the fish and crabs. Take everything else with you.

Weather radio channel WX 1: The signal is spotty. If necessary, walk along the dock with a handheld VHF until you find reception, or use the computer in The Shack to check the forecast online.

④ **Darke Waters Inn & Adventure Lodge.** (250) 289-3585; darkewaters@xplornet.ca; www.darkewaters.com. Rob & Corrina Darke took over the old hospital building across from the marine ways building, a right turn and a short walk from the the docks. Darke Waters offers lodging, hot showers, and coin laundry. Meals are offered with advance notice. The building is currently for sale but is open during the boating season. Additional lodging can be found at Martin River Lodge, which offers fishing charters and B&B guest rooms in nearby Martin Valley.

Lama Passage. Lama Passage leads westward and northward from Fisher Channel to New Bella Bella and Shearwater. Cruise ships and BC Ferries use this passage regularly. Keep a sharp lookout ahead and astern.

Fancy Cove. Fancy Cove is on the south shore of Lama Passage and is a delightful little anchorage. Don and Reanne Douglass write about the cove in their book *Exploring the North Coast of British Columbia*. This nearly landlocked cove is well protected. Anchor in 10 to 25 feet.

Fannie Cove. Fannie Cove is in Cooper Inlet on the south shore of Lama Passage. It's a beautiful little spot, with an obvious anchoring nook on its eastern shore just inside the entrance. Unfortunately, the holding ground is only fair. We tried twice to get a good set in the little nook and once farther out, but each time we dragged without much effort. We would overnight in settled weather only. Study the chart before entering. Leave Gus Island and the little dot islet west of Gus Island to port as you approach.

Lizzie Cove. Monitors VHF 10. Their hospitality has been a favorite of cruisers in these parts for years. Pete and Rene Darwin moved their floats, BBQ shelter, and gift shop from Namu to Lizzie Cove in 2013. Tucked inside the southeast end of Lizzie Cove, Pete and Rene offer ample side-tie moorage for visitors and overnight guests. No power or water at the docks. Don't miss the gift shop filled with custom-made wood working items and other crafts. Their self-sufficient gardens are impressive and include a hothouse with fruit trees and a chicken.

Enter Lizzie Cove leaving Gus Island to port, then turn northwest and wrap around the 41 meter island. Private red and green buoys mark the channel. Shoals extend nearly 100 meters north from the 41 meter island, so don't cut too close.

Jane Cove. Jane Cove, on the south shore of Lama Passage in Cooper Inlet, offers shelter

The once charming homes of Ocean Falls are now in disrepair.

Browse the distinctive hand-made items at Lizzie Cove's Gift Shop

See Area Map Page 412- Maps Not for Navigation   NORTHERN B.C. COAST

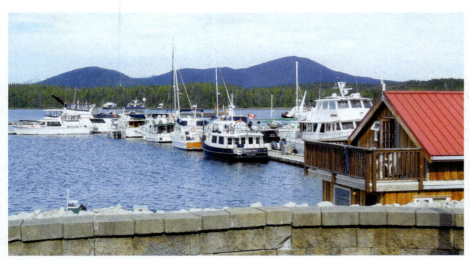
Busy docks at Shearwater Resort

but lacks scenic quality. Study the chart carefully before entering to avoid shoals and rocks. Fannie Cove, despite its marginal holding, or Fancy Cove, which is spectacular by comparison, are preferred.

⑤ **New Bella Bella.** New Bella Bella (Waglisla) is a major Native village, with gasoline and diesel, potable water, garbage drop, and a good grocery store and nice cafe; cell phone service is good. The village has a hospital. The closest laundromat is at Shearwater. The fuel dock attendants are courteous, but religious about their lunch hour. You may have to be patient. The fuel pumps and meters are on the wharf above the fuel float. They extend a hose down to the fuel dock. New Bella Bella's water treatment plant provides a steady stream of clear, potable water at the fuel dock.

A new large grocery store was completed in 2017 and includes a bakery and meat department. This is a fun place to shop for gifts and food items to re-stock your galley. The supply barge arrives weekly on Sundays. Just north of this store is the Waglisla Senior Centre, with native artwork. The locals are friendly and eager to share their stories. Visitors are also welcome to tour the K-12 Bella Bella Community School.

Guests at Shearwater can take the water taxi to New Bella Bella to shop at the band store or to drop off or pick up passengers or parts from the airport. Scheduled airline service runs throughout the day.

The New Bella Bella airport is about 2 miles from the village. You can walk along the road or take a taxi. The taxi is often standing by before or after a flight or call (250) 957-2582 or on VHF channel 14. They know the schedules. Wilderness Seaplanes serves New Bella Bella with multiple flights per day.

Bella Bella. Bella Bella (Old Bella Bella) is on Denny Island on the northeastern shore of Lama Passage. The excellent docks and lovely buildings ("Whistler North") house the Coast Guard Search and Rescue vessel *Cape Farewell*, its crew and support staff, and Fisheries and Oceans personnel. No transient moorage.

Kliktsoatli Harbour. Shearwater Resort & Marina is located in Kliktsoatli Harbour, 2 miles east of New Bella Bella on the north side of Denny Island. Good anchorage can be found on the eastern shore.

⑥ **Shearwater Resort & Marina.** (250) 957-2666; moorage@shearwater.ca; hotel@shearwater.ca; www.shearwater.ca. Monitors VHF 06 & 66A, the fuel dock monitors VHF 08. Open all year, 1500 feet of guest moorage, 15, 30 & 50 amp power all the way out the main float, free Wi-Fi and for-fee premium Wi-Fi. Potable water is available on the guest docks and at the fuel dock. During prime season, register and pay for moorage at the dockside harbourmaster's office, or at the hotel during shoulder season. Moorage reservations are highly recommended during the busy summer months. If the main docks are full, you can moor on the inside of the breakwater docks, no power or water. Cellular service is good. 200 additional feet of guest moorage was added in 2018.

The fuel dock has diesel, gasoline, lubricants, propane, and Avgas and Jet A. On shore you'll find an ATM, washrooms, showers, laundry, ice, restaurant, pub, haulout, launch ramp, and facilities for waste oil dump. Garbage drop and the recycling center. There is a small fee for recycling to cover the costs of barging the material to Richmond B.C. A well-stocked grocery store, liquor store, and marine supply store are on site along with a post office, coffee pastry bar, and gift shop.

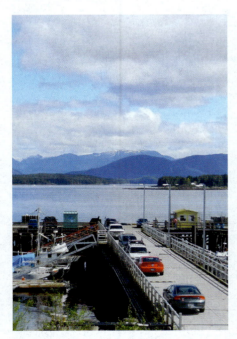
Native village of New Bella Bella is accessible by water taxi or dinghy.

Shearwater Marine Resort

2018 WAGGONER CRUISING GUIDE

NORTHERN B.C. COAST See Area Map Page 412 - Maps Not for Navigation

The sculptures commemorate the areas' war veterans. *The coffee bar is a new addition at Shearwater.*

The showers and laundry room, in the building across from the store, are excellent.

The popular pub, with live entertainment, has a nice deck for outdoor dining. It's a great place to meet other boaters and locals, who often share a table. The pub has a new look for 2018, a new menu, and has been expanded with a variety of seating options. New for 2018 is a fine-dining venue located above the pub with outstanding views; open Friday and Saturday by reservation.

Shearwater is the most complete marine facility between Campbell River and Prince Rupert. The shipyard can haul boats to 70 tons and handle almost anything, from toilet repairs to electronics to repowers. They can order parts for you and coordinate their arrival by air if needed. Shearwater has its own 3,000-foot airstrip for private aircraft. Scheduled airline service to Port Hardy and Vancouver is available at New Bella Bella. Shearwater is also a stop for the BC Ferries system. Shearwater Helicopter Tours (778-899-0513) can provide airport transfers and sightseeing excursions. The Sea-Bus water taxi connects Shearwater and New Bella Bella (Waglisla) with a 10-minute, 2.5-mile ride. In calm weather you can scoot over in a dinghy.

Shearwater is the crossroads of the northern coast and gets a full range of visitors.

The marina is the site of a WWII Royal Canadian Air Force seaplane base. The large historic hangar now serves as the shop. In 2013, Craig Widsten, the principal owner of this family-owned resort, created two special tributes to the heritage of Shearwater and the surrounding area. When a wall of the shop needed replacement, Craig had it rebuilt and commissioned muralist Paul Gartua to paint the images of seventeen people who had an impact on the growth and development of Shearwater. They include tribal leaders, medi-

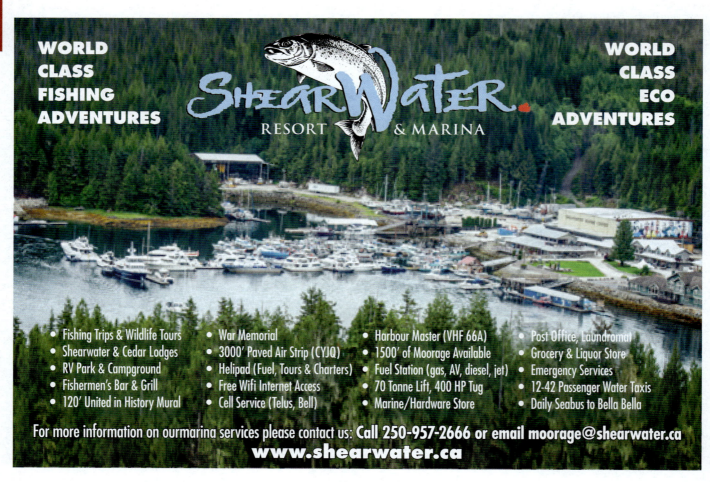

cal professionals, the original manager of the Hudson's Bay Co. outpost, and even Craig's father, Andrew, the founder of Shearwater. Measuring 120 feet wide and 22 feet tall, the mural is quite striking.

Craig also installed a cenotaph to commemorate Shearwater and New Bella Bella residents' war service. He commissioned the casting of a 17-foot scale replica of the Stranraer flying boat that was based at Bella Bella during WWII. Nearby, a newly carved Eagle pole commemorates First Nations veterans. An obelisk commemorates other veterans from the area. A new gazebo and additional landscaping are other delights you will find at Shearwater in 2018 along with new totems created by carver, Larry Campbell.

Kakushdish Harbour. Kakushdish Harbour, long and narrow, extends into Denny Island immediately east of Kliktsoatli Harbour (Shearwater). An overhead power cable with 23 meters (75 feet) vertical clearance crosses the entrance. "We favored the north shore through the entrance bar and saw a minimum depth of 11 feet, zero tide. Anchor in 20 to 25 feet, good holding in mud. The anchorage was surprisingly deserted and tranquil." [*Hamilton*]

LOCAL KNOWLEDGE

NAVIGATION NOTES: The trickiest spot in Gunboat Passage is the narrow fairway between Denny Point and Maria Island. Use caution to navigate away from the rocks. A second tricky spot is the reef that extends from the southern shore toward Dingle Island. Watch the currents in this area. A red nun buoy marks the outer end of this reef. Red, Right, Returning assumes you are returning eastbound, from the sea. The third tricky spot is the range at the west end of Gunboat Passage. Entering or departing, stay on the range.

Gunboat Passage. Gunboat Passage connects Seaforth Channel with Fisher Channel and is a scenic route between Ocean Falls and New Bella Bella/Shearwater. The passage is littered with reefs and rocks, but well marked with aids to navigation.

Beales Bay. The entrance looks tricky on the chart, but if you leave the small islet to port as you enter, you'll have good water. Anchor inside in 30 to 40 feet. Stay well clear of the mouth of Beales Lagoon. At least two detached drying rocks lie in the cove off the lagoon's mouth. Excellent protection.

Gosse Bay. Gosse Bay is west of Maria Island, a good anchorage on the west side of the westernmost cove.

Forit Bay. Forit Bay, on the eastern approach to Gunboat Passage, is an excellent, protected anchorage in 15 to 25 feet. The entrance, however, is encumbered by a large rock between Flirt Island and the point of land that marks the inner part of the bay. The rock is not visible at high tide, but is visible through the water at a little less than half tide.

Enter Forit Bay by wrapping around the north tip of Flirt Island, leaving the island to port.

BURKE CHANNEL, DEAN CHANNEL, BELLA COOLA

Important chart note: In October, 2011, Canadian Hydrographic Service (CHS) released new Chart 3974 and cancelled Charts 3729 and 3730. All coverage of this area is now shown on 3900-series charts—Chart 3936 for the mouth and western portion of Burke Channel, and Chart 3939 for the mouth and western portion of Dean Channel.

Burke Channel and Dean Channel border the south and north sides of King Island and plunge deep into the Coast Range mountains. We had been told that this is some of the most beautiful and awe-inspiring country imaginable, but after seeing so much beautiful country all along the B.C. coast, we expected it to be just more of the same. We were wrong. A circumnavigation of King Island will astonish you. Gone is the raw coast with its low, wave-pounded islands. A short distance up either channel puts you inland, bounded on each side by high mountains. If you're going to spend some time on this coast, see these waters.

LOCAL KNOWLEDGE

EBB CURRENT: On warm summer days, heating of inland air produces an up-channel sea breeze in Burke Channel that can begin as early as 10:00 a.m. and blow strongly until sundown. Make your runs early and find shelter before the wind starts blowing.

TIDE-RIPS: The surface water in Burke Channel is often in an almost constant ebb, the result of fresh water flowing toward the sea. When this surface ebb meets a spring flood, tide-rips, whirlpools, and general confusion results.

Burke Channel. Burke Channel leads 38 miles inland, beginning at Edmund Point, just north of Namu. From Edmund Point to Restoration Bay, the lower reaches of Burke Channel are subject to strong tidal currents and heavy tide-rips, but in the upper reaches the tidal streams are weak.

The north end of Burke Channel divides into South Bentinck Arm and North Bentinck Arm (Bella Coola is at the head of North Bentinck Arm), and Labouchere Passage, which leads to Dean Channel. When the ebb current is flowing and the up-channel sea breeze is blowing, expect rough seas at the confluence of these channels. Early morning, before the B.C. Interior heats up, is often the calmest time of day.

All these cautions make Burke Channel sound impenetrable, which isn't the case. The prudent skipper simply will avoid being out there in the wrong conditions.

The best anchorage along Burke Channel is at the head of Kwatna Inlet, with a second-best choice being the small cove just north of Cathedral Point.

Fougner Bay. Fougner Bay is near the mouth of Burke Channel on the south side, just east of Edmund Point. The outer part the bay is somewhat protected, with anchorage in 40 to 60 feet. To us it feels uninviting. An inner cove, however, is a perfect spot.

Find the 4.1-meter sounding back in the bay. That's the cove. To get in, the chart shows good water by leaving the + symbol (indicating a dangerous underwater rock 2 meters or less at zero tide) to starboard. Once clear of the rock, loop into the back cove. Very cozy and protected. Study the chart carefully before entering Fougner Bay. The rocks off the entry are easy to avoid, but you want to know where they are and where you are.

Kwatna Inlet. Kwatna Inlet extends some 12 miles into the mainland and is too deep for anchoring until near the head. Watch carefully for the drying flats at the head. We are told by several people that it is an excellent place to put the hook down.

Cathedral Point. Cathedral Point, a weather reporting station, marks the north entrance to Kwatna Inlet, and is easily identified by its white building and tower. Just north of the point, a tiny cove with dramatic granite walls makes a good anchorage in 25 feet. The cove has excellent protection from up-channel winds, but the mass of large logs on the south beach suggests that down-channel winds and seas blow right in. We patrolled the cove but did not stay. Early Correspondent Bill Hales, from Victoria, anchored for the night and reported a pleasant experience.

South Bentinck Arm. South Bentinck Arm, 25 miles long, lies between high mountains. The relatively few cruisers who have gone all the way up the arm say it is beautiful. We have gone as far as Larso Bay, which has good anchorage in 35 to 70 feet. The mountains across from Larso Bay are beautiful. Correspondent Gil Flanagan found one of the largest red cedars in B.C. by walking about 1 km up a logging road that begins in the north part of the bay. The tree is on the right side of the road, marked with a plaque.

Tallheo Hot Springs. Tallheo Hot Springs is about one-quarter mile north of the mouth of Hotsprings Creek on the west shore of South Bentinck Arm, a short distance south of Bensins Island. Anchorage is exposed.

North Bentinck Arm. The water in North Bentinck Arm is green and milky, the result of the Bella Coola River emptying into the head of the arm. We found no good anchorages, so

NORTHERN B.C. COAST   See Area Map Page 412 - Maps Not for Navigation

The Bella Coola docks look more spacious in this photo than when we were trying to raft off in 20-knot winds.

you have to hope for room at the Bella Coola docks. Watch for drift. Windy Bay is on the south side of North Bentinck Arm, near the junction with Burke Channel. When we crossed the mouth of Windy Bay in early afternoon we learned how it got its name. Whew!

LOCAL KNOWLEDGE

WEATHER TIP: The wind can blow almost constantly at Bella Coola, making for rough seas going in or out. There aren't many places to hide from the weather, either. Be aware of the tendency for strong inflow and outflow winds before deciding to go to Bella Coola.

⑦ **Bella Coola.** Bella Coola is seldom visited by yachts but interesting nonetheless. The government floats are run by the Bella Coola Harbour Authority, and they are making improvements. Water is available all the way out the docks, with 20 & 30 amp power. Showers and washrooms are at the head of the ramp.

The Columbia Fuels fuel dock is adjacent to the public floats.

Correspondent Gil Flanagan says the best way to visit is to overnight in Larso Bay in South Bentinck Arm or Eucott Bay on Dean Channel, and come over in the morning. A visitor at the Seattle Boat Show recommended anchoring in Bryneldsen Bay, near the north end of Labouchere Channel, and going to Bella Coola early the next morning. Use Chart 3974. Bryneldsen Bay is behind the thumb of land that extends southeast, approximately 0.8 miles from Ram Bluff. The bay is not labeled, but Chart 3974 does show an anchor symbol beside it.

The town of Bella Coola is 3 kilometers (about 2 miles) from the dock. Taxis may be available. When we visited in 2013, the taxi service was not operating. We walked instead, and the lush vegetation, waterfalls beside the road, and the Bella Coola River Estuary made for a beautiful stroll. Stay on the water side of the road, since it's wider and safer for walking.

We urge you to see the Bella Coola Museum, housed in buildings dating from 1892 and 1898. It is on the edge of town along the road from the marina. Bella Coola is where, in 1793, Alexander Mackenzie touched saltwater on his transcontinental crossing of Canada. Much of the museum's display is about Mackenzie. We bought a booklet of Mackenzie's journal entries (including comment about the unrelenting wind) in the Bella Coola and Dean Channel area.

The town has provincial and federal government offices, a post office, hospital, motel, liquor store, laundromat, showers, and a well-stocked co-op grocery store and Moore's Organic Market. Take a tour of the area on the Bella Coola Valley Bus for $2.50; call (250) 799-0079 before 8:00 p.m. the day before you want to ride the bus.

Correspondents Bruce and Margaret Evertz add the following: "A worthwhile attraction in this area are the petroglyphs. The Native band wants them preserved, so they are not marked on any maps. Guides may be available. You can get information about them at the museum."

Correspondents Gil and Karen Flanagan report that rental cars are available (Bella Coola Vehicle Rentals 250-957-7072). "We put about 150 miles on a Dodge Caravan, all on good paved roads. The spectacular drive to Tweedsmuir Park inland is rated as one of the 10 most scenic drives in Canada."

Bella Coola is the B.C. Interior's window on the coast. Each year, a remarkable number of boats are trailered from the Interior to Bella Coola, where they stay the summer, either tied to the dock or on trailers.

⑦ **Bella Coola Harbour Authority.** P.O. Box 751, Bella Coola, BC V0T 1C0; (250) 799-5633; bellacoolaharbour@gmail.com. They try to monitor VHF channels 06 & 16. Open all year with guest moorage. Facilities include 20 & 30 amp power (20 amp shore power breakers have 20 amp receptacles—bring adaptor), water, washrooms, laundry and showers (showers closed November through March), tidal grid, garbage drop, waste oil drop, pumpout, launch ramp, pay phones, Wi-Fi. Fuel dock adjacent. The harbor office is at the head of the pier. Office hours June through September 8:00 a.m. to 6:00 p.m. and off season Monday through Saturday 8:00 a.m. to 12:00 p.m.

Float "A" is dedicated for visiting pleasure craft 14 meters and longer. The float is exposed to westerly winds. Smaller boats can tie up there, but if a boat 14 meters or longer arrives, the smaller boats will have to move.

Bella Coola is a popular launch point for trailerable boats. The Harbour Authority has added additional boat launch floats to make launching and retrieving easier.

The marina is tight and the wind can blow almost constantly. Rafting is required. If necessary, take temporary moorage at the loading zone. Put out lots of fenders, both sides. Of all the places we have landed, Bella Coola is one of the most challenging.

The floats are located south of a rock breakwater, behind a floating log breakwater. They are home port to a large number of commercial fish

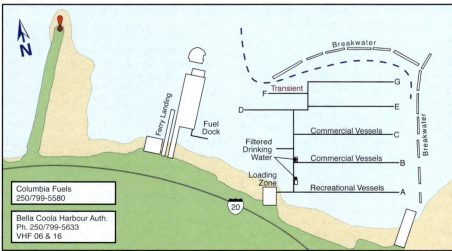

Bella Coola

424   www.WaggonerGuide.com

boats. All of A dock and the south side of B dock are reserved for pleasure craft, however. You may have to raft to a permanent boat. The channel on the land side of A dock is narrow, especially at low tide. Feel your way in and find a spot.

Now that the local Harbour Authority is running the facility more interest is devoted to visiting boaters. Even so, Bella Coola is not a "resort marina." Self-reliance is the key.

Columbia Fuels Fuel Dock. (250) 799-5580. Open Monday through Friday 9:00 a.m. to 4:00 p.m. all year. Call (250) 305-8333 for off-hours service. Gasoline, diesel, lubricants. Dwayne Saugstad is the manager. Dwayne's great-great-grandfather led the original band of Norwegian settlers to Bella Coola. Dwayne's great-grandfather remained, as did Dwayne's grandfather, Dwayne's father, and now Dwayne and his two children. All have called or presently call Bella Coola their home. Six generations.

Labouchere Channel. Labouchere Channel connects the north end of Burke Channel with Dean Channel. **Mesachie Nose**, at the confluence of the two channels, is a magnificent glacier-smoothed rock prominence on the north shore. Tidal currents combined with winds and surface water runoff can create very difficult seas in this area. If the water is flat, see Mesachie Nose up close. In 2013, we noticed someone had painted a cartoon character and graffiti on a small section of the rocks near the waterline. This unfortunate act of vandalism has visually scarred the area.

The waters of Labouchere Channel itself are generally smooth and wind-free. The scenery, with waterfalls spilling from high mountains, is fabulous. Our notes say, "So many waterfalls!"

LOCAL KNOWLEDGE

WEATHER TIP: Strong up-channel sea breezes can develop when warm temperatures in the Interior heat the air and suck cold ocean air up the various inlets. This sea breeze can begin as early as 10:00 a.m. and last until sundown. Because summertime freshets often create a nearly permanent ebb surface current, an ugly chop can develop when the wind blows against the current.

Dean Channel. Dean Channel connects with Fisher Channel at the mouth of Cousins Inlet (Ocean Falls) and continues 53 miles northward It is bordered on both sides by high mountains; Burke Channel offers some of the finest scenery along the coast. In Dean Channel we felt as if we were high up in the mountains on a huge lake, like we should be chewing gum to clear our ears. The concept of being at sea level in these surroundings was hard to grasp.

The principal points of interest on Dean Channel are Elcho Harbour, Sir Alexander Mackenzie Rock, and Eucott Bay and hot springs. Cascade Inlet is stunning, but not a good place to anchor.

This monument marks Sir Alexander Mackenzie Rock, where Mackenzie ended his westward explorations in 1793.

Jenny Inlet. If Jenny Inlet were someplace else it might be interesting. But we found it ordinary, too deep for anchoring, with a logging camp near the head. Elcho Harbour, 8 miles farther up Dean Channel, or Cousins Inlet (Ocean Falls), 5 miles down-channel, are better choices.

Elcho Harbour. If you are looking for a scenic spot, Elcho Harbour qualifies. It's stunning. The inlet reaches a little more than 2 miles back between steep high mountains, and appears perfectly protected from all winds. Waterfalls plummet from the sides. A lovely bowl is at the head of the inlet, with the obligatory stream that creates an estuary and mudflat. Anchor in 90 to 110 feet off a delightful waterfall on the west side, about one-third of the way in. Or anchor at the head in 90 feet before it shelves up to mudflat. Take the dinghy back out to Sir Alexander Mackenzie Rock for a little history.

Sir Alexander Mackenzie Rock. Sir Alexander Mackenzie Rock is marked by a cairn at the mouth to Elcho Harbour. On 22 July 1793 Mackenzie completed his overland journey across Canada to the Pacific Ocean, and marked his accomplishment with ochre paint on the rock. Later, the inscription was carved into the stone. You can bring the boat right up to the monument, watching for underwater rocks close to shore, and take your own picture of it. Or you can anchor out and dinghy ashore, leaving somebody aboard in case the wind kicks up.

Apparently, Mackenzie ended his westward trek here because the waters beyond were Bella Bella Indian country, and his Bella Coola Indian guides could not guarantee safety. A few miles west on the north side of Dean Channel, ochre pictographs on white cliffs are thought to be boundary markers. They are a short distance east of Frenchman Creek. We found the pictographs and took the lat/lon coordinates off the GPS: 52°20.44'N/127°29.07'W.

Eucott Bay. Eucott Bay is a gorgeous spot, about as pretty as any we have anchored in. The mountains along the eastern and northeastern sides remind us of Yosemite. Photographers, bring your camera—half-dome exists in Eucott Bay. Eucott Hot Springs is near the head of the bay, inshore of a line of pilings. The hot springs have been improved with concrete to make an excellent soaking basin. The water used to be too hot for soaking, but now the temperature can be adjusted.

Craig Widsten, principal owner of Shearwater Marine Resort, told us that in 1948 his father and he journeyed to Eucott Bay to pack mud and hot spring water for sale to health and beauty fanatics in Europe. We're sure it was elegant—hot spring water and mud from the remote Canadian coast, to smooth away the wrinkles and cure what ails you.

Enter Eucott Bay along the east (starboard) side. We are told the entrance has silted up, and is much shallower than charted. Once inside, a large basin unfolds. Find a good spot in the middle and put the hook down. Take the dinghy up to the hot springs. Insect repellant might be needed to protect against deer flies ("those man-eating winged demons," one reader wrote). At low tide wear boots. The beach is muddy.

Nascall Bay. Nascall Hot Springs is near the mouth of Nascall Bay. You'll recognize the buildings by their blue roofs. Previous owners had ambitious development plans, but they didn't work out. The facility is private with posted No Trespassing signs.

SEAFORTH CHANNEL, MILBANKE SOUND, FINLAYSON CHANNEL

LOCAL KNOWLEDGE

Navigation Note: Although Seaforth Channel is connected with the sea, west of Lama Passage the buoyage system defines "returning from the sea" as returning from south to north, not west to east. If you are outbound in Seaforth Channel, west of Lama Passage you will leave red aids to navigation (buoys, beacons, lights) to starboard (Red, Right, Returning from the

NORTHERN B.C. COAST

south). If you are inbound in Seaforth Channel, west of Lama Passage, leave red aids to navigation to port.

"Returning from the sea" changes at Lama Passage. East of Lama Passage, inbound vessels will leave red buoys, beacons and lights to starboard.

Seaforth Channel. Seaforth Channel connects the New Bella Bella/Shearwater area with Milbanke Sound to the west and is part of the Inside Passage route. Ivory Island is at the western entrance.

Troup Passage. Troup Passage runs between Chatfield Island and Cunningham Island, and leads to Roscoe Inlet. Troup Narrows is at the northern end. Near the southern end of Troup Passage an unnamed bay sometimes called Discovery Cove is an excellent anchorage.

Discovery Cove. Discovery Cove at lat 52°13.50'N, unnamed on the charts, is the only major indent of Cunningham Island from Troup Passage. It was first recommended to us by John and Evonne MacPherson, who spent many summers cruising the coast in their perfectly-maintained 45-foot Grenfell, *Malacandra*. The chart shows rocks on the southwest shore of the entry, but if you go in along the northeast shore you'll have no problems. This is one of the most beautiful coves on the coast. It is surrounded by mountains and seemingly immune to any storm winds that might be about. Anchor in either of the two nooks along the north shore or the area to the east.

Troup Narrows. Troup Narrows, with maximum tidal currents of only about 2 knots, is easily run. Assuming a passage from south to north, identify the reef that dries 15 feet near the south entrance to the narrows. Leave the reef to port, and slide west to the beautiful rock cliffs of Chatfield Island. Stay on the Chatfield Island side until the point of land on Cunningham Island is abeam, then trend east to the far shore of Cunningham Island to avoid the reef that extends from the 65-meter island. Study the chart to find the rocks you must avoid.

Roscoe Inlet. Roscoe Inlet is drop-dead beautiful. Beginning where Johnson Channel meets Return Channel, Roscoe Inlet winds some 21 miles back through high mountains that plunge straight down into the sea. Exquisite bowls and valleys lead into the mountains. Sheer cliffs tower overhead. In some places you can bring the boat alongside a vertical granite wall that rises to a mountain peak 3600 feet above and still have more than 450 feet of water below. Dramatic.

Good anchorages are scarce. For a day trip, we suggest motoring up in the morning, dropping the hook for lunch at the head of the inlet, and motoring back in the afternoon. You can overnight, of course.

Other than the head of the inlet, in our opinion **Boukind Bay** is the easiest anchorage along the way. A large, 25- to 30-foot-deep area allows plenty of room to swing. If an inflow wind is blowing, however, it might be a little bouncy. **Quartcha Bay** is a visually stunning anchorage, although deep until close to the sides or the mud flats at the head. Waterfalls tumble down the mountain sides. From near the head you can look back into two glacier-polished bowls of rock (called *cirques*) and extensive meadows. Correspondent Gil Flanagan reports that evidence of ancient fish traps can be found on the large tide flats. **Shack Bay** and **Ripley Bay** are exposed to inflow winds, and deep until very close to shore. We didn't like them. **Clatse Bay**, at the south end of Roscoe Inlet, is a good anchorage. Go all the way to the head and anchor in 40 to 50 feet.

Bugs: Several readers have warned about ravenous deer flies. Bring insect repellant.

Morehouse Bay. Morehouse Bay, indenting Chatfield Island off Return Channel, has a lovely one-boat anchorage (more, if all are stern-tied to shore) in a cove at the very back, or room for more boats in 60-foot depths outside the back cove. To enter the outer anchorage, leave the 53-meter island to port and the 44- and 59-meter islands to starboard. The more secluded back cove is in the south part of the bay, behind the 59-meter island. Leave a large rock, shown as a 1.2-meter depth, to starboard as you enter. The entry is easy—just be sure you know where that rock is. Anchor in 25 to 35 feet.

Wigham Cove. Wigham Cove, on the south shore of Yeo Island, is a popular anchorage and an excellent place to overnight before transiting Seaforth Channel. Favor the west shore as you enter, until abeam the islets in the middle of the bay. Then turn to pass north of the islets to the favored anchorage in the northeast nook of the cove. This nook has room for several boats. We have shared this anchorage with a 60-footer and a 43-footer with no crowding at all. An 80-footer was anchored in the southeast cove.

Dangerous rock: Be careful if you enter the southernmost nook of Wigham Cove. A dangerous underwater rock with a depth of 0.5 meters at zero tide is reported lying close to and just east of the northernmost of the three drying rocks that extend from the eastern shore of

Ivory Island Lighthouse marks the decision point, a northeast turn to protected Reid Passage, or continue west up Milbanke Sound.

CHARTS

3910 Plans	Milbanke Sound and Beauchemin Channel, 1:20,000
3911 Plans	Vicinity of Princess Royal Island (1:25,000)
3728	Milbanke Sound and Approaches (1:76,600)
3936	Fitz Hugh Sound to Lama Passage (1:40,000)
3938	Queens Sound to Seaforth Channel (1:40,000)
3939	Fisher Channel to Seaforth Channel and Dean Channel (1:40,000); Troupe Narrows (1:6000)
3940	Spiller Channel & Roscoe Inlet (1:40,000)
3941	Channels Vicinity of Milbanke Sound (1:40,000)
3942	Mathieson Channel Northern Portion (1:40,000)
3945	Approaches to Douglas Channel (1:40,000)

Roscoe Inlet has some of the most awe-inspiring scenery on the coast.

the entrance to Wigham Cove. When entering this nook, favor the islets to the east.

Spiller Channel. Spiller Channel and Bullock Channel run north from Seaforth Channel on either side of Yeo Island and lead to famed Ellerslie Lagoon, whose entrance rocks have bumped many a boat. Neither run is particularly scenic. Compared with other areas, the hillsides are low.

Neekas Cove, across the channel from the north tip of Yeo Island, is the only easy anchorage in the southern part of Spiller Channel. Yeo Cove, near the south entrance to Spiller Channel, has a rock-studded entry and only limited anchorage deep in the southeast corner. Tate Lagoon, which leads into Don Peninsula, has a treacherous entrance. This lagoon is shown as unnamed on Chart 3940. Douglass describes both places, but we're not brave or determined enough to do them ourselves.

The top of Spiller Channel is a little better. The hidden anchorage Douglass calls "Nash Narrows Cove" is lovely. Decent anchorage can be found in the bay immediately south of Ellerslie Lagoon.

Neekas Cove. Neekas Cove is opposite the north tip of Yeo Island in Spiller Channel. The cove is narrow and pretty, but deep until close to the head, where the bottom shelves rapidly. Anchor in 50 feet (zero tide) if cautious; 35 feet if braver; less, at your peril. Watch for bears on the shore here.

Nash Passage. Nash Passage (Douglass' name for this otherwise unnamed winding channel), separates Coldwell Peninsula from a good-sized unnamed island on the approach to Ellerslie Bay, just before Spiller Inlet. The chart shows rocks, but the ones to watch out for dry at 4.3 meters, so they should be visible much of the time.

Nash Narrows Cove (Douglass' name again), is the little cove at the turn of Nash Passage. It is beautiful, and would be a good spot to put the hook down.

A peninsula separates Ellerslie Lagoon from a substantial bay immediately to the south. Anchorage is in the inner bay, east of an islet in the middle of the fairway. Pass either side of the islet. Our preferred spot is in 60 feet (zero tide) on the south side, under a towering cliff. The north side of the bay might get down to 40-foot depths, but isn't as protected or cozy feeling.

Ellerslie Lagoon. Because of dangerous rocks, a spring tide high water entry is called for. Two sets of narrows lead in. Ellerslie Lake pours a lot of water into the lagoon; expect the outflowing current through the narrows to last longer than usual.

Spiller Inlet. Spiller Inlet extends northward from the top of Spiller Channel. The sides are steep and the water is deep until near the head, where the depths shoal rapidly to a shelf. Near the head of the inlet, the granite cliff on the east side has fractured and fallen away to create Weeping Woman, a Picasso-like natural sculpture on the mountainside. It's quite dramatic.

Bullock Channel. Bullock Channel is a straight run between Return Channel and the top of Yeo Island. Study the chart and favor the Coldwell Peninsula side of the channel. The shoal areas on the Yeo Island side have a tendency to be right where you think you should be going.

The only good Bullock Channel anchorages are on the Coldwell Peninsula side—one at the south end, the other at the north end (where we overnighted). We checked the purported anchorages on the Yeo Island side, but they weren't satisfactory. We found poor holding in the northernmost anchorage, and rock, rock, rock in the bight a little south of the north anchorage.

The water is warm near the top of both channels. In colder waters we like our cabin heat in the morning, but we had no need for it there. [*Hale*]

Bullock Channel North Cove. This is Douglass' name for the otherwise unnamed anchorage behind the 39-meter island at the north end of Bullock Channel, on the Coldwell Peninsula side. We found excellent overnight holding in 50 feet (zero tide) opposite the west opening to the cove. The chart shows a rock awash at zero tide in this west opening. Enter and depart this cove from the north.

Bullock Spit Cove. Again, Douglass' name for this unnamed anchorage located inside the 70-meter island on the Coldwell Peninsula side, near the south entrance to Bullock Channel. As the chart shows, you don't want to go very far in or you'll run aground. We found good holding in 35 feet just south of the tip of the island.

Kynumpt Harbour. Kynumpt Harbour indents the north tip of Campbell Island, east of Raymond Passage. Sailing Directions says the local name is Strom Bay. The entrance is open and easy, but study the chart carefully to identify and avoid rocks on the western and southern shores. The northernmost indent on the eastern shore is reported to be a good anchorage, as is Strom Cove, the arm that extends to the southeast. We poked around Strom Cove to find a good lunch stop, but saw mostly 55 to 75 feet on the sounder. At those depths, even a 3:1 scope would swing us too close to rocks near shore, so we anchored in the outer bay, 40 feet, west of Spratt Point.

Dufferin Inlet. Dundivan Inlet indents Dufferin Island west of Raymond Passage. It's a pretty spot with several islets to break up the scenery, but the water is deep except near hazards. Two arms make up Lockhart Bay, near the head. The western arm is the more attractive anchorage. For overnight we would run a stern-tie to a tree. The eastern arm is deep (60 feet) until very near the head and requires a stern-tie. Dundivan Inlet would not be our first choice unless weather was ugly and we were looking for a place to hole up.

Raymond Passage. Raymond Passage connects Seaforth Channel with Queens Sound and sees few pleasure craft. The passage is open, free of hazards, and connects with Codfish Passage at the south end. If you're looking for a raw and exposed wilderness experience and have the boat and navigation skills to manage it, Raymond Passage is a good choice.

Thompson Bay. Thompson Bay is on the west side of Potts Island. Examine the area on your chartplotter or study Chart 3938. This entire area is beautiful and seldom visited. At the northeast corner of Thompson Bay an excellent, protected cove indents Potts Island. Enter the cove from the north, at 52°09.75′N/128°20.75′W.

To get from Raymond Passage to Thompson Bay, run a course of approximately 239° magnetic from the southern tip of Alleyne Island

NORTHERN B.C. COAST

See Area Map Page 412 - Maps Not for Navigation

This photo at low tide shows you should pass to the east of Carne Rock in Reid Passage.

to the 45-meter island, then turn to a course of approximately 292° magnetic to Agnew Islet. You will leave Seen Island approximately one-quarter mile to the south. Rocks will be all around you, but stay in the pass and you will have water.

St. John Harbour. Enter from the north, leaving red buoy E46, marking Rage Reefs, to starboard. Several floating fishing resorts are around Dyer Cove. We prefer the back cove; be sure to avoid the drying shoal. The shallowest point of the channel is at least 7 feet deep. Holding is good.

Milbanke Sound. Milbanke Sound is the shortest route north or south for boats trying to make time along the Inside Passage. In quiet conditions Milbanke Sound is easy. But if the wind is blowing the crossing can be brutal.

From Seaforth Channel to Finlayson Channel, leave Ivory Island to starboard and lay a course that passes north of Susan Rock and west of Vancouver Rock Buoy E54. From there, lay a course to the mouth of Finlayson Channel. Our course took us fairly close to Jorkins Point and the east side of Swindle Island. Total distance was about 12 miles. We've seen boats pass east of Vancouver Rock and take Merilia Passage. This saves about a mile.

Tuno Creek Anchorage. "At the south end of Reid Passage, Blair Inlet extends nearly 2 miles eastward into the Don Peninsula. Tuno Creek empties into the head of Blair Inlet. Anchor south of the creek in 25 to 30 feet, good holding over mud. Strong westerly winds probably will reach the anchorage, but wind protection is good from other directions." [Hamilton]

Reid Passage & Port Blackney. If there's much wind at all, most pleasure craft headed north or south will avoid Milbanke Sound and use the Reid Passage route east of Ivory Island. Chart 3710 makes navigation straightforward. At the south end, be sure to identify all the rocks and islets, and Buoy E50. In the middle of Reid Passage, pass to the east of Carne Rock. Port Blackney, at the north end of Reid Passage, has two anchorages, Boat Inlet and Oliver Cove, that can be used before crossing to Perceval Narrows.

Boat Inlet. Boat Inlet, at the southwest corner of Port Blackney, has a delightful basin for anchorage, with an untouched feeling. The passage that leads to the basin is shallow, however, and rocks encumber the south shore and middle of the channel. Favor the north shore all the way in, with an alert lookout for underwater rocks. The little bay on the north shore at the east end of the passage is shallow and rocky. Stay out. Depending on your vessel's draft, wait for half tide or higher before running Boat Inlet.

Oliver Cove. Oliver Cove Marine Provincial Park, on the east side of Port Blackney, is a safe and pretty anchorage. Enter carefully, avoiding a charted rock in the middle of the fairway and another on the south side. Put the hook down in 35 feet. A few years ago we saw a bear and her cubs on the rocky shore.

Perceval Narrows. The Inside Passage route leads across Mathieson Channel between Port Blackney and Perceval Narrows. Tidal current predictions are found as a secondary station under Prince Rupert in Tide and Current Tables, Vol. 7 and Ports and Passes. From south to north, lay a course that gives Cod Reefs a good offing to port as you leave Port Blackney. Then turn to approximately 270° magnetic and cross Mathieson Channel toward Martha Island, leaving Lizzie Rocks to starboard. We found turbulence in Mathieson Channel off Lizzie Rocks on an ebb tide.

Cockle Bay/Lady Douglas Island. Cockle Bay, a short distance north of Perceval Narrows, has a beautiful beach and good protection from westerlies. You can find 30- to 35-foot depths along the south shore and 60 to 90 feet in the middle, as shown on the chart.

Tom Bay. Tom Bay is on the east side of Mathieson Channel at lat 52°24.20'N. It's a good anchorage, though scarred by recent logging. As with most bays on this coast, Tom Bay shoals at the head. Anchor in 60 to 70 feet.

Dowager Island & Arthur Island. The coves north of Arthur Island, approximately 1.5 miles

---

FULL MOON PARTY AND THE MESS AFTERWARDS

On June 23rd I was moored at Rescue Bay. As night fell, a particularly bright full moon rose from the horizon: the supermoon. When a full moon coincides with the moon's closest pass to Earth, the moon appears particularly large. Thus, the term *supermoon*.

During this celestial event, tides are at their absolute peak. This means currents are particularly strong, but more importantly, any buoyant material sitting below the highest high tide line will be washed into the water.

On June 24th the seas were calm.

Mathieson Channel, Perceval Narrows and Seaforth Channel were packed with logs and there was no wind to push the logs and other debris back to shore. All day I dodged log after

log. Some were rafted together, others floated independently. One thing was for sure: the supermoon party was over, but someone forgot to clean up the mess.

– Mark Bunzel

south of Oscar Passage on the west side of Mathieson Channel, are mentioned in Sailing Directions as a small boat anchorage. Neither cove is very scenic and driftwood clogs the eastern cove. We would choose Rescue Bay on Susan Island, Salmon Bay to the north, or Tom Bay to the south.

Salmon Bay. Salmon Bay is on the east side of Mathieson Channel, opposite the mouth of Oscar Passage. It is deep until the very head, where the bottom comes up to 50 to 60 feet. The bay is cozy and we heard a loon—always a soothing sound.

Oscar Passage. Oscar Passage is the wide-open Inside Passage route between Mathieson Channel and Finlayson Channel. On an ebb, however, the seas can heap up where Oscar Passage joins Finlayson Channel, the result of swells from Milbanke Sound meeting outflowing current. Larger vessels often use Oscar Passage rather than Jackson Passage.

Rescue Bay. Rescue Bay is the most popular anchorage in this area. It is well protected with good holding, and has room for many boats. Study the chart carefully before entering, and steer a determined mid-channel course between the two islands and their reefs that mark the entrance. Once inside Rescue Bay, scout around with the depth sounder and pick your spot carefully. We saw one boat on the western side find the bottom at low tide, after being too eager to get the anchor down.

Note the drying rock in the southeast corner of the bay. Note also the drying reef that extends from the east side of the bay, south of the round islet. The reef covers at high water, and we anchored a little close to it. After checking things out by dinghy and seeing how near the reef was, we re-anchored farther out. At low water the reef showed itself. We were glad we had moved.

Jackson Passage. Jackson Passage is the scenic route between Mathieson Channel and Finlayson Channel. The passage is easily navigated, except for a tight spot at Jackson Narrows at the eastern end, where the depth shows as low as 12 feet on the charts. The fairway through the eastern end of Jackson Narrows is quite narrow and shallow; kelp marks the rocks. Larger vessels may prefer Oscar Passage to the south. While neither the chart nor Sailing Directions shows the current directions, our observations from several transits indicate the flood current sets east and the ebb current sets west.

Jackson Narrows is blind. Before entering, either direction, it's a good idea to call ahead on VHF channel 16, low power, to announce your intentions (*Securité, securité, this is the 34-foot motor vessel* Happy Days, *about to enter Jackson Narrows westbound. Any eastbound traffic please advise, channel one-six*). One year, to our astonishment, a boat approaching from the other end called back on channel 16. Since we were about to enter, the other boat waited until we got through. Strongly favor the *south shore* all the way through the

At anchor in Rescue Bay on the east end of Jackson Passage

narrows, and keep a sharp lookout. A transit near high water slack would be the least anxious, although we have gone through at low water slack with no difficulty.

James Bay. James Bay, on the west side of Mathieson Channel, is open to southerly winds, but gets you out of the chop in the channel. It is a pretty spot, but the bottom shoals abruptly in the northwest corner. Anchor in 75 feet, where the little anchor symbol is on the chart.

FIORDLAND RECREATION AREA

The Fiordland Recreation Area was established in 1987, and is some of the most striking country on the coast. The mountains are sheer and beautiful and the wildlife abundant, but anchorages are just about nonexistent. Fortunately, good anchorage can be found in Windy Bay, only a short distance away.

Fiordland begins just east of Bolin Bay at the north end of Sheep Passage, and includes Mussel Inlet and Kynoch Inlet. We include Bolin Bay in this section because it is so pretty, and Windy Bay because it is the best anchorage near Fiordland.

Windy Bay. Windy Bay is on the south shore of Sheep Passage, near the eastern end. The chart shows anchorage in the middle, but more protected anchorage is in 60 feet in what we call Cookie Cove, just east of the little island at the northeast corner of the bay. Excellent holding.

Bolin Bay. Bolin Bay is set in a bowl of sheer rock mountains with a beautiful drying flat at the head. We didn't anchor, but we did find a few spots with depths of 35 to 60 feet near the head of the bay. With care you might get a safe amount of scope out and stay off the flats. Windy Bay is a better choice.

Oatwish Bay. Oatwish Bay is at the north end of Mussel Inlet. Amazing Lizette Falls will have you reaching for the camera. The bay is too deep for anchoring. We enjoyed lunch there, drifting, engines off.

Poison Cove. At the northeast end of Mussel Inlet lies Poison Cove and Mussel Cove/Mussel River. This is a protected wildlife area for bears and mountain goats which is jointly monitored by BC Parks and the Mussel River Watchmen program. When arriving at the area, boaters should contact the Watchmen on VHF Channel 06. A maximum number of people/boats are allowed in the area at one time. For more information go to www.env.gov.bc.ca/bcparks/explore/parkpgs/fiordland/. The run to the east of Mussel Inlet to Poison Cove left us awestruck. Our notes say, "Poison Cove dwarfed us. I run out of superlatives."

Kynoch Inlet & Culpepper Lagoon. Kynoch Inlet is off Mathieson Channel. On a coast filled with unspeakable beauty, no places we have seen surpass Kynoch Inlet. Most fall well short. Words such as amazing, awesome, incomparable and magnificent suggest but do not capture the grandeur of this inlet. Black rock mountains rise straight up and lead away into bowls of rock. Waterfalls spill down the faces of the mountains. One waterfall shoots out into the channel. The inlet is so narrow and the sides are so steep that our GPS lost its satellites. Anchor at the head of the inlet off the drying flats of Lard Creek or continue into Culpepper Lagoon.

Culpepper Lagoon. Enter or depart Culpepper Lagoon around slack water. Bill Hales, one of our early correspondents, says the current in the entrance turns 15 to 30 minutes before high or low water at Bella Bella, with a least depth of 10 to 15 feet. Gil Flanagan, another of our excellent correspondents, adds to those thoughts, along with personal experience in the narrows

The size, scale and grandeur of Fiordland is awe inspiring.

Waterfalls abound in Kynoch Inlet.

when they are running.

Flanagan went into Culpepper Lagoon around high slack without difficulty. Coming out the next morning was a different matter. They departed on a falling tide, an hour or two before low water slack. Flanagan reports: "We could hear the roar of the rapids well before we could see the narrows in the fog. I went for it, but it was quite a ride. We estimated the current in the narrows at 7.5 knots, and we are sure we dropped more than a foot. The depth sounder was unusable because of the turbulence. We didn't have time to look at it, anyway. There was no turning back. Just steer the sled to the bottom of the hill and hope we miss the Kainet Creek mudflats. Yahoo!"

After comparing Bella Bella tides with Hiekish Narrows current predictions, Flanagan thinks Hiekish Narrows might be a better predictor of slack water. At this point the Waggoner draws no conclusions, except to arrive early and—unlike our correspondent—wait for slack water before going through.

On our own visit to Culpepper Lagoon we went through the narrows an hour after low water at Bella Bella with no difficulty at all. We tried to anchor off Riot Creek, where an old cabin is shown on the chart. We didn't see the cabin (Douglass, in the 2nd Edition of his North Coast book, says the cabin has burned down), and couldn't find a place we liked to put the hook down. Flanagan anchored south of the Lard Creek mudflats at the head of Culpepper Lagoon, inshore from the 60-foot sounding. He saw a sailboat anchored southwest of the Lard Creek mouth. In our case, down at the Riot Creek cabin site it was growing late and we were tired. So we left and motored to Rescue Bay for the night. It was probably a mistake to give up so easily.

FINLAYSON CHANNEL TO PRINCE RUPERT

Nowish Cove. Nowish Cove is on the east side of Finlayson Channel, south of Jackson Passage, at the entrance to Nowish Inlet. Despite being shown as an anchorage, we weren't impressed. The bottom is 85 feet deep and currents from Nowish Narrows swirl through the bay. If protection is needed from a southerly storm, we would consider this cove. Otherwise, if we were looking for a place to hide and had the time, Bottleneck Inlet, 11 miles farther north, is a better choice.

⑧ **Klemtu.** The fuel dock and Kitasoo band store are at the north end of town. Both are open Monday through Saturday, closed for lunch 12:00 p.m. to 1:00 p.m., limited hours Sundays. Boaters may tie-up at the fuel dock when shopping for groceries at the band store as space permits. The band store has an ATM. You'll find gasoline, diesel, propane, stove oil, and ample clear water from the village's water treatment system. The fuel dock faces the channel and wakes from passing boat traffic are apt to bounce you against the dock. Be sure you are well-tied and well-fendered. If the attendant is not in the office shack on the pier, try calling First Nations Fuel on VHF 06 or ask someone in town what the fuel situation is. The fuel dock is closed Sundays, but someone might be available to turn on the pumps.

Klemtu is the last fuel stop until Hartley Bay, approximately 65 miles north. In several recent instances, Hartley Bay has temporarily run out of fuel. Choose fuel stops accordingly.

BC Ferries and Wilderness Seaplanes have scheduled service into Klemtu.

An 11-foot-wide, 210-foot-long concrete dock has been installed in the bay near the village. The dock has no power. The docks can get crowded with local fishing boats and nets are often stacked on the floats. Be prepared to anchor, being mindful of large drying shoals on the south and west sides of the bay.

The village has a K-12 school, good cell phone coverage, two nurses, a post office and three stores. We have shopped in two of the stores: the band store at the fuel dock, and Robinson-Mason General Store in the village.

The band store at the head of the fuel dock pier has been improved and carries a good selection of groceries and other essentials (no liquor), but the stock can thin a few days after the ferry delivered it. On our last visit, we watched the last gallon of milk get snatched up. A small restaurant with breakfast, burgers, and Chinese food is in the entry to the store. You can dine in or order takeout. A pay telephone is just outside the store.

If you'd like to see the extraordinary Big House overlooking the harbor, contact George Robinson on VHF channel 06. Tours are $10 per person. George is delightful. A boardwalk runs around the harbor from the fuel dock to the long house. In 2017 we were surprised to see a medium sized cruise ship stopped at Klemtu. It waited near the ferry landing while its tender shuttled passengers to the Big House and Cultural Center.

Clothes Bay. Clothes Bay is south of Klemtu on the west side of the channel between Swin-

CHARTS

3908	Kitimat Harbour (1:15,000)	3945	Approaches to Douglas Channel (1:40,000)
3977	Douglas Channel (1:80,000)	3946	Grenville Channel (1:40,000) (Replaces Chart 3772)
3911 Plans	Vicinity of Princess Royal Island (1:25,000)	3947	Grenville Channel to Chatham Sound (1:40,000) (Replaces Chart 3773)
3978	Bonilla Island to Edye Passage (1:80,000)	3955 Plans	Prince Rupert Harbor, Venn Passage
3938	Queens Sound to Seaforth Channel (1:40,000)	3957	Approaches to Prince Rupert Harbour (1:40,000)
3941	Channels Vicinity of Milbanke Sound (1:40,000)	3958	Prince Rupert Harbour (1:20,000)
3944	Princess Royal Channel (1:40,000) (Replaces Chart 3739)		

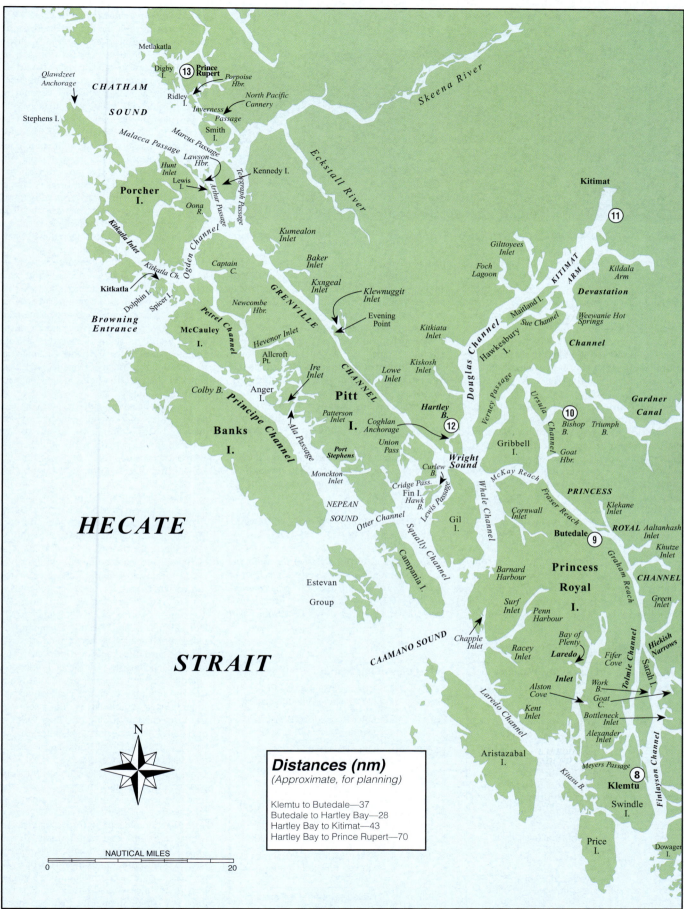

NORTHERN B.C. COAST   See Area Map Page 431 - Maps Not for Navigation

The Native village of Klemtu has a Band Grocery and fuel dock.

dle Island and Cone Island. The bay is well protected except from southeasterly winds. We anchored for the night behind the north tip of Star Island at the mouth of the bay. At low tide, we discovered that the charted "something," extending from Base Point north of us, was a substantial drying reef. The bay has good holding but limited room for only a couple of boats. Being near Klemtu, there is cell phone service in the bay.

Alexander Inlet. Alexander Inlet extends 5 miles into Princess Royal Island, beginning where Meyers Passage and Tolmie Channel meet. If you're fed up with the throngs of boaters and crowded anchorages on this part of the coast (we're joking), here is where you can escape. The early sections of Alexander Inlet are bordered by steep mountains, and are beautiful. The head, however, is surrounded by low hills and is rather ordinary. But, being 5 miles off the beaten path, chances are you'll be the only boat.

The chart shows the inlet well. The only tricky part is near Bingham Narrows. After clearing the drying reef before you reach Bingham Narrows, sag to the west shore to avoid the drying rocks, marked by kelp, just before the narrows themselves.

The head of the inlet is wide open, with ample room to avoid the rock that dries at 2.4 meters lying off the west shore. Anchor in 30 to 35 feet with outstanding holding.

One of the hilltops looks like the profile of a woman lying on her side, and we called it Sleeping Woman. See if you agree. We saw a pair of birds that our field guide identified as red-throated loons, not seen as often as common loons. A lagoon pours into the very head of the inlet, making fluffs of white foam on the water's surface. We rowed over and took pictures, but didn't take the time to explore further. It's very pretty.

The next morning our final note, written after the previous day's notes called the head of Alexander Inlet rather ordinary, reads, "This is a neat spot." [*Hale*]

OUTSIDE ROUTE – PRINCESS ROYAL ISLAND & PITT ISLAND

At this point we step away from the main Inside Passage route to describe the routes west of Princess Royal and Pitt Islands. Those continuing through Finlayson or Tolmie Channels, past Butedale, and through Grenville Channel will find that information resuming on page 436.

Without question, the preferred Inside Passage route to Prince Rupert and beyond is through Finlayson or Tolmie Channels (past Klemtu), past Butedale, and up through Grenville Channel. The waters are protected, the scenery is outstanding, and there's enough boat traffic that if you have a problem, somebody will be along to help out.

An alternate route is on the outside of Princess Royal and Pitt Islands. This route is popular with sailors and adventuresome power boaters. It's as beautiful as the traditional route, but wilder and much less traveled, with more islands and anchorages but fewer waterfalls. Sailors will find more consistent and stronger winds due to the wider channels and lower hills. There's even room for tacking. Because of their remoteness, we recommend these passages for more experienced cruisers only.

From south to north, the outside route first leads up the west side of Princess Royal Island. It begins by running west through Meyers Passage (near Klemtu), then through Laredo Channel and Whale Channel, and rejoins the Inside Passage at Wright Sound. To cruise the outside of Pitt Island, the route runs west from Wright Sound (south end of Grenville Channel), and north through Principe Channel and Petrel Channel, then east through Ogden Channel to rejoin the Inside Passage.

On the outside of either island you could travel all day and only see one or two other pleasure boats, although you're sure to see a few fish boats, perhaps a tug and barge or even a cruise ship. You'll find good anchorages on the outside. In many cases you'll be the only boat.

Weather permitting, you could travel the traditional Inside Passage going one way and all or part of the outside route going the other. The inside and outside routes are roughly the same distance. However, if you take only part of the outside route, going back and forth between the inside and the outside, your total trip will be longer. If you are considering the outside route, carry Sailing Directions PAC 206, and *Exploring the North Coast of B.C.*, by Don Douglass and Réanne Hemmingway-Douglass. The Waggoner Guide describes only the most direct outside routes and focuses on good anchorages. The other books cover a wider area and describe places that require caution and may be more challenging than some skippers would like. If you have the desire for a coastal cruising challenge, with the boat and skills to meet that challenge, the west coast of Princess Royal Island and Pitt Island are excellent cruising areas.

If winds are favorable, sailboats (or slower powerboats) can cut almost a day off their time on the outside route with an open water passage that avoids Klemtu and Meyers Passage. Northbound exit Seaforth Channel, cross Milbanke Sound, and transit Catala Passage. Or, go around McInnes Island, then north up Laredo Sound to Laredo Inlet. This open water route has no stops until you reach Higgins Passage, so pick your weather window carefully. Pay careful attention to your navigation in Catala Passage. The islands and rocks are

CHARTS

West Side of Princess Royal Island	
3721	Harbours on the West Coast of Pitt Island, Mink Trap Bay & Adjacent Inlets, Port Stephens & Monckton Inlet, Buchan Inlet (1:18,300)
3737	Laredo Channel Including Surf Inlet (1:77,400)
3910 Plans	Milbanke Sound and Beauchemin Channel (1:20,000)
3911 Plans	Vicinity of Princess Royal Island (1:25,000)
3943	Finlayson Channel and Tolmie Channel (1:40,000)

West Side of Pitt Island	
3721	Harbours on the West Coast of Pitt Island (Various scales)
3741	Otter Passage to Bonilla Island (1:72,900)
3742	Otter Passage to McKay Reach (1:72,900)
3978	Bonilla Island to Edye Passage (1:80,000)
3945	Approaches to Douglas Channel (1:40,000)
3984	Principe Channel (1:40,000)
3985	Principe Channel Central Portion & Petrel Channel (1:40,000)
3987	Kitkatla Channel & Porcher Inlet (1:40,000)

easily confused, especially in fog. Watch for cruise ships and freighters that occasionally use Laredo Sound.

WEST SIDE OF SWINDLE ISLAND

Higgins Passage. Higgins Passage connects the north end of Milbanke Sound to Laredo Sound, between Swindle and Price Islands. The middle section of the passage, however, has strong currents, many turns, and dries on a six foot tide.

Anchorage can be found in the western end of Higgins Passage. From Laredo Sound, enter Higgins Passage south of Kipp Islet. **Grant Anchorage** is deep and not well protected from southeast winds. Proceed through the anchorage and anchor in 30 to 40 feet on the west side of **Lohbrunner Island**. This anchorage is well protected from all winds, mud bottom.

Kitasu Bay. Kitasu Bay is between Wilby Point and Meyers Passage. Several anchorages are available, ranging from good to excellent. The bay itself is exposed to northwesterly winds, which blow straight down Laredo Channel into **Parson's Anchorage**. In southeasterly or southwesterly weather, however, Parson's Anchorage provides good holding.

The **Marvin Islands** provide shelter from northwest winds. Anchor on the southeast side of the islands in about 50 feet. Several boats can anchor in this location and be protected from moderate winds. Gale force northwesterly winds can make this anchorage uncomfortable.

Jamieson Point Anchorage (also known as Coward's Cove) is just east of Jamieson Point and provides total protection from all winds. Stay mid-channel when entering to avoid a rock on the west side of the entrance. This rock is usually marked by kelp. Once inside, anchor in 30 to 40 feet over a sticky mud bottom.

The eastern basin of **Osment Inlet** provides good anchorage in most weather but the bottom is rocky and irregular.

WEST SIDE OF PRINCESS ROYAL ISLAND

NAVIGATION NOTE: Red spar Buoy *E70* is in the middle of the tight spot in Meyers Passage. Pass north of the buoy, midway between the buoy and the north shore. Currents to 3 knots flood east and ebb west. Sailing Directions says least depth at zero tide is 4 feet. Kelp shows the places to avoid.

Meyers Passage. Meyers Passage separates Swindle Island and Princess Royal Island and is the low-anxiety way to travel between Finlayson Channel and Laredo Sound. The only tricky spot is kelp-choked Meyers Narrows. Although the narrows are not difficult to run, the kelp may cause concern the first time through. Current can run to 3 knots in the narrows.

We went through slowly, avoiding the kelp as best we could. When we got through we said, "Piece of cake."

Although we have not tried it, our fisherman friend Mike Guns says there's good anchorage in 45 feet in the bay on the south shore of the passage.

Laredo Channel. Laredo Channel separates Princess Royal Island and Aristazabal Island, and connects Laredo Sound at the south end with Caamaño Sound and Campania Sound at the north end. Aristazabal Island, on the west side of Laredo Channel, is incompletely charted and considered extremely challenging.

While several inlets lead off Laredo Channel into Princess Royal Island, Laredo Inlet at the south end and Surf Inlet at the north end are the major indents.

INACCURATE CHART: We've heard reports that Chart 3737 is based on an unknown datum, resulting in significant inaccuracies. Electronic charts based on Chart 3737 have similar inaccuracies.

Laredo Inlet. Laredo Inlet is about 10 miles long, and is well protected from westerly storms. If you're approaching from the south, such as from Meyers Passage, the closest entry is through **Thistle Passage**. Rocks extend first from the east side of the narrows, then from the west side. They aren't shown well on the chart. We went through at the top of a 12.8-foot tide. We didn't see any sign of the rocks and they were not marked by kelp. Caution advised. The chart shows 4½ fathoms least depth at the north end of the narrows.

Palmer Anchorage. Fisherman Mike Guns suggests Palmer Anchorage at the south end of Thistle Passage as a good wait-and-see temporary anchorage in a northwest gale, but it's deep, and not what we'd select as the best overnight cruising anchorage.

While several overnight anchorages are available in Laredo Inlet, we think you'll be choosing between Quickly Creek Cove, Alston Cove, Bay of Plenty, and perhaps Fifer Cove. We spent the night in Alston Cove and explored Fifer Cove and Bay of Plenty.

Quigley Creek Cove. From the top of Thistle Passage, turn east just beyond the first small island, leaving the remaining islands to port, then follow the shore into a landlocked basin at the mouth of Quigley Creek. The basin has a depth of about 60 feet at zero tide. A beautiful spot, protected by surrounding islands from wind and waves. This is one of the few outer channel anchorages that you might share with another boat.

Alston Cove. Mouth 52°45.10'N/128°45.75'W. Lovely Alston Cove is easy to enter and is surrounded by mountain peaks. We put the hook down in sticky brown mud just onto the 6½-fathom area on the north side of the cove, near the flats. When we departed the next morning we were glad to have the anchor washdown system. It took a long time to hose the chain and anchor clean.

Fifer Cove. Mouth 52°52.15'N/128°45.15'W. Fifer Cove is surrounded by mountain peaks and is very scenic, but most of the cove is too deep for easy anchoring. To enter, wrap around Tuite Point, leaving it to starboard. We found 40- to 50-foot depths near the head of the cove, off the stream mouth. Correspondents James and Jennifer Hamilton report the creek shoals out much farther than the chart indicates or they expected, and holding was poor.

Kohl Island Anchorage. "Kohl Island is in Weld Cove, directly south of Bay of Plenty. The bight at the northwest tip of Kohl Island is a sheltered anchorage with mountain views. Approach between Kohl and Pocock Islands and turn west when clear of the rocks off the north tip of Kohl Island. The anchorage is at 52°49.00'N/128°46.09'W between two uncharted rocks. One rock rarely covers and the other is awash at 12 feet. We dropped the anchor between the rocks and pulled back 150 feet to stern-tie onto Kohl Island. Holding was good in 10 to 20 feet over mud and shell." [*Hamilton*]

Bay of Plenty. Bay of Plenty was recommended to us by Correspondents Mike Guns and Laurie and Anita Dowsett. On our chart, Guns drew the entrance channel south of the 120-foot island, and north of the little islet in the middle of the Bay. Anchor in 30 feet, short of the flats. Those flats, by the way, come out a long way. The bay is open to southwest storms.

Correspondent Jim Norris reports good anchorage, but his empty crab pot had him renaming this spot "Bay of Not so Much."

Buie Creek. "A spectacular two-level waterfall is a short distance up Buie Creek at the head of Laredo Inlet. To visit, anchor temporarily off the head of Laredo Inlet at 52°58.128'N/128°39.763'W in 90 feet with a 250-foot swing radius, moderate holding." [*Hamilton*]

Kent Inlet. Kent Inlet is on the east side of Laredo Channel. Once inside, Kent Inlet is scenic and appears to be well protected. To get inside, however, you must go through Philip Narrows, which is guarded by rocks. Sailing Directions says currents through Philip Narrows run to 8 knots at spring tides, and recommends a transit at slack water only.

We arrived at Kent Inlet near high water slack, so we went in. Kelp marked the rocks at the entrance, off Laredo Channel, and they were not a problem. Kelp did *not* mark the rocks a short distance east of Loap Point. Rocks are out in the middle, exactly where you think you want to be. Stay south of those rocks. Give them room.

At slack water Philip Narrows was easy. Correspondents Laurie and Anita Dowsett

These extraordinary falls are at the head of Surf Inlet.

recommended anchoring either near the west shore immediately inside Phllip Narrows, or in the back basin off the tidal waterfall. Favor the north shore to get to the back basin. Note the rocks on the south side when entering the back basin. The water in Kent Inlet was dark with rain runoff when we visited; we couldn't see more than a foot or two into it. We had good depths all around the point that defines the back basin. This anchorage is beautiful, marred only by many diseased trees.

LOCAL KNOWLEDGE

CHARTPLOTTER ERRORS: In Surf Inlet, one of our chartplotters placed our boat several hundred feet from where it actually was. Navigate cautiously in this area.

Surf Inlet. Beautiful Surf Inlet stretches 13 miles into Princess Royal Island at the north end of Laredo Channel, ending at a stunning waterfall over a dam that separates Bear Lake from the inlet.

An abandoned concrete power house is on a point below the dam at the head of Surf Inlet. A road leads to a point below the falls. We've been told that if you can get a dinghy or kayak up to the dam (the road looks like the way to go), you can go up Bear Lake to an old mining camp that is surprisingly intact.

Chapple Inlet, at the mouth of Surf Inlet, has a few anchorage possibilities, but Surf Inlet itself has only one, Penn Harbour.

Penn Harbour. Penn Harbour is beautiful and spacious, with a straightforward entry and ample anchoring room in 40 to 50 feet near the head. A stream cascades into the east end and makes little white icebergs of foam on the surface—except that on the night of our visit the icebergs weren't white, they were tan. The water was brown and the anchor turned brown as it penetrated the surface. It disappeared altogether within a foot or two.

Chapple Inlet. Chapple Inlet leads north from the mouth of Surf Inlet, and has anchorage possibilities. These include a little nook on the west shore at Doig Anchorage, another nook behind Chettleburgh Point, and in Kiln Bay. Entry to Chapple Inlet is easy at Mallandaine Point. Follow a midchannel course along the east shore.

At **Doig Anchorage**, try the area just north of the point at 52°55.10'N/ 129°07.80'W. We didn't verify the depths, but we saw three rafted powerboats anchored and stern-tied to shore.

Behind **Chettleburgh Point**, we would anchor in 60 feet, with ample swinging room. This is where you will appreciate an all-chain anchor rode so you can swing in a smaller circle on shorter scope. If you move closer in for shallower water, you'll probably want to run a stern-tie to shore.

In **Kiln Bay**, anchor in 60 feet, north of the little island.

LOCAL KNOWLEDGE

CHARTPLOTTER ERRORS: In Emily Carr Inlet, one of our chartplotters placed our boat several hundred feet from where it actually was. Navigate cautiously in this area.

Emily Carr Inlet. Emily Carr Inlet is on the north side of Surf Inlet, right at the mouth. The inlet is beautiful, and the main body of the inlet is open. With close attention it should present no problems. A reef, however, extends from Webber Island nearly across Holgate Passage, making the entry from Chapple Inlet a little tricky.

We went through Emily Carr Inlet from north to south, then turned northeast to complete our circumnavigation of Princess Royal Island. Although the winds were light, we got into a nasty tide-rip off the 207-foot island south of Duckers Island and wet the boat down pretty thoroughly. It wasn't fun. We crowded over close to Duckers Island and found calmer water. [*Hale*]

Barnard Harbour. Mouth, west side of Borde Island, 53°04.90'N/129°07.75'W; east side of Borde Island, 53°05.20'N/129°06.65'W. Barnard Harbour is shown on planning Charts 3737 and 3742, see Chart 3911 for detail.

Barnard Harbour is big, open, and beautiful. It was a center for fly-in sport fishing, lodges, but these lodges have since moved. Anchor in Cameron Cove along the west shore in 30 to 35 feet or in 40 to 60 feet off the mouth of Barnard Creek.

Campania Island. Campania Island, with its bald, knobby mountaintops, is recognizable from miles away. Several inlets on Campania Island's west shore provide sheltered anchorages, interesting views, and opportunities for exploration by kayaks and dinghies. All are well charted; use Charts 3724 and 3912.

McMicking Inlet. McMicking Inlet, in Estevan Sound on the west side of Campania Island, is one of the few places in the outer channels where, at least in July and August, you might have competition for the best anchoring spots. The looming granite mass of Pender Mountain makes for a dramatic anchorage, and twisted cedars growing among the rocks add to the scenic character. Use Charts 3724 and 3912. Although the entrance to McMicking Inlet is open to the south, islets, rocks and reefs diminish any swells. Enter south and east of a chain of islets and drying reefs extending from the south end of Jewsbury Peninsula. Anchor north of the narrows.

Dunn Passage. Use Charts 3742 and 3912. Dunn Passage, in Estevan Sound on the west side of Campania Island, provides good shelter from all weather. Anchor at the head of Dunn Passage and explore a labyrinth of rocks and islands by dinghy or kayak.

Weinburg Inlet. Inside Dunn Passage, Weinburg Inlet has granite domes and stacks, creating an intriguing and picturesque anchorage. Correspondent Jim Norris reports spending three nights anchored here in 2016, waiting out a southeast gale, with good holding but limited swing room on a 5 to 1 scope.

WEST SIDE OF PITT ISLAND

This route leads from the south end of Grenville Channel.

Otter Channel. Two possible anchorages appear to be available on the south tip of Pitt Island (the north side of Otter Channel). The first is Dillon Bay, where we saw a sailboat anchored. The second is Saycuritay Cove.

Saycuritay Cove. "Securitay Cove is the of-

Knobby Campania Island

Patterson Inlet, Princess Diana Cove

ficial name, not labeled on the chart, for the small cove east of Fleishman Point on the southwest corner of Pitt Island. Approach from 53°12.67'N/129°33.54'W, heading north. Favor the Pitt Island shore beyond the islet at the entrance, and wrap around the north side of the first of the three small islets inside. Minimum depth on entry is 10 feet. Anchor in 25 feet with room to swing between the first and second of the three small islets. Holding is good over a soft bottom, with reasonable wind protection and views out between the islets. Good anchoring depths also are at the 6-fathom sounding on the chart. The ruins of an old settlement, now a kayaker camp, are on the east shore of the bight in the north side of the large islet that makes up the south shore of the cove." [*Hamilton*]

Monckton Inlet. Monckton Inlet indents Pitt Island at lat 53°18.65'N. The inlet is well protected, with three anchorage possibilities. The first is in 60 feet on the back side of Monckton Point, a short distance inside the inlet on the north side. If you can get in and out near high water, this would be a marvelous, snug anchorage. With propellers and rudders hanging down, however, low water access is scary.

The second anchorage is about three-quarters of the way into the inlet in the bay that extends north almost a mile behind Roy Island. Go up near the head, past the two rocks marked with a + on the chart. Anchor with lots of room in 40 to 50 feet, mud bottom. We tried to find the two rocks mentioned above, but didn't see them. They were not marked by kelp. Be aware.

The third anchorage is at the very head of Monckton Inlet in 50 to 60 feet, mud bottom. It's not very interesting.[*Hale*]

Kooryet Bay. Kooryet Bay, on Banks Island, roughly across Principe Channel from Monkton Inlet, can provide a convenient escape when fog sets in or winds kick up in Principe Channel. Inside the bay you'll have a good vantage point for watching changing conditions in the channel. In southerly winds, anchor in the south cove. In northerly winds, anchor off the creek bed or northwest of Kooryet Island.

Patterson Inlet/Princess Diana Cove. Patterson Inlet is narrow, beautiful, and appears well protected. The head of the inlet divides into a north arm and a south arm. The south arm is very pretty, with a stunning rock wall on the north side near the entry. The bottom is 90 feet deep, though, and a grown-over log booming ground is near the head. We see no need to anchor in the south arm.

The north arm is known as Princess Diana Cove. We overnighted there. It was a perfect anchorage, 25 to 30 feet deep, thick mud bottom. Anchor in the middle. Rocks and reefs sneak up along the shores.

Note: A reader tells us this bay was not good in a southeast gale.

Ire Inlet. Ire Inlet is entered from Ala Passage at latitude 53°30'N. The entry is narrow and quite dramatic, but the fairway is clear. The hillsides are covered with remarkable trees, tall and straight with very short limbs. They look like green pipe cleaners. The trees on top of the rock mountain on the north side of Ire Inlet are twisted and have few limbs. From our distance they looked like bonsai trees.

The little cove on the south shore has rocks as shown on Chart 3984 but not on 3741. Not a good spot. A much better anchorage is between the little islet and the head of the inlet in 20 to 25 feet. Pass north of the little islet. Rocks lie off the south side, and a large drying shoal extends from the south shore of the inlet.

If you visit Ire Inlet (recommended), study the chart carefully before entering Ala Passage. A number of islets and drying rocks must be identified and located. Know where you are at all times and check for fallen trees before entering.

Azimuth Island. Mike Guns put us onto this one. A small unnamed island lies southwest of Azimuth Island, and a convenient anchorage is behind that island at 53°31.45'N/129°59.50'W on the chart. Anchor in 60 to 65 feet. Be sure to enter this anchorage from the north. The southern entry is foul with rocks.

Tangent Island. Tangent Island lies in a cluster of islands located north of Anger Island, near the intersection of Petrel and Principe Channels. The cove on the east side of Tangent Island provides good protection, with a view to the mountains of Pitt Island to the east. Although the anchorage is 100 feet deep, it has good holding and is well protected. Tangent Island also provides an opportunity to refresh your high school math. Enter via Markle Passage, passing between Sine Point to the west, Tangent Point to the east and Logarithm Point to the south.

Colby Bay. Colby Bay is on Banks Island, the west side of Principe Channel, at latitude 53°32.10'N. Go down the middle and anchor in 30 feet where the bay opens up. You'll be surrounded by mountains and protected from northwest or southeast gale winds in Principe Channel. Mike Guns, who first recommended Colby Bay to us, called this spot "a joy."

Petrel Channel. Petrel Channel begins at the south tip of McCauley Island and winds along the west side of Pitt Island to Captain Cove. It has four anchorages, all on the Pitt Island side.

Allcroft Point. Just south of Allcroft Point, at lat 53°35.65'N, is an unnamed bay that gets you off Petrel Channel. Anchor in 75 to 90 feet when you get to the wide spot. The chart shows a rock awash at zero tide obstructing access to the back cove. You may prefer Hevenor Inlet.

Hevenor Inlet. Hevenor Inlet stretches 5 miles into Pitt Island's mountains and you have to go all the way to the head of the inlet for suitable anchorage. The hills on both sides have been clearcut, but already are green again. Anchor in 35 to 60 feet off the falls (you'll see them) or off the mouth of the lagoon.

Newcombe Harbour. Newcombe Harbour is a fine, well-protected anchorage. Motor straight in and anchor off the drying flats in 40 to 50 feet. We wouldn't bother with the little nook on the east shore, a short distance inside the entrance. It is rather tight and not that exciting. With such good, easy anchorage only a little farther in, it's not worth the effort. The log booms reported in the Douglass *Exploring the North Coast of British Columbia* were not there when we visited.

Signs like this one at Newcombe Harbour mark several anchorages.   *The public dock in Kitkatla. When maneuvering, stay close to the dock.*

Captain Cove. Captain Cove is a cozy, protected anchorage at the northwest corner of Pitt Island, near the south entrance to Ogden Channel. Anchor in 60 to 80 feet in the large basin behind the 84-foot island, or in the 5-fathom basin along the south shore, behind the little dot islet. We have anchored twice in the 5-fathom basin and once behind the 84-foot island. If you don't mind 70 to 80 feet, the anchorage behind the island is excellent.

Kitkatla. (250) 848-2214. Kitkatla is a Native village on the north end of Dolphin Island, west of Ogden Channel. The dock has 20 & 30 amp power but no other amenities. Most of the dock is taken by local boats. Fuel is available by jerry jug; pay in advance at the band office.

Kitkatla is a pleasant community. Ann's B&B and gift shop has cedar weaving for sale—small baskets to conical hats. Several small convenience stores operate out of homes.

Don't plan to stop at Kitkatla on weekends. Most of the village goes shopping in Prince Rupert.

We left Bully Island to port and went up Kitkatla Channel, leaving the Kitkatla Islands to starboard. Sailing Directions says a church spire is a significant Kitkatla landmark from the water, but new construction makes the spire less significant. Green Buoy *E95* marks the end of a rocky shoal when you get close to the moorage area, and a little island lies beyond. Leave Buoy *E95* to port and turn toward shore. Head for the large loading dock, leaving the little island to starboard. Go slowly. Kelp marks the shallow spots. Once past the island, run right along the public dock or as close as the rafted boats allow. Rocks lie along the island.

Deep draft boats beware: Depth alongside the dock is approximately 6.5 feet at zero tide.

Spicer Islands. Located off Beaver Passage, between Spicer Island and South Spicer Island. Follow the channel to the well-protected, roomy basin. Anchor in 25 feet, good holding.

Larsen Harbour. Larsen Harbour, at the northwest corner of Banks Island, is a scenic anchorage. Low-lying rocks surround the anchorage and storm-battered trees line the shore. Correspondent Jim Norris reports that there is no significant kelp blocking the entrance and that the anchorage is well-protected from swells originating in the Hecate Strait but not from northwest winds which can build steep waves at the entrance. Jim also reports that there are no buoys in the harbour, contrary to some other guidebooks.

Conditions on Hecate Strait are visible from within the anchorage, making it a good place to stage a trip across the strait to Haida Gwaai. Anchor in 15-25 feet, with fair holding on a rocky bottom with patchy kelp.

Welcome Harbour. Welcome Harbour is on the east side of Henry Island. A maze of rocks and islets guard the entrance; navigate carefully. The channel on the west side of Dancey Island leads to Secret Cove. Welcome Harbour is a favorite of many Prince Rupert boaters.

INSIDE PASSAGE ROUTE, CONTINUED

Mary Cove. Mary Cove is on the east side of Finlayson Channel across from Klemtu. It is a pleasant little cove, but it appears open to southwest winds. Anchor in 50 to 55 feet inside. A salmon stream empties into Mary Cove.

Bottleneck Inlet. Bottleneck Inlet, at latitude 52°42.8'N on the east side of Finlayson Channel, is an outstanding anchorage. It is protected and beautiful, and large enough for a number of boats. The north side of the inlet has superb rock walls. The chart shows a least depth of just over a fathom in the narrow entry, and a rock shelf extends from the south shore at the narrow part. Favor the north shore. Deeper draft vessels should enter cautiously at low tide. The chart fails to show a 13-15 fathom hole a short distance inside the entry sill. The bottom then comes up to 25-30 feet.

Although we have anchored in Bottleneck Inlet several times now, one night in particular was memorable. That was the night a forewarned on-shore gale struck the coast. Four people died in that storm. At 1:30 a.m. the winds hit. We could see clouds racing overhead and hear the wind roaring in the trees above us, but except for four tongues of strong wind that slammed into our boat between 1:30 a.m. and 4:00 a.m., the air around us was almost calm. [*Hale*]

Goat Cove. Goat Cove indents the eastern shore near the north end of Finlayson Channel. An inner basin is reached by running through a narrow neck. Inside, Sailing Directions says good anchorage can be had in 17 fathoms, which is pretty deep. Don Douglass likes this inner basin, too, and would anchor near the head in 36 feet. We don't like it at all. We went in during a gather-

The view out the mouth of Bottleneck Inlet the morning after a storm. At high tide the entry looks wide, but a rock ledge extends from the south shore.

ing storm, and wind gusts found their way to us with nothing to stop them. The bottom shoaled too quickly for us to anchor in 36 feet and pay out scope to stand up to the wind. "Oversold!" we decided, and left. We must add that since then, we have met other cruisers who like Goat Cove, so perhaps it comes down to what the weather is doing. [*Hale*]

Work Bay. Work Bay is on the west side of Finlayson Channel near the north end. The bay appears open to southerly winds, but we anchored there in the southerly storm that chased us out of Goat Cove, and found no wind and only remnants of a few rollers from Finlayson Channel. In our opinion Work Bay has room for just one boat at anchor unless all boats stern-tie to trees. The bay is 40 to 50 feet deep. With only a 3:1 scope (150 feet) of anchor rode out, you must be in the center or you will swing onto shore or onto the drying shelf at the head of the bay.

Lime Point Cove. Lime Point Cove, on Griffin Passage, is an indentation just south of the north end of Pooley Island. For years it has been passed by after the area above the cove was logged. New growth has filled in and once again it is a quiet, scenic anchorage, although exposed to southerlies passing up through Griffin Passage. Anchor in the shallow areas of the cove in 36 to 70 feet.

Carter Bay. Carter Bay is on the north side of Sheep Passage at the east entry to Hiekish Narrows. The bones of the steamship *Ohio*, which ran up on Ohio Rock in 1909, are there. Knowing he was sinking, the captain of the *Ohio* made it across the mouth of the narrows and into Carter Bay, where he grounded the ship. Of the 135 passengers and crew, only four were lost.

Hiekish Narrows. Hiekish Narrows connects with Sheep Passage and Finlayson Channel at the south end, and Graham Reach, the continuation of the Inside Passage, at the north end. Current predictions are given under Hiekish Narrows in Ports and Passes and Canadian Tide and Current Tables, Vol. 7. Currents run to 4.5 knots on the flood, 4 knots on the ebb. The flood sets north. The water behind Hewitt Island appears to be a possible anchorage, but the current runs strongly through it.

Graham Reach & Fraser Reach. Graham Reach and Fraser Reach are wide, straight and deep, and lined with beautiful waterfalls. Cruise ships make this their highway. The principal stopping point for pleasure craft is Butedale.

Horsefly Cove. Horsefly Cove is a short distance inside the mouth of Green Inlet on the east side of Graham Reach. The cove is cozy and protected, but 80 to 90 feet deep. You may have to stern-tie to shore to restrict your swing.

Swanson Bay. Swanson Bay is on the east side of Graham Reach. This bay is exposed, but

This humpback was spotted in Fraser Reach just a few miles from Butedale.

interesting. Ruins of an old sawmill and pulp mill are on the beach and back in the trees. A 3-story concrete building is just inside the treeline. Farther back, a tall red brick chimney is hidden in the trees. Although the chart shows the chimney as a landmark, summer foliage has almost obscured it from view.

We had trouble finding a comfortable place to anchor at Swanson Bay, settling finally for the shallower water off the creek mouth. Current from the creek kept the boat from swinging. Ashore are the ruins of what once was a formidable shipping center. We have seen a photo of a long wharf at Swanson Bay, with a large square-rigger tied alongside. The wharf is gone, and only a few pilings remain. Unfortunately, the dense forest inhibited our exploration on land.

Our notes, written at Ocean Falls, say that Swanson Bay shipped its first load of pulp in 1909, and in the 1920s had a population of 500. Its last shipment was in 1934. For some reason the notes don't show the source of this information, so no guarantees as to accuracy.

A few years ago we saw a black-colored wolf on the south shore of Swanson Bay. It watched as our boat slowly approached. Then, with a dismissive, air it ambled back into the forest. [*Hale*]

Khutze Inlet. Khutze Inlet stretches eastward from Graham Reach nearly 5 miles and rewards visitors with a stunning anchorage near the head. From there you can look across the drying flats of the Khutze River into a broad valley with mountains on both sides. Don't get too close to the flats. The water can be murky and the bottom comes up sharply. A long and beautiful waterfall tumbles down the mountain to your right. The outfall stream forms an alluvial fan off its mouth. We've seen boats anchored there, and earlier editions suggested that you could find a good spot on that fan to put the hook down. A few years ago, however, a 42-foot boat anchored in that location, but swung too close to shore and went aground.

We have anchored toward the river mouth in 90 to 100 feet, and between the river mouth and the waterfall in 60 feet. Approach the drying flats slowly until you reach your depth, and put the anchor down. Note that a drying spit extends from the south shore of the Khutze River into the bay. You want to anchor on the south side of that spit.

You can also anchor behind Green Spit near the mouth of the inlet. One good spot is along the south shore, just west of the stream mouth. The chart shows the right spot.

⑨ **Butedale.** The historic Butedale cannery ruins are located on Princess Royal Island, at the south end of Fraser Reach. The waterfalls are beautiful but the site is in an advanced state of disrepair. Anchorage is possible, though the bottom near the dock may be foul with cable.

A new owner purchased Butedale in 2013 with plans to redevelop the property. Limited cleanup and stabilization efforts have taken place, but the bulk of the work is still to come, possibly next season. Officially Butedale is closed for business, and signs on the dock warn visitors that visiting is at their own risk. However, boaters seeking shelter or wanting to visit won't be turned away. In 2015, a new aluminum ramp to shore was installed and the floats were resurfaced. The concrete dock was cleared to make a heliport in 2017, just in case you need to land there. The docks are still primitive, but they're the only docks between Klemtu and Hartley Bay. Untreated water is available on the dock. The caretaker welcomes visitors and can be contacted on VHF 66A. Spirit Bears have been spotted in this area.

See www.WaggonerGuide.com for updates.

⑩ **Bishop Bay Hot Springs.** Bishop Bay Hot Springs is located at the head of Bishop Bay, on the east side of Ursula Channel. This is one of the don't-miss stops along the northern B.C. coast. Local residents have done an outstanding job building and maintaining the bathhouse and boardwalk. A voluntary use fee was initiated in 2017 with an honor box on the way to the hot springs. At the bathhouse, the hot spring water is an agreeable temperature and odor-free. The boardwalk parallels the shoreline through fabulous, moss-covered and moss-hung forest.

The dock is small, maximum boat size is 30 feet, and plan on rafting. In 2015, the ramp connecting the float to shore was missing. It was replaced in 2016. Anchoring is only fair to poor, because the bottom slopes quickly to deep water. A stern-tie would

NORTHERN B.C. COAST   See Area Map Page 431 - Maps Not for Navigation

Boats moored at the improved log-float at Butedale

make anchoring more comfortable. A short distance south of the dock a shoal, not shown on the charts, extends into the bay from the shoreline. Be aware of that shoal and plan your swing to stay well off it. The three mooring buoys marked "Private" actually are for public use, use at your own risk.

Verney Passage. Verney Passage, along the west side of Gribbell Island, must be one of the more beautiful places on earth. It is lined, both sides, with raw, polished rock mountains, 3500 feet high. Great glacier-carved bowls, called cirques, are hollowed into the mountains. From the water you can see their forested floors and sheer rock walls. Especially on a sunny day, a visit to Bishop Bay Hot Springs should include a circumnavigation of Gribbell Island, to see Verney Passage.

Weewanie Hot Springs. Midway up Devastation Channel, Weewanie Hot Springs is a beautiful small bay, surrounded by sheer rock walls and forest. One mooring buoy was available in 2015.

Though the anchorage is beautiful, the hot springs on shore are the primary attraction. The Kitimat Aquanauts Scuba Club built a rustic bathhouse and soaking tubs. Land a dinghy on the rocky beach and follow the trail past a campsite to the bathhouse. Or, land the dinghy on the rocks just below the bathhouse, tie to a log ashore, and climb up to the bathhouse. We've found Weewanie Hot Springs quiet and tranquil, less crowded than popular Bishop Bay.

Proper hot spring etiquette is to pull the plug on the lower tub, drain, then replug. The tub will fill again from the hose connected to the underground hot springs.

⑪ **Kitimat.** Kitimat, pop. 10,000, is a small city located at the head of Douglas Channel. While it has shopping for nearly everything one might need, the town itself is located about 5 miles from the nearest marina, MK Bay Marina. Taxi service (Coastal Taxis, 250-632-7250), if available, is about $25 each way. We suspect a person needing to get to town for shopping could find a ride.

Kitimat is a classic company town, built by Alcan in the 1950s to make aluminum. In the middle of the shopping area, the small Kitimat Museum and Archives has several exhibits that show how the town was built, including the massive tunnels and hydroelectric power dam for the smelting plant. The Alcan plant was one of the largest non-defense construction projects of the 1950s. Today, new owners continue updating and operating the plant.

Just a few miles west on Douglas Channel you can see the clearing and construction for a Liquid Natural Gas plant planned for sometime in the future. When completed, this will be the terminus for an LNG pipeline beginning in the Interior. The gas will be processed, chilled into liquid form, and loaded on ships for distribution.

⑪ **MK Bay Marina.** 4935 Kitimat Village Rd, Kitimat, BC V8C 2G7; (250) 632-6401; contact@mkbay.ca; www.mkbaymarina.ca. Monitors VHF 68. Open all year, 420 feet of guest side-tie moorage on D-dock and occasional slip moorage. 20, 30 & 50 amp power, water, washrooms, showers, laundry, and Wi-Fi. Store with fishing supplies, ice, and a deli. Gas and diesel fuel, haulout to 20 tons, and launch ramp. The marina is on the east side of Kitimat Arm.

Boats on the seaward side of the dock should consider extra fenders. Inflow winds, common in the afternoon, produce significant chop. The marina is co-owned by The Mill Bay Group and Haisla Nation. Facility upgrades are planned for 2017/2018. An overnight guest house is available at the marina. The marina does not take reservations but they recommend calling ahead, especially larger vessels..

LOCAL KNOWLEDGE

WEATHER TIP: When crossing Wright Sound in an outflow wind in Douglas Channel, it is better to lay a course to Juan Point, at the north end of Gil Island. We tried this route in an outflow wind, and found it much smoother than our previous crossing, in which we tried a direct (and wet) route between Point Cumming and Cape Farewell.

Wright Sound. Wright Sound is at the junction of Grenville Channel, Douglas Channel, Verney Passage and McKay Reach. All these passages pour their currents into Wright Sound, where the waters collide and mix. Especially on an ebb, not much wind is needed to make conditions ugly.

Coghlan Anchorage. Coghlan Anchorage is behind Promise Island, and is connected by Stewart Narrows with Hartley Bay. The anchorage is open to the south, but still decently protected. There are no mooring buoys in the anchorage. One year we anchored briefly in 35 to 40 feet just north of Brodie Point. The protection and holding ground were excellent, if not scenic. Anchorage is also possible on the shore opposite Brodie Point, off Otter Shoal. [*Hale*]

⑫ **Hartley Bay.** Band Office, 320 Hayimi-isaxaa Way, Hartley Bay, BC V0V 1A0; (250)

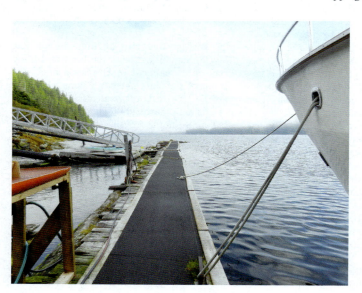

A new ramp now leads from the shore to the dock at Butedale.

438   www.WaggonerGuide.com

See Area Map Page 431- Maps Not for Navigation   NORTHERN B.C. COAST

Hartley Bay is a pleasant boardwalk community.

Beautiful Devastation Channel connects Verney Passage to Kitimat Arm. Weewanie Hot Springs is on the east side.

841-2500; hbvc@gitgaat.ca. Open all year. Gasoline and diesel, pure water (from the water treatment plant) at the fuel dock, 30 amp power on the floats. Garbage drop, but only separated recycling accepted. Major credit cards accepted.

Hartley Bay, near the south end of Douglas Channel, is a friendly and modern-looking Native village, population 160-200, with a no-charge government dock behind a rock breakwater. The Cultural Centre is in a new building near the fuel dock. No liquor. No pay phone, but cell phones work. A medical clinic has two nurses and a visiting doctor.

Fuel dock hours are Monday through Thursday 8:00 a.m. to 12:00 p.m., and 1:00 p.m. to 5:00 p.m.; Friday through Sunday on call, VHF 06, Hartley Bay Fuel. Hartley Bay has run out of fuel several times in recent years. Boats that must take on fuel at Hartley Bay should call ahead to ensure availability. It is a pleasure to walk the Native village of Hartley Bay where homes and public buildings are all connected by a series of wide, substantial boardwalks. There are no roads in town per sey except for the wide boardwalks used occasionally by ATV's and Smart Cars; residents generally get around by bicycle or on foot. For supplies and groceries locals must ride the foot ferry to Prince Rupert, an 80-mile journey one way. This interesting community has a small fishing fleet and a fish hatchery. A trail along Kukayu River leads to the fish hatchery, where visitors are welcome. Continuing further along the trail we discovered the "local swimming hole" where you can hike down the stairs to enjoy a natural pool. Rumor has it that locals know where you might see a "Spirit Bear," stop by the Band Office for more information. Marven Robinson serves as a local "Spirit Bear" guide and is available August through September.

Fin Island. Fin Island lies between Lewis Passage and Cridge Passage, immediately west of Gil Island. Fin Island is fairly low and not particularly interesting, but it has two workable anchorages, Curlew Bay and Hawk Bay. Hawk Bay is the better of the two.

Curlew Bay. Curlew Bay indents the northeast corner of Fin Island. It isn't a destination anchorage by any means, but it will do in settled weather or a southerly. The bay appears open to a northerly and to outflow winds from Douglas Channel. The chart shows shoaling a short distance west of the narrows. We anchored in 20 feet at the east end of the narrows. The anchor bumped twice on what felt like rock, then set solidly. [Hale]

Hawk Bay. Hawk Bay, on the west side of Fin Island, is more scenic and has more room than Curlew Bay. The anchorage is somewhat open to westerly winds and you'll swing around if it's blowing. Anchor in the middle in 60 feet.

LOCAL KNOWLEDGE

STRONG CURRENTS: Sailing Directions says Grenville Channel currents run to a maximum of 2 knots, but the channel narrows between Lowe Inlet and Evening Point, creating stronger currents. We've seen 3 to 4 knots of current in this stretch, on the flood and the ebb.

When headed north, you can save time and fuel by riding an afternoon or early evening flood part way in, then overnighting in one of Grenville Channel's excellent anchorages. Then ride a morning ebb out.

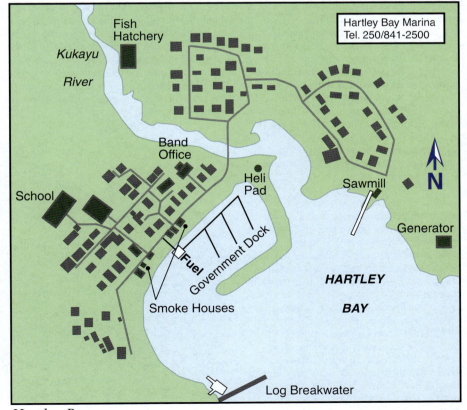

Hartley Bay

2018 Waggoner Cruising Guide

NORTHERN B.C. COAST See Area Map Page 431 - Maps Not for Navigation

Village of Hartley Bay with entrance to Government Dock behind the breakwater to the right.

Grenville Channel. Though sometimes called "The Ditch," Grenville Channel is a straight, beautiful, and unobstructed 45-mile-long channel running between Wright Sound in the south and Arthur Passage in the north. Tidal currents flow in and out of each end. Currents run more strongly in the narrower south half than in the wider north half. Flood currents meet in the area of Evening Point, about 25 miles from the south entrance. Ebb currents divide about 1.5 miles north of Evening Point.

The tide & current tables show no current predictions for Grenville Channel, but corrections for high and low tides are shown for Lowe Inlet as a secondary port under Bella Bella in Ports and Passes and the Canadian Tide and Current Tables, Vol. 7 (Index No. 9195).

Be sure to give Morning Reef, north of Evening Point, a wide berth.

Grenville Channel is a major waterway on the Inside Passage. You may see tugs with tows, all types of fish boats and large commercial vessels, the BC Ferries, and cruise ships. In limited visibility, radar is essential and AIS is helpful. We monitor Prince Rupert Vessel Traffic Service on VHF 11. Large vessels have Call-in Points shown on the charts. Their check-ins with VTS will help you develop a mental picture of the large vessels that may be a factor on your passage, especially those approaching from ahead or overtaking from astern.

Union Passage. Union Passage, on the west side of Grenville Channel, is served by Hawkins Narrows from Grenville Channel, and Peters Narrows from the south. It is one of those places people talk about but not many visit. The problem is the two sets of narrows. The chart shows 8-knot currents in Hawkins Narrows and 7-knot currents in Peters Narrows. Hawkins Narrows slack is shown as 5 minutes in duration. Neither the chart nor Sailing Directions say much about Peters Narrows. Once inside, the scenery is not remarkable.

The currents often are much less than shown, and the window of least current much wider than 5 minutes. We entered Union Passage through Hawkins Narrows at low water slack, poked around for a few minutes, then departed the way we came. The day was windy, rainy and cold. Our spirit was with the great explorers, but our resolve that day was weak. [*Hale*].

The entrance to Hawkins Narrows is at latitude 53°22'N. The channel is open until the inner end is approached. There, a rock awash at zero tide lies off the eastern shore. Favor the western shore to avoid it.

Lowe Inlet (Verney Falls). Lowe Inlet, a provincial park 14.5 miles from the southern entrance to Grenville Channel, is an excellent spot to overnight. You can anchor either in the outer basin or in Nettle Basin, the cozier inner cove. Walt Woodward, in his book *How to Cruise to Alaska Without Rocking the Boat Too Much*, recommends anchoring directly in front of Verney Falls where they pour into Nettle Basin. Current holds the boat in place, and you are treated to a wonderful view of the falls. Depending on the time of year, you may see bears fishing in the falls. Holding ground is only fair, so be sure the anchor is well set and you have ample scope for high tide. An alternative is to anchor far enough from the falls that the current, while still enough to hold the boat steady, is not very strong.

Douglass, in *Exploring the North Coast of British Columbia*, likes the Verney Falls anchorage, but also suggests an anchorage along the south shore of Nettle Basin, off the shelf formed by a creek that empties into that area. We tried to put the hook down in 60 feet off that shore, but found that we would swing too close to the shelf. After two tries in wind squalls and heavy rain showers, we moved out to the middle and anchored in 100 feet with 300 feet of rode out. Shortly after we were settled another boat came in, tried to anchor as we earlier tried, then moved out to the middle as we had. Our holding ground was excellent. We had trouble tripping the anchor the next morning.

Lowe Inlet is beautiful. Our notes read, "If you're looking for a scenic spot, this is it." [*Hale*]

Klewnuggit Inlet. At approximately 120 feet, Klewnuggit Inlet is too deep for most boats to anchor. We talked with some folks, however, who found excellent crabbing near the head of the inlet.

East Inlet. East Inlet is adjacent to Klewnuggit Inlet. The inner cove of East Inlet is a superb anchorage, surrounded by high mountains and protected from seas. In a storm, however, winds might swirl through. Anchor near the head of the inner basin in 50 to 55 feet. You can also find anchorage in the little cove on the south shore, just inside the entrance to the inner basin.

We anchored at the head of East Inlet, a perfect night in a perfect place. Mountains reflected in the calm water. A small stream drained from a lake into the head of the inlet, and waterfalls poured down from the sides. We found an inukshuk, a small, stonehenge-like marker, next to the stream mouth. [*Hale*]

Kxngeal Inlet. Kxngeal Inlet, on the north side of Grenville Channel approximately 4 miles northwest of Klewnuggit Inlet, is a beautiful bowl in the mountains. Favor either shore

Mountains tower over Grenville Channel.

as you enter to avoid a nasty rock that dries 16 feet in the entrance. The inlet is at least 130 feet deep until it shelves at the head, and when it shelves, it shelves *right now*. Trees are at the head of the inlet, with logged areas on each side. The shelf is on a line with the points where the trees begin. Anchor in 90 feet.

Watts Narrows. Watts Narrows is a short passage that connects Baker Inlet with Grenville Channel. A dogleg turn near the inner entrance makes the passage blind. Before entering, either direction, announce your intentions on VHF 16, low power. Sound the ship's horn as you approach the turn. The current runs swiftly through the narrows, but people tell us they have gone through in the presence of current without trouble. We have waited for slack water, which occurs about the times of high and low water at Prince Rupert. As the chart shows, the narrows are narrow, but they are deep. A mid-channel course will get you through safely.

Baker Inlet. Baker Inlet, entered through Watts Narrows, is wonderful. The best overnights are at the head of the inlet, 60 feet, good bottom, mountains all around. Beautiful.

Kumealon Island/Kumealon Inlet. The little cove behind Kumealon Island is a good anchorage for a small number of boats. The much larger Kumealon Inlet, immediately south, also is good. Behind Kumealon Island, anchor in 15 to 25 feet north of the island, near the head.

Kumealon Inlet is well protected and has beautiful scenery. Anchor in the inner basin, behind the little island. Find a good spot and put the hook down in 50 to 70 feet. A reader reported that two uncharted rocks lie close to shore near the southeast corner.

Oona River. The village of Oona River, a tiny Swedish fishing and boatbuilding community, indents Porcher Island at the east end of Ogden Channel. A public dock is behind a stone breakwater, and is served by a narrow channel through drying mudflats. From the white buoy, line up on the private range markers on the rock jetty and proceed along the markers set in the entrance. Use caution, but depths should be adequate for most pleasure vessels. Call "Oona River" on VHF channel 06 for additional information, though you may not always get an answer.

Cell phones work near Oona River.

Arthur Passage to Chatham Sound. Assuming a northbound route, begin your run west of Watson Rock (west of Gibson Island) at the northern entrance to Grenville Channel. Continue north to a waypoint off the flashing light on the southwest shore of Kennedy Island. Then turn westward slightly to run past the southwest corner of Hanmer Island and leave Bell Buoy *D9*, marking Cecil Patch, to port. Continue to a waypoint in the passage west of Genn Island, then to a waypoint east of Holland Rock.

From Holland Rock, run to a waypoint west of Barrett Rock at the entrance to Prince Rupert Harbour. The entire area is well-buoyed, but it is easy to get the buoys confused.

Bears search for food along the shore.

LOCAL KNOWLEDGE

WEATHER TIP: Chatham Sound can be downright ugly when the wind blows. Especially on an ebb, when the onshore wind meets the combined ebb current and Skeena River runoff, seas can get high, steep and close together. On the VHF weather channel, listen to the hourly updates for Holland Rock. If it's blowing at Holland Rock, conditions can be rough when you try to cross.

Lawson Harbour/Kelp Passage. Kelp Passage is on the west side of Lewis Island, across Arthur Passage from Kennedy Island.

Lawson Harbour indents the top of Lewis Island. Neither would be our first choice for scenery, but each serves as an anchorage if needed. A reef extends from the western shore inside Lawson Harbour. Anchor near the south end of the reef in 35 to 40 feet.

In Kelp Passage, anchor in the area marked 8.8 meters on Chart 3947, mud bottom. The small basin at the south end of Kelp Passage provides good protection in a northerly wind.

Qlawdzeet Anchorage. A large bay on the north end of Stephens Island, well protected from all but northerly winds. This anchorage is often used by fishing vessels and has plenty of room for a number of boats. Anchorage can be found in the main bay or tucked into small bights. Use Chart 3909.

Porpoise Harbour. (250) 628-9220; info@peharbour.ca. Located at Port Edward, Porpoise Harbour gives priority to long-term year-round customers. Transient moorage available on first-come, first-served basis, best to call ahead, 15

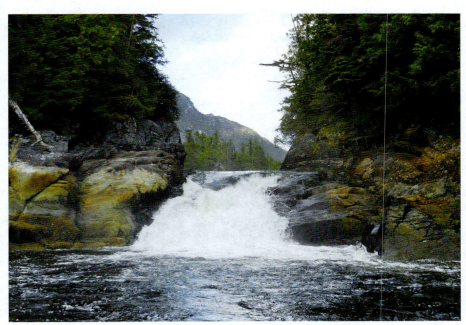
Small boats can anchor just beneath Verney Falls where the current prevents you from swinging into the rocks. If the salmon are running the bear viewing is fantastic.

NORTHERN B.C. COAST See Area Map Page 431 - Maps Not for Navigation

& 30 amp power, water, garbage drop, washrooms, showers, laundry. Approach using the range south of Ridley Island marked with a buoy for Porpoise Channel.

The harbor is close to the North Pacific Cannery, a museum showing what cannery life was all about. Bus service to Prince Rupert is available.

North Pacific Cannery Dock. (250) 628-3538; www.northpacificcannery.ca info@northpacificcannery.ca. Hours: 10:00 a.m. to 5:00 p.m., May-September, max. 4-hour stay. Located on the north shore of Inverness Passage, the North Pacific Cannery National Historic Site/Museum has a concrete 45-foot day-use dock available for boaters visiting this interesting, picturesque historic cannery. Available on a first-come, first-serve basis, no charge for use of the dock. Located about 5 miles up the Inverness Passage from Chatham Sound, a short side-trip on your way to or from Prince Rupert. Inverness Passage is well charted but open to river flow from the Skeena River which can carry wood debris. To minimize river flow influence, time your visit around high tide. Follow the west side of Smith Island to enter Inverness Passage, use Charts 3947 and 3958. Fender and secure well as current runs past the dock. A boomstick was recently attached to the up-river corner of the dock to deflect some of the windfall debris coming down the Skeena River.

The North Pacific Cannery is the oldest standing cannery on the West Coast and is a National Historic Site. The cannery operated from 1889 to 1968. Visitors can tour the cannery buildings including the processing plant, check in at the museum entrance. Guided tours are available three times daily, July through September; and Tuesday through Sunday during May and June. Tour boats occasionally reserve the dock, call ahead for availability.

LOCAL KNOWLEDGE

SPEED LIMIT: A 5-knot speed zone in Prince Rupert Harbour is enforced within 600 yards of the Prince Rupert shore. It is up to you to gauge the distance as there are no speed limit buoys.

⑬ **Prince Rupert.** As you approach Prince Rupert, it's a good idea to monitor Prince Rupert Traffic (VTS) on VHF 11 in case a large ship decides to depart while you're coming in. The fairway gets narrow in places. This is especially important in poor visibility.

As you approach, the large coal and grain loading areas are part of the Port of Prince Rupert's Ridley Terminals. From Barrett Rock at the entrance to Prince Rupert Harbour, it is another 5.5 miles of slow speed travel to town. Four marinas serve Prince Rupert: Fairview at the south end, the new Cow Bay Marina in front of Atlin Terminal, Prince Rupert Rowing and Yacht Club in the middle, and Rushbrooke at the north end.

Rushbrooke Floats, Fairview Small Craft Docks, and Porpoise Harbour are all managed by the Port Edward Harbour Authority, (250) 628-9220.

Fairview is primarily a commercial boat moorage, although some pleasure boats do tie up there. It is fairly far from downtown, with limited bus service. Rushbrooke, at the north end, has better facilities for pleasure boats, but during the commercial fishing months many fish boats occupy the slips. The walk from Rushbrooke to town is long but manageable. Most pleasure boats go directly to the Cow Bay Marina and the Prince Rupert Rowing and Yacht Club, located at Cow Bay. In the past the

---

NORTH PACIFIC CANNERY
A CENTURY OF SALMON

Imagine a century ago, when hundreds of fishing boats would be out on the Skeena and Nass Rivers for 4-5 days per week, 24 hours per day during the salmon runs, in all kinds of weather and sea conditions. Tender boats would shuttle the salmon catch back to the docks of the North Pacific Cannery. Imagine a dock with thousands of silvery salmon being cued up for processing. It was tough work done by specialists of different ethnic backgrounds. In the beginning the work was all manual, even the cans were made by hand. As time went on, new machines and processes improved the efficiency and ability to can more salmon.

The North Pacific Cannery was more than just a cannery. It was a small town, processing salmon for over 90 continuous years from 1889 to 1968, and remains the oldest standing cannery on the West Coast. A tour of the North Pacific Cannery is a glimpse back in time,

where you get a sense of how these hardy people fished, processed the salmon, and lived in different housing areas onsite. As you tour the buildings and grounds, you can almost hear and feel what it must have been like.

The North Pacific Cannery museum captures what cannery life was like for the Japanese, Chinese, First Nations, and Europeans working in this plant. You can walk from building to building and see how a cannery worked, see the company store, office building, and rows of houses. You can tour the cannery on your own, or take one of the group tours to learn more about the canning process and the social aspects of life here.

The North Pacific Cannery is located 22 km south of Prince Rupert. You can rent a car in town or take the local bus which stops right in front of the cannery. Allow about 3 hours for a docent's tour of the facility. The Crew Kitchen, a small café at the cannery, sells baked goods and is open for lunch. Don't forget to stop by the gift shop.

The North Pacific Cannery is accessible by boat, 5 miles up Inverness Passage from Chatham Sound. The cannery has a 45-foot guest dock for stays up to 4 hours on a first-come, first serve basis. It's best to time your visit around high tide to minimize the effects of river flow from the Skeena River.

The green "Lightering Dock" is for Customs check-in and clearance.

Cow Bay Marina opened in 2016 and offers 51 slips and side-tie moorage.

Prince Rupert Rowing and Yacht Club would quickly fill during the summer months. New in the 2016 season is the Cow Bay Marina, with 51 slips and linear moorage for boats to 100 feet. Cow Bay Marina has new shower and laundry facilities, a welcome addition to Cow Bay. This is a secure marina with keys issued to overnight guests. Good anchorage is in Pillsbury Cove, across the harbor. Northwest Fuels operates a large fuel dock in Cow Bay.

Prince Rupert ("Rainy Rupert"), population 12,500, is a complete city. With a large fishing fleet to support, you can find anything you need for your boat. What isn't there can be flown in. Fuel and waste oil disposal are available at Northwest Fuels in Cow Bay.

A shopping mall is a pleasant walk uptown, or you can take a cab. A Wal-Mart is now located in the mall. A large Safeway is located between the yacht club and the mall. The Save-On-Foods market (formerly Overwaitea market), farther uptown, is another option for provisions, and will deliver to the docks for a fee. The provincial liquor store is between the Safeway and the yacht club. A smaller, private liquor store is at Cow Bay.

The Museum of Northern British Columbia is excellent, and sponsors a variety of informative day and evening programs during the summer. Highly recommended. Several restaurants are in town, some of them quite good. The Port Interpretive Centre, located on street level in Atlin Terminal, gives free tours about the past, present and future of the Port of Prince Rupert. Recommended.

Located above Cow Bay, Sea Sport Outboard Marina and Clothing has an excellent selection of clothing, fishing equipment, safety gear, and marine parts. They also have a machine shop on site.

The King Coin laundromat in the center of town will do your laundry for a reasonable charge. It's a treat for us to leave all the ship's sheets, towels and dirty clothes at the laundromat and go for dinner at one of the local restaurants. A few hours later we pick up the laundry, clean, dry, and neatly folded.

Up at 617 2nd Avenue, just beyond the mall, we found Gary's Lock and Security Shop Ltd., a lock shop with a twist. Gary Weick, the longtime owner, collects things. His shop is a museum. In the window were wonderful toys from the 1930s and 40s, Canadian Pacific Railroad conductors' caps, old photos–and a stuffed and mounted *fur-bearing trout*, very rare. It was caught in Lake Superior, from depths so great trout grow fur to keep warm. This trout's fur is white. Everything is explained on the sign next to the specimen. You have to see it.

If you have time, take the bus to Port Edward for a tour of the North Pacific Cannery, now a museum. You'll see how the workers lived and worked.

Prince Rupert was hurt by the decline of the commercial fishing and forest industries, and then the pulp mill closed. The town lost about one-third of its population. In the last eight years it has become a major deepwater seaport, in heavy competition with Vancouver, Puget Sound and California. Prince Rupert is closer to Asia than any other west coast port, and CN Rail owns tracks from Prince Rupert to Memphis, Tennessee. Transit time

Prince Rupert Harbour

NORTHERN B.C. COAST   See Area Map Page 431 - Maps Not for Navigation

Cow Bay shops and restaurants near Cow Bay Marina and Rowing Club

from Asia to the heartland of the U.S. is cut by at least two days. Not only can Prince Rupert handle the largest container ships now afloat, it will be able to handle the largest on the drawing board.

Prince Rupert is the last major city in British Columbia before transiting Dixon Entrance on the way to Ketchikan and Southeast Alaska. While there is good shopping and a liquor store in Prince Rupert, vessels bound for Alaska may want to wait to provision until Ketchikan to avoid customs issues with liquor, produce, and meat. On the way south from Alaska, Prince Rupert is the best place to stock up on produce, meat and liquor.

Customs clearance. Tie up at the 100-foot-long green-painted "Lightering Dock," where a dedicated toll-free phone for customs clearance is installed. The dock is located beneath the large shopping mall building at the top of the hill. The railroad museum building is near the shore, and a whale sculpture. Lat/Lon 54°18.827'N/130°19.930'W. Touch-and-go for customs clearance only. A locked gate prevents shore access.

You can also clear customs by telephone at Rushbrooke, the Prince Rupert Rowing and Yacht Club, Cow Bay Marina and Fairview Government Dock by calling 888-226-7277, or on a dedicated phone at each of the three marinas. Calls now go to a call center in Hamilton, Ontario. Agents have the option of calling out a local customs agent for an inspection.

Car Rentals. National, (250) 624-5318. Located on the west end of town in the Highline Hotel.

Cruise Ships. A cruise ship will call once or twice a week during the summer. When a ship is in town, the streets and stores are apt to be crowded.

Golf. The Prince Rupert Centennial Golf Course is a good 18-hole course. Call (250) 624-2000. You'll probably take a cab. In early evening the no-see-ums can be thick and ravenous. Cover up.

Fairview Small Craft Harbour. (250) 624-3127; info@peharbour.ca. Open 7 days a week 5:00 a.m. to 8:00 p.m. during the summer; 8:30 a.m. to 5:00 p.m. Monday through Friday the rest of the year. This is the first set of docks as you approach Prince Rupert. Commercial vessels primarily, but sometimes room for a few pleasure boats. Water, 15 & 30 amp power, garbage drop, washrooms. First-come, first-served.

⑬ **Cow Bay Marina.** (250) 622-2628; www.cowbaymarina.ca. Monitors VHF 66A. Open all year with moorage for boats up to 80 feet and can accommodate larger yachts up to 120 feet on the breakwater docks, 30, 50 & 100 amp power, washrooms, showers, laundry, water, garbage drop, recycling, and Wi-Fi. Reservations are accepted. This is a new 51-slip marina located in Cow Bay in front of the Atlin Terminal building, which opened in 2016. Be sure to fender well as wakes from passing boats find their way into the marina despite the posted "no wake" sign. A pub and microbrewery is nearby and the marina is close to the center of town. Cow Bay Marina is a welcome addition to the previously tight moorage options at Prince Rupert and offers clean, modern shower and laundry facilities for visiting boats.

⑬ **Prince Rupert Rowing and Yacht Club.** P.O. Box 981, 121 George Hills Way, Prince Rupert, BC V8J 1A3; (250) 624-4317; info@prryc.com. Monitors VHF 73. Open all year, 30 & 50 amp power, new washroom and shower, recycling, water, pay phone, garbage drop, Wi-Fi, fish-cleaning station. Waste oil dump at the Northwest Fuels facility next door.

Historically, this has been the preferred pleasure craft moorage in Prince Rupert, more of a marina than a traditional yacht club. There is no reciprocal moorage. Although reservations are not accepted, visitors are encouraged to call at least 24 hours ahead to get on a wait list. Cell phones work for calling the Yacht Club from Hartley Bay and Oona River. As you approach, call on VHF 73. The dock staff can be busy.

The yacht club docks are strong and safe, but well used. The main dock has been replaced, and more replacements are planned. New docks or old, be aware that you will be squeezed in more tightly than at most marinas. If the commercial salmon fishing fleet is in the midst of an opening, the boats will come and go all night, and moorage at the outermost docks can be pretty bouncy. Put

Cow Bay Marina is just one block from shops and restaurants and three blocks up to town.

out lots of fenders.

A new club house and facilities were under construction in 2017, slated to be completed for the 2018 boating season.

The yacht club is close to good dining in Cow Bay or you can walk or take a cab uptown. Moorage is open to all.

⑬ **Northwest Fuels Ltd.** (250) 624-4106. Located in Cow Bay next to the Yacht Club. Monitors VHF 71. Open every day, extended hours in summer. Petro Canada gasoline, diesel, lubricants, washrooms and showers. Block, cube and salt ice. Small convenience store on the pier with a surprising number of marine and fishing tackle items. Garbage drop, waste oil disposal. Propane is available a few blocks away. This fuel dock is often busy; be prepared to wait for a space to clear.

⑬ **Rushbrooke Floats Small Craft Harbour.** (250) 624-9400; info@peharbour.ca. Open all year, water, 15 amp power, washrooms, showers. Commercial vessels have priority in the summer, but there can be room for pleasure craft too. Rafting required. Located about a mile north of town. Rushbrooke has the only launch ramp in Prince Rupert. First-come, first-served.

Pillsbury Cove. Pillsbury Cove, on the west side of Prince Rupert Harbour, is an excellent anchorage: level bottom, great holding, beaches and tide pools, and lots of crab. If the marinas in Prince Rupert are all full or you prefer anchoring, this is a good choice. Prince Rupert is a 3-mile dinghy ride away. Correspondent Jim Norris notes that entering Pillsbury Cove can be intimidating due to the extensive aquaculture floats crowding the east side of the entrance channel; hug close to these floats on your starboard side as you enter.

THINGS TO DO

1. **Cow Bay.** Several good restaurants and shops. One casual favorite is Cowpuccino's for coffee, fresh baked goods and excellent Wi-Fi.

2. **Khutzeymateen Sanctuary.** Also called "Valley of the Grizzly," this is the only park of its kind in Canada. It contains one of the largest populations of grizzly bears–about 50 –in British Columbia. Located 45 km NE of Prince Rupert.

3. **North Pacific Cannery.** The oldest, most completely preserved cannery remaining of 200-or-so that once dotted B.C.'s northwest coast. Now a bus or car ride away from town.

4. **Museum of Northern British Columbia.** An impressive collection about the northwest coast. A First Nations longhouse describes the history of the people and area going back to the last ice age. It contains well-preserved, historical Tsimshian and other First Nations works of art, clothing, baskets and more. A short walk from the marinas.

5. **Firehall Museum.** Focused on the history of the local fire department since 1908. A rebuilt red fire truck from 1925 sits in the middle of the museum.

6. **Kwinitsa Railway Museum.** Authentic railway station with artifacts from the early 1900s, the heyday of the Grand Trunk Pacific Railway. On the waterfront, near the Lightering Dock.

7. **Farmer's Market.** In town on Sunday afternoons during the summer season.

8. **Earl Mah Aquatic Center.** A short walk from Cow Bay.

9. **Seafest.** The town's biggest annual festival, held each June.

10. **Port Interpretive Centre.** Free guided tours about the Port of Prince Rupert. Informative and hands-on activities let visitors explore the growth of the Prince Rupert's commerce including, containers, coal and grain.

Prince Rupert Waterfront

Haida Gwaii

CHAPTER 17

GRAHAM ISLAND
Masset • Port Clements • Skidegate • Queen Charlotte

MORESBY ISLAND, HEADING SOUTH
Sandspit Harbour • Louise Narrows • Skedans Bay • Dana Passage • Hoya Bay

GWAII HAANAS NATIONAL PARK RESERVE
Tanu Island • Louise Narrows • Hoya Bay • Hotspring Island • Rose Inlet

ANTHONY ISLAND (SGANG GWAAY)
Nan Sdins • Grays Cove

HAIDA GWAII

Located 130 miles north of Vancouver Island and 65 miles west of the B.C. coast's mainland islands, Haida Gwaii offers some of the Northwest's most spectacular cruising. Haida Gwaii, formerly called the Queen Charlotte Islands, is an archipelago of over 150 islands, best explored by boat. It is remote and pristine with a unique geological history. Glaciers once covered this area and receded 2,000 years before the rest of British Columbia, resulting in an ecosystem with some species of plants and animals not seen anywhere else. It has been referred to as the "Galapagos of the Northwest" with hundreds of species of birds, unique species of bears and many trees and plants growing in areas from the rain forests of the western coast to the dry forests on the eastern coast.

Haida Gwaii means "Islands of the People" in the language of the first people to settle here. The Haida were revered and respected along the coast as ambassadors and warriors, with a unique culture. The islands had a population of more than 10,000 until the 1800s when many succumbed to smallpox and other diseases from Europe. By 1900, only 350 remained. A visit to Haida Gwaii and the Gwaii Haanas National Park will take you to a place where you can see what remains of this once great culture. As you walk the trails through the rain forest and moss-covered rock canyons around the old villages you may even feel the presence of the people who inhabited this rugged and beautiful area.

Haida Gwaii experienced the impact of an imbalance caused by western man. In the 1800s sea otters were hunted almost to extinction. Their pelts were highly valued around the world and greed took over. In time the sea urchin population grew out of control without the sea otters to keep them in check. Later, the health of the kelp beds was affected by the overabundance of sea urchins. Nature's balance was thrown off. Today the symbol of Haida Gwaii is the sea otter and the sea urchin, a reminder to keep the ecosystem in balance. The sea otter population is now continuing to make a steady recovery.

Buddy-boating helps with difficult anchorages at Gwaii Haanas Watchmen Sites.

Permits. The Gwaii Haanas National Park Reserve, a Protected Area, was created in 1987 and encompasses the southern third of the archipelago. The Reserve is jointly managed by the Haida and the government of Canada. It is unique in Canada, covering both land and sea. A visit to Gwaii Haanas requires a permit for the time you will be in protected areas, and payment of a daily fee for a maximum stay of six days within the Park boundary. The daily fee is $49.00 for families (up to 7 people, max of 2 people over 18), $19.60 for adults, $16.60 for seniors (65 and over), and $9.80 for youths (6 to 16 years).

Only 100 people are permitted in Gwaii Haanas National Park Reserve at once. Advance reservations are recommended to ensure you'll get a permit. An orientation is required for all visitors, either in advance by DVD or at the **Haida Heritage Centre** in Skidegate. The Heritage Centre has a gift ship and museum displays. Orientation sessions are typically at 9:00 a.m. Monday-Friday in June and after mid-August, and Monday-Saturday July to mid-August. Orientation sessions can be scheduled by appointment if staff is available. Reserving space for scheduled orientations is not required. A permit tag is issued at the time of orientation and must be carried ashore within the Park Reserve. The excellent orientation covers the history of Gwaii Haanas as well as the procedures to visit the different sites within the park. All protected sites are managed by Haida Watchmen. They can be reached on VHF 06 prior to going ashore at each site. They manage the number of people on shore at a time. They also provide interpretive talks about the site and are very welcoming.

A fee is not required between October 1st and April 30th, but visitors must register and attend an orientation session. Check the Parks Canada Gwaii Haanas web site for more information. Call (877) 559-8818 (8:30 a.m. to 4:30 p.m. Monday through Friday after April 1st) for more information or to arrange for a permit (www.pc.gc.ca/gwaiihaanas). As a convenience, orientation sessions are generally offered in the Spring in Vancouver BC and Victoria, check their website for the year's schedule.

Getting to Haida Gwaii. Separated from mainland British Columbia by Hecate Strait, and from Vancouver Island by Queen Charlotte Sound, getting to Haida Gwaii by boat requires crossing some of the Northwest's most feared bodies of water.

Hecate Strait is notorious for rough water. With shallow depths, ranging from 50 to 115 feet, winds can quickly whip up uncomfortable seas. Early morning crossings, when winds are typically lighter, are usually recommended. Tides move large volumes of water through Hecate Strait. When wind blows against current, dangerous conditions can result. Particularly during spring tides, be mindful of possible wind-against-current situations. Despite Hecate Strait's reputation for rough water, we've had smooth crossings.

CHARTS

3002	Queen Charlotte Sound to Dixon Entrance (1:525,000)	3855	Houston Stewart Channel (1:20,000)
3800 Plans	Dixon Entrance	3857	Louscoone Inlet (1:18,275)
		3868	Port Louis to Langara Island (1:72,921)
3807	Atli Inlet to Selwyn Inlet (1:37,500)	3890	Approaches to Skidegate (1:40,000)
3808	Juan Perez Sound (1:37,500)	3891	Skidegate Channel (1:40,000)
3809	Carpenter Bay to Burnaby Island (1:37,500)	3892	Masset Harbour and Naden Harbour (1:40,000)
3811	Harbours in Queen Charlotte Islands (1:18,315)	3894	Selwyn Inlet to Lawn Point (1:73,026)
3825	Princess Royal Channel (1:40,000) (Replaces Chart 3739)	3895 Plans	Selwyn Inlet to Lawn Point (1:73,026)
L/C3853	Cape St. James to Cumshewa Inlet and Tatsu Sound (1:150,000)	L/C3902	Hecate Strait (1:250,000)

2018 WAGGONER CRUISING GUIDE

Haida Gwaii

Reference Only – Not for Navigation

HAIDA GWAII

Many boats depart for Haida Gwaii from Prince Rupert. This route offers the shortest crossing (roughly 60 to 65 miles of open water), allowing boaters to minimize their exposure to potentially hazardous weather. Prince Rupert is a major city, and has anything a cruising boater might need before heading out to explore Haida Gwaii. With fuel, provisions, and internet access for weather information, it makes a logical departure point.

After leaving Prince Rupert, several anchorages provide a place to spend the night and wait for better weather before crossing Hecate Strait. Larsen Harbour, the Spicer Islands, and Welcome Harbour are good choices.

In the past we have been warned of extreme kelp in Larsen Harbour. More recently we have been told that Larsen Harbour is easily navigable. It is the shortest point of crossing to Lawn Point.

Boats returning to British Columbia from Alaska may be tempted to cross Dixon Entrance to Masset instead of Prince Rupert. Unfortunately, the Canadian Government no longer operates a customs office in Masset. Boats southbound from Alaska must first clear customs in Prince Rupert.

Haida Gwaii can also be accessed from Vancouver Island to the south. The trip is long—about 160 nautical miles—and exposed to the full brunt of the open Pacific Ocean. Sailboats and slow powerboats will have to make an overnight passage. For faster boats in settled weather, the trip can be completed in a very long day. Keep in mind, however, that sea conditions may not be conducive to high-speed operation. Also remember that fuel is not available anywhere south of Sandspit.

During our recent trip, we traveled from Prince Rupert to an anchorage between the Spicer Islands. For our early morning departure we listened for the wind and wave report from the North Hecate Strait weather buoy Station 46183 and navigated directly across Hecate Strait, passing the buoy on the way to Lawn Point. Note the shoal area leading north from the entrance to Skidegate Inlet. If headed to Sandspit Harbour or Queen Charlotte, follow the deeper channel to Skidegate Inlet or Shingle Bay. In settled conditions and higher tides, we have crossed just north or south of Bar Rocks near the green can buoy.

From the south, plot a route from the area north of Vancouver Island or from Hakai Pass. The open water crossing to Houston Stewart Channel will be about 110 miles. Use West Sea Otter weather buoy, Station 46204, and the South Hecate Strait weather buoy Station 46185 for wind and wave reports for the area. This might also be your return route when leaving Haida Gwaii for points south.

Fuel. Fuel is available at Masset on the north end of Graham Island, at Skidegate, and at Sandspit. Cruising in Haida Gwaii is wilderness cruising with no major repair services or boatyards. Be prepared.

Water. Masset, Port Clements, Sandspit, and Queen Charlotte have potable water. Parks Canada maintains fresh water hoses at Shuttle Island and Louscoone Inlet, but the water is untreated.

Garbage Drops. In the remote and protected areas all trash must be carried out with you.

Insurance. Not all vessel insurance policies cover Haida Gwaii, check with your insurance agent to ensure that you have coverage for this area.

Provisioning. Groceries are available in Masset, Skidegate, Queen Charlotte, and Sandspit. Deliveries are usually once a week. Selection may be limited.

Trailering. BC Ferries serve Masset, Skidegate, Sandspit, and Alliford Bay. Check www.bcferries.com for schedules and rates. Boat launches are located at Alliford Bay, Sandspit, Masset, and Copper Bay. Trailering small boats to Haida Gwaii may save time and money and can minimize weather delays.

Resources. Don and Reanne Douglass's *Exploring the North Coast of British Columbia* is the most complete cruising guide for Haida Gwaii. It has been updated in 2017. See www.WaggonerGuide.com.

Protected moorage at Sandspit Harbour, northeast end of Moresby Island

Masset Harbour

HAIDA GWAII

See Area Map Page 448 - Maps Not for Navigation

Queen Charlotte Harbour Authority floats, with Bearskin Bay anchorage in the background

GRAHAM ISLAND

① **Masset.** During the summer months, Masset, the northernmost community on Haida Gwaii, is a hub of sport fishing operations. The local airport offers regular flights to Vancouver, and floatplanes run regularly from Prince Rupert. You'll find restaurants, a liquor store, three grocery stores, a hardware store, pubs, car rentals and an internet cafe.

Local businesses cater to tourists, with sightseeing trips and fishing charters. Hikes give boaters the opportunity to stretch their legs and see a different side of Haida Gwaii. The 9-hole Dixon Entrance Golf Club is 5 kilometers outside of town. The Dixon Entrance Maritime Museum showcases the maritime history of the area.

① **North Arm Transportation.** (250) 626-3328; nat@northarm.bc.ca; www.northarm.bc.ca. Open all year. Located at the government dock. Gas, diesel, and lubricants available.

① **Delkatla Slough Harbour Authority.** (250) 626-5487. Open all year, first-come, first-served, primarily a commercial boat facility. Power and water on the docks, garbage drop, tidal grid. Rafting required.

Refuge Cove. Known locally as 7-mile Cove, Refuge Cove provides good protection from weather and has 600 feet of dock space. This is a good place to wait out a storm, or to wait for favorable currents to enter Masset. Use caution entering Refuge Cove. The fairway is narrow, about 100 feet wide, with 6-foot depths at zero tide. In stormy conditions, swells can break across the entrance channel, making it impassable. Fishing outside Refuge Cove is reportedly excellent.

Skidegate Inlet

Traditional Haida war canoes traveled as far as the coast of California.

Langara Island. Langara Island, the northernmost island in the archipelago, is known for its exceptional salmon fishing. Sport fishing lodges on the island cater to fly-in guests. Several anchorages are available, although they are typically busy with sport fishing boats.

Masset Sound. Masset Sound connects Masset to Port Clements and Masset Inlet. Currents run to 5.5 knots, although the Douglasses report little turbulence. Boats, particularly slow boats, should use caution when transiting the area. Vessels entering Masset Sound should do so on a flood, and exit on an ebb.

② **Port Clements.** Port Clements is a small town south of Masset. It has a grocery store, post office, health clinic, liquor store, restaurants, and a pub. A museum showcases the history of logging on Haida Gwaii. Local businesses offer sightseeing tours and fishing trips.

Several miles from town, a hiking trail leads to the Golden Spruce heritage site, where a sacred, golden-colored Sitka Spruce tree stood until a logger-turned-conservationist famously cut it down to protest logging. John Vaillant's book *The Golden Spruce* tells this story with a lot of interesting facts about Haida Gwaii..

② **Port Clements Small Craft Harbour.** P.O. Box 198, Port Clements, BC V0T 1R0; (250) 557-4295; www.portclements.ca. Open all year. Transient moorage, 20 & 30 amp power, garbage drop, unpaved boat launch. First-come, first-served, rafting required. Register at office three blocks away. Ice, a pay phone and groceries are available at the nearby Bayview Market.

SKIDEGATE, QUEEN CHARLOTTE, AND SANDSPIT

③ **Skidegate.** Skidegate offers lodging, restaurants, groceries, and shops with local crafts. The small public float next to the ferry dock was not installed when we visited in July 2015. In fair weather boats can anchor offshore and dinghy in. Visiting cruisers may want to visit Skidegate by road from Queen Charlotte.

④ **Queen Charlotte.** Queen Charlotte, on the south end of Graham Island, has many services and supplies. Groceries, restaurants, pubs, a liquor store, ATM, marine supplies, a hardware store, rental cars, lodging, a post office, and an internet café are available. Local outfitters offer guided tours which can be an option to see the protected areas.

A visitor center is just east of the Harbour Authority floats. The staff is friendly and can answer most questions about the area. Many summer events are hosted at a "square" just below the visitor center.

The grocery store is located approximately ½ mile west of the Harbour Authority. It is restocked each Monday. The post office, laundromat, and liquor store are in the same complex. A farmers market is held each Saturday near the community center and library.

Anchorage, in 20-35 feet, is good in Bearskin Bay, although it is open to wind and chop from the east.

④ **Queen Charlotte Harbour Authority.** P.O. Box 68, Queen Charlotte, BC V0T 1S0; (250) 559-4650; harbour@qcislands.net. Open all year with moorage, 15 & 30 amp power, and garbage drop. A tidal grid is available for haulouts, and nearby there is a boat launch for trailerable boats. Water is available, but not on all docks.

④ **Haida Gwaii Fuels.** (250) 559-4527; fastfuel@qcislands.net. Located at the Inland Air pier. Open 9:00 a.m. - 5:00 p.m. mid-June to late August, open all year for call outs. Gas and diesel. Call ahead for lubricants.

Skidegate Channel. Skidegate Channel is the narrow, shallow, and winding channel between Graham and Moresby Islands, connecting Hecate Strait with the Pacific Ocean.

EXPLORING GRAHAM ISLAND BY CAR

We wanted to visit the north end of Graham Island, but the 90-mile trip up the east coast and around Rose Spit didn't fit our schedule. Instead, we rented a car in Queen Charlotte City and drove north. National Car Rental and several local companies offer rentals, but availability is limited. It's best to reserve well in advance.

We only had the car for one day but managed to visit many sights. Our first stop was the remains of the golden spruce, a once sacred tree to the Haida. This tree was tragically cut down in an act of protest against the logging industry. John Valliant's compelling book, *The Golden Spruce,* tells what is known about the mysterious story.

Our next stop was a bit farther up the logging road. A short trail leads into the woods to the site of an abandoned, partially carved Haida canoe. A prominent sign at the trailhead marks the turn-off to the trailhead.

Continuing north to Port Clement, we stopped in a little museum with steam donkeys and local historical memorabilia, including a stuffed raven. From there we drove into Masset for a quick and delicious lunch at Pearl's Dining Room. The museum in Old Masset is now closed, but we drove through town to see the many carved poles sprinkled throughout the village. Sarah's Haida Arts in Old Masset has a beautiful selection of Haida jewelry, carvings and artwork. It is next door to a traditional dance house that the community is restoring after a fire.

We continued along the coast road to Agate Beach, where we picked up dozens of luminous, pale honey-colored Queen Charlotte agates, each rounded and smoothed to a frosted polish. Tow Hill soared above the booming surf ahead of us. We wished we had enough time to hike the trail that leads to an observation deck that seems to touch the clouds. On a clear day, Alaska is almost visible from here.

As the light faded we passed the wide, sandy beaches of Graham's east coast, then the fascinating shops and galleries of Tlell. Eventually we made it back to Queen Charlotte City. The short car rental opened up a vast amount of Haida Gwaii we couldn't have seen from the boat. Still, we'll be back to see the rest.

– *Lydia McKenzie*

HAIDA GWAII

See Area Map Page 448 - Maps Not for Navigation

East and West Narrows are particularly challenging, though daybeacons make transiting easier than in the past. Because of the difference in tidal swings on the Pacific and Hecate Strait sides of Haida Gwaii, tides and currents in Skidegate Channel are complex and difficult to predict. It's best to plan on arriving at McLellan Point roughly three hours after low water in Queen Charlotte.

⑤ **Sandspit.** Sandspit, on the northeast end of Moresby Island, is a settlement with a launch ramp and well-protected marina, restaurants, pubs, liquor store, lodging, post office, car rentals and laundromat. The grocery store, about 4 km northeast from the marina, is restocked each Monday and Friday.

Sandspit has hiking and biking trails, the Willows Golf Course, (Haida Gwaii's only 18-hole golf course), and an airport with scheduled commercial service to Vancouver.

JUAN JOSE PEREZ HERNANDEZ (1725-1775)

Juan Perez was an early Spanish explorer and was the first European to discover the islands of Haida Gwaii off the coast of present-day British Columbia. Like other explorers of his time, he was sent from San Blas, New Spain to discover possible Russian and British settlements with instructions to treat the Native people he encountered with respect. In command of the ship Santiago, Perez reached the north tip of Langara Island in Haida Gwaii where he had interactions with a group of Haida natives, but did not go ashore due to the crew's poor health, most of whom were suffering from scurvy. Reaching Nootka Sound on August 7, 1774, he engaged in the first European trade of goods with the Nootka; but once again, neither Perez nor his crew had gone ashore. Although the Viceroy of New Spain instructed Perez to reach 60 degrees north latitude (Cordova), he turned south and arrived at Monterey on August 28, 1774. After a brief respite, he reached San Blas in early November 1774. A second expedition was organized in 1775 under Bruno de Heceta and Juan Bodega y Quadra. Perez served as pilot of Heceta's ship, the Santiago. As fate would have it, Perez died on November 3, 1775 during the return trip to San Blas. Juan Perez Sound on the east coast of Moresby Island in Haida Gawaii is named in his honor.

Taxi service is no longer available to take you to the airport or the BC Ferry to Skidegate. Ask the marina about alternate transportation. From Skidegate, a larger BC Ferry runs to Prince Rupert several days a week.

⑤ **Sandspit Harbour.** P.O. Box 477, Sandspit, BC V0T 1T0; (250) 637-5700; sandspitharbour2@outlook.com; www.sandspitharbour.com. Monitors VHF 06, 08, 09, 73. Open all year with guest moorage to 100 feet, 15, 30, 50 & 100 amp power, seasonal water, pumpout, pay phone, showers, washroom, garbage drop, launch ramp and free Wi-Fi. Marina office hours are the same as the Fuel Dock hours listed below. This is the most modern marina in Haida Gwaii. Reservations strongly recommended in the summer for vessels over 45 feet. Bridgeview Marine for repairs is located across the road.

⑤ **Sandspit Harbour Fuel Dock.** Operated by and located at Sandspit Harbour. Open June through August 7:00 a.m. to 9:00 a.m. and 6:00 p.m. to 9:00 p.m. Open September, through May 9:00 a.m. to 12:00 p.m. Gas and diesel available.

⑤ **Bridgeview Marine.** 537 Beach Road, Sandspit, BC V0T 1T0; (250) 637-5432; www.bridgeviewmarine.com. Open all year 8:00 a.m. to 5:00 p.m., Monday to Friday. Haulout to 36 feet. Marine supplies, mechanics with extensive outboard and stern drive experience, limited diesel and inboard experience.

Moresby Camp. Moresby Camp has road access to Sandspit, a public float, and a boat launch.

Gordon Cove. Gordon Cove, just south of Moresby Camp, is a an excellent anchorage. Good holding in 15-30 feet.

Louise Narrows. The small boat passage at Louise Narrows is scenic, shallow and narrow, only 30 feet across in some places. It is best to travel through the passage before high water and while the gravel banks are still visible. This way, you can see the channel, and if you inadvertently run aground, the rising tide will

Louise Narrows

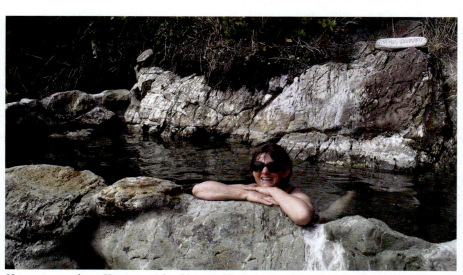

Hot spring pools on Hotspring Island have refilled after earthquake-induced disruption.

float you off.

When we transited we saw depths of less than five feet under the keel. It was manageable, but added a bit of excitement to the passage. Given the limited space for maneuvering within the narrows, boats transiting Louise Narrows should make a sécurité call on VHF 16 low power before entering.

Skedans Bay. Skedans (or K'uuna Llnagaay) is situated on the the eastern tip of Louise Island. It faces south onto Skedans Bay from a crescent beach that forms the neck of a small peninsula. As the furthest north of all the Watchmen sites, its relative accessibility makes it one of the most often visited. Skedans Bay is within the protected area of the Gwaii Haanas National Park Reserve and requires a permit when visiting. The procedure for visiting all sites within the protected areas is to contact the Haida Watchmen on VHF 06 before coming ashore. If the site already has visitors, the Watchmen will ask you to stand by on board until the next group can come ashore. K'uuna Llnagaay means Village at the Edge, but it was also known by the Haida as Grizzly-Bear-Town because of the large number of grizzly bear carvings found there. Visiting traders named it Skedans, a corruption of the name of its chief, Gida'nsta.

In the mid-1800s almost 450 Haida lived here in about 26 longhouses. Records show there were 56 monumental cedar sculptures, including frontal poles, single and double mortuary poles, memorial poles and mortuary figures.

K'uuna Llnagaay is one of the few remaining village sites with some standing poles and remnants of large longhouses. Crests featured on the poles, such as rainbow, frog, eagle, beaver, and two-finned killer whale, signify which families lived there. A path winding through the old village allows you to appreciate the artistry of the poles, now in varying stages of decay, and provide a glimpse of what Haida life might have been like many years ago.

We anchored in 45 feet, about one mile southeast of the Watchmen site, and took the dinghy to shore. The anchorage immediately south of the Watchmen site was smaller and more exposed to northerly wind than we liked.

Thurston Harbour. Thurston Harbour on Talunkwan Island is a well-protected anchorage conveniently located between Skedans Watchmen site to the north and Tanu Watchmen site to the south. Anchor here following an afternoon visit to Skedans and get an early morning start to visit Tanu. There is plenty of room and good holding. While located near Gwaii Haanas Park, this anchorage is outside the park boundary and does not require a reservation or daily fee.

Dana Passage. Dana Passage is a narrow and scenic route between Talunkwan and Moresby Islands. At the narrowest section, the passage is only about 100 feet wide, but depths are at least 30 feet throughout.

GWAII HAANAS NATIONAL PARK RESERVE

Tanu Island. The beautiful and haunting village of T'aanuu Llnagaay is located on the east shore of Tanu Island, on Laskeek Bay. T'aanuu means eelgrass, which commonly grows in shallow water around the village. T'aanuu Llnagaay follows the shoreline of two beaches divided by a rocky shoal. In the mid-1800s the village population was about 550, with 25 longhouses, 31 mortuary columns, and 15 mortuary houses. Present-day visitors notice the many logs on the ground and may mistake them for windfalls; these, however, are the posts and beams of old longhouses. The longhouses faced the shoreline, and were dug into the ground for protection from the weather. Large, rectangular pits mark their locations. Though there are no standing poles here, on close inspection you can see ancient carvings made smooth by time and furred by moss. Walking amidst the ruins, surrounded by the protective rainforest, one gets a strong sense of the people who lived there. Contact the Haida Watchmen on VHF 06 for permission before coming ashore.

Fair weather anchorage can be found just off the landing beach, in 35-50 feet. Holding is marginal and currents run strongly. When

Totem honoring the Eagle Clan

the wind is blowing from the north, swells roll in from Hecate Strait.

Crescent Inlet. The head of secluded Crescent Inlet has sheltered anchorage with good holding. The inlet has beautiful views of mountains and old growth forest. Bears frequent the meadow at the head of the inlet. Moresby Explorers, a tour company, maintains a small floating lodge in Crescent Inlet. The inlet is outside the protected area, anchorage here does not require a reservation or payment.

Anna Inlet. Beautiful, knobby mountains surround Anna Inlet. The narrow entrance is difficult to see but easily navigated. Steering a mid-channel course, we never saw depths less than 35 feet at zero tide. Anchor in 50-60 feet at the head of the inlet.

Hoya Passage. Currents run to 2 knots, flooding north and ebbing south.

Hoya Bay. Hoya Bay, also known as Freshwater Cove, has a public float with untreated fresh water available. For overnight stays, anchor out or use one of the two public mooring buoys.

De la Beche Inlet. According to Douglass, De la Beche Inlet has two interesting anchorages, De la Beche Cove and Sac Bay. De la Beche Cove is a small nook on the south shore of De la Beche Inlet, landlocked by an island. Douglass reports adequate holding at the head of the bay.

Sac Bay. Sac Bay juts out to the south from De la Beche Inlet, good holding and spectacular mountain scenery.

⑥ Hotspring Island. Hotspring Island has been one of the most popular stops in Haida Gwaii. The hot springs, located on the south side of the island, were some of the finest on the coast. A magnitude 7.7 earthquake shook the area in October of 2012, and appeared to change mother nature's plumbing. For several years, the flow of hot water ceased entirely. In 2015, pools of hot water appeared below the high tide line and in 2016 some of the pools

Hotspring Island

Trail leading through the forest and rock to Nan Sdins

began filling again. Correspondents Stephen and Debbie Gratton report that three pools were full in 2017, the hottest one is near the Watchmen dwelling, and the other two nearby pools are linked by a new boardwalk. In addition to the fabulous boardwalk, changing facilities and a bathhouse were added at the site.

Haida Watchmen are on site and require boaters to call on VHF channel 06 before coming ashore. The anchorage directly off the hot springs is exposed, with marginal holding on a rocky bottom. A better anchorage is between Hotspring and House islands.

Ramsay Passage Cove. Fairly well-protected alternative to Hotspring Island anchorages, but requires a 1.5-mile dinghy ride.

Dolomite Narrows. Dolomite Narrows is narrow, shallow, and poorly charted. One section dries completely on a 2-foot tide. Currents run to several knots. Small, privately maintained range markers show the route the locals take. We explored by dinghy and opted for the longer, more exposed route around Burnaby Island rather than chance grounding.

Bag Harbour. Bag Harbour is a secure anchorage at the south end of Dolomite Narrows. It's a good place to wait for appropriate conditions for a northbound transit of Dolomite Narrows, or relax after a transit.

Ikeda Cove. Ikeda Cove is a lovely, protected anchorage with excellent holding. A grassy meadow is a haven for wildlife. We spotted deer, a bear and cub, and a pair of sandhill cranes. Remains of cabins, wharves and machinery can be found on shore.

Collison Bay. Collison Bay offers good protection, easy anchoring depths, and good holding. The Douglasses report watching bears turn over rocks in search of food.

Windy Bay. Windy Bay, or Hlk'yah Gaaw-Ga, is a fair weather anchorage used to visit the historic fishing village called Hlk'yah Llnagaay (Falcon Town). Near here in 1985, the Haida blocked logging roads in their protest to put an end to logging on Lyell Island and protect the area that became Gwaii Haanas. The longhouse is named "Looking Around and Blinking House" to honor this victory. An old growth forest contains trees over 1000 years old and more than 200 feet tall. A trail leads through huge Sitka spruce and western red cedar trees, draped with mosses and lichens. The Haida Watchmen can point out culturally modified trees where the bark was stipped for making baskets or hats. Some of these trees show where test holes were cut in them to check their suitability for making a canoe or carving a pole.

In August 2013, the Legacy Pole, the first new monumental pole in 130 years, was raised in Windy Bay. This pole was carved to celebrate the 20 years of co-management of the Reserve by the Haida Nation and the government of Canada. It is visible from the water.

We anchored just offshore from the Watchmen cabin, on the 3.7 meter sounding, in 20-30 feet, fair holding on a rocky bottom. Contact the Haida Watchmen on VHF 06 before coming ashore.

⑦ **Rose Harbour.** Once a bustling whaling station, Rose Harbour is now a small, quiet community and the only piece of privately owned land within Gwaii Haanas. Remnants of the old whale rendering facilities can still be seen on the shoreline. Local residents provide bed and breakfast style lodging, tours, and meals; try contacting Susan on VHF 06. No fuel, water, or services available. This is a favorite stop for kayakers.

Louscoone Inlet. Louscoone Inlet at the south end of Moresby Island has several possible anchorages. Small Cove, east of Crooked Point, is reportedly rocky and filled with kelp. Etches Point Cove, between two unnamed islands northwest of Etches Point, is the best anchorage. The Douglasses report another small and unnamed cove with limited swinging room 1 mile northwest of Etches Point Cove and 0.4 mile north of Cadman Point.

Untreated fresh water is available from a buoy on the west side side of Louscoone Inlet, west of Skindaskun Island.

⑧ **Anthony Island.** Anthony Island or **SGang Gwaay**, on the northwest side of Kunghit Island, is recognized worldwide as a historic UNESCO World Heritage Site. Nan Sdins (also known as Ninstints) is a former Haida village and the major attraction. Filled with the largest collection of original Haida heraldic and mortuary poles, Nan Sdins offers a remarkable look into the Haida culture. The poles at Nan Sdins have been reset upright for the last time. Going forward, when a pole naturally falls it will be left to decay, following the tradition of the memory fading for the chief or family depicted by the pole, and for whom it was created.

Anchorage is not permitted directly off the totem park. Instead, anchor off the Watchmen cabin (exposed), in Grays Cove, or in the cove on the northwest corner of the island. If anchored in the northwest cove, look for the bright orange fishing floats on the beach. These floats mark the boardwalk trail through the woods to the Watchman cabin for check-in. Call the Haida Watchmen on VHF 06 for permission to come ashore.

SGang Gwaay and the Nan Sdins Village Site is one of the top 10 places to visit on the entire coast. You might feel the spirits of the Haida as you walk through the woods to Nan Sdins. You emerge from the wood into a grove of carved poles. From the beach you can see what it must have been like when the Haida pulled their long war canoes up in front of the village. Nan Sdins should not be missed.

⑧ **Grays Cove.** Grays Cove, on the eastern shore of SGang Gwaay, is about a quarter-mile south of Nan Sdins. This anchorage is not well protected, however, and has only marginal holding. David Hoar, an experienced Haida Gwaii cruiser, writes, "We have NEVER (8 or 9 attempts) hooked the bottom here." Use caution.

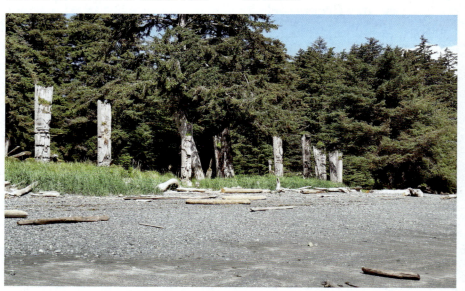

Mortuary Poles on SGang Gwaay (Anthony Island)

Crossing Dixon Entrance

CHAPTER 18

VENN PASSAGE TO METLAKATLA BAY
Du Vernet Pt. • Metlakatla

PORTLAND INLET AND TONGASS PASSAGE ROUTE
Port Simpson • Tongass Passage • Lincoln Channel

NORTH DUNDAS ISLAND ROUTE
Green Island • Holliday Passage • Danger Passage

FOGGY BAY OR MARY ISLAND TO KETCHIKAN
Revillagigedo Channel • Tongass Narrows

CROSSING DIXON ENTRANCE

On to Southeast Alaska! This chapter covers the departure routes from Prince Rupert and Chatham Sound, the options for the open water crossing of Dixon Entrance, and the approach to Ketchikan.

The distance from Prince Rupert to Ketchikan (via Venn Passage) is 82 nautical miles. Depending on the speed of your vessel, the weather and sea conditions, a stop in Prince Rupert before crossing Dixon Entrance might be required. Foggy Bay is 50 miles from Prince Rupert and could be an option for an overnight stop. It's a beautiful anchorage with good protection.

Ketchikan is a required stop for customs clearance into the U.S. in Alaska. Vessels that overnight in Foggy Bay before clearing customs in Ketchikan must first receive permission by calling U.S. Customs and Border Protection (907-225-2254). Permission is always granted for one day.

Before leaving British Columbia, however, consider some of the excellent cruising in Portland Inlet and Portland Canal, just north of Prince Rupert. Portland Canal is one of the longest fjords in North America and defines the border between the U.S. and Canada. It is beautiful and remote. Farther up the canal, the water becomes increasingly opaque, almost milky, the result of glacial run-off. The outpost of Stewart, B.C., with Bear Glacier just above town, has a public dock, a "yacht club," and other services. Stewart, B.C. is so remote that there is no VHF weather radio reception.

Hyder, Alaska is on the other side of the canal, less than a mile from Stewart. Hyder does not have a U.S. Customs office for clearance. Ketchikan is the closest CBP office. The typical strategy is to explore British Columbia on the way north, then go to Ketchikan for customs clearance. When headed home from Southeast Alaska, explore the areas south of Ketchikan, such as Misty Fjord or Hyder. Then go to Prince Rupert for customs clearance into Canada.

Both the United States and Canada require vessels to check in with customs authorities prior to anchoring, mooring, or going ashore.

In addition to Portland Canal, Observatory Inlet has a number of good anchorages. This area was the base camp for Captain George Vancouver when his expedition explored this area in 1793.

CHARTS	
17434	Revillagigedo Channel, Ruys & Foggy Bays, Duke I. (1:80,000)
17435	Harbors in Clarence Strait Various
17428	Revillagigido Channel, Nichols Pass. & Tongass Narrows (1:40,000)
3955 Plans	Prince Rupert Harbour
3957	Approaches to Prince Rupert Harbour (1:40,000)

Foggy Bay is a good anchorage, strategically located between Prince Rupert and Ketchikan.

Cruising in Portland Canal is covered in detail by Don and Reanne Douglass in their cruising guide, *Exploring the North Coast of British Columbia*, published by FineEdge.com.

Guidebook: For cruising in Alaska we recommend Don and Reanne Douglass' excellent guide, *Exploring Southeast Alaska*, 3rd Ed. Full disclosure: our sister company, Fine Edge, is the publisher. For 2018 the Southeast Alaska book was extensively updated by Reanne Douglass and her staff. It is the only comprehensive cruising guide for Southeast Alaska and includes additional tips for crossing Dixon Entrance and arriving in Ketchikan.

Crossing Dixon Entrance: Heading North. Several options exist for transiting Chatham Sound and crossing the open water of Dixon Entrance.

Understanding how to read the weather, sea conditions, and currents is critical to planning a safe and comfortable passage. Good planning for the crossing starts with examining the weather forecast and course options.

A stop at Prince Rupert can be a welcome break after the long passage up Grenville Channel and through northern British Columbia. Prince Rupert is the last fuel stop in Canada, and some boats may need to take on fuel before proceeding the 82 miles to Ketchikan.

If conditions are favorable, many boats bypass Prince Rupert entirely on their way north. This saves several hours of transit time. Anchorages are available in the Moffatt Islands, Qlawdzeet Anchorage on Stephens Island, and Brundige Inlet on Dundas, or in Foggy Bay after crossing Dixon Entrance (with a call to U.S. Customs and Border Protection in Ketchikan, (907) 225-2254).

The first route option is the shortest but the most exposed. From Venn Passage steer towards the northeast tip of Dundas Island. Then set a course past Cape Fox (leave plenty of sea room) to Mary Island and up Revillagigedo Channel.

A second route is a variation on the first: Cross Chatham Sound on a northwest heading and pass through the Moffatt Islands. They're beautiful and protected, but require good situational awareness to navigate among the many small islands, islets, and rocks. Several anchorages are tucked among the islands, pleasant enough for an overnight at anchor. At Dundas Island cross to Cape Fox and follow the coastline to Foggy Bay to overnight. The next morning continue up Revillagigedo Channel to Ketchikan.

The third choice is a longer route. First travel along the east side of Chatham Sound, then cross Portland Inlet. Sometimes referred to as the "mainland route," it offers some protection, and minimizes the open water crossing by harbor hopping along the shoreline. Attention needs to be focused on the effect of outflow wind and current from Portland Inlet.

The longer routes offer more shelter and duck-in points. The best choice depends on weather and current conditions. It is critical to develop a good picture of the currents, wind speed and direction, and ocean swells from the Environment Canada and NOAA weather forecasts, buoy reports, and lightstation reports. Monitoring these resources for several days prior to crossing Dixon Entrance can give a skipper a good understanding of what to expect during a crossing. Once headed up Revillagigedo Channel, instructions for clearing U.S. Customs and arriving in Ketchikan are covered in the Ketchikan chapter.

Weather planning. Planning a Dixon Entrance crossing starts with NOAA and Environment Canada forecasts. Use NOAA's "Dixon Entrance to Cape Decision" forecast and Environment Canada's "Dixon Entrance East," forecast.

Given a favorable forecast, several weather reporting stations are useful in determining if conditions are acceptable. The Central Dixon Entrance Buoy (Buoy 46145) provides regularly updated wind speed, direction and sea state information. This information can be accessed by listening to the continuous marine broadcast, using the Dial-a-Buoy service (888-701-8992), or checking online at www.ndbc.noaa.gov.

Automated, land-based weather stations at

CROSSING DIXON ENTRANCE — Reference Only – Not for Navigation

Dixon Entrance

Lucy Island, Grey Islet, and Rose Spit provide wind speed and direction, updated hourly. The Green Island and Triple Island lightstations are staffed with lightkeepers year round. These lightkeepers provide updated weather observations every three hours, including wind and sea conditions. Listen for their reports on the continuous marine broadcast, or visit www.weather.gc.ca. You may also be able to call them directly on VHF 82.

The NOAA Ocean Prediction Center, Pacific Marine section website has extensive forecast information (www.opc.ncep.noaa.gov/Pac_tab.shtml). The 24, 48, and 96 hour wind and wave forecast charts are a valuable resource for a graphical look at upcoming weather systems and conditions. Mariners are also using Apps like PredictWind.com, SailFlow.com, and Windy.com which give visual representations of forecast winds and sea conditions to judge the open ocean crossing. These Apps require a good internet connection.

Consider reading a weather book or taking a weather course to help understand and interpret weather data. Much data is available, even if the only source is the VHF continuous marine broadcast. The key is to understand the information as it streams by, and to use reports from multiple stations to paint a complete picture for the area you are interested in. An outflow wind from Portland Inlet blowing against a flood current, for example, will make for rough conditions as far away as Dundas Island. Even with the best preparations, conditions can change. Have a backup plan, such as using Brundige Inlet as a duck-in point before crossing. Be sure your vessel and crew are ready for changing weather conditions.

① **Venn Passage to Metlakatla Bay.** Venn Passage and the route through Metlakatla Bay is suitable for recreational boats of 75 feet or less. The route through Venn Passage is narrow and twisting, with shoals on each side. Buoys and range markers help navigation. Depths can be less than 10 feet, so some skippers time their passage for mid- or high-tide.

This route saves about 12 miles, compared with going south from Prince Rupert Harbour and rounding Digby Island. It's the channel favored by the fishing fleet, and it can be busy with fish boats. The route requires careful situational awareness and attention to the depth sounder and chartplotter. Even the buoys are suspect. In the past some have been dragged hundreds of yards out of position by log tows. Use caution when passing the landing for the ferry to the airport at Du Vernay Point. It is a regularly enforced no-wake zone. A no-wake zone in front of the village of Metlakatla is also enforced. Spend time studying the charts or your chartplotter to understand this route before attempting.

From Prince Rupert, head west to Grindstone Point and enter the channel. Follow the buoys and range markers. Note when heading west through Venn Passage, the range markers will be astern (back ranges). You will need either a clear view astern, or a stern watch with clear communication to the helm. At Tugwell Island, a turn to the north takes you into Chatham Sound toward Dundas Island, or along a route that follows the shoreline toward Port Simpson and Portland Inlet.

Dundas Island Route. The shortest route across Dixon Entrance is to depart Metlakatla Bay, take a direct course towards Green Island, then head up Holliday Passage. Round the top of Dundas Island and turn toward Mary Island. Proceed via Tongass Narrows to Ketchikan. If Dixon Entrance is too rough, you can anchor in protected Brundige Inlet on the north end of Dundas Island and remain in Canadian waters. If conditions allow a crossing of Dixon Entrance late in the day you can proceed to Foggy Bay for the night. The next day go from Foggy Bay to Ketchikan via Revillagigedo Channel and Tongass Narrows.

For planning purposes, it's about 26 miles from Metlakatla to Brundige Inlet. It's an additional 22 miles from Brundige Inlet to Foggy Bay through mainly open water. Foggy Bay to Ketchikan is 32 miles. The total distance from Prince Rupert to Ketchikan is 82 miles—a long day for a displacement-speed cruising boat. There are no services along this route.

② **Moffatt Islands.** For an interesting and scenic passage, depart Metlakatla Bay and head west to Melville Island. Carefully pick your way through the channel between Dunira Island and the Moffatt Islands. Cross to Dundas Island and Holliday Passage and proceed to the north end of Dundas Island. Several small anchorages are along the way in the Moffatt Islands. Canadian Sailing Directions cautions against this route without local knowledge. We found it easy enough to follow with good charts or a chartplotter.

③ **Brundige Inlet.** Brundige Inlet extends for about 2.5 miles. Enter at Prospector Point. The inlet is well protected, though windblown and barren in areas. Some have advised of vicious black flies on the island. Not the prettiest anchorage, but a good protected departure point to cross Dixon Entrance.

④ **Foggy Bay.** Foggy Bay is a well-protected stopping place between Prince Rupert and Ketchikan. For those headed north, it can provide an escape from rough conditions in Dixon Entrance. Headed south, it is a good overnight anchorage to shorten the leg to Prince Rupert and allows for an early morning departure to cross Dixon Entrance. Most boats anchor in the "inner cove," which provides a view of the conditions in Foggy Bay and Dixon Entrance. Uncharted rock awash reported at 54° 57.518'N , 130° 57.280' W. If you want privacy in a remote environment, cruise deep into Very Inlet to the "north basin." Use the Douglass' *Exploring Southeast Alaska* for detailed information on the anchorage in Foggy Bay and other interesting anchorages in the area.

LOCAL KNOWLEDGE

Fishing Nets: From Cape Fox to Tree Point, you may encounter many gillnet fish boats. Gillnets can extend up to 1800 feet from the boat (mostly from the stern, but sometimes from the bow) and show hard-to-see small white floats along the top of the net. The end is marked by an orange float, which is often difficult to see in choppy seas. They sometimes monitor VHF 16 when their nets are set.

Navigating the challenging well-marked Venn Passage

Dundas Island anchorage

CROSSING DIXON ENTRANCE See Area Map Page 458 - Maps Not for Navigation

Entering Inner Foggy Bay looks tricky, but the area is well charted.

Foggy Bay or Mary Island to Ketchikan. This route appears to be a straight shot up Revillagigedo Channel to Ketchikan, although weather conditions can vary from one side of the channel to the other. You might also encounter changing conditions as you pass Behm Canal, Thorne Arm or other inlets, depending on the wind direction and speed. Expect to see more recreational vessels, fish boats, tugs with tows and even large cruise ships maneuvering in Tongass Narrows as you approach Ketchikan.

Note the location of Behm Canal as you pass. Later in the trip you might want to visit some of the majestic cruising areas in Misty Fjords. For now, continue to Ketchikan to clear customs.

Danger Pass. At the south end of Mary Island and off Edge Point, this narrow passage will allow you to move out of the main channel and along the back side of Mary Island. Depending on the wind direction this route allows you to travel in the lee of Mary Island.

Portland Inlet & Tongass Passage Route. This route is preferred when northern outflow winds from Portland Inlet create a sharp chop in Chatham Sound. It reduces the open water across Portland Inlet to less than 5 miles. The total distance from Metlakatla Bay to Foggy Bay is about 50 miles.

If planning to overnight in Foggy Bay, the skipper must call U.S. Customs and Border Protection (907-225-2254) in Ketchikan and inform them. You may call CBP while in Prince Rupert. Cell phone towers on Cape Fox provide some phone coverage while enroute. No cell phone coverage in Foggy Bay. You are now in the United States, which requires clearing with CBP before anchoring, mooring, or going ashore. Proceed to Ketchikan and clear customs as soon as possible.

⑤ **Port Simpson.** North of Metlakatla Bay, Port Simpson can be used as a jumping-off point for crossing Portland Inlet. Port Simpson is a tribal village protected behind Rose Island. There are several floats, though they're often filled with commercial and fishing vessels, requiring rafting. A small store is in the village.

⑥ **Lincoln Channel.** Lincoln Channel, between Tongass Island and Kanagunut Island on the west and Sitklan Island and the mainland on the east, provides an interesting stop with easy access for boats coming from either Ketchikan, or Nichols Bay on Prince of Wales Island. The south end of Lincoln Channel is only two miles from the Canadian border and 38 miles from Prince Rupert, making it a good departure point for vessels heading south.

This is a popular anchorage for fish boats during the gillnet season. Several fishermen keep float houses here. Tongass Island was the site of Fort Tongass, the first U.S. Customs office in Alaska, and a major Tlingit village. The rocky shores of Kanagunut Island contain interesting rock formations. You may even find garnets near Garnet Point on the south tip of the island.

Enter at either the north or south end of the channel, or between Tongass Island on the north and Kanagunut Island on the south. If entering between Tongass and Kanagunut, follow Chart 17437 or your chartplotter carefully and watch for rocks. The best anchorage is north of a small unnamed island in 80-100 feet. Anchorage can also be found off Tongass Island or, in northerly winds, south of the unnamed island.

Crossing Dixon Entrance: Heading South. Southbound vessels coming from Southeast Alaska must clear Canadian Customs if they intend to stop or anchor in British Columbia. If transiting non-stop between Ketchikan and the U.S., as delivery captains or fish boats often do, customs clearance is not required. Most recreational boats will stop along the way and thus require clearance into Canada in Prince Rupert.

Approach Prince Rupert through Metlakatla Bay and Venn Passage, or continue down the west side of Digby Island and enter through Prince Rupert Harbour.

Once in the harbor, proceed to the designated customs dock or one of the four marinas where customs reporting is allowed by telephone: Fairview Terminal, the new Cow Bay Marina at Atlin Terminal, Prince Rupert Rowing & Yacht Club, or Rushbrooke Floats.

The customs dock, or "lightering dock," is painted green and located west of the Cow Bay area and below a shopping mall on shore. Call customs from the dedicated phone on the dock. The gate to the street is locked.

If clearing customs at another facility, call by cell phone (888) 226-7277.

Until cleared, all crew must remain on the boat. Canadian Customs may send agents to your boat for an inspection. Once cleared, you will be given a clearance number to post on the dockside window of your vessel and record in the ship's log.

If the weather deteriorates and you must anchor in Canadian waters before clearing customs in Prince Rupert, call Canadian Customs by phone, or notify the Canadian Coast Guard on VHF 16.

Note: All calls to Canadian Customs are directed to a call center in Hamilton, Ontario. While the customs agents on the phone are not located in Prince Rupert, they can still call out local agents if a clearance requires an inspection.

GEORGE DIXON (1748-1795)

George Dixon was a sea captain and fur trader who also served as a Royal Navy officer. He began his service on the HMS Resolution under Captain Cook during Cook's third voyage of exploration (1776-1779). George Dixon was later asked by the Director of the East India Company to participate in a voyage to the Pacific Northwest for the fur trade. Dixon helped promote interest in the Northwest fur trade among English merchants, which led to the formation of the Etches consortium. In 1785, Dixon in command of the Queen Charlotte, and Nathaniel Portlock in command of the King George, sailed from England for the Pacific Northwest. During the summers of 1786 and 1787, Dixon explored the coast of present-day British Columbia and Southeast Alaska with a focus on the Queen Charlotte Islands and Queen Charlotte Sound, Yakutat Bay (Port Mulgrave), Sitka Sound (Norfolk Bay), and his namesake, Dixon Entrance. After selling his cargo in China, Dixon returned to England in 1788 and published his book, *A Voyage Round the World*.

Arriving in Ketchikan

CHAPTER 19

KETCHIKAN
Thomas Basin • Casey Moran • Bar Harbor North & South

KETCHIKAN

Ketchikan. Tongass Narrows is the transition from crossing Dixon Entrance to arrival in a bustling maritime city. The transition begins at Mountain Point, and the closer you get to the city, the more signs of humanity you see. Overhead, float planes take summer tourists to Misty Fjords and other sites. The shoreline changes from remote and pristine to a few homes, then a few more, and eventually a developed roadway. Soon, cars are whizzing by. Off in the distance, up Tongass Narrows, the shapes of what seems to be a major city appear. In reality, they are the profiles of cruise ships lined up at the docks, towering 10 stories high, dwarfing the buildings below.

We enjoy visiting Ketchikan. Shopping is good. Several restaurants serve excellent food. The airport is convenient for exchanging crew or flying home. Boat repairs can be arranged, although the local mechanics cater mostly to the fishing fleet. The Fourth of July parade and fireworks are a favorite.

Cruise ships frequent Ketchikan. Three to four cruise ships are typically moored in Ketchikan during the day, their passengers touring the city, shopping, or just hanging out and absorbing their first (or last) stop in Alaska. You may encounter one of the cruise ships headed towards you, an imposing sight. Remember that federal law requires boats stay at least 100 yards from cruise ships. Occasionally the Coast Guard will escort cruise ships in and out of town and require 200 yards of separation. Listen to VHF channel 16 or 13 for Securité calls from cruise ships (and other commercial ships) as they prepare to get underway, and be prepared to alter course to maintain adequate separation.

Ketchikan calls itself "Alaska's First City"—the first city visitors see when they arrive in Southeast Alaska by boat. The cruise ships

Entrance to Thomas Basin with downtown Ketchikan in the background

CHARTS	
17428	Revillagigedo Channel, Nichols Passage & Tongass Narrows (1:40,000)
17430	Ketchikan Harbor (1:10,000)
17434	Revillagigedo Channel, Ruys & Foggy Bays, Duke I. (1:80,000)

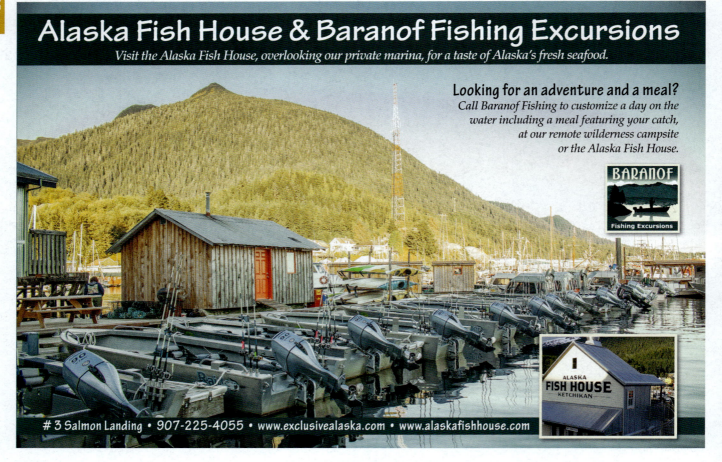

Reference Only – Not for Navigation **KETCHIKAN**

typically arrive early in the morning and depart by mid-afternoon or early evening. During the day the town can be bursting with 10,000 visitors if several cruise ships are docked. When the ships leave, usually in late afternoon or early evening, the tourist shops close and Ketchikan returns to a sleepy little Alaskan town.

Ketchikan has three public marinas and two private marinas for transient moorage, each with its own advantages, disadvantages, and personality.

A Walmart, north of town and Bar Harbor, runs a free shuttle between their store and the cruise ship docks. Ketchikan has several options for provisioning and picking up parts and marine hardware.

Ketchikan also has a number of local attractions and museums, including the Totem Heritage Center, the Southeast Alaska Discovery Center, and the Tongass Historical Museum. All are within walking distance of the marinas. Totem Bight State Park and Saxman Native Village are accessible by bus. The buses

run every 30-45 minutes.

Ketchikan has a good public bus system, the Ketchikan Gateway Borough Bus, that shuttles passengers to the main attractions, or from the airport ferry to downtown. Individual rides are $2; a day pass is $5. The bus also runs to several places you may want to visit, such as Totem Bight State Park, Saxman Native Village, and additional shopping farther from the waterfront. Taxis are also available, though they seem to use "cruise ship flat rate pricing" to some destinations. The bus is convenient and low cost, with stops near the three marinas. Schedule posted at bus stops.

Customs Clearance. Vessels entering Alaska from B.C. are required to clear customs in Ketchikan. When headed north to Southeast Alaska, it may be necessary to anchor for the night due to approaching darkness or worsening weather conditions. Technically, vessels are not allowed to drop anchor or land in Alaska until they have checked in at a U.S. Customs reporting station.

U.S. Customs and Border Protection (CBP) typically allows arriving vessels to stay one night in Foggy Bay before proceeding to Ketchikan. The procedure is to call (907) 225-2254 and advise CBP of your plans. Many crews will call from Prince Rupert. For most U.S. cell phone carriers, coverage begins at Cape Fox with fairly good coverage in Dixon Entrance. We haven't found cell phone coverage in Foggy Bay.

Assuming a good phone connection, a CBP agent will take all of the necessary information about your vessel and crew. Be ready with your information when you call. The next day when you arrive in Ketchikan, the agent will have this information when he or she comes to your boat. At this point all they need to do is verify ID with your passport photo.

In the past Ketchikan CBP has had a 100% boarding policy, even for Nexus and I-68 holders. Beginning in 2015, Ketchikan CBP began accepting Nexus and I-68 on a case-by-case basis. Nexus and I-68 holders should contact Ketchikan CBP when entering Alaska and follow the instructions provided.

On a recent trip, we knew we would arrive in Ketchikan after normal office hours. We called the CBP office from the water several hours ahead and the CBP agent took all of our information. When we arrived at our slip in Thomas Basin we called CBP again to inform them of our arrival and location. Although it was after office hours, an agent met us at our boat and we received our clearance number within five minutes. He had all the information on a computer printout and needed only to verify and inspect our passports. CBP officers do check the marinas to confirm that all vessels have checked in.

You'll pass two fuel docks as you approach Ketchikan. Upon request, and if workload allows, CBP may meet you at the fuel dock for clearance, allowing you to refuel and clear customs at the same time. Call first to see if this is possible.

Non-U.S. flagged vessels that don't already have a Cruising License (including Canadian vessels), may request a Cruising License upon clearing customs; a Cruising License reduces the cost and complexity for foreign-flagged vessels. See the Cruising License section under U.S./Canada Border Crossings in Chapter 1. Cruising Licenses do not affect customs reporting requirements.

Note: U.S. flagged vessels that have departed from a U.S. port without stopping or clearing Canada customs do not need to clear customs in Ketchikan.

Time change. Ketchikan is in Alaska Time Zone, one hour earlier than Seattle and British Columbia. Set clocks back one hour when you arrive.

Alaska Pilotage Requirements. Non-U.S. flagged vessels longer than 65 feet must employ an Alaska Marine Pilot when operating in Alaskan waters or apply for and receive an exemption. For more information visit www.commerce.alaska.gov.

Ketchikan Ports and Harbors Tel. 907-228-5632 VHF 73
U.S. Customs (CBP) Tel. 907-225-2254
Petro Marine Services Tel. 907-225-2106 VHF 16
Anderes Oil Tel. 907-225-2163
Anderes Service Tel. 907-225-1985
Doyon's Landing Tel. 907-225-5155
Ketchikan Moorage Tel. 907-225-8285

Tongass Narrows

DON'T MISS MISTY FJORDS NATIONAL MONUMENT

Misty Fjords National Monument is among the most breathtaking places on the coast. Sheer granite walls plunge into the water from thousands of feet above and waterfalls gush from the snowcapped peaks. It's like Princess Louisa Inlet, only bigger and seldom visited by cruising boats.

Misty Fjords is on the west side of Behm Canal, which winds around Revillagigedo Island, and is entered either south or north of Ketchikan. Boats arriving from British Columbia typically pass the southern entrance, but because they have not yet cleared customs they are not allowed to visit. Thus, visiting Misty Fjords National Monument requires a bit of backtracking from Ketchikan.

Due to this backtracking, many save Misty Fjords for the end of their Southeast Alaska cruise. Upon exciting Behm Canal, they can overnight in Foggy Bay or clear Canadian Customs.

Some cruisers visit Misty Fjords by circumnavigating Revillagigedo Island. The downside is the relatively boring western section. An alternative is to head southeast from Ketchikan for about 20 miles. Then turn north into Behm Canal.

Smeaton Bay is the first bay and is not visited often. Rudyerd Bay is the next bay, just past New Eddystone Rock. New Eddystone has a sandy beach and a remarkable tree covered spire of rock jutting 200 feet into the air. Rudyerd Bay is probably the most visited area of Misty Fjords National Monument. Punchbowl Cove, the first anchorage, juts off to the south. It's deep and astoundingly beautiful. Think Yosemite, multiply by 3 or 4, and fill the valleys with water. A steep muddy trail leads to a lake about 1000 feet above sea level.

Don't expect to be alone in Punchbowl Cove. Tour boats and floatplanes bring cruise ship passengers from Ketchikan to Misty Fjords. We were shocked at how many camera flashes we saw going off as they passed our boat!

– *Mark Bunzel*

KETCHIKAN MARKETPLACE

RESTAURANTS, SHOPS & SERVICES

ALASKA EAGLE ARTS
Alaska Eagle Arts Gallery features contemporary Native artist Marvin Oliver. Established in 1991 by Brigette Ellis (granddaughter of legendary aviator Bob Ellis of Ellis Airlines). This fine art gallery features Marvin's work in glass, bronze, steel, wood, paper and more!
907.225.8365 • #5 Creek Street
info@marvinoliver.com • www.alaskaeaglearts.com

ALASKA FISH HOUSE
Come and visit us, in the heart of downtown Ketchikan, for a taste of fresh, locally caught, Alaskan seafood. Cozy up around the fireplace and enjoy the view overlooking our private marina. If you prefer a more exclusive dining experience, call us to reserve our captain's room and customize your menu.
907.225.4055 • # 3 Salmon Landing • www.alaskafishhouse.com

BARANOF FISHING EXCURSIONS
Let Baranof introduce you to Ketchikan's world renowned fishing waters. Enjoy halibut and salmon fishing, bottom fishing, dungeness crabbing and seafood dining at our remote wilderness campsite. We are happy to help create the perfect Alaska Fishing adventure for you and your group.
907.225.4055 • www.exclusivealaska.com
 # 3 Salmon Landing (below the Alaska Fish House)

CRAZY WOLF STUDIO
Authentic, traditional NW Coast Native art by Ketchikan Tsimshian Ken Decker and other regional artists. Local native owned and operated store. Masks, paddles, bentwood boxes, drums, prints, ivory, argillite, apparel, and handcarved native jewelry.
907.225.9653 • 633 Mission St. • www.crazywolfstudio.com

PACIFIC PRIDE OF ALASKA
Locally owned commercial and sport fishing gear store. We pride ourselves in a large inventory to keep you on the water catching fish. Stop in and see why we're the name fish fear most.
907.225.3135 • 1050 Water Street

PARNASSUS BOOKS AND GIFTS
For three decades, Parnassus Books and Gifts has specialized in books about Alaska from around the world. We also have an outstanding handpicked selection of general stock, best-sellers, gift items, chocolate and local handcrafted arts and crafts.
907.225.0870 • 105 Stedman St. • parnassusak@gmail.com

SOHO COHO
A contemporary art and craft gallery featuring local artists and natural history items. Located on Creek Street, the Soho Coho is also a planetary headquarters of Ketchikan artist Ray Troll.
907.225.5954 • 5 Creek Street • www.trollart.com

TIMBER & MARINE SUPPLY INC.
Located in the heart of Bar Harbor for over 40 years. We are a marine hardware retail store. We sell and service Honda and Suzuki outboard motors, and are a Lund Boat and Achilles Inflatable dealer.
907.225.6644 • 2547 Tongass Ave. • www.timberandmarine.com

KETCHIKAN

Moorage. The waterfront is managed by the City of Ketchikan's Port & Harbors department. Thomas Basin and Bar Harbor slips are permanently assigned, with waiting lists for vacancies. Visiting boats are hot-berthed. When a local boat goes out, the harbor notes the vacancy and rents the slip. It usually works well. Sometimes, though, a permanent tenant will return to their slip unannounced. If this happens, the office will assign the visiting boat to a new slip. Harbor staffers are on the docks often, checking the status of slips. They work hard to accommodate everyone. Limited options for long-term moorage.

Thomas Basin, the first major marina you'll see when approaching from the south, is at the foot of Creek Street in the heart of the tourist district. It's an easy walk to groceries, local shops, and attractions. Ketchikan Yacht Club is in the red building on float 2, with some transient (no reciprocal) moorage available. The members are friendly, helpful, and a good source of local knowledge.

Casey Moran Harbor, formerly known as (and still often called) "City Floats," is next. It's small and in the middle of downtown, right in the shadow of the cruise ships. Moorage is first-come, first-served anywhere with unpainted bull rails.

Bar Harbor North and South are about a mile north of the center of Ketchikan. A Safeway, shopping mall, and chandlery are a short walk away.

During a stay in Ketchikan, you may be directed by Ketchikan Ports and Harbors to move between marinas, from Thomas Basin to say, Bar Harbor. It is also possible that you may be assigned a slip without power. When your crew goes out touring or shopping, they could come back to find the boat has moved to a new moorage a mile away. It helps to have a communication plan in case things change.

The Port & Harbors office does not take reservations. Things change by the hour; the office will work with you to find moorage. For many first-time visitors, especially with large boats, not having a reservation is disconcerting. The staff is good at fitting everyone in. Call on VHF 73 (preferred), VHF 16, or phone (907) 228-5632. Moorage is paid by calling the harbor office with credit card information, or in person at the harbor office in the middle of Bar Harbor marina. The office is open 8:00 a.m. to 5:00 p.m. seven days a week during summer months, and 8:00 a.m. to 5:00 p.m. Monday through Friday during winter. The harbormaster is available from 6:00 a.m. to 10:00 p.m. during summer months.

First-come, first-served open moorage can be found at Casey Moran, and in designated areas of Thomas Basin and Bar Harbor Basin. In these areas, take an unoccupied space and then register and pay at the office. See maps or www.city.ketchikan.ak.us for designated open moorage.

Shore power has been upgraded to GFI-protected circuits at Thomas Basin and Float 9 at Bar Harbor.

Two private marinas, Doyon's Landing and Ketchikan Moorage (Ellis Floats), cater primarily to larger yachts, with limited moorage for other boats.

Thomas Basin, as seen from a cruise ship. Cruise ships moor just north (left in this photo) of the entrance to Thomas Basin.

Weather. Ketchikan gets more than 150 inches of rain each year. Its driest month (July) is wetter than Seattle's wettest month (November). Daytime summer temperatures typically range from the high 40s to the mid 60s, but occasionally reach into the 80s. Rain boots, better known as "Alaska Sneakers," are readily available in local stores. Locals swear by the brown XtraTuf brand.

Airport. The Ketchikan Airport is convenient for visitors and crew. Alaska Airlines and Delta Airlines each have several daily flights to Seattle. The airport is located across Tongass Narrows on Gravina Island, and connects with Ketchikan by a ferry that departs and arrives just north of Bar Harbor Marina. The ferry leaves the airport terminal every hour and half-hour, daily. The ferry leaves the Ketchikan side on the quarter hours. Crossing time is approximately 10 minutes. If flying out, allow time for the ferry schedule and walk to the airport.

Stairs and ramps connect the airport terminal with the ferry. If you have considerable luggage, it's best to take an airport shuttle van that will deliver you and your luggage door-to-door. On the airport side of the narrows, a small dock, north of the ferry dock and connected to the float plane dock, is below the covered stairway. Dinghies and boats under 35 feet can tie-up to drop off or pick up guests and luggage. The modest short-term moorage fee is paid in an honor box on the dock.

Doyon's Landing. 1716 South Tongass Highway, Ketchikan, AK 99901; (907) 225-5155; moorage@mistyfjords.com; www.doyonslanding.com. Power, water, 24-hour security, internet. Reservations encouraged. This is a full service marina that caters to large yachts. Located south of town near the Coast Guard station.

Petro Marine Services. 1100 Stedman St., P.O. Box 7398, Ketchikan, 99901; (800) 478-7277; (907) 225-2106; www.petromarineservices.com. Monitors VHF 16. Located on Tongass Narrows next to the U.S. Coast Guard station (buildings with red roofs). In summer, open 7 days a week from 7:00 a.m. to 7:00 p.m. In winter, Monday through Saturday, 8:00 a.m. to 5:00 p.m. and Sunday 9:00 a.m. to 5:00 p.m. Gasoline, diesel, propane, lubricants, restrooms, showers, garbage, and waste oil disposal.

Anderes Oil Inc. 900 Stedman St., P.O. Box 5858, Ketchikan, AK 99901; (907) 225-2163; www.anderesoil.com. Monitors VHF 16. Open summers: Monday through Friday 7:00 a.m. to 7:00 p.m., Saturday 7:00 a.m. to 6:00 p.m., and Sunday 8:00 a.m. to 5:00 p.m. Winter hours vary. Located on Tongass Narrows. Gasoline, diesel, propane, lubricants.

Thomas Basin. (907) 228-5632; www.city.ketchikan.ak.us. Monitors VHF 73. Moorage for boats to 60 feet, call ahead as all slips are reserved. Water, pumpout, garbage and waste oil disposal, tidal grid to 100 tons (reserva-

Port of Ketchikan, Thomas Basin

KETCHIKAN   See Area Map Page 463 - Maps Not for Navigation

tions required for grid). Power varies from slip to slip, check with the harbor office and inform them of power requirements when requesting a slip. All power is ELCI-protected. A hot berth system is maintained. You may be asked to move if the owner of a slip returns sooner than scheduled. Supermarket, restaurants, shops, and bars nearby. Located at the foot of Creek Street. Many attractions within walking distance. Local bus and taxi available on nearby Steadman Street.

Ketchikan Yacht Club. Clubhouse phone (907) 225-3262 relays the Port Captain's number; info@ketchikanyachtclub.com; ketchikanyachtclub.org/blog. On float 2 in Thomas Basin, with guest moorage when a member's slip is not being used. Pick an empty slip that fits your boat and check the whiteboard at the head of the slip for the return date of the slip holder. South side: boats 36-45 feet. North side: boats 24-39 feet. Slips cannot be reserved. Moorage is paid in the honor box at the yacht club. Power is 30 & limited 50 amp. A keycode to the clubhouse is available for guest boats. The clubhouse has Wi-Fi, restrooms, showers, laundry, kitchen, barbecue and social area. Guests are welcome to use the facility.

Casey Moran. (907) 228-5632; www.city.ketchikan.ak.us. Monitors VHF 73. Open moorage for boats to 90 feet, 30 & 50 amp power, water, garbage drop, pumpout, and waste oil disposal. White bull rails designate loading, blue designates handicap access. Unpainted bull rails show open moorage area, rafting is allowed. Close to all downtown attractions and in the shadow of cruise ships during the day. Restaurants, bars, and marine supplies nearby. Bus and taxi service are on the busy street above the marina.

Ketchikan Moorage (Locally known as Ellis Floats). (907) 225-8285; info@ketchikanmoorage.com; www.ketchikanmoorage.com. Moorage for boats to 170 feet, 30, 50 &

Small Shops line Creek Street

100 amp power, water, garbage drop, free Wi-Fi and secure gate. Reservations encouraged. This is a full service marina that caters to larger yachts with a limited number of slips.. Located north of Casey Moran and south of Bar Harbor.

Bar Harbor North and South. (907) 228-5632; www.city.ketchikan.ak.us. Monitors VHF 73A. Open moorage available on the ends of floats 3 - 5; 9 - 15; and the north side of float 7. All slips reserved. Do not moor in a slip without authorization from harbormaster. Limited power (some of the docks are old). Power on dock 9 has been upgraded to ELCI-protected. Pumpout, water, restrooms, showers (8 minutes for $2 in quarters, change available in harbor office), garbage and waste oil disposal at the head of the dock. Tidal grid available by reservation. Restaurants, groceries, laundry, chandlery and shopping mall nearby. The marina is walking distance to the Alaska Marine Highway ferry terminal and the local ferry to the airport. The downtown area is about a 1.5 mile walk. Bus and taxi service available. The harbor office, with restrooms and showers, is in the green building between the north and south areas of the harbor.

Anderes Service. 4161 Tongass Avenue, Ketchikan, AK 99901; (907) 225-1985; www.anderesoil.com. Located on Tongass Narrows just south of the airport ferry. Gasoline, diesel, and lubricants. In summer, staffed 7 days a week, 8:00 a.m. to 6:00 p.m. In winter, Monday through Friday, 8:00 a.m. to 5:00 p.m. A card lock/credit card payment system is on the dock for after hours payment. It stops at $75, but can be used three times. Historically the Anderes Oil location south of town has the best prices.

Port of Ketchikan. Bar Harbor Basin

Port of Ketchikan, Casey Moran

THINGS TO DO

1. Totem Heritage Center. Located Northeast of Thomas Basin and within walking distance. Great display of historic old totems.

2. Saxman Native Village and Totem Bight State Park. A glimpse into the traditions of the Tlingit culture. Both can be reached by bus. Saxman has tours and ceremonial dances, Totem Bight has 14 poles and a longhouse.

3. Southeast Alaska Discovery Center. Located just above Thomas Basin. This National Park Service museum includes exhibits and interactive displays about the land, people, and culture of Southeast Alaska.

4. Creek Street. Just above Thomas Basin. Cute shops and galleries, though a little touristy. Still fun to stroll.

5. Tongass Historical Museum. Located at the top of Creek Street. This is the town museum; small and well done, covering the history of Ketchikan.

6. Float Plane to Misty Fjords. A number of operators along the waterfront offer breathtaking tours of Behm Canal and Misty Fjords. Tip: Ask for the "local rate."

7. Rent a Car. You can tour the area in a standard rental car, or a classic 1950s rental car. You won't be going far, though, since there aren't many roads around Ketchikan.

8. Tongass Trading Company. Above the Casey Moran Floats. A large store with souvenirs and gifts on the first floor. The good stuff is on the second floor, including an extensive selection of boots, jackets, marine, and fishing supplies.

9. Catch a Salmon. Charter a fishing boat from one of the many outfits in town. Local guides know the waters and can take care of your license.

10. Bear watching at Herring Bay in August and September.

INDEX

A

A History of The Waggoner 9
About Anchoring 28, 29
About the Waggoner Cruising Guide 8
Acland Islands 229
Actaeon Sound 339
Active Cove 201
Active Pass 222
Active Pass Auto & Marine 223
Actress Passage 339
Admiralty Inlet 128
Adventure Cove 383
Agamemnon Channel 279
Agate Passage 114
Ahclakerho Channel 405
Ahousat 382
Ajax Cafe 131
Alaska Pilotage Requirements 463
Alberni Inlet 391
Alderbrook Resort & Spa 122
Aleck Bay 180
Alert Bay 350
Alert Bay Boat Harbour 350
Alexander Inlet 432
Allan Island 159
Allcroft Point 435
Allies Island 297
Allison Harbour 402
Allyn Waterfront Park (Port of Allyn) 80
Alston Cove 433
Amos Island 370
Amphitrite Point 388
Amsterdam Bay 80
Anacortes 150
Anacortes Marina 156
Anderes Oil Inc 465
Anderes Service 466
Anderson Bay 258
Andrews Bay 109
Angler's Anchorage Marina 232
Anna Inlet 453
Annette Inlet 229
Anthony Island 454
April Point Resort, Spa & Marina 306
Arabella's Landing 88
Arran Rapids 318
Arthur Passage to Chatham Sound 441
Atkins Cove 364
Atkinson Island 338
Azimuth Island 435

B

B.C. Maritime Museum 208
Bacchante Bay 382
Backeddy Resort & Marina 279
Bag Harbour 454
Bainbridge Island 114
Baker Inlet 441
Balch Passage 80
Ballard 104
Ballard Locks 101
Ballard Mill Marina 104
Ballet Bay 282
Bamfield 394
Bamfield Fuel Barge 394
Bamfield Inlet 393
Bar Harbor North and South 466
Barb's Buns 226

Bargain Bay 275
Barkley Sound 388
Barkley Sound To Becher Bay 394
Barlow Bay 180
Barnard Harbour 434
Barnes and Clark Islands 198
Barnes Bay 304
Baronet Passage 344
Barter Cove 370
Bathgate General Store, Resort & Marina 280
Battle Bay 367
Bauza Cove 346
Bay Of Plenty 433
Baynes Sound 253
Bayshore West Marina 266
Bayview Marina 88
Bazett Island 390
Beach Gardens Resort & Marina 285
Beales Bay 423
Bear Cove 355
Bear watching 466
Beaumont/Mount Norman Park 218
Beaux Arts Village 108
Beaver Cove 347
Beaver Harbour 353
Beaver Inlet 320
Becher Bay 396
Becher Bay Marina & Campground 396
Bedwell Bay 268
Bedwell Harbour 216
Belcarra 268
Belfair State Park 124
Bell Harbor Marina 99
Bella Bella 421
Bella Coola 424
Bella Coola Harbour Authority 424
Belleisle Sound 336
Bellevue Marina 108
Bellingham 160
Bellingham Farmers Market 161
Bellingham Railway Museum 160
Bend Island 342
Bennett Bay 223
Benson Island 392
Berth Marina 285
Bessborough Bay 321
Beware Cove 343
Beware Passage 342
Bickley Bay 319
Big Bay (Stuart Island) 314
Big Frypan Bay 410
Big Salmon Resort 171
Billy Proctor's Museum 333
Birch Bay 164
Birds Eye Cove Marina 235
Bishop Bay Hot Springs 437
Blackfish Archipelago 341
Blaine 164
Blaine Harbor/Port of Bellingham 165
Blaine Marina Inc 165
Blair Island 338
Blake Island Marine State Park 96
Blakely Harbor 116
Blakely Island 181
Blakely Island Store & Marina 181
Blenkinsop Bay 322
Blind Bay (San Juans) 182
Blind Bay (Sunshine Coast) 282
Blind Channel Resort 320

Blind Island Marine State Park 182
Bliss Landing Estates 289
Bloedel Floral Conservatory 264
Blubber Bay 258
Blue Lips Cove 370
Blue Pacific Yacht Charters 265
Bluenose Marina 234
Blunden Harbour 402
Boardings 62
Boat Harbour 243
Boat Inlet 428
Boat Pass 221
Boating From Inn to Inn 48, 49
Bockett Islets 327
Bodega Cove 376
Bold Island Anchorage 301
Bolin Bay 429
Bond Sound 330
Bones Bay 342
Booker Lagoon 340
Booker Passage 340
Boot Cove 221
Bootleg Bay 341
Boston Harbor 77
Boston Harbor Marina 78
Bottleneck Bay (Coyote Cove) 381
Bottleneck Inlet 436
Boughey Bay 327
Boukind Bay 426
Boundary Bay 260
Bowen Island 269
Bowen Island Marina 270
Bowman Bay (Reservation Bay) 149
Bowman Bay 149
Breakwater Marina 88
Breezy Bay 221
Bremerton 110
Bremerton Marina 110
Brentwood Bay 232
Brentwood Bay Resort & Marina 232
Bridgeview Marina 111
Bridgeview Marine 452
Brigade Bay 271
Brigantine Bay 177
Broad Spit Park 120
Broken Group 392
Brooks Bay 365
Brooks Peninsula 366
Broughton Archipelago 340
Broughton Lagoon 336
Broughton Street Wharf - GVHA 208
Browning Harbour Public Wharf 219
Browning Inlet 363
Browning Passage and Tsapee Narrows 384
Brown's Bay Marina & RV Park 311
Browns Point Park 94
Brownsville 112
Brundige Inlet 459
Brydon Anchorage 415
Brydon Channel 415
Buccaneer Bay 274
Buccaneer Marina & Resort Ltd 275
Budd Inlet 74
Buie Creek 433
Bull Harbour 360
Bull Passage 258
Bullock Channel 427
Bullock Channel North Cove 427
Bullock Spit Cove 427

2018 Waggoner Cruising Guide

INDEX

Bunsby Islands 367
Buoys, Beacon and Ranges 61
Burdwood Bay 301
Burdwood Group 333
Burfoot County Park 77
Burgoyne Bay 234
Burial Cove 327
Burke Channel 423
Burly Bay 338
Burnaby 268
Burrard Civic Marina 264
Burrows Island State Park 159
Butchart Cove 232
Butchart Gardens 232
Bute Inlet 302
Butedale 437
Bywater Bay 118

C

Cabbage Island 222
Cable Ferry 255
Cachalot 371
Cadboro Bay 210
Call Inlet 327
Calm Channel 301
Calmus Passage to Heynen Channel 383
Cama Beach State Park 142
Camano Island State Park 142
Cameleon Harbour 319
Campania Island 434
Campbell Bay 223
Campbell River 307
Cannery Bay 384
Canoe Bay 214
Canoe Cove Marina & Boatyard 216
Canoe Passage (Fraser River) 260
Canoe Passage (Broughtons) 342
Cap Sante 156
Cap Sante Marina 156
Cape Beale 394
Cape Caution 398
Cape Cockburn 282
Cape Cook & Solander Island 366
Cape Lazo 257
Cape Mudge 305
Cape Scott 360
Cape Scott to Quatsino Sound 362
Cape Sutil to Cape Scott 360
Captain Coupe Park 143
Captain Cove 436
Captain's Cove Marina 262
Carillon Point Marina 108
Carr Inlet 81
Carriden Bay 338
Carrie Bay 341
Carrington Bay 300
Carter Bay 437
Carter Passage 340
Cartwright Bay 337
Casey Moran 466
Castle Island 180
Catala Island Provincial Park 371
Cates Park 268
Cathedral Point 423
Cattle Pass 184
Caulfeild Cove 269
Causeway Floats - GVHA 208
Caution Cove 343
Cellular, Internet and Satellite Communications 42-44

Center For Wooden Boats 97
Center Island 177
Central Puget Sound 84
Centre Bay 270
Chained Islands 311
Chandler's Cove 105
Chapple Inlet 434
Charles Bay 320
Chatham Channel 327
Checleset Bay 367
Chemainus 236
Chemainus Municipal Dock 237
Chettleburgh Point 434
Chiefs Bathtub 342
Children's Museum of Tacoma 92
China Creek Marina & Campground 391
Chinook Landing Marina 94
Chonat Bay 304
Choquer & Sons Ltd 281
Chuckanut Bay 160
Church House 301
Cigarette Cove 390
City of Des Moines Marina 96
City of Richmond Imperial Landing 261
City of White Rock Pier 260
Clallam Bay 170
Clam Bay 241
Clam Cove 360
Clark Island Marine State Park 198
Clarke Island 392
Clatse Bay 426
Claydon Bay 338
Clayoquot Sound 380
Clayoquot Sound to Ucluelet 386
Clear Passage 357
Clear Passage to Tatchu Point 371
Clerke Point 367
Clio Channel 342
Clo-oose 396
Clothes Bay 430
Clutesi Haven 392
Coal Harbour 357, 365
Coal Harbour Chevron 266
Coal Harbour Marina 266
Coast Marina 308
Coast Victoria Harbourside Hotel 209
Coastal Mountain Fuels (Bear Cove) 355
Cockburn Bay 282
Cockle Bay/Lady Douglas Island 428
Codville Lagoon 418
Coghlan Anchorage 438
Colby Bay 435
Coles Bay 232
Collison Bay 454
Columbia Cove 367
Columbia Fuels Fuel Dock 425
Colvos Passage 94
Commencement Bay 88
Comox 255
Comox Bar 255
Comox Harbour 257
Comox Municipal Marina 257
Comox Valley Harbour Authority 257
Comox Valley Marina 256
Conover Cove 241
Contact Phone Numbers & Web Addresses 69
Conversion Tables 71, 72
Copeland Islands 289
Cordero Lodge 320

Cormorant Channel Marine Park 347
Cornet Bay 145, 149
Cortes Bay 299
Cortes Island 299
Coulter Bay 300
Coupeville 143
Coupeville Wharf 143
Courtenay 257
Cousins Inlet 418
Cow Bay 445
Cow Bay Marina 444
Cowichan Bay 233
Cowichan Bay Fishermen's Wharf Association 234
Coyote Cove 381
Cozy Cove and Fairweather Bay 108
Crab Cove 417
Cracroft Inlet 342
Crawford Anchorage 320
Creek Street 466
Crescent Bay 170
Crescent Beach 260
Crescent Beach Marina Ltd 260
Crescent Harbor 145
Crescent Inlet 453
Critter Cove 377
Critter Cove Marina 377
Crofton Public Wharf 235
Crossing Dixon Entrance 457, 460
Crossing the Strait of Georgia 250
Crossing the Strait of Juan de Fuca 172
Cruising with a Charter Boat 34, 35
Cufra Inlet 241
Cullen Harbour 340
Culpepper Lagoon 429
Curlew Bay 439
Curley's Resort 170
Curme Islands 293
Customs, Canadian and U.S. 20
Customs - Entering Canada 204
Customs Clearance 463
Cutter Cove 328
Cutts Island Marine State Park 81
Cypress Harbour 336
Cypress Head 159
Cypress Island 159

D

Dabob Bay 120
Dana Passage 453
Danger Pass 460
Darby Channel (Schooner Pass) 409
D'Arcy Island 210
Dark Cove 284
Darke Waters Inn & Adventure Lodge 420
Dash Point State Park 95
Dave's Parking 288
Davis Bay 339
Dawsons Landing 409
Days Island 84
De Courcy Group 242
De la Beche Inlet 453
Dead Point 344
Dean Channel 425
Decatur Island 177
Deception Pass 149
Deception Pass Marina 149
Deception Pass Marine State Park 149
Deep Bay 253

468

INDEX

Deep Bay Harbour Authority 253
Deep Cove 231
Deep Cove 268
Deep Cove North Shore Marina 268
Deep Cove Public Wharf 268
Deep Harbour 340
Deepwater Bay 159
Deepwater Bay 310
Deer Harbor 193
Deer Harbor Marina 193
Degnen Bay 243
Degnen Bay Public Wharf 243
Delin Docks 94
Delkatla Slough Harbour Authority 450
Denham Bay 318
Denman Island 255
Dent Island Lodge 317
Dent Rapids 318
Departure Bay Gas N Go 248
Des Moines 96
Developing an Itinerary to
    Delight the Entire Crew 50
Dickson Island 340
Differences Between U.S. & Canadian Charts 26, 27
Dinghy Dock Pub 247
Dinner Bay 222
Dinner Rock 287
Dionisio Point Park 242
Discovery Bay 168
Discovery Cove 426
Discovery Harbour Authority
    Small Craft Harbours 310
Discovery Harbour Fuels 310
Discovery Harbour Marina 310
Discovery Island Marine Park 210
Discovery Passage 305
Dixie Cove 370
Dock Street Marina 94
Dock Street North Pier 94
Dockton Park 95
Doctor Bay 297
Dodd Narrows 245
Doe Bay Resort and Retreat 198
Doe Island Marine State Park 197
Dogfish Bay 243
Doig Anchorage 434
Dolomite Narrows 454
Dosewallips State Park 122
Dowager Island & Arthur Island 428
Doyon's Landing 465
Draney Narrows & Draney Inlet 408
Drayton Passage 80
Drew Harbour/Rebecca Spit Marine 304
Drumbeg Provincial Park 243
Drury Inlet 339
Dsulish Bay 405
Duck Bay 236
Dufferin Inlet 427
Duncanby Lodge & Marina 406
Dundas Island Route 459
Dungeness Marina 234
Dungeness Spit 168
Dunn Passage 434
Dyes Inlet 111

E

Eagle Harbor (Bainbridge Island) 115
Eagle Harbor (Cypress Island) 159
Eagle Harbor Marina 116

Eagle Harbor Waterfront Park 115
Eagle Harbour 269
Eagle Island Marine State Park 80
Eagle Marine, Ltd./Columbia Fuels 389
Eagle nook resort and Spa (Vernon Bay) 391
East Bamfield Public dock 394
East Channel Bridge 108
East Cove 363
East Inlet 440
East of Eden (lady Boot Cove) 340
East Passage 95
East Sound 196
East Waterway 99
Eastern Barkley Sound 393
Eastsound 196
Echo Bay (Broughtons) 331
Echo Bay (San Juans) 200
Echo Bay Marine Park 333
Edmonds 137
Edward Channel 414
Effingham Bay 392
Effingham Inlet 390
Egmont 279
Egmont Public Wharf 280
Elcho Harbour 425
ELCI Protected Shore Power 30-32
Eld Inlet 78
Elger Bay 142
Ellerslie Lagoon 427
Elliott Bay 97
Elliott Bay Marina 98
Ellis Floats 466
Elworthy Island 296
Embe Bakery 226
Embley Lagoon 338
Emily Carr Inlet 434
English Camp 186
English Camp national Historical Park 192
Entrance Inlet 390
Erie Street Wharf (Fisherman's) - GVHA 208
Esperanza Inlet 371
Espinosa Inlet 373
Esquimalt Harbour 207
Estero Basin 318
Estevan Point 357, 378
Ethel Cove 405
Eucott Bay 425
Eveleigh Island 295
Evening Cove 238
Everett 138
Everett Marine Park 141
Ewin Inlet 377
Ewing Cove 200
Exploring Graham Island by Car 451

F

Fair Harbor 79
Fair Harbor Marina 80
Fair Harbour 370
Fair Harbour Marina & Campground 370
Fairhaven Moorage 160
Fairview Small Craft Harbour 444
Fairwinds Marina at Schooner Cove 251
False Bay 258
False Creek 263, 265
False Creek Fuels 264
False Creek Harbour Authority
    Fishermen's Wharf 265
False Creek Yacht Club 265

False Narrows 245
Fancy Cove 420
Fannie Cove 420
Fanny Bay 255
Fanny Bay 319
Fanny Island 321
Farewell Harbour 342
Fay Bainbridge Park 115
Fernwood Public Wharf 231
Fidalgo Marina 158
Fife Sound 340
Fifer Bay 410
Fifer Cove 433
Filucy Bay 80
Fin Island 439
Finis Nook 405
Finlayson Arm 233
Finlayson Channel to Prince Rupert 430
Finn Bay 410
Fiordland Recreation Area 429
Fish Creek 184
Fish Egg Inlet 410
Fish Trap Bay 411
Fisher Channel 417
Fisherman Bay 179
Fisherman Harbor 120
Fishermans Cove 269
Fisherman's Harbour 392
Fisherman's Resort & Marina 277
Fisherman's Wharf
    (Campbell River Harbour Authority) 307
Fisherman's Wharf
    (Port Hardy Harbour Authority) 355
Fishermen's Terminal 104
Fishing Nets 459
Fitz Hugh Sound 413
Flat Top Islands 243
Fleming Beach at Macaulay Park 207
Fleming Island 393
Fletcher Bay 113
Float Plane to Misty Fjords 466
Floatplane Travel Along the Inside Passage 18-19
Flounder Bay 158
Fly Basin 405
Foggy Bay 459
Foggy Bay or Mary Island to Ketchikan 460
Ford Cove 253
Ford Cove Harbour Authority 253
Forit Bay 423
Fort Casey State Park 137
Fort Ebey State Park 137
Fort Flagler Marine State Park 133
Fort Rupert 353
Fort Townsend Marine State Park 135
Fort Ward Park 109
Fort Worden Marine State Park 135
Fortune Channel 383
Forward Harbour 321
Foss Harbor Marina 94
Foss Waterway Seaport 92
Fossil Bay 200
Fougner Bay 423
Fox Cove 200
Fox Island 82
Frances Bay 301
Francisco De Eliza 172
Fraser River 261
Frederick Arm 318
Freeman Island 201
Fremont Bridge 105

2018 Waggoner Cruising Guide

469

INDEX

French Creek Harbour Authority 252
Fresh seafood on the dock 247
Freshwater Marina and Boatyard 310
Friday Harbor 185
Friday Harbor Seafood 186
Friendly Cove 377
Friendly Dolphin Cove 382
Frye Cove County Park 78
Frypan Bay 410
Fulford Harbour 224
Fulford Harbour Marina 224
Fulford Inner Harbour 224
Fulford Outer Harbour 224
Fury Cove 410

G

Gabriola Passage 243
Gabriola Sands Park 246
Galiano Oceanfront Inn & Spa 223
Galley Bay 293
Gambier Island 270
Ganges 224
Ganges Breakwater Float 226
Ganges Centennial Wharf 226
Ganges Kanaka Wharf 226
Ganges Marina 228
Garden Bay 277
Garden Bay Hotel Marina & Pub 277
Garrison 192
Garrison Bay 191
Gas N Go Marine Ltd 256
Gedney Island 138
Gene Coulon Memorial Beach Park 108
Genoa Bay 234
Genoa Bay Marina 234
George Dixon 460
Georgeson Passage 222
Georgia 287
Gerrans Bay 278
Getting to Haida Gwaii 447
Gibson Cove 383
Gibson Marine Park 383
Gibsons 272
Gibsons Landing Harbour Authority 272
Gibsons Marina and Fuel Dock 272
Gig Harbor 84
Gig Harbor Marina and Boatyard 88
Gilford Island 334
Gillam Channel 371
Gillard Passage 317
Glen Cove 81
Glendale Cove 329
Glenthorne Passage 229
Goat Cove 436
Goat Island Anchorage 341
God's Pocket 359
Gods Pocket 383
God's Pocket Resort 359
Goldstream Boathouse 233
Goldstream Harbour 414
Goletas Channel 359
Good Hope Cannery 409
Goose Bay 408
Goose Bay Cannery Dock 408
Gordon Cove 452
Gorge Harbour 300
Gorge Harbour Marina Resort 300
Gorge Harbour Public Dock 300
Gosse Bay 423

Gossip Island 202
Gowlland Harbour 306
Grace Harbour 292
Graham Island 450
Graham Reach & Fraser Reach 437
Granite Bay 311
Granite Falls 269
Granite Point 311
Grant Anchorage 433
Granville Island Boat Yard 265
Granville Market 263
Grappler Inlet 393
Grappler Sound 338
Grays Cove 454
Greater Victoria Harbour Authority - GVHA 208
Grebe Cove 341
Green Bay 279
Green Island Anchorage 413
Greene Point Rapids 320
Greenway Sound 336
Greenway Sound Marine Resort 337
Grenville Channel 440
Grief Point 285
Griffin Bay 184
Griffin Bay Park 184
Grindstone Harbor 196
Grocery & Shopping 190
Growler Cove 344
Guemes Channel 158
Guemes Island 158
Guise Bay 362
Gulf Islands National Park Reserve 204
Gunboat Bay 278
Gunboat Passage 423
Gunner Inlet 384
Guthrie Bay 196
Gwaii Haanas National Reserve Park 453

H

H.C. Henry Marina 105
Haida Gwaii Fuels 451
Haida Heritage Centre 447
Haithayim Provincial Marine Park (Von Donop) 301
Hakai Beach Institute 413
Hakai Luxvbalis Conservancy Area 413
Hakai Passage 414
Hale Passage 82
Halfmoon Bay 274
Halkett Bay 270
Hammersley Inlet 78
Hammersley Inlet and Shelton 78
Handfield Bay 319
Hankin Cove 370
Hansen Bay 362
Hanson Island 344
Harbor Island Marina 100
Harbour Authority of Pender Harbor 278
Harbour Authority of Salt Spring Island 224, 226
Harbour Authority of Squamish Boat Harbour 271
Harbour Marina 116
Harbour Quay 391
Harbourside Lodge 394
Hardy Bay 354
Hardy Bay to Cape Scott 359
Hardy Island Marine Park 283
Harmony Islands Marine Park 283
Harper State Park 95
Harstine Island 79
Harstine Island State Park 80

Hartley Bay 438
Harwood Point Regional Park 258
Havannah Channel 327
Hawk Bay 439
Hayden Passage 382
Hayle Bay 335
Health Bay 341
Heather Civic Marina 265
Heelboom Bay 384
Helen Bay 339
Helmcken Island 322
Hemasila Inlet 408
Hemming Bay 319
Henderson Inlet 82
Henry Island 192
Herb Beck Marina 122
Herbert Inlet 383
Heriot Bay 304
Heriot Bay Inn & Marina 305
Heriot Bay Public Wharf 305
Hernando Island 287
Herring Bay 242
Herron Island 80
Hesquiat Harbour 378
Hevenor Inlet 435
Hicks Bay 182
Hidden Basin 282
Hidden Cove 115
Hiekish Narrows 437
Higgins Passage 433
Hiking 190
Hill Island 301
Hilton Harbor Marina 164
Hiram Chittenden Locks 101
Hisnit Inlet 377
Hjorth Bay 301
Hoeya Sound 329
Holberg Inlet 365
Hole in the Wall 303
Holmes Harbor 143
Holmes Inlet Nook 381
Home Bay 406
Homeland Security 63
Homeport Marina 106
Homfray Channel 296
Homfray Lodge 296
Honeymoon Bay 143
Hood Canal Floating Bridge 118
Hood Canal Marina 122
Hood Head 118
Hoodsport 122
Hootla-Kootla Bay 381
Hope Bay Public Wharf 221
Hope Island 145
Hope Island Marine State Park 78
Hopetown Passage 338
Hornby Island 252
Horsefly Cove 437
Horsehead Bay 82
Horseshoe Bay 269
Horseshoe Bay Public Wharf 269
Horton Bay 222
Hoskyn Channel 301
Hospital Bay 276
Hospital Bay Public Wharf 277
Hot Springs Cove 379
Hotham Sound 283
Hotspring Island 453
How to Cruise the Pacific Northwest 11-17

INDEX

Howe Sound 269
Hoy Bay 338
Hoya Bay 453
Hoya Passage 453
Huckleberry Island 150
Hughes Bay 180
Humchitt Island 417
Hunter Bay 178
Hurricane anchorage 416
Hylebos Waterway 94

I

Iceberg Island 180
Ikeda Cove 454
Illahee Marine State Park 112
Illahie Inlet 411
Inati Bay 164
Indian Arm 268
Indian Arm Marine Park 268
Indian Cove 182
Indianola 114
Inner Boat Basin 247
Inner Port Madison 115
Interpreting Northwest Weather 56-59
Ire Inlet 435
Irish Bay 221
Iroquois Passage 214
Irvines Landing Marina & Pub 276
Isabella Island 224
Island Cove 384
Island West resort 389
Islands Marine Center 179
Island's West Coast 338
Isle-de-Lis at Rum Island 211

J

Jack's Boatyard (Finn Cove) 288
Jackson Passage 429
James Bay (Gulf Islands) 229
James Bay (Northern BC) 429
James Island Marine State Park 177
Jamieson Point Anchorage 433
Jane Bay/Franks Bay 390
Jane Cove 420
Jarrell Cove 79
Jarrell Cove Marine State Park 79
Jarrell's Cove Marina 79
Jedediah Island 258
Jennis Bay 339
Jennis Bay Marina 339
Jenny Inlet 425
Jerisich Dock 88
Jervis Inlet 281, 283
Jetty Island 141
Joe Cove 340
Joemma Beach State Park 80
Joe's Bay 411
John Henry's 277
John Passage 214
John Wayne Marina 168
Johnny's Dock 94
Johns Pass 202
Johnson Point 82
Johnson Street Float-GVHA 209
Johnston Bay 408
Johnstone Strait 321
Jones Cove 405

Jones Island Marine State Park 192
Jones Marine Services Ltd 237
Joseph Whidbey State Park 137
Juan Jose Perez Hernandez 452
Julian Cove 363

K

Kakushdish Harbour 423
Kamils Anchorage 370
Kanish Bay 311
Kayak Point County Park 141
Kayaking & Whale Watching 190
Kelsey Bay 322
Kenary Cove 243
Kenmore 105
Kenmore Air Tour 98
Kennedy Cove 384
Kenneth Passage 338
Kent Inlet 433
Ketchikan 462
Ketchikan Yacht Club 466
Ketron Island 82
Keyport 113
Khutze Inlet 437
Khutzeymateen Sanctuary 445
Kiket Island 145
Kildidt Narrows 415
Kildidt Sound 415
Kilisut Harbor 131
Kiln Bay 434
Kiltik Cove 417
Kingcome Inlet 336
Kingston 126
Kinnaird Island 338
Kirkland 106
Kisameet Bay 417
Kitasu 433
Kitimat 438
Kitkatla 436
Kitsap Memorial Marine State Park 118
Klaoitsis Island 342
Klaskino Inlet 365
Klaskish Inlet 366
Klemtu 430
Klewnuggit Inlet 440
Kliktsoatli Harbour 421
Knight Inlet 329
Knox Bay 321
Koeye River 417
Kohl Island Anchorage 433
Kooryet Bay 435
Kopachuck Marine State Park 81
Koprino Harbour 363
Koskimo Bay 363
Koskimo Islands 363
Kukutali Preserve 145
Kumealon Island/Kumealon Inlet 441
Kumlah Island Anchorage 330
Kwakshua Channel 413
Kwakume Inlet 416
Kwatna Inlet 423
Kwatsi Bay 330
Kwatsi Bay Marina 331
Kwinitsa Railway Museum 445
Kxngeal Inlet 440
Kynoch Inlet 429
Kynumpt Harbour 427
Kyuquot Sound 368

Kyuquot Sound to Esperanza Inlet 371

L

La Conner 149
La Conner Landing Marine Services 150
La Conner Marina 150
Labouchere Channel 425
Lacy Falls 331
Ladner 261
Ladner Yacht Club 262
Ladysmith 239
Ladysmith Community Marina 239
Ladysmith Fisherman's Wharf 239
Ladysmith Harbour 238
Ladysmith Marina 239
Lagoon Cove 329
Lagoon Cove Marina 329
Lake Union 104
Lake Washington 105
Lake Washington Ship Canal 100
Lakebay 81
Lakebay Marina & Resort 81
Lakewood Moorage 109
Lama Passage 420
Lancelot Inlet 293
Langara Island 451
Langley 142
Langley Boat Harbor 142
Langus Waterfront Park 141
Laredo Channel 433
Laredo Inlet 433
Larrabee State Park 159
Larsen Harbour 436
Lasqueti Island 257
Laura Bay 335
Laura Cove 296
Lawson Harbour/Kelp Passage 441
Lemmens Inlet 357, 383
Lemmens Northwest Cove 383
Leone Island 341
Lewall Inlet 414
Lewis Channel 298
Liberty Bay 113
Lieber Haven Resort 197
Lighthouse Marine County Park 166
Lighthouse Pub & Marina 281
Lime Kiln Point 192
Lime Kiln Point State Park 185
Lime Point Cove 437
Limestone Bay 393
Lincoln Channel 460
Lions Bay Marine Ltd 271
Little Bull Passage 258
Little Nimmo Bay 338
Little Patos 198
Little River 257
Lizzie Cove 420
Locator Maps 4, 5
Lohbrunner Island 433
Long Harbour 229
Long Point Cove 418
Longbranch Improvement Club Marina 80
Lopez Island 177
Lopez Islander Resort & Marina 180
Lopez Pass 177
Lopez Sound 178
Loughborough Inlet 320
Louise Narrows 452

2018 Waggoner Cruising Guide

471

INDEX

Louscoone Inlet 454
Lowe Inlet (Verney Falls) 440
Lower Rapids 304
Lucky Creek 390
Lummi Island 164
Lummi Island Recreation Site 164
Lund 287
Lund Automotive & Outboard Ltd 288
Lund Hotel 288
Lund Small Craft Harbour 288
Lund Water Taxi 288
Luther Burbank Park 108
Lyall Harbour 221
Lyall Harbour Public Wharf 221
Lynnwood Marina 268

M

Mabbott Island 363
Mackaye Harbor 180
Mackenzie Sound 338
Madeira Marina 278
Madeira Park Public Wharf 278
Madiera Park 278
Mahatta Creek 363
Main Arm 260
Mainland Route 399
Maintaining Your Boat Like a Pro 36, 37
Makah Marina 171
Malaspina Inlet 292
Malaspina Strait 285
Malcolm Island Lions Harbour Authority 351
Malibu Rapids 284
Manchester State Park 109
Mansons Landing 300
Mansons Landing Marine Park 300
Mantrap Inlet 410
Manzanita Bay 113
Maple Bay 234
Maple Bay Marina 235
Maple Bay Public Wharf 235
Marble Cove 393
Margaret Bay 405
Marina Mart 105
Marina Park 106
Marine Servicenter 158
Marktosis 383
Marvin Islands 433
Mary Cove 436
Massacre Bay Rocks 195
Masset 450
Masset Sound 451
Matia Island 199
Matilda Inlet 382
Matilpi 327
Matlset Narrows 383
Mats Mats Bay 130
Mattson's Bay Marine 114
Maury Island Marine Park 96
Mayne Passage (Blind Channel) 320
Mayo Cove 81
McArdle Bay 180
Mcbride Bay 405
Mcintosh Bay 335
McKay Bay Lodge 394
Mclane Cove 79
Mcmicken Island Marine State Park 80
Mcmicking Inlet 434
Meay Inlet 414
Melanie Cove 296

Menzies Bay 310
Mesachie Nose 425
Metcalf Island 304
Meydenbauer Bay 108
Meyers Passage 433
Middle Arm Fraser River 262
Milbanke Sound 428
Miles Inlet 402
Mill Bay 233
Mill Bay Community Wharf 233
Mill Bay Marina 233
Millbrook Cove 406
Miller Bay 114
Mills Landing & Marina 247
Miners Bay 223
Mink Island 293
Minstrel Island Resort 328
Mistaken Island 252
Mitchell Bay (North Vancouver) 352
Mitchell Bay (San Juans) 192
Mitlenatch Island 287
MK Bay 209
Mk Bay Marina 438
Moffatt Islands 459
MOHI Docks 105
Monckton Inlet 435
Monday Anchorage 340
Monks' Wall 343
Montague 229
Montague Harbour 229
Montague Harbour Marina 230
Montague Harbour Marine Park 230
Montague Harbour Public Wharf 230
Montlake Bridge 105
Montlake Cut 105
Morehouse Bay 426
Moresby Camp 452
Morgan's Landing Retreat 317
Morrison's North Star Marine 104
Mosquito Creek Marina 268
Mosquito Harbour 384
Mosquito Pass 191
Mound Island 342
Mount Gardner Park Public Dock 270
Moutcha Bay resort 377
Mowgli Island 241
Mud Bay 178
Mudge Boatworks 305
Muirhead Islands 339
Mukilteo 138
Murden Cove 115
Murray Labyrinth 402
Museum Of Glass 92
Museum Of Northern British Columbia 445
Musgrave Landing 234
Mystery Bay Marine State Park 133

N

Nahwitti Bar 360
Nahwitti Bar Inner Route 360
Nakwakto Rapids 403
Nalau Passage 415
Namu 417
Nanaimo 246
Nanaimo Bastion 247
Nanaimo Museum 247
Nanaimo Port Authority 247
Nanoose Harbour 251
Narrows Inlet 281

Narrows Marina 83
Narvaez Bay 222
Nascall Bay 425
Nash Narrows Cove 427
Nash Passage 427
Native Anchorage 342
Nautical Landing Marina 105
Naval Base Kitsap (Bangor) 120
Neah Bay 170
Neekas Cove 427
Nepah Lagoon 338
Neroutsos Inlet 364
Nettle Island 392
New Bella Bella 421
New Vancouver 342
New Westminster 262
Newcastle Island 247
Newcastle Island Marine Park 248
Newcombe Harbour 435
Newport Shores 108
Newton Cove Resort 373
Nimmo Bay Wilderness Resort 339
Nisqually 82
Nisqually Reach 82
Nitinat Narrows 395
Nodales Channel 319
Nootka Light Station 378
Nootka Sound 377
Nootka Sound Resort 377
Nootka Sound to Hot Springs Cove 357
North Arm Fraser River 262
North Arm Transportation 450
North Bentinck Arm 423
North Cove 241
North Galiano 242
North Harbour 363
North Island Marina 353
North Lake Marina 105
North Pacific Cannery 445
North Pacific Cannery Dock 442
North Saanich Marina 214
Northeast Puget Sound 137, 143
Northpoint Landing 76
Northumberland Channel 245
Northwest Fuels Ltd 445
Northwest Mcconnell Rock 192
Nuchatlitz Inlet 371
Nuchatlitz Provincial Park 371
Nuttal Bay 252

O

Oak Bay 130
Oak Bay 210
Oak Bay County Park 130
Oak Bay Marina 210
Oak Harbor 143
Oak Harbor Marina 143
Oakland Bay 78
Oakland Bay Marina (Port of Shelton) 78
Oatwish Bay 429
O'brien Bay 335
Obstruction 382
Obstruction Pass 181
Obstruction Pass State Park 197
Ocean Falls (Cousins Inlet) 418
Ocean Falls Small Craft Harbour 418
Oceanfront Suites at Cowichan Bay 234
Octopus Islands Marine Park 303
Odlin Park 180

INDEX

Okeover Harbour Authority 292
Okisollo Channel 302
Old Town Dock 89
Oleo's 318
Olga 197
Oliver Cove 428
Olson's Resort 170
Olympia 74
Oona River 441
Open Bight 406
Orcas Island 193
Orcas Landing 195
Oro Bay 80
Oscar Passage 429
Osment Inlet 433
Ostrich Bay 111
Otter Bay 220
Otter Bay Marina 220
Otter Channel 434
Otter Island 295
Outer Islands 392
Outpost at Winter Harbour, Grant Sales Ltd. 363
Outside Route to Princess Royal Island
      & Pitt Island 432
Overflow Basin 338
Owen Bay 304
Oyster Bay (Puget Sound) 111
Oyster Bay (Northern B.C. Coast) 410
Oyster River 257

P ☐

Pacific Boulevard Marina 266
Pacific Gateway Marina 395
Pacific Playgrounds Resort & Marina 257
Padilla 146
Padilla Bay 150
Page Passage 214
Page Point Marina Inc 239
Page's Resort & Marina 244
Painted Boat Resort Spa & Marina 279
Palmer Anchorage 433
Pamphlet Cove 363
Panther Point 242
Parks Bay 182
Parksville 252
Parson's Anchorage 433
Patos Island 201
Patricia Bay 232
Patterson Inlet/princess Diana Cove 435
Peale Passage 78
Pearse Islands
      (Cormorant Channel Marine Park) 347
Peavine Pass 181
Pedder Bay 396
Pedder Bay Marina 396
Pelican Bay Marina 265
Pelican Beach Recreation Site 159
Pelindaba Lavender Farms 186
Pender Canal 218
Pender Harbour 275
Pender Harbour Hotel & Grasshopper 278
Pender Harbour Resort and Marina 276
Pendrell Sound 296
Peninsula Yacht Basin 88
Penn Cove 143
Penn Harbour 434
Penrose Bay 292
Penrose Point Marine State Park 81
Perceval Narrows 428

Percival Landing Park 76
Peter Cove 218
Petrel Channel 435
Petro Marine Services 465
Petro-Canada Coastal Mountain Fuels 248
Petroglyph Cove (Blue Lips Cove) 370
Petroglyph Provincial Park 247
Philip Inlet 410
Phillips Arm 319
Phinney Bay 111
Pickering Passage 78
Picnic Cove 184
Pier 66 and Pier 67 Marina 234
Pier 73 Marina & Yacht Club 262
Pierce Bay 410
Pierre's Echo Bay - The Cliffside 333
Pierre's Echo Bay Lodge & Marina 333
Piers Island Public Wharf 216
Pillar Point 170
Pillsbury Cove 445
Pilot Bay 246
Pine Island Route 398
Pinkerton Islands 390
Pipestem Inlet 390
Pirates Cove 242
Pirates Cove Marine Park 242
Pitt Passage 81
Pleasant Harbor 122
Pleasant Harbor Marina 122
Pleasant Harbor Marine State Park 122
Plumper Bay 310
Plumper Cove Marine Park 271
Poets Cove Marina 218
Poett Nook Marina & Campground 393
Point Atkinson to Horseshoe Bay 269
Point Defiance 88
Point Defiance Boathouse Marina 88
Point Grey 263
Point Hudson 134
Point Hudson Marina & RV Park 134
Point No Point 128
Point Roberts 165
Point Roberts Marina Resort 165
Point Robinson 96
Point Wilson 135
Poise Cove Marina 281
Poison Cove 429
Pole Pass 194
Polkinghorne Islands 340
Porlier Pass 242
Porpoise Bay Government Wharf 281
Porpoise Harbour 441
Port Alberni 391
Port Alberni yacht Club 393
Port Alexander 359
Port Alice 364
Port Alice Yacht Club 364
Port Angeles 168
Port Angeles Boat Haven 170
Port Angeles City Pier 170
Port Blackney 428
Port Browning 218
Port Browning Marina 219
Port Clements 451
Port Clements Small Craft Harbour 451
Port DeSire 393
Port Elizabeth 330
Port Gamble 118
Port Gardner Landing 140
Port Graves 270

Port Hadlock and Irondale 131
Port Hadlock Marina 131
Port Hardy 354
Port Hardy Harbour Authority 355
Port Harvey 327
Port Harvey Marine Resort 327
Port Interpretive Centre 445
Port Ludlow 128
Port Ludlow Resort and Marina 128
Port Madison 114
Port McNeill 352
Port McNeill Harbour 352
Port Moody 268
Port Neville 322
Port of Allyn Hood Canal 124
Port of Anacortes 156
Port of Bellingham 161
Port of Brownsville 112
Port of Edmonds 137
Port of Everett Marina 140
Port of Friday Harbor 186
Port of Friday Harbor Fuel Pier 189
Port of Hoodsport 122
Port of Keyport Marina 113
Port of Kingston 126
Port of Manchester 109
Port of Olympia 74
Port of Port Townsend Boat Haven 134
Port of Poulsbo 114
Port of Shelton 78
Port of Silverdale 111
Port of South Whidbey/Langley Boat Harbor 142
Port Orchard 109
Port Orchard Marina 109
Port Plaza Dock 76
Port Renfrew Community Dock 395
Port San Juan 395
Port Sidney Marina 213
Port Simpson 460
Port Susan 141
Port Townsend 133
Port Townsend Boat Haven Marina & Boat Yard 133
Port Townsend Canal 130
Port Washington Public Wharf 221
Portage Bay 105
Porteau Cove 271
Portland Inlet & Tongass Passage Route 460
Portland Island 216
Portside Marina 232
Posey Island Marine State Park 191
Possession Sound 138
Potable Water, Can I Drink It? 55
Potlatch Marine State Park 122
Potts Lagoon 342
Poulsbo 113
Poulsbo Marina 113
Powell River 285
Preedy Harbour 240
Prevost Harbor 202
Prevost Island 229
Prideaux Haven 295
Prince Rupert 442
Prince Rupert Rowing and Yacht Club 444
Princesa Channel 376
Princess Cove 242
Princess Louisa Inlet 284
Princess Louisa Society 284
Princess Royal Island 433
Provisioning Your Boat for a Well Fed
      and Happy Crew 52-54

2018 Waggoner Cruising Guide

INDEX

Pruth Bay 413
Pulteney Point to Jeanette Islands Route 398
Pylades Island 242
Pym Rocks 333

Q

Qlawdzeet Anchorage 441
Quadra Island, South 304
Quait Bay 383
Quarry Bay 281
Quartcha Bay 426
Quarterdeck Inn & Marina Resort 355
Quartermaster Harbor 95
Quartermaster Marina 95
Quartz Bay 301
Quathiaski Cove 306
Quathiaski Cove Public Wharf 306
Quatsino First Nations dock 365
Quatsino Narrows 364
Quatsino Sound 362
Quatsino Village 365
Quayside Marina 265
Queen Charlotte 451
Queen Charlotte Harbour Authority 451
Queen Charlotte Strait 346
Queen Cove 373
Quigley Creek Cove 433
Quilcene Bay 122

R

Raft Island 81
Rainier Beach 109
Ramsay Passage Cove 454
Raymond Passage 427
Reach Island 79
Read Island 301
Reads Bay 177
Reads Bay Island 177
Rebecca Spit Provincial Park 305
Redonda Bay 301
Redondo 95
Reed Point Marina 268
Refuge Cove (Desolation Sound) 298
Refuge Cove (Haida Gwaii) 450
Refuge Cove General Store 298
Refuge Island 390
Reid Bay 335
Reid Harbor 202
Reid Passage 428
Rendezvous Islands 301
Rescue Bay 429
Resolution Cove 377
Retreat Cove 242
Retreat Passage 341
Rich Passage 109
Richmond Chevron 262
Riley Cove 381
Ripley Bay 426
Rivers Inlet 406
Robbers Passage 393
Roberts Bay 211
Robson Bight 322
Roche Harbor 190
Roche Harbor Marina 190
Roche Harbor Mausoleum 186
Rock Bay Marine Park (Otter Cove) 311
Rock Inlet 417
Rocky Bay (San Juans) 189
Rocky Bay (South Sound) 80

Rocky Point 145
Roesland/Roe Lake 220
Roffey Island 296
Rolfe Cove 199
Rolling Roadstead
    (Catala Island Provincial Park) 371
Rosario Resort & Spa 196
Roscoe Bay/Roscoe Bay Marine Park 296
Roscoe Inlet 426
Rose Harbour 454
Rosedale 81
Royal Reach Marina & Hotel 281
Ruckle Park 224
Rugged Point Marine Park 370
Rumble Beach Marina 364
Rupert Inlet 365
Rushbrooke Floats Small Craft Harbour 445
Russell Island 223
Ruston 89
Ruxton Island 242

S

Saanich 213
Saanich Inlet 231
Sac Bay 453
Saddlebag Island Marine State Park 150
Safety Cove 413
Saint Edward State Park 106
Salmon Bay (Puget Sound) 102
Salmon Bay (Northern B.C. Coast) 429
Salmon Bay Marina 102
Salmon Bay Marine Center 102
Salmon Inlet 281
Salmon Point Resort 257
Salsbury Point County Park 118
Salt Spring Island 234
Salt Spring Island Cheese Company 226
Salt Spring Island Community 224
Salt Spring Island Saturday Market 226
Saltery Bay 283
Saltery Bay Provincial Park 283
Saltery Bay Public Wharf 283
Saltspring Marina 228
Saltwater Marine State Park 95
San Josef Bay 362
San Juan County Park 192
San Juan Island 184
Sand Heads 260
Sand Point 105
Sandell Bay 409
Sandspit 452
Sandspit Harbour 452
Sandspit Harbour Fuel Dock 452
Sandwell Park 246
Sandy Island Marine Provincial Park 255
Sandy Point 164
Sansum Narrows 234
Santa Gertrudis Cove 377
Sarah Point 285, 292
Saratoga Passage 141
Sargeaunt Passage 330
Satellite Island East Cove 202
Saturna Island Family Estate 221
Saturna Point Store & Fuel 222
Savary Island 287
Saxman Native Village and Totem Bight 466
Saycuritay Cove 434
Scenic Beach State Park 120
Schooner Channel 403

Schooner Cove 251
Schooner Pass 409
Schooner Reef 252
Scott Cove 331
Sea Otter Cove 362
Sea Otter Inlet 417
Seabeck Bay 120
Seabreeze Cove 341
Seafest 445
Seaforth Channel 426
Seagate T-Floats
    (Port Hardy Harbour Authority) 355
Seascape Waterfront Resort 307
Seattle 97
Seattle Aquarium 97
Seattle Boat-Newport 108
Sechelt Inlet 279-280
Sechelt Rapids 281
Second Narrows 268
Secret Cove 275
Secret Cove Marina 275
Secret Cove Public Wharf 275
Secretary Islands 241
Sekiu 170
Selby Cove 229
Selma Park 272
Semiahmoo Marina 165
Sequim Bay 168
Sequim Bay Marine State Park 168
Serpent Group 415
Seward Park 109
Sewell's Marina Ltd 269
Seymour Narrows 310
SGang Gwaay 454
Shack Bay 426
Shallow Bay 199
Shark Creek 382
Sharpe Cove 149
Sharpe's Landing 289
Shaw General Store 182
Shaw Island 181
Shaw Ocean Discovery Centre in Sidney 211
Shawl Bay & Moore Bay 335
Shawl Bay Marina 335
Shearwater 421
Shearwater Resort & Marina 421
Shelter Bay Marina 149
Shelter Inlet 382
Shelter Island Marina Inc 262
Shelter Sheds 367
Shelton 78
Shilshole Bay 100
Shilshole Bay Fuel Dock 100
Shilshole Bay Marina 100
Shine Tidelands State Park 118
Shingle Bay 220
Ship Canal 100
Ship Point Floats - GVHA 208
Shoal 116
Shoal Bay (San Juans) 179
Shoal Bay (Discovery Passage) 319
Shoal Bay Pub 319
Shoal Channel (The Gap) 271
Shoal Harbour 333
Shushartie Bay 360
Sibell 239
Sidney 211
Sidney Bay 320
Sidney Beacon Ave. Public Wharf 213
Sidney Spit 210

INDEX

Silva Bay 244
Silva Bay Resort & Marina 244
Silva Bay Shipyard 245
Silverdale 109
Silverdale Marina (Port of Silverdale) 111
Similk Bay 145
Simoom Sound 335
Sinclair and Eliza Islands 159
Sinclair Inlet 111
Sir Alexander Mackenzie Rock 425
Sir Edmund Bay 335
Skagit Bay 145-146
Skagit Cycle 156
Skagit Island 145
Skedans Bay 453
Skidegate 451
Skidegate Channel 451
Skookumchuck 279
Skull Cove 402
Skull Island 195
Skyline Marina 158
Skyline Marina 262
Slingsby Channel 403
Slo-cat Harbour 276
Small Inlet 311
Smelt Bay Provincial Park 300
Smith Cove 364
Smith Sound 405
Smuggler Cove 274
Smuggler's Villa Resort 198
Snohomish River Delta 141
Snoring Bay 200
Snow Creek Resort 172
Snug Cove 270
Snug Cove Public Wharf 270
Snug Harbor Resort 192
Sointula 351
Sooke And Becher Bay 395
Sooke Harbour 395
Sooke Harbour Authority 396
Sooke Harbour Resort & Marina 395
South Arm Fraser River 260
South Bentinck Arm 423
South Whidbey State Park 137
Southeast Alaska Discovery Center 466
Southeast Cove 390
Southey Bay 241
Southgate Group 402
Souvenir Passage 411
Spanish Bank 263
Spencer Spit Marine State Park 178
Spicer Islands 436
Spider Island Area 415-416
Spiller Channel 427
Spiller Inlet 427
Spitfire Channel 416
Spitfire North Anchorage 416
Spitfire West Anchorage 416
Spring Island 236
Squalicum Harbor/Port of Bellingham 161
Squamish 271
Squamish Harbor 118
Squirrel Cove 299
Squirrel Cove Public Wharf 299
Squirrel Cove Store 299
Squirrel Cove Trading Co. Ltd 299
Squitty Bay 258
St. John Harbour 428
St. Roch Dock 267

St. Vincent Bay 283
Stanley Park 263, 266
State and Provincial 64
Steamboat Bay 338
Steamer Cove 381
Steep Island Lodge 306
Steilacoom 83
Steps dock 389
Steveston 261
Steveston Chevron 261
Steveston Harbour 261
Steveston Harbour Authority Wharf 261
Stones Marina 248
Stopper Islands 390
Strathcona 268
Strawberry Island State Park 159
Stretch Island 79
Stretch Point Marine State Park 79
Stuart Channel 236
Stuart Island 201
Stuart Island Community Dock 314
Stuart Narrows 339
Studio Tour 226
Sturdies Bay 223
Sturt Bay 258
Subtle Islands 300
Sucia Island 199
Sullivan Bay Marina Resort 337
Sulphur Passage 382
Summer weather pattern 172
Summertide Resort & Marina 124
Sunday Harbour 340
Sunderland Channel 321
Sunny Shores Resort & Marina 396
Sunrise Motel & Resort 122
Sunset Marina Ltd 269
Sunshine Bay 410
Sunshine Coast Resort & Marina 278
Suquamish 114
Surf Inlet 434
Surge Narrows & Beazley Passage 303
Surge Narrows 302
Surprise Island 370
Sutil Point 300
Sutlej Channel 336
Swanson Bay 437
Swantown Marina 77
Swartz Bay Public Wharf 216
Swifts Bay 178
Swinomish Channel 146
Sydney Inlet 380
Sydney Inlet Unnamed Cove 380
Sylvan Cove 177

T ||

Table Island 405
Tacoma Area 88
Tacoma Art Museum 92
Tacoma Fuel Dock 94
Tacoma Narrows 83
Tahsis 375
Tahsis Inlet 375
Tahsis Narrows 375
Taku Resort & Marina 305
Talbot Cove 299
Tallheo Hot Springs 423
Tangent Island 435
Tanglewood Island 82
Tanu Island 453

Taylor Bay 408
Taylor Bay 80
Teakerne Arm 298
Telegraph Cove 346
Telegraph Cove Marina 347
Telegraph Cove Resort 347
Telegraph Harbour 240
Telegraph Harbour Marina 240
Telescope Passage 283
Tenedos Bay 293
Tent Island 240
Texada Island 258
Thatcher Pass 177
The Blow Hole 329
The Cut 241
The Fish'n' Hole 134
The Narrows 82
The Pilothouse Marina 278
The Trap 418
The Whale Museum 185
Thea Foss Waterway 89
Theodosia Inlet 293
Thetis Island Marina 240
Thistle Passage 433
Thomas Basin 465
Thompson Bay 427
Thompson Sound 330
Thornbrough Bay 271
Thorndyke Bay 118
Thrasher Rock Light 243
Thunder Bay 283
Thunderbird Marina 269
Thurston Bay Marine Park 319
Thurston Harbour 453
Tidal Current Turbine Generator 320
Timeline of Northwest Explorers 8
Titlow Park 84
Toba Inlet 297
Toba Wilderness Marina 297
Tod Inlet 233
Tofino 357, 384
Tofino Harbour Authority 4th Street 385
Tofino Harbour Authority Crab Dock 386
Tofino Inlet 384
Tofino Resort & Marina 386
Tolmie Marine State Park 82
Tom Bay 428
Tongass Historical Museum 466
Tongass Trading Company 466
Topaze Harbour 321
Toquaht Bay Marina 390
Totten Inlet 78
Tracey Harbour 340
Trail Bay 272
Tramp Harbor 96
Tranquilito Cove 384
Treadwell Bay 403
Trevenen Bay 292
Tribune Bay 252
Tribune Channel 330
Trinka Rock 195
Triton Cove State Park 122
Triton Head 122
Troup Narrows 426
Troup Passage 426
Tsakonu Cove 329
Tsehum Harbour 213
Tsehum Harbour Public Wharf 214
Tsowwin Narrows 375
Tugboat Passage 318

INDEX

Tulalip Bay 138
Tulalip Casino Resort 140
Tumbo Island 222
Tuno Creek Anchorage 428
Turn Island 321
Turn Island State Park 184
Turnbull Cove 338
Turret Island 392
Turtle Bay 392
Twanoh Marine State Park 124
Twin Islands 300
Twin Islands and Racoon Island 268
Twin Rocks 197
Tyee 116
Tyee Marina 94
Tzartus Cove 393
Tzoonie Narrows Park 281

U

U.S. and Canadian Customs Information 20-24
Ucluelet 388
Ucluelet Small Craft Harbour 389
Uganda Passage 300
U'mista Cultural Centre 350
Union Bay 105
Union Passage 440
Union Steamship Co. Marina 270
Unnamed Island #119 184
Unnamed Island #3 (Reads Bay Island) 177
Unnamed Island #80 (Massacre Bay) 195
Unnamed Island #81 (Trinka Rock) 195
Upper Barkley Sound 390
Upper Rapids 303
Upright Channel Park 180
Useless Inlet 391

V

Van Isle Marina 213
Van Riper's Resort 170
Vananda/Sturt Bay Public Wharf 258
Vancouver Aquarium 263
Vancouver Boating Welcome Centre 264
Vancouver Harbour (North) 267
Vancouver Harbour (South) 266
Vancouver Marina 262
Vancouver Maritime Museum 263-264
Varney Bay 365
Vaughn Bay 80
Vendovi Island 159
Venn Passage to Metlakatla Bay 459
Verney Passage 438
Vernon Bay 391
Vessel Traffic System Radio Channels 66, 67
Vesuvius 235-236
VHF Channels for Pleasure Craft 70
VHF Radio Procedures 39-41
Victim Island 195
Victoria 207
Victoria Inner Harbour 208
Victoria International Marina 209
Victoria Mandatory Traffic Lanes 207
Victoria Marine Fuels Ltd 209
Village Bay 222
Village Island 342
Village Of Steveston 261
Village of Zeballos Municipal Wharf 375
Viner Sound 331
Volcanic Cove 370

Von Donop Inlet 301
Von Geldern Cove 81

W

W.E. Mills Landing & Marina 247
Waddington Bay 341
Waddington Channel 296
Wahkana Bay 331
Wahshihlas Bay 329
Waiatt Bay 303
Wakeman Sound 336
Wakes Cove 243
Waldron Island 201
Walker Hook 230
Wallace Island Marine Park 241
Walsh Cove Marine Park 297
Walters Cove 368
Walters Cove Resort 370
Ward Channel 414
Warrior Cove 417
Washington Narrows 111
Washington Park 158
Washington State Capital Museum 76
Washington State Capitol 76
Washington State History Museum 92
Wasp Islands 192
Waterfall Inlet 411
Waterfront Suites & Marina 248
Watmough Bay 180
Watson Cove 331
Watts Narrows 441
We Are All Explorers 7
Weewanie Hot Springs 438
Weinburg Inlet 434
Welbourn Cove 278
Welcome Harbour 436
Welcome Passage 274
Wellbore Channel 321
Wells Passage 340
Wells Passage to Blunden Harbour 402
West Bamfield Public dock 394
West Bay 270
West Bay Marina 77
West Beach Resort 201
West Coast Wilderness Lodge 280
West Marina Place 98
West Side of Pitt Island 434
West Side of Princess Royal Island 433
West Side of Swindle Island 433
West Sound 194
West Sound Marina 194
West Waterway 99
West Whidbey Island 137
West Whitepine Cove 383
Westbay Marina 210
Westcott 192
Westcott Bay 191
Westcott Bay Shellfish Co 191
Western Barkley Sound 390
Westminster 260
Westminster Street 285
Westport Marina 214
Westview Fuels 287
Westview Harbour 286
Westview Marina & Lodge 375
Westview/Powell River 285
Whaleboat Island 242
Whaleboat Island Marine Park 242
Whaler Bay 223

Whaler Bay Public Wharf 223
Whaletown 300
Wharf Street Floats - GVHA 209
What Recreational Boaters
   Need to Know About VTS 65
What's New in the 2018 Waggoner Cruising Guide?
Whirlpool Rapids 321
Whiskey Golf 250
Whiskey Landing 389
Whiskey Slough Public Wharf 279
White Rock 260
White Rock to Vancouver 260
Whiterock Passage 301
Wigham Cove 426
Wigwam Inn 269
Windy Bay 384
Windy Bay 429
Windy Bay 454
Winslow Wharf Marina 115
Winter Cove 221
Winter Harbour 357, 363
Winter Harbour Authority 363
Wollochet Bay 82
Wooden Boat Building 131
Woods Bay 338
Work Bay 437
Wouwer Island 393
Wright Sound 438

Y

Yaculta 305
Yaculta Public Dock 305
Yaletown 264
Yarrow Bay Marina 108
Yellow Island 192
Yorke Island 322
Young Bay 380
Yuculta Rapids 314
Yukon Harbor 96

Z

Zeballos 373
Zeballos Fuel dock Inc 375
Zeballos Small Craft Harbour 375
Zittel's Marina 75
Zittel's Marina Inc 82

ADVERTISER INDEX

49th Parallel Grocery and Café 238

A

AAA Yachtfinders 11
Ace Hardware Anacortes and
    Friday Harbor 152, 188
Achilles Inflatables 23
Alaska Boat Brokers 32
Alaska Eagle Arts 464
Alaska Fish House 462, 464
Alert Bay Visitor Centre 348
Alexander Marine Inside, Front Cover
Alfred's 93
All Bay Marine Ltd. 211
All Things Marine Thrift Store 217
ALT Insurance Group 152
American Tug 2
Anacortes Brewery 152
Anacortes Chamber of Commerce 155
Anacortes Marine Electronics 152, 156
Anacortes Marine Insurance 152
Anacortes Rigging & Yacht Services 152
Anacortes Yacht Charters 24
Anthony's at Cap Sante Marina 152
Anthony's at Gig Harbor 85, 88
Anthony's at Point Defiance 88
Anthony's at Sinclair Inlet 111
Anthony's at Squalicum 163
Anthony's Beach Café - Edmonds 138
Anthony's Cabana - Anacortes 156
Anthony's Chinook's - Salmon Bay 104
Anthony's Hearthfire Grill - Bellingham 161, 163
Anthony's Hearthfire Grill - Olympia 77
Anthony's Home Port - Anacortes 156
Anthony's Home Port - Bellingham 161
Anthony's Home Port - Des Moines 96
Anthony's Home Port - Edmonds 138
Anthony's Home Port - Everett 139, 140
Anthony's Home Port - Kirkland 108
Anthony's Home Port - Olympia 76
Anthony's Pier 66 & Bell Street Diner 99
Anthony's Restaurants 53
Anthony's The Cabana 152
Anthony's Woodfire Grill - Everett 139, 140
Arabella's Landing 87
Aspen Power Catamarans 1

B

Backdoor Kitchen 188
Baranof Fishing Excursions 464
Bayside Marine and Dry Stack 139
Beach Gardens Resort & Marina 285
Bell Harbor Marina 99
Bellhaven Yacht Sales and Charters 163
Black Sheep Books 225
Blackline Marine Inc. 217
Blaine Harbor 164
Blind Channel Resort 321

Boat Insurance Agency 98
Book Nook, The 355
Bremerton Marina 111
Brown Latern Ale House, The 152
Butchart Gardens 10

C

Cafe Guido 355
Canoe Cove Marina & Boatyard 217
Cap Sante Inn 152
Cap Sante Marina 157
Cap Sante Marine 23, 151, 152
Captain's Supplies 27
Children's Museum of Tacoma 90, 93
Chinook's at Salmon Bay 104
Classic Marine Ltd 233
Coal Harbour Marina 267
Comox Valley Harbour Authority
    (Fisherman's Wharf) 256
Cow Bay Marina 444
Cowichan Bay Fisherman's Wharf Association 234
Crazy Wolf Studio 464
Crows Nest Yacht Sales 30
Cruisers College 17, 154
Cutwater Boats 480

D

Dawsons Landing General Store 409
Deer Harbor Marina 193
Delta Marine Service 212
Dent Island Lodge 317
Desolation Sound Yacht Charters 255
Devlin Designing Boat Builders 65
Devoted Kiss Café 85
Discovery Harbour Marina & Fuels 309
Doc's Marina Grill 131
Dock Street Marina 93
Dreamspeaker Series 44, 389

E

Eagle Eye Marine 225
Elevated Ice Cream & Candy Shop 132
Elliott Bay Marina 97, 98
Elsie Hulsizer - Glaciers Bears and Totems 40
Emerald Harbor Marine 98, 103
Everett Marina 138
Everett Yacht Service 139
Exploring Series Guidebooks 67

F

Fairwinds-Schooner Cove 254
False Creek Harbour Authority 262
Fine Edge Publishing 22, 44, 67
Fisheries Supply 45
Fisherman's Wharf
    (Campbell River Harbour Authority) 308
Fisherman's Wharf
    (Comox Valley Harbour Authority) 256

Fishermen's Terminal 106
Flagship Maritime Training 31
Foss Waterway Seaport 90, 93
Fountain Café, The 132
Fox & Hounds 238
Fresh Water Marina 307
Friday Harbor Marine 186

G

Garden Bay Hotel, Marina & Pub 277
Garmin 15
Gig Harbor Marina & Boatyard 84, 85
Gig Harbor, City of 83
Gourmet's Galley 188
Greater Victoria Harbour Authority 207

H

H2O 152
Harbor History Museum 85
Hasse & Company/Port Townsend Sails 131
Helsman Trawlers 42
Heritage Distilling 85

I

IGA (Madeira Park Pender Harbour) 280
Irwin Yacht Sales 16
Island Marine Instrument 13
Islands Marine Center 179
Ivar's Salmon House 108

J

J & G Marine Supply 92
Jarrell's Cove Marina 79
Jesperson Boat Builders 217
John Henry's Marina Inc. 276
JW Timber Company (Fresh Water Marina) 307

K

Kenmore Air 19
Kings Marine Center 185, 188

L

La Conner Brewing Company 148
La Conner Chamber of Commerce 148
La Conner Channel Lodge & County Inn 148
La Conner Landing Fuel Dock 148
La Conner Marina 147
La Conner Maritime Service 13, 147, 148
Ladysmith Chamber of Commerce
    and Visitor Centre 238
Ladysmith Community Marina 238
Ladysmith Marina 238
Lagoon Cove Marina 328
Lavendera Massage 188
LeMay - America's Car Museum 90, 93
LFS Marine & Outdoor 160, 163
Li Read Sea to Sky Premier Properties 225
Lopez Islander Resort 180

2018 Waggoner Cruising Guide

ADVERTISER INDEX

M

M. Morgan Warren Studio 217
Madeira Marina 280
Malcolm Island Lions Harbour
    Authority/Sointula 351
Marine Thrift 132
Martin Marine 269
Method Marine Supply 385
Milltech Marine 110
Moby's Pub 223, 225
Monkey Fist Marine 98, 106
Montague Harbour Marina 230
Museum of Glass 90, 93
Museum of Nothwest Art 148

N

Nanaimo Port Authority 246
Nordhavn Yachts Northwest 51, 98
Nordic Yachts Northwest 38
North Harbor Diesel & Yacht Service 153, 154
North Harbor Yacht Brokers 154
North Island Boat Company 154, 159
North Island Marina 352
North Saanich Marina - OBMG 211
Northwest Maritime Center 130
Northwest Yachts 46
Northwest Yachtnet Brokerage 93
NW Explorations 36, 163

NW Explorations - Brokerage 35
NW Explorations - Chartering 34
NW Seaplanes 18
NW Yachts 46

O

Oak Bay Marina 209
Oak Bay Marine Group 204
Ocean Falls 418
Ocean Pacific Marine Store 310
Ocens 39
Olsson Mfg. Inc. 63
Otter Bay Marina 220
Outer Reef Yachts 25

P

Pacific Fiberglass 106
Pacific Pride of Alaska 464
Page's Resort & Marina 244
Palisade Restaurant 98
Parnassus Books and Gifts 464
Pedder Bay Marina - OBMG 396
Pharmasave Ladysmith 238
Philbrook's Boatyard 212
Pierre's Echo Bay Lodge & Marina 332
Pleasant Harbor Marina & Golf Resort 123
Poets Cove Resort & Spa 219
Point Hudson Marina and RV Park 134

Point Roberts Marina Resort 166
Port Angeles Boat Haven 169
Port Harvey Marine Resort 327
Port Ludlow Resort & Marina 129
Port McNeill Habour Authority 353
Port of Anacortes 157
Port of Bellingham- Blaine Harbor 164
Port of Bellingham-Squalicum Harbor 161
Port of Bremerton-Bremerton Marina 111
Port of Bremerton-Port Orchard Marina 110
Port of Edmonds 137
Port of Everett Marina 138
Port of Friday Harbor 187
Port of Kingston 126
Port of Olympia/Swantown Marina 77
Port of Port Angeles 169
Port of Port Townsend/Boat Haven 133
Port of Port Townsend/Point Hudson 134
Port of Seattle/Bell Harbor 99
Port of Seattle/Fishermen's Terminal 106
Port of Seattle/Shilshole Bay Marina 100
Port of Silverdale/Silverdale Marina 112
Port of Skagit/La Conner Marina 147
Port Orchard Marina 110
Port Sidney 209
Port Townsend's Boat Haven 133
Ports & Passes 351
Ports & Passes Skipper's Logbook 341

LOCAL KNOWLEDGE INDEX

Backeddy Marina - Dangerous Rocks 279
Backeddy Marina - Strong Currents 279
Bangor Naval Station - Restricted Area 118
Baronet Passage - Current Flow Directions 344
Baynes Sound - Cable Ferry Signal Lights 255
Bella Coola - Weather / Wind Tip 424
Blind Channel Resort - Strong Currents 320
Blind Island - Dangerous Rocks 181
Booker Lagoon - Uncharted Rock 340
Bremerton Marina - Strong Current 110
Brentwood Bay - Dangerous Rocks 232
Burke Channel - Ebb Current 423
Burke Channel - Tide-Rips 423
Cameleon Harbour - Dangerous Rock 319
Cape Mudge - Tide-Rips 305
Cattle Pass - Tide-Rips 172
Chatham Sound - Weather Tip 441
CHS Chart 3737 - Inaccurate Chart 433
Comox Bar - Navigation Tip 255
Contacting Coast Guard by Cell Phone 41
Dean Channel - Weather / Wind Tip 425
Deception Pass - Strong Currents 149
Deep Bay, Baynes Sound - Navigation Note 253
Dixon Entrance - Fishing Nets 459
Eagle Harbor - No Anchoring Zone 115
Emily Carr Inlet - Chartplotter Errors 434

First and Second Narrows - Strong Currents 266
Fisherman Bay - Entry Shoal 179
Foss Waterway - Strong Current 89
Ganges Harbour - Safe Entrance Channel 224
Ganges Harbour - Two Dangerous Rocks 228
Gig Harbor - Speed Limit 84
Grenville Channel - Strong Currents 439
Gunboat Passage - Navigation Notes 423
Hood Canal Bridge - Rocks 118
Hopetown Passage - Dangerous Currents 338
Illahee park - Rock 112
Jerrell Cove - Shallow Area 79
Lagoon Cove - Caution Shoal Area 328
Little Sucia Island - Dangerous Reef 199
Mayne Passage - Anchored Turbine Generator 320
Meyers Passage - Naviation Note 433
Monahan's - Johnstone Strait Currents 316
Oak Harbor - Entrance Channel Shoals 143
Okisollo Channel Rapids - Dangerous Currents 303
Owen Bay Area - Strong Currents 303
Peavine and Obstruction Passes - Tide-Rip 181
Pendrell Sound - Speed Limit 296
Pirates Cove - Dangerous Reefs 242
Point Atkinson - Tide-Rips 269
Point Wilson - Tide-Rip 135
Pole Pass Area - Speed Limit 194

Port Hardy - Floatplane Operations Lights 354
Port Ludlow - Navigation Note 128
Prince Rupert Harbour - Speed Limit 442
Rich Passage - Heavy Traffic 109
Robson Bight - Ecological Restricted Area 322
Scott Cove - Powell Rock Warning 331
Seaforth Channel - Navigation Note 425
Sechelt Rapids - Dangerous Currents 281
Sechelt Rapids - Incorrect Tide Data 281
Semiahmoo Bay - Entry Shoal 164
Sequim Bay - Shoal Area 168
Shilshole Bay - Shallow Area 100
Ship Canal - Bridge Openings 100
Silva Bay - Dangerous Rock 243
Slingsby Channel - Tide-Rip 403
Snohomish River - Strong Currents 138
Squalicum Harbor - Shallow Area 161
Surf Inlet - Chartplotter Errors 434
Telegraph Harbour - Safe Entrance Channel 240
Thatcher Pass - Tide-Rip 177
Van Isle Marin - Rocks 213
Victoria Harbor - Mandatory Traffic Lanes 207
Von Donop Inlet - Dangerous Rock 301
Wasp Islands - Dangerous Reefs 192
Welcome Passage - Strong Currents 272
Wright Sound - Weather Tip 438

www.WaggonerGuide.com

ADVERTISER INDEX

Pro-Tech Yacht Services 29
Pump Me Out 149

R

Ranger Tugs, Inside Back Cover
Raven Marine 217
Refuge Cove 298
Resort at Port Ludlow The 129
Roche Harbor Marine 189
Roche Harbor Resort & Marina 190
Rock The Dock 93
Rockfish Grill 152
Rosario Resort 196
Roskelley / Olsson Davits 63

S

S3 Maritime 15, 37, 55
SailTime 43
Salamander Books 238
Salish Marine 154
Saltspring Marina 228
San Juan Islands Museum of Art 188
San Juan Sailing 163
Scan Marine 33
Scuttlebutt Brewing Company 139
Sea Grant 12
SEA Marine Yacht Services 135
Sea Recovery Watermakers 55
Sea Sport Clothing 443
Sea Sport Outboard Marina Ltd 443
Seafood Cookbook - House Ad 54
Seattle Yachts 46, 47, 154
Seaview Boatyard North 162, 163
Seaview Boatyard West 103
Seaworthy Yachts and Brokerage 32
Secret Cove Marina 274
Shaw General Store 182
Shearwater Resort & Marina 422
Shilshole Bay Marina 100
Ship to Shore Marine & Kayak 85, 87
Silverdale Marina 112
Skyline Marine Center (Skyline Marina) 158
Soho Coho 464
Sointula Harbour 351
Spectra Watermakers 103
Squalicum Harbor 161
Squirrel Cove Store 299
Steveston Marine & Hardware 262
Storm Light Outfitters 385
Sullivan Bay Marina Resort 337
Sure Marine Service Inc. 63
Susie's Mopeds 188
Swan Hotel and Cottages, The 132
Swantown Marina 77

T

Tacoma Art Museum 90, 93
Taku Resort & Marina 305
Thetis Island Resort 240
Tides of Anacortes 154
Tides Tavern 84
Timber & Marine Supply 464
Toba Wilderness Marina 297
Total Boat Marine Surveyors 217
Tri-County Diesel 163

U

U'Mista Cultural Center 348
Union Steamship 271
Union Steamship, Back Cover
Union Tavern 154

V

Van Isle Marina 214
Vector Yacht Services 68, 210, 217
Victoria Harbour Authority 207
Victoria International Marina 20

W

Waggoner Cruising Guide 154, 228, 411
Waggoner Flotillas 121
Washington State History Museum 90, 93
Waterfront Suites & Marina 247
Waterline Boats 42
West Coast Community Craft Shop 355
West Sound Marina 195
Westview Fuels 286
Whale Museum 188
Wine Seller, The 132
Wooden Boat Chandlery 132

Y

Yanmar 68

NW MARITIME EXPLORERS INDEX

Alessandro Malaspina 288
Charles William Barkley 392
Dionisio Alcala Galiano 231
Early Explorers Timeline 8
Francisco de Eliza 172
George Dixon 460
George Vancouver 289
James Cook 129
Jose Maria Narvaez 282
Joseph Whidbey 143
Juan de Fuca 171
Juan Francisco de la Bodega y Quadra 303
Juan Jose Perez Hernandez 452
Martinez and the Nootka Crisis 380
Peter Puget 114
Salvador Fidalgo 150
Sir Francis Drake 411
William Robert Broughton 334

SIDEBAR INDEX

Alert Bay - The Spirit of U'mista 349
Be Whale Wise 183
Boardwalk Planks At Hot Springs Cove 378
Canada - U.S. Border Dispute At Dixon Entrance 26
Cape Scott 361
Caution In Rosario Strait 177
Close Encounter In Fitz Hugh Sounds 406
Don't Miss Misty Fjords National Monument 464
Exploring Graham Island By Car 451
First-Aid Supplies & Preparedness 396
Flag Etiquette 334
From The Lighthouse 386
Full Moon Party And The Mess Afterwards 428
Ganges & Salt Spring Island - Foodie Heaven! 227

Hakai Beach Institute - Pruth Bay 414
Happy Hour Pot Luck Favorites 290
Hiram M. Chittenden Locks 101
History of the Waggoner 9
How You Can Help The Orcas 187
Large Scale, Large Detail 27
Nakwakto Rapids And Belize Inlet 404
Ocean Falls 419
Past & Present: Sea Otter Cove 362
Planning For Happy Hour 336
Radio Check 39
Resources For Cruising Hams 41
Running In Fog 60
Running The Rapids 315

Scolding On The Radio 40
Securite Call Instead of Big Wake Scold 40
Seymour Narrows 311
Stern Ties 28
Swimming Pools Of The Inside Passage 215
Swinomish Channel 146
Tacoma Reborn 91
The End Of Paper Charts? 26
The Point Wilson Rip 173
The Surprise On Knight Inlet 329
Turn Point Special Operating Area 200
Watch For Ferry Traffic 175

2018 Waggoner Cruising Guide

CUTWATER
DISCOVER YOUR INNER EXPLORER

CutwaterBoats.com

2016 Cutwater Cruise • Montague Harbour Marina, Galiano Island, BC